Make government
COME ALIVE

with GLENCOE'S

TECHNOLOGY TOOLS

Students can review
lesson content, take notes,
and build vocabulary at
StudentWorks™ Plus!

Help students learn
key vocabulary with
eFlashcards!

Bring the sights
and sounds
of government to
your classroom
with Spotlight
Videos, rich
with primary
source images!

Challenge students
with games and
activities (that are
great on Interactive
White Boards)!

**Students can find maps in motion, interactive graphic organizers, and
more technology tools on StudentWorks™ Plus or online at glencoe.com.**

QuickPass™
More Than a Textbook

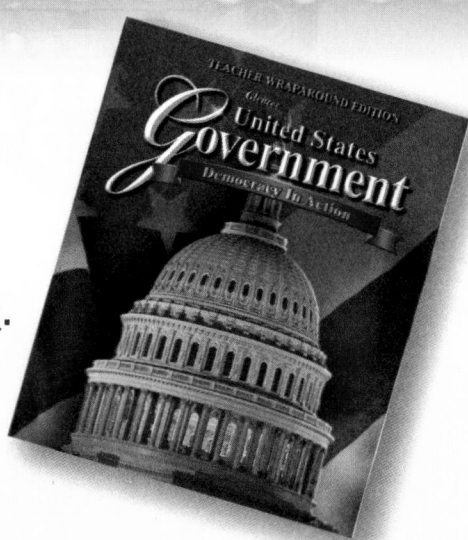

- ## More online resources
  Go to Government ONLINE at glencoe.com.

- ## More convenient
  Enter a QuickPass™ chapter code to go directly to the chapter resources you need.

Student QuickPass™

> Key in chapter number.

Enter student code USG9822c1 to access these resources:

- StudentWorks™ Plus Online
- Chapter Spotlight Video
- Chapter Overview
- Study-to-Go
- Chapter Audio
- In Motion Animations
- Student Web Activity
- Self-Check Quiz
  ...and more

Teacher QuickPass™

> Key in chapter number.

Enter teacher code USG9085c1T to access these resources:

- All student materials
- Web resources
- Teacher resources
  ...and more

You can easily launch a wide rang[e] from your computer's desktop wit[h] Social Studies widget.

Table of Contents

▼ U.S. legislators during a joint session of Congress in the chamber of the U.S. House of Representatives

▶ Senate flag

▲ The Supreme Court

Table of Contents

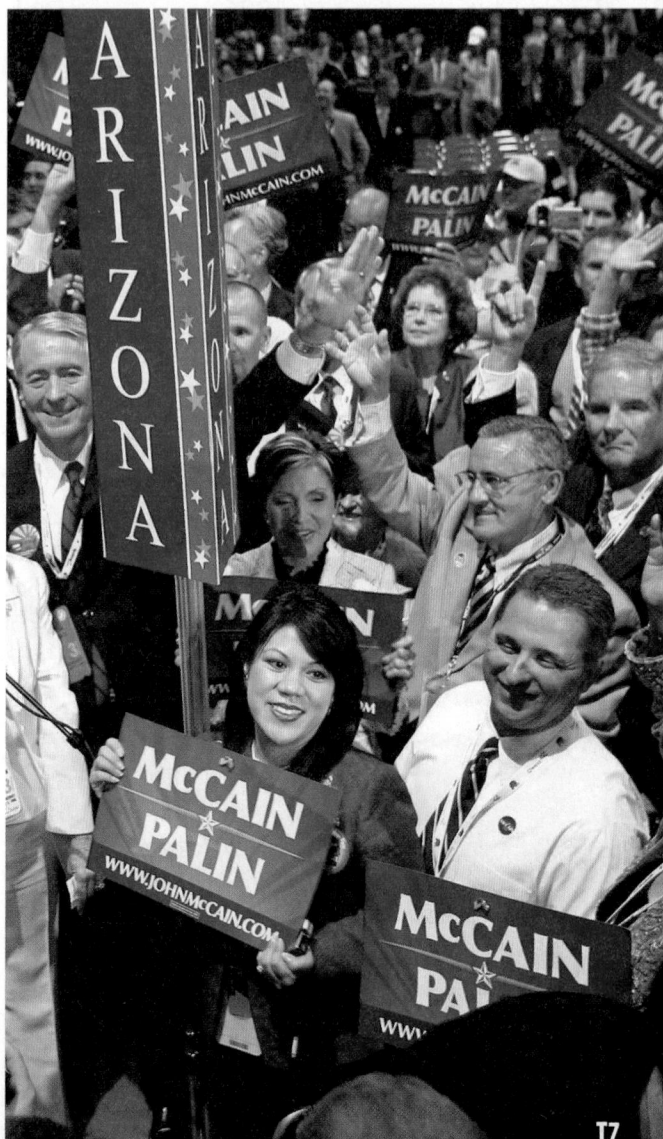

▶ Delegates from Arizona at the Republican National Convention

Table of Contents

Supreme Court Cases to Debate

ISSUES to Debate

Government Skills

◀ Registering to vote

TIME
For the Record

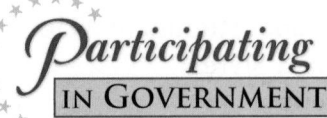

Participating
IN GOVERNMENT

▲ Thurgood Marshall and Daisy Bates (both center) and the "Little Rock Nine"

We the People

Making a Difference

Table of Contents

Charts, Graphs, and Maps

Graphs In MOtion

Entries in blue indicate In Motion graphics. These graphs, charts, and maps have been specially enhanced on the StudentWorks™ Plus CD-ROM and on glencoe.com.

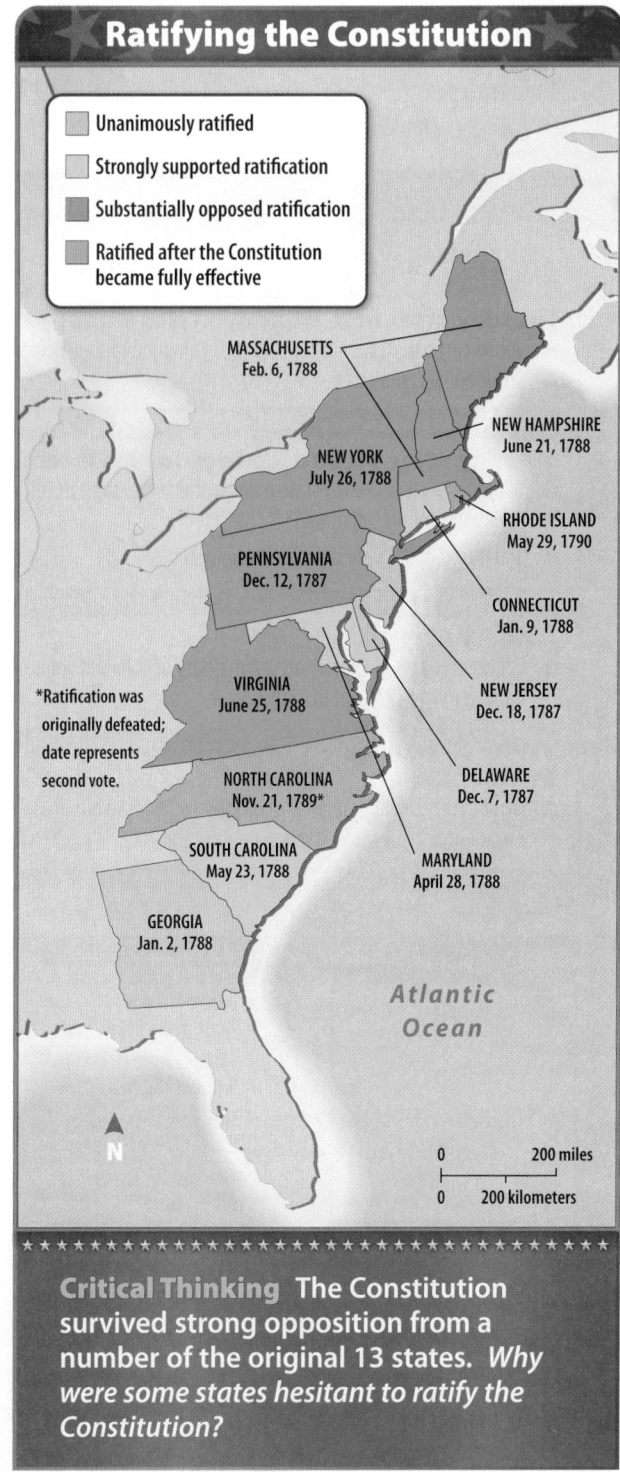

Ratifying the Constitution

- Unanimously ratified
- Strongly supported ratification
- Substantially opposed ratification
- Ratified after the Constitution became fully effective

MASSACHUSETTS
Feb. 6, 1788

NEW HAMPSHIRE
June 21, 1788

NEW YORK
July 26, 1788

RHODE ISLAND
May 29, 1790

PENNSYLVANIA
Dec. 12, 1787

CONNECTICUT
Jan. 9, 1788

*Ratification was originally defeated; date represents second vote.

VIRGINIA
June 25, 1788

NEW JERSEY
Dec. 18, 1787

DELAWARE
Dec. 7, 1787

NORTH CAROLINA
Nov. 21, 1789*

SOUTH CAROLINA
May 23, 1788

MARYLAND
April 28, 1788

GEORGIA
Jan. 2, 1788

Atlantic Ocean

N

0   200 miles

0   200 kilometers

Critical Thinking The Constitution survived strong opposition from a number of the original 13 states. *Why were some states hesitant to ratify the Constitution?*

Table of Contents

The Electoral College System

Presidential Election Year

Tuesday after first Monday in November
- Voters cast ballots for a slate of electors pledged to a particular presidential candidate.

Monday after second Wednesday in December
- Winning electors in each state meet in their state capitals to cast their votes for president and vice president.
- Statement of the vote is sent to Washington, D.C.

January 6
- Congress counts electoral votes. A majority of electoral votes is needed to win (270 out of 538).

January 20
- Candidate receiving majority of electoral votes is sworn in as president of the United States.

Election	Candidates (presidents in red)	Electoral Vote	Percentage of Popular Vote***
1824	John Q. Adams* Andrew Jackson	84 99	30.5% 43.1%
1876	Rutherford B. Hayes** Samuel Tilden	185 184	48.0% 51.0%
1888	Benjamin Harrison Grover Cleveland	233 168	47.9% 48.6%
2000	George W. Bush Albert Gore	271 266	47.9% 48.4%

* Clay and Crawford also received electoral votes. The election was determined in the House of Representatives.
** Hayes was awarded the disputed electoral votes of three states by a special commission. *** Percentages do not add up to 100 percent due to votes for other candidates.
Source: Atlas of U.S. Presidential Elections: http://uselectionatlas.org.

Critical Thinking The writers of the Constitution chose the Electoral College system as a compromise between selection by Congress and election by popular vote. *How many weeks pass between the presidential election and the inauguration? Is this time necessary? Why?*

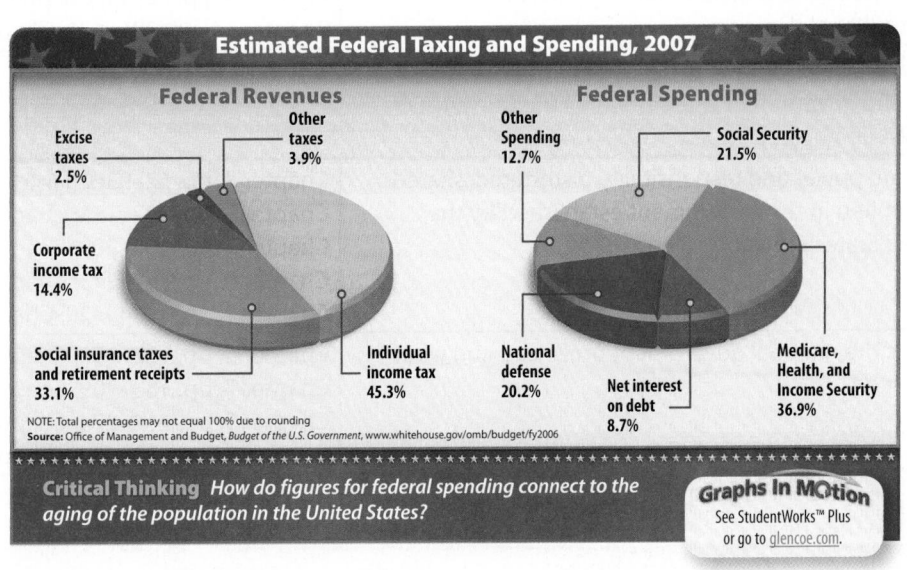

Estimated Federal Taxing and Spending, 2007

Federal Revenues

Excise taxes 2.5%

Other taxes 3.9%

Corporate income tax 14.4%

Social insurance taxes and retirement receipts 33.1%

Individual income tax 45.3%

Federal Spending

Other Spending 12.7%

Social Security 21.5%

National defense 20.2%

Net interest on debt 8.7%

Medicare, Health, and Income Security 36.9%

NOTE: Total percentages may not equal 100% due to rounding
Source: Office of Management and Budget, *Budget of the U.S. Government,* www.whitehouse.gov/omb/budget/fy2006

Critical Thinking *How do figures for federal spending connect to the aging of the population in the United States?*

Graphs In MOtion
See StudentWorks™ Plus or go to glencoe.com.

United States Government: Democracy In Action
to the National Standards for Civics and Government

National Standards for Civics and Government	Student Pages
Standard 1 What are civic life, politics, and government?	
I.A. What is civic life? What is politics? What is government? Why are government and politics necessary? What purposes should government serve?	Chapter 1, pp. 4–33; Chapter 13, pp. 354–385; Chapter 14, pp. 392–397
I.B. What are the essential characteristics of limited and unlimited government?	Chapter 1, pp. 5–11; Chapter 25, pp. 688–701
I.C. What are the nature and purposes of constitutions?	Chapter 2, pp. 48–61; Chapter 3, pp. 62–93
I.D. What are alternative ways of organizing constitutional governments?	Chapter 1, pp. 12–25; Chapter 2, pp. 48–61; Chapter 3, pp. 62–93; Chapter 25, pp. 688–701
Standard 2 What are the foundations of the American political system?	
II.A. What is the American idea of constitutional government?	Chapter 2, pp. 53–61; Chapter 3, pp. 62–93
II.B. What are the distinctive characteristics of American society?	Chapter 13, pp. 354–385; Chapter 14, pp. 386–413; Chapter 15, pp. 422–449; Chapter 16, pp. 452–473; Chapter 17, pp. 474–501; Chapter 18, pp. 502–525; Chapter 19, pp. 526–551; Chapter 20, pp. 554–573; Chapter 21, pp. 574–605; Chapter 22, pp. 606–633
II.C. What is American political culture?	Chapter 16, pp. 452–473; Chapter 17, pp. 474–501; Chapter 18, pp. 502–525; Chapter 19, pp. 526–551
II.D. What values and principles are basic to American constitutional democracy?	Chapter 3, pp. 62–93; Chapter 13, pp. 354–385; Chapter 14, pp. 386–421; Chapter 15, pp. 422–449
Standard 3 How does the government established by the Constitution embody the purposes, values, and principles of American democracy?	
III.A. How are power and responsibility distributed, shared, and limited in the government established by the United States Constitution?	Chapter 3, pp. 62–93; Chapter 4, pp. 94–119; Chapter 5, pp. 122–155; Chapter 6, pp. 156–179; Chapter 7, pp. 180–209; Chapter 8, pp. 212–243; Chapter 9, pp. 244–273; Chapter 10, pp. 274–301; Chapter 11, pp. 304–329; Chapter 12, pp. 330–351
III.B. How is the national government organized and what does it do?	Chapter 5, pp. 122–155; Chapter 6, pp. 156–179; Chapter 7, pp. 180–209; Chapter 8, pp. 212–243; Chapter 9, pp. 244–273; Chapter 10, pp. 274–301; Chapter 11, pp. 304–329; Chapter 12, pp. 330–351
III.C. How are state and local governments organized and what do they do?	Chapter 23, pp. 636–661; Chapter 24, pp. 662–685

National Standards for Civics and Government	Student Pages
III.D. What is the place of law in the American constitutional system?	Chapter 15, pp. 422–449
III.E. How does the American political system provide for choice and opportunities for participation?	Chapter 16, pp. 452–473; Chapter 17, pp. 474–501; Chapter 18, pp. 502–525; Chapter 19, pp. 526–551
Standard 4 What is the relationship of the United States to other nations and to world affairs?	
IV.A. How is the world organized politically?	Chapter 25, pp. 688–715
IV.B. How do the domestic politics and constitutional principles of the United States affect its relations with the world?	Chapter 22, pp. 606–633; Chapter 25, pp. 688–715
IV.C. How has the United States influenced other nations, and how have other nations influenced American politics and society?	Chapter 22, pp. 606–633; Chapter 25, pp. 688–715; Chapter 26, pp. 716–739
Standard 5 What are the roles of the citizen in American democracy?	
V.A. What is citizenship?	Chapter 14, pp. 386–413
V.B. What are the rights of citizens?	Chapter 14, pp. 386–413
V.C. What are the responsibilities of citizens?	Chapter 14, pp. 386–413
V.D. What civic dispositions or traits of private and public character are important to the preservation and improvement of American constitutional democracy?	Chapter 14, pp. 386–413
V.E. How can citizens take part in civic life?	Chapter 16, pp. 452–473; Chapter 17, pp. 474–501; Chapter 18, pp. 502–525; Chapter 19, pp. 526–551

Using the Teacher Wraparound Edition

To Teachers:

Welcome to the Teacher Wraparound Edition of *United States Government: Democracy In Action*. We have created this teacher edition based on input from experienced teachers and educational consultants. Our goal is to provide you with teaching strategies and activities, which are labeled for you at point of use. The following pages will show the structure of the Teacher Wraparound Edition.

Student-Based Instruction

Point-of-Use
- Strategies and activities apply directly to student content.

Differentiated Instruction
- Leveled activities and options for differentiated instruction help meet the needs of all your students, including English Language Learners.

Review and Reinforcement
- Reading and critical thinking skills are reinforced throughout the lesson.

Assessment and Intervention
- Chapter Assessments gauge student mastery of content.
- Additional resources provide intervention options.

Planning and Teaching the Unit

Planning pages appear at the beginning of each unit.

Pacing Chart

Provides time management suggestions for teaching the unit

Author Note

Highlights author's ideas for teaching the time period

Teacher to Teacher

Includes activities from the classrooms of successful teachers

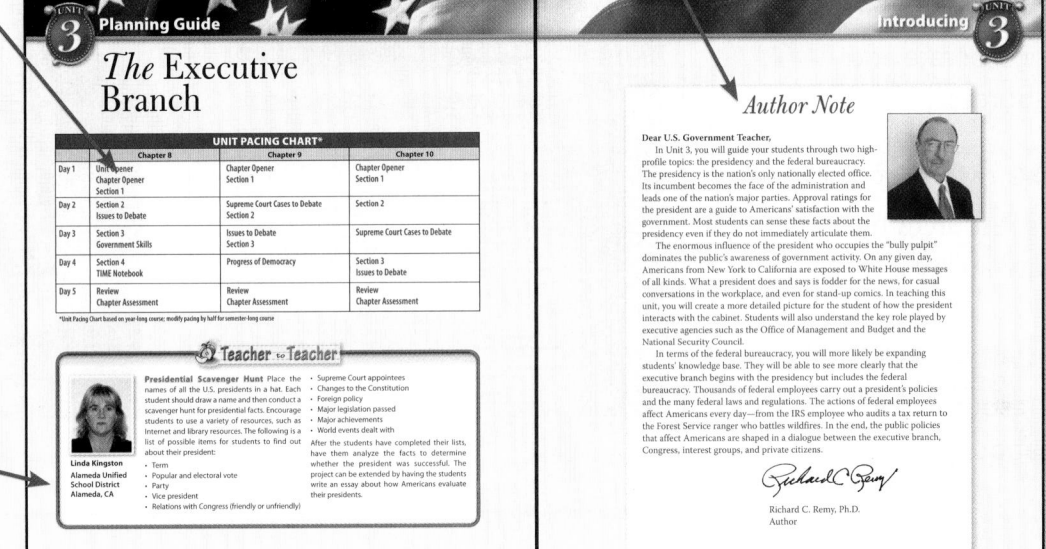

Making It Relevant

Provides a question or activity to help students discover why the events they will study are important

Skill Practice

Point-of-use skill-based activities help students practice analysis and geography skills

Launching the Unit Activity

Introduce the unit by relating government to other disciplines

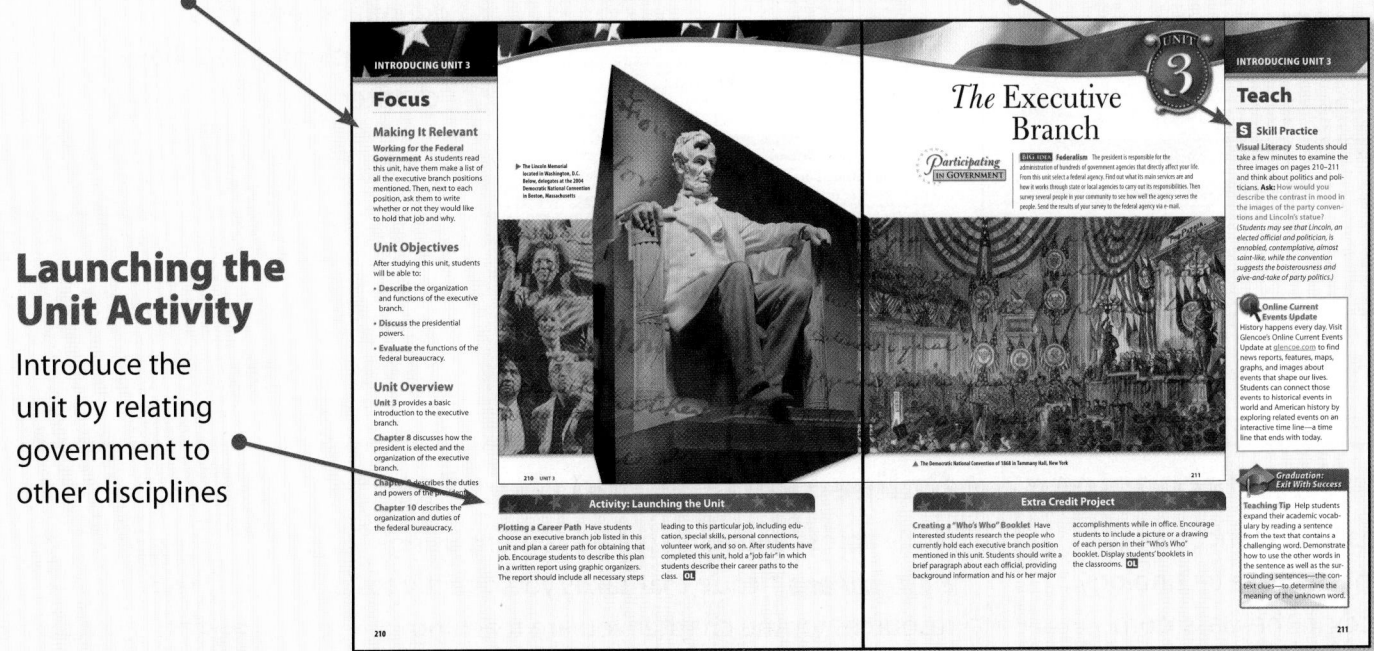

Planning the Chapter

Chapter Planning Guides provide a snapshot of the scope of resources available to enhance and extend learning in each chapter.

Incorporating Resources

Utilizes a structured lesson plan to incorporate additional resources

Leveled Activities

Organizes resources by appropriate ability levels

*Spanish Resources

Provides resources for English Language Learners

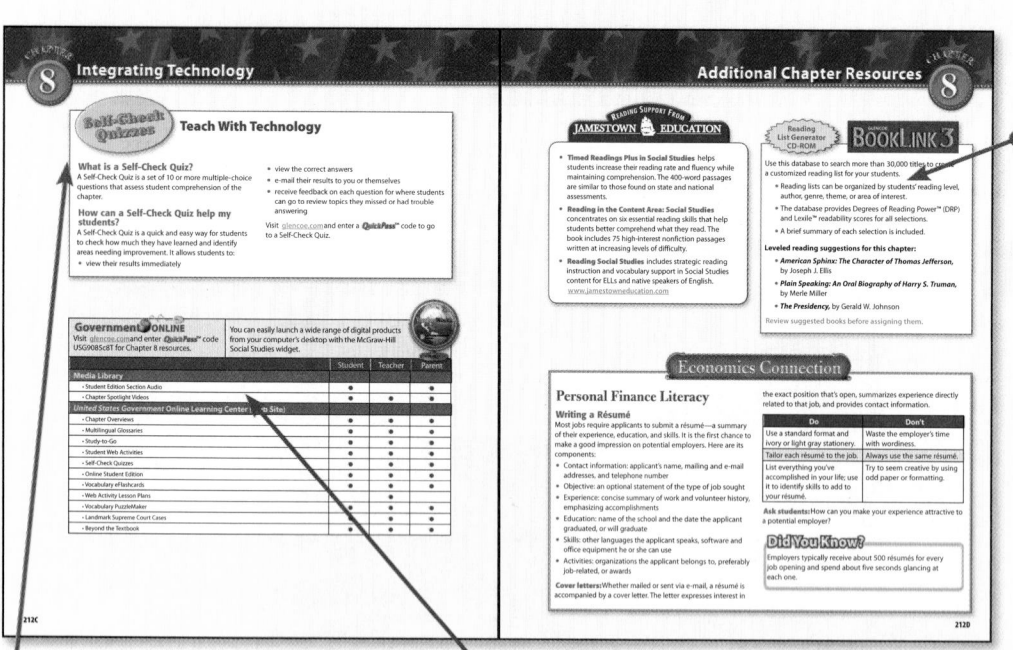

Additional Resources

Identifies resources for supplementing the chapter

Teach With Technology

Explains how to incorporate different Glencoe technology resources in the classroom

Online Learning and *QuickPass*™

Easily access engaging online content using a *QuickPass*™ code that takes you directly to resources for the chapter you are teaching

Teaching the Chapter

The Big Ideas and Essential Question at the beginning of the chapter help you teach the most important chapter content.

Essential Question

Introductory questions lead to an exploration of big ideas. These questions activate students' prior knowledge and lead students to see not only the "big picture," but also the relevancy of what they are learning. These lesson launcher activities compel students to consider the Big Idea for each chapter.

Chapter Spotlight Video

Engages students with the content using a short BBC video

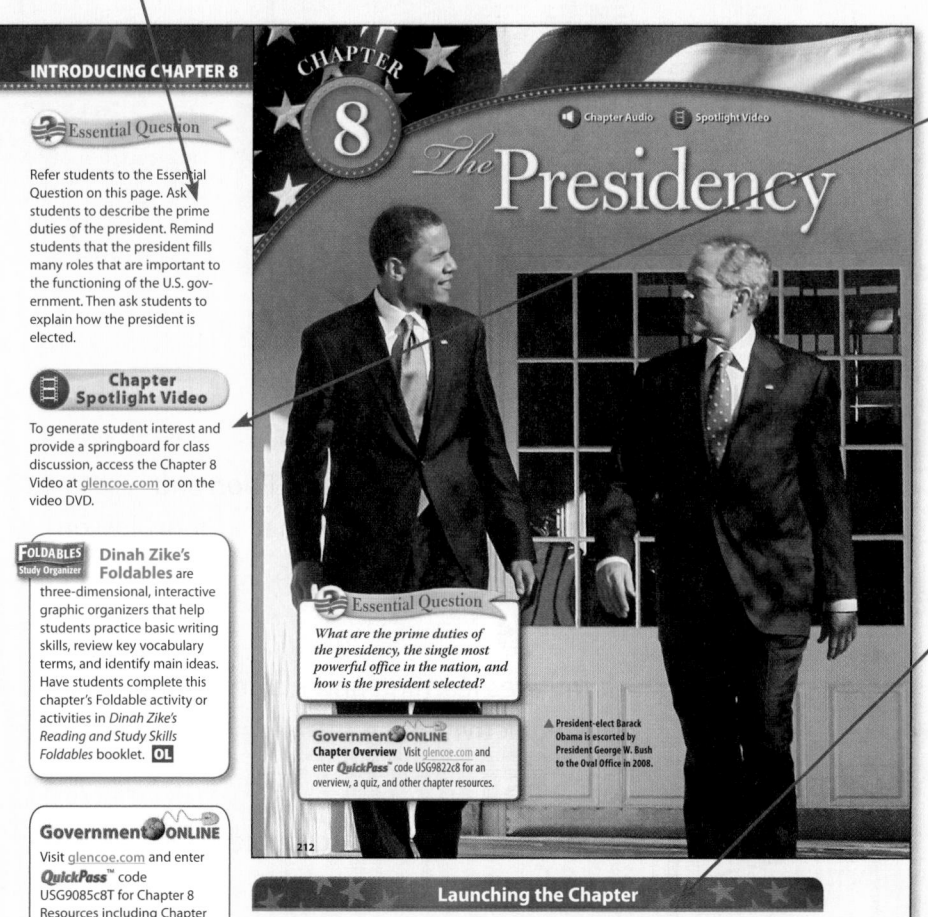

Launching the Chapter Activity

Introduce the chapter by activating students' prior knowledge. Each activity includes an Essential Question that is thought-provoking, challenges old assumptions, and stimulates classroom discussion. Student activities throughout the chapter will refer back to the Essential Question, leading to a greater comprehension of chapter themes.

Lesson Structure

Each lesson in *United States Government: Democracy In Action* is presented in a structured lesson plan: Focus, Teach, Assess, and Close.

FOCUS

Includes a Bellringer activity to help your students think about the lesson topic

Reader's Guide

Provides pre-reading strategies to improve comprehension

Resource Manager

Provides a list of teacher edition and supplemental resources that support lesson content and reinforce skills

TEACH

Stimulates learning and interest using leveled activities

ASSESS

Identifies assessment resources

CLOSE

Gauges comprehension of section content

Answers

Lists the answers to Student Edition questions

Understanding the Brackets and Letters

Brackets

Brackets on the reduced Student Edition page correspond to teaching strategies and activities in the Teacher Wraparound Edition. As you teach the section, the brackets show you exactly where to teach these strategies and activities.

Letters*

The letters on the reduced Student Edition page identify the type of strategy or activity. See the key below to learn about the different types of strategies and activities.

KEY for Using the Teacher Wraparound Edition

R **Reading Strategies** activities help you teach reading skills and vocabulary.

C **Critical Thinking** strategies help students apply and extend what they have learned.

D **Differentiated Instruction** activities provide differentiated instruction for students learning to speak English, along with suggestions for teaching various types of learners.

S **Skill Practice** strategies help students practice historical analysis and geography skills.

W **Writing Support** activities provide writing opportunities to help students comprehend the text.

* Letters are followed by a number when there is more than one of the same type of strategy or activity on the page.

Hands-On Chapter Projects

Extend student learning with unique interactive projects in each chapter. The Hands-On Chapter Projects allow students to take concepts and put them to practical use. Activities are progressive and require teamwork. Students conceptualize, plan, and execute their vision in a hands-on approach that makes history come alive.

Steps

Each lesson includes a self-contained activity, with one lesson building on knowledge gained from previous lessons.

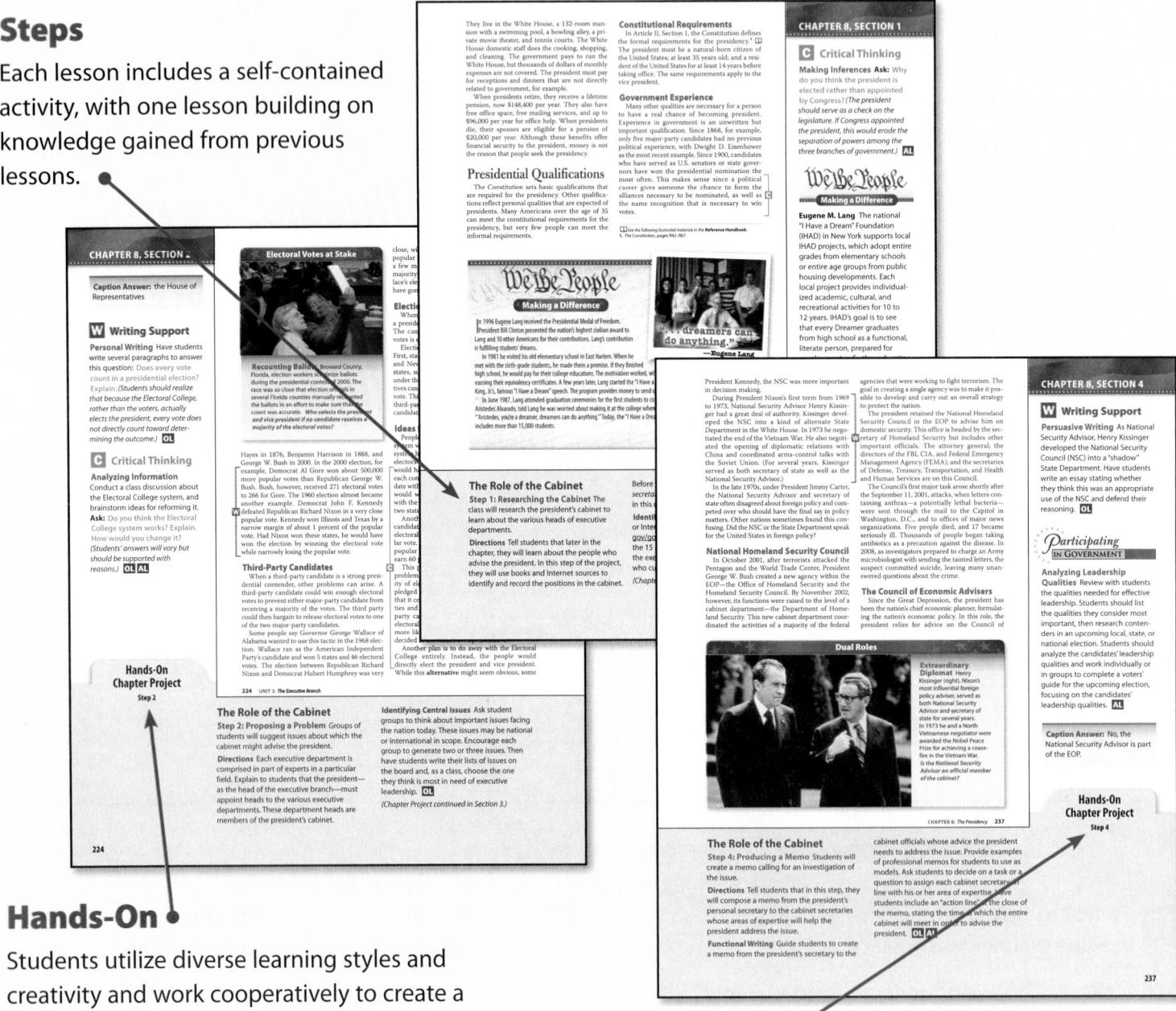

Hands-On

Students utilize diverse learning styles and creativity and work cooperatively to create a final project for each lesson.

Results

The Hands-On project culminates in a summary activity that ties the other activities in the chapter together.

Differentiated Instruction

Each section of the Teacher Wraparound Edition of *United States Government: Democracy In Action* provides differentiated instruction activities to meet the diverse needs of every student.

Differentiated Instruction

Innovative ideas meet each student's interests and learning styles through point-of-use activities.

Additional Resources

Provides suggestions for incorporating additional resources based on students' different learning abilities

Leveled Activities

Extends instruction beyond the text by suggesting activities related to content on the page

Dynamic Features

Use the creative features in the textbook to dig deep into the fascinating issues and people covered in the text.

Supreme Court Cases to Debate

Teaches students to analyze Supreme Court decisions by revisiting real cases

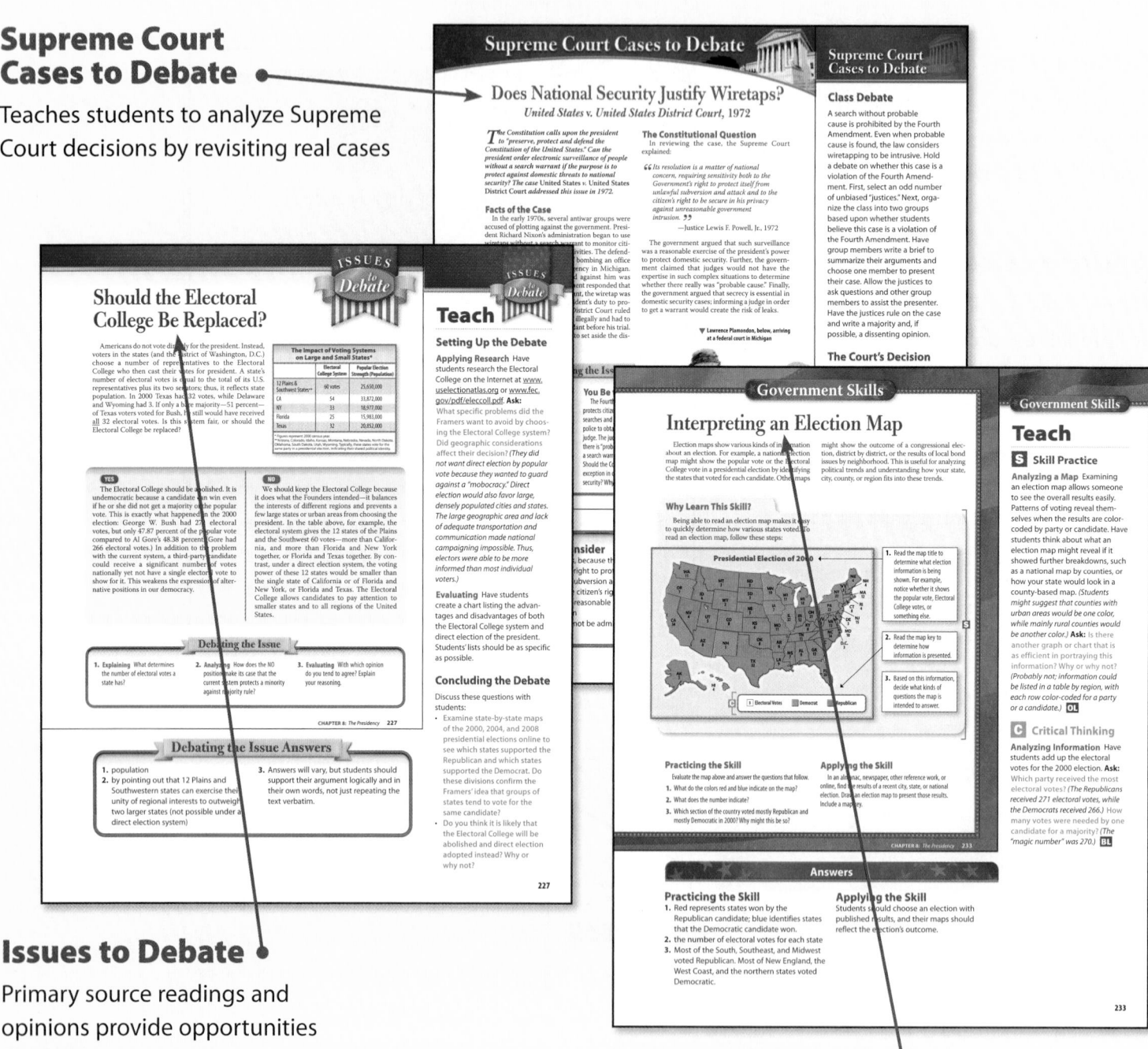

Issues to Debate

Primary source readings and opinions provide opportunities for analysis and classroom discussion on political issues

Government Skills

Each unit-based Critical Thinking skill provides a lesson and activity that is useful for studying government and other disciplines

Chapter Summary and Assessment

Chapter Assessment

Each assessment features questions that incorporate analysis and identify potential pitfalls and challenges.

Chapter Summary

Helps students to synthesize major chapter themes

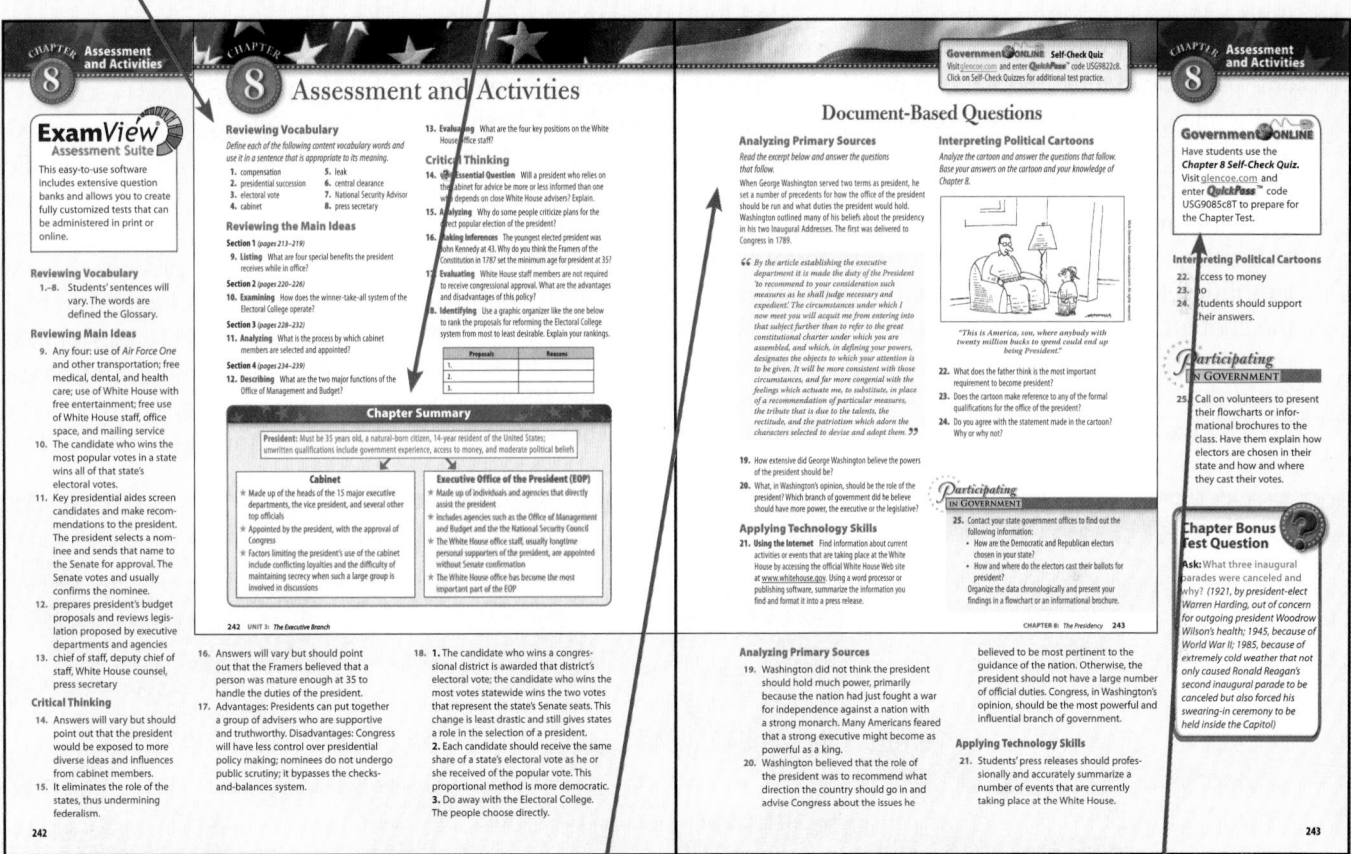

Critical Thinking and Document-Based Questions

Extend answers and analysis through document and graphic assessment

Government Online

Provides additional assessment opportunities

Academic Vocabulary

How Can I Help My Students Learn Academic Vocabulary?

What Is Academic English?

Academic English is the language used in academics, business, and courts of law. It is the type of English used in textbooks, and it contains linguistic features associated with academic disciplines such as social studies. Proficiency in reading and using academic English is especially related to long-term success in all parts of life.

By reinforcing academic English, teachers can help learners to access authentic, academic texts—not simplified texts that "dumb down" the content. In this way, they can provide information that will help build their students' background knowledge rapidly.

What Is Academic Vocabulary?

Academic vocabulary is based on academic English. By the time children have completed elementary school, they must have acquired the knowledge needed to understand academic vocabulary. How many words should they acquire to be able to access their textbooks? A basic 2,000-word vocabulary of high-frequency words makes up 87% of the vocabulary of academic texts. Eight hundred other academic words comprise an additional 8% of the words. Three percent of the remaining words are technical words. The remaining 2% are low-frequency words. There may be as many as 123,000 low-frequency words in academic texts.

Why Should Students Learn Academic Vocabulary?

English learners who have a basic 2,000-word vocabulary are ready to acquire most general words found in their texts.

Knowledge of academic words and general words can significantly boost a student's comprehension level of academic texts. Students who learn and practice these words before they graduate from high school are likely to master academic material with more confidence and speed. They waste less time and effort in guessing words or

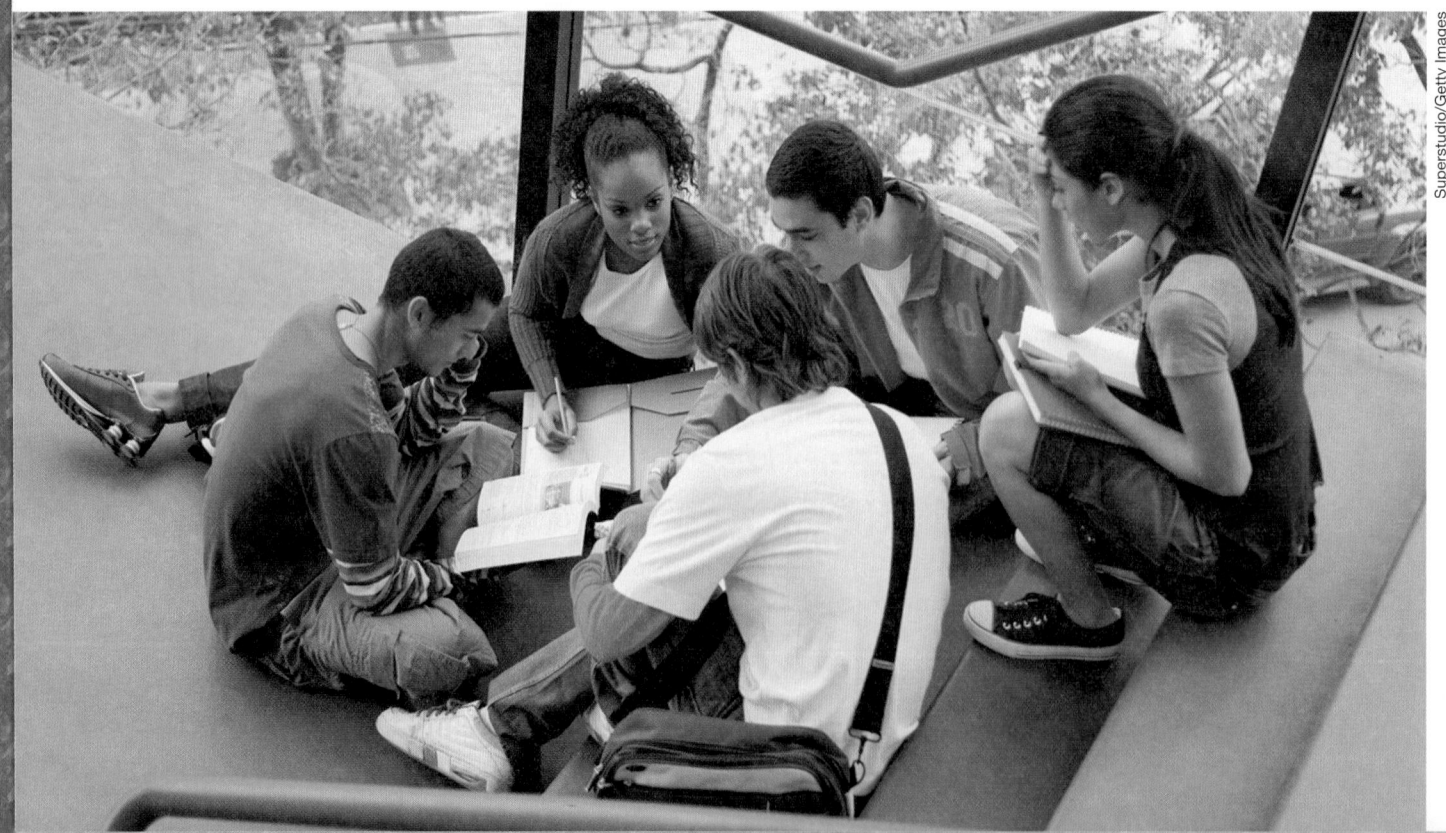

Superstudio/Getty Images

consulting dictionaries than those who know only the basic 2,000 words that characterize general conversation.

How Do I Include Academic Vocabulary and Academic English in My Teaching?

Teachers can provide students with academic vocabulary and help students understand the academic English of their text.

To develop academic English, learners must have already acquired basic proficiency in the grammar of everyday English.

Academic English should be taught within contexts that make sense. In terms of instruction, teaching academic English includes providing students with access to core curriculum—in this case social studies.

Academic English arises in part from social practices in which academic English is used. The acquisition of academic vocabulary and grammar is necessary to advance the development of academic English.

Tips for Teaching Academic Vocabulary:

✔ **Expose Students to Academic Vocabulary**
You do not need to call attention to words students are learning because they will acquire them subconsciously.

✔ **Do Not Correct Students' Mistakes When Using the Vocabulary Words**
All vocabulary understanding and spelling errors will disappear once the student reads more.

✔ **Help Students Decode the Words Themselves** Once they learn the alphabet, they should be able to decode words. Decoding each word they don't recognize will help them more than trying to focus on sentence structure. Once they can recognize the words, they can read "authentic" texts.

✔ **Do Not Ignore the English Learner in This Process** They can learn academic vocabulary before they are completely fluent in oral English.

✔ **Helping Students Build Academic Vocabulary Leads to Broader Learning** Students who have mastered the basic academic vocabulary are ready to continue acquiring words from the rest of the groups. To help determine which words are in the 2,000-word basic group, refer to *West's General Service List of English Words*, 1953. The list is designed to serve as a guide for teachers and as a checklist and goal list for students. For additional information about the list, visit: http://www.vuw.ac.nz/lals/research/awl.

Guidelines for Teaching Academic Vocabulary

1. Direct and planned instruction
2. Models that have increasingly difficult language
3. Attention to form, pointing out linguistic features of words
4. Practice
5. Motivation
6. Instructional feedback
7. Assessment on a regular basis

Classroom Activity

Writing About Modern America

Give students a brief writing assignment. Ask them to write a short essay about one of the topics listed below in the left column. Have students use as many of the academic vocabulary words in the right column as they can in their essay. When completed, ask student volunteers to share their writing. Note what academic vocabulary words they use.

Topic	Academic Vocabulary
The challenges of reducing poverty in America	sufficient
	minimum
	medical
	income
Recent technological advances	innovate
	technology
	media
	potential
	data
	transmit

Meeting the Diverse Needs of Our Students

by Douglas Fisher, Ph.D.

Today's classroom contains students from a variety of backgrounds with a variety of learning styles, strengths, and challenges. As teachers we are facing the challenge of helping students reach their educational potential. With careful planning, you can address the needs of all students in the social studies classroom. The basis for this planning is universal access. When classrooms are planned with universal access in mind, fewer students require specific accommodations.

What Is a Universal Access Design for Learning?

Universal design was first conceived in architectural studies

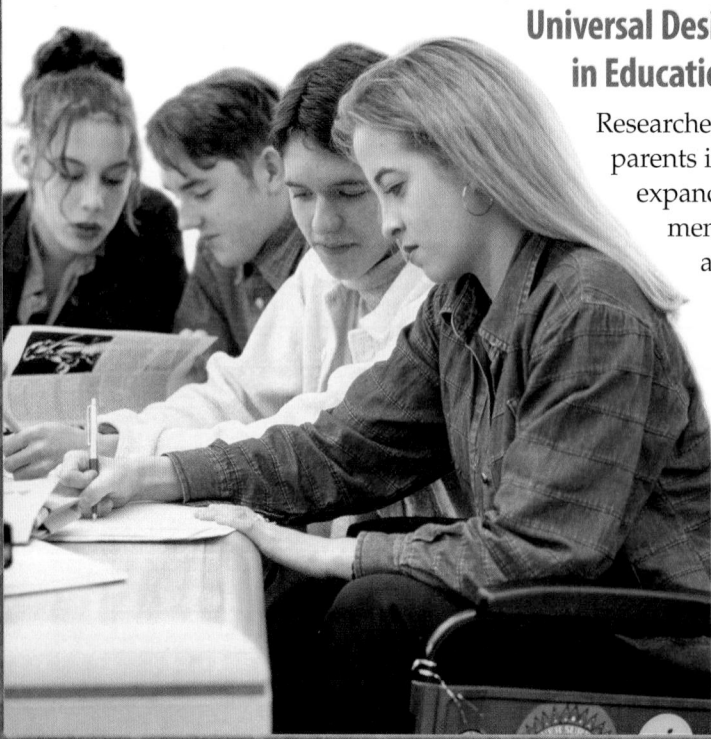

when businesspeople, engineers, and architects began making considerations for physical access to buildings. The idea was to plan the environment in advance to ensure that everyone had access. As a result, the environment would not have to be changed later for people with physical disabilities, people pushing strollers, workers who had injuries, or others for whom the environment would be difficult to negotiate. The Center for Universal Design at www.design.ncsu.edu/cud defines Universal Design as:

The design of products and environments to be usable by all people, to the greatest extent possible, without the need for adaptation or specialized design.

Universal Design and Access in Education

Researchers, teachers, and parents in education have expanded the development of built-in adaptations and inclusive accommodations from architectural space to the educational experience, especially in the area of curriculum.

In 1998, the National Center to Improve the Tools of Educators (NCITE),

Ian Shaw/Getty Images

with the partnership of the Center for Applied Special Technology (CAST), proposed an expanded definition of universal design focused on education:

In terms of learning, universal design means the design of instructional materials and activities that allows the learning goals to be achievable by individuals with wide differences in their abilities to see, hear, speak, move, read, write, understand English, attend, organize, engage, and remember.

How Does Universal Design Work in Education?

Universal design and access, as they apply to education and schooling, suggest the following:

✔ **Inclusive Classroom Participation** Curriculum should be designed with all students and their needs in mind. The Glencoe/McGraw-Hill social studies texts and materials were designed with a wide range of students in mind. For example, understanding that English learners and students who struggle with reading would be using this textbook, vocabulary is specifically taught and reinforced. Similarly, the teacher-support materials provide multiple instructional points to be used depending on the needs of the students in the class. Further, the text is written such that main ideas are identified for all learners. Activating prior knowledge is also taken into consideration by the text. Connections between what students know and think about are made within the text.

✔ **Maximum Text Readability** In universally designed classrooms that provide access for all students, texts use direct language, clear noun-verb agreements, and clear construct-based wording. In addition to these factors, the Glencoe social studies text uses embedded definitions for difficult terms, provides for specific instruction in reading skills, uses a number of visual representations, and includes note-taking guides.

✔ **Adaptable and Accommodating** The content in this textbook can be easily translated, read aloud, or otherwise changed to meet the needs of students in the classroom. The section and end-of-chapter assessments provide students with multiple ways of demonstrating their content knowledge while also ensuring that they have practice with thinking in terms of multiple-choice questions. Critical thinking and analysis skills are also practiced.

How Is Differentiated Instruction the Key to Universal Access?

To differentiate instruction, teachers must acknowledge student differences in background knowledge and current reading, writing, and English language skills. They must also consider student learning styles, preferences, interests, and needs and react accordingly. There are a number of general guidelines for differentiating instruction in the classroom to reach all students, including:

✔ **Link Assessment With Instruction** Assessments should occur before, during, and after instruction to ensure that the curriculum is aligned with what students do and do not know. Using assessments in this way allows you to plan instruction for whole groups, small groups, and individual students. Backward planning, where you establish the assessment before you begin instruction, is also important.

✔ **Clarify Key Concepts and Generalizations** Students need to know what is essential and how this information can be used in their future learning. In addition, students need to develop a sense of the **Big Ideas**—ideas that transcend time and place.

✔ **Emphasize Critical and Creative Thinking** The content, process, and products used or assigned in the classroom should require that students think about what they are learning. While some students may require support, additional motivation, varied tasks, materials, or equipment, the overall focus on critical and creative thinking allows for all students to participate in the lesson.

✔ **Include Teacher- and Student-Selected Tasks** A differentiated classroom includes both teacher- and student-selected activities and tasks. At some points in the lesson or day, the teacher must provide instruction and assign learning activities. In other parts of the lesson, students should be provided choices in how they engage with the content. This balance increases motivation, engagement, and learning.

How Do I Support Individual Students?

The vast majority of students will thrive in a classroom based on universal access and differentiated instruction. However, wise teachers recognize that no single option will work for all students and that there may be students who require unique systems of support to be successful.

Classroom Activity

Display a map of imperialism in Africa around 1914. Discuss with students the map's general information and have them list each country under the European power that controlled it.

To differentiate this activity:

- Have students imagine they are living in the early 1900s. Have them write a letter to a British newspaper about colonial rule in Africa.
- Have students record the number of African countries under European rule. Have them take the data and create a bar graph that shows which European powers were the most active colonizers at the time.
- Have students compose a song or poem about European rule in Africa, from an African's point of view.
- Have students choose a country of modern Africa to research. Have them write a three-page paper discussing how that country was affected by colonialism and how it has changed since the days of European rule.

Tips For Instruction

The following tips for instruction can support your efforts to help all students reach their maximum potential.

✔ Survey students to discover their individual differences. Use interest inventories of their unique talents so you can encourage contributions in the classroom.

✔ Be a model for respecting others. Adolescents crave social acceptance. The student with learning differences is especially sensitive to correction and criticism, particularly when it comes from a teacher. Your behavior will set the tone for how students treat one another.

✔ Expand opportunities for success. Provide a variety of instructional activities that reinforce skills and concepts.

✔ Establish measurable objectives and decide how you can best help students meet them.

✔ Celebrate successes and make note of and praise "work in progress."

✔ Keep it simple. Point out problem areas if doing so can help a student effect change. Avoid overwhelming students with too many goals at one time.

✔ Assign cooperative group projects that challenge all students to contribute to solving a problem or creating a product.

How Do I Reach Students With Learning Disabilities?

✔ Provide support and structure. Clearly specify rules, assignments, and responsibilities.

✔ Practice skills frequently. Use games and drills to help maintain student interest.

✔ Incorporate many modalities into the learning process. Provide opportunities to say, hear, write, read, and act out important concepts and information.

✔ Link new skills and concepts to those already mastered.

✔ If possible, allow students to record answers on audiotape.

✔ Allow extra time to complete assessments and assignments.

✔ Let students demonstrate proficiency with alternative presentations, including oral reports, role plays, art projects, and musical presentations.

✔ Provide outlines, notes, or tape recordings of lecture material.

✔ Pair students with peer helpers, and provide class time for pair interaction.

How Do I Reach Students With Behavioral Challenges?

✔ Provide a structured environment with clear-cut schedules, rules, seat assignments, and safety procedures.

✔ Reinforce appropriate behavior and model it for students.

Comstock/CORBIS

✔ Cue distracted students back to the task through verbal signals and teacher proximity.

✔ Set goals that can be achieved in the short term. Work for long-term improvement in the big areas.

How Do I Reach Students With Physical Challenges?

✔ Openly discuss with the student any uncertainties you have about when to offer aid.

✔ Ask parents or therapists and students what special devices or procedures are needed and whether any special safety precautions need to be taken.

✔ Welcome students with physical challenges into all activities, including field trips, special events, and projects.

✔ Provide information to assist class members and adults in their understanding of support needed.

How Do I Reach Students with Visual Impairments?

✔ Facilitate independence. Modify assignments as needed.

✔ Teach classmates how and when to serve as visual guides.

✔ Limit unnecessary noise in the classroom if it distracts the student with visual impairments.

✔ Provide tactile models whenever possible.

✔ Foster a spirit of inclusion. Describe people and events as they occur in the classroom. Remind classmates that the student with visual impairments cannot interpret gestures and other forms of nonverbal communication.

✔ Provide taped lectures and reading assignments for use outside the classroom.

✔ Team the student with a sighted peer for written work.

How Do I Reach Students With Hearing Impairments?

✔ Seat students where they can see your lip movements easily and where they can avoid any visual distractions.
✔ Avoid standing with your back to the window or light source.
✔ Use an overhead projector so you can maintain eye contact while writing information for students.
✔ Seat students where they can see speakers.
✔ Write all assignments on the board, or hand out written instructions.
✔ If the student has a manual interpreter, allow both student and interpreter to select the most favorable seating arrangements.
✔ Teach students to look directly at each other when they speak.

How Do I Reach English Learners?

✔ Remember, students' ability to speak English does not reflect their academic abilities.
✔ Try to incorporate the students' cultural experience into your instruction. The help of a bilingual aide may be effective.
✔ Avoid any references in your instruction that could be construed as cultural stereotypes.
✔ Preteach important vocabulary and concepts.
✔ Encourage students to preview text before they begin reading, noting headings.
✔ Remind students not to ignore graphic organizers, photographs, and maps since there is much information in these visuals.
✔ Use memorabilia and photographs whenever possible to build background knowledge and understanding. An example of this would be coins in a foreign currency or a raw cotton ball to reinforce its importance in history.

How Do I Reach Gifted Students?

✔ Make arrangements for students to take selected subjects early and to work on independent projects.
✔ Ask "what if" questions to develop high-level thinking skills. Establish an environment safe for risk taking in your classroom.
✔ Emphasize concepts, theories, ideas, relationships, and generalizations about the content.
✔ Promote interest in the past by inviting students to make connections to the present.
✔ Let students express themselves in alternate ways such as creative writing, acting, debates, simulations, drawing, or music.
✔ Provide students with a catalog of helpful resources, listing such things as agencies that provide free and inexpensive materials, appropriate community services and programs, and community experts who might be called upon to speak to your students.
✔ Assign extension projects that allow students to solve real-life problems related to their communities.

image100/CORBIS

Douglas Fisher is a professor at San Diego State University, San Diego, CA.

Classroom Activity

Students respond eagerly to a subject when they can relate it to their own experiences. With the growing number of students who come from other world regions, explaining geography through a global theme (such as volcanoes) can give them a worldwide as well as a regional perspective. To develop this awareness, display a large world map. Have students use the library or the Internet to research the latitude and longitude of 15 major volcanoes around the world. Ask them to mark these locations on the map and answer the following questions:
• What patterns do you see in volcanic activity?
• What causes volcanic activity?
• Where in the world are volcanoes most active?
As a follow-up, suggest students go to http://volcano.und.nodak.edu/vwdocs/kids/legends.html to find legends about the origins of some of the world's volcanoes. Encourage students to share what they find with the class.

Teaching Maps, Graphs, and Charts

How Can I Use Visuals to Improve Students' Reading Comprehension?

Maps, graphs, and charts are visual tools. By using images rather than words, these tools present complex information in an easy-to-understand format. Teach students the following generalized viewing strategies, and encourage them to apply these strategies as they study each chapter.

✔ **Asking Questions** Students should start by looking over the graphic and asking themselves questions, such as "What is my purpose in looking at this image?" Then students can identify questions they hope to answer, such as "What is being compared?" or "What are the most important features?"

✔ **Finding Answers** Next, students should use the graphic's features, such as the title, labels, colors, and symbols, to help them find answers to their questions. If the source of the graphic is available, students should also determine its reliability.

✔ **Drawing Conclusions** After studying the visual, students should summarize its main points and draw conclusions.

✔ **Connecting** Students also should relate what they learned from the visual with what they gained from reading the text selection. Students can examine how the visual supports or extends the meaning of the text.

Maps

Maps show the relative size and location of specific geographic areas. Two of the most common general purpose maps are political maps and physical maps.

Parts of Maps

All maps contain parts that assist in interpreting the information. Help students learn to identify the following map parts.

✔ **Title** The map title identifies the area shown on the visual. The title can also identify a map's special focus.

✔ **Map Key** The map key, or legend, explains the symbols presented on the map, thus unlocking the map's information.

✔ **Compass Rose** A compass rose is a direction marker. It is a symbol that points out where the cardinal directions—north, south, east, and west—are positioned.

✔ **Scale** A measuring line, often called a scale bar, indicates the relationship between the distances on the map and the actual distances on Earth.

✔ **Latitude and Longitude** Mapmakers use lines of latitude and longitude to pinpoint exact locations on maps and globes. The imaginary horizontal lines that circle the globe from east to west are lines of latitude, also called parallels. The imaginary vertical lines are lines of longitude, also called meridians. Both parallels and meridians are measured in degrees.

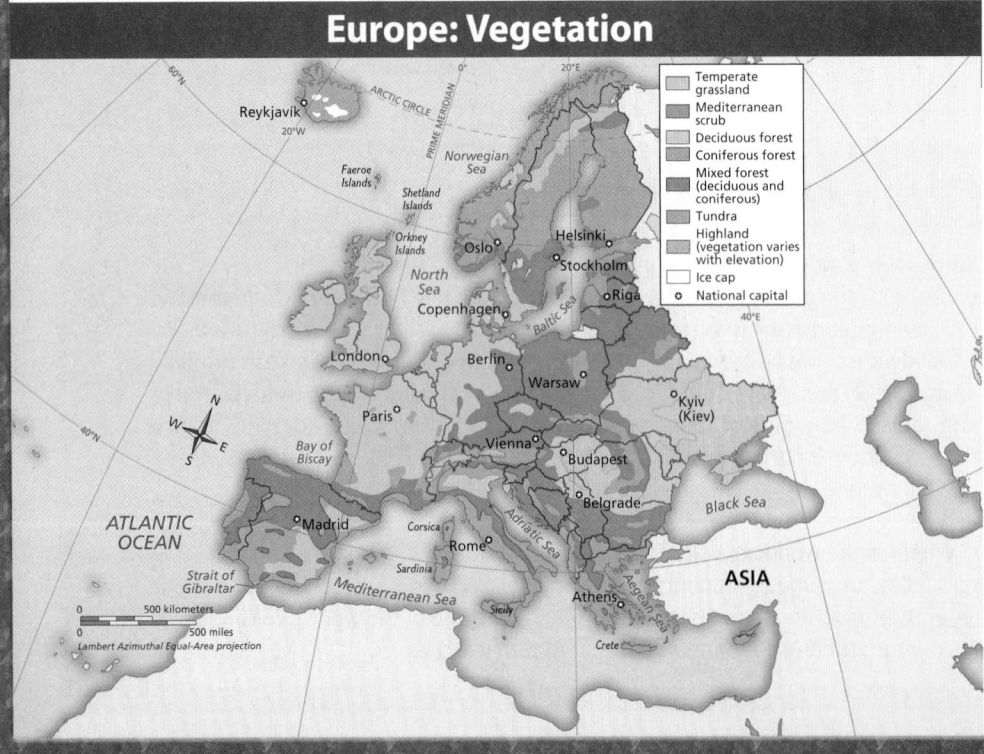

Europe: Vegetation

Temperate grassland
Mediterranean scrub
Deciduous forest
Coniferous forest
Mixed forest (deciduous and coniferous)
Tundra
Highland (vegetation varies with elevation)
Ice cap
○ National capital

Graphs

Graphs are a way of showing numbers or statistics in a clear, easy-to-read way. Because graphs summarize and present information visually, readers have an easier time understanding the data and drawing conclusions. The most common types of graphs are bar graphs, line graphs, circle graphs, and pictographs.

✔ **Bar Graphs** A bar graph shows how two or more subjects or statistics compare. It provides information along two sides or axes. The horizontal axis is the line across the bottom of the graph. The vertical axis is the line along the side. The bars may be either vertical or horizontal. In most cases the labels on one axis show quantity, while the labels on the opposite axis show the categories of data being compared.

✔ **Line Graphs** A line graph shows change over time. Like a bar graph, it organizes information along the horizontal and vertical axes. The horizontal axis usually shows passing time, such as months, years, or decades. The vertical axis usually shows quantity or amount. Sometimes more than one set of data is shown in a line graph. A double-line graph, for instance, plots data for two related quantities, which may be represented in different colors or patterns.

✔ **Circle Graphs** A circle graph, also called a pie graph, shows how each part or percentage relates to the whole. A circle graph enables a viewer to make comparisons between parts and to analyze the relationship of each part to the whole.

✔ **Pictograph** A pictograph uses rows of small symbols or pictures, each representing a particular amount. Like a bar graph, a pictograph is useful for making comparisons.

Charts

While all charts present information or data in a visual way, the type of chart is often dictated by the nature of the information and by the chart-maker's purposes.

✔ **Tables** Tables show information, including numerical data, in columns and rows. This organized arrangement facilitates comparisons between categories of information. Labels are usually located at the top of each column and on the left-hand side of the table.

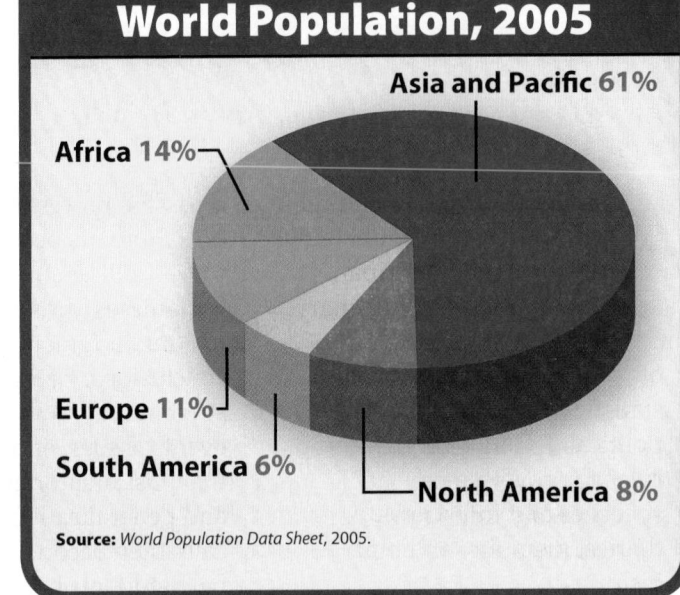

World Population, 2005

Asia and Pacific 61%

Africa 14%

Europe 11%

South America 6%

North America 8%

Source: *World Population Data Sheet*, 2005.

✔ **Diagrams** Diagrams are specialized drawings. They can show stages or steps in a process; point out parts of an object, organization, or idea; or show how something works. Arrows or lines may join parts of a figure and can show relationships between parts or the flow of sequential steps.

Classroom Activity

Create a Graph

Graphs can be difficult to interpret and understand. Help students by having them create their own graphs. First, separate students into small groups. Then have each group take a survey of classmates and make a graph to show their results. Suggest that students select a bar graph, line graph, circle graph, or pictograph to show their data. To prompt students' thinking, ask the following questions.

- *Do you play on a sports team? Which sport(s)?*
- *What do you plan to do after high school?*
- *About how much time do you spend watching TV each day? About how much time did you spend on TV when you were 10 years old? When you were 5 years old?*

After students have these graphs completed, invite each group to share its work. Discuss the types of graphs students made and their reasons for choosing them. Each group should then take the graph done by another group and transfer the information to another type of graph.

Primary Source Strategies

How Do I Use Primary Sources in My Classroom?

A primary source is an oral or written account obtained from actual participants in an event. Examples of primary sources include the following:

- ✔ official documents (records, statistics)
- ✔ political declarations, laws, and rules for governance
- ✔ speeches and interviews
- ✔ diaries, memoirs, and oral histories
- ✔ autobiographies
- ✔ recipes and cookbooks
- ✔ advertisements and posters
- ✔ letters
- ✔ physical objects such as tools, dishes, fine art, photographs, maps, films, and videotapes
- ✔ songs and audio recordings

Why Use Primary Sources in Your Classroom?

Using primary sources transforms the study of social studies from a passive process to an active one. Students become investigators—finding clues, formulating hypotheses, drawing inferences, making judgments, and reaching conclusions. Using primary sources, students can think critically about events, issues, and concepts rather than just memorizing dates, names, and generalizations. Thinking critically then becomes a habit that can help students become good citizens.

How Do I Introduce Students to Primary Sources?

Carefully explain the nature of primary sources to students. Alert students to the fact that primary sources contain biases and prejudices and must be approached with caution. Every primary source reflects the creator's point of view. Students must consider the authorship and why the primary source was originally written.

Choosing Primary Sources

Expose students to a variety of sources, including historical photographs, folk or popular music, financial records, letters, journals, and other historical documents.

When choosing print sources, consider the interests and reading levels of your students. Many texts contain challenging vocabulary and unfamiliar sentence structure. You may need to create a reader's guide that defines key vocabulary words and paraphrases the main points of the reading.

Some documents may be too long. Decide whether using an excerpt will provide enough information for students to draw conclusions. You also may need to provide different primary sources to expose students to a variety of perspectives.

Decide how students will access the primary sources: through the Internet, the library, a museum, or other print resources. Consider the possibility of an Internet virtual field trip for students. Students can visit museum sites and other Web pages to view artifacts, interpret data, and read journals, letters, and official documents.

Interpreting a Primary Source

Before students interpret a primary source, they need to know the source's context. Then they can use guidelines, such as those below, to help them analyze and interpret the primary source's content.

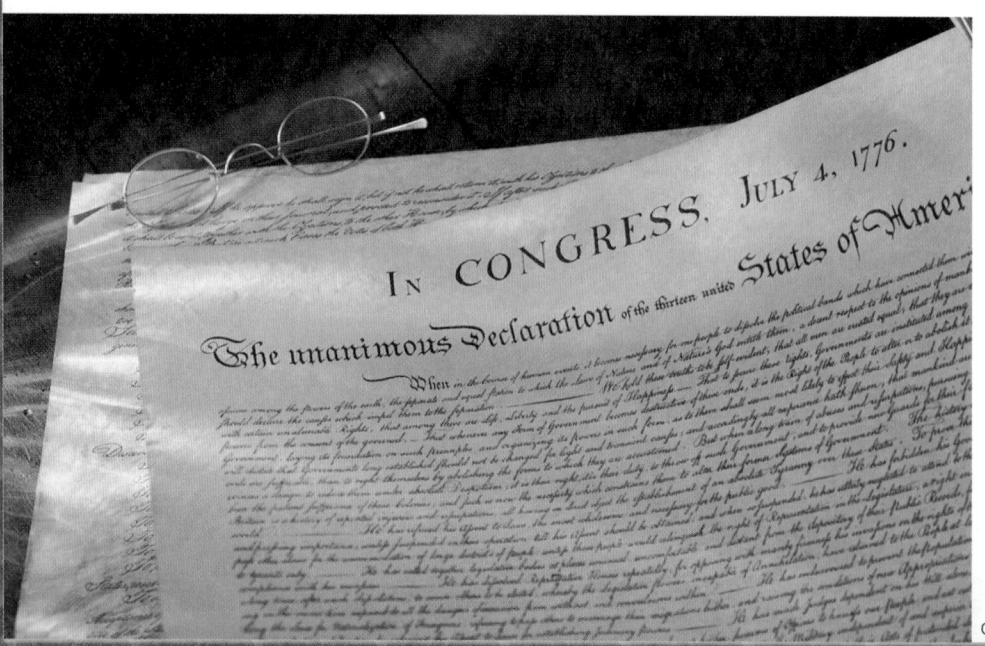

Comstock/PunchStock

Interpreting a Primary Source

Print Sources
- Who created the source, and what was the purpose for doing so?
- Did the writer personally experience or witness the event(s)?
- Who was the intended audience?
- Was the writer trying to record facts, express an opinion, or persuade others to take action?
- What bias does it reflect?
- What information about the topic can you gather from this document?
- Compare this document with what you already know about the topic. Does it confirm your ideas or introduce a new perspective?
- How might other accounts about this topic support or modify the message this source delivers?

Visual Sources
- Who created the source, and what was the purpose for doing so?
- What does the image show?
- Who or what dominates the image or catches your eye?
- How does the view impact the message the image conveys?
- What is excluded from view?
- What bias does the visual source reflect?
- What information about the topic can you gather from this visual?
- How might other visual images about this topic support or modify the message this one delivers?

Audio Sources
- Who created the source? What was the purpose for creating this source?
- What is the main idea of the audio message?
- What bias does the audio text reflect?
- What information about the topic can you gather from this audio source?
- Compare the information in this source with what you already know about the topic. Does it confirm those ideas or introduce a new perspective?
- How might other sources about this topic support or modify the message that this one delivers?

Exploring Information

Provide a variety of primary sources related to a topic or time period. Have students compare and contrast the items, analyzing the information, making inferences, and drawing conclusions about the period.

Prereading Activities

Present a primary source for students to study at the beginning of a new chapter or topic. Have students analyze the source, using the questions and guidelines presented above. Then have students make predictions about what they might learn in the upcoming lessons.

Evaluation Activities

Have students evaluate a primary source and tell how it supports or refutes what they learned in the textbook. Or have students read a primary source document that provides one perspective on a topic, and then have students write their own account, presenting another perspective or opinion.

Classroom Activity

Use this activity to explore the use of primary sources. This activity is especially beneficial when a less-proficient reader is paired with a more-proficient reader.
1. Before class make a list of student reading partners. Make sure one of the two is a good reader.
2. Have students read a primary source document, taking turns as they go. They should "mark" any words that they do not understand.
3. After each paragraph, the student pair should stop and restate what it says in their own words.
4. Students should look up unfamiliar words they've marked and create an illustrated dictionary entry for each term.
5. Ask student pairs to present their paraphrased primary source to the rest of the class.

Participating IN GOVERNMENT

Exploring the BIG IDEAS

Why does government matter? People fight and die for political beliefs. Governments influence the purity of the food you eat, your personal safety, your education, and your right to voice an opinion. The success of the United States as a representative democracy and a leading voice for freedom in the world depends on your positive and informed participation in government.

Find resources for each activity by visiting glencoe.com and entering the activity's *QuickPass*™ code.

Foundations *of* American Government

BIG IDEA **Comparative Government** Knowledge of other government types promotes an understanding of democracy.

Government Role Plays Divide into three groups to create three mini-productions demonstrating the key concepts of three government types: absolute monarchy, Soviet dictatorship, and the American republic. For each production, groups will divide activities as follows: a) Researchers and writers who will create a short script for the chosen government example (e.g., the absolute rule of the French king, Louis XIV); b) Actors for various roles (e.g., Madison and Hamilton discussing the early American republic); c) Production staff (e.g., a director or students to create a simple set).

Use *QuickPass*™ code USG9085c1T.

The Legislative Branch

BIG IDEA **Political Processes** The procedures for governing the nation on a daily basis are known as political processes.

Drafting a Proposal Draft a proposal with your classmates to revise your school's senior curriculum. The proposal should meet state standards or propose a realistic revision of them. All classmates should agree on the proposed changes. Separate groups will: a) Research state standards for your grade; b) Survey class opinions for ideas; c) Vote on a process for reaching agreement on one revision; and d) Polish and present a draft proposal for the administration.

Use *QuickPass*™ code USG9085c5T.

The Executive Branch

BIG IDEA **Federalism** American democracy functions through a sharing of power between the federal and state governments.

Researching Federal Implementation Identify a recent law in an area of your interest, such as college tuition grants; and identify the federal and state or local agencies that are involved in implementing the law. Present your findings to the class by creating a flow chart to illustrate this implementation.

Use *QuickPass*™ code USG9085c8T.

The Judicial Branch

BIG IDEA **Civil Rights** The U.S. Supreme Court functions to guarantee equality under the law.

Discussing a Supreme Court Case Use the format of high school debate to mimic the discussion and debate of Supreme Court justices as they deliberate on a case involving civil rights. Standard debate rules can be modified to achieve a sense of the way justices engage in debate to delineate a case's critical points.

Use *QuickPass*™ code USG9085c11T.

Liberty *and* Justice *for* All

BIG IDEA **Public Policy** Public policy can affect all branches of government, including the judiciary.

Simulating Sentencing In the American criminal justice system, guilty verdicts are followed by sentencing. A judge usually uses state guidelines to sentence a person. Sentencing can be controversial if the public believes a sentence is too harsh or lenient; thus, public policy can change sentencing rules. The class will divide into two groups. One person in each can be the sentencing judge, while others research sentencing rules or the crime. (Find a serious crime reported in newspapers.) One group will use standard sentencing rules, while the second will use an alternative method, such as the Three Strikes law.

Use *QuickPass*™ code USG9085c13T.

Participating *in* Government

BIG IDEA **Civic Participation** Understand why participating in campaigns, caucuses, and elections are basic to our democracy.

Organizing an Election Campaign Hold a mock election to gain insights into organizing a base of support, caucusing, and voting in an election. As a class, choose to hold an election for your class, local school board, congressional district, or a national presidential election. Select sets of candidates. The remaining part of the class will represent the electorate. Conduct the campaign and hold the election. Analyze the results.

Use *QuickPass*™ code USG9085c16T.

Public Policies *and* Services

BIG IDEA **Checks and Balances** Checks and balances operate when one branch of government uses its constitutional authority to affect the actions of another.

Analyzing GAO Functions The Government Accountability Office (formerly the Government Accounting Office) is a nonpartisan independent agency that works for Congress. It investigates and reports to Congress on how taxpayer dollars are spent. Explore a GAO report at the GAO Web site and summarize it for the class. (To make a full and complete report, conduct additional research at the extensive GAO site or other government Web sites.)

Use *QuickPass*™ code USG9085c20T.

State *and* Local Government

BIG IDEA **Cultural Pluralism** Understand how groups in our multicultural society organize to exercise their political power.

Grassroots Organizing A grassroots movement starts at the local level to get all groups active in a campaign to change the system. Grassroots campaigns typically have the goal of representing people from all ethnic, racial, and economic backgrounds—people who may often be left out of the political process because they are not part of an already well-established lobby like business or labor. As a class, agree on a reform achievable at the city or state level. Then lay out steps for a grassroots campaign.

Use *QuickPass*™ code USG9085c23T.

Political *and* Economic Systems

BIG IDEA **Global Perspectives** Understand why political and trade issues today are influenced by a new and broader context.

Visualizing Trade Arguments Debates over free trade continue to engage the public as global trade grows and nations like China and India flex their economic muscle. Divide into two teams. Each team will design storyboards for short television ads—one supporting NAFTA (North American Free Trade Agreement) and one against it. Each team should create eight storyboards that consist of one image per storyboard. Then each team should write accompanying narration.

Use *QuickPass*™ code USG9085c25T.

Foundations *of* American Government

UNIT PACING CHART*				
	Chapter 1	**Chapter 2**	**Chapter 3**	**Chapter 4**
Day 1	Unit Opener Chapter Opener Section 1	Chapter Opener Section 1	Chapter Opener Section 1	Chapter Opener Section 1
Day 2	Section 2	Supreme Court Cases to Debate	Section 2	Section 2
Day 3	Section 3 Supreme Court Cases to Debate	Section 3	Section 3 TIME Notebook	Section 3 Supreme Court Cases to Debate
Day 4	Section 4 Government Skills	Section 4 Government Skills	Section 4 Supreme Court Cases to Debate	Section 4 Supreme Court Cases to Debate
Day 5	Review Chapter Assessment	Review Chapter Assessment	Review Chapter Assessment	Review Chapter Assessment

*Unit Pacing Chart based on year-long course; modify pacing by half for semester-long course

 Teacher *to* Teacher

Benecia Tuthill

South Panola
Consolidated
School System
Batesville, MS

A Forum on Federalism Have one student act as a moderator for a forum on federalism. This student will give a description of the evolution of federalism.

Fourteen student panelists will answer several questions. Two students will answer each question, each presenting an opposing view.

- Should the federal government or the state governments be supreme?
- Was FDR justified in arguing that since the Great Depression was a national crisis, the solutions also needed to be national?
- Did FDR overstep the powers of the federal government in creating New Deal programs?

- Did FDR pave the way to our present-day welfare state, or does that credit lie with Lyndon Johnson?
- Do federal grants requiring matching funds cause state and local governments to spend money wastefully, or do the benefits of matching funds outweigh the costs?
- Should the decision to control grant money be left to the states or the federal government?
- What are the advantages and disadvantages of so-called marble cake federalism?

Author Note

Dear U.S. Government Teacher,

This unit lays the groundwork for the entire course in American government. The chapters of the unit cover two overarching themes:

- first, the origins of government and the basic purposes any government serves;
- second, the history of the American republic, its underlying constitutional principles, and the essential features of our federal system.

You may find that your students are eager to discuss current controversies or a recent election. Yet a student's ability to analyze a current political problem depends on an understanding of the principles of government and the U.S. Constitution. No matter what political or social issue faces us, the solution will be worked out through a political process that has proved itself over time. Will we retain a volunteer army? Should student loan funding be expanded? The final decision will be the product of a multifaceted process: citizens, lobbyists, legislators, and political leaders interacting within the federal system.

Federalism is certainly one of the most important features of American politics that students should understand. The subject is addressed at length in Chapter 4. The United States had the first federal system in the world, and it remains a distinctive part of our political process. The Founders intended for federalism to divide power between the states and the federal government. The tension that federalism creates between levels of government is one more way that the rights of individuals and of groups are protected.

Finally, the unit's overview of other types of governments and economies has particular relevance today. The global economy and international relations are more important than ever. The unit's overview on these topics will give you a point of departure for Chapters 25 and 26 that examine political and economic systems around the world.

Richard C. Remy

Richard C. Remy, Ph.D.
Author

Focus

Making It Relevant

Ask: How would you feel about running for political office? Explain. *(Answers will vary.)* Ask students if they would rather participate in national or state and local governments. Discuss students' opinions on the subject.

Unit Objectives

After studying this unit, students will be able to:

- **Discuss** the history and purpose of government.

- **Analyze** ideas and historical documents and events that shaped the U.S. Constitution.

- **Describe** structural features of the Constitution.

- **Explain** how the U.S. system of government is a federal one.

Unit Overview

Unit 1 provides a basic introduction to the foundations of American government.

Chapter 1 focuses on identifying the essential features of a state and describes theories about the origin of government and economic systems.

Chapter 2 discusses the weaknesses and achievements of the Articles of Confederation and the development of the Constitution.

Chapter 3 describes the structure of and the principles behind the Constitution.

Chapter 4 focuses on the development of national and state powers.

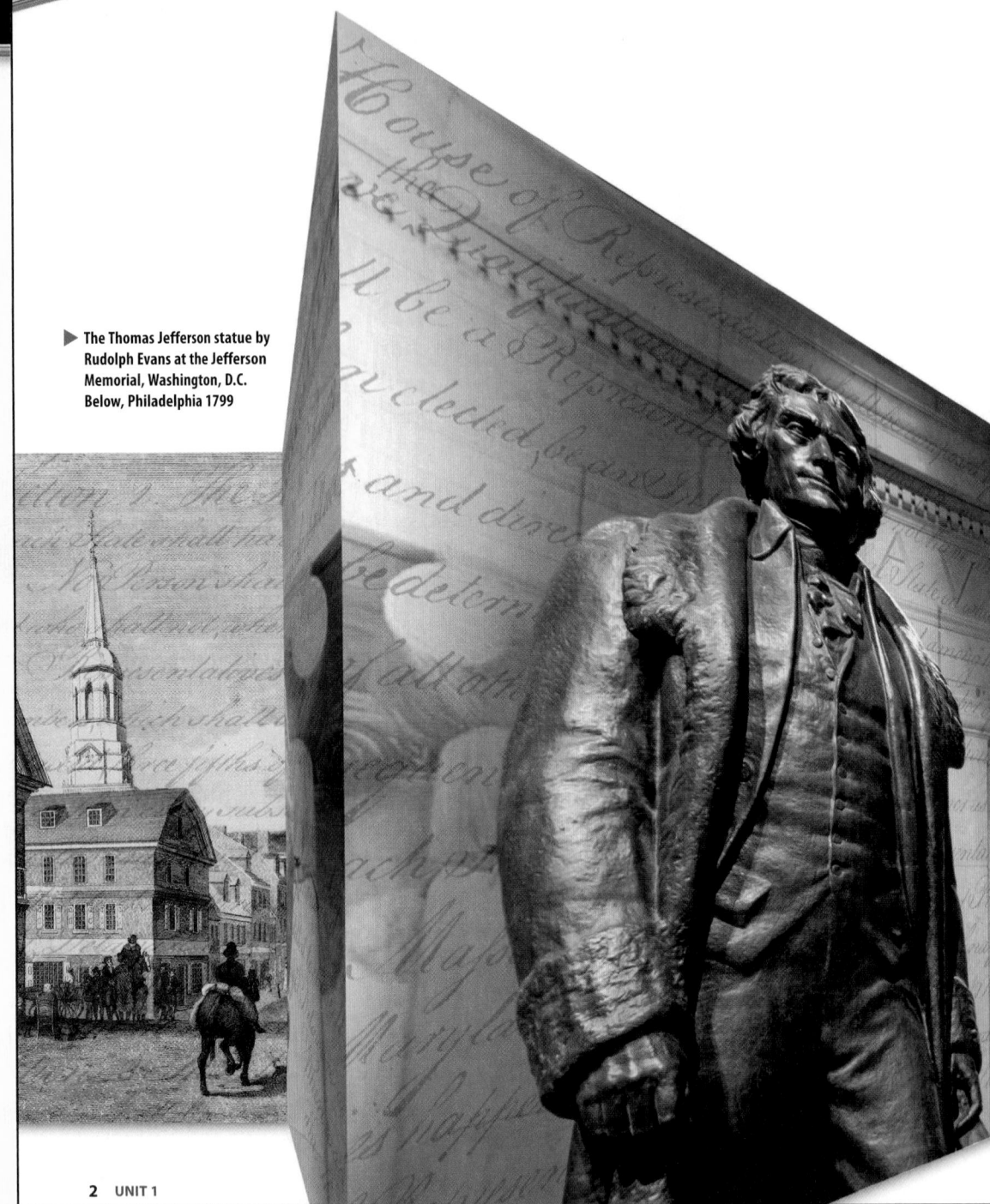

▶ The Thomas Jefferson statue by Rudolph Evans at the Jefferson Memorial, Washington, D.C. Below, Philadelphia 1799

2   UNIT 1

★ ★ ★ Activity: Launching the Unit ★ ★ ★

Analyzing Historical Documents Have students work cooperatively or individually to develop an illustrated handbook of documents on which the U.S. government is based. Suggest that students include such documents as the Magna Carta, Petition of Right, English Bill of Rights, Mayflower Compact, Fundamental Orders of Connecticut, Declaration of Independence, and Articles of Confederation. For each document, students should provide a summary of the most important provisions, a brief history of the document, and an explanation of its connection to the U.S. system of government. **OL**

Foundations *of* American Government

UNIT 1

Participating IN GOVERNMENT

BIG IDEA **Comparative Government** Follow news coverage online or on television of a foreign government that is not a democracy. Take notes on how this government functions, especially if it strikes you as different from the United States. Based on what you learn, create a table comparing the government of the United States and the country in question; use the table to stimulate a class discussion.

▲ Signing of the U.S. Constitution, 1787

3

Planning Guide

Key to Ability Levels
- **BL** Below level
- **OL** On level
- **AL** Above level
- **ELL** English Language Learners

Key to Teaching Resources
- Print Material
- CD-ROM or DVD
- Transparency

Levels					Resources	Chapter Opener	Section 1	Section 2	Section 3	Section 4	Chapter Assess
BL	OL	AL	ELL								
FOCUS											
BL	OL	AL	ELL	▣	Section Focus Transparencies		1-1	1-2	1-3	1-4	
TEACH											
BL	OL		ELL	📁	Reading Essentials and Study Guide (and Answer Key)		p. 1	p. 4	p. 7	p. 10	
BL	OL		ELL	📁	Guided Reading Activities		p. 1	p. 2	p. 3	p. 4	
BL	OL		ELL	📁	Vocabulary Activities		p. 1				
BL	OL	AL	ELL	📁	Chapter Summaries					p. 1	
BL	OL			📁	American Biographies				p. 28		
BL	OL	AL	ELL	📁	Cooperative Learning Activities						
	OL	AL	ELL	📁	Government Simulations and Debate		p. 1				
BL	OL	AL	ELL	📁	Historical Documents and Speeches					p. 4	
BL	OL	AL	ELL	📁	Interpreting Political Cartoons			p. 1			
BL	OL		ELL	📁	Skill Reinforcement Activities		p. 1				
BL	OL	AL	ELL	📁	Source Readings					p. 1	
BL	OL			📁	Supreme Court Case Studies				p. 61		
BL	OL	AL	ELL	📁	Participating in Government Activities				p. 1		
BL	OL		ELL	📁	Spanish Declaration of Independence and U.S. Constitution	✓	✓	✓	✓	✓	✓
BL	OL	AL	ELL	📁	NGS World Atlas, Spanish	✓	✓	✓	✓	✓	✓
BL	OL	AL	ELL	▣	Unit Overlay Transparencies, Strategies, and Activities	✓	✓	✓	✓	✓	✓
BL	OL		ELL	▣	Making It Relevant Transparencies	✓	✓	✓	✓	✓	✓
BL	OL	AL	ELL	▣	High School Writing Process Transparencies, Strategies, and Activities	✓	✓	✓	✓	✓	✓
BL	OL	AL		▣	American Art & Architecture Transparencies, Strategies, and Activities	✓	✓	✓	✓	✓	✓

✓ Chapter- or unit-based activities applicable to all sections in this chapter

Teacher Works™ Plus

All-In-One Planner and Resource Center

- Interactive Lesson Planner
- Interactive Teacher Edition
- Fully editable blackline masters
- Chapter Spotlight Videos Launch

- Differentiated Lesson Plans
- Printable reports of daily assignments
- Standards tracking system

Levels					Resources	Chapter Opener	Section 1	Section 2	Section 3	Section 4	Chapter Assess
BL	OL	AL	ELL								
TEACH *(continued)*											
BL	OL			⊙	American Music: Hits Through History	✓	✓	✓	✓	✓	✓
BL	OL		ELL	📁	Reading Strategies for the Social Studies Classroom	✓	✓	✓	✓	✓	✓
			ELL	📁	English Language Learner Handbook	✓	✓	✓	✓	✓	✓
BL	OL		ELL	📁	Writer's Guidebook for Social Studies	✓	✓	✓	✓	✓	✓
BL	OL	AL	ELL	📁	Living Constitution, SE	✓	✓	✓	✓	✓	✓
BL	OL	AL	ELL	📁	Living Constitution, TAE	✓	✓	✓	✓	✓	✓
BL	OL			📁	NGS World Atlas, English	✓	✓	✓	✓	✓	✓
BL	OL		ELL	📁	The Constitution and You (poster set)	✓	✓	✓	✓	✓	✓
BL	OL	AL	ELL	📁	Spanish Chapter Summaries					p. 1	
BL	OL	AL	ELL	📁	Spanish Vocabulary Activities		p. 1				
BL	OL		ELL	📁	Spanish Reading Essentials and Study Guide (and Answer Key)		p. 1	p. 4	p. 7	p. 10	
BL	OL	AL	ELL	⊙	PresentationPlus! with MindJogger CheckPoint	✓	✓	✓	✓	✓	✓
ASSESS											
BL	OL	AL	ELL	⊙	*ExamView® Assessment Suite*		1-1	1-2	1-3	1-4	Ch. 1
BL	OL	AL	ELL	📁	Authentic Assessment with Rubrics			p. 8			p. 8
BL	OL	AL	ELL	📁	Section Quizzes and Chapter Tests		p. 1	p. 2	p. 3	p. 4	pp. 5–12
BL	OL	AL	ELL	📁	Spanish Section Quizzes and Tests		p. 1	p. 2	p. 3	p. 4	pp. 5–12
CLOSE											
BL			ELL	📁	Reteaching Activities			p. 1			p. 1
BL	OL	AL	ELL	⊙	StudentWorks™ Plus with Audio Summaries	✓	✓	✓	✓	✓	✓
BL	OL		ELL	🖐	Graphic Organizer Transparencies		✓	✓	✓	✓	
BL	OL		ELL	📁	High School Government Reading and Study Skills Foldables®		p. 19	p. 19	p. 19	p. 19	

Teach with Technology

What is a QuickPass™ code?

A **QuickPass**™ code is a shortcut that takes students and teachers from glencoe.com directly to resources for each chapter in this book. You can enter a QuickPass™ code at glencoe.com or with the McGraw-Hill Social Studies widget.

How can a QuickPass™ code help my students and me?

A QuickPass™ code takes you directly to each chapter's resources. QuickPass™ codes in the Student Edition go directly to student resources, and codes in the Teacher Wraparound Edition go to teacher resources. The *T* at the end of the code indicates a teacher version.

Find a QuickPass™ code on the Chapter Opener pages of the textbook. Visit glencoe.com and enter a QuickPass™ code to go directly to resources for each chapter.

Government ONLINE

Visit glencoe.com and enter **QuickPass**™ code USG9085c1T for Chapter 1 resources.

You can easily launch a wide range of digital products from your computer's desktop with the McGraw-Hill Social Studies widget.

	Student	Teacher	Parent
Media Library			
• Student Edition Section Audio	●		●
• Chapter Spotlight Videos	●	●	●
***United States Government* Online Learning Center (Web Site)**			
• Chapter Overviews	●	●	●
• Multilingual Glossaries	●	●	●
• Study-to-Go	●	●	●
• Student Web Activities	●	●	●
• Self-Check Quizzes	●	●	●
• Online Student Edition	●	●	●
• Vocabulary eFlashcards	●	●	●
• Web Activity Lesson Plans		●	
• Vocabulary PuzzleMaker	●	●	●
• Landmark Supreme Court Cases	●	●	●
• Beyond the Textbook	●	●	●

READING SUPPORT FROM
JAMESTOWN EDUCATION

- **Timed Readings Plus in Social Studies** helps students increase their reading rate and fluency while maintaining comprehension. The 400-word passages are similar to those found on state and national assessments.

- **Reading in the Content Area: Social Studies** concentrates on six essential reading skills that help students better comprehend what they read. The book includes 75 high-interest nonfiction passages written at increasing levels of difficulty.

- **Reading Social Studies** includes strategic reading instruction and vocabulary support in Social Studies content for ELLs and native speakers of English. www.jamestowneducation.com

Reading List Generator CD-ROM

GLENCOE BOOKLINK 3

Use this database to search more than 30,000 titles to create a customized reading list for your students.

- Reading lists can be organized by students' reading level, author, genre, theme, or area of interest.

- The database provides Degrees of Reading Power™ (DRP) and Lexile™ readability scores for all selections.

- A brief summary of each selection is included.

Leveled reading suggestions for this chapter:

- from **"Civil Disobedience,"** by Henry David Thoreau
- *On Liberty,* by John Stuart Mill
- selected works of Marcus Tullius Cicero

Review suggested books before assigning them.

Economics Connection

Personal Finance Literacy

Starting a Business

A basic principle of capitalism is that anyone can start his or her own business and succeed or fail based on skill, perseverance, and/or market conditions. Teenagers start their own businesses every day. Five students at Baltimore's Digital Harbor High School, for example, received a $5,000 loan from a local bank to start a school store by presenting a business plan to the bank.

Some teen businesses provide spending money or help pay for college; some succeed and grow into permanent companies. Others fail financially but teach valuable business lessons.

Tell students: If you want to be your own boss, now is the perfect time to try it. Whatever the result, becoming an entrepreneur (a person who owns his or her own business) impresses college admissions officers and job interviewers. How do you start? Think of something you do or use. How could it be improved or made more convenient? Do you already have a skill or a job you could expand? Before you start, you will need a plan for your business. Here are some of the questions you will need to answer:

- What will you sell, and what need does it fill?
- Who are your potential customers, and how will you reach them?
- Why will people buy your product or service rather than a competitor's?
- How much should you charge?
- Where will you get the money to start your business?
- Are you willing to give up leisure time to run a business? Who will help you?

For ideas, advice, and stories about teenage entrepreneurs, check out the Web sites of the Small Business Administration and Junior Achievement.

Did You Know?

Elkhart Lake High School student Ian Abston started "2 Buff Guys," providing lawn care and handyman services. He and his partner netted nearly $10,000 one summer, and then hired more workers to keep up with the demand for subcontractors by established landscaping businesses.

Essential Question

Assessing Prior Knowledge
Refer students to the Essential Question on this page. Ask students to name some of the ways that governments are formed and write their responses on the board. Ask students to name specific contemporary or historical examples of such governments. Which ones would they describe as governments created *by* the people? Which ones were imposed *on* the people?

 Chapter Spotlight Video

To generate student interest and provide a springboard for class discussion, access the Chapter 1 Video at glencoe.com or on the video DVD.

FOLDABLES **Dinah Zike's**
Study Organizer **Foldables** are three-dimensional, interactive graphic organizers that help students practice basic writing skills, review key vocabulary terms, and identify main ideas. Have students complete this chapter's Foldable activity or activities in *Dinah Zike's Reading and Study Skills Foldables* booklet. **OL**

Government ONLINE
Visit glencoe.com and enter *QuickPass*™ code USG9085c1T for Chapter 1 Resources including Chapter Overview, Student Web Activity, Self-Check Quiz, and other materials for students and teachers.

CHAPTER

1

🔊 Chapter Audio   🎬 Spotlight Video

People *and* Government

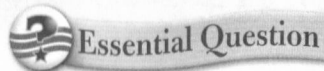

Fourth of July parade

Essential Question

What are the basic ways that governments are formed, and how do they serve the people who live under them?

Government ONLINE
Chapter Overview Visit glencoe.com and enter *QuickPass*™ code USG9822c1 for an overview, a quiz, and other chapter resources.

4   UNIT 1: *Foundations of American Government*

Launching the Chapter

Summarizing News Articles Have each student find a news article pertaining to some topic covered in the chapter, write a summary of the article, and explain how it relates to the chapter. Then have students write three questions that are answered in the article. Post students' articles, summaries, and questions on the bulletin board and have the class vote to choose the five that are most clearly related to the chapter. **Essential Question:** How does the information in the news article relate to the chapter? *(Answers will vary. Students should supply evidence to support their opinions.)* **OL**

Principles of Government

Reader's Guide

Content Vocabulary
* ★ state *(p. 5)*
* ★ sovereignty *(p. 6)*
* ★ nation *(p. 6)*
* ★ nation-state *(p. 6)*
* ★ consensus *(p. 6)*
* ★ government *(p. 8)*
* ★ social contract *(p. 8)*

Academic Vocabulary
* ★ philosopher *(p. 5)*
* ★ affect *(p. 6)*
* ★ theory *(p. 8)*

Reading Strategy
Use a circle diagram similar to the one below to help you take notes about the four essential features of a state.

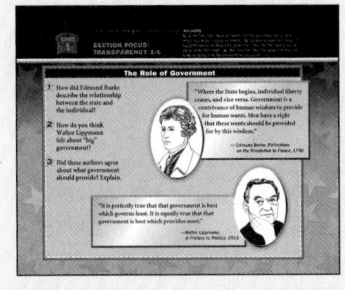
People in the News

For decades, older women have worked the polls on Election Day, but the tradition does not seem to have passed down to the next generation of wives and mothers. Many states and localities are having a harder time staffing the polls on election days. One of their solutions to filling the gap left by aging poll workers is to replace them with trained high school students 17 and older. In Columbus, Ohio, "Kids Vote," a civics education group, helped recruit the students. With the new touch-screen voting machines, teens' comfort level with technology has been a bonus. But the real bonus is civic participation. "They're really excited to know they can be involved in the process," said Joetta Bradley Gregory, a teacher at Columbus Africentric Secondary School.

▲ Students can be poll workers.

In 1972 for the first time, many 18-year-olds were allowed to vote. Since then, getting eligible young voters to exercise the franchise has been a concern. The "Kids Vote" project is just one of many that aim to do that. In a large country, it is not always easy to understand why voting is important or why and how government affects each person's life. People have asked questions about government for centuries. What is its proper function, and what form will work best? How did governments begin?

What Is the State?

The Greeks were the first serious students of politics and government. In the Western world, scholars look to the ancient Greek **philosopher** Aristotle. Aristotle, who famously wrote that "man is a political animal," carefully analyzed what he observed in society. For example, in a democracy:

> ❝ He who has the power to take part in the deliberative or judicial administration of any state is said by us to be a citizen of that state. ❞
>
> —*Politics II*, Aristotle

For Aristotle, the state meant the Greek city-state, the territory of a town and its surrounding area where face-to-face communication was possible. In the modern world, the word **state** identifies a political community in a precise territory.

Teach

C Critical Thinking

Predicting Consequences
Ask: Why did so many African Americans leave the South between 1941 and 1945? *(World War II created more job opportunities; factories that once refused to hire minorities began to drop such policies.)* **Ask:** How do you think this migration affected politics in this country? *(Students should mention an increase in African American political participation.)* **OL**

W Writing Support

Expository Writing Have students locate the terms *state*, *nation*, and *nation-state* in the text and ask someone to read the definition of each. Write the definitions on the board and review the characteristics of each. Have students write sentences using the terms. Ask volunteers to read their sentences. **BL**

Additional Support

Changing Population and State Power

◄ **Past** Between 1941 and 1945 more than 700,000 African Americans moved from one part of the United States to another seeking opportunity for a better life.

▼ **Present** As people seek a better life, the population of the United States changes, sometimes straining existing facilities, as illustrated in this overcrowded classroom in San Antonio, Texas.

Political Processes
How can shifting population affect the political power of the states?

A state has **sovereignty**—that is, its government makes and enforces its own laws without approval from any other authority. Many basic concepts of the Greeks came down to us through the Romans. The Romans had a republic, meaning the government was representative of certain groups, but it was not a democracy.

The United States is one of 193 sovereign states recognized by the United Nations. In the American context, state also refers to 50 states in our federal system. In 1776 when the thirteen American colonies declared independence, each thought of itself as being sovereign. They later joined together as one nation, but the term *state* survived to describe our main political units.

The term **nation** is often used for state, but strictly speaking, it means a sizable group of people who believe themselves united by common bonds of race, language, custom, or religion. In modern times, states have often been created by such groups, but not every citizen of a modern state shares this kind of identity. For example, although not all citizens of France are of French descent, the territories of both the nation of France and the state of France coincide. The term **nation-state** is often used for such a country.

Some national groups do not have a state but would like to have one. Some French-speaking Catholics of Quebec province, for example, would like to break away from Canada and its British heritage. Some African states are made up of several different nations or tribal groups. This blending in certain African states came about during the colonial era when Western imperialist nations drew the boundaries of areas they ruled. In most cases, the words *state*, *nation*, and *country* are used interchangeably.

Essential Features of a State

The states that make up today's political world share four essential features: population, territory, sovereignty, and government.

Population

The most obvious essential for a state is people. The nature of a state's population **affects** its stability. States where the people share a **consensus,** or agreement, about basic beliefs and values have the most stable governments. The United States is relatively stable because most Americans believe in a democratic system.

Another way that population affects a state and its activities is through its distribution. A state that is mostly urban is likely to have different policies than one that is mostly rural. Shifts in the population influence a state's political organization, too. In recent decades, millions of Americans have moved to Texas, California, Nevada, and Arizona, shifting political power from the

Activity: Collaborative Learning

Preparing a Teaching Booklet Ask: What are the four purposes of government? *(maintaining social order, providing public services, providing national security, and making economic decisions)* Have students work in small groups, each of which is to prepare a booklet for sixth graders that explains one of the four purposes of government. Some students should prepare the written expla-

nations, while others should find newspaper or magazine pictures that show examples of the chosen purpose. Students may also create illustrations. One student per group should be assigned as editor, to make sure students have used standard grammar, spelling, sentence structure, punctuation, and vocabulary that is appropriate to sixth graders. **OL**

Northeast to the Southwest. States that have lost population now have fewer representatives in Congress, while states with a growing population have gained representatives. At the local level, population shifts have also affected political life. The suburbs or exurbs (commuter towns beyond the suburbs) have more political clout than inner cities that have lost residents and businesses.

Territory

A state has established boundaries. The United States's continental boundaries are the Atlantic Ocean, the Pacific Ocean, and recognized borders with its two continental neighbors, Canada and Mexico. The exact location or shape of political boundaries is often a source of conflict among states. Territorial boundaries may change as a result of war, negotiations, or purchase. The territory of the United States, like that of some other states, has grown considerably since it declared independence. By purchase, negotiation, and war, the United States extended its territory to the Pacific Ocean.

Sovereignty

The key characteristic of a state is sovereignty. Political sovereignty means the state has supreme and absolute authority within its boundaries. It has complete independence and power to make laws, foreign policy, and determine its course of action. In theory, at least, no state has the right to interfere with the internal affairs of another state.

Because every state is considered sovereign, every state is equal with respect to legal rights and duties—at least in theory. In practice, of course, states with great economic strength and military capabilities have more power than other states.

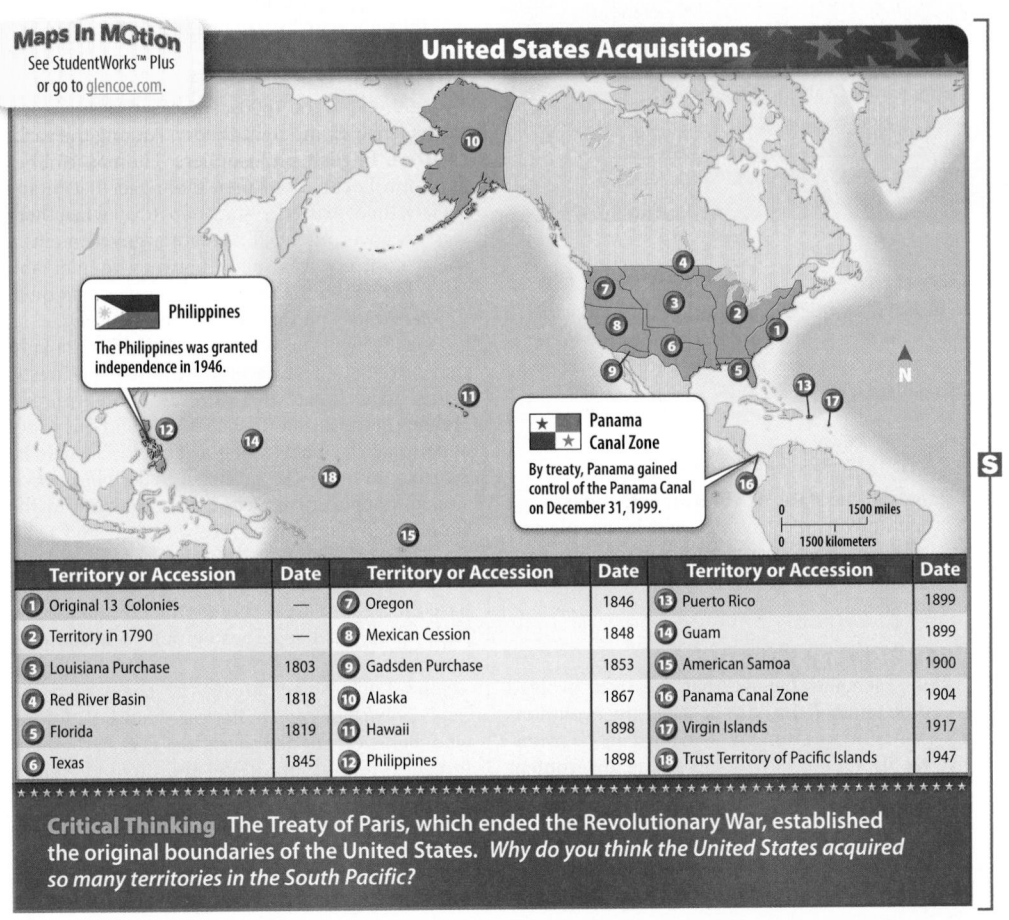

Maps In Motion See StudentWorks™ Plus or go to glencoe.com.

United States Acquisitions

Philippines The Philippines was granted independence in 1946.

Panama Canal Zone By treaty, Panama gained control of the Panama Canal on December 31, 1999.

Territory or Accession	Date	Territory or Accession	Date	Territory or Accession	Date
① Original 13 Colonies	—	⑦ Oregon	1846	⑬ Puerto Rico	1899
② Territory in 1790	—	⑧ Mexican Cession	1848	⑭ Guam	1899
③ Louisiana Purchase	1803	⑨ Gadsden Purchase	1853	⑮ American Samoa	1900
④ Red River Basin	1818	⑩ Alaska	1867	⑯ Panama Canal Zone	1904
⑤ Florida	1819	⑪ Hawaii	1898	⑰ Virgin Islands	1917
⑥ Texas	1845	⑫ Philippines	1898	⑱ Trust Territory of Pacific Islands	1947

Critical Thinking The Treaty of Paris, which ended the Revolutionary War, established the original boundaries of the United States. *Why do you think the United States acquired so many territories in the South Pacific?*

D Differentiated Instruction

English Learners Have students use magazines or newspapers to find evidence of the four essential features of a state. Students should look for photographs or illustrations to describe population, territory, sovereignty, and government. Below each illustration, have students write a sentence describing the nature and quality of the evidence they find. **ELL**

S Skill Practice

Using Geography Skills Refer students to the map on this page. **Ask:** In what year did the United States make the Gadsden Purchase? *(1853)* **BL**

Critical Thinking

Answer: Let students know that in the early 1800s, a high-pressure steam engine was developed. The United States acquired territories in the South Pacific to use as fueling stations for ships making the long journey across the ocean.

Additional Support

Activity: Economics Connection

Making Generalizations Have students select and investigate a particular benefit the federal government provides—national defense, environmental protection, aid to farmers, and so on. Ask students to research the costs of the benefit over the past 50 years and then use the figures they find to prepare a line graph. **Ask:** What generalizations can be made based on the graphs? *(Answers will vary. If possible, have all students use the same scale for their graphs so that comparisons can be made on spending for various purposes.)* **OL**

C Critical Thinking

Comparing and Contrasting Ask: What is the biggest difference between the social contract theory of Thomas Hobbes and that of John Locke? *(Hobbes believed that as long as a government maintained order and security in exchange for freedom, people had no right to rebel; Locke believed that a government should protect people's natural rights—life, liberty, and property. If it did not do so, the people were justified in rebelling.)* **OL**

CURRICULUM **CONNECTION**

Literature In William Golding's *Lord of the Flies* a group of schoolboys has crashed on a deserted island. Their attempts to set up a democratic society fail, and one boy, Jack, seizes power. Golding's premise that humans are fundamentally savage is revealed in Jack's brutal reign of terror.

Hands-On Chapter Project
Step 1

Creating a Nation

Step 1: Defining the Population
Students will decide on the population demographics of a theoretical nation.

Directions For the project, students will create a theoretical nation, decide on the characteristics of its population, and decide how it should be governed.

Divide the class into groups of four or five students. Tell them they will be creating a theoretical nation and must begin by

66 . . . and it is not without reason that [man] seeks out, and is willing to join in society with others . . . for the mutual preservation of their lives, liberties, and estates, which I call by the general name property. 99

—from Book II, Chapter 9,
Two Treatises of Government

Critical Thinking Locke suggested with these words one reason governments were formed. *Why did Locke think property motivated people to join into a society?*

Government

Government is the institution through which a state maintains social order, provides public services, and enforces decisions that are binding on all its residents.

Origins of the State

How did the state, or government, come to be? No one knows precisely how or why people created the earliest governments, but scholars have constructed **theories** to explain the origins of the state.

Evolutionary Theory

Some scholars believe that the state evolved from the family—this idea is called the evolutionary theory of government. The head of the primitive family supposedly served as the government authority. An extended family might include hundreds of people. Abraham's descendants in the Old Testament of the Christian Bible are given as an example of the theory. Gradually, it is theorized, the extended family needed more organization.

Force Theory

In early civilizations, people cooperated to survive. For example, they built walled cities to keep out enemies. Some scholars point to this behavior as proof that the state was born of force—that is, the state would not exist except for the need to resist an enemy. A state emerged when everyone in an area was brought under the authority of one person or group.

Divine Right Theory

The idea that certain people are chosen by a god or gods to rule is very old. The ancient Egyptians, Chinese, and Aztec believed that their rulers were descendants of gods or chosen by them. The term *divine right,* however, refers particularly to European monarchs in the 1600s and 1700s who proclaimed that their right to rule came from God alone. To oppose the monarch was to oppose God, and thus not only treasonous but sinful.

Social Contract Theory

Beginning in the 1600s, some Europeans began to challenge divine right theory. Among the earliest were English philosophers Thomas Hobbes and John Locke. Both men theorized that in any society, there existed a "state of nature" when there was no government. To create a government, a social contract was made between a ruler and the ruled. Hobbes and Locke, however, had quite different views on the terms of this contract.

Hobbes, who was writing in the 1650s, thought that in the state of nature, life would be "nasty, brutish, and short." In this often-quoted phrase, Hobbes emphasized his belief that without order and protection, no decent life of any kind would be possible. In the **social contract** that Hobbes envisioned, people surrendered their freedom to the state, but in return, they received order and security. Hobbes believed that as long as the government was maintaining order, the people did not have the right to break this contract. Claiming any such rights was dangerous because it would only lead to chaos.

John Locke lived during the time when the English Parliament challenged James II, a king who believed in divine right. The Parliament forced him out of office and invited Prince William and Mary of Orange to rule according to a constitution. In his writings, Locke defended Parliament's overthrow of the king. The reason? Unlike Hobbes, Locke thought that in the state of nature, men and women had certain natural

creating a profile of the demographics and characteristics of their nation.

Some of the characteristics they should determine include:

Is their country primarily urban or rural?

Is the population made up primarily of one ethnic group, or is it a multiethnic population with a large immigrant population? Is one dominant language spoken?

Is it a youthful or an aging population? What is the average age of its citizens?

On what is the economy based? Agriculture? Industry? Services?

Summarizing Have students create graphs and charts representing the characteristics of their nation. Encourage students to add other defining characteristics that they consider important. **OL**

(Chapter Project continued in Section 2.)

rights—the rights to life, liberty, and property. As he explained in the *Two Treatises of Government* (1690):[1] 📖

   ❝ *Men being, as has been said, by nature, all free, equal, and independent, no one can be put out of this estate, and subjected to the political power of another, without his own consent. The only way whereby any one divests himself of his natural liberty, and puts on the bonds of civil society, is by agreeing with other men to join and unite into a community. . . .* ❞

               —John Locke, 1690

Locke's social contract was made between the people and a government that promised to preserve these natural rights. According to Locke, if it did not do so, the people were justified in rebelling. Nearly a century later, the American colonies revolted against King George III, citing Locke's political philosophy of natural rights.

Purposes of Government

Modern governments have several functions:
- to maintain social order
- to provide public services
- to provide security and defense
- to provide for the economy

To fulfill these functions, governments make rules that everyone must follow—and they have the authority to punish those who do not follow them.

Governments derive their authority from two sources—their legitimacy and their ability to use force. Legitimacy means the willingness of citizens to obey the government. In democratic countries, legitimacy is based on the consent of the people as expressed through the vote. Americans know that if their elected officials fail to respond to their interests, they can be voted out of office. Therefore, the people trust their government with power.

📖 *See the following footnoted materials in the* **Reference Handbook:**
1. *Two Treatises of Government, page R74.*

R

R **Reading Strategy**

Taking Notes Have students create a chart listing the four bulleted points on the page and then list government functions under the appropriate heading. **BL**

Government *and* You

More About Government in Daily Life In the last few decades, state and federal governments have passed laws aimed at protecting Americans' health. Examples are the Clean Water Act of 1987, which authorized spending $18 billion through 1994 for the construction of sewer plants and cleanup of toxic "hot spots," and the Beach Program, which was established in 1997 to detect harmful contaminants in the water of the nation's beaches. Information about the water quality at beaches and potential health risks is available on the Beach Watch Internet site.

Additional Support

Government *and* You

Government in Daily Life

Government is much closer than the officials working in Washington, D.C., your state capital, or even city hall. Many things that Americans take for granted result from services and protections offered by government.

The roads on which you drive are constructed and maintained by state and/or local governments. Traffic laws dictate how you drive on those roads. When you go to the store, government regulations make it likely that the groceries you buy will not poison you. Your hairstylist and dentist are expected to be skilled professionals because government licenses them and sets minimum standards. Turn on your radio or TV. The program you receive will be clear because government prevents stations from interfering with each other's signals. All in all, the presence of government in daily life is greater than you may think.

▶ Ensuring traffic safety

Participating IN GOVERNMENT ACTIVITY

Solving Problems Assume you serve on your city council. A group of citizens has petitioned the city to change the speed limit on all nonresidential streets from 35 mph to 50 mph. Brainstorm the advantages and disadvantages of each alternative and how it would affect citizens. Recommend what speed limit should be in effect and why.

Activity: Interdisciplinary Connection

Health Have students find out about the many ways in which government, especially the federal government, is involved in public health and safety. Students may present their findings in chart form or as a written report. Some students may wish to take a historical approach to the subject to find out what conditions prompted government involvement. (A common example is the history of meatpacking regulation, but many others can be found.) Other students may investigate conditions in countries in which the government is less involved in health and safety. **OL**

Linking Past & Present

During the Great Depression, President Franklin D. Roosevelt delivered weekly radio addresses that became known as fireside chats. In his address of September 30, 1934, Roosevelt quoted Abraham Lincoln's words about the "legitimate object of government." The main point of his speech was to drum up support for the New Deal, specifically for the National Recovery Administration (NRA). The NRA was created to bring about economic recovery, which it failed to do.

Caption Answer: He says their gills are gummed and they'll have to "walk on their fins and get woefully weary."

Government ONLINE

Objectives and answers to the Student Web Activity can be found in the **Web Activity Lesson Plan** at glencoe.com. Enter **QuickPass**™ code USG9085c1T.

Differentiated Instruction

Fire on the Cuyahoga River, November 2, 1952

Providing Services Government enacts laws to help fight pollution and prevent disasters such as this fire on the Cuyahoga River and Lake Erie. Dr. Seuss's *The Lorax* referred to the problem:

You're glumping the pond where the Humming-Fish hummed
No more can they hum, for their gills are all gummed
So I'm sending them off. O their future is dreary
They'll walk on their fins and get woefully weary
In search of some water that isn't so smeary
I hear things are just as bad up in Lake Erie.

How does Dr. Seuss dramatize pollution's effect on fish?

Force, the second source of government authority, derives from certain institutions of the state: the police, the judiciary, and the military. The government can force people to pay taxes and can punish offenders by imposing fines or imprisonment.

Maintaining Social Order

According to the social contract theory, people need government to maintain order because human groups do not know how to live in peace. There are many sources of conflict. Two neighbors may argue over their property lines or parents may argue about policies at a PTA meeting. In any group, some will try to take advantage of others. Conflict seems to be an inescapable part of life.

Governments provide ways of resolving conflicts among people, thus helping to maintain social order. Governments also make and enforce laws. They can require people to do things they might not do voluntarily, such as pay taxes or serve in the army. Governments also provide the structures that are necessary to help resolve disagreements in an orderly process. The judicial system is the prime example of this function.

Without government, civilized life would be impossible. Government controls and contains conflict between people by placing limits on what individuals are permitted to do. Government provides a group with law and order. An effective government allows citizens to plan for the future, get an education, raise a family, and live orderly lives.

Providing Public Services

One of the obvious functions of government is to provide the services that no one person could provide. Abraham Lincoln described this function in these words:

The legitimate object of government, is to do for a community of people, whatever they need to have done, but cannot do, at all, *or can not so well do, for themselves—in their separate, and individual capacities. In all that people can individually do for themselves, government ought not to interfere.*

—Abraham Lincoln, 1854

Providing essential services is an important purpose of government that makes community life possible and promotes the general welfare. Building sewer systems, laying utility lines, paving roads and creating a water supply system are examples of government projects that individuals could not or would not do on their own.

Government ONLINE

Student Web Activity Visit glencoe.com and enter **QuickPass**™ code USG9822c1. Click on Student Web Activity and complete the activity about principles of government.

Leveled Activities

BL Guided Reading Activities, p. 1

OL Interpreting Political Cartoons, p. 1

AL Source Readings, p. 1

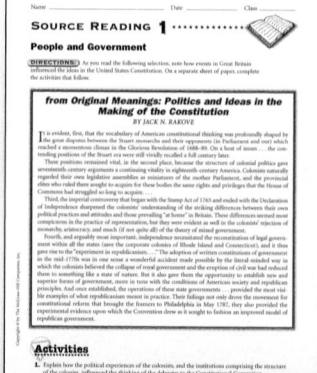

ELL Vocabulary Activities, p. 1

Many other government services promote public health and safety. For example, government inspectors enforce housing codes, check meat, and oversee restaurant operations. State legislators pass laws that require drivers to pass a driving test.

Providing National Security

A third task of government is to protect the people against attack by other states or from threats such as terrorism. Protecting its national security is a major concern of each sovereign state. In today's world of nuclear weapons, spy satellites, international terrorists, and huge armies, it is a complex and demanding task to provide for the safety of a nation's citizens.

In addition to protecting the nation from attack, government handles the day-to-day relations with other nations. The U.S. Constitution gives the federal government a monopoly over the nation's relations with foreign countries. Thus, the federal government has the exclusive power to make treaties with other nations.

Government helps provide economic security by signing trade agreements with other countries. Some state governments have informal relations with other nations to increase their trade or cultural exchange, but the national government can place limitations on these relations.

Making Economic Decisions

Nations vary greatly in their ability to provide their citizens with economic opportunities or resources. No country provides its citizens with everything they need or desire. Even in a wealthy country like the United States, many people are poorly clothed, housed, and fed. The problem of scarcity is far greater in many other nations.

Throughout history, poverty and scarce resources have been a basic cause for conflict in a society or between countries. When the income gap between social groups is great, civil conflict is likely. Poverty has also contributed to full-blown revolutions. Leaders understand this, so they often try to reduce economic conflict by intervening in the economic system.

Governments do not intervene only in domestic crises. They might intervene in the economic affairs of another nation to promote their own national security. After World War II, the United States funded the Marshall Plan because it was worried that economic distress would lead to Communist revolutions.

In all nations, governments pass the laws that shape the economic environment. These laws could be as limited as providing a national currency or as broad as controlling individual economic decisions.

Governments also make choices that distribute benefits and services among citizens. For example, the government can make payments to farmers who raise certain crops or allow tax advantages to certain industries. The government's decision to build a veterans' hospital in a certain town benefits some people but not others. Governments usually try to stimulate economic growth and stability by controlling inflation, encouraging trade, and regulating the development of natural resources.

CHAPTER 1, SECTION 1

R Reading Strategy

Identifying Ask: What are some economic decisions that a government must make? *(when to intervene to avoid economic conflict—both domestically and abroad; how to distribute benefits and services)* **Why have poverty and scarce resources historically led to conflict?** *(Students may mention that when there are not enough resources, people become impoverished and may need to fight for the resources they need.)* **AL**

Assess

Assign the Section 1 Assessment as homework or as an in-class activity, or have students take Section Quiz 1–1 from *Section Quizzes and Chapter Tests*.

Close

Making Generalizations Have students read Lincoln's quote on page 10. **Ask: Have popular attitudes toward government changed since Lincoln's time? Why or why not?** *(Students should note that many people, especially political conservatives today, would agree with Lincoln's statement.)* **OL**

Section 1 Review

SECTION 1 Review

Vocabulary

1. **Explain** the significance of: state, sovereignty, nation, nation-state, consensus, government, social contract.

Main Ideas

2. **Summarizing** What are the divine right and social contract theories?

3. **Describing** How can one sovereign state have more power and influence compared to another state?

Critical Thinking

4. **Making Comparisons** Hobbes and Locke subscribed to the social contract theory of government. Analyze their views of that theory.

5. **Organizing** In a graphic organizer similar to the one below, identify four major purposes of government and give an example of each.

Purpose	Example

Writing About Government

6. **Descriptive Writing** Read news articles concerning decisions made by foreign governments. Classify those decisions that you believe are making life better for their citizens and those you believe are making life worse.

CHAPTER 1: *People and Government* 11

Answers

1. All definitions can be found in the section and the Glossary.
2. The divine right theory holds that the state comes from a god and that rulers are descended from or chosen by a god. The social contract theory says people give power to the state so the state may preserve order and rights.
3. States with great economic strength and military capabilities have more power than other states.
4. Both believed that people surrendered to the state the power needed to maintain order, but Locke believed that people had the right to break that contract when government failed to preserve the rights of the people. Hobbes did not believe the people had that right.
5. Answers might include: maintain social order—police and courts; provide public services—highways and firefighters; provide national security—army and navy; establish and regulate an economic system—banks and currency.
6. Students should be able to defend their classifications.

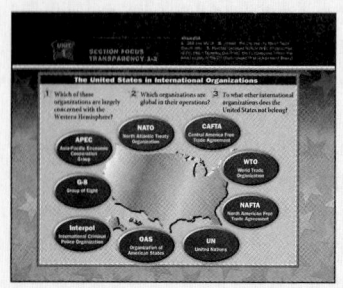
The Formation of Governments

Reader's Guide

Content Vocabulary
- ★ unitary system (p. 12)
- ★ federal system (p. 13)
- ★ confederacy (p. 13)
- ★ constitution (p. 13)
- ★ constitutional government (p. 13)
- ★ preamble (p. 14)
- ★ constitutional law (p. 14)
- ★ politics (p. 14)
- ★ industrialized nation (p. 16)
- ★ developing nation (p. 16)

Academic Vocabulary
- ★ goal (p. 14)
- ★ amend (p. 14)
- ★ benefit (p. 15)

Reading Strategy
Use a graphic organizer similar to the one below to identify the causes and results of interdependence among nations.

Causes		Results
	→	

Issues in the News

The headline for an article on the European Union read, "EU Federal Superstate Becoming a Reality." In the article, reporter Steve Watson was writing about a proposed constitution for the EU. The proposed constitution would make the EU much more than an economic pact—this was how the organization originated in the 1950s. According to Watson, under the proposed constitution, the EU would have primacy over the laws of individual countries—an upsetting prospect for many nationalists. "This means that were it to be implemented, countries would lose control of foreign policy and defence [defense] and would be stripped of their sovereign power to legislate in almost all areas of national life."

▲ Slovenia's Dimitrij Rupel, who served on the Council of the European Union with Condoleezza Rice, U.S. Secretary of State

The EU debate highlights some of the basic questions a nation faces when it decides on a constitution. Each nation has certain characteristics stemming from its history and so may have different goals. All governments, however, must organize to carry out their functions. Most large countries have several levels of government—a central or national government, as well as smaller divisions such as states, counties, and towns.

Government Systems

The relationship between a nation's central government and its smaller government divisions can be described as either a unitary system or a federal system. The differences are discussed in this section.

Unitary System

A **unitary system** of government gives all key powers to the central government. This does not mean that only one level of government exists, but rather that the central government is the unit with the power to create state, provincial, or other local governments. It may also limit their sovereignty. Great Britain, Italy, and France developed unitary governments when they emerged from smaller kingdoms. Other states employed a system of government based on shared powers.

Federal System

A **federal system** of government divides the powers of government between the national and state or provincial government. Each level of government has sovereignty in some areas. The United States developed a federal system after the thirteen colonies became states.

To begin with, the United States formed a **confederacy,** or confederation—a loose union of independent states. When the confederacy failed to provide an effective national government, the Constitution made the national government supreme while preserving some powers for the state governments. Today, other countries with federal systems include Canada, Switzerland, Mexico, Australia, India, and Russia.

Constitutions and Government

A **constitution** is a plan that provides the rules for government. A constitution serves several major purposes: (l) it sets out ideals that the people bound by the constitution believe in and share, (2) it establishes the basic structure of government and defines the government's powers and duties, and (3) it provides the supreme law for the country. Constitutions provide rules that shape the actions of government and politics, much as the rules of basketball define the action in a basketball game.

Constitutions may be written or unwritten; however, in most modern states, constitutions are written. The United States Constitution, drawn up in 1787, is the oldest written constitution still serving a nation today. Other nations with written constitutions include France, Kenya, India, and Italy. Great Britain, on the other hand, has an unwritten constitution based on hundreds of years of legislative acts, court decisions, and customs.

All governments have a constitution in the sense that they have some plan for organizing and operating the government. In this sense, the People's Republic of China has a constitution. The term **constitutional government,** however, has a special meaning. It refers to a government in which a constitution has authority to place clearly recognized limits on the powers of those who govern. Thus, constitutional government is *limited* government. Despite having a written constitution, the People's Republic of China does not have constitutional government. In that country, there are

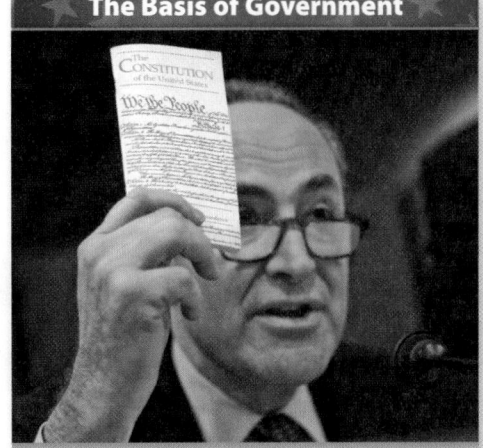

The Basis of Government

Making a Point Senator Charles Schumer (D-N.Y.) holds a copy of the U.S. Constitution. *How is the United States Constitution different from other countries' constitutions?*

few limits on the powers of the government. The same was true for the former Soviet Union.

Incomplete Guides

Constitutions are important but incomplete guides to how a country is actually governed. They are incomplete for two reasons. First, no written constitution can possibly spell out all the laws, customs, and ideas that grow up around the document. In the United States, for example, until Franklin D. Roosevelt was elected president four times, it was custom, rather than law, that no person should be elected president more than twice. Only when the Twenty-second Amendment went into effect was a president limited by law to two elected terms.

Second, a constitution does not always reflect actual government practice. The People's Republic of China, for example, has a written constitution filled with statements about the basic rights, freedoms, and duties of citizens. Yet, for years the Chinese government has maintained an extensive police force to spy on Chinese citizens. Citizens whose ideas are not acceptable to the state are punished. The government relaxed some restrictions in the late 1980s, but authorities crushed a pro-democracy movement in 1989. Tensions continue between pro-democracy forces and the state.

Teach

C Critical Thinking

Making Connections Have students speculate about why it might be important for a country to have a written constitution. Write their ideas on the board. **Ask:** What might happen if a country does not have a written constitution? *(Laws would not be consistent, the government might assume too much power, and the people would not know their civil rights.)* OL

Caption Answer: It is the oldest written national constitution, and as such, a model for many other nations.

 James Madison (1751–1836)

As the primary designer of the Virginia Plan, upon which the Constitution is based, Madison became an important member of the Constitutional Convention. He also kept diligent records of the proceedings. Published 50 years after the convention, his notes provide the main source of information about the convention.

Additional Support

Activity: Collaborative Learning

Taking Part in Politics Organize the class into small groups, each of which is to choose a local issue or benefit that they believe the government should provide, such as constructing a new playground or ballfield, widening a narrow road, or installing a traffic light at a dangerous intersection. Have some group members prepare a position statement explaining why action is needed. Others should research the probable costs of the project and suggest sources of revenue to pay for these costs. Students also should design and make posters in support of the cause. Have a representative from each group present the project to the rest of the class. BL

R Reading Strategy

Reading Primary Sources
Have students read and discuss Breaking Precedent at the top of the page. Ask students to examine the poster. **Ask:** What is this poster implying? (*Uncle Sam does not like the idea of third terms, implying it is un-American.*) **Ask:** What does the fact that this poster represents the views of Democrats suggest about popular opinion about third terms? (*Even within political parties there was controversy about how long one person should lead the nation.*) **AL**

D Differentiated Instruction

English Learners Ask students to read the Preamble of the U.S. Constitution. Help them with any vocabulary words they may find difficult. Then have them identify which purpose of government is most important to them personally. **ELL**

Differentiated Instruction

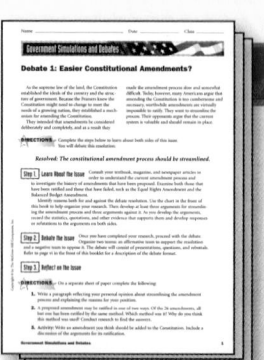

Government Simulations and Debates p. 1

Breaking Precedent

Constitutional Interpretations
Wendell Lewis Willkie became the Republican nominee for president in 1940 when Franklin D. Roosevelt ran for an unprecedented third term. Roosevelt violated George Washington's precedent that limited presidents to two terms. *How did George Washington's precedent reflect the idea of limited government?*

A Statement of Goals

Most constitutions contain a statement that sets forth the **goals** and purposes that the government will serve. This statement is called the **preamble.** The Preamble to the U.S. Constitution lays out the major goals for the government of the United States:

> 66 *We the people of the United States, in Order to form a more perfect Union, establish Justice, insure domestic Tranquility, provide for the common defence [defense], promote the general Welfare, and secure the Blessings of Liberty to ourselves and our Posterity, do ordain and establish this Constitution for the United States of America.* 99
> —Preamble to the Constitution, 1787

A Framework for Government

The main body of a constitution sets out the plan for government. In federal states, such as the United States, the constitution also describes the relationship between the national government and state governments. Most written constitutions also describe the procedure for **amending,** or changing, the constitution.

The main body of a constitution is usually divided into parts, called articles and sections. The U.S. Constitution has 7 articles containing a total of 21 sections. The French constitution has 89 articles grouped under 16 titles. The Indian constitution, the longest in the world, consists of hundreds of articles.

The Highest Law

A constitution provides the supreme law for a state. It is usually accepted as a morally binding force, drawing its authority from the people or from an assembly chosen by the people. **Constitutional law** is the field of law that studies questions on how to interpret the Constitution—how far government power extends, for example.

Politics and Government

The effort to control or influence the conduct and policies of government is called **politics.** The Constitution did not prevent the development of politics because politics and government are closely related. In fact, a major political struggle developed over the ratification of the Constitution. Within a few years, major political parties played key roles in elections.

People are taking part in politics when they join a citizens' group protesting higher taxes or when they meet with the mayor to ask the city to repave the streets in their neighborhood. Legislators are acting politically when they vote to have government buildings constructed in the districts they represent.

Seeking Government Benefits

People participate in politics because they realize that government has the potential to influence their lives in many ways. Different individuals and different interest groups make different demands on government. Construction workers may want government to support the building of new highways to create jobs. Conservationists may

---

Easier Constitutional Amendments?

Objective: To understand the process for amending the U.S. Constitution

Focus: Assign students Step 1: "Learn More About the Issue."

Teach: Choose a moderator and proceed with the debate (Step 2).

Assess: Evaluate students' performances in the debate.

Close: Have students complete Step 3, "Reflect on the Issue."

Differentiated Instruction Strategies

BL Have students debate whether it is too hard to amend the Constitution.

AL Have students research a proposed amendment and decide if the process for amendments is working.

ELL Ask students to diagram the two procedures for amending the Constitution.

want the government to spend its money on mass transit and public parks instead. Others who favor lower taxes may want neither the new highways nor more public parks.

In a large, diverse nation like the United States, a continual struggle occurs over what **benefits** and services government should provide, how much they should cost, and who should pay for them. Through politics, individuals and groups seek to maximize the benefits they get from government while they try to reduce the costs of these benefits. Through politics, people also seek to use government to turn their values and beliefs into public policy. One group, for example, tries to influence government to ban smoking in public places. Other people pressure government not to restrict smoking in any way.

Importance of Politics

Through politics, conflicts in society are managed. As people seek rewards and benefits, politics provides a peaceful way for them to compete with one another and come up with compromises that everyone can accept. The outcomes of politics—the struggle to control government—affect such key matters as the quality of air and water, economic conditions, peace and war, and the extent of citizens' rights and freedoms.

Special Interests

The Constitution states that the government should promote the *general* welfare, that is, the welfare of the society as a whole. The Framers believed government should operate in the interests of *all* the people and not favor any special group or person.

One important issue that concerned the Framers was the possibility that groups of people, united by special political interests, would hinder the launching of the new government. James Madison explained his concerns in a series of articles called *The Federalist*:

> 66 *Among the numerous advantages promised by a well constructed Union. . . [is] its tendency to break and control the violence of faction. . . . By a faction, I understand a number of citizens . . . who are united and actuated [moved] by some common impulse of passion, or of interest, adverse to the rights of other citizens, or to the permanent and aggregate interests of the community.* 99
> —James Madison, 1787

Some people equate politics with bribery or corruption. They believe the general welfare may be sacrificed to the desires of a special-interest group. The misuse of politics, however, should not obscure the value of a political system.

We the People
Making a Difference

Laura Epstein did not plan to stir her community to action when she spent the summer of 1996 with a paintbrush. She and eight other young people only wanted to paint over graffiti-covered walls to help beautify downtown Seattle.

Working with Seattle's waste department, Laura and her team painted murals on many of the city's graffiti-covered walls. Laura was surprised when the graffiti-erasing campaign turned into a creative project for the community. "That was the best part—having the neighborhood kids help us paint and get involved," she said, adding that kids can say, "Hey, I helped make that!"

The anti-graffiti project is just one of hundreds of projects being carried out by teams who are members of the Youth Volunteer Corps of America (YVCA). The federal government funds YVCA to give young people a way to get involved in their communities.

"Hey, I helped make that!"
—Laura Epstein

W Writing Support

Persuasive Writing Have students read James Madison's essay No. 10 from *The Federalist*. (See pp. R80–R81 for a longer excerpt.) Have students write a letter to Madison, explaining why they do or do not agree with his philosophy. Suggest that they incorporate present-day examples to support their point of view. **AL**

We the People
Making a Difference

Laura Epstein The YVCA is just one of many programs for young volunteers. In Boston, for example, young people can volunteer for City Year, a program whose aim is to carry on the legacy of the civil rights movement. Youths of all ethnic backgrounds can earn $100 per week from September to June by cleaning parks and playgrounds, planting trees, working as teachers' aides, and staffing after-school programs for children. At the end of the service, they receive a $5,000 award in the form of a scholarship or savings certificate.

Activity: Ask students to consider creating programs that are similar to the YVCA. **OL**

Hands-On Chapter Project
Step 2

Creating a Nation

Step 2: Deciding on the Government's Functions Students will decide on the functions and duties for which their government is responsible.

Directions Students will need to decide what functions their government will perform. Groups should take into account their country's demographics and characteristics as they prepare a detailed list of the various responsibilities of their government. (If they have a young population, for example, they need to consider how they will educate their children.)

Have students consider the various functions of government discussed in Section 1 (maintaining social order, providing public services, providing national security, and making economic decisions). Then have each group prepare an annotated list that explains how their government will address these various needs.

Summarizing Groups should now have a well-developed profile of their society and the type of government it needs. **OL**

(Chapter Project continued in Section 3.)

W Writing Support

Expository Writing In addition to the global links provided by multinational corporations, links also result from international sporting events and organizations. Probably the best-known event is the Olympics, but many others exist. Have students research a sport of their choice and give a brief description of the international organization involved and the events that it sponsors. Students should include a map showing member nations and locations of recent events. **OL**

Caption Answer: Developing nations are more interested in providing jobs and strengthening the economy. Industrialized nations can focus on protecting the environment. Tensions occur when economic progress in developing nations threatens the environment. For example, clearing South American rain forests may contribute to the growth of South American economies, but it creates far-reaching environmental concerns.

Additional Support

Destruction and Development

Inequalities Among Countries
Nations must cooperate to solve global concerns. Today the increasing demands for natural resources threaten many tropical rain forests, like this one in South America. *What tensions occur between nations over the destruction of the rain forests?*

Governing in a Complex World

The United States government conducts policy in a complex world. Changing relationships challenge the policies of every nation. It is not easy to define the boundaries of government.

Major Inequalities Among States

Because of great inequalities among countries, the world today is full of contrasts. The United States and about 20 other states, such as Japan, Canada, Australia, and France, are **industrialized nations.** Industrialized nations have generally large industries and advanced technology that provide a more comfortable way of life than developing nations have. **Developing nations** are only beginning to develop industrially. More than 100 developing nations have average per capita, or per person, incomes that are a fraction of those of industrialized nations. In the poorest countries,

starvation, disease, and political turmoil are a way of life. Many states of Africa south of the Sahara and of Southeast Asia are developing nations. Between these two levels of nations are many newly industrialized nations such as Mexico, South Korea, Singapore, Malaysia, Algeria, and Kenya.

Growing Interdependence

Although each state is sovereign, nations today are interdependent. This means that nations must interact or depend upon one another, especially economically and politically.

Global interdependence is increasing due to growing industrialization and rapid technological advances in manufacturing, transportation, and telecommunications. The Internet is linking billions of people, and soon half the world's population will have access to the Web. Global interdependence affects developed and developing states. For example, Canada, Mexico, and the United States are developing greater economic, political, and social ties through the North American Free Trade Agreement (NAFTA), signed in 1993.

International Organizations

In today's world, many groups play a role in the international scene. Although all of these groups are active on a worldwide basis, their goals and activities can be very different—it is because they operate beyond national boundaries that they are grouped together. The types of international organizations are as follows:

- National liberation organizations
- Terrorist organizations
- Multinational corporations
- Organizations of states of the world
- Nongovernmental organizations (NGOs)

National liberation organizations aim to establish an independent state for a particular ethnic or religious group, often through terrorism. The Irish Republican Army (IRA) is one example. For decades, its goal was to integrate Ireland and Northern Ireland into a single country under one Irish government. The Palestine Liberation Organization (PLO) used hijackings and murder in an effort to replace Israel with a Palestinian state.

In recent decades, terrorist organizations have grown in international influence. These groups have a quasi-military organization; that is, there is a chain-of-command from top to bottom, and orders must be obeyed. Al-Qaeda, the group that staged the September 11, 2001, attacks on the United

---

★ Activity: Interdisciplinary Connection ★

Speech Have students write a speech to present before the United Nations. Ask them to assume they are ambassadors from developing countries. Have students explain in their speeches the positive and negative effects that global interdependence has had on the people in their countries. Some effects may involve multinational corporations, trade agreements, economic aid, international communications, and changes in culture and living standards. **OL**

States, is probably the most familiar terrorist organization. It is comprised mostly of Islamic radicals drawn largely from countries in the Middle East.

Multinational corporations are huge companies with offices and factories in many countries. In 1989 Richard Holder, the president of Reynolds Metals Company, emphasized how integrated such companies are. "Every decision . . . is considered in the light of a worldwide system," Holder said.

The biggest multinationals are sometimes referred to as "stateless" because they are so international in ownership, management, and workforce that it is hard to identify them with a single nation. Because of the wealth they generate, such companies have enormous influence on international policies and on the domestic policies in their host countries. Well-known examples of multinationals include General Motors, American Telephone and Telegraph, Nabisco, and British Petroleum.

Organizations whose members are nations are another type of international organization. They serve a variety of purposes and tend to use the same methods: building coalitions and partnerships with other nations and negotiating policies at home that promote agreed-upon goals. The World Trade Organization (WTO) is a leading example of such an organization. It is comprised of more than 150 nations that negotiate trade matters. The premiere organization of this type is the United Nations. Virtually all recognized states in the world belong to it. Its members discuss many thorny

Environmental Concerns During a 2007 UN conference in Indonesia on climate change, one group showed its concern dramatically. *What special problem do less developed nations have with pollution controls?*

international problems and provide disaster relief and peacekeeping forces among other functions.

Finally, there are the nongovernmental organizations (NGOs)—organizations that private groups set up to achieve a goal that affects multiple nations. In Doctors Without Borders, doctors and nurses from many countries work to provide medical and health services to people suffering from civil wars, epidemics, or natural disasters. Greenpeace campaigns to change policies on global warming and other environmental issues.

SECTION 2 Review

Vocabulary

1. Explain the significance of: unitary system, federal system, confederacy, constitution, constitutional government, preamble, constitutional law, politics, industrialized nation, developing nation.

Main Ideas

2. Analyzing How do recent events in the Middle East illustrate economic interdependence?

3. Contrasting Explain how a unitary system of government differs from a federal system.

Critical Thinking

4. Analyzing James Madison wanted to prevent "factions," or special-interest groups. Would it be possible to have government without special-interest groups? Explain.

5. Organizing In a Venn diagram like the one below, show the similarities and differences between a constitutional government and a government that merely has a constitution.

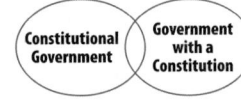

Constitutional Government   Government with a Constitution

Writing About Government

6. Expository Writing Choose five foreign nations, and find out about the basic government structure of each one. When was its constitution adopted? Is the government democratic? Obtain information from a local library or on the Internet. Write a brief summary on each nation.

CHAPTER 1: *People and Government*   **17**

CHAPTER 1, SECTION 2

S Skill Practice

Conducting Research Have students work in pairs to research a nongovernmental organization. Each pair must identify the organization's name, mission, funding source, location, and other relevant information. **OL**

Caption Answer: They want to catch up to industrialized nations and are, therefore, less concerned about pollution. They may think it is unfair for industrialized nations to now impose controls on pollution.

Assess

Assign the Section 2 Assessment as homework or as an in-class activity, or have students take Section Quiz 1–2 from *Section Quizzes and Chapter Tests*.

Close

Evaluating Have students restate in their own words the Preamble of the U. S. Constitution (page 14). Then have them evaluate how the federal government serves the purposes it sets forth. **OL**

Section 2 Review

Answers

1. All definitions can be found in the section and the Glossary.
2. The United States and other nations rely on oil from the Middle East and have intervened militarily and diplomatically to protect oil supplies and maintain order.
3. A unitary system of government gives all powers to the national government; a federal system divides governmental powers between the national and state or provincial governments.
4. In a democratic society, government without special-interest groups is probably impossible because people want to influence government for their own benefit or that of their communities. In a totalitarian state, most political activity is repressed.
5. Constitutional government: Constitution authorizes the government to operate within limits set by the Constitution. Government with a constitution: Government operates by its own authority with few limits. Both: A written plan exists for organizing and operating the government.
6. Students' responses depend on the nations they choose.

Focus

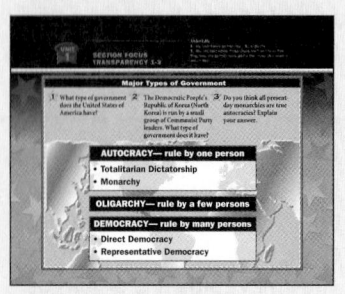
Reader's Guide

Answers to Graphic:

Type of Government	Feature
autocracy	rule by one person
oligarchy	rule by a few
democracy	rule by many

Resource Manager

Types of Government

Reader's Guide

Content Vocabulary
- ★ autocracy *(p. 19)*
- ★ monarchy *(p. 19)*
- ★ oligarchy *(p. 20)*
- ★ democracy *(p. 20)*
- ★ republic *(p. 20)*
- ★ political party *(p. 23)*
- ★ free enterprise *(p. 24)*

Academic Vocabulary
- ★ authority *(p. 19)*
- ★ assembly *(p. 20)*
- ★ institution *(p. 21)*

Reading Strategy
Create a table that highlights the *distinguishing feature* of these forms of government: direct democracy, representative democracy, and republic.

Type of Government	Feature

Issues in the News

Saffron-robed Buddhist monks caught the world's attention in the late summer of 2007. Thousands of them went out into the streets to protest the military leadership of the country of Myanmar. Myanmar (formerly Burma) has been under military rule for most of the past 40 years. The government quickly resorted to harsh measures to repress the protests. According to a United Nations report, many monks were held in deplorable conditions and offered food only at the time when their religion expressly forbids eating. One monk said many died not from injuries, but from confinement and torture. The UN called on Myanmar to "release all those detained or imprisoned merely for the peaceful exercise of their right to freedom of expression, assembly and association."

▲ Buddhist monks protest in Myanmar.

The monks and other demonstrators in Myanmar wanted "government of the people, by the people, and for the people." In 1990 a small military group refused to give up power to the party that won the elections. Today Myanmar remains under military rule. Increasingly, however, most governments are democratic.

Over the centuries, people have organized their governments in many different ways. In Saudi Arabia, for example, the ruling royal family controls the government and its resources. Family members choose the king from among themselves.

Thousands of miles away, in Burkina Faso, a small nation in west central Africa, a small group of wealthy landowners and military officers has been in power since the late 1980s. In Sweden the people elect the Riksdag, which is the name for the Swedish national legislature. In turn, the Riksdag selects the prime minister to carry out the laws.

Major Types of Government

Governments can be classified in many ways. The most time-honored system comes from the ancient Greek philosopher Aristotle. It is based on

---

R Reading Strategies	**C** Critical Thinking	**D** Differentiated Instruction	**W** Writing Support	**S** Skill Practice
Teacher Edition • Activating Prior Knowledge, p. 19 • Identifying, p. 22 • Reading Primary Sources, p. 24 **Additional Resources** • Quizzes/Tests, p. 3 • Guid. Read. Act., p. 3	**Teacher Edition** • Analyzing, p.23 **Additional Resources** • Read. Essen., pp. 7–9 • Supreme Ct. Case Studies, pp. 63–64	**Teacher Edition** • Visual/Spatial, p. 20 **Additional Resources** • Part. in Gov. Act., pp. 1–2	**Teacher Edition** • Personal Writing, p. 21 • Expository Writing, p. 23 **Additional Resources** • Supreme Ct. Case Studies, pp. 61–62	**Teacher Edition** • Visual Literacy, p. 19 **Additional Resources** • Am. Biographies, p. 28

a key question: Who governs? In Aristotle's view, all governments belong to one of three major groups:

- autocracy—rule by one person
- oligarchy—rule by a few persons
- democracy—rule by many persons

These three groups are helpful for looking at actual governments, although additional terms have been added to Aristotle's list in the modern period. The choice of which term is appropriate for a government often depends on the historical era and the kind of society that existed at that time. One could never use the term *totalitarian*, for example, for an ancient society. Totalitarian rulers could develop only in the twentieth century when modern communications and transportation systems gave them some of the tools needed to achieve total control.

Autocracy

An **autocracy** is the system of government in which one person has all the **authority** and power to rule. The term is used for dynastic kings and emperors who exercised personal rule and maintained their power through army and police powers. The last true autocrats were the czars of Russia who ruled until 1918, when the Russian Revolution occurred. No group of nobles or church leaders had any power to check the czar's will.

Monarchy is another form of government in which one person has great power; a king, queen, or emperor inherits the throne and heads the state. Autocracy and kingship originated in ancient times when rulers were considered sacred or sanctioned by religion. Unlike an autocrat, however, a monarch's power has often been limited in some way by tradition or law. Medieval kings, for example, were expected to consult with a council of nobles. In France, a body of noble judges was supposed to review the king's laws to give them formal sanction.

A new type of monarchy developed in France in the 1660s, however, that was very important in European history. Louis XIV, the famous king who built the Palace of Versailles, became an absolute monarch—his power was unlimited. In practice, this was the same as autocracy.

Today monarchies still exist in the world, but almost all of them are limited or constitutional monarchies—the king or queen is limited by the law. Examples include Great Britain, Sweden, Japan, and the Netherlands. Their rulers either share power with elected legislatures or serve merely as ceremonial figures.

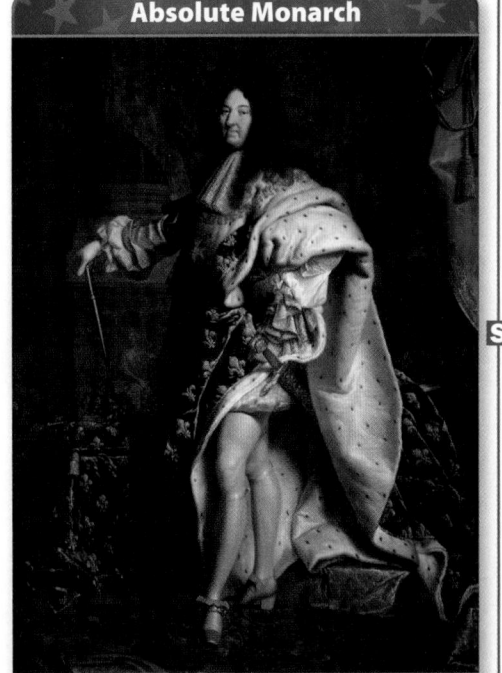

Absolute Monarch

Absolute Power The power of King Louis XIV of France, who reigned from 1660–1714, was absolute, that is, unchecked by other nobles or law courts. *What technological advances allow modern dictators to have more practical power over a country than Louis XIV did?*

A dictator is also a single ruler, but this term emphasizes the fact that this person rules by force and by dictate alone. No support is found in custom or religion for a dictatorship. In modern times, dictatorship is often the result of a military coup, or seizure of power.

Finally, totalitarianism is a special type of single-ruler government. Here the ruler attempts to control the *total* society (thus the term *totalitarianism*). Both Adolf Hitler in Nazi Germany and Joseph Stalin in Soviet Russia tried to control civil society completely, that is, every aspect of civilian life, not just government institutions. Hitler, for example, created Nazi youth groups and social groups of all kinds. A political term for totalitarianism is *fascism*. The name comes from Benito Mussolini's Fascist Party in Italy from 1922 through 1943.

CHAPTER 1: *People and Government* **19**

Teach

S Skill Practice

Visual Literacy Ask students to study the portrait of Louis XIV. Then, have them make a list of items or symbols in the picture that reflect his power as monarch. **OL**

Caption Answer: Radio, television, and other mass communication advances; these allow police and military communication, as well as electronic surveillance.

R Reading Strategy

Activating Prior Knowledge Ask students what they know about the current British monarchy. What functions does the monarch perform? What responsibilities go with the crown? Do students think the monarchy still serves a purpose, or should it be abolished? **AL**

Additional Support

Activity: Collaborative Learning

Setting Up a Government Organize the class into three groups. Ask each to imagine that it has been marooned on a deserted island in the ocean and needs to set up a society and adopt rules and regulations. Assign each group a major type of government: autocracy, oligarchy, or democracy. Have the group plan how its government will distribute jobs, build shelters, and gather food. What will it do about education and health care? Will there be any police or military? Have each group present its plans for a society to the rest of the class. After students hear each plan, have them decide the one under which they would like to live. **OL**

Comparing Governments

D Differentiated Instruction

Visual/Spatial Divide the class into six groups, and assign each group one of the flags in the chart. Have students do library or Internet research to find out the significance of the symbols on the flag. Then have each group create a poster that explains the symbols. **OL**

Hands-On Chapter Project

Step 3

Creating a Nation

Step 3: Creating a Constitution Students will create a framework of government.

Directions Taking into account the governmental responsibilities they decided upon in Step 2, students will develop a constitution for their nation.

Use this as an opportunity to review the outline and structure of the U.S. Constitution. Point out that the first three articles define the responsibilities of the

---

Comparing Governments
Government Systems

		Unitary	Federal	Confederacy
	People's Republic of China 1949–Present	★		
	Republic of Cuba 1959–Present	★		
	Russian Federation 1991–Present		★	
	United States 1788–Present		★	
	United States Articles of Confederation 1781–1788			★
	European Union 1993–Present			★

A **unitary system** gives all key powers to the national or central government.

A **federal system** divides the powers of government between the national government and state or regional governments.

A **confederal system**, or confederacy, is a union of independent sovereign states, joined together by a central government that has limited powers over them.

Critical Thinking *Explain why a dictatorship will always have a unitary system but a unitary system does not have to be a dictatorship.*

Charts In MOtion
See StudentWorks™ Plus or go to glencoe.com.

Source: Clement, *Clement's Encyclopedia of World Governments* (Dallas: Political Research Inc., 1996).

Oligarchy

An **oligarchy** is any system of government in which a small group holds power. Some scholars have said that the ancient Roman Republic was really an oligarchy because a few prominent Roman families dominated the Roman Senate. For the same reasons, the leaders of Japan in the late 1800s are often referred to as an oligarchy. Oligarchs derive their power from their wealth, social position, military power, or a combination of these factors. China's Communist leaders could be called an oligarchy, too.

Dictators or oligarchs might claim that they rule in the people's interest to give the impression that

---

the people have some control. They might also hold elections, but only one candidate is on the ballot. If there is a legislature, it is only able to approve policies. As in a dictatorship, oligarchies often suppress opposition—sometimes ruthlessly.

Democracy

A **democracy** is a system of government in which rule is by the people, either through representatives or directly. The word *democracy* comes from the Greek *demos* meaning "the people" and *kratia* meaning "rule." The ancient Greeks used democracy to mean government by the many rather than a small elite. Pericles, a great leader of ancient Athens, declared, "Our constitution is named a democracy because it is in the hands not of the few, but of the many." This does not mean that everyone in Athens could vote. Only citizens could vote, and many people, including women, foreign residents, and slaves, were not citizens.

It was only in the early 1800s that some educated people in Western Europe began to believe that every adult should have the right to vote—and these people were often seen as radicals. Before that time, only a landowner, merchant, or professional person with significant wealth was able to vote. This was true even in the European country with the most progressive government, Great Britain. By degrees, however, modern governments became more democratic. First workers, and later minorities and women, were given the vote.

Democracies can be direct or representative. A direct democracy is a government in which all citizens cast a vote directly on government issues and laws. Such a government can exist only in a small society where it is practical for everyone to assemble, discuss, and vote. The ancient Athenians had a direct democracy, but in modern times one can find something like it only in some New England town meetings and the smaller states, or cantons, of Switzerland.

In an indirect or representative democracy, the people elect representatives to make laws and conduct government. An **assembly** of the people's representatives may be called a council, a legislature, a congress, or a parliament. It is the most efficient way to ensure that the rights of individual citizens, who are part of a large group, are represented.

In a **republic,** the head of state is not a king or queen, and voters elect representatives to run the nation's government. In a republic, only a small percentage of the people might be empowered to vote.

---

three branches of government (Article I, legislative; Article II, executive; and Article III, judicial).

First, instruct groups to write a preamble for their constitution. The preamble should describe the basic purposes and ideals of their government and nation. Also have them choose a name for their country that reflects its ideals.

Then have students create a constitution for their government. It should describe the structure of their government. Does

it have different branches? If so, how are responsibilities divided among them? These responsibilities should be presented in a detailed outline.

Summarizing Groups have now created a government that should be prepared to serve its people. Have students summarize their government's structure in a brief paragraph. **OL**

(Chapter Project continued in Section 4.)

The need for citizen participation in a republic was highlighted by Benjamin Franklin as he was leaving the Constitutional Convention in Philadelphia. A woman approached him and asked, "What kind of government have you given us, Dr. Franklin? A republic or a monarchy?" Franklin answered, "A republic, Madam, if you can keep it."

In the United States, we have a democracy that is a republic, but not every democracy is a republic. Great Britain, for example, is a democracy but not a republic because Queen Elizabeth, a constitutional monarch, is the head of state.

Characteristics of Democracy

A number of countries call their governments "democratic" or "republican" when they are not. Their leaders may want to convey the idea that the people back those in power, but it is clear that their government **institutions** do not meet the definition of a democracy. The government of North Korea, for example, is called the Democratic People's Republic of Korea, but it is an oligarchy because a few Communist Party leaders run it. A true democracy has certain key characteristics: individual liberty, majority rule with minority rights, free elections, and competing political parties.

Individual Liberty

No individual, of course, can be completely free to do absolutely anything he or she wants. Rather, the goal of democracy is that all people be as free as possible to develop their talents.

Majority Rule with Minority Rights

Democracy also requires that government decisions be based on the will of the majority. A representative democracy is one in which elected representatives enact laws that reflect the will of the majority of lawmakers. Because these lawmakers are elected by the people, the laws are accepted by the people.

At the same time, the American concept of democracy includes a concern about the tyranny of the majority. The Constitution protects the rights of those in the minority as well. Respect for minority rights can be difficult to maintain, especially when society is at war or under other great stress. During World War II, the government imprisoned more than 100,000 Japanese Americans in relocation camps because it feared they would be disloyal. The relocation program deprived many Japanese American citizens of their basic liberties. Even so, the government's action was upheld by the Supreme Court in 1944 in *Korematsu* v. *United States.*[1] 📖

📖 *See the following footnoted materials in the* **Reference Handbook:**
1. *Korematsu* v. *United States* case summary, page R29.

Relocation and Discrimination

Civil Liberties More than 100,000 people of Japanese descent were placed in camps during World War II—about 70,000 of these were American-born citizens. *What kind of compensation did internment victims receive in the 1980s?*

W

W **Writing Support**

Personal Writing Have students research the relocation camps. Encourage them to read personal narratives. Then have them write one-page editorials, expressing their opinions about the internment camps. **AL**

Did You Know?

In 1942 Toyosaburo Korematsu refused to leave San Leandro, California, which had been designated a "military area" by executive order. He was found guilty in a federal district court of violating Civilian Exclusion Order No. 34. Korematsu petitioned the Supreme Court to review the decision. The Court ruled that although exclusion orders based on race are constitutionally suspect, the government is justified in time of "emergency and peril" to suspend citizens' civil rights.

Caption Answer: Congress acknowledged the "grave injustice" and offered payments of $20,000 to Japanese Americans still living who had been interned.

Additional Support

Activity: Interdisciplinary Connection

Speech Write the following statement on the board: "The Constitution established a republic, effectively limiting the power of government and preserving individual liberty to this day." Ask students to decide whether they agree or disagree with the statement and to jot down a few reasons in support of their opinions. Then ask for volunteers to present their positions to the class. Finally, have students vote on the most persuasive speaker. Did anyone change his or her mind after listening to reasons given by others? **OL**

R Reading Strategy

Identifying Ask: How were voting rights restricted in American history? *(The right to vote was limited to white males. In some places, individuals were required to own a certain amount of property or wealth in order to vote.)* **OL**

🏛 Landmark Case

See *Regents of the University of California v. Bakke and Kaiser Aluminum and Chemical Corporation v. Weber* in the Supreme Court Summaries in the **Reference Handbook** and Case Studies 61 and 63 in the Supreme Court Case Studies booklet.

Participating
IN GOVERNMENT

The larger the sampling of people students survey, the more representative of the population their results will be. Suggest that students allow people to respond privately so they will feel freer to be completely honest.

Activity: Provide class time for compilation of all students' results. Do students agree with the majority responses? **OL**

Additional Support

Ex Parte Endo v. *United States*

🏛 **Landmark Case** That same session, the Court took a different stance. A woman named Mitsuye Endo, a native-born citizen, was fired from a California state job in 1942 and sent to a relocation camp. Her lawyer challenged the government. The Court agreed that she could no longer be held:

> 66 *[D]etention in Relocation Centers of persons of Japanese ancestry regardless of loyalty is not only unauthorized by Congress or the Executive but is another example of the unconstitutional resort to racism inherent in the entire evacuation program. . . . [R]acial discrimination of this nature bears no reasonable relation to military necessity and is utterly foreign to the ideals and traditions of the American people.* 99
> —Justice Frank Murphy, 1944

In recent decades, the treatment of Japanese Americans during World War II has been seen as a denial of individual rights—and as proof that tyranny can occur in a democracy. In 1988 Congress recognized the "grave injustice" that was done and offered payments of $20,000 to the surviving Japanese Americans who had been relocated.

Free Elections

As we have seen, democratic governments receive their legitimacy by the consent of the governed. The authority to create and run the government rests with the people. All genuine democracies have free and open elections. Free elections give people the chance to choose their leaders and to voice their opinions on various issues. Free elections also help ensure that public officials pay attention to the wishes of the people.

In a democracy, several characteristics mark free elections. First, everyone's vote carries the same weight—a principle expressed by the phrase "one person, one vote." Second, all candidates have the right to express their views freely, giving voters access to competing ideas. Third, citizens are free to help candidates or support issues. Fourth, the legal requirements for voting, such as age, residence, and citizenship, are kept to a minimum. Thus, racial, ethnic, religious, or other discriminatory tests cannot be used to restrict voting. Fifth, citizens vote by secret ballot without coercion or fear of punishment for their decisions.

Participating
IN GOVERNMENT — Determining the Social Consensus

Democracy depends, in part, on a social consensus. It stabilizes democracy when a majority of the people share ideas, values, and beliefs. To find out the shared values of your community, ask a variety of people whether they agree or disagree with the following statements:

- Everyone should be able to get a free public education.
- Burning the American flag as a protest should be a crime.
- The wealthy people should pay a higher tax on their income.
- Dumping trash on public property should be a punishable offense.
- Scientists should not experiment on animals for any reason.

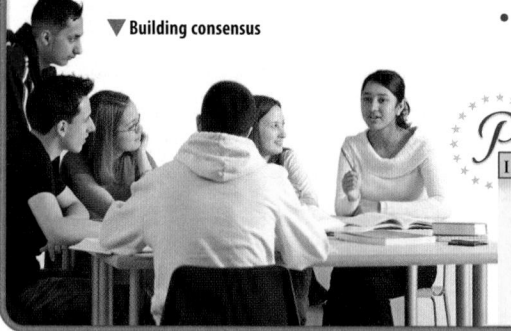
▼ **Building consensus**

Participating
IN GOVERNMENT ACTIVITY

Compile and analyze the responses to your survey and create a poster illustrating the social consensus of your survey group.

Activity: Interdisciplinary Connection

The Arts President Ronald Reagan signed into law the bill that gave $20,000 tax-free in reparations to each of the 60,000 still-living Japanese Americans who were interned during World War II. This was a victory for Senators Daniel Inouye and Spark Matsunaga of Hawaii, who were leaders in fighting for the bill's passage. Interested students might read one of the fictionalized accounts of families who were interned and present to the class dramatizations based on their reading. Program notes or a follow-up to the presentation should discuss the role of the two senators and the bill they fought for. **AL**

Prerequisites of Democracy: An Educated Public

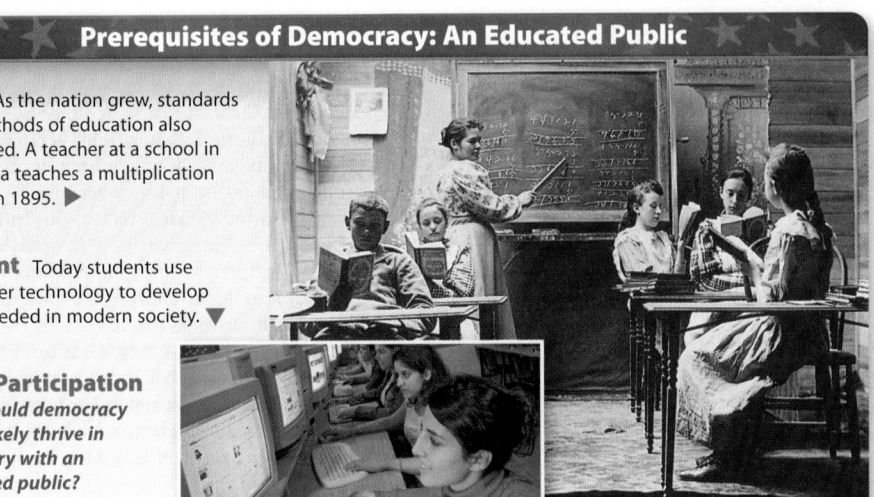

Past As the nation grew, standards and methods of education also expanded. A teacher at a school in Nebraska teaches a multiplication lesson in 1895. ▶

Present Today students use computer technology to develop skills needed in modern society. ▼

Civic Participation *Why would democracy more likely thrive in a country with an educated public?*

Competing Political Parties

Political parties are an important element of democratic government. A **political party** is a group of individuals with broad common interests who organize to nominate candidates for office, win elections, conduct government, and determine public policy.

In the United States, any number of political parties may compete. In the 2000 presidential election, for example, votes for the Green Party candidate, Ralph Nader, played a significant role in the outcome. Yet for most of its history, the United States has had a two-party system. Since the mid-1800s, these parties have been the Republicans and the Democrats.

Rival parties make elections meaningful because they give voters a choice. Parties have another function in a democracy: They focus voters' attention on the issues by debating them publicly. Finally, in democracies, the political party or parties that are out of power serve as a "loyal opposition." That is, by criticizing the policies and actions of the party in power, they help make the party in power more responsible to the people.

Essential Elements for a Democracy

Until recent centuries, democracies were rare. Democracy calls for certain conditions that have only developed since the Industrial Revolution. Industrialized societies allowed many people to have a decent standard of living and enough education to demand the vote. To sustain a democracy, five elements are essential: citizen participation, a favorable economy, widespread education, a strong civil society, and a social consensus.

Citizen Participation

Democracy requires citizens who are willing to participate in civic life. A strong democracy is best maintained in nations where citizens inform themselves, actively participate in political campaigns, vote, and serve on juries.

A Favorable Economy

A second factor for a successful democracy is a prosperous economy that distributes wealth to many members of society. Having a large middle class signals this kind of economy.

The connection between people's economic status and their involvement in government can be seen by looking at history. Representative government first began in England because landowning nobles who ran their local counties felt they had a right to share power with the king. Later, the same feeling arose among the middle classes. In other words, anyone who owns property of any kind wants to have some say in government.

There is another way of looking at the connection between economic status and government. If people

CHAPTER 1: *People and Government* **23**

C Critical Thinking

Analyzing Have students research elections in which a third party has influenced the outcome or an established major party has splintered into factions. Divide the class into five groups, and assign each group one of the following elections to research: 1860, 1912, 1948, 1968, or 2000. **OL**

Caption Answer: An educated electorate can more effectively understand issues and evaluate candidates. Democracy requires that the public or representatives of the people create and enforce laws that are wise and just.

W Writing Support

Expository Writing Inform students that political philosopher John Locke wrote that all people have a "natural right" to life, liberty, and property. Have students write an essay in which they explain the connection between the ownership of property and representative government. **OL**

Additional Support

Extending the Content

Growth of Democracy The late 1980s and early 1990s brought a tremendous move toward more democratic governments in totalitarian nations. The Solidarity movement won democratic elections in Poland. Chinese students held demonstrations in Tiananmen Square in Beijing. Czechoslovakians in 1989 voted to end communism in the government. That year, the Berlin Wall came down and the following year Germany was reunited. Free multiparty elections took place in Romania in 1990. Many Soviet republics followed the Baltic states in announcing their independence from the Soviet Union, which dissolved in 1991.

R Reading Strategy

Reading Primary Sources
Have students reread the quote by Thaddeus Stevens. **Ask:** What connection does he draw between education and democratic government? *(A democratic republic needs well-informed citizens who can make wise choices; it is the responsibility of a democratic republic to ensure that the population is educated.)* **OL**

Assess

Assign the Section 3 Assessment as homework or as an in-class activity, or have students take Section Quiz 1-3 from *Section Quizzes and Chapter Tests.*

Close

Making Connections
John F. Kennedy stated one of democracy's basic ideals when he said: "Ask not what your country can do for you; ask what you can do for your country." Discuss the quotation, and ask students what they can do for their country now and in the future. **OL**

Section 3 Review

---

do not control their economic lives, they probably will not be free to make political decisions.

In the West, and in the United States especially, voters endorse the free enterprise system. **Free enterprise** is the freedom of private business to operate with minimal government regulation.

Countries with stable economies are better able to support democratic governments. During severe depressions, dictators have often come to power because they promised citizens jobs. Unemployed people tend to worry about eating and feeding their families more than their political rights.

Widespread Education

Democracy is also more likely to succeed in countries where most people are educated. The debate over public education in America was settled in the 1830s. For example, in 1835 Pennsylvania voted to fund public schools. Thaddeus Stevens, speaking to the Pennsylvania state legislature in favor of the funding legislation, said:

> **R** 66 *If an elective Republic is to endure for any great length of time, every elector must have sufficient information . . . to direct wisely the legislature, the ambassadors, and the Executive of the Nation. . . . [I]t is the duty of Government to see that the means of information be diffused to every citizen.* 99
> —Thaddeus Stevens, April 1835

A Strong Civil Society

Democracy is not possible without a civil society. Civil society refers to private, nongovernmental society. Civil society is made up of a complex network of voluntary associations—economic, political, charitable, religious, and many other kinds of groups that exist outside government.

The United States has thousands of such groups—the American Red Cross, the Humane Society, the Sierra Club, the National Rifle Association, your local church and newspaper, labor unions, and business groups.

It is through these organizations that citizens often organize and make their views known. Such groups give citizens a means to take responsibility for protecting their rights, and to learn about democracy by participating in it at the grass roots level.

A Social Consensus

Democracy also prospers where most people accept democratic values such as individual liberty and equality for all. Such countries are said to have a social consensus. People also must generally agree about the purpose and limits of government.

History shows that conditions in the American colonies favored the growth of democracy. Many individuals had an opportunity to get ahead economically, and the colonists were among the most educated people of the world at the time.

Their English heritage provided a consensus of political and social values. In time, the benefits of democracy would extend to all Americans.

SECTION 3 Review

Vocabulary

1. **Explain** the significance of: autocracy, monarchy, oligarchy, democracy, republic, political party, free enterprise.

Main Ideas

2. **Identifying** What characteristics of democracy distinguish it from other forms of government?

3. **Describing** What five criteria help democracy succeed?

Critical Thinking

4. **Distinguishing Fact from Opinion** Suppose you are assigned to interview the president of the Republic of Mauritania. What questions would help you determine if democracy exists there?

5. **Classifying** Using a graphic organizer similar to the one below, show who rules the state in each of Aristotle's three classifications of government.

Classification	Ruler(s)

Writing About Government

6. **Expository Writing** How are the rights of the minority protected under our system of government? In a short essay, paraphrase the concerns of the Founders about minority rights. Then give evidence from current events to illustrate how they are protected.

Answers

1. All definitions can be found in the section and the Glossary.
2. individual liberty, majority rule with minority rights, free elections with secret ballots, rival political parties
3. active citizen participation; a favorable economy with a large middle class; an educated public; civil society—or a network of organizations that exist independently of government and help protect their rights; and a social consensus or a general agreement of the limitations and purposes of government

4. Answers may include: How many political parties are there? Do people vote by secret ballot? Do all people have an equal opportunity to develop their talents? How are minority rights protected?
5. autocracy—one person; oligarchy—few people; democracy—many people
6. Students should organize the information they gather in an orderly way so it will be easy to present to the class.

Do Noise Ordinances Infringe on First Amendment Rights?

Ward v. *Rock Against Racism*, 1989

*F*reedom of speech is a fundamental American right. At the same time, a legitimate purpose of government is to maintain public order, including protecting citizens from unwelcome and excessive noise. Does the First Amendment allow a city to regulate the sound level at rock concerts held in a public park?

Factors of the Case

Rock concerts are regularly held in New York City's Central Park. Area residents had complained of too much noise at some events. At other events, audiences complained that the sound was not loud enough. In 1986 the city passed a regulation requiring performing groups to use a sound system provided and operated by the city.

For a number of years, Rock Against Racism, an anti-racist rock group, sponsored annual concerts in Central Park. The group had always used their own sound equipment and sound technician. Rock Against Racism charged that the city's new regulation violated their rights to free speech under the First Amendment. It won a lower federal court case, and in 1989, the Supreme Court agreed to hear the case.

The Constitutional Question

Music has long been considered a form of protected speech under the First Amendment. The courts do allow governments to make regulations, however, that happen to limit speech in the process of trying to accomplish a legitimate government end. Thus, in several cases the Supreme Court had ruled that the government can limit the time, place, and manner of speech if the aim is not to censor the content of the speech but rather to promote people's health and safety.

Rock Against Racism argued that the regulation violated the First Amendment by giving city officials artistic control over performers in the park. The group claimed the regulation was not narrowly focused and gave city officials the chance to select poor equipment or to modify the sound when they did not like the message. The city responded that it had a legitimate purpose in protecting citizens from excessive noise and that its guidelines were focused on controlling noise levels in a way that was fair to the audience, the performers, and citizens living nearby.

Debating the Issue

Questions to Consider

1. Do musicians have a free-speech right to play as loudly as they want in a public space, or is the regulation a proper exercise of the government's power to maintain order?

2. If officials did not like the message in the music, could they use the regulation to control the content? Explain.

You Be the Judge

The Court established that governments can enforce regulations that limit speech if there is a legitimate government purpose. What was the city's goal in drawing up the regulation?

Was there another, less intrusive way the city could have handled this issue? Design an alternative plan and present it to the class.

▼ **A concert in Central Park**

Class Debate

Organize the class into three groups: one group representing Rock Against Racism, another representing the city, and the third to act as a jury. Have the first two groups prepare their cases and present them to the jury. After the jury has deliberated, have a representative read the opinion to the class.

The Court's Decision

The lower court decided that the city did not use the most effective and least intrusive method to prevent the sound from disturbing others. The U.S. Supreme Court reversed the lower court's decision, saying that the regulation is not required to be the most effective or efficient means. It also found that the regulation did not violate free speech because it did not regulate the content of the concert or even the type, but merely the volume of the sound. The issue in this case illustrates the tension in democracies between the need to give government enough power to promote the common good and the need to limit government's power and protect individual rights.

Debating the Issue Answers

Questions to Consider

1. Answers will vary, but students should explain the rationale behind their opinion.
2. The regulation could be fairly easily abused by biased officials.

You Be the Judge

The city wanted to protect the rights of residents near the park. Perhaps the city could have passed regulations on the loudness level without insisting on providing its own technicians.

Focus

Bellringer

Section Focus Transparencies 1-4

Reader's Guide

Answers to Graphic: private ownership and control of property and economic resources, free enterprise, competition, freedom of choice, and the possibility of profits

Resource Manager

Economic Theories

Reader's Guide

Content Vocabulary
* economics *(p. 26)*
* capitalism *(p. 27)*
* free market *(p. 27)*
* laissez-faire *(p. 27)*
* socialism *(p. 28)*
* proletariat *(p. 29)*
* bourgeoisie *(p. 29)*
* communism *(p. 29)*
* command economy *(p. 30)*

Academic Vocabulary
* consumer *(p. 27)*
* regulation *(p. 28)*
* capacity *(p. 28)*

Reading Strategy
Create a graphic organizer like the one below to explain the five characteristics of capitalism.

Issues in the News

The products and services that have made many millionaires might not be known to most of us. But that can't be said of Mark Zuckerberg. Zuckerberg is the man behind Facebook, the social networking site he founded when he was a student at Harvard. When he launched the site, more than half of Harvard's students signed up in a matter of weeks. The operation soon spread to other colleges, welcomed by a "Facebook generation" willing to share their personal lives online. Privacy issues can be tricky, though. Some customers have rebelled at Zuckerberg's plan to link their online purchases to their personal profile. The struggles and challenges seem to be worth it: Still in his early 20s, Zuckerberg is said to be the youngest billionaire in American history.

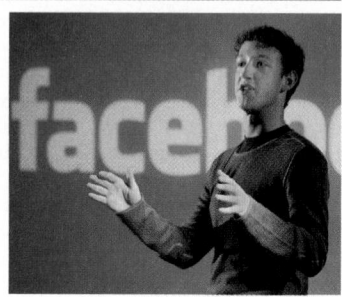
▲ **Facebook founder Mark Zuckerberg**

Facebook offers a social networking service that is free to users. It makes money the same way television does—by selling advertisements. In our market economy, producers use ads to inform consumers about their products.

Economics is the study of how limited resources are used to satisfy people's seemingly unlimited wants. Resources include natural materials such as land and water, as well as human resources like knowledge and labor. Because there are never enough resources to produce everything people could want, societies have to decide how resources will be used. This allocation occurs through a society's political system. Some political systems let a free market determine how resources are used. Other political systems use government regulation or control to allocate resources.

Economic systems are classified in two ways. One way looks at how economies actually work. The second way looks at the political ideology that is connected to an economy.

Someone who classifies economies by how they work will use these three categories: a traditional or pre-modern economy, a market economy, and a command economy. Someone who groups economies according to the related political belief will use the terms *capitalism, socialism,* and *communism.*

R Reading Strategies	**C** Critical Thinking	**D** Differentiated Instruction	**W** Writing Support	**S** Skill Practice
Additional Resources • Read. Essen., pp. 10–12 • Quizzes/Tests, p. 4 • Guid. Read. Act., p. 4	**Teacher Edition** • Comparing and Contrasting, p. 27 • Identifying Points of View, p. 29 **Additional Resources** • Ch. Summaries, pp. 1–3	**Teacher Edition** • Gifted and Talented, p. 28 **Additional Resources** • Source Readings, p. 1	**Teacher Edition** • Personal Writing, p. 28 **Additional Resources** • Foldables, p. 19	**Additional Resources** • Quizzes/Tests, pp. 5–12

The Role of Economic Systems

All economic systems must answer three key questions: What and how much should be produced? How should goods and services be produced? Who gets the goods and services that are produced?

Different peoples in different historical circumstances have answered these questions in various ways. Societies with more political freedom tend to have relatively free or unregulated economies. Societies with relatively less political freedom have economies that are under more government control.

Capitalism

Capitalism is an economic system in which freedom of choice and individual incentive for workers, investors, **consumers,** and business enterprises are emphasized. The government assumes that society is best served by whatever productive activity individuals choose. Pure capitalism has five characteristics: private ownership and control of property and economic resources, free enterprise, competition, freedom of choice, and the possibility of profits.

Origins of Capitalism

No one person invented capitalism. The word *capital* means "money or wealth that is invested to make more money." Such investment could not take place until people were producing enough to have extra to invest. A market system in which buyers and sellers compete to make money is at the heart of capitalism. In Europe, capitalism began to develop around 1200. Explorers and merchants opened trade routes to Asia. They needed long-term investors to carry out their projects. As trade increased, people made more money and reinvested it in other moneymaking schemes.

By the 1700s, Europe had national states, a wealthy middle class familiar with banks and markets, and an aggressive attitude toward work and wealth. Europeans valued progress, invention, and the free market—a **free market** meant that the government placed no limits on the freedom of buyers and sellers to make economic decisions.

In 1776 Adam Smith, a Scottish philosopher and economist, provided a philosophy for free trade. Smith opposed what many nations at the time were doing regulating trade in a variety of ways, such as taxing imports. In his famous book *The Wealth of Nations,*[1] Smith said that the government should leave the economy alone as much as possible—he wanted a **laissez-faire** economy. (*Laissez-faire* is French for "to let alone.") The market would act as an "invisible hand" guiding economic choices for the best possible results. It is the action of buyers and sellers, not the government, that determines what is produced and bought.

Competition plays a key role in this kind of economy because sellers compete over resources to produce goods and services at the most reasonable price. At the same time, consumers compete over limited products to buy what they want and need. Finally, these same consumers in their role as workers try to sell their skills and labor for the best wages or salaries they can get.

See the following footnoted materials in the **Reference Handbook:**
1. *The Wealth of Nations*, page R75.

Tools of Capitalism

Free Enterprise Teens possess increased buying power and are a target audience for businesses. *How does the free enterprise system contribute to the idea of individual rights and freedoms?*

Teach

C Critical Thinking

Comparing and Contrasting Organize students into pairs. Have one student in each pair use library and Internet resources to find more information about Karl Marx and his views on communism. Have the second student in each pair find more about Adam Smith and capitalism. Have pairs create charts comparing and contrasting the two men's philosophies. Have pairs of students present their charts to the class. **OL**

Caption Answer: In a free enterprise system, decisions are made by buyers and sellers. Individuals are free to buy and sell the products and services they want.

GO TO To enrich the study of chapter content, remind students that footnoted materials appear in the **Reference Handbook.**

Additional Support

★ Activity: Interdisciplinary Connection ★

Geography and Cultures Ask: What countries have moved or are moving toward a free market economy? Then organize the class into small groups to make a bulletin board illustrating the changes in these countries. One group should be responsible for providing a map for the center of the bulletin board, with affected countries outlined in red. Other groups should find magazine and newspaper articles about each transition country. Have group members write summaries of the articles to post around the map. Students also should include photographs and other visuals. New summaries may be added as events occur. Use yarn to connect summaries and visuals to the appropriate countries. **BL**

Differentiated Instruction

D

Gifted and Talented Have students research early twentieth-century ads for patent medicines and compare them to ads for present-day medicines. How are they similar? How are they different? What restrictions does the Food and Drug Administration place on advertisements for prescription drugs? **AL**

Writing Support

W

Personal Writing Have students respond to the following questions. **Ask:** Do you agree with Marx's opinion that there is a repeating pattern of class struggles between workers and those in charge? Is it possible to have a functioning society with only one class? (Students must defend their responses.) **OL**

Reading Strategy

R

Identifying Ask: What are the main characteristics of a mixed economy as it concerns the United States? (rooted deeply in individual initiative, all persons have the right to own property, freedom to make economic decisions) **BL**

Additional Support

Free Enterprise in the United States

A pure capitalist system is theoretical—it does not exist in reality. The American economy, however, is one of the most capitalistic in the world today. Although the United States has significant government **regulation,** its economic policies aim to preserve a free market.

Since the early 1900s, however, the government's role in the economy has steadily increased. First, as the federal government has grown, it has become the single largest buyer of goods and services. Second, the federal government has regulated the economy more and more in the interest of consumer health and product safety. The Meat Inspection Act and the Pure Food and Drug Act, both passed in 1906, were early examples of this kind of regulation. Third, the Great Depression of the 1930s created an emergency that propelled government action. With millions of Americans out of work, the government created programs to provide basic economic security. For example, it set up the Social Security system. It even set up a public corporation, the Tennessee Valley Authority, that competed with private companies to provide electricity.

Since then, many laws have been passed giving the government a role in such areas as labor-management relations, environmental regulation, and control over financial institutions.

Mixed Economies

Economists describe the American economy and many others in the world today as mixed economies. "Mixed" economies mix elements of capitalism and socialism. Even though it is a mixed economy, the American economy is basically identified with a capitalist economy. It is rooted deeply in the value of individual initiative—that each person knows what is best for himself or herself. Further, it respects the right of all persons to own private property. Finally, it recognizes that freedom to make economic choices is a part of individual freedom. Regulation is usually embraced reluctantly and only when necessary to protect public welfare.

Socialism

The second type, **socialism,** is an economic system in which the government owns the basic means of production, determines the use of resources, distributes the products and wages, and provides social services such as education, health care, and welfare.

Socialism developed in the early 1800s after the Industrial Revolution began. Industrialization

resulted in modern economies that were vastly more productive, but it also created a great deal of suffering. During the early stages of the Industrial Revolution, workers lived in terrible poverty, working 12 hours per day, six days per week. They lived in slums and had no power to bargain with employers.

Social reformers believed that with so much productive **capacity,** no one should have to suffer or starve. They wanted the government to direct the economy to distribute goods and wealth more equally. Some socialists rejected capitalism and believed that only a violent revolution would bring about change. Others believed reforms could be made peacefully and gradually by organizing the working class and voters. Still others tried to build ideal communities, or communes, where people were supposed to share in all things.

Opponents of socialism say that it stifles individual initiative. They also claim that under a socialist government, high tax rates hinder economic growth. Further, some people argue that because socialism requires increased governmental regulation, it helps create big government and thus can lead to dictatorship.

Democratic Socialism

Socialists who are committed to democracy in the political sphere but want better distribution of economic goods are called democratic socialists. Under this kind of system, citizens have basic democratic rights like free speech and free elections, but in the economic sphere, the government owns key large industries and makes economic decisions to benefit everyone.

Denmark, Norway, and Sweden are sometimes seen as practicing democratic socialism. In the decades after World War II, democratic socialist countries kept a sharp focus on retaining control of key industries like steel mills, shipyards, railroads, and airlines. These governments also provided extensive welfare benefits to their citizens, such as health and medical care and old-age pensions.

In recent decades, these countries have lessened government control of many economic activities, but they have continued to provide generous social benefits. In 2008 Denmark, Sweden, and Norway all had prosperous economies.

Communism

Karl Marx was a German philosopher, writer, and reformer. He lived from 1818–1883 and saw firsthand both early industrialization and political

Activity: Collaborative Learning

Visual/Spatial Have students work in pairs to create a chart that compares capitalist, communist, and socialist economic systems. Each chart should contain the following information about each economy:
- Who owns the means of production?
- Who makes the economic decisions?
- Is there competition and profit motive?

Some pairs may wish to expand their chart by naming a few countries for each type of economy. **ELL** rebellion. He concluded that the capitalist system would collapse. He first published his ideas in 1848 in a pamphlet called *The Communist Manifesto.* Later, Marx expanded his ideas about capitalism in a multivolumed work, *Das Kapital,* whose first volume came out in 1867.

Marx saw that the Industrial Revolution had brought about dramatic economic change. Workers were now concentrated in factories and no longer owned their tools. Marx referred to this industrial working class as the **proletariat.** The other important class in an industrial society was the **bourgeoisie.** For Marx, this term did not just mean the middle class, but the middle class as owners of industrial capital—the means necessary to produce industrial goods, such as factories, land, water rights, or other necessary resources.

Capitalists were the ruling class because they had so much power over resources. Meanwhile, workers were paid a low hourly wage. They did not receive the full value of their labor because owners paid them a subsistence wage and pocketed the profits. In a capitalist system, Marx said, wages would never rise above a subsistence level—just barely enough to survive.

Class Struggles

Marx interpreted all human history as a class struggle between the workers and the owners of the means of production. In *The Communist Manifesto,* Marx claimed that there had always been a struggle between lord and master, feudal servant and feudal lord, but that in the end, this struggle brought progress. For example, bourgeois merchants had opposed the interests of old feudal aristocrats. In the process, these bourgeois merchants created industrial wealth.

Marx predicted that the same thing would happen again, but this time the struggle would be between the bourgeois owners of capital and the workers. Over time, industries would consolidate so that a small number of capitalists would own everything. These capitalists would expropriate, or rob, workers of more and more of the fruits of their labor. Finally, the workers would overthrow the capitalists. The goal of their revolution was socialism, or government ownership of the means of production and distribution. Karl Marx called his ideas "scientific socialism." He thought it was scientific fact that communism would develop—inevitable according to the laws of history.

What would a future communist society be like? Here Marx had less to say. Under **communism,** Marx predicted that there would be only one class, the working class. All property would be held in common, and, finally, there would be no need for a government.

Marx claimed that the coming of communism was a matter of scientific fact, yet he wrote about it with an almost religious passion:

> 66 *In short, Communists everywhere support every revolutionary movement against the existing social and political order of things. . . . Let the ruling class tremble at the communist revolution. The proletarians have nothing to lose but their chains. [Working men] of all countries, unite!* 99
> —*The Communist Manifesto,* 1848

Glorification of the Proletariat

Comparative Government
This painting, *The Cultivation of Cotton* by Aleksandr Volkov, is a propaganda piece exalting workers and the virtues of hard work. *Analyze the message this painting is supposed to send to citizens laboring under a Communist government.*

C **Critical Thinking**

Identifying Points of View
Since the fall of the Soviet Union, the Russian economy has often teetered on the brink of disaster. People have lost their jobs, a large homeless population exists, and organized crime has increased rapidly. Faced with this situation, some people long for the "good old days" of communism. Others point to hopeful signs in the economy and the growth of private enterprise, saying that this is a transitional period and that conditions will improve. Have students choose a side and prepare an argument in support of their choice. Have volunteers present their arguments to the class. **OL**

Caption Answer: Through hard work and unity, workers can achieve progress. Remind students that this message is neither truth nor lies, but propaganda used to influence the opinion of the working class.

Hands-On Chapter Project

Step 4

Creating a Nation

Step 4: Presenting the Project Groups will present their projects to the class.

Directions Students will prepare a presentation of their project to present to the class.

Tell students that they will need to decide how best to present their project. Encourage groups to make a multimedia presentation. Groups can create visuals, such as a map of their country or a diagram of the structure of its government.

They might also choose to include music, perhaps composing a national anthem for their country and performing it for the class.

Groups also should decide how they will organize their presentation. Each member of the group should be responsible for some aspect of the oral presentation. Allow 10 to 15 minutes for each group to present.

Summarizing Each group should follow their presentation with a question-and-answer session involving the rest of the students in the class. Encourage questions about the choices the group made in organizing their government. **OL**

Caption Answer: The man who is carrying a sign protests the individualistic system of capitalism; at the same time, he is marketing his services like any entrepreneur in a capitalist system.

Assess

Assign the Section 4 Assessment as homework or as an in-class activity, or have students take Section Quiz 1-4 from *Section Quizzes and Chapter Tests*.

Close

Speculating Marx predicted that communist revolutions would come first to industrialized nations. In fact, though, they came to countries that were largely agricultural. Ask students to speculate on why that was the case. *(Agricultural nations tend to be poorer and historically they had no tradition of representative government.)*

Section 4 Review

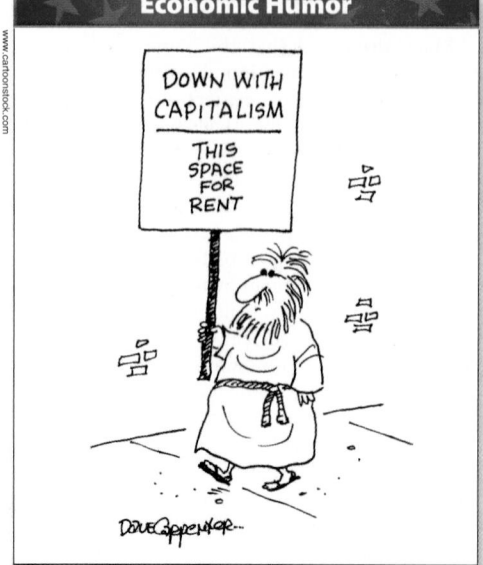

Economic Humor

DOWN WITH CAPITALISM

THIS SPACE FOR RENT

Opposing Economies Capitalism and socialism promote opposing economic systems—a market economy rewarding individual enterprise or a command economy to ensure the welfare of all. *How does the cartoonist use this information to make a joke?*

Communism, a Command Economy

In communist nations, government planners decide how much to produce, what to produce, and how to distribute the goods and services produced. This system is called a **command economy** because decisions are made at the upper levels of government and handed down to managers. In communist countries, the state owns the land, natural resources, industry, banks, and transportation facilities. The state controls mass communication including newspapers, magazines, television, radio, the Internet, and the movie industry.

Today only a handful of communist states exist in the world, most of them in Asia. Like capitalist states, communist states vary in how much of the economy is state-controlled. In the People's Republic of China, established in 1949, the government had tight control of the economy for decades. The Chinese government used five-year plans to set precise goals for every facet of production in the nation. It specified, for example, how many new housing units would be produced over the next five years, where houses would be built, who could live in them, and how much the rent would be.

Mao Zedong was the historic founder of the Chinese Communist Party. Since his death in 1976, China's economy has changed significantly. Today, it, too, has a mixed economy, with a number of capitalist elements in its socialist system. Political freedom is still very limited, however, and for that reason, economic freedom remains limited as well.

SECTION 4 Review

Vocabulary

1. **Explain** the significance of: economics, capitalism, free market, laissez-faire, socialism, proletariat, bourgeoisie, communism, command economy.

Main Ideas

2. **Identifying** What are the three main goals of a socialist economic system?

3. **Explaining** What did Marx believe would happen in a true communist economy?

Critical Thinking

4. **Making Inferences** What ideas by Marx appealed to people in nations where wealth was unevenly distributed?

5. **Organizing** In a graphic organizer similar to the one below, identify three functions of economic systems.

Economic Systems

Writing About Government

6. **Persuasive Writing** Find advertisements in newspapers that illustrate various kinds of economic competition. Display these ads on a bulletin board and include a brief written summary of your findings. Should the government regulate prices? Why or why not?

Answers

1. All definitions can be found in the section and the Glossary.
2. Socialism's goals include the distribution of wealth and economic opportunities equally among the people; society's control, through the government, of all major decisions of production; and public ownership of land, factories, and other means of production.
3. Government would not be needed.
4. Workers would revolt against capitalists, property would be held in common, and one class would evolve.

5. Economic systems decide what is produced, how it is produced, and who gets what is produced.
6. Ads should be those that openly compare one product with another, those that do it more subtly ("better than the leading brand"), or those that do it by inference ("best product for the job"). Students should discuss the advantages and disadvantages of competition.

Interpreting Political Cartoons

You have probably heard the saying: "A picture is worth a thousand words." Political cartoonists agree. They use drawings to express opinions about public figures, political issues, or economic social conditions. Their goal is to convince readers of the cartoonist's or the publication's opinion in an amusing way.

Why Learn This Skill?

Knowing how to interpret political cartoons is useful because it helps you put issues and candidates in perspective.

1. Read the title, caption, conversation balloons, and other text to identify the topic of the cartoon.

2. Identify the characters, people, or symbols shown. Ask yourself: What action is occurring? Who is taking the action?

3. Determine the cartoonist's purpose: Is it to persuade, criticize, or just make people think? What idea is the cartoonist trying to get across? Is the publication or the cartoonist expressing bias?

OKAY, TAKE BOTH FEET OFF THE BRAKE...

PUTIN

DEMOCRACY

THE DRIVING LESSON

Practicing the Skill

1. What is the topic of this cartoon?

2. Who are the participants and what are they doing?

3. Does the cartoon express a favorable or unfavorable view of each leader?

Applying the Skill

Find political cartoons in newspapers or magazines. Then enlarge them and bring them to class. Attach them to the wall and explain the cartoons, including any bias you may detect.

Teach

S₁ Skill Practice

Visual Literacy Ask: Is this cartoon effective in conveying the message intended by the cartoonist? *(Students may answer yes or no but must defend their answer.)* **OL**

S₂ Skill Practice

Visual Literacy Ask: How important are dialogue and labels in this cartoon? *(Very important; the cartoon would not make sense without them.)* Have students locate a political cartoon that has either no dialogue or no labels. **Ask:** How is this cartoon able to get its point across without using dialogue/labels? *(Answers will vary but should mention that the meaning comes from the drawing.)* **OL**

Answers

Practicing the Skill

1. Russia's progress toward democracy
2. President George W. Bush is teaching Russian president Vladimir Putin how to be a democratic leader;—how to "drive" democracy.
3. Answers will vary; students may mention that Bush seems to be confident as a leader of democracy (favorable) and that Putin appears to be unwilling to move toward democracy (unfavorable).

Applying the Skill

Students should express a well-reasoned opinion and be able to support it by citing characteristics of the cartoon.

CHAPTER 1 — Assessment and Activities

ExamView® Assessment Suite

This easy-to-use software includes extensive question banks and allows you to create fully customized tests that can be administered in print or online.

Reviewing Vocabulary

1. state
2. sovereignty
3. democracy
4. constitution
5. autocracy
6. republic
7. capitalism
8. free market
9. communism
10. command economy

Reviewing Main Ideas

11. To establish their sovereignty when declaring independence from Great Britain; at that time, each state considered itself a country.
12. Political movements, such as national liberation organizations, maintain diplomatic relations with many states; multinational corporations have offices and factories in many states—they carry out activities on a global scale; international organizations undertake a variety of tasks, often to serve the needs of member states.
13. In a direct democracy, the people govern themselves by voting on issues individually at meetings that all citizens may attend. In a republic, people elect representatives to govern for them.
14. The government avoids interfering except to ensure that free competition exists in the marketplace.

Critical Thinking

15. Governments help maintain social order, provide public services, provide for national security and common defense, and provide for and control the economic system. Governments can enforce their decisions by legitimacy and coercive force.
16. Without education, people do not have the skills and knowledge to make informed, intelligent choices.

CHAPTER 1 — Assessment and Activities

Reviewing Vocabulary

Insert the content vocabulary word(s) below into the paragraph at right to describe the nature of government and differing political and economic systems. Each word or phrase should be used only once.

constitution, sovereignty, democracy, communism, autocracy, capitalism, state, free market, republic, command economy

Chapter Summary

Purposes of Government
★ Maintain social order
★ Provide public services
★ Provide national security
★ Make economic decisions

Government Systems
★ Unitary System—National or central government holds all key powers
★ Federal System—Power is divided between the national government and state or provincial governments

Characteristics of Democracy
★ Individual liberty
★ Majority rule with minority rights
★ Free elections
★ Competing political parties

Economic Theories
★ Capitalism—Emphasis on freedom of choice and individual incentive
★ Socialism—Government owns means of production, decides how to use resources, and distributes wealth more equally among people
★ Communism—No recognized social classes; all property is held in common; government is unnecessary

32 UNIT 1: *Foundations of American Government*

Every (1) has a form of government that has (2) within its territorial boundaries. A (3) is a government of and by the people that may have a (4) that protects the rights of the people—unlike an (5) that concentrates power in the hands of one person. The United States is a (6) with elected representation. It has a mixed economy based on (7). The (8) allows buyers and sellers to make economic decisions about what to produce, how much to produce, and who gets the goods and services produced. In contrast, under (9), the People's Republic of China and other states have operated a (10) with government planning.

Reviewing Main Ideas

Section 1 *(pages 5–11)*

11. Why did the thirteen American colonies become known as "states"?

Section 2 *(pages 12–17)*

12. Describe three kinds of non-state groups that influence national politics.

Section 3 *(pages 18–24)*

13. How is a direct democracy different from a representative democracy?

Section 4 *(pages 26–30)*

14. What is the role of government in a laissez-faire economic system?

Critical Thinking

15. **Essential Question** What are the major purposes of government, and how do governments enforce their decisions?

16. **Understanding Cause and Effect** Why is widespread educational opportunity necessary for a nation to develop a democratic system?

17. **Making Comparisons** In a Venn diagram like the one below, show how capitalism, democratic socialism, and communism are alike and different.

17.

Capitalism	Democratic Socialism	Communism
Private property, Business competition, Profit motive	Peaceful change, Freedom of choice, Government with basic industries, provides social services	No private property, Violent revolution

Government ONLINE **Self-Check Quiz**
Visit glencoe.com and enter *QuickPass*™ code USG9822c1.
Click on Self-Check Quizzes for additional test practice.

Document-Based Questions

Analyzing Primary Sources

Read the excerpt below and answer the questions that follow.

The Declaration of Independence is not part of the U.S. Constitution and is not considered a legal document upon which the government of the United States is based. It did, however, put into simple terms the reasons why the original thirteen colonies were seeking to form their own nation.

66 *We hold these truths to be self-evident, that all men are created equal, that they are endowed by their Creator with certain unalienable Rights, that among these are Life, Liberty, and the pursuit of Happiness. . . . That whenever any Form of Government becomes destructive of these ends, it is the Right of the People to alter or to abolish it, and to institute new Government, . . . as to them shall seem most likely to effect their Safety and Happiness. . . .*

Such has been the patient sufferance of these Colonies; and such is now the necessity which constrains them to alter their former Systems of Government. The history of the present King of Great Britain is a history of repeated injuries and usurpations, . . .

He has dissolved Representative Houses repeatedly, . . .

He has kept among us, in times of peace, Standing Armies without the Consent of our legislatures.

For quartering large bodies of troops among us: . . .

For imposing Taxes on us without our Consent: . . . 99

18. How does the Declaration of Independence echo the ideas of John Locke?

19. Why do you think the Founders did not include the Declaration of Independence within the constitutional plans for the new federal government?

Interpreting Political Cartoons

Analyze the cartoon and answer the questions that follow. Base your answers on the cartoon and your knowledge of Chapter 1.

"Founding Fathers! How come not Founding Mothers?"

20. What is the subject of the painting in the cartoon?

21. According to the painting, who were the Founders of the United States?

22. What message is the cartoonist trying to communicate?

23. Do you think women influenced the creation of the United States government? Why or why not?

Participating IN GOVERNMENT

24. Constitutions provide a plan for organizing and operating governments. What plan provides the rules for your local government? Does your local government operate under a constitution? Contact a local government official to find out about the basic plan of your city or town. Where did it originate? Present your findings in a diagram to share with the class.

Participating IN GOVERNMENT

24. Diagrams will vary according to the type of local government and with students' choice of diagramming method.

Chapter Bonus Test Question

Ask: Why does Delaware call itself the First State? *(It was the first state to ratify the Constitution.)*

Analyzing Primary Sources

18. Answers should discuss Locke's ideas about the pursuit of life, liberty, and property and might talk about why Jefferson used the word *happiness* rather than *property*.

19. Answers should include the idea that the Founders did not want to make it simple to change the government at will or for selfish purposes, but only when the majority of people were being oppressed by an unfair system.

Interpreting Political Cartoons

20. It shows the writers of the Constitution, the Founders of the United States.

21. men

22. the absence of women among the Founders

23. Possible answer: Yes, although women were treated as second-class citizens, they still influenced society at that time, and thus affected the ideas of the Founders.

Planning Guide

Key to Ability Levels

BL Below level	**AL** Above level
OL On level	**ELL** English Language Learners

Key to Teaching Resources

Print Material   Transparency

CD-ROM or DVD

Levels					Resources	Chapter Opener	Section 1	Section 2	Section 3	Section 4	Chapter Assess
BL	OL	AL	ELL								
					FOCUS						
BL	OL	AL	ELL	📽	Section Focus Transparencies		2-1	2-2	2-3	2-4	
					TEACH						
BL	OL		ELL	📁	Reading Essentials and Study Guide (and Answer Key)		p. 13	p. 16	p. 19	p. 22	
BL	OL		ELL	📁	Guided Reading Activities		p. 5	p. 6	p. 7	p. 8	
BL	OL		ELL	📁	Vocabulary Activities		p. 2				
BL	OL	AL	ELL	📁	Chapter Summaries			p. 4			
BL	OL			📁	American Biographies					p. 11	
BL	OL	AL	ELL	📁	Cooperative Learning Activities					p. 1	
	OL	AL	ELL	📁	Government Simulations and Debate		p. 3				
BL	OL	AL	ELL	📁	Historical Documents and Speeches			p. 2			
BL	OL	AL	ELL	📁	Interpreting Political Cartoons		p. 3				
BL	OL		ELL	📁	Skill Reinforcement Activities				p. 2		
BL	OL	AL	ELL	📁	Source Readings		p. 2				
BL	OL			📁	Supreme Court Case Studies						
BL	OL	AL	ELL	📁	Participating in Government Activities						
BL	OL		ELL	📁	Spanish Declaration of Independence and U.S. Constitution	✓	✓	✓	✓	✓	✓
BL	OL	AL	ELL	📁	NGS World Atlas, Spanish	✓	✓	✓	✓	✓	✓
BL	OL	AL	ELL	📽	Unit Overlay Transparencies, Strategies, and Activities	✓	✓	✓	✓	✓	✓
BL	OL		ELL	📽	Making It Relevant Transparencies	✓	✓	✓	✓	✓	✓
BL	OL	AL	ELL	📽	High School Writing Process Transparencies, Strategies, and Activities	✓	✓	✓	✓	✓	✓
BL	OL	AL		📽	American Art & Architecture Transparencies, Strategies, and Activities	✓	✓	✓	✓	✓	✓

✓ Chapter- or unit-based activities applicable to all sections in this chapter

TeacherWorks™ Plus
All-In-One Planner and Resource Center

- Interactive Lesson Planner
- Interactive Teacher Edition
- Fully editable blackline masters
- Chapter Spotlight Videos Launch
- Differentiated Lesson Plans
- Printable reports of daily assignments
- Standards tracking system

Levels BL	OL	AL	ELL		Resources	Chapter Opener	Section 1	Section 2	Section 3	Section 4	Chapter Assess
TEACH *(continued)*											
BL	OL			◉	**American Music: Hits Through History**	✓	✓	✓	✓	✓	✓
BL	OL		ELL	📁	**Reading Strategies for the Social Studies Classroom**	✓	✓	✓	✓	✓	✓
			ELL	📁	**English Language Learner Handbook**	✓	✓	✓	✓	✓	✓
BL	OL		ELL	📁	**Writer's Guidebook for Social Studies**	✓	✓	✓	✓	✓	✓
BL	OL	AL	ELL	📁	**Living Constitution, SE**	✓	✓	✓	✓	✓	✓
BL	OL	AL	ELL	📁	**Living Constitution, TAE**	✓	✓	✓	✓	✓	✓
BL	OL			📁	**NGS World Atlas, English**	✓	✓	✓	✓	✓	✓
BL	OL		ELL	📁	**The Constitution and You (poster set)**	✓	✓	✓	✓	✓	✓
BL	OL	AL	ELL	📁	**Spanish Chapter Summaries**			p. 4			
BL	OL	AL	ELL	📁	**Spanish Vocabulary Activities**		p. 2				
BL	OL		ELL	📁	**Spanish Reading Essentials and Study Guide (and Answer Key)**		p. 13	p. 16	p. 19	p. 22	
BL	OL	AL	ELL	◉	**PresentationPlus! with MindJogger CheckPoint**	✓	✓	✓	✓	✓	✓
ASSESS											
BL	OL	AL	ELL	◉	*ExamView® Assessment Suite*		2-1	2-2	2-3	2-4	Ch. 2
BL	OL	AL	ELL	📁	**Authentic Assessment with Rubrics**				p. 9		p. 9
BL	OL	AL	ELL	📁	**Section Quizzes and Chapter Tests**		p. 13	p. 14	p. 15	p. 16	pp. 17–24
BL	OL	AL	ELL	📁	**Spanish Section Quizzes and Tests**		p. 13	p. 14	p. 15	p. 16	pp. 17–24
CLOSE											
BL			ELL	📁	**Reteaching Activities**					p. 2	p. 2
BL	OL	AL	ELL	◉	**StudentWorks™ Plus with Audio Summaries**	✓	✓	✓	✓	✓	✓
BL	OL		ELL	🖥	**Graphic Organizer Transparencies**		✓	✓	✓	✓	
BL	OL		ELL	📁	**High School Government Reading and Study Skills Foldables®**		p. 45	p. 45	p. 45	p. 45	

Teach With Technology

What is a widget?
The McGraw-Hill Social Studies widget is a program for any computer with Internet access that acts as a one-stop launching pad for software- and online-based programs.

How can the widget help my students and me?
The widget is a convenient way for you and your students to access McGraw-Hill's software-based and online technology tools. Some of the features of the widget include:

- customizable links to frequently used Glencoe Web pages
- recognition of, and compatibility with, Glencoe DVD and CD-ROM programs
- QuickPass™ entry for fast access to chapter content and activities

Visit glencoe.com to download the free student and teacher versions of the McGraw-Hill Social Studies widget.

Government ONLINE
Visit glencoe.com and enter *QuickPass*™ code USG9085c2T for Chapter 2 resources.

You can easily launch a wide range of digital products from your computer's desktop with the McGraw-Hill Social Studies widget.

	Student	Teacher	Parent
Media Library			
• Student Edition Section Audio	●		●
• Chapter Spotlight Videos	●	●	●
***United States Government* Online Learning Center (Web Site)**			
• Chapter Overviews	●	●	●
• Multilingual Glossaries	●	●	●
• Study-to-Go	●	●	●
• Student Web Activities	●	●	●
• Self-Check Quizzes	●	●	●
• Online Student Edition	●	●	●
• Vocabulary eFlashcards	●	●	●
• Web Activity Lesson Plans		●	
• Vocabulary PuzzleMaker	●	●	●
• Landmark Supreme Court Cases	●	●	●
• Beyond the Textbook	●	●	●

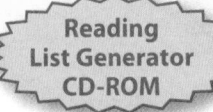

READING SUPPORT FROM
JAMESTOWN EDUCATION

- **Timed Readings Plus in Social Studies** helps students increase their reading rate and fluency while maintaining comprehension. The 400-word passages are similar to those found on state and national assessments.

- **Reading in the Content Area: Social Studies** concentrates on six essential reading skills that help students better comprehend what they read. The book includes 75 high-interest nonfiction passages written at increasing levels of difficulty.

- **Reading Social Studies** includes strategic reading instruction and vocabulary support in Social Studies content for ELLs and native speakers of English.
www.jamestowneducation.com

Reading List Generator CD-ROM

GLENCOE BookLink 3

Use this database to search more than 30,000 titles to create a customized reading list for your students.

- Reading lists can be organized by students' reading level, author, genre, theme, or area of interest.

- The database provides Degrees of Reading Power™ (DRP) and Lexile™ readability scores for all selections.

- A brief summary of each selection is included.

Leveled reading suggestions for this chapter:

- *Citizen Tom Paine,* by Howard Fast
- *Founding Mothers: Women of America in the Revolutionary Era,* by Linda Grant De Pauw
- *The Young United States, 1783–1830,* by Edwin Tunis

Review suggested books before assigning them.

Economics Connection

Personal Finance Literacy

Who Pays Taxes?

As the colonists formed a new nation, they wanted to establish a way to fund the government that was fairer than the taxation without representation they had endured under British rule.

Today, most federal revenue comes from income taxes. The U.S. tax system is called "progressive" because it is structured so that people pay a progressively larger percentage in taxes as their incomes increase. Some countries have a flat tax—the same percentage for everyone.

Effects of Tax Cuts on After-Tax Incomes	
Income level	**Percentage change**
Bottom fifth	+0.3%
Middle fifth	+2.5%
Top fifth	+4.1%
Top 1 percent	+5.4%

Source: Tax Policy Center.

From time to time, Congress passes legislation that affects the federal tax structure. The table on the left shows how tax cuts enacted from 2001 to 2006 affected the 2006 incomes of several income groups.

Ask students: What other taxes do citizens pay? Students might mention income taxes assessed by states, municipalities, and some school districts; sales taxes; or property taxes. Explain that excise taxes also are levied on nonessential consumer goods and services such as guns, gambling, alcohol, tobacco, airline tickets, and motor fuel. There are state and federal taxes on motor fuel. In 2008 state gasoline taxes ranged from 4 to 37 cents per gallon, and the federal tax on gasoline was 18.4 cents per gallon. The petroleum industry also pays other taxes. In mid-2008, the average total tax imposed on gasoline was 49.4 cents per gallon.

Did You Know?

The gap between the incomes of the wealthiest and the poorest U.S. citizens in 2008 was greater than at any time since 1929.

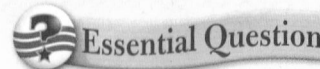 **Essential Question**

Assessing Prior Knowledge
Refer students to the Essential Question on this page. Ask students to list the major events and turning points in the Revolution and write their responses on the board. Ask students to name specific people who were involved in these events. Which individuals were leaders?

Chapter Spotlight Video

To generate student interest and provide a springboard for class discussion, access the Chapter 2 Video at glencoe.com or on the video DVD.

 Dinah Zike's Foldables are three-dimensional, interactive graphic organizers that help students practice basic writing skills, review key vocabulary terms, and identify main ideas. Have students complete this chapter's Foldable activity or activities in *Dinah Zike's Reading and Study Skills Foldables* booklet. **OL**

Government ONLINE

Visit glencoe.com and enter *QuickPass*™ code USG9085c2T for Chapter 2 Resources including Chapter Overview, Student Web Activity, Self-Check Quiz, and other materials for students and teachers.

CHAPTER 2

Chapter Audio   Spotlight Video

The Origins of American Government

Benjamin Franklin, John Adams, and Thomas Jefferson working on a draft of the Declaration of Independence.

Essential Question

How did the critical period of the Revolution and the early years of the republic define our basic government institutions?

Government ONLINE
Chapter Overview Visit glencoe.com and enter *QuickPass*™ code USG9822c2 for an overview, a quiz, and other chapter resources.

34   UNIT 1: *Foundations of American Government*

Launching the Chapter

Accessing Prior Knowledge Discuss with students what they know about early colonial life in North America. For example, they may know that the first permanent English settlement was at Jamestown or that the oldest European settlement still in existence is St. Augustine, Florida. Have students suggest some of the challenges explorers and settlers faced when they arrived. **Essential Question: How might these challenges have influenced the structure of the U.S. government?** *(Answers will vary. Students should draw connections between the challenges facing settlers and basic government institutions.)* **AL**

The Colonial Period

Reader's Guide

Content Vocabulary
★ limited government (p. 36)
★ representative government (p. 37)
★ separation of powers (p. 40)

Academic Vocabulary
★ establish (p. 36)
★ contract (p. 37)
★ revolutionary (p. 38)

Reading Strategy
As you read, create a time line that reflects basic English and American documents on representative government.

1215   1619 1620   1628   1639   1688 1690

Issues in the News

Only in the 1990s did archaeologists discover that the original fort at Jamestown was not washed away in the James River. Today, workers are still digging to uncover all they can about Jamestown, the first English settlement in North America. So far they have found more than 250 feet (76 m) of the lines marking the defensive walls, as well as the east cannon projection, three filled-in cellars, and many artifacts. The original colony grew slowly and in 1618 the Virginia Company tempted new settlers with reforms: easier land ownership, the use of English common law in the courts, and an elected assembly, the House of Burgesses.

▲ The Living History Museum at the Jamestown Settlement

An English Political Heritage

Every year thousands of tourists flock to Virginia to visit Jamestown. Ruins of the old church tower mark the site that many Americans visit with a sense of reverence.

The decaying brick and mortar make a striking contrast to the principles of self-government first exercised here. This legacy of self-government allows Americans today to voice their opinions without fear of reprisal, to choose their leaders, and to take an active role in shaping the nation and communities in which they live.

During the 1600s, people from all over Europe immigrated to North America. Most colonists, however, came from England, and English people settled villages and carried on the bulk of the trade and farming. It was the English who filled the offices for all of the original thirteen colonies along the Atlantic coast. Their political views are at the heart of the American system of government.

The English colonists brought ideas about government that had been developing in England for centuries. Two basic principles are key to English political thought: limited government and representative government. These greatly influenced colonial governments and the Founders during the revolutionary period.

Limited Government

By the time the first colonists settled North America, the idea of limited government was accepted in England. The seeds for the idea first appeared in the Magna Carta[1] of 1215. 📖

📖 See the following footnoted materials in the **Reference Handbook:**
1. *Magna Carta*, page R70.

CHAPTER 2: *Origins of American Government* **35**

Focus

Bellringer
Section Focus Transparencies 2-1

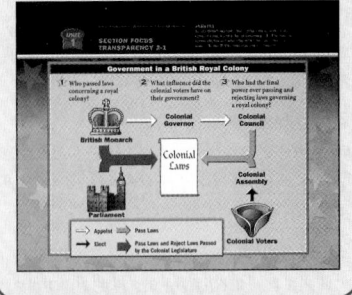

Reader's Guide

Answers to Graphic:
1215—Magna Carta;
1619—Virginia House of Burgesses;
1620—The Mayflower Compact;
1628—Right of Petition;
1636—General Fundamentals;
1639—Fundamental Orders of Connecticut;
1689—The English Bill of Rights

Resource Manager

R Reading Strategies	C Critical Thinking	D Differentiated Instruction	W Writing Support	S Skill Practice
Teacher Edition • Comparing and Contrasting, p. 40 **Additional Resources** • Quizzes/Tests, p. 13 • Guid. Read. Act., p. 5	**Teacher Edition** • Analyzing Information, p. 36 **Additional Resources** • Read. Essen., pp. 13–15	**Teacher Edition** • English Learners, p. 38 **Additional Resources** • Vocab. Act., p. 2	**Teacher Edition** • Narrative Writing, p. 38 **Additional Resources** • Gov. Sims. and Debates, pp. 3–7	**Teacher Edition** • Reading Primary Sources, p. 39 **Additional Resources** • Inter. Poli. Cartoons, pp. 3–4

Teach

C Critical Thinking

Analyzing Information
Discuss the Magna Carta, Petition of Right, and English Bill of Rights. **Ask:** How did these documents build upon one another? How did they later contribute to the revolutionary ideas of the American colonists? (*The Magna Carta established the first principles of a limited government. The Petition of Right granted more powers to Parliament. The English Bill of Rights spelled out rights upon which the monarch could not impose. The colonists modeled their government on aspects of these documents.*) **OL**

Participating
IN GOVERNMENT

Volunteering More than half the teenagers in the United States do volunteer work.

Activity Ask students what benefits there are in volunteering. To help them focus on a type of volunteer work they might enjoy, have them list their interests and skills. **BL**

Hands-On Chapter Project
Step 1

Designing a Film Treatment

Step 1: Seeing the "Big Picture" Have students work in groups to develop a film treatment of the chapter content.

Essential Question: How did the complaints that American colonists had about British rule lead to the American Revolution?

Directions Tell students that they are going to plan a film treatment of the events leading to the Constitutional Convention and the subsequent fight for ratification.

English nobles who were upset with the policies of King John forced him to sign a document recognizing their rights. The nobles did not think the Magna Carta **established** permanent principles of government, nor were they thinking of the rights of common people. As the centuries passed, however, the English came to regard the Magna Carta as the beginning of the idea of **limited government**—the concept that the monarch's power, or government, was limited, not absolute. They believed it protected people from unjust punishment and the loss of life, or the levying of taxes without popular consent. Over time, opponents of absolute monarchy used the Magna Carta to gain more political liberties and build support for true constitutional government.

Petition of Right

In the centuries after the Magna Carta, the English monarchy remained strong, but the Parliament, England's assembly of nobles, was also influential. Monarchs like Queen Elizabeth I (1588–1603) often consulted Parliament and gave it a sense that it ruled with the monarch.

This situation changed in 1625 when Charles I took the throne. Charles wanted to be as powerful as Louis XIV, the absolute monarch of France, and acted that way. This angered English nobles, and when Charles called Parliament into session in 1628, it forced him to agree to the Petition of Right. This limited his power in a number of ways. For example, he could not collect taxes without Parliament's consent. The king and Parliament continued to fight over power, and in the 1640s a war broke out. When Parliament's troops won, Charles was beheaded. After a decade or more of chaos, the monarchy was restored.

English Bill of Rights

Although the monarchy was restored, the same old conflicts occurred between the king and Parliament. The underlying question was: who has the final authority in the kingdom? By 1688, Parliament reached a consensus, and King James II was removed from the throne with little resistance. Parliament then invited William III and Mary II (daughter of the English king) to be the new monarchs. This peaceful transfer of power came to be called the Glorious Revolution. William and Mary recognized Parliament as supreme, and in 1689 the Parliament passed the English Bill of Rights. The English Bill of Rights sets clear limits on the monarch.

Participating
IN GOVERNMENT Being Represented

One reason for the American Revolution was that Britain was depriving the colonists, who saw themselves as British citizens, of representation. By being represented in some organizations in your community, you can provide input to them from a student's perspective. Organizations such as crime patrols, community development groups, youth associations, environmental groups, and volunteer organizations hold regular committee meetings that make decisions that affect you. What can you do to be represented in these organizations?

▼ **Participating in their community**

Participating
IN GOVERNMENT ACTIVITY

1. Call your chamber of commerce or local government offices and ask for a listing of such organizations mentioned.
2. After you have decided on an issue and a committee that interests you, ask to become a part of the committee. You are more likely to serve as a student adviser than as a voting member. As an adviser, though, you will still have the ability to influence decisions and to provide ideas for the future plans of the committee.
3. Attend meetings and ask questions when there are issues that you do not understand. Provide suggestions for getting things done.

First, have groups discuss the structure of the film. Will it be told from the point of view of specific individuals, such as leaders, soldiers, or citizens? Remind students as they read the chapter to look for events and ideas that have the most conflict and dramatic "punch." Each section of the film should correspond to a section of the chapter and include at least one dramatic event.

Next, have group members divide the responsibilities for planning the film.

Each group will need people to create a storyboard and to outline a script. Groups should choose scene designers, costume designers, and sound designers. Location scouts will identify settings for the film.

Putting It Together Ask each group to report on the preliminary choices they have made. **OL**

(Chapter Project continued in Section 2.)

Beginnings of Representative Government in America

▲ The House of Burgesses was the first elected lawmaking body in the English colonies. The royal governor of Jamestown, Sir George Yeardley, allowed the men of the colony to elect representatives to the assembly.

▼ This report of the Virginia General Assembly contains a partial list of the 22 men who hoped to be elected to serve as burgesses. The burgesses made local laws for the colony.

Growth of Democracy
What aspects of the English government influenced the creation of the House of Burgesses?

Linking ☆ Past & Present

John Locke Locke's purpose for writing *Two Treatises of Government* was to show that the English people had a right to dethrone James II in 1688. He argued that God gave people reason so they would know their natural rights and so they could devise a government to protect these rights. Citizens today still base their notions of government on Locke's ideas.

Did You Know?

By the end of the 1600s, several colonies had at least one printing press, which published broadsides, almanacs, pamphlets, and books. During this time, the most widely read authors were clergy who published sermons.

Additional Support

What were the major principles of this influential document? They can be summarized this way:

- Monarchs do not have absolute authority, but rule with the consent of the people's representatives in Parliament;
- The monarch must have Parliament's consent to suspend laws, levy taxes, or maintain an army;
- The monarch cannot interfere with parliamentary elections and debates;
- The people have a right to petition the government and to have a fair and speedy trial by a jury of their peers;
- The people should not be subject to cruel and unusual punishments or to excessive fines and bail.

The influence of the English Bill of Rights was felt directly in the American colonies. The colonists believed the document applied to them and that they had the same rights as people living in Britain. The problem was that the king had a different idea—he saw colonials as *subjects* of the British Empire. These differing ideas were a major cause for the rebellion.

Representative Government

The colonists firmly believed in **representative government,** a government in which people elect delegates to make laws and conduct government. Britain's Parliament was a representative assembly with the power to enact laws. It had two chambers. The members of the upper chamber, the House of Lords, were the first sons of noble families. The lower chamber, or House of Commons, was elected, but few people could vote. Most people elected to the Commons were the younger sons of noble families or wealthy commoners. American colonial legislatures followed the English model.

New Political Ideas

European ideas on government deeply influenced the American colonists. During the late 1600s and 1700s, a major intellectual movement known as the Enlightenment occurred. Enlightenment writers stressed that society and social relations should be based on reason. Educated American colonists were familiar with Enlightenment ideas.

Two thinkers they read closely were John Locke, an English philosopher, and Jean-Jacques Rousseau, a leading writer during the French Enlightenment. Both men had theories about a social **contract** among the governed. Locke spelled out his political ideas in *Two Treatises of Government,*[1] which was first published in 1690.

Locke reasoned that before governments came about, a "state of nature" existed. In this state of nature, people were free, equal, and independent. In his view, people were born with natural rights—the right to life, liberty, and property. He theorized that people made a contract among themselves, a social contract, to create a government to protect their natural rights.

📖 *See the following footnoted materials in the* **Reference Handbook:**
1. *Two Treatises of Government,* page R74.

★ Activity: Interdisciplinary Connection

Music Choral reading can be a stirring way to dramatize some of the documents in our heritage. Have interested students browse through some of the documents discussed in the section—such as the Petition of Right and the English Bill of Rights—and put together a medley of passages to present to the class. Caution students that it takes a fair amount of practice to get the group speaking in unison and that unless they do so, the dramatic effect will be lost. **OL**

D Differentiated Instruction

English Learners Have students work with a proficient student to check their pronunciation for each of the names of the thirteen colonies. If necessary, have partners create phonetic spellings. **ELL**

W Writing Support

Narrative Writing Ask students to assume that they are Virginia colonists. Have them write letters to relatives in England explaining how American colonial government is similar to and different from English government. Additional research might be necessary. Students might want to enliven their letters by describing an imaginary situation in which a friend presented a hotly-debated issue before the House of Burgesses or in which a friend ran afoul of the law. **OL**

Critical Thinking

Answer: They shared the legacy of political representation from England, especially the ideas of John Locke.

Additional Support

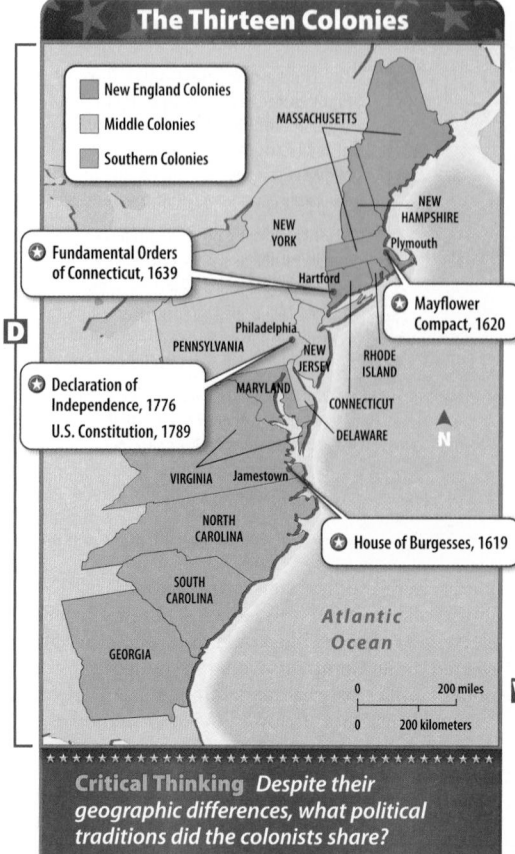

The Thirteen Colonies

Legend:
- New England Colonies
- Middle Colonies
- Southern Colonies

Map labels: MASSACHUSETTS, NEW HAMPSHIRE, NEW YORK, Plymouth, Fundamental Orders of Connecticut, 1639, Hartford, Mayflower Compact, 1620, Philadelphia, PENNSYLVANIA, NEW JERSEY, RHODE ISLAND, Declaration of Independence, 1776, U.S. Constitution, 1789, MARYLAND, CONNECTICUT, DELAWARE, VIRGINIA, Jamestown, NORTH CAROLINA, House of Burgesses, 1619, SOUTH CAROLINA, GEORGIA, Atlantic Ocean, N

0   200 miles
0   200 kilometers

Critical Thinking *Despite their geographic differences, what political traditions did the colonists share?*

If, however, a government failed to protect these rights, people were justified in rebelling and changing that government.

These political theories were **revolutionary** in an age when monarchs still claimed they ruled by divine right. Locke denied that people were obliged to obey such monarchs. Instead, he insisted that:

> ❝ *Whenever the legislators endeavour to take away and destroy the property of the people, or to reduce them into slavery under arbitrary power, they put themselves into a state of war with the people who are thereupon absolved from any further obedience, and are left to the common refuge which God has provided for all men against force and violence.* ❞
>
> —from *The Second Treatise of Government*, 1690

For Locke, government was legitimate only as long as the people continued to consent to it. The Declaration of Independence, the Constitution, and the ideas behind the French Revolution reflected this principle.

Colonial Governments

The English founded thirteen colonies along the eastern coast of North America between 1607 and 1733—from the New England colonies in the north to the Carolinas and Georgia in the south. From these colonies the present system of American government evolved.

Each English colony had its own government consisting of a governor, a legislature, and a court system. These colonial institutions did exercise a certain amount of authority. Nevertheless, the British believed that all colonists owed allegiance to the monarch. For many years the colonists seemed to be loyal subjects, but there were few occasions when the relationship between the monarch and the colonists was put to the test.

Democratic ideas grew rapidly in all the colonies, but it certainly was not democracy as we know it today. Democracy at this time meant that it was possible for a working farmer, for example, to have his views heard in local meetings or to vote on certain issues in some colonies. Women and enslaved persons could not vote, and every colony had some type of property qualification for voting. Nine of the thirteen colonies had an official or established church, and many colonists remained intolerant of religious dissent. In Puritan town meetings, for example, voting was originally reserved for members of the community church.

Despite such shortcomings, colonial governments established practices that became a key part of the nation's system of government. Chief among these practices were:

- a written constitution,
- a legislature of elected representatives, and
- the separation of powers between the executive and the legislature.

Written Constitutions

A key feature of the colonial period was government according to a written plan. The Mayflower Compact[1] that the Pilgrims signed in 1620 was the first of many colonial plans for self-government. 📖

📖 *See the following footnoted materials in the **Reference Handbook**:*
1. *The Mayflower Compact,* page R72.

Activity: Collaborative Learning

Holding a Town Meeting Organize the class into small groups. Ask them to identify school rules or practices that they would like to see changed. Have each group member think of at least two examples. Then have group members meet to discuss their responses. With one group member acting as a recorder, have the groups put together a descriptive listing of their ideas to present to the class for discussion. After all groups have made their presentations, have students compile a master list representing all the accepted ideas. Finally, initiate a class "town meeting" to determine what steps should be taken to make the recommended changes. **OL**

Men of the Pilgrim families drew up the document in the tiny cabin of their ship, the *Mayflower,* anchored off the New England coast. The Pilgrim leaders realized they needed rules to govern themselves if they were to survive in the new land. Through the Mayflower Compact, they agreed to:

" *[S]olemnly and mutually in the Presence of God and one of another, covenant [pledge] and combine ourselves together into a civil Body Politick, for our better Ordering and Preservation, and Furtherance of the Ends aforesaid.* "
—The Mayflower Compact, 1620

The Pilgrims also agreed to choose their own leaders and to make their own laws, which they would design for their own benefit.

In the 1620s, new Puritan immigrants established the Massachusetts Bay Colony and added many towns to the original Plymouth settlement. In 1636 the colony adopted the General Fundamentals, the first system of laws in the English colonies.

In 1639 Puritans from the Massachusetts Bay Colony established yet another colony in Connecticut. They then drew up America's first formal constitution, or charter, called the Fundamental Orders of Connecticut.[1] It gave the people the right to elect the governor, judges, and representatives to make laws. Soon after, other English colonies created their own charters with similar provisions.

Colonial Legislatures

Representative assemblies also became firmly established in the colonies. The Virginia House of Burgesses, the first legislature in America, was established in 1619, only 12 years after the settlement of Jamestown. Farther north, religious beliefs played a key role in how representative assemblies developed. In England, the king was the head of the Church of England and therefore appointed bishops and clergy. American Puritans rejected this idea. They believed that each congregation should choose its ministers. Many Puritans migrated to America to gain the freedom to organize their churches as they chose. Puritan congregations in the colonies came to believe that church members should also elect their government—again, the elective principle was reinforced in colonial life.

In 1636 Puritans in Massachusetts forced their leaders to allow each town to elect two members of the General Court, the colony's legislature. By the mid-1700s, most colonial legislatures had been operating for more than 100 years. As a result, representative government was an established tradition in America well before the colonists declared their independence from Great Britain in 1776.

[1] *See the following footnoted materials in the* **Reference Handbook:**
1. *Fundamental Orders of Connecticut,* page R73.

Forming a Government

Political Processes
Tompkins H. Matteson painted *Signing the Compact on Board the Mayflower.* In the compact, the Pilgrims pledged to obey the laws passed "for the general good of the colony." *Why did the colonists believe they needed to draw up the Mayflower Compact?*

S Skill Practice

Reading Primary Sources
Ask: How does the phrase "better Ordering and Preservation" reflect the purpose of the Mayflower Compact? *(It was created to establish an orderly society so the Pilgrims could survive.)* **OL**

Did You Know?

Puritans placed a high value on education. In 1642 the Massachusetts legislature required parents and ministers to teach all children to read so they could understand the Bible. Five years later, the legislature ordered towns with at least 50 families to establish an elementary school and those with 100 families or more to set up secondary schools. Soon afterward, other New England colonies adopted similar legislation.

Caption Answer: They knew they would need rules to govern themselves if they were to survive.

Additional Support

Activity: Interdisciplinary Connection

Technology In colonial times, most work was done with hand tools. Today people are more likely to use power machinery and equipment. Organize the class into groups to make a bulletin board display comparing colonial and modern technology. Each group should work on a different category, such as kitchen implements, shop tools, cloth-making equipment, and farm tools. Students may draw the equipment or cut pictures from old magazines. Have students label their work. **OL**

R Reading Strategy

Comparing and Contrasting
The idea of natural rights and responsible government became the basis of protest and revolt in the colonies. Have students work in small groups to learn more about the ideas of Locke, Rousseau, and Montesquieu. Students should prepare a report comparing the ideas of these three important Enlightenment figures. Students' reports should also discuss their influence on the men who wrote the U.S. Constitution. **OL**

Assess

Assign the Section 1 Assessment as homework or as an in-class activity, or have students take Section Quiz 2-1 from *Section Quizzes and Chapter Tests*.

Close

Analyzing Note that the Mayflower Compact was not a constitution. **Ask:** Why was the Mayflower Compact important? *(It bound colonists to set up self-government—an important step on the road to democracy.)* **OL**

Section 1 Review

TIME
For the Record

Best Bird The bald eagle became our national bird in 1782. What did this raptor have going for it? The bird is native to the United States, and to the Founders it symbolized courage, strength, freedom, and immortality. Benjamin Franklin, however, disagreed with the other Founders. He thought the bald eagle was too aggressive and preferred the turkey. After a six-year debate, Franklin was outvoted, which no doubt ruffled his feathers.

The legislative bodies of colonial government were dominant in political life. The rapidly growing colonies constantly needed new laws to cope with new circumstances. For example, they had to control the distribution of land, which could be very controversial. They had to lay out plans for public buildings. They also had to build roads and ferries that were vital to the economy, and set up schools and courts.

Compared to Europe, a relatively large percentage of the male population could vote. There were property qualifications for voting, but land was abundant and cheap, enabling many colonists to own land and thus vote. As a result, colonial legislatures had to develop policies that received the consent of the governed.

Separation of Powers

Colonial charters divided the power of government. The governor, the king's agent in the colonies, had executive power, while the legislative assembly had the power to pass laws. Colonial courts heard cases. The idea of **separation of powers** had been written about by Charles-Louis Montesquieu, an Enlightenment thinker, in *The Spirit of Laws*. Colonists were familiar with Montesquieu's ideas.

R The actions of colonial legislatures and courts could be reviewed by a committee of the king's Privy Council, but the colonies practiced a great deal of self-government. Their legislatures became the training grounds for the political leaders who wrote the Constitution. Many of them were active in colonial politics and had served in colonial legislatures. Thus, the combination of their English heritage and colonial experience in representative self-government made them leaders in what one historian called "the seedtime of the republic."

SECTION 1 Review

Vocabulary

1. **Explain** the significance of: limited government, representative government, separation of powers.

Main Ideas

2. **Analyzing** How did John Locke's natural law argument apply to the social contract theory?

3. **Describing** What were two key ideas from the Magna Carta that were used in the English Bill of Rights?

Critical Thinking

4. **Identifying Central Issues** The idea of limited government, first established by the Magna Carta, is an important principle of American government. Why must government be limited?

5. **Organizing** In a graphic organizer similar to the one below, list three practices that were established by colonial governments and became a key part of the nation's system of government.

Key Practices of American Government

Writing About Government

6. **Expository Writing** Review the key ideas of the English Bill of Rights outlined on page 37. Then review the Bill of Rights in the U.S. Constitution. Create a table showing the similarities in the two documents, and accompany it with a short explanatory essay.

40   UNIT 1: *Foundations of American Government*

Answers

1. All definitions can be found in the section and the Glossary.
2. Locke believed "natural law" provided the right to life, liberty, and property and that people form a social contract with government to protect these natural rights.
3. The monarch does not have absolute power; must have consent of Parliament to suspend laws, levy taxes, and maintain an army; and cannot interfere with parliamentary elections. The people have a right to a speedy trial and a jury of peers. The people are not subject to cruel and unusual punishments or excessive fines or bail.
4. Answers should explain that a government of unlimited power would be more prone to abuse that power, rulers could become tyrants, many groups would not be represented, and civil liberties/natural rights would be endangered.
5. Answers might include a written constitution, a legislature of elected representatives, and separation of powers.
6. Students' essays should note the rights granted by the English Bill of Rights. Students' reasons are more important than the rights they choose. Students should use standard grammar, spelling, sentence structure, and punctuation.

Does the First Amendment Protect Symbolic Speech?

Texas v. *Johnson*, 1989

The First Amendment protects free speech, one of the nation's key freedoms. Is any and all speech allowed, however? What about speech that offends or provokes others? In this case, symbolic speech (conduct that conveys a message) was the type of speech at issue.

Facts of the Case

In 1984 Gregory Lee Johnson set fire to an American flag during a protest at the Republican National Convention in Dallas, Texas. No one was injured, but many witnesses were outraged. Johnson was arrested and charged with violating a Texas law that made it illegal to "intentionally or knowingly desecrate . . . a state or national flag." He was convicted, sentenced to a year in prison, and fined $2,000.

Johnson appealed his conviction to the Texas Court of Criminal Appeals, the highest criminal court in the state, contending that the law violated his First Amendment right to free expression. His conviction was overturned. The State of Texas then asked the United States Supreme Court to review the case.

The Constitutional Question

The Supreme Court has long held that the right to free speech is not absolute. A person does not have the right, for example, to "cry fire in a crowded theater" because that could cause a dangerous panic. Nor are "fighting words"—speech intended to provoke violence—a protected form of speech. Can expressive actions that may offend many people—such as burning the American flag—be restricted?

In siding with Johnson, the Texas Court of Criminal Appeals held that Johnson's conviction violated his First Amendment rights. The court ruled that in burning the flag, Johnson was engaged in "symbolic speech." In other words, the court held that his action constituted an expression of opinion protected by the First Amendment.

In the U.S. Supreme Court case *Texas* v. *Johnson*, the state made two arguments. First, Texas argued that the state had an interest in preserving the flag as a symbol of national unity. Second, Texas argued that it had a right to ban flag burning as part of its duty to maintain order. The burning of an American flag, argued the state, could be so offensive that it could incite violence or a breach of the peace.

Debating the Issue

Questions to Consider

1. What is symbolic speech? How can an action be considered speech?

2. Which do you believe is more important—a citizens' right to express themselves or the government's need to keep order? Explain.

You Be the Judge

Under what circumstances, if any, should the government be able to restrict free speech? Should the First Amendment protect symbolic speech? Does the U.S. flag, or any other venerated symbol, deserve constitutional protection?

▶ Gregory Lee Johnson

Debating the Issue Answers

Questions to Consider

1. Symbolic speech is an action that expresses an idea. A person may convey a message through actions such as wearing a protest button or an arm band, participating in a sit-in, or waving (or burning) a flag.

2. Students should explain the rationale behind their opinions.

You Be the Judge

In their responses, students should address each question. Consider using their responses as a starting point for class debate.

Teach

Class Debate

Organize students into three groups: one group to argue that a flag-burning amendment to the Constitution is necessary, one group to refute that view, and a third group to act as a jury. After the jury has deliberated, have a representative read the opinion to the class. OL

The Court's Decision

In a 5 to 4 ruling, the Supreme Court declared the Texas law unconstitutional. The Court ruled that Johnson's act of burning the flag was expressive conduct protected by the First Amendment. The state could not justify infringing upon First Amendment rights by claiming a need to preserve national unity. By arresting and convicting him of flag burning, Texas violated Johnson's right to express political dissent. (He had been participating in a protest of policies of the Reagan administration.)

The Court also rejected Texas's argument that the statute was necessary to avoid breaches of the peace. Johnson's act did not lead to any such breach of the peace. No one was injured, and no property besides the flag was damaged. The Court noted that another Texas law existed under which the state could prosecute breaches of the peace—if, for example, a riot had ensued—without violating a person's right to free expression.

Focus

Bellringer

Section Focus Transparencies 2-2

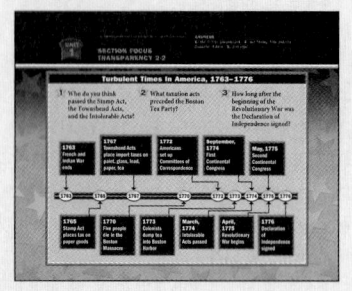

Reader's Guide

Answers to Graphic:

French and Indian War →
   Colonists taxed to pay for war

Stamp Act → Colonists
   boycotted British goods

Other taxes → Boston Tea Party

Boston Tea Party → Coercive
   Acts

Coercive Acts → First
   Continental Congress

Resource Manager

Uniting for Independence

Reader's Guide

Content Vocabulary	Academic Vocabulary	Reading Strategy
★ revenue (p. 43) ★ embargo (p. 44)	★ dramatically (p. 42) ★ draft (p. 46) ★ constitution (p. 47)	Create a graphic organizer like the one below. Track the actions of the British government and American colonists to illustrate how their relations weakened.

Causes	Results

Issues in the News

Lexington, Massachusetts, has the nation's longest tradition of reenacting historic events. It was in Lexington that the famed minutemen gathered in April 1775 to let off "the shot heard round the world"—setting off the American Revolution. A 2004 documentary highlighted the reenactors' efforts to get every detail right, even the exact type of linen used in uniforms. "It itches and scratches—I not only look like this individual, I feel like him," one participant said. For her part, filmmaker Marian Marzynski was most impressed with the men's "far-from-textbook passion for history."

▲ Reenacting the Battle of Lexington

How did the Battle of Lexington come about? For more than a century, relations between the colonies and Great Britain were peaceful. The colonies developed their political institutions without much interference.

By the 1760s, however, things changed **dramatically** because the British government—for reasons of its own—began to tighten control of the colonies and raise taxes in North America.

The Colonies on Their Own

As British subjects, the colonists in North America owed allegiance to the monarch and the British government. As with other parts of the British Empire, the colonies were supposed to serve as a source of raw materials and a market for British goods. Thus, in the eyes of the British crown, the American colonies existed for the economic benefit of Great Britain.

In practice, during the 150 years following the settling of Jamestown in 1607, the colonies in America did pretty much as they pleased. The colonies were more than 3,000 miles (4,828 km) from Great Britain. Orders from the monarch took two months or more to get across the Atlantic Ocean.

Given this distance, only the governors of the colonies and the colonial legislatures were actually in a position to deal with the everyday problems facing the colonies. As a result, the colonists grew accustomed to governing themselves through their representatives.

Until the mid-1700s, the British government was generally satisfied with this arrangement. The colonies added to British wealth. In addition, the British needed the colonists' loyalty to counter the threat of the French in Canada. The colonists remained loyal in return for a large measure of self-rule and protection from the French.

R Reading Strategies	**C** Critical Thinking	**D** Differentiated Instruction	**W** Writing Support	**S** Skill Practice
Teacher Edition • Identifying, p. 47 **Additional Resources** • Quizzes/Tests, p. 14 • Guid. Read. Act., p. 6	**Teacher Edition** • Drawing Conclusions, p. 43 **Additional Resources** • Read. Essen., pp. 16–18 • Ch. Summaries, pp. 4–6	**Teacher Edition** • Kinesthetic, p. 44 • Verbal/Linguistic, p. 46 **Additional Resources** • Source Readings, p. 2	**Additional Resources** • Hist. Docs. and Speeches, p. 2	**Additional Resources** • Am. Biographies, p. 45

Britain Tightens Control

Two events greatly changed the relationship between the colonies and Britain. First, in the French and Indian War, the British defeated the French, eliminating their power in North America. Second, George III became king in 1760. He had different ideas about how the colonies should be governed.

The French and Indian War started as a struggle between the French and British over lands in western Pennsylvania and Ohio. By 1756, several other European countries became involved. Great Britain won the war in 1763 and gained complete control of the eastern third of the continent.

The defeat of France meant American colonists no longer needed the British to protect them from the French. The real impact of the war, however, was the cost to the British. Left with a huge war debt, Britain's leaders believed the colonists had an obligation to pay up—and that was how all the trouble started.

Taxing the Colonies

When George III became king, he was determined to deal firmly with the American colonies. To help pay for the war, the king and his ministers levied taxes on tea, sugar, glass, paper, and other products. The Stamp Act of 1765 imposed the first direct tax on the colonists. It required them to pay a tax on legal documents, pamphlets, newspapers, and even dice and playing cards. Parliament also passed laws regulating colonial trade in ways that benefited Great Britain but not the colonies.

Britain's **revenue**—the money a government collects from taxes or other sources—from the colonies increased. Colonial resentment, however, grew along with the revenues. Political protests began to spread throughout the colonies. Colonists refused to buy British goods.

The protests led to the repeal of the Stamp Act, but the British passed other tax laws to replace it. The situation reached a boiling point in 1773.

We the People

Making a Difference

"With a firm reliance on the protection of divine Providence, we mutually pledge to each other our Lives, our Fortunes, and our Sacred Honor." With these words, the signers of the Declaration of Independence launched their nation's bid for freedom. For many, that goal came at great cost. Four signers were taken prisoner while fighting in South Carolina. Another signer, Richard Stockton of New Jersey, was taken prisoner, beaten, and held for several years. His health ruined, he died soon after being released.

The New York home of signer Francis Lewis was plundered and his wife taken prisoner. Badly mistreated, she died a few years after her release. Altogether 14 signers had their homes invaded and were forced to flee with their families.

Carter Braxton of Virginia lost his merchant ships to the British. Robert Stockton was probably the only signer to die as a direct result of the war, but all of the signers were willing to risk everything for freedom. Without their courage, independence could not have been achieved.

▲ The signers of the Declaration

66 . . . we mutually pledge to each other our Lives, our Fortunes, and our Sacred Honor. 99

Teach

C Critical Thinking

Drawing Conclusions Discuss with students the excerpt from the last paragraph of the Declaration of Independence and the events that followed its signing. **Ask:** Did the signers stand by their words? Do you think their sacrifices were worth the effort? Would the results have been the same without those sacrifices? *(Generally, yes, the signers stood by their words; students may answer yes or no.)* **OL**

Making a Difference

George Mason In 1787 Mason was one of three delegates at the Constitutional Convention who refused to approve the Constitution. He was disappointed that the document failed to deal with slavery. Washington felt betrayed by Mason's refusal to sign, and the longtime friends never visited again.

Activity: Have students investigate the lives of other Americans who paid a price for taking an unpopular stand. **AL**

Additional Support

Activity: Collaborative Learning

Understanding Points of View Explain to students that Loyalists were American colonists who remained loyal to Great Britain and opposed the Revolution. Organize the class into small groups to consider the Loyalist point of view of pre-Revolutionary events. Have each group assume that it is a committee of Loyalists living in the colonies. Each committee should discuss relations between Great Britain and the colonies and prepare a list of policy recommendations for King George III. One person in each group should take notes of the discussion and record the group's recommendations. Have another member of each group present its list to the class. Ask students to compare the lists to identify common solutions and innovative approaches to resolving the crisis. **OL**

D Differentiated Instruction

Kinesthetic Have students design and make a monument to a person or an event discussed under the heading *Colonial Unity*, such as Benjamin Franklin, Patrick Henry, Samuel Adams, Richard Henry Lee, George Washington, the Boston Tea Party, or the signing of the Declaration of Independence. Encourage students to do research as necessary to make their monuments authentic. Leave the choice of materials—clay, wood, paper, cardboard, and so on—to the students. Each monument should have a plaque identifying the person or event honored and giving a brief explanation of the monument's significance. **OL**

Caption Answer: the right to representation, self-government, individual liberty, and equality under British law

Hands-On Chapter Project

Step 2

Designing a Film Treatment

Step 2: Making Key Decisions
Students will begin making some crucial decisions based on what they have learned in Section 1.

Directions At this stage, groups will need to identify the film's main characters. Suggest that students find ways to incorporate the speakers of primary source quotations as characters in the film. Then have them discuss possible actors to play

those roles. At this point, groups will have to make final, firm decisions about the structure and point of view of the film—the storyboard and outline should begin to take shape, and key scenes should be identified. Costume and scene designers will make some preliminary sketches, and background music and sound effects will be chosen. (Students may enjoy researching these period details.) Location scouts will explain where various scenes might be filmed. Remind students that although they have specific responsibilities, they should keep

---

Growing Distrust

Civic Rights New British laws caused discontent among colonists who believed their civic rights were being denied. *Which civic rights do you think Britain denied the colonists?*

A group of colonists, dressed as Mohawk Indians, dumped 342 chests of British tea into Boston Harbor. This protest became known as the Boston Tea Party. In retaliation Parliament passed the Coercive Acts, which the colonists called the Intolerable Acts. One of these acts closed Boston Harbor. Another of the Coercive Acts withdrew the right of the Massachusetts colony to govern itself. By the early 1770s, events clearly showed that revolution was not far off.

Colonial Unity

D Before the mid-1770s, most colonists thought of themselves as British subjects. At the same time, each of the colonies developed largely on its own. Thus, most colonists also thought of themselves as Virginians or New Yorkers or Georgians. Indeed, early attempts to unite the colonies had failed.

In response to French attacks on the frontier, in 1754 Benjamin Franklin proposed a plan for uniting the colonies—the Albany Plan of Union. The colonies rejected the plan, however, because it gave too much power to an assembly made up of representatives from all thirteen colonies.

By the 1760s, the harsh new British policies spurred an American sense of community. A growing number of colonists began to think of themselves as Americans united by their hostility toward British authority. At the same time, colonial leaders began to work together to take political action against what they felt was British oppression.

Taking Action

In 1765 nine colonies sent delegates to a meeting in New York called the Stamp Act Congress. This was the first meeting organized by the colonies to protest King George's actions. Delegates to the Congress sent a petition to the king, arguing that only colonial legislatures could impose direct taxes such as the Stamp Tax.

By 1773, organizations called committees of correspondence were urging resistance to the British. These committees consisted of colonists who wanted to keep in touch with one another as events unfolded. Samuel Adams established the first committee in Boston. The idea spread quickly, and within a few months, Massachusetts alone had more than 80 such committees. Virginia and other colonies soon joined in this communication network. Two prominent members of the Virginia committee of correspondence were Thomas Jefferson and Patrick Henry.

The First Continental Congress

The Intolerable Acts prompted Virginia and Massachusetts to call a general meeting of the colonies. Delegates from all the colonies except Georgia met in Philadelphia on September 5, 1774, for the First Continental Congress. Key colonial leaders such as Patrick Henry, Samuel Adams, Richard Henry Lee, and George Washington attended. The delegates debated what to do about the relationship with Great Britain. They finally imposed an **embargo,** an agreement prohibiting trade, on Britain and agreed not to use British goods. They also proposed a meeting the following year if Britain did not change its policies.

Events then moved quickly. The British adopted stronger measures. "The New England governments are in a state of rebellion," George III firmly announced. "Blows must decide whether they are to be subject to this country or independent."

The first blow fell early on the morning of April 19, 1775. British Redcoats clashed with colonial minutemen at Lexington and Concord in Massachusetts. This skirmish was the first battle of the Revolutionary War.

---

the overall project in mind and contribute their ideas about areas that are not their primary responsibility.

Putting It Together Have students share preliminary storyboards, outlines, and sketches. As a group, have students evaluate the progress they have made toward completion of the film treatment. Discuss any key events in Sections 1 and 2 that they have difficulty conveying. **OL**

(Chapter Project continued in Section 3.)

The Second Continental Congress

Within three weeks, delegates from all thirteen colonies gathered in Philadelphia for the Second Continental Congress. The Continental Congress immediately assumed the powers of a central government. It chose John Hancock of Massachusetts as president. Hancock was a well-known colonial leader, but he was also a wealthy merchant and thus well-placed for helping to raise funds for an army. The next critical steps were to organize an army and navy, to issue money, and to appoint George Washington as commander of the Continental Army.

Although it had no constitutional authority, the Second Continental Congress served as the acting government of the colonies throughout the war. It purchased supplies, negotiated treaties, and rallied support for the colonists' cause.

Independence

As the Congress set to work, the independence movement was growing rapidly. A brilliant pamphlet titled *Common Sense*, written by Thomas Paine, influenced many colonists. Paine, a onetime British corset maker, argued that monarchy was a corrupt form of government and that George III was an enemy to liberty:

66 *The powers of governing still remaining in the hands of the [king], he will have a negative over the whole legislation on this continent. And as he hath shown himself such an inveterate enemy to liberty, and discovered such a thirst for arbitrary power; is he, or is he not, a proper man to say to these colonies, 'You shall make no laws but what I please.'* 99
—Thomas Paine

Comparing Governments

Critical Thinking

Answer: World War II set off a series of events that led to independence movements in Asian nations.

Research Activity Have each student choose a country (other than the United States) on the chart to research. Ask questions such as the following: Was the country a colony, a territory, or a mandate of another country before independence? If so, which country? Did the country fight a war for independence? Did the country establish a democratic government upon achieving independence? If so, does it still have such a government? What kind of government does the country have now? OL

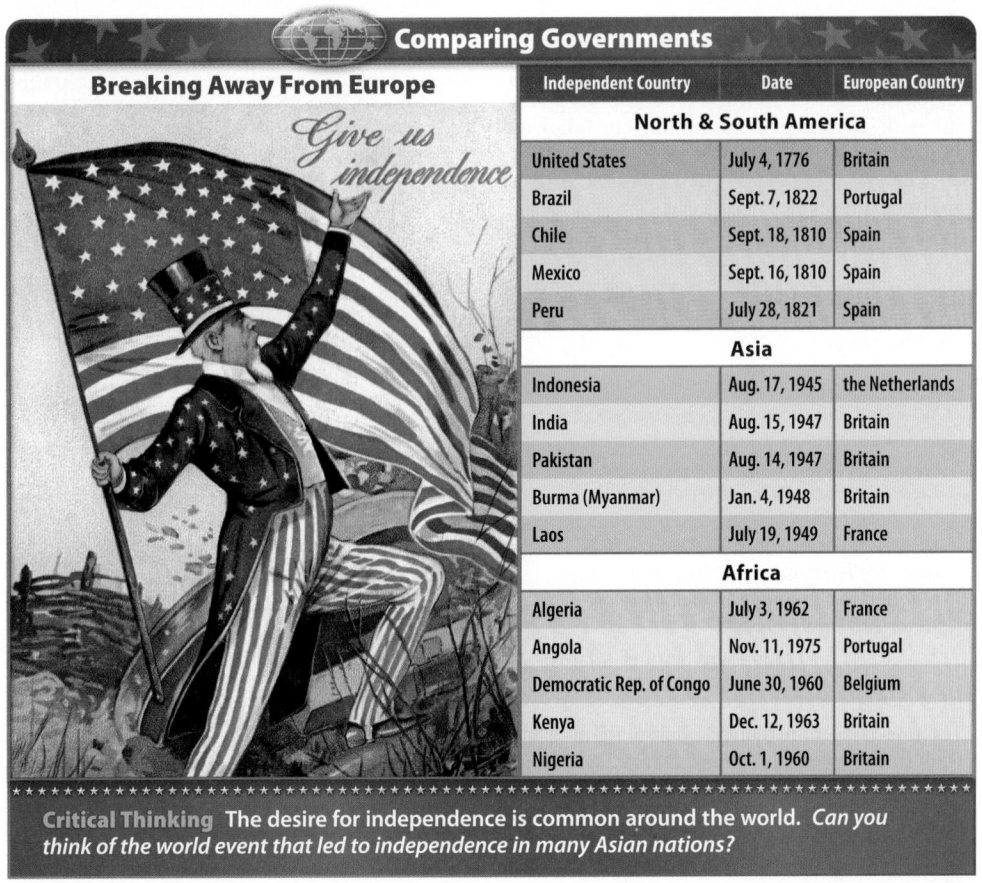

Comparing Governments

Breaking Away From Europe

Give us independence

Independent Country	Date	European Country
North & South America		
United States	July 4, 1776	Britain
Brazil	Sept. 7, 1822	Portugal
Chile	Sept. 18, 1810	Spain
Mexico	Sept. 16, 1810	Spain
Peru	July 28, 1821	Spain
Asia		
Indonesia	Aug. 17, 1945	the Netherlands
India	Aug. 15, 1947	Britain
Pakistan	Aug. 14, 1947	Britain
Burma (Myanmar)	Jan. 4, 1948	Britain
Laos	July 19, 1949	France
Africa		
Algeria	July 3, 1962	France
Angola	Nov. 11, 1975	Portugal
Democratic Rep. of Congo	June 30, 1960	Belgium
Kenya	Dec. 12, 1963	Britain
Nigeria	Oct. 1, 1960	Britain

Critical Thinking The desire for independence is common around the world. *Can you think of the world event that led to independence in many Asian nations?*

Additional Support

Activity: Collaborative Learning

Analyzing Primary Sources The middle section of the Declaration of Independence lists abuses suffered by the colonists under King George III. Divide the class into groups, and assign three of those abuses to each group to restate in their own words. For each abuse, have a representative of each group read aloud their version. Have the class decide which group's version is most clearly worded. As an extension, ask the class to decide whether the abuses can be classified in any way; for example, they could be classified as abuses of laws, abuses of personal property, and so on. OL AL

Caption Answer: Students may answer yes or no. The colonies were established under the British monarchy and were, therefore, subject to its laws, so making the Declaration was an illegal action. However, the colonists justified their actions under natural law, so to them making the Declaration was legal.

D Differentiated Instruction

Verbal/Linguistic Have students rewrite the Samuel Adams excerpt in their own, more modern sounding, words. Encourage students to look up unfamiliar words in a dictionary or thesaurus. **Ask:** When this complicated excerpt is broken down, does it make more sense?

GO TO To enrich study of chapter content, remind students that footnoted materials appear in the **Reference Handbook.**

Additional Support

Growth of Democracy

In *Pulling Down the Statue of George III*, William Walcutt depicted Americans celebrating their independence by tearing down the statue of King George III in New York City on July 9, 1776. The statue was later melted down into bullets to be used against the king's troops. *Was the Declaration of Independence a legal act?*

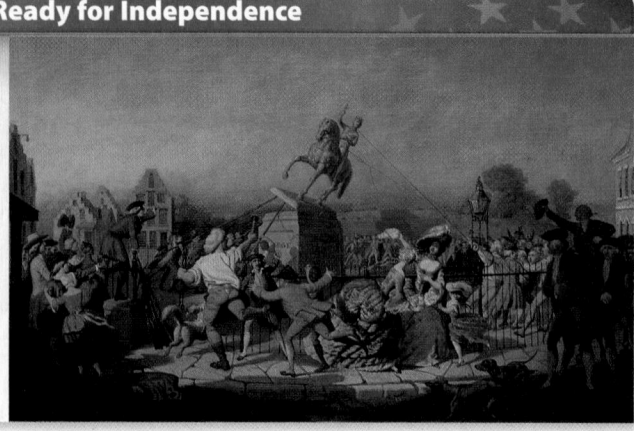

The views of patriot Samuel Adams of Boston also had a powerful influence on the colonists. Adams, who grew up in a middle-class family, was trained in the law, but he had little interest in the law or in anything that made him focus on making money. Adams was a natural-born politician with an independent mind. He followed the debates about colonial liberties closely and wrote essays, letters, and articles on the struggle with the British.

By April 1776, the war had been going on for almost a year, yet no declaration of independence had been made. Adams was bewildered and frustrated by this situation. In a letter to a friend, he wrote:

> 66 *Is not America already independent? Why then not declare it? . . . Can Nations at War be said to be dependent either upon the other? . . . Upon what Terms will Britain be reconciled with America? . . . [S]he will be reconciled upon our abjectly submitting to Tyranny, and asking and receiving Pardon for resisting it. Will this redound to the Honor or the Safety of America? Surely no.* 99
>
> —Letter from Samuel Adams,
> April 3, 1776

In June 1776, more than a year after fighting had begun in the colonies, Richard Henry Lee of Virginia did declare independence. Lee introduced a resolution in the Continental Congress "[t]hat these United Colonies are, and of right ought to be, free and independent states."

The Declaration of Independence

After Lee's resolution, the Congress promptly named a committee of John Adams, Benjamin Franklin, Thomas Jefferson, Robert Livingston, and Roger Sherman to prepare a written declaration of independence. The committee asked Thomas Jefferson, a Virginia planter known for his writing skills, to write the **draft.** On June 28 the committee submitted the edited draft to the Congress.

On July 2, 1776, the Congress approved Lee's resolution. The colonies officially broke with Great Britain. The Congress then turned its attention to Jefferson's draft. After considerable debate, a few passages were removed and some editorial changes were made. On July 4, the Congress approved the final draft. John Hancock, the president of the Congress, was the first to sign the document, which eventually held the signatures of all 56 delegates. It explained the reasons for declaring independence. Its actual title was "The unanimous declaration of the thirteen United States of America."

Key Parts of the Declaration

The American Declaration of Independence[1] is one of the most famous documents in history. In the Declaration, Jefferson drew on the ideas of Locke and other philosophers to explain the colonists' need for freedom.

The Declaration explained the reasons the American colonies were angry at the British government. It confirmed why revolution was justified

See the following footnoted materials in the **Reference Handbook:**
1. *Declaration of Independence,* pages R38–R41.

Activity: Interdisciplinary Connection

Daily Life People sometimes think with nostalgia of earlier, simpler times. From a public health standpoint, however, colonial times were anything but "the good old days." Colonists commonly emptied their chamber pots directly into the street. Other household wastes, dead animals, and wastes from butcher shops were also dumped into the streets. Drains and open sewers carried the smelly mess into harbors, creating an unbearable stench as refuse rotted in summer at low tide. Runoff also polluted the groundwater, and epidemics caused by drinking such water from public wells were common. Have students find out about the advantages and disadvantages of colonial life and decide whether they would choose to live in colonial times. As a class, discuss students' opinions and reasons for them. **OL**

and laid down the founding principles of the new nation. In later years, Jefferson wrote:

> " I did not consider it any part of my charge to invent new ideas, . . . but to place before mankind the common sense of the subject, in terms so plain and firm as to command their assent. . . . It was intended to be an expression of the American mind. "
>
> —Thomas Jefferson

The revolutionary document stirred the hearts of the American people. No government at the time had been founded on the principles of human liberty and consent of the governed. The Declaration won praise the world over and influenced the French Revolution of 1789. Over the years many nations, particularly in Latin America, have used it as a model in their own efforts to gain freedom.

The Declaration has three parts. It begins with a statement of purpose and basic human rights:

> " We hold these Truths to be self-evident, that all Men are created equal, that they are endowed by their Creator with certain unalienable Rights, that among these are Life, Liberty and the Pursuit of Happiness. That to secure these Rights, Governments are instituted among Men, deriving their just Powers from the Consent of the Governed. . . . "
>
> —Declaration of Independence

The middle section of the Declaration lists specific complaints against George III. Each item describes a violation of the colonists' political, civil, and economic liberties. These paragraphs were designed to justify the break with Great Britain.

The conclusion states the colonists' determination to separate from Great Britain. Their efforts to reach a peaceful solution had failed, leaving them no choice but to declare their independence.

The First State Constitutions

The Declaration of Independence recognized the changes taking place in the colonies. One of the most important of these was the transformation of the colonies into states subject to no higher authority. Thus, the states saw themselves as "states" in the sense in which this term is used in Chapter 1.

About two months before the Declaration of Independence, the Second Continental Congress had instructed the colonies to form "such governments as shall . . . best conduce [lead] to the happiness and safety of their constituents." By the end of 1776, 10 states had adopted written **constitutions.** Within a few years, each state had a new constitution or had converted old colonial charters into a constitution.

Most of the new constitutions contained a bill of rights defining citizens' personal liberties. All recognized the people as the sole source of authority in a limited government.

Government ONLINE

Student Web Activity Visit glencoe.com and enter *QuickPass*™ code USG9822c2. Click on Student Web Activity and complete the activity about uniting for independence.

CHAPTER 2, SECTION 2

R Reading Strategy

Identifying Have students create a chart listing the four sections of the Declaration of Independence and provide a brief summary and explanation of the purpose of each section. **OL**

Assess

Assign the Section 2 Assessment as homework or as an in-class activity, or have students take Section Quiz 2-2 from *Section Quizzes and Chapter Tests.*

Government ONLINE

Objectives and answers to the Student Web Activity can be found in the *Web Activity Lesson Plan* at glencoe.com. Enter *QuickPass*™ code USG9085c2T.

Close

Drawing Conclusions Ask: Do you think the colonists or the British were more responsible for the breakup leading to American independence? *(Prompt students to explain their reasoning.)* **OL**

Section 2 Review

SECTION 2 Review

Vocabulary

1. **Explain** the significance of: revenue, embargo.

Main Ideas

2. **Examining** What actions did George III take to make the Americans pay for the French and Indian War?

3. **Describing** Who were members of the committees of correspondence, and what was their primary goal?

Critical Thinking

4. **Analyzing** Why did Jefferson's principles and ideas in the Declaration of Independence support separation from England?

5. **Listing** In a graphic organizer similar to the one below, identify the series of events that led the colonies to declare their independence.

```
                                    ┌─────────────┐
                                    │ Declaration of │
                                    │ Independence │
                                    └─────────────┘
```

Writing About Government

6. **Persuasive Writing** Identify a recent government action or policy with which you disagree. Decide on a written format that would best express your disagreement, such as a letter to a newspaper editor, an e-mail to your congressperson, or a government agency official. Then write your complaint or grievance.

CHAPTER 2: *Origins of American Government* **47**

Answers

1. All definitions can be found in the section and the Glossary.
2. levied taxes on tea, sugar, glass, paper, and other products; the Stamp Act and other laws
3. Colonists who wanted to resist the British formed organizations to communicate with other colonists.
4. The principles of liberty, equality, and consent of the governed were not being recognized by the British government.
5. Events should include the French and Indian War, Stamp Act, Boston Tea Party, Coercive Acts, Continental Congress
6. Students' letters should demonstrate an understanding of the protest method chosen.

Focus

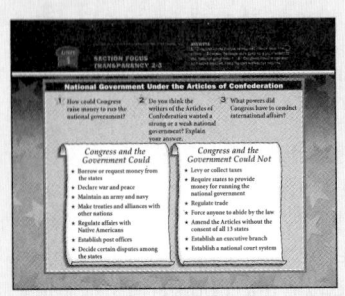
Reader's Guide

Answers to Graphic:

I. A.
1. Unicameral legislature
2. Legislature chose executive
3. Congress settled disputes among the states
4. Each state had one vote in Congress

B.
1. Congress could not collect taxes or regulate trade
2. Congress could not force anyone to follow laws
3. No executive branch

Resource Manager

The Articles of Confederation

Reader's Guide

Content Vocabulary
★ ratify (p. 48)
★ unicameral (p. 48)
★ cede (p. 50)
★ ordinance (p. 50)

Academic Vocabulary
★ legislature (p. 48)
★ levy (p. 49)
★ precedent (p. 50)

Reading Strategy
Use a graphic organizer similar to the one to the right to help take notes on the Articles of Confederation.

The Articles of Confederation
I. Government Under the Articles of Confederation
   A.
   B.
II. Weaknesses of the Articles
   A.
   B.

Issues in the News

When Americans celebrate national independence, they might look at today's world to see how hard it is to set up a new government. In Iraq, after U.S. and coalition forces defeated Saddam Hussein, the first thing that happened was that an interim government was set up. A major roadblock was deep religious and political differences among Sunnis, Shias, and Kurds. Voters finally approved a new constitution for Iraq in December 2005. Yet three years later, the government created by the new constitution continued to have serious problems. The first American constitution, the Articles of Confederation, had its own problems. It lasted only seven years.

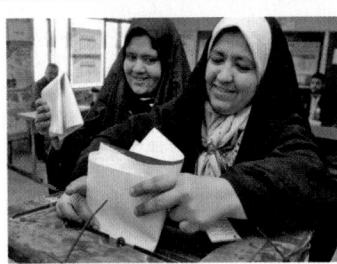
▲ Iraqi women voting in 2005

When Richard Henry Lee proposed his resolution for independence in June 1776, he also asked that a "plan for confederation" be prepared for the colonies. In 1777 a committee appointed by Congress presented the Articles of Confederation.[1] 📖 The Articles basically continued the structure and operation of the government that had been set up by the Second Continental Congress. It created a confederation, or "league of friendship," among the 13 states rather than a strong central government. By March 1781, all 13 states had **ratified,** or approved, the Articles.

📖 See the following footnoted materials in the **Reference Handbook:**
1. Articles of Confederation, pages R76–R79.

Government Under the Articles of Confederation

Under the Articles, the plan for the central government was simple. It included a **unicameral,** or single-chamber, **legislature.** Executive leaders were chosen from the legislature. When the legislature or Congress was not in session, the government was run by a Committee of the States made up of one delegate from each state. There was no federal court system, and Congress settled disputes among the states. Each state had one vote in Congress, no matter what its size or population. Every state legislature selected its own representatives to Congress, paid them, and could recall them at any time.

R **Reading Strategies**	C **Critical Thinking**	D **Differentiated Instruction**	W **Writing Support**	S **Skill Practice**
Teacher Edition • Determining Importance, p. 50 **Additional Resources** • Quizzes/Tests, p. 15 • Guid. Read. Act., p. 7	**Teacher Edition** • Determining Cause and Effect, p. 49 • Problem Solving, p. 51 **Additional Resources** • Read. Essen., pp. 19–21	**Teacher Edition** • Visual/Spatial, p. 50 **Additional Resources** • Foldables, p. 45	**Additional Resources** • Authentic Assess., p. 9	**Teacher Edition** • Reading a Chart, p. 49 **Additional Resources** • Making It Rel. Trans., pp. 3–4

Congress had only those powers specifically mentioned in the Articles. It could make war and peace, send and receive ambassadors, make treaties, raise and equip a navy, maintain an army by asking states for troops, appoint top military officers, fix weights and measures, regulate Indian affairs, set up post offices, and decide some state disputes.

Weaknesses of the Articles

Although the Articles of Confederation gave Congress power, they created an ineffective national government. Because each state had no intention of giving up its sovereignty to a central government, the Articles had serious weaknesses.

First, Congress did not have the power to **levy** or collect taxes. It could raise money only by borrowing or requesting money from the states. Each state had to collect taxes from its citizens and turn the money over to the national treasury.

Congress could do little, however, if a state refused to provide the money.

Second, Congress did not have the power to regulate trade. Economic disputes among the various states and difficulty in making business arrangements with other countries resulted. Third, Congress could not force anyone to obey the laws it passed or to abide by the Articles of Confederation. Congress could only advise and request that the states comply.

Fourth, laws needed the approval of 9 of the 13 states. Usually, delegates from only 9 or 10 states were in Congress at any time, making it difficult to pass laws. Also, each state had only a single vote. The votes of any 5 of the smaller states could block a measure that 8 of the larger states wanted.

Fifth, amending, or changing, the Articles required all states to agree. In practice this was impossible. As a result the Articles were never amended.

Charts In MOtion
See StudentWorks™ Plus or go to glencoe.com.

Government Under the Articles of Confederation

The Articles of Confederation		The Federal Constitution
One—the Confederation Congress	How Many Houses In the Legislature?	Two—the House of Representatives and the Senate
Members of Congress appointed annually by state legislatures	How Are Delegates Chosen?	Representatives elected every two years by voters; senators originally chosen by state legislatures for a six-year term (today voters elect senators as well)
No separate executive; members of the Congress elect a president annually; government departments are run by committees created by the Congress	How Is Executive Power Exercised?	Separate executive branch; president elected every four years by Electoral College; president conducts policy, selects officers to run government departments, appoints ambassadors and judges
Judical matters left to the states and local courts; the Congress acts as a court for disputes between states	How Is Judicial Power Exercised?	Separate judicial branch with a Supreme Court and lower courts created by Congress; judges appointed by the president but confirmed by the Senate
Only states can levy taxes	What Taxes Can Be Levied?	Federal government can levy taxes
The Congress regulated foreign trade but had no power to regulate interstate trade	Can Trade Be Regulated?	Federal government regulates both interstate commerce and foreign commerce

Critical Thinking The Articles of Confederation established a league of cooperation among the 13 states, but the national government had only limited powers and was dependent on the states for revenue, soldiers, and law enforcement. *How was trade regulated under the Articles of Confederation compared to the Constitution?*

Teach

C Critical Thinking

Determining Cause and Effect Organize the class into small groups. Pass a single sheet of paper around in each group. Each group member should take a turn writing first a weakness of the Articles of Confederation and then an example of how the weakness caused a later problem. Have the groups share and analyze weaknesses and examples with the class. **OL**

S Skill Practice

Reading a Chart Have students study the chart on this page. **Ask:** What are three differences between the Articles of Confederation and the U.S. Constitution? *(Answers will vary, but students should prove that they can read the table accurately.)* **BL**

Critical Thinking

Answer: Under the Articles of Confederation, Congress could regulate foreign trade but not trade among states. Under the Constitution, the federal government could regulate both.

Hands-On Chapter Project

Step 3

Designing a Film Treatment

Step 3: Complete the Film Treatment
Students will put the finishing touches on their film treatment.

Directions Have each group member display and describe his or her contribution. At this point, all members of the group should see sketches, the storyboard, and the outline and provide their summaries of details such as

music, sound effects, and location. Have them agree upon a title for their film.

Putting It Together Ask students to describe which parts of the film treatment they think are strongest and which ones need to be expanded, revised, or cut. More research might be necessary to improve certain scenes. **OL**

(Chapter Project continued in Section 4.)

Differentiated Instruction

D **Differentiated Instruction**

Visual/Spatial Have students choose one weakness of the Articles of Confederation and draw a political cartoon illustrating that weakness. Have them study paintings and costume books so they can use period dress on any figures in the cartoon. Students might want to look at examples of political cartoons of the time for ideas on drawing styles. **ELL**

R **Reading Strategy**

Determining Importance
Ask: What was the most important achievement of the Articles of Confederation? *(the establishment of a fair and consistent policy for settling and developing the lands west of the Appalachian Mountains)* **BL**

Government and You

More About Passports
Passports have been in use for centuries throughout the world. Excluding the Civil War period, travelers to the United States did not need passports until 1918, following World War I.

Sixth, the central government did not have an executive branch. The Confederation government carried on much of its business, such as selling western lands and establishing a postal system, through congressional committees. Without an executive, however, there was no unity in policy making and no way to coordinate the work of the different committees.

D Finally, the government had no national court system. Instead, state courts enforced and interpreted national laws. The lack of a court system made it difficult for the central government to settle disputes among the states. A legislator from North Carolina described the powerlessness of the Confederation in a speech to his legislature in 1787:

66 *The general government ought . . . to possess the means of preserving the peace and tranquility of the union. . . . The encroachments of some states, on the rights of others, and of all on those of the confederacy, are incontestible [cannot be denied] proofs of the weakness and imperfection of that system.* 99
—William Davie, 1787

Achievements

R Despite its weaknesses, the Confederation made some important contributions to the new nation. Its greatest success was in establishing a fair and consistent policy for settling and developing the lands west of the Appalachian Mountains. What to do with the western lands was one of the most hotly debated issues of the era. These lands represented the future of the nation because land was the basis of most wealth in an agricultural society.

The solution was that individual states **ceded,** or yielded, their land claims in the West to the central government so that the Congress could make a national plan for the area. Congress then passed two land **ordinances,** or laws that set out how the lands would be organized: the Ordinance of 1785, and the Northwest Ordinance of 1787. The Ordinance of 1785 provided for the surveying and division of the territory. Among other things, the Northwest Ordinance of 1787 supported a principle advocated by Thomas Jefferson. Once territories reached a certain population, they could achieve statehood on an equal basis with the original thirteen states.

Another important achievement was a 1783 peace treaty with Britain. Under its terms, Britain recognized American independence. Land acquired from Britain greatly enlarged the nation's boundaries, including all land from the Atlantic coast to the Mississippi River and from the Great Lakes and Canada to the present-day boundary of Florida.

Congress also set up the departments of Foreign Affairs, War, Marine, and the Treasury, each under a single permanent secretary. This development set a **precedent** for the creation of cabinet departments under the Constitution of 1787.

Government and You

Applying for a Passport

Planning a trip overseas? If so, you will need a passport—an official document that grants a citizen the right to travel to another country. United States passports are issued by the Department of State in Washington, D.C.

A passport application can be obtained from your post office or from any federal or state court. A fee is required, and two current, identical photos of your full face are needed to help prove who you are. You will also need a document, such as a birth certificate, to prove that you are a U.S. citizen. Instructions on the application detail the types of proof of citizenship that are acceptable.

It might take several weeks to receive your passport in the mail, so apply well in advance of your trip. Your passport will be valid for 5 or 10 years, depending on your age.

▲ A United States passport

Participating
IN GOVERNMENT ACTIVITY

Investigate Further Search the Internet using the word *passport* to determine which foreign countries have additional requirements for visitors.

Differentiated Instruction

Leveled Activities

ELL Interpreting Political Cartoons, p. 3

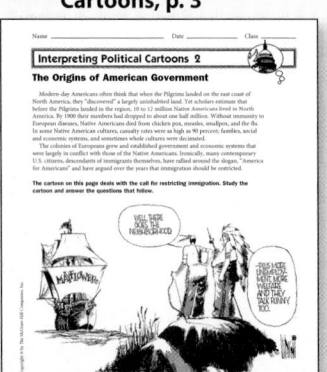

BL Guided Reading Activities, p. 7

OL Skill Reinforcement Activities, p. 2

AL Authentic Assessment with Rubrics, p. 9

Growing Unrest

Shays's Rebellion
Government authorities often jailed debtor farmers or seized their property. Shays led armed men to capture and close the courts, stopping land confiscations.
How do you think Americans viewed the government after Shays's Rebellion?

C Critical Thinking

Problem Solving Shays's Rebellion was an important factor in convincing leaders of the need for a stronger government. In that sense, it led to the Constitutional Convention of 1787. Some people, however, think that the use of force is rarely, if ever, justified. Ask students to brainstorm a number of alternative strategies for the angry farmers led by Daniel Shays. You might want to extend the discussion by relating it to current or recent examples of the use of force, either in the world at large or in students' lives. **AL**

To encourage cooperation among the states, the Articles provided that each state give "full faith and credit" to the legal acts of the other states and treat one another's citizens without discrimination. This provision, often ignored, was carried over to the Constitution, under which it could be enforced.

The Need for Stronger National Government

Despite its achievements, the Confederation had difficulty dealing with many of the problems facing the nation. The structure of the central government simply could not effectively coordinate the actions of the states.

Growing Problems

Soon after the war, the states began to quarrel. As might be expected in such a young nation, many of the quarrels were over borders, tariffs and taxes on goods from another state. New Jersey farmers, for example, had to pay fees to sell their vegetables in New York. Each state thought of itself as sovereign, that is, independent. Some states even began to deal directly with foreign nations. Congress could do little or nothing about these matters.

Even worse, the new nation faced serious money problems. By 1787, the government owed $40 million to foreign governments and to American soldiers who were still unpaid after the Revolutionary War. Unfortunately, the Articles of Confederation did not allow the central government to impose taxes. Without money, the Congress could not maintain an army for the defense of the states.

States, too, were financially strapped. Many had accumulated considerable debt during the war years. By 1786, an economic depression left many farmers and merchants angry and in debt.

Shays's Rebellion

Economic troubles led to rebellion. Armed groups of farmers forced several courts to close to prevent farm foreclosures. The farmers hoped the state would pass laws allowing them to keep their farms. Daniel Shays, a former captain in the Revolutionary Army, led a band that closed the Massachusetts state supreme court. When the justices refused to help, Shays gathered a force of 1,200 men and advanced on the federal arsenal in Springfield. **C**

The Massachusetts militia put down the rebellion, but the unrest frightened American leaders. Henry Knox, later the nation's first secretary of war, echoed the opinion of a growing number of Americans who were ready to agree to a strong

CHAPTER 2: *Origins of American Government* **51**

Additional Support

Activity: Economics Connection

Economic Relationships Invite an economics teacher or an economist to speak to the class about the relationship among taxes, inflation, and the issuance of currency. If possible, ask the speaker to provide an activity or pretest that the students can complete

before he or she comes to speak. After the presentation, have students use a graphic organizer to summarize the information. Then have students discuss how these economic concepts and interactions affect their daily lives. **OL**

Did You Know?

Shays's Rebellion was not the only act of defiance at this time. Unrest also occurred in New Jersey and Rhode Island, where riots broke out because storekeepers would not accept the unreliable, state-issued paper money.

Assess

Assign the Section 3 Assessment as homework or as an in-class activity, or have students take Section Quiz 2-3 from *Section Quizzes and Chapter Tests.*

Close

Synthesizing Ask: Why have the years between 1781 and 1787 been called a critical period in American history?
(Disagreements about the national government were stressful for the young states. It could have torn the nation apart for good, but it did not.) OL

Section 3 Review

---

national government. In a letter to George Washington, Knox wrote:

> 66 *This dreadful situation has alarmed every man of principle and property in New England. [People wake] as from a dream, and ask what has been the cause of our delusion? [W]hat is to afford us security against the violence of lawless men? Our government must be [strengthened], changed, or altered to secure our lives and property.* 99
>
> —Henry Knox

The Annapolis Convention

The Constitutional Convention grew out of two earlier meetings. Washington, now retired, was concerned about problems that had arisen between Maryland and his home state of Virginia. In 1785 he invited representatives from both states to his home in Mount Vernon to discuss their differences over currency, import duties, and navigation on the Potomac River and Chesapeake Bay. This successful meeting inspired Virginia's representatives to call, for all states, a convention the following year in Annapolis, Maryland, to discuss trade.

Only five states sent delegates; among them were Alexander Hamilton of New York and James Madison of Virginia. Both men favored a stronger national government. With Shays and his followers threatening the government of Massachusetts, Hamilton persuaded the other delegates to call for another convention in Philadelphia in May 1787.

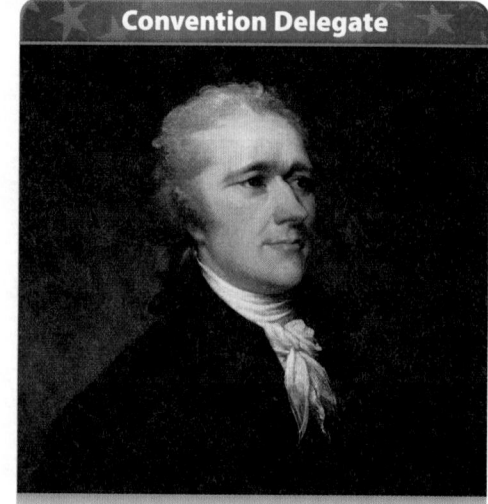

Convention Delegate

New York Delegate Alexander Hamilton supported strong national government and robust commerce. *Why did he want to amend the Articles of Confederation?*

Its purpose was to regulate commerce among the states and to propose changes to make the national government more effective.

After some hesitation, the Congress gave its consent to hold the Philadelphia convention "for the sole and express purpose of revising the Articles of Confederation." The stage was now set for what has been called the "miracle at Philadelphia."

SECTION 3 Review

Vocabulary

1. **Explain** the significance of: ratify, unicameral, cede, ordinance.

Main Ideas

2. **Explaining** How was the original government under the Articles of Confederation organized?

3. **Describing** What were two financial problems that could not be resolved under the Articles of Confederation?

Critical Thinking

4. **Identifying Central Issues** What problems did Shays's Rebellion reveal?

5. **Listing** Use a graphic organizer to list the major weaknesses and achievements of the Articles of Confederation.

Articles of Confederation	
Weaknesses	Achievements

Writing About Government

6. **Descriptive Writing** The plan for confederation ratified a "league of friendship" among the 13 independent states. What are some examples of interstate cooperation today? Find a recent example of state cooperation on a given problem and write several paragraphs describing how the states are working together.

Answers

1. All definitions can be found in the section and the Glossary.
2. It had a single-chamber Congress. Instead of an executive, a Committee of the States made up of one delegate from each state managed the government when Congress was not in session. Disputes between states were settled by Congress rather than by a federal court.
3. The national government could not levy taxes directly or regulate interstate commerce.
4. the lack of security and strength in the national government
5. Weaknesses include: no power to levy or collect taxes, no power to regulate trade, no power to enforce laws, laws needed approval of nine states, amendments required all states to agree, no executive branch or national court system. Achievements include: established a fair policy for developing western lands, negotiated a peace treaty with Great Britain, set a precedent for the creation of cabinet departments, established "full faith and credit" among states.
6. Students should describe a current example of interstate cooperation.

The Constitutional Convention

Focus

Reader's Guide

Content Vocabulary
★ interstate commerce (p. 55)
★ extralegal (p. 57)
★ anarchy (p. 57)

Academic Vocabulary
★ advocate (p. 54)
★ modification (p. 54)
★ publish (p. 58)

Reading Strategy
Use a graphic organizer similar to the one at the right to list the issues at the Constitutional Convention and how they were settled.

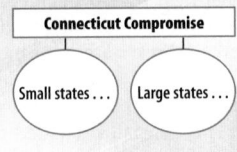

Connecticut Compromise

Small states . . .   Large states . . .

Bellringer

Section Focus Transparencies 2-4

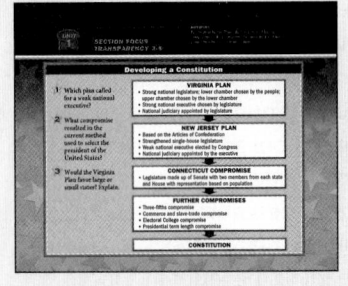

Issues in the News

Amendments to require balancing the national budget were proposed in 1982, 1992, 1997, and 2005. During the 1992 argument, House Republican Charles Stenholm, who led that campaign, insisted that a balanced budget amendment was necessary. "We got carried away with tax cuts and we've paid a high price for that mistake," Stenholm said. Another member of Congress, Democrat Mike Synar of Oklahoma, was just as certain a balanced budget amendment would be foolish. He called the proposal "the constitutional equivalent of hanging garlic in the window to ward off vampires."

▲ Representative Charles Stenholm who retired in 2005

Reader's Guide

Answers to Graphic: Small states: unicameral legislature with one vote for each state, weak central government, New Jersey Plan; Large states: strong bicameral national legislature—lower chamber is representative of population and also elects the upper chamber, national legislature can bar state laws found to be unconstitutional, Virginia Plan

Modern-day efforts to pass just one amendment to the Constitution like the balanced budget amendment are good reminders of how difficult it was for our early political leaders to craft a constitution. It takes imagination to understand how hard the work was. After all, they had no existing document to work with, and the rules for the process did not yet exist.

In May 1787, the Constitutional Convention began this daunting task. State legislatures were allowed to send 74 delegates, but only 55 attended. In the end, 39 of them signed the final draft.

The Convention Begins

The delegates did have a great deal of practical experience in politics. Seven had served as governors of their states. Thirty-nine had served in the Congress. Many had helped write their state constitutions. Eight had signed the Declaration of Independence, and six delegates had signed the Articles of Confederation.

Several men stood out as leaders. The presence of George Washington ensured that many people would trust the convention's work. Benjamin Franklin, world famous as a scientist and diplomat, was now 81 years old, yet he played an active role in the debates.

Two other Pennsylvanians also played key roles. James Wilson often read Franklin's speeches and did important work on the details of the Constitution. Gouverneur Morris, an eloquent speaker and writer, wrote the final draft of the Constitution.

Resource Manager

R Reading Strategies	C Critical Thinking	D Differentiated Instruction	W Writing Support	S Skill Practice
Teacher Edition	**Teacher Edition**	**Teacher Edition**	**Teacher Edition**	**Teacher Edition**
• Inferring, p. 56	• Contrasting, p. 56	• Visual/Spatial, p. 58	• Persuasive Writing, pp. 55, 57	• Analyzing Maps, p. 57
Additional Resources	**Additional Resources**	**Additional Resources**	**Additional Resources**	**Additional Resources**
• Quizzes/Tests, p. 16	• Read. Essen., pp. 22–24	• Reteaching Act., p. 2	• Coop. Learning Act., pp. 1–2	• Skill Reinforce. Act., p. 2
• Guid. Read. Act., p. 8				

Teach

Alexander Hamilton (1755–1804), owed his success in part to a hurricane. Hamilton was born in the British West Indies, where his father was a trader. When the business hit hard times, young Hamilton had to give up school and go to work. After the hurricane struck, he wrote a letter describing the destruction on the island of St. Croix. After reading the letter in a local newspaper, several plantation owners were so impressed with his talent that they decided to send him to college in New York. His promising career ended when he was killed in a duel with Aaron Burr.

Participating IN GOVERNMENT

Getting Out the Vote Civic organizations and people running for office often have volunteers telephoning registered voters to urge them to get to the polls on Election Day. Have interested students find out how to get involved and volunteer their services for this task on the next Election Day. **OL**

Differentiated Instruction

Historical Documents and Speeches, p. 3

James Madison was the delegate from Virginia. Madison, a relatively young man in his mid-thirties, was a brilliant **advocate** of a strong national government. His careful notes are the major source of information about the convention's work. Madison is often called the Father of the Constitution because he was the author of the basic plan of government that the convention eventually adopted.

Organization

The convention began by unanimously choosing George Washington to preside over the meetings. It also decided that each state would have one vote on all questions. A simple majority vote of those states present would make decisions. No meetings could be held unless delegates from at least 7 of the 13 states were present.

The delegates decided to keep the public and press from attending the sessions. This was a key decision because it made it possible for the delegates to talk freely.

Key Agreements

Although the delegates originally came together to revise the Articles, they eventually agreed to abandon the former government and begin again. The delegates reached a consensus on many basic issues. All favored the idea of limited and representative government. They agreed that the powers of the national government should be divided among legislative, executive, and judicial branches. They all believed it was necessary to limit the power of the states to coin money or to interfere with creditors' rights. And all of them agreed that they should strengthen the national government.

The great debates and compromises of the Convention were not over these fundamental questions. Rather, they dealt with how to put these ideas into practice.

Decisions and Compromises

After the rules were adopted, the convention opened with a surprise. It came from the Virginia delegation, who presented a plan for a strong national government.

The Virginia Plan

On May 29 Edmund Randolph of Virginia introduced 15 resolutions that James Madison had drafted. They came to be called the Virginia Plan. The plan proposed a government based on three principles: (1) a strong national legislature with two chambers, the lower one to be chosen by the people and the upper chamber to be chosen by the lower. The legislature would have the power to bar any state laws it found unconstitutional; (2) a strong national executive to be chosen by the national legislature; and (3) a national judiciary to be appointed by the legislature.

The introduction of the Virginia Plan was a brilliant political move on the part of the nationalists. By offering a complete plan at the very start, the nationalists set the direction and agenda for the rest of the convention. Eventually, and after much discussion by delegates who required a number of **modifications,** the Virginia Plan became the basis of the new Constitution.

The delegates debated the Virginia Plan for more than two weeks. Delegates from the smaller states soon realized that the larger, more populous states would be in control of a strong national government under the Virginia Plan. The smaller states wanted a less-powerful government with more independence for the states.

The New Jersey Plan

On June 15, the delegates from the small states, led by William Paterson of New Jersey, made a counterproposal. The New Jersey Plan called for government based on keeping the major feature of the Articles of Confederation, a unicameral legislature, with one vote for each state. Congress, however, would be strengthened by giving it the power to impose taxes and regulate trade. A weak executive, consisting of more than one person would be elected by Congress. A national judiciary with limited power would be appointed by the executive.

Paterson argued that the convention should not deprive the smaller states of the equality they had under the Articles. Thus, his plan was designed simply to amend the Articles. The central government was to continue as a confederation of sovereign states. After some discussion, the New Jersey Plan was rejected. The delegates returned to considering the Virginia Plan.

As the summer grew hotter, so did the delegates' tempers. Soon the convention was deadlocked over the question of the representation of states in Congress. Should the states be represented on the basis of population (favored by the large-state delegations), or should they be represented equally, regardless of population (favored by the small-state delegations)? The debate was bitter, and the convention was in danger of dissolving.

The Constitution

Objective: To understand Thomas Jefferson's critique of the merits and shortcomings of the Constitution.

Focus/Teach: Review the compromises reached at the Constitutional Convention. Then have students read Jefferson's letter to Madison.

Assess: Have students complete the questions in the activity.

Close: Ask students how accurate they believe Jefferson's critique turned out to be.

Differentiated Instruction Strategies

BL Have students list the positive and negative points Jefferson made.

AL Have students take on the role of James Madison and write a letter in which they respond to Jefferson's critique.

ELL Help students rewrite portions of the letter using simpler, contemporary language.

The Three-Fifths Compromise

Constitutional Ideals By accepting the Three-Fifths Compromise, the Framers, in essence, condoned slavery. Leaders like Thomas Jefferson accepted slavery as a social norm. Isaac Jefferson (below) was an enslaved worker at Jefferson's home, Monticello (right). *How does slavery clash with the ideals of the Revolution?*

The Connecticut Compromise

Finally, a special committee designed a compromise. Called the Connecticut Compromise because the delegation from that state played a key role on the committee, this plan was adopted after long debate. The compromise suggested that the legislative branch have two parts: (1) a House of Representatives, with state representation based on population. All revenue laws—concerning spending and taxes—would begin in this house; and (2) a Senate, with two members from each state. State legislatures would elect senators.

The larger states would have an advantage in the House of Representatives, where representation was to be based on population. The smaller states would be protected in the Senate, where each state would have equal representation.

The Three-Fifths Compromise

A second compromise settled a disagreement over how to determine how many representatives each state would have in the House. Almost one-third of the people in the Southern states were enslaved African Americans. These states wanted enslaved persons to be counted the same as free people to give the South more representation. At the same time, the Southern states did not want enslaved persons counted at all for the purpose of levying taxes. Because the North did not have many enslaved persons, Northern states took the opposite position. They wanted the enslaved persons counted for tax purposes but did not think they should be counted for representation.

The Three-Fifths Compromise settled this deadlock. Instead of counting all of the enslaved people, only three-fifths were to be counted for both tax purposes and for representation.

Commerce and the Slave Trade

A third compromise resolved a dispute over commerce and the slave trade—not slavery, but the continuing trade of enslaved people. The Northern states wanted the government to have complete power over trade with other nations. The Southern states depended heavily on agricultural exports. They feared that business interests in the North might have enough votes in Congress to impose taxes on exports or to ratify trade agreements that would hurt the South. They also feared the North might interfere with the slave trade.

Again, a compromise settled the issue. The delegates determined that Congress could not ban the slave trade until 1808. At the same time, they gave Congress the power to regulate both **interstate commerce,** or trade among the states, and foreign commerce. To protect the South's exports, however, Congress was forbidden to impose export taxes. As a result, the United States is one of the few nations in the world today that does not tax the goods that it exports.

CHAPTER 2: *Origins of American Government* **55**

W Writing Support

Persuasive Writing Have students reread the paragraphs under "The Connecticut Compromise" and write a speech for Roger Sherman in which he sets forth his arguments for the Great Compromise. Encourage students to review the information about the Virginia Plan and the New Jersey Plan so they can include specific details in their speech. Their speeches should directly address the fears and concerns of the delegates. **OL**

Hands-On Chapter Project

Step 4

Designing a Film Treatment

Step 4: Make a Pitch to a Producer
Students will synthesize what they have learned in Steps 1, 2, and 3 by pitching their film treatment to a producer.

Directions Write the Essential Question (on page 36) on the board, and have students evaluate how well they have answered this question in their film treatment. Ask volunteers from each group to discuss the most interesting and challenging elements of the project and describe the choices the group made to address these elements.

Putting It Together Have one group member assume the role of a film producer. He or she should ask questions, make suggestions, interview each contributor, and evaluate the pitch. **OL**

The Slavery Question

Although the Constitution includes these compromises, the only place where slavery is mentioned is Article IV, Section 2. In this section, the Constitution notes that enslaved people who escaped to free states were to be returned to their holders.[1] 📖 At that time, a number of Northern states were beginning to think about abolishing slavery. Massachusetts, Delaware, Connecticut, Pennsylvania, and Rhode Island were all working on plans to reach this goal. In the end, most states decided to gradually eliminate the practice. Most Northern states did not completely abolish slavery until the early 1800s.

Whatever their personal beliefs about slavery, the delegates knew that the Southern states would never accept the Constitution if it interfered with slavery. Thus, in order to create the badly needed new government, the Founders compromised on slavery. Their refusal to deal with slavery left it to later generations of Americans to resolve.

Independence Hall

Making History During the hot summer of 1787, it is said that delegates nailed the windows shut for privacy. *Why might they have done this?*

Other Compromises

The delegates compromised on several other issues to complete the Constitution. The debate over how to elect the president centered on whether the president should be elected directly by the people, by the Congress, or by state legislatures. As a compromise, the delegates finally settled on the present Electoral College system. In this system, each state selects electors to choose the president. Similarly, the president's four-year term was a compromise between those wanting a longer term and those who feared a long term would give the president too much power.

On September 8, 1787, a Committee of Style and Arrangements began polishing the final draft. By September 17 the document was ready. Thirty-nine delegates stepped forward to sign the Constitution. The aging Ben Franklin had to be helped to the table to sign. As others went up to sign, Franklin remarked that during the long debates he had often looked at the sun painted on the back of General Washington's chair and wondered whether it was rising or setting. "[B]ut now at length I have the happiness to know," he said, "it is a rising and not a setting Sun."

Ratifying the Constitution

For the new Constitution to become law, 9 of the 13 states had to ratify it. The political debate over ratification lasted until May 29, 1790, when Rhode Island finally voted for approval. The Constitution, however, actually went into effect on June 21, 1788, when New Hampshire became the ninth state to ratify it.

The Federalists and Anti-Federalists

The great debate over ratification quickly divided the people in the states. Fervent debates broke out in the newspapers. One group, known as the Federalists, favored the Constitution and was led by many of the Founders. Their support came mainly from merchants and others in the cities and coastal regions. The other group, called the Anti-Federalists, opposed the new Constitution. They drew support largely from the inland farmers and laborers, who feared a strong national government. The lines of support, however, were not clearly drawn, and many city

📖 *See the following footnoted materials in the Reference Handbook:*
1. *The Constitution,* pages R42–R47.

Activity: Collaborative Learning

Illustrating the Bill of Rights Organize the class into eight groups, and assign each group one of the first eight amendments in the Bill of Rights. Have some students in each group analyze and write the amendment in their own words. Other group members should be responsible for illustrating the effect of the amendment on our lives today. Display the results on the bulletin board. **OL**

dwellers and businesspeople agreed with the opponents of the Constitution.

The Anti-Federalists criticized the Constitution for having been drafted in secret. They claimed the document was **extralegal,** not sanctioned by law, because Congress authorized the Convention only to revise the old Articles. They further argued that the Constitution took important powers from the states.

The Anti-Federalists' strongest argument, however, was that the Constitution lacked a Bill of Rights. The Convention had, in fact, considered adding this kind of bill. In their discussions, they concluded logically that it was not necessary to have a bill of rights. After all, the Constitution did not authorize the government to violate the rights of the people.

This was not good enough for the Anti-Federalists. This group warned that without a bill of rights, a strong national government might take away the rights that were won in the Revolution. They demanded that the new Constitution clearly guarantee the people's freedoms.

One of the strongest opponents of the Constitution was Patrick Henry, the passionate delegate from Virginia. He voiced his position eloquently:

> 66 *The necessity of a Bill of Rights appears to me to be greater in this government than ever it was in any government before.... [A]ll rights not expressly and unequivocally reserved to the people are impliedly and incidentally relinquished to rulers.... If you intend to reserve your unalienable rights, you must have the most express stipulation; for ... [I]f the people do not think it necessary to reserve them, they will be supposed to be given up.* 99
>
> —Patrick Henry, 1788

The Federalists, on the other hand, argued that without a strong national government, **anarchy,** or political disorder, would triumph. They claimed that only a strong national government could protect the nation from enemies abroad and solve the country's internal problems. The Federalists had yet another argument. They pointed out that eight states already had such bills in their state constitutions. Eventually, however, the Federalists promised to add a bill of rights as the first order of business when the new government met.

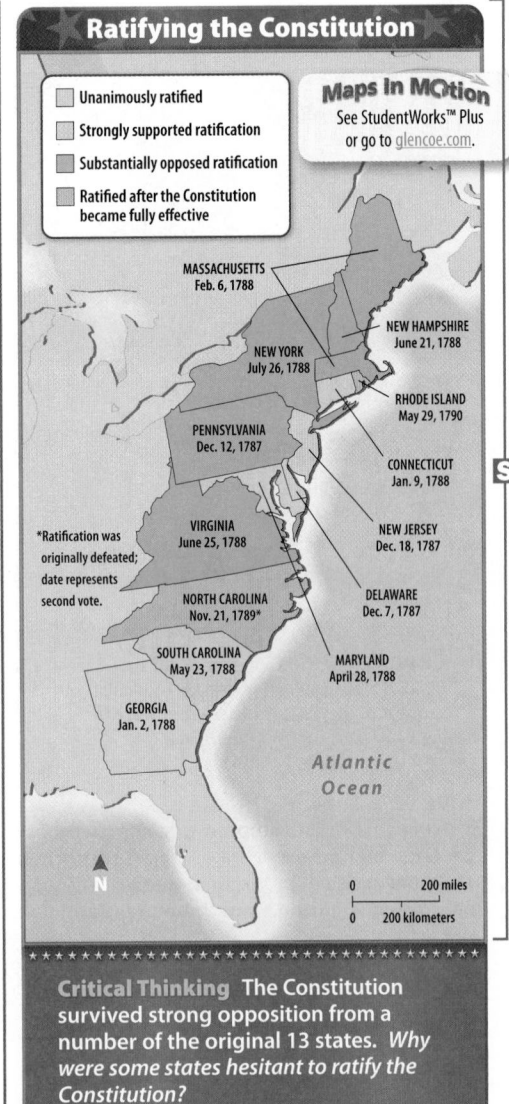

Ratifying the Constitution

Maps In Motion
See StudentWorks™ Plus or go to glencoe.com.

- ☐ Unanimously ratified
- ☐ Strongly supported ratification
- ☐ Substantially opposed ratification
- ☐ Ratified after the Constitution became fully effective

MASSACHUSETTS
Feb. 6, 1788

NEW HAMPSHIRE
June 21, 1788

NEW YORK
July 26, 1788

RHODE ISLAND
May 29, 1790

PENNSYLVANIA
Dec. 12, 1787

CONNECTICUT
Jan. 9, 1788

*Ratification was originally defeated; date represents second vote.

VIRGINIA
June 25, 1788

NEW JERSEY
Dec. 18, 1787

NORTH CAROLINA
Nov. 21, 1789*

DELAWARE
Dec. 7, 1787

SOUTH CAROLINA
May 23, 1788

MARYLAND
April 28, 1788

GEORGIA
Jan. 2, 1788

Atlantic Ocean

N

0   200 miles
0   200 kilometers

Critical Thinking The Constitution survived strong opposition from a number of the original 13 states. *Why were some states hesitant to ratify the Constitution?*

Progress Toward Ratification

With the promise of a bill of rights, the tide turned in favor of the Constitution. Many small states ratified it quickly because they were pleased with equal representation in the new Senate. Although the Constitution went into effect when New Hampshire ratified it, the legislatures in Virginia and New York had not yet held a vote on the new Constitution.

W Writing Support

Persuasive Writing Review the arguments of the Federalists and Anti-Federalists. Have each student write a newspaper editorial that might have been published during that time, either supporting or opposing the Constitution. Encourage students to write their editorials from the point of view of one of the colonists, such as a merchant in a coastal city or a large landowner. **OL**

S Skill Practice

Analyzing Maps Point out that most of the people who lived on the Atlantic Coast voted for ratification. Ask students to discuss why this was the case. *(Students may suggest that coastal cities, most vulnerable to outside attack, wanted guaranteed federal protection as soon as possible.)* **Ask:** Which states' delegates voted unanimously for ratification? *(New Jersey, Delaware, and Georgia)* **OL BL**

Caption Answer: They feared a strong central government and wanted a bill of rights added to the Constitution.

Additional Support

Activity: Interdisciplinary Connection

Language Arts Ask a language arts teacher to instruct students on the elements of a persuasive essay. Then ask students to assume the role of an American just after the Constitution was ratified. Have each student write a one-page amendment that he or she would want to have added at that time. The amendment should have a title and an explanation regarding why it should be added to the Constitution. **OL**

Teacher Tip

Choosing a Topic Remind students to identify the purpose of their essay before they begin writing. What exactly will their amendments accomplish?

D Differentiated Instruction

Visual/Spatial Have students select a point made by the Federalists or Anti-Federalists and draw a cartoon making their point. Suggest that they look at a variety of political cartoons to get ideas. **ELL OL**

Caption Answer: A strong government is necessary to ensure political order, protect the nation from enemies abroad, and solve the country's internal problems.

Assess

Assign the Section 4 Assessment as homework or as an in-class activity, or have students take Section Quiz 2-4 from *Section Quizzes and Chapter Tests.*

Close

Predicting Ask students to suggest ways in which history would have been different if the Framers had not succeeded in drafting a working constitution. **OL**

Section 4 Review

The Constitutional Debate

Choosing Sides The woodcut shows the "Ship of State" being paraded by Federalists in support of the Constitution. *What were the key arguments of the Federalists?*

Everyone knew that without the support of those two large and powerful states, the Constitution would not succeed. In Virginia, George Washington, James Madison, and Edmund Randolph

argued in favor of the new Constitution, and their efforts helped Federalists win a close vote on June 25, 1788.

In New York, Alexander Hamilton argued the case for six weeks. To help win the battle in New York, Hamilton, Madison, and John Jay **published** more than 80 essays defending the new Constitution. Hamilton and James Madison wrote most of the essays, which were later collected in a book called *The Federalist.*[1] Madison brilliantly answered the opposition's fears that a republic had to be a small government. In *The Federalist,* No. 10, he wrote: "Extend the sphere, and you take in a greater variety of parties and interests; you make it less probable that a majority of the whole will have a common motive to invade the rights of other citizens." On July 26, the Federalists in New York won by three votes.

Washington was elected president and John Adams vice president. Voters also elected 22 senators and 59 representatives. On March 4, 1789, Congress met for the first time in Federal Hall in New York City, the temporary capital. Washington took the oath of office as president on April 30. To fulfill the promises made during the fight for ratification, James Madison introduced a set of amendments during the first session. Congress approved 12 amendments and the states ratified 10 of them in 1791. These first 10 amendments became known as the Bill of Rights.

See the following footnoted materials in the **Reference Handbook:**
1. *The Federalist,* No. 10, pages R80–R82 and *The Federalist,* No. 51, pages R83–R84.

SECTION 4 Review

Vocabulary

1. **Explain** the significance of: interstate commerce, extralegal, anarchy.

Main Ideas

2. **Listing** What were the key issues on which the delegates to the Constitutional Convention agreed?

3. **Identifying** Who were the authors of *The Federalist,* and what was the purpose for writing it?

Critical Thinking

4. **Analyzing** Evaluate the impact of the Federalists and Anti-Federalists on the Constitution.

5. **Organizing** Use a graphic organizer to analyze how the Connecticut Compromise provided fair treatment for both large and small states.

Issues	Resolutions
1.	
2.	
3.	

Writing About Government

6. **Descriptive Writing** The Bill of Rights continues to be a strong foundation of the American political system. Find a news story that reflects a civil liberties issue, and then write a short essay explaining how it does so.

Answers

1. All definitions can be found in the section and the Glossary.
2. limited and representative government; division of government into legislative, executive, and judicial branches; limited power of states to coin money; need for a stronger national government
3. Alexander Hamilton, James Madison, and John Jay wrote the essays to encourage New York to ratify the Constitution.
4. Federalists, such as Hamilton and Madison, led the campaign to adopt the Constitution, while the Anti-Federalists insisted on a bill of rights.

Both groups contributed to the political development of constitutional government.
5. Issues: How to balance the interests of small states versus large states. Resolutions: Small states are protected in the Senate. Large states have an advantage in the House.
6. Students' essays should include references to the issues they find in the news and liberties found in the Bill of Rights.

Interpreting Political Points of View

If you ask friends about a new movie, their opinions might range from "terrific" to "boring." People have different opinions about the same people, events, or issues because they look at them from different points of view. Many factors influence a person's point of view, including experience, gender, age, racial or ethnic background, economic status, religion, and education.

To judge the accuracy or objectivity of an argument, you must first identify the speaker's or writer's point of view. This skill helps you determine which issues to support and which candidates share your goals and values.

Why Learn This Skill?

Read the following excerpt from Senator John McCain's speech to the Republican National Convention in 2004 about the "war on terror." Then answer the questions below it.

It's a fight between a just regard for human dignity and a malevolent force. . . . It's a fight between right and wrong, good and evil. And should our enemies acquire for their arsenal the . . . weapons they seek, this war will become a much bigger thing. . . . It is, whether we wished it or not, that we have come to the test of our generation, to our rendezvous with destiny. And much is expected of us. We are engaged in a hard struggle against a cruel and determined adversary. Our enemies have made clear the danger they pose to our security and to the very essence of our culture—liberty. Only the most deluded of us could doubt the necessity of this war . . . we must fight. We must.

1. To interpret point of view in written material, gather background information on the author. Does he or she represent an organization, political party, or special-interest group?

2. Notice what points are emphasized or excluded.

3. Look for emotionally charged words such as *vicious, drastic, heartwarming,* or *evil.* Notice metaphors and analogies that imply an opinion, such as, "If this budget can work, then pigs can fly."

Practicing the Skill

1. What subject is McCain addressing? For what purpose is he speaking?

2. What is his point of view?

3. What emotionally charged words and phrases reveal McCain's point of view?

Applying the Skill

Find an editorial or letter to the editor in a newspaper or magazine that expresses a point of view on an issue. Then write a paragraph analyzing the author's point of view and compare it to your own. Make sure to explain why you agree or disagree with the author.

Answers

Practicing the Skill

1. McCain is addressing the U.S. invasion of Iraq. He is speaking in support of the reelection of George W. Bush, who authorized the war as president in 2003.

2. McCain believes that war is the only possible response to terrorism.

3. malevolent, evil, cruel, rendezvous with destiny

Applying the Skill

Answers should express a reasoned opinion supported with facts or statements from the letter or editorial.

S Skill Practice

Recognizing Bias Have students analyze several letters to the editor expressing different points of view. **Ask:** Which of the letters conflict most with each other? Which letter most effectively expresses the author's point of view? Why? *(Answers will vary.)* **OL**

C Critical Thinking

Comparing Have students write an essay comparing McCain's speech with the "Four Freedoms" speech delivered by President Franklin D. Roosevelt a few months before the United States entered World War II:

"In the future days, which we seek to make secure, we look forward to a world founded upon four essential human freedoms.

"The first is freedom of speech and expression—everywhere in the world.

"The second is freedom of every person to worship God in his own way—everywhere in the world.

"The third is freedom from want—which . . . will secure to every nation a healthy peacetime life for its inhabitants—everywhere in the world.

"The fourth is freedom from fear—which, translated into world terms, means a worldwide reduction of armaments to such a point and in such a thorough fashion that no nation will be in a position to commit an act of physical aggression against any neighbor—anywhere in the world." *(Students' essays should use evidence to support their comparisons.)* **AL**

59

CHAPTER
2

Assessment and Activities

ExamView®
Assessment Suite

This easy-to-use software includes extensive question banks and allows you to create fully customized tests that can be administered in print or online.

Reviewing Key Terms

1.–8. Students' paragraphs will vary. All the words used in this exercise are defined in the Glossary.

Reviewing Main Ideas

9. any three: monarch must rule with consent of governed; monarch must have legislature's consent to suspend laws, levy taxes, or maintain army; monarch may not interfere with legislative elections or debates; people have right to petition government and to fair and speedy trials by juries of peers; no cruel and unusual punishment or excessive fines or bails

10. consent of the people

11. separation of powers between governor and legislature, legislature of elected representatives, written constitution guaranteeing basic liberties and limiting power of government

12. acted as a central government, organized an army and a navy, issued money to pay for a war, named George Washington as commander of army, purchased supplies, negotiated treaties with other countries, rallied support for colonists' cause

13. It called for a country whose government was founded on

Reviewing Vocabulary

Write a paragraph that summarizes the key points of this chapter. Use all of the following content vocabulary word(s).

1. limited government
2. cede
3. representative government
4. revenue
5. ratify
6. anarchy
7. ordinance
8. interstate commerce

Reviewing Main Ideas

Section 1 *(pages 35–40)*

9. **Identifying** What are three key ideas found in the English Bill of Rights?

10. **Analyzing** According to John Locke, what fundamental element made government legitimate?

11. **Describing** What practices established by colonial governments became a basic part of our system of government?

Chapter Summary

English Traditions
★ The Magna Carta established the principle of **limited government**
★ The **English Bill of Rights** limited the powers of the monarch
★ House of Commons exemplified **representative government**

Colonial Independence
★ **Declaration of Independence** formally separated colonies from England
★ **Articles of Confederation** emphasized state governments over a strong federal government

New Constitutional Government
★ New government **balanced** need for strong central government with continued state power
★ Inclusion of **Bill of Rights** ensured ratification of new government

60   UNIT 1: *Foundations of American Government*

Section 2 *(pages 42–47)*

12. **Summarizing** What tasks did the Second Continental Congress accomplish?

13. **Describing** Why was the Declaration of Independence a revolutionary document?

Section 3 *(pages 48–52)*

14. **Examining** What achievements were made under the Articles of Confederation?

Section 4 *(pages 53–58)*

15. **Interpreting** State the position of small states in the debate over representation in Congress.

16. **Explaining** What issue did the Convention delegates refuse to settle in 1787?

Critical Thinking

17. 🇺🇸 **Essential Question** What new political ideas influenced the American colonists?

18. **Making Connections** Analyze the impact of the English political heritage on the United States and its importance to the Declaration of Independence.

19. **Evaluating** In your opinion, why were the Articles of Confederation an unworkable or unrealistic plan of government?

20. **Summarizing** Why did the Anti-Federalists insist on a bill of rights?

21. **Understanding Cause and Effect** Use a graphic organizer like the one below to analyze the cause for each effect listed.

Cause	Effect
	a strong central government
	compromises in the Constitution

22. **Synthesizing** How do you account for the contradiction between the constitutional acceptance of slavery and the ideals set forth in both the Declaration of Independence and the Constitution?

principles of human liberty and consent of the governed, the world's first such country.

14. established fair policy for development of western lands; concluded peace treaty with Great Britain; established departments of Foreign Affairs, War, Marine, and Treasury; provided that states recognize legal acts of other states and treat one another's citizens without discrimination

15. Small states favored equal representation with large states; large states wanted representation based on population.

16. slavery

Critical Thinking

17. Colonists began to believe that people should form governments to protect their natural rights and that all people were born free, equal, and independent.

18. Ideas expressed in Magna Carta and English Bill of Rights, principles of limited government and representative government, ideas of John Locke

19. It lacked power to enforce its laws, and it lacked power over the states.

20. to prevent government from violating individual rights

Government ONLINE **Self-Check Quiz**
Visit glencoe.com and enter *QuickPass*™ code USG9822c2.
Click on Self-Check Quizzes for additional test practice.

CHAPTER
2
Assessment and Activities

Document-Based Questions

Analyzing Primary Sources

Read the excerpt below and answer the questions that follow.

Inspired by the American Revolution, the French people revolted against the crown in 1789. They created a written document similar to the U.S. Declaration of Independence, specifying the rights for which French citizens were fighting.

❝ *Approved by the National Assembly of France, August 26, 1789*

The representatives of the French people, organized as a National Assembly, believing that the ignorance, neglect, or contempt of the rights of man are the sole cause of public calamities and of the corruption of governments, have determined to set forth in a solemn declaration the natural, unalienable, and sacred rights of man, . . . in order that the grievances of the citizens, based hereafter upon simple and incontestable principles, shall tend to the maintenance of the constitution and redound to the happiness of all. Therefore the National Assembly recognizes and proclaims, . . . the following rights of man and of the citizen:

Articles:

1. Men are born and remain free and equal in rights.

2. The aim of all political association is the preservation of the natural and imprescriptible rights of man. These rights are liberty, property, security, and resistance to oppression.

3. The principle of all sovereignty resides essentially in the nation. No body nor individual may exercise any authority which does not proceed directly from the nation. ❞

23. How is the preamble to this document similar to the U.S. Declaration of Independence?

24. Why do you think the French people used the Declaration of Independence as a model for their own document?

Interpreting Political Cartoons

Analyze the cartoon and answer the questions that follow. Base your answers on the cartoon and your knowledge of Chapter 2.

THE HORSE AMERICA, *throwing his Master.*

25. What symbol represents the colonies in this 1779 cartoon?

26. Who do you think the rider on the horse is?

27. What is the message of this cartoon?

Applying Technology Skills

28. **Using the Internet** Use the Library of Congress Web site to research political cartoons. Then create a political cartoon that might have appeared in a colonial newspaper. The cartoon should illustrate the colonists' feelings toward Great Britain.

Participating IN GOVERNMENT

29. Investigate the history of your local government. Visit local government offices to find out about your community's origins and early leaders. From your research you should be able to describe how the government grew and changed over the years. Prepare a brochure about the early governments of your community with the class.

Government ONLINE

Have students use the ***Chapter 2 Self-Check Quiz.*** Visit glencoe.com and enter *QuickPass*™ code USG9085c2T to prepare for the Chapter Test.

24. Students might answer that the French Revolution was inspired by the American Revolution because France contributed soldiers who fought in the United States and brought American ideas of liberty home with them. The Declaration was used as a model first because of its clear and concise writing style, but also because it echoed and synthesized other written documents like the Magna Carta and the ideas of John Locke, which were already in existence.

Interpreting Political Cartoons

25. the bucking horse
26. King George III, British leaders
27. America is breaking its relationship with Great Britain by getting rid of its master, King George III.

Applying Technology Skills

28. Display students' cartoons. Students should use information from the chapter to create their cartoons.

Participating IN GOVERNMENT

29. Brochures should include details about the early history of students' community government.

21. Causes: the states' common goals, such as national protection; differences among the states

22. People who favored slavery did not consider slaves to be entitled to the same rights as whites. People who opposed slavery compromised their beliefs in order to establish a much-needed government.

Analyzing Primary Sources

23. Like the American Declaration of Independence, the French Declaration of the Rights of Man was inspired by the writings of Thomas Paine and John Locke (specifically, the idea that the power of government comes from the governed). It models the wording of the U.S. Declaration in that its preamble specifically states why the French were rebelling against their king and the exact rights they expect their government to protect. The wording of the first three articles is quite similar, echoing Jefferson's ideas that "all men are created equal" and that they have the "unalienable right to life, liberty, and the pursuit of happiness."

Levels (BL OL AL ELL)					Resources	Chapter Opener	Section 1	Section 2	Section 3	Section 4	Chapter Assess
BL	OL	AL	ELL		**FOCUS**						
BL	OL	AL	ELL	🖨	**Section Focus Transparencies**		3-1	3-2	3-3	3-4	
					TEACH						
BL	OL		ELL	📁	**Reading Essentials and Study Guide (and Answer Key)**		p. 25	p. 28	p. 31	p. 34	
BL	OL		ELL	📁	**Guided Reading Activities**		p. 9	p. 10	p. 11	p. 12	
BL	OL		ELL	📁	**Vocabulary Activities**						
BL	OL	AL	ELL	📁	**Chapter Summaries**						
BL	OL			📁	**American Biographies**				p. 10		
BL	OL	AL	ELL	📁	**Cooperative Learning Activities**						
	OL	AL	ELL	📁	**Government Simulations and Debate**		p. 3				
BL	OL	AL	ELL	📁	**Historical Documents and Speeches**						
BL	OL	AL	ELL	📁	**Interpreting Political Cartoons**				p. 5		
BL	OL		ELL	📁	**Skill Reinforcement Activities**					p. 3	
BL	OL	AL	ELL	📁	**Source Readings**		p. 3				
BL	OL			📁	**Supreme Court Case Studies**		p. 1	p. 3			
BL	OL	AL	ELL	📁	**Participating in Government Activities**			p. 5			
BL	OL		ELL	📁	**Spanish Declaration of Independence and U.S. Constitution**	✓	✓	✓	✓	✓	✓
BL	OL	AL	ELL	📁	**NGS World Atlas, Spanish**	✓	✓	✓	✓	✓	✓
BL	OL	AL	ELL	🖨	**Unit Overlay Transparencies, Strategies, and Activities**	✓	✓	✓	✓	✓	✓
BL	OL		ELL	🖨	**Making It Relevant Transparencies**	✓	✓	✓	✓	✓	✓
BL	OL	AL	ELL	🖨	**High School Writing Process Transparencies, Strategies, and Activities**	✓	✓	✓	✓	✓	✓
BL	OL	AL		🖨	**American Art & Architecture Transparencies, Strategies, and Activities**	✓	✓	✓	✓	✓	✓

✓ Chapter- or unit-based activities applicable to all sections in this chapter

TeacherWorks Plus™
All-In-One Planner and Resource Center

- Interactive Lesson Planner
- Interactive Teacher Edition
- Fully editable blackline masters
- Chapter Spotlight Videos Launch

- Differentiated Lesson Plans
- Printable reports of daily assignments
- Standards tracking system

Levels BL	OL	AL	ELL		Resources	Chapter Opener	Section 1	Section 2	Section 3	Section 4	Chapter Assess
					TEACH (continued)						
BL	OL			💿	American Music: Hits Through History	✓	✓	✓	✓	✓	✓
BL	OL		ELL	📁	Reading Strategies for the Social Studies Classroom	✓	✓	✓	✓	✓	✓
			ELL	📁	English Language Learner Handbook	✓	✓	✓	✓	✓	✓
BL	OL		ELL	📁	Writer's Guidebook for Social Studies	✓	✓	✓	✓	✓	✓
BL	OL	AL	ELL	📁	Living Constitution, SE	✓	✓	✓	✓	✓	✓
BL	OL	AL	ELL	📁	Living Constitution, TAE	✓	✓	✓	✓	✓	✓
BL	OL			📁	NGS World Atlas, English	✓	✓	✓	✓	✓	✓
BL	OL		ELL	📁	The Constitution and You (poster set)	✓	✓	✓	✓	✓	✓
BL	OL	AL	ELL	📁	Spanish Chapter Summaries						
BL	OL	AL	ELL	📁	Spanish Vocabulary Activities						
BL	OL		ELL	📁	Spanish Reading Essentials and Study Guide (and Answer Key)		p. 25	p. 28	p. 31	p. 34	
BL	OL	AL	ELL	💿	PresentationPlus! with MindJogger CheckPoint	✓	✓	✓	✓	✓	✓
					ASSESS						
BL	OL	AL	ELL	💿	*ExamView® Assessment Suite*		3-1	3-2	3-3	3-4	Ch. 3
BL	OL	AL	ELL	📁	Authentic Assessment with Rubrics			p. 10			p. 10
BL	OL	AL	ELL	📁	Section Quizzes and Chapter Tests		p. 25	p. 26	p. 27	p. 28	pp. 29–36
BL	OL	AL	ELL	📁	Spanish Section Quizzes and Tests		p. 25	p. 26	p. 27	p. 28	pp. 29–36
					CLOSE						
BL			ELL	📁	Reteaching Activities		p. 3				p. 3
BL	OL	AL	ELL	💿	StudentWorks™ Plus with Audio Summaries	✓	✓	✓	✓	✓	✓
BL	OL		ELL	🖥	Graphic Organizer Transparencies		✓	✓	✓	✓	
BL	OL		ELL	📁	High School Government Reading and Study Skills Foldables®		p. 46	p. 46	p. 46	p. 46	

Teach With Technology

What are Reproducible Lesson Plans?

Reproducible Lesson Plans (RLPs) are detailed lesson plans that teachers can use to prepare their lessons throughout the year.

How can RLPs help me teach?

RLPs are organized by chapter and also by section, suggesting where the wide variety of technology and ancillary products can be used within the book. RLPs are organized in two ways:

- Teaching activities and ancillaries are presented using the FOCUS, TEACH, ASSESS, CLOSE organization of the Teacher Wraparound Edition.
- Teaching activities and ancillaries are also grouped by skill level, which helps you identify the activities that are appropriate for the students in your classroom.

RLPs are available on TeacherWorks™ Plus.

Government ONLINE
Visit glencoe.com and enter *QuickPass*™ code USG9085c3T for Chapter 3 resources.

You can easily launch a wide range of digital products from your computer's desktop with the McGraw-Hill Social Studies widget.

	Student	Teacher	Parent
Media Library			
• Student Edition Section Audio	●		●
• Chapter Spotlight Videos	●	●	●
***United States Government* Online Learning Center (Web Site)**			
• Chapter Overviews	●	●	●
• Multilingual Glossaries	●	●	●
• Study-to-Go	●	●	●
• Student Web Activities	●	●	●
• Self-Check Quizzes	●	●	●
• Online Student Edition	●	●	●
• Vocabulary eFlashcards	●	●	●
• Web Activity Lesson Plans		●	
• Vocabulary PuzzleMaker	●	●	●
• Landmark Supreme Court Cases	●	●	●
• Beyond the Textbook	●	●	●

READING SUPPORT FROM
JAMESTOWN EDUCATION

- **Timed Readings Plus in Social Studies** helps students increase their reading rate and fluency while maintaining comprehension. The 400-word passages are similar to those found on state and national assessments.

- **Reading in the Content Area: Social Studies** concentrates on six essential reading skills that help students better comprehend what they read. The book includes 75 high-interest nonfiction passages written at increasing levels of difficulty.

- **Reading Social Studies** includes strategic reading instruction and vocabulary support in Social Studies content for ELLs and native speakers of English. www.jamestowneducation.com

Reading List Generator CD-ROM

GLENCOE BookLink 3

Use this database to search more than 30,000 titles to create a customized reading list for your students.

- Reading lists can be organized by students' reading level, author, genre, theme, or area of interest.

- The database provides Degrees of Reading Power™ (DRP) and Lexile™ readability scores for all selections.

- A brief summary of each selection is included.

Leveled reading suggestions for this chapter:

- *A Convention of Delegates: The Creation of the Constitution,* by Denis J. Hauptly

- *The First Book of the Founding of the Republic,* by Richard B. Morris

- *George Washington's World,* by Genevieve Foster

Review suggested books before assigning them.

Economics Connection

Personal Finance Literacy

Taxing Your Paycheck?

Tell students that money they earn is taxable, including wages, tips, interest earned by bank accounts, and profits from the sale of property such as real estate or stocks. When they get a paycheck, the attached pay stub will list the amounts that are withheld for several purposes:

- **Federal taxes:** Employers withhold part of an employee's pay based on a table from the IRS. Employees can request extra deductions to be sure they do not owe more income tax in April.

- **State and local taxes:** The amount varies by state and municipality.

- **Social Security:** Employers withhold part of their employees' pay—and match that amount—throughout a person's working life. In this way, everyone contributes to the financial safety net that will provide income when workers retire or are disabled.

- **Medicare:** Everyone who receives Social Security benefits automatically receives Medicare Part A benefits to partially cover the cost of hospital stays or skilled nursing facilities.

Medicare taxes are withheld from employees' paychecks, and employers match the employees' tax payment.

- **Optional withholdings:** Employees may have employers deduct money for other purposes, such as health insurance, automatic savings plans, or retirement plans—some of which are matched by employers.

Typical Payroll Deductions

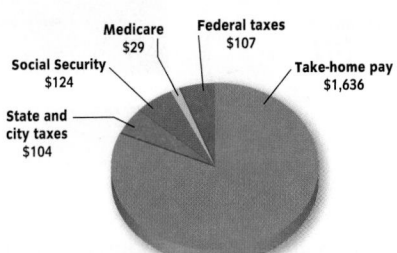

Medicare $29
Federal taxes $107
Social Security $124
Take-home pay $1,636
State and city taxes $104

Did You Know?

Your starting salary after college will be affected as much by the school you attend and where you live as by your college major.

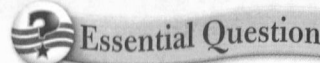

Essential Question

Refer students to the Essential Question on this page. Ask students whether they can name the three branches of government. Have them speculate in which order the branches are discussed in the Constitution. *(Article I, legislative; Article II, executive; Article III, judicial)* Then, ask them whether they think the Framers of the Constitution deliberately put them in order according to how important they thought each branch of the new government should be.

Chapter Spotlight Video

To generate student interest and provide a springboard for class discussion, access the Chapter 3 Video at glencoe.com or on the video DVD.

FOLDABLES Dinah Zike's **Foldables** are three-dimensional, interactive graphic organizers that help students practice basic writing skills, review key vocabulary terms, and identify main ideas. Have students complete this chapter's Foldable activity or activities in *Dinah Zike's Reading and Study Skills Foldables* booklet. **OL**

Government ONLINE

Visit glencoe.com and enter *QuickPass*™ code USG9085c3T for Chapter 3 Resources including Chapter Overview, Student Web Activity, Self-Check Quiz, and other materials for students and teachers.

CHAPTER 3

Chapter Audio   **Spotlight Video**

The Constitution

Constitution Hall in Washington, D.C.

Essential Question

How do the specific parts of the Constitution work to create limited government and an effective democracy?

Government ONLINE
Chapter Overview Visit glencoe.com and enter *QuickPass*™ code USG9822c3 for an overview, a quiz, and other chapter resources.

62

Launching the Chapter

Comparing Constitutions The average national constitution contains about 26,500 words—more than three times as many as the U.S. Constitution. Yet, the U.S. Constitution has provided a stability that few other nations have enjoyed. (France, for example, has had 16 constitutions since 1789). Have students research and write a brief report comparing the U.S. Constitution with the constitutions of several other nations. Suggest that students focus on such points as length, time in use, and values reflected in the documents. **Essential Question:** How do other countries' constitutions address limited government and effective democracy? Compare and contrast your findings with the U.S. Constitution. *(Answers will vary. Students should draw connections between how other countries' constitutions have, or have not, established limited government and democracy.)* **OL**

Structure and Principles

Focus

Reader's Guide

Content Vocabulary
★ article *(p. 64)*
★ jurisdiction *(p. 64)*
★ supremacy clause *(p. 65)*
★ amendment *(p. 65)*
★ popular sovereignty *(p. 65)*
★ federalism *(p. 65)*
★ separation of powers *(p. 66)*
★ checks and balances *(p. 66)*
★ veto *(p. 66)*
★ judicial review *(p. 66)*

Academic Vocabulary
★ principle *(p. 63)*
★ procedure *(p. 64)*
★ dynamic *(p. 67)*

Reading Strategy
Use a graphic organizer similar to the one below to list the six major principles of government.

Major Principles

Bellringer
Section Focus Transparencies 3-1

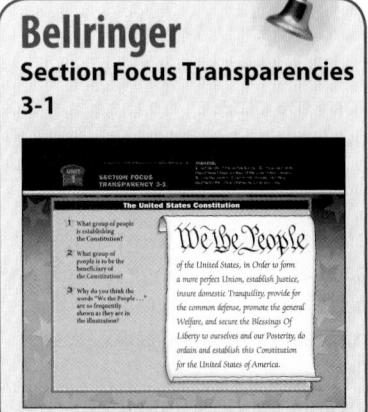

Reader's Guide

Answers to Graphic:
popular sovereignty
federalism
separation of powers
checks and balances
judicial review
limited government

Issues in the News

As head of the executive branch, the president usually resists any effort by the legislative branch to gain access to the president's records. In the aftermath of the al-Qaeda attacks of September 11, 2001, however, the relationship between these two branches of government briefly changed. During this national tragedy, a rare spirit of unity transcended the usual feeling that each branch must guard its rights closely. When a special congressional committee investigating the attacks asked for access to national security files of the executive branch, the president agreed.

▲ After the September 11, 2001, attacks, a feeling of national unity emerged.

Dividing power among the three branches of government is a key **principle** of the U.S. Constitution. Its authors feared the tyranny of government. If a government's powers were concentrated, or consolidated into a single executive branch, it would be deadly to individual freedom.

They therefore established three separate branches of government. Each of them—a legislative, an executive, and a judicial branch—would have significant power and thus be able to check each other's use of power. This concept of divided power was inspired by their view of British government in which the Parliament and monarch were able to counter one another.

The Constitution also established a republic. A republic has no monarch. Instead, it is the voters who have authority through their elected representatives. Finally, the Constitution lays out citizens' rights and what they can expect of their government.

A republican form of government depends on informed and active citizens. To understand how American government functions on a daily basis, it is necessary, first of all, to understand these constitutional principles.

Structure

Compared with the constitutions of some other countries, the U.S. Constitution is relatively simple and brief. It sets out the structure and powers of government, yet it does not spell out every detail of how the government should work. The Founders left it to future generations of Americans to work out the practical mechanics according to the situation. The Constitution is divided into three parts—the Preamble, the articles, and the amendments. All together, it contains about 7,000 words. (For the entire text, see the Reference Handbook, pages R42–R67).

Resource Manager

R Reading Strategies	**C** Critical Thinking	**D** Differentiated Instruction	**W** Writing Support	**S** Skill Practice
Teacher Edition • Identifying, p. 64 **Additional Resources** • Quizzes/Tests, p. 25 • Guid. Read. Act., p. 9	**Additional Resources** • Read. Essen., pp. 25–27 • Supreme Ct. Case Studies, pp. 1–2	**Teacher Edition** • Academic Vocabulary, p. 65 **Additional Resources** • Reteaching Act., p. 3	**Teacher Edition** • Personal Writing, pp. 64, 65 **Additional Resources** • Source Readings, p. 3	**Teacher Edition** • Visual Literacy, p. 66 **Additional Resources** • Skill Reinforce. Act., p. 3

Teach

W Writing Support

Personal Writing Have students copy the phrase "We the People of the United States." Have them free-write for two minutes, listing words or phrases they associate with the phrase. Then have them choose partners and exchange ideas. Have pairs write a few sentences that summarize their ideas. As a class, use students' ideas to discuss the meaning of these important words. **OL**

R Reading Strategy

Identifying Ask: In which article of the Constitution would you find the powers held by the president? What are some specifics of this article? *(Article II details the powers and duties of the president, describes qualifications for the office and procedures for electing the president, and provides for a vice president.)* **BL**

Critical Thinking

Answer: trial by jury, due process, no excessive bail or fines

Additional Support

The Preamble

In the Preamble, or introduction, the authors of the Constitution explain why it was written and the purposes of government. The words of the Preamble are as follows:

> 66 *We the People of the United States, in Order to form a more perfect Union, establish Justice, insure domestic Tranquility, provide for the common defence, promote the general Welfare, and secure the Blessings of Liberty to ourselves and our Posterity, do ordain and establish this Constitution for the United States of America.* 99
>
> —The Preamble

Seven Articles

The Constitution contains seven divisions called **articles.** Each article covers a general topic. For example, Articles I, II, and III create the three branches of the national government—the legislative, executive, and judicial branches. Most of the articles are divided into sections.

Article I establishes the legislative branch. Section 1 of Article I creates the United States Congress. Sections 2 and 3 set forth details about the two houses of Congress—the House of Representatives and the Senate. Other sections of Article I spell out the **procedures** for making laws, list the types of laws Congress may pass, and specify the powers that Congress does not have.

Article II creates an executive branch to carry out laws passed by Congress. Article II, Section 1, begins: "The executive Power shall be vested in a President of the United States of America." This section and those that follow:

- detail the powers and duties of the presidency,
- describe qualifications for the office and procedures for electing the president, and
- provide for a vice president.

Article III, Section 1, establishes a Supreme Court to head the judicial branch. The section also gives the national government the power to create lower federal courts. Section 2 outlines the **jurisdiction,** or the authority, of the Supreme Court and other federal courts to rule on cases. Section 3 defines treason against the United States.

Article IV explains the relationship of the states to one another and to the national government.

Foundations of Personal Liberties				
Rights and Freedoms	**Magna Carta (1215)**	**English Bill of Rights (1689)**	**Virginia Declaration of Rights (1776)**	**Bill of Rights (1791)**
Trial by jury	★	★	★	★
Due process	★	★	★	★
Private property	★		★	★
No unreasonable searches or seizures	★		★	★
No cruel and unusual punishment	★	★	★	★
No excessive bail or fines	★	★	★	★
Right to bear arms		★ limited		★
Right to petition		★		★
Freedom of speech		★ limited		★
Freedom of the press			★	★
Freedom of religion		★ limited	★	★

Critical Thinking The Bill of Rights, the first ten amendments to the Constitution, provided a number of personal liberties that expanded on the liberties granted by the other documents. *Which three categories of rights were extended by all four documents?*

Teacher Tip

Class Participation Encourage student participation in the class question-and-answer period by having members of each group pose a question you select to the class. The student who reads the question to the class should be prepared to state the answer if needed.

Activity: Collaborative Learning

Holding a Town Meeting Organize the class into seven groups, and assign each group one of the seven articles of the U.S. Constitution. Ask the groups to write as many questions and answers about their assigned article as they can in a 10-minute period. Suggest that each group divide its task by assigning each member specific sections of the article. Collect all the groups' papers, and select questions to ask the class. **OL**

This article requires each state to give citizens of other states the same rights as its own citizens, addresses admitting new states, and guarantees that the national government will protect the states against invasion or domestic violence.

Article V spells out the ways that the Constitution can be amended, or changed. Article VI contains the **supremacy clause,** establishing that the Constitution, laws passed by Congress, and treaties of the United States "shall be the supreme Law of the Land." Finally, Article VII addresses ratification and declares that the Constitution would take effect after it was ratified by nine states.

The Amendments

The third part of the Constitution consists of **amendments,** or changes. The Constitution has been amended 27 times throughout the nation's history. The amendment process provides a way this document, written more than two centuries ago, can remain responsive to the needs of a changing nation.

Major Principles

The Constitution rests on six major principles of government: popular sovereignty, federalism, separation of powers, checks and balances, judicial review, and limited government. These principles continue to influence the character of American government.

Popular Sovereignty

The Constitution is based on the concept of **popular sovereignty**—rule by the people. United States government is based upon the consent of the governed; the authority for government flows from the people.

Federalism

The terms *federalism* and *federal system* describe the kind of structure that exists in American government. These terms should not be confused with the term *federal government,* which simply refers to the national government in Washington, D.C. So what is meant by federalism? Under **federalism,** power is divided between national and state governments. Both levels have their own agencies and officials, and both pass laws that directly affect citizens.

Why did the Founders create such a complex system of government? Why did they choose it instead of a unitary form of government in which the central government has all the major powers? In 1787 there seemed to be no other choice—a middle way involving a sharing of power was the

only form of government the states would agree to support. Although the Articles of Confederation[1] had not worked very well, the men drafting the Constitution also feared the consequences of giving all power to a central government.

The solution of federalism represented a way to forge a union and yet limit central power. Federalism gives the United States a flexible system of government under which the national government has the power to act for the country as a whole, while states have power over many local matters.

Separation of Powers

In addition to creating a federal system, the Constitution also limits the central government by dividing power among the legislative, executive, and

See the following footnoted materials in the **Reference Handbook:**
1. *The Articles of Confederation,* pages R76–R79.

Major Principles of the Constitution

⭐ **Popular Sovereignty**
People are the source of government power.

⭐ **Federalism**
In this governmental system, power is divided between national and state governments.

⭐ **Separation of Powers**
Each of the three branches of government has its own responsibilities.

⭐ **Checks and Balances**
Each branch of government holds some control over the other two branches.

⭐ **Judicial Review**
Courts have power to declare laws, and actions of Congress and the president, unconstitutional.

⭐ **Limited Government**
The Constitution limits the powers of government by making explicit grants of authority.

Critical Thinking The principles outlined in the Constitution were the Framers' solution to the complex problems of a representative government. *Which principle allows the president to veto legislation?*

W Writing Support

Personal Writing Have students keep a log or diary of their activities for one week. **Ask:** What activities would be restricted or impossible under a repressive government or a government that does not have a constitution based on the ideas listed in the table entitled "Major Principles of the Constitution"? Which principles or provisions of the Constitution allow students to carry out their daily activities without fear of punishment? *(Answers will vary depending on the students' activities; popular sovereignty and limited government.)* **OL**

Critical Thinking

Answer: checks and balances

D Differentiated Instruction

Academic Vocabulary Review the term *federal* with students. To help students remember its meaning, point out its relation to the word *federation,* a union of organizations. **ELL**

Differentiated Instruction

Leveled Activities

BL Skill Reinforcement Activities, p. 3

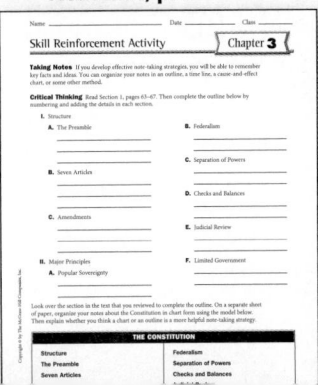

OL Interpreting Political Cartoons, p. 5

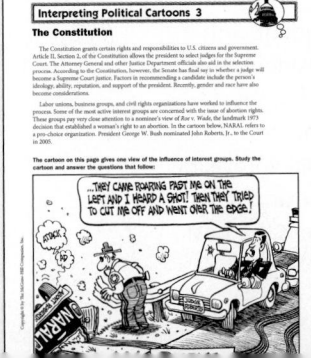

AL Authentic Assessment with Rubrics, p. 10

ELL Vocabulary Activities, p. 3

S Skill Practice

Visual Literacy Have students review the diagram. **Ask:** What are the three branches of government? *(legislative, executive, and judicial)* What do the arrows on the diagram represent? *(They show the ways in which the three branches of government can check each other's power.)* **OL**

Critical Thinking

Answer: Congress can impeach judges, create lower federal courts, set the size of the Supreme Court, confirm or deny appointments to the Court, and determine judicial salaries.

Participating IN GOVERNMENT

Popular Sovereignty Among those with the lowest voter participation rates are 18- to 25-year-olds. Have students brainstorm ways to improve this rate. **OL**

Hands-On Chapter Project

Step 1

Creating a Class Constitution

Step 1: Electing a President and Vice President Have students place their names on a sheet of paper. Collect and randomly draw three names. These students will be the "candidates" for president. If the students who were chosen do not want to participate, draw again. The rest of the class will serve as delegates.

Directions Give candidates a day to campaign. Construct a ballot listing the candidates' names. Each candidate gives

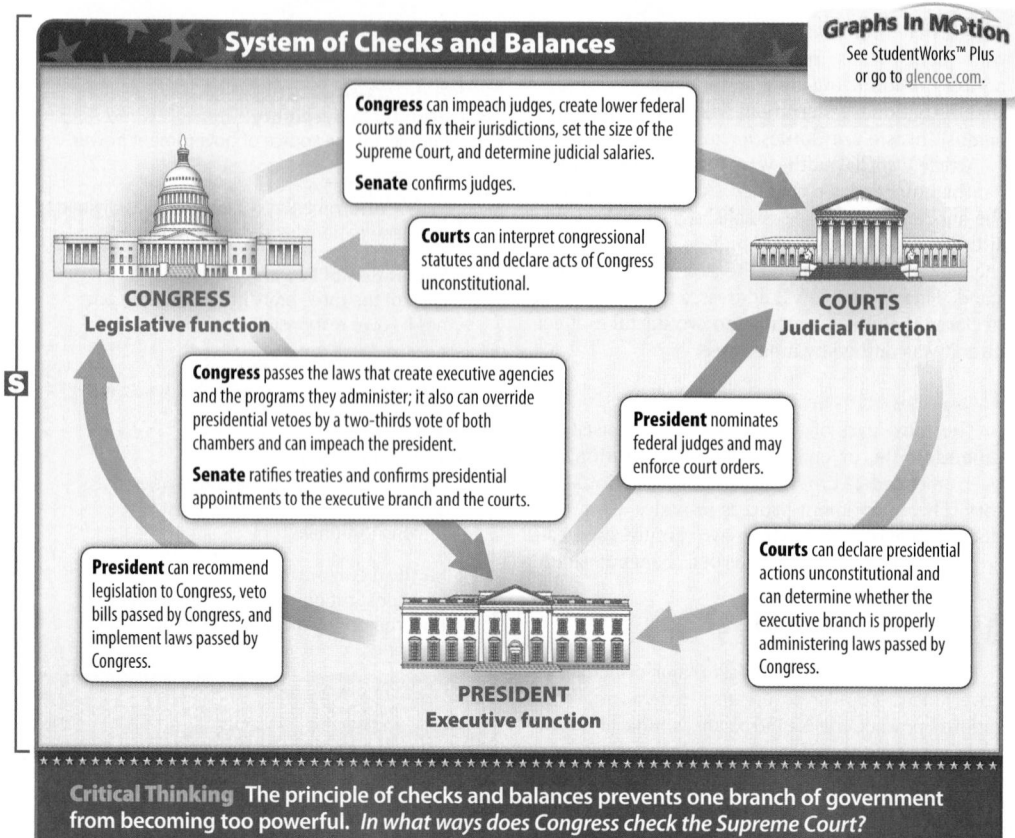

System of Checks and Balances

Graphs In Motion See StudentWorks™ Plus or go to glencoe.com.

Congress can impeach judges, create lower federal courts and fix their jurisdictions, set the size of the Supreme Court, and determine judicial salaries.
Senate confirms judges.

Courts can interpret congressional statutes and declare acts of Congress unconstitutional.

CONGRESS Legislative function

COURTS Judicial function

Congress passes the laws that create executive agencies and the programs they administer; it also can override presidential vetoes by a two-thirds vote of both chambers and can impeach the president.
Senate ratifies treaties and confirms presidential appointments to the executive branch and the courts.

President nominates federal judges and may enforce court orders.

President can recommend legislation to Congress, veto bills passed by Congress, and implement laws passed by Congress.

Courts can declare presidential actions unconstitutional and can determine whether the executive branch is properly administering laws passed by Congress.

PRESIDENT Executive function

Critical Thinking The principle of checks and balances prevents one branch of government from becoming too powerful. *In what ways does Congress check the Supreme Court?*

judicial branches. Under **separation of powers,** each branch has duties, a system that our early leaders hoped would prevent any single branch from gaining too much power.

Checks and Balances

To the principle of separation of powers the Founders added a system of **checks and balances,** whereby each branch of government exercises some control over the others. This system works in several ways.

Congress, for example, passes laws. The president can check Congress by rejecting—**vetoing**—its legislation. This veto power is balanced, however, by the power of Congress to override the veto by a two-thirds vote of each house. The federal courts restrain Congress by ruling on the constitutionality of laws. This power of the judicial branch is balanced by the power of the president to appoint federal judges. This presidential power is balanced,

in turn, by the Constitution's requirement that the Senate approve appointments. Checks and balances create a system of shared powers.

Judicial Review

Judicial review is the power of the courts to say that laws and actions of local, state, or national governments are invalid because they conflict with the principles of the Constitution.

All federal courts have the power to declare a law unconstitutional. A case involving a constitutional issue can be appealed, however, all the way to the highest court in the land, the Supreme Court. The Supreme Court is the final authority on the meaning of the Constitution. Any acts the Court declares contrary to the Constitution are void.

Given the importance of judicial review, it is noteworthy that the Constitution does not actually mention a specific power of judicial review. But Article III of the Constitution states that

a five-minute speech prior to the election. Remind the delegates that they can choose only one person. Students should vote for the person they believe will do the best job.

Putting It Together The student with the most votes becomes president. The student receiving the second-highest number of votes becomes the vice president. In the case of a split vote, allow the tied candidates to debate and have each one state why he or she is the best

person for the job. Then the delegates vote again. The rest of the class become members of Congress. (Divide the group in half and assign each half to either the House or the Senate.) **OL**

(Chapter Project continued in Section 2.)

"the judicial power shall extend to all cases . . . arising under this Constitution." The principle of judicial review was clearly established by the Supreme Court in its decision in the 1803 case of *Marbury* v. *Madison*.[1] 📖

The principle of judicial review is very important. A Supreme Court decision can only be changed in two ways: first, if the Court itself changes its views, and second, if the Congress—the people's representatives—proposes an amendment to the Constitution, which is then ratified by the states.

Limited Government

How is the principle of limited government reflected in the Constitution? It is reflected by the fact that the Constitution specifically lists the powers the government is allowed as well as the powers that are prohibited to it.

The first 10 amendments set specific limits in the areas of freedom of expression, personal security, and fair trials. We know these amendments, of course, as the Bill of Rights.

The Constitution safeguards the nation against abuse of power. In 1974 when President Richard Nixon resigned in the face of evidence that he had acted illegally, President Gerald Ford said:

❝ *My fellow Americans, our long national nightmare is over. Our Constitution works; our great Republic is a government of laws and not of men. Here the people rule.* ❞
—Gerald Ford, 1974

'It works!'

Checks and Balances During the Watergate crisis of 1973–1974, Congress found evidence that President Nixon had directed the break-in of the Democratic Party's headquarters in Washington. *What mood is the cartoonist conveying about this national crisis?*

Although the principles that President Ford described have existed for more than 200 years, the Constitution has not become dated. It remains a flexible and **dynamic** instrument for meeting the changing needs of government.

📖 *See the following footnoted materials in the Reference Handbook:*
1. *Marbury* v. *Madison* case summary, page R30.

SECTION 1 Review

Vocabulary

1. **Explain** the significance of: article, jurisdiction, supremacy clause, amendment, popular sovereignty, federalism, separation of powers, checks and balances, veto, judicial review.

Main Ideas

2. **Discussing** Explain the importance of *Marbury* v. *Madison*.

3. **Identifying** What are the six underlying principles of the Constitution?

Critical Thinking

4. **Analyzing** What is the relationship between the principles of federalism and the separation of powers detailed in the Constitution?

5. **Organizing** Using a graphic organizer like the one below, show how the Constitution divides the powers of the federal government.

```
                    ┌──────────┐
                    └──────────┘
┌────────────┐      ┌──────────┐
│  Federal   ├──────┤          │
│ Government │      └──────────┘
└────────────┘      ┌──────────┐
                    └──────────┘
```

Writing About Government

6. **Expository Writing** The principle of checks and balances limits the power of each branch of government. To help you understand this principle, research the powers of your local government. Create a diagram to show any system of checks and balances that operates at the local level, and write a brief summary of your findings.

Did You Know?

Gerald Ford is the only person who has become president as a result of the Twenty-fifth Amendment. When Vice President Spiro Agnew resigned amid scandal in 1973, President Nixon appointed Ford as his replacement. A year later, Nixon resigned during the Watergate scandal, and Ford became president.

Caption Answer: one of surprise and happiness at the effectiveness of the Constitution

Assess

Assign the Section 1 Assessment as homework or as an in-class activity, or have students take Section Quiz 3-1 from *Section Quizzes and Chapter Tests.*

Close

Analyzing Primary Sources
Ask: What did Gerald Ford mean when he said that the U.S. government is a "government of laws, and not of men"? *(Leaders are not above the law.)* **AL**

Section 1 Review

Answers

1. All definitions can be found in the section and the Glossary.
2. *Marbury v. Madison* established the precedent for judicial review. The Supreme Court could declare laws and actions of the local, state, or national governments unconstitutional.
3. popular sovereignty, federalism, separation of powers, checks and balances, judicial review, limited government
4. In both cases, power is distributed. In federalism, it is distributed between state and national governments; in separation of powers, it is distributed among the executive, legislative, and judicial branches.
5. Boxes should list executive, judicial, and legislative branches.
6. Diagrams will vary but should illustrate the principle of checks and balances in local government.

Focus

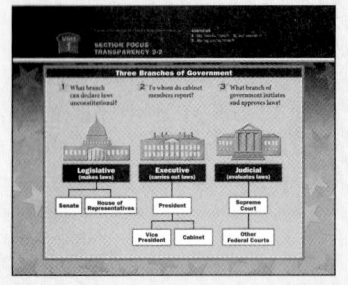
Reader's Guide

Answers to Graphic:

legislative: to make laws;
executive: to enforce laws;
judicial: to interpret laws

Resource Manager

Three Branches of Government

Reader's Guide

Content Vocabulary	Academic Vocabulary	Reading Strategy

Content Vocabulary
- ★ expressed powers *(p. 69)*
- ★ enumerated powers *(p. 69)*
- ★ elastic clause *(p. 69)*
- ★ federal bureaucracy *(p. 72)*

Academic Vocabulary
- ★ concept *(p. 68)*
- ★ contrast *(p. 72)*
- ★ initiative *(p. 73)*

Reading Strategy
Use a graphic organizer similar to the one below to list the functions of each branch of the federal government.

Legislative	Executive	Judicial

Issues in the News

In recent years, the Miller Center for Public Affairs at the University of Virginia has prepared annotated transcripts of tapes made by presidents from Franklin D. Roosevelt to Richard Nixon. Today, presidents who tape their conversations are probably more cautious of what they say than President Nixon was. In August 1974, Nixon chose to resign from office rather than face an impeachment trial. Such a trial was certain once Congress subpoenaed the tapes that would confirm the Watergate crimes. At the time, people referred to the tapes as "the smoking gun," meaning they were unquestionable evidence that a crime had been committed.

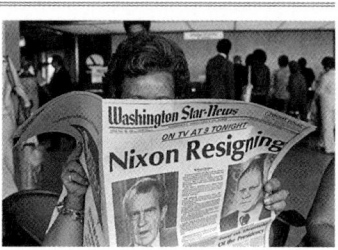

▲ A newspaper headline announces the end of the Watergate crisis.

The Watergate crisis of the early 1970s was important in American history because it showed a necessity for an independent legislative branch. (For more on Watergate, see Chapter 6, Section 1.) How were the three branches established by the Constitution?

Article I of the Constitution created a legislature of two houses: the Senate and the House of Representatives. The House was the voice of the people, chosen by popular vote. The Senate represented the broad interests of states. In many ways, the Senate and House had equal powers.

Article II created the executive branch. The presidency was a new **concept** in 1787, and the Founders hotly debated whether the office was needed. Compromises shaped the provisions for a four-year term, for the president's power to appoint, for control of the armed forces, and for foreign policy. An impeachment clause was added to ensure that the president's powers were limited.

Article III established the judicial branch. The Constitution established only one court, the Supreme Court. Congress had the authority to set up other courts as needed. State courts were already operating, so the Constitution limited federal jurisdiction to cases arising under the Constitution, the laws of the United States, or to controversies that went outside the jurisdiction of state courts.

R Reading Strategies	**C** Critical Thinking	**D** Differentiated Instruction	**W** Writing Support	**S** Skill Practice
Teacher Edition • Identifying, p. 71 **Additional Resources** • Quizzes/Tests, p. 26 • Guid. Read. Act., p. 10	**Teacher Edition** • Drawing Conclusions, p. 69 • Analyzing, pp. 70, 71 • Determining Cause and Effect, p. 74 • Analyzing Primary Sources, p. 75 **Additional Resources** • Read. Essen., pp. 28–30	**Teacher Edition** • English Learners, p. 69 **Additional Resources** • Part. in Gov. Act., pp. 5–6	**Teacher Edition** • Personal Writing, p. 72 **Additional Resources** • Authentic Assess., p. 10	**Teacher Edition** • Visual Literacy, p. 70 **Additional Resources** • Supreme Ct. Case Studies, pp. 3–4

The Legislative Branch

The Founders believed that passing laws was important and expected Congress to become the most important branch of government. At the same time, they feared it might abuse power the way they believed the British Parliament had. For that reason, the powers they gave Congress, unlike those enjoyed by the president and the Supreme Court, are **expressed powers,** powers directly stated in the Constitution.

Enumerated Powers

Most of the expressed powers of Congress are itemized in Article I, Section 8. These powers are also called **enumerated powers** because they are specified by number, 1 through 18. Five of the enumerated powers deal with economic matters—the power to levy taxes, to borrow money, to regulate commerce, to coin money, and to punish counterfeiting. Seven enumerated powers provide for defense, including the power to declare war, to raise and support armed forces, and to organize the militia. In addition, Section 8 provides for naturalizing citizens and establishing post offices and courts.

The final enumerated power is the **elastic clause.** As the name suggests, this clause lets Congress stretch its powers to meet situations the Founders could not anticipate. The clause says that Congress can make all laws "necessary and proper" to carrying out the powers expressed in Article I. The meaning of the phrase "necessary and proper" quickly became a subject of dispute. How far could Congress stretch its powers? Was "necessary and proper" to be interpreted broadly or more strictly?

The dispute was first addressed in 1819 in the case of *McCulloch* v. *Maryland,*[1] when the Supreme Court ruled for a broad interpretation. The Court supported the idea that the elastic clause gave Congress the right to make any laws necessary to carry out its other powers.

Congress Then and Now

The first home of Congress was Federal Hall in lower Manhattan, New York. The House of Representatives met downstairs; the Senate met on the upper floor. Under the direction of Speaker Fredrick A. Muhlenberg, the House named a committee to establish rules and procedures. As soon as the Senate had its twelfth member—a quorum—it informed the House that it was ready for a joint session to count electoral votes. House members climbed the stairs and helped count the votes. George Washington and John Adams became the first president and vice president elected under the new Constitution.

📖 *See the following footnoted materials in the* **Reference Handbook:**
1. *McCulloch* v. *Maryland* case summary, page R30.

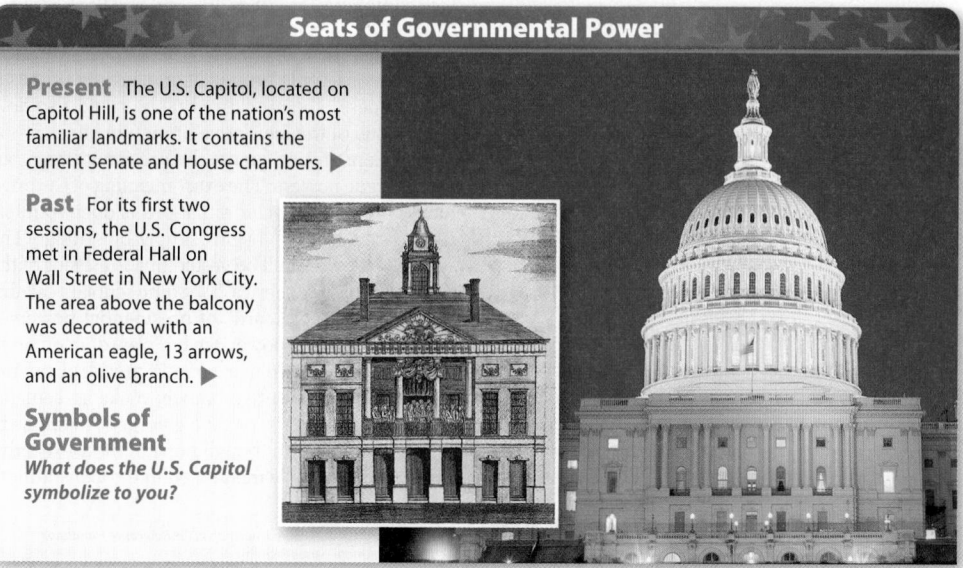

Seats of Governmental Power

Present The U.S. Capitol, located on Capitol Hill, is one of the nation's most familiar landmarks. It contains the current Senate and House chambers. ▶

Past For its first two sessions, the U.S. Congress met in Federal Hall on Wall Street in New York City. The area above the balcony was decorated with an American eagle, 13 arrows, and an olive branch. ▶

Symbols of Government
What does the U.S. Capitol symbolize to you?

Teach

D Differentiated Instruction

English Learners Ask: What does the word expressed mean in this context? *(Answers may include the word stated, written, or explicit.)* **ELL**

C Critical Thinking

Drawing Conclusions
Organize students into groups of five to consider one of the expressed powers of Congress: taxing and spending; regulating commerce, foreign policy, and national defense; or providing for the nation's growth. Have each group discuss why the power it selected was delegated to Congress rather than to the executive branch. Then ask each group to share its answers. **AL**

Caption Answer: Answers may include freedom, democracy, representative government, and ideals of the nation.

Additional Support

Activity: Collaborative Learning

Understanding Points of View Organize the class into small groups to create a bulletin-board display showing the history of the executive branch. Some group members can do the necessary research, others can create illustrations and charts, and still others can write captions for the visuals. Topics for comparison include the president's daily schedule, salary, staff, housing, number of cabinet departments, means of travel, and so on. **OL**

A Strong Executive

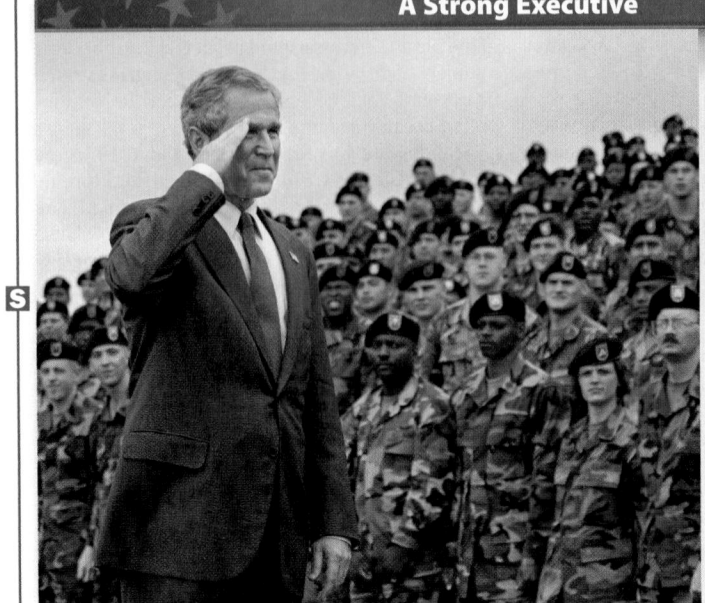

S

Commander in Chief
Executive power is strongest in foreign policy and defense. Presidents can negotiate with foreign leaders and make executive agreements with them without Congress's approval. Presidents can also send troops into conflicts without Congress declaring war. As shown after the September 11, 2001, attacks, the president has far-reaching powers to direct the military's actions. *Why might the Framers have wanted the president's power in foreign affairs to be so broad?*

Once the structure of the House and Senate was in place, each body began to work on legislation. By 1795, members of Congress had created four permanent committees.

Numbers alone tell the story that it was a smaller country and a simpler society. In the first Congress, the Senate introduced only 24 bills, and the House 143. By comparison, today a total of about 10,000 bills are introduced yearly.

Attendance in legislative sessions was only a part-time job for many years. Members had other jobs or were wealthy enough not to work. Congress did not sit in continuous session until the mid-twentieth century. Today members of Congress live and work nearly year-round in Washington, D.C.

C

The Executive Branch

The office of the presidency was initiated in response to the weakness of the Articles of Confederation. It was significant that the office was described in the second, not the first, article of the Constitution. Like those of Congress, presidential responsibilities and powers have grown enormously since George Washington took office in 1789.

Broad Powers
The president is head of the executive branch. The Founders recognized the need for a strong executive to carry out the acts of Congress. They also distrusted direct participation of the people in decision making, fearing that mass democratic movements might try to take the property of the wealthy and give it to poorer members of society. The executive branch, they believed, could protect liberty, private property, and business. The executive branch could also hold the actions of the legislative branch in check.

The Constitution grants the president broad but rather vague powers. The exact meaning of the president's power in specific situations is open to interpretation. Article II[1] begins simply by stating: "The executive Power shall be vested in a President of the United States of America." Some scholars call this sentence the "wild card" of presidential powers—meaning executive power can be "played" in different ways, like a wild card in a game. A president can fire officials in the executive branch, make agreements with foreign nations, or take emergency actions to save the nation even though none of these executive actions is specifically mentioned in the Constitution.

*See the following footnoted materials in the **Reference Handbook:*** **1.** *The Constitution, pages R42–R67.*

Specific Powers

Sections 2 and 3 of Article II define all the specific powers of the presidency. It is important to understand that the extent of presidential power in the twenty-first century has expanded on these powers considerably. In these articles, the president (1) is commander in chief of the armed forces and the state militias (National Guard); (2) with the consent of the Senate, appoints heads of executive departments, such as the Department of Labor; (3) can pardon people convicted of federal crimes, except in cases of impeachment, or reduce a person's sentence or fine; (4) makes treaties with foreign nations, again with the Senate's advice and consent; (5) with the Senate's consent, appoints ambassadors, federal court judges, and other top officials; (6) delivers an annual State of the Union message to Congress and sends Congress other messages from time to time; (7) calls Congress into special session when necessary; (8) meets with heads of state, ambassadors, and other foreign officials; (9) commissions all military officers of the United States; and (10) ensures that the laws Congress passes are "faithfully executed."

The Presidency Then and Now

In 1789 presidential government was a novel idea. Much depended on the character of the first president. Everyone knew that George Washington was the likely choice, but he, the aging general and "father of his country," was not enthusiastic about becoming president at this time of his life. In a letter to the Marquis de Lafayette, the French general who aided the Americans in the Revolution, Washington wrote:

> 66 *All that it will be necessary to add, my dear Marquis, in order to show my decided predilection [preference], is, that, (at my time of life and under my circumstances) the increasing infirmities of nature and the growing love of retirement do not permit me to entertain a wish beyond that of living and dying an honest man on my own farm.* 99
> —George Washington

A Changing Office

Presidential Leadership
George Washington set many precedents as president. Washington, although a brilliant leader, was cautious. During the Civil War, President Abraham Lincoln boldly used measures to quiet opposition, even though such measures violated constitutional guarantees of free speech, press, and assembly. After the September 11, 2001, attacks, President Bush started many new surveillance activities in the U.S. and abroad. *What outside forces shaped Washington's, Lincoln's, and Bush's views of the presidency?*

C Critical Thinking

Analyzing Ask students to discuss why the Framers of the Constitution made the president commander in chief. *(The Framers wanted to ensure civilian control of the military.)* OL

R Reading Strategy

Identifying Have students reread the powers granted to the president by Sections 2 and 3 of Article II. **Ask:** Even though the presidency is the highest government position in the country, is the president's power limited? Does the president have to answer to anyone? *(The president needs the Senate's consent to appoint heads of executive departments, make treaties with foreign nations, and appoint ambassadors, federal judges, and other top officials.)* BL

Caption Answer: Washington was influenced by the recent break from Great Britain. Lincoln felt the need to be a strong leader to hold the nation together during the Civil War. Bush was influenced by the September 11, 2001, terrorist attacks.

Additional Support

Activity: Interdisciplinary Connection

Political Science Until 1951, when the Twenty-second Amendment was adopted, it was legal for a president to be elected to more than two terms in office, although only one president (Franklin D. Roosevelt) served more than two terms. Ask students to discuss the pros and cons of term limits. *(Pros include the benefits of experience; a president would not have to waste time learning what to do. Cons include the danger of a president gaining too much power, becoming too inflexible, and being unwilling to accept new ideas.)* OL

W Writing Support

Personal Writing Ask: How do you think President Washington would feel about the national government today? *(Students might speculate that Washington would be unhappy with the national government today. Political parties are strong and often antagonistic, and the United States is very involved with foreign nations.)* **OL**

Making a Difference

Sam and Geeta Dardick The Department of Justice enforces the Americans with Disabilities Act (ADA). One ADA supporter summarized that task: "Now every day we must fight to make sure that the words in the law . . . become reality for 49 million Americans with disabilities. . . ."

Activity Have students take a tour of their homes and assess what would need to be done to allow access for someone who uses a wheelchair. *(Stairs are an obvious problem, but remind students that wheelchair users also need wider doorways, lower sinks, and so on.)* **OL**

Additional Support

When Washington was pressed into serving as president, he fulfilled his duties carefully, knowing that he would serve as a model for the future. His wisdom about the future is summarized in his Farewell Address, written in 1796 when he retired. Washington warned Americans against being too attached to their own region or to one political party. He also warned against becoming too involved in the affairs of other nations.

Early presidents would not recognize the office today. President Washington had so little to do on some days that he advertised in the newspaper the times when he would entertain visitors. He held tea parties for anyone "properly attired" on Friday evenings. He had only a handful of advisers and staff. By 1800, when President Adams moved to Washington, D.C., the second president's papers were packed in only seven boxes.

By **contrast,** modern presidents' schedules are timed by the minute. They have a White House staff numbering in the hundreds, a military force of millions, and a vast **federal bureaucracy** made up of all executive branch employees. A fleet of airplanes and helicopters stands ready to carry the president and close advisers to any part of the nation or the world.

The Judicial Branch

If judged by the length of Article III, the judicial branch appears to be the weakest of the branches of government. After naming the Supreme Court, the Constitution allows Congress to establish all "inferior" courts. The Framers were not concerned about the power of the justices, allowing them to hold office for life.

Jurisdiction of Federal Courts

The American judiciary is made up of two different court systems. One is the federal court systems, whose powers derive from the Constitution and federal laws. The second system includes the courts of the 50 states whose powers derive from the various state constitutions and their laws. Some have described the two-court systems existing side by

Making a Difference

Sam Dardick, who had polio as a child, has a permanent physical disability and must use a wheelchair. Every day he faced obstacles most people never did. Climbing stairs or boarding a bus was a huge challenge.

In the 1960s, Sam married. His wife, Geeta, who does not have a disability, saw her husband's challenges firsthand. At the time there were no national laws requiring businesses to make their services and buildings accessible. "Sam's wheelchair was a problem for both of us. We'd try to rent an apartment and find that 100 percent of them had stairs." When the Dardicks lived in California in the 1970s, they worked to see that the state's access laws were enforced and to raise public awareness.

In 1990 the Dardicks saw the fruits of their campaigning when Congress passed the Americans with Disabilities Act—the first national civil rights law for people with disabilities. Today, most Americans expect public places to be accessible for all, but there is still work to be done. Kevin McGuire, a New York lawyer who is physically disabled, works to make sure that theater and sporting events are fairly handled. He remembers in school having to ride with food deliveries in the freight elevator but is confident that when today's children grow up, "they're not going to be like I was. They're not going to ride the freight elevator anymore."

" . . . they're not going to be like I was."

—**Kevin McGuire**

Activity: Interdisciplinary Connection

Architecture Have students find out about the history and architectural style of one of Washington, D.C.'s government buildings, such as the Supreme Court Building, the Capitol, the Smithsonian, the National Archives, the Library of Congress, or the White House.

Information about many of these sites can be found on Web sites maintained by the National Park Service at www.nps.gov. Have them present their findings in an illustrated report. Some students might want to work together in pairs for this project. **OL**

The Early Presidency

The Roles of the President Shown here in *The Republican Court* by Daniel Huntington, the president held this reception in New York City in 1789 to honor his wife, Martha. In his spare time, Washington often entertained guests. *Why have the president's duties increased over the past 200 years?*

side as a dual-court system. Every court has the authority to hear only certain kinds of cases. This authority is known as the court's jurisdiction.

Two factors determine federal jurisdiction—the subject matter of the case and who is involved in it. For example, federal courts try cases that involve federal laws, foreign treaties, international law, bankruptcy cases, and interpretations of the Constitution.

Federal Courts Then and Now

In 1800 when the federal government moved to Washington, D.C., the capital architects forgot to design a building for the Supreme Court! Two weeks before the start of its term, the Court was assigned a small chamber on the main floor of the Capitol.

In the beginning, its justices were assigned to "ride circuit"—when the Supreme Court was not in session, they traveled by horseback to hear appeals in different district courts. It was such an exhausting job that the first chief justice declined an invitation to serve again. It was not until 1891 that Congress created the modern federal court system. The Court did not even have its own building until 1935.

The Supreme Court's history may seem humble. Nevertheless, the Supreme Court is a powerful branch of government and has had a significant impact on American history. It has carved out power in a number of landmark cases beginning with *Marbury* v. *Madison* in 1803. As discussed in the previous section, the case established the principle of judicial review. The case concerned the Judiciary Act of 1789. Chief Justice John Marshall decided that this law gave the Court more power than was

constitutionally allowed. Judicial review, established clearly for the first time with this case, elevated the Supreme Court to a status that balanced the other two branches of government.

When it rules on constitutional issues, the Supreme Court cannot be overturned except by a constitutional amendment. But Congress can effectively overturn a Supreme Court decision on a federal statute by enacting a new law.

Shared Power and Conflict

When the Constitution created three separate branches of government, it also defined areas in which they would cooperate—areas like passing legislation, conducting war, and spending money. Many of the working relationships among the branches are not mentioned in the Constitution; they have developed over time.

The President as Legislator

The executive and legislative branches must work together for legislation to become actual policy. Without cooperation, government can do little to address the nation's needs.

In practice, the executive branch provides plans for many of the laws that Congress considers. The presidential **initiative** in lawmaking is mentioned in Article II, Section 3, of the Constitution where it states that the president will recommend to Congress "such measures as he shall judge necessary and expedient. . . ." A great deal of the president's power comes from the fact that the president proposes the

In *The Federalist,* No. 78, written to persuade voters to ratify the Constitution, Alexander Hamilton implied that judicial review was to be expected:

"The interpretation of the laws is the proper and peculiar province of the courts. A constitution is . . . a fundamental law. It therefore belongs to them to ascertain its meaning, as well as the meaning of any particular act proceeding from the legislative body. If there should happen to be an irreconcilable variance between the two, that which has the superior obligation and validity ought, of course, to be preferred; or, in other words, the Constitution ought to be preferred to the statute. . . ."

Caption Answer: Students may mention an increase in the complexity of foreign and domestic problems, an increase in international communications and relations, an increase in population and needs of that population, and so on.

Additional Support

Activity: Collaborative Learning

The Cabinet George Washington started the tradition of holding cabinet meetings in which the heads of the executive departments were called upon to give their advice on various matters. The first cabinet consisted of Thomas Jefferson (secretary of state), Alexander Hamilton (secretary of the treasury), Henry Knox (secretary of war), and Edmund Randolph (attorney general). Today the cabinet has 15 departments (State, Treasury, Defense [formerly War], Justice, Interior, Agriculture, Commerce, Labor, Housing and Urban Development, Transportation, Energy, Education, Health and Human Services, Veterans Affairs, and Homeland Security). Have small groups of students each research a different cabinet department and give a short presentation on its function and history. **OL**

C Critical Thinking

Determining Cause and Effect Discuss examples showing the increase in presidential power during the twentieth and twenty-first centuries. For example, increasing globalization has expanded the president's foreign relations responsibilities, such as waging "undeclared wars." Write the following statement on the board: "The increase in presidential power has been related to crises, whether domestic or foreign." **Ask:** Do you think this is the true cause of the increase in presidential power? Why or why not? If not, what do you think caused the increase? *(Some students might agree that globalization is the cause of increased presidential importance. Others might point to the role of the media in focusing attention on one governing individual.)* **AL**

Caption Answer: Members of Congress might have been desperate for change. They might have allowed Roosevelt more freedom to institute programs because they thought it ultimately would revitalize the economy.

Hands-On Chapter Project

Step 2

Creating a Class Constitution

Step 2: Running the Office Students will decide which rules and consequences will be in the class constitution. For example, students might allow chewing gum or eating snacks during class. If wrappers, gum, or food are found in the classroom, however, the rule would be reviewed.

Directions To explain the bills (proposed laws), students should create a poster, pamphlet, or other means of describing

A Time of Crisis

Separation of Powers
New Yorkers hoist the flag of the federal National Recovery Administration (NRA) at its New York headquarters. In 1933, the NRA was created to regulate business as a solution to the Depression. In 1935, however, the Supreme Court said the NRA law was unconstitutional. It said Congress had given too much power to the executive branch because President Franklin D. Roosevelt could issue regulatory codes. *Why would the Great Depression have made Congress more likely to approve President Roosevelt's programs?*

legislative agenda and spells out the details of how programs enacted into law will be carried out. In order for programs to be effective, the executive branch must have the power to carry out legislative enactments. This often involves creation of a bureaucracy to carry out the details of policy.

The President Versus Congress

Even though cooperation is essential, there is often conflict between the executive and legislative branches—the principle of separation of powers intends that there will be some conflict as a way to ensure liberty.

One source of conflict is that the presidency has expanded dramatically in modern times, yet there was never any formal change in the Constitution. At times, the power of the modern presidency has troubled Congress. On the other hand, presidents have sometimes charged Congress with trying to encroach upon the proper powers of the executive to lead and protect the nation.

Another source of conflict stems from congressional responsibility to monitor how the executive branch enforces the laws. Sometimes the two branches quarrel over the way the president interprets the will of Congress in the bills it has passed. When this happens, the federal courts may be called upon to interpret the intent of Congress on a case-by-case basis.

Occasionally, Congress has been accused of yielding too much power to the president. For example, in 1935 the Supreme Court nullified the law creating the National Recovery Administration (NRA). In the majority opinion, Chief Justice Hughes said:

> 66 *Congress cannot delegate legislative power to the President to exercise an unfettered discretion to make whatever laws he thinks may be needed or advisable for the rehabilitation and expansion of trade or industry.* 99
> —Charles Evans Hughes, 1935

Finally, political parties have been a source of conflict. Obviously if the executive office is controlled by one party and the legislature is controlled by another, cooperation will be difficult. Each party tends to have different goals, different constituents to please, and a different philosophy of government.

At best, different parties in each branch can craft careful compromises. At worst, there is "gridlock"—a political traffic jam in which all forward progress comes to a halt.

Congress Versus the Courts

Under the Constitution, Congress can create lower federal courts and limit the Supreme Court's jurisdiction. Yet Congress has hesitated to use this

the importance of each one. Bills created by members of the House must pass the House by a majority vote. Then the bill is passed to the Senate for approval. If it fails in the Senate, it is returned to the House for revision and can be resubmitted. Bills originating in the Senate are approved first in the Senate and then in the House. Each bill must be approved individually. The bills that are passed by Congress with a majority vote are given to the president for review. The bill must be passed by Congress and the president. If a proposed

law is vetoed by the president, Congress can approve it with a two-thirds majority vote. After they are approved, the bills become law and can be amended using the same procedure.

Putting It Together Have Congress and the president sign the final draft of the constitution, showing their approval and understanding that it is a living document that can be amended. **OL**

(Chapter Project continued in Section 3.)

authority because it would challenge the independence of the judicial branch. In 1964 when the Supreme Court ruled that state legislatures must reapportion seats according to population, some members of Congress were outraged. The House passed a bill to strip federal courts of jurisdiction in such matters. Ultimately the Senate killed the bill.

The Supreme Court Versus the President

Some Supreme Court decisions require the president to take action in order for its decision to be carried out. In rare cases, a president has refused to enforce the Court's decision.

The most famous example of a president who ignored the ruling of the Supreme Court came in the 1830s. President Andrew Jackson defied the Court in an issue involving the rights of the Cherokee in Georgia. In 1830 President Jackson pushed the Indian Removal Act through Congress. This law met the demands of white Americans and provided money to relocate Native Americans to the Great Plains.

In 1832 the Cherokee in Georgia were living on land that had been guaranteed to them by treaty. The state of Georgia wanted this land and tried to subject the Cherokee to state law. The Cherokee sued, and in *Worcester* v. *Georgia*, the Supreme Court ruled in favor of the Cherokee. President Jackson's angry reaction to its decision was to comment: "John Marshall has made his opinion. Now let him enforce it." This conflict underscores

Quiet, Please! The delegates to the Constitutional Convention in Philadelphia really needed to concentrate on writing the Constitution. The sound of carriages and carts passing back and forth on cobblestone streets outside the Pennsylvania State House bothered the delegates. Therefore, they hired people to shovel dirt onto the street outside to muffle the noise.

the kinds of power the two branches have—the judiciary has great authority, but the executive commands the military. This was an issue that Alexander Hamilton, the main author of the Federalist Papers, focused on in *The Federalist*, No. 78.

In another example from history, President Franklin Roosevelt indicated he would not obey pending decisions in two Court cases. This time, however, the Court avoided outright conflict by ruling in favor of the president.

SECTION 2 Review

Vocabulary

1. **Explain** the significance of: expressed powers, enumerated powers, elastic clause, federal bureaucracy.

Main Ideas

2. **Identifying** What are five powers of the president?

3. **Listing** What two systems of courts make up the judiciary of the United States?

4. **Discussing** How can Supreme Court decisions be overturned?

Critical Thinking

5. **Making Comparisons** What information would you need to determine which branch of the federal government has the greatest power? Formulate questions to obtain needed information.

6. **Organizing** Using a Venn diagram, analyze the different functions of the president and Congress in passing legislation and the functions they share.

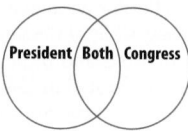

Writing About Government

7. **Expository Writing** One Supreme Court case led to a decision that televised court proceedings do not necessarily deny defendants a fair trial. Conduct an opinion poll to find out whether people favor or oppose televised trials. Chart the responses and then write a report summarizing your poll results.

C Critical Thinking

Analyzing Primary Sources
Have students reread President Andrew Jackson's reaction to the Supreme Court decision in *Worcester* v. *Georgia*. **Ask:** Do you think this is an appropriate reaction? *(Prompt students to explain their answers.)* **AL**

Assess

Assign the Section 2 Assessment as homework or as an in-class activity, or have students take Section Quiz 3-2 from *Section Quizzes and Chapter Tests*.

Close

Reading Primary Sources
Ask students to explain this quote from James Madison: "If men were angels, no government would be necessary. If angels were to govern men, neither external nor internal controls on government would be necessary. In framing a government which is to be administered by men over men, the great difficulty lies in this: you must first enable the government to control the governed; and in the next place oblige it to control itself." **OL**

Section 2 Review

Answers

1. All definitions can be found in the section and the Glossary.
2. any five of the following: serves as commander in chief of armed forces; appoints heads of executive departments; may pardon people convicted of federal crimes; makes treaties with the advice and consent of the Senate; with consent of Senate, appoints ambassadors, federal court judges, and other top officials; delivers annual State of the Union message to Congress; calls Congress into special session; meets with heads of state and other foreign officials; commissions military officers; ensures
that laws Congress passes are "faithfully executed"
3. federal courts and courts of each of the 50 states
4. by a constitutional amendment or by the Supreme Court itself
5. Students' questions should focus on checks and balances and past uses of power.
6. The president enforces laws. Congress makes and passes laws. Both propose laws.
7. Students should indicate the number of people polled, the characteristics of the polled groups, and the questions asked.

Focus

Amending the Constitution

Bellringer

Section Focus Transparencies 3-3

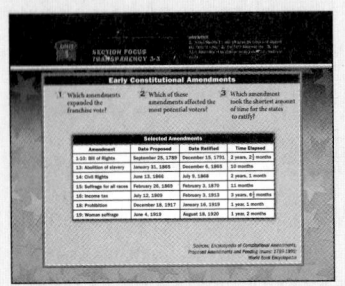

Reader's Guide

Answers to Graphic:

1. amendments
2. interpretation
3. court rulings
4. custom and use

Reader's Guide

Content Vocabulary

★ ratify *(p. 76)*
★ petition *(p. 77)*
★ balanced budget *(p. 77)*
★ impeach *(p. 79)*
★ treaty *(p. 79)*
★ executive agreement *(p. 80)*
★ judicial restraint *(p. 80)*
★ judicial activism *(p. 80)*

Academic Vocabulary

★ adapt *(p. 76)*
★ convention *(p. 77)*
★ conduct *(p. 79)*

Reading Strategy

Complete a graphic organizer similar to the one below to explain the kinds of presidential acts that have resulted in changes to the Constitution.

Cause	Effect
1.	Changes to the Constitution
2.	
3.	

People in the News

While researching a paper, a 20-year-old student at the University of Texas discovered a constitutional amendment that James Madison proposed in 1789. The student, Greg Watson, thought the idea sounded like a good one. Madison proposed that members of Congress shouldn't be able to raise their own pay. The Twenty-seventh Amendment to the Constitution was ratified by Michigan, the necessary 38th state in May 1992, more than 203 years after it was first proposed.

James Madison first proposed what later became the Twenty-seventh Amendment. ▶

In 1787, the year the Constitution was written, the nation consisted of fewer than 4 million people living in 13 agricultural states along the Atlantic coast. More than two centuries later, the Constitution is the basis for governing an advanced nation of more than 300 million people in 50 states. The Constitution has been flexible enough to meet the needs of a changing society while at the same time preserving the basic institutions and principles of the government the Framers created in 1787. As long ago as 1819, the Chief Justice of the Supreme Court, John Marshall, stated his conviction that the Constitution's flexibility was necessary and something that the Framers intended:

❝ *We must never forget that it is . . . a Constitution intended to endure for ages to come, and consequently to be adapted to the various crises of human affairs.* ❞
—John Marshall, 1819

The Amendment Process

The Founders created a Constitution that could be **adapted** to an unknown future. One way they provided for change was to describe how Congress and the states could amend the Constitution. Article V states that amendments may deal with any topic, but that no state can lose its Senate representation without the state's consent.

Amendments may be proposed and **ratified,** or approved, in two ways. Both methods illustrate the federal system of American government. An amendment is proposed at the national level but is ratified in a state-by-state process.

Proposing Amendments

One method of proposing an amendment is by a two-thirds vote in the House and Senate—the only method successfully used to date. Dozens of proposals are made every year. In recent years, suggestions

Resource Manager

R Reading Strategies	**C** Critical Thinking	**D** Differentiated Instruction	**W** Writing Support	**S** Skill Practice
Teacher Edition • Identifying, p. 81 **Additional Resources** • Quizzes/Tests, p. 27 • Guid. Read. Act., p. 11	**Teacher Edition** • Theorizing, p. 77 **Additional Resources** • Read. Essen., pp. 28–30	**Teacher Edition** • Visual/Spatial, p. 80 **Additional Resources** • Foldables, p. 46	**Teacher Edition** • Expository Writing, p. 79 **Additional Resources** • Inter. Poli. Cartoons, pp. 5–6	**Additional Resources** • Am. Biographies, p. 10

have been made to limit income taxes, to limit the tenure of Supreme Court justices, and to give states complete control of oil deposits in their borders. None have won the necessary two-thirds vote.

The other way to propose an amendment is for two-thirds of the states to ask Congress to call a **convention.** This method was tried twice. In 1963 states began to **petition,** or appeal to, Congress for a convention because they wanted to overturn a Supreme Court decision affecting state elections. (Only 33 state legislatures—1 short of the required two-thirds—voted for a convention.)

Then in the 1980s and early 1990s, 32 state legislatures petitioned Congress for a convention to propose a **balanced budget** amendment—one in which federal spending cannot exceed its income. Recent deficits have revived interest in such an amendment.

Calling a constitutional convention is controversial because other issues might be taken up. In the 1970s, President Jimmy Carter cautioned that a convention for a balanced budget amendment might be "completely uncontrollable."

Ratifying Amendments

When an amendment is proposed, Congress chooses one of two methods for obtaining state approval. The legislatures in three-fourths of the states can ratify the amendment. The other method is for the states to hold special conventions and then to have three-fourths of the conventions approve it. If an amendment is rejected using the first method, the state legislators can reverse their decision later. Suppose, however, that a state's legislators try to revoke their approval of an amendment. This situation arose over the proposed Equal Rights Amendment (ERA) to bar sex discrimination. Five of the 35 states that approved it later tried to take back their ratification. The amendment failed anyway, but the courts have never resolved the issue.

The other ratification method—state ratifying conventions—has been used only once. That occurred when conventions ratified the Twenty-first Amendment. It repealed the Eighteenth Amendment (1919) banning the sale of alcoholic beverages. Congress let each state legislature determine how delegates would be elected to the ratifying conventions.

Teach

C Critical Thinking

Theorizing Ask: Why do you think the method of ratifying by special state constitutional conventions has rarely been used? *(Answers may mention that the process for creating special constitutional conventions is less clearly defined in the Constitution or that going through the legislatures is simpler because they are already elected sitting bodies.)* **AL**

Linking ★ Past & Present

ERA The earliest version of the ERA was proposed in 1923. Every year for the next 49 years, some version of the amendment was introduced in Congress. It was not discussed by the legislature until 1967. It passed Congress in 1972 but failed to be ratified by the states by the July 1982 deadline.

Critical Thinking

Answer: because the method does not limit the convention to the consideration of just one amendment

Additional Support

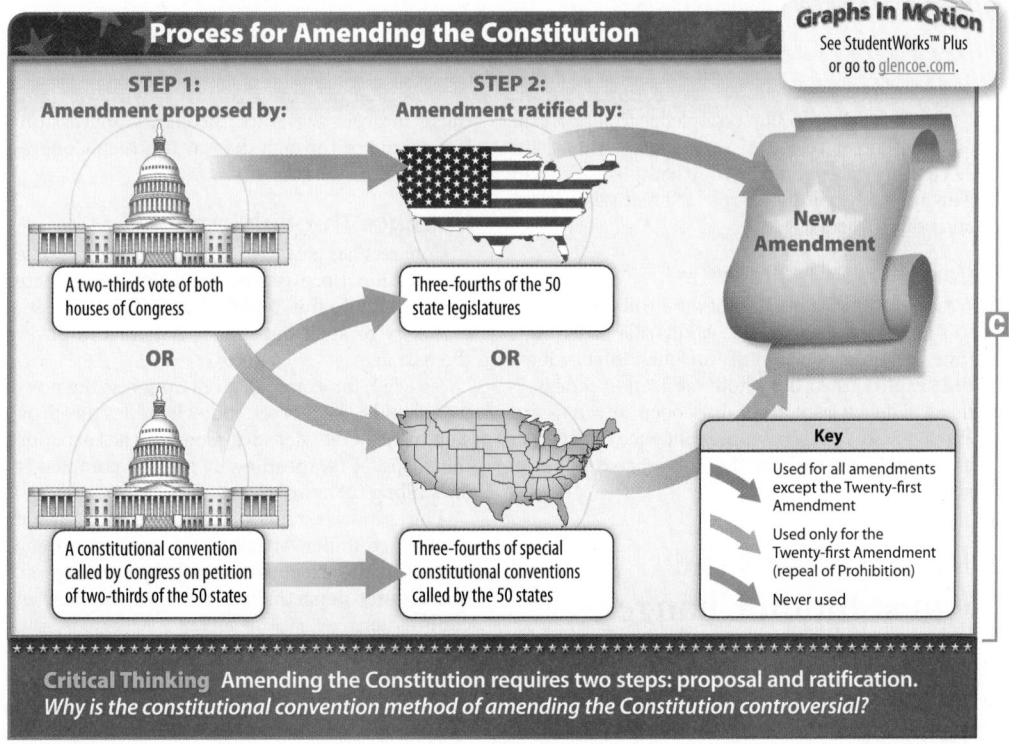

Process for Amending the Constitution

Graphs In Motion See StudentWorks™ Plus or go to glencoe.com.

STEP 1: Amendment proposed by:

A two-thirds vote of both houses of Congress

OR

A constitutional convention called by Congress on petition of two-thirds of the 50 states

STEP 2: Amendment ratified by:

Three-fourths of the 50 state legislatures

OR

Three-fourths of special constitutional conventions called by the 50 states

New Amendment

Key
Used for all amendments except the Twenty-first Amendment

Used only for the Twenty-first Amendment (repeal of Prohibition)

Never used

Critical Thinking Amending the Constitution requires two steps: proposal and ratification. *Why is the constitutional convention method of amending the Constitution controversial?*

CHAPTER 3: *The Constitution* **77**

Activity: Collaborative Learning

Creating and Debating an Amendment

Have the class select a topic for an amendment that might be proposed. Then organize the class into three groups. Have Group 1 draft the wording of the amendment, Group 2 develop arguments for the amendment, and Group 3 develop arguments against it. You might want to have some students in Groups 2 and 3 create posters and campaign buttons in support of their groups' positions. Have Group 1 write their amendment on the board, and have Groups 2 and 3 debate it. Next, have Group 1 work with the entire class to reword the amendment to satisfy objections. Finally, have a ratification vote. **OL**

Skill Practice

Conducting Research Have students research the history of the Equal Rights Amendment by finding the arguments for and against the amendment. Students should write an essay supporting or opposing the amendment. **OL**

Critical Thinking

Inferring Ask: Why would Congress want to set a time limit on how long states have to ratify an amendment? *(Possible answers include: to make states act quickly or to reduce uncertainty over the status of old amendments.)* **OL**

Caption Answer: Possible answers: Yes, amending the Constitution should not be easy, but it does not need to be as difficult as it is; no, the difficulty ensures that only the most worthy amendments are passed.

Additional Support

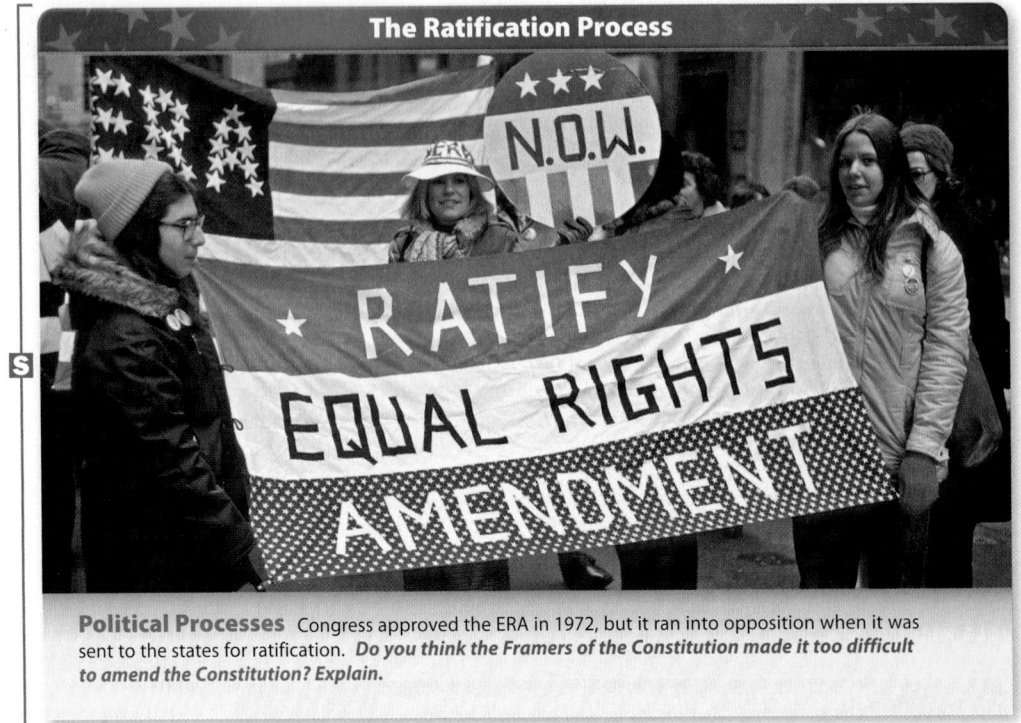

The Ratification Process

Political Processes Congress approved the ERA in 1972, but it ran into opposition when it was sent to the states for ratification. *Do you think the Framers of the Constitution made it too difficult to amend the Constitution? Explain.*

Delegates ran for election on a pledge to support the amendment or reject it. At the conventions, the elected delegates voted as they had pledged to do. This method gave the people a direct voice in the amending process.

Congress Sets the Rules

Congress sets a number of other rules that apply to the ratification process. A key rule is setting a time limit for states to ratify an amendment—if the time expires, then the whole ratification process is dead. The current limit has been seven years. Placing a time limit has a big influence on whether an amendment can get the necessary number of states to pass.

Indirect Ways the Constitution Changes

Amending the Constitution is a direct method of adapting it to modern times. But the Constitution can also be adapted to the needs of changing times in a number of indirect ways. Principally these indirect ways are through Congressional lawmaking or through the way in which Congress interprets certain of its powers.

Changes Through Law

Congress has passed many laws that have clarified constitutional provisions. The Founders expected Congress to do this, and they gave it the necessary authority to spell out practical details to govern the nation.

Article I, for example, gives Congress the power to "lay and collect taxes." But what does this provision mean? Over decades, Congress has expanded the scope of its meaning by passing complex tax laws filling many volumes.

The same is true of the executive branch established under Article II. Congress has greatly expanded the executive branch by creating various cabinet departments, agencies, boards, and commissions.

In Article III, the Founders created "one Supreme Court" and other courts "as the Congress may . . . establish." Congress completed the judicial branch by passing the Judiciary Act of 1789.

Activity: Interdisciplinary Connection

Music Challenge students to compose a song in support of or opposing an amendment. They may choose an existing amendment, the Equal Rights Amendment, the amendment created by the class in the Collaborative Learning Activity on page 77, or an amendment that they would propose if they could.

Songs may be in the rap style or set to the tune of an existing song or to a tune students create themselves. Encourage students who are musically inclined (guitar players, "beat-boxers," and so on) to perform for the class. Some students might want to work with partners or with small groups. **AL**

Over the years, Congress has changed the structure and organization of the judicial branch many times. As the nation expanded, Congress created new federal courts and rules.

Changes Through Practices

Congress has also shaped the Constitution by the way it has used its other powers. In other words, by finding a method to implement a constitutional provision, Congress defines that power for the future. For example, under the Constitution, the House may **impeach,** or accuse, federal officials—including the president—while it is up to the Senate to conduct an impeachment trial. Article II of the Constitution states that an official can be removed from office if he or she is convicted of "treason, bribery, or other high Crimes and Misdemeanors." In this article, the meanings of treason and bribery are clear, but what is meant by "high crimes and misdemeanors"? By deciding this issue and other ones like it, Congress is adapting the Constitution.

Congress has investigated more than 60 people on impeachment charges, including three presidents—Andrew Johnson, Richard Nixon, and Bill Clinton. The Senate voted against convicting Johnson and Clinton. President Nixon chose to resign during the Watergate crisis of the 1970s rather than face trial.

Informal Presidential Changes

The actions of presidents have also affected the interpretion of the Constitution, especially the powers of the presidency and the workings of the executive branch.

Presidential Succession

In 1841 William Henry Harrison became the first president to die in office. As provided in the Constitution, Vice President John Tyler assumed the powers of president. But did Tyler actually become president, or did he merely act as president until the next election?

Tyler took the presidential oath of office. Many officials opposed Tyler's interpretation of the Constitution, but no one successfully challenged him. Not until 1967, when the Twenty-fifth Amendment clarified presidential succession, was Tyler's precedent formally endorsed in the Constitution.

Foreign and Domestic Affairs

Modern presidents often **conduct** foreign affairs by executive agreement, instead of the **treaty** process specified in the Constitution. The main difference is that a treaty, an agreement between nations,

Participating IN GOVERNMENT Proposing an Amendment

Anyone can initiate an amendment simply by sending a written proposal for amending the Constitution to a member of Congress.

Senator Paul Simon, author of a balanced budget amendment in the 1990s ▶

Participating IN GOVERNMENT ACTIVITY

Propose an amendment you think is necessary. Use existing amendments as guides for form and language. Follow these guidelines when writing your proposal:

- Explain what your proposed amendment will do.
- Explain why you believe it is needed and how the nation will benefit if it is ratified.
- Indicate what opposition you expect there to be to your amendment and why.
- Suggest arguments that could be used to reply to criticism of your amendment.

Submit your proposed amendment in a letter to a member of Congress.

CHAPTER 3: *The Constitution* **79**

Hands-On Chapter Project
Step 3

Creating a Class Constitution

Step 3: Impeaching the President

If at any time the president is accused of wrongdoing, an impeachment process will begin.

Directions Arrange with the president of the class that he or she will visibly break a rule in the classroom. Decide with the president whether the offense will be major or minor. If the president is accused of wrongdoing, and commits a major offense, such as throwing a pencil, the Congress then decides whether the offense was serious enough to warrant impeachment.

If impeachment occurs, randomly choose a student to serve as chief justice to the Supreme Court to preside over the hearing. Accusing members of the House present the allegations. If the majority of the House decides the offense warrants impeachment, the Senate will conduct a trial at which the chief justice presides. At the trial, the allegations are once again presented. The president admits wrongdoing or defends himself or herself. A two-thirds Senate vote is needed for conviction and removal from office.

In the case of impeachment, the vice president becomes president, and selects a new vice president pending approval by both houses of Congress.

Putting It Together As a class, discuss what differentiates minor and major offenses. Does the office of the person committing the offense lessen or worsen the consequences? Why or why not? **OL**

(Chapter Project continued in Section 4.)

D Differentiated Instruction

Visual/Spatial Have students work in groups to find photos and create a photo-essay about the Watergate scandal. Encourage students to use photographs and captions to tell how the Watergate scandal started, who was involved, when it happened, and how it concluded. **OL**

Government ONLINE

Objectives and answers to the Student Web Activity can be found in the **Web Activity Lesson Plan** at glencoe.com. Enter *QuickPass*™ code USG9085c3T.

Caption Answer: A flood is sweeping away Nixon and the Oval Office. Students might mention that Nixon's expression in the photo, and the image of him sprawled on the desk in the cartoon, make him look defeated—as if he knows he was wrong.

Additional Support

The Watergate Crisis

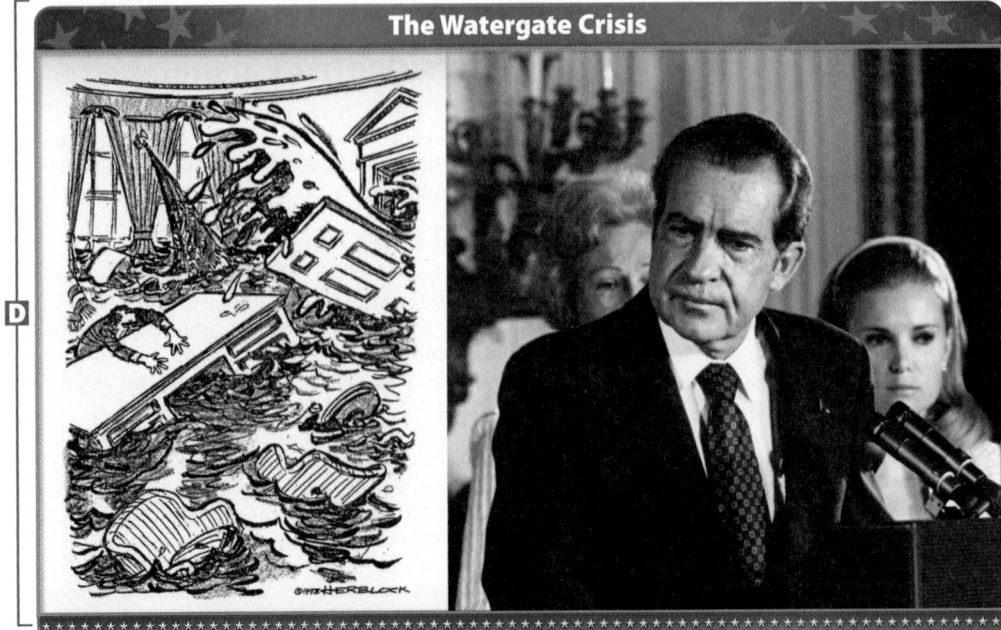

Critical Thinking The cartoon and photo both represent the final period of the Watergate crisis that engulfed the nation. *What does the cartoonist use to symbolize the Watergate scandal? How does the image of Nixon compare with the photo to the right?*

requires Senate approval, **executive agreements** do not. Executive agreements are made between heads of states, not their nations.

In the domestic arena, the Founders thought the executive branch would be concerned mostly with carrying out laws initiated by Congress. Yet in this century, presidents have been aggressive in requesting legislation from Congress. In this way and others, the president plays a far bigger role than most of the Founders ever imagined.

Court Decisions

When federal courts settle cases, they are usually interpreting the meaning of words and phrases in the Constitution that may not be very precise. The Supreme Court plays the key role in this process.

Judicial Review

The most important device the Court uses to interpret the Constitution is judicial review. Although the principle of judicial review is well established, people continue to disagree over how

the Court should use this power. Some advocate judicial restraint; others argue for judicial activism. What do these phrases mean?

Those who support **judicial restraint** believe that the Court should avoid taking the initiative on social and political issues. They believe the Court should uphold acts of Congress unless the acts clearly violate a specific constitutional provision. In other words, the Court should leave policy making to others.

Those who support **judicial activism** believe the opposite: that the Court should actively help settle the difficult social and political questions of the day. Under Earl Warren, chief justice from 1953 to 1969, for example, the Court decided many controversial cases involving the civil rights of minorities.

Government ONLINE

Student Web Activity Visit glencoe.com and enter *QuickPass*™ code USG9822c3. Click on Student Web Activity and complete the activity about amending the Constitution.

80   UNIT 1: *Foundations of American Government*

★ Activity: Interdisciplinary Connection

Geography Have students consider what would happen to representation in the House of Representatives if membership were allocated by a state's geographic size. Have students list the top 10 states by size (area) and population in descending order. Have them compare the rank in area with the rank in population. Students should see that the huge

state of Alaska would end up with the most representatives even though it has one of the smallest populations. They should also note that a small state such as New Jersey would have fewer representatives despite its large population. Ask what might happen to the number of representatives from the students' state. **BL**

Because of the kinds of cases the Warren Court decided, people tend to think that judicial activism means the court is active on civil rights or social issues. But judicial activism can also serve conservative goals. In the 1930s, for example, conservative justices often took activist positions against New Deal programs intended to regulate the economy. In general, however, liberals have been more likely to support judicial activism, and conservatives have supported judicial restraint.

Changing Court Rulings

Changing social and political conditions affect how the Court interprets the Constitution. In 1896 the Court ruled that separate public facilities for African Americans were constitutional as long as those facilities were equal. More than a half century later, in 1954, the Court reversed its position when it decided that "separate educational facilities are inherently unequal."

Changes Through Custom and Use

The Constitution has also been changed informally through customs that have developed over time. Political parties are a good example. The Constitution does not mention political parties, but parties developed soon after the government was organized. They play an important role in elections and shape how Congress conducts its business.

The amendments added to the Constitution and the changes achieved through precedent and practice have created a government that can respond to the needs of the times—to the era of the horse and buggy, as well as the era of space exploration and the Internet. Thus, this short, simple document has continued for more than two centuries to serve as the supreme law of the land.

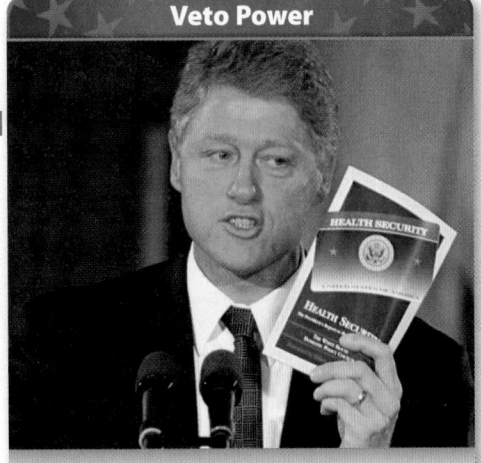

Veto Power

Presidential Influence President Bill Clinton warned Congress that if they did not "send me legislation that guarantees every American private health insurance . . . you will force me to take this pen [and] veto the legislation." *How does the influence modern presidents have on legislation differ from what the Founders intended?*

R Reading Strategy

Identifying Ask: How could judicial activism infringe on powers given to Congress in the Constitution? *(The Supreme Court could, through its decisions, force changes that otherwise would require legislation to be passed by Congress.)* **AL**

Caption Answer: Modern presidents have been aggressive in requesting legislation. Today presidents play a far greater role in government than the Founders intended.

Assess

Assign the Section 3 Assessment as homework or as an in-class activity, or have students take Section Quiz 3-3 from *Section Quizzes and Chapter Tests.*

Close

Synthesizing Ask: Is it effective to limit the amount of time allowed for ratification of an amendment? *(Answers will vary. Students should be able to defend their positions.)* **OL**

Section 3 Review

✦ SECTION 3 Review ✦

Vocabulary

1. **Explain** the significance of: ratify, petition, balanced budget, impeach, treaty, executive agreement, judicial restraint, judicial activism.

Main Ideas

2. **Identifying** What are two methods of ratifying amendments?

3. **Examining** How can Congress make informal changes to the Constitution?

Critical Thinking

4. **Analyzing** How have the four informal methods of amending the Constitution affected the executive branch?

5. **Organizing** Using a graphic organizer like the one below, describe at least one way Congress and the Supreme Court each have changed the Constitution.

Changes in the Constitution	
By Congress	
By Supreme Court	

Writing About Government

6. **Descriptive Writing** Do you think the Founders were correct in allowing the Constitution to be amended? Write a letter to the editor of a local newspaper explaining your position on this issue.

CHAPTER 3: *The Constitution* **81**

Focus

S Skill Practice

Have students review the quotes in the Verbatim section and discuss each item as it relates to the people and themes found in their textbooks. Then have students research the debate over the ratification of the Constitution. They should create a list of quotations about the issue along with a brief statement explaining the quote, identifying the person quoted, and describing how the quote relates to the issue. Ask students to share their lists in a class discussion. **OL**

Teach

C Critical Thinking

Differentiating Pros and Cons
Have students consider the following questions: Should the president be allowed to assert special powers and declare war? Have students evaluate the pros and cons of the issue and write a brief essay defending their point of view. **BL**

Additional Support

CONSIDERING THE CONSTITUTION

THE CONSTITUTION ALLOWS CONGRESS TO IMPEACH THE PRESIDENT. **BARBARA JORDAN,** the first African American woman elected to the Texas State Senate, was serving on the House Judiciary Committee in 1974. This committee was considering the impeachment of Richard Nixon for "high crimes and misdemeanors." Jordan examined how our Constitution has changed and expanded over the years. Here is part of her speech on this issue:

AP Images
MS. JORD

"Mr. Chairman . . . Earlier today we heard the beginning of the Preamble to the Constitution of the United States, 'We, the people.' It is a very eloquent beginning. But when the document was completed on the 17th of September, 1787, I was not included in that 'We, the people.' I felt somehow for many years that George Washington and Alexander Hamilton just left me out by mistake. But through the process of amendment, interpretation, and court decision, I have finally been included in 'We, the people.'"

SPECIAL POWERS?

Article 1, Section 8 of the Constitution states that "Congress shall have the power to declare war." But it is the president, claiming special powers from the Constitution, who often declares war. Which of the wars from the past 100 years listed below were declared by Congress?

1 World War II
2 Korean War
3 Vietnam War
4 The war in Grenada
5 Persian Gulf War
6 The war in Afghanistan
7 The war in Iraq

We the People of the United States, in order to form a more perfect Union, establish Justice, insure domestic Tranquility, provide for the common defence, promote the general Welfare, and secure the Blessings of Liberty to ourselves and our Posterity, do ordain and establish this Constitution for the United States of America.

Article I.

The Granger Collection, New York

82

MILESTONES

ACCEPTED, MAY 7, 1992. THE TWENTY-SEVENTH AMENDMENT to the Constitution was ratified 203 years after it was first proposed. The amendment states that raises for members of Congress will take effect only after the subsequent congressional election.

Robyn Beck/AFP/Getty Images

RESTORED, 2002. TWO LARGE MURALS in the National Archives Building in Washington, D.C. This building, the home of the Constitution, is where artist Barry Frank painted the murals in 1936. They depict fictional scenes of the presentation of the Constitution and the Declaration of Independence. The murals were painstakingly restored over a two-year period.

★ Activity: Collaborative Learning ★

Proposing an Amendment Organize the class into groups of three or four students to discuss and debate issues that they believe warrant an amendment to the Constitution. Encourage students to think in terms of human or inalienable rights. After students in each group have agreed upon an issue, have them write a proposal for a constitutional amendment and persuasively present their proposal to the class. Following each presentation, have the class vote on whether or not to approve the suggested amendment. **OL**

VERBATIM

WHAT PEOPLE SAID

❝The people made the Constitution, and the people can unmake it. It is the creature of their will, and lives only by their will.❞

U.S. Supreme Court Chief Justice **John Marshall**, *1821*

❝I would rather have a King, a House of Lords and Commons than the new government.❞

The patriot **Patrick Henry**, *in support of his stand against the establishment of the Constitution in 1788*

❝Setting up White House operatives who secretly decide to fight dirty little wars is a direct assumption of war powers expressly forbidden by the Constitution.❞

Journalist **Bill Moyers**, *writing about the Iran-Contra affair, when the Reagan administration attempted to bypass Congress in the name of national security*

❝The Constitution I interpret is not living, but dead.... Our first responsibility is to not make sense of the law—our first responsibility is to follow the text of the law.❞

Antonin Scalia, *nominated by President Reagan to be an associate justice of the Supreme Court in 1986*

❝The happy union of these states is a wonder; their constitution a miracle; their example the hope of liberty throughout the world.❞

James Madison, *sometimes called the "Father of the Constitution," 1829*

Daren Fentiman/ZUMA

REMAIN SILENT

The Supreme Court's ruling in *Miranda* v. *Arizona* (1966) said that people who are arrested must be informed of their constitutional rights before being questioned by the police. This requirement is known as "Miranda rights." Here's one script police officers use to inform people of their Miranda rights:

1. You have the right to remain silent.

2. Anything you say can and will be used against you in a court of law.

3. You have the right to have an attorney present now and during any future questioning.

4. If you cannot afford an attorney, one will be appointed to you free of charge if you wish.

NUMBERS

28" by 23 5/8"

The measurements of each of the four sheets of the U.S. Constitution

Burke/Triolo/Brand X Pictures/Jupiter Images

$30 Amount paid to Jacob Shallus, who transcribed the words of the Constitution in "fancy handwriting" in preparation for its signing

9 The number of states that needed to ratify the Constitution in order for it to go into effect. This happened in June 1788, when New Hampshire became the 9th state to ratify.

12 Number of amendments originally proposed to the Constitution. Ten of these were accepted and are known as the Bill of Rights.

CORBIS

39 Number of signers of the Constitution

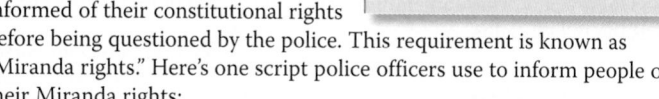

Bettmann/CORBIS

1 Number of amendments that have been repealed. The Eighteenth Amendment, which dealt with Prohibition, was repealed in 1933.

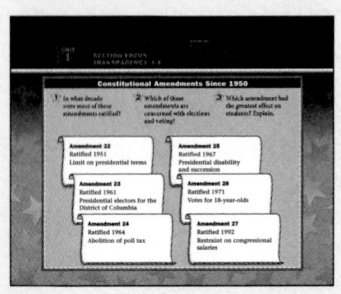
SECTION 4

The Amendments

Reader's Guide

Content Vocabulary	Academic Vocabulary	Reading Strategy
★ incorporation doctrine *(p. 84)* ★ prior restraint *(p. 85)* ★ probable cause *(p. 86)* ★ search warrant *(p. 86)* ★ arrest warrant *(p. 86)*	★ due process *(p. 86)* ★ eminent domain *(p. 86)* ★ lame duck *(p. 90)* ★ poll tax *(p. 90)* ★ demonstration *(p. 85)* ★ location *(p. 87)* ★ reverse *(p. 89)*	In a table, categorize the 27 amendments into the three major groups described in this section. **Constitutional Amendments**

Issues in the News

In 2006 a piece of parchment documenting New York State's approval of the Bill of Rights was shown in public for the first time since March 27, 1790, the day it was signed. This rare item was removed from the National Archives and put on display at Federal Hall on Wall Street in New York City. During the week of the exhibit, 80 new citizens were sworn in at the hall. "It's an even more important day because part of the Bill of Rights is here," said one woman, Natella O'Bryant. "When I read the Bill of Rights, I realize that they are not on paper but live in reality."

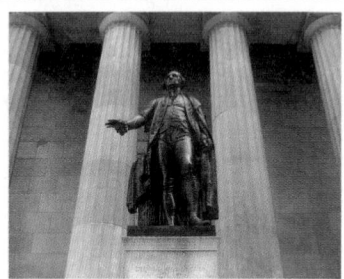

▲ **Federal Hall in New York City**

The Bill of Rights that so moved Natella O'Bryant exists because in 1788, political leaders in Massachusetts and Virginia refused to support ratification of the new Constitution without it. To ensure ratification in these major states, supporters of the Constitution promised to add a list of basic rights to the Constitution. In 1791 the states ratified 10 amendments that described these rights. These amendments became known as the Bill of Rights.

The Bill of Rights

The Bill of Rights protects individual rights by limiting government powers. When the Constitution was adopted, some state constitutions had bills of rights. Thus, many felt that the new national government should be limited in the same way.

Originally the Bill of Rights applied only to the national government, but almost all its provisions have been "incorporated" into the states through court decisions, meaning its protections cover state laws. Scholars call this the **incorporation doctrine.**

The First Amendment

One of the most important amendments in the Bill of Rights, the First Amendment states:

> ❝ *Congress shall make no law respecting an establishment of religion, or prohibiting the free exercise thereof; or abridging the freedom of speech, or of the press; or the right of the people peaceably to assemble, and to petition the Government for a redress of grievances.* ❞
>
> —First Amendment, 1791

R Reading Strategies	C Critical Thinking	D Differentiated Instruction	W Writing Support	S Skill Practice
Teacher Edition • Reading Primary Sources, p. 85 • Making Connections, p. 87 **Additional Resources** • Quizzes/Tests, p. 28 • Guid. Read. Act., p. 12	**Teacher Edition** • Analyzing Primary Sources, p. 87 • Drawing Conclusions, p. 88 **Additional Resources** • Read. Essen., pp. 34–36 • Ch. Summaries, pp. 7–9	**Teacher Edition** • Interpersonal, p. 85 **Additional Resources** • Hist. Docs. and Speeches, p. 3	**Teacher Edition** • Narrative Writing, p. 86 • Expository Writing, p. 90 **Additional Resources** • Quizzes/Tests, pp. 29–36	**Teacher Edition** • Conducting Research, p. 89 **Additional Resources** • Making It Rel. Trans., pp. 5–6

The First Amendment protects the right of Americans to worship as they please, or, if they prefer, to have no religion at all. These principles are known as freedom of religion and separation of church and state. The First Amendment also protects freedom of speech and freedom of the press. The government cannot prevent individuals from freely expressing their opinions. Citizens thus have the right to criticize the government and to spread unpopular ideas.

The First Amendment also protects the expression of ideas in newspapers, books, radio, television, and, to some extent, movies and the Internet. Unlike in some countries, the American press is not subject to **prior restraint**—that is, government cannot censor information before it is published or broadcast.

Freedom of speech is not unlimited. For example, laws prohibit slander and libel. Slander is false speech intended to damage a person's reputation. Libel is similar to slander, except that it applies to written or published statements. There are also other unprotected forms of speech. Endangering the nation by giving away military secrets or calling for the violent overthrow of the government are examples of unprotected speech. Courts have also held that speech should be responsible. The classic example is that no one has the right to cry "Fire!" in a crowded theater just to see what happens.

The First Amendment also protects the right to assemble in groups and hold **demonstrations.** People may pass out pamphlets, hold meetings, and peaceably advertise their beliefs, but courts have ruled that they can require a group to obtain a permit before holding meetings or demonstrations.

Finally, the First Amendment protects the right to criticize government officials and their actions. The rights to sign petitions in support of an idea, to present those petitions to government officials, and to send letters to those officials are all protected.

The Second Amendment

This amendment ensures citizens and the nation the right to security. It states:

> 66 *A well regulated Militia, being necessary to the security of a free State, the right of the people to keep and bear Arms, shall not be infringed.* 99
>
> —Second Amendment, 1791

The Second Amendment was intended originally to prevent the national government from repeating actions that the British took. Before the Revolution, the British tried to take weapons away from colonial militia, or armed forces of citizens.

This amendment seems to support the right to own firearms, but it does not prevent Congress from regulating the interstate sale of weapons. Further, the Second Amendment is one of the few which the Court has not yet incorporated into state law. Many state constitutions guarantee the right to keep and bear arms.

Law and Libel

The Limits of Free Expression A Manhattan lawyer brought a libel case against the television series *Law and Order*. The lawyer said that the plot of one episode implied false things about him that harmed his reputation—the definition of libel. Even a fictional drama can be charged with libel if friends and family of the subject recognize that the TV character was meant to be that person. *Which amendment is concerned with libel?*

Teach

D Differentiated Instruction

Interpersonal As a class, list First Amendment issues facing your school. Start a petition to enact change in the school based on one or more of those issues. Discuss as a class how and when signatures may be obtained and why the method of petitioning is important to the validity of the claim. **OL**

R Reading Strategy

Reading Primary Sources Discuss the meaning and importance of the Second Amendment. Have students summarize the meaning in their own words. **Ask:** Is this amendment still as relevant today as it was in Revolutionary times? *(Answers will vary, but students should base their answers on the prevalence, necessity, and danger of firearms.)* **OL**

Caption Answer: the First Amendment

Hands-On Chapter Project
Step 4

Creating a Class Constitution

Step 4: Amending the Constitution
Students will synthesize what they have learned in Steps 1, 2, and 3 by evaluating the class constitution.

Ask: Are the laws set forth in the constitution being carried out? Do any of the laws need to be amended? Are the president and vice president and members of Congress performing their jobs properly? Do any laws need to be added to the constitution?

Putting It Together If students feel that changes need to be made, follow the protocol outlined in Step 2 to make the changes. **OL**

W Writing Support

Narrative Writing Have students write a creative short story about a society in which the government has suspended the Bill of Rights. Some questions their stories might address include: Why did the government suspend the Bill of Rights? What changes occur in everyday life? Do groups of people revolt? What happens to the freedoms that you and your friends enjoy when there is no guaranteed individual protection from the government? Encourage students to focus on the suspension of one or two amendments and the effects they see on their lives, their friends' lives, or society in general. **AL**

Additional Support

The Bill of Rights

1. Guarantees freedom of religion, speech, assembly, and press, and the right of people to petition the government

2. Protects the right of states to maintain a militia and of citizens to bear arms

3. Restricts quartering of troops in private homes

4. Protects against "unreasonable searches and seizures"

5. Assures the right not to be deprived of "life, liberty, or property, without due process of law," including protections against double jeopardy, self-incrimination, and government seizure of property without just compensation

6. Guarantees the right to a speedy and public trial by an impartial jury

7. Assures the right to a jury trial in cases involving the common law (the law established by previous court decisions)

8. Protects against excessive bail and cruel and unusual punishment

9. Provides that people's rights are not restricted to those specified in Amendments 1–8

10. Restates the Constitution's principle of federalism by providing that powers not granted to the national government nor prohibited to the states are reserved to the states and to the people

Critical Thinking The Bill of Rights was not part of the original Constitution. *For what purpose were the first 10 amendments added to the Constitution?*

The Third Amendment

This amendment prohibits the government from forcing people to provide shelter for soldiers in their homes, another British practice before the Revolution. In times of war, however, Congress may require a home owner to house soldiers but only under conditions clearly spelled out by law.

The Fourth Amendment

The Fourth Amendment reflects the early Americans' desire to protect their privacy. Britain used writs of assistance—general search warrants—to enter private residences in search of smuggled goods. The Fourth Amendment limits the government's power to conduct searches and seizures by protecting the right to privacy. Authorities must have a specific reason for a search or to seize evidence or people. The police cannot conduct a search or seizure hoping to find evidence or arrest people on the chance they might have committed a crime.

To be lawful, a search or an arrest must be based on **probable cause**—a reasonable basis to believe a person or premises are linked to a crime. A search or an arrest usually requires a **search warrant** or an **arrest warrant.** These are orders signed by a judge describing the place to be searched for specific items, or else naming the person to be arrested for a specific crime.

The Fifth Amendment

This amendment contains four important protections for people accused of crimes. First, no one can be tried for a serious crime unless a grand jury has decided there is enough evidence to justify a trial. Second, a person found innocent may not be tried again for the same offense. This clause prevents harassment of people to convict them of a crime for which they were already found innocent. Third, no one may be forced to testify against himself or herself. People questioned by the police, standing trial, or testifying before a congressional hearing can refuse to answer questions if their answers would connect them with a crime. The burden of conviction is on the government; people cannot be forced to convict themselves.

Finally, the Fifth Amendment states that no one can be deprived of life, liberty, or property without **due process** of the law. Thus the government must follow constitutional procedures in all actions against individuals. The Fifth Amendment also defines government's right of **eminent domain**—the power of government to take private property for public use. The government must pay a fair price for the property and must use it to benefit the public.

The Sixth Amendment

The Sixth Amendment gives an accused person several important rights. A basic protection is the right to a speedy, public trial by an impartial jury. Thus, the authorities cannot purposely hold a person for an unnecessarily long time while awaiting trial.

★ Activity: Interdisciplinary Connection ★

Law Provide the following hypothetical case, and ask students to indicate which amendment is involved, the exact words that apply to the case, and whether the amendment has been violated: The police think John Smith might be storing stolen property in his house because they believe some of his friends have broken into neighborhood houses. They go to his house when his 10-year-old sister is the only person home and tell her that they are checking houses to find a gas leak. While they are there, they look around and find the stolen property in John's room, seize it, and arrest John when he returns. *(The Fourth Amendment has been violated; a search or arrest must be based on probable cause, and a search requires a warrant. The police have conducted an unreasonable search and seizure.)* **OL**

Amendments in Practice

Present In 1993, 80 people died in a fire at the compound of the Branch Davidians, a religious cult, when their leader, David Koresh, refused to let federal agents serve him with a legal warrant. ▶

Past In the 1920s, Prohibition agents often destroyed illegal kegs in public. ▶

Enforcing Laws
Explain why the Eighteenth Amendment may have been more difficult to enforce than the Fourth Amendment.

C

This protection prevents government from silencing its critics, as often happens under dictatorships. A public trial assures that justice is carried out in full view of the people. The right to a court trial under this amendment has been extended by the Supreme Court to people charged with crimes subject to the state courts.

The Sixth Amendment provides for trial by jury. An accused person could, however, ask to be tried by a judge alone—that is a constitutional right, too.

The accused also may ask to have the trial moved to another community. A change of venue, or new trial **location,** is sometimes requested when unfavorable publicity makes it unlikely the defendant can receive a fair trial in the original location.

The Sixth Amendment gives accused persons the right to know the charges against them, so that they can prepare a defense. They also have the right to hear and question all witnesses against them and the right to compel witnesses to testify in court for them. In addition, accused persons have the right to be defended by a lawyer.

The Seventh Amendment

The Seventh Amendment provides for the right to a jury trial in federal courts to settle all disputes about property worth more than $20. When both parties in a conflict agree, however, a judge rather than a jury may hear evidence and settle the case.

The Eighth Amendment

This amendment prohibits excessive bail—money or property that the accused deposits with the court to gain release from jail until the trial. The judge sets bail in an amount that ensures the accused will appear for trial. When the trial ends, bail is returned. If the accused does not appear, bail is forfeited.

The Eighth Amendment also prevents judges from ordering someone convicted of a crime to pay an excessive fine. Fines for serious crimes may be higher than those for less serious ones. If someone is too poor, he or she cannot be imprisoned for longer than the maximum sentence to "work off" the fine.

Finally, the Eighth Amendment bans "cruel and unusual punishment" for crimes. These are punishments that are out of proportion to the crime committed. For example, 20 years in prison for stealing a candy bar would be cruel and unusual punishment. The Eighth Amendment also has been used to limit the use of the death penalty in some circumstances.

The Ninth Amendment

The Ninth Amendment states that all other rights not spelled out in the Constitution are "retained by the people." This amendment prevents government from claiming that the only rights people have are those listed in the Bill of Rights. The amendment protects all basic or natural rights not specifically noted in the Constitution.

Caption Answer: The Fourth Amendment had more public support than the Eighteenth Amendment, which was repealed in 1933.

C **Critical Thinking**

Analyzing Primary Sources Have students examine the photographs and captions on this page. **Ask:** Why do you think Prohibition agents destroyed illegal alcohol in public? *(probably to make an example of it; to demonstrate to onlookers and to the media that they were serious about prohibiting the manufacture, sale, and transportation of liquor)* **BL**

R **Reading Strategy**

Making Connections Have students use a graphic organizer or Foldable such as the Layered-Look book to collect information about the Sixth, Seventh, and Eighth Amendments to the Constitution. **Ask:** How do these amendments build upon one another? Is it possible to have one without the others? *(Answers will vary. Ask students to cite specific details when they answer.)* **OL**

Differentiated Instruction

Constitutional Photo-Essay

Participating in Government Activities, p. 5

Objective: To understand how the Constitution affects daily life within students' communities.

Focus/Teach: Review the background with students, and have them answer the "Questions to Consider."

Assess: Have students complete the activity.

Close: Complete the "Follow-Up" activity.

Differentiated Instruction Strategies

BL Have students rank, in order of personal importance, each of the 27 constitutional amendments.

AL Have students write a Twenty-eighth Amendment that addresses an issue about which they feel strongly.

ELL Encourage students to label every photo as accurately as possible.

Did You Know?

Some people want an amendment to limit the terms of members of Congress. Other Americans demand a victims' rights amendment to guarantee that the victim in every criminal prosecution will be granted the right to be present and heard at all critical stages of judicial proceedings. Still others want to establish an amendment setting a legal definition of marriage.

C Critical Thinking

Drawing Conclusions Discuss the victims' rights amendment. **Ask:** Do you think a victims' rights amendment would be good for the justice system? Would it conflict with any of the other amendments? *(Answers will vary, but students should point out that a presentation by the victim might influence a jury's opinion, which would be unfair to the defendant. It might conflict with the Sixth Amendment.)* **AL**

Critical Thinking

Answer: the Thirteenth, Fourteenth, and Fifteenth Amendments

Additional Support

The Tenth Amendment

Unlike the other amendments, the Tenth Amendment did not add any new rights, but clarified that if some power was not specifically delegated or if it was not actually forbidden to be held by the states, then that power belonged to the states and the people. In the words of the amendment: "powers not delegated to the United States . . . nor prohibited . . . to the States, are reserved to the States respectively, or to the people."

Other Amendments

The 27 amendments fall into three major groups. The first group includes the Bill of Rights, which we have just discussed in detail. It was added between 1791 and 1804 to put the finishing touches on the original Constitution. The Eleventh and Twelfth Amendments also belong to this group.

Article III, Section 1, of the Constitution gave the federal courts jurisdiction in cases arising

Other Constitutional Amendments

Amendments	Date	Purpose
11	1795	Removed cases in which a state was sued without its consent from the jurisdiction of the federal court
12	1804	Required presidential electors to vote separately for president and vice president
13	1865	Abolished slavery and authorized Congress to pass legislation implementing its abolition
14	1868	Granted citizenship to all persons born or naturalized in the United States; banned states from denying any person life, liberty, or property without due process of law; and banned states from denying any person equal protection under the laws
15	1870	Extended voting rights to African American males by outlawing denial of the right to vote on the basis of race, color, or previous condition of servitude
16	1913	Empowered Congress to levy an income tax
17	1913	Provided for the election of U.S. senators by direct popular vote instead of by the state legislatures
18	1919	Authorized Congress to prohibit the manufacture, sale, and transportation of liquor
19	1920	Extended the right to vote to women
20	1933	Shortened the time between a presidential election and inauguration by designating January 20 as Inauguration Day; set January 3 as the date for the opening of a new Congress
21	1933	Repealed the Eighteenth Amendment and empowered Congress to regulate the liquor industry
22	1951	Limited presidents to two full terms in office
23	1961	Granted voters in the District of Columbia the right to vote for president and vice president
24	1964	Forbade requiring the payment of a poll tax to vote in a federal election
25	1967	Provided for succession to the office of president in the event of death or incapacity and for filling vacancies in the office of vice president
26	1971	Extended the right to vote to 18 year olds
27	1992	Banned Congress from increasing its members' salaries until after the next election

Key

- Amendments changing the powers of the national and state governments
- Amendments changing government structure or function
- Amendments extending the suffrage and power of voters

Critical Thinking The United States Constitution is the oldest, active, written constitution of any nation in the world, yet it has been amended only 27 times. *Which amendments are known as the Civil War amendments?*

Activity: Interdisciplinary Connection

Political Science The constitutions of most of the world's countries contain a section describing the rights of individual citizens. The U.S. Constitution and the constitutions of most European democracies describe the political rights and civil liberties of citizens. Some constitutions include rights related to education and welfare. During the era of communism, the constitutions of Communist countries emphasized economic and social rights, such as the right to work, the right to choose an occupation, and the right to leisure. Have students research Japan's constitution and find where it guarantees academic freedom. *(Article XXIII)* **OL**

between states, between citizens of different states, or between a state and citizens of another state. In 1795 the Eleventh Amendment was added to prohibit a state from being sued in federal court by citizens of another state or of another nation.

In 1793 two South Carolina citizens sued Georgia in the Supreme Court over property confiscated during the Revolution. Georgia maintained that a sovereign state could not be summoned into federal court and ordered to defend itself. When Georgia officials refused to appear for the trial, the Supreme Court decided against the state. Although Georgia lost the court case, it won its power struggle with the federal judiciary. The day after the Supreme Court announced its decision in *Chisholm* v. *Georgia*,[1] Congress introduced an amendment to limit the jurisdiction of the federal courts. 📖

The Twelfth Amendment, added in 1804, corrected a problem in how the president and vice president were elected. This amendment fixed the problem with a simple change. The amendment said that the Electoral College would use *separate* ballots in voting for president and vice president.

Civil War Amendments

The second group of amendments—Thirteen, Fourteen, and Fifteen—are often called the Civil War amendments because they were the result of that conflict. The Thirteenth Amendment (1865) outlawed slavery, and the Fourteenth Amendment (1868) intended to protect the legal rights of the freed enslaved people and their descendants. Today the Fourteenth Amendment serves to protect the rights of all citizens. It prohibits a state from depriving a person of life, liberty, or property 🅂 without "due process of law." The Fourteenth Amendment also says that all citizens have the right to equal protection of the law in all states. The Fifteenth Amendment (1870) prohibits the government from denying a person's right to vote on the basis of race.

The Later Amendments

All of the amendments in the third group were added in the twentieth century. These amendments deal with a range of topics that reflect some of the changes that occurred in American society in that time period—advances in the status of workers, African Americans, and women to mention a few.

📖 *See the following footnoted materials in the* **Reference Handbook:**
1. *Chisholm* v. *Georgia* case summary, page R25.

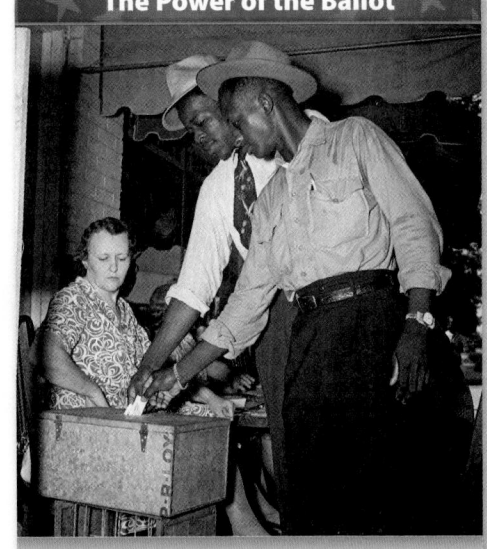

The Power of the Ballot

Civil Rights The Fifteenth Amendment enfranchised African Americans but they were often unable to vote in Southern states until the 1960s because of poll taxes and other state requirements. *Which political party did African Americans support after the Civil War?*

The Sixteenth Amendment (1913) gives Congress the power to levy individual income taxes. In 1895 the Supreme Court **reversed** a previous decision and declared a federal income tax unconstitutional. This prevented passage of another income tax law until the Constitution was amended in 1913.

The Seventeenth Amendment (1913) says that the people, not state legislatures, elect United States senators directly. Congress tried to pass this amendment several times, but in 1912, scandals involving charges of vote buying in state legislatures helped the amendment pass.

The Eighteenth Amendment (1919) prohibits the manufacture, sale, or transportation of alcoholic beverages, concluding a crusade to abolish the use of liquor that began in the 1830s.

The Nineteenth Amendment (1920) guaranteed women the right to vote. By 1920 women had already won the right to vote in many state elections, but the amendment established their right to vote in all state and national elections.

Caption Answer: In the 1860s, African Americans supported the Republican Party (Abraham Lincoln's party).

🅂 Skill Practice

Conducting Research Divide the class into six groups. Assign each group one amendment from the Fourteenth to the Nineteenth. Each group will create a poster or pamphlet explaining the amendment and its importance. Allow ample time for research, creation, and presentation. **OL**

POLITICAL PROFILES **Alice Paul** (1885–1977) was born in Moorestown, New Jersey. She was the founder of the Congressional Union for Woman Suffrage, later the National Woman's Party. Paul devoted her life to women's rights, leading the campaign for suffrage that resulted in the Nineteenth Amendment. She wrote the first version of the Equal Rights Amendment.

Additional Support

Activity: Collaborative Learning

The Fourteenth Amendment This amendment has been the basis of more Supreme Court rulings than any other part of the Constitution. The constitutional provisions protecting personal liberties have been tested many times. One such test occurred during World War II, when more than 100,000 Japanese and Japanese Americans were put into relocation camps. Divide students into two groups. Each side will debate for or against the issue. **Ask:** In times of crisis, should the government be allowed to suspend personal liberties? Allow time for the groups to create their arguments and select a spokesperson to serve during the debate. Then hold a debate in which the arguments chosen by each side are presented and each group has time to respond to the other's points. **OL**

W Writing Support

Expository Writing Write the following statement on the board: "That the people of Washington, D.C., have no representation in Congress is a violation of their democratic rights." Ask students to write a one-page paper expressing their feelings and point of view on this statement. **OL**

Assess

Assign the Section 4 Assessment as homework or as an in-class activity, or have students take Section Quiz 3-4 from *Section Quizzes and Chapter Tests*.

Close

Determining Importance

Ask: Which three amendments (excluding those in the Bill of Rights) do you consider most important? Ask volunteers to share their choices with the class and explain why they chose the amendments they did. **OL**

Section 4 Review

The Twentieth Amendment (1933) sets new dates for when the president and vice president are inaugurated and when Congress begins its term. Originally, elected officials who retired or who were defeated remained in office for several months. For the outgoing president, this period ran from November until March. Outgoing officials had little influence and accomplished little—they were nicknamed **"lame ducks"** because they were so ineffective. The amendment addressed this problem by ending the terms of senators and representatives on January 3, and the president's term on January 20 in the year following a presidential election.

The Twenty-first Amendment (1933) repeals the unsuccessful Eighteenth Amendment. The Twenty-first Amendment, however, continued to ban the transport of alcohol into any state where its possession violated state law.

The Twenty-second Amendment (1951) limits presidents to a maximum of two elected terms. It was passed in reaction to Franklin D. Roosevelt's election to four terms between 1933 and 1945.

W Before the Twenty-third Amendment (1961) was passed, citizens living in Washington, D.C., the nation's capital, were denied the right to vote for president and vice president because they did not live in a state. This amendment gave the District of Columbia three presidential electors, the number to which it would be entitled if it were a state.

The Twenty-fourth Amendment (1964) prohibits poll taxes in federal elections. **Poll taxes** are taxes that are paid in order to vote. After the Civil War, some Southern states created poll taxes to keep poor African Americans from voting.

The Twenty-fifth Amendment (1967) establishes a process for the vice president to take over the office of president if that person is disabled. The amendment also lays down the process for filling the vice presidency if that office becomes vacant.

How does the nation determine when a president can no longer fulfill the duties of the office? This delicate issue is addressed by the amendment. In the past, this problem arose several times. Should the vice president take over the duties of chief executive if the president is ill?

The amendment says that the vice president immediately becomes acting president if the president or the vice president informs Congress that the president cannot perform duties of the office. A cabinet majority must agree. The information must be sent in a letter to the Speaker of the House and also to the highest-ranking senator, called the "president pro tem." If there is a conflict between the president and the vice president, Congress decides who will act as president.

The Twenty-sixth Amendment (1971) lowers the voting age in federal and state elections to 18.

The Twenty-seventh Amendment (1992) makes congressional pay raises effective during the term following their passage. Originally proposed as part of the Bill of Rights in 1789, it did not have sufficient votes for ratification. A campaign to pass it began in the 1980s, and it became law in 1992.

SECTION 4 Review

Vocabulary

1. **Explain** the significance of: incorporation doctrine, prior restraint, probable cause, search warrant, arrest warrant, due process, eminent domain, lame duck, poll tax.

Main Ideas

2. **Describing** What does the Twenty-fifth Amendment establish?

3. **Identifying** Which twentieth-century amendments deal with voting rights?

Critical Thinking

4. **Analyzing** How do the amendments to the Constitution preserve individual rights?

5. **Categorizing** Use a graphic organizer to list the five civil liberties protected by the First Amendment.

Writing About Government

6. **Expository Writing** Amendments often reflect a change in society or a need for change in the structure of government. Write a report that identifies the reasons and events that led to the adoption of one of the 27 amendments. Present your findings to the class.

Answers

1. All definitions can be found in the section and the Glossary.
2. freedoms of religion, speech, and press; rights of assembly and petition
3. Nineteenth, Twenty-third, Twenty-fourth, and Twenty-sixth
4. The amendments protect civil rights, increase opportunities for participation in government, and limit the power of government.
5. freedom of religion, freedom of speech, freedom of the press, freedom of assembly, and freedom of petition
6. Students' reports should focus on the change resulting from the amendment.

Supreme Court Cases to Debate

Does Mandatory Drug Testing Violate Students' Civil Rights?

Board of Education of Pottawatomie County v. Earls, 2002

The Fourth Amendment protects against "unreasonable searches." Is a school policy that requires drug testing for extracurricular activities an "unreasonable search"?

Facts of the Case

In the fall of 1998, the Pottawatomie school district in Oklahoma said that there would be random drug testing for any middle or high school student who wanted to participate in extracurricular activities. Lindsay Earls, a National Honor Society student active in many such activities, objected. She and her family sued, saying the drug tests violated her constitutional right against unreasonable searches. The U.S. District Court dismissed her challenge, but the U.S. Court of Appeals for the Tenth Circuit reversed that decision. It stated that before setting up a "suspicionless" drug test program, the school must show there is a drug abuse problem among those to be tested so that the testing would actually address the problem. The Supreme Court agreed to review the case.

The Constitutional Question

In a previous case, *Vernonia School District* v. *Acton* (1995), the Supreme Court upheld a policy under which a school randomly tested high school athletes for drug use. The Court found that the Vernonia policy was "reasonable." Student athletes faced exceptional temptations to take steroids. Furthermore, the Court ruled that student athletes had already given up much of their privacy because of physicals and medical testing they must undergo.

Attorneys for the Pottawatomie school district argued that it is legal to test students who participate in extracurricular activities. Those students represent the school in competition in the same way sports teams do. The policy is a "natural, local, rational" application of the principles in the *Vernonia* case.

Attorneys for the Earls argued that such testing is against the Fourth Amendment. They also argued that the school board failed to identify a special need for testing students who participate in extracurricular activities. Furthermore, the drug testing policy "neither addresses a proven problem nor promises to bring any benefit to students or the school."

Debating the Issue

Questions to Consider

1. Does mandatory drug testing deter drug use? Explain.
2. Define "suspicionless testing" in your own words.
3. If you are tested based on what others think you are taking, is this an "improper search and seizure"?

You Be the Judge

In your opinion, did the school board's policy violate the ban on unreasonable searches? Explain.

Lindsay Earls with an attorney ▶

Teach

Class Debate

Organize students into three groups. One group will argue that random drug testing is reasonable and legal; another group will claim that it violates students' rights under the Fourth Amendment; and a third group will act as a jury. After the jury has deliberated, have a representative read the opinion to the class. **OL**

The Court's Decision

In a 5 to 4 ruling, the Supreme Court held that the random drug testing of students at Tecumseh High School in Pottawatomie County was constitutional. The use of urine samples to test for drugs, ruled the Court, was minimally intrusive and did not violate students' Fourth Amendment rights. The Court reasoned: "Within the limits of the Fourth Amendment, local school boards must assess the desirability of drug testing school-children. In upholding the constitutionality of the Policy, we express no opinion as to its wisdom. Rather, we hold only that Tecumseh's Policy is a reasonable means of furthering the School District's important interest in preventing and deterring drug use among its schoolchildren."

Debating the Issue Answers

Questions to Consider

1. Answers will vary, but students should provide a rationale for their opinions.
2. Definitions will vary, but encourage students to think of specific examples. One answer may be "drug tests given when there is no reason to believe drugs have been taken."
3. Answers will vary. Follow this question by asking students who agree that it would be an improper search and seizure to list some specific types of suspicious behavior they would require before they would consider drug testing to be justified and constitutional.

You Be the Judge

Consider using students' responses as a starting point for class debate.

ExamView®
Assessment Suite

This easy-to-use software includes extensive question banks and allows you to create fully customized tests that can be administered in print or online.

Reviewing Vocabulary

1. separation of powers
2. expressed powers
3. eminent domain
4. judicial activism

Reviewing Main Ideas

5. popular sovereignty, federalism, separation of powers, checks and balances, judicial review, limited government
6. separation of powers
7. the right to make all laws necessary and proper to carry out the powers expressed in the other clauses of Article 1
8. proposed—by two-thirds vote in each house of Congress or by national convention called by Congress at the request of two-thirds of the states; ratified—by legislatures of three-fourths of the states or by special conventions in three-fourths of the states
9. Through a series of court decisions, the Bill of Rights was applied to the states as well as the national government.

Critical Thinking

10. The Constitution has listed powers that the government does and does not have. It has set specific limits in the

CHAPTER
3 Assessment and Activities

Reviewing Vocabulary

Choose the italicized content vocabulary word or phrase that best completes each of the following sentences.

1. The national government is divided into three branches according to the principle of *judicial restraint/separation of powers.*
2. All powers of Congress specifically listed in the Constitution are *expressed powers/reserved powers.*
3. According to the principle of *judicial review/eminent domain,* the government can force someone to sell his or her home to make way for a highway.
4. The idea that the Supreme Court should play an active role in shaping politics reflects the philosophy of *judicial restraint/judicial activism.*

Reviewing Main Ideas

Section 1 *(pages 63–67)*

5. **Identifying** What are the six major principles of government on which the Constitution is based?
6. **Explaining** What is the constitutional principle illustrated by the division of the national government into three branches?

Section 2 *(pages 68–75)*

7. **Summarizing** In the Constitution, what right does the final enumerated power give Congress?

Section 3 *(pages 76–81)*

8. **Describing** How are amendments to the Constitution proposed and ratified?

Section 4 *(pages 84–90)*

9. **Synthesizing** How did the Bill of Rights become applicable to the states?

Critical Thinking

10. **Essential Question** Examine the U.S. Constitution and describe how it has created a limited government.
11. **Understanding Cause and Effect** Use the graphic organizer to show two results of having a brief Constitution rather than a detailed plan of government.

| Brief Constitution | → | Result |
| | | Result |

12. **Predicting** How would the federal system work if the Supreme Court did not have judicial review?

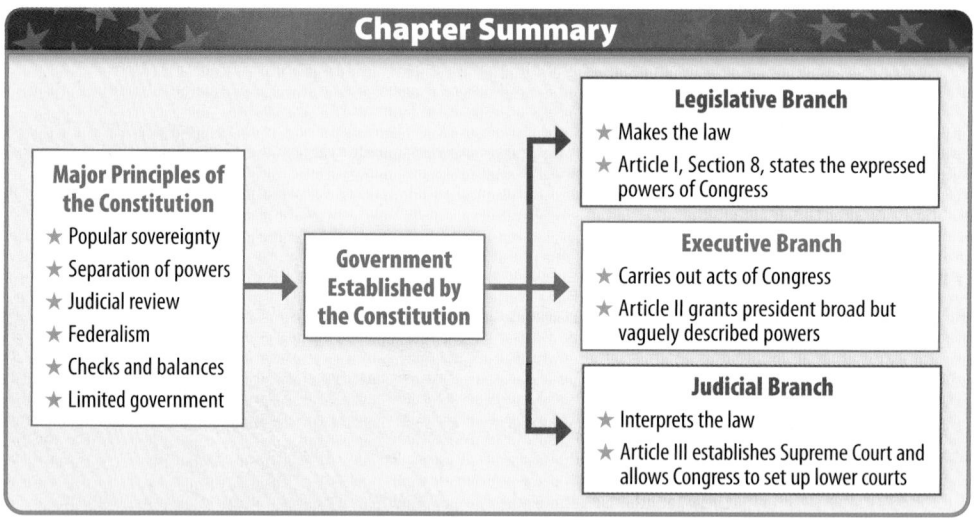

Chapter Summary

Major Principles of the Constitution
★ Popular sovereignty
★ Separation of powers
★ Judicial review
★ Federalism
★ Checks and balances
★ Limited government

→ **Government Established by the Constitution** →

Legislative Branch
★ Makes the law
★ Article I, Section 8, states the expressed powers of Congress

Executive Branch
★ Carries out acts of Congress
★ Article II grants president broad but vaguely described powers

Judicial Branch
★ Interprets the law
★ Article III establishes Supreme Court and allows Congress to set up lower courts

areas of freedom of expression, personal security, and fair trials with the Bill of Rights. Other answers may apply.

11. Answers might include flexible government and few amendments.

12. Answers may suggest that the legislative branch would gain more power than the judicial branch or that it would make the system of checks and balances less effective.

Government ONLINE Self-Check Quiz
Visit glencoe.com and enter *QuickPass™* code USG9822c3.
Click on Self-Check Quizzes for additional test practice.

CHAPTER
3
Assessment
and Activities

Document-Based Questions

Analyzing Primary Sources

Read the excerpt below and answer the questions that follow.

In October 1787, one of the Anti-Federalists argued that the proposed Constitution needed to include a bill of rights *before* being ratified, not *after*.

❝ *No measures can be taken towards amendments, unless two-thirds of the congress, or two-thirds of the legislatures of the several states shall agree. . . . But when power is once transferred from the many to the few, all changes become extremely difficult. . . . I am sensible, thousands of men in the United States, are disposed to adopt the proposed constitution, though they perceive it to be essentially defective, under an idea that amendments of it, may be obtained when necessary. This is a pernicious [very harmful] idea, it argues a servility of character totally unfit for the support of free government; it is very repugnant to that perpetual jealousy respecting liberty, so absolutely necessary in all free states. . . .* ❞

—Letter from "Federal Farmer"

13. What point does "Federal Farmer" make about the amendment process to convince his readers of his position?

14. What does he imply about any citizen who thinks it is okay to ratify the current draft and avoid the work of fighting for a bill of rights?

Applying Technology Skills

15. **Primary Sources on the Internet** Go to http://thomas.loc.gov/home/histdox/fed_85.html and find *The Federalist*, No. 85, the last of the series written by Alexander Hamilton. Hamilton wrote it as a "letter to the people of New York." Read the last paragraph and write two questions for another student to answer about Hamilton's words in that paragraph.

Interpreting Political Cartoons

Analyze the cartoon and answer the questions that follow. Base your answers on the cartoon and your knowledge of Chapter 3.

"Let's never forget that the constitution provides for three equally important branches of government; the legislative and the other two."

16. Which branch of government does the cartoonist imply the speaker believes is the most important?

17. Do you think the writers of the Constitution believed one branch of government was more important? Explain your answer.

Participating
IN GOVERNMENT

18. The First Amendment guarantees freedom of assembly. Contact your local government to find out its rules about holding assemblies, such as political rallies, meetings, or parades. Find out what restrictions the community places on where and when the assemblies take place.

CHAPTER 3: *The Constitution* **93**

Government ONLINE

Have students use the **Chapter 3 Self-Check Quiz.** Visit glencoe.com and enter *QuickPass™* code USG9085c3T to prepare for the Chapter Test.

Interpreting Political Cartoons

16. the legislative branch

17. Probably, the Framers created a legislature in the first article of the Constitution; they attached great importance to lawmaking.

Participating
IN GOVERNMENT

18. Answers will vary. Students should explain the rules for assembly as defined by their local governments.

Chapter Bonus Test Question

Ask: Which president was the only one who was elected to more than two terms? *(Franklin D. Roosevelt was elected to four terms.)*

Analyzing Primary Sources

13. that it is extremely difficult and time-consuming and therefore, much easier to get a bill of rights during the drafting process than later

14. He calls them servile; they lack the character needed to protect liberty and freedom.

Applying Technology Skills

15. Students' questions should be relevant, thought provoking, and answerable.

Planning Guide

Levels BL	OL	AL	ELL		Resources	Chapter Opener	Section 1	Section 2	Section 3	Section 4	Chapter Assess
					FOCUS						
BL	OL	AL	ELL	🖨	Section Focus Transparencies		4-1	4-2	4-3	4-4	
					TEACH						
BL	OL		ELL	📁	Reading Essentials and Study Guide (and Answer Key)		p. 37	p. 41	p. 43	p. 46	
BL	OL		ELL	📁	Guided Reading Activities		p. 13	p. 14	p. 15	p. 16	
BL	OL		ELL	📁	Vocabulary Activities			p. 4			
BL	OL	AL	ELL	📁	Chapter Summaries					p. 10	
BL	OL			📁	American Biographies						
BL	OL	AL	ELL	📁	Cooperative Learning Activities						
	OL	AL	ELL	📁	Government Simulations and Debate						
BL	OL	AL	ELL	📁	Historical Documents and Speeches				p. 4		
BL	OL	AL	ELL	📁	Interpreting Political Cartoons		p. 7				
BL	OL		ELL	📁	Skill Reinforcement Activities					p. 4	
BL	OL	AL	ELL	📁	Source Readings				p. 4		
BL	OL			📁	Supreme Court Case Studies		p. 3	p. 3		p. 7	
BL	OL	AL	ELL	📁	Participating in Government Activities			p. 7			
BL	OL		ELL	📁	Spanish Declaration of Independence and U.S. Constitution	✓	✓	✓	✓	✓	✓
BL	OL	AL	ELL	📁	NGS World Atlas, Spanish	✓	✓	✓	✓	✓	✓
BL	OL	AL	ELL	🖨	Unit Overlay Transparencies, Strategies, and Activities	✓	✓	✓	✓	✓	✓
BL	OL		ELL	🖨	Making It Relevant Transparencies	✓	✓	✓	✓	✓	✓
BL	OL	AL	ELL	🖨	High School Writing Process Transparencies, Strategies, and Activities	✓	✓	✓	✓	✓	✓
BL	OL	AL		🖨	American Art & Architecture Transparencies, Strategies, and Activities	✓	✓	✓	✓	✓	✓

✓ Chapter- or unit-based activities applicable to all sections in this chapter

All-In-One Planner and Resource Center

- Interactive Lesson Planner
- Interactive Teacher Edition
- Fully editable blackline masters
- Chapter Spotlight Videos Launch
- Differentiated Lesson Plans
- Printable reports of daily assignments
- Standards tracking system

BL	OL	AL	ELL		Resources	Chapter Opener	Section 1	Section 2	Section 3	Section 4	Chapter Assess
					Levels						
					TEACH (continued)						
BL	OL			💿	**American Music: Hits Through History**	✓	✓	✓	✓	✓	✓
BL	OL		ELL	📁	**Reading Strategies for the Social Studies Classroom**	✓	✓	✓	✓	✓	✓
			ELL	📁	**English Language Learner Handbook**	✓	✓	✓	✓	✓	✓
BL	OL		ELL	📁	**Writer's Guidebook for Social Studies**	✓	✓	✓	✓	✓	✓
BL	OL	AL	ELL	📁	**Living Constitution, SE**	✓	✓	✓	✓	✓	✓
BL	OL	AL	ELL	📁	**Living Constitution, TAE**	✓	✓	✓	✓	✓	✓
BL	OL			📁	**NGS World Atlas, English**	✓	✓	✓	✓	✓	✓
BL	OL		ELL	📁	**The Constitution and You (poster set)**	✓	✓	✓	✓	✓	✓
BL	OL	AL	ELL	📁	**Spanish Chapter Summaries**					p. 10	
BL	OL	AL	ELL	📁	**Spanish Vocabulary Activities**			p. 4			
BL	OL		ELL	📁	**Spanish Reading Essentials and Study Guide (and Answer Key)**		p. 37	p. 41	p. 43	p. 46	
BL	OL	AL	ELL	💿	**PresentationPlus! with MindJogger CheckPoint**	✓	✓	✓	✓	✓	✓
					ASSESS						
BL	OL	AL	ELL	💿	*ExamView® Assessment Suite*		4-1	4-2	4-3	4-4	Ch. 4
BL	OL	AL	ELL	📁	**Authentic Assessment with Rubrics**				p. 11	p. 11	p. 11
BL	OL	AL	ELL	📁	**Section Quizzes and Chapter Tests**		p. 37	p. 38	p. 39	p. 40	pp. 41–48
BL	OL	AL	ELL	📁	**Spanish Section Quizzes and Tests**		p. 37	p. 38	p. 39	p. 40	pp. 41–48
					CLOSE						
BL			ELL	📁	**Reteaching Activities**		p. 4				p. 4
BL	OL	AL	ELL	💿	**StudentWorks™ Plus with Audio Summaries**	✓	✓	✓	✓	✓	✓
BL	OL		ELL	🖥	**Graphic Organizer Transparencies**		✓	✓	✓	✓	
BL	OL		ELL	📁	**High School Government Reading and Study Skills Foldables®**		p. 47	p. 47	p. 47	p. 47	

Lesson Planner   Teach With Technology

What is the Lesson Planner?

The TeacherWorks™ Plus Lesson Planner is a practical tool for creating and organizing daily lesson plans using an interactive calendar.

How can the Lesson Planner help me?

The Lesson Planner makes it easy to see, at a glance, the resources you have chosen to use for each class on any given day. Using a simple drag-and-drop format, you can generate lesson plans using any number of ancillary titles included in the TeacherWorks™ Plus software, as well as Internet links, documents, files, and programs of your choosing. Once a lesson plan is created, the Lesson Planner serves as a launching point for these resources.

The Lesson Planner is a feature of TeacherWorks™ Plus.

Government ONLINE

Visit glencoe.com and enter *QuickPass*™ code USG9085c4T for Chapter 4 resources.

You can easily launch a wide range of digital products from your computer's desktop with the McGraw-Hill Social Studies widget.

	Student	Teacher	Parent
Media Library			
• Student Edition Section Audio	●		●
• Chapter Spotlight Videos	●	●	●
***United States Government* Online Learning Center (Web Site)**			
• Chapter Overviews	●	●	●
• Multilingual Glossaries	●	●	●
• Study-to-Go	●	●	●
• Student Web Activities	●	●	●
• Self-Check Quizzes	●	●	●
• Online Student Edition	●	●	●
• Vocabulary eFlashcards	●	●	●
• Web Activity Lesson Plans		●	
• Vocabulary PuzzleMaker	●	●	●
• Landmark Supreme Court Cases	●	●	●
• Beyond the Textbook	●	●	●

- **Timed Readings Plus in Social Studies** helps students increase their reading rate and fluency while maintaining comprehension. The 400-word passages are similar to those found on state and national assessments.

- **Reading in the Content Area: Social Studies** concentrates on six essential reading skills that help students better comprehend what they read. The book includes 75 high-interest nonfiction passages written at increasing levels of difficulty.

- **Reading Social Studies** includes strategic reading instruction and vocabulary support in Social Studies content for ELLs and native speakers of English. www.jamestowneducation.com

Reading List Generator CD-ROM

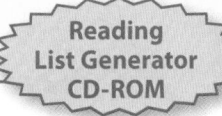

GLENCOE
BOOKLINK 3

Use this database to search more than 30,000 titles to create a customized reading list for your students.

- Reading lists can be organized by students' reading level, author, genre, theme, or area of interest.

- The database provides Degrees of Reading Power™ (DRP) and Lexile™ readability scores for all selections.

- A brief summary of each selection is included.

Leveled reading suggestions for this chapter:

- *The Great Depression and the New Deal: America's Economic Collapse and Recovery,* by Anne E. Schraff

Review suggested books before assigning them.

Economics Connection

Personal Finance Literacy

Life of a Check

A check is a written order directing your bank to transfer money from your account to the account of whomever receives your check. Millions of checks are moved around the country, sorted, tabulated, and credited or debited to the accounts of financial institutions. Federal, state, and private institutions are all involved in the cashing of a check. To help students understand the collaboration among federal, state, and private financial institutions, present the following steps in a chart or a cyclical diagram.

1. Jennifer has a checking account with Home Bank of Detroit, Michigan. She sends a $100 check to Midwest Magazines for a year-long subscription.

2. Midwest Magazines deposits the check in its account with City Bank of Toledo. City Bank credits Midwest Magazines' account + $100.

3. City Bank of Toledo sends the check electronically to the Federal Reserve Bank of Chicago to be cleared.

4. Federal Reserve Bank of Chicago credits City Bank of Toledo (Midwest Magazines' financial institution) + $100.

5. After processing, Federal Reserve Bank of Chicago sends the check to Home Bank (Jennifer's financial institution).

6. Home Bank then pays Federal Reserve Bank of Chicago $100, and it reduces (debits) Jennifer's account by $100. She receives a summary statement.

Did You Know?

The first printed checks were made in England in 1762. They might have been called "checks" because the serial numbers on them were used to keep track of them.

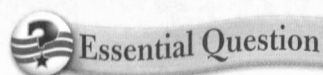

Essential Question

Accessing Prior Knowledge
Ask students to name some of the powers of the national government and the states and start a list on the board. Are there any powers that the national government and the states both possess? Which powers are unique to the national government and which are unique to the states? Is this distinction necessary? If so, why?

Chapter Spotlight Video

To generate student interest and provide a springboard for class discussion, access the Chapter 4 Video at glencoe.com or on the video DVD.

FOLDABLES
Study Organizer
Dinah Zike's Foldables are three-dimensional, interactive graphic organizers that help students practice basic writing skills, review key vocabulary terms, and identify main ideas. Have students complete this chapter's Foldable activity or activities in *Dinah Zike's Reading and Study Skills Foldables* booklet. **OL**

Government ONLINE

Visit glencoe.com and enter **QuickPass**™ code USG9085c4T for Chapter 4 Resources including Chapter Overview, Student Web Activity, Self-Check Quiz, and other materials for students and teachers.

CHAPTER 4

🔊 Chapter Audio   🎬 Spotlight Video

The Federal System

▶ Massachusetts State House, Boston

Essential Question

How does the overall power of the national government compare to that of the states?

Government ONLINE
Chapter Overview Visit glencoe.com and enter **QuickPass**™ code USG9822c4 for an overview, a quiz, and other chapter resources.

Launching the Chapter

Researching Court Cases Have students research and write about two Supreme Court cases: *Fletcher* v. *Peck* and *Missouri* v. *Holland*. Have students research one of the cases to find (1) the essential facts and background of the case, (2) the central issue, and (3) the Supreme Court's decision.

Essential Question: What did these two cases establish about federal and state powers?

(Fletcher v. Peck *was the first case in which the Supreme Court found a state law to be unconstitutional.* Missouri v. Holland *established that the federal government's power to make treaties does not infringe upon the rights reserved to the states. Students' answers will vary but should mention that certain powers can be exercised only by the federal government.)* **OL**

National and State Powers

Reader's Guide

Content Vocabulary
★ delegated powers (p. 95)
★ expressed powers (p. 95)
★ implied powers (p. 96)
★ elastic clause (p. 96)
★ inherent powers (p. 96)
★ reserved powers (p. 96)
★ supremacy clause (p. 97)
★ concurrent powers (p. 97)
★ enabling act (p. 99)

Academic Vocabulary
★ authority (p. 96)
★ affect (p. 101)
★ amendment (p. 102)

Reading Strategy
As you read, create a graphic organizer like the one below to keep track of national powers and state powers.

National Powers	State Powers

Focus

Bellringer
Section Focus Transparencies 4-1

Issues in the News

When Hurricane Katrina swamped New Orleans a few years ago, the Federal Emergency Management Agency (FEMA) was supposed to coordinate the federal, state, and local responses. In a federal system, the national and state governments need to cooperate especially closely in times of disaster, but the dividing lines for their roles are not easy to define. As the Katrina disaster grew, one federal official told a congressional committee, "My biggest mistake was not recognizing by Saturday that Louisiana was dysfunctional." The Louisiana governor shot back that that official was "either out of touch with the truth or reality."

▲ Hurricane Katrina victims in flooded New Orleans

Reader's Guide

Answers to Graphic: National powers—expressed, implied, and inherent powers; State powers—reserved powers

During a natural catastrophe, the relationships between state, local, and national government are easily seen. Those relationships are critical to the everyday workings of government, too. Since the earliest days of the republic, they have been continually redefined through conflict, compromise, and cooperation. How do these different levels of government work together?

The Division of Powers

The Constitution divided government authority by giving the national government certain specified powers, reserving all other powers to the states or to the people. In addition, the national and state governments share some powers. Finally, the Constitution specifically denied some powers to each level of government.

The Constitution has preserved the basic design of federalism, or the division of government powers,

over the years. The American concept of federalism, however, has changed greatly since 1787.

Federalism is not a static relationship between different levels of government. It is a dynamic concept that affects everyday decisions at all levels. An understanding of federalism must begin with the Constitution.

National Powers

The Constitution grants three types of power to the national government: expressed, implied, and inherent powers. Collectively, these powers are known as **delegated powers,** powers the Constitution grants or delegates to the national government.

Expressed Powers

The **expressed powers** are those powers directly expressed or stated in the Constitution by the Founders. Most of these powers are found in the

Resource Manager

R Reading Strategies	**C** Critical Thinking	**D** Differentiated Instruction	**W** Writing Support	**S** Skill Practice
Teacher Edition • Identifying, p. 96 • Summarizing, p. 97 **Additional Resources** • Quizzes/Tests, p. 37 • Guid. Read. Act., p. 13	**Teacher Edition** • Analyzing Primary Sources, p. 99 **Additional Resources** • Read. Essen., pp. 37–40	**Teacher Edition** • English Learners, pp. 96, 102 • Using Technology, p. 101 **Additional Resources** • Reteaching Act., p. 4 • Foldables, p. 47	**Teacher Edition** • Expository Writing, p. 100 **Additional Resources** • Supreme Ct. Case Studies, pp. 3–4	**Teacher Edition** • Reading a Venn Diagram, p. 97 • Conducting Research, p. 100 **Additional Resources** • Inter. Poli. Cartoons, pp. 7–8

Teach

R Reading Strategy

Identifying Ask: What is another name for the necessary and proper clause? Why is it often known as this? *(the elastic clause; because it allows the powers of Congress to stretch)* **BL**

D Differentiated Instruction

English Learners Have students try to come up with synonyms for the word *inherent*. Then have them look up the word in the dictionary. Ask them if there is a better term for *inherent powers*. If not, why is *inherent* the perfect descriptor? *(Synonyms include: basic, fundamental, inalienable, intrinsic, and so on.)* **ELL**

Participating IN GOVERNMENT

Flag Research The flag is flown at half-staff for the death of a government official and on Memorial Day.

Activity: Have students debate whether flag-burning should be protected by the First Amendment. **OL**

Additional Support

first three articles of the Constitution. This constitutional **authority** includes the power to levy and collect taxes, to coin money, to make war, to raise an army and navy, and to regulate commerce among the states. Expressed powers are also called enumerated powers.

Implied Powers

The authority that the national government requires to carry out the powers that are expressly defined in the Constitution are called **implied powers.** Although not specifically listed, implied powers spring from and depend upon the expressed powers. For example, the power to draft people into the armed forces is implied by the power given to the government to raise an army and navy.

The basis for the implied powers is the necessary and proper clause (Article I, Section 8). Often called the **elastic clause** because it allows the powers of Congress to stretch, it says:

> ❝ [Congress shall] . . . make all Laws which shall be necessary and proper for carrying into Execution the foregoing Powers, and all other Powers vested by this Constitution in the Government of the United States. . . . ❞
> —Article I, Section 8

Implied powers have helped the national government strengthen and expand its authority to meet many problems the Founders did not foresee. Thus, Congress has used the implied powers to regulate nuclear power plants and to develop the space program.

Inherent Powers

Those powers that the national government may exercise simply because it is a government are its **inherent powers.** For example, the national government must control immigration and establish diplomatic relations with other countries, even though these powers are not spelled out in the Constitution.

The States and the Nation

Some people believed that the Constitution granted too much power to the national government. In *The Federalist*, No. 45, James Madison argued that in fact it granted few and limited powers to the national government while the states' powers were many and broadly drawn. The Constitution also reserves certain powers strictly to the states. These are called **reserved powers.** While the Constitution does not list these powers

---

★★★★★★★ **Government *and* You** ★★★★★★★

Displaying the Flag

Whether you display the American flag every day or only for special occasions, certain rules and customs govern its use. In general, the flag is flown only from dawn to dusk, and it should be lighted if it is displayed at night. The flag is flown at half-staff on the death of a government official and until noon on Memorial Day. Indoors, the flag may hang flat against the wall behind a speaker, with the stars on the left. If the flag is on a staff, it should be seen to the viewers' left. Other flags should be placed to the right. The flag is never flown upside down except to signal distress.

As the symbol of the United States, the flag should be treated with respect. Never let it touch the ground, and if it becomes too worn to display, it should be destroyed in a dignified way, preferably by burning.

▲ Proudly displaying the flag

Participating IN GOVERNMENT ACTIVITY

Flag Research When is the flag flown at half-staff? When was the last time a flag flew at half-staff over your school?

★ ★ ★ **Activity: Collaborative Learning** ★ ★ ★

Researching Government Organize the class into small groups and have each group choose some aspect of their daily lives: buying food or clothing, driving a car, eating in a restaurant, watching television, and so on. Have students find out how each level of government affects that activity. Aspects to consider include government inspection, taxes, licensing, standards, and regulation. Some students may interview local business owners and government workers, while others may gather information by writing, e-mailing, or calling other government offices. **OL**

Division of Federal and State Powers

NATIONAL GOVERNMENT
(Expressed, Implied, and Inherent Powers)

- Regulate foreign and interstate commerce
- Coin money
- Provide an army and navy
- Declare war
- Establish federal courts below the Supreme Court
- Conduct foreign relations
- Exercise powers implied from the expressed powers

NATIONAL and STATE GOVERNMENTS
(Concurrent Powers)

- Levy taxes
- Borrow money
- Spend for general welfare
- Establish courts
- Enact and enforce laws

STATE GOVERNMENTS
(Reserved Powers)

- Regulate intrastate commerce
- Establish local government systems
- Administer elections
- Protect the public's health and welfare

Critical Thinking The Constitution established a detailed plan for the distribution of power between the federal and state governments. *What powers are shared by the national and state governments?*

Graphs In MOtion
See StudentWorks™ Plus or go to glencoe.com.

---

specifically, it grants to the states those powers "not delegated to the United States by the Constitution, nor prohibited by it to the states." Thus, the states have authority over matters not found in the Constitution, such as the regulation of public school systems.

The Supremacy Clause

What happens when states exceed their reserved powers and pass laws that conflict with national laws? Which law is supreme? Article VI, Section 2, makes the acts and treaties of the United States supreme. For this reason, this Article is called the **supremacy clause.** It states:

> 66 *This Constitution, and the Laws of the United States which shall be made in Pursuance thereof; and all Treaties made . . . under the Authority of the United States, shall be the supreme Law of the Land; and the Judges in every State shall be bound thereby.* 99
>
> —Article VI, Section 2

No state law or state constitution may conflict with any form of national law. Article VI also requires that all national and state officials and judges be bound to support the Constitution. State officials are not permitted to use their state's reserved powers to interfere with the Constitution.

States create local governments such as those of cities and counties. As such, local governments get their powers from the states. Hence, local governments are also bound by the Constitution's supremacy clause—if a state is denied a certain power, so, too, are the local governments within the state.

Concurrent Powers

The federal government and the states also have certain concurrent powers. **Concurrent powers** are those powers that the national government and the states both have. Each level of government exercises these powers independently. Examples of concurrent powers are the power to tax, to maintain courts and define crimes, and to appropriate private property for public use. Concurrently with the national government, the states may exercise any power not reserved by the Constitution for the national government. Of course, state actions must not conflict with any national laws.

S Skill Practice

Reading a Venn Diagram
Ask: What is the purpose of overlapping circles in this Venn diagram? *(The part that overlaps signifies the powers that are common to national and state governments.)* **BL**

R Reading Strategy

Summarizing Have students reread "The Supremacy Clause" section. Summarize this section by answering the question: Why is Article VI, Section 2, of the Constitution called the supremacy clause? *(The Constitution states that the laws of the United States "shall be the supreme Law of the Land." All state and local laws and constitutions are bound to support the U.S. Constitution.)* **OL**

Critical Thinking

Answer: The powers to levy taxes, borrow money, spend for general welfare, establish courts, and enact and enforce laws are shared by national and state governments (concurrent powers).

Differentiated Instruction

Activity: Multiple Learning Styles

Auditory/Musical Have students assume that they must teach the content of the section to someone who is visually challenged. Ask pairs of students to come up with an oral presentation, complete with a review quiz that would accomplish the task. Tell them they must provide something other than a recorded reading of the text or at least a plan that would augment such a recording. **AL**

POLITICAL PROFILES

Dwight D. Eisenhower
(1890–1969)

During World War II, Dwight D. Eisenhower, better known as Ike, had a variety of command roles. In January 1944, he was named Supreme Commander of the Allied Expeditionary Force in Western Europe. In 1945 he became Chief of Staff of the U.S. Army. During his presidency, he sent some 1,000 U.S. paratroopers to Little Rock, Arkansas, following riots protesting the integration of Central High School. He also put the Arkansas National Guard under federal command. In doing so, he became the first president since Reconstruction to use the military to protect the rights of African Americans.

 To enrich the study of chapter content, remind students that footnoted materials appear in the *Reference Handbook.*

Additional Support

Federal and State Cooperation

Concurrent Powers Members of both the Noble County Sheriff's Department and FBI agents lead convicted terrorist Timothy McVeigh out of an Oklahoma courthouse. McVeigh was convicted (and ultimately executed) for his role in the 1995 bombing of a federal office building in Oklahoma City, which killed 168 people. *Why did federal and state authorities have to cooperate after the bombing of the federal building in Oklahoma City?*

Denied Powers

Finally, the Constitution specifically denies some powers to all levels of government. Article I, Section 9,[1] enumerates those things the national government cannot do. 📖 For example, the national government cannot tax exports, and it cannot interfere with the ability of states to carry out their responsibilities.

Article I presents a long list of powers denied to the states. No state can make treaties or alliances with foreign governments. Nor can states coin money, make any laws impairing the obligation of contracts or grant titles of nobility. And states must have congressional permission to collect duties on exports or imports, or to make agreements—called compacts—with other states.

Consistent with the belief in the sovereignty of the people, the Constitution applies important limitations to both the national and state governments. These restrictions, designed to protect individual liberties such as free speech and the rights of the accused, are set forth in Article I, Section 9, in the Bill of Rights and in several other amendments.

Guarantees to the States

The Constitution obliges the national government to do three things for the states. These three obligations are outlined in Article IV, Sections 3 and 4.[2] 📖

Republican Form of Government

First, the national government must guarantee each state a republican form of government. Enforcement of this guarantee has become a congressional responsibility. When Congress allows senators and representatives from a state to take their seats in Congress, it is in effect ruling that the state has a republican form of government.

The only extensive use of this guarantee came just after the Civil War. At that time, some Southern states refused to ratify the Civil War amendments granting citizenship rights to African Americans. Congress ruled that these states did not have a republican form of government. It refused to seat senators and representatives from those states until the states ratified the Civil War amendments and changed their laws to recognize African Americans' rights.

Protection

Second, the national government must protect states from invasion and domestic violence. An attack by a foreign power on one state is considered an attack on the United States.

Congress has given the president authority to send federal troops to put down domestic disorders when state officials ask for help. In the summer of 1967, for example, President Lyndon Johnson sent troops to Detroit to help control racial unrest and rioting. Johnson did so after Michigan's governor declared that the Detroit police and the Michigan National Guard could not cope with the widespread violence.

When national laws are violated, federal property is threatened, or federal responsibilities are interfered with, the president may send troops to a state without the request of local authorities—

📖 *See the following footnoted materials in the* ***Reference Handbook:***
1. *The Constitution,* pages R42–R67.
2. *The Constitution,* pages R42–R67.

Activity: Collaborative Learning

Predicting Consequences The third part of Article I, Section 10, of the Constitution prohibits states from engaging in war, except under certain conditions. Have students research what those conditions are *(when a state is attacked or when imminent danger will not allow delay).* Divide the class into groups of three or four students and have them imagine two scenarios: one that illustrates what might have happened if the states were allowed to declare war and one in which a state took advantage of the second exception. Allow students to present their scenarios in a method of their own choosing. **OL**

or even over local objections. In 1894, for example, President Grover Cleveland sent federal troops to Chicago to restore order during a strike of railroad workers even though the governor of Illinois objected. During the strike, rioters had threatened federal property and interfered with mail delivery.

During the 1950s and 1960s, Presidents Dwight Eisenhower and John F. Kennedy used this power to stop state officials from blocking the integration of Southern schools and universities. Eisenhower sent troops to Little Rock, Arkansas, in 1957 when local officials failed to integrate public schools. Kennedy used troops at the University of Mississippi in 1962 and the University of Alabama in 1963.

The national government has extended its definition of domestic violence to include natural disasters such as earthquakes, floods, hurricanes, and tornadoes. When one of these disasters strikes, the president often orders troops to aid disaster victims. The government also provides low-cost loans to help people repair damages.

Territorial Integrity

Finally, the national government has the duty to respect the territorial integrity of each state. The national government cannot use territory that is part of an existing state to create a new state unless the national government has permission from the legislature of the state involved. The admission of West Virginia as a state in 1863 may be considered an exception to this rule.

Admission of New States

Thirty-seven states have joined the Union since the original 13 formed the nation. Most of these states became territories before taking steps to gain statehood. What procedures do these territories then follow to become states?

Congress Admits New States

The Constitution gives Congress the power to admit new states to the Union. There are two restrictions on this power. First, as noted earlier, no state may be formed by taking territory from one or more states without the consent of the states involved and of Congress. Second, acts of admission, like all laws, are subject to presidential veto.

The procedure for admission begins when Congress passes an **enabling act.** An enabling act, when signed by the president, enables the people of the territory interested in becoming a state to prepare a constitution. Then, after the constitution has been drafted and approved by a popular vote in the area, it is submitted to Congress. If Congress is still agreeable, it passes an act admitting the territory as a state.

Since the original 13 states formed the Union, Congress has admitted new states under a variety of circumstances. Five states—Vermont, Kentucky, Tennessee, Maine, and West Virginia—were created from existing states. Two states, West Virginia and Texas, were admitted under unusual circumstances.

C **Critical Thinking**

Analyzing Primary Sources
According to Article IV, Section 3, of the U.S. Constitution, no state may be formed by taking territory from one or more states without the consent of the states involved and of Congress. Divide students into five groups. Assign each group one of the five states created from existing states. Have groups use official documents (available online) to identify the rationale for taking land from one state to form another. Allow time for research and presentation of the findings. If time permits, analyze the details for each state, looking for common threads in rationale. **AL**

Caption Answer: State authorities were defying a federal court order; the president was enforcing the Constitution.

C

Federal Troops Enforce the Constitution

Federal and State Struggles After members of the Arkansas National Guard prevented Elizabeth Ann Eckford from attending Little Rock High School on September 4, 1957, President Eisenhower sent federal troops to forcibly integrate the school. *Analyze the role of the executive branch in protecting individual rights. What authority did the president have to send federal troops to Little Rock?*

Hands-On Chapter Project
Step 1

National Governors' Conference

Step 1: Research and Petition Divide the class into groups of two or three students. Each group will research the responsibilities of the governor of one state and the issues that affect that state. Groups will prepare a petition describing their state's concerns and requesting federal assistance to be presented to a mock national governors' conference.

Directions Begin by having each group choose one state to research. Have students use the Internet to find information from state government Web sites about the duties of the governor of that state and political and economic issues currently affecting that state.

Organizing Have groups list four or five specific duties of their selected state's governor under the appropriate column heading: *Executive, Legislative,* or *Judicial.* Students will use their charts in Step 2. **OL**

(Chapter Project continued in Section 2.)

S Skill Practice

Conducting Research Texas draws on a rich history that includes having been part of Mexico and an independent country. Have students research the various flags that have flown over Texas throughout its history. Have students use their findings to prepare displays showing each flag, and explain when and why it was used. Ask students to share their displays with the class. **OL**

W Writing Support

Expository Writing Have students research and write a report on Puerto Rico's political status. **Ask:** What disadvantages and advantages are there in Puerto Rico becoming a state? Do you predict Puerto Rico will become a state in the future? Why or why not? *(Students should demonstrate an understanding of Puerto Rico's political status and back up their assertions with evidence from research.)* **AL**

Additional Support

Inaugurating a New Policy

New Federalism
President Ronald Reagan, seen here during his 1981 inaugural celebration, is associated with "New Federalism," a policy aimed at reducing government and shrinking government spending. The military budget was an exception. *What happened to the federal deficit during Reagan's presidency?*

West Virginia was created from 40 western counties of Virginia that broke away when Virginia seceded from the Union. Some people have argued that the admission of West Virginia was a violation of the Constitution because the Virginia legislature did not give its consent. Congress, however, accepted the decision of the minority of the Virginia legislature that represented the 40 western counties. It held that the western representatives were the only legal acting Virginia legislature at that time.

Texas won independence from Mexico and sought annexation to the United States for several years before being admitted. Antislavery members of Congress opposed creation of a new slaveholding state. Texas was annexed to the United States by a joint resolution of Congress in 1845. The joint resolution provided for immediate statehood, allowing Texas to skip the territorial period. It also stated that Texas could be divided into as many as five states with the approval of both Texas and the United States.

The last two states admitted, Alaska and Hawaii, each adopted a proposed constitution without waiting for an enabling act. Both were admitted in 1959.

Residents of Puerto Rico, a commonwealth under the American government, have voted at various times on whether to become a state. In 1998

46.5 percent voted for statehood, but the future status of Puerto Rico remains unsettled.

Conditions for Admission

Congress or the president may impose certain conditions before admitting a new state, including requiring changes in the drafted constitution submitted by a territory. In 1911 President William H. Taft vetoed the congressional resolution admitting Arizona because he objected to a section in the Arizona constitution dealing with the recall of judges. Arizona then modified the constitution, and the next year it became the forty-eighth state. When Alaska entered the union in 1959, it was prohibited from ever claiming title to any lands legally held by Native Americans or Aleuts in Alaska. Ohio was admitted in 1803 on the condition that for five years it not tax any public lands sold by the national government within its borders.

The Supreme Court has ruled that the president or Congress may impose conditions for admission of a state. Once a state is admitted, however, those conditions may be enforced only if they do not interfere with the new state's authority to manage its own internal affairs. In the case of Arizona, once it was admitted as a state, it promptly amended its constitution to restore provisions about the recall of judges that Taft had requested be deleted.

100 UNIT 1: *Foundations of American Government*

Extending the Content

U.S. Territories A territory is a region that belongs to or is controlled by a nation. In 1901 the Supreme Court distinguished between incorporated and unincorporated territories. All rights guaranteed by the Constitution applied in incorporated territories; in unincorporated territories, only fundamental rights applied. Congress decides whether a territory is incorporated or unincorporated. Incorporated territories may become states; unincorporated territories cannot. A third class of territories includes wholly organized and unincorporated territories, which are controlled by executive branch officials, not by Congress. **Ask:** What were the last two fully incorporated U.S. territories? What are some unincorporated territories? *(Alaska and Hawaii were the last fully incorporated U.S. territories. The Virgin Islands, Puerto Rico, and Guam are unincorporated.)*

When Oklahoma was admitted in 1907, Congress forbade it to move its capital from the city of Guthrie until 1913. The Supreme Court, however, upheld the right of Oklahoma to move the capital to Oklahoma City in 1911. The Court declared:

❝ *The power to locate its own seat of government and to determine when and how it shall be changed from one place to another, and to appropriate its own public funds for that purpose, are essentially and peculiarly state powers. . . . Has Oklahoma been admitted upon an equal footing with the original States? If she has . . . [Oklahoma] may determine for her own people the proper location of the local seat of government.* ❞

—Justice Horace H. Lurton, 1911

Equality of the States

Once admitted to the Union, each state is equal to every other state and has rights to control its internal affairs. No state has more privileges or fewer obligations than any other. Each state is also legally separate from every other state in the Union. All states in the Union are bound to support the Constitution.

National Governors' Association

The National Governors' Association (NGA) supports federalism by helping governors in state policy making and in influencing national policy. In 1908 President Theodore Roosevelt first called the nation's governors together to discuss conservation. After that the governors began to meet regularly as the Governors' Conference to deal with a variety of issues. In the 1960s, the governors set up a permanent organization with an office in Washington, D.C.

In the 1970s, the renamed National Governors' Association focused on helping governors to be successful in their own states. It held seminars and published materials on subjects like how to organize the governor's office, deal with the press, or organize relations with other government units. In one series of publications, the NGA focused on the growing influence of state initiatives and of governors who led innovative programs. Through the NGA, states shared ideas on how to solve problems.

Beginning in the 1980s, governors began working to effect national policies that **affect** state budgets like education, welfare, and health. In July 2007, for example, the NGA wrote a letter to President George W. Bush, urging him to increase

D

D Differentiated Instruction

Using Technology The National Governors' Association has a Web site covering the group from its founding in 1908 to today. Have students use the Web site www.nga.org to investigate the NGA, its founding, and its continued efforts. **Ask:** Is it important for the governors of all 50 states to communicate and work together? Explain why or why not. *(Students may say it is important for consistency among the states and to affect national policies, or they may suggest that each state has individual needs.)* **OL**

Participating IN GOVERNMENT

Participating in Government Public interest groups, such as the Christian Coalition and NOW, use grassroots movements and aggressive advertising to gain the support of politicians to further their causes through legislation.

Activity: Have students develop a mock campaign to influence local, state, or federal officials to pass favorable legislation. **OL**

Differentiated Instruction

Participating IN GOVERNMENT — Working Within the System

Do we really have government by and for the people? If so, how can you work for change by making your opinion known about a law you believe is unjust?

Your opinion is more likely to be heard if you join with others. Choose an appropriate means of expressing your views: to challenge a local ordinance, attend a city council meeting; to challenge a state law, write to your state legislator. Petitions—formal requests for a specific change in the law signed by many people—are also effective. You could write letters to the editor or prepare an editorial for a local radio or television broadcast. The Internet also offers an avenue through which citizens can speak out on an issue.

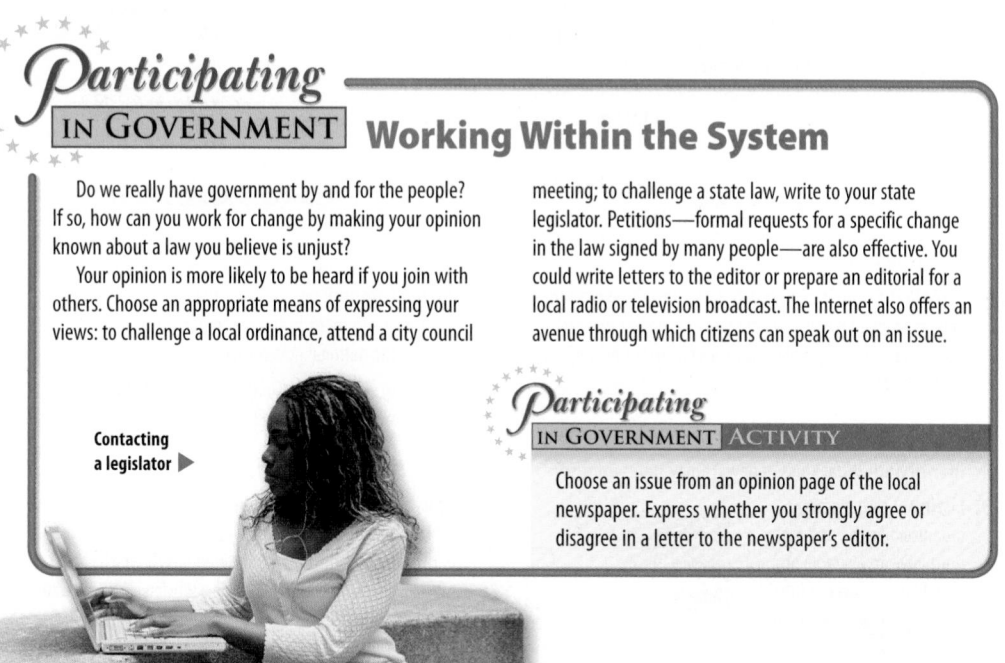

Contacting a legislator ▶

Participating IN GOVERNMENT ACTIVITY

Choose an issue from an opinion page of the local newspaper. Express whether you strongly agree or disagree in a letter to the newspaper's editor.

Leveled Activities

BL Vocabulary Activities, p. 4

OL Authentic Assessment with Rubrics, p. 11

AL Participating in Government Activities, p. 7

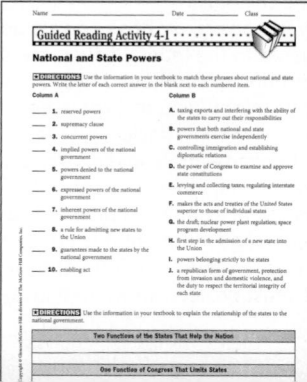

ELL Guided Reading Activities, p. 13

D Differentiated Instruction

English Learners To help students understand the umpire analogy, explain that an umpire judges the outcome of plays based on the rules of baseball. Present a scenario such as a student complaining about a classmate who constantly bumps into the desk when passing, and ask one group of students to serve as umpire. Have other students represent both sides of the scenario and present their side to the "umpire." The umpire should then decide who is right and who is wrong. **ELL**

Assess

Assign the Section 1 Assessment as homework or as an in-class activity, or have students take Section Quiz 4-1 from *Section Quizzes and Chapter Tests*.

Close

Inferring Ask: Why is the federal court system called the "umpire"? *(The federal court system is called upon to settle disputes between national and state governments; they are the final authority.)* **OL**

Section 1 Review

---

support for the federal State Children's Health Insurance Program. The NGA has also actively campaigned against "unfunded mandates," that is, to have more federal funding for programs that national laws require the states to provide. By joining together, the governors have become a bigger part of national policy-making.

Obligations of the States

The states perform two important functions for the national government. First, state and local governments conduct and pay for elections of all national government officials—senators, representatives, and presidential electors. The Constitution gives state legislatures the power to fix the "times, places, and manner" of election of senators and representatives (Article I, Section 4). Under the same provision, Congress has the authority to alter state election laws should it so desire.

In addition, the states play a key role in the process of amending the Constitution. According to the Constitution, no **amendment** can be added to it unless three-fourths of the states approve it.

The Courts as Umpire

Because federalism divides the powers of government, conflicts often arise between national and state governments. By settling such disputes, the federal court system, particularly the Supreme Court, plays a key role of umpire for our federal system.

The question of national versus state power arose early in our history. In 1819, in the landmark case of *McCulloch* v. *Maryland*,[1] the Supreme Court ruled on a conflict between a state government and the national government. It held that when the national government and a state government come into conflict, the national government is supreme.

Since *McCulloch,* the Supreme Court has ruled many times on the constitutional issue of how powers should be divided between state and national governments. Through the years, the Court's view has shifted in response to national trends and according to the makeup of the Court.

Early on, the Court usually favored the state. Then during the Great Depression of the 1930s and the civil rights movement of the 1960s, the Court tended to favor a strong national government. Since the 1990s, a narrow majority of conservative justices has again usually ruled in favor of the states. For example, in *United States* v. *Lopez* (1995), the Court held that Congress was exceeding its authority over the states when it passed a law banning gun possession in or near schools.

Federal judges also serve as umpires for the federal system when they review the actions of state and local governments. In recent decades, such review powers of federal judges have increased because of how the Fourteenth Amendment is being interpreted. That Amendment prohibits states from depriving any person of life, liberty, or property without "due process of law." A broad interpretation of these words makes it possible for a judge to question nearly every action of a state or local official.

📖 *See the following footnoted materials in the* **Reference Handbook:**
1. *McCulloch* v. *Maryland* case summary, page R30.

★★★ SECTION 1 Review ★★★

Vocabulary

1. **Explain** the significance of: delegated powers, expressed powers, implied powers, elastic clause, inherent powers, reserved powers, supremacy clause, concurrent powers, enabling act.

Main Ideas

2. **Identifying** What kinds of powers may states exercise?

3. **Listing** Using a graphic organizer like the one at the right, give an example of each kind of power granted to the national government.

Expressed	
Implied	
Inherent	

Critical Thinking

4. **Making Comparisons** How do the obligations of the national government to states compare to obligations of states to the national government?

5. **Analyzing** How did *McCulloch* v. *Maryland* affect the powers of the national government?

Writing About Government

6. **Expository Writing** New states coming into the Union have had to follow a process established by Congress. Create a flow chart that shows the dates and conditions by which your state was admitted to the Union. Include a written summary that describes the process.

Answers

1. All definitions can be found in the section and the Glossary.
2. reserved powers, or those powers not delegated to the federal government by the Constitution or prohibited by it to the states
3. Answers might include: Expressed—levy taxes, coin money, declare war, raise an army. Implied—draft soldiers, regulate nuclear power. Inherent—control immigration, establish diplomatic relations.
4. The federal government must guarantee each state a republican form of government, must protect states from invasion

and internal violence, and must respect the territorial integrity of each state. The states conduct and pay for elections of all national officials, and the states must approve constitutional amendments before they can become law.

5. It established that when the national government and a state government come into conflict, the national government is supreme.
6. Students' charts should clearly outline the steps involved in admitting new states as described in the section. Flowchart should

include: people of the territory prepare a constitution; constitution is approved by popular vote; constitution is submitted to Congress; Congress approves of constitution; and territory becomes a state.

Relations Among the States

Focus

Reader's Guide

Content Vocabulary
* extradite *(p. 103)*
* civil law *(p. 103)*
* interstate compact *(p. 105)*

Academic Vocabulary
* interact *(p. 103)*
* license *(p. 103)*
* residency *(p. 104)*

Reading Strategy
As you read, use a cause-and-effect diagram to think about issues that lead states to make interstate compacts.

→ Interstate Compacts

Bellringer
Section Focus Transparencies 4-2

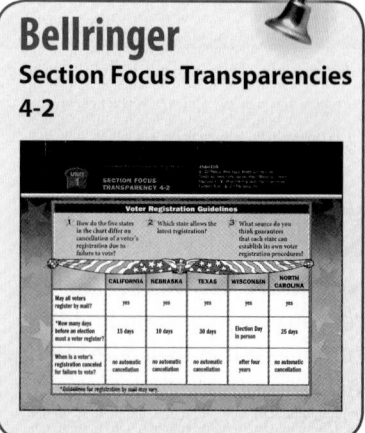

Reader's Guide

Answers to Graphic: air and water pollution, pest control, toll bridges, transportation, waste disposal

---

People in the News

On February 14, 2008, a campus security officer pulled Nicholas Weaver out of his science class at Adelphi University and promptly turned him over to Nassau County police on Long Island. The Adelphi University student was accused of murdering an 18-year-old five years ago. The crime occurred in Baltimore, and Maryland authorities were waiting for an extradition hearing. Weaver, however, waived the hearing because, his attorney said, he wanted to return to Maryland to stand trial and clear his name.

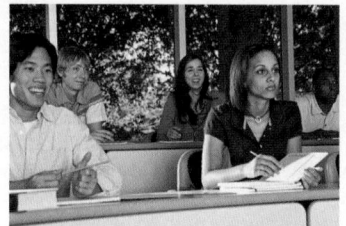

▲ Out-of-state students involved in a crime might be subject to extradition.

The case of Nicholas Weaver shows what happens when one state asks another to forcibly return a person to its jurisdiction. This is an example of how states must **interact.** In setting up our federal system, the Constitution strengthened the national government and set legal ground rules for state relations. Although each state has considerable independence, these rules promote cooperation.

Interstate Relations

Article IV of the Constitution requires the states to do the following: (1) give "full faith and credit" to the laws, records, and court decisions of other states; (2) give each other's citizens all the "privileges and immunities" of their own citizens; and (3) **extradite**—that is, return to a state—criminals and fugitives who flee across state lines to escape justice.

Full Faith and Credit

The Constitution says that "full faith and credit" shall be given in each state to the public acts, records, and judicial proceedings of every other state. Thus each state must recognize, for example, a car registration issued in another state. This clause applies only to **civil law,** or laws relating to disputes between individuals, groups, or with the state. States cannot enforce another state's criminal laws. The need for this kind of rule in the federal system is obvious. Without it, each state could treat all other states like foreign countries. Each state could become a haven for people who moved to another state to avoid their legal obligations.

The "full faith and credit" rule is quite broad. *Public acts* refers to civil laws passed by state legislatures. *Records* means such documents as mortgages, wills, marriage **licenses,** car registrations, and birth certificates. *Judicial proceedings* refers to court actions affecting civil matters.

CHAPTER 4: *The Federal System* **103**

Resource Manager

R Reading Strategies	C Critical Thinking	D Differentiated Instruction	W Writing Support	S Skill Practice
Teacher Edition • Summarizing, p. 104 **Additional Resources** • Quizzes/Tests, p. 38 • Guid. Read. Act., p. 14	**Teacher Edition** • Making Inferences, p. 104 **Additional Resources** • Read. Essen., pp. 41–42	**Teacher Edition** • Special Education, p. 105 **Additional Resources** • Vocab. Act., p. 4 • Foldables, p. 47	**Additional Resources** • Part. in Gov. Act., pp. 7–8	**Additional Resources** • Making It Rel. Trans., p. 8

Teach

R Reading Strategy

Summarizing Have students read Article IV, Section 2, and summarize it in their own words. **Ask:** Does this article of the Constitution support states' rights? *(It supports states' rights by ensuring that criminals can be brought back to face the consequences.)* **BL**

C Critical Thinking

Making Inferences Suggest that students consider the case of a runaway enslaved person who has fled to a free state. Article IV supports the rights of the state from which the enslaved person escaped. **Ask**: By allowing the enslaved person to be captured and returned, are the rights of the free state violated? *(Students may consider the perspective of the free state or the slave state.)* **AL**

Hands-On Chapter Project

Step 2

National Governors' Conference

Step 2: Identifying State Issues Student groups continue to prepare for the national governors' conference by researching current state issues.

Directions Have student partners use the Internet to research current issues of concern in their state. Explain that state

---

Examples of Interstate Compacts

Compact	Purpose	Member States
Columbia River Compact	Provides for regulation, preservation, and protection of fish in the Columbia River	OR, WA
Gulf States Marine Fisheries Compact	Promotes better use and protection of fisheries of the Gulf of Mexico seaboard	AL, FL, LA, MS, TX
Interstate Forest Fire Suppression Compact	Enables member states to use prison inmates in forest firefighting units from another state to fight fires	ID, OR, WA
Interstate Wildlife Violator Compact	Member states can suspend the wildlife license privileges of a person who has violated the wildlife laws of another member's state	AZ, CO, IA, ID, IN, GA, MD, MT, NM, ND, OR, UT, WA, WV, WY
Pacific Marine Fisheries Compact	Promotes the conservation, development, and management of Pacific coast fishery resources through research, monitoring, and use	AK, CA, ID, OR, WA

Source: Council of State Governments Web site.

Critical Thinking *Why are waterways and forests likely subjects for interstate compacts?*

Judicial decisions in civil matters in one state will be honored and enforced in all states. If, for example, a person in Texas loses a lawsuit requiring a specific payment and moves to Illinois to avoid paying the money, Illinois courts will enforce the Texas decision.

Privileges and Immunities

The Founders knew that when citizens traveled between states, they might face problems. Someone from Delaware, for example, might be treated as an alien in Virginia or Maryland. To solve this problem, the Constitution provides that "the Citizens of each State shall be entitled to all Privileges and Immunities of Citizens in the several States."

As interpreted by the Supreme Court, this clause means that one state cannot discriminate unreasonably against citizens of another state—they must have the same privileges and immunities as citizens of that state.

The courts have never given a complete listing of all possible "privileges and immunities." Examples, however, include the right to pass through or live in any state; to use the courts; to make contracts; and to buy, sell, and hold property.

Under the Constitution, states can treat out-of-state residents differently than residents if the distinction is reasonable. It is reasonable for states to require people to be residents if they are to vote in a state, serve on its juries, or use public institutions that are supported by state taxes. Nonresidents, for example, do not have the same access to state colleges or state hospitals as residents do. State colleges and universities can, and usually do, charge higher tuition to students from other states than they do to in-state students.

Whether a person is considered a resident depends on how a state defines **residency.** Some states require someone to live in a state for a certain period of time before being able to vote there. States can also require people to establish residency before they can practice a profession like law, medicine, or dentistry there.

Extradition

Because states are basically independent of one another, some means is needed to prevent criminals from escaping justice simply by going from one state to another. The Constitution provides:

> ❝ A Person charged in any State with Treason, Felony, or other Crime, who shall flee from Justice, and be found in another State, shall on demand of the executive Authority of the State from which he fled, be delivered up, to be removed to the State having Jurisdiction of the Crime. ❞
> —Article IV, Section 2

---

newspapers are a good source of online information about problems that state and local governments face. Ask students to identify three issues in the state and to categorize them as either executive, legislative, or judicial problems.

Focusing on a Problem Have groups select one state problem that could be resolved with help from the federal government. Ask partners to list solutions the state has tried and barriers to the

solutions, such as funding, federal regulations, and so on. Students will use the information in Step 3. **OL**

(Chapter Project continued in Section 3.)

This clause provides for the extradition of fugitives. Congress has made the governor of the state to which fugitives have fled responsible for returning them.

The Supreme Court has softened the meaning of extradition by ruling that a governor does not have to return a fugitive to another state. Although extradition is routine in the vast majority of cases, occasionally a governor will refuse. For example, a Michigan governor once refused to return a fugitive to Arkansas because, the governor said, prison conditions in Arkansas were inhumane. Arkansas officials could do nothing about the governor's decision. In recent years, Congress has acted to close the extradition loophole by making it a federal crime to flee from one state to another in order to avoid prosecution for a felony.

Interstate Compacts

The Constitution requires the states to settle their differences with one another peacefully. The principal way states settle disagreements is by negotiating compacts. **Interstate compacts** are written agreements between two or more states. The national government or foreign countries may also be part of an interstate compact.

Congress must approve interstate compacts. This requirement prevents states from threatening the Union by making alliances among themselves. Once a compact has been signed and approved by Congress, it is binding; its terms are enforceable by the Supreme Court.

Before 1900, only 13 interstate compacts had received congressional approval. Most involved boundary disputes. As society has become more complex, the number of compacts has increased. Today nearly 200 compacts are in force. (See chart, p. 104.)

States use compacts to deal with air and water pollution, pest control, toll bridges, and transportation. New Jersey and New York started this trend in 1921 when they created the Port of New York Authority to develop and manage harbor facilities in the area. Many compacts today deal with natural resources; others deal with how hazardous waste should be transported and disposed of. Interstate compacts have become an important way for the states to deal with regional problems.

Lawsuits Between States

Sometimes states are unable to resolve their disputes using these or other methods. Since 1789 more than 220 disputes between states have ended in court. Suits among two or more states are heard in the U.S. Supreme Court—the only court where one state can sue another.

States bring one another to court for a variety of reasons. Cases in the West often involve water rights. Arizona, California, and Colorado have gone to the Court in disputes over water from the Colorado River. Other cases have involved state conflict over the sewage from one state polluting the water of another. Still other cases are disputes over boundary lines. Arkansas and Tennessee had such a dispute as recently as 1970.

SECTION 2 Review

Vocabulary

1. **Explain** the significance of: extradite, civil law, interstate compact.

Main Ideas

2. **Examining** What three constitutional provisions are aimed at promoting cooperation among the states?

3. **Describing** How does the "full faith and credit" clause affect individuals?

Critical Thinking

4. **Understanding Cause and Effect** What environmental problems could interstate compacts address, and what solutions could they achieve?

5. **Displaying** In a chart similar to the one below, list three ways that states treat nonresidents differently or similarly to their residents.

Treated Differently	Treated Similarly
1.	
2.	
3.	

Writing About Government

6. **Expository Writing** Imagine you have moved to a new state. Find out if and how you would change your driver's license, automobile registration, and voting registration. Write a report on your findings.

Special Education Work with students to make a chart of the key points under the heading "Interstate Compacts." Have students suggest creative ideas for a new heading. **BL**

Assess

Assign the Section 2 Assessment as homework or as an in-class activity, or have students take Section Quiz 4-2 from *Section Quizzes and Chapter Tests*.

Close

Ask: What are some examples of the public acts, records, and judicial proceedings to which the "full faith and credit" rule refers? *(Possible answers include, but are not limited to: civil laws passed by state legislatures, mortgages, deeds, leases, wills, marriage licenses, car registrations, birth certificates, and judgments to pay a debt.)* **OL**

Section 2 Review

Answers

1. All definitions can be found in the section and the Glossary.
2. States must give "full faith and credit" to the laws of other states, give citizens from every state the same privileges and immunities, and extradite fugitives who cross state lines.
3. It allows individuals to move across state lines without worrying about the validity of their contracts and licenses. Individuals cannot move to avoid paying civil suits.
4. Problems include the transportation of hazardous wastes or garbage, problems dealing with water pollution of rivers or

lakes, acid rain, and so on. Solutions could impose restrictions at the source and require compensation for damage.

5. Answers might include: Treated Differently: one must establish residency before voting, holding public office or practicing medicine, dentistry, or law; nonresidents pay higher fees for hunting and fishing licenses; nonresidents pay higher tuition. Treated Similarly: right to pass through or live in any state, right to use the courts, right to make contracts.

6. Students should do research on voter registration, automobile registration, and driver's licensing requirements for their state as well as a second state prior to preparing their reports.

Focus

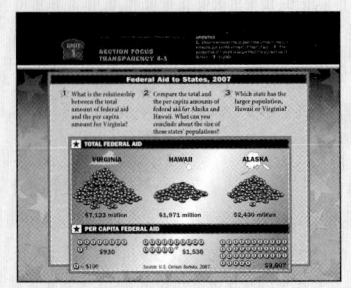
Reader's Guide

Answers to Graphic:

	States' Rightists	Nationalists
Relation of Government to People	National government heavy-handed and a threat to liberty	National government stands for all the people
Relevant Constitutional Provision or Court Case	Tenth Amendment	McCulloch v. Maryland

Resource Manager

Developing Federalism

Reader's Guide

Content Vocabulary
- ★ states' rights position (p. 107)
- ★ nationalist position (p. 107)
- ★ income tax (p. 108)
- ★ preemption (p. 109)

Academic Vocabulary
- ★ convince (p. 106)
- ★ subordinate (p. 107)
- ★ allocate (p. 109)

Reading Strategy
As you read, use a table like the one below to track the positions of states' rightists and nationalists.

	States' Rightists	Nationalists
Relation of Government to People		
Relevant Constitutional Provision or Court Case		

Issues in the News

In recent years, South Carolina took a states' rights position over its right to sell the information that drivers supply when they apply for a driver's license. For many years, departments of motor vehicles in various states have sold this kind of information to businesses and marketers who want to contact drivers with customized solicitations. In the 1990s, Congress passed a law to prevent this activity unless the driver consents. South Carolina fought this law and was upheld in lower courts. Attorney General Janet Reno then took the case to the Supreme Court, which upheld the federal law in 2000. Why? Because drivers' information that is sold becomes part of the "stream of interstate commerce"; as such, it can be regulated by Congress.

▲ Attorney General Janet Reno

What are the roles of state and national government officials in a federal system? The answers to this question have come about gradually in two centuries of American government.

Early supporters of federalism like John Jay and Alexander Hamilton had to **convince** state leaders that the federalism of the new Constitution would be better than the old confederation under the Articles. Federalists were certain that the nation needed a strong central government to survive, but they knew many Americans were suspicious of central government. Hadn't they just thrown off tyrannical British rule? Why would they want to replace that with a strong central government? In his writings, Hamilton went out of his way to explain that the Constitution would respect the power of state governments:

> 66 *The proposed Constitution, so far from implying an abolition of the State Governments, makes them constituent parts of the national sovereignty by allowing them a direct representation in the Senate, and leaves in their possession certain exclusive and very important portions of sovereign power. This fully corresponds . . . with the idea of a Federal Government.* 99
> —Alexander Hamilton, 1787

The core of Hamilton's definition is still true, but interpretations of federalism have changed since 1787 and will probably continue to do so.

R Reading Strategies	**C** Critical Thinking	**D** Differentiated Instruction	**W** Writing Support	**S** Skill Practice
Teacher Edition • Outlining, p. 107 **Additional Resources** • Quizzes/Tests, p. 39 • Guid. Read. Act., p. 15	**Teacher Edition** • Making Inferences, p. 108 **Additional Resources** • Read. Essen., pp. 43–45	**Teacher Edition** • Interpersonal, p. 107 **Additional Resources** • Hist. Docs. and Speeches, p. 4 • Foldables, p. 47	**Teacher Edition** • Personal Writing, p. 109 **Additional Resources** • Source Readings, p. 4	**Teacher Edition** • Conducting Research, p. 109 • Map Skills, p. 110 **Additional Resources** • Skill Reinforce. Act., p. 4

States' Rightists and Nationalists

In the history of the United States, there have been two quite different views of how federalism should operate. One view—the **states' rights position**—favors state and local action in dealing with problems. A second view—the **nationalist position**—favors national action in dealing with these matters.

The States' Rights Position

The states' rights view is that the Constitution is a compact among the states. States' rightists argue that the states created the national government and gave it only certain limited powers. Any doubt about whether a power belongs to the national government or is reserved to the states should be settled in favor of the states. Because the national government is an agent of the states, all of its powers should be narrowly defined.

States' rightists believe state governments are closer to the people and can better reflect their wishes than the national government. They tend to see the government in Washington, D.C., as heavy-handed and a threat to individual liberty.

At various points in the nation's history, the Supreme Court has accepted this view. Under Chief Justice Roger B. Taney (1836–1864), the Court often supported the states in opposition to the national government. The same was true from 1918 to 1936. In this period, the Court ruled that various federal laws intended to regulate child labor, industry, and agriculture were unconstitutional. It was an era when the Court largely ignored John Marshall's principle of implied powers set out in *McCulloch* v. *Maryland.* Instead, the Court focused on the Tenth Amendment, which states that powers not delegated to the national government are reserved to the states or the people.

The Nationalist Position

The nationalist position rejects the idea of the Constitution as merely a compact among the states. Nationalists deny that the national government is an agent of the states. They argue that it was the *people,* not the states, who created both the national government and state governments. Therefore, the national government is not **subordinate** to the states.

Nationalists believe the powers expressly delegated to the national government should be expanded as necessary to carry out the people's will. They hold that the "necessary and proper" clause of the Constitution means that Congress has the right to adopt any means that are convenient and useful to carry out its delegated powers. They also claim that the reserved powers of the states should not act as a brake on how the national government uses its own powers.

Nationalists believe the national government stands for all the people, while each state speaks for only part of the people. They look to the national government to take the lead in solving major social and economic problems facing the nation.

The nationalist position was first set out in 1819 in the *McCulloch* v. *Maryland* case, but it really gained ground during the late 1930s. At that time, the Great Depression gripped the nation. President Franklin D. Roosevelt's New Deal initiated many new social welfare and public works programs. At first, the Court ruled these programs were unconstitutional, but as the financial and economic crisis intensified, the Court changed its

TIME For the Record

The 51st State? Puerto Ricans hotly debate their political future. Though they are U.S. citizens and must follow U.S. laws, they lack some rights of mainland Americans, such as the right to vote in presidential elections. If Puerto Rico became a state, residents would have to pay federal income taxes, but they would also acquire all the rights U.S. citizens have. Those in favor of Puerto Rican independence fear that statehood would force them to speak English and could weaken their heritage. Some claim that commonwealth status gives Puerto Ricans the best of both worlds. They are U.S. citizens and have military protection, but they retain their rich Spanish culture. In the past 30 years, public support for statehood has increased on the island.

Teach

R Reading Strategy

Outlining Have students create an outline for the states' rights and nationalist positions. Tell students this information will be used in a roundtable discussion (see activity below). Remind students to be as thorough as possible. **OL**

D Differentiated Instruction

Interpersonal Have students choose a position: pro-states' rights, pro-nationalist, or middle-of-the-road. Ask students to be prepared to defend their positions in roundtable discussions. After the discussions, ask whether any students would like to change their positions. **Ask:** What made you change your mind? **OL**

Differentiated Instruction

Activity: Multiple Learning Styles

Kinesthetic States' rights proponents and nationalist proponents can sometimes be very vehement about their beliefs. Have students choose one point of view to advocate or to oppose. Then ask them to create a statue or other three-dimensional piece representing that point of view. Creations may be caricatures or serious pieces. For example, a caricature of a states' rights position might be an animal with many legs, each going in a different direction. **ELL**

C Critical Thinking

Making Inferences The textbook states that "in modern times, creating a national defense system is complex. The national government can rightly claim that it needs to be active in education and the economy to ensure that the nation is strong enough to defend itself." **Ask:** In what ways might these complexities affect national defense? *(Answers might include: a strong economy would be able to produce war materials relatively easily, whereas a weak economy would have problems doing so; well-educated fighters would be able to understand and use today's high-tech weapons and equipment and probably would respond better to situations requiring sound reasoning and decision making.)* **Ask:** What other factors might affect the nation's military capabilities? *(Possible answers may include the number of military commitments or where training bases are located.)* **AL**

Caption Answer: Racial discrimination makes travel difficult and thus restricts the flow of interstate commerce, which Congress has the power to regulate.

Hands-On Chapter Project

Step 3

---

view, supporting an expansion of the national government's powers to address the problems.

Growing National Government

The growth in the power of the national government has shifted the balance in the federal system: The expansion of the national government has come largely at the expense of the states.

Why has the national government been able to expand? A key reason is the adaptability of the Constitution. This has allowed the Supreme Court, Congress, and the president to stretch the powers of the central government to meet the needs of a modern industrial nation. To accomplish this goal, three provisions of the Constitution have been applied in most cases:

- the war powers,
- the power to regulate interstate commerce, and
- the power to tax and spend.

War Powers

The national government has been given the authority to wage war. In modern times, creating a national defense system is complex. The national government can rightly claim that it needs to be active in education and the economy to ensure that the nation is strong enough to defend itself. The fact that the United States is a superpower providing security for many tense global conflicts has reinforced the argument that there must be a strong national government.

Commerce Power

Supreme Court decisions have expanded the constitutional power of the national government to regulate commerce. The Court has interpreted the term *commerce* to mean almost any activity connected with producing, buying, selling, and transporting goods. For example, Congress used the commerce clause for the authority behind the Civil Rights Act of 1964 that prohibited racial discrimination in hotels, restaurants, and other public accommodations. The Court reasoned as follows:

- If restaurants and hotels discriminate against African Americans or any group of Americans, it restricts interstate commerce.
- Congress has the power to regulate commerce.
- Therefore, Congress may pass laws against racial discrimination.

Taxing Power

Congress has no specific constitutional authority to pass laws to promote the general welfare, but it does have the authority to raise taxes and spend money for that purpose.

The Sixteenth Amendment (1913) gave Congress the power to levy an **income tax.** The tax on individual income has become the major source of revenue for the national government, giving it far greater resources than state or local governments.

Integration of Interstate Travel

Freedom Riders' Bus
In 1961 "Freedom Riders" rode buses to the South to pressure the federal government to enforce integration. At rest stops, the white "Riders" went into blacks-only areas while African American Riders did the opposite. This bus was set on fire by white segregationists in Alabama, but the strategy worked. *Based on the information above, how might the commerce clause be interpreted to end segregation on buses?*

108 UNIT 1: *Foundations of American Government*

National Governors' Conference

Step 3: Preparing Presentations

Groups will prepare their issues of concern for presentation at the national governors' conference.

Directions Ask groups to create a computer presentation that focuses on the state problem identified in Step 2 of this activity. Student presentations should include a minimum of five slides with a title slide and a concluding slide. The title slide should include a visual that displays what the governor would like the federal government to do to help the state with its problem. The following slides should present the problem, explain how it affects citizens of the state, and suggests ways in which the federal government can help. The concluding slide should summarize the presentation in a dramatic way. **OL**

(Chapter Project continued in Section 4.)

Finally, Congress has used its taxing power to increase the national government's authority in two ways. First, taxes are sometimes used to regulate businesses as when Congress heavily taxes a dangerous product so that it is not profitable to make. Second, Congress can use taxes to influence states to adopt certain programs. For example, employers are allowed to deduct from their federal taxes any state taxes paid to support state unemployment programs. This tax break has persuaded the states to set up their own unemployment insurance programs.

Federal Aid to the States

As the national government has grown and enlarged its powers, Congress has developed two major ways to influence the policies of state and local governments:

- by providing federal grants of money, and
- by mandating, or requiring, state and local governments to follow certain policies.

Types of Federal Aid

The national government has always provided different types of aid to the states. In 1862, for instance, Congress passed a law giving nearly 6 million acres of public land to the states for support of colleges. Since the 1950s, federal aid to state and local governments has increased tremendously.

The main way the national government provides money to the states is through federal grants—sums of money given to state or local governments for specific purposes. For example, federal money might go to a city to help improve airport runways or to a state to build new roads.

Federal grants redistribute income among the **S** states. Taxes are collected by the federal government from citizens in all 50 states. This money is then **allocated** through grants to people in many states. Thus, grants often help reduce inequalities among wealthy and less wealthy states. The process of deciding how grant money is allocated can be very political, with states competing fiercely in Washington to get as large a share of funds as possible.

Funds come at a price, however. State and local governments have learned that along with aid comes federal control and red tape—federal money is granted only if the state and localities are willing to meet certain conditions.

Preemption Laws

Since the mid-1960s, Congress has used **preemption.** In government terms, preemption is

Preemption in Education Signed into law in 2002, the No Child Left Behind act passed by Congress set out a number of requirements for teachers, schools, and students. The law can decrease federal funds for schools that do not meet the law's goals. *How might states argue against this law?*

the federal government's ability to take over a state government function. For example, when Congress passed the 1990 Nutritional Labeling and Education Act, states were no longer allowed to set their own food labeling standards, even when they were higher than the new national standards.

Preemption laws can limit state and local authority either by restraining their power or by mandating them to do certain things. The Americans with Disabilities Act, for example, required **W** state and local governments to build ramps and alter curbs on sidewalks. Preemption laws have dealt with many issues. They have protected the civil rights of women and African Americans, set environmental standards, and required the nation's schools to meet testing standards in math and reading.

Advocates of states' rights dislike preemption because it takes away state and local authority to make their own laws and policies. In the process, preemption can interfere with the ability of local and state governments to set priorities for their

Caption Answer: No federal funds were provided to carry out the new law, passing the burden of paying for the mandate to the states.

S Skill Practice

Conducting Research Have students research a federal grant by finding all relevant information including eligibility requirements, guidelines, time frames, amount of money available, and so on. Each student should create a pamphlet for the grant, advertising it to the other students. All necessary information must be present in the pamphlet. **OL**

W Writing Support

Personal Writing Have students give their personal opinion about the federal government's right to create preemption laws. Ask students to consider that many preemptive laws relate to issues that are clearly defined as states' rights in the Constitution. **Ask:** Do preemption laws violate states' rights? *(Students may answer yes or no, but they should defend their position.)* **OL**

Additional Support

Activity: Collaborative Learning

Spending Grant Money Organize the class into small groups, each of which is to make a plan for spending a block grant from the federal government. The only string attached is that it be spent on improving education. Each group's share of the money is $100,000. Have each group discuss ways to spend the money. Then ask group members to investigate further by interviewing curriculum specialists, department heads, and other staff members. Students may also interview their parents or guardians on the matter. Next, students need to find out costs for various items. When all groups have finalized their plans, have each group present its plan to the rest of the class. Have the class vote on the best plan. **AL**

S Skill Practice

Map Skills Ask: For each dollar of federal taxes sent to Washington, D.C., how much federal spending does your state receive in return? *(Answers will vary.)* **BL**

Assess

Assign the Section 3 Assessment as homework or as an in-class activity, or have students take Section Quiz 4-3 from *Section Quizzes and Chapter Tests.*

Close

Summarizing Have students rewrite the quote from Alexander Hamilton (page 106) in their own words. **OL**

Section 3 Review

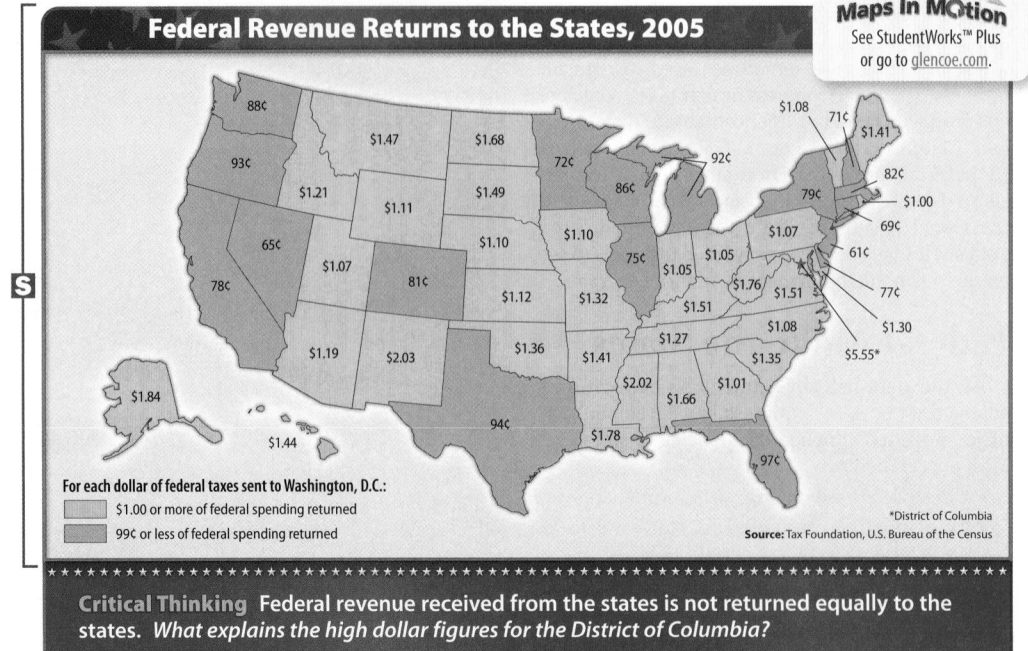

Maps In Motion
See StudentWorks™ Plus or go to glencoe.com.

Federal Revenue Returns to the States, 2005

For each dollar of federal taxes sent to Washington, D.C.:
- $1.00 or more of federal spending returned
- 99¢ or less of federal spending returned

*District of Columbia
Source: Tax Foundation, U.S. Bureau of the Census

Critical Thinking Federal revenue received from the states is not returned equally to the states. *What explains the high dollar figures for the District of Columbia?*

own budgets. From this perspective, the worst kind of preemption law is one that provides no federal funds to carry out a policy—Congress is not required to pay for new mandates and can pass the burden of paying for them to the states.

At different times, the balance of power in the federal system has shifted. In the 1980s, Republican president Ronald Reagan endorsed the policy of "new federalism," meaning his administration worked to return more power and responsibility to state and local governments. His successor, President George H.W. Bush, also followed new federalism. Since the 1990s, however, new federalism has weakened. The federal-state relationship is a dynamic one and is affected by the sitting president and Congress.

SECTION 3 Review

Vocabulary

1. **Explain** the significance of: states' rights position, nationalist position, income tax, preemption.

Main Ideas

2. **Examining** In what two ways has Congress used its taxing power to increase the national government's authority?

Critical Thinking

3. **Making Comparisons** Analyze the major difference between the states' rights and the nationalist views of federalism.

4. **Organizing** Using a graphic organizer like the one below, identify three constitutional provisions that have been the basis for the tremendous growth of the national government.

National Government		

Writing About Government

5. **Persuasive Writing** Write an opinion paper stating your position on the following question: Should the national government distribute money to states with "no strings attached," or should the grant have stipulations? Explain your position.

Answers

1. All definitions can be found in the section and the Glossary.
2. to regulate businesses and to influence states to adopt certain kinds of programs
3. The states' rights position favors state and local action in dealing with social and economic problems. The nationalist position favors national government action in dealing with these matters.
4. Answers might include war powers, regulation of interstate commerce, and power to tax and spend.
5. Opinion papers will vary, but students should demonstrate sound reasoning in explaining their positions.

Does the Commerce Clause Have Limits?

Philadelphia v. New Jersey, 1978

Americans take it for granted that they can travel from state to state and take any purchase they make back home without paying any fee. But are there limits to how products can move across state lines?

Facts of the Case

The disposal of solid and liquid wastes is a problem for cities. As available sites for landfills shrink, some cities have shipped their wastes across state lines. In the early 1970s, the volume of waste being shipped from Philadelphia, Pennsylvania, into New Jersey was increasing rapidly.

New Jersey legislators believed that these shipments posed a threat to its environment. In 1973 they prohibited the importation of solid or liquid waste that came from outside the state.

A lawsuit was then filed by private landfill owners and by several cities that had contracts with those owners for waste disposal. The suit claimed that the New Jersey law was unconstitutional because it violated their right to ship materials across state lines under the Constitution's commerce clause.

▼ Landfill in New Jersey

The Constitutional Question

In the United States, power is divided among the national government, the state governments, and the people. The Constitution gave the national government power to regulate interstate commerce—trade that crosses state lines. In the New Jersey case, the issue was whether liquid and solid wastes could be defined as interstate commerce according to the Constitution.

Over the course of American history, the Supreme Court has expanded the definition of interstate commerce. In an 1824 case, *Gibbons v. Ogden*, the Court said that travel by ship on the Hudson River between New York and New Jersey was interstate commerce. In the 1930s, the Court upheld legislation that expanded the meaning of interstate commerce in another way—the Wagner Act allowed Congress to regulate business and labor relations across states. In the 1960s, the Court again applied a broad definition of commerce when it upheld the new Civil Rights Act of 1964. In several cases, the Court ruled that the federal government could use the commerce clause to regulate restaurants serving mostly interstate travelers. Thus, these restaurants could no longer discriminate against African American customers.

Debating the Issue

Questions to Consider

1. Why was new legislation passed in New Jersey in 1973?
2. Why do waste haulers consider their shipments a form of commerce?
3. What national impact might this decision have?

You Be the Judge

Many states are facing the same issues that New Jersey did. What would be the long-term results if the Court decided in favor of New Jersey? In favor of the landfill owners? Does the commerce clause apply in this case? Why or why not?

Teach

Class Debate

Organize the class into groups based on students' leanings (pro-New Jersey or pro-Philadelphia). Have each group discuss the issues and list as many supporting arguments as possible. Then have each group present its position to the class.

The Court's Decision

In a 7 to 2 decision, the Court found for the city of Philadelphia. It argued that the actual transportation of wastes was not harmful, that the wastes were potentially harmful only after disposal, and that at that point there was no difference to the environment whether the wastes came from in state or out of state. The Court pointed out that it had historically found legislation similar to that passed by New Jersey to be invalid: A state cannot isolate itself from the national economy. A state also cannot accord its own citizens preferred right of access over consumers from other states. Justices William Rehnquist and Warren Burger dissented on the grounds that New Jersey's need to dispose of its own wastes does not mean that it must serve as a depository for other states' wastes.

Debating the Issue Answers

Questions to Consider

1. As volumes of waste coming into the state increased, the state legislature believed that the treatment and disposal of waste materials posed a threat to the quality of the state's environment.
2. They believed the material they were shipping across state lines had commercial value.
3. All 50 states would have to abide by the ruling. An immediate end to all interstate transportation of solid waste could occur, or there could be a great increase in the interstate transportation of such materials.

You Be the Judge

There would be an end to the interstate transportation of solid wastes. There would be an increase in the interstate transportation of solid wastes. Students should provide logical responses that make reference to the language of the commerce clause and examples provided elsewhere in the textbook.

Focus

Bellringer

Section Focus Transparencies 4-4

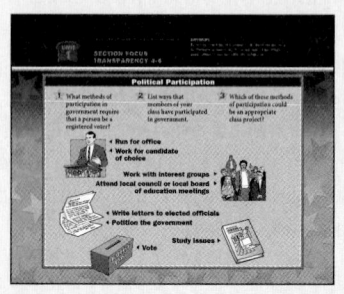

Reader's Guide

Answers to Graphic:

more people have the opportunity to hold political office

more access to political leaders

frequent elections/more opportunities to vote

more opportunities to influence/petition government political leaders

Resource Manager

Federalism and Politics

Reader's Guide

Content Vocabulary	Academic Vocabulary	Reading Strategy	
★ sunset law *(p. 112)* ★ sunshine law *(p. 113)* ★ bureaucracy *(p. 115)*	★ role *(p. 112)* ★ community *(p. 113)* ★ analyst *(p. 115)*	As you read, fill in a graphic organizer like the one to the right to show how federalism affects political participation.	**How Federalism Affects Participation**

Public Policy in the News

What would happen if a national health emergency occurred—an outbreak of bird flu, or terrorists releasing anthrax into the air? Would the federal Centers for Disease Control (CDC) take charge, or would state governments do so? Some experts like Professor Lawrence Gostin at Georgetown Law School worry about a lack of organization and coordination. "They are pushing a national plan for how states should deal with an emergency. Supporters of state leadership say a federally dictated plan would give government bureaucrats the ability to declare a state of emergency when it pleases them . . . , to destroy property, and incarcerate people."

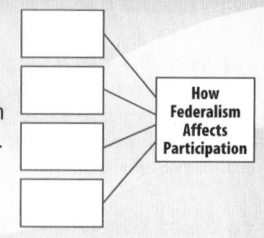

▲ Health workers test specimens suspected of being connected to a virus outbreak.

Debates over state and federal **roles** are common in our federal system. That is because carrying out most policies requires a degree of shared responsibility. As in the scenario of a bird flu emergency, both levels of government often believe they have the right to play the lead role.

Federalism and Public Policy

What do we mean exactly when we talk about a *policy*? A policy is a stated course of action for addressing certain problems or issues. A high school principal may say, "It's our policy that students not park in the teachers' parking lot." A sign in a local store often reads: "It's our policy to prosecute all shoplifters." In both cases, people are

defining the actions they will take in response to a recurring problem or situation.

When a government settles on a course of action, we call it *public policy*. Federalism influences public policy in two important ways. First, it influences how and where policies are made. Second, it places certain limits on policy making.

The United States has many different units of government—50 state governments and thousands of local governments. This fact promotes experimentation in policy-making. States and localities can serve as proving grounds for the development and testing of new policies.

Georgia, for example, was the first state to allow 18-year-olds to vote. Colorado pioneered the use of the sunset laws now found in many states. (A **sunset law** is a provision in a law that sets an automatic end date for the law: Lawmakers are forced

R Reading Strategies	**C** Critical Thinking	**D** Differentiated Instruction	**W** Writing Support	**S** Skill Practice
Teacher Edition • Using Word Parts, p. 115 **Additional Resources** • Quizzes/Tests, p. 40 • Guid. Read. Act., p. 16	**Teacher Edition** • Making Connections, p. 115 **Additional Resources** • Read. Essen., pp. 46–48 • Quizzes/Tests, pp. 41–48	**Teacher Edition** • English Learners, p. 113 **Additional Resources** • Ch. Summaries, pp. 10–12	**Teacher Edition** • Persuasive Writing, p. 116 **Additional Resources** • Authentic Assess., p. 11	**Additional Resources** • Supreme Ct. Case Studies, pp. 7–8

to review the need for continuing the law beyond that date.) In California, local groups pressured the state to pass laws to control air pollution. Their laws became models for federal air-pollution laws. In 1967 Florida legislators were the first in the nation to pass a sunshine law, or open meetings law. **Sunshine laws** prohibit public officials from holding closed meetings. Since then, many states have adopted sunshine laws.

Very often policy originates at the national level. Congress can impose policies on states if local groups resist a federal law that infringes on people's basic rights. This happened most dramatically in the 1950s and 1960s during the African American struggle for civil rights. Led by Martin Luther King, Jr., African Americans in Southern states demonstrated peacefully to be able to exercise their constitutional right to vote. They faced violence and resistance in Selma, Alabama, and many other **communities.** Gradually the civil rights movement attracted substantial media attention and public support. The federal government then used federal troops to pressure the states to enforce the law.

Federalism and Political Parties

Rival political parties are a key element of democratic government. Because of federalism, politics in the United States is not a desperate all-or-nothing struggle for control of the national government. Federalism makes it possible for different parties to be victorious in state, local, and

> **Government ONLINE**
> **Student Web Activity** Visit glencoe.com and enter *QuickPass*™ code USG9822c4. Click on Student Web Activity and complete the activity about federalism and politics.

We the People
Making a Difference

David Levitt was only a sixth grader when he decided to do something about the 30 million people in the United States who go to bed hungry every day. So he asked the principal of his middle school whether he could start a program to distribute cafeteria leftovers. The principal pointed out that previously served food could not be distributed under the current health regulations in the district. David's mother encouraged David to find a way around this problem. First, he made his case before the Pinellas County (Florida) school board. After the board gave its approval, he worked to satisfy state health department requirements.

Since its beginnings in the mid-1990s, David's program has distributed almost a million pounds of food to shelters and food banks in this Florida county. David's efforts to help the people of his state did not stop with distributing food. When he was in high school, David worked on state legislation to protect donors of surplus food from liability lawsuits. Most important, David's efforts have drawn attention to a significant problem and shown that there is food available in communities that can be used to feed the hungry.

In 1996 David was awarded a Points of Light medal in a White House ceremony. During the ceremony, he demonstrated the kind of thinking that got him there in the first place. Meeting then First Lady Hillary Clinton, he immediately asked her what the White House did with its leftovers.

"What one can do, another can be inspired to do."
—Points of Light Foundation

Teach

D Differentiated Instruction

English Learners Refer students to the term *sunshine law.* Point out the use of the word *sunshine* to connote "out in the open" or "visible" (as opposed to meeting secretly and keeping voters "in the dark"). **ELL**

> **Government ONLINE**
> Objectives and answers to the Student Web Activity can be found in the **Web Activity Lesson Plan** at glencoe.com. Enter *QuickPass*™ code USG9085c4T.

We the People
Making a Difference

Activity: Have students find out how people qualify for food stamps, and the types of items that may be bought with the stamps. **OL**

Additional Support

★ Activity: Collaborative Learning ★

Recycling The issue of recycling is important in many communities. Although most programs began when residents voluntarily took recyclables to a central gathering place, many communities have now initiated curbside pickup, and some communities have assigned penalties for disposing of recyclables in the regular trash. Have students investigate local recycling programs. **Ask:** What items can be recycled in each? How is recycling carried out? Would cooperation among groups of communities work? Would statewide recycling laws help get other materials out of the trash stream? Have small groups of students investigate these questions and propose plans for more effective and comprehensive recycling. **OL**

The Federal System and Political Parties

Caption Answer: Competition between political parties may ensure that no one group becomes too powerful, encourage compromise and diversity, and offer more points of access for citizens.

ISSUES to Debate

Influencing Government Policies Americans may participate in politics by joining an interest group that tries to influence public policy. Have students choose an established interest group. Encourage students to research its goals and methods. **Ask:** Do you agree with the group's goals? What methods does this group use to try to influence policy? Does this group concentrate its efforts on local, state, or national policy matters? Would you participate in the activities of this group? Why or why not? *(Students' answers should be based on their research.)* **OL**

The Federal System and Political Parties

Impact of Parties
Federalism increases political participation at the party level. Each state sends delegates to a national convention to nominate the party's presidential candidate. Here the delegates from Arizona cast their votes for John McCain's nomination at the 2008 Republican National Convention. *How does the structure of political parties reflect federalism?*

federal elections. Federalism lessens the risk of one party having a monopoly of political power.

After the Civil War, for example, the Democratic Party went into a long period of decline on the national level. Yet the party survived because Democratic candidates managed to maintain control of many state and local offices in the Southern states. With such state and local bases, the party developed new policies and new leadership with which to challenge the majority party.

The Democratic Party controlled the White House for only 5 of the 14 presidential terms between 1952 and 2008. Democratic organization at the state and local level, however, allowed the Democrats to win a majority in Congress during most of that time period.

Political Participation

Federalism increases opportunities for American citizens to participate in politics. A citizen can choose to run for local office, to lobby the state government, or to campaign for a candidate for national office.

Many Opportunities

Because federalism provides for several levels of government, people have relatively easy access to political office. The road to national office often begins at the local or state level. This aspect of federalism has tended to preserve political organization from the bottom up.

American federalism gives citizens many points of access to government leaders and increases their opportunities for influencing public policy. A noted political scientist believed the two-party system contributes to this access:

> ❝ *The lack of party discipline produces an openness in the system that allows individuals, groups, and institutions (including state and local governments) to attempt to influence national policy at every step of the legislative . . . process.* ❞
> —Morton Grodzins, 1966

Americans have the chance to vote fairly often. They elect governors, state lawmakers, mayors, council members, school board members, county prosecutors, and many other state and local officials such as the judges that sit on the municipal, county, and state courts. They also vote on specific local issues—whether to build a mass transit system in their city, whether to outlaw smoking in public places, or whether to increase property taxes for schools.

Citizens may also work with special-interest groups to influence national policies and state and local government agencies. A group of concerned neighbors can petition the county zoning board to set aside nearby land for a public playground, or members of a local labor union may work together to support their union's efforts to influence passage of a law in the state legislature.

Hands-On Chapter Project

Step 4

National Governors' Conference

Step 4: Delivering the Presentations
Groups will deliver their presentations at the mock governors' conference.

Directions Set up a laptop computer with a video projector for students to use as they deliver their presentations. Give each group an opportunity to introduce their state and to show their presentations of state issues or concerns. After each presentation, allow other class members

to ask questions. Have students take notes on each issue and the proposed government remedies. At the end of the presentations, ask students to discuss common themes within the different state issues. Record the themes on the board. Then, reconvene groups and have each group—acting as representatives of the national governors' conference—create a proclamation addressed to the president of the United States. Help groups get started by providing text to begin their proclamation:

WHEREAS, the governors of these United States have met to discuss common state issues, and

WHEREAS, the states enjoy a cooperative relationship with the government of the United States of America, and

WHEREAS, the national government has historically granted funds to promote the welfare of these states and their citizens,

THEREFORE, these states request assistance to remedy the following issues of concern: **OL**

Increasing Chances of Success

A related effect of federalism is an increased chance that one's political participation will have some practical impact on policy. And because that is true, people are more likely to become involved in political activity. In a campaign for city council in a smaller town, for example, someone working in the campaign has to persuade relatively few voters to elect the candidate of his or her choice.

Federalism's Bureaucrats

Since the 1960s, more and more public policy has been initiated by people in government service. The great increase in federal programs beginning in the mid-1930s called for a large **bureaucracy,** or organization of government administrators, to carry out legislation. As these bureaucrats gained expertise, they offered more and more ideas. Political writer Samuel H. Beer described their results this way:

> 66 *In the fields of health, housing, urban renewal, transportation, welfare, education, poverty, and energy, it has been . . . people in government service . . . acting on the basis of their specialized and technical knowledge, who first perceived the problem, conceived the program, initially urged it on the President and Congress, went on to help lobby it through to enactment, and then saw to its administration.* 99
> —Samuel H. Beer, 1978

Some political **analysts** have used the term *technocracy* to refer to bureaucrats making policy in this type of process. For example, someone working in the Department of Health and Human Services may have training in nursing, a degree in health planning, or a medical degree in a specific area. Thus, government policies are made in a system that is influenced greatly by the technical expertise of government "technocrats."

The increase in federal programs has also changed how state and federal officials relate to one another. As mayors and state officials sought to take advantage of the new federal programs, they were forced to work more closely with federal officials. Organizations such as the United States Conference of Mayors established headquarters in Washington, D.C., to keep up with events and to stay in touch with lawmakers. In time, officials representing the mayors acquired much more political influence at the national level.

Differences Among the States

Federalism allows for real economic and political differences among the states because it permits each state considerable freedom in arranging its own internal affairs. As a result, some states do more than others to regulate business and industry, and some states concentrate their resources on providing more health services. Other notable differences are that some states have stricter criminal laws, and some have higher taxes.

Because states create different economic and political environments, Americans can choose among a range of conditions under which they want to live. They might want to live in a state with lower taxes or one with better schools. Because of these differences, this means that when people cross a state boundary, they become members of a different political system with its own officials, taxes, and laws.

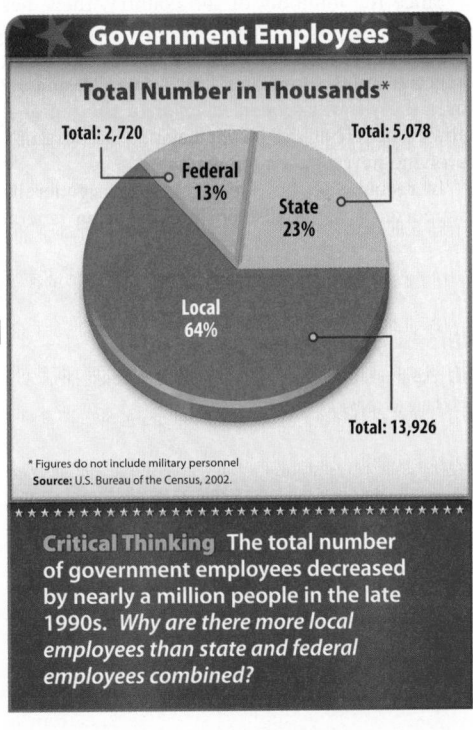

Government Employees

Total Number in Thousands*

Total: 2,720

Federal 13%

Total: 5,078

State 23%

Local 64%

Total: 13,926

* Figures do not include military personnel
Source: U.S. Bureau of the Census, 2002.

Critical Thinking The total number of government employees decreased by nearly a million people in the late 1990s. *Why are there more local employees than state and federal employees combined?*

C Critical Thinking

Making Connections Ask: What political development of the 1960s expanded the role of the federal government in public policy? *(the Great Society and War on Poverty programs)* What political development of the 1930s led to a dramatic increase in the federal bureaucracy? *(the New Deal)* **OL**

R Reading Strategy

Using Word Parts Point out the word *bureaucracy*. Tell students that *bureau-* derives from the French word for "office" (literally meaning "desk") and *-cracy* originates from the Greek word *kratos,* meaning "strength" or "power." Then, point students to the word *technocracy* and ask them to guess that word's etymology. (*Techno-* refers to technical or technology.) **OL**

Caption Answer: Local governments are far more numerous than state and federal governments.

Differentiated Instruction

Historical Documents and Speeches, p. 21

Social and Domestic Policy

Objective: To understand and evaluate the goals of President Lyndon Johnson's Great Society.

Focus/Teach: Review the historical context, and then discuss the goals mentioned in the speech.

Assess: Have students respond to the "Activity" questions.

Close: Discuss the connection between the Great Society and the federal government's role in public policy.

Differentiated Instruction Strategies

BL Have students make a list of the goals Johnson mentioned in his speech.

AL Ask students to research which federal programs today originated as part of the Great Society.

ELL Divide students into pairs, and have each pair paraphrase a single paragraph of the speech.

W Writing Support

Persuasive Writing Have students respond to this statement: "The highway speed limit in this state should be lowered because it would reduce the number of accidents and save gasoline." *(Students should defend their positions logically.)* **OL**

Assess

Assign the Section 4 Assessment as homework or as an in-class activity, or have students take Section Quiz 4-4 from *Section Quizzes and Chapter Tests.*

Close

Intrapersonal Invite a local government employee to visit and discuss his or her job. Have students ask questions about the kinds of skills, education, and training the job requires. Have students write a short explanation of why they would or would not like to have that job. **OL**

Section 4 Review

Accepting New Responsibilities

State-Federal Expertise
Louisiana governor Bobby Jindal is the nation's first Indian American governor. Jindal is a good example of someone who is comfortable in leadership roles at both the state and the national level. Before being elected governor in 2007, he served in the U.S. Department of Health and Human Services and on a national bipartisan committee. *How is Governor Jindal's experience with different levels of government an advantage?*

The Direction of Federalism

Since the founding of the country, there has always been a debate about what the proper division of powers between the national government and the states should be. The general tendency over the years has been in favor of the national government, but the power balance is constantly evolving in response to new issues.

In recent decades, Democrats have generally supported a nationalist position favoring federal grants targeted at specific issues. Republicans have preferred relying upon the judgment of state and local authorities. Because of the relatively even distribution of party seats in recent Congresses, legislation has reflected both positions. For example, Congress has given states more power to control how they spend money for development in rural areas, permitted states to set their own highway speed limits, and acquire more responsibility for social welfare programs. On the other hand, Congress has strengthened national control of food safety standards and the regulation of telecommunications.

SECTION 4 Review

Vocabulary

1. **Explain** the significance of: sunset law, sunshine law, bureaucracy.

Main Ideas

2. **Analyzing** How did African Americans influence state and local policy in the 1950s and 1960s?

3. **Describing** How does federalism affect the two-party system in the United States?

Critical Thinking

4. **Making Inferences** How does federalism allow for political and economic diversity among the states?

5. **Organizing** Using a graphic organizer like the one below, show two ways that federalism influences public policy making.

Writing About Government

6. **Descriptive Writing** Federalism gives people easier access to public office and more chances to influence government policy. Find out what state and local offices a person living in your community can run for. Write slogans and brief text for a poster for an imaginary campaign.

116 UNIT 1: *Foundations of American Government*

Answers

1. All definitions can be found in the section and the Glossary.
2. They called national attention to local discrimination and restriction of civil rights. National pressure caused the federal government to pass legislation that affected those areas.
3. By providing each party with many choices for election victories, federalism helps lessen the risk of one political party gaining a monopoly on political powers.
4. Each state has internal sovereignty, which allows it to adopt policies that fit its individual needs.
5. Answers might include: determines how and where policies are made, limits government policy making.
6. Students' posters should illustrate the various elected offices at the state and local levels.

Can States Be Sued in Federal Court?

Seminole Tribe of Florida v. Florida, 1996

The Eleventh Amendment (1795) was originally passed after a Supreme Court ruling allowed a South Carolina man to sue the state of Georgia. The amendment protects states from being sued in federal courts by "Citizens of another State, or by citizens or Subjects of any Foreign State." In different eras, the Court has viewed the amendment differently.

Facts of the Case

In the 1980s, several Native American groups started gambling operations on reservation lands. To regulate such activities, Congress enacted the Indian Gaming Regulatory Act in 1988. Under it, Native Americans could operate casinos on reservations if casino gambling was legal in the state *and* if they negotiated an agreement with the state.

The Seminoles tried to negotiate an agreement with Florida. When they could not, they filed suit in federal court, arguing that the state had not negotiated in good faith. Florida argued that the case should be dismissed, citing the Eleventh Amendment's protection against states being sued in federal courts.

The Constitutional Question

How does the commerce clause affect the interpretation of the Eleventh Amendment? The commerce clause of the Constitution gives the federal government the power to regulate commerce "with foreign Nations, and among the several States, and with the Indian Tribes." To what extent does the Eleventh Amendment make states immune from lawsuits in federal courts? Can a state be forced, through a suit filed in federal court, to obey federal regulations?

One interpretation—the one favored by the Seminoles—granted the federal courts jurisdiction in the case. According to this view, the federal government's power to regulate commerce with Native Americans outweighed Florida's assertion that the Seminoles had no right to sue the state in federal court.

Florida, however, argued that states have "sovereign immunity" from being sued in federal court. The state claimed the Eleventh Amendment took precedence over Congress's powers under the commerce clause.

Teach

Class Debate

Organize the class into groups based on students' leanings (pro-Seminole or pro-Florida). Have each group discuss the issues and list as many supporting arguments as possible. Have each group present its position to the class.

The Court's Decision

The Supreme Court ruled 5 to 4 that the provision of the Indian Gaming Regulatory Act that gave the Seminole Tribe the authority to sue the state in federal court was unconstitutional. Although the federal government, not the states, has the constitutional authority to make laws regarding Native American affairs, a state cannot be sued in federal court unless it consents. The decision limited the federal government's ability to force states to comply with federal legislation enacted through its authority to regulate commerce.

Debating the Issue

Questions to Consider

1. Why did Congress pass the Indian Gaming Regulatory Act?

2. How was Florida's claim of "sovereign immunity" a declaration of states' rights?

3. If the Court sided with Florida, how might that affect a citizen's ability to sue for damages when a state is at fault?

You Be the Judge

Does the fact that the commerce clause predates the Eleventh Amendment give it more authority, less authority, or is it irrelevant? Why or why not?

▼ A signing ceremony with a group of Seminoles

Debating the Issue Answers

Questions to Consider

1. Congress passed the law to allow states some authority to regulate gambling on reservations within their borders.

2. Florida expressed a states' rights position because it was a declaration that the federal government had no authority to compel a state to defend itself in federal court. Explain that sovereign immunity refers to a doctrine that holds that a state (sovereign) cannot be sued without its consent.

3. The citizen might have no legal recourse if the state were at fault.

You Be the Judge

Students may take a states' rights position—agreeing with Florida's claim of state sovereignty–or a nationalist position—believing the federal government has the power to compel states to abide by federal laws. Answers should express an opinion on whether the Eleventh Amendment supersedes the commerce clause.

ExamView®
Assessment Suite

This easy-to-use software includes extensive question banks and allows you to create fully customized tests that can be administered in print or online.

Reviewing Vocabulary

1.–8. National Government— implied powers, expressed powers, inherent powers, elastic clause, concurrent powers, delegated powers; State Government—extradite, reserved powers, concurrent powers

Reviewing Main Ideas

9. supremacy clause, Article VI, Section 2

10. It gives nonresidents all the "privileges and immunities" of state citizens.

11. the Supreme Court's broad interpretation of interstate commerce

12. income taxes

13. It increases peoples' opportunities for political participation because people may participate or influence the government at national, state, or local levels. It increases the possibility that a person's participation will have some practical effect.

14. state and local governments

Critical Thinking

15. *Reserved* means "set aside," and those are the powers that are set aside for the people and the states.

16. They believe the states created the national

Reviewing Vocabulary

On a sheet of paper, write the headings "National Government" and "State Government." Group the terms below under the appropriate heading.

1. implied powers   **5.** reserved powers
2. expressed powers   **6.** elastic clause
3. inherent powers   **7.** concurrent powers
4. extradite   **8.** delegated powers

Chapter Summary

Federal System
★ The Constitution delegates certain powers to national government
★ Some powers are shared by the federal government and states
★ All other powers are reserved to the states or the people

Developing Federalism
★ States' rights position favors the power of states over national government
★ Nationalist position favors supremacy of national government over states
★ Size and power of national government expanded over the years to meet the needs of a modern industrial nation
★ Today states are gaining responsibility as federal government loosens regulations

Federalism and Politics
★ Federalism determines whether public policy originates at local, state, or national level
★ Federalism lessens the risk of one political party monopolizing power
★ Federalism gives citizens greater opportunities to participate in politics

Reviewing Main Ideas

Section 1 *(pages 95–102)*

9. Naming What clause of the Constitution resolves conflicts between state law and national law?

Section 2 *(pages 103–105)*

10. Explaining What rights does the "privileges and immunities" clause provide for nonresidents traveling between states?

Section 3 *(pages 106–110)*

11. Describing How did Congress gain power to regulate farm production, child labor, and wages?

12. Identifying What is the major source of income for the national government?

Section 4 *(pages 112–116)*

13. Explaining How does the federalist system affect political participation?

14. Examining Who pays for elections of senators, representatives, and presidential electors?

Critical Thinking

15. Essential Question Why does the Tenth Amendment use the term *reserved* to describe the powers that belong to the people and the states?

16. Expressing On what historical basis do states' rights supporters argue that the national government is only an agent of the states?

17. Analyzing Experts in government agencies initiate many national laws in health, the environment, energy, welfare, education, and business. Why do these bureaucrats have great influence on legislation and decision making?

18. Making Comparisons Use a graphic organizer to compare President Ronald Reagan's concept of federalism with President Franklin D. Roosevelt's.

Concepts of Federalism	
Roosevelt	Reagan

government and gave it limited powers. Because the Constitution is a compact among the states, the national government is an agent of the states.

17. Bureaucrats have the expertise to identify problems, suggest solutions, and follow the implementation of those solutions.

18. Roosevelt supported the expansion of the national government's powers. Reagan believed in returning power to state and local governments.

Government ONLINE Self-Check Quiz
Visit glencoe.com and enter QuickPass™ code USG9822c4.
Click on Self-Check Quizzes for additional test practice.

CHAPTER
4
Assessment
and Activities

Document-Based Questions

Analyzing Primary Sources

Read the excerpt below and answer the questions that follow.

In 1964 Lyndon B. Johnson declared his desire to create a Great Society that would use the nation's wealth to meet the needs of all of its people:

❝ *The Great Society rests on abundance and liberty for all. It demands an end to poverty and racial injustice, to which we are totally committed in our time. But that is just the beginning. . . .*

So I want to talk to you today about three places where we begin to build the Great Society—in our cities, in our countryside, and in our classrooms. . . .

The catalog of ills is long: there is the decay of the centers and the despoiling of the suburbs. There is not enough housing for our people or transportation for our traffic. . . . But I do promise this: We are going to assemble the best thought and the broadest knowledge from all over the world to find those answers for America. I intend to establish working groups to prepare a series of White House conferences and meetings—on the cities, on natural beauty, on the quality of education, and on other emerging challenges. And from these meetings . . . we will begin to set our course toward the Great Society. ❞

—President Lyndon B. Johnson, May 1964
at the University of Michigan

19. Based on this excerpt, did President Johnson interpret the Constitution's "necessary and proper" clause loosely or strictly?

20. Do you believe Johnson was acting within his power to enact a program like the Great Society? Explain.

Interpreting Political Cartoons

Analyze the cartoon and answer the questions that follow. Base your answers on the cartoon and your knowledge of Chapter 4.

"Look, the American people don't want to be bossed around by federal bureaucrats. They want to be bossed around by state bureaucrats."

21. How does this cartoon demonstrate the states' rights position of federalism?

22. How are the American people "bossed around" by federal bureaucrats?

23. Is the speaker probably a state or federal official? Why?

𝒫*articipating* IN GOVERNMENT

24. Congress has the power to add new states to the Union. Find out how and when your state was first settled, developed government, and was admitted to the Union. Use research materials from your school or local library and present your findings in an illustrated report. Create a time line that includes important governmental developments.

Government ONLINE

Have students use the **Chapter 4 Self-Check Quiz.** Visit glencoe.com and enter **QuickPass**™ code USG9085c4T to prepare for the Chapter Test.

Interpreting Political Cartoons

21. It states that the American people prefer state and local action in dealing with problems.

22. Americans must follow the rules and regulations set and enforced by federal, state, and local bureaucrats.

23. He is probably a state official. The speaker implies that Americans prefer state rules and regulations or state governments that are closer to the people than the federal government.

𝒫*articipating* IN GOVERNMENT

24. Answers will vary. Have students present their reports and time lines to the class.

Chapter Bonus Test Question

Ask: According to the Constitution, a state can split into two states only with the consent of which two parts of the government? *(the state legislature and Congress)*

Analyzing Primary Sources

19. Students might answer that Johnson was taking a loose interpretation of the necessary and proper clause. The clause was primarily aimed at Congress, because at the time a constitutional government was established, the executive and judicial branches of the government did not have as much power as they do today. Today, the necessary and proper clause can be applied to all branches of government.

20. Answers will vary, but students should know the difference between a states' rights interpretation of the Constitution and a nationalist interpretation and should also be able to discuss whether enacting the Great Society programs was an expressed, inherent, or implied power of the executive branch. They might also discuss which branch of government they believe was most appropriate to introduce such an agenda—the executive, legislative, or judicial branch.

The Legislative Branch

	UNIT PACING CHART*		
	Chapter 5	**Chapter 6**	**Chapter 7**
Day 1	Unit Opener Chapter Opener Section 1	Chapter Opener Section 1	Chapter Opener Section 1
Day 2	Supreme Court Cases to Debate Section 2	Supreme Court Cases to Debate	Section 2 Supreme Court Cases to Debate
Day 3	Section 3 Section 4	Section 2	Section 3 Issues to Debate
Day 4	Section 5 Issues to Debate TIME Notebook	Section 3 Issues to Debate	Section 4 Progress of Democracy
Day 5	Review Chapter Assessment	Review Chapter Assessment	Review Chapter Assessment

*Unit Pacing Chart based on year-long course; modify pacing by half for semester-long course

 Teacher *to* Teacher

Alisa Nazelli

**Lakewood
School District
Lakewood, OH**

Passing a Bill Give students a copy of a bill such as one creating a national park. After students have looked over the bill, assign them roles. One student will act as president. A group of students will act as a congressional committee. Two other groups will be lobbyists—one group in favor of the bill and the other against it.

A representative of the lobby supporting the bill will identify a member of Congress to introduce the bill. Members of the congressional committee will then debate the bill and decide on a course of action, either sending it to a floor vote or killing it in committee. If the bill passes the committee and floor votes, the president may either sign or veto the bill.

Have students discuss the results of the activity. Did the lobbyists sway their opinions? How much debate went on concerning this bill? Did anyone try to stop the bill? On what basis did committee members and the president make their decisions?

Author Note

Dear U.S. Government Teacher,

In Unit 2, your students will be focusing on the U.S. Congress—its organization, its powers and relations with the executive branch, and finally, in Chapter 7, the "ins and outs" of how Congresspersons work to pass bills and serve their constituents.

You might say that this unit is the core of a course on government; your students' representatives are the engine of government! Yes, the executive branch has gained power in modern times, and yes, a president's administration promotes policies and a legislative agenda. But Congress must pass the laws; Congress must balance competing interests so that a law is fair and represents the public interest; and Congress must investigate wrongdoing, scandal, and new social problems that emerge. These are not mere abstractions but are actual problems reflected in the nightly news reports. Is the American automobile industry in trouble? Are environmentalists fighting with Western ranchers over the preservation of an animal habitat? Are products toxic to children being imported? Any and all of these problems might come to the attention of a member of Congress. And if they do, the subject will be vetted in a House or Senate committee where interested citizens and lobbyists can weigh in.

Immersing your students in the legislative process is one of the best things you can do for them as future citizens. They will then be able to understand how democracy works from the grass roots right up to the halls of Congress. They will be prepared to participate in numerous ways when their own interests are at stake.

Richard C. Remy

Richard C. Remy, Ph.D.
Author

Focus

Making It Relevant

Who Makes the Laws? Have students imagine a large country that is a direct democracy—that is, all matters are decided directly by a ballot of all eligible voters. Discuss the problems involved in enacting a piece of legislation under such a system.

Unit Objectives

After studying this unit, students will be able to:

- **Describe** the organizational structure, support systems, and leadership systems of Congress.

- **Discuss** the powers of Congress and the relationship between Congress and the executive branch.

- **Analyze** the lawmaking process, the factors involved in the passage of legislation, and the interaction between members of Congress and their constituents.

Unit Overview

Unit 2 provides a basic introduction to the legislative branch.

Chapter 5 discusses how members are elected to Congress and how the House and Senate are organized.

Chapter 6 discusses the history of the U.S. Congress and its present-day powers.

Chapter 7 describes how Congress goes about its daily business.

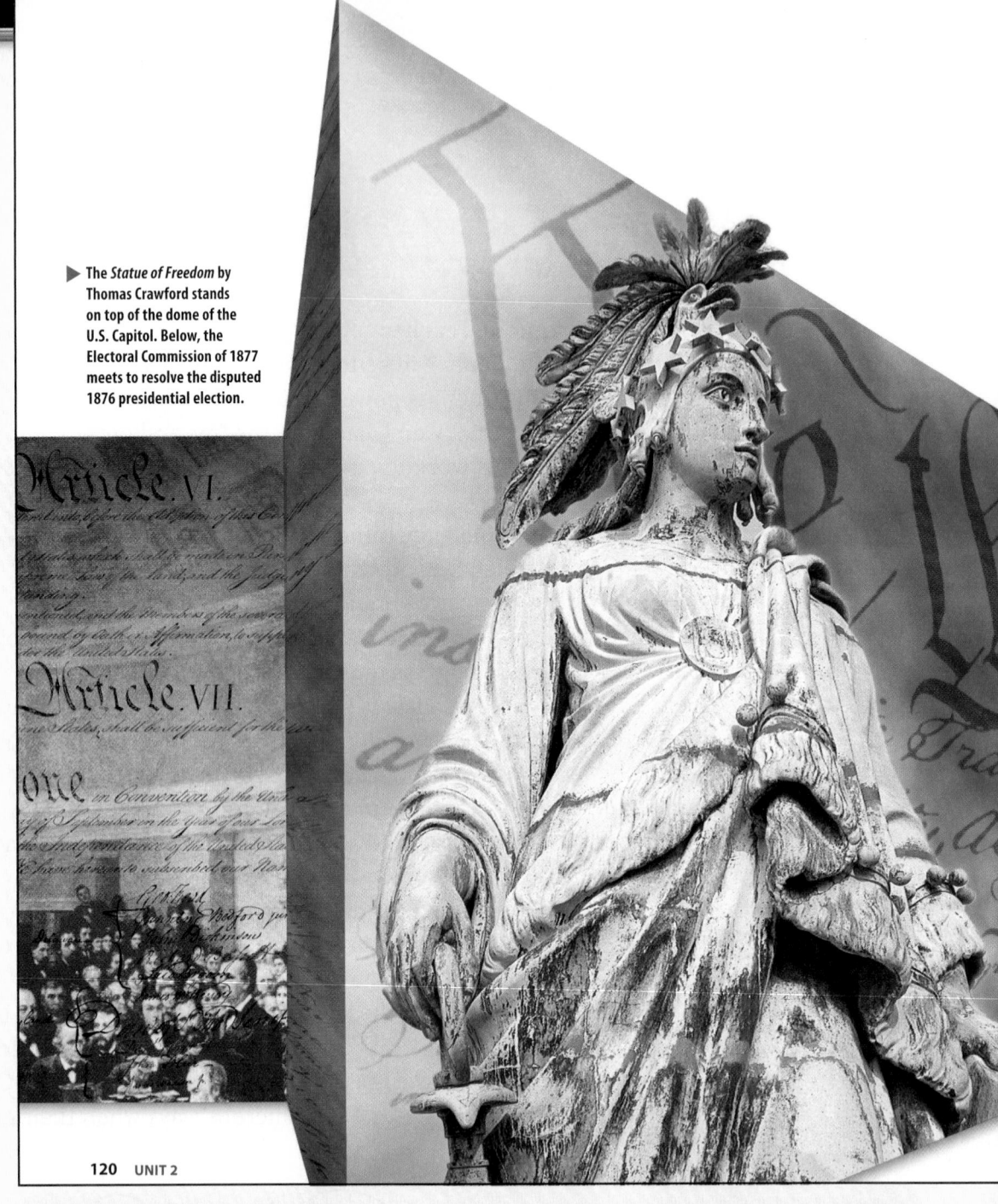

► The *Statue of Freedom* by Thomas Crawford stands on top of the dome of the U.S. Capitol. Below, the Electoral Commission of 1877 meets to resolve the disputed 1876 presidential election.

120   UNIT 2

Activity: Launching the Unit

Analyzing Congressional Memoirs Many former members of Congress have published their memoirs. Have students locate and read a congressional memoir such as *Balance of Power: Presidents and Congress From the Era of McCarthy to the Age of Gingrich,* by former Speaker of the House Jim Wright (Atlanta: Turner Publishing, 1996), which focuses on the often-stormy relationship between Congress and nine presidents of the recent past. Have students write a brief report on the books they read, sharing the authors' insights into the life of a member of Congress and offering their own thoughts about the effectiveness of the writing. **OL**

The Legislative Branch

Participating IN GOVERNMENT

BIG IDEA **Political Processes** How well does your member of Congress represent your interests? Find your representative at www.house.gov. Then search for bills passed that relate to an issue that interests you. Search for "energy" at http://thomas.loc.gov to learn about bills on this issue. Use the bill number at your representative's site to see how he or she voted. Poll student opinions on the bill and e-mail your representative about the results.

▲ Henry Clay proposes the Compromise of 1850 to the U.S. Senate

121

Teach

S Skill Practice

Visual Literacy Give students a few minutes to examine the statue on page 120. **Ask:** What do you think was the sculptor's intent in designing the head-dress on the Statue of Freedom at the far right? *(Students might suggest that the feathered head-dress is a reference to Native American culture.)*

Online Current Events Update

History happens every day. Visit Glencoe's Online Current Events Update at glencoe.com to find news reports, features, maps, graphs, and images about events that shape our lives. Students can connect those events to historical events in world and American history by exploring related events on an interactive time line—a time line that ends with today.

Graduation: Exit With Success

Teaching Tip Wherever possible, give students the opportunity to use Internet search engines and electronic databases to extend their learning on topics about which they are especially interested and to make interdisciplinary connections between United States Government and other subject areas.

Extra Credit Project

Passing Legislation Have students read the chapter on how a bill becomes a law. Have students create visuals illustrating each step of the process. Then have them write an essay explaining why each step in the process exists.

Students should also come up with suggestions to change the lawmaking process, and explain why their changes should be made. If students can formulate no suggestions, ask them if the current system is perfect as-is. **OL**

Planning Guide

Levels					Resources	Chapter Opener	Section 1	Section 2	Section 3	Section 4	Section 5	Chapter Assess
BL	OL	AL	ELL									
					FOCUS							
BL	OL	AL	ELL	🖨	Section Focus Transparencies		5-1	5-2	5-3	5-4	5-5	
					TEACH							
BL	OL		ELL	📁	Reading Essentials and Study Guide (and Answer Key)		p. 49	p. 52	p. 55	p. 57	p. 60	
BL	OL		ELL	📁	Guided Reading Activities		p. 17	p. 18	p. 19	p. 20	p. 21	
BL	OL		ELL	📁	Vocabulary Activities			p. 5				
BL	OL	AL	ELL	📁	Chapter Summaries					p. 13		
BL	OL			📁	American Biographies							
BL	OL	AL	ELL	📁	Cooperative Learning Activities				p. 3			
	OL	AL	ELL	📁	Government Simulations and Debate							
BL	OL	AL	ELL	📁	Historical Documents and Speeches		p. 5					
BL	OL	AL	ELL	📁	Interpreting Political Cartoons					p. 9		
BL	OL		ELL	📁	Skill Reinforcement Activities				p. 5			
BL	OL	AL	ELL	📁	Source Readings			p. 5				
BL	OL			📁	Supreme Court Case Studies		pp. 83, 93, 95					
BL	OL	AL	ELL	📁	Participating in Government Activities				p. 9		p.9	
BL	OL		ELL	📁	Spanish Declaration of Independence and U.S. Constitution	✓	✓	✓	✓	✓	✓	✓
BL	OL	AL	ELL	📁	NGS World Atlas, Spanish	✓	✓	✓	✓	✓	✓	✓
BL	OL	AL	ELL	🖨	Unit Overlay Transparencies, Strategies, and Activities	✓	✓	✓	✓	✓	✓	✓
BL	OL		ELL	🖨	Making It Relevant Transparencies	✓	✓	✓	✓	✓	✓	✓
BL	OL	AL	ELL	🖨	High School Writing Process Transparencies, Strategies, and Activities	✓	✓	✓	✓	✓	✓	✓
BL	OL	AL		🖨	American Art & Architecture Transparencies, Strategies, and Activities	✓	✓	✓	✓	✓	✓	✓

✓ Chapter- or unit-based activities applicable to all sections in this chapter

All-In-One Planner and Resource Center

- Interactive Lesson Planner
- Interactive Teacher Edition
- Fully editable blackline masters
- Chapter Spotlight Videos Launch
- Differentiated Lesson Plans
- Printable reports of daily assignments
- Standards tracking system

Levels BL	OL	AL	ELL		Resources	Chapter Opener	Section 1	Section 2	Section 3	Section 4	Section 5	Chapter Assess
					TEACH (continued)							
BL	OL			⦿	**American Music: Hits Through History**	✓	✓	✓	✓	✓	✓	✓
BL	OL		ELL	🗀	**Reading Strategies for the Social Studies Classroom**	✓	✓	✓	✓	✓	✓	✓
			ELL	🗀	**English Language Learner Handbook**	✓	✓	✓	✓	✓	✓	✓
BL	OL		ELL	🗀	**Writer's Guidebook for Social Studies**	✓	✓	✓	✓	✓	✓	✓
BL	OL	AL	ELL	🗀	**Living Constitution, SE**	✓	✓	✓	✓	✓	✓	✓
BL	OL	AL	ELL	🗀	**Living Constitution, TAE**	✓	✓	✓	✓	✓	✓	✓
BL	OL			🗀	**NGS World Atlas, English**	✓	✓	✓		✓	✓	✓
BL	OL		ELL	🗀	**The Constitution and You (poster set)**	✓	✓	✓	✓	✓	✓	✓
BL	OL	AL	ELL	🗀	**Spanish Chapter Summaries**					p. 13		
BL	OL	AL	ELL	🗀	**Spanish Vocabulary Activities**			p. 5				
BL	OL		ELL	🗀	**Spanish Reading Essentials and Study Guide (and Answer Key)**		p. 49	p. 52	p. 55	p. 57	p. 60	
BL	OL	AL	ELL	⦿	**PresentationPlus! with MindJogger CheckPoint**	✓	✓	✓	✓	✓	✓	✓
					ASSESS							
BL	OL	AL	ELL	⦿	*ExamView® Assessment Suite*		5-1	5-2	5-3	5-4	5-5	Ch. 5
BL	OL	AL	ELL	🗀	**Authentic Assessment with Rubrics**			p. 12				p. 12
BL	OL	AL	ELL	🗀	**Section Quizzes and Chapter Tests**		p. 51	p. 52	p. 53	p. 54	p. 55	pp. 57–64
BL	OL	AL	ELL	🗀	**Spanish Section Quizzes and Tests**		p. 51	p. 52	p. 53	p. 54	p. 55	pp. 57–64
					CLOSE							
BL			ELL	🗀	**Reteaching Activities**		p. 5			p. 5		p. 5
BL	OL	AL	ELL	⦿	**StudentWorks™ Plus with Audio Summaries**	✓	✓	✓	✓	✓	✓	✓
BL	OL		ELL	✋	**Graphic Organizer Transparencies**		✓	✓	✓	✓		
BL	OL		ELL	🗀	**High School Government Reading and Study Skills Foldables®**		p. 48	p. 48	p. 48	p. 48	p. 48	

CHAPTER 5

Integrating Technology

Teach With Technology

What is StudentWorks™ Plus Online?

StudentWorks™ Plus Online is a powerful learning and teaching tool that offers the entire textbook online in an interactive, searchable format. It provides links to student workbooks, audio recordings of the textbook, audio summaries in Spanish, In Motion animations, and links to Section Spotlight Videos.

How can StudentWorks™ Plus Online help my students and me?

StudentWorks™ Plus Online helps students learn and master the material in the textbook. Students can go to a specific chapter and read the text, listen to audio of the text, and type and print their answers on workbook pages. While reading about a topic, students can quickly search the entire text and the glossary for a key term. You can project StudentWorks™ Plus Online during a classroom lecture and launch Section Spotlight Videos directly.

Visit glencoe.com and enter a *QuickPass*™ code to go to StudentWorks™ Plus Online.

Government ONLINE

Visit glencoe.com and enter *QuickPass*™ code USG9085c5T for Chapter 5 resources.

You can easily launch a wide range of digital products from your computer's desktop with the McGraw-Hill Social Studies widget.

	Student	Teacher	Parent
Media Library			
• Student Edition Section Audio	●		●
• Chapter Spotlight Videos	●	●	●
***United States Government* Online Learning Center (Web Site)**			
• Chapter Overviews	●	●	●
• Multilingual Glossaries	●	●	●
• Study-to-Go	●	●	●
• Student Web Activities	●	●	●
• Self-Check Quizzes	●	●	●
• Online Student Edition	●	●	●
• Vocabulary eFlashcards	●	●	●
• Web Activity Lesson Plans		●	
• Vocabulary PuzzleMaker	●	●	●
• Landmark Supreme Court Cases	●	●	●
• Beyond the Textbook	●	●	●

READING SUPPORT FROM JAMESTOWN EDUCATION

- **Timed Readings Plus in Social Studies** helps students increase their reading rate and fluency while maintaining comprehension. The 400-word passages are similar to those found on state and national assessments.

- **Reading in the Content Area: Social Studies** concentrates on six essential reading skills that help students better comprehend what they read. The book includes 75 high-interest nonfiction passages written at increasing levels of difficulty.

- **Reading Social Studies** includes strategic reading instruction and vocabulary support in Social Studies content for ELLs and native speakers of English. www.jamestowneducation.com

Reading List Generator CD-ROM

Use this database to search more than 30,000 titles to create a customized reading list for your students.

- Reading lists can be organized by students' reading level, author, genre, theme, or area of interest.

- The database provides Degrees of Reading Power™ (DRP) and Lexile™ readability scores for all selections.

- A brief summary of each selection is included.

Economics Connection

Personal Finance Literacy

Protecting Your Identity

The federal government and numerous states have passed laws to protect victims of identity theft. What is identity theft? It's the use of another person's name and personal information, such as a Social Security number, bank credit card number, or driver's license, for personal gain. Thieves use the information to buy goods, take out loans, get medical treatment or prescription drugs, access or open bank accounts or credit cards. Some even buy cars, boats, and houses with phony identities.

For victims, identity theft is like being mugged on paper. They typically lose between $1,000 and $5,000, plus extensive time spent proving to creditors that their identity was stolen and replacing cards and documents. Perhaps most serious is the damage the theft does to the victim's credit rating. This crime is often not detected for months, until the victim receives "overdue" notices for bills he or she has not incurred.

Ask students: What steps can you take to prevent someone from stealing your identity?

Ways to Guard Against Identity Theft

- Don't give your Social Security, bank account, or credit card numbers to anyone who contacts *you.*

- Carry only the identification and credit card(s) you will need that day. When you buy something, watch to see that the card is not copied and get it back as quickly as possible. Consider not using credit cards in restaurants, since the card is often out of sight for a period of time.

- Don't use links in an e-mail to get to a Web page. Type the address in your browser.

- Check your credit report regularly for charges you don't recognize.

- Report lost or stolen credit cards immediately to one of the credit reporting companies: Equifax, Experian, or TransUnion. If theft is established, file a police report and an ID Theft Complaint form with the Federal Trade Commission (available at the FTC Web site or a library).

Did You Know?

In the 12 months prior to March 2007, 15 million Americans were victims of identity theft—the nation's fastest-growing crime.

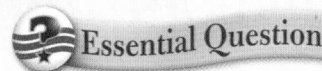

🔊 Chapter Audio   📼 Spotlight Video

The Organization *of* Congress

▸ The United States Capitol

Essential Question

Refer students to the Essential Question on this page. Ask students if they can describe the basic structure and organization of Congress. Remind students that the Constitution outlines the basis of representation in the House of Representatives and the Senate. Ask students to hypothesize how this structure helps members of Congress represent the interests of the voters. **OL**

Chapter Spotlight Video

To generate student interest and provide a springboard for class discussion, access the Chapter 5 Video at glencoe.com or on the video DVD.

FOLDABLES Study Organizer **Dinah Zike's Foldables** are three-dimensional, interactive graphic organizers that help students practice basic writing skills, review key vocabulary terms, and identify main ideas. Have students complete this chapter's Foldable activity or activities in *Dinah Zike's Reading and Study Skills Foldables* booklet. **OL**

Government ONLINE

Visit glencoe.com and enter *QuickPass*™ code USG9085c5T for Chapter 5 Resources including Chapter Overview, Student Web Activity, Self-Check Quiz, and other materials for students and teachers.

Essential Question

What is the basic structure and organization of Congress as it represents the interests of the voters?

Government ONLINE
Chapter Overview Visit glencoe.com and enter *QuickPass*™ code USG9822c5 for an overview, a quiz, and other chapter resources.

122

Launching the Chapter

Following Local Coverage of Congress
Have each student begin the chapter by watching a local 30-minute evening news program (not national or cable news) and noting any stories relating to members of Congress. During the course of the chapter, students should continue to watch the same local news and write down relevant stories. **Essential Questions:** Overall, about how much of the local coverage mentioned the work of members of Congress? How much coverage was given to the members that represent your district or state? Have students respond to these questions in a class discussion. Then ask students if they would change the coverage of Congress in the local news. Have student volunteers give their reasons. **OL**

Congressional Membership

Reader's Guide

Content Vocabulary
- ★ bicameral legislature *(p. 123)*
- ★ session *(p. 123)*
- ★ census *(p. 124)*
- ★ reapportionment *(p. 124)*
- ★ redistrict *(p. 125)*
- ★ gerrymander *(p. 126)*
- ★ at-large *(p. 127)*
- ★ censure *(p. 128)*
- ★ incumbent *(p. 129)*

Academic Vocabulary
- ★ formulate *(p. 123)*
- ★ occur *(p. 124)*
- ★ trace *(p. 126)*

Reading Strategy
As you read, complete a table like the one below to help you compare the qualifications for representatives and senators.

Qualifications	
Senator	Representative

Public Policy in the News

Congress members have certain "perks"—short for *perquisites,* or privileges. Perks have been cut back in recent years, but some remain, like the ability to use the House or Senate gym. Former members of Congress keep these perks for life. Thus, if a former congressperson becomes a lobbyist, he or she has special access to these areas and can use that access to make contacts in an effort to argue for or against a bill. In 2005 one lobbyist who is not a former Congress member said: "Why should they have any more of a privilege than I have to go into the House gym? As a matter of principle, it's wrong."

▲ Senate members, here in session, retain some of their privileges for life.

The Founders did not intend to make Congress a privileged group, but they intended to give it more power than any other branch of government. The Constitution emphasized the importance of the lawmaking branch by describing Congress in Article I. As James Madison said, Congress is "the First Branch of this Government."

The U.S. Congress is a **bicameral legislature,** meaning that it is made up of two houses—the Senate and the House of Representatives. In 1787 most delegates to the Constitutional Convention agreed that a bicameral legislature was best. These colonial legislatures were following the model of the English Parliament with its House of Lords and House of Commons.

Today, Congress plays a central role in **formulating** national policies. It initiates and approves laws that deal with everything from health care to changes in our taxes.

Congressional Sessions

Each term of Congress begins on January 3 in years ending in an odd number and lasts for two years. For example, the 109th Congress began its term in January 2005, and the 110th Congress began in January 2007. Each Congressional term is two **sessions,** or meetings. A session lasts one year and includes breaks for holidays and vacations. Until the Twentieth Amendment was ratified in 1933, Congressional sessions did not formally end until March, which left a four-month period between the election and when new members began to serve. This time delay was shortened when the session start date was moved to January.

Congress remains in session until its members vote to adjourn. Neither the House nor the Senate can adjourn for more than three days without the approval of the other house. If the Congress does

Focus

Bellringer
Section Focus Transparencies 5-1

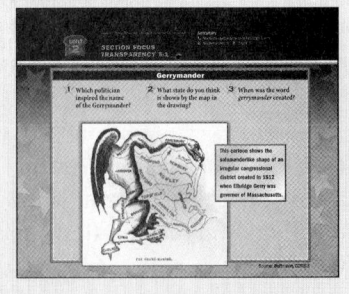

Reader's Guide

Answers to Graphic: Senator: at least 30 years old, U.S. citizen for 9 years before election, legal resident of state he or she represents; Representative: at least 25 years old, U.S. citizen for 7 years, legal resident of state he or she represents (and usually lives in the district he or she represents)

Resource Manager

R Reading Strategies	C Critical Thinking	D Differentiated Instruction	W Writing Support	S Skill Practice
Teacher Edition • Inferring, p. 124 • Summarizing, p. 125 • Analyzing Primary Sources, p. 128 **Additional Resources** • Quizzes/Tests, p. 51 • Guid. Read. Act., p. 17	**Teacher Edition** • Comparing and Contrasting, p. 127 • Identifying Central Issues, p. 127 **Additional Resources** • Read. Essen., pp. 49–51	**Teacher Edition** • Logical/Mathematical, p. 128 • Verbal/Linguistic, p. 129 **Additional Resources** • Foldables, p. 48 • Hist. Docs. and Speeches, p. 5	**Additional Resources** • Supreme Ct. Case Studies, pp. 83–84, 93–94, 95–96	**Teacher Edition** • Reading a Map, pp. 125, 126 • Visual Literacy, p. 129 **Additional Resources** • Reteaching Act., p. 5

Teach

R Reading Strategy

Inferring Ask students to read the text and then explain how population growth in the United States affects membership in the House of Representatives. **OL**

Caption Answer: The division aids the Speaker in identifying members and their parties who want to speak.

Did You Know?

What's in a Name? The Founders named the U.S. Senate after ancient Rome's highest political body. At the time, nine of the thirteen colonies named their upper bodies "senate." The House of Representatives lacked such a grand, historic origin. "House" simply refers to a legislative body or assembly of representatives. The Founders may have borrowed the name from the Virginia House of Burgesses.

Additional Support

Teacher Tip

Collaborative Learning
Because this activity is completed by groups, it offers an opportunity to team students of different skill levels. Form student teams according to needs and ability levels.

Division of the House

◄ **Past** As this photo shows, in the British House of Commons, the governing party and the opposition sit on opposite sides of the Parliament. Here William Pitt, prime minister during the Napoleonic Wars, is speaking at the left. The bewigged man in the center is the speaker, who presides over debate.

▼ **Present** British procedures have some influence on the U.S. House of Representatives. Each party sits on one side of the chamber, although they face the Speaker, who is on a raised platform at the front. *How does the physical division into political groups help the Speaker of the U.S. Congress moderate debates?*

---

adjourn, the president has the authority to call it back for a special session if necessary.

Membership of the House

With 435 members, the House of Representatives is larger than the Senate. The Constitution does not set the number of representatives in the House. It simply states that House seats must be apportioned, or divided, among the states on the basis of population. Each state is entitled to at least one seat in the House, no matter how small its population is.

Qualifications and Term of Office

The Constitution sets the qualifications for election to the House of Representatives. Representatives must be at least 25 years old, be citizens of the United States for at least 7 years, and be legal residents of the state that elects them. Traditionally, representatives also live in the district they represent.

Members of the House of Representatives are elected for two-year terms. Elections are held in November of even-numbered years—for example, 2004, 2006, and 2008. Representatives begin their term of office on January 3 following the November election. This means that every two years, all 435 members of the House must run for reelection. It also means that the House reorganizes itself every two years. Because more than 90 percent of all representatives are reelected, however, the

House has great continuity. If a representative dies or resigns in the first session of Congress, the state must hold a special election to fill that vacancy. Procedures for filling vacancies that **occur** during the second session vary from state to state.

Representation and Reapportionment

In order to assign representatives on the basis of population, the Census Bureau takes a national **census,** or population count, every 10 years. The first census was taken in 1790, and each state was apportioned its representatives. The next census will be in 2010. Each state's population determines the number of representatives it will have for the next 10 years—a process called **reapportionment.** States with slow growth or a population decrease can lose representatives, while states with strong population growth can gain seats. For example, by 2008, it was predicted that both Minnesota and Iowa would each lose a seat in the 2010 census, thus lessening Midwestern influence on farm issues.

Originally the House had only 64 members. As the population of the nation grew, the number of representatives increased. After the 1810 census, the House had 186 members. By 1911, the House had 435 members. In 1929 Congress capped the number of House members at 435. Now each census decides how these seats will be divided among the states.

Activity: Collaborative Learning

Redefining Congressional Qualifications Organize students into groups of citizens who want to redefine the qualifications for membership in the House of Representatives. Have the groups review the current qualifications for membership. Then discuss which qualifications they want to keep, revise, or delete, and which new ones they might add and why. Each

group should make one student responsible to lead the discussion and one to be the group's reporter. Ask group reporters to present the groups' revised lists of qualifications and explain the reasons for the changes. After all groups have presented, try to achieve a class consensus on qualifications for membership in the House of Representatives. **OL AL**

Congressional Redistricting

After the states find out their new representation for the next 10 years, each state legislature draws the boundaries for the congressional districts—one for each representative. Representatives are elected from these districts. If a state is entitled to only one representative, it has one congressional district. The process of setting up new district lines after reapportionment has been completed is called **redistricting.**

In 2006 the Supreme Court decided a case that allowed states to modify this time-honored procedure. In *League of United Latin American Citizens, et al* v. *Perry,* the Court ruled that state legislators may redraw congressional districts in the middle of a decade rather than only after a U.S. census.

Over the years, some state legislatures abused the redistricting power. They did so in two ways— by creating congressional districts of very unequal populations or by gerrymandering. During the early 1960s, for example, there were some states in which the largest district in the state had twice the population of the smallest district.

Redistricting Cases

In a series of decisions in the 1960s, the Supreme Court ruled on reapportionment issues in three different states: Tennessee, Georgia, and Alabama. In a 1962 Tennessee case, *Baker* v. *Carr,*[1] the Court held that federal courts could decide conflicts over drawing district boundaries.

See the following footnoted materials in the **Reference Handbook:**
1. *Baker* v. *Carr* case summary, page R23.

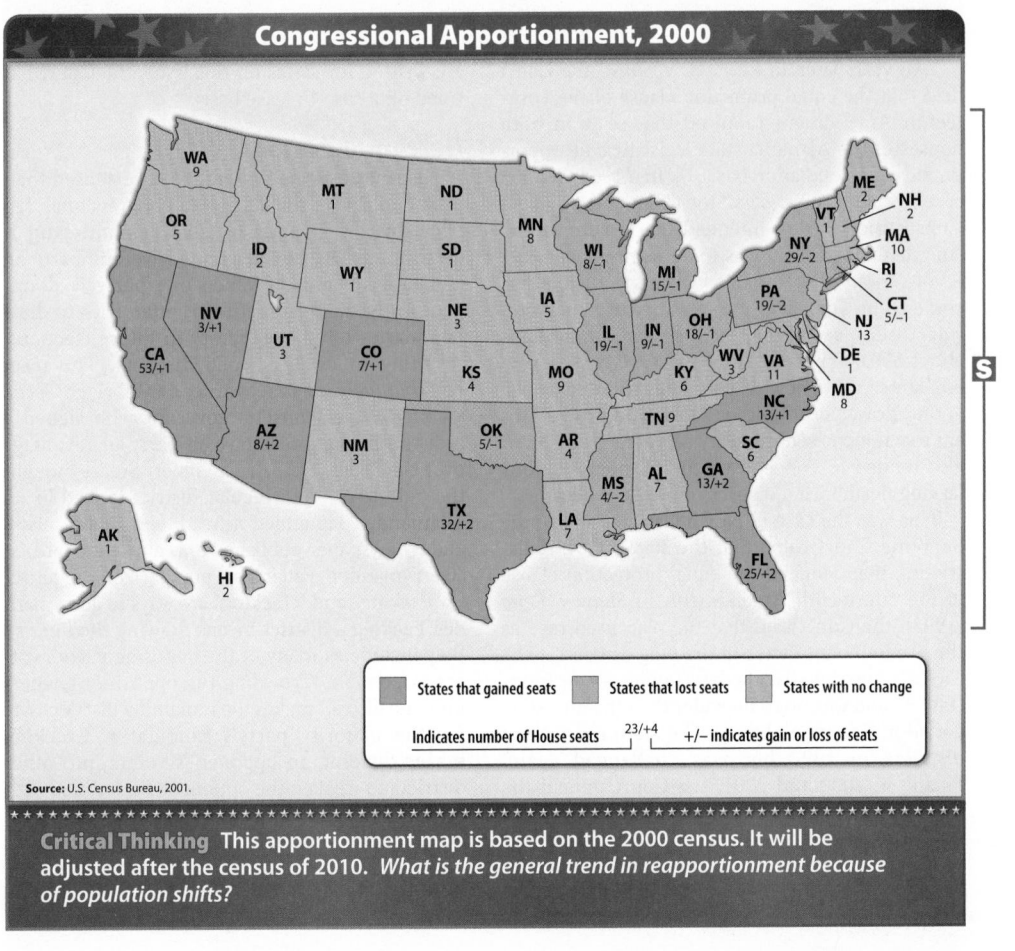

Congressional Apportionment, 2000

WA 9	MT 1	ND 1	MN 8			ME 2
OR 5	ID 2	SD 1	WI 8/–1	MI 15/–1	NY 29/–2	NH 2
	WY 1	NE 3	IA 5		PA 19/–2	VT 1 MA 10

NV 3/+1 · CA 53/+1 · UT 3 · CO 7/+1 · KS 4 · MO 9 · IL 19/–1 · IN 9/–1 · OH 18/–1 · KY 6 · WV 3 · VA 11 · RI 2 · CT 5/–1 · NJ 13 · DE 1 · MD 8

AZ 8/+2 · NM 3 · OK 5/–1 · AR 4 · TN 9 · NC 13/+1 · SC 6

TX 32/+2 · LA 7 · MS 4/–2 · AL 7 · GA 13/+2

AK 1 · HI 2 · FL 25/+2

Legend:
States that gained seats · States that lost seats · States with no change
Indicates number of House seats — 23/+4 — +/– indicates gain or loss of seats

Source: U.S. Census Bureau, 2001.

Critical Thinking This apportionment map is based on the 2000 census. It will be adjusted after the census of 2010. *What is the general trend in reapportionment because of population shifts?*

R Reading Strategy

Summarizing Have students read the text and then describe congressional redistricting in their own words. **BL**

S Skill Practice

Reading a Map Ask: Which areas of the country are experiencing population growth? *(the Southeast and Southwest)* **Ask:** What is the general population trend of the Great Lakes states? *(The population is decreasing.)* **OL**

Critical Thinking

Answer: The Southeast and the Southwest gained seats while the Midwest lost seats.

Landmark Case

See *Baker* v. *Carr* in the Supreme Court Case Summaries in the **Reference Handbook** and Case Study 42 in the *Supreme Court Case Studies* booklet.

Hands-On Chapter Project
Step 1

Mock Senate

Step 1: Identifying Bills Organize students into four groups. Each group will conduct research to determine the topic for a bill they will write to introduce on the Senate floor. The bills should focus on issues that affect young people or families, or on other issues to which students can relate.

Directions Begin by having each group research bill ideas by searching for legislation before the current Congress at the Web site of the Library of Congress, thomas.loc.gov. After each group has determined the topic of its bill, they should research the issue they have selected: its history, facts, existing controversies, and the people most affected (senior citizens, teens, criminals, etc.). Remind students to consider the powers given to Congress as they propose solutions. **AL**

(Chapter Project continued in Section 2.)

S Skill Practice

Reading a Map Have students study the map on this page. **Ask:** How can you tell that some gerrymandering might have occurred? (*Most of the districts are compact and fairly uniform in shape. However, the 1st and 12th districts have irregular shapes, suggesting that their boundaries might have been drawn to take in certain residents and omit others.*) **OL** **AL**

Critical Thinking

Answer: The Supreme Court holds that the equal protection clause of the Fourteenth Amendment requires seats to be apportioned based on population.

🏛 Landmark Case

See *Reynolds* v. *Sims* and *Wesberry* v. *Sanders* in the Supreme Court Case Summaries in the **Reference Handbook** and Case Studies 47 and 48 in the *Supreme Court Case Studies* booklet.

Additional Support

North Carolina Congressional Districts, 2002

The 12th District

The 1st and 12th districts have been redrawn several times because of legal challenges that these districts artificially increase African American representation.

Source: North Carolina General Assembly Web site, www.ncleg.net

Critical Thinking Which group has the final authority to determine whether legislative districts are constitutional?

Two years later, in *Reynolds* v. *Sims*,[1] the Court held that the equal protection clause of the Fourteenth Amendment required that seats in both houses of the Alabama state legislature be apportioned on a population basis. 📖 In a 1964 Georgia case, *Wesberry* v. *Sanders*,[2] the Court ruled that the Constitution clearly intended that a vote in one congressional district was to be worth as much as a vote in another district. 📖 This principle has come to be known as the "one-person, one-vote" rule. Today, each congressional district contains about 650,000 people. After the 1990 census, several states drew new district lines to increase the voting power of ethnic or racial minorities. This approach increased minority representation, but it also tended to concentrate the Democratic vote, leaving neighboring districts more Republican.

This was the case in North Carolina where the Supreme Court ruled that the state's 1992 redistricting map violated the equal protection clause of the Fourteenth Amendment. In *Shaw* v. *Reno* (1993), the Court said that the plan used race as the predominant factor in drawing districts. (The Twelfth District stretched 160 miles along Interstate 85 and was often no wider than the interstate corridor. See map above.) The state redrew the districts in 1997 but was challenged again. Finally in 2000 and 2001, the Court upheld the new redistricting plan. Because no clear guidelines

📖 *See the following footnoted materials in the* **Reference Handbook:**
1. *Reynolds* v. *Sims* case summary, page R33.
2. *Wesberry* v. *Sanders* case summary, page R36.

are written for states on this issue, the Court has ruled on a case-by-case basis.

Gerrymandering

Historically, state legislatures have abused their power to divide the state into congressional districts by gerrymandering. **Gerrymandering** is drawing district boundaries to give one party an electoral advantage. When one party is dominant in the state legislature, it often tries to draw boundaries to ensure victory in future elections, resulting in oddly shaped districts. The term *gerrymandering* has been **traced** to Elbridge Gerry, an early Massachusetts governor who signed a redistricting plan that gave his party an advantage over the Federalists. Artist Gilbert Stuart thought the outline of one irregular district looked like a salamander. He added a head, wings, and claws and a newspaper published it as a cartoon labeled "Gerrymander." Federalists popularized the term.

"Packing" and "cracking" are ways to gerrymander. Packing a district means drawing the lines so they include as many of the opposing party's voters as possible. Crowding the opposition's voters into one district makes the remaining districts safe for the majority party's candidates. Cracking means dividing an opponent's voters into other districts to weaken the opponent's voter base.

The Supreme Court has ruled that congressional districts must be compact and contiguous, or physically adjoining. This requirement, plus the one-person, one-vote ruling, has cut down on some of the worst examples of gerrymandering.

126 UNIT 2: *The Legislative Branch*

Activity: Collaborative Learning

Setting Boundary Lines Remind students that state legislatures have the power to set the boundary lines for congressional districts—and that, in the past, state legislatures sometimes have abused this power. **Ask:** How would anyone know if a state legislature was abusing this power? Organize students into small groups, and have them respond by preparing a list of questions that would help

make that determination. Tell students that questions might include the following: *How many representatives does the state have based on the latest census? How do the districts compare in population? What do each district's boundaries look like?* As you call on groups to present their questions to the class, note the questions that appear on the lists most often. **OL** **AL**

Nevertheless, the competitive struggle of the two-party system continues to fuel the practice of gerrymandering. Many districts today are still drawn in irregular shapes for political reasons.

Membership of the Senate

According to the Constitution, the Senate "shall be composed of two senators from each state." Thus, each state is represented equally. Today's Senate includes 100 members—2 from each of the 50 states.

Qualifications and Term of Office

The Constitution provides that senators must be at least 30 years old, citizens of the United States for 9 years before election, and legal residents of the state they represent. All voters of each state elect senators **at-large,** or statewide—they have no particular district.

Like those of the House, Senate elections are held in November during even-numbered years. Senators, too, begin their terms on January 3 after the election of the previous November. The Constitution provided for Senate continuity by giving senators six-year terms and providing that only one-third of the senators run for reelection every two years. In fact, the Senate has more continuity than the Framers planned because most senators win reelection.

If a senator dies or resigns before the end of the term, the state legislature can authorize the governor to appoint a person to fill the vacancy until the next election. The governor can choose instead to call a special election to fill the seat.

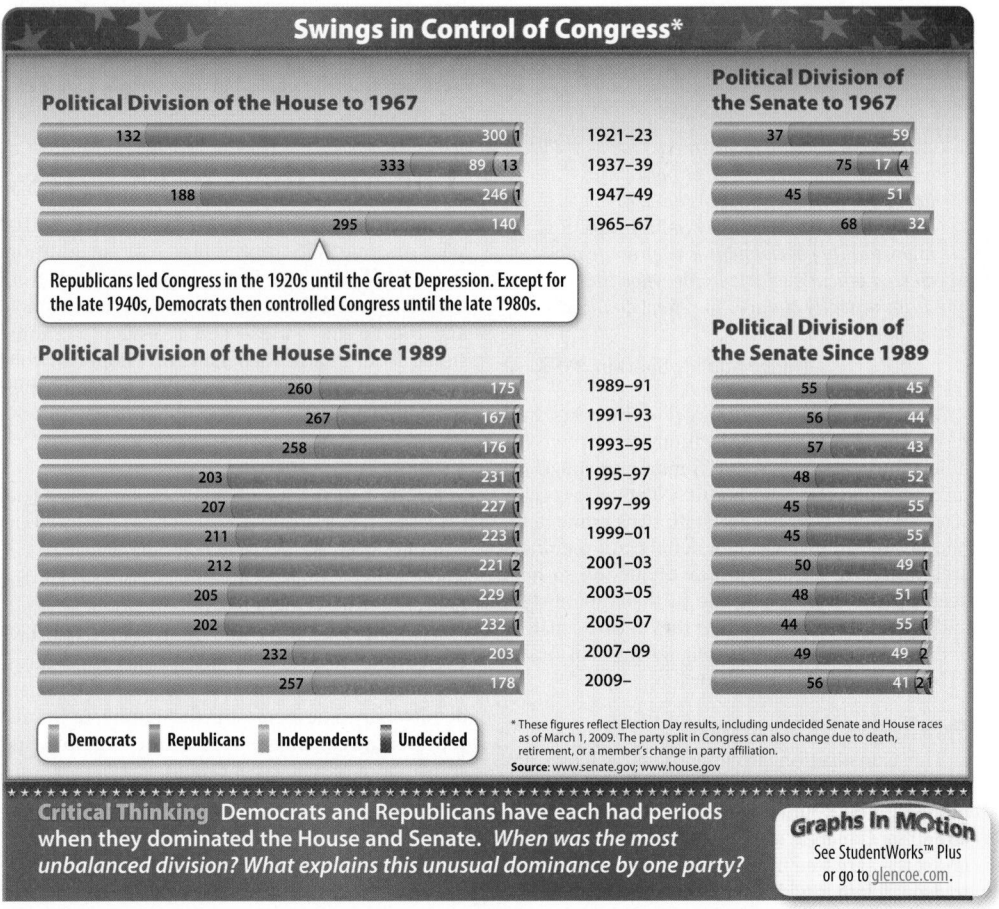

Swings in Control of Congress*

Political Division of the House to 1967

Year	Democrats	Republicans
1921–23	132	300
1937–39	333	89 13
1947–49	188	246
1965–67	295	140

Republicans led Congress in the 1920s until the Great Depression. Except for the late 1940s, Democrats then controlled Congress until the late 1980s.

Political Division of the House Since 1989

Year	Democrats	Republicans
1989–91	260	175
1991–93	267	167
1993–95	258	176
1995–97	203	231
1997–99	207	227
1999–01	211	223
2001–03	212	221 2
2003–05	205	229
2005–07	202	232
2007–09	232	203
2009–	257	178

Political Division of the Senate to 1967

Year	Democrats	Republicans
1921–23	37	59
1937–39	75	17 4
1947–49	45	51
1965–67	68	32

Political Division of the Senate Since 1989

Year	Democrats	Republicans
1989–91	55	45
1991–93	56	44
1993–95	57	43
1995–97	48	52
1997–99	45	55
1999–01	45	55
2001–03	50	49 1
2003–05	48	51 1
2005–07	44	55 1
2007–09	49	49 2
2009–	56	41 2 1

Democrats **Republicans** **Independents** **Undecided**

* These figures reflect Election Day results, including undecided Senate and House races as of March 1, 2009. The party split in Congress can also change due to death, retirement, or a member's change in party affiliation.
Source: www.senate.gov; www.house.gov

Critical Thinking Democrats and Republicans have each had periods when they dominated the House and Senate. *When was the most unbalanced division? What explains this unusual dominance by one party?*

Graphs In MOtion
See StudentWorks™ Plus
or go to glencoe.com.

C₁ Critical Thinking

Comparing and Contrasting
Ask: How does the composition of the Senate differ from that of the House? *(The Constitution states that the Senate will have two senators from each state and that House seats must be apportioned among the states based on population.)* **OL**

C₂ Critical Thinking

Identifying Central Issues
Explain that members in both houses of Congress can serve for an unlimited number of terms and that the issue of term limits has been debated since the founding of the nation. Then organize students into two teams—one in favor of term limits and the other against them—and have the teams debate the issue. Ask listeners to note the key points in each side's argument for follow-up discussion. **OL**

Critical Thinking

Answer: 1937–1939; due to support of the Democratic president during the troubled times of the Great Depression

Additional Support

Activity: Interdisciplinary Connection

Geography Demographics are a factor in congressional elections. For example, students might read that a candidate for the Senate has a high approval rating among inner-city families or that an incumbent's appeal to older voters has slipped. Have students complete one of the following demographic activities and share the results.

• Using newspapers, newsmagazines, and the Internet, find statements in which a candidate's chances are evaluated on the basis of demographics.

• Make a list of demographic groups in your community that probably exercise influence at election time and another list of groups that you think should have more influence. **AL**

R **Reading Strategy**

Analyzing Primary Sources
Have students read the statement
from Judge Stanley Sporkin. **Ask:**
Why do you think Judge Sporkin
ruled that the Twenty-seventh
Amendment allows for salary
increases to match the cost of
living? *(The Twenty-seventh
Amendment prohibits any law
varying the compensation for the
services of legislators. It does not
mention cost-of-living
increases.)* **OL**

D **Differentiated
Instruction**

Logical/Mathematical Ask
students to use the data provided
about female representatives in
the House to create a line graph
or a bar graph. After students
have completed their graphs, **ask:**
By how much did the number of
women in the House increase
between 1957 and 2009? *(There
were 61 more women in 2009 than
there were in 1957.)* **BL ELL**

**Additional
Support**

Salary and Benefits

The Senate and the House set their own salaries. In 1789 salaries were $6 per day. This low pay
deterred some people from running for Congress.
Congress has voted itself periodic salary increases.
In 1991 it voted for a pay hike of $23,000, but it
also included a provision that prohibited hono-
raria—money paid for speeches.

Meanwhile, a constitutional amendment on salaries for legislators was being considered. Originally
proposed by James Madison in 1789, the Twenty-
seventh Amendment was finally ratified by the
required 38 states on May 7, 1992. The amendment
says that Congress cannot give itself a pay raise; the
raise becomes effective only after another election.

With the new amendment on the books, a group
of plaintiffs then challenged the cost-of-living
increases in salary that Congress members regularly received. These plaintiffs argued that even a
cost-of-living increase was prohibited by the new
amendment. A U.S. district court judge, however,
ruled that salary increases to match the cost of living were allowed:

> **R** 66 *Automatic annual adjustments to
> congressional salaries meet both the
> language and the spirit of the 27th
> Amendment. . . . One way to maintain
> high-quality government is to provide our
> elected officials with a living wage that
> automatically changes to reflect changed
> economic conditions.* 99
>
> —Judge Stanley Sporkin, 1992

Members enjoy a number of benefits and
resources. These include stationery, postage for
official business (called the "franking privilege"), a
medical clinic, and a gymnasium. They also receive
large allowances to pay for staff, trips home, telephones, telegrams, and newsletters. All members
are entitled to an income tax deduction to help
keep up two residences, one in their home state
and one in the capital. When they retire, senators
and representatives may be eligible for pensions of
$150,000 or more per year for life.

Privileges of Members

The Constitution provides members of Congress with certain protections so they can carry
out their public duties. For example, when they are
attending Congress or on the way to or from Congress, they are free from arrest "in all cases except
treason, felony, and breach of the peace."

Members also cannot be sued for anything they
say on the House or Senate floor. This privilege
does not cover what members say outside of Congress, however. This fact was established in a 1979
court case when the Court ruled that members of
Congress can be sued for libel for statements in
news releases or newsletters.

Another privilege of members of Congress is
that both the Senate and the House may judge the
qualifications of new members and decide whether
to seat them. Each house may refuse to seat an
elected member by a majority vote. This power of
exclusion was later defined in the Supreme Court
case, *Powell* v. *McCormack.* (See the Supreme
Court Case to Debate on page 131.)

Finally each house may punish its own members for disorderly behavior by a majority vote and
expel a legislator by a two-thirds vote. Only the
most serious offenses, such as treason or accepting bribes, are grounds for expulsion. Members
who are guilty of lesser offenses may be censured.
Censure is a vote of formal disapproval of a member's actions.

The Members of Congress

Congress includes 535 voting members—100
senators and 435 representatives. In addition,
there are 4 delegates in the House—1 each from
the District of Columbia, Guam, American Samoa,
and the Virgin Islands—and 1 resident commissioner from Puerto Rico, none of whom can vote.
However, they do attend sessions, introduce bills,
speak in debates, and vote in committees.

Characteristics

Nearly half the members of Congress are lawyers. Lawyers are well prepared to understand the
complex legal issues that may affect legislation.
Many other Congress members come from the
fields of business, banking, or education.

Typically, senators and representatives have
been white, middle-aged males. Slowly Congress
has begun to reflect more racial, ethnic, and gender diversity. The increase in the number of women
representatives in the House, for example, has
come about only in recent times:

- 1957–1959: 15 women (3 percent)
- 1987–1989: 24 women (5.5 percent)
- 1997–1999: 57 women (13 percent)
- 2007–2009: 76 women (17 percent)

Extending the Content

Drawing Conclusions At one time,
a citizen could have been represented by
more than one House representative.
Some states had multimember districts,
making it possible to have more than
one representative. The number of representatives allotted to states remained the
same whether they had single or multimember districts, but voters in multimember districts elected two or more

representatives instead of just one. Congress banned this practice in 1842. In the
mid-1990s, though, the concept was
debated again as a means to increase the
voting power of African Americans and
other minorities. **Ask:** Do you agree with
the policy of multiple representation?
Why or why not? *(Students' opinions
will vary but should be supported.)* Have
students research the arguments in favor

of and the arguments against multimember districts (also known as proportional representation). Ask students to
share their findings in a class discussion.

Reelection to Congress

Membership in Congress tends to change slowly because officeholders seldom lose reelection. One representative put it simply: "All members of Congress have one primary interest—to be reelected." Since Franklin Roosevelt's landslide presidential victories in the 1930s, incumbency helped Democrats dominate Congress in all but a few years until 1990.

Between 1945 and 1990, about 90 percent of all **incumbents,** members who were already in office, won reelection. In some elections, many seats went unchallenged because opponents knew that they would have little or no chance of winning. One analyst said that winning an election to Congress for most members was like removing olives from a bottle—"after the first one, the rest come easy."

Incumbents are reelected in part because they can raise campaign funds more easily through personal contacts they made while representing their district. Second, many districts have been gerrymandered in the incumbent party's favor. Third, incumbents are better known to voters, who see them on television and read about them regularly in news stories. Fourth, incumbents use their position to solve the problems of voters, who are then grateful. Finally, incumbents may simply win because most voters believe they best represent their views.

Campaigning Online

While TV and radio remain the dominant campaign technologies, the Internet is being used more and more to win office. Challengers for open seats and incumbents in very competitive races use the Web the most. Nearly all candidates now have election Web sites that serve as electronic brochures. A typical site offers a biography of a candidate, press releases, upcoming campaign events, and positions on hot issues. Web sites are also used to recruit volunteers and raise campaign funds. A few candidates have used their Web sites to broadcast, in real time, campaign events such as speeches.

Candidates have begun to take advantage of the interactive capacities of the Internet. A few years back, only a small percentage of people who were running for office conducted town hall-like

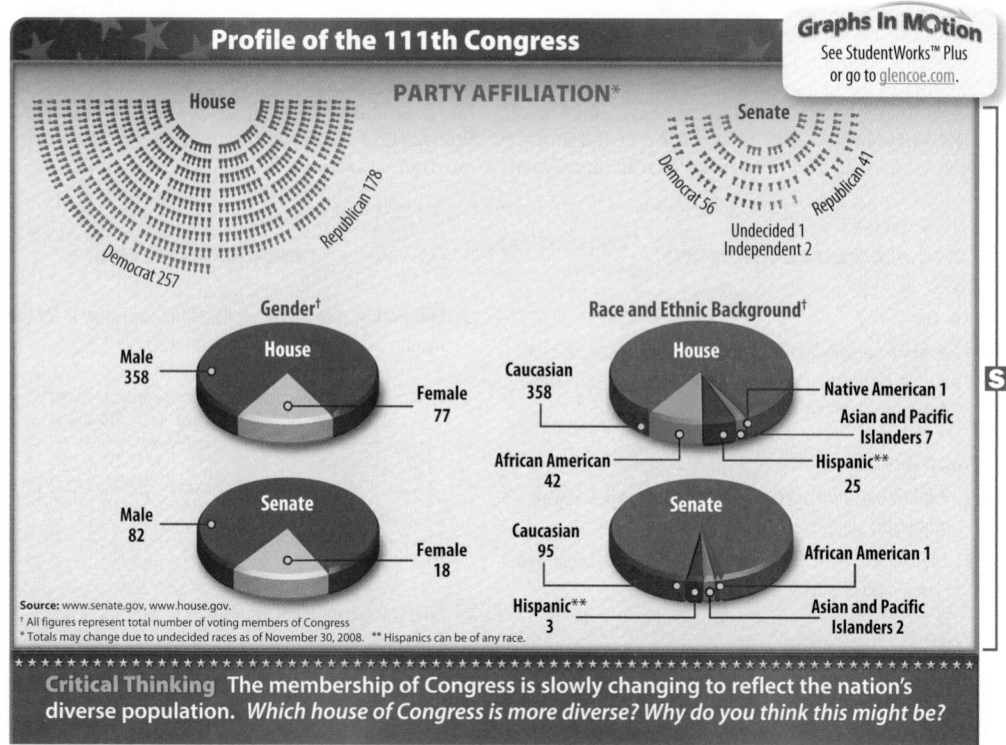

Profile of the 111th Congress

Graphs In MOtion
See StudentWorks™ Plus
or go to glencoe.com.

PARTY AFFILIATION*

House
Democrat 257
Republican 178

Senate
Democrat 56
Republican 41
Undecided 1
Independent 2

Gender†

House
Male 358
Female 77

Senate
Male 82
Female 18

Race and Ethnic Background†

House
Caucasian 358
African American 42
Native American 1
Asian and Pacific Islanders 7
Hispanic** 25

Senate
Caucasian 95
Hispanic** 3
African American 1
Asian and Pacific Islanders 2

Source: www.senate.gov, www.house.gov.
† All figures represent total number of voting members of Congress
* Totals may change due to undecided races as of November 30, 2008. ** Hispanics can be of any race.

Critical Thinking The membership of Congress is slowly changing to reflect the nation's diverse population. *Which house of Congress is more diverse? Why do you think this might be?*

CHAPTER 5, SECTION 1

D Differentiated Instruction

Verbal/Linguistic If students were running for Congress, which would they rather be—incumbents or challengers? Have students choose and then consider how they would present themselves and their qualifications to voters. Encourage students to focus on personal strengths rather than criticism of the opponent. Ask each student to create a slogan that summarizes the advantages that he or she offers to voters. If possible, have students make and display bumper stickers with their slogans. **OL AL**

S Skill Practice

Visual Literacy Ask: How many more Democrats than Republicans are there in the 111th Congress? *(97)* What percentage of senators are women? *(17%)* **OL**

Critical Thinking

Answer: the House of Representatives because it reflects the demographics of individual districts

Additional Support

Activity: Technology Connection

Identifying Discuss with students how the Internet promotes interdependence, interaction, and integration of people around the world. Have students find recent or current election Web sites of local, state, and national candidates and review each site. **Ask:** What did you like about the site? What did you dislike about the site? Would the site influence your vote? Have student volunteers share their findings with the class. Then discuss the advantages and the disadvantages of using the Internet as part of a political campaign in the United States today. **BL OL**

Critical Thinking

Answers: Incumbents are better known to voters and can continue with legislative work from term to term. They also have more political connections and experience. In addition, many districts have been gerrymandered to favor the incumbent's party. Having incumbents in office might hurt the lawmaking process if the incumbents become complacent or corrupt.

Assess

Assign the Section 1 Assessment as homework or as an in-class activity, or have students take Section Quiz 5-1 from *Section Quizzes and Chapter Tests.*

Close

Explaining Discuss with students why the Founders established a bicameral legislature. Remind students that, with differences in service terms, qualifications, perspectives, and leadership, a two-house system is more likely to consider various viewpoints and to protect the interests of minorities. **OL**

Section 1 Review

The Power of Incumbency

Longest-Serving Senators

Rank	Name	Seniority Date	Rank	Name	Seniority Date	Rank	Name	Seniority Date
1	Robert Byrd (D-WV)	January 3, 1959	11	Chuck Grassley (R-IA)	January 3, 1981	21	Harry Reid (D-NV)	January 6, 1987
2	Ted Kennedy (D-MA)	November 7, 1962	12	Arlen Specter (R-PA)	January 3, 1981	22	Kit Bond (R-MO)	January 6, 1987
3	Daniel Inouye (D-HI)	January 3, 1963	13	Jeff Bingaman (D-NM)	January 3, 1983	23	Kent Conrad (D-ND)	January 6, 1987
4	Patrick Leahy (D-VT)	January 3, 1975	14	John Kerry (D-MA)	January 2, 1985	24	Herb Kohl (D-WI)	January 3, 1989
5	Richard Lugar (R-IN)	January 4, 1977	15	Tom Harkin (D-IA)	January 3, 1985	25	Joe Lieberman (ID-CT)	January 3, 1989
6	Orrin Hatch (R-UT)	January 4, 1977	16	Mitch McConnell (R-KY)	January 3, 1985	26	Daniel Akaka (D-HI)	May 16, 1990
7	Max Baucus (D-MT)	December 15, 1978	17	Jay Rockefeller (D-WV)	January 15, 1985	27	Dianne Feinstein (D-CA)	November 10, 1992
8	Thad Cochren (R-MS)	December 17, 1978	18	Barbara Mikulski (D-MD)	January 6, 1987	28	Byron Dorgan (D-ND)	December 15, 1992
9	Carl Levin (D-MI)	January 3, 1979	19	Richard Shelby (R-AL)	January 6, 1987	29	Barbara Boxer (D-CA)	January 3, 1993
10	Chris Dodd (D-CT)	January 3, 1981	20	John McCain (R-AZ)	January 6, 1987	30	Judd Gregg (R-NH)	January 3, 1993

Critical Thinking *How could having so many members serving long terms help the Senate with lawmaking? How might it hurt the process?*

meetings for voters on their Web sites, but many more are beginning to do so. Experts predict that candidates for Congress will increasingly use Web technologies—search engines, portals, and e-mail lists—to identify voters who are interested in specific issues like gun control or health care. Once they have this information, they can contact these voters with specially targeted e-mails or Web sites on a given issue. Finally, experts anticipate that more candidates will make the fullest use of the Internet to improve communication in their campaign organizations.

SECTION 1 Review

Vocabulary

1. **Explain** the significance of: bicameral legislature, session, census, reapportionment, redistrict, gerrymander, at-large, censure, incumbent.

Main Ideas

2. **Explaining** How does Congress reapportion House seats among the states every 10 years?

3. **Identifying** When does each term of Congress begin, and how long does it run?

Critical Thinking

4. **Making Inferences** Members of Congress spend part of their time working for reelection. Which house has a greater percentage of its time remaining for legislative work? Why?

5. **Comparing** Use a table similar to the one below to list the number of seats up for election each year.

	2008	2010	2012
House			
Senate			

Writing About Government

6. **Expository Writing** What percentage of people think that their representative does not listen to them? Formulate a questionnaire that surveys voters about this issue.

Answers

1. The terms are defined in the section and the Glossary.
2. Following the Census, each state's population determines how the House seats are reapportioned.
3. on January 3 in years ending in odd numbers; each term is divided into two sessions that are each one year long
4. The Senate has more time because senators come up for reelection only every six years. Members of the House face reelection every two years.
5. House: (2008) 435, (2010) 435, (2012) 435; Senate: (2008) 33, (2010) 33, (2012) 33
6. Students' questions should follow a format that can be marked and easily read. Have students comment on the responses.

Can Congress Determine Who Is Qualified to Be a Member?

Powell v. *McCormack*, 1969

The Constitution establishes requirements for membership in the House and Senate, but does it allow Congress to add to those requirements?

Facts of the Case

In 1966 Adam Clayton Powell, Jr., was reelected to the House of Representatives, but the House charged him with misusing funds during his previous terms in office and refused to seat Powell. In March 1967, Congress declared the seat vacant and notified New York's governor to order a new election. Powell countered that the House could not unseat him since he met the requirements of age, citizenship, and residence of Article I, Section 2, of the Constitution. He then brought suit in the federal courts, naming the Speaker of the House among the defendants. The federal district court dismissed the complaint on the grounds that it did not have jurisdiction. The U.S. Court of Appeals for the District of Columbia refused to hear the case on the grounds that it was essentially a political question.

The Constitutional Question

Despite lower court rulings, the Supreme Court agreed to review the case. While the suit was proceeding, Powell was reelected in 1968 and seated in the 91st session of Congress. His lawyers now asked the Court for back salary for the two years he was denied his seat. The Court had to determine whether it could decide the case. The defendants held that the Court could not because the Constitution gave Congress, not the Court, power to judge members' qualifications. They also argued that it was a political question and thus belonged to the legislative branch to decide. Powell's lawyers believed Congress did not have the power to judge a member's moral qualifications. The Court referred to debates at the Constitutional Convention that related to giving Congress power to judge its members' qualifications.

Debating the Issue

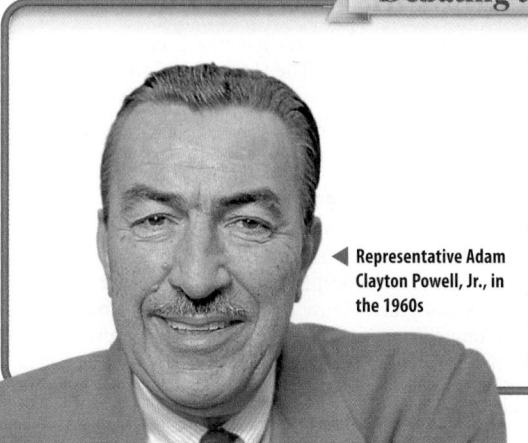

◄ **Representative Adam Clayton Powell, Jr., in the 1960s**

Questions to Consider

1. **Predicting** What might be a far-reaching result if the Court decided in favor of the Speaker?

2. **Analyzing** What might be a far-reaching result if the Court decided in favor of Adam Clayton Powell, Jr.?

You Be the Judge

Must Congress accept a member if he or she meets the three basic tests—age, citizenship, and residency? Did Adam Clayton Powell, Jr., deserve back pay and restoration of his seniority rights?

CHAPTER 5: *The Organization of Congress*   **131**

Supreme Court Cases to Debate

Class Debate

Organize the class into three groups. Group A will represent Adam Clayton Powell, Jr., Group B will represent Speaker John McCormack, and Group C will represent the Supreme Court. Have all three groups study this case and then complete the tasks below.

Groups A and B: Write briefs detailing why the Constitution supports their client.

Group A: Select an "attorney" to present Powell's case and develop its arguments.

Group B: Select an "attorney" to present McCormack's defense and develop its arguments.

While Groups A and B present their arguments, Group C may interrupt to ask questions. Afterward, the justices will meet to issue a written opinion.

The Court's Decision

In *Powell* v. *McCormack*, the Supreme Court found in Powell's favor. It ruled that the Court of Appeals was wrong in holding that the dispute was not justiciable, because the case arises under Article III of the Constitution. The House could not expel Powell because he had met all the constitutional qualifications, and the Constitution does not give the House unrestricted power to judge its members' qualifications.

Debating the Issue Answers

Questions to Consider

1. Possible answer: Future Speakers of the House could gain more power because they could expel political opponents from Congress for minor or false violations.

2. Possible answer: More people with questionable ethics could run for Congress, claiming that the only thing that matters is that they meet the qualifications outlined in the Constitution.

You Be the Judge

Encourage students to review the arguments they made during the classroom debate about *Powell* v. *McCormack*. Answers will vary, with some students taking a strict interpretation of the constitutional tests and others arguing from a point of view based more on ethics. Students should support their opinions.

Focus

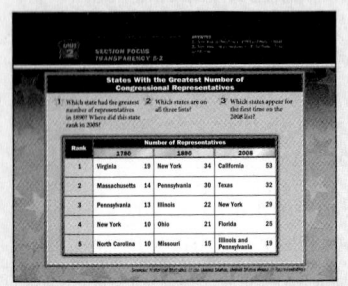
Resource Manager

The House of Representatives

Reader's Guide

Content Vocabulary
★ constituent (p. 133)
★ caucus (p. 134)
★ majority leader (p. 134)
★ whip (p. 135)
★ bill (p. 135)
★ calendar (p. 136)
★ quorum (p. 137)

Academic Vocabulary
★ available (p. 133)
★ parallel (p. 135)
★ constitute (p. 137)

Reading Strategy
Use a graphic organizer similar to the one below to help you take notes about the organization of leaders in the House.

```
              Speaker of the House
          ┌──────────────────┴──────────────────┐
    majory _____.                  minority _____.
    majority _____.                minority _____.
```

Issues in the News

Voters have complained in recent years about bitterness between the parties, but only rarely does conflict become physical. However, this happened in 1997 when Democrat David Obey and Republican Tom Delay got into a pushing and shoving match in the main aisle over a newspaper article that criticized Delay. In 1995 committee members had a "brawl in the hall," as news stories referred to it—a yanked necktie was as violent as it got. Today's Congress is quite civil compared to earlier centuries. As an example, men's walking sticks were used as weapons as in 1798, when the Vermont and Connecticut representatives got into a fight.

▲ In the early days of the Republic, party bitterness sometimes led to physical fighting.

Political divisions are unavoidable in a democracy. Legislators must be free to express their opinions. Rules are needed to help ensure fairness and to protect the minority. Article I, Section 51, of the Constitution says: "Each House may determine the Rules of its Proceedings." Thomas Jefferson stressed the importance of rules when he was vice president.

> 66 *It is much more material that there be a rule to go by, than what that rule is; that there may be a uniformity of proceeding in business not subject to the caprice [whims] of the Speaker or captiousness [criticisms] of the members.* 99
>
> —Thomas Jefferson, 1797

Rules for Lawmaking

The main task of each house of Congress is the same—to make laws. The House and Senate differ in many ways; each house has organized itself in a way that will help it carry out its chief obligations of making the laws.

Complex Rules

Each chamber has scores of precedents based on past rulings that serve as a guide to conducting business. The House and Senate each print their rules every two years. House rules are generally aimed at defining the actions an individual representative can take, such as limiting representatives to speaking for five minutes or less during a debate.

R Reading Strategies	**C** Critical Thinking	**D** Differentiated Instruction	**W** Writing Support	**S** Skill Practice
Teacher Edition • Using Context Clues, p. 135 • Academic Vocabulary, p. 137 **Additional Resources** • Quizzes/Tests, p. 52 • Guid. Read. Act., p. 18	**Teacher Edition** • Analyzing, p. 134 • Comparing and Contrasting, p. 136 **Additional Resources** • Read. Essen., pp. 52–54	**Teacher Edition** • English Learners, p. 133 • Interpersonal, pp. 134, 136 **Additional Resources** • Foldables, p. 48 • Source Readings, p. 5	**Additional Resources** • Authentic Assess., p. 12	**Additional Resources** • Vocab. Act., p. 5

The complex rules in the House are geared toward moving legislation quickly once it reaches the floor. House debates rarely last more than one day. Moreover, leaders of the House of Representatives have more power than leaders in the Senate. For example, the rules of the House allow its leaders to make key decisions about legislative work without consulting other House members.

Committee Work

It is the committees of Congress that perform most legislative activity. In the House, committee work is even more important than in the Senate. The reason has to do with size. Membership in the House is so large that members organize into committees. They can have more influence than on the House floor, plus they have the time to study and shape bills.

In addition, representatives tend to specialize in a few issues that are important to their **constituents**—the people in the districts they represent. For example, Major R. Owens, a representative who served from the 1980s until 2007, was the only trained librarian in Congress. He often emphasized that libraries were important for promoting literacy. As an African American, Owens also supported the funding of African American colleges and aid for underprivileged students.

Another member, Texas representative Sheila Jackson Lee from Houston, spends time promoting a health project for African Americans. Lee believes good health will strengthen communities in her district: The project, she said:

> ❝ . . . gives families an opportunity to learn about important health issues, speak with experts, and explore **available** resources. ❞
>
> —Sheila Jackson Lee

Finally, because members represent districts, they serve on committees that are important to their constituents. As Richard Durbin, of Illinois, said of his interest in the Agriculture Committee:

> ❝ [A]griculture plays a key role in our local economy. . . . The constituents who I will serve are most concerned about agricultural issues. . . . ❞
>
> —Richard Durbin

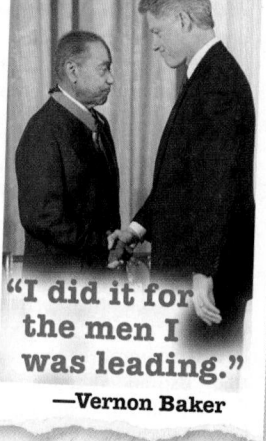

We the People
Making a Difference

In 1944 Vernon Baker, a 25-year-old army second lieutenant serving in World War II, was shot in the wrist by a German sniper. He spent two months in a segregated hospital, and then returned to lead his men into battle. On the morning of April 5, 1945, Baker destroyed two enemy bunkers, an observation post, and three machine gun nests. His company was nearly wiped out, but he ordered the seven remaining men to retreat while he drew enemy fire. Somehow, amid exploding shells, Lieutenant Baker escaped.

Although the army segregated African Americans during the war, Baker and his men fought like heroes. Asked why he fought so courageously for a country that treated him like a second-class citizen, Baker replied, "I was a soldier with a job to do, and I did it for the men I was leading."

Presented with the Distinguished Service Cross for his service in Italy, Baker remained in the military after the war. When he retired from the army in 1968, he took a job with the American Red Cross, counseling military families in need.

In 1990 army officials reexamined their records, looking for congressional Medal of Honor candidates among African Americans with outstanding service in World War II. Fifty years after his act of bravery, Vernon Baker accepted the medal in a White House ceremony. "It's a great day. We've all been vindicated," he said.

"I did it for the men I was leading."
—Vernon Baker

Teach

D Differentiated Instruction

English Learners Ask: Which English word helps explain the meaning of *constituent?* What does this word mean? (constitute; it means "to make up, form, or compose.") **ELL**

We the People
Making a Difference

Vernon Baker In 1996 the Pentagon leadership conceded that racism was the reason that no African Americans had been awarded the Medal of Honor in World War II. President Clinton awarded Baker the medal, announcing, "Today we fill the gap in that picture and give a group of heroes who also loved peace—but adapted themselves to war—the tribute that has always been their due."

Activity Have groups of students research the history of discrimination in the U.S. armed forces and then present their findings in a time line. **OL**

Hands-On Chapter Project

Step 2

Mock Senate

Step 2: Writing Bills Student groups continue the lawmaking process begun in Step 1.

Directions After each group has determined the topic for its bill, have the group write its bill, using bills found on the Library of Congress Web site as models. In addition, you may provide students with the blank bill document available from the Web site of the Center on Congress at Indiana University. See "Teaching About Congress": http://congress.indiana.edu/pdf/best_practices.pdf. **AL**

(Chapter Project continued in Section 3.)

Differentiated Instruction

D Differentiated Instruction

Interpersonal The House of Representatives operates under an extremely detailed set of rules intended to help it function in an effective, orderly way. To reinforce the importance of these rules to the orderly and efficient conducting of business, discuss with students daily life situations in which various kinds of rules make cooperation more efficient and more pleasant. **BL**

C Critical Thinking

Analyzing Remind students that Article I, Section 2, Clause 5 of the U.S. Constitution does not state that the Speaker has to be a member of the House. **Ask:** What is the benefit of having a House member as Speaker? *(Answers may include that the Speaker may be better equipped to handle the presidency in the event of the president's death or incapacity, and the Speaker would have the authority to cast votes on legislation.)* **AL**

TIME
For the Record

Speaking Frankly Members of Congress don't need stamps for their official mail: their signature, real or printed, is known as a frank and is accepted by the Post Office. Franking cannot be used for personal business or for political campaigns. It can be used only on letters mailed to constituents. Because this privilege gives incumbents an advantage during an election year, members of Congress can't send out large volumes of franked mail right before an election.

Importance of Party Affiliation

Many procedures in Congress are organized around one political party. Party distinctions are physically obvious: In both the House and Senate, the Republicans sit on the right side of the chamber, and the Democrats sit on the left. In each house, the majority party gets to select the leaders of that body, to control the flow of legislative work, and to appoint the chairs of all the committees.

The power to organize the House explains why some conservative Democrats switched to the Republican Party when it became the majority party in Congress after the 1994 election. When that happened, they began to make sweeping changes of the House rules in 1995. In their campaigning, the Republicans made a "contract with America," promising to make the House more accountable.

Their new rules concentrated more power in the speaker's office, provided for fewer committees and fewer staff members, and limited the terms of committee chairs and of the Speaker. New rules also ended absentee voting in committees. Despite strong resistance from the Democratic leaders in the House, the new Republican majority was able to push through the changes.

House Leadership

Leaders of the House coordinate the work of this large body of 435 individual members. It is helpful to think of the work of the leadership as meeting six kinds of goals:

- Organizing and unifying party members
- Scheduling work
- Making certain that lawmakers are present for key floor votes
- Distributing and collecting information
- Keeping the House in touch with the president
- Influencing lawmakers to support their party's positions

The Constitution provides only for the presiding officer of the House. Other than that, the House chooses all of its leaders.

The Speaker of the House

The Speaker of the House is the presiding officer and its most powerful leader. The Constitution states that the House "shall choose their Speaker and other officers." A **caucus,** or closed meeting, of the majority party chooses the House Speaker at the start of each session of Congress, and the entire House membership approves the choice of Speaker.

As both the presiding officer of the House and the leader of the majority party, the Speaker has great power. Presiding over the sessions of the House, the Speaker can influence proceedings by deciding which members to recognize first. The Speaker also appoints the members of some committees, schedules bills for action, and refers bills to the proper House committee. Finally, the Speaker of the House follows the vice president in the line of succession to the presidency.

Today, Speakers rely as much on persuasion as on their formal powers to influence other members. On a typical day, the Speaker may talk with dozens of members. Often the Speaker does so just to hear their requests for a favor. As former Speaker Thomas P. "Tip" O'Neill once put it, "The world is full of little things you can do for people." In return, the Speaker expects representatives' support on important issues.

House Floor Leaders

The Speaker's top assistant is the **majority leader.** The majority leader's job is to help plan the party's legislative program, steer important bills through the House, and make sure the chairpersons of the many committees finish work on bills that are important to the party. The majority leader is the floor leader of his or her political party in the House and, like the Speaker, is elected by the majority party. Thus, the majority leader is not a House official but rather a party official.

Authentic Assessment with Rubrics, p. 12

Congressional Firsts

Objective: Research the history of congressional representation in the United States.

Focus/Teach: Ask students to work together in groups to create a time line of "congressional firsts."

Assess: Have student groups present their completed time lines to the class, explaining why they selected the milestones on their time lines.

Close: Ask students to give their opinions on whether Congress truly represents the U.S. population.

Differentiated Instruction Strategies

BL Have students research to find images or symbols to illustrate the time line.

AL Have students write the time line entries based on their research. The entries should be brief and to the point.

ELL Ask students to create the structure of the time line by determining how it will be displayed and in what time intervals.

The majority leader has help from the majority **whip** and deputy whips. These whips serve as assistant floor leaders in the House. The majority whip's job is to watch how majority-party members intend to vote on **bills,** to persuade them to vote as the party wishes, and to see that party members are present to vote.

The minority party in the House elects its own leaders—the minority leader and the minority whip. Their responsibilities **parallel** the duties of the majority party, except that they have no power over scheduling work in the House.

Lawmaking in the House

On a typical day, the House of Representatives might look a bit disorganized—representatives are talking in small groups, reading newspapers, or constantly walking in and out of the chamber. Most representatives are not even on the floor but are in committee meetings, talking with voters, or in their offices. Representatives reach the floor quickly, however, when it is time for debate or a vote on proposed bills.

Usually, the House starts its floor sessions at noon or earlier. Buzzers ring in members' offices in the House office buildings, committee rooms, and in the Capitol to call representatives to the chamber. The House is normally in session from Monday through Friday. Mondays are for routine work. Not much is done on Friday because many representatives leave to go to their home districts over the weekend. Thus, most of the House's important work is done from Tuesday through Thursday.

How House Bills Are Scheduled

All laws start as bills. A proposed law is called a bill until both houses of Congress pass it and the president signs it. According to the procedure that is currently in place, to introduce a bill in the House, representatives drop it into the hopper, a mahogany box that is accessible to all near the front of the chamber.

After a bill is introduced, the Speaker of the House sends it to the appropriate committee for study, discussion, and review. Of the thousands of bills and resolutions that are introduced during each legislative term of Congress, only about 10 to

Historic First

Madame Speaker With the Democratic victory in the 2005 midterm elections, Nancy Pelosi of California became the first woman ever to become Speaker of the House. Here Pelosi joins hands with other Democrats during the news conference announcing her leadership. *Why is the Speaker of the House a powerful position?*

Participating IN GOVERNMENT

Parliamentary Procedure

Parliamentarians in Congress advise the presiding officers of the House and Senate about parliamentary rules and procedures. They also counsel members of Congress on procedures for routing legislation and decide which committees have jurisdiction over bills.

D Differentiated Instruction

Interpersonal Discuss why parliamentarians would be considered powerful employees of Congress and how the student parliamentarian (in the activity) influenced the class meeting. **OL**

C Critical Thinking

Comparing and Contrasting Have students suggest bills they would want to propose to their House representatives, choose two on very different topics, and write a sentence to summarize each. Then have the class compare the bills. **Ask:** Which bill might the House be more likely to consider? Which would be more appropriate for presentation to the Senate first? **AL**

Additional Support

Participating IN GOVERNMENT — Parliamentary Procedure

Like Congress, all deliberative assemblies need rules to conduct business in a fair and impartial way. Rules of order have their origin in early British Parliaments. Thomas Jefferson's *Manual of Parliamentary Practice* (1801) provided rules for the new U.S. government. Many groups use *Robert's Rules of Order*, first published in 1876 by U.S. Army officer Henry M. Robert. *Robert's Rules* addresses such issues as:

1. How to make a motion and how to amend a motion
2. What rank or precedence various kinds of motions have
3. How to table or suspend a motion
4. How to close or extend debate
5. How to raise the question of consideration and how to vote
6. The duties and powers of the presiding officer

Activity

1. Obtain a copy of *Robert's Rules of Order*. Appoint a small group to find rules that pertain to the items listed above. Discuss the needs of a small group meeting (about the size of your class). Write rules for such a meeting based on these needs.
2. Choose a presiding officer for a meeting of your government class and a parliamentarian to enforce the rules. Hold a meeting in which the class determines an issue to discuss, hears opinions from the floor, and decides whether to take any action.

Participating IN GOVERNMENT ACTIVITY

D Find a copy of *Robert's Rules of Order*. Write Robert's rules for the items listed above. Then choose a presiding officer for a meeting of your government class as well as a parliamentarian to enforce them. Hold a meeting to discuss and take action on an issue that is of interest to all students.

---

20 percent ever go to the full House for a vote. Bills that survive the committee process are put on one of the House calendars. **Calendars** list bills that are up for consideration.

The House has five calendars. Three are used to schedule different kinds of bills for consideration. The Union Calendar lists bills that deal with money issues. Most other public bills are on the House Calendar. The Private Calendar lists bills that deal with individual people or places. If the House consents unanimously to debate a bill out of regular order, it is listed on the Consent Calendar. Finally, the Discharge Calendar is used for petitions to discharge a bill from a committee.

The House Rules Committee

C The Rules Committee is extremely important because it is a "traffic officer," helping to direct the flow of major legislation. It is one of the oldest and the most powerful House committees. The representative who chairs this committee has great influence over legislative activity and how bills progress through Congress. After a committee has considered and approved a major bill, it usually goes to the Rules Committee. The Rules Committee can move bills ahead quickly, hold them back, or stop them completely.

The power of the Rules Committee has often been the focus of political battles. From 1858 to 1910, the Speaker of the House chaired this committee and dominated the flow of legislation. In 1911 the House revolted against Speaker Joseph G. Cannon's authoritarian leadership and removed him from the Rules Committee.

Party battles over the Speaker's power also have arisen in relatively recent times. In 1975 Democratic majorities in the House once again placed the Rules Committee under the control of the Speaker. The Democratic Caucus gave the Speaker the power to appoint all majority members of the Rules Committee, subject to caucus ratification.

In 1995 Republicans became the majority party in the House. Despite two ethics investigations, they maintained the majority for the next decade. Recently, an ethics investigation took place when House Majority Leader Tom Delay was accused of using illegal corporate contributions in a Texas election. Delay resigned in 2006 before the investigation was completed and was replaced by John Boehner of Ohio.

Activity: Interdisciplinary Connection

Daily Life What is an "average day" for a member of the House of Representatives? Challenge students, working independently or collaboratively, to supplement the details in this section with some original research and then to create a one-day schedule (divided into 15-minute increments) for a representative.

Remind students that part of the day might be spent dealing with office staff, constituents, or lobbyists—and that the representative might have family responsibilities as well. As students share their schedules, invite them to compare the representative's "average day" with their own. **OL AL**

Function of the Rules Committee

Major bills that reach the floor of the House do so by a rule—or special order—from the Rules Committee. As major bills come out of committee, they are entered on either the Union Calendar or the House Calendar in the order in which they are received.

Calendars have so many bills on them that if they were taken up in calendar order, many would never reach the floor before the session ended. To solve this problem, the chairperson of the committee that sent the bill to the Rules Committee can ask for it to move ahead of other bills. The Rules Committee can also say how long the bill can be debated and revised.

The Rules Committee also settles disputes among other House committees. For example, the Armed Services Committee may consider a bill that involves a subject that also is covered by the Veterans' Affairs Committee. The Rules Committee can help resolve any dispute between the two committees.

Finally, the Rules Committee often delays or blocks bills that representatives and House leaders do not want to come to a vote on the floor. In this way, it can draw criticism away from members who might have to take an unpopular stand on a bill if it did reach the floor.

A Quorum for Business

A **quorum** is the minimum number of members needed for official legislative action. For a regular session, a quorum requires a majority of

House Rules Committee Chair
Representative Louise Slaughter has represented New York's 28th District in upstate New York for many years. She chairs the House Rules Committee that directs the flow of legislation. *Why do you think this committee is so important?*

218 members. When the House meets to debate and amend legislation, it often sits as a Committee of the Whole. In that case, 100 members **constitutes** a quorum. This procedure helps speed consideration of important bills, but the Committee of the Whole cannot pass a bill. Instead, it reports the measure back to the full House with any revisions it makes. The House then passes or rejects the bill.

CHAPTER 5, SECTION 2

R Reading Strategy

Academic Vocabulary Ask:
What are some synonyms for the word *constitutes*? *(makes up, comprises, forms, composes)* **OL**

Caption Answer: The House Rules Committee is important because it helps direct the flow of major legislation.

Assess

Assign the Section 2 Assessment as homework or as an in-class activity, or have students take Section Quiz 5-2 from *Section Quizzes and Chapter Tests.*

Close

Speculating Call on volunteers to name what they think would be the most satisfying aspect and the most frustrating aspect of serving in Congress. Have them draw upon details in this section to support their answers. **BL OL**

Section 2 Review

SECTION 2 Review

Vocabulary

1. **Explain** the significance of: constituent, caucus, majority leader, whip, bill, calendar, quorum.

Main Ideas

2. **Analyzing** What is the role of House committees?

3. **Describing** How does a representative introduce a bill?

4. **Identifying** What is the primary function of the Rules Committee?

Critical Thinking

5. **Understanding Cause and Effect** Why are changes in House rules more likely to occur when political control of the House shifts to another party?

6. **Organizing** Use a graphic organizer to list three ways in which the Rules Committee controls legislation.

Rules Committee	

Writing About Government

7. **Expository Writing** Browse through current newspapers and magazines to find out what laws the majority party in the House is trying to pass. Make a chart of the key legislation, and find out where each bill is in the legislative process. Follow its progress online for several weeks. Write a short summary report of the progress you noted.

Answers

1. The terms are defined in the section and the Glossary.
2. Committees allow House members to accomplish their work efficiently with more influence as a group than they could have as individuals on the House floor.
3. The representative drops a copy of the bill into the "hopper."
4. The Rules Committee determines which bills reach the floor of the House for debate and for a vote.
5. Answers will vary, but students may suggest that once a party gains majority power it will want to do things its own way, so it will establish its own rules.
6. Answers might include: directs flow of legislation; may limit debate on bills; specifies how much a bill may be amended.
7. Students' charts should make following the progress of the selected legislation an easy task and should provide enough annotation for viewers to understand what has happened to the legislation during the process.

Focus

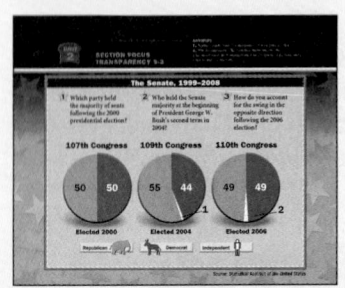
Reader's Guide

Answers to Graphic: Possible answer: Only a few senators attend sessions; rules are more flexible to give senators freedom to express their ideas; the Senate has no Speaker.

Resource Manager

The Senate

Reader's Guide

Content Vocabulary
- ★ president pro tempore *(p. 139)*
- ★ filibuster *(p. 139)*
- ★ cloture *(p. 140)*

Academic Vocabulary
- ★ specific *(p. 138)*
- ★ assistant *(p. 138)*
- ★ devote *(p. 139)*

Reading Strategy
Use a graphic organizer like the one below to list the differences in the everyday operations of the House and the Senate.

Differences between the House and the Senate

People in the News

In the 2006 midterm elections, opposition to President George W. Bush's policies in Iraq helped Democrats gain Senate seats. A prime example was Sherrod Brown's victory in Ohio over the otherwise-popular Republican Mike DeWine. Brown hit the Iraq issues hard. "We went to war on false pretenses, without a plan for withdrawal, and without the proper body armor and vehicles our troops need," he said on the campaign trail. Brown's victory put the Democrats up five seats compared to the previous session.

▲ Senator Sherrod Brown's victory was fueled by opposition to the war in Iraq.

The Senate is called a deliberative body because it deliberates, or formally discusses, public policies. Senators handle issues that are of **specific** interest to their committees, but they address many other issues, too. Because two senators represent an entire state, they are expected to be knowledgeable about many issues from national defense to farming.

The Senate at Work

Visitors going from the House to the Senate are often startled by the difference between the two chambers. The Senate is smaller, and usually only a few senators attend sessions. The Senate chamber has 100 desks (one per senator) facing a raised platform where the president pro tempore and another senator preside. Party leaders or their **assistants** stay in the Senate at all times to keep the work moving and to look after their party's interests. In the Senate, the rules are more flexible than in the House to give all senators maximum freedom to express their ideas. For example, the Senate usually allows unlimited debate on bills. Senate rules are spelled out in about 100 pages, allowing a relatively informal atmosphere. Senators can debate a proposal on and off for weeks or even months.

Senate Leaders

Leadership in the Senate closely parallels leadership in the House, but the Senate has no Speaker. The vice president presides but cannot vote except to break a tie. Senate procedures also allow senators more freedom. Thus, Senate party leaders do not usually have as much influence over members as their counterparts in the House.

The Vice President

The Constitution names the vice president as the Senate's president, but he or she does not have

---

R Reading Strategies	**C** Critical Thinking	**D** Differentiated Instruction	**W** Writing Support	**S** Skill Practice
Teacher Edition • Taking Notes, p. 139 **Additional Resources** • Quizzes/Tests, p. 53 • Guid. Read. Act., p. 19	**Additional Resources** • Read. Essen., pp. 55–56	**Additional Resources** • Foldables, p. 48 • Coop. Learning Act., pp. 3–4	**Teacher Edition** • Expository Writing, p. 139 **Additional Resources** • Part. in Gov. Act., pp. 9–10	**Additional Resources** • Skill Reinforce. Act., p. 5

the same role or power as the Speaker of the House. The vice president may recognize members and put questions to a vote, but he or she is not an elected representative so this person may not take part in Senate debates or cast a vote except in the event of a tie. The vice president may, however, influence members through personal contact. Most vice presidents find Senate duties unchallenging and **devote** more time to executive duties. In the absence of the vice president, the **president pro tempore**—"pro tem" for short—presides. (The term means "for the time being.") The Senate elects this leader from the majority party. Usually, it is that party's longest-serving member.

Majority and Minority Leaders

The Senate's most important officers are the majority and minority leaders. Elected by party members, these are officials of the party, not of the Senate. The job of the majority leader is to steer the party's bills through the Senate, which is done by planning the work schedule and agenda in consultation with the minority leader. The majority leader also makes sure that party members attend important sessions and gets support for key bills.

The minority leader has a different job—critiquing the majority party's bills and keeping his or her own party united. As in the House, whips and assistant whips are very important because they do the detailed work that supports leaders. A key job is making sure that legislators are present in the chamber when key votes come up.

How Senate Bills Are Scheduled

As in the House, any senator can introduce a bill, but procedures for moving a bill through the Senate are less formal than in the House. Because it is smaller, the Senate has never needed a committee like the House Rules Committee. Instead, Senate leaders control the flow of bills to committees and to the floor. They do this by consulting closely with one another. The Senate has only two calendars—the Calendar of General Orders, which lists all the bills the Senate will consider, and the Executive Calendar, which schedules treaties and nominations.

The Senate brings bills to the floor by unanimous consent, a motion by all members present to set aside formal rules and consider a bill from the calendar. This procedure has not changed much through the years.

The Filibuster

Because Senate rules usually allow unlimited debate on any bill, one way for senators to defeat a bill they oppose is to filibuster against it. To **filibuster** means to extend debate to prevent a bill from coming to a vote. A senator or group of senators could use a filibuster to extend debate for

A Hollywood View of Congressional Debate

A Movie Filibuster
The film classic *Mr. Smith Goes to Washington* had actor James Stewart engaging in a filibuster to prevent passage of a corrupt land bill in a Western state. Stewart's character wanted to set up a boys' ranch on the land. Smith's heroism so impressed the corrupt senator played by Claude Rains (left) that he confessed his misdeeds. ***How is cloture related to the filibuster?***

CHAPTER 5, SECTION 3

Teach

R Reading Strategy

Taking Notes Have students create a list of the Senate majority leader's duties and a list of the Senate minority leader's duties. **BL**

W Writing Support

Expository Writing Have students write a paragraph explaining how Senate bills are scheduled and how the process differs from bills in the House. **OL**

Caption Answer: Senators will filibuster, or extend debate, to prevent a bill from coming to vote. Cloture limits debate by allowing each senator to speak for only one hour. However, 60 senators must vote for cloture.

Hands-On Chapter Project

Step 3

Mock Senate

Step 3: Introducing Bills Student groups continue the lawmaking process begun in Step 1.

Directions Have each group choose one member to introduce the bill. Ask groups to identify the standing committee to which their bills will be sent. Each group will then become a standing committee. Do not assign a bill to its originating group.

Deliberation Have students read and research the bill. Are there any points they think should be added to the bill? Are there portions of the bill they think should be deleted or amended? Groups will have to deliberate and reach a consensus on these points. Senate committees have the power to kill bills, but for the purpose of this activity, committees are to revise their assigned bills to prepare them for consideration on the Senate floor. Have committees prepare a new bill that reflects their markups. Students will be using these bills in Step 4. **AL**

(Chapter Project continued in Section 4.)

Caption Answer: When Democrats and Republicans are evenly divided, it is nearly impossible to get the necessary 60 votes for cloture.

Government ONLINE

Objectives and answers to the Student Web Activity can be found in the **Web Activity Lesson Plan** at glencoe.com. Enter **QuickPass**™ code USG9085c5T.

Assess

Assign the Section 3 Assessment as homework or as an in-class activity, or have students take Section Quiz 5-3 from *Section Quizzes and Chapter Tests.*

Close

Analyzing Share this comment from Daniel Webster to his Senate colleagues in 1820: "This is a hall for mutual consultation and discussion; not an arena for the exhibition of champions." Have students use this section to support or challenge Webster's statement. **OL**

Section 3 Review

Historic Filibuster Senator Strom Thurmond led the longest filibuster ever against the Civil Rights Act of 1957. **Why can cloture be hard to achieve?**

weeks or even months, perhaps by reciting Shakespeare as Huey Long did in the 1930s, or by just reading the phone book. In the 1970s, the rules were changed so that such drama was avoided. Only 41 senators had to say they intended to filibuster for it to accomplish its purpose.

Why is the mere threat of a filibuster as good as an actual one? The rules say that once a filibuster is on, it can be stopped only by a vote for cloture. **Cloture** limits the debate by allowing each senator only one hour for speaking on a bill, but 60 senators must vote for cloture. When Democrats and Republicans are evenly divided, it is nearly impossible to get the necessary 60 votes.

Bitter conflict between the parties in the last decade meant that many occasions arose when filibusters were threatened to prevent action on bills and many motions were made to stop them. One analysis found that in 2007, more than 70 motions were made to stop filibusters, most on the war in Iraq. Opinion polls showed that many Americans were upset at this degree of congressional gridlock where it seemed impossible to enact proposals or reforms.

In 2005 the issue of filibusters arose over President George W. Bush's appointments to federal judgeships. Democrats used the threat of the filibuster to hold up some appointments. Republicans then threatened the "nuclear option," meaning they intended to get majority support for a new rule that filibusters could not be used on judicial appointments in the current Senate. The fight ended when moderates in both parties compromised. As long as Democrats and Republicans have sharp differences, the issue of how and when a filibuster should be threatened is likely to linger.

Politics

As in the House, Senate procedures are organized around party affiliations. Republicans sit on the right side of the chamber and Democrats on the left. More importantly, the majority party controls the flow of bills.

Government ONLINE
Student Web Activity Visit glencoe.com and enter **QuickPass**™ code USG9822c5. Click on Student Web Activity and complete the activity about the U.S. Senate.

SECTION 3 Review

Vocabulary

1. **Explain** the significance of: president pro tempore, filibuster, cloture.

Main Ideas

2. **Contrasting** How does the Calendar of General Orders differ from the Executive Calendar?

3. **Explaining** How does the Senate bring bills to the floor?

Critical Thinking

4. **Making Comparisons** Compare the rules and procedures of the House with those of the Senate.

5. **Organizing** In a graphic organizer, analyze the relationship between the Senate majority and minority leaders, and whips and assistant whips.

Majority	Minority

Writing About Government

6. **Persuasive Writing** Search through a reference work of historic Senate speeches. Use one of them as a model for a persuasive speech of your own.

Answers

1. The terms are defined in the section and the Glossary.
2. The Calendar of General Orders lists all the bills the Senate will consider, while the Executive Calendar schedules treaties and nominations.
3. Through unanimous consent, all senators present agree to consider a bill from the calendar.
4. The Senate has a more informal atmosphere than the House and follows more flexible rules; furthermore, senators generally can act more independently than members of the House.
5. From top to bottom: majority leader, majority whip, assistant majority whip; minority leader, minority whip, assistant minority whip
6. Students should be ready to explain why they chose the passage they did. Their presentation should be clear and natural, not overdramatized.

Congressional Committees

Reader's Guide

Content Vocabulary
- ★ standing committee *(p. 142)*
- ★ subcommittee *(p. 142)*
- ★ select committee *(p. 143)*
- ★ joint committee *(p. 143)*
- ★ conference committee *(p. 144)*
- ★ seniority system *(p. 145)*

Academic Vocabulary
- ★ issue *(p. 141)*
- ★ investigation *(p. 141)*
- ★ temporary *(p. 143)*

Reading Strategy
Use the graphic organizer below to take notes about the different types of congressional committees.

Types of Committees

Issues in the News

Ads for R-rated films shown during television programs with a large percentage of viewers under age 17 sparked a Senate investigation in 2000. Around this time, a federal report also found that underage teenagers were easily sneaking into R-rated movies. Many people in Hollywood are suspicious about the timing of the hearings—less than two months before a national election. "I think it's a bunch of weasels scrambling for votes," said Larry Kasanoff, who heads a company that makes movies based on action-oriented video games.

▲ Studio executives testifying to Congress, promising to limit marketing of R-rated movies to minors

While the subject of R-rated movies made for a dramatic hearing, the detailed work of debating and crafting bills is usually not very exciting. It occurs in floor debates after the hearings or in committee meetings away from the lights of television cameras.

Purposes of Committees

Both the House and Senate depend upon committees to consider the thousands of bills that are proposed each session. Committees help ease the workload and are the key power centers in Congress.

The committee system serves several important purposes. First, it allows members of Congress to divide their work among many smaller groups. Lawmakers can become specialists, over their years of service, on the **issues** that their committees consider. This system is the only practical way for Congress to operate because no lawmaker can possibly know the details of each of the thousands of bills that are introduced in each term of Congress.

Second, from the huge number of bills that are introduced in each Congress, committees select those few that are to receive further consideration. Committees are the places in which lawmakers listen to supporters and opponents of a bill. It is in committees where they work out compromises and decide which bills will or will not have a chance to become law. Most bills never get beyond the committee stage.

Third, by holding public hearings and **investigations,** committees help the public learn about key problems and issues facing the nation. Congressional committees have called the public's attention to such issues as organized crime, the safety of prescription drugs, hunger in America, airline safety, and many other concerns that have confronted the nation.

Focus

Bellringer
Section Focus Transparencies 5-4

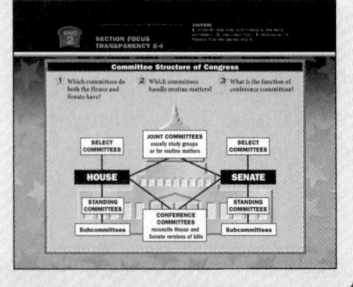

Reader's Guide

Answers to Graphic: standing committees (with subcommittees), select committees, joint committees, conference committees

Resource Manager

R Reading Strategies	**C** Critical Thinking	**D** Differentiated Instruction	**W** Writing Support	**S** Skill Practice
Teacher Edition • Making Connections, p. 142 **Additional Resources** • Quizzes/Tests, p. 54 • Guid. Read. Act., p. 20	**Teacher Edition** • Identifying Central Issues, p. 144 • Predicting Consequences, p. 145 **Additional Resources** • Read. Essen., pp. 57–59	**Teacher Edition** • Kinesthetic, p. 143 **Additional Resources** • Foldables, p. 48	**Additional Resources** • Inter. Poli. Cartoons, pp. 9–10	**Teacher Edition** • Visual Literacy, p. 143 **Additional Resources** • Ch. Summaries, pp. 13–15

Teach

Reading Strategy

Making Connections How does the word *standing* help describe standing committees and what they do? *(Standing committees are permanent groups that oversee bills dealing with certain issues. The word* standing *is a synonym for the word* permanent.*)* **OL**

The Law *and* You

More About Emerging Music Formats and Copyright Law In recent years, technology—principally computers and the ability to download materials from the Internet—has raised ethical and legal issues. The courts have ruled that the law prohibits the copying of copyrighted music using digital technology that stores songs on computers or handheld players.

Hands-On Chapter Project

Step 4

Kinds of Committees

Congress has four basic kinds of committees: (1) standing committees, (2) select committees, (3) joint committees, and (4) conference committees. Congress always has the right, however, to change the method of committee organization and the number of committees.

Standing Committees

Early in its history, Congress set up permanent groups to oversee bills that dealt with certain kinds of issues. These are called **standing committees**—they stand, or continue, from one Congress to the next. The House and Senate each create their own standing committees and control their areas of jurisdiction, occasionally adding or eliminating a standing committee when necessary.

The majority party has the power to write the rules in Congress. Republicans made changes in the structure and titles of several committees when they became the majority in 1995. They also set six-year term limits for committee chairpersons. The last major realignment of standing committees in the Senate took place in 1977.

Because the majority party in each house controls the standing committees, it selects a chairperson for each from among its party members. The majority of the members of each standing committee are also members of the majority party. Party membership on committees is usually divided in direct proportion to each party's strength in each house. For example, if 60 percent of the members of the House are Republicans, then 60 percent of the members of each House standing committee will be Republicans. Thus, a 10-member committee would have 6 Republicans and 4 Democrats. However, the party in power in the House will often have a supermajority on the most important committees.

Subcommittees

Nearly all standing committees have several **subcommittees.** Each subcommittee specializes in a subcategory of its standing committee's responsibility. Like committees, they usually continue from one Congress to the next, although the majority party can make changes. For example, House Republicans in the 104th Congress limited most committees to no more than 5 subcommittees.

The Law *and* You

Emerging Music Formats and Copyright Law

The law and technology are butting heads and the arena is copyright law. What is copyright law? Copyright laws protect the authors of "original works of authorship"—intellectual property as lawyers refer to it—from having their works copied without credit or payment. Musical compositions are intellectual property, and in the Internet age, copyright law is struggling to keep up with real world practices.

Every day, countless songs are downloaded from person-to-person (P2P) file-sharing Web sites like Limewire, BearShare and Direct Connect. The record industry's trade group, Recording Industry Association of America (RIAA), has cracked down on these sites in the last decade and more, even seizing personal computers of people who download a large volume of copyrighted music.

Many established artists are as upset with file sharing as the recording industry is, but for someone like Jonathan Coulton, it is a different story. Coulton's music is not only freely available, but fans can use it creatively. A 2007 *New York Times* feature reported that more than 50 fans created music videos using Coulton's songs and then posted them on YouTube. One woman used his song, "Someone Is Crazy" as the background for a collection of scenes from anime cartoons spliced together.

▶ **Jonathan Coulton**

Exploring the Law Activity

Analyzing Do you think the government has an obligation to enforce copyright laws against file-sharing individuals? Analyze the issue and present your view.

Mock Senate

Step 4: Debating the Bills Groups will present their bills to the class, which will convene as the mock Senate.

Directions Students will act as senators; the teacher will preside as president of the Senate. Have each committee present its bill to the class while fellow "senators" take notes. Debate each bill, asking volunteers to share their comments. Have students cast their votes and tell students that all bills will be passed and forwarded to the House of Representatives. You should then revise each bill as if it were a version passed by the House of Representatives. Be sure to include some significant changes that must be resolved in committee. Students will work on compromise bills in conference committees in Step 5. **AL**

(Chapter Project continued in Section 5.)

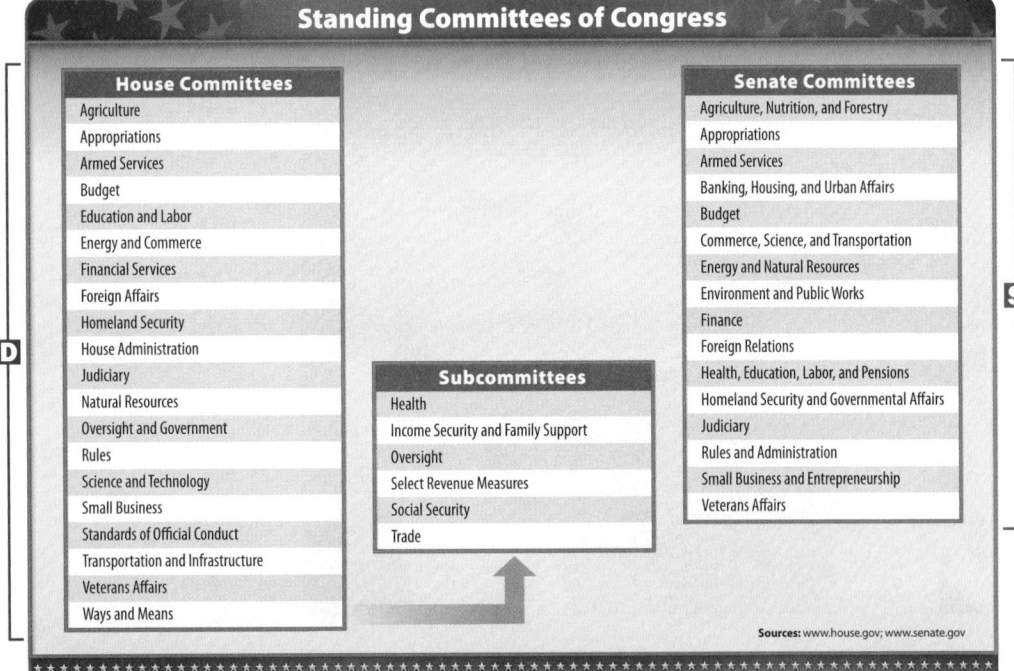

Standing Committees of Congress

House Committees
- Agriculture
- Appropriations
- Armed Services
- Budget
- Education and Labor
- Energy and Commerce
- Financial Services
- Foreign Affairs
- Homeland Security
- House Administration
- Judiciary
- Natural Resources
- Oversight and Government
- Rules
- Science and Technology
- Small Business
- Standards of Official Conduct
- Transportation and Infrastructure
- Veterans Affairs
- Ways and Means

Subcommittees
- Health
- Income Security and Family Support
- Oversight
- Select Revenue Measures
- Social Security
- Trade

Senate Committees
- Agriculture, Nutrition, and Forestry
- Appropriations
- Armed Services
- Banking, Housing, and Urban Affairs
- Budget
- Commerce, Science, and Transportation
- Energy and Natural Resources
- Environment and Public Works
- Finance
- Foreign Relations
- Health, Education, Labor, and Pensions
- Homeland Security and Governmental Affairs
- Judiciary
- Rules and Administration
- Small Business and Entrepreneurship
- Veterans Affairs

Sources: www.house.gov; www.senate.gov

Critical Thinking Congressional committees have changed in recent decades. The House rules adopted in the 104th Congress limited most standing committees to no more than five subcommittees. *What is the difference between standing committees and select committees?*

The exceptions were Appropriations (13 subcommittees), Oversight and Government Reform (7 subcommittees), and Transportation and Infrastructure (6 subcommittees).

Select Committees

From time to time, each house of Congress has created **temporary** committees. Usually, these committees, called **select committees,** study one specific issue and report their findings to the Senate or the House. These issues can include matters of great public concern at a given time, such as the cost of gasoline, problems that have been neglected for a while, or the problems of interest groups that are saying that Congress is not meeting their needs. Select committees usually cannot submit bills to their parent chamber, however.

Select committees were set up to last for no more than one term of Congress. In practice, however, select committees may be renewed and continue to meet for several terms of Congress. For this reason, both the House and Senate have reclassified several select committees, such as the Select Intelligence Committee, as standing committees. In the early 1990s, the House also terminated four select committees.

Joint Committees

Made up of members from both the House and Senate, **joint committees** can be temporary or permanent. Both parties are represented on them, just like other committees. These committees usually act as a kind of study group that reports back to the House and Senate on a topic or bill. For example, the Joint Economic Committee might report on the economic impact of the war in Iraq or the income trends for average Americans.

In theory, joint committees coordinate the work of the two houses of Congress, but they do not have the authority to deal directly with bills or to propose laws to Congress. In practice, lawmakers usually limit joint committees to handling routine matters such as are handled by the Joint Committee on Printing or the Joint Committee on the

CHAPTER 5: *The Organization of Congress* **143**

D Differentiated Instruction

Kinesthetic The standing committees of the Senate and the House address a variety of topics that are important to life in the United States. Ask students to collect and display some items that represent these topics (for example, an apple for Agriculture). Call on volunteers to pick up various items from the display, identify a standing committee that the item suggests, and explain why the committee is important and why it is appropriate for the committee to be a standing committee. **BL OL**

S Skill Practice

Visual Literacy Ask students to name two House committees whose work does not seem to be paralleled by a Senate committee. *(Answers include Education and the Workforce, House Administration, Resources, Science, Standards of Official Conduct, and Ways and Means.)* **OL**

Critical Thinking

Answer: Standing committees are permanent, but select committees are established temporarily, as the need arises.

Differentiated Instruction

Leveled Activities

ELL Vocabulary Activities, p. 5

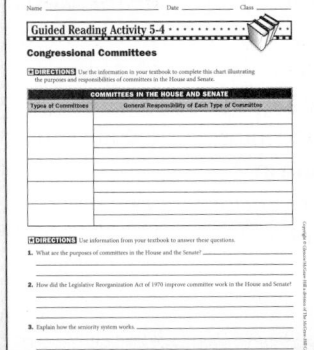

BL Guided Reading Activities, p. 20

OL Interpreting Political Cartoons, p. 9

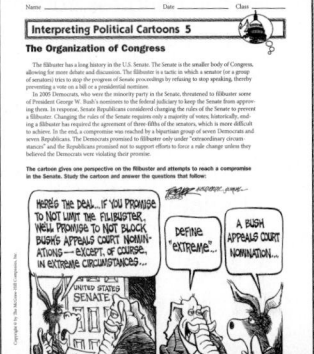

AL Participating in Government Activities, p. 9

C Critical Thinking

Identifying Central Issues

Organize the class into three groups—one that will function as the Senate, one that will function as the House, and one that will function as a conference committee. Have the Senate and House groups go through the process of passing the same school or classroom rule, with each group following the committee rules of its group. Each group will then turn over its rule (bill) to the conference committee group. This group will resolve the differences between the two versions of the rule (bill). **Ask:** What are the strengths and weaknesses of the Senate operating procedures? The House operating procedures? How did the conference committee resolve the differences between the two versions of the rule (bill)? **OL** **AL**

Caption Answer: Traditionally, committee chairs have been selected by seniority. In recent decades, they have been elected through a secret ballot.

Additional Support

A Chair's Influence

The Benefit of Experience
Longtime Michigan Senator Carl Levin (left) chairs the Armed Services Committee. A *TIME* magazine profile said he spends as many as 20 hours to prepare for hearings so he can get accurate testimony from witnesses who are appearing before the committee. Here he is conferring with Senator John McCain. *How does a member get the job of chairing a committee in the House or Senate?*

Library of Congress; some joint committees study more volatile matters, such as atomic energy, defense, or tax reform.

Conference Committees

No bill can be sent from Congress to the president until both houses have passed it in identical form. A **conference committee** is a temporary committee that is set up when the House and Senate have passed different versions of a bill. Its members, called conferees, usually come from the House and Senate standing committees that handled the bill. Democrats and Republicans are represented in the same way as on other committees.

The job of the conference committee is to resolve the differences between the two versions of the bill. Conference committees play a key role because they work out a bill that both houses will accept and can then send to the president to be signed. To get such a bill, the conferees bargain over each section of the bill. A majority of the conferees from each house must accept the final compromise bill—called a conference report—before it can be sent to the floor of the House and Senate. When the conference committee's report reaches the floor of each house, it must be considered as a whole and cannot be amended. It must be accepted or rejected as it is.

Choosing Committee Members

The career of a Congress member can be greatly influenced by the committees he or she is assigned. Assignment to the "right" committee can help a member's career in several ways. First, membership on some committees can increase a lawmaker's chances for reelection because it puts a congressperson in position to act on bills that are important to their constituents. A freshman representative from a farm state, for example, might be eager to serve on the House Committee on Agriculture.

Second, membership on some committees can mean the lawmaker will be able to influence national policies. Committees that often help formulate national policies include those dealing with education, the budget, health, the judiciary, and foreign policy. Third, some committees allow a member to influence many other members because they affect matters that are important to everyone in Congress. The House Rules Committee is an obvious example of a committee with wide powers.

In the House, the key committees are Rules, Ways and Means, and Appropriations. In the Senate, the most prestigious committees are Foreign Relations, Finance, and Appropriations.

144 UNIT 2: *The Legislative Branch*

Activity: Collaborative Learning

Role Play Select a bill that is currently being considered in Congress. You might want to choose a controversial bill that has recently been at the center of considerable media coverage. Have a group of student volunteers research the bill, gathering background information and facts that would help them in deciding whether they would be for or against passage. Ask the volunteers to present their findings to the class. Then organize a House or a Senate committee hearing and floor debate on the bill. For the hearing, assign some students to be committee members and others to be expert witnesses. Have committee members question the witnesses about their views on the bill. After members make revisions on the bill, send it to the full House (the class) for a floor debate and a vote. **OL**

Assignment to the Foreign Relations Committee, for example, will give a lawmaker a chance to influence American foreign policy directly. Senators on this committee usually receive a great deal of publicity, which is helpful in being reelected.

Assignment to Committees

In both the House and Senate, the parties have the job of assigning members to the standing committees. Newly elected members of Congress or veteran lawmakers who want to transfer to another committee approach party leaders when they want to seek a certain assignment that matches their interest. Each member can serve on only a limited number of standing committees and subcommittees.

The Role of the Committee Chair

Along with party leaders, the chairpersons of standing committees are the most powerful people in Congress. They make the key decisions about the work of committees, such as when committees will meet, which bills they will consider, and for how long. They decide when hearings will be held and which witnesses will be called to testify for or against a bill. Chairpersons also hire staff members for committees and to control its budget. Finally, chairs manage floor debates that take place on the bills that come from their committees.

Since the 1970s, the powers of committee chairpersons have been limited somewhat. The Legislative Reorganization Act of 1970 made a number of changes that made the committee system more democratic:

- A majority of committee members can call a meeting without the chair's approval.
- Committee members who disagree with the chair must be given time to present their views.
- Reasonable notice must be given for all committee hearings.

Changes in 1995 carried this democratic trend further by prohibiting the chair from casting an absent vote and requiring committees to publish all members' votes.

The Seniority System

The unwritten rule of seniority has guided the selection of chairpersons in the past. This meant that the majority party member with the longest uninterrupted service on a committee was appointed leader of that committee.

The **seniority system** has been criticized for giving a few congresspersons too much power. As a result, changes were made so that chairs are elected through a secret ballot. In 1971 House Republicans adopted this procedure, and in 1973 the Democrats followed suit. In a historic action in 1975, House Democrats voted to replace three senior committee chairs. Then in 1995, several senior Republicans were passed over as chairs in their elections. In the same year, Republicans decided that the chairs of House committees could not serve for more than three consecutive terms. For the most part, however, members tend to cast their ballots for the longest-serving members to chair committees.

C Critical Thinking

Predicting Consequences
Explain to students that incumbents are occasionally defeated when trying to get reelected. **Ask:** How will this affect the district or the state that the legislator represents? *(If the defeated incumbent had been a senior member of Congress and a member of important standing committees, it is unlikely that the newly elected junior legislator will automatically serve on the incumbent's committees.)* **AL**

Assess

Assign the Section 4 Assessment as homework or as an in-class activity, or have students take Section Quiz 5-4 from *Section Quizzes and Chapter Tests.*

Close

Hypothesizing Discuss why members of Congress might seek particular committee assignments. *(Certain committee memberships may help members with reelection by allowing them to work on bills that will benefit their district or state and help influence national policy making.)* **OL**

Section 4 Review

SECTION 4 Review

Vocabulary

1. Explain the significance of: standing committee, subcommittee, select committee, joint committee, conference committee, seniority system.

Main Ideas

2. Identifying What are the key committees in the House?

3. Classifying List the four important powers of a committee chairperson.

Critical Thinking

4. Making Inferences Why did Republicans, when they won control of Congress in 1995, institute many rule changes?

5. Contrasting In a Venn diagram like the one below, show how a conference committee and a joint committee are alike and how they are different.

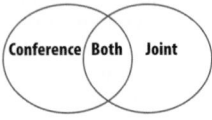

Writing About Government

6. Persuasive Writing Watch coverage of a congressional committee on television, or read about it in a newspaper. Outline the major issues presented in the testimony before the committee. Write a position paper in which you agree or disagree with a witness.

Answers

1. The terms are defined in the section and the Glossary.
2. Rules, Ways and Means, and Appropriations
3. Any four: makes key decisions about committee work, decides when hearings will be held and which witnesses will be called, hires committee staff members, controls the committee budget, manages floor debates over the bills from the committee
4. Possible answer: The majority party can set the rules, and the Republicans wanted to do things in ways that were more comfortable for them or that they considered to be more efficient.
5. Conference committees resolve differences between conflicting versions of a bill. Joint committees act as study groups. Both have members from the Senate and the House.
6. Students' analyses should focus on how well the witnesses made and supported their points. You might have students watch the same testimony and give their responses in the form of an informal debate.

Focus

Bellringer
Section Focus Transparencies 5-5

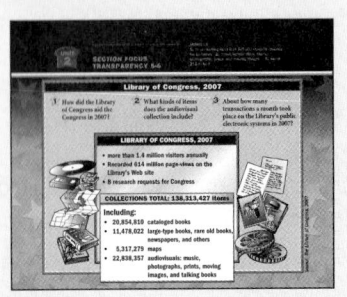

Reader's Guide

Answers to Graphic: Personal Staff: work directly for individual senators and representatives; run the lawmaker's office; research and draft bills; attend committee meetings; prepare speeches; handle requests for help from constituents.
Committee Staff: work for many House and Senate committee members; draft bills, study issues; collect information; plan committee hearings; write memos; prepare committee reports.

Resource Manager

Staff and Support Agencies

Reader's Guide

Content Vocabulary
★ personal staff (p. 147)
★ committee staff (p. 147)
★ administrative assistant (p. 148)
★ legislative assistant (p. 148)
★ caseworker (p. 148)

Academic Vocabulary
★ complex (p. 146)
★ expert (p. 147)
★ coordinate (p. 149)

Reading Strategy
As you read, create a table like the one below to describe the functions of congressional support staff.

Personal Staff	Committee Staff

Issues in the News

Voters sometimes complain about the cost of congressional staffs to the taxpayer. Few question another resource for Congress members: the Library of Congress. Its prime mission remains serving Congress's research needs, but its vast collection serves citizens and, for that matter, the world. In 2007 the Library of Congress announced that it would cooperate in the World Digital Library. This will join several nations' libraries in an effort to make rare artifacts available on the Web. One oral history connects directly to President Thomas Jefferson, whose many books increased the size of the early collections in the Library of Congress. "My grandfather belonged to Thomas Jefferson," one man says over the hiss of an old recording. "My grandfather was 115 years old when he died . . . . I am 101 years old."

▲ Thomas Jefferson played a role in establishing the Library of Congress.

The work of Congress is so extensive and **complex** that lawmakers have many resources to meet their obligations, including supporting agencies like the Library of Congress.

Its key resource, however, is trained staff that can help them draw up bills, be informed on issues, and represent their constituents. Members rely heavily on staff in their committee work. Staff members research issues and topics on the committees' agenda and schedule witnesses for hearings.

Since World War II, the size of staff has grown, often because the legislative branch believed it needed more staff to match the resources of the executive branch. After the Republican victories in the 1994 election, however, the House leadership cut staff to reflect their promise to reduce the overall size of government. Total committee staff was cut by one-third in the House and by 15 percent in the

Senate. Congress also adopted a resolution to cut the budgets of the legislative branch of the Government Accountability Office. Such staff reductions are rare.

Congressional Staff Role

When Lowell Weicker of Connecticut was in the Senate, a woman wrote to him complaining about the way an airline had handled her dog. The dog, shipped as animal cargo, died during the flight. One of the senator's secretaries mentioned the letter to the press secretary, who thought that the incident had news value. He phoned the Federal Aviation Agency and other government offices and found many similar cases. After informing the senator, the secretary wrote a draft of a bill to authorize the Transportation Department to regulate air transport of animals. Senator Weicker

R Reading Strategies	C Critical Thinking	D Differentiated Instruction	W Writing Support	S Skill Practice
Teacher Edition • Taking Notes, p. 148 • Identifying, p. 149 **Additional Resources** • Quizzes/Tests, pp. 55–64 • Guid. Read. Act., p. 21	**Teacher Edition** • Comparing and Contrasting, p. 147 • Drawing Conclusions, p. 150 **Additional Resources** • Read. Essen., pp. 60–62	**Teacher Edition** • Interpersonal, p. 147 **Additional Resources** • Foldables, p. 48	**Teacher Edition** • Persuasive Writing, p. 149	**Additional Resources** • Part. in Gov. Act., pp. 9–10

later introduced the legislation on the floor of the Senate. The story became headlines in Weicker's home state, and he received many letters of appreciation.

This story illustrates that staffers do much of the important work on legislation. Lawmakers rely on staffers to help them handle the growing workload of Congress, communicate with voters, run committee hearings and floor sessions, draft new bills, write committee reports, and attend committee meetings. Staffers also help lawmakers get reelected. Staffers help members of Congress get publicity, keep an eye on political developments back home, and write speeches and newsletters. They also help raise funds for election campaigns and meet with lobbyists and visitors from home.

Congressional Staff Growth

Congress has not always relied on staff to accomplish its work. For almost 100 years, senators and representatives had no personal aides. Occasionally they might hire assistants out of personal funds, but Congress provided no paid staff. Inadequate staffing became an urgent complaint by the time Congress considered the Legislative Reorganization Act in 1946. After that the number of staff members increased dramatically. The House and Senate employed 2,000 personal staff members in 1947, but more than 11,500 in 1990.

Committee staff increased from 400 to more than 3,000 in that same period.

Congressional staffs grew as lawmaking became more complex after the early 1900s. Lawmakers could not be **experts** on all the issues that came before their committees or that they needed to vote on in Congress. The demands that constituents placed on lawmakers also increased over the years. Members of Congress needed a large office staff simply to deal with the many letters from people in their states or congressional districts.

Voters do more than write to representatives to voice their opinions. Sometimes constituents expect their representatives to help them solve a specific problem. One legislator commented that more than half his total staff time is devoted to resolving problems that come up between individual citizens and state or federal government.

Personal Staff

Congress includes two types of staffs: **personal staff** and **committee staff.** Personal staff members work directly for individual senators and representatives. Committee staff members work for the many House and Senate committees.

The size of senators' personal staffs varies because the allowances to pay for them are based on the population of the senators' state and distance from the capital. Senators each receive a yearly budget to operate their offices. Most of this goes for staff salaries. About one-third of personal staffers work in

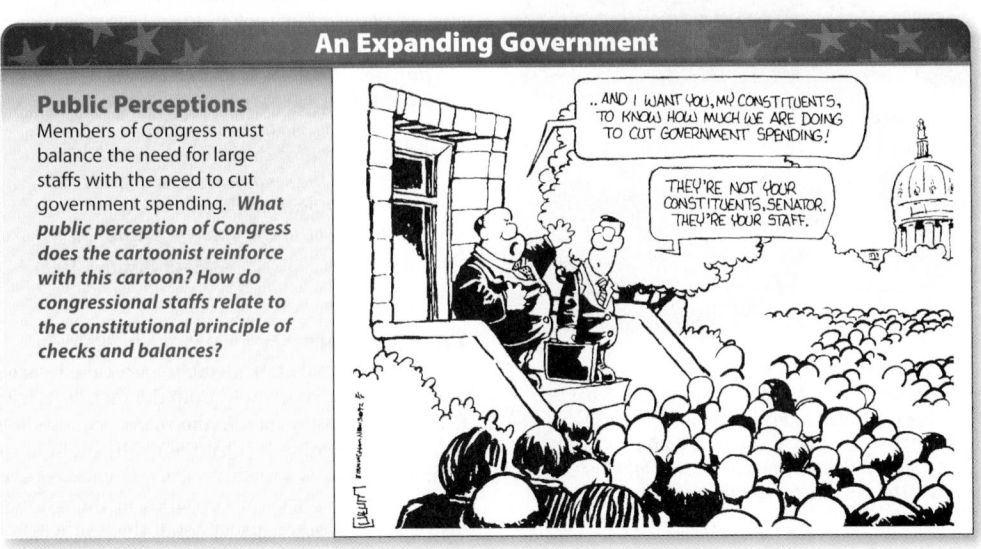

An Expanding Government

Public Perceptions
Members of Congress must balance the need for large staffs with the need to cut government spending. *What public perception of Congress does the cartoonist reinforce with this cartoon? How do congressional staffs relate to the constitutional principle of checks and balances?*

..AND I WANT YOU, MY CONSTITUENTS, TO KNOW HOW MUCH WE ARE DOING TO CUT GOVERNMENT SPENDING!

THEY'RE NOT YOUR CONSTITUENTS, SENATOR. THEY'RE YOUR STAFF.

CHAPTER 5: *The Organization of Congress* **147**

Teach

C Critical Thinking

Comparing and Contrasting
Have students brainstorm a list of responsibilities associated with the work of a member of Congress. **Ask:** If each member of Congress had to do this work alone, could the work of Congress be handled efficiently? (*No, there is too much work.*) What kind of help is needed? (*Assistants handle some less important responsibilities.*) BL OL

D Differentiated Instruction

Interpersonal Organize students into two groups—one to study personal staff and one to study committee staff. Have each group summarize the purpose of that kind of assistance and list several of the tasks that might be handled. AL

Caption Answer: It suggests that members of Congress are isolated from the public and that congressional staffs have grown too large. Staff help the lawmaking branch keep up with the expanding powers of the executive branch.

Hands-On Chapter Project
Step 5

Mock Senate

Step 5: Drafting a Compromise Bill
Groups conclude the lawmaking process.

Directions Have groups convene as conference committees, and compare the bill they approved and the bill passed by the House of Representatives. Then ask committees to draft a new compromise bill. After the compromise bills are complete, provide students with copies of each compromise bill and have them individually evaluate the bills. Reconvene the class, and then ask volunteers to share their comments about the class as a model Senate.

Evaluation Evaluations should consider the following:
1. Were the bill sponsors prepared to answer questions during floor debate? Were they able to support their views with facts and logic?
2. Were you prepared to question or challenge other bill sponsors? What helped you prepare? What might you have done differently?
3. Did you change any of your votes as a result of the floor debate? If so, what persuaded you to vote differently?
4. How well did your group work together? Explain your response. AL

R **Reading Strategy**

Taking Notes As they read, have students make a list of the three types of personal staff members lawmakers usually have in their offices. Have students write a brief description of each type of staff member when they have finished reading this page. **BL** **ELL**

Caption Answer: Students might suggest that legislative assistants wield influence by controlling the research and the reports on committee meetings.

Differentiated Instruction

---

the legislators' home states. The rest work in the capital. Each House member has an allowance to pay for a personal staff. The House and Senate employ thousands of personal staff aides. Lawmakers can hire and fire staff members at will.

Administrative Assistants

Lawmakers usually have three types of personal staff members in their offices. The **administrative assistant,** called an AA, is an important legislative aide. The AA runs the lawmaker's office, supervises the lawmaker's schedule, and gives advice on political matters. A good AA also deals with influential people from the lawmaker's congressional district or state, which may influence the lawmaker's reelection.

Legislative Assistants

Legislative assistants, or LAs, are a second type of personal staff member. An LA makes certain that the lawmaker is well informed about the many bills with which she or he must deal. An LA does research, drafts bills, studies bills that are currently in Congress, and writes speeches and articles for the lawmaker.

Another important part of the LA's job is to assist the lawmaker in committee meetings and to attend them when the lawmaker cannot be present. Senators and representatives cannot possibly attend all the committee and subcommittee meetings they are assigned to. When they do attend, they often arrive at the last minute and briefly talk with their LA to find out what has taken place. The LA, who has followed the meeting and studied the bill in question, may have prepared a short speech for the lawmaker or made up a list of questions for the lawmaker to ask witnesses. Often the senator or representative has not seen the speech or the questions but relies on the LA's judgment.

LAs keep track of what is happening on the floor of Congress and of any bills that are in committee. While routine legislative business goes on, the lawmaker may be in a committee meeting or talking with voters. When the buzzer rings, signaling time for a vote, lawmakers rush to the floor of the Senate or House from their offices or committee rooms. They might not know what the vote is about unless it involves a major bill that has been scheduled far in advance. As they walk, they look for their LAs.

In his book *In the Shadow of the Dome,* Mark Bisnow, a former legislative assistant, described the scene:

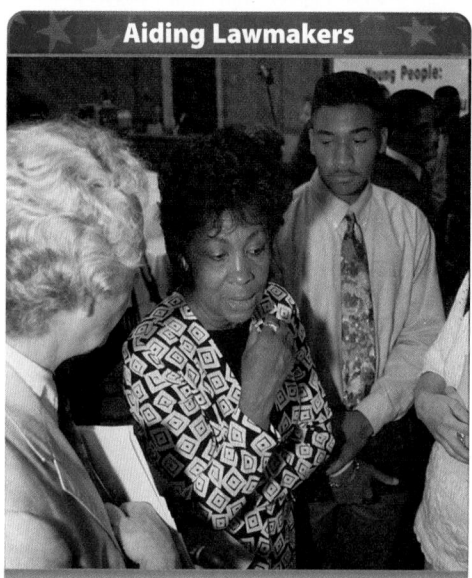

Aiding Lawmakers

Influencing Congress Democratic Congresswoman Maxine Waters (center) has been serving Los Angeles and nearby areas since 1991, often focusing on housing and community development. *How might her legislative assistants influence her work?*

❝ *As the door of the "Senators Only" elevator opened, their bosses would pour out. . . . If they did not know what they were voting on (votes occurred frequently throughout the day, and it was hard to keep track), . . . they would glance to the side to see if someone were waiting. A staffer might wave and run up for a huddled conference behind a pillar; or if the senator were in a hurry . . . he [or she] might simply expect a quick thumbs-up or thumbs-down gesture.* ❞

—Mark Bisnow, 1990

Caseworkers

Some personal staff members are called **caseworkers,** a term borrowed from the social services field, because they handle the many requests for help from a member's constituents. In addition to their offices in Washington, D.C., lawmakers are likely to have offices in key cities in their home district. Caseworkers usually staff these offices.

148 UNIT 2: *The Legislative Branch*

★ ★ ★ Activity: Multiple Learning Styles ★ ★ ★

Gifted and Talented Encourage students to consider the changes in the workload of Congress by asking the following questions: How have the increases in population affected Congress? How have the increases in the demands of constituents affected Congress? Do you think that these trends will continue, or do you foresee a change in this trend? Why? How might technological advances affect the workload of Congress? Do you consider changes in this area likely? Have students debate their answers to these questions and support their opinions with reasons and examples. **AL**

Committee Staff

Every committee and subcommittee in Congress has a staff. The larger a committee is, the more staff people it usually has. The committee chairperson and the senior minority party member of the committee are in charge of these staff members. Committee staffers draft bills, study issues, collect information, plan committee hearings, write memos, and prepare committee reports. They are largely responsible for the work involved in making laws.

Some senior committee staff members are very experienced and are experts in the area their committee covers, whether it is tax policy, foreign affairs, or health care. Laurence Woodworth, who spent 32 years on staff of the Joint Committee on Internal Revenue Taxation, is a good example of such an expert. As the committee's staff director for 14 years, he was largely responsible for all changes in the tax laws. Later, Woodworth left the committee to become assistant secretary of the treasury.

Do Staffers Have Too Much Power?

Staffers are not elected, yet they play a key role in the House and the Senate. Some lawmakers think staffers have too much influence, but others disagree. They say that the staff is only collecting information and developing alternative courses of action for them. In the end, the lawmakers make the judgment calls and direct the next steps to be taken.

Support Agencies

Several agencies in the legislative branch of government provide services that support the Congress. Some of their services are available to the other two branches of government and to American citizens, too. The four important support agencies created by Congress are discussed below.

The Library of Congress

Early in the nation's history, Congress created the Library of Congress to purchase such books as may be necessary for the use of Congress and to serve as the research arm of Congress. Much of the library was destroyed when the British burned the capital during the War of 1812. Congress then authorized the purchase of Thomas Jefferson's more than 6,000 books to rebuild the collection. Today, the Library

Congressional Research The Library of Congress owns more than 80 million items including 4 million maps and 6 million pieces of music. It contains 532 miles of bookshelves. *Why would members of Congress require research materials?*

of Congress is the largest library in the world, containing more than 100 million books, journals, music pieces, films, photographs, and maps.

The Library is the administrator of the copyright law; as a result, it receives two free copies of most published works copyrighted in the United States.

The Library of Congress has a Congressional Research Service (CRS) with hundreds of employees. Every year, CRS answers thousands of requests for information from lawmakers, congressional staff, and committees. CRS workers will check out anything from the number of kangaroos in Australia to the crime rates in urban areas. Congress members use the CRS to research matters related to bills that are before Congress and to answer requests from voters.

Congressional Budget Office (CBO)

Congress established the CBO in 1974 to **coordinate** the budget work of Congress, to study the budget proposals put forward by the president each year, and to project the costs of proposed

W Writing Support

Persuasive Writing Tell students that the employees of staff and support agencies will be more efficient at their jobs if they have a clear understanding of what a member of Congress needs. Ask students to write memos in which the member of Congress asks for a specific kind of help from a staff member or an employee of a support agency. **OL** **AL**

R Reading Strategy

Identifying Have students identify which agency should be consulted for information in the following cases:

- How much money a congressional committee is spending (*Congressional Budget Office*)
- The crime rate for the three largest U.S. cities (*Library of Congress*)
- When copies of a House floor speech made yesterday will be available (*Government Printing Office*) **OL**

Caption Answer: to become better educated about the bills before Congress and to answer requests for information from voters

Additional Support

Activity: Collaborative Learning

Team Quiz Organize the class into five teams of students. Assign each team one of the five sections in Chapter 5. Each team should create a 10-question quiz on the material covered in their assigned section. Before having the teams administer their quizzes to the class, you might want to review the questions to rule out trick questions or those that are overly complex. A main benefit of the activity will come from having student teams review the material to form 10 questions with correct answers. **OL**

Critical Thinking

Drawing Conclusions Ask:
Do you think that congressional staff and supporting agencies aid or impede the democratic process? Have students share their responses in a class discussion. **OL**

Assess

Assign the Section 5 Assessment as homework or as an in-class activity, or have students take Section Quiz 5-5 from *Section Quizzes and Chapter Tests.*

Close

Making Generalizations Have students complete these sentences and then discuss their responses.

• Congressional staff and support agencies have grown because

_____.

• Because congressional staff and support agencies have grown,

_____. **OL**

Section 5 Review

---

programs. The CBO counterbalances the president's elaborate budget organization, the Office of Management and Budget. CBO staffers study economic trends, track how much congressional committees are spending, and report on the budget each April. They also calculate how budget decisions might affect the economy.

Government Accountability Office (GAO)

Established in 1921, this agency is the nation's watchdog over how the funds Congress appropriates are spent. A comptroller general appointed to a 15-year term directs the GAO. The agency has a professional staff of about 3,000 people. They review the financial management of government programs that Congress creates, collect government debts, settle claims, and provide legal service.

Many GAO staff members answer requests for information about specific programs from lawmakers and congressional committees. They also prepare reports on various federal programs for lawmakers, testify before committees, develop questions for committee hearings, and provide legal opinions on bills that are under consideration. Almost one-third of the GAO's work now comes from congressional requests for information.

Government Printing Office (GPO)

The Government Printing Office is the largest multipurpose printing plant in the world. It does the printing for the entire federal government.

Every day the GPO prints the Congressional Record, a daily record of all the bills introduced in both houses and of the speeches and testimony presented in Congress. Members can amend the speeches they have made before they are printed in the *Congressional Record.* They can also have speeches they never actually made in the House or Senate printed there.

Congressional staffers spend a good deal of time preparing speeches for legislators because those words will be published in the *Record.* When voters ask about the lawmaker's position on a particular issue, the staff can send a copy of the *Record* containing a speech the lawmaker made on that issue to the constituent who is making the request.

Another valuable publication of the Government Printing Office is the *Statistical Abstract of the United States,* which has been updated and printed every year since 1878 and is now available online. Published by the Bureau of the Census, it gives a wealth of information about various topics related to the United States—population statistics, government expenditures, average personal income, levels of education, business, agriculture, law enforcement, elections, and many other topics. It is an invaluable source of data for congressional staff as well as the general public.

These support agencies are vital for the Congress to function. They have helped the legislative **C** branch become less dependent on the executive branch for information. This has helped Congress regain some of the power it held in earlier years.

SECTION 5 Review

Vocabulary

1. **Explain** the significance of: personal staff, committee staff, administrative assistant, legislative assistant, caseworker.

Main Ideas

2. **Analyzing** Why did the numbers of congressional staff increase rapidly after 1900?

3. **Examining** What is the primary task of the Congressional Research Service?

Critical Thinking

4. **Demonstrating Reasoned Judgment** Why do you think the comptroller general who oversees the Government Accountability Office is appointed for a 15-year term?

5. **Organizing** In the table below, describe the functions of support agencies for Congress.

Support Agency	Function

Writing About Government

6. **Persuasive Writing** Create a political cartoon with a caption about the role of committee staff in Congress. Take a position on whether staff members have too much power.

Answers

1. The terms are defined in the section and the Glossary.
2. Staff grew to cope with the growing complexity of lawmaking and increasing numbers of constituents.
3. The Congressional Research Service researches matters related to bills that are before Congress and also addresses research requests from voters.
4. Possible answer: The comptroller general needs to serve a long term to trace the ways in which Congress appropriates and spends funds.

5. The Library of Congress: serves as the research arm of Congress; Congressional Budget Office: coordinates the budget work of Congress; Government Accountability Office: watches how funds Congress appropriates are spent; Government Printing Office: does the printing for the entire federal government
6. Students' political cartoons should express an opinion about the power of staff members. Have students write their captions on a separate piece of paper. Prior to having each student read his or her caption, other class members can suggest captions for each cartoon.

Should the U.S. Adopt Proportional Representation?

Most democracies use proportional representation to elect their legislators. Legislators are elected from multi-seat districts in proportion to the votes they receive. A district might be represented by two members from one party and three from another. In the United States, the candidate with the largest number of votes represents the entire district. Should this winner-take-all system be replaced by proportional representation?

 YES Lani Guinier, Professor of Law, University of Pennsylvania

Primary Source

❝ [The current] system crudely overcompensates the majority: a candidate who wins with even 50.5 percent of the vote gets 100 percent of the power. . . .

All voters, not just black voters, are affected by this. In cities, heavily Democratic voting districts often submerge Republican voters; in Republican-dominated suburbs, the voices of Democratic voters cannot be heard. All political constituencies suffer. Women cannot join forces with like-minded voters who don't live in their neighborhood. . . .

Choice—so highly valued in the commercial marketplace—is even more important in the marketplace of ideas. Where elections do not result in only one winner, diverse viewpoints can be represented. ❞

—"Don't Scapegoat the Gerrymander," The *New York Times Magazine*, January 8, 1995

NO Abigail M. Thernstrom, Senior Fellow, the Manhattan Institute

Primary Source

❝ [T]he purpose of an electoral system is not to mirror the population precisely, but to produce officials who can govern. The current system not only creates incentives for reaching across racial and ethnic lines . . . but also forces compromise among various political factions. From multimember districts, the next step . . . will encourage a multiplicity of parties. . . . There will be a David Duke party and a black nationalist party, and blacks and whites will both be the losers. In order to govern, representatives from a variety of warring parties will have to create shifting coalitions, [which] will inject instability into a system that now works well. ❞

—Statement before a subcommittee of the U.S. House of Representatives, September 23, 1999

Debating the Issue

1. **Contrasting** How do the proportional representation and the winner-take-all systems differ?

2. **Analyzing** According to Professor Guinier, what is wrong with the winner-take-all system?

3. **Theorizing** Which system do you think would produce a better government? Why?

▶ A voter in Germany where proportional representation is used

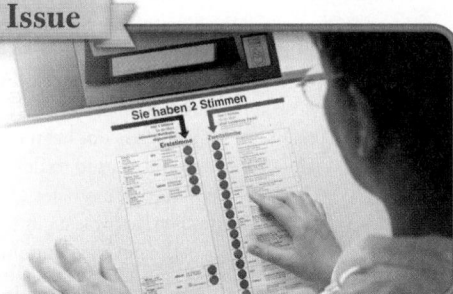

Teach

Setting Up the Debate

Analyzing Help students focus on the issue of proportional representation as it relates to electing legislators. **Ask:** What is proportional representation? (*Proportional representation is a system in which several officials are elected to represent the same area in proportion to the votes each party's candidate receives.*)

Evaluating Have students conduct research to identify instances outside of the United States in which proportional representation is used to elect legislatures. Have students on the panel meet to build their arguments for and against the system of proportional representation. Urge both groups to consider their findings about the use of proportional representation in other countries as well as current issues involving its use.

Concluding the Debate

Discuss these questions with the participants:

- What standards did you set in identifying evidence either for or against the use of proportional representation?
- What arguments would you have used in response to information provided by the opposing view on the issue?

Debating the Issue Answers

1. In a proportional representation system, legislators are elected from multi-seat districts in proportion to the number of votes they receive. In a winner-take-all system, the candidate with the largest number of votes represents the entire district.

2. Professor Guinier believes that the winner-take-all system "crudely overcompensates the majority," which stifles the voices of the minority.

3. Students' answers will vary but should be supported with logical explanations.

TIME NOTEBOOK

Focus

R₁ Reading Strategy

Questioning Read aloud this description of the Johnson treatment: "Its tone could be supplication, accusation, cajolery, exuberance, scorn, tears, complaint, the hint of threat. . . . Its velocity was breathtaking. . . . [Johnson] moved in close, his face a scant millimeter from his target. . . . [It] was an almost hypnotic experience and rendered the target stunned and helpless." Discuss students' reactions to this description, as well as their opinions on effective styles of leadership. **OL**

Teach

R₂ Reading Strategy

Reading Primary Sources Have students read the quotes in the Verbatim section and then conduct a class discussion about each item as it relates to the people and themes found in the textbook. **OL**

Additional Support

THE JOHNSON TREATMENT

LYNDON B. JOHNSON, Senate leader from 1955 to 1961, had a unique way of persuading colleagues to see his point of view. He would lean in close, cajole, and sometimes touch the other person for emphasis—techniques some might refer to as gentle bullying. **R₁**

Senator Johnson gives Senator Theodore Francis Green "the treatment."

SYMBOLS IN THE HOUSE AND SENATE

THE MACE is made up of 13 ebony rods tied together with silver string and topped by a globe upon which sits a silver eagle with outstretched wings. This nearly four-foot high bundle is placed at the right of the Speaker's desk at the beginning of each House session. If a member becomes unruly, the sergeant at arms has been known to place the mace in front of that person—or march up and down the aisle with the mace until people calm down.

THE GAVEL is a symbol of authority used by both the House and the Senate. The Senate has a fondness for a certain silver-capped ivory gavel that is placed on the vice president's desk at the opening of each Senate session. This gavel has not been used since 1954, when it started to deteriorate; it has since been replaced by a replica that was a gift from the government of India.

Courtesy U.S. House of Representatives

VERBATIM

WHAT PEOPLE SAID

❝I think it is high time we remembered that the Constitution speaks not only of the freedom of speech but also of trial by jury instead of trial by accusation....❞

Senator Margaret Chase Smith *of Maine, standing up to Senator Joseph McCarthy during his anti-Communist crusade in 1950*

❝Members of the Congress, the Constitution makes us not rivals for power but partners for progress. We are all trustees for the American people, custodians of the American heritage.❞

President John F. Kennedy, *in a 1962 State of the Union Address* **R₂**

❝It is the duty of every member of this House to act upon his conscience and his sense of duty. It is his business to be right, careless of what may happen to him in consequence thereof.❞

Representative Thomas Brackett Reed, *in an 1884 speech in the House of Representatives*

❝Congress is the great commanding theater of this nation.❞

Thomas Jefferson, *in an 1808 letter to William Wirt, a lawyer and statesman*

Collaborative Learning

Creating a Handbook Have students work cooperatively to create a "Who's Who" handbook of members of Congress from their state. Students should divide up research tasks. Suggest that for each representative and senator students include some background information, length of service, committee and subcommittee membership, and major accomplishments while in office. Students from states with fewer than 12 representatives and senators might want to make their handbook a historical "Who's Who," focusing on leading members of Congress of the past. Have students display their handbooks for other government classes. **BL OL**

MILESTONES

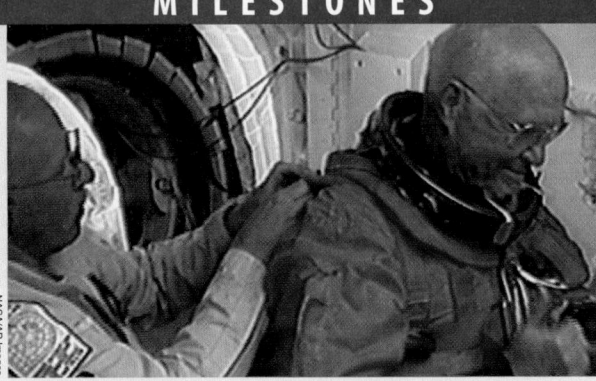

LAUNCHED, 1998. JOHN GLENN, former Ohio senator and the first American to orbit Earth, became the oldest person to travel in space as a passenger aboard a NASA space shuttle. He was 77.

APPOINTED, 1971. TWO 16-YEAR-OLD GIRLS became the first females to serve as Senate pages. In the 1830s, Senator Daniel Webster had appointed a 9-year-old boy to run errands and deliver messages for him—and the tradition of Senate pages was born, an all-male tradition that was not broken for more than 130 years.

TALKED THE TALK, 1957. SENATOR STROM THURMOND of South Carolina set a filibuster record by refusing to give up the Senate floor. He talked for 24 hours and 18 minutes.

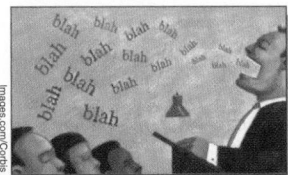

UNSEATED, 1926. SMITH BROOKHART became the only person in U.S. history to be unseated in the Senate following a recount of votes. After a long dispute, the Senate recounted all 900,000 votes from a 1924 race in Iowa—and realized that the wrong man was currently serving. In 1926 it awarded the Senate seat to the true winner, Daniel Steck.

TIE BROKEN, 2001. VICE PRESIDENT DICK CHENEY used his powers as president of the Senate (a position given to every U.S. vice president) to break a tie vote. Cheney's move approved an amendment to a resolution that allowed up to $300 billion to be spent on Medicare prescription drug coverage.

NUMBERS

1st In 1968 Shirley Chisholm became the first African American woman elected to Congress. Four years later, the New York state resident was the first African American and first woman to enter the race for her party's nomination for president of the United States.

#1

1st In 1992 Carol Mosley-Braun became the first African American woman elected to the United States Senate.

1st Ben Nighthorse Campbell was the first Native American to chair the Senate Indian Affairs Committee. Judo champ, gold medalist at the Pan American Games, jewelry designer, rancher—all these titles fit this versatile senator.

1 The number of votes in the Senate by which Texas squeaked into the Union in 1845. (Other senators were holding out, thinking Texas should be carved up into four separate states.)

1 The number of votes by which the Senate approved the purchase of Alaska from Russia for around $7 million.

W Writing Support

Narrative Writing Have students research one of the following people: John Glenn, Strom Thurmond, Shirley Chisholm, Margaret Chase Smith, Carol Mosley-Braun, or Ben Nighthorse Campbell. Ask students to write a one-page essay about the person's place in history. **OL AL**

S Skill Practice

Locating Have students use library and Internet resources to find at least five other significant "firsts" pertaining to Congress. Examples include the first woman elected to the Senate, the first African American elected to Congress, etc. **BL ELL**

Close

Have students select one of the people mentioned on pages 152–153. Ask each student to learn one new thing about the person selected. Have volunteers share their findings with the class.

Additional Support

Extending the Content

Congressional Pages Today, about 100 young adults serve as congressional pages at any given time. House and Senate pages must be high school juniors and at least 16 years old. They live in supervised housing near the Capitol and earn salaries at the annual rate of about $19,400. Pages, who must be appointed and sponsored by a member of Congress, serve for one or two semesters of a school year or a summer session. Pages who serve during the school year are educated at special schools in Washington, D.C.

CHAPTER
5 Assessment and Activities

Assessment and Activities

ExamView®
Assessment Suite

This easy-to-use software includes extensive question banks and allows you to create fully customized tests that can be administered in print or online.

Reviewing Vocabulary

1. c
2. c
3. a
4. b
5. c
6. c
7. a
8. a
9. c
10. c

Reviewing Main Ideas

11. Incumbents find it easier to raise campaign funds; they often represent districts that have been gerrymandered in their party's favor; they are better known to voters; they use their positions and office staff to help solve problems for voters.
12. House Rules Committee
13. Senate rules are more flexible than House rules. Senate rules are designed to give all senators maximum freedom to express their ideas. House rules are more complex and are designed to move legislation quickly once it reaches the floor.
14. Health, Income and Family Support, Oversight, Select Revenue Measures, Social Security, and Trade
15. The Congressional Budget Office coordinates the budget work of Congress (the Senate and the House), while the Office of

Reviewing Vocabulary

Match each content vocabulary word below with one of the following terms:

   a. House   **b.** Senate   **c.** Both chambers

  1. bill   **6.** joint committee
  2. majority leader   **7.** redistrict
  3. gerrymander   **8.** reapportionment
  4. filibuster   **9.** censure
  5. constituent   **10.** incumbent

Reviewing Main Ideas

Section 1 *(pages 123–130)*

11. Describing What are four advantages that incumbents have in running for office?

Section 2 *(pages 132–137)*

12. Identifying Which is the most powerful committee in the House of Representatives?

Section 3 *(pages 138–140)*

13. Contrasting How do House rules differ from Senate rules?

Section 4 *(pages 141–145)*

14. Analyzing What are the six subcommittees of the House Ways and Means Committee?

Section 5 *(pages 146–150)*

15. Summarizing How does the Congressional Budget Office differ from the Office of Management and Budget?

Critical Thinking

16. 🎖 **Essential Question** Why does the Constitution provide for free and unlimited debate in Congress?

17. Explaining How does the census affect the reapportionment of the House?

18. Making Comparisons In a graphic organizer, compare the duties of a congressional administrative assistant with those of a legislative assistant.

administrative	legislative

Chapter Summary

Congress

	Senate	House of Representatives
Presiding officer	Vice president	Speaker of the House
Qualifications	30 years old, U.S. citizen for 9 years, legal resident of the state where elected	25 years old, U.S. citizen for 7 years, legal resident of the state where elected
Terms of office	6 years	2 years
Number of members	100 voting representatives—two from each state	435 voting representatives
Annual salary	$169,300	$169,300

Committees	Staff	Support Agencies
★ Needed to manage the thousands of bills proposed	★ Personal staff work for individual senators and representatives	★ Help Congress carry out its powers
★ Include standing, select, joint, and conference committees	★ Committee staff work for particular committees	★ Some services also available to other branches and the public

Management and Budget is involved with the president's budget organization.

Critical Thinking

16. to ensure that legislators would have the freedom to express their ideas and opinions
17. A state's population determines its number of House members.
18. Administrative: run the lawmaker's office; supervise schedules; give advice on political matters. Legislative: attend committee meetings; keep track of work on floor of Congress; keep the lawmaker informed.

Government ONLINE **Self-Check Quiz**
Visit glencoe.com and enter *QuickPass*™ code USG9822c5.
Click on Self-Check Quizzes for additional test practice.

CHAPTER **5** **Assessment and Activities**

Document-Based Questions

Analyzing Primary Sources

Read the excerpt below and answer the questions that follow.

In 1775, at the request of the Continental Congress, John Adams wrote *Thoughts on Government,* in which he detailed what he believed would be the components of an ideal form of government. He advocated, among other things, a bicameral legislature.

❝ *A representation of the people in one assembly being obtained, a question arises, whether all the powers of government, legislative, executive, and judicial, shall be left in this body? I think a people cannot be long free, nor ever happy, whose government is in one assembly....*

[L]et a distinct assembly be constituted, as a mediator between the two extreme branches of the legislature, that which represents the people, and that which is vested with the executive power.

Let the representative assembly then elect by ballot, from among themselves or their constituents, or both, a distinct assembly, which, for the sake of perspicuity, we will call a council. It ... should have a free and independent exercise of its judgment, and consequently a negative voice in the legislature. ❞

19. John Adams advocated a bicameral legislature with an upper house that would be appointed by leaders and a lower house that would be elected by the population. What are the benefits of having a legislative body that is arranged in this manner?

20. Even though Adams believed that one section of the legislative branch should be appointed, both houses of the U.S. Congress are directly elected. What are the benefits of direct elections of representatives?

Interpreting Political Cartoons

Analyze the cartoon and answer the questions that follow. Base your answers on the cartoon and your knowledge of Chapter 5.

21. What is the subject of this cartoon?
22. What do the roots of the tree trunk symbolize?
23. According to this cartoon, how difficult is it to unseat an incumbent in Congress?

Participating IN GOVERNMENT

24. The idea of a constitutional amendment requiring term limits for members of Congress has been debated in recent years. What are the arguments for and against a constitutional amendment on term limits? What is your view? Research this issue and write a letter to the editor of your local paper expressing your opinion for or against term limits. Be sure to include at least three arguments that support your position in the letter.

CHAPTER 5: *The Organization of Congress* **155**

Government ONLINE

Have students use the *Chapter 5 Self-Check Quiz.* Visit glencoe.com and enter *QuickPass*™ code USG9085c5T to prepare for the Chapter Test.

Interpreting Political Cartoons

21. incumbent members of Congress
22. The roots represent the network of support that incumbents build—a network that makes it hard for them to be "uprooted" by a challenger at election time.
23. It is extremely difficult.

Participating IN GOVERNMENT

24. Students' letters to the editor should reflect research, and students should support their opinions with facts.

Chapter Bonus Test Question

Ask: What is the House mace, and has it ever been used? *(The mace is a 46-inch-long staff topped by a silver globe and an eagle with outstretched wings. The sergeant-at-arms has used the mace to restore order on several occasions. Sometimes the Speaker has ordered the sergeant-at-arms to parade it up and down aisles to quiet agitated members.)*

Analyzing Primary Sources

19. Answers might include the idea that the houses could balance each other if conflict arose during lawmaking. Having two houses prevents any one section of the legislative body from gaining too much power. A bicameral legislature ensures that discussion of most important matters will take place, because one house will generally always act as a "negative" or dissenting voice in the discussion.

20. Students should note that direct election helps guard against corruption in the government because constituents can always remove a particular candidate from office through their voting power. Also, the people can more easily voice their opinions on certain matters through the direct election of their representatives.

155

Key to Ability Levels	
BL Below level	**AL** Above level
OL On level	**ELL** English Language Learners

Key to Teaching Resources	
📁 Print Material	🖦 Transparency
💿 CD-ROM or DVD	

| Levels | | | | | Resources | Chapter Opener | Section 1 | Section 2 | Section 3 | Chapter Assess |
BL	OL	AL	ELL							
					FOCUS					
BL	OL	AL	ELL	🖦	Section Focus Transparencies		6-1	6-2	6-3	
					TEACH					
BL	OL		ELL	📁	Reading Essentials and Study Guide (and Answer Key)		p. 63	p. 66	p. 68	
BL	OL		ELL	📁	Guided Reading Activities		p. 22	p. 23	p. 24	
BL	OL		ELL	📁	Vocabulary Activities			p. 6		
BL	OL	AL	ELL	📁	Chapter Summaries				p. 16	
BL	OL			📁	American Biographies					
BL	OL	AL	ELL	📁	Cooperative Learning Activities					
	OL	AL	ELL	📁	Government Simulations and Debate					
BL	OL	AL	ELL	📁	Historical Documents and Speeches		p. 6			
BL	OL	AL	ELL	📁	Interpreting Political Cartoons				p. 9	
BL	OL		ELL	📁	Skill Reinforcement Activities			p. 6		
BL	OL	AL	ELL	📁	Source Readings			p. 6		
BL	OL			📁	Supreme Court Case Studies		pp. 7, 97	p. 75		
BL	OL	AL	ELL	📁	Participating in Government Activities		p. 11	p. 7		
BL	OL		ELL	📁	Spanish Declaration of Independence and U.S. Constitution	✓	✓	✓	✓	✓
BL	OL	AL	ELL	📁	NGS World Atlas, Spanish	✓	✓	✓	✓	✓
BL	OL	AL	ELL	🖦	Unit Overlay Transparencies, Strategies, and Activities	✓	✓	✓	✓	✓
BL	OL		ELL	🖦	Making It Relevant Transparencies	✓	✓	✓	✓	✓
BL	OL	AL	ELL	🖦	High School Writing Process Transparencies, Strategies, and Activities	✓	✓	✓	✓	✓
BL	OL	AL		🖦	American Art & Architecture Transparencies, Strategies, and Activities	✓	✓	✓	✓	✓

✓ Chapter- or unit-based activities applicable to all sections in this chapter

TeacherWorks™ Plus

All-In-One Planner and Resource Center

- Interactive Lesson Planner
- Interactive Teacher Edition
- Fully editable blackline masters
- Chapter Spotlight Videos Launch
- Differentiated Lesson Plans
- Printable reports of daily assignments
- Standards tracking system

Levels					Resources	Chapter Opener	Section 1	Section 2	Section 3	Chapter Assess
BL	OL	AL	ELL							
TEACH *(continued)*										
BL	OL			💿	**American Music: Hits Through History**	✓	✓	✓	✓	✓
BL	OL		ELL	📁	**Reading Strategies for the Social Studies Classroom**	✓	✓	✓	✓	✓
			ELL	📁	**English Language Learner Handbook**	✓	✓	✓	✓	✓
BL	OL		ELL	📁	**Writer's Guidebook for Social Studies**	✓	✓	✓	✓	✓
BL	OL	AL	ELL	📁	**Living Constitution, SE**	✓	✓	✓	✓	✓
BL	OL	AL	ELL	📁	**Living Constitution, TAE**	✓	✓	✓	✓	✓
BL	OL			📁	**NGS World Atlas, English**	✓	✓	✓	✓	✓
BL	OL		ELL	📁	**The Constitution and You (poster set)**	✓	✓	✓	✓	✓
BL	OL	AL	ELL	📁	**Spanish Chapter Summaries**				p. 16	
BL	OL	AL	ELL	📁	**Spanish Vocabulary Activities**			p. 6		
BL	OL		ELL	📁	**Spanish Reading Essentials and Study Guide (and Answer Key)**		p. 63	p. 66	p. 68	
BL	OL	AL	ELL	💿	**PresentationPlus! with MindJogger CheckPoint**	✓	✓	✓	✓	✓
ASSESS										
BL	OL	AL	ELL	💿	*ExamView® Assessment Suite*		6-1	6-2	6-3	Ch. 6
BL	OL	AL	ELL	📁	**Authentic Assessment with Rubrics**				p. 13	p. 13
BL	OL	AL	ELL	📁	**Section Quizzes and Chapter Tests**		p. 65	p. 66	p. 67	pp. 69–76
BL	OL	AL	ELL	📁	**Spanish Section Quizzes and Tests**		p. 65	p. 66	p. 67	pp. 69–76
CLOSE										
BL			ELL	📁	**Reteaching Activities**		p. 6			p. 6
BL	OL	AL	ELL	💿	**StudentWorks™ Plus with Audio Summaries**	✓	✓	✓	✓	✓
BL	OL		ELL	🖨	**Graphic Organizer Transparencies**		✓	✓	✓	
BL	OL		ELL	📁	**High School Government Reading and Study Skills Foldables®**		p. 49	p. 49	p. 49	

Teach With Technology

What is *ExamView® Assessment Suite?*

Glencoe's *ExamView® Assessment Suite* is a powerful assessment tool that enables you to create and customize tests for your students. Tests can be printed or administered online.

How can *ExamView® Assessment Suite* help me?

ExamView® allows you to create test questions or choose from existing, fully editable banks of questions that are customized for this book. Question formats include true/false, multiple choice, completion, matching, short answer, and essay, and many questions are

based on documents, maps, or graphs. Each question includes reteach information where students can go for more help on the topic. The flexibility of *ExamView®* allows you to develop testing materials that:

- focus on specific skills or competencies
- address state or national standards
- are leveled for different abilities
- can be translated to Spanish in one click

ExamView® Assessment Suite is one of Glencoe's technology resources available for teachers.

Government ONLINE

Visit glencoe.com and enter *QuickPass*™ code USG9085c6T for Chapter 6 resources.

You can easily launch a wide range of digital products from your computer's desktop with the McGraw-Hill Social Studies widget.

	Student	Teacher	Parent
Media Library			
• Student Edition Section Audio	●		●
• Chapter Spotlight Videos	●	●	●
***United States Government* Online Learning Center (Web Site)**			
• Chapter Overviews	●	●	●
• Multilingual Glossaries	●	●	●
• Study-to-Go	●	●	●
• Student Web Activities	●	●	●
• Self-Check Quizzes	●	●	●
• Online Student Edition	●	●	●
• Vocabulary eFlashcards	●	●	●
• Web Activity Lesson Plans		●	
• Vocabulary PuzzleMaker	●	●	●
• Landmark Supreme Court Cases	●	●	●
• Beyond the Textbook	●	●	●

READING SUPPORT FROM
JAMESTOWN EDUCATION

- **Timed Readings Plus in Social Studies** helps students increase their reading rate and fluency while maintaining comprehension. The 400-word passages are similar to those found on state and national assessments.

- **Reading in the Content Area: Social Studies** concentrates on six essential reading skills that help students better comprehend what they read. The book includes 75 high-interest nonfiction passages written at increasing levels of difficulty.

- **Reading Social Studies** includes strategic reading instruction and vocabulary support in Social Studies content for ELLs and native speakers of English. www.jamestowneducation.com

Reading List Generator CD-ROM
GLENCOE BookLink 3

Use this database to search more than 30,000 titles to create a customized reading list for your students.

- Reading lists can be organized by students' reading level, author, genre, theme, or area of interest.

- The database provides Degrees of Reading Power™ (DRP) and Lexile™ readability scores for all selections.

- A brief summary of each selection is included.

Leveled reading suggestions for this chapter:

- *If You Were There When They Signed the Constitution,* by Elizabeth Levy

- *The United States Constitution,* by Kristal Leebrick

Review suggested books before assigning them.

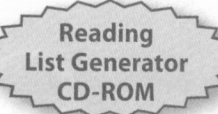

Economics Connection

Personal Finance Literacy

Living on a Budget

In 2007 the federal government had to borrow $162 billion because it spent more than the revenue it took in. That year American consumers owed nearly $2.5 trillion in non-mortgage debt, about 14 percent of their disposable after-tax income. Median credit-card debt by mid-2008 was $1,673.

Why do we spend more money than we have? Many people have no idea where their money goes. It just seems to disappear. In hard times, we need credit to pay for necessities, such as food and transportation. But most debt is caused by overspending on things we *want*—but do not actually *need*. It may seem fun to splurge on impulse purchases, but those splurges prevent you from saving money for important things, such as education, a car, and, eventually, a home and retirement. The best way to avoid overspending is to establish a budget—and stick to it.

Ask students: What did you buy last month that you did not need? Have them complete "Wants" and "Needs" lists on the whiteboard.

Practice budgeting: Have students create budgets by first writing down the amount of money they earn monthly (or a fictitious amount) above a 4-column table or spreadsheet:

- **Column 1, Spending Categories:** Food, Transportation, Entertainment, Personal Care (clothes, shoes, haircuts, cosmetics, accessories), Savings, Utilities (gas and electricity), Medical/Dental (if they contribute), Donations to Charity, Miscellaneous, Total

- **Column 2, Current Expenses:** the amount currently spent for each category

- **Column 3, New Budget:** the amount they *plan* to spend on each category

- **Column 4, Cuts:** ways they could trim expenses in each category

Did You Know?

American households spent an average of $2,694—almost half their food dollars—eating out an average of 5.8 times per week in 2006.

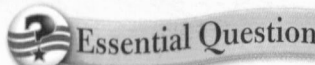

Essential Question

Refer students to the Essential Question on this page. Ask students if they can list the responsibilities of Congress. Have them group these powers into categories. Explain that the Constitution defines the powers of Congress, but those of the president and Supreme Court are not fully outlined. Ask students to hypothesize why the Framers of the Constitution might have detailed the powers of Congress so specifically.

Chapter Spotlight Video

To generate student interest and provide a springboard for class discussion, access the Chapter 6 Video at glencoe.com or on the video DVD.

Dinah Zike's Foldables are three-dimensional, interactive graphic organizers that help students practice basic writing skills, review key vocabulary terms, and identify main ideas. Have students complete this chapter's Foldable activity or activities in *Dinah Zike's Reading and Study Skills Foldables* booklet. **OL**

Government ONLINE

Visit glencoe.com and enter *QuickPass™* code USG9085c6T for Chapter 6 Resources including Chapter Overview, Student Web Activity, Self-Check Quiz, and other materials for students and teachers.

CHAPTER

6

Chapter Audio   Spotlight Video

Development of Congressional Powers

The Capitol

Essential Question

What powers did the Constitution give to the Congress, and how have these developed over time?

Government ONLINE
Chapter Overview Visit glencoe.com and enter *QuickPass™* code USG9822c6 for an overview, a quiz, and other chapter resources.

Launching the Chapter

Researching Congressional Power
Have students check recent news coverage about the powers of Congress (the power to tax and spend, to regulate interstate and foreign commerce, to approve presidential appointments, to conduct investigations, to practice legislative oversight, and so on). **Essential Question:** As students read the chapter, they should summarize what each set of powers involves. Then ask them to find newspaper and newsmagazine articles that deal with congressional actions. Have them summarize the articles and indicate which type of power Congress exercised in each case. Review the articles and summaries. If you choose, post them on a bulletin board under appropriate headings. **OL**

Constitutional Powers

Reader's Guide

Content Vocabulary
- ★ expressed powers (p. 157)
- ★ necessary and proper clause (p. 157)
- ★ implied powers (p. 157)
- ★ revenue bill (p. 158)
- ★ appropriations bill (p. 160)
- ★ interstate commerce (p. 161)
- ★ impeachment (p. 164)

Academic Vocabulary
- ★ initiate (p. 157)
- ★ major (p. 158)
- ★ bond (p. 160)

Reading Strategy
Use a graphic organizer to list the powers denied to Congress by the Constitution.

Congress cannot . . .

Issues in the News

More than once during the Iraq war, Congress and the president quarreled over war powers. The Constitution made the president commander in chief and gave Congress the power to declare war, but this has not been enough to solve disputes. In 2007 law professor Noah Feldman noted that the Constitution does not give any guidance "on the question of winding down hostilities. . . ." Can Congress "undeclare" a war? Congress holds the purse strings, so could it legally have withheld funding for President George W. Bush's troop surge in 2007? Feldman thinks Congress will always hesitate to step in once a war is on.

▲ A controversial surge in U.S. troops in Iraq began in the summer of 2007.

Can a president **initiate** military action without a declaration of war? The Constitution lays down many important principles, but it is not an exact blueprint. The Constitution is, in fact, unclear on many questions about how the president and Congress share power.

Nearly half of its text, however, is on the legislative branch of Article I. This suggests the Framers wanted Congress, the branch that directly represents the people, to play the central governmental role.

Constitutional Provisions

The Constitution describes the legislative powers of Congress in Article I, Section 8, Clauses 1–18.[1] 📖 These **expressed powers** of Congress are sometimes called the enumerated powers. The last clause (18) of Section 8 gives Congress power to do whatever is "necessary and proper" to carry out its other powers. This **necessary and proper clause** implies that Congress has powers beyond those in the first 17 clauses. Because these **implied powers** have allowed Congress to expand its role to meet the nation's needs, the "necessary and proper clause" has often been called the elastic clause.

Conflicting Interpretations

Because of the far-reaching implications of the expanding power of Congress, the Supreme Court has often had to resolve conflicts over what is

📖 See the following footnoted materials in the **Reference Handbook:**
1. The Constitution, pages R42–R67.

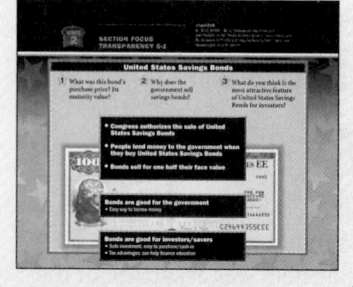

Teach

C Critical Thinking

Analyzing Primary Sources
Have students read the quote from John Marshall. **Ask:** Which side was supported in this ruling? *(the federal government or loose constructionists)* **OL**

S Skill Practice

Visual Literacy In 2004 Secretary of Defense Donald Rumsfeld was asked about the condition of military supplies and whether there was a military equipment shortage. His response was: "You go to war with the army you have, not the army you might want or wish to have at a later time." Discuss how this cartoon applies to the issue of military equipment and funding the war in Iraq. **Ask:** What do each of the characters represent? *(The father is Congress, the son is the military, and the mouse is Rumsfeld.)* **OL**

Caption Answer: Students may suggest that the cartoonist sympathizes with the military that now finds itself without any financial support.

Additional Support

"necessary and proper" legislation. The first **major** conflict was between supporters of "strict construction," or interpretation, of the Constitution and those who believed in a "loose construction."

When the Second Bank of the United States was created in 1816, the strict constructionists said Congress had no right to charter the Bank. They backed the state of Maryland when it taxed the notes of the Bank. A federal bank teller named James McCulloch then issued notes without paying the state tax, and Maryland sued.

When the state won in its own courts, the U.S. government appealed to the Supreme Court. Its majority opinion, written by Chief Justice John Marshall, supported the position of the loose constructionists:

> **C** 66 *The result of the most careful and attentive consideration bestowed upon this clause is, that if it does not enlarge, it cannot be construed to restrain the powers of Congress, or to impair the right of the legislature to exercise its best judgment in the selection of measures to carry into execution the constitutional powers of the government.* 99
> —John Marshall

Power of the Purse This early 2007 cartoon used a domestic family situation to comment on a current issue: whether Congress should withhold funding in the middle of the Iraq war. *What side is the cartoonist taking on that debate? Why do you think so?*

Powers Denied

The powers of Congress, like those of the other government branches, are limited. One very important constitutional limit is the Bill of Rights, but Article I, Section 9, of the Constitution also denies certain powers to Congress. It may not suspend the writ of habeas corpus—a court order to release a person accused of a crime to court to determine whether he or she has been legally detained. Congress may not pass bills of attainder—laws that establish guilt and punish people without a trial. Congress is also prohibited from passing ex post facto laws; that is, they cannot make an act criminal that was legal when it was committed. Article I, Section 9, also denies Congress a number of other powers, including the power to tax exports.

Legislative Powers

Congress has both legislative and non-legislative powers. Non-legislative powers include the power to confirm or deny presidential appointments, which is a power of the Senate. Congress has expanded the domain of its legislative powers—the power to pass laws—as the nation has grown. The most significant expansion of congressional legislative power is in its control over the economy—taxing, spending, and regulating commerce.

The Taxing and Spending Power

Perhaps the most important power of Congress is the power to levy taxes to provide for the general welfare. Sometimes this is called "the power of the purse." It allows Congress to influence policy because no government agency can spend money without its authorization. This broad authority to provide for the general welfare allows Congress to impose many taxes. For example, taxes on narcotics are meant to protect public health.

Article I, Section 7, says "All Bills for raising Revenue shall originate in the House of Representatives." **Revenue bills,** laws for raising money, start in the House and then go to the Senate. This provision was adopted at the Constitutional Convention because the more populous states, such as Virginia and Pennsylvania, insisted on having a greater voice in tax policy than the smaller states. Because representation in the House was to be based on population, the Founders agreed that any revenue bills introduced in Congress would originate there.

Activity: Collaborative Learning

Understanding Congressional Powers
Help students distinguish between expressed (enumerated) powers and implied powers. Organize students into an even number of groups. Half the groups should focus on the expressed powers of Congress (begin by listing the powers outlined in Article I, Section 8, of the Constitution). The other half should focus on the implied powers (with some members focusing on the expressed powers from which various implied powers arose). Each set of groups can assign its members tasks in the preparation of reports, diagrams, charts, and so on. Group representatives can review the powers and comment upon the importance of each power. **OL**

Charts In Motion
See StudentWorks™ Plus or go to glencoe.com.

The Powers of Congress

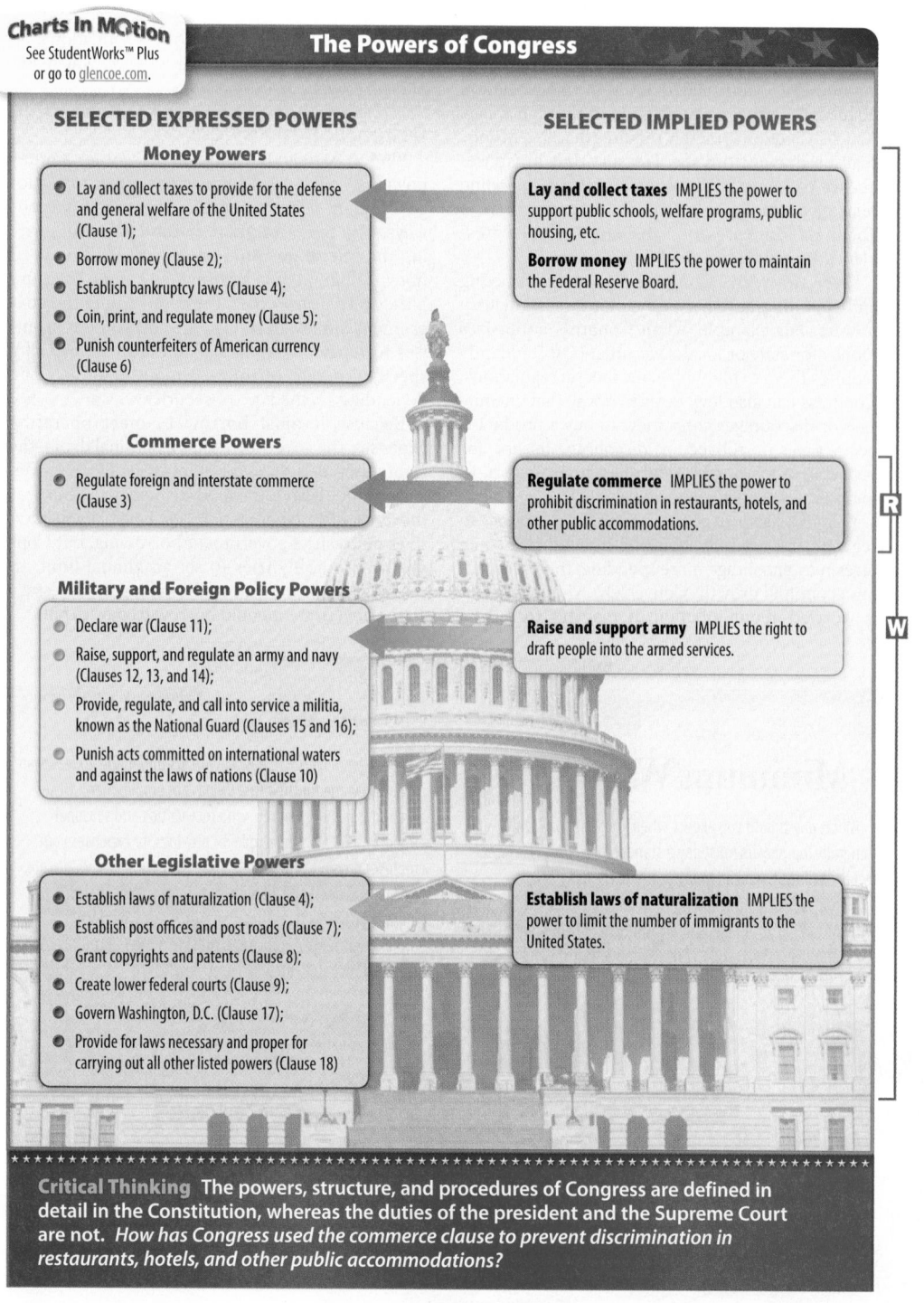

SELECTED EXPRESSED POWERS

Money Powers
- Lay and collect taxes to provide for the defense and general welfare of the United States (Clause 1);
- Borrow money (Clause 2);
- Establish bankruptcy laws (Clause 4);
- Coin, print, and regulate money (Clause 5);
- Punish counterfeiters of American currency (Clause 6)

Commerce Powers
- Regulate foreign and interstate commerce (Clause 3)

Military and Foreign Policy Powers
- Declare war (Clause 11);
- Raise, support, and regulate an army and navy (Clauses 12, 13, and 14);
- Provide, regulate, and call into service a militia, known as the National Guard (Clauses 15 and 16);
- Punish acts committed on international waters and against the laws of nations (Clause 10)

Other Legislative Powers
- Establish laws of naturalization (Clause 4);
- Establish post offices and post roads (Clause 7);
- Grant copyrights and patents (Clause 8);
- Create lower federal courts (Clause 9);
- Govern Washington, D.C. (Clause 17);
- Provide for laws necessary and proper for carrying out all other listed powers (Clause 18)

SELECTED IMPLIED POWERS

Lay and collect taxes IMPLIES the power to support public schools, welfare programs, public housing, etc.

Borrow money IMPLIES the power to maintain the Federal Reserve Board.

Regulate commerce IMPLIES the power to prohibit discrimination in restaurants, hotels, and other public accommodations.

Raise and support army IMPLIES the right to draft people into the armed services.

Establish laws of naturalization IMPLIES the power to limit the number of immigrants to the United States.

Critical Thinking The powers, structure, and procedures of Congress are defined in detail in the Constitution, whereas the duties of the president and the Supreme Court are not. *How has Congress used the commerce clause to prevent discrimination in restaurants, hotels, and other public accommodations?*

R Reading Strategy

Inferring Discuss how the power to regulate commerce allows Congress to ban discrimination in public places. **Ask:** How could discrimination hinder commerce? *(Answers will vary. Students might mention that not everyone would be allowed to shop in certain stores or stay in certain hotels.)* **OL**

W Writing Support

Personal Writing Have students discuss the difference between expressed and implied powers. Ask students to write about whether they think implied powers can be abused. **Ask:** Do you think the Framers of the Constitution intended for the powers of Congress to be implied or expressed? *(Answers will vary. Students should mention Clause 18 of Section 8.)* **OL**

Critical Thinking

Answer: Congress has determined that since such places receive business from various states, they are subject to Congress's power to regulate interstate commerce.

Additional Support

Activity: Interdisciplinary Connection

Political Science Ask students who have an affinity for environmental issues to consider the following questions:
- How might Congress use its power to tax to help the environment?
- Has Congress's attempt to lower the national debt turned its attention away from environmental concerns? Explain.

- Why might a specific environmental issue be related to interstate commerce?
- How does Congress address environmental needs as it governs federal property?

Encourage students to share their responses individually or collaboratively. **AL**

CURRICULUM CONNECTION

Economics The colonies had laws against counterfeiters. Offenders could be sentenced to death. Engraver James Mar, facing execution for counterfeiting, was granted clemency after the women of the community presented the governor with a petition.

The Law *and* You

More About Minimum Wage Laws The first minimum wage laws in the United States were enacted by state governments and applied only to women and minors. In 1923 the Supreme Court declared such laws unconstitutional. The Court also invalidated the federal government's first attempt to establish minimum wage scales for men and women in 1933. Not until 1938, with the enactment of the Fair Labor Standards Act, was a national minimum wage fixed—25¢ per hour for workers in interstate commerce.

Additional Support

The legislative process for **appropriations bills**—meaning, laws proposed to authorize spending money—is not spelled out in the Constitution. Instead, the process has developed through usage. Article I, Section 9, merely requires that "No Money shall be drawn from the Treasury, but in Consequence of Appropriations made by Law." Spending requests generally come from the executive branch. Today, most are presented to Congress in the president's annual budget proposal.

Over the years, Congress has used its taxing and spending authority to expand its regulatory powers. For example, when Congress authorizes money for state or local governments, it frequently requires them to follow specific federal regulations. Congress can also levy taxes in a way that encourages or discourages consumers to buy a product—heavy taxes on tobacco to discourage its use, for instance, or tax breaks to farmers who use corn to make ethanol, an alternative fuel.

Congress also uses the power of the purse to regulate the economy. Cutting individual income taxes may encourage more spending, thus stimulating economic growth. Conversely, when Congress is worried about inflation, it may try to reduce federal spending. (Generally, however, inflation is an issue addressed by the Federal Reserve, which sets interest rates.)

Other Money Powers

Under Article 1, Congress has other money powers. A big one is its power to borrow to pay for government costs. Congress does this in various ways. The most common method is by authorizing the sale of government securities—**bonds** or notes. When people buy savings bonds, Treasury bills, or Treasury notes, they are lending the government money. In return, the government promises to repay buyers with interest at the end of a specified period of time—3 months to 30 years, depending on the type of security.

Because it must borrow to meet operating expenses, the government has a national debt—the total amount the government owes at any given time. This debt, almost $1 trillion in 1980, was more than $9 trillion in 2007. The Constitution does not restrict government borrowing, but Congress periodically tries to set an annual limit. In recent years, it has raised the ceiling as necessary so the government could borrow to pay its bills.

The Law *and* You

Minimum Wage Laws

What pay should you expect when you look for a job? Generally, employers must pay a standard minimum wage set by federal law. However, many exceptions exist.

If you are a student working for a retail business, in an agricultural job, or for a school's vocational education program, your employer is not required to pay minimum wage. In addition, employers can pay all workers under age 20 less than minimum wage for their first 90 days of employment. Other exceptions include workers who receive tips and seasonal employees. Meals your employer provides, or expenses your employer pays on your behalf, can also reduce your wage rate.

Finally, federal law allows states to pass laws that can be more generous than the minimum wage. Your local employment services office can provide more information about wage laws in your state.

▼**Earning a wage**

Exploring the Law Activity

Conduct Research Find out how the minimum wage affects jobs in your community. Gather information online, at the local library, or through interviews with local officials or businesspeople. Summarize what you learn in a letter to the local paper.

Extending the Content

National Debt Explain that two possible ways to reduce the national debt are (1) to increase taxes or (2) to decrease spending. **Ask:** What are the arguments, pro and con, for each of these solutions? What kind of opposition would each solution be likely to face in Congress? *(Answers will vary. Students might say that increasing taxes provides the government with more funding for programs but reduces the income of citizens. By decreasing spending, the support that government programs can provide citizens is reduced, but citizens will pay less in taxes.)* Help students use their own words to express the dilemma caused when citizens oppose more taxes but also oppose reductions in benefits that the government provides them—entitlements paid for with tax revenues and borrowed money.

As part of Congress's money powers, the Constitution gives the legislative branch the power to coin money and to regulate its value. All currency issued by the federal government is legal tender, meaning that it must be accepted as payment.

The money powers also allow Congress to make laws on bankruptcy—legal proceedings to administer the assets of a person or business that cannot pay its debts. For nearly a century, Congress generally left these matters to the states. In 1898 it passed the federal bankruptcy law that, with later amendments, remains in force.

In 2005 the Bush administration was successful in getting more revisions to the law. They made it harder for consumers to avoid paying debt when they file for bankruptcy—a provision that allowed filers to get a "fresh start." Opponents of the bill said credit card companies were partly responsible because they were giving out credit cards too easily.

The Commerce Power

Article I, Section 8, Clause 3, the so-called "commerce clause" of the Constitution, authorizes Congress to regulate foreign commerce and **interstate commerce,** or commerce among the states.[1] In this clause, the Founders provided what has become one of the most sweeping powers of government. The Supreme Court has promoted the expansion of this power by consistently ruling that the meaning of commerce—whether international or interstate—far exceeds the mere buying and selling of goods and services.

Gibbons v. Ogden

🏛 **Landmark Case** The first decision on the breadth of the commerce powers did not come until 1824 when the Court decided the landmark case *Gibbons v. Ogden.* The case came about because American inventor Robert Fulton and his business partner got a license from the state of New York to be the exclusive operator of a steamboat in New York waters. In 1807 the steamboat began carrying passengers regularly between New York City and Albany. The company then granted Aaron Ogden a permit for steamboat operation across the Hudson River between New York state and New Jersey.

Controversy began in the following years as others challenged this monopoly. One entrepreneur, Thomas Gibbons, started a competing line that operated boats between New York and New Jersey. Gibbons had no New York permit, but he

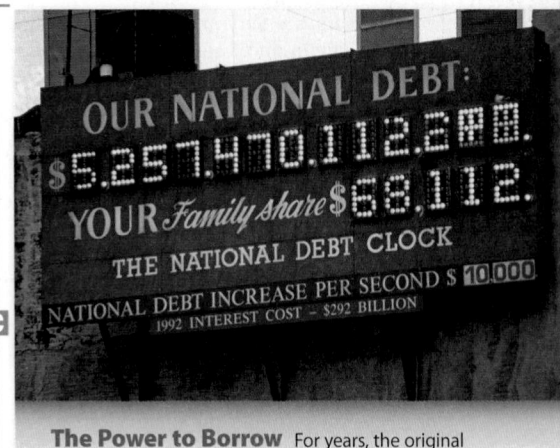

The Power to Borrow For years, the original national debt clock in Manhattan kept a running tab of the nation's debt. Seymour Durst, a concerned citizen, invented the computer-operated clock to dramatize the problem. *Do you think the now nearly $10 trillion national debt is meaningful to average citizens?*

had received a license from the federal government. An angry Ogden then sued Gibbons, and New York upheld Ogden's position.

Gibbons, who felt his federal license gave him a solid claim, appealed the case. He argued that Congress, not New York, had the power to regulate commerce. New York meanwhile argued that federal commerce powers only covered the regulation of products, not navigation. Justice John Marshall disagreed emphatically:

> 66 *The subject to be regulated is commerce; . . . it becomes necessary to settle the meaning of the word. The counsel for the appellee [Ogden] would limit it to traffic, to buying and selling, or the interchange of commodities, and do not admit that it comprehends navigation. . . . Commerce, undoubtedly, is traffic, but it is something more; it is intercourse. . . . The mind can scarcely conceive a system for regulating commerce between nations, which shall exclude all laws concerning navigation. . . .* 99
> —John Marshall, 1824

📖 See the following footnoted materials in the **Reference Handbook:**
1. *The Constitution,* pages R42–R67.

Caption Answer: Answers will vary. Students may say that they disapprove of such a high national debt and that the money to pay it back eventually will be taken out of their pockets in the form of taxes.

C Critical Thinking

Drawing Conclusions Have students research the current amount of the national debt. Assign students to research current legislative action by the Senate, House of Representatives, or executive branch to address the national debt. Discuss students' findings. **Ask:** Do you think it is more important to reduce the debt or to stop adding to it? Why? *(Students should provide reasoned opinions.)* **OL**

 To enrich study of chapter content, remind students that footnoted materials appear in the *Reference Handbook.*

🏛 **Landmark Case**

See *Gibbons v. Ogden* in the Supreme Court Summaries in the *Reference Handbook* and Case Study 4 in the *Supreme Court Case Studies* booklet.

Additional Support

★★★ Activity: Interdisciplinary Connection ★★★

History Share these quotations about taxes and taxation, expressed by past leaders:

Benjamin Franklin: "In this world nothing is certain, except death and taxes."

Oliver Wendell Holmes, Jr.: "Taxes are what we pay for civilized society."

Calvin Coolidge: "Collecting more taxes than is absolutely necessary is legalized robbery."

Have students discuss the meaning of each quotation, relating it to Congress's "power of the purse" and its tendency to use taxation as a regulatory power. **OL**

POLITICAL PROFILES Jeannette Rankin (R-Montana), the first woman elected to Congress, was a pacifist who once commented, "You can no more win a war than you can win an earthquake." She voted against the United States's entry into World War I and was the only member of Congress to vote against the United States's entry into World War II.

S Skill Practice

Using a Line Graph Have students examine the line graph. **Ask:** What was the first year in which a majority of Americans was opposed to the Vietnam War? *(1968)* **OL**

Critical Thinking

Answer: Answers will vary. Students might suggest that presidential war powers should be contingent on the consensus of opinion of the citizens.

Additional Support

Over the years, the Supreme Court has further expanded its definition of commerce. Any widespread activity that can possibly be considered interstate commerce has been made subject to federal control—broadcasting, banking and finance, and air and water pollution.

This broad interpretation of commerce has allowed Congress to set policy in many areas. For example, Congress has required businesses engaged in interstate commerce to pay their employees a minimum wage. Because almost all businesses deal in some way with another state, Congress has been able to regulate working conditions across the nation.

Heart of Atlanta Motel v. United States

One of the most significant applications of the commerce clause has been in the area of civil rights. The Supreme Court intentionally used the commerce clause to uphold federal laws intended to protect equal rights in the United States.

In 1964 Congress passed major civil rights legislation: the Civil Rights Act. Among other things, this 1964 legislation had a law that applied to public accommodations. It prohibited discrimination in restaurants, hotels, and motels.

Many Southern states encountered resistance to the goals of this legislation. A Georgia motel owner who refused to serve African Americans as required by the new federal law immediately attacked the law. He claimed that his motel was a local business and therefore not part of the interstate commerce described in the Civil Rights Act.

When the case was appealed to the Supreme Court, the justices disagreed with the motel owner's stand. In *Heart of Atlanta Motel* v. *United States* (1964), the Court noted that public places of accommodation served travelers who crossed state boundaries. Such places also sold food that had crossed state lines.[1] If African Americans were unable to find decent places to stay or eat, how would interstate commerce be able to take place?

❝ *We, therefore, conclude that the action of Congress in the adoption of the Act as applied here to a motel which concededly serves interstate travelers is within the power granted it by the Commerce Clause of the Constitution, as interpreted by this Court for 140 years.* ❞

—Justice Tom C. Clark, 1964

📖 *See the following footnoted materials in the* **Reference Handbook:**
1. *Heart of Atlanta Motel v. United States* case summary, page R28.

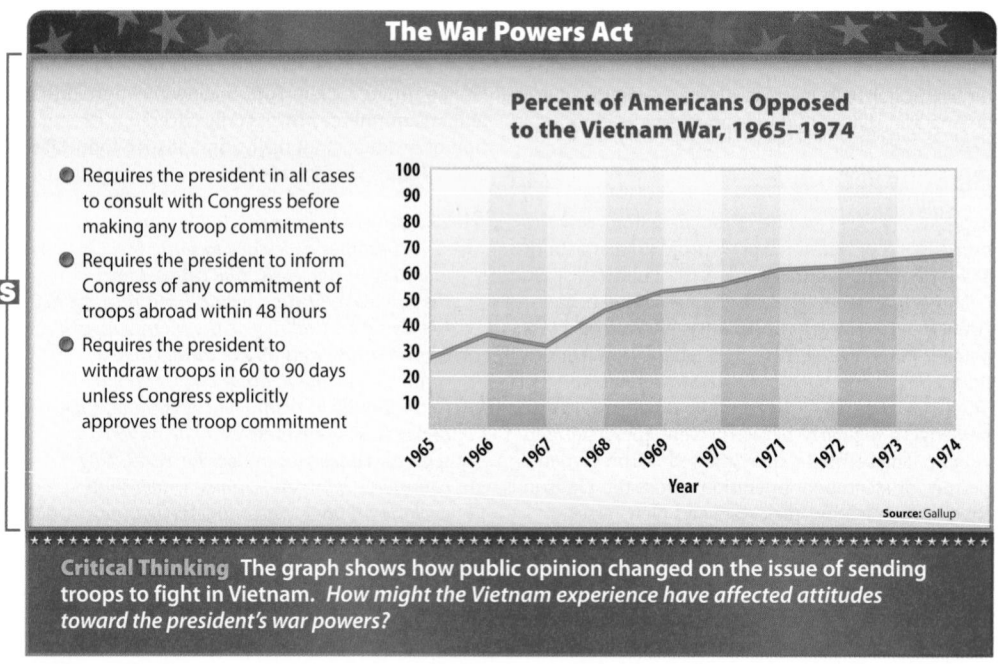

The War Powers Act

- Requires the president in all cases to consult with Congress before making any troop commitments
- Requires the president to inform Congress of any commitment of troops abroad within 48 hours
- Requires the president to withdraw troops in 60 to 90 days unless Congress explicitly approves the troop commitment

Percent of Americans Opposed to the Vietnam War, 1965–1974

Year

Source: Gallup

Critical Thinking The graph shows how public opinion changed on the issue of sending troops to fight in Vietnam. *How might the Vietnam experience have affected attitudes toward the president's war powers?*

Extending the Content

A Busy Day A survey by the House of Representatives reveals that wielding congressional power requires an average member to work 11 hours and 26 minutes each day, about 39 percent—4 hours and 25 minutes—of which is spent on the House floor or in committee and subcommittee meetings. Of 3 hours and 19 minutes of office time, nearly 2 hours are spent meeting constituents, answering letters, and making phone calls. Another hour is given to personal and committee staff meetings. The remaining time goes for reading and writing speeches and legislation. A further 3 hours and 42 minutes are spent around town at various meetings and special events. **Ask:** Do you think the average representative focuses his or her time and attention efficiently? How would you restructure the day of representatives? Allow students time to share schedules and discuss.

The Court clearly supported Congress's use of the commerce powers when the economic issue was not the motive for the case. Since then, the commerce power has been used to support federal laws aimed at racketeering and arson, too.

Foreign Policy Powers

Congress shares power with the president to make foreign and national defense policy. Congress has the power to approve treaties, to declare war, to create and maintain an army and navy, to make rules governing land and naval forces, and to regulate foreign commerce.

Historically Congress generally has let the president take the lead in these areas. As commander in chief, the president often sends troops on missions around the world without a declaration of war. Congress has declared war only five times, but the president has used troops in more than 200 international conflicts. Two major conflicts in the twentieth century, the Korean War and the Vietnam War, were fought without a declaration of war.

Because the Vietnam War was costly and lost public support over time, Congress looked closely at how the United States was drawn into the Southeast Asian conflict. Specifically, it focused on the actions of President Lyndon Johnson that led to American troops being sent to Vietnam. Congress concluded that the Constitution did not intend the president to have this kind of power.

In 1973, over President Richard Nixon's veto, Congress passed the War Powers Act. Under this law, the president must notify Congress within 48 hours of any commitment of troops abroad and must withdraw them in 60 to 90 days unless Congress explicitly approves the action. Since the act's passage, both Republican and Democratic presidents have protested its constitutionality.

Presidents have continued to send American troops abroad without a declaration of war by Congress. Troops were sent to Cambodia in 1975; to Iran, Lebanon, Grenada, Libya, the Persian Gulf, and Panama in the 1980s; to the Balkans and Somalia in the 1990s; and to Afghanistan and Iraq in the 2000s. Many of these incidents were not sustained actions, but in most cases the president adhered to the provisions of the War Powers Act.

Providing for the Nation's Growth

The Constitution gives Congress power over naturalization, the process by which immigrants become citizens. (See Chapter 14.) Under Article IV, Section 3, Congress also has the power to admit new states and govern any territories. Today, American territories such as Puerto Rico, Guam, the Virgin Islands, and Wake Island fall under this provision. Finally, Article I and Article IV give Congress the power to pass laws to govern federal property. When the Constitution was written, the Founders were thinking of military bases and government buildings, but today federal property also includes national parks, historic sites, and public lands.

Other Legislative Powers

Article I, Section 8, Clause 8, gives Congress the power to grant copyrights and patents.[1] A copyright is the exclusive right to publish and sell a literary, musical, or artistic work for a specified period of time. Under the present law, this period is the lifetime of the creator plus 70 years. A patent is the exclusive right of an inventor to manufacture, use, and sell his or her invention for a specific period, currently 20 years, after which a patent may be renewed.

Article I, Section 8, grants Congress the power to establish a post office and federal courts. Congress has also used its postal power to combat criminal activity; using the mail for any illegal act is a federal crime.

Nonlegislative Powers

In carrying out their legislative powers, the two Houses of Congress perform the same basic tasks—considering, amending, and voting on bills. Most non-legislative functions require cooperation between the houses, but each house usually plays a distinct role in exercising these powers.

The Power to Choose a President

The Constitution requires Congress to hold a joint session to count the Electoral College votes for a new president. If no candidate has a majority, the House chooses the president from the three candidates with the most electoral votes. Each state has one vote in the House. For the vice presidency, a tie would be broken by a majority vote in the Senate from the top two vote-getters. It is, therefore, possible that the vice president could be from a different party than the president.

See the following footnoted materials in the **Reference Handbook:**
1. *The Constitution*, pages R42–R67.

Did You Know?

Patent "Open and available to anyone's study" is the meaning of the adjective *patent*. Its legal use comes from the fact that the legal papers giving someone the right to make and sell a new invention for a set number of years once were written on open sheets of parchment (called letters patent), with the authorizing seal at the bottom.

C Critical Thinking

Analyzing Information Have students read about and discuss Foreign Policy Powers. **Ask:** Does the president need a declaration of war from Congress in order to deploy troops? *(No, the president needs to notify Congress within 48 hours of deployment.)* **Ask:** Do you think the War Powers Act is unconstitutional? **OL**

S Skill Practice

Conducting Research Have each student choose an everyday household item and use the Internet to find out whether the patent for the item is still current or when it expired. Allow time to share findings. **OL**

Additional Support

Extending the Content

The Impeachment of Andrew Johnson

In addition to being upset by his suspension of Secretary of War Edwin Stanton, Congress was angered by Johnson's appointment of generals whom the Radical Republicans opposed as commanders of Southern military districts. Johnson's impeachment trial began in March 1868 and lasted for three months. One of Johnson's strongest supporters was Samuel J. Tilden, a Democrat from New York, who claimed that Congress was trying to remove the president from office without accusing him of a crime "or anything more than a mere difference of opinion." **Ask:** For what offenses do you think a president should be impeached? *(Possible answers include lying under oath, insider trading, campaign fraud, or other illegal activities.)*

Caption Answer: Andrew Johnson was impeached in 1868.

D Differentiated Instruction

Logical/Mathematical
Have students read about the impeachment process. President Clinton was impeached by the House in 1998. The Senate then found him not guilty. **Ask:** What vote in the Senate would have removed Clinton from office? *(67 to 33; needs to be approved by a two-thirds majority)* **OL**

C Critical Thinking

Hypothesizing Ask: Why do you think the Framers granted the House "the sole Power of Impeachment" but gave the Senate "the sole Power to try all impeachments"? *(Answers will vary. Students may mention the principle of separation of powers. They might also note that the Senate is better suited to conduct trials because it has fewer members and senators serve longer terms.)* **AL**

Hands-On Chapter Project

Step 1

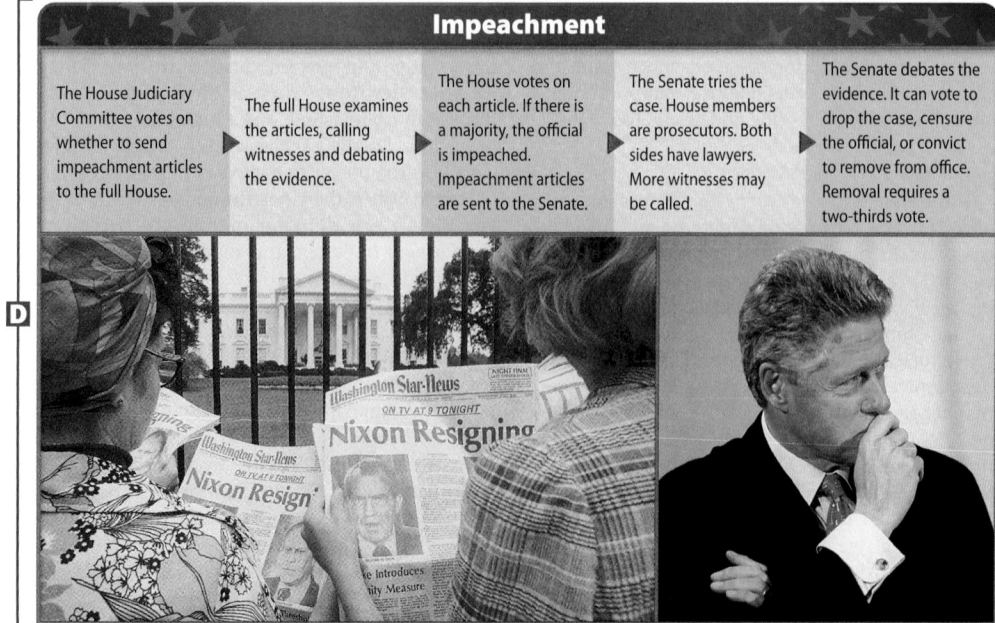

Impeachment

The House Judiciary Committee votes on whether to send impeachment articles to the full House.

The full House examines the articles, calling witnesses and debating the evidence.

The House votes on each article. If there is a majority, the official is impeached. Impeachment articles are sent to the Senate.

The Senate tries the case. House members are prosecutors. Both sides have lawyers. More witnesses may be called.

The Senate debates the evidence. It can vote to drop the case, censure the official, or convict to remove from office. Removal requires a two-thirds vote.

National Crises In August 1974, President Nixon resigned after a year-long ordeal. The House impeached President Clinton (right) in December 1998; the Senate found him not guilty in February 1999. *Which Civil War-era president was impeached?*

Graphs In MOtion
See StudentWorks™ Plus or go to glencoe.com.

Only twice in American history has no presidential candidate captured a majority of electoral votes, requiring the election to be settled by these rules. In 1800 the House elected Thomas Jefferson over Aaron Burr, and in 1824 it chose John Quincy Adams over Andrew Jackson.

Two amendments to the Constitution address situations related to the presidency. The Twentieth Amendment, ratified in 1933, moved up the inauguration of a new president from March to January 20. This leaves less time when the old president is a "lame duck," unable to rule effectively because he or she will be leaving office soon. The Twenty-fifth Amendment, ratified in 1965, clearly lays out what happens if a president, vice president, or elected candidate dies or is incapacitated.[1] 📖

The Removal Power

The Constitution gives Congress the power to remove any federal official from office. The House

📖 *See the following footnoted materials in the Reference Handbook:*
1. *The Constitution, pages R42–R67.*

is the chamber with power over **impeachment**— the formal accusation of misconduct in office. If a majority of the House votes to impeach an official, the Senate then conducts a trial. A two-thirds vote of the senators present is required to convict and thus remove someone from office. If a president is impeached, the chief justice presides.

Since 1789, several federal judges, a Supreme Court justice, a cabinet secretary, and two presidents have been impeached. Several officials have been convicted by the Senate, but no presidents have been convicted. President Andrew Johnson came the closest, escaping conviction by only one vote.

In 1972 and 1973 two reporters, Bob Woodward and Carl Bernstein, published a series of stories linking President Richard Nixon's administration to burglars who broke into Democratic Party offices in the Watergate Hotel. A Senate committee investigating the incident discovered other illegal activities, as well as evidence that the president had helped to cover up the crimes. When it was clear he would be impeached, Nixon resigned—the first president in American history to do so.

Conducting an Opinion Poll

Step 1: Preparing the Poll Tell students they will be conducting an opinion poll on the performance of the current Congress.

Directions Divide the class into groups of four or five. Have students use newspapers, magazines, and the Internet to research legislation that has been enacted or is being considered by the current Congress. Ask groups to compose five statements about the performance of the current Congress. The poll should give respondents five options, ranked by number: (1) strongly disagree; (2) disagree; (3) neutral; (4) agree, or (5) strongly agree. **OL**

(Chapter Project continued in Section 2.)

Many attributed the Watergate crisis to an imbalance among the three branches: The executive, they said, had grown too strong, too "imperial." In disputes between Congress and the president since Watergate, Congress often voices this complaint.

In 1998 President Bill Clinton was impeached by a narrow margin in the House. Clinton was charged with perjury and obstruction of justice because he lied under oath about his relationship with a White House intern. The Senate votes on the charges were well short of the two-thirds majority needed to remove the president from office. For many senators, the charges did not constitute "Treason, Bribery, or other high Crimes and Misdemeanors."

The Confirmation Power

The Senate must approve presidential appointments to office. Often, Senate action is only a formality, but the Senate looks more closely at several hundred nominations to cabinet positions for regulatory agencies, major diplomatic and military posts, and the judiciary. Supreme Court nominees receive the most scrutiny. The Senate has rejected about 20 percent of Court nominations.

The Ratification Power

The Senate must also ratify formal treaties with other nations. To ratify a treaty, two-thirds of the senators present must vote for it. Senate action on treaties has usually not been a major factor in American foreign policy. In recent years, presidents have often bypassed the need for a treaty.

Instead, they have negotiated executive agreements that do not require Senate approval.

The Amendment Power

Congress and state legislatures share the power to propose amendments to the Constitution. Amendments can be proposed by a two-thirds vote of both houses of Congress, or by a convention called by the legislatures of two-thirds of the states.

The second method has never been used, but it raises this constitutional question: Can a constitutional convention called to propose a certain amendment and then propose other amendments in addition to the one in the states' original petition? Some people fear that once delegates meet, they might propose revisions on long-established provisions. Congress has considered, but not acted on, measures to prevent this from happening. Finally, Congress also has the power to determine whether state conventions or state legislatures will ratify a proposed amendment.

To date, all of the constitutional amendments added to the Constitution have started in Congress. The states have approved 27 proposed amendments and have failed to ratify only 6. Congress has required all amendments—except the Twenty-first Amendment (1933), which repealed the Eighteenth Amendment on Prohibition—to be ratified by state legislatures. Advocates of the Twenty-first Amendment believed they would have better support in conventions than in state legislatures because many of these bodies were dominated by "Drys"—representatives who favored Prohibition.

CHAPTER 6, SECTION 1

R **Reading Strategy**

Determining Relationships
Have students discuss similarities and differences in the confirmation and ratification powers of Congress. **Ask:** How are amendment powers similar to confirmation and ratification powers? *(A two-thirds majority must approve the amendment.)*
Ask: How can states propose constitutional amendments? *(A convention is called by the legislatures of two-thirds of the states.)* **BL**

Assess

Assign the Section 1 Assessment as homework or as an in-class activity, or have students take Section Quiz 6-1 from *Section Quizzes and Chapter Tests*.

Close

Drawing Conclusions **Ask:** Which legislative power of Congress has had the most impact on American life? Which nonlegislative power? *(Take a class vote and discuss the results.)* **OL**

Section 1 Review

SECTION 1 Review

Vocabulary

1. **Explain** the significance of: expressed powers, necessary and proper clause, implied powers, revenue bill, appropriations bill, interstate commerce, impeachment.

Main Ideas

2. **Describing** What are the foreign policy powers of Congress, and how are they shared with the president?

3. **Analyzing** Who participates in the impeachment and trial of a member of the executive or judicial branch?

Critical Thinking

4. **Drawing Conclusions** What case provided a basis for the ruling in *Heart of Atlanta Motel v. United States*? Explain.

5. **Organizing** In a chart like the one below, list two or more examples of powers the Constitution expresses, implies, and denies to Congress.

Expressed	Implied	Denied

Writing About Government

6. **Descriptive Writing** Research legislation that Congress passed in a recent session. Identify any bills that you believe were based on the power to regulate interstate commerce. Draw a political cartoon supporting or criticizing the legislation. Explain your cartoon in one or two paragraphs.

CHAPTER 6: *Development of Congressional Powers* **165**

Answers

1. All definitions can be found in the section and the Glossary.
2. Congress has the power to approve treaties, to declare war, to create and maintain an army and a navy, to make rules governing land and naval forces, to regulate foreign commerce; the president must notify Congress about committing troops abroad, and Congress must approve of any long-term military engagements.
3. the House Judiciary Committee, the House of Representatives, and the Senate

4. *Gibbons* v. *Ogden*; when the Court decided that customers were interstate commerce in the *Gibbons* case, it established a basis for ruling that a hotel serving interstate travelers was engaging in interstate commerce.
5. Examples might include: Expressed: levying taxes; declaring war; regulating commerce; coining money; granting copyrights and patents; Implied: supporting public schools; maintaining the Federal Reserve Board; drafting people into the armed services;

limiting immigration; Denied: suspending writ of habeas corpus; passing bills of attainder; passing ex post facto laws.
6. Students' cartoons should indicate issues relating to interstate commerce.

Teach

Caption Answer: Congress can uncover problems and abuses in executive branch agencies.

C Critical Thinking

Distinguishing Fact From Opinion Organize the class into two groups. One group should focus on the power of Congress to conduct investigations. The other group should focus on the power of Congress to conduct legislative oversight. Have each student write one fact and one opinion about the power assigned to his or her group. Have students read their statements aloud. Listeners should determine whether each statement is a fact or an opinion. **OL**

Did You Know?

Actor Fred Thompson, a Republican, served as minority counsel on the Watergate Committee (seated third from left in photo). He later served two terms (1994–2003) as a U.S. senator from Tennessee.

Hands-On Chapter Project
Step 2

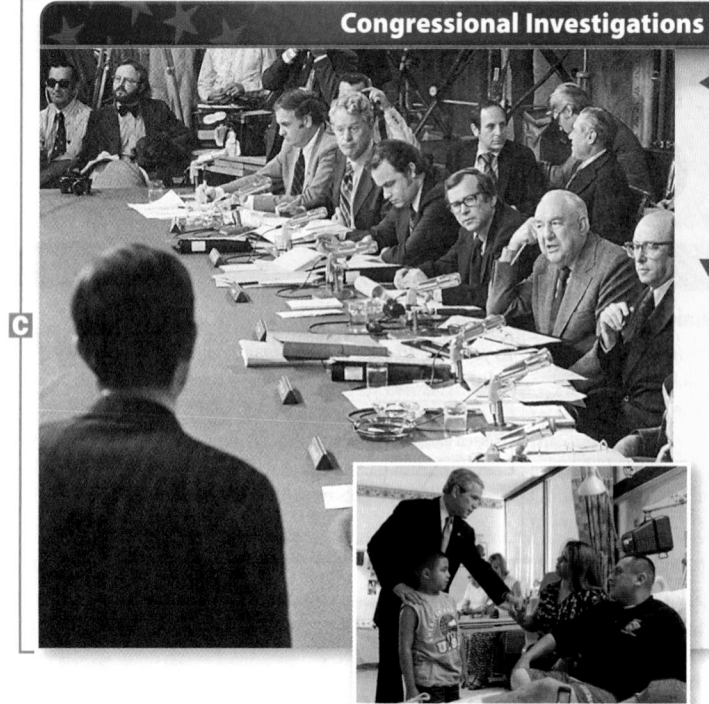

Congressional Investigations

◄ **Past** The Senate's Select Committee on Presidential Campaign Activities investigated the Watergate break-in in the 1970s. Its investigation led to President Richard Nixon's resignation.

▼ **Present** A 2007 *Washington Post* story on poor treatment for veterans of the war in Iraq at Walter Reed Hospital in Washington, D.C., sparked a congressional hearing on leadership at the Veterans Administration.

Checks and Balances
How does Congress's power to investigate strengthen the system of checks and balances?

Congressional investigations occur for many reasons. Most get little notice, but a few have become media events. In 1998 the Senate Finance Committee opened hearings into the collection methods of the Internal Revenue Service (IRS). The televised testimony of witnesses about the strong-arm tactics of the federal agency led to a 97 to 0 Senate vote to reform the IRS.

More than once in the 1990s, Congress investigated allegations against its own members. While some of these complaints were politically motivated, several members were indicted and one senator resigned to avoid being expelled. In 2003 an investigation began into possible abuse, torture, and brutality against Iraqi prisoners by American troops at Abu Ghraib.

One of the biggest investigations in recent years was of Jack Abramoff, a lobbyist convicted of corrupting public officials. Others were convicted as result of his **schemes,** including the deputy of a cabinet member and Representative Bob Ney (R-OH). In federal court, Ney admitted that he had done favors for lobbyists in exchange for campaign contributions, expensive meals, expensive travel, and sports tickets.

Investigations can lead to new laws to deal with a problem, reforms in a government program, or to officials being fired. Sometimes, however, they damage the reputations of innocent people.

Rights of Congressional Witnesses

Although congressional investigations are not trials, Congress has several powers that help committees collect evidence. Like courts, congressional committees have the power to subpoena witnesses. A **subpoena** is a legal order that requires a person to appear or produce requested documents. Congress makes frequent use of this power.

Like courts, congressional committees can require witnesses to testify under oath. Witnesses who do not tell the truth can be criminally prosecuted for **perjury,** or lying under oath. Committees may also punish those who refuse to testify or otherwise will not cooperate by holding them in **contempt** of Congress, meaning that they are willfully obstructing its work. Persons found in contempt of Congress can be arrested and jailed. The Constitution does not grant this power to Congress, but court decisions have generally upheld it.

168 UNIT 2: *The Legislative Branch*

Conducting an Opinion Poll
Step 2: Conducting the Poll

Directions Each student in each group should arrange to talk with at least three people who are registered voters. The student should then read each of the statements composed in Step 1 and ask the respondent for his or her opinion on the issue. Encourage students to ask follow-up questions to learn why the respondent has that opinion. Have students keep track of answers to the follow-up questions in a table or graphic organizer. **OL**

(Chapter Project continued in Section 3.)

Until the mid-twentieth century, witnesses who testified before a congressional committee had few rights. In 1948, for example, the chairperson of a House committee told one witness: "The rights you have are the rights given you by this committee. We will determine what rights you have and what rights you do not have before the committee."

The situation today is very different, and witnesses before congressional committees have important rights. In the case of *Watkins* v. *United States* (1957), the Supreme Court ruled that Congress must respect witnesses' constitutional rights just as a court does.[1] In the Court's words:

66 *Witnesses cannot be compelled to give evidence against themselves. They cannot be subjected to unreasonable search and seizure. Nor can the First Amendment freedoms of speech, press, religion, or political belief and association be abridged.* 99
—Chief Justice Earl Warren, 1957

One way congressional committees have gotten around this requirement to observe First Amendment rights is by giving witnesses immunity. **Immunity** is freedom from prosecution for people whose testimony ties them to criminal acts. Of course, the Fifth Amendment states that people cannot be forced to testify against themselves. If witnesses are granted immunity, however, they can be required to testify. Those who refuse may be held in contempt of court and jailed.

A 1987 case illustrates how immunity works. A Senate committee investigated charges against officials in the Reagan administration. They were charged with selling arms to Iran and using the money to finance a war in Nicaragua. The committee granted immunity to Colonel Oliver North and compelled him to testify. North, who worked for the National Security Council, implicated the national security adviser as well as others. North was tried and convicted. His conviction was later overturned because the evidence was obtained *only* as a result of testimony he gave while under immunity.

Legislative Oversight

Most congressional investigations are related to another power that Congress has developed over

See the following footnoted materials in the **Reference Handbook:**
1. *Watkins v. United States* case summary, page R36.

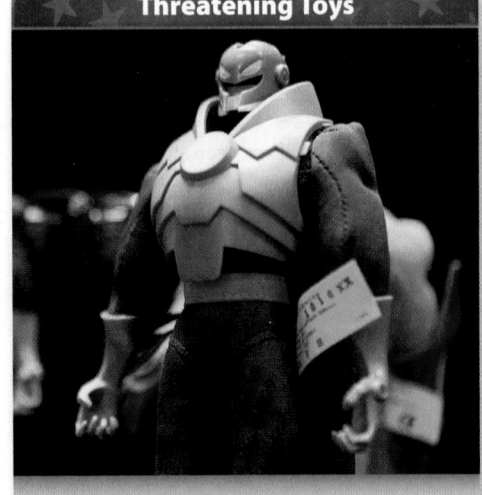

Threatening Toys

Products Under Scrutiny In early 2008, a Senate subcommittee asked the Senate to investigate how imported toys, especially those from China, are regulated. A four-year-old boy from Minnesota died after he swallowed a lead-tainted charm that came with athletic shoes from China. *What government branch has authority over regulatory agencies?*

the years—the power of legislative oversight. As the word suggests, oversight is the power to review executive branch activities on an ongoing basis.

In modern American government, the executive carries out those laws through a huge bureaucracy of multiple agencies and hundreds of public officials. Thus, the oversight power of Congress can be focused on a wide array of programs and officials.

Oversight and Checks and Balances

Legislative oversight is a good example of how checks and balances work. Congress makes the laws, and the executive branch carries them out. As it does so, the executive branch interprets what the laws mean in a practical sense. Later Congress can check how the executive branch has administered the law and decide whether it met the law's goals.

Congress defined oversight functions in several places. The 1946 Legislative Reorganization Act asks Congress to exercise "continuous watchfulness" over executive agencies. A 1970 act gave each standing committee oversight authority for the areas of its responsibility.

D **Differentiated Instruction**

Auditory/Musical Show students video excerpts from a historic congressional investigation. Tell students to listen to the kinds of questions raised and how they are addressed to the witnesses. **Ask:** Who sounded more confident—the congressional investigators or the witnesses? Why was the questioning effective or ineffective? What did you learn about the investigative power of Congress?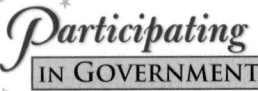

Caption Answer: the executive branch

Participating **IN GOVERNMENT**

Local Courts Students probably will never be involved in a congressional investigation, but they should know about aspects of such investigations at the state level. Have students research witness rights. How would a court in your state go about issuing a subpoena or granting immunity? **AL**

Additional Support

Activity: Collaborative Learning

Enacting a Historic Moment The power to conduct investigations has made Congress part of several moments of historic impact. Have groups of students prepare and present skits about the following events:
- the decision to investigate possible links between labor unions and organized crime;
- criticism of Senator Joseph McCarthy's investigation of communism in the government;

- the moment that might have prompted *Watkins* v. *United States.*

Each group should choose a director and a secretary. Encourage the actors to try different roles in the skit before choosing characters to portray. **OL**

R Reading Strategy

Activating Prior Knowledge
Ask: What law prohibits discrimination against persons with disabilities in employment, transportation, and public education? *(the Americans with Disabilities Act)* **OL**

We the People

Making a Difference

Jim Langevin The story of Jim Langevin is exceptional, but it has a parallel—that of Max Cleland, who served in the U.S. Senate from 1996 to 2003. Cleland, a decorated veteran of the Vietnam War, lost both legs and an arm in the war. When he was elected in 1996, the Capitol architect had to take steps to modify the Senate chamber. Ramps had to be constructed in many hearings rooms and to give him access to the dais where senators' desks are located. Antiquated subways in the Capitol complex and bathrooms posed other challenges for Capitol staff.

Activity: Have students research legislation sponsored by Representative Jim Langevin or Senator Max Cleland and write a 1–2 paragraph summary about the proposed legislation. **AL**

Additional Support

Although lawmakers have broad oversight powers, they use them inconsistently. Vice President Hubert Humphrey once said that Congress "sometimes gets in the habit of 'pass it and forget it' lawmaking." Legislative oversight tends to occur on a "hit-and-miss" basis as congressional staffs and committees go about their business. Why?

First, lawmakers do not have enough staff, time, or money to keep track of everything going on in the executive branch. Second, lawmakers know that oversight does not interest many voters, unless it uncovers a scandal or major problem. Third, some legislation and regulations are so vague that it is difficult to know exactly what they mean. Without clear objectives, lawmakers have little means of judging whether the executive branch is doing its job.

Finally, committees sometimes come to favor the federal agencies they are supposed to oversee. Lawmakers and the officials who work for a federal agency often become well-acquainted because they spend long hours working together. This creates the possibility that committee members will not be objective when assessing the performance of people who work at the agency.

How Congress Limits the Executive

Congress exercises oversight in several ways. It requires executive agencies to report to it. The 1946 Employment Act, for example, requires the president to send Congress an annual report on the nation's economy. During a recent congressional term, federal agencies submitted more than 1,000 reports to Congress. Keeping up with the reports, especially those that relate to a member's committee assignment, is an important job.

A second oversight technique is for Congress to ask one of its support agencies, like the Government Accountability Office (GAO), to study an agency's work. The GAO typically examines the finances of federal agencies to see if public money is being spent appropriately and legally.

Obviously, the power of the purse gives Congress another means of overseeing the executive branch. Each year Congress reviews the budgets of all agencies in the executive branch. Congress can then decide to expand, reduce, or eliminate certain programs in the budget.

For years, Congress exercised oversight power by using the **legislative veto.** Congress put provisions

We the People

Making a Difference

R Congressperson Jim Langevin of Rhode Island has championed the rights of the disabled. He played a key role in revising the 1990 Americans with Disabilities Act. As the first paraplegic elected to the House, Langevin understands disabilities as well as anyone. He is quick to point out, however, that such issues are not "what defines Jim Langevin," and that he works hard on many other constituent concerns.

Langevin was 16 and a police cadet when his life changed overnight. In a police locker room, a member of a SWAT team pulled the trigger on a semiautomatic pistol, believing it was unloaded. The gun discharged and a bullet ricocheted off a locker, hitting Langevin and severing his spinal cord. The accident "thrust me into a public life, whether I liked it or not. . . . this devastating accident . . . changed the course of my life."

Langevin became the youngest person ever at 30 to serve as Rhode Island's secretary of state. Six years later, he was elected to Congress, where officials had to quickly make the cloakroom, phones, and restrooms accessible to him.

The Americans with Disabilities Act was groundbreaking for the disabled, but it had loopholes that eliminated some disabled people from coverage. The 2008 law has fixed that. For example, now an impairment that is sporadic is still considered a disability if it seriously restricts someone when it occurs. In Langevin's words, the law "reaffirms . . . the ideals of equality and opportunity on which this country was founded."

"... the new law reaffirms ... the ideals of equality and opportunity on which this country was founded."
—**Jim Langevin**

Activity: Interdisciplinary Connection

Writing Former Senator William S. Cohen noted that "The danger inherent in . . . a congressional committee investigation is that the person under scrutiny will not survive with his reputation intact or unstained. . . . Acts of innocence or error when magnified under the microscope of the committee and the . . . national television networks will emerge as calculated wrongdoing." Ask students to think about how their lives might change if they were the focus of the media during such an investigation. Would their reputations remain "intact or unstained"? Have students write a personal narrative discussing the consequences. As time permits, encourage sharing and explanations. **AL**

into some laws that allowed it to review and cancel actions of the executive agencies carrying out those laws. In effect, Congress was claiming authority over officials who worked in the executive branch. In 1983 the Supreme Court ruled in *Immigration and Naturalization Service* v. *Chadha* that the legislative veto was unconstitutional because it violated the separation of powers.

Independent Counsel

In 1978, largely as a result of the Watergate experience, Congress passed the Ethics in Government Act. The law provided that in certain cases, Congress could demand the appointment of a special prosecutor, called the independent counsel.

After this law was passed, some 20 investigations occurred using a special prosecutor, or independent counsel. One of these was led by special prosecutor, attorney Kenneth Starr, who was appointed to the position in 1994. Four years later, in 1998, Starr's investigations led to the impeachment of President Clinton.

After a lengthy and costly investigation, the Senate voted against convicting Clinton. Public support for the independent counsel law faded after this long ordeal. Many complained that the law had resulted in too much party prejudice in the process. In 1999 Congress let the law expire and gave the attorney general sole power to conduct ethics investigations of top officials.

This power was used to dramatic effect in 2003 when Special Counsel Patrick Fitzgerald investigated a CIA leak. Fitzgerald convinced a grand jury

Independent Counsel An independent counsel investigated Lewis Libby's role in the leaking of a CIA agent's identity. Libby was convicted in March 2007 for lying to a grand jury. *Why did Congress abandon the use of special prosecutors?*

to charge Vice President Dick Cheney's top staff person with five counts of perjury, obstruction of justice, and making false statements. The man, Lewis "Scooter" Libby, was subsequently convicted on four of the five counts and sentenced to 30 months in federal prison.

Government ONLINE
Student Web Activity Visit glencoe.com and enter *QuickPass*™ code USG9822c6. Click on Student Web Activity and complete the activity about Congress.

Assess

Assign the Section 2 Assessment as homework or as an in-class activity, or have students take Section Quiz 6-2 from *Section Quizzes and Chapter Tests.*

Government ONLINE
Objectives and answers to the Student Web Activity can be found in the *Web Activity Lesson Plan* at glencoe.com. Enter *QuickPass*™ code USG9085c6T.

Close

Drawing Conclusions Have students review this section by discussing whether immunity advances justice or is an obstacle to it. **OL**

Section 2 Review

SECTION 2 Review

Vocabulary

1. **Explain** the significance of: subpoena, perjury, contempt, immunity, legislative veto.

Main Ideas

2. **Explaining** How does congressional oversight reflect the checks and balances principle in American government?

3. **Discussing** Name three congressional investigations that were focused on the executive branch.

Critical Thinking

4. **Synthesizing** How does the use of a subpoena assist legislators in the committee hearing process?

5. **Identifying** Using a graphic organizer like the one shown, identify the steps Congress can take if a witness at a congressional investigation cites Fifth Amendment protection and refuses to testify.

Writing About Government

6. **Expository Writing** Suppose you are a reporter assigned to cover a recent congressional investigation. Prepare a news report in which you analyze the purpose of the investigation and its findings.

CHAPTER 6: *Development of Congressional Powers* **171**

Answers

1. All definitions can be found in the section and the Glossary.
2. Congressional oversight gives Congress (the legislative branch) the responsibility of keeping members of the executive and judicial branches from abusing their power.
3. Any three: leadership in the Veterans Administration, Watergate investigation, Iran-Contra Affair investigation, CIA identity leak involving Scooter Libby

4. A subpoena helps ensure that needed witnesses or evidence will be available during investigations.
5. 1. Grant the witness immunity from prosecution. 2. Hold the witness in contempt.
6. Have students present their news broadcasts. Hold a class discussion about the effects of the various congressional investigations.

Focus

Resource Manager

Congress and the President

Reader's Guide

Content Vocabulary	Academic Vocabulary	Reading Strategy
★ national budget *(p. 175)* ★ impoundment *(p. 175)*	★ revise *(p. 173)* ★ period *(p. 174)* ★ transportation *(p. 174)*	Create a graphic organizer like the one below to take notes on how the Congressional Budget and Impoundment Control Act affected the president.

Cause		Effect
Congress passed the Congressional Budget and Impoundment Control Act	→	

Issues in the News

In March 2007, Congress and Republican President George W. Bush locked horns once more. This time it was over the firing of a number of federal prosecutors in the middle of their terms. Democrats in Congress said it was because the prosecutors resisted political pressure from Republicans and demanded internal documents from the White House. Republicans countered that Attorney General Gonzales had legal authority to fire the prosecutors. When the administration offered to talk privately with members about the firings, Senator Leahy of Vermont shot back, "It is not constructive, and it is not helpful to be telling the Senate how to do our investigation. . . ."

▲ Attorney General Alberto Gonzales testifies before the Senate Judiciary Committee on why he dismissed several U.S. attorneys.

When the Founders established the principle of separation of powers, they probably did not envision that it could lead to a shutdown of the federal government. The checks and balances system they created, however, can often result in a government stalemate. Many of the president's most important duties are shared with the Congress, including making treaties, appointing federal officials and judges, and paying the expenses of the executive branch. When Congress refuses to cooperate, the president may be frustrated.

Likewise, all the bills Congress passes require the executive's cooperation—the president must sign them before they become law. Further, the president has another legislative weapon: He or she can veto a bill or threaten to veto it. For Congress to override a presidential veto, it requires a two-thirds majority vote in each house of Congress, which is usually difficult to obtain. Thus, the president can play a major role in the legislative process. Finally, modern presidents are expected to develop a legislative program and secure its adoption by Congress.

Cooperation and Conflict

The level of cooperation between Congress and the president has varied throughout history. Usually, the best relations exist between the two branches when the president makes few demands on Congress. Less active presidents, who do not take the lead in shaping legislation, may get along well with Congress. Those who propose major new programs will almost surely come into conflict with the legislative branch for any number of reasons that will be discussed next. Recent presidents have frequently found it hard to work with Congress.

Constituents and Conflict

The national electorate chooses presidents they believe will carry out policies that are in the best interests of the nation. Voters in states and districts, however, elect members of Congress who represent their particular interests. Since senators and representatives represent these narrower interests, they often differ with the president about public policy.

Checks and Balances

The system of checks and balances gives Congress and the president the power to counteract each other. For example, the president may threaten a veto, arguing that a bill spends too much money and would spur inflation, which is harmful to the national economy. Some members of Congress may cooperate in attempting to amend the bill or override a veto because their states or districts would benefit from the bill. Historian James MacGregor Burns argues that the system is "designed for deadlock and inaction" and that it is really "President versus Congress" in our government.

Party Politics

Partisan politics (politics driven mostly by party loyalty) can also affect relations between the president and Congress. This is most obvious if one party controls the White House and the other controls the House and the Senate. In recent decades the president's party has rarely controlled Congress. Thus, conflict has increased between the president and Congress. It was pronounced in the 1990s when President Clinton, a Democrat, faced Republican majorities in Congress, and again from 2006 to 2008 when Republican George W. Bush had a Congress with a slight Democratic majority. As legislative progress slowed, the press often referred to "gridlock."

> 66 The question in the next two years, will be whether that lack of mandate for either side will foster cooperation to get things done or positioning to do battle in the next election. 99
>
> —Curtis B. Gans, political analyst

Organization as a Cause of Conflict

The organization of Congress gives many weapons to members who want to resist a proposal of the president. Rules of procedure, such as the Senate's unlimited debate rule, can be used to block legislation. Even when congressional leaders support the president, they may have to struggle to get presidential initiatives through Congress.

Because the basic shape of legislation is set in committees and subcommittees, the committee system also may be a weapon against the president. Committee chairpersons are powerful members of Congress, and they use their positions to influence bills. Conflicts in government occur when a president wants a major proposal approved and a committee tries to delay, **revise,** or defeat it.

Different Political Timetables

Conflicts may also occur because the president and Congress have different political timetables. Presidents have a little more than three years to develop, present, and move their programs through Congress before they have to busy themselves running for reelection. At best, they have only eight years to accomplish their agenda.

By contrast, senators and representatives are not limited to two terms in office. Most members can look forward to being reelected for several terms. Thus, they have a much longer political timetable than the president. Representatives, who serve only two-year terms, are always running for reelection.

Gridlock Haunts the Capital

Distributed by King Features Syndicate

The Miami Herald

YESS BAAAAACK!

GRIDLOCK

President and Congress Clash
Gridlock occurs when the president and parties in Congress cannot agree on legislation. *According to the cartoon, is gridlock a problem that is quickly or easily resolved? Explain.*

Teach

Caption Answer: Point out that the cartoonist's perception that gridlock is a huge problem represents only one view of the issue. The principle of separation of powers is designed to slow down the legislative process. Have students debate whether gridlock is good or bad and whether they prefer that laws be made quickly or slowly.

C Critical Thinking

Predicting Ask students to predict how a sharp increase in inflation might affect the following people:

- a person who has just withdrawn a large sum from a savings account (*The money may have less value than when it was initially saved.*)

- a retiree on a fixed pension (*The person will have less purchasing power.*)

- a borrower repaying a loan (*The value of the money being repaid will be less than it was when it was borrowed.*) **OL**

Differentiated Instruction

Interpreting Political Cartoons, p. 13

Congress at Work

Objective:	Analyze a political cartoon.
Focus/Teach:	Review the advantages of being an incumbent.
Assess:	Evaluate answers to the activity questions.
Close:	Have students find out how many incumbents currently serve in Congress.

Differentiated Instruction Strategies

BL Describe incumbents' financial advantages.

AL List ideas for evening the playing field for candidates who challenge incumbents.

ELL Review the definitions of the terms in the cartoon.

D Differentiated Instruction

Logical/Mathematical Ask: Which president had the most vetoes? Why do you think he had so many? *(Franklin D. Roosevelt; He served for longer than any other president. He was president during the Great Depression and World War II; these were critical periods during which Congress produced a high volume of legislation.)* **OL**

R Reading Strategy

Academic Vocabulary Review the definition of *imperial* with students. *(related to, or befitting, an emperor)* **OL**

Critical Thinking

Answer: Yes; a president can exercise the veto only if a bill goes through both houses; Congress tends to be very active during times of national crisis.

Chart Skills Practice
Which two presidents vetoed the most bills? *(Franklin D. Roosevelt and Grover Cleveland)*

Hands-On Chapter Project

Step 3

Presidential Vetoes

President	All Bills Vetoed	Regular Vetoes	Pocket Vetoes	Vetoes Overridden
Washington	2	2	0	0
J. Adams	0	0	0	0
Jefferson	0	0	0	0
Madison	7	5	2	0
Monroe	1	1	0	0
J.Q. Adams	0	0	0	0
Jackson	12	5	7	0
Van Buren	1	0	1	0
W.H. Harrison	0	0	0	0
Tyler	10	6	4	1
Polk	3	2	1	0
Taylor	0	0	0	0
Fillmore	0	0	0	0
Pierce	9	9	0	5
Buchanan	7	4	3	0
Lincoln	7	2	5	0
A. Johnson	29	21	8	15
Grant	93	45	48	4
Hayes	13	12	1	1
Garfield	0	0	0	0
Arthur	12	4	8	1
Cleveland (1st term)	414	304	110	2
B. Harrison	44	19	25	1
Cleveland (2d term)	170	42	128	5
McKinley	42	6	36	0
T. Roosevelt	82	42	40	1
Taft	39	30	9	1
Wilson	44	33	11	6
Harding	6	5	1	0
Coolidge	50	20	30	4
Hoover	37	21	16	3
F. Roosevelt	635	372	263	9
Truman	250	180	70	12
Eisenhower	181	73	108	2
Kennedy	21	12	9	0
L. Johnson	30	16	14	0
Nixon	43	26	17	7
Ford	66	48	18	12
Carter	31	13	18	2
Reagan	78	39	39	9
G.H.W. Bush	46	29	17	1
Clinton	37	36	1	2
G.W. Bush*	9	8	1	1
Total	2,561	1,492	1,069	107

Source: thomas.loc.gov
* As of May 2008
*A pocket veto occurs when the president exercises a veto so late in a session that Congress has no time to override it.

Critical Thinking The average annual number of vetoes was highest during the years of the New Deal and World War II. *Could the number of vetoes partly be a function of how many bills reach the president's desk? Why?*

Senators, whose terms are six years, can be more patient in handling controversial bills. For various reasons then, lawmakers in both houses may not be eager to act on legislation that does not benefit their constituents directly. President Lyndon Johnson, who had served as Senate majority leader, complained about the conflict of interests:

> ❝ You've got to give it all you can that first year. . . . You've got just one year when they treat you right, and before they start worrying about themselves. The third year, you lose votes. . . . The fourth year's all politics. You can't put anything through when half the Congress is thinking how to beat you. ❞
>
> —Lyndon Johnson

The Struggle for Power

For most of the first 150 years of the Republic, Congress dominated policy making. At times, however, strong presidents such as Andrew Jackson, Abraham Lincoln, and Franklin D. Roosevelt challenged congressional supremacy. They increased presidential powers as they dealt with changing social, political, and economic conditions.

The system of checks and balances makes it likely that the president and Congress will always compete for power. Which branch will dominate in a **period** depends on many factors, including the political issues of the time, the political savvy of congressional leaders, and the popularity of the president. Strong presidential leadership during the Depression of the 1930s and the Cold War made the president more powerful compared to the Congress.

After the Watergate crisis, many members of Congress concluded that President Nixon tried to create an "imperial presidency" and that the executive was too strong. Congress worked to regain its power and influence. Specifically, they restricted the president's war-making and budgetary powers and exercised the legislative veto more often.

Curbing Emergency Powers

In times of crisis, Congress has given extra powers to the president. Presidents have declared martial law, seized property, and controlled **transportation** and communications.

President Franklin D. Roosevelt had vast authority during the Depression and World War II. In 1933 Congress empowered him to close the

---

Conducting an Opinion Poll

Step 3: Analyzing the Findings

Directions Have groups calculate the average response to each of their statements. Then, students individually should write a brief essay corresponding to each question in which they interpret their findings. They should incorporate respondents' comments in their essays. Have students share their results with the rest of the class. **Ask:** Did Congress get a more favorable review in some groups' polls than others? Did it depend on the topic of the questions asked? Did it depend on whom they interviewed? **OL**

nation's banks. When Pearl Harbor was bombed, another national emergency was proclaimed, giving Roosevelt broader control over the economy. Provisions of this grant were later cancelled, but some provisions were left in place. In 1950 President Truman proclaimed a national emergency in response to the Korean conflict, and President Nixon exercised this authority twice in the 1970s.

During the Vietnam War, congressional leaders felt that the president's emergency powers had helped deepen the nation's involvement in Asia. (Before this time, many members of Congress were not aware that, legally, many emergency powers had been on the books since the 1930s.) To correct this situation, Congress passed an act in 1976 to restrict the president's emergency powers.

The National Emergencies Act ended the decades-long state of emergency and set down procedures for how and when a state of emergency exists. Presidents had to notify Congress when they intended to declare a national emergency, and it could not last more than one year unless the president repeated the process. Congress could also end a state of emergency by passing legislation.

In 2001 President George W. Bush used his authority under this act to selectively suspend, if necessary, the law that permitted a miliary officer to retire.

Controlling Budget Power

Over the years, presidents have assumed more responsibility for planning the **national budget,** the yearly financial plan for the national government. Because of this, by the early 1970s Congress had slipped into the role of merely reacting to budget proposals.

To increase its role in budgeting, Congress passed the Congressional Budget and Impoundment Control Act in 1974. The act did several things: it established a permanent budget committee for each house; it set up the Congressional Budget Office (CBO) to provide financial expertise for Congress, and it limited the president's ability to impound funds. **Impoundment** is the president's refusal to spend money Congress has voted for a program. This law required the president to spend appropriated funds unless Congress agreed with the president that the monies be impounded.

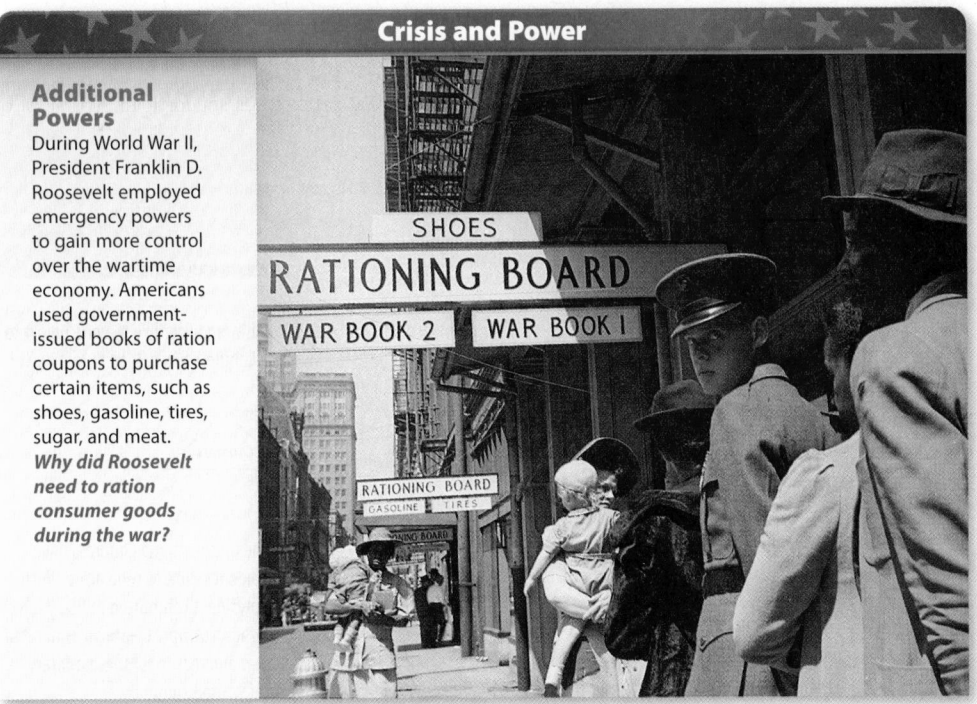

Crisis and Power

Additional Powers
During World War II, President Franklin D. Roosevelt employed emergency powers to gain more control over the wartime economy. Americans used government-issued books of ration coupons to purchase certain items, such as shoes, gasoline, tires, sugar, and meat. *Why did Roosevelt need to ration consumer goods during the war?*

SHOES
RATIONING BOARD
WAR BOOK 2   WAR BOOK I

RATIONING BOARD
GASOLINE   TIRES

ISSUES to Debate

The Legislative Veto Review the term *legislative veto* and the ways in which Congress used that power before it was declared unconstitutional in 1983. **Ask:** Does the legislative veto violate the principle of separation of powers, or is it an important part of the system of checks and balances?

W **Writing Support**

Personal Writing In addition to rationing, FDR used the federal government to regulate wages and prices on certain products. Have students write essays in which they respond to the following question. **Ask:** Do you think the government should strictly regulate the economy during wartime? *(Students may suggest that the world was different then, but now such a move by the government would not be acceptable.)* OL

Caption Answer: Supplying the troops and the war effort had priority, and keeping those supplies flowing meant asking American consumers to conserve or do without.

Differentiated Instruction

Leveled Activities

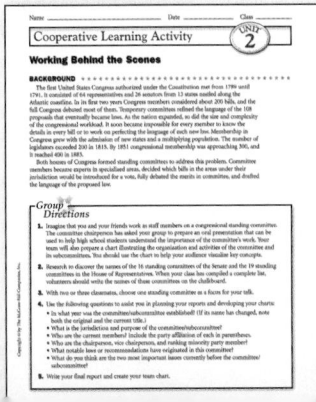

Summarizing Have students write brief essays in which they explain, in their own words, the Supreme Court's rationale for declaring the line-item veto unconstitutional. **OL** **BL**

Caption Answer: It is unusual for Congress to have the votes to override a presidential veto.

Assess

Assign the Section 3 Assessment as homework or as an in-class activity, or have students take Section Quiz 6-3 from *Section Quizzes and Chapter Tests.*

Close

Making Decisions Have students review the comment by President Lyndon Johnson on page 174, and then use details from this section to help them explain why they agree or disagree with it. **OL**

Section 3 Review

Trumping Executive Power

"Well, I guess they had the votes to override your veto after all, didn't they?"

Critical Thinking What does the cartoon suggest about how often a presidential veto is overridden?

Legislative and Line-Item Vetoes

Between 1932 and 1983, when the legislative veto was declared unconstitutional, Congress used it to negate executive actions many times. The legislative veto was used most often in the 1970s, when Congress was feeling that the executive branch had grown too powerful. Presidents, of course, believed that the legislative veto infringed upon their constitutional authority, and in a 1983 Supreme Court case, the Court struck down the legislative veto.

The line-item veto allowed a president to veto parts, or lines, in a bill. (This is a power that many state governors have, but the Constitution only provides for presidents to veto an entire bill.) Many presidents have asked Congress to enact a line-item veto and in 1996, Republicans in Congress passed a bill authorizing the veto of spending items and certain tax breaks.

In early 1997, Congress passed the Line Item Veto Act. It said that if Congress could get a two-thirds vote from both the House and the Senate, it could put the line items back into a bill. That summer, President Bill Clinton became the first president to use the line-item veto. Supporters of the line-item veto wanted the president to curb spending; critics said Congress, not the president, should control spending.

In 1998 challenges to the Line Item Veto Act reached the Supreme Court, which struck it down, saying that it circumvented the legislative procedures set out in Article I of the Constitution. In the words of Justice John Paul Stevens: "If there is to be a new procedure in which the President will play a different role . . . such change must come not by legislation but through the amendment procedures set forth in Article V of the Constitution."

SECTION 3 Review

Vocabulary

1. **Explain** the significance of: national budget, impoundment.

Main Ideas

2. **Explaining** How does the system of checks and balances lead to conflict between the president and Congress?

3. **Discussing** Why does the party system contribute to conflict between the president and Congress?

Critical Thinking

4. **Synthesizing** The constitutional system between Congress and the president has been described as "an invitation to struggle." Is this description accurate? Explain.

5. **Organizing** Use a graphic organizer like the one below to identify three ways that Congress has gained or lost power.

```
+ ————————————————— -
        /\
       /Congress\
```

Writing About Government

6. **Expository Writing** The president and Congress have had conflict over the president's right to send armed forces overseas. When has the president committed military forces overseas without a declaration of war? Create an annotated time line showing the year and reason for these military involvements with a brief written summary.

Answers

1. All definitions can be found in the section and the Glossary.
2. Because the Constitution intentionally gave each branch the power to check the other, each has a degree of independent authority and tends to use it for its own political goals.
3. When different parties control Congress and the White House, party politics adds to congressional opposition to the president's proposals.
4. Because the Constitution requires that Congress share powers with the executive branch and because Congress has developed the power to oversee the executive branch, the relationship is marked by conflict.
5. Gained: federal budget, legislative veto, limits on emergency powers of the president. Lost: emergency powers to close banks, control wages and prices, rationing of consumer goods.
6. Students' time lines should be accurate and thorough.

Should the President Be Able to Keep All Communications With Advisers Secret?

Executive privilege is the doctrine stating that the executive branch can withhold information on its decision making from Congress and the courts. Presidents have often invoked this doctrine on sensitive issues. President George W. Bush did so in 2002 when the General Accountability Office (GAO) wanted to learn whether Enron, an energy trading company that engaged in illegal accounting practices, served on an energy task force led by Vice President Dick Cheney. The White House refused to name the task force members, claiming executive privilege.

NO

Executive privilege should not be absolute. It is not mentioned in the Constitution and Congress needs to have access to important information. The Supreme Court has already held in *United States* v. *Nixon* (1972) that the president must reveal confidential information when presidential privilege is outweighed by other constitutional requirements. In this case, the GAO needs certain information to help Congress frame new laws to protect the public. Vice President Dick Cheney's refusal to hand over the documents also weakens public confidence in government because it implies that the White House has something to hide.

YES

To be an effective leader, the president must be able to communicate in confidence with advisers. If Vice President Cheney cannot keep minutes of the energy task force meetings secret, it is unlikely that he will receive frank advice from expert advisers in the future. Not only that, but key advisers will hesitate to give the president the full benefit of their thinking in the future. They will always be worried that something said in confidence will eventually become public. The GAO is infringing on the authority of the executive branch.

Debating the Issue

1. **Analyzing** How does executive privilege contribute to the independence of the executive branch of government?

2. **Explaining** How does the idea of separation of powers support the claim for executive privilege?

3. **Deciding** How should the courts determine when executive privilege should or should not be used?

▶ **President George W. Bush and Vice President Dick Cheney**

Teach

Setting Up the Debate

Analyzing Help students focus on the issue of confidentiality in regard to presidential communications. **Ask:** What is executive privilege? (*Executive privilege is a doctrine stating that the executive branch can withhold information on its decision making from Congress and the courts.*)

Evaluating Have students research instances in which executive privilege has been used and identify the pros and cons of each use. Have students on the panel meet to build their arguments for and against the use of executive privilege. Urge both groups to consider the historic arguments about the use of executive privilege as well as current issues involving its use.

Concluding the Debate

Discuss these questions with the participants:

- What standards did you set for identifying evidence either for or against the use of executive privilege?

- What arguments would you have used in response to information provided by the opposing view on the issue?

Debating the Issue Answers

1. Executive privilege allows the executive branch to seek advice and information from sources freely and securely. Without the fear of conversations becoming public, these resources might be more likely to offer candid and honest information.

2. Separation of powers ensures that no one branch of the government is more powerful than the others. If the legislative branch were allowed to require the executive branch to divulge all its information and sources, the legislative branch would be more powerful than the executive branch.

3. Students' answers will vary, but ask them to explain the rationale behind their answers.

ExamView®
Assessment Suite

This easy-to-use software includes extensive question banks and allows you to create fully customized tests that can be administered in print or online.

Reviewing Vocabulary

1. d
2. a
3. f
4. b
5. c

Reviewing Main Ideas

6. Implied powers are necessary to carry out expressed powers.

7. It has expanded to give Congress authority over virtually everything that crosses state lines.

8. Congress may subpoena witnesses, require witnesses to testify under oath, prosecute witnesses for perjury, and indict individuals who do not cooperate with contempt of Congress.

9. requiring executive agencies to report on their activities, asking the congressional support agencies to study an agency's work, and reviewing each agency's budget

10. paying expenses, appointing officials, and making treaties

11. The Supreme Court claimed it is an unconstitutional violation of the separation of powers principle.

Critical Thinking

12. Congress has the power to collect taxes, to borrow and print money, to regulate foreign and interstate commerce, to declare war,

---

Reviewing Vocabulary

Match each of the descriptions below with the content vocabulary word(s) it describes. Not every word or phrase will have a description.

a. appropriations bill
b. impoundment
c. immunity
d. implied powers
e. legislative veto
f. subpoena

Chapter Summary

Selected Powers of Congress

Legislative Powers

★ Taxing and Spending Power—Congress has great control over national policy, as no agency can spend money without congressional approval

★ Commerce Power—Congress regulates foreign commerce and trade between the states

Non-Legislative Powers

★ Ratification Power—Congress accepts or rejects treaties negotiated between the president and a foreign country

★ Confirmation Power—Both houses of Congress confirm or deny presidential appointments

★ Power to Choose Presidents—The House selects the president if no candidate wins a majority of votes in the Electoral College

★ Removal Power—Both houses of Congress play a role in the removal of a president from office due to misconduct

Investigative Powers

★ The Constitution does not specifically state this power, but the legislature's role as a people's body made this power necessary

★ Congress investigates the operation of government agencies and the actions of individual government personnel

---

1. Powers not specified in the Constitution
2. Grants money to carry out programs
3. Compels a witness to appear
4. Refusing to spend funds
5. Freedom from prosecution

Reviewing Main Ideas

Section 1 *(pages 157–165)*

6. **Describing** How are expressed powers and implied powers related?

7. **Summarizing** Why has the power to regulate interstate commerce become such an important power of Congress?

Section 2 *(pages 167–171)*

8. **Describing** What powers does Congress use to collect evidence for congressional investigations?

9. **Examining** What are three methods that Congress uses to oversee the executive branch?

Section 3 *(pages 172–176)*

10. **Identifying** List three powers that Congress and the president share.

11. **Interpreting** On what grounds did the Supreme Court declare the legislative veto unconstitutional?

Critical Thinking

12. **Essential Question** What were some enumerated powers given to Congress by the Constitution? How have these powers developed over time?

13. **Evaluating** Explain how the Constitution's commerce clause has helped African Americans obtain equal rights.

14. **Theorizing** What arguments might be made to support a legislative veto power for Congress?

15. **Understanding Cause and Effect** In a graphic organizer like the one below, indicate how the power struggle between the president and Congress strengthens or weakens the government.

Power Struggle	
Strengthening Effects	Weakening Effects

---

to maintain an army and navy, to establish laws of naturalization, and to provide for laws necessary and proper for carrying out all other powers; many implied powers have risen from the enumerated powers over time.

13. Congress has used this power to outlaw racial discrimination by businesses that are in any way part of interstate commerce. This use of the commerce clause has ranged from serving travelers who cross state lines to businesses that get supplies of products from other states.

14. Answers will vary but should focus on the right of Congress to make sure that the intents of the laws it passes are carried out.

15. Graphic organizers will vary, but those indicating a stronger government may note a distribution of power (i.e., checks and balances). Those indicating a weaker government may note deadlock and inaction (i.e., political party gridlock).

Government ONLINE Self-Check Quiz
Visit glencoe.com and enter QuickPass™ code USG9822c6.
Click on Self-Check Quizzes for additional test practice.

CHAPTER
6
Assessment
and Activities

Document-Based Questions

Analyzing Primary Sources

Read the excerpt below and answer the questions that follow.

In 1964 Congress granted President Lyndon B. Johnson the power to send troops into Vietnam without an official declaration of war and without notification to Congress. Congress later enacted a law requiring the president to notify and consult with Congress anytime soldiers are to be stationed in conflicts overseas. This law is known as the War Powers Act.

> *SEC. 3. The President in every possible instance shall consult with Congress before introducing United States Armed Forces into hostilities or into situations where imminent involvement in hostilities is clearly indicated by the circumstances, and after every such introduction shall consult regularly with the Congress until United States Armed Forces are no longer engaged in hostilities or have been removed from such situations.*

16. How is the 1973 War Powers Act a check on presidential power?

17. What are the benefits or drawbacks of requiring the president to notify Congress before sending troops into conflict?

Applying Technology Skills

18. Creating a Multimedia Presentation Study the list below of topics dealing with Congress. Choose one of the topics, and create a presentation using at least three types of media to teach the topic to your class.
- The national debt and Congress's attempts to limit it
- The War Powers Act and the relationship between Congress and the president
- The power of Congress to propose amendments
- A congressional investigation
- Congressional term limits

Interpreting Political Cartoons

Analyze the cartoon and answer the questions that follow. Base your answers on the cartoon and your knowledge of Chapter 6.

OPTIMIST   PESSIMIST   ADMINISTRATION SPOKESMAN

MANKOFF

"Half full."   "Half empty."   "Half empty due to congressional inaction and half full due to the tireless efforts of the President."

19. What is happening in this cartoon?

20. Which side does the administration spokesperson support? Explain.

21. Is the administration spokesperson an objective judge? What biases might he have?

Participating IN GOVERNMENT

22. Because members of Congress represent the interests of individual states and congressional districts, their ideas are often different from the president's, which promote policies for the entire nation. Find out about an important issue in your state that has been reflected in a bill debated in Congress. See how your senators and representatives voted on the bill. Do you agree or disagree with the senator's or representative's position? Write an opinion paper supporting or criticizing your lawmaker's position.

Government ONLINE

Have students use the **Chapter 6 Self-Check Quiz.** Visit glencoe.com and enter **QuickPass**™ code USG9085c6T to prepare for the Chapter Test.

finds a way to promote the president at the same time.

20. The spokesperson supports the president by linking the president with the "half-full" view and speaking of the president's "tireless efforts."

21. No, he is employed to support the president. He probably has biases that favor executive policies and treats other points of view as obstacles or even enemy ideas.

Participating IN GOVERNMENT

22. Papers should discuss a specific bill, how the senators and representatives voted, and the student's opinion.

Chapter Bonus Test Question

Ask: If Congress never issued a declaration of war, how did the United States wind up sending troops to fight in Vietnam? (*Congress passed the Gulf of Tonkin Resolution that gave President Lyndon Johnson the power to "take all necessary measures" to protect American forces.*)

Analyzing Primary Sources

16. The War Powers Act prevents the executive branch from sending soldiers overseas without consulting with Congress at regular intervals during the conflict, particularly if involvement is expected to be longer than 60 days.

17. The drawback is that if the president waits to consult with Congress, he or she may not be able to act quickly enough in an emergency. On the other hand, it prevents the president from utilizing the military as a personal military force.

Applying Technology Skills

18. Students' presentations should be thorough, should be concise, and should use three different types of media creatively.

Interpreting Political Cartoons

19. Three speakers are evaluating a glass with liquid in it. The optimist and pessimist describe it as "half full" and "half empty," respectively, but the administration spokesperson describes it as both, and

179

Key to Ability Levels
- **BL** Below level
- **OL** On level
- **AL** Above level
- **ELL** English Language Learners

Key to Teaching Resources
- 📁 Print Material
- 💿 CD-ROM or DVD
- 🖨 Transparency

Levels					Resources	Chapter Opener	Section 1	Section 2	Section 3	Section 4	Chapter Assess
BL	OL	AL	ELL								
FOCUS											
BL	OL	AL	ELL	🖨	Section Focus Transparencies		7-1	7-2	7-3	7-4	
TEACH											
BL	OL		ELL	📁	Reading Essentials and Study Guide (and Answer Key)		p. 71	p. 75	p. 77	p. 80	
BL	OL		ELL	📁	Guided Reading Activities		p. 25	p. 26	p. 27	p. 28	
BL	OL		ELL	📁	Vocabulary Activities				p. 7		
BL	OL	AL	ELL	📁	Chapter Summaries					p. 19	
BL	OL			📁	American Biographies						
BL	OL	AL	ELL	📁	Cooperative Learning Activities			p. 3			
	OL	AL	ELL	📁	Government Simulations and Debate				p. 8		
BL	OL	AL	ELL	📁	Historical Documents and Speeches		p. 7				
BL	OL	AL	ELL	📁	Interpreting Political Cartoons				p. 8		
BL	OL		ELL	📁	Skill Reinforcement Activities		p. 7				
BL	OL	AL	ELL	📁	Source Readings						
BL	OL			📁	Supreme Court Case Studies						
BL	OL	AL	ELL	📁	Participating in Government Activities			p. 13			
BL	OL		ELL	📁	Spanish Declaration of Independence and U.S. Constitution	✓	✓	✓	✓	✓	✓
BL	OL	AL	ELL	📁	NGS World Atlas, Spanish	✓	✓	✓	✓	✓	✓
BL	OL	AL	ELL	🖨	Unit Overlay Transparencies, Strategies, and Activities	✓	✓	✓	✓	✓	✓
BL	OL		ELL	🖨	Making It Relevant Transparencies	✓	✓	✓	✓	✓	✓
BL	OL	AL	ELL	🖨	High School Writing Process Transparencies, Strategies, and Activities	✓	✓	✓	✓	✓	✓
BL	OL	AL		🖨	American Art & Architecture Transparencies, Strategies, and Activities	✓	✓	✓	✓	✓	✓

✓ Chapter- or unit-based activities applicable to all sections in this chapter

TeacherWorks™ Plus
All-In-One Planner and Resource Center

- Interactive Lesson Planner
- Interactive Teacher Edition
- Fully editable blackline masters
- Chapter Spotlight Videos Launch

- Differentiated Lesson Plans
- Printable reports of daily assignments
- Standards tracking system

Levels					Resources	Chapter Opener	Section 1	Section 2	Section 3	Section 4	Chapter Assess
BL	OL	AL	ELL								
					TEACH (continued)						
BL	OL			⊙	**American Music: Hits Through History**	✓	✓	✓	✓	✓	✓
BL	OL		ELL	🗀	**Reading Strategies for the Social Studies Classroom**	✓	✓	✓	✓	✓	✓
			ELL	🗀	**English Language Learner Handbook**	✓	✓	✓	✓	✓	✓
BL	OL		ELL	🗀	**Writer's Guidebook for Social Studies**	✓	✓	✓	✓	✓	✓
BL	OL	AL	ELL	🗀	**Living Constitution, SE**	✓	✓	✓	✓	✓	✓
BL	OL	AL	ELL	🗀	**Living Constitution, TAE**	✓	✓	✓	✓	✓	✓
BL	OL			🗀	**NGS World Atlas, English**	✓	✓	✓	✓	✓	✓
BL	OL		ELL	🗀	**The Constitution and You (poster set)**	✓	✓	✓	✓	✓	✓
BL	OL	AL	ELL	🗀	**Spanish Chapter Summaries**					p. 19	
BL	OL	AL	ELL	🗀	**Spanish Vocabulary Activities**				p. 7		
BL	OL		ELL	🗀	**Spanish Reading Essentials and Study Guide (and Answer Key)**		p. 71	p. 75	p. 77	p. 80	
BL	OL	AL	ELL	⊙	**PresentationPlus! with MindJogger CheckPoint**	✓	✓	✓	✓	✓	✓
					ASSESS						
BL	OL	AL	ELL	⊙	*ExamView® Assessment Suite*		7-1	7-2	7-3	7-4	Ch. 7
BL	OL	AL	ELL	🗀	**Authentic Assessment with Rubrics**					p. 14	p. 14
BL	OL	AL	ELL	🗀	**Section Quizzes and Chapter Tests**		p. 77	p. 78	p. 79	p. 80	pp. 81–88
BL	OL	AL	ELL	🗀	**Spanish Section Quizzes and Tests**		p. 77	p. 78	p. 79	p. 80	pp. 81–88
					CLOSE						
BL			ELL	🗀	**Reteaching Activities**		p. 7				p. 7
BL	OL	AL	ELL	⊙	**StudentWorks™ Plus with Audio Summaries**	✓	✓	✓	✓	✓	✓
BL	OL		ELL	✋	**Graphic Organizer Transparencies**		✓	✓	✓	✓	
BL	OL		ELL	🗀	**High School Government Reading and Study Skills Foldables®**		p. 50	p. 50	p. 50	p. 50	

Chapter Spotlight Video

Teach With Technology

What are Chapter Spotlight Videos?

Chapter Spotlight Videos are one of the digital media associated with your textbook. They present a topic specific to each chapter of the textbook.

How can Chapter Spotlight Videos help my students?

Chapter Spotlight Videos generate student interest and provide a springboard for classroom discussion. Students can watch videos from their classroom computer screen or review chapter content while on their home computer.

Visit glencoe.com to access the Media Library, and enter a **QuickPass**™ code to go to Chapter Spotlight Videos. These videos can also be launched from StudentWorks™ Plus Online or PresentationPlus! with MindJogger CheckPoint.

Government ONLINE
Visit glencoe.com and enter **QuickPass**™ code USG9085c7T for Chapter 7 resources.

You can easily launch a wide range of digital products from your computer's desktop with the McGraw-Hill Social Studies widget.

	Student	Teacher	Parent
Media Library			
• Student Edition Section Audio	●		●
• Chapter Spotlight Videos	●	●	●
***United States Government* Online Learning Center (Web Site)**			
• Chapter Overviews	●	●	●
• Multilingual Glossaries	●	●	●
• Study-to-Go	●	●	●
• Student Web Activities	●	●	●
• Self-Check Quizzes	●	●	●
• Online Student Edition	●	●	●
• Vocabulary eFlashcards	●	●	●
• Web Activity Lesson Plans		●	
• Vocabulary PuzzleMaker	●	●	●
• Landmark Supreme Court Cases	●	●	●
• Beyond the Textbook	●	●	●

READING SUPPORT FROM
JAMESTOWN EDUCATION

- **Timed Readings Plus in Social Studies** helps students increase their reading rate and fluency while maintaining comprehension. The 400-word passages are similar to those found on state and national assessments.

- **Reading in the Content Area: Social Studies** concentrates on six essential reading skills that help students better comprehend what they read. The book includes 75 high-interest nonfiction passages written at increasing levels of difficulty.

- **Reading Social Studies** includes strategic reading instruction and vocabulary support in Social Studies content for ELLs and native speakers of English. www.jamestowneducation.com

Reading List Generator CD-ROM

GLENCOE
BOOKLINK 3

Use this database to search more than 30,000 titles to create a customized reading list for your students.

- Reading lists can be organized by students' reading level, author, genre, theme, or area of interest.

- The database provides Degrees of Reading Power™ (DRP) and Lexile™ readability scores for all selections.

- A brief summary of each selection is included.

Leveled reading suggestions for this chapter:

- *First Woman in Congress: Jeannette Rankin,* by Florence Meiman White

- *Senator: A Profile of Bill Bradley in the U.S. Senate,* by William Jaspersohn

Review suggested books before assigning them.

Economics Connection

Personal Finance Literacy

Federal Revenues and Expenditures

When the nation was young, the government needed money mostly for the military. The 1789 budget was $1.7 million—about $20 million in today's dollars. Over the years, government expanded to fund functions such as public health, highways, and veterans' benefits. Various presidents have had different priorities. In the 1930s Franklin Roosevelt's New Deal aided those thrown into poverty by the Depression. In the 1980s Ronald Reagan's priority was weapons.

Today, a $2.9 trillion budget is supported by tax dollars: individual income (45%); payroll (35%); corporate income (15%); customs, excise, estate (6%). Federal revenue in 2007 was $2.6 trillion, but the government spent $162 billion more. To make up the difference—the deficit—the government borrows from businesses, individuals, and other governments. Just as consumers pay interest on credit cards, the government pays interest to its creditors. The total accumulated debt the government owed in mid-2008—the national debt—was $9.5 trillion.

The graph shows how federal funds are spent (percentage excludes nuclear weapons, military operations in Iraq and Afghanistan, and other defense-related funding).

Federal Government Outlays, 2007

- Natural Resources and Environment 1%
- Other 16%
- Social Security 22%
- Education, Training, Employment, and Social Services 3%
- Health 10%
- National Defense 20%
- Medicare 14%
- Income Security 13%

Total Outlays $2,730.2 billion

Note: Percentages may not equal 100 due to rounding.

Ask students: Which spending categories do you think should get a larger or a smaller share—and why?

■) **Chapter Audio**   ▦ **Spotlight Video**

CHAPTER 7

Congress *at* Work

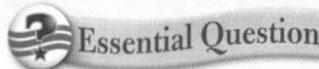 **Essential Question**

Members of Congress can sponsor bills to represent voters' interests. They are bound by the rules of the House or Senate. Rules range from processes for assigning bills to particular committees to congressional ethics. Have students brainstorm reasons why Congress is subject to so many different rules and responsibilities.

▦ **Chapter Spotlight Video**

To generate student interest and provide a springboard for class discussion, access the Chapter 7 Video at glencoe.com or on the video DVD.

FOLDABLES **Dinah Zike's**
Study Organizer **Foldables** are three-dimensional, interactive graphic organizers that help students practice basic writing skills, review key vocabulary terms, and identify main ideas. Have students complete this chapter's Foldable activity or activities in *Dinah Zike's Reading and Study Skills Foldables* booklet. **OL**

 Government ONLINE

Visit glencoe.com and enter *QuickPass*™ code USG9085c7T for Chapter 7 Resources including Chapter Overview, Student Web Activity, Self-Check Quiz, and other materials for students and teachers.

Essential Question

What types of actions can members of Congress take to represent voters' interests, and what rules govern congressional activities?

Government ONLINE
Chapter Overview Visit glencoe.com and enter *QuickPass*™ code USG9822c7 for an overview, a quiz, and other chapter resources.

▲ **Nancy Pelosi, Speaker of the House**

180

Launching the Chapter

Researching Court Cases During the course of Chapter 7, have students collect newspaper or magazine articles that relate to the legislative process. Examples may include hearings on a current bill, the introduction of new bills, or an interview with the president regarding the veto of recently proposed legislation. Alternatively, students may record such stories from radio or television news broadcasts. Ask each student to

select one news item and summarize it, indicating how it relates to the chapter.
Essential Question: Did the process for considering the bill(s) follow a standard procedure? Which of the steps in the legislative process did the bill go through? *(Answers should make a connection between the bill students studied and the information presented in this chapter.)* **OL**

How a Bill Becomes a Law

Reader's Guide

Content Vocabulary
★ private bill *(p. 181)*
★ public bill *(p. 182)*
★ simple resolution *(p. 182)*
★ rider *(p. 183)*
★ hearing *(p. 184)*
★ veto *(p. 187)*
★ pocket veto *(p. 187)*

Academic Vocabulary
★ labor *(p. 181)*
★ interactive *(p. 184)*
★ challenge *(p. 188)*

Reading Strategy
As you read, create a flowchart to analyze the major stages by which a bill becomes a law.

☐ → ☐ → ☐ → ☐ →

Issues in the News

In late 2005, Senator Russ Feingold of Wisconsin threatened to filibuster the renewal of the Patriot Act. First passed in 2001, the act gives the government special powers in investigating possible terrorists but critics say citizens' basic civil rights are being infringed upon unnecessarily. Feingold, the lone vote against the 2001 act, has gained more support this time for his opposition. The new act added a few more protections of individual rights, but the Federal Bureau of Investigations (FBI) still has broad powers to search telephone, e-mail and financial records without a court order. When it was clear the measure would pass with only these moderate revisions, Feingold showed his anger by reading the Constitution on the Senate floor.

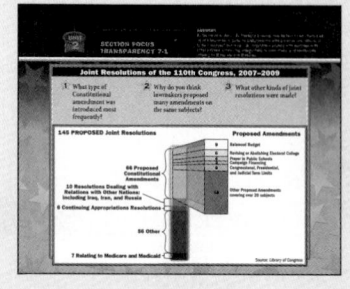

▲ Senator Russ Feingold of Wisconsin opposed the USA Patriot Act renewal in 2006 with a filibuster.

In 2006 the USA Patriot Act was one of many bills introduced in Congress. Unlike most that year, it passed, although echoes of Feingold's criticisms surfaced later. During each two-year term, thousands of bills are introduced in Congress. Why are there so many? Congress is a forum for all Americans who want things from the government. The president, federal agencies, **labor** unions, business groups, and individuals all look to Congress to pass laws reflecting their interests.

Of the thousands of bills introduced each session, only a few hundred become law. Most die in Congress, and some are vetoed by the president. If a bill is not passed before the end of the term, it has to be introduced again in the next Congress to be given further consideration.

In this section, you will look at the different forms new legislation takes, and the steps a bill must go through to become a law.

Types of Bills and Resolutions

Two types of bills are introduced in Congress: private bills and public bills. **Private bills** deal with individual people or places. They often involve claims against the government or a person's immigration problem. Private bills used to make up a significant percentage of congressional bills, but not lately. In a recent Congress, only a few hundred of almost 12,000 bills introduced were private ones.

Focus

Bellringer
Section Focus Transparencies 7-1

Reader's Guide

Answers to Graphic:
introduced →
committee action →
floor action →
conference action →
sent to president →

Resource Manager

R **Reading Strategies**	C **Critical Thinking**	D **Differentiated Instruction**	W **Writing Support**	S **Skill Practice**
Teacher Edition • Comparing and Contrasting, p. 182 • Inferring, p. 186 **Additional Resources** • Quizzes/Tests, p. 77 • Guid. Read. Act., p. 25	**Teacher Edition** • Drawing Conclusions, p. 183 • Making Inferences, p. 187 **Additional Resources** • Read. Essen., pp. 71–74	**Teacher Edition** • English Learners, p. 187 **Additional Resources** • Reteaching Act., p. 7 • Foldables, p. 50	**Teacher Edition** • Expository Writing, p. 183 **Additional Resources** • Hist. Docs. and Speeches, p. 7	**Teacher Edition** • Reading a Flow Chart, p. 185 • Using a Database, p. 188 **Additional Resources** • Skill Reinforce. Act., p. 7

Teach

R Reading Strategy

Comparing and Contrasting
Ask: In what way is a joint resolution different from other resolutions? *(It is passed by both houses of Congress.)* **BL**

Participating IN GOVERNMENT

More About Initiating Legislation Before writing a description of a bill, students should evaluate their ideas carefully, perhaps starting with questions such as the following:

- How do I know that current laws are ineffective in dealing with this issue?

- What do other people think of my idea?

- What objections might people have to my idea?

- If my idea became law, how easy would it be to enforce? **OL**

Additional Support

On the other hand, **public bills** deal with general matters and apply to the entire nation. They are often controversial since it is hard to shape policies that touch many people. Public bills might address tax cuts, national health insurance, gun control, civil rights, or abortion. The press covers major bills heavily and they may be debated for months before becoming law. Major public bills like these account for about 30 percent of all bills passed.

Resolutions

Besides passing laws, Congress can also pass resolutions to make policy on an unusual or temporary matter. There are three kinds of resolutions: simple, joint, and concurrent.

A **simple resolution** covers matters affecting only one house of Congress and is passed by that house alone. If a new rule or procedure is needed, it is adopted in the form of a resolution. Because it is an internal matter, it does not have the force of law and is not sent to the president for signature.

A joint resolution is a resolution passed in the same form by both houses. When a joint resolution is signed by the president, it has the force of law. Joint resolutions are often used to correct an error in an earlier law or to appropriate money for a special purpose. The joint resolution is also used if Congress wants to propose a constitutional amendment, but this does not require the president's signature. (See page 77 for the amendment process.)

Concurrent resolutions cover matters requiring the action of the House and Senate but on which a law is not needed. For example, a concurrent resolution might set the date for adjourning Congress or express Congress's opinion on an issue. Both houses of Congress must pass concurrent resolutions. They do not require the president's signature, and they do not have the force of law.

Earmarks

Earmarks are a way that members of Congress can specify that some part of a funding bill will go toward a certain purpose. Sometimes earmarks are included in the text of a bill, but many earmarks appear only in the committee reports explaining a measure. An earmark might say, for example, that $490,000 of monies for the state of California will be set aside for the Los Angeles County Fire Museum. Critics see earmarks as allowing members of Congress to direct money to their own pet projects. Often earmarks add money to appropriations bills.

In March 2008, Congress defeated a proposal to put a one-year moratorium on earmarks. One member said earmarks are acceptable because they allow Congress to direct the spending of funds.

Participating IN GOVERNMENT — Initiating Legislation

Have you ever said, "There ought to be a law!" when observing an apparent injustice? Some acts of Congress originate with private individuals or groups. If you see a need for a law, you can write a bill and ask a representative or senator to introduce it for consideration.

Rarely, if ever, does a bill begin this way. However, a representative may agree to sponsor your bill. A sponsor will work to put your bill in the proper form for introduction.

The sponsor may also make changes in your bill's content to increase its chances for passage.

After your bill is introduced, if you are considered an expert on the subject of the bill, you may be asked to testify before a congressional committee. You may also contact other members of Congress to request their support for your legislation. Finally, if Congress passes your bill, be prepared for an invitation to the White House to participate in the president's signing ceremony!

◀ Proposing a law

Participating IN GOVERNMENT ACTIVITY

Writing Legislation Most legislation develops from a problem that people cannot resolve themselves. Brainstorm to identify a problem that national legislation might solve and describe it in a few paragraphs.

Activity: Interdisciplinary Connection

Logic Read aloud the following hypothetical situations to students and have them work together to decide whether each action exemplifies a private bill, a public bill, a resolution, a joint resolution, or a concurrent resolution.

- speeding overdue Social Security payments to a needy recipient *(private bill)*

- changing the vacation schedule of the House *(resolution)*
- raising taxes on luxury items *(public bill)*
- reintroducing the Equal Rights Amendment *(joint resolution)* **OL**

Otherwise, she said, "the agencies allocate the dollars rather than members of Congress."

Riders

Bills and resolutions usually deal with only one subject. However, sometimes a rider is attached to a bill. A **rider** is a provision on a subject other than the one covered in the bill. Lawmakers attach riders to bills that are likely to pass. Presidents sometimes veto bills because of a rider they oppose. Lawmakers sometimes attach many riders to a bill for a variety of constituents—the bill then resembles a Christmas tree loaded with ornaments. The bill might still pass because of its core subject.

Why So Few Bills Become Law

Fewer than 10 percent of all bills introduced in Congress become public laws. Why is this true? One reason is that creating law is a long and complicated process—as many as 100 steps can be involved. There are many points at which a bill can be delayed, killed, or amended. Thus a bill's opponents have many opportunities to defeat a bill.

Second, because there are so many steps, a bill's sponsors must be willing to bargain and compromise with others. Compromise is the only way to get enough support to move a bill from one step to the next—major bills have little chance of passage without strong support. Bills opposed by powerful interest groups are not likely to pass.

Another reason so few bills "make it" is that members introduce many bills knowing they have no chance of becoming law. In other words, they are introduced as a symbolic gesture. A member might introduce a bill to show support for a policy, to attract media attention to an issue, or to satisfy an important group of voters. When reelection comes around, legislators can say they have taken action and they can blame a committee or Congress for the bill's failure to pass.

Introducing a Bill

The Constitution sets forth only a few of the many steps a bill must go through to become law. The remaining steps have developed as Congress has grown and the number of bills has increased.

How Bills Are Introduced

The first step in the process is to introduce a bill. Ideas for bills come from citizens, interest groups, or the executive branch. The executive branch initiates roughly half of all bills passed.

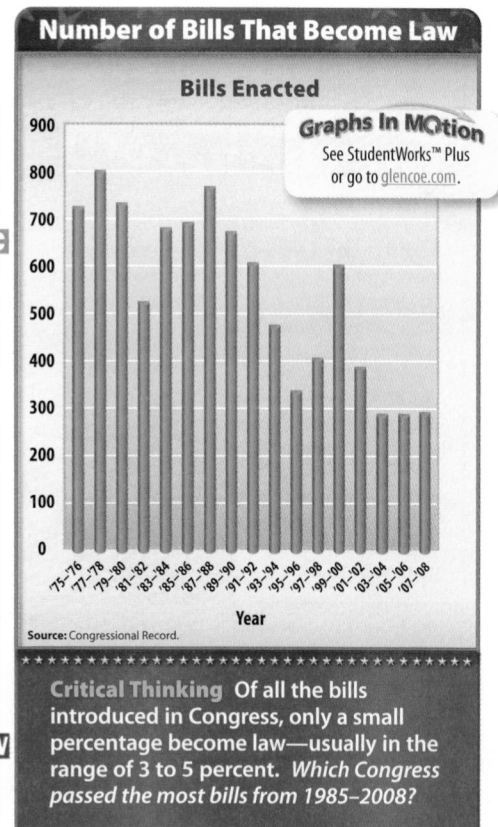

Number of Bills That Become Law

Bills Enacted

Graphs In Motion
See StudentWorks™ Plus
or go to glencoe.com.

Source: Congressional Record.

Critical Thinking Of all the bills introduced in Congress, only a small percentage become law—usually in the range of 3 to 5 percent. *Which Congress passed the most bills from 1985–2008?*

Bills may be drafted by legislators, their staffs, lawyers for a Senate or House committee, or an interest group. But only a member of Congress can actually introduce a bill. Lawmakers who sponsor a major bill usually find cosponsors to show that the bill has wide support.

To introduce a bill in the House, a member drops the bill into the hopper, a box near the clerk's desk. To introduce a bill in the Senate, the presiding officer must first recognize the senator, who then formally presents the bill.

As soon as a bill is introduced, it is given a title and number and then printed and distributed to lawmakers. (The first bill in a Senate session is S.1, and the first bill in the House is H.R.1.) These steps make up the first reading of the bill.

Committee Action

For both houses of Congress, bills are sent to the committees that deal with their subject.

CHAPTER 7: *Congress at Work* **183**

Critical Thinking

Answer: the '87–'88 Congress

C Critical Thinking

Drawing Conclusions Ask: Should Congress allow riders? *(Students might believe that riders are wrong because they allow Congress to pass bills that might not pass on their own. Others might feel that riders are time savers, passing needed legislation without introducing a separate bill.)* **OL**

W Writing Support

Expository Writing Have students look at some of the bills being considered in the House and Senate. They can locate information at the THOMAS site maintained by the Library of Congress (thomas.loc.gov). Ask students to focus on one House bill and one Senate bill. They may call the offices of senators and representatives to get information about the origin of the bill, its purpose, and the legislator's stand. Have students write essays describing their findings. **Ask:** What effect would passage of the bill have on the community in which it applies? *(Answers will depend on the type of bill.)* **AL**

Additional Support

Creating a Board Game Organize the class into groups, with each group assigned the task of creating a board game about how a bill becomes a law. Have each group choose a name for the game and discuss how it will be played. Ask each group to assign the following tasks to its members: drawing a game board background; designing a route for players to follow; writing the rules of the game; creating playing pieces; and designing playing cards. After each group has completed its game, have it play another group's game. **OL**

Teacher Tip

Drawing Conclusions Help students evaluate their games by asking them the following questions:

- Does playing the game help you better understand how a bill becomes a law?
- How would you improve the game?

Did You Know?

Pigeonholing The origin of the term *pigeonholing* is related to early American furniture. Desks had small compartments, or "pigeonholes," into which paper could be stuffed, often to be lost or forgotten.

Participating
IN GOVERNMENT

Types of Testimony People who testify during the hearings on a bill may come from universities, businesses, Hollywood—just about anywhere. Have students follow the hearings on a specific bill and note who gives testimony. As a class, discuss the following questions. **Ask:** Who can speak with authority about the facts under consideration? Why might the publicity that comes from celebrity testimony be valuable? *(They are experts on the subject matter; publicity can influence public opinion for or against a bill.)* **OL**

Differentiated Instruction

Participating in Government Activities, p. 13

184

TIME
For the Record

Follow the Leader In Congress, whips are not there to speed up the process of government. Rather, whips are leaders who make sure party members vote along with the rest of the party on bills. The term was originally used in the British House of Commons. The term comes from fox hunting, in which a person, known as a "whipper-in," whips the dogs to keep them running in a pack.

Committee chairs may then send a bill to a subcommittee. If a committee wants to reject a bill, it can ignore it and simply let the bill "die," a process called "pigeonholing," or the committee can "kill" it by a majority vote. A committee can completely rewrite a bill, amend it, or recommend that it be adopted as it is before sending it back to the House or Senate for action. Committee members and staff are considered experts in their areas. If they reject a bill, other lawmakers will usually agree with them. Time is also a factor. Lawmakers have heavy workloads and must depend on the judgment of their peers.

Committee Hearings

When a committee decides to act on a bill, it holds hearings. During a **hearing,** the committee listens to testimony from experts on the bill's subject, from government officials, and from interest groups that are concerned with the bill. Hearings allow a committee to gather information, but most information usually comes from their staff research.

Hearings can be very important in their own right, however. Skillful chairs can use hearings to influence public opinion for or against a bill or to test its political acceptability. Hearings can also focus public attention on a problem or give interest groups a chance to present their perspective.

184 UNIT 2: *The Legislative Branch*

Finally, hearings are often the best time for outside groups to influence the bill. Citizens can write letters, make phone calls, or send e-mails to express their opinions.

To improve the legislation process, many congressional committees have begun using the Internet in connection with hearings on a bill. The Internet has been used for the following:

- **interactive** hearings using expert witnesses from outside Washington
- broadcast hearings, thus giving citizens the chance to e-mail questions to committee members
- report on a bill's contents or status on their Web home pages
- make information available in a second language

For Spanish speakers, the House Education and Labor Committee was the first with a Web site that informed them of former president George W. Bush's education programs.

Markup Session

After the hearings are over, the committee meets in a markup session—marking up the bill—to decide what changes, if any, to make to the bill. Committee members go through the bill section by section, making any changes they think the bill needs. A majority vote of the committee is required for all changes made to the bill.

Reporting a Bill

When all the changes have been made, the committee votes either to kill the bill or to report it. To report the bill means to send it to the House or Senate for action. Along with the revised bill, the committee will send to the House or Senate a written report prepared by the committee staff. This report is important. It explains the committee's actions, describes the bill, lists the major changes the committee has made, and gives opinions on the bill. The report is often the only document available to lawmakers or their staffs as they decide how to vote on a bill.

The committee report may recommend passage of the bill, or it may report the bill unfavorably. Why would a committee report a bill, but not recommend passage? This happens extremely rarely. A committee may believe the full House should have the opportunity to consider a bill even though the committee does not support it.

Congressional Petition

Objective: Write a petition.

Focus/Teach: Discuss problems in your school or community and write petitions.

Assess: Evaluate students' petitions.

Close: Have students send their petitions to their member of Congress and discuss the responses they receive.

Differentiated Instruction Strategies

BL Have students list community problems and then poll other students about the issues.

AL Encourage students to write a letter to the editor of the local newspaper.

ELL Research the name and address of the representative from their congressional district.

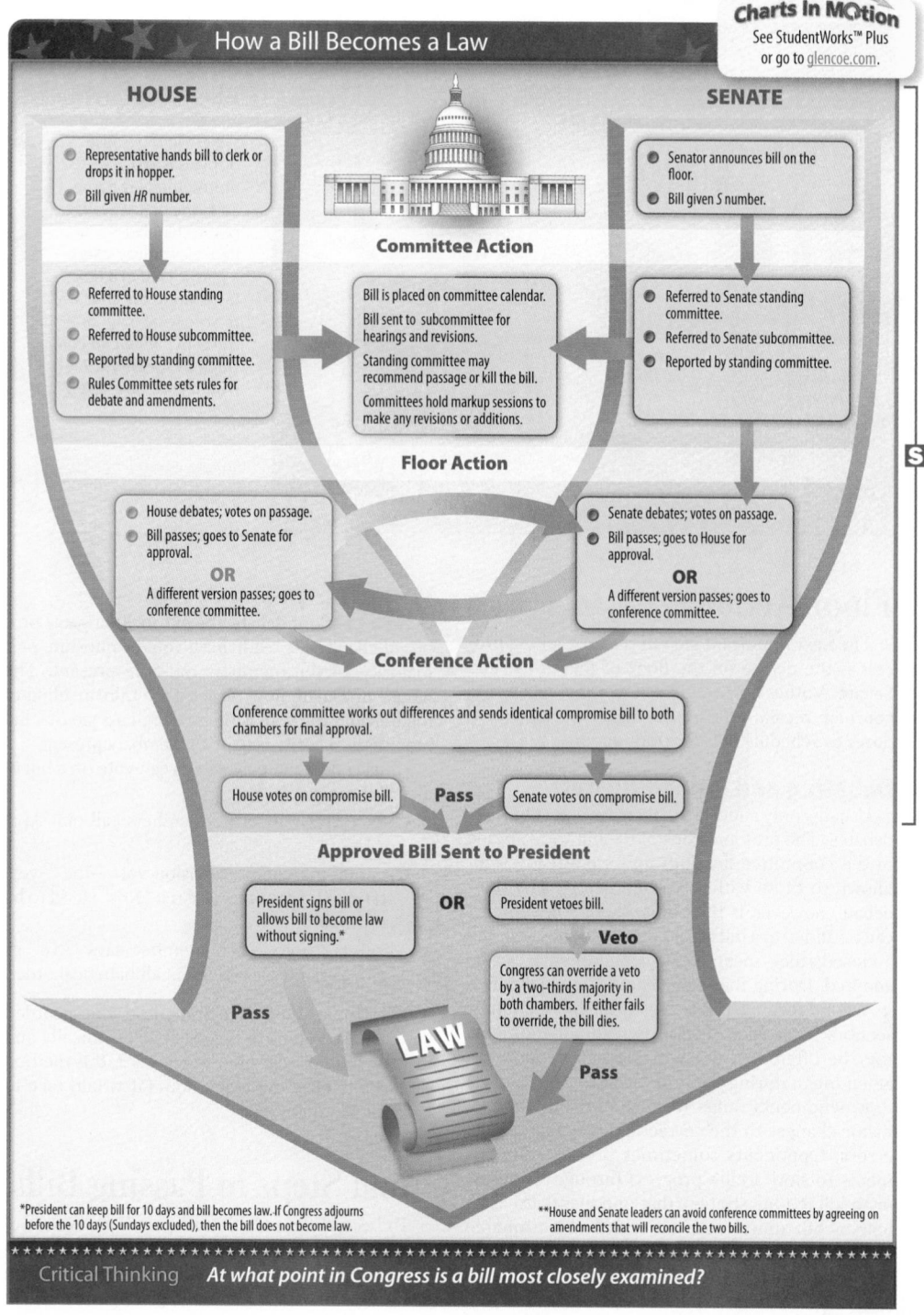

How a Bill Becomes a Law

Charts in Motion See StudentWorks™ Plus or go to glencoe.com.

HOUSE

- Representative hands bill to clerk or drops it in hopper.
- Bill given *HR* number.

- Referred to House standing committee.
- Referred to House subcommittee.
- Reported by standing committee.
- Rules Committee sets rules for debate and amendments.

SENATE

- Senator announces bill on the floor.
- Bill given *S* number.

- Referred to Senate standing committee.
- Referred to Senate subcommittee.
- Reported by standing committee.

Committee Action

Bill is placed on committee calendar.

Bill sent to subcommittee for hearings and revisions.

Standing committee may recommend passage or kill the bill.

Committees hold markup sessions to make any revisions or additions.

Floor Action

- House debates; votes on passage.
- Bill passes; goes to Senate for approval.
  OR
  A different version passes; goes to conference committee.

- Senate debates; votes on passage.
- Bill passes; goes to House for approval.
  OR
  A different version passes; goes to conference committee.

Conference Action

Conference committee works out differences and sends identical compromise bill to both chambers for final approval.

House votes on compromise bill. **Pass** Senate votes on compromise bill.

Approved Bill Sent to President

President signs bill or allows bill to become law without signing.* **OR** President vetoes bill.

Veto

Congress can override a veto by a two-thirds majority in both chambers. If either fails to override, the bill dies.

Pass

LAW

Pass

*President can keep bill for 10 days and bill becomes law. If Congress adjourns before the 10 days (Sundays excluded), then the bill does not become law.

**House and Senate leaders can avoid conference committees by agreeing on amendments that will reconcile the two bills.

Critical Thinking *At what point in Congress is a bill most closely examined?*

S Skill Practice

Reading a Flow Chart Ask: According to the chart, do the House and Senate work on bills independently, jointly, or both? *(both)* **OL**

Linking ★ Past & Present

Civil Rights Act of 1964

Riders are usually used to get an unpopular proposal enacted by attaching it to a bill that is likely to pass. A bill's opponents, if they cannot muster the votes to defeat it, may attach a rider to make the bill undesirable to some of its supporters. In 1964 Senate opponents of the Civil Rights Act tried to kill it by adding a rider to prohibit gender discrimination in the workplace. To their surprise, both bill and rider passed, giving the nation a law against racial and gender discrimination at the same time.

Critical Thinking

Answer: during the period of committee action

Additional Support

Activity: Collaborative Learning

Culture Students might be surprised to realize how much influence Congress has upon some aspects of contemporary culture. Have students work with partners or in small groups to explore how Congress has acted—or has attempted to act—in relation to one of the following topics:

- establishing a rating system for movies, television programs, or musical recordings;

- designating funds for support of the arts;
- banning certain kinds of advertising (the content or the approach) from certain media.

Have students report on their findings in a format of their choice. **Ask:** Is it appropriate for Congress to regulate these aspects of cultural life? *(Answers will vary. Students should defend their positions.)* **AL**

Caption Answer: A representative may vote "present" when the House is checking to see whether a quorum exists, or when a representative does not want to vote on an issue but still wants to be recorded as present.

Did You Know?

If a lawmaker must be absent during a vote, he or she sometimes will try to "pair off" with an opposition colleague who also will be absent. The "paired" votes, which are listed in the *Congressional Record*, thus cancel out each other and do not affect the result. (If one of the lawmakers is in attendance for the vote, the colleagues are called a "live pair.")

R Reading Strategy

Inferring Ask: Why would the strategy to "load a bill down with so many objectionable amendments that it dies" not work for a popular bill? *(If a bill is popular, opponents of the bill would have a difficult time garnering the majority vote needed to amend it.)* **OL**

Additional Support

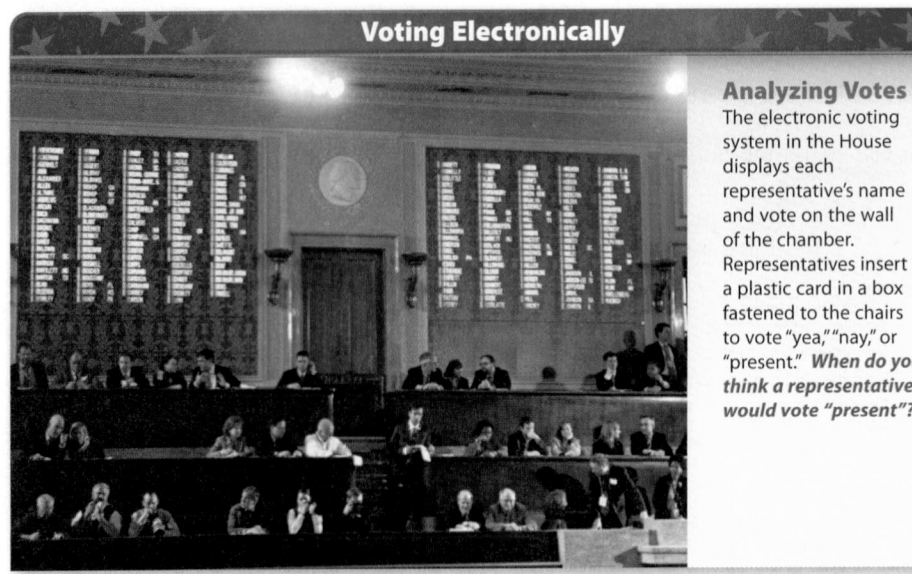

Voting Electronically

Analyzing Votes
The electronic voting system in the House displays each representative's name and vote on the wall of the chamber. Representatives insert a plastic card in a box fastened to the chairs to vote "yea," "nay," or "present." ***When do you think a representative would vote "present"?***

Floor Action

The next important step in the lawmaking process is the debate on the floor of the House and Senate. Voting on the bill follows the debate. As you may recall, both houses have special procedures to schedule bills for floor action.

Debating and Amending Bills

Usually, only a few lawmakers take part in floor debates. The pros and cons of the bill were argued in the committee hearings and are already well-known to those with a strong interest. The floor debate, however, is the point where amendments can be added to a bill unless the House has adopted a closed rule—meaning no amendments can be adopted. During the floor debate, the bill receives its second reading. A clerk reads the bill section by section. After each section is read, amendments may be offered. Any lawmaker can propose an amendment during the floor debate.

R Amendments range from the introduction of major changes to the correction of typographical errors. Opponents sometimes propose amendments to slow a bill's progress through Congress or to kill it. One strategy that opponents use is to load a bill down with so many objectionable amendments that it dies. In both the House and the Senate, it takes a majority vote of members present to amend a bill.

Voting on Bills

After the floor debate, the bill, including any proposed changes, is ready for a vote. A quorum, or a majority, of the members must be present. The House or Senate now receives the third reading of the bill, and the vote is then taken. Passage of a bill requires a majority vote of all members present.

House and Senate members can vote on a bill in one of three ways:

- Voice vote—together members call out "Aye" or "No";
- A standing vote, or division vote—the "Ayes" stand to be counted, and the "Nos" stand to be counted;
- Roll-call vote—each member says "Aye" or "No" as names are called in alphabetical order.

The House uses a fourth method, the recorded vote, where votes are recorded electronically and displayed on panels. Used since 1973, this method saves the House the many hours it would take to roll-call 435 members.

Final Steps in Passing Bills

To become law, a bill must pass both houses of Congress *in identical form.* A bill passed in the House of Representatives often differs at first from a Senate's bill on the same subject.

Extending the Content

Markup Sessions The importance of markup sessions is often overlooked. A markup session is a meeting held after the hearings, when a bill is revised before it is sent to the floor. (The term comes from the time when original bills were literally "marked up" with changes.) Many congressional observers maintain that the markup of a bill is not merely a step in the legislative process—rather, for most bills it *is* the legislative process. Later approval by the full committee and on the floor is, for many bills, a formality. There might be debate and opposition, but the outcome of a bill on the floor is usually predictable.

Conference Committee Action

If one house will not accept the version passed by the other house, a conference committee must work out the differences the two chambers have. Members of the conference committee are called conferees or managers. They usually come from the House and Senate committee members that handled the bill originally.

The conferees work out the differences by finding compromises, supposedly only on the parts of the bill where the two houses disagree. But sometimes the conference committee will make changes that neither chamber has considered before. Finally, a majority of the conferees from each house drafts the final bill, called a conference report. Once accepted, it can be submitted to each house of Congress for final action.

Presidential Action on Bills

Article I[1] of the Constitution states that: 📖

66 *Every Bill which shall have passed the House of Representatives and the Senate, shall, before it becomes a Law, be presented to the President of the United States. . . .* 99

—Article I, Section 7

After both houses have approved an identical bill, it is sent to the president. If he or she signs the bill, it becomes law. The president can also keep the bill for 10 days without signing it. If Congress **C** is in session, the bill then becomes law without the president's signature. Usually, however, presidents sign the bills that are sent to them.

Vetoing Bills

The president can also reject a bill by using the **veto.** If a president vetoes a bill, it returns to the house where it originated, along with an explanation of why the president vetoed it. The president can also kill a bill using the so-called **pocket veto.** This means that the president refuses to act on a bill passed during the last 10 days of **D** the session. By failing to send it back before the session ends, the president effectively kills the bill for that session.

Congressional Override of a Veto

Congress can override a president's veto with a two-thirds vote in both houses. If this happens, the bill becomes law. It is usually difficult, however, to get two-thirds of the members in both houses to vote against the president's position.

Roll-Call Vote

Senate Calls Roll on Iraq War Two senators, Joe Biden and John Kerry, consulted closely before the Senate vote on a joint resolution authorizing the use of American troops in Iraq. It passed 77 to 23. **Why did the Senate call the roll for this vote?**

Thus, Congress seldom overrides presidential vetoes.

Line-Item Veto

Presidents since Ronald Reagan have sought the power of the line-item veto, a tool used by many state governors. The line-item veto allows a leader to reject specific lines or items in a bill while accepting the rest of the bill. Granting a true line-item veto to the president, however, requires an amendment to the Constitution because of the Supreme Court's position. (See page 188.) In 1996 Congress tried to avoid this obstacle by passing a special bill that gave the president some of the powers of a line-item veto. The bill allowed the president to veto individual spending and tax items from bills.

📖 *See the following footnoted materials in the* ***Reference Handbook:*** **1.** *The Constitution, pages R42–R67.*

C Critical Thinking

Making Inferences **Ask:** Why might the president hold a bill for 10 days, allowing it to become law? *(The president might not personally agree with the bill but might believe that it is necessary or that it will pass with a congressional override.)* **AL**

Caption Answer: Making the decision to go to war is serious, and members of Congress wanted their votes to be on the record.

D Differentiated Instruction

English Learners **Ask:** From the description of a *pocket veto,* why is this term appropriate? *(Because the bill is shelved and forgotten, it is as if it has been placed in someone's pocket, out of sight.)* **ELL**

Hands-On Chapter Project

Step 1

Creating a Public Interest Campaign

Step 1: Identifying the Issues Have groups of students identify and select an issue of either school, local, or national interest to them.

Directions Tell student groups to prepare a short statement expressing their point of view on the issue they selected. The statement should include an explanation of their issue. It should describe the group's point of view on the issue and explain why the group holds its particular point of view.

Summarizing Ask volunteers to read each group's statement to the class. Encourage the class to question groups about their positions. **OL**

(Chapter Project continued in Section 2.)

S Skill Practice

Using a Database Have students go to the Library of Congress's THOMAS site (thomas. loc.gov) and find a bill that their representative in Congress is currently sponsoring. Choose one or two bills and encourage students to debate whether or not they support it. **OL**

Assess

Assign the Section 1 Assessment as homework or as an in-class activity, or have students take Section Quiz 7-1 from *Section Quizzes and Chapter Tests.*

Close

Speculating Have students list the ways bills can be blocked or hindered. **Ask:** Do you think it would be beneficial or harmful to democracy in the United States if passing laws were an easier process? *(Ways to block bills include pigeonholing, vetoes, pocket vetoes, and so on. Students should cite logical reasons for their decisions.)* **OL**

Section 1 Review

President Bill Clinton first used the new veto power in August 1997 to cancel a provision of the Balanced Budget Act of 1997 and parts of the Taxpayer Relief Act of 1997. New York **challenged** the veto because it reduced Medicaid funding to the state's hospitals. Farmers in Idaho also challenged the line-item veto when Clinton used it to eliminate a tax break for them in the Taxpayer Relief Act. The Supreme Court ruled in *Clinton* v. *City of New York* (1998) that the Line Item Veto Act was unconstitutional.

Registering Laws

After a bill becomes law, it is registered with the National Archives and Records Service. The law is labeled as a public or private law and assigned a number that identifies the Congress that passed it and the number of the law for that term. For example, Public Law 187 under the 105th Congress is registered as PL105-187—it was the 187th bill passed by the 105th Congress. The law is then added to the U.S. Code of current federal laws.

Tracking Legislation on the Internet

To find out about all legislation Congress is considering, one can go to an online information resource called THOMAS, after Thomas Jefferson. THOMAS allows those who are interested to search by either the bill number or a subject keyword; this will call up the full text of all versions of House and Senate bills. Another section of the database shows the full text of the *Congressional Record,* committee reports, summaries of bills, and updates on their status as they move through the legislative process. The history of bills is also searchable.

Not everything about legislation appears on THOMAS, however. Bills do not appear in the database until they are published in an official version by the Government Printing Office, so certain things are not available—drafts of bills, committee recommendations, and the "chairman's mark," the version of a bill as it goes through a markup session.

THOMAS was designed to open up the complex lawmaking process to citizens, who can then voice their opinions, offsetting the power of lobbyists and special interests. When Speaker of the House Newt Gingrich unveiled THOMAS at a 1995 press conference, he said:

❝ [K]nowledge is power. . . . If every citizen had the access to the information that Washington lobbyists have, we will have changed the balance of power in America [towards] the citizens and out of the Beltway. ❞

—Newt Gingrich

There are other Web sites that provide information on Congress. Among the best known is the Congressional Quarterly (CQ) Web site found at www.cq.com. CQ, a private nonprofit company, has published news on Congress since 1945, including books, magazines, and newsletters. It has a large staff of reporters and researchers who supply the information for its various publications. Yet another Internet source is the online version of the newspaper *Roll Call. Roll Call* has been a newspaper for members of Congress since the 1950s. Its Web site requires a subscription and provides news and commentary on whatever is happening on Capitol Hill.

SECTION 1 Review

Vocabulary

1. **Explain** the significance of: private bill, public bill, simple resolution, rider, hearing, veto, pocket veto.

Main Ideas

2. **Explaining** Why do so few bills become laws?

3. **Analyzing** How do the president's veto powers reflect the checks and balances system of the Constitution?

Critical Thinking

4. **Drawing Conclusions** Is it possible for all members of Congress to keep abreast of all bills under consideration? Support your answer.

5. **Organizing** Create a graphic organizer like the one below to list the types of resolutions passed by Congress.

Types of Resolutions

Writing About Government

6. **Descriptive Writing** Imagine that you are asked to help younger children learn how laws are made in the United States. Create a poster, using cartoon-like illustrations, to show how a bill becomes a law.

Answers

1. All definitions can be found in the section and the Glossary.
2. The process provides many opportunities to kill a bill. Many bills are introduced that have little chance of becoming law in the first place.
3. The executive branch retains some power over the legislative process, which mainly resides with Congress.

4. Possible answer: Because the task is impossible to complete single-handedly, Congress has the subcommittee system, aides, party leaders, and so on.
5. Joint, Concurrent, and Simple
6. You may arrange to display students' posters in middle school classes that are studying history or government.

Taxing and Spending Bills

Reader's Guide

Content Vocabulary
★ tax (p. 189)
★ closed rule (p. 190)
★ appropriation (p. 191)
★ authorization bill (p. 191)
★ entitlement (p. 192)

Academic Vocabulary
★ revenue (p. 189)
★ consequence (p. 191)
★ facility (p. 192)

Reading Strategy
Create a graphic organizer to show the role of Congress in making and passing tax laws.

House | Both | Senate

Issues in the News

For years, the late Senator William Proxmire of Wisconsin awarded his Golden Fleece Award to call attention to wasteful government spending—the first "honoree" was the National Science Foundation for an $84,000 grant to find out why people fall in love. In 2000 Taxpayers for Common Sense revived Proxmire's award and in 2005, presented it to Alaskan Republican Don Young for a bridge project he sponsored—the "bridge to nowhere," as the Taxpayers' group called it. Young proposed to spend $315 million to link the tiny town of Ketchikan, Alaska, to the airport. Young said the bridge was a necessity although a seven-minute ferry ride can take Ketchikan residents to the airport on Gravina Island.

▲ The Ketchikan, Alaska, ferry takes seven minutes to reach the airport on Gravina Island.

Pork barrel projects like the Ketchikan bridge project add excess to today's huge government budget. Total operating costs for the national government in 2010 are expected to reach $3.2 trillion (a trillion equals 1,000 times a billion). The Constitution gives Congress the authority to decide where this money will come from and how it will be spent. Passing laws to raise and spend money is one of the most important jobs Congress has. The government could not operate without money to carry out its programs and provide services.

Making Decisions About Taxes

The national government gets most of its **revenues** from taxes. **Taxes** are money that people

and businesses pay to support the government. The Constitution states:

> 66 *The Congress shall have the Power To Lay and collect Taxes, Duties, Imposts and Excises, to pay the Debts and provide for the common Defence and general Welfare of the United States. . . .* 99
> —Article I, Section 8

House Power Over Revenue Bills

The Constitution gives the House of Representatives the exclusive power to start all revenue measures. Almost all important work on tax laws occurs in the House Ways and Means Committee. The Ways and Means Committee decides whether to go along with presidential requests for tax cuts or increases. It also makes the numerous rules and

---

Focus

Bellringer
Section Focus Transparencies 7-2

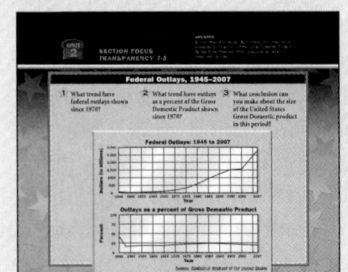

Reader's Guide

Answers to Graphic:
House: starts all revenue bills
Senate: (The Senate has no exclusive role in enacting laws; Senate circle should be empty.)
Both: propose amendments to revenue bills

Resource Manager

R Reading Strategies	**C** Critical Thinking	**D** Differentiated Instruction	**W** Writing Support	**S** Skill Practice
Additional Resources • Quizzes/Tests, p. 78 • Guid. Read. Act., p. 25	**Teacher Edition** • Drawing Conclusions, p. 190 **Additional Resources** • Read. Essen., pp. 75–76	**Teacher Edition** • Interpersonal, p. 191 **Additional Resources** • Coop. Learning Act., pp. 3–4 • Foldables, p. 50	**Additional Resources** • Part. in Gov. Act., pp. 13–14	**Teacher Edition** • Inferring From Charts, p. 190 **Additional Resources** • Making It Rel. Trans., pp. 13–17

Teach

S Skill Practice

Inferring From Charts Have students select one country from the chart to research (other than the United States). What programs does this country fund by taxation? How does the funding for these programs compare with the funding of such programs in the United States? **Ask:** Based on the information in this chart, in what part of the world do you expect taxes to take the largest "bite" out of your wallet? *(Europe, especially northern Europe)* **OL**

C Critical Thinking

Drawing Conclusions Ask: Why do you suppose the House of Representatives has a closed rule but the Senate does not? *(The House, with 435 members, is a much larger body than the Senate. This makes debating issues or amendments in a forum of all House members more cumbersome.)* **AL**

Critical Thinking

Answer: the belief in the free enterprise system

Additional Support

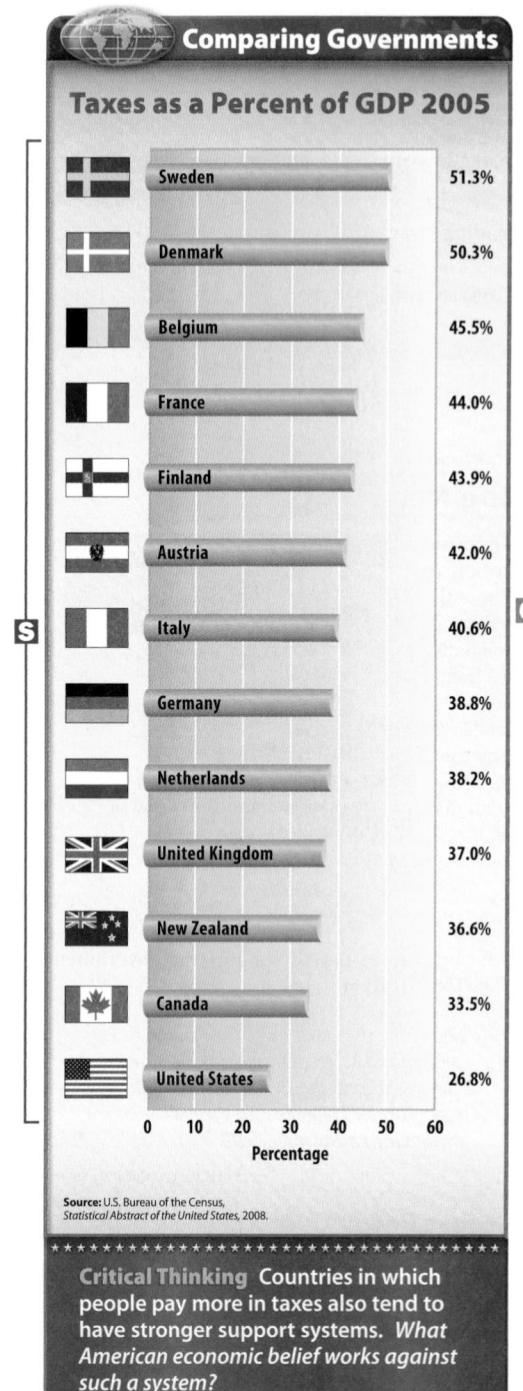

Comparing Governments

Taxes as a Percent of GDP 2005

Country	Percentage
Sweden	51.3%
Denmark	50.3%
Belgium	45.5%
France	44.0%
Finland	43.9%
Austria	42.0%
Italy	40.6%
Germany	38.8%
Netherlands	38.2%
United Kingdom	37.0%
New Zealand	36.6%
Canada	33.5%
United States	26.8%

0   10   20   30   40   50   60
Percentage

Source: U.S. Bureau of the Census, *Statistical Abstract of the United States,* 2008.

Critical Thinking Countries in which people pay more in taxes also tend to have stronger support systems. *What American economic belief works against such a system?*

regulations that determine who will pay how much tax. Some of these rulings are very simple while others are more complex. This committee, for example, influences how much of a tax deduction parents are allowed on their income tax for each child living at home. It also decides what kind of tax benefit businesses can claim for building new factories.

For many years, the committee's tax bills were debated on the House floor under a closed rule. A **closed rule** forbids members from offering any amendments to a bill from the floor. This rule meant that only members of the Ways and Means Committee had a direct hand in writing a tax bill.

Other House members accepted this procedure on tax bills for several reasons. House leaders claimed that tax bills were too complicated to be easily understood outside the committee. Leaders also warned that representatives could come under great pressure from special interests if tax bills could be revised from the floor. Floor amendments, they argued, might upset the fair and balanced perspective of the committee.

In the 1970s, House members began to rebel against the closed rule system. In 1973 House members were allowed to amend a tax bill from the floor. In 1974 members forced Wilbur Mills, the powerful chair of the Ways and Means Committee, to resign after a personal scandal. Critics charged that tax bills soon became a collection of amendments written to please special interests.

In the Senate, no closed rule exists, and tax bills often do become collections of amendments. Many tax bills are amended so often on the Senate floor that they become "Christmas tree" bills similar to the appropriations bills decorated with many riders.

The Senate Role in Tax Laws

All tax bills start in the House. Article I, Section 7, of the Constitution, however, says, "The Senate may propose . . . amendments. . . ."[1] 📖 This provision gives the Senate the authority to amend tax bills passed by the House. This is why many people view the Senate as the place where special-interest groups are able to get tax provisions they oppose taken out of a House bill.

In the Senate, the Committee on Finance has primary responsibility for tax matters. Like the House Ways and Means Committee, this committee

📖 *See the following footnoted materials in the **Reference Handbook:***
1. *The Constitution,* pages R42–R67.

Activity: Collaborative Learning

Fill in the Blank Organize the class into groups of five to seven students each. Have the groups consider this fill-in-the-blank statement: The congressional power to tax and spend is important because _____. Ask everyone in each group to provide one original answer—for example, various programs and services that depend upon congressional funding, ways in which this power can promote or frustrate presidential wishes, and so on. *(Answers may include: It determines who pays how much tax, it gives the government money to spend on public uses, and so on.)* Have each group elect a leader to supervise the activity and a spokesperson to present the responses to the class. As a class, look for common elements in the responses. **OL**

is powerful. Although the Senate Finance Committee has subcommittees, the full committee does most of the work. This makes its chair an extremely important figure.

Appropriating Money

Besides passing revenue bills, Congress has another important power over government spending. The power of **appropriation,** or approval of government spending, belongs to Congress. In Article I, Section 9, the Constitution states, "No money shall be drawn from the Treasury, but in **consequence** of appropriations made by law."[1] Thus, Congress must pass laws to appropriate money for the federal government. Congress must approve spending before the departments and agencies of the executive branch, such as the Department of Defense, can actually spend money.

How Congress Appropriates Money

Congress follows a two-step procedure in appropriating money—an authorization bill and an appropriations bill. Suppose the president signs a bill to build recreational facilities in inner cities. This first step in the legislative process is an authorization bill. An **authorization bill** sets up a federal program and specifies how much money can be appropriated for it. For example, the law has a provision limiting the amount of money that can be spent to $30 million per year. The recreation bill also states that the Department of Housing and Urban Development (HUD) will administer the program. HUD, however, does not yet actually have any money to carry out the program.

The second step in the appropriations procedure comes when HUD requests that Congress provide the $30 million it authorized. This kind of bill is an appropriations bill. HUD's request for the $30 million will be only one small item in the multibillion-dollar budget HUD will send to Congress for that year. HUD's budget, in turn, will be part of the president's total annual budget for the executive branch.

Each year the president presents a budget to Congress. The appropriations committees create their own appropriations bills. Congress might decide to grant HUD only $15 million to carry out the building program. In the following year, HUD would have to ask for another appropriation in order to continue the program.

📖 *See the following footnoted materials in the **Reference Handbook:***
1. *The Constitution,* pages R42–R67.

Managing the Nation's Purse

Congressional Funding Supported by government funds during the Great Depression, an artist created this painting of California's multiethnic workforce. Congress appropriated funds for the Works Progress Administration (WPA) to provide relief for the unemployed, including artists. WPA artists created hundreds of artworks documenting the times. *The WPA administrator had to testify before an appropriations committee to receive funding. Why?*

D Differentiated Instruction

Interpersonal Divide the class into pairs in which one student assumes the role of an interviewer and the other takes the role of a Depression-era citizen. Each interviewer should construct three or four questions regarding the WPA. Citizens should respond by expressing any opinion that they believe large numbers of Americans would have held. Encourage students to consider congressional appropriations in their questions and answers. **AL**

Caption Answer: Agency heads must explain their budget and answer specific questions about it for Congress to appropriate a specific level of funding. It is possible that all of the money authorized in legislation will not be appropriated.

📖 **GO TO** To enrich study of chapter content, remind students that footnoted materials appear in the ***Reference Handbook.***

Hands-On Chapter Project
Step 2

Creating a Public Interest Campaign

Step 2: Speaking Out Have groups of students collaborate on an editorial based on the short statement they prepared in Step 1.

Directions Tell student groups to use their short statements as the basis for an editorial. Have students do research to find information to back up their point of view. Each editorial should include at least two statistics and one concrete example that support their point of view. Remind groups to include the sources they used for the information in their editorial.

Summarizing Ask for volunteers to read each group's editorial. Encourage groups to share what they learned about their issue and any challenges they encountered in writing the editorial. **OL**

(Chapter Project continued in Section 3.)

Assess

Assign the Section 2 Assessment as homework or as an in-class activity, or have students take Section Quiz 7-2 from *Section Quizzes and Chapter Tests.*

Close

Making Inferences Tell students when Representative Wilbur Mills (R-Arkansas, whose 1974 resignation is mentioned on page 190) considered entering the 1972 presidential race, a colleague asked, "Wilbur, why do you want to run for president and give up your grip on the country?" Discuss what that question implies about the power of Congress, especially in matters of taxing and spending. **OL**

Section 2 Review

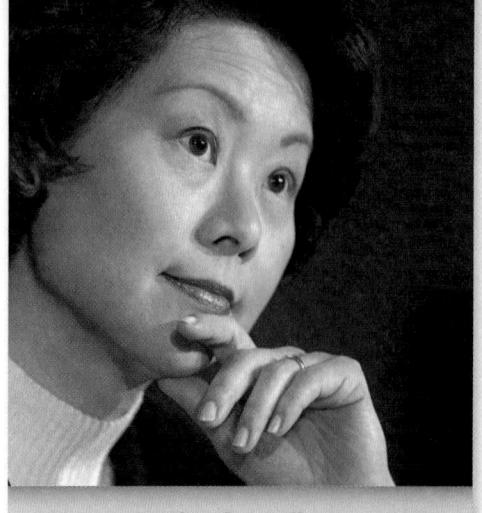

Accounting for the Dollars Secretary of Labor Elaine Chao appeared before a congressional subcommittee to present her department's budget in March 2008. *How do such appearances help Congress make informed decisions?*

The Appropriations Committees

The House and the Senate have committees dedicated to appropriations bills. Both the House and Senate appropriations committees have 12 subcommittees covering the same policy areas. Thus, the same appropriations subcommittees in both chambers would review the HUD budget, including its recreational **facility** program.

Every year, department heads and program directors answer questions about their budgets in hearings of the appropriations subcommittees. These officials explain why they need the money they have requested. Each year, officials must return to Congress to request the money they need to operate in the coming year. In this way, lawmakers become familiar with federal programs.

Appropriations subcommittees often develop close relationships with certain agencies and tend to favor them in appropriating funds. Powerful special-interest groups also try to exercise influence with the appropriations subcommittees. For example, a private aeronautics firm might try to influence an appropriations subcommittee so that the Defense Department has money in its budget to have a certain kind of aircraft built.

Uncontrollable Expenditures

The House and Senate appropriations committees do not have a voice in all current spending of the federal government. Earlier legislation, such as the laws establishing Medicare, represent about 70 percent of federal government spending each year. Since the government is already legally committed to these expenditures, the committees cannot control them and they are termed *uncontrollables.* Such required spending includes Social Security payments, interest on the national debt, and federal contracts that already are in force. Some of these expenditures are known as **entitlements** because they are social programs that entitle individuals to a certain program or monetary benefit— Social Security payments are entitlements.

★★★★★★★★★★★★★★★★★★★★★★★ 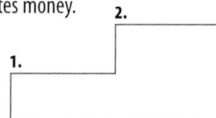 **SECTION 2 Review** ★★★★★★★★★★★★★★★★★★★★

Vocabulary

1. **Explain** the significance of: tax, closed rule, appropriation, authorization bill, entitlement.

Main Ideas

2. **Describing** What control does the House Ways and Means Committee exert over presidential requests for changes in tax laws?

3. **Analyzing** When do agencies and lobbyists have a chance to influence the amount of a department's budget?

Critical Thinking

4. **Synthesizing** Do you think Congress should have the power to raise and to spend money? Support your answer.

5. **Labeling** Using a graphic organizer like the one below, show the two-step procedure that Congress follows when it appropriates money.

Writing About Government

6. **Expository Writing** Using the library or the Internet, research the major categories of revenues and expenditures in the current federal budget. Find out what amounts of money the government plans to raise and spend in each category. Create an illustrated report with graphs and charts.

Answers

1. All definitions can be found in the section and the Glossary.
2. It decides whether to go along with presidential requests for tax cuts or increases.
3. at hearings of the appropriations subcommittees
4. Answers will vary. Students who agree may suggest that the checks and balances provided are sufficient to prevent abuse of the power and that Congress, as the branch of government closest to the people, is perhaps the most appropriate body to make those decisions.
5. 1. authorization bill; 2. appropriations bill
6. Suggest that students arrange to talk to a reference librarian to locate information about the federal budget. Students should include relevant, understandable graphs or charts with their reports.

Can Members of Congress Be Sued for Defamation?

Hutchinson v. Proxmire, 1979

According to the U.S. Constitution, members of Congress cannot be sued for statements made during legislative debate. This protection allows members to express themselves freely. Does this protection for members extend beyond the halls of Congress?

Facts of the Case

In the 1970s, U.S. Senator William Proxmire of Wisconsin began bestowing a "Golden Fleece of the Month Award" to publicize projects receiving federal grants that he deemed unnecessary or wasteful. He gave one such award to a government study of aggression in monkeys, publicly attacking research scientist Dr. Ronald Hutchinson for having "made a fortune from his monkeys and in the process made a monkey out of the American taxpayer." Proxmire ridiculed Hutchinson on the floor of the Senate, in newsletters he published, and in a press release. Hutchinson sued for defamation, accusing Proxmire of libel (false written statements intended to damage someone's reputation). He asked for damages of $8 million for the harm done to his professional reputation.

The Constitutional Question

Article I, Section 6, of the U.S. Constitution declares that "for any Speech or Debate in either House" of Congress, members "shall not be questioned in any other Place." This meant that Hutchinson had no right to sue for Proxmire's Senate comments. Less clear was the question of whether he was protected from defamation charges for statements made in other situations—in this case statements made in a press release and newsletters. Was it part of his duties to his constituents to share his views with them and thereby protected speech?

Another key issue was Hutchinson's right to sue for defamation. A "public figure" may do so only if he or she is attacked with "actual malice," that is, "with knowledge that [a statement] was false or [with] reckless disregard of whether it was false or not." Actual malice is difficult to prove, and defamation suits filed by public figures are often dismissed before trial. Hutchinson accepted public funds for his research. Did this make him a public figure, limiting his right to sue? Or, was he a "private person" who did not have to prove malice?

Debating the Issue

◄ Senator William E. Proxmire

Questions to Consider

1. Was Senator Proxmire performing a public duty by drawing attention to what he viewed as wasteful spending?
2. Why is it harder for a public figure to sue for defamation?
3. Should his acceptance of public funds have made Hutchinson a "public figure"?

You Be the Judge

Was Proxmire's right to inform the public of alleged wasteful spending more important than Hutchinson's right to protect his reputation? Explain how you would have ruled if you had been on the Supreme Court.

Class Debate

Organize the class into groups based on students' leanings (pro-Hutchinson or pro-Proxmire). Have each group discuss the issues and list as many supporting arguments as possible. Have each group present its position to the class.

The Court's Decision

In an 8-to-1 ruling, the Supreme Court ruled for Hutchinson. The majority ruled:

1. "There is nothing in the history of the [Speech or Debate] Clause or its language suggesting any intent to create an absolute privilege from liability or suit for defamatory statements made outside the legislative Chambers . . ."
2. "Neither the newsletters nor the press release here was 'essential to the deliberation of the Senate,' and neither was part of the deliberative process . . ."
3. "The newsletters and press release were not privileged as part of the 'informing function' of Members of Congress to tell the public about their activities. . . ."
4. "[Ronald Hutchinson] is not a public figure so as to make the 'actual malice' standard of proof . . . applicable."

Debating the Issue Answers

Questions to Consider

1. Most students probably will say that Proxmire was doing a public service by highlighting wasteful spending.
2. Public figures, such as politicians, must prove actual malice to win a defamation suit. The rationale lies in the need for a free press and free society to be able to criticize public figures without fear of costly lawsuits.
3. Students' answers will vary, but ask them to explain the rationale behind their answers.

You Be the Judge

Students who would have sided with Proxmire probably will mention that, as a member of Congress, Proxmire was supposed to serve the public. Thus, informing the public of wasteful spending was part of his job.

Students who would have sided with Hutchinson may argue that the attack was unfair because Hutchinson was performing government research and was singled out for public ridicule.

Focus

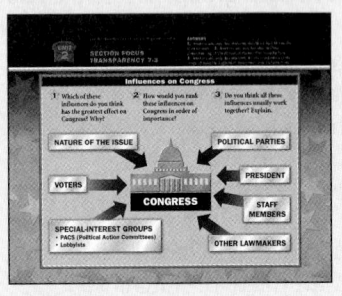
Reader's Guide

Answers to Graphic: Influences on Congress: concerns of the voters, party positions, the president, special-interest groups

Resource Manager

Influencing Congress

Reader's Guide

Content Vocabulary
★ lobbyist (p. 198)
★ lobbying (p. 198)

Academic Vocabulary
★ aware (p. 195)
★ contribute (p. 196)
★ unaffected (p. 197)

Reading Strategy
As you read, fill in a chart like the one below to list the different influences on lawmakers in Congress.

> **Influences on Congress**

People in the News

What a difference one vote makes! In 2001 Republican Senator Jim Jeffords left his party and became an independent. Single-handedly, he shifted party control in the Senate. It had been 50 Republicans and 50 Democrats (with a Republican vice president to break tie votes), but now it was 50 Democrats, 49 Republicans—with the independent Jeffords leaning toward the Democrats. One analyst blamed the White House for ignoring moderate Republicans' opinions and assuming they would display "absolute party loyalty." The one-vote shift meant that Democrats now headed Senate committees, and that had results. Democrat Patrick Leahy now chaired the Judiciary Committee, and he was able to stall the president's conservative nominees to judgeships.

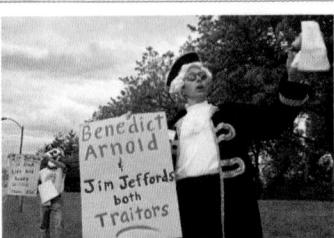

▲ Senator Jeffords's decision to leave the Republican Party prompted some of his constituents to compare him to Benedict Arnold, a traitor during the American Revolutionary period.

Senator Jeffords was faced with an especially difficult decision, but members of Congress make hard decisions every day. They decide which policies they will support and when to yield to political pressure from their constituents, their party, or the president. They must also decide when to make speeches explaining their views. In a single session, members may cast votes on a thousand issues. Their speeches and actions influence government policy and shape the public's views on bills and issues before Congress. What forces influence lawmakers?

Influences on Lawmakers

A great many factors influence how a lawmaker votes. One is temperament. Some members are more willing to take risks, while others might "play it safe." The nature of the issue also plays a role in how a lawmaker votes. For example, on a controversial issue, such as gun control, a lawmaker might adhere closely to the positions of the voters back home, no matter what his or her own beliefs may be. On an issue that has little direct effect on their constituents, however, lawmakers tend to rely on their own beliefs or the advice of other lawmakers.

Congressional staffers also influence decisions. Often, they do so because they research the information a lawmaker ends up seeing on an issue. Staffers also have influence by setting a member's daily calendar—they influence who he or she will meet with and which committee meetings the member attends. They may also influence which issues a member chooses to present or comment on in committee meetings.

R Reading Strategies	**C** Critical Thinking	**D** Differentiated Instruction	**W** Writing Support	**S** Skill Practice
Additional Resources • Quizzes/Tests, p. 79 • Guid. Read. Act., p. 27	**Teacher Edition** • Recognizing Issues, p. 195 **Additional Resources** • Read. Essen., pp. 77–79	**Teacher Edition** • Verbal/Linguistic, p. 198 **Additional Resources** • Vocab. Act., p. 7 • Foldables, p. 50	**Teacher Edition** • Personal Writing, p. 197 **Additional Resources** • Gov. Sims. and Debates, pp. 8–14	**Teacher Edition** • Researching, p. 195 **Additional Resources** • Inter. Poli. Cartoons, pp. 13–14

Thus, many factors affect a lawmaker's decision. Perhaps most lawmakers would rank the most important influences on their votes in this order: the concerns of their voters, their party's positions on issues, the president, and, finally, special-interest groups.

The Influence of Voters

The political careers of all lawmakers depend upon how the voters back home feel about the lawmaker's job performance. Only very unusual lawmakers would regularly vote against the wishes of the people in their home states or districts.

What Voters Expect

Experienced lawmakers know that their constituents expect them to pay a great deal of attention to their needs. Voters usually expect their representatives to put the needs of their district ahead of nationwide needs. But what if a conflict arises between what the lawmaker thinks is needed and what constituents want? In a national opinion survey, most people still said their lawmaker should "follow what people in the district want."

It is not surprising that most members' votes often reflect their constituents' opinions. Especially on issues that affect constituents' daily lives, such as civil rights and social welfare, lawmakers usually go along with voter preferences. In contrast, on issues where constituents have less information or interest, such as foreign affairs, lawmakers often make up their own minds.

Voters have said that they want and expect their representatives to follow their wishes. Still most voters do not take the time to find out how members vote. Voters may not be **aware** of all the issues lawmakers are considering. Why, then, do voting records count in a reelection?

The answer is that in an election campaign, candidates will bring up their opponent's record. They may demand that their opponent explain the votes that turned out to be unpopular. A good example of this is congressional support for the Iraq war. In October 2002, by a margin of roughly two-to-one, Congress passed a joint resolution to authorize military force against Iraq. When support for the war faded, Hillary Clinton, a Democratic presidential candidate in 2008, had to defend her Iraq vote many times on the campaign trail. The opposite is also true: If a legislator has voted for measures important to some group, he or she will remind those voters about that during a campaign.

Influencing Policy Makers

"Whose conscience are we voting today?"

Influencing Government Lawmakers represent the citizens of their districts and their own political parties. At election time, these groups will hold lawmakers accountable for their votes. *What is the cartoonist saying about who influences a legislator's vote?*

In this way, campaigns inform voters about the voting record of their representative. Lawmakers know that this will happen. Thus, well before they run for reelection, they work to find out what voters back home are concerned about.

Visits to the District

Most lawmakers use several methods to try to keep track of their constituents' opinions. One method is making frequent trips home to learn the local voters' concerns. Senators and representatives make dozens of trips to their home districts each year. During their visits, they try to speak with as many voters as possible about issues of concern.

Messages from Home

Lawmakers also pay attention to the messages pouring into their offices every day. Staff members screen the mail to learn what issues concern voters most—for example, the closing of a plant in a community would probably get a lawmaker's attention.

Teach

C Critical Thinking

Recognizing Issues Make a list of factors that influence a legislator's decisions (personal beliefs, voters' wishes, and so on). Have students give at least one example of how each factor can influence a member of Congress. **OL**

Caption Answer: The legislators are concerned with satisfying an outside influence. The legislators are not discussing their views on the issue that is up for vote.

S Skill Practice

Researching Ask: If voters think their member of Congress is not acting in their interests, can they "fire" him or her? *(It depends where the voters live. In some states, voters can start a recall petition. If a certain percentage of the electorate signs it, a recall election takes place, and voters can choose whether to keep or "fire" their representative.)* Have students research which public officials, if any, can be recalled by voters in your state. **AL**

Additional Support

Activity: Cooperative Learning

Planning a Strategy Assign each of six groups one of these roles: a legislator, his or her constituents, his or her staff, congressional colleagues, a special-interest group, and the president. Assign a bill to the groups. Have groups choose leaders and assign other tasks as they see fit. Each group then should develop ways to encourage the legislator to vote for or against the bill. Have a representative from each group present the group's case to the legislator group. Have the legislator group keep track of the major arguments made by each group and then tell how the legislator has decided to vote and why. **OL**

Participating
IN GOVERNMENT

Conducting a Poll Have students poll five people about the influences upon their representatives, asking each respondent to rank these influences from most influential to least influential (in the respondent's opinion). Have students present their findings in a graph for classroom display. **AL**

Linking★
Past & Present

The Folks Back Home More than a century ago, Representative J. Proctor Knott of Kentucky was asked whether he thought that *Hamlet* or *Macbeth* was the better play. Knott replied, "Friend, don't ask me that question. I am a politician, and a candidate for reelection to Congress. My district is about equally divided. Hamlet has his friends down there, and Macbeth his, and I am unwilling to take any part between them!"

Caption Answer: foreign policy

Differentiated Instruction

Grassroots Campaigns

Rousing the Faithful This cover of *AARP: the Magazine*, represents one means for AARP to organize a grassroots campaign. AARP, formerly called the American Association of Retired Persons, but now known simply as AARP, is one of the most effective groups at getting elderly constituents to contact their representatives in Congress. In 2008 concerns about increases in Medicare premiums generated more than 300,000 signed petitions that were sent to Senate offices. AARP is often involved when seniors contact Congress about an issue. *What factors do you think make members of Congress respond to constituent contacts?*

Not all messages carry equal weight. Lawmakers are usually interested only in messages from their constituents or from special-interest groups relevant to their district or state. The form of the message is also important. Personal letters, visits, and phone calls traditionally were the best way to make one's point-of-view known. Today, e-mails have become so common that lawmakers may view them just as seriously as older forms of communication.

Surveys and Polls

Many lawmakers send questionnaires to their constituents asking for their opinions on various issues. Increasingly, lawmakers use Web sites and e-mail to get feedback on key issues. Before an election, lawmakers will often hire professional pollsters to conduct opinion surveys on issues.

Key Supporters

Finally, all lawmakers pay close attention to the ideas of their rain-or-shine supporters—people who regularly work in their campaigns and **contribute** money to win their reelection. As one lawmaker put it, "Everybody needs some groups which are strongly for him." These supporters also help lawmakers keep in touch with events back home.

The Influence of Parties

Almost every member of Congress is either a Republican or a Democrat. Both political parties take stands on major issues and come out for or against certain legislation. Party identification is one of the most important influences on a lawmaker's voting behavior. Knowing which political party a member belongs to often predicts how he or she will vote.

Party Voting

Both Democrats and Republicans tend to vote with their parties. In the House of Representatives, members vote with their party more than 70 percent of the time. Senators are generally more independent and less likely to follow their party's position.

Party voting is much stronger on some issues than others. On economic issues, party members tend to vote together. Party voting is also strong on farm issues and on social welfare issues. It is usually weaker on foreign policy because the parties do not often have fixed positions in this area.

The Importance of Parties

Why do parties often vote together? The obvious answer is that party members tend to share the same political outlook. As a group, Democrats are more likely to favor social welfare programs, job programs, tax laws that help people with lower incomes, and government regulation of business. In general, Republicans are likely to support lower taxes, less social welfare spending, less business regulation, and limited intervention in the economy.

Another reason for party voting is that many lawmakers do not have strong opinions on every issue.

Leveled Activities

BL Guided Reading Activities, p. 27

OL Authentic Assessment with Rubrics, p. 14

AL Government Simulations and Debates, p. 8

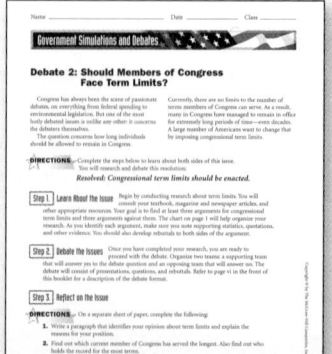

ELL Skill Reinforcement Activities, p. 7

Since they cannot know enough to make informed decisions on every bill, they will get advice from party members on it.

On some issues, party leaders put pressure on members to vote according to the party position. If the president is of the same party, a party leader will urge members to support the president's program. Likewise, leaders of the opposing party often vote against the president's program and seek to make their opposition a political issue. The party leaders, the Senate majority leader, and the Speaker of the House usually use the power of persuasion and work hard to influence lawmakers to support the party's position. Gaining party members' support is one of the main jobs of a party leader. Very few issues are **unaffected** by party identity.

Other Influences on Congress

Other than voter preferences and parties, there are two other influences on Congress—the president and various interest groups.

The Influence of the President

Every president tries to influence Congress to pass the bills he or she supports. Some presidents work harder than others at this task—and some are more successful in getting programs passed.

Members of Congress often complain that presidents have more ways to influence legislation and policy than they do. Through White House speeches or television appearances, the president has the best stage for influencing public opinion. In 1990, for example, when Iraq invaded the small nation of Kuwait, President George H.W. Bush sent U.S. troops to nearby Saudi Arabia. A military buildup followed as the U.S. government tried to force Iraq out of Kuwait. The president took every opportunity to express his belief that military action against Iraq was necessary. With public support growing, Congress did vote for military action in the Persian Gulf.

Presidents can also influence individual members of Congress by supporting their legislative goals. In the 1960s, for example, Senator Frank Church of Idaho criticized President Lyndon Johnson's conduct of the Vietnam War. To support his

We the People
Making a Difference

While she is not a lobbyist or a member of a political action committee, Arlys Endres of Phoenix, Arizona, has already made her mark in Congress. In 1996, when she was 10 years old, Endres wrote a school report on suffragist Susan B. Anthony. Endres later discovered that a statue of Anthony and two other famous suffragists was given to Congress in 1921. It was briefly displayed in the Capitol Rotunda but then moved permanently to the first floor below the Rotunda.

"I was furious about this," the precocious girl told an interviewer. She decided to campaign to have the statue moved back to a place of prominence. "If it weren't for her, I wouldn't have the right to vote, the right to hold public office, the right to own property, or the right to keep my children after a divorce."

She discovered that women in the Congress were already working on the issue, but money was needed for the move. Endres mailed at least 2,000 letters and raised almost $2,000. Her efforts also took her to Washington, D.C., to see the statue and speak at a "Raise the Statue" rally.

Her campaign did not go unnoticed by national legislators. The U.S. Congress unanimously voted to reinstall the statue in the Capitol Rotunda in 1996.

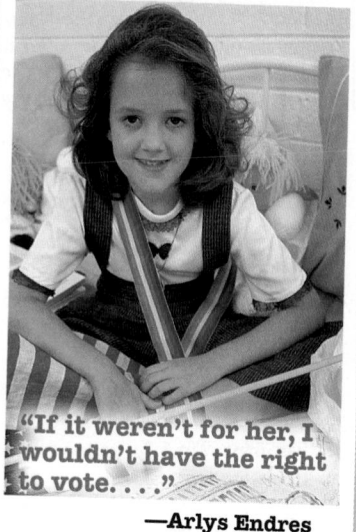

"If it weren't for her, I wouldn't have the right to vote...."
—Arlys Endres

W **Writing Support**

Personal Writing Have students write one paragraph explaining whether they think it is more important for members of Congress to vote according to their consciences or to back their party's position on an issue. **OL**

Making a Difference

Arlys Endres The statue for which Endres campaigned was commissioned to celebrate the passage of the Nineteenth Amendment and was created by sculptor Adelaide Johnson. Before Congress passed the relocation resolution, Representative Constance Morella (R-Maryland) said, "When schoolchildren from around the Nation come to visit Washington, . . . they will see in the rotunda a statue that not only honors the women who marched for the vote but a statue that also underscores the importance of the right to vote in our American democracy, a right that today so many of us take for granted."

Activity: Have students suggest ways in which they might work in their community to raise funds for a national project or cause. **OL**

Hands-On Chapter Project
Step 3

Creating a Public Interest Campaign

Step 3: Working Together Have groups of students create a public interest group on behalf of the issue they identified in Step 1.

Directions Discuss the ways that interest groups attempt to influence government policy. Have groups create a name for their interest group, and have them plan a peaceful demonstration to promote their agenda. Ask students to consider to whom they most want to communicate their concerns: the government or the public. They should consider which activity and location would best communicate their concerns.

Summarizing Have groups share their demonstration plans in class. Then have volunteers share what they learned while collaborating on their plans. Encourage the class to discuss the effectiveness of the campaigns. **OL**

(Chapter Project continued in Section 4.)

D Differentiated Instruction

Verbal/Linguistic Ask:

Where do you suppose the term lobbyist came from? *(The term lobbyist was first used in the 1830s to describe people who waited in the lobbies of statehouses to ask politicians for favors.)* **ELL**

Assess

Assign the Section 3 Assessment as homework or as an in-class activity, or have students take Section Quiz 7-3 from *Section Quizzes and Chapter Tests*.

Government ONLINE

Objectives and answers to the Student Web Activity can be found in the **Web Activity Lesson Plan** at glencoe.com. Enter *QuickPass*™ code USG9085c7T.

Close

Summarizing Ask students to describe methods they would use to keep informed of constituent concerns if they were political representatives. **OL**

Section 3 Review

---

viewpoint, Church showed President Johnson a newspaper column written by journalist Walter Lippmann criticizing the war. "All right," Johnson said, "the next time you need a dam for Idaho, you go ask Walter Lippmann."

Since the early 1900s, many presidents have tried to increase their influence over Congress and the lawmaking process, and they have succeeded. In more recent years, Congress has taken steps to limit the president's influence, letting Congress remain a more autonomous legislative body.

The Influence of Interest Groups

The representatives of interest groups, called **lobbyists,** are another important influence on Congress. Lobbyists try to convince members of Congress to support policies favored by the groups they represent. Their efforts to persuade officials to support their point of view is called **lobbying.** The largest and most powerful lobbies have their own buildings and full-time professional staffs in the nation's capital.

Lobbyists represent a wide variety of interests such as business organizations, labor unions, doctors, lawyers, education groups, minority groups, and environmental organizations. In addition, lobbyists work for groups that sometimes form to support or to oppose a specific issue.

Lobbyists use many methods to influence members of Congress. They offer lawmakers data and case studies on policies they support or oppose. They visit lawmakers in their offices or in the lobbies of the Capitol to try to persuade them to support their position. They encourage citizens to write to members of Congress on the issues they favor or oppose.

Interest groups and their lobbyists also focus their attention on congressional committees. For example, farm groups concentrate their attention on influencing the committees responsible for laws on agriculture. Labor unions focus their effort on committees dealing with labor legislation and the economy.

Political Action Committees

Some observers believe that the importance of individual lobbyists has declined in recent years, while the influence of political action committees (PACs) has increased.

PACs are political fund-raising organizations established by corporations, labor unions, and other special-interest groups. PAC funds come from voluntary contributions by employees, stockholders, and union members. A PAC uses the money it raises to support lawmakers who agree with their outlook.

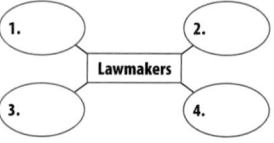

Government ONLINE
Student Web Activity Visit glencoe.com and enter *QuickPass*™ code USG9822c7. Click on Student Web Activity and complete the activity about influencing Congress.

SECTION 3 Review

Vocabulary

1. **Explain** the significance of: lobbyist, lobbying.

Main Ideas

2. **Examining** On which type of issues do lawmakers tend to pay less attention to voter opinion?

3. **Describing** What influence does the president have on Congress?

Critical Thinking

4. **Making Inferences** Why do some people think that PACs now have more influence over members of Congress and the process of congressional legislation than do individual lobbyists?

5. **Identifying** Using a graphic organizer like the one below, identify four ways lawmakers can keep in touch with voters' opinions.

```
   ( 1. )          ( 2. )
        \          /
        [ Lawmakers ]
        /          \
   ( 3. )          ( 4. )
```

Writing About Government

6. **Political Processes** Contact a special-interest group to request literature on the group's purpose and activities. Summarize how the group attempts to influence legislators. Post the literature and your summary on a bulletin board.

Answers

1. All definitions can be found in the section and the Glossary.
2. issues in which voters have less information or interest
3. Presidents can use the media to rally public opinion for or against a policy. They can also grant or withhold support for projects that are important to a lawmaker's constituents.
4. PACs often are better organized and better funded than individual lobbyists.
5. Answers might include: 1. trips home; 2. screening mail; 3. questionnaires; 4. opinion surveys
6. Students should summarize their efforts and show the literature they collected.

Should Robots, Not Humans, Explore Space?

The debate over how to conduct space exploration is as old as the space program. This debate is continuously revisited when U.S. Congress members vote on whether to provide the funding necessary for more expensive crewed space exploration. The case for crewed space exploration boils down to the argument over human versus artificial intelligence. Computer-controlled robotic missions can gather enormous amounts of data, and they cost much less money. But robot "explorers" are not nearly as good as humans at evaluating data.

YES

Robots would be better because the cost of sending humans into space far exceeds the benefits. Each shuttle launch costs more in public funds than any exploration carried out by uncrewed spacecraft. One space shuttle launch alone could pay for two or three uncrewed missions. Crewed missions are also inefficient—the supplies and protection humans need weigh so much, they prevent the craft from going most places in space. The space shuttle ends up being a limited vehicle, capable of reaching only a low orbit, which is not ideal for scientific research. The hazards to crewed space exploration present other drawbacks. Solar radiation can kill an unprotected space walker, and collisions with small space flotsam can bring down a shuttle. It is better to lose machinery than human life, and relatively inexpensive robotic missions could continue the nation's quest for knowledge without any risk to human life.

NO

People are more useful than machines when it comes to space exploration. Humans are needed to make most repairs in space. Although robots can gather important data, much of it is vague because robots do not have the ability to do follow-up tests right away. They can miss important clues and waste time on unproductive lines of study. A human still has much more acute vision than even the best video camera and can process data better than a computer. For example, a geologist can apply all of his or her senses to quickly make determinations as to what to study and what to ignore. Furthermore, the publicity given to human space disasters has covered up the much higher failure rate of uncrewed missions. For example, the Mars uncrewed exploration programs have failed roughly two out of three times since 1960. Compare that to the high success rates of astronaut-crewed missions at almost 90 percent. It is worth the added cost to the government to fund crewed space exploration.

Debating the Issue

1. **Analyzing** Why would Congress be reluctant to allocate funds for space exploration?

2. **Explaining** What are the benefits and costs of a crewed space exploration?

3. **Deciding** If you were a member of Congress would you vote to fund crewed space exploration? Explain your reasoning.

▶ An astronaut repairing the Hubble Space Telescope

Teach

Setting Up the Debate

Analyzing Help students focus on the issue of space exploration. **Ask:** What are the benefits to using robots in space? *(It is less expensive, and they can gather enormous amounts of data.)* **OL**

Evaluating Have students research the results of some crewed and uncrewed missions and identify the pros and cons of each mission. Have students on the panel meet to build their arguments for and against the use of crewed missions. Urge both groups to consider historic as well as current missions. **AL**

Concluding the Debate

Discuss these questions with the participants:

- What standards did you set in identifying evidence either for or against the use of crewed space missions?

- What arguments would you have used in response to the information provided by the opposing view on the issue? **OL**

Debating the Issue Answers

1. Possible answers include: the more money Congress spends on exploring space, the less money there is to spend on issues people really care about. Elections are not decided on the issue, so Congress would rather spend time on those issues.

2. Benefits: People are better at judging what to look at and what to follow up on than are machines. People are necessary to make repairs. Costs: It is expensive and inefficient to put people into space. If a catastrophe happens, it is much worse if human lives are lost than if a few robots are destroyed, regardless of the cost.

3. Students' answers will vary, but they should explain the rationale behind their answers.

SECTION 4

Focus

Bellringer

Section Focus Transparencies 7-4

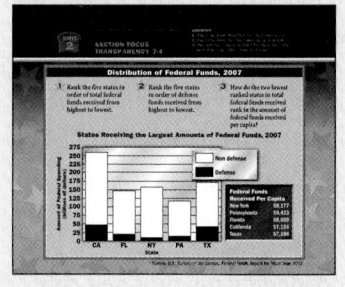

Reader's Guide

Answers to Graphic: to help lawmakers get reelected, to help Congress monitor the performance of the executive branch, and to provide ways that average citizens can cope with the huge federal government

Helping Constituents

Reader's Guide

Content Vocabulary	Academic Vocabulary	Reading Strategy
★ casework (p. 200) ★ pork-barrel legislation (p. 202) ★ logrolling (p. 202)	★ involve (p. 200) ★ source (p. 203) ★ assign (p. 203)	As you read, complete the cause-and-effect chart to detail the purposes of casework. **Purposes of Casework**

Economics in the News

When the I-35 bridge collapsed just outside downtown Minneapolis in 2007, state representative Jim Oberstar was in the perfect place to propose a federal solution. Oberstar chairs the House's Transportation and Infrastructure Committee. In hearings, experts told Oberstar and other committee members that as many as one in eight bridges are unsound. Oberstar proposed a 5 cent increase to the federal gasoline tax, which has not increased since the early 1990s. But Oberstar's proposal has captured little interest in a time when gas prices are already high.

▲ When this Minnesota bridge collapsed, hearings were held to highlight problems with the nation's infrastructure.

Representative Oberstar's experience mirrors what many seasoned lawmakers have learned—they are expected to do more in Congress for their constituents than debate great issues. To be reelected, they must spend much of their time on two important tasks. First, they must act as problem solvers for voters who have difficulties with federal departments or agencies. Second, they must make sure that their district or state gets its share of federal money for projects such as new post offices, highways, and contracts.

These two congressional duties are not new, but as the national government has grown, they have become a very time-consuming part of the lawmaker's job.

Handling Problems

Helping constituents with problems is called **casework.** All lawmakers today are **involved** with casework. One House member put it this way: "Rightly or wrongly, we have become the link between the frustrated citizen and the very involved federal government in citizens' lives. . . . We continually use more and more of our staff time to handle citizens' complaints."

Many Different Requests

Lawmakers respond to thousands of requests from voters for help in dealing with executive agencies. Here are some typical requests: A soldier would like the Army to move him to a base close to home because his parents are ill; a local businessperson claims the Federal Trade Commission (FTC) is treating her business unfairly and she wants to meet with top FTC officials; a veteran has had his GI life insurance policy canceled by a government agency, which states that the veteran failed to fill out a certain form (the veteran says he never got the form); a new high school graduate wants help in finding a government job in Washington.

Resource Manager

R Reading Strategies	**C** Critical Thinking	**D** Differentiated Instruction	**W** Writing Support	**S** Skill Practice
Teacher Edition • Organizing, p. 201 **Additional Resources** • Quizzes/Tests, p. 80 • Guid. Read. Act., p. 28	**Teacher Edition** • Defending, p. 202 **Additional Resources** • Read. Essen., pp. 80–81 • Quizzes/Tests, pp. 81–88	**Teacher Edition** • Verbal/Linguistic, p. 202 **Additional Resources** • Ch. Summaries, pp. 19–21 • Foldables, p. 50	**Additional Resources** • Authentic Assess., p. 14	**Additional Resources** • Unit Overlay Trans., pp. 3–4

Many lawmakers complain that voters will say they want less government in their lives, but in fact, they demand more from their representatives. Sometimes voters make unreasonable requests or ask for help a lawmaker is unwilling to deliver. A representative from New York, for example, was asked to fix a speeding ticket. Another member received a call asking what the lawmaker was going to do about the shortage of snow shovels at a local hardware store during a blizzard.

Who Handles Casework

All lawmakers have staff members called case-workers to handle constituent problems. Usually, the caseworkers can handle the requests on their own—the problem can be solved simply by having a caseworker clarify matters with the agency involved. At other times, however, the senator or representative may have to get directly involved.

Purposes of Casework

Why do lawmakers spend so much time on casework? Casework serves three important purposes. First, it gets lawmakers reelected. Helping voters with problems is part of what lawmakers are supposed to do. "I learned soon after coming to Washington," a Missouri lawmaker once said, "that it was just as important to get a certain document for somebody back home as for some European diplomat—really, more important, because that little guy back home votes."

As a result, many lawmakers actually look for casework. One lawmaker, for example, regularly sent invitations to almost 7,000 voters in his district asking them to bring their problems to a town meeting that his staff runs. Today lawmakers may encourage voters to communicate with them by e-mail. Many representatives have vans that drive through their districts as mobile offices to keep watch on problems back home.

Second, casework is one way in which Congress monitors the performance of the executive branch. Casework brings problems with federal programs to the attention of Congress. Lawmakers and their staffs are getting a closer look at how well executive agencies handle such federal programs as Social Security and veterans' benefits.

Third, casework provides a way for the average citizen to cope with the huge national government. Before the national government grew so large, most citizens with a problem turned to their local politicians—called ward heelers—for help. One member of Congress explained:

Longevity and Its Rewards Senator Robert Byrd of West Virginia has served in the Senate longer than anyone in American history. He has held many leadership positions in the Senate, including majority whip. Byrd is well-known for bringing many federal dollars to his home state. *Why does longevity help a representative in the competition for federal projects?*

❝ *In the old days, you had the ward heeler who cemented himself in the community by taking care of everyone. . . . Now the Congressman plays the role of ward heeler—wending his way through the bureaucracy, helping to cut through red tape and confusion.* ❞

—Les Aspin

Helping the District or State

Besides providing constituent services, members try to bring federal projects to their districts and states. They do this in three ways: through pork-barrel legislation, winning federal grants and contracts, and by working to keep existing federal projects.

Public Works Legislation

Every year, through public works bills, Congress appropriates billions of dollars for local projects. Examples are post offices, dams, military bases, river improvements, federally funded highways, veterans' hospitals, pollution-treatment centers, and mass-transit system projects.

CHAPTER 7: *Congress at Work* **201**

CHAPTER 7, SECTION 4

Teach

R **Reading Strategy**

Organizing Have students make a list of the types of casework members of Congress handle. Then have students write an explanation of the purpose served by each example. **OL**

Caption Answer: because a long-standing member wins coveted chair positions on committees that have a strong role in shaping legislation and dealing with the White House

Subcommittees
Read the following quotation from Tad Szulc: "The subcommittee system . . . has smothered or splintered legislation more often than it has expedited it. The 96th Congress has inherited 29 standing committees and 151 subcommittees in the House, 21 committees and 112 subcommittees in the Senate. . . . The average representative sits on three subcommittees, the average senator, five. . . ." Have students debate the value of subcommittees. **AL**

Additional Support

★ Activity: Collaborative Learning ★

Recycling Have groups of students prepare and present skits on any of the following situations:

- A small business owner calls the "hot line" his senator has established.
- A caseworker calls the Environmental Protection Agency on behalf of a constituent.
- Lawmakers spend time "logrolling" in hopes of getting federal projects for their states.

- A representative decides whether or not to apply for a federal grant for her district.

Each group should choose a director and a secretary; encourage the actors to try different roles in the skit before choosing the characters they will portray. **OL**

D Differentiated Instruction

Verbal/Linguistic This section introduces congressional slang such as *logrolling, pork-barrel, red tape,* and *ward heeler.* Have students work individually or with partners to clarify the meanings of these terms by brainstorming words and images that they associate with each term. Encourage additional research, if students choose; also allow students to draw as well as list the images that come to mind. Call on volunteers to share their comments about these terms as you introduce or review this section. **BL**

C Critical Thinking

Defending Ask: What defense can be given for pork-barrel projects? *(Students may note that these projects benefit people who live in a particular state or district.)* **BL**

Hands-On Chapter Project

Step 4

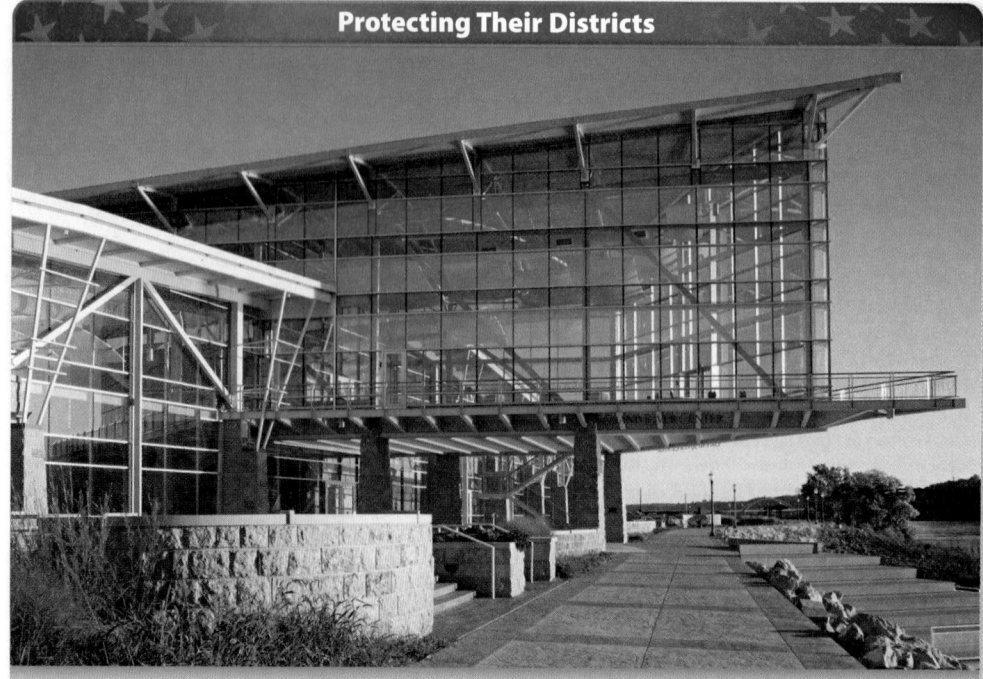

Protecting Their Districts

Constituent Services Senator Tom Harkin (D-Iowa) helped bring funds to Iowa for the Mississippi Discovery Center in Dubuque, Iowa. Harkin says it is proper for him to use his influence to direct funds to his home state. In fact, he refers not to "pork" or "earmarks," but "directed spending." *How might critics of pork respond to Harkin's argument?*

Projects like these bring jobs and money into a state or district. For example, Senator Robert Byrd's pet project, the Appalachian Regional Commission, oversaw more than a billion dollars' worth of government spending in its first three years. In 1989 Byrd used his position as chair of the Appropriations Committee to transplant federal agencies to his home state of West Virginia. For example, agencies or divisions of the FBI, CIA, Internal Revenue Service, and even the Coast Guard were moved from Washington to Byrd's state.

When Congress passes laws to appropriate money for such local federal projects, it is often called **pork-barrel legislation.** The idea is that a member of Congress has dipped into the "pork barrel," meaning the federal treasury, and pulled out a piece of "fat," a federal project for his or her district. This kind of legislation often draws criticism. Referring to Robert Byrd's project, a Maryland congresswoman claimed she was "afraid to go to sleep at night for fear of waking up and finding another agency has been moved to West Virginia."

More often, lawmakers take the view that if "you scratch my back, I'll scratch yours." They share the belief that getting federal projects for the home state is a key part of their job, so they often help each other. When two or more lawmakers agree to support each other's bills, it is called **logrolling.**

Winning Grants and Contracts

Lawmakers also try to make sure their districts or states get their fair share of the available federal grants and contracts that are funded through the national budget. A senator from Colorado put it this way: "If a program is to be established, the state of Colorado should get its fair share."

Federal grants and contracts are very important to lawmakers and their districts or states.

202 UNIT 2: *The Legislative Branch*

Creating a Public Interest Campaign

Step 4: Demonstrating Concern Have each group stage a demonstration using the plan they developed in Step 3.

Directions Discuss different ways that interest groups draw attention to their issues. Using the plan they developed in Step 3, have groups of students incorporate posters, music, movement, and/or a skit that dramatizes their cause.

Summarizing Have groups stage their demonstrations in class. Encourage the class to discuss whether or not the demonstrations successfully communicated the concerns of each interest group. **OL**

These contracts are a vital **source** of money and jobs and can radically affect the economy of a state. Every year, federal agencies like the Department of Defense spend billions of dollars to carry out hundreds of government projects and programs. For example, when the Air Force decided to locate a new project at one of its bases in Utah, almost 1,000 jobs and millions of dollars came into the state. Lawmakers compete for such valuable federal grants and contracts: Several states wanted the Air Force project, but Utah's lawmakers got the prize.

Behind the Scenes

Lawmakers do not vote on grants and contracts as they do on pork-barrel legislation. Instead, executive branch agencies like the Defense Department or the Department of Labor award them. Lawmakers, however, try to influence agency decisions in several ways. They may pressure agency officials to give a favorable hearing to their state's request for a grant. They may also encourage their constituents to write, telephone, or e-mail agency officials with their requests. If problems come up when someone from the state is competing for a grant or contract, lawmakers may step in to help.

Many lawmakers **assign** one or more staffers to act as specialists in this area. These staff members become experts on how individuals, businesses, and

local governments can qualify for federal money. They help constituents apply for contracts and grants because the lawmaker wants to make sure they continue to flow to their state or district.

Distributing the Pork

Eric Allie, Caglecartoons.com

Bad Examples "The Alaskan bridge to nowhere," as the media nicknamed it, became a symbol of wasteful "pork." Senator Robert Byrd, often seen as the king of pork, initially tried to save the project but Alaskan representatives withdrew it because of criticism. *What factors make "pork" continue to work?*

Caption Answer: public works projects such as post offices, dams, military bases, harbor improvements, highways, and so on

Assess

Assign the Section 4 Assessment as homework or as an in-class activity, or have students take Section Quiz 7-4 from *Section Quizzes and Chapter Tests.*

Close

Explaining Ask: Why do casework and pork-barrel legislation provide a huge boost for incumbents at election time? *(They help "prove" that the incumbent is working for his or her constituents in a way that a challenger cannot match.)* **OL**

★ SECTION 4 Review ★

Vocabulary

1. Explain the significance of: casework, pork-barrel legislation, logrolling.

Main Ideas

2. Explaining Why do lawmakers get involved in casework?

3. Listing What three ways can lawmakers bring federal projects to their states?

4. Defining Which branch of government awards federal grants and contracts?

Critical Thinking

5. Drawing Conclusions Why do you think the size of the lawmakers' staff has increased in recent years?

6. Organizing Use a graphic organizer like the one below to explain how allocation of grants and contracts is different from pork-barrel legislation.

Grants/Contracts	
Pork	

Writing About Government

7. Descriptive Writing Look through several editions of your local paper to find examples of federal money spent in your state or community. Present your findings in the form of a written summary for a radio news broadcast. Your broadcast should explain how pork-barrel legislation has benefited your state or local community.

Section 4 Review

★ Answers ★

1. All definitions can be found in the section and the Glossary.
2. Casework helps lawmakers get reelected, allows Congress to oversee the executive branch, and provides a way for the average citizen to cope with the huge national government.
3. pork-barrel legislation, federal grants and contracts, and keeping federal projects
4. the executive branch
5. Answers might include keeping up with growing federal agencies and a complicated bureaucracy.
6. Grants/contracts: lawmakers appeal to agencies of the executive branch. Pork barrel: Congress appropriates money.
7. Students' broadcasts should identify the pork-barrel legislation and its benefits to the state or local community.

Focus

Introducing the Topic

Ask students to read through the United States Congress time line of events. Have them determine whether each event increased or decreased Congress's power of representation. If the event decreased Congress's representative power, have them determine why that change was necessary.

Teach

C Critical Thinking

Drawing Conclusions Ask: Should the minority in Congress have the right to block a bill by using a filibuster? *(If students answer yes, ask them what limits there should be on the filibuster; for example, a time limit, a certain number of votes to overcome it, and so on. If students answer no, ask them if the minority should have any rights at all to block legislation.)* **OL**

Additional Support

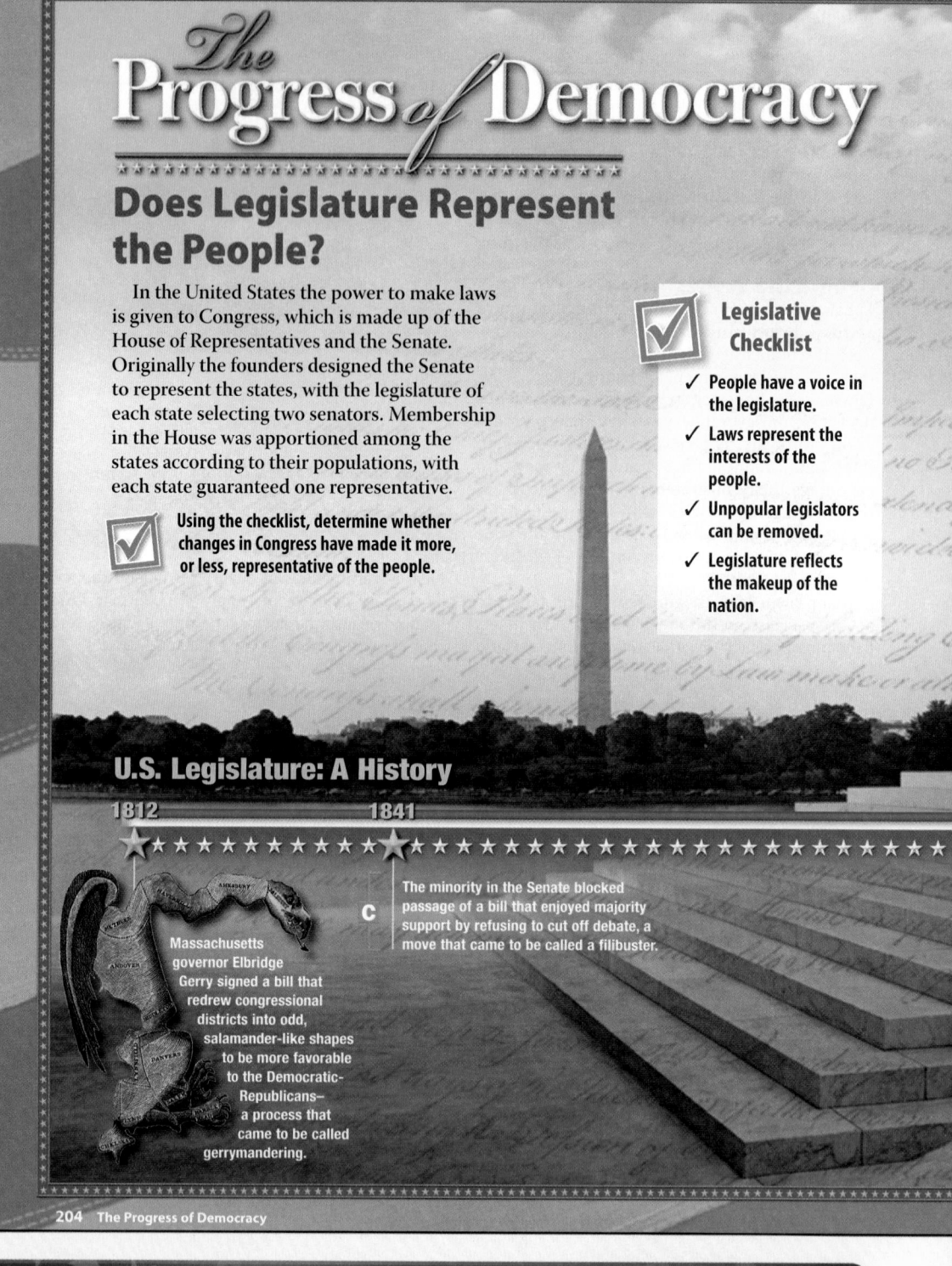

The Progress *of* Democracy

Does Legislature Represent the People?

In the United States the power to make laws is given to Congress, which is made up of the House of Representatives and the Senate. Originally the founders designed the Senate to represent the states, with the legislature of each state selecting two senators. Membership in the House was apportioned among the states according to their populations, with each state guaranteed one representative.

☑ Using the checklist, determine whether changes in Congress have made it more, or less, representative of the people.

☑ **Legislative Checklist**

✓ People have a voice in the legislature.

✓ Laws represent the interests of the people.

✓ Unpopular legislators can be removed.

✓ Legislature reflects the makeup of the nation.

U.S. Legislature: A History

1812

Massachusetts governor Elbridge Gerry signed a bill that redrew congressional districts into odd, salamander-like shapes to be more favorable to the Democratic-Republicans— a process that came to be called gerrymandering.

1841

C The minority in the Senate blocked passage of a bill that enjoyed majority support by refusing to cut off debate, a move that came to be called a filibuster.

204   The Progress of Democracy

Extending the Content

Gerrymandering The use of gerrymandering to give one party an advantage over another party has been a controversial technique in legislative elections for nearly 200 years. With the advent of GIS (geographic information systems) and other mapping programs, partisans have been able to draw reliably safe seats for themselves. Some politicians, such as California governor Arnold Schwarzenegger, have tried to establish nonpartisan commissions to draw districts without considering the ramifications on partisan politics. So far their efforts have been unsuccessful.

Have students research your congressional district. **Ask:** Was it drawn naturally, or was it drawn by gerrymandering?

The House of Representatives refused to seat Victor Berger as a member due to his conviction for espionage.

Strom Thurmond tries to delay the passage of a civil rights bill by filibustering for more than 24 hours. The bill passed two hours after he yielded the floor.

The Supreme Court rules in *Shaw* v. *Reno* that districts drawn based on race are unconstitutional. **W**

1913 1919   1929   1957   1964   1993
★★★

The Seventeenth Amendment gives people the right to elect senators directly.

The number of representatives in the House is capped at 435. **C**

The Supreme Court rules in *Wesberry* v. *Sanders* that the voting population of each congressional district must be as equal as possible.

POLITICAL PROFILES **Victor Berger** (1860–1929) was a Socialist representative from Wisconsin convicted in 1919 under the Espionage Act for his vocal opposition to World War I. In spite of his conviction, he was elected to the House but was refused his seat. In a runoff election, he won again, and again the House refused to seat him. Berger's conviction was overturned by the Supreme Court in 1921, and he was allowed to take his seat in 1922.

C Critical Thinking

Making Inferences Ask: Why do you think Congress capped the number of representatives at 435? Should that number be increased? Why or why not? *(Students may suggest that with too many lawmakers it would be hard to get things done.)* **OL**

W Writing Support

Persuasive Writing Ask students to review the Supreme Court opinion in *Shaw* v. *Reno* that race-based districts are unconstitutional and write an essay arguing for or against the ruling. **OL**

Additional Support

Extending the Content

The Longest Filibuster To prepare for his filibuster, Strom Thurmond gathered a wide variety of materials to ensure he had plenty to speak about. He brought with him the voting rights laws of every state, the Declaration of Independence, and a history of Anglo-Saxon juries. He also brought throat lozenges and milk tablets to help save his voice. He was allowed to sit for short periods of time, while sympathetic colleagues made short remarks. He was also allowed to quickly eat a sandwich. His filibuster lasted 24 hours and 18 minutes, the longest filibuster in U.S. history.

The Progress of Democracy

Does Legislature Represent the People?

Around the world countries have set up their legislatures in a variety of ways. Most countries have tried to make their legislatures as representative as possible. However, some countries' legislatures are not representative because of historical, political, or cultural reasons.

Use the checklist to determine whether legislatures around the world represent the people.

Legislative Checklist

✓ People have a voice in the legislature.
✓ Laws represent the interests of the people.
✓ Unpopular legislators can be removed.
✓ Legislature reflects the make-up of the nation.

Japan
Democratic Party candidate Yumiko Himei celebrates an electoral victory. The Democratic Party of Japan gets most of its support from heavily populated urban areas. However, a majority of the seats in the legislature represent rural areas.

Activity: Collaborative Learning

Creating a Time Line Organize students into five groups and assign one of the countries from the feature to each group. Have students research the history and current makeup of the country's legislature. Have students make a time line of changes in the legislature in the country selected. Have groups present their findings to the class and explain whether the changes made the legislature more or less representative.

Great Britain

Membership in the United Kingdom's upper house, the House of the Lords, is by appointment, and its members serve life terms.

Lebanon

Druze protesters march in support of the government of Lebanon. After Lebanon's religious civil war, Christians and Muslims were each guaranteed half the seats in Parliament.

Spain

Spain's lower house, the Congress of Deputies, is elected by a party list system. Rather than pick a specific representative, Spanish voters choose which party they would like to control Congress. Representatives are then chosen based on the percentage of votes their party received.

United Arab Emirates

Half of the Federal National Council (FNC), the legislature of the United Arab Emirates, is elected, and the other half is appointed by the rulers of the Emirate. The FNC is only a consultative body; it has no power to pass laws.

Critical Thinking

Representative Legislatures

1. How does the United States Congress compare to other legislatures around the world? What changes could make Congress more representative?

2. Which countries above do not have representative legislatures? Which criteria do they fail to meet?

3. Select a country and research its legislature. Does its legislature represent the people? What changes could be made to make it more representative? How does that country compare to other countries around the world?

Did You Know?

The House of Lords has undergone a gradual reduction in its power. It has lost the ability to reject certain bills, for example, and can only delay the passage of most bills by a year at most. The House of Lords cannot introduce bills concerning finances. The British government is considering reducing the powers of the House of Lords even further.

C Critical Thinking

Drawing Conclusions The Lebanese civil war was fought between Christians, Shia Muslims, Sunni Muslims, and the Druze Muslim group. To guarantee equal power between the groups, equal seats in Parliament were guaranteed for Christians and Muslims. **Ask:** Should different groups of people be guaranteed representation in the legislature to prevent unrest? *(Students' answers may vary. Possible answers: Yes—they may not be represented otherwise. No—the legislature should represent the majority.)* **OL**

Additional Support

Critical Thinking Answers

1. Students' answers should include details on how the United States Congress compares to other countries around the world.

2. Great Britain: members of the House of Lords are not elected and cannot be removed; UAE: half the members are appointed, and they have no power to make laws.

3. Students' research should include information on the country's legislature, and their findings should reflect what changes could be made to make it more representative.

This easy-to-use software includes extensive question banks and allows you to create fully customized tests that can be administered in print or online.

Reviewing Vocabulary

1. a
2. f
3. b
4. e
5. d
6. g
7. c

Reviewing Main Ideas

8. The president may sign the bill into law, veto the bill, pocket veto the bill, or leave the bill unsigned and allow it to become law after 10 days if Congress is still in session.
9. It initiates and reviews all the tax laws.
10. Possible answers include the nature of the issue, voters at home, other lawmakers, staff members, political parties, the president, special-interest groups, and the lawmaker's beliefs.
11. logrolling

Critical Thinking

12. Possible answers: Without special-interest groups, lawmakers would not be pressured to vote according to the demands of the special-interest groups but would vote in the best interest of their constituents; enough other influences will continue to have an impact on lawmakers' activities.

Assessment and Activities

Reviewing Vocabulary

Fill in the blank with the letter of the correct content vocabulary word(s) listed below.

a. tax
b. rider
c. pocket veto
d. closed rule
e. entitlements
f. casework
g. pork-barrel legislation

1. A(n) ____ is money that citizens and businesses pay to support the government.
2. ____ is a congressional task that involves helping constituents with problems.
3. A(n) ____ is an often controversial provision tacked on to a bill pertaining to a different subject.
4. Interest on the national debt and Social Security payments are examples of ____.
5. Under a(n) ____, House members were forbidden to offer amendments to tax bills from the floor.
6. Laws passed by Congress to appropriate money for local and federal projects are known as ____.
7. The president exercises a(n) ____ by not signing a bill by the last 10 days Congress is in session.

Reviewing Main Ideas

Section 1 *(pages 181–188)*

8. **Analyzing** What are four actions a president may take on a bill?

Section 2 *(pages 189–192)*

9. **Defining** What role does the House Ways and Means Committee play in tax legislation?

Section 3 *(pages 194–198)*

10. **Summarizing** What factors influence lawmakers when they consider legislation?

Section 4 *(pages 200–203)*

11. **Explaining** What key tool do lawmakers use to secure the passage of public works legislation?

Critical Thinking

12. **Essential Question** Would lawmakers' activities be different if there were no special-interest groups?

13. **Analyzing** What procedure is Congress supposed to use to fund its programs and control its expenses?

14. **Making Inferences** Use the graphic organizer to show three characteristics of a successful bill.

15. **Drawing Conclusions** Why is Congress reluctant to appropriate the full amount of money an agency requests?

Chapter Summary

Congress at Work

Bills	**Money**	**Constituents**
★ Bills pass through many steps before becoming law ★ Congress considers new bills in committee and then debates and votes on them ★ Bills must be signed by president to become law; Congress can override presidential veto with a two-thirds vote in both houses	★ House of Representatives has sole power to start revenue measures ★ Congress has power to appropriate, or approve, government spending	★ Lawmakers spend time doing casework, helping constituents with problems ★ Lawmakers pass public works bills to appropriate money for projects in their home districts or states

---

13. Congress funds its programs with tax money and uses appropriations to control how much can be spent on each program.
14. Characteristics might include clearly written, obvious goals, and wide public support.
15. Congress might want an agency to avoid wasteful spending or force an agency to concentrate its allotted spending on the most effective measures.

Government ONLINE **Self-Check Quiz** Go to glencoe.com and enter **QuickPass™** code USG9822c7. Click on Self-Check Quizzes for additional test practice.

CHAPTER
7
Assessment and Activities

Document-Based Questions

Analyzing Primary Sources

Read the excerpt below and answer the questions that follow.

During the 1930s, President Franklin D. Roosevelt used his power as chief executive to propose a record number of laws to deal with the Great Depression. In the "fireside chat" excerpted below, Roosevelt explains why the New Deal did not take power away from Congress.

> ❝ *A prompt program applied as quickly as possible seemed to me not only justified but imperative to our national security. . . . The members of Congress realized that the methods of normal times had to be replaced in the emergency by measures which were suited to the serious and pressing requirements of the moment. There was no actual surrender of power, Congress still retained its constitutional authority. . . . The function of Congress is to decide what has to be done and to select the appropriate agency to carry out its will. . . . The only thing that has been happening has been to designate the President as the agency to carry out certain of the purposes of the Congress.* ❞

16. Where did many proposals for New Deal legislation originate, and why was this important?

17. Why do you think the president was careful to specify that Congress had not surrendered its constitutional power?

18. Applying Technology Skills The inaugural speeches of the nation's presidents are available at a Yale Law School Web site, the Avalon project: www.yale.edu/lawweb/avalon/presiden/inaug/inaug.htm. Choose the Inaugural Addresses of two presidents that interest you. Read them closely, even placing them side-by-side. Then write a short analysis that compares and contrasts the two addresses on whatever characteristics you choose— length, theme, structure, language, style, or specific content.

Interpreting Political Cartoons

Analyze the cartoon and answer the questions that follow. Base your answers on the cartoon and your knowledge of Chapter 7.

"Someone called from a Political Inaction Committee to speak to you on behalf of apathetic voters. He said he might call back."

19. What is the "Political Inaction Committee" referred to in the cartoon?

20. How is the "Political Inaction Committee" different from other special-interest groups?

21. Why is this situation unrealistic?

Participating IN GOVERNMENT

22. Obtain a copy of a bill being considered in your state from your state representative or senator. Decide what changes you would suggest in the bill. Forward these suggestions to your representative or senator and ask for a response.

Interpreting Political Cartoons

19. It is an interest group.

20. It represents apathetic voters—those who do not care about issues being debated in the Capitol.

21. Members of interest groups are not indifferent voters. They care enough about an issue to lobby lawmakers.

Participating IN GOVERNMENT

22. Call on volunteers to indicate the bill that they obtained and their suggestions for change. Ask students to share responses they receive from their state representative or senator.

Chapter Bonus Test Question

Ask: What are caucuses, and what role do they play in the work of Congress? *(Caucuses are groups that consist of members of Congress with a common interest—for example, the Congressional Black Caucus—who meet privately to discuss and plan legislation relating to causes that they want to support.)*

Analyzing Primary Sources

16. President Roosevelt introduced hundreds of bills to deal with the Great Depression, whereas up until that time new legislation generally had originated in Congress. Roosevelt explained that although he proposed many of the bills, Congress had not stopped doing its job. This was also important because Congress has the power to appropriate funds for new programs.

17. In an emergency situation like the Great Depression, there may be fear that a strong president might seize power and take over the governing of the nation from Congress.

Applying Technology Skills

18. Students' analyses should thoughtfully and effectively compare and contrast characteristics of the presidential addresses.

The Executive Branch

UNIT PACING CHART*			
	Chapter 8	**Chapter 9**	**Chapter 10**
Day 1	Unit Opener Chapter Opener Section 1	Chapter Opener Section 1	Chapter Opener Section 1
Day 2	Section 2 Issues to Debate	Supreme Court Cases to Debate Section 2	Section 2
Day 3	Section 3 Government Skills	Issues to Debate Section 3	Supreme Court Cases to Debate
Day 4	Section 4 TIME Notebook	Progress of Democracy	Section 3 Issues to Debate
Day 5	Review Chapter Assessment	Review Chapter Assessment	Review Chapter Assessment

*Unit Pacing Chart based on year-long course; modify pacing by half for semester-long course

 Teacher to Teacher

Linda Kingston
Alameda Unified
School District
Alameda, CA

Presidential Scavenger Hunt Place the names of all the U.S. presidents in a hat. Each student should draw a name and then conduct a scavenger hunt for presidential facts. Encourage students to use a variety of resources, such as Internet and library resources. The following is a list of possible items for students to find out about their president:

• Term
• Popular and electoral vote
• Party
• Vice president
• Relations with Congress (friendly or unfriendly)

• Supreme Court appointees
• Changes to the Constitution
• Foreign policy
• Major legislation passed
• Major achievements
• World events dealt with

After the students have completed their lists, have them analyze the facts to determine whether the president was successful. The project can be extended by having the students write an essay about how Americans evaluate their presidents.

Author Note

Dear U.S. Government Teacher,

In Unit 3, you will guide your students through two high-profile topics: the presidency and the federal bureaucracy. The presidency is the nation's only nationally elected office. Its incumbent becomes the face of the administration and leads one of the nation's major parties. Approval ratings for the president are a guide to Americans' satisfaction with the government. Most students can sense these facts about the presidency even if they do not immediately articulate them.

The enormous influence of the president who occupies the "bully pulpit" dominates the public's awareness of government activity. On any given day, Americans from New York to California are exposed to White House messages of all kinds. What a president does and says is fodder for the news, for casual conversations in the workplace, and even for stand-up comics. In teaching this unit, you will create a more detailed picture for the student of how the president interacts with the cabinet. Students will also understand the key role played by executive agencies such as the Office of Management and Budget and the National Security Council.

In terms of the federal bureaucracy, you will more likely be expanding students' knowledge base. They will be able to see more clearly that the executive branch begins with the presidency but includes the federal bureaucracy. Thousands of federal employees carry out a president's policies and the many federal laws and regulations. The actions of federal employees affect Americans every day—from the IRS employee who audits a tax return to the Forest Service ranger who battles wildfires. In the end, the public policies that affect Americans are shaped in a dialogue between the executive branch, Congress, interest groups, and private citizens.

Richard C. Remy

Richard C. Remy, Ph.D.
Author

Focus

Making It Relevant

Working for the Federal Government As students read this unit, have them make a list of all the executive branch positions mentioned. Then, next to each position, ask them to write whether or not they would like to hold that job and why.

Unit Objectives

After studying this unit, students will be able to:

- **Describe** the organization and functions of the executive branch.

- **Discuss** the presidential powers.

- **Evaluate** the functions of the federal bureaucracy.

Unit Overview

Unit 3 provides a basic introduction to the executive branch.

Chapter 8 discusses how the president is elected and the organization of the executive branch.

Chapter 9 describes the duties and powers of the president.

Chapter 10 describes the organization and duties of the federal bureaucracy.

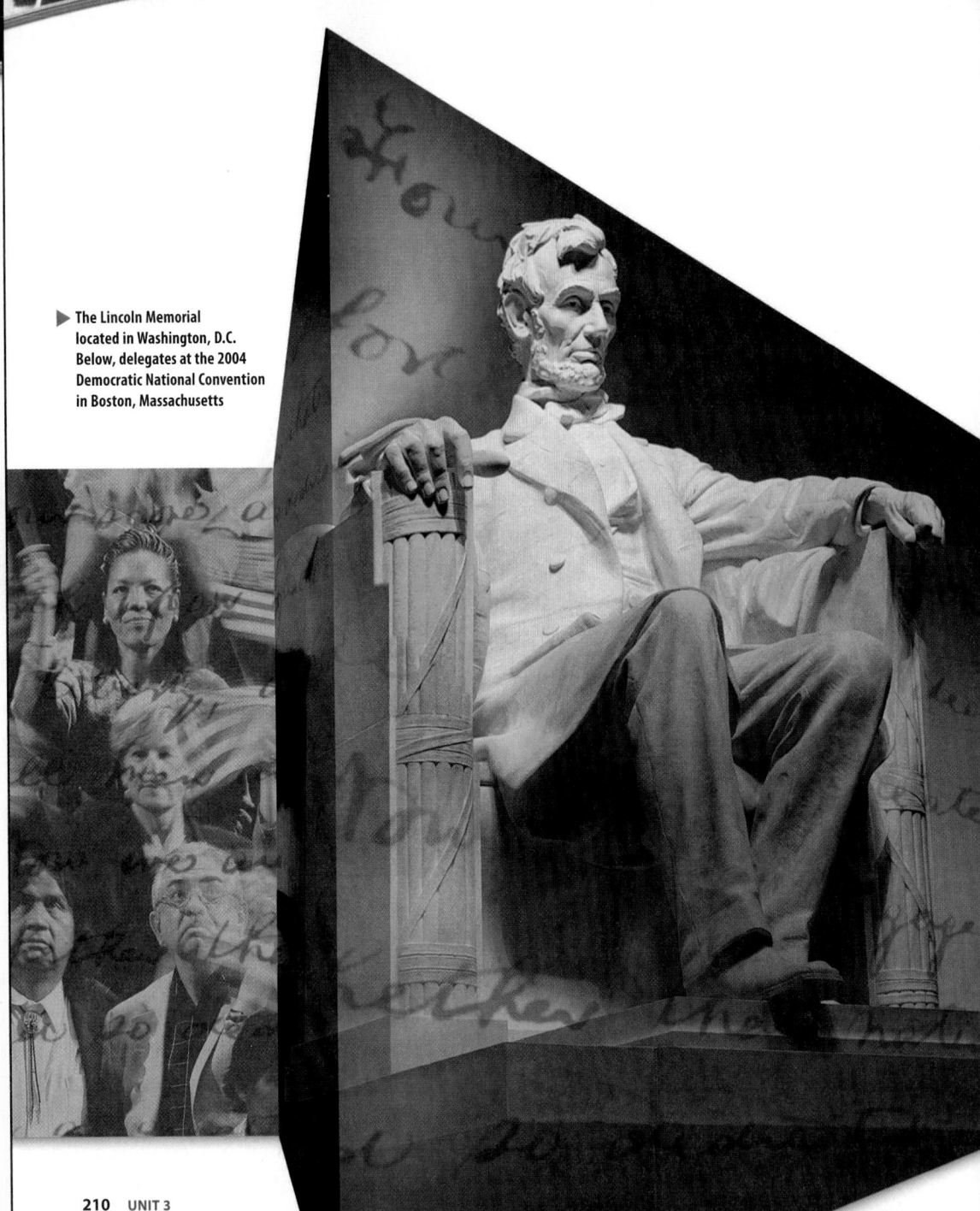

► The Lincoln Memorial located in Washington, D.C. Below, delegates at the 2004 Democratic National Convention in Boston, Massachusetts

210 UNIT 3

Activity: Launching the Unit

Plotting a Career Path Have students choose an executive branch job listed in this unit and plan a career path for obtaining that job. Encourage students to describe this plan in a written report using graphic organizers. The report should include all necessary steps leading to this particular job, including education, special skills, personal connections, volunteer work, and so on. After students have completed this unit, hold a "job fair" in which students describe their career paths to the class. **OL**

The Executive Branch

Participating IN GOVERNMENT

BIG IDEA **Federalism** The president is responsible for the administration of hundreds of government agencies that directly affect your life. From this unit select a federal agency. Find out what its main services are and how it works through state or local agencies to carry out its responsibilities. Then survey several people in your community to see how well the agency serves the people. Send the results of your survey to the federal agency via e-mail.

▲ The Democratic National Convention of 1868 in Tammany Hall, New York

211

Teach

S Skill Practice

Visual Literacy Students should take a few minutes to examine the three images on pages 210–211 and think about politics and politicians. **Ask:** How would you describe the contrast in mood in the images of the party conventions and Lincoln's statue? (*Students may see that Lincoln, an elected official and politician, is ennobled, contemplative, almost saint-like, while the convention suggests the boisterousness and give-and-take of party politics.*)

Online Current Events Update

History happens every day. Visit Glencoe's Online Current Events Update at glencoe.com to find news reports, features, maps, graphs, and images about events that shape our lives. Students can connect those events to historical events in world and American history by exploring related events on an interactive time line—a time line that ends with today.

Graduation: Exit With Success

Teaching Tip Help students expand their academic vocabulary by reading a sentence from the text that contains a challenging word. Demonstrate how to use the other words in the sentence as well as the surrounding sentences—the context clues—to determine the meaning of the unknown word.

Extra Credit Project

Creating a "Who's Who" Booklet Have interested students research the people who currently hold each executive branch position mentioned in this unit. Students should write a brief paragraph about each official, providing background information and his or her major accomplishments while in office. Encourage students to include a picture or a drawing of each person in their "Who's Who" booklet. Display students' booklets in the classrooms. **OL**

Planning Guide

Key to Ability Levels

BL Below level   **AL** Above level

OL On level   **ELL** English Language Learners

Key to Teaching Resources

📁 Print Material   🖶 Transparency

💿 CD-ROM or DVD

BL	OL	AL	ELL		Resources	Chapter Opener	Section 1	Section 2	Section 3	Section 4	Chapter Assess
					FOCUS						
BL	OL	AL	ELL	🖶	Section Focus Transparencies		8-1	8-2	8-3	8-4	
					TEACH						
BL	OL		ELL	📁	Reading Essentials and Study Guide (and Answer Key)		p. 82	p. 86	p. 89	p. 92	
BL	OL		ELL	📁	Guided Reading Activities		p. 29	p. 30	p. 31	p. 32	
BL	OL		ELL	📁	Vocabulary Activities		p. 8				
BL	OL	AL	ELL	📁	Chapter Summaries					p. 22	
BL	OL			📁	American Biographies				pp. 71, 73		
BL	OL	AL	ELL	📁	Cooperative Learning Activities			p. 5		p. 5	
	OL	AL	ELL	📁	Government Simulations and Debate					pp. 16–21	
BL	OL	AL	ELL	📁	Historical Documents and Speeches			p. 8			
BL	OL	AL	ELL	📁	Interpreting Political Cartoons				p. 15		
BL	OL		ELL	📁	Skill Reinforcement Activities			p. 8			
BL	OL	AL	ELL	📁	Source Readings				p. 8		
BL	OL			📁	Supreme Court Case Studies						
BL	OL	AL	ELL	📁	Participating in Government Activities			p. 15			
BL	OL		ELL	📁	Spanish Declaration of Independence and U.S. Constitution	✓	✓	✓	✓	✓	✓
BL	OL	AL	ELL	📁	NGS World Atlas, Spanish	✓	✓	✓	✓	✓	✓
BL	OL	AL	ELL	🖶	Unit Overlay Transparencies, Strategies, and Activities	✓	✓	✓	✓	✓	✓
BL	OL		ELL	🖶	Making It Relevant Transparencies	✓	✓	✓	✓	✓	✓
BL	OL	AL	ELL	🖶	High School Writing Process Transparencies, Strategies, and Activities	✓	✓	✓	✓	✓	✓
BL	OL	AL		🖶	American Art & Architecture Transparencies, Strategies, and Activities	✓	✓	✓	✓	✓	✓

✓ Chapter- or unit-based activities applicable to all sections in this chapter

TeacherWorks™ Plus

All-In-One Planner and Resource Center

- Interactive Lesson Planner
- Interactive Teacher Edition
- Fully editable blackline masters
- Chapter Spotlight Videos Launch
- Differentiated Lesson Plans
- Printable reports of daily assignments
- Standards tracking system

Levels					Resources	Chapter Opener	Section 1	Section 2	Section 3	Section 4	Chapter Assess
BL	OL	AL	ELL								
					TEACH (continued)						
BL	OL			⊙	**American Music: Hits Through History**	✓	✓	✓	✓	✓	✓
BL	OL		ELL	📁	**Reading Strategies for the Social Studies Classroom**	✓	✓	✓	✓	✓	✓
			ELL	📁	**English Language Learner Handbook**	✓	✓	✓	✓	✓	✓
BL	OL		ELL	📁	**Writer's Guidebook for Social Studies**	✓	✓	✓	✓	✓	✓
BL	OL	AL	ELL	📁	**Living Constitution, SE**	✓	✓	✓	✓	✓	✓
BL	OL	AL	ELL	📁	**Living Constitution, TAE**	✓	✓	✓	✓	✓	✓
BL	OL			📁	**NGS World Atlas, English**	✓	✓	✓	✓	✓	✓
BL	OL		ELL	📁	**The Constitution and You (poster set)**	✓	✓	✓	✓	✓	✓
BL	OL	AL	ELL	📁	**Spanish Chapter Summaries**					p. 22	
BL	OL	AL	ELL	📁	**Spanish Vocabulary Activities**		p. 8				
BL	OL		ELL	📁	**Spanish Reading Essentials and Study Guide (and Answer Key)**		p. 82	p. 86	p. 89	p. 92	
BL	OL	AL	ELL	⊙	**PresentationPlus! with MindJogger CheckPoint**	✓	✓	✓	✓	✓	✓
					ASSESS						
BL	OL	AL	ELL	⊙	*ExamView® Assessment Suite*		8-1	8-2	8-3	8-4	Ch. 8
BL	OL	AL	ELL	📁	**Authentic Assessment with Rubrics**		p. 15				p. 15
BL	OL	AL	ELL	📁	**Section Quizzes and Chapter Tests**		p. 91	p. 92	p. 93	p. 94	pp. 95–102
BL	OL	AL	ELL	📁	**Spanish Section Quizzes and Tests**		p. 91	p. 92	p. 93	p. 94	pp. 95–102
					CLOSE						
BL			ELL	📁	**Reteaching Activities**				p. 8		p. 8
BL	OL	AL	ELL	⊙	**StudentWorks™ Plus with Audio Summaries**	✓	✓	✓	✓	✓	✓
BL	OL		ELL	🖥	**Graphic Organizer Transparencies**		✓	✓	✓	✓	
BL	OL		ELL	📁	**High School Government Reading and Study Skills Foldables®**		p. 51	p. 51	p. 51	p. 51	

Teach With Technology

What is a Self-Check Quiz?
A Self-Check Quiz is a set of 10 or more multiple-choice questions that assess student comprehension of the chapter.

How can a Self-Check Quiz help my students?
A Self-Check Quiz is a quick and easy way for students to check how much they have learned and identify areas needing improvement. It allows students to:

- view their results immediately

- view the correct answers
- e-mail their results to you or themselves
- receive feedback on each question for where students can go to review topics they missed or had trouble answering

Visit glencoe.com and enter a **QuickPass**™ code to go to a Self-Check Quiz.

Government ONLINE
Visit glencoe.com and enter **QuickPass**™ code USG9085c8T for Chapter 8 resources.

You can easily launch a wide range of digital products from your computer's desktop with the McGraw-Hill Social Studies widget.

	Student	Teacher	Parent
Media Library			
• Student Edition Section Audio	●		●
• Chapter Spotlight Videos	●	●	●
United States Government Online Learning Center (Web Site)			
• Chapter Overviews	●	●	●
• Multilingual Glossaries	●	●	●
• Study-to-Go	●	●	●
• Student Web Activities	●	●	●
• Self-Check Quizzes	●	●	●
• Online Student Edition	●	●	●
• Vocabulary eFlashcards	●	●	●
• Web Activity Lesson Plans		●	
• Vocabulary PuzzleMaker	●	●	●
• Landmark Supreme Court Cases	●	●	●
• Beyond the Textbook	●	●	●

READING SUPPORT FROM JAMESTOWN EDUCATION

- **Timed Readings Plus in Social Studies** helps students increase their reading rate and fluency while maintaining comprehension. The 400-word passages are similar to those found on state and national assessments.

- **Reading in the Content Area: Social Studies** concentrates on six essential reading skills that help students better comprehend what they read. The book includes 75 high-interest nonfiction passages written at increasing levels of difficulty.

- **Reading Social Studies** includes strategic reading instruction and vocabulary support in Social Studies content for ELLs and native speakers of English. www.jamestowneducation.com

Reading List Generator CD-ROM — GLENCOE BOOKLINK 3

Use this database to search more than 30,000 titles to create a customized reading list for your students.

- Reading lists can be organized by students' reading level, author, genre, theme, or area of interest.

- The database provides Degrees of Reading Power™ (DRP) and Lexile™ readability scores for all selections.

- A brief summary of each selection is included.

Leveled reading suggestions for this chapter:

- *American Sphinx: The Character of Thomas Jefferson,* by Joseph J. Ellis

- *Plain Speaking: An Oral Biography of Harry S. Truman,* by Merle Miller

- *The Presidency,* by Gerald W. Johnson

Review suggested books before assigning them.

Economics Connection

Personal Finance Literacy

Writing a Résumé

Most jobs require applicants to submit a résumé—a summary of their experience, education, and skills. It is the first chance to make a good impression on potential employers. Here are its components:

- Contact information: applicant's name, mailing and e-mail addresses, and telephone number
- Objective: an optional statement of the type of job sought
- Experience: concise summary of work and volunteer history, emphasizing accomplishments
- Education: name of the school and the date the applicant graduated, or will graduate
- Skills: other languages the applicant speaks, software and office equipment he or she can use
- Activities: organizations the applicant belongs to, preferably job-related, or awards

Cover letters: Whether mailed or sent via e-mail, a résumé is accompanied by a cover letter. The letter expresses interest in the exact position that's open, summarizes experience directly related to that job, and provides contact information.

Do	Don't
Use a standard format and ivory or light gray stationery.	Waste the employer's time with wordiness.
Tailor each résumé to the job.	Always use the same résumé.
List everything you've accomplished in your life; use it to identify skills to add to your résumé.	Try to seem creative by using odd paper or formatting.

Ask students: How can you make your experience attractive to a potential employer?

Did You Know?

Employers typically receive about 500 résumés for every job opening and spend about five seconds glancing at each one.

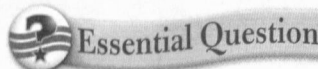

Essential Question

Refer students to the Essential Question on this page. Ask students to describe the prime duties of the president. Remind students that the president fills many roles that are important to the functioning of the U.S. government. Then ask students to explain how the president is elected.

Chapter Spotlight Video

To generate student interest and provide a springboard for class discussion, access the Chapter 8 Video at glencoe.com or on the video DVD.

FOLDABLES Study Organizer **Dinah Zike's Foldables** are three-dimensional, interactive graphic organizers that help students practice basic writing skills, review key vocabulary terms, and identify main ideas. Have students complete this chapter's Foldable activity or activities in *Dinah Zike's Reading and Study Skills Foldables* booklet. **OL**

Government ONLINE

Visit glencoe.com and enter *QuickPass*™ code USG9085c8T for Chapter 8 Resources including Chapter Overview, Student Web Activity, Self-Check Quiz, and other materials for students and teachers.

CHAPTER

8

🔊 Chapter Audio   📼 Spotlight Video

The Presidency

Essential Question

What are the prime duties of the presidency, the single most powerful office in the nation, and how is the president selected?

Government ONLINE
Chapter Overview Visit glencoe.com and enter *QuickPass*™ code USG9822c8 for an overview, a quiz, and other chapter resources.

▲ President-elect Barack Obama is escorted by President George W. Bush to the Oval Office in 2008.

212

Launching the Chapter

Understanding the Presidency Explain to students that although the U.S. president holds one of the most powerful and important elective offices in the world, the Framers did not state specifically in the Constitution what the role of the president should be. The nation's first president, George Washington, established many traditions that shaped the presidency. Every president since Washington has followed and built upon these traditions, refining the president's role within the government. **Essential Question:** What does each president have the obligation and the opportunity to do? (*Answers may include that each president must abide by the U.S. Constitution and that each has the opportunity to shape the office for those who will follow and to respond to the current national needs.*) **OL**

President and Vice President

Reader's Guide

Content Vocabulary
★ compensation (p. 214)
★ presidential succession (p. 217)

Academic Vocabulary
★ assist (p. 214)
★ fund (p. 216)
★ recover (p. 218)

Reading Strategy
As you read, use a chart like the one below to list the constitutional requirements for president and vice president.

Constitutional Requirements	
President	Vice President

Issues in the News

The duties of the chief executive are never so obvious as when the life of the president is threatened. In March 1981, Vice President George H.W. Bush rushed back to Washington, D.C., from Texas after President Ronald Reagan was shot. If Reagan's wounds made him unable to govern, Bush would have had to assume the duties of the office. For a day, in fact, Bush filled in for the president at various meetings, but no official steps were taken to designate him as acting president. The next day, Reagan was alert enough to make presidential decisions from his hospital bed.

▲ Chaos ensued outside the Washington, D.C., Hilton hotel when John Hinckley, Jr., shot President Reagan.

A vice president suddenly stepping into a president's shoes faces a daunting assignment. When President Harry S. Truman took office the day Franklin B. Roosevelt died, he told the press:

> ❝ I don't know whether you fellows ever had a load of hay fall on you, but when they told me yesterday what had happened, I felt like the moon, the stars, and all the planets had fallen on me. ❞
>
> —Harry S. Truman, 1945

The office of the president has been developing for more than 200 years. As the nation has grown, so has the power of the executive. Today, the president of the United States is one of the most powerful individuals in the world.

Duties of the President

The constitutional duties of the nation's first president, George Washington, and those of a modern president are much the same, but today's presidents have much greater power and responsibility. For example, the Constitution makes the president the commander in chief of the armed forces. In Washington's time, this meant calling on 15,000 volunteers to lead them against rebellious whiskey distillers. Today the president oversees a military that is divided into four major units, stations hundreds of thousands of troops at bases around the world, and manages a defense budget estimated in 2009 at more than $500 billion.

The Constitution also gives the president the authority to appoint—with the Senate's consent—heads of executive departments, federal court

Focus

Bellringer
Section Focus Transparencies 8-1

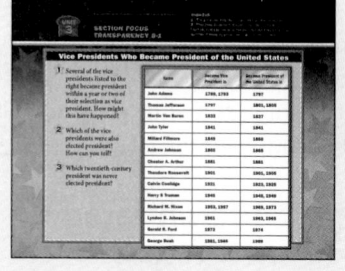

Reader's Guide

Answers to Graphic: The requirements for president and vice president are the same: natural-born U.S. citizen, at least 35 years old, and a resident of the United States for at least 14 years before taking office.

Resource Manager

R Reading Strategies	**C** Critical Thinking	**D** Differentiated Instruction	**W** Writing Support	**S** Skill Practice
Teacher Edition • Making Connections, p. 216 • Analyzing Primary Sources, p. 217 • Questioning, p. 218 **Additional Resources** • Guid. Read. Act., p. 29 • Quizzes/Tests, p. 91	**Teacher Edition** • Making Inferences, p. 215 • Drawing Conclusions, p. 218 **Additional Resources** • Read. Essen., pp. 82–85	**Teacher Edition** • Visual/Spatial, p. 214 • Logical/Mathematical, p. 214 • Kinesthetic, p. 217 **Additional Resources** • Foldables, p. 51	**Teacher Edition** • Expository Writing, p. 219 **Additional Resources** • Authentic Assess., p. 15	**Additional Resources** • Vocab. Act., p. 8

Teach

D₁ Differentiated Instruction

Visual/Spatial Ask students to draw a caricature of the ideal president and label the qualities they think are the most necessary to make an effective president. Encourage students to share their drawings with the class. **ELL OL**

D₂ Differentiated Instruction

Logical/Mathematical Ask:
By how much did the president's annual salary increase between 2000 and 2001? *(by $200,000 per year)* **BL OL**

Caption Answer: Public transportation could be dangerous, and the Secret Service is better equipped to protect the president by using private vehicles.

GO TO To enrich study of chapter content, remind students that footnoted materials appear in the *Reference Handbook.*

Additional Support

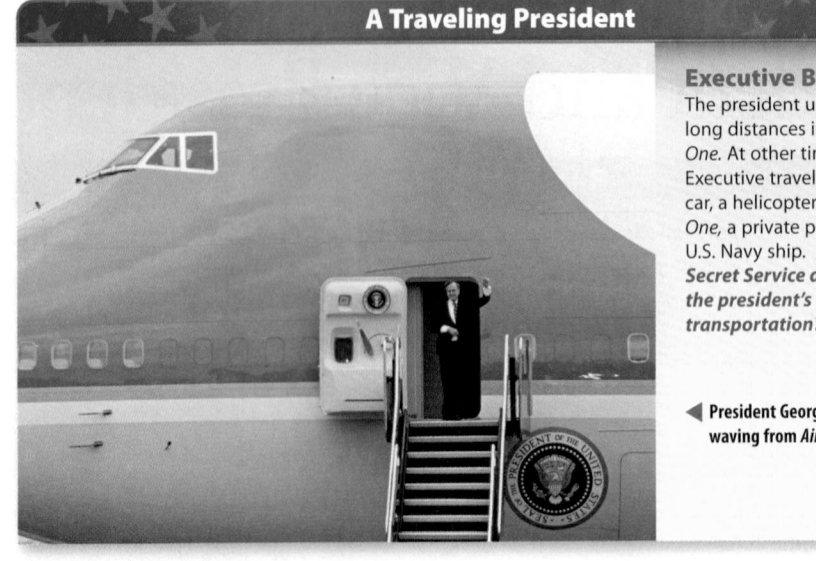

A Traveling President

Executive Benefits
The president usually flies long distances in *Air Force One.* At other times, the Chief Executive travels in an official car, a helicopter called *Marine One,* a private plane, or a U.S. Navy ship. *Why does the Secret Service discourage the president's use of public transportation?*

◄ **President George H.W. Bush waving from *Air Force One* in 1992**

---

judges, and other top officials. In conducting foreign policy, the president makes treaties with the advice and consent of the Senate, meets with heads of state, hosts foreign officials, and appoints ambassadors to other nations.

The most important duty of the president might be to ensure that all the laws of the United States are faithfully executed. A vast bureaucracy **assists** the president in this task. A president has the power to pardon people who have been convicted of federal crimes, except in cases of impeachment, or to reduce a person's jail sentence or fine.

The president has lawmaking power. Each year the president delivers a State of the Union message to Congress, in addition to other messages from time to time. Today, Congress expects a president to propose policy changes.

The President's Term and Salary

Originally, the Constitution did not specify how many four-year terms a president could serve. George Washington set a long-held precedent when he served for eight years and then refused to run for a third term. The tradition of serving only two terms lasted for 150 years. Then in 1940 on the eve of World War II and again in 1944, during the war, Franklin D. Roosevelt broke tradition, running successfully for a third and a fourth term.

The Twenty-second Amendment

Reaction to Roosevelt's four terms in office and concern over too much executive power led to passage of the Twenty-second Amendment in 1951.[1] It confirmed that a president would be limited to two terms. It also allowed a vice president who takes over in the middle of a presidency and serves no more than two years to serve two more terms. Thus, one person could be president for 10 years.

Salary and Benefits

The Constitutional Convention determined that presidents should receive compensation but left it up to Congress to decide the amount of **compensation,** or salary. Between 1969 and 2001, the president's salary was $200,000 per year in taxable salary and $50,000 per year for expenses. In 1999 Congress raised it to $400,000, starting with the new president in 2001. The Executive Office of the President also provides a nontaxable travel allowance of up to $100,000 per year. Congress cannot increase or decrease the salary during a president's term.

Other benefits, some necessary for security reasons, are provided to the president. For example, *Air Force One,* a specially equipped jet, as well as other planes, helicopters, and limousines are made available to the president and top assistants. Presidents receive free medical, dental, and health care.

*See the following footnoted materials in the **Reference Handbook:** 1. The Constitution, pages R42–R67.*

Activity: Collaborative Learning

Role Playing Organize the class into groups of four to role-play an interview with the president and vice president. Encourage groups to brainstorm a list of qualities and experiences they think are important for presidents and vice presidents. Then ask each group to write 10 questions, using their lists as a guide, for a reporter to ask at an interview.

Have group members choose who will role-play the president, vice president, and reporter. The fourth person in the group will create props and costumes to make the role play realistic. Based on the role play, challenge the class to identify the qualities and experiences portrayed. **OL**

They live in the White House, a 132-room mansion with a swimming pool, a bowling alley, a private movie theater, and tennis courts. The White House domestic staff does the cooking, shopping, and cleaning. The government pays to run the White House, but thousands of dollars of monthly expenses are not covered. The president must pay for receptions and dinners that are not directly related to government, for example.

When presidents retire, they receive a lifetime pension, now $148,400 per year. They also have free office space, free mailing services, and up to $96,000 per year for office help. When presidents die, their spouses are eligible for a pension of $20,000 per year. Although these benefits offer financial security to the president, money is not the reason that people seek the presidency.

Presidential Qualifications

The Constitution sets basic qualifications that are required for the presidency. Other qualifications reflect personal qualities that are expected of presidents. Many Americans over the age of 35 can meet the constitutional requirements for the presidency, but very few people can meet the informal requirements.

Constitutional Requirements

In Article II, Section 1, the Constitution defines the formal requirements for the presidency.[1] 📖 The president must be a natural-born citizen of the United States, at least 35 years old, and a resident of the United States for at least 14 years before taking office. The same requirements apply to the vice president.

Government Experience

Many other qualities are necessary for a person to have a real chance of becoming president. Experience in government is an unwritten but important qualification. Since 1868, for example, only five major-party candidates had no previous political experience, with Dwight D. Eisenhower as the most recent example. Since 1900, candidates who have served as U.S. senators or state governors have won the presidential nomination the most often. This makes sense since a political career gives someone the chance to form the alliances necessary to be nominated, as well as the name recognition that is necessary to win votes. **C**

📖 See the following footnoted materials in the **Reference Handbook:**
1. The Constitution, pages R42–R67.

Making a Difference

In 1996 Eugene Lang received the Presidential Medal of Freedom. President Bill Clinton presented the nation's highest civilian award to Lang and 10 other Americans for their contributions. Lang's contribution is fulfilling students' dreams.

In 1981 he visited his old elementary school in East Harlem. When he met with the sixth-grade students, he made them a promise. If they finished high school, he would pay for their college educations. The motivation worked, with 75 percent of the class graduating or earning their equivalency certificates. A few years later, Lang started the "I Have a Dream" Foundation, named for Martin Luther King, Jr.'s, famous "I Have a Dream" speech. The program provides money to send underprivileged young people to college.

In June 1987, Lang attended graduation ceremonies for the first students to come through the program. One of them, Aristedes Alvarado, told Lang he was worried about making it at the college where he had been accepted. Lang told him, "'Aristedes, you're a dreamer, dreamers can do anything.'" Today, the "I Have a Dream" program has spread to 59 cities and includes more than 15,000 students.

" . . . dreamers can do anything."
—Eugene Lang

C Critical Thinking

Making Inferences Ask: Why do you think the president is elected rather than appointed by Congress? *(The president should serve as a check on the legislature. If Congress appointed the president, this would erode the separation of powers among the three branches of government.)* **AL**

Making a Difference

Eugene M. Lang The national "I Have a Dream" Foundation (IHAD) in New York supports local IHAD projects, which adopt entire grades from elementary schools or entire age groups from public housing developments. Each local project provides individualized academic, cultural, and recreational activities for 10 to 12 years. IHAD's goal is to see that every Dreamer graduates from high school as a functional, literate person, prepared for employment or further education.

Activity Have students use IHAD's home page at www.ihad.org to find out how individual projects are funded and how a young person can become a Dreamer.

Hands-On Chapter Project
Step 1

The Role of the Cabinet

Step 1: Researching the Cabinet The class will research the president's cabinet to learn about the various heads of executive departments.

Directions Tell students that later in the chapter, they will learn about the people who advise the president. In this step of the project, they will use books and Internet sources to identify and record the positions in the cabinet.

Before they begin, explain the use of the title *secretary* and the meaning of the word *cabinet* in this context.

Identifying Have students use library books or Internet sources such as www.whitehouse.gov/government/cabinet.html to learn about the 15 cabinet positions. Tell students to list the executive departments and the person who currently heads each department. **OL AL**

(Chapter Project continued in Section 2.)

Government ONLINE

Objectives and answers to the Student Web Activity can be found in the **Web Activity Lesson Plan** at glencoe.com. Enter *QuickPass*™ code USG9085c8T.

R Reading Strategy

Making Connections Ask:
What American ideal does this widening field of presidential candidates reflect? *(equal opportunity for all, regardless of race, religion, or gender)* **AL**

Did You Know?

In the 1800s, the president received a salary of $25,000 per year and paid for everything except for the maintenance of the White House. By the twentieth century the president paid only his valet, his wife's maid, and any child care providers his children might need. Today the White House staff are federal employees, but they serve at the pleasure of the president, without the job protection of the civil service.

Differentiated Instruction

Importance of Money

Running for the presidency demands large amounts of money—from supporters and from one's own finances. Paying for television time, hiring campaign staff and consultants, and sending out mailings costs tens of millions of dollars.

The figures for expenditures for the 2008 presidential campaign demonstrate how important it is that a candidate have access to huge sums of money. The Federal Elections Commission (FEC) tracks campaign spending based on reports required by the candidates. According to the FEC, individual contributions alone tracked through June of 2008 were as follows:

- $269,985,803 for the top four Republican candidates
- $588,443,633 for the top four Democratic candidates

Personal wealth is a great asset for any candidate as well. Governor Mitt Romney spent approximately $44 million of his own money on his campaign in 2008.

The Bipartisan Campaign Reform Act (BCRA) of 2002 attempted to reform campaign fundraising. It adjusted limits on the amount of money candidates can receive from individual donors; it also described how political parties could spend **funds** during a campaign. The BCRA allows presidential candidates to accept public financing if they agree to limit their spending—$37.3 million

Historic Victory Barack Obama, with wife Michelle and daughters, celebrating his election in November 2008 as the first African American president in the nation's history.

Government ONLINE

Student Web Activity Visit glencoe.com and enter *QuickPass*™ code USG9822c8. Click on Student Web Activity and complete the activity about the president and vice president.

for the primaries and $74.6 million for the general election. In 2008 Republican John McCain accepted public funding and was thus limited in his spending. Democrat Barack Obama turned down public financing and raised much more money from private sources.

Political Beliefs

Extremely liberal or conservative candidates have little chance of being elected, and the major parties usually choose candidates who are moderate. Exceptions do occur. In 1964 Barry Goldwater, a very conservative Republican, became his party's nominee for the presidency. In 1972 a very liberal Democrat, George McGovern, won his party's nomination. Both men were defeated.

Personal Characteristics

What kind of person becomes president? In the past, most presidents have come from northern European backgrounds. A few have been from poor families—Abraham Lincoln, Harry S. Truman, and Bill Clinton, for example. Several have come from wealthy families like Franklin D. Roosevelt and John F. Kennedy, but most have been middle class. Most presidents have been male, white, married, Protestant, and financially successful. John F. Kennedy, elected in 1960, was the first Roman Catholic president. A historic milestone was reached in 2008, when the two leading Democratic candidates were a woman, Senator Hillary Clinton, and an African American, Senator Barack Obama. When Obama became the first African American president, it represented a sea of change in American politics. A racial barrier had been broken. In his campaign, Obama, who grew up in Hawaii and Indonesia, stressed the need for unity among all ethnic, racial, and religious groups.

Personal Growth

When politicians hold the office of president, it underscores their personal strengths and weaknesses. Harry S. Truman, who became president

---

Activity: Multiple Learning Styles

Intrapersonal Discuss the role of today's vice president. Ask the following questions:
- What are the constitutional duties of the vice president?
- What might be some informal or implied duties of the vice president?
- Why would a presidential candidate choose a particular person as a running mate?

Have each student write a personal résumé detailing experiences and character traits that would convince the president to choose that student as a vice-presidential running mate. Encourage students to research the incumbent president's stand on current issues and to write a cover letter matching their abilities to the president's needs. **OL** after Roosevelt died, explained why the office tests one's strength of character:

> *The presidency of the United States carries with it a responsibility so personal as to be without parallel. . . . No one can make decisions for him. . . . Even those closest to him . . . never know all the reasons why he does certain things and why he comes to certain conclusions. To be President of the United States is to be lonely, very lonely at times of great decisions.*
>
> —Harry S. Truman

Although he had never expected to reach the Oval Office, Truman went on to become a successful president. He learned firsthand about the difficult decisions a president faces, having had to make the decision to drop atomic bombs on Japan and to commit the nation to war in Korea. Truman was known for the motto displayed on his desk in the White House: "The Buck Stops Here."

Presidential Succession

Eight presidents have died in office. Four were assassinated, and four died of natural causes. After John F. Kennedy was assassinated in 1963, the nation realized that the Constitution's rules for **presidential succession** were inadequate.[1]

In 1967 the Twenty-fifth Amendment was ratified to clarify the succession to the presidency and the vice presidency.

> *Section 1. In case of the removal of the President from office or of his death or resignation, the Vice President shall become President.*
>
> *Section 2. Whenever there is a vacancy in the office of the Vice President, the President shall nominate a Vice President who shall take office upon confirmation by a majority vote of both Houses of Congress.*
>
> —Twenty-fifth Amendment, 1967

The amendment was first applied in 1973 when Spiro Agnew resigned as President Richard Nixon's vice president. Nixon then nominated Gerald Ford as vice president, and Congress approved the nomination. Less than a year later, when President Nixon resigned due to the Watergate scandal,

Ford became president. Ford then nominated Nelson Rockefeller as vice president, and Congress again approved the nomination. These events marked the only time in American history that neither the president nor the vice president was elected.

What would happen if the offices of president and vice president both became vacant at the same time? The Succession Act of 1947 established the order of presidential succession. According to this law, the next in line for the presidency is the Speaker of the House. The president pro tempore of the Senate follows the Speaker. Next in line are the cabinet officers, starting with the secretary of state.

---

[1] See the following footnoted materials in the **Reference Handbook:**
1. *The Constitution*, pages R42–R67.

Line of Presidential Succession

- ★ Vice President
- ★ Speaker of the House
- ★ President pro tempore of the Senate
- ★ Secretary of State
- ★ Secretary of the Treasury
- ★ Secretary of Defense
- ★ Attorney General
- ★ Secretary of the Interior
- ★ Secretary of Agriculture
- ★ Secretary of Commerce
- ★ Secretary of Labor
- ★ Secretary of Health and Human Services
- ★ Secretary of Housing and Urban Development
- ★ Secretary of Transportation
- ★ Secretary of Energy
- ★ Secretary of Education
- ★ Secretary of Veterans Affairs
- ★ Secretary of Homeland Security

Source: thomas.loc.gov.

Critical Thinking The Succession Act of 1947 established the order of succession if the offices of the president and vice president are vacant at the same time. Why do you think the secretaries of state and treasury were put ahead of other cabinet officers?

R **Reading Strategy**

Analyzing Primary Sources Have students read the quote from Harry S. Truman. **Ask:** Why do you think Truman felt this way about the presidency? Do you agree or disagree? (*Answers may include the view that no one else could understand the pressure that such responsibility brings.*) **OL**

D **Differentiated Instruction**

Kinesthetic Use the chart to assign roles to students for each office listed. Ask those students to assemble in the order in which they would succeed the president. Then allow the other students to correct any misplaced successors. **Ask:** What is the likelihood that the secretary of one of the more recently created cabinet departments will become president? (*The odds are extremely slim.*) **BL**

Critical Thinking

Answer: They were the first cabinet departments created.

Additional Support

Activity: Interdisciplinary Connection

Business How do the president's salary and responsibilities compare to those of a chief executive officer (CEO) in the private sector? Have students make a chart with the following headings: Name, Company, Salary, Bonuses, Travel, Health Care, Housing, and Miscellaneous. Then have students use the Internet to find information about the five highest-paid CEOs in the United States and complete the chart. Allow students to share information. Discuss with the class how the president's compensation compares to that of these CEOs, considering the responsibilities each job requires. **Ask:** Do you think the president's compensation is sufficient for the job's responsibilities? **OL**

Caption Answer: the Twenty-fifth Amendment

R Reading Strategy

Questioning Ask: What would happen if the president were temporarily unconscious because of injury or illness? *(The vice president would assume the president's responsibilities until the president was well again.)* **BL**

C Critical Thinking

Drawing Conclusions Ask: What was the purpose of the Twenty-fifth Amendment? *(It clarified the succession to the presidency and the vice presidency.)* **OL**

Did You Know?

In 1989 Dan Quayle became the first vice president to be sworn in by a woman, Sandra Day O'Connor, the first female justice of the Supreme Court. Quayle served as vice president from 1989 to 1993 under President George H.W. Bush.

Differentiated Instruction

Participating in Government Activities, p. 15

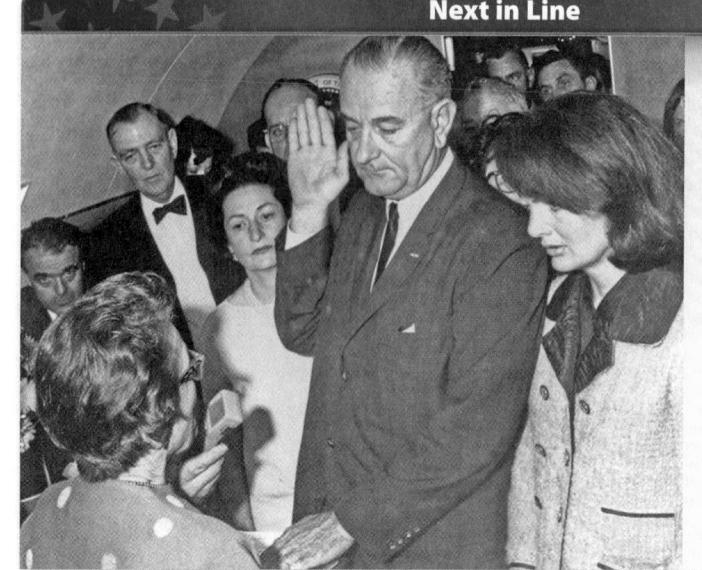

Next in Line

Aftermath of Assassination On November 22, 1963, after President Kennedy was shot, Vice President Lyndon B. Johnson was sworn into the presidency onboard *Air Force One* in Dallas. First Lady Jacqueline Kennedy is to the right of him. His wife, Lady Bird Johnson, is to his left. *Which amendment established the line of succession to the nation's highest office?*

The other 14 department heads follow in the order in which Congress created the departments.

Presidential Disability

What happens if a president becomes seriously disabled while in office? Several presidents have not been able to fulfill their responsibilities. President James Garfield lingered between life and death for 80 days after he was shot in 1881, but no one was officially named to fulfill his duties. Just after World War I, a stroke disabled President Woodrow Wilson—his wife often performed his duties. In 1955 President Dwight D. Eisenhower had a heart attack. He was completely disabled for several days and had limited energy for several months. During that time, his assistants ran the executive branch.

The Twenty-fifth Amendment describes what should be done when a president is disabled. It provides that the vice president becomes acting president under one of two conditions: if the president informs Congress of an inability to perform in office and, second, if the vice president and a majority of the cabinet or another legally authorized body informs the Congress that the president is disabled. This second provision takes effect when a disabled president is unwilling or unable to inform Congress of a disabling condition.

The Twenty-fifth Amendment also spells out how a president can resume the powers and duties of the office. This can happen at any time if the president informs Congress that a disability no longer exists. If, however, the vice president and a majority of the cabinet or another authorized body think the president has not **recovered,** Congress must settle the dispute within 21 days. The president can resume office unless two-thirds of the Congress agrees with the vice president's position.

The Vice President's Role

The Constitution gives the vice president only two duties. First, the vice president presides over the Senate and votes in that body in case of a tie. Most vice presidents spend very little time in this job. Second, under the Twenty-fifth Amendment, the vice president helps decide whether the president is disabled and acts as president should that happen. Fourteen vice presidents have become president. Of these, nine vice presidents have succeeded to the office upon the death or resignation of the president.

Modern Responsibilities

A vice president's work and power can be much greater than the narrow formal responsibilities mentioned in the Constitution. It all depends upon the duties the president assigns. As Hubert Humphrey, Lyndon B. Johnson's vice president,

Presidential Poll

Objective: To get an idea of the president's popularity in your area

Focus/Teach: Have students read the Background and discuss the Questions to Consider.

Assess: Have students conduct the poll, tabulate their results, and compare their findings.

Close: Complete and discuss the Follow-Up activity. Were the results surprising?

Differentiated Instruction Strategies

BL Have students brainstorm different ways to present their poll results.

AL Discuss with students what they believe is a good-sized sample.

ELL Explain to students why a large, random sample is essential for getting accurate polling results.

said, "The only authority he [the Vice President] has is what the President gives him. He who giveth can taketh away."

Before the Eisenhower administration (1953–1961), presidents generally ignored their vice presidents. The vice presidency was almost a purely ceremonial office, with vice presidents attending events in place of the president and making goodwill tours to foreign countries.

Today, a vice president's role is much more significant. Vice presidents now often participate in policy meetings or undertake special assignments, such as giving speeches to promote the president's policies, or taking on a project of their own interest, such as Al Gore's work on streamlining the bureaucracy. Often vice presidents are involved not merely in ceremonial visits abroad but in serious diplomatic efforts. Vice presidents are also members of the National Security Council and take part in its policy deliberations.

During the presidency of George W. Bush, his vice president, Richard Cheney, had greater responsibility than most vice presidents. Some political analysts even claimed he was the real policymaker during this administration. Cheney consulted closely with President Bush and represented him in cabinet meetings with cabinet officers, legislators, and foreign dignitaries. One senator reported the president as saying: "When you're talking to Dick Cheney, you're talking to me. When Dick Cheney's talking, it's me talking." Whether the Bush-Cheney model is followed in future presidencies remains to be seen.

Executive Powers John Adams, president from 1797 to 1801, was famously argumentative with his vice president, Thomas Jefferson, but then Jefferson and he were from different parties. *What does this tell you about the Framers' view of political parties?*

SECTION 1 Review

Vocabulary

1. **Explain** the significance of: compensation, presidential succession.

Main Ideas

2. **Examining** What did the Twenty-second and Twenty-fifth Amendments establish?

3. **Identifying** Who are the first four officers in the line of succession to the presidency?

Critical Thinking

4. **Drawing Conclusions** Why do you think presidential candidates who represent moderate views usually win elections?

5. **Categorizing** Using a graphic organizer like the one below, show three constitutional requirements and three informal requirements of a president.

Constitutional	Informal
1.	
2.	
3.	

Writing About Government

6. **Expository Writing** Conduct a survey using the following questions: In your opinion, when will the United States have its first female president? Tabulate the results on graphs and summarize your findings in a one-page report.

W **Writing Support**

Expository Writing Read the following quote from John Adams to students: "I am Vice President. In this I am nothing, but I may be everything." Then have students write a paragraph explaining what they think Adams meant by this statement. *(The vice president does not have much official power, but if he became president, he would have great power.)* **OL AL**

Caption Answer: The Framers did not want or anticipate political parties.

Assess

Assign the Section 1 Assessment as homework or as an in-class activity, or have students take Section Quiz 8-1 from *Section Quizzes and Chapter Tests*.

Close

Determining Importance Challenge students to choose the most important quality for a vice president. Tally students' choices on the board. **OL**

Section 1 Review

Answers

1. All definitions can be found in the section and the Glossary.
2. The Twenty-second and Twenty-fifth Amendments established a two-term limit for the U.S. presidency and a presidential order of succession, respectively.
3. vice president, Speaker of the House, president pro tempore of the Senate, secretary of state
4. Answers will vary but should point out that most voters hold moderate views; if candidates express extreme views, they may isolate themselves from the majority of voters.
5. Answers might include: Constitutional—natural-born citizen of United States; at least 35 years old; U.S. resident for 14 years. Informal—experience in government; moderate position on most issues; access to large amounts of money.
6. Students' graphs will vary but should include numbers and dates for the first female president. Students should write a brief analysis of the results of their public opinion surveys.

Focus

Bellringer

Section Focus Transparencies 8-2

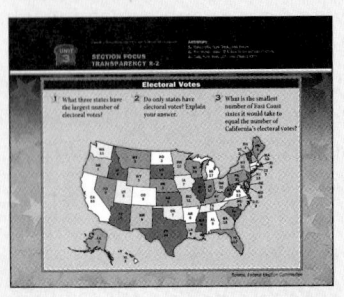

Reader's Guide

Answers to Graphic: winner takes all, third-party candidates, election by the House of Representatives

Resource Manager

Electing the President

Reader's Guide

Content Vocabulary
★ elector (p. 220)
★ electoral vote (p. 220)

Academic Vocabulary
★ majority (p. 221)
★ margin (p. 222)
★ alternative (p. 224)

Reading Strategy
Complete a graphic organizer similar to the one below to list the weaknesses of the Electoral College system.

Weaknesses of the Electoral College

Issues in the News

As Americans know from the controversial 2000 election, our system for choosing a president is intricate. In 2000 Al Gore, the winner of the popular vote, lost the election to George W. Bush, who won the Electoral College vote. Early in our history, an even more unusual situation occurred. In 1824 no candidate received a majority of the popular vote or the Electoral College vote, so the House of Representatives made the choice. It chose John Quincy Adams, despite the fact that Andrew Jackson had the highest percentage of the popular and Electoral College vote, though not a majority vote. Jackson said the outcome was the result of a "corrupt bargain."

▶ In 1824 John Quincy Adams was chosen as the sixth president by the House of Representatives.

The method for selecting the president was debated at length during the Constitutional Convention. At first, the Founders proposed that the Congress choose the president. They gave up this idea, however, because it violated the principle of separation of powers—if Congress chose the president, it could control the executive branch.

The Founders then turned to the idea of a direct vote by the people, but these educated men feared that citizens might make poor choices. In colonial times, no national news media, radio, or television existed so candidates were almost unknown to voters. Some leaders also believed that candidates who were popular with average voters might not be the best presidents.

After weeks of debate, the Founders settled on a compromise that Alexander Hamilton introduced.

It set up the Electoral College, which elected the president indirectly. With a few changes, that system is still in use today.

The Original System

Article II, Section 1, established the Electoral College.[1] 📖 Each state legislature would set up a method for choosing people who would be the electors. (The number of electors for a state would equal its number of senators and representatives in Congress.) At election time, the **electors** would meet in their state and cast their **electoral vote** for president. In early elections, the people did not vote for president.

📖 See the following footnoted materials in the **Reference Handbook:**
1. The Constitution, pages R42–R67.

R Reading Strategies	**C** Critical Thinking	**D** Differentiated Instruction	**W** Writing Support	**S** Skill Practice
Teacher Edition • Summarizing, p. 221 • Identifying, p. 226 **Additional Resources** • Guid. Read. Act., p. 30 • Quizzes/Tests, p. 92	**Teacher Edition** • Identifying Alternatives, p. 223 • Analyzing Information, p. 224 **Additional Resources** • Read. Essen., pp. 86–88	**Additional Resources** • Foldables, p. 51 • Hist. Docs. and Speeches, p. 8	**Teacher Edition** • Personal Writing, p. 224 **Additional Resources** • Part. in Gov. Act., pp. 15–16	**Teacher Edition** • Researching, p. 225 **Additional Resources** • Skill Reinforce. Act., p. 8

Electoral votes from all the states would be counted in a joint session of Congress. The candidate receiving a **majority** would become president, and the candidate with the second-highest number—also a majority—would become vice president. In case of a tie, or if no one received a majority, the House of Representatives would choose the president or vice president, with each state having one vote.

As expected, the Electoral College unanimously chose George Washington as the nation's first president in 1789 and again in 1792. After President Washington retired, however, parties began to play an important role in elections. They had an unexpected and profound impact on the Electoral College system.

The Impact of Political Parties

By 1800, two national parties had formed: the Federalists and the Democratic-Republicans. Each party nominated its own candidate for president and vice president. Each party also nominated candidates for electors in every state. It was understood that if they were chosen, these electors would vote for their party's candidates.

In the election of 1800, the Democratic-Republicans won a majority of electoral votes. As agreed, each Democratic-Republican elector cast one vote for each of the party's candidates—Thomas Jefferson and Aaron Burr, but not specifying which office each man was to fill. Most electors wanted Jefferson to be president, but both Jefferson and Burr received 73 votes. The tie meant that the House of Representatives had to decide the winner.

The opposing party, the Federalists, controlled the House of Representatives. Popular opinion in the nation supported Jefferson, but many Federalists in the House favored Burr. The House debated day and night for six days. Thirty-six ballots were taken before Jefferson was finally elected president and Burr vice president. The 1800 election clearly demonstrated the need for a change in the rules before the next election.

To solve the problem, the Twelfth Amendment was added to the Constitution in 1804. It requires that the electors cast separate ballots for president and vice president. The amendment also provides that if no candidate receives a majority of the electoral votes, the House chooses from the three candidates who have the largest number of electoral

The First President

Political Symbols Frederick Kemmelmeyer created this reverential painting to honor Washington, our nation's only unanimously elected president. *What symbols did the artist use in this painting, and how do they convey his attitude toward Washington?*

votes. If no candidate for vice president gets a majority of electoral votes, the Senate chooses from the top two candidates for vice president.

In the 1820s, states began to place presidential candidates on the ballot. Since then political parties have chosen electors by popular vote. Parties also changed their method of nominating presidential candidates, giving the people more of a voice. The Electoral College system adapted to the growth of democracy.

The Electoral College System Today

The Electoral College is still the method for choosing the president and vice president of the United States. Parties choose their nominees for president in conventions held in late summer. Voters cast their ballots for president every four years

Teach

R Reading Strategy

Summarizing Ask students to summarize how the Electoral College system "adapted to the growth of democracy." *(The role of electors has been diminished as the U.S. political system has become more democratic.)* **OL**

Caption Answer: The artist used symbols including an eagle, stars, flags, the Declaration of Independence, and bugles to signify a great respect for the first president and his achievements.

Did You Know?

Political cartoonist Thomas Nast popularized the donkey and elephant as national political party symbols in *Harper's Weekly* in the late 1870s.

Additional Support

Activity: Collaborative Learning

Creating a Map Organize the class into groups of three to create maps of presidential election results. Assign each group an election to research. Then have students in each group choose from the following tasks: research the popular and electoral vote for each state; draw an outline map of the United States on poster board to show the electoral and/or popular vote; and determine the major campaign issues. Have members work together to fill in the popular and electoral vote on the map and brainstorm reasons for these election results. Have each group write a paragraph explaining the election results. Ask each group to present the completed poster and paragraph to the class. Discuss the results of each election. **ELL**

Linking Past & Present

Election by Commission The 1876 presidential election was the only time the presidency was decided by a special commission. Democrat Samuel J. Tilden won the popular vote and needed only 1 more electoral vote to capture the presidency. Two sets of election returns existed—one from the Democrats and one from the Republicans. Unable to decide, Congress established a 15-member, "nonpartisan" commission, which accepted the Republicans' count, giving Rutherford B. Hayes the presidency.

Differentiated Instruction

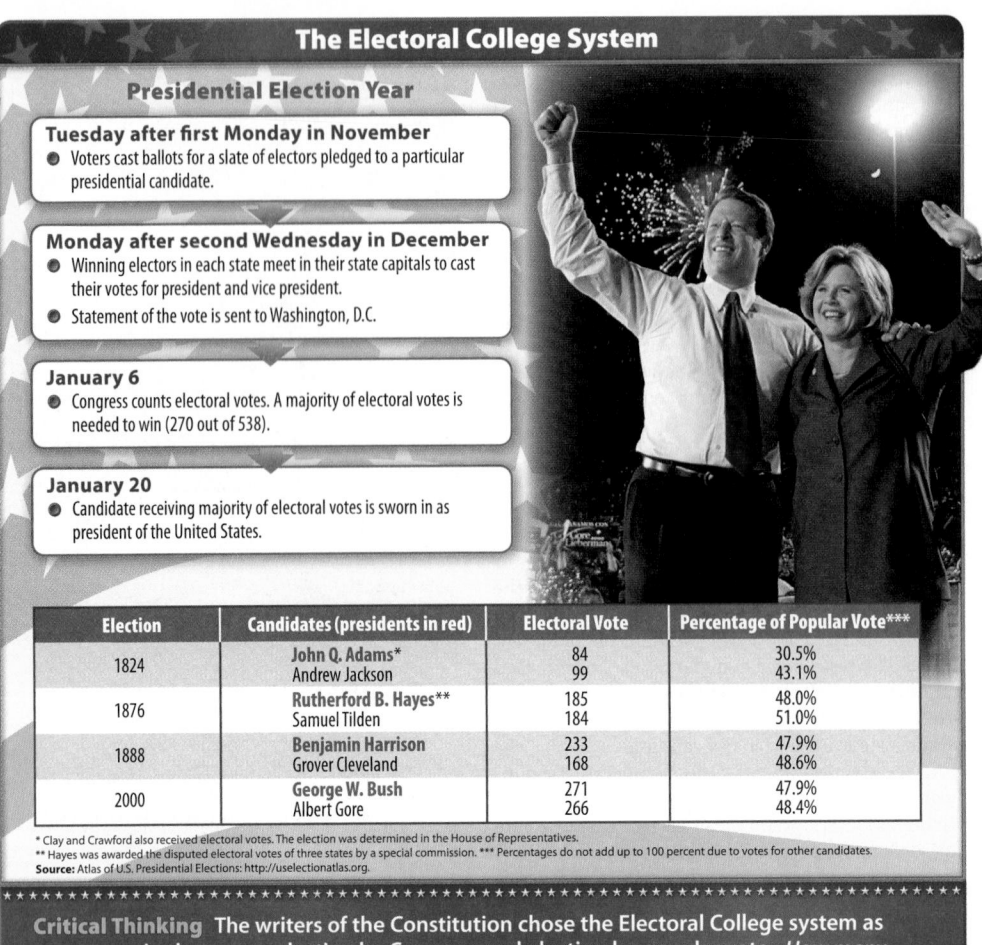

The Electoral College System

Presidential Election Year

Tuesday after first Monday in November
● Voters cast ballots for a slate of electors pledged to a particular presidential candidate.

Monday after second Wednesday in December
● Winning electors in each state meet in their state capitals to cast their votes for president and vice president.
● Statement of the vote is sent to Washington, D.C.

January 6
● Congress counts electoral votes. A majority of electoral votes is needed to win (270 out of 538).

January 20
● Candidate receiving majority of electoral votes is sworn in as president of the United States.

Election	Candidates (presidents in red)	Electoral Vote	Percentage of Popular Vote***
1824	John Q. Adams* Andrew Jackson	84 99	30.5% 43.1%
1876	Rutherford B. Hayes** Samuel Tilden	185 184	48.0% 51.0%
1888	Benjamin Harrison Grover Cleveland	233 168	47.9% 48.6%
2000	George W. Bush Albert Gore	271 266	47.9% 48.4%

* Clay and Crawford also received electoral votes. The election was determined in the House of Representatives.
** Hayes was awarded the disputed electoral votes of three states by a special commission. *** Percentages do not add up to 100 percent due to votes for other candidates.
Source: Atlas of U.S. Presidential Elections: http://uselectionatlas.org.

Critical Thinking The writers of the Constitution chose the Electoral College system as a compromise between selection by Congress and election by popular vote. *How many weeks pass between a presidential election and inauguration? Is this time necessary? Why?*

(2000, 2004, 2008, and so on) on the Tuesday after the first Monday in November. While the candidates' names are printed on the ballot, it is important to understand that voters are not voting directly for president and vice president. Rather, American citizens are voting for all of their party's electors—the slate of electors—in their state. In December, these electors cast the official vote for president and vice president. Thus, a vote for the Democratic candidate is a vote for the Democratic electors, and a vote for the Republican candidate is a vote for the Republican electors.

The Electoral College includes 538 electors—a number determined by the total of House and Senate members plus 3 for the District of Columbia. Each state has as many electors as it has senators and representatives in Congress. Wyoming with 1 representative and 2 senators has 3 electoral votes. California, the most populous state, with 53 representatives and 2 senators has 55 electoral votes.

To be elected president or vice president, a candidate must win at least 270 of the 538 votes. The Electoral College is a winner-take-all system with the exception of Maine and Nebraska. The party whose candidate receives the largest popular vote in any state wins all its electoral votes even if the **margin** of victory is only a single popular vote.

Activity: Multiple Learning Styles

Verbal/Linguistic Historically, in the Inaugural Address the president speaks words of encouragement, inspiration, and healing to the American people. Presidents often ask notable literary figures to read a poem or tell a story to help set the tone for their new administration. Have students imagine that they have been asked by the president-elect to write a poem to read at the inauguration. Encourage students to consider the present state of the country and decide what would encourage and inspire the American people. After students have written their poems, call on volunteers to do dramatic readings for the class. **OL**

The winning presidential candidate is usually announced on the same evening as the popular election because popular-vote counts indicate who won each state. The formal election by the Electoral College, however, begins on the Monday following the second Wednesday in December when the electors meet in each state capital and cast their ballots. The electoral ballots from each state are sealed and mailed to the president of the Senate for a formal count. On January 6, both houses of Congress meet in the House of Representatives to open and count the ballots. Congress then officially declares the winning president.

Most states do not legally require electors to vote for the candidate who wins the popular vote, but electors usually do so. A few electors, however, have ignored this tradition. In 1976 an elector from the state of Washington voted for Ronald Reagan, even though Gerald Ford won the majority of popular votes in the state. In 2004 an elector from Minnesota voted for John Edwards, the Democratic vice presidential candidate, for both president and vice president. Over the years, nine other electors have broken with custom.

Electoral College Issues

The Electoral College system works well in most elections. However, the call for reform is heard **C** after every closely contested election. Critics point to three major weaknesses in the system that could affect the outcome of an election.

Winner Take All

In all but two states, Maine and Nebraska, if a candidate wins the largest number of popular votes, that person receives all the state's electoral votes. Critics argue that this system is unfair to those who voted for a losing candidate. For example, in 1992 more than 2 million Texans voted for Bill Clinton, but he did not receive any of Texas's electoral votes.

The winner-take-all system makes it possible for a candidate who loses the popular vote to win the electoral vote. This usually happens when a candidate wins several large states by narrow margins. Four times in American history, the candidate who lost the popular vote won the election: in the elections of John Quincy Adams in 1824, Rutherford B.

C Critical Thinking

Identifying Alternatives
Organize the class into two groups. Have one group determine the advantages of the Electoral College system and the other group determine the disadvantages. Allow time for each group to brainstorm and make a list. Discuss within each group how to reform, abolish, or retain the present system. Then have each group share its conclusions with the other group. Take a class vote on whether the Electoral College system should be retained, abolished, or reformed. **OL**

Government and You

Electing Your President

Young people are less likely to vote than any other age group. However, Music Television (MTV) and Rock the Vote hope to draw more young voters into the political process.

Rock the Vote is a nonprofit organization dedicated to educating and involving young people. It conducts voter registration drives at concerts and on radio stations. It can even register voters over the Internet.

During presidential campaigns, Rock the Vote and MTV distribute a free election guide for young voters at record stores across the nation. MTV also airs a voter education series called *Choose or Lose*. MTV personalities interview the candidates about issues that are of interest to young voters. Televised MTV forums allow young people to express their concerns directly to the candidates. MTV Online makes election information available on the Internet. The presidential candidates have Internet home pages that you also can contact for information.

▼ The Rock the Vote bus

Participating IN GOVERNMENT ACTIVITY

Measuring Success How successful was Rock the Vote in the last presidential election? Gather information through magazine articles in *Readers' Guide to Periodical Literature*. Create a graphic reflecting your findings.

Government and You

More About Rock the Vote
In response to what they considered political attacks on freedom of speech and artistic expression, members of the recording industry founded Rock the Vote in 1990. This group focused on registering young people to vote and getting them to participate in the political process. In 1991 the organization expanded, advocating legislation that would have a positive effect on 18- to 24-year olds.

Additional Support

Extending the Content

Electors In the beginning of the United States, members of the Electoral College were usually appointed by the state legislatures. By 1836, the choosing of electors by popular vote had become the rule in every state except South Carolina. Each elector was listed on the ballot; as the population grew, the list became long and unwieldy. In 1892 many states grouped electors by political party, requiring only a single vote. The names of presidential candidates began to appear on ballots along with the electors in 1897. A few years later, because of space limitations on voting machines, Iowa and Nebraska set the precedent of listing only the presidential and vice-presidential candidates' names, dropping the electors' names completely. A vote for a party's candidate was taken as a vote for the electors of that party.

Caption Answer: to help facilitate a smooth and peaceful transition of power

R Reading Strategy

Identifying Ask: What do you think is the purpose of an Inaugural Address? *(Answers may include that an Inaugural Address gives insight into the new president's policies and focuses on the current state of the country.)* **OL**

Assess

Assign the Section 2 Assessment as homework or as an in-class activity, or have students take Section Quiz 8-2 from *Section Quizzes and Chapter Tests.*

Close

Predicting Have students predict the future of the Electoral College in presidential elections. **OL**

Section 2 Review

Peaceful Succession Above, Franklin D. Roosevelt is congratulated by Herbert Hoover in 1933; at left, Ronald Reagan congratulates the new president, George H.W. Bush. *Why do you think these cordial greetings are important?*

the Capitol for the inauguration when the chief justice administers the oath of office. The new president then gives an Inaugural Address.

Several Inaugural Addresses have become part of the nation's heritage. During the Great Depression, Franklin D. Roosevelt lifted American spirits with the words: "The only thing we have to fear is fear itself." In 1961 John F. Kennedy inspired a generation when he said: "Ask not what your country can do for you—ask what you can do for your country." Members of Congress, foreign diplomats, and thousands of citizens attend the inauguration. After the speech, a parade goes from the Capitol to the White House. That evening parties are held to celebrate the new administration and to thank political supporters.

SECTION 2 Review

Vocabulary

1. **Explain** the significance of: elector, electoral vote.

Main Ideas

2. **Analyzing** Why do presidential candidates spend more time in states with large populations?

3. **Explaining** What does the phrase "winner take all" mean in presidential elections?

Critical Thinking

4. **Evaluating** In judging the Electoral College, how important is it to know that on several occasions an elector broke with custom and voted independently?

5. **Organizing** Using a graphic organizer such as the one below, describe the ceremonial events that usually occur when a new president takes office.

Writing About Government

6. **Persuasive Writing** Imagine that you are a member of an interest group. Choose a position for your group: keep the Electoral College or abolish it. Then write a persuasive speech explaining your position.

226 UNIT 3: *The Executive Branch*

Answers

1. All definitions can be found in the section and the Glossary.
2. States with large populations have more electoral votes, and the candidate with the most popular votes in a given state wins all of that state's electoral votes.
3. The party whose candidate wins the most popular votes in a state takes all of that state's electoral votes
4. Answers should point out that in most states, electors are not bound by law to vote for the winner of the popular vote and therefore can affect the election outcome if enough electors break with custom. Though this has happened in the past, it has never made a difference in the outcome of an election.
5. Answers might include: inaugural speech, oath of office; parade to the White House; inaugural parties.
6. Students' speeches should reflect one of the following positions on the Electoral College: keep it, abolish it, or change it.

Should the Electoral College Be Replaced?

Americans do not vote directly for the president. Instead, voters in the states (and the district of Washington, D.C.) choose a number of representatives to the Electoral College who then cast their votes for president. A state's number of electoral votes is equal to the total of its U.S. representatives plus its two senators; thus, it reflects state population. In 2000 Texas had 32 votes, while Delaware and Wyoming had 3. If only a bare majority—51 percent—of Texas voters voted for Bush, he still would have received <u>all</u> 32 electoral votes. Is this system fair, or should the Electoral College be replaced?

The Impact of Voting Systems on Large and Small States*		
	Electoral College System	Popular Election Strength (Population)
12 Plains & Southwest States**	60 votes	25,650,000
CA	54	33,872,000
NY	33	18,977,000
Florida	25	15,983,000
Texas	32	20,852,000

* Figures represent 2000 census year.
**Arizona, Colorado, Idaho, Kansas, Montana, Nebraska, Nevada, North Dakota, Oklahoma, South Dakota, Utah, Wyoming. Typically, these states vote for the same party in a presidential election, indicating their shared political identity.

YES

The Electoral College should be abolished. It is undemocratic because a candidate can win even if he or she did not get a majority of the popular vote. This is exactly what happened in the 2000 election: George W. Bush had 271 electoral votes, but only 47.87 percent of the popular vote compared to Al Gore's 48.38 percent (Gore had 266 electoral votes.) In addition to the problem with the current system, a third-party candidate could receive a significant number of votes nationally yet not have a single electoral vote to show for it. This weakens the expression of alternative positions in our democracy.

NO

We should keep the Electoral College because it does what the Founders intended—it balances the interests of different regions and prevents a few large states or urban areas from choosing the president. In the table above, for example, the electoral system gives the 12 states of the Plains and the Southwest 60 votes—more than California, and more than Florida and New York together, or Florida and Texas together. By contrast, under a direct election system, the voting power of these 12 states would be smaller than the single state of California or of Florida and New York, or Florida and Texas. The Electoral College allows candidates to pay attention to smaller states and to all regions of the United States.

Debating the Issue

1. **Explaining** What determines the number of electoral votes a state has?

2. **Analyzing** How does the NO position make its case that the current system protects a minority against majority rule?

3. **Evaluating** With which opinion do you tend to agree? Explain your reasoning.

Debating the Issue Answers

1. population
2. by pointing out that 12 Plains and Southwestern states can exercise their unity of regional interests to outweigh two larger states (not possible under a direct election system)

3. Answers will vary, but students should support their argument logically and in their own words, not just repeating the text verbatim.

Teach

Setting Up the Debate

Applying Research Have students research the Electoral College on the Internet at www.uselectionatlas.org or www.fec.gov/pdf/eleccoll.pdf. **Ask:** What specific problems did the Framers want to avoid by choosing the Electoral College system? Did geographic considerations affect their decision? *(They did not want direct election by popular vote because they wanted to guard against a "mobocracy." Direct election would also favor large, densely populated cities and states. The large geographic area and lack of adequate transportation and communication made national campaigning impossible. Thus, electors were able to be more informed than most individual voters.)*

Evaluating Have students create a chart listing the advantages and disadvantages of both the Electoral College system and direct election of the president. Students' lists should be as specific as possible.

Concluding the Debate

Discuss these questions with students:

- Examine state-by-state maps of the 2000, 2004, and 2008 presidential elections online to see which states supported the Republican and which states supported the Democrat. Do these divisions confirm the Framers' idea that groups of states tend to vote for the same candidate?

- Do you think it is likely that the Electoral College will be abolished and direct election adopted instead? Why or why not?

Focus

Bellringer
Section Focus Transparencies
8-3

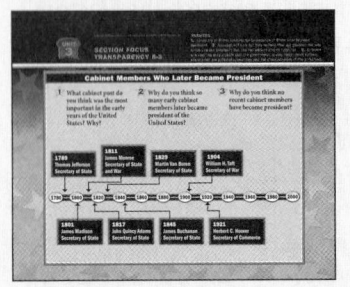

Reader's Guide

Answers to Graphic:
compatibility with department
ability to satisfy interest groups
administrative skills and
     experience
race, gender, and ethnic
     background

Resource
Manager

The Cabinet

Reader's Guide

Content Vocabulary
★ cabinet (p. 228)
★ leak (p. 230)

Academic Vocabulary
★ gender (p. 228)
★ media (p. 230)
★ relevant (p. 230)

Reading Strategy
Create a graphic organizer like the one below to list the major factors that a president must address when appointing cabinet members.

Major Factors

Issues in the News

In June 2002, President George W. Bush told the nation that a new cabinet department was essential because of its "titanic struggle against terror." The Department of Homeland Security combined multiple government agencies with a total workforce of almost 170,000 employees. In his address, Bush argued for a need to better coordinate department efforts: "We are now learning that before September 11, the suspicions and insights of some of our front-line agents did not get enough attention."

▲ Airport security was one of the first high-profile programs of the new Department of Homeland Security.

The Department of Homeland Security is the fifteenth cabinet-level department to be created in the executive branch. The earliest departments were created in 1789, soon after President George Washington's election: the Department of State, the Department of War, the Department of the Treasury, and the Attorney General's office. (See Chapter 10, Section 1, for more discussion of cabinet departments.)

President Washington met regularly with his department heads to get their advice on policy matters. The newspapers of the time called this group Washington's *cabinet*, the general term for the advisers around any head of state. The name stuck.

One of the first responsibilities of a president is to organize and staff the executive branch of government. In fact, the president-elect often has selected most of his nominees for cabinet appointments before taking office.

Today, the president appoints the secretaries that head the 15 major executive departments. Each appointee must be approved by the Senate. The 15 secretaries, the vice president, and several other top officials make up the **cabinet.** Cabinet secretaries advise the president, but they also serve as the administrators of large bureaucracies.

Selection of the Cabinet

In selecting their department heads, presidents must balance a great many political, social, and management considerations. Secretaries should have some credible expertise in the policy areas their departments will manage. Appointees must be acceptable to all groups that have political power. They should provide geographic balance as well as racial and **gender** representation. Patronage and party loyalty also are important.

R Reading Strategies	C Critical Thinking	D Differentiated Instruction	W Writing Support	S Skill Practice
Teacher Edition • Taking Notes, p. 231 **Additional Resources** • Guid. Read. Act., p. 31 • Quizzes/Tests, p. 93	**Teacher Edition** • Evaluating, p. 229 • Analyzing Information, p. 231 **Additional Resources** • Read. Essen., pp. 89–91	**Teacher Edition** • Interpersonal, p. 230 **Additional Resources** • Foldables, p. 51 • Source Readings, p. 8	**Teacher Edition** • Personal Writing, p. 229 **Additional Resources** • Inter. Poli. Cartoons, pp. 15–16	**Teacher Edition** • Researching, p. 232 **Additional Resources** • Reteaching Act., p. 8

Factors in Making Appointments

The selection of a president's cabinet is largely a political process. An appointee usually will have a background that is compatible with the department he or she will head. The secretary of the interior, for example, typically is someone from a western state who has experience in land policy and conservation issues. Generally, the secretary of housing and urban development (HUD) is usually from a large city and the secretary of agriculture is from a farm state. This qualification also can bring some geographic balance to the cabinet.

Equally important is the president's need to satisfy powerful interest groups that have a stake in a department's policies. The secretary of labor, therefore, generally is someone who is acceptable to labor unions. The secretary of commerce will have a good reputation with business and industry. The secretary of the treasury will often be a banker or someone with close ties to the financial community.

In addition, it is important that appointees have high-level administrative skills and experience. Cabinet officers are responsible for huge departments that employ thousands of people and spend billions of dollars each year. If inefficiency or scandal should result, blame will fall on the secretary and on the president.

As women and minority groups have gained political power, presidents have considered the race, gender, and ethnic background of candidates when making their appointments. In 1966 Lyndon B. Johnson named the first African American department secretary, Robert Weaver, to lead HUD. Franklin D. Roosevelt appointed the first woman to the cabinet, Secretary of Labor Frances Perkins, in 1933. Women in the cabinet remained rare until 1975, when President Gerald Ford appointed Carla Hills as HUD secretary. Since then, every president's cabinet has included women and African Americans. President Ronald Reagan named the first Latino, Lauro F. Cavazos, as secretary of education in 1988.

In 1997 President Bill Clinton appointed the first woman to the prestigious cabinet position of secretary of state. In fact, Clinton's cabinet became the most gender and racially balanced team to date. President George W. Bush, too, had a woman as secretary of state, Condoleezza Rice.

Even after people are selected, obstacles can arise. Faced with giving up a secure career for a possible short-term appointment, many qualified candidates find the pay, the work, or life in Washington politics unattractive. Almost all modern presidents have been turned down by some of the people they have invited to join their cabinets.

Background of Cabinet Members

What kind of person accepts appointment to the cabinet, and why? Almost without exception, cabinet members are college graduates. Many have

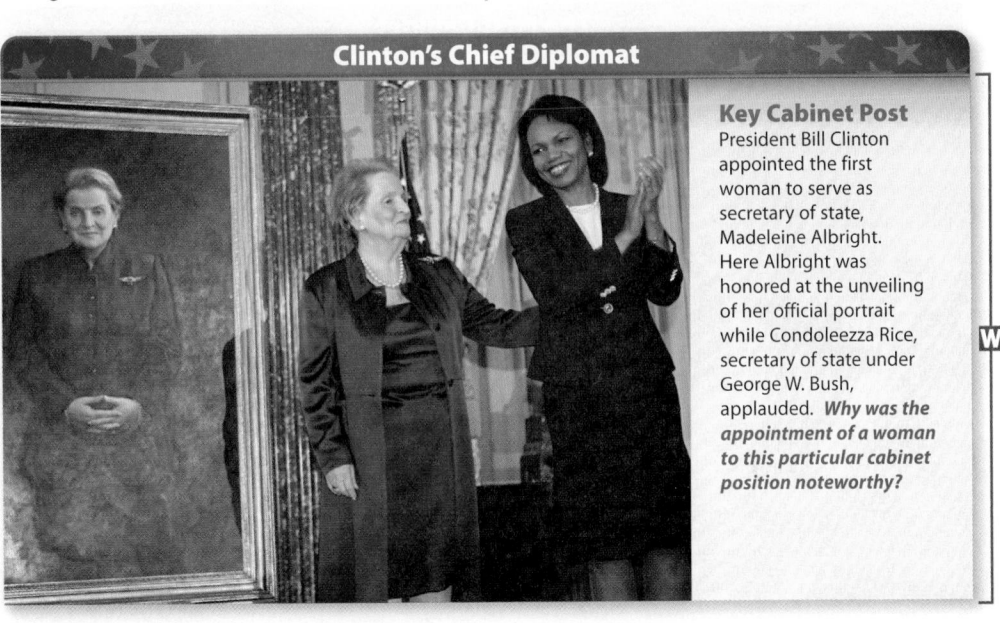

Clinton's Chief Diplomat

Key Cabinet Post
President Bill Clinton appointed the first woman to serve as secretary of state, Madeleine Albright. Here Albright was honored at the unveiling of her official portrait while Condoleezza Rice, secretary of state under George W. Bush, applauded. *Why was the appointment of a woman to this particular cabinet position noteworthy?*

Teach

C Critical Thinking

Evaluating Have students scan this section or use outside research to analyze a cabinet office or an official of their choice. Students should ask, "Is the cabinet position effective? What can be done to improve the cabinet's effectiveness?" Then have them list ways in which the cabinet could be improved. Call on volunteers to share their evaluations with the class. **OL**

Caption Answer: Madeleine Albright was the first female secretary of state in U.S. history.

W Writing Support

Personal Writing The replacement of a cabinet member's portrait is a ceremonial event to bid farewell to the outgoing secretary and welcome the new one. Have students write a short essay describing their feelings during the unveiling of their portrait at the welcoming ceremony. **OL**

Additional Support

Activity: Collaborative Learning

Creating a Time Line Organize the class into groups of three to create a time line showing when various cabinet offices were created. Have groups research and list all the titles of the cabinet offices and the years the offices were created. Then have one group member design a poster-sized time line, another use index cards to write out the cabinet officer's title and a short description of the cabinet duties, and the third design graphics illustrating each cabinet office, to be placed on the date of origination. Have members assemble the time line. Ask volunteers to present their time lines to the class and discuss the different cabinet offices and their duties. **OL**

Senate Confirmation Throughout history, the Senate has rarely rejected cabinet nominees. Because the press scrutinizes and reports on nominees, the public also judges their qualifications. Encourage students to research recent Senate confirmation hearings. Then hold an open-forum debate on whether the Senate should continue to hold this check. **AL**

Caption Answer: the cabinet

D Differentiated Instruction

Interpersonal Ask students to scan the section to find the reasons that the cabinet is not a powerful advisory body. Discuss these reasons with the class. Have students work in small groups to brainstorm recommendations for changes in the cabinet (such as the appointment process, job descriptions, and so on) that would make it more effective. Allow groups to share their recommendations with the class. Discuss the feasibility of each recommendation. **OL**

Differentiated Instruction

---

advanced degrees. Most are leaders in the fields of business, industry, law, science, and education.

Cabinet secretaries earn $191,300 per year. For many, this salary represents only half of what they could earn in the private sector. Some take their posts out of a deep sense of public service. Typically they move in and out of government posts from positions in private industry or the legal, financial, or educational fields.

Nominations and Confirmation

The selection process for a new president's cabinet begins long before Inauguration Day. The president-elect draws up a list of candidates after consulting with campaign advisers, congressional leaders, and representatives of interest groups. Key campaign staffers meet with potential candidates to discuss the issues facing the department they may be asked to head. Before making final decisions, members of the president-elect's team may **leak,** or deliberately disclose, some candidates' names to the news **media.** They do this to test the reaction of Congress, interest groups, and the public.

The Senate holds confirmation hearings on the president's nominees for cabinet posts. Nominees answer questions about their views and background before the Senate committee that is **relevant** to the cabinet position. Since cabinet members are viewed as part of the president's official family, the Senate is usually willing to routinely confirm most of the president's nominees. Of more than 500 cabinet appointments since the time of George Washington, the Senate has rejected only a handful.

Appointments are not automatic, however. President Bill Clinton was in office for less than a month when his nominee for attorney general, Zoë Baird, had to bow out of the confirmation process. In the midst of Senate hearings, a newspaper reported that in the past, Baird had hired undocumented workers for household work. An outpouring of public opinion derailed the nomination.

The Role of the Cabinet

Each cabinet member is responsible for the executive department that he or she heads. As a group, the cabinet is intended to serve as an advisory body to the president. Yet most presidents have been reluctant to give the cabinet a major advisory role.

The cabinet meets when the president calls it together. Meetings might be held once a week or more or less frequently depending on the preference and the needs of a president. Meetings take place in the cabinet room of the White House and are usually closed to the public and the press.

The First Cabinet

Advising the President President George Washington (at far left), with his cabinet: Henry Knox, Secretary of War; Alexander Hamilton, Secretary of the Treasury; Thomas Jefferson, Secretary of State; and Edmond Randolph, the Attorney General. *How do we refer to these positions as a group today?*

Activity: Multiple Learning Styles

Verbal/Linguistic Organize the class into small groups. Assign each group a cabinet position. Have group members brainstorm a list of five examples of advice or policy recommendations that their cabinet member might make to the president. Have groups write each example on an index card and include the name of the cabinet post. Collect all the completed cards and shuffle them. Read each recommendation aloud and have the class guess which cabinet member would most likely make that recommendation. **OL**

The Cabinet in History

From the beginning, the cabinet's role in decision making depended on the president's wishes. Strong presidents, like Andrew Jackson, Abraham Lincoln, and Franklin Roosevelt, paid relatively less attention to their cabinet. Jackson relied on a small group of friends instead. Since they often met in the White House kitchen, they became known as the Kitchen Cabinet. During the Great Depression, Roosevelt often relied on a group of university professors nicknamed the "brain trust." His wife, Eleanor, was also a frequent adviser.

Some members of Lincoln's cabinet thought he was weak and that they would run the government. They soon learned otherwise. Secretary of State William Seward acknowledged: "The President is the best of us. There is only one vote in the Cabinet, and it belongs to him." Lincoln's treatment of his cabinet is typical of many American presidents. Before he issued the Emancipation Proclamation, Lincoln simply called his cabinet together to inform them that he intended to end slavery:

> 66 *I have got you together to hear what I have written down. I do not wish you to advise about the main matter for that I have determined myself.* 99
>
> —Abraham Lincoln, 1862

The Modern Cabinet

Several recent presidents have attempted to increase the cabinet's role, but in the end, most have given up and turned elsewhere for advice. After President Kennedy was assassinated, Lyndon B. Johnson was anxious to get along with Kennedy's cabinet. He wanted a smooth transition of power and needed their information on the state of affairs. Soon, however, Johnson called on them less often. When a meeting occurred, it was generally to give department heads what one assistant called their "marching orders." Johnson's cabinet fared better than Richard Nixon's, however. Some of Nixon's cabinet members did not see him for months.

At the start of his presidency, Ronald Reagan also pledged to make greater use of the cabinet. He stated that his department heads would be his "inner circle of advisers." In an attempt to improve its usefulness, Reagan divided the cabinet into smaller groups, with each responsible for a broad policy area. After only a year in office, however, Reagan began to rely mainly on his White House aides for advice. George

H.W. Bush and Clinton used their cabinets as sounding boards for ideas, not as the advisory body that President George Washington envisioned.

The Influence of Cabinet Members

Some cabinet members have greater influence because their departments are concerned with the most sensitive national issues. The secretaries of state, defense, and the treasury, as well as the attorney general fill this role in most administrations. These officials are sometimes called an "inner

Historical and Political Reasons for Cabinet Status

Inner Cabinet	
State, 1789	Founding of a Sovereign Nation
Treasury, 1789	Founding of a Sovereign Nation
Justice (Attorney General), 1789	Founding of a Sovereign Nation
Defense (originally, the War Department), 1789	Founding of a Sovereign Nation

Outer Cabinet	
Interior, 1849	Westward expansion
Agriculture, 1889	Land grant legislation; interest in scientific agriculture
Commerce, 1913	Economic influence of manufacturing and business
Labor, 1913	Industrial workforce, unions, and concern with welfare of workers
Health and Human Services (originally Health, Education and Welfare), 1953	The belief, reinforced by the New Deal, that government should play a role in social welfare
Housing & Urban Development, 1966	Concern with condition of inner cities during the War on Poverty
Transportation, 1966	Burgeoning travel and transport: need to coordinate multiple air, sea, and highway agencies
Energy, 1977	Development of nuclear energy in the 1940s and the extended energy crisis of the 1970s
Education, 1980	Need for strong science and math education to compete with Soviets; desire to improve education for minorities
Veterans Affairs, 1988	Recognition that Veterans Administration, one of the largest federal agencies, deserved cabinet status
Homeland Security, 2003	Response to terrorist attacks; need to coordinate multiple agencies that focus on security

Critical Thinking *Do you think the cabinet will continue to grow in the future? Why or why not?*

C Critical Thinking

Analyzing Information Discuss with students the following paradox: the cabinet was created as a close advisory body but has become an aloof, bureaucratic one. Most presidents try to increase the role of the cabinet, then turn elsewhere for advice. **Ask:** Should presidents rely more on the cabinet for advice? *(Answers will vary.)* **AL**

R Reading Strategy

Taking Notes Have students use the chart to create flashcards for the different cabinet departments. Students should write the function of the department on one side and the department's name on the other side. Students should identify the title of the department by reading the description, and vice versa. **BL**

Critical Thinking

Answer: Students might answer that the cabinet will continue to grow due to growth in population, technology, and a global economy; or that bureaucracies are too big already and should be consolidated.

Hands-On Chapter Project
Step 3

The Role of the Cabinet

Step 3: Choosing an Adviser Groups of students will investigate the areas of expertise of cabinet members and decide who should advise the president on the problem.

Directions Divide the class into five groups, and assign three cabinet departments to each group.

Interpersonal Have students use library books or online sources such as http://www. whitehouse.gov/government/cabinet.html to learn the area of expertise of each secretary

and his or her department. Students should list the areas of national and international interest for which each secretary is responsible. Then the whole class should review the issue that students chose in Step 2. Ask the class to determine which secretaries should be assigned to gather information and then advise the president on the issue. Students should be prepared to explain why they have included or excluded a secretary. **OL AL**

(Chapter Project continued in Section 4.)

Section 3 Review

S **Skill Practice**

Researching Have students use library or Internet resources to research arguments, disagreements, or even fights that have occurred among cabinet members. **Ask:** What are some reasons for these disagreements? Did collateral damage ever result? Did the president have to intervene? *(Conflicting loyalties are often the cause.)* **AL**

Assess

Assign the Section 3 Assessment as homework or as an in-class activity, or have students take Section Quiz 8-3 from *Section Quizzes and Chapter Tests.*

Close

Drawing Conclusions Ask students to choose which cabinet office they think has had the most influence on the history of the United States. **OL**

---

cabinet." Other secretaries, the "outer cabinet," head departments that represent narrower interests such as agriculture or veterans' affairs. They tend to have less direct access to the president and less influence.

Factors Limiting the Cabinet's Role

Why have presidents been reluctant to rely more on their cabinet for advice and assistance? There are several factors that limit the president's use of the cabinet for key decisions or help in running the executive branch. Understanding these factors helps explain why presidents rely most on assistants in the Executive Office of the President, a presidential advisory agency established by Congress.

Conflicting Loyalties

No president commands the complete loyalty of cabinet members. Even though the president appoints them, cabinet officials have loyalties to three other constituencies: long-term officials in their own department, members of Congress, and **S** special-interest groups. Each of these groups has a stake in the department's programs. Each may push the secretary in directions that do not always agree with the president's plans and policies—or with each other.

Sometimes disagreements arise among different cabinet secretaries. These might be a result of loyalty to their department's programs, to its constituent groups, or to personal animosity. Secretaries might also have a natural preference to compete over the control of a given program. President Reagan's Secretary of State George Schulz and Secretary of Defense Caspar Weinberger battled to influence the president on arms control and foreign policy for almost two years before Weinberger finally resigned in 1987. More recently, during George W. Bush's first term, notable disagreements arose between Colin Powell, the secretary of state, and Donald Rumsfeld, the secretary of defense. Their disagreements created some confusion about national policy; in the end, Powell resigned in 2005.

Secrecy and Trust

A second factor that reduces the cabinet's usefulness is the difficulty of maintaining secrecy when 15 cabinet secretaries are involved in a discussion of sensitive topics. The result is that cabinet debates are sometimes leaked to the press.

Presidents naturally prefer to discuss tough problems with people they know and trust. Yet because of the political factors that must be considered, presidents can end up appointing relative strangers to their cabinets. President Kennedy, for example, never met his secretary of defense and secretary of the treasury before he appointed them. For these reasons, presidents have increasingly turned to the Executive Office of the President and to their White House staff for help.

SECTION 3 Review

Vocabulary

1. **Explain** the significance of: cabinet, leak.

Main Ideas

2. **Summarizing** What five factors do presidents consider when choosing cabinet officers?

3. **Explaining** How did the decline of the cabinet as an advisory body to the president weaken the system of checks and balances?

Critical Thinking

4. **Theorizing** What could a president do when choosing cabinet members to increase their value as advisers?

5. **Organizing** Using a graphic organizer like the one at right, show which cabinet members often form an "inner circle" that is closer to the president and which have less direct contact.

Writing About Government

6. **Expository Writing** Search library and Internet resources for information about the major responsibilities of one of the 15 executive departments. Then prepare a list of interview questions that you think would help determine the competence of a potential secretary of the executive department you chose.

Answers

1. All definitions can be found in the section and the Glossary.
2. compatible background; geographic balance; acceptability to interest groups; high level of administrative skills and experience; race, ethnicity, and gender balance; party loyalty
3. reduces Congress's ability to influence presidential policy making by eliminating its control of the cabinet through its oversight, appropriations, and confirmation powers
4. Answers will vary but should address the politics of the selection process and suggest that personal ties and loyalty be a bigger factor in selection.
5. Closely work with president: secretaries of state, defense, treasury, and attorney general. Not as close: secretaries of the interior, housing, education, agriculture, commerce, labor, energy, and veterans' affairs
6. You might have students work together to conduct the interview. Hold a class discussion to evaluate interview questions.

Interpreting an Election Map

Election maps show various kinds of information about an election. For example, a national election map might show the popular vote or the Electoral College vote in a presidential election by identifying the states that voted for each candidate. Other maps might show the outcome of a congressional election, district by district, or the results of local bond issues by neighborhood. This is useful for analyzing political trends and understanding how your state, city, county, or region fits into these trends.

Why Learn This Skill?

Being able to read an election map makes it easy to quickly determine how various states voted. To read an election map, follow these steps:

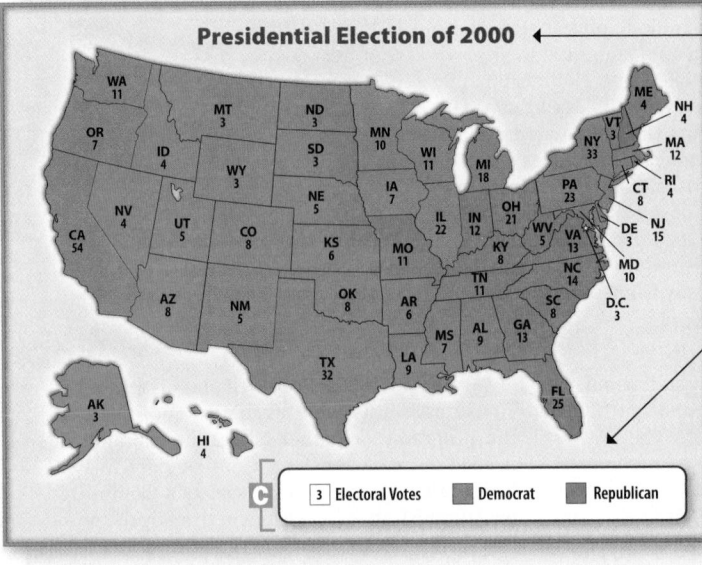

1. Read the map title to determine what election information is being shown. For example, notice whether it shows the popular vote, Electoral College votes, or something else.

2. Read the map key to determine how information is presented.

3. Based on this information, decide what kinds of questions the map is intended to answer.

Practicing the Skill

Evaluate the map above and answer the questions that follow.

1. What do the colors red and blue indicate on the map?

2. What does the number indicate?

3. Which section of the country voted mostly Republican and mostly Democratic in 2000? Why might this be so?

Applying the Skill

In an almanac, newspaper, other reference work, or online, find the results of a recent city, state, or national election. Draw an election map to present those results. Include a map key.

Teach

S Skill Practice

Analyzing a Map Examining an election map allows someone to see the overall results easily. Patterns of voting reveal themselves when the results are color-coded by party or candidate. Have students think about what an election map might reveal if it showed further breakdowns, such as a national map by counties, or how your state would look in a county-based map. (*Students might suggest that counties with urban areas would be one color, while mainly rural counties would be another color.*) **Ask:** Is there another graph or chart that is as efficient in portraying this information? Why or why not? (*Probably not; information could be listed in a table by region, with each row color-coded for a party or a candidate.*) **OL**

C Critical Thinking

Analyzing Information Have students add up the electoral votes for the 2000 election. **Ask:** Which party received the most electoral votes? (*The Republicans received 271 electoral votes, while the Democrats received 266.*) How many votes were needed by one candidate for a majority? (*The "magic number" was 270.*) **BL**

Answers

Practicing the Skill

1. Red represents states won by the Republican candidate; blue identifies states that the Democratic candidate won.
2. the number of electoral votes for each state
3. Most of the South, Southeast, and Midwest voted Republican. Most of New England, the West Coast, and the northern states voted Democratic.

Applying the Skill

Students should choose an election with published results, and their maps should reflect the election's outcome.

Focus

Bellringer

Section Focus Transparencies 8-4

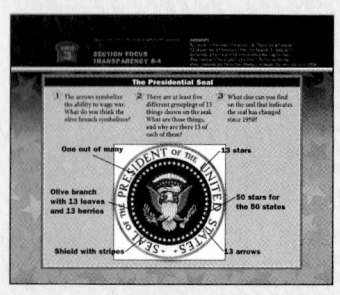

Reader's Guide

Answers to Graphic:

1939: Reorganization Act passed, Bureau of the Budget moved into the EOP

1946: Council of Economic Advisers created

1947: NSC created

Resource Manager

The Executive Office

Reader's Guide

Content Vocabulary	**Academic Vocabulary**	**Reading Strategy**
★ central clearance *(p. 236)* ★ National Security Advisor *(p. 236)* ★ press secretary *(p. 239)*	★ accessible *(p. 234)* ★ professional *(p. 235)* ★ conclude *(p. 238)*	Create a time line like the one below to organize the important events in the history of the Executive Office.

1939   1946 1947

Issues in the News

These days one goal of U.S. Trade Representative Susan Schwab is to help American companies sell their products in China. In 2007 she negotiated a deal with China that eliminated some subsidies China gives its exporters. "This outcome represents a victory for U.S. manufacturers and their workers," Schwab said. American companies were not as optimistic, arguing that the two nations are far from having a "level playing field." A key obstacle is that the Chinese government keeps the value of its currency artificially low. This raises the price of American goods by comparison. Chinese consumers still buy mostly Chinese products.

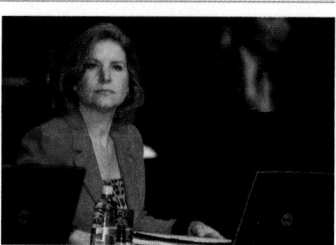

▲ U.S. Trade Representative Susan Schwab at a trade summit with Asian nations in 2007

Susan Schwab was one of many staff people in the Executive Office of the President (EOP) of President George W. Bush. The EOP is made up of people and agencies that directly assist the chief executive with advice and information. Modern presidents also use the EOP to help them implement decisions and to maintain control over the entire executive branch.

Executive Office Agencies

Created by President Franklin D. Roosevelt in 1939, the Executive Office of the President has grown to serve the needs of each administration. Roosevelt, who took office during the Great Depression, immediately proposed many federal programs to deal with the country's serious economic problems. As Congress passed one special program after another, the size of the national government grew rapidly.

By the mid-1930s, Roosevelt and his few White House assistants were unable to coordinate all the programs or gather all the information he needed to make decisions. Consequently, in 1936 Roosevelt appointed the President's Committee on Administrative Management to study the problem. In its report, the Committee recommended that a personal staff be "installed in the White House itself, directly **accessible** to the president." This staff was to assist the president in:

❝ [O]btaining quickly and without delay all pertinent information . . . so as to guide him in making his responsible decisions; and then when decisions have been made, to assist him in seeing to it that every administrative department and agency affected is promptly informed. ❞

—The President's Committee on Administrative Management, 1937

R Reading Strategies	**C** Critical Thinking	**D** Differentiated Instruction	**W** Writing Support	**S** Skill Practice
Teacher Edition • Summarizing, p. 236 **Additional Resources** • Quizzes/Tests, pp. 94–102 • Guid. Read. Act., p. 32	**Teacher Edition** • Drawing Conclusions, p. 235 • Making Inferences, p. 236 • Evaluating Information, p. 238	**Teacher Edition** • Interpersonal, p. 239 **Additional Resources** • Foldables, p. 51	**Teacher Edition** • Persuasive Writing, p. 237 **Additional Resources** • Coop. Learning Act., pp. 5–6	**Additional Resources** • Ch. Summaries, pp. 22–24

In response, Congress passed the Reorganization Act of 1939, which created the Executive Office of the President. At the same time, President Franklin D. Roosevelt moved the Bureau of the Budget out of the Treasury Department into the EOP, where it would be more responsive and where he could stay informed of its activities. As another part of the EOP, he established the White House Office, which he intended to be a small group of advisers who work directly with the president on day-to-day matters.

Organization and Growth

Today the EOP consists of the White House Office and several specialized agencies that report directly to the president. Agency staffs include attorneys, scientists, social scientists, and other highly technical or **professional** personnel. The EOP currently has more than 1,500 full-time employees, many of whom work in the west wing of the White House.

The Executive Office of the President has grown rapidly for three reasons. First, every president has reorganized it, adding new agencies or expanding existing ones in response to the problems of the day. For example, after an American-sponsored invasion of Cuba failed in 1961, President Kennedy enlarged the National Security Council staff.

Second, because some problems facing the nation's industrial society are so complex, presidents have wanted experts available to advise them about issues related to those problems. The Council of Economic Advisers was created for this reason.

Third, many of today's huge federal programs require that several executive departments and agencies work together. EOP staff members have been added to coordinate these efforts. For example, President Ronald Reagan created the Office of National Drug Control Policy in 1988. This department coordinated the activities of more than 50 federal agencies involved in the war on drugs.

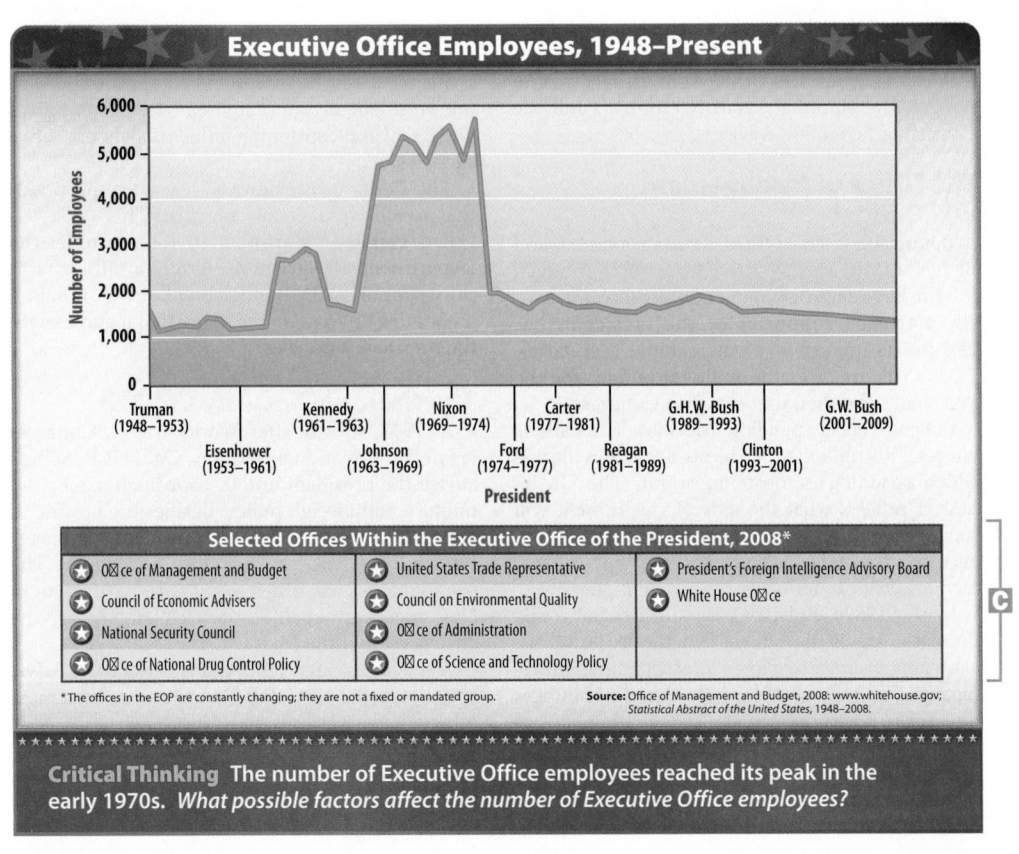

Executive Office Employees, 1948–Present

Number of Employees (vertical axis: 0 to 6,000)

Presidents (horizontal axis):
Truman (1948–1953), Eisenhower (1953–1961), Kennedy (1961–1963), Johnson (1963–1969), Nixon (1969–1974), Ford (1974–1977), Carter (1977–1981), Reagan (1981–1989), G.H.W. Bush (1989–1993), Clinton (1993–2001), G.W. Bush (2001–2009)

Selected Offices Within the Executive Office of the President, 2008*

★ Office of Management and Budget	★ United States Trade Representative	★ President's Foreign Intelligence Advisory Board
★ Council of Economic Advisers	★ Council on Environmental Quality	★ White House Office
★ National Security Council	★ Office of Administration	
★ Office of National Drug Control Policy	★ Office of Science and Technology Policy	

* The offices in the EOP are constantly changing; they are not a fixed or mandated group.

Source: Office of Management and Budget, 2008: www.whitehouse.gov; *Statistical Abstract of the United States, 1948–2008.*

Critical Thinking The number of Executive Office employees reached its peak in the early 1970s. *What possible factors affect the number of Executive Office employees?*

CHAPTER 8, SECTION 4

Teach

C Critical Thinking

Drawing Conclusions Ask students to list the people they would appoint to each of the offices listed in the table and explain why they would choose that person. **OL**

Critical Thinking

Answer: Factors may include the addition of new agencies, the reorganization of existing ones, and the size of each agency's budget.

Graph Skills Practice
Which president had the most executive employees? *(President Richard Nixon)* **OL**

Rahm Emanuel (1959–present) was appointed chief of staff by President-elect Obama. Emanuel was a chief political adviser for President Clinton and was elected to Congress in 2003 from Illinois. He chaired the Democratic Congressional Campaign Committee in 2006 and was head of the Democratic Caucus.

Additional Support

Activity: Collaborative Learning

Creating a Board Game Organize the class into groups of three, each of which will create a board game called "Executive Office of the President," illustrating how this part of the executive branch works. Have groups of students write the rules of the game and choose the agencies and White House staff represented in the game. Then have students in each group select and carry out one of the following tasks: design the game board, design playing pieces for each staff member, design playing cards for events during the game, and other tasks as necessary. Have each group assemble the game, play their own game, and adjust any part of the game that could be improved. Then have groups trade games to play and critique. **OL**

R Reading Strategy

Summarizing How does the Office of Management and Budget give the president influence over policy? *(The OMB sets the budget for all other agencies. By setting spending priorities, presidents can steer funding toward some goals and away from others.)* BL

C Critical Thinking

Making Inferences Ask: Why does the president need information about foreign governments? *(Answers may include that other countries could harm U.S. interests while pursuing their own aims.)* AL

Did You Know?

Although it was built of gray Virginia freestone, the president's home was painted white to cover smoke stains after the British partly burned it in 1814. President Theodore Roosevelt made the name *White House* official when he had it printed on stationery after 1901.

Differentiated Instruction

The National Budget

The Defense Budget
The defense budget usually represents about 20 percent of the national budget. *Looking at the cartoon, would you say the cartoonist believes that the size of the defense budget is justified?*

"Put simply, the mission is to discover a potential enemy who could justify our three-hundred-billion-dollar defense budget."

Three of the oldest agencies in the EOP have played the greatest role in presidential decision making. They are the Office of Management and Budget, the National Security Council, and the Council of Economic Advisers.

The Office of Management and Budget

Before 1970, the Office of Management and Budget (OMB) was called the Bureau of the Budget. It is the largest agency in the EOP. Its director, usually a trusted supporter of the president, has become as important as the cabinet secretaries. The OMB prepares the national budget for the president, who then presents it to Congress.

Budgets reflect spending priorities. The nation's budget is not unlimited, so the president must decide which spending is most important. The OMB's budget reflects what the federal government will spend money on and how much. A president's influence over the budget is thus one important way that the president can influence government policy.

In the 1980s, President Ronald Reagan made dramatic use of the budget function to fulfill his campaign promise to trim federal spending. Immediately after taking office, he ordered his budget director to prepare detailed plans to cut billions of dollars from government programs. The budget director has continued to shape national policy.

Each year all executive agencies submit their budgets to the OMB. OMB officials then review them and recommend where to make cuts in each agency's budget. If an agency head wants to challenge a cut, he or she must appeal directly to the president or a top adviser. This system gives OMB real and continuing influence over executive agencies.

The OMB also reviews all legislative proposals that executive agencies prepare. This review is called **central clearance.** If, for example, the Department of Agriculture drafts a bill on farm price supports, OMB officials will review it before it goes to Congress to make sure that it agrees with the president's policies.

The National Security Council

In 1947, shortly after World War II, Congress created the National Security Council (NSC) to advise the president and to coordinate American military and foreign policy. Besides the president, the council includes the vice president, the secretary of state, and the secretary of defense. The president can ask other advisers to participate in NSC meetings, such as the CIA director or the chairperson of the Joint Chiefs of Staff.

A special assistant, the **National Security Advisor,** directs the NSC staff. Perhaps more than most other advisory groups, the importance of the NSC has varied with the president's use of it. Truman did little with the NSC. Eisenhower held frequent NSC meetings, but he relied more on the advice of his secretary of state, John Foster Dulles. Under

Activity: Multiple Learning Styles

Verbal/Linguistic Assign each student a particular position in the Executive Office of the President. Ask students to imagine they must relay key information to the president about a current issue. Have each student write a detailed memo providing advice and background information for the president. Ask volunteers to read their memos aloud, discussing the issue in question and the quality and reliability of the advice given to the president. AL

President Kennedy, the NSC was more important in decision making.

During President Nixon's first term from 1969 to 1973, National Security Advisor Henry Kissinger had a great deal of authority. Kissinger developed the NSC into a kind of alternate State Department in the White House. In 1973 he negotiated the end of the Vietnam War. He also negotiated the opening of diplomatic relations with China and coordinated arms-control talks with the Soviet Union. (For several years, Kissinger served as both secretary of state as well as the National Security Advisor.)

In the late 1970s, under President Jimmy Carter, the National Security Advisor and secretary of state often disagreed about foreign policy and competed over who should have the final say in policy matters. Other nations sometimes found this confusing. Did the NSC or the State Department speak for the United States in foreign policy?

National Homeland Security Council

In October 2001, after terrorists attacked the Pentagon and the World Trade Center, President George W. Bush created a new agency within the EOP—the Office of Homeland Security and the Homeland Security Council. By November 2002, however, its functions were raised to the level of a cabinet department—the Department of Homeland Security. This new cabinet department coordinated the activities of a majority of the federal agencies that were working to fight terrorism. The goal in creating a single agency was to make it possible to develop and carry out an overall strategy to protect the nation.

The president retained the National Homeland Security Council in the EOP to advise him on domestic security. This office is headed by the secretary of Homeland Security but includes other important officials. The attorney general; the directors of the FBI, CIA, and Federal Emergency Management Agency (FEMA); and the secretaries of Defense, Treasury, Transportation, and Health and Human Services are on this Council.

The Council's first major task arose shortly after the September 11, 2001, attacks, when letters containing anthrax—a potentially lethal bacteria—were sent through the mail to the Capitol in Washington, D.C., and to offices of major news organizations. Five people died, and 17 became seriously ill. Thousands of people began taking antibiotics as a precaution against the disease. In 2008, as investigators prepared to charge an Army microbiologist with sending the tainted letters, the suspect committed suicide, leaving many unanswered questions about the crime.

The Council of Economic Advisers

Since the Great Depression, the president has been the nation's chief economic planner, formulating the nation's economic policy. In this role, the president relies for advice on the Council of

Dual Roles

Extraordinary Diplomat Henry Kissinger (right), Nixon's most influential foreign policy adviser, served as both National Security Advisor and secretary of state for several years. In 1973 he and a North Vietnamese negotiator were awarded the Nobel Peace Prize for achieving a cease-fire in the Vietnam War. *Is the National Security Advisor an official member of the cabinet?*

W **Writing Support**

Persuasive Writing As National Security Advisor, Henry Kissinger developed the National Security Council (NSC) into a "shadow" State Department. Have students write an essay stating whether they think this was an appropriate use of the NSC and defend their reasoning. **OL**

Participating IN GOVERNMENT

Analyzing Leadership Qualities Review with students the qualities needed for effective leadership. Students should list the qualities they consider most important, then research contenders in an upcoming local, state, or national election. Students should analyze the candidates' leadership qualities and work individually or in groups to complete a voters' guide for the upcoming election, focusing on the candidates' leadership qualities. **AL**

Caption Answer: No, the National Security Advisor is part of the EOP.

Hands-On Chapter Project
Step 4

The Role of the Cabinet

Step 4: Producing a Memo Students will create a memo calling for an investigation of the issue.

Directions Tell students that in this step, they will compose a memo from the president's personal secretary to the cabinet secretaries whose areas of expertise will help the president address the issue.

Functional Writing Guide students to create a memo from the president's secretary to the cabinet officials whose advice the president needs to address the issue. Provide examples of professional memos for students to use as models. Ask students to decide on a task or a question to assign each cabinet secretary, in line with his or her area of expertise. Have students include an "action line" at the close of the memo, stating the time at which the entire cabinet will meet in order to advise the president. **OL AL**

238

Did You Know?

User fee became the political doublespeak for "tax" when the Office of Management and Budget (OMB) first called a four-cents-a-gallon increase in the federal gasoline tax a "user's fee."

Additional Support

Economic Advisers, an office that was created in 1946. The Council assesses the nation's economic health, predicts future economic conditions, and supports other executive agencies that are involved in economic planning. It also proposes solutions to specific problems, such as unemployment or inflation. It has access to any information a federal agency gathers on the American economy. The Council also prepares an annual report that the president gives Congress on the state of the economy.

Other EOP Agencies

The number and size of EOP agencies can vary because presidents can have different priorities. For example, President Lyndon B. Johnson's War on Poverty involved many different programs to fight unemployment and other social problems in the inner cities and among all Americans. He therefore set up an Office of Economic Opportunity to track some of these programs. His successor, President Richard Nixon, opposed many of Johnson's policies, so Nixon eliminated this office.

The Domestic Policy Council focuses on advising the president on domestic policies like farming and energy. The Office of Environmental Policy advises the president on environmental issues and works closely with the Environmental Protection Agency and the departments of Interior, Agriculture, and Energy. The Office of Science and Technology Policy advises the president on all scientific and technological matters that can affect the nation. The Office of the United States Trade Representative works to negotiate trade agreements with other nations.

The White House Office

The nation's first presidents had no personal staff. George Washington hired his nephew at his own expense to be his personal secretary. When James Polk was president from 1845 to 1849, his wife, Sarah, was his secretary. During the 1890s, two presidents, Grover Cleveland and William McKinley, personally answered the White House telephone. As late as the 1930s, Herbert Hoover's personal staff consisted of a few secretaries, several administrative assistants, and a cook.

A 1937 study of the executive branch **concluded** that:

> 66 *The President needs help. His immediate staff assistance is entirely inadequate. He should be given a small number of executive assistants who would be his direct aides in dealing with the managerial agencies and administrative departments of the Government.* 99
>
> —The President's Committee on Administrative Management, 1937

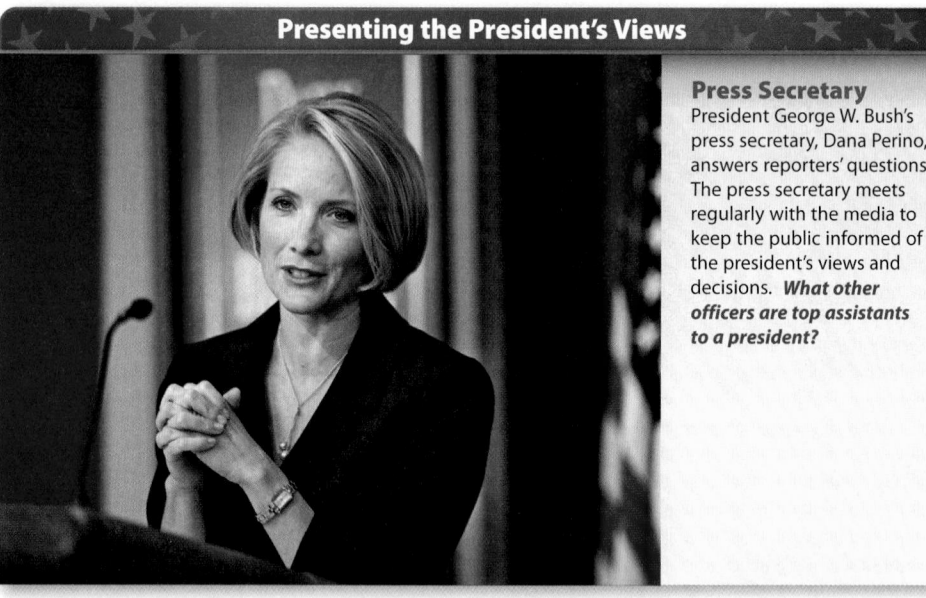

Presenting the President's Views

Press Secretary
President George W. Bush's press secretary, Dana Perino, answers reporters' questions. The press secretary meets regularly with the media to keep the public informed of the president's views and decisions. *What other officers are top assistants to a president?*

★ Activity: Interdisciplinary Connection ★

Technology The purpose of the Executive Office of the President is to provide specialized information and advice so that the president can make informed decisions quickly and accurately. Discuss with students how modern technology has provided speedy and abundant information but not necessarily more accurate information. Have students research the difference between accessing information from a book or an article and from online sources. Discuss students' findings, pointing out differences in the information's currency, reliability, accuracy, and accessibility. **AL**

Organization and Growth

Unlike cabinet members, the White House staff can be chosen without Senate confirmation. Key aides usually are longtime personal supporters of the president. Many are newcomers to Washington. They do not usually have large constituencies of their own, which is true for some cabinet officers.

The White House Office has become the most important part of the EOP. From about 50 people under Roosevelt, the Executive Office of the President grew to almost 600 staffers under Nixon. Clinton's White House Office consisted of about 380 people, while George W. Bush's staff numbered about 430 in 2006.

Only a small number of this staff can report directly to the president, but these top assistants—including the chief of staff, deputy chief of staff, and White House counsel—become a kind of inner circle around the president. A popular television series, *West Wing,* set out to dramatize the daily lives of this inner circle. Episodes focused on the personal and political battles of those working close to a fictional president, Jed Bartlett, played by Martin Sheen.

Duties of the White House Staff

White House aides perform whatever duties the president assigns them. Some aides can become very influential. One former adviser confided to an interviewer: "I had more power over national affairs in a few years in the White House than I could if I spent the rest of my life in the Senate."

One job of White House staff is to gather information and provide advice about key issues. Some staffers specialize in policy areas such as foreign affairs or energy issues. Others focus on political strategy, analyzing how a policy decision will affect the attitudes of voters and members of Congress. For the legal consequences of a policy, the president looks to the White House counsel.

Top staff members also work to make sure the executive agencies and departments carry out the president's directives. As Bill Moyers, press secretary to President Johnson, put it: "The job of the White House assistant is to help the president impress his priorities on the Administration."

Other White House staffers present the president's views to the public. The **press secretary** heads a staff that handles relations with the press corps, sets up press conferences, and issues public statements. Still other staffers work with members of Congress. The chief assistant for legislative affairs, for example, advises the president about possible reactions in Congress to a policy and lobbies lawmakers to win support.

Executive departments and agencies write the president thousands of reports and memos. Meanwhile a steady stream of people from inside and outside government want to see the president. Which people and which issues get through to the president is decided largely by White House aides.

Recent presidents have given top White House staff more authority over policymaking. Today, more policy decisions are being made in the White House than in executive agencies.

SECTION 4 Review

Vocabulary

1. **Explain** the significance of: central clearance, National Security Advisor, press secretary.

Main Ideas

2. **Listing** What are three reasons why the EOP has grown?

3. **Identifying** What are the three oldest agencies in the EOP, and what roles do they play?

Critical Thinking

4. **Synthesizing** How does the influence of key presidential aides affect the checks and balances established by the Constitution?

5. **Categorizing** Use a Venn diagram to show how the functions of the White House Office and the cabinet are alike and how they are different.

White House Office — Both — Cabinet

Writing About Government

6. **Expository Writing** Find out who the following presidential advisers are: chief of staff, deputy chief of staff, White House counsel, and press secretary. Research the background of each adviser and present your findings in a chart with a written summary.

D Differentiated Instruction

Interpersonal Organize students into small groups, and assign each group a different department in the Executive Office. Have each group write a policy paper to be presented to the president. **AL**

Assess

Assign the Section 4 Assessment as homework or as an in-class activity, or have students take Section Quiz 8-4 from *Section Quizzes and Chapter Tests.*

Close

Analyzing Discuss the relationships of the EOP and the cabinet with the president, and then debate the advantages and disadvantages each body has in helping to shape and implement policy. **OL**

Section 4 Review

Answers

1. All definitions can be found in the section and the Glossary.
2. Each president has reorganized it; presidents wanted experts to advise them on complex issues; and huge federal programs required several executive agencies.
3. OMB: reviews executive agencies' budgets, prepares national budget; Council of Economic Advisers: assesses current and future economic conditions, advises president; National Security Council: coordinates military and foreign policy

4. The growing power of appointees reduces the influence Congress has over presidential decision making.
5. White House Office: inner circle of advisers, no Senate confirmation, does whatever the president asks; Cabinet: heads of individual departments, confirmed by Senate; Both: advise the president
6. Students should list names and backgrounds of current key presidential advisers.

Focus

S Skill Practice

Have students review the quotes in the Verbatim section and discuss each item as it relates to the people and themes found in their textbooks. Have them create a list of additional quotations about other presidents, along with a brief statement explaining the quote, identifying the person quoted, and describing how the quote relates to the issue. Ask students to share their lists in a class discussion. **OL**

Teach

C Critical Thinking

Comparing and Contrasting
Have students use library and Internet resources to find full transcripts of President Roosevelt's address to the nation after the attack on Pearl Harbor on December 7, 1941, and President Bush's address following the terrorist attacks on September 11, 2001. Ask students to create a chart or write a brief essay comparing and contrasting the tone, content, and delivery of the two messages. **AL**

Additional Support

TIME NOTEBOOK

WASHINGTON TRADITIONS

"I DO SOLEMNLY SWEAR (or affirm) that I will faithfully execute the Office of President of the United States, and will to the best of my ability, preserve, protect and defend the Constitution of the United States."

Every American president since **GEORGE WASHINGTON** has taken this same oath of office. Presidents also follow these traditions set by Washington:

- Bowing in greeting (replaced later by Thomas Jefferson with shaking hands);
- Deciding who will join the cabinet;
- Giving an Inaugural Address and annual State of the Union messages, as well as a Farewell Address when leaving office;
- Attending the inauguration of the succeeding president.

COMFORTING A NATION

The American people turn to the president for leadership, strength, and comfort in times of national tragedy. On September 11, 2001, President George W. Bush spoke to the nation after one of the greatest tragedies in American history. Here is part of his speech:

"Today, our fellow citizens, our way of life, our very freedom came under attack in a series of deliberate and deadly terrorist acts. The victims were in airplanes, or in their offices; secretaries, businessmen and women, military and federal workers; moms and dads, friends and neighbors. Thousands of lives were suddenly ended by evil, despicable acts of terror. . . .

"A great people has been moved to defend a great nation. Terrorist attacks can shake the foundations of our biggest buildings, but they cannot touch the foundation of America. These acts shattered steel, but they cannot dent the steel of American resolve. . . ."

NAMED, 1901. THE WHITE HOUSE received its official name from President Theodore Roosevelt. The president's residence has also been called the President's Palace, the Executive Mansion, and the President's House.

TOSSED, APRIL 14, 1910. THE FIRST BASEBALL of the season was thrown out by President William Taft in Washington, D.C. Other presidents have continued this tradition, including John F. Kennedy, who wanted to make a good showing and secretly practiced his throw on the White House grounds.

WIRED, 2001. A WHITE HOUSE WEB SITE with news and information about the First Family's life in their famous residence was introduced by George W. Bush's administration. The site even includes a video tour conducted by the Bush's Scottish terrier, Barney.

Collaborative Learning

Creating a Magazine Spread Organize the class into groups of three or four students. Ask each group to create a two-page magazine spread on U.S. presidents. Each group's spread should feature about five presidents and be organized around a particular theme, such as "Presidential Legacies," "Least-Remembered Presidents," or "Plagued by Scandal." Students should look at current magazines and books for ideas about page design. This activity can be completed using desktop publishing software or the more traditional cut-and-paste method. **OL**

VERBATIM

WHAT PEOPLE SAID

"We have talked long enough in this country about equal rights. We have talked 100 years or more. It is time now to write the next chapter, and to write it in the books of law."

President Lyndon Johnson, *1963, shortly before getting Congress to pass the Civil Rights Act of 1964, which banned racial segregation and discrimination in employment*

Harry Truman

"I am not a crook."

President Richard Nixon *in 1973, months before being forced to resign over the Watergate scandal*

"Let freedom reign!"

President George W. Bush, *after being told that sovereign power in Iraq had officially passed from the U.S.-led coalition to the Iraqis in June 2004*

"I believe that it must be the policy of the United States to support free peoples who are resisting attempted subjugation by armed minorities or by outside pressure."

President Harry Truman, *announcing the Truman Doctrine to Congress in 1947*

"The basis of our government being the opinion of the people, the first object shall be to keep that right; and were it left for me to decide whether we should have a government without newspapers, or newspapers without government, I should not hesitate a moment to choose the latter."

Thomas Jefferson, *as he discussed the role of the newspapers and fears that the American press might have too much freedom, in 1787*

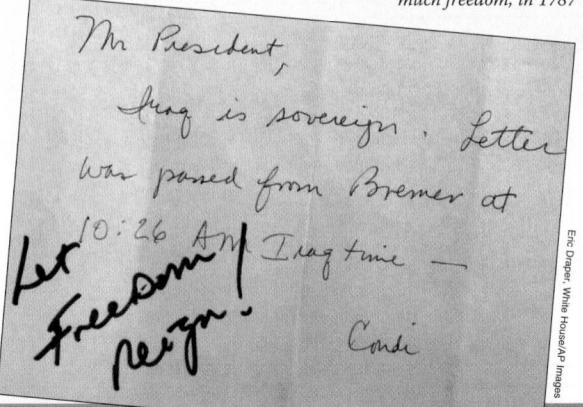

Mr President,
Iraq is sovereign. Letter was passed from Bremer at 10:26 AM Iraq time —
Condi
Let Freedom reign!

NUMBERS

2 The number of presidents who are the sons of former presidents. They are George W. Bush and John Quincy Adams.

50 The least number of dogs that have lived in the White House as the commander in chief's best friend.

30 The approximate number of years that Ronald Reagan worked as a Hollywood actor before becoming president.

1 The number of presidents to resign from office. Richard Nixon has this dubious honor.

4 The number of terms Franklin D. Roosevelt served as president—the only president to do so before the Twenty-second Amendment to the Constitution limited presidents to two terms of office.

0 Amount of money Herbert Hoover accepted as his salary for being president

Did You Know?

When Marian Anderson was denied the use of Constitution Hall for a concert because of her race, Eleanor Roosevelt arranged for her to sing at the Lincoln Memorial. The concert drew more than 75,000 people.

D Differentiated Instruction

Logical/Mathematical Have students research the salaries of the president and vice president over time. Based on the information, have students create a line graph that shows the changes in the salaries. Ask students if they think today's salaries for these offices reflect the importance of the job. Encourage students to explain their reasoning. **OL**

Close

Have students work in small groups to discuss the qualities they feel are most important in a president. Then ask students to list interview questions they would ask a presidential candidate and share their responses. **OL**

Additional Support

Extending the Content

The Civil Rights Act After the assassination of President Kennedy, civil rights leaders were concerned about whether his successor, Lyndon B. Johnson, a Texan, would support equal rights for African Americans as Kennedy had. Johnson's proposed Civil Rights Act of 1964 answered their question. Although the bill was easily passed by the House, the real challenge was in the Senate, where in the past Southerners had staged filibusters to block civil rights legislation. President Johnson had civil rights leaders launch a massive lobbying campaign at the Capitol and used his own considerable influence to win passage of the bill in the Senate. He signed the bill into law on July 2, 1964.

ExamView® Assessment Suite

This easy-to-use software includes extensive question banks and allows you to create fully customized tests that can be administered in print or online.

Reviewing Vocabulary

1.–8. Students' sentences will vary. The words are defined the Glossary.

Reviewing Main Ideas

9. Any four: use of *Air Force One* and other transportation; free medical, dental, and health care; use of White House with free entertainment; free use of White House staff, office space, and mailing service

10. The candidate who wins the most popular votes in a state wins all of that state's electoral votes.

11. Key presidential aides screen candidates and make recommendations to the president. The president selects a nominee and sends that name to the Senate for approval. The Senate votes and usually confirms the nominee.

12. prepares president's budget proposals and reviews legislation proposed by executive departments and agencies

13. chief of staff, deputy chief of staff, White House counsel, press secretary

Critical Thinking

14. Answers will vary but should point out that the president would be exposed to more diverse ideas and influences from cabinet members.

15. It eliminates the role of the states, thus undermining federalism.

Reviewing Vocabulary

Define each of the following content vocabulary words and use it in a sentence that is appropriate to its meaning.

1. compensation
2. presidential succession
3. electoral vote
4. cabinet
5. leak
6. central clearance
7. National Security Advisor
8. press secretary

Reviewing the Main Ideas

Section 1 *(pages 213–219)*

9. Listing What are four special benefits the president receives while in office?

Section 2 *(pages 220–226)*

10. Examining How does the winner-take-all system of the Electoral College operate?

Section 3 *(pages 228–232)*

11. Analyzing What is the process by which cabinet members are selected and appointed?

Section 4 *(pages 234–239)*

12. Describing What are the two major functions of the Office of Management and Budget?

13. Evaluating What are the four key positions on the White House Office staff?

Critical Thinking

14. 🌐 **Essential Question** Will a president who relies on the cabinet for advice be more or less informed than one who depends on close White House advisers? Explain.

15. Analyzing Why do some people criticize plans for the direct popular election of the president?

16. Making Inferences The youngest elected president was John Kennedy at 43. Why do you think the Framers of the Constitution in 1787 set the minimum age for president at 35?

17. Evaluating White House staff members are not required to receive congressional approval. What are the advantages and disadvantages of this policy?

18. Identifying Use a graphic organizer like the one below to rank the proposals for reforming the Electoral College system from most to least desirable. Explain your rankings.

Proposals	Reasons
1.	
2.	
3.	

Chapter Summary

President: Must be 35 years old, a natural-born citizen, 14-year resident of the United States; unwritten qualifications include government experience, access to money, and moderate political beliefs

Cabinet

★ Made up of the heads of the 15 major executive departments, the vice president, and several other top officials

★ Appointed by the president, with the approval of Congress

★ Factors limiting the president's use of the cabinet include conflicting loyalties and the difficulty of maintaining secrecy when such a large group is involved in discussions

Executive Office of the President (EOP)

★ Made up of individuals and agencies that directly assist the president

★ Includes agencies such as the Office of Management and Budget and the the National Security Council

★ The White House office staff, usually longtime personal supporters of the president, are appointed without Senate confirmation

★ The White House office has become the most important part of the EOP

---

16. Answers will vary but should point out that the Framers believed that a person was mature enough at 35 to handle the duties of the president.

17. Advantages: Presidents can put together a group of advisers who are supportive and truthworthy. Disadvantages: Congress will have less control over presidential policy making; nominees do not undergo public scrutiny; it bypasses the checks-and-balances system.

18. 1. The candidate who wins a congressional district is awarded that district's electoral vote; the candidate who wins the most votes statewide wins the two votes that represent the state's Senate seats. This change is least drastic and still gives states a role in the selection of a president. **2.** Each candidate should receive the same share of a state's electoral vote as he or she received of the popular vote. This proportional method is more democratic. **3.** Do away with the Electoral College. The people choose directly.

Government ONLINE Self-Check Quiz
Visit glencoe.com and enter QuickPass™ code USG9822c8.
Click on Self-Check Quizzes for additional test practice.

CHAPTER 8 Assessment and Activities

Document-Based Questions

Analyzing Primary Sources

Read the excerpt below and answer the questions that follow.

When George Washington served two terms as president, he set a number of precedents for how the office of the president should be run and what duties the president would hold. Washington outlined many of his beliefs about the presidency in his two Inaugural Addresses. The first was delivered to Congress in 1789.

> " *By the article establishing the executive department it is made the duty of the President 'to recommend to your consideration such measures as he shall judge necessary and expedient.' The circumstances under which I now meet you will acquit me from entering into that subject further than to refer to the great constitutional charter under which you are assembled, and which, in defining your powers, designates the objects to which your attention is to be given. It will be more consistent with those circumstances, and far more congenial with the feelings which actuate me, to substitute, in place of a recommendation of particular measures, the tribute that is due to the talents, the rectitude, and the patriotism which adorn the characters selected to devise and adopt them.* "

19. How extensive did George Washington believe the powers of the president should be?

20. What, in Washington's opinion, should be the role of the president? Which branch of government did he believe should have more power, the executive or the legislative?

Applying Technology Skills

21. Using the Internet Find information about current activities or events that are taking place at the White House by accessing the official White House Web site at www.whitehouse.gov. Using a word processor or publishing software, summarize the information you find and format it into a press release.

Interpreting Political Cartoons

Analyze the cartoon and answer the questions that follow. Base your answers on the cartoon and your knowledge of Chapter 8.

"This is America, son, where anybody with twenty million bucks to spend could end up being President."

22. What does the father think is the most important requirement to become president?

23. Does the cartoon make reference to any of the formal qualifications for the office of the president?

24. Do you agree with the statement made in the cartoon? Why or why not?

Participating IN GOVERNMENT

25. Contact your state government offices to find out the following information:
- How are the Democratic and Republican electors chosen in your state?
- How and where do the electors cast their ballots for president?

Organize the data chronologically and present your findings in a flowchart or an informational brochure.

Government ONLINE

Have students use the **Chapter 8 Self-Check Quiz.** Visit glencoe.com and enter QuickPass™ code USG9085c8T to prepare for the Chapter Test.

Interpreting Political Cartoons

22. access to money

23. no

24. Students should support their answers.

Participating IN GOVERNMENT

25. Call on volunteers to present their flowcharts or informational brochures to the class. Have them explain how electors are chosen in their state and how and where they cast their votes.

Chapter Bonus Test Question

Ask: What three inaugural parades were canceled and why? *(1921, by president-elect Warren Harding, out of concern for outgoing president Woodrow Wilson's health; 1945, because of World War II; 1985, because of extremely cold weather that not only caused Ronald Reagan's second inaugural parade to be canceled but also forced his swearing-in ceremony to be held inside the Capitol)*

Analyzing Primary Sources

19. Washington did not think the president should hold much power, primarily because the nation had just fought a war for independence against a nation with a strong monarch. Many Americans feared that a strong executive might become as powerful as a king.

20. Washington believed that the role of the president was to recommend what direction the country should go in and advise Congress about the issues he believed to be most pertinent to the guidance of the nation. Otherwise, the president should not have a large number of official duties. Congress, in Washington's opinion, should be the most powerful and influential branch of government.

Applying Technology Skills

21. Students' press releases should professionally and accurately summarize a number of events that are currently taking place at the White House.

Key to Ability Levels

- **BL** Below level
- **OL** On level
- **AL** Above level
- **ELL** English Language Learners

Key to Teaching Resources

- 📁 Print Material
- 💿 CD-ROM or DVD
- 🖪 Transparency

Levels					Resources	Chapter Opener	Section 1	Section 2	Section 3	Chapter Assess
BL	OL	AL	ELL							
FOCUS										
BL	OL	AL	ELL	🖪	Section Focus Transparencies		9-1	9-2	9-3	
TEACH										
BL	OL		ELL	📁	Reading Essentials and Study Guide (and Answer Key)		p. 95	p. 98	p. 102	
BL	OL		ELL	📁	Guided Reading Activities		p. 33	p. 34	p. 35	
BL	OL		ELL	📁	Vocabulary Activities			p. 9		
BL	OL	AL	ELL	📁	Chapter Summaries					
BL	OL			📁	American Biographies					
BL	OL	AL	ELL	📁	Cooperative Learning Activities					
	OL	AL	ELL	📁	Government Simulations and Debate				p. 15	
BL	OL	AL	ELL	📁	Historical Documents and Speeches					
BL	OL	AL	ELL	📁	Interpreting Political Cartoons			p. 17		
BL	OL		ELL	📁	Skill Reinforcement Activities		p. 9			
BL	OL	AL	ELL	📁	Source Readings				p. 9	
BL	OL			📁	Supreme Court Case Studies		pp. 1, 161		p. 117	
BL	OL	AL	ELL	📁	Participating in Government Activities			p. 17		
BL	OL		ELL	📁	Spanish Declaration of Independence and U.S. Constitution	✓	✓	✓	✓	✓
BL	OL	AL	ELL	📁	NGS World Atlas, Spanish	✓	✓	✓	✓	✓
BL	OL	AL	ELL	🖪	Unit Overlay Transparencies, Strategies, and Activities	✓	✓	✓	✓	✓
BL	OL		ELL	🖪	Making It Relevant Transparencies	✓	✓	✓	✓	✓
BL	OL	AL	ELL	🖪	High School Writing Process Transparencies, Strategies, and Activities	✓	✓	✓	✓	✓
BL	OL	AL		🖪	American Art & Architecture Transparencies, Strategies, and Activities	✓	✓	✓	✓	✓

✓ Chapter- or unit-based activities applicable to all sections in this chapter

All-In-One Planner and Resource Center

- Interactive Lesson Planner
- Interactive Teacher Edition
- Fully editable blackline masters
- Chapter Spotlight Videos Launch

- Differentiated Lesson Plans
- Printable reports of daily assignments
- Standards tracking system

Levels					Resources	Chapter Opener	Section 1	Section 2	Section 3	Chapter Assess
BL	OL	AL	ELL							
	TEACH *(continued)*									
BL	OL			💿	**American Music: Hits Through History**	✓	✓	✓	✓	✓
BL	OL		ELL	📁	**Reading Strategies for the Social Studies Classroom**	✓	✓	✓	✓	✓
			ELL	📁	**English Language Learner Handbook**	✓	✓	✓	✓	✓
BL	OL		ELL	📁	**Writer's Guidebook for Social Studies**	✓	✓	✓	✓	✓
BL	OL	AL	ELL	📁	**Living Constitution, SE**	✓	✓	✓	✓	✓
BL	OL	AL	ELL	📁	**Living Constitution, TAE**	✓	✓	✓	✓	✓
BL	OL			📁	**NGS World Atlas, English**	✓	✓	✓	✓	✓
BL	OL		ELL	📁	**The Constitution and You (poster set)**	✓	✓	✓	✓	✓
BL	OL	AL	ELL	📁	**Spanish Chapter Summaries**					
BL	OL	AL	ELL	📁	**Spanish Vocabulary Activities**			p. 9		
BL	OL		ELL	📁	**Spanish Reading Essentials and Study Guide (and Answer Key)**		p. 95	p. 98	p. 102	
BL	OL	AL	ELL	💿	**PresentationPlus! with MindJogger CheckPoint**	✓	✓	✓	✓	✓
	ASSESS									
BL	OL	AL	ELL	💿	*ExamView® Assessment Suite*		9-1	9-2	9-3	Ch. 9
BL	OL	AL	ELL	📁	**Authentic Assessment with Rubrics**		p. 16			p. 16
BL	OL	AL	ELL	📁	**Section Quizzes and Chapter Tests**		p. 103	p. 104	p. 105	pp. 107–114
BL	OL	AL	ELL	📁	**Spanish Section Quizzes and Tests**		p. 103	p. 104	p. 105	pp. 107–114
	CLOSE									
BL			ELL	📁	**Reteaching Activities**		p. 9			p. 9
BL	OL	AL	ELL	💿	**StudentWorks™ Plus with Audio Summaries**	✓	✓	✓	✓	✓
BL	OL		ELL	🖨	**Graphic Organizer Transparencies**		✓	✓	✓	
BL	OL		ELL	📁	**High School Government Reading and Study Skills Foldables®**		p. 52	p. 52	p. 52	

Teach With Technology

Section Audio

What is Section Audio?
Section Audio is a recording of each section of the textbook. It helps students learn the content in the textbook.

How can Section Audio help my students?
Section Audio allows students to:

- read and listen simultaneously to improve content comprehension
- practice reading skills

- review important concepts for struggling readers
- improve listening comprehension

Visit glencoe.com to access the Media Library, and enter a *QuickPass*™ code to go to Section Audio recordings.

Government ONLINE
Visit glencoe.com and enter *QuickPass*™ code USG9085c9T for Chapter 9 resources.

You can easily launch a wide range of digital products from your computer's desktop with the McGraw-Hill Social Studies widget.

	Student	Teacher	Parent
Media Library			
• Student Edition Section Audio	●		●
• Chapter Spotlight Videos	●	●	●
***United States Government* Online Learning Center (Web Site)**			
• Chapter Overviews	●	●	●
• Multilingual Glossaries	●	●	●
• Study-to-Go	●	●	●
• Student Web Activities	●	●	●
• Self-Check Quizzes	●	●	●
• Online Student Edition	●	●	●
• Vocabulary eFlashcards	●	●	●
• Web Activity Lesson Plans		●	
• Vocabulary PuzzleMaker	●	●	●
• Landmark Supreme Court Cases	●	●	●
• Beyond the Textbook	●	●	●

READING SUPPORT FROM JAMESTOWN EDUCATION

- **Timed Readings Plus in Social Studies** helps students increase their reading rate and fluency while maintaining comprehension. The 400-word passages are similar to those found on state and national assessments.

- **Reading in the Content Area: Social Studies** concentrates on six essential reading skills that help students better comprehend what they read. The book includes 75 high-interest nonfiction passages written at increasing levels of difficulty.

- **Reading Social Studies** includes strategic reading instruction and vocabulary support in Social Studies content for ELLs and native speakers of English. www.jamestowneducation.com

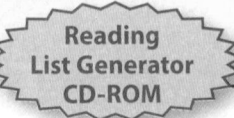

Reading List Generator CD-ROM

GLENCOE BookLink 3

Use this database to search more than 30,000 titles to create a customized reading list for your students.

- Reading lists can be organized by students' reading level, author, genre, theme, or area of interest.

- The database provides Degrees of Reading Power™ (DRP) and Lexile™ readability scores for all selections.

- A brief summary of each selection is included.

Leveled reading suggestions for this chapter:

- *Abraham Lincoln: The Writer,* by Harold Holzer
- *Kennedy,* by Theodore D. Sorensen
- *Leader by Destiny: George Washington, Man and Patriot,* by Jeannette Eaton

Review suggested books before assigning them.

Economics Connection

Personal Finance Literacy

Acing an Interview

Applicants for civil service and other jobs complete applications, but whether a person is applying for a government job or a civilian one, the interview is the most important step. Tell students: Prepare by researching the company's products, history, financial status, and so on. Use the Internet or ask the human resources department for brochures. Practice answering questions such as "Why do you want to work here?" If you are asked, "What are your weaknesses?" be prepared with one that would not interfere with doing a good job.

Appearance is important, so dress neatly and appropriately for the job or one level up. Ask the receptionist what the dress code is. If it is "business casual," do not wear jeans and a T-shirt or a double-breasted suit. Shake hands firmly with the interviewer and address the person as Mr. or Ms. unless told otherwise. Be enthusiastic, maintain eye contact, and answer questions honestly. Focus on how you can meet the needs of the *company*—not on yourself. After the interview, shake hands and give the interviewer a typed list of references.

Do	Don't
Arrive early	Say anything negative about former employers
Be polite to everyone you meet in the office	Look disinterested
Ask questions showing interest in the company	Mention salary until the interviewer does
Follow up with a thank-you note; briefly state your interest in the job and your qualifications	Chew gum, eat, leave your cell phone or pager on, talk about your personal life

Ask students: How many of you have had job interviews? What was your experience like, and did you get the job?

Did You Know?

In a recent survey, hiring managers cited these reasons for not hiring applicants: 51% inappropriate dress, 49% badmouthing a former employer, 44% arrogance, 30% insufficient answers.

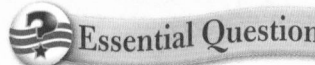

9

Chapter Audio   Spotlight Video

Presidential Leadership

Essential Question

Refer students to the Essential Question on this page. Ask students if they can list the powers of the president. Have them determine which of those powers affect the other two branches of government. Ask students if they think the president has too much or too little power over the other branches.

Chapter Spotlight Video

To generate student interest and provide a springboard for class discussion, access the Chapter 9 Video at glencoe.com or on the video DVD.

FOLDABLES
Study Organizer

Dinah Zike's Foldables are three-dimensional, interactive graphic organizers that help students practice basic writing skills, review key vocabulary terms, and identify main ideas. Have students complete this chapter's Foldable activity or activities in *Dinah Zike's Reading and Study Skills Foldables* booklet. **OL**

▶ President John F. Kennedy

Essential Question

What basic powers of the presidency directly affect the other two branches of government—the legislature and the judiciary?

Government ONLINE
Chapter Overview Visit glencoe.com and enter *QuickPass*™ code USG9822c9 for an overview, a quiz, and other chapter resources.

244

Visit glencoe.com and enter *QuickPass*™ code USG9085c9T for Chapter 9 Resources including Chapter Overview, Student Web Activity, Self-Check Quiz, and other materials for students and teachers.

Launching the Chapter

Evaluating The president of the United States must assume many roles while in office. Each role requires him or her to perform different duties. The president is the nation's chief diplomat, economic planner, head of state, chief legislator, party leader, commander in chief, and chief executive. **Essential Question:** What qualities and skills should a president possess to fulfill these roles? *(Allow students to brainstorm ideas. Then, discuss which presidents have best demonstrated those qualities.)* **OL**

Presidential Powers

Focus

Reader's Guide

Content Vocabulary
★ mandate *(p. 248)*
★ forum *(p. 249)*

Academic Vocabulary
★ enforce *(p. 245)*
★ annual *(p. 247)*
★ medium *(p. 249)*

Reading Strategy
Create a graphic organizer like the one at the right to list some of the powers given to the president by the Constitution.

Powers of the President

Bellringer
Section Focus Transparencies 9-1

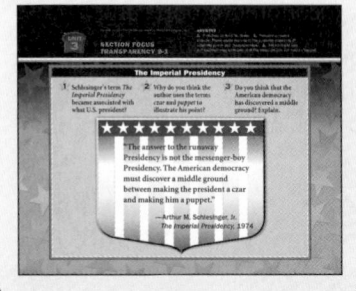

Issues in the News

In October 2007 Rep. John Yarmuth (D-KY) gave fellow House members buttons saying "Article 1." It was his way of reminding them that the Constitution gives the executive branch very limited powers. Yarmuth is worried because President George W. Bush has used "signing statements" far more than any other president. Signing statements are a president's official notes on bills signed into law that assert that the president has a right not to enforce it—at least, under his or her interpretation of the Constitution. Some scholars say Bush was merely making a statement about executive power and that the president would not actually instruct federal agencies not to obey the law. Others say there is no way to be sure.

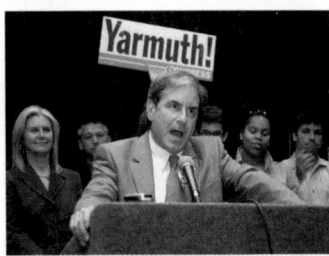

▲ Representative John Yarmuth wants House members to remember the limits on executive power.

Reader's Guide

Answers to Graphic:
• controls armed forces
• proposes legislation
• vetoes legislation
• appoints executive officials
• appoints judges
• issues pardons
• conducts foreign policy

Like signing statements, many presidential powers are not mentioned in the Constitution. Instead, they have developed over time, reflecting the changing national needs and the personalities of the presidents. The Founders crafted the office carefully, relying on their understanding of human nature and on their experience with the British king and his officials. The Founders also realized that the executive office would reflect the personal characteristics of a particular president.

The sources of presidential power and the limitations on the office have interacted throughout American history. The office may have been defined by the Constitution narrowly, but many factors have shaped it into its modern form—the immediate needs of the nation, the personal energy and influence of each president, and popular support for a president's programs.

Constitutional Powers

The Founders made the president the head of the executive branch. Having fought a revolution against the hated king of Britain, the Framers of the Constitution did not want the leader of the new executive branch to become a tyrant. However, despite these concerns, there were two reasons to give the national government a strong executive.

Need for a Strong Executive

First, the Founders knew that one of the main weaknesses of the Articles of Confederation was its lack of an independent executive. Without an executive, the government had no one to carry out the acts of Congress. Moreover, this made it difficult for the government to respond quickly to problems and to **enforce** laws.

Resource Manager

R Reading Strategies	C Critical Thinking	D Differentiated Instruction	W Writing Support	S Skill Practice
Teacher Edition • Organizing, p. 246 • Using Context Clues, p. 247 **Additional Resources** • Quizzes/Tests, p. 103 • Guid. Read. Act., p. 33	**Teacher Edition** • Drawing Conclusions, p. 250 **Additional Resources** • Read. Essen., pp. 95–97 • Supreme Ct. Case Studies, pp. 161–162	**Additional Resources** • Foldables, p. 52 • Reteaching Act., p. 9	**Additional Resources** • Supreme Ct. Case Studies, pp. 1–2 • Authentic Assess., p. 16	**Teacher Edition** • Creating a Cause-and-Effect Chart, p. 249 **Additional Resources** • Skill Reinforce. Act., p. 9

Teach

R Reading Strategy

Organizing Instruct students to create a graphic organizer showing the presidential powers. Ask volunteers to share their organizers with the class. Discuss the effectiveness of each power. **BL**

Comparing Governments

Answer: French presidential powers include appointing the prime minister, dissolving the legislature, and suspending rights, whereas the U.S. president is not authorized to perform these functions.

Research Activity: Assign one of the nations listed in the chart to each of seven groups. Have each group make a graphic organizer illustrating the assigned nation's presidential election process, as well as the length of service and constitutional powers of the president. **OL**

Additional Support

Second, many of the Founders distrusted direct participation by the people in decision making. They feared that mass democratic movements might try to redistribute personal wealth and threaten private property. Consequently, they wanted a strong executive branch that would protect liberty, private property, and businesses and would hold the legislature (the branch that directly represents popular opinion) in check.

Presidential Powers in Article II

Article II of the Constitution grants the president broad but vaguely described powers, simply stating that, "The Executive Power shall be vested in a President of the United States of America."

Sections 2 and 3 of Article II define the president's powers.[1] As commander in chief of the armed forces, the president is mainly responsible for the nation's security. As head of the executive branch, the president appoints, and the Senate confirms, the heads of executive departments. The chief executive also conducts foreign policy, making treaties with the advice and consent of the Senate, and appointing ambassadors. In addition, the president has some power over the judiciary. He or she appoints federal court judges, can pardon people convicted of federal crimes (except in cases of impeachment), and can reduce a person's jail sentence or fine.

See the following footnoted materials in the **Reference Handbook:**
1. *The Constitution, pages R42–R67.*

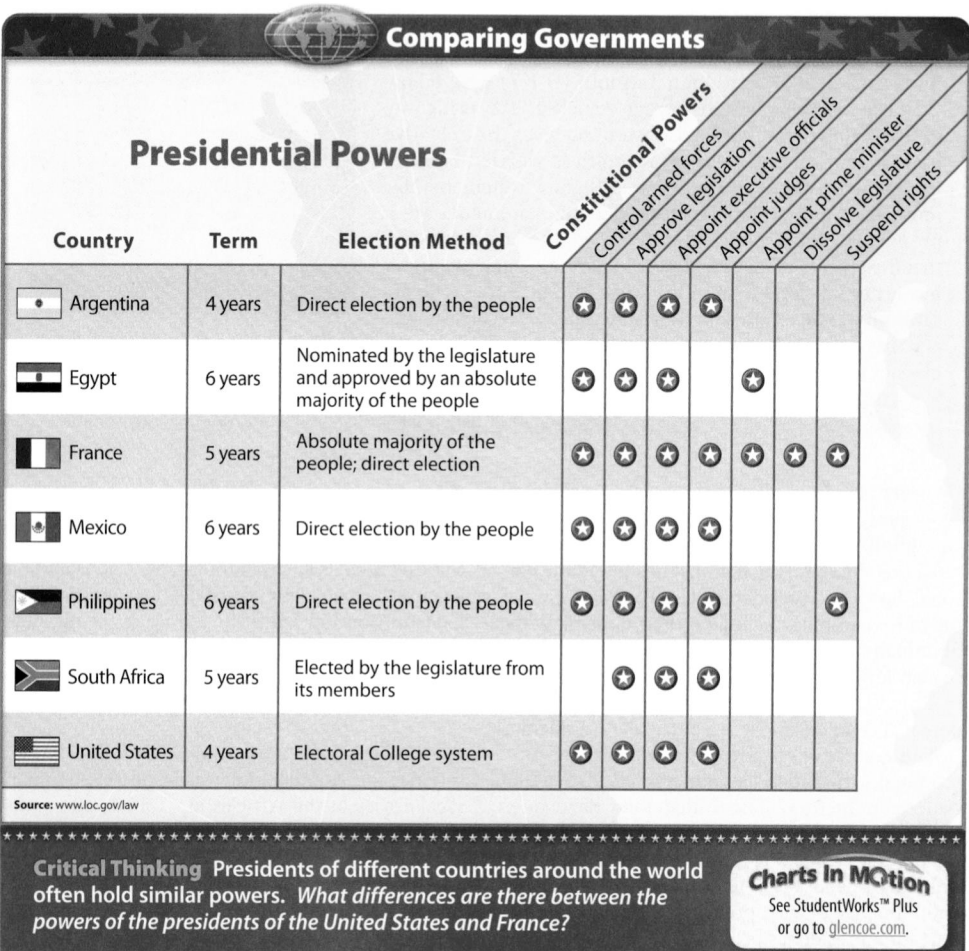

Comparing Governments

Presidential Powers

Country	Term	Election Method	Constitutional Powers						
			Control armed forces	Approve legislation	Appoint executive officials	Appoint judges	Appoint prime minister	Dissolve legislature	Suspend rights
● Argentina	4 years	Direct election by the people	★	★	★	★			
▬ Egypt	6 years	Nominated by the legislature and approved by an absolute majority of the people	★	★	★		★		
▮ France	5 years	Absolute majority of the people; direct election	★	★	★	★	★	★	★
▬ Mexico	6 years	Direct election by the people	★	★	★	★			
▶ Philippines	6 years	Direct election by the people	★	★	★	★			★
▬ South Africa	5 years	Elected by the legislature from its members		★	★	★			
▬ United States	4 years	Electoral College system	★	★	★	★			

Source: www.loc.gov/law

Critical Thinking Presidents of different countries around the world often hold similar powers. *What differences are there between the powers of the presidents of the United States and France?*

Charts In Motion
See StudentWorks™ Plus or go to glencoe.com.

Activity: Collaborative Learning

Polling Popularity The Gallup presidential approval survey is an important measure of the president's standing with the public. It tells whether the public approves or disapproves of the president's handling of the job. Have students create and conduct a presidential poll. Organize the class into groups of three to compile a list of five questions about an issue that the president has recently addressed. Each student in a group should be responsible for polling peers, school faculty members, or community members. Each group should tabulate its results and present its findings. After groups present their findings to the class, discuss what the polls revealed about how the public views the president's recent decisions. **OL**

Presidential Decisions

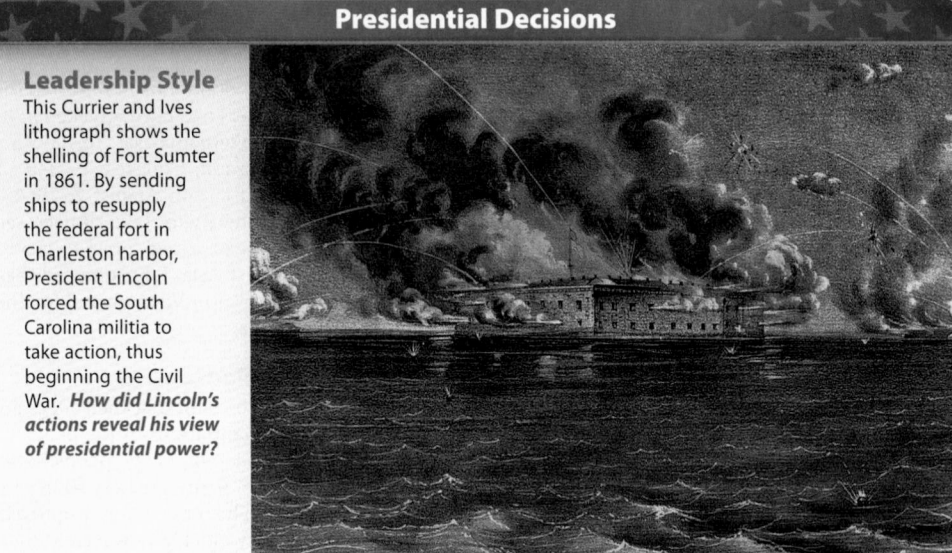

Leadership Style This Currier and Ives lithograph shows the shelling of Fort Sumter in 1861. By sending ships to resupply the federal fort in Charleston harbor, President Lincoln forced the South Carolina militia to take action, thus beginning the Civil War. *How did Lincoln's actions reveal his view of presidential power?*

R **Reading Strategy**

Using Context Clues Have students read the quote from Theodore Roosevelt. **Ask:** Using context clues, can you figure out the meaning of *usurpation*? *(taking something by force or without right)* **ELL**

Did You Know?

After the fall of Fort Sumter, President Lincoln called for 75,000 volunteers to serve in the military for 90 days. This created a crisis in the Upper South. Many people there did not want to secede, but faced with the prospect of civil war, believed they had no choice but to leave the Union. Virginia seceded on April 17, 1861. By early June, Arkansas, North Carolina, and Tennessee had also seceded.

Additional Support

Working with the legislature, the president ensures that the laws Congress passes are "faithfully executed." The president delivers an **annual** State of the Union message to Congress, proposes legislation, and can call Congress into special session when necessary.

Informal Sources of Power

The Constitution's list of presidential powers is brief and simple, but ever since George Washington's presidency, the list has expanded greatly. Today, these powers come from several sources besides the Constitution.

Personal Exercise of Power

Over the years, some presidents have added to the power of the presidency simply by how they have handled the job. Each president has defined the office in unique ways. A number of presidents have expanded the powers of the executive because of their beliefs about the office.

In 1803 Thomas Jefferson made the decision to purchase the Louisiana Territory from France. Nothing in the Constitution, however, stated that a president had the power to acquire territory. Jefferson decided that the presidency had inherent powers, or powers attached to the office itself. These were powers the Constitution did not specifically define but

that Article II implied. The Senate agreed with Jefferson and ratified the Louisiana Purchase treaty.

Theodore Roosevelt expressed the broad view of presidential power, explaining that it was both the president's right and duty to "do anything that the needs of the Nation demanded, unless such action was forbidden by the Constitution or by the laws." In a letter to a contemporary historian, Roosevelt explained:

> ❝ *I have used every ounce of power there was in the office and I have not cared a rap for the criticisms of those who spoke of my 'usurpation of power'; . . . I believe that the efficiency of this Government depends upon its possessing a strong central executive. . . .* ❞ **R**
> —Theodore Roosevelt, 1908

Immediate Needs of the Nation

During the Civil War, Abraham Lincoln took actions that led some people to call him a dictator. He suspended the writ of habeas corpus and jailed opponents of the Union without a trial or the legal authority to do so. He raised an army before getting Congress's approval. He took illegal action against the South by blockading its ports. Lincoln claimed the Constitution gave him the authority to do what was necessary to preserve the Union. In the end, the nation agreed with the president.

Activity: Interdisciplinary Connection

Mathematics When Franklin D. Roosevelt became president in 1933, about 600,000 people worked for the federal government. By 1945 the federal government employed more than 3 million workers. Have students research the number of people who worked for the government at the end of each decade from 1940 to the present. Have students plot the information on a graph. Encourage students to be creative in their choice of graph styles, colors, and graphics. Display completed graphs, and discuss the changes in the number of workers. **OL**

POLITICAL PROFILES

Theodore Roosevelt
(1858–1919)

President Theodore Roosevelt raised a ruckus with the press in 1906 when he ordered the government printer to abide by a list of 300 words to be spelled according to the Simplified Spelling Board guidelines. Funded by millionaire industrialist and philanthropist Andrew Carnegie, the organization crusaded for respellings that deleted, for example, the *u* in *honour* and *parlour,* the standard British spellings. The press challenged the president's power to change American orthography, and Congress instructed the printing office that all the material sent to its chambers maintain standard British spellings. Roosevelt regretfully withdrew his order in response to the public outcry. The changes eventually came into general usage anyway.

Caption Answer: Students may note that a president might not be able to get his or her point of view across effectively and might have difficulty getting policies enacted.

Hands-On Chapter Project
Step 1

Presidential Rhetoric

Step 1: Selecting the Speech

Directions Divide the class into groups. Have students choose a speech from a list of notable twentieth-century presidential addresses. The list might include: FDR, first Inaugural Address, March 4, 1933; FDR, "Four Freedoms," January 6, 1941; DDE, "Farewell Address," January 17, 1961; JFK, Inaugural Address, January 21, 1961; JFK, call for a civil rights bill, June 11, 1963; LBJ,

call for a voting rights bill, March 15, 1965; Nixon, "Silent Majority," November 3, 1969; Ford, address on taking office, August 9, 1974; and Reagan, "The Evil Empire," March 8, 1983.

Ideally students will analyze an audio or video recording of the speech. Some sources are *The Library of Congress Presents Historical Presidential Speeches* (audiobook), *The Greatest Speeches of All Time* (DVD), and the Vincent Voice Library at Michigan State University (online). Recordings of the speeches are also available from a variety of Internet sources.

Researching Before they listen to the speech, have students research the subject and historical context of the speech. **AL**

(Chapter Project continued in Section 2.)

Franklin D. Roosevelt used the power of the presidency to expand the role of the federal government in the economy. The economic crisis of the Great Depression was severe, with 25 percent of the population without jobs. Roosevelt persuaded Congress to create many new programs to provide income for the elderly, supply people with jobs, regulate banks, and set up the federal agencies to run these programs. After Roosevelt, Americans expected their presidents to take a firm hand in directing the nation's economy.

In 2001 the terrorist attacks on New York City and Washington, D.C., transformed the presidency of George W. Bush. He had gained office nine months earlier in a close, bitterly contested election. A poll at the time showed that 40 percent of the public did not believe Bush won the election fairly. The terrorist attacks, however, changed everything. Americans now looked to the president for leadership. Bush responded by declaring that the "war on terrorism" would be the focus of his presidency. "I will not yield; I will not rest; I will not relent in waging this struggle for freedom and security for the American people." During this crisis, he gained sweeping authority from Congress to fight terrorism, and his public approval ratings temporarily soared to 90 percent.

Although Congress sometimes complains about presidential power, it often grants a president special powers during emergencies. In 1964, for example, President Lyndon Johnson reported that two American destroyers had been attacked in the Gulf of Tonkin off the Vietnam coast. To allow him to cope with the situation, Congress passed the Gulf of Tonkin Resolution on August 7, 1964. It gave the president authority to "take all necessary steps, including the use of armed force" to protect Americans in Southeast Asia. Johnson used these powers to expand the war in Vietnam and in other parts of Southeast Asia.

Mandate of the People

All presidents like to claim that their ideas and policies represent a **mandate** from the people. A mandate—the expressed will of the people, often in an election—is one of the greatest sources of presidential power. The president's popularity ratings can change very quickly, however. Modern presidents have thus learned to use the mass media to communicate their message and to gain popular support for what they want to do.

Today, television gives presidents even greater power to convey their ideas and personalities directly to the American people. The media called

The Bully Pulpit

Great Communicators
In the early 1900s, President Theodore Roosevelt referred to the "bully pulpit"—his forum for persuading citizens and advocating his agenda. President Franklin D. Roosevelt, seen here with radio microphones, unified the nation during the Depression with his "fireside" chats. In the 1980s, Ronald Reagan was known for being able to connect with a national television audience through his speeches. *What repercussions might follow for a president who is not a good communicator?*

President Ronald Reagan "the Great Communicator" partly because of his ability to deliver his message directly to the people through television. People often judge a president's ideas by how appealing he or she appears on television, a fact presidents know very well and try to use.

Major newspapers, magazines, and the Internet also provide a **forum,** or **medium** for discussion, for presidential messages. The print media assign reporters to cover the president full-time. White House staff make sure these reporters receive a steady flow of information about the president's activities and ideas. One of the staff's objectives is to create the image of a president as an active, personable servant of the people.

Limits on Executive Power

The Founders built significant safeguards into the Constitution against the possibility that presidents would abuse their lawful powers. Congress and the courts are able to limit the president's authority. Besides these constitutional limitations, the president's actions can be limited in a number of other ways.

Limitation by Congress

The Constitution gives Congress the power to pass legislation even after a president has vetoed it. This power to override a president's veto limits executive power. For example, in 1973, President Richard Nixon vetoed the War Powers Act, but Congress overrode his veto. The War Powers Act prevented presidents from committing troops to combat for more than 60 days without congressional approval. Congress felt that Nixon and Lyndon B. Johnson abused their powers as commander in chief by committing American troops to fighting a long, undeclared war in Vietnam.

What other ways can Congress limit a president? First, the Senate must confirm a president's appointees. Second, the House of Representatives must approve the budget. Third, the House and Senate can use the impeachment process to remove the president from office.

In the nation's history, the House of Representatives has initiated impeachment proceedings against three presidents. In 1868, just after the end of the Civil War, the House impeached President Andrew Johnson over issues related to how southern states would be reconstructed. The Senate acquitted him by one vote. In 1974 the House prepared impeachment charges against President Richard Nixon, but

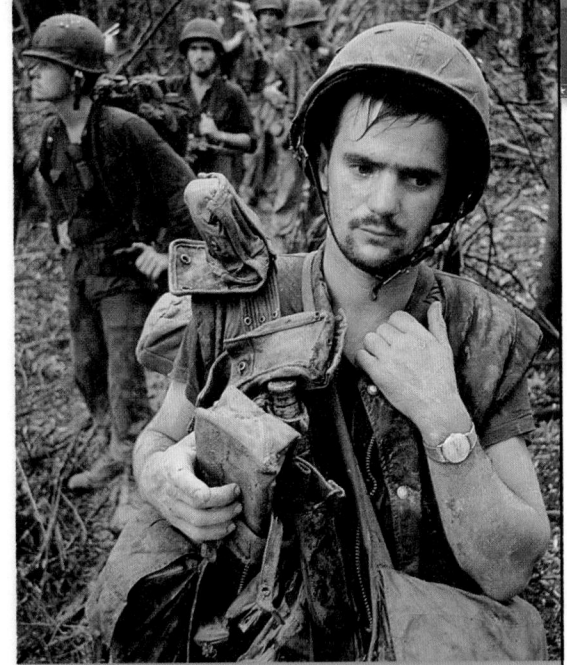

Checks and Balances Congress concluded that American involvement in the Vietnam War was a result of an abuse of presidential power. It proposed the War Powers Act in 1973 to limit the president, even mustering the necessary votes to override the president's veto. *How does the War Powers Act reflect the principle of checks and balances?*

he resigned before they could be voted on by the full House. In 1999 the House brought two charges of impeachment against President Bill Clinton, but after a short trial, the Senate acquitted him.

Limitation by the Federal Courts

Because of a historic Supreme Court decision, the federal courts also have the power to limit a president. In *Marbury* v. *Madison*[1] (1803), the Court said that it had the right to the final interpretation of whether an act of the legislature or the president violates the Constitution. This happened several times during the Great Depression, when the Supreme Court ruled that some of President Franklin D. Roosevelt's New Deal legislation was unconstitutional.

📖 *See the following footnoted materials in the **Reference Handbook:***
1. *Marbury* v. *Madison,* page R30.

CHAPTER 9, SECTION 1

S **Skill Practice**

Creating a Cause-and-Effect Chart Have students make a cause-and-effect chart showing the relationship between the Vietnam War and the War Powers Act. (*Charts should show that the War Powers Act was a response to the fact that Johnson and Nixon committed troops to fight in Vietnam without an explicit declaration of war by Congress.*) **OL**

Caption Answer: Congress was able to override the president's veto of the War Powers Act and assert its role as the branch of government with the power to declare war, thereby balancing the power of the president as commander in chief.

GO TO To enrich study of chapter content, remind students that footnoted materials appear in the *Reference Handbook.*

Additional Support

Activity: Interdisciplinary Connection

Daily Life Have students use a variety of news sources to chart the president's activities over a two-week period. Have students create charts with the following headings: *Activity, Power Exercised,* and *Limits.* For each presidential activity, direct students to write a brief statement describing the powers being exercised and the limitations being imposed. Be sure students include media coverage and public opinion as limitations. Call on volunteers to evaluate the limitations and the powers of the president. **AL**

C Critical Thinking

Drawing Conclusions Ask: How did the Supreme Court's decision in *Hamdi* v. *Rumsfeld* demonstrate the principle of checks and balances? *(The Court checked the power of the executive branch by requiring the government to grant detainees a judicial hearing.)* **OL**

Assess

Assign the Section 1 Assessment as homework or as an in-class activity, or have students take Section Quiz 9-1 from *Section Quizzes and Chapter Tests.*

Close

Drawing Conclusions

Ask: What kind of limits on presidential power are the most effective? *(Take a class vote and discuss the results.)* **OL**

Section 1 Review

Youngstown Sheet and Tube Company v. Sawyer (1952)

This 1950s case focused on an important issue. Could the president act in areas of authority that the Constitution delegates to Congress if the Congress failed to act? Before this decision, a president's action in similar situations was challenged only if Congress passed a law assuming its authority.

In 1952 President Harry S. Truman, believing a strike by steelworkers could threaten national security, ordered his secretary of commerce to seize and operate most of the nation's steel mills. The president reported all of this to Congress, but Congress failed to take action. In earlier cases, Congress had provided procedures for dealing with similar situations.

The steel companies resisted a government takeover of their mills by suing Commerce Secretary Charles Sawyer. The case eventually reached the Supreme Court. Writing for the majority, Justice Hugo Black noted that no statute authorized the president to take over the mills. Black argued that just because Congress had not exercised its powers to seize the mills did not mean that the president could do so: "The Founders of this Nation entrusted the lawmaking power to the Congress alone in both good and bad times."

Following the attacks of September 11, 2001, President George W. Bush attempted to expand presidential powers as a way to fight terrorism. This led to several Supreme Court decisions limiting the president's ability to undertake sweeping new anti-terrorism measures.

In 2004, for example, the Court ruled in *Hamdi* v. *Rumsfeld* that the president cannot indefinitely lock up foreigners or U.S. citizens without giving them a chance to challenge their detention in court. In 2006 the justices rejected the Bush administration's use of specially created courts called military tribunals to try suspected terrorists.

Limitation by the Bureaucracy

The federal bureaucracy sometimes limits presidential powers. Bureaucrats can obstruct presidents' programs unintentionally by failing to provide needed information, by misinterpreting instructions, and by not completing a task properly. Bureaucrats have some discretion to interpret laws, and at times their interpretations may not reflect the president's priorities either intentionally or unintentionally.

Limitation by Public Opinion

Public opinion can also affect a president. In 1968 public dissatisfaction with President Johnson's conduct of the Vietnam War convinced him to retire instead of running for reelection. Without favorable public opinion, no president can carry out a political program. For example, in 1993 President Clinton proposed major changes to the nation's health-care system. Various interests groups, including insurance companies and doctors, began to campaign against the president's proposal. When public opinion turned against the plan, Congress decided not to act on Clinton's proposal.

SECTION 1 Review

Vocabulary

1. **Explain** the significance of: mandate, forum.

Main Ideas

2. **Summarizing** In what three ways have former presidents expanded the power of their office?

3. **Explaining** Why, during Lyndon B. Johnson's presidency, did Congress pass the Gulf of Tonkin Resolution?

Critical Thinking

4. **Distinguishing Fact from Opinion** President Woodrow Wilson said that the president "is at liberty, both in law and conscience . . . to be as big a man as he can." Explain whether this statement is fact or opinion.

5. **Listing** Using a graphic organizer like the one below, list two or more constitutional limits and three other limits on presidential power.

Constitutional Limits	Other Limits

Writing About Government

6. **Descriptive Writing** Determine whether you think there should be greater limits on the president's power. Compose several catchy slogans supporting your view and create signs or buttons that might be used in a rally.

Answers

1. All definitions can be found in the section and the Glossary.
2. Any three of the following: Thomas Jefferson's purchase of the Louisiana Territory, Theodore Roosevelt's broad interpretation of presidential power, Abraham Lincoln's actions during the Civil War, Franklin D. Roosevelt's expansion of the government's role in the economy.
3. to give the president the authority to defend U.S. forces from armed attack in Southeast Asia
4. Some students may say it is opinion because many presidents believed the Constitution

limited their power. Others may say fact because other presidents molded the office to their own interpretations of the Constitution.
5. Answers might include: Constitutional limits: congressional veto override; Senate's confirmation power; the power to impeach. Other limits: federal courts; the bureaucracy; public opinion.
6. Slogans should illustrate whether the president's power should be limited.

Does National Security Justify Wiretaps?

United States v. United States District Court, 1972

The Constitution calls upon the president to "preserve, protect and defend the Constitution of the United States." Can the president order electronic surveillance of people without a search warrant if the purpose is to protect against domestic threats to national security? The case United States v. United States District Court *addressed this issue in 1972.*

Facts of the Case

In the early 1970s, several antiwar groups were accused of plotting against the government. President Richard Nixon's administration began to use wiretaps without a search warrant to monitor citizens they suspected of such activities. The defendant in the case was accused of bombing an office of the Central Intelligence Agency in Michigan. He argued that evidence used against him was obtained illegally. The government responded that although it did not have a warrant, the wiretap was lawful because it was the president's duty to protect national security. A U.S. District Court ruled that the evidence was gathered illegally and had to be made available to the defendant before his trial. The attorney general filed suit to set aside the district court's order.

The Constitutional Question

In reviewing the case, the Supreme Court explained:

> 66 *Its resolution is a matter of national concern, requiring sensitivity both to the Government's right to protect itself from unlawful subversion and attack and to the citizen's right to be secure in his privacy against unreasonable Government intrusion.* 99
>
> —Justice Lewis F. Powell, Jr., 1972

The government argued that such surveillance was a reasonable exercise of the president's power to protect domestic security. Further, the government claimed that judges would not have the expertise in such complex situations to determine whether there really was "probable cause." Finally, the government argued that secrecy is essential in domestic security cases; informing a judge in order to get a warrant would create the risk of leaks.

▼ **Lawrence Plamondon, below, arriving at a federal court in Michigan**

Debating the Issue

Questions to Consider

1. Should domestic security cases be handled differently than other types of crimes?

2. What could be the consequences of allowing the wiretapping in such cases without a warrant?

3. Does the government need a search warrant to wiretap in domestic security cases?

You Be the Judge

The Fourth Amendment protects citizens from "unreasonable searches and seizures" by requiring police to obtain a warrant from a judge. The judge must decide if there is "probable cause" before a search warrant can be issued. Should the Court make an exception in cases of national security? Why or why not?

Class Debate

A search without probable cause is prohibited by the Fourth Amendment. Even when probable cause is found, the law considers wiretapping to be intrusive. Hold a debate on whether this case is a violation of the Fourth Amendment. First, select an odd number of unbiased "justices." Next, organize the class into two groups based upon whether students believe this case is a violation of the Fourth Amendment. Have group members write a brief to summarize their arguments and choose one member to present their case. Allow the justices to ask questions and other group members to assist the presenter. Have the justices rule on the case and write a majority and, if possible, a dissenting opinion.

The Court's Decision

In *United States* v. *United States District Court* (1972), the Supreme Court unanimously rejected the government's claim that it did not need a search warrant. Justice Lewis Powell stated, "We do not think a case has been made for the requested departure from the Fourth Amendment standards. The circumstances described do not justify complete exemption of domestic security surveillance from prior judicial scrutiny [a search warrant]."

Debating the Issue Answers

Questions to Consider

1. Possible answers: yes, because the government has the right to protect itself from unlawful subversion and attack; no, due to the citizen's right to privacy against unreasonable government intrusion

2. The evidence would not be admissible in court.

3. According to the ruling in this case, yes; students should support their opinions.

You Be the Judge

Answers will vary, but students should defend their answers. Students' answers should be based on the special circumstances involved and whether Fourth Amendment rights were violated.

Focus

Bellringer

Section Focus Transparencies 9-2

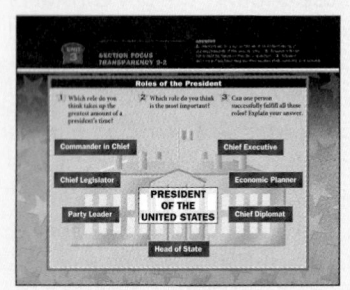

Reader's Guide

Answers to Graphic:

Head of State: directs government, represents nation

Chief Executive: carries out laws

Chief Legislator: proposes legislation

Economic Planner: submits economic reports and prepares budget

Party Leader: fund-raises, appoints party members to office, plans election strategies

Chief Diplomat: directs foreign policy

Commander in Chief: controls armed forces

Resource Manager

Roles of the President

Reader's Guide

Content Vocabulary
- ★ executive order *(p. 253)*
- ★ impoundment *(p. 253)*
- ★ reprieve *(p. 254)*
- ★ pardon *(p. 254)*
- ★ amnesty *(p. 254)*
- ★ patronage *(p. 256)*
- ★ treaty *(p. 257)*
- ★ executive agreement *(p. 257)*

Academic Vocabulary
- ★ design *(p. 253)*
- ★ submit *(p. 256)*
- ★ inspect *(p. 259)*

Reading Strategy
Create a table to identify the different roles and duties of the president.

Role	Duties

Issues in the News

In the early 1970s, President Richard Nixon directed cabinet members not to spend certain funds appropriated by Congress, arguing that the programs were wasteful. Nixon withheld $8.7 billion designated for programs he believed were useless. Previous presidents had occasionally impounded, or withheld, smaller amounts of appropriated monies for a short time, but no president had used this power on such a large scale. Congress fought back and passed the Impoundment Control Act in 1974. The act established rules regarding when, and for how long, a president can impound funds.

▲ Nixon impounding program funds

When President Richard Nixon impounded funds, it raised a major issue about the exact power and duties of a president. What are the roles of the president? The president has seven key duties, and five are specified in the Constitution: serving as head of state, chief executive, chief legislator, chief diplomat, and commander in chief. Two other duties—economic planner and political party leader—are not implied in the Constitution but have developed over time.

Head of State

As head of state, the president represents the nation and performs many ceremonial roles. Serving as host to visiting kings, queens, and heads of governments, the president is the nation's chief diplomat. Other ceremonial duties are less vital but are often covered in the press. In a tradition dating back to the early 1900s, many presidents throw out the first pitch to begin the baseball season, light the nation's Christmas tree on the White House lawn, or meet public figures or give awards to distinguished business leaders, actors, or artists. These activities are considered a part of the president's role.

The president is both head of state and chief executive. In most countries, these two duties are distinct. One person, a king or queen, or a president without substantial powers, is the ceremonial head of state, while another person, a prime minister or premier, directs the government.

This difference is important. Much of the mystique of the presidency exists because presidents are more than politicians. To millions around the world and to millions at home, the president is the symbol for the United States. As a living symbol of the nation, the president is not just a single individual, but the collective image of the United States.

R Reading Strategies	**C** Critical Thinking	**D** Differentiated Instruction	**W** Writing Support	**S** Skill Practice
Teacher Edition • Activating Prior Knowledge, p. 255 **Additional Resources** • Quizzes/Tests, p. 104 • Guid. Read. Act., p. 34 • Vocab. Act., p. 9	**Teacher Edition** • Evaluating, p. 258 • Drawing Conclusions, p. 259 **Additional Resources** • Read. Essen., pp. 98–101	**Teacher Edition** • Visual/Spatial, p. 253 **Additional Resources** • Foldables, p. 52 • Hist. Docs. and Speeches, p. 9	**Teacher Edition** • Personal Writing, pp. 253, 254 • Persuasive Writing, p. 257 **Additional Resources** • Part. in Gov. Act., pp. 17–18	**Teacher Edition** • Interpreting Visuals, p. 255 **Additional Resources** • Inter. Poli. Cartoons, pp. 17–18

Chief Executive

As the nation's chief executive, the president sees that the laws of Congress are carried out. These laws range over a great many areas of public concern from Social Security, taxes, housing, flood control, and energy to civil rights, health care, education, and environmental protection.

The executive branch employs more than 2 million people to enforce the many laws and programs Congress establishes.[1] The president is in charge of these employees and the federal departments and agencies for which they work. Of course, no president could directly supervise the daily activities of all these people. At best, presidents can try to influence the way laws are implemented so the laws follow that president's own philosophy of government.

Tools of Influence

Presidents have several tools to influence how laws are carried out. One is the ability to issue **executive orders,** or rules that have the force of law. This power is implied by the Constitution because it charges the presidency with making certain that "the laws be faithfully executed." Thus, executive orders are issued to detail the specific actions federal agencies must take to implement a law. For example, President Jimmy Carter used an executive order to put thousands of acres of land in Alaska under the control of the National Park Service.

Executive orders have also been used, however, to make dramatic new policy. President Harry S. Truman used an executive order in 1948 to integrate the armed forces, while President Franklin D. Roosevelt used one to place Japanese Americans in internment camps during World War II. (See image above.)

Another presidential tool is the power to appoint people to important offices in the executive branch. Besides cabinet members, presidents appoint ("with the advice and consent of the Senate") about 2,200 top-level federal officials—agency directors, deputy directors, and their assistants. Presidents try to appoint officials who share their political beliefs because they will be committed to carrying out their goals.

A third tool that presidents can use is the right to fire officials they have appointed. President Nixon fired his secretary of the interior for opposing his Vietnam policies. It is not always easy, however, to remove a popular official who has

A Wartime Order Wartime fears of the Japanese led President Roosevelt to issue an executive order in early 1942. It authorized the military to round up Japanese Americans, including American citizens, and place them in camps for the duration of the war. *Why do executive orders have the force of law?*

congressional and public support. J. Edgar Hoover was the director of the Federal Bureau of Investigations for 48 years. Several presidents had doubts about his capacities and conduct, but Hoover was too popular to fire and held the position until his death in 1972.

Using a fourth tool, **impoundment** of funds, a president can refuse to allow a federal department or agency to spend money Congress has appropriated. Presidents have practiced impoundment for years. In 1803 President Thomas Jefferson did not spend money Congress set aside for new gunboats until less costly **designs** were found. Most impoundments have been for routine matters or specific items. Sometimes that money is appropriated, but later the president impounds the money because spending needs have changed. The Congress might agree with the president's judgment.

📖 *See the following footnoted materials in the **Reference Handbook:***
1. For number of employees by department, see *United States Data Bank,* page R100.

Teach

D Differentiated Instruction

Visual/Spatial Ask students to create a montage illustrating the five presidential tools of influence. Display completed montages and allow students to vote on the montage that most effectively depicts these roles. **BL**

Caption Answer: Presidents have the power to make sure laws are executed faithfully. Executive orders detail how federal agencies should implement the law.

W Writing Support

Personal Writing Ask students to imagine themselves in the position of one of the Japanese Americans pictured on this page. Then, have them write a one-page essay in which they describe how they would feel about being sent to a relocation camp. Would they feel more determined to prove their loyalty to the United States, or would they feel resentful or hostile? **OL**

Additional Support

Activity: Collaborative Learning

Media Coverage of Presidential Roles
In small groups, have students scan recent newsmagazines or the Internet for examples of the president functioning in the various roles listed in the textbook. Groups should find an example of each of the president's roles. After articles have been identified, tell groups to analyze how each role was portrayed in the media; for example, the photographs used, the tone of the article, and so on. Groups should present their findings and address the following questions: Which roles of the president receive the most news coverage? Why do you think this occurs? In which role does the current president spend the most time? **OL**

Caption Answer: Students may mention that Ford believed that pardoning Nixon would help the country move past the Watergate scandal or that he wished to avoid the national division that Nixon's trial could have created.

POLITICAL PROFILES

Gerald R. Ford (1913–2006) In an effort to put the Watergate scandal to rest, President Gerald Ford pardoned former president Richard Nixon. The pardon created a backlash. Ford's popularity rating plunged from 71 percent to 50 percent. People suspected that Ford had struck a bargain with Nixon: Nixon would resign; Ford would become president and pardon Nixon.

W Writing Support

Personal Writing Review the facts concerning the Watergate scandal and the possible involvement of President Richard Nixon. Ask students to decide what they would have done concerning Nixon if they had succeeded him as president. Challenge students to write speeches in which they explain their decisions to the American people. **OL**

Hands-On Chapter Project

Step 2

Presidential Rhetoric

Step 2: Analyzing the Speech

Directions Provide groups with a list of questions before they listen to the speech. The list could include the following questions:

- Who is the audience for the speech?
- What is the topic?
- Is it a speech intended to persuade its audience to take action on an issue? How effective is it as a call to action?

★ **Presidential Pardon** ★

Reactions to the President Gerald Ford entered the presidency hoping to pull a troubled country together. His pardon of Nixon, however, outraged many Americans who believed the president should be held accountable to the laws of the land. **Why do you think Ford pardoned Nixon?**

President Richard Nixon used this tool in a more radical manner by impounding huge sums —$13 billion in a single year—for broad social programs he opposed. Groups that would have benefited from the programs took Nixon to court. The court then ordered the president to spend the appropriated money. In response, Congress passed legislation to prevent such wholesale impounding.

Yet another tool is the power of the president to appoint officials to the judiciary. With Senate approval, the president appoints all federal judges, including the justices of the Supreme Court. By appointing justices with particular points of view on constitutional and other issues, presidents are

able to influence government and society. In 2005 President George W. Bush appointed two justices to the Supreme Court: John G. Roberts, Jr., as chief justice, and Samuel Alito. Both appointments were expected to shift the court's balance to a more conservative view.

Reprieves and Pardons

As chief executive, the president also can grant "reprieves and pardons for offenses against the United States." A **reprieve** grants a postponement of legal punishment. A **pardon** is a release from legal punishment. People who receive them have usually been convicted of a federal crime. An exception was in 1974 when President Gerald Ford granted Richard Nixon a full pardon before he could be indicted for any crimes he might have committed during the Watergate scandal. The pardon was very controversial, but it was fully within President Ford's power to grant it.

Amnesty

Finally, the president may grant **amnesty.** Amnesty is a group pardon to people for an offense against the government, often in a military situation. President Jimmy Carter granted amnesty to young men who evaded the draft during the Vietnam War. Another controversy involving amnesty arose in 2007. Some legislators from both parties proposed amnesty for undocumented workers who had lived in the United States for a long time. The proposal was part of a bill to address many sides of the illegal immigration problem.

Presidential amnesties can be controversial. Many citizens were angry over Carter's amnesty grant. Opposition also arose over President Bill Clinton's use of pardons on his last day in office. In particular, Clinton pardoned a wealthy business leader indicted for fraud whose ex-wife had donated money to Clinton's presidential library.

Chief Legislator

Congress expects the executive branch to propose legislation it wishes to see enacted. This was clarified when President Dwight D. Eisenhower once wanted Congress to act on a particular problem he was concerned about. The White House, however, neglected to draft a bill to deal with the situation. A member of Congress scolded the president's staff: "Don't expect us to start from scratch on what you people want. You draft the bills, and we work them over."

- Does the president use historical or symbolic references in the speech? If so, for what purpose?
- Does he use body language to accentuate his message?
- Does he emphasize points with his intonation or volume of speaking?
- Is his style folksy or scholarly?
- Does he have an accent? If so, does it add to or detract from his message?

Students should listen to the speech and respond to the questions.

Discussing Each group should discuss the speech and compile their answers to the questions. **OL**

(Chapter Project continued in Section 3.)

The President's Legislative Program

Usually the president describes a legislative program in the annual State of the Union message to Congress. It calls attention to the president's ideas about how to solve key problems facing the country. A detailed legislative program presented to Congress during the year reflects the president's values and political beliefs.

The president has a large staff to help write legislation. This legislation determines much of what Congress will do each year. The president's office also presents to Congress a suggested budget and an annual economic report.

Taking office after the assassination of President John F. Kennedy, Lyndon B. Johnson called upon Congress to enact Kennedy's programs:

> 66 I believe in the ability of the Congress, despite the divisions of opinions which characterize our Nation, to act—to act wisely, to act vigorously, to act speedily when the need arises. The need is here. The need is now. 99
>
> —Lyndon B. Johnson, 1963

Congress responded by passing a host of new domestic legislation that the administration proposed.

Tools of Presidential Lawmaking

When the president and the majority of Congress are from different political parties, the president must work harder to influence Congress to support the administration's programs. Presidents often meet with members of Congress to share their views. They also appoint several staff members to work closely with Congress on new laws.

Presidents may hand out political favors to get congressional support. They may visit the home state of a member of Congress to support his or her reelection. Or, a president may start a new federal project that will bring money and jobs to a member's home state or district.

An important presidential tool in lawmaking is the veto power. Each bill Congress passes is sent to the president for approval. The president may sign the bill, veto the bill, or lay it aside. Presidents sometimes use the threat of a veto to force Congress to stop a bill or change it to fit his or her wishes. The threat of a veto may succeed because Congress generally finds it very difficult to gather enough votes to override a veto.

Unlike most state governors, the president does not have the power to veto selected items in a bill. Congress attempted to give the president some power over individual items by passing the Line Item Veto Act in 1996. President Clinton began to use the new power almost immediately, but the law was challenged as soon as it went into effect. The law survived the initial challenges, but the Supreme Court agreed to hear appeals of two cases on the new veto power in 1998. In *Clinton v. City of New York*,[1] the Supreme Court struck down the law as unconstitutional. 📖

📖 *See the following footnoted materials in the **Reference Handbook:***
1. *Clinton v. City of New York* case summary, page R25.

★ Presidential Lawmaking ★

Maestro of the 88   **By Karl Hubenthal**

Political Strategy Soon after becoming president, Lyndon Johnson used his 22 years of congressional experience and skill as a legislator to persuade Congress to pass his "Great Society" programs. *How does the cartoonist depict President Johnson's abilities and success as chief legislator?*

R Reading Strategy

Activating Prior Knowledge
Ask students if they recall reading about the presidential line item veto in Chapter 6. **Ask:** Why did the U.S. Supreme Court rule the Line Item Veto Act unconstitutional? *(Article I of the U.S. Constitution gives Congress the sole power to write legislation. The president can only approve a bill in its entirety or veto it entirely. Approving parts of a bill and vetoing other parts would unconstitutionally give the executive branch authority that belongs solely to the legislative branch.)* **AL**

S Skill Practice

Interpreting Visuals Have students search newspapers and the Internet to find editorial cartoons about the current president. Then have them choose one and summarize the cartoon's message and the symbols or imagery the artist used to convey that message. **OL**

Caption Answer: Johnson is presented as the maestro of the 88th Congress, skillfully "playing" Congress to push through a variety of bills.

Additional Support

★ Activity: Collaborative Learning ★

Identifying Central Issues As chief diplomat, the president decides whether to recognize the governments of other countries. Have students research and list countries whose governments are not recognized by the United States and the reasons the president might have for not acknowledging those governments. Call on volunteers to name a country and the possible reasons its government is not recognized by the United States. After discussing the main issues, take a class vote to decide if the students agree or disagree with the president. **AL**

Participating
IN GOVERNMENT

AmeriCorps members help provide services, including housing renovation, child immunization, and neighborhood policing. They also address community needs in education, public safety, human services, and the environment. They may tutor teens, teach elementary school students, assist crime victims, start neighborhood crime watches, help turn vacant lots into neighborhood parks, provide assistance and companionship to the elderly or those with disabilities, lead community health awareness campaigns, restore coastlines, or respond to natural disasters with emergency relief for victims.

Activity: Discuss the mission of AmeriCorps and the services its members may provide to their communities. Ask students to work in small groups to create a list of local community needs that AmeriCorps volunteers might meet. Have groups share their lists with the class. Make a class list on the board of the top community needs. Encourage volunteers to propose effective methods to meet those needs. **OL**

Additional Support

Economic Planner

The president's role as chief economic planner has grown rapidly since Franklin D. Roosevelt's New Deal. The Employment Act of 1946 gave new duties to the president. This law directed the president to **submit** an annual economic report to Congress. The law also created a Council of Economic Advisers to study the economy and help prepare a report for the president. In the law, it was declared for the first time that the federal government was responsible for promoting high employment, production, and purchasing power.

Since 1946, Congress has continued to pass laws giving presidents the power to deal with economic problems. In 1970 Congress gave President Nixon power to control prices and wages. One year later, the president put a 90-day freeze on all prices, rents, wages, and salaries. (The law expired and was not renewed.)

One of the president's economic duties is to prepare an annual budget. The president supervises this work and spends many months with budget officials deciding which government programs to support and which programs to cut back. Decisions on the size of the budget, the deficit, and where monies will be spent all affect the nation's economy.

Party Leader

The president's political party expects the chief executive to be a party leader. The president may give speeches to help party members who are running for office or may attend fund-raising activities to help raise money for the party. The president also selects the party's national chair and often helps plan future election strategies.

Presidents are expected to appoint members of their party to government jobs. These appointments ensure that supporters will remain committed to a president's programs. Political **patronage,** or appointment to political office, rewards the people who have helped get a president elected.

Being a political party leader can be a difficult role for a president. People expect a president, as head of the government, to represent all Americans. Political parties, however, expect presidents to provide leadership for their own political party. Sometimes these conflicting roles cause problems. When President Bill Clinton compromised with the Republican Congress to enact legislation in 1996, he was criticized by the more liberal members of his party. If a president appears to act in a partisan way, that is, in a way that favors his or her party, the media and the public can be critical.

Participating
IN GOVERNMENT AmeriCorps

Joining AmeriCorps lets a student help society at the same time that he or she earns money to pay for further education. AmeriCorps is a federal program that allows young people to earn up to $4,725 for college or graduate school, or to pay for school loans in return for one year's service. Volunteers also receive living allowances and health care services.

AmeriCorps has many local projects for volunteers, but there are also two national programs. One is a conservation program, AmeriCorps-NCCC. People from ages 18 to 24 live at regional campuses and work in teams on community projects. The second program, AmeriCorps-VISTA, allows members to work on their own for other organizations. They can train community volunteers or help set up neighborhood programs, for example. This approach expands the number of people who volunteer and helps more people.

◄ **Volunteer at work**

256

Participating
IN GOVERNMENT ACTIVITY

1. Gather more information about AmeriCorps by writing to the Corporation for National & Community Service at 1201 New York Avenue, NW, Washington, D.C., 20525, or visit its Web site at www. nationalservice.org.

2. Prepare a report on your findings to share with the class.

★ Activity: Interdisciplinary Connection ★

Literature Many past presidents have written memoirs about their experiences in the White House. Ulysses S. Grant finished his memoirs just four days before he died in 1885. In *Personal Memoirs of Ulysses S. Grant,* the former president focused mainly on his military career, especially his service in the Mexican War and the Civil War. The book became a best seller. Have students select the memoirs of a president and skim or read the book. Then have them write flap copy for the book jacket. **OL**

Chief Diplomat

The president directs the foreign policy of the United States, making key decisions about the relations the United States has with other countries in the world. In this role, the president is the nation's chief diplomat.

Because Congress also has powers related to foreign policy, a struggle continues between the president and Congress over who will exercise control of the country's foreign policy. Presidents have an advantage in this struggle because they have access to more information about foreign affairs than most members of Congress do. The administration sometimes classifies this information as secret. The Central Intelligence Agency (CIA), the State Department, the Defense Department, and the National Security Council (NSC) constantly give the president the latest information needed to make key foreign-policy decisions. Skilled presidents use this information to plan and justify actions they want to take. Members of Congress who lack access to this information often find it difficult to challenge the president's decisions.

In addition, the ability to take decisive action has added greatly to the power of the presidency in foreign affairs. Unlike Congress, where the individual opinions of 435 representatives and 100 senators must be coordinated, the executive branch is headed by a single person. In a national emergency, the responsibility for action rests with the president.

The Power to Make Treaties

As chief diplomat, the president has sole power to negotiate and sign **treaties**—formal agreements between the governments of two or more countries. As part of the constitutional system of checks and balances, however, two-thirds of the Senate must approve all treaties before they can go into effect.

The Senate takes its constitutional responsibility about treaties very seriously. Sometimes the Senate will refuse to approve a treaty. After World War I, the Senate rejected the Treaty of Versailles, the agreement to end the war and to make the United States a member of the League of Nations. More recently, in 1978, only after lengthy debates and strong opposition did the Senate approve two treaties giving eventual control of the Panama Canal to the government of Panama.

The Power to Make Executive Agreements

The president also has the authority to make **executive agreements** with other countries. Executive agreements are pacts between the president and the head of a foreign government. These agreements have the same legal status as treaties, but they do not require Senate consent.

Most executive agreements involve routine matters, but some presidents have used executive agreements to conclude more serious arrangements with other countries. Franklin D. Roosevelt lent American ships to the British in exchange for leases on British military bases. At the time, the British were fighting Nazi Germany, but the United States had not yet entered the war. Roosevelt knew that the strongly isolationist Senate would not ratify a treaty. He therefore negotiated an executive agreement.

Some presidents have kept executive agreements secret. To prevent this, Congress passed a law in 1972 requiring the president to make public all executive agreements signed each year. Some presidents have ignored the law and kept secret those agreements they considered important to national security. In 1969 Congress discovered that several presidents had kept secret many executive agreements giving military aid to South Vietnam, Laos, Thailand, and the Philippines.

Recognition of Foreign Governments

As chief diplomat, the president decides whether the United States will recognize governments of other countries. This power means the president determines whether the government will acknowledge the legal existence of another government and have dealings with that government. Presidents sometimes use recognition as a foreign-policy tool. For example, since 1961, presidents have refused to recognize the Communist government of Cuba. This action indicates American opposition to the policies of the Cuban government.

Government ONLINE
Student Web Activity Visit glencoe.com and enter **QuickPass™** code USG9822c9. Click on Student Web Activity and complete the activity about the roles of the president.

Did You Know?

Commander in Chief In the capacity of commander in chief, U.S. presidents have committed military forces to almost 200 overseas conflicts, both large and small. Only five of these were formally declared wars by Congress. The five "official wars" were the War of 1812, the Mexican War, the Spanish-American War, World War I, and World War II.

W Writing Support

Persuasive Writing Have students learn more about U.S. relations with Cuba. Then ask each student to write a letter to the president that supports maintaining the embargo against Cuba or calls for its repeal. **OL**

Government ONLINE
Objectives and answers to the Student Web Activity can be found in the **Web Activity Lesson Plan** at glencoe.com. Enter **QuickPass™** code USG9085c9T.

Differentiated Instruction

Leveled Activities

BL Reteaching Activities, p. 9

OL Vocabulary Activities, p. 9

AL Authentic Assessment with Rubrics, p. 16

ELL Skill Reinforcement Activities, p. 9

Commanding the Military

Some presidents, such as Bill Clinton, have had no military experience. In fact, during the 1992 presidential campaign, critics accused Clinton of cutting ethical corners to avoid the draft during the Vietnam War. Discuss the assets and liabilities of having a president with a military background and one who has not served in the military.

Caption Answer: Modern presidents are still the commander in chief, but rely heavily on the expertise of top military advisers, including members of the Joint Chiefs of Staff.

C Critical Thinking

Evaluating Ask: Do you think the president's power to make war should be restricted? Why or why not? (Answers will vary.) How can Congress "check" the power of the president to wage war? (Students should refer to Congress's power of the purse and the War Powers Act.) **OL**

Additional Support

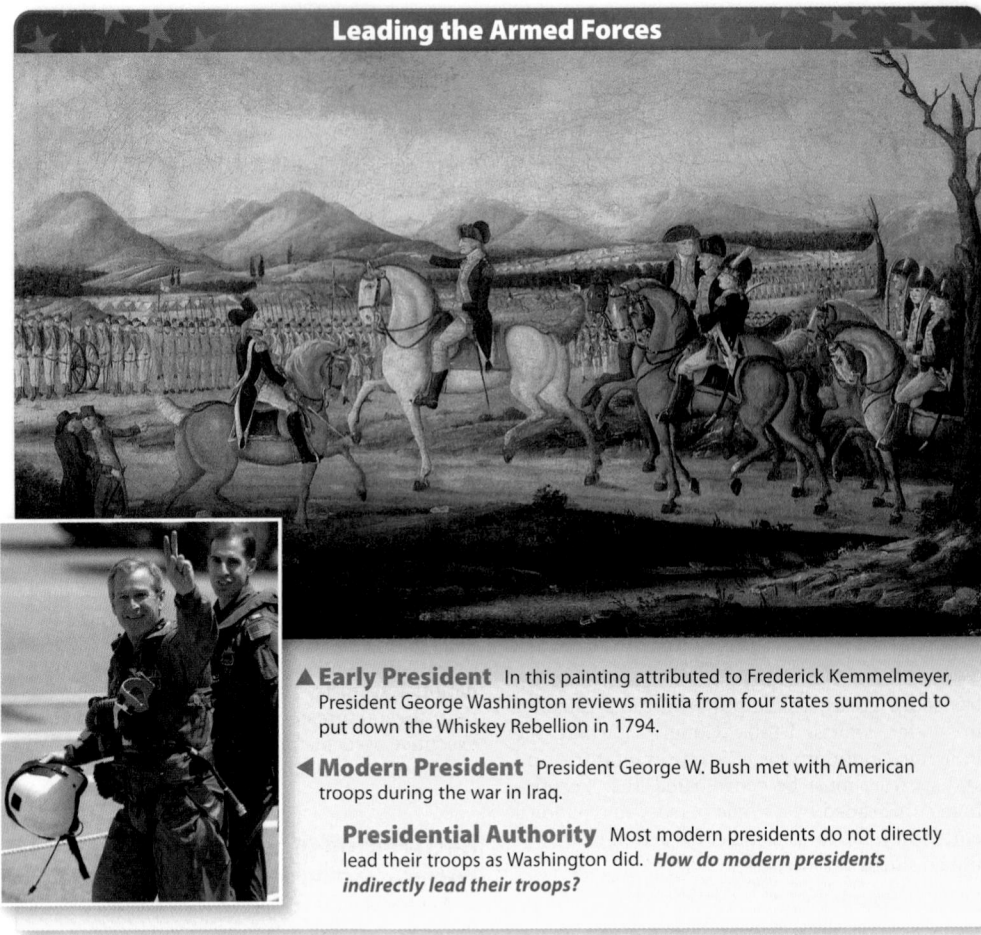

Leading the Armed Forces

▲ **Early President** In this painting attributed to Frederick Kemmelmeyer, President George Washington reviews militia from four states summoned to put down the Whiskey Rebellion in 1794.

◄ **Modern President** President George W. Bush met with American troops during the war in Iraq.

Presidential Authority Most modern presidents do not directly lead their troops as Washington did. *How do modern presidents indirectly lead their troops?*

Commander in Chief

Presidents can back up their foreign-policy decisions with military force when needed. The Constitution makes the president commander in chief of the armed forces of the United States.

Power to Make War

The president shares with Congress the power to make war. In January 1991, President George H.W. Bush received congressional approval for military action in Iraq before he ordered a massive air strike. His actions prevented a serious constitutional issue that might have divided the nation if the president had sent troops without congressional approval as he was prepared to do.

Several other presidents have sent American forces into action without a formal declaration of war. In the early 1900s, several presidents sent forces into Latin America to support leaders who were friendly to the United States. In the late twentieth century, when President George H.W. Bush ordered an invasion of Panama to overthrow the dictator Manuel Noriega, he did not seek congressional approval.

In 2001 President George W. Bush began his "war on terrorism" by sending troops to Afghanistan without asking Congress for a declaration of war. Subsequently, Bush asked for congressional approval for a much larger military action against Iraq. The president claimed Iraq had weapons of mass destruction and "gathers the most serious

Extending the Content

A Plural Executive? The executive branch would have been headed by three people, not one president, if Edmund Randolph and George Mason had persuaded other members of the Constitutional Convention to accept this idea in 1787. Randolph suggested that the dangers of monarchy could be averted by a plural executive. Moreover, people from different sections of the country could be appointed to give all regions representation in the executive branch. Eventually this proposal was defeated.

dangers of our age in one place." In October 2002 Congress passed a resolution that authorized the president to use the U.S. armed forces in Iraq "as he deems necessary and appropriate."

Military Operations and Strategy

Generals, admirals, and other military leaders run the armed forces on a day-to-day basis. The president, however, is responsible for the key military decisions that represent overall policy and strategy.

In 1794 President George Washington exercised his constitutional authority over the military when defiant whiskey distillers in western Pennsylvania refused to pay the federal tax on their product. It was Secretary of the Treasury Alexander Hamilton who urged the president to take action against the rebels by mobilizing some 15,000 state militia troops. Hamilton rode west with the troops, while Washington went to Pennsylvania to **inspect** them. When the troops arrived in Pittsburgh, the rebels retreated in the face of this convincing show of strength.

Several presidents have had a military background. Besides Washington, they have included Andrew Jackson, William H. Harrison, Zachary Taylor, Ulysses S. Grant, Theodore Roosevelt, and Dwight D. Eisenhower.

Neither Woodrow Wilson nor Franklin D. Roosevelt, presidents during World War I and World War II had any military experience. Some presidents with limited military experience have had to command military operations. Presidents Lyndon B. Johnson and Richard Nixon, for example, made key military decisions in the Vietnam War. President Jimmy Carter sent a special military force into Iran in 1980 to try to rescue American hostages. In 2001 terrorist attacks on New York City and Washington, D.C., led President George W. Bush to launch a military campaign against terrorist groups in several countries. Bush sent troops into Afghanistan, Iraq, the Philippines, and other terrorist-training areas.

As commander in chief, the president has the authority to order the use of atomic weapons, a daunting responsibility. President Nixon said, "I can walk into my office, pick up the telephone, and in twenty minutes 70 million people will be dead."

As commander in chief, the president has more than military duties. During a war, Congress is likely to give the president special powers at home as well as abroad. During World War II, Franklin D. Roosevelt demanded and received from Congress power over price controls, gas and food rationing, and the industries needed to produce tanks, guns, and other war materials.

The president may also use the military to control serious turmoil in the nation. Presidents have used federal troops to control rioting in American cities. In case of a natural disaster, such as a flood, the president may send needed supplies or troops to help keep order.

All these roles combined—head of state, chief executive, chief legislator, economic planner, party leader, chief diplomat, and commander in chief—make the president of the United States the most powerful person in the world.

SECTION 2 Review

Vocabulary

1. Explain the significance of: executive order, impoundment, reprieve, pardon, amnesty, patronage, treaty, executive agreement.

Main Ideas

2. Describing Which three foreign relations duties of the president are based on the Constitution?

3. Identifying Which officials may the president appoint?

Critical Thinking

4. Understanding Cause and Effect Which decisions by a president affect the direction of the nation's economy?

5. Organizing Using a graphic organizer like the one below, describe the different duties of the president's roles as head of state and chief executive.

Head of State	Chief Executive

Writing About Government

6. Expository Writing Imagine a typical day in the life of an American president. Prepare an agenda for the president's day. Be sure to keep the seven duties of the president in mind when creating your agenda.

C Critical Thinking

Drawing Conclusions Ask:
Why did Washington and his advisers believe it was important to send the message that the government would use force if necessary to maintain order? *(to prevent future rebellions, to establish the authority and power of the new government, and to keep the new nation unified)* **OL**

Assess

Assign the Section 2 Assessment as homework or as an in-class activity, or have students take Section Quiz 9-2 from *Section Quizzes and Chapter Tests.*

Close

Drawing Conclusions
Challenge students to choose the presidential role that they think is the most important for creating an effective leader and have them defend their choice. **OL**

Section 2 Review

Answers

1. All definitions can be found in the section and the Glossary.
2. The president as head of state performs ceremonial duties. As chief diplomat he or she directs foreign policy; and as commander in chief, he or she directs the armed forces.
3. cabinet members, agency directors, deputy directors and their assistants, and federal judges
4. The president gives an annual economic report to Congress, prepares the federal budget, and proposes economic legislation.

5. Answers might include: Head of state— ceremonial duties; Chief Executive—executive orders, impoundment of funds, granting amnesty.
6. Students' presidential agendas should relate to the seven major roles of the president.

ISSUES
to
Debate

Teach

Setting Up the Debate

Analyzing Help students focus on the constitutionality of the War Powers Act.

Ask: What is the War Powers Act? *(The act sets deadlines for the president to notify and get congressional approval for sending troops abroad.)*

Evaluating Have students research the history of the War Powers Act and identify reasons why it does or does not violate the president's constitutional war-making powers. Have students on the panel meet to build their arguments for and against the constitutionality of the War Powers Act. Urge both groups to consider historic examples of the president's war-making powers, as well as current issues involving its use.

Concluding the Debate

Discuss these questions with the participants:

- What standards did you set for identifying evidence either for or against the constitutionality of the War Powers Act?
- What arguments would you have used in response to information provided by the opposing view on the issue?

Is the War Powers Act Constitutional?

The War Powers Act of 1973 was inspired by the Vietnam War. Many believed the president should not have sent so many American soldiers to Vietnam without a formal declaration of war. Congress wanted to prevent this from happening again. The act sets various deadlines for the president to notify and get congressional approval for sending troops abroad. Since the Constitution gives both the president and Congress war-making powers, the act remains controversial.

YES

The War Powers Act is constitutional. The legislation was necessary to maintain a proper balance of power between the executive and legislative branches. The Framers of the Constitution gave Congress the power to declare war, or ultimately decide whether to enter a war. As commander in chief, the president has the power to lead U.S. forces only after the decision to wage war has been made by Congress. It is dangerous to encourage presidents to act alone, assuming that Congress will rally around the president after he has committed a sufficient number of troops to combat. The president can commit troops in an emergency, but the Framers never intended them to be committed indefinitely—or for so long that war is really inevitable. The War Powers Act provides some real control for Congress by setting clear time limits and improves communication between the president and Congress in a crisis. The War Powers Act also promotes stability because it moderates a president's response to a crisis since he or she knows that actions may ultimately be vetoed by Congress.

NO

The War Powers Act interferes with the president's authority as commander in chief. It restricts the president's effectiveness in foreign policy and should be repealed. The act restricts a president's power to send troops into action in an international crisis. If the president wants to conduct the best foreign policy—and use American military superiority to help solve world crises—he or she needs flexibility. The time limits in the act highlight the fact that the War Powers Act is unconstitutional as well as impractical. Further, the obligation of a deadline presents the image of a divided nation to the world. It gives the enemy hope that the president will be forced by domestic pressure to withdraw troops after a short period. This can actually increase the risk to American soldiers who are sent into action. As stated in the Constitution, the president is meant to command the armed forces, thus he or she must be able to commit troops without interference.

Debating the Issue

1. **Analyzing** Why would the time limit provision be a cause for controversy?
2. **Explaining** How does the War Powers Act attempt to balance power?
3. **Deciding** With which opinion do you tend to agree? Explain your reasoning.

▶ **President Lyndon B. Johnson** signs the Gulf of Tonkin Resolution, which gave him power to increase U.S. involvement in the Vietnam War.

Debating the Issue Answers

1. It could cause the withdrawal of troops in a volatile situation, risking American lives and objectives.
2. It allows the president to send troops into combat for limited engagements, but long-term engagements require the approval of Congress.
3. Students' answers will vary, but ask them to explain the rationale behind their answers.

Styles of Leadership

Focus

Reader's Guide

Content Vocabulary
* ★ de facto (p. 266)
* ★ covert (p. 266)
* ★ executive privilege (p. 266)

Academic Vocabulary
* ★ survey (p. 261)
* ★ tension (p. 261)
* ★ generate (p. 262)

Reading Strategy

As you read, create a graphic organizer like the one below to list the reasons for presidential isolation.

Reasons for Presidential Isolation

Bellringer
Section Focus Transparencies 9-3

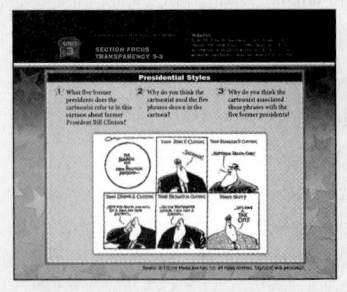

Issues in the News

"This is a problem that must have started with George Washington," said an aide to Richard Nixon when asked about the president's isolation. "If everybody went in immediately whenever he needed something, the White House wouldn't work." Some senators were so desperate for attention that they blurted out ideas in White House reception lines. President Dwight Eisenhower was known for letting his chief of staff serve as a buffer, while President Lyndon B. Johnson was just the opposite. Johnson saw or telephoned hundreds of people almost daily—but he did most of the talking.

▲ President Nixon in a quiet moment

Reader's Guide

Answers to Graphic:
* special treatment
* people do not voice opinions freely
* access to the president is limited

Every president has a unique style of leadership. In the summer of 1981, President Ronald Reagan and his assistants prepared complex legislation to cut federal taxes. One day the president's secretary of the treasury was working out details of the tax bill with key congressional leaders. At one point, the president stopped by to see how things were going. "Would you like to join us?" the secretary asked with a smile. "Heck, no," the president replied, "I'm going to leave this to you experts. I'm not going to get involved in details."

Reagan's response illustrated one aspect of his leadership style. He focused on what his aides called the "big picture" and let others in the Executive Office work out policy details. President Jimmy Carter, Reagan's predecessor, took a different approach. He spent many hours studying policy details and often became directly involved with his assistants to sort through them.

Increased Responsibilities

When the Founders wrote the Constitution, they were thinking that Congress, not the president, would lead the nation. At best, the president was to be the nation's chief administrator and, in time of war, its commander in chief. Instead the powers and duties of the president have grown steadily over the years. Public opinion **surveys** clearly show that Americans look to the president to keep the peace and to solve economic and social problems.

Sometimes presidents demonstrate leadership by introducing bold new policies. President Truman did this in 1948 when he announced measures to end discrimination against African Americans. More often, presidents demonstrate leadership by responding to crises, problems, or opportunities as they occur. President Richard Nixon took advantage of **tensions** between the

Resource Manager

R **Reading Strategies**	C **Critical Thinking**	D **Differentiated Instruction**	W **Writing Support**	S **Skill Practice**
Teacher Edition • Identifying, p. 262 **Additional Resources** • Quizzes/Tests, pp. 105–114 • Guid. Read. Act., p. 35	**Teacher Edition** • Predicting Consequences, p. 266 **Additional Resources** • Read. Essen., pp. 103–105	**Teacher Edition** • Verbal/Linguistic, p. 266 **Additional Resources** • Foldables, p. 52 • Gov. Sims. and Debates, pp. 15–16	**Teacher Edition** • Persuasive Writing, p. 266 **Additional Resources** • Supreme Ct. Case Studies, pp. 117–118	**Additional Resources** • Source Readings, p. 9 • Making It Rel. Trans., pp. 17–18

Teach

R Reading Strategy

Identifying Why is understanding the public an important leadership quality? *(A president with strong public support can more easily influence Congress.)* **AL**

POLITICAL PROFILES **Lyndon B. Johnson** (1908–1973)

President Johnson liked to nap every day after lunch and sometimes invited reporters to interview him right up until he fell asleep. These interviews usually began with an impromptu invitation to join him for lunch in the family quarters. Johnson would give an off-the-record talk throughout the meal. Then he would signal the reporters to follow him to his bedroom, where he would change for his nap, talking all the while. Finally the president fell asleep and the reporters rushed off to report what he had said.

Additional Support

Styles of Presidential Leadership

Different Styles President George W. Bush meets with Democratic leaders Nancy Pelosi and Harry Reid to discuss funding for the war in Iraq. Bush combined promises to compromise with veto threats to get legislation passed. ▶

President Lyndon Johnson's leadership style was often called the "Johnson Treatment." It involved flattering, cajoling, and arm-twisting to persuade others. Here he discusses strategy with Supreme Court Justice Abe Fortas. ▶

Presidential Relationships *Which president's leadership style do you think is most effective? Explain.*

Soviet Union and China to open diplomatic relations between the People's Republic of China and the United States. President Bill Clinton made the difficult decision to intervene in a civil war in Bosnia.

Leadership Qualities and Skills

What kinds of qualities and skills do presidents need to lead the nation? Several qualities common to all good administrators can be identified. Many presidents have more than one of these qualities, and a number of great presidents have had them all.

Understanding the Public

A president must know and understand the American people. The most successful presidents have a genuine feel for the hopes, fears, and moods of the nation. Understanding the people is necessary to gain and hold their support.

Public support, in turn, can give a president real leverage in influencing lawmakers. Since Congress is a representative body, it is very sensitive to the amount of public support a president can **generate.** When a president is popular, presidential proposals

and policies are better received by Congress than when the public holds a president in low regard. When Lyndon B. Johnson succeeded to the office of president, Congress passed his Great Society legislation. However, when Johnson became unpopular during the Vietnam War, he encountered fierce opposition in Congress. His effectiveness as a leader was almost destroyed.

Failure to understand the public mood can prove disastrous for a president. In 1932, when the nation was mired in the Great Depression, President Herbert Hoover believed that the public did not want government to take an active role in confronting the nation's economic problems. Actually, with millions out of work, Americans wanted their problems solved by any means, including federal intervention. Hoover's failure to understand people's attitude cost him the presidency. In 1932 he lost to the Democratic candidate, Franklin D. Roosevelt, in a landslide.

Ability to Communicate

Successful presidents must be able to communicate effectively and to present their ideas in a way that inspires public support. President Herbert Hoover met infrequently with the press and only answered questions that were written in advance.

Activity: Collaborative Learning

Role Playing Organize the class into groups of five to role-play participants in a television talk show. Have group members choose from the roles of talk show host, Republican member of Congress, Democratic member of Congress, president's press secretary, and journalist. Discuss Lyndon Johnson's stand during the Vietnam War, Clinton's decision to intervene in Bosnia's civil war, or a current issue. Have each group prepare a 10-minute talk show segment with each guest trying to sway the opinion of the others. **OL**

In contrast, Franklin D. Roosevelt was a master at communicating with the public. He held weekly press conferences during which he answered all questions. After his famous "fireside chats" over the radio, Roosevelt received as many as 50,000 letters of public support per day.

A president who cannot communicate effectively will have a hard time being a strong leader. President Carter, for example, did not win much support for his policies. President Reagan, on the other hand, was a very effective communicator. The press dubbed him "the Great Communicator" because of his ability to sell his ideas to the public.

Sense of Timing

A successful president must know when the time is right to introduce a new policy, to make a key decision, or to delay such actions. During the crisis in the former Soviet Union in the early 1990s, President George H.W. Bush agreed that American economic aid would help encourage democratic reforms there. He decided to delay acting on this policy, however, until the Soviet political situation was clearer and more stable. On the other hand, when some Soviet republics declared independence, Bush was quick to recognize their sovereignty.

Skillful presidents often use their assistants or cabinet secretaries to test a position on a controversial issue. One way is to deliberately leak information to the press about something that is being considered. Another device is to have a cabinet secretary or an aide make a statement about the issue or give a speech on it. If public and congressional responses are favorable, the president then supports the position and may implement the policy. If reaction is unfavorable, the idea may be quietly dropped, or the president may begin a campaign to shape public opinion on the issue.

Openness to New Ideas

Good leadership also requires the capacity to be flexible and open to new ideas. As events in Eastern Europe and the Soviet Union demonstrated in the early 1990s, situations can change rapidly in the modern world. Consequently, an effective president must be receptive to new solutions to problems.

Presidents who are flexible are willing to engage in informal give-and-take sessions with their advisers. Presidents Franklin D. Roosevelt and John F. Kennedy liked to hear their staffs argue differing positions. In contrast, President Ronald Reagan

A United Military Throughout much of U.S. history, the armed forces were segregated. During World War II, nearly one million African American men and women served their country in segregated military units. In 1948 President Harry S Truman issued an executive order that forced the military to integrate African American and white units. African American and white soldiers first fought together during the Korean War.

did not tolerate serious dissension among his staff. President Bill Clinton was known for liking to listen to all kinds of opinions, too, as well as for getting involved with details. George W. Bush has been described as someone who acted more on instinct. He preferred to get brief summaries of policy options and make quick decisions. "He never thought about reversing course," one former adviser said.

Ability to Compromise

A successful president must be able to compromise. The nature of politics is such that even the president must be willing to give up something to get something in return. Presidents who are successful leaders are able to recognize that sometimes they have to settle for legislation that provides only part of the programs they want. Presidents who will not compromise risk accomplishing nothing at all.

A famous dispute at the end of World War I between President Woodrow Wilson and the Congress is often cited as an example of a president refusing to compromise and losing everything in the end. Wilson had represented the nation at the Paris Peace Conference negotiations to end the war. He lobbied the other nations involved with the treaty to include a plan for a League of Nations, a global organization whose goal was to prevent war.[1]

See the following footnoted materials in the **Reference Handbook:**
1. *The Fourteen Points,* page R90.

Did You Know?

President Franklin D. Roosevelt assembled a group of advisers who became known as the Brain Trust. The Brain Trust included Columbia University professors Rexford Tugwell, Raymond Moley, and Adolf A. Berle. They led a faction that thought the Depression could be solved by instituting public planning and strong corporate regulations. In contrast, another group of advisers, led by Harvard University law professor Felix Frankfurter, opposed centralized planning, distrusted big corporations, and thought the New Deal should do more to help the "little guy." This group pushed for programs that would increase business competition and create social programs to help those who were most hurt by the Depression.

Roosevelt tended to do what was expedient, trying different policies and waiting to see what worked. The result, however, was that the New Deal lacked a coherent economic philosophy and New Deal programs often served seemingly overlapping or contradictory purposes.

Differentiated Instruction

Activity: Multiple Learning Styles

Verbal/Linguistic Franklin D. Roosevelt inspired public support through his "fireside chats," which were broadcast over the radio. Arrange students into groups, and have them choose a current issue that the president faces and write a fireside chat rallying people to support a position related to that issue. Remind students that a successful president must be able to communicate ideas clearly to gain public support. Have the groups present dramatic readings of their fireside chats. **OL**

Caption Answer: By not allowing any criticism of his opinions, Nixon isolated himself from outside ideas and public opinion.

Participating
IN GOVERNMENT

National and Community Issues Often national issues spring from community issues. For example, in 1997 President Bill Clinton launched a national forum on the issue of race relations by visiting local communities.

Activity: Ask students to identify possible issues in their community or state that might have an impact on the entire nation. Students should then identify how best to deal with those issues. For example, should the president get personally involved in resolving these issues? If so, what specific actions should the president take? Should state or local leaders, such as a state governor or city mayor, deal with these issues? What local actions should be taken? Students should work individually or in groups to create proposals for dealing with a community issue. **AL**

Hands-On Chapter Project

Step 3

An Inaccessible President

An Imperial Presidency Here President Nixon makes a rare trip to the White House gates to greet citizens. Nixon surrounded himself with aides who agreed with him, creating an atmosphere in which all opinions reflected his own. Nixon thrived on the power of the presidency, and critics dubbed him "King Richard." *How might Nixon's attitude have limited his ability to govern?*

When the treaty came before the Senate for ratification, many senators opposed it. They did not want permanent ties of any kind to Europe and its problems. They specifically objected that the League of Nations plan would take away the right of Congress to declare war. (The League called for members to take collective action against any aggressor nation.)

Faced with these objections, President Wilson still refused to modify the treaty. Wilson faced a significant problem, however: If changes were made to the treaty to please the Senate, it would also have to be renegotiated with foreign powers. An angry Wilson decided to go on a public speaking tour to build support for the treaty. The tour ended suddenly when Wilson suffered a stroke. The Senate rejected the treaty, and the United States never joined the League of Nations.

Political Courage

Successful presidents need political courage because sometimes they have to go against public opinion to do what they think is best. It takes courage to make decisions that will be unpopular.

President Abraham Lincoln made this kind of decision during the Civil War. The early years of the war went very badly for the North. Despite some Union victories, casualties were very high, and the war's end seemed nowhere in sight. As time passed, the war became increasingly unpopular, and the president came under intense public and political pressure to negotiate peace. Despite his belief that his decision would mean his defeat in the 1864 election, Lincoln chose to continue the war to preserve the Union.

Presidential Isolation

Information and realistic advice are key ingredients for successful decision making. As presidents have become more dependent on the White House staff, however, the danger is that they will become isolated from solid information and sound advice.

Special Treatment

Modern presidents get very special treatment. One adviser to President Johnson noted:

66 *The life of the White House is the life of a court. It is a structure designed for one purpose and one purpose only—to serve the material needs and desires of a single man. . . . He is treated with all the reverence due a monarch. . . . No one ever invites him to 'go soak your head' when his demands become petulant and unreasonable.* 99

—George Reedy, 1970

In this kind of atmosphere, it is easy for presidents to see themselves as deserving only praise and to consider their ideas above criticism.

Presidential Rhetoric

Step 3: Presenting the Analysis

Directions Each group should prepare a presentation of their analysis. Presentations should include an overview of the subject of the speech and its historical context. If the technology is available, encourage groups to select key sections of the speech and play them for the class. Presentations should also discuss the rhetorical devices the president employed.

Summarizing Wrap up the projects by facilitating a discussion in which students compare and contrast the speaking styles of the various presidents. **OL**

Voicing Opinions

Presidents can easily discourage staff members from disagreeing with them or giving unpleasant advice. Lincoln once asked his cabinet for advice on a proposal he favored. Every member of the cabinet opposed it—to which Lincoln responded, "Seven nays, one aye; the ayes have it."

No matter how well advisers know the president personally, many advisers stand in awe of the office of the president. A close adviser and friend of President Kennedy put it this way: "I saw no halo, I observed no mystery. And yet I found that my own personal, highly informal relationship with him changed as soon as he entered the Oval Office." An assistant to President Nixon had similar feelings. He explained that even after working closely with Nixon, "I never lost my reverent awe of the president, or the presidency, which for me were synonymous." Such feelings can make it difficult for staff to stand up to the president or voice criticism. In the end, this may mean that the president does not hear all sides of an issue.

Access to the President

A veteran political observer once noted that "power in Washington is measured in access to the president." Top White House staff are closer to the president than any other government officials. Presidents have different styles of managing staff. Franklin D. Roosevelt liked having staff members who had different ideas and would fight for them. Lyndon B. Johnson was much less open to dissent.

William Safire, one of the speechwriters for President Nixon, tells a story that shows what can happen to the careless staffer who happens to disagree with the president. Safire once challenged the accuracy of a statement that Nixon made. When Nixon insisted that he was correct, Safire produced evidence to show that the president was wrong. As a result, Safire recalls, "For three solid months I did not receive a speech assignment from the president, or a phone call, or a memo, or a nod in the hall as he was passing by."

Woodrow Wilson's closest adviser, Colonel Edward House, admitted that he constantly praised his boss. As for bad news, one presidential adviser explained that the strategy everyone followed was "to be present either personally or by a proxy piece of paper when 'good news' arrives and to be certain that someone else is present when the news is bad."

We the People
Making a Difference

Jimmy Carter served as president of the United States from 1977 to 1981. After leaving office, he continued to work on domestic and international problems like global health and human rights. For his peacemaking efforts, Carter has been nominated seven times for a Nobel Peace Prize. He was awarded the prize in 2002. The focal point of Carter's efforts is his Carter Center in Atlanta, founded in 1982. He has traveled to Ethiopia, Sudan, North Korea, and Bosnia to promote peace.

Carter and his wife, Rosalynn, are working to eradicate a deadly disease called guinea-worm disease that affects people in India, Pakistan, and 16 African countries. By teaching people to filter their water, the death rate from this disease has decreased.

At home, Carter and his wife are involved in Habitat for Humanity, building houses for the poor with other volunteers. Carter, who is now in his eighties, says, "To work for better understanding among people, one does not have to be a former president. . . . Peace can be made in the neighborhoods, the living rooms, the playing fields, and the classrooms of our country."

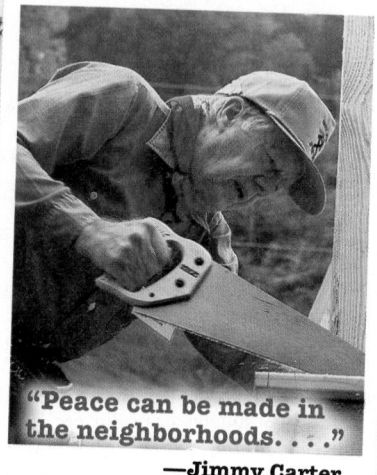

"Peace can be made in the neighborhoods. . . ."
—Jimmy Carter

Making a Difference

Jimmy Carter Former President Jimmy Carter and his wife Rosalynn committed to working with Habitat for Humanity in 1984. The Carters tackle projects for Habitat under the Jimmy Carter Work Project (JCWP). The Carters stress that Habitat is not a give-away program. The JCWP owns the houses, and the partner families make payments to the JCWP that go to a local building fund for Habitat for Humanity.

Activity: Ask students to think about Carter's statement: "To work for better understanding among people, one does not have to be a former president. . . ." Encourage students to work individually or in groups to identify misunderstandings or problems in their community. Students should then present proposals to resolve the misunderstandings or problems. **OL**

Additional Support

★ Activity: Interdisciplinary Connection ★

History President Woodrow Wilson refused to accept any changes to his plan for the United States to join the League of Nations. Because Wilson was unwilling to compromise, Congress voted not to join the League. Organize the class into small groups to review Wilson's plan to join the League of Nations. Have each group identify points on which Wilson might have compromised and then propose suitable compromises. After all groups have shared their compromises with the class, choose the most effective from those presented, and write a plan that might have led the United States to join the League of Nations. **AL**

C Critical Thinking

Predicting Consequences

Ask: Why might it be dangerous for the president to become isolated? *(The president might not get an accurate picture of a situation, or advisers could filter or skew information to suit their own agendas.)* **OL**

D Differentiated Instruction

Verbal/Linguistic Point out that *de facto* refers to how something functions in practice, although it is not sanctioned by law. Explain that *de jure* refers to something that is formally based on law. Brainstorm situations in which the law or the rules dictate that somezthing should be done one way, but in practice it is done differently. **OL**

W Writing Support

Persuasive Writing Have students write a brief essay in which they argue for or against executive privilege. **OL**

Differentiated Instruction

Interpreting Political Cartoons, p. 17

266

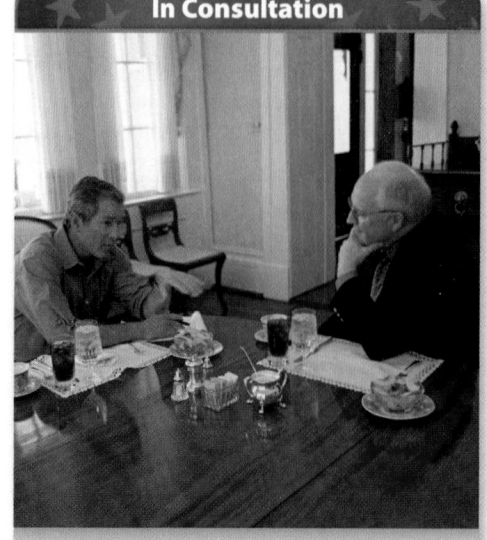

In Consultation

Executive Privilege Presidents need confidential discussions with their advisers, as George W. Bush seems to be having with his vice president here. *How does the Congress view executive privilege?*

The Dangers of Isolation

Not only do top staffers have easy access to the president, but they also use their closeness to control others' access. Few messages of any kind reached President Dwight D. Eisenhower unless his chief of staff, Sherman Adams, saw them first. H.R. Haldeman played a similar role for President Nixon.

President Reagan at first depended heavily on several top advisers. During his second term, however, his new chief of staff, Donald Regan, severely restricted access to the president. One Reagan staffer called Regan the **de facto** president, meaning that although Regan did not legally hold the office, he exercised power as if he were president. Like Nixon, President Reagan became increasingly isolated. This isolation made it more believable when the president claimed he was unaware of the **covert**, or secret, activities of his National Security Council staff in the Iran-Contra affair.

Perhaps in response to the events of the Nixon and Reagan presidencies, President George H.W. Bush tried to reverse the trend to consolidate power in the White House. His chief of staff, however, was very strong and restricted access. Although most presidents appoint their close friends to the White House staff, Bush appointed them to the cabinet instead. As one presidential aide explained, "The cabinet has played a very important role in all major decisions. [The president] wants them to be running things—not the White House staff."

Many observers believed that the leadership changes Bush made were positive. They argue that by listening to officials not so closely tied to White House operations, the president heard a greater variety of views.

Staying in Touch

Most political observers warn that despite a president's best intentions, power inevitably drifts toward the White House. Keeping in direct touch with the public can be very difficult, if not impossible, for a modern president. The need for cabinet members to protect the interests of their departments and the constituent groups they serve always influences the advice they give.

In 1993 President Clinton brought plans for major domestic legislation to Washington. Dealing with White House staff problems became a major distraction, however. The president relied on key staffers for input in brainstorming sessions that could last for hours. Many sessions were inconclusive, and the president's agenda lost momentum. To increase efficiency, the president found it necessary to reorganize the staff.

Executive Privilege

Presidents do not want the information from their advisers to become public while they are still deciding on policies. To keep their White House discussions confidential, modern presidents have sometimes used **executive privilege.** Executive privilege is the right of the president and other high-ranking executive officers, with the president's consent, to refuse to provide information to Congress or a court.

Although the Constitution does not mention executive privilege, the concept rests on the principle of separation of powers. Presidents since George Washington have claimed that executive privilege is implied in the powers granted in Article II. Congress has disputed executive privilege. Members claim that their oversight powers give them the right to get all necessary information from the president.

Presidential Leadership

Objective: Analyze a political cartoon.

Focus/Teach: Review presidential responsibilities in terms of foreign policy.

Assess: Evaluate answers to the activity questions.

Close: Have students research the president's involvement with foreign policy.

Differentiated Instruction Strategies

BL List qualities that are desirable in a president.

AL Determine the most important presidential quality and construct an argument in favor of it.

ELL Review the definitions of the terms in the cartoon.

Limits of Executive Privilege

Presidents have long claimed that executive privilege is necessary for another reason—it protects their communication with executive branch staff. Without this protection, they argue that they would be unable to get frank advice from their assistants.

Until recently, neither Congress nor the courts had much need to question members of the White House staff. These presidential aides traditionally had little influence on policy-making. The various cabinet departments made key policy decisions, and Congress could call department heads to testify as part of its oversight function. But as more policy has been made in the Executive Office of the President, the constitutionality and limits of executive privilege have become controversial.

United States v. *Nixon*

Landmark Case In 1974 the Supreme Court decided a major case on executive privilege. President Nixon had secretly tape-recorded his conversations with key aides about the Watergate cover-up. In *United States* v. *Nixon,* the Court unanimously ruled that the president had to surrender the tapes to the special prosecutor investigating the scandal. Although the Court rejected Nixon's claim of executive privilege in this case, it ruled that executive privilege is supported by the Constitution. In Chief Justice Warren Burger's words:

66 *A President and those who assist him must be free to explore alternatives in the process of shaping policies and making decisions, and to do so in a way many would be unwilling to express except privately.* 99
—Chief Justice Warren Burger, 1974

The Court's decision did not end the controversy. Although executive privilege is legally recognized, the question of how far it extends to presidential advisers has gone unanswered.

President George W. Bush invoked executive privilege many times, four times just in the summer of 2007 alone. In one instance, Congress wanted information on the firing of eight federal prosecutors. Democrats believed the prosecutors were fired because they were not sympathetic to the administration's positions on the Iraq war. Congress subpoenaed the former White House counsel and another top staffer to testify before the House Judiciary Committee on the matter. When they refused, the committee brought suit in a federal court to force them to appear. As this back-and-forth struggle suggests, arguments over executive privilege will likely continue to cause conflict between the president and Congress. In the words of Justice Kennedy:

66 *Once executive privilege is asserted, coequal branches of the Government are set on a collision course.* 99
—Justice Anthony Kennedy, 2004

CHAPTER 9, SECTION 3

Landmark Case

See *United States* v. *Nixon* in the Supreme Court Summaries in the **Reference Handbook** and case study 59 in the *Supreme Court Case Studies* booklet.

Assess

Assign the Section 3 Assessment as homework or as an in-class activity, or have students take Section Quiz 9-3 from *Section Quizzes and Chapter Tests.*

Close

Drawing Conclusions Ask students which president they think was the most effective leader. Discuss the leadership qualities that enabled that president to fulfill the office effectively. **OL**

SECTION 3 Review

Vocabulary

1. **Explain** the significance of: de facto, covert, executive privilege.

Main Ideas

2. **Analyzing** How do presidents test public opinion before announcing new policies?

3. **Explaining** How do good communication skills help a president gain public support?

Critical Thinking

4. **Synthesizing** How can a president's willingness to let staff express disagreements on issues help the president make better decisions?

5. **Organizing** Using a graphic organizer like the one below, identify six qualities of presidential leadership and give an example of each.

Qualities	Examples

Writing About Government

6. **Persuasive Writing** Suppose that you are the president's chief assistant for legislative affairs. The president has asked for your advice on whether the opinions of interest groups should be a factor in making policy decisions. Write a memo supporting your position.

Section 3 Review

Answers

1. All definitions can be found in the section and the Glossary.
2. A presidential aide leaks information about an issue to the press so the president can observe public reaction before announcing the policy.
3. Good communication skills help presidents explain their policies clearly and inspire public support.
4. That willingness may lead to a well-informed decision and allow the president to see all points of view.
5. Answers might include: political courage—Abraham Lincoln; ability to compromise—Woodrow Wilson; understanding the public—F.D.R.; openness to new ideas—John F. Kennedy; ability to communicate—Ronald Reagan; sense of timing—George H.W. Bush.
6. Student memos will vary but should include supporting statements for the position taken.

Focus

Introducing the Topic

Ask students to read through the time line of changes in United States presidential elections. Have them explain how each event made the elections more or less free or fair. If the event made the elections less fair, ask students why that change may have been made.

Teach

C Critical Thinking

Drawing Conclusions Because of the Electoral College, votes in smaller states carry more weight than votes in larger states. **Ask:** Why would the Founders set up the system this way? *(to prevent larger states from dominating the presidential election)* **OL**

S Skill Practice

Reading a Time Line Ask: During which 50-year period were most of the changes in presidential elections made? *(1950–2000)* **BL**

Additional Support

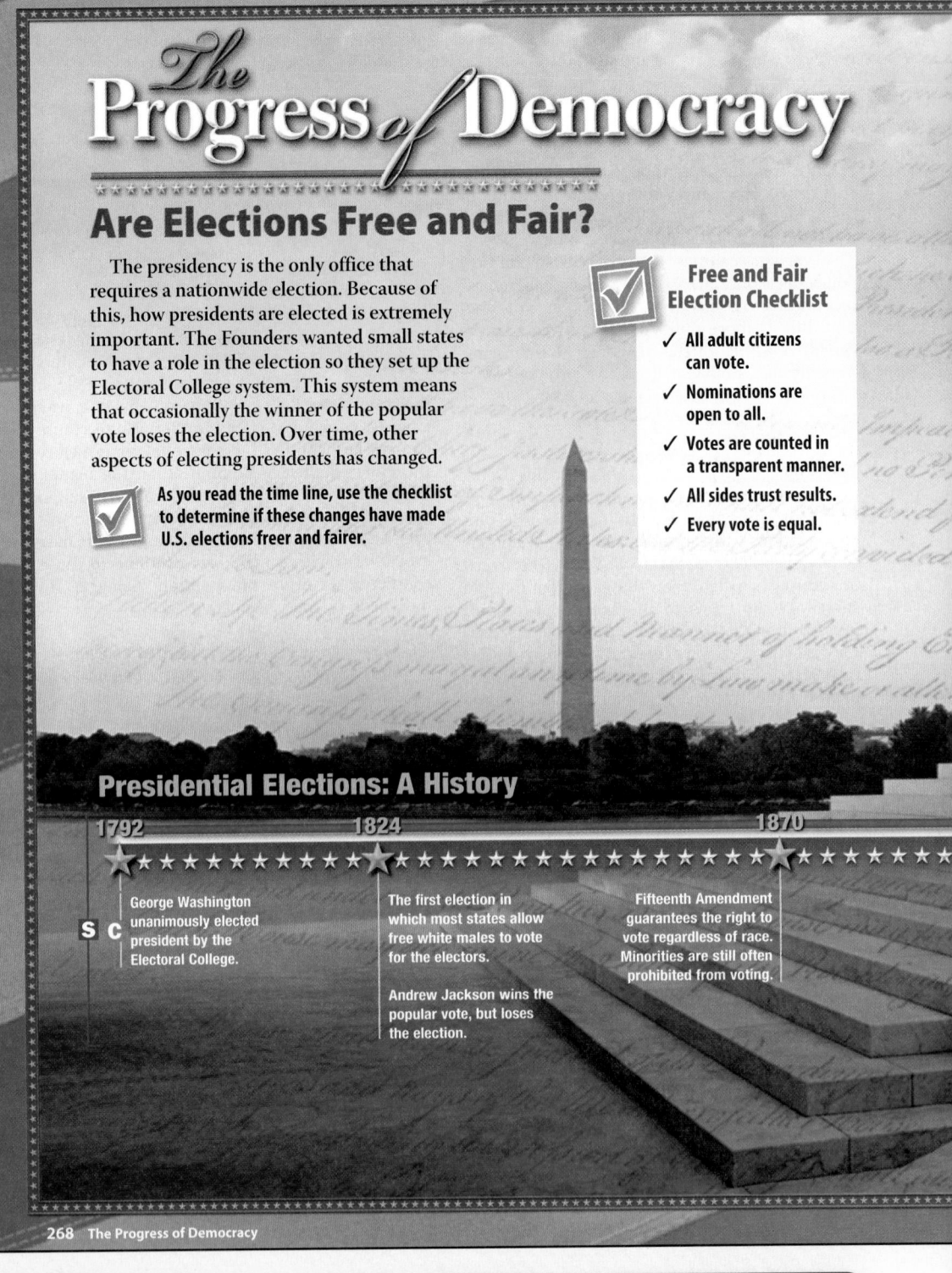

The Progress of Democracy

Are Elections Free and Fair?

The presidency is the only office that requires a nationwide election. Because of this, how presidents are elected is extremely important. The Founders wanted small states to have a role in the election so they set up the Electoral College system. This system means that occasionally the winner of the popular vote loses the election. Over time, other aspects of electing presidents has changed.

✓ As you read the time line, use the checklist to determine if these changes have made U.S. elections freer and fairer.

✓ Free and Fair Election Checklist

✓ All adult citizens can vote.

✓ Nominations are open to all.

✓ Votes are counted in a transparent manner.

✓ All sides trust results.

✓ Every vote is equal.

Presidential Elections: A History

1792

S C George Washington unanimously elected president by the Electoral College.

1824

The first election in which most states allow free white males to vote for the electors.

Andrew Jackson wins the popular vote, but loses the election.

1870

Fifteenth Amendment guarantees the right to vote regardless of race. Minorities are still often prohibited from voting.

Activity: Collaborative Learning

Exploring the Impact of Government Action Explain to students that the way elections are held in the United States is still changing. Organize students in groups. Ask them to use the information from the time line and their knowledge of U.S. presidential elections to decide what additional changes should be made in the voting process. Have students in each group discuss how these proposed changes make elections more free and/or fair. If any of the changes make the elections less free or fair, they should defend their reasoning. **OL**

African Americans vote in a Mississippi primary.

The Fifteenth Amendment and the Voting Rights Act ensured that minorities have the right and the opportunity to vote.

A Florida election official manually examines a ballot for irregularities after the 2000 presidential election. The U.S. Supreme Court later held that the recount was unconstitutional, violating the Fourteenth Amendment, because ballots were not treated the same throughout the state.

Voting Rights Act outlaws poll taxes, literacy tests, and other methods of preventing people from voting.

1920   **1951**   **1965 1971**   **2000 2008**

Nineteenth Amendment guarantees the right of women to vote.

Franklin D. Roosevelt was elected president four times. After his death, the 22nd Amendment was passed to prevent any president from maintaining power for so long. The Twenty-second Amendment limits presidents to two terms in office. **C**

Twenty-sixth Amendment lowers the voting age to 18. Many states' voting age had been 21.

Supreme Court rules that requiring a state I.D. to vote is not an undue burden on voting. **W**

We Want F.D.R. Again

The Progress of Democracy   269

Extending the Content

Voting Restrictions Before the passage of the Voting Rights Act, a variety of methods were used to prevent African Americans from voting. One method used to restrict voting rights was the grandfather clause, which prevented people from voting whose grandfathers were not allowed to vote. This meant slaves and immigrants were disenfranchised. Another method used to prevent African Americans from voting was the poll tax, or a sum of money to be paid to vote. This prevented poor African Americans from voting. Literacy tests were also used to disenfranchise African Americans.

The Progress *of* Democracy

C₁ Critical Thinking

Making Inferences Ask: Why might Saddam Hussein have held elections, even though it is questionable how free and fair they were? *(Students' answers may vary. Possible answers: he felt it gave him more legitimacy, he wanted to show how powerful his rule over the country was, he hoped observers would accept the process as democratic.)* **OL**

C₂ Critical Thinking

Identifying Central Issues
Have students look through the Free and Fair Election Checklist. Have them think of other items that may be necessary for free and fair elections. **Ask:** Are any of the items currently on the list not necessary for free and fair elections? *(Students' answers will vary.)* **AL**

Additional Support

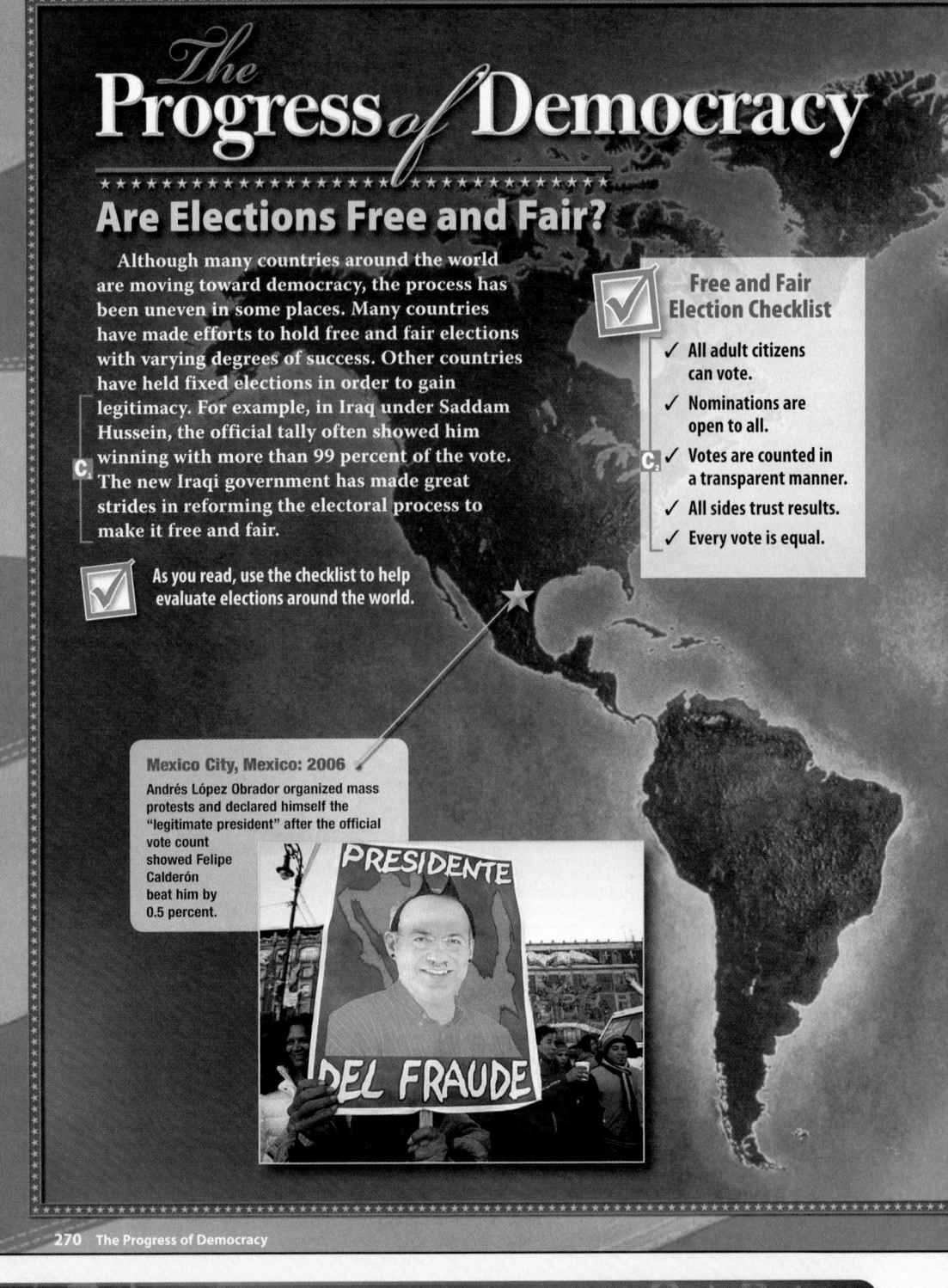

The Progress *of* Democracy

Are Elections Free and Fair?

Although many countries around the world are moving toward democracy, the process has been uneven in some places. Many countries have made efforts to hold free and fair elections with varying degrees of success. Other countries have held fixed elections in order to gain legitimacy. For example, in Iraq under Saddam Hussein, the official tally often showed him winning with more than 99 percent of the vote. The new Iraqi government has made great strides in reforming the electoral process to make it free and fair.

As you read, use the checklist to help evaluate elections around the world.

Free and Fair Election Checklist

✓ All adult citizens can vote.
✓ Nominations are open to all.
✓ Votes are counted in a transparent manner.
✓ All sides trust results.
✓ Every vote is equal.

Mexico City, Mexico: 2006
Andrés López Obrador organized mass protests and declared himself the "legitimate president" after the official vote count showed Felipe Calderón beat him by 0.5 percent.

PRESIDENTE
DEL FRAUDE

Extending the Content

Mexico's Election Despite massive protests in Mexico, a plurality of Mexicans felt that Calderón was the legitimate winner of the election. However, even among those who thought that Obrador was the legitimate winner, most Mexicans felt that the mass protests should end. Mexican business groups stated that blockades from the protests cost their businesses over 35 million U.S. dollars.

Beijing, China: 2007

Former vice president Zeng Qinghong casts a ballot for the new leadership of the Communist Party of China. The Communist Party controls China's political systems and media outlets.

Seoul, South Korea: December 2007

Lee Myung-bak was elected president after defeating his closest competitor by 22 percent. Some Koreans were disappointed that only 62.9 percent of the people turned out to vote, an all-time low.

Luanda, Angola: September 2008

The political party Unita accepted defeat in the first Angolan election since 1992. In the previous election, Unita did not accept the official tally leading to a resumption of the civil war.

Harare, Zimbabwe: June 2008

Morgan Tsvangirai, shown here at a pre-election rally, withdrew from a run-off election after many of his voters were beaten and killed by supporters of President Robert Mugabe.

Did You Know?

Despite the fact that many Koreans were disappointed, 62.9 percent turnout would be unusually high in many other countries around the world. In the United States voter turnout is often near 50 percent. In Switzerland voter turnout is sometimes as low as 36 percent.

C Critical Thinking

Drawing Conclusions Despite controlling the army and the media and even after resorting to widespread intimidation of Morgan Tsvangirai's supporters, Robert Mugabe failed to win a plurality of the vote, forcing a run-off with Tsvangirai. **Ask:** Why do you think Mugabe failed to win outright despite having so many built-in advantages? *(Students' answers may vary. One possible answer: He might have been so unpopular that even with unfair electoral advantages he came close to losing.)* OL

Critical Thinking

Free and Fair Elections

1. Which countries above do not meet the criteria of having free and fair elections? Which criteria do they fail to meet?

2. Select a country and research its most recent election. Was that election free and fair? What changes could be made to make the election free and fair?

Additional Support

Critical Thinking Answers

1. Mexico: All sides do not trust in the results; China: Communists control the media and political systems; Zimbabwe: Voter intimidation prevented people from voting and undermined trust in the results.

2. Students' research should include information on a country's electoral system, and what changes could be made to make it more free and more fair.

CHAPTER
9

Assessment and Activities

ExamView®
Assessment Suite

This easy-to-use software includes extensive question banks and allows you to create fully customized tests that can be administered in print or online.

Reviewing Vocabulary

1. d	5. a
2. j	6. b
3. g	7. c
4. f	8. i

Reviewing Main Ideas

9. limitations by Congress, federal courts, federal bureaucracy, and public opinion

10. helps party members who are running for office, helps raise funds for the party, selects the national chair-person, and helps plan election strategies

11. The president might lose public support. Without public support, relations with Congress will be diffcult, and the president's effectiveness will diminish.

12. Most information comes through close aides who screen what they do not want the president to hear. Thus, the flow of information and ideas to the president may be severely limited. Also, presidents might isolate themselves by discouraging opposing opinions or unwanted advice.

Critical Thinking

13. Possible answers: The president nominates justices for federal courts and the Supreme Court. The

Reviewing Vocabulary

On a separate sheet of paper, choose the letter of the content vocabulary word(s) defined in each phrase.

- **a.** executive order
- **b.** reprieve
- **c.** de facto
- **d.** mandate
- **e.** pardon
- **f.** amnesty
- **g.** line-item veto
- **h.** treaty
- **i.** covert
- **j.** forum

Chapter Summary

Presidential Powers

★ Formal powers are granted in Article II of the Constitution.

★ Informal sources of power include the president's personal exercise of power, the immediate needs of the nation, and public mandates.

★ Powers can be limited by Congress, the federal courts, the bureaucracy, and by public opinion.

Roles of the President

★ Head of State—Performs ceremonial roles

★ Chief Executive—Sees that laws of Congress are carried out

★ Chief Legislator—Proposes legislation

★ Economic Planner—Prepares federal budget

★ Party Leader—Supports party members

★ Chief Diplomat—Directs foreign policy

★ Commander in Chief—Commands armed forces of the United States

Presidential Leadership Skills

★ Understanding of the public

★ Ability to communicate

★ Sense of timing

★ Openness to new ideas

★ Ability to compromise

★ Political courage

1. expressed will of the people
2. medium of discussion of presidential messages
3. the power to accept or to reject only parts of a congressional bill
4. expunging someone from legal punishment
5. presidential decree that has the force of law
6. postponement of a person's legal punishment
7. existing "in fact" rather than officially or legally
8. something that is secret

Reviewing Main Ideas

Section 1 *(pages 245–250)*

9. **Listing** What are four limits on presidential power?

Section 2 *(pages 252–259)*

10. **Explaining** What is the president's role as party leader?

Section 3 *(pages 261–267)*

11. **Interpreting** Why can failing to understand the public's mood weaken a president's power?

12. **Analyzing** How do presidents become isolated?

Critical Thinking

13. **Essential Question** Give examples of how the president has influence over the other two branches of government.

14. **Synthesizing** When has Congress allowed expansion of a president's economic power?

15. **Discussing** Why is compromise such a vital ingredient for a president to be able to maintain support of the people?

16. **Analyzing** How could Congress have prevented President Thomas Jefferson from purchasing the Louisiana Territory?

17. **Drawing Conclusions** What are the dangers in depending only on the cabinet for advice? Only on presidential aides?

18. **Understanding Cause and Effect** Use a graphic organizer to show why President Lyndon B. Johnson chose not to run for reelection in 1968.

president signs or vetoes legislation from Congress.

14. In 1970 Congress gave President Nixon the power to control prices and wages. The president used this power to put a 90-day freeze on all prices, rents, wages, and salaries.

15. A president needs the support of many different interests to get a new program accepted by Congress. Compromise is often necessary to build support. Presidents who will not compromise risk accomplishing nothing at all.

16. by refusing to ratify the treaty or refusing to raise the money for the purchase of the Louisiana Territory

17. By depending only on the cabinet, the president would be exposed to the influence of interest groups and the self-interest of departments. By relying only on aides, the president would risk isolation and little open exchange of ideas.

Government ONLINE Self-Check Quiz
Visit glencoe.com and enter QuickPass™ code USG9822c9.
Click on Self-Check Quizzes for additional test practice.

CHAPTER 9 Assessment and Activities

Document-Based Questions

Analyzing Primary Sources

Read the excerpt below and answer the questions that follow.

George Washington knew that his two terms as the nation's first president would set the precedent for future officeholders. Washington's Farewell Address, written near the end of his second term in 1796, gives his ideas on presidential duties and powers regarding both domestic and foreign policy.

On office terms:

> 66 *The period for a new election of a citizen to administer the executive government of the United States being not far distant, and the time actually arrived when your thoughts must be employed in designating the person who is to be clothed with that important trust, it appears to me proper, especially as it may conduce to a more distinct expression of the public voice, that I should now apprise you of the resolution I have formed, to decline being considered among the number of those out of whom a choice is to be made.* 99

On foreign policy:

> 66 *In the execution of such a plan, nothing is more essential than that permanent, inveterate antipathies against particular nations, and passionate attachments for others, should be excluded; and that, in place of them, just and amicable feelings towards all should be cultivated.* 99

19. What is the first precedent that George Washington set in declining to run for another term of office? Why do you think he did this?

20. George Washington also warned against carrying grudges against other nations. What does this warning say about the developing powers of the presidency?

Interpreting Political Cartoons

Analyze the cartoon and answer the questions that follow. Base your answers on the cartoon and your knowledge of Chapter 9.

IF ELECTED, I PROMISE TO FLY FASTER THAN A SPEEDING BULLET, LEAP TALL BUILDINGS IN A SINGLE BOUND, AND PERSONALLY SAVE THE EARTH!

21. According to the cartoon, what do the American people expect of their president?

22. How must presidential candidates present themselves to the public?

Participating IN GOVERNMENT

23. Like the nation's president, city mayors must know how residents view their policies. Design a poll to find out what people in your town think of the mayor's recent decisions. Then explain your poll results in a report.

CHAPTER 9: *Presidential Leadership* **273**

Government ONLINE

Have students use the **Chapter 9 Self-Check Quiz.** Visit glencoe.com and enter **QuickPass**™ code USG9085c9T to prepare for the Chapter Test.

States's own interests and to avoid alliances with other countries that might harm the nation as a whole.

Interpreting Political Cartoons

21. to be "Superman," performing amazing, superhuman feats

22. as capable of performing any feat that is humanly possible

Participating IN GOVERNMENT

23. Students' reports should reflect the results of a poll in the community concerning the mayor's recent actions. Call on volunteers to read their survey questions and hold a class discussion to evaluate the questions. Discuss the results of students' polls.

---

18. Cause: Public opinion turned against Johnson and made a strong campaign impossible.
Effect: Vice President Hubert Humphrey was nominated by the Democratic Party and lost to Nixon.

Analyzing Primary Sources

19. Washington set the precedent for presidents to serve no more than two terms in office. All presidents until Franklin D. Roosevelt followed this precedent, and after Roosevelt's four terms, the Twenty-second Amendment to the Constitution established a two-term limitation. Washington believed that a president who served too many terms would come too close to being a monarch.

20. The president, in Washington's view, was the chief diplomat of the country, representing the nation to the world. Additionally, Washington thought that the president's role was to act as a diplomat to keep peace by balancing the interests of other nations against the United

Chapter Bonus Test Question

Ask: Which president holds the record for writing the most (3,522) executive orders? *(Franklin D. Roosevelt, who also served the longest as president)*

Key to Ability Levels

BL Below level   **AL** Above level
OL On level   **ELL** English Language Learners

Key to Teaching Resources

📁 Print Material   🖶 Transparency
💿 CD-ROM or DVD

Levels					Resources	Chapter Opener	Section 1	Section 2	Section 3	Chapter Assess
BL	OL	AL	ELL		**FOCUS**					
BL	OL	AL	ELL	🖶	**Section Focus Transparencies**		10-1	10-2	10-3	
					TEACH					
BL	OL		ELL	📁	**Reading Essentials and Study Guide (and Answer Key)**		p. 106	p. 110	p. 113	
BL	OL		ELL	📁	**Guided Reading Activities**		p. 36	p. 37	p. 38	
BL	OL		ELL	📁	**Vocabulary Activities**		p. 10			
BL	OL	AL	ELL	📁	**Chapter Summaries**				p. 28	
BL	OL			📁	**American Biographies**					
BL	OL	AL	ELL	📁	**Cooperative Learning Activities**					
	OL	AL	ELL	📁	**Government Simulations and Debate**					
BL	OL	AL	ELL	📁	**Historical Documents and Speeches**			p. 10		
BL	OL	AL	ELL	📁	**Interpreting Political Cartoons**			p. 19		
BL	OL		ELL	📁	**Skill Reinforcement Activities**		p. 10			
BL	OL	AL	ELL	📁	**Source Readings**		p. 10			
BL	OL			📁	**Supreme Court Case Studies**					
BL	OL	AL	ELL	📁	**Participating in Government Activities**			p. 19		
BL	OL		ELL	📁	**Spanish Declaration of Independence and U.S. Constitution**	✓	✓	✓	✓	✓
BL	OL	AL	ELL	📁	**NGS World Atlas, Spanish**	✓	✓	✓	✓	✓
BL	OL	AL	ELL	🖶	**Unit Overlay Transparencies, Strategies, and Activities**	✓	✓	✓	✓	✓
BL	OL		ELL	🖶	**Making It Relevant Transparencies**	✓	✓	✓	✓	✓
BL	OL	AL	ELL	🖶	**High School Writing Process Transparencies, Strategies, and Activities**	✓	✓	✓	✓	✓
BL	OL	AL		🖶	**American Art & Architecture Transparencies, Strategies, and Activities**	✓	✓	✓	✓	✓

✓ Chapter- or unit-based activities applicable to all sections in this chapter

CHAPTER 10

TeacherWorks™ Plus
All-In-One Planner and Resource Center

- Interactive Lesson Planner
- Interactive Teacher Edition
- Fully editable blackline masters
- Chapter Spotlight Videos Launch
- Differentiated Lesson Plans
- Printable reports of daily assignments
- Standards tracking system

Levels					Resources	Chapter Opener	Section 1	Section 2	Section 3	Chapter Assess
BL	OL	AL	ELL							
TEACH *(continued)*										
BL	OL			💿	American Music: Hits Through History	✓	✓	✓	✓	✓
BL	OL		ELL	📁	Reading Strategies for the Social Studies Classroom	✓	✓	✓	✓	✓
			ELL	📁	English Language Learner Handbook	✓	✓	✓	✓	✓
BL	OL		ELL	📁	Writer's Guidebook for Social Studies	✓	✓	✓	✓	✓
BL	OL	AL	ELL	📁	Living Constitution, SE	✓	✓	✓	✓	✓
BL	OL	AL	ELL	📁	Living Constitution, TAE	✓	✓	✓	✓	✓
BL	OL			📁	NGS World Atlas, English	✓	✓	✓	✓	✓
BL	OL		ELL	📁	The Constitution and You (poster set)	✓	✓	✓	✓	✓
BL	OL	AL	ELL	📁	Spanish Chapter Summaries				p. 28	
BL	OL	AL	ELL	📁	Spanish Vocabulary Activities		p. 10			
BL	OL		ELL	📁	Spanish Reading Essentials and Study Guide (and Answer Key)		p. 106	p. 110	p. 113	
BL	OL	AL	ELL	💿	PresentationPlus! with MindJogger CheckPoint	✓	✓	✓	✓	✓
ASSESS										
BL	OL	AL	ELL	💿	*ExamView® Assessment Suite*		10-1	10-2	10-3	Ch. 10
BL	OL	AL	ELL	📁	Authentic Assessment with Rubrics		p. 17		p. 17	p. 17
BL	OL	AL	ELL	📁	Section Quizzes and Chapter Tests		p. 115	p. 116	p. 117	pp. 119–126
BL	OL	AL	ELL	📁	Spanish Section Quizzes and Tests		p. 115	p. 116	p. 117	pp. 119–126
CLOSE										
BL			ELL	📁	Reteaching Activities				p. 10	p. 10
BL	OL	AL	ELL	💿	StudentWorks™ Plus with Audio Summaries	✓	✓	✓	✓	✓
BL	OL		ELL	🖨	Graphic Organizer Transparencies		✓	✓	✓	
BL	OL		ELL	📁	High School Government Reading and Study Skills Foldables®		p. 53	p. 53	p. 53	

Chapter Overviews

Teach With Technology

What is a Chapter Overview?

A Chapter Overview provides an online, section-by-section summary of the content of each chapter. It can help students review—or preview—chapter content to increase comprehension of main ideas.

How can a Chapter Overview help my students and me?

A Chapter Overview helps you and your students review the main points from each chapter section by section. It can help:

- students preview chapter content
- students focus on the main ideas
- students review chapter content
- students practice reading and comprehension skills
- you devise discussion points
- you summarize the chapter for your students

Visit glencoe.com and enter a *QuickPass*™ code to go to a Chapter Overview.

Government ONLINE
Visit glencoe.com and enter *QuickPass*™ code USG9085c10T for Chapter 10 resources.

You can easily launch a wide range of digital products from your computer's desktop with the McGraw-Hill Social Studies widget.

	Student	Teacher	Parent
Media Library			
• Student Edition Section Audio	●		●
• Chapter Spotlight Videos	●	●	●
***United States Government* Online Learning Center (Web Site)**			
• Chapter Overviews	●	●	●
• Multilingual Glossaries	●	●	●
• Study-to-Go	●	●	●
• Student Web Activities	●	●	●
• Self-Check Quizzes	●	●	●
• Online Student Edition	●	●	●
• Vocabulary eFlashcards	●	●	●
• Web Activity Lesson Plans		●	
• Vocabulary PuzzleMaker	●	●	●
• Landmark Supreme Court Cases	●	●	●
• Beyond the Textbook	●	●	●

- **Timed Readings Plus in Social Studies** helps students increase their reading rate and fluency while maintaining comprehension. The 400-word passages are similar to those found on state and national assessments.

- **Reading in the Content Area: Social Studies** concentrates on six essential reading skills that help students better comprehend what they read. The book includes 75 high-interest nonfiction passages written at increasing levels of difficulty.

- **Reading Social Studies** includes strategic reading instruction and vocabulary support in Social Studies content for ELLs and native speakers of English. www.jamestowneducation.com

Reading List Generator CD-ROM

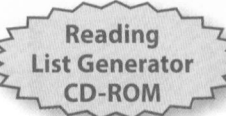

GLENCOE
BOOKLINK 3

Use this database to search more than 30,000 titles to create a customized reading list for your students.

- Reading lists can be organized by students' reading level, author, genre, theme, or area of interest.

- The database provides Degrees of Reading Power™ (DRP) and Lexile™ readability scores for all selections.

- A brief summary of each selection is included.

Leveled reading suggestions for this chapter:

- *Apollo and the Moon Landing,* by Gregory Vogt

- *Black Stars in Orbit: NASA's African American Astronauts,* by Khephra Burns and William Miles

- *Living in Space,* by Larry Kettelkamp

Review suggested books before assigning them.

Economics Connection

Personal Finance Literacy

Getting a Job

Civil servants rarely have to search for jobs because their positions are generally protected by the civil service system. Most Americans, however, change careers three to five times during their working lives and job hunt six times in each career. Searching for a job *is* a job. It takes skill, hard work, and persistence. Here are some sources for students seeking part-time or summer jobs:

- **"Help Wanted" signs:** As you walk in business districts, dress appropriately and be ready to complete applications in case you get an on-the-spot interview.

- **Newspaper and Internet ads:** Remember that competition for jobs advertised in these sources is stiff; hundreds of people respond to newspaper ads and thousands respond to Internet ads. So they should not be the only job-hunt sources.

- **Networking:** The best way to find leads is to let friends and relatives know you are job hunting.

- **Placement agencies:** Free state agencies match applicants with available jobs. Private agencies charge a fee to applicants or employers.

- **Informational interviews:** Many people in business who have no current job openings will still be willing to spend a few minutes giving you information about their field. This is a good way for students to gain interviewing experience, contacts, and possibly leads on upcoming jobs there or in other companies. Remind students to send thank-you notes.

Ask students: What jobs—paid or unpaid—have you done, and what did the experience tell you about the type of job you would or would not like in the future?

Did You Know?

Many young people start their own businesses. Five students at Baltimore's Digital Harbor High School received a $5,000 loan from a local bank to start a school store by presenting a business plan to the bank's loan committee. Refer students to the Web sites of Junior Achievement and the Small Business Administration for ideas.

CHAPTER 10

The Federal Bureaucracy

🎬 **Essential Question**

The federal bureaucracy is organized into departments, agencies, boards, commissions, corporations, and advisory committees. Most agencies report to the president, but some report to Congress. Have students individually list as many federal departments or agencies as they can think of and reward the student who compiles the most complete list.

Chapter Spotlight Video

To generate student interest and provide a springboard for class discussion, access the Chapter 10 Video at glencoe.com or on the video DVD.

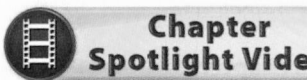
Dinah Zike's Foldables are three-dimensional, interactive graphic organizers that help students practice basic writing skills, review key vocabulary terms, and identify main ideas. Have students complete this chapter's Foldable activity or activities in *Dinah Zike's Reading and Study Skills Foldables* booklet. **OL**

Government ONLINE

Visit glencoe.com and enter *QuickPass*™ code USG9085c10T for Chapter 10 Resources including Chapter Overview, Student Web Activity, Self-Check Quiz, and other materials for students and teachers.

▶ Aerial view of the Capitol and nearby government buildings

🎬 **Essential Question**

How is the federal bureaucracy organized to serve Americans, and how do federal agencies carry out their missions?

Government ONLINE
Chapter Overview Visit glencoe.com and enter *QuickPass*™ code USG9822c10 for an overview, a quiz, and other chapter resources.

Launching the Chapter

Making Connections Help students understand the importance of the federal bureaucracy by highlighting the ways it affects them individually. Point out, for example, that the food they eat is subject to regulation and inspection by the Food and Drug Administration and that the U.S. Postal Service is a government-owned corporation. **Essential Question:** How else does the federal bureaucracy affect you as individuals? *(Answers will vary.)* How would your lives be different if there were no federal bureaucracy? *(Prompt students to provide specific examples.)* **OL**

Bureaucratic Organization

Reader's Guide

Content Vocabulary
★ bureaucrat *(p. 275)*
★ embassy *(p. 276)*
★ government corporation *(p. 279)*
★ deregulate *(p. 281)*

Academic Vocabulary
★ register *(p. 277)*
★ data *(p. 277)*
★ innovative *(p. 280)*

Reading Strategy
As you read, use a graphic organizer similar to the one below to list the effects of the Republicans pushing for deregulation in the 1990s.

Cause		Effect
Republicans push for deregulation.	→	

Issues in the News

Having Internet access in government offices raised the same issue that cropped up when another new invention was introduced—the telephone! At first, only managers had them because they worried that workers would waste time chatting with friends. The Internet poses many other challenges, however, such as how to keep workers from using inappropriate sites. In 2006 one Department of the Interior employee commented that so far, that goal has not been met. "They chose a filtering product that was designed for ease of administration rather than precision or accuracy, and they've been flailing about . . . trying to determine which categories should be blocked and which shouldn't. . . ."

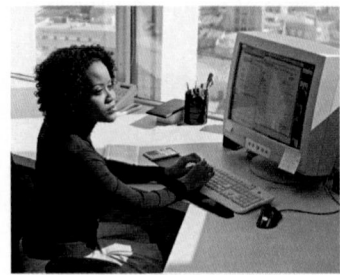
▲ An office worker with Internet access

Hundreds of agencies like the Department of the Interior make up the federal bureaucracy. Their staff are called **bureaucrats,** or civil servants. The federal bureaucracy is organized into departments, agencies, boards, commissions, corporations, and advisory committees. Most belong to the executive branch, which carries out laws passed by Congress. Most agencies report to the president, although some report to Congress. Almost all were created by an act of Congress. In an indirect way, the Constitution provided for the bureaucracy. Article II, Section 2, states that

❝ he [the president] may require the Opinion, in writing, of the principal Officer in each of the executive Departments, upon any Subject relating to the Duties of their respective Offices, . . . ❞
—The Constitution

Article II also gives the president the power to appoint the heads of those departments. Thus, the Founders anticipated the need for creating federal agencies that would carry on the day-to-day business of government. Yet the Founders would no doubt be shocked by the size and scope of today's federal bureaucracy.

In the early years of the republic, the federal bureaucracy was quite small. When Thomas Jefferson became president in 1801, the federal government employed only 2,120 people. These employees were mainly commissioners of Native American affairs, postmasters, customs collectors, tax collectors, marshals, and clerks.

Today, nearly 3 million civilians work for the federal government. Federal agencies are located in more than 440,000 buildings scattered across the nation and around the world.

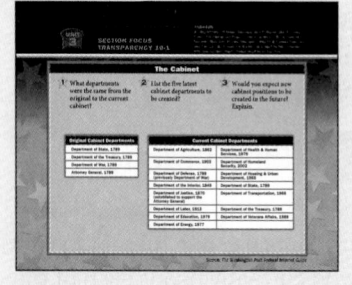

Teach

R Reading Strategy

Activating Prior Knowledge
Ask: Who was the first secretary of state? *(Thomas Jefferson)* Who was the first secretary of the treasury? *(Alexander Hamilton)* **OL**

S Skill Practice

Conducting Research Have students use the Internet to learn who currently heads each of the cabinet departments listed in the table and what former occupation, training, or education prepared each department head for his or her current position. **OL**

Answer: Students should note in their answers that the secretary of transportation would be able to police any air, ocean, or land traffic.

Table Skills Practice
What is the newest cabinet department? *(Department of Homeland Security)*

Additional Support

The Cabinet Departments

The 15 cabinet departments are a major part of the federal bureaucracy. One of President George Washington's first acts in 1789 was to ask Congress to create the departments of Treasury, State, and War, and the office of attorney general. Since 1789, 11 additional departments have been created. A secretary who is a member of the president's cabinet heads each of the departments in the executive branch. Departments usually have a second in command, called the deputy secretary or undersecretary. In addition, departments have assistant secretaries. The president appoints all these officials.

The next level under these top officials includes the directors of the major units that make up the cabinet department, along with their assistants. These units have various names, including bureau, agency, office, administration, or division. Overall policy is set by the top officials in each department—

secretaries, directors, deputy directors, and their assistants. These top leaders rely on ideas and information from career officials who are specialists and business managers in each department. Often, these career civil servants, who have many years of experience, do the research on the policy options that leaders will consider.

State

The secretary of state is one of the president's most trusted advisers. The Department of State is responsible for implementing the foreign policy of the United States. It also protects the rights of United States citizens traveling in foreign countries. It has several key functions. It staffs **embassies,** or offices of ambassadors in foreign countries. It analyzes issues related to American interests in other countries. Finally, it represents American positions to the United Nations (UN) through the ambassador to the UN, who is appointed by the president.

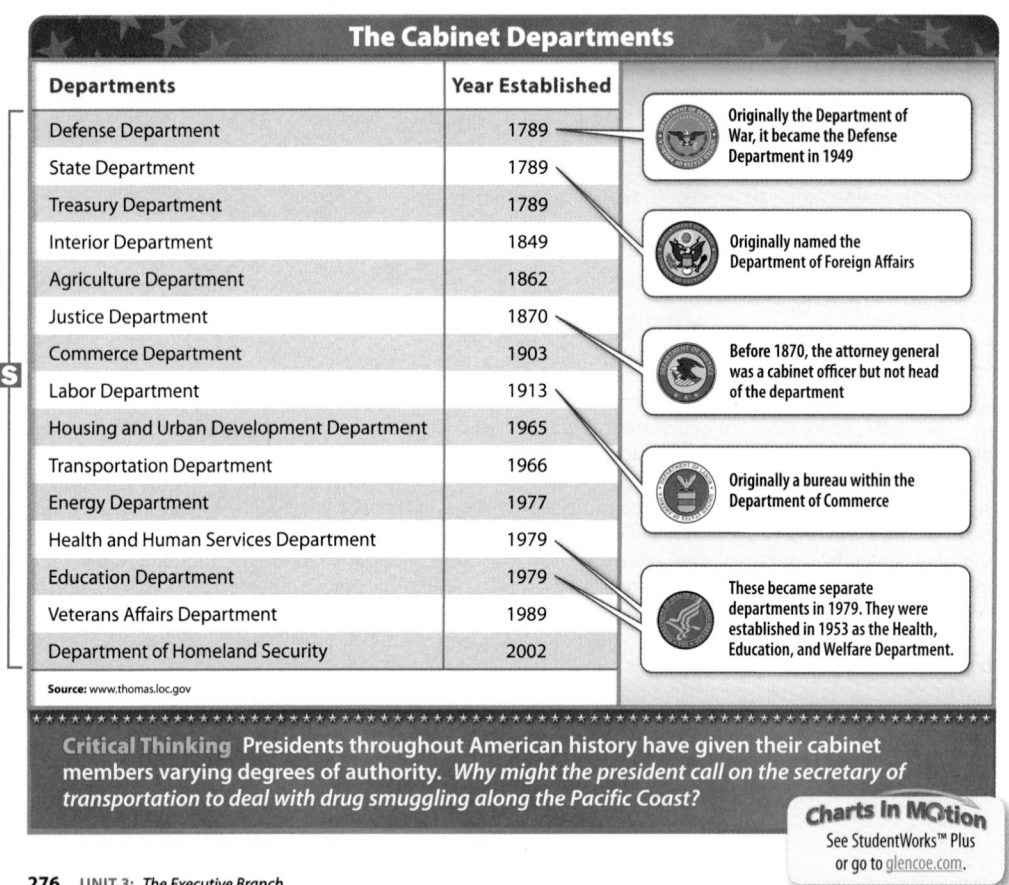

The Cabinet Departments

Departments	Year Established
Defense Department	1789
State Department	1789
Treasury Department	1789
Interior Department	1849
Agriculture Department	1862
Justice Department	1870
Commerce Department	1903
Labor Department	1913
Housing and Urban Development Department	1965
Transportation Department	1966
Energy Department	1977
Health and Human Services Department	1979
Education Department	1979
Veterans Affairs Department	1989
Department of Homeland Security	2002

Source: www.thomas.loc.gov

Originally the Department of War, it became the Defense Department in 1949

Originally named the Department of Foreign Affairs

Before 1870, the attorney general was a cabinet officer but not head of the department

Originally a bureau within the Department of Commerce

These became separate departments in 1979. They were established in 1953 as the Health, Education, and Welfare Department.

Critical Thinking Presidents throughout American history have given their cabinet members varying degrees of authority. *Why might the president call on the secretary of transportation to deal with drug smuggling along the Pacific Coast?*

Charts in MOtion
See StudentWorks™ Plus or go to glencoe.com.

Activity: Collaborative Learning

Creating a Public Awareness Booklet
Organize the class into groups of four to create a public awareness booklet illustrating the functions of each cabinet department. Assign each group a different cabinet department to portray. Allow group members to choose from the following tasks: design the cover and write the table of contents, write the cabinet

secretary's job description, write background information about the department, and make drawings or find pictures to illustrate the department including captions for each illustration. After groups assemble the information into a booklet and present it to the class, discuss each cabinet department's function and accomplishments. **OL**

Treasury

Managing the monetary resources of the United States is the main duty of the Department of the Treasury. Within the department, the Bureau of the Mint manufactures coins, and the Bureau of Engraving and Printing produces paper money.

The largest bureau in the department is the Internal Revenue Service (IRS). The IRS creates the nation's tax code and collects taxes paid by American citizens and businesses each year. Finally, the Bureau of Public Debt is in charge of borrowing any money needed to operate the federal government.

Interior

This department protects public lands and natural resources and oversees relations with Native Americans. Congress established the Department of the Interior in 1849. The Bureau of Mines in this department oversees the mining of natural resources. The National Park Service manages national monuments, historic sites, and national parks.

Agriculture

Created to help farmers improve their incomes and expand their markets, the Department of Agriculture develops conservation programs and provides financial credit to farmers. It also safeguards the nation's food supply.

Justice

Congress created the office of attorney general in 1789 to oversee the nation's legal affairs. The Department of Justice, which carries out these same duties, was created in 1870. Among its well-known agencies are the Federal Bureau of Investigation (FBI), the U.S. Marshals Service, and the Drug Enforcement Administration (DEA). The Antitrust Division of the department enforces antitrust laws. The Civil Rights Division helps enforce civil rights legislation.

Commerce

To promote and protect the industrial and commercial segments of the American economy, the Department of Commerce was founded in 1903. Three agencies of this department carry out constitutional directives. The Bureau of the Census counts the population every 10 years. Census figures are used to redraw congressional district boundaries. The Patent and Trademark Office issues patents for new inventions and **registers** trademarks. The National Institute of Standards and Technology provides uniform standards for weights and measurements.

Labor

Congress created the Department of Labor in 1913. Charged with protecting American workers, the department ensures safe working conditions, safeguards a minimum wage, and protects pension rights. The Bureau of Labor Statistics analyzes **data** on employment, wages, and compensation. The Office of the American Workplace encourages cooperation between labor and management.

Defense

In 1947 Congress merged the Department of War, which managed the army, with the Department of the Navy. In 1949 this new department was named the Department of Defense. The civilian officials in the Defense Department work with the Joint Chiefs of Staff—the leaders of the Army, Navy, Marines, and Air Force—to manage the armed forces of the United States. The government cut back the Defense Department's budget after the Cold War ended, but budgets have since increased due to the struggle against terrorism.

Health and Human Services

This department is concerned with public health and social services. It manages the federal Medicare and Medicaid programs. It also helped less-fortunate Americans through the Social Security Administration until it was made an independent agency in 1995. Perhaps the most visible agency in the department has been the Public Health Service. This agency helps implement a national health policy, funds medical research, and ensures the safety of food and drugs. The Food and Drug Administration inspects food- and drug-processing plants and must approve all new drugs before they can be sold.

Housing and Urban Development

This department was created in 1965 to ensure Americans of equal housing opportunities. The Government National Mortgage Association helps make mortgage money available for people to buy homes.

Transportation

The Department of Transportation is divided into separate agencies to help it regulate all aspects of American transportation needs, policy development, and planning. The Federal Aviation Administration regulates air travel. The Federal Railroad Administration oversees the nation's railroads. The highways that crisscross the country are regulated

Did You Know?

The cabinet meets around a big mahogany table in the Cabinet Room, which is next to the president's Oval Office in the West Wing of the White House. This room faces the Rose Garden and is furnished with draperies, brass chandeliers, and chairs replicated in eighteenth-century style. Portraits of former presidents hang throughout the room.

POLITICAL PROFILES

Donna Shalala (1941–) With a doctorate in political science, Donna Shalala became the highest ranking political scientist in government since President Woodrow Wilson. In 1993 she was appointed Secretary of Health and Human Services by Bill Clinton. She was also the first woman to head a Big Ten university, the University of Wisconsin. As a child, she played baseball on a youth team coached by George Steinbrenner.

Additional Support

Activity: Collaborative Learning

Drawing Conclusions Organize the class into two groups to debate government regulation of business. Have one group represent a heavily regulated industry, such as the airline industry, and the other group represent a regulatory agency, such as the Federal Aviation Administration (FAA). Ask students to research information on specific industry regulations and, if possible, to interview people who work in that field.

A good source for research on regulations is *Basic Principles of American Government* by William R. Sanford and Carl R. Green. Allow one group to describe a particular regulation that they research. Then let each group state its case for or against the regulation. After each debate, let the class vote on whether regulation of the specified industry should be continued as is, decreased, or increased. **AL**

Did You Know?

The first predecessor to the U.S. Coast Guard was established in 1790, although the organization did not get its modern name until 1915. During peacetime, it is part of the Department of Homeland Security. When war is declared or the president orders troops into combat, the Coast Guard operates under the authority of the Deparment of the Navy (within the Defense Department).

C Critical Thinking

Assessing Ask: Should the federal government promote policies to encourage energy conservation? Or, should energy prices and energy consumption be left to the free market? *(Prompt students to explain their responses.)* **OL**

Critical Thinking

Answer: the U.S. Coast Guard

Chart Skills Practice
How many subdivisions fall under Emergency Preparedness and Response? *(seven)*

Additional Support

by the Federal Highway Administration, and the Federal Transit Administration is responsible for the nation's mass transit.

Energy

The Department of Energy was created in 1977 in response to the nation's first major energy shortage. The department gathered together a number of separate policy groups. Some of these groups sprang from the Manhattan Project, which developed and tested the nation's first atomic bomb. The Department of Energy plans energy policy and researches and develops energy technology.

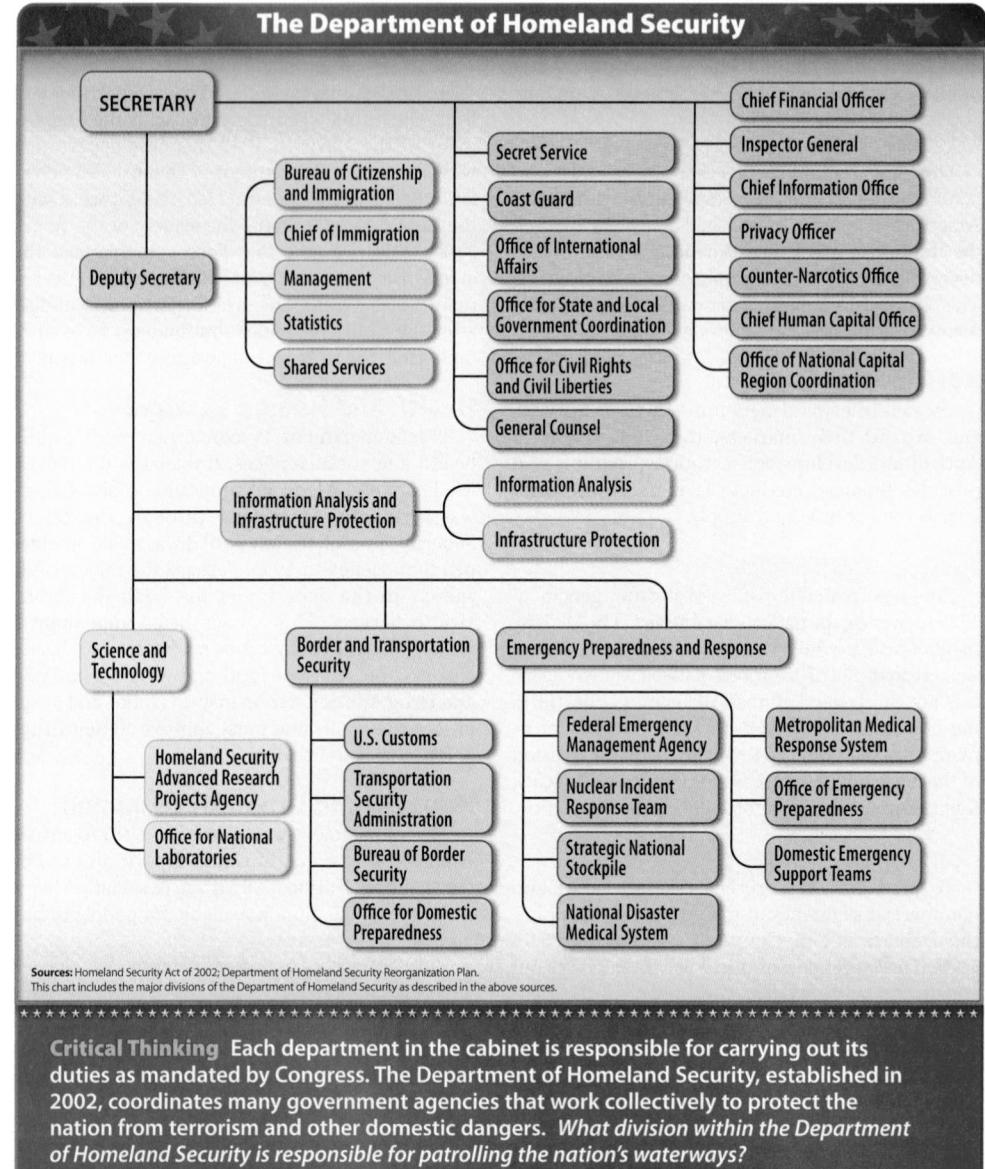

The Department of Homeland Security

SECRETARY

Deputy Secretary
- Bureau of Citizenship and Immigration
- Chief of Immigration
- Management
- Statistics
- Shared Services

- Secret Service
- Coast Guard
- Office of International Affairs
- Office for State and Local Government Coordination
- Office for Civil Rights and Civil Liberties
- General Counsel

- Chief Financial Officer
- Inspector General
- Chief Information Office
- Privacy Officer
- Counter-Narcotics Office
- Chief Human Capital Office
- Office of National Capital Region Coordination

Information Analysis and Infrastructure Protection
- Information Analysis
- Infrastructure Protection

Science and Technology
- Homeland Security Advanced Research Projects Agency
- Office for National Laboratories

Border and Transportation Security
- U.S. Customs
- Transportation Security Administration
- Bureau of Border Security
- Office for Domestic Preparedness

Emergency Preparedness and Response
- Federal Emergency Management Agency
- Nuclear Incident Response Team
- Strategic National Stockpile
- National Disaster Medical System
- Metropolitan Medical Response System
- Office of Emergency Preparedness
- Domestic Emergency Support Teams

Sources: Homeland Security Act of 2002; Department of Homeland Security Reorganization Plan. This chart includes the major divisions of the Department of Homeland Security as described in the above sources.

Critical Thinking Each department in the cabinet is responsible for carrying out its duties as mandated by Congress. The Department of Homeland Security, established in 2002, coordinates many government agencies that work collectively to protect the nation from terrorism and other domestic dangers. *What division within the Department of Homeland Security is responsible for patrolling the nation's waterways?*

Activity: Collaborative Learning

Problem Solving Organize the class into small groups to inspect the community for pollution problems. Have each group make a list of specific problems. Then have group members write to the Environmental Protection Agency (EPA) for information about ways to correct each problem. Encourage students to talk to city officials about possible solutions to these local pollution problems. Ask each group to write a description of the problem and a recommended solution to present to the class. Discuss the problems and evaluate the effectiveness of proposed solutions. **OL**

Education

In 1979 Congress created the Department of Education to coordinate federal assistance programs for public and private schools. Today the department oversees programs to help students with limited English proficiency as well as programs for physically challenged students.

Veterans Affairs

Founded in 1989, this department was formerly known as the Veterans Administration. It administers several hospitals as well as educational and other programs for veterans and their families.

Homeland Security

The terrorist attacks of September 11, 2001, led to the creation of this department in 2002. It controls the Coast Guard, the Border Patrol, the Immigration and Naturalization Service, the Customs Service, the Federal Emergency Management Agency, and many other agencies. It also analyzes information collected by the FBI and the Central Intelligence Agency (CIA).

Independent Agencies

The federal bureaucracy also includes more than 100 independent organizations that are not part of these departments. The president appoints the heads of these agencies. A few of these agencies are almost as large and well-known as cabinet departments. Examples include the National Aeronautics and Space Administration (NASA) and the Social Security Administration. Most independent agencies have few employees, small budgets, and little publicity. Few Americans, for example, have heard of the American Battle Monuments Commission.

Assisting the Executive Branch

Some independent agencies perform services for the executive branch. The General Services Administration (GSA) and the Central Intelligence Agency (CIA) are examples. The GSA is responsible for constructing and maintaining all government buildings and supplying equipment for federal offices. The National Archives and Records Administration maintains government records and publishes all rules applying to various federal agencies.

The CIA provides a very different kind of service. It gathers information about what is going on in other countries, evaluates it, and passes it on to the president and other foreign-policy decision makers. The CIA uses its own secret agents,

Aid to Veterans Tammy Duckworth, who ran for the U.S. House of Representatives in 2006, lost both her legs in the war with Iraq when the helicopter she was copiloting was hit. Veterans receive rehabilitation services from the Veterans Affairs department. *How likely is it that the Veterans Affairs budget will be cut in times of war?*

paid informers, foreign news sources, and friendly governments to collect such information.

Government Corporations

Some independent agencies, such as the Small Business Administration, directly serve the public. Many major agencies are **government corporations,** or businesses, that the federal government runs. Today, the executive branch has at least 60 government corporations. The Tennessee Valley Authority (TVA) is one. The TVA has built dams and supplies electric power for an eight-state area.

The Federal Deposit Insurance Corporation (FDIC) is also a government corporation. It insures bank accounts up to a certain amount. If a bank fails, the FDIC takes it over and repays the depositors.

Caption Answer: Students should recognize that it is very unlikely that the Veterans Affairs budget would be cut during a time of war.

Linking ☆ Past & Present

During World War II, the Joint Chiefs of Staff created the Office of Strategic Services (OSS) to oversee espionage activities and collect intelligence information. The OSS was abolished at the end of the war, but its successor, the Central Intelligence Agency (CIA), was established by the National Security Act of 1947. As defined by that law, the purpose of the CIA is to gather and disseminate intelligence and "perform other such functions and duties related to intelligence affecting the national security." In 2004 the Intelligence Reform and Terrorism Prevention Act created the position of Director of National Intelligence to whom the directors of the CIA and the National Counterterrorism Center report.

Additional Support

★ Activity: Technology Connection ★

USAJOBS What does it take to become a federal bureaucrat, or civil servant, and what kinds of jobs do federal bureaucrats perform? Have students research civil service careers at www.usajobs.gov. Guide students to choose a job they are interested in and find out what qualifications they would need as young adults applying for that job. Provide students with a simple job application form to practice filling out. Discuss the importance of beginning to gather references, knowledge, and experience as soon as possible. **OL**

Caption Answer: Such achievements provide visible evidence that shows that tax dollars are well spent. They raise the prestige of NASA in the public's view, which might lead to increased funding for the agency.

W **Writing Support**

Persuasive Writing Have students write an editorial in which they defend or rebut this statement: "Space exploration, although interesting, is an unnecessary luxury that the federal government, with its enormous debt, cannot afford." **AL**

C **Critical Thinking**

Differentiating Ask: How is a government corporation similar to and different from a private corporation? *(Whereas a private corporation relies on money from investors, a government corporation depends on money allocated by Congress. Both have a board of directors and executive officers and attempt to make money to reinvest in the "business.")* **BL**

Differentiated Instruction

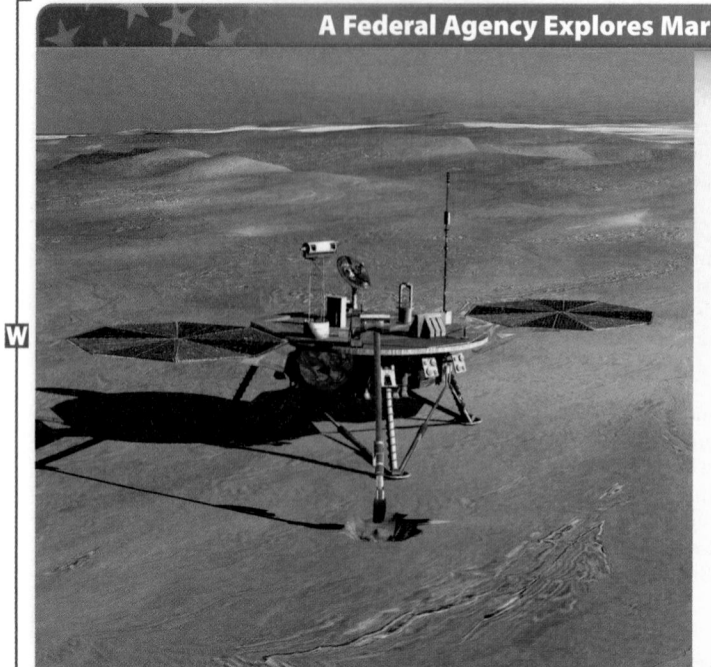

A Federal Agency Explores Mars

NASA Returns to Mars NASA is perhaps the most famous independent government agency. Its space program has landed astronauts on the moon and sent uncrewed probes across the solar system. In June 2008, NASA achieved another major success with the landing of the Phoenix spacecraft (shown in an artist's rendering at left) near the north pole of Mars. Large quantities of water ice are located nearby. The mission is to analyze Martian soil for signs of life. *Why is it important for federal agencies to have high profile achievements, such as the Phoenix mission?*

The best known of the government corporations is the United States Postal Service (USPS). Originally an executive department called the Post Office Department, the USPS became a government corporation in 1970. As an executive department, the post office consistently lost money. Since becoming a corporation, the USPS has done a better job of balancing its budget. This is, in part, because Congress passed legislation giving the USPS "the exclusive right, with certain limited exceptions, to carry letters for others." Only the USPS may deliver first-class mail.

Government corporations are organized somewhat like private businesses. Each has a board of directors and executive officers who direct the day-to-day operations. Government corporations are supposed to be more flexible than regular government agencies. They are more likely to take risks and to find **innovative** solutions to the challenges they confront. Most of the corporations earn money that is put back into the "business." Unlike private businesses, however, money from Congress—not funds from private investors— supports government corporations.

Regulatory Commissions

Regulatory commissions occupy a special place in the federal bureaucracy. They are independent of all three branches of the national government. To keep the regulatory commissions impartial, Congress has been careful to protect them from political pressure. Each commission has from 5 to 11 commissioners, whom the president appoints with Senate consent. The terms of office of these board members are long—in some cases, as long as 14 years—and the starting dates for terms are staggered. Unlike other bureaucrats, these commissioners do not report to the president, nor can the president fire them.

Purpose of the Commissions

The independent regulatory commissions were created to make rules for large industries and businesses that affect the public. Commissions also regulate the conduct of these businesses and industries. Regulatory agencies decide such questions as who will receive a government license to operate a radio station or to build a natural gas pipeline to serve a large city. The commissions can also act as

280 UNIT 3: *The Executive Branch*

Authentic Assessment with Rubrics, p. 17

Cutting Through the Red Tape

Objective: Create an organizational chart.

Focus/Teach: Review the distinctions among cabinet departments, independent agencies, and regulatory commissions.

Assess: Evaluate charts on accuracy and thoroughness.

Close: Display charts in the classroom.

Differentiated Instruction Strategies

BL List the cabinet departments, and write a brief description of each department's purpose.

AL Annotate graphs showing how the number of employees or the size of the budget has changed over time.

ELL Make a bilingual chart.

a court—investigating businesses, holding hearings, and setting penalties for businesses that may have violated the rules.

Some Problems

The decisions of these commissions can have a huge impact on business profits. For that reason, business lobbyists often pressure regulatory agencies. Commission critics have noted that lawyers for a business sometimes try to go in the "back door" to argue their position privately with agency officials.

Critics also charge that commissions and the industries they are supposed to regulate can develop a close relationship because of the "revolving door" in top positions in a business and the commission that regulates it. Because of their knowledge of an industry, commissioners are often former executives in the industry being regulated. A commissioner may leave that position to accept high-paying jobs in that industry. Will a commissioner regulate an industry without bias, or will he or she be too sympathetic to its interests because of the possibility of a future job? Some argue that the public's interest suffers due to this revolving door, but others say most agencies have a good record and that inside knowledge of an industry is necessary to regulate it.

In 2007 a major crisis erupted in the home mortgage industry and many people lost their homes.

In response, political leaders began proposing changes to agencies that regulate financial institutions, including the Securities and Exchange Commission. Reformers did not attribute the crisis to a conflict of interest on the part of regulators, but they did argue for stronger and improved regulation.

How much regulation is needed is often debated. Typically when there is a crisis—food contamination, consumer fraud, unethical business practices about assets—the public will call on Congress for more regulation.

Deregulation or Regulation?

In a 1976 campaign speech, presidential candidate Jimmy Carter called for a reduction in the number of federal agencies. He said it was difficult to track how effective existing federal agencies are. According to Carter:

> 66 We need increased program evaluation. Many programs fail to define with any specificity what they intend to accomplish. Without that specification, evaluation by objective is impossible.... 99
> —Jimmy Carter, 1976

In recent years, Congress has responded to complaints of overregulation by trying to **deregulate,** or reduce the powers of regulatory agencies.

CHAPTER 10, SECTION 1

S Skill Practice

Paraphrasing Have students read the quote from Jimmy Carter and ask them to restate his message in their own words. **BL**

Participating IN GOVERNMENT

More About Social Security
Social Security is the largest government entitlement program, meaning citizens become eligible for benefits by meeting specific requirements, such as age or disability. As people are living longer, benefits might have to be reduced or the retirement age might need to be raised.

Additional Support

Government and You

Social Security

If you have a part-time job, 6.2 percent of your pay is probably being deducted for Social Security taxes. Your deductions fund programs that benefit workers and their families.

Eligibility for Social Security benefits depends on how much you earn and how long you contribute to the system. For example, to receive monthly payments when you retire, you must accumulate at least 40 work credits. You can receive up to 4 credits per year, based on your earnings. Currently, Social Security retirement benefits provide about 40 percent of a worker's salary.

In addition, statistics show that you have about a 3-in-10 chance of becoming unable to work before you reach age 65. If you are disabled for a year or longer, Social Security will pay monthly benefits to help make up for your loss of income. In many cases, minor children of disabled, deceased, or retired workers are also eligible for benefits.

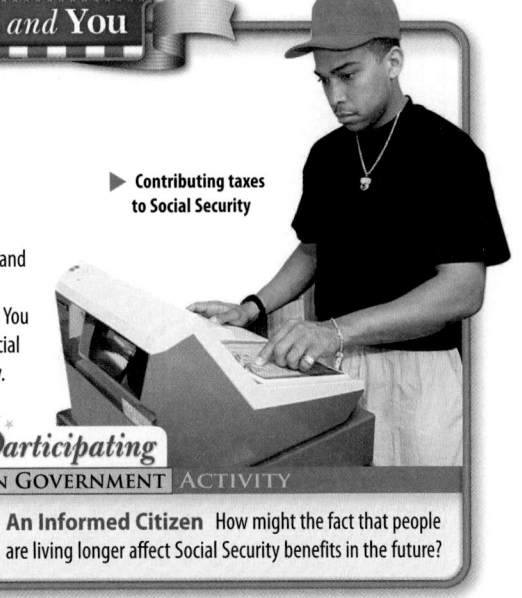

▶ **Contributing taxes to Social Security**

Participating IN GOVERNMENT ACTIVITY

An Informed Citizen How might the fact that people are living longer affect Social Security benefits in the future?

CHAPTER 10: *The Federal Bureaucracy* **281**

Extending the Content

The Origins of Social Security A major New Deal program was the Social Security Act, which provided a variety of benefits to many retired, disabled, or unemployed workers. The original Social Security program did not cover agricultural or domestic workers. In 1940

Ida Fuller became the first recipient of Social Security retirement benefits in the United States. By the time Fuller died at age 100, she had contributed about $22 into the Social Security fund and had received more than $20,000 in benefits.

Did You Know?

Established in 2002, the USA Freedom Corps was an initiative of President George W. Bush. The agency promotes volunteer networks that help individuals find volunteer service opportunities and works with existing national service organizations. It also created the USA Freedom Corps for Kids Web site to encourage young people to participate in volunteer projects in their communities.

D Differentiated Instruction

Gifted and Talented Have students select one independent agency or government corporation and prepare a report on its history and purpose. Reports should also discuss any recent changes in the organization or current controversies. Have students present their reports. **AL**

Critical Thinking

Answer: Government corporations are funded by Congress, not by private investors.

Hands-On Chapter Project
Step 1

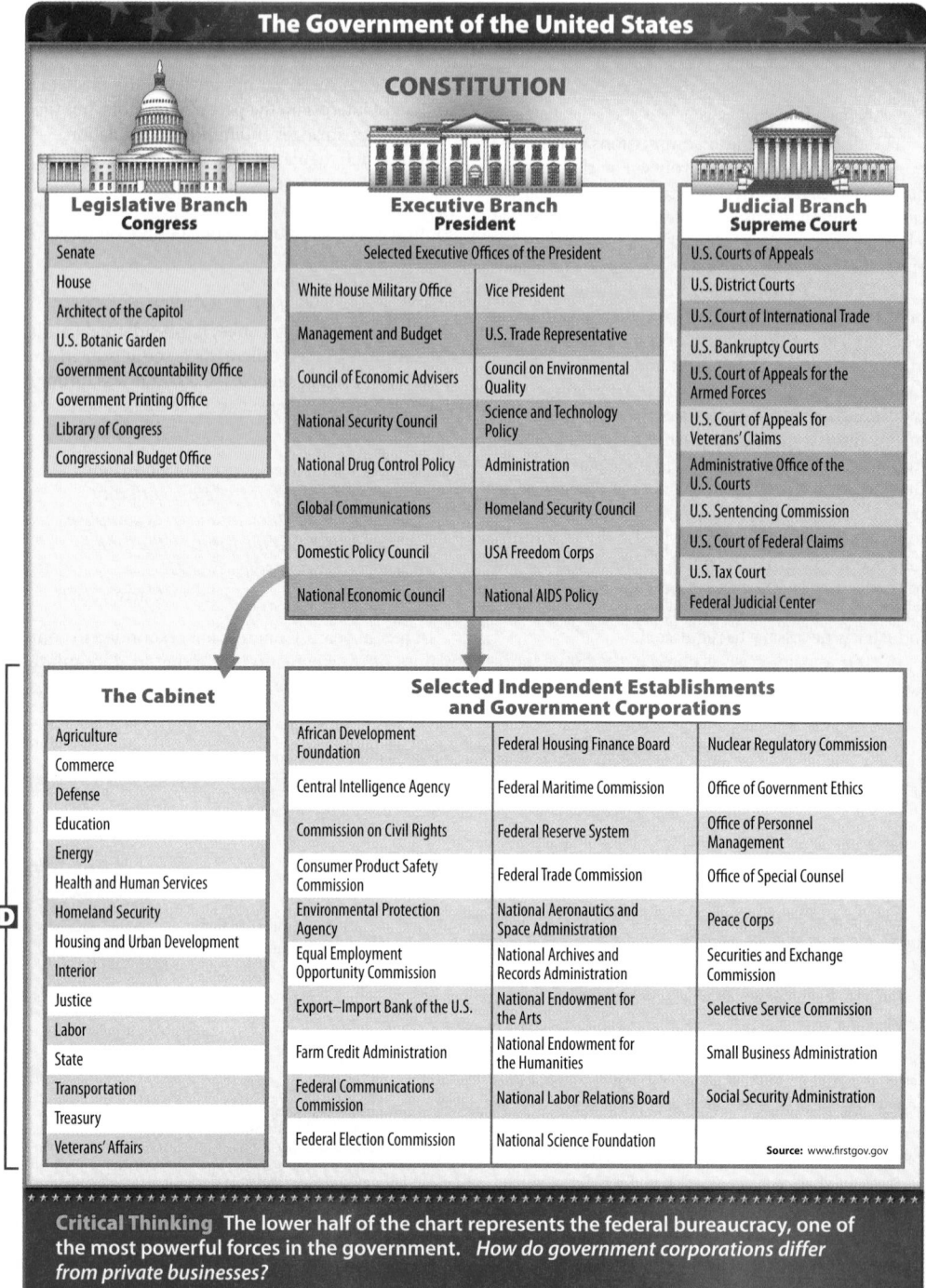

The Government of the United States

CONSTITUTION

Legislative Branch
Congress

- Senate
- House
- Architect of the Capitol
- U.S. Botanic Garden
- Government Accountability Office
- Government Printing Office
- Library of Congress
- Congressional Budget Office

Executive Branch
President

Selected Executive Offices of the President

White House Military Office	Vice President
Management and Budget	U.S. Trade Representative
Council of Economic Advisers	Council on Environmental Quality
National Security Council	Science and Technology Policy
National Drug Control Policy	Administration
Global Communications	Homeland Security Council
Domestic Policy Council	USA Freedom Corps
National Economic Council	National AIDS Policy

Judicial Branch
Supreme Court

- U.S. Courts of Appeals
- U.S. District Courts
- U.S. Court of International Trade
- U.S. Bankruptcy Courts
- U.S. Court of Appeals for the Armed Forces
- U.S. Court of Appeals for Veterans' Claims
- Administrative Office of the U.S. Courts
- U.S. Sentencing Commission
- U.S. Court of Federal Claims
- U.S. Tax Court
- Federal Judicial Center

The Cabinet

- Agriculture
- Commerce
- Defense
- Education
- Energy
- Health and Human Services
- Homeland Security
- Housing and Urban Development
- Interior
- Justice
- Labor
- State
- Transportation
- Treasury
- Veterans' Affairs

Selected Independent Establishments and Government Corporations

African Development Foundation	Federal Housing Finance Board	Nuclear Regulatory Commission
Central Intelligence Agency	Federal Maritime Commission	Office of Government Ethics
Commission on Civil Rights	Federal Reserve System	Office of Personnel Management
Consumer Product Safety Commission	Federal Trade Commission	Office of Special Counsel
Environmental Protection Agency	National Aeronautics and Space Administration	Peace Corps
Equal Employment Opportunity Commission	National Archives and Records Administration	Securities and Exchange Commission
Export–Import Bank of the U.S.	National Endowment for the Arts	Selective Service Commission
Farm Credit Administration	National Endowment for the Humanities	Small Business Administration
Federal Communications Commission	National Labor Relations Board	Social Security Administration
Federal Election Commission	National Science Foundation	**Source:** www.firstgov.gov

Critical Thinking The lower half of the chart represents the federal bureaucracy, one of the most powerful forces in the government. *How do government corporations differ from private businesses?*

Preparing a Report to Congress

Step 1: Identifying Policy Influences

Have students review the various departments, commissions, and councils that comprise the federal bureaucracy, such as the Department of Agriculture, the U.S. Postal Service, and the Federal Election Commission.

Directions Tell student groups to select an agency to research. Each group will prepare a statement explaining to the class what the responsibilities of its chosen agency are and listing current issues that relate to that agency. Let students know that later in the project, they will select one of these issues and prepare a report to "Congress" (the class) about it.

Summarizing Ask volunteers to read each group's statement to the class. Encourage questions. **OL**

(Chapter Project continued in Section 2.)

In 1978 Congress ordered the Civil Aeronautics Board (CAB) to simplify its procedures and cut back on regulation. Congress also said that the CAB was to go out of business in 1985. Deregulation was a major issue in the 1980s and 1990s. Republicans wanted less regulation, and in 1993 Democratic president Bill Clinton met them halfway. He signed an executive order saying the benefits of burdensome regulations should be proven.

Since 2001, the pendulum has swung back toward more regulation. Terrorist threats are one reason—in the name of national security, individuals and businesses have been required to submit to more regulation. The 2001 Enron scandal is another reason for more regulation. Investors lost billions of dollars because Enron used accounting tricks that misrepresented the company's real value. As a result, laws were passed requiring stricter accounting rules.

Cutting the Federal Workforce

One way to cut costs is to cut the number of federal workers. After a study by Vice President Al Gore, the Clinton administration proposed to reduce the federal workforce by 252,000 employees in six years. Congress passed a bill requiring the reductions and provided cash incentives for workers to resign. It wrote into law a bill that would reduce the size of the Department of Agriculture, cutting 7,500 jobs by 1999. The number of federal employees, which peaked in 1990, was reduced substantially by 1995 and has stayed approximately the same since.

Promoting Competition

In most cases, the president and Congress support the idea that competition is good for consumers. If industries are regulated, Americans often see regulation as a last resort.

In certain industries, competition would not serve the public good. For example, it would not be cost-effective to have competing bus companies or subways. Economists refer to industries like these as "natural monopolies." Where a natural monopoly exists, however, it is expected that the government will make sure the company does not take advantage of its position and raise prices too high.

In the past, telecommunications was seen as a natural monopoly. In the 1980s, however, Congress deregulated the industry. As a result, AT&T's historic monopoly over telephone services ended. Competition became intense because of technological advances. Internet-based technologies for communication have proliferated, and they have made most government regulation outmoded. To take just one example, geographic boundaries are largely unrelated to the cost of Internet services.

The Telecommunications Act of 1996 reflected this new spirit of competition, but industry developments have been too difficult to predict—and thus for the government to influence. Major players in the industry merged or "bundled" and "unbundled" services frequently to get a larger share of the market. Many analysts are doubtful that older methods of regulation can be effective in the new age of global communications.

SECTION 1 Review

Vocabulary

1. **Explain** the significance of: bureaucrat, embassy, government corporation, deregulate.

Main Ideas

2. **Identifying** What are the responsibilities of the Department of State and the Department of the Treasury?

3. **Examining** How are cabinet departments organized?

Critical Thinking

4. **Making Inferences** Why is it important that regulatory commissions be free from political pressures?

5. **Organizing** Using a Venn diagram like the one below, analyze how regulatory commissions and independent agencies are alike and how they are different.

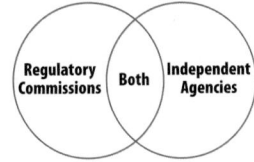

Regulatory Commissions | Both | Independent Agencies

Writing About Government

6. **Persuasive Writing** Imagine that you serve on a task force to set up a new executive agency. Think of an issue the nation faces. Then research it and write a report on why a new agency is needed.

C Critical Thinking

Predicting Consequences
Ask: Why do federal agencies regulate businesses? What might happen if no regulation occurred? *(Students might note that consistency is helpful for interstate and international businesses, and if unregulated, some businesses would cease to be vigilant about issues of quality and safety. Point out that lacking regulation is partially responsible for the Enron scandal.)* **AL**

Assess

Assign the Section 1 Assessment as homework or as an in-class activity, or have students take Section Quiz 10-1 from *Section Quizzes and Chapter Tests.*

Close

Analyzing Ask students to choose which cabinet departments they think are the most important and the least important. Discuss students' choices and explanations. **OL**

Section 1 Review

Answers

1. All definitions can be found in the section and the Glossary.

2. State: implements foreign policy, protects rights of citizens abroad, staffs embassies, and represents United States at the UN
   Treasury: manages monetary resources, manufactures coins and paper money, collects taxes, and borrows money to operate the government

3. A secretary heads each department. The second in command is the deputy secretary or undersecretary; assistant secretaries are next in line. Under these top officials are the directors of the departments' major units and their assistants.

4. so they can be impartial about policies, subject to fewer influences, and regulate what they were created to control

5. Regulatory commissions: make rules for businesses; do not report to the president
   Independent commissions: serve the government or the public
   Both: part of the bureaucracy

6. Students should consider whether an existing department could deal with the issue.

Focus

The Civil Service System

Bellringer

Section Focus Transparencies 10-2

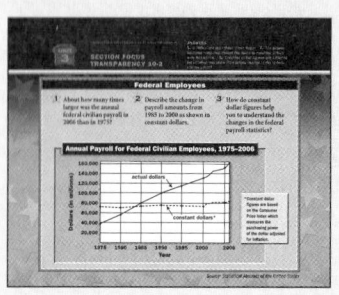

Reader's Guide

Answers to Graphic:

Causes: inefficiency, employees lack skills their jobs require, corruption, assassination of President Garfield

Effects: Pendleton Act, creation of the civil service system

Resource Manager

Reader's Guide

Content Vocabulary	Academic Vocabulary	Reading Strategy
★ spoils system (p. 285) ★ civil service system (p. 286)	★ percent (p. 284) ★ ignore (p. 285) ★ neutral (p. 287)	As you read, create a graphic organizer similar to the one below to list the causes and effects of the calls to reform the federal bureaucracy in the 1850s.

Cause		Effect
	→	

Individual Rights in the News

In early 2008, the U.S. Office of Special Counsel began to investigate three federal employees who allegedly violated the Hatch Act by engaging in political activities while on the job. The three were suspected of using government e-mail accounts to spread false statements about presidential candidate Barack Obama. "Quick access to the Internet from work makes it easier for people to make the mistake," said one official in the Special Counsel office. "Now people can step into trouble very easily just by forwarding a message that someone else sent to them." In fact, the e-mail at issue was forwarded by another federal employee to soldiers and army personnel worldwide.

▲ A federal worker at her computer

Many people think of a federal bureaucrat as a pencil pusher shuffling papers in Washington, D.C. Yet only 11 **percent** of all federal employees actually work in Washington, D.C. The rest work in offices across the United States and the world. In addition, many federal employees do little paperwork—FBI agents, forest rangers, and air-traffic controllers among many others.

Federal employees are vital to the smooth functioning of the American government. President Dwight Eisenhower commented on their role when he said:

❝ *The government of the United States has become too big, too complex, and too pervasive in its influence on all our lives for one individual to pretend to direct the details of its important and critical programming. Competent assistants are mandatory.* ❞

—Dwight D. Eisenhower

Who makes up the federal bureaucracy? The typical man or woman in federal service is more than 40 years old and has worked for the government for about 15 years. The majority of the civilian employees earn between $25,000 and $50,000 per year.

In terms of ethnic and gender profile, about 30 percent of federal workers are members of minority groups (compared to 22 percent in the private sector); women make up about 44 percent of federal workers—roughly the same percentage as in the private sector. A recent survey found that 30 percent of all federal employees had family members who also worked for the government.

About half of the federal employees are administrative and clerical workers. The government also employs doctors, veterinarians, lawyers, cartographers, scientists, engineers, accountants, and many other professionals.

R Reading Strategies	**C** Critical Thinking	**D** Differentiated Instruction	**W** Writing Support	**S** Skill Practice
Teacher Edition • Identifying, p. 285 **Additional Resources** • Quizzes/Tests, p. 116 • Guid. Read. Act., p. 37	**Teacher Edition** • Drawing Conclusions, p. 288 **Additional Resources** • Read. Essen., pp. 110–112	**Teacher Edition** • English Learners, p. 289 **Additional Resources** • Part. in Gov. Act., pp. 19–20 • Foldables, p. 53	**Teacher Edition** • Narrative Writing, p. 285 • Personal Writing, p. 288 **Additional Resources** • Hist. Docs. and Speeches, p. 10	**Teacher Edition** • Problem Solving, p. 287 **Additional Resources** • Inter. Poli. Cartoons, pp. 17–18

A Federal Bureaucrat

Not Your Typical Office
This National Park Service ranger is actually a federal bureaucrat. A ranger's office may be a national park, a national monument, or a national historic site. Park rangers patrol the parklands to protect them from damage and to help visitors. *Besides park rangers, what are some other jobs in the federal bureaucracy that are not located in Washington, D.C.?*

Teach

Caption Answer: Answers may include FBI agents, air traffic controllers, doctors, and so on.

R Reading Strategy

Identifying Ask: Is the spoils system a good method for filling bureaucratic positions? Why or why not? *(No; the spoils system fosters inefficiency because appointees are often unqualified, and can lead to corruption because appointees tend to use their jobs for personal gain.)* **OL**

W Writing Support

Narrative Writing Ask students to imagine that they have been elected to a high-ranking government position. Have them write a narrative essay in which they discuss the people whom they would appoint to the cabinet and other government positions. **Ask:** Why did you choose these people? Are they qualified for their new positions? **OL**

Additional Support

Origins

Today almost all federal jobs are filled through competitive exams, but this method was not used when our government was established.

The Spoils System

George Washington declared that he appointed government officials according to "fitness of character." At the same time, however, he favored members of the Federalist Party.

When Thomas Jefferson entered the White House, he found most federal workers opposed him and his political ideas. Consequently, Jefferson fired hundreds of workers who were Federalists. He replaced these workers with people from his own political party, the Democratic-Republican Party.

By the time Andrew Jackson became president in 1829, the federal government had begun to grow. Jackson fired about 1,000 federal workers and gave their jobs to his own political supporters. **R** Jackson defended his actions by arguing that it was more democratic to have rotation in office. Long service in the same jobs by any group of workers, he claimed, would only promote tyranny.

A New York senator defended Jackson's actions by stating, "To the victor belong the spoils." The **spoils system** became the phrase used to describe Jackson's method of appointing federal workers. Today, the term *spoils system* refers to the practice of victorious politicians rewarding their followers with government jobs.

For the next 50 years, national, state, and local politicians used the spoils system to fill bureaucratic positions. Political supporters of candidates expected to be rewarded with jobs if their candidate won. As the federal government grew larger, the spoils system flourished.

Calls for Reform

The spoils system fostered inefficiency and corruption. Inefficiency grew because as government became more complex, many jobs required specific skills, yet most federal workers were not experts in their jobs. Their skills were in working in election campaigns to secure victory for their candidates.

Corruption developed as people used their jobs for personal gain. Government employees did special favors for special-interest groups in return for political support for their candidates. Jobs were often bought and sold. People made large profits from government contracts. Bureaucrats regularly gave jobs to friends rather than to the lowest bidder. **W**

Calls for reform began in the 1850s. Newspapers and magazines described the problems with the spoils system. In 1871 Ulysses S. Grant, whose own administration was filled with corruption, persuaded Congress to set up the first Civil Service Commission. In 1875, however, reform efforts faltered when Congress failed to appropriate money for the new commission.

It took a tragedy to restart reforms. In 1881 President James A. Garfield **ignored** Charles Guiteau's requests for a job in the diplomatic service. Infuriated, Guiteau shot Garfield at a Washington railway station on July 2, 1881. Garfield died 80 days later.

Activity: Collaborative Learning

Writing a Newspaper Organize the class into groups of five to write the front page of a newspaper. Have groups choose a current issue or one from the past that exposes corruption in the federal government. Allow each group to choose a name for their newspaper and each member to choose from the following tasks: write an article exposing the corruption; draw a political cartoon illustrating the main reason that the corruption occurred; create the front-page layout including date and placement of articles, weather information, and so on; find or draw pictures pertaining to the news item and write captions; write a biography of the main person(s) involved in the scandal. Ask volunteers to present their front-page stories to the class. Discuss how the media helped or will help influence political change. **AL**

Did You Know?

Turkey is the term used for a nonperforming federal bureaucrat. It is said that they are "sent to the turkey farm" because they do almost nothing yet continue to collect salaries. Why do turkeys exist? It is nearly impossible to fire someone from a government job. Of approximately 2.75 million current federal workers, only 12,000–30,000 are fired each year (less than one percent). As President Jimmy Carter remarked, it is "easier to promote and transfer incompetent employees than to get rid of them."

Differentiated Instruction

A System of Corruption

Patronage System
Politicians often bestowed "political plums" in the form of federal jobs on friends and family, as suggested by this cartoon of the late nineteenth century. Many of these people were ill-equipped for their jobs and interested mainly in their salary. *What does the umbrella in the cartoon symbolize?*

"PUBLIC OFFICE IS A 'FAMILY SNAP'."

The Pendleton Act

The public was outraged. Chester Arthur, the new president, pushed hard for reform. In 1883 Congress passed the Pendleton Act, creating the present federal **civil service system.** The civil service system is the principle and practice of government employment on the basis of open, competitive exams and merit. The law set up the Civil Service Commission to administer exams and supervise the operation of the new system.

The Civil Service Commission operated for 95 years. In 1979 two new agencies replaced it. The Office of Personnel Management handles recruitment, pay, retirement policy, and exams for federal workers. The Merit System Protection Board settles job disputes and investigates complaints from federal workers.

The Civil Service Today

Has the present civil service system created new problems while solving those problems linked with the spoils system?

Getting a Job

Competition for federal jobs today is stiff. In recent years, every job opening has had in the range of 80 applicants. This competition will probably continue. While the federal bureaucracy is huge, the number of federal jobs has not changed much since 1950. Yet the number of people wanting federal jobs continues to increase.

The Office of Personnel Management, along with individual agencies, is responsible for filling federal jobs. Job notices are usually posted in post offices, newspapers, and online at USAJOBS (www.usajobs.gov).

Most secretarial and clerical jobs require the applicant to take a written examination. For other jobs such as accountants, social workers, and project managers, applicants are evaluated on their training and experience. Veterans are given special preference.

Benefits and Problems

Government jobs are attractive because of the many benefits they offer. Salaries are competitive with those in private industry. Federal workers get from 13 to 26 days of paid vacation every year, depending on the length of their service. They have good medical insurance plans and 13 days of sick leave every year. Many government workers may retire at age 55. If they retire before then, their monthly benefit payment is reduced.

Each government job is assigned a certain grade ranging from GS-l, the lowest level, to GS-15, the highest. All civil service workers have job security. They may be fired, but only for specific reasons and only after a very long, complex series of hearings. Many supervisors and top officials find it

Activity: Multiple Learning Styles

Interpersonal Why are so many people interested in working for the federal government? Ask students to interview several local federal government employees, such as postal employees, forest rangers, national park workers, air-traffic controllers, or IRS employees. Encourage students to ask about the following: number of years worked, number of raises, average percentage raise per year, amount of vacation time, type of work, whether any family members hold or held a government position, retirement plan, and any other information that students consider important. Have students share their findings with the class. After they complete their research, ask students to discuss the advantages and disadvantages of working for the federal government. **OL**

is easier to put up with an incompetent worker than to document the reasons to fire one.

Thus, an ironic situation has developed. On the one hand, the civil service was designed to hire federal workers based on merit and protect them from being fired for political reasons. In achieving this goal, however, the system also helps protect a small number of incompetent and inefficient employees.

The Hatch Act

The Hatch Act limits how involved federal government employees can become in elections. In 1939 Congress passed this law—named after its chief sponsor, Senator Carl Hatch—to prevent a political party from using federal workers in election campaigns. If that happened, it would raise the dangerous possibility that workers' promotions and job security could depend on their support of candidates from the party in power.

The law has been controversial since its passage, and its constitutionality has been the subject of two Supreme Court decisions. Many federal workers dislike the Hatch Act, arguing that the law violates freedom of speech. They also claim that the act discourages political participation by people who may be well informed about political issues.

Supporters of the Hatch Act believe it is needed to keep the federal civil service politically **neutral.** They argue that the act protects workers from political pressure from superiors, and that it prevents employees from using their government positions to punish or influence people for political reasons. A high-profile example of how political prejudice can affect bureaucratic decisions occurred in 2008. Charges were made that Secretary of Housing and Urban Development Alphonso Jackson canceled a housing grant to someone who said he did not like President George W. Bush. Secretary Jackson **S** resigned following press reports of the charges.

In 1993 Congress revised the Hatch Act to address criticisms. The amended law prohibits federal workers from engaging in political activities during work hours, including wearing a campaign button. When they are not at work, they can hold office in a political party, participate in political campaigns and rallies, publicly endorse candidates, and raise funds from within their government agency's political action committee. They cannot run for an elective office, however, or solicit public contributions.

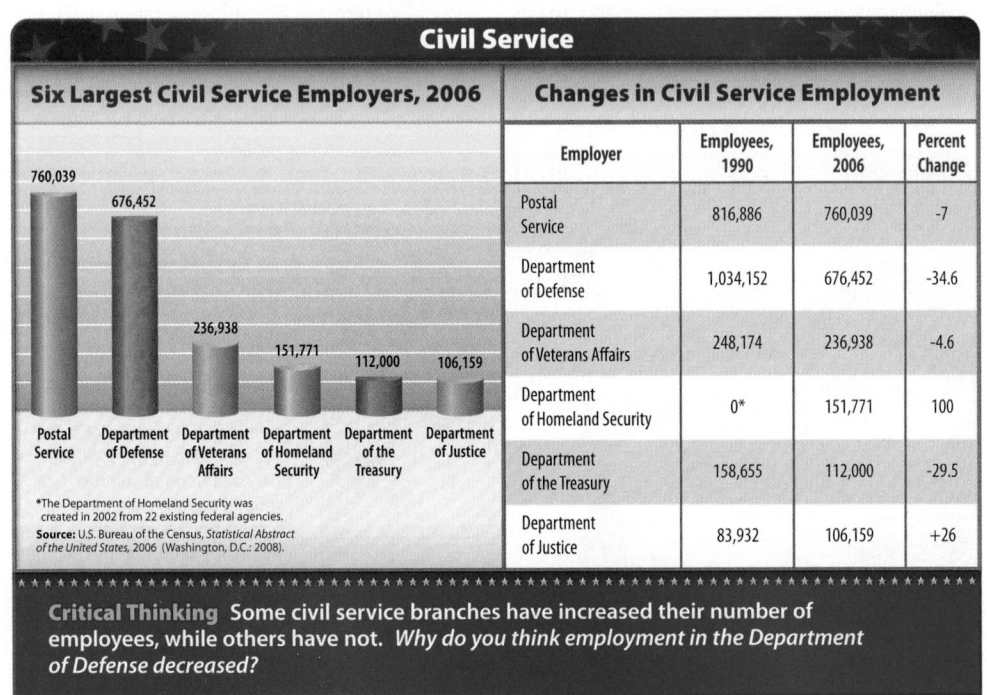

Civil Service

Six Largest Civil Service Employers, 2006

- Postal Service: 760,039
- Department of Defense: 676,452
- Department of Veterans Affairs: 236,938
- Department of Homeland Security: 151,771
- Department of the Treasury: 112,000
- Department of Justice: 106,159

Changes in Civil Service Employment

Employer	Employees, 1990	Employees, 2006	Percent Change
Postal Service	816,886	760,039	-7
Department of Defense	1,034,152	676,452	-34.6
Department of Veterans Affairs	248,174	236,938	-4.6
Department of Homeland Security	0*	151,771	100
Department of the Treasury	158,655	112,000	-29.5
Department of Justice	83,932	106,159	+26

*The Department of Homeland Security was created in 2002 from 22 existing federal agencies.
Source: U.S. Bureau of the Census, *Statistical Abstract of the United States, 2006* (Washington, D.C.: 2008).

Critical Thinking Some civil service branches have increased their number of employees, while others have not. *Why do you think employment in the Department of Defense decreased?*

S Skill Practice

Problem Solving The civil service system was created to resolve problems inherent to the spoils system, but it has its own set of problems. Have students review the basics of the civil service system to identify problems. Ask students to list the problems on one side of a sheet of paper and list suggested resolutions to the problems on the other side. Call on volunteers to share their suggestions. **OL**

Caption Answer: Students might suggest that the creation of the Department of Homeland Security caused redundancies, that budget cuts led to massive layoffs, or that the end of the Cold War in the early 1990s led to the elimination of certain positions.

Table Skills Practice
Which civil service employer had the most employees in 1990? In 2006? *(Department of Defense; Postal Service)*

Hands-On Chapter Project
Step 2

Preparing a Report to Congress

Step 2: Researching an Issue Have each group select an issue that relates to the agency they chose in Step 1. Explain that Congress will be considering legislation on that issue and that the group will present a report to Congress. For example, Congress might ask the Environmental Protection Agency to prepare facts about the advantages and disadvantages of drilling for oil in the Arctic National Wildlife Refuge. The report will present various sides of the issue but make a recommendation for congressional action. **Directions** Groups will research the issue they select, using the Internet and other resources, including government Web sites and those of special-interest groups. Assuming the role of an employee of the agency, each group member will research some aspect of the issue and become an "expert" who is prepared to give testimony about it. In the example above, one member might be an expert on fuel consumption needs, one on animal habitat, and another on the geology of the arctic region. Students will compile statistics, facts, and quotations and will print or photocopy their sources.

Putting It Together Have each group prepare posters or a multimedia presentation showing the key facts they found: graphs, flowcharts, bulleted lists, annotated photos, or other visual aids that will support their report to Congress in Step 3. **OL**

(Chapter Project continued in Section 3.)

Political Appointees in Government

In each presidential election year, the House or Senate publishes a book known by Washington insiders as the plum book. The word *plum* can mean something good—a tasty sweet—given in return for a favor. When we are talking about government, it means a political plum, that is, a job the new president can award to supporters. The plum book lists all such jobs.

On taking office, every president has the chance to fill about 2,200 top-level jobs in the federal bureaucracy. These jobs are outside the civil service system. This means that a person does not have to take a competitive civil service exam to win the position. The people who fill these jobs are sometimes called unclassified employees, as opposed to the classified employees hired by the civil service system.

About 10 percent of the jobs in the executive branch are filled by presidential appointees. These jobs include very important, high-profile posts, such as the 15 cabinet secretaries, about 300 top-level bureau and agency heads, and more than 170 ambassadors to foreign countries. The appointments also include about 1,700 aide and assistant positions.

Filling these jobs gives presidents a chance to put loyal supporters in key positions. These political appointees head agencies, offices, and bureaus, and they will make key political decisions. They are expected to try to implement the president's policies. Unlike career civil service workers, their employment usually ends when a new president is elected. Who are the people with these "plum" jobs? Beyond their loyalty to the president, what kind of qualifications do they usually have?

People at the Top

The people appointed to the non-civil service positions are first and foremost the president's political supporters. Most are well educated. Nearly all are college graduates. The majority have advanced degrees, and a significant percentage are usually lawyers. Others are successful businesspeople or other professionals. Yet the people in these positions are not typically experts in the specialized work of the agency they are appointed to. They may well have served in government before. Almost certainly they will have administrative or managerial experience. When the president leaves office, most of them return to jobs outside the government.

A Short Tenure

Many new people enter the bureaucracy by presidential appointment, but unless a president serves two terms, a new administration will come in and they will be replaced. Thus, they often have only a few years in which to learn their jobs.

Blowing the Whistle

Protections for Civil Servants Federal laws protect "whistle-blowers" from being punished if they "blow the whistle" on problems or wrongdoing in their agencies. After Frederic Whitehurst (left) reported scientific misconduct at the FBI crime lab in the 1990s, he was forced to sue the federal government for attempting to retaliate against him for his whistle blowing. *Why do you think laws to protect "whistle-blowers" are appropriate for federal jobs?*

288 UNIT 3: *The Executive Branch*

 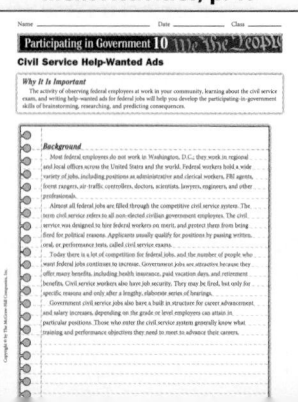

A Ballooning Federal Bureaucracy

Paring Down Government
Historically the federal bureaucracy has expanded to meet the increasing complexities and issues facing the government. *How do you think the increasing size of the federal bureaucracy affects the president's control of the government?*

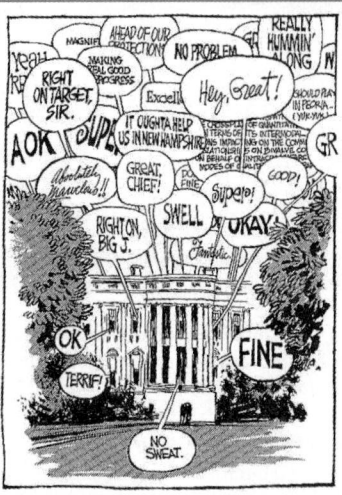

Most federal agencies are very large and have multiple departments and divisions. The complexity of the federal government makes it especially difficult for presidential appointees to learn their jobs in the short time they usually have. It can take the head of a large agency a year or more to learn about all the issues, programs, procedures, and personalities involved. "I was like a sea captain who finds himself on the deck of a ship that he has never seen before," one new appointee said. "I did not know the mechanism of my ship, I did not know my officers—and I had no acquaintance with the crew."

The result of these short tenures is that much of the real power over daily operations stays with the career civil service officials. Their day-to-day decisions do not often make headlines or the nightly newscast, but they do shape the national policy on key problems.

SECTION 2 Review

Vocabulary

1. **Explain** the significance of: spoils system, civil service system.

Main Ideas

2. **Describing** What was the Pendleton Act?

3. **Identifying** What two agencies now make up the former Civil Service Commission?

Critical Thinking

4. **Synthesizing Information** Why do you think political supporters are so eager to fill the plum jobs?

5. **Analyzing** How did the spoils system foster inefficiency and corruption?

6. **Organizing** Using a graphic organizer like the one below, note the advantages and disadvantages of the spoils system and the civil service system.

	Advantages	Disadvantages
Spoils		
Civil Service		

Writing About Government

7. **Expository Writing** Imagine that you are considering a civil service job. Find a specific position at www.USAJobs.gov, the general U.S. government job Web site. Once you have read about the position, evaluate its negative and positive aspects. Create a document that lists the pros and cons of the position. At the bottom of the document, summarize your overall assessment.

Caption Answer: Answers should mention that the president has less control as the bureaucracy grows. Some students might think that the government has grown too large for one person to manage effectively.

D Differentiated Instruction

English Learners Review the quote with English learners to make sure they understand the analogy about the sea captain. **ELL**

Assess

Assign the Section 2 Assessment as homework or as an in-class activity, or have students take Section Quiz 10-2 from *Section Quizzes and Chapter Tests.*

Close

Analyzing Primary Sources
Discuss the following quote by James F. Byrnes, a former secretary of state: "The nearest approach to immortality on earth is a government bureau." **OL**

Section 2 Review

Answers

1. All definitions can be found in the section and the Glossary.
2. The Pendleton Act created the federal civil service system, which established the principle of government employment on the basis of merit.
3. the Office of Personnel Management and the Merit System Protection Board
4. They seek the challenge of such jobs, might want to be close to the center of power, make key political decisions, and meet influential people.

5. Inefficiency was caused by government positions being filled by unqualified appointees. Corruption developed as appointees used their jobs for personal gain; government employees did favors in return for political support, took bribes, and gave jobs to friends rather than the lowest bidder.
6. Spoils: advantages—allows victorious politicians to reward their followers; disadvantages—inefficiency, corruption, government workers without needed expertise

Civil service: advantages—competitive salaries, paid vacations, health insurance, early retirement, job security; disadvantages—difficult to fire incompetent and inefficient workers
7. Students should discuss the pros and cons of a career in the civil service.

Class Debate

Ask students to form two groups based on their opinion about what the Supreme Court's ruling on this case should be. Then have each group write a majority opinion and a dissenting opinion. Have each group argue its case, and then ask students to reevaluate their opinions. Have students re-form groups based on their reevaluations. Ask students who changed their minds to explain why.

The Court's Decision

In the case of *Civil Service Commission* v. *Letter Carriers,* the Supreme Court, by a 6-to-3 vote, upheld the constitutionality of the Hatch Act. The Court said that the law was not too broad and that in passing the law, Congress was responding to an important government need that outweighed the limitations on speech in the law. Justice Byron White wrote in the majority opinion: "It is in the best interest of the country, indeed essential, that federal service should depend upon meritorious performance rather than political service." The Court also noted that Congress could change the law in the future to suit new circumstances. In 1993 Congress did make substantial changes in the law.

Can Federal Employees Participate in Partisan Politics?

U.S. Civil Service Commission v. *National Association of Letter Carriers, 1973*

Should federal employees be free to engage in partisan political activities, or can Congress limit such participation?

Facts of the Case

The Hatch Act of 1939 barred federal workers from campaigning for a political party, raising funds for a party, or running for political office. Workers still had the right to vote, join a political party, attend political rallies, and express their opinions. In 1972 six federal employees, a union, and local Democratic and Republican Party officials argued that the act violated the First Amendment. A district court recognized a "well-established governmental interest in restricting political activities by federal employees," but said the law was unconstitutional because it was too vague. The court held that free speech was so important that laws limiting speech had to be clear and precise. The Hatch Act was amended in 1993, allowing federal workers to engage in more political activity.

The Constitutional Question

There was no question that the Hatch Act put restrictions on free speech, but were such restrictions justified? Over the years, the Supreme Court developed the principle that the right to free speech was not absolute; Congress could put some limits on speech when it was necessary to protect the public good. Was this one of those situations? The Court also asked whether the restrictions in the law were applied evenly and not aimed at particular political parties, groups, or points of view.

In its 1973 decision, the Court referenced the 1947 case of *United Public Workers of America* v. *Mitchell.* In that case, George Poole, a federal worker, lost his job for serving as a Democratic ward committeeperson and working as a poll watcher. The Court upheld the law's limitations on political activity, stating that Congress had the power to pass a law "to promote efficiency and integrity in the public service." Justice Hugo Black, in a strong dissent, stated that any law limiting speech must be "narrowly drawn to meet the evil aimed at."

Debating the Issue

Questions to Consider

1. What problem did the Hatch Act address?
2. Would allowing government employees to become involved in political campaigns and activities have positive or negative consequences?
3. Did the law's aim outweigh free speech rights?

You Be the Judge

Should the Court's earlier decision on the Hatch Act be overturned? Or was that decision an acceptable limitation on free speech?

▶ A federal employee

Debating the Issue Answers

Questions to Consider

1. Federal employees participating in political activities; it sought to protect democracy from the influence of partisan government employees.
2. Students should choose positive or negative consequences and defend their choices.
3. Possible answers: Yes; it is important that government service be based solely on merit; No; freedom of speech is a fundamental right that should not be compromised.

You Be the Judge

Answers will vary, but students should decide whether they agree or disagree with the Court's original ruling on the constitutionality of the Hatch Act. Students should decide whether the Hatch Act violates the First Amendment.

The Bureaucracy at Work

Reader's Guide

Content Vocabulary
* ★ client group (p. 295)
* ★ liaison officer (p. 296)
* ★ injunction (p. 297)
* ★ iron triangle (p. 297)

Academic Vocabulary
* ★ implement (p. 291)
* ★ guideline (p. 292)
* ★ technical (p. 292)

Reading Strategy
As you read, create a graphic organizer similar to the one on the right to take notes about three groups who work together to keep government moving.

Issues in the News

Recently, the federal Food and Drug Administration (FDA) filed criminal charges against executives at two American companies for importing Chinese toothpaste containing "a poison used in some antifreeze," a city attorney for Los Angeles reported. Attorney Rocky DelGadillo worked with the FDA on the case. DelGadillo said a chemical analysis of the toothpaste uncovered that Chinese manufacturers substituted glycerin with diethylene glycol, a product that can lead to kidney damage and liver disease; in toothpaste it becomes a thickening agent. Last year almost a million tubes of Chinese-made toothpaste were recalled in 34 countries.

▲ FDA officials questioned this toothpaste.

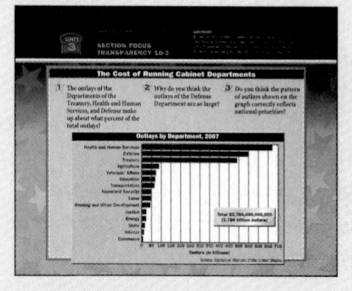
Public policy is whatever action the government chooses to take or not to take. Or, it can be actions the government requires or forbids. If Congress decides, for example, to beef up FDA staff so it can investigate foreign imports like Chinese toothpaste, that is a public-policy decision. The decision of the president to refuse to send military aid to a Latin American country is also public policy. Requiring federal contractors to submit certain kinds of reports is also public policy.

In theory, federal bureaucrats only carry out the policies the president and Congress make, but in practice they also make public policy. They often play key roles in choosing goals the government will try to meet and in selecting programs to meet those goals. Should people who were not elected make policy? Administering federal programs seems to demand that they do. In recent years,

federal agencies have made key decisions about many policy issues. For example, they have established safety requirements for nuclear power plants and set fuel-efficiency targets for automakers.

Influencing Policy

Federal bureaucrats help make policy in several ways. The most important of these involves administering the hundreds of programs that affect almost all aspects of national life. Administering these programs requires federal bureaucrats to write rules and regulations and to set standards to **implement** laws.

Making Rules

When Congress passes a law, it cannot spell out exactly what needs to be done to enforce it. The bureaucracy shapes what the law actually means.

Teach

R Reading Strategy

Organizing Have students create a graphic organizer to illustrate how the federal bureaucracy makes public policy and what influences its decision making. After students have presented their graphic organizers to the class, discuss the five reasons why a growing bureaucracy has assumed an important role in public policy making. **BL**

C Critical Thinking

Making Inferences Ask: Why do you suppose HUD has guidelines for contractors who hire minority employees? *(Students may note that HUD wants to ensure that contractors do not practice racial discrimination.)* **OL**

Caption Answer: The staff and budget of the Department of Veterans Affairs go up to meet the needs of new veterans.

Additional Support

The chief way federal agencies do this is by issuing rules and regulations designed to translate the law into action. One study has shown that, on an average, the bureaucracy formulates 20 rules or regulations to carry out each law.

In 1935 Congress passed the Social Security Act establishing the Social Security system. The act makes it possible for disabled workers to receive payments from the government. What does the word *disabled* mean? Are workers considered to be disabled if they can work only part-time? Are they disabled if they can work, but not at the job they once had?

R The Social Security Administration has developed 14 pages of rules and regulations describing disability. Someone who is "visually impaired" is defined, for example, as someone with no better than 20/70 vision in his or her better eye (with correction). The measure for being considered "legally blind" is corrected vision of 20/200 or lower in the better eye. Rules help ensure that only eligible people receive benefits.

C Often, rule making by federal agencies is considered the same as lawmaking. For example, the Department of Housing and Urban Development (HUD) has created **guidelines** for building contractors who hire minority employees. Unless contractors follow these guidelines, they cannot bid on federally-funded construction projects. In effect, the HUD guidelines have the force of law.

Paperwork

Until the mid-1990s, the number of rules and regulations federal agencies issued grew. Agency regulations totaled more than 50,000 printed pages per year. Along with more regulations came more paperwork. More than 2 billion forms were filled out and submitted to the federal government each year. The Small Business Administration estimated that companies spent at least 1 billion hours per year filling out forms—at a cost of about $100 billion annually.

In 1995 a law was enacted to reduce the amount of federal paperwork. The law required the Office of Management and Budget (OMB) director to set a goal for reducing federal paperwork: The OMB goal had to be a reduction of at least 10 percent of existing paperwork in each of the first two years and then 5 percent per year until 2001.

Involvement in Lawmaking

The bureaucracy also shapes public policy by helping draft new bills for Congress, testifying about legislation, and providing lawmakers with **technical** information they might not otherwise have. Besides, lawmakers know that it can be difficult to pass major bills unless they have gotten the advice of the federal agencies that are concerned with them.

Often, the ideas for new laws come from within the bureaucracy. Lawyers within the Justice

Bureaucratic Policy Making

Veterans Affairs
The mission of civil servants at the Department of Veterans Affairs becomes more challenging during a war. Veterans of the war in Iraq such as this man have required physical rehabilitation, treatment for post-traumatic stress disorder, and job and housing services.
What happens to staff and budget needs at Veterans Affairs during and after a war?

Activity: Collaborative Learning

Awarding Waste Former Senator William Proxmire's "Golden Fleece Award" became a well-known means of calling attention to waste within government agencies. Organize the class into groups of three to award four "Golden Fleece Awards" for examples of waste in the local community. Have members choose from the following tasks: research and describe the wastefulness of the "Golden Fleece Award" recipients, create a mock award for each recipient, or write a paragraph stating the reasons for choosing each award recipient. **OL**

Department, for example, drafted the Safe Streets Act of 1968, which created a new division within the Justice Department—the Law Enforcement Assistance Administration—that existed into the 1980s. In the same way, bureaucrats in what is now the Department of Health and Human Services, along with some hospital administrators and labor unions, worked hard and over a long period of time for the law that set up the Medicare program.

Settling Disputes

Some federal agencies shape policy by deciding disputes over how a law or set of rules should be applied. Agencies that do this act almost as courts. The regulatory commissions in particular make government policy in this way. They have the authority to resolve disputes among parties that come under their regulatory power. The rulings of these agencies have the same legal status as those of courts.

Providing Advice

Bureaucrats also help shape public policy by providing top political decision makers with information and advice. Many career bureaucrats are experts in their areas. In addition, federal agencies collect information on an incredible variety of subjects. The U.S. Fish and Wildlife Service in the Department of the Interior has data on the number of bald eagles in the United States. The Surgeon General's office in the Health and Human Services Department has scientific data on the influence of 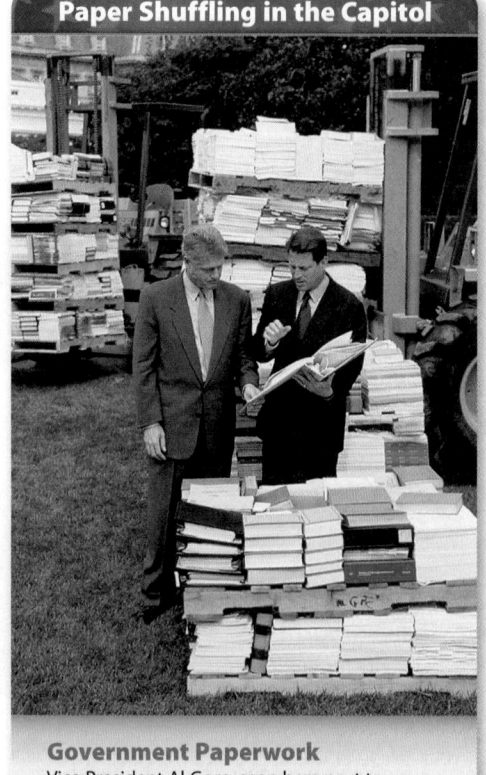secondhand smoke on newborns.

Federal agencies often use their information to support or oppose a particular public policy. Several years ago, studies by the Public Health Service on the effects of smoking led to new laws and regulations that were designed to cut down on the use of cigarettes.

Thus, the federal bureaucracy does more than fill in the details of laws. The bureaucracy plays a role in determining what those policies will be.

Why the Bureaucracy Makes Policy

A number of forces have driven the growth in size and importance of the federal bureaucracy: (1) growth in the nation's population, (2) international crises, (3) economic problems at home, (4) citizens' demands for action, and (5) the nature of bureaucracy itself.

Paper Shuffling in the Capitol

Government Paperwork

Vice President Al Gore, seen here next to President Clinton, was identified (as was President Reagan in the 1980s) with a project to reduce paperwork. In 1995 Congress passed the Paperwork Reduction Act. *How might the governments' need to monitor for fraud affect this mission to eliminate paperwork?*

National Growth and Technology

Bureaucratic growth has mirrored the growth of the American population. For almost 60 years, the three original cabinet departments and the attorney general's office handled the work of the executive branch. As the population grew, so did the government. The same number of officials who ran a country of 50 million people cannot govern a country of more than 250 million.

Growth in numbers is not the only way in which the nation has changed. We now live in an urban, highly technological society. A single president and 535 lawmakers in Congress cannot possibly have the knowledge and time required to deal with

POLITICAL PROFILES

William Proxmire
(1915–2005)

A U.S. senator from Wisconsin, William Proxmire assumed a watchdog role, hunting out waste and wrongdoing in government agencies. He championed the "Golden Fleece Award," which spotlighted wasteful spending. In 1979 Proxmire gave the award to Congress for the growth of its staff bureaucracy. The award made the headlines and helped initiate improvements in the organization that received the award.

Caption Answer: Minimizing paperwork could allow some fraud to go undetected by reducing the paper trail. It could also make some fraud easier to detect by making it easier to obtain documents.

W Writing Support

Persuasive Writing Have students explore the Web site of the Office of the Surgeon General at www.surgeongeneral.gov. Then have students create posters to promote public awareness of health risks or to promote healthful habits. **OL**

Additional Support

Activity: Collaborative Learning

Making Policy Organize the class into small groups to define a specific public policy dilemma such as the following: the definition of *disabled*; guidelines for a building contractor when hiring minorities; safety requirements for nuclear power plants; or eligibility requirements for federal health and welfare programs. Discuss the process involved in defining these policies. Call on volunteers to share their definitions. **AL**

S Skill Practice

Researching Point out to students that since the space race began, government-assisted research in the space program has produced more than 1,300 technological developments that have transferred to the private sector. Space-program spin-offs have led to the development or improvement of commercial products and services in consumer goods, industry, medicine, computer technology, and the environment. Examples include cordless power tools and appliances, athletic shoe design, the CAT scanners and MRI technology used in hospitals, and a new type of artificial heart. Have students research and identify one or more such spin-offs and write a brief report. You might point them to the NASA publication *Spinoff* or its Web site at www.sti.nasa.gov/tto. **OL**

Additional Support

National Security Needs Expand the Government

Department of Homeland Security Total Budget Authority (in billions)

Year	Budget
2004	35.6
2005	38.5
2006	40.5
2007	43.1

Source: U.S. Bureau of the Census, *Statistical Abstract of the United States,* 2008

Critical Thinking In March 2003 the Department of Homeland Security combined many existing federal agencies, including the Coast Guard (seen here in a rescue operation), Citizenship and Immigration Services, and the Federal Emergency Management Agency. *What kind of information would you want if you had to analyze increases in the department's budget?*

the many complex issues at hand. Nuclear power, education reform, cancer research, health care, and world financial markets are just a few of the issues the government must consider.

Issues that are broad in scope are especially challenging since they involve multiple federal agencies. Global warming illustrates this point. If public concern about global warming grows, the government will likely respond with new laws and policies, but imagine how many agencies could potentially be pulled into the policy circle. Policy roles might be played by federal agencies dealing with the following: home builders (to have them build energy-efficient homes), farmers (to promote growing corn for ethanol), manufacturers (to have them contain emissions from their plants), and automakers (to get them to build more fuel-efficient cars).

International Crises

Competition with the Soviet Union and international crises during the Cold War promoted the expansion of the federal bureaucracy. The Cold War lasted from the end of World War II in 1945 to the dissolution of the Soviet Union in 1991. During

the Cold War, the two superpowers were in a race to increase their military and weapons programs. They competed to persuade other countries to join their side by giving them huge sums of money for military and other projects.

The Department of Defense (DOD) was a direct result of the Cold War. In 1947 DOD was created by combining the Departments of War and Navy. After the end of the Cold War, efforts were made to reduce its budget. The DOD budget shrank somewhat in size during the 1990s, but after the terrorist attacks of September 11, 2001, President George W. Bush began to build it up again.

The Cold War had other effects on American spending priorities. When the Soviet Union launched *Sputnik I,* the first space satellite, in 1957, the federal government strengthened educational programs in science and mathematics. A similar impact could be seen in 1958 when President Dwight D. Eisenhower established a new agency to direct the nation's space exploration, NASA. Several other agencies were created as a result of the Cold War: the Central Intelligence Agency, the Arms Control and Disarmament Agency, the United States Information Agency, and the Peace Corps.

Activity: Collaborative Learning

Formulating Questions Discuss the difference between objective and subjective tests. An objective test, such as a multiple-choice test, is one that can be scored with a single answer key. Scorers seldom disagree as to whether responses are right or wrong. In contrast, a subjective test, such as an essay exam, can be scored differently by different

scorers. Explain how to construct closed-ended, unambiguous questions with only one correct answer. Ask pairs of students to create a 10-question, multiple-choice quiz covering the content of this chapter. Have pairs exchange and take the quizzes. Have the pair that created the quiz grade it and discuss wrong answers with the pair who took the quiz. **OL**

The Korean War in the early 1950s and the Vietnam War in the 1960s and early 1970s involved millions of American soldiers. Both wars led to the continued need for the Veterans Administration. President Reagan elevated it to cabinet level in 1989 and renamed it the Department of Veterans Affairs. It is one of the largest federal agencies.

Economic Problems

The president most associated with expanding the federal bureaucracy is Franklin D. Roosevelt. In coping with the Great Depression during the 1930s, Roosevelt created many new agencies. Some administered relief programs, some put men and women to work, and some created brand new social services programs like Social Security. By 1940, the number of federal workers had almost doubled.

Before the Depression, most Americans had not expected the government to provide any level of economic security. After the crisis of the Depression and the many social programs that were introduced as a result, Americans thought about their government in a new way. They now believed it should play an important role in helping the sick, people with disabilities, and the elderly. Today, the federal government spends billions of dollars each year on assistance programs.

The Depression years also led to the idea that the federal government has a responsibility to stimulate the economy or to regulate unfair business practices. This has led to a larger mission for an agency like the Department of Commerce, which helps businesses, and for the Federal Trade Commission, whose mission is to administer laws that protect consumers. In 2008 significant numbers of people lost their homes in the mortgage crisis, and many Americans demanded that the government step in to help them keep their homes and to regulate the mortgage industry more closely.

Citizen Demands

The bureaucracy has also grown in response to issues raised by various interest groups within the country. This is not a new phenomenon. Congress created the Departments of Agriculture (1862), Commerce (1903), and Labor (1913) partly as a result of demands from farmers, businesspeople, and workers, respectively.

After it is established, each agency has client groups that it serves. **Client groups** are the individuals and groups who work with the agency and are most affected by its decisions. The client groups of the Department of Defense, for example,

include the contractors who make weapons and supplies for the armed forces. The client groups of the Department of Agriculture are the farmers and others in the business of agriculture.

Client groups often lobby both Congress and the relevant agency for more programs and services. Often competition develops. If business leaders have "their" people in the Commerce Department, labor leaders want "their" people in the Labor Department to make sure they get treated fairly.

The Nature of Bureaucracy

The number of federal agencies increases, too, because the country's needs change—and once created, federal agencies almost never die. Some years back, Congress created the Federal Metal and Non-Metallic Safety Board of Review. A bureaucrat named Jubal Hale was appointed as its director. The board never received any cases to review, and Hale had no work to do. He spent the next four years

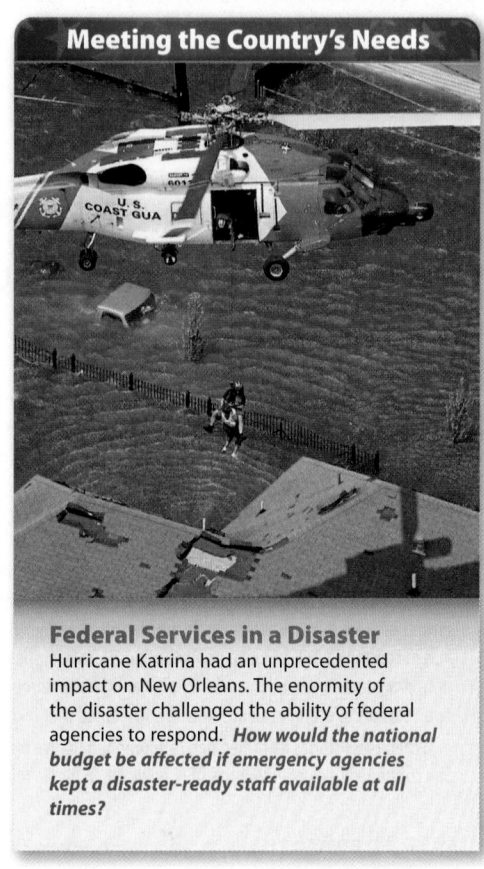

Meeting the Country's Needs

Federal Services in a Disaster
Hurricane Katrina had an unprecedented impact on New Orleans. The enormity of the disaster challenged the ability of federal agencies to respond. *How would the national budget be affected if emergency agencies kept a disaster-ready staff available at all times?*

**Linking ★
Past & Present**

The Bureaucratic Third
A maxim dating to President Franklin D. Roosevelt's administration is that bureaucrats believe they can ignore a president's first two requests because he always asks a third time. President John F. Kennedy learned this bitter truth when he ordered the removal of a sign that identified the secret location of the CIA's Virginia headquarters. It was not until his third try, when Kennedy called the person in charge, that he got the sign removed.

Caption Answer: The budget would have to increase to account for the additional staff and equipment.

Additional Support

★ Activity: Interdisciplinary Connection ★

Science In 1957 after the Soviet Union launched *Sputnik I,* the federal government began a program to improve science and mathematics instruction in the United States. Have students work in small groups to research their state or local Scholastic Assessment Test (SAT) verbal and math scores from 1960 to the present in five-year increments. (The SAT measures current verbal and math skills

against the skills needed to be successful in first-year-level college course work. The highest possible score is 1600.) As a class, make a line graph illustrating the information. Evaluate whether the SAT scores in math improved over the verbal scores and whether the government spending was effective. Discuss the benefits and liabilities of government funding of education. **AL**

ISSUES to Debate

Bureaucratic Reform Is the federal bureaucracy an asset or a liability? Critics of the bureaucracy abound, but others come to its defense. Ask students to write an opinion paper defending or criticizing the bureaucracy. Then have each student read the paper to the class. Allow the other students to pose questions to the reader in the same format that news reporters use to pose questions to the president after a speech. **AL**

Making a Difference

Heidi Landgraf Her role in a famous international drug money laundering sting operation made Heidi Landgraf famous. A film studio bought the rights to her true-life exploits as a Drug Enforcement Agency (DEA) heroine to make a motion picture.

Activity: Ask students to imagine life as an undercover DEA agent. Have them write a first-person narrative describing how they feel working undercover. Encourage them to describe their fears, challenges, exploits, and so on.

Additional Support

reading and listening to music in his office. Finally, Hale suggested the agency be abolished, and it was. Former president Gerald Ford put it this way:

> 66 *One of the enduring truths of the nation's capital is that bureaucrats survive. Agencies don't fold their tents and quietly fade away after their work is done. They find Something New to Do.* 99
>
> —Gerald Ford

These observations are what led to reform. President Bill Clinton's "reinventing government" and the Republican Congress's "Contract With America" both targeted government waste.

Influencing Bureaucratic Decisions

The federal bureaucracy does not make public policy in isolation; it is influenced by the president, Congress, the courts, and client groups.

The Influence of Congress

Bureaucrats carefully build relationships with the congressional committees that have authority over their agencies. Each cabinet department has **liaison officers** who help promote good relations with Congress. Liaison officers keep track of bills moving through Congress that might affect the agency and respond to lawmakers' requests for information.

The two tools Congress uses most to influence federal agencies are new legislation and the budget. Lawmakers can pass laws to change the rules or regulations a federal agency establishes, or they can limit an agency in other ways. In 1979, for example, the Internal Revenue Service ruled that donations to private schools were not tax deductible unless the schools enrolled a certain number of minority students. The ruling angered many, and Congress overturned it with new legislation.

Congress has also tried to hold agencies more accountable for what they do by passing the Government Performance and Results Act. This law requires federal agencies to write strategic plans, set annual performance goals, and then collect data to measure how well the goals are being met. Starting in 2000, each agency began publishing reports on their performance. Over time these reports are supposed to allow lawmakers and taxpayers to determine which programs produce the best results for the money spent.

We the People

Making a Difference

Hearing the words "My name is Heidi Landgraf. I'm an agent with the DEA," two drug cartel bosses stared in disbelief. The drug bosses were the victims of a sting operation of the Drug Enforcement Administration (DEA). Landgraf was at the center of Operation Green Ice, playing the part of a drug lord's daughter for two years. Green Ice was a large operation, involving Landgraf and more than 100 other federal agents worldwide. The operation led to the arrest of about 140 suspects and a seizure of $50 million.

With the use of tax returns, credit cards, and a passport, Landgraf was turned into "Heidi Herrera." Although she was watched by fellow agents, she was in constant danger. From a phony business location, she collected cash from drug dealers around the country and laundered it through banks. After two years of collecting evidence, the DEA scheduled the "takedown."

When press stories identified her, Landgraf had to give up being an undercover agent. She continued to work within the DEA, however, in media relations and drug prevention.

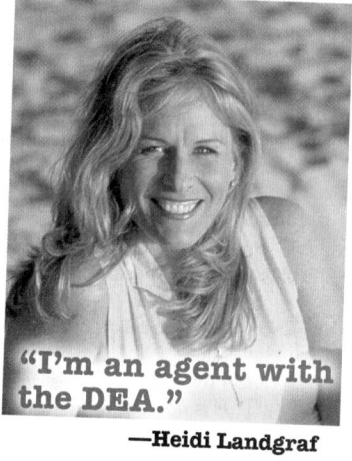

"I'm an agent with the DEA."

—Heidi Landgraf

Extending the Content

Measuring Bureaucratic Red Tape How lengthy is the so-called bureaucratic red tape? One way to measure it is by tallying the pages of the *Federal Register,* which is where all new regulations are published. In 1940 the *Register* totaled 5,307 pages; it grew to 87,012 pages by 1980. In 1990, due mostly to the government's decreased regulation of the economy, the total was down to 53,618 pages. However, by 2000 the *Register* contained 83,293 pages.

Congress's major power over the bureaucracy is the power of the purse–Congress controls each agency's budget. It can add to or cut an agency's budget and, in theory at least, refuse to appropriate money for the agency. What usually happens, however, is that Congress threatens to eliminate programs that are important to an agency.

Even the power of the purse has limits in influencing agency decisions. In some cases, a big part of an agency's budget is for entitlement programs—basic services the agency must provide by law, such as Social Security, pensions for retired government workers, or payments to disabled veterans. Such services are almost impossible for Congress to cut.

If budget cuts must be made, agencies might intentionally target the cuts in the districts or states of key representatives who have the political power to restore the cuts. In 1975, for example, when Congress wanted to reduce the budget for Amtrak passenger trains, the agency announced plans to comply by cutting train service in the districts of key congressional leaders. The announcements had the desired effect: Most Amtrak funds were restored.

The Influence of the Courts

Federal courts do not actively seek to influence the bureaucracy. The courts, however, can have an important impact on policy making. The Administrative Procedures Act of 1946 allows citizens who are directly affected by the actions of federal agencies to challenge those agencies' actions in court. A federal court may issue an **injunction**—an order that will stop an action or enforce a rule or regulation.

Success in Court Cases

The courts can have a real impact on the bureaucracy, but citizens are not usually successful at fighting the bureaucracy in court. One study showed that the courts rarely reverse decisions of federal regulatory commissions. About 90 percent of the time, for example, the Federal Energy Regulatory Commission and the Federal Trade Commission win the cases they argue before the Supreme Court. The National Labor Relations Board and the Internal Revenue Service have a "win" rate of 75 percent.

The Influence of Client Groups

As already explained, each agency has client groups. The Department of Education spends much of its time dealing with school administrators.

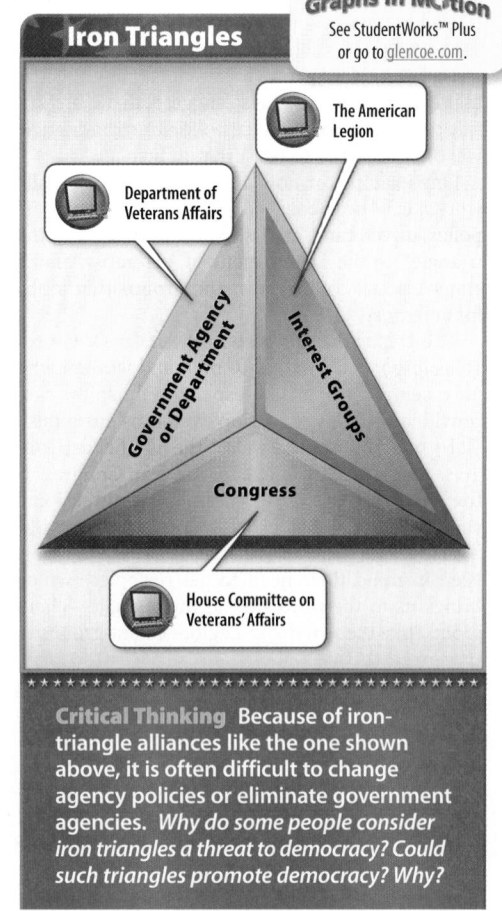

Iron Triangles

Graphs In Motion
See StudentWorks™ Plus or go to glencoe.com.

The American Legion

Department of Veterans Affairs

Government Agency or Department

Interest Groups

Congress

House Committee on Veterans' Affairs

Critical Thinking Because of iron-triangle alliances like the one shown above, it is often difficult to change agency policies or eliminate government agencies. *Why do some people consider iron triangles a threat to democracy? Could such triangles promote democracy? Why?*

The Food and Drug Administration works closely with major drug companies.

Client groups often attempt to influence agency decisions through lobbyists. Lobbyists want to get their cases heard. They will often testify at agency hearings, write letters, track agency decisions and report them to their clients, and take many other steps to support their groups' interests.

Iron Triangles

Congressional committees, client groups, and a federal department or agency often cooperate closely to make public policy. When agencies, congressional committees, and client groups continually work together, such cooperation creates what analysts have called an **iron triangle.** The term is used because together the three groups provide all that is needed by any one of them. The word *iron*

Critical Thinking

Answer: Critics believe that iron triangles allow interest groups to have undue influence on public policy. Because these subgovernments operate outside the control of the executive branch, Congress has been urged to pass laws regulating interest groups that support iron triangles. Students' answers will vary but they should support their answers.

Chart Skills Practice

Which three groups make up an iron triangle for veterans' affairs? *(Department of Veterans Affairs, the American Legion, and the House Committee on Veterans' Affairs)*

R Reading Strategy

Activating Prior Knowledge Have students create a list of other client-group relationships in addition to those mentioned on this page. *(Answers might include the Federal Aviation Administration and airplane manufacturers, the Department of Defense and weapons companies, and so on.)* **BL**

Hands-On Chapter Project

Step 3

Preparing a Report to Congress

Step 3: Giving a Report Have groups organize the information they gathered in Step 2 and prepare an oral report to Congress that presents the facts of the issue, supported by the visual aids they created. One member will call on the others and summarize the group's recommendation for congressional action. Group members will make name cards to place on their desks during the report, including the title they assumed, such as "Jane Smith, Chief Geologist."

Directions Tell the class that they are now senators. Have a volunteer convene a session of Congress to hear testimony about each group's issue. Each group member will present one aspect of the report orally, using the visual aids created in Step 2 as support. Encourage class members to ask questions.

Summarizing Ask the class to rate the groups' presentations in three categories: (1) organization, (2) presentation skills, and (3) content. **OL**

Assess

Assign the Section 3 Assessment as homework or as an in-class activity, or have students take Section Quiz 10-3 from *Section Quizzes and Chapter Tests.*

Close

Analyzing Ask students to write a brief essay opposing or supporting the federal bureaucracy's increased role in making public policy. **OL**

Section 3 Review

---

is used because the relationship is strong and self-supporting. Thus, it becomes a self-sufficient three-way relationship that proves difficult for any outsider to break into. The term also suggests that if an outside group tries to influence policy, the iron triangle will bond together to resist that influence.

One example of how an iron triangle typically works can be observed by looking at public policy in veterans' affairs. The three sides of the triangle are the Department of Veterans Affairs, congressional committees, and groups that lobby for veterans.

The Department of Veterans Affairs (VA) provides important services to men and women who have served the nation, especially hospital care provided through the nation's veterans' hospitals.

To provide these services, the VA needs Congress to approve its budget every year. Congress is the second side of the triangle. Congressional committees responsible for veterans' affairs review VA budget requests; when they do this, they must keep in mind their need to get reelected, which brings us to the third side of the triangle—client groups like the American Legion. Client groups in turn need the VA's goods and services to satisfy the demands of their members. It is the working combination of these three groups that largely determines the policy of the national government toward veterans.

Similar iron triangles operate in many policy areas such as agriculture, business, labor, and national defense. People often move from one side of the triangle to another. In the area of national defense, for example, a general in the Department of Defense might retire and become a Washington lobbyist for a defense contractor that sells weapons to the Department of Defense. A staff member of the Senate Armed Services Committee might leave Congress to work in the Defense Department. Later, the same person might take a job with a defense contractor. Many critics believe that because iron triangles allow interest groups undue influence outside the control of the executive branch, Congress should pass laws to regulate them.

Agencies Influence One Another

Interactions among agencies can also influence policy making in the bureaucracy. For example, rules made by the Occupational Safety and Health Administration about noise standards in factories might contradict regulations established by the Environmental Protection Agency. Decision makers in each agency could try to influence one another. Often, such disputes are settled by interagency task forces or committees.

SECTION 3 Review

Vocabulary

1. **Explain** the significance of: client group, liaison officer, injunction, iron triangle.

Main Ideas

2. **Describing** What kind of influence does the court system have on the federal bureaucracy?

3. **Examining** What are five reasons that the federal bureaucracy has assumed an important role in making public policy?

Critical Thinking

4. **Making Inferences** Do you think that iron triangles undermine or serve the public interest? Explain your answer.

5. **Organizing** Using a graphic organizer like the one below, identify two ways Congress influences federal agencies and two ways federal agencies contribute to legislation.

Congress	1. 2. →	Federal Agencies
	← 1. 2.	

Writing About Government

6. **Expository Writing** In theory, federal agencies regulate or shape policy for groups in the private sector, yet these groups lobby agencies to influence that policy. Research two or three client groups of one federal agency. Write a short report that explains the client groups' interest in the agency and the client groups' probable message to the agency.

298 UNIT 3: *The Executive Branch*

Answers

1. All definitions can be found in the section and the Glossary.
2. The court system can hear challenges to federal agency actions by those who are affected by them and can issue injunctions to stop an action.
3. national growth and technology, international crises, economic problems at home, citizens' demands, and the nature of bureaucracy; so that they can be impartial about policies, subject to fewer influences, and regulate what they were created to control

4. Students should support their opinions. Students may note the cooperation of the groups or the undue influence of interest groups.
5. Answers might include: Congress: new legislation, the budget; Federal agencies: draft bills, testify about legislation
6. Students should research at least two groups and write an essay on their interests in the federal agency.

Should the FDA Bureaucracy Be Expanded?

The Food and Drug Administration (FDA) is a federal agency that regulates the purity and safety of food, drugs, cosmetics, and medical devices. Traditionally, Americans have not supported strong government regulation, preferring to let the market work. Many regulatory agencies tend to work closely with the industry they regulate. The very idea of a large government inspection force of any kind is not popular. Recently, a wave of tainted foods and unsafe products has raised the question of whether stronger regulation is needed to make American life safer and healthier.

YES

The free market and free enterprise are at the heart of the American economic system, but the public needs to have its health and safety protected. It is the government's duty to make sure citizens have pure food, medicines that do not make them sicker, and products that do not cause accidents. The average citizen has no way of knowing whether foods and other products are safe. Presidents and Congress were too eager to trim government costs and to deregulate every industry in recent decades. Now we see the results—people suffering from E. coli infections from contaminated spinach, pets who die of tainted dog food, and children exposed to lead in their toys. Congress needs to expand the budget for FDA research and for its inspection staff. The agency's computer systems, vital to any large scale effort to track agricultural and other products from all over the world, need to be upgraded.

NO

There has rarely been a time when spending money on a larger bureaucracy has solved a problem. True, when there are problems like an E. coli outbreak or tainted aspirin scare, the public would like Congress to "throw money at the problem," but this is not really effective. Industry acts quickly when there is a problem because it knows the public will refuse to buy its products. If we were to increase FDA regulations and inspections, it would simply burden companies who are researching and developing new products. Does anyone think that a few government inspectors can adequately assess a trial drug that a company has already been testing for a decade? (As it is, new drugs have to wait longer in the United States to go on the market than in most Western nations.) The solution to any specific problems will come from doctors, patients, and consumers—not the government.

Debating the Issue

1. **Determining Cause and Effect** What developments have led to calls for FDA reform?
2. **Analyzing** What is the key argument for each position?
3. **Evaluating** With which viewpoint do you tend to agree? Explain your reasoning.

▶ The FDA linked an E. coli outbreak to bagged spinach, here being removed from grocery shelves.

Teach

Setting Up the Debate

Analyzing Remind students that much of the food they eat each day is regulated or inspected in some way by the FDA. **Ask:** Should the FDA regulate food and drugs more closely? *(Prompt students to explain their responses.)*

Evaluating Have students research the arguments for and against tighter FDA regulations. Students should find specific examples to support both points of view. They might, for example, cite incidents of deaths and illnesses caused by contaminated foods or life-saving medicines that were slow to be approved.

Concluding the Debate

Discuss these questions with students:
- What standards would you set to ensure that foodstuffs and medicines are safe?
- Should the additional costs associated with tighter regulations be a consideration when setting standards?

Debating the Issue Answers

1. E. coli infections, tainted pet food, toys with lead paint
2. Yes; the government should be responsible for protecting Americans from harmful food and medicines. No; the free market can do a better job of ensuring safe food and medicine than government can.
3. Students' answers will vary, but ask them to explain the rationale behind their answers.

This easy-to-use software includes extensive question banks and allows you to create fully customized tests that can be administered in print or online.

Reviewing Vocabulary

1. f
2. h
3. c
4. i
5. g
6. d
7. a
8. b
9. e

Reviewing Main Ideas

10. cabinet departments, independent agencies, and regulatory commissions
11. They make rules for large industries and businesses that affect public interest and operate independently of the national government.
12. to replace the widespread inefficiency and corruption of the spoils system; to make government employment available on the basis of open, competitive examinations and merit
13. through lobbyists who influence agency officials and through iron triangles

Critical Thinking

14. Advantages: New people bring new ideas; they are supportive of the new administration; they can urge the bureaucracy to implement new programs. Disadvantages: New people might be inexperienced and not

---

Reviewing Vocabulary

Fill in the blank with the letter of the content vocabulary word(s) listed below.

a. injunction
b. liaison officer
c. government corporation
d. client group
e. iron triangle
f. bureaucrat
g. embassy
h. spoils system
i. deregulate

1. A government official who works for a federal agency is a(n) _____.
2. Before the civil service system, many people got government jobs through the _____.
3. Some people work for a(n) _____, such as the U.S. Postal Service.

Chapter Summary

1750

The Spoils System

1789 ★ Victorious candidates rewarded political supporters and friends with jobs

Need for Reform

1800

★ Spoils system led to government inefficiency and corruption

★ As government operations became more complex, staff employees needed specific expertise

1850

1871 ★ First Civil Service Commission was created in 1871 but had no effective power

1881 ★ President James A. Garfield's assassination by an ignored job seeker renewed calls for reform

1900

Changes

1883 ★ The Pendleton Act created a federal employment system based on competitive examinations and individual merit

1950

1979 ★ In modern times, the Office of Personnel Management and the Merit System Protection Board split the functions of the original Civil Service Commission

2000

---

4. Some people lost their jobs when Congress began to _____ the Civil Aeronautics Board and cut down on its procedures.
5. A(n) _____ is the office of an ambassador in a foreign country.
6. A(n) _____, such as a special-interest group, is a key factor in influencing public policy.
7. In some cases, a court will issue a(n) _____ to stop a particular action.
8. A(n) _____ helps promote good relations among Congress and cabinet departments.
9. When congressional committees, federal agencies, and client groups work together it is called a(n) _____.

Reviewing Main Ideas

Section 1 *(pp. 275–283)*

10. **Identifying** What three types of agencies make up the federal bureaucracy?

11. **Summarizing** What is the special role of independent regulatory commissions in the federal bureaucracy?

Section 2 *(pp. 284–289)*

12. **Describing** Why was the civil service system created?

Section 3 *(pp. 291–298)*

13. **Analyzing** How do client groups attempt to influence the decisions that government agencies make?

Critical Thinking

14. **Essential Question** With every new administration, new people are named to hold top positions. Explain the advantages and disadvantages of this system.

15. **Making Inferences** Why might a strong president rely less on the cabinet's advice than a weak president would?

16. **Organizing** Use an outline like the one below to organize a paper that would explain why the federal bureaucracy has grown. Use facts from the text and charts in Chapter 10.

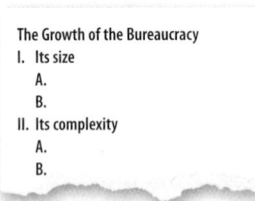

The Growth of the Bureaucracy
I. Its size
  A.
  B.
II. Its complexity
  A.
  B.

---

understand how the bureaucracy works; political appointees might be more interested in serving political advantages rather than the public.

15. A strong president probably would have decided already which policies he or she wants to follow.

16. Outlines might include:
  I. Its size
    A. national growth
    B. citizens' demands
    C. nature of bureaucracies to perpetuate selves
  II. Its complexity
    A. technology
    B. international crises
    C. economic problems at home

Government ONLINE **Self-Check Quiz**
Visit glencoe.com and enter *QuickPass*™ code USG9822c10.
Click on Self-Check Quizzes for additional test practice.

Document-Based Questions

Analyzing Primary Sources

Read the excerpt below and answer the questions that follow.

The Social Security Act (1935) was the first government program of its kind to ensure retirement and unemployment income. Social Security payments are funded by taxes on employers' and employees' incomes. Social Security funds are administered by the Treasury Department. The excerpt below is from a Social Security Administration publication.

> ❝ *YOUR CARD shows you have an insurance account with the U.S. Government, under the old-age, survivors and disability insurance system provided for in the Social Security Act.*
>
> *YOUR ACCOUNT is a record of the pay you receive which counts toward old-age and survivors insurance benefits. The size of benefits will depend upon the amount of wages credited to your account.* ❞

17. What do you think are some of the benefits of having a social insurance program? Why is it beneficial to have this program administered by the Treasury Department (a part of the federal bureaucracy) and not directly by the federal government (Congress)?

18. Although programs like Social Security were not outlined in the Constitution, they are part of the growing bureaucracy of the federal government. What are some of the positive and negative effects of this growth?

Applying Technology Skills

19. Many analysts predict that Social Security and Medicare payments will be a burden to future generations. Research this topic at a nonprofit, nonpartisan site like http://www.ncpa.org/abo/ or at http://www.ssa.gov/. Then summarize the conclusions they reach.

Interpreting Political Cartoons

Analyze the cartoon and answer the questions that follow. Base your answers on the cartoon and your knowledge of Chapter 10.

"Don't Touch Medicare! . . ."

20. What is the warning each of these people is giving?

21. How do you think these people's attitudes affect the size of the federal bureaucracy?

22. What governmental dilemma does this cartoon emphasize?

23. Does the cartoonist imply that special-interest groups are to blame for Congress's failure to balance the budget by cutting programs?

✯ *Participating* IN GOVERNMENT

24. You can find jobs within the government bureaucracy in all levels of government. This allows a greater number of citizens the opportunity to participate in political life. Using your local library or the Internet, research the different types of government jobs available in your community. Find out the procedure for applying for these jobs, the qualifications required, and the salaries. Present your findings in an illustrated pamphlet.

Government ONLINE

Have students use the **Chapter 10 Self-Check Quiz.** Visit glencoe.com and enter *QuickPass*™ code USG9085c10T to prepare for the Chapter Test.

Interpreting Political Cartoons

20. Do not touch government funding for that group.

21. Answers should point out that each group defends its own territory and, therefore, the bureaucracy continues to grow.

22. Tax cuts are extremely difficult to make because Americans will try to protect the programs that affect them, yet the government cannot equally please every interest group.

23. Congress must decide whether to raise taxes or to cut federal spending.

✯ *Participating* IN GOVERNMENT

24. Students' illustrated pamphlets should list government jobs that are available in their community and for each job describe the application procedure, the qualifications required, and the salary.

Analyzing Primary Sources

17. Answers may include that a social insurance program provides a safety net for workers who become unemployed or who cannot afford to save for retirement. Having Social Security administered by the Treasury Department is beneficial because Congress would not have the time to oversee the programs or might withhold funds for political purposes.

18. Positive: The government now provides more public services and more returns for people's tax dollars.
Negative: A number of seemingly unnecessary jobs could be taken care of by people in the private sector.

Applying Technology Skills

19. Students should accurately summarize their findings.

Chapter Bonus Test Question

Ask: What is the oldest federal government departmental headquarters? *(the Treasury Building)*

The Judicial Branch

UNIT PACING CHART*		
	Chapter 11	**Chapter 12**
Day 1	Unit Opener Chapter Opener Section 1	Chapter Opener Section 1
Day 2	Supreme Court Cases to Debate	Section 2
Day 3	Section 2 TIME Notebook	Supreme Court Cases to Debate
Day 4	Section 3 Government Skills	Section 3 Issues to Debate
Day 5	Review Chapter Assessment	Review Chapter Assessment

*Unit Pacing Chart based on year-long course; modify pacing by half for semester-long course

Teacher to Teacher

**David Badger,
Ph.D.**

**Benedictine
High School
Detroit, MI**

Let's Talk About the Federal Court System Have students create a mock talk show about the federal court system. To set up the talk show, assign individual students to research a single court system in the vast array of federal courts in our country, such as tax courts, military courts, territorial, claims, or bankruptcy courts. Explain to students that they need to be well versed in the workings of their particular court system because they will be interviewed by the talk show host, who has also researched the court system. Set up a talk show format and have the host-student interview guest-students who have researched the history, processes, and daily routine of a specific federal court system.

To extend the learning process, select nine students, one to act as a chief justice and the others to act as associate justices of the Supreme Court. Props such as a gavel and black graduation or choir robes can make the experience more realistic. With the help of the student researchers, design a fictitious court case that will be appealed to the U.S. Supreme Court for a mock trial.

Author Note

Dear U.S. Government Teacher,

Unit 4 focuses on the judicial branch of government. You may want to begin the unit by looking at *The Federalist*, No. 78, with students (a long excerpt of this document can be found in the back of the student text). In this article, Alexander Hamilton did a superb job of sketching out the unique position of the judiciary in the American federal system. You will also want to focus students' attention on judicial review, which was introduced in Chapter 3 and is taken up again in Chapter 11. The story of how this critical power was established is one of the most gripping episodes in our constitutional history.

Many students will have some grasp of the importance of the Supreme Court, if only because they have heard its more controversial decisions mentioned so often in newscasts. A useful way to involve students is to follow the political struggles over the confirmation of new justices to the Court. Profiling current judges, their judicial philosophy, and why they were appointed to the bench is a good way to humanize this topic. The Supreme Court is a revered institution, but it is also a political one, as the chart in Section 2 makes clear.

The phrase *due process* is critical to American democracy, and the ultimate stage for testing due process is the court system. The organization of the federal court system is diagrammed for students in the first section. While students may not easily remember the hierarchy of the court system, they should grasp the most important point—that jurisdiction is all, and a clearly defined process determines how a suit of a citizen or group will be heard—even to the highest court in the land.

Richard C. Remy

Richard C. Remy, Ph.D.
Author

Focus

Making It Relevant

Supreme Court Pages Like Congress, the Supreme Court has pages who run errands and deliver messages. Have students find out how to become a page; where the pages go to school; what the dress code is, if any (for years it was black or dark blue knickers with long black stockings); what the age and gender requirements have been and are now; and what kinds of tasks pages perform. Have students present their findings in a brief report.

Unit Objectives

After studying this unit, students will be able to:

- **Describe** the jurisdiction of federal courts and the method of selecting judges for them.

- **Explain** the workings of the Supreme Court, how it shapes public policy, and the forces that shape its decisions.

Unit Overview

Unit 4 provides a basic introduction to the judicial branch.

Chapter 11 describes the organization, jurisdiction, and powers of the federal court system.

Chapter 12 describes how the Supreme Court makes decisions.

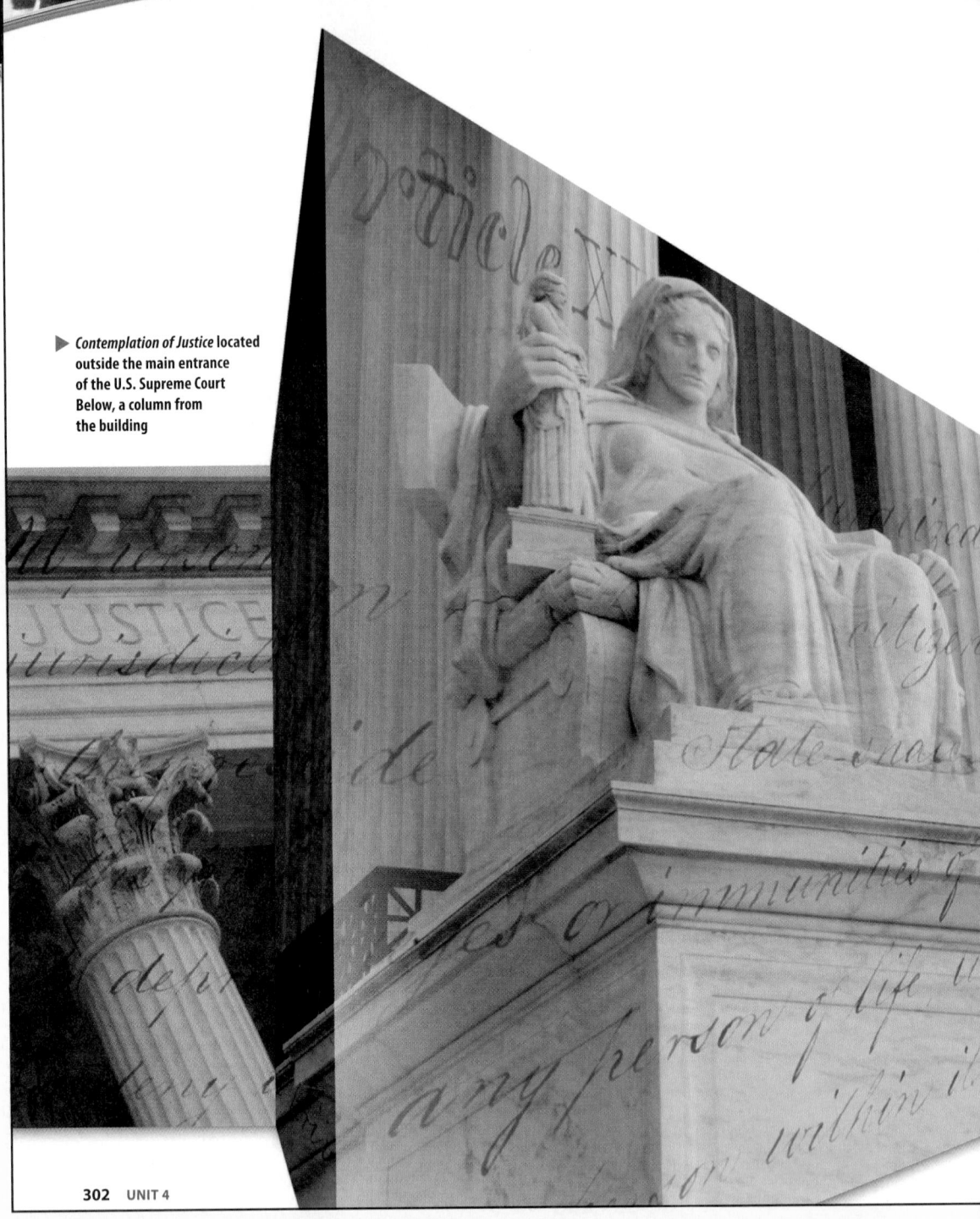

▶ *Contemplation of Justice* located outside the main entrance of the U.S. Supreme Court Below, a column from the building

Activity: Launching the Unit

Literature and History Have students find and read the short story "The Devil and Daniel Webster" by Steven Vincent Benét. It is available either online or through a local library. Originally published by the *Saturday Evening Post* in 1938, it tells the story of how Daniel Webster helps a New Hampshire man who has sold his soul to the devil to get out of a contract. The short story won the 1938 O. Henry Award. Have students work in small groups to interpret the political significance of the short story as it relates to fundamental freedoms in the United States and our notion of equal justice under the law. **OL**

UNIT 4

The Judicial Branch

Participating IN GOVERNMENT

BIG IDEA **Civil Rights** Research a current case before the Supreme Court by watching for coverage of the Court in the media. Write a summary of the case and circulate it among a group of classmates and your teacher. Ask your teacher to lead a class discussion of the issues before the Court and have a follow-up discussion when the Court has made its decision.

▲ Ben Shahn's *Supreme Court Integration,* 1954

303

303

Planning Guide

Key to Ability Levels
BL	Below level	AL	Above level
OL	On level	ELL	English Language Learners

Key to Teaching Resources
📁 Print Material   🖨 Transparency
💿 CD-ROM or DVD

Levels					Resources	Chapter Opener	Section 1	Section 2	Section 3	Chapter Assess
BL	OL	AL	ELL							
FOCUS										
BL	OL	AL	ELL	🖨	Section Focus Transparencies		11-1	11-2	11-3	
TEACH										
BL	OL		ELL	📁	Reading Essentials and Study Guide (and Answer Key)		p. 117	p. 120	p. 123	
BL	OL		ELL	📁	Guided Reading Activities		p. 39	p. 40	p. 41	
BL	OL		ELL	📁	Vocabulary Activities		p. 11			
BL	OL	AL	ELL	📁	Chapter Summaries				p. 31	
BL	OL			📁	American Biographies				p. 68	
BL	OL	AL	ELL	📁	Cooperative Learning Activities				p. 7	
	OL	AL	ELL	📁	Government Simulations and Debate					
BL	OL	AL	ELL	📁	Historical Documents and Speeches					
BL	OL	AL	ELL	📁	Interpreting Political Cartoons				p. 21	
BL	OL		ELL	📁	Skill Reinforcement Activities					
BL	OL	AL	ELL	📁	Source Readings			p. 11		
BL	OL			📁	Supreme Court Case Studies		pp. 1, 3, 5, 7, 11, 23, 25, 27, 73		p. 115	
BL	OL	AL	ELL	📁	Participating in Government Activities			p. 21		
BL	OL		ELL	📁	Spanish Declaration of Independence and U.S. Constitution	✓	✓	✓	✓	✓
BL	OL	AL	ELL	📁	NGS World Atlas, Spanish	✓	✓	✓	✓	✓
BL	OL	AL	ELL	🖨	Unit Overlay Transparencies, Strategies, and Activities	✓	✓	✓	✓	✓
BL	OL		ELL	🖨	Making It Relevant Transparencies	✓	✓	✓	✓	✓
BL	OL	AL	ELL	🖨	High School Writing Process Transparencies, Strategies, and Activities	✓	✓	✓	✓	✓
BL	OL	AL		🖨	American Art & Architecture Transparencies, Strategies, and Activities	✓	✓	✓	✓	✓

✓ Chapter- or unit-based activities applicable to all sections in this chapter

All-In-One Planner and Resource Center

- Interactive Lesson Planner
- Interactive Teacher Edition
- Fully editable blackline masters
- Chapter Spotlight Videos Launch

- Differentiated Lesson Plans
- Printable reports of daily assignments
- Standards tracking system

Levels					Resources	Chapter Opener	Section 1	Section 2	Section 3	Chapter Assess
BL	OL	AL	ELL							
TEACH *(continued)*										
BL	OL			◉	**American Music: Hits Through History**	✓	✓	✓	✓	✓
BL	OL		ELL	📁	**Reading Strategies for the Social Studies Classroom**	✓	✓	✓	✓	✓
			ELL	📁	**English Language Learner Handbook**	✓	✓	✓	✓	✓
BL	OL		ELL	📁	**Writer's Guidebook for Social Studies**	✓	✓	✓	✓	✓
BL	OL	AL	ELL	📁	**Living Constitution, SE**	✓	✓	✓	✓	✓
BL	OL	AL	ELL	📁	**Living Constitution, TAE**	✓	✓	✓	✓	✓
BL	OL			📁	**NGS World Atlas, English**	✓	✓	✓	✓	✓
BL	OL		ELL	📁	**The Constitution and You (poster set)**	✓	✓	✓	✓	✓
BL	OL	AL	ELL	📁	**Spanish Chapter Summaries**				p. 31	
BL	OL	AL	ELL	📁	**Spanish Vocabulary Activities**		p. 11			
BL	OL		ELL	📁	**Spanish Reading Essentials and Study Guide (and Answer Key)**		p. 117	p. 120	p. 123	
BL	OL	AL	ELL	◉	**PresentationPlus! with MindJogger CheckPoint**	✓	✓	✓	✓	✓
ASSESS										
BL	OL	AL	ELL	◉	*ExamView® Assessment Suite*		11-1	11-2	11-3	Ch. 11
BL	OL	AL	ELL	📁	**Authentic Assessment with Rubrics**			p. 18		p. 18
BL	OL	AL	ELL	📁	**Section Quizzes and Chapter Tests**		p. 129	p. 130	p. 131	pp. 133–140
BL	OL	AL	ELL	📁	**Spanish Section Quizzes and Tests**		p. 129	p. 130	p. 131	pp. 133–140
CLOSE										
BL			ELL	📁	**Reteaching Activities**				p. 11	p. 11
BL	OL	AL	ELL	◉	**StudentWorks™ Plus with Audio Summaries**	✓	✓	✓	✓	✓
BL	OL		ELL	🖐	**Graphic Organizer Transparencies**		✓	✓	✓	
BL	OL		ELL	📁	**High School Government Reading and Study Skills Foldables®**		p. 54	p. 54	p. 54	

Teach With Technology

What is StudentWorks™ Plus Online?

StudentWorks™ Plus Online is a powerful learning and teaching tool that offers the entire textbook online in an interactive, searchable format. It provides links to student workbooks, audio recordings of the textbook, audio summaries in Spanish, In Motion animations, and links to Chapter Spotlight Videos.

How can StudentWorks™ Plus Online help my students and me?

StudentWorks™ Plus Online helps students learn and master the material in the textbook. Students can go to a specific chapter and read the text, listen to audio of the text, and type and print their answers on workbook pages. While reading about a topic, students can quickly search the entire text and the glossary for a key term. You can project StudentWorks™ Plus Online during a classroom lecture and launch Section Spotlight Videos directly.

Visit glencoe.com and enter a *QuickPass*™ code to go to StudentWorks™ Plus Online.

Government ONLINE
Visit glencoe.com and enter *QuickPass*™ code USG9085c11T for Chapter 11 resources.

You can easily launch a wide range of digital products from your computer's desktop with the McGraw-Hill Social Studies widget.

	Student	Teacher	Parent
Media Library			
• Student Edition Section Audio	●		●
• Chapter Spotlight Videos	●	●	●
***United States Government* Online Learning Center (Web Site)**			
• Chapter Overviews	●	●	●
• Multilingual Glossaries	●	●	●
• Study-to-Go	●	●	●
• Student Web Activities	●	●	●
• Self-Check Quizzes	●	●	●
• Online Student Edition	●	●	●
• Vocabulary eFlashcards	●	●	●
• Web Activity Lesson Plans		●	
• Vocabulary PuzzleMaker	●	●	●
• Landmark Supreme Court Cases	●	●	●
• Beyond the Textbook	●	●	●

READING SUPPORT FROM
JAMESTOWN EDUCATION

- **Timed Readings Plus in Social Studies** helps students increase their reading rate and fluency while maintaining comprehension. The 400-word passages are similar to those found on state and national assessments.

- **Reading in the Content Area: Social Studies** concentrates on six essential reading skills that help students better comprehend what they read. The book includes 75 high-interest nonfiction passages written at increasing levels of difficulty.

- **Reading Social Studies** includes strategic reading instruction and vocabulary support in Social Studies content for ELLs and native speakers of English. www.jamestowneducation.com

Reading List Generator CD-ROM

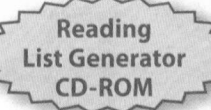

GLENCOE
BookLink 3

Use this database to search more than 30,000 titles to create a customized reading list for your students.

- Reading lists can be organized by students' reading level, author, genre, theme, or area of interest.

- The database provides Degrees of Reading Power™ (DRP) and Lexile™ readability scores for all selections.

- A brief summary of each selection is included.

Leveled reading suggestions for this chapter:

- ***Little Rock: The Desegregation of Central High,*** by Laurie A. O'Neill

- ***Mississippi Challenge,*** by Mildred Pitts Walter

Review suggested books before assigning them.

Economics Connection

Personal Finance Literacy

Determining Averages

Tell students that the most common way to summarize statistics is the average. There are two types of averages: mean and median. Suppose you want to determine the average age of Supreme Court justices. In 2008 the justices were John Paul Stevens, 88; Ruth Bader Ginsburg, 75; Antonin Scalia, 72; Anthony Kennedy, 71; Stephen Breyer, 69; David Souter, 68; Clarence Thomas, 60; Samuel Alito, 58; and John Roberts, 53.

To find the *mean,* we add the ages and then divide that sum by the number of justices: $614 \div 9 = 68.2$. The mean, or average, age is slightly over 68.

In cases when a few of the numbers at the top or bottom are much higher or lower than most of the other numbers, the mean may be misleading. For example, if one student received 100 on a test and 20 others received a 40, the mean would be 70—but that does not give an accurate picture of the class's scores. The median would show that 40 was the most common score.

To determine the *median* age of Supreme Court justices, we would list all the ages and then find the number in the middle—the one with the same number of ages below and above it. In our example, 4 justices are older than 69 and 4 are younger than 69—so the median age is 69. The calculation for this example is easy because we're dealing with an uneven total number of justices' ages—9 justices. If even numbers of statistics are being compared—for example, 10 justices' ages instead of 9—we could find the median by adding the two middle numbers and dividing that sum by 2.

Ask students for examples of times when a mean or a median would be useful. As an exercise, you may want to have them vote on their favorite movie. Then have each student state the number of times they have seen that movie. Students will write down all the responses and find the median.

Did You Know?

The salary of an associate justice of the Supreme Court in 2008 was $145,981; the chief justice, $160,579. The administrative budget of the Supreme Court and state court system was $44.6 million. Seven of the nine current justices were appointed by Republican presidents.

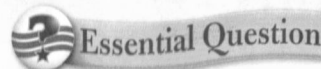

CHAPTER 11

The Federal Court System

🔊 Chapter Audio   ▶ Spotlight Video

Essential Question

In the U.S. Constitution, the federal judiciary is the least clearly defined branch of government. Article III vests judicial authority in a "Supreme Court and in such inferior Courts as the Congress may from time to time ordain and establish." Thus, one of the first acts of the First Congress was to enact the Judiciary Act of 1789, which outlined the makeup of the Supreme Court and established the lower federal courts.

🎬 Chapter Spotlight Video

To generate student interest and provide a springboard for class discussion, access the Chapter 11 Video at glencoe.com or on the video DVD.

Dinah Zike's Foldables are three-dimensional, interactive graphic organizers that help students practice basic writing skills, review key vocabulary terms, and identify main ideas. Have students complete this chapter's Foldable activity or activities in *Dinah Zike's Reading and Study Skills Foldables* booklet. **OL**

Government ONLINE

Visit glencoe.com and enter *QuickPass*™ code USG9085c11T for Chapter 11 Resources including Chapter Overview, Student Web Activity, Self-Check Quiz, and other materials for students and teachers.

Essential Question

How does the Constitution define the powers of the federal courts, and how are the various courts related to one another?

Government ONLINE
Chapter Overview Visit glencoe.com and enter *QuickPass*™ code USG9822c11 for an overview, a quiz, and other chapter resources.

▲ **U.S. courthouse in New York City**

304   **UNIT 4:** *The Judicial Branch*

Launching the Chapter

Hammurabi's Code One of the world's earliest codes of laws was that of the Babylonian king Hammurabi. To govern the various peoples in his empire, he set up a uniform code of laws, which he had inscribed on a stone pillar, or stela. Students may find it interesting to learn about these laws, some of which include punishments that might seem barbaric compared to today's standards. Have students choose five laws and punishments from Hammurabi's Code and present them in a chart that compares them with today's laws.
Essential Question: What would the United States be without a judicial system or a way of enforcing laws? *(People would not necessarily be treated fairly when they broke the law, and laws might not be applied equally. With no one to enforce or interpret laws, the passage of laws would be futile.)* **OL**

Powers of the Federal Courts

Focus

Reader's Guide

Content Vocabulary

★ concurrent jurisdiction (p. 306)
★ original jurisdiction (p. 307)
★ appellate jurisdiction (p. 307)
★ litigant (p. 307)
★ due process clause (p. 309)

Academic Vocabulary

★ derive (p. 306)
★ overlap (p. 306)
★ emphasize (p. 308)

Reading Strategy

As you read, create a Venn diagram like the one below to list the jurisdictional authority for state and federal courts.

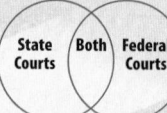

State Courts | Both | Federal Courts

Bellringer

Section Focus Transparencies 11-1

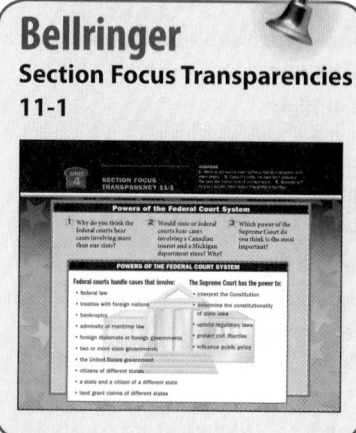

People in the News

The chief justice of the Supreme Court, John Roberts, helped celebrate the 100th anniversary of Rhode Island's federal courthouse in 2008. In a speech to a Providence audience, Roberts said, "Throughout our nation's history, federal and state courthouses have been, both literally and figuratively, the center of civic life." The speech Roberts gave did not stray from the theme of celebration for the nation's judiciary. But because Roberts is a powerful symbol of that branch of government, demonstrators gathered outside to voice protests against some of the positions he has taken.

▲ As chief justice, John Roberts, Jr., symbolizes the powerful role of the Supreme Court.

Reader's Guide

Answers to Graphic:

State Courts: cases involving state laws
Federal Courts: cases involving federal laws; treaties with foreign nations; interpretations of the Constitution; bankruptcy; admiralty laws; representatives of foreign governments; two or more states; U.S. government offices and agencies; citizens of more than one state; and citizens of the same state who claim land grants in other states.
Both: civil cases involving citizens of different states

It is not surprising to us that some citizens might protest the public appearance of the chief justice of the Supreme Court. In the early days of the nation, however, it would have been shocking. Although the Constitution called for an independent judiciary to balance the other two branches, the Supreme Court played only a minor role in government until 1801. In that year, Chief Justice John Marshall was appointed. Marshall, a major figure in the growing power of the Court, served until 1835.

Over the years, the expansion of the Supreme Court's power has met serious challenges, as one historian of the Court noted:

66 *Nothing in the Court's history is more striking than the fact that, while its significant and necessary place in the Federal form of Government has always been recognized by thoughtful and patriotic men, nevertheless, no branch of the Government and no institution under the Constitution has sustained more continuous attack or reached its present position after more vigorous opposition.* 99
—Charles Warren, 1924

Today, the judiciary is well established as a branch equal to the legislative and executive branches.

Resource Manager

R Reading Strategies	**C** Critical Thinking	**D** Differentiated Instruction	**W** Writing Support	**S** Skill Practice
Teacher Edition • Paraphrasing, p. 307 • Summarizing, p. 308 **Additional Resources** • Quizzes/Tests, p. 129 • Guid. Read. Act., p. 39	**Teacher Edition** • Drawing Conclusions, p. 307 **Additional Resources** • Read. Essen., pp. 117–119	**Teacher Edition** • Kinesthetic, p. 309 **Additional Resources** • Foldables, p. 54 • Supreme Ct. Case Studies, pp. 1–2, 3–4, 5–6, 7–8, 11–12, 23–24, 25–26, 27–28, 73–74	**Teacher Edition** • Personal Writing, p. 310 **Additional Resources** • Making It Rel. Trans., pp. 21–22	**Teacher Edition** • Reading Charts, p. 306 **Additional Resources** • Vocab. Act., p. 11

Teach

S Skill Practice

Reading Charts **Ask:** What is the highest court to which a case can be appealed? (*U.S. Supreme Court*) From which courts will the U.S. Supreme Court hear direct appeals? (*highest state courts, U.S. Courts of Appeals, U.S. Court of Appeals for the Federal Circuit, and U.S. Court of Appeals for the Armed Forces*. Note: the orange boxes are courts not belonging to the federal court system.) **BL**

Did You Know?

By the twentieth century, the Supreme Court was so powerful that Justice Charles Evans Hughes boasted: "We are under a Constitution, but the Constitution is what the judges say it is, . . ." Hughes was chief justice from 1930 to 1941, during which period the justices struck down many laws as unconstitutional.

Hands-On Chapter Project

Step 1

The Federal Court System

Charts In Motion See StudentWorks™ Plus or go to glencoe.com.

The United States Supreme Court

- U.S. Court of Appeals for the Armed Forces
- 12 U.S. Courts of Appeals
- U.S. Court of Appeals for the Federal Circuit

- Military Courts
- U.S. Tax Court
- 94 District Courts (including 1 in the District of Columbia and 4 Territorial Courts)
- U.S. Court of international Trade
- U.S. Claims Court
- U.S. Court of Veterans' Appeals

- Appeals from Highest State Courts
- Appeals from Federal Regulatory Agencies

Source: Squire and Lindsey, et al., *Dynamics of Democracy*, 2d. ed. (Madison, WI: Brown & Benchmark, 1997).

Critical Thinking The U.S. Constitution gives Congress the authority to create lower federal courts. *Which court has jurisdiction over a case involving a United States veteran?*

Jurisdiction of the Courts

The United States judiciary consists of parallel systems of federal and state courts. Each of the 50 states has its own system of courts whose powers **derive** from state constitutions and laws. The federal court system consists of the Supreme Court and lower federal courts established by Congress. Federal courts derive their powers from the Constitution and federal laws.

Federal Court Jurisdiction

The authority to hear certain cases is called the jurisdiction of the court. In the dual-court system, state courts have jurisdiction over cases involving state laws, while federal courts have jurisdiction over cases involving federal laws. Sometimes the jurisdiction of the state courts and the jurisdiction of the federal courts **overlap.**

The Constitution gave federal courts jurisdiction in cases that involve United States laws, treaties with foreign nations, or interpretations of the Constitution. Federal courts also try cases involving bankruptcy and cases involving admiralty or maritime law.

Federal courts also have jurisdiction to hear a case if certain parties or persons are involved. These include:

- ambassadors and other representatives of foreign governments;
- two or more state governments;
- the U.S. government or one of its offices or agencies;
- citizens who are residents of more than one state; and
- citizens who are residents of the same state but claim land grants in other states.

Concurrent Jurisdiction

In most cases, the difference between federal and state court jurisdiction is clear. In some instances, however, both federal and state courts have jurisdiction, a situation known as **concurrent jurisdiction.** Concurrent jurisdiction exists, for example, in a case involving citizens of different states in a dispute concerning more than $75,000. In such a case, a person may sue in either a federal or a state court. If the person being sued insists, however, the case must be tried in a federal court.

306 UNIT 4: *The Judicial Branch*

Debating Judicial Activism

Step 1: Researching

Directions Begin by defining *judicial activism* and *judicial restraint*. Work with students to reach a consensus on the definitions. Have students consult the textbook, other books, periodicals, and other sources to find at least three arguments for judicial activism and three arguments for judicial restraint.

Taking Notes Tell students to take notes of the statistics, quotations, and other evidence that support each argument. Remind them that they should be prepared to refute the arguments for both sides. **AL**

(Chapter Project continued in Section 2.)

Original and Appellate Jurisdiction

The court in which a case is originally tried is known as a trial court. A trial court has **original jurisdiction.** In the federal court system, the district courts as well as several other lower courts have only original jurisdiction.

When people lose a case in a trial court and wish to appeal the decision, they may take the case to a court with **appellate jurisdiction.** The federal court system provides courts of appeals with appellate jurisdiction. A party may appeal a case from a district court to a court of appeals. If that party loses in the court of appeals, he or she may appeal the case to the Supreme Court, which has original jurisdiction for some types of cases and appellate jurisdiction for others.

Developing Supreme Court Power

Since 1789, the Supreme Court has become very powerful. It may also be the least understood institution of American government. The role of the Court has developed from custom, usage, and history.

Early Precedents

Certain principles were established early in the Court's history. Neither the Supreme Court nor any federal court can initiate action. A judge or justice cannot seek an issue and ask people to bring it to court. The courts must wait for **litigants,** or people engaged in a lawsuit, to come before them.

A second principle is that federal courts only decide cases involving actual conflicts between two or more people. They do not answer a general legal question, regardless of how significant the issue or who asks the question. In July 1793, at the request of President George Washington, Secretary of State Thomas Jefferson wrote to Chief Justice John Jay asking the Court for advice. Jefferson submitted 29 questions dealing with American neutrality during the war between France and England. Three weeks later, the Court refused to answer the questions with a polite reply:

66 *We exceedingly regret every event that may cause embarrassment to your administration, but we derive consolation from the reflection that your judgment will discern what is right.* 99

Marbury v. Madison

🏛 **Landmark Case** In an 1803 case, the Court did not hesitate to be assertive. In this landmark case, it asserted that the Court had the power of judicial review—the power to determine whether a law or government action is constitutional. Some of the Founders argued for judicial review in the Federalist Papers, especially Alexander Hamilton's *The Federalist,* No. 80, but until this court case, judicial review was not clearly established.

Just before President Adams's term expired in 1801, Congress passed a bill enabling the president to appoint 42 justices of the peace. The Senate quickly confirmed the nominees. The secretary of

Judicial Review

Constitutional Interpretations On his last night in the White House, John Adams stayed up signing judicial commissions for his party members, the Federalists, who were defeated in the 1800 elections. The new president, Thomas Jefferson, angrily called these appointees "midnight judges." Adams's actions led to the landmark case *Marbury* v. *Madison,* which secured the power of judicial review for the Supreme Court. *Why is judicial review a key feature of the United States governmental system?*

C Critical Thinking

Drawing Conclusions Ask: Why was it significant that the Supreme Court declined to respond to Secretary of State Thomas Jefferson's request for advice? *(It established the principle that the federal courts will only make rulings on particular cases; they will not provide general legal advice.)* **OL**

R Reading Strategy

Paraphrasing After reading the section on *Marbury* v. *Madison,* have students work in pairs to write a sentence that explains the main idea of the ruling. Remind them to use their own words. **ELL BL**

🏛 **Landmark Case**

See *Marbury* v. *Madison* in the Supreme Court Case Summaries in the **Reference Handbook** and Case Study 1 in the *Supreme Court Case Studies* booklet.

Caption Answer: It gives the Supreme Court the power to check Congress; the Supreme Court is the final authority on the meaning of the Constitution.

Differentiated Instruction

Activity: Multiple Learning Styles

Verbal/Linguistic Have students read in the **Reference Handbook** the case summaries of each case mentioned in the section. Then have students write a headline and an accompanying introductory paragraph that might have appeared in a newspaper when a decision was announced. Remind students of the reporter's five *W*'s and one *H*—*who, what, where, when, why,* and *how.* After they have completed their articles, have students exchange papers and edit each other's work. **OL**

R Reading Strategy

Summarizing Ask: Why did the U.S. Supreme Court rule that the Second Bank of the United States was immune from taxation? *(The Bank was immune because it was an institution of the federal government. In a federal-state conflict, the state must yield. The power to tax is the power to destroy; therefore, Congress had a right to take necessary steps to preserve an institution it had created).* **OL**

🏛 Landmark Case

See *McCulloch v. Maryland, Gibbons v. Ogden,* and *Dred Scott v. Sandford* in the Supreme Court Case Summaries in the **Reference Handbook** and Case Studies 2, 4, and 6 in the *Supreme Court Case Studies* booklet.

Government ONLINE

Objectives and answers to the Student Web Activity can be found in the **Web Activity Lesson Plan** at glencoe.com. Enter **QuickPass™** code USG9085c11T.

Additional Support

---

state delivered all but four of the commissions by the day Thomas Jefferson took office. Jefferson stopped delivery of the remaining commissions. William Marbury, one of those who did not receive his commission, filed suit in the Supreme Court under a provision of the Judiciary Act of 1789.

In his 1803 ruling, Chief Justice John Marshall said that Marbury's appointment was legal but that he could not sue for it because the law he used to bring the suit to the Court, the Judiciary Act of 1789, was unconstitutional. The ruling established the power of the judiciary to review laws and decide whether they were constitutional. It expanded the principle of limited government—courts too, should serve as a check on the legislature.

In two other decisions under Marshall, the Court further expanded its power. In *Fletcher v. Peck*[1] (1810), the Court held that a Georgia state law violated the Constitution's protection of contracts. 📖 The case established the Court's power to review state laws. In *Dartmouth College v. Woodward*[2] (1819), the Court applied the protection of contracts to corporate charters as well. 📖

McCulloch v. Maryland

🏛 **Landmark Case** In *McCulloch v. Maryland*[3] (1819), the Court established that the federal government was "supreme in its sphere of action." 📖 The state of Maryland had tried to tax the Bank of the United States, but Marshall said that the power to tax was the power to destroy. A state should not be able to interfere with federal actions that were "necessary and proper" to carrying out its constitutional powers. Creating a national bank was "necessary and proper" because Congress had the power to borrow money, collect taxes, and raise an army.

Gibbons v. Ogden

🏛 **Landmark Case** In the 1824 case of *Gibbons v. Ogden,*[4] the Court again delivered a strong message about the power of the national government. 📖 This time it used the Constitution's commerce clause. Basically the Court broadened the definition

Government ONLINE

Student Web Activity Visit glencoe.com and enter **QuickPass™** code USG9822c11. Click on Student Web Activity and complete the activity about the powers of the federal courts.

of interstate commerce in a way that again increased the power of the federal government.

The case concerned a steamboat monopoly that New York had granted to Robert Fulton. Fulton licensed Aaron Ogden to carry passengers between New York City and New Jersey. Meanwhile Thomas Gibbons, owner of a competing steamboat line, wanted to carry passengers between New Jersey and Manhattan. Gibbons challenged New York's right to control river travel. The Court agreed with Gibbons because otherwise no real commerce could develop.

❝ *Rivers and bays, in many cases, form the divisions between States; and thence it was obvious, that if the States should make regulations for the navigation of these waters, and such regulations should be repugnant and hostile, embarrassment would necessarily happen to the general intercourse of the community.* ❞
—Chief Justice John Marshall

By 1825, the Court had declared at least one law in each of 10 states unconstitutional.

Dred Scott v. Sandford

🏛 **Landmark Case** When Chief Justice Marshall died in 1835, President Andrew Jackson nominated Roger Taney to succeed him. Jackson also named seven justices to the Supreme Court during his eight years in office, and the Court reflected his views. Society was becoming more democratic as more men gained the right to vote. The Court began to **emphasize** the rights of the states and of citizens.

In the 1840s, states' rights became tied directly to the slavery issue. In *Dred Scott v. Sandford* (1857), the Court declared that African Americans could not be citizens, that the Missouri Compromise of Congress was unconstitutional—in effect, Congress was powerless to stop the spread of slavery. The national uproar over the *Scott* case damaged the Court.

Due Process

After the Civil War, the Supreme Court issued rulings on the Thirteenth, Fourteenth, and Fifteenth Amendments.[5] 📖 These are known as the Reconstruction amendments because they are part of the

📖 *See the following footnoted materials in the Reference Handbook:*
1. *Fletcher v. Peck* case summary, page R27.
2. *Dartmouth College v. Woodward* case summary, page R26.
3. *McCulloch v. Maryland* case summary, page R30.
4. *Gibbons v. Ogden* case summary, page R27.
5. *The Constitution*, pages R42–R67.

Activity: Collaborative Learning

Formulating Questions Debate continues over the following issue: How should judges interpret the Constitution—on the basis of the Framers' original intent or on the basis of today's values and principles? Have groups of two or three formulate questions they would ask of proponents of each position. For example, students might ask constitutional-basis supporters: "How do we know what the Framers really meant? What if the Framers had different reasons for their support of certain constitutional provisions?" Questions that might be asked of someone supporting the use of today's principles include: "How should judges decide which contemporary principles to follow? Should they follow their personal views or the views of the majority of citizens?" **AL**

Protector of Civil Liberties

Fighting Segregation Linda Brown (on the left), shown here with her family, was one of several students whose families were recruited in a national campaign to end segregated schools. The National Association for the Advancement of Colored People (NAACP) asked the Brown family and 12 other families in Topeka, Kansas, to take part in a legal suit that was also being fought in other states. When the case reached the Supreme Court, it came to be known as *Brown* v. *Board of Education of Topeka. What legal doctrine dating from 1896 did the Brown case overturn?*

effort to "reconstruct" the United States. They were intended to ensure the rights and liberties of newly freed African Americans. The Fourteenth Amendment contains the **due process clause,** which says that no state may deprive any person of life, liberty, or property without due process of law. In this era, the Court did not strongly apply the clause when individuals challenged business or state interests.

Early Due Process Cases

The first significant ruling on the Fourteenth Amendment came in 1873 with the Slaughterhouse Cases. Louisiana had granted a monopoly in the slaughtering business to one company. Competing butchers challenged this grant, arguing that it denied them the right to practice their trade. They claimed that the Fourteenth Amendment guaranteed the privileges and immunities of U.S. citizenship, equal protection of the laws, and due process. The Court ruled for Louisiana, saying that the Fourteenth Amendment only extended protection to rights, privileges, and immunities that had their source in federal citizenship, not state citizenship.

Plessy v. Ferguson

Landmark Case In 1896 the Court upheld a Louisiana law requiring railroads in the state to provide separate cars for white and African American passengers. In *Plessy* v. *Ferguson* the Court said that this was a reasonable exercise of state police power to preserve peace and order. "Legislation is powerless to eradicate racial instincts or to abolish

distinctions," it concluded. The lone dissenter, Justice John Harlan, said this decision was "inconsistent with the personal liberty of citizens, white and black." The case established the "separate but equal" doctrine, which held that if facilities for both races were equal, they could be separate. This ruling was not completely overturned until the 1950s.

The Court and Business

The Court refused to broaden federal powers to enforce individual rights. Yet it seemed willing to broaden the police power of the states to protect consumers from the expanding power of businesses and corporations.

In the 1870s, in a group of cases known as the Granger Cases, the Court rejected a challenge to state regulatory laws. It held that some private property, such as a railroad, was invested with a public interest. It was, therefore, proper for a state to exercise its power to regulate the railroads.

Most of the time, however, the Court sided with business interests as the nation industrialized. In the 1890s, in *United States* v. *E.C. Knight & Co.*[1] and other cases, the Court ruled to uphold the monopoly of business trusts. In *Debs* v. *United States,*[2] it upheld the contempt conviction of labor leader Eugene V. Debs, who disobeyed an order to call off a strike against a railroad company. During the Progressive Era, the Court upheld several federal

*See the following footnoted materials in the **Reference Handbook:***
1. *United States* v. *E.C. Knight and Co.,* case summary, page R35.
2. *Debs* v. *United States* case summary, page R26.

Activity: Collaborative Learning

Separate but Equal Organize the class into two groups to research the "separate but equal" doctrine. One group should research *Plessy* v. *Ferguson,* which set the legal precedent for "separate but equal" schools. The other group should research *Brown* v. *Board of Education of Topeka, Kansas,* which overturned the "separate but equal" doctrine. Groups should then come together for a class discussion of their findings—or group spokespersons may be selected for class presentations. **OL**

W Writing Support

Personal Writing Ask: If you could ask a nominee for the Supreme Court about his or her position on one issue, what would it be? Why? *(Students should explain why they consider the issue to be crucial.)* **OL**

🏛 Landmark Case

See *Schechter Poultry Corp.* v. *United States* and *Brown* v. *Board of Education of Topeka* in the Supreme Court Case Summaries in the **Reference Handbook** and Case Studies 25 and 37 in the *Supreme Court Case Studies* booklet.

Assess

Assign the Section 1 Assessment as homework or as an in-class activity, or have students take Section Quiz 11-1 from *Section Quizzes and Chapter Tests.*

Close

Analyzing Ask students to explain briefly the significance of each Supreme Court case discussed in the section. **OL**

> ### Section 1 Review

Pioneering Decision Thurgood Marshall argued the *Brown* case before the Supreme Court and later became the first African American appointed to the Supreme Court. **What was the basic argument of the Court in this decision?**

and state laws regulating business, but it returned to its support for business by the 1920s.

A major constitutional crisis arose in the 1930s over the question of federal and state regulation of the economy. President Franklin D. Roosevelt was angered by the Court's decision in *Schechter Poultry Corporation* v. *United States*[1] and a number of other cases. 📖 To find a way around the Court's

decisions, Roosevelt proposed increasing the number of Supreme Court justices so he could appoint men who supported his policies. Congress defeated Roosevelt's proposal to "pack the court," but it did begin to shift its views and to uphold laws regulating business.

Brown v. Board of Education

🏛 **Landmark Case** The dramatic role of the Court in protecting civil liberties did not begin until Earl Warren became chief justice. Warren served as chief justice from 1953 to 1969. In *Brown* v. *Board of Education of Topeka*, the Court outlawed segregation in public schools. In several other cases during the Warren era, the Court issued rulings that extended equal protection in voting rights and in apportioning representation in Congress or state legislatures. In other cases, the Warren Court applied due process and Bill of Rights protections to people accused of crimes. Although the Court since then has not been as active in advancing civil liberties, it has not made any major revisions to the decisions of the Warren Court.

As the twentieth century drew to a close, it was apparent that the Supreme Court had carved out considerable power to influence policy in the United States. The legal views of the justices and their opinions on the various cases put before them would determine how the Court uses that power.

📖 *See the following footnoted materials in the **Reference Handbook**:*
1. *Schechter Poultry Corporation v. United States* case summary, page R34.

SECTION 1 Review

Vocabulary

1. **Explain** the significance of: concurrent jurisdiction, original jurisdiction, appellate jurisdiction, litigant, due process clause.

Main Ideas

2. **Identifying** What are the different jurisdictions of federal and state courts?

3. **Analyzing** What doctrine was established by the ruling in *Plessy* v. *Ferguson*?

Critical Thinking

4. **Synthesizing** What choice of jurisdiction would be available to a person who was being sued by a citizen of another state for damages of at least $75,000?

5. **Organizing** Use a graphic organizer like the one below to show how the Supreme Court extended civil liberties in the 1950s and 1960s.

Cause	Effect/Cause	Effect
"Separate but Equal" doctrine		

Writing About Government

6. **Expository Writing** Choose one of the cases discussed in Section 1 or another case that contributed to developing the power of the Supreme Court. Research the details of the case, including the background, the ruling, and the reasons for the ruling. Write a newspaper article that reports on the effects of the ruling.

Answers

1. All definitions can be found in the section and the Glossary.
2. State courts have jurisdiction over state laws; federal courts have jurisdiction over U.S. laws, treaties, the Constitution, bankruptcy, and maritime laws.
3. "separate but equal" doctrine, which held that if facilities for both races were equal, they could be separate

4. The person being sued could choose to have the case tried in the state court or in a federal court.
5. Effect/Cause: *Brown* v. *Board of Education of Topeka, Kansas;* Effect: outlawed segregation in public schools
6. Newspaper articles should be concise, and they should answer the questions *who, what, when, where, why,* and *how.*

Does a Male-Only Admissions Policy Violate Women's Constitutional Rights?

United States v. *Virginia*, 1996

Governments often make distinctions among groups, such as providing medical benefits only for military veterans. Does a state college's policy of admitting only men violate the constitutional rights of women?

Facts of the Case

Virginia Military Institute (VMI), a state-supported college, was created in 1839 as an all-male institution. Since then, VMI's distinctive mission was to produce "citizen soldiers," men prepared for leadership in civilian and military life. VMI's "adversative" approach to education required student cadets to wear uniforms, live in barracks, and participate in tough physical training. New VMI students, called "rats," were exposed to a seven-month experience similar to Marine Corps boot camp. In 1990 the U.S. government sued Virginia and VMI at the request of a female high school student seeking admission. After a long process of appeals, the Supreme Court finally took the case in 1996.

The Constitutional Question

The U.S. government claimed that by denying women the unique educational opportunity offered to men at VMI, the state of Virginia was making a classification that violated the Fourteenth Amendment's guarantee of "equal protection of the law." Under the equal protection clause, governments can treat different groups of people differently only if such a classification serves an important governmental objective such as promoting safety.

VMI explained that its policy should be allowed under the Constitution's equal protection principle because its male-only school brought a healthy diversity to the state of Virginia's otherwise coeducational system. Further, VMI argued that if women were admitted, the school would have to change housing and physical training requirements, and that such modifications would fundamentally change its distinctive approach to education.

Finally, VMI offered to establish a separate program called the Virginia Women's Institute for Leadership (VWIL) at a small, private women's college. The women's college would not offer engineering, advanced math, or physics, and its students had SAT scores about 100 points lower than VMI's students. The VWIL program would not involve the tough physical training, uniforms, or barracks life. VMI cited "important differences between men and women in learning and developmental needs" as the reason for the alternative program.

Class Debate

Organize the class into three groups: one to represent VMI's lawyers, one to represent the U.S. government's lawyers, and a third group to represent the Supreme Court justices. Allow class time for the development of arguments, and then have each side present its case. Have the justices' decision and any dissenting opinions read aloud.

The Court's Decision

The Court voted 7 to 1 that VMI's admissions policy denied women equal protection of the laws and was thus unconstitutional. Justice Ruth Bader Ginsburg wrote for the majority that the Court found no evidence that male-only admissions furthered the state of Virginia's policy of diversity in education. Further, the Court found no evidence that admitting women would destroy VMI's adversative approach to education and no inherent gender differences that could justify denying women the opportunity for VMI's unique approach to education for citizen soldiers. The Court then ruled that the proposed VWIL alternative program did not settle the constitutional violation because VMI had not presented a good reason to withhold its program from women, and the VWIL alternative program was not substantially equivalent. Thus, the Constitution required VMI to admit, on an equal basis with men, women who could meet all requirements.

Debating the Issue

Questions to Consider

1. Did VMI's male-only policy violate the equal protection clause?

2. Was VMI's proposed remedy of a separate program a legally acceptable alternative?

◀ **A female cadet endures VMI traditions.**

You Be the Judge

In your opinion, was VMI's goal of educating citizen soldiers unsuitable for women? Was VMI's men-only policy unconstitutional? If so, what remedy should be offered?

Debating the Issue Answers

Questions to Consider

1. Whichever side students choose should be well-defended.

2. Students should be able to provide logical defenses for their positions.

You Be the Judge

Whichever position students choose should be well-defended. Possible answer: Since women have the right to equal educational opportunities, the only remedy is to admit qualified women.

Focus

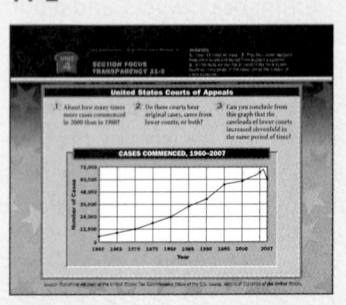
Reader's Guide

Answers to Graphic:

Cause: A person loses a case in a district court.

Effect: The person appeals to a federal court of appeals.

Resource Manager

Lower Federal Courts

Reader's Guide

Content Vocabulary
★ grand jury (p. 312)
★ indictment (p. 313)
★ petit jury (p. 313)
★ judicial circuit (p. 313)
★ senatorial courtesy (p. 317)

Academic Vocabulary
★ network (p. 312)
★ sufficient (p. 313)
★ panel (p. 313)

Reading Strategy
As you read, create a graphic organizer to list the possible effects when a person loses a case in a district court.

Cause		Effect
A person loses a case in a district court.	→	

Public Policy in the News

In 1969 fifteen-year-old Ricky Wyatt, labeled a "juvenile delinquent," was placed in Bryce State Mental Hospital in Tuscaloosa, Alabama, even though he had no signs of mental illness. Bryce was used as "dumping grounds" for those with mental illness or retardation. "Anybody who was unwanted was put in Bryce," said one attorney who worked on the court case. Once confined, patients got little or no treatment, and basic conditions at Bryce were substandard. Wyatt's attorneys filed a lawsuit holding Alabama responsible for the conditions at Bryce. In 1971 a federal district court judge ruled that patients who were involuntarily committed to Alabama mental institutions have a constitutional right to humane treatment. Later court actions led the state to monitor conditions and develop a plan for improvement. In 2003 a federal court dismissed the *Wyatt* case because it determined that treatment standards were being met.

▲ Bryce State Mental Hospital today

District courts like the one that handled *Wyatt v. Stickney* are part of a **network** of federal courts that serve the nation. The Constitution created the Supreme Court but Congress used its authority to set up these lower federal courts, beginning with the Judiciary Act of 1789. These courts are of two basic types—constitutional federal courts and legislative federal courts.

Constitutional Courts

Courts established by Congress under the provisions of Article III of the Constitution are constitutional courts. These courts include the federal district courts, the federal courts of appeals, and the United States Court of International Trade.

Federal District Courts

Congress created district courts in 1789 to serve as trial courts. These districts followed state boundary lines. As the population grew and cases multiplied, Congress divided some states into more than 1 district. Today the United States has 94 districts, with each state having at least 1 district court. Large states—California, New York, and Texas—each have 4 district courts. Washington, D.C., and Puerto Rico also have 1 district court each. More than 550 judges preside over the district courts.

United States district courts are the trial courts for both criminal and civil federal cases. District courts use two types of juries in criminal cases. A **grand jury,** which usually includes 16 to 23 people, hears charges against a person suspected of having

R Reading Strategies	**C** Critical Thinking	**D** Differentiated Instruction	**W** Writing Support	**S** Skill Practice
Teacher Edition • Predicting, p. 317 **Additional Resources** • Quizzes/Tests, p. 130 • Guid. Read. Act., p. 40	**Teacher Edition** • Synthesizing, p. 315 **Additional Resources** • Read. Essen., pp. 120–122	**Teacher Edition** • Visual/Spatial, p. 313 **Additional Resources** • Foldables, p. 54	**Teacher Edition** • Persuasive Writing, p. 317 **Additional Resources** • Part. in Gov. Act., pp. 21–22 • Authentic Assess., p. 18	**Teacher Edition** • Using Geography Skills, p. 314 **Additional Resources** • Source Readings, p. 11

Rulings of Federal Courts

Settling Disputes
To protect consumers, New York passed an Airline Passenger Bill of Rights to fine airlines when they do not supply water, fresh air, power, and working rest rooms to passengers during long delays. In 2008 a U.S. Court of Appeals ruled that New York had overstepped its regulatory authority. *Why do you think the court ruled against the state in this case?*

committed a crime. If the grand jury believes **sufficient** evidence is available to bring the person to trial, it issues an **indictment**—a formal accusation charging a person with a crime. If the jury believes the evidence is insufficient, the charges are dropped.

A **petit jury,** which usually consists of 6 or 12 people, is a trial jury. Its function is to weigh the evidence presented at a trial in a criminal or civil case. In a criminal case, a petit jury renders a verdict of guilty or not guilty. In a civil case, the jury finds for either the plaintiff, the person bringing the suit, or the defendant, the person against whom the suit is brought. If the parties do not want a jury trial, a judge or a **panel** of three judges weighs the evidence.

District courts hear hundreds of thousands of cases each year. This caseload represents more than 80 percent of all federal cases. District courts have jurisdiction to hear cases involving federal questions: issues of federal statutory or constitutional law. They can also hear some cases involving citizens of different states. In the vast majority of their cases, district courts render the final decision. Few are appealed. One scholar explained:

❝ *Trial judges, because of the multitude of cases they hear which remain unheard or unchanged by appellate courts, as well as because of their fact- and issue-shaping powers, appear to play an independent and formidable part in the policy impact of the federal court system upon the larger political system.* ❞

—Kenneth M. Dolbeare, 1969

Officers of the Court

Many appointed officials provide support services for district courts. Each district has a United States attorney to represent the United States in all civil suits brought against the government and to prosecute people charged with federal crimes. Each district court appoints a United States magistrate who issues arrest warrants and helps decide whether the arrested person should be held for a grand jury hearing. A bankruptcy judge handles bankruptcy cases for each district. A United States marshal carries out such duties as making arrests, securing jurors, and keeping order in the courtroom. With the help of deputy clerks, bailiffs, and a stenographer, a clerk keeps records of court proceedings.

Federal Courts of Appeals

Good records are important because a person or group that loses a case in a district court may appeal to a federal court of appeals or, in some instances, directly to the Supreme Court. Congress created the United States courts of appeals in 1891 to ease the appeals workload of the Supreme Court. The caseload of appellate courts has increased dramatically since 1980, climbing from 23,200 cases to nearly 60,000 in 2007.

The appellate level includes 13 United States courts of appeals. The United States is divided into 12 **judicial circuits,** or regions, with 1 appellate court in each circuit. The thirteenth court is a special appeals court with national jurisdiction. Usually, a panel of three judges sits on each appeal. All of the circuit judges may hear a major case.

CHAPTER 11: *The Federal Court System* **313**

Teach

Caption Answer: Although New York's Airline Passenger Bill of Rights makes a lot of sense, it would have given all states the green light to institute potentially conflicting fines and policies, causing chaos.

D Differentiated Instruction

Visual/Spatial Challenge students to create a political cartoon about one or more of the appointed officials mentioned in the section "Officers of the Court." Suggest that students attempt to portray the relationships between the appointed officials and the United States or individual districts. Before students begin, you might want to have them review the political cartoons in the textbook, in magazines such as *Newsweek,* or in other available resources. Choose a few of the best cartoons, post them on the bulletin board, and have students give an explanation, orally or in writing, of each displayed cartoon. **AL**

Additional Support

Activity: Collaborative Learning

Writing a Newspaper Have students review the criteria that are usually considered by presidents in making appointments to the federal bench. Then organize the class into groups of six. Tell groups that they are charged with designing a system for improving the method of appointing federal judges. Have groups brainstorm criteria for nominating federal judges and a procedure for presidents to follow to identify possible appointees. Have group representatives present their ideas to the class. One or more members from each group should make charts or other visuals to illustrate the presentation. **OL**

Using Geography Skills Ask students to identify the states within each district. Using what they know about each state's population, what generalization could they make about how the states were divided into circuits? *(With the exception of the ninth district, the districts vary in land area but have similar populations.)* **OL**

Critical Thinking

Answer: federal civil and criminal cases

Linking ☆ Past & Present

Circuit Courts Before 1891, when Congress created circuit courts of appeals, each Supreme Court justice traveled to a specific region of the nation to hear appeals from the federal district courts. Officially renamed courts of appeals in 1948, these appellate courts are often still called circuit courts. Although they have their own federal judges, a Supreme Court justice remains assigned to each court of appeals.

Hands-On Chapter Project

Step 2

Debating Judicial Activism

Step 2: Conducting the Debate

Directions After students have completed their research, organize two teams. One will support judicial activism and the other will oppose it.

Debating Use the following format for the debate:

1. Affirmative speaker presents speech arguing for judicial activism (5 minutes).
2. Negative speaker asks questions of affirmative speaker (2 minutes).

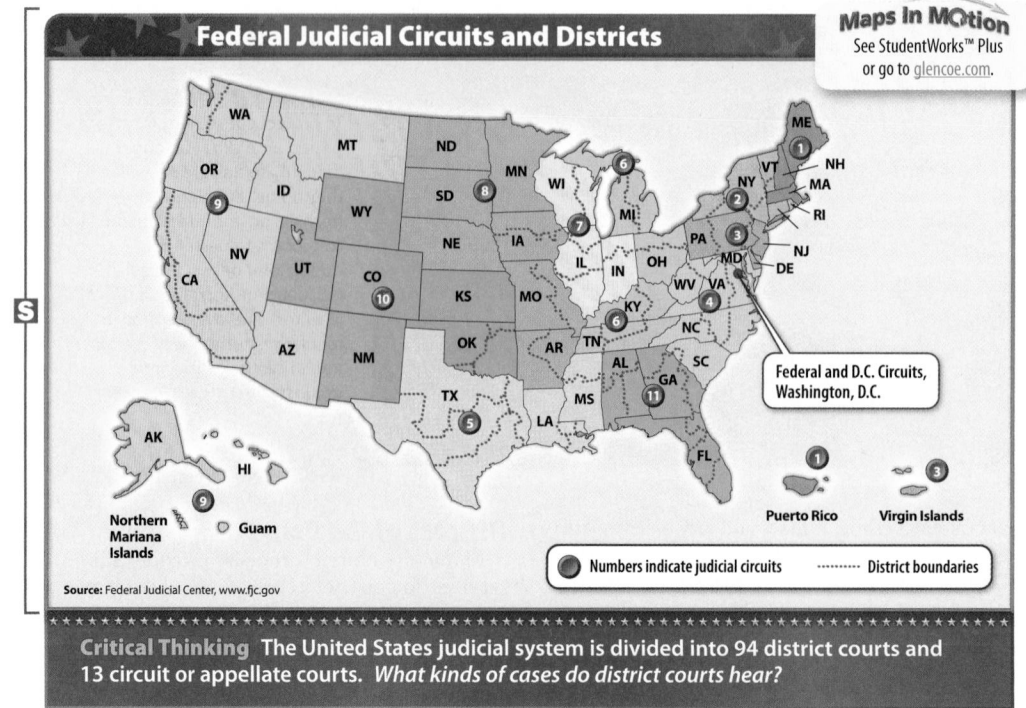

Federal Judicial Circuits and Districts

Maps in Motion
See StudentWorks™ Plus
or go to glencoe.com.

Federal and D.C. Circuits, Washington, D.C.

Puerto Rico   Virgin Islands

Northern Mariana Islands   Guam

● Numbers indicate judicial circuits   ········· District boundaries

Source: Federal Judicial Center, www.fjc.gov

Critical Thinking The United States judicial system is divided into 94 district courts and 13 circuit or appellate courts. *What kinds of cases do district courts hear?*

As their name implies, the courts of appeals have only appellate jurisdiction. Most appeals arise from decisions of district courts, the U.S. Tax Court, and various territorial courts. These courts also hear appeals on the rulings of various regulatory agencies, such as the Federal Trade Commission and the Federal Communications Commission.

The courts of appeals may decide an appeal in one of three ways: uphold the original decision, reverse that decision, or send the case back to the lower court to be tried again. Unless appealed to the Supreme Court, decisions of the courts of appeals are final.

In 1982 Congress set up a special court of appeals, called the United States Circuit Court of Appeals for the Federal Circuit. This court hears cases from a federal claims court, the Court of International Trade, the United States Patent Office, and other executive agencies. The court's headquarters are in Washington, D.C., but it sits in other parts of the country as needed.

The Court of International Trade

Formerly known as the United States Customs Court, this court has jurisdiction over cases dealing with tariffs. Citizens who believe that tariffs are too high bring most of the cases heard in this court.

The Court of International Trade is based in New York City, but it is a national court. The judges also hear cases in other major port cities around the country such as New Orleans and San Francisco. The Circuit Court of Appeals for the Federal Circuit hears decisions appealed from this court.

Legislative Courts

Along with the constitutional federal courts, Congress has created a series of courts referred to as legislative courts. As spelled out in Article I[1] of the Constitution, the legislative courts help Congress exercise its powers. Thus, it was the power of Congress to tax that led to the creation of the United States Tax Court. The congressional power of regulating the armed forces led to the formation of the Court of Appeals for the Armed Forces. The duty of Congress to govern overseas territories such as Guam and the Virgin Islands led to the creation of

---

📖 *See the following footnoted materials in the* **Reference Handbook:**
1. *The Constitution,* pages R42–R67.

3. Negative speaker presents prepared speech against judicial activism (5 minutes).
4. Cross examination: affirmative speaker asks questions of negative speaker (2 minutes).
5. Negative speaker refutes affirmative arguments (3 minutes).
6. Affirmative speaker refutes negative arguments (3 minutes).
7. Classmates ask questions of both sides (10 minutes).
8. Classmates vote to determine the winner. **AL**

(Chapter Project continued in Section 3.)

territorial courts. Similarly, congressional supervision of the District of Columbia led to the establishment of a court system for the nation's capital.

Federal Claims Court

Established in 1982, the U.S. Court of Federal Claims is a court of original jurisdiction that handles claims against the United States for money damages. A person who believes that the government has not paid a bill for goods or services may sue here. Its headquarters are in Washington, D.C., but it hears cases throughout the country. The Circuit Court of Appeals for the Federal Circuit hears any appeals from the Claims Court.

The Tax Court and the Appeals Court for the Armed Forces

Congress established the Tax Court in 1969 to hear cases from citizens who disagree with the Internal Revenue Service or other Treasury Department agencies about their federal taxes. Based in Washington, D.C., it can hear cases all over the United States. A federal court of appeals handles appeals cases.

The U.S. Court of Appeals for the Armed Forces was established in 1950; it is the armed forces' highest appeals court. It hears appeal cases of members of the armed forces convicted of breaking military law. This court is sometimes called the "GI Supreme Court." The U.S. Supreme Court can review the decisions of this court.

Territorial Courts

Congress has created a territorial court system for the Virgin Islands, Guam, the Northern Mariana Islands, and Puerto Rico. These courts are roughly similar to district courts in how they operate. They handle civil and criminal cases, and constitutional cases. Appeals from this system are heard by the U.S. Courts of Appeals.

Courts of the District of Columbia

Because the District of Columbia is a federal district, Congress has developed a judicial system for the nation's capital. Along with a federal district court and a court of appeals, various local courts handle both civil and criminal cases that need to be heard within the District of Columbia.

C **Critical Thinking**

Synthesizing Ask students to differentiate between constitutional and legislative courts. **Ask:** Which court would handle each of the following cases?

a. A man challenges an IRS ruling disallowing a deduction on his tax return. *(legislative court, Tax Court)*

b. The man above loses his case and appeals. *(constitutional court, court of appeals)*

c. A woman is arrested for robbery in Washington, D.C. *(legislative court, District of Columbia courts)*

d. A man challenges the denial of a patent. *(constitutional court, court of appeals)* **OL**

The Law *and* You

Serving on a Jury

If you are registered to vote or have a driver's license, you may be called for jury duty. To serve on a jury you must be a U.S. citizen, at least 18 years old, understand English, and never have been convicted of a felony.

If you are summoned for jury duty, you must respond since failure to do so is a crime. Once you are called, you become part of a jury pool—actual jurors are selected during the voir dire, a Latin-based term that refers to a questioning process conducted by the attorneys for each side, or the judge. The goal of the voir dire is to eliminate anyone whose knowledge or personal views might prevent them from deciding the case only on the evidence presented in court. Although it is possible to be excused from jury duty for certain reasons, it is an important responsibility of American citizenship.

Suspect John Allen Muhammad, listening to his lawyers as they make their final juror selections in the 2002 case of sniper ◀ killings in the Washington, D.C. area.

Exploring the Law Activity

Interview a Juror Find people from your school or city who have been jurors. Ask them about their experiences and then report your findings to the class.

CHAPTER 11: *The Federal Court System* **315**

The Law *and* You

Jury Duty In some states, jurors serve for a given length of time and must report to the courthouse each day or until they have been chosen for a jury. In some states, jurors who are not chosen on the first day are dismissed and do not have to report to the courthouse again. Most states set a limit on how often people may be called to serve on a jury.

Differentiated Instruction

Jury Selection

Participating in Government Activities, p. 21

Objective: Find out how juries are selected in your local trial court.

Focus/Teach: Have students do research and answer the questions in the activity.

Assess: Have students summarize the information in a written report.

Close: Discuss the strengths and weaknesses of jury trials.

Differentiated Instruction Strategies

BL Interview someone who has served on a jury.

AL Analyze statistics about the strengths and weaknesses of jury trials.

ELL Discuss the reasons why a person might be excluded from a jury and whether students think those reasons are fair.

CURRICULUM CONNECTION

Law In the United States and other countries whose legal systems are based on English common law, an accused person is presumed innocent until proven guilty. In countries whose legal systems are based on Roman law, an accused person is presumed guilty. The principle of presumed innocence balances the rights of the accused and the accuser. On the accuser's side stand law enforcement officials, the court system, and law-abiding citizens. The accused stands alone but, if presumed innocent, has equal rights under the law.

Critical Thinking

Answer: The percentages are strongly correlated to the party of the president in office.

Additional Support

The Court of Appeals for Veterans

In 1988 Congress created the United States Court of Appeals for Veterans to hear appeals from the Board of Veterans' Appeals in the Department of Veterans Affairs. This court handles cases arising from unsettled claims for benefits and other veterans' problems.

Foreign Intelligence Surveillance Court

Congress created this court in 1978 as part of the Foreign Intelligence Surveillance Act (FISA). The FISA court operates in secret. It consists of a panel of federal judges who govern the process of eavesdropping on citizens and foreigners inside the United States in national security cases. The law has been amended many times, in part to keep up with changes created by cell phones, e-mails, and the Web. Originally it required intelligence services like the CIA or FBI to get a warrant from the FISA Court within 72 hours after wiretapping began. Starting in 2007, federal agents were allowed under certain circumstances to intercept phone calls and e-mails without a FISA Court warrant.

Selection of Federal Judges

Article II, Section 2, of the Constitution provides that the president, with the advice and consent of the Senate, appoints all federal judges. The legal profession regards a position on the federal bench as recognition of a lawyer's high standing in the profession. Judges in the constitutional courts serve for life. A life term grants judges freedom from public or political pressures when deciding cases.

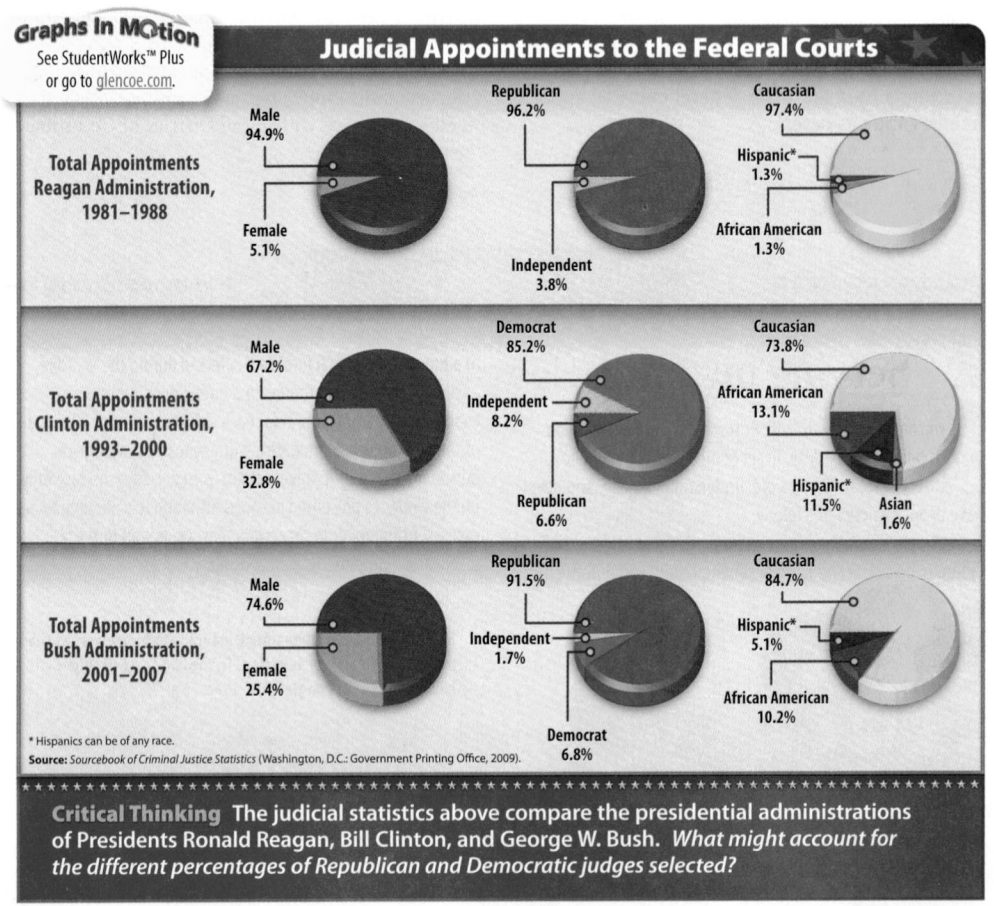

Graphs In Motion See StudentWorks™ Plus or go to glencoe.com.

Judicial Appointments to the Federal Courts

Total Appointments Reagan Administration, 1981–1988
- Male 94.9%
- Female 5.1%
- Republican 96.2%
- Independent 3.8%
- Caucasian 97.4%
- Hispanic* 1.3%
- African American 1.3%

Total Appointments Clinton Administration, 1993–2000
- Male 67.2%
- Female 32.8%
- Democrat 85.2%
- Independent 8.2%
- Republican 6.6%
- Caucasian 73.8%
- African American 13.1%
- Hispanic* 11.5%
- Asian 1.6%

Total Appointments Bush Administration, 2001–2007
- Male 74.6%
- Female 25.4%
- Republican 91.5%
- Independent 1.7%
- Democrat 6.8%
- Caucasian 84.7%
- Hispanic* 5.1%
- African American 10.2%

* Hispanics can be any race.
Source: *Sourcebook of Criminal Justice Statistics* (Washington, D.C.: Government Printing Office, 2009).

Critical Thinking The judicial statistics above compare the presidential administrations of Presidents Ronald Reagan, Bill Clinton, and George W. Bush. *What might account for the different percentages of Republican and Democratic judges selected?*

★ ★ Activity: Interdisciplinary Connection ★ ★

Language Arts Have students choose a biography of a Supreme Court justice or of another person in the legal profession. After reading the biography, students should prepare a book report presenting highlights, interesting facts or trivia, level of reading difficulty, and an evaluation of the author's style. The language arts teacher might have a style guide for book reports that students can follow. One possible biography is *America's First Woman Lawyer: The Biography of Myra Bradwell* by Jane M. Friedman. **OL**

Party Affiliation

Presidents favor judges who belong to their own political party. In recent years, the percentage of appointed federal judges who belong to the president's party has ranged from 81 percent in the case of President Gerald Ford's appointments to a high of 95 percent in President Jimmy Carter's case.

Another factor that emphasizes the political nature of court appointments is the power of Congress to increase the number of judgeships. Studies have shown that when one party controls both the presidency and Congress, it is more likely to increase the number of judicial posts. When President John F. Kennedy was elected in 1960, the Democratic Congress immediately passed a new omnibus judgeship bill creating 71 new positions for the president to fill.

Judicial Philosophy

Because judges are appointed for life, presidents view judicial appointments as a means of perpetuating their political views even after they have left office. This has made judicial appointments a political issue rather than a matter of assessing a judicial candidate's qualifications. Voters are strongly divided on controversial issues, such as abortion rights, marriage rights, and affirmative action. They put enormous pressure on presidents and senators to select and approve judges who will agree with them on key constitutional issues.

Senatorial Courtesy

In naming judges to trial courts, presidents customarily follow the practice of **senatorial courtesy.** Under the senatorial courtesy system, a president submits the name of a judicial candidate to the senators from the candidate's state before submitting it for formal Senate approval. If either or both senators oppose the nominee, the president usually withdraws the name and nominates another candidate.

The practice of senatorial courtesy applies only to the selection of judges for district courts and other trial courts. It is not followed for nominations to the courts of appeals and the Supreme Court because those appointments are for judicial positions with a much wider area of responsibility than just one state.

The Background of Federal Judges

Almost all federal judges have had legal training and have held a variety of positions in law or government including service as law school professors, members of Congress, leading attorneys, and federal district attorneys. More than one-third of district court judges have served as state court judges.

Until very recently, few women, African Americans, and Latinos were appointed as judges in the lower federal courts. President Jimmy Carter did much to change this situation in his court appointments. President Lyndon Johnson appointed Thurgood Marshall, the first African American justice to the Supreme Court. President Ronald Reagan appointed Sandra Day O'Connor, the first female justice to the Supreme Court.

SECTION 2 Review

Vocabulary

1. **Explain** the significance of: grand jury, indictment, petit jury, judicial circuit, senatorial courtesy.

Main Ideas

2. **Summarizing** What two major divisions of federal courts has Congress created?

3. **Describing** In what two ways do political parties influence the federal court system?

Critical Thinking

4. **Demonstrating Reasoned Judgment** Judges who share a president's views on various issues when they are first appointed may change their views when making decisions on the bench. Why?

5. **Organizing** Use a graphic organizer like the one shown to identify the three options a court of appeals has when deciding a case.

Court of Appeals

Writing About Government

6. **Political Processes** Review the criteria used by presidents to appoint federal judges. Develop any additional criteria that you think should be used for nominating judges. Prepare the criteria in the form of a checklist.

W Writing Support

Persuasive Writing Have students write a paragraph stating their position on life tenure for federal judges. **OL**

R Reading Strategy

Predicting **Ask:** What is the practice of senatorial courtesy? What might happen to judicial nominations if this practice were not followed? *(Nominees for judgeships would be rejected more frequently by the Senate.)* **OL**

Assess

Assign the Section 2 Assessment as homework or as an in-class activity, or have students take Section Quiz 11-2 from *Section Quizzes and Chapter Tests.*

Close

Evaluating **Ask:** What qualifications do you think a judge should have? *(Answers might include honesty, moral fiber, excellent education, legal experience, and so on.)* **OL**

Section 2 Review

Answers

1. The terms are defined in the Glossary and in the section.
2. constitutional courts and legislative courts
3. Presidents choose mainly members of their own party for judges; when one party controls the presidency and Congress, Congress often increases the number of judgeships.
4. People's views sometimes change over time, and because justices are appointed for life, they often have plenty of time to change their opinions. Also, because of their lifetime tenure, judges enjoy independence from political pressures.
5. uphold the original decision, reverse the decision, send the case back to the lower court
6. Call on students to present their checklists and compile a class checklist of criteria for appointing judges.

Focus

S₁ Skill Practice

Researching Issues Have students review the quotes in the Verbatim section and discuss each item as it relates to the people and themes found in their textbooks. Have students research a current or historical issue pertaining to the Supreme Court and its justices. Have them create a list of quotations about the issue along with a brief statement explaining the quote, identifying the person who is quoted, and describing how the quote relates to the issue. Ask students to share their lists in a class discussion. **OL**

Teach

C Critical Thinking

Making Connections Have students research information on Moses, Confucius, and Solon and then write a paragraph explaining why each of these figures is depicted on the pediment on the east side of the Supreme Court Building. Students may also include explanations of other figures or symbolism that is incorporated into the building's design. **AL**

Differentiated Instruction

TIME NOTEBOOK

VERBATIM   MILESTONES

WHAT PEOPLE SAID

❝I guess this is the end of our friendship.❞
President Lyndon Johnson *to Thurgood Marshall, after saying he was going to appoint Marshall to the Supreme Court, in 1967*

❝Women's equality under the law does not effortlessly translate into equal participation in the legal profession.❞
Sandra Day O'Connor, *first female Supreme Court justice, in 1985* **S**

❝[Those who won our independence] believed that freedom to think as you will and to speak as you think are means indispensable to the discovery and spread of political truth. . . .❞
Justice Louis D. Brandeis, *from his opinion in* Whitney v. California, *in 1927*

❝Why, to improve my mind.❞
Retired Supreme Court Justice **Oliver Wendell Holmes, Jr.,** *then 92, in response to Franklin Roosevelt's question about why he was reading Plato in the Greek language, in 1933*

ASSEMBLED, FEBRUARY 2, 1790. The **FIRST MEETING** of the U.S. Supreme Court justices took place in New York City one day later than originally planned because Chief Justice John Jay was delayed by transportation problems. At the time, there were six justices. In 1869 the number was settled permanently at nine.

SETTLED IN, OCTOBER 7, 1935. **THE SUPREME COURT** moved into its current building. For the previous 145 years, the Court had moved from building to building, sharing space with other government agencies.

SWORN IN, OCTOBER 2, 1967. THURGOOD MARSHALL became the first African American to be sworn in as a justice of the Supreme Court.

SUPREME HANDSHAKE, LATE 1800S. CHIEF JUSTICE MELVILLE FULLER started the tradition of having each Supreme Court justice shake hands with the other eight justices before the start of a private conference where decisions are discussed. It serves as a reminder that the justices are unified in purpose even if they have differences of opinion. **S**

Evan Vucci/AP Images

318 **UNIT 4:** *The Judicial Branch*

★ Activity: Multiple Learning Styles ★

Visiting a Court Although a visit to the U.S. Supreme Court Building probably will not be practical for most classes, it might be possible to visit your state's high court. Have students prepare for the trip by learning what they can from the local library and other resources. If students will be able to see the court in session or hear the reading of a decision, have them research the case ahead of time. After the trip, students should write a report summarizing what they saw and learned. **OL**

DECIDING OUR FUTURE

DOES SEGREGATION—AND ITS corresponding ideas of "separate but equal"—contradict the tenets of the Constitution? This hotly debated question came to the U.S. Supreme Court in the case of *Brown* v. *Board of Education*. On May 17, 1954, Chief Justice Earl Warren delivered the decision of the Court. Here is part of what he said:

"Today, education is perhaps the most important function of state and local governments. Compulsory school attendance laws and the great expenditures for education both demonstrate our recognition of the importance of education to our democratic society. It is required in the performance of our most basic public responsibilities, even service in the armed forces. It is the very foundation of good citizenship. Today it is a principal instrument in awakening the child to cultural values, in preparing him for later professional training, and in helping him to adjust normally to his environment. In these days, it is doubtful that any child may reasonably be expected to succeed in life if he is denied the opportunity of an education. Such an opportunity, where the state has undertaken to provide it, is a right which must be made available to all on equal terms.

"We come then to the question presented: Does segregation of children in public schools solely on the basis of race, even though the physical facilities and other 'tangible' factors may be equal, deprive the children of the minority group of equal educational opportunities? We believe that it does."

Index Stock Imagery/Photolibrary

A SLICE OF JUSTICE

The Supreme Court cannot hear all the cases that are brought before it—there's not enough time. Here's how the numbers break down:

5,000
Approximate number of cases the Court is petitioned to review each year.

250
Approximate number of cases it actually hears.

25
Approximate number of cases that come to the Court on appeal, such as when a state or lower federal court declares a federal law unconstitutional.

CORBIS

NUMBERS

9 The number of Supreme Court aides, who run errands and deliver mail. There is one aide for each justice.

2nd The floor where Ruth Bader Ginsburg chose to have her chambers because her room there is larger than those of the rest of the justices who have chambers on the first floor.

Najlah Feanny/CORBIS

0 The number of term limits imposed on a justice (as long as he or she exhibits "good behavior").

188 The number of seats open to the public in the visitors' section to watch public oral arguments. Seating is on a first-come, first-served basis.

5 The number of minutes left for a lawyer making oral arguments before the Supreme Court to wrap up his or her argument once a small white light on the lectern turns on.

$94,000 The amount returned to the U.S. Treasury upon the completion of the Supreme Court building, which cost less than the $9,740,000 Congress had authorized for its construction.

Extending the Content

The *Brown* Case Some misconceptions persist today regarding the landmark *Brown* case. Oliver Brown, on behalf of his daughter Linda, was not the only plaintiff in the case. *Brown* v. *Board of Education* came before the Supreme Court as a combination of five cases from around the country, representing almost 200 plaintiffs. Another myth is that Brown's name was used in the *Topeka* case because it came first alphabetically among the 13 *Topeka* plaintiffs. In fact, legal strategists wanted to have a man at the top of the roster, and Oliver Brown was the only male plaintiff.

Focus

Reader's Guide

Answers to Graphic:

Characteristics of Justices:

- a law degree and considerable legal experience
- experience as a judge or attorney general
- usually age 50 or older
- usually upper socioeconomic background
- usually native-born

Qualifications for Presidential Choices:

- same party affiliation
- share the president's views

Resource Manager

The Supreme Court

Reader's Guide

Content Vocabulary	**Academic Vocabulary**	**Reading Strategy**
★ riding the circuit *(p. 320)* ★ opinion *(p. 322)*	★ unconstitutional *(p. 321)* ★ violated *(p. 321)* ★ objectivity *(p. 322)*	As you read, create a table similar to the one below to identify the characteristics of most Supreme Court justices and the qualifications presidents look for when nominating justices.

Characteristics of Justices	Qualifications for Presidential Choices

People in the News

In *Riegel v. Medtronic, Inc.* (2008), the U.S. Supreme Court ruled that individuals cannot sue manufacturers of medical devices that were approved by the Food and Drug Administration (FDA). It was an 8 to 1 decision, but Justice Ruth Bader Ginsburg, the single dissenter, showed the independence typical of Supreme Court justices. She argued that FDA approval should not stand in the way of people being paid for injuries from devices later found to be unsafe. Ginsburg believed it is the job of the Court to "pass on controversies, to see that matters are settled peacefully . . . and that people don't settle their differences by . . . coming to blows."

▲ Justice Ruth Bader Ginsburg views the Court's role as seeing "that matters are settled peacefully."

Ruth Bader Ginsburg and the other eight justices of the Supreme Court are at the top of the American legal system. Article III of the Constitution created the Supreme Court as one of three coequal branches of the national government, along with Congress and the president.

The Supreme Court is the court of last resort in all questions of federal law. The Court is not required to hear all cases presented before it, and it carefully chooses the cases it will consider. It has final authority in any case involving the Constitution, acts of Congress, and treaties with other nations. Most of the cases the Supreme Court hears are appeals from lower courts. The decisions of the Supreme Court are binding on all lower courts.

Nomination to the Supreme Court today is a very high honor. It was not always so. Several of George Washington's nominees turned down the job. Until 1891, justices earned much of their pay while **riding the circuit,** or traveling to hold court in their assigned regions. One justice, after a painful stagecoach ride in 1840, wrote to his wife:

> ❝ *I think I never again, at this season of the year, will attempt this mode of journeying. . . . I have been elbowed by old women—jammed by young ones—suffocated by cigar smoke—sickened by the vapours of bitters and w[h]iskey—my head knocked through the carriage top by careless drivers and my toes trodden to a jelly by unheeding passengers.* ❞
> —Justice Levi Woodbury, 1840

Today the Court hears all its cases in the Supreme Court building in Washington, D.C., in a large, first-floor courtroom that is open to the public. Nearby is a conference room where the justices meet privately to discuss and decide cases.

R **Reading Strategies**	**C** **Critical Thinking**	**D** **Differentiated Instruction**	**W** **Writing Support**	**S** **Skill Practice**
Teacher Edition • Taking Notes, p. 321 • Making Connections, p. 324 **Additional Resources** • Quizzes/Tests, pp. 133–140 • Guid. Read. Act., p. 41	**Teacher Edition** • Drawing Conclusions, p. 322 • Determining Cause and Effect, p. 323 **Additional Resources** • Read. Essen., pp. 123–125 • Reteaching Act., p. 11	**Teacher Edition** • Visual/Spatial, p. 325 **Additional Resources** • Foldables, p. 54 • Coop. Learning Act., pp. 7–8	**Teacher Edition** • Expository Writing, p. 321 **Additional Resources** • Inter. Poli. Cartoons, pp. 21–22 • Supreme Ct. Case Studies, pp. 115–116	**Teacher Edition** • Creating a Time Line, p. 322 • Drawing a Circle Graph, p. 326 **Additional Resources** • Ch. Summaries, pp. 31–33 • Am. Biographies, p. 68

Supreme Court Jurisdiction

The Supreme Court has both original and appellate jurisdiction. Article III, Section 2, of the Constitution sets the Court's original jurisdiction.[1] This article and section address two types of cases: (1) cases involving representatives of foreign governments, and (2) certain cases in which a state is a party. Congress is not permitted to expand or curtail the Court's original jurisdiction.

Many original jurisdiction cases have involved two states or a state and the federal government. When Maryland and Virginia argued over oyster fishing rights, and when a dispute broke out between California and Arizona over the control of water from the Colorado River, the Supreme Court had original jurisdiction.

The Supreme Court's original jurisdiction cases form a very small part of its yearly workload—an average of fewer than five such cases per year. Most of the cases the Court decides fall under the Court's appellate jurisdiction—appellate comes from the word *appeal*. Under its appellate jurisdiction, the Court hears cases appealed from lower courts of appeals, or it may hear cases from federal district courts where an act of Congress was held **unconstitutional.**

The Supreme Court can also hear cases appealed from the highest court of a state if claims under federal law or the Constitution are involved.

In such cases, however, the Supreme Court has the authority to rule only on the federal issue involved, not on issues of state law.

For example, suppose that a state court tried a person charged with violating a state law. Yet during the trial, the accused claimed that the police **violated** his or her Fourteenth Amendment rights by illegally searching his or her home at the time of the arrest. This defendant could appeal to the Supreme Court on this particular constitutional issue. The Supreme Court would have no jurisdiction for ruling on the state issue—whether the accused actually violated state law. The Court would decide only whether Fourteenth Amendment rights were violated.

Supreme Court Justices

The Supreme Court is comprised of nine justices: the chief justice of the United States and eight associate justices. Congress sets this number and has the power to change it. Over the years it has varied from 5 to 10, but it has been 9 since 1869. In 1937 President Franklin D. Roosevelt attempted to gain greater control of the Court by asking Congress to increase the number of justices. Congress refused, in part because the number 9 was well established.

📖 See the following footnoted materials in the **Reference Handbook:**
1. The Constitution, pages R42–R67.

The Highest Court in the Land

Judicial Ideals The nine justices meet regularly in the Supreme Court building in Washington, D.C. Architect Cass Gilbert worked in the style of a classical Greek temple to blend with nearby buildings. Marble from Georgia, Vermont, and Italy was used in the building, completed in just three years in 1935. *Why do you think court buildings are built with such impressive architecture?*

CHAPTER 11, SECTION 3
★★★★★★★★★★★★★★★★★★★★★★★★

Teach

R Reading Strategy

Taking Notes Have students make a chart of Supreme Court jurisdiction with the headings "Original Jurisdiction" and "Appellate Jurisdiction." **BL**

W Writing Support

Expository Writing Organize the class into small groups, and assign each group one or more of the most influential Supreme Court justices, such as John Marshall, Benjamin Cardozo, Hugo Black, William O. Douglas, Earl Warren, or Thurgood Marshall. Have students prepare biographical sketches including birthplace, education, experience, ethnic origin, and famous opinions. Some students in each group should do the research and writing, and others can act as editors and illustrators. **OL**

Caption Answer: to reflect the value society places upon the law

Additional Support

Extending the Content

The Court-Packing Plan In March 1937, President Franklin D. Roosevelt sent Congress a bill to increase the number of justices on the Supreme Court. It proposed that if any justice had served for 10 years and did not retire within six months after reaching the age of 70, the president could appoint an additional justice. Since four justices were in their 70s and two more were in their late 60s, the bill, if passed, would allow FDR to appoint as many as six new justices.

The court-packing plan, as the press called it, was FDR's first serious political mistake. Although Congress had the power to change the Court's size, the scheme created the impression that the president was trying to undermine the Court's independence.

Despite the uproar, FDR's actions appeared to force the Supreme Court to back down. In April 1937, the Court upheld the constitutionality of the Wagner Act by a vote of five to four. In May, the Court narrowly upheld the Social Security Act.

In mid-July the Senate quietly killed the court-packing bill without bringing it to a vote.

The Justices of the Supreme Court

Ruth Bader Ginsburg | **John Paul Stevens** | **Stephen Breyer** | **David Hackett Souter**

Interpreters of the Law U.S. Supreme Court justices are pictured from left to right to suggest where they stand politically compared to one another. Justices on the right side of the spectrum tend to vote more conservatively, while justices to the left tend to vote more liberally. *Why are citizens interested in which president gets to nominate justices to the Supreme Court?*

In 2008 the eight associate justices received annual salaries of $208,100. The chief justice was paid a salary of $217,400. Congress sets the justices' salaries, and it may not reduce them.

Under the Constitution, Congress may remove Supreme Court justices through impeachment for and conviction of "treason, bribery, or other high crimes and misdemeanors." No Supreme Court justice has ever been removed from office through impeachment, however. The House of Representatives impeached Justice Samuel Chase in 1804 because of his participation in partisan political activities, but the Senate found him not guilty.

Duties of the Justices

The Constitution does not describe the duties of the justices. Instead, the duties have developed from laws, through tradition, and as the needs and circumstances of the nation have developed. The main duty of the justices is to hear and rule on cases. This duty involves them in three decision-making tasks: deciding which cases to hear from among the thousands appealed to the Court each year; deciding the case itself; and determining an explanation for the decision, called the Court's **opinion.**

The chief justice has several additional duties. The person filling this position must preside over sessions and conferences at which the justices discuss cases. The chief justice assigns the writing of the Court's opinion to one of the justices who voted for the ruling. The chief justice also helps administer the federal court system.[1]

The justices also have limited duties related to the 12 federal judicial circuits. One Supreme Court justice is assigned to each federal circuit. Three of the justices handle two circuits each. The justices are responsible for requests for special legal actions that come from their circuit.

In 1980, for example, a lower federal court ruled against the federal government's program of draft registration. Lawyers for the federal government then requested that the Supreme Court temporarily set aside the lower court's decision. The Supreme Court justice who was responsible for the federal judicial circuit in which the issue arose heard this request.

Occasionally, justices might take on other duties if their workload permits. In 1945 Justice Robert Jackson was the chief prosecutor at the Nuremberg trials of Nazi war criminals. In 1963 Chief Justice Earl Warren headed a special commission investigating President Kennedy's assassination.

To maintain their **objectivity** on the bench, justices are careful not to become involved in any activities that might prevent them from dealing fairly with one side or the other on a case. If justices have any personal or business connection with either of the parties in a case, they usually disqualify themselves from participating in that case.

*See the following footnoted materials in the **Reference Handbook:***
1. *Leaders of Government,* page R11.

Activity: Multiple Learning Styles

Logical/Mathematical Have students use the 2010 U.S. Census to find out what percentage of the population is made up of women, African Americans, Asian Americans, Native Americans, and Latino Americans. Then have students describe the makeup of the Supreme Court if justices were representative of the population. For example, if 12 percent of the population is African American, then the Court would need one African American justice. Students will find that some groups, such as Native Americans, are too small to be represented in a Court of only nine justices. Have students suggest ways of getting around that problem—increase the size of the Court, combine ethnic groups, and so on. **AL**

Anthony Kennedy

Chief Justice John Roberts

Samuel Alito

Antonin Scalia

Clarence Thomas

Date of Appointment and Appointing President

1975, John Paul Stevens (Ford)	1990, David Souter (G.H.W. Bush)	1994, Stephen Breyer (Clinton)
1986, Antonin Scalia (Reagan)	1991, Clarence Thomas (G.H.W. Bush)	2005, John Roberts (G.W. Bush)
1988, Anthony Kennedy (Reagan)	1993, Ruth Bader Ginsburg (Clinton)	2006, Samuel Alito (G.W. Bush)

Law Clerks

In 1882 Justice Horace Gray hired the first law clerk—mainly to be his servant and barber. Today the Court's law clerks assist the justices with many tasks, enabling the justices to concentrate on their pressing duties. Law clerks read all the appeals filed with the Court and write memos summarizing the key issues in each case. When cases are decided, the clerks help prepare the Court's opinions by doing research and sometimes writing first drafts of the opinions.

The justices each hire a few law clerks from among the top graduates of the nation's best law schools. These young men and women usually work for a justice for one or two years. After leaving the Court, many clerks go on to distinguished careers as judges, law professors, and even become Supreme Court justices, too.

Background of the Justices

Throughout the Court's history, more than 100 men and 2 women have served as justices. What sort of people become the top judges in the nation? Although it is not a formal requirement, a justice usually has a law degree and considerable legal experience. Most justices have been state or federal court judges, or have held other court-related positions such as attorney general. One former president, William Howard Taft, served as chief justice. Younger people are not usually appointed to the Court. Most of the justices selected in the twentieth century were

in their fifties when they were appointed to the Court. Ten were younger than 50, and the remainder were more than 60 years old.

Justices have not been representative of the general population in social class, background, gender, and race. Most justices have come from upper socioeconomic levels. To date, only two African American justices, Thurgood Marshall and Clarence Thomas, and only two women, Sandra Day O'Connor and Ruth Bader Ginsburg, have been appointed to the Court.

The Constitution does not require justices to be native-born Americans. Six Supreme Court justices have been born outside the United States. Of these, three were appointed by George Washington.

Appointing Justices

Justices reach the Court through appointment by the president with Senate approval. The Senate usually grants such approval, and presidents with strong support in the Senate are less likely to have their candidates rejected, but there is no guarantee. The Senate even chose to reject one of President Washington's nominees. During the nineteenth century, more than 25 percent of the nominees failed to win Senate approval. By contrast, during the early part of the twentieth century, the Senate was much more supportive of presidential choices. More recently, the Senate rejected two of President Nixon's nominees and

C Critical Thinking

Determining Cause and Effect Ask: What societal and political pressures were at play when Thurgood Marshall and Sandra Day O'Connor were appointed to the Supreme Court? *(The movement for civil rights in the 1950s and 1960s resulted in the appointment of Marshall. The women's movement of the seventies led to the appointment of O'Connor.)* OL

ISSUES to Debate

Composition of the Court Organize the class into groups to debate the question of whether the composition of the Supreme Court should represent the composition of the United States in terms of ethnicity, geography, and gender. Before debating the issue, each student should list at least two arguments in support of his or her position. Then ask groups to meet to combine their lists and choose the strongest arguments. OL

Differentiated Instruction

Leveled Activities

ELL Interpreting Political Cartoons, p. 21

BL Skill Reinforcement Activities, p. 11

OL Cooperative Learning Activities, p. 7

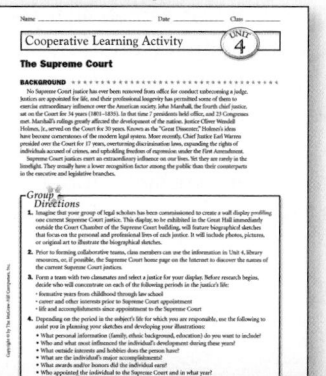

AL Historical Documents and Speeches, p. 11

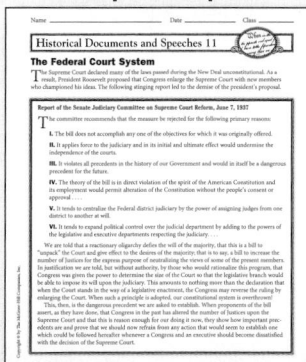

323

R Reading Strategy

Making Connections Earl Warren became chief justice in 1953. During the following year, the Supreme Court handed down a landmark decision that signaled that the Warren Court would be liberal and activist. **Ask:** What landmark case did the Supreme Court rule on in 1954? (Brown *v.* Board of Education of Topeka) Inform students that President Eisenhower, who nominated Warren, never strongly endorsed the *Brown* ruling publicly; in private, he expressed concern that forced desegregation would provoke massive resistance and violence in the South. **OL**

Making a Difference

Reneé Askins Biologists monitoring wildlife in Yellowstone National Park have found that the park's canine hierarchy is changing. Since their reintroduction, wolves have accounted for scores of coyote deaths. Specialists expect wolves and coyotes to survive, but no one knows how a reduced coyote population will affect the park's ecosystem.

Additional Support

President Reagan's nomination of Robert Bork in 1988. The Senate closely scrutinized Justice Clarence Thomas's nomination in 1991 but finally accepted the nomination by a vote of 52 to 48.

As with lower court judges, political considerations often affect a president's choice of a nominee to the Court. Usually presidents will choose someone from their own party, sometimes as a reward for faithful service to the party. But presidents must be careful to nominate people who are likely to be confirmed by the Senate.

President Clinton had to decide among several choices in 1994. Bruce Babbitt was thought to be the likely nominee. However, Babbitt had some powerful enemies among Western senators because of his decisions as secretary of the interior. So the president chose a federal judge, Stephen Breyer, who had friends among Democrats and Republicans. He was a safe choice and was easily confirmed.

In 2005 President George W. Bush nominated his chief counsel Harriet Miers to fill the seat of retiring justice Sandra Day O'Connor. Opposition to Miers began to build from several groups: those who thought she did not have enough experience in constitutional law and those who thought she was not conservative enough on abortion. Miers withdrew

when it looked as if she would not get Senate approval. Ultimately Samuel Alito, a judge with conservative views, was approved to fill the vacancy.

Presidents prefer to nominate candidates whose political beliefs are similar to their own. However, several presidents have discovered that it is difficult to predict how an individual will rule on issues once he or she becomes a member of the Court. After securing the nomination of Tom Clark, President Harry S. Truman expressed his displeasure:

> 66 *Tom Clark was my biggest mistake. No question about it. . . . I don't know what got into me. He was no . . . good as Attorney General, and on the Supreme Court . . . he's been even worse. He hasn't made one right decision that I can think of.* 99
>
> —Harry S. Truman

R When President Dwight Eisenhower named Earl Warren as chief justice in 1953, he expected Warren to continue to support the rather conservative positions he had taken as governor of California. Under Warren's leadership, however, the Court began an era of unprecedented liberal decisions.

Making a Difference

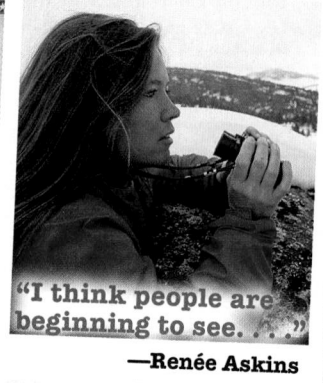

"I think people are beginning to see. . . ."
—Reneé Askins

Wildlife ecologist Reneé Askins has been a leader in the fight to reintroduce the gray wolf into Yellowstone National Park. This fight has been going on for some time. By the 1930s, all the wolves in Yellowstone had been killed. In 1973 the Endangered Species Act required the federal government to reintroduce the wolf. Ranchers and farmers went to court to stop the program, fearing that wolves would kill their livestock.

Askins looks at the issue very differently. "We exterminated the wolf to take control. I think people are beginning to see we've taken too much control," she said. In 1986 she created the Wolf Fund in Moose, Wyoming, to raise money and support.

In 1995 a federal judge refused ranchers' requests and a small number of wolves were released in the park and in Idaho. Then, in 1997, a district court in Wyoming ordered that the wolves be removed. Due to an appeal, the wolves were allowed to remain. Finally, on January 13, 2000, Denver's 10th Circuit Court of Appeals overturned the lower court ruling so the wolves, by that time numbering more than 300, were allowed to remain. Courts and legislatures continue to battle over this issue.

Extending the Content

Sandra Day O'Connor Sandra Day O'Connor was named an associate justice of the U.S. Supreme Court by President Ronald Reagan in 1981. Until the appointment of Ruth Bader Ginsburg in 1993, she was the only woman to serve on the Court. O'Connor was a lawyer, an assistant attorney general, a state senator, and a court of appeals judge, all in Arizona, before being named to the high court. She occasionally dealt with her isolation on the bench with humor. In 1991 during a prison-rights case hearing, a lawyer representing Louisiana said to the justices, "I would like to remind you gentlemen of an important legal point." Leaning forward, O'Connor responded, "Would you like to remind me, too?"

Selecting Justices

Political Processes
President George W. Bush (left) chose John Roberts, Jr., to serve as chief justice in 2005 when the sitting chief justice, William Rehnquist died. Roberts, joined here by his wife, Jane, and Justice John Paul Stevens, is the youngest chief justice to be appointed in two centuries. *Why is the age of a new appointee important to the nation?*

How does the president go about identifying and choosing candidates to the Court? The president usually turns to the attorney general and other Justice Department officials for advice. In turn, the attorney general consults with the legal community. The attorney general then comes up with a list of candidates for the president. In making the final selection, the president and the attorney general may also check with leading members of Congress. In addition, they hear from several different groups that have a special interest in the selection of a justice.

In 1932 faculty members of the nation's leading law schools, labor and business leaders, judges, and senators all urged Republican President Herbert Hoover to appoint Democrat Benjamin Cardozo to the Supreme Court. Cardozo was chief judge of the New York Court of Appeals. The support for Cardozo was so great that Hoover nominated Cardozo, who was confirmed without opposition.

The American Bar Association's Role

The American Bar Association (ABA) is the largest national organization of attorneys. Since 1952, the ABA's Committee on the Federal Judiciary has been consulted by every president concerning almost every federal judicial appointment. The role of the ABA is solely to evaluate the professional qualifications of candidates for all Article III judicial positions—the Supreme Court, the United States Courts of Appeals, and the United States District

Courts. The committee rates nominees as either "well qualified," "qualified," or "not qualified." The ABA rating is advisory, and neither the president nor the Senate is required to follow it. In 2001 President George W. Bush attempted to reduce the ABA's role, arguing that it is a liberal-oriented organization that plays too large a part in the confirmation process. Democrats, on the other hand, contend that the ABA provides a fair appraisal of candidates.

The Role of Other Interest Groups

Interest groups that have a stake in Supreme Court decisions may attempt to influence the selection process. Generally, these groups make their positions on nominees known through their lobbyists, or agents, and the media. Strong opposition to a nominee by one or more major interest groups may influence the senators who vote on the nominee.

Labor unions, for example, may oppose a nominee if the nominee's previous court decisions or writings suggest an antilabor outlook. Similarly, the National Organization for Women (NOW) or the National Right to Life might oppose a nominee based upon a nominee's interpretation of *Roe* v. *Wade*,[1] the historic case that sets down the conditions under which a woman can legally obtain an abortion. 📖

📖 *See the following footnoted materials in the* **Reference Handbook:**
1. *Roe* v. *Wade* case summary, page R33.

CHAPTER 11: *The Federal Court System* **325**

D Differentiated Instruction

Visual/Spatial Have students work in pairs to create a word web showing factors that can influence the selection of a nominee for the Supreme Court. They can write *Influencing Factors* in the center oval. Have them discuss why or how each factor might influence a president's choice. **ELL** **BL**

Participating IN GOVERNMENT

Qualifications of Federal Judges As a class, brainstorm a list of qualifications that the ideal federal judge might possess. Critique the list and pare it down to a reasonable number of attributes. Discuss why qualifications are important. **OL**

Hands-On Chapter Project

Step 3

Debating Judicial Activism

Step 3: Reflecting on the Issue

Directions Have each student write a paragraph that identifies his or her opinion about judicial activism and explains why it was important to define the meaning of the phrase before beginning the debate.

Evaluating Follow up this activity by having students locate news reports on a recent court decision. Have students cut out or copy the article and write a report about the ruling in which they explain why it is an example of either judicial activism or judicial restraint. **AL**

In recent years, interest groups have looked closely at the attitudes of potential justices to *Roe v. Wade.* This occurred in 2005 when President George W. Bush nominated John Roberts as the new chief justice of the United States, and Harriet Miers and Samuel Alito as associate justices. (Miers withdrew her candidacy, partly as a result of pressures related to her position on abortion.) Civil rights groups are also usually active during the selection process. Groups such as the National Association for the Advancement of Colored People (NAACP) and the National Organization for Women carefully examine nominees' views on racial integration and women's rights.

Although presidents have withdrawn nominees who were unpopular, most of those actually nominated have won Senate approval. A study by the Congressional Research Service reported that between 1789 and 2004, only 34 failed to win nomination out of a total of 154 nominations. In the twentieth century, 6 nominees failed to win confirmation.

The Role of the Justices

Members of the Supreme Court sometimes have considerable influence in the selection of new justices. As leaders of the Court, chief justices have often been very active in the selection process. Justices who must work with the newcomers often participate in selecting candidates. They may write letters of recommendation supporting candidates who have been nominated, or they may lobby the president for a certain candidate.

Three-Way Contest During George W. Bush's presidency, the legal status of suspected terrorists detained at Guantanamo prison ("Gitmo" in the cartoon) was in dispute for several years. Did prisoners have the right to challenge their detention in federal courts? Could the president and Congress create special military courts to try them? *What does the cartoonist imply about the attitude of Congress?*

William Howard Taft, who was chief justice between 1921 and 1930, intervened frequently in the nominating process. Chief Justice Warren Burger suggested the name of Harry Blackmun, who was ultimately confirmed. Knowing a member of the Court personally helped Sandra Day O'Connor. She received a strong endorsement from former law school classmate Justice William Rehnquist in 1981.

SECTION 3 Review

Vocabulary

1. **Explain** the significance of: riding the circuit, opinion.

Main Ideas

2. **Describing** Under what conditions can a case be appealed from a state court to the Supreme Court?

3. **Summarizing** In your opinion, should politics influence the selection of Supreme Court justices? Explain.

Critical Thinking

4. **Understanding Cause and Effect** Supreme Court justices have often been active in the selection of new justices. Do you think this is appropriate? Explain your answer.

5. **Organizing** Use a graphic organizer like the one below to identify two kinds of cases where the Supreme Court has original jurisdiction and two kinds that may be appealed from a state court.

Original	Appeal

Writing About Government

6. **Descriptive Writing** Prepare a script for an imaginary interview with a Supreme Court justice. The script should cover questions related to the justice's personal and professional background, the justice's outlook on the Court's role in society, and the justice's position on a few important political or social issues.

Creating Multimedia Presentations

Multimedia presentations combine several media, such as text, photographs, illustrations, animation, diagrams, videos, or sound recordings. Most multimedia presentations are now created on computers, using graphic tools, drawing and animation programs, and authoring systems that tie everything together. They are often created using multimedia software such as PowerPoint®, combined with MP3 downloads, DVDs, podcasts, Web casts, or other media.

Why Learn This Skill?

A multimedia presentation enables you to teach, tell a story, persuade people, or make points by using the media most appropriate to your purpose. Use the following steps when creating a multimedia presentation:

1. Decide on the topic you want to cover and which points you want to make.

2. Organize the information using an outline or graphic organizer.

3. Determine what media equipment is available to you. What computer software can you use?

4. Decide which medium is most appropriate for each point you are making (ex: video, sound, animation, text, photographs, or graphics).

5. Create your presentation and then review it to make sure there are no factual or technical errors.

Practicing the Skill

Assume you are creating a multimedia presentation about a court case involving the rights of persons with disabilities, and answer these questions:

1. How could you personalize the case?

2. What would determine the media used for the presentation? Would the media be different if you were creating a biography?

3. Name three types of media that would effectively present the case. Explain your reasons for choosing them.

Applying the Skill

Choose a U.S. Supreme Court judge or case since 1900 and create a multimedia presentation on the topic. Use as many different media as possible. If you choose a judge, include his or her background and opinions on major cases. If you choose a court case, explain its background, the issues involved, and the Court's ruling. Show your presentation to the class.

Teach

S Skill Practice

Utilizing Multimedia Students are becoming increasingly accustomed to using multimedia options. Point out that using multimedia resources not only makes classes more interesting, but also will help students as they enter the workplace.

Be prepared to demonstrate some media applications. For example, you might find an audio file online of a famous congressional speech or show some presidential campaign commercials on YouTube. **Ask:** What are some possible forms of media that could be used in a multimedia presentation? *(Answers might include PowerPoint® with embedded audio and/or video files, YouTube, DVDs, MP3 downloads, podcasts, Web casts, and so on.)*

You also may bring in a team teacher or guest speaker to demonstrate the development of multimedia presentations on a computer. If necessary, schedule computer lab time so students can sample software they might use to build their presentations. **OL**

Answers

Practicing the Skill

1. Answers will vary but may include using photographs, video, or recorded interviews with people who will be affected by the Court's ruling.

2. The media used would depend on the content of the presentation. If students are able to procure interviews, video or audio files would be appropriate. Students can also create a photo slideshow when relevant.

3. Answers will vary but should demonstrate an understanding of why the media suggested would be effective.

Applying the Skill

Presentations should incorporate a variety of media and should address a Supreme Court justice or case thoroughly.

Reviewing Vocabulary

1.–7. Sentences will vary. The terms are defined in the sections and the Glossary.

Reviewing Main Ideas

8. federal courts and state courts

9. judicial review—the power to review acts of Congress, executive actions, and state laws against the Constitution to see what might violate constitutional provisions

10. The grand jury hears charges against a person suspected of having committed a crime, decides whether there is sufficient evidence and, if so, issues an indictment.

11. cases dealing with tariffs

12. A life term permits judges to be more insulated from political pressures.

13. deciding which cases to hear, deciding individual cases, determining an explanation for the decision of the Court

14. Any three: hearing and ruling on cases, presiding over public sessions of the Court, exercising leadership in judicial work of the Court, administering the federal court system

Critical Thinking

15. The court in which a case is originally tried has original jurisdiction. A court that

---

CHAPTER

11 Assessment and Activities

Reviewing Vocabulary

Define each of the following content vocabulary word(s) and use it in a sentence.

1. concurrent jurisdiction
2. appellate jurisdiction
3. litigant
4. grand jury
5. indictment
6. petit jury
7. riding the circuit

Chapter Summary

Lower Federal Courts

Constitutional courts

★ Established by Congress under the provisions of Article III of the Constitution

★ Include federal district courts, federal courts of appeals, and United States Court of International Trade

Legislative courts

★ Created by Congress under provisions in Article I of the Constitution to help Congress carry out its powers

★ Include United States Tax Court, U.S. Court of Appeals for the Armed Forces, Court of Appeals for Veterans, and others

The Supreme Court

★ Original jurisdiction in cases involving representatives of foreign countries and certain cases in which a state is a party

★ Appellate jurisdiction in cases that are appealed from lower courts of appeals or from a state's highest court, as well as certain cases from federal district courts in which an act of Congress was held unconstitutional

★ Justices appointed by president with Senate approval

Development of Supreme Court Power

★ 1801–1883: Marshall Court extended power of Supreme Court and strengthened federal power over the states

★ 1803: *Marbury* v. *Madison* established power of judicial review

★ 1953–1969: Warren Court adopted a more liberal view on civil rights and public-policy issues

---

Reviewing Main Ideas

Section 1 *(pp. 305–310)*

8. **Listing** What are the two systems of courts in the United States?

9. **Describing** What principle resulted from the ruling in *Marbury* v. *Madison*?

Section 2 *(pp. 312–317)*

10. **Examining** What are the duties of a grand jury in a criminal case?

11. **Identifying** What kinds of cases are heard by the Court of International Trade?

12. **Stating** Why do federal judges serve for life?

Section 3 *(pp. 320–326)*

13. **Describing** What are the three decision-making tasks of a Supreme Court justice?

14. **Classifying** What are three duties of the chief justice of the United States?

Critical Thinking

15. **Essential Question** What is the difference between courts with original jurisdiction and courts with appellate jurisdiction?

16. **Defending** If the issue is whether a person's civil rights were violated in a court decision, through what levels of courts might that person appeal?

17. **Evaluating** Federal district judges generally represent the values of the states they serve. How can a president assure appointees meet this criterion?

18. **Identifying** Use a graphic organizer to identify two solutions for the Court's high caseload. Explain.

Solution 1	Solution 2

19. **Synthesizing** What factors determine whether a case will be tried in a state court or a federal court?

20. **Analyzing** When the Supreme Court rules on an appeal from a state court, what restriction applies to the Court's ruling?

---

hears an appeal of a trial court ruling has appellate jurisdiction.

16. federal district court, federal courts of appeals, Supreme Court

17. The president first submits the candidate's name to the senators from the candidate's state in a practice called senatorial courtesy.

18. Solution 1: Hire more clerks to do everyday tasks. This would give the justices more time to make important decisions; Solution 2: Limit the number of cases.

This may limit the Court's influence and be unfair to many applicants.

19. The subject matter of a case and the parties involved; examples might include: subject—interpretation of the Constitution, a federal law, a treaty with a foreign nation; parties might include: ambassadors, two or more state governments, citizens of different states

20. The Court may rule only on the issue involving the Constitution or a federal law. The Court cannot rule on a state law.

Government ONLINE Self-Check Quiz
Visit glencoe.com and enter QuickPass™ code USG9822c11.
Click on Self-Check Quizzes for additional test practice.

CHAPTER
11
Assessment
and Activities

Document-Based Questions

Analyzing Primary Sources

Read the excerpt below and answer the questions that follow.

Chief Justice Thurgood Marshall was the first African American to serve on the Supreme Court (1967–1991). Prior to this, he was the legal director of the NAACP. This excerpt, from a 1981 speech to the American Bar Association, details Marshall's ideas about the purpose of the Supreme Court.

❝ *But the framers of the Constitution recognized that responsiveness to the will of the majority might, if unchecked, become a tyranny of the majority. They therefore created a third branch—the judiciary—to check the actions of the legislature and the executive. In order to fulfill this function, the judiciary was intentionally isolated from the political process and purposely spared the task of dealing with changing public concerns and problems. . . . Finally, the constitutional task we are assigned as judges is a very narrow one. We cannot make laws, and it is not our duty to see that they are enforced. We merely interpret them through the painstaking process of adjudicating actual 'cases or controversies' that come before us.*

We have seen what happens when the courts have permitted themselves to be moved by prevailing political pressures and have deferred to the mob rather than interpret the Constitution. Dred Scott, Plessy, Korematsu, and the trial proceedings in Moore v. Dempsey, *come readily to mind as unfortunate examples.* ❞

21. What, in Marshall's opinion, is the purpose of the Supreme Court? What is the Court not allowed to do?

22. What does Marshall believe will happen to the Court if it does allow itself to become affected by the changing moods of public opinion?

Interpreting Political Cartoons

Analyze the cartoon and answer the questions that follow. Base your answers on the cartoon and your knowledge of Chapter 11.

ED FISCHER

"okay—fair is fair... you can help select judges— pick one"

www.cartoonstock.com

23. Why has the cartoonist made the nominees to the Supreme Court identical in appearance?

24. The Constitution states that the president nominates justices for vacancies to the Supreme Court and the U.S. Senate has the power of confirming them. What does the cartoonist imply about the nomination process at the time the cartoon was created?

Participating IN GOVERNMENT

25. Using your local library or the Internet, research the kinds of courts located in or near your community. Find out the following:

- Are they part of the federal or state system?
- Where are the nearest federal district courts located?
- Where is the nearest appeals court located?

After gathering this information, create a "court directory" map of your community area and share your findings with the class.

Interpreting Political Cartoons

23. The cartoonist is insinuating that all Supreme Court nominees are essentially the same—none of them has an advantage over any other one.

24. that the executive branch and the opposing party in the Senate are not inclined to compromise in the process of naming new justices to the Court

Participating IN GOVERNMENT

25. Students should accurately answer the questions concerning the location of courts.

Chapter Bonus Test Question

Ask: Who was the only chief justice to have been impeached by the House but acquitted by the Senate? *(Samuel Chase in 1804)*

Analyzing Primary Sources

21. According to Marshall, the Court cannot make laws; it can only interpret them. Also, the Court is not supposed to pander to public opinion or enforce the laws. Students might also mention that the Court's function includes balancing the will of the majority against the rights of the minority, and it also serves as a check on the legislative and executive branches.

22. Marshall believes that the Court's opinions can become tainted and that the Court might eventually begin to interpret the Constitution to serve the needs of public opinion rather than remaining impartial. When this happens, he believes that the Court interprets the laws incorrectly, and he cites examples like *Plessy* v. *Ferguson* (legalized segregation) or *Korematsu* (which allowed the incarceration of Japanese Americans during World War II) to show how deferring to public opinion can be harmful to the Supreme Court's powers and rulings.

329

Key to Ability Levels

- **BL** Below level
- **OL** On level
- **AL** Above level
- **ELL** English Language Learners

Key to Teaching Resources

- 📁 Print Material
- 💿 CD-ROM or DVD
- 🖨 Transparency

Levels (BL / OL / AL / ELL)		Resources	Chapter Opener	Section 1	Section 2	Section 3	Chapter Assess
FOCUS							
BL OL AL ELL	🖨	Section Focus Transparencies		12-1	12-2	12-3	
TEACH							
BL OL ELL	📁	Reading Essentials and Study Guide (and Answer Key)		p. 126	p. 129	p. 132	
BL OL ELL	📁	Guided Reading Activities		p. 42	p. 43	p. 44	
BL OL ELL	📁	Vocabulary Activities				p. 12	
BL OL AL ELL	📁	Chapter Summaries				p. 33	
BL OL	📁	American Biographies					
BL OL AL ELL	📁	Cooperative Learning Activities					
OL AL ELL	📁	Government Simulations and Debate			p. 22		
BL OL AL ELL	📁	Historical Documents and Speeches		p. 12			
BL OL AL ELL	📁	Interpreting Political Cartoons			p. 23		
BL OL ELL	📁	Skill Reinforcement Activities		p. 12			
BL OL AL ELL	📁	Source Readings			p. 12		
BL OL	📁	Supreme Court Case Studies			pp. 1, 11, 13, 73, 99, 103		
BL OL AL ELL	📁	Participating in Government Activities				p. 23	
BL OL ELL	📁	Spanish Declaration of Independence and U.S. Constitution	✓	✓	✓	✓	✓
BL OL AL ELL	📁	NGS World Atlas, Spanish	✓	✓	✓	✓	✓
BL OL AL ELL	🖨	Unit Overlay Transparencies, Strategies, and Activities	✓	✓	✓	✓	✓
BL OL ELL	🖨	Making It Relevant Transparencies	✓	✓	✓	✓	✓
BL OL AL ELL	🖨	High School Writing Process Transparencies, Strategies, and Activities	✓	✓	✓	✓	✓
BL OL AL	🖨	American Art & Architecture Transparencies, Strategies, and Activities	✓	✓	✓	✓	✓

✓ Chapter- or unit-based activities applicable to all sections in this chapter

All-In-One Planner and Resource Center

- Interactive Lesson Planner
- Interactive Teacher Edition
- Fully editable blackline masters
- Chapter Spotlight Videos Launch

- Differentiated Lesson Plans
- Printable reports of daily assignments
- Standards tracking system

Levels					Resources	Chapter Opener	Section 1	Section 2	Section 3	Chapter Assess
BL	OL	AL	ELL							
TEACH *(continued)*										
BL	OL			💿	American Music: Hits Through History	✓	✓	✓	✓	✓
BL	OL		ELL	📁	Reading Strategies for the Social Studies Classroom	✓	✓	✓	✓	✓
			ELL	📁	English Language Learner Handbook	✓	✓	✓	✓	✓
BL	OL		ELL	📁	Writer's Guidebook for Social Studies	✓	✓	✓	✓	✓
BL	OL	AL	ELL	📁	Living Constitution, SE	✓	✓	✓	✓	✓
BL	OL	AL	ELL	📁	Living Constitution, TAE	✓	✓	✓	✓	✓
BL	OL			📁	NGS World Atlas, English	✓	✓	✓	✓	✓
BL	OL		ELL	📁	The Constitution and You (poster set)	✓	✓	✓	✓	✓
BL	OL	AL	ELL	📁	Spanish Chapter Summaries				p. 33	
BL	OL	AL	ELL	📁	Spanish Vocabulary Activities				p. 12	
BL	OL		ELL	📁	Spanish Reading Essentials and Study Guide (and Answer Key)		p. 126	p. 129	p. 132	
BL	OL	AL	ELL	💿	PresentationPlus! with MindJogger CheckPoint	✓	✓	✓	✓	✓
ASSESS										
BL	OL	AL	ELL	💿	*ExamView® Assessment Suite*		12-1	12-2	12-3	Ch. 12
BL	OL	AL	ELL	📁	Authentic Assessment with Rubrics		p. 19			p. 19
BL	OL	AL	ELL	📁	Section Quizzes and Chapter Tests		p. 141	p. 142	p. 143	pp. 145–152
BL	OL	AL	ELL	📁	Spanish Section Quizzes and Tests		p. 141	p. 142	p. 143	pp. 145–152
CLOSE										
BL			ELL	📁	Reteaching Activities				p. 12	p. 12
BL	OL	AL	ELL	💿	StudentWorks™ Plus with Audio Summaries	✓	✓	✓	✓	✓
BL	OL		ELL	🖌	Graphic Organizer Transparencies		✓	✓	✓	
BL	OL		ELL	📁	High School Government Reading and Study Skills Foldables®		p. 55	p. 55	p. 55	

Teach With Technology

What is *ExamView® Assessment Suite?*
Glencoe's *ExamView® Assessment Suite* is a powerful assessment tool that enables you to create and customize tests for your students. Tests can be either printed or administered online.

How can *ExamView® Assessment Suite* help me?
ExamView® allows you to create your own test questions or choose from existing, fully editable banks of questions customized for this book. Question formats include true/false, multiple choice, completion, matching, short answer, and essay, and many questions are based on documents, maps, or graphs. Each question includes reteach information where students can go for more help on the topic. The flexibility of *ExamView®* allows you to develop testing materials that:

- focus on specific skills or competencies
- address state or national standards
- are leveled for different abilities
- can be translated to Spanish in one click

ExamView® Assessment Suite is one of Glencoe's technology resources available for teachers.

Government ONLINE
Visit glencoe.com and enter *QuickPass*™ code USG9085c12T for Chapter 12 resources.

You can easily launch a wide range of digital products from your computer's desktop with the McGraw-Hill Social Studies widget.

	Student	Teacher	Parent
Media Library			
• Student Edition Section Audio	●		●
• Chapter Spotlight Videos	●	●	●
***United States Government* Online Learning Center (Web Site)**			
• Chapter Overviews	●	●	●
• Multilingual Glossaries	●	●	●
• Study-to-Go	●	●	●
• Student Web Activities	●	●	●
• Self-Check Quizzes	●	●	●
• Online Student Edition	●	●	●
• Vocabulary eFlashcards	●	●	●
• Web Activity Lesson Plans		●	
• Vocabulary PuzzleMaker	●	●	●
• Landmark Supreme Court Cases	●	●	●
• Beyond the Textbook	●	●	●

READING SUPPORT FROM JAMESTOWN EDUCATION

- **Timed Readings Plus in Social Studies** helps students increase their reading rate and fluency while maintaining comprehension. The 400-word passages are similar to those found on state and national assessments.

- **Reading in the Content Area: Social Studies** concentrates on six essential reading skills that help students better comprehend what they read. The book includes 75 high-interest nonfiction passages written at increasing levels of difficulty.

- **Reading Social Studies** includes strategic reading instruction and vocabulary support in Social Studies content for ELLs and native speakers of English. www.jamestowneducation.com

Reading List Generator CD-ROM

GLENCOE BookLink 3

Use this database to search more than 30,000 titles to create a customized reading list for your students.

- Reading lists can be organized by students' reading level, author, genre, theme, or area of interest.

- The database provides Degrees of Reading Power™ (DRP) and Lexile™ readability scores for all selections.

- A brief summary of each selection is included.

Leveled reading suggestions for this chapter:

- *America's Courts on Trial: Questioning Our Legal System,* by Elaine Pascoe

- *The Supreme Court,* by Ann E. Weiss

- *The Supreme Court of the United States,* by David Heath

Review suggested books before assigning them.

Economics Connection

Personal Finance Literacy

Renting an Apartment

The U.S. Supreme Court heard cases on rent laws as early as 1921, when the Court ruled that an emergency must exist for there to be a legal basis for rent control (a ruling amended in 1934 to "rational basis"). Today, renting an apartment is still not a simple process, but following some basic steps can save time and money, and lead to a more pleasant renting experience.

1. **Calculate the total cost:** Along with rent, tenants usually pay for heat, air conditioning, electricity, and sometimes water. Many landlords expect the first and last months' rent in advance, plus a security deposit they hold until tenants move. If the tenant damages the property, the deposit is used to pay for repairs. Tenants may want to obtain renter's insurance for any expensive items.

2. **Make basic decisions:** Figure out how close you want to live to school or a job, if you will have roommates, how much space you need, and what else is important to you, such as security, noise, level, light, storage, nearby shopping, or laundry facilities.

3. **Gather information:** Begin your search with friends, newspaper ads, the Internet, bulletin boards, and/or rental agencies. Before making appointments to see several apartments, be sure you have identification, your Social Security number, proof of income and employer's name and phone number, and contact numbers for references.

4. **Walk through:** Before signing a rental agreement, visit the apartment with the landlord. Take dated photos of anything in disrepair. Most cities have a tenants' rights organization to assist renters with landlord disputes.

5. **Clarify roommate arrangements:** If you will have roommates, make a clear agreement about what happens if one of you moves out, and have all roommates sign the rental agreement. Remember that, if there is a lease, the person whose name is on the lease is responsible for paying the rent for the duration of the lease—even if that person moves out before the lease period has ended.

Did You Know?

It is illegal for landlords to discriminate because of race, disability, color, gender, religion, familial status, or national origin. To learn more about your rights as a tenant, you may want to join a local tenants union.

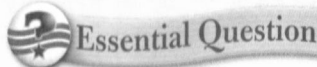

Essential Question

Some cases are first heard in the Supreme Court because they fall under its original jurisdiction. Most cases, however, are selected from writs of certiorari or appeals. The Court is influenced by briefs, oral arguments, and conferences.

Chapter Spotlight Video

To generate student interest and provide a springboard for class discussion, access the Chapter 12 Video at glencoe.com or on the video DVD.

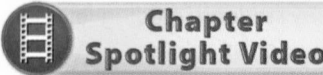

Dinah Zike's Foldables are three-dimensional, interactive graphic organizers that help students practice basic writing skills, review key vocabulary terms, and identify main ideas. Have students complete this chapter's Foldable activity or activities in *Dinah Zike's Reading and Study Skills Foldables* booklet. **OL**

Government ONLINE

Visit glencoe.com and enter *QuickPass*™ code USG9085c12T for Chapter 12 Resources including Chapter Overview, Student Web Activity, Self-Check Quiz, and other materials for students and teachers.

CHAPTER

12

🔊 Chapter Audio   📽 Spotlight Video

Supreme Court Decision Making

The Supreme Court building

Essential Question

How do cases come before the Supreme Court, and what factors influence the decisions the Court makes?

Government ONLINE
Chapter Overview Visit glencoe.com and enter *QuickPass*™ code USG9822c12 for an overview, a quiz, and other chapter resources.

330 UNIT 4: *The Judicial Branch*

Launching the Chapter

Drawing Conclusions Before Chief Justice John Roberts, Jr., was appointed to the Supreme Court, the average age of the justices was 70. Roberts, age 50, replaced William Rehnquist, age 80, who died after serving 33 years on the Court. Before 1970, a justice on the Supreme Court served, on average, about 15 years. Since 1970, the average has increased to about 25 years. Some people question whether there should be term limits for Supreme Court justices, claiming that the Framers of the Constitution did not intend for anyone to hold such a powerful office for such a long time. **Essential Question:** Should there be term limits for Supreme Court justices? *(Prompt students to explain their opinions.)* **OL**

The Supreme Court at Work

Reader's Guide

Content Vocabulary
★ writ of certiorari *(p. 332)*
★ per curiam opinion *(p. 333)*
★ brief *(p. 333)*
★ amicus curiae *(p. 333)*
★ majority opinion *(p. 335)*
★ dissenting opinion *(p. 335)*

Academic Vocabulary
★ periodic *(p. 331)*
★ accompany *(p. 332)*
★ initial *(p. 335)*

Reading Strategy
Use a flowchart similar to the one below to list the steps that the Supreme Court uses to decide major cases.

☐ → ☐ → ☐ → ☐

Focus

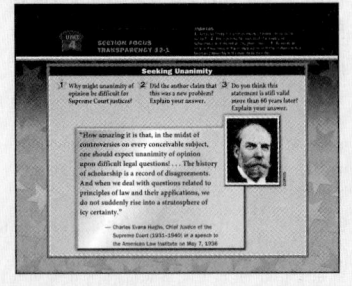

Bellringer
Section Focus Transparencies 12-1

Reader's Guide

Answers to Graphic:
submitting briefs →
oral arguments →
the conference →
writing the opinion

Public Policy in the News

In 2008 the U.S. Supreme Court was still considering damages to be paid from the oil spill from *Exxon Valdez,* a 1989 accident that occurred off the Alaskan coast. Exxon Mobil is urging the Court to reverse a lower court's ruling that the company should pay a total of $2.5 billion to Alaskan fishers, cannery workers, and other groups affected by the spill. By running aground on a reef, the tanker released 11 million gallons of oil into Prince William Sound. The oil spread over 1,500 miles of shoreline and killed thousands of birds, fish, and other sea animals. Commercial fisher Tom Copeland said his family business has never recovered and that Exxon Mobil "needs to get told they need to be a better corporate citizen."

▲ Rescue workers in Prince William Sound

The *Exxon Valdez* case is just one example of Supreme Court cases that have a major impact on American society. Traditionally, the Court met for about nine months each year. Each term began the first Monday in October and ran for as long as business demanded. Since 1979, however, the Court has been in continuous session, taking only **periodic** recesses. The 2007 term began in October and did not adjourn until the first Monday in October 2008.

The Court's Procedures

During the term, the Court sits for two consecutive weeks each month. At these sittings, the justices listen to oral arguments from lawyers for each side.

Later they announce their opinions. The Court hears oral arguments from Monday through Wednesday. On Wednesdays and Fridays the justices meet in secret conferences to decide cases.

After a two-week sitting, the Court recesses and the justices work privately on paperwork. They consider arguments in cases they have heard and study petitions from plaintiffs who want the Court to hear their cases. They also work on opinions—written statements on cases they have already decided.

More than 8,800 cases were appealed to the Supreme Court in 2006. However, the Court has time to grant review to only about 1 percent of these cases. The Court may decide several hundred cases, but it gave full hearings and signed opinions in only 83 cases in 2000. That number

R Reading Strategies	**C** Critical Thinking	**D** Differentiated Instruction	**W** Writing Support	**S** Skill Practice
Teacher Edition • Using Context Clues, p. 332	**Teacher Edition** • Analyzing, p. 333 • Evaluating, p. 334	**Additional Resources** • Foldables, p. 55 • Hist. Docs. and Speeches, p. 12	**Teacher Edition** • Expository Writing, p. 335	**Teacher Edition** • Reading a Graph, p. 332
Additional Resources • Quizzes/Tests, p. 141 • Guid. Read. Act., p. 42	**Additional Resources** • Read. Essen., pp. 126–128		**Additional Resources** • Authentic Assess., p. 19	**Additional Resources** • Skill Reinforce Act., p. 12

Teach

S Skill Practice

Reading a Graph **Ask:** What is the approximate percentage of signed opinions compared to the number of cases appealed in 2005? In 1995? In 1985? In 1955? *(0.7%, 1%, 2.8%, 10%; students should divide the number of signed opinions by the number of cases.)* What is the general trend in the number of cases that have been appealed since 1955? *(The number of cases that are appealed has increased.)* **OL**

R Reading Strategy

Using Context Clues What is a synonym for *docket*? *(caseload, agenda, calendar)* **OL**

Additional Support

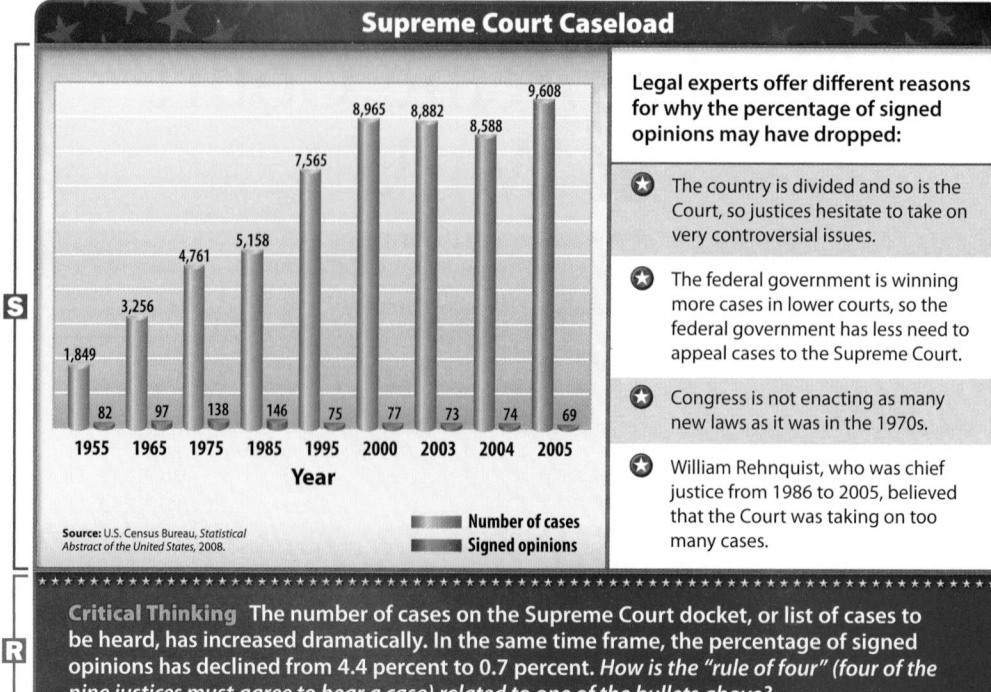

Supreme Court Caseload

Legal experts offer different reasons for why the percentage of signed opinions may have dropped:

⭐ The country is divided and so is the Court, so justices hesitate to take on very controversial issues.

⭐ The federal government is winning more cases in lower courts, so the federal government has less need to appeal cases to the Supreme Court.

⭐ Congress is not enacting as many new laws as it was in the 1970s.

⭐ William Rehnquist, who was chief justice from 1986 to 2005, believed that the Court was taking on too many cases.

Source: U.S. Census Bureau, *Statistical Abstract of the United States,* 2008.

■ Number of cases
■ Signed opinions

Critical Thinking The number of cases on the Supreme Court docket, or list of cases to be heard, has increased dramatically. In the same time frame, the percentage of signed opinions has declined from 4.4 percent to 0.7 percent. *How is the "rule of four" (four of the nine justices must agree to hear a case) related to one of the bullets above?*

dropped to 67 cases by 2006. In the opinions that **accompany** this small number of cases, the Court sets out general principles that apply to the nation as well as to the specific parties in the case. It is mainly through these cases that the Court interprets the law and shapes public policy.

Getting Cases to the Court

Some cases begin at the Supreme Court because they fall under its original jurisdiction. The vast majority of cases, however, reach the Supreme Court only as appeals from lower court decisions. These cases come to the Supreme Court in one of two ways—by **writ of certiorari** or on appeal.

Writ of Certiorari

The main route to the Supreme Court is by a writ of certiorari (suhr • shee • uh • RAR • ee)—an order from the Court to a lower court to send up the records on a case for review. The party seeking review petitions the Court for certiorari and must argue either that the lower court made a legal error

in handling the case or that the case raises a significant constitutional issue.

The Supreme Court is free to choose which cases it will consider, and it rejects more than 90 percent of requests for certiorari. Denial of certiorari does not necessarily mean that the justices agree with the lower court's decision. Instead, they may see the case as not being important enough to the public welfare to reconsider. Whatever the reason, when the Court denies certiorari, the lower court's decision stands.

On Appeal

Certain cases reach the Court on appeal, meaning that a request has been made to review the decision of a lower federal or state court. In most cases, an appeal results from instances in which a lower court has ruled a law unconstitutional or dismissed the claim that a state law violates federal law or the Constitution.

Few cases actually arrive on appeal, and the Court dismisses many of them. The Court will generally dismiss a case if it has procedural defects or does not involve federal law. When a case is dismissed, the decision of the lower court becomes final.

Activity: Collaborative Learning

Holding a Mock Appeal Have the class conduct a mock Supreme Court appeal. Select a case from the *Supreme Court Case Studies* booklet to provide background for the appeal. Have nine students serve as justices and others assist them as law clerks. Organize the remainder of the class into plaintiff and

defense teams to prepare written briefs for the Court. On hearing day, give a spokesperson for each team 15 minutes to present its case. Allow the justices to interrupt with questions and challenges. Before the justices rule, have all students write opinions. **OL**

The Solicitor General

Close to half of the cases decided by the Supreme Court involve the federal government in the suit. The solicitor general is appointed by the president and represents the federal government before the Supreme Court. The solicitor general serves as a link between the executive branch and the judicial branch. Presidents expect the solicitor general to support the administration's views on legal questions.

The solicitor general plays a key role in setting the Court's agenda by determining whether the federal government should appeal lower federal court decisions to the Supreme Court. Lawyers on the solicitor general's staff do most of the research for Supreme Court cases that involve the federal government. This staff also prepares written and oral arguments to support the government's position on the case.

Selecting Cases

Justice William O. Douglas once called the selection of cases "in many respects the most important and interesting of all our functions." When petitions for certiorari come to the Court, the justices or their clerks identify cases worthy of serious consideration, and the chief justice puts them on a "discuss list" for all the justices to consider.

Almost two-thirds of all petitions for certiorari never make it to the discuss list. At the Court's Friday conferences, the chief justice reviews the cases on the discuss list. Then the justices—armed with memos from their clerks, other information on the cases, and various law books—give their views. In deciding to accept a case, the Court operates by the "rule of four." If four of the nine justices agree to accept the case, the Court will do so.

When the justices accept a case, they also decide whether to ask for more information from the opposing lawyers or to rule quickly on the basis of written materials that are already available. If the Court rules without consulting new information, the ruling may be announced with a **per curiam** (puhr KYUR • ee • ahm) **opinion**—a brief, unsigned statement of the Court's decision.

Steps in Deciding Major Cases

The Supreme Court follows a set procedure when hearing important cases. Much of this activity goes on behind the scenes, with only a small part taking place in an open courtroom.

Submitting Briefs

After the Court accepts a case, the lawyers on each side of the case submit a **brief.** A brief is a written statement setting forth the legal arguments, relevant facts, and precedents supporting one side of a case.

Parties who are not directly involved in the case but who have an interest in its outcome may also submit written briefs. Called **amicus curiae** (uh • mee • kuhs KYUR • ee • eye)—or "friend of the court"—briefs, they come from individuals, interest

Clerking for the Court

Behind the Scenes
U.S. Supreme Court Justice Clarence Thomas (right) shares a relaxing moment with three of his law clerks in his chambers. Law school graduates compete strenuously to clerk for a Supreme Court justice. They gain invaluable experience by researching and making recommendations on cases on the Court's docket. *What is the "discuss list" and why is it important?*

C Critical Thinking

Analyzing Point out that the increasing workload of the Supreme Court has led to several proposals to change the structure of the Court. One proposal calls for a screening board to review the cases that are submitted to the Court and to select those that the Court should hear. Another recommends increasing the size of the Court's staff. Ask students to work individually or in groups to state and defend which proposal they prefer or to create proposals of their own. **OL**

Opinions of the Court Call on students to contrast majority opinion, concurring opinion, and dissenting opinion. **Ask:** Does the practice of publishing dissenting opinions demonstrate a weakness or a strength in the judicial system? **OL**

Caption Answer: It is the list that identifies cases that are worthy of serious consideration. It is from this list that the Supreme Court votes whether or not to hear a case.

Differentiated Instruction

Activity: Multiple Learning Styles

Visual/Spatial Have students create a flowchart to illustrate what happens to appeals cases that are submitted to the Supreme Court. *(Cases reach the Court on appeal or by writ of certiorari; cases are reviewed; some are accepted; most are rejected. Worthy cases are put on a "discuss list," and justices decide whether to accept them. About half of accepted cases are decided on the basis of written materials that are already available; the remaining cases receive full consideration. Lawyers' briefs and amicus curiae briefs are submitted, and oral arguments are presented. Justices study the case, discuss it, write opinions, and announce the decision.)* **BL**

C Critical Thinking

Evaluating Ask: What problems might a person have while defending himself or herself in court? (*A defendant might not know about proper court procedures, legal precedents, or the importance of various pieces of evidence.*) **BL**

We the People
Making a Difference

Clarence Gideon Justice Black reasoned that "Governments, both state and federal, quite properly spend vast sums of money to establish machinery to try defendants accused of crime. Lawyers to prosecute are everywhere deemed essential to protect the public's interest. . . ." That being the case, the right to counsel is a fundamental right for the defendant as well as the prosecution.

Activity: Gideon based his appeal on the Sixth Amendment as well as on the Fourteenth. Have students find the relevant wording in the Sixth Amendment. (*"In all criminal prosecutions, the accused shall enjoy the right to . . . have the Assistance of Counsel for his defense."*) **OL**

Hands-On Chapter Project

Step 1

---

groups, or government agencies claiming to have information they believed would be useful to the Court's consideration of the case. Sometimes the briefs present new ideas or information. More often, however, they are most useful for indicating which interest groups are on either side of an issue.

Oral Arguments

After briefs are filed, a lawyer for each side is asked to present an oral argument before the Court. Each side is allowed 30 minutes to summarize the key points of its case. Justices often interrupt the lawyer during his or her oral presentation, sometimes challenging a statement or asking for further information. The lawyer speaks from a lectern that has a red light and a white light. The white light flashes 5 minutes before the lawyer's time is up. When the red light comes on, the lawyer must stop talking immediately.

The Conference

On Wednesdays and Fridays the justices meet to discuss the cases they have heard. The nine justices come into the conference room and, by tradition, each shakes hands with the other eight. Everyone else leaves. Then one of the most secret meetings in Washington, D.C., begins.

For the next several hours, the justices debate the cases. No meeting minutes are kept. The chief justice presides over the discussion of each case and usually begins by summarizing the facts of the case and offering recommendations for handling it.

In the past, the justices discussed cases in detail. Today the Court's heavy caseload allows little time for debate. Instead, each decision gets about 30 minutes of discussion. Cases being considered for future review get about 5 minutes. The chief justice asks each associate justice, in order of seniority, to give his or her views and conclusions. Then the justices vote. Each justice's vote carries the same weight.

A majority of justices must be in agreement to decide a case, and at least six justices must be present for a decision. If a tie occurs, the lower court decision is left standing. The Court's vote at this stage, however, is not necessarily final.

We the People
Making a Difference

One morning in 1961, police officers arrested Clarence Earl Gideon for a burglary the previous night, despite his pleas of innocence. Gideon, a poor man, could not afford to hire a lawyer.

On August 4, Gideon's trial began in the Circuit Court of Bay County, Florida. Gideon addressed the judge, saying, "I request this court to appoint counsel to represent me." The judge explained that the Supreme Court had ruled that states must provide lawyers for poor people only if they were charged with serious crimes, like murder. Without a lawyer's help, Gideon was found guilty.

Gideon appealed his conviction, claiming, "I knew the Constitution guaranteed me a fair trial, but I didn't see how a man could get one without a lawyer to defend him." The state supreme court refused to review Gideon's case. Gideon appealed his case to the Supreme Court.

Although the jail had no resources, no law library or attorneys to consult, and not even a typewriter, Gideon studied law and pursued his goal. The justices finally agreed to let Gideon have his day in court.

In 1963 the Court ruled in Gideon's favor. Justice Hugo Black explained that the Fourteenth Amendment requires states to grant citizens those rights considered "fundamental and essential to a fair trial." Those who are too poor to hire their own attorneys must be provided one by the state. A book was written about Gideon's case.

C

"I knew the Constitution guaranteed me a fair trial. . . ."

—**Clarence Gideon**

A Day in Court

Step 1: Getting Started Begin by having students review and complete the questions for case study 31, *Endo* v. *United States,* in the *Supreme Court Case Studies* booklet. During a mock trial, students will assume the roles and responsibilities of the people who were involved in Mitsuye Endo's court case, starting at the district level and moving through the appeals court and ultimately to the U.S. Supreme Court.

Directions Divide the class into thirds. To each group assign one of the levels of federal courts. Explain that they will be working on Mitsuye Endo's case.

Setting a Purpose Tell groups to research the Executive Orders that Roosevelt enacted that made possible the internment of Mitsuye Endo. Groups will use this information in Section 2 to decide how they plan to present their case in court. **OL**

(Chapter Project continued in Section 2.)

Writing the Opinion

For major cases, the Court issues at least one written opinion. The opinion states the facts of the case, announces the Court's ruling, and explains its reasoning. These written opinions are as important as the decision itself. Not only do they set precedent for lower courts to follow in future cases, but they also are the Court's way to communicate with Congress, the president, and the public.

The Court issues four kinds of opinions. In a unanimous opinion, all justices vote the same way. About one-third of the Court's decisions are unanimous. A **majority opinion** expresses the views of the majority of the justices on a case. One or more justices who agree with the majority's conclusions about a case, but do so for different reasons, write a concurring opinion. A **dissenting opinion** is the opinion of justices on the losing side in a case. Because the Court sometimes does change its mind on issues, a dissenting opinion may even become the majority opinion on a similar issue many years later. Chief Justice Charles Evans Hughes expressed this in a frequently quoted defense of dissenting opinion:

Rules of the Court This secret photograph of the Supreme Court in session in 1935 may be the only photo ever taken during a case hearing before the Court. *Why might Supreme Court sessions be closed to cameras?*

> 66 *A dissent in a court of last resort is an appeal to the brooding spirit of the law, to the intelligence of a future day, when a later decision may possibly correct the error into which the dissenting judge believes the court to have been betrayed.* 99

If the chief justice has voted with the majority, he or she assigns someone in the majority to write the opinion. When the chief justice holds the minority opinion, the most senior associate justice among the majority assigns a justice to write the majority opinion. Since public policy established by a case will be guided by the majority opinion, chief justices often assign opinions in important cases to themselves. The law clerks for a justice usually help write a first draft of an opinion. Other justices may accept it, suggest revisions, or reject it.

When the justices do not accept the **initial** draft of a majority opinion, a bargaining process begins. New versions of the opinion may be written as justices try to influence one another. Weeks or even months may go by as the justices bargain and rewrite their opinions. Finally, the case is settled and the decision is announced during a sitting. All the while, the Court is selecting and hearing new cases.

W **Writing Support**

Expository Writing Have students select a case in which they disagree with the majority ruling from the Supreme Court Case Summaries in the *Reference Handbook.* Then have them write a dissenting opinion that explains why they believe the Court's ruling was incorrect or unjust. **AL**

Assess

Assign the Section 1 Assessment as homework or as an in-class activity, or have students take Section Quiz 12-1 from *Section Quizzes and Chapter Tests.*

Close

Theorizing Ask: If the Supreme Court were to reverse most of the lower court decisions it receives, what would be the effect on the American system of justice? **OL**

SECTION 1 Review

Vocabulary

1. **Explain** the significance of: writ of certiorari, per curiam opinion, brief, amicus curiae, majority opinion, dissenting opinion.

Main Ideas

2. **Describing** What steps does the Supreme Court take in selecting, hearing, and deciding cases?

3. **Listing** What are four kinds of Supreme Court opinions?

Critical Thinking

4. **Analyzing** Do you believe it is proper that the Court's deliberations are secret and that no minutes are kept? Explain.

5. **Identifying** Use a graphic organizer like the one below to identify the three ways cases reach the Supreme Court.

Writing About Government

6. **Expository Writing** Find out how many cases were sent to the Supreme Court in each of the past 10 years and the number of cases about which an opinion was issued. Write a short report summarizing what you learn.

Section 1 Review

CHAPTER 12: *Supreme Court Decision Making* **335**

Answers

1. All definitions can be found in the section and the Glossary.
2. Justices discuss cases and accept those involving important constitutional questions. The Court receives briefs, listens to lawyers' oral arguments, discusses the cases in private, votes on the cases, and writes opinions and its decisions.
3. majority opinion, dissenting opinion, unanimous opinion, and concurring opinion
4. Answers will vary. Students should cite the relationship between secrecy, judicial independence, and political or public pressure.
5. original jurisdiction, on appeal, writ of certiorari
6. Students should complete their research and submit a report detailing the results.

Focus

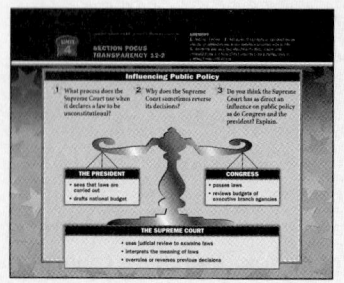
Reader's Guide

Answers to Graphic:

Decision must make a difference and cannot be advisory.

Real harm must be done.

The case must involve a federal question.

The case must not be about a strictly political question.

Resource Manager

Shaping Public Policy

Reader's Guide

Content Vocabulary

★ judicial review (p. 336)
★ impound (p. 337)
★ stare decisis (p. 338)
★ precedent (p. 338)
★ advisory opinion (p. 339)

Academic Vocabulary

★ policy (p. 336)
★ suspension (p. 337)
★ interpretation (p. 338)

Reading Strategy

As you read, create a graphic organizer similar to the one below to list the criteria the Court uses to decide which cases to hear.

> Criteria to Hear Cases

Public Policy in the News

In a unanimous decision, the Supreme Court has ruled that individual workers have the right to sue employers and recover losses when their 401(k) retirement accounts have been mishandled. The justices' action came in a case brought by James LaRue, who accused his employer, DeWolff, Boberg & Associates, of failing to make the investment changes he requested, resulting in a profit loss of $150,000. The question in the LaRue case was whether a federal law—the Employee Retirement Income Security Act—recovered money only for the "plan" or whether it also allowed participants to sue as individuals. The Court stated that, for individuals, such lawsuits are permitted under the act. Companies, the Court ruled, are in a position of trust and have a legal obligation to run a 401(k) plan in the best interest of individual participants.

▲ James LaRue with his wife

The Supreme Court is both a political and a legal institution. It is a legal institution because it is ultimately responsible for settling disputes and interpreting the meaning of laws. The Court is a political institution because when it applies the law to specific disputes, it often determines what national **policy** will be. For example, when the Court rules that certain provisions of the Social Security Act must apply to men and women equally, it is determining government policy.

Tools for Shaping Policy

Congress makes policy by passing laws. The president shapes policy by carrying out laws and by drawing up the national budget. As the Supreme Court decides cases, it determines policy in three ways. These include: (1) using **judicial review**, (2) interpreting the meaning of laws, and (3) overruling or reversing its previous decisions.

Under Chief Justice Earl Warren in the 1950s, the Court took a stand that was far in advance of public opinion. The cases seemed to contain more and more public policy. It seemed that the Court had become the agent of change that Justice Oliver Wendell Holmes, Jr., had envisioned in 1913:

> ❝ We too need education in the obvious—to learn to transcend our own convictions and to leave room for much that we hold dear to be done away with short of revolution by the orderly change of law. ❞
>
> —Justice Oliver Wendell Holmes, Jr.

R Reading Strategies	**C** Critical Thinking	**D** Differentiated Instruction	**W** Writing Support	**S** Skill Practice
Teacher Edition • Predicting, p. 341	**Teacher Edition** • Analyzing, p. 337	**Teacher Edition** • Kinesthetic, p. 337	**Teacher Edition** • Expository Writing, p. 340	**Teacher Edition** • Researching, p. 338
Additional Resources • Quizzes/Tests, p. 142 • Guid. Read. Act., p. 43	**Additional Resources** • Read. Essen., pp. 129–131	**Additional Resources** • Foldables, p. 55 • Source Readings, p. 12	**Additional Resources** • Gov. Sims. and Debates, pp. 22–28 • Supreme Ct. Case Studies, pp. 1–2, 11–12, 13–14, 73–74, 99–100, 103–104	**Additional Resources** • Inter. Poli. Cartoons, pp. 23–24

Judicial Review

The Supreme Court's power to examine the laws and actions of local, state, and national governments and to cancel them if they violate the Constitution is called judicial review. The Supreme Court first assumed the power of judicial review and ruled an act of Congress unconstitutional in the case of *Marbury* v. *Madison*[1] in 1803. 📖 Since then, the Court has invalidated about 150 provisions of federal law. This number may seem insignificant when compared to the thousands of laws Congress has passed, but when the Court declares a law unconstitutional, it often discourages the passage of similar legislation for years. In addition, some of these rulings have had a direct impact on the nation's future. For example, in the *Dred Scott*[2] case (1857), the Court ruled that the Missouri Compromise, which banned slavery in some territories, was unconstitutional. 📖 This decision added to the tensions leading to the Civil War.

Judicial Review and Civil Rights

The Supreme Court may also review presidential policies. In the classic case of *Ex parte Milligan*[3] (1866), the Court ruled that President Lincoln's **suspension** of certain civil rights during the Civil War was unconstitutional. 📖 More recently, in the case of *Train* v. *City of New York*[4] (1975), the Court limited the president's power to **impound**, or refuse to spend, money that Congress has appropriated. 📖

The Supreme Court exercises judicial review most frequently at the state and local levels. Since 1789, the Court has overturned more than 1,270 state and local laws. In recent years, the Court has used judicial review to significantly influence public policy at the state level in the areas of racial desegregation, reapportionment of state legislatures, and police procedures.

Judicial review of state laws and actions may have as much significance as the Court's activities at the federal level. In *Brown* v. *Board of Education of Topeka*[5] (1954), the Court held that laws requiring or permitting racially segregated schools in four states and the District of Columbia were unconstitutional. 📖 The *Brown* decision cleared the way for the end of segregated schools throughout the nation. In *Miranda* v. *Arizona*[6] (1966), the Court ruled that police had acted unconstitutionally and had violated a suspect's rights. 📖 The *Miranda* decision brought major changes in law enforcement policies and procedures across the nation.

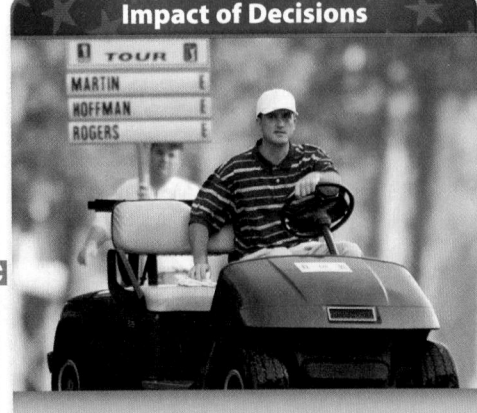

★ **Impact of Decisions** ★

Judicial Review Casey Martin (shown above) took his case to the Supreme Court. A decision of the Court affects the entire country. *Why would the PGA Tour, Inc. case not have come to the Court for a decision before the 1990s?*

Interpretation of Laws

Another way that the Court shapes public policy is by interpreting existing federal laws. Congress often uses very general language in framing laws, leaving it to the executive or judicial branch to apply the law to a specific situation. For example, the Americans with Disabilities Act of 1990 prohibits discrimination on the basis of disability in jobs, housing, and "places of public accommodation."

Did such language mean that the Professional Golfers' Association (PGA) had to provide special tournament arrangements for disabled participants in the same manner it did spectators? In *PGA Tour, Inc.* v. *Martin*[7] (2001), the Court ruled that the PGA must accommodate Casey Martin, a professional golfer who was disabled by a degenerative condition in his right leg, allowing him to ride in a golf cart rather than walk the course as required by PGA rules. 📖 The *Martin* decision could influence who participates in a variety of sports competitions.

A similar law, the Civil Rights Act of 1964, prohibits discrimination based on "race, color, or national origin" in any program receiving federal aid.

📖 *See the following footnoted materials in the* **Reference Handbook:**
1. *Marbury* v. *Madison* case summary, page R30.
2. *Dred Scott* v. *Sandford* case summary, page R26.
3. *Ex parte Milligan* case summary, page R27.
4. *Train* v. *City of New York* case summary, page R34.
5. *Brown* v. *Board of Education of Topeka* case summary, page R24.
6. *Miranda* v. *Arizona* case summary, page R30.
7. *PGA Tour, Inc.* v. *Martin* case summary, page R32.

CHAPTER 12: *Supreme Court Decision Making* **337**

Teach

Caption Answer: The Americans with Disabilities Act was only passed in 1990.

C Critical Thinking

Analyzing Discuss how the Supreme Court shapes government policy and the limits on its powers. As students note each tool for shaping policy and each limit, list it on the board. Ask volunteers to give examples. **BL**

D Differentiated Instruction

Kinesthetic Without realizing it, students may be familiar with the results of the *Miranda* case from seeing movies and television shows in which police arrest a suspect. Provide students with the text of the *Miranda* decision and have them find the wording in the opinion that is used almost verbatim by police. Then organize the class into small groups to prepare skits showing two possible outcomes of an arrest: one in which the suspect was told of his or her rights and the other in which the same suspect was not told. **OL**

Differentiated Instruction

Supreme Court Case Studies, p. 13

★ **Rights of Citizens During Wartime** ★

Objective: Understand legal precedents for presidential powers during wartime.

Focus/Teach: Explain the background of the case and have students read excerpts from the ruling.

Assess: Assign the Case Analysis Questions.

Close: Discuss the ruling's relevance for today.

Differentiated Instruction Strategies

BL Ask students to describe instances in which it would be appropriate to declare martial law; discuss different scenarios.

AL Study the issue of presidential powers during wartime in other historical contexts.

ELL Discuss the circumstances that prompted President Abraham Lincoln to suspend the writ of habeas corpus.

S Skill Practice

Researching In 1998 the U.S. Department of Justice filed suit against the Microsoft Corporation for engaging in monopolistic behavior in violation of the Sherman Antitrust Act of 1890. Have students investigate the facts of *United States* v. *Microsoft Corporation,* the settlement of the case, and its impact on the computer software business. As a class, discuss the relevance of the Sherman Antitrust Act in the twenty-first century. **AL**

GO TO To enrich the study of chapter content, remind students that footnoted materials appear in the *Reference Handbook.*

Differentiated Instruction

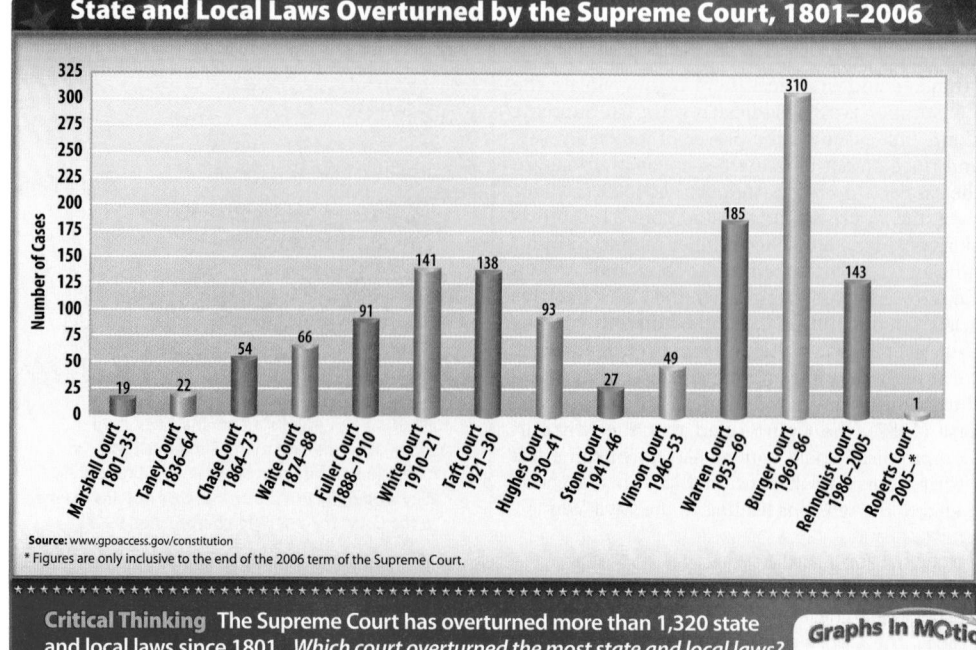

State and Local Laws Overturned by the Supreme Court, 1801–2006

Number of Cases

Court	Cases
Marshall Court 1801–35	19
Taney Court 1836–64	22
Chase Court 1864–73	54
Waite Court 1874–88	66
Fuller Court 1888–1910	91
White Court 1910–21	141
Taft Court 1921–30	138
Hughes Court 1930–41	93
Stone Court 1941–46	27
Vinson Court 1946–53	49
Warren Court 1953–69	185
Burger Court 1969–86	310
Rehnquist Court 1986–2005	143
Roberts Court 2005–*	1

Source: www.gpoaccess.gov/constitution
* Figures are only inclusive to the end of the 2006 term of the Supreme Court.

Critical Thinking The Supreme Court has overturned more than 1,320 state and local laws since 1801. *Which court overturned the most state and local laws?*

Graphs In Motion
See StudentWorks™ Plus or go to glencoe.com.

In *Lau* v. *Nichols*[1] (1974), the Court interpreted the law to require schools to provide special instruction in English to immigrant students.

Legislatures nationwide interpreted the Court's ruling to mean that classes must be taught in Spanish for Latino students whose native language is not English. Congress may not have considered this **interpretation** when it wrote the Civil Rights Act. The Supreme Court, in the end, decides what Congress means, and the impact of its rulings is felt across the nation.

Major acts of Congress, such as the Interstate Commerce Act and the Sherman Antitrust Act, have come before the Court repeatedly in settling disputes. Chief Justice John Roberts, in his confirmation hearing, described the constitutional role of Supreme Court justices as similar to:

S *❝ . . . umpires. Umpires don't make the rules; they apply them. The role of an umpire and a judge is critical. They make sure everybody plays by the rules. But it is a limited role. . . . it's my job to call balls and strikes . . . not to pitch or bat. ❞*

—Justice John Roberts

Overturning Earlier Decisions

One of the basic principles of law in making judicial decisions is **stare decisis** (stehr • ee dih • SY • suhs)—a Latin term that means "let the decision stand." Under this principle, once the Court rules on a case, its decision serves as a **precedent,** or model, on which to base other decisions in similar cases. This principle is important because it makes the law predictable. If judges' decisions were unpredictable from one case to another, what is legal one day could be illegal the next.

On the other hand, the law needs to be flexible and adaptable to changing times, social values and attitudes, and circumstances. Flexibility exists partly because justices sometimes change their minds. As one noted justice said, "Wisdom too often never comes, and so one ought not to reject it merely because it comes late."

More often, the law is flexible because of changes in the Court's composition. Justices are appointed for life, but they do not serve forever.

See the following footnoted materials in the *Reference Handbook:*
1. *Lau* v. *Nichols* case summary, page R29.

Activity: Multiple Learning Styles

Interpersonal Show the film *Twelve Angry Men.* Before the jury takes its second vote on the case, stop the film. Organize the class into small groups. Have students in each group decide which juror they believe will be next to change his vote. Next, have students answer the following question: If all jurors switched their votes, which juror would be the last to change to a "not guilty" vote? Have each group present its ideas. Show the rest of the film and discuss its outcome. **OL**

As justices die or retire, the president appoints replacements. New justices may bring different legal views to the Court and, over time, shift its position on some issues.

In 1928, for example, the Court ruled in *Olmstead* v. *United States*[1] that wiretaps on telephone conversations were legal because they did not require police to enter private property. Almost 40 years later, however, the Court's membership and society's values changed. In *Katz* v. *United States*[2] (1967), the Court overturned the *Olmstead* decision, ruling that a wiretap is a search and seizure under the Fourth Amendment and requires a court order.

Limits on the Supreme Court

Despite its importance, the Court does not have unlimited powers. Restrictions on the types of issues and kinds of cases the Court will hear, limited control over its own agenda, lack of enforcement power, and the system of checks and balances curtail the Court's activities.

Limits on Types of Issues

Despite the broad range of its work, the Court does not give equal attention to all areas of national policy. For example, the Court has played only a minor role in making foreign policy. Over the years, most Supreme Court decisions have dealt with civil liberties, economic issues, federal legislation and regulations, due process of law, and suits against government officials.

Civil liberties cases tend to involve constitutional questions and make up the bulk of the Court's cases. Appeals from prisoners to challenge their convictions, for example, account for about one-fourth of the Court's decisions. Most of these cases concern constitutional issues, such as the right to a fair trial and the proper use of evidence. Many of the Court's other cases deal with economic issues such as government regulation of business, labor-management relations, antitrust laws, and environmental protection. The Court also spends time resolving disputes between the national government and the states or between two states.

Limits on Types of Cases

The Supreme Court has developed many rules and customs over the years. As a result, the Court will hear only cases that meet certain criteria.

Government ONLINE
Student Web Activity Visit glencoe.com and enter **QuickPass**™ code USG9822c12. Click on Student Web Activity and complete the activity about shaping public policy.

First, the Court will consider only cases in which its decision will make a difference. It will not hear a case merely to decide a point of law. Thus, the Court refused to decide whether the state of Idaho could retract its ratification of the Equal Rights Amendment (ERA). Not enough states had ratified the amendment, and the deadline had already expired. Whether or not Idaho could change its vote on the ERA made no difference. Further, unlike courts in some countries, the Supreme Court will not give an **advisory opinion**—a ruling on a law or action that has not been challenged.

Second, the plaintiff—the person or group bringing the case—must have suffered real harm.

See the following footnoted materials in the **Reference Handbook:**
1. *Olmstead* v. *United States* case summary, page R31.
2. *Katz* v. *United States* case summary, page R29.

Gradual Changes

Judicial Processes Fast-moving national and state governments often "bump up" against the slower-moving, deliberative Supreme Court. *Why would states want the Court's decision making to move more quickly?*

Government ONLINE
Objectives and answers to the Student Web Activity can be found in the **Web Activity Lesson Plan** at glencoe.com. Enter **QuickPass**™ code USG9085c12T.

POLITICAL PROFILES **Louis Brandeis** (1856–1941) Louis Brandeis was a Supreme Court justice from 1916 to 1939. As an attorney, he transformed legal practice by introducing sociological and economic factors in his arguments before the Supreme Court. Criticized for taking a short vacation before an important trial he explained he needed the rest, and said, "I find that I can do a year's work in eleven months, but I can't do it in twelve."

Caption Answer: Societal norms and expectations often change faster than the Court can overturn laws. Local, state, and national governments must enforce controversial or outdated laws.

Hands-On Chapter Project

Step 2

A Day in Court

Step 2: Preparing the Case Groups of students continue the work that they began in Section 1 to prepare for the mock trial.

Directions Tell the groups that they must research their local district or appellate court. Refer them to the Web site www.uscourts.gov/courtlinks/. They can use their zip code to locate the nearest court. Each group should use the Web site as a resource to help them prepare for

their day in court. **Ask:** What information can you find on this Web site that might help you prepare your case? (*There are instructions to the jury and forms for filing civil and criminal cases; local and federal rules are explained; appellate and district courts are distinguished, and so on.*)

Researching Review the facts of Mitsuye Endo's case. Forced to leave her job and her home, she was detained in a prison camp for months but was never charged for violating any law. Explain that *habeas*

corpus comes from the Latin phrase, *you should have the body.* Discuss what it meant for Mitsuye Endo to petition for a writ of habeas corpus. (*It gave her the right to a court hearing.*) **Ask:** Why is the right to petition for a writ of habeas corpus often referred to as the "centerpiece of our liberty"? (*It protects against unlawful imprisonment.*) **OL**

(*Chapter Project continued in Section 3.*)

Expository Writing Ask students to research the Texas legislative redistricting controversy that went all the way to the Supreme Court. In *League of United Latin American Citizens* v. *Perry* (2006), the Court considered whether a Texas redistricting plan violated the Voting Rights Act by diluting the votes of minorities. In an essay, have students summarize the Court's ruling and explain why they agree or disagree with it. **AL**

The Law *and* You

More About Privacy on the Phone Scanners make it possible for people to eavesdrop on conversations on wireless phones and other devices. Speaker of the House Newt Gingrich found to his dismay that some people listen to and tape calls to use illegally. In 1996 a conference call in which Gingrich was seemingly reneging on a promise to the House Ethics Committee was taped and handed over to a committee member of the opposing party (in violation of federal law).

Additional Support

It is not enough for people merely to object to a law or an action because they think it is unfair. Plaintiffs must show that the law or action being challenged has harmed them.

Third, the Court accepts only cases that involve a substantial federal question. The legal issues in dispute must affect many people or the operation of the political system.

Finally, the Court has traditionally refused to deal with political questions—issues the Court believes the executive or legislative branches should resolve. For the first time, in the 2000 presidential election, the Court heard two cases involving the recounting of votes in the state of Florida.[1] 📖 No clear line separates political questions from the legal issues the Court will hear. In the 1840s, two groups each claimed to be the legal government of Rhode Island. The Supreme Court decided the dispute was political rather than legal and that Congress should settle it. In the end, the difference between a political question and a legal question is whatever the Court determines it to be.

Limited Control Over Agenda

A third limit on the Supreme Court's power to shape public policy is that with few exceptions, it can decide only cases that come to it from elsewhere in the legal system. As a result, events beyond the Court's control shape its agenda. For example, when Congress abolished the draft in the mid-1970s, it ended the Court's ability to decide religious freedom cases involving refusal to serve in the military. On the other hand, passage of the 1964 Civil Rights Act and similar laws created a large volume of civil liberties cases for the Court to decide.

The Court can and does signal its interest in a subject by deliberately taking on a specific case. **W** In 1962, for example, the Court entered the area of legislative apportionment by agreeing to hear *Baker* v. *Carr*.[2] 📖 In that Tennessee case, the

---

📖 *See the following footnoted materials in the* **Reference Handbook:**
1. *Bush* v. *Gore* case summary, page R25; *Bush* v. *Palm Beach County* case summary, page R24.
2. *Baker* v. *Carr* case summary, page R23.

The Law *and* You

Privacy on the Phone

Innovations in telephone technology have made communication much more convenient. Cordless, cellular, and digital phones allow varying degrees of mobility while talking on the telephone. When you use such phones, however, you are transmitting signals through the air that are similar to a radio

◀ **Girl making a phone call**

broadcast. Anyone with a receiver tuned to the right frequency can overhear your conversation. Digital phones offer the most protection against eavesdropping, but special decoders can convert even digital transmissions into voice audio.

Federal laws offer some protection of telephone privacy. While it might not be unlawful to overhear a phone call, it is against the law to divulge the conversation or to use it for someone's benefit. The manufacture or sale of scanning devices that can intercept cellular or digital calls is also illegal. With some exceptions, the recording of telephone conversations without the knowledge or consent of both parties is a violation of federal and state law.

Exploring the Law Activity

Survey Your Class How many people in the class use a cordless, cellular, or digital phone regularly? How many people are concerned that their conversations might not be private? Contact the Federal Communications Commission to obtain more information about laws protecting telephone use.

340

Activity: Interdisciplinary Connection

History The quotation by Andrew Jackson on page 341 was in reference to the outcome of the case *Worcester* v. *Georgia* (1832) in which the Court ruled that the Cherokee Nation was not subject to the laws of Georgia. That case and a previous one, *Cherokee Nation* v. *Georgia,* were part of the Cherokee Nation's attempt to retain its lands, which the state of Georgia wanted to take over. In the end, the Cherokee were forced to move to Indian Territory in what is now Oklahoma. Have students research the Cherokee Trail of Tears and this period of history, and present their findings in written or oral reports. **AL**

Court reversed its 1946 position that drawing state legislative districts was a political issue. As a result of the *Baker* decision, many cases challenging the makeup of legislative districts were brought to the Court. Still, even when the Court wishes to rule in an area, it may have to wait years for the right case in the proper context to come along.

Lack of Enforcement Power

A fourth factor limiting the Court's power to shape public policy is the Court's limited ability to enforce its rulings. President Andrew Jackson recognized this limitation when he refused to **R** carry out a Court ruling he disliked, reputedly saying: "[Chief Justice] John Marshall has made his decision, now let him enforce it."

Noncompliance may occur in several ways. Lower court judges may simply ignore a Supreme Court decision. During the 1960s, many state court judges did not strictly enforce the Court's decisions banning school prayer. During the same time period, some officials, ranging from school principals to judges to governors, sought ways to avoid Court rulings on integrating schools. Moreover, the Supreme Court simply is not able to closely monitor the millions of trial decisions throughout the United States to make sure its rulings are followed. Nevertheless, most Court decisions are accepted and generally enforced.

Checks and Balances

The Constitution provides that the legislative and executive branches of the national government have several ways to try to influence or check

Civil Rights and the Courts Thurgood Marshall (center), the lead attorney in *Brown v. Board of Education of Topeka,* is seen with civil rights activist Daisy Bates (to his right) and some of the Central High School students who integrated the school in Little Rock, Arkansas. *Why did the civil rights movement increase the Supreme Court caseload?*

the Supreme Court's power. These checks include the president's power to appoint justices, the Senate's power to approve appointments, and Congress's power to impeach and remove justices. The system of checks and balances is a process that the Framers intended would both monitor and protect the integrity of the Court.

R Reading Strategy

Predicting Point out President Jackson's statement. **Ask:** How do you think Congress and the public would react if the president made such a statement today? *(Answers will vary.)* Should a constitutional amendment be written that would compel the president to enforce all Supreme Court rulings? *(Prompt students to consider its potential impact on the system of checks and balances.)* **OL**

Assess

Assign the Section 2 Assessment as homework or as an in-class activity, or have students take Section Quiz 12-2 from *Section Quizzes and Chapter Tests.*

Close

Analyzing Have students discuss this quote from the Greek lawgiver Solon: "Wrongdoing can only be avoided if those who are not wronged feel the same indignation at it as those who are." **OL**

Section 2 Review

SECTION 2 Review

Vocabulary

1. **Explain** the significance of: judicial review, impound, stare decisis, precedent, advisory opinion.

Main Ideas

2. **Identifying** What are four reasons why the Supreme Court's power to shape public policy is limited?

3. **Examining** In what three ways can the Supreme Court determine public policy?

Critical Thinking

4. **Drawing Conclusions** How would the Court's power be enhanced or diminished if it gave advisory opinions?

5. **Organizing** Use a graphic organizer like the one below to compare the power of the Supreme Court with its constitutional limitations.

Power	Limitations

Writing About Government

6. **Descriptive Writing** Research the supreme courts of Canada and Mexico. Find out how these courts select which cases they will hear. Write a brief summary that compares the selection process of these other supreme courts with that of the United States Supreme Court.

CHAPTER 12: *Supreme Court Decision Making* **341**

Answers

1. All definitions can be found in the section and the Glossary.

2. any four: restrictions on issues it will hear, limits on cases it can or will hear, limited control over its agenda, lack of enforcement powers, checks and balances

3. through judicial review, interpretation of laws, and overturning earlier decisions

4. Answers will vary. If the opinions influenced executive or legislative actions, its power would grow. If its advice was ignored, its power would diminish.

5. Power: judicial review, interpretation of laws, overturning earlier decisions
   Limitations: president's power to appoint judges; Congress's power to approve appointments and to impeach/remove judges, lack of enforcement power

6. Call on students to present their summaries and discuss the similarities and differences.

Class Debate

Have students read the text and answer the Questions to Consider. Allow students time to discuss their ideas with a partner. Then organize the class into groups and have each group answer the questions in You Be the Judge. After a representative from each group has presented its position, hold a class discussion about which were the most effective points.

The Court's Decision

In a complicated per curiam decision, seven justices held that the lack of uniform standards for recounting punch-card ballots violated the Fourteenth Amendment's guarantee of equal protection of the laws: "The 'intent of the voter' . . . is unobjectionable as an abstract proposition and a starting principle. The problem lies in the absence of specified standards to ensure its equal application." Five justices ruled that there was not sufficient time to remedy the problem before the federal deadline for choosing electors, which effectively awarded Florida's 25 electoral votes and the presidency to George W. Bush. Four justices dissented, holding that the Court overreached its authority by agreeing to decide the case.

Should All Ballots Be Treated Equally?

George W. Bush et al. v. *Albert Gore, Jr., et al.,* 2000

The Supreme Court sometimes takes a case to clarify the meaning of the Constitution on an important issue. This happened during the presidential election of 2000, one of the closest in the nation's history.

Facts of the Case

The outcome of the 2000 presidential election hinged on Florida's 25 electoral votes. When the polls closed on November 7, Democrat Al Gore had captured 267 of the 270 votes needed, and Republican George W. Bush had won 246. The vote in Florida was so close—Bush led by 1,784 out of more than 6 million votes cast—that it triggered an automatic recount to ensure an accurate result.

When ballots were again run through tabulation machines, Bush's margin shrank to fewer than 200 votes. Gore requested hand recounts of ballots in four predominantly Democratic counties where thousands of punch-card ballots had recorded no vote for president. Bush asked a U.S. District Court to block any further recounts, and a legal battle began.

While the manual recount was still in progress, the Florida Secretary of State certified Bush as the winner by 537 votes. Gore appealed this action to the Florida circuit court and then to the Florida Supreme Court, which authorized manual recounts of disputed ballots to begin immediately. Bush appealed the ruling to the Supreme Court, which ordered the recount to stop.

The Constitutional Question

The Florida Supreme Court ordered any recounts to use a general standard set forth in Florida law to discern "the intent of the voter." The ballots required voters to punch out small squares called chads. On some ballots, the chad was still partly attached. The machine did not count it, so that ballot was uncounted. In a manual recount, how would the recounters interpret the voter's intent when a chad was left hanging by one or two corners and was not cleanly removed?

Lawyers for Gore argued that examining ballots by hand inevitably requires personal judgments about a voter's intent. Lawyers for Bush argued that such a general standard violates the Fourteenth Amendment guarantee of equal protection. Without uniform standards regarding what constitutes a legal vote, it is impossible to ensure that each person's vote is treated the same.

Debating the Issue

Questions to Consider

1. Did the Florida Supreme Court's standard for recounting disputed punch-card ballots result in one person's vote being valued more than another's?

2. What might be the consequences of using a very specific standard to determine which votes count?

You Be the Judge

Review the meaning of the Fourteenth Amendment. In your opinion, did the Florida Supreme Court's method for recounting votes violate the Fourteenth Amendment's guarantee of equal protection under the law? Explain.

 ▶ George W. Bush

 ▶ Albert Gore, Jr.

Debating the Issue Answers

Questions to Consider

1. Some students might say that allowing counties to choose their own standard could give an advantage to one candidate. For example, a liberal standard in a heavily Democratic county and a strict standard in a Republican county would result in more Democratic votes. Other students might say that standards need to be loose enough to allow for unforeseen problems.

2. Many ballots might be disqualified, which could mean that some voters would not have their votes counted. If a county did not have the money or technology to provide accurate voting methods, the voters of that county might be at a disadvantage.

You Be the Judge

Answers will vary. Have students compare their answers with the actual decision. You might want to debate whether the state judge monitoring the recount or the U.S. Supreme Court was in a better position to judge the fairness of the recount.

Influencing Court Decisions

Reader's Guide

Content Vocabulary
★ bloc (p. 344)
★ swing vote (p. 344)

Academic Vocabulary
★ foundation (p. 343)
★ function (p. 344)
★ inherently (p. 347)

Reading Strategy
As you read, create a table similar to the one below to identify the forces inside and outside the Court that influence its decisions.

Influences Inside the Court	Influences Outside the Court

People in the News

One of the Supreme Court's most outspoken members, Antonin Scalia, sized up the current atmosphere for appointing justices to the Court in the early twenty-first century. In his address to students at Roger Williams University Law School, Scalia said he doubted he could win confirmation to the Court today. (He was confirmed by a 98–0 vote of the Senate in 1986.) Scalia, who usually votes with the conservative wing of the Court, believes that justices should stick close to the original text of the Constitution and not interpret what the Founders meant for changing times. "You don't like the death penalty? Persuade your fellow citizens it's a bad idea and repeal it." Scalia summed up his judicial philosophy for an appreciative audience this way: "I am a textualist, I am an originalist. I am not a nut."

▲ Since his appointment in 1986, Justice Scalia has been known for his outspoken views inside and outside the Court.

W hy do justices decide cases as they do? What factors influence how each votes on a case? Five forces shape the decisions the Court makes. They are (1) existing laws, (2) the personal views of the justices, (3) the justices' interactions with one another, (4) social forces and public attitudes, and (5) Congress and the president.

Basing Decisions on the Law

Law is the **foundation** for deciding cases that come before the Supreme Court. Justices, like other people, often hold strong opinions on these issues, however, they must base their decisions on the principles of law, and not on their own opinions.

Laws and the Constitution, however, are not always clear in their meaning. The First Amendment, for example, prohibits any law "abridging freedom of speech," but does this right provide absolute freedom or do limits exist? Does freedom of speech mean that a person has the right to falsely cry "Fire" in a crowded theater? The Fourth Amendment prohibits unreasonable searches and seizures, but what is unreasonable? Can tapping a person's telephone be considered an unreasonable search?

Most of the cases the Supreme Court is asked to rule on involve difficult questions like these. When the meaning of a statute or a provision of the Constitution is not clear, the justices of the Court must interpret the language, determine what it means, and apply it to the circumstances of the case.

CHAPTER 12: *Supreme Court Decision Making* **343**

Focus

Bellringer
Section Focus Transparencies 12-3

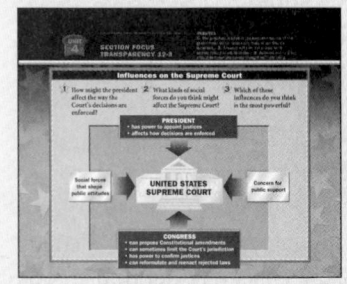

Reader's Guide

Answers to Graphic:
Influences Inside the Court: existing laws, the personal views of the justices, justices' interactions with one another
Influences Outside the Court: social forces and public attitudes, Congress, and the president

Resource Manager

R Reading Strategies	C Critical Thinking	D Differentiated Instruction	W Writing Support	S Skill Practice
Additional Resources • Quizzes/Tests, pp. 143–152 • Guid. Read. Act., p. 44 • Ch. Summaries, pp. 33–36	**Teacher Edition** • Drawing Conclusions, p. 346 **Additional Resources** • Read. Essen., pp. 132–134	**Teacher Edition** • Visual/Spatial, p. 346 **Additional Resources** • Foldables, p. 55	**Teacher Edition** • Expository Writing, p. 347 **Additional Resources** • Part. in Gov. Act., pp. 23–24	**Teacher Edition** • Interpreting, p. 348 **Additional Resources** • Reteaching Act., p. 12 • Vocab. Act., p. 12

Teach

POLITICAL PROFILES

William H. Rehnquist
(1924–2005)

Nominated by President Richard Nixon, William H. Rehnquist took his seat as an associate justice on the U.S. Supreme Court in 1972. He quickly became a leading voice for conservatism on the Court and, in 1973, was one of two dissenters in the Court's ruling in *Roe* v. *Wade,* in which the majority based a woman's right to an abortion on the right to privacy implicit in the Bill of Rights. In a variety of cases, Justice Rehnquist exhibited a strong states' rights stance, narrowly interpreting the powers of the federal government. In 1986 President Ronald Reagan nominated him to replace Warren Burger as chief justice. During his tenure, Rehnquist remained a staunch conservative and greatly improved the efficiency of the Court.

Differentiated Instruction

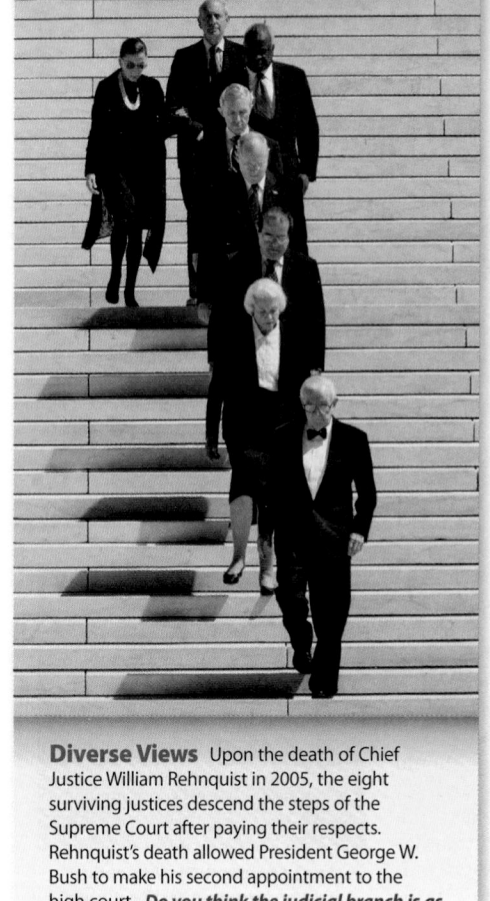

Diverse Views Upon the death of Chief Justice William Rehnquist in 2005, the eight surviving justices descend the steps of the Supreme Court after paying their respects. Rehnquist's death allowed President George W. Bush to make his second appointment to the high court. *Do you think the judicial branch is as political as the other branches? Why or why not?*

In interpreting the law, however, justices are not free to give it any meaning they wish. Justices must relate their interpretations logically to the Constitution, to statutes that are relevant to the case, and to legal precedents. The Court explains, in detail, the legal principles behind any new interpretation of the law.

Views of the Justices

Supreme Court justices, like other political figures, are people with active interests in important issues. Some justices, for example, believe that individual rights must be protected at almost all costs, even if that means a few criminals go unpunished. Other justices might be more concerned about rising crime rates. They might believe that a little loss of freedom from wiretaps or stop-and-frisk laws is acceptable if it helps curb crime.

Over the years, some justices become identified with specific views on certain issues. Justice William O. Douglas, for example, was known as a consistent supporter of the rights of the underprivileged during his 36 years on the Court. Because, like Douglas, most justices take consistent positions in areas of personal concern, voting blocs, or coalitions of justices, exist on the Court on certain kinds of issues. In recent years, one group of justices has consistently tended toward liberal positions on civil rights and economic issues. A different bloc has consistently tended to take more conservative positions on the same issues.

When justices retire and new appointees take their places, the size and power of each bloc may change. A majority bloc on certain issues might gradually become the minority **bloc.** If the Court is badly split over an issue, a justice whose views are not consistent with either bloc might represent a **swing vote,** or the deciding vote. When new justices are appointed, the Court sometimes overturns precedents and changes direction in its interpretations.

Relations Among the Justices

In the early years of the Supreme Court, the justices lived and ate together in a Washington boardinghouse during the Court's term. Because the term was fairly short, they did not move their families to Washington, D.C. Justice Joseph Story described life at the boardinghouse:

> ❝ Judges here live with perfect harmony, and as agreeably as absence from friends and from families could make our residence. . . . [O]ur social hours when undisturbed with the labors of law, are passed in gay and frank conversation. ❞
>
> —Justice Joseph Story, 1812

Today the justices work almost the entire year and live with their families in or near Washington, D.C. In 1976 Justice Lewis F. Powell said, "As much as 90 percent of the time we **function** as nine small, independent law firms," meeting as a group only for the oral argument sessions and conferences. The justices, he added, communicate with one another mostly in writing: "Indeed, a justice may go through

---

Leveled Activities

ELL Vocabulary Activities, p. 12

BL Interpreting Political Cartoons, p. 23

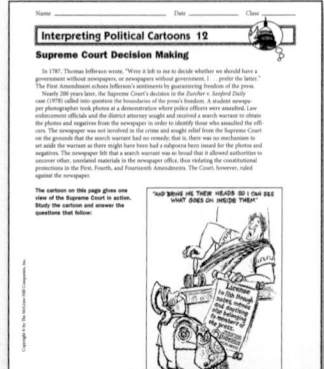

OL Authentic Assessment with Rubrics, p. 19

AL Source Readings, p. 12

an entire term without being once in the chambers of all the other eight members of the Court."

Harmony or Conflict

Despite the lack of frequent interaction, the quality of personal relations among the justices influences the Court's decision making. A Court marked by harmony is more likely to agree on decisions than one marked by personal antagonisms. Justices who can work easily with one another will be more likely to find common solutions to problems.

Even when justices are at odds with one another, they will try to avoid open conflict. A news reporter once asked a justice why he did not complain about certain actions of the chief justice, whom he disliked. The justice replied, "YOU don't have to live here for the rest of your life."

Relatively good personal relations among justices who disagreed strongly on legal issues marked some modern Courts. At other times, severe personal conflicts have seriously divided the Court.

Influence of the Chief Justice

The chief justice has several powers that can be used to influence the Court's decisions. In presiding over the Court during oral arguments and in conference, the chief justice can direct discussion and frame alternatives. In addition, the chief justice makes up the first version of the discuss list and assigns the writing of opinions to the justices.

These advantages do not necessarily guarantee leadership by a chief justice. Supreme Court chief justices must make skillful use of the tools of influence available to them if they are to be effective leaders and shape the Court's decisions. The chief justice can also influence the amount of personal conflict that exists on the Court.

The Court and Society

Harold Burton was appointed to the Supreme Court in 1945, after having served in Congress. When asked what the switch was like, he replied, "Have you ever gone from a circus to a monastery?"

Justice Burton's remark illustrates that, unlike Congress, the Court is fairly well insulated from public opinion and daily political pressures. The insulation results from the lifetime tenure of the justices and from rules that limit the way interest groups may try to influence the Court.

Still, the Supreme Court does not exist in a vacuum. The justices are interested in the Court's

TIME
For the Record

Flipping Their Wigs When the first Supreme Court convened in 1790, almost no justice followed the English tradition of wearing a wig in court. Instead they followed the advice of Thomas Jefferson, who had said, "For heaven's sake, discard the monstrous wig which makes the English judges look like rats peeping through bunches of oakum."

prestige and in maintaining as much public support as possible. In addition, the justices are part of society and are affected by the same social forces that shape public attitudes.

Concern for Public Support

As already noted, the Court relies on the cooperation and goodwill of others to enforce its decisions. The justices recognize that the Court's authority and power depend in part on public acceptance of and support for its decisions. They know that when the Court moves too far ahead or lags too far behind public opinion, it risks losing valuable public support and may weaken its own authority. For example, in one ruling against voter discrimination in the South, Justice Felix Frankfurter, a Northerner, was assigned to write the Court's opinion. After thinking it over, the Court reassigned the opinion to Justice Stanley Reed, a Southerner. The justices hoped this change would ease the resentment that they believed was almost inevitable in the South.

Influence of Social Forces

The values and beliefs of society influence Supreme Court justices. As society changes, attitudes and practices that were acceptable in one era may become unacceptable in another. In time, the Court's decisions will usually reflect changes in American society, providing another reason why the Court sometimes reverses its earlier decisions. Two major decisions on racial segregation provide an example of how the Court changes with the times.

CHAPTER 12: *Supreme Court Decision Making* **345**

Did You Know?

The highest court in most states is also called the supreme court. In Maine and Massachusetts, however, it is called the supreme judicial court. In New York and Maryland, it is the court of appeals. West Virginia's highest court is the supreme court of appeals.

Participating IN GOVERNMENT

Contacting a Justice Have a student representative find out who the current justices are and write a letter to one of them asking about some aspect of his or her work. The student might ask what the justice likes and dislikes most about serving on the Court, or about the most difficult or interesting case that the justice has heard while serving on the Court. Encourage the student to share the response with the class. **BL**

Differentiated Instruction

Activity: Multiple Learning Styles

Gifted and Talented A good example of how the system of checks and balances influences the work of the Supreme Court is illustrated by the 1984 *Grove City College* v. *Bell* decision. This case involved gender discrimination in schools that receive federal aid. The Court's decision had the effect of narrowing or weakening four federal civil rights laws that

barred discrimination on the basis of race, gender, or national origin. Civil rights groups and members of Congress began a four-year battle to reverse the Court's ruling, and a new law was passed in 1988 over President Ronald Reagan's veto. Have students research this decision, the reaction to it, and the legislative battle to reverse it. **AL**

Caption Answer: The societal values of justices change along with those of other Americans. Their decisions reflect such changes. Also, if the Supreme Court failed to react to changes in values, their rulings might be ignored.

D Differentiated Instruction

Visual/Spatial Have students collect images of segregation in the South from different time periods. Have groups work together to create a collage of images accompanied by captions. **ELL**

C Critical Thinking

Drawing Conclusions Ask: What was the significance of the Supreme Court's decision in *Brown* v. *Board of Education of Topeka, Kansas?* (Brown v. Board of Education *was significant because it challenged the entire system of segregation by overturning the precedent of "separate but equal." It also invigorated the civil rights movement by inspiring more African Americans to organize in opposition to other forms of discrimination.)* **BL**

Hands-On Chapter Project

Step 3

A Day in Court

Step 3: Presenting the Case Groups continue their work preparing the cases that they began in Section 1.

Directions Discuss court procedures for each group to present its case. Explain that one must apply to the Supreme Court for a writ of certiorari. If at least four justices agree that the case merits review, then the Supreme Court will direct the lower court to send the records.

Acknowledging Changes in Society

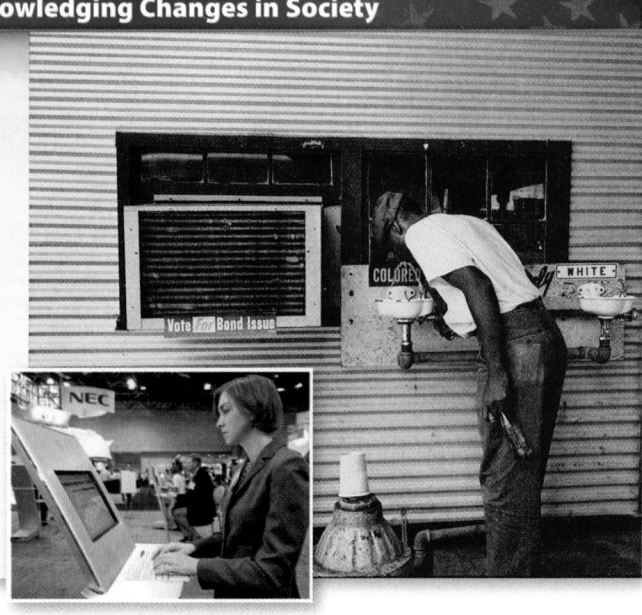

Societal Norms Changes in societal values forced the Supreme Court to declare segregated facilities, like these drinking fountains for African Americans and whites in New Orleans, unconstitutional. ▶

The Internet The Internet has more than 1 billion users with more added daily. A wired world not only changes our lives but also creates many new issues for the Supreme Court to resolve. For example, is speech in e-mail protected by the First Amendment? ▶

Evaluating Change *Why must the Supreme Court react to changes in American values?*

Plessy v. Ferguson

Landmark Case In the 1890s, many restaurants, schools, and trains were segregated. In Louisiana, Homer Plessy attempted to sit in a section of a train marked "For Whites Only." When he refused to move, Plessy was arrested and convicted of violating Louisiana's segregation law that required "equal but separate" accommodations based on race. Plessy appealed his conviction to the Supreme Court, which in 1896 upheld the Louisiana law as constitutional in the case of *Plessy* v. *Ferguson*.

The Court ruled that the equal protection clause of the Fourteenth Amendment permitted a state to require separate facilities for African Americans as long as those facilities were equal to the facilities available to whites. In reality, the facilities for African Americans were not truly equal, but few whites at the time were concerned about the needs of African Americans. The *Plessy* decision served as a legal justification for racial segregation for the next half century.

By the 1950s, society's attitudes toward race relations were beginning to change. World War II made it harder to support segregation openly because many African Americans had fought and died for American ideals. In addition, social science research began to document the damaging effects segregation had on African American children. Civil rights groups were demanding an end to racial discrimination.

Overturning Plessy

These social forces helped persuade the Supreme Court to overturn the precedent established in the *Plessy* case. During its 1952 term, in *Brown* v. *Board of Education of Topeka*, the Court heard a challenge to its 56-year-old interpretation of the Fourteenth Amendment. In 1954 the Court ruled unanimously that "separate but equal" educational facilities were unconstitutional.

In writing the Court's opinion, Chief Justice Earl Warren clearly recognized that social change was important in deciding the case. He reviewed the history of American education in the late 1800s. He then added:

> ❝ *Today, education is perhaps the most important function of state and local governments. . . . In these days, it is doubtful that any child may reasonably be expected to succeed in life if he is denied the opportunity of an education. Such an opportunity . . . is a right which must be made available to all on equal terms.* ❞
> —Chief Justice Earl Warren, 1954

346 UNIT 4: *The Judicial Branch*

Ask: What has to happen in order for Mitsuye Endo's case to be reviewed by the Supreme Court? *(Her lawyers must first petition the Supreme Court to review her case. Then, if all goes well, the Supreme Court presents a writ of certiorari to the lower court.)* How many justices must vote to hear and rule on a case? *(Four out of nine justices must vote to hear a case.)*

Concluding Student attorneys prepare their briefs and present their arguments to the Court. Have student justices confer, decide on the case, and write their opinions. Next, launch a class discussion about the decision. Point out to students that Mitsuye Endo was confined for more than two years without being charged of any crime. She believed in her cause, so she held firm until she won her case. Ask students how they would react to waiting for so long to achieve such a goal. Begin a discussion about what it takes to stand up for what you believe is right. **OL**

Chief Justice Warren declared that separate was **inherently** unequal, and that it violated the equal protection clause of the Fourteenth Amendment. Times had changed, and so had the Court's position. **W**

Balancing the Court's Power

The judicial branch, like the two other branches of the national government, operates under two related principles: separation of powers, and checks and balances. Thus, the powers of Congress and the president affect the Supreme Court and its decisions.

The President's Influence

A president's most important influence over the Court is the power of the chief executive to appoint justices—with Senate consent. Presidents generally use this appointment power to choose justices who seem likely to bring the Court closer to their own philosophy.

Every full-term president except Jimmy Carter has made at least one appointment to the Supreme Court. (Because justices are appointed for life, the number of appointments a president can make depends on whether a justice retires or dies during a given administration.) President Richard Nixon appointed four justices, including a chief justice, and President Ronald Reagan appointed three—all sharing the conservative philosophies of these presidents. Presidents Bill Clinton and George W.

Bush each made two appointments. The importance of being able to make even a single appointment can be noteworthy because in many decisions, the votes of only one or two justices can determine which way the vote goes. The vote of Justice Sandra Day O'Connor, who retired in 2006, was frequently referred to as a swing vote.

Presidents may also exercise influence with the Court in less formal ways. As head of the executive branch, the president plays a role in enforcing Court decisions. Executive departments and agencies must enforce Court decisions in such areas as integration and equal employment opportunity if they are to have any impact. An administration may enforce such Court decisions vigorously or with little enthusiasm, depending on its views on these issues.

The Influence of Congress

The system of checks and balances can also be used to try to shape the Court's decisions. One method Congress has used is to try to control whether the Court is able to hear certain cases from appellate courts. In the late 1950s, for example, some members of Congress were angry at Court decisions on subversive activities so they tried to pass a law that ended the Court's authority to hear such cases. (The attempt failed.) Congress can also pass laws aimed at limiting the Court's options to order a legal remedy in a case. This happened in the early 1980s, when some members of Congress were frustrated by how the Court was ruling on issues affecting school busing and abortion. They introduced hundreds of bills to limit the Court's remedies.

President's Appointment Power

An Acceptable Nominee
President Bill Clinton appointed Stephen Breyer to the Court in 1994. Breyer enjoys a reputation as a moderate who has an unusual ability to bring about agreement among his colleagues. Breyer's moderate views assured his confirmation. *Why do particular groups oppose some nominees?*

CHAPTER 12: *Supreme Court Decision Making* **347**

Activity: Interdisciplinary Connections

Health Today medical science can cure people of once-fatal diseases and has all but eliminated other diseases. That same knowledge, however, allows doctors to maintain life in people who have no hope of recovery, who may be in great pain, who are in a permanent state of unconsciousness, or who are suffering from senility. This ability has given rise to moral, ethical, legal, and religious questions about withholding or withdrawing

medical treatment in terminal cases. The first Supreme Court case involving the issue was *Cruzan v. Director, Missouri Department of Health* (1990). Have students investigate that case and the issue in general. A straightforward, clear presentation geared for young people is found in *Euthanasia: The "Right to Die" Issue,* by Daniel Jussim (Hillside, N.J.: Enslow Publishers, 1993). **AL**

Caption Answer: The public was strongly opposed to Roosevelt's court-packing plan.

S Skill Practice

Interpreting Have students write a description of the editorial cartoon about the court-packing plan. Encourage them to pick out symbols the artist used and explain their meanings. *(The donkey, a symbol of the Democratic Party, kicks up a storm and the dove of peace flies off, dropping the olive branch.)* **OL AL**

Assess

Assign the Section 3 Assessment as homework or as an in-class activity; or have students take Section Quiz 12-3 from *Section Quizzes and Chapter Tests.*

Close

Analyzing Discuss the meaning of the quote from Justice Harold Burton (page 345). **Ask:** How is the Supreme Court like a monastery? How is it different? **OL**

Section 3 Review

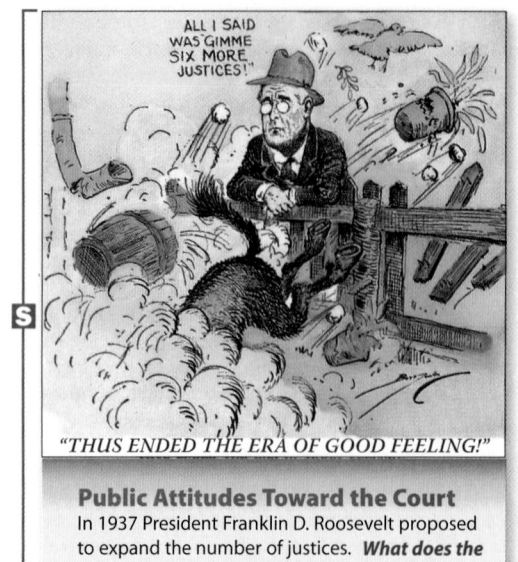

"THUS ENDED THE ERA OF GOOD FEELING!"

Public Attitudes Toward the Court
In 1937 President Franklin D. Roosevelt proposed to expand the number of justices. **What does the cartoonist imply about the public's reaction?**

In 1793 the Court ruled in *Chisholm* v. *Georgia*[1] that a citizen of another state could sue a state in federal court. To counter this decision, Congress passed, and the states approved, the Eleventh Amendment that prohibited such action. In an 1895 case, the Court ruled that a tax on incomes was unconstitutional. The Sixteenth Amendment, ratified in 1913, allowed Congress to levy an income tax.

Another way that Congress exercises power over the Court is through its right to set the justices' salaries. Congress cannot reduce the justices' salaries, but it has shown its disapproval of the Court by refusing raises for them.

Congress also sets the number of justices on the Court. In 1937, when President Franklin D. Roosevelt wanted to add six justices to the Court to prevent it from declaring New Deal legislation unconstitutional, even lawmakers from the president's party rejected the proposal.

Finally, the Senate can use its power to confirm nominees to shape the Court's outlook. The Senate scrutinizes the nominee's attitudes about sensitive social issues. Two of President George H.W. Bush's appointees, David Souter and Clarence Thomas, were questioned intensely in Senate confirmation hearings about their views on abortion. To avoid this kind of controversy, President Bill Clinton tried to choose nominees who had strong support in the Senate. Presidents know that their nominees will be closely questioned in confirmation hearings and often can be expected to name judges who do not hold extreme views.

If the Court rejects a law as unconstitutional, Congress can reenact it in a different form. In the 1930s, Congress passed laws to regulate industry as part of a program to lift the economy out of the Depression. After the Court rejected the National Industrial Recovery Act in 1935, Congress reenacted essentially the same law but limited it to the coal industry. This law was upheld in 1937.

Congress can also propose a constitutional amendment to overturn a Court ruling, a strategy that has been used successfully several times.

See the following footnoted materials in the **Reference Handbook:**
1. *Chisholm* v. *Georgia* case summary, page R25.

SECTION 3 Review

Vocabulary

1. **Explain** the significance of: bloc, swing vote.

Main Ideas

2. **Expressing** On what factors do Supreme Court justices base their decisions?

3. **Describing** How do personal relationships among Supreme Court justices affect decision making?

Critical Thinking

4. **Making Inferences** Why did the Supreme Court overturn a precedent in deciding the *Brown* case?

5. **Organizing** Use a graphic organizer like the one on the right to show five forces that shape Supreme Court decisions.

Supreme Court Decisions

Writing About Government

6. **Public Policy** Although the Supreme Court sets policy, its decisions are affected by the powers of Congress and the president. Create a diagram that illustrates how Congress and the president check the powers of the Supreme Court. Display and discuss your diagram.

Answers

1. All definitions can be found in the section and the Glossary.
2. relevant laws, precedents, the Constitution
3. Severe personal conflicts may divide the Court. Good personal relations promote solutions to problems.
4. The Court overturned the "separate but equal" doctrine upheld by *Plessy* v. *Ferguson* because of a societal shift in race relations, and the Court's opinion that *separate* is inherently *unequal*.
5. existing laws, justices' personal views, interactions among justices, social forces and public attitudes, Congress and the president
6. Display and discuss students' diagrams.

Should Supreme Court Justices Have Limited Terms of Office?

Unless they are impeached for bad behavior, Supreme Court justices are appointed for life. Recently some law professors and scholars have argued that the Court's justices should serve a limited term. Justices are now living longer and critics question whether it is a good thing to have elderly justices. In 2005, when Chief Justice William Rehnquist died in office at the age of 81, the issue seemed more relevant than ever. Diagnosed with cancer in 2004, Rehnquist was reluctant to retire. Although he continued to work from his home, he missed more than 40 oral arguments over a several-month period.

YES

We need to limit the terms Supreme Court justices serve for at least two reasons. First, the length of their term in office has grown: According to one study, from 1789 to 1970, justices served, on average, for just under 15 years. Since 1970, however, justices have served for about 26 years. It is likely that some justices stay on the Court even when their mental and physical powers are weakened, relying instead on talented law clerks. There is an even more important reason for establishing term limits, however. When vacancies occur so infrequently due to the long tenures, the battles over appointments to the Court tend to become bitter and divisive to the nation. Finally, because such long tenures are possible, a president is tempted to appoint a relatively young judge. A young judge may not be as seasoned as he or she should be to sit in this high position. Yet the president may urge such a person because a young judge can represent the president's point of view on the Court for a very long time—as long as 30 years.

NO

Alexander Hamilton is the Founder who is most closely connected with life tenure for Supreme Court justices. In his *The Federalist*, No. 78, Hamilton quoted a great French thinker, the baron de Montesquieu, who understood the importance of an independent judiciary: "There is no liberty if the power of judging be not separated from the legislative and executive powers." Anything less than life tenure will make a justice vulnerable to political influence. As for the older age of justices, if judges are living longer, so too is the population in general. Critics have not pointed to any specific Supreme Court decisions as flawed because a justice was old or feeble. The confirmation process is highly politicized, it is true, but it could be just as politicized under a new system. The real key to the confirmation process is how well the two parties can cooperate, not how often vacancies occur. The current system has stood the test of time, and there is no reason to change it.

Debating the Issue

1. **Analyzing** What are the three reasons critics use to back their argument for limiting tenures?
2. **Explaining** How did the baron de Montesquieu connect an independent judiciary to life tenure?
3. **Evaluating** Which position is more convincing to you? Why?

▶ The Supreme Court building

Teach

Setting up the Debate

Analyzing Remind students that John Paul Stevens, the longest-serving current justice, was appointed by Gerald Ford in 1975. **Ask:** Is it a problem that justices serve such long terms? *(Prompt students to explain their responses.)*

Evaluating Have students research the arguments for and against term limits for Supreme Court justices. Students should find specific examples to support both points of view. They might cite examples from states where justices serve shorter terms to bolster their argument.

Concluding the Debate

Discuss these questions with students:
- If term limits were set for Supreme Court justices, how long should they serve?
- Is it true that anything less than life tenure will make a justice vulnerable to political influence?

Debating the Issue Answers

1. Justices are serving longer. Battles over appointments have become bitter. Presidents are inclined to nominate younger candidates.
2. If judges do not have life tenure, they will be vulnerable to political influence.
3. Students should state a position and clearly defend it.

CHAPTER 12

Assessment and Activities

ExamView®
Assessment Suite

This easy-to-use software includes extensive question banks and allows you to create fully customized tests that can be administered in print or online.

Reviewing Vocabulary

1. writ of certiorari
2. state decisis
3. amicus curiae
4. per curiam opinion
5. precedent
6. brief
7. majority opinion
8. dissenting opinion

Reviewing Main Ideas

9. After the Court accepts a case, the lawyers for each side submit a brief. The lawyers then present oral arguments. The justices meet in conference to discuss the case. They vote on the decision and an opinion is written to explain the majority position.

10. It instructs lower courts on how to act in the future and communicates the Court's thinking to government, interest groups, and the public.

11. The dissenting opinion might become the basis for a majority opinion if the Court later changes its position.

12. Society's attitudes and values change over time, as do those of the justices. What was once acceptable might have changed over time.

13. limits on the types of issues, limits on the types of cases, limited control over its agenda, lack of enforcement

Reviewing Vocabulary

Match each of the following content vocabulary word(s) with the description below that correctly identifies it.

amicus curiae, precedent, stare decisis, dissenting opinion, brief, majority opinion, per curiam opinion, writ of certiorari

1. order to lower court for records on a case to be handed up for review
2. lets a decision stand
3. an interested party that is not directly involved in a case
4. short, unsigned statement of the Supreme Court's decision
5. earlier decision on similar cases
6. sets forth facts and legal arguments to support one side of a case
7. sets forth reasons for a Supreme Court decision
8. sets forth reasons for disagreeing with a Supreme Court decision

Reviewing Main Ideas

Section 1 *(pages 331–335)*

9. **Specifying** What procedure do the justices follow to reach a decision in a case?

10. **Assessing** What is the importance of a Supreme Court majority opinion?

11. **Describing** What is the importance of a dissenting opinion?

Section 2 *(pages 336–341)*

12. **Explaining** Why does the Supreme Court sometimes overturn its earlier decisions?

13. **Identifying** What are the four limits that restrict the power of the Supreme Court?

Section 3 *(pages 343–348)*

14. **Examining** How does the Supreme Court remain insulated from public opinion and political pressures?

15. **Summarizing** How can Congress try to shape decisions or limit the Supreme Court's powers?

Critical Thinking

16. **Analyzing** Why does the Supreme Court refuse to hear so many cases?

17. **Synthesizing** In a chart, identify factors that affect how the Supreme Court shapes public policy, and name a major case that illustrates each factor.

How the Court Shapes Policy	
Factor	Example

Chapter Summary

How the Court Shapes Public Policy

★ Judicial review: Court may decide whether government laws are constitutional
★ Interpreting the meaning of laws: Court takes the general language of laws and applies it to specific cases
★ Overruling or reversing previous Court decisions to reflect changing social values and laws.

Limits on the Court's Shaping of Public Policy

★ Types of issues: Court deals mostly with civil liberties, economic issues, federal laws, and suits against government officials
★ Types of cases: Court hears only cases that meet certain criteria
★ Agenda: Generally can decide only cases that come to it from elsewhere in the legal system
★ Enforcement power: Court has limited ability to enforce its rulings

Influences on Supreme Court Decisions

★ Existing laws: Court interprets and applies laws to individual cases
★ Personal views of the justices: Political ideology
★ Justices' ability to work together
★ Social forces and public attitudes
★ Congress and the president: Judicial branch works as part of the system of checks and balances

14. Justices have life tenure, and rules limit the ways in which outside groups can influence the Court.

15. Congress can pass new laws to limit judicial remedies, revise laws that were declared unconstitutional, propose constitutional amendments, refuse to raise justices' salaries, and add new justices to the Court.

Critical Thinking

16. The Court may decline to hear a case because it does not involve an important constitutional issue or is not the best case for deciding an issue; also the Court may not want to take a position on a political issue.

17. Factor—judicial review: *Marbury v. Madison, Dred Scott, Ex parte Milligan, Train v. City of New York, Brown v. Board of Education of Topeka, Miranda v. Arizona*
Example—interpreting the meaning of laws:
Lau v. Nichols
reversing previous decisions:
Katz v. United States

Government ONLINE **Self-Check Quiz**
Visit glencoe.com and enter *QuickPass*™ code USG9822c12.
Click on Self-Check Quizzes for additional test practice.

Document-Based Questions

Analyzing Primary Sources

Read the excerpt below and answer the questions that follow.

President Harry S. Truman established the President's Committee on Civil Rights in 1946. The committee issued a report on its findings about the state of civil rights and its recommendations for improving their protection.

> ❝ The Court has announced a new doctrine that when a law appears to encroach upon a civil right . . . the presumption is that the law is invalid, unless its advocates can show that the interference is justified because of the existence of a 'clear and present danger' to the public security. These new developments have resulted in a striking increase in the number of civil rights cases heard by the Supreme Court. . . .
>
> It is not too much to say that during the last 10 years, the disposition of cases of this kind has been as important as any work performed by the Court. As an agency of the federal government, it is now actively engaged in the broad effort to safeguard civil rights. ❞

18. According to the report, how did the Court's role in regard to civil rights change during the first years of the civil rights movement?

19. To what do you attribute the increased number of cases heard by the Supreme Court in the late 1940s, when this report was released?

Applying Technology Skills

20. Using the Internet Search the Internet for a Web site that has extended quotations on a recent case heard by the Supreme Court. Write a summary of the ruling, the majority opinion, and the dissenting opinion. Try to use ordinary language to express your sense of the main emphasis of the ruling and opinions.

Interpreting Political Cartoons

Analyze the cartoon and answer the questions that follow. Base your answers on the cartoon and your knowledge of Chapter 12.

21. How would you characterize the attitude of the cartoonist of the Supreme Court, and is this the attitude of the average American? Explain.

22. How does the cartoonist illustrate the importance of the fact that there are nine (not eight) justices on the Supreme Court?

23. Why is one justice singled out in the cartoon by name and why does he look flustered?

24. Is the nature of the Court—as presented in this cartoon—beneficial to American society? Why or why not?

Participating IN GOVERNMENT

25. As you have learned, public opinion does have some influence on Supreme Court decisions. Survey members of your community about a current case on the Supreme Court's docket. Chart the responses you receive about the issues in the case.

Government ONLINE

Have students use the Chapter 12 Self-Check Quiz. Visit glencoe.com and enter *QuickPass*™ code USG9085c12T to prepare for the Chapter Test.

how the average American views the Supreme Court.

22. If all the justices vote, a tie cannot occur.

23. Justice Anthony Kennedy (known as a swing voter) is uncertain whether to side with Republicans or Democrats on the Court.

24. Answers will vary, but encourage students to provide thoughtful responses.

Participating IN GOVERNMENT

25. Tabulate the various opinions students gather. Ask students whether they agree with those opinions and to analyze how those opinions might affect the Court's ruling, or enforcement of the ruling.

Chapter Bonus Test Question

Ask: Which Supreme Court justice served the longest? (William O. Douglas, 1939–1975)

Analyzing Primary Sources

18. This report indicates that the Court became more inclined to invalidate laws that appeared to encroach upon civil rights, and civil rights cases became the largest portion of its work. The Supreme Court became a more political body of the government because of the civil rights movement and its legal challenges to segregation.

19. Public pressure, particularly from the NAACP, brought civil rights cases to the

Supreme Court, making it the protector and promoter of civil rights.

Applying Technology Skills

20. Compile students' information in a class chart. Encourage students to share the addresses of interesting and informative Web sites concerning the Supreme Court.

Interpreting Political Cartoons

21. The cartoonist believes the Court is very politicized. Students may disagree about

Liberty *and* Justice *for* All

UNIT PACING CHART*			
	Chapter 13	**Chapter 14**	**Chapter 15**
Day 1	Unit Opener Chapter Opener Section 1	Chapter Opener Section 1	Chapter Opener Section 1
Day 2	Section 2 Supreme Court Cases to Debate	Section 2	Supreme Court Cases to Debate Section 2
Day 3	Section 3 Section 4	Section 3 Supreme Court Cases to Debate	Issues to Debate Section 3
Day 4	Section 5 Government Skills	Section 4 Issues to Debate	Section 4 Progress of Democracy
Day 5	Review Chapter Assessment	Review Chapter Assessment	Review Chapter Assessment

*Unit Pacing Chart based on year-long course; modify pacing by half for semester-long course

 Teacher *to* Teacher

Earnestine Gordon

Riverview Gardens School District St. Louis, MO

Eulogy of a Suffragist Have students compose eulogies for suffragists. As a class, students should compile a list of women who were important to the suffrage movement. Organize the students into groups of three. Each group will research one of the women on the list. Make sure each group picks a different woman. One member of each group will play the role of newspaper reporter, one will be a designer and artist, and the third will be an orator.

One student will write an article about the woman the group chose to study. Another student will design and create a poster to illustrate that person's life and achievements, and a third student will present the poster and article to the class. Encourage students to look not only at what each woman did for the women's rights movement, but also at the things she sacrificed and the life she led outside of the movement.

To conclude each presentation, have each student orator tell why voting is an important privilege.

Author Note

Dear U.S. Government Teacher,

In Unit 5, "Liberty and Justice for All," the textbook addresses those unalienable rights guaranteed by the Bill of Rights, paying particular attention to freedom of religion, freedom of speech, freedom of the press, and freedom of assembly. People around the world identify these rights with American democracy, as do Americans themselves.

In each section of Chapter 13, these core freedoms are addressed through discussions of landmark Supreme Court decisions. In addition, you will be introducing students to the incorporation doctrine. Over time, this important doctrine has applied most of the Bill of Rights to the states.

In Chapter 14, students will explore the very nature of citizenship. Who is a citizen and how does one acquire citizenship? Because global migration will most likely continue and possibly increase, a knowledge and appreciation of our nation's history of immigration is essential.

Citizens have the right to equal protection of the law. The vigilance required to guarantee equal protection involves all of us. Students who know and understand these rights and how they have been expanded will be in a better position to participate in a democracy and to protect their own rights or the rights of others. In the words of famed abolitionist Wendell Phillips, "Eternal vigilance is the price of liberty."

In the end, democratic freedoms rest on a system of laws. Chapter 15 gives students a brief history in the development of legal systems, highlighting the legal heritage of the Anglo-American world that was developed by Britain. In separate sections, students will learn the basic categories of civil law and criminal law. In the last section of the chapter, the basic rights of the accused—another cornerstone of democracy—are laid out and explained through reference to significant court cases.

Richard C. Remy

Richard C. Remy, Ph.D.
Author

Focus

Making It Relevant

Understanding an Event
Have students look at the photograph of the March on Washington on this page and share what they know about this landmark event. Then point out the title of this unit—"Liberty and Justice for All." Discuss how this event has symbolized the progress of freedom in the United States and ways in which it expresses the goal of justice and equal treatment for all Americans.

Unit Objectives

After studying this unit, students will be able to:

- **List** an American citizen's basic civil liberties and review the constitutional protections provided for each.

- **Discuss** the nature, rights, and responsibilities of U.S. citizenship.

- **Explain** the foundations of the U.S. legal system and the basic procedures of civil and criminal law.

Unit Overview

Unit 5 describes the rights and responsibilities of American citizens.

Chapter 13 describes the basic freedoms granted by the Constitution.

Chapter 14 describes gaining citizenship and the rights and responsibilities of citizens.

Chapter 15 describes the sources of American law and the differences between civil and criminal law.

352

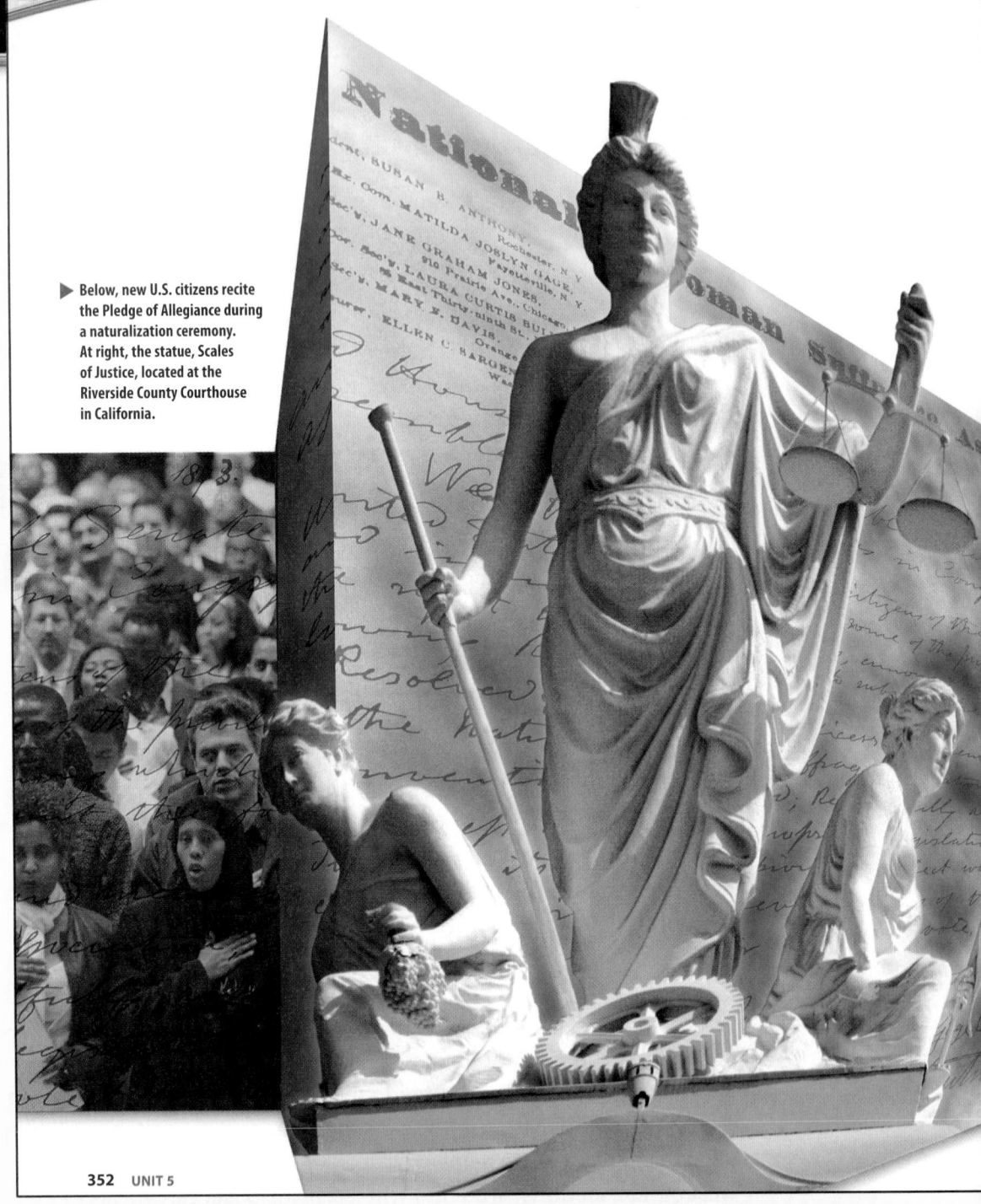

▶ Below, new U.S. citizens recite the Pledge of Allegiance during a naturalization ceremony. At right, the statue, Scales of Justice, located at the Riverside County Courthouse in California.

Activity: Launching the Unit

Preparing a Student Guide Have groups of students develop a guide to the constitutional rights and responsibilities enjoyed by 18-year-old students in the United States. The guide should take the form of a four-page, illustrated pamphlet entitled *Know Your Rights.* Group members should share the tasks involved in developing the pamphlet, and so on. Have groups create enough copies of their pamphlets that each group member has a copy; then have groups display their pamphlets for other government and civics classes. **OL**

UNIT 5

Liberty *and* Justice *for* All

Participating IN GOVERNMENT

BIG IDEA **Public Policy** Providing equal treatment for all is a main goal of the American system of justice. Read a newspaper or visit a Web site and find a civil or criminal case before local or state courts. Identify the main constitutional or legal issue the case reflects. Ask yourself: Is this an issue that is affected by changes in public policy? If so, why do you think so? If not, why?

▲ Martin Luther King, Jr., at the March on Washington, August 28, 1963

353

Teach

S Skill Practice

Visual Literacy Ask students to consider the photo on page 353 of Martin Luther King, Jr., at the March on Washington. **Ask:** What details help to make this photo good for symbolizing this historic event? *(Students may comment on King's posture—encompassing the thousands who attended, how he stands out as a silhouette in his robes before so many, or the perspective that suggests how many thousands attended, seeming to stretch to the Washington Monument in the distance.)*

Online Current Events Update

History happens every day. Visit Glencoe's Online Current Events Update at <u>glencoe.com</u> to find news reports, features, maps, graphs, and images about events that shape our lives. Students can connect those events to historical events in world and American history by exploring related events on an interactive time line—a time line that ends with today.

Graduation: Exit With Success

Teaching Tip Help students become more proficient at understanding phonics by modeling for them how to sound out difficult names or words.

Extra Credit Project

History of American Law Have interested students interview a local attorney or a historian about how laws have changed over the course of our nation's history. Some examples of laws that have changed might include immigration laws; laws that restricted voting, such as the poll tax; Prohibition; drunk-driving laws; the juvenile justice system; divorce and child custody laws; laws that allowed people to buy their way out of the draft; laws that segregated or allowed segregation of citizens by race or gender; and so on. Have students write a report about their interview. **OL**

	Key to Ability Levels		Key to Teaching Resources	
BL Below level	**AL** Above level		Print Material	Transparency
OL On level	**ELL** English Language Learners		CD-ROM or DVD	

Levels					Resources	Chapter Opener	Section 1	Section 2	Section 3	Section 4	Section 5	Chapter Assess
BL	OL	AL	ELL									
FOCUS												
BL	OL	AL	ELL	📠	Section Focus Transparencies		13-1	13-2	13-3	13-4	13-5	
TEACH												
BL	OL		ELL	📁	Reading Essentials and Study Guide (and Answer Key)		p. 135	p. 137	p. 140	p. 143	p. 146	
BL	OL		ELL	📁	Guided Reading Activities		p. 45	p. 46	p. 47	p. 48	p. 49	
BL	OL		ELL	📁	Vocabulary Activities					p. 13		
BL	OL	AL	ELL	📁	Chapter Summaries		p. 37					
BL	OL			📁	American Biographies							
BL	OL	AL	ELL	📁	Cooperative Learning Activities							
	OL	AL	ELL	📁	Government Simulations and Debate				p. 22			
BL	OL	AL	ELL	📁	Historical Documents and Speeches					p. 13		
BL	OL	AL	ELL	📁	Interpreting Political Cartoons						p. 25	
BL	OL		ELL	📁	Skill Reinforcement Activities			p. 13				
BL	OL	AL	ELL	📁	Source Readings						p. 13	
BL	OL			📁	Supreme Court Case Studies		p. 39	pp. 17, 67, 85, 113	pp. 39, 69, 77, 105, 129, 131		p. 51	
BL	OL	AL	ELL	📁	Participating in Government Activities				p. 25			
BL	OL		ELL	📁	Spanish Declaration of Independence and U.S. Constitution	✓	✓	✓	✓	✓	✓	✓
BL	OL	AL	ELL	📁	NGS World Atlas, Spanish	✓	✓	✓	✓	✓	✓	✓
BL	OL	AL	ELL	📠	Unit Overlay Transparencies, Strategies, and Activities	✓	✓	✓	✓	✓	✓	✓
BL	OL		ELL	📠	Making It Relevant Transparencies	✓	✓	✓	✓	✓	✓	✓
BL	OL	AL	ELL	📠	High School Writing Process Transparencies, Strategies, and Activities	✓	✓	✓	✓	✓	✓	✓
BL	OL	AL		📠	American Art & Architecture Transparencies, Strategies, and Activities	✓	✓	✓	✓	✓	✓	✓

✓ Chapter- or unit-based activities applicable to all sections in this chapter

All-In-One Planner and Resource Center

- Interactive Lesson Planner
- Interactive Teacher Edition
- Fully editable blackline masters
- Chapter Spotlight Videos Launch

- Differentiated Lesson Plans
- Printable reports of daily assignments
- Standards tracking system

Levels BL	OL	AL	ELL		Resources	Chapter Opener	Section 1	Section 2	Section 3	Section 4	Section 5	Chapter Assess
TEACH *(continued)*												
BL	OL			◉	American Music: Hits Through History	✓	✓	✓	✓	✓	✓	✓
BL	OL		ELL	📁	Reading Strategies for the Social Studies Classroom	✓	✓	✓	✓	✓	✓	✓
			ELL	📁	English Language Learner Handbook	✓	✓	✓	✓	✓	✓	✓
BL	OL		ELL	📁	Writer's Guidebook for Social Studies	✓	✓	✓	✓	✓	✓	✓
BL	OL	AL	ELL	📁	Living Constitution, SE	✓	✓	✓	✓	✓	✓	✓
BL	OL	AL	ELL	📁	Living Constitution, TAE	✓	✓	✓	✓	✓	✓	✓
BL	OL			📁	NGS World Atlas, English	✓	✓	✓		✓	✓	✓
BL	OL		ELL	📁	The Constitution and You (poster set)	✓	✓	✓	✓	✓	✓	✓
BL	OL	AL	ELL	📁	Spanish Chapter Summaries		p. 37					
BL	OL	AL	ELL	📁	Spanish Vocabulary Activities					p. 13		
BL	OL		ELL	📁	Spanish Reading Essentials and Study Guide (and Answer Key)		p. 135	p. 137	p. 140	p. 143	p. 146	
BL	OL	AL	ELL	◉	PresentationPlus! with MindJogger CheckPoint	✓	✓	✓	✓	✓	✓	✓
ASSESS												
BL	OL	AL	ELL	◉	*ExamView® Assessment Suite*		13-1	13-2	13-3	13-4	13-5	Ch. 13
BL	OL	AL	ELL	📁	Authentic Assessment with Rubrics		p. 20					p. 20
BL	OL	AL	ELL	📁	Section Quizzes and Chapter Tests		p. 155	p. 156	p. 157	p. 158	p. 159	pp. 161–168
BL	OL	AL	ELL	📁	Spanish Section Quizzes and Tests		p. 155	p. 156	p. 157	p. 158	p. 159	pp. 161–168
CLOSE												
BL			ELL	📁	Reteaching Activities						p. 13	p. 13
BL	OL	AL	ELL	◉	StudentWorks™ Plus with Audio Summaries	✓	✓	✓	✓	✓	✓	✓
BL	OL		ELL	🖨	Graphic Organizer Transparencies		✓	✓	✓	✓		
BL	OL		ELL	📁	High School Government Reading and Study Skills Foldables®		p. 56	p. 56	p. 56	p. 56	p. 56	

Teach With Technology

Chapter Spotlight Video

What are Chapter Spotlight Videos?
Chapter Spotlight Videos are one of the digital media associated with your textbook and present a topic specific to each chapter of the textbook.

How can Chapter Spotlight Videos help my students?
Chapter Spotlight Videos generate student interest and provide a springboard for classroom discussion. Students can watch videos from their classroom computer screen or review for a test while on their home computer.

Visit glencoe.com to access the Media Library, and enter a *QuickPass*™ code to go to Chapter Spotlight Videos. These videos can also be launched from StudentWorks™ Plus Online or PresentationPlus! with MindJogger CheckPoint.

Government ONLINE
Visit glencoe.com and enter *QuickPass*™ code USG9085c13T for Chapter 13 resources.

You can easily launch a wide range of digital products from your computer's desktop with the McGraw-Hill Social Studies widget.

	Student	Teacher	Parent
Media Library			
• Student Edition Section Audio	●		●
• Chapter Spotlight Videos	●	●	●
***United States Government* Online Learning Center (Web Site)**			
• Chapter Overviews	●	●	●
• Multilingual Glossaries	●	●	●
• Study-to-Go	●	●	●
• Student Web Activities	●	●	●
• Self-Check Quizzes	●	●	●
• Online Student Edition	●	●	●
• Vocabulary eFlashcards	●	●	●
• Web Activity Lesson Plans		●	
• Vocabulary PuzzleMaker	●	●	●
• Landmark Supreme Court Cases	●	●	●
• Beyond the Textbook	●	●	●

TeacherWorks

READING SUPPORT FROM
JAMESTOWN EDUCATION

- **Timed Readings Plus in Social Studies** helps students increase their reading rate and fluency while maintaining comprehension. The 400-word passages are similar to those found on state and national assessments.

- **Reading in the Content Area: Social Studies** concentrates on six essential reading skills that help students better comprehend what they read. The book includes 75 high-interest nonfiction passages written at increasing levels of difficulty.

- **Reading Social Studies** includes strategic reading instruction and vocabulary support in Social Studies content for ELLs and native speakers of English. www.jamestowneducation.com

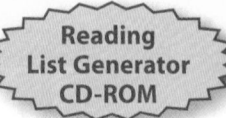

Reading List Generator CD-ROM

GLENCOE
BOOKLINK 3

Use this database to search more than 30,000 titles to create a customized reading list for your students.

- Reading lists can be organized by students' reading level, author, genre, theme, or area of interest.
- The database provides Degrees of Reading Power™ (DRP) and Lexile™ readability scores for all selections.
- A brief summary of each selection is included.

Leveled reading suggestions for this chapter:

- *Great Lives: Human Rights,* by William Jay Jacobs
- *Martin Luther King, Jr. and the Freedom Movement,* by Lillie Patterson
- *Thurgood Marshall: Champion of Justice,* by G.S. Prentzas

Review suggested books before assigning them.

Economics Connection

Personal Finance Literacy

College Costs

An educated citizenry is essential in a democracy. Equal educational opportunity was one of the rights sought by the civil rights movement. In today's global environment, higher education increasingly is associated with the economic competitiveness of the nation, as well as greater individual wealth, civic participation, and better health.

Everyone knows college is expensive, but the average college graduate earns considerably more over a lifetime than a high-school graduate earns. Over the years the government has established programs designed to make a college education accessible to more people. The Higher Education Act of 1965 (HEA) provides federal funds for loans, grants, and scholarships. State governments also offer similar, smaller programs.

College costs vary widely from school to school, but in recent years have tended to increase by about 6 percent per year. The good news is that about $130 billion in financial aid is available in the form of grants, scholarships, tax benefits, and low-interest loans. Between 2007 and 2008, estimated grants and tax benefits averaged $2,040 per student at public two-year colleges, about $3,600 at public four-year colleges, and about $9,300 per student at private four-year colleges. The chart shows costs for tuition and fees—but not for room and board.

Average 2007–2008 1-Year College Costs	
Type of Institution	**Tuition and Fees**
Public 4-year	$6,185*
Private 4-year	$23,712
2-year community	$2,361

*Out-of-state students add an average of $10,455
Source: The College Board

Did You Know?

About two-thirds of full-time undergraduate students receive grant aid. Almost three-fourths attend public two- or four-year colleges and universities rather than private schools.

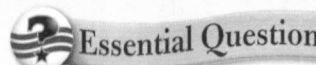

CHAPTER 13

🔊 Chapter Audio   📺 Spotlight Video

Constitutional Freedoms

Freedom of speech is subject to some limitations. Speech that is defamatory, that is likely to provoke violence, or that presents a clear and present danger can be regulated. Student speech can also be regulated. Have students brainstorm about limits to other constitutional freedoms.

📽 Chapter Spotlight Video

To generate student interest and provide a springboard for class discussion, access the Chapter 13 Video at glencoe.com or on the video DVD.

FOLDABLES
Study Organizer

 Dinah Zike's Foldables are three-dimensional, interactive graphic organizers that help students practice basic writing skills, review key vocabulary terms, and identify main ideas. Have students complete this chapter's Foldable activity or activities in *Dinah Zike's Reading and Study Skills Foldables* booklet. **OL**

Government ONLINE

Visit glencoe.com and enter **QuickPass**™ code USG9085c13T for Chapter 13 Resources including Chapter Overview, Student Web Activity, Self-Check Quiz, and other materials for students and teachers.

▶ **The Liberty Bell Center, Philadelphia, Pennsylvania**

 Essential Question

Freedom of speech is one of Americans' most valued liberties, but are there limits to this and other basic freedoms under the Constitution?

Government ONLINE
Chapter Overview Visit glencoe.com and enter **QuickPass**™ code USG9822c13 for an overview, a quiz, and other chapter resources.

354

Launching the Chapter

Depicting Many events discussed in this chapter are filled with drama. Invite students to select one such moment to depict artistically. Here are a few ideas:
- James Madison introducing the amendments that became the Bill of Rights
- students or parents demonstrating against a Court ruling (as in a school prayer or Bible-study case)

- a student newspaper staff learning that their publication is being censored

As time permits, you may wish to work with students to prepare a classroom display of the individual works.

Essential Question: What makes these scenes moving and dramatic? *(Answers will vary, but help students make the connection between constitutional rights and fundamental human rights.)* **OL**

Constitutional Rights

Reader's Guide

Content Vocabulary
★ human rights *(p. 355)*
★ incorporation *(p. 357)*

Academic Vocabulary
★ guarantee *(p. 355)*
★ deny *(p. 357)*
★ pursue *(p. 357)*

Reading Strategy
As you read, create a graphic organizer similar to the one below to describe the freedoms guaranteed by the First Amendment.

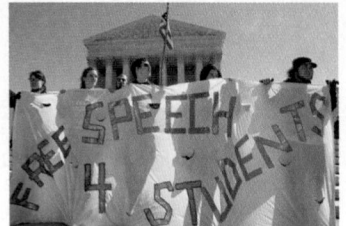

Issues in the News

When school officials disciplined Andrew Smith for an editorial he wrote in the school paper, the California student took his case to court. The court of appeals supported Smith's claim that his free speech rights had been violated. When the school appealed the decision to the Supreme Court, it refused to review the decision, meaning the court of appeals decision was final. In the words of Judge Linda Gemello, writing for the appeals court: "A school may not prohibit student speech simply because it presents controversial ideas and opponents of the speech are likely to cause disruption."

▲ Students demonstrating for free speech at the Supreme Court

The belief in **human rights,** or fundamental freedoms, lies at the heart of the American political system. Citizens and noncitizens alike have the right to speak freely, to read and write what they choose, and to worship as they wish or to not worship at all.

The Constitution guarantees the rights of U.S. citizens. Along with these rights comes a responsibility to protect them. As the Preamble states, "We, the people" adopted the Constitution, and in many ways, United States citizens remain the keepers of their own rights. Rights and responsibilities cannot be separated. Judge Learned Hand expressed this well when he observed:

❝ Liberty lies in the hearts of men and women; when it dies there, no constitution, no law, no court can save it; no constitution, no law, no court can even do much to help it. ❞
—Judge Learned Hand

As citizens, people share a common faith in the power they have to steer the course of government. If people do not carry out their responsibilities as citizens, the whole society suffers.

Constitutional Rights

The Constitution of the United States **guarantees** certain basic rights in the Bill of Rights, comprised of the first 10 amendments, and in several additional amendments. The Framers of the Constitution believed that people had rights simply because they were people. In the words of the Declaration of Independence, people "are endowed by their Creator with certain unalienable rights." The Constitution and the Bill of Rights inscribe into law those rights that really belong to everyone. The Bill of Rights, in particular, stands as a written guarantee that government cannot abuse the rights of individuals.

CHAPTER 13: *Constitutional Freedoms* **355**

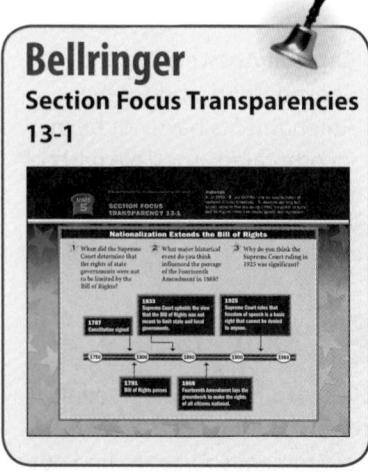

Teach

S Skill Practice

Researching Have students use the Internet and several government sources to find out how the Supreme Court has interpreted the Fourteenth Amendment over the years, beginning with *Gitlow* v. *New York* (1925). Have students research the following cases: *Near* v. *Minnesota*, *DeJonge* v. *Oregon*, *Wolf* v. *Colorado*, *Pointer* v. *Texas*, and *Benton* v. *Maryland*. Students will present their findings in a chart.

Ask: Should all the protections and rights guaranteed by the Bill of Rights apply to state governments as well as the national government? Do you think the Framers of the Constitution wanted the states to grant all of the rights listed in the Bill of Rights? **AL**

Hands-On Chapter Project

Step 1

Guaranteed Freedoms

Free Speech Champions Supreme Court Justices Oliver Wendell Holmes (left) and Louis Brandeis are pictured together in a 1931 photo. Six years earlier, in *Gitlow* v. *New York*, the pair dissented with the majority, saying that Benjamin Gitlow's writing about socialist revolution was too abstract to be truly dangerous. The case's real impact was that it helped incorporate the Bill of Rights into the laws of all the states. *Has the entire Bill of Rights been incorporated into state and local laws?*

The language of the Bill of Rights is very important, beginning with the words "Congress shall make no law. . . ." Today the Bill of Rights offers protection not only from congressional actions, but also from acts by state and local governments that may threaten people's basic rights.

The Bill of Rights was originally intended to offer protection against the actions of the federal government. The Constitution drafted in 1787 did not include a bill of rights. Because most of the state constitutions of the time contained a bill of rights, the Framers believed it unnecessary to include another such list of rights in the national Constitution.

Many state leaders, however, were suspicious of the new Constitution. When it was submitted to the states for ratification, a number of states refused to

approve it unless a bill of rights was added. When the first Congress met in 1789, James Madison introduced a series of amendments that became the Bill of Rights in 1791. These amendments placed certain limitations on the national government to prevent it from controlling the press, restricting speech, establishing or prohibiting religion, and limiting other areas of personal liberty.

The Bill of Rights was not intended to limit state and local governments. An important 1833 Supreme Court case, *Barron* v. *Baltimore*,[1] upheld this view. Chief Justice John Marshall, speaking for the Court, ruled that the first 10 amendments "contain no expression indicating an intention to apply them to the state governments."

The Fourteenth Amendment

As times changed, so did the Constitution. The addition of the Fourteenth Amendment in 1868 paved the way for a major expansion of individual rights. The Fourteenth Amendment[2] not only defined citizenship (a person born or naturalized in the United States is a citizen of the nation and of the state of residence), it also laid the groundwork for making individual rights national. In part, the amendment states:

> 66 *No State shall make or enforce any law which shall abridge the privileges or immunities of citizens of the United States; nor shall any State deprive any person of life, liberty, or property without due process of law. . . .* 99
> —Fourteenth Amendment, 1868

The Supreme Court has interpreted the due process clause of the Fourteenth Amendment to apply the guarantees of the Bill of Rights to state and local governments. The Supreme Court has interpreted the word *liberty* in that amendment to include all First Amendment freedoms. Thus, no state can deprive any person of freedom of speech, press, religion, assembly, or petition because these freedoms are essential to liberty.

The Supreme Court interpreted the words *due process* to include other protections of the Bill of Rights—protection from unreasonable search and seizure, the right of the accused to have a lawyer, and protection from cruel and unusual

---

See the following footnoted materials in the **Reference Handbook:**
1. *Barron v. Baltimore* case summary, page R23.
2. *The Constitution*, pages R42–R67.

Creating a Class Poster

Step 1: Listing Constitutional Rights
Students will work in small groups to contribute to a poster entitled "Constitutional Rights: Here and There." Each group will create one panel of the poster, which will be displayed in a prominent position in the school.

Directions Have students use copies of the Constitution to remind them of the rights

Americans have. Ask them to make lists of these rights in their own words. For extra credit, someone might want to make a panel for the poster listing these rights.

Evaluating Ask: Which constitutional right do you consider most important? Discuss their answers. **OL**

(Chapter Project continued in Section 2.)

punishment. These rights have also been applied to the states through the Fourteenth Amendment. Because of how the Supreme Court has interpreted the Fourteenth Amendment, the Bill of Rights has been applied to all levels of government. In *Gitlow v. New York*[1] (1925), the Court ruled that freedom of speech is a basic right no state government could **deny** to a person. 📖 The process by which the Bill of Rights was extended to the states and localities is **incorporation.**

Incorporation occurs through Supreme Court cases that raise a specific issue. Since the 1920s, almost all of the amendments in the Bill of Rights have been incorporated. The exceptions are the Second, Third, and Tenth Amendments, the excessive bails and fines prohibition of the Eighth Amendment, and two judicial procedures in the Fifth and Seventh Amendments. As a result, states are not required to use a grand jury to bring formal charges for serious crimes, nor are they required to have a trial by jury in civil cases involving more than $20.

The Importance of Incorporation

The incorporation of the Bill of Rights means that United States citizens in every part of the country have the same basic rights. On the face of it, incorporation may not seem significant because state constitutions contain bills of rights. Yet in the past, state governments have ignored individual rights, denied voting rights to minority citizens, and practiced various forms of discrimination. As a result of incorporation, the Bill of Rights becomes a final safeguard when personal rights are threatened, proving that the Constitution is a living document.

District of Columbia v. Heller In a 2008 case, the Court addressed the District of Columbia's ban on firearms, ruling that it was unconstitutional. One of the petitioners, Dick Heller (right), stands before the Supreme Court with Robert Levy, who organized the suit. ***Does a Court ruling automatically incorporate a decision into state constitutions?***

In practice, nationalization means that citizens who believe that a state or local authority has denied them their basic rights may take their case to a federal court. If the decision of a lower federal court goes against them, they may **pursue** their claim all the way to the Supreme Court.

📖 *See the following footnoted materials in the **Reference Handbook:***
1. *Gitlow v. New York* case summary, page R27.

SECTION 1 Review

Vocabulary
1. Explain the significance of: human rights, incorporation.

Main Ideas
2. Analyzing Explain the impact of the incorporation of the Bill of Rights.

3. Examining Which branch of government has been primarily responsible for the incorporation of the Bill of Rights?

Critical Thinking
4. Making Inferences When it came time to submit the new Constitution to the states for ratification, why do you think state leaders insisted on a national Bill of Rights?

5. Organizing Use a graphic organizer like the one below to show the effects of incorporation on the scope of the Bill of Rights.

Cause: Incorporation of Bill of Rights	→	Effect:

Writing About Government
6. Persuasive Writing Some people have argued that all Americans should be required to perform some type of compulsory public service. Write an editorial for a newspaper either supporting or opposing the idea.

CHAPTER 13: *Constitutional Freedoms* 357

Answers

1. All definitions can be found in the section and the Glossary.
2. Incorporation extended the Bill of Rights to protect citizens from all levels of government in the United States.
3. the judicial branch (the Supreme Court)
4. They feared the potential power and abuses of the national government.
5. Effect: The Bill of Rights grew to protect citizens on the state level as well as the federal level.
6. Students' editorials should discuss the reasons that they support or oppose compulsory public service.

Focus

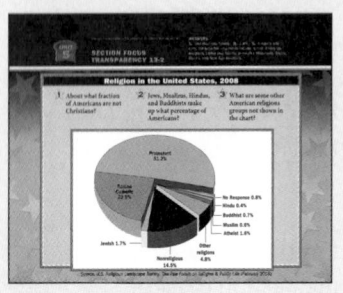
Reader's Guide

Answers to Graphic: Tables should include the following:
Establishment Clause: *Everson v. Board of Education, Wolman v. Walter, Lemon v. Kurtzman, Mitchell v. Helms, Zorach v. Clauson, Engel v. Vitale, Edwards v. Aguillard*
Free Exercise Clause: *Reynolds v. United States, Wisconsin v. Yoder, Minersville School District v. Gobitis, West Virginia State Board of Education v. Barnette*

Resource Manager

SECTION 2

Freedom of Religion

Reader's Guide

Content Vocabulary
★ establishment clause *(p. 358)*
★ free exercise clause *(p. 358)*
★ parochial school *(p. 359)*
★ secular *(p. 360)*
★ abridge *(p. 363)*
★ precedent *(p. 364)*

Academic Vocabulary
★ significant *(p. 358)*
★ acknowledge *(p. 361)*
★ justify *(p. 363)*

Reading Strategy
As you read, create a table similar to the one below to list the cases that are related to the establishment clause and the free exercise clause.

Establishment Clause Cases	Free Exercise Clause Cases

Issues in the News

In 2008 Gene R. Nichol, president of the College of William and Mary, resigned his position after a heated dispute over the display of a cross in the college's chapel. Deciding that the cross should be on display only during Christian services, Nichol said he was protecting the First Amendment and the separation of church and state. Some alumni of the college disagreed. They started Web sites to rally support for displaying the cross. Under pressure from these groups, the government board of the college told Nichol his contract would not be renewed. In a final defense of his action, Nichol stated his principles: "We are charged, as state actors, to respect and accommodate all religions, and to endorse none."

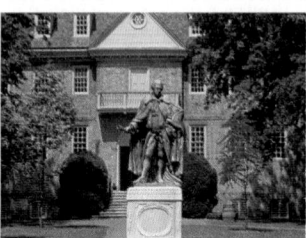

▲ The dispute at the College of William and Mary highlights a debate over the role of religion that has been going on since the nation's founding.

As this college chapel dispute suggests, debate over the public role of religion can be intense. But few would disagree that religion has always been a **significant** part of American life. About 85 percent of Americans identify with a religion. Religious tolerance developed slowly in the American colonies, but soon after the Constitution was adopted the nation guaranteed religious freedom in the First Amendment.[1] 📖

The first clause of the amendment, known as the **establishment clause,** states that "Congress shall make no law respecting an establishment of religion." The second clause—the **free exercise clause**—prohibits government from unduly interfering with the free exercise of religion. The precise meaning of these clauses has been the subject of continuing debate in American politics.

The Establishment Clause

In 1801 Baptists in Connecticut—a state where the Congregational Church was the official church—wrote to Thomas Jefferson asking his views about religious liberty. Jefferson wrote back strongly supporting the First Amendment. He stated that by passing the First Amendment, Americans had "declared that their legislature should 'make no law respecting an establishment of religion or prohibiting the free exercise thereof,' thus building a wall of separation between Church and State."

The phrase "wall of separation" that Jefferson used is not in the Constitution. He appears to have

📖 *See the following footnoted materials in the* **Reference Handbook:**
1. *The Constitution,* pages R42–R67.

R Reading Strategies	**C** Critical Thinking	**D** Differentiated Instruction	**W** Writing Support	**S** Skill Practice
Teacher Edition • Organizing, p. 360 • Evaluating, p. 363 **Additional Resources** • Guid. Read. Act., p. 46 • Quizzes/Tests, p. 156	**Teacher Edition** • Defending, p. 359 **Additional Resources** • Read. Essen., pp. 137–139	**Additional Resources** • Foldables, p. 56	**Teacher Edition** • Expository Writing, p. 363 **Additional Resources** • Supreme Ct. Case Studies, pp. 17–18, 67–68, 85–86, 87–88, 113–114	**Additional Resources** • Skill Reinforce. Act., p. 13

Constitutional Interpretations

The Establishment Clause Soldiers of the U.S. Army 1st Infantry take part in a benediction ceremony as they replace an outgoing unit for duty in Tikrit, Iraq, in 2004. *Why would this religious service not be considered a violation of the establishment clause?*

used the phrase to stress that the government should not establish an official church or restrict worship. Over time, the idea of a "wall of separation" has been expanded and become very controversial. How high does the "wall of separation" go? Does it mean that the state and any church or religious group should have no contact with each other?

Religion in Public Life

In practice, religion has long been part of public life in the United States. Although Article VI of the Constitution bans any religious qualification to hold public office, most government officials take their oaths of office in the name of God. Since 1864, most of the nation's coins have carried the motto "In God We Trust." The Pledge of Allegiance includes the phrase "one nation under God." Many public meetings, including daily sessions of Congress and most state legislatures, open with a prayer.

In some ways, the government encourages religion. For example, chaplains serve with the armed forces. In addition, most church property and contributions to religious groups are tax-exempt.

Attempting to define church-state relations often leads to controversy. Under the Constitution, the task of resolving these controversies falls on the Supreme Court. The Court had ruled on several religious freedom cases, but did not hear one on the establishment clause until 1947 when it decided *Everson* v. *Board of Education.* Since then, the Court has ruled many times on this clause. Most of these cases have involved some aspect of religion and education.

Everson v. Board of Education

This 1947 case involved a challenge to a New Jersey law allowing the state to pay for busing students to **parochial schools,** schools operated by a church or religious group. The law's critics contended that the law amounted to state support of a religion, which is in violation of the establishment clause. Writing the Court's decision, Justice Hugo H. Black defined the establishment clause:

> 66 *Neither a state nor the Federal Government can set up a church. Neither can pass laws which aid one religion, aid all religions, or prefer one religion over another. . . .* 99
> —Justice Hugo L. Black, 1947

The Court ruled, however, that the New Jersey law was constitutional. The Court determined that the law benefited students rather than aiding a religion directly. Although this 1947 decision still guides the Court, the *Everson* case illustrated uncertainty over just how high Jefferson's "wall of separation" should be. That uncertainty continues today both in the Court and among the American people.

State Aid to Parochial Schools

Some of the most controversial debates over church-state relations have focused on what kind of aid the government can give parochial schools. Since *Everson*, more than two-thirds of the states have given parochial schools aid ranging from driver education classes to subsidized lunches. The Court has found some programs constitutional and some not.

CHAPTER 13: *Constitutional Freedoms* **359**

Teach

Caption Answer: The religion practiced in the photo is not state supported but voluntary. The Supreme Court also ruled that government-related activities, such as the activities of the armed forces, are not violated by prayer because adults are less "susceptible to religious indoctrination."

C Critical Thinking

Defending Ask: Do you think parochial schools should get any form of state aid? Why or why not? *(Insist that students defend their opinions.)* If you think they should be able to receive state aid, what kinds of aid should they get? *(Students might mention funds for busing, school lunches, or direct financial aid.)* **AL**

Landmark Case

See *Everson* v. *Board of Education* in the Supreme Court Case Summaries in the *Reference Handbook* and Case Study 33 in the *Supreme Court Case Studies* booklet.

Additional Support

Activity: Collaborative Learning

Round-Robin Wrap-Up Organize students into small groups. Have a scribe for each group write each of these statements at the top of a sheet of paper:

• Freedom of religion means that I can

_____.

• Freedom of religion means that I cannot

_____.

Ask the groups to circulate each paper among their members, with every member providing a response to each question. Continue circulating the papers until every student has given at least two responses to each question. Complete the activity by having a volunteer from each group present the responses to the class and asking the class to look for common elements among the responses. **BL**

R Reading Strategy

Organizing Have students create a chronological chart of the Supreme Court decisions regarding the separation of church and state that are discussed in this chapter. Instruct students to include all the decisions that are mentioned in this section and to supplement that information with details from the Supreme Court Case Summaries in the **Reference Handbook. OL**

Differentiated Instruction

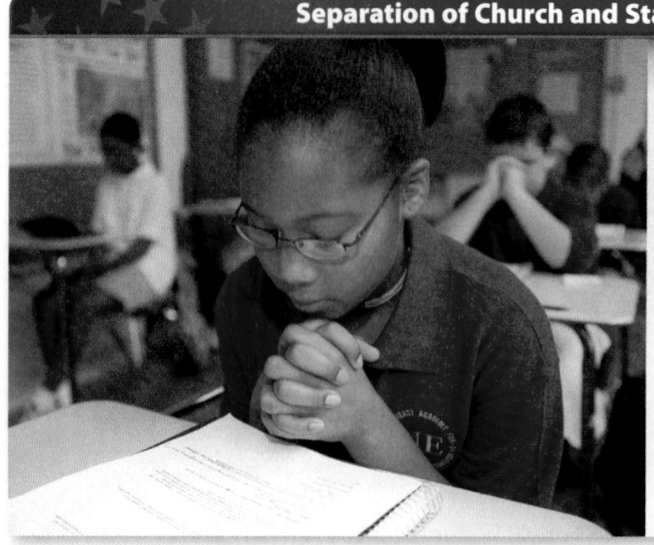

Separation of Church and State

Constitutional Principles The Constitution lays down the principle of separation of church and state. Thus, teaching religion to students in public schools has often raised controversy, yet the House of Representatives opens every session with a prayer. *Does a constitutional conflict exist when the state aids parochial schools? How has the Supreme Court addressed this conflict? Explain.*

For example, in *Board of Education* v. *Allen*[1] (1968) the Court upheld state programs that provide **secular,** or nonreligious, textbooks to parochial schools. 📖 Although the *Everson* decision permitted state-supported bus transportation to and from school, *Wolman* v. *Walter*[2] (1977) banned its use for field trips. 📖

Why are some forms of aid constitutional but not others? The answer is in the so-called Lemon test. Since the 1971 case of *Lemon* v. *Kurtzman*,[3] the Court has used a three-part test to decide whether such aid violates the establishment clause. 📖 To be constitutional, state aid to church schools must:

• have a clear secular, nonreligious purpose;

• in its main effect neither advance nor inhibit religion; and

• avoid "excessive government entanglement with religion."

In a 1973 case, *Levitt* v. *Committee for Public Education*,[4] the Court voided a New York plan to help pay for parochial schools to develop testing programs. 📖 In yet another case in 1980, *Committee for Public Education* v. *Regan*,[5] the Court permitted New York State to pay parochial schools to administer and grade tests. 📖 In this case the state's department of education prepared the tests. In the 1973 case, the tests were prepared by teachers, which the Court considered part of religious instruction.

In *Mueller* v. *Allen*[6] (1983), the Court upheld a Minnesota law allowing parents to deduct tuition, textbooks, and transportation to and from school from their state income tax. 📖 Public schools charge little or nothing for these items, because taxes are used to pay for them. Parents whose children attend parochial schools benefited from the deduction. But because the law permitted parents of all students to take the deduction, it passed the Court's three-part test.

In a similar case in 2000, *Mitchell* v. *Helms*,[7] the Court ruled that taxpayer funds could be used to provide religious schools with equipment—for example, computers, library books, projectors, and televisions—so long as the equipment is not used for religious purposes. 📖 This continued the Court's recent pattern of expanding government aid for parochial schools.

Conflicts over state aid to church schools are not confined to Christian schools. In *Kiryas Joel* v. *Grumet*[8] (1994), the Court ruled that the state of New York could not create a public school district solely to benefit a community of Hasidic Jews. 📖

📖 *See the following footnoted materials in the **Reference Handbook:***
1 *Board of Education* v. *Allen* case summary, page R24.
2. *Wolman* v. *Walter* case summary, page R37.
3. *Lemon* v. *Kurtzman* case summary, page R29.
4. *Levitt* v. *Committee for Public Education* case summary, page R30.
5. *Committee for Public Education* v. *Regan* case summary, page R25.
6. *Mueller* v. *Allen* case summary, page R31.
7. *Mitchell* v. *Helms* case summary, page R31.
8. *Kiryas Joel* v. *Grumet* case summary, page R29.

★ Activity: Multiple Learning Styles ★

Kinesthetic Many elements of faith are symbolized in religious objects and art. Ask students to collect and display pictures or items that they consider symbolic of various religions as well as of elements that are common to many religions—prayer (for example, a rosary or a picture of someone in prayer), moral living in accordance with one's faith (for example, a candle or religious literature), special observances (for example, a menorah or a picture of a Christmas tree), and so on. Call on volunteers to pick up various items from the display. Have each volunteer describe the item and comment upon it, perhaps explaining why it is protected by the First Amendment. **BL ELL**

Release Time for Students

Can public schools release students from school to attend classes in religious instruction? The Court first dealt with this question in *McCollum* v. *Board of Education*[1] (1948). 📖 The public schools in Champaign, Illinois, had a program in which religion teachers came into the schools once a week and gave instruction to students who desired it. The Court declared this program unconstitutional because school classrooms—tax-supported public facilities—were being used for religious purposes. Justice Hugo Black wrote that the program used tax-supported public schools "to aid religious groups to spread their faith."

Four years later in *Zorach* v. *Clauson*,[2] however, the Court accepted a New York City program that allowed religious instruction during the school day but away from the public schools. 📖 The Court ruled that a release-time program of religious instruction was constitutional if carried on in private rather than public facilities.

School Prayer Cases

In 1962 and 1963, the Court handed down three controversial decisions affecting prayer and Bible reading in public schools. The first was *Engel* v. *Vitale*,[3] a school prayer case that began in New York State. 📖 The New York Board of Regents composed a nondenominational prayer that it urged schools to use: "Almighty God, we **acknowledge** our dependence upon Thee, and we beg Thy blessings upon us, our parents, our teachers, and our country." In New Hyde Park, parents of 10 students challenged the prayer in court. In 1962 the Court declared the regents' prayer unconstitutional, interpreting the First Amendment to mean the following:

> 66 *[I]n this country it is no part of the business of government to compose official prayers for any group of the American people to recite as a part of a religious program carried on by government.* 99
> —Justice Hugo H. Black, 1962

In his lone dissent from the *Engel* decision, Justice Potter Stewart argued that the New York prayer was no different from other state-approved religious expression, such as referring to God in the Pledge of Allegiance.

School prayer has been addressed in a number of other important cases. In 1963 the Court combined a Pennsylvania case—*Abington School District* v. *Schempp*[4]—and one from Maryland—*Murray* v.

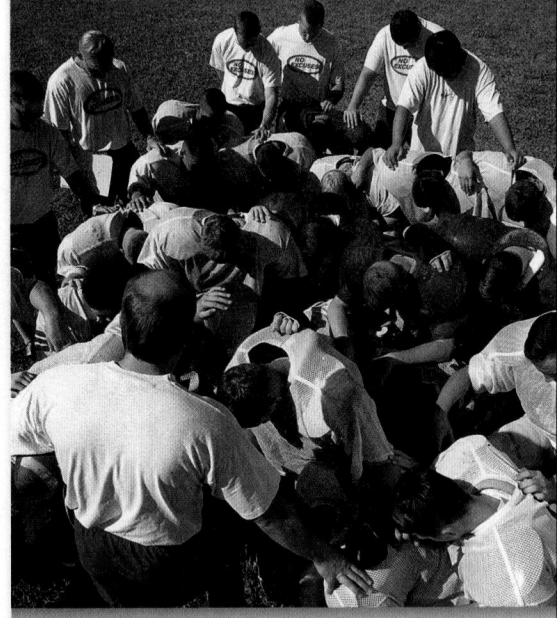

Prayer in Sports A San Marcos, Texas, public high school football team voluntarily prays before a game. *On what grounds does the Supreme Court reject mandatory prayers in public schools?*

Curlett—for another major decision on school prayer. 📖 In these cases, the Court banned school-sponsored Bible reading and recitation of the Lord's Prayer in public schools. Because teachers whose salaries were paid with tax dollars conducted the activities in public buildings, the Court reasoned that these acts violated the First Amendment.

In 1985, in *Wallace* v. *Jaffree*, the Court struck down an Alabama law requiring teachers to observe a moment of silence for "meditation or voluntary prayer" at the start of each school day. The Court ruled that the law's reference to prayer made it an unconstitutional endorsement of religion. In 1992 the Court also prohibited clergy-led prayers at public school graduations.

Then, in *Santa Fe Independent School District* v. *Doe*[5] (2000), the Supreme Court ruled that public school districts cannot let students lead stadium crowds in prayer before football games. 📖

📖 *See the following footnoted materials in the **Reference Handbook:***
1. *McCollum v. Board of Education* case summary, page R30.
2. *Zorach v. Clauson* case summary, page R37.
3. *Engel v. Vitale* case summary, page R26.
4. *Abington School District v. Schempp* case summary, page R23.
5. *Santa Fe Independent School District v. Doe* case summary, page R33.

Caption Answer: In *Engel* v. *Vitale,* the Court declared mandatory school prayer to be unconstitutional. In later rulings, the Court continued to rule that school-sponsored prayer constituted an establishment of religion.

CURRICULUM CONNECTION

Law The Supreme Court decision in *Abington School District* v. *Schempp* banned the reading of the Lord's Prayer and sections from the Bible, but it did not rule against teaching about religion in public schools. The ruling noted: "Nothing we have said here indicates that . . . study of the Bible or religion, when presented objectively as part of a secular program of education, may not be effected consistently with the First Amendment."

🏛 Landmark Case

See *Engel* v. *Vitale* and *Abington School District* v. *Schempp* in the Supreme Court Case Summaries in the **Reference Handbook** and Case Studies 43 and 44 in the *Supreme Court Case Studies* booklet.

Hands-On Chapter Project

Step 2

Creating a Class Poster

Step 2: Researching Events Students will do research for the poster.

Directions Tell students that not all countries offer the same rights. Ask each group to choose a different constitutional right of U.S. citizens to research. Each member of the groups will use his or her knowledge of history, current events, or other sources to find examples of events that demonstrate the lack of that right in another country. Students should look for specific examples of individuals or groups that have been denied a right at specific times. A fictitious example might be: **Date:** July 1992; **Location:** New South Wales, Australia; **Event:** A number of Aborigines are imprisoned for peacefully protesting against selling kangaroo meat; **Right denied:** Freedom of assembly.

Improving Research Skills Discuss any problems students might be having in searching for examples. **OL**

(Chapter Project continued in Section 3.)

Caption Answer: yes, if the items are publicly funded; the Supreme Court has ruled that such displays are permissible if they contain secular as well as religious symbols

ISSUES to Debate

Civil Liberties

Most Americans believe that one of the principal functions of government is to protect the rights of the governed. Among the rights that Americans want government to secure are the freedoms of religion, speech, press, and assembly. These civil liberties are expressly granted by the First Amendment. Although the Constitution grants these liberties, government can restrict or limit them when the well-being of the general public is at stake. Encourage students to debate these issues by agreeing or disagreeing with the following statement: "In a democracy, guaranteed rights must be accompanied by a means to restrict those rights." **AL**

Additional Support

Church and State

A Delicate Balance
Over the annual holiday season, the nation's Christmas tree and a large menorah are on view near the White House. Jews use the menorah in their celebration of Hanukkah, which commemorates the rededication of the Temple of Jerusalem in ancient times. *Does the establishment clause apply to these practices?*

According to Justice John Paul Stevens, such prayers "over the school's public address system by a speaker representing the student body" violated the separation of government and religion.

Public reaction to the Court's rulings has been both divided and heated. Although many people support the Court's stance, others are bitterly opposed. About half of the states have passed moment-of-silence laws that make no mention of prayer. Congress has considered several constitutional amendments to overturn these Court decisions, but has not produced the two-thirds majority needed to propose an amendment.

Equal Access Act

An exception to the Court's imposed limits on prayer in public schools is the Equal Access Act passed by Congress in 1984. The act allows public high schools receiving federal funds to permit student religious groups to hold meetings in the school. The bill's sponsors made it clear that they intended to provide opportunity for student prayer groups in public schools, a position that received overwhelming support in Congress.

In 1990 the Court ruled the law constitutional in a case that arose in Nebraska. Students at Westside High School in Omaha, Nebraska, asked to form a club for Bible study and prayer. Student organizers said that membership would be completely voluntary and that it would be open to students of any religion. When school officials refused to let the group meet in the school like other clubs,

the students sued. In *Westside Community Schools v. Mergens*[1] (1990), the Court ruled as follows:

> *Although a school may not itself lead or direct a religious club, a school that permits a student-initiated and student-led religious club to meet after school, just as it permits any other student group to do, does not convey a message of state approval or endorsement of the particular religion.*
>
> —Justice Sandra Day O'Connor

Teaching the Theory of Evolution

The Supreme Court has also applied the establishment clause to classroom instruction. In *Epperson v. Arkansas*[2] (1968), the justices voided an Arkansas law that banned teaching evolution in public schools. The Court ruled that "the state has no legitimate interest in protecting any or all religions from views distasteful to them."

Some state legislatures passed laws that required schools to teach the Bible's account of creation along with the theory of evolution as an alternative viewpoint in science classes. In 1987, however, the Court struck down these laws. In *Edwards v. Aguillard*,[3] the Court ruled that a law requiring the teaching of creationism violated the establishment clause because its primary purpose was "to endorse a particular religious doctrine."

See the following footnoted materials in the **Reference Handbook:**
1. *Westside Community Schools v. Mergens* case summary, page R36.
2. *Epperson v. Arkansas* case summary, page R26.
3. *Edwards v. Aguillard* case summary, page R26.

Activity: Interdisciplinary Connection

History The establishment clause of the First Amendment reflects a basic principle that brought many colonists to America. Freedom of religion has always been considered a primary right of citizens in a democracy. Have students imagine that they are part of a group of lawmakers in 1789 who are writing the amendment that protects freedom of religion. Ask students to reenact the debate—expressing both pro and con arguments—over the establishment clause. Have groups present their debates to the rest of the class. **ELL**

Other Establishment Issues

Not all establishment clause issues concern education. For example, the Supreme Court has also applied the separation of church and state to public Christmas displays, which have caused controversy in some communities. In *Lynch* v. *Donnelly*[1] (1984), the Court allowed the city of Pawtucket, Rhode Island, to display a Nativity scene with secular items such as a Christmas tree and a sleigh and reindeer. In 1989 the Court ruled that a publicly funded Nativity scene by itself violated the Constitution in *Allegheny County* v. *ACLU*.[2] The justices upheld placing a menorah—a candelabrum with seven or nine candles that is used in Jewish worship—alongside a Christmas tree at city hall the same year, however.

The Court has also ruled that the school prayer ban does not apply to government meetings. In *Marsh* v. *Chambers*[3] (1983), the justices noted that prayers have been offered in legislatures since colonial times, and that, unlike students, legislators are not "susceptible to religious indoctrination."

The Free Exercise Clause

In addition to banning an established church, the First Amendment forbids laws "prohibiting the free exercise" of religion. But in interpreting this free exercise clause, the Supreme Court makes an important distinction between belief and practice. The Court has ruled that the right to religious belief is absolute. It has applied some restrictions, however, to the practice of those beliefs.

Religious Practice May Be Limited

The Supreme Court has never permitted religious freedom to **justify** any behavior, particularly when religious practices conflict with criminal laws. The Court first dealt with this issue in the case of *Reynolds* v. *United States*[4] (1879). George Reynolds, a Mormon who lived in Utah, had two wives and was convicted of polygamy. Reynolds's religion permitted polygamy, but federal law prohibited it. He appealed his conviction to the Supreme Court, claiming that the law **abridged,** or limited, freedom of religion.

*See the following footnoted materials in the **Reference Handbook**:*
1. *Lynch* v. *Donnelly* case summary, page R30.
2. *Allegheny County* v. *ACLU* case summary, page R23.
3. *Marsh* v. *Chambers* case summary, page R30.
4. *Reynolds* v. *United States* case summary, page R33.
5. *Jacobson* v. *Massachusetts* case summary, page R29.
6. *Oregon* v. *Smith* case summary, page R32.
7. *City of Boerne, Texas* v. *Flores* case summary, page R25.
8. *Wisconsin* v. *Yoder* case summary, page R36.

The Court, however, upheld his conviction. The *Reynolds* case established that people are not free to worship in ways that violate laws that protect the health, safety, or morals of the community.

Over the years, the Supreme Court has consistently followed this principle, upholding a variety of restrictive laws. In 1905, in *Jacobson* v. *Massachusetts*,[5] the Court upheld compulsory vaccination laws, even though some religions prohibit it. In *Oregon* v. *Smith*[6] (1990), the Court denied unemployment benefits to a worker who was fired for using drugs as part of a religious ceremony.

In 1993 the Religious Freedom Restoration Act was passed to overturn the principle set forth in the *Smith* case. The act stated that people can perform religious rituals unless they are prohibited by a narrowly tailored law and that Congress can set aside state laws that violate this principle. The Restoration act did not survive long. In June 1997, the Court ruled in *City of Boerne, Texas* v. *Flores*[7] that the act was unconstitutional on several grounds.

While government may limit some religious practices, the Court also has ruled that a number of other restrictions violate the free exercise clause. For example, in *Wisconsin* v. *Yoder*[8] (1972), the Court decided that the state could not require Amish parents to send their children to public school beyond the eighth grade. To do so, the Court ruled, would violate long-held Amish religious beliefs that were "intimately related to daily living" and would present "a very real threat of undermining the Amish community."

Religious Expression and the Flag

Two of the most-discussed free exercise cases have to do with whether children could be forced to salute the American flag. In 1936 Lillian and William Gobitis were expelled from school for refusing to salute. As Jehovah's Witnesses, the children and their parents believed saluting the flag violated the Christian commandment against worshiping graven images. In *Minersville School District* v. *Gobitis* (1940), the Court upheld the school regulation. The flag was a patriotic symbol, the Court ruled, and requiring the salute did not infringe on religious freedom.

Government ONLINE

Student Web Activity Visit glencoe.com and enter **QuickPass**™ code USG9822c13. Click on Student Web Activity and complete the activity about constitutional rights.

W Writing Support

Expository Writing When the Supreme Court issued its ruling in *Wisconsin* v. *Yoder*, some legal experts criticized it for yielding too much authority to a religious group and weakening the state's power to regulate education. Have students write essays in which they explain why they agree or disagree with these criticisms. Refer students to *Wisconsin* v. *Yoder* in the **Reference Handbook** for more details on the case. **AL**

R Reading Strategy

Evaluating Tell students that "under God" was not part of the Pledge of Allegiance as originally written in 1892. It was added in 1954 during the Cold War. **Ask:** Should the phrase "under God" be deleted from the Pledge of Allegiance? Why or why not? **OL**

Government ONLINE

Objectives and answers to the Student Web Activity can be found in the **Web Activity Lesson Plan** at glencoe.com. Enter **QuickPass**™ code USG9085c13T.

Additional Support

Extending the Content

Conscientious Objectors Another application of the free exercise clause becomes evident during wartime. Conscientious objectors—people who oppose war on moral grounds—may be exempted from military service. Although they still must register, they may fulfill their term of service in certain civilian jobs, or they may choose to be inducted and serve in a noncombatant position. During the Vietnam War, boxer Cassius Clay (known today as Muhammad Ali), a member of the Nation of Islam (Black Muslims), refused to be inducted into military service because of his religious beliefs. He was fined and sentenced to prison, but the Supreme Court overturned the conviction. Although religious affiliation is not required for conscientious objector status, most conscientious objectors are members of religious groups that are known for pacifist views.

Caption Answer: In 1943 the Court concluded that patriotism could be achieved without violating religious beliefs.

Landmark Case

See *West Virginia State Board of Education* v. *Barnette* in the Supreme Court Case Summaries in the **Reference Handbook** and Case Study 30 in the *Supreme Court Case Studies* booklet.

Assess

Assign the Section 2 Assessment as homework or as an in-class activity, or have students take Section Quiz 13-2 from *Section Quizzes and Chapter Tests.*

Close

Inferring Ask: What might life be like if the First Amendment did not guarantee freedom of religion? *(Encourage students to consider government-regulated religious practices, people practicing different religions in secret for fear of persecution, and so on.)* **OL**

Section 2 Review

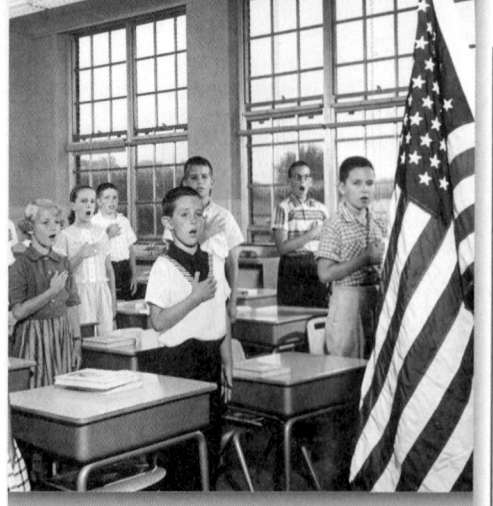

Interpreting the First Amendment
Saluting the flag and reciting the Pledge of Allegiance have been traditional in schools as it was for these 1965 grade-schoolers, but the custom infringes on some students' beliefs. *In 1943, how did the Supreme Court change its interpretation of the First Amendment right of free exercise of religion?*

After the *Gobitis* decision, the West Virginia legislature passed an act requiring public schools in the state to conduct classes in civics, history, and the federal and state constitutions. The state board of education followed this legislation by directing that all students and teachers salute the flag and recite the Pledge of Allegiance as part of regular school activities. Failure to comply would lead to expulsion from school, and a student would be treated as a delinquent. Uncooperative parents of such students were liable to prosecution and a penalty of 30 days in jail as well as a $50 fine.

When a member of Jehovah's Witnesses appealed this requirement of West Virginia, the Court overruled the *Gobitis* decision and held such laws to be an unconstitutional interference with the free exercise of religion. The Court concluded in *West Virginia State Board of Education* v. *Barnette* (1943) that patriotism could be achieved without forcing people to violate their religious beliefs:

> 66 *To believe that patriotism will not flourish if patriotic ceremonies are voluntary and spontaneous instead of a compulsory routine is to make an unflattering estimate of the appeal of our institutions to free minds.* 99
> —Justice Robert Jackson, 1943

Flag salute cases illustrate how the Supreme Court can change its interpretation of the Constitution. The Court usually follows **precedent,** decisions made on the same issue in earlier cases. As one justice put it, however, "when convinced of former error, this Court has never felt constrained to follow precedent."

SECTION 2 Review

Vocabulary

1. **Explain** the significance of: establishment clause, free exercise clause, parochial school, secular, abridge, precedent.

Main Ideas

2. **Examining** What test does the Court use to determine if state aid to parochial education is constitutional?

3. **Describing** How was *West Virginia State Board of Education* v. *Barnette* different from the *Gobitis* case?

Critical Thinking

4. **Analyzing** Do you think that prayer in public schools is permitted or disallowed by the establishment clause and/or the free exercise clause of the First Amendment? Explain.

5. **Organizing** Use a Venn diagram to show the similarities and differences between the establishment clause and the free exercise clause.

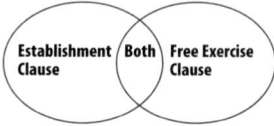

Writing About Government

6. **Cultural Pluralism** Study the free exercise and establishment clauses. Take a position on the following: Government buildings should be allowed to place the motto "In God We Trust" in public view. Write a brief position paper in which you clearly outline the reasons for your position.

Answers

1. All definitions can be found in the section and the Glossary.
2. Aid must have a clearly secular purpose, must neither advance nor inhibit religion, and must not involve "excessive government entanglement with religion."
3. The *Gobitis* ruling was reversed by the ruling in *West Virginia State Board of Education* v. *Barnette.*
4. Answers will vary. Some students may contend that if such prayers neither favor nor discriminate against specific religions, church and state separation is maintained. Other students may argue that any religious activity in public schools destroys that separation.
5. Establishment Clause: government must remain neutral, not supporting religion or nonreligion. Both: wall of separation between church and state; Free Exercise Clause: the right to hold any religious beliefs is absolute
6. Call on volunteers to explain their positions. Discuss students' reasons with the class.

Can a Group Use Public Campgrounds for a Political Protest?

Clark v. Community for Creative Non-Violence, 1984

Demonstrations can bring the need for public order into conflict with the rights of free speech and free assembly. Does the First Amendment give groups the right to use public parks to promote political ideas?

Background of the Case

In 1982 a group, the Community for Creative Non-Violence (CCNV), applied to the National Park Service (NPS) for a permit to conduct round-the-clock demonstrations in Lafayette Park and the Mall in Washington, D.C. The CCNV wanted to set up 60 large tents for overnight camping in both parks to call attention to the problems of the homeless. The NPS issued the permit but refused to allow the CCNV to sleep overnight in tents. Camping in national parks is permitted only in campgrounds designated for that purpose, and no such campgrounds had ever been set up in either Lafayette Park or the Mall. The CCNV filed suit claiming a violation of their First Amendment rights. A district court ruled in favor of the NPS; the court of appeals then ruled for the CCNV. The case went to the Supreme Court.

The Constitutional Issue

The Supreme Court stated, "The issue in this case is whether a National Park Service regulation prohibiting camping in certain parks violates the First Amendment when applied to prohibit demonstrators from sleeping in Lafayette Park and the Mall." The CCNV argued that sleeping in the tents was essential to convey to people "the central reality of homelessness." Further, the group said the poor and homeless would not participate without the incentive of sleeping space and a hot meal. The CCNV also claimed that while the camping might interfere with some park use, the NPS did not have a truly substantial governmental interest in banning camping.

The NPS countered that the regulation against sleeping except in designated campsites was not targeted against the CCNV's message about the homeless. The government did have a substantial interest in keeping the parks attractive and available to the public. If non-demonstrators were not allowed to camp in the two parks, demonstrators should not be treated any differently, especially when they could use other ways to get their political message across to the public.

Debating the Issue

Questions to Consider

1. What was the government's "substantial interest" in this case?

2. Was the regulation intended to suppress the CCNV's message?

3. What could be the far-reaching consequence of allowing the CCNV to camp in the parks?

You Be the Judge

In your opinion, did the NPS regulation violate the First Amendment or did a substantial governmental interest justify their ban?

▶ **Lafayette Park statue**

Debating the Issue Answers

Questions to Consider

1. The government's interest was in enforcing NPS regulations and in keeping Lafayette Park and the Mall available to and clean for visitors, interests that camping onsite would compromise.

2. It had nothing to do with the CCNV's message—it was "content neutral."

3. Possible answers: Any part of the National Park System in which camping is restricted could be opened up for camping. Excessive camping might damage those sites. Other regulations might be ignored.

You Be the Judge

It is likely that not all students will agree that allowing camping at these two sites would have violated a "substantial governmental interest."

Class Debate

Organize the class into three groups. Group A will represent the Community for Creative Non-Violence, Group B will represent the National Park Service, and Group C will represent the Supreme Court. Have all three groups study this case and then complete the following tasks:

Groups A and B: Write briefs detailing why the Constitution supports their respective positions.

Group A: Select an "attorney" to present the CCNV's case and develop its arguments—in particular, why sleeping in the park would convey a message that could not be expressed in any other way.

Group B: Select an "attorney" to present the NPS's defense—that its regulation was not intended to target the CCNV or any other group with a "message"—and develop its arguments.

Group C: Be prepared to interrupt the presentations to ask questions or request clarifications. After the presentations, meet and issue a written opinion.

The Court's Decision

Provide students with the following information about the Court's actual decision.

The Court ruled 7 to 2 to uphold the NPS ban on camping as a reasonable restriction on the way in which First Amendment rights could be exercised. Justice Byron White, writing the majority opinion, stated: "The regulation is neutral with regard to the message presented, and leaves open ample alternative methods of communicating the intended message. . . ."

Focus

Bellringer
**Section Focus Transparencies
13-3**

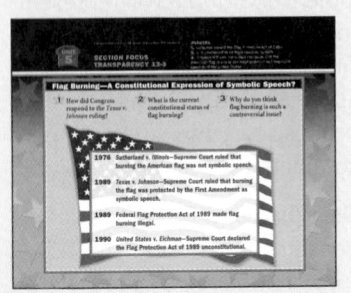

Reader's Guide

Answers to Graphic:
Protected: pure speech, some symbolic speech
Not Protected: seditious speech, speech that presents a clear and present danger, defamatory speech, fighting words, student speech

Resource Manager

Freedom of Speech

Reader's Guide

Content Vocabulary	Academic Vocabulary	Reading Strategy
★ pure speech *(p. 366)* ★ symbolic speech *(p. 366)* ★ seditious speech *(p. 368)* ★ defamatory speech *(p. 369)* ★ slander *(p. 369)* ★ libel *(p. 369)*	★ categories *(p. 366)* ★ require *(p. 367)* ★ presumed *(p. 369)*	As you read, use a graphic organizer similar to the one below to list the types of speech that are protected and that are not protected by the First Amendment.

Protected	Not Protected

Issues in the News

Can the department of motor vehicles prevent you from expressing your opinion on your license plate? Not according to a federal appeals court. In an Arizona case, the court ruled that state officials had violated the free expression rights of an antiabortion group, Arizona Life Coalition. The group wanted to order a license plate reading "Choose Life" from the state. When the state refused, the group sued. The state argued that it had the right to control expression on state-issued plates, but the appeals court disagreed. In the 3 to 0 ruling, a judge said that the state "clearly denied the application based on the nature of the message."

▲ A state motor vehicle office where plate requests are processed

The Arizona case underscores an important point. Democratic government demands that everyone have the right to speak freely. Most Americans agree with this principle and certainly they want freedom of speech for themselves. When it comes to opinions they disagree with, however, they may be tempted to deny freedom of speech.

The First Amendment exists to protect the expression of unpopular ideas—popular ideas need little protection. Those who support democracy value the right of expression for people with different opinions from their own.

Types of Speech

What is meant by the word *speech* when we talk about freedom of speech? Clearly, talking with neighbors or addressing the senior class in a school assembly is speech. Are students who wear black armbands to protest a school policy engaging in an act of "speech" that is protected by the First Amendment? Is demonstrating in front of a government building to protest a new law a form of speech? To answer these questions, the Supreme Court has distinguished two **categories** of speech that the First Amendment protects.

Pure speech, the verbal expression of thought and opinion before an audience that has chosen to listen, is the most common form of speech. Pure speech may be delivered calmly in the privacy of one's home or passionately in front of a crowd. Because pure speech relies only on the power of words to communicate ideas, the Supreme Court traditionally has provided the strongest protection for pure speech against government control.

Symbolic speech—sometimes called expressive conduct—involves the use of actions and symbols, in addition to or instead of words, to express opinions.

R Reading Strategies	**C** Critical Thinking	**D** Differentiated Instruction	**W** Writing Support	**S** Skill Practice
Teacher Edition • Identifying, p. 367 **Additional Resources** • Guid. Read. Act., p. 47 • Quizzes/Tests, p. 157	**Teacher Edition** • Differentiating, p. 367 **Additional Resources** • Read. Essen., pp. 140–142	**Teacher Edition** • Interpersonal, p. 368 **Additional Resources** • Foldables, p. 56 • Gov. Sims. and Debates, pp. 22–28	**Teacher Edition** • Personal Writing, p. 369 **Additional Resources** • Supreme Ct. Case Studies, pp. 39–40, 69–70, 77–78, 105–106, 129–130, 131–132	**Additional Resources** • Part. in Gov. Act., pp. 25–26

During the Vietnam War, for example, protestors burned their draft cards or burned the American flag to express opposition to the war. Because symbolic speech involves actions, the government can sometimes restrict it in ways that do not apply to pure speech—for example, if it endangers public safety.

An early case on symbolic speech arose in 1931 at a time when some Americans were concerned about communism. A California state law prohibited public display of a red flag (associated with communism) "as a sign, symbol or emblem of opposition to organized government." This part of the state law did not **require** that the flag's display incite violence. The Court's decision in *Stromberg v. California* struck down the state law, saying it was so vague that it could lead to punishing legal opposition to government.

In addressing symbolic speech, the Court has generally followed a three-part test established in 1968 in *United States* v. *O'Brien.* The government upheld the arrest of four young men who burned their draft cards to protest the Vietnam War.[1] The Court ruled that a government can regulate or forbid expressive conduct if the regulation (1) falls within the constitutional power of government, (2) is narrowly drawn to further a substantial government interest unrelated to the suppression of free speech, and (3) leaves ample alternative communication outlets.

Since this decision, the Court has made several rulings that protect symbolic speech. In *Tinker* v.

Des Moines School District[2] (1969), it said students had the right to wear black armbands in school to protest the Vietnam War.

In *Texas* v. *Johnson*[3] (1989), the Court held that flag burning was protected symbolic speech. On the same principle, the Court said in *United States* v. *Eichman*[4] (1990) that the federal Flag Protection Act of 1989, which made flag burning a crime, was unconstitutional. In other cases, the Court came down on the other side, saying that the right to privacy was more important than the right to expressive speech. In *Frisby* v. *Schultz*[5] (1988), the Court held that a city can limit protestors from picketing in front of a private residence. In *Hill* v. *Colorado* (2000), the Court upheld a Colorado law prohibiting groups from approaching individuals within 100 feet of a health facility to speak to them or give them literature. Groups may take such actions only if they are given consent to do so.

Regulating Speech

Because free speech must be balanced against the need to protect society, some restraints on pure speech do exist. Congress and state legislatures,

See the following footnoted materials in the **Reference Handbook:**
1. *United States* v. *O'Brien* case summary, page R35.
2. *Tinker* v. *Des Moines School District* case summary, page R34.
3. *Texas* v. *Johnson* case summary, page R34.
4. *United States* v. *Eichman* case summary, page R35.
5. *Frisby* v. *Schultz* case summary, page R27.

Symbolic Speech

Demonstrative Actions During the Vietnam War, thousands of defiant young people challenged the idea that citizens have a military obligation to their country. Many young Americans burned their draft cards in protest. *What methods of symbolic speech are used today?*

Teach

C Critical Thinking

Differentiating Have students propose situations involving the two types of speech (pure and symbolic) and write them on index cards. Collect the cards, read aloud several examples, and have the class determine the type of speech that each example represents. **OL**

R Reading Strategy

Identifying Ask: According to the three-part test established in *United States* v. *O'Brien,* when can the government regulate or forbid expressive conduct? *(The regulation must satisfy all three of the following: falls within the constitutional power of the government; furthers a substantial government interest unrelated to free speech; and leaves sufficient communication alternatives.)* **BL**

Caption Answer: Answers might include wearing armbands or buttons, flag burning, wearing ribbons or certain colors of clothing, and so on.

Additional Support

Activity: Collaborative Learning

Classifying Organize students into two groups—one to represent actions that freedom of speech guarantees and one to represent actions that freedom of speech does not protect. Have students in both groups choose one of the following tasks: summarize the guarantee or lack thereof, choose examples and classify each example as pure speech or symbolic speech, explain how Supreme Court rulings have defined such actions, or relate the group's category to student rights and freedoms. **OL**

D Differentiated Instruction

Interpersonal People who enjoy having the right of free speech for themselves sometimes wish that the same freedom was not available to people whose views they find distasteful. Have students prepare and present skits on one of the following situations:

- a Vietnam War protester being confronted by a war veteran,

- a reporter's reaction to the Court's ruling in *Schenck* or *Yates,*

- a city council meeting at which a radically right-wing or left-wing group's petition for a parade permit is being discussed, or

- a school principal discussing "appropriate" speech with a guest speaker.

Follow up the skit presentations with class discussion. **OL**

Caption Answer: The terrorist attacks on September 11, 2001; students should suggest that the devastation of the attacks led people to believe that more should be done to stop terrorism.

Differentiated Instruction

---

for example, have outlawed **seditious speech**—speech urging resistance to lawful authority or advocating the overthrow of the government. How far can government go in limiting free speech? When does speech lose the protection of the First Amendment? Different philosophies about free speech have emerged as the Court has wrestled with the issue. During the twentieth century, the Court has developed three constitutional tests, or general guidelines, to use in examining free speech cases. They are: (1) the "clear and present danger" rule, (2) the bad tendency doctrine, and (3) the preferred position doctrine.

Clear and Present Danger

When the speech in question clearly presents an immediate danger, the First Amendment does not protect it. If a conflict between free expression and public safety occurs, judges often rely on this test. Justice Oliver Wendell Holmes, Jr., developed the "clear and present danger" test in *Schenck* v. *United States* (1919). During World War I, Charles Schenck, a member of the Socialist Party, was convicted of printing and distributing leaflets that urged draftees to obstruct the war effort. The government claimed

Civil Liberties and Terrorism

Survey Question: Do We Need to Sacrifice Some Civil Liberties to Curb Terrorism?*

	Yes	No	Don't Know
Mid-September 2001	55	35	10
June 2002	49	45	6
August 2003	44	50	6
July 2004	38	56	6
July 2005	40	53	7
September 2006	43	50	7
January 2007	40	54	6

*Adapted From Pew Research Center, Trends in Political Values and Core Attitudes: 1987-2007

Critical Thinking *What event in 2001 correlates with the highest percentage for a "yes" answer to the survey? Can you suggest why?*

---

that his actions violated the 1917 Espionage Act, a law that made it a crime to "willfully utter, print, write, or publish any disloyal, profane, scurrilous or abusive language" about the government. Schenck said his actions were protected by the First Amendment.

The Court upheld the conviction. It said that ordinarily the First Amendment would protect Schenck's expression, but not during wartime:

> ❝ *The question in every case is whether the words used are used in such circumstances and are of such a nature as to create a clear and present danger that they will bring about the substantive evils that Congress has a right to prevent. . . . When a nation is at war many things that might be said in time of peace . . . will not be endured [and] . . . no Court could regard them as protected by any constitutional right.* ❞
> —Justice Oliver Wendell Holmes, Jr., 1919

Later that same year, Justice Holmes interpreted things differently in another case. A man named Abrams and two of his friends were arrested for distributing leaflets condemning President Woodrow Wilson for sending troops to fight in the Russian civil war against communist revolutionaries. In *Abrams* v. *United States,* the Court's majority ruled again that the Espionage Act was constitutional—Abrams could not criticize the government because he was presenting a clear and present danger.

In his dissent, Justice Holmes refined the standard for clear and present danger. He argued that Abrams was not really hurting the war effort. Holmes did not give the Court an easy test for future cases, but his defense of free speech is justly famous. People will come to understand, he wrote, that the good is better reached by a free trade in ideas and:

> ❝ *. . . that the best test of truth is the power of the thought to get itself accepted in the competition of the market, and that truth is the only ground upon which their wishes safely can be carried out. That at any rate is the theory of our Constitution. It is an experiment, as all life is an experiment.* ❞
> —Justice Oliver Wendell Holmes, 1919

The Bad Tendency Doctrine

Some Supreme Court justices did not think that the "clear and present danger" principle was enough to protect the government's interests and wanted a more restrictive standard. In 1925 the Court held

---

Leveled Activities

ELL Interpreting Political Cartoons, p. 25

BL Reading Essentials and Study Guide, p. 140

OL Supreme Court Case Studies, p. 37

AL Source Readings, p. 13

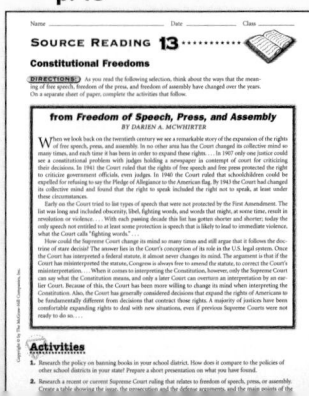

in *Gitlow* v. *New York*[1] that speech could be restricted even if it had only a tendency to lead to illegal action, establishing the "bad tendency doctrine." Since the 1920s, the Supreme Court has not often used this doctrine. Some Americans do argue, however, that society's need for order justifies any damage to basic freedoms.

The Preferred Position Doctrine

Developed in the 1940s, the preferred position doctrine holds that First Amendment freedoms are more fundamental than other freedoms because they provide the basis of all liberties. Thus, First Amendment freedoms hold a preferred position over competing interests. Any law limiting these freedoms should be **presumed** unconstitutional unless it can be shown to be absolutely necessary.

Sedition Laws

The Espionage Act of 1917 expired at the end of World War I. Later, in the 1940s and 1950s, Congress passed three sedition laws that applied in peacetime as well as during war. One of these, the Smith Act, made it a crime to advocate revolution. In *Dennis* v. *United States*[2] (1951), the Court applied the "clear and present danger" test to uphold the conviction of 11 Communist Party leaders under the act. In later cases, however, the Court sharply narrowed its definition of seditious speech.

In *Yates* v. *United States*[3] (1957), the Court overturned convictions of several other Communist Party members. It decided that it cannot be illegal merely to say that the government should be overthrown and distinguished between urging people to believe an action was necessary and urging them to take that action. In *Brandenburg* v. *Ohio*[4] (1969), the Court further narrowed its definition of seditious speech. A Ku Klux Klan leader, Clarence Brandenburg, was arrested for giving a speech at a Klan rally where he said that some "revengeance" against the government might occur if it continued to "suppress the white, Caucasian race. . . ." The Court ruled in favor of Brandenburg, declaring that under the First Amendment he was free to advocate force as he did. If his speech incited people to use force, then his speech could be suppressed.

Other Unprotected Speech

Other forms of speech, less protected than so-called seditious speech, are not protected by the First Amendment. **Defamatory speech** and

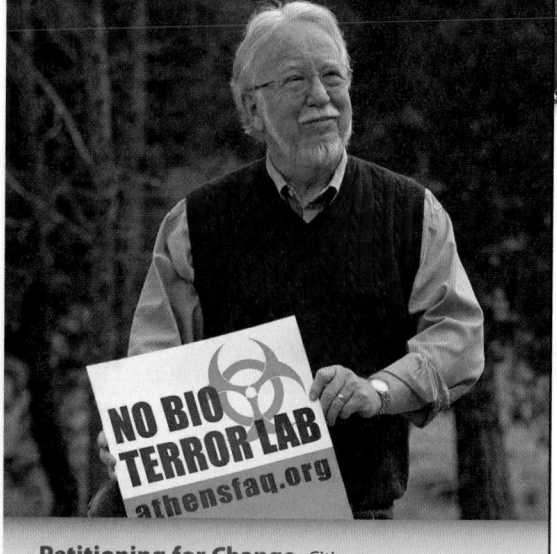

Petitioning for Change Citizens can express their opinion by signing petitions on a public issue. Grady Thrasher of Athens, Georgia, started a petition drive in 2008 against having a federal animal research lab in his community. *What did the Supreme Court say about free speech in its preferred position doctrine?*

"fighting words" fall outside the First Amendment, as do some forms of student speech.

Defamatory Speech

The First Amendment does not protect defamatory speech, or false speech that damages a person's good name, character, or reputation. Defamatory speech falls into two categories. **Slander** is spoken; **libel** is written. Someone who commits slander or libel may be sued in a civil court and ordered to pay damages for making false, damaging statements about someone else.

The Court has limited the right of public officials, however, to recover damages for defamation. In *New York Times Co.* v. *Sullivan*[5] (1964), the Court determined that even if a newspaper story about an Alabama police commissioner was false, it was protected speech unless the statement was made with the knowledge that it was false, or with reckless disregard for whether or not it was false.

See the following footnoted materials in the *Reference Handbook:*
1. *Gitlow* v. *New York* case summary, page R27.
2. *Dennis* v. *United States* case summary, page R26.
3. *Yates* v. *United States* case summary, page R37.
4. *Brandenburg* v. *Ohio* case summary, page R24.
5. *New York Times Co.* v. *Sullivan* case summary, page R31.

CHAPTER 13: *Constitutional Freedoms* **369**

Caption Answer: According to the preferred position doctrine, free speech is a fundamental freedom. Any law limiting free speech should be presumed unconstitutional unless the government can prove that the law is absolutely necessary.

W Writing Support

Personal Writing Have students write an essay in which they explain whether they believe it is ever acceptable for the government to restrict free speech. If students think it is sometimes acceptable, they should explain under what circumstances. If they think it is never acceptable, they should explain why they believe government should never be allowed to abridge freedom of speech. **OL**

Landmark Case

See *Gitlow* v. *New York* and *Dennis* v. *United States* in the Supreme Court Case Summaries in the *Reference Handbook* and Case Studies 20 and 35 in the *Supreme Court Case Studies* booklet.

Hands-On Chapter Project

Step 3

Creating a Class Poster

Step 3: Organizing Information Students will summarize their findings.

Directions Ask students to condense their research into concise entries for the poster, similar to the fictitious example used in Step 2. If they have not located photos for the examples, they should do so in Step 3.

Putting It Together Ask three volunteers to design a format for the entire poster and have

the class vote on the one they prefer. The designs can be submitted as sketches for one panel, using imaginary text, but should show the sizes and locations of text and photos. Each panel should list the constitutional right as its title and include for each event the date, location, event summary, right denied, and one or two photos. **OL**

(Chapter Project continued in Section 4.)

Did You Know?

In *Morse* v. *Frederick* (better remembered as the "BONG HITS 4 JESUS" case, for the banner that got the student into trouble), the Supreme Court ultimately ruled in favor of the school principal, noting: "The First Amendment does not require schools to tolerate at school events student expression that contributes to [the dangers of illegal drug use]."

Assess

Assign the Section 3 Assessment as homework or as an in-class activity, or have students take Section Quiz 13-3 from *Section Quizzes and Chapter Tests*.

Close

Summarizing Have students use the content vocabulary terms in this section to explain the difference between speech that is protected and speech that is not protected under the First Amendment. **OL**

Section 3 Review

The Court allowed some defamatory speech about public officials. It was afraid that if people could be sued for their statements, it might silence criticism of government. Since the 1960s, the justices have extended this protection to statements about public figures in general. Political candidates are included, but so are professional entertainers and athletes as well as private citizens who become newsworthy. In *Hustler Magazine* v. *Falwell*[1] (1988), for example, the Court ruled that Reverend Jerry Falwell, a well-known conservative minister, could not collect damages for words that might intentionally inflict emotional distress. 📖

"Fighting Words"

In 1942 the Supreme Court ruled that some words are so insulting that they provoke immediate violence. Such "fighting words" do not constitute protected speech. The Court upheld a state law that prohibited any person from speaking "any offensive, derisive, or annoying word to any other person who is lawfully in any street or public place." In *Chaplinsky* v. *New Hampshire*[2] (1942), the Court held that certain well-defined and narrow classes of speech, such as "the lewd and obscene, the profane, the libelous, and the insulting" or "fighting words," have never been seen as a constitutional issue because such speech tends to "incite an immediate breach of the peace." 📖

📖 *See the following footnoted materials in the* **Reference Handbook:**
1. *Hustler Magazine* v. *Falwell* case summary, page R28.
2. *Chaplinsky* v. *New Hampshire* case summary, page R25.
3. *Hazelwood School District* v. *Kuhlmeier* case summary, page R28.
4. *Bethel School District* v. *Fraser* case summary, page R23.

Student Speech Cases

🏛 **Landmark Case** Two landmark cases have addressed how the First Amendment is applied to student speech. In the 1969 case of *Tinker* v. *Des Moines*, the Court said that students do not give up all their free speech rights while in high school. A later case, *Hazelwood School District* v. *Kuhlmeier*[3] (1988), however, limited student speech in schools. 📖 The Court held that school officials have broad authority to regulate student speech in school-sponsored newspapers, theatrical productions, and other activities. Justice Byron White drew a distinction between "a student's personal expression"—which is protected—and speech that occurs "as part of the school curriculum." Another decision that had the effect of narrowing students' First Amendment rights and expanding the authority of school officials was *Bethel School District* v. *Fraser*[4] (1986). 📖 In *Bethel*, the Court ruled that the First Amendment does not prevent school officials from suspending students for lewd or indecent speech at school events even though the same speech would be protected outside the school. The Court held that school officials can decide "what manner of speech in the classroom or in school assembly is appropriate." More recently, the Court placed further limits on students' free speech rights. In *Morse* v. *Frederick* (2007), the Court ruled that school officials may punish students for displaying a banner at a school-sponsored event that officials believed condoned the use of illegal drugs.

SECTION 3 Review

Vocabulary

1. **Explain** the significance of: pure speech, symbolic speech, seditious speech, defamatory speech, slander, libel.

Main Ideas

2. **Identifying** What three tests does the Supreme Court use to set limits on free speech?

3. **Describing** What types of speech does the First Amendment not protect?

Critical Thinking

4. **Making Comparisons** How does freedom of speech in the United States differ in wartime and in peacetime? Refer to Supreme Court decisions in your answer.

5. **Organizing** Use a diagram like the one shown here to explain the difference between slander and libel.

6. **Persuasive Writing** The Supreme Court has held that First Amendment freedoms are more fundamental than others. Read a Court decision in this chapter and write a brief outline of the case you would present if you were going to argue the case before the Court. Take whichever side of the argument you wish. You might also want to do additional research to strengthen your position.

Writing About Government

Answers

1. All definitions can be found in the section and the Glossary.
2. clear and present danger—speech presenting immediate danger is not protected; bad tendency—speech can be restricted even if it only tends to lead to illegal action; preferred position—speech should not be limited unless absolutely necessary
3. seditious speech, defamatory speech, "fighting words," and certain types of student speech

4. Speech that is considered seditious during war [*Schenck* v. *U.S.* (1919), *Abrams* v. *U.S.* (1919), and *U.S.* v. *O'Brien* (1968)] was protected in peacetime [*Yates* v. *U.S.* (1957) and *Brandenburg* v. *Ohio* (1969)].
5. Slander: spoken
   Libel: written
6. Evaluate outlines according to their level of detail.

Freedom of the Press

Focus

Reader's Guide

Content Vocabulary
★ prior restraint (p. 371)
★ sequester (p. 373)
★ gag order (p. 373)
★ shield laws (p. 374)

Academic Vocabulary
★ outcome (p. 372)
★ exclusion (p. 373)
★ transmission (p. 374)

Reading Strategy
As you read, create a graphic organizer similar to the one below to analyze how trial judges deal with the conflict between freedom of the press and a defendant's right to a fair trial.

Freedom of the Press | Right to a Fair Trial

Issues in the News

Recently, a new twist arose in a case that focused on the First Amendment. A Web site, Wikileaks, published documents claiming to reveal unethical behavior at a bank, but the bank said the Web site violated the bank's right to privacy. When a judge issued a restraining order shutting down the site, several groups complained. They said the judge's order amounted to prior restraint—restraining expression before any actual violation of free speech occurs, a violation of the First Amendment. In the words of the groups' lawyer, Paul Levy, "the court had muzzled a very important voice in the fight against corporate and government misdeeds." The bank's lawyer was equally assertive: ". . . individual privacy rights outweigh the right of the press. . . . If financial industry customers do not think their information is protected, [banks] can go out of business."

▲ As in the *Wikileaks* case, freedom of the press sometimes conflicts with other rights.

As the *Wikileaks* case shows, the right of the press to gather and publish information can conflict with other important rights. Most of the time, freedom of the press is protected because it is closely related to freedom of speech. It moves free speech one step further by allowing opinions to be written and circulated or broadcast. In today's world, the press includes magazines, radio, television, the Internet, and newspapers because of their roles in spreading news and opinions.

Prior Restraint Forbidden

In many nations, **prior restraint**—censorship of information before it is published—is a common way for government to control information and limit

freedom. In the United States, the Supreme Court has ruled that the press may be censored in advance only in cases relating directly to national security. Two Court decisions illustrate this principle.

Near v. Minnesota

This 1931 case concerned a Minnesota law prohibiting the publication of any "malicious, scandalous, or defamatory" newspapers or magazines. An acid-tongued editor of a Minneapolis paper had called local officials "gangsters" and "grafters." Acting under the state's law, officials obtained a court injunction to halt publication.

By a 5 to 4 vote, the Supreme Court lifted the injunction. The Court ruled the Minnesota law unconstitutional because it involved prior restraint.

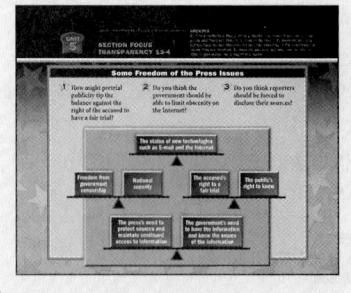

Teach

C Critical Thinking

Drawing Conclusions Write *censorship* on the board. Invite students to share their thoughts about this word and its negative connotations. **Ask:** In what kinds of situations, if any, do you think it might be reasonable to consider censoring information or opinions? **BL**

S Skill Practice

Researching Have students locate and read the *New York Times* issues in which the excerpts from the Pentagon Papers appeared. **Ask:** Having read the leaked material, do you think the public had a right to this information? Why or why not? **AL**

Caption Answer: It ruled that the government could not stop publication.

📜 Landmark Case

See *New York Times Co. v. United States* in the Supreme Court Case Summaries in the **Reference Handbook** and Case Study 55 in the *Supreme Court Case Studies* booklet.

Additional Support

For years the *Near* case defined the Supreme Court's position on censorship. The Court stressed that a free press means freedom from government censorship.

New York Times Co. v. United States

The Supreme Court reaffirmed its position in *New York Times Co. v. United States* (1971)—widely known as the Pentagon Papers case. In 1971 a former Pentagon employee leaked to the *New York Times* a secret government report outlining the history of American involvement in the Vietnam War. This report, which became known as the Pentagon Papers, contained many government documents, including secret cables and memos.

Believing the Pentagon Papers showed that government officials had lied about the war, the *New York Times* began to publish parts of the report. The government tried to stop publication of the papers, arguing that national security was at risk and that the documents had been stolen. The Court rejected the government's claims. It ruled that stopping publication would be prior restraint. Justice William O. Douglas noted that "the dominant purpose of the First Amendment was to prohibit the widespread practice of governmental suppression of embarrassing information." Justice Hugo L. Black added:

> ❝ *The press [is] to serve the governed, not the governors. . . . The press was protected so that it could bare the secrets of government and inform the people.* ❞
> —Justice Hugo L. Black, 1971

Fair Trials and Free Press

Conflicts have also occurred between the First Amendment's freedom of the press and the Sixth Amendment's right to a fair trial. Can the press publish information that might influence the **outcome** of a trial? Can courts issue orders that limit news gathering to increase the chances of a fair trial and protect a jury's deliberations? Can reporters withhold sources of information that might be important to a trial?

Sheppard v. Maxwell

Pretrial publicity and news stories about a crime can make it difficult to obtain a jury capable of fairly deciding the case. Sensational crimes and cases involving celebrities are particularly subject to this problem. In *Sheppard* v. *Maxwell* (1966), the Supreme Court overturned the 1954 conviction of Samuel H. Sheppard for just such reasons.

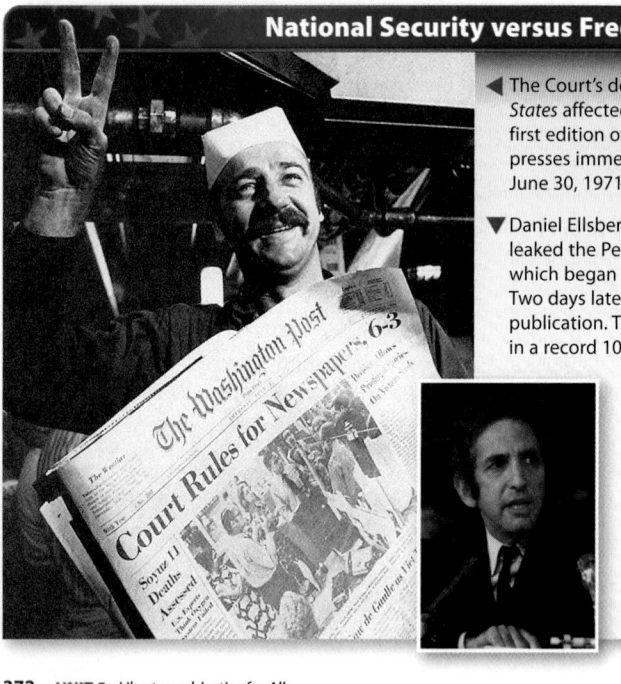

National Security versus Free Press

◀ The Court's decision in *New York Times Co. v. United States* affected newspapers nationwide. Here the first edition of *The Washington Post* rolls off the presses immediately after the Court's decision on June 30, 1971.

▼ Daniel Ellsberg, a Department of Defense employee, leaked the Pentagon Papers to the *New York Times*, which began publishing them on June 13, 1971. Two days later, the government halted their publication. The case reached the Supreme Court in a record 10 days.

Press Responsibility
What did the Supreme Court say about the government's actions in the Pentagon Papers case?

★ Activity: Collaborative Learning ★

Illustrating Organize students into small groups to create a mural depicting freedom of the press at work in American life today. Encourage students to use library resources and information from the Internet to find additional information and illustrations for inspiration. Groups should choose different elements of the print, radio, television, and motion picture media to illustrate. It might be a good idea to have delegates from each group meet initially to make an overall plan for the mural and to delegate such tasks as researching, sketching, coloring, lettering, and so on. Have group representatives explain various elements of the finished mural to the class. **OL**

A Free but Restricted Press

Justice and the Media

One of the most highly publicized trials of the 1950s was that of Sam Sheppard, a Cleveland doctor accused of murdering his pregnant wife (the movie *The Fugitive* is loosely based on this case). Sheppard's conviction was overturned in 1966 because of biased pretrial press coverage. In 2000 Sheppard's son tried to have his deceased father's name cleared, but the jury did not find enough evidence to do so. *Why would a judge bar the press from a courtroom or have a jury sequestered?*

A prominent Cleveland physician, Sheppard was convicted of killing his wife. The case attracted sensational press coverage. Pretrial news reports practically called Sheppard guilty. During the trial, reporters interviewed witnesses and published information that was damaging to Sheppard.

The Supreme Court ruled that press coverage interfered with Sheppard's right to a fair trial. Sheppard was later found not guilty. In the *Sheppard* decision, the Court described several measures judges might take to restrain coverage of a trial. They could: (1) move the trial to reduce pretrial publicity; (2) limit the number of reporters in the courtroom; (3) control reporters' conduct in the courtroom; (4) isolate witnesses and jurors from the press; and (5) have the jury **sequestered,** or kept isolated, until the trial ends.

Gag Orders Unconstitutional

After the *Sheppard* case, judges began to use "gag orders" to restrain the press. A **gag order** is an order by a judge barring the press from publishing certain types of information about a pending court case.

In October 1975, a man killed six members of a Nebraska family. Details of the crime were so sensational that a local judge prohibited news stories about the pretrial hearing. The gag order was challenged and eventually came to the Supreme Court as *Nebraska Press Association* v. *Stuart*[1] (1976). The Court ruled that the Nebraska gag order was too vague and too broad to satisfy the First Amendment.

Press Access to Trials

In the Nebraska case, reporters were permitted in court, even though the trial judge forbade the press to report on the proceedings. In *Gannett Co., Inc.* v. *DePasquale*[2] (1979), the Supreme Court ruled that the public and press could be barred from certain pretrial hearings if the trial judge found a "reasonable probability" that publicity would harm the defendant's right to a fair trial. Since then, the Court has modified the *Gannett* decision, limiting the **exclusion** of the press to only pretrial hearings on the suppression of evidence. In *Richmond Newspapers, Inc.* v. *Virginia*[3] (1980) and later cases, the Court ruled that trials, jury selections, and preliminary hearings must be open to the press and the public except under limited circumstances.

Protecting News Sources

Many reporters argue that to protect their confidential sources, they have the right to refuse to testify in court. But what if a reporter has information the defense or the government needs? In three 1972 cases that were considered together, the Supreme Court said that reporters have to surrender evidence because the First Amendment does not give them special privileges. The Court added that special exemptions must come from Congress and the

---

*See the following footnoted materials in the **Reference Handbook:***
1. *Nebraska Press Association* v. *Stuart* case summary, page R31.
2. *Gannett Co., Inc.* v. *DePasquale* case summary, page R27.
3. *Richmond Newspapers, Inc.* v. *Virginia* case summary, page R33.

CHAPTER 13: *Constitutional Freedoms* **373**

Activity: Multiple Learning Styles

Linking Past & Present

The Colonial Press Freedom of the press was an important issue in the British North American colonies. The libel trial of John Peter Zenger in 1735 set a precedent for this freedom. Zenger, the publisher of the *New York Weekly Journal,* accused the governor of New York of corruption. As a result, Zenger was arrested and charged with seditious libel. English common law called for criminal punishment of anyone who published statements that undermined the government, regardless of their truthfulness. Zenger's attorney, Alexander Hamilton, argued that Zenger was not guilty because the accusations were true and free speech was a basic right of the British people. The judge instructed the jury that truth was not a defense to seditious libel, but the jury disagreed and found Zenger not guilty.

Hands-On Chapter Project

Step 4

The Constitution and the Press

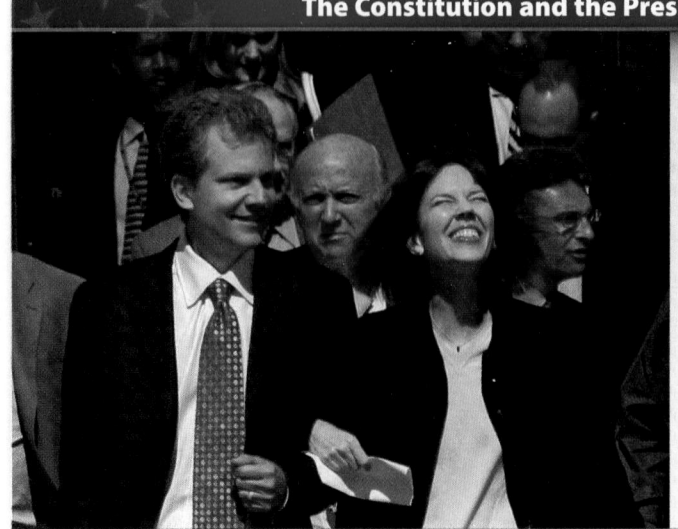

Shield Laws Reporter
Judith Miller walks with *New York Times* publisher Arthur Sulzberger, Jr., after testifying to a grand jury in 2005. Miller's case was not clear-cut because some questioned her actions, but it alarmed many journalists who urged the passage of a federal shield law. *What factors might influence a grand jury to force a reporter to name a source?*

states. To date, 30 states have passed **shield laws**—laws that give reporters some protection from disclosing their sources in state courts.

In 2005 new issues were raised about whether reporters can be forced to disclose their notes when national security is at stake. Judith Miller, a *New York Times* journalist, was jailed for refusing to reveal the sources of certain stories. The stories were about an investigation into a leak that might have revealed the identity of an active Central Intelligence Agency (CIA) agent. After almost three months in jail, Miller was released because she agreed to testify: Miller's explanation was that her source had finally told her she was free to do so.

There is no federal shield law, but even state shield laws set limits on reporters. In the *Miller* case, issues were muddied because the original source of the leak was not immediately known. Many people also doubted Miller's decision not to testify, believing she was more interested in publicity than principle.

Free Press Issues

In writing the First Amendment, the Founders thought of the press as printed material like books, newspapers, and pamphlets. They could not foresee the growth of technology that has created new instruments of mass communication—and new issues regarding freedom of the press.

Radio, Television, and Movies

Because radio and broadcast television use public airwaves, they do not enjoy as much freedom as other press media. Stations must obtain a license from the Federal Communications Commission (FCC), a government agency that regulates their actions. Although Congress has denied the FCC the right to censor programs before they are broadcast, the FCC can require that stations observe certain standards. In addition, it can punish stations that broadcast obscene or indecent language.

Although cable television does not use public airwaves, in *Turner Broadcasting System, Inc.* v. *FCC*[1] (1997), the Court ruled that cable operators are also not entitled to maximum First Amendment protections because typically only one cable company is operating in a community. 📖 The ruling states that cable operators deserve more First Amendment protection than other broadcasters, but less than newspaper and magazine publishers.

In 2000 the Court struck down the part of the Telecommunications Act of 1996 that required cable television to block or limit **transmission** of sexually oriented programs to protect young viewers. In *United States* v. *Playboy,*[2] the Court decided that the cable operators' First Amendment rights were violated because the law was too restrictive. 📖

📖 *See the following footnoted materials in the **Reference Handbook:***
1. *Turner Broadcasting System, Inc.* v. *FCC* case summary, page R35.
2. *United States* v. *Playboy* case summary, page R35.

Creating a Class Poster

Step 4: Presenting Information Visually Students will use the format they selected for the poster to produce their panels.

Directions Provide each group with poster paper. Have students type and print their entries, photocopy the photos in the assigned format, and assemble their panels.

Analyzing Processes **Ask:** What have you learned about working in groups during this project? **OL**

(Chapter Project continued in Section 5.)

Movies were the subject of a 1952 case, *Burstyn v. Wilson*.[1] The Court held that "liberty of expression by means of motion pictures is guaranteed by the First and Fourteenth Amendments." The Court has also ruled, however, that movies can be treated differently than books or newspapers.

E-mail and the Internet

The Supreme Court has always given the highest level of free speech protection to print media. In *Reno v. American Civil Liberties Union*[2] (1997), the Court made a significant ruling that concerned the Internet. The Court ruled that speech on the Internet was closer to print media than to broadcast media. It determined, therefore, that Internet speech deserves the same level of First Amendment protection. In the *Reno* decision, the Court declared unconstitutional a federal law against sending pornographic material online in a way that makes it available to children. The Court agreed that protecting children is important, but said: "The interest in encouraging freedom of expression in a democratic society outweighs any theoretical but unproven benefit of censorship."

Obscenity

The Supreme Court and most other courts have supported the principle that society has the right to protection from obscene speech, pictures, and written material. After many attempts to define obscenity, the Court finally ruled in *Miller v. California*[3] (1973) that, in effect, local communities should set their own standards for obscenity.

In the *Miller* ruling, the Court stated:

❝ It is neither realistic nor constitutionally sound to read the First Amendment as requiring that the people of Maine or Mississippi accept . . . conduct found tolerable in Las Vegas, or New York City. ❞
—Chief Justice Warren Burger

Since the *Miller* decision, however, the Court has stepped in to overrule specific acts by local authorities, making it clear that communities have limits on the right to censor.

Advertising

Advertising is considered "commercial speech"—speech that has a profit motive—and is given less protection under the First Amendment than purely political speech. In fact, advertisers have long faced strong government regulation and control. In the mid-1970s, however, the Supreme Court began to relax controls. In *Bigelow v. Virginia*[4] (1975), the justices permitted newspaper advertisements for abortion clinics. Since then the Court has voided laws that ban advertising medical prescription prices, legal services, and medical services. It has also limited regulation of billboards, "for sale" signs, and lawyers' advertisements.

📖 *See the following footnoted materials in the* **Reference Handbook:**
1. *Burstyn v. Wilson* case summary, page R24.
2. *Reno v. American Civil Liberties Union* case summary, page R33.
3. *Miller v. California* case summary, page R30.
4. *Bigelow v. Virginia* case summary, page R24.

SECTION 4 Review

Vocabulary

1. **Explain** the significance of: prior restraint, sequester, gag order, shield laws.

Main Ideas

2. **Describing** When can the government exercise prior restraint on the press?

3. **Explaining** What measures may a court take to restrain press coverage in the interest of a fair trial?

Critical Thinking

4. **Evaluating** Are there any circumstances under which reporters should be required to reveal or protect their confidential information or sources? Explain your answer.

5. **Analyzing** Use a graphic organizer like the one shown to analyze the importance of the Supreme Court's ruling in *Turner Broadcasting System, Inc.* v. *FCC.*

Communications Decency Act	
Issue at Stake	Court's Ruling

Writing About Government

6. **Expository Writing** The issue of freedom of the press traces back to the *New York* v. *John Peter Zenger* case. Research this case and explain how the results of this case relate to freedom of the press issues today. Present your findings in a written summary and a comparison chart.

Answers

1. All definitions can be found in the section and the Glossary.
2. only in those cases relating directly to national security
3. Courts may move or delay the trial to reduce pretrial publicity, limit the number of reporters in the courtroom or place strict controls on their conduct, isolate witnesses and jurors from the press, and sequester the jury.
4. Some students might believe that when national security, public safety, or individual rights are

jeopardized, reporters should not be shielded from mandatory disclosure. Others might argue that information that endangers someone should not be revealed.

5. Issue at stake: freedom of speech and safeguards on other media, such as the Internet; Court's ruling: Speech on the Internet is constitutionally protected.

6. Ask students to share their charts and summaries with the class.

W Writing Support

Expository Writing In *Reno* v. *ACLU*, the ACLU challenged the constitutionality of the Communications Decency Act of 1996. Have students write an essay in which they agree or disagree with the ACLU's argument that the government "cannot constitutionally reduce the adult population to reading and viewing only what is appropriate for children." **OL**

Assess

Assign the Section 4 Assessment as homework or as an in-class activity, or have students take Section Quiz 13-4 from *Section Quizzes and Chapter Tests.*

Close

Analyzing Ask students to complete the following statements in as many ways as they can: **Because the Constitution guarantees a free press, _____.**

The Constitution guarantees a free press because _____.

Section 4 Review

Focus

Bellringer

Section Focus Transparencies 13-5

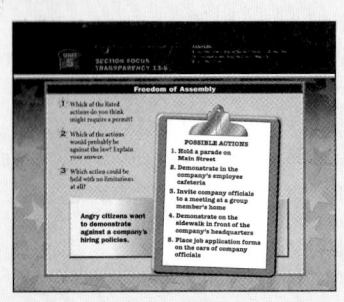

Reader's Guide

Answers to Graphic:

Regulations:

permits may be required

limits can be placed on protests on public property not usually open to public access

demonstrations that disrupt others can be banned

restrictions must apply to all groups

Resource Manager

Freedom of Assembly

Reader's Guide

Content Vocabulary	Academic Vocabulary	Reading Strategy
★ picketing (p. 378)	★ potential (p. 377)	As you read, create a graphic organizer similar to the one below to list the ways government can regulate freedom of assembly.
★ heckler's veto (p. 379)	★ ensure (p. 377)	
	★ survivor (p. 379)	

Issues in the News

In Wilkes-Barre, Pennsylvania, the city council decided they would charge $20 to anyone wanting to demonstrate on public property. Many townspeople think the new ordinance is unconstitutional. Says resident Walter Griffin: "If I'm not in favor of something that happens here and I want to picket in front of this building, I can't do that. . . . I don't think that's fair to me as a taxpayer or as a citizen of the United States." Bill Vinsko of the city's solicitor's office defends the ordinance, saying it is intended only to make sure adequate police protection is available for any demonstration or rally. "If you apply for a permit, you're going to get a permit." Vinsko added that the ordinance was proposed after a disturbance at a St. Patrick's Day parade.

▲ Picketing is a right that is protected under the First Amendment, which guarantees the right to petition the government for redress of grievances.

The right at issue in Wilkes-Barre is in the First Amendment, which guarantees "the right of the people peaceably to assemble, and to petition the Government for a redress of grievances." The right applies not only to meetings in private homes but also to public meetings. It protects the right to make views known to public officials and others by such means as petitions, letters, lobbying, carrying signs in a parade, and marching.

Protecting Freedom of Assembly

Freedom of assembly is a right that is closely related to freedom of speech because most gatherings, no matter how large or small, involve some form of protected speech. Without this basic freedom, no political parties and no special-interest groups could exist to influence the actions of government.

DeJonge v. Oregon

One of the Supreme Court's first major decisions on freedom of assembly came in 1937 in the case of *DeJonge* v. *Oregon*. Dirk DeJonge was convicted for conducting a public meeting sponsored by the Communist Party. He claimed he was innocent because he had not advocated any criminal behavior but had merely discussed public issues. Voting unanimously to overturn DeJonge's conviction, the Court ruled Oregon's law unconstitutional. Chief Justice Charles Evans Hughes wrote that under the First Amendment, "peaceable assembly for lawful discussion cannot be made a crime."

R Reading Strategies	**C** Critical Thinking	**D** Differentiated Instruction	**W** Writing Support	**S** Skill Practice
Teacher Edition	**Teacher Edition**	**Teacher Edition**	**Teacher Edition**	**Teacher Edition**
• Academic Vocabulary, p. 382	• Analyzing Information, p. 377	• Visual/Spatial, p. 379	• Persuasive Writing, p. 378	• Summarizing, p. 380
Additional Resources	**Additional Resources**	**Additional Resources**	**Additional Resources**	**Additional Resources**
• Guid. Read. Act., p. 49	• Read. Essen., pp. 146–148	• Foldables, p. 56	• Source Readings, p. 13	• Inter. Poli. Cartoons, pp. 25–26
• Quizzes/Tests, pp. 159–168		• Supreme Ct. Case Studies, pp. 51–52		• Reteaching Act., p. 13

The *DeJonge* case established two legal principles. The Court determined that the right of assembly is as important as the rights of free speech and free press. Also, the Court ruled that the due process clause of the Fourteenth Amendment protects freedom of assembly from state and local governments. In other words, this case was the one that incorporated freedom of assembly to all levels of government.

Assembly on Public Property

Freedom of assembly includes the right to parade and demonstrate in public. Because these forms of assembly usually occur in parks, in streets, or on sidewalks, they could interfere with the rights of others to use the same facilities.

Conflicts also arise when parades and demonstrations advocate unpopular causes. Demonstrations have a high **potential** for violence because those with opposite views may launch counterdemonstrations. The two sides may engage in heated verbal or physical clashes. For this reason, parades and demonstrations can be subject to greater government regulation than exercises of pure speech and other kinds of assembly.

Limits on Demonstrations

To provide for public order and safety, many states and cities require that groups wanting to parade or demonstrate first obtain a permit. The precedent for such regulation was set in *Cox* v. *New Hampshire*[1] (1941). Cox was one of several Jehovah's Witnesses convicted of violating a law requiring a parade permit. He challenged his conviction on the grounds that the permit law restricted his rights of free speech and assembly.

The Court voted to uphold the law, ruling that the law was not designed to silence unpopular ideas, but to **ensure** that parades would not interfere with public use of the streets. In part, the decision said:

> ❝ The authority of a municipality to impose regulations in order to assure the safety and convenience of the people in the use of public highways has never been regarded as inconsistent with civil liberties. ❞
>
> —Chief Justice Charles Evans Hughes, 1941

Other Limits on Public Assembly

For public demonstrations in some public facilities—airports, libraries, courthouses, schools, and swimming pools—the Court has set additional limits. For example, in *Adderly* v. *Florida*[2] (1966), the Court held that demonstrators could not enter the grounds of a county jail without permission. The Court ruled that, while the jail was public property, it was not usually open to public access. The state has the power, the Court reasoned, "to preserve the property under its control for the use to which it is lawfully dedicated."

More restrictions on peaceable public assembly can apply, too, if the right of assembly clashes with the rights of others. In *Cox* v. *Louisiana*[3] (1965), the Court upheld a law banning demonstrations and parades near courthouses if they might interfere with trials. In *Grayned* v. *City of Rockford*[4] (1972) the justices upheld a ban on demonstrations that were intended to disrupt school classes.

📖 *See the following footnoted materials in the* **Reference Handbook:**
1. *Cox* v. *New Hampshire* case summary, page R25.
2. *Adderly* v. *Florida* case summary, page R23.
3. *Cox* v. *Louisiana* case summary, page R25.
4. *Grayned* v. *City of Rockford* case summary, page R28.

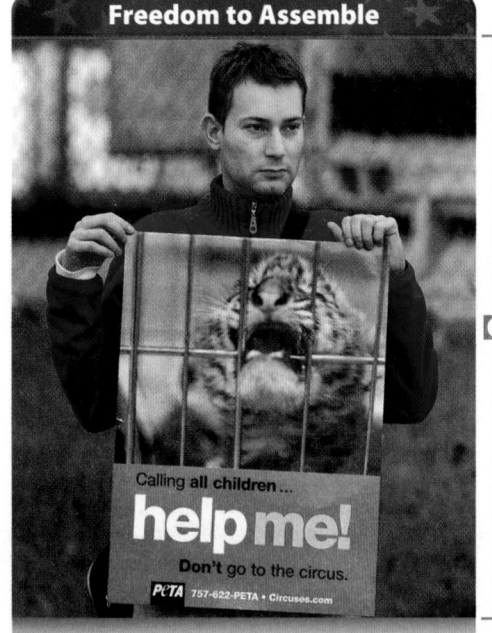

Freedom to Assemble ★ ★ ★

Persuading Others Tony Madson was just one of those assembling to oppose the Ringling Bros. circus coming to town in Chicago in 2005. Freedom of assembly brings minority opinions before fellow citizens where they can compete in the marketplace of ideas. *If there were no right to assemble, what would be the impact on democracy?*

Teach

C Critical Thinking

Analyzing Information Ask students to read "Issues in the News" on the previous page. **Ask:** Do you see any lapse of logic in the arguments given by Walter Griffin or the city council? *(Mr. Griffin complains that a $20 charge prevents him from demonstrating but does not say how. The city council did not say it banned picketing—only that it would charge $20. The city council's response also is unclear because a $20 fee would not cover the cost of "adequate police protection.")* **OL** **AL**

Caption Answer: People would not be able to demonstrate their opposition to government actions or their support for popular or unpopular causes. This would limit the people's ability to influence their government.

Additional Support

Activity: Collaborative Learning ★ ★ ★

Reviewing Key Concepts This activity can reinforce discussion of the freedom of assembly. Organize students into groups, and assign each group one of the following topics: protections for the freedom of assembly, limits on public assembly, labor picketing, or freedom of association. Each member of the group should become an "expert" on the group's topic. Students should summarize the text's discussion of the topic (including relevant Supreme Court cases), exchanging and answering questions within the group, considering "what if . . ." situations, and so on. Then form new groups, making sure that at least one representative from each "topic" group is in each new group, and have the "experts," in turn, teach their topics to fellow group members. **OL**

Still other Supreme Court decisions have made it clear that restrictions on freedom of assembly must be precisely worded and apply equally to all groups. In *Police Department of Chicago v. Mosley*[1] (1972), the Court voided a city law that banned all demonstrations near school buildings except in the case of labor union **picketing**—patrolling an establishment to convince workers and the public not to enter it.

Assembly and Property Rights

The right to assemble does not allow a group to convert private property to its own use, even if the property is open to the public. In *Lloyd Corporation v. Tanner*[2] (1972), the Court ruled that a group protesting the Vietnam War did not have the right to gather in a shopping mall.

In recent years, some right-to-life demonstrators blocked the entrances of private abortion clinics. The Court appeared unwilling to protect this type of assembly. In *New York State NOW v. Terry* (1990) and *Hirsch v. Atlanta* (1990), the justices refused to hear appeals of bans on such demonstrations. In 1993, however, the Court ruled that an 1871 civil rights law could not be applied against these demonstrators. In the 1997 case of *Schenck v. Pro-Choice Network of Western New York,*[3] the Court upheld parts of an injunction that created a fixed buffer zone around abortion clinics. At the same time, the Court struck down "floating buffer zone" laws that attempted to keep a few feet of distance between a demonstrator and a moving person who might be approaching a clinic.

Assembly and Disorder

A basic principle of democracy is that people have the right to assemble regardless of their views. Police, however, sometimes have difficulty protecting this principle when public assemblies threaten public safety.

*See the following footnoted materials in the **Reference Handbook:***
1. *Police Department of Chicago v. Mosley* case summary, page R32.
2. *Lloyd Corporation v. Tanner* case summary, page R30.
3. *Schenck v. Pro-Choice Network of Western New York* case summary, page R34.

The Law *and* You

How to Find a Supreme Court Decision

A law library or even the library in your local courthouse can have more than 1,000 volumes on law cases. Vance Cheek, Jr., the mayor of Johnson City, Tennessee, relies on his extensive library in his law practice.

How can a nonlawyer find out about a certain Supreme Court case? If you know the person or group involved in a case, you can look in a digest of cases. If you look up "Olmstead," for example, you will find "*Olmstead* v. *United States, 277 U.S. 438.*" This means that the report of the *Olmstead* decision begins on page 438 of volume 277 of the United States Reports. These reports are published by the government several times each year and date back to the very first year of the Court.

It is probably easier to learn about a case on the Internet. Two up-to-date, reliable sites are www.oyez.org and www.findlaw.com. Both are searchable using the names of the parties. Often it is enough to search the approximate year in which the case was decided.

◀ **Mayor Vance Cheek, Jr.**

Exploring the Law Activity
Researching a Case Choose an interesting case from this chapter and research it. Take notes and prepare to share what you find with the class.

The Nazis in Skokie

In 1977 the American Nazi Party, a small group patterned after Adolf Hitler's German Nazi Party, announced plans to hold a rally in Skokie, Illinois, a largely Jewish suburb of Chicago. Skokie residents were outraged. Many were **survivors** of the Holocaust, the mass extermination of Jews by the Nazis during World War II. Other residents were relatives of the Jews who were killed in Nazi death camps.

Skokie officials, citizens, and many others argued that the Nazis should not be allowed to march. They claimed that the march would cause great pain to residents and would attract a counterdemonstration. To prevent the march, the city required the Nazis to post a $350,000 bond to get a parade permit. The Nazis claimed the high bond interfered with free speech and assembly.

The Skokie case illustrates a free speech and assembly problem that some scholars have called the **heckler's veto.** The public vetoes the free speech and assembly rights of unpopular groups by claiming that demonstrations will result in violence. Such claims may be effective because government officials will almost always find it easier to curb unpopular demonstrations than to take measures to prevent violence. This dilemma leads to two related questions: Does the Constitution require the police to protect unpopular groups when their demonstrations incite violence? Can the police order demonstrators to disperse in the interest of public peace and safety?

Feiner v. New York

In 1950, speaking on a sidewalk in Syracuse, New York, Irving Feiner verbally attacked President Harry S. Truman, the American Legion, and the mayor of Syracuse. He also urged African Americans to fight for civil rights. As Feiner spoke, a larger and larger crowd gathered. When the crowd grew hostile, someone called the police. Two officers arrived to investigate, and an angry man in the audience told them that if they did not stop Feiner, he would. The police asked Feiner to stop speaking. When he refused, the police arrested him; he was convicted of disturbing the peace.

The Supreme Court upheld Feiner's conviction, ruling that the police had not acted to suppress speech but to preserve public order. Chief Justice Fred M. Vinson spoke for the majority of the Court:

Demonstrating for Civil Liberties

Freedom of Assembly Randy Wegerski, a four-year-old Tuscarora Native American, joins a picket line in 1958. The protestors gathered to block a state survey of reservation land that had been seized for a power project. *Do you think government officials should be able to limit demonstrations that interfere with government work?*

    ❝ *It is one thing to say that the police cannot be used as an instrument for the suppression of unpopular views, and another to say that, when as here the speaker passes the bounds of argument or persuasion and undertakes incitement to riot, they are powerless to prevent a breach of the peace.* ❞
—Chief Justice Fred M. Vinson, 1951

Gregory v. City of Chicago

The *Feiner* case stands as a precedent that the police may disperse a demonstration and limit the freedom of assembly if it threatens the peace.

CHAPTER 13: Constitutional Freedoms **379**

Caption Answer: Students may note that groups have a right to resist what they consider to be injustices, but the government must be able to perform its duties.

Participating IN GOVERNMENT

Students on Parade Ask students to think of a parade they would like to organize and then find out how they would apply for a parade permit. After they share their findings with the class, discuss whether some kinds of parades are more "welcome" in the community than others. If so, which ones? **OL**

D Differentiated Instruction

Visual/Spatial **Ask:** What message does the photo on this page convey? What elements make it effective? *(The sign reminds us that the government has already taken many things from Native Americans. The fact that it is carried by a child reminds us that the problem has lasted for generations. The boy's clothing says "I am part of a tradition.")* **ELL** **BL** **OL**

Hands-On Chapter Project
Step 5

Creating a Class Poster

Step 5: Discussing the Project Students will discuss what they have learned about constitutional rights.

Directions Have a member of each group show the panels to the class and read the entries. Encourage a class discussion or debate following each presentation that focuses on citizens' constitutional rights.

Putting It Together **Ask:** What have you learned during this project about citizens' rights in other countries? Have students assemble the poster and its title and display it in a hallway or some other prominent place. **OL**

S Skill Practice

Summarizing Create a class time line entitled "American Protests and Strikes," using a tick mark for each decade of the past century. Divide the class into 10 groups—one for each decade. Groups will research one strike or protest that occurred during their assigned decade. Groups will write summaries that include the date of the event, the type of event, location, issue, and the demographics of participants. **Ask:** How did the event affect individual participants and the nation? *(Answers should demonstrate an understanding of the issues.)* **ELL** **BL** **OL**

Additional Support

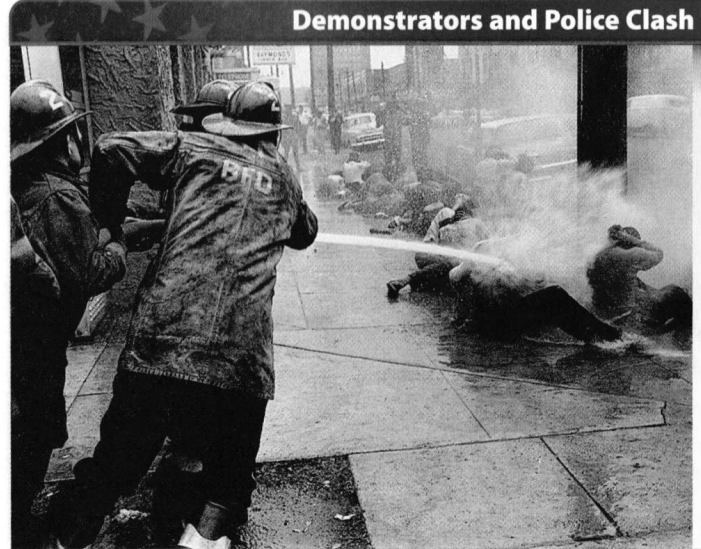

Demonstrators and Police Clash

Voices of Protest
As a wave of civil rights activity swept across the nation in the 1960s, some government officials and police tried to preserve laws that supported segregation by attempting to restrict demonstrations. Police in Birmingham, Alabama, used high-pressure water hoses against marchers in the spring of 1963. **Which Supreme Court decisions might apply to this kind of police action?**

A federal appeals court ruled that the need to keep the peace was not a valid reason to deny a parade permit. Since then, the Court has overturned the convictions of people whose only offense has been to demonstrate peacefully in support of unpopular causes.

The case of *Gregory* v. *City of Chicago* (1969) is a good example of the Court's thoughts on this matter. Dick Gregory, an entertainer and African American activist, led a group of marchers from the city hall in downtown Chicago to the mayor's home to demand the dismissal of the school superintendent for failing to desegregate schools. About 180 police officers were on hand to provide protection. Hostile onlookers from the all-white neighborhood began to throw rocks and eggs at the marchers. After a time, the police decided that violence was imminent and ordered the marchers to disperse. When the marchers refused, they **S** were arrested and later convicted of disorderly conduct. In a departure from the *Feiner* case, the Court overturned this conviction, saying the marchers had done no more than exercise their First Amendment right of assembly and petition.

A related case on the First Amendment right to assembly was decided in *City of Chicago* v. *Morales* (1999). This case tested the constitutionality of a Chicago Police Department anti-loitering ordinance. The ordinance said that if police saw a person whom officers believed to be a gang member

loitering in a public place with one or more persons, these people could be ordered to disperse—if they then failed to disperse, they could be arrested. The Court ruled that the law was too vague. It gave police no standards by which to determine when someone was loitering, that is, when they had no apparent purpose for standing on the street. The Chicago law was struck down.

Protecting Labor Picketing

Workers who are on strike or other demonstrators often organize picket lines. For many years the Supreme Court has debated how much protection the First Amendment gives picketers. Picketing conveys a message and is, therefore, a form of speech and assembly. But labor picketing, unlike most other kinds of demonstrations, tries to persuade customers and workers not to deal with a business. Many people will not cross a picket line, depriving a business of its workers and customers.

Through much of American history, courts have supported many kinds of restraints on labor picketing. Then, in *Thornhill* v. *Alabama*[1] (1940), the Supreme Court ruled that peaceful picketing was a form of free speech. It reflected the growing strength of the labor movement in American life.

*See the following footnoted materials in the **Reference Handbook**:*
1. *Thornhill* v. *Alabama* case summary, page R34.

Activity: Interdisciplinary Connection

The Arts Songs about causes and reforms have long been a part of the United States's tradition of protest. Have students choose one of these two activities:

- Find recordings of three of the songs that were part of the civil rights movement in the United States—for example, "Keep Your Eyes on the Prize," "We Shall Not Be Moved," and "We Shall Overcome." After sharing the

music, explain the meaning and importance of each of the songs.

- Artists today often perform together to raise awareness of social problems and to raise funds to help effect change. Research one such concert (and, if possible, show a video clip from it), when and where it was held, what cause was spotlighted, who performed, and how effectively it got its message across. **OL**

In later decisions, however, the Court severely limited the position it took in the *Thornhill* case. In *Hughes* v. *Superior Court*[1] (1950), the Court refused to overturn a California court's ban on picketing at a supermarket to force it to hire African American workers. 📖 The Court wrote:

> 66 While picketing is a mode of communication it is inseparably something more and different. . . . [T]he very purpose of a picket line is to exert influences, and it produces consequences, different from other modes of communication. 99
>
> —Justice Felix Frankfurter, 1950

The Court further limited picketing in *International Brotherhood of Teamsters, Local 695* v. *Vogt*[2] (1957). 📖 The Court upheld a Wisconsin law that prohibited picketing a business unless there was a labor dispute.

📖 *See the following footnoted materials in the Reference Handbook:*
1. *Hughes* v. *Superior Court* case summary, page R28.
2. *International Brotherhood of Teamsters, Local 695* v. *Vogt* case summary, page R29.
3. *DeJonge* v. *Oregon* case summary, page R26.

Freedom of Association

Does the First Amendment protect an individual's right to join an organization that the government considers subversive?

In a 1937 case, *DeJonge* v. *Oregon*,[3] the Supreme Court extended the right to freely assemble to protect the right of individuals to freedom of association. 📖 (Freedom of association means the right to join a political party, interest group, or other organization.) Can the government restrict the right of assembly and association in order to protect the nation's security?

Whitney v. California

In 1927 the Supreme Court reviewed the case of Charlotte Anita Whitney, who attended a convention where the Communist Labor Party was organized. Because the party advocated workers using violent means to take over control of property, Whitney was convicted of breaking a California law concerning violent actions. The prosecution successfully argued that membership in the party indicated that she had committed a crime.

We the People
Making a Difference

USAS With the help of successful campaigns like the one against BJ&B, USAS has been able to spread the Designated Supplier Program (DSP) to universities across the country. Under the DSP: "university licensees are required to source most university logo apparel from supplier factories that have been determined by universities . . . to be in compliance with their obligation to respect the rights of the employees— including the right to organize and bargain collectively and the right to be paid a living wage."

Activity: Have students research the universities that have adopted or are working to adopt the Designated Suppliers Program. **Ask:** How do university students attempt to educate people about DSP? (*mostly through demonstrations and rallies*) **OL**

We the People
Making a Difference

College students are known for their idealism and willingness to campaign for social justice. As the Internet heightens their awareness of global problems, some students have begun campaigning on behalf of workers in other countries. United Students Against Sweatshops (USAS) protests American firms that have factories abroad that exploit foreign workers. (In sweatshops, workers have few if any rights and face unhealthy working conditions.)

The main weapon of USAS is the threat of a boycott of any T-shirts or other college paraphernalia produced in sweatshops. USAS works to inform the student body about the issue and how college-branded clothes are made.

One successful campaign was against the BJ&B company that made baseball caps for Nike, Reebok, and others in a free trade zone in the Dominican Republic. It was a long battle, and ultimately Nike and Reebok worked with the college students and other labor activists to improve labor conditions for workers.

"I never thought a group of students, thousands of them, could put so much pressure on these brands," said Ignacio Hernández, the general secretary of the Federation of Free Trade Zone Unions. "We were determined to win, but without them it would have taken us five more years. And it would have been more traumatic without them because all we would have was the pressure to strike."

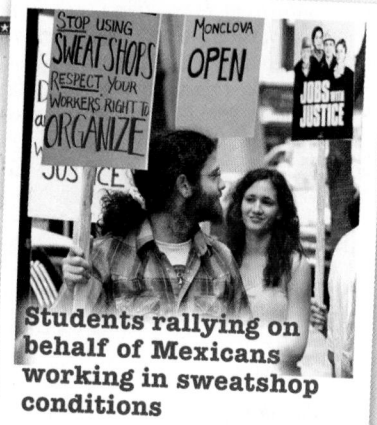

Students rallying on behalf of Mexicans working in sweatshop conditions

Guaranteeing Fundamental Rights

Objective: Prepare a seminar on First Amendment rights.

Focus/Teach: Research the principles of the First Amendment in practice.

Assess: Review reports and student lesson plans.

Close: Have students present the seminars they prepared.

Differentiated Instruction Strategies

BL Make graphic organizers showing each right listed in the First Amendment and how it applies today.

AL Have students research a recent court case involving the First Amendment.

ELL Discuss how the American colonial experience influenced the First Amendment.

R **Reading Strategy**

Academic Vocabulary Ask students to discuss the various meanings of the word *alien,* including its use in relation to immigration and the Smith Act. **ELL** **OL**

Assess

Assign the Section 5 Assessment as homework or as an in-class activity, or have students take Section Quiz 13-5 from *Section Quizzes and Chapter Tests.*

Close

Summarizing Review the types of assembly and reasons for assembly that are discussed in this section. Have students identify and explain ways in which teenagers might participate in various assemblies—and their First Amendment right to protection when doing so. **OL**

Section 5 Review

Registering Aliens, 1940

R

The Smith Act In New York City, people who were not citizens stood in line in August 1940 to get forms related to the Smith Act, or the Alien Registration Act. The act made advocating the forcible overthrow of the American government a crime. *Could international tensions influence the Court's ruling in this area?*

In *Whitney* v. *California* (1927), the Supreme Court decided that:

> [A]lthough the rights of free speech and assembly are fundamental, they are not in their nature absolute. Their exercise is subject to restriction, if the particular restriction proposed is required in order to protect the state from destruction. . . . [T]he necessity which is essential to a valid restriction does not exist unless speech would produce, or is intended to produce, a clear and imminent danger of some substantive evil which the state constitutionally may seek to prevent.
> —Justice Louis Brandeis, 1927

*See the following footnoted materials in the **Reference Handbook:*** **1.** *Dennis* v. *United States* case summary, page R26.

In the 1950s, as the Cold War with the Soviet Union intensified and fears of communism increased, this clear and present danger doctrine became a major issue. The government began to arrest and convict accused subversives, primarily Communist Party members. In 1940 the Alien Registration Act, known as the Smith Act, was passed in anticipation of the United States's possible entry into World War II. (The Smith Act contained a section that made advocating forcible overthrow of any government in the United States illegal.) In 1951, under this act, the Supreme Court upheld convictions of 11 leaders of the American Communist Party in *Dennis* v. *United States*[1] (1951). In later cases, however, the Court ruled that only actual preparations for the use of force against the government were in fact punishable.

SECTION 5 Review

Vocabulary

1. **Explain** the significance of: picketing, heckler's veto.

Main Ideas

2. **Identifying** What two principles were established by the *DeJonge* decision?

3. **Describing** How did the Court use the clear and present danger doctrine in the 1950s?

Critical Thinking

4. **Analyzing** Should more restrictions apply if a parade supports an unpopular cause? Support your answer.

5. **Organizing** Use a graphic organizer like the one below to identify two reasons the right to assemble is important to preserve in a democracy and two reasons it can be limited.

To Preserve	To Limit

Writing About Government

6. **Persuasive Writing** Imagine that you are the mayor of a town where a citizen is planning a rally to protest the government's environmental policies. Write a letter to the city council explaining the constitutional issues and the public welfare concerns that they should consider before allowing the rally.

Answers

1. All definitions can be found in the section and the Glossary.
2. The right of assembly is as important as free speech; the Fourteenth Amendment protects the right of assembly from infringement by state and local governments.
3. People who advocated the overthrow of the U.S. government were imprisoned.
4. Answers may vary but should balance the rights of assembly with concern for maintaining order.
5. To Preserve: It allows political parties and interest groups to exist, and it protects organized dissent against the government. To Limit: Local governments may require permits for organized parades and demonstrations, and restrictions may be set if the right of assembly clashes with the rights of other people.
6. Have students read letters aloud.

Analyzing News Media

Every citizen should be aware of current issues and events in order to make good decisions when exercising citizenship rights. To stay informed, people use a variety of news sources, including print, broadcast, and electronic media.

Why Learn This Skill?

To get an accurate picture of current events, you must be able to think critically about the news. To analyze news media, read the excerpt and perform the steps that follow it.

❝ *Bill Pierce, teacher, engineer, and entrepreneur has recently announced his candidacy to challenge [Sen. Mike] DeWine for the Republican Senatorial primary in Ohio. Pierce is friendly and engaging and his passion for governmental reform and a return to governance as intended by our constitution resonates with his every word. . . . On the issues, Pierce is solidly conservative. Local conservative groups are asking for meetings with Pierce and are anxious to support him and there is also evidence that county level Republican leaders are realizing that it may be time to move on from DeWine and support a true conservative like Pierce.* ❞

—Tim Holloway,
American Conservative
Union Foundation, 2005

1. Ask yourself: Is this story being reported because it is important for the public to know about it—or because it is entertaining?

2. As you watch, listen, or read, ask yourself whether the story is being presented objectively. Does it present both sides of an issue? Look for any evidence of bias. Is the publication, radio station, television channel, or reporter known for evenhanded, accurate news reporting?

3. Think about the source of the news story. Reports that reveal sources are more reliable than those that do not. If you know the sources, you can evaluate them. How many sources are used? The more sources that are cited, the more reliable it usually is.

Practicing the Skill

After reading the excerpt above, answer the following questions:

1. To what political party do both people mentioned in the passage belong?

2. Do you detect any evidence of bias in the passage? If so, give examples.

3. Did the writer support his points with sources?

Applying the Skill

Find two articles that discuss an issue in which public opinion is divided. Write a brief report covering these points:

• What points did the articles try to make? Were the articles successful?

• Can the facts be verified?

• Did either of the articles reflect bias, or do they represent both sides fairly? If you detect bias, give examples.

• List any unsupported statements.

• List the sources you can identify in the articles.

CHAPTER 13: *Constitutional Freedoms* **383**

Teach

C Critical Thinking

Analyzing Sources The Internet and cable television have made news more readily accessible for many people. This frequently means people are getting more news and have even more reason to analyze the content. Ask students to compare a cable news broadcast on a given topic with its coverage on two different Web sites. Have them present their comparisons to the class. **OL**

R Reading Strategy

Reading Primary Sources Have students read excerpts from two different news resources. One should be a conservative publication (such as www. conservativetruth.org), and the other should be liberal (such as www.trueblueliberal.com). Have students use the skill-set questions on this page to identify any biases and determine overall reliability.
Ask: Why do you think bipartisanship can affect biases, and thus the reliability of an article? *(News articles are sometimes written with a personal or political agenda as the motivating factor.)* **AL**

★★★★★★★★★★★★★★★★★★★★★★★★★★★★★ **Answers** ★★★★★★★★★★★★★★★★★★★★★★★★★★★★★

Practicing the Skill

1. Republican

2. Holloway calls Pierce friendly and engaging and passionate. He refers to "a return to governance as intended."

3. no; this sometimes can mean a less-than-reliable news source

Applying the Skill

Students should carefully go through the articles and fully answer each question.

ExamView®
Assessment Suite

This easy-to-use software includes extensive question banks and allows you to create fully customized tests that can be administered in print or online.

Reviewing Vocabulary

1. heckler's veto
2. prior restraint
3. symbolic speech
4. libel
5. picketing
6. seditious speech
7. pure speech
8. shield laws

Reviewing Main Ideas

9. The Fourteenth Amendment defined citizenship and laid the groundwork for making individual rights national.
10. Possible answers: Most government officials take their oaths of office in the name of God. The nation's coins carry the motto "In God We Trust." The Pledge of Allegiance contains the phrase "one nation under God." Daily sessions of Congress open with a prayer.
11. protected—pure speech, symbolic speech; not protected—seditious speech, defamatory speech, "fighting words"
12. The press might print or broadcast information that could influence witnesses' testimony, prejudice jurors or prospective jurors, or otherwise influence the trial's outcome.
13. so that authorities can make arrangements for the public's welfare, safety, and protection

Reviewing Vocabulary

From the following list, choose the content vocabulary word(s) that fits each situation described.

shield laws
pure speech
prior restraint
libel

heckler's veto
seditious speech
picketing
symbolic speech

1. Spectators threaten violence against demonstrators and authorities break up the demonstration.
2. A government official tells a reporter that she cannot publish a story that might compromise national security.
3. A group burns an American flag to show its objection to a government policy.
4. A newspaper publishes an untrue story that damages the reputation of a local resident.

Chapter Summary

The First Amendment Freedom of . . .

Religion	The **establishment clause** prevents government from promoting or sponsoring religion. The **free exercise clause** prevents government from impeding the religious beliefs of Americans.
Speech	**Protected:** pure speech and symbolic speech (in most cases) **Not protected:** seditious speech (treasonous speech), defamatory speech (slander and libel), and "fighting words"
Press	A free press is invaluable in a democracy to ensure that citizens remain well informed. The press can be regulated in matters of national security or to ensure a fair trial.
Assembly	The right of assembly is protected but permits are often required to assemble in public places.
Petition	The right to petition the government for redress of grievances is guaranteed.

5. Animal rights activists parade outside a store that sells furs and attempt to convince customers not to enter.
6. An individual urges a group to fight the police rather than obey a police order to disperse.
7. A person stands in front of a group and states her opinion on an issue.
8. A reporter is protected against being forced to disclose a source of information in court.

Reviewing Main Ideas

Section 1 *(pages 355–357)*

9. **Explaining** What did the Fourteenth Amendment do for citizens and individual rights?

Section 2 *(pages 358–364)*

10. **Listing** What are four examples of how religion remains part of government?

Section 3 *(pages 366–370)*

11. **Identifying** What types of speech does the First Amendment protect and what types does it not protect?

Section 4 *(pages 371–375)*

12. **Speculating** How might freedom of the press interfere with an individual's right to a fair trial?

Section 5 *(pages 376–382)*

13. **Assessing** Why might government require that groups first obtain permits to parade or demonstrate?

Critical Thinking

14. **Essential Question** Should the First Amendment protect those who publish stolen government documents? Explain.
15. **Evaluating** Analyze the Supreme Court's decision in *Gitlow* v. *New York*. How did it support the intent of the Fourteenth Amendment on citizenship?
16. **Making Comparisons** Use a graphic organizer to compare the three sedition tests.

Limits on Seditious Speech		
Relaxes Limits	Sets Standard	Toughens Limits

Critical Thinking

14. Answers will vary but should include references to Supreme Court decisions on this issue, such as the *Pentagon Papers* case. Students should attempt to balance the interests of national security and government suppression of embarrassing information.
15. Possible answers: The Court's decision that freedom of speech is a basic, undeniable right promotes an atmosphere in which citizens can speak their

minds about issues that matter to them but cannot advocate the violent overthrow of the government. The ruling determined that no state government can deny basic rights and liberties to any person.

16. Relaxes Limits: preferred position; Sets Standard: clear and present danger; Toughens Limits: bad tendency

Government ONLINE Self-Check Quiz
Visit glencoe.com and enter *QuickPass*™ code USG9822c13.
Click on Self-Check Quizzes for additional test practice.

CHAPTER 13 **Assessment and Activities**

Document-Based Questions

Analyzing Primary Sources

Read the excerpt below and answer the questions that follow.

Civil rights leader Malcolm X advocated a more directly confrontational approach to acquiring African American rights. In this 1964 speech, he discussed how African Americans would gain their full constitutional right to vote.

> 66 *If we don't do something real soon, I think you'll have to agree that we're going to be forced either to use the ballot or the bullet. It's one or the other in 1964. It isn't that time is running out—time has run out! 1964 threatens to be the most explosive year America has ever witnessed. . . . We will work with anybody, anywhere, at any time, who is genuinely interested in tackling the problem head-on, nonviolently as long as the enemy is nonviolent, but violent when the enemy gets violent.* 99

17. In this excerpt, is Malcolm X advocating a violent overthrow of the government? If so, is his right to say this protected by the constitutional right to free speech?

18. If Malcolm X's speech had led to a violent uprising or an attempt to overthrow the government, would you consider him responsible? Would the Court?

Applying Technology Skills

19. Using a Web Site Locate the Web site for the Journalism Education Association at www.jea.org/resources/index. Research the association's position on student press rights. Summarize and discuss these rights with your classmates.

20. Exploring the First Amendment Visit www.newseum.org, the Web site for a Washington, D.C., museum that opened in 2008. The site states that the museum aims to present a history of the First Amendment and the media. Explore the site, then answer the following questions: 1) What organization operates the museum? 2) What are some examples of exhibits at the Newseum? 3) Offer your assessment of whether the exhibits reflect the stated mission of the museum.

Interpreting Political Cartoons

Analyze the cartoon and answer the questions that follow. Base your answers on the cartoon and your knowledge of Chapter 13.

21. Whom do you think the person in the cartoon is representing? Why?

22. What is this person doing?

23. What do his thoughts suggest about the nature of an individual's constitutional rights?

Participating IN GOVERNMENT

24. Locate a copy of your state's constitution, particularly the bill of rights. Compare the rights guaranteed in the First Amendment of the U.S. Constitution with the rights protected by your state's bill of rights. Prepare a chart or graphic organizer that identifies the similarities and the differences between the two documents.

CHAPTER 13: *Constitutional Freedoms* **385**

Government ONLINE

Have students use the **Chapter 13 Self-Check Quiz.** Visit glencoe.com and enter *QuickPass*™ code USG9085c13T to prepare for the Chapter Test.

20. The Freedom Forum funds and operates the Newseum. Answers to parts 2 and 3 will vary.

Interpreting Political Cartoons

21. one of the Framers of the Constitution, because his clothing, hairstyle, and writing materials suggest the time when the Constitution was written

22. drafting the Constitution or the Bill of Rights

23. They suggest how the Framers had to create a balance between freedom and rights and the limits to them.

Participating IN GOVERNMENT

24. Have students refer to their charts or other graphic organizers as they discuss similarities and differences in the documents.

Analyzing Primary Sources

17. Students' responses may vary. Some may say that Malcolm X was advocating violence, but others may point out that he was only advocating violence as a reaction to violations of voting rights. Either way, Malcolm X's right to make this speech is protected by the Constitution because he was criticizing the government, an action that is specifically protected, and because he was not advocating direct violence, force, or lawless action.

18. Again, students' answers will vary, but they may include the idea that the Court could determine that Malcolm X was guilty of inciting violence under *Gitlow* v. *New York* (1925), which prohibited speech that had a tendency to lead to illegal action.

Applying Technology Skills

19. Discuss student press rights with the class. You might focus on how the rights are expressed in the print or broadcast media of your school.

Chapter Bonus Test Question

Ask: What are three major religions practiced in the United States today? *(any three of Christianity, Judaism, Buddhism, Islam, and Hinduism)*

Key to Ability Levels

BL Below level		**AL** Above level	
OL On level		**ELL** English Language Learners	

Key to Teaching Resources

Print Material   Transparency

CD-ROM or DVD

Levels					Resources	Chapter Opener	Section 1	Section 2	Section 3	Section 4	Chapter Assess
BL	OL	AL	ELL								
FOCUS											
BL	OL	AL	ELL		Section Focus Transparencies		14-1	14-2	14-3	14-4	
TEACH											
BL	OL		ELL		Reading Essentials and Study Guide (and Answer Key)		p. 149	p. 152	p. 156	p. 159	
BL	OL		ELL		Guided Reading Activities		p. 50	p. 51	p. 52	p. 53	
BL	OL		ELL		Vocabulary Activities					p. 14	
BL	OL	AL	ELL		Chapter Summaries						
BL	OL				American Biographies				p. 65		
BL	OL	AL	ELL		Cooperative Learning Activities						
	OL	AL	ELL		Government Simulations and Debate						
BL	OL	AL	ELL		Historical Documents and Speeches		p. 14				
BL	OL	AL	ELL		Interpreting Political Cartoons						
BL	OL		ELL		Skill Reinforcement Activities					p. 14	
BL	OL	AL	ELL		Source Readings				p. 14		
BL	OL				Supreme Court Case Studies				p. 27	pp. 115, 121	
BL	OL	AL	ELL		Participating in Government Activities			p. 27			
BL	OL		ELL		Spanish Declaration of Independence and U.S. Constitution	✓	✓	✓	✓	✓	✓
BL	OL	AL	ELL		NGS World Atlas, Spanish	✓	✓	✓	✓	✓	✓
BL	OL	AL	ELL		Unit Overlay Transparencies, Strategies, and Activities	✓	✓	✓	✓	✓	✓
BL	OL		ELL		Making It Relevant Transparencies	✓	✓	✓	✓	✓	✓
BL	OL	AL	ELL		High School Writing Process Transparencies, Strategies, and Activities	✓	✓	✓	✓	✓	✓
BL	OL	AL			American Art & Architecture Transparencies, Strategies, and Activities	✓	✓	✓	✓	✓	✓

✓ Chapter- or unit-based activities applicable to all sections in this chapter

All-In-One Planner and Resource Center

- Interactive Lesson Planner
- Interactive Teacher Edition
- Fully editable blackline masters
- Chapter Spotlight Videos Launch
- Differentiated Lesson Plans
- Printable reports of daily assignments
- Standards tracking system

Levels BL	OL	AL	ELL		Resources	Chapter Opener	Section 1	Section 2	Section 3	Section 4	Chapter Assess
TEACH *(continued)*											
BL	OL			💿	**American Music: Hits Through History**	✓	✓	✓	✓	✓	✓
BL	OL		ELL	📁	**Reading Strategies for the Social Studies Classroom**	✓	✓	✓	✓	✓	✓
			ELL	📁	**English Language Learner Handbook**	✓	✓	✓	✓	✓	✓
BL	OL		ELL	📁	**Writer's Guidebook for Social Studies**	✓	✓	✓	✓	✓	✓
BL	OL	AL	ELL	📁	**Living Constitution, SE**	✓	✓	✓	✓	✓	✓
BL	OL	AL	ELL	📁	**Living Constitution, TAE**	✓	✓	✓	✓	✓	✓
BL	OL			📁	**NGS World Atlas, English**	✓	✓	✓	✓	✓	✓
BL	OL		ELL	📁	**The Constitution and You (poster set)**	✓	✓	✓	✓	✓	✓
BL	OL	AL	ELL	📁	**Spanish Chapter Summaries**						
BL	OL	AL	ELL	📁	**Spanish Vocabulary Activities**						
BL	OL		ELL	📁	**Spanish Reading Essentials and Study Guide (and Answer Key)**		p. 149	p. 152	p. 156	p. 159	
BL	OL	AL	ELL	💿	**PresentationPlus! with MindJogger CheckPoint**	✓	✓	✓	✓	✓	✓
ASSESS											
BL	OL	AL	ELL	💿	*ExamView® Assessment Suite*		14-1	14-2	14-3	14-4	Ch. 14
BL	OL	AL	ELL	📁	**Authentic Assessment with Rubrics**		p. 21				p. 21
BL	OL	AL	ELL	📁	**Section Quizzes and Chapter Tests**		p. 169	p. 170	p. 171	p. 172	pp. 173–180
BL	OL	AL	ELL	📁	**Spanish Section Quizzes and Tests**		p. 169	p. 170	p. 171	p. 172	pp. 173–180
CLOSE											
BL			ELL	📁	**Reteaching Activities**						
BL	OL	AL	ELL	💿	**StudentWorks™ Plus with Audio Summaries**	✓	✓	✓	✓	✓	✓
BL	OL		ELL	🖨	**Graphic Organizer Transparencies**		✓	✓	✓	✓	
BL	OL		ELL	📁	**High School Government Reading and Study Skills Foldables®**		p. 57	p. 57	p. 57	p. 57	

Teach With Technology

What is a Self-Check Quiz?

A Self-Check Quiz is a set of 10 or more multiple-choice questions that assess student comprehension of the chapter.

How can a Self-Check Quiz help my students?

A Self-Check Quiz is a quick and easy way for students to check how much they have learned and identify areas needing improvement. It allows students to:

- view their results immediately
- view the correct answers
- e-mail their results to you or themselves
- receive feedback on each question for where students can go to review topics they missed or had trouble answering

Visit glencoe.com and enter a *QuickPass*™ code to go to a Self-Check Quiz.

Government ONLINE

Visit glencoe.com and enter *QuickPass*™ code USG9085c14T for Chapter 14 resources.

You can easily launch a wide range of digital products from your computer's desktop with the McGraw-Hill Social Studies widget.

	Student	Teacher	Parent
Media Library			
• Student Edition Section Audio	●		●
• Chapter Spotlight Videos	●	●	●
***United States Government* Online Learning Center (Web Site)**			
• Chapter Overviews	●	●	●
• Multilingual Glossaries	●	●	●
• Study-to-Go	●	●	●
• Student Web Activities	●	●	●
• Self-Check Quizzes	●	●	●
• Online Student Edition	●	●	●
• Vocabulary eFlashcards	●	●	●
• Web Activity Lesson Plans		●	
• Vocabulary PuzzleMaker	●	●	●
• Landmark Supreme Court Cases	●	●	●
• Beyond the Textbook	●	●	●

READING SUPPORT FROM
JAMESTOWN EDUCATION

- **Timed Readings Plus in Social Studies** helps students increase their reading rate and fluency while maintaining comprehension. The 400-word passages are similar to those found on state and national assessments.

- **Reading in the Content Area: Social Studies** concentrates on six essential reading skills that help students better comprehend what they read. The book includes 75 high-interest nonfiction passages written at increasing levels of difficulty.

- **Reading Social Studies** includes strategic reading instruction and vocabulary support in Social Studies content for ELLs and native speakers of English. www.jamestowneducation.com

Reading List Generator CD-ROM

GLENCOE BOOKLINK 3

Use this database to search more than 30,000 titles to create a customized reading list for your students.

- Reading lists can be organized by students' reading level, author, genre, theme, or area of interest.

- The database provides Degrees of Reading Power™ (DRP) and Lexile™ readability scores for all selections.

- A brief summary of each selection is included.

Leveled reading suggestions for this chapter:

- *Choice: A Tribute to Dr. Martin Luther King, Jr.,* by Alice Walker

- *Pathways to Freedom,* by Edwin D. Hoffman

- *Telephone Conversation,* by Wole Soyinka

Review suggested books before assigning them.

Economics Connection

Personal Finance Literacy

Education: A Jumpstart for Your Future

Remind students that, besides its other benefits, a college education is an economic advantage. The average college graduate earns 60 to 80 percent more over a lifetime than a high school graduate.

The choice of a college is important and should be based on finances; career goals (some schools are better in certain fields); location (out-of-state tuition is higher than in-state tuition); and income potential of the career (high-paying careers justify more expensive schools).

Students can cut college costs by taking advanced placement classes in high school, scoring high on the College-Level Examination Program test, or attending an in-state school. Financial aid is available to most students, based on need, merit, or membership (theirs or a parent's) in certain groups—military, churches, or others. Students should apply for all types of aid for which they're eligible.

Financial Aid Tips

- Begin searching for financial aid sources as early as the junior year of high school.

- Students must contribute about one-third of their savings toward tuition, so they should use savings to pay down as much credit card debt as possible before applying for financial aid.

- To apply for state or federal government grants, scholarships, and loans, students should get the Free Application for Federal Student Aid (FAFSA) form, available online and in libraries.

- For most aid, students need: proof of income—theirs and parents' or guardians'; family assets and expenses; number of college students in the family; a high school transcript.

Did You Know?

Students are not expected to pay back the principal on college loans until after they leave school, but interest on some loans accumulates while they're still in school.

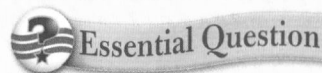

🔊 Chapter Audio   🎬 Spotlight Video

 Essential Question

The United States has been shaped by waves of immigrants from all around the world. Our rights of citizenship come from the Constitution.

🎬 **Chapter Spotlight Video**

To generate student interest and provide a springboard for class discussion, access the Chapter 14 Video at glencoe.com or on the video DVD.

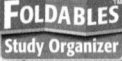 **FOLDABLES™** Study Organizer **Dinah Zike's Foldables** are three-dimensional, interactive graphic organizers that help students practice basic writing skills, review key vocabulary terms, and identify main ideas. Have students complete this chapter's Foldable activity or activities in *Dinah Zike's Reading and Study Skills Foldables* booklet. **OL**

Government ONLINE

Visit glencoe.com and enter *QuickPass*™ code USG9085c14T for Chapter 14 Resources including Chapter Overview, Student Web Activity, Self-Check Quiz, and other materials for students and teachers.

Citizenship *and* Equal Justice

Essential Question

How has the United States been shaped by its immigrant history, and how do we determine the rights of citizenship?

Government ONLINE
Chapter Overview Visit glencoe.com and enter *QuickPass*™ code USG9822c14 for an overview, a quiz, and other chapter resources.

▲ Dr. Martin Luther King, Jr., during the March on Washington, August 28, 1963

386

Launching the Chapter

Identifying Points of View Ask students to keep a series of journal entries throughout this chapter, noting their thoughts as they place themselves in the following roles:

- an illegal alien or refugee who desires citizenship
- an African American who was denied citizenship prior to ratification of the Fourteenth Amendment

- a worker who claims to have been overlooked for a promotion because of affirmative action
- an American who is trying to prove intent to discriminate

Students may share their entries if they want to or use the comments as an informal study guide.

Essential Question: What is the meaning of *citizenship*? *(Prompt students to consider both the rights and the duties of citizenship.)* **OL**

A Nation of Immigrants

Focus

Reader's Guide

Content Vocabulary
* ★ amnesty (p. 390)
* ★ alien (p. 391)
* ★ resident alien (p. 391)
* ★ nonresident alien (p. 391)
* ★ enemy alien (p. 391)
* ★ refugee (p. 391)
* ★ undocumented alien (p. 391)

Academic Vocabulary
* ★ symbol (p. 387)
* ★ formula (p. 389)
* ★ shift (p. 389)

Reading Strategy
As you read, use a chart like the one below to track changes in American immigration policy.

Major Immigration Legislation	Basic Features of Law
1886 Chinese Exclusion Act	Restricted Chinese immigration, barred citizenship
Immigration Act of 1924	

Bellringer
Section Focus Transparencies 14-1

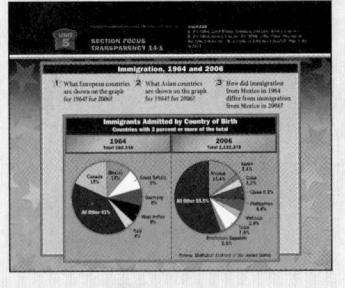

Issues in the News

In November 2007, the Department of Homeland Security (DHS) was ahead of schedule in building a 12 to 15-foot-tall steel fence to stop people from crossing the Mexican border illegally. Political pressure to "fast-track" the project led DHS to make an unusual land swap with the U.S. Fish and Wildlife Service. Environmentalists criticized the fence because it disrupted the habitat of jaguars and pygmy owls. "This is another example of the federal government riding roughshod over America's treasured lands and legal process in its rush to complete a highly ineffective and controversial border wall," one critic said.

▲ The border fence between the United States and Mexico

Few American **symbols** are as beloved as the Statue of Liberty, who holds aloft her torch to welcome the "huddled masses yearning to breathe free." Yet the fence project sets a different mood. Because many Americans are concerned about the number of undocumented immigrants, they worry about immigration overall and how it may change the society they know.

Immigration Policy

For much of our history, Americans have cherished the belief that we are a nation of immigrants—a melting pot of many ethnicities and races. It might be said that the first immigrants were the nomadic people who crossed the land bridge between Asia and Alaska in prehistoric times. Much later, the Spanish populated the Southwest, while the British settled along the East Coast. Between 1815 and 1914, waves of Germans, Irish, Italians, Russians, and other Europeans arrived. Most of the immigrants settled in large cities, especially in the Northeast and Midwest.

Sometimes Americans were afraid that immigrants would change their world. Prejudice was often involved. In the 1840s, many Americans were upset when large numbers of Irish Catholics arrived. A strong anti-immigrant movement developed in the period between 1880 to 1910 when there was a huge influx of Catholic and Jewish immigrants from southern and eastern Europe and Russia.

In the 1960s, Latinos and Asians began to make up a big percentage of the immigrant population. Latinos, who can be of any race, have become the largest group of immigrants. This is partly because the term *Latino* covers immigrants from many countries—Mexico, Cuba, and all the countries of Central and South America.

Reader's Guide

Answers to Graphic:

Immigration Act of 1924: lowered number of immigrants admitted annually; established the national origins system.

Immigration Reform Act of 1965: abolished national origins system; gave preference to family members and skilled workers and professionals.

Immigration Reform and Control Act of 1986: amnesty for undocumented immigrants who arrived before 1982, established penalties for employers who knowingly hire illegal workers.

Resource Manager

R Reading Strategies	**C** Critical Thinking	**D** Differentiated Instruction	**W** Writing Support	**S** Skill Practice
Teacher Edition • Academic Vocabulary, p. 390 **Additional Resources** • Guid. Read. Act., p. 50 • Quizzes/Tests, p. 170	**Teacher Edition** • Making Connections, p. 388 **Additional Resources** • Read. Essen., pp. 149–151	**Teacher Edition** • Kinesthetic, p. 391 **Additional Resources** • Foldables, p. 57	**Teacher Edition** • Personal Writing, p. 389 • Persuasive Writing, p. 390 **Additional Resources** • Authentic Assess., p. 21	**Teacher Edition** • Charting Information, p. 389 **Additional Resources** • Hist. Docs. and Speeches, p. 14

Teach

C Critical Thinking

Making Connections Ask:
Why did these states attract so many unauthorized immigrants? (*Answers might include: available jobs, established presence of many immigrants, lax enforcement of immigration laws.*) **OL**

Did You Know?

In the 1800s anti-Catholic prejudice was strong. Many Protestants thought Catholicism was incompatible with American values. In 1894 the American Protective Association, an anti-Catholic organization, declared: "We unite to protect our country and its free institutions against the secret, intolerant, and aggressive efforts that are persistently being set forth by . . . [the Catholic Church] to control the government of the United States and destroy our blood-bought civil and religious liberty."

Additional Support

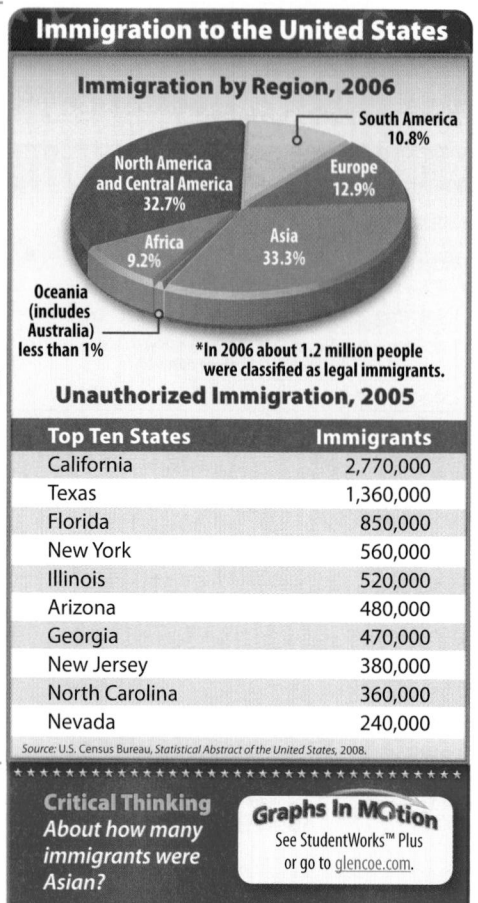

Immigration to the United States

Immigration by Region, 2006

- South America 10.8%
- Europe 12.9%
- North America and Central America 32.7%
- Asia 33.3%
- Africa 9.2%
- Oceania (includes Australia) less than 1%

*In 2006 about 1.2 million people were classified as legal immigrants.

Unauthorized Immigration, 2005

Top Ten States	Immigrants
California	2,770,000
Texas	1,360,000
Florida	850,000
New York	560,000
Illinois	520,000
Arizona	480,000
Georgia	470,000
New Jersey	380,000
North Carolina	360,000
Nevada	240,000

Source: U.S. Census Bureau, *Statistical Abstract of the United States, 2008.*

Critical Thinking
About how many immigrants were Asian?

Graphs In Motion
See StudentWorks™ Plus or go to glencoe.com.

Today immigration is again a major political issue, but the concerns are somewhat different. The big difference is that now many undocumented immigrants are living here—perhaps 12 million in 2008. A second reason is terrorism. Remembering the attacks of September 11, 2001, Americans are more nervous about the fact that so many people can enter the country illegally. Finally, the issue has become more prominent because significant numbers of immigrants are moving to states like Iowa, Montana, and North Carolina. These states do not have a long experience with immigrants and tend to be more fearful about how immigrants may change their communities. Competition for jobs has always driven fears of immigrants, but today we face new challenges in a global economy. We are importing more than we export at the same time that some American firms are exporting, or outsourcing, jobs to India and China. Technology and the Internet have also presented new challenges for economic competition in the world.

Early Restrictions

The Constitution clearly gives Congress the power to make immigration policy. Early in the nation's history, Congress declared a preference for immigrants from Europe. In 1790, it passed a law defining who could become a citizen if a person was not born here: Citizenship was possible only for someone who was "a free white person." As that term was then understood, this barred any African or Asian immigrant from becoming a citizen. After the Civil War, this law was revised to allow people born in Africa to become citizens, but Asian immigrants were still excluded from citizenship.

The first major law on immigration was passed in the late 1800s. Since then, several stages of immigration policy have occurred. In 1882 Congress passed the first major law that barred entrance to specific groups because the California Gold Rush and railroad building had attracted many immigrants. Of the men who built the Central Pacific Railroad, the vast majority were Chinese. By the 1870s, Chinese workers made up almost half of the workforce in San Francisco.

San Franciscans and other Californians began to rally against the Chinese. According to one account at the time, white American miners:

> 66 . . . accused them of stealing their wealth. They boldly asserted that California's gold belonged to them. The cry of 'California for the Americans' was raised and taken up on all sides. 99
> —from *The Story of California* (1924)

In 1882 Congress responded by passing the Chinese Exclusion Act. It said that no Chinese laborer could enter the United States for 10 years. (Chinese professionals were still allowed to immigrate.) Renewed several times, the act was in force until World War II. In that conflict, China was an American ally and Congress repealed the law.

One of the heaviest periods of immigration in American history came between 1880 and 1920 when some 25 million immigrants arrived. Most came from the countries of Southern and Eastern Europe—parts of the world that were unfamiliar to many Americans. They saw these new immigrants as very different from themselves.

Activity: Collaborative Learning

Producing a Documentary Organize students into small groups to research and produce a videotaped documentary about immigrant groups. Have group representatives plan together what immigrant groups they want to study, what information they want to gather, and what kind of presentation they want to prepare. Within each group, students should delegate tasks such as preparing interview questions, contacting interview subjects, conducting and taping the interviews, preparing background research about the various countries and cultures represented, creating visuals to clarify the information, choosing appropriate music, narrating the documentary, and so on. Another meeting of group representatives, for sharing ideas, can help each group polish its video. When the documentaries are completed, have students present them. **BL**

National Origins Quota System

In 1924 Congress took a more drastic step. The Immigration Act of 1924 introduced a quota system by country: Each country's immigrants were limited to 2 percent of foreign-born residents from that country listed in the U.S. Census of 1890. This **formula** favored groups that had been in the United States for a long time. For example, Great Britain would have a high quota because there were many British-born residents in the United States in 1890. By contrast, the Italian quota would be low because Italians only began migrating to the United States in large numbers in the late 1800s. During the next 40 years, immigration dropped sharply.

Immigration Reform Act of 1965

The next major policy **shift** was inspired largely by the civil rights movement and its ideal of equality and social justice. In 1965 Congress passed the Immigration Reform Act, abolishing the quota system based on national origin. When he signed the reform bill, President Lyndon B. Johnson referred to the old system as "un-American."

The new law was driven by two principles: reunifying families and giving priority to certain skills. The law also set up annual limits: 170,000 immigrants from the Eastern Hemisphere (Europe, Asia, and Africa) and 120,000 from the Western Hemisphere (Canada, Mexico, and Central and South America).

The family preference system gave top priority to unmarried children of U.S. citizens. After that, preference was given to (1) husbands, wives, and unmarried children of permanent residents; (2) doctors, lawyers, scientists and other professionals; (3) married children of U.S. citizens; (4) siblings of U.S. citizens; (5) workers whose occupations are needed; and (6) refugees. Some analysts say that the emphasis on reuniting families meant the annual limits were being filled by immigrants bringing in their relatives, so others did not have much chance to immigrate.

Immigration Reform and Control Act of 1986

President Ronald Reagan's Immigration and Reform Control Act (IRCA) had a dual purpose. First, Reagan wanted to slow illegal immigration by punishing employers who knowingly hired undocumented immigrants. Second, he wanted to offer a way for long-term, undocumented immigrants to become legal. If they could show they had entered the United States before January 1982 and lived here continuously, they could apply for amnesty. Eligible workers could be granted temporary and then permanent residency. After five years, they could apply for citizenship.

A Major Policy Shift

Lifting Quotas
On October 3, 1965, President Lyndon B. Johnson gave a major speech on a milestone immigration law at Liberty Island (seen in the distance, with Ellis Island in the foreground). *What was the major difference between this law and previous immigration policy?*

66 *[The national origins system] violated the basic principle of American democracy—the principle that values and rewards each man on the basis of his merit as a man. It has been un-American in the highest sense. . . . Today, with my signature, this system is abolished.* 99

S **Skill Practice**

Charting Information To help students understand the long-term impact of the Immigration Reform Act of 1965, provide them with statistics on the immigrant population in 1960 and the immigrant population in later years. Then, have students create graphs or charts showing country of origin, number of immigrants, and so forth. The information can be found in the *Statistical Abstracts* prepared by the U.S. Census Bureau. (www.census.gov). **AL**

W **Writing Support**

Personal Writing About 12 million immigrants passed through Ellis Island between 1892 and 1954. Explain to students that some new arrivals were denied admittance for medical or other reasons, which could have divided families. Have students write about how they would feel if they had to cope with such a dilemma. **OL** **BL**

Caption Answer: This law gave priority to relatives and skilled, educated people, rather than focusing on the country of origin.

Differentiated Instruction

Authentic Assessment with Rubrics, p. 21

A Nation of Immigrants

Objective: Prepare illustrated reports on immigration.

Focus/Teach: Research current trends in immigration and determine the countries from which the largest immigrant groups come.

Assess: Review reports and assess visual supplements.

Close: Display graphs and maps in the classroom.

Differentiated Instruction Strategies

BL Color maps showing the native countries of the top immigrant groups.

AL Have students compare the immigrant population in your community with the immigrant population nationwide.

ELL Discuss programs that are available to help new immigrants assimilate into American society.

Highlights of American Immigration Policy, 1880s–Present

Stage 1: Early Restrictions	1880s:	Chinese laborers cannot immigrate; foreign-born Chinese cannot become citizens; "paupers, ex-convicts, [and] mental defectives" are barred.
Stage 2: National Origins Quota System	1921:	Congress sets up quotas favoring immigrants from northwestern Europe; the Immigration Act of 1924 expands the quota system: immigration from any country is limited to 2 percent of its total numbers in the 1890 census.
Stage 3: System of Skills and Family Preferences	1965:	The Immigration Reform Act throws out the national origins system; now preference is given first to reunifying families and second to people whose skills help the United States.
Stage 4: Reforms of the 1980s and 1990s	1986:	The Immigration Reform and Control Act penalizes employers for knowingly hiring undocumented immigrants, but it gives amnesty to some undocumented immigrants, allowing them a path to eventually apply for citizenship.
	1996:	A new law expands the U.S. Border Patrol and stiffens penalties for false papers.

Critical Thinking *What waves of immigration were behind the pressures that led Congress to pass the quota system?*

Critical Thinking

Answer: immigrants from Southern and Eastern Europe

R Reading Strategy

Academic Vocabulary The term *amnesty* dates to about 1580. It refers to a collective pardon given to a large group of people. It partly shares its etymology with the word *amnesia*, which refers to a loss of memory. Both terms stem from a Greek word meaning "forgetfulness." **OL**

W Writing Support

Persuasive Writing Have students write an editorial supporting or criticizing proposals to grant amnesty to unauthorized immigrants. **OL**

Employers who violated the law paid penalties ranging from $250 to $2,000 for each undocumented worker they hired. If they continued to break the law, they could be imprisoned. Employers had the duty to find out if workers were qualified to work in the United States. None of these provisions slowed the stream of illegal immigration. Critics pointed out that the penalties were not severe enough and enforcement was lax.

Later Immigration Acts

By 1990, more than 80 percent of American immigrants came from Asia and Latin America. Congress wanted to prevent any one country from making up most of the immigrants to the United States. In order to accomplish this, it passed the Immigration Act of 1990, which said that no country could account for more than 7 percent of total immigrants. The law also considered a person's education and skills. In addition, the 1990 law set up special categories for war refugees or close relatives of American citizens.

In 1996 concerns about the continuing problem of illegal immigration led Congress to pass yet another immigration law. It increased the border patrol staff and stiffened penalties for creating false citizenship papers or smuggling undocumented workers.

Current Political Debate

As illegal immigration continues across the southwestern border, the debate continues. Employers in agriculture and construction do not want the flow of low-cost labor stopped. Others, often Americans with few skills, worry that a steady stream of undocumented workers will depress their wages.

Late in his presidency, in June 2007, President George W. Bush committed himself to backing a bill to address all immigration issues. Bush's bill proposed to fill short-term labor needs through a guest worker program and strengthened border control. Yet Bush argued that his bill was also realistic because it did not propose to track down and deport millions of undocumented workers who were already here.

The bill also would have fined undocumented immigrants and required them to fulfill certain obligations before they could apply for citizenship—what the administration called "a path to citizenship." Many, especially Republicans, charged that the penalties were not harsh enough and the bill really amounted to **amnesty,** or forgiveness. In late June 2007, the Senate voted the bill down, ending any chance of solving the immigration issue during Bush's presidency.

During the 2008 presidential primaries, immigration was a "hot-button" issue—political analysts called it a no-win issue. If an immigration proposal pleased one group, it seemed certain to ignite bitter opposition in another. Questions on immigration peppered the televised presidential debates. For example, Republican candidate Mitt Romney criticized fellow candidate Mike Huckabee for approving in-state tuition for the children of undocumented immigrants. Democratic candidate Hillary Clinton was criticized for initially backing a

---

Hands-On Chapter Project

Step 1

Discrimination

Step 1: Understanding the Issues To provide insight into the effects of discrimination, the class will experience minor examples of discrimination in the classroom. In Step 1, they will participate in an exercise that demonstrates discrimination in educational opportunity. In Step 4, they will write an essay expressing their thoughts and feelings about the experience.

Directions Divide the class into two groups: "Us" and "Them." Have members of

"Them" turn their desks facing away from the front of the class and put away their pens. Give "Them" pencils that are not sharp, and do not allow "Them" to sharpen the pencils or use their pens. Write some facts about segregation on the board closest to the "Us" group and erase it quickly. Give a short quiz on the facts. Ask students for their reactions to the discrimination they just witnessed or experienced—but do not call on "Them."

Taking Notes Have all students jot down their immediate reactions to the discrim-

ination they just experienced or observed. Explain that they will use these reactions in the introductory statement of the essay they will write later. To help students visualize the five parts of an essay, you might compare it to a cheeseburger. Tell them that their introductory statement is like the top of the bun. **OL**

(Chapter Project continued in Section 2.)

proposal to allow undocumented immigrants to get a driver's license to increase highway safety.

Some anti-immigration groups raised fears by using words like *anchor baby* or *chain migration.* These phrases refer to the fact that since the 1960s, a new citizen can send for children, spouses, parents, and siblings, who can later apply for citizenship. Many immigrants are family-sponsored, but any chain process takes a long time. The first immigrant might take five years to become a citizen, and it usually takes 15 to 20 years for an adult relative to gain entry.

The Republican Party tends to take a more restrictive stance on undocumented immigrants, but many Democrats responded to polls showing that they, too, were upset over illegal immigration. Yet politicians must consider that the number of Latino voters is increasing and that many Latinos have been citizens for generations. Some Latino voters feel that racism is the real reason for the opposition to illegal immigration. They also claim that new Latino immigrants are doing work that other Americans will not do for the low wages offered.

As one Democratic analyst warned: "Getting on the wrong side of a demographic trend, like the growing Latino electorate, can make a political party a minority party for a long time."

Aliens

An **alien** is the term for someone who lives in a country where he or she is not a citizen. Immigrants are aliens before they become citizens.

Under the law, there are five categories of aliens. A **resident alien** is a foreigner who has established permanent residency in the United States. (Resident aliens can stay in the United States as long as they want without becoming American citizens.) **Nonresident aliens** are people who expect to stay for a short, specified time—a foreign journalist covering an election, for example. A third category, **enemy aliens,** represents citizens of nations that are at war with the United States. A fourth type is **refugees,** or people who are fleeing persecution or danger from their home country. Finally there are **undocumented aliens,** people here illegally. Most of these people crossed the border illegally, but some are foreigners whose permits have expired.

It is important to know that the Bill of Rights protects anyone living in the United States, even enemy aliens. The Supreme Court has often struck down state government laws that tried to limit aliens' rights. Like citizens, aliens may own homes, attend public schools, and use public facilities.

Aliens also have many of the same responsibilities as citizens. They must pay taxes and they must obey the law. They cannot vote, of course, and usually are exempt from military or jury duty.

In wartime, aliens might be prohibited from traveling freely. Even in peacetime, they must notify the U.S. Bureau of Citizenship and Immigration Services if they change their residence.

D Differentiated Instruction

Kinesthetic Ask students to find photographs of Americans from as many countries of origin as possible. Have them cut out the photographs and glue them onto a poster for a collage entitled "America's Diverse Population." Tell students to include the names of the countries of origin and facts about immigrants in the collage. **BL**

Assess

Assign the Section 1 Assessment as homework or as an in-class activity, or have students take Section Quiz 14-1 from *Section Quizzes and Chapter Tests.*

Close

Analyzing Lead a discussion that evaluates immigration policy as it affects communities and states. **OL**

Section 1 Review

SECTION 1 Review

Vocabulary

1. **Explain** the significance of: amnesty, alien, resident alien, nonresident alien, enemy alien, refugee, undocumented alien.

Main Ideas

2. **Listing** What are the five categories of aliens according to U.S. law?

3. **Analyzing** What trend inspired the immigration policies in the 1980s and 1990s?

Critical Thinking

4. **Making Inferences** How does the Immigration Reform Act of 1965 reflect the overall values of the 1960s?

5. **Organizing** Use a graphic organizer like the one below to analyze the main features of the Immigration Reform and Control Act of 1986.

Immigration Reform and Control Act of 1986

Writing About Government

6. **Descriptive Writing** When did people of various ethnic and racial backgrounds move into your town or city? Research this question at your local library. Write a report describing each group in a paragraph or two. Add a time line to the report to track your community's ethnic history.

CHAPTER 14: *Citizenship and Equal Justice* **391**

Answers

1. All definitions can be found in the section and the Glossary.
2. resident alien, nonresident alien, enemy alien, refugee, undocumented alien
3. In the 1980s and 1990s, laws were passed to crack down on illegal immigration.
4. In the 1960s, the emphasis was turning away from where one was from and turning toward favoring relatives and educated and skilled people.

5. stem the tide of illegal immigrants, provide a way for undocumented immigrants to become residents, punish employers of undocumented immigrants
6. You may arrange to display students' time lines in the classroom and hold a class discussion about the topic.

Focus

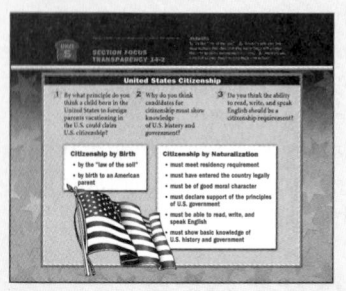
Reader's Guide

Answers to Graphic:

Sources: born on American soil, naturalized, born to a U.S. citizen

Responsibilities: knowledge of laws, participation in political process

Resource Manager

The Basis of Citizenship

Reader's Guide

Content Vocabulary
- ★ naturalization *(p. 392)*
- ★ jus soli *(p. 393)*
- ★ jus sanguinis *(p. 394)*
- ★ collective naturalization *(p. 395)*
- ★ expatriation *(p. 395)*
- ★ denaturalization *(p. 395)*

Academic Vocabulary
- ★ core *(p. 392)*
- ★ process *(p. 392)*
- ★ automatic *(p. 393)*

Reading Strategy

As you read, create a graphic organizer like the one below to describe the conditions of American citizenship.

Sources in 14th Amendment	Responsibilities

Issues in the News

When he first came to the United States, the prize-winning novelist Ha Jin did not expect to stay. He wanted to study American literature and then return to his native China to teach. While he was enrolled at a Massachusetts university, news of the Tiananmen Square student protests and the ensuing violence broke. "I was glued to the TV for three days . . . I was in shock." Ha Jin extended his visa and eventually became a citizen. Today, he would like to visit China but cannot imagine living there again. "The social fabric is very different from America. To live in China is hard. You have to learn to lie and give bribes. It would be very hard for me to learn to do these things again."

▲ Novelist Ha Jin

Citizens are members of a political society—a nation. American citizens, whether they are born here or naturalized like Ha Jin, have certain rights. The Declaration of Independence describes the **core** rights of a citizen when it states that "all men are created equal, that they are endowed by their Creator with certain unalienable Rights," the rights of life, liberty, and the pursuit of happiness. The government exists to secure these fundamental rights and equality under the law.

Citizens also have duties and responsibilities. These include obeying the law, paying taxes, and being loyal to the nation and its principles. As participants in government, citizens have the duty to be informed, to vote, and to respect the rights and property of others, as well as their opinions and ways of life. Citizens should be willing to exercise both their responsibilities as well as their rights.

Who Determines Citizenship?

Over the years, the basis of American citizenship has changed significantly. Today citizenship has both a national and a state dimension. This was not always true. The articles of the Constitution mention citizenship only as a qualification for holding national office.

The Founders assumed that the states would decide who was or was not a citizen and that state citizens would then automatically be citizens of the nation. Originally, this rule had two exceptions: African Americans and immigrants who became U.S. citizens through **naturalization**—the legal **process** by which someone who was not born in the United States is granted citizenship.

R **Reading Strategies**	**C** **Critical Thinking**	**D** **Differentiated Instruction**	**W** **Writing Support**	**S** **Skill Practice**
Teacher Edition • Organizing, p. 395 **Additional Resources** • Guid. Read. Act., p. 51 • Quizzes/Tests, p. 171	**Teacher Edition** • Evaluating, p. 396 **Additional Resources** • Read. Essen., pp. 152–155	**Teacher Edition** • Auditory/Musical, p. 393 • Intrapersonal, p. 396 **Additional Resources** • Foldables, p. 57	**Teacher Edition** • Personal Writing, p. 393 • Persuasive Writing, p. 394 **Additional Resources** • Part. in Gov. Act., pp. 27–28	**Additional Resources** • Inter. Poli. Cartoons, pp. 27–28

Dred Scott v. Sandford (1857)

Landmark Case Just before the Civil War, a Supreme Court case highlighted the issue of whether enslaved African Americans were citizens. Dred Scott was an enslaved African American in Missouri, a slaveholding state. But Scott had also lived with his slaveholder in the free state of Illinois and in the Wisconsin territory, where slavery was forbidden. Scott sued for his freedom, claiming that his residence in a free state and a free territory made him a free citizen. A state court ruled in Scott's favor, but the Missouri Supreme Court reversed the decision.

At that point, Scott's lawyers took the case to the U.S. Supreme Court. The Court ruled that Scott could not sue in a federal court because African Americans, whether enslaved or free, were not U.S. citizens when the Constitution was adopted. Only descendants of people who were state citizens at that time, or immigrants who became citizens through naturalization, were U.S. citizens. Inflaming the debate over slavery, the Court also said that Congress could not forbid slavery in U.S. territories.

The Fourteenth Amendment

The *Dred Scott* decision, regarded today as one of the worst decisions the Court ever made, caused great outrage at the time. It also helped intensify the emotions that led to the Civil War. The African American abolitionist Frederick Douglass hoped that the case would begin a chain of events that would produce a "complete overthrow of the whole slave system."

When the Civil War was over, the Fourteenth Amendment was one of three amendments to the Constitution that were passed. The Fourteenth Amendment overruled the *Dred Scott* decision and clearly established what constitutes citizenship at both the national and state levels:

> 66 *All persons born or naturalized in the United States, and subject to the jurisdiction thereof, are citizens of the United States and of the State wherein they reside. No State shall make or enforce any law which shall abridge [deprive] the privileges or immunities of citizens of the United States.* 99
>
> —Fourteenth Amendment, 1868

The Fourteenth Amendment was a major milestone in American history. It established that people of all races, excluding Native Americans,

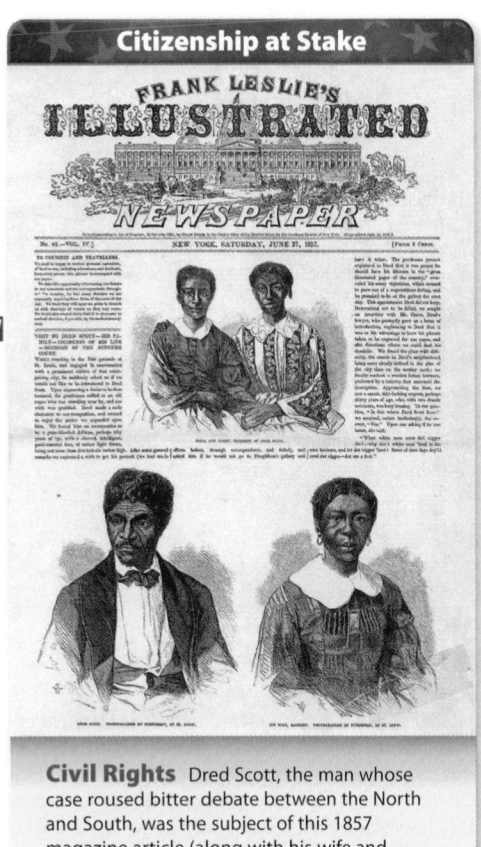

Citizenship at Stake

Civil Rights Dred Scott, the man whose case roused bitter debate between the North and South, was the subject of this 1857 magazine article (along with his wife and daughters). The article described Scott as having a "shrewd, intelligent, good-natured face." *Do you think the reporter was a Northerner or a Southerner? Why?*

were citizens and that state citizenship was an **automatic** result of national citizenship.

Gaining Citizenship

The Fourteenth Amendment set forth two of the three bases for U.S. citizenship—birth on American soil and naturalization. The third basis for citizenship is being born to a U.S. citizen.

Citizenship by Birth

Like most other nations in the world, the United States follows the principle of **jus soli** (YOOS SOH • lee), a Latin phrase for "law of the soil." Jus soli, the most common basis for citizenship, focuses on

Teach

Caption Answer: The reporter was likely a Northerner, because he portrayed Scott in a positive light. Also, the magazine was published in New York.

D **Differentiated Instruction**

Auditory/Musical Have students write a script for a "You Are There" radio program on reactions to the *Dred Scott* decision. Suggest that the scripts include background information and interviews with Dred Scott, John F.A. Sanford, other eyewitnesses at the court, and various experts on the Supreme Court. Encourage students to "broadcast" their scripts for the rest of the class on the Web, DVDs, or other presentation tools. **OL**

W **Writing Support**

Personal Writing Have students write a personal response paper to the Court's *Dred Scott* ruling. Ask them to include their thoughts about the case's effect on the nation and on the slaveholding controversy. **OL**

Additional Support

Activity: Collaborative Learning

Making a Flowchart Have groups of students create an illustrated flowchart that presents the various roads to acquiring U.S. citizenship as responses to a series of "yes/no" questions. Offer these questions to get students thinking about how they might set up the flowchart:

- Was I born in the United States?
- Are both of my parents U.S. citizens?

- Can I read, write, and speak English?
- Have I lived in the United States for five consecutive years?

Have students choose their role in the project—checking facts, drawing the chart, preparing the illustrations, writing captions, and so on. Post the finished flowcharts for class review. **BL**

Did You Know?

A citizen born in the United States can become a citizen of another country—that is, hold dual citizenship—by birth, by marriage, or by naturalization. For example, a baby born to French parents in the United States would have French citizenship by jus sanguinis and U.S. citizenship by jus soli. In some countries, a woman gains citizenship by marrying a citizen. If a country does not require naturalized citizens to renounce their previous citizenship, they may claim dual citizenship.

W Writing Support

Persuasive Writing Children born to foreigners on American soil are U.S. citizens. Have students write one paragraph agreeing or disagreeing with this principle. **OL**

Differentiated Instruction

Gaining Citizenship

African Americans Fight Many African Americans joined the Union Army during the Civil War. Their bravery and commitment aided those who argued that African Americans should be citizens. After the Civil War, a constitutional amendment established that everyone born in the United States is an American citizen. *Which amendment made all African Americans citizens?*

where a person is born. Almost anyone born in the United States or in American territories is an American citizen. An exception would be a baby born in this country to foreign diplomats. The child is not a citizen because his or her parents are not subject to U.S. laws. However, a baby born to foreigners who happen to be in this country is a citizen.

Another basis for automatic citizenship focuses not on place of birth, but rather on parentage. This principle is called **jus sanguinis** (YOOS SAHN • gwuh • nuhs), which means the "law of blood." The rules governing jus sanguinis are complex. If a child is born abroad and both parents are U.S. citizens, the child is a citizen so long as one parent lived in and was a legal American resident at some point.

If only one parent is an American citizen, however, another rule applies. The parent who is a citizen must have lived in the United States or an American possession for at least 5 years, 2 of which had to occur after the age of 14.

Citizenship by Naturalization

All immigrants who want to become American citizens must go through naturalization. The federal government grants citizenship and takes it away. (A state government can deny a convicted criminal some privileges of citizenship like voting, but it cannot deny citizenship itself.) At the end of the naturalization

process, a person will have almost all of the rights and privileges of a citizen who was born here. The main exception is that he or she cannot serve as president or vice president of the United States.

Congress has defined a number of steps that immigrants must take before they can even apply to become citizens. The U.S. Citizenship and Immigration Services, a bureau of the Department of Homeland Security, is the federal agency that administers most of the naturalization process. Five broad requirements for naturalization must be met. Certain people, such as draft evaders or military deserters, are usually denied citizenship.

Winning and Losing Citizenship

To apply for citizenship, a person must be at least 18 years old, have lived in the United States as a legal resident alien for 5 years, been physically present for half of that period, and lived in the state where the petition is filed for at least 3 months. (Only 3 years of residency is necessary for someone who is married to a citizen.)

During the naturalization process, the witnesses must appear to testify to the applicant's moral character. Applicants may be asked to show their grasp of English or to answer basic questions about American government, such as "What is the highest court in the land?" If applicants make it

---

Activity: Multiple Learning Styles

Auditory/Musical Have students read aloud the oath of allegiance that new citizens take:

"I hereby declare, on oath, that I absolutely and entirely renounce and abjure all allegiance and fidelity to any foreign prince, potentate, state or sovereignty, of whom or which I have heretofore been a subject or citizen; that I will support and defend the Constitution and laws of the United States of America against all enemies, foreign and domestic; that I will bear

true faith and allegiance to the same; that I will bear arms on behalf of the United States when required by the law; that I will perform work of national importance under civilian direction when required by the law; and that I take this obligation freely without any mental reservation or purpose of evasion; so help me God."

Have students comment on any words that caught their attention. **BL** through the first hearing, they attend a final hearing, usually in a federal district court. The judge administers an oath of allegiance to the United States and its laws and then issues a naturalization certificate declaring the person a citizen.

Most people go through this type of naturalization—individual naturalization. There is also a process called **collective naturalization,** however. As the term implies, collective naturalization is a process under which an entire group of people become citizens by a treaty or by an act of Congress.

In the entire history of the nation, Congress has used collective naturalization five times to grant citizenship to people living in a territory that was annexed or gained by treaty. One example of a collective naturalization process occurred when President Thomas Jefferson signed a treaty with France to acquire the nearly 1 million square miles that made up the Louisiana Purchase. All of the people who were living in this territory were collectively naturalized.

Other exceptions to individual naturalization can be seen in the history of Native Americans in this country. Most of them were not allowed to be citizens even when their land was annexed. In 1868, for example, Congress stated that the citizenship guarantees of the Fourteenth Amendment did not apply to them. Congress later offered citizenship to a Native American who would give up his or her traditional culture. Finally, in 1924 Congress made all Native Americans U.S. citizens.

Losing one's citizenship is something that can occur in three ways. The first is through **expatriation,** meaning that a person gives up his or her citizenship by the act of leaving the United States and becoming a citizen of another country.

The second way to lose citizenship is by being convicted of certain serious federal crimes, such as treason, or participating in a rebellion.

Finally, a naturalized citizen can lose his or her citizenship in an administrative process of **denaturalization.** This occurs when it is proved that fraud, deception, or error occurred during the original naturalization.

Citizen Responsibilities

The ability to exercise one's rights depends on being aware of those rights. A constitutional democracy, therefore, needs citizens who are knowledgeable about the laws that govern society and their legal rights. Respect for the law is crucial in modern society, but this respect depends on knowledge of the law.

In addition to schools, a number of organizations help citizens learn more about their rights, laws, and government: legal aid societies, consumer

Making a Difference

In 1995 Irena Sliskovic came to the United States to escape the Bosnian War. She lost many of her friends when the Bosnian city of Sarajevo was under siege. Then when she was 10 months from finishing high school, she heard that an American program allowed Bosnian students to stay with American families and complete their education. Sliskovic remembers thinking: "I'm going far away to peace and freedom."

She had to sneak out of the city at night—and almost didn't make it. Five minutes from the border she was stopped and ordered to go back, but she escaped and crossed the border into Croatia. In the United States, she lived with a family in Kentucky. After finishing high school, she enrolled in a Kentucky college. She later served as an interpreter for others who were fleeing the conditions of her home region.

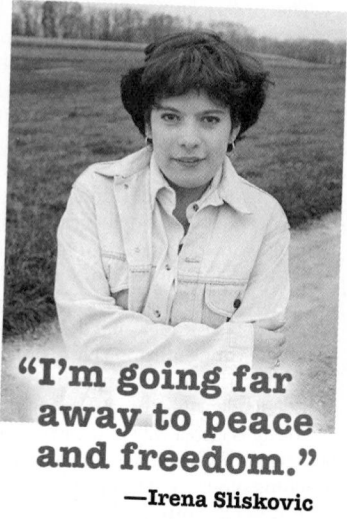

"I'm going far away to peace and freedom."
—Irena Sliskovic

R **Reading Strategy**

Organizing Draw three columns on the board. **Ask:** What are the three ways in which a person can lose his or her citizenship? *(expatriation, conviction of certain serious federal crimes, or denaturalization)* Have students provide details that explain each process. **BL**

Making a Difference

Irena Sliskovic By 1995, the year that Sliskovic came to the United States, some 2,000 Bosnian students had left their war-torn homeland to pursue an education elsewhere. Most of the students found schools in other parts of Europe, with Austria hosting the largest number of refugee students from Bosnia.

Activity: Have students imagine hosting a foreign student who is a refugee. Ask for ideas about helping the foreign-born student get used to life in the United States and deal with his or her sadness over the situation that was left behind. **OL**

Additional Support

Activity: Interdisciplinary Connection

Science/Technology Many scientific and technological advances have come from Americans who were born in other lands. Have students research the contributions of any of the following immigrants and present their findings in a format of their own choosing:

- Alexis Carrel (France)
- George Cotzias (Greece)
- Albert Einstein (Germany)
- Leo Esaki (Japan)
- Enrico Fermi (Italy)
- Conrad Hubert (Russia)
- Chao Hao Li (China)
- Karl Landsteiner (Austria)
- Jan Earnest Matzeliger (Suriname)
- Severo Ochoa (Spain)
- Wernher von Braun (Germany) **OL**

Critical Thinking

Answer: Answers should note that the government wants citizens to take an active, positive role in how the United States is governed.

D Differentiated Instruction

Intrapersonal Ask students to ask themselves how well informed they are. Do they know what the public issues are and have opinions about them? If there is an upcoming election, do they know who the candidates and issues are? Have students rate themselves on their knowledge of public issues and candidates and cite at least one way to stay informed. **OL**

C Critical Thinking

Evaluating Have students discuss the reasons given for people not voting and the reasons voting is important. Call on volunteers to state one of these reasons, from the "I" point of view: Examples: *"I do not vote because I do not meet state voting requirements"* or *"I vote because voting gives me a chance to choose my government leaders."* **OL**

Hands-On Chapter Project
Step 2

Discrimination

Step 2: Researching Students will research a contemporary or historical example of discrimination in the United States.

Directions Ask students to select a group that has been subjected to discrimination. Students will do some research and write a paragraph that (a) identifies the group, (b) explains the type of discrimination, (c) discusses how the discrimination might have affected the group, and (d) mentions

Responsible Citizens

Naturalization

Naturalization is the process by which someone becomes a citizen of another country sometime after birth. To become a U.S. citizen, usually one must:

★ Enter the United States legally

★ Be of good moral character

★ Declare support for American government principles

★ Prove English literacy (exceptions for some older, long-term immigrants)

★ Know the basics of U.S. history and government

Critical Thinking A member of this family completed the steps to become a naturalized citizen. *Why do you think the government requires a person to declare support for principles of American government to become naturalized?*

protection groups, and tenants' rights organizations. Moreover, many states now require that government regulations be written in everyday language so people can understand them.

Citizen Participation

The American ideal has always been to stress each citizen's duty to participate in political life. By doing this, citizens are governing themselves. Each individual learns to put aside personal concerns and preferences and to consider the political goals and needs of others. The hope is that in the process, policies will be shaped that are in the general public interest. Thus, participation teaches people about the key elements of a democratic society—majority rule, individual rights, and the rule of law.

Voting is the most common way that a citizen participates in political life. By casting their ballots, citizens choose leaders and direct the course of government. Voting affirms a basic principle of American political life that was inscribed in the Declaration of Independence—"the consent of the governed."

Voting is also a way to express one's support for democracy. When a person casts a vote, he or she is joining other citizens in a common effort at self-government. Voting allows Americans to share responsibility for how their society is governed. By contrast, anyone who does not vote could be implying that he or she does not support democracy.

Voters' Impact

Why doesn't everyone vote? Some people say they do not vote because they are not interested in politics. Others fail to vote because they do not think a single vote can affect who wins. Yet, many examples exist of close elections in American history at all levels of government.

In recent years, the most notable example of the impact of just a few voters was the 2000 presidential election when the final outcome turned on voters in Florida. That state's 25 electoral votes would determine the president of the United States. George W. Bush was declared the winner by only 537 votes out of almost 6 million cast in the state.

Very close votes also figured in the 2006 by-elections. A number of races in the House of Representatives were decided by small margins, and some were decided only in a recount as in Ohio. There, Republican Deborah Pryce won by about 1,000 votes—less than half of 1 percent of all the votes cast.

Government ONLINE
Student Web Activity Visit glencoe.com and enter *QuickPass*™ code USG9822c14. Click on Student Web Activity and complete the activity about the basis of citizenship.

any legislation that addressed the issue or, in the case of contemporary discrimination, legislation that they believe is still needed.

Summarizing Explain that this paragraph will be the first of three supporting paragraphs for their essays that support the theme of the essay—the "condiments on the cheeseburger." At this point, you might want to have them draw a cheeseburger and label the parts, top to bottom: Top bun, "introductory statement"; condiments, "supporting paragraph 1";

cheese, "supporting paragraph 2"; burger, "supporting paragraph 3"; bottom bun, "summary." **OL**

(Chapter Project continued in Section 3.)

Making One's Voice Heard

Participating in Campaigns During the Democratic primaries, Barack Obama (center) enlisted the support of the Culinary Workers Union in Las Vegas for his candidacy. *Why would an interest group pressure candidates for their cause?*

Caption Answer: in order to gain their support in passing legislation they favor

Government ONLINE
Objectives and answers to the Student Web Activity can be found in the *Web Activity Lesson Plan* at glencoe.com. Enter *QuickPass*™ code USG9085c14T.

Assess

Assign the Section 2 Assessment as homework or as an in-class activity, or have students take Section Quiz 14-2 from *Section Quizzes and Chapter Tests.*

Close

Inferring Have students review this section by discussing ways in which feelings about citizenship might be different among people who are born citizens and those who are naturalized citizens. **OL**

Besides voting, citizens can affect the political system by campaigning for a candidate, distributing leaflets on an issue, or working at the polls on Election Day.

The rights and privileges of citizenship also include activities outside the elections. A veteran might lobby to improve health care for disabled soldiers. Students might sign a petition to submit to the local school board on school safety issues. A group of mothers might contact officials in their state in order to discuss the need for a program for senior citizens in their community. Single parents who must care for a disabled child might lobby for a program that would provide respite care—short-term care that gives hard-pressed parents some much-needed time of their own.

Sharing your opinions through writing letters to newspapers and magazines has always been an important way to participate in politics. (The Federalist Papers was a written form of activism.) Today e-mails, blogging, personal Web sites, and other Internet activities offer citizens chances to express his or her political opinions and to influence the opinions of their fellow citizens.

SECTION 2 Review

Vocabulary
1. **Explain** the significance of: naturalization, jus soli, jus sanguinis, collective naturalization, expatriation, denaturalization.

Main Ideas
2. **Identifying** What was the *Dred Scott* decision?
3. **Listing** What are the five requirements for becoming a naturalized citizen?

Critical Thinking
4. **Synthesizing** Why does the United States require citizenship applicants to speak English and have knowledge of the American government?
5. **Listing** Use a graphic organizer similar to the one below to list the ways an American can lose his or her citizenship.

Ways to Lose Citizenship

Writing About Government
6. **Expository Writing** The Fourteenth Amendment extends the "privileges and immunities" of each state to all American citizens. Write a summary of the privileges that you believe your state should provide to out-of-state persons and those that should apply only to state residents. You can accompany your summary with a chart if it is helpful.

CHAPTER 14: *Citizenship and Equal Justice* **397**

Section 2 Review

Answers

1. All definitions can be found in the section and the Glossary.
2. The *Dred Scott* decision stated that persons of African descent were not U.S. citizens.
3. Applicants must have entered the United States legally; be of good moral character; declare their support of the principles of American government; prove that they can read, write, and speak English; and show some basic knowledge of American history and government.
4. Possible answer: Since the United States is based on self-government, it is vital that new citizens understand and support the principles of government and speak the dominant language in order to participate.
5. expatriation, punishment for treason, denaturalization
6. Students' summaries will vary. Encourage students to explain their suggestions and to work together to come up with a master chart.

Focus

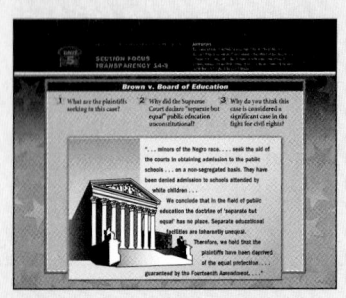
Reader's Guide

Answers to Graphic:

1963: Equal Pay Act

1964: Civil Rights Act

1965: Voting Rights Act

1967: Age Discrimination Act

1968: Civil Rights Act, Title VIII

1972: Higher Education Act, Title IX

1974: Housing and Community Development Act

Resource Manager

Equal Protection of the Law

Reader's Guide

Content Vocabulary	Academic Vocabulary	Reading Strategy
★ suspect classification (p. 399) ★ fundamental right (p. 399) ★ discrimination (p. 399) ★ Jim Crow laws (p. 400) ★ "separate but equal" doctrine (p. 400) ★ civil rights movement (p. 401)	★ illegal (p. 399) ★ motivate (p. 399) ★ impact (p. 399)	As you read, create a time line of major 1960s and 1970s civil rights laws, beginning with the Equal Pay Act in 1963.

```
        1964      1967              1972    1974
   1963      1965        1968
```

Issues in the News

High-tech companies are noted for their youthful workforce and trendy work environment—with jeans and T-shirts, every day is casual-dress day. In late 2007, Brian Reid was able to continue his legal battle against Google™ for age discrimination when a court in San Jose, California, accepted his appeal. In his original lawsuit, Reid, 54, said he had never received a negative review, but was told when he was let go that he was not a "cultural fit." Reid also alleged that only a very small percentage of Google employees were over 40 years old.

▲ Google offices in California

Many forms of discrimination, including age discrimination, are illegal. The Declaration of Independence affirmed an ideal of American democracy when it stated "all men are created equal." This statement does not mean that everyone is born with the same characteristics or will remain equal. What it means is that all people are entitled to equal rights and treatment before the law.

What Is Equal Protection?

The Fourteenth Amendment says that no state can "deny to any person within its jurisdiction the equal protection of the laws." Equal protection is also addressed by the Fifth Amendment.

The general meaning of the equal protection clause is that state and local governments cannot draw unreasonable distinctions among different groups. The key word is *unreasonable*. All governments must draw some distinctions among people in legislation.

If a citizen challenges a law, the issue is not whether a classification is being made, but whether it is reasonable. The Supreme Court has developed three basic guidelines for considering whether a law or an action violates the equal protection clause.

The rational basis test asks if the classification is reasonably related to an acceptable government goal. A law stating that people with red hair can not drive would fail this test because no relationship exists between red hair and safe driving. In *Wisconsin* v. *Mitchell*[1] (1993), however, the Supreme Court upheld a state law that imposed longer prison sentences on people who commit hate crimes, crimes motivated by prejudice. Unless special circumstances exist, the Court said that the people challenging a law must prove that it is unreasonable.

📖 *See the following footnoted materials in the **Reference Handbook:***
1. *Wisconsin* v. *Mitchell* case summary, page R37.

R Reading Strategies	**C** Critical Thinking	**D** Differentiated Instruction	**W** Writing Support	**S** Skill Practice
Teacher Edition • Organizing, p. 399 **Additional Resources** • Guid. Read. Act., p. 52 • Quizzes/Tests, p. 172 • Reteaching Act., p. 14	**Teacher Edition** • Drawing Conclusions, p. 399 **Additional Resources** • Read. Essen., pp. 156–158	**Teacher Edition** • Auditory/Musical, p. 401 **Additional Resources** • Foldables, p. 57 • Am. Biographies, p. 65	**Additional Resources** • Supreme Ct. Case Studies, pp. 27–28	**Teacher Edition** • Using Geography Skills, p. 402 **Additional Resources** • Source Readings, p. 14

The second test the Court uses takes place when special circumstances are involved. Special circumstances exist when the Court decides that a state law involves a "suspect classification." A suspect classification is a classification made on the basis of race or national origin. Such classifications are "subject to strict judicial scrutiny," according to the Supreme Court. A law requiring only African Americans to ride in the back of buses is a suspect classification.

If a case involves a suspect classification, the Court reverses the normal presumption that the law is constitutional. It is no longer enough for the state to show that the law is reasonable: It must also show the Court that there is "some compelling public interest" to justify its classifications.

The third test the Court uses is **fundamental rights**—rights that go to the heart of the American system or are indispensable to a just system. The Court closely scrutinizes any state law dealing with fundamental rights. For example, it has ruled that fundamental rights are the right to travel freely between the states, the right to vote, and all First Amendment rights—freedom of religion, freedom of speech and assembly, the right to petition, and for a free press. Laws that violate these fundamental rights are unconstitutional.

Proving Intent to Discriminate

Laws that classify people unreasonably are said to discriminate. **Discrimination** exists when individuals are treated unfairly solely because of their race, gender, ethnic group, age, physical disability, or religion. Such discrimination is **illegal,** but it can be difficult to prove.

What happens if a law does not classify people directly, but it still classifies them? For example, suppose a law requires that applicants for police jobs take a test. Suppose members of one group usually score better than members of another group. Can discrimination be proven simply by showing that the law has a different impact on people of different races, genders, or national origins?

Showing Intent to Discriminate

In *Washington* v. *Davis*[1] (1976), the Supreme Court ruled that to prove discrimination in a state law, one must prove that the state was **motivated** by an intent to discriminate. The case arose when two African Americans challenged the District of

Columbia police department's requirement that all recruits pass a verbal ability test. They said that the requirement was unconstitutional because more African Americans than whites failed the test.

The Court said that this **impact** on African Americans did not automatically make the test unconstitutional. The crucial issue was that the test was not designed to discriminate. As the Court said in a later case, "The Fourteenth Amendment guarantees equal laws, not equal results."

Since the *Washington* case, the Court has applied the "intent to discriminate" principle to other areas. For example, in an Illinois town, a zoning law permitted only single-family homes. This had the effect of barring low-cost housing projects. The Court ruled the ordinance constitutional, even though it effectively kept minorities from moving into the city. The Court reasoned that there was no intent to discriminate against minorities.

📖 *See the following footnoted materials in the* **Reference Handbook:**
1. *Washington* v. *Davis* case summary, page R36.

Civil Rights Champions A civil rights bill was first introduced by President John F. Kennedy. *How did President Lyndon Johnson (right), seen here consulting with Martin Luther King, Jr., use Kennedy's death to advance the bill?*

Teach

Caption Answer: He used emotional appeals and invoked the language of civil rights activists.

R Reading Strategy

Organizing Have groups of students create a problem/solution chart. In the left column, they should list problems that revealed the presence of discrimination in the United States. In the right column, they should note how the Supreme Court attempted to resolve each problem. **BL**

C Critical Thinking

Drawing Conclusions Review the concept of "intent to discriminate," in the case of *Washington* v. *Davis*. Then have students suggest situations in which they would suspect some "intent to discriminate." For each suggested situation, have students define the bias and propose a change that they think would bring it into compliance with the Fourteenth Amendment. **OL**

Additional Support

Activity: Collaborative Learning

Contrasting Points of View Help students focus on the "separate but equal" doctrine by organizing the class into four groups—two to develop arguments showing why people thought the doctrine was fair and two to develop arguments explaining why it was unfair. Some group members can do research, others can prepare key statements, others can speak for the group before the class, one can

monitor the progress of the various tasks, and so on. Urge students to analyze Supreme Court decisions in their arguments. After a representative from each group has reported on the group's work to the entire class, conduct a class discussion to summarize and contrast the two points of view that students have presented. **OL**

CURRICULUM CONNECTION

Law In *Plessy* v. *Ferguson,* the Supreme Court declared: "The object of the [Fourteenth] amendment was undoubtedly to enforce the absolute equality of the two races before the law, but . . . it could not have been intended to abolish distinctions based upon color, or to enforce social, as distinguished from political, equality, or a commingling of the two races upon terms unsatisfactory to either. . . . We cannot say that a law which authorizes or even requires the separation of the two races in public conveyances is unreasonable."

Justice John Marshall Harlan, a Kentucky native and former slaveholder, was the sole dissenter on the Court. He predicted that the *Plessy* ruling would prove "quite as pernicious" as the *Dred Scott* (1857) decision had been.

Differentiated Instruction

The Struggle for Equality Under the Law

Silent Protest
In early 1960, college students from North Carolina A&T began their "sit-in" campaign at a Greensboro lunch counter reserved for whites—six months later, service was integrated. *Why might they have chosen this tactic?*

The Equal Rights Struggle

The Fourteenth Amendment, guaranteeing equal protection, was ratified in 1868, shortly after the Civil War. Yet for almost a century the courts made no decisions prohibiting discrimination against and segregation of African Americans. (Racial discrimination is treating people differently simply because of their race; segregation is separating people from the larger group in society.) By the late 1800s, about half the states had adopted **Jim Crow laws**— state and local laws in mostly Southern states that required racial segregation in places like schools, public transportation, and hotels.

Plessy v. Ferguson

(Landmark Case) In 1896 the Supreme Court upheld the constitutionality of Jim Crow laws in *Plessy* v. *Ferguson.*[1] The Court said that the Fourteenth Amendment allowed separate facilities for different races as long as those facilities were equal. Justice Harlan disagreed in his dissent:

    ❝ *I deny that any legislative body or judicial tribunal may have regard to the race of citizens when the civil rights of those citizens are involved. . . . Our Constitution is colorblind, and neither knows nor tolerates classes among citizens. In respect of civil rights, all citizens are equal before the law.* ❞
—Justice John Marshall Harlan, 1896

Nevertheless, for the next 50 years the **"separate but equal" doctrine** was used to justify segregation. In the 1930s and the 1940s, the Supreme Court began to chip away at the doctrine in a series of decisions that have had far-reaching implications. The most important decision came in 1954 in a case involving an African American student in Topeka, Kansas.

Brown v. Board of Education

(Landmark Case) In the 1950s, the schools of Topeka were racially segregated. Linda Carol Brown, an eight-year-old African American, was denied admission to an all-white school near her home and had to attend a distant all-black school. With the help of the National Association for the Advancement of Colored People (NAACP), Linda's family sued the Topeka Board of Education. The NAACP successfully argued that segregated schools could never be equal and were, therefore, unconstitutional.

In 1954 the Court ruled on this case and similar cases filed in Virginia, Delaware, and South Carolina. In *Brown* v. *Board of Education of Topeka* (the short name for this decision), the Court unanimously overruled the "separate but equal" doctrine. This decision marked the beginning of a long struggle to desegregate public schools.

See the following footnoted materials in the **Reference Handbook:**
1. *Plessy* v. *Ferguson* case summary, page R32.

Activity: Interdisciplinary Connection

Rhetoric Encourage students to take a closer look at the speeches and writings of Martin Luther King, Jr. Students can find collections of his work at the local library or on the Internet, including the following:
• "The Montgomery Story" (1956)
• "Letter From a Birmingham Jail" (1963)

• "I Have a Dream" (1963)
• "I've Been to the Mountaintop" (1968)

Have students report on one or more selections and share their conclusions about why King had such an impact on the civil rights movement. **OL**

The *Brown* decision set a precedent that has guided other rulings. For example, although the Court ruled against school segregation, housing patterns produced segregated schools. Thus in many areas, school districts reflected neighborhoods and were largely either African American or white. The Court's remedy to this situation came in *Swann* v. *Charlotte-Mecklenburg Board of Education* (1971). Again unanimously, the Court declared that children should be bused to schools outside their neighborhoods to combat these housing patterns and to ensure integrated schools.

The Civil Rights Movement

After the *Brown* decision, many African Americans and whites worked together in the **civil rights movement** to end segregation. Throughout the United States, but mostly in the South, African Americans organized nonviolent protests against laws supporting racial segregation. Some held sit-ins at restaurant lunch counters that served only whites; that is, they sat in seats reserved for whites and refused to move. When arrested for breaking the law, they were almost always found guilty. They could then appeal, challenging the constitutionality of the laws.

The most important civil rights leader was Dr. Martin Luther King, Jr. King, a Baptist minister, led nonviolent protest marches and demonstrations against segregation. He understood the importance of the courts in trying to win equal rights and sought to stir the nation's conscience.

New Civil Rights Laws

Influenced by the civil rights movement, Congress began to act. In 1964 and 1965, it passed key civil rights legislation, barring discrimination and ensuring the right to vote. The 1965 law was introduced just after the nation saw TV coverage of police violence aimed at peaceful demonstrators in Selma, Alabama. President Lyndon Johnson made a dramatic plea on television to Congress, asking it to work long hours to pass the bill quickly:

66 . . . I don't make that request lightly, for, from the window where I sit, with the problems of our country, I recognize that from outside this chamber is the outraged conscience of a nation, the grave concern of many nations . . . 99

—President Lyndon Johnson

Selected Major Civil Rights Legislation

Charts In Motion
See StudentWorks™ Plus or go to glencoe.com.

Year	Act	Major Provisions
1875	Civil Rights Act	Bans discrimination in places of public accommodation (declared unconstitutional in 1883)
1957	Civil Rights Act	Makes it a federal crime to prevent a person from voting in a federal election
1963	Equal Pay Act	Bans wage discrimination based on race, gender, color, religion, or national origin
1964	Civil Rights Act	Bans discrimination in places of public accommodation, federally funded programs, and private employment; authorizes Justice Department to bring school integration suits
1965	Voting Rights Act	Allows federal registrars to register voters and ensure that those who are registered can exercise their right to vote without qualifications
1967	Age Discrimination Act	Bans discrimination in employment based on age
1968	Civil Rights Act, Title VIII	Bans racial discrimination in sale or rental of housing
1972	Higher Education Act, Title IX	Forbids discrimination based on gender by universities and colleges receiving federal aid
1974	Housing and Community Development Act	Bans housing discrimination based on gender
1990	Americans With Disabilities Act	Bans discrimination in employment, transportation, public accommodations, and telecommunications against persons with physical or mental disabilities

Critical Thinking Ratified in 1868, the Fourteenth Amendment was passed to protect the rights of formerly enslaved persons. It was not until 1964, however, that racial segregation in public places was made illegal. *Which civil rights act eliminated voting qualifications such as the literacy test?*

Critical Thinking

Answer: Voting Rights Act of 1965

Chart Skill Practice
Which civil rights law was declared unconstitutional? *(the Civil Rights Act of 1875)*

D Differentiated Instruction

Auditory/Musical Play a recording of Martin Luther King, Jr.'s, "I Have a Dream" speech for students. **Ask:** What words and phrases are used repeatedly? Why? *(one hundred years later; we cannot be satisfied; I have a dream; let freedom ring; free at last)* In what other ways does King appeal to listeners' emotions? *(Possible answer: by mentioning the Declaration of Independence)* Ask them how listening to the speech makes them feel. **OL** **AL**

Landmark Case

See *Brown* v. *Board of Education* in the Supreme Court Case Summaries in the **Reference Handbook** and Case Study 37 in the *Supreme Court Case Studies* booklet.

Hands-On Chapter Project
Step 3

Discrimination

Step 3: Adding Examples Students will research two more examples of discrimination.

Directions Have students select two groups other than the one they researched in Step 2 and write a paragraph about each, including the same type of information they researched in Step 2.

Summarizing Explain that these two paragraphs will be supporting paragraphs 2 and 3 in their essays—the "cheese and burger." Discuss any questions or problems students are having in doing their research. **OL**

(Chapter Project continued in Section 4.)

S Skill Practice

Using Geography Skills Have students refer to a map or globe to locate the countries from which the Latino population originated. **BL**

Assess

Assign the Section 3 Assessment as homework or as an in-class activity, or have students take Section Quiz 14-3 from *Section Quizzes and Chapter Tests*.

Close

Analyzing Discuss whether legislation can end discrimination. **Ask:** What do you think would have to happen for discrimination to come to a complete end? Take a class vote and discuss the results. **OL**

Section 3 Review

Latinos and Civil Rights

Following a Model
African American leaders inspired other groups to work for their civil rights, including women, Latinos, and Native Americans. Among the first well-known Latino groups **S** was the United Farm Workers. The UFW are seen here at a 1979 rally in California. *What kinds of strategies do you think other minority groups would tend to copy from African Americans?*

At regular intervals of this historic speech, President Johnson repeated the anthem of the civil rights movement—"We Shall Overcome." In August 1965, the bill passed by a healthy majority.

Some years later, John Lewis, a civil rights leader who watched the speech with Martin Luther King, Jr., commented on how King reacted to the president's speech, especially when he heard the president use King's own language of "we shall overcome." Lewis reported that King had cried from joy because at last he was confident that the movement had turned the corner.

Historians recognize that King's leadership was critical in persuading all Americans that reforms were needed. Historians also comment on how the 1960s civil rights legislation led to many other groups organizing to ensure equality of opportunity. Among women, prominent leaders were Bella Abzug and Gloria Steinem. Among Latinos, César Chávez and Dolores Huerta were active. Among Native Americans, Dennis Banks and Russell Means led the American Indian Movement to urge an end to discriminatory practices.

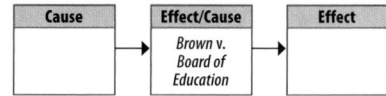

SECTION 3 Review

Vocabulary

1. **Explain** the significance of: suspect classification, fundamental right, discrimination, Jim Crow laws, "separate but equal" doctrine, civil rights movement.

Main Ideas

2. **Listing** What are three guidelines or tests the Supreme Court uses to evaluate cases involving equal protection under the law?

3. **Explaining** What was the impact of *Washington* v. *Davis*?

Critical Thinking

4. **Evaluating** Was Chief Justice Earl Warren's opinion in *Brown v. Board of Education of Topeka* consistent with Justice Harlan's dissenting opinion in *Plessy v. Ferguson*? Explain your answer.

5. **Analyzing** Use the graphic organizer below to analyze why the Supreme Court overturned the "separate but equal" doctrine and what effects followed that decision.

Cause	Effect/Cause	Effect
	Brown v. Board of Education	

Writing About Government

6. **Expository Writing** Find information about the following: Civil Rights Act of 1964, Voting Rights Act of 1965, Equal Employment Opportunities Act of 1972, Education Amendment of 1972, Voting Rights Act of 1975, and Americans with Disabilities Act of 1990. Prepare an informational brochure that describes these acts.

Answers

1. All definitions can be found in the section and the Glossary.
2. rational basis test, suspect classifications, fundamental rights
3. If laws were not designed to discriminate, they are constitutional even if they produce unequal results.
4. Yes, both Warren and Harlan wrote that equal protection of the laws meant that racial segregation was unconstitutional.
5. Cause: Separate facilities are inherently unequal. Effect: School districts redrew boundaries, reassigned pupils, and bused students to desegregate; courts heard cases to desegregate parks, prisons, and libraries.
6. Discuss with students how each piece of legislation has attempted to end discrimination. Students' brochures should show research and creativity.

Can a Judge Determine What Is a Hate Crime?

Apprendi v. New Jersey, 2000

The Fourteenth Amendment requires that an accused person receive due process when tried for breaking a state law. The Sixth Amendment guarantees those accused of a crime the right to a trial by jury. How do these amendments affect sentencing for "hate crimes" for which a state law may require harsher punishments?

Facts of the Case

On December 22, 1994, Charles Apprendi fired several gunshots into an African American family's home in Vineland, New Jersey. He confessed to the shooting and said he did not want the family in the neighborhood "because they are black in color." Later, Apprendi took back his statement. He pleaded guilty to possession of a firearm for unlawful purposes. At the evidence hearing, the judge ruled that the shooting was motivated by racial prejudice. Apprendi was sentenced to 12 years, which exceeded the usual 10-year maximum. Apprendi appealed, claiming that the extended sentence violated his rights under the Sixth and Fourteenth Amendments because the judge, not a jury, decided his crime was motivated by racial hatred. In 2000 the U. S. Supreme Court reviewed the case.

The Constitutional Question

During the 1990s, many people became alarmed about violent crimes whose victims were chosen because they were members of certain groups. State legislatures responded by passing hate crime laws. These laws carry extended sentences when a court determines that a convicted person committed the crime because of prejudice.

Hate crime laws were passed with good intentions. Establishing that prejudice is a criminal's main motive can be difficult to prove in most cases. The judge in the *Apprendi* case based his decision on the "preponderance of evidence"—which seems to be a reasonable way to determine whether or not a crime is a hate crime. And judges, not juries, often choose a sentence from a range of punishments prescribed for a certain crime.

The crime for which Apprendi pleaded guilty, however, was not designated a hate crime in the indictment. Apprendi's case raised the issue of whether a defendant has the right to have a jury—rather than a judge—determine whether a crime was, beyond a reasonable doubt, motivated by prejudice.

Debating the Issue

Questions to Consider

1. Which amendments guarantee trial by jury and due process of law?

2. How would a Supreme Court decision in Charles Apprendi's favor affect other cases in which extended sentences have been handed down by judges rather than juries?

You Be the Judge

Does the deterrent posed by hate crime laws justify the use of the "preponderance of evidence" standard rather than the "proof beyond a reasonable doubt" standard? Is a defendant denied his or her rights if a judge, not a jury, decides on an extended sentence?

▶ Charles Apprendi

403

Debating the Issue Answers

Questions to Consider

1. the Sixth Amendment and the Fourteenth Amendment

2. Answers will vary, but students should recognize that similar cases will be seen in a new light and that many convicted criminals might try to overturn their convictions or at least shorten their sentences.

You Be the Judge

Encourage students to draw upon the points raised in the classroom debate as they consider these questions. As students respond, have them explain which point or points they believed were most persuasive.

Class Debate

Organize the class into two teams—one team to argue that judges have the right to determine the defendant's motive and base sentencing on his or her determination and the other team to argue that under due process, only a jury can determine if a crime was motivated by prejudice and sentence the defendant accordingly. Have each team list the points in its favor. Ask team secretaries to record what each group believes are its five strongest points.

Have each team elect three of its members to serve as a "jury." Ask team reporters to state the strongest points of each team's argument. After allowing the "jury" to ask questions, have it deliberate and announce a decision.

The Court's Decision

Provide students with the following information about the Court's decision.

On June 26 in a 5-to-4 ruling, the Court struck down New Jersey's procedure. According to the justices, it allowed a judge to impose a greater punishment than the jury had authorized. Justice John Paul Stevens wrote in the majority opinion: "The New Jersey procedure is an unacceptable departure from the jury tradition that is an indispensable part of our criminal justice system."

With four justices dissenting, the decision caused controversy. Justice Sandra Day O'Connor argued that the Court had upheld the laws in other cases in which judges had imposed "enhanced" sentences.

Focus

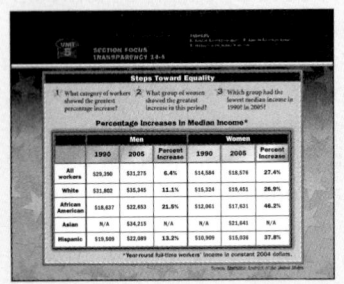
Reader's Guide

Answers to Graphic:
affirmative action
discrimination against women
freedom of information
right to privacy

Resource Manager

Civil Liberties Challenges

Reader's Guide

Content Vocabulary	Academic Vocabulary	Reading Strategy
★ affirmative action *(p. 404)* ★ security classification system *(p. 408)*	★ diverse *(p. 405)* ★ integrate *(p. 405)* ★ arbitrary *(p. 407)*	As you read, create a graphic organizer similar to the one below to list current issues involving civil liberties.

Challenges for Civil Liberties

Issues in the News

Music sharing on the Internet often violates copyright laws, but many students do it anyway. In its fight to stop the practice, the recording industry has sued many students. In December 2007, the industry filed a court action against the University of Oregon for failing to help identify the students. The university argued that industry tactics were violating privacy by unearthing information that was not related to copyrighted material. Lawyers for the record company angrily responded that when students are breaking the law, the university has no right to talk about privacy and due process.

▲ Some downloading is illegal, but some college students do not see it that way.

An American family living on the Western frontier might have worried about roving outlaws or whether the sheriff was doing his job, but they did not worry if someone was watching how they used the Internet. As society changes, so do the issues affecting our civil liberties. From the 1960s through the 1990s, concerns about civil rights often involved racial or gender discrimination. Those issues remain, but other civil liberties concerns have arisen since the September 11, 2001, terrorist attacks: Where is the dividing line between protecting individual liberties and the government's need to protect national security?

Affirmative Action

Affirmative action is a set of policies developed in the 1960s to remedy past discrimination. The policies are carried out by federal, state, and local governments, as well as by private employers with government contracts. Often the policies involve the targeted recruitment of women and minorities. The hope is that these groups will then be represented in jobs and in higher education in roughly the same proportion that they are in the population. Most affirmative action is required by the federal government or the courts, but many businesses use it voluntarily. Today some people argue that affirmative action has served its purpose and should end. Others say it is still needed so everyone will have an equal opportunity to use their talents and to get ahead. Many cases were fought in court over specific affirmative action policies. As more conservatives have been appointed to the Supreme Court, more affirmative action policies have been ruled as violating the protection of individual rights.

Affirmative Action in Education

Affirmative action has had a major impact on college admissions. In a 1978 case, a white male

---

student named Allan Bakke sued because he was twice rejected for medical school. He claimed that the University of California had practiced reverse discrimination because a certain number of slots were guaranteed to minorities. In *Regents of the University of California v. Bakke,*[1] the Court ruled that colleges and universities could not use a quota system, although they could consider race in admissions. 📖 After the *Bakke* decision, many colleges were considering race to achieve a **diverse** student body.

In the mid-1990s, opponents of affirmative action began a fight to eliminate any use of race by public institutions—in college admissions or in state-agency hiring. Ward Connerly, an African American member of the University of California's Board of Regents, led the fight. Later Connerly and others succeeded in getting Proposition 209 on the ballot, and voters passed the measure. It amended California's constitution; the state was barred from favoring applicants on the basis of race, gender, ethnicity, or national origin.

Michigan has also seen major battles over affirmative action. In *Grutter v. Bollinger*[2] (2003), the Court upheld a University of Michigan admissions policy that gave preference to minorities who applied to its law school. 📖 The Court said universities could treat race as a "plus factor" in admitting students. It added that universities serve a special role because they make it possible for people of all backgrounds to compete at all levels of society. In another Michigan case, however, the Court ruled against an admission policy to increase diversity. In *Gratz v. Bollinger* (2003),[3] the Court said that it was unconstitutional to use a system that automatically gave extra points to minority applicants for admission. 📖 In November 2006, Michigan voters supported Proposal 2, a ballot initiative similar to California's that makes preferential treatment in admissions and hiring illegal. So far the Court has rejected attempts to appeal this new law.

In recent years, a more conservative Supreme Court has also questioned integration plans of elementary and high schools that were adopted after 1954. In accordance with the *Brown* decision, many schools redrew district lines, bused students, and created magnet schools. Yet in 2007, the Supreme Court struck down the policies of two school districts. (The case was *Parents Involved in Community Schools v. Seattle School District No. 1.*) To achieve more **integrated** schools, the schools involved in the case sometimes limited

Affirmative Action Suits Barbara Grutter (left) and Jennifer Gratz brought suit in separate cases in 2003 against the University of Michigan. Undergraduate admissions policies that awarded points based on race were struck down. *Why might the Supreme Court object to a system that gave extra points to minorities?*

transfer students on the basis of race, or they used race as a tiebreaker when choosing among students for certain schools. The justices were bitterly divided over this decision. Speaking for the majority, Chief Justice John Roberts argued that the 1954 *Brown* decision meant that schools should be color-blind:

> ❝ The way to stop discrimination on the basis of race is to stop discriminating on the basis of race. ❞
>
> —Chief Justice John Roberts

The dissenting justices contended that his argument was a "cruel irony." The real goal of *Brown v. Board of Education,* they said, was to integrate schools, even if taking account of race is necessary to accomplish this.

📖 *See the following footnoted materials in the **Reference Handbook:***
1. *Regents of the University of California* v. *Bakke* case summary, page R33.
2. *Grutter* v. *Bollinger* case summary, page R28.
3. *Gratz* v. *Bollinger* case summary, page R28.

Teach

Caption Answer: Favoring minorities denies nonminority students equal protection of the law, which is in violation of the Fourteenth Amendment.

CURRICULUM CONNECTION

Law In the *Bakke* case, the Supreme Court ruled that "the purpose of helping certain groups whom the [University of California] perceived as victims of 'societal discrimination' does not justify a classification that imposes disadvantages upon persons like [Bakke], who bear no responsibility for whatever harm the beneficiaries of the special admissions program are thought to have suffered. To hold otherwise would be to convert a remedy heretofore reserved for violations of legal rights into a privilege that all institutions throughout the Nation could grant at their pleasure to whatever groups are perceived as victims of societal discrimination."

Additional Support

Activity: Collaborative Learning

Exploring the Impact of Government Action Explain to students that access to information about what the government is doing is an essential part of a democracy. Organize students into small groups. **Ask:** How can Americans become more aware of actions taken by government that affect their lives? Have each group select a student to

report responses to the class. *(A basic answer should include references to the Freedom of Information Act and the Sunshine Act.)* Then have each group select another student to work with students from other groups to list the provisions of the two acts to present to the class. **OL**

★ ★
Critical Thinking

Answer: The greatest increase occurred between 1989 and 1997. Students may note a greater acceptance of women in power, thanks to earlier civil rights victories.

W Writing Support

Persuasive Writing Ask students to consider whether they think affirmative action policies are a fair way to address past discrimination. Then, have students write letters to the editor explaining their opinions. **OL**

Did You Know?

In *United States* v. *Paradise* (1987), the Supreme Court ruled on a plan to encourage promotion of African American state troopers in Alabama, based upon a quota of "one black for one white." The Court declared that the quota was justified, given the fact that it was "narrowly tailored" and temporary and given the "long and shameful record of delays and resistance" shown toward African American employment on the state police force.

Differentiated Instruction

Early Struggles

Women in Congress	
1917–1919	1
1937–1939	9
1947–1949	8
1957–1959	15
1977–1979	21
1987–1989	24
1997–1999	66
2007–2009	92

Critical Thinking When the first woman ran in the Boston Marathon in 1967, the act outraged a male trainer. *Based on the chart, in which years did women see the greatest increase in the number of female Congress members? Why do you think these increases occurred?*

Affirmative Action in Other Areas

Outside of the educational sphere, the use of affirmative action has also been mixed. In a 1987 trucking industry case, the Supreme Court upheld a plan by a state transportation agency to take account of gender in promotions if the candidates for a position were equally qualified. Then in 1995, in *Adarand Constructors, Inc.* v. *Peña,*[1] the Court overturned earlier decisions by saying that federal agencies could not automatically favor minority-based companies for federal contracts. 📖

W An Ongoing Debate

As the previous discussion shows, the affirmative action debate continues to this day. Supporters argue that minorities and women have been so disadvantaged in the past that they may be viewed as inferior candidates compared to white men. Supporters also argue that affirmative action should continue because it is an important social goal to increase the number of minorities and women in desirable jobs.

Opponents say that any discrimination is wrong, even if it is practiced to correct past injustices. They want merit to be the only basis for hiring. To favor a minority over a white candidate, they say, is reverse discrimination.

📖 *See the following footnoted materials in the* **Reference Handbook:**
1. *Adarand Constructors, Inc.* v. *Peña* case summary, page R23.

Discrimination Against Women

Women did not win the right to vote until 1920 when the Nineteenth Amendment was adopted. In the 1960s and 1970s, women challenged discrimination in employment and in other areas.

Before the 1970s, the Supreme Court usually said that laws discriminating against women did not violate the Fourteenth Amendment. Often the reasoning was that these laws protected the "weaker sex" from night work, heavy lifting, or "bad elements" in society. In the 1950s, for example, the Court upheld an Ohio law forbidding any woman other than the wife or daughter of a tavern owner from working in a bar.

A historic change came in 1971, when the Court held that a state law was unconstitutional because it discriminated against women. In *Reed* v. *Reed*, the Court said that a law that automatically preferred a father over a mother as executor of a son's estate violated the Fourteenth Amendment:

❝ *To give a mandatory preference to members of either sex over members of the other . . . is to make the very kind of arbitrary legislative choice forbidden by the Equal Protection Clause.* ❞
—Chief Justice Warren Burger

Activity: Multiple Learning Styles

Interpersonal Have each student choose a person from the section and write two or three diary entries that the person might have made. In addition to the people mentioned by name in the section, such as Allan Bakke, allow students to choose the role of one of the many unnamed people involved in these issues—for example, the director of admissions to a law school, a woman applying to a state-supported, all-male military college, a specialist in Internet security, and the like. Before they write their entries, encourage students to think about how their chosen character might have felt in a situation that challenged civil liberties and how they themselves would have felt in the same situation. Also assure students that they need not write fluently and that they can include sketches and other diagrams to express their thoughts. **ELL**

Reasonableness Standard

The *Reed* decision created a new standard of reasonableness for sex discrimination cases. In this case, the Supreme Court said that any law that classifies people on the basis of gender "must be reasonable, not **arbitrary,** and must rest on some ground of difference." If a real ground of difference exists, then the court must make two other determinations:

- that recognizing the difference serves "important governmental objectives" and
- that the law or practice is substantially related to those objectives.

In a 1977 case, the Court wrote that treating women differently from men cannot be based merely on "old notions" about women and "the role-typing society has long imposed on women."

Substantial Interest Standard

Since the *Reed* decision, federal courts have decided that some distinctions are not substantially related to important government goals, but here are some examples of distinctions that are prohibited:

- States cannot set different ages at which men and women become legal adults.

- States cannot set different ages for when men and women can buy alcohol.
- States cannot exclude women from juries.
- Girls cannot be kept off Little League baseball teams.
- Community service groups cannot exclude women from membership.
- Employers must pay women the same retirement benefits as men.

Sometimes the courts have decided that gender distinctions are allowable because they are substantially related to public policy goals; for example, the following are legal:

- All-male or all-female schools
- Having only male staff in all-male prisons
- Barring fathers from the delivery room during Caesarean sections

Laws on Gender Discrimination

Since the 1960s, Congress has passed several important laws to protect women from discrimination. The Civil Rights Act of 1964 banned job discrimination based on gender. In 1972 the Equal Employment Opportunity Act strengthened

C Critical Thinking

Making Inferences Ask: What might be the "public policy goals" that justify single-sex schools? *(Answers will vary.)* **OL**

Participating IN GOVERNMENT

In addition to handling complaints, the U.S. Commission on Civil Rights evaluates federal laws and policies that relate to discrimination, serves as a clearinghouse for information on the issue, and keeps the issue before Americans in the form of public service announcements. Students can find out more about the commission by visiting its Web site at www.usccr.gov.

Activity: Review the key elements of a formal civil rights complaint (the date and place, plus how to contact witnesses to the discrimination). You might want to have students work with partners on this activity; be prepared to offer advice about the best place to direct specific complaints. To extend this activity, have volunteers share their complaints, and have the class discuss how they think the government should respond. **OL**

Hands-On Chapter Project

Step 4

Participating IN GOVERNMENT Filing a Civil Rights Complaint

If you believe you have been treated unfairly because of gender, race, color, national origin, religion, or disability, you can make a formal complaint that your civil rights have been violated.

The complaint must be in writing, be signed and dated, and include your name, address, and phone number. It must include the name and address of the person or establishment that is the subject of the complaint. The complaint must describe the act and the type of discrimination (gender, race, and so on). It must include the date and place the act occurred and the names, addresses, and phone numbers of any witnesses. No other documents are necessary.

▶ **Filing a complaint**

Generally, a complaint must be filed with the appropriate agency within 180 days of the discrimination it alleges. Discrimination in employment, education, housing, credit, and public services are handled by various state or federal government agencies. The Complaints Referral Office of the U.S. Commission on Civil Rights in Washington, D.C., gives advice on where to file a complaint.

Participating IN GOVERNMENT ACTIVITY

1. Investigate the state or federal agencies that handle various civil rights complaints. Use the telephone directory to make a list of the agencies that are concerned with the following areas: employment, housing, credit, education, public facilities.
2. Create an imaginary civil rights complaint following the guidelines above. Include the name and address of the agency where you would file your complaint.

CHAPTER 14: *Citizenship and Equal Justice* **407**

Discrimination

Step 4: Putting It Together Students will use the information they gathered in Steps 1 through 3 to write their essays.

Directions Ask students to use the notes they took in Steps 1 through 3 to write a one-page essay that includes:

- an introductory statement summarizing how the classroom experience in Step 1 affected them and led them to consider the effects of discrimination on various groups;

- a supporting paragraph for each of the three examples of discrimination that they researched; and
- a summary paragraph—the "bottom bun on the cheeseburger"—explaining why they believe discrimination is unacceptable in a democracy.

Summarizing Ask volunteers to share portions of their essays and display them in the room so that the class can read them. **OL**

Caption Answer: The Court would claim that this gender classification is constitutional because it serves important governmental objectives. In the past, the draft has been used to enlist enough men for combat during war. Women are excluded from frontline combat positions, so there is no reason to draft them.

Participating IN GOVERNMENT

Women in the Military Ask students to gather information about military service from the school guidance office or from armed forces recruiting stations. Have them report and comment upon opportunities that are available to women in the military.

R Reading Strategy

Drawing Conclusions In the *Griswold* decision, the Supreme Court noted that the First, Third, Fourth, and Fifth Amendments recognize a right to privacy. Review each of these amendments and ask students to brainstorm about how they recognize a right to privacy. **AL**

Differentiated Instruction

★ Reasonable Distinctions ★

Women in the Armed Forces
Although many women are enlisted in the armed forces, the Supreme Court ruled in 1981 that Congress could exclude women from registering for the draft. *Why would the Court allow Congress to adopt this policy?*

---

earlier laws on discrimination in hiring and firing practices, promotion, pay, and other employment actions. During the same year, Congress passed a comprehensive education law that included provisions referred to as Title IX.

Patsy Mink, the first Asian American woman elected to Congress, was a primary sponsor of Title IX. Mink, who began representing Hawaii in 1965, faced discrimination as a girl and as an Asian American in high school and in later years. One of Title IX's most obvious visible effects was in school athletics: Any school that received federal money had to give boys and girls an equal chance to participate.

Finally, in 1972, Congress made its boldest effort R to ban gender discrimination by proposing to amend the Constitution. The Equal Rights Amendment (ERA) stated: "Equality of rights under the law shall not be denied or abridged by the United States or by any state on account of sex." A total of 35 states supported the ERA, but 38 states were necessary for passage. Since the defeat, women have relied on the Fourteenth Amendment's equal-protection clause to address discrimination.

Citizens' Right to Know

The right of citizens and the press to know what the government is doing is essential. Only informed citizens can make a democracy. Government officials, however, are often reluctant to share information. Since 1917, the government has used a **security classification system** that permits it to keep information that is important to national security or foreign policy secret. Each year, the government determines that millions of documents are classified, and as such, unavailable to the public.

In 1966 Congress increased the public's access to government by passing the Freedom of Information Act (FOIA). FOIA requires federal agencies to give citizens access to unclassified records on request. If people are denied access to information, they can sue the government to get it. Most FOIA requests come from veterans and senior citizens who want to know about their service records or benefits, but journalists often use the act to investigate stories. In 2005, for example, reporters for the *Dayton Daily News* sued to get information on the safety of Peace Corps volunteers abroad.

Another way citizens exercise their right to know is by attending government meetings. Before 1976, many government meetings or hearings were closed. The Sunshine Act of 1976 helped correct this. About 50 federal agencies, boards, and commissions must now give notice of meetings and open them to the public. If a closed session is permissible, a record must be kept and made available to the public.

Citizens' Right to Privacy

The Constitution does not mention a right to privacy. In 1965, however, in *Griswold* v. *Connecticut*, the Court interpreted that taken together the First, Third, Fourth, and Fifth Amendments recognize an area of privacy. The Ninth Amendment protects this right because it says, in effect, that just because the Constitution names certain specific rights does R not mean that people do not have other rights.

In the *Griswold* case, the Court said that Connecticut could not outlaw access to contraception because it would violate the privacy of married couples. Since the *Griswold* decision, the Court has upheld a right to privacy in a number of cases involving personal matters—child rearing, abortion, and intimate relationships within the home. This privacy right is not unlimited. The Court can limit it if the state needs to protect the larger society.

★ Activity: Interdisciplinary Connection ★

Daily Life Have students work together to plan and present a TV news special—"Civil Liberties Every Day." Students can report on the impact of civil legislation on such daily activities as the following:

- being considered for a job or a promotion
- playing on a school sports team
- applying for a loan

- visiting a doctor
- applying to a specialized college program
- speaking with a guidance counselor
- serving on a jury

Have each group conclude with a commentary explaining why Americans need to be aware of their civil liberties. **OL**

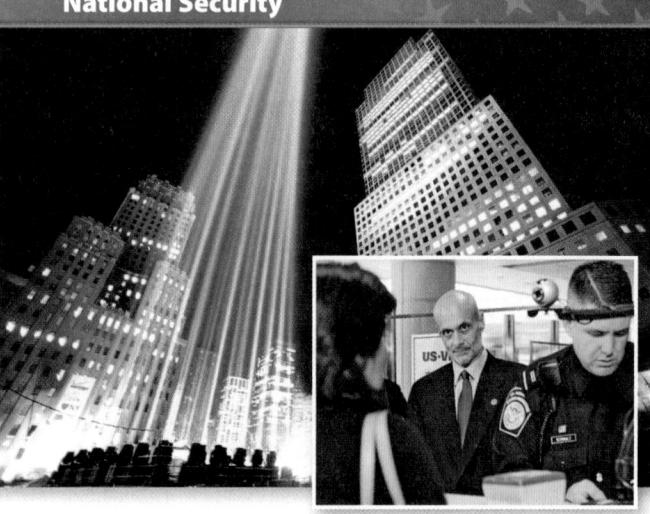

National Security

Emergency Measures
The "Tribute of Light" in New York City memorializes the victims of the September 11, 2001, terrorist attacks, a national crisis that led to passage of the USA Patriot Act. At right, Michael Chertoff (center) of the Department of Homeland Security observes security checks at Dulles International Airport. *Have any Patriot Act provisions been criticized?*

Roe v. Wade

Landmark Case In 1973 the landmark *Roe* v. *Wade*[1] decision established a woman's right to get an abortion during the first six months of her pregnancy, but individual states could prohibit abortion in the last three months.

Before 1973, many states outlawed abortion completely unless the life of the mother was at stake. In *Roe,* the Court noted that it was necessary to balance a woman's right to privacy of her body with the rights of the unborn child. It also noted that there was no clear agreement among medical and philosophical experts on exactly when life begins.

Since the 1970s, abortion has remained very controversial. Many Americans see it as morally wrong and want the government to make it a criminal act. Others may also see it as a moral wrong but believe that women and families have the right to decide the issue for themselves.

A more conservative Supreme Court began restricting access to abortion in the 1990s. In a 1992 case, for example, the Court ruled that Pennsylvania could require a woman who wants an abortion to first get counseling—even counseling that is aimed at persuading her against having an abortion.

Antiabortion and pro-life activists continue to keep the issue in the public eye. In 2003 Congress passed a federal law banning a particular method of late-term abortion, and in 2007, the Court upheld the law. Some legal experts wondered whether this decision was a sign that *Roe* v. *Wade* might be overturned or at least restricted further.

Internet Issues

Internet use is creating new challenges to the right to privacy. One concern is government surveillance. The Federal Bureau of Investigation (FBI), for example, uses wiretapping technology to intercept Internet e-mails or to target suspect words or phrases in messages.

Online privacy is also threatened by Web sites and hackers that gather information on people who are surfing the Web. By "spying" on your online activity, marketers can create a profile of individuals that includes their age, income, recent purchases, music preferences, and political party. More and more, personal information is being collected in "data warehouses" where it is for sale to businesses, current or potential employers—or nearly anyone else who is willing to pay for it.

Identity theft is another phenomenon that has increased with the Internet and that threatens individuals. The sheer volume of personal information in online databases has made many people fear for their privacy. Government agencies and businesses devote many resources to finding ways to increase security.

Government Surveillance

War and the threat of terrorism create tension in a democracy between citizens' privacy rights and national security needs. Currently two laws

See the following footnoted materials in the **Reference Handbook:**
1. *Roe* v. *Wade* case summary, page R33.

Caption Answer: Many Patriot Act provisions have been criticized for allowing the U.S. government to expand the standards for probable cause.

D Differentiated Instruction

English Learners Point out the phrase *data warehouses.* Tell students that *data* means "information" and that a *warehouse* is a place where business owners store merchandise. Point out that *warehouse* is made up of *ware* and *house.* Note that other phrases such as *Web site* and *database* are also metaphors for locations on the Internet. **ELL**

S Skill Practice

Making a Fact/Opinion Chart Help students make a chart that identifies the statements under "Government Surveillance" as facts or opinions. *(Charts should include points such as: Facts: The NSA can monitor e-mail messages. President Bush secretly ordered the NSA to eavesdrop on U.S. citizens. Opinions: The Iraq War Resolution authorized the president to act outside FISA. The threat of terrorism justifies monitoring private citizens.)* **OL**

Differentiated Instruction

Leveled Activities

ELL Vocabulary Activities, p. 14

BL American Biographies, p. 62

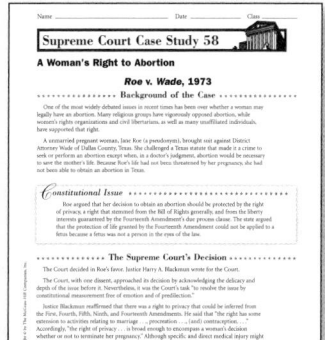

OL Supreme Court Case Studies, p. 115

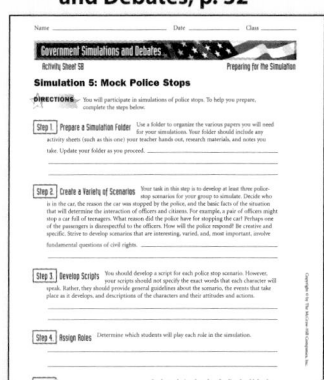

AL Government Simulations and Debates, p. 32

409

📜 Landmark Case

See *Roe* v. *Wade* in the Supreme Court Case Summaries in the **Reference Handbook** and Case Study 58 in the *Supreme Court Case Studies* booklet.

Assess

Assign the Section 4 Assessment as homework or as an in-class activity, or have students take Section Quiz 14-4 from *Section Quizzes and Chapter Tests*.

Close

Summarizing Have students use the information under the main headings of this section to write newspaper headlines that summarize the section's major ideas. Have students share their headlines with the class. **OL**

Section 4 Review

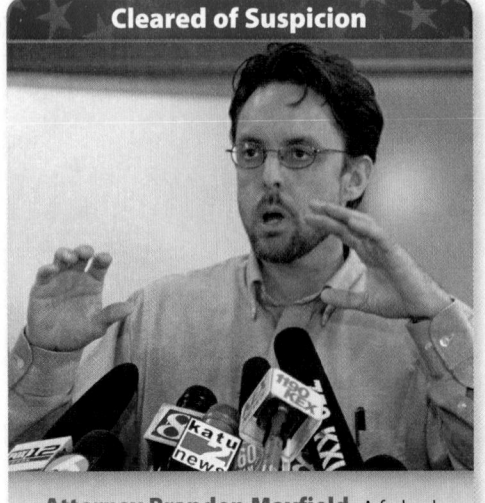

Cleared of Suspicion

Attorney Brandon Mayfield A federal court found that the FBI used flawed evidence to justify its surveillance of Mayfield and his family. *What amendment requires a warrant to search an individual's home?*

lay down the guidelines for government surveillance in national security cases: the 1978 Foreign Intelligence Surveillance Act (FISA), and the 2001 Patriot Act. FISA originally required federal agents to get a warrant from a special FISA court before tapping domestic phone and computer lines.

In 2005 the law became controversial when it was learned that shortly after the September 11, 2001, terrorist attacks, President George W. Bush secretly ordered the National Security Agency (NSA) to monitor the phone calls of millions of citizens without a FISA warrant. President Bush asserted that Congress had, in effect, given him the power to act outside FISA when it passed the Iraq War Resolution. Critics said he overstepped his authority. Under pressure, the attorney general told Senate leaders in early 2007 that the president would carry out future surveillance under FISA guidelines.

The Patriot Act and its revisions broadened the definition of who could be seen as a terrorist and expanded the government's power to detain, investigate, and prosecute suspected terrorists. Federal agencies can monitor Internet messages and tap phones, usually with a warrant from the FISA court, and they can use broader standards for "probable cause." In the case of attorney Brandon Mayfield, however, a federal court found that the FBI went too far. The FBI used flawed fingerprint evidence to connect Mayfield to a terrorist bombing in Spain and then began intense surveillance on him. When he brought suit, the FBI's mishandling of evidence was discovered. A federal court ruled that the surveillance was conducted without sufficient probable cause. The FBI formally apologized and paid Mayfield $2 million.

Most citizens supported the Patriot Act when it was passed. Since then, many legal experts have warned that some of its provisions could threaten civil liberties. The law's supporters counter that the latest versions contain many safeguards and that the law has been an asset in protecting the nation.

SECTION 4 Review

Vocabulary

1. **Explain** the significance of: affirmative action, security classification system.

Main Ideas

2. **Describing** How does the Supreme Court apply the reasonableness standard in judging discrimination against women?

3. **Identifying** What is the key provision of the Freedom of Information Act?

Critical Thinking

4. **Analyzing** Based on Supreme Court decisions, give examples of permitted actions that allow for gender differences.

5. **Listing** Use a graphic organizer like the one below to list arguments for and against affirmative action programs.

For	Against

Writing About Government

6. **Expository Writing** Write a magazine article about affirmative action and describe the ways it was intended to deal with discrimination. Then explain both sides of the ongoing debate.

Answers

1. All definitions can be found in the section and the Glossary.
2. The Court looks closely at laws that classify on the basis of gender. Such a law "must be reasonable, not arbitrary, and must rest on some ground of difference" serving "important governmental objectives."
3. The act requires federal agencies to provide citizens with access to public records on request.
4. All-boy and all-girl public schools are allowed; women can be prohibited from working in all-male prisons.
5. Answers might include: For—programs help remedy the effects of past discrimination that put minorities at a disadvantage; increasing minority representation in desirable jobs is an important social goal. Against—programs may result in reverse discrimination against qualified individuals.
6. Students' articles should fully explain both sides of the affirmative action debate.

Should Undocumented Workers Be Licensed to Drive?

Today it is estimated that anywhere from 12 to 20 million people in the United States are here illegally. There have been many proposals for how to address this problem in the long term, but a controversial proposal by a New York governor triggered debates among the 2008 presidential candidates. He recommended that undocumented workers be able to apply for New York driver's licenses. Although his proposal was withdrawn, debate continues about how to achieve greater safety and security.

 YES **William Bratton, former New York Police Commissioner**

Primary Source

❝ As former Commissioner of the New York City Police Department and now Chief of the Los Angeles Police Department, I support efforts that have the potential to solve crimes and improve traffic safety. That's why I backed legislation in California that would give undocumented immigrants the ability to get a driver's license once they have provided proof of their identification. It is my belief that by doing that you would reduce the number of hit and runs and increase the number of insured motorists on the road. We would also now have undocumented immigrants' identifying information on record such as photographs and addresses which could prove helpful in the fight against crime and terrorism. ❞

—in a press release, October 2007

 NO **Dan Stein, President of the Federation for American Immigration Reform**

Immigration Reform

❝ If [the governor's] plan is implemented, future terrorists in need of a valid U.S. identity document will be able to get one simply by proving that they can parallel park.... [His] rationalization is essentially the same one President Bush used in seeking amnesty for illegal aliens. Rather than enforce laws against illegal immigrants, President Bush argued that we must give-in to them and grant them legal status.... [The governor] is seeking to reward illegal alien scofflaws [contemptuous lawbreakers] with the privilege of driving and a U.S. identity document. The American public rejected the idea of amnesty for illegal aliens, and New Yorkers firmly reject the notion of licenses for people who have no right to be in the country. ❞

—in a testimony before the New York State Senate, October 15, 2007

Debating the Issue

1. **Identifying** What is the main reason Chief Bratton supports the proposal?

2. **Explaining** Why does Stein fear granting driver's licenses to illegal aliens?

3. **Evaluating** Both Bratton and Stein justify their positions by pointing to security needs. Which person is more persuasive on this point and why?

▼ Protesters

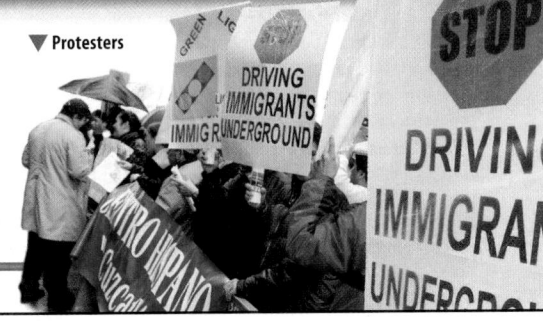

Debating the Issue Answers

1. It would help solve crimes and improve traffic safety.
2. It would reward people who broke the law, undermine the law, and hurt security.

3. Students should state a position and clearly defend it.

ExamView®
Assessment Suite

This easy-to-use software includes extensive question banks and allows you to create fully customized tests that can be administered in print or online.

Reviewing Vocabulary

1. double jeopardy
2. naturalization
3. nonresident alien
4. resident alien
5. undocumented alien
6. counsel
7. exclusionary rule
8. Jim Crow laws
9. affirmative action
10. security classification system

Reviewing Main Ideas

11. An immigrant enters a new country intending to live there permanently and become a citizen, whereas an alien is a temporary resident and may not intend to become a citizen of the country.
12. The Constitution spoke of citizenship only as a qualification for holding office in the federal government.
13. *Swann* v. *Charlotte-Mecklenburg Board of Education* (1971) declared that children should be bused to schools outside their neighborhoods to combat these housing patterns and ensure integrated schools.
14. the Voting Rights Act of 1965
15. In *Griswold* v. *Connecticut,* the Supreme Court ruled that personal privacy is one of the rights guaranteed by the Constitution.

412

Reviewing Vocabulary

Match the following content vocabulary word(s) with the descriptions that follow.

Affirmative action, resident alien, undocumented alien, Jim Crow laws, security classification system, naturalization, nonresident alien

1. the process of gaining citizenship
2. person from a foreign country who expects to stay in the United States for a short, specified period of time
3. person from a foreign country who establishes permanent residence in the United States
4. person who comes to the United States without legal permits

---

Chapter Summary

Citizenship

★ A person who is born on American soil, born to a parent who is a U.S. citizen, or naturalized is a U.S. citizen.
★ A person can lose citizenship through expatriation, by being convicted of certain crimes, or through denaturalization.
★ Responsibilities of citizens include knowing about rights and laws, participating in political life, and voting.

Challenges for Civil Liberties

★ Affirmative action debate over whether minorities should be compensated for past injustices continues.
★ Efforts to stop discrimination against women and minorities in employment, housing, and credit policies continue.
★ Citizens' right to know sometimes clashes with government's need for security.
★ Citizens' right to privacy sometimes clashes with state's need to protect society.

Equal Protection of the Law

★ The Supreme Court uses three tests—rational basis, suspect classifications, and fundamental rights—to determine violations of equal protection.
★ *Brown* v. *Board of Education of Topeka* (1954) overruled the "separate but equal" doctrine.
★ Civil rights movements throughout the 1960s and 1970s sought to end segregation and discrimination.

---

5. laws that discriminated against African Americans
6. policy giving preference to minorities
7. how government documents are kept secret

Reviewing Main Ideas

Section 1 *(pages 387–391)*

8. **Differentiating** What is the difference between an immigrant and an alien?

Section 2 *(pages 392–397)*

9. **Analyzing** How did the Constitution address the issue of citizenship?

Section 3 *(pages 398–402)*

10. **Evaluating** How did the Court remedy the problem of housing patterns creating segregated school districts?
11. **Listing** Which civil rights act allows federal registrars to register voters?

Section 4 *(pages 404–410)*

12. **Stating** Which Supreme Court ruling set the precedent for the right to privacy?
13. **Summarizing** What are the provisions of the Freedom of Information Act?

Critical Thinking

14. 🏛 **Essential Question** What are the three basic sources of U.S. citizenship?
15. **Drawing Conclusions** Why did the Court rule that wiretapping without a warrant was an illegal search and thus a violation of the Fourth Amendment?
16. **Predicting** Use a graphic organizer like the one below to show what might happen if no formal procedures were in place for becoming an American citizen.

Cause		Effect
No naturalization	→	

---

16. It required federal agencies to provide citizens with access to public records on request with exemptions for national defense materials, confidential personnel and financial data, and law-enforcement files.

Critical Thinking

17. jus soli, jus sanguinis, naturalization
18. The Court ruled that the Fourth Amendment protects people, not simply areas, from search and seizure.
19. Effect: The country would be flooded with immigrants and refugees who could not participate in government.

Government ONLINE Self-Check Quiz
Visit glencoe.com and enter QuickPass™ code USG9822c14.
Click on Self-Check Quizzes for additional test practice.

CHAPTER 14 Assessment and Activities

Document-Based Questions

Analyzing Primary Sources

Read the excerpt below and answer the questions that follow.

Jane Addams was a prominent social reformer and advocate for woman suffrage. In a 1906 newspaper editorial, Addams discussed her arguments for giving women the vote.

66 *Logically, their electorate should be made up of those who . . . in the past have at least attempted to care for children, to clean houses, to prepare foods, to isolate the family from moral dangers; those who have traditionally taken care of that side of life which inevitably becomes the subject of municipal consideration and control as soon as the population is congested. . . . These problems must be solved, if they are solved at all, not from the military point of view, not even from the industrial point of view, but from a third . . . the human-welfare point of view.* 99

17. What is the basis of Jane Addams's argument for giving women the vote?

18. Can you see any problems with granting women the right to vote based on these reasons? Why do you suppose, using the reasons listed above, that it took so long for women to get the right to vote?

Applying Technology Skills

19. Using the Internet The Sixth Amendment guarantees the right to counsel only in criminal cases, but there are civil cases that can have serious consequences for a person. For example, a case involving a person's immigrant status or job discrimination. For people who qualify as low-income, legal aid societies provide assistance in such cases. Explore the Web sites of legal aid societies in your own state and one other state. Then report briefly on the mission of legal aid societies, the clientele they serve, and types of cases handled—or other pertinent information that reflects their activities.

Interpreting Political Cartoons

Analyze the cartoon and answer the questions that follow. Base your answers on the cartoon and your knowledge of Chapter 14.

20. Who are the people grouped on the left of the cartoon?

21. What is the meaning of the comment made by the person on the right?

22. How is the term *illegal immigrants* being defined by the cartoonist?

Participating IN GOVERNMENT

23. Find out about or visit one of the citizenship classes offered to immigrants in your community. Find out what material is covered in courses designed to prepare immigrants for becoming U.S. citizens. What obstacles do immigrants have to overcome to be successful in these classes? Who sponsors and pays for these classes? Share your findings with the class in a brief oral presentation.

CHAPTER 14: *Citizenship and Equal Justice* **413**

25. In the cartoon, the term *illegal immigrants* applies to both groups on the left. The cartoonist implies that "illegal immigrants" are those who came to the Americas and took Native Americans' lands.

Participating IN GOVERNMENT

26. Call on volunteers to present their findings in an oral report.

Chapter Bonus Test Question

Ask: Which Supreme Court justice earned the title "Mr. Civil Rights" before his Court appointment? (*Thurgood Marshall, who, as an NAACP lawyer, argued the* Brown *case before the Supreme Court.*)

Analyzing Primary Sources

20. Addams argued that women should be given the vote because they are inherently more moral than men and would, therefore, be better able to vote for issues that would improve society's problems.

21. Students might answer that women, when given the vote under those conditions, could be held to higher and, therefore, unequal standards than men, which could theoretically be discriminatory.

Applying Technology Skills

22. Students' reports should logically and concisely discuss their findings.

Interpreting Political Cartoons

23. They are depicted as Latino Americans.

24. Native Americans, whose presence in the Americas dates back thousands of years, are the only non-immigrants. The man in the middle is a descendant of immigrants.

Planning Guide

Key to Ability Levels
- **BL** Below level
- **OL** On level
- **AL** Above level
- **ELL** English Language Learners

Key to Teaching Resources
- 📁 Print Material
- 💿 CD-ROM or DVD
- 🖨 Transparency

Levels				Resources	Chapter Opener	Section 1	Section 2	Section 3	Section 4	Chapter Assess
BL	OL	AL	ELL							
				FOCUS						
BL	OL	AL	ELL	🖨 Section Focus Transparencies		15-1	15-2	15-3	15-4	
				TEACH						
BL	OL		ELL	📁 Reading Essentials and Study Guide (and Answer Key)		p. 149	p. 152	p. 156	p. 159	
BL	OL		ELL	📁 Guided Reading Activities		p. 54	p. 55	p. 56	p. 57	
BL	OL		ELL	📁 Vocabulary Activities					p. 14	
BL	OL	AL	ELL	📁 Chapter Summaries						
BL	OL			📁 American Biographies				p. 65		
BL	OL	AL	ELL	📁 Cooperative Learning Activities						
	OL	AL	ELL	📁 Government Simulations and Debate						
BL	OL	AL	ELL	📁 Historical Documents and Speeches		p. 14				
BL	OL	AL	ELL	📁 Interpreting Political Cartoons				p. 27		
BL	OL		ELL	📁 Skill Reinforcement Activities					p. 14	
BL	OL	AL	ELL	📁 Source Readings				p. 14		
BL	OL			📁 Supreme Court Case Studies				p. 27	pp. 115, 121	
BL	OL	AL	ELL	📁 Participating in Government Activities			p. 27			
BL	OL		ELL	📁 Spanish Declaration of Independence and U.S. Constitution	✓	✓	✓	✓	✓	✓
BL	OL	AL	ELL	📁 NGS World Atlas, Spanish	✓	✓	✓	✓	✓	✓
BL	OL	AL	ELL	🖨 Unit Overlay Transparencies, Strategies, and Activities	✓	✓	✓	✓	✓	✓
BL	OL		ELL	🖨 Making It Relevant Transparencies	✓	✓	✓	✓	✓	✓
BL	OL	AL	ELL	🖨 High School Writing Process Transparencies, Strategies, and Activities	✓	✓	✓	✓	✓	✓
BL	OL	AL		🖨 American Art & Architecture Transparencies, Strategies, and Activities	✓	✓	✓	✓	✓	✓

✓ Chapter- or unit-based activities applicable to all sections in this chapter

All-In-One Planner and Resource Center

- Interactive Lesson Planner
- Interactive Teacher Edition
- Fully editable blackline masters
- Chapter Spotlight Videos Launch

- Differentiated Lesson Plans
- Printable reports of daily assignments
- Standards tracking system

Levels					Resources	Chapter Opener	Section 1	Section 2	Section 3	Section 4	Chapter Assess
BL	OL	AL	ELL								
TEACH *(continued)*											
BL	OL			⊙	American Music: Hits Through History	✓	✓	✓	✓	✓	✓
BL	OL		ELL	📁	Reading Strategies for the Social Studies Classroom	✓	✓	✓	✓	✓	✓
			ELL	📁	English Language Learner Handbook	✓	✓	✓	✓	✓	✓
BL	OL		ELL	📁	Writer's Guidebook for Social Studies	✓	✓	✓	✓	✓	✓
BL	OL	AL	ELL	📁	Living Constitution, SE	✓	✓	✓	✓	✓	✓
BL	OL	AL	ELL	📁	Living Constitution, TAE	✓	✓	✓	✓	✓	✓
BL	OL			📁	NGS World Atlas, English	✓	✓	✓	✓	✓	✓
BL	OL		ELL	📁	The Constitution and You (poster set)	✓	✓	✓	✓	✓	✓
BL	OL	AL	ELL	📁	Spanish Chapter Summaries						
BL	OL	AL	ELL	📁	Spanish Vocabulary Activities						
BL	OL		ELL	📁	Spanish Reading Essentials and Study Guide (and Answer Key)		p. 149	p. 152	p. 156	p. 159	
BL	OL	AL	ELL	⊙	PresentationPlus! with MindJogger CheckPoint	✓	✓	✓	✓	✓	✓
ASSESS											
BL	OL	AL	ELL	⊙	*ExamView® Assessment Suite*		15-1	15-2	15-3	15-4	Ch. 15
BL	OL	AL	ELL	📁	Authentic Assessment with Rubrics		p. 21				p. 21
BL	OL	AL	ELL	📁	Section Quizzes and Chapter Tests		p. 181	p. 182	p. 183	p. 184	pp. 185–192
BL	OL	AL	ELL	📁	Spanish Section Quizzes and Tests		p. 181	p. 182	p. 183	p. 184	pp. 185–192
CLOSE											
BL			ELL	📁	Reteaching Activities				p. 14		p. 14
BL	OL	AL	ELL	⊙	StudentWorks™ Plus with Audio Summaries	✓	✓	✓	✓	✓	✓
BL	OL		ELL	🔨	Graphic Organizer Transparencies		✓	✓	✓	✓	
BL	OL		ELL	📁	High School Government Reading and Study Skills Foldables®		p. 57	p. 57	p. 57	p. 57	

Teach With Technology

What is Section Audio?
Section Audio is a recording of each section of the textbook. It helps students learn the content in the textbook.

How can Section Audio help my students?
Section Audio allows students to:
- read and listen simultaneously to improve content comprehension
- practice reading skills
- review important concepts for struggling readers
- improve listening

Visit glencoe.com to access the Media Library, and enter a *QuickPass*™ code to go to Section Audio recordings.

Government ONLINE
Visit glencoe.com and enter *QuickPass*™ code USG9085c15T for Chapter 15 resources.

You can easily launch a wide range of digital products from your computer's desktop with the McGraw-Hill Social Studies widget.

	Student	Teacher	Parent
Media Library			
• Student Edition Section Audio	●		●
• Chapter Spotlight Videos	●	●	●
***United States Government* Online Learning Center (Web Site)**			
• Chapter Overviews	●	●	●
• Multilingual Glossaries	●	●	●
• Study-to-Go	●	●	●
• Student Web Activities	●	●	●
• Self-Check Quizzes	●	●	●
• Online Student Edition	●	●	●
• Vocabulary eFlashcards	●	●	●
• Web Activity Lesson Plans		●	
• Vocabulary PuzzleMaker	●	●	●
• Landmark Supreme Court Cases	●	●	●
• Beyond the Textbook	●	●	●

READING SUPPORT FROM
JAMESTOWN EDUCATION

- **Timed Readings Plus in Social Studies** helps students increase their reading rate and fluency while maintaining comprehension. The 400-word passages are similar to those found on state and national assessments.

- **Reading in the Content Area: Social Studies** concentrates on six essential reading skills that help students better comprehend what they read. The book includes 75 high-interest nonfiction passages written at increasing levels of difficulty.

- **Reading Social Studies** includes strategic reading instruction and vocabulary support in Social Studies content for ELLs and native speakers of English. www.jamestowneducation.com

Reading List Generator CD-ROM

GLENCOE BOOKLINK 3

Use this database to search more than 30,000 titles to create a customized reading list for your students.

- Reading lists can be organized by students' reading level, author, genre, theme, or area of interest.

- The database provides Degrees of Reading Power™ (DRP) and Lexile™ readability scores for all selections.

- A brief summary of each selection is included.

Leveled reading suggestions for this chapter:

- *Choosing a Career in Law Enforcement,* by Claudine G. Wirths

- *Computer Crime,* by Robert L. Perry

- *Hidden Evidence: Forty True Crimes and How Forensic Science Helped Solve Them,* by David Owen

Review suggested books before assigning them.

Economics Connection

Personal Finance Literacy

Consumer Protection: Lemon Laws

Tell students that the Federal Trade Commission monitors commerce and some consumer protection laws. One of these is the Magnusson-Moss Warranty Act, which protects buyers of autos called "lemons." A lemon is a vehicle that continues to have a defect that substantially impairs its use, value, or safety after a reasonable number of attempts to fix it. Most states also have enacted lemon laws, which vary. Some define a lemon as a car repaired unsuccessfully four or more times for the same defect within the warranty period. In some states, lemon laws also exist for RVs, boats, motorcycles, wheelchairs, and computers.

Checklist for Buying a Vehicle

- Have a reliable technician inspect the vehicle, whether it is used or new.
- Notice what is covered by the service warranty. A used car may still be covered by the manufacturer's warranty or by a limited used-car warranty offered by some dealers.
- Check the reputation of various dealers' service departments. Warranties usually allow repairs by any dealer selling that make of vehicle.

Ask students to research their state's lemon law.

Documenting Repairs

- Keep a record of every repair visit. Include any Warranty Repair Orders and notes: whom you talk to, what is said, dates, and times. Even if there were no charges, get a copy of the invoice.

- Be sure the dealer records your complaint on the Warranty Repair Order exactly as you describe it. To document a lemon, you must describe the defect the same way at each repair visit.

- Record date, time in, odometer reading, and pick-up date and time. Cumulative time in the repair shop affects lemon-law coverage.

Did You Know?

Ralph Nader's 1965 book, *Unsafe at Any Speed,* championed safety improvements to U.S. vehicles and highways. In that year $320 million was spent beautifying highways, but just $500,000 on safety.

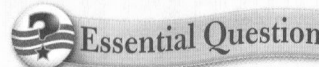

Essential Question

Although the American legal system derives from many sources, it most directly reflects the United States's British colonial heritage. English notions regarding common law and notions of the rights of citizens are embedded in the American legal system and the U.S. Constitution. In addition to common law, the legal system recognizes constitutional law, statutory law, and administrative law.

Chapter Spotlight Video

To generate student interest and provide a springboard for class discussion, access the Chapter 15 Video at glencoe.com or on the video DVD.

Dinah Zike's Foldables are three-dimensional, interactive graphic organizers that help students practice basic writing skills, review key vocabulary terms, and identify main ideas. Have students complete this chapter's Foldable activity or activities in *Dinah Zike's Reading and Study Skills Foldables* booklet. **OL**

Government ONLINE

Visit glencoe.com and enter **QuickPass**™ code USG9085c15T for Chapter 15 Resources including Chapter Overview, Student Web Activity, Self-Check Quiz, and other materials for students and teachers.

CHAPTER 15

🔊 **Chapter Audio**   📽 **Spotlight Video**

Law in America

▶ An Orleans Parish Criminal District Courtroom in New Orleans

Essential Question

What are the major sources for American law, and what key principles guide our legal system?

Government ONLINE

Chapter Overview Visit glencoe.com and enter **QuickPass**™ code USG9822c15 for an overview, a quiz, and other chapter resources.

414

Launching the Chapter

The Legal System in the News
Supplement students' reading and discussion of Chapter 15 by having them collect and study newspaper or magazine clippings that show the American legal system at work. For example, one day's newspaper might run a front-page article about a lawsuit being brought by a well-known person or against a well-known business; another day's issue might find letters to the editor praising or protesting a proposed change in a local law; an interview with a criminal attorney might appear in a regional or national magazine, and so forth. Ask students to select one clipping, summarize its content, and indicate how that content relates to the legal issues discussed in Chapter 15. **Essential Question: What is justice, and how does the American legal system serve that goal? OL**

Sources of American Law

Focus

Reader's Guide

Content Vocabulary
- ★ law *(p. 415)*
- ★ constitutional law *(p. 416)*
- ★ statute *(p. 417)*
- ★ ordinance *(p. 417)*
- ★ statutory law *(p. 417)*
- ★ administrative law *(p. 417)*
- ★ common law *(p. 418)*
- ★ equity *(p. 418)*
- ★ due process *(p. 419)*
- ★ substantive due process *(p. 419)*
- ★ procedural due process *(p. 419)*
- ★ adversary system *(p. 419)*
- ★ voir dire *(p. 420)*
- ★ presumed innocence *(p. 420)*

Academic Vocabulary
- ★ invoke *(p. 415)*
- ★ code *(p. 415)*
- ★ contradict *(p. 417)*

Reading Strategy
As you read, use a time line similar to the one below to list the sources of American law.

A.D. 534 — 1804
1792 B.C. — 1776

Bellringer
Section Focus Transparencies 15-1

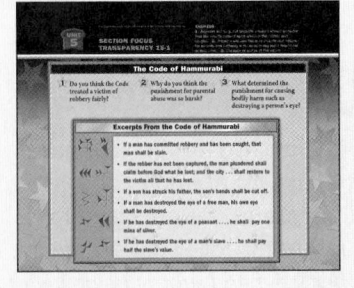

Reader's Guide

Answers to Graphic:

1792 B.C.: Hammurabi's Code

A.D. 534: Justinian Code

before 1776: English common law established in the American colonies

1804: Napoleonic Code

Issues in the News

Does due process protect grade school students from paddling? That is what some parents are saying as they file suit to stop teachers from disciplining their children physically. "Almost every democracy in the world has bans on corporal punishment—we're going in the opposite direction," one Ohio parent said. The practice remains legal in more than 20 states, but the parents of two students in one school are suing the school board. They argue that paddling violates the guarantee of equal protection. If it is illegal for those in authority to hit prisoners or nursing home residents, they say, then it is illegal to hit schoolchildren.

▲ **Does equal protection apply to disciplining in school?**

The due process these parents are **invoking** is a cornerstone of American **law.** Law is the set of rules and standards by which a society governs itself. In democratic societies, law resolves conflict between and among individuals and groups and protects the individual against government power. It defines criminal acts and determines the punishments for them. These are only some of its many functions. Laws affect nearly every part of our daily lives—the food we eat, how we drive our cars, how we buy and sell things, and even what happens when we are born or die.

A hallmark of democracy is the principle that no one is above the law, including government officials. Government policies and actions are to follow established laws and not merely reflect the whim of an individual.

Early Systems of Law

The earliest known written laws or rules were based on practices in tribal societies. The most well-known is the Code of Hammurabi, laws collected by Hammurabi, king of Babylonia from 1792 to 1750 B.C. The **code** categorized crimes and provided 282 examples and their punishments. Today we would refer to these categories as criminal law, property law, and family law, to name a few examples.

The Ten Commandments were one of the sources of law for the ancient Israelites. According to the Hebrew Bible, Moses received these commandments from God on Mount Sinai. The Ten Commandments' emphasis on social justice and individual and communal responsibility has become a model for ethical laws. These ideals have been adopted by much of the world.

Resource Manager

R Reading Strategies	C Critical Thinking	D Differentiated Instruction	W Writing Support	S Skill Practice
Teacher Edition • Supporting Key Ideas, p. 416 • Activating Prior Knowledge, p. 419 **Additional Resources** • Guid. Read. Act., p. 54 • Quizzes/Tests, p. 183	**Teacher Edition** • Categorizing, p. 417 **Additional Resources** • Read. Essen., pp. 163–165	**Teacher Edition** • Gifted and Talented, p. 419 **Additional Resources** • Foldables, p. 58 • Source Readings, p. 15	**Additional Resources** • Authentic Assess., p. 15	**Teacher Edition** • Interviewing, p. 420 **Additional Resources** • Hist. Docs. and Speeches, p. 15

Teach

R Reading Strategy

Supporting Key Ideas Have students list examples of constitutional and statutory laws that support the following statement: *Liberty depends upon the power of laws. (Examples include: Constitutional laws preserve individual rights and freedoms; statutory laws establish the age at which one can be licensed to drive.)* **OL**

Linking ★ Past & Present

Lord Coke and Common Law
Lord Edward Coke (1552–1634) helped establish the tradition of common law. He reinterpreted the Magna Carta, claiming that it embodied "the immemorial common law" of England and implied support for his views. For generations afterward, "the immemorial common law" was a catchphrase for the custom of English law.

Additional Support

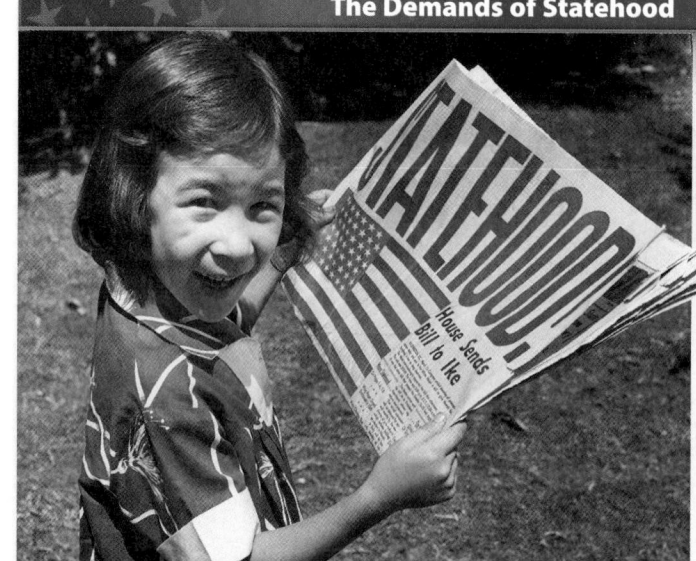

The Demands of Statehood

Constitutional Conventions
Hawaiians celebrated when Hawaii became a state in 1959, but in 1978 they convened to revise the state constitution. The new constitution included provisions to preserve Hawaiian culture. *Why do you think the new constitution reflected this goal?*

Our Legal Heritage

The laws that govern our lives and protect our rights can be classified as follows: **constitutional law** (the basic foundation law of a society), statutory law, administrative law, common law, and equity. We will look at each group below. These laws are addressed in state and federal constitutions, in legislation, in the regulations of administrative agencies, and in court interpretations of the law.

Constitutional Law

The Constitution is the most fundamental and important source of law in the United States. It establishes our country as a representative democracy, lays out the basic structure of the government, and sets forth basic rights. The Constitution is the supreme law of the land—the standard against which all other laws are judged. Both federal and state courts look to the Constitution to guide their decisions.

The term *constitutional law* applies to laws that interpret state and national constitutions—first and foremost cases involving the limits of government power and the rights of the individual. How we interpret the Constitution is influenced by the day-to-day decisions of the president, Congress, and other public officials. In the end, however, the courts, especially the Supreme Court, are the main

guide to the meaning and interpretation of constitutional law.

One example of a constitutional law issue would be a battle between the president and Congress over executive privilege—how much information the president must share with Congress on certain issues. That is because it involves separation of powers. This issue arose in 2007 when President George W. Bush at first claimed he did not have to tell Congress all the details of why certain federal prosecutors were fired.

What is the role of state constitutions in our system? In the United States, state constitutions were the first to be placed in writing. Of the original 13 states, 11 adopted written constitutions in the years between 1776 and 1780. Because state constitutions are easier to amend than the national Constitution, they are more likely to reflect changes in public concerns and public opinion. Some state constitutions also set forth rights that do not appear in the U.S. Constitution.

If a court case concerns an issue addressed in the state constitution, then a state court decides it. State courts usually use the Supreme Court's rulings on the Constitution as a guide for interpreting their own constitutions, but they do not have to.

Let us suppose that a person loses a case over a state constitutional issue in a state court. He or she could then appeal to the Supreme Court.

★ Activity: Collaborative Learning ★

Depicting a Theme Ask one or more groups of students to create murals that illustrate the theme "Sources of American Law." Have students divide the work so that everyone brainstorms and chooses what to show about ancient (Hammurabi's Code and the Ten Commandments) and more recent (constitutional, statutory, common, and administrative) sources of law. Some students can work on the layout; some students can supplement the text's discussion with additional research for artistic accuracy; some students can provide sketches and lettering; and everyone should color and provide finishing touches. Invite group representatives to explain the finished murals to the class. **OL**

Essentially that person would be claiming that the state constitution violated the U.S. Constitution. In short, the Supreme Court has the final word on what is lawful—no state constitution can be in conflict with it.

Statutory Law

Another source of American law is statutory law. A **statute** is a law that is written by a legislative branch of government. Statutory law is the body of all such laws passed by the U.S. Congress, state legislatures, and other governing bodies. (Statutes passed by city councils are called **ordinances.**) Here are some examples of citizen rights and limitations specified by statutes:

- a senior citizen's right to a Social Security check,
- a veteran's right to hospital care,
- a consumer's right to return merchandise,
- speed limits,
- food inspections, and
- minimum working age.

Most federal court decisions, including those of the Supreme Court, are related to **statutory law.** In these cases, the courts are deciding not only what a statute means but also whether it deprives a person of a basic constitutional right.

Statutory law is sometimes called Roman law because in some ways it resembles how ancient Romans made their laws. Rome's plebeians, or the common people, first demanded that the laws be written down so that everyone might know and understand them. As a result, the government published the Twelve Tables (for the tablets on which they were written) in about 450 B.C. The tables focused on different areas of law, such as family or criminal law.

As the Roman Empire spread, laws were continuously added so that the body of law became very complex and difficult to follow—some laws might **contradict** provisions of other laws. Emperor Justinian had scholars reorganize and simplify all the laws into a final Roman legal code, the Justinian Code, which was completed in A.D. 534.

The Justinian Code was one of Rome's greatest contributions to civilization. Many countries have written legal codes that reflect ideas in the Justinian Code. The most important was the Napoleonic Code created by French emperor Napoleon Bonaparte in 1804. It is still in force in France today. It was the model for legal systems in many European countries, in parts of Africa, in most of Latin

Loopy Laws Justice is blind—and sometimes strange. Some actual state laws and local statutes might make you wonder. In Alabama, you may not have an ice cream cone in your back pocket. People in Boston are not allowed to eat peanuts in church. Residents of Idaho may not fish from the back of a giraffe. Yamhill, Oregon, prohibits people from predicting the future.

America, and in Japan. In North America, both the state of Louisiana and the Canadian province of Quebec—once French colonies—have a system of laws based on the Napoleonic Code.

Administrative Law

Over the decades, government agencies have tended to multiply. Today all government levels have a large number of agencies that administer programs and provide services. The agencies range in size and power from the expansive Social Security Administration to the little-known Food and Nutrition Service. **Administrative law** spells out their authority level and procedures.

During the 1930s, when the nation suffered the Great Depression, many new federal agencies were created in an effort to provide American citizens with basic security, health, and unemployment insurance. Since then, administrative agencies have created a significant portion of our laws. Some legal scholars believe that this type of law is as important in regulating American society as statutory laws.

Administrative laws often affect people very directly. Will a social welfare agency decide that a certain family is eligible for Medicaid? Is a person who is laid off from work eligible for unemployment benefits? Because of their direct impact, people often dispute administrative laws in court. They might dispute their basic fairness or how these laws are being applied.

ISSUES to Debate

Administrative Authority Explain that many people who think that the federal government exercises too much control over a community or an individual often target administrative agencies as examples. Have students do some research into the size and power of administrative agencies and the laws to which those agencies are subject. **Ask:** Do current administrative laws allow federal agencies to have too much power over communities and individuals? **OL**

C Critical Thinking

Categorizing Read the following hypothetical situations to students and have them decide whether each situation is an example of statutory law or administrative law.

- the minimum age at which a person can be licensed to drive *(statutory)*
- the rules concerning the processing of applications for parade permits *(administrative)*
- the procedure by which an inquiry regarding a veteran's benefits would be investigated *(administrative)* **BL**

Hands-On Chapter Project

Step 1

Writing a News Report

Step 1: Planning a News Report Students will work in groups to prepare a television news report about an important Supreme Court decision. One member of each group will act as a television news anchor and give the report to the class.

Directions Have groups select a major Supreme Court case—recent or historical— and research the background of the justice who wrote the opinion. Tell them that they will use the information later to write a television news report, so they should take notes.

Presenting Ask students: What experience prepared this justice for his or her appointment to the Court? **OL**

(Chapter Project continued in Section 2.)

417

The Law *and* You

More About Choosing a Lawyer In general, a lawyer cannot practice law in a state until he or she has been recognized by that state's body of lawyers—its "bar." Most states require lawyers to pass a written bar examination (in most places, the Multistate Bar Examination) and sometimes a written ethics examination (such as the Multistate Professional Responsibility Examination). In most states, before a lawyer takes the bar exam, he or she must have had at least three years of college education and must have graduated from a law school approved by the American Bar Association. A person seeking the services of a lawyer would probably want to include these minimum standards as he or she considers the competency of the lawyer.

Additional Support

Common Law

The single most important basis of the American legal system is **common law,** also called case law. It is law made by judges as they resolve individual cases. It originated in England in the eleventh century as kings sent judges throughout the nation to hold trials. Judges began to record the facts of the cases and their decisions in yearbooks.

Eventually, judges began comparing facts and rulings from earlier cases to a current case. When a new case was similar to ones in the yearbooks, the judges followed the earlier ruling, or precedent. This was the origin of stare decisis (literally, it means "let the decision stand"), a basic principle guiding the judges' decisions. In cases without precedent, judges use common sense and customs, which creates precedents for future cases.

In the American colonies, English colonists used the common law they were familiar with. When they trained, colonial lawyers also studied English sources, especially the important four-volume work by William Blackstone. Blackstone's *Commentaries on the Laws,* which focused on the vast body of English common law, was published between 1765 and 1769. As a young lawyer,

Thomas Jefferson studied the *Commentaries,* as did other Founders of the American Republic.

After the American Revolution, Americans had to choose which parts of English law they would keep. Many states attempted to resist English influences, but English common law remained in force. State constitutions today and the U.S. Constitution are worded in language that reflects English common law. The practice of common law continues except in Louisiana, where legal procedures based on the Napoleonic Code persist.

Equity

Equity is a certain set of legal rules or principles that developed over time to supplement and sometimes overrule common law or statutory law in a decision. The word *equity* means "fairness," but this does not give one the key to understanding legal equity principles or imply that somehow statutory law or common law is not fair.

Principles of equity began to develop during medieval times. Defendants would appeal their cases to special courts of the king when a judgment under common law went against them. If the king's court felt that common law principles led to a

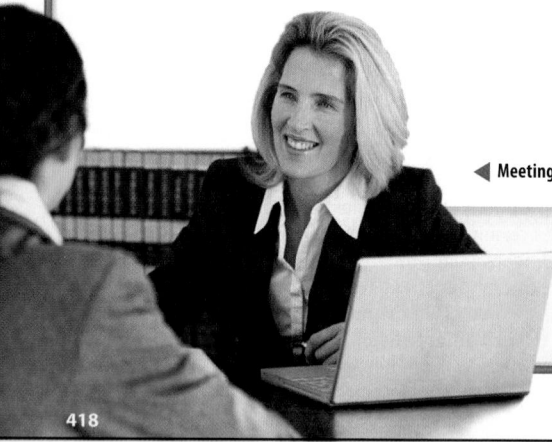

The Law *and* You

Choosing a Lawyer

You might want to hire a lawyer for many reasons. For example, if you were asked to sign a document that you did not completely understand, you would want to have a lawyer present. Some lawyers are general practitioners who take on many types of cases. Others specialize in a particular area, such as personal injury, divorce, or criminal cases. If you ever need an attorney, look for one who handles the kind of problem you have.

One of the best ways to choose a lawyer is to ask relatives and friends who have had a reason to use one. Another good source is the *Martindale-Hubbell Law Directory* in the library of your local courthouse. (A version of this directory also can be found online at www.martindale.com.) *Martindale-Hubbell* lists nearly every American lawyer by his or her specialty. Your county bar association also can refer you to a competent attorney.

Talking to more than one lawyer before hiring one is a good idea. Many lawyers will not charge for the first meeting.

◀ **Meeting with a lawyer**

Exploring the Law Activity
Make a List Imagine a situation that would require you to hire a lawyer. Prepare a list of questions for your first consultation with a lawyer.

418

Activity: Collaborative Learning

Drawing Conclusions In pairs, have students complete the following sentences. Students should be prepared to defend their statements based upon facts from this section:

- Within four years after the Declaration of Independence was signed, 11 of the 13 colonies adopted state constitutions. These constitutions reflected American legal principles by _____.

- Common-law decisions were an important part of England's legal system. They continue to influence the American legal system by _____.
- In American courtrooms, the adversary system of justice prevails. Although imperfect, it is the best system to carry out justice because _____.
- Proving an accused person's guilt is the responsibility of the prosecution. The

presumption of innocence is vital to ensuring the fairness of the legal system because _____.

Students may extend the activity by choosing other facts and drawing reasonable conclusions from them. **AL** harsh and unjustified result, that court could overrule the result. In time, certain principles of equity developed.

Today, when civil lawsuits are decided on principles of equity, it often means that the remedy fashioned by the court includes an injunction—a court order to do or not to do something—because a money payment would not fairly compensate the injured party. For example, a court might tell your neighbor that he or she cannot build a fence across your property: Merely having a payment from the neighbor would not get rid of the fence. In the 1800s, American equity and common law merged. Today a single court can administer both common law principles and principles of equity.

Legal System Principles

Four basic principles underlie how both federal and state courts operate. These principles are:

- equal justice under the law,
- due process of law,
- an adversary system of justice, and
- the presumption of innocence.

Equal Justice Under the Law

This principle states that the goal of the American court system is to treat all persons alike. Every person, regardless of wealth, social status, ethnic group, gender, or age, is entitled to the law's full protection. The equal justice principle grants all Americans the same rights, such as the right to a trial by a jury of one's peers. The Fifth through the Eighth Amendments to the Constitution spell out these guarantees.

Due Process of Law

This principle is closely related to the principle of equal justice. **Due process** has two parts: a substantive part and a procedural part. **Substantive due process** is a kind of shorthand for rights that are specified or implied in the Constitution, such as free speech or the right of privacy. Examples of laws that the Supreme Court has found to violate substantive due process include a law limiting dwellings to single families, thus preventing grandparents from living with their grandchildren, and a school regulation preventing a female teacher from returning to work sooner than three months after her child was born. **Procedural due process** concerns fairness in the way a case is handled. It prohibits arbitrary enforcement of the law and provides safeguards to

make sure that law enforcement is constitutional. At the most basic level, procedural due process requires (1) notice to a person that he or she is accused of wrongdoing and that the government intends to take action against that person, and (2) giving the affected person the right to respond or to be heard on the accusation.

The Adversary System

American courts operate under an **adversary system** of justice. This means that the courtroom

Due Process

Pretrial Release Lisa Nowak wept at the conclusion of her pretrial hearing in Florida in 2007. The former NASA astronaut was accused of stalking a female colleague, who was the girlfriend of another NASA employee. Nowak was approved for release before her trial only on the condition that she wear a tracking bracelet. *Why do you think being free before trial is important to a defendant's due process?*

R **Reading Strategy**

Activating Prior Knowledge
Ask: What rights are guaranteed by the Fifth through Eighth Amendments? *(If students have trouble answering, refer them to the **Reference Handbook** to review these amendments.)* **OL**

Caption Answer: A defendant can prepare his or her defense and maintain employment and family ties; it also reflects the accused person's right to a presumption of innocence.

D **Differentiated Instruction**

Gifted and Talented *Due process* refers to something to which people feel rightly entitled. Tell students that due process refers to *how* (procedural) and *why* (substantive) laws are enforced. The *how* aspect applies to issues such as: Is the legal system applying the same rules evenly to everyone? The *why* aspect concerns issues such as: Is the law reasonable and fair? Have students list legal scenarios that they believe would violate procedural or substantive due process. **AL**

Additional Support

Activity: Interdisciplinary Connection

History Share these quotations about the nature and purpose of laws:

- "The law is not an end in itself, nor does it provide ends. It is preeminently a means to serve what we think is right."—William J. Brennan
- "One with the law is a majority."—Calvin Coolidge

- "Our defense is not in armaments, nor in science, nor in going underground. Our defense is in law and order."—Albert Einstein

Have students discuss the meaning of each quotation, relating it to the power of laws and the extent to which laws govern various aspects of American life. **OL**

Caption Answer: because all defendants are entitled to the presumption of innocence

S Skill Practice

Interviewing Ask students to talk to adults who have served on jury duty and find out what types of questions potential jurors were asked during voir dire. Did the potential jurors believe that their answers influenced whether they were selected to be on a jury? **OL**

Assess

Assign the Section 1 Assessment as homework or as an in-class activity, or have students take Section Quiz 15-1 from *Section Quizzes and Chapter Tests*.

Close

Determining Cause and Effect Have students complete these cause-and-effect sentences in as many ways as they can. Discuss their responses.

• We have laws because _____.

• Because we have laws, _____. **OL**

Section 1 Review

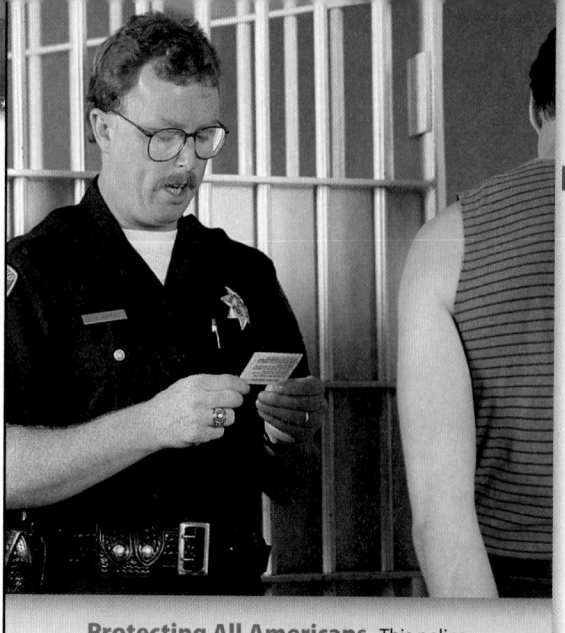

Protecting All Americans This police officer reads a suspect his rights. Proper procedures must be followed when police arrest and the courts try suspected offenders. *Why should the rights of people who may be criminals be protected?*

is an arena in which lawyers for the opposing sides are adversaries and that the lawyer who makes the better case will win. Lawyers on each side will try to present their best legal arguments in order to win. Part of what helps a lawyer win a case is doing a good job during **voir dire**, the jury selection process in which lawyers on both sides interview potential jurors. In the American tradition, lawyers are expected to do all that is legally allowed to win the case. The judge in the court should be impartial—as fair as possible to both sides.

Some observers have attacked the adversary system. They claim that it encourages lawyers to ignore evidence that is not favorable to their side and to be more concerned about victory than about justice. Supporters answer that the adversary system is the best way to bring out all the facts.

Presumption of Innocence

The fourth basic principle of the American justice system is that people who are charged or accused are presumed to be innocent until the state proves that they are guilty. Although the idea of **presumed innocence** is not mentioned in the Constitution, it is deeply rooted in the English legal heritage. The burden of proving an accusation falls on the prosecution—defendants do not have to prove their innocence.

Since the state's police and prosecutorial powers are so great, this principle has the effect of creating a more balanced fight between prosecution and defense. Unless the prosecution can prove the accusation, the court must declare that the defendant is not guilty.

SECTION 1 Review

Vocabulary

1. **Explain** the significance of: law, constitutional law, statute, ordinance, statutory law, administrative law, common law, equity, due process, substantive due process, procedural due process, adversary system, voir dire, presumed innocence.

Main Ideas

2. **Analyzing** Explain the differences among constitutional law, statutory law, and administrative law.

3. **Describing** Why is common law, or case law, the most important basis of the American legal system?

Critical Thinking

4. **Synthesizing** If a rental agency refuses to rent to families with children, what kind of due process is violated?

5. **Categorizing** In a graphic organizer, identify the major sources of American law and the key principles of the American legal system.

American Law	
Sources	Principles

Writing About Government

6. **Expository Writing** Laws affect nearly everything people do. Laws change to meet the needs of the times. Work with a partner to brainstorm new laws or to identify laws that should be repealed. Write a one-page summary identifying a situation that requires a new law to be established or an existing law to be repealed.

Answers

1. All definitions can be found in the section and the Glossary.
2. Constitutional law applies to the branch of law that deals with interpretation of the Constitution; statutory law deals with laws written by a legislative branch of the government; and administrative law details the procedures to be followed by local, state, and federal government agencies and the rules and regulations issued by these agencies.
3. Common law is law made by judges in the process of resolving individual cases. Judges use facts and rulings from earlier cases as precedents for deciding new cases.
4. As an unreasonable regulation, it would violate substantive due process.
5. Sources: United States Constitution, statutory law, administrative law, common law; Principles: rule of law, equal justice under the law, due process, adversary system, presumed innocence
6. Students' skits might suggest laws that deal with genetic engineering, space exploration, DNA testing, and so on.

Can a Method of Capital Punishment Constitute Cruel and Unusual Punishment?

Baze et al. v. *Rees*, 2008

The death penalty has been outlawed in a number of states, but this case tested whether a particular method of capital punishment was unconstitutional. Did Kentucky's method of lethal injection cause such pain that it violated the Eighth Amendment?

Facts of the Case

In 2007 Ralph Baze and another inmate on Kentucky's death row asked the Supreme Court to review the state's method of lethal injection. Baze and the second inmate, both convicted of double murders, first appealed to the Kentucky Supreme Court, which upheld the state's method. Although they had not yet been given an execution date, they argued that the state's method violated the Eighth Amendment's prohibition of cruel and unusual punishment. Lethal injection was adopted in the late 1970s as a method that was considered more humane than the electric chair, the gas chamber, or other methods. Lethal injection is used by the federal government and in more than 30 states. Most of them use the same three-drug "cocktail" as Kentucky: one drug induces unconsciousness, the second mainly causes paralysis, and the third causes cardiac arrest.

The Constitutional Issue

Lawyers for the inmates argued that the specific Kentucky formula presented an "unnecessary risk of inflicting needless pain and suffering"—especially since the second paralyzing drug made it impossible to discern the inmates' suffering. Further they said that the state standards were wide-ranging in describing what represented acceptable suffering in an execution; thus, the Court needed to establish a consistent standard. Finally, they said that there was no reason for the state not to use other available drug combinations that would reduce the risk of suffering.

Kentucky countered with three main arguments. First, the risk of any inmate being conscious during an execution was very remote. Second, the lethal injection method the state used did not expose inmates to a substantial risk of wanton or unnecessary pain. Finally, Kentucky said that the standard the inmates wanted would lead to endless litigation tying up the courts. Death row inmates would constantly be asking for changes in the injection drugs used. They also would be filing lawsuits based on whether a state was using the best procedures to guarantee an uncomplicated execution.

Debating the Issue

◀ Ralph Baze during an interview in the Kentucky State Penitentiary

Questions to Consider

1. Explain why the state wants to use a standard of "substantial risk" and why the inmates' lawyers want the standard of "unnecessary risk."

2. What objection did Kentucky raise about the future impact of overthrowing the three-drug "cocktail" currently in use?

You Be the Judge

In your opinion, does Kentucky's method of lethal injection violate the Eighth Amendment? Should the Court create a specific method of lethal injection and guarantee that individuals who are being executed not suffer unnecessary pain?

CHAPTER 15: *Law in America* **421**

Debating the Issue Answers

Questions to Consider

1. The state wants a weaker standard to avoid endless and costly litigation. The inmates' lawyers want a stricter test to delay the execution and to be sure that it is done in a manner that is pain-free.

2. Execution methods would be challenged and changed constantly.

You Be the Judge

Answers will vary, but students should decide whether they agree or disagree with the Court's ruling on the constitutionality of Kentucky's method of lethal injection. Students should decide whether or not the Court should select a specific method of lethal injection.

Class Debate

Ask students to form two groups based on their opinion about what the Supreme Court's ruling on this case should be. Then have each group write a majority opinion and a dissenting opinion. Have each group argue its case, and then ask students to reevaluate their opinions. Have students form new groups based on their reevaluations. Ask students who changed their minds to explain why they did so.

The Court's Decision

In the case of *Baze et al.* v. *Rees*, the Supreme Court, by a 7-to-2 vote, upheld the constitutionality of Kentucky's lethal injection protocol. The Court said that there was no Eighth Amendment requirement that executions be administered pain-free. All that the Eighth Amendment requires is that there be no "substantial or objectively intolerable risk of serious harm." Chief Justice John Roberts wrote in the majority opinion: "He must show that the risk is substantial when compared to the known and available alternatives." The Court also noted that the Eighth Amendment did not require execution methods to change every time a marginally safer alternative was identified, stating: "Permitting an Eighth Amendment violation to be established on such a showing would threaten to transform courts into boards of inquiry charged with determining 'best practices' for executions."

Focus

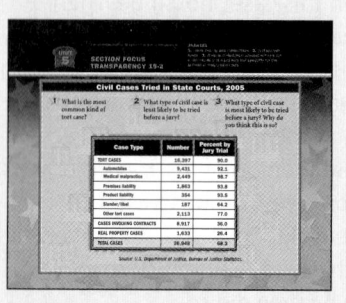
Reader's Guide

Answers to Graphic:
hiring a lawyer →
filing the complaint →
pretrial discovery →
resolution without trial

Resource Manager

Civil Law

Reader's Guide

Content Vocabulary
★ civil law (p. 422)
★ contract (p. 422)
★ expressed contract (p. 422)
★ implied contract (p. 422)
★ real property (p. 423)
★ personal property (p. 423)
★ mortgage (p. 423)
★ tort (p. 423)
★ plaintiff (p. 424)
★ defendant (p. 424)
★ injunction (p. 424)
★ complaint (p. 425)
★ summons (p. 425)
★ answer (p. 425)
★ discovery (p. 425)
★ mediation (p. 425)
★ affidavit (p. 426)

Academic Vocabulary
★ phase (p. 422)
★ circumstance (p. 422)
★ explicit (p. 423)

Reading Strategy
As you read, create a graphic organizer similar to the one below to list the steps in a civil case that does not go to trial.

☐ → ☐ → ☐ → ☐

Issues in the News

Accidents will happen, but when are accidents predictable? If an accident is predictable, could it have been prevented? If a flying hockey puck hits you in the head during the game, is the team or stadium owner responsible? This is the situation that occurred in 2002 when a young girl who was attending an ice hockey game in Columbus, Ohio, was hit and subsequently died. Was it just a "freak accident"? The father of the girl believed otherwise. "A freak accident is a meteor falling out of the skies and striking you. I call this a preventable accident."

▲ Ice hockey manager Doug MacLean spoke to the media about a tragic hockey puck accident in 2002.

If an injured fan were to sue a sports team, it would be a civil case. Civil law concerns disputes among two or more people, or between individuals and the government. Civil cases arise when people believe they have suffered an injury or want to prevent a harmful action.

Types of Civil Law

Civil law touches nearly every **phase** of daily life—from buying a house to getting married. About 90 percent of state court cases are civil cases. There are four important types of civil law:

- contracts,
- property,
- family relations, and
- torts (civil injuries to a person or property).

Contracts

A **contract** is a set of voluntary promises, enforceable by the law, between parties who agree to do or not to do certain things. We enter into contracts all the time: when we join a health club, buy a car on credit, marry, or agree to do a job. That is why so many civil suits involve disputes over a contract. In an **expressed contract,** the terms are specifically stated by the parties, usually in writing. In an **implied contract,** the terms are not stated but can be inferred from what people do and the **circumstances.**

What makes a contract valid? First, each party must be mentally competent. Usually they must be adults, and finally, the contract's terms cannot involve any illegal activity. Typically a contract has three basic elements: an offer, an acceptance, and a consideration (money paid for the offer).

R Reading Strategies	C Critical Thinking	D Differentiated Instruction	W Writing Support	S Skill Practice
Teacher Edition • Accessing Prior Knowledge, p. 425 **Additional Resources** • Guid. Read. Act., p. 55 • Quizzes/Tests, p. 184	**Teacher Edition** • Drawing Conclusions, p. 426 **Additional Resources** • Read. Essen., pp. 166–169	**Additional Resources** • Foldables, p. 58 • Coop. Learning Act., pp. 9–10	**Teacher Edition** • Expository Writing, pp. 423, 424 **Additional Resources** • Part. in Gov. Act., pp. 29–30	**Teacher Edition** • Using the Internet, p. 427 **Additional Resources** • Inter. Poli. Cartoons, pp. 29–30

For instance, the auto shop says that it will repair your smashed bumper for $500—this is the offer. If you agree in writing or orally to have the bumper fixed, that is the acceptance. Finally, the auto shop owner and you exchange something of value—$500 in return for a repaired bumper.

Property Law

As the name implies, property law is civil law that deals with the use and ownership of property. The U.S. Constitution **explicitly** established the right of individuals to own, buy, and sell property in the Fifth and Fourteenth Amendments. The courts have defined property as either:

- **Real property**—land and whatever is attached to or growing on it (houses, trees, etc.), or
- **Personal property**—all other property, including movable items like clothes and cars and intangible items like stocks and bonds.

Many legal disputes concern property. Owners of houses might fail to repair them or discriminate against minorities when they rent or sell property. Buying a house is the biggest financial investment most Americans can make. Thus, the federal and state governments have passed many laws to ensure that discrimination does not prevent any American from obtaining a **mortgage**—a loan to pay for the house. The key law prohibiting discrimination on the basis of race, religion, gender, or national origin is the federal Fair Housing Act passed in 1968.

Family Law

Another branch of civil law deals with family relationships, including marriage, divorce, child custody and child support issues. The family courts that handle such matters are some of the busiest in the nation.

In the United States, family law developed outside of religion because there is no state church. Marriage became a civil contract with the requirements set by each state. In the 1800s, two forms of marriage were possible in the United States—the civil ceremony under the authority of the individual state and common-law marriage. Because many men and women lived in rural areas where there were no clergy, many marriages were agreements that had no religious or official sanction. The law recognizes such marriages as valid. Common-law marriages are still valid in some states, but most marriages are civil contracts.

Family law is changing rapidly as the meaning of the family changes. In a number of states, same-sex unions are recognized, but in other states, they are not. This has meant that gay couples have gone to court to adopt children or to ensure that both people in the relationship can have rights as parents.

Torts or Civil Wrongs

A **tort** is any wrongful act (other than breaking a contract) for which an injured person can sue for damages in a civil court. What are examples of torts? Suppose that neighbors did not clear ice

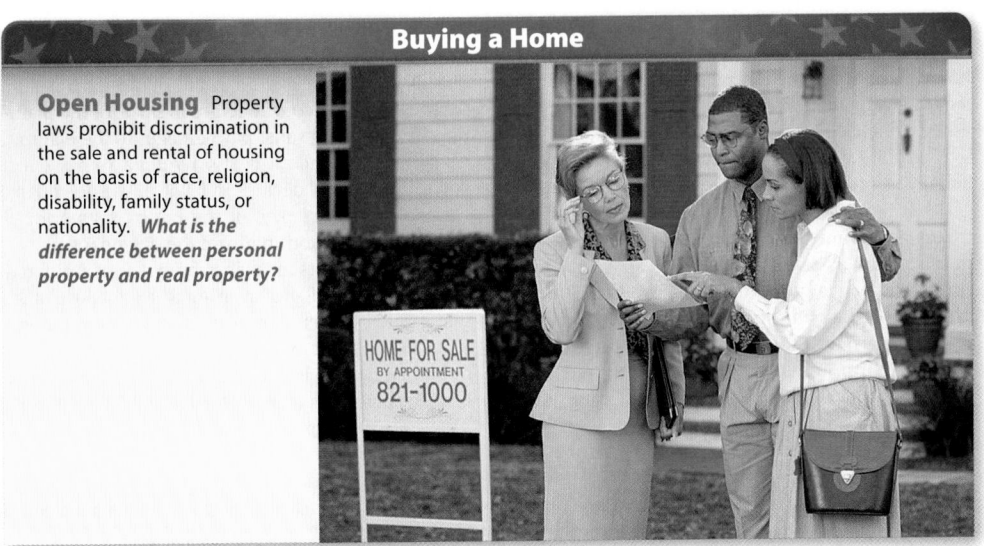

Buying a Home

Open Housing Property laws prohibit discrimination in the sale and rental of housing on the basis of race, religion, disability, family status, or nationality. *What is the difference between personal property and real property?*

HOME FOR SALE
BY APPOINTMENT
821-1000

Teach

W Writing Support

Expository Writing Have students research the laws regarding marriage in your state. Then have students write essays that address issues such as the minimum age at which a minor can be married with parental or guardian consent, prerequisites to being married, and laws regarding same-sex unions. **OL**

Did You Know?

Contracts often are classified as unilateral or bilateral. In a unilateral contract, one party agrees to pay (or give other consideration to) the other for meeting the obligations established in the contract. In a bilateral contract, each party promises something to the other.

Caption Answer: Personal property includes movable things and intangible items; real property refers to land and whatever is attached to it.

Hands-On Chapter Project

Step 2

Writing a News Report

Step 2: Analyzing a Court Opinion Have the groups analyze the Court's ruling in the case they selected in Step 1. They will use their analysis to write the news report.

Directions Ask students to answer these questions about the opinion in note form:
- What was the basis for the Court's decision?
- Is the language eloquent, memorable, and clear? What sections of the opinion are appropriate to use in a news report?

- Was there a dissenting opinion? If so, what was the dissenting justices' reason for disagreeing with the majority?
- What group of citizens will the Court's ruling affect, and how?

Summarizing Have students discuss the elements of Court opinions. **OL**

(Chapter Project continued in Section 3.)

CURRICULUM CONNECTION

Law Equity law developed in England when the common law system became so technical that it could not deal with cases that did not meet its rules precisely. As a result, a litigant had to be sure that he or she was bringing a complaint to the right court—the court of law or the court of equity. In the United States, the two kinds of court systems were combined under the Code of Civil Procedure, written in 1848. England unified its two-court system in the mid-1870s.

W Writing Support

Expository Writing Have students write a paragraph explaining why the law would force the plaintiff to pay court costs if he or she loses the case. Include at least one benefit and one drawback to this legal requirement. **BL**

Differentiated Instruction

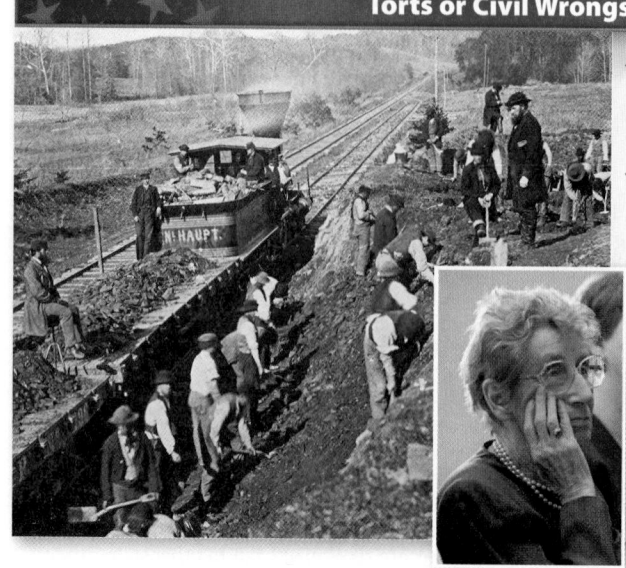

Torts or Civil Wrongs

◀ **Past** Difficult and dangerous conditions for early railway construction led to an increase in tort cases in the 1800s.

▼ **Present** In a famous tort case, Stella Liebeck sued McDonald's for third-degree burns she received from their coffee. Jurors heard that 180-degree coffee would produce third-degree burns in 12 to 15 seconds; lowering the temperature a few degrees would allow for a margin of safety.

Laws Through the Ages
What factors might a jury look at in a complex tort case?

from the sidewalk in front of their house and your mother fell and broke her hip. Your mother could sue in civil court for reasonable costs associated with the injury. She could even ask for more money to punish the neighbors to ensure that they would clear sidewalk ice in the future—the additional money is referred to in the courts as punitive damages.

Before the Industrial Revolution, tort law was not well-developed. In the late 1800s, almost every leading case had to do with railroads. Courts hesitated to award damages to injured workers because they feared doing so would hurt businesses. By the 1900s, however, the state and federal governments began to issue safety regulations for industry, and courts established a doctrine of liability for industrial hazards.

There are two major kinds of torts—intentional and unintentional. An intentional tort is a deliberate act that harms a person or property. Slander and assault and battery are intentional torts that are tried in civil courts. (Assault and battery can also be tried under criminal law, but then the burden of proof is greater, as is the punishment.) An unintentional tort is doing harm without intending to, but still the resulting harm was predictable. For example, some kinds of practical jokes might obviously carry a risk of injuring someone.

Negligence is an unintentional tort that involves careless or reckless actions. A person is negligent when he or she fails to do something a reasonable person would have done, or does something a prudent person would not have done. Leaving a sharp kitchen knife where small children could easily reach it or not having the brakes checked on an old car with high mileage are examples of negligence that could result in legal liability if someone were injured.

Steps in a Civil Case

Civil cases are called lawsuits. The **plaintiff** is the person who brings charges in a lawsuit, called the complaint. The person against whom the suit is brought is the **defendant.** The plaintiff in a civil suit usually seeks damages, an award of money from the defendant. If the court decides in favor of the plaintiff, the defendant must pay damages to the plaintiff. Usually the defendant is also required to pay court costs. If the court decides in favor of the defendant, the plaintiff must pay all the court costs and, of course, receives nothing from the defendant.

In some lawsuits involving equity, the plaintiff may ask the court to issue an **injunction,** a court order that forbids a defendant from taking or continuing a certain action. For example, suppose a company plans to build a factory in the middle of a residential area. Citizens believe that the factory would pollute the air. They take the factory owner to court and argue that residents would suffer serious health problems if the factory is constructed. If the citizens win this suit under equity principles, the judge issues an injunction ordering the company not to build its factory.

424 UNIT 5: *Liberty and Justice for All*

Activity: Multiple Learning Styles

Interpersonal Mediation can keep many civil disputes from going to trial. A mediator must be skilled in dealing with people and understanding how opposing parties think. Ask students with strong interpersonal skills to write or talk about what they think a mediator might say to persuade the opposing parties in any of the following situations to settle their civil dispute out of court:

• A person who is denied a loan believes that she has been the victim of discrimination.

• A customer wants compensation for fracturing an arm when he fell on a wet floor in a supermarket.

• Family members are debating the distribution of a deceased person's personal belongings.

• A married couple is seeking a divorce. **OL**

Lawsuits are the ultimate way to settle disputes, but they can be time-consuming and expensive with no guarantee of success. There are standard stages in how lawsuits proceed:

- hiring a lawyer,
- filing a complaint,
- pretrial discovery,
- resolution without trial,
- trial, and
- the award.

Hiring a Lawyer

To start a lawsuit, a person almost always needs a lawyer. Lawyers can work for a contingency fee (typically from one-fifth to one-half of the money won in the lawsuit) or for an hourly fee. The lawyer gets nothing if the plaintiff and attorney agreed to a contingency fee and the case is lost. However, the plaintiff pays for court costs such as copying documents or fees for experts.

Filing the Complaint

The plaintiff sets forth the charges against the defendant in a **complaint,** a legal document filed with the court that has jurisdiction. (Unless a case involves the U.S. Constitution or a federal matter, lawsuits are filed in state courts.) The complaint states what the defendant allegedly did wrong, allowing the defendant to mount a defense. The defendant receives a **summons,** an official notice with the date, time, and place of the initial court appearance.

The defendant's lawyer may file a motion to dismiss, asking the court to end the suit. If the court says no, the defendant must then file an **answer,** or formal response to the charges within a certain time, usually 10 to 60 days. Failure to answer gives the plaintiff a victory by default. The defendant can also respond by filing a counterclaim, or lawsuit against the plaintiff in which the defendant asserts that the plaintiff did something wrong.

Pretrial Discovery

The next step, **discovery,** occurs when both sides prepare for trial by checking facts and gathering evidence for their case. The attorneys and private investigators in major cases interview witnesses, examine records and photos, and file motions against the other side. Discovery can be very expensive as well as time-consuming. In complex cases, it can take months or years.

Resolution Without Trial

Ninety percent of all civil lawsuits are settled before trial through one of several techniques, including settlement, **mediation,** and arbitration.

First, either party in a lawsuit can come to a settlement at any time, even during the trial. It often happens during the discovery phase because costs accumulate and influence the parties to compromise. Judges may encourage people to settle by calling a pretrial conference to talk things over. The court can even require people to settle out of court.

Belva Lockwood

(1830–1917) From humble beginnings, Belva Lockwood went on to pave the way for female lawyers in the United States. After completing her legal studies, Lockwood was able to get her law degree only after presenting her complaint to President Ulysses S. Grant. She then spent years working for the passage of laws that would require federal courts to accept female attorneys, a victory that was achieved in 1879. Lockwood also ran twice for president (in 1884 and 1888) as the candidate of the Equal Rights Party. In 1906 she became the first female attorney to argue before the Supreme Court.

R Reading Strategy

Accessing Prior Knowledge
Ask: Why does Louisiana not follow common-law principles? *(It was once French territory, and its legal system is based on the Napoleonic Code.)* **OL**

Caption Answer: Common-law principles still apply in the United States because they are based on custom and precedent.

Additional Support

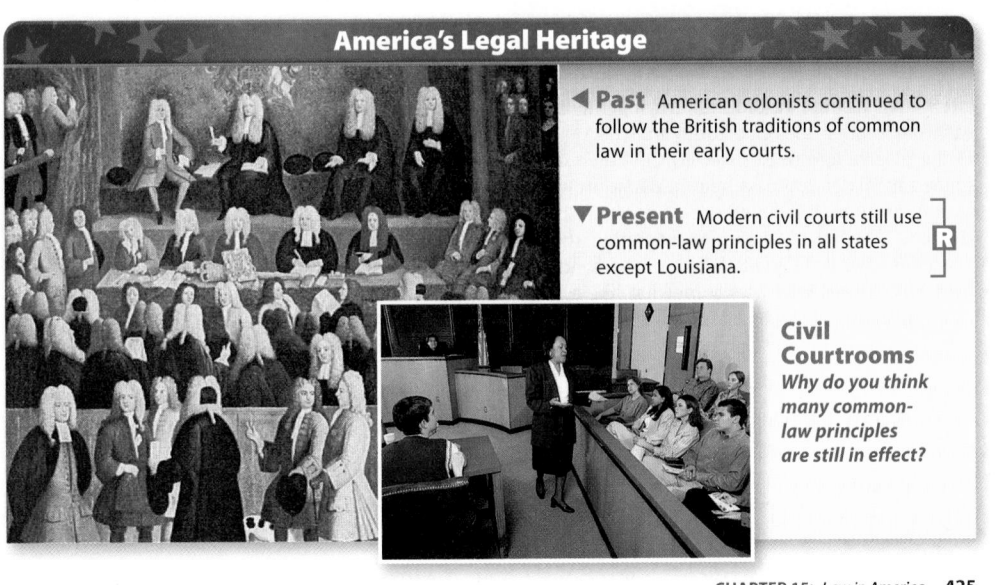

America's Legal Heritage

◄ **Past** American colonists continued to follow the British traditions of common law in their early courts.

▼ **Present** Modern civil courts still use common-law principles in all states except Louisiana.

Civil Courtrooms
Why do you think many common-law principles are still in effect?

CHAPTER 15: *Law in America* **425**

Activity: Collaborative Learning

Formulating Questions Discuss the difference between objective and subjective tests. An objective test, such as a multiple-choice test, is one that can be scored with a single answer key. Unless a scoring mistake is made, scores will be the same no matter who scores the test. A subjective test, on the other hand, can be scored differently by different scorers. Explain how to construct closed-ended, unambiguous questions from which respondents can choose only one correct answer. Then have each student create a 10-question, multiple-choice quiz covering the discussion of civil law in this section. Pair off students to take each other's quizzes. Have the student who created the quiz grade it and discuss incorrect answers with the student who took the quiz. Allow each student to critique the other's questions. **OL**

C Critical Thinking

Drawing Conclusions In criminal cases, the prosecutor must prove that a defendant is guilty "beyond a reasonable doubt." In civil cases, the plaintiff only has to present "a preponderance of evidence" to demonstrate that the defendant *more likely than not* was responsible for the incident that caused the damages or injury. **Ask:** Why is the burden of proof higher in criminal cases? *(The consequences of a criminal conviction are much more serious; a higher standard of proof is required before someone is sentenced to prison or even to death.)* **OL**

Additional Support

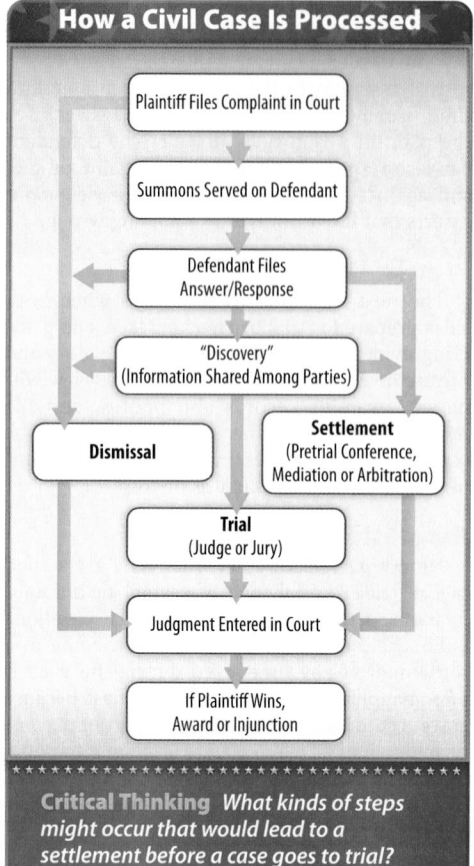

How a Civil Case Is Processed

Plaintiff Files Complaint in Court

Summons Served on Defendant

Defendant Files Answer/Response

"Discovery" (Information Shared Among Parties)

Dismissal

Settlement (Pretrial Conference, Mediation or Arbitration)

Trial (Judge or Jury)

Judgment Entered in Court

If Plaintiff Wins, Award or Injunction

Critical Thinking *What kinds of steps might occur that would lead to a settlement before a case goes to trial?*

Mediation and arbitration are both types of alternative dispute resolution. During mediation, each side is given the opportunity to explain its side of the dispute and must listen to the other side. A trained mediator acts as a neutral party, promoting communication, but he or she does not impose a solution. If both parties agree to arbitration, the process is somewhat different. Arbitration is conducted by a professional who acts somewhat like a judge. The arbitrator reviews evidence and decides on a solution; the decision usually applies to everyone.

Trial

C If all else fails, lawsuits go to trial, although the courts are so crowded that this can take years. Civil trials, like criminal trials, may be heard by a judge only or by a jury of 6 to 12 people. Plaintiffs give their side first, followed by the defendants.

Both sides summarize their cases, and the judge or jury renders a verdict.

The Award

As was discussed in Section 1, common-law courts and equity courts have merged. (See page 418.) This means that a court can use either case law or the equity principles when a case is decided. Judges also have more flexibility to adjust jury decisions.

When the plaintiff wins a case, the court can award monetary damages, issue an injunction, or both. (Punitive damages are another possible type of award. These are awarded not to compensate the plaintiff but to reform the defendant's practices in an attempt to prevent similar suits in the future.)

An award might be more or less than the plaintiff wanted. A judge can also modify a jury's award if he or she believes it is out of line. In the McDonald's coffee case referred to on page 424, the judge reduced the punitive damages that the jury recommended from $2.7 million to $640,000. However, he agreed that it "was appropriate to punish and deter" McDonald's from continuing their current method of coffee preparation.

Even after an award is made, the case may continue if the loser appeals the judgment or refuses to pay the damages. If the defendant refuses to pay, the plaintiff can get a court order to enforce the payment in one of several ways—taking money from a paycheck or savings account, or by seizing property.

Small Claims Court

Most states have created small claims courts as a legal alternative to the expensive and lengthy trial process. In small claims courts, no lawyers are necessary because judges decide the cases. The fees for filing a claim are only $10 or $15 and the application to file is simple. The defendant, or person the claim is filed against, has from two to four weeks to respond, and then a court date is set.

Small claims courts hear civil cases involving claims ranging from $1,000 to $5,000. A typical case might be someone who files a claim saying a tenant in an apartment damaged property worth $1,000. The plaintiff, or person who is making the charge, brings evidence to court and explains the case. The evidence might include testimony from witnesses or their affidavits. An **affidavit** is a statement that is written and sworn to in the presence of an authorized person, such as a notary public. If a defendant fails to appear for the hearing, the plaintiff usually wins the claim.

Activity: Interdisciplinary Connection

Health Have students work individually or collaboratively to show how some civil disputes might arise from health issues. Offer the following mini-projects, or let students choose their own:

- Locate an advertisement for a piece of exercise equipment or a nutritional supplement for which the promised results seem suspect. What legal action might an unsatisfied customer take?

- Talk to someone who has joined a gym. Does that person believe that the contract was fair?

- Look in the Yellow Pages for listings of specialists in family law. Might a divorced parent want to consult one of these specialists if he or she believed that the child's custodial parent was not providing proper medical attention for their son or daughter?

- Under what circumstances might a person sue a nursing-care facility? **OL**

E-Filing Court Cases

1. Inform us about your problem
2. Choose your filing place
3. Answer basic questions
4. EZLegalFile will complete your court forms
5. Review your forms. Print and mail or bring your forms to the court. E-Delivery coming soon
6. Court notifies you about your appearance date

Source: California Superior Court.

Critical Thinking The diagram above is similar to the one used on the state of California's Web site explaining how residents can file a case for the state court system online. *What issues do you think some people might have with filing online? Would different income groups react differently to this method of filing?*

Charts In MOtion See StudentWorks™ Plus or go to glencoe.com.

Critical Thinking

Answer: People might be concerned about how secure information submitted electronically would be. Others might lack the necessary computer skills or not have Internet access.

S Skill Practice

Using the Internet Have students search the Internet to find the Web site for your state's court system and assess how helpful and user-friendly it is. **OL**

Assess

Assign the Section 2 Assessment as homework or as an in-class activity, or have students take Section Quiz 15-2 from *Section Quizzes and Chapter Tests*.

Close

Thinking Hypothetically Ask students to imagine that they are about to appear in small claims court. Call on volunteers to explain the nature of their hypothetical case, their decision to settle the matter in this fashion, and their desired results. **OL**

Winning a judgment in small claims court does not guarantee the collection of a payment. If the defendant is unwilling or unable to pay, the plaintiff can get a court order requiring payment and give it to the police or sheriff to enforce the order.

One trend the National Association for State Courts has noted is an increase in the handling of cases electronically. In the 10 years, between 1997 and 2007, half of all states made e-filing an option for **S** self-litigators, people who are handling their own lawsuits in a court. When courts first began to create Web sites, they provided basic information, such as directions to the courthouse. More and more, however, the goal of court Web sites has been to increase access to justice for self-litigants and to provide access to information for anyone in the community who wants to know about a case or an issue. Another goal has been to cut costs by offering downloadable forms and the ability to assemble case documents.

Web technology is expected to help lawyers and court staff, too, through the use of "RSS" feeds (Really Simple Syndication). These could give court customers real-time alerts to content in their specific area of expertise or interest.

SECTION 2 Review

Section 2 Review

Vocabulary

1. **Explain** the significance of: civil law, contract, expressed contract, implied contract, real property, personal property, mortgage, tort, plaintiff, defendant, injunction, complaint, summons, answer, discovery, mediation, affidavit.

Main Ideas

2. **Describing** What do four of the most important branches of civil law deal with?

3. **Analyzing** What is the difference between intentional tort and negligence tort?

Critical Thinking

4. **Drawing Conclusions** Should mediation and arbitration be used to settle most civil lawsuits? Explain.

5. **Organizing** Use a graphic organizer like the one below to show the five steps in a civil lawsuit.

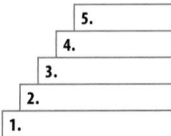

Writing About Government

6. **Expository Writing** Interview an individual who has been involved in a lawsuit or in small claims court. Find out the nature of the dispute and how the lawsuit was resolved. Make sure you get the individual's permission before discussing the case in class. Write a brief summary of your findings to the class.

CHAPTER 15: *Law in America* **427**

Answers

1. All definitions can be found in the section and the Glossary.
2. contracts, property, family relations, torts
3. An intentional tort involves a deliberate act that results in harm to a person or property; negligence involves careless or reckless behavior in which a person fails to do something that a reasonable person would have done.
4. Answers will vary. Students might be in general agreement in favoring resolutions without trials, but some students might stress that going to trial should remain an option.
5. 1. hiring a lawyer; 2. complaint; 3. discovery; 4. trial; 5. award
6. Students' findings will vary.

Teach

Setting Up the Debate

Accessing Prior Knowledge
Have students brainstorm alternate ways to encourage better services and practices without lawsuits. **Ask:** Are any of these alternatives better than the current tort laws? Discuss the pros and cons of each. *(Students should discuss the pros and cons of different methods of encouraging better services, and so on.)*

Evaluating Have students research the arguments for and against reforming tort laws. Students should give specific arguments to support both points of view.

Concluding the Debate

Discuss these questions with students:

- Are too many frivolous and unfounded lawsuits filed?
- What are your state's laws on punitive damages? Should those damages be capped?

Should Tort Laws Be Reformed?

The American legal system has long allowed someone to sue a person or a business for tort, or personal injury. People sue for damages, usually a monetary payment, to compensate them for financial suffering due to a physical injury (a workplace injury or medical malpractice, for example). The possibility of being sued is meant to encourage better services and products, but are too many unfounded lawsuits filed? Do such lawsuits drive up the costs of services and professional practices for everyone?

YES

The federal government needs to intervene to reform tort law because the costs of frivolous, or unfounded, lawsuits are out of control. Successful lawsuits often involve not only awards for losses and medical costs, but additional punitive awards for pain and suffering. While they are meant to punish the injurer, they are often excessive because lawyers play upon the jurors' sympathies. To avoid high damage awards, companies often settle with a plaintiff before a trial can begin. This may prevent a large settlement, but it only encourages more lawsuits. Torts have had an especially bad effect on the health care industry. Excessive damage awards have led to high rates for malpractice insurance. These high costs, in turn, are passed on to consumers. The federal government should set limits on damages in order to discourage frivolous lawsuits.

NO

People who have suffered injury should be able to seek justice without restrictions. This goal is met by the current system. Tort suits force the injurer to reexamine and improve the safety of products and practices. Also, there is no real proof that the number of lawsuits has risen. In fact, statistics suggest that many more people suffer from medical malpractice than ever go to court—the media mislead the public by focusing on a few outlandish cases. Although the number of medical malpractice lawsuits has dropped in some states where payouts are capped, this does not prove that there were too many frivolous lawsuits. It might just mean lawyers are less willing to represent someone until they know they can win back their costs—and it costs quite a bit to challenge doctors or lawyers in court. As it is, low-income people have a hard time finding lawyers. Reforms that cap punitive damages will just increase the imbalance in the system.

Debating the Issue

1. **Explaining** How do both sides view the issue, especially as it relates to medical malpractice?
2. **Deciding** With which opinion do you tend to agree? Explain your reasoning.

▶ The Herrera family received a large settlement when relatives were killed by a drunk driver.

428 **UNIT 5:** *Liberty and Justice for All*

Debating the Issue Answers

1. One side views the costs as out of control, needlessly driving up the price of insurance and services, and encouraging more lawsuits. The other side views the costs as necessary to allow low-income people to find lawyers who are willing to represent them, and people who have suffered from malpractice should be compensated for it.
2. Students should state a position and clearly defend it.

Criminal Law

Reader's Guide

Content Vocabulary
* ★ criminal law *(p. 429)*
* ★ criminal justice system *(p. 429)*
* ★ petty offense *(p. 430)*
* ★ misdemeanor *(p. 430)*
* ★ felony *(p. 430)*
* ★ arrest warrant *(p. 430)*
* ★ grand jury *(p. 431)*
* ★ indictment *(p. 431)*
* ★ information *(p. 432)*
* ★ plea bargaining *(p. 432)*
* ★ jury *(p. 433)*

* ★ verdict *(p. 433)*
* ★ hung jury *(p. 434)*
* ★ sentence *(p. 434)*

Academic Vocabulary
* ★ method *(p. 429)*
* ★ citation *(p. 430)*
* ★ obvious *(p. 432)*

Reading Strategy
Create a two-column table. In the first column, list the steps in a criminal case; in the second column, write a brief description of what happens at each step.

8 Steps in Criminal Cases	
Key Steps	**Key Features**
1. Investigation and Arrest	Police gather evidence and arrest suspect
2. Initial Court Appearance	
3. Preliminary Hearing or Grand Jury	

Focus

Bellringer
Section Focus Transparencies
15-3

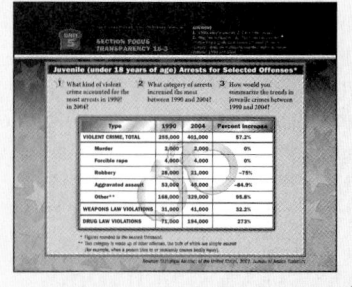

Issues in the News

Students of crime control sat up and took notice when New York City's raging crime rate dropped dramatically from 1991 through 2004. What caused it? According to a law professor who published a book on the subject, "The most important lesson of the 1990s was that major changes in rates of crime can happen without major changes in the social fabric." Population, schools, and the economy—these did not change. But "relatively small improvements in policing" made a difference, among them, a larger police force and more aggressive law enforcement.

▲ Officer Eric Perez patrolling New York's Washington Heights neighborhood in the late 1990s

Reader's Guide

Answers to Graphic:

Key Steps
1. Investigation & Arrest
2. Initial Court Appearance
3. Preliminary Hearing or Grand Jury
4. Plea Bargaining
5. Arraignment and Pleas
6. The Trial
7. The Decision
8. Sentencing

Key Features can be found on pages 430–435.

Every society needs to protect people from crime and invest resources into policing. In modern times, societies also devote resources to address indirect causes for crime such as poverty and unemployment. Still **criminal law** is the most direct **method** for controlling crime because it defines criminal acts and spells out punishments for them.

In criminal law cases, the government charges a person with a crime: The government is always the prosecutor, and the defendant is the person charged. A crime is an act that breaks the law and harms someone or society in general. Not doing something also can be defined as a crime— for example, not reporting child abuse if state law requires it. Most crimes in the nation break state laws and are tried in state courts, but there has been an increase in federal criminal cases, such as tax fraud, selling narcotics, counterfeiting, and kidnapping.

The **criminal justice system** is the system of state and federal courts, judges, lawyers, police, and prisons responsible for enforcing criminal law. There is a separate juvenile justice system with special rules and procedures for handling juveniles, who in most states are people under the age of 18.

Types of Crime

Each state has its own penal code, written laws that spell out what constitutes a crime and the punishments that go with it. Crimes may be classified in three groups: petty offenses, misdemeanors, and felonies.

Resource Manager

R Reading Strategies	**C** Critical Thinking	**D** Differentiated Instruction	**W** Writing Support	**S** Skill Practice
Teacher Edition • Using Word Parts, p. 433 **Additional Resources** • Guid. Read. Act., p. 56 • Quizzes/Tests, p. 185 • Reteaching Act., p. 14	**Teacher Edition** • Drawing Conclusions, pp. 430, 434 • Comparing, p. 433 **Additional Resources** • Read. Essen., pp. 170–173	**Additional Resources** • Foldables, p. 58	**Teacher Edition** • Personal Writing, p. 435 **Additional Resources** • Ch. Summaries, pp. 43–45	**Teacher Edition** • Using Map Skills, p. 434 **Additional Resources** • Skill Reinforce. Act., p. 15

Teach

C Critical Thinking

Drawing Conclusions Ask:
Why might people convicted of felonies lose certain civil rights even after they have served their prison sentences? *(Some crimes are so severe that a loss of civil rights can be considered part of the punishment for the crimes.)* Do you think this is just or unjust? **OL**

Comparing Governments

Critical Thinking

Answer: No, it could mean that Canada has a good reporting system, while in Colombia, a great deal of crime is not reported at all.

Research Activity: Have students look for news articles about crimes that are committed in other countries. As students share their findings, encourage them to suggest comparisons they might make between law enforcement in the United States and in other countries. **OL**

Additional Support

Petty offenses are minor crimes such as parking illegally, littering, disturbing the peace, minor trespassing, and driving over the speed limit. The punishment for a petty offense is often a ticket, or **citation,** rather than arrest. If a person does not challenge the citation, he or she might only have to pay a fine. (Not paying the fine is usually considered a more serious crime.)

Misdemeanors represent more serious crimes such as vandalism, stealing inexpensive items, writing bad checks for modest amounts of money, or being drunk and disorderly. Punishments for misdemeanors can be fines or jail sentences, usually for a year or less. (Sometimes, the more serious the offense, a misdemeanor can be treated as a felony, especially when a person has committed the same offense more than once.)

Felonies are serious crimes such as burglary, kidnapping, arson, rape, fraud, forgery, murder, or manslaughter (killing someone but less serious than murder, for example, if it occurs in the heat of passion or through recklessness). For a felony, someone can be imprisoned for a year or more. In the case of murder, the punishment could be death, often referred to as capital punishment. (The word *capital* came about because centuries ago, people might be decapitated for murder. See Section 4 for a detailed discussion of capital punishment.) People who are convicted of felonies might lose basic rights to vote, possess a firearm, or serve on a jury. They also might lose the chance to be a lawyer or a teacher, or to serve in the military or police departments.

Steps in Criminal Cases

Nearly every criminal case is handled through the same basic steps. At each step, defendants are protected by due process, which is guaranteed in the Bill of Rights. The prosecutor is a government lawyer who is responsible for bringing and proving the case against the person who is charged, the defendant. The prosecutor must prove beyond a reasonable doubt that the defendant violated the law.

Investigation and Arrest

The first step in a criminal case occurs when police begin to investigate what appears to be a crime. The police goal is to gather enough evidence to convince a judge to issue a warrant to arrest a suspect. A valid **arrest warrant** lists the suspect's

Comparing Governments

Crime and Law Enforcement, 2004

Graphs In Motion
See StudentWorks™ Plus or go to glencoe.com.

Country	Total	Murder	Assault	Burglary	Auto Theft
Australia	7,003	3.7	708.5	2,926.2	684.8
France	6,097	3.4	162.7	632.4	511.0
Canada	8,121	4.0	140.3	1,044.4	529.4
Colombia	790	56.3	61.8	57.9	75.3
Israel	6,254	2.2	491.8	990.1	501.7
Japan	1,773	1.0	16.0	206.0	34.0
The Netherlands	7,808	10.9	242.8	3,100.4	239.0
United States	5,374	9.0	430.2	1,041.8	591.2

Offenses Reported to the Police (per 100,000 population)

Population per Police Officer

630, 534, 438, 420, 480, 510, 210, 318

Source: Encyclopaedia Britannica, *2005 Book of the Year* (Chicago, IL: Encyclopaedia Britannica, 2006). Canadian Statistics at www.statcan.ca

Critical Thinking The chart shows that Canada has many more offenses reported than Colombia. *Does this mean Canada has more crime? Why or why not?*

Activity: Collaborative Learning

Creating a Board Game Organize the class into groups. Ask each group to create a board game that illustrates the procedures followed in a criminal trial, with the goal of the defendant's acquittal. Each group should choose a name for its game and discuss how the game will be played, including such factors as the severity of the crime, the methods of examining and cross-examining witnesses, and the ways in which a player could be ejected from the game (for example, by plea bargaining or having a mistrial declared). Group members should assume the following tasks: draw a game board background, design a route for players to follow, write the game rules, create playing pieces, design playing cards. After each group has completed its game, have the group play another group's game and compare. How many of the events in the game could be expected in a real criminal trial? **OL**

name and the alleged crime. Police also can arrest people without warrants if they catch them committing a crime. In certain circumstances, it is enough if the police have only a reasonable suspicion that a person has broken the law.

The arrested person is taken to a police station where the charges are "booked," or recorded. The suspect may be fingerprinted, photographed, or put in a lineup to be identified by witnesses. Police may administer a blood test (usually this takes a court order) or take a handwriting sample. These procedures do not violate a person's constitutional rights and lawyers do not have to be present, but a suspect has the right to ask for a lawyer before answering any questions.

Initial Appearance

Whenever someone is arrested, he or she must be brought before a judge as quickly as possible to be charged—usually within 24 hours. The judge explains the charges to the defendant and reads the person his or her rights. If the charge is a misdemeanor, the defendant can plead guilty and the judge will decide on a penalty. If the defendant pleads not guilty, a date is set for a trial.

For a felony, the defendant is not usually asked to enter a plea. Instead the judge sets a date for a preliminary hearing, and the process of determining if the charges have merit begins. The judge may also decide whether the suspect will be released or "held to answer." If the judge thinks a person is a good risk to return, a suspect will be released on his or her own recognizance (meaning the suspect has officially recognized the duty to return to court for trial). If the person is not a good risk, the judge will require bail, a sum of money the accused leaves with the court until he or she returns. According to the Eighth Amendment,[1] the bail amount should fit the severity of the charge but cannot be excessive. If the defendant is likely to flee the country, bail may be denied.

Preliminary Hearing or Grand Jury

The next step in the process varies among states and also between state and federal governments. In federal courts and in many state courts, cases will go to a **grand jury.** A grand jury is a group of citizens who review the charges to determine whether there is enough evidence to "hand up" an **indictment,** or formal criminal charge.

Grand jury hearings are conducted in secret and may consider types of evidence not allowed in trials. Defendants are not entitled to have an attorney

Hard Lessons

Raising Public Awareness Millie Webb, who served as national president of Mothers Against Drunk Driving (MADD), holds a photo of her daughter Lori, who was killed at the age of four when the car in which she was riding was hit by a drunk driver. *What might constitute a reasonable suspicion for a police officer to stop a driver to test him or her for driving under the influence of alcohol or drugs?*

represent them, although their attorney can often observe the proceedings.

If a preliminary hearing is used instead of a grand jury, the prosecution presents its case to a judge. The defendant's lawyer also may present certain kinds of evidence. If the judge believes there is a reason to believe the defendant committed the crime, the case moves to the next stage. If the judge decides the government does not have enough evidence, the charges are dropped. In some states, the prosecutor is allowed to try to get a grand jury indictment if the judge dismissed a case at the preliminary hearing.

See the following footnoted materials in the **Reference Handbook:**
1. *The Constitution,* pages R42–R67.

Participating IN GOVERNMENT

Under Arrest Help interested students arrange to tour a city precinct station or police headquarters to ask questions about how an arrested person is booked and prepared to be brought before a judge. Have students share and comment on what they learned.

Caption Answer: A driver might be driving erratically, swerving, or going unusually fast or extremely slowly.

Did You Know?

The grand jury has historically served as the guardian of the rights of the innocent. If a majority of the grand jurors are not convinced that sufficient evidence has been presented by the prosecutor, an indictment will not be given, and the complaint against the accused will be dismissed. This protects people from being unfairly harassed by the government.

Differentiated Instruction

Leveled Activities

431

ELL Chapter Summaries, p. 45

BL Vocabulary Activities, p. 15

OL Historical Documents and Speeches, p. 15

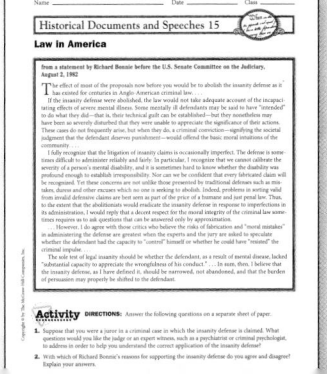

AL Authentic Assessment with Rubrics, p. 22

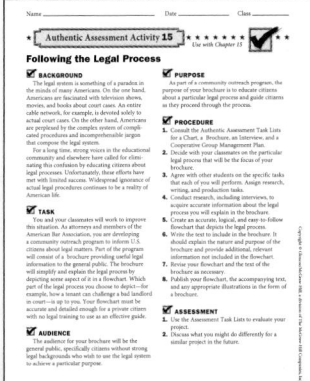

We the People
Making a Difference

Mary Ellen Beaver The sugar-cane company that Beaver targeted also sued Florida Rural Legal Services to keep Beaver off its property, but Beaver's employer countersued—and won. A tireless worker, Beaver has traveled thousands of miles each year to help migrant workers. Her supervisor says: "Her energy is enormous. . . . She is working at a very tough job at an age when most people are getting ready to retire." Beaver's motivation, however, is simple. "I do it," she explains, "because I believe defrauding a laborer of wages is a great sin."

Research Activity Analyze the impact of Mary Ellen Beaver's efforts on state policies.

Government **ONLINE**

Objectives and answers to the Student Web Activity can be found in the **Web Activity Lesson Plan** at glencoe.com. Enter **QuickPass**™ code USG9085c15T.

Hands-On Chapter Project

Step 3

Writing a News Report

Step 3: Writing the News Groups will use the information they gathered in Steps 1 and 2 to write and present their news reports.

Directions Have each group collaborate to write a news report in a feature style that might be presented on an all-news channel. The report will announce the Court's decision as if it just happened, briefly explain the case, use bits of the majority opinion (and dissenting opinion,

---

We the People
Making a Difference

Mary Ellen Beaver has developed a reputation that has earned her the nickname "Fighting Grandma." Since 1969 Beaver worked hard to help migrant workers understand their legal rights and improve their working conditions.

Beaver began her campaign after seeing groups of poorly dressed tomato pickers pass by her Pennsylvania farm each day in run-down buses. "I was outraged. They had no rights and were being exploited," she said.

Beaver collected clothing to take to the workers and organized a group of churches to help provide support. Her work helped convince Pennsylvania legislators to pass the state's 1978 Farm Labor Law. She also created a support group for workers called Friends of Farm Workers. For her dedication and hard work, she earned a humanitarian medal from Pope John Paul II in 1984.

Other states have benefited from Beaver's efforts. After leaving Pennsylvania, she worked with the Neighborhood Legal Assistance Program in South Carolina to monitor migrant working conditions in the state's peach orchards. She also worked for the Florida Rural Legal Services, which provides legal support to Florida's migrant workers. In a lawsuit filed against a sugarcane company, Florida cane workers were awarded $51 million in back wages.

Beaver says the reward for her work is "when a worker comes up to me and says, 'No one has ever treated me with respect before.'"

" . . . They had no rights and were being exploited."

—**Mary Ellen Beaver**

Convening a grand jury is time-consuming and expensive. Today, in misdemeanor cases and in many felony cases, courts use an **information** rather than a grand jury indictment. An information is a sworn statement by the prosecution asserting that enough evidence exists to go to trial. Grand juries usually follow the recommendations of the prosecution. Some people believe that a grand jury is an unnecessary expense; others see it as a unique citizen-based check against the power of the government.

Plea Bargaining

In about 90 percent of all criminal cases, the process comes to an end with a guilty plea because of **plea bargaining.** In this pretrial process, the prosecutor, defense lawyer, and police work out an agreement through which the defendant pleads guilty to a lesser crime (or fewer crimes) in return for the government not prosecuting the more serious (or additional) crime with which the defendant was originally charged. In many courts, the judge also participates in the process, especially if the length of the sentence is part of the negotiation. Plea bargaining has become very widely used as a way to handle the tremendous volume of criminal cases the courts must process every year.

Supporters of the process claim that it is efficient and saves the state the cost of a trial in situations where guilt is **obvious,** as well as those where the government's case may have weaknesses. Some opponents argue "copping a plea" allows criminals to get off lightly. Others say that it encourages people to give up their rights to a fair trial. The Supreme Court in several decisions has approved the process as constitutional. In *Santobello* v. *New York*[1] (1971), the Court said plea bargaining was "an essential component of the administration of justice. Properly administered, it is to be encouraged."

See the following footnoted materials in the **Reference Handbook:**
1. *Santobello* v. *New York* case summary, page R33.

Government ONLINE
Student Web Activity Visit glencoe.com and enter **QuickPass**™ code USG9822c15. Click on Student Web Activity and complete the activity about criminal law.

---

if any) to show the basis for the ruling, mention the background of the justice who wrote the majority opinion, and discuss the ruling's likely effect on citizens.

Analyzing Information Ask students to take notes as groups give their reports so that they can later evaluate each presentation. Tell them to consider these criteria:

• Is the issue that is involved explained clearly? What is it?
• Are the selections from the Court's

majority and dissenting opinions well chosen? Which words or phrases stand out?
• Does the presentation summarize the justice's background well?
• Can you summarize the effect the ruling is likely to have on citizens? **OL**

(Chapter Project continued in Section 4.)

Arraignment and Pleas

After the indictment by a grand jury, a preliminary hearing, or an information, the next step is the arraignment. At the arraignment, the judge reads the formal charge against the defendant in court. The defendant is represented by an attorney. During this process, the judge may ask the defendant questions to make sure the person understands everything about the charges and the process. A copy of the charges is given to the defendant, and the judge asks whether the defendant pleads guilty or not guilty.

The defendant then enters one of four pleas:

- not guilty,
- not guilty by reason of insanity,
- guilty, or in some states,
- no contest, or nolo contendere.

The nolo contendere plea comes from the Latin for "I do not contend or contest" the charge. It means that the defendant indirectly admits guilt, but this is not recorded as a guilty plea. Since the person is giving up the right to a defense, the judge decides the punishment—the defendent could be sent to prison immediately.

The Trial

If the plea is "not guilty," the next stage is the trial. The Sixth Amendment[1] guarantees that defendants have a speedy trial, but the courts are so crowded that long delays before a trial begins are common. (In fact, court dockets, or lists of cases on the court calendar, have become so long that some question whether justice is being compromised.)

Defendants accused of a felony have a right to choose between the two types of trials: a jury trial or a bench trial (before the judge only). In a bench trial, the judge hears all the evidence and determines guilt or innocence. Experience has shown that judges are more likely to find defendants guilty than juries.

A **jury** is a group of citizens who hear evidence during a trial to decide on guilt or innocence. How is the jury chosen? The attorneys for both sides select jurors from a large pool of residents from the court's jurisdiction. During the selection process, each attorney can ask potential jurors questions and decide whether they might be favorable or unfavorable to the defense or prosecution. Both sides try to avoid jurors who might be unfavorable to their side.

After the jury is chosen, the trial begins with the prosecution presenting its case. Witnesses are called, and evidence is presented. The defense attorney has the right to cross-examine witnesses. Each side can object to statements or actions by the other side. Next, the defense has its turn and may call witnesses, with the prosecution doing the cross-examination.

Under the Fifth Amendment,[2] defendants do not have to testify against themselves, and refusal to testify cannot be taken as a sign of guilt. At the end, both attorneys make closing arguments that summarize their case.

The Decision

The last step is the decision, or **verdict,** in the case. After closing arguments, the judge instructs

See the following footnoted materials in the **Reference Handbook:**
1. *The Constitution,* pages R42–R67.
2. *The Constitution,* pages R42–R67.

R Reading Strategy

Using Word Parts The term *arraignment* might be unfamiliar to many students. To help them understand the term, have them look it up in a dictionary that gives word origins. (Arraign *comes from the Latin* adrationare, *meaning* "to call to account.") **OL**

C Critical Thinking

Comparing Ask: What is the difference between a jury trial and a bench trial? *(A jury trial usually has 12 people deciding a case; a bench trial has only the judge.)* **BL**

Caption Answer: Voir dire is the process in which opposing lawyers question each prospective juror to discover any prejudices or preconceived opinions he or she might have concerning the case. As a class, discuss the qualities that students believe would make them more receptive to a lawyer's arguments.

Additional Support

The Right to a Jury Trial

The Art of Persuasion
A lawyer's ability to win a jury case depends on persuading the jury. Lawyers are required to be persuasive. Much depends on a lawyer's ability to connect with jurors during the voir dire. (See pages 315 and 420.) *What is voir dire? If you were a juror, what qualities would make you consider a lawyer's arguments favorably?*

Activity: Interdisciplinary Connection

Literature Increased media attention to high-profile cases has turned some criminal lawyers into heroes (or villains) of the popular culture. Interested students might enjoy reading memoirs by these attorneys connected with the O.J. Simpson case (or other attorneys) and sharing insights that the memoirs gave them into the system of criminal law in the United States:

- Marcia Clark with Teresa Carpenter, *Without*

a Doubt (New York: Viking Press, 1997)
- Johnnie L. Cochran, Jr., with Tim Rutten, *Journey to Justice* (New York: Ballantine Books, 1996)
- Christopher Darden with Jess Walter, *In Contempt* (New York: HarperCollins, 1996)
- Robert L. Shapiro with Larkin Warren, *The Search for Justice: A Defense Attorney's Brief on the O.J. Simpson Case* (New York: Warner Books, 1996) **AL**

S Skill Practice

Using Map Skills **Ask:** What region of the country has the highest incarceration rate? *(the South)* What conclusions could you draw from this? *(Possible answers include that these states have higher crime rates or that they are more likely to sentence convicted criminals to extended prison terms.)* **OL**

C Critical Thinking

Drawing Conclusions Have students consider the factors that a judge takes into account when deciding on a sentence. **Ask:** How might these factors affect the severity of the sentence? *(The judge can give a more severe sentence if the defendant has been in trouble previously or a lighter sentence if the defendant is needed at home and this is a first-time offense.)* **BL**

Additional Support

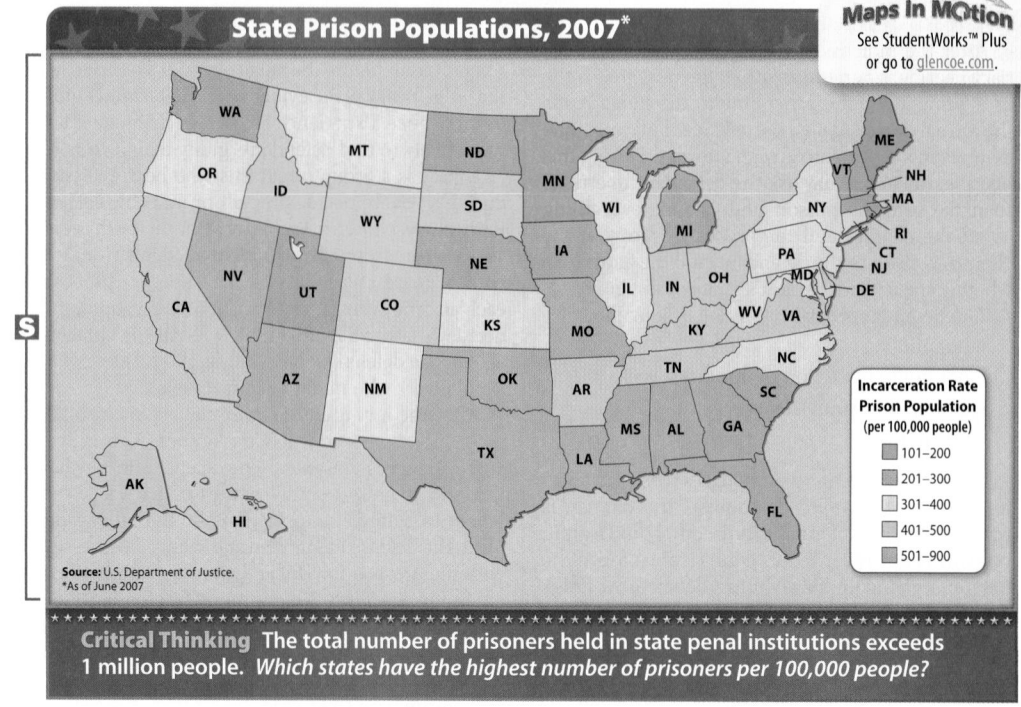

State Prison Populations, 2007*

Maps In Motion
See StudentWorks™ Plus or go to glencoe.com.

Source: U.S. Department of Justice.
*As of June 2007

Incarceration Rate
Prison Population
(per 100,000 people)
- 101–200
- 201–300
- 301–400
- 401–500
- 501–900

Critical Thinking The total number of prisoners held in state penal institutions exceeds 1 million people. *Which states have the highest number of prisoners per 100,000 people?*

the jury on legal procedures and on the law they must apply to the evidence. The jurors then go to a room where they select a foreperson to lead discussions on the case. Jury deliberations are secret and have no set time limit. During its deliberations, the jury may ask questions of the judge or ask to review evidence. To decide on a guilty verdict, the jury must find the evidence convincing "beyond a reasonable doubt." Nearly all criminal cases require a unanimous vote for a guilty verdict. If the jury cannot agree on a verdict, there is a **hung jury,** and the court usually declares a mistrial. A new trial with another jury may be scheduled later.

Sentencing

When the verdict is "not guilty," the defendant is released immediately. With very few exceptions, a person cannot be tried again for the same crime.

If the verdict is "guilty," the judge usually determines the **sentence,** or punishment for the offender. Sentences may require time in prison, the payment of a fine, or a number of hours of community service. In a few states, jurors play a role in sentencing, particularly in cases in which the death penalty is a possibility. Today, victims of the crime are often allowed

to make statements about the sentence, and judges can take these statements into consideration.

People who are convicted of misdemeanors and felonies have the right to appeal their cases to a higher court, although this right to appeal is not a constitutional one.

The law usually sets minimum and maximum penalties for a crime, but what determines whether someone receives the minimum or maximum sentence, or something in-between? A judge might decide that the person's background or the particular circumstances of the crime should affect the severity of the sentence. The judge can also hold hearings to consider how to weigh these factors. In death penalty cases, the Constitution requires such a hearing.

In the 1990s, many citizens became frustrated with the short sentences some serious criminals were receiving and with the number of repeat offenders. Beginning with the state of Washington in 1993, many states passed a three-strikes law—a nickname referring to the baseball phrase "three strikes, you're out." These laws typically impose an automatic minimum sentence of 25 years or life imprisonment when a person is convicted of a serious offense for the third time.

434 UNIT 5: *Liberty and Justice for All*

Activity: Economics Connection

The Economics of Incarceration
Ask: Why are judges permitted so many sentencing options that do not include prison time? Explain to students that one important reason is the economics of incarceration. It is expensive to operate a prison and provide food, clothing, and a safe and secure environment for prisoners. Tell students that the United States has the

highest incarceration rate in the world; in many states, expenditures for correctional facilities have become the single largest item in the budget.

Organize the class into three groups. Ask each group to research and prepare a report on one of the following: (1) causes of growing prison costs; (2) efforts that are being made to reduce costs; and

(3) recommendations to keep prison costs affordable for state and federal governments.

Have groups present their findings to the class in the form of oral reports. **AL**

Deadlocked Jury

High Stakes Emotions ran high during the trial and sentencing of Terry Nichols. An army veteran, Nichols was convicted in 2004 of conspiring with Timothy McVeigh in 1995 to blow up a federal government building in Oklahoma City. The bombing killed 168 people. The jury determined a guilty verdict relatively quickly, but after three days, the jury announced it was deadlocked over the question of whether he should be put to death. Thus, the death penalty was no longer an option, and the judge sentenced him to multiple life terms without the possibility of parole. *How might the statements in court of a victim's family affect the sentencing phase of a trial?*

Three-strikes laws are controversial. Opponents argue that they can be unfair. For example, what happens if one of the three offenses is serious but not violent? (A violent felony would be murder, robbery, or rape.) People who support the three-strikes laws argue that the states that have adopted the three-strikes approach have seen a drop in serious crime.

A prominent court case challenging California's three-strikes law involved Gary Ewing, a man who stole three golf clubs from a pro shop in El Segundo, California. Because of Ewing's many previous crimes, the judge in the case stated that stealing the clubs was a third strike. In *Ewing* v. *California*, the Supreme Court decided that the three-strikes law was constitutional, and Ewing was sentenced to 25 years to life.

SECTION 3 Review

Vocabulary

1. **Explain** the significance of: criminal law, criminal justice system, petty offense, misdemeanor, felony, arrest warrant, grand jury, indictment, information, plea bargaining, jury, verdict, hung jury, sentence.

Main Ideas

2. **Identifying** What are three classifications of crimes?

3. **Explaining** Why do courts use an information rather than a grand jury indictment for misdemeanors and some felonies?

Critical Thinking

4. **Demonstrating Reasoned Judgment** Should people who are charged with violent crimes be allowed to post bail? Why?

5. **Organizing** Use a Venn diagram like the one here to show the differences and similarities between the steps in criminal and civil lawsuits.

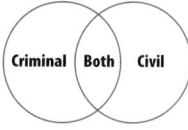

Criminal | Both | Civil

Writing About Government

6. **Expository Writing** Create a slide presentation that illustrates how the criminal justice system balances the rights of the accused and the rights of society. You can use clip art or visual symbols to accompany your brief descriptions.

CHAPTER 15: *Law in America* **435**

Answers

1. All definitions can be found in the section and the Glossary.
2. petty offenses, misdemeanors, and felonies
3. Convening a jury is time-consuming and expensive; an information allows a sworn statement by the prosecution to assert that enough evidence exists to go to trial—forgoing the time and expense of convening a grand jury.
4. Answers will vary. Students who think that the accused should be allowed to raise bail might suggest that not releasing the accused violates the principle of innocent until proven guilty.

Students who think otherwise might suggest that setting the accused free is too risky and that such a person might commit a violent crime again.
5. Criminal: investigation, arrest, initial appearance, hearing or grand jury, plea bargaining or arraignment and plea, decision, sentencing. Civil: hiring a lawyer, complaint, discovery, award. Both: trial.
6. Follow up with a class discussion of how the criminal justice system attempts to balance the rights of the accused against the rights of society.

Focus

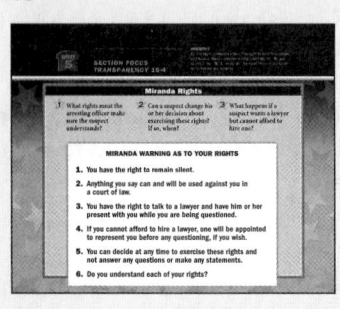
Reader's Guide

Answers to Graphic:

- No Unreasonable Search and Seizure—the police must obtain a warrant

- Guarantee of Counsel—the accused has the right to an attorney

- No Self-Incrimination—confessions cannot be obtained by force or violence

- Double Jeopardy—no person may be tried for the same crime twice

- Cruel and Unusual Punishment—no cruel and unusual punishments

Resource Manager

Rights of the Accused

Reader's Guide

Content Vocabulary	Academic Vocabulary	Reading Strategy
★ exclusionary rule (p. 437) ★ counsel (p. 439) ★ self-incrimination (p. 440) ★ double jeopardy (p. 441)	★ evidence (p. 436) ★ precise (p. 436) ★ reluctant (p. 439)	As you read, create a table similar to the one below to list the rights of the accused and a brief description about each right.

Right of the Accused	Description

Issues in the News

An appeal was filed in September 2007 in Washington, D.C., having to do with a local police tactic called a "jump out." A group of police officers in several unmarked vehicles suddenly emerge to confront a suspect. The suit alleges that the tactic represents unlawful search and seizure. They argue that it is more like a "paramilitary operation used against suspects in the drug war." They also argued that it was used regularly in inner city neighborhoods without sufficient cause, making some people flee in fear.

▲ Police work is often dangerous and, at times, controversial.

The "jump out" case illustrates a major challenge in a democracy—dealing with crime and with criminals. On the one hand, one of the first duties of a government is to protect society against criminals. On the other hand, in a nation committed to individual rights, the government must protect those rights. Justice in a democracy means protecting the innocent from police power as well as punishing the guilty.

In the Constitution and the Bill of Rights, the Founders attempted to meet this challenge by setting out principles that would guard the rights of the accused as well as the rights of society. Laws were to be carefully interpreted, trial procedures fair and impartial, and punishments reasonable. Later, the Fourteenth Amendment described the specific rights of the accused in the same place that it defined national citizenship.[1] 📖

📖 See the following footnoted materials in the **Reference Handbook:**
1. The Constitution, pages R42–R67.

Searches and Seizures

The police need **evidence** to accuse people of committing crimes, but getting evidence often requires searching people or their homes, cars, and offices. To protect the innocent from searches, the Fourth Amendment specifies that people have the right to be "secure in their persons, houses, papers, and effects, against unreasonable searches and seizures." But what constitutes unreasonable searches and seizures? Because no **precise** definition has been established, the courts deal with this issue on a case-by-case basis.

Today the police must state under oath that they have probable cause to suspect that someone has committed a crime. This probable cause justifies the police search. Usually police must get a warrant from a court official before searching for evidence or making an arrest. The warrant must describe the place to be searched and the person or things to be seized.

R Reading Strategies	**C** Critical Thinking	**D** Differentiated Instruction	**W** Writing Support	**S** Skill Practice
Teacher Edition • Summarizing, p. 437 **Additional Resources** • Guid. Read. Act., p. 57 • Quizzes/Tests, pp. 186–194 • Reteaching Act., p. 15	**Teacher Edition** • Making Generalizations, p. 441 **Additional Resources** • Read. Essen., pp. 174–176 • Supreme Ct. Case Studies, pp. 99–100, 119–120, 143–144	**Teacher Edition** • Visual/Spatial, p. 440 **Additional Resources** • Foldables, p. 58	**Teacher Edition** • Expository Writing, p. 440 **Additional Resources** • Supreme Ct. Case Studies, pp. 47–48, 57–58, 89–90	**Teacher Edition** • Using Map Skills, p. 442 **Additional Resources** • Vocab. Act., p. 15

Before 1980, more than 20 states had search laws that permitted police to enter a home without a warrant if they had reason to believe the occupant had committed a felony, or major crime. In *Payton* v. *New York*[1] (1980), the Supreme Court ruled that, except in a life-threatening emergency, the Fourth Amendment forbids searching a home without a warrant. 📖 In *Florida* v. *J.L.*[2] (2000), the Court strengthened Fourth Amendment protections further by ruling that an anonymous tip that a person is carrying a gun does not give police the right to stop and frisk that person. 📖

Special Situations

Certain situations do not require warrants. The police do not need one to search and arrest someone seen breaking the law, even minor infractions of the law. In *Whren* v. *United States*[3] (1996), the Court held that the police could seize drugs found in a suspect's vehicle that was stopped for a traffic violation. 📖 In *Atwater* v. *City of Lago Vista*[4] (2001), the Court found that the Fourth Amendment did not prevent the police from arresting a woman who was driving her children in a car in which no one was wearing a seat belt. 📖

The police also do not need a warrant to search garbage placed outside a home for pickup, as was decided in *California* v. *Greenwood*[5] (1998). 📖 Also since the 1980s, the Court has considered certain drug tests to be searches not requiring a warrant if the tests are judged to protect public safety.

The Exclusionary Rule

As the name suggests, the **exclusionary rule** excludes illegally obtained evidence from trial. The rule was first established for federal courts in *Weeks* v. *United States*[6] (1914). 📖 The rule was not applied to state courts until *Mapp* v. *Ohio*[7] (1961). 📖

Some people have criticized the exclusionary rule. They ask whether criminals should go free

📖 *See the following footnoted materials in the* **Reference Handbook:**
1. *Payton* v. *New York* case summary, page R32.
2. *Florida* v. *J.L.* case summary, page R27.
3. *Whren* v. *United States* case summary, page R36.
4. *Atwater* v. *City of Lago Vista* case summary, page R23.
5. *California* v. *Greenwood* case summary, page R25.
6. *Weeks* v. *United States* case summary, page R36.
7. *Mapp* v. *Ohio* case summary, page R30.
8. *United States* v. *Leon* case summary, page R35.
9. *Nix* v. *Williams* case summary, page R31.

Deciding Vote Supreme Court Justice Hugo Black, seen here in a 1958 photo, had the deciding vote in *Mapp* v. *Ohio*. This 1961 case completed the process of incorporation. ***What is incorporation, and why is it so important?***

simply because the police made a mistake in collecting evidence. In *United States* v. *Leon*[8] (1984), the Court ruled that as long as the police act in good faith when they ask for a warrant, the evidence they collect may be used in court even if the warrant turns out to be flawed. 📖

That same year, the Court also approved another exception to the exclusionary rule— "inevitable discovery." In *Nix* v. *Williams*[9] (1984), the Court held that evidence obtained in violation of a defendant's rights can be used at trial "if the prosecutor can show that the evidence eventually would have been discovered by legal means. 📖

CHAPTER 15: *Law in America* **437**

Teach

Caption Answer: Students first read about incorporation in Chapter 13. Remind them that it is the process through which the Bill of Rights was extended to state and local governments.

R Reading Strategy

Summarizing Ask: What is the exclusionary rule, and how does it work? *(Evidence obtained illegally cannot be used in court.)* What are some arguments in favor of the rule? Against the rule? *(It means that police cannot violate a person's rights in order to obtain evidence; it sometimes means that a guilty person can go free if evidence is suppressed.)* **OL**

🏛 Landmark Case

See *Weeks* v. *United States* and *Mapp* v. *Ohio* in the Supreme Court Case Summaries in the ***Reference Handbook*** and Case Studies 18 and 41 in the *Supreme Court Case Studies* booklet.

Additional Support

★ Activity: Collaborative Learning

Applying Landmark Cases Organize three groups of students to analyze the exclusionary rule, the right to counsel, and the protection against self-incrimination. Have pairs of students in each group read Supreme Court Cases 37 *(Escobedo* v. *Illinois)* and 41 *(Miranda* v. *Arizona)* in the *Supreme Court Case Studies*

booklet. After each pair summarizes the case for its group, ask each group to decide how the case fits the category that it is investigating. Have each group appoint a spokesperson to share its findings on these cases with the class. **OL**

Linking ☆ Past & Present

Punishing the Guilty

Sentencing criminals to prison is a relatively recent form of punishment. In earlier times, physical punishment was the most common way of dealing with criminals. Tormenting the body through physical pain was considered necessary to cleanse the criminal's soul of sins.

Did You Know?

In *Vernonia School District v. Acton,* the U.S. Supreme Court ruled 6 to 3 that the school district's drug testing policy was reasonable and, therefore, constitutional. According to the Court, student athletes are children and, therefore, they lack some basic rights. The Court held that the intrusion of privacy was negligible. Further, discouraging drug use was important enough to justify the drug testing.

Differentiated Instruction

Search and Seizure for Students
Court cases have limited some student rights at school. *What might be reasonable suspicion for a locker search?*

Finally, in 2006 the Court held that evidence seized at a home could be used in a trial even if the police entered the home without knocking and announcing their presence (*Hudson* v. *Michigan*). The Court said the exclusionary rule did not apply as long as the police had a valid search warrant.

California v. Acevedo

In a 1987 case, *California* v. *Acevedo,* the Supreme Court overturned an earlier decision and set a new precedent for automobile searches. The case involved the police search of a car driven by Charles Acevedo, whom police witnessed leaving a drug house. Acevedo's attorney argued that the marijuana found in the car could not be used as evidence since the police had no warrant, but the trial court disagreed. The case went to the Supreme Court, which ruled that the police were free to "search an automobile and the containers within it where they have probable cause to believe contraband or evidence is contained."

High Schools and Search and Seizure

In the high school setting, courts have ruled that the Fourth Amendment protections can be limited.

In *New Jersey* v. *T.L.O.*[1] (1985), the Supreme Court ruled that school officials do not need warrants or probable cause to search students or their property. They only need a reasonable suspicion that a student has broken school rules.

The New Jersey case arose when an assistant principal searched the purse of a student he suspected had been smoking tobacco in a rest room. The search turned up not only cigarettes but marijuana. The student was suspended from school and prosecuted by juvenile authorities. The Court probably would have ruled in favor of the student if a police officer had conducted the search, but school officials were not under the same restraints when they had a reasonable suspicion of misconduct.

In 1995 the Court further limited privacy protections in high schools where drug use was at issue. In *Vernonia School District* v. *Acton*[2] (1995), the Court upheld the ruling that all students in competitive school athletics could be required to have drug tests even if there was no specific reason to suspect the use of drugs.

Wiretaps and Electronic Surveillance

The Supreme Court views wiretapping, eavesdropping, and other means of electronic surveillance to be search and seizure.

The Court first dealt with wiretapping in *Olmstead* v. *United States*[3] (1928). For four months, federal agents had tapped individuals' telephones to get evidence to convict them of bootlegging. The Court upheld the conviction, ruling that wiretapping did not violate the Fourth Amendment. The Court said that no warrant was needed to wiretap because the agents had not actually entered anyone's home.

This precedent stood for almost 40 years. Then in 1967, in *Katz* v. *United States,*[4] the Court overturned the *Olmstead* decision. The case concerned Charles Katz, a Los Angeles gambler, who was using a public phone booth to place bets across state lines. Without a warrant, the FBI put a microphone outside the booth to gather evidence that was later used to convict Katz. In reversing his conviction, the Court said that the Fourth Amendment "protects people—and not simply 'areas'" against unreasonable searches and seizures. The ruling extended Fourth Amendment protections by prohibiting wiretapping without a warrant.

See the following footnoted materials in the **Reference Handbook:**
1. *New Jersey* v. *T.L.O.* case summary, page R31.
2. *Vernonia School District 47J* v. *Acton* case summary, page R35.
3. *Olmstead* v. *United States* case summary, page R31.
4. *Katz* v. *United States* case summary, page R29.

Activity: Multiple Learning Styles

Visual/Spatial Have students draw a political cartoon dealing with some aspect of this section. Offer these topics or allow students to select their own:

- reaction to a school search-and-seizure activity
- the need for a prohibition against wiretapping

- the importance of an accused person's right to counsel
- a Supreme Court ruling in a matter relating to self-incrimination

Work with students to prepare a classroom display of the finished cartoons, captioning each cartoon with some background information about the topic. **AL**

In 1968 Congress passed a law that set up new rules for most wiretaps. The Omnibus Crime Control and Safe Streets Act said that almost all federal, state, and local authorities had to get a court order in order to conduct a wiretap. In 1978 Congress extended this same protection to wiretapping and bugging in national security cases when it passed the Foreign Intelligence Surveillance Act (FISA). These two laws, along with the Patriot Act, limit the circumstances under which the government can use electronic surveillance without a warrant.

Writ of Habeas Corpus

One of the most important constitutional rights related to criminal procedure is the writ of habeas corpus (Latin for "you have the body"). This writ is a court order that directs an official who has a person in custody to bring the prisoner to court and to explain to a judge why the person is being held. A prisoner must be released unless sufficient cause can be shown to detain him or her. Article I, Section 9, of the Constitution guarantees this right and says it cannot be suspended except in cases of rebellion or invasion.

Today habeas corpus is typically used in criminal cases by persons serving sentences in state and federal prisons to reopen their cases on the grounds of illegal detention. People in jail may appeal to a judge stating why they think their rights were violated before or during their trial. The judge then asks the jailer or a lower court to show cause why a writ should not be issued. If a judge finds the prisoner was detained unlawfully, the judge may order his or her immediate release.

Habeas corpus was the issue in a major Supreme Court case stemming from the Bush administration's fight against terrorists. After the September 11, 2001, terrorist attacks, President Bush decided that U.S. citizens and foreign nationals detained on suspicion of terrorism would be designated "unlawful enemy combatants" and could be imprisoned indefinitely without judicial hearings at the U.S. naval base at Guantánamo Bay, Cuba. The administration also created military tribunals to try some of the detainees and convinced Congress to pass a law in 2006 stripping detainees of their right to habeas corpus.

In *Boumediene* v. *Bush* (2008), the Supreme Court ruled 5 to 4 that all Guantánamo Bay prisoners, including foreigners, have a constitutional right to seek a writ of habeas corpus in a federal court. The Court said that the military tribunals hearing detainee cases failed to offer "the fundamental procedural protections of habeas corpus." Writing for the majority, Justice Kennedy declared: "The laws and constitution are designed to survive and, remain in force, in extraordinary times." In a strongly worded dissent, Justice Scalia said: "The nation will live to regret what the Court has done today." Observers noted that the Court has historically been **reluctant** to rule against a president in times of armed conflict.

Guarantee of Counsel

The Sixth Amendment guarantees a defendant the right "to have the assistance of counsel for his defense." In federal cases, the courts provided the **counsel,** or an attorney, but for years, people could be tried in state courts without a lawyer. As a result, defendants who could pay hired the best lawyers and stood a better chance of acquittal, while poorer defendants were often convicted because they did not understand the law.

Early Rulings on Right to Counsel

The Supreme Court first dealt with the right to counsel in state courts in *Powell* v. *Alabama*[1] (1932). Nine African American youths were convicted of assaulting two white girls in Alabama. The accused were sentenced to death. The Court reversed the conviction, ruling that the state had to provide a lawyer in cases involving the death penalty.

Ten years later, in *Betts* v. *Brady*[2] (1942), the Court held that states did not have to provide a lawyer in cases that did not involve the death penalty. The Court said that appointment of counsel was "not a fundamental right, essential to a fair trial" for state defendants unless special circumstances, such as illiteracy or mental incompetence, required one to get a fair trial.

For the next 20 years, under the *Betts* rule, the Supreme Court struggled to determine when the circumstances in a case were special enough to require a lawyer. Then in 1963 Clarence Earl Gideon, a drifter from Florida, won a landmark case that ended the *Betts* rule.

Gideon v. Wainwright

Landmark Case Gideon was charged with breaking into a pool hall with the intent to commit a crime—a felony. Because he was too poor to hire

---

See the following footnoted materials in the **Reference Handbook:**
1. *Powell* v. *Alabama* case summary, page R32.
2. *Betts* v. *Brady* case summary, page R24.

POLITICAL PROFILES

George Sutherland
(1862–1942)

Justice George Sutherland joined the Supreme Court in 1922. During Franklin D. Roosevelt's presidency, Sutherland was dubbed—along with three other conservative justices—one of the "Four Horsemen" of the Court. The Four Horsemen were known for adopting strong stands against New Deal legislation. Justice Hugo Black quoted Sutherland when writing the unanimous Court decision in *Gideon* v. *Wainwright*: "The right to be heard would be, in many cases, of little avail if it did not comprehend the right to be heard by counsel. Even the intelligent and educated layman has . . . sometimes no skill in the science of law. . . . Without [the guiding hand of counsel], though he be not guilty, he faces the danger of conviction because he does not know how to establish his innocence."

Landmark Case

See *Powell* v. *Alabama, Betts* v. *Brady,* and *Gideon* v. *Wainwright* in the Supreme Court Case Summaries in the **Reference Handbook** and Case Studies 24, 29, and 45 in the *Supreme Court Case Studies* booklet.

Hands-On Chapter Project
Step 4

Writing a News Report

Step 4: Writing the News The class will evaluate the news reports presented in Step 3.

Directions On the board, draw a table with the Court cases presented by each group across the top row. Along the left side, list the criteria on which the class took notes during the reports. Ask the class to use the notes they took to complete the table for each presentation in which they were not involved.

Evaluating Students will discuss which presentations were most effective. They should also ask groups follow-up questions, such as: What has been the long-term impact or significance of the ruling? In other cases or contexts, has this ruling affected citizens and/or the way the justice system functions? **OL**

S Skill Practice

Using Map Skills In which parts of the continental United States do most states have no death penalty? *(the Northeast and the northern Midwest)* **BL**

Uniform Penalties Have students explore the issue of uniform penalties for similar crimes in all states. **Ask:** Would uniform penalties better extend equal protection of the law? *(Students might indicate that a uniform code could make it more difficult to consider the individual circumstances of each case; on the other hand, students might discuss the fairness of discrepant sentences, or might consider whether differences in sentences are related to the economic or ethnic backgrounds of the accused.)* **OL**

Differentiated Instruction

Supreme Court Case Studies, p. 99

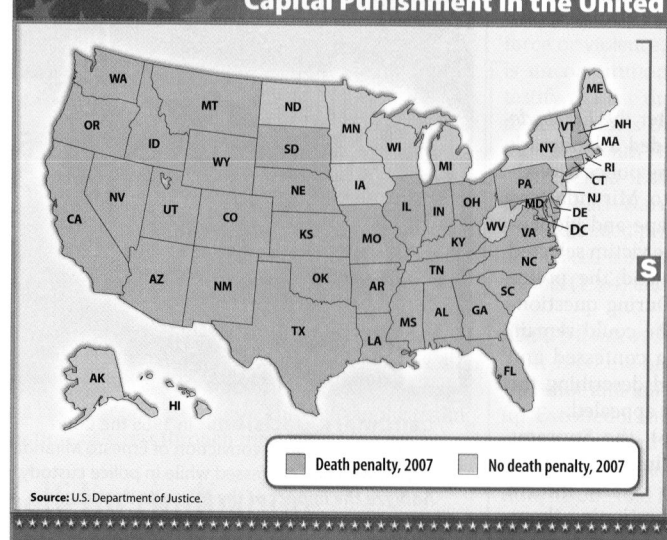

Capital Punishment in the United States

Source: U.S. Department of Justice.

Legend: ■ Death penalty, 2007   ■ No death penalty, 2007

Support For The Death Penalty

	% Oppose	% Favor*
Total	32	62
White	27	68
Black	51	40
Hispanic	45	49
Other	47	48
Conservative Republican	14	82
Mod/Liberal Republican	25	74
Independent	33	60
Mod/Conserv. Democrat	37	57
Liberal Democrat	53	41
White Protestant	23	71
White, non-Hispanic Catholic	28	67
Unaffiliated	36	59

*The columns across do not add to 100 percent because neutral responses are not shown.
Source: Pew Research Center, 2007.

Critical Thinking In December 2007, New Jersey abolished the death penalty, leaving 37 states where it is still legal. *Which phrase in the Eighth Amendment has required states to reexamine their methods of execution?*

People can, however, face criminal charges even if they have paid a civil fine for violating government regulations. This was the ruling in *Hudson* v. *United States*[1] (1997), a case against officials who violated banking regulations.

Double jeopardy does not apply in several other situations. If a crime violates both state and federal law, the case can be tried at both government levels. If a single act involves more than one offense, double jeopardy does not apply—stealing a car and selling it, for example, involves theft and the sale of stolen goods. Double jeopardy also does not apply when a trial jury fails to agree on a verdict—the accused could have to stand trial again. Finally, double jeopardy does not apply if a defendant makes an appeal in a higher court.

Debating the Death Penalty

The Eighth Amendment forbids cruel and unusual punishment. It is the only place in the Constitution where criminal penalties are specifically limited. The Supreme Court has rarely found that a penalty is cruel and unusual. In *Rhodes* v. *Chapman*[2](1981), for example, the Court ruled that putting two prisoners in a cell built for one is not cruel and unusual punishment.

Ever since the 1970s, however, there has been debate over whether the death penalty—also called capital punishment—should be considered "cruel and unusual punishment." In *Furman* v. *Georgia*[3] (1972), the Supreme Court did not outlaw the death penalty, but it struck down existing death penalty statutes. The reason, the Court explained, was that the death penalty was being administered arbitrarily; that is, in an illogical and inconsistent manner. It was imposed mainly on African Americans and applied to a wide variety of cases.

In 1976 the Court allowed executions to resume. In 35 states, new death penalty laws were passed. Some states hoped to eliminate arbitrary decisions by making the death penalty mandatory, or required, for certain crimes. The Court did not accept this solution either. It ruled in *Woodson* v. *North Carolina*[4] (1976) that a mandatory law is unconstitutional because it does not allow a jury to take into account circumstances that might lead to a lesser sentence.

See the following footnoted materials in the **Reference Handbook:**
1. *Hudson* v. *United States* case summary, page R28.
2. *Rhodes* v. *Chapman* case summary, page R33.
3. *Furman* v. *Georgia* case summary, page R27.
4. *Woodson* v. *North Carolina* case summary, page R37.

The Rights of the Accused

Objective: Learn about Fifth Amendment rights.

Focus/Teach: Have students read the activity and discuss *Miranda* v. *Arizona*.

Assess: Assign the Case Analysis Questions.

Close: Discuss and evaluate the long-term impact of the ruling.

Differentiated Instruction Strategies

BL Review the wording of the Fifth Amendment and have students paraphrase its meaning.

AL Have students research cases in which a suspect's Fifth Amendment rights might have been violated.

ELL Select phrases from the ruling and help students learn new vocabulary terms.

Other states addressed the problem by establishing new court procedures to reduce arbitrary decisions and racial prejudice. In *Gregg* v. *Georgia*[1] (1976), the Court upheld Georgia's law. This decision made it clear that the Court did not view the death penalty itself as cruel and unusual punishment.

Since then the Court has issued a series of decisions upholding the death penalty while at the same time limiting the ultimate punishment to a small category of offenders. Thus in *Atkins* v. *Virginia* (2002), the Court said the death penalty could not be used for mentally disabled defendants. In *Roper* v. *Simmons* (2005), the death penalty was narrowed further when it was ruled it should not apply to defendants who were under 18 when they committed a crime. Then in *Kennedy* v. *Louisiana* (2008), the justices rejected it for child rapists, saying that the death penalty should apply only to murder in crimes against individuals. (The justices added that this ruling did not apply to crimes against the government, such as espionage or terrorism.)

The American Bar Association (ABA) has called for a moratorium, or temporary halt, to the death penalty to study these issues. In 2000 Illinois governor George Ryan called for a death penalty moratorium there, saying that there was a flaw in the system. Campaigns against the death penalty have gained ground partly because of DNA testing. In 2007 it was reported that 200 people were freed from prison through DNA tests proving their innocence. For many defendants, however, no DNA

See the following footnoted materials in the **Reference Handbook:**
1. *Gregg* v. *Georgia* case summary, page R28.

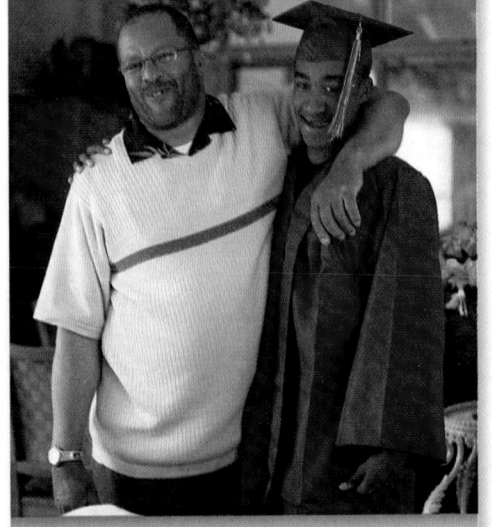

Impact of DNA Testing Ricky Walker (left) is seen here with his nephew. Walker served 12 years in prison before being freed. A pro bono lawyer worked for the DNA testing that proved Walker was innocent. *How do such cases influence the capital punishment debate?*

evidence is involved or DNA is no longer available. In late 2007, New Jersey abolished the death penalty; it was the first state to do so in four decades.

Court cases continue on aspects of the death penalty. In mid-2008, the Supreme Court heard *Baze* v. *Rees* and ruled on one method of lethal injection. (See page 421 for facts of the case.) By its nature, the death penalty remains controversial.

Landmark Case

See *Gregg* v. *Georgia* in the Supreme Court Case Summaries in the **Reference Handbook** and Case Study 60 in the *Supreme Court Case Studies* booklet.

Assess

Assign the Section 4 Assessment as homework or as an in-class activity, or have students take Section Quiz 15-4 from *Section Quizzes and Chapter Tests*.

Close

Drawing Conclusions Ask: Do you agree or disagree with the opinion that Americans who are accused of crimes have too many legal rights? Invite discussion, encouraging students to draw upon details from the section to support their views. **OL**

SECTION 4 Review

Vocabulary

1. **Explain** the significance of: exclusionary rule, counsel, self-incrimination, double jeopardy.

Main Ideas

2. **Analyzing** What procedure must police follow to make a lawful search?

3. **Examining** What does the Sixth Amendment guarantee, and how did *Gideon* v. *Wainwright* set a standard?

Critical Thinking

4. **Identifying** What decisions must the accused make when he or she hears the Miranda warning?

5. **Organizing** Use a graphic organizer like the one below to analyze the significance of the *Gideon, Escobedo,* and *Miranda* cases.

Gideon	Escobedo	Miranda

Writing About Government

6. **Descriptive Writing** Would you be willing to undergo routine random drug testing or locker searches in your school? Create a slogan explaining your position, and use it to create a one-page advertisement for your position.

CHAPTER 15: *Law in America* **443**

Section 4 Review

Answers

1. All definitions can be found in the section and the Glossary.
2. Police must state under oath that they have probable cause to search, and then they must obtain a warrant. Special warrantless situations also exist.
3. The Sixth Amendment guarantees a defendant the right to counsel; until *Gideon,* defendants in state courts could be tried without an attorney until the case established the rule that whenever a jail sentence of six months or more is possible,

the accused has a right to a lawyer at public expense.
4. An accused person has to decide whether to say anything or remain silent. If the accused decides to talk, he or she must decide whether or not to ask for an attorney to be present.
5. *Gideon:* guaranteed the right to counsel; *Escobedo:* limited self-incrimination; *Miranda:* expanded protection of the accused
6. Students' slogans and posters should indicate their positions.

Focus

Introducing the Topic

Ask students to read through the time line of changes in the United States judiciary and explain how each event made the judiciary either more independent or less independent. If the event made the judiciary less independent, have students determine why that change may have been made.

Teach

C Critical Thinking

Drawing Conclusions **Ask:** Why would the Constitution ban the Supreme Court from hearing suits against the states? *(Many Americans were afraid states would lose much of their authority if they could be sued in federal courts.)* **OL**

Additional Support

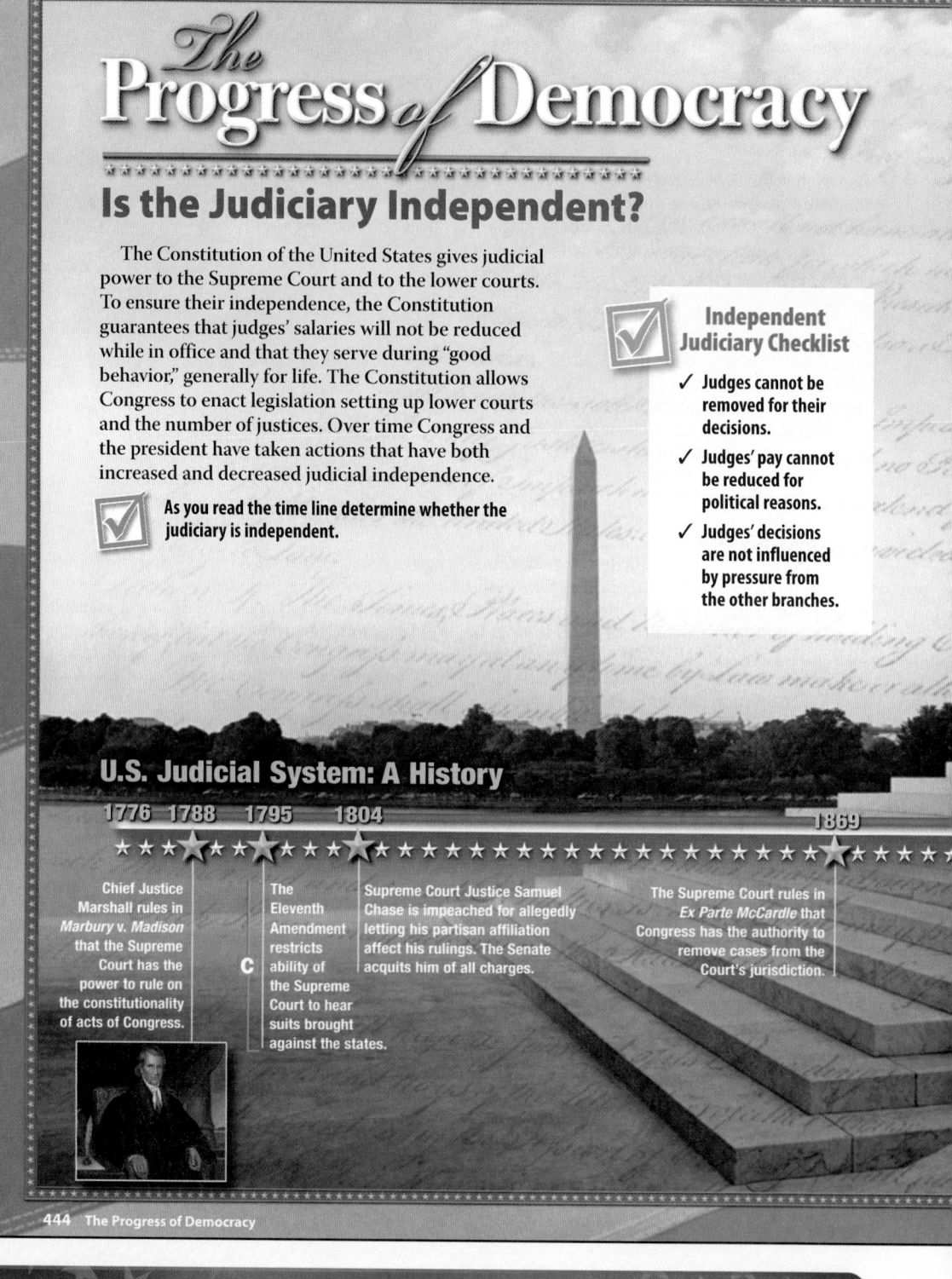

The Progress of Democracy

Is the Judiciary Independent?

The Constitution of the United States gives judicial power to the Supreme Court and to the lower courts. To ensure their independence, the Constitution guarantees that judges' salaries will not be reduced while in office and that they serve during "good behavior," generally for life. The Constitution allows Congress to enact legislation setting up lower courts and the number of justices. Over time Congress and the president have taken actions that have both increased and decreased judicial independence.

☑ As you read the time line determine whether the judiciary is independent.

Independent Judiciary Checklist

✓ Judges cannot be removed for their decisions.

✓ Judges' pay cannot be reduced for political reasons.

✓ Judges' decisions are not influenced by pressure from the other branches.

U.S. Judicial System: A History

1776 1788 1795 1804   1869

Chief Justice Marshall rules in *Marbury* v. *Madison* that the Supreme Court has the power to rule on the constitutionality of acts of Congress.

C

The Eleventh Amendment restricts ability of the Supreme Court to hear suits brought against the states.

Supreme Court Justice Samuel Chase is impeached for allegedly letting his partisan affiliation affect his rulings. The Senate acquits him of all charges.

The Supreme Court rules in *Ex Parte McCardle* that Congress has the authority to remove cases from the Court's jurisdiction.

Extending the Content

Partisanship on the Supreme Court
Samuel Chase signed the Declaration of Independence and was appointed to the Supreme Court by George Washington. On the Court he gained a reputation as a strong supporter of the Federalists. The Democratic-Republican-led Congress filed impeachment articles against him, arguing that he let his political leanings affect his cases. He was impeached by the House and acquitted by the Senate. The acquittal set a precedent that judges could not be removed based on their performance on the bench. Chase is the only Supreme Court justice ever to be impeached.

In *Hamdan* v. *Rumsfeld* the Supreme Court rules it can hear cases from detainees in Guantanamo Bay despite legislation that stripped federal courts of jurisdiction.

1937   1986   2006

After several elements of the New Deal were declared unconstitutional, President Franklin D. Roosevelt proposed adding six new justices to the Court.

C

The Anti-Drug Abuse Act enacts federally mandated minimum sentences that must be imposed for certain crimes.

LET ME MOVE OVER!

U.S. SUPREME COURT

A FREE AND INDEPENDENT JUDICIARY

C Critical Thinking

Making Inferences Explain to students that the Constitution allows Congress to set the number of judges on the Supreme Court. **Ask:** Why does Congress not add more sympathetic justices to the Court when the Court declares a law unconstitutional? *(Students may suggest that citizens or the opposition party might get angry and retaliate if Congress appeared to be manipulating the courts to achieve political results.)* **OL**

Did You Know?

Salim Hamdan was a chauffeur for Osama bin Laden. He was captured by a militia group in Afghanistan and imprisoned at the U.S. naval base at Guantanamo Bay, Cuba. After the Supreme Court invalidated his conviction by a U.S. military commission, Congress set up a new method of trying enemy suspects. Hamdan was convicted of illegal enemy activity by a military jury and sentenced to five and a half years imprisonment.

Differentiated Instruction

Activity: Multiple Learning Styles

Visual/Spatial Have students create political cartoons of Franklin D. Roosevelt's plan to pack the court with six additional associate justices. When creating their cartoons, students should decide whether or not they support Roosevelt's plan and what facts shaped their opinions.

Their cartoons should reflect their opinions and highlight significant aspects of the controversy. Display students' completed cartoons in the classroom and invite students to interpret the artwork.

R Reading Strategy

Using Context Clues Ask: How are members of Venezuela's Supreme Tribunal of Justice likely to feel about a recall of President Chavez? *(Since most of the members were appointed by pro-Chavez legislators, they are unlikely to support a recall.)* **BL**

C Critical Thinking

Identifying Central Issues Have students look through the independent Judiciary Checklist. Ask them to think of other items that may be necessary for an independent judiciary. **Ask:** Are any of the items currently on the list not necessary for an independent judiciary? *(Students' answers will vary.)* **AL**

W Writing Support

Persuasive Writing Unlike the United States, where the legislative branch enacts disciplinary measures on judicial branch officials, Colombia's judiciary is in charge of disciplining itself. Have students decide which method is better and then write a persuasive essay explaining why. **OL**

Additional Support

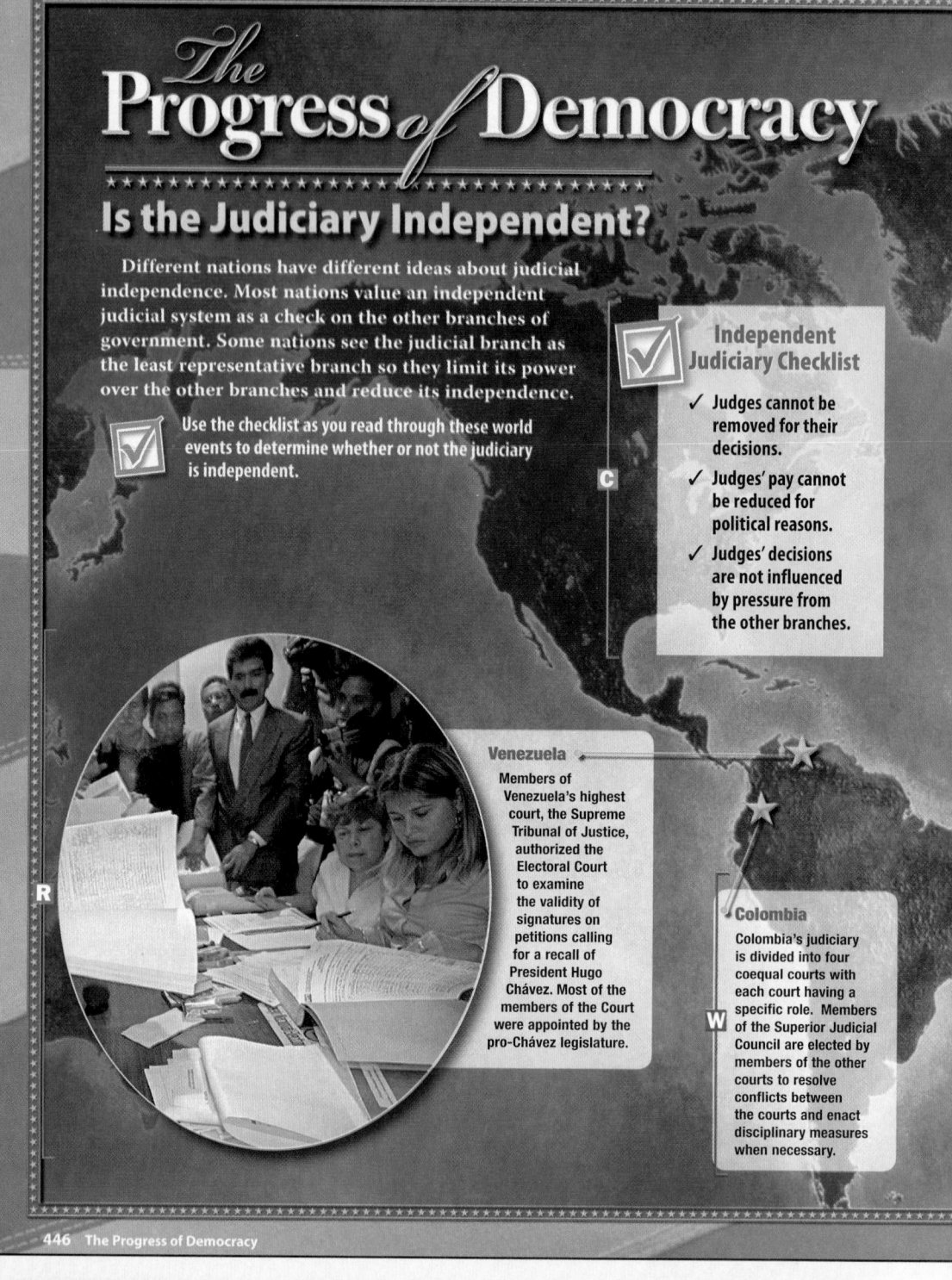

The Progress of Democracy

★★★★★★★★★★★★★★★★★★★★★★

Is the Judiciary Independent?

Different nations have different ideas about judicial independence. Most nations value an independent judicial system as a check on the other branches of government. Some nations see the judicial branch as the least representative branch so they limit its power over the other branches and reduce its independence.

Use the checklist as you read through these world events to determine whether or not the judiciary is independent.

Independent Judiciary Checklist

✓ Judges cannot be removed for their decisions.

✓ Judges' pay cannot be reduced for political reasons.

✓ Judges' decisions are not influenced by pressure from the other branches.

Venezuela

Members of Venezuela's highest court, the Supreme Tribunal of Justice, authorized the Electoral Court to examine the validity of signatures on petitions calling for a recall of President Hugo Chávez. Most of the members of the Court were appointed by the pro-Chávez legislature.

Colombia

Colombia's judiciary is divided into four coequal courts with each court having a specific role. Members of the Superior Judicial Council are elected by members of the other courts to resolve conflicts between the courts and enact disciplinary measures when necessary.

446   The Progress of Democracy

Activity: Collaborative Learning

Creating a Time Line Organize students into five groups and assign each group one of the countries from the feature. Have students research the history of the country's judicial branch. Have students make a time line of changes in the judiciary in the country, including its historical origins. Have groups present their finding to the class and explain whether each of the changes made the judiciary more or less independent.

Afghanistan

President Hamid Karzai is responsible for selecting members of the Afghani Supreme Court. His selections must be approved by the legislature. Justices serve 10-year terms.

France

Laws passed by the French legislature are subject to judicial review only before they are signed by the president.

Pakistan

In 2007 President Pervez Musharraf declared emergency rule and fired the Chief Justice of the Supreme Court. Thousands of Pakistani lawyers demonstrated in the streets in protest.

W

D

Critical Thinking

Independent Judiciaries

1. How does the United States judicial system compare to judicial systems around the world? What changes could make the judiciary more independent?

2. Which countries above do not have independent judiciaries? Which criteria do they fail to meet?

3. Select a country and research its judicial system. Is its judiciary independent? What changes could be made to make it more independent? How does that country compare to other countries around the world?

POLITICAL PROFILES **Hamid Karzai** (1957–) is the current president of Afghanistan. In the 1980s, he fought against Soviet troops and helped remove them from Afghanistan. In the 1990s, he lived in exile in Pakistan. After the U.S. invasion, Karzai was appointed the interim president, and in 2004 he was elected president.

W ## Writing Support

Narrative Writing Ask students to imagine that they are lawyers in Pakistan. Have them research Musharraf's reasons for firing the chief justice and write an essay describing what actions they are taking as a result. **AL**

D ## Differentiated Instruction

Visual/Spatial Have students examine the photo of Pakistani lawyers. **Ask:** What does their hand gesture mean? Has it meant different things in other times and places? *(the peace sign; during World War II, Winston Churchill popularized it as a 'V' for 'victory'; they may suggest that it means the same today in Pakistan as in the United States.)* **BL**

Answers

1. Students' answers should include details on how the United States judiciary compares to other countries around the world.
2. France: Judicial review extremely limited; Pakistan: Chief Justice fired by the President
3. Students' research should include information on a country's judiciary and what changes could be made to make it more independent.

ExamView® Assessment Suite

This easy-to-use software includes extensive question banks and allows you to create fully customized tests that can be administered in print or online.

Reviewing Vocabulary

1. f
2. a
3. h
4. g
5. b
6. i
7. e
8. c
9. d
10. j

Reviewing Main Ideas

11. Hammurabi's Code divided laws into different categories. The Ten Commandments established principles of moral and ethical laws.
12. Almost 90 percent of cases heard in state courts involve civil cases, such as buying a house or getting married.
13. civil cases and criminal cases
14. Prior to any questioning, the person must be warned that he or she has the right to remain silent, that any statement he or she makes may be used as evidence against him or her in court, and that he or she has the right to the presence of an attorney.

Critical Thinking

15. All people are equal before the court, even if they have little money or little political power.

CHAPTER 15 Assessment and Activities

Reviewing Vocabulary

On a separate sheet of paper, choose the letter of the content vocabulary word(s) identified in each statement below.

a. administrative law
b. verdict
c. indictment
d. contract
e. statute
f. misdemeanor
g. common law
h. tort
i. adversary system
j. injunction

1. a minor or less serious crime
2. the procedures of and rules issued by government agencies
3. any wrongful act, other than breach of contract, for which the injured party has the right to sue for damages in a civil court
4. law made by judges in resolving individual cases
5. decision of a jury in a criminal case
6. a judicial system in which lawyers for the opposing sides present their cases in court
7. a law written by a legislative branch
8. a charge by a grand jury that a person committed a particular crime
9. a set of voluntary promises, enforceable by the law, between parties to do or not to do something
10. a court order that forbids a defendant from taking or continuing a certain action

Reviewing Main Ideas

Section 1 *(pages 415–420)*

11. **Identifying** What were two early systems of laws and what principles did they establish?

Section 2 *(pages 422–427)*

12. **Expressing** What type of court cases are heard most often in state courts?

Section 3 *(pages 429–435)*

13. **Analyzing** What two kinds of cases do courts in the American legal system hear?

Section 4 *(pages 436–443)*

14. **Listing** What are the three Miranda rules?

Critical Thinking

15. **Essential Question** How has the principle of "equal justice under law" been applied in key Court cases?

16. **Making Comparisons** What is the difference between procedural due process and substantive due process?

17. **Demonstrating Reasoned Judgment** Use a graphic organizer to show positions on plea bargaining.

Plea Bargaining	
For	Against

Chapter Summary

Sources of Law

★ **Constitutional law** studies and interprets the Constitution and resolves the tension between individual rights and government powers.
★ **Statutory law** is created by a governing legislature.
★ **Administrative law** governs the authority and procedures practiced by government agencies.
★ **Common law** is the historical body of legal decisions that provide the basis for current and future decisions.
★ **Equity law** is a system of legal actions based on the principle of fairness.

Kinds of Law

Civil Law
★ Concerns disputes among two or more individuals or between individuals and the government
★ Makes up 90 percent of the cases heard in state courts
★ Deals with contracts, property law, family law, and torts

Criminal Law
★ Concerns acts that cause injury or harm to people or to society in general
★ The government charges someone with a crime and serves as the prosecution
★ Includes petty offenses, misdemeanors, and felonies

---

16. Procedural due process deals with the way in which a law is carried out; substantive due process deals with the content of the law.
17. Answers might include—For: avoids a lengthy and expensive trial; makes sure that a person receives some kind of punishment. Against: a serious crime may get a light sentence; encourages people to give up their right to a fair trial.

Government ONLINE Self-Check Quiz
Visit glencoe.com and enter QuickPass™ code USG9822c15.
Click on Self-Check Quizzes for additional test practice.

CHAPTER 15 Assessment and Activities

Document-Based Questions

Analyzing Primary Sources

Read the excerpt below and answer the questions that follow.

Hammurabi's Code was the world's first written code of law, compiled by the king of Babylonia in the 1700s B.C. The principles expressed in the code share many parallels with the principles of the modern legal system.

> 66 *9. If any one lose an article, and find it in the possession of another: if the person in whose possession the thing is found say 'A merchant sold it to me, I paid for it before witnesses,' and if the owner of the thing say, 'I will bring witnesses who know my property,' then shall the purchaser bring the merchant who sold it to him, and the witnesses before whom he bought it, and the owner shall bring witnesses who can identify his property. The judge shall examine [the witnesses'] testimony. . . . The merchant is then proved to be a thief and shall be put to death. The owner of the lost article receives his property, and he who bought it receives the money he paid from the estate of the merchant.* 99

18. What parallels can be drawn between this particular code and modern U.S. trial procedures?

19. How do you think Hammurabi's Code would treat the guilt or innocence of the accused? Is this similar to or different from American laws?

Applying Technology Skills

20. **Using the Internet** Locate a Web site on the Internet that deals with criminal law. Find pending federal criminal cases and the issues involved in these cases. Write a short report summarizing the main issues of one case, and share your findings with the class.

Interpreting Political Cartoons

Analyze the cartoon and answer the questions that follow. Base your answers on the cartoon and your knowledge of Chapter 15.

Cartoonists & Writers Syndicate

"Do you swear to tell your version of the truth as you perceive it, clouded perhaps by the passage of time and preconceived notions?"

21. What is occurring in this cartoon?

22. How do you think the cartoonist feels about the reliability of witnesses' testimony during court trials?

23. Do you believe that the current trial system ensures justice? Explain.

Participating IN GOVERNMENT

24. The government must provide a lawyer for defendants in criminal cases who cannot afford one. This is not true of civil cases. Thus, many lawyers donate their time to helping poor people with lawsuits. Find out about the work of a legal aid society in your community. Report your findings to the class.

Interpreting Political Cartoons

21. Someone is being sworn in to give testimony at a trial.

22. The cartoonist is suggesting that testimony may not be reliable. Students may note that testimony could be affected by cloudy memories, points of view, feelings, and so on.

23. Students should provide answers based on information from the chapter. Students also might point out how the current trial system could be improved.

Participating IN GOVERNMENT

24. Call on volunteers to report on the work of a legal aid society in your community. Ask students to report on the kinds of lawsuits that the society generally deals with.

Analyzing Primary Sources

18. First, the accuser must prove his or her case against the accused. Next, the case in this code must be heard by an impartial judge. Finally, the code sets out clear steps through which the trial is to proceed. (In due process, a person must be notified that he or she has done something wrong and that the government will take action; the affected person has the right to respond or be heard on the accusation.)

19. Implicit in this code is an assumption of innocence until guilt is proven. This is the basis of the American legal system, in which the defendant is presumed innocent and the burden of proof is on the prosecution.

Applying Technology Skills

20. Students' reports should logically and concisely discuss the main issues of the case they have chosen.

Chapter Bonus Test Question

Ask: What is a docket, and how does it relate to court activity? *(A docket can be either the cases listed on a court's calendar or the daily summary of the court's action. Both meanings suggest the importance of scheduling and documentation.)*

Participating *in* Government

UNIT PACING CHART*

	Chapter 16	Chapter 17	Chapter 18	Chapter 19
Day 1	Unit Opener Chapter Opener Section 1	Chapter Opener Section 1	Chapter Opener Section 1	Chapter Opener Section 1
Day 2	Section 2	Issues to Debate Section 2	Section 2	Section 2 Issues to Debate
Day 3	Issues to Debate	Supreme Court Cases to Debate Voter's Handbook	Section 3 Supreme Court Cases to Debate	Supreme Court Cases to Debate
Day 4	Section 3 Government Skills	Section 3 TIME Notebook	Section 4 Government Skills	Section 3
Day 5	Review Chapter Assessment	Review Chapter Assessment	Review Chapter Assessment	Review Chapter Assessment

*Unit Pacing Chart based on year-long course; modify pacing by half for semester-long course

 Teacher to Teacher

Chris Staggs
East Baton Rouge
Parish Schools
Zachary, LA

Staging a Presidential Election Show students how political parties work by staging a mock presidential election. Organize the class into two parties, and have each party decide on a candidate for president. Next, subdivide the parties by organizing students into groups of two or three, and outline the tasks for the group members. Each group will write a position paper on an issue such as welfare, education, immigration, or taxes. Students will create campaign posters and campaign ads, each using one type of propaganda. The groups will all write campaign slogans. After the small groups complete their tasks, they should convene again as parties to combine their position papers and develop a party platform.

Each party will then submit a position paper addressing certain basic issues. Both candidates can give campaign speeches to the class. The party should help write the speech, making sure that important platform issues are covered. Students then elect the president of their classroom. Extra credit can be given for dressing as the part, creating campaign buttons, and so on.

Author Note

Dear U.S. Government Teacher,

Vigorous debate has characterized American democracy since the early republic, and many of these debates have occurred through the political party system. How parties originated and developed is the subject of Chapter 16, the first of four chapters in Unit 6. In the United States, two parties dominate our political life, unlike the multi-party or one-party systems of many other nations.

American parties serve to aggregate citizens and interest groups of various outlooks. Your students should be able to draw the conclusion that a significant result of the two-party system is a process which forces compromise on any individual or group that hopes to win broad political support.

Chapter 17 includes a virtual voter's handbook. Section 4 analyzes various voter influences, for example, a family's voting history. Today's U.S. Government student is tomorrow's voter. By making students aware of campaign tactics and how voters have historically shaped their political identity, you are increasing their self-awareness as citizens. When they do go to the polls—next year or even sooner—they will be in a better position to know why they are casting their vote as they are.

Historically, our political culture has been marked by the instinct to join with others to reach a goal. The French writer Alexis de Tocqueville commented on this trait more than 150 years ago. Interest groups employing lobbyists are a modern-day manifestation of this phenomenon. Chapter 18 makes it clear, however, that interest groups do not comprise only the well-funded lobbyists of large corporations but also include small, local grassroots organizations. Public opinion factors heavily into national debates as analysts and pollsters try to track the volatile yet influential element of popular sentiment in national conversations.

Richard C. Remy

Richard C. Remy, Ph.D.
Author

Focus

Making It Relevant

Forming a Political Party
Have students work in small groups to create their own political party to serve an unfulfilled local need. Have groups create a party logo, slogan, song, and political poster illustrating the party platform. After groups have presented their new party to the class, have students vote on the party "most likely to succeed."

Unit Objectives

After studying this unit, students will be able to:

- **Identify** the function of political parties.

- **Analyze** the importance of an informed electorate.

- **Evaluate** the effect of interest groups on the government.

- **Explain** the power of mass media as it relates to individuals, interest groups, and the government.

Unit Overview

Unit 6 discusses the different ways that people can participate in government.

Chapter 16 describes the development and role of political parties.

Chapter 17 describes election campaigns and the influence of voters on the electoral process.

Chapter 18 describes how interest groups shape public policy and opinion.

Chapter 19 discusses how the mass media and the Internet impact government.

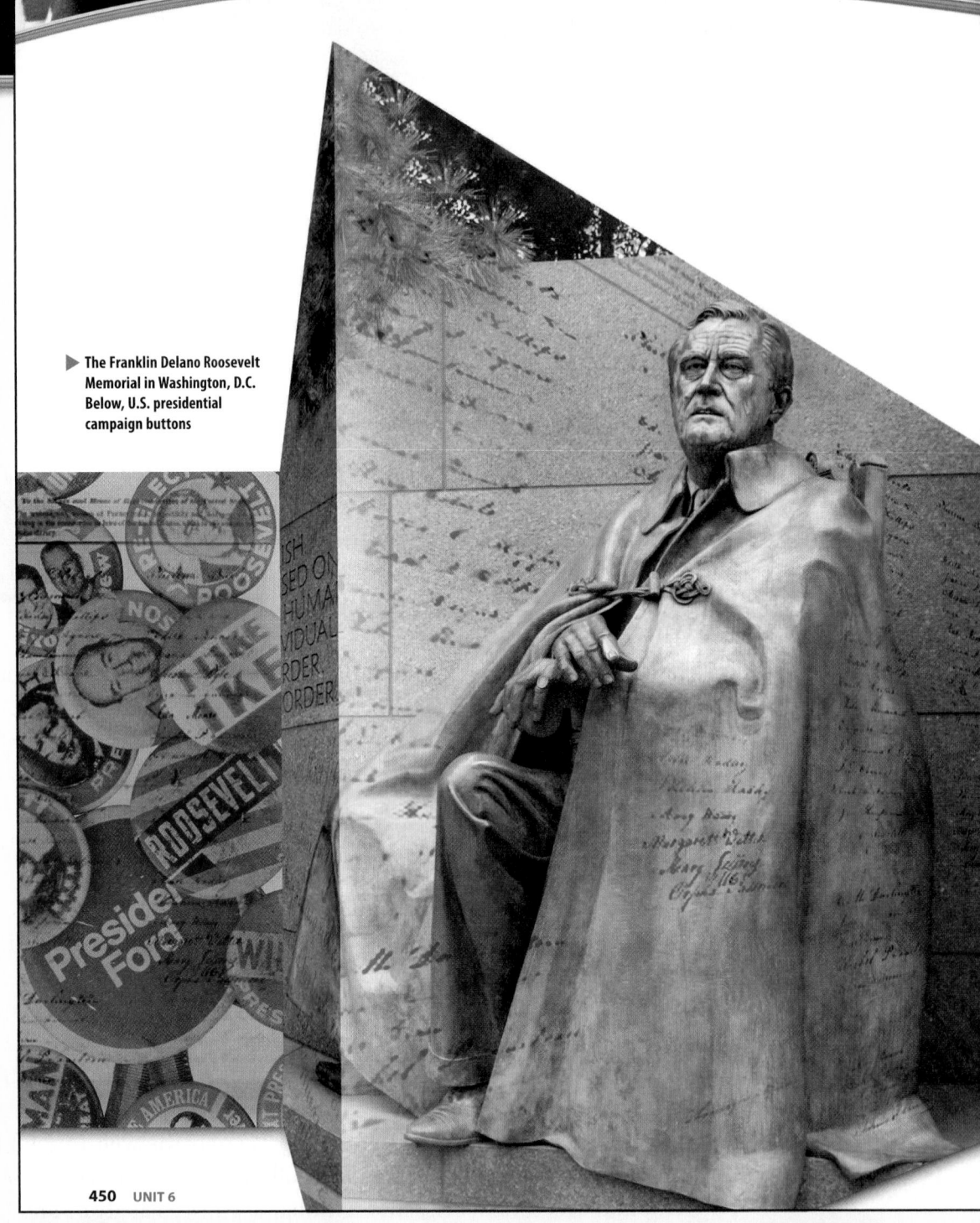

▶ The Franklin Delano Roosevelt Memorial in Washington, D.C. Below, U.S. presidential campaign buttons

450   UNIT 6

Activity: Launching the Unit

Writing Letters Have students write a series of letters, one for each chapter. **Chapter 16:** Write a letter to a political party that students are interested in joining. Ask if there is a local party office, and inquire about membership requirements. **Chapter 17:** Write to a candidate for public office to ask about his or her stand on specific issues of interest to students. **Chapter 18:** Inquire about joining an interest group or a political action committee, and ask for information that details the group's mission and main issues. **Chapter 19:** Write to a mass media public relations office requesting information regarding policies on endorsement of public officials, interest groups, and public policies. As students receive responses to their letters, have them share the information with the class. **OL**

Participating *in* Government

Participating IN GOVERNMENT

BIG IDEA **Civic Participation** With classmates, conduct a survey of more than 100 adults. (Track respondents by an assigned number only.) Respondents will indicate their age, gender, ethnic or racial identity, education, and occupation. Ask the following: Do you consider yourself a Democrat, Republican, or independent? Did you vote in the last election? Then analyze the results by correlating age or other characteristics with their answers.

▲ Journalists watch the first presidential debate in 2000 between former vice president Al Gore and then Texas governor George W. Bush.

451

Teach

S Skill Practice

Visual Literacy Have students study the photo on page 451 and think about the role of the media in the election process. **Ask:** Why does the photo do a good job of suggesting how voters rely on the media? *(It shows reporters and writers busily writing their observations and comments on the candidates' performances and that many voters will be influenced by these media assessments.)*

Online Current Events Update
History happens every day. Visit Glencoe's Online Current Events Update at glencoe.com to find news reports, features, maps, graphs, and images about events that shape our lives. Students can connect those events to historical events in world and American history by exploring related events on an interactive time line—a time line that ends with today.

 Graduation: Exit With Success

Teaching Tip Modeling can help students learn how to develop comprehension skills such as making inferences. Read aloud an excerpt from the textbook, and model what you are thinking as you read and the inferences you are making.

Extra Credit Project

Polling the Community Have interested students poll 10 people in the community as to whether or not they voted in the last election. If the person did not vote, the student should then ask for the main reason why. Have students make a list of the reasons people gave for not voting and then share their information with the class. You might want to make a class list to tally the main reasons why people do not vote. **OL**

Key to Ability Levels

BL Below level   AL Above level
OL On level   ELL English Language Learners

Key to Teaching Resources

📁 Print Material   🖨 Transparency
💿 CD-ROM or DVD

Levels					Resources	Chapter Opener	Section 1	Section 2	Section 3	Chapter Assess
BL	OL	AL	ELL							
FOCUS										
BL	OL	AL	ELL	🖨	**Section Focus Transparencies**		16-1	16-2	16-3	
TEACH										
BL	OL		ELL	📁	**Reading Essentials and Study Guide (and Answer Key)**		p. 177	p. 181	p. 183	
BL	OL		ELL	📁	**Guided Reading Activities**		p. 58	p. 59	p. 60	
BL	OL		ELL	📁	**Vocabulary Activities**		p. 16			
BL	OL	AL	ELL	📁	**Chapter Summaries**					
BL	OL			📁	**American Biographies**				p. 74	
BL	OL	AL	ELL	📁	**Cooperative Learning Activities**					
	OL	AL	ELL	📁	**Government Simulations and Debate**			p. 36		
BL	OL	AL	ELL	📁	**Historical Documents and Speeches**		p. 16			
BL	OL	AL	ELL	📁	**Interpreting Political Cartoons**				p. 31	
BL	OL		ELL	📁	**Skill Reinforcement Activities**			p. 16		
BL	OL	AL	ELL	📁	**Source Readings**		p. 16			
BL	OL			📁	**Supreme Court Case Studies**					
BL	OL	AL	ELL	📁	**Participating in Government Activities**				p. 31	
BL	OL		ELL	📁	**Spanish Declaration of Independence and U.S. Constitution**	✓	✓	✓	✓	✓
BL	OL	AL	ELL	📁	**NGS World Atlas, Spanish**	✓	✓	✓	✓	✓
BL	OL	AL	ELL	🖨	**Unit Overlay Transparencies, Strategies, and Activities**	✓	✓	✓	✓	✓
BL	OL		ELL	🖨	**Making It Relevant Transparencies**	✓	✓	✓	✓	✓
BL	OL	AL	ELL	🖨	**High School Writing Process Transparencies, Strategies, and Activities**	✓	✓	✓	✓	✓
BL	OL	AL		🖨	**American Art & Architecture Transparencies, Strategies, and Activities**	✓	✓	✓	✓	✓

✓ Chapter- or unit-based activities applicable to all sections in this chapter

TeacherWorks™ Plus
All-In-One Planner and Resource Center

- Interactive Lesson Planner
- Interactive Teacher Edition
- Fully editable blackline masters
- Chapter Spotlight Videos Launch

- Differentiated Lesson Plans
- Printable reports of daily assignments
- Standards tracking system

Levels					Resources	Chapter Opener	Section 1	Section 2	Section 3	Chapter Assess
BL	OL	AL	ELL							
TEACH *(continued)*										
BL	OL			⊙	**American Music: Hits Through History**	✓	✓	✓	✓	✓
BL	OL		ELL	📁	**Reading Strategies for the Social Studies Classroom**	✓	✓	✓	✓	✓
			ELL	📁	**English Language Learner Handbook**	✓	✓	✓	✓	✓
BL	OL		ELL	📁	**Writer's Guidebook for Social Studies**	✓	✓	✓	✓	✓
BL	OL	AL	ELL	📁	**Living Constitution, SE**	✓	✓	✓	✓	✓
BL	OL	AL	ELL	📁	**Living Constitution, TAE**	✓	✓	✓	✓	✓
BL	OL			📁	**NGS World Atlas, English**	✓	✓	✓	✓	✓
BL	OL		ELL	📁	**The Constitution and You (poster set)**	✓	✓	✓	✓	✓
BL	OL	AL	ELL	📁	**Spanish Chapter Summaries**					
BL	OL	AL	ELL	📁	**Spanish Vocabulary Activities**		p. 16			
BL	OL		ELL	📁	**Spanish Reading Essentials and Study Guide (and Answer Key)**		p. 177	p. 181	p. 183	
BL	OL	AL	ELL	⊙	**PresentationPlus! with MindJogger CheckPoint**	✓	✓	✓	✓	✓
ASSESS										
BL	OL	AL	ELL	⊙	*ExamView® Assessment Suite*		16-1	16-2	16-3	Ch. 16
BL	OL	AL	ELL	📁	**Authentic Assessment with Rubrics**					
BL	OL	AL	ELL	📁	**Section Quizzes and Chapter Tests**		p. 195	p. 196	p. 197	pp. 199–206
BL	OL	AL	ELL	📁	**Spanish Section Quizzes and Tests**		p. 195	p. 196	p. 197	pp. 199–206
CLOSE										
BL			ELL	📁	**Reteaching Activities**				p. 16	p. 16
BL	OL	AL	ELL	⊙	**StudentWorks™ Plus with Audio Summaries**	✓	✓	✓	✓	✓
BL	OL		ELL	🖥	**Graphic Organizer Transparencies**		✓	✓	✓	
BL	OL		ELL	📁	**High School Government Reading and Study Skills Foldables®**		p. 59	p. 59	p. 59	

Integrating Technology

Chapter Overviews · Teach With Technology

What is a Chapter Overview?

A Chapter Overview provides an online section-by-section summary of the content of each chapter. It can help students review—or preview—chapter content to increase comprehension of main ideas.

How can a Chapter Overview help my students and me?

A Chapter Overview helps you and your students review the main points from each chapter section-by-section. It can help:

- students preview chapter content
- students focus on the main ideas
- students review chapter content
- students practice reading and comprehension skills
- you devise discussion points
- you summarize the chapter for your students

Visit glencoe.com and enter a *QuickPass*™ code to go to a Chapter Overview.

Government ONLINE

Visit glencoe.com and enter *QuickPass*™ code USG9085c16T for Chapter 16 resources.

You can easily launch a wide range of digital products from your computer's desktop with the McGraw-Hill Social Studies widget.

	Student	Teacher	Parent
Media Library			
• Student Edition Section Audio	●		●
• Chapter Spotlight Videos	●	●	●
***United States Government* Online Learning Center (Web Site)**			
• Chapter Overviews	●	●	●
• Multilingual Glossaries	●	●	●
• Study-to-Go	●	●	●
• Student Web Activities	●	●	●
• Self-Check Quizzes	●	●	●
• Online Student Edition	●	●	●
• Vocabulary eFlashcards	●	●	●
• Web Activity Lesson Plans		●	
• Vocabulary PuzzleMaker	●	●	●
• Landmark Supreme Court Cases	●	●	●
• Beyond the Textbook	●	●	●

READING SUPPORT FROM
JAMESTOWN EDUCATION

- **Timed Readings Plus in Social Studies** helps students increase their reading rate and fluency while maintaining comprehension. The 400-word passages are similar to those found on state and national assessments.

- **Reading in the Content Area: Social Studies** concentrates on six essential reading skills that help students better comprehend what they read. The book includes 75 high-interest nonfiction passages written at increasing levels of difficulty.

- **Reading Social Studies** includes strategic reading instruction and vocabulary support in Social Studies content for ELLs and native speakers of English.
www.jamestowneducation.com

Reading List Generator CD-ROM

GLENCOE BOOKLINK 3

Use this database to search more than 30,000 titles to create a customized reading list for your students.

- Reading lists can be organized by students' reading level, author, genre, theme, or area of interest.

- The database provides Degrees of Reading Power™ (DRP) and Lexile™ readability scores for all selections.

- A brief summary of each selection is included.

Economics Connection

Personal Finance Literacy

Saving and Investing: Growing Money
Explain that saving and investing are not just for older or rich people. They are the keys to building wealth. By starting early, a person can amass huge amounts of money. Why? Because, unlike money you spend, money saved or invested *grows*. Think of it this way: It's money you don't have to work for.

Saving: A savings account provides a safety net for emergencies and improves your credit rating. But there is an even better reason to save as early as possible: an important concept called *compounding*—the process of interest earning interest. Money in a savings, certificate of deposit, or money market account earns interest. That interest is added to the original amount, or principal, and the sum of the two continues to earn more interest for as long as the money stays in the account. A parent who saves $75 a month at 5 percent from the day a child is born will have more than $24,000 when the child is ready for college.

Annual Percentage Rates
When choosing an account, check the annual percentage rate, or APR—the rate of interest earned in a year. For example, if $10,000 is deposited in an account with an APR of 5 percent, at the end of the year the money has earned $500 ($10,000 × 5% = $500). That's if compounding is done only once per year. But most accounts are compounded more often, so the $10,000 principal grows faster.

Investing: About 19 percent of U.S. students in grades 8–12 own stocks or bonds. Some even manage their families' investments. Even spare change can reap rewards if invested consistently and well in stocks, bonds, or mutual funds. Since the market fluctuates, the key is to leave money invested for a long time—at least 10 years.

5 Rules for Becoming a Millionaire

1. Start young and save often.

2. Save as much as you can.

3. Get compound interest, calculated as often as possible.

4. Earn a high interest rate.

5. Leave the money in the account as long as possible.

Did You Know?

Looking rich and being rich are not the same. Most millionaires buy used cars, live in modest houses, and don't wear expensive clothes. They save at least 15 percent of their earned income.

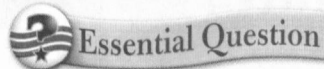 **Essential Question**

Political parties help people who have broad common interests organize to win elections. By getting large numbers of party members elected, they can play a larger role in shaping government.

Chapter Spotlight Video

To generate student interest and provide a springboard for class discussion, access the Chapter 16 Video at glencoe.com or on the video DVD.

 Dinah Zike's Foldables are three-dimensional, interactive graphic organizers that help students practice basic writing skills, review key vocabulary terms, and identify main ideas. Have students complete this chapter's Foldable activity or activities in *Dinah Zike's Reading and Study Skills Foldables* booklet. **OL**

Government ONLINE

Visit glencoe.com and enter *QuickPass*™ code USG9085c16T for Chapter 16 Resources including Chapter Overview, Student Web Activity, Self-Check Quiz, and other materials for students and teachers.

CHAPTER 16

Chapter Audio · Spotlight Video

Political Parties

John McCain, and his wife Cindy, during his 2008 bid for the Republican presidential nomination

Essential Question

How do political parties play a large role in the decisions made by government? By answering this question, it may also help you identify your own political beliefs.

Government ONLINE
Chapter Overview Visit glencoe.com and enter *QuickPass*™ code USG9822c16 for an overview, a quiz, and other chapter resources.

452

Launching the Chapter

Identifying Points of View Have interested students create a table outlining other nations' systems of government. Use the following headings for the table: Country, Form of Government, Type of Political Party System, and Name of Political Party(ies). As students read the chapter, have them list all nations that are mentioned and fill in the table with the appropriate information. Encourage students to research other nations that are not mentioned in the chapter. Discuss the information gathered with the class and compare other countries' governments and political party systems with those of the United States.
Essential Question: What role do political parties have in shaping governments? **OL**

Development of Parties

Reader's Guide

Content Vocabulary
* ★ political party (p. 453)
* ★ theocracy (p. 454)
* ★ ideologies (p. 454)
* ★ coalition government (p. 454)
* ★ third party (p. 455)
* ★ single-member district (p. 457)
* ★ proportional representation (p. 457)

Academic Vocabulary
* ★ thereby (p. 453)
* ★ revolution (p. 453)
* ★ range (p. 454)

Reading Strategy
As you read the section, create a table similar to the one below to help you take notes on the role of minor political parties.

Types of Third Parties	Description of Party Goals	Party Example

Focus

Bellringer
Section Focus Transparencies 16-1

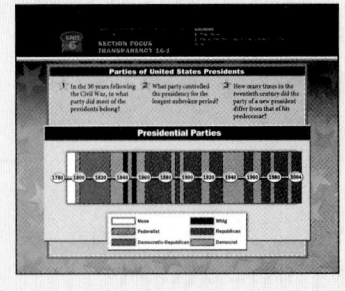

Issues in the News

After failing to form a government, Italy's President Giorgio Napolitano dissolved parliament in February 2008, preparing the way for new elections. His decision came after the legislature voted that they had no confidence in the current administration. Political instability, however, is nothing new to Italians. Since World War II, Italy has had a total of 61 governments. One reason for the political turmoil is Italy's election law, which reformers have tried to change for years. The law gives small parties in Italy's parliament potentially the same power as the largest parties when it comes to forming governments. Observers say that the squabbling and bickering that come with the constant creation and dissolution of governments have made many Italians cynical about politics.

▲ Italian President Giorgio Napolitano (left)

Reader's Guide

Answers to Graphic: Types of Third Parties: single-issue; ideological; splinter

Description of Party Goals: focus on one major social, economic, or moral issue; particular set of ideas to be enacted; disagreement with one aspect of a major party's policy

Party Example: Liberty Party; Libertarian Party; Bull Moose Party

Unlike Italy, the structure of the government in the United States does not require a coalition of political parties for the government to operate. That does not mean, however, that political parties do not exist in the United States.

Parties and Party Systems

A **political party** is a group of people with broad common interests who organize to win elections, control government, and **thereby** influence government policies. Although most nations have one or more political parties, the role that parties play differs with each nation's political system.

One-Party Systems

In a one-party system, that party *is* the government and party leaders set government policy. In some one-party nations, political differences arise within the party because the government tolerates no other opposition.

One-party systems are usually found in nations with authoritarian governments. Such governments are formed when political parties or the military take power by force. For example, a **revolution** in 1917 brought the Communist Party to power in Russia. Today Cuba, Vietnam, North Korea, and China are among the few nations that remain one-party Communist governments.

Resource Manager

R Reading Strategies	**C** Critical Thinking	**D** Differentiated Instruction	**W** Writing Support	**S** Skill Practice
Teacher Edition • Making Connections, p. 455 **Additional Resources** • Guid. Read. Act., p. 58 • Quizzes/Tests, p. 195	**Teacher Edition** • Analyzing Information, p. 456 • Predicting, p. 457 **Additional Resources** • Read. Essen., pp. 177–179	**Teacher Edition** • Logical/Mathematical, p. 454 **Additional Resources** • Foldables, p. 59 • Source Readings, p. 16	**Additional Resources** • Authentic Assess., p. 23	**Teacher Edition** • Creating a Time Line, p. 454 **Additional Resources** • Vocab. Act., p. 16

Teach

D Differentiated Instruction

Logical/Mathematical **Ask:** Why are two-party systems more efficient than multiparty systems? *(In a multiparty system, one party seldom gets a majority of the votes. Decisions are delayed until parties form coalitions to gain a majority.)* **AL**

S Skill Practice

Creating a Time Line Ask students to work in small groups to create illustrated time lines of the history of political parties in the United States. After groups have shared their time lines with the class, discuss why the two-party system has dominated and third parties have not won a national election. **BL**

Additional Support

One-party systems also exist in some non-Communist countries such as Iran where religious leaders dominate government. A government run by religious officials is known as a **theocracy.** The Muslim clergy controls the Islamic Republican Party. All major opposition parties have been outlawed or are inactive. After briefly experimenting with democratic elections in the mid-1990s, Russia has evolved into a one-party system. Vladimir Putin, who served as the president from 1999 to 2008, has created an authoritarian system in which no political parties are able to effectively compete against his United Russia Party, a powerful group of political elites loyal to Putin.

Multiparty Systems

In nations that allow more than one political party, the most common political system today is the multiparty system. France, for example, has 5 major parties, and Italy has more than 10. In such countries, voters have a wide **range** of choices on election day. The parties in a multiparty system often represent widely differing **ideologies,** or basic beliefs about government.

In a multiparty system, one party rarely gets enough support to control the government. Several parties often combine forces to obtain a majority and form a **coalition government.** When groups with different ideologies share power, coalitions often break down as disputes arise, and new elections are required. Thus, many nations with multiparty systems are politically unstable.

Two-Party Systems

Only about a dozen nations have systems in which two major parties compete for power, although minor parties exist. In the United States, the major parties are the Republican Party and the Democratic Party.

Rise of American Parties

Many of the Founders distrusted factions, or groups with differing political views. In *The Federalist,* No. 10¹, James Madison observed: 📖

> 66 [T]he public good is disregarded in the conflicts of rival parties; and . . . measures are too often decided, not according to the rules of justice, and the rights of the minor party, but by the superior force of an interested and overbearing majority. 99
>
> —James Madison, 1787

In his Farewell Address of 1796, President George Washington warned against the "baneful [very harmful] effects of the spirit of party." Even so, by the end of President Washington's second term, two political parties had organized in opposition to one another. The Federalists called for a strong central government. The Democratic-Republicans believed that the states should have more power than the central government.

Parties Before the Civil War

After the Federalists elected John Adams president in 1796, their power quickly declined. Thomas Jefferson won the presidency under the Democratic-Republican banner in 1800 and in 1804. The Democratic-Republicans dominated politics into the 1820s. Conflicts over banking, tariffs, and slavery later shattered the party. By 1828, when Andrew Jackson won the presidency, the Democratic-Republicans were splitting into two parties. Jackson aligned with the group called Democrats. The other group called itself the National Republicans, or the Whigs.

By the 1850s, the debate over slavery had created divisions within both parties. The Democrats split into Northern and Southern factions. Many Whigs joined a new party that opposed the spread of slavery—the Republican Party.

Parties After the Civil War

By the end of the Civil War, two major parties dominated the national political scene. The Republicans remained the majority party from the Civil War until well into the twentieth century. Democrats held the presidency for only four terms between 1860 and 1932.

Parties in the Great Depression and After

In 1932 the Democratic Party won the White House and assumed control of Congress. For most of the next 60 years, Democrats were the majority party. Beginning in 1968, Republicans controlled the White House for six of the next nine

📖 *See the following footnoted materials in the **Reference Handbook:***
1. *The Federalist,* No. 10, pages R80–R82.

Activity: Collaborative Learning

Creating a Third Party Organize the class into groups of five. Each group should function as a third party for the next presidential election. Have each group decide which type of third party they will develop—single-issue, ideological, or splinter—and then determine the party platform. Allow members to choose from the following tasks: design a party symbol, create a campaign poster, write a campaign speech, create a bumper sticker, or design a campaign button. After all groups have presented their new party to the class, have students vote for the party they think best represents the most viable third party. Discuss why that party won. **OL**

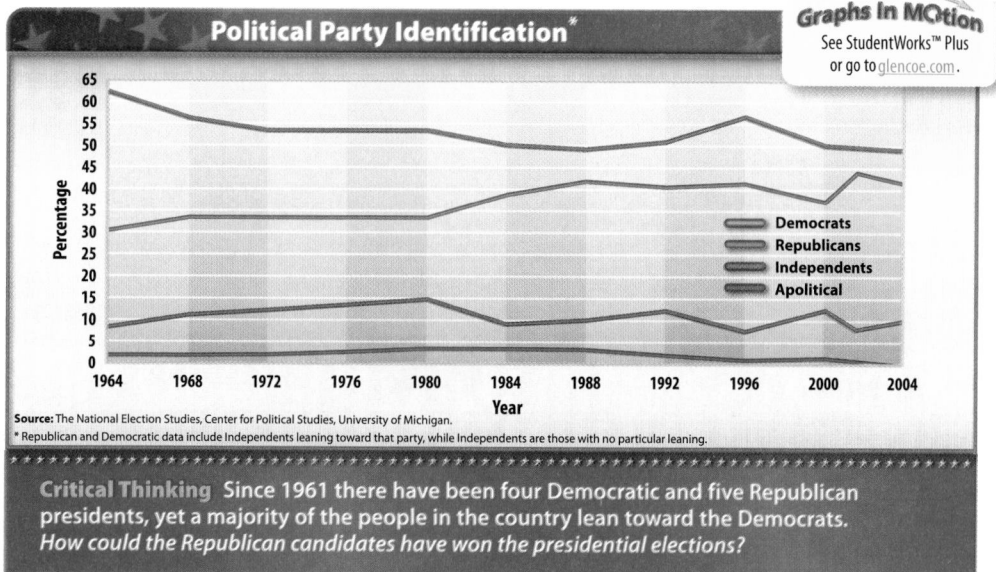

Political Party Identification*

See StudentWorks™ Plus or go to glencoe.com.

Source: The National Election Studies, Center for Political Studies, University of Michigan.
* Republican and Democratic data include Independents leaning toward that party, while Independents are those with no particular leaning.

Critical Thinking Since 1961 there have been four Democratic and five Republican presidents, yet a majority of the people in the country lean toward the Democrats. How could the Republican candidates have won the presidential elections?

Critical Thinking

Answer: If Democrats had a lower turnout at the polls, if Democrats did not vote their party preference, or if the independent vote went mostly Republican

Graph Skills Practice

In which year was the percentage of Democrats the highest? Republicans? *(1964; 2002)*

Did You Know?

The third-party candidates who received the most votes in U.S. history were Theodore Roosevelt in 1912 (27.4 percent), Millard Fillmore in 1856 (21.6 percent), and Ross Perot in 1992 (18.9 percent). Perot's total was the highest in history for a candidate who was not a former president.

R Reading Strategy

Making Connections **Ask:** On what national concern does the Libertarian Party primarily focus? *(government interference in private enterprise)* **OL**

Differentiated Instruction

---

presidential terms. After losing the White House to Bill Clinton in 1992, Republicans won the 1994 mid-term elections, taking both houses of Congress for the first time in 42 years. Beginning in 1995, for the first time since Truman, a Democratic president worked with a Republican Congress.

The Role of Minor Parties

Despite the dominance of the two major parties, third parties have been part of the American political scene since the early days of the Republic. A **third party** is any party other than one of the two major parties. In any election, more than one party may run against the major parties, yet each of them is labeled a "third" party. Because they rarely win major elections, third parties are also called minor parties.

Although they are motivated by a variety of reasons, third parties have one thing in common: They believe that neither major party is meeting certain needs. A third party runs candidates who propose ways to remedy this situation.

Types of Third Parties

Although some exceptions and overlapping can be found, minor parties generally fall into one of three categories. The single-issue party focuses exclusively on one major social, economic, or moral issue. For example, in the 1840s the Liberty Party and the Free Soil Party formed to take stronger stands against slavery than either the Democrats or the Whigs had taken. A single-issue party generally is short-lived. It might fade away when an issue ceases to be important, or a party with a popular issue might become irrelevant if one of the major parties adopts the issue.

Another type of third party is the ideological party, which has a particular set of ideas about how to change society overall rather than focusing on a single issue. Ideological parties such as the Socialist Labor Party and the Communist Party USA advocate government ownership of factories, transportation, resources, farmland, and other means of production and distribution. The Libertarian Party calls for drastic reductions in the size and scope of government in order to increase personal freedoms.

The third type of minor party is the splinter party, which splits away from one of the major parties because of some disagreement. Such disputes frequently result from the failure of a popular figure to gain the major party's presidential nomination. The most notable occurrence was in 1912, when former president Theodore Roosevelt led a group out of the Republican Party to form the Progressive Party, also known as the Bull Moose Party. Splinter parties typically fade away with the defeat of their candidate. The Bull Moose Party disappeared after Roosevelt lost the election in 1912.

CHAPTER 16: *Political Parties* **455**

Activity: Multiple Learning Styles

Logical/Mathematical Poll students in the class by secret ballot as to their party preference. Have volunteers tally the results on the board. Then have each student use the information given to create a graph showing the poll results. Instruct students to calculate what percentage of the class is represented by each party. Compare the results of the class poll with those of the most recent election. Do the election results reflect the same outcome as the class poll? **BL**

Graph Skills Practice
The Democratic Party is about how many years older than the Republican Party? *(25 years)*

C Critical Thinking

Analyzing Information Ask each student to choose one of the third parties mentioned in this section and analyze why that party failed to gain widespread public support. Allow students some time to research their chosen party. After students have determined why the third party failed, encourage them to critique the party, determining what could have been done to prevent the party's demise. Invite volunteers to explain their party's downfall and share their critiques with the class. **AL**

Hands-On Chapter Project

Step 1

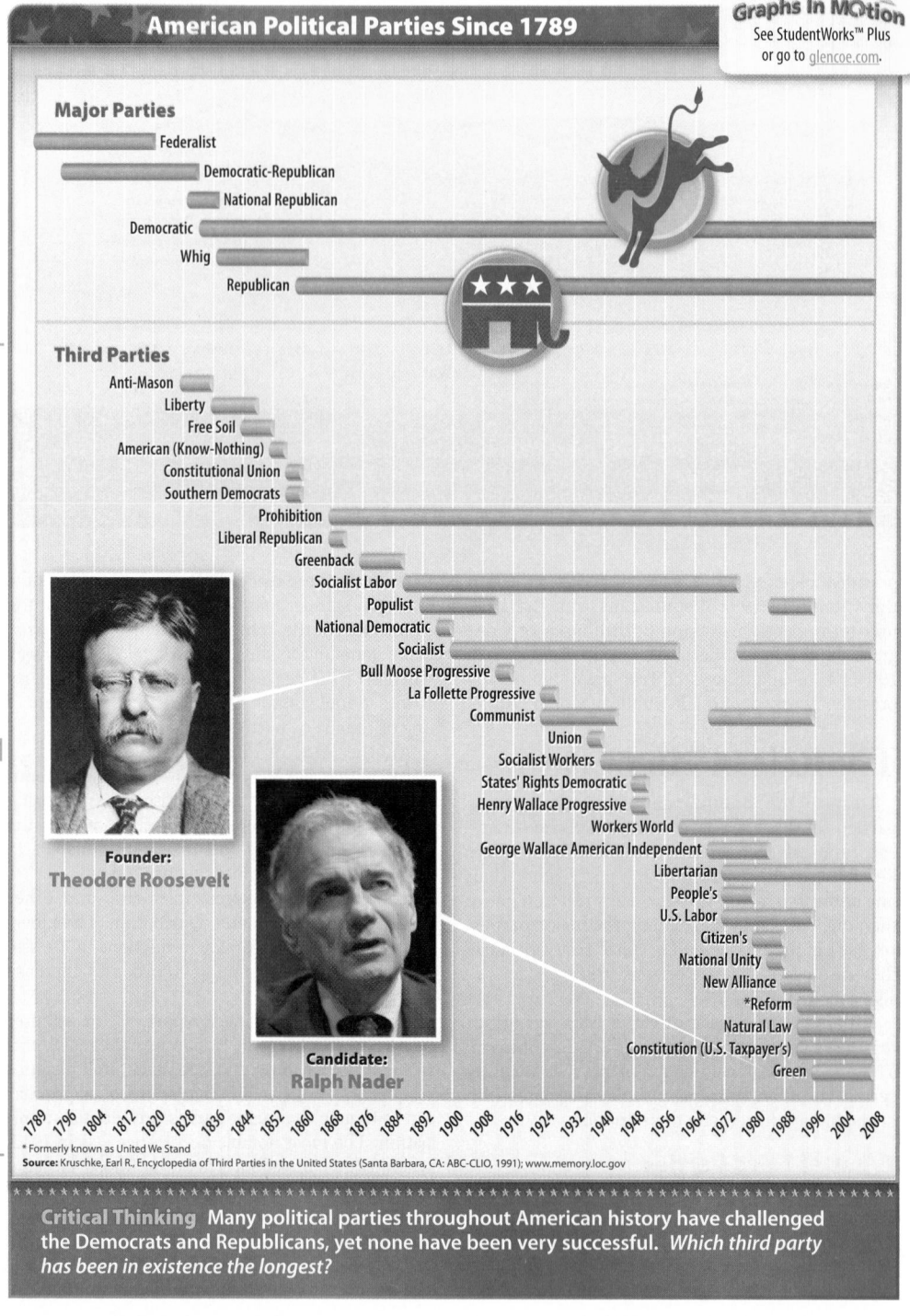

American Political Parties Since 1789

Graphs In Motion
See StudentWorks™ Plus
or go to glencoe.com.

Major Parties

Federalist
Democratic-Republican
National Republican
Democratic
Whig
Republican

Third Parties

Anti-Mason
Liberty
Free Soil
American (Know-Nothing)
Constitutional Union
Southern Democrats
Prohibition
Liberal Republican
Greenback
Socialist Labor
Populist
National Democratic
Socialist
Bull Moose Progressive
La Follette Progressive
Communist
Union
Socialist Workers
States' Rights Democratic
Henry Wallace Progressive
Workers World
George Wallace American Independent
Libertarian
People's
U.S. Labor
Citizen's
National Unity
New Alliance
*Reform
Natural Law
Constitution (U.S. Taxpayer's)
Green

Founder:
Theodore Roosevelt

Candidate:
Ralph Nader

1789 1796 1804 1812 1820 1828 1836 1844 1852 1860 1868 1876 1884 1892 1900 1908 1916 1924 1932 1940 1948 1956 1964 1972 1980 1988 1996 2004 2008

* Formerly known as United We Stand
Source: Kruschke, Earl R., *Encyclopedia of Third Parties in the United States* (Santa Barbara, CA: ABC-CLIO, 1991); www.memory.loc.gov

Critical Thinking Many political parties throughout American history have challenged the Democrats and Republicans, yet none have been very successful. *Which third party has been in existence the longest?*

Creating a Political Party

Step 1: Seeing the "Big Picture" Students will work in groups to create their own political parties.

Directions Divide the class into several groups and tell them they are going to create a new political party. In Step 1, they will select a party name and a symbol that communicates their viewpoint. Tell the groups that they will be

developing a party platform, and refer them to the Internet for examples they will use in Step 2.

Explain that their platforms will be shorter than the examples they will find.

Putting It Together Ask each "party" to report on the preliminary choices they have made. **OL**

(Chapter Project continued in Section 2.)

The Impact of Third Parties

Minor parties have influenced the outcome of national elections. Theodore Roosevelt's Bull Moose Party drew so many Republican votes from President William Howard Taft in 1912 that Democratic candidate Woodrow Wilson was elected. In 1968 the American Independent Party won 13.5 percent of the vote, and some think this helped the Republican candidate Richard Nixon to win. Some also think that Ross Perot's independent candidacy helped Bill Clinton win in 1992.

Third parties often influence politics by promoting new ideas. If they gain support, the major parties adopt their issues. For example, it was third parties that first proposed the minimum wage, the five-day workweek, and unemployment and health insurance.

Obstacles to Third Parties

As a result of the two-party tradition, minor parties face difficulties in getting on the ballot in all 50 states. The names of Republicans and Democrats are automatically on the ballot in many states, but third-party candidates are required to obtain a large number of voter signatures in a short time.

Another difficulty for third-party candidates is that nearly all elected officials in the United States are selected by **single-member districts.** Under this system, no matter how many candidates compete in a district, only one will win. Because most voters support a major party, the winner has almost always been a Democrat or a Republican. By contrast, many nations use an election system based on **proportional**

Third Parties Sway Elections

Trying to Build a Third Party Ross Perot is seen on a video screen at the Reform Party's convention in 1999. *How did Perot's candidacy help one of the major party candidates?*

representation. In this system, several officials are elected to represent voters in an area. Offices are filled in proportion to the votes that each party's candidates receive. Such a system encourages minority parties.

Third parties often have problems with financing and appealing to a broad cross section of voters. Campaigns require a lot of money, and because many voters do not believe a third-party candidate can win, they are reluctant to contribute to the campaign or vote for the candidate.

Caption Answer: Many of Ross Perot's supporters likely would have voted for George H.W. Bush, therefore Perot's candidacy may have helped Clinton.

C Critical Thinking

Predicting **Ask:** Do you think a third-party candidate will ever be elected president? *(Students should support their answers.)* **BL**

Assess

Assign the Section 1 Assessment as homework or as an in-class activity, or have students take Section Quiz 16-1 from *Section Quizzes and Chapter Tests.*

Close

Evaluating Evaluate the following 1789 quote by Thomas Jefferson: "If I could go to heaven but with a party, I would not go there at all." **OL**

SECTION 1 Review

Vocabulary

1. **Explain** the significance of: political party, theocracy, ideologies, coalition government, third party, single-member district, proportional representation.

Main Ideas

2. **Contrasting** How are the Bull Moose Party and the American Independent Party different?

3. **Identifying** What are three obstacles facing third parties?

Critical Thinking

4. **Making Inferences** Why might the National Organization for Women want to choose and run a third-party candidate?

5. **Organizing** Use a graphic organizer like the one below to identify three types of political party systems and how they affect governing.

Party System	Effects

Writing About Government

6. **Persuasive Writing** Imagine you have been named to a committee to plan a new government for a former colony. The structure of this government will influence the development of political parties. Consider the advantages and disadvantages of no parties, one-party, two-party, and multiparty systems. Write a speech explaining your choice.

CHAPTER 16: *Political Parties* **457**

Section 1 Review

Answers

1. All definitions can be found in the section and the Glossary.
2. The Bull Moose Party attracted Republican votes, and the American Independent Party attracted Democratic votes.
3. getting on the ballots, single-member districts, and obtaining financing
4. They might run a third-party candidate if they believed that neither party met needs that the organization believed were important.

5. One-party—lack of differences, lack of choices; Two-party—stability, fewer choices; Multiparty—diverse ideologies represented, instability when coalitions disagree
6. Speeches should note students' choice of form of government and, as a result, their choice of political party system, if any.

Focus

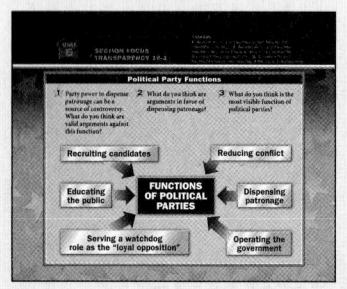
Reader's Guide

Answers to Graphic:

Recruiting Candidates, Educating the Public, Operating the Government, Dispensing Patronage, The Loyal Opposition, Reduction of Conflict

Resource Manager

Party Organization

Reader's Guide

Content Vocabulary
★ independent (p. 459)
★ precinct (p. 459)
★ precinct captain (p. 459)
★ ward (p. 459)
★ state central committee (p. 460)
★ national convention (p. 460)
★ national committee (p. 460)
★ patronage (p. 462)

Academic Vocabulary
★ cooperate (p. 458)
★ compromise (p. 462)
★ stability (p. 462)

Reading Strategy
As you read, create a graphic organizer similar to the one below to identify several important functions that political parties perform.

Functions of Political Parties

Issues in the News

The Idaho Democratic Party primary caucus had a record turnout in 2008, and young people were visible participants. In Bingham County, five teenagers and a high school teacher were among the eight delegates who went to the state Democratic Convention in June in Boise, the state capital. Bingham County has had teenage political delegates before, but never so many. In the words of student Amy Homer: "People are asking me, 'So you're a delegate—what does that mean? Oh, your vote matters.' And I say, 'Yeah, my vote matters.'" At the Boise convention, Amy joined other delegates to select 23 super delegates, who attended the Democratic National Convention in Denver in August 2008.

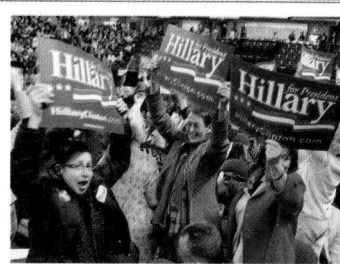

▲ A young supporter of presidential candidate Senator Hillary Clinton at a county Democratic caucus in Boise, Idaho

In order to succeed, a political party must have a dedicated core of willing volunteers like Amy Homer of Idaho. Both major parties employ small paid staffs in permanent party offices at the county, state, and national levels. Between elections these employees carry out the day-to-day business, but at campaign time parties also use volunteers to perform many tasks. Volunteers obtain campaign contributions, publicize candidates, send out campaign literature, canvass voters, and watch at the polls on Election Day. Parties also seek the help of various professionals to win elections: media experts to prepare television commercials, pollsters to take opinion polls, and writers to prepare speeches for the candidates.

In addition, to be successful, a party needs strong leadership and good organization at every level.

Membership and Organization

Democrats and Republicans are organized into 50 state parties and thousands of local parties that operate independently of the national organization. Although the three levels generally **cooperate**, separate authority exists at each level. Local, state, and national parties select their own officers and raise their own funds. The national party cannot give orders to the state or local parties.

R Reading Strategies	**C** Critical Thinking	**D** Differentiated Instruction	**W** Writing Support	**S** Skill Practice
Teacher Edition • Activating Prior Knowledge, p. 459 **Additional Resources** • Guid. Read. Act., p. 59 • Quizzes/Tests, p. 196	**Teacher Edition** • Comparing, p. 461 **Additional Resources** • Read. Essen., pp. 181–182	**Teacher Edition** • Kinesthetic, p. 460 **Additional Resources** • Foldables, p. 59 • Hist. Docs. and Speeches, p. 16	**Teacher Edition** • Persuasive Writing, p. 462 **Additional Resources** • Gov. Sims. and Debates, pp. 36–42	**Teacher Edition** • Understanding a Flowchart, p. 459 **Additional Resources** • Skill Reinforce. Act., p. 16

Party Membership

How does a voter join a political party, and what does it mean to belong? In many states, citizens must declare their party preference when they register to vote or when they vote in certain kinds of elections. Joining a political party, however, is not required in the United States. A voter may declare that he or she is an **independent,** not supporting any particular party.

People who belong to a political party generally do so because they support most of its ideas and candidates. Both the Republican and Democratic Parties do everything they can to attract supporters. In this sense, the two major parties are open parties, welcoming anyone who wishes to belong and accepting whatever degree of involvement these individuals choose. Party membership involves no duties or obligations beyond voting. Members do not have to attend meetings or contribute to the party if they choose not to do so. Most people who consider themselves Democrats or Republicans do nothing more than vote for the party's candidates.

Some citizens, however, become more involved in the political process. They might support a party by contributing money or by doing volunteer work for the party or its candidates. In most states, one must be a party member in order to hold an office in a party or to be its candidate for a public office. Thus, party membership provides a way for citizens to increase their influence on government. The parties, in turn, depend on citizen involvement, especially at the local level, to carry out activities and accomplish goals.

Local Party Organization

The basic local unit is the **precinct,** a voting district ranging in size from just a few voters to more than 1,000 voters, all of whom cast their ballots at the same polling place.

In a precinct, each party has a volunteer **precinct captain,** who organizes party workers to distribute information about the party and its candidates and to attract voters to the polls. Several adjoining precincts comprise a larger district called a **ward.** Party members in each ward select a person, also unpaid, to represent the ward at the next level of party organization—the party's county committee.

The county committee selects a chairperson to handle the county party's daily affairs. The party county chairperson usually has a great deal of political power in the county. He or she is very often the key figure in determining which candidate receives the party's support. If the state's governor, or

a U.S. senator, is from the same party, he or she might seek recommendations from the county chairperson when appointing judges and administrative officials.

At the same time, however, local parties, because of the nature of their membership, are the weakest link in the organizational chain. One study of political parties concluded the following:

> 66 *The vast majority of local parties are essentially voluntary organizations. . . . They have the least influence and the fewest resources. The combination of . . . reliance on volunteers in an era when volunteers are hard to find, complex campaign finance regulations, and the general low regard in which parties are held combine to discourage the best leadership or the greatest participation.* 99
> —Xandra Kayden and Eddie Mahe, Jr., 1985

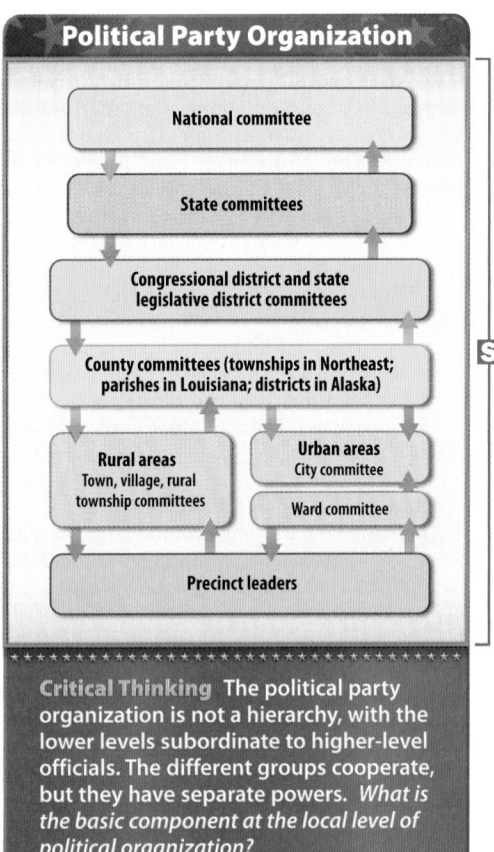

Political Party Organization

National committee

State committees

Congressional district and state legislative district committees

County committees (townships in Northeast; parishes in Louisiana; districts in Alaska)

Rural areas
Town, village, rural township committees

Urban areas
City committee

Ward committee

Precinct leaders

Critical Thinking The political party organization is not a hierarchy, with the lower levels subordinate to higher-level officials. The different groups cooperate, but they have separate powers. *What is the basic component at the local level of political organization?*

Teach

R Reading Strategy

Activating Prior Knowledge
Have students brainstorm ways in which volunteers can support a political party. (*Answers might include encouraging people to register to vote, door-to-door recruiting and donation gathering, working at a voting booth, and so on.*) **OL**

Critical Thinking

Answer: the precinct

Chart Skills Practice
Describe the organization of county committees. (*townships in the Northeast, parishes in Louisiana, districts in Alaska*)

S Skill Practice

Understanding a Flowchart
Ask: What do the arrows in the flowchart represent? (*The arrows represent cooperation among the different levels of the political party organization.*) **BL**

Additional Support

Activity: Cooperative Learning Activity

Designing a Party Function Booklet
Organize the class into six groups to create an illustrated booklet of the party functions mentioned in the section (recruiting candidates, educating the public, operating the government, dispensing patronage, the loyal opposition, and reduction of conflict). Have members collectively design a cover and create a title for their booklet. Then allow

each member to choose one of the party functions mentioned and create a page for the booklet. Each page should include an explanation of the party function and examples of how this function is carried out. Encourage students to be creative in designing their page by using photographs, drawings, clip art, and other graphic images. Display completed booklets in the classroom. **OL**

State Party Organization

In each state, the most important part of a party is the **state central committee,** which usually is comprised largely of representatives from the party's county organizations. The state central committee chooses the party state chairperson. In selecting this person, however, the committee generally follows the wishes of the governor, a U.S. senator, or some other party leader who is powerful in state politics.

A main function of the state central committee is to help elect the party's candidates for state government offices. In addition, the state central committee may provide assistance to local parties and candidates and may help coordinate the activities of the local parties. The committee also works hard at raising money.

National Party Organization

The national party organization has two main parts—the **national convention** and the **national committee.** The national convention is a gathering of party members and local and state party officials. It meets every four years, primarily to nominate the party's presidential and vice-presidential candidates. Beyond this function, it has very little authority.

Between conventions, the party's national committee, a large group comprised mainly of representatives from the 50 state party organizations, runs the party. Some members of Congress and some state and local elected officials also may sit on the national committee, as may other selected party members.

The party national chairperson, elected by the national committee, manages the daily operations of the national party. Usually the person selected is the choice of the party's presidential candidate. The national chairperson also raises money for the party; touts its achievements; and promotes national, state, and local party cooperation.

Both the Democrats and the Republicans also have independent campaign committees for Congress. These committees provide assistance to senators and representatives who are running for reelection. Each party's committee also provides resources to help challengers defeat senators and representatives from the other party.

Political Party Functions

The Constitution does not provide for political parties or even mention them, yet political parties are an essential part of the American democratic system. Through the election process, the people select the officials who will govern them. As part of this process, political parties perform several important functions. No other body or institution in American government performs these tasks.

Government *and* You

Running for Office

The most direct way of being involved in government is to hold elected office. The procedures and requirements for becoming a political candidate vary somewhat from state to state. However, in most cases you must file an official petition, signed by the required number of registered voters, with the appropriate local or state election board before a specified deadline. If other members of your political party have filed petitions for the same office, you may have to win a primary election to become the candidate.

Among the resources you will need in your campaign are time, money, and volunteers. Running for political office takes a great deal of personal time. Loans and donations from supporters will pay for brochures, TV and radio spots, and other devices to promote your candidacy. Volunteers can help get your message out to voters by distributing your materials. You may also need expert volunteer help to file the campaign finance reports required under state and federal law.

▲ John McCain during his presidential campaign

Participating **IN GOVERNMENT** ACTIVITY

Candidate Qualifications Contact your local board of elections to determine the qualifications, requirements, and procedures for running for office in your community.

Recruiting Candidates

Political parties seek men and women who appear to have a good chance of being elected. Selecting candidates for public office and presenting them to the voters for approval is the major function of political parties. It is often said that political parties are election-oriented rather than issues-oriented. This characteristic helps the Republicans and the Democrats maintain their status as major parties.

Educating the Public

Despite efforts to avoid division within their party, political parties bring important issues to the public's attention. Each party publishes its position on important issues such as inflation, military spending, taxes, pollution, energy, and the environment. Candidates present these views in pamphlets, press conferences, speeches, and television, radio, and newspaper advertisements.

The Republican and Democratic Party national organizations as well as third parties also maintain Web sites to raise money for their candidates, keep supporters informed about party positions on key issues, and recruit volunteers. The Democratic National Committee site (www.democrats.org) presents information about current campaigns, new legislation, important policy issues, and local party organizations. The Republican National Committee site (www.rnc.org) contains similar material, along with video news briefs, a "week in review" feature, and special reports.

Sometimes major party candidates feel safer attacking their opponent's views rather than stating their own. As a result, important issues can become lost in a sea of personal attacks. When major party candidates fail to address issues, a minor party candidate may force debate on these subjects. In 1992 and 1996, Ross Perot brought his concern for the national debt and the nation's economic problems to the campaign agenda. In 2000, 2004, and 2008 Ralph Nader championed consumer and environmental issues as an independent candidate.

Unfortunately, many Americans are not well-informed about important issues or the background of candidates. Political parties simplify elections by helping such people decide how to vote. By supporting a candidate just because he or she is a Democrat or a Republican, the voter knows generally how the candidate stands on key issues. Political party affiliation helps voters assess which candidate will be more acceptable.

The Cost of Campaigning

An Alternative Model Unlike other candidates, Republican Mike Huckabee ran his 2008 presidential campaign on a shoestring budget but managed to win significant support. *What factors might make up for a relatively small campaign budget?*

Operating the Government

Political parties also play a key role in running and staffing the government. Congress and the state legislatures are organized and carry on their work on the basis of party affiliation. Party leaders in the legislatures make every effort to see that their members support the party's position when considering legislation.

A party also acts as a link between a legislature and a chief executive. A chief executive works through his or her party leaders in the legislature to promote the administration's program. For most of the past 30 years, however, one party has controlled the White House and the other has controlled one or both houses of Congress. In recent years, the same situation has developed between governors and legislatures in more than half the states.

C Critical Thinking

Comparing Have students create tables comparing the current platforms of the Democratic and Republican Parties. (This information is easily obtained on the Internet at the Democratic National Committee and the Republican National Committee Web sites or by calling or writing to local party headquarters.) Ask students to identify specific issues in their tables such as inflation, military spending, taxes, pollution, energy, and the environment, noting each party's stand on each issue. After students have completed their tables, create a class table merging students' results. Discuss each party's general platform. Students might want to add a column to their tables identifying their stand on each issue to determine which party they most closely identify with. **OL**

Caption Answer: Factors might include charisma, the "common touch," or standing out from a field of candidates because of one's positions on a single high-profile issue.

Differentiated Instruction

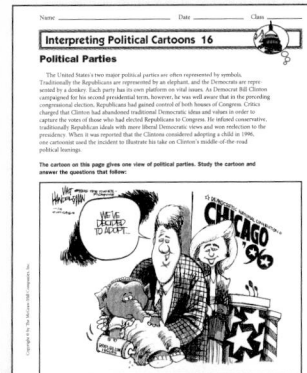

W Writing Support

Persuasive Writing Have students assume the hypothetical role of the loyal opposition, or "watchdog" to the current presidential administration. Have them write research-based essays in which they attempt to persuade the American people that the current administration is failing (even if they do not believe it to be true). **AL**

Assess

Assign the Section 2 Assessment as homework or as an in-class activity, or have students take Section Quiz 16-2 from *Section Quizzes and Chapter Tests.*

Close

Analyzing Information Let students know that candidates for the U.S. presidency must express their policy goals to the public. Have students work in groups to identify a specific policy position of a recent presidential candidate. Groups should then analyze how the candidate's policy position impacts special-interest groups and the candidate's ability to finance his or her campaign. **AL**

Section 2 Review

TIME For the Record

It's a Zoo In 1874 Thomas Nast drew a cartoon in *Harper's Weekly* that used an elephant, about to fall into a chasm, as the symbol of the Republican Party. The Republicans were expected to lose seats in Congress. The symbol stuck and the party put a spin on it. For Republicans, the elephant is strong and intelligent; the Democrats chose the donkey as clever and brave.

Dispensing Patronage

Political parties also dispense **patronage,** or favors given to reward party loyalty, to their members. These favors often include jobs, contracts, and appointments to government positions. Business executives or labor unions that contribute heavily to a political party, for example, may expect government to be sympathetic to their problems if that party comes to power. They might be awarded contracts to provide government with goods or services. Loyal party workers might be placed in government jobs. Although laws and court decisions have limited patronage in recent years, the practice remains a major way that parties control and reward their supporters.

The Loyal Opposition

The party that is out of power in the legislative or executive branch assumes the role of "watchdog" over the government. It observes the party that is in power, criticizes it, and offers solutions to political problems. If the opposition party does this successfully, public opinion might swing in its favor and return it to power in a future election. Concern about this makes the party in power more sensitive to the will of the people.

Reduction of Conflict

In a complex society, conflict among groups with differing interests is inevitable. To win an election, a political party must attract support from many different groups. To accomplish this, a party encourages groups to **compromise** and work together. A key outcome of this process is that parties encourage government to adopt moderate policies with mass appeal.

Parties contribute to political **stability** in another way, too. When one party loses control of the government, the transfer of power takes place peacefully. No violent revolutions occur after elections, as they do in some nations. In the United States, the losing party accepts the outcome of elections because it knows that the party will continue to exist as the opposing party and someday will return to power.

SECTION 2 Review

Vocabulary

1. **Explain** the significance of: independent, precinct, precinct captain, ward, state central committee, national convention, national committee, patronage.

Main Ideas

2. **Identifying** What are the responsibilities of the party county chairperson, party state chairperson, and party national chairperson?

3. **Analyzing** What are the roles of political parties at the national, state, and local levels?

Critical Thinking

4. **Understanding Cause and Effect** What are the advantages and the disadvantages of the system of patronage?

5. **Organizing** Use a graphic organizer like the one below to show the three levels at which each major political party functions.

Writing About Government

6. **Persuasive Writing** Prepare for a debate on the following statement: The two-party system has outlived its usefulness. Choose either the pro or con side of the issue, and prepare arguments for the side you chose. Pair up with a classmate who has prepared arguments that oppose yours and debate the issue.

Answers

1. All definitions can be found in the section and the Glossary.
2. Party county chairperson—handles the county party's daily affairs, key figure in determining which candidate receives the party's support; party state chairperson—helps elect party's candidates for state offices, provides assistance to local parties and candidates, helps coordinate activities of local parties; party national chairperson—manages the daily operations of the national party; raises money for the party; touts its achievements; promotes national, state, and local party cooperation.
3. On all levels, political parties recruit volunteers, select candidates to run for office, and raise money.
4. Possible advantages: parties can reward and control their supporters, people who contribute time and money will be rewarded; Possible disadvantages: political favors are dispensed to reward party loyalty and are not given on the basis of merit, can lead to corruption
5. from the inside out: local or county; state; national
6. Students should choose the pro or con side of the statement and prepare an argument defending their stand with facts and supporting arguments. Then they should pair up with a classmate who holds the opposing viewpoint and debate the issue.

Should There Be Limits On Campaign Spending?

Although there are limits to how much individuals and groups can contribute to a federal candidate, there are no limits on how much money a candidate can raise or spend. In the 2004 presidential election, candidates spent more than $650 million on their campaigns. In the 2008 election, candidates spent well over $1 billion.

 YES

Campaign spending should be limited. While individual political contributions are limited, overall contributions are not. Candidates still spend large amounts of time fund-raising rather than meeting with and serving the public. Fundraising itself has become another race at which the candidate must succeed.

Furthermore, large corporations and other special-interest groups have more money to spend on contributions, which gives them a greater opportunity to meet with candidates and influence political outcomes. The costs of campaigning are increasing with every election. It seems quite possible that soon only the wealthy or someone who is backed by one of the two major parties will have any chance of being elected to a government office.

 NO

Campaign spending should not be limited. Campaigning is expensive, and to successfully present their qualifications and ideas, candidates need considerable funds. In 1976 the Supreme Court considered the issue of putting a cap on campaign spending. It ruled that setting limits on an individual's campaign spending was unconstitutional because it violated the right of free speech.

There is a second reason to worry about imposing limits on spending. If this happens, incumbents will have an edge because of their name recognition—opponents need large amounts of money to generate an equivalent kind of name recognition and thus the ability to get opposing ideas noticed. Finally, large donors might pose the problem of influencing candidates, and money cannot buy an election. As long as contributions are controlled and reported, corruption will not be a problem.

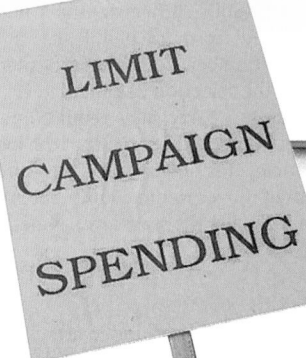

Debating the Issue

1. **Identifying** How did the Supreme Court rule on limiting campaign spending in 1976?
2. **Explaining** How do both sides view the issue of large donations from corporations and special-interest groups and the issue of limits on campaign spending?
3. **Deciding** With which opinion do you tend to agree? Explain your reasoning.

Debating the Issue Answers

1. It ruled that limits on campaign spending violated the candidates' constitutional right to free speech.
2. One side views donations from corporations and outside groups as undue outside influence and believes that campaign spending should be limited. The other side believes that as long as outside contributions are controlled and reported and corruption is eliminated, then campaign spending should not be limited.
3. Students should state a position and clearly defend it.

ISSUES to Debate

Teach

Setting up the Debate

Speculating Discuss with students the importance of spending money in an election. Have students create a list of potential campaign expenditures. *(frequent transportation, food for candidates and campaign workers, cost of venues, and so on)* **Ask:** What might be some positive and negative effects of a spending cap? *(Positive—elections are accessible to more candidates, lowered risk of corruption, fewer "smear" ads; negative—fewer campaign stops, increased advantage to incumbents)*

Evaluating Have students research the arguments for and against limiting campaign spending. Students should give specific arguments to support both points of view.

Concluding the Debate

Discuss these questions with students:

• Should limits on campaign spending be related, in any way, to the sources of funds? Should independently wealthy candidates be subject to different limits?
• Are there any positive or negative externalities to enormous campaign spending? In other words, how are people who are not involved with campaigns affected by their spending?

Focus

Nominating Candidates

Bellringer

**Section Focus Transparencies
16-3**

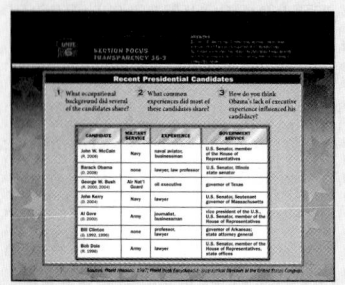

Reader's Guide

Answers to Graphic:

Caucuses

Nominating conventions

Primary elections

Petition

Resource Manager

Reader's Guide

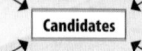

Content Vocabulary

★ caucus (p. 464)
★ nominating convention (p. 464)
★ boss (p. 465)
★ direct primary (p. 465)
★ closed primary (p. 465)
★ open primary (p. 465)
★ plurality (p. 465)
★ runoff primary (p. 465)
★ ticket (p. 466)
★ platform (p. 469)
★ plank (p. 469)

Academic Vocabulary

★ vary (p. 464)
★ file (p. 465)
★ eliminate (p. 468)

Reading Strategy

As you read, create a graphic organizer like the one below to list the ways that candidates are selected to run for office.

Candidates

Issues in the News

About 45,000 people—including delegates, volunteers, guests, and members of the media—attended the four-day 2008 Republican National Convention in Minneapolis-St. Paul, Minnesota. The main convention site was the Xcel Energy Center, an entertainment and sports complex that opened in 2000 in downtown St. Paul. As with past political conventions, the host city benefited economically. Minneapolis-St. Paul took in an estimated $155 million from the big political event. The convention was only the second time in history that the Republicans have met in Minnesota. The first time was in 1892 when the city hosted the Republican convention that nominated Benjamin Harrison for the presidency.

▲ The Republican National Convention met in St. Paul in 2008.

National conventions are the climax of a long process of choosing a party's presidential and vice-presidential candidates. To win elections, a party must offer appealing candidates and conduct expensive campaigns. Party nominations are often hard-fought contests.

Selecting Candidates

Although election laws **vary** greatly from state to state, all candidates reach the ballot through one or more of these methods: (1) caucus, (2) nominating convention, (3) primary election, or (4) petition.

Caucuses

Early in our nation's history, caucuses—private meetings of party leaders—chose nearly all candidates for office. As the nation became more democratic in the 1800s, however, the caucus began to be criticized. To many people, caucuses seemed undemocratic because most party members had no say in the selection of candidates.

In modern caucuses, party rules require openness with the selection process starting at the local level. Selecting delegates starts at the neighborhood level and then moves to the county, congressional district, and finally the state level. Nineteen states use caucuses today.

Nominating Conventions

As political caucuses came under attack, the **nominating convention,** an official public meeting of a party to choose candidates for office, became popular. Under this system, local party

---

R Reading Strategies	C Critical Thinking	D Differentiated Instruction	W Writing Support	S Skill Practice
Teacher Edition • Identifying Central Issues, p. 469 **Additional Resources** • Guid. Read. Act., p. 60 • Quizzes/Tests, p. 197 • Reteaching Act., p. 16	**Teacher Edition** • Making Inferences, p. 465 • Analyzing, p. 466 **Additional Resources** • Read. Essen., pp. 183–186	**Teacher Edition** • Visual/Spatial, p. 468 **Additional Resources** • Foldables, p. 57 • Am. Biographies, p. 74	**Additional Resources** • Part. in Gov. Act., pp. 31–32	**Additional Resources** • Inter. Poli. Cartoons, pp. 31–32

organizations send representatives to a county nominating convention that selects candidates for county offices and chooses delegates to go to a state nominating convention. The state convention selects candidates for statewide office and chooses delegates to go to the national convention.

In theory, the convention system was more democratic than party caucuses because power would flow upward from the people. As the convention system developed, however, powerful party leaders, called **bosses,** began to choose the delegates and take control of the conventions. Public reaction against the bosses in the 1900s convinced many states to begin using primary elections to select candidates.

Primary Elections

The method most commonly used today to nominate candidates is the **direct primary,** an election in which party members select people to run in the general election. Two types of primary elections are held. Most states hold a **closed primary,** in which only members of a political party can vote. Thus, only Democrats pick Democratic candidates for office, and only Republicans can vote in the Republican primary. In an **open primary,** all voters may participate, even if they do not belong to the party, but they can vote in only one party's primary.

Primary elections are conducted according to state law and are held at regular polling places just as general elections are. Each state sets the date of its primary, provides the ballots and poll workers, and counts the votes. In most states a primary candidate does not need a majority to win, but only a **plurality,** or more votes than any other candidate. In a few states, if no one receives a majority, a **runoff primary** is held. The runoff is a second primary election between the two candidates who received the most votes in the first primary. The person who wins may then be a contender for the party's nomination at the national convention.

In most states today, candidates for governor and for the House, Senate, other state offices, and most local offices are selected in primary elections. In many states, however, party caucuses and nominating conventions continue to exist alongside primaries.

Petition

Under the petition method, a person announces his or her candidacy and files petitions that a specified number of voters have signed in order to be placed on the ballot. Some states require that all candidates **file** petitions.

Making a Difference

Loretta and Linda Sanchez, typical sisters in many ways, are sharing a unique and historic experience in Washington, D.C.: They are the first sisters ever to serve in Congress together. Loretta, the older of the two members of the House of Representatives, was first elected from California's 47th district in 1996. Linda was elected in 2002 to represent California's 39th district.

Both sisters credit their mother for their success. Maria Sanchez helped all of her children make it to college before she enrolled herself, while in her forties, and earned a college degree in bilingual education. "She's an incredible woman," says Linda Sanchez. "She was very involved in the local community and always taught us to stand up for what was right."

Although they are both members of the Democratic Party, the sisters are not exactly alike. "My sister is more liberal than I," says Loretta. "We approach issues from a different perspective." Loretta earned an MBA degree and had a career in financial consulting before entering public service. Linda studied law and served as a labor leader and civil rights lawyer before entering into politics.

"She . . . always taught us to stand up for what was right."
—Linda Sanchez

Teach

C Critical Thinking

Making Inferences Discuss the logic behind the closed primary. **Ask:** Why do you think closed primaries allow only Democrats to choose Democratic candidates and only Republicans to choose Republican candidates? *(Students might point out that if Democrats could vote for Republicans and vice versa, they might attempt to sabotage the opposing party by voting for the weakest candidate.)* **AL**

Making a Difference

Linda Sanchez served on the House Judiciary Committee. Loretta Sanchez has focused much of her attention on issues such as economic development, crime reduction, protections for senior citizens, and education.

Activity: Have students create an illustrated time line showing the growing diversity of representation in Congress. Students should note how growing diversity has affected Congress and legislative policies. **OL**

Additional Support

Activity: Collaborative Learning

Designing a Poster Organize the class into groups of four to design posters depicting the four methods by which individuals have historically been able to seek nomination for public office. Allow each group member to choose and illustrate one of the following:

caucus, nominating convention, primary election, or petition. Have groups divide the poster into four sections to show how each method of nominating a candidate works. Encourage students to note states that use the method they have chosen to depict. **OL**

POLITICAL PROFILES

Woodrow Wilson
(1856–1924)

Woodrow Wilson won the 1912 Democratic nomination on the 46th ballot. Wilson wrote about his grueling experience: "There ought never to be another Presidential nominating convention. The nomination should be made directly by the people." Wilson supported a direct national primary.

Caption Answer: The poster calls Andrew Jackson a "Man of the People" and states that the presidency should be "derived from the PEOPLE!" It appeals to the electorate's sense of democracy.

C Critical Thinking

Analyzing Ask: Why do you think that voters had less say over presidential nominees in the early 1800s? *(Answers will vary. Students might note that news traveled more slowly, and voters had less information available to them to make informed decisions.)* **OL**

Differentiated Instruction

Jackson Forever!
The Hero of Two Wars and of Orleans!
The Man of the People!
HE WHO COULD NOT BARTER NOR BARGAIN FOR THE
PRESIDENCY!

Who, although *"A Military Chieftain,"* valued the purity of Elections and of the Electors, MORE than the Office of PRESIDENT itself! Although the greatest in the gift of his countrymen, and the highest in point of dignity of any in the world,

BECAUSE
It should be derived from the
PEOPLE!

No Gag Laws! No Black Cockades! No Reign of Terror! No Standing Army or Navy Officers, when under the pay of Government, to browbeat, or

KNOCK DOWN
Old Revolutionary Characters, or our Representatives while in the discharge of their duty. To the Polls then, and vote for those who will support

OLD HICKORY
AND THE ELECTORAL LAW.

Broad Appeal Andrew Jackson, president from 1829 to 1837, benefited from the fact that all but three states allowed universal white male suffrage. *How does this poster reflect the expanded electorate of the 1830s?*

In a primary contest, the party-backed candidate has an advantage because party workers will circulate petitions. The party also will use its financial and organizational resources to back its choice. Candidates without caucus or convention support have serious obstacles to overcome. If such a candidate poses a serious threat, however, party leaders frequently are willing to make a deal. They might offer the challenger party support for another office or appointment to a government post to avoid a primary. Political analyst Theodore H. White once explained why:

> ❝ [E]stablished leaders hate primaries for good reason; they are always, in any form, an appeal from the leaders' wishes to the people directly. Primaries suck up and waste large sums of money from contributors who might better be tapped for the November finals; the charges and countercharges of primary civil war provide the enemy party with ammunition it can later use with blast effect against whichever primary contender emerges victorious. ❞
> —Theodore H. White, 1961

Presidential Nominations

The most exciting and dramatic election in American politics is the presidential election. Every four years, each major party gathers during July or August in a national convention. Elected or appointed delegates representing the 50 states, Guam, Puerto Rico, the Virgin Islands, American Samoa, and the District of Columbia attend the convention. The task of the delegates is to select a **ticket**—candidates for president and vice president—that will win in the November general election. Because this ticket, if elected, can change history and affect every American's life, millions of Americans watch the televised coverage of the conventions. The drama and spectacle of a convention, however, have not always been so open to the public's view. Likewise, presidential nominations have not always been as democratic as they are today.

The History of Presidential Nominations

Before national nominating conventions, congressional caucuses chose presidential candidates. From 1800 to 1824, congressional leaders from each party met in secret and selected their party's ticket. In the presidential election of 1824, Andrew Jackson made the caucus system an issue, declaring that a small group of representatives did not speak for the nation. Although Jackson lost the election, his revolt against "King Caucus," as he called it, discredited the caucus system and led to the eventual adoption of the nominating convention.

A minor political party, the Anti-Masons, held the first national convention in 1831, and the two major parties quickly copied the idea. Since 1832, a convention of party members has chosen major party presidential candidates. To make these conventions more democratic, by 1916 almost half the states were choosing convention delegates in presidential primary elections.

For years, when citizens voted in a presidential primary, they really were choosing among groups of party members who pledged to support specific candidates. The group pledged to the winning candidate became that state's delegation to the national convention.

In the 1970s, however, both major parties provided a more democratic nomination process. For example, new party rules encouraged that women, minorities, and young people be included as convention delegates. By 1996, presidential primaries existed in 44 states and were part of the selection

---

★ Activity: Multiple Learning Styles ★

Verbal/Linguistic Have students imagine that they have been selected to give the nominating speech at the national convention of the Democratic Party or the Republican Party. Students can choose their own presidential candidate or use the candidates from an upcoming or recent election. Remind students that the nominating speech sets the tone for the convention and outlines what the party

and the selected presidential candidate support. Encourage students to use quotes, poems, literature, and other sources in their speeches to rally support for their candidate. After students have presented their nominating speeches to the class, have the class vote on which candidate they would nominate from each political party. **AL** process for about three-fourths of the delegates to the two national conventions.

Presidential Primaries Today

Like other primary elections, presidential primaries operate under a wide variety of state laws. In addition, each party frequently changes its rules regarding delegate selection. Even in the same state, each party's primary may operate under different procedures. The following three generalizations, however, can be made about presidential primaries: (1) They may be a delegate selection process or a presidential preference poll, or both; (2) Either the candidate who wins the primary gets all the state's convention delegates (called "winner-take-all"), or each candidate gets delegates based on how many popular votes he or she receives in the primary; (3) Delegates selected on the basis of the popular vote may be required to support a certain candidate at the national convention, or they may be uncommitted.

Many presidential primaries were originally winner-take-all. The Democrats now use proportional representation. Under this system, a state's delegates must represent the candidates in proportion to the popular vote each receives in the primary once a certain threshold is reached. The Republicans allow both winner-take-all and proportional systems.

Although proportional representation was intended to make a party's nomination process more democratic, in many states it had an unanticipated result. Combined with the other rules for state delegations, proportional representation made delegate selection almost impossibly complicated. Today only a few of the states with presidential primaries hold "beauty contests." These are preference polls where voters indicate which candidate they would like to be the nominee. Caucuses later choose the actual delegates.

Criticisms of Presidential Primaries

While most people agree that the presidential primary system is a great improvement over the previous methods of selecting convention delegates, it has its critics. A major criticism is that the primaries extend too long in an election year. With the first primary held in February and the last in June, seeking a party's nomination is a very long, costly, and exhausting process.

Another criticism is that the primaries seem to make the image of the candidates more important than the issues. The news media's coverage of primary campaigns tends to play up candidates' personalities rather than their positions on important questions. Also, relatively few people vote in primaries. Thus, the winner of a primary might not be as popular as the victory would indicate.

Candidates who win the early primaries capture the media spotlight. Often the other candidates are saddled with a "loser" image that makes it difficult for them to raise campaign contributions. Some are forced to drop out before the majority of voters in either party have the chance to pick their choice for the nominee.

Did You Know?

With such a small number of delegates at stake (30 Democratic and 12 Republican), New Hampshire's primary is largely a media event. Why? Conventional wisdom once held that the candidate who lost in the New Hampshire primary would lose the presidency. That is the way events unfolded for 40 years until 1992, when Bill Clinton lost in the primary but won the presidency. Another reason New Hampshire has attracted media attention is that it has traditionally held the first presidential primary. But in 2000, two states, Iowa and Alaska, upstaged New Hampshire. Iowa held its presidential caucus on January 24, the same day that Alaska held its presidential primary.

Caption Answer: States continue to experiment with ways to make the primaries more democratic and fair.

Running for the Nomination

Primary Elections
New York senator Hillary Clinton made a strong showing in the 2008 Democratic primaries. However, she did not win enough votes to gain her party's nomination at the national convention in the fall of 2008. Illinois senator Barack Obama outran her in the contest to gain the number of delegates needed to win the nomination. *Why do states continue to experiment with the structure of primaries?*

Hands-On Chapter Project

Step 3

Creating a Political Party

Step 3: Presenting the Party Parties will use the platform they developed in Step 2 to create posters for class presentations.

Directions Have each party create a poster based on the platform they developed in Step 2. They will then select a party chairperson to present the platform to the class. Not all details of the party's plans for tackling the issues have to be on the poster, but they should be discussed by the presenter or another member of the party.

Presenting Information Ask the class to discuss how effective the presentations were and to vote for the party whose candidate they would elect president. **OL**

Linking ★ Past & Present

Political Slogans Many political campaign slogans are more memorable than the candidates themselves. Calvin Coolidge's slogan "Keep Cool with Coolidge" lives on. In 1932 Herbert Hoover promised "A Chicken in Every Pot, a Car in Every Garage." Bill Clinton's reminder to the Republicans helped him win the election by noting that "It's the Economy, Stupid."

D Differentiated Instruction

Visual/Spatial Have students work in pairs to create charts illustrating a historical presidential election. Ask each pair to use graphic layouts of their choice showing the names of the political parties involved, the main election issues, the candidates, and other images that illustrate the campaign. Display completed projects in the classroom and discuss which ones are historical issues and which are contemporary ones. **OL**

Differentiated Instruction

Participating in Government Activities, p. 31

468

In 2008 more than 17 states moved their presidential primaries or caucuses forward on the calendar as they competed with each other to play a more important role in determining who got the nomination. This put even greater pressure on candidates to raise money quickly and to do well at the very start of the process.

Because primaries **eliminate** many opponents, they often result in one-sided convention victories for particular candidates. Some observers believe that the nominating convention has become simply a rubber-stamp operation. If the primary winners come to the convention with enough delegate votes to win the nomination, they ask, why hold the nominating convention at all? Of course, it is possible that in the future, primary election support for contenders will be more equally divided, in which case the convention will once again be an arena of debate for the presidential nomination.

The National Convention

D From February to June, the candidates crisscross the country competing for delegate support. Meanwhile, the national committee staff is preparing for the convention to be held in late summer.

Preconvention Planning

Long before its convention meets, the national committee of each major party chooses the site and dates. After the city and dates are chosen, the national committee tells each state party organization how many votes the state will have at the convention. In the past, states had the same number of convention votes as they had electoral votes. At recent conventions, however, the parties have used complicated formulas to determine the number of votes each state will have.

Assembling the Convention

From across the country, thousands of delegates assemble in the convention city, accompanied by a mass of spectators, protesters, and news media representatives. When the delegates arrive, many are already pledged to a candidate, but others are not. All the candidates actively woo these uncommitted delegates, especially if the presidential nomination is still in doubt. As rumors of political deals circulate, candidates hold news conferences and reporters mill about in search of stories. One writer described a national convention as:

❝ . . . *an American invention as native to the U.S.A. as corn pone or apple pie. . . . [I]t has something of the . . . gaiety of a four-ring circus, something of the . . . sentiment of a class reunion, and something of the tub-thumping frenzy of a backwoods camp meeting.* ❞

—Theodore H. White

The noise and confusion subside as the party chairperson calls the opening session to order. On the evening of the opening day, the keynote speech is delivered. It is an address by an important party member that is intended to unite the party for the coming campaign. The delegates then approve the convention's four standing committees—rules and order of business, credentials, permanent organization, and platform and resolutions—which have been at work for several weeks.

Because in recent conventions, little suspense has remained about who would be either party's candidate, the only real conflict has involved committee reports. The convention spends the second and third days, or even longer, listening to these reports and to speeches about them.

The Rules Committee

Each party's rules committee governs the way its convention is run. The committee proposes rules for convention procedure and sets the convention's order of business. The delegates must approve any proposed changes in the rules from the last convention. Although the rules committee report is usually accepted, at times real battles have developed over it. The outcome of a rules fight can be vital to a candidate for the presidential nomination. For example, at the 1980 Democratic convention, Senator Edward Kennedy was eager to capture the nomination, even though President Jimmy Carter had won a majority of the delegates in the primaries.

Thinking that many of the Carter delegates were not strong supporters of the president, Kennedy sought to defeat a rule binding delegates to vote for the candidate who won their state primary. If the rule were defeated, the Carter delegates would be free to support whomever they wished. Kennedy felt that many of the Carter delegates would then switch to him. When Kennedy lost this rules vote, he also lost his chance to win the nomination.

The Committee on Permanent Organization

This committee selects the permanent chairperson and other officials for the convention.

Objective: Learn about local political party organizations.

Focus/Teach: Have students read the activity and discuss local political parties.

Assess: Review reports and experiences.

Close: Discuss the "Activity" bullet points and the "Follow Up" activity.

Differentiated Instruction Strategies

BL How do the platforms of Republicans and Democrats differ?

AL Determine with which political party you most closely align yourself. Why?

ELL What are the two main political parties? Are there other parties?

Crowning Moment

Democrats Prepare
After a tight race for the presidential nomination, Democrats gathered in Denver in August 2008 for their convention. The campaign for the nomination was historic. For the first time, a major party selected an African American, Barack Obama, as their nominee. Also for the first time, a woman, Hillary Clinton, ran a very close second. *Why do the parties strive to hold entertaining national conventions?*

 POLITICAL PROFILES **Fannie Lou Hamer** (1917–1977)
Fannie Lou Hamer testified before the credentials committee at the 1964 Democratic National Convention, saying "I question America." Hamer and members of the Mississippi Freedom Democratic Party challenged the all-white delegation sent by the regular Mississippi Democratic Party.

R **Reading Strategy**

Identifying Central Issues
Organize students into small groups to serve as the platform committee for the political party of their choice. Have students write a statement of the party's principles, beliefs, and positions on vital issues and spell out how the party intends to implement them. Remind students that a platform should appeal to all factions at the convention. Call on volunteers to read their platforms to the class and have the class identify the central issues of the platforms. **AL**

Additional Support

After it reports, the delegates elect the permanent convention officials who take control of the day-to-day aspects of the convention from the temporary officials.

The Credentials Committee

The credentials committee must approve the delegations from each state. Sometimes disputes arise over who the proper delegates are. Candidates who trail in delegate support may challenge the credentials of their opponents' delegates. Two entire rival delegations may even appear at the convention, each claiming to be a state's official delegation. It is up to the credentials committee to determine which delegates should be seated. Although the committee's decisions may be appealed on the convention floor, the delegates generally accept its report without changes.

Fights over credentials often have been livelier than rules fights at national conventions. In 1964, for example, African Americans at the Democratic convention charged that an all-white Mississippi delegation had excluded them, giving the African American citizens of Mississippi no representation at the convention. The credentials committee allowed some African Americans to be seated in the Mississippi delegation. In 1968 the same situation occurred. The committee refused to seat another all-white Mississippi delegation, and this time replaced it with an integrated rival delegation.

The Platform Committee

The platform committee, as its name suggests, is assigned an important task—the writing of the party's **platform**, a statement of its principles, beliefs, and positions on vital issues. It also spells out how the party intends to deal with these issues. The party must try to adopt a platform that appeals to all factions, or divisions, at the convention. This is not always an easy task.

Part of the difficulty in getting platforms accepted is that individual parts of the platform, called **planks**, may divide the delegates. In 1968, for example, a pro-Vietnam War plank angered Democrats who wanted the United States to withdraw from that conflict. In 1980 the Republican platform contained a plank opposing the Equal Rights Amendment. Although this plank was controversial, the platform passed. **R**

Because the party's presidential candidate must support the party platform, all contenders try to get their points of view into the platform. Rival candidates with opposing views will often create a fight within the party over the platform. The danger is that a platform fight might divide the party. If the fight is bitter, as it was for Democrats in 1968, the party could become so divided that it loses the election.

Nominating the Candidates

After each committee's reports are adopted, it is time to select the party's candidate for president.

CHAPTER 16: Political Parties 469

Extending the Content

Female Political Party Nominees In 1964 Senator Margaret Chase Smith of Maine declared her candidacy for the Republican nomination for president. She received 27 votes at the Republican National Convention but lost the nomination to Senator Barry Goldwater of Arizona. In 1984 Representative Geraldine Ferraro of New York became the first woman to be nominated for vice president, serving as Walter Mondale's running mate on the Democratic ticket. In 2008 Governor Sarah Palin of Alaska was nominated as John McCain's vice-presidential running mate on the Republican ticket.

Assess

Assign the Section 3 Assessment as homework or as an in-class activity, or have students take Section Quiz 16-3 from *Section Quizzes and Chapter Tests.*

Close

Analyzing Have students work in groups to brainstorm reasons why the presidential primaries might not create a truly democratic pool of candidates from which to choose. **OL**

Section 3 Review

From the opening day, the leading contenders work hard to hold onto their delegates and to gain the support of uncommitted delegates.

In recent years, however, the front-runners have won enough committed delegates in the primaries to take the suspense out of the nominating process. Even so, the nominating speech for each candidate sets off a demonstration, as supporters parade around the convention hall. After the nominating speeches and all the seconding speeches that follow are made, the balloting starts.

The convention chairperson instructs the clerk to read an alphabetical roll call of the states, and the chairperson of each state delegation calls out the delegates' votes. The candidate who receives a majority becomes the nominee. If no candidate wins the majority, then further roll calls are taken until one delegate changes his or her vote or drops out.

In recent conventions, most candidates were selected on the first ballot. This is partly because rising campaign expenses have narrowed the field of candidates in the primaries. Candidates who win few delegates in the early primary states quickly drop out because they will not be able to raise the money they need to continue campaigning. By the time of the convention, there is no mystery about who will be nominated.

Party leaders benefit from the early victory of one candidate, having more time to plan the convention and unify the party. The convention can then become a scripted television event. However, with the mystery removed from the nominating process, a convention might not attract a large television audience. This is one reason why the major television networks have reduced their coverage.

The Vice-Presidential Nomination

The vice-presidential nomination, which normally takes place on the last day of the convention, may create some suspense. Usually, the party's presidential nominee selects a running mate, and the convention automatically nominates the person chosen. A vice-presidential candidate is sometimes selected to balance the ticket, meaning that he or she has a personal, political, and geographic background that is different from the presidential nominee. This balance is designed to make the ticket appeal to as many voters as possible.

In 1960 John F. Kennedy, a young Catholic senator from Massachusetts, chose Lyndon B. Johnson, an older Protestant senator from Texas, as his running mate. In 1984 Minnesota senator Walter F. Mondale made New York representative Geraldine Ferraro the first female vice-presidential major party candidate.

Adjournment

With the nomination of the presidential and vice-presidential candidates, the convention is almost over. These major nominees appear before the delegates and make their acceptance speeches. These speeches are intended to bring the party together, to attack the opposition party, to sound a theme for the upcoming campaign, and to appeal to a national television audience. The convention then adjourns.

SECTION 3 Review

Vocabulary

1. **Explain** the significance of: caucus, nominating convention, boss, direct primary, closed primary, open primary, plurality, runoff primary, ticket, platform, plank.

Main Ideas

2. **Describing** How do states deal with the situation in which no primary candidate wins a majority of votes?

3. **Explaining** How is each major party's presidential candidate chosen at its national nominating convention?

Critical Thinking

4. **Making Generalizations** What changes in society have influenced presidential nominating methods?

5. **Organizing** Use a chart like the one below to show four ways candidates for office can get on the ballot and why each method has drawn criticism.

Method	Criticism

Writing About Government

6. **Descriptive Writing** Write a letter to the editor that presents a democratic and cost-efficient system for selecting nominees for president. Clearly explain your plan and how it differs from the current system.

Answers

1. All definitions can be found in the section and the Glossary.
2. In most states, the winner of the plurality vote is selected. In some states, the top two candidates compete in a runoff election.
3. In an alphabetical roll call, each state delegation calls out the delegates' votes. The candidate with the majority becomes the nominee. If no one wins a majority, additional roll calls are taken.
4. Generalizations should point out that as American society became more democratic, so did nominating methods.
5. Caucuses—considered undemocratic; Nominating conventions—subject to control by bosses; Primary elections—extend over too long a time, candidates' image seems more important than the issues; Petition—advantage to party-backed candidates
6. Students' letters should outline a democratic and cost-efficient system for selecting nominees for president of the United States.

Evaluating a Political Web Site

Politicians, political parties, lobbies, and many other organizations have Web sites that provide information about legislation under consideration, voting records, news, and positions on various issues. These Web sites are a convenient way to learn about issues and candidates, and some of them offer objective information. It is important to understand, however, that because they support specific candidates and issues, many sites present information from a certain point of view.

Why Learn This Skill?

Knowing how to evaluate a political Web site enables you to identify its point of view. Following the steps on the right can help:

Web site 1

The Healthy Forests Initiative is providing public land managers the tools to undertake commonsense management of our forests and woodlands. The initiative focuses on reducing the risk of catastrophic fire by thinning dense undergrowth and brush in priority locations that are collaboratively selected by Federal, state, tribal, and local officials and communities. . . . The initiative also provides for more timely responses to disease and insect infestations that threaten to devastate forests.

—www.whitehouse.gov

Web site 2

Under the guise of "fuel reduction," the U.S. Forest Service issues a draft plan to resume the logging of giant ancient sequoia trees in the Giant Sequoia National Monument and two national forests in California's Sierra Nevada mountain range. The plan would sidestep wildlife and watershed protections to allow logging companies to cut down enough of the nation's oldest and grandest trees to fill more than 2,000 log trucks every year.

—www.greenpeace.org

1. Notice who owns the Web site. Ask yourself: What is the site owner's motivation? You will get different opinions about prescription drug legislation, for example, from pharmaceutical companies' Web sites than from those representing senior-citizen groups.

2. Ask yourself: Are sources provided for facts cited? If so, are the sources reliable? Does the quality of the writing instill confidence? Are the site's positions supported by groups or individuals you trust?

3. To get both sides of an issue, check several sites that offer different opinions. Then decide for yourself.

Practicing the Skill

Read the excerpts above and answer the questions that follow.

1. What issue are the two passages discussing?

2. Do any words or phrases in each passage indicate bias?

3. What do you think the motivations are behind each of the passages?

4. Are facts provided? If so, are they supported by reliable sources?

Applying the Skill

Find the Web sites of two opposing political candidates from a recent election. Analyze the sites, and write a brief report covering these points:

- The candidates' names, office sought, and party affiliation
- Techniques used to promote the candidate
- Were the facts presented on the site accurate? Verify with reliable sources.
- Which site was more effective? Why?

CHAPTER 16: *Political Parties* 471

Teach

C Critical Thinking

Analyzing Sources Inform students that virtually anyone can create and post a Web page. This means that when you search for information on the Internet, it is likely that your results will include some authoritative and some less reliable sites. Ask students to find examples of authoritative sites and less reliable sites about a political topic. Have them print the home page of each site and write a brief explanation of why one is authoritative and the other is less reliable. **OL**

R Reading Strategy

Comparing and Contrasting Have students locate a political news article and a political opinion piece (about the same topic if possible) online. **Ask:** How do the writing styles of the two articles differ? Is anything similar about the articles? *(Students should look for sentences that begin "I think" or "I feel," or opinion-charged words that cannot be proven, such as stupid, irresponsible, brilliant, and so on. These words probably will not be present in the news article.)* **OL**

Answers

Practicing the Skill

1. a forest management plan
2. Some biased words include *commonsense, guise,* and *grandest.*
3. The White House Web site wants to show the benefits of the bill and get credit for helping forests. The Native Forest site wants to prevent logging in national forests.
4. Native Forest provides a fact about logging trucks but does not provide a supporting source.

Applying the Skill

Students should go through the Web sites carefully and answer each question fully.

Assessment and Activities

ExamView®
Assessment Suite

This easy-to-use software includes extensive question banks and allows you to create fully customized tests that can be administered in print or online.

Reviewing Vocabulary

1. (1) ideology
   (2) plank
   (3) platform
   (4) national convention
   (5) ticket
2. (6) national convention
   (7) caucus
   (8) ticket
   (9) bosses

Reviewing Main Ideas

3. selecting candidates for public office and presenting them to the voters for approval
4. A precinct captain organizes party workers to distribute information about the party and its candidates and to get voters to the polls.
5. In a closed primary, only members of a particular party can vote in that party's primary. In an open primary, all voters can vote in any party's primary, but each voter can vote in only one primary.
6. Party caucuses involved only party leaders and became controlled by party bosses. Primary elections allow all interested voters to vote and are, therefore, more democratic.

Reviewing Vocabulary

Insert the correct content vocabulary words into the sentences. Some terms will be used more than once.

bosses	ticket
plank	national convention
ideology	platform
caucus	

1. A political party's **(1)** is expressed in each **(2)** of the **(3)** that it adopts at the **(4)** to select its **(5)**.
2. Although the **(6)** replaced the party **(7)** in choosing its **(8)**, the party's **(9)** continued to influence the nomination process.

Reviewing Main Ideas

Section 1 *(pages 453–457)*

3. **Describing** What is the main function of the two major political parties?

Section 2 *(pages 458–462)*

4. **Explaining** What are the responsibilities of a precinct captain within a political party?

Section 3 *(pages 464–470)*

5. **Differentiating** What is the difference between open primaries and closed primaries?
6. **Assessing** Why is a primary election better than a party caucus for selecting candidates?

Critical Thinking

7. **Essential Question** Since there are only two major parties in the United States, what kind of strategy do they have to follow in order to win elections?
8. **Analyzing** Why are many Americans uninformed about the issues in a campaign?
9. **Predicting Consequences** Use a chart to analyze the advantages and disadvantages of using a national primary to nominate each party's presidential candidate.

Advantages	Disadvantages

Chapter Summary

Party Development	Party Organization and Functions	Party Nominations
★ Late 1700s: Despite Washington's warnings, two political parties—Federalists and Democratic-Republicans—form	★ Political parties are organized at the local, state, and national levels	★ Caucuses—private meetings of party leaders; used early in our nation's history and in some states today
★ Pre-Civil War: Conflicts over issues such as slavery cause divisions within nation's political parties; Democratic-Republicans split into Democrats and the Whigs	★ Functions of political parties include recruiting candidates for public office, educating the public about issues, running and staffing the government, rewarding party loyalists with favors, watching over the party in power, and encouraging compromise and moderate government policies	★ Nominating conventions—official public meetings of a party to choose candidates for office
★ Post-Civil War: Republicans and Democrats emerge as the two dominant political parties		★ Primary elections—party members select people to run in the general election; method most commonly used today
★ Third Parties: Continue to impact the political scene, despite obstacles presented by the two-party tradition		★ Petitions—candidate is placed on the ballot if a certain number of voters signs a petition

Critical Thinking

7. They must be relatively inclusive and represent a fairly wide range of interest groups and viewpoints.
8. Primary elections have made the image of the candidates more important than the issues, and media coverage tends to play up candidates' personalities rather than their positions on important questions. Also, political parties simplify elections by helping uninformed people decide how to vote.
9. Advantages: reduce campaign costs and time; focus on national issues. Disadvantages: weaken parties and federalism; focus even more on national media coverage.

Government ONLINE Self-Check Quiz
Visit glencoe.com and enter QuickPass™ code USG9822c16.
Click on Self-Check Quizzes for additional test practice.

CHAPTER
16
Assessment
and Activities

Document-Based Questions

Analyzing Primary Sources

Read the excerpt below and answer the questions that follow.

William Jennings Bryan's famous "Cross of Gold" speech was made at the 1896 Democratic National Convention, which focused that year on the issue of monetary standards. The speech gained Bryan the nomination as the Democratic presidential candidate that year, although he lost the election to Republican William McKinley.

❝ [W]e care not upon what lines the battle is fought. If they say bimetallism is good, but that we cannot have it until other nations help us, we reply that, instead of having a gold standard because England has, we will restore bimetallism, and then let England have bimetallism because the United States has it. If they dare to come out into the open field and defend the gold standard as a good thing, we will fight them to the uttermost. Having behind us the producing masses of this nation and the world, the laboring interests, and the toilers everywhere, we will answer their demand for a gold standard by saying to them: You shall not press down upon the brow of labor this crown of thorns; you shall not crucify mankind upon a cross of gold! ❞

10. To what demographic of American society does Bryan seem to be appealing?

11. Bryan's speech focused primarily on one issue—monetary standards. Can you see any harm in having an election or a party based around a single political issue?

Applying Technology Skills

12. Using the Internet Using the Internet, find current information about the Democratic and Republican Parties and write an informational pamphlet about ways that citizens can participate in political parties at the national, state, and local levels.

Interpreting Political Cartoons

Analyze the cartoon and answer the questions that follow. Base your answers on the cartoon and your knowledge of Chapter 16.

WEEEEEEEEEEEEE!

U.S. SENATE SEATS

Manny Francisco, Manila, The Philippines/Cagle Cartoons

13. What is the cartoonist saying about the party balance in the U.S. Senate?

14. Do you think that the cartoonist believes this constant "teetering" is good, bad, or does not matter, for the American political system?

15. Can you relate the subject of this cartoon to the idea of political gridlock?

Participating IN GOVERNMENT

16. The method by which delegates are selected to national nominating conventions depends on party rules and on the laws of each state. Work with a partner to determine the process in your state. Contact each party's county and state organizations and the local board of elections to find out the following information: how many delegates are sent to the national convention from your state, the selection process for those delegates, and whether there have been any special laws or rules applied to the selection process. When all of the information has been gathered and analyzed, present your findings to the class.

CHAPTER 16: *Political Parties* **473**

---

and Republican Party and write informational pamphlets about the ways in which citizens can participate in state political parties.

Interpreting Political Cartoons

13. It has shifted to the Democrats.

14. Answers may vary, but students should defend their answers.

15. Constant teetering between parties in the Senate can make it hard to pass legislation as the parties try to gain more control.

Participating IN GOVERNMENT

16. Student pairs should contact each party's county and state organizations and local board of elections. Pairs should report about the number of delegates, how the number is determined, how delegates are selected, and any special laws or rules that apply.

Chapter Bonus Test Question

Ask: Which minor political party has been the most persistent, offering candidates in every election since 1872? (*Prohibitionists*)

Analyzing Primary Sources

10. Bryan is addressing laborers and the working-class people of society, as indicated by the phrases "producing masses of this nation" and "the laboring interests and the toilers everywhere."

11. Some students might answer that having an election or a party based on one issue can lead to less power for that party, because it cannot appeal to a broad array of people and tends to alienate those who do not support its stand on this particular issue. In addition, after the issue is resolved, it can be difficult for that party to maintain power or cohesion because its reason for existence might have disappeared. Also, having one candidate tied too much to one cause can prevent that candidate from forming a political identity separate from that particular cause.

Applying Technology Skills

12. Students should use the Internet to find information about the Democratic Party

Key to Ability Levels
BL Below level   **AL** Above level
OL On level   **ELL** English Language Learners

Key to Teaching Resources
📁 Print Material   🖨 Transparency
💿 CD-ROM or DVD

Levels					Resources	Chapter Opener	Section 1	Section 2	Section 3	Chapter Assess
BL	OL	AL	ELL							
FOCUS										
BL	OL	AL	ELL	🖨	Section Focus Transparencies		17-1	17-2	17-3	
TEACH										
BL	OL		ELL	📁	Reading Essentials and Study Guide (and Answer Key)		p. 187	p. 190	p. 197	
BL	OL		ELL	📁	Guided Reading Activities		p. 61	p. 62	p. 63	
BL	OL		ELL	📁	Vocabulary Activities		p. 17			
BL	OL	AL	ELL	📁	Chapter Summaries			p. 49		
BL	OL			📁	American Biographies					
BL	OL	AL	ELL	📁	Cooperative Learning Activities				p. 11	
	OL	AL	ELL	📁	Government Simulations and Debate			p. 33		
BL	OL	AL	ELL	📁	Historical Documents and Speeches			p. 17		
BL	OL	AL	ELL	📁	Interpreting Political Cartoons				p. 33	
BL	OL		ELL	📁	Skill Reinforcement Activities			p. 17	p. 17	
BL	OL	AL	ELL	📁	Source Readings		p. 17			
BL	OL			📁	Supreme Court Case Studies					
BL	OL	AL	ELL	📁	Participating in Government Activities					
BL	OL		ELL	📁	Spanish Declaration of Independence and U.S. Constitution	✓	✓	✓	✓	✓
BL	OL	AL	ELL	📁	NGS World Atlas, Spanish	✓	✓	✓	✓	✓
BL	OL	AL	ELL	🖨	Unit Overlay Transparencies, Strategies, and Activities	✓	✓	✓	✓	✓
BL	OL		ELL	🖨	Making It Relevant Transparencies	✓	✓	✓	✓	✓
BL	OL	AL	ELL	🖨	High School Writing Process Transparencies, Strategies, and Activities	✓	✓	✓	✓	✓
BL	OL	AL		🖨	American Art & Architecture Transparencies, Strategies, and Activities	✓	✓	✓	✓	✓

✓ Chapter- or unit-based activities applicable to all sections in this chapter

TeacherWorks Plus™
All-In-One Planner and Resource Center

- Interactive Lesson Planner
- Interactive Teacher Edition
- Fully editable blackline masters
- Chapter Spotlight Videos Launch
- Differentiated Lesson Plans
- Printable reports of daily assignments
- Standards tracking system

Levels					Resources	Chapter Opener	Section 1	Section 2	Section 3	Chapter Assess
BL	OL	AL	ELL							
TEACH *(continued)*										
BL	OL			●	American Music: Hits Through History	✓	✓	✓	✓	✓
BL	OL		ELL	📁	Reading Strategies for the Social Studies Classroom	✓	✓	✓	✓	✓
			ELL	📁	English Language Learner Handbook	✓	✓	✓	✓	✓
BL	OL		ELL	📁	Writer's Guidebook for Social Studies	✓	✓	✓	✓	✓
BL	OL	AL	ELL	📁	Living Constitution, SE	✓	✓	✓	✓	✓
BL	OL	AL	ELL	📁	Living Constitution, TAE	✓	✓	✓	✓	✓
BL	OL			📁	NGS World Atlas, English	✓	✓	✓	✓	✓
BL	OL		ELL	📁	The Constitution and You (poster set)	✓	✓	✓	✓	✓
BL	OL	AL	ELL	📁	Spanish Chapter Summaries			p. 49		
BL	OL	AL	ELL	📁	Spanish Vocabulary Activities		p. 17			
BL	OL		ELL	📁	Spanish Reading Essentials and Study Guide (and Answer Key)		p. 187	p. 190	p. 197	
BL	OL	AL	ELL	●	PresentationPlus! with MindJogger CheckPoint	✓	✓	✓	✓	✓
ASSESS										
BL	OL	AL	ELL	●	*ExamView® Assessment Suite*		17-1	17-2	17-3	Ch. 17
BL	OL	AL	ELL	📁	Authentic Assessment with Rubrics		p. 24			p. 24
BL	OL	AL	ELL	📁	Section Quizzes and Chapter Tests		p. 207	p. 208	p. 209	pp. 211–218
BL	OL	AL	ELL	📁	Spanish Section Quizzes and Tests		p. 207	p. 208	p. 209	pp. 211–218
CLOSE										
BL			ELL	📁	Reteaching Activities					
BL	OL	AL	ELL	●	StudentWorks™ Plus with Audio Summaries	✓	✓	✓	✓	✓
BL	OL		ELL	🖨	Graphic Organizer Transparencies		✓	✓	✓	
BL	OL		ELL	📁	High School Government Reading and Study Skills Foldables®		p. 60	p. 60	p. 60	

Combined Vocabulary Products

Teach With Technology

What Glencoe technology products improve students' vocabulary?

Vocabulary eFlashcards, ePuzzles and Games, and **Vocabulary PuzzleMaker** all build students' vocabulary and help students understand key words and concepts from the textbook.

How can these products help my students?

Vocabulary eFlashcards help students review and test their recall of content vocabulary, academic vocabulary, and people, places, and events for each chapter.

ePuzzles and Games are an entertaining way for students to study the key facts, concepts, and

vocabulary introduced in each chapter. The **Vocabulary PuzzleMaker** lets you quickly create word searches, crosswords, and jumbles that students can use to practice vocabulary from each chapter.

For **Vocabulary eFlashcards** and **ePuzzles and Games,** visit glencoe.com and enter a student **QuickPass**™ code to go directly to student resources for the chapter. For **Vocabulary PuzzleMaker,** enter a teacher code to go to teacher resources.

Government ONLINE

Visit glencoe.com and enter **QuickPass**™ code USG9085c17T for Chapter 17 resources.

You can easily launch a wide range of digital products from your computer's desktop with the McGraw-Hill Social Studies widget.

	Student	Teacher	Parent
Media Library			
• Student Edition Section Audio	●		●
• Chapter Spotlight Videos	●	●	●
***United States Government* Online Learning Center (Web Site)**			
• Chapter Overviews	●	●	●
• Multilingual Glossaries	●	●	●
• Study-to-Go	●	●	●
• Student Web Activities	●	●	●
• Self-Check Quizzes	●	●	●
• Online Student Edition	●	●	●
• Vocabulary eFlashcards	●	●	●
• Web Activity Lesson Plans		●	
• Vocabulary PuzzleMaker	●	●	●
• Landmark Supreme Court Cases	●	●	●
• Beyond the Textbook	●	●	●

- **Timed Readings Plus in Social Studies** helps students increase their reading rate and fluency while maintaining comprehension. The 400-word passages are similar to those found on state and national assessments.

- **Reading in the Content Area: Social Studies** concentrates on six essential reading skills that help students better comprehend what they read. The book includes 75 high-interest nonfiction passages written at increasing levels of difficulty.

- **Reading Social Studies** includes strategic reading instruction and vocabulary support in Social Studies content for ELLs and native speakers of English. www.jamestowneducation.com

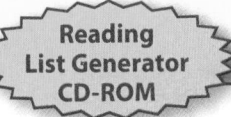

Reading List Generator CD-ROM

GLENCOE BOOKLINK 3

Use this database to search more than 30,000 titles to create a customized reading list for your students.

- Reading lists can be organized by students' reading level, author, genre, theme, or area of interest.
- The database provides Degrees of Reading Power™ (DRP) and Lexile™ readability scores for all selections.
- A brief summary of each selection is included.

Leveled reading suggestions for this chapter:

- *The Day the Women Got the Vote,* by George Sullivan
- *Elections in the United States,* by David Heath
- *Forward Into Light: The Struggle for Women's Suffrage,* by Madeleine Myers

Review suggested books before assigning them.

Economics Connection

Personal Finance Literacy

Reading Stock Reports

Tell students that presidential elections affect the stock market. It usually rises just before and just after elections and fluctuates during election years. Explain to students: If you want to buy and sell stocks someday, you will have to be able to read a stock market report. Reports are updated throughout every day that the stock market is open, from "opening bell" until "closing bell." (A bell is actually rung at U.S. stock exchanges.) The first half of a stock report includes this data:

Did You Know?

David Leung, of Palos Verdes, CA, started investing gifts and earnings at age 10. By the time he was 17, his investments were worth nearly half a million dollars.

1. Locate stock in the alphabetical list. Names are

3. Note the ticker symbol.

5. Check yield—the return on investment per share (calculated by dividing dividend by closing price).

7. Compare day's closing price with prior business day's closing price. Positive numbers mean a price increase; negative,

Stock Quotations

52 Weeks		Stock	Sym	Div	Yld %	PE	Vol 100s	Hi	Lo	Close	Net Chg
Hi	Lo										
86.40	47.87	AppleComp	AAPL	2.22	2.9	34.96	391290	77.78	76.10	77.74	+ 1.86
475.11	290.69	Google	GOOG	6.82	1.7	59.68	51928	407.68	401.77	406.99	+ 3.01
27.49	16.75	Intel	INTC	1.10	5.5	18.15	939098	19.98	19.32	19.96	+ 0.55

2. Check high & low prices for the past 52 weeks.

4. Evaluate annual dividend or the per-share payment

6. Read price/earnings ratio. Low ratios usually mean

8. Examine a day's high, low, and closing price.

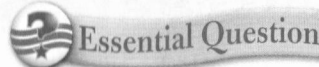

Essential Question

Our electoral system contains mechanisms for campaign strategy, advertising, financing, voting procedures, the Electoral College, and so on. Some factors that influence public choices are personal background, party loyalty, issues, public image, propaganda, and so on.

Chapter Spotlight Video

To generate student interest and provide a springboard for class discussion, access the Chapter 17 Video at glencoe.com or on the video DVD.

FOLDABLES
Study Organizer

Dinah Zike's Foldables are

three-dimensional, interactive graphic organizers that help students practice basic writing skills, review key vocabulary terms, and identify main ideas. Have students complete this chapter's Foldable activity or activities in *Dinah Zike's Reading and Study Skills Foldables* booklet. **OL**

Government ONLINE

Visit glencoe.com and enter **QuickPass**™ code USG9085c17T for Chapter 17 Resources including Chapter Overview, Student Web Activity, Self-Check Quiz, and other materials for students and teachers.

CHAPTER 17

◀ Chapter Audio   Spotlight Video

Elections and Voting

▲ Delegate at the 2008 Democratic National Convention in Denver, Colorado

Essential Question

What are the basic mechanisms of our electoral system, and what factors shape public choices at the polls?

Government ONLINE
Chapter Overview Visit glencoe.com and enter *QuickPass*™ code USG9822c17 for an overview, a quiz, and other chapter resources.

474

Launching the Chapter

The Electoral College Explain that the 538 Electoral College votes represent one vote for each legislator in Congress, plus three electoral votes from Washington, D.C. A candidate must win at least 270 electoral votes to become president. A candidate can ensure a victory by winning the 11 states with the largest number of electoral votes. Give each student a blank U.S. map and a chart showing how many electoral votes each state has. Have students color in the 11 states that total 270 electoral votes. **Essential Question:** Why is it unlikely that a single candidate would win all of these 11 states? *(California almost always votes Democratic, and Texas almost always votes Republican.)* **ELL OL**

Election Campaigns

Reader's Guide

Content Vocabulary
★ campaign manager (p. 476)
★ image (p. 476)
★ political action committee (p. 478)
★ soft money (p. 479)

Academic Vocabulary
★ intense (p. 475)
★ strategy (p. 476)
★ distribute (p. 476)

Reading Strategy
As you read, create a table similar to the one below to list the ways the Federal Election Campaign Act of 1971 changed campaign finance rules.

Sources of Campaign Funds Before 1971	Sources of Campaign Funds After 1971

Focus

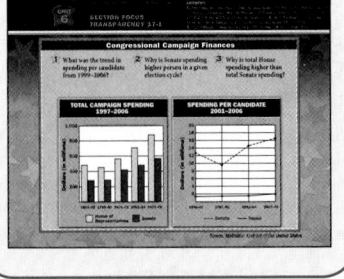

Bellringer
Section Focus Transparencies 17-1

Economics in the News

The 2008 presidential primaries may have been the most expensive in the nation's history. Candidates spent millions of dollars in hotly contested races in Iowa, in New Hampshire, and in other states. Democrat Barack Obama collected an amazing $36 million in one month, mostly from small online donations. Also in a single month, Republican Mitt Romney was said to have raised more than $1.4 million from Web donors, while Republican John McCain raised $12 million after surprise victories in New Hampshire and South Carolina. Obama, McCain, and Hillary Clinton decided not to accept federal matching funds, a decision that allowed them to ignore the spending limits those federal monies require. Ironically, both McCain and Obama championed public campaign funding as a way to ensure that all candidates are on a level playing field.

▲ Republican candidate Mitt Romney spent record sums of his personal money in the 2008 campaign.

Reader's Guide

Answers to Graphic:
Sources of Campaign Funds Before 1971: businesses, labor unions, individuals, parties, special-interest groups
Sources of Campaign Funds After 1971: individuals, parties, special-interest groups, federal government

Elections are an ongoing part of American life. Every two years, national elections are held to select all representatives and one-third of the senators. Senators and representatives spend a significant amount of their time and resources raising money for campaigns. For the presidency, an election is held every four years, and candidates must spend hundreds of millions of dollars to run. This lengthy and expensive campaign leads, of course, to the most powerful political office in the land.

Electing the President

Candidates for president begin organizing their campaigns more than a year before the election. Primary races in the spring help narrow the field of candidates. After late-summer national conventions, the presidential campaigns become **intense.** They end on Election Day, which is always the Tuesday after the first Monday in November. During the campaign's final two months, candidates spend long hours traveling from state to state, taping television messages, shaking hands, making speeches, and giving interviews. Exhausted candidates may greet the people of Denver with a "Hello, Dallas." That kind of slipup will likely be reported on the nightly news.

Electoral Votes and the States

To be elected president, a candidate must win 270 of the 538 available electoral votes—a simple majority. The electoral vote is equal to the number of representatives and senators from all the states,

Resource Manager

R Reading Strategies	**C** Critical Thinking	**D** Differentiated Instruction	**W** Writing Support	**S** Skill Practice
Teacher Edition • Inferring, p. 479 **Additional Resources** • Guid. Read. Act., p. 61 • Quizzes/Tests, p. 207	**Teacher Edition** • Making Connections, p. 476 **Additional Resources** • Read. Essen., pp. 167–189	**Teacher Edition** • Interpersonal, p. 476 • Logical/Mathematical, p. 478 **Additional Resources** • Foldables, p. 60 • Source Readings, p. 17	**Teacher Edition** • Personal Writing, p. 477 **Additional Resources** • Authentic Assess., p. 24	**Teacher Edition** • Researching, p. 477 **Additional Resources** • Vocab. Act., p. 17

Teach

Caption Answer: The system is complex, with multiple primaries using different state rules. This, coupled with the Electoral College system in the general election, means a campaign has to make many calculations to have effective support from various groups.

D Differentiated Instruction

Interpersonal Have groups devise a campaign plan for a presidential candidate, including a personal appearance schedule and media ads. Students might identify geographic areas and plan strategies to maximize attendance at campaign rallies in those areas. They should choose famous landmarks as rally sites and identify issues to be discussed. **OL** **AL**

C Critical Thinking

Making Connections Explain that before television, voters only saw candidates in person or heard them on the radio. **Ask:** How do you think television has changed elections? **BL**

Additional Support

Key Strategist

Low-Profile Adviser
Valerie Jarrett, the senior strategist for Barack Obama and a longtime friend, is seen here on the campaign train during the Pennsylvania primary. Many analysts said the campaign's organization was exceptional and made skillful use of the Internet. *Why does the American electoral system require a high level of organization?*

plus 3 votes from the District of Columbia. Each state's electoral vote equals the total number of its senators and representatives in Congress.

The candidate who wins the greatest number of popular votes in any state usually receives all of that state's electoral votes. To win the presidency, a candidate must pay special attention to those states with large populations, such as California, Texas, New York, and Florida. The larger a state's population is, the more electoral votes it has. A presidential candidate who won the electoral votes of the 11 largest states would obtain the 270 votes necessary to win the presidency.

A candidate needs to win as many states as possible, so he or she must appeal to a broad range of voters across the nation. A candidate who runs on a single issue or appeals only to a certain region of the country will find it much harder to win the necessary number of electoral votes. This need for broad appeal works against third-party candidates, who usually do not have the money or the political organization that is available to Democrats and Republicans.

Campaign Strategy and Organization

Planning how to capture key states is only one of many decisions a presidential candidate must make. For example, should the candidate wage an aggressive, all-out attack on an opponent, or would a low-key campaign be a better **strategy?** What theme should the campaign strike? What slogan will catch people's attention, and what issues should be stressed? How much money should be spent on television commercials compared to radio and newspaper ads?

A strong organization is essential to running a presidential campaign. Heading the organization is a **campaign manager,** who is responsible for overall strategy and planning. In the national office, individuals handle relations with television, radio, and the print media and manage finances, advertising, opinion polls, and campaign materials.

On the state and local levels, the state party chairperson usually coordinates a campaign. Local party officials and field workers contact voters, hold local rallies, and **distribute** campaign literature. The field workers, who are usually volunteers, ring doorbells, canvass voters by telephone, and do whatever they can do to make sure voters turn out to vote on Election Day.

Using Television

The most important communication tool for a presidential candidate is television. Watching television is the main way that many citizens find out about a candidate and the way a campaign is progressing. The **image** voters have of a candidate has proven to be extremely important for their voting decisions. Thus, a campaign organization spends significant resources on trying to "package" a candidate for television appearances.

Political commercials are one of the possibilities that television offers for a candidate to shape his or her image to the voters. Appearances on television news shows are equally important. Compared to all other sources, television has now become the single most common news source for most Americans.

Candidates also use this medium in televised debates. Debates usually come later in a campaign

---

Activity: Collaborative Learning

Creating a Viral Video Organize the class into groups of four to create a made-for-YouTube presidential campaign ad. Encourage students to consider the concept of "viral" videos. Assign each group a past presidential campaign to model. Have students in each group divide up or work together on the following tasks: write and present a brief statement that reflects the candidate's stand on an important issue, design the graphics and setting for the ad, decide what the tone or mood of the ad should be, and videotape the ad. After the groups have videotaped their ads, play them for the class and have the class vote for the best one. **AL**

and can have a big impact on undecided voters. Political parties know these voters can determine the outcome of the election. In 2008 the debate between the rival vice presidential candidates, Democrat Joe Biden and Republican Sarah Palin, captured a huge audience of 70 million people. Analysts attributed the audience to curiosity about Palin, a newcomer to the national political scene.

Using the Internet

Candidates running for nearly every office from the president to county clerk are making increasing use of the Internet. Howard Dean, Democratic presidential candidate in 2004, was the first to raise significant contributions on the Web and to gain support through www.Meetup.com.

Since then the Web has become key to fundraising and persuading voters. The public can use Web sites to learn all about a candidate. Some sites list contributors or have a newsletter offering e-mail updates on a candidate's activities.

In the 2008 presidential race, the Internet's impact was obvious. Political pundits said Democrat Barack Obama revealed something about himself through his Web style—he was more of a "Mac" guy, it was said, while Hillary Clinton was more of a "PC" person. More importantly, Obama's campaign tapped into the youth vote by making

the fullest use of social networking on the Internet. He launched his own social network and also made use of Facebook and YouTube.

Financing Campaigns

Running for political office is very expensive. In the 2008 elections, presidential and congressional candidates spent more than $4 billion. Candidates need money for such things as office space, staff salaries, travel, and especially television advertising. Money can contribute to a broader political debate, but there is also the possibility that once elected, candidates will feel the need to give favors to those who contributed heavily to their campaign.

Regulating Campaign Financing

Today campaign financing is heavily regulated. The Federal Election Campaign Act (FECA) of 1971 and its amendments in 1974, 1976, and 1979 provide regulations that apply to campaign financing. This law and its amendments require public disclosure of each candidate's spending, provide federal funding for presidential elections, prohibit labor unions and business organizations from making direct contributions, and limit how much individuals and groups can contribute. At first, the

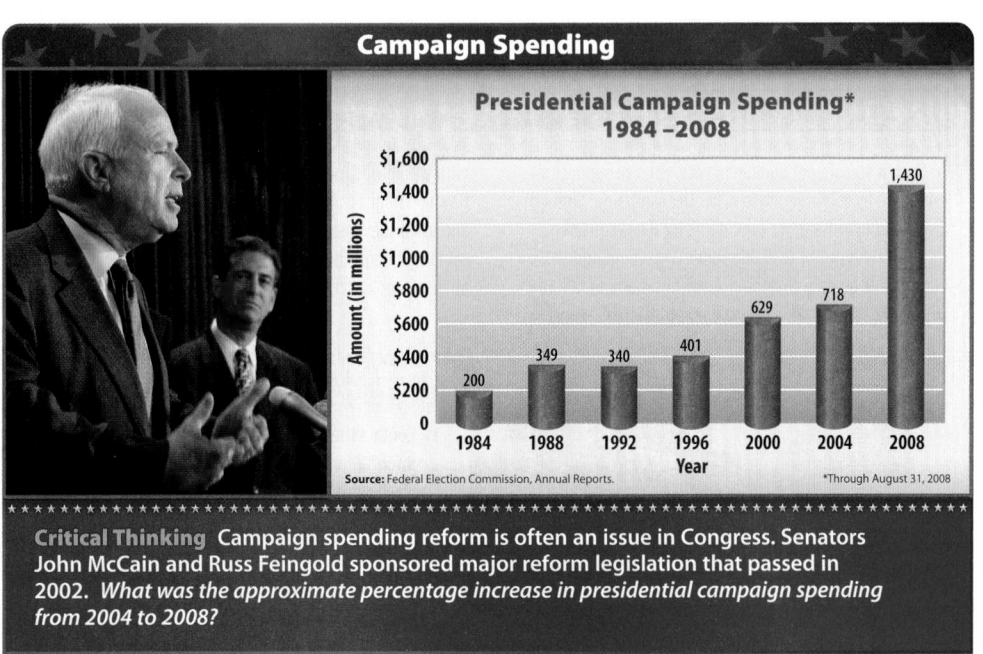

Campaign Spending

Presidential Campaign Spending*
1984–2008

Year	Amount (in millions)
1984	200
1988	349
1992	340
1996	401
2000	629
2004	718
2008	1,430

Source: Federal Election Commission, Annual Reports. *Through August 31, 2008

Critical Thinking Campaign spending reform is often an issue in Congress. Senators John McCain and Russ Feingold sponsored major reform legislation that passed in 2002. *What was the approximate percentage increase in presidential campaign spending from 2004 to 2008?*

S Skill Practice

Researching Tell students that Barack Obama made extensive use of the Internet in the 2008 presidential campaign. The Internet had first been used as a central campaign strategy in Howard Dean's bid for the Democratic presidential nomination in 2004. Ask students to research President Obama's campaign and create a graphic organizer that illustrates the campaign methods he used in 2008. **OL**

W Writing Support

Personal Writing Ask students to write blog entries expressing their support for a political candidate. Blogs should discuss at least one campaign issue and the student's reasons for supporting the candidate. **AL**

Critical Thinking

Answer: about 100%

Graph Skills Practice
Between which two presidential election years did presidential campaign spending decrease? *(1988 and 1992)* **OL**

Hands-On Chapter Project
Step 1

Analyzing an Election Campaign

Step 1: Seeing the "Big Picture"
Working in groups, students will select and research a presidential campaign they have heard or read about.

Directions Tell students they will be analyzing various components of the campaign throughout the chapter. Have them brainstorm what resources they

might use. Then organize the class into several groups, and have each group select one candidate—recent or historical—to research. In Step 1, they will find three examples of their candidate's rhetoric from sections of campaign speeches and analyze the style and content.

Putting It Together Ask each group to present their findings to the class. **Ask:** What effect do you think this candidate's rhetoric had on the campaign? Does it

make the candidate's position on an issue clear? What does it tell you about the candidate? Have students share their responses. **OL**

(Chapter Project continued in Section 2.)

477

D Differentiated Instruction

Logical/Mathematical In the 2008 presidential election, the majority of money raised by Barack Obama came from individuals who donated $200 or less. In contrast, most of the money raised by John McCain came from persons who donated $2,300 or more. As of mid-July, the Obama campaign had raised more than $287 million and the McCain campaign $120 million. **Ask:** What does this tell you about the voters who supported each candidate? **OL**

Participating IN GOVERNMENT

Volunteerism Explain that volunteerism is an important part of the American democratic system. Discuss former president George H.W. Bush's attempt to rally Americans to volunteer through his "Thousand Points of Light" program.

Activity Have students choose an organization they believe supports an important cause and find out how to volunteer for this organization.

Differentiated Instruction

regulations also tried to limit how much candidates could spend in a campaign.

The 1974 amendment to the law created the Federal Election Commission (FEC) as an independent agency in the executive branch to administer federal election laws. Records of campaign contributions must be kept, and all contributions of more than $100 must be reported to the FEC. Any citizen can gain access to the FEC's records to inspect them.

In 1976 the Supreme Court ruled that even though limiting individual contributions to candidates did not violate the First Amendment, an overall limit on the total cost of a campaign was unconstitutional. As a result, some candidates have spent huge sums of money. In 2000 Democrat Jon S. Corzine used $65 million of his own money to finance his campaign for a seat in the New Jersey Senate.

Public Funding

The 1974 campaign finance law established public funding for presidential campaigns. Presidential candidates can accept federal funding from the Presidential Election Campaign Fund for the primary campaigns and the general election but must agree to limit their total campaign spending. From 1976 to 2004, all major party candidates accepted these funds for the general election. Third-party presidential candidates can also receive federal funds. In order to do so, however, their party must have received at least 5 percent of the vote in the previous presidential election.

Private Funding

In every election, most campaign funding comes from private sources, such as individual citizens, parties, corporations, and special-interest groups. The passage of FECA in 1974 limited direct donations by an individual to $1,000.

Direct donations to candidates or parties also come from **political action committees,** or PACs. PACs are established by interest groups to raise money to support candidates or parties. Like individuals, PACs are limited by FECA in how much they can donate directly to a single candidate in one election cycle. An election cycle includes the primary and general election.

Political parties have used loopholes in FECA regulations to maximize their campaign contributions. One way to bypass campaign spending limits is to place ads that advocate a position on an issue. Interest groups often pay for issue ads to urge voters to support a certain position on gun control, health care, or some other issue. Since

Participating IN GOVERNMENT **Working in a Campaign**

Even if you are not eligible to vote, you can support a candidate by volunteering in his or her campaign. Sign up by calling or visiting the candidate's local headquarters.

Volunteers might stuff envelopes with campaign literature or go door to door in a neighborhood to talk to voters. You might staff a phone bank; that is, call voters with a prepared message about the candidate. On Election Day, you might call selected voters to remind them to vote and ask if they need a ride to the polls. Volunteering in a campaign helps the candidate you favor. It also gives you an inside look at the election process.

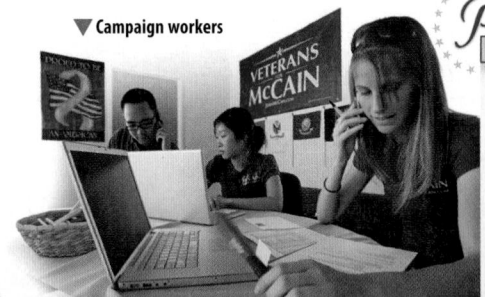

▼ Campaign workers

Participating IN GOVERNMENT ACTIVITY

1. Contact the local branch of a political party to get information on volunteering. Share it with your classmates.

2. For an upcoming election, gather information on the candidates. Then summarize each candidate's position on the issues and explain which candidate you support and why.

Activity: Multiple Learning Styles

Verbal/Linguistic Have the class work in pairs to role-play a campaign volunteer during a presidential election campaign. Assign each pair a different candidate from a past election. Have one student imagine he or she is answering phones while the other student is a caller with questions about the candidate. Allow students time to research their candidate before role-playing for the class a three-to-five-minute, question-and-answer phone conversation. Ask students not to reveal the candidate's name. Have the class speculate on which candidate is being portrayed. **ELL OL**

they do not ask for support for a candidate, they are not regulated, but these ads often contain a candidate's name. They can be a powerful way to support a candidate or target one they oppose. The top 10 advertisers on issues spent about $2.39 million during the 2000 election.

In 2002 Senators John McCain and Russ Feingold sponsored a bill to place new controls on campaign spending. The Bipartisan Campaign Reform Act (BRCA) targeted issue advertising and soft money donations to national political parties. (Soft money donations are contributions that are given directly to a party by PACs or individuals for general purposes, such as voter registration drives and party mailings.) In past elections, this money was spent by political parties to benefit the campaigns of candidates without ever giving the money directly to the candidates. FECA did not limit **soft money,** and in the 2000 election, each party raised more than $250 million in soft money contributions. The BRCA banned soft money donations to national political parties, but it raised the limit for individual direct donations to $2,000. It also prohibited unions, corporations, and nonprofit groups from running issue ads within 30 days of a primary election and 60 days of a general election. This law was challenged as an unconstitutional restriction on free speech, but in 2003 it was largely upheld by the Supreme Court.

Campaign Law and the Internet

Most campaign finance regulations were written before the use of the Internet. The FEC has issued rulings on how election laws apply to the Internet.

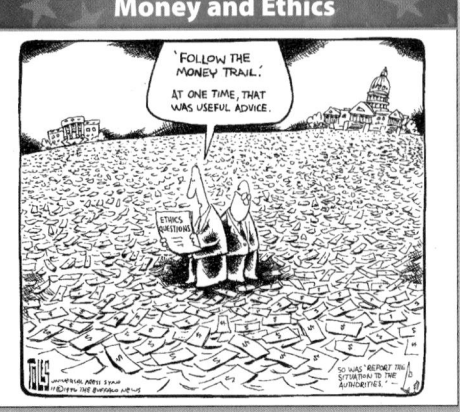

Money and Ethics

Campaign Reform Questionable campaign funding has dominated partisan battles on Capitol Hill. *According to the cartoonist, how has the high cost of running for public office affected the ethics of campaign fund-raising?*

Web site operators must identify themselves online, even if they are individual citizens. Web sites working independently of official campaigns must register with the FEC if they spend $250 or more on the site; this includes the equipment and Internet connections used to maintain it. Official candidate and party sites receive contributions electronically and must follow reporting procedures.

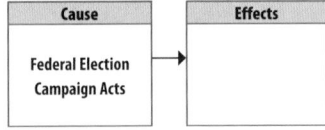

SECTION 1 Review

Vocabulary

1. **Explain** the significance of: campaign manager, image, political action committee, soft money.

Main Ideas

2. **Describing** How can third-party candidates qualify for federal funds for a presidential campaign?

3. **Analyzing** What are some rules that the FEC has issued on how federal election laws apply to the Internet?

Critical Thinking

4. **Synthesizing** PACs can contribute to as many political candidates as they wish. Why might they contribute to all major candidates in a presidential campaign?

5. **Organizing** Use a graphic organizer to show the effects of the Federal Election Campaign Acts on campaign financing.

Cause		Effects
Federal Election Campaign Acts	→	

Writing About Government

6. **Descriptive Writing** Imagine that you are running for political office. Prepare a campaign strategy for your election. Explain what campaign tools you would use and how you would finance your campaign. Write an outline detailing your strategy.

CHAPTER 17: *Elections and Voting* **479**

R Reading Strategy

Inferring Ask: Why are Web site operators required to register with the FEC when they spend more than $250 on a campaign site? *(because their work is considered a contribution to the campaign they are supporting)* OL

Caption Answer: Money might be coming in from many different sources, some of which are ethically questionable.

Assess

Assign the Section 1 Assessment as homework or as an in-class activity, or have students take Section Quiz 17-1 from *Section Quizzes and Chapter Tests.*

Close

Evaluating Have students suggest what controls, if any, they would place on the financing and running of election campaigns. OL

Section 1 Review

Answers

1. All definitions can be found in the section and the Glossary.
2. by winning more than 5 percent of the popular vote in the current or previous presidential election
3. Web site operators must identify themselves online; Web sites that spend more than $250 on an independent campaign Web site must register with the FEC.
4. They might think that contributing to all candidates will assure a friendly reception to their positions.
5. Effects—prohibited business organizations and unions from contributing directly to campaigns; individuals could contribute up to $1,000 to any candidate or general election campaign; encouraged the growth of PACs
6. Students' illustrated posters should outline their campaign strategies.

Teach

Setting Up the Debate

Applying Research Have students research the 2008 presidential primaries. **Ask:** How many candidates were running in January of 2008? How many were still running in June or July? What do these dwindling numbers of candidates say about the selection process? *(Students should point out that candidates are forced to withdraw from the race for a variety of reasons including lack of money and support.)*

Evaluating Have students research the arguments for and against a national presidential primary. Students should give specific arguments to support both points of view.

Concluding the Debate

Discuss these questions with students:

- What might be some negative effects of a national presidential primary? Positive effects?
- Would you vote in a presidential primary? If there were a national presidential primary, would you be more likely to vote knowing that your vote might be more meaningful?
- What is the purpose of voting in a presidential primary?

Should We Have a National Presidential Primary?

In a presidential primary election, voters go to the polls to choose among a party's presidential candidates. By custom and party rule, Iowa and New Hampshire hold the first caucus and primary, respectively, of the campaign season. In recent years, some states have tried to increase their influence on the outcome by moving up the dates of their primaries. In 2008 the Republican and Democratic Parties held primaries in more than 40 states, including the District of Columbia and Puerto Rico.

YES

We need to have a national primary in which all states hold their primary elections on the same day. Right now, with the first primaries in January and the last in June or July, the primary process is too drawn out. A more serious problem is the fear that the votes of many Americans do not matter. In 2000, for example, George W. Bush and Al Gore had all but locked up their party's nominations before 33 states had even held their primaries. A national primary would accomplish three things. It would simplify the system. It would avoid placing too much emphasis on one or two states. And finally, it would increase turnout and make all votes meaningful.

NO

A national primary has several flaws. It favors candidates with the most money and name recognition. Campaigns would be waged primarily through the media, making it nearly impossible for a candidate without a personal fortune to compete. By contrast, a staggered primary season is more democratic. It gives greater voice to lesser-known and underfunded candidates. Campaigning in Iowa and New Hampshire allows these candidates to present their message directly to the voters, gain momentum from early successes, and build grassroots support to continue their campaign.

Debating the Issue

1. **Explaining** Why have some states moved the date of their presidential primary?

2. **Analyzing** What does the schedule of primary elections mean for the candidates? For the voters?

3. **Deciding** With which opinion do you tend to agree? Explain your reasoning.

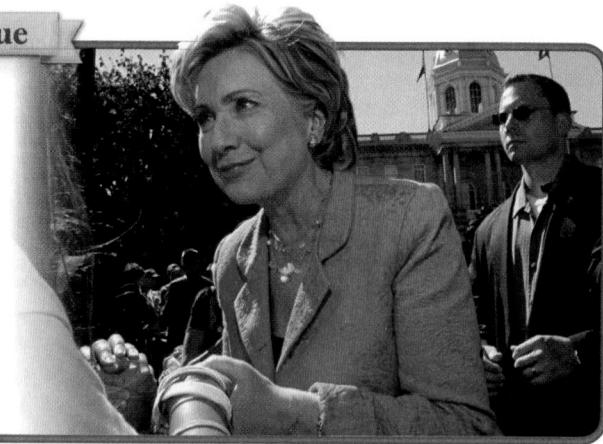

▶ Democrat Hillary Clinton at a 2007 rally in New Hampshire, the state whose dominance in the primaries is being challenged

Debating the Issue Answers

1. to increase their influence on the primary's outcome
2. A spread-out schedule of primaries gives candidates with less money more of an opportunity to campaign, but it tends to give voters who participate in later primaries less influence.

3. Students should support their opinion with references to the quotes or individual research and logical arguments.

Expanding Voting Rights

Focus

Content Vocabulary	Academic Vocabulary	Reading Strategy
★ suffrage (p. 482)	★ dominant (p. 481)	As you read, create a graphic organizer similar to the one below to help you take notes on expanding voting rights.
★ grandfather clause (p. 483)	★ device (p. 483)	
★ poll tax (p. 483)	★ diminish (p. 484)	

Effects of the Voting Rights Acts

Individual Rights in the News

For the March 2008 primary, some 1,000 students from Texas A&M University at Prairie View marched from campus to the polls at the Waller County courthouse. They carried "Register to Vote" signs, and their T-shirts read "It is 2008. We will vote." The students were protesting the failure of officials to provide an early voting site on campus. Freshman Brittney Veasey, a first-time voter, commented: "Instead of making it inconvenient, students should be encouraged to vote." Prairie View Mayor Frank Johnson praised the students. "Until they spoke up, there was only one early voting place in the entire county."

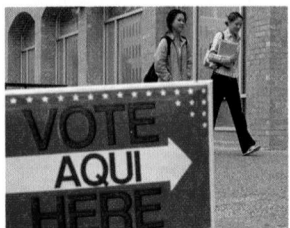

▲ Unlike the Prairie View students in the 2008 primary, students in Austin, Texas, had a campus polling location.

Bellringer

Section Focus Transparencies 17-2

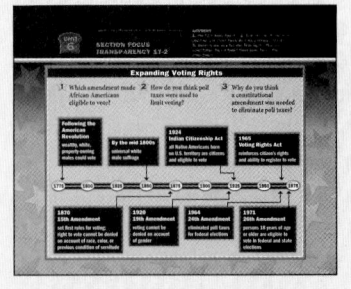

Reader's Guide

Answers to Graphic:

ended practices limiting voting participation by African Americans, outlawed the division of election districts in order to diminish the impact of minorities, appointment of poll watchers required ballots to be printed in minorities' languages

The students' march in Prairie View underscored the fact that voting is not a privilege, but a right. Voting is vital to the success of American democracy. After all, democracy means rule by the people—only through voting can democracy become a reality. Americans have the power to select more than 500,000 government officials at all levels of government.

Today, almost all citizens 18 years old or older can exercise the right to vote. Like other rights, the right to vote is not absolute, but subject to regulations and restrictions. For example, the right to vote for those over the age of 18 did not always exist. During the Vietnam War era, student activism led to the adoption of the Twenty-sixth Amendment to the Constitution, which was ratified in 1971: 18 years of age was established as the age limit for voting. During periods of American history, law, custom, and even violence prevented certain groups of people from voting.

Early Voting Limitations

Before the American Revolution, the colonies placed many restrictions on who had the right to vote. Women and most African Americans were not allowed to vote; neither were white males who did not own property or pay taxes. In some colonies, only members of the **dominant** religious group could vote. As a result, only about 5 or 6 percent of the adult population was eligible to vote.

These restrictions existed because educated white men of the time did not believe in mass democracy. Most believed that voting was best left to wealthy, white, property-owning males. As John Jay, the first chief justice of the United States, put it: "The people who own the country ought to govern it."

During the first half of the 1800s, state legislatures gradually abolished property requirements and religious restrictions for voting. By the mid-1800s,

Resource Manager

R Reading Strategies	C Critical Thinking	D Differentiated Instruction	W Writing Support	S Skill Practice
Teacher Edition • Identifying, p. 483 **Additional Resources** • Guid. Read. Act., p. 62 • Quizzes/Tests, p. 208	**Teacher Edition** • Making Inferences, p. 484 **Additional Resources** • Read. Essen., pp. 190–192	**Teacher Edition** • Intrapersonal, p. 482 **Additional Resources** • Foldables, p. 60 • Hist. Docs. and Speeches, p. 17	**Teacher Edition** • Personal Writing, p. 483 **Additional Resources** • Gov. Sims. and Debates, pp. 33–34	**Additional Resources** • Skill Reinforce. Act., p. 17 • Ch. Summaries, pp. 49–51

Teach

D Differentiated Instruction

Intrapersonal The Fifteenth Amendment banned racial qualifications for voters, but it did not guarantee the right to vote to all citizens. Have students imagine that it is 1876 and they are either an African American living in the South or a white woman in the North. Have them write five diary entries in which they describe their feelings about the obstacles that keep them from voting and how they would try to overcome these obstacles. **OL**

We the People
Making a Difference

Condoleezza Rice Under President George H.W. Bush, Condoleezza Rice drew on her political science background as senior director for Soviet affairs at the National Security Council. In that role, she helped bring democratic reforms to Poland and to develop many of the Bush administration's policies toward the former Soviet Union.

Hands-On Chapter Project
Step 2

---

the country achieved universal white adult male **suffrage,** or the right to vote. Neither women nor African Americans could vote, however.

Woman Suffrage

The fight for woman suffrage dates from the mid-1800s. Woman suffrage groups grew in number and effectiveness in the last half of the century, and by 1914 they had won the right to vote in 11 states, all of them west of the Mississippi. Not until after World War I, when the Nineteenth Amendment was ratified, was woman suffrage put into effect nationwide. The Nineteenth Amendment states:

> 66 *The right of citizens of the United States to vote shall not be denied or abridged by the United States or by any State on account of sex.* 99
>
> —Nineteenth Amendment, 1920

African American Suffrage

When the Constitution went into effect in 1789, African Americans, both enslaved and free, made up about 20 percent of the U.S. population. Yet nowhere were enslaved persons permitted to vote, and free African Americans who were allowed to vote could do so in only a few states.

The Fifteenth Amendment

The first effort to extend suffrage to African Americans nationwide came shortly after the Civil War, when the Fifteenth Amendment[1] was ratified **D** in 1870. The amendment provided that no state can deprive any citizen of the right to vote on account of race, color, or previous condition of servitude. This amendment was also important because for the first time, the national government

*See the following footnoted materials in the **Reference Handbook:**
1. The Constitution, pages R42–R67.

We the People
★ Making a Difference ★

Did you know that Condoleezza Rice once intended to study music in college? Did you know that she has an oil tanker named after her?

Rice grew up in Birmingham, Alabama, during the early years of the civil rights movement. Her family was the third generation to have gone to college. Her parents were teachers and taught her that education is the best defense against segregation and prejudice. "I can remember my parents taking me to watch the [civil rights] marchers," she once said. Rice firmly believes that in the United States, "[I]t really does not matter where you come from. It matters where you are going."

Rice served as National Security Advisor for President George W. Bush during his first term. In 2004 he appointed her to be the secretary of state. Her academic background includes graduate study in international relations. One of her college courses was taught by Josef Korbel, the father of the first female secretary of state, Madeleine Albright.

In the early 1980s, she was on the political science faculty of Stanford University, rising to the post of university provost. Rice has also served on the boards of directors for a number of major corporations. A devoted fan of football, she has said that someday she would love to be the commissioner of the National Football League.

"[I]t really does not matter where you come from. It matters where you are going."
—**Condoleezza Rice**

Analyzing an Election Campaign

Step 2: Identifying the Issues Students will research their candidate's position on key campaign issues and notice how difficult it is to find clear statements about issues.

Directions Have students identify two of the campaign's most important issues. Each group will create a graphic organizer showing the issues, their candidate's position on each issue, and the groups that were likely to support that position.

Explaining Have groups discuss their graphic organizers and display them in the classroom. **OL**

(Chapter Project continued in Section 3.)

Overcoming Obstacles

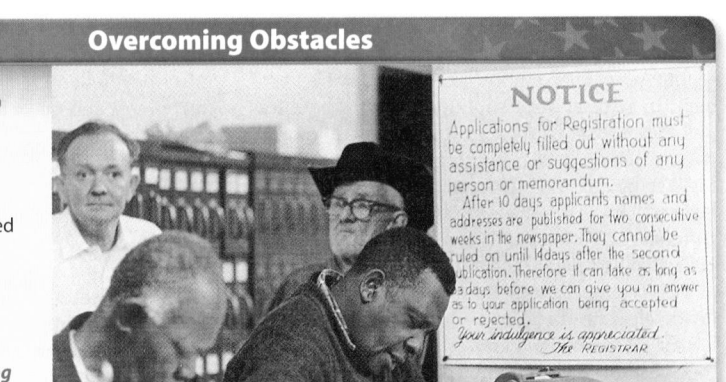

Tools of Citizenship Throughout the South, African Americans faced intimidating rules and regulations as late as the 1960s when they attempted to register to vote or cast their ballots. Even after the Voting Rights Act of 1965 was passed, some encountered obstacles to voting. *How did the Voting Rights Act of 1965 address these problems?*

set rules for voting, a power that only the states had previously exercised.

Grandfather Clause

Although the Fifteenth Amendment was an important milestone on the road to full suffrage, it did not result in complete voting rights for African Americans. Southern states set up a number of roadblocks to limit and discourage the participation of African American voters.

One such roadblock was the **grandfather clause.** It was incorporated in the constitutions of some Southern states. The grandfather clause provided that only voters whose grandfathers had voted before 1867 were eligible to vote without paying a certain tax or passing a literacy test. The grandfathers of most African American Southerners had been enslaved and were not permitted to vote, so this clause prevented most of them from voting. In 1915 the Supreme Court declared the grandfather clause unconstitutional.

Literacy Test

Until recent years, many states required citizens to pass a literacy test to qualify to vote. Some Southern states used the literacy tests to keep African Americans from the polls. In many cases white voters were judged literate if they could write their names, but African American voters were often required to do much more. For example, they were frequently asked to explain a complicated part of the state or national constitution. The Voting Rights Acts of 1965 and 1970, and later additions to these laws, outlawed literacy tests.

Poll Tax

Another **device** that was designed to discourage African American suffrage was the poll tax. A **poll tax** was an amount of money—usually one or two dollars—that a citizen had to pay before he or she could vote. The poll tax had to be paid not only for the current year but also for previous unpaid years as well. It was a financial burden for poor citizens of all ethnic backgrounds. In addition, the tax had to be paid well in advance of Election Day, and the poll-tax payer had to present a receipt showing payment before being permitted to enter the voting booth. Voters who did not have their receipts were barred from voting. Thousands of African Americans in the states with poll taxes were excluded from the polls.

In 1964 the Twenty-fourth Amendment outlawed the poll tax in national elections. The use of the poll tax in state elections was not eliminated until a 1966 Supreme Court decision.

The Voting Rights Acts

Despite the elimination by the early 1960s of many discriminatory practices, African American participation in elections was still limited, particularly in the South.

It took the civil rights movement of the 1960s to create the political pressure to pass new voting laws. These laws reformed state practices that stood in the way of African Americans voting. The Voting Rights Act of 1965 was the centerpiece of these civil rights laws. How did this law work?

In the American political system, states run the electoral process. With the Voting Rights Act of

---

Caption Answer: The Voting Rights Act gave the federal government the power to register voters in places where less than half of the adult population was registered to vote.

R Reading Strategy

Identifying Ask students to list and describe the roadblocks devised to prevent African Americans from voting. **BL** **ELL**

W Writing Support

Personal Writing Have students research the different kinds of literacy tests that were used to keep African Americans from voting. **Ask:** Did African Americans and whites have the same literacy tests? Were the tests difficult? Would *you* be able to pass one of these tests? **OL**

Differentiated Instruction

Participating in Government Activities

Participating in Government Activities, p. 34

Objective: To understand the "ins and outs" of voter registration in your community

Focus/Teach: Have students read the background material and answer the Questions to Consider.

Assess: Complete the Activity, and discuss students' results.

Close: Have each student compile all of the information and materials needed to register to vote.

Differentiated Instruction Strategies

BL Have students create a poster encouraging students to register to vote.

AL Have students find out the percentage of eligible voters in your community who are registered to vote.

ELL Have students find out where eligible voters can register in your community.

C Critical Thinking

Making Inferences Ask: What is the youth vote, and why is it important in elections? *(Voters between 18 and 29 years old; young voters are often more malleable in terms of political beliefs.)* **ELL OL**

Assess

Assign the Section 2 Assessment as homework or as an in-class activity, or have students take Section Quiz 17-2 from *Section Quizzes and Chapter Tests*.

Close

Defining Ask students to choose which amendment or federal law they think helped expand voting rights to the greatest number of people in the United States. Discuss students' answers. **OL**

Government ONLINE

Objectives and answers to the Student Web Activity can be found in the *Web Activity Lesson Plan* at glencoe.com. Enter *QuickPass*™ code USG9085c17T.

Section 2 Review

1965, however, the federal government entered directly into the electoral process. The Voting Rights Act of 1965 empowered the federal government to register voters in any district where less than 50 percent of African American adults were on the voting lists. The government could also register voters in districts where it appeared that local officials were discriminating against African Americans. Voting rights laws of 1970, 1975, and 1982 also broadened the federal role in elections.

The voting rights laws also made it illegal to divide election districts in order to **diminish** the impact of minority voters. The laws provided for poll watchers to be appointed to see that all votes were properly counted. Literacy tests were abolished. The laws also required that ballots be printed in Spanish for Spanish-speaking communities or in other minority languages where appropriate. The Voting Rights Acts resulted in a dramatic increase in African American voter registration. In 1960 only 29 percent of all African Americans in the South were registered. By 2000, the figure rose to more than 64 percent.

Within a few years of the passage of the 1965 Voting Rights Act, more than 1,000 African Americans were elected to political office. In the North, the civil rights movement and the Voting Rights Acts led to the election of many African American mayors—Cleveland, Ohio, and Gary, Indiana, were the first. Within a decade, about 200 African American mayors served in cities of all sizes.

Recent efforts at voting reform include the Help America Vote Act of 2002. Under this act, states must meet federal requirements to reform the voting process and make it as consistent and inclusive as possible.

Twenty-sixth Amendment

For many years, the minimum voting age in most states was 21. In the 1960s, when many young Americans were fighting in Vietnam, a movement to lower the voting age to 18 began. The basic argument was that if individuals were old enough to be drafted and fight for their country, they were old enough to vote. The Twenty-sixth Amendment ended this debate, stating that:

C

❝ *The right of citizens of the United States, who are eighteen years of age or older, to vote shall not be denied or abridged by the United States or by any State on account of age.* ❞
—Twenty-sixth Amendment, 1971

Thus, more than 10 million citizens between the ages of 18 and 21 gained the right to vote.

Government ONLINE
Student Web Activity Visit glencoe.com and enter *QuickPass*™ code USG9822c17. Click on Student Web Activity and complete the activity about voting rights.

SECTION 2 Review

Vocabulary

1. **Explain** the significance of: suffrage, grandfather clause, poll tax.

Main Ideas

2. **Describing** What did the Twenty-fourth Amendment outlaw?

3. **Summarizing** What were the provisions of the Voting Rights Acts, and why were they so important?

Critical Thinking

4. **Making Inferences** John Jay said, "The people who own the country ought to govern it." Explain the impact of the extension of voting rights on the meaning of Jay's statement.

5. **Organizing** Use a chart to explain the changes brought about by the Fifteenth, Nineteenth, and Twenty-sixth Amendments.

15th	19th	26th

Writing About Government

6. **Expository Writing** Create an illustrated time line that focuses on major events in the extension of voting rights in the United States. Include events between 1791 and the present and write a brief description of how voting rights have changed over time.

Answers

1. All definitions can be found in the section and the Glossary.
2. the poll tax in federal elections
3. The provisions of the Voting Rights Act empowered the federal government to prevent voting rights discrimination at the state level. It also resulted in an increased number of minority voters and African American participation in the political process.
4. Answers should point out that Jay believed, like many others of his time, that only property owners should have the right to

vote. The extension of voting rights allowed all Americans to participate and "own" their country.

5. Fifteenth: African American men were given the right to vote nationwide, the first time that the national government set rules for voting; Nineteenth: women were given the right to vote nationwide; Twenty-sixth: voting age lowered from 21 to 18

6. Students' time lines should cite specific events, and descriptions should be logical.

When Do Voter ID Laws Restrict the Right to Vote?

Crawford v. Marion County Election Board, 2008

For the right to vote to be preserved, the electoral process must guarantee access to the polls while protecting against voter fraud— only eligible voters are permitted to vote. This case examined the constitutionality of a new voter ID law in Indiana.

Facts of the Case

In 2005 the Republican-controlled legislature of Indiana passed a law that set more strict requirements for identifying Indiana voters at the polls. They require a voter to present an ID issued by the state or the federal government that includes a photo. Usually only a current driver's license or a passport qualifies. The state will issue a photo ID card for nondrivers, but obtaining it requires a person to provide a birth certificate, a passport, or another primary document.

The Indiana Democratic Party, among other groups, challenged the law on two grounds. First, it said that there was no proven voter fraud to justify a need for the new requirement. Second, it said the law placed a special burden on people with no driver's license. A higher number of nondrivers are poor, elderly, or disabled. Finally, plaintiffs pointed out that the voter ID law was the strictest in the nation and that it had been passed by Republican legislators with not a single Democratic vote.

The Constitutional Issue

The justices attempted to judge whether a new state law aimed at preventing voting fraud was reasonable. Was the state's interest in electoral integrity enough to justify new forms of identification for voters? The plaintiffs said that the new law would make it harder for some citizens to exercise the right to vote. The plaintiffs further noted that the problem of voter fraud had not been proven, but was only a *potential* danger. They also wanted the law overturned before it went into effect. (Waiting to see if it harmed some voters would mean that that election would be unfair.)

The state argued that the new ID card was free and that going to the Bureau of Motor Vehicles for it was not any more burdensome than the ordinary inconvenience of voting. Was the law too burdensome and was the goal of the law justified? The justices had to decide the case without evidence of voter fraud and without evidence that the new law might hinder access to the polls.

Debating the Issue

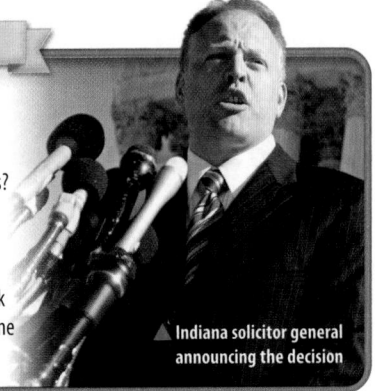

▲ Indiana solicitor general announcing the decision

Questions to Consider

1. What was the legislative background of the voter ID law?

2. Why did the Democratic Party enter into the lawsuit against state election officials?

3. What two factors did the justices weigh?

You Be the Judge

How burdensome does the new law seem to you as a potential voter? Do you think that someone without a car or who works unconventional hours might face an extreme burden? Do you think the justices' decision might influence other states?

Debating the Issue Answers

Focus

Bellringer

Write the following list on the board:

1. Register
2. Become informed
3. Cast your ballot
4. Monitor results

To vote, people must register with their local board of elections. To make sure their votes reflect their views, citizens must inform themselves about candidates and the issues being debated. They should also know about the mechanics of voting in their particular polling place. After the election, citizens should check on results to figure out how their community voted and why.

Reader's Guide

Answers to Graphic:
- Voters' Information Bulletin
- political party literature
- interest groups (American Conservative Union, AFL-CIO)
- print and television media

Resource Manager

Voter's Handbook

Voting is a basic political right of all citizens in a democracy who meet certain qualifications set by law. Voting allows citizens to take positive actions to influence or control government.

Reader's Guide

Content Vocabulary
★ canvass *(p. 487)*
★ register *(p. 487)*
★ polling place *(p. 488)*
★ precinct *(p. 488)*
★ office-group ballot *(p. 488)*
★ ticket-splitting *(p. 488)*
★ party-column ballot *(p. 489)*
★ canvassing board *(p. 490)*
★ absentee ballot *(p. 491)*

Academic Vocabulary
★ confirm *(p. 487)*
★ beneficiary *(p. 488)*
★ traditional *(p. 491)*

Reading Strategy
Complete a graphic organizer similar to the one below to explain the different sources of information about candidates.

```
→  Candidates  ←
```

New voters registering in Las Vegas, Nevada

486

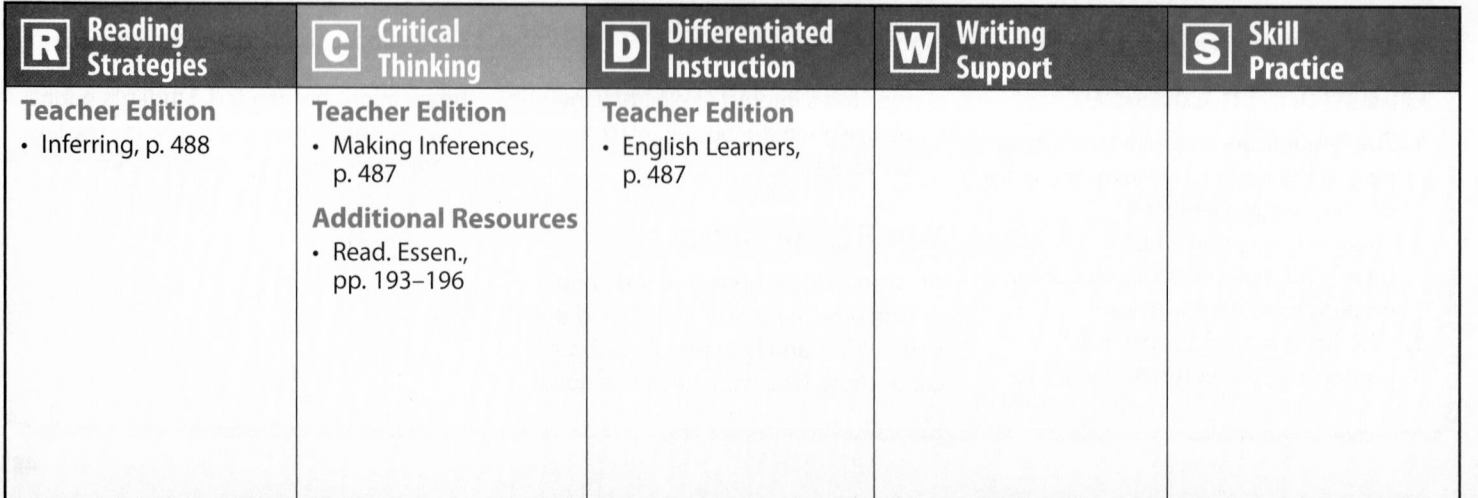 **R** Reading Strategies	**C** Critical Thinking	**D** Differentiated Instruction	**W** Writing Support	**S** Skill Practice
Teacher Edition • Inferring, p. 488	**Teacher Edition** • Making Inferences, p. 487 **Additional Resources** • Read. Essen., pp. 193–196	**Teacher Edition** • English Learners, p. 487		

Qualifications to Vote

Today you are qualified to vote if you are (1) a citizen of the United States, (2) at least 18 years old, and (3) not a convicted felon or legally insane. Most states also require that you be a resident of the state for a specified period and that you register or enroll with the appropriate local government.

Who sets the qualifications to vote?

Originally, under Article I, Section 2, the Constitution left voting qualifications entirely to the states. The Constitution gave to Congress only the power to pick the day on which presidential electors would gather and to fix "the Times, Places, and Manner of holding elections" of members of Congress.

Since the end of the Civil War, Congress and the federal courts have imposed national standards on state-run elections. A series of constitutional amendments, federal laws, and Supreme Court decisions forced the states to conduct elections without discrimination because of race, creed, color, or gender. Even with such federal requirements, however, the registration of voters and the regulation of elections are primarily state powers.

Will my vote count?

Each person's vote counts. If you doubt it, think about the times when a few votes have decided elections. In the 2000 election, more than 5.8 million votes were cast in the state of Florida. When the vote tally was completed, George W. Bush won the state's 25 electoral votes, and therefore the presidency by a margin of only 537 votes!

When Milton R. Young, a Republican, ran for the Senate in North Dakota, he led his challenger by fewer than 200 votes out of more than 236,000 cast. The official **canvass,** the vote count by the official body that tabulates election returns and certifies the winner, finally **confirmed** Young's victory. Sometimes victory hinges on a single vote. In a Cincinnati, Ohio, suburb, a candidate for the town council was suddenly hospitalized and unable to vote. When the votes were counted, he had lost by 1 vote.

Registering to Vote

Americans must take the initiative if they want to vote. Unlike in many countries, in the United States you must **register,** or enroll with the appropriate local government.

Expanding Democracy

FRANK LESLIE'S ILLUSTRATED NEWSPAPER

Western Pioneers Western states and territories like Wyoming led the way in granting women the vote. Here women cast their votes in Cheyenne, Wyoming, in 1888. *Can you think of social factors that might have encouraged this to happen?*

Registration became common in the late 1800s as a way to stop voting fraud. In those days, the slogan "Vote Early and Often" was not a joke. In Denver in 1900, for example, one man confessed to having voted 125 times on Election Day!

Reformers saw registration as a way to stop such abuses and clean up elections by giving officials a list of who could legally vote. Many of these reforms came during the Progressive Era in American history, from about 1890 to 1920. Meanwhile in the South, registration laws were being used in a negative way to stop African Americans and poor whites from voting.

Registration requirements are set by state law and differ from state to state. Telephone your local board of elections or county or city government

Teach

D Differentiated Instruction

English Learners Have students bring voter registration applications to class. Discuss voter requirements. Then have students complete the application form. (Students who are at least 18 years old could send in their completed application forms if they are not already registered.)

C Critical Thinking

Making Inferences Ask students to explain why the victory of the North in the Civil War led to national standards for state-run elections. Have students consider consequences of the abolition of slavery. **AL**

Caption Answer: Because the West required pioneer women to exercise initiative and even to fill traditionally male roles, their communities were more open to allowing women to vote. **OL**

Differentiated Instruction

Activity: Multiple Learning Styles

Visual/Spatial Organize the class into groups to create pictograph posters on voter participation. (Explain that a pictograph is a diagram representing statistical data by pictorial forms.) Have each group poll 30 people of legal voting age to ask if they voted in the most recent presidential election. Have them note each interviewee's gender, race, education level, and age. The information should be tallied for each characteristic. Then members in each group should choose one category and create a pictograph to report it. Finally, one member in each group can create a graph showing overall voter participation. Put completed pictographs on a bulletin board and discuss the results. **BL**

Did You Know?

In 1913 thousands of suffragists marched in a parade through Washington, D.C. In 1917 they set up a daily picket line outside the White House. Because their protest continued after the country entered World War I, the suffragists were accused of being traitors. The same accusation was made against veterans protesting the Vietnam War.

Caption Answer: Yes, more people registered in 1996 than in 1992. The act failed to accomplish its ultimate purpose, however, because fewer registered voters actually voted. Other factors might include the perception that candidates and issues did not seem important.

Additional Support

to check on your state's requirements. Registration forms typically ask for your name, address, place and date of birth, gender, Social Security number, and party affiliation. One important requirement is to sign your name—when you go to the polls, a poll worker will check your signature as a way of authenticating your vote.

Usually, you must register to vote 15 to 30 days before an election. Only three states currently allow you to register on Election Day—Maine, Minnesota, and Wisconsin.

The National Voter Registration Act that took effect in 1995 requires states to make registration forms available not only at motor vehicle departments but also at numerous state offices, welfare offices, and agencies that serve the disabled. It also requires states to allow mail-in registration. It permits, but does not require, states to use information from change-of-address forms filed with the U.S. Postal Service to update voter lists. Driver's license applicants are required to fill out a separate form for registering to vote. Public agencies must make it clear to **beneficiaries** that registering to vote is optional and that not registering will not affect the amount of assistance they receive.

Supporters of the National Voter Registration law believed that it would add 50 million citizens to the voting rolls when the changes went into effect. Many more citizens did register. However, the ease of registration did not help voter turnout in the 1996 election. Less than half the voting-age population participated, one of the lowest turnouts in history.

Voting Procedures

You vote at a **polling place** in your home **precinct.** A precinct is a voting district. Each city or county is usually divided into precincts containing from 200 to 1,000 voters.

Generally, before the date of the election you will receive notification of where you are to vote. Procedures will vary slightly at different polling places. Look over the sample ballot posted on a wall near the entryway. Then: (1) Go to the clerk or election judge's table and sign in by writing your name and address on an application form. (2) The clerk will read your name aloud and pass the application to a challenger, a local election official representing a political party. (3) The challenger compares your signature with your voter registration form. If they match, the challenger initials your form and returns it to you. (4) Give your form to one of the judges and enter the booth to vote.

You cannot be stopped from voting because of your race, gender, religion, income, or political beliefs. You can be challenged, however, if your registration or identification is in question.

What will the ballot look like?

Two forms of ballots are generally used. An **office-group ballot** lists all candidates together by the office for which they are competing. Their party is listed next to their name. Many believe this ballot type encourages **ticket-splitting,** voting for candidates from different parties for different offices.

The National Voter Registration Act and Presidential Elections

	1992	1996	2000	2004
Voting Age Population (VAP)	189,044,500	196,511,000	205,815,000	221,287,328
Voters Registered	133,821,178	146,211,960	156,421,311	174,804,298
Turnout	104,405,155	96,456,345	105,586,274	122,000,000
Turnout as % of VAP	55%	49%	51%	55%
Turnout as % of Those Registered	78%	66%	67%	70%

Source: U.S. Election Assistance Commission (www.eac.gov) and Federal Election Commission (www.fec.gov)   *Figures current as of late 2008.

Critical Thinking The National Voter Registration Act of 1994, implemented in 1995, aimed to register more voters in hopes of increasing turnout. *Using the table above, can you conclude that the legislation accomplished its purpose? Are there other factors that might explain why people decide to vote or not to vote in an election?*

Extending the Content

The Closest and the Smallest Elections
The closest final vote in a Senate campaign was recorded in Nevada in 1964, when Howard Cannon defeated Paul Lexalt by only 84 votes. Earlier in Nevada in 1912, Key Pittman, a Democrat, won with the smallest number of total votes—7,942—in Senate history. Pittman was not actually elected until January 28, 1913, when the Nevada legislature, which had agreed to select whichever candidate won the popular referendum, voted him in. The Seventeenth Amendment, ratified on April 8, 1913, marked the direct election of senators.

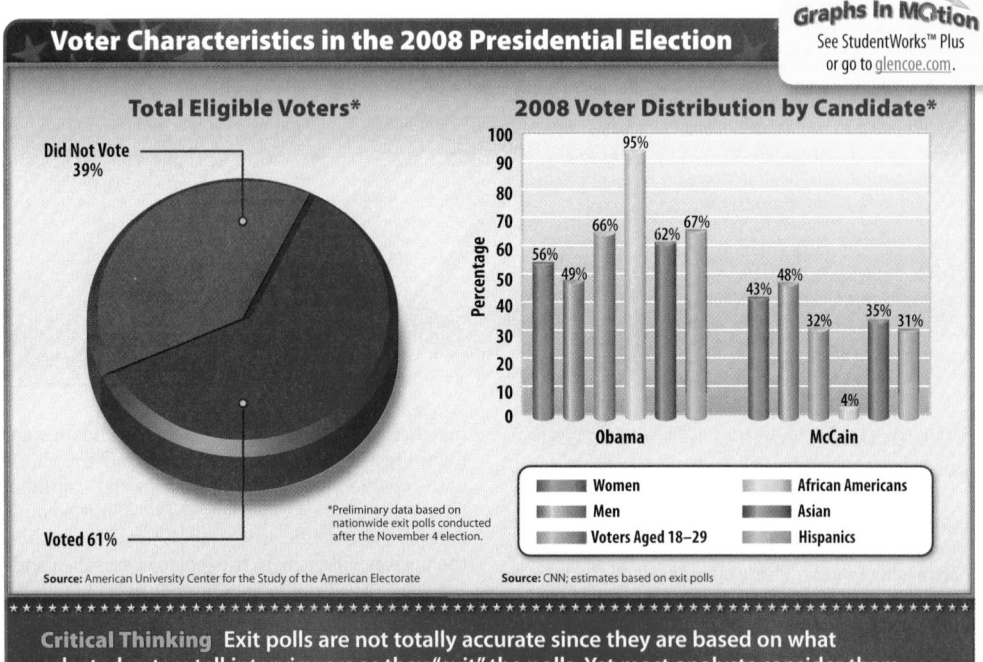

Voter Characteristics in the 2008 Presidential Election

Graphs In Motion
See StudentWorks™ Plus
or go to glencoe.com.

Total Eligible Voters*

Did Not Vote 39%

Voted 61%

Source: American University Center for the Study of the American Electorate

2008 Voter Distribution by Candidate*

Obama — Women 56%, Men 49%, Voters Aged 18–29 66%, African Americans 95%, Asian 62%, Hispanics 67%

McCain — Women 43%, Men 48%, Voters Aged 18–29 32%, African Americans 4%, Asian 35%, Hispanics 31%

Legend: Women, Men, Voters Aged 18–29, African Americans, Asian, Hispanics

*Preliminary data based on nationwide exit polls conducted after the November 4 election.

Source: CNN; estimates based on exit polls

Critical Thinking Exit polls are not totally accurate since they are based on what selected voters tell interviewers as they "exit" the polls. Yet most analysts consider them a good rough guide to how different segments of the population voted. *Based on the bar graph, which two groups showed the highest percentage voting for Barack Obama?*

The second type, a **party-column ballot,** lists each party's candidates in a column under the party's name. A square or circle is usually set at the top of each party's column. By putting one mark in the square or circle, you can vote a straight ticket for all the party's candidates. You can also vote for each office individually by marking one box in each column. You may also write in the name of someone who is not listed on the ballot.

How do I use the voting machine?

As a result of incorrectly marked ballots during the 2000 presidential election, many states are modernizing their voting machines. Besides newer touch-screen systems, the most common voting systems are the punch-card machine and the lever machine.

If you are given a punch-card ballot, insert it in the voting machine and line up the ballot with the names of the candidates. Punch holes in the appropriate places on the ballot with the provided stylus. Put your card in its envelope and give it to the election judge.

To use the lever machine, pull the large lever to one side to close the booth's curtain. The ballot is part of the machine facing you. Vote by pulling down the small levers beside the names of the candidates you are choosing. Then pull the large lever again to record your vote and reset the machine.

Touch-screen systems display the ballot on a computer screen. You vote by touching the box beside a candidate's name. Problems can occur with any method. In Ohio, the manufacturer of the touch-screen voting machines admitted in 2008 that a source-code error had led to votes being dropped in some counties in recent elections.

Will my vote be a secret?

The law entitles you to a secret ballot. Borrowed from a procedure developed in Australia in 1856, the Australian ballot was printed at government expense. The ballot listed all candidates, was given out only at the polls on Election Day, was marked in secret, and was counted by government officials. By 1900, nearly all states had adopted this system.

CHAPTER 17: *Elections and Voting* **489**

Linking Past & Present

Secret Ballots Today we see the secret ballot as a protection of our right to make electoral choices without fear. When it was first introduced, however, some Southern states used it to deny voting rights to African Americans. Illiteracy rates were high among African Americans at the time, and to cast a secret ballot a voter had to be able to read.

Did You Know?

The National Voter Registration law registered 13.5 million new voters between 1993 and 1996 as they applied for driver's licenses. In addition, more than 1 million immigrants gained voting rights in 1996. Why, then, did the 1996 election attract fewer than 50 percent of eligible voters to the polls? A strong economy, excessive polling, negative advertising, and bland issues were reasons given for not voting.

Activity: Multiple Learning Styles

English Learners Discuss with students ways in which they can prepare themselves to vote in an upcoming election. One way would be to compare the candidates' stands on issues that are important to the student. Instruct students to make a two-column table and write the names of the two major candidates in an upcoming election at the top. Then have students research each candidate's stand on important issues and list each candidate's position in the appropriate column. Have students compare the candidates' positions and decide which candidate would get their vote. **OL**

Did You Know?

After the presidential election of 2000, television networks became much more cautious in calling the results of elections. In that historic contest, the networks first announced that Florida's electoral votes would go to Democrat Al Gore, then switched to Republican George Bush, then declared that it could not be called. A weeks-long battle followed that hinged on how Florida's votes would be counted and authenticated.

CURRICULUM CONNECTION

Geography and Cultures
Maine, Minnesota, and Wisconsin consistently turn out 60 percent of the voters in presidential elections, compared to a national average in the 50s. One of the explanations appears to be that these states allow people to register at the voting place on Election Day.

Additional Support

Securing the Vote

Monitoring Democracy
In one Ohio county, the board of elections struggled to determine why election results from a touch-screen system were not uploaded to a server. A member of the Board of Elections looks on in the background. *What group in the state can certify the winner of an election?*

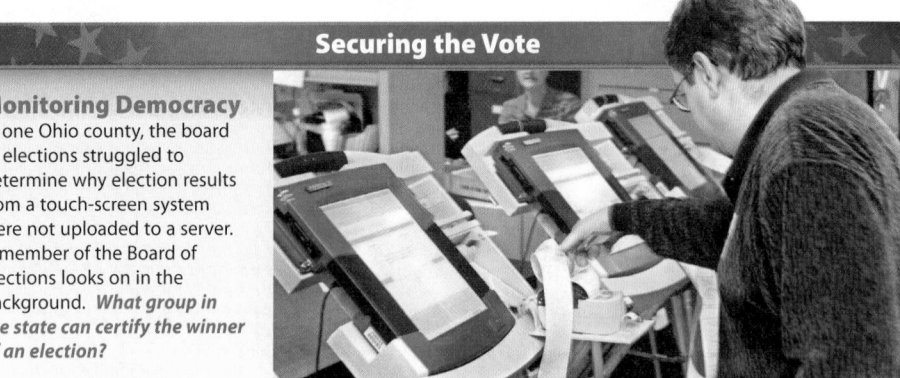

Who actually counts the votes and certifies a winner?

A **canvassing board,** or an official body that is bipartisan, counts votes. As soon as the polls close, precinct ballots are forwarded to city or county canvassing boards. These boards put all the returns together and send them to the state canvassing authority. Within days of the election, this authority certifies the election of the winner. Each winner gets a certificate of election from the county or state canvassing board.

Through television and radio, people usually know the winners before canvassing boards certify them. In close elections, the result might depend upon the official vote count and certification.

How can I prepare to vote?

The best way to prepare to vote is to stay informed about candidates and public issues. As Election Day nears, newspapers, TV, radio, and newsmagazines will carry useful information. You might also try the following: (1) The local League of Women Voters may publish a Voters' Information Bulletin, a fact-filled, nonpartisan rundown on candidates and issues. (2) Each political party has literature and other information about its candidates and will be eager to share it with you. (3) Many interest groups such as the American Conservative Union or the AFL-CIO Committee on Political Education rate members of Congress on their support for the group's programs. If you agree with the views of an interest group, check its ratings of candidates.

How can I choose a candidate?

Everyone has different reasons for supporting one candidate over another. Asking these questions may help you decide: (1) Does the candidate stand for things I think are important? (2) Is the candidate reliable and honest? (3) Does the candidate have relevant past experience? (4) Will the candidate be effective in office? Look for the resources the person will bring to the job. (5) Does the candidate have good political connections? (6) Does the candidate have a real chance of winning? You have a tough choice to make if it appears that your favorite candidate has a slim chance of winning. You may want to vote for a losing candidate to show support for a certain point of view. You might also want to vote for someone who has the greatest chance of beating the candidate you like the least.

Special Circumstances

With so many millions of voters, election officials have always had to consider how special circumstances might affect the ability of some voters to get to the polls. Over the years, special procedures and protections were developed to ensure every citizen's right to exercise the franchise. Recently, however, states have significantly loosened the guidelines for early voting. In some states, in fact, a voter needs no special reason or excuse to vote early. Early voting can occur in two ways:

- In-person voting
- Absentee voting

In-Person Voting

In recent years, the trend in many states has been to provide significant opportunities to vote early. A major reason for the trend is that states want to reduce the pressure placed on precincts on Election Day. For these early voters, new campaign ads or late political developments will not

490 UNIT 6: *Participating in Government*

Activity: Collaborative Learning

Role-Playing Have students work in pairs to explain the voting process in the United States. Have one student imagine that he or she is a newly naturalized citizen. Have the other student imagine that he or she works for a voter registration office. Ask the voter registration worker to explain the registration qualifications and the voting process in this country to the naturalized citizen. Then have that "new citizen" repeat what he or she learned. Rotate roles and replay the tasks. Ask each pair to write a paragraph about how they felt as a new citizen in this country attempting to register to vote. **OL**

matter. Most sources predicted that about one-third of the electorate cast their ballot before Election Day in 2008.

Absentee Ballot Voting

An **absentee ballot** allows you to vote without going to the polls. You must obtain an absentee ballot within a specified time before an election, fill it out, and return it (usually by mail). Deadlines vary by state.

Traditionally, you could vote absentee if you will be out of town or hospitalized on Election Day, have a disability or an illness that makes it difficult to go to the polls, cannot vote on Election Day for religious reasons, or will be in jail for a misdemeanor or awaiting trial.

Currently, many states' rules have been adjusted so that no excuse is needed—a voter can simply ask for an absentee ballot with no excuse needed. To do so, you must request an absentee ballot in person or by mail from your local board of elections or similar office.

Special Assistance

Any voter who needs help voting is entitled to receive it. In the case of voters with disabilities, some states allow you to pick the person to assist you. Other states require that only officials at the polling place can help. To protect voters with disabilities from pressure, some states require that two election officials from opposite parties be

Michigan Voting Issues Running for secretary of state, Democrat Carmella Sabaugh promised same-day registration and no-reason absentee voting in a recent race. *Why would these propositions appeal to retirees?*

present during voting. Non-English-speaking voters are also entitled to special assistance under the Voting Rights Act of 1975. Ballots and related election materials must be printed in the language of voting minorities, but this provision applies only where illiteracy in English is high or recent voter turnout was unusually low. In many parts of Florida, Texas, and California, election materials are available in both Spanish and English. In Hawaii, election materials have been printed in Cantonese, Ilocano, and Japanese as well as in English.

Handbook Assessment

Vocabulary

1. **Explain** the significance of: canvass, register, polling place, precinct, office-group ballot, ticket-splitting, party-column ballot, canvassing board, absentee ballot.

Main Ideas

2. **Summarizing** What are two requirements to vote in the United States?

3. **Describing** What is the Australian ballot, and why was it important in the United States?

Critical Thinking

4. **Making Inferences** Why do you think the secret ballot was adopted?

5. **Organizing** Use a graphic organizer like the one below to show some circumstances in which a voter would choose to cast an absentee ballot.

If		Then
	→	Absentee Ballot

Writing About Government

6. **Expository Writing** Citizens must prepare to vote. Walking into a voting booth without being prepared makes voting a meaningless activity. What should a person know in order to be an informed voter? Create a pamphlet describing the kinds of things voters should know in order to make their vote count.

Caption Answer: Retirees might have limited mobility. Absentee ballots would make voting less stressful.

CURRICULUM CONNECTION

Technology The news media interviews people exiting the voting booth. Using these "exit poll" results, television networks are able to project winners long before all the votes are counted. In the 1980 election, President Jimmy Carter conceded to Ronald Reagan while the polls were still open in California. Many Californians who were waiting in line went home after hearing the news.

Assess

Assign the Handbook Assessment as homework or as an in-class activity.

Close

Describing Have students write a paragraph discussing how they would feel if they lost the right to vote. **OL**

Voter's Handbook Review

Answers

1. All definitions can be found in the section and the Glossary.
2. Voters must satisfy all of the following: citizen of the United States, at least 18 years old, and neither a convicted felon nor legally insane.
3. The Australian ballot is the secret ballot; it reflected a belief that elections should be fair.
4. to prevent intimidation of voters by employers, unions, and former plantation owners (in the case of those who were formerly enslaved)
5. out of town, hospitalized, physically disabled, observing a religious holiday, in jail for a misdemeanor or awaiting trial
6. Students' pamphlet will vary; completeness, logical order, and an appealing format will characterize the best pamphlets.

Focus

Bellringer
Section Focus Transparencies 17-3

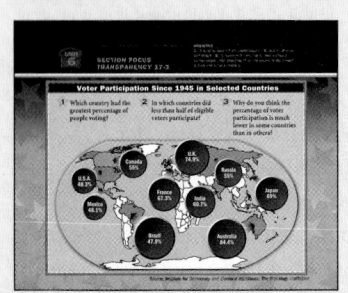

Reader's Guide

Answers to Graphic: family, age, income level, outlook on life, education, religion, racial/ethnic background

Resource Manager

Influences on Voters

Reader's Guide

Content Vocabulary	Academic Vocabulary	Reading Strategy
★ cross-pressured voter *(p. 493)* ★ straight party ticket *(p. 493)* ★ propaganda *(p. 495)*	★ occupation *(p. 492)* ★ predict *(p. 493)* ★ perceive *(p. 495)*	Create a graphic organizer similar to the one below to identify the ways voters' personal backgrounds influence their behaviors.

Background Influences

People in the News

A record number of young people voted in the 2008 election season. Many asked what drove the high youth turnout. Was it dissatisfaction with the state of the world or the appeal of the first African American and the first female candidates? Diane M. Phillips, a journalism professor at St. Joseph's University in Philadelphia, said young Americans tend to "favor authentic candidates—those who stick by their beliefs." Another analyst argues that the major influences on young people are family and significant others. Experts may differ, but given young people's unusual interest, candidates crafted their political messages to include this segment of the electorate.

▲ A young adult voting

Whether voters are young or old, five major factors tend to drive their choices:
- personal background of the voter,
- degree of loyalty to a party,
- issues in the campaign,
- voters' image of the candidates, and
- propaganda.

The first critical decision voters make, however, is whether they will vote on Election Day.

Personal Background of Voters

Voters' personal backgrounds affect their decisions. A person's background includes such things as upbringing, family, age, **occupation,** income level, and even general outlook on life.

Age

Consider, for example, how a person's age might affect his or her vote. A 68-year-old senior citizen would probably favor a candidate who promised an increase in Social Security payments, provided, of course, that the other positions of the candidate did not offend the voter. On the other hand, a voter who is 23 might resent the prospect of having more money deducted from his or her paycheck for Social Security. Younger voters might very well decide to vote against a candidate who wants to increase Social Security payments.

Other Background Influences

Voters' education, religion, and racial or ethnic background also affect their attitudes toward the candidates. For example, an African American might favor a candidate who supports strong antidiscrimination measures in education and

---

R Reading Strategies	**C** Critical Thinking	**D** Differentiated Instruction	**W** Writing Support	**S** Skill Practice
Teacher Edition • Identifying, p. 497 **Additional Resources** • Guid. Read. Act., p. 63 • Quizzes/Tests, pp. 209–218	**Teacher Edition** • Debating, p. 495 **Additional Resources** • Read. Essen., pp. 197–200	**Teacher Edition** • Interpersonal, p. 493 **Additional Resources** • Foldables, p. 60	**Teacher Edition** • Expository Writing, p. 494 • Persuasive Writing, p. 496 **Additional Resources** • Coop. Learning Act., pp. 11–12	**Teacher Edition** • Visual Literacy, p. 495 **Additional Resources** • Skill Reinforce. Act., p. 17 • Inter. Poli. Cartoons, pp. 33–34

employment. A Jewish voter might not vote for a candidate with strong reservations about American support of Israel.

It is important to understand that people's backgrounds influence them in a certain direction. Yet individuals do not always vote the way their backgrounds might **predict.** Will labor union members always vote for the Democratic presidential candidate, as they have for many decades? The large number of union members who voted for Republican Ronald Reagan in 1980 confirms that they do not. Will college-educated voters, most of whom usually vote Republican, always give their votes to the Republican candidate? The landslide vote by which Lyndon B. Johnson, a Democrat, defeated Republican Barry Goldwater in 1964 indicates that this is not always true.

One reason why voters' backgrounds do not give a ready answer to how they will vote is that many voters fall into two or more categories. These categories may pressure voters to vote in different ways. These **cross-pressured voters** face conflicting pressures from different elements of their identity—their religion, income level, and peer group. For example, Catholics are generally more inclined to vote Democratic than Republican. Yet, suppose a Catholic voter is also a wealthy business executive. Well-to-do businesspeople are usually Republicans, and many of this voter's close friends are Democrats. How will this person vote? Like millions of other voters, this person's background has conflicting elements: Issues, a candidate's profile, and personality may influence a voter in opposite ways.

Loyalty to Political Parties

Another influence on voters' decisions is their loyalty—or lack of it—to one of the political parties. The majority of American voters consider themselves either Republicans or Democrats, and most vote for their party's candidates.

Strong Versus Weak Party Voters

Not all voters who consider themselves Republicans or Democrats support their party's candidates with the same degree of consistency. Strong party voters are those who select their party's candidates in election after election. Strong party voters tend to see party as more important than the issues or the candidates. In the voting booth, they usually vote a **straight party ticket,** meaning they always choose to vote for the candidates of their party.

Unlike strong party voters, weak party voters are more likely to switch their votes to the rival party's candidates from time to time. For example, in 1980, 27 percent fewer Democrats voted for Carter than had voted for him in 1976. Weak party voters are more influenced by issues and the candidates than they are by party loyalty.

Independent Voters

Another important group of voters are the independents, those who do not identify themselves as either Republican or Democrat. Even when independents lean toward one party, their party loyalty is weak.

The number of independent voters has increased somewhat since the 1970s. This increase of independent voters has become an important factor in presidential elections. Together, independents and weak party voters may determine who wins the right to occupy the White House every four years.

In 1992 Ross Perot, an independent candidate, won many of these votes. President Bill Clinton and Republican Bob Dole adjusted their message and strategy to appeal to these voters in 1996. Eventually, Perot's support declined to less than half its 1992 level.

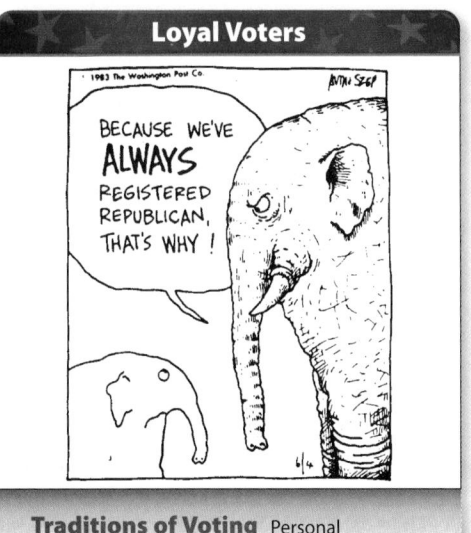

Loyal Voters

Traditions of Voting Personal associations with family, friends, and coworkers influence voting decisions. *What is the cartoonist suggesting about voters who regularly vote for one party? Do you agree with this statement on party voters?*

Teach

D Differentiated Instruction

Interpersonal Students will create a matrix with cells for each factor mentioned in this section that influences voting preferences. Then they will conduct a poll of 10 people, asking what factors influence their votes in a national election. Have students tally the responses on their matrices and give short reports to the class on the results. **Ask** Might the results of the poll cause people to vote against their usual party affiliation? *(Answers will vary.)* **OL**

Caption Answer: That they do so simply because that is what they have always done or because that was their parent's party affiliation. Students should decide whether they agree or disagree with that implication.

Hands-On Chapter Project

Step 3

Analyzing an Election Campaign

Step 3: Detecting Propaganda
Students will analyze the propaganda techniques used in campaigns.

Directions First mention the controversies surrounding famous ads that have been credited with tilting election results, such as the Willie Horton ad that helped George H.W. Bush defeat Michael Dukakis in 1988 or the Swift Boat ad that swayed some voters in George W. Bush's defeat of John Kerry in 2004. Direct students to the Propaganda Techniques table in this section. Have groups use the campaign they are researching to find examples of each technique. They may print out or photocopy ads, summarize television ads, or select sections of speeches, position statements, or other information. They also will note how the candidate's personality and appearance affected the campaign and the overall image that was presented to the electorate.

Putting It Together Ask groups to present their findings to the class. Ask students to explain why they think this candidate was successful (or unsuccessful). **OL AL**

Answer: in the South and the upper Plains states; in the Northeast, the Great Lakes states, and the West Coast

Chart Skills Practice
In which presidential election year listed on the chart was the voter turnout percentage the highest? The lowest?
(1964, 1996) **BL**

W **Writing Support**

Expository Writing Ask students to select one of the issues that was important to the 2008 presidential campaign. Then have them research both candidates' positions on the issue and their voting records relevant to it. Students will write a one-paragraph report explaining their findings. **OL**

Differentiated Instruction

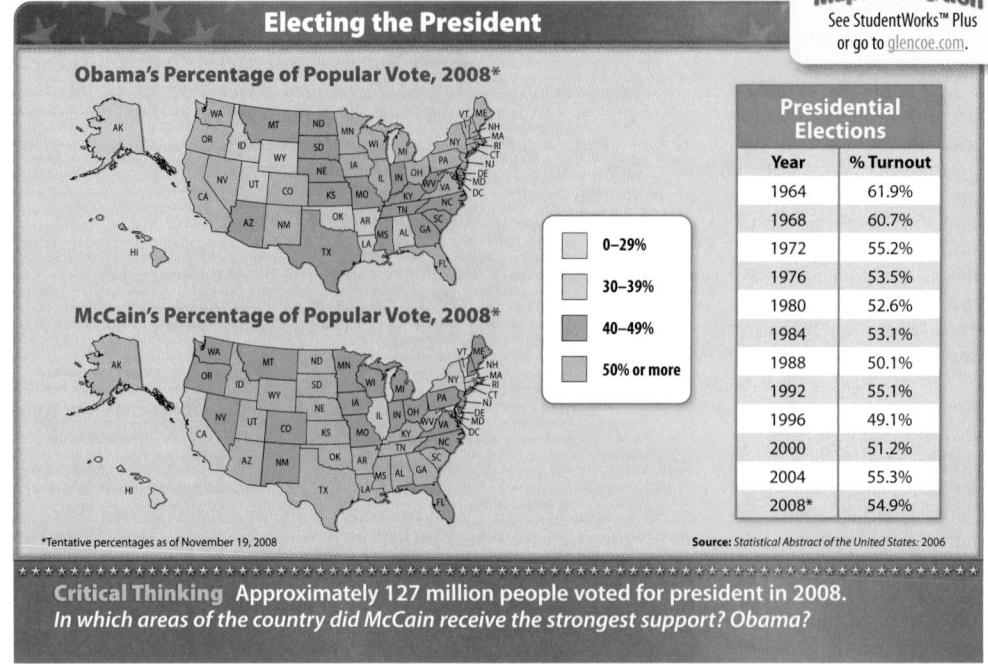

Electing the President

Obama's Percentage of Popular Vote, 2008*

McCain's Percentage of Popular Vote, 2008*

- 0–29%
- 30–39%
- 40–49%
- 50% or more

*Tentative percentages as of November 19, 2008

Maps In Motion
See StudentWorks™ Plus or go to glencoe.com.

Presidential Elections	
Year	% Turnout
1964	61.9%
1968	60.7%
1972	55.2%
1976	53.5%
1980	52.6%
1984	53.1%
1988	50.1%
1992	55.1%
1996	49.1%
2000	51.2%
2004	55.3%
2008*	54.9%

Source: *Statistical Abstract of the United States: 2006*

Critical Thinking Approximately 127 million people voted for president in 2008. In which areas of the country did McCain receive the strongest support? Obama?

Some experts believe that the number of weak party voters and independent voters will continue to increase. In the 2008 election, it was estimated that roughly 40 percent of the electorate were either independent or only weakly identified with a major party. If this trend continues, presidential candidates will no longer be able to rely on party loyalty for victory. Instead, campaign issues, the image and character of a candidate, and probably the amount of money spent, will be more and more decisive in electing the nation's president.

Issues in Election Campaigns

W Many voters are not well-informed about all of the issues discussed in campaigns. Still, today's voters are better informed than the voters of earlier years. Several reasons account for this change.

First, television has brought the issues into almost every home in the country. Second, voters today are better educated than in the past. A third reason is that certain issues are having a greater impact on the lives of voters than at any time since the Great Depression. These issues include Social Security, health care, taxes, education, affirmative action, abortion, gun rights, and the environment.

The 1980 election illustrates that *when* issues arise can be critical for a presidential candidate. In 1980 many Americans blamed President Jimmy Carter for inflation, high energy costs, and unemployment. Carter had been unable to turn the economy around and his Republican challenger Ronald Reagan used the issues to his benefit. At the end of a televised debate, he asked: "Are you better off than you were four years ago?" For most Americans the answer to this question was "no" and millions switched their support to the Republican candidate.

During the 2008 campaign, the war in Iraq was an important issue early on. For some voters, Republican John McCain, with his military background, seemed a better choice to deal with foreign conflicts. Meanwhile Democrat Barack Obama focused on economic issues, and those issues began to take center stage in early 2008 when gas prices rose over $3 a gallon. Home foreclosures and job losses reinforced unease about the economy. Then in late August, a major financial crisis began. Investment companies went bankrupt, and banks were refusing to lend money. This crisis favored Obama, since McCain had to defend the economic policies of Republican George W. Bush.

Leveled Activities

ELL Vocabulary Activities, p. 17

BL Guided Reading Activities, p. 63

OL Interpreting Political Cartoons, p. 33

AL Authentic Assessment with Rubrics, p. 24

The Candidate's Image

Just as important as the issues is the way the voters **perceive** the issues. If, for example, they believe that an administration is dealing effectively with the economy, they may reward the president with their votes. Conversely, if they believe an administration's measures are ineffective, voters may punish the president by voting for the other candidate.

Certainly, most Americans want a president who seems to be a strong and trustworthy leader. All candidates try to convey this image to the public, but not everyone is successful in doing so. Gerald Ford, running for president in 1976, struck many voters as well-meaning but dull. Adlai Stevenson, who lost to Dwight D. Eisenhower in 1952 and 1956, was perceived by many voters as too intellectual to be president.

Many voters select candidates on image alone—for the personal qualities they perceive them to have. In 1964 President Lyndon B. Johnson had the image of a peacemaker, while his opponent, Barry Goldwater, was viewed as more willing to lead the nation into war. At the very least, a candidate must be viewed as competent to handle the problems of the day. Many voters rejected Michael Dukakis in 1988 because they believed he was unqualified to deal with the nation's problems. President Harry S. Truman cited the danger of getting this image when he said:

> 66 [B]eing a president is like riding a tiger. A man has to keep riding it or be swallowed. . . . [A] president is either constantly on top of events or, if he hesitates, events will soon be on top of him. 99
> —Harry S. Truman

A candidate, then, must convey the impression of having the qualities voters expect in a president.

Propaganda

Political parties, interest groups, and businesses need to convince people of the value of their candidates, ideas, goods, or services. Americans are used to hearing hundreds of such messages every day. Many of these messages could be classified as propaganda. **Propaganda** involves using ideas, information, or rumors to influence opinion. Propaganda is not necessarily lying or deception; however, neither is it objective. Propaganda uses information in any way that supports a predetermined objective.

Typical Party Positions in 2008

Issue	The Democrat	The Republican
Health Care	Government should play a bigger role in providing health care for everyone.	It is better and cheaper to rely on private insurance plans for most of our health care.
Health & Social Welfare	Government should shoulder more of the burden of providing a "safety net" for the poorest citizens.	Government assistance should be difficult to get since it can weaken people's self-reliance and work ethic.
The Economy	Increase tax burden on wealthier classes, raise minimum wage periodically, and support policies for the average worker.	Keep government regulation of business at a minimum, and lower taxes on corporations and businesses that are the prime creators of wealth.
The Environment	Government should set strict standards for auto emissions, promote alternative energy sources, and lead the world in meeting global environmental standards.	Government should avoid regulation when possible and instead give businesses incentives for energy efficiency; regulations should not hinder growth; other nations should agree to global standards before the U.S. adopts them.
Immigration	Offer long-term illegal residents a path to citizenship ("amnesty" for their past illegal residence); work to secure the border.	Secure the border first; against "blanket amnesty" for undocumented workers.

Critical Thinking The positions here are general tendencies in each party. *Do you think political identification is also related to people's feelings about perceived party values?*

S Skill Practice

Visual Literacy Have students collect several pictures from magazines or newspapers of past presidential candidates and paste them on a sheet of paper. Under each picture, have students write their impression of the candidate's image. Is this a person they would vote for as their nation's leader? Have students trade papers to see if they have the same impression of the candidate's image. Discuss with the class the importance of portraying a candidate as competent and trustworthy. **BL**

C Critical Thinking

Debating Have students reread the issues in the table and choose a position for each. Then have students pair up and debate with classmates whose opinions differ from their own. For example, students who lean mostly Democratic should debate with students who lean mostly Republican. **OL**

Critical Thinking

Answer: Students' answers will vary but may include that some people do identify strongly with a party's values.

Additional Support

Activity: Collaborative Learning

Designing a Newspaper Page Organize students into groups of four to create the front page of a newspaper covering a recent local, state, or national election. As a group, have students think of a name for the newspaper. Then have each group member choose one of the following tasks: design an advertisement for a particular candidate; write a letter to the editor critically examining how each candidate is running his or her campaign; write a front-page news story on a major campaign issue; or draw a political cartoon depicting the candidates' stands on a major issue. Have each group lay out the newspaper either on newsprint or using desktop publishing software. After groups display their completed front pages to the class, have the class identify the issues covered and the type of election it reflects. **OL**

POLITICAL PROFILES **Ronald Reagan** (1911–2004) was a master at image making. With years of experience on the radio, as a television host, and in movies, Reagan used the media to his advantage as a candidate and during his presidency. Candidate Reagan portrayed a youthful image, which helped him get elected and become—at age 69— the oldest American ever to be elected to the presidency.

Propaganda techniques were initially used on a mass scale by commercial advertisers. As political campaigns adapted to television, campaign managers developed sophisticated messages using seven propaganda techniques.

One popular technique called "Plain folks" has been used since Andrew Jackson won the White House in 1828. The technique that asks a person to "jump on the bandwagon" came soon after. When a party's convention is all decked out in patriotic symbols, it is using "transfer" to influence viewers. A Hollywood actor or a popular musician who speaks for a candidate is giving a "testimonial," or endorsement. Republicans used the term *liberal* as a negative label for Democrats beginning in the 1980s. Democrats often refer to conservative Republican candidates as "right wing" politicians. A debate is a good place to identify "card stacking" when candidates quote only favorable statistics.

When political propaganda becomes obviously misleading, people become skeptical of politicians. Name calling can override the important issues of a campaign. Voters say they do not appreciate that approach, and some analysts believe the result can be reduced voter participation.

Profile of Regular Voters

Citizens who vote regularly have certain positive attitudes toward government and citizenship.

According to researchers, education, age, and income are important factors in predicting which citizens will vote. The more education a citizen has, the more likely it is that he or she will vote regularly. Middle-aged citizens have the highest voting turnout of all age groups. Voter regularity also increases with income—the higher a person's income is, the more regularly that person votes.

Profile of Nonvoters

Due to the civil rights movement, more Americans have the right to vote than ever before. Yet many Americans still do not go to the polls. Why is this?

Some citizens do not vote because they do not meet state voting requirements. Almost all states have three basic requirements—U.S. citizenship, residency, and registration. A voter who does not fulfill all of these requirements is not permitted to vote.

All states limit the right to vote to American citizens. Even people who have lived in this country for many years cannot vote if they have not formally become U.S. citizens.

Most states require voters to be residents of the state for a certain period of time before they are allowed to vote. When a voter moves to a new state, he or she needs time to become informed about local and state issues and candidates. Before 1970, the period of required residence ranged from

Propaganda Techniques	
Technique	**How to Recognize It**
Labeling	Name calling; identifying a candidate with a term such as *un-American*
Spin	Interpreting a political event or statement from a particular point of view
Card Stacking	Giving only one side of the facts to support a candidate's position
Transfer	Associating a patriotic symbol with a candidate
Plain Folks	Identifying the candidate as "just one of the common people"
Testimonial	A celebrity endorses a candidate
The Bandwagon	Urging voters to support a candidate because everyone else is

Critical Thinking Campaigns use different techniques to promote the best interests of their candidates. *Which techniques would an incumbent candidate most likely use? Why?*

3 months to 2 years. The Voting Rights Act of 1970, however, along with two Supreme Court decisions, created a residence period of 30 days in all elections. Some states have no required residency period at all.

Except for North Dakota, all states require voters to register or record their names officially with local election boards. On Election Day, an election official must check voters' names. Voters whose names are on the list sign in by writing their names on a form. Registration is a way to prevent voter fraud and dishonest elections. All voter registration is permanent, and a voter, once registered, remains on the list unless he or she dies, moves, or fails to vote within a certain number of years.

One problem in meeting residency and registration standards is that Americans are highly mobile. Almost one-fifth of them move to a new location every five years. A new resident may forget to register or believe that the registration offices are open at inconvenient times.

Complicated registration procedures and residency requirements can also be a barrier to voting. In recent decades, these requirements have become less burdensome, although voter turnout still has remained relatively low. Beginning in 2005, however, several states seemed to be reversing that trend by adopting stricter requirements to prevent voter fraud. In one of these states, Indiana, the new law was challenged in court. The Supreme Court upheld the state's law in *Crawford* v. *Marion County Election Board* (2008).

Voter Participation

The percentage of Americans voting in presidential elections declined from about 62 percent in 1960 to just over 50 percent in 2000. Even fewer Americans voted in congressional, state, and local elections. In 2004, however, voter participation jumped to about 55 percent in the hotly contested race between incumbent George W. Bush and Massachusetts Senator John Kerry. The election ended in Bush's victory over Kerry. Some voters in key battleground states waited for hours to vote. Each candidate received more votes than any presidential candidate had ever received before.

Heightened voter interest continued during the 2008 presidential campaign. Higher-than-expected turnout was forecast in many primaries where record numbers of voters cast their votes. This was especially notable in the race for the Democratic nomination.

Increasing Voter Turnout

People who are concerned about the number of nonvoters have called for reforms to make voting more convenient. For example, one suggestion is to shift Election Day from Tuesday to Sunday, so that citizens do not have to take time off from work to vote. Another idea is to have a national registration system, so that people's registrations will follow them when they move to a new state. Making it easier for more people to votes by absentee ballot or extending the deadlines for an absentee ballot are other reforms that are already in place in some states.

CHAPTER 17, SECTION 3

R Reading Strategy

Identifying Ask: What are some potential ways to increase voter turnout? *(Shift Election Day from Tuesday to Sunday. Institute a national registration system. Make absentee voting easier.)* **BL**

Assess

Assign the Section 3 Assessment as homework or as an in-class activity, or have students take Section Quiz 17-3 from *Section Quizzes and Chapter Tests.*

Close

Making Generalizations Ask: Is it a right, a duty, or a privilege to vote? Discuss personal and civic responsibilities with the class. **OL**

Section 3 Review

SECTION 3 Review

Vocabulary

1. **Explain** the significance of: cross-pressured voter, straight party ticket, propaganda.

Main Ideas

2. **Identifying** What is an independent voter?

3. **Analyzing** What factors in a voter's personal background might influence that individual's vote?

Critical Thinking

4. **Demonstrating Reasoned Judgment** What qualities of competence and leadership do you think are important for a presidential candidate to have?

5. **Organizing** Use a graphic organizer like the one below to show how parties try to influence voters.

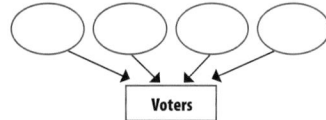

Writing About Government

6. **Narrative Writing** Voter apathy is an issue in the United States today. Draw a political cartoon that depicts a reason people give for not voting. Write a brief description of the cartoon and how it represents your personal opinion.

CHAPTER 17: *Elections and Voting* **497**

Answers

1. All definitions can be found in the section and the Glossary.
2. a voter who does not identify himself or herself as either a Democrat or a Republican (or any other party)
3. Students should identify any or all of the following factors: upbringing, family, age, occupation, income level, general outlook on life, education, religion, and racial or ethnic background.

4. Answers will vary, but students should identify personal qualities and leadership skills worthy of presidential candidates.
5. appealing to members' loyalty, addressing issues, building candidate's image, using propaganda techniques
6. Students' political cartoons should depict one reason why people do not vote.

TIME NOTEBOOK

Focus

S₁ Skill Practice

Researching Ask students to review the quotes in the Verbatim section. Then have students research a current or a historical issue pertaining to the Supreme Court and its justices and create a list of quotations about the issue along with a brief statement explaining the quote, identifying the person quoted, and describing how the quote relates to the issue. Ask students to share their lists in a class discussion. **OL**

Teach

S₂ Skill Practice

Participating in Government Have students research the improvements in voting machines and voter registration implemented by their state since the 2000 election. What changes have been made? What issues still need to be addressed? As a class, have students draft a letter that outlines their concerns over voting procedures. Then have them mail the letter to their state board of elections. **AL**

Additional Support

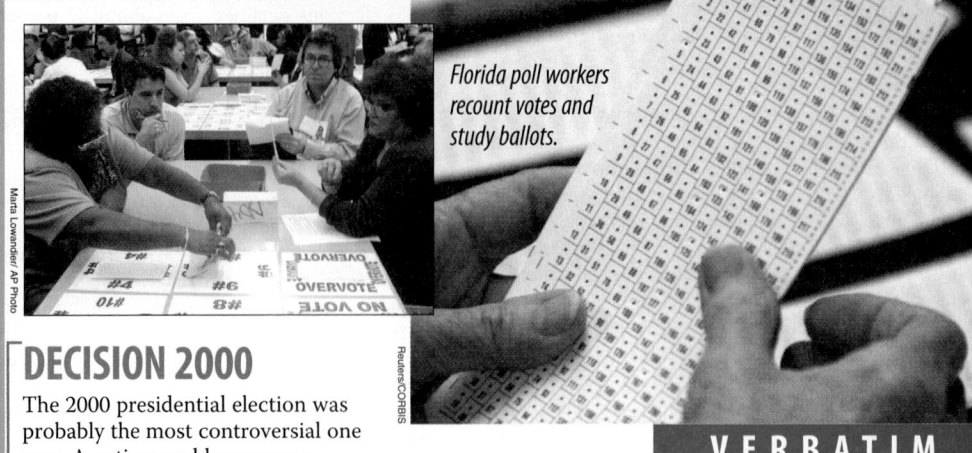

Florida poll workers recount votes and study ballots.

Marta Lowander/ AP Photo

Reuters/CORBIS

DECISION 2000

The 2000 presidential election was probably the most controversial one ever. A voting card known as a **BUTTERFLY BALLOT** caused a lot of controversy that still lingers in the minds of many Americans. Some people in Florida found the butterfly ballot confusing and felt that they may have accidentally voted for the wrong person. Adding to the mix-up, some ballots had incomplete perforations (known as "hanging chads") or just slight indentations. In these cases, counting machines might not have counted the votes.

DATE WITH DESTINY

In 1845 Congress went through a process of elimination in order to set **ELECTION DAY**. It settled on the Tuesday after the first Monday in November in even-numbered years. Why did the members choose a Tuesday? Why not just November 1? Here's what they were thinking:

Images.com/CORBIS

NO to Monday (first day of the work week)
NO to Friday (last day of the week)
NO to Saturday (shopping/religious day)
NO to Sunday (shopping/religious day)
NO to Thursday (British election day)
MAYBE Wednesday (no major conflicts)
MAYBE Tuesday (no major conflicts)

Congress didn't want to set Election Day as November 1. Why? It might disrupt the business of shopkeepers and accountants who had to take care of October books. So, it finally chose the Tuesday after the first Monday. (Whew!)

VERBATIM

WHAT PEOPLE SAID

Bettmann/CORBIS

❝I will never pay a dollar for your unjust fine.❞

Susan B. Anthony, *referring to the $100 fine she received for voting in the 1872 presidential election. At that time, it was illegal for women to vote.*

❝During the last presidential race, I had the privilege of traveling the country and meeting vast numbers of young people. I cannot express how impressed I was. With energy and passion as contagious as it was inspiring, these young Americans confided their dreams and shared their aspirations, not for themselves alone, but for their country.❞

Senator John McCain, *who ran for the Republican presidential nomination in 2000*

❝A chicken in every pot and a car in every garage.❞

Herbert Hoover, *making a promise during his 1928 presidential campaign*

★ Activity: Collaborative Learning ★

Who Will Vote? Many students and their classmates are or soon will be old enough to vote in elections—but will they take advantage of this right? Organize the class into groups of three or four students. Have students research and discuss the issue of voter participation among young voters. Then have each group design and create a poster that will encourage young people to vote. Display the posters in the classroom or elsewhere in the school. **OL**

PARTY ANIMALS

During Andrew Jackson's 1828 presidential campaign, opponents portrayed him as stubborn, not very bright, and similar to a DONKEY. Rather than get upset, Jackson thought it would be a good idea to put the strong-willed animal on his campaign posters. Later, a cartoonist named Thomas Nast made the symbol famous by using it in newspaper cartoons. In 1877, after the Republicans lost the White House to the Democrats, Nast drew a cartoon of a trap set by a donkey with an ELEPHANT walking right into it—and the Republican Party symbol was born! Nast chose the elephant because elephants are intelligent but easily controlled.

Today, Democrats use the words "smart" and "brave" to describe the donkey, and Republicans say the elephant is "strong" and "brave."

The Granger Collection, New York

MILESTONES

The Granger Collection, New York

BUTTONED UP, 1896. CAMPAIGN BUTTONS were first used in the presidential race between William McKinley and William Jennings Bryan. There were no catchy slogans—just photos of the candidates, their names, and a few words, such as "For President."

NAMED, LATE 1700S. "His highness the President of the United States of America and Protector of their Liberties." This mouthful is how a Senate committee wanted to address **PRESIDENT WASHINGTON** and all future presidents. The House thought this title was too royal and reduced it to merely "the President of the United States." The Senate agreed, and the name has stuck ever since.

Comstock/Alamy Images

NUMBERS

1 The number of people to serve as both vice president and president without actually being elected to do so. Gerald Ford was appointed vice president by President Nixon after Spiro Agnew stepped down in 1973. Ford then became president when Nixon resigned in 1974.

Bettmann/CORBIS

1 The number of vice presidents to win a presidential election since Martin Van Buren in 1836. Former vice president George H.W. Bush was elected president in 1988.

5 The number of votes in the Electoral College that made up George W. Bush's margin of victory in the 2000 election.

17 The number of people to become president after governing a state. George W. Bush is the 17th, after serving as governor of Texas.

1st Geraldine Ferraro, a congressional representative from New York, was the first woman to run for vice president on a major party ticket. She and running mate Walter Mondale lost the race in 1984.

Roger Ressmeyer/CORBIS

D **Differentiated Instruction**

Visual/Spatial Have students use library and Internet resources to research presidential candidate buttons, bumper stickers, and slogans. Each student should choose one that he or she finds the most effective and/or inspirational and share it with the class. **OL**

W **Writing Support**

Expository Writing History has had mixed reactions to Gerald Ford's pardon of Richard Nixon for his involvement in the Watergate scandal. Have students use library and Internet resources to research the background of and various opinions on Ford's decision. Then ask students to write a brief essay explaining why they either support Ford's decision or believe he made an error in judgment. **OL**

Close

Have students select one of the presidents or presidential candidates mentioned on pages 498–499. Ask each student to learn one new thing about the person selected and share his or her findings with the class.

Additional Support

Extending the Content

Thomas Nast The influence of Thomas Nast's political cartoons lends credence to the adage "a picture is worth a thousand words." One of his cartoons is said to have helped President Lincoln win reelection in 1864, and President Grant attributed his 1868 election "to the sword of [General Phil] Sheridan and the pencil of Nast." When Nast used his political cartoons to draw attention to the corruption in the New York City administration of William Magear "Boss" Tweed, legend says that Tweed commanded his underlings to "Stop them . . . pictures. I don't care what the papers write about me. My constituents can't read. But . . . they can see the pictures."

ExamView®
Assessment Suite

This easy-to-use software includes extensive question banks and allows you to create fully customized tests that can be administered in print or online.

Reviewing Vocabulary

1. political action committees
2. suffrage
3. straight-party ticket
4. soft money
5. grandfather clause
6. cross-pressured voter

Reviewing Main Ideas

7. Larger states with more electoral votes get more attention from candidates.
8. those between 18 and 21 years old
9. Television has brought the issues into almost every home. It has also increased the importance of a candidate's image.

Critical Thinking

10. Answers may indicate that younger voters have a more parochial viewpoint, are not as concerned with national issues, are more involved in their daily lives, have not been influenced by either major party, and so on.
11. Although the Fifteenth Amendment granted voting rights, Southern states set up many roadblocks designed to limit and discourage African American voters. The Voting Rights Acts empowered the federal government to extend voting rights to all eligible African Americans.

Assessment and Activities

Reviewing Vocabulary

Write the content vocabulary word(s) that best completes each sentence.

political action committees	cross-pressured voter
soft money	suffrage
straight party ticket	grandfather clause

1. Political candidates often receive campaign contributions and support from ____.
2. Women in the United States gained ____ in 1920.

Chapter Summary

Expanding Voting Rights
★ Fifteenth Amendment grants African American males right to vote
★ Nineteenth Amendment grants women right to vote
★ Twenty-fourth Amendment outlaws poll taxes
★ Twenty-sixth Amendment lowers voting age to 18

Financing Campaigns
★ The Federal Election Commission (FEC) administers federal election laws.
★ The Federal Election Campaign Act of 1971 set up a new system for financing federal elections.
★ New laws led to growth of political action committees (PACs) and the raising of huge amounts of soft money.
★ Efforts to reform campaign finance have met with only limited success.

Influences on Voters
★ Personal background (age, religion, education, ethnicity)
★ Loyalty to political parties (strong, weak, or independent)
★ Knowledge of campaign issues
★ Candidate's image
★ Propaganda

3. Most independent voters do not vote a ____.
4. Political parties can raise unlimited amounts of money for general purposes, not designated to particular candidates, through ____.
5. The ____ was a roadblock to voting for most African American Southerners.
6. One cannot be sure how a ____ will vote because that person has conflicting interests.

Reviewing Main Ideas

Section 1 *(pages 475–479)*

7. **Summarizing** How does the number of electoral votes of a state affect presidential campaigning?

Section 2 *(pages 481–484)*

8. **Identifying** Which group of Americans gained the right to vote under the Twenty-sixth Amendment?

Section 3 *(pages 492–497)*

9. **Describing** What effects has television had on presidential elections?

Critical Thinking

10. 🗳 **Essential Question** In terms of percentage, far fewer members of the 18–21 age bracket exercise their right to vote than is the case with any other age group. How might you explain this?
11. **Explaining** Why were the Voting Rights Acts necessary?
12. **Analyzing** Individuals have suggested extending public financing of election campaigns to include congressional campaigns. Explain the advantages and disadvantages of this idea.
13. **Predicting** Identify at least three consequences that could result from limiting the amount of money any individual could give to a political campaign.
14. **Organizing** Use a graphic organizer like the one below to list three ways of increasing voter turnout.

1.
2.
3.

---

12. Possible advantages: enable more people to run for office, diminish candidates' "selling" themselves for campaign contributions, diminish the power wealth has on candidates; Possible disadvantages: more taxpayer dollars spent on campaigning, congressional candidates should not be responsible to federal influence but to state influence, Congress might vote themselves more money.
13. Possible consequences may include: diminish the influence of wealthy individuals in government, force political

parties to find funds elsewhere such as from PACs, federal funding may become more important, individuals may lose interest if they cannot contribute, other PAC-type organizations may form, soft money may play an even greater role, and so on.
14. Answers might include: shift Election Day from Tuesday to Sunday; have national registration rather than state or local; allow voters to register on Election Day

Government ONLINE Self-Check Quiz
Visit glencoe.com and enter QuickPass™ code USG9822c17.
Click on Self-Check Quizzes for additional test practice.

CHAPTER **17** **Assessment and Activities**

Document-Based Questions

Analyzing Primary Sources

Read the excerpt below and answer the questions that follow.

Civil rights activist Anne Moody participated in massive drives in Southern states to register African American voters in what was called the "Freedom Summer" of 1964. The registration drives were violent, and immensely successful, registering millions of voters. Some of these voters had never before been able to vote because of strict voting laws in Southern states. The excerpt below is from Moody's autobiography.

❝ *Suddenly we began to get quite a lot of support from the local Negroes. . . . Every day now we managed to send a few Negroes to the courthouse. . . . But the registrar was flunking them going and coming. Sometimes out of twenty or twenty-five Negroes who went to register, only one or two would pass the test. Some of them were flunked because they used a title (Mr. or Mrs.) on the application blank; others because they didn't. And most failed to interpret a section of the Mississippi constitution to the satisfaction of Foote Campbell, the Madison County circuit clerk.* ❞

15. What kinds of voting restrictions were being placed on the voters Anne Moody was trying to register?

16. Why would the restrictions make it difficult for African Americans in the South in the early 1960s to register to vote? What types of laws make this illegal today?

Applying Technology Skills

17. Creating a Spreadsheet Find out the percentage of registered voters who voted in the most recent presidential election at census.gov. Organize the eligible voters into age groups and by region. Then create a table illustrating this information and present a brief written analysis of your results.

Interpreting Political Cartoons

Analyze the cartoon and answer the questions that follow. Base your answers on the cartoon and your knowledge of Chapter 17.

"AND THEY WONDER WHY WE DON'T VOTE...."

18. According to the cartoonist, why don't some people vote?

19. How does the cartoonist exaggerate campaign advertising?

20. Should Americans rely on television advertisements to gather information on candidates? Why or why not?

21. How has campaign advertising changed with the expansion of the Internet? How would you change this cartoon to include the Internet as a medium?

Participating IN GOVERNMENT

22. Find out what the voter registration laws are in your community. Contact your local election board for this information. Present the information on an illustrated poster. Include information about local residency requirements, the procedure for registering, the time and location in which people can register, and the types of identification needed to register.

CHAPTER 17: *Elections and Voting* **501**

Government ONLINE
Have students use the **Chapter 17 Self-Check Quiz.** Visit glencoe.com and enter QuickPass™ code USG9085c17T to prepare for the Chapter Test.

19. The cartoonist portrays campaign advertising as only negative. Candidates criticize opponents without noting their own accomplishments.

20. Answers will vary. Students may note that voters should gain reliable information from newspaper and magazine articles, political party brochures, TV or radio news, or other organizations.

21. "Smear" campaigns translate for the Internet as well as TV, although a single Web site might not reach as large an audience. The couple could be seated at a computer.

Participating IN GOVERNMENT

22. Students should find out the voter registration laws in their community and present the information on a poster.

Analyzing Primary Sources

15. Voters were being denied registration approval for not filling out applications correctly. They were also being given literacy tests in which they were required to interpret the state constitution.

16. Registration was at the discretion of the circuit clerk, who could decide whether an application was filled out properly or whether the interpretation of the constitution was correct. The Voting Rights Acts of 1965 and 1970 and the voting rights laws of 1970, 1975, and 1982 make this illegal today.

Applying Technology Skills

17. Tables should be organized and presented logically.

Interpreting Political Cartoons

18. Americans are discouraged by negative campaign ads that criticize candidates.

Chapter Bonus Test Question

Ask: Which presidential candidate won the biggest landslide victory in presidential history? (*Lyndon Johnson over Barry Goldwater in 1964*)

Key to Ability Levels

| BL | Below level | AL | Above level |
| OL | On level | ELL | English Language Learners |

Key to Teaching Resources

Print Material   Transparency
CD-ROM or DVD

| Levels | | | | | Resources | Chapter Opener | Section 1 | Section 2 | Section 3 | Section 4 | Chapter Assess |
BL	OL	AL	ELL								
					FOCUS						
BL	OL	AL	ELL	🖳	**Section Focus Transparencies**		18-1	18-2	18-3	18-4	
					TEACH						
BL	OL		ELL	📁	**Reading Essentials and Study Guide (and Answer Key)**		p. 177	p. 205	p. 208	p. 211	
BL	OL		ELL	📁	**Guided Reading Activities**		p. 64	p. 65	p. 66	p. 67	
BL	OL		ELL	📁	**Vocabulary Activities**		p. 18				
BL	OL	AL	ELL	📁	**Chapter Summaries**					p. 52	
BL	OL			📁	**American Biographies**						
BL	OL	AL	ELL	📁	**Cooperative Learning Activities**					p. 11	
	OL	AL	ELL	📁	**Government Simulations and Debate**			p. 40			
BL	OL	AL	ELL	📁	**Historical Documents and Speeches**			p. 18			
BL	OL	AL	ELL	📁	**Interpreting Political Cartoons**				p. 35		
BL	OL		ELL	📁	**Skill Reinforcement Activities**			p. 18			
BL	OL	AL	ELL	📁	**Source Readings**			p. 18			
BL	OL			📁	**Supreme Court Case Studies**						
BL	OL	AL	ELL	📁	**Participating in Government Activities**				p. 35		
BL	OL		ELL	📁	**Spanish Declaration of Independence and U.S. Constitution**	✓	✓	✓	✓	✓	✓
BL	OL	AL	ELL	📁	**NGS World Atlas, Spanish**	✓	✓	✓	✓	✓	✓
BL	OL	AL	ELL	🖳	**Unit Overlay Transparencies, Strategies, and Activities**	✓	✓	✓	✓	✓	✓
BL	OL		ELL	🖳	**Making It Relevant Transparencies**	✓	✓	✓	✓	✓	✓
BL	OL	AL	ELL	🖳	**High School Writing Process Transparencies, Strategies, and Activities**	✓	✓	✓	✓	✓	✓
BL	OL	AL		🖳	**American Art & Architecture Transparencies, Strategies, and Activities**	✓	✓	✓	✓	✓	✓

✓ Chapter- or unit-based activities applicable to all sections in this chapter

All-In-One Planner and Resource Center

- Interactive Lesson Planner
- Interactive Teacher Edition
- Fully editable blackline masters
- Chapter Spotlight Videos Launch

- Differentiated Lesson Plans
- Printable reports of daily assignments
- Standards tracking system

Levels					Resources	Chapter Opener	Section 1	Section 2	Section 3	Section 4	Chapter Assess
BL	OL	AL	ELL								
TEACH *(continued)*											
BL	OL			💿	**American Music: Hits Through History**	✓	✓	✓	✓	✓	✓
BL	OL		ELL	📁	**Reading Strategies for the Social Studies Classroom**	✓	✓	✓	✓	✓	✓
			ELL	📁	**English Language Learner Handbook**	✓	✓	✓	✓	✓	✓
BL	OL		ELL	📁	**Writer's Guidebook for Social Studies**	✓	✓	✓	✓	✓	✓
BL	OL	AL	ELL	📁	**Living Constitution, SE**	✓	✓	✓	✓	✓	✓
BL	OL	AL	ELL	📁	**Living Constitution, TAE**	✓	✓	✓	✓	✓	✓
BL	OL			📁	**NGS World Atlas, English**	✓	✓	✓	✓	✓	✓
BL	OL		ELL	📁	**The Constitution and You (poster set)**	✓	✓	✓	✓	✓	✓
BL	OL	AL	ELL	📁	**Spanish Chapter Summaries**					p. 52	
BL	OL	AL	ELL	📁	**Spanish Vocabulary Activities**		p. 18				
BL	OL		ELL	📁	**Spanish Reading Essentials and Study Guide (and Answer Key)**		p. 177	p. 205	p. 208	p. 211	
BL	OL	AL	ELL	💿	**PresentationPlus! with MindJogger CheckPoint**	✓	✓	✓	✓	✓	✓
ASSESS											
BL	OL	AL	ELL	💿	*ExamView® Assessment Suite*		18-1	18-2	18-3	18-4	Ch. 18
BL	OL	AL	ELL	📁	**Authentic Assessment with Rubrics**		p. 25				p. 25
BL	OL	AL	ELL	📁	**Section Quizzes and Chapter Tests**		p. 219	p. 220	p. 221	p. 222	pp. 223–230
BL	OL	AL	ELL	📁	**Spanish Section Quizzes and Tests**		p. 219	p. 220	p. 221	p. 222	pp. 223–230
CLOSE											
BL			ELL	📁	**Reteaching Activities**				p. 18		p. 18
BL	OL	AL	ELL	💿	**StudentWorks™ Plus with Audio Summaries**	✓	✓	✓	✓	✓	✓
BL	OL		ELL	🖨	**Graphic Organizer Transparencies**		✓	✓	✓	✓	
BL	OL		ELL	📁	**High School Government Reading and Study Skills Foldables®**		p. 61	p. 61	p. 61	p. 61	

Teach With Technology

What is the Media Library?

The Media Library is an all-in-one online resource center that provides students with access to digital media associated with the textbook.

How can the Media Library help my students?

The Media Library contains Section Audio and Chapter Spotlight Videos. Section Audio can help struggling readers and English language learners better comprehend the textbook. Chapter Spotlight Videos engage visual learners and generate student interest. Students can download audio to their digital media player or listen from their computer screen.

Visit glencoe.com and enter a *QuickPass*™ code to go to the Media Library.

Government ONLINE

Visit glencoe.com and enter *QuickPass*™ code USG9085c18T for Chapter 18 resources.

You can easily launch a wide range of digital products from your computer's desktop with the McGraw-Hill Social Studies widget.

	Student	Teacher	Parent
Media Library			
• Student Edition Section Audio	●		●
• Chapter Spotlight Videos	●	●	●
***United States Government* Online Learning Center (Web Site)**			
• Chapter Overviews	●	●	●
• Multilingual Glossaries	●	●	●
• Study-to-Go	●	●	●
• Student Web Activities	●	●	●
• Self-Check Quizzes	●	●	●
• Online Student Edition	●	●	●
• Vocabulary eFlashcards	●	●	●
• Web Activity Lesson Plans		●	
• Vocabulary PuzzleMaker	●	●	●
• Landmark Supreme Court Cases	●	●	●
• Beyond the Textbook	●	●	●

READING SUPPORT FROM
JAMESTOWN EDUCATION

- **Timed Readings Plus in Social Studies** helps students increase their reading rate and fluency while maintaining comprehension. The 400-word passages are similar to those found on state and national assessments.

- **Reading in the Content Area: Social Studies** concentrates on six essential reading skills that help students better comprehend what they read. The book includes 75 high-interest nonfiction passages written at increasing levels of difficulty.

- **Reading Social Studies** includes strategic reading instruction and vocabulary support in Social Studies content for ELLs and native speakers of English. www.jamestowneducation.com

Reading List Generator CD-ROM

GLENCOE BOOKLINK 3

Use this database to search more than 30,000 titles to create a customized reading list for your students.

- Reading lists can be organized by students' reading level, author, genre, theme, or area of interest.
- The database provides Degrees of Reading Power™ (DRP) and Lexile™ readability scores for all selections.
- A brief summary of each selection is included.

Leveled reading suggestions for this chapter:

- *Anarchy, State, and Utopia,* by Robert Nozick
- *The Animal Rights Controversy,* by Laurence Pringle
- *Caretakers of the Earth,* by Kathlyn Gay

Review suggested books before assigning them.

Economics Connection

Personal Finance Literacy

Understanding Percentages

Tell students that there are many times when knowing how to calculate and understand percentages comes in handy. For example, candidates for public office need to know what percentage of the voters are in favor of an issue or of the job they are doing. The most common use of percentages is while shopping. Suppose you see a "30% Off Sale" sign and want to know how much the items cost now. The basic step for calculating a percentage is to convert the percentage to a decimal (e.g., 10 percent to .10) and then multiply a number by the decimal.

Calculating Percentages

1. Multiply the number by the percentage:

Regular price of shoes	$57.00
Sale 30% as decimal	× .30
Dollar discount	$17.10

2. To find the current price, subtract the discount amount from the original price:

Regular price of shoes	$57.00
Discount	− 17.10
Sale price	$39.90

3. Alternatively, you could simply subtract the percentage discounted from 100 percent and multiply the regular price by the remainder:

Regular percentage	100%
Sale percentage	− 30%
Percentage you pay	70%

Regular price of shoes	$57.00
Percentage you pay	× .70
Price you pay	$39.9000, or $39.90

Did You Know?

In most recent polls, the percentage of people who had confidence in the economy progressively decreased among lower-income groups and increased among groups with higher incomes. Fuel costs, inflation, and defense spending were cited as reasons for economic concerns.

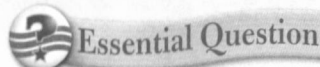

Essential Question

If public opinion on an issue is strong enough, it will shape the government's response to it because of politicians' desire to be reelected. Interest groups organize like-minded people into a large voting block and lobby Congress.

Chapter Spotlight Video

To generate student interest and provide a springboard for class discussion, access the Chapter 18 Video at glencoe.com or on the video DVD.

FOLDABLES Study Organizer

Dinah Zike's Foldables are three-dimensional, interactive graphic organizers that help students practice basic writing skills, review key vocabulary terms, and identify main ideas. Have students complete this chapter's Foldable activity or activities in *Dinah Zike's Reading and Study Skills Foldables* booklet. **OL**

Government ONLINE

Visit glencoe.com and enter **QuickPass**™ code USG9085c18T for Chapter 18 Resources including Chapter Overview, Student Web Activity, Self-Check Quiz, and other materials for students and teachers.

🔊 Chapter Audio   📹 Spotlight Video

Interest Groups *and* Public Opinion

Essential Question

How does public opinion influence government, and what do interest groups do to ensure that their policy positions have the most impact?

Government ONLINE

Chapter Overview Visit glencoe.com and enter *QuickPass*™ code USG9822c18 for an overview, a quiz, and other chapter resources.

Special-interest group demonstrating for better health care

502

Launching the Chapter

Tocqueville's *Democracy in America*
Alexis de Tocqueville was a noted French thinker who traveled in the United States during the era of Jacksonian democracy. Tocqueville saw that ordinary men were expanding their political power in the 1830s and noted the absence of any aristocracy. The political power of common people was due, he said, to the fact that it was relatively easy for a man to own land. Broad land ownership and a culture of equality led to suspicion and contempt for elites. Tocqueville argued that the nation's equality was achieved at the price of excellence in social and political life. **Essential Question:** From your observation of the impact of public opinion today on government, what comment would you make about Tocqueville's ideas on equality and the supremacy of the common man? **OL**

Interest Group Organization

Reader's Guide

Content Vocabulary
* interest group (p. 503)
* public-interest group (p. 506)

Academic Vocabulary
* equip (p. 504)
* commodity (p. 505)
* target (p. 507)

Reading Strategy
Create a graphic organizer similar to the one below to categorize different interest groups.

Business Interest Groups	Labor Interest Groups	Agricultural Interest Groups

Focus

Bellringer
Section Focus Transparencies 18-1

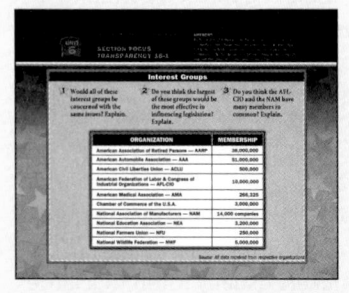

Reader's Guide

Answers to Graphic:

Business Interest Groups: National Association of Manufacturers, U.S. Chamber of Commerce, Business Roundtable

Labor Interest Groups: AFL-CIO, United Auto Workers, United Mine Workers, Teamsters, Committee on Political Education

Agricultural Interest Groups: American Farm Bureau Federation, National Farmers Union, Patrons of Husbandry (the Grange)

Issues in the News

Mothers Against Drunk Driving (MADD) has given its three-mile walks to raise funds a new name. Instead of Strides for Change, it's now Walk like MADD. Every year, more than 30 American cities hold the MADD walks. MADD national president Glynn Birch explained the prevalence of the walks by saying that drunk driving affects all walks of life. "By walking we can do more to fight for victims' and survivors' rights, . . . and support . . . new technologies to keep drunk drivers off our streets." In most places where the walks are held, participants hear live music and learn about new technology, such as an ignition interlock that makes cars inoperable by a drunk driver.

▲ MADD's Glynn Birch

MADD is just one of countless interest groups in the United States that influence public policy. Along with political parties, special-interest groups have long been a feature of American political life. An **interest group** is a group of people who share common goals and organize to influence government.

Many early leaders in the United States believed that interest groups could make governing difficult. In *The Federalist,* No. 10,[1] James Madison referred to "factions" as groups of people who are united to promote special interests that were "adverse to the rights of other citizens, or to the permanent and aggregate interests of the community." Madison explained that removing the causes of factions was not as acceptable as removing their effects. He believed that the Constitution would be a sufficient safeguard against the potential abuses of these interest groups.

Whether the Constitution has eliminated the harmful effects of interest groups is still debated. Today Americans have organized to pressure all levels of government through interest groups. These groups spend much time and money in organized efforts to influence officeholders to support laws that the groups feel will be beneficial. Do these groups endanger the rights of other citizens, as Madison thought they might? Or do they play an important role in helping people interact with their government?

Power of Interest Groups

Alexis de Tocqueville, a French traveler in the United States in the early 1800s and author of

See the following footnoted materials in the **Reference Handbook:**
1. *The Federalist,* No. 10, pages R80–R82.

Resource Manager

R Reading Strategies	**C** Critical Thinking	**D** Differentiated Instruction	**W** Writing Support	**S** Skill Practice
Teacher Edition • Creating a Graphic Organizer, p. 504 **Additional Resources** • Guid. Read. Act., p. 64 • Quizzes/Tests, p. 221	**Teacher Edition** • Analyzing Information, p. 506 **Additional Resources** • Read. Essen., pp. 202–204	**Additional Resources** • Foldables, p. 61 • Source Readings, p. 18	**Teacher Edition** • Expository Writing, p. 505 **Additional Resources** • Authentic Assess., p. 25	**Teacher Edition** • Visual Literacy, p. 504 **Additional Resources** • Vocab. Act., p. 18

Teach

R Reading Strategy

Creating a Graphic Organizer
Instruct students to create a graphic organizer illustrating the main categories of interest groups. **BL**

Caption Answer: Public rallies demonstrate the level of public support by the number of people who turn out. Lawmakers usually listen to a large public showing of support.

S Skill Practice

Visual Literacy Examine the images on this page. The group demonstrating, AARP, formerly the American Association of Retired Persons, has a naturally large constituency. **Ask:** Based on what you know about the political power of interest groups, how strong do you think their influence is on Medicare? *(Very strong—this is a large group with a direct interest in this issue. As a group, they are likely to be retired and thus able to focus on representing themselves.)* **AL**

Additional Support

Democracy in America, recognized Americans' tendency toward group membership:

> 66 *In no country of the world has the principle of association been more successfully used, or . . . applied to a greater multitude of . . . objects, than in America. . . . [I]n the United States associations are established to promote public order, commerce, industry, morality, and religion.* 99
> —Alexis de Tocqueville, 1835

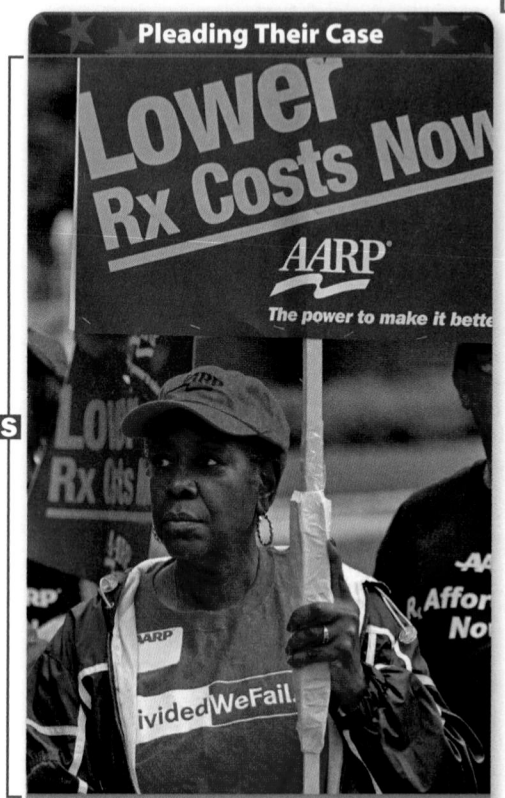

Pleading Their Case

Interest Group Politics Members of AARP, formerly known as the American Association of Retired Persons, an association representing older Americans, rallied in Albany, New York, to urge state legislators to do something about the ballooning costs of prescription drugs. *Explain why a public rally like this one is more likely to sway a lawmaker's position than a one-on-one meeting.*

Defining Interest Groups

Political parties nominate candidates for office and try to win elections to gain control of the government. Interest groups may support candidates who favor their ideas, but they do not nominate candidates for office. Instead, interest groups try to influence government officials to support certain policies.

Another difference between interest groups and political parties is that interest groups usually are concerned with only a few issues or specific problems. They do not try to gain members with different points of view. Political parties, on the other hand, are broad-based organizations. They must attract the support of many opposing groups to win elections. They also must consider conflicting issues and problems that affect all Americans, not just certain groups.

Finally, most interest groups are organized on the basis of common values, rather than on geographic location. Political parties elect officials from geographic areas to represent the interests of people in those areas. National interest groups unite people with common attitudes from every region of the country.

The Purpose of Interest Groups

Interest groups help bridge the gap between the citizen and the government. Through interest groups, citizens communicate their "wants," or policy goals, to government leaders, such as the president, Congress, city council, or state legislators. When lawmakers begin to address the vital concerns of an interest group, its members swing into action.

Political Power

Interest groups follow the old principle "There is strength in numbers." By representing more than one individual, an interest group has a stronger bargaining position with leaders in government, but only proportionally. Officials in a small community, for example, will listen to a 100-member group of citizens that has organized into a Local Safety Association, but officials in a large city might not.

On the state and national levels, an interest group draws from the financial resources and expertise of its many members. Organized and **equipped** with sufficient resources, an interest group can exert influence far beyond the power of its individual members.

Activity: Collaborative Learning

Identifying Points of View Organize the class into groups of four, and assign each foursome an interest group mentioned in this section. Explain that each group is to publicize its assigned interest group. Allow groups to research their interest group to analyze its mission, goals, and main concern. Then have group members plan a publicity strategy. Students should choose from the following publicity tasks: write a letter to a government official to promote awareness, create a flyer to publicize the concerns to the community, design a bumper sticker to raise community awareness, or give a one-minute speech to the class on the major issues of the interest group. Allow each group time to present its publicity campaigns to the class. **OL**

Leadership and Membership

Interest group leaders strengthen the political power of the group by unifying its members. They keep members informed of the group's activities through newsletters, mailings, and telephone calls. They act as speakers for their group and try to improve its image in the media. They plan the group's strategy, raise money to run the organization, and oversee all financial decisions of the group.

Why do people join an interest group? Usually, the first reason is to protect or promote their economic self-interest. A labor union works for higher union wages and other job benefits, while businesses work to ensure favorable tax laws. People join to get their beliefs translated into policy. They also join for social reasons; socializing promotes a group unity that is vital to achieving political goals.

Since political decisions are made primarily through competing interest groups, people who do not belong to an interest group are at a disadvantage. Often these are poorer Americans. It could be said that lower-income Americans who might benefit the most from having an interest group are the least likely to create one.

Business and Labor Groups

Nearly all Americans have economic interests and concerns about taxes, food prices, housing, inflation, and unemployment. As a result, many interest groups are concerned with economic issues. These business and labor interest groups seek to convince lawmakers of policies that they feel will strengthen the economy.

Business-Related Interest Groups

Business-related interest groups are among the oldest and largest in the nation. The National Association of Manufacturers (NAM) works to lower individual and corporate taxes and to limit government regulation of business. The U.S. Chamber of Commerce speaks on behalf of smaller businesses. A third group is the Business Roundtable, which is comprised of executives from the largest and most powerful corporations.

Labor-Related Interest Groups

The American Federation of Labor and Congress of Industrial Organizations (AFL-CIO) is the largest and most powerful labor organization today. Among the many unions in the AFL-CIO

Issues and the Candidates During the presidential campaign of 2008, Republican candidate John McCain spoke on the issue of immigration reform at a town hall meeting. *Would this issue be difficult for a candidate to take a stand on with two different interest groups, business and labor?*

are the United Auto Workers (UAW), United Mine Workers (UMW), and the International Brotherhood of Teamsters. A separate organization called The Committee on Political Education (COPE) directs the AFL-CIO's political activities. COPE's major goals include fund-raising, holding voter-registration drives, and providing support for political candidates.

Agricultural Groups

Three major interest groups represent almost 6 million American farmers. The largest of these groups is the American Farm Bureau Federation, which speaks for the larger, more successful farmers and is closely associated with the federal Department of Agriculture.

The National Farmers' Union (NFU) draws its membership from smaller farmers and favors higher price supports for crops and livestock. The group also has supported laws protecting migrant farmworkers. The oldest farm group is the Patrons of Husbandry, known as the Grange. Although this group is more of a social organization than an interest group, it has been very outspoken in advocating price supports for crops.

Just as important are **commodity** associations representing groups such as dairy farmers and potato growers. Congressional subcommittees dealing with agriculture are organized around commodity lines.

Caption Answer: Yes, because business groups tend to support higher levels of immigration. Labor groups tend to want more immigration restrictions.

W Writing Support

Expository Writing Instruct students to read newspapers or watch television newscasts and note any recent actions of interest groups. Students should then document the names of the groups, analyze the main issues being covered, and write a report on how often interest groups appeared in the news and what issues were covered. **OL**

Did You Know?

The largest national organization, after the Roman Catholic Church, is AARP, formerly known as the American Association of Retired Persons. With over 39 million members, it has defined the term *gray power*. The AARP receives so much mail that its building in Washington, D.C., has its own zip code.

Differentiated Instruction

Activity: Multiple Learning Styles

Kinesthetic Write the names and purpose of an interest group on an index card for as many interest groups as possible. Then have a student choose a card at random and act out the group's purpose. Have the class identify the purpose and the interest group being portrayed. The first student to make a correct identification of either the purpose or the name of the interest group gets to choose the next card. As each interest group is identified, write its name, its purpose, its central issue, and the main heading under which the interest group can be categorized—such as business, education, labor, or agriculture—on the board. Discuss with students the variety of interest groups represented and the issues covered. **OL**

POLITICAL PROFILES **Ralph Nader** (1934–) Ralph Nader founded and then led the movement for what he called "economic self-determination." In 1965 he forced General Motors to acknowledge and correct the safety-deficient Corvair. He has outlasted several presidents and numerous Congresses with his philosophy, "You've got to keep the pressure on, even if you lose. The essence of the citizens' movement is persistence."

C Critical Thinking

Analyzing Information
Instruct students to research an interest group they might identify with and create a booklet that tells about the group. The booklet should include information about who started the group and when, what influenced the group to form, its original and current size, the source of the group's funding, and the policies the group has influenced. **AL**

Hands-On Chapter Project

Step 1

Other Interest Groups

C Besides purely economic interest groups, there are countless other kinds of interest groups. These range from professional and environmental organizations to governmental and public-interest groups.

Professional Associations

The American Bar Association (ABA) and the American Medical Association (AMA) are examples of interest groups that represent specific professions. Basically, these two groups influence the licensing and training of lawyers and doctors. Professional associations also represent bankers, teachers, college professors, police officers, and hundreds of other professions. These associations are concerned primarily with the standards of their professions, but they also try to influence government policy on issues important to them.

Environmental Interest Groups

Concerns about the environment and the impact of environmental regulation have led to the founding of many interest groups, both liberal and conservative. Their goals include conserving resources, protecting wildlife, and reversing the trend toward global warming. Among these interest groups are the Sierra Club, the National Wildlife Federation, the Environmental Defense Fund, and the Friends of the Earth.

Public-Interest Groups

Groups that are concerned about the public interest work to achieve policy goals that they believe will benefit American society. The name itself, **public-interest groups,** signals the fact that they are not dedicated to representing a single interest group. Rather they claim to represent policy positions that will be in the best interests of all.

For example, Ralph Nader's Public Citizen, Inc., devotes itself to consumer and public safety issues that affect the general population. Another well-known public-interest group is Common Cause, founded in 1970. This public-interest group focuses its energy on trying to reform aspects of the American political system.

Interest Groups in Government

Organizations and leaders in American government can also act as interest groups. Two prime examples of interest groups made up of government employees are the National Conference of State Legislators and the National Governors' Association.

Concerts for a Cause

◀ Crowds gather at Live Earth at Aussie Stadium in Sydney, Australia, on July 7, 2007.

▼ Alicia Keys performs during the Live Earth concert at Giants Stadium, on July 7, 2007, in East Rutherford, New Jersey.

Environmental Interest Groups Young people sometimes voice their political opinions through concerts. Live Earth, a 2007 event, was unusual because it organized performers in a simulcast on seven continents to urge solutions to global warming. *Why did the global concert suit the perceived problem? Do you think legislators in individual countries would be very likely to respond to this rally? Why or why not?*

Exploring the "Blogosphere"

Step 1: Making a Blog Chart Groups of students will use a blog search engine to search the Internet and identify a variety of blogs. They will chart the information.

Directions Tell groups of students to use a blog search engine to find blogs on different topics. Groups will then chart the information they have collected in three columns. The first column will give the name and Web address of the site. The second column will describe the topic covered by the site. Topics may cover a range of subjects from politics to pop culture. The third column will state what kind of blog it is (private, political, or commercial) and its creator's name.

Summarizing Have students share what they learned about how people use the Internet to communicate. Encourage the class to speculate about the goals of each of the blogs on their charts. **OL AL**

(Chapter Project continued in Section 2.)

Typically, state and local government officials who belong to an interest group will try to influence Congress or the president because they want to receive a bigger share of federal aid.

Additional Groups

Thousands of interest groups represent diverse interests and factions in the American population. Some seek to influence public policy, and others organize to support larger segments of the population, or to protect civil rights.

Foreign governments and private interests of foreign nations also seek to influence government in the United States. Foreign-interest groups might seek military aid, economic aid, or favorable trade agreements. They might make political donations in an effort to sway political decisions. All foreign agents must register with the U.S. government.

The possible influence of foreign donations on the 1996 presidential election was one **target** of congressional hearings. Committee members heard a number of charges for how this might have occurred. For example, it was said that some foreigners bought access to American political leaders and that their contributions were then "laundered" by various bookkeeping tactics to evade campaign finance laws. The national committees of both the Democrats and the Republicans returned questionable donations, many from lobbyists for Asian interests. In the 2008 presidential campaign, several aides of the Republican presidential nominee resigned because they had ties to foreign governments and businesses.

Product Safety Pioneer Ralph Nader, a third-party candidate for president in several recent elections, first made his mark in public-interest groups as a critic of the auto industry. *What difficulties might an activist like Nader face in trying to influence Congress?*

The idea that foreign lobbyists might be influencing Congress upsets many Americans, but since many laws and proposals can powerfully affect other nations, it is predictable that such lobbying will occur. Currently the Foreign Agents Registration Act requires foreign lobbyists or foreign officials in the United States to inform the Department of Justice. There has been some controversy over whether this law is rigorous enough.

Caption Answer: Answers will vary, but he might be up against larger and better-funded opposition groups that want to influence Congress in the opposite direction.

Assess

Assign the Section 1 Assessment as homework or as an in-class activity, or have students take Section Quiz 18-1 from *Section Quizzes and Chapter Tests.*

Close

Evaluating Ask students to evaluate which type of interest group they think has had the most influence on public policy making. **OL**

SECTION 1 Review

Vocabulary

1. **Explain** the significance of: interest group, public-interest group.

Main Ideas

2. **Summarizing** Why are interest groups more effective in influencing the government than individual citizens are?

3. **Listing** What are the six categories of interest groups?

4. **Describing** What are three reasons why citizens join interest groups?

Critical Thinking

5. **Analyzing** Do interest groups help make representative government truly "government by the people"? Explain.

6. **Comparing** Use a Venn diagram like the one below to compare the goals of an interest group and a political party.

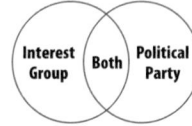

Writing About Government

7. **Persuasive Writing** Create a promotional brochure describing an interest group that you would like to see formed to address some interest or concern that you have. Include a description of the concern or interest, goals of the group, the kinds of people likely to be members of the group, and the methods your group would use to attain its goals.

CHAPTER 18: *Interest Groups and Public Opinion* **507**

Section 1 Review

Answers

1. All definitions can be found in the section and the Glossary.
2. They represent more than one person, are organized, and are equipped with sufficient resources.
3. business, labor, agricultural, professional associations, environmental, public interest
4. to help promote an individual's self-interests, to support a certain political principle, and to be social
5. "Yes" answers may point out that interest groups help citizens to be heard; "No" answers may point out that interest groups might not represent the will of the people.
6. Interest groups—influence public officials to support certain policies, concerned with a few issues
   Political parties—nominate candidates to win elections, concerned with a broad base of issues
   Both—work to help their constituents
7. Brochures should thoroughly describe an interest group.

Focus

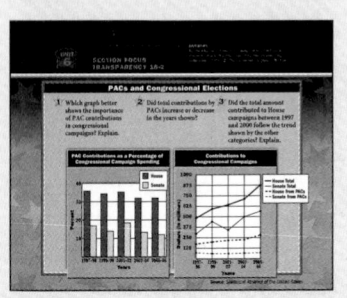
Reader's Guide

Answers to Graphic:
face-to-face, congressional testimony, drafting bills

Resource Manager

SECTION 2

Affecting Public Policy

Reader's Guide

Content Vocabulary	Academic Vocabulary	Reading Strategy
★ lobbying (p. 508) ★ lobbyist (p. 508)	★ technique (p. 508) ★ retain (p. 508) ★ abstract (p. 513)	Create a graphic organizer similar to the one below to list the ways lobbyists provide useful information to members of Congress and government officials.

Information From Lobbyists

Issues in the News

To promote their causes, interest groups hire representatives called lobbyists to make direct contact with lawmakers. Concerned about openness in government, 19 states and the federal government require lobbyists to report their incomes. Louisiana is now considering this step. The state legislature is debating a law to make the state's 1,000 registered lobbyists report monthly on how much money they are paid and by whom. Lobbyists opposing the bill call it an invasion of privacy. "Whatever contractual arrangement I have with my client as a private businessman is my business," said Alton Ashy, a lobbyist who represents video poker businesses. "It's not the government's business."

▲ Alton Ashy, Louisiana lobbyist

Meeting with elected officials on the state or national level is only one way that interest groups influence public policy. They may also employ television, radio, magazine, and newspaper advertising to create public support for their causes. They also may resort to court action or seek a constitutional amendment to achieve their goals.

The Work of Lobbyists

Most interest groups try to influence government policy by making direct contact with lawmakers or other government leaders. This process of direct contact is called **lobbying** because of the practice of approaching senators and representatives in the outer room or lobby of a capitol. The representatives of interest groups who do this kind of work are called **lobbyists.** Lobbying is one of the most widely used and effective **techniques** available to interest groups.

Who Are Lobbyists?

In 1995 Congress redefined *lobbyists* to mean anyone who:

- is employed or **retained** by a client,
- makes more than one contact for the client, and
- spends more than 20 percent of his or her time serving the client.

Why was such a specific definition necessary? The new Lobbying Disclosure Act of 1995 was intended to close loopholes in the 1946 Federal Regulation of Lobbying Act, which allowed most lobbyists to avoid registering with Congress.

R Reading Strategies	**C** Critical Thinking	**D** Differentiated Instruction	**W** Writing Support	**S** Skill Practice
Additional Resources • Guid. Read. Act., p. 65 • Quizzes/Tests, p. 222	**Teacher Edition** • Synthesizing Information, p. 511 **Additional Resources** • Read. Essen., pp. 205–207	**Teacher Edition** • Gifted and Talented, p. 509 • Visual/Spatial, p. 510 • Naturalist, p. 510 **Additional Resources** • Foldables, p. 61 • Hist. Docs. and Speeches, p. 18	**Teacher Edition** • Persuasive Writing, p. 512 **Additional Resources** • Gov. Sims. and Debates, pp. 40–42	**Additional Resources** • Skill Reinforce. Act., p. 18

Celebrity Lobbyists

Popularity and Political Causes In recent decades, film and music celebrities have used their popularity to try to influence public policy. Here the Irish rock star Bono meets with Delaware senator Joseph Biden in the halls of Congress. Known for working to address poverty in Africa, Bono toured the continent in 2002 with Secretary of the Treasury Paul O'Neill. **Can you think of a reason why some people might be critical of celebrity campaigns of this kind?**

The goal was to make sure that all lobbyists were registered. That way, their activities could be monitored, thus preventing illegal influence on members of Congress. There has been a rapid growth in Washington lobbying in recent years. Currently, there are more than 37,000 registered lobbyists—nearly double the number reported in 2000. The money lobbyists are spending has also grown dramatically, increasing from about $800 million in 1996 to more than $2.2 billion today.

Under current law, registered lobbyists must file semiannual reports with the Clerk of the House and the Secretary of the Senate. These reports must reveal the issues or laws being lobbied, the government branches and agencies being contacted, and an estimate of the money being paid by the client.

What kinds of people are lobbyists? Many are former government officials. They usually have friends in Congress and the executive branch and know the intricacies of Washington politics. Lobbying has proved to be an attractive second career for many members of Congress. In the 1980s, one national newsmagazine reported that many in Congress were cashing in on their connections: "For many, public service has become a mere internship for a lucrative career as a hired gun for special interests." Congress placed a time requirement on how soon former senators and representatives may become lobbyists—they must wait one year after retirement.

Besides former government officials or members of Congress, lobbyists are often lawyers or public relations experts. Understanding the government and how it works is vital for a lobbyist to be successful and effective.

Providing Useful Information

One of the important ways that lobbyists make their case is by providing a member of Congress with facts and data about the policy they want. When they do this, lobbyists will often try to meet face-to-face with members of Congress and other government officials—at the Capitol, in a member's office, over lunch, or even on a golf course. The information lobbyists provide legislators comes in many forms—pamphlets, reports, and statistical and trend data.

In this process of contacting legislators, lobbyists might end up paying for lunch or giving them something else of value. House and Senate rules, however, restrict the gifts lobbyists can give lawmakers. Senators and their staff cannot accept any gift (including meals and entertainment) of more than $50 from a lobbyist. The Senate and House also have $100 limits on gifts from any single source.

How much do members of Congress rely on information presented by lobbyists? Legislators realize that lobbyists can be biased. A lobbyist who intentionally misrepresents the facts runs the risk of losing a legislator's trust and permanently losing access to him or her.

CHAPTER 18: *Interest Groups and Public Opinion* **509**

Teach

Caption Answer: Celebrities are not experts in the fields of policy where they try to use their influence.

D Differentiated Instruction

Gifted and Talented Organize the class into groups of four to role-play lobbyists debating an issue mentioned in this section, such as school prayer, the budget, an official national language, term limits for members of Congress, flag burning, victims' rights, or campaign financing. Allow time to research the issue. Have group members choose from the following roles: a lobbyist supporting the issue, a lobbyist opposing the issue, a government official asking questions about the issue, and a recorder logging the information presented in the role play. Allow time for groups to role-play for the class. At the end of each role play, ask the recorder to review the main arguments for and against the issue; then ask the class to vote on the most persuasive argument. **AL**

Differentiated Instruction

Congress at Work

Source Readings, p. 18

Objective: To understand how major interest groups historically tried to influence American politics.

Focus/Teach: Have students do research to answer the activity's questions.

Assess: Have students summarize their answers in a written report.

Close: Discuss the strengths and weaknesses of interest groups and lobbyists in today's political system.

Differentiated Instruction Strategies

BL Identify a major organization that would likely have several paid lobbyists.

AL Conduct research to find loopholes in the Endangered Species Act.

ELL Have students make a list of endangered species. Why might endangered species need lobbyists?

D₁ Differentiated Instruction

Visual/Spatial Have students draw a political cartoon reflecting the influence of a particular political action committee (PAC). Have students trade their cartoons with a partner. Have partners identify the PAC illustrated and evaluate the student-artist's bias. **BL**

D₂ Differentiated Instruction

Naturalist Organize the class into small groups to brainstorm environmental issues that would warrant the support of a special-interest group. Encourage students to research their neighborhood to discover environmental problems that need to be addressed. Have groups make lists of neighborhood environmental concerns and rank them according to importance. **OL**

Differentiated Instruction

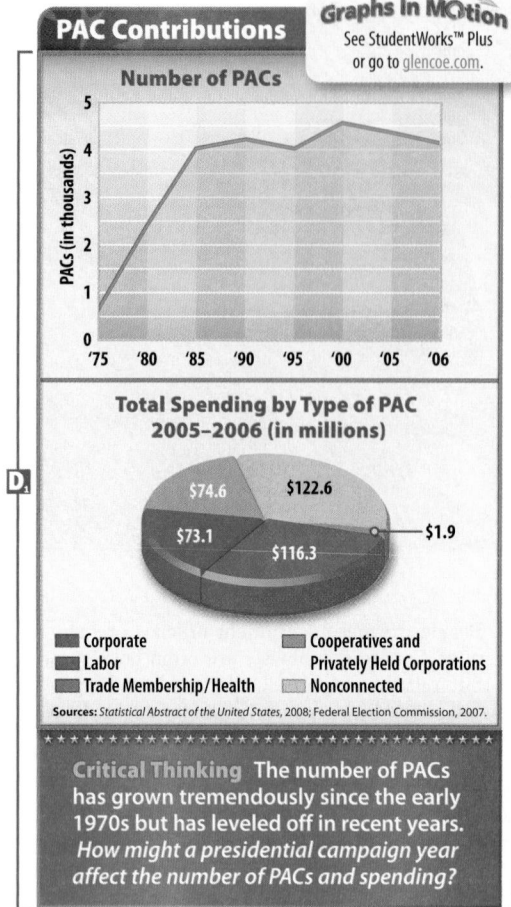

Graphs In Motion
See StudentWorks™ Plus or go to glencoe.com.

PAC Contributions

Number of PACs

Total Spending by Type of PAC 2005–2006 (in millions)

$74.6 $122.6
$73.1 $116.3 $1.9

- Corporate
- Labor
- Trade Membership/Health
- Cooperatives and Privately Held Corporations
- Nonconnected

Sources: *Statistical Abstract of the United States*, 2008; Federal Election Commission, 2007.

Critical Thinking The number of PACs has grown tremendously since the early 1970s but has leveled off in recent years. *How might a presidential campaign year affect the number of PACs and spending?*

Besides personally contacting legislators, lobbyists provide information in congressional testimony. Usually when Congress is considering a bill, lobbyists are invited to testify because of their expertise. For example, lobbyists representing the oil industry may testify before a committee considering a law to tax oil profits. Finally, when a bill comes to the floor in either house, lobbyists continue to work hard to influence lawmakers' votes.

Drafting Bills

Besides providing information to lawmakers, lobbyists and interest groups might help write bills. Many well-organized interest groups have research staffs that help members of Congress draft proposed laws. Studies have shown that interest groups and their lobbyists draft parts of or entire bills for almost 50 percent of all legislation.

Interest Groups Seek Support

Interest groups run publicity campaigns to win support for their policies. A wide range of techniques is available to interest groups in their effort to influence policy makers.

Media Campaigns

Interest or pressure groups use the mass media—television, newspapers, magazines, and radio—to inform the public and to create support for their views. For example, when Congress considered changes to the nation's health-care system in the 1990s, the American College of Surgeons used advertising to explain its position on patient choice. Environmentalists have run television and magazine ads to dramatize pollution and the hazards it poses, just as senior citizens campaign actively when changes in Medicare are before Congress.

Letter Writing

Many interest groups urge their members to write letters or e-mails to government officials to demonstrate broad support for or against a policy. For example, the National Rifle Association (NRA) can deliver hundreds of thousands of letters from its members. Although members of Congress know that the NRA represents many voters, they also must take into account the view of other groups. Such campaigns make officials aware of an issue, but they do not always produce results.

Limitations

The public tends to believe that interest groups are well financed and carry a great deal of weight with Congress. Does this public perception match reality? Do lobbyists determine public policy?

Interest groups provide representation for Americans in addition to the representation they have in Congress. They allow Americans to be represented according to their economic, social, or occupational interests. Interest groups also act as watchdogs and protest government policies that harm their members.

Several factors limit the effectiveness of interest groups. Different interest groups compete for power and influence, keeping any single group from controlling lawmakers and other public officials. Generally, the larger the group, the more diverse the interests of its members are. This diversity has meant that nationally organized interest groups might be unable to adopt broad policy goals.

Leveled Activities

ELL Interpreting Political Cartoons, p. 35

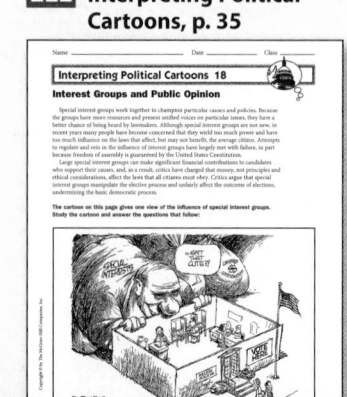

BL Reteaching Activities, p. 18

OL Cooperative Learning Activities, p. 11

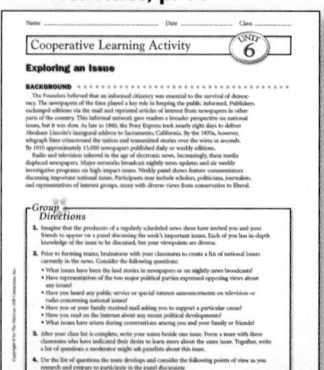

AL Government Simulations and Debates, p. 39

As a result, smaller interest groups or those that unite people who have narrower aims have been most effective in shaping policy.

While large interest groups have membership that provides an impressive financial base, most organizations struggle to pay small staffs. In recent years, however, the greatest concern about the power of interest groups has been their financial contributions to political campaigns.

The Rise of Political Action Committees

Lobbying is just one method interest groups use to influence lawmakers. These groups also provide a large percentage of the funds used in candidates' election campaigns. Most of these funds come from political action committees (PACs), or organizations that are specifically designed to collect money and provide financial support for a political candidate. A Washington lobbyist admitted: "I won't even take a client now unless he's willing to set up a political action committee and participate in the [campaign contribution] process."

How PACs Began

Before 1974, wealthy individuals gave large sums to finance political campaigns. Then the federal government passed laws to reform campaign finance. The new laws limited the amounts that individuals could contribute to federal candidates. While federal law prevented corporations and labor unions from making direct contributions to any federal candidate, the law permitted their political action committees to do so.

Laws Governing PACs

At the beginning of this period, the government set rules regulating political action committees. The main federal laws governing PACs are the Federal Election Campaign Act (FECA) of 1971; the amendments to it passed in 1974, 1976, and 1979; and the Revenue Act of 1971. Under these laws, a PAC must register with the government six months before an election. It must raise money from at least 50 contributors and give to at least 5 candidates in a federal election. PACs also must follow strict accounting rules.

PACs can give $5,000 directly to each candidate per election. The government, however, has not limited the total amount a PAC can spend on a candidate's campaign as long as the PAC does not work directly with the candidate.

In 1976 the Supreme Court ruled that any independent group can give money to a political candidate as long as the group is not legally tied to that candidate. PAC spending climbed from $52.9 million in the 1975–1976 election cycle to about $279 million in 2005–2006. PACs gave about $63 million to Senate candidates and $225 million to House candidates in 2003–2004.

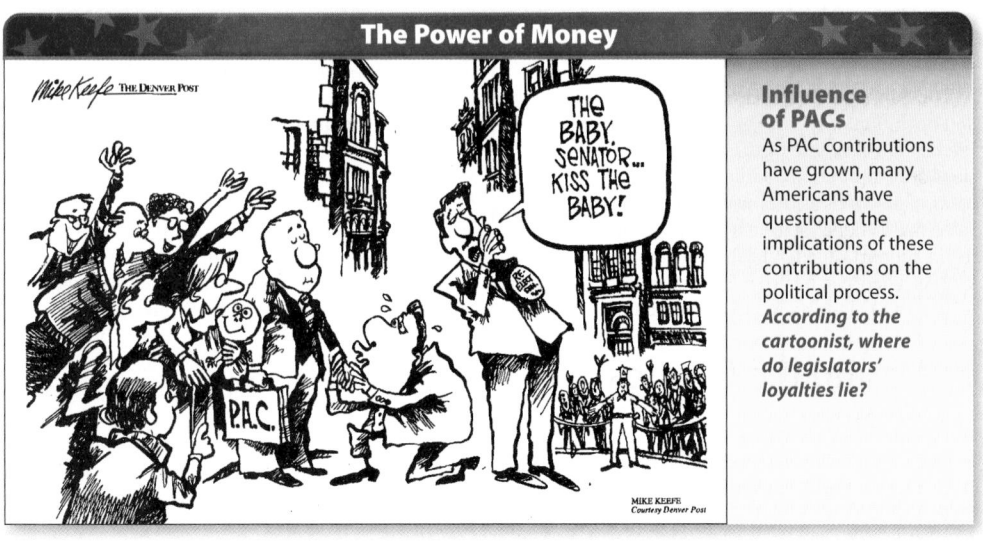

The Power of Money

Mike Keefe THE DENVER POST

THE BABY. SENATOR... KISS THE BABY!

P.A.C.

MIKE KEEFE
Courtesy Denver Post

Influence of PACs
As PAC contributions have grown, many Americans have questioned the implications of these contributions on the political process. *According to the cartoonist, where do legislators' loyalties lie?*

CHAPTER 18: *Interest Groups and Public Opinion* **511**

C Critical Thinking

Synthesizing Information
Have students design graphic organizers depicting the methods used by special-interest groups to influence public policy, such as advertising, bumper stickers, flyers, protest marches, and so on. Encourage students to be creative, using colors and pictures. **OL**

ISSUES to Debate

Tactics of Interest Groups
Discuss the most effective tactics of interest groups.
Start the discussion by pointing out the following strategies: Go on the attack—make public officials fear you; concede only when you have to; manipulate the media to present your case in a positive way; overwhelm the opposition with information—seize control of discussion of the issues. Taking each tactic in turn, ask students: How effective is this approach? Would you be swayed by it? Why or why not? **OL**

Caption Answer: Legislators' loyalties lie with the PACs.

Hands-On Chapter Project
Step 2

Exploring the "Blogosphere"

Step 2: Blog Quotes Students will make posters using quotes from blogs selected from the chart they compiled in Step 1.

Directions Have student groups select a quote from three of the blogs found on their charts. Ask students to make a poster for each quote. Each poster should include the quote in large enough type to be easily read. The posters should also include photographs from newspapers, magazines, and the Internet that illustrate the meaning of the quote.

Summarizing Have students present their posters to the class. Ask the class to match the posters to blogs on the chart that they compiled in Step 1. Have them discuss in what ways, if any, the blogs from which they have quoted strengthen or threaten democracy. **OL AL**

(Chapter Project continued in Section 3.)

We the People
Making a Difference

David Laughery The Pennsylvania helmet law states that "A person under 12 years of age shall not operate a pedalcycle or ride as a passenger on a pedalcycle unless the person is wearing a pedalcycle helmet. . . ." It identifies the penalty for failure to comply as ". . . punishable by a fine, including all penalties, assessments and court costs imposed on the convicted person not to exceed $25."

Activity: Have students write what the last quote from David Laughery about rights and responsibilities means to them.

W Writing Support

Persuasive Writing Ask students to develop an argument about why it is that nonconnected PACs should not be subjected to any kind of regulation. *(Students should be able to see that these organizations operate through direct-mail campaigns to anyone who is interested in an issue. Thus, they are viewed by Congress as being part of the American democratic process; as a result, their voices should not be regulated or restricted in any way.)* **OL**

Additional Support

We the People
Making a Difference

Pennsylvania teacher David Laughery believes that people of any age can make a difference if they make their voices heard. "My students first made their voices heard when they decided to . . . lobby for the adoption of a citywide helmet ordinance," Laughery said. The students in Laughery's class joined five other classes to develop a plan to lobby their township's Board of Supervisors. Students gathered statistics on bike-related injuries and deaths.

Armed with their research data and a prepared speech, the students presented their recommendation to their local township board. The board agreed to review their request for a helmet law in the Hershey, Pennsylvania, community.

Just a few weeks later, Pennsylvania state legislators passed a statewide helmet law. The students believed they performed a valuable service. "For the first time in their lives, these kids realized that they, too, are citizens who not only have rights, but also responsibilities," Laughery said.

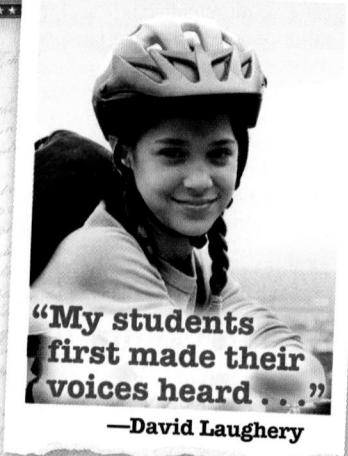

"My students first made their voices heard . . ."
—David Laughery

Federal Election Commission

The Federal Election Commission (FEC) issues regulations and advisory opinions that control PAC activities. In 1975 the FEC ruled that corporations can use their own money to administer their PACs and also can use payroll deductions to raise money from employees of a PAC. The FEC's decision stimulated the growth of PACs among business interests. In the decade after the ruling, the number of corporate PACs increased by more than 1,000 percent.

Supreme Court Decisions

The Supreme Court has also affected the growth and operation of PACs. For example, in a 1976 case, *Buckley* v. *Valeo*,[1] the Court ruled that different divisions of a corporation or different union locals can set up as many PACs as they want. In 1996 the Court ruled that national, state, and local committee spending in support of federal candidates is a form of free speech. There can be no spending limit. Spending for federal campaigns soared to more than $1.6 billion.

PACs and the Groups They Serve

PACs can be classified into two categories according to the groups they serve—affiliated or independent.

Affiliated and Nonconnected PACs

PACs tied to corporations, labor unions, trade groups, or health organizations are called affiliated PACs. Comprising about 70 percent of all PACs, they raise funds through voluntary contributions from corporate executives, union officials, workers, and stockholders. Examples of affiliated PACs are the Sun Oil Corporation's SunPAC, the Realtors' Political Action Committee, and the Cattlemen's Action Legislative Fund (CALF).

Groups interested in a particular cause can set up PACs that are not connected to any existing interest group. Nonconnected or independent PACs make up about 25 percent of all PACs. Some nonconnected PACs are organized mainly to participate in elections. Examples include Americans for Free International Trade, Council for a Livable World, the National Abortion Rights Action League PAC, and the National Right to Life PAC.

Nonconnected PACs raise money largely through direct mail appeals. They are very successful and usually raise more money than business or labor PACs. They spend less on political campaigns than affiliated PACs, however, because massive direct-mail fund-raising is very costly.

See the following footnoted materials in the **Reference Handbook:**
1. *Buckley* v. *Valeo* case summary, page R24.

★ ★ Activity: Interdisciplinary Connection ★ ★

Daily Life Studies show that historically, a typical lobbyist is a white male, of Protestant faith, living in a metropolitan area, whose father worked as a professional or manager. Have students scan the section to note the different roles a lobbyist plays in influencing government. Then, using the information gathered, have them draw political cartoons reflecting the typical lobbyist today. **ELL**

Thus, much of the money raised goes for postage, for staff workers, and to purchase mailing lists of potential contributors.

527 Organizations

In the 2004 election, a new kind of political influence group appeared: the 527 organization, named for the part of the tax code that gives an exemption to certain groups. While these groups can have a PAC wing, the term is usually defined as a group that does not directly urge citizens to vote for a specific candidate. Instead they focus on advocating an issue. The issue may easily be associated with a candidate, but by avoiding any mention of a candidate, 527s escape regulation. The Swift Boat Veterans and MoveOn.org are examples of 527 groups.

Strategies for Influence

Political action committees generally follow two strategies to influence public policy. They use their money to gain access to lawmakers and to influence election outcomes directly.

Interest groups can promise campaign support for legislators who favor their policies, or they can threaten to withhold support. (Campaign contributions were exempted from the 1995 Lobbying Disclosure Act, which restricts gifts to members of Congress.) Loss of a sizable contribution can affect a candidate's chances of winning. Other interest groups with comparable political strength who support opposite goals, however, might back the candidate.

Interest groups, especially PACs, raise much of the money used in political campaigns. They realize that making a campaign contribution does not guarantee that a candidate, if elected, will always vote the way they wish. Such groups, however, know that campaign contributions will at least assure access to the officials they help elect. Busy lawmakers are more likely to set aside time in their crowded schedules to meet with a group that has given money. As a result, PACs may give donations to lawmakers who do not always support the views of the PACs.

PACs generally support incumbents, or government officials already in office. In recent elections, 88 percent of corporate and trade PAC donations went to incumbents in House campaigns (with only 12 percent going to challengers). In Senate elections, more than 65 percent of PAC donations went to incumbents.

PAC support for incumbents has the expected result. Incumbents in both the House and Senate have a good chance of winning reelection. In some cases, challenging an incumbent is so difficult that no challengers come forward. Joan Claybrook, president of Public Citizen, Inc., an interest group that Ralph Nader founded, said: "That these PACs feel compelled to contribute to lawmakers who have no opponent shows that what is being sought is access and influence."

Some members of Congress admit to the power of the PACs. Representative Barney Frank once said: "We are the only human beings in the world who are expected to take thousands of dollars from perfect strangers and not be affected by it." Others disagree. Representative Dan Glickman said: "I do not think any member of Congress votes because of how a PAC gives him money on El Salvador, or the MX missiles, or . . . broader, **abstract** national issues."

Did You Know?

The political action committee of the National Education Association—a teachers' union—is one of the largest in the nation. Founded in 1857, the NEA currently claims more than 2.7 million members.

Assess

Assign the Section 2 Assessment as homework or as an in-class activity, or have students take Section Quiz 18-2 from *Section Quizzes and Chapter Tests.*

Close

Evaluating Have students evaluate the ethical issues surrounding PACs. **OL**

SECTION 2 Review

Section 2 Review

Vocabulary

1. **Explain** the significance of: lobbying, lobbyist.

Main Ideas

2. **Identifying** What are political action committees?

3. **Describing** What kinds of backgrounds do people who become lobbyists often have?

Critical Thinking

4. **Making Generalizations** What qualities of a lobbyist would make that person successful in furthering the goals of democratic government?

5. **Organizing** Use a graphic organizer like the one below to list two methods lobbyists and PACs use to influence public policy.

Lobbyists	PACs
1.	
2.	

Writing About Government

6. **Persuasive Writing** Members of Congress rely on lobbyists to provide them with information. Write a job description for a professional lobbyist. Include the skills and experience required for the position and a list of duties the position will require.

CHAPTER 18: *Interest Groups and Public Opinion* **513**

Answers

1. All definitions can be found in the section and the Glossary.
2. PACs are organizations that are specifically designed to collect money and provide financial support for a political candidate or a political issue.
3. former government officials, people who have friends in government, and those who know Washington politics
4. Answers should describe qualities such as the ability to represent the majority view while protecting minority rights, to listen to all citizens, to inform the public, and so on.
5. lobbyists—provide information to legislators, help write bills; PACs—use money to gain access to lawmakers, use money to directly influence election outcomes
6. Students' job descriptions should list the characteristics of a strong lobbyist.

Focus

Reader's Guide

Answers to Graphic:

Liberals: government should actively promote health, education and justice; willing to curtail economic freedom in exchange for equality; government should not restrict individual freedoms in social matters

Moderates: hold beliefs common to both conservative and liberal ideologies

Conservatives: government's role in economy and in solving social problems should be limited; government should have some say about morality

Resource Manager

Shaping Public Opinion

Reader's Guide

Content Vocabulary
★ public opinion *(p. 514)*
★ peer group *(p. 515)*
★ mass media *(p. 515)*
★ political culture *(p. 516)*

Academic Vocabulary
★ factor *(p. 514)*
★ communicate *(p. 515)*
★ affect *(p. 515)*

Reading Strategy
As you read, create a Venn diagram similar to the one below and identify the ideological beliefs of liberals, moderates, and conservatives.

Liberals — Moderates — Conservatives

Issues in the News

On the air since 1989, Channel One Network® in New York City provides 10,000 schools across the United States with televisions, satellite dishes, and other technology. In exchange, each school contracts to show the 12-minute Channel One news program. In 2007 the program sparked controversy when parents and other groups objected to the number of ads being broadcast—40 percent of air time for ads was too much for a captive student audience, parents said. In response, the owner, Alloy Media and Marketing, promised to improve programming through a partnership with NBC. Alloy's Matt Diamond said the NBC connection would give Channel One "more in-depth coverage." He also promised to make ads appropriate for classrooms and to give teachers a chance to preview them.

▲ Students watching a newscast

Channel One is just one example of the thousands of media outlets in the nation. To a great extent, the media both reflect and direct what Americans are thinking about. As a result, public officials rely on the media for clues to what the public is thinking. Even before the advent of television and radio, elected officials wanted to know what the public is thinking. "What I want," Abraham Lincoln once declared, "is to get done what the people desire to have done, and the question for me is how to find that out exactly." Today the president watches and reads the same news as everyone else. With television, radio, and the Internet easily accessible, public officials can gain perspectives into the opinions of ordinary citizens quickly and efficiently.

The Nature of Public Opinion

Most Americans have opinions or preferences about many matters that affect their lives. These range from preferences about the best baseball players to favorite television programs. Few such opinions, however, have much effect on government. Yet one form of opinion, public opinion, has an enormous influence on government. **Public opinion** includes the ideas and attitudes that a significant number of Americans hold about government and political issues. Three **factors** characterize the nature of public opinion.

R Reading Strategies	**C** Critical Thinking	**D** Differentiated Instruction	**W** Writing Support	**S** Skill Practice
Teacher Edition • Identifying, p. 515 **Additional Resources** • Guid. Read. Act., p. 66 • Quizzes/Tests, p. 223	**Additional Resources** • Read. Essen., pp. 208–210	**Teacher Edition** • Verbal/Linguistic, p. 516 **Additional Resources** • Foldables, p. 61	**Teacher Edition** • Persuasive Writing, p. 517 **Additional Resources** • Part. in Gov. Act., pp. 35–36	**Additional Resources** • Inter. Poli. Cartoons, pp. 35–36

Diversity

Public opinion is varied. In a nation as vast as the United States, it is unlikely that all citizens will think the same way about any political issue. Because of the diversity of American society, different groups of people hold different opinions on almost every issue.

Communication

People's ideas and attitudes must in some way be expressed and **communicated** to government. Unless Americans make their opinions on important issues clear, public officials will not know what people are thinking. Accordingly, officials will not be able to weigh public opinion when making decisions. Interest groups communicate the opinions of many individuals. Officials also rely on opinion polls and private letters and e-mails to know what people are thinking.

Significant Numbers

The phrase "a significant number of Americans" in the definition of public opinion means that enough people must hold a particular opinion to make government officials listen to them. For example, perhaps the most important reason President Lyndon B. Johnson decided not to run for reelection in 1968 was because so many people opposed his conduct during the Vietnam War.

Political Socialization

Personal background and life experiences exert important influences on opinion formation. Individuals learn their political beliefs and attitudes from their family, school, friends, and coworkers in a process called political socialization. This process begins early in life and continues throughout adulthood.

Family and Home Influence

Political socialization begins within the family. Children learn many of their early political opinions from their parents. In most cases, the political party of the parents becomes the party of their children. A study of high school seniors showed that only a small minority differed in party loyalty from their parents. As adults, more than two-thirds of all voters continue to favor the political party their parents supported.

Schools and Peer Groups

School also plays an important part in the political socialization process. In the United States, all

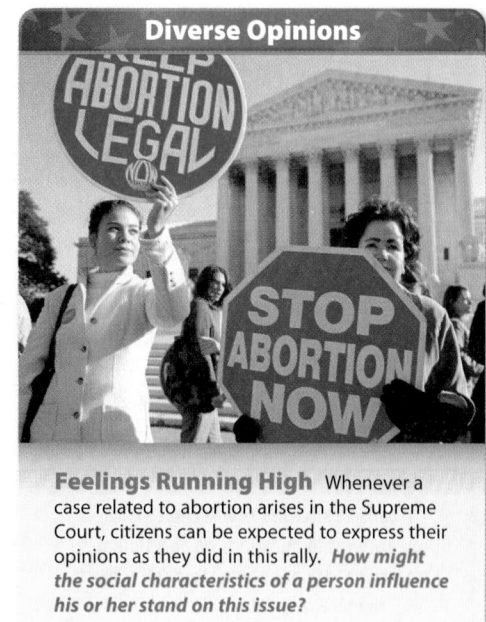

Diverse Opinions

Feelings Running High Whenever a case related to abortion arises in the Supreme Court, citizens can be expected to express their opinions as they did in this rally. *How might the social characteristics of a person influence his or her stand on this issue?*

students learn about their nation, its history, and its political system. Democratic values are also learned in school clubs and through school rules and regulations.

An individual's close friends, religious group, clubs, and work groups—called **peer groups**—are yet another factor in the political socialization process. A person's peer groups often influence and shape opinions. For example, a member of a labor union whose closest friends belong to the same union is likely to have political opinions similar to theirs.

Social Characteristics

Economic and social status is another aspect of political socialization. Whether a person is young or old, rich or poor, rural or urban, from the East coast or from the South, African American or white, a male or a female may **affect** personal political opinions.

The Mass Media

The Internet, television, radio, newspapers, magazines, movies, and books—the **mass media**—play an important role in political socialization. Both the Internet and television provide political information and images that can directly influence

Teach

R Reading Strategy

Identifying Draw six columns on the board and label each with a factor that influences political socialization. Ask students for specific examples of how each factor can influence their opinions. Write students' answers in the appropriate columns. Discuss with students how they would rank each factor in order of importance. **OL**

Caption Answer: A person's religion, age, education, experience, or gender might affect his or her opinion on abortion.

Participating IN GOVERNMENT

Political Culture Ask students to work in small groups to create lists of 10 widely shared political values. Then have members interview 10 people about their feelings toward each value. Have groups share their findings with the class.

Additional Support

Activity: Collaborative Learning

Designing a Game Organize the class into groups of six to design a Jeopardy®-style game reflecting influences on public opinion, such as cultural background, life experiences, political beliefs, family influence, peer groups, economic or social status, and so on. Remind students that Jeopardy® is a game in which the answer is given first and the question is then asked by the contestant. Each group should design a set of 20 cards with the question on one side and the answer on the other side. Then have groups exchange cards to play the game. Group members should choose from the following roles: three contestants, host, timer, and judge. Have groups take turns playing the game and keeping score. Award the group with the most correct answers first place. **OL**

D Differentiated Instruction

Verbal/Linguistic Have students reread the quote by Ralph Waldo Emerson that expresses his beliefs concerning liberty and freedom as one of the key elements of American national identity. Then encourage each student to write a poem that expresses his or her basic values and beliefs within the American political culture. Remind students that support of the Bill of Rights and the Constitution are also examples of widely shared political values in this country. **OL**

Caption Answer: Based on the chart, African Americans are typically more conservative, and women are less conservative on this particular measure of conservatism. The older an African American woman is, the more conservative she is likely to be, based on the responses measured for the over-65 age group.

Hands-On Chapter Project

Step 3

Conservative and Liberal Differences

Who Is Conservative On Social and Cultural Issues*

	High	Medium	Low
Men	31	35	34
Women	25	33	42
White	26	34	40
Black	40	36	24
18–29 Years of Age	23	27	50
65+	37	38	25
College Grad	18	30	52
High School or Less	33	38	29
Republicans	44	34	22
Democrats	23	35	42

*A conservative index was created based on answers to questions on abortion, gay marriage, gay adoption, stem cell research, and the morning-after pill.

Source: Pew Research Center, data from a 2006 survey.

Critical Thinking This survey measured how conservative different Americans were on a grouping of related social and cultural issues. *Based on the data, would you expect an African American woman to be highly conservative? Would her age make a difference?*

political attitudes. For example, broadcasts of a rally against a Supreme Court decision or videos on the Internet of a riot outside an American embassy can help shape viewers' opinions.

Movies, recordings, novels, and television entertainment also affect opinions. Showing police as heroes or as criminals, for example, can shape attitudes toward authority. The way the media depict different groups—men, women, African Americans, Asian Americans, Latinos, or immigrants—can discredit stereotypes or reinforce them.

Other Influences

Government leaders also play an important role in political socialization. The president especially has **D** a tremendous influence on people's opinions. The news media provides almost continuous reports on the president's activities and policy proposals.

Like the president, members of Congress try to influence opinions. They frequently go to their home states or home districts to talk to their constituents. Many legislators send newsletters or write personal letters to voters. They also appear on television programs and give newspaper interviews on timely issues. Lawmakers who come across as sincere, personable, and intelligent are particularly effective in influencing opinions on major issues. At the state and local levels, lawmakers also use the media to gain public support for their views.

At the same time, interest groups try to shape public opinion. If an interest group can win enough support, public opinion might pressure legislators to accept the group's goals. Churches and other religious organizations also affect people's political opinions.

Political Efficacy

Most people are unaware that political socialization occurs in their lives because it is a slow process that begins in childhood and continues over a lifetime. Similarly, people do not often see that this socialization directly affects their feelings of political efficacy.

Political efficacy refers to a person's belief that he or she has an impact on politics. Some people are socialized to believe that they cannot impact the system. Others are brought up to believe that their actions can be effective and lead to changes that are important to them. Feelings of political efficacy are vital in a democracy. Without citizen participation, democracies would be unable to realize the concept of government "of the people, by the people, and for the people."

Political Culture

A **political culture** is a set of basic values and beliefs about a nation and its government that most citizens share. For example, a belief in liberty and freedom is one of the key elements of the American political culture. Ralph Waldo Emerson expressed this value when he wrote:

> 66 *The office of America is to liberate, to abolish kingcraft, priestcraft, caste, monopoly, to pull down the gallows, to burn up the bloody statute-book, to take in the immigrant, to open the doors of the sea and the fields of the earth.* 99
> —Ralph Waldo Emerson

Exploring the "Blogosphere"

Step 3: Blogging Students will work in groups to create their own blog.

Directions Remind students that they have the responsibility to practice free speech in a constructive manner. Any criticism they make should be useful and not abusive. Have student groups use the charts and posters they created in Steps 1 and 2 to brainstorm ideas for a blog topic. Remind students that the content

of their blog must adhere to school standards. When students have selected a topic and a name for their blogs, have them collaborate on writing the first entries for their blog.

Summarizing Have students read their blog entries to the class. Encourage the class to discuss how they chose their blog topics and if school standards influenced what they wrote. **OL AL**

(Chapter Project continued in Section 4.)

Additional examples of widely shared political values include support for the Constitution and Bill of Rights, commitment to the idea of political equality, belief in the value of private property, and an emphasis on individual achievement. The American political culture helps shape public opinion in the United States in two ways.

The political culture sets the general boundaries within which citizens develop and express their opinions. For example, Americans will disagree over how much the federal government should regulate the airline industry. Very few Americans, however, would urge that government eliminate regulations altogether or, conversely, that it take over and run the industry.

A nation's political culture also influences how its citizens interpret what they see and hear every day—the political culture colors how Americans see the world. An American citizen and a Russian citizen probably would interpret the same event quite differently. If shown a photo of people in line outside a grocery store, the Russian citizen might think there was a food shortage, but an American citizen might conclude there was a sale.

Ideology and Public Policy

An ideology is a set of basic beliefs about life, culture, government, and society. One's political ideology provides the framework for looking at government and public policy. However, Americans tend to determine their positions on an issue-by-issue basis rather than following a strict ideology. Polls show that many people express inconsistent opinions on issues. For example, most people favor lower taxes, but they also want better schools and increased government services. In the United States, the main ideologies are liberals, conservatives, moderates, and libertarians.

A liberal believes the government should actively promote health, education, and justice. Liberals are willing to curtail economic freedom to increase equality, for example, by regulating business to protect consumers. In social matters, however, liberals believe the government should not restrict most individual freedoms.

A conservative believes in limiting the government's role in the economy and in solving social problems. Recently, however, some conservatives have supported a government role to protect what they see as a moral lifestyle. For example, they have supported prayer in the schools and restricting access to abortion.

Moderates fall somewhere between liberals and conservatives. For example, a moderate might want the government to regulate business and support traditional values. Libertarians support both economic and social freedoms including free markets and unrestricted speech.

Government ONLINE

Student Web Activity Visit glencoe.com and enter **QuickPass™** code USG9822c18. Click on Student Web Activity and complete the activity about shaping public opinion.

CHAPTER 18, SECTION 3

W Writing Support

Persuasive Writing Have students determine which of the four main U.S. ideologies they *least* believe in. Then have each student write a short essay in which he or she argues *in favor* of that ideology's principles. Encourage Internet research to learn more about each ideology. **AL**

Assess

Assign the Section 3 Assessment as homework or as an in-class activity, or have students take Section Quiz 18-3 from *Section Quizzes and Chapter Tests*.

Close

Visual/Spatial Have students draw a caricature of themselves illustrating the most influential factors involved in their political socialization. **OL**

Government ONLINE

Objectives and answers to the Student Web Activity can be found in the *Web Activity Lesson Plan* at glencoe.com. Enter **QuickPass™** code USG9085c18T.

Section 3 Review

SECTION 3 Review

Vocabulary

1. **Explain** the significance of: public opinion, peer group, mass media, political culture.

Main Ideas

2. **Describing** How do individuals learn their political beliefs?

3. **Summarizing** What five social characteristics can influence the opinions a person holds?

Critical Thinking

4. **Making Generalizations** Do you think that the mass media have too much influence on American public opinion? Explain why or why not.

5. **Organizing** Use a graphic organizer like the one below to contrast liberal and conservative ideologies.

	Social Policy	Economic Policy
Liberals		
Conservatives		

Writing About Government

6. **Expository Writing** Use library resources or the Internet to find examples of situations in which public opinion has caused an elected official to change his or her position on an issue. Present your findings in the form of a poster along with a written summary to your classmates.

Answers

1. All definitions can be found in the section and the Glossary.
2. family influences, schools, peer groups, economic status, social status, and the mass media
3. age, level of wealth, geographical location, gender, race
4. Possible "yes" answers may include that the media control public opinion by what they choose to tell the public; possible "no" answers may point out that the media are biased, but the public can filter the news accordingly.

5. Social Policy: Liberals favor individual freedom; conservatives favor government support of traditional moral values.
   Economic Policy: Liberals are willing to curtail economic freedom to increase equality; conservatives oppose government limitations on businesses.
6. Students' posters should illustrate examples of such a situation.

Class Debate

Ask students to form two groups based on their opinion about what the Supreme Court's ruling on this case should be. Then have each group write a majority opinion and a dissenting opinion. Have each group argue its case and then ask students to reevaluate their opinions. Have students re-form groups based on their reevaluations. Ask students who changed their minds to explain why they did so.

The Court's Decision

In the case of *Massachusetts, et al. v. EPA,* the Supreme Court, by a 5-to-4 vote, ruled that the EPA may not decline to issue emissions standards for greenhouse gases. The majority opinion, written by Justice Stevens, ruled that the Clean Air Act's language was written to include as broad a definition of pollutants as possible, including greenhouse gases. The dissenting opinions stated that Massachusetts had no standing to sue, because it could not show any concrete injury suffered from the EPA's inaction. Justice Scalia maintained that the Clear Air Act was limited to traditional pollutants and not greenhouse gases.

Does the EPA Have the Power to Regulate Greenhouse Gases?

Massachusetts et al. v. *Environmental Protection Agency,* 2007

The Clean Air Act authorizes the Environmental Protection Agency (EPA) to regulate "any air pollutant" that may "reasonably be anticipated to endanger public health or welfare." Does the EPA have the statutory authority to regulate greenhouse gas emissions from new vehicles?

Facts of the Case

In 1999 environmentalists who were concerned about global warming petitioned the EPA to regulate carbon dioxide emissions and other greenhouse gases from new cars and trucks. In 2003 the EPA denied their request, arguing that the agency did not have the authority to regulate these gases and emissions. Further, the officials said that there was no conclusive evidence connecting greenhouse gases and global warming.

Joined by some state and local governments, the environmentalist groups then asked the U.S. Court of Appeals for the Washington, D.C., Circuit to review the EPA decision. In July 2005, the court upheld the EPA's ruling. On further appeal, the Supreme Court accepted the case for review.

The Constitutional Question

The Court is sometimes called upon to interpret the meaning of federal laws such as the Clean Air Act. In *Massachusetts, et al.* v. *Environmental Protection Agency,* the Court considered two questions: (1) Does the Clean Air Act give the EPA the authority to regulate greenhouse gases, specifically the exhaust emissions of new cars and trucks? (2) Was the EPA correct to deny the petition to regulate these emissions?

The EPA argued that the amended 1990 Clean Air Act did not give it the power to regulate because it did not include a proposal to set limits on emissions. Instead, Congress authorized further study of the emissions issue. The EPA reasoned that it had no choice but to deny the petition.

The petitioners argued that EPA's refusal to regulate carbon dioxide led to "actual" and "imminent" harm: Massachusetts, California, and other states would lose hundreds of miles of their coastlines to rising seas. The petitioners also argued that the EPA had "abdicated its responsibility under the Clean Air Act to regulate the emissions of four greenhouse gases, including carbon dioxide."

Debating the Issue

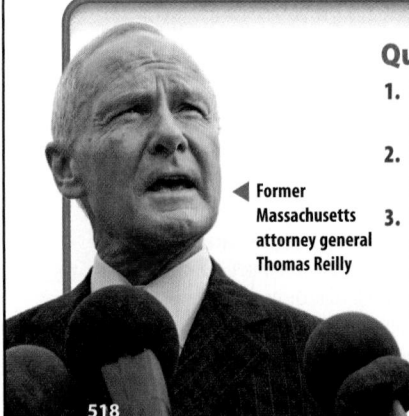

◄ **Former Massachusetts attorney general Thomas Reilly**

518

Questions to Consider

1. Why did environmentalist groups petition the EPA?

2. On what grounds did the EPA refuse the petition?

3. What could be the long-term consequences of the Supreme Court ruling for the petitioners? Against the petitioners?

You Be the Judge

In law, *standing* means that a plaintiff has the necessary status or qualification to bring a legal issue before a court. The courts have ruled that a plaintiff who has suffered or is exposed to actual injury (physical, economic, or other) has standing. A plaintiff who cannot show injury does not have standing and, therefore, cannot sue. In your opinion, did the plaintiffs in the *Massachusetts* case have standing? Explain.

Debating the Issue Answers

Questions to Consider

1. They wanted the EPA to regulate greenhouse gases.

2. It did not have the power to regulate greenhouse gases under the Clean Air Act.

3. Answers will vary. If the court rules for the petitioners, the EPA would be forced to set emissions standards for greenhouse gases. If the court rules against the petitioners, the EPA could continue to refuse to regulate greenhouse gases; however, Congress could amend the Clean Air Act to force the EPA to act.

You Be the Judge

Answers will vary, but students should decide whether they think the plaintiffs have standing and clearly explain their answers.

Measuring Public Opinion

Focus

Reader's Guide

Content Vocabulary
★ biased sample (p. 520)
★ universe (p. 520)
★ representative sample (p. 520)
★ random sampling (p. 521)
★ sampling error (p. 521)
★ cluster sample (p. 521)

Academic Vocabulary
★ access (p. 519)
★ indication (p. 520)
★ variation (p. 521)

Reading Strategy
As you read, complete a graphic organizer similar to the one below to help you take notes about the disadvantages of using mail and phone polls to gauge public opinion.

Disadvantages of Mail Polls	Disadvantages of Phone Polls

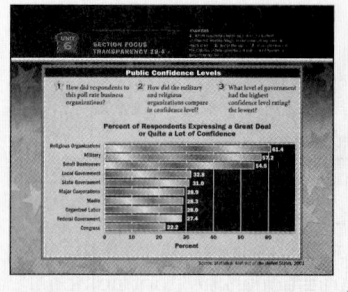

Bellringer
Section Focus Transparencies 18-4

Issues in the News

Polling was rampant in 2008, a presidential election year, but polling is common in the United States at almost any time. A poll is usually conducted by asking 1,000 or more people a series of questions on a certain topic. The answers provide insight into public opinion. In a recent poll by the Pew Research Center on the economy, for example, polled Americans identified their top economic worry as the cost of energy and health care: 24 percent of those surveyed gave this answer. The second-most-important concern was "jobs—unemployment, low wages, and outsourcing" at 18 percent. Elected officials often look at polls to give them direction for their legislative priorities.

▲ A woman polling individuals at a street fair

Reader's Guide

Answers to Graphic:

Disadvantages of Mail Polls: only 10–15 percent respond, pollsters cannot control respondents' careless or confusing replies

Disadvantages of Phone Polls: pollsters might fail to reach the person being called, people might refuse to answer questions

Americans express their opinions at the ballot box. Between elections, officials want to know what the public is thinking. Over the years, the methods and technology to **access** and tabulate public opinion have changed.

Nonscientific Methods

Elected officials use a number of sources or channels to stay abreast of public opinion:

- political parties and interest groups,
- mass media,
- letters and e-mails or faxes,
- straw polls, and
- political Web sites and blogs.

Party organizations have long been a reliable source of information about public opinion. Party officials were in close touch with voters in their hometowns, cities, counties, and states. National leaders, in turn, communicated regularly with Republican and Democratic Party bosses in cities such as New York, Chicago, Philadelphia, and Detroit. If the two major parties did not respond to issues quickly, support for third parties increased. In the early 1900s, political reforms designed to curb the abuses of city party bosses and the party "machines" weakened the role of parties. As a result, their ability to provide information on voters' attitudes declined.

Interest groups, too, provide elected officials with an easy way to find out about the opinions of interested citizens. Interest groups, however, often represent the attitudes of a vocal minority that is concerned with specific issues such as gun control, health care, or auto safety. They are not a good measure of broader public opinion.

The mass media often measures public attitudes fairly well because they speak to a broad audience.

Resource Manager

R Reading Strategies	**C** Critical Thinking	**D** Differentiated Instruction	**W** Writing Support	**S** Skill Practice
Teacher Edition • Outlining, p. 520 **Additional Resources** • Guid. Read. Act., p. 67 • Quizzes/Tests, pp. 224–232 • Reteaching Act., p. 18	**Teacher Edition** • Making Inferences, p. 522 **Additional Resources** • Read. Essen., pp. 211–213	**Additional Resources** • Foldables, p. 61	**Additional Resources** • Coop. Learning Act., pp. 11–12	**Additional Resources** • Ch. Summaries, pp. 52–54

Teach

R Reading Strategy

Outlining Have students scan the section to outline the traditional and nontraditional measures of public opinion. Ask them to include examples of each measure in their outlines. Discuss the various ways of measuring public opinion. Evaluate which measures are most reliable. **BL**

Linking ★ Past & Present

The First White House Pollster
President Lyndon B. Johnson was the first president to hire a pollster, Albert Cantril, for the White House staff. Cantril provided President Johnson with polling data from every state. Johnson used the polls to defend his escalation of the Vietnam War and his decision in 1968 not to seek another term in the face of mounting opposition to the war.

Additional Support

Polling Voters

Perils of Exit Polls Historically, exit polls—surveys taken to learn voters' choices as they leave the polling place—have been misleading. *Why might a person's answer to an exit poll be suspect, and how does the cartoonist make a point about exit polls?*

Newspapers, magazines, and television and radio programs reflect the interests of the public. For example, if a news program gets higher audience ratings by covering a certain issue, it is an **indication** of strong public interest in that issue. To know what the public is thinking about, politicians keep an eye on newspaper headlines, magazine cover stories, editorials, radio talk shows, and television newscasts.

These sources of information, however, may give a distorted view of public opinion. The mass media's focus on news that has visual appeal or shock value, such as stories about violent crime, distorts the public perception of reality. People who watch television news as their only source of news, for example, tend to be more pessimistic about the nation than those who also use other sources for information.

One time-honored form of expressing opinion in a democracy is to write letters to elected officials. The first major letter-writing campaign convinced George Washington to seek a second term as president in 1792. Letter writing increases in times of national crisis or major government decisions. The president might even request letters from the public to indicate support for a new policy. Lawmakers may do the same. Today, interest groups often stage massive letter-writing campaigns using mass e-mail chains. Officials,

however, might give such letters less attention than personal letters from individual constituents.

In recent years, people have been more likely to contact legislators by e-mail or faxes. This allows citizens to react almost immediately on an issue, while legislators, too, can use electronic means to quickly respond to citizen concerns on their Web sites.

Another method of gauging opinion is the straw poll. This is an unscientific attempt to measure public opinion. Newspapers might print "ballots" in the paper and ask people to "vote." Television and radio stations ask questions—"Should the mayor run for reelection?" Members of Congress often send their constituents questionnaires. Straw polls do not use scientific procedures to choose the respondents. Instead, the people who respond to a straw poll have chosen to respond voluntarily. This self-selection mechanism means that straw polls are always a **biased sample** of the population.

Finally, elected officials and their staff keep track of opinions about current issues expressed on political Web sites and blogs. These places are rapidly becoming major forums for political expression. Reviewing the discussions on such sites helps officials gauge what an important segment of the public thinks about issues and can alert leaders to emerging problems that have yet to be covered by the traditional mass media.

Scientific Polling

Almost everyone involved in politics today uses scientific polls to measure public opinion. Scientific polling involves three basic steps: selecting a sample of the group to be questioned, presenting carefully worded questions to the individuals in the sample, and interpreting the results.

Sample Populations

In conducting polls, the group of people that is to be studied is called the **universe.** A universe might be all the seniors in a high school, all the people in the state of Texas, or all women in the United States. Since it is not possible to actually interview every person in Texas or every woman in the United States, pollsters question a **representative sample,** or a small group of people who are typical of that universe.

Most pollsters are able to use samples of only 1,200 to 1,500 adults to accurately measure the opinions of all adults in the United States—more than 208 million people. Such a small group is a

---

Activity: Collaborative Learning

Creating an Overhead Transparency
Organize the class into groups to design an overhead transparency that reflects influences on the outcome of an election. Students in each group should choose political parties, interest groups, mass media, or public opinion

and then create an overhead transparency to list the ways in which one of these forces can influence an election outcome. Allow groups to display their completed overheads on an overhead projector. **OL**

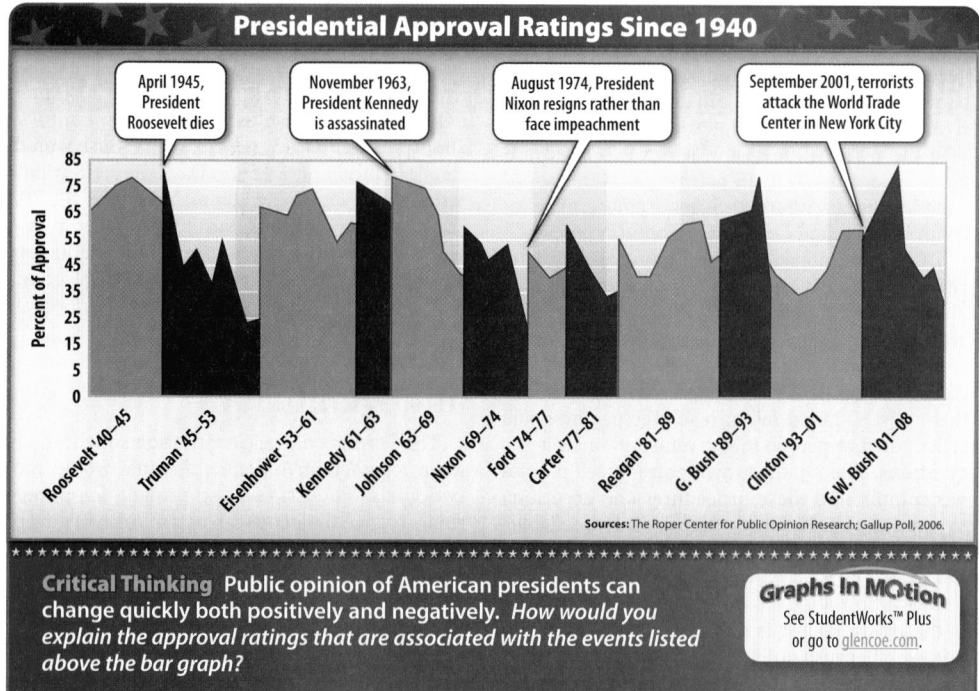

Presidential Approval Ratings Since 1940

April 1945, President Roosevelt dies

November 1963, President Kennedy is assassinated

August 1974, President Nixon resigns rather than face impeachment

September 2001, terrorists attack the World Trade Center in New York City

Percent of Approval: 85, 75, 65, 55, 45, 35, 25, 15, 5, 0

Roosevelt '40–45, Truman '45–53, Eisenhower '53–61, Kennedy '61–63, Johnson '63–69, Nixon '69–74, Ford '74–77, Carter '77–81, Reagan '81–89, G. Bush '89–93, Clinton '93–01, G.W. Bush '01–08

Sources: The Roper Center for Public Opinion Research; Gallup Poll, 2006.

Critical Thinking Public opinion of American presidents can change quickly both positively and negatively. *How would you explain the approval ratings that are associated with the events listed above the bar graph?*

Graphs In MOtion
See StudentWorks™ Plus or go to glencoe.com.

Critical Thinking

Answer: When a big event happened, approval ratings went up.

Graph Skills Practice
Which president shown had the highest approval rating? *(G. W. Bush)*

Did You Know?

One of the most important traditional measures of the president's standing with the public is the Gallup presidential approval survey. Since 1945 the Gallup Organization has polled members of the public monthly—and sometimes more often—about whether they approve or disapprove of the president's handling of the job.

---

representative sample because pollsters use **random sampling,** a technique in which everyone in that universe has an equal chance of being selected.

Sampling Error

A **sampling error** is a measurement of how much the sample results might differ from the sample universe. Sampling error decreases as the sample size becomes larger. Most national polls use 1,200 to 1,500 people; this number represents the characteristics of any size population, with an error of only plus or minus 3 percent. If a poll says that 65 percent of Americans favor tougher pollution laws, with a 3 percent sampling error, between 62 and 68 percent of the entire population favor such laws. When one interprets a poll, it is important to know the sampling error. During the 1976 presidential race, for example, one poll said Jimmy Carter was behind Gerald Ford by 48 percent to 49 percent. With a sampling error of 3 percent, Carter could have been ahead. As it turned out, Carter won the election.

Sampling Procedures

A random sample of the entire population can be drawn in a number of ways. One method, a

cluster sample, organizes, or clusters, people by geographical divisions. The clusters may be counties, congressional districts, or census tracts (regions established by the Census Bureau). At times, pollsters adjust or weight the results of a poll to overcome defects in sampling. Pollsters may adjust a poll to take into account **variations** in race, gender, age, or education. For example, if pollsters found that not enough Americans over the age of 65 were interviewed, they might give extra weight to the opinions of the senior citizens who were interviewed.

Poll Questions

The way a question is phrased can greatly influence people's responses and, in turn, poll results. In 1971 the Gallup Poll asked whether people favored a proposal "to bring home all American troops from Vietnam before the end of the year." Two-thirds of those polled answered yes. Then the Gallup Poll asked the question differently: "Do you agree or disagree with a proposal to withdraw all U.S. troops by the end of the year regardless of what happens there [in Vietnam] after U.S. troops leave?" When the question was worded this way, fewer than half the respondents agreed.

CHAPTER 18: *Interest Groups and Public Opinion* **521**

Exploring the "Blogosphere"

Step 4: Responding to Blogs Student groups respond to blog entries created in Step 3.

Directions Have student groups trade the blogs they created in Step 3. As a group, have students write a response to the blog entry. Remind students that readers contribute to blogs in many ways. They may rebut opinions stated in blogs. They sometimes add helpful

information such as hyperlinks. They may point out errors in information and make corrections. Sometimes, they simply express admiration for the blog. Have students weigh their right to free speech with their responsibility to be civil as they respond to each other's blogs.

Summarizing Have groups share their blog responses with the class. Encourage the class to discuss what they learned as they explored the "blogosphere." **OL AL**

Hands-On Chapter Project
Step 4

C Critical Thinking

Making Inferences This chapter concludes by saying that public opinion is "not the only influence on public policy." It then lists a number of "other" influences, such as interest groups, political parties and activists. **Ask:** What can you infer about the relationship between "public opinion" and the "other groups" mentioned? *(When people say public opinion they are referring to unorganized opinion of the general public. An advanced student might question whether there is a good deal of ambiguity in the use of the term public opinion.)* **AL**

Assess

Assign the Section 4 Assessment as homework or as an in-class activity; or have students take Section Quiz 18-4 from *Section Quizzes and Chapter Tests.*

Close

Drawing Conclusions Ask students to assess whether measuring public opinion provides an important check on all branches and levels of government. **OL**

Section 4 Review

Mail and Phone Polls

In recent years, many public opinion polls have been conducted by mail or by telephone, largely because interviewing people in their homes is expensive. Although the mail questionnaire is cheaper than the personal interview, it has two disadvantages. First, only 10 to 15 percent of the questionnaires are usually returned. Second, pollsters cannot control respondents' careless or confusing replies.

Telephone interviews are now used in many national polls. To create a reliable telephone poll, pollsters use random digit dialing: They select an area code and the first three local digits. Then a computer randomly chooses and dials the last four digits. The drawbacks to telephone interviews are that pollsters might fail to reach the person being called, or that people might refuse to answer the questions. The rapidly growing use of cell phones has complicated these procedures and according to some experts has made such polls less reliable.

Interpreting Results

Scientific polling has improved since its first use in the 1930s. Polling is never completely accurate, however, because pollsters can never be sure that the people they are interviewing are being honest. Still, major polling organizations have learned how to conduct polls that are usually reliable within a few percentage points.

Serious problems occurred, however, during the elections of 2000 and 2002. In these election years, the Voter News Service (VNS), a polling service created by six major news organizations, experienced a great deal of difficulty forecasting accurate election results. The flawed data gathered by the VNS during exit polling for the 2000 presidential election resulted in extensive confusion about whether Al Gore or George W. Bush won the state of Florida on Election Day. The VNS tried to redesign its data collection technique for the 2002 congressional elections, but it again failed to provide accurate exit polling data for the media services that were tracking the results of the election.

Public Opinion and Democracy

C The Framers of the Constitution sought to create a representative democracy that would meet two goals. The first was to provide for popular rule—to give the people an active voice in government. The people were supposed to have control over the lawmakers who represented them. The Framers' second goal was to insulate government from the shifting whims of an ill-informed public. The system the Framers created has worked well. Research shows that the government is responsive to public opinion—the wishes of the people.

At the same time, public opinion is not the only influence on public policy. Interest groups, political parties, the mass media, other institutions of government, and the ideas of activists and public officials also help shape public policy.

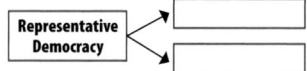

SECTION 4 Review

Vocabulary

1. **Explain** the significance of: biased sample, universe, representative sample, random sampling, sampling error, cluster sample.

Main Ideas

2. **Identifying** What are seven sources that public officials use to determine public opinion?

3. **Listing** Why might poll results not accurately reflect public opinion?

Critical Thinking

4. **Making Inferences** Why do politicians pay closer attention to the results of polls conducted through personal interviews rather than through the mail?

5. **Organizing** Use a graphic organizer like the one below to identify two goals the Framers of the Constitution wanted to meet by creating a representative democracy.

Representative Democracy → ☐ ☐

Writing About Government

6. **Expository Writing** Find a public opinion poll in a newspaper or newsmagazine. Analyze the poll by focusing on the following questions: How many people were contacted? Does the poll include a random or representative sampling? What is the sampling error? Are the questions presented in an unbiased and effective way? Present your answers in an analytical report.

Answers

1. All definitions can be found in the section and the Glossary.
2. political parties, interest groups, mass media, letter writing, electronic access, straw polls, scientific polling
3. sample might not be representative of the population, questions might be interpreted differently, questionnaires are not returned, pollsters may fail to reach the person being called, interviewer's appearance or tone of voice can influence answers, individuals sometimes answer the way they think they should, the respondent may know little about the topic
4. Mail interviews are not as reliable as personal interviews because only 10 to 15 percent of mail recipients respond, and their replies cannot be clarified.
5. provide for popular rule; insulate government from shifting whims of public opinion
6. Students should analyze a public opinion poll by answering the questions.

Interpreting Opinion Polls

Well-designed public opinion polls give us accurate representation of what people think at a given time. They are also used by politicians to identify trends and gauge public support for various issues and legislation. Although objective polls can be useful, some polls are designed to get answers that support the opinion of the group conducting (or paying for) the poll. For example, a poll of dog owners is likely to result in less favorable opinions of leash laws than a poll of the general population. For this reason, interpreting poll results takes some analytical skill.

Why Learn This Skill?

Knowing how to read data from public opinion polls will help you to understand what your fellow citizens are thinking. The poll below was conducted in April 2007 and sampled 2,012 adult Americans, with a margin of error of plus or minus 2.2 percent. To analyze the results of polls, follow the steps at the right:

Taxation Poll*

Poll Question: Do you consider the amount of federal income tax you have to pay as too high, too low, or about right?

Too high	58%
Too low	3%
About right	32%

*Percentages do not total 100%; 7% had no response to this question.

1. Look at the title and date of the poll to determine a context for what you read.

2. Note who was interviewed and the size of the sample, or the number of people polled. The higher the sample size, the more reliable the poll.

3. Notice what questions were asked and whether they are phrased in an unbiased way. Questions should be phrased to neither encourage nor discourage a given answer.

4. State the results in sentence form, indicating how the poll data reflects Americans' thoughts about the topic.

Practicing the Skill

Examine the poll results above and answer the questions that follow.

1. What is this poll about?

2. What was the size of the polling sample and what was the margin of error?

3. State the results of the poll in sentence form.

Applying the Skill

Select an issue that interests you and decide what you want to know about it. Develop an unbiased question to poll opinions about the issue. Randomly select a sample group from the population you have decided to poll. Record your answers. Present your results to the class in a chart. Include your sample size and a brief summary.

Teach

S Skill Practice

Creating a Poll Analyze and evaluate the reliability and validity of different types of public opinion polls. Review the steps to analyzing a public opinion poll. Then have students exchange with a partner the public opinion poll they created in the Applying the Skill activity. Ask students to use the steps listed on this page to analyze their partner's public opinion poll. Finally, ask partners to share their analyses and discuss any problems they discovered. **OL**

C Critical Thinking

Analyzing Information Ask: Why would someone design a poll that was not objective? *(A group might want to use the results of the poll to help convince politicians to pass legislation that is favorable to them.)* **OL**

Answers

Practicing the Skill

1. opinions on federal income taxes
2. The size of the sample was 2,012 Americans; the margin of error was plus or minus 2.2%.
3. Fifty-eight percent of adult Americans believed their federal income taxes were too high; only 3% believed their taxes were too low. Thirty-two percent of adult Americans believed they paid about the right amount of taxes.

Applying the Skill

Students should select an issue that is of concern to them and to other students. Then they should develop a nonbiased question to poll a selected sample and record the sample population's answers. Students should present the results of their poll in a chart, including their sample size and a brief summary.

523

Assessment Suite

This easy-to-use software includes extensive question banks and allows you to create fully customized tests that can be administered in print or online.

Reviewing Vocabulary

1. lobbyist
2. random sampling
3. interest group
4. political culture
5. representative sample
6. public opinion
7. sampling error
8. universe

Reviewing Main Ideas

9. to help promote an individual's economic self-interests; because a group shares an individual's beliefs, values, or attitudes; for social reasons
10. They run mass media and letter-writing campaigns.
11. family and home, schools, peer groups, economic and social status, mass media, government leaders, and interest groups
12. Any or all of the following reasons: sample may not be representative of the population as a whole, questions on poll may be interpreted differently by different people, question-naires are not returned, pollsters may fail to reach the person being called, the interviewer's appearance or tone of voice can influence answers, individuals sometimes answer the way they think they should, the respondent might not know anything about the topic.

524

Reviewing Vocabulary

Match the following content vocabulary word(s) with each of the descriptions provided:

interest group · political culture
lobbyist · universe
random sampling · sampling error
public opinion · representative sample

1. representative of an interest group
2. everyone in the sampled group has an equal chance of being selected

Chapter Summary

Interest Groups

★ **Who** Interest groups are groups of people who share common goals and organize to influence government.

★ **What** Major categories of interest groups include business and labor groups, agricultural groups, environmental groups, public-interest groups, government groups, and professional associations.

★ **How** Most groups try to influence government policy by lobbying lawmakers, running publicity campaigns, and providing funds for candidates' election campaigns.

Public Opinion

★ **What** The ideas and attitudes a significant number of Americans hold about government and politics; factors such as family, schools, peer groups, economic and social status, the mass media, and government leaders shape one's political beliefs.

★ **Who** In America, most people fall into the categories of liberal, conservative, or moderate, depending on their basic beliefs about government and society.

★ **How** Officials measure public opinion by meeting with leaders of interest groups and talking with voters, as well as through scientific polling methods.

3. people who share common policy goals and organize to influence government
4. basic values and beliefs about a nation and its government that most citizens share
5. small group of people who are typical of the universe
6. the ideas and attitudes that a significant number of Americans hold about certain issues
7. measurement of how much the sample results might differ from the universe being sampled
8. group of people from which samples are taken for polls or statistical measurements

Reviewing Main Ideas

Section 1 *(pages 503–507)*

9. **Identifying** What are three reasons or concerns that cause people to join interest groups?

Section 2 *(pages 508–513)*

10. **Describing** How do interest groups try to influence public opinion to support their policies?

Section 3 *(pages 514–517)*

11. **Listing** What seven forces influence a person's political socialization?

Section 4 *(pages 519–522)*

12. **Assessing** Why might the results of scientific polls not be accurate?

Critical Thinking

13. 🇺🇸 **Essential Question** How can an interest group influence national and local government?
14. **Understanding Cause and Effect** Why do you think that people in lower socioeconomic levels are less likely to contribute to, lead in, or even join special-interest groups?
15. **Making Comparisons** Use a graphic organizer like the one below to compare the AFL-CIO with an environmental interest group in the areas of size, composition of membership, and methods used to accomplish their goals.

	AFL-CIO	Other
Size		
Members		
Methods		

13. A local interest group can unite large numbers of people to attend a local meeting to influence government policy. Specific examples may include parents attending a school board meeting, children and parents attending a planning meeting for a new town park, and so on.
14. Answers may include that people of lower socioeconomic levels have less leisure time than other groups, may not have the financial resources needed to participate, may be less informed about issues, have

to worry more about basic needs than political needs, and so on.
15. Answers may include: AFL-CIO—largest labor organization, membership includes union workers with economic interests from many industries, holds fund-raisers and voter registration drives and supports political candidates; Sierra Club—small size, interested in the environment, monitors the environment and brings lawsuits against those who violate regulations.

Government ONLINE Self-Check Quiz
Visit glencoe.com and enter QuickPass™ code USG9822c18.
Click on Self-Check Quizzes for additional test practice.

CHAPTER
18
Assessment
and Activities

Document-Based Questions

Analyzing Primary Sources

Read the excerpt below and answer the questions that follow.

The National Grange is the oldest agricultural interest group in the United States. Below is the 2004 National Grange Blueprint for Rural America, the organization's political issues platform.

> 66 *America's family farmers and ranchers face challenges regarding food security, contract agriculture, agribusiness consolidations, trade negotiations and low prices. Federal farm programs should encourage increased participation in the agricultural sector by the largest number of individuals and families. . . . Instead, federal farm policies discourage innovative farm practices. . . . The government depresses farm income by selling surplus agricultural products and allowing imports of milk protein concentrates. All dairy farmers and all consumers deserve to benefit from regional dairy programs and continued financial assistance for moderate-sized dairy farms. The U.S. faces hostile multilateral trade negotiations where the goal of our trading partners is to decrease U.S. farm income.*
>
> *Access to telecommunications services such as telephone, cell phone, television, radio, Internet, satellite and cable are important to rural America. This access is threatened by government regulations that allow large conglomerates to control multiple media venues while restricting entry of new and medium-sized media companies. . . . Advanced telecommunications technologies must be available in every rural community at affordable costs.* 99

16. Based on this excerpt, how is a farming interest group like the National Grange different from a political party?

17. What key issues does the Grange promote? Is their membership based in certain regions, or is it nationwide?

Interpreting Political Cartoons

Analyze the cartoon and answer the questions that follow. Base your answers on the cartoon and your knowledge of Chapter 18.

18. What do the oxen's words suggest about politicians?

19. What is going to happen in the cartoon?

20. What does the choice of a wagon and oxen suggest about the cartoonist's viewpoint?

Applying Technology Skills

21. Using E-mail Use library or Internet resources to research an interest group that you might like to join. Locate an e-mail address for the group and compose a letter requesting information about the group—its purpose, activities, dues, and number of members. Produce a class pamphlet titled "Interest Groups to Join."

Participating IN GOVERNMENT

22. Arrange an interview with a public official in your local government. Ask how that official finds out what issues are important to the public, and how he or she measures public opinion on those issues. Present your findings in class.

CHAPTER 18: *Interest Groups and Public Opinion* **525**

Interpreting Political Cartoons

18. They are uncertain about their direction and believe that lobbyists will show them what to do.

19. The lobbyists are about to crack the whip to steer politicians.

20. The cartoon suggests that politicians are yoked to and work for lobbyists.

Applying Technology Skills

21. Students should combine their findings in a class pamphlet titled "Interest Groups to Join."

Participating IN GOVERNMENT

22. Students should interview a local government official and report to the class about how that official finds out what issues are important and how he or she measures public opinion.

Analyzing Primary Sources

16. Students might answer that a political party runs candidates for specific offices; an interest group tries to influence those officials to vote for issues the interest group promotes. These groups do this through writing letters or lobbying key officials to take note of their causes. Finally, the Grange is attempting only to recruit people with similar interests, whereas a political party tries to build a broader support base.

17. The Grange in this instance is promoting government withholding of farm surpluses to drive the price of certain items up on the world market and discouraging imports of farm products. Additionally, the Grange would like to have legislation to dissuade agricultural consolidations as well as looser trade negotiations with foreign nations. The organization is nationwide rather than regionally based, because it seeks to include farmers across America and not just in key regions such as the South or the West.

Chapter Bonus Test Question

Ask: Which Supreme Court case became the basis for many campaign finance loopholes? *(Buckley v. Valeo)*

Levels					Resources	Chapter Opener	Section 1	Section 2	Section 3	Chapter Assess
BL	OL	AL	ELL							
FOCUS										
BL	OL	AL	ELL	📠	**Section Focus Transparencies**		19-1	19-2	19-3	
TEACH										
BL	OL		ELL	📁	**Reading Essentials and Study Guide (and Answer Key)**		p. 214	p. 218	p. 221	
BL	OL		ELL	📁	**Guided Reading Activities**		p. 68	p. 69	p. 70	
BL	OL		ELL	📁	**Vocabulary Activities**		p. 19			
BL	OL	AL	ELL	📁	**Chapter Summaries**					
BL	OL			📁	**American Biographies**				p. 74	
BL	OL	AL	ELL	📁	**Cooperative Learning Activities**					
	OL	AL	ELL	📁	**Government Simulations and Debate**				p. 37	
BL	OL	AL	ELL	📁	**Historical Documents and Speeches**		p. 19		p. 4	
BL	OL	AL	ELL	📁	**Interpreting Political Cartoons**			p. 37		
BL	OL		ELL	📁	**Skill Reinforcement Activities**					
BL	OL	AL	ELL	📁	**Source Readings**					
BL	OL			📁	**Supreme Court Case Studies**			p. 109		
BL	OL	AL	ELL	📁	**Participating in Government Activities**			p. 37		
BL	OL		ELL	📁	**Spanish Declaration of Independence and U.S. Constitution**	✓	✓	✓	✓	✓
BL	OL	AL	ELL	📁	**NGS World Atlas, Spanish**	✓	✓	✓	✓	✓
BL	OL	AL	ELL	📠	**Unit Overlay Transparencies, Strategies, and Activities**	✓	✓	✓	✓	✓
BL	OL		ELL	📠	**Making It Relevant Transparencies**	✓	✓	✓	✓	✓
BL	OL	AL	ELL	📠	**High School Writing Process Transparencies, Strategies, and Activities**	✓	✓	✓	✓	✓
BL	OL	AL		📠	**American Art & Architecture Transparencies, Strategies, and Activities**	✓	✓	✓	✓	✓

✓ Chapter- or unit-based activities applicable to all sections in this chapter

Teacher Works™ Plus

All-In-One Planner and Resource Center

- Interactive Lesson Planner
- Interactive Teacher Edition
- Fully editable blackline masters
- Chapter Spotlight Videos Launch

- Differentiated Lesson Plans
- Printable reports of daily assignments
- Standards tracking system

Levels					Resources	Chapter Opener	Section 1	Section 2	Section 3	Chapter Assess
BL	OL	AL	ELL							
TEACH *(continued)*										
BL	OL			💿	**American Music: Hits Through History**	✓	✓	✓	✓	✓
BL	OL		ELL	📁	**Reading Strategies for the Social Studies Classroom**	✓	✓	✓	✓	✓
			ELL	📁	**English Language Learner Handbook**	✓	✓	✓	✓	✓
BL	OL		ELL	📁	**Writer's Guidebook for Social Studies**	✓	✓	✓	✓	✓
BL	OL	AL	ELL	📁	**Living Constitution, SE**	✓	✓	✓	✓	✓
BL	OL	AL	ELL	📁	**Living Constitution, TAE**	✓	✓	✓	✓	✓
BL	OL			📁	**NGS World Atlas, English**	✓	✓	✓	✓	✓
BL	OL		ELL	📁	**The Constitution and You (poster set)**	✓	✓	✓	✓	✓
BL	OL	AL	ELL	📁	**Spanish Chapter Summaries**					
BL	OL	AL	ELL	📁	**Spanish Vocabulary Activities**					
BL	OL		ELL	📁	**Spanish Reading Essentials and Study Guide (and Answer Key)**		p. 214	p. 215	p. 216	
BL	OL	AL	ELL	💿	**PresentationPlus! with MindJogger CheckPoint**	✓	✓	✓	✓	✓
ASSESS										
BL	OL	AL	ELL	💿	*ExamView® Assessment Suite*		19-1	19-2	19-3	Ch. 19
BL	OL	AL	ELL	📁	**Authentic Assessment with Rubrics**		p. 26			p. 26
BL	OL	AL	ELL	📁	**Section Quizzes and Chapter Tests**		p. 231	p. 232	p. 233	pp. 235–242
BL	OL	AL	ELL	📁	**Spanish Section Quizzes and Tests**		p. 231	p. 232	p. 233	pp. 235–242
CLOSE										
BL			ELL	📁	**Reteaching Activities**		p. 19			
BL	OL	AL	ELL	💿	**StudentWorks™ Plus with Audio Summaries**	✓	✓	✓	✓	✓
BL	OL		ELL	🖋	**Graphic Organizer Transparencies**		✓	✓	✓	
BL	OL		ELL	📁	**High School Government Reading and Study Skills Foldables®**		p. 62	p. 62	p. 62	

Teach With Technology

What is PresentationPlus! with MindJogger CheckPoint?

Glencoe's PresentationPlus! with MindJogger CheckPoint offers ready-made presentations and review activities for each chapter or section in the textbook.

How can PresentationPlus! help me?

PresentationPlus! allows you to create your presentations quickly and includes links to glencoe.com, In Motion animations (maps, graphs, and charts), and a selection of transparencies that enhance the classroom discussion. Additionally, MindJogger CheckPoint offers entertaining ask-the-audience games that review content and generate student interest.

PresentationPlus! with MindJogger CheckPoint is one of Glencoe's technology resources available for teachers.

Government ONLINE

Visit glencoe.com and enter *QuickPass*™ code USG9085c19T for Chapter 19 resources.

You can easily launch a wide range of digital products from your computer's desktop with the McGraw-Hill Social Studies widget.

	Student	Teacher	Parent
Media Library			
• Student Edition Section Audio	●		●
• Chapter Spotlight Videos	●	●	●
***United States Government* Online Learning Center (Web Site)**			
• Chapter Overviews	●	●	●
• Multilingual Glossaries	●	●	●
• Study-to-Go	●	●	●
• Student Web Activities	●	●	●
• Self-Check Quizzes	●	●	●
• Online Student Edition	●	●	●
• Vocabulary eFlashcards	●	●	●
• Web Activity Lesson Plans		●	
• Vocabulary PuzzleMaker	●	●	●
• Landmark Supreme Court Cases	●	●	●
• Beyond the Textbook	●	●	●

READING SUPPORT FROM JAMESTOWN EDUCATION

- **Timed Readings Plus in Social Studies** helps students increase their reading rate and fluency while maintaining comprehension. The 400-word passages are similar to those found on state and national assessments.

- **Reading in the Content Area: Social Studies** concentrates on six essential reading skills that help students better comprehend what they read. The book includes 75 high-interest nonfiction passages written at increasing levels of difficulty.

- **Reading Social Studies** includes strategic reading instruction and vocabulary support in Social Studies content for ELLs and native speakers of English. www.jamestowneducation.com

Reading List Generator CD-ROM

GLENCOE

Use this database to search more than 30,000 titles to create a customized reading list for your students.

- Reading lists can be organized by students' reading level, author, genre, theme, or area of interest.
- The database provides Degrees of Reading Power™ (DRP) and Lexile™ readability scores for all selections.
- A brief summary of each selection is included.

Leveled reading suggestions for this chapter:

- *The Internet,* by Kerry Cochrane
- *Should Schools be Wired to the Internet?,* by Al Gore and David Gelemter
- *Who's to Know: Information, the Media, and Public Awareness,* by Ann E. Weiss

Review suggested books before assigning them.

Economics Connection

Personal Finance Literacy

Shopping on the Internet

Like television, the Internet is a medium that can be used to influence government, entertain, educate, and sell products and services. Before the Internet existed, many people bought by telephone goods they saw on television shopping networks.

Online shopping has increased in popularity in recent years: $26 billion in 2007 U.S. sales alone. Reasons for Internet shopping's popularity include convenience and savings of time and money. Shoppers enjoy the convenience of clicking a mouse and pressing a few computer keys from home, at any time. Online goods are often less expensive because manufacturers don't have to pay the overhead costs of retail outlets.

Online shopping does, however, have a greater potential for consumer fraud than retail shopping. Some 36 percent of the National Consumer League's fraud complaints in 2007 were about goods purchased online and never delivered or misrepresented. Online shopping also requires the use of a credit card, something that always presents the danger of theft or fraud.

Tips for Safer Online Shopping

- **Reputable sellers:** Check consumer protection agencies and the Better Business Bureau to see if complaints have been made against the company. Before buying, get a physical address and phone number.

- **Credit cards:** You have a legal right to dispute charges for goods not received, not ordered, or misrepresented. Single-use cards protect your real account number from hackers.

- **Secure sites:** Look for a padlock symbol on the Web site; don't buy if the lock is broken.

- **Full information:** Know the price, product description, delivery date, warranty, and return policy. Keep a copy of the order.

Ask: What are the advantages and disadvantages of online shopping?

Did You Know?

A recent survey found that more men than women shop online. Men said they know what they want and want to buy it quickly. Women often preferred the tactile and visual experience of shopping in stores.

🔊 **Chapter Audio** 📹 **Spotlight Video**

Mass Media
and the Internet

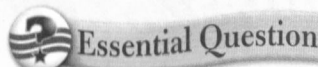

Essential Question

The media offer biased and unbiased points of view toward political affairs, both of which help shape our opinions of politicians, parties, and so on. The Internet has helped streamline the way everyday citizens participate in and express opinions about politics and government. Governments and politicians save time and money by advertising and conducting business online, and interest groups have found new ways to disseminate their messages.

Chapter Spotlight Video

To generate student interest and provide a springboard for class discussion, access the Chapter 19 Video at glencoe.com or on the video DVD.

FOLDABLES
Study Organizer

Dinah Zike's Foldables are three-dimensional, interactive graphic organizers that help students practice basic writing skills, review key vocabulary terms, and identify main ideas. Have students complete this chapter's Foldable activity or activities in *Dinah Zike's Reading and Study Skills Foldables* booklet. **OL**

A 2008 Republican presidential primary debate in California.

526

Essential Question

How do the media affect our political life, and how has the Internet opened up new paths of communication for citizens, government, and interest groups?

Government ONLINE
Chapter Overview Visit glencoe.com and enter *QuickPass*™ code USG9822c19 for an overview, a quiz, and other chapter resources.

Government ONLINE

Visit glencoe.com and enter *QuickPass*™ code USG9085c19T for Chapter 19 Resources including Chapter Overview, Student Web Activity, Self-Check Quiz, and other materials for students and teachers.

Launching the Chapter

Researching The mass media—television, radio, and the Internet—have a central role in shaping opinion. Their role can be critical during times of crisis or rapid change, such as during an election, a war, or a social protest. Have students survey the media's role in a recent presidential campaign. Help them refine their research by assigning a specific political party, a specific medium (television, for instance), or a specific time period (the election of 2000, for example). **Essential Question:** During an election, how do the mass media operate to mobilize voters around a candidate or for a particular issue? *(Answers should include informing voters about candidates and their positions.)* **OL**

How Media Impact Government

Focus

Reader's Guide

Content Vocabulary	Academic Vocabulary	Reading Strategy
★ mass media *(p. 527)*	★ expose *(p. 529)*	As you read, create an outline similar to the one at the right to help you take notes about how the media impact government.
★ news release *(p. 528)*	★ commentator *(p. 530)*	
★ news briefing *(p. 528)*	★ link *(p. 532)*	
★ leak *(p. 529)*		
★ media event *(p. 529)*		
★ front-runner *(p. 531)*		
★ spot advertising *(p. 531)*		

How Media Impact Government
I. The President and the Media
   A. News Releases and Briefings
   B.
   C.
   D.
II. Media and Presidential Campaigns

Issues in the News

When President George W. Bush was ready to travel to Africa in early 2008, it was White House Press Secretary Dana Perino who announced the trip: "The trip will be an opportunity for the president to review firsthand the significant progress . . . in efforts to increase economic development and fight HIV/AIDS . . . as a result of United States . . . programs." Since fall 2007, Perino had been the face of the Bush administration, providing daily press briefings and answering reporters' questions. Perino's interest in government goes back to her childhood. She told interviewers that at age six, she stood on a milk crate, held up an American flag, and told her parents that she was going to work in the White House. Despite the new and potent role of the Internet in political communication, the president's press secretary is still a key gatekeeper for conveying White House policy to the public.

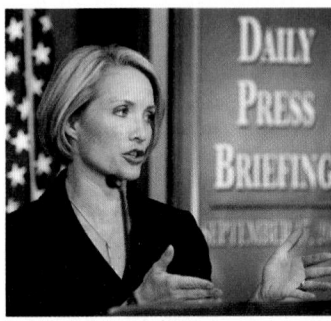

▲ White House Press Secretary Dana Perino at an official press briefing

The **mass media** include all the means for communicating information to the general public. Traditionally, two types of mass media have existed: print media such as daily newspapers and popular magazines, and the broadcast media comprised of radio and television. The Internet has recently emerged as a powerful new interactive medium for transmitting words, sounds, and images. Supreme Court Justice Lewis F. Powell explained the vital contribution of media to a democratic society:

66 *An informed public depends upon accurate and effective reporting by the news media.*

No individual can obtain for himself the information needed for the intelligent discharge of his political responsibilities. For most citizens the prospect of personal familiarity with newsworthy events is hopelessly unrealistic. In seeking out the news the press therefore acts as an agent of the public at large. It is the means by which the people receive that free flow of information and ideas essential to intelligent self-government. 99

—Lewis F. Powell, 1974

Reader's Guide

Answers to Graphic:
Students' organizers should resemble the one below:
I. How Media Impact Government
   A. The President and the Media
      1. News Releases and Briefings
      2. Press Conferences
      3. Other Means of Sharing Information
      4. Media Events

Resource Manager

R Reading Strategies	**C** Critical Thinking	**D** Differentiated Instruction	**W** Writing Support	**S** Skill Practice
Teacher Edition	**Teacher Edition**	**Teacher Edition**	**Additional Resources**	**Additional Resources**
• Reading Primary Sources, p. 528 • Analyzing Text Structure, p. 532	• Drawing Conclusions, p. 534	• Verbal/Linguistic, p. 528	• Authentic Assess., p. 26	• Vocab. Act., p. 19 • Reteaching Act., p. 19
Additional Resources	**Additional Resources**	**Additional Resources**		
• Guid. Read. Act., p. 68 • Quizzes/Tests, p. 233	• Read. Essen., pp. 214–217	• Foldables, p. 62 • Hist. Docs. and Speeches, p. 19		

Teach

Caption Answer: whether it is formal or informal, whether the president answers hard questions and allows follow-up questions

D Differentiated Instruction

Verbal/Linguistic Discuss the purpose and effectiveness of President Franklin D. Roosevelt's fireside chats. Then have students choose a contemporary topic and write a fireside chat. Remind students that Roosevelt's fireside chats were given to rally the American public during a difficult time. Call on volunteers to perform their fireside chats for the class. **AL**

R Reading Strategy

Reading Primary Sources Have students analyze Senator Fulbright's statement. **Ask:** What would such an amendment encroach upon? *(separation of powers, checks and balances)* What is the senator implying? *(that the media increase the president's power dangerously)* **OL** **AL**

Hands-On Chapter Project

Step 1

Political Processes George W. Bush, not known for holding frequent press conferences in Washington, D.C., often met with the press at his Crawford, Texas, ranch. *What do you think makes a reporter rate a press conference as worthwhile?*

The relationship between the media and U.S. government officials, however, is complex. They need to work together, but their jobs often place them in adversarial positions. Politicians want to use the mass media to help them reach their goals, such as getting reelected and convincing the public that their policies are worthwhile. Politicians also want the media to pass on their messages just as the politicians present them.

The President and the Media

The president and the mass media, especially television, have a mutually beneficial relationship. As one of the most powerful government officials in the world, the president is a great source of news. Almost 80 percent of all U.S. television coverage of government officials focuses on the president. The mass media, in turn, offer presidents the best way to "sell" their ideas and policies to the public.

D Franklin D. Roosevelt was the first president to master the use of broadcast media. Broadcast television did not exist at the time of his presidency, and most newspaper owners did not support him. Therefore, Roosevelt presented his ideas directly to the people with "fireside chats" over the radio. Roosevelt had an excellent speaking voice. Journalist David Halberstam later described the impact of a Roosevelt fireside chat:

> *He was the first great American radio voice. For most Americans of this generation, their first memory of politics would be of sitting by a radio and hearing that voice, strong, confident, totally at ease. . . . Most Americans in the previous 160 years had never even seen a President; now almost all of them were hearing him, in their own homes. It was . . . electrifying.*
> —David Halberstam, 1979

The era of television politics really began with the 1960 presidential debate between Nixon and Kennedy. All presidents since that time have paid great attention to their television image and their use of that medium. In 1970 Senator J. William Fulbright of Arkansas told Congress:

> *Television has done as much to expand the powers of the President as would a constitutional amendment formally abolishing the co-equality of the three branches of government.*
> —J. William Fulbright, 1970

The White House staff media advisers try to manage relations with the mass media by controlling the daily flow of information about the president. To do so, they use news releases and briefings, press conferences, background stories, leaks, and media events.

News Releases and Briefings

A government **news release** is a ready-made story prepared by officials for members of the press. It can be printed or broadcast word-for-word or used as background information. A news release usually has a dateline that states the earliest time it can be published.

During a **news briefing,** a government official makes an announcement or explains a policy, a decision, or an action. Briefings give reporters the chance to ask officials about news releases. The president's press secretary meets daily with the press to answer questions and to provide information on the president's activities.

Press Conferences

A press conference involves the news media's questioning of a high-level government official. Presidents have held press conferences since the days of Theodore Roosevelt.

Analyzing the Media

Step 1: Analyzing Editorials Students will select an issue that is of current importance and analyze the coverage of the issue by several media. They will collect printed examples and notes from broadcast media for inclusion in a folder.

Directions Ask students to list on the board issues that are of national or international importance. Each student will select one of the issues to research and begin compiling a folder of media coverage of the issue. Then have

students find a newspaper or a newsmagazine editorial about the issue and print or photocopy it. Next to the editorial, they should write a paragraph that discusses the writer's point of view, the facts used to support the point of view, how objective the editorial is, and how effective it is.

Analyzing a Source Stimulate a class discussion by asking several students to share their paragraphs. **OL** **AL**

(Chapter Project continued in Section 2.)

Over the years, most presidential press conferences have been carefully planned events. In preparation for a press conference, the president often studies briefing books that identify potential questions. In addition, the White House can limit questions to certain topics, and aides may have friendly reporters ask specific questions that they want the president to address.

Other Means of Sharing Information

Sometimes the president or another top official, such as the secretary of state, will give reporters important pieces of information called *backgrounders.* Reporters can use the information in a story, but they cannot reveal their source. Reporters will make this kind of information public by saying, "Government sources said . . ." or "A senior White House official said . . ."

Backgrounders give government officials the opportunity to test new ideas or to send unofficial messages to other policy makers or even foreign governments. The media can, in this manner, make information public without making it official.

When officials give the media information that is totally off the record, reporters cannot print or broadcast the information. Off-the-record meetings can still be useful, however. Officials often establish valuable connections with newspapers in this way, and journalists might receive some tips to assist during their news coverage.

Another way top officials try to influence the flow of information to the press is through a **leak,** or the release of secret information to the media by anonymous government officials. These officials might be seeking public support for a policy that others in the government do not like. Sometimes low-level officials leak information to **expose** corruption or to get top officials to pay attention to a problem.

Media Events

Modern presidents often stage a **media event,** a visually interesting event designed to reinforce the president's position on some issue. A president who takes a strong stand against pollution, for example, makes a stronger statement by standing in front of a state-of-the-art, administration-supported manufacturing plant than by remaining in the Oval Office.

Media and Presidential Campaigns

Television impacts presidential campaigns. The first televised political advertisements appeared in the 1952 presidential campaign between Dwight Eisenhower and Adlai Stevenson. Since then, television has greatly influenced who runs for office, how candidates are nominated, how election campaigns are conducted, and how political parties fit into the election process.

Linking ★ Past & Present

Fireside Chats President Franklin Delano Roosevelt tried to give the people the feeling that they were participating in the government's decision-making process. He did this by taking his programs to the people via radio in the form of "fireside chats." On Sunday evening, March 12, 1933, just eight days after his inauguration, President Roosevelt broadcast his first fireside chat to announce the reopening of the banks. He began his chats with "my friends" and then proceeded to seemingly open his heart to millions of Americans. A Brooklyn, New York, resident described Roosevelt's chats as making him feel ". . . that he [Roosevelt] walked into my home, sat down, and in plain and forceful language explained to me how he was tackling the job I and my fellow citizens gave him."

Caption Answer: No, more likely they appeal to people with more extreme views or to those who "live and breathe" politics.

Talking Heads

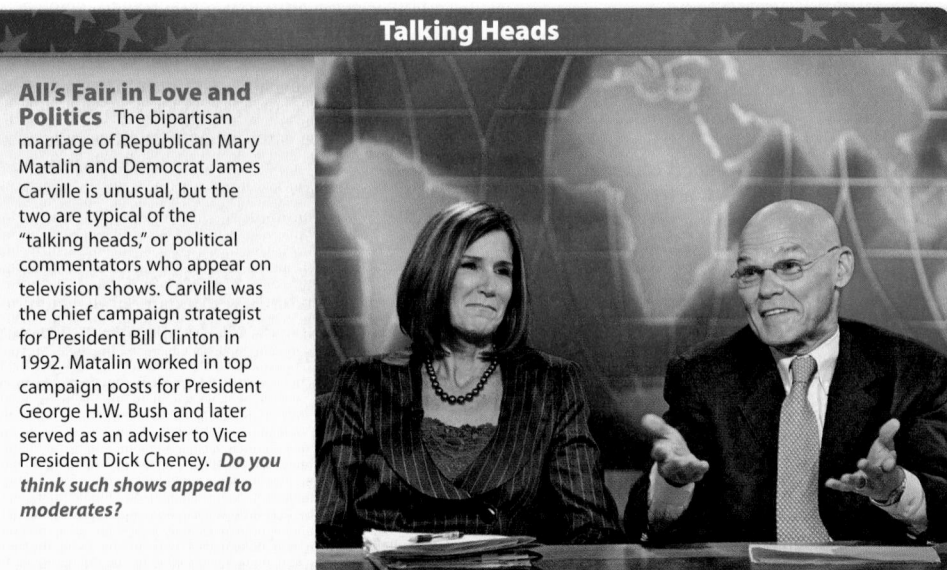

All's Fair in Love and Politics The bipartisan marriage of Republican Mary Matalin and Democrat James Carville is unusual, but the two are typical of the "talking heads," or political commentators who appear on television shows. Carville was the chief campaign strategist for President Bill Clinton in 1992. Matalin worked in top campaign posts for President George H.W. Bush and later served as an adviser to Vice President Dick Cheney. *Do you think such shows appeal to moderates?*

CHAPTER 19: *Mass Media and the Internet* **529**

Differentiated Instruction

Activity: Multiple Learning Styles

Verbal/Linguistic Have students imagine that they are news reporters attending a press conference given by the president of the United States on a current topic. Students should list five questions they would ask of the president at the press conference. Remind students that questions should not only be difficult and answerable, but also potentially controversial and politically charged. Call on volunteers to read their questions aloud and to explain why each question is important. You might want to elaborate on this activity by having individuals or groups of students take turns playing the role of the president to answer students' questions. **OL**

We the People
Making a Difference

Lloyd Newman and LeAlan Jones LeAlan Jones and Lloyd Newman's year-long investigation of the Eric Morse murder included interviews with the prosecutors and public defenders who were involved in the case. They also interviewed the head of the Chicago Housing Authority and housing security officers who knew the killer. *Our America* draws from more than 100 hours of taped interviews, conversations, and monologues that were not included in the original National Public Radio (NPR) documentaries.

Activity: Have students write an outline for a book they would propose to publish. Ask pairs to identify issues they could write about from firsthand experience to use as the topic of the book. Encourage students to think of issues that are likely to interest readers. **OL**

We the People
Making a Difference

When LeAlan Jones and Lloyd Newman were both 13 years old, a producer from National Public Radio (NPR) approached them and asked them to document what it was like to live among the poverty and violence of Chicago's South Side. Armed with tape recorders, the two friends interviewed people who lived in and around the Ida B. Wells housing project and also recorded their own experiences. The result was a 30-minute radio documentary titled "Ghetto Life 101." The documentary won many national and international awards.

In 1994 Newman and Jones created another documentary to tell the tragic story of a murder in the Ida B. Wells housing project: Two young boys threw Eric Morse, a 5-year-old boy, out of a 14-story window when he refused to steal candy for them. Jones said their goal was "to expose how violence has spread to younger age groups and to find ways to prevent this kind of crime from recurring." In the documentary, titled "Remorse: The 14 Stories of Eric Morse," the two teens interviewed friends and neighbors who knew the victim and the suspects. They also recorded an interview with Eric Morse's mother, who refused to talk to anyone in the media except them. Their second documentary won another series of awards, including the prestigious Robert F. Kennedy Journalism Award and the Peabody Award.

The two teens have given a voice to the people of Chicago's projects. In 1997 they published their first book, *Our America: Life and Death on the South Side of Chicago.*

> "[Our goal was] to find ways to prevent this kind of crime from recurring."
> —LeAlan Jones

Identifying Candidates

Television has influenced the types of candidates who run for office in several ways. First, candidates for major offices must be "telegenic"—that is, they must project a pleasing appearance and performance on camera. John F. Kennedy and Ronald Reagan were examples of good candidates for the television age. They had strong features and good speaking voices, and they projected the cool, low-key style that goes over well on television.

Second, television has made it much easier for people who are political unknowns to gain exposure and quickly become serious candidates for major offices. For example, Bill Clinton was not well-known when he addressed a national television audience at the Democratic convention in 1988. Four years later, as governor of Arkansas, he ran successfully for the Democratic nomination. In 1992 his campaign organization made skillful use of television. By the time the nominating convention met, Clinton had won enough primary elections to capture his party's nomination.

Third, television has encouraged celebrities from a wide variety of fields to enter politics. In recent years, actors, astronauts, professional athletes, and television **commentators** have run successfully for Congress and for governorships. Since voters are familiar with such people from seeing them on television, these candidates have instant name recognition, which often aids them greatly in getting elected.

The Presidential Nominating Process

The mass media have fundamentally changed the nomination process for president through horse-race coverage of elections, especially primaries. This approach focuses on winners and losers, and on who is ahead nearly as much as on issues and policy positions.

Early presidential primaries are critically important to a candidate's chances, even though the voters in these primaries represent only a small fraction of the national electorate. The media declare a candidate who wins an early primary,

---

★ ★ Activity: Interdisciplinary Connection ★ ★

Technology Make available to students a copy of the Morse code alphabet and current newspaper articles. Have each student use the Morse code alphabet to tap out a brief sentence from an article for the class to interpret. Discuss with students the communications process and its difficulties. Then compare the telegraph with current communications technology such as cellular phones, the Internet, and so on. **OL**

Additional Support

even if by a very small margin, a **front-runner,** or early leader. The press largely determines the weight attached to being a front-runner. The label carries great significance, however, because it is much easier for front-runners to attract the millions of dollars in loans and campaign contributions as well as the volunteer help they need to win the long, grueling nominating process.

The last time a party gathered for its nominating convention without knowing for certain who its nominee would be was in 1976, when Republican incumbent president Gerald Ford narrowly won a first-ballot nomination over Ronald Reagan. In 2008 Arizona Senator John McCain won enough primaries by March to become the presumptive nominee of the Republican Party. Senators Hillary Clinton and Barack Obama staged a tough primary campaign for the Democratic nomination. Even so, Obama locked up the nomination several months before their party's convention in August.

With the nominees in place, convention planners have time to produce a huge, made-for-television production. Both Democrats and Republicans run carefully scripted programs with celebrities, music, and videos. Because the drama of choosing a nominee is missing, however, television audience ratings have fallen. As a result, the networks have decided to carry less convention coverage because the conventions are not "news."

Campaign Advertising

Television also has affected how candidates communicate with the voters. The first candidates in American history did little campaigning; they left such work to political supporters. Andrew Jackson's election started the "torchlight era," in which candidates gave stump speeches and provided parades and expensive entertainment for voters and supporters. Around 1900, candidates began using advertisements in newspapers and magazines and mass mailings of campaign literature. In 1924 candidates began radio campaigning, and in 1952 television campaigning began with Eisenhower.

Television campaigns use **spot advertising,** the same basic technique that television uses to sell other products. Spot advertisements are brief (30 seconds to 2 minutes), frequent, positive descriptions of the candidate or the candidate's major platform points. Advertisements also might present negative images of the opposing candidate.

Financing TV Advertising

The television advertising that has become such a necessary part of a political campaign is not cheap. Candidates rely on extensive fund-raising efforts to afford the huge fees needed to pay for sophisticated television advertising campaigns. One 30-second commercial in a medium-size market can cost

Government ONLINE
Student Web Activity Visit glencoe.com and enter **QuickPass**™ code USG9822c19. Click on Student Web Activity and complete the activity about how media impact government.

Internet Political Influence

An Informed Electorate?
In its advertisements, YouTube tells readers to "Broadcast Yourself." The ability to do so has given a new dimension to political campaigns. *How does the cartoonist view the YouTube audience and its effect on the electorate? Do you agree with the characterization?*

ISSUES to Debate

Television and Elections Much of the money spent on political campaigns pays for television advertising and program time. Campaigns seek to get the candidate featured on the nightly news by staging media events. Have students discuss whether controls ought to be placed on television or on campaigns using television. If so, discuss what types of controls might be implemented and how such controls should be enforced. Be sure to provide equal time for those students who do not believe in controls to state and argue their positions. **AL**

Government ONLINE
Objectives and answers to the Student Web Activity can be found in the **Web Activity Lesson Plan** at glencoe.com. Enter **QuickPass**™ code USG9085c19T.

Caption Answer: The audience and electorate are seen as more interested in entertainment than issues. Students should defend their answers.

Additional Support

Extending the Content

Freedom of the Media Only about one-fifth of the world's people live in countries where the news media are free from government control. In most countries, the government owns at least one television and radio network, but in free societies most government-owned stations have nearly complete freedom in presenting news. All governments keep some material secret for national security reasons. Most governments around the world regulate the media. For example, Iran outlaws "insult to religion" and "propaganda against the state." China directly controls the press through its Central Propaganda Department and extensive regulations. Brazil restricts criticism of politicians.

Linking ★ Past & Present

The McCarthy Hearings The first major congressional event to be televised live was the McCarthy hearings, which took place from April 22 to June 17, 1954. Joseph R. McCarthy, a second-term Republican senator from Wisconsin, began his quest to ferret out Communists in the government by claiming that he had a list of 205 State Department employees who were members of the Communist Party. However, his televised emotional outburst convinced Americans that McCarthy was a bully and an extremist.

R Reading Strategy

Analyzing Text Structure
Have students use the Internet to find an excerpt of a speech or statement by Joseph McCarthy and find the words, phrases, or statements that demonstrate bias, an emotional "pitch," or faulty logic. An excellent place to start is the Web site http://historymatters. gmu.edu/d/6456. **Ask:** What words, phrases, or statements give you clues to McCarthy's methods? Why? *(Answers will vary depending on the excerpt.)* **OL**

Differentiated Instruction

Cooperative Learning Activities, p. 11

---

several thousand dollars. It has been estimated that a senator must raise more than $7,500 per week for six years to pay for a reelection campaign. Most of the money goes to television ads. Reed Hundt, chairperson of the Federal Communications Commission, summed up the problem:

❝ *The cost of TV time-buys makes fundraising an enormous entry barrier for candidates for public office, an oppressive burden for incumbents who seek reelection, a continuous threat to the integrity of our political institutions, and a principal cause of the erosion of public respect for public service.* ❞
—Reed Hundt, 1995

Political Parties

Television has weakened the role of political parties as the key **link** between politicians and the voters in national politics. It also has made candidates less dependent on their political party organization. Today it is television rather than political parties that provides most of the political news for people who are interested in politics. Voters can get the information they need to decide how to vote without depending on the party organization.

Television also lets candidates appeal directly to the people, bypassing party leadership. Should a candidate do well in the primary elections, the political party has little choice but to nominate him or her even if party leaders would rather nominate someone else. Finally, television advertising requires so much money that candidates cannot depend solely on their party to provide needed campaign funds. They must approach other donors if they are to run a competitive campaign and win an election.

Congress and the Media

Thousands of reporters have press credentials to cover the House and Senate. Several hundred spend all their time on Congress. Most congressional coverage focuses on individual lawmakers and is published mainly in their home states. The news stories usually feature the local angle of national news stories.

Nearly every member of Congress has a press secretary to prepare press releases, arrange interviews, and give out television tapes. Congress, however, gets less media coverage than the president because of the nature of its work. Most important congressional work takes place in committees and subcommittees over long periods of time. Congress's

---

slow, complicated work rarely meets television's requirements for dramatic, entertaining news.

Of course, no single congressional leader can speak for all 535 members of Congress. Nationally known lawmakers often are seen as spokespersons for their political party rather than for Congress. When Congress is in the news, newspapers and television reporters tend to focus on a controversial issue, such as confirmation hearings, oversight activities, or the personal lives of members.

Confirmation Hearings

The Constitution requires Congress to confirm presidential appointments to high government posts. The Senate usually holds hearings to review such nominations. The most controversial hearings attract wide media coverage. Sometimes the media uncover damaging information about an appointee. In 1989, for example, President George H.W. Bush nominated former senator John Tower to be his secretary of defense. Media investigations contributed to harsh criticism of Tower's alleged alcoholism and marital problems. Despite having a solid legislative record, Tower became the first cabinet nominee to be rejected by the Senate in 30 years.

Oversight Activities

In its oversight role, Congress has the power to review how the executive branch enforces laws and carries out programs. Oversight is handled through routine hearings, but sometimes lawmakers uncover a major scandal. Such investigations have become some of the biggest stories in American politics. In 1987, for example, Congress created a committee to investigate the secret sale of arms to Iran by Reagan White House aides and the use of money from the arms sale to support the contras, a rebel group in Nicaragua. Millions of viewers watched the nationally televised hearings.

Personal Business

The media also look for scandals in the personal lives of members of Congress. Until recently, the media usually overlooked personal problems of lawmakers. Now, however, even powerful lawmakers might not escape media attention. For example, under media scrutiny, in 1994 future Speaker of the House Newt Gingrich returned to the publisher a large cash advance for a book he was writing.

C-SPAN Television

By the late 1970s, congressional leaders realized that they were losing to presidents in the never-

---

Exploring an Issue

Objective: Get students to see how political "talk shows" are structured to explore an issue from different points of view.

Focus/Teach: Have students carry out the group activity.

Assess: Have students complete the Group Process Questions on page 12.

Close: Ask students to discuss their perceptions of such TV shows now that the activity is completed.

Differentiated Instruction Strategies

BL Ask students to identify two political talk shows and the guests who appeared on them in a given week.

AL Ask students to compare the political point of view of two separate talk shows.

ELL Ask students to identify and try to define the words common to political debate on a given issue.

Setting the Agenda

Press Influence The book *Setting the Agenda* by Maxwell McCombs describes how the press influences what people will think *about* (not *what* they will think). Television journalists like CNN's Wolf Blitzer (right) and PBS's Gwen Ifill (left) often set the agenda. *How might journalistic standards influence agenda setting?*

setting the agenda
the mass media and public opinion

maxwell mccombs

POLITICAL PROFILES **Lucinda Frank** (1946–) was the first woman to receive the Pulitzer Prize for national reporting. A freelance writer, she shared the 1971 Pulitzer with journalist Thomas Powers for "The Making of a Terrorist." At the time Franks received the award, she was also the youngest person to ever win it.

Did You Know?

The term *fourth estate* is sometimes used to describe the media. This name comes from the three estates of feudal Europe: the clergy, the nobility, and the commoners. This term dates back to the eighteenth century when it was coined by Edmund Burke, a British political philosopher. He observed that in the reporters' gallery of the British Parliament, "there sat a Fourth Estate more important by far than them all."

ending struggle for more media coverage, especially on television. In 1979 the House began allowing closed-circuit television coverage of floor debates, and in 1986 the Senate began allowing television coverage of Senate debates. The floor proceedings of the House and Senate are now regularly broadcast to lawmakers' offices and to cable television subscribers across the nation via Cable-Satellite Public Affairs Network (C-SPAN).

Congressional Recording Studios

Both the House and Senate have extensive recording studios so lawmakers can prepare broadcasts. The tapes that are made are then sent to the lawmakers' hometown stations for local news or public affairs programs.

The Court and the Media

Most Americans depend upon the mass media to learn about Supreme Court decisions. Yet the Supreme Court and lower federal courts receive much less media coverage than Congress or the president. During a recent Supreme Court term, for example, the *New York Times* reported on only three-fourths of the Court's decisions. Other newspapers covered fewer than half of the Court's cases.

Major newspapers and television and radio networks assign reporters to cover the Supreme Court. However, the judicial branch gets less coverage because of the remoteness of judges and the technical nature of the issues with which the Court deals. Broadcast media are even less likely to report court decisions than newspapers because broadcast news does not allow time to explain issues in depth, and television news must be highly visual. Furthermore, since no broadcast cameras or microphones are allowed inside the Supreme Court, the broadcast media are unable to obtain images and footage of proceedings to show their audience.

Remoteness of Judges

Since they are appointed officials, Supreme Court justices and other federal judges do not need publicity like elected politicians. Judges must remain unbiased, and publicity might interfere with their objectivity. They rarely appear on radio or television, although Justice Clarence Thomas often appears on C-SPAN to talk about how the Court works.

Technical Issues

The Court receives less coverage than other branches of government for another reason. The Supreme Court handles issues that are complex

Additional Support

Extending the Content

Coverage of Congress In the early days of Congress, no reliable account was kept of House or Senate speeches. Newspapers or shorthand companies reported the debates only sporadically. Both chambers now make available gavel-to-gavel television coverage of floor activity. Television viewers get an entirely different picture than do readers of the *Congressional Record,* which has kept a substantially verbatim account since 1873.

C Critical Thinking

Drawing Conclusions
Students can understand the concept of agenda setting by exploring a current issue in the news. Students should get teacher approval of an issue they will monitor on three television news shows for a week. **Ask:** What agenda was the media setting on this particular issue? Did you see a common theme among the different stations? *(Answers will vary, but students should correctly connect agenda setting to the television treatment.)* **AL**

Assess

Assign the Section 1 Assessment as homework or as an in-class activity, or have students take Section Quiz 19-1 from *Section Quizzes and Chapter Tests.*

Close

Outlining Ask students to create a graphic organizer illustrating the media's relationship to different sectors of government. **OL**

Section 1 Review

and abstract, which means that many of the issues interest only a small minority. The Court also has a tradition that its judicial opinions must speak for themselves. Thus, justices do not hold news conferences to explain their rulings and answer questions.

Setting the Public Agenda

The mass media play an important role in setting the public agenda, a list of societal problems that both political leaders and citizens agree need government attention. The wars in Iraq and Afghanistan, aid to the homeless, long-term health care for children and the elderly, teenage substance abuse, and high crime rates are all problems that have been part of the public agenda.

The media's role in setting the public agenda is not to determine how these social problems will be solved but to bring these issues to the attention of the public and the government. The media highlight the importance of some problems over others. In this way, the media help determine which political issues the American people and their leaders will be discussing.

Networks and the Issues

How do the media decide what to cover? The likely size of the audience is part of the answer. This is especially true for television. Each network competes to attract the biggest audience in a viewing market since a larger audience allows it to charge higher advertising rates. Thus, a network might cover a high-profile political scandal instead of the federal budget because they know most people will quickly switch to another channel if they report on budget details at length.

In turn, the extent of media coverage will influence how the public ranks the importance of an issue to the nation. As Bernard Cohen, a foreign policy expert, noted in 1963: "The mass media may not be successful in telling their audience what to think, but the media are stunningly successful in telling their audience what to think about." A study of media coverage of the Vietnam War, for example, found that the content of news stories on the war had less impact on people than the sheer amount of coverage. Thus, the study suggested that opinion on the war was not based on a complete understanding but rather on the media's focus on the war.

Attitudes and Values

The media have an even more basic effect on political attitudes and values. First, they play a role in political socialization, the process through which people form such values and attitudes. Although most of a person's political socialization comes from family, social class, and peer groups, the media, especially television, convey messages about war and peace, crime, and many other topics. Second, media reporting is usually on negative events like political corruption or party wrangling. For this reason, viewers may get a negative view of politics. In fact, some observers refer to "television malaise," a feeling of cynicism toward government. People who rely on television as their main news source have more negative attitudes toward government and politics than people who do not.

SECTION 1 Review

Vocabulary

1. **Explain** the significance of: mass media, news release, news briefing, leak, media event, front-runner, spot advertising.

Main Ideas

2. **Describing** How has the mass media changed the presidential nominating process with horse-race coverage?

3. **Summarizing** Why are television networks reducing coverage of nominating conventions?

Critical Thinking

4. **Formulating Questions** Write three questions that should be asked in order to determine whether the media challenges government actions effectively.

5. **Organizing** Use a graphic organizer like the one below to identify how media impact government.

	Impact of Media
1. President	
2. Congress	
3. Courts	

Writing About Government

6. **Descriptive Writing** Create a political cartoon that describes the role of the mass media in forming ideas about government, politicians, and national and international events. Then examine another student's cartoon and write a brief summary of the similarities and differences between the two cartoons.

Answers

1. All definitions can be found in the section and the Glossary.
2. Declaring winners of early primaries as front-runners, even if their margin of victory is small, helps those early winners gain campaign contributions and national attention.
3. Because the nominees are already chosen before the convention, the networks believe the conventions are not "news" and, therefore, deserve less coverage than they used to get.

4. Questions will vary but should ask whether the media inform the public truthfully, protect public interest, influence public opinion, provide a fairly unbiased viewpoint, serve as many people as possible, and so on.
5. Answers might include: President—media shape image, communications with public, and campaigns; Congress—media coverage of congressional hearings and debates helps members be aware of constituents'

concerns; Court—largely independent of media coverage and public opinion
6. Students' cartoons will vary but should clearly demonstrate their personal views and should consider all forms of media mentioned in the activity.

Should News Programs Adhere to Journalistic Standards?

When the major networks dominated television in the 1960s and 1970s, news programs reflected a commitment to the same goals and standards of accuracy and fairness as daily newspapers. Television airtime focused on major political developments or breaking world news. It was relatively rare to see human interest or celebrity stories, and the difference between news and entertainment was clear. Today's news organizations increasingly feature entertainment that critics have dubbed "infotainment"—their name for what they see as entertainment disguised as news. Defenders say current programs are providing what the public wants—more topics that are relevant to their personal lives, including health and consumer news, as well as information about sports and movies. Critics say this "soft" journalism weakens democracy.

YES

News publishers and broadcasters have enormous power to determine what the public will think about. By the topics they choose to cover, they set the public agenda and determine which of the nation's problems get attention. For example, how campaigns are financed has a huge impact on who is elected, but news programs do not devote much time to the subject. In the 1990s, people thought the crime rate was rising, not falling, just because crimes were played up in the news. "Infotainment" does not train citizens how to think seriously about national policy. Instead we have "chatfests"—a show like *The View*, hosted by Barbara Walters, is a perfect example. Democracy cannot survive without a free press. The media have an obligation to provide the balanced news reports that help citizens govern themselves.

NO

If people want "hard" news, they can find it. What people say the media *should* present and what they will actually watch or read are two different things. The only thing that gets a bigger audience than sex, violence, or the paranormal is a scandal that includes all three—preferably involving a celebrity. This has been true for as long as public media have existed. Even in the 1700s in England, there was a popular scandal-sheet called the *National Tattler*. It is human nature to want to be entertained and not just informed, especially after a hard day's work. Competition from cable television and the Internet means that the major networks must aggressively pursue the ratings that will get them advertising revenues. Media companies are businesses whose goal is to make a profit. "Infotainment" sells.

Debating the Issue

1. **Identifying** Why does the "Yes" argument say the media use "infotainment"? How does the "No" argument counter that claim?

2. **Summarizing** Summarize the argument against "infotainment."

3. **Deciding** With which opinion do you agree? Explain your reasoning, and give examples of the difference between "infotainment" and hard news.

▶ Cast of *The View*

Debating the Issue Answers

1. The "Yes" argument does not cite a reason for infotainment; it only refers to "chatfests" such as *The View*. The "No" argument states simply that infotainment sells. The news is a business, and programmers are in it to make money.

2. The mass media have an obligation to present a balanced report of the most important news stories to help train the public how to think critically about national policy. Infotainment merely entertains and does not educate.

3. Students should state a position and clearly defend it.

Teach

Setting Up the Debate

Speculating Have students compile a list of "infotainment" sources and a list of "hard" news sources. **Ask:** Is there any shortage of either one? *(Students probably will have no problem finding many sources for both kinds of news.)* Now have students read or watch a couple of stories or segments from an infotainment source and from a hard news source. **Ask:** What is different about the subject matter in each? Is anything similar? *(Students might point out that infotainment often features stories about celebrities, and hard news usually features politics, global economics, and so on.)*

Evaluating Have students research the arguments for and against adherence to journalistic standards. Students should give specific arguments to support both points of view.

Concluding the Debate

Discuss these questions with students:

- Have students brainstorm two lists of topics: (1) the stories that should be covered in hard news programs, and (2) the stories that should be covered in infotainment programs. Are there stories that could be common to both? Is there any way to generalize the subject matter for each list?

- Why do violence and celebrities tend to attract larger audiences than campaign spending, political debates, and public policy?

535

Focus

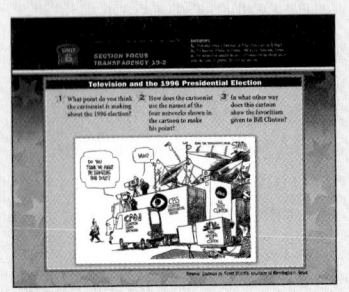
Reader's Guide

Answers to Graphic:

Regulating Broadcast Media: fining stations, granting licenses, ensuring diverse ownership of media

Resource Manager

Regulating Print and Broadcast Media

Reader's Guide

Content Vocabulary
★ prior restraint *(p. 537)*
★ libel *(p. 537)*
★ shield law *(p. 537)*
★ fairness doctrine *(p. 538)*

Academic Vocabulary
★ source *(p. 537)*
★ via *(p. 539)*
★ format *(p. 540)*

Reading Strategy
As you read, create a table similar to the one below to list the ways the Federal Communications Commission regulates broadcast media.

Regulating Broadcast Media

Issues in the News

Congress and the Federal Communications Commission (FCC) set in motion a technological change that affected all Americans. Beginning in June 2009, Congress decreed that all television stations had to switch from analog to digital broadcasting. It was one of the rare times that the government's power over communications was obvious. Why the change? The FCC wanted to free up the analog broadcast frequencies for improved wireless services and emergency communications. In fact, only a minority of citizens who relied on over-the-air signals (through rabbit ears or rooftop aerials) were affected. For them, it meant buying a set-top converter box and the government offered coupons to help cover the cost of the equipment.

▲ The FCC logo

Despite the regulatory powers of the federal government, the mass media in the United States have more freedom than anywhere else in the world. Such freedom has given rise to many diverse avenues of expression. Of these, Internet communications and cable television are among the fastest growing. The goal of government regulations is to provide order, fairness, and access to the mass media.

Protecting the Media

The First Amendment says in part that "Congress shall make no law . . . abridging the freedom . . . of the press." The guarantee of this freedom is fundamental to democracy. Thomas Jefferson described the importance of a free press when he argued:

> 66 *The people are the only censors of their governors. . . . [T]he only safeguard of the public liberty . . . is to give them full information of their affairs [through] the channel of the public papers, & to contrive that those papers should penetrate the whole mass of the people.* 99

—Thomas Jefferson, 1787

R Reading Strategies	C Critical Thinking	D Differentiated Instruction	W Writing Support	S Skill Practice
Teacher Edition • Outlining, p. 539 **Additional Resources** • Guid. Read. Act., p. 69 • Quizzes/Tests, p. 234	**Teacher Edition** • Evaluating, p. 537 **Additional Resources** • Read. Essen., pp. 218–220	**Teacher Edition** • Verbal/Linguistic, p. 538 **Additional Resources** • Foldables, p. 62 • Supreme Ct. Case Studies, pp. 109–110	**Teacher Edition** • Expository Writing, p. 537 **Additional Resources** • Part. in Gov. Act., pp. 37–38	**Teacher Edition** • Interviewing, p. 537 **Additional Resources** • Inter. Poli. Cartoons, pp. 37–38

Free Press Guaranteed

In the United States, the First Amendment means that print media are free from **prior restraint,** or government censorship of information before it is published. Over the years, the Supreme Court has struck down attempts to give government prior restraint powers. These decisions mean that editors and reporters have freedom to decide what goes in or stays out of their publications.

Libel

Freedom of the press, however, is not absolute. Falsely written statements intended to damage a person's reputation are called **libel.** People who believe that falsehoods in a published story have damaged their careers or reputations may sue for libel. However, it is almost impossible for a public official to win a libel suit. The reason, in part, is because there is no law against criticizing government officials.

Public figures who believe they have been libeled may file a libel suit to discourage the press from continuing to write stories about them. If taken to court, publishers must prove that they intended to tell the truth. Defending against a libel suit can be very expensive. Also, public officials who file libel suits may win sympathy from the public, who sometimes resent the way journalists report the news.

The Right to Gather Information

Freedom for the media to publish whatever they want means little if they cannot collect information about government actions and decisions. If government officials tell lies, hold secret meetings, or try to limit reporters' access to information in other ways, the media may not be able to provide the information citizens need. Does the First Amendment give the media special rights of access to courtrooms or government offices? Further, does it give reporters special protection for their news **sources**—the people they consult to get information?

The Right of Access

The press has gone to court many times to fight for its right of access to information on the decisions of government. The results have been mixed. Generally the Supreme Court has rejected the idea that the media have special rights of access. In 1965, for example, in *Zemel* v. *Rusk,*[1] the Court ruled that "the right to speak and publish does not

carry with it the unrestrained right to gather information." A similar ruling came down in 1972 in *Branzburg* v. *Hayes*[2] when the Court decided that "the First Amendment does not guarantee the press a constitutional right of special access to information not available to the public generally."

The lower courts have been more supportive of the right of access. In the last decade, the media filed more than 200 right-of-access lawsuits. They won access in about 60 percent of these cases.

Despite such victories in the lower courts, authorities do not have to give the media special right of access to crime or disaster sites if the general public is excluded, although they usually do. Reporters may be kept out of legislative sessions that are closed to the general public. Neither do reporters have special access to grand jury proceedings.

Protection of Sources

Reporters often need secret informants when investigating government officials, political radicals, or criminals. Success in gathering news may depend on getting information from people who do not want their names made public. If the courts, the police, or legislatures force reporters to name their sources, these sources of information may vanish. On the other hand, criminals may go unpunished if reporters do not give police information about them.

The press and the U.S. government have fought many battles over the media's right to keep sources secret. As you read in Chapter 13, more than half the states have **shield laws** to protect reporters from having to reveal their sources. While no federal shield law exists, the Privacy Protection Act of 1980 prevents all levels of government from searching for and seizing source documentation, except in a few circumstances.

Regulating Broadcast Media

In the United States, most mass media are private, money-making businesses. Like other businesses, they are subject to some government regulation. The federal government has more power to regulate the broadcast media than the print media largely because broadcast media must share public airwaves.

See the following footnoted materials in the **Reference Handbook:**
1. *Zemel* v. *Rusk* case summary, page R37.
2. *Branzburg* v. *Hayes* case summary, page R24.

Teach

C Critical Thinking

Evaluating Ask: Do you think that public figures should have a harder time winning a libel suit than the average person? Why or why not? (*Answers will vary. Students should defend their answers.*) **OL**

S Skill Practice

Interviewing Ask students to interview reporters who cover the political beat for local newspapers, radio stations, or television stations. Interview questions should elicit answers that will provide a description of the day-to-day life of a political reporter. **OL**

W Writing Support

Expository Writing Tell students that journalists have at times faced a jail sentence to protect the identity of a source. Have students research a case in which a journalist refused to reveal his or her source. Ask students to write a one-page report on the case. **OL**

Additional Support

★ Activity: Collaborative Learning ★

Role Playing a Court Hearing Organize the class into groups of four to role-play a court hearing concerning a libel suit against a newspaper reporter. Have students choose from the following roles: newspaper reporter, plaintiff who is a major public figure, the judge, and court reporter. Have groups write a dialogue for the court hearing in which the judge will read the case aloud, and the reporter and the plaintiff will each tell their side of the story. The defendant and the plaintiff should cite a law or an amendment to support their sides of the story. Have the class act as the jury to rule on the case. Allow the court reporter to read back any information the jury needs to make its decision. **OL**

ISSUES to Debate

Regulation versus Deregulation

Discuss the benefits and liabilities of government regulation of an industry that is of interest to students, such as video games. Then allow students to choose sides and debate the issue of government regulation of mass media. **AL**

D Differentiated Instruction

Verbal/Linguistic Have students conduct interviews of two different age groups to test public opinion on network coverage. As background, discuss the fairness doctrine and explain how the expansion of media outlets (cable and satellite stations, for example) led the FCC to end this rule. Then have students identify four younger people and four older people to interview about their perceptions. Finally, craft the questions with students. **OL**

Additional Support

The Value of Public Pressure

Broadcasting Standards
In 2007 the Rutgers women's basketball team—all freshmen—went all the way to the championship final. A radio talk show host who commented negatively on their accomplishment was fired because of public disapproval. *How do advertisers play a role when the public makes its opinions clear as it did in this situation?*

The Federal Communications Commission

In 1934 Congress created the Federal Communications Commission (FCC). The FCC is a government agency with authority to regulate interstate and international communications by radio, television, telephone, telegraph, cable, and satellite. The FCC has five commissioners appointed by the president with Senate approval. Each commissioner serves a five-year term.

The FCC has broad powers to make rules that require stations to operate in the public interest. The most important power is the power to grant licenses to all radio and television stations in the country. The FCC's two major regulatory activities deal with the content of broadcasts and with ownership of the media.

Content Regulation

The FCC cannot censor broadcasts. It can, however, influence the content of broadcasts by fining stations that violate rules and by threatening not to renew a station's license. Over the years, the extent of FCC content regulation has varied in response to developments in technology, court rulings, and changes in political ideas about the proper role of government.

For example, during Ronald Reagan's presidency in the 1980s, the FCC took many steps to deregulate broadcasting by cutting hundreds of content rules. Rules limiting the amount of advertising were ended, and bans on commercials during children's shows were removed. Requirements that

stations devote 10 percent of programming to news and public affairs also were eliminated.

Perhaps the most controversial change was removal of the **fairness doctrine.** This rule was established in 1949. It required broadcasters to provide airtime to both sides of a controversial issue. The doctrine was supposed to discourage one-sided coverage of issues and encourage stations to present a range of views.

The Supreme Court upheld the doctrine in 1969 in *Red Lion Broadcasting Co. v. FCC.*[1] The Court stated that the doctrine protected a "[free] marketplace of ideas in which truth will ultimately prevail." The Court added that this type of regulation was justified in the broadcast media because the airwaves are scarce. If print media such as newspapers presented one-sided coverage, the Court said, anyone could start another paper.

Some broadcasters and political activists claimed that the fairness doctrine was actually censorship. They argued that it caused stations to avoid reporting on any type of controversy. In 1987 the FCC decided to drop the fairness doctrine. Congress passed a law requiring the FCC to keep it, but President Reagan vetoed the bill, saying:

> 66 *This type of content-based regulation by the Federal Government is, in my judgment, antagonistic to the freedom of expression guaranteed by the First Amendment.* 99
> —President Ronald Reagan

See the following footnoted materials in the **Reference Handbook:**
1. *Red Lion Broadcasting Co. v. FCC* case summary, page R32.

Activity: Interdisciplinary Connection

Geography Have students choose a foreign country and research restrictions on the media in that country. Have each student report to the class what government regulations they found concerning radio broadcasting, television reporting, or newspaper or magazine journalism. **Ask:** How do other countries' restrictions compare with those placed on the media in the United States? **AL**

Reagan said the growth of cable television had added so many new outlets for different ideas that the scarcity argument no longer mattered.

Ownership Regulation

Given the power of the press, the federal government is also concerned with who owns media outlets. Owners can influence the messages their media present. The ownership issue is especially important for television, radio, and newspapers.

Shortly after its creation in 1934, the FCC began creating a complex set of rules to prevent the ownership of media from being concentrated in the hands of a few. For example, in 1941 the FCC said a company could not own more than eight radio stations in a single large market like Chicago or New York. In 1975 the FCC limited cross-ownership of media by stating that companies could no longer own both a newspaper and a television or radio station in the same market.

Those who supported these limits on ownership argued that democracy requires citizens to be exposed to a wide array of ideas. They also claimed that these limits promoted competition, which would make the industry more cost-efficient and affordable to consumers.

By the mid-1990s, however, attitudes about media ownership were changing dramatically. Emerging technologies made new business relationships in telecommunications possible. Telephone lines could carry the same signals that cable companies carried, and cable companies might eventually offer phone service. Both could offer Internet service, videoconferencing, and other services. Voice, data, video, and images could be transmitted **via** broadcast, narrowcast, or point-to-point services. Phone companies realized that if government policy permitted, their lines could carry many additional information services. Broadcasters had already invested in cable and wanted to expand.

Broadcast owners and many other communications interests pressured Congress to review media communications policy. Congress agreed that the time had come to review telecommunications regulations, and in 1996, it passed the Telecommunications Act.

Telecommunications Act of 1996

This law ended or relaxed many FCC limits on media ownership. For instance, the law removed any national limits on radio station ownership. It also removed limits on how many television stations a

Comparing Governments

Media Access, 2007*

Country	Televisions per 1,000 people	Radios per 1,000 people	Telephone Lines in Millions	Newspapers circulating per 1,000 people	Internet Users in millions
China	291	342	350.4	59.3	111
Iraq	82	229	1	N/A	0.036
Israel	328	524	3	N/A	3.2
Mexico	272	329	19.5	93.5	17
Russia	421	417	40.1	N/A	23.7
United States	844	2,116	177.9	196.3	203.8
Thailand	274	234	7	196.9	8.4
United Kingdom	661	1,437	33.7	326.4	37.8

* While figures are taken from a 2007 source, the statistics for each heading represent the most recent information cited in that source.   N/A = not available
Source: World Almanac Book of Facts, 2007.

Critical Thinking The United States leads the world in the number of televisions and radios per 1,000 people. *Which two countries have more newspapers circulating per 1,000 people than the United States?*

Participating
IN GOVERNMENT

Regulating Electronic Media
After students have read the provisions of the Telecommunications Act of 1996, have them evaluate what changes should be added to the act to bring it up to date with advances in technology. Ask students to write their recommended changes in the form of an amendment to the act. **OL**

R Reading Strategy

Outlining Ask students to make a chart listing the five issues the Telecommunications Act of 1996 addressed and how the provisions of the act resolved these issues. **BL**

Critical Thinking

Answer: Thailand and the United Kingdom

Research Activity
Have students research statistics on media access in five additional countries and create a graph or a table displaying the information. **OL**

Hands-On Chapter Project
Step 2

Analyzing the Media

Step 2: Comparing Broadcast Media
Remind students that about three-fourths of adults get their news primarily from television and radio. Students will compare broadcast media with opposing views of the issue they selected in Step 1.

Directions Ask students to add to their folders by watching or listening to two broadcast media and taking notes. One should be a conservative radio station; the other should be a public radio or television station, or one that takes an opposing view of the issue. Their notes should include the same elements as in Step 1: point of view, facts used to support it, objectivity, and effectiveness.

Comparing Have students write a paragraph in their folders comparing the two media, and ask several students to share their comparisons with the class. **OL AL**

(Chapter Project continued in Section 3.)

539

Linking ☆ Past & Present

Real-Life Television The 1980s and 1990s television public clamored for slice-of-life television, which mixes news with sensational journalism. Such shows as *Cops, Rescue 911,* and *America's Most Wanted* helped law enforcement officials track down hundreds of fugitive felons. Other mixed fact-with-fiction types of television shows were semi-biographical, made-for-television movies. Such movies as *The People vs. Jean Harris* (1981) and *Baby M* (1988) were based on subjects taken from headline news, often before all the facts of the case were revealed. Fictional dramas such as *Hill Street Blues* and *NYPD Blue* even began using facts from real-life events as the basis for their story lines.

Additional Support

The Internet and War Reporting

Defining News The Internet has changed reporting for journalists, but its availability allowed many American soldiers to blog and post images (some graphic) of their wartime experiences. *Is it logical for the public to conclude that a soldier's blog or images, rather than another media source, represent a more realistic assessment of how a war is going?*

company could own as long as the company controlled no more than 35 percent of the national market. It allowed cross-ownership of cable and broadcast stations and dropped some of the rate regulations for cable systems. Finally, Congress required the FCC to review ownership rules every two years. Since then the FCC has been conducting regular studies on ownership issues.

It can be difficult to predict the longer-term consequences of a new law. This is especially true for communications technology. The Telecommunications Act of 1996 is a prime example. One of its key objectives was to increase competition, yet contrary to what many predicted, it appears to have led to an even greater concentration of media ownership.

Since the 1996 Telecommunications Act, several media companies have merged to create communications giants. In 2000 America Online (AOL), the nation's largest Internet service provider, merged with Time Warner, the nation's second-largest cable system. Some critics worried because the merger gave the company nearly half the U.S. Internet market and more than 12 million cable subscribers. Ultimately the deal became known as a poor business move because AOL was already losing its appeal in the Internet market. In early 2008, Time Warner appeared to be moving toward spinning off the AOL segments of its business to cut its losses.

Media concentration in the wake of the 1996 legislation was greater in radio. Now only four companies claim two-thirds of all the listeners of news radio stations.

Policy makers and interest groups often disagree about whether the consequences of a new law are good or bad. Has consolidation in the radio broadcasting business given listeners more variety? Some say yes because companies that buy several stations eliminate duplication in reaching many different audiences. Others claim listeners have fewer choices. They note that today's pop music radio **formats** overlap—stations labeled rock, pop, or alternative actually play many of the same songs.

One goal of the Telecommunications Act was to combat the growth of violent and obscene content in the mass media. It prohibited obscene or harassing conversation on any telecommunications facility. The law also ordered the broadcast industry to rate objectionable programming so that parents could use the V-chip to block objectionable programs from their homes. All new televisions sold in the United States had to have the V-chip. But a number of studies have concluded that the V-chip approach has failed so far because parents either do not know they have a V-chip, they do not know how to use it, or they are not motivated to use it. The Telecommunications Act included a provision to amend the federal criminal code so that obscenity laws applied to Internet users. This part of the act, however, was struck down by the Supreme Court as an undue limitation on free speech.

Concerns with obscenity during the George W. Bush administration led to passage of the Broadcast Decency Enforcement Act of 2005, signed into law in 2006. It dramatically increased the penalties for obscene language, but as with any law, the question is how often such penalties are actually imposed. Thus far, no wholesale use of this penalty power of the FCC has occurred.

Activity: Interdisciplinary Connection

Cultural Life Have students research one type of media to locate a cultural issue that is currently being covered. Have them state what media is being used and outline the cultural nature of the issue, where the issue is taking place, and the effects of the actions being taken concerning the issue. Call on volunteers to give an overview of the information gathered and the effectiveness of the media through which it was gathered. **OL**

Media and National Security

Tension often arises between the government's need for secrecy in national security matters and the citizens' need for information. This is most obvious in foreign and military affairs where intelligence information is involved. The government controls this information by classifying some information as secret and by limiting press coverage of military actions. The government classifies many government documents as "secret." During the Vietnam War, for example, the *New York Times* published a secret Defense Department study on how the United States became involved in the war. The government tried to stop the publication. In *New York Times Co.* v. *United States*[1] (1971), the Supreme Court ruled that the publication did not harm national security. 📖

Government restriction on media coverage during wartime has varied. During the Vietnam War, there were few limits. Reporters roamed freely across combat zones, sometimes hitching rides on Army helicopters to get to a battle. During the 1991 Persian Gulf War, the Defense Department limited coverage to a small group of reporters, with most having to depend on official briefings for information. When the war in Iraq began in 2003, the Pentagon allowed 500 reporters to accompany troops into battle. These "embedded" journalists reported live on encounters, but they did not have complete freedom: They could not announce their exact location or where they were traveling. If they

War Reporting Jill Carroll, an embedded journalist during the war in Iraq, was well-known because, for a time, she was held hostage by enemy insurgents. *Are there drawbacks to embedded journalism?*

did, the military removed their embedded status. Critics worried that any reporter who shared the army life and grew close to the troops could lose objectivity. One journalism professor argued that growing close to soldiers can inhibit a reporter's ability to write anything negative about the war.

📖 *See the following footnoted materials in the **Reference Handbook**:*
1. *New York Times Co.* v. *United States* case summary, page R31.

SECTION 2 Review

Vocabulary

1. **Explain** the significance of: prior restraint, libel, shield law, fairness doctrine.

Main Ideas

2. **Explaining** Why does the federal government regulate broadcast media more than print media?

3. **Analyzing** Why have regulations on media ownership relaxed in recent decades?

Critical Thinking

4. **Synthesizing** Why might the need for national security conflict with the First Amendment protections that are usually given to the media?

5. **Organizing** Use a graphic organizer like the one below to show how the Telecommunications Act of 1996 affected the FCC.

```
Telecommunications
Act of 1996  →  [   ]
                [   ]
```

Writing About Government

6. **Expository Writing** Interview, write, or e-mail a local newspaper editor to find out what precautions the newspaper takes to prevent libel suits. Share the information you obtain with your classmates.

Answers

1. All definitions can be found in the section and the Glossary.
2. The federal government has more power to regulate broadcast media because it involves the use of public airwaves.
3. Advancing technology has forced the loosening of regulations.
4. Students' answers will vary but should focus on the tension between the need to protect national security and the need in a free society for people to send and to receive open and accurate information.
5. Answers might include that the FCC's regulation of media ownership was greatly relaxed and that the FCC was required to conduct studies on media ownership every two years.
6. Students should report their findings to the class.

Caption Answer: Answers will vary. Some drawbacks include the danger that embedded journalists face, the possibility that the government only embeds journalists in areas that are going well, and the inability to report all the facts freely.

🏛 **Landmark Case**

See *New York Times* v. *United States* in the Supreme Court Case Summaries in the **Reference Handbook** and Case Study 55 in the *Supreme Court Case Studies* booklet.

Assess

Assign the Section 2 Assessment as homework or as an in-class activity, or have students take Section Quiz 19-2 from *Section Quizzes and Chapter Tests*.

Close

Analyzing Challenge students to consider whether they think it is possible for a news report to be completely unbiased. Discuss the factors that lead to bias in the news. **OL**

Section 2 Review

Supreme Court Cases to Debate

Class Debate

Organize students into three groups. One group will argue that censorship of the Internet infringes upon First Amendment rights, and that such restrictions will have a stifling effect on the free exchange of ideas. Have another group argue that the government needs to regulate or censor the Internet to prevent children from being exposed to inappropriate content. The third group will serve as the jury and decide which side has made the more persuasive argument. **OL**

The Court's Decision

In the case of *Reno v. American Civil Liberties Union,* the Supreme Court unanimously ruled that parts of the CDA violated the First Amendment. The Court held that the act violated the First Amendment because it was a content-based ban on speech, and Congress failed to narrowly define "indecent" speech. The Court also held that the factors that allowed the government to subject radio and television to censorship did not apply in the case of the Internet.

Can the Government Regulate the Internet?
Reno v. American Civil Liberties Union, 1997

The First Amendment protects the right of freedom of speech, but that right is not absolute. Should the Internet be regulated to protect children from some material?

Facts of the Case

As access to the Internet became more widespread, some people believed it needed to be regulated to protect children from exposure to inappropriate material. In response, Congress passed the Communications Decency Act (CDA) in 1996. The CDA prohibited transmitting "patently offensive" or "indecent" material "in a manner available to a person under 18 years of age." A person found guilty of violating the law could be imprisoned for up to two years and fined up to $250,000.

The American Civil Liberties Union (ACLU) and several other groups argued that the law would have a chilling effect on free speech and violated the First Amendment rights of adults. Language or material that might be inappropriate for children could still be constitutionally protected speech.

The Constitutional Question

Broadcast radio and television have long been subject to censorship. The rationale behind the restrictions on broadcast media was that they were widely available to children who could happen across unsuitable or harmful content. Supporters of the CDA believed the Internet should be similarly censored. The ACLU challenged the constitutionality of the law before it could go into effect.

On June 13, 1996, a special Federal District Court declared that major parts of the CDA violated the First Amendment. The judges described the Internet as "the most participatory form of mass speech yet developed" and held that it deserved "the highest protection from governmental intrusion." The Justice Administration, headed by Attorney General Janet Reno, appealed.

Before the U.S. Supreme Court, the Justice Department argued that the Internet gives children "a free pass into the equivalent of every adult bookstore and every adult video store in the country," thus making "irrelevant all prior efforts" to shield children from such material. The ACLU argued that the CDA violated the First Amendment, insisting that the government "cannot constitutionally reduce the adult population to reading and viewing only what is appropriate for children."

Debating the Issue

Questions to Consider

1. Why did Congress pass the Communications Decency Act?
2. How might the CDA have a "chilling effect" on free speech?

You Be the Judge

Should government censor or regulate the Internet in order to protect children from sexually explicit or otherwise unsuitable content? Why or why not? If you do not believe the government should police the Internet, how do you suggest parents shield their children from inappropriate material?

▼ A cartoonist's view of the debate over Internet censorship

Debating the Issue Answers

Questions to Consider

1. to prevent children from accessing indecent material on the Internet
2. It would prevent adults from freely creating and reading content on the Internet out of fear that the material might be inappropriate for children.

You Be the Judge

Answers will vary, but students should decide whether they agree or disagree with the government's efforts to censor the Internet. Students should decide on a method to help parents shield their children from inappropriate material.

The Internet and Democracy

Reader's Guide

Content Vocabulary
* partisan (p. 544)
* electronic mailing list (p. 545)
* action alert (p. 546)
* electronic petition (p. 546)

Academic Vocabulary
* site (p. 544)
* global (p. 544)
* journal (p. 547)

Reading Strategy
As you read, use a graphic organizer to analyze the impact of the Internet on citizen participation.

Internet and Citizenship

Issues in the News

Some people argue that technology has strengthened democracy because it creates a direct link between politicians and voters. This effect was clear during the 2008 presidential race when candidates made a major push to raise funds and campaign online. Instead of direct-mail campaigns, candidates relied on e-mails to attract small donations. Almost all the candidates for president had links to their own Facebook, MySpace, and YouTube site. "You have an inexpensive way to have a conversation with people. . . ." said Rich Davies, an adviser to Republican John McCain. Certainly Internet campaigning was the key to Barack Obama's success with young voters. Obama's critical win in the Iowa caucus was attributed to his strong base of technology-savvy young voters.

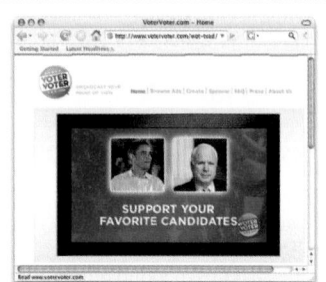

▲ Campaign ads have plugged into the Internet such as on the VoterVoter.com Web site.

In recent years, the Internet has had a major impact on American government and politics. As one experienced presidential campaign manager explains, "Day-to-day life is happening on the Internet and the political world is catching up."

Key Features of the Internet

The Internet offers several distinctive benefits for politics and government.

Widespread Audience

The Internet is rapidly developing an audience large enough to rival older forms of mass media. Web traffic has been growing by 100 percent per year, as compared to less than 10 percent for phone networks. In 2006 about 73 percent of Americans reported using the Internet. By 2010, it is likely that the figure will be more than 80 percent. Many of these users also will be new voters.

Interactivity

Traditional mass media are unidirectional, meaning the communication goes in one direction. Radio, television, and newspapers provide a shared experience for huge audiences, but they do so mainly through one-way transmission of images and ideas. By contrast, the Internet supports interactive communications. This allows activists or anyone else to find people with similar interests and views easily and quickly mobilize them to organize a campaign or to contact government officials.

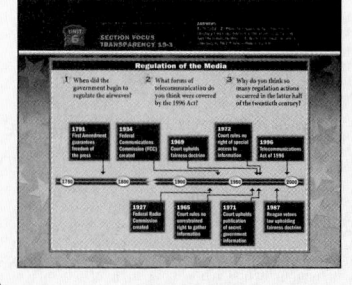

Teach

S Skill Practice

Conducting Polls Ask students to poll family members and friends on the following:

1. How many hours each week do you spend watching television? How much of this time is devoted to each of the following: news, entertainment, sports?

2. How many hours each week do you spend reading a newspaper? What subjects do you spend the most time reading—news, sports, business, or arts and entertainment?

Have students collate their results and create a report that makes several generalizations based on their findings. **OL**

Critical Thinking

Answer: Households that earn more than $40,000, those with a college degree, and young adults; those groups are the most likely to be able to afford high-speed Internet, and young adults are more likely to be up-to-date on technology than older adults.

Differentiated Instruction

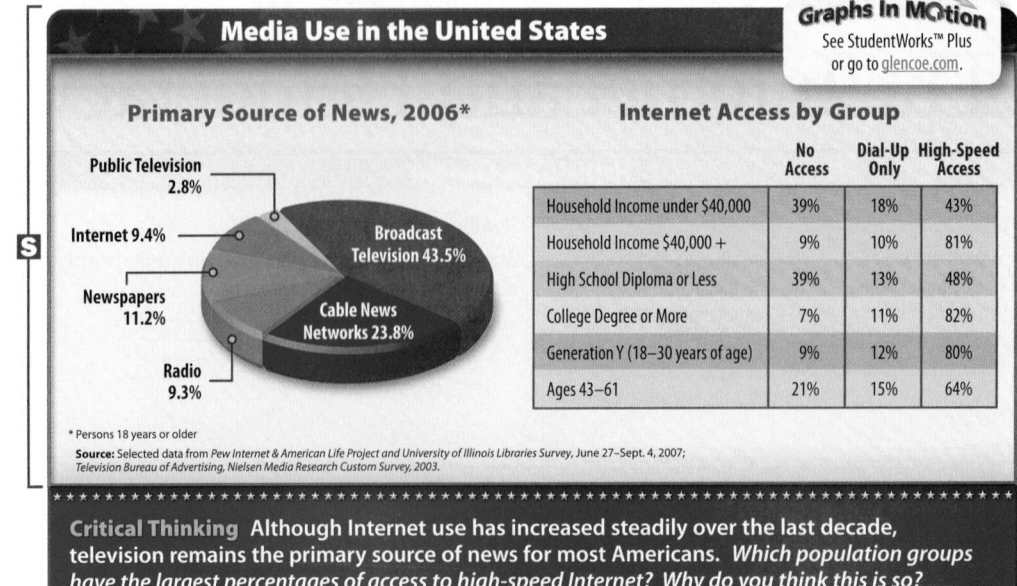

Graphs In Motion
See StudentWorks™ Plus or go to glencoe.com.

Media Use in the United States

Primary Source of News, 2006*

- Public Television 2.8%
- Internet 9.4%
- Newspapers 11.2%
- Radio 9.3%
- Broadcast Television 43.5%
- Cable News Networks 23.8%

Internet Access by Group

	No Access	Dial-Up Only	High-Speed Access
Household Income under $40,000	39%	18%	43%
Household Income $40,000 +	9%	10%	81%
High School Diploma or Less	39%	13%	48%
College Degree or More	7%	11%	82%
Generation Y (18–30 years of age)	9%	12%	80%
Ages 43–61	21%	15%	64%

* Persons 18 years or older

Source: Selected data from *Pew Internet & American Life Project and University of Illinois Libraries Survey*, June 27–Sept. 4, 2007; *Television Bureau of Advertising, Nielsen Media Research Custom Survey*, 2003.

Critical Thinking Although Internet use has increased steadily over the last decade, television remains the primary source of news for most Americans. *Which population groups have the largest percentages of access to high-speed Internet? Why do you think this is so?*

Global Scope

The Internet is a worldwide collection of Web **sites** and computer servers that is accessible to people all around the world. The Internet's **global** nature ensures that this medium represents a wide range of content and opinions; this diversity is one of the Internet's major strengths. At the same time, the Internet is a decentralized medium with few rules.

Since Internet communications extend around the world, it is not clear which national law should govern them. For example, one music-swapping service, KaZaA, distributes its software from the South Pacific island nation of Vanuatu, is managed from Australia, and uses computer servers in Denmark. This makes it very difficult for Hollywood media companies to try to sue KaZaA for violating U.S. copyright law.

Gathering Information

Every day, more and more Americans are using the Internet for information on political issues and to access government at all levels.

Political Web Sites

Web sites devoted to political issues are everywhere on the Internet. All of the major newspapers and newsmagazines, such as *Time* and the *New York Times*, have Web sites and maintain archives, or files, of older stories. Television and radio networks like NBC, CNN, and National Public Radio (NPR) also have sites.

Thousands of Web sites are devoted to politics and government. These sites are sponsored by government agencies, Congress, political parties, universities, and various interest groups such as the Sierra Club and the National Rifle Association. Public Agenda (www.publicagenda.org) is an example of a site that offers balanced information on major issues such as the economy and foreign policy. The site presents articles, data, and in-depth coverage of both sides of many other issues.

Keep in mind, however, that many Web sites are **partisan,** meaning they offer information and ideas that support only their own point of view on issues. A good Web site will tell you who owns and maintains it and when it was last updated. Ultimately, it is the responsibility of the user to evaluate the information on a Web site and determine whether or not it is reliable, accurate, and up-to-date.

Tracking Legislation

A Web site named after Thomas Jefferson provides the public with access to a great deal of information about the federal legislature and its daily activities. THOMAS (www.thomas.loc.gov) allows

Activity: Multiple Learning Styles

Verbal/Linguistic Help students use their prior knowledge by going through the list of Key Terms at the beginning of the section. Go through the list as a class and ask student volunteers to share what they know about each term. Encourage other classmates to confirm or clarify information. Then review

with students the meaning of each Key Term. Have students use each term in a sentence that explains the meaning of the term. Call on students to take turns reading one sentence aloud to the class, leaving the term out of the sentence. Allow the class to determine which term is being described. **ELL** users to search for all versions of House and Senate bills by either bill number or key word. The "Daily Digest" section of the *Congressional Record* is also available online. It provides a brief summary of each day's activities during each current congressional session. Reports filed by the committees within the Senate and the House of Representatives are also available on the database. The Library of Congress hosts and updates the Web site on a daily basis with the help of the Government Printing Office. THOMAS is also a useful place to find contact information for members of Congress and other offices that work within the legislative branch.

Electronic Mailing Lists

Those who are interested in political issues can subscribe to **electronic mailing lists.** These are automated e-mail notifications that provide subscribers with current information on a topic. Mailing list owners or operators conduct research on the issue upon which their list focuses, such as gun control, civil liberties, or copyright laws.

Receiving these updates is a good way to stay informed about political issues as they are being discussed in the public or considered by Congress or other government agencies. To subscribe to an electronic mailing list, you need to provide an e-mail address. Several Web-based directories can help you find a variety of lists on many different issues. The easiest way to find a Web-based list that suits your interests is to conduct an Internet search using key terms such as *political listservs* or *political discussion groups*. In addition, the national offices of the Republican and Democratic Parties operate several mailing lists that provide information about issues, candidates, press briefings, and upcoming events.

E-Government

All levels of government now provide services and information over the Internet. For example, residents of Vilas County, deep in the north woods of Wisconsin, are going online to access property tax bills, get forms for marriage licenses, or find town board meeting times. Across the nation, people are using their local and state government Web sites to pay parking tickets, report abandoned cars or illegal dumping, register to vote, get absentee ballots, view the state budget, or obtain a hunting or fishing license, among many other activities. Jane Hague, a city councilmember in King County, Washington, put it this way: "The motto for the twenty-first century for government should be 'On line, and not in line.'"

Did You Know?

The first televised presidential debate took place during the 1960 election campaign between candidates Richard Nixon, a Republican, and John Kennedy, a Democrat. Most television viewers believed that Kennedy won the crucial first debate over a nervous-looking Nixon. Radio listeners were not influenced by appearances and often scored Nixon higher than Kennedy.

CURRICULUM CONNECTION

Technology Television coverage of the Vietnam War fed public antagonism toward the war. Graphic color images of devastation and carnage shown live on television news brought the war into Americans' living rooms. In January 1991, millions of Americans watched Operation Desert Storm and kept track of progress in the Persian Gulf War. News coverage of this war brought a display of high-tech weaponry in action, while viewers watched, glued to their television sets.

Additional Support

Activity: Collaborative Learning

Communicating a Political Message

Organize the class into groups of four to plan a talk-radio program with a political message. Have students in each group choose from the following roles: talk-show host, interviewee who represents a government official, and a call-in listener to ask questions of the government official. The fourth student should broadcast a brief commercial break that would reflect an advertiser who supports the political message being aired. Allow students time to research and rehearse their talk-show segment. Then have them role-play the segment for the class. **OL**

Linking ★ Past & Present

The Internet When the Internet was created in 1969, it consisted of four connected computers. It was founded as part of the quest to ensure that communication could continue during and after a nuclear war. In 1990 the Federal Networking Council modified the Internet membership policy from only organizations with sponsorship by a U.S. government agency to anyone who wanted membership. This opened the door to commercialization of the Internet and resulted in its exponential growth.

W Writing Support

Persuasive Writing Have students come up with an issue that they care about, and have them write a petition urging a government or school official to take action. Issues might deal with funding for extracurricular activities or school lunches, saving a town landmark from being demolished or a park from being paved, and so on. Then have them post their petitions online or circulate them around the school. **AL**

Hands-On Chapter Project
Step 3

Federal government Web sites contain vast amounts of information. However, accessing the information electronically can be difficult. Separate federal agencies have different, often poorly organized sites, some of which are not user friendly. In 2002 Congress passed the E-Government Act to address such problems. This law established the Office of Electronic Government to help federal agencies work together to provide better online service to the public.

The federal government also provides and maintains an official Web site, www.usa.gov. This site offers access to a wide variety of governmental information, including statistical data, contacts and directories within government agencies, forms and applications for government services, laws and regulations, and historical documents. The site also provides links to information on all 50 states and many local organizations, and it offers an easy and convenient way to contact local, state, and federal representatives by e-mail or telephone. Many of the links on the USA.gov site are available in a variety of languages.

Impact on Citizen Participation

In recent years, the Internet has become a powerful tool for citizen activism. It helps people connect with like-minded individuals who share information. They can then build consensus on issues among a group and put pressure on government officials.

Communicating With Officials

Telling legislators and other government officials what you think is one of the most basic ways individual citizens can participate in representative democracy. E-mail has become the most widely used Internet tool for contacting officials. Congress, for example, receives about 12 e-mail messages every second, adding up to more than a million per day. Many Web sites offer interactive message boards and e-mail directories that make it easy to send electronic messages day or night to members of Congress, state legislators, your mayor, or a local school board member. You can even send e-mail messages directly to the president!

Action Alerts and Petitions

Political organizers have developed several tools that take advantage of the Internet's power to spread

information very quickly in many directions. One such tool is an **action alert.** This is a message from an interest group to its members that calls upon each member to respond immediately by telephone, fax, or e-mail to a specific lawmaker, group of lawmakers, or other officials. An alert might instruct you, for example, to contact a lawmaker to tell him or her that you support or oppose a bill on gun control that his or her committee will be considering. Action alerts usually give background on the issue, a date by which you must send your message, and clear instructions on what to ask for.

Another tool is an **electronic petition.** This is a message that asks you, along with many other people, to "sign" your name electronically to a request that is going to an official. Net users send their electronic signatures via e-mail to a collection point. The petition organizers check the signatures, removing those that seem questionable, and organize and print the results. They then give the results to officials via mail or in person. The goal of an electronic petition drive is to show lawmakers that a large number of people agree on how an issue should be decided.

Grassroots Web Sites

The 2000 election saw a new development—individual citizens setting up their own independent Web sites in support of their favorite candidates. Creating such sites gives citizens an opportunity to become involved in election politics at many levels of government without ever leaving home. Experts have noted that for many people, grassroots Web sites are the electronic way of putting a bumper sticker on a car or posting a sign in a front yard.

Candidates and major political parties are discovering, however, that independent Web sites can also cause problems. These sites may present misleading information about a candidate. They may also have links to extremist groups that the candidate would not want to be associated with. Further, even with new Federal Election Commission disclosure requirements, it can be difficult for visitors to tell the difference between official and unofficial Web sites.

Volunteering

Donating your time and effort to an election campaign or political cause can be a highly effective way to participate in politics. Election candidate Web sites usually give you information on how to sign up for such jobs as working on a telephone bank, going door-to-door for the candidate,

Analyzing the Media

Step 3: Comparing Internet Sites
Students will compare Internet sites' coverage of their issue.

Directions Ask students to locate two Internet sites of organizations that are likely to disagree about the issue they are researching. As in Steps 1 and 2, they will take notes on point of view, facts used to support it, objectivity, and effectiveness. They will then write a paragraph comparing the two sites' coverage of the issue.

Putting It Together Ask: What have you learned about the media? What does this tell you about how citizens can stay informed about important issues? **OL**

Growing Influence of Blogs

Not Your Average Blogger A widely read blog, "Talking Points Memo," was created by former *New York Times* reporter Joshua Micah Marshall. Marshall is the first blogger to win a major journalism award. His reporting on the firing of attorneys in the U.S. Attorney General's office led to wider media coverage and ultimately to the resignation of the attorney general. *Can you suggest how an Internet user can learn whether a blogger is a reliable news source?*

or mailing brochures. Further, many people have started "cybervolunteering." This process involves volunteer activities that can be done only on the Internet. One popular activity is to send an electronic postcard provided by the candidate you support to a friend, usually with a personalized message from you. Another method is to put a banner ad supporting a candidate or an issue on your own personal Web site.

In the months leading up to the 2004 presidential primaries, Democrat Howard Dean became the first major candidate to effectively employ a campaign Web site. Dean used his site to register more than 500,000 volunteers and to raise several million dollars in campaign funds. In 2008 Barack Obama's skill in using the Internet to campaign was a key factor in his upset over Senator Hillary Rodham Clinton for the Democratic Party's nomination.

Political Blogs

Blogging, an online personal **journal,** gives people and groups a new way to participate in politics both during and between elections. Anyone can create a blog and publish material about politics for millions of others to read and comment upon. Political blogs are being widely used. People express their **D** opinions about candidates and issues, they evaluate government performance, and they uncover stories that were missed by the major media. In a 2006 primary election in Connecticut, bloggers were credited with helping an unknown challenger defeat the Democratic candidate Joe Lieberman, an incumbent senator who had been the party's candidate for vice president in 2000. In the 2008 presidential race, the importance of bloggers was enough that Republican candidate John McCain held a weekly conference call with interested bloggers.

Blogging has the potential to give nearly every American, regardless of his or her status, a voice in American political life. At the same time, there is nothing to prevent bloggers from publishing inaccurate information or even lies.

Electronic Voting

The growth of the Internet, along with the disputed Florida ballot count in the 2000 presidential election, has led to calls for online voting. In 2002 Congress passed the Help America Vote Act, which required states to replace old voting methods such as punch cards. Since then a number of states along with the Department of Defense have been experimenting with e-voting. Proponents of electronic voting claim it makes it easier and more efficient to vote.

Others, however, are concerned about sabotage, vote stealing by hackers, and the lack of an easily countable printed record in case of a recount. Lawsuits were filed in at least six states to stop the purchase or use of computerized machines. Defenders of the new systems argue most problems occur because of lack of training for poll workers or hasty set-up prior to elections.

Activity: Collaborative Learning

Designing a Magazine Cover Organize the class into groups of three to design newsmagazine covers. As a group, students should choose a name for the magazine that will reflect the views covered. Then have students choose to design a picture for the cover or write caption titles for articles covered in the magazine. Display completed magazine covers in the classroom. Analyze the possible bias of each magazine and what the cover shows that makes students feel that way. **BL**

C Critical Thinking

Drawing Conclusions Discuss with students the many different pieces of legislation that have sought to restrict or ban offensive content on the Internet. **Ask:** Why is it so difficult for the legislative branch to pass these laws? *(The legislation must be worded carefully so as not to infringe upon Internet users' First Amendment right to free speech.)* **OL**

GO TO To enrich the study of chapter content, remind students that footnoted materials appear in the *Reference Handbook.*

Differentiated Instruction

Connectivity at the Library

The Diffusion of Knowledge More and more, libraries offer Internet access to patrons or students. In addition, library collections are becoming digital. *What challenges do you think librarians face in keeping up with a digital source like Wikipedia (a collaborative Web site that allows anyone to edit, delete, or modify its content)?*

Challenges for Public Policy

The rise of a major technology like the Internet creates a need for new laws to deal with its impact on politics, business, and people's lives. Everyone from lawmakers in Congress to local school board officials has struggled to keep up with the legal implications of the Internet.

Offensive Content

The Internet gives anyone with a personal computer the ability to spread his or her ideas to a global audience. This has led to an explosion of creativity and new opportunities for civic participation. However, it has also allowed anyone, anywhere, to gain access to obscene content in the privacy of their own homes.

The Supreme Court ruled in *Reno v. American Civil Liberties Union*[1] (1997) that the First Amendment guarantees freedom of expression on the Internet. As a result, Congress has struggled with how to protect children from online pornography while at the same time upholding constitutional protections of free speech.

The first attempt by Congress, the 1996 Communications Decency Act, made publishing "indecent" or "patently offensive" material on the Internet a federal offense. The Supreme Court ruled that such limits interfered with the free speech rights of adults. Congress then responded with the 1998 Child Online Protection Act. This law ordered Web site operators to require an adult identification device, such as a credit card, before granting access to material that could be considered harmful to minors. So far the Court has blocked this law from taking effect by sending it back to a lower federal court for review.

In 2000 Congress passed the Children's Internet Protection Act. This law requires public libraries that accept federal funds to install anti-pornography filters on computers used by the public. The filters block Web sites that present offensive content by using key words or lists. One argument employed against the use of such filtering software was that the filters sometimes block nonobscene sites.

In 2003 the Supreme Court ruled in the case of *United States* v. *American Library Association* that the law's filter requirement does not violate the First Amendment rights of library users. While the Supreme Court justices agreed that the software can make mistakes, they emphasized that adults could ask to have a filter turned off if it prevented them from accessing sites they wanted to see.

In 2008 the Court ruled on the issue of restricting sexual content on the Internet. The case arose as a result of a federal law passed in 2003 that made it a crime to advertise or solicit online images of child pornography. In *United States* v. *Williams*, the Court said the law was carefully written and that it did not violate First Amendment free speech guarantees. Justice Scalia emphasized that the First Amendment does not cover child pornography.

See the following footnoted materials in the *Reference Handbook:*
1. *Reno v. American Civil Liberties Union* case summary, page R33.

Leveled Activities

ELL Chapter Summaries, p. 57

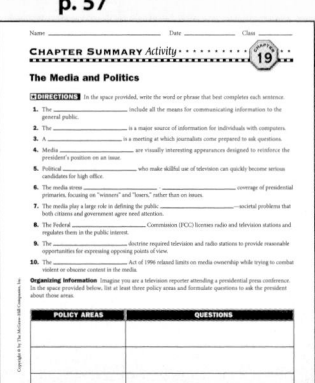

BL Historical Documents and Speeches, p. 19

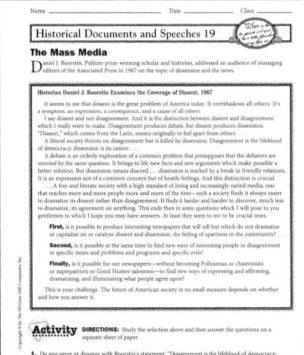

OL Skill Reinforcement Activities, p. 19

AL Authentic Assessment with Rubrics, p. 26

Graphs In Motion
See StudentWorks™ Plus
or go to glencoe.com.

E-Commerce: Online Retail Sales

Projected Sales in Billions of Dollars

2007

$19.0 $19.0
$16.4 $12.5
   $9.9
$80.6

2011

$31.4 $27.8
$28.2 $23.0
   $17.6
$143.1

- Apparel/accessories/footwear
- Auto parts
- Computer hardware/software
- Home furnishings
- Music/videos
- Other products/services

Source: Forrester Research, Inc., Cambridge, MA, *US eCommerce: Five-Year Forecast and Data Overview,* October 12, 2006.

Critical Thinking *What challenges might the growth of e-commerce sales pose for state and federal taxes?*

D **Differentiated Instruction**

Gifted and Talented Have students work in groups to develop plans for a fair state and local tax system for online merchants. **AL**

Assess

Assign the Section 3 Assessment as homework or as an in-class activity, or have students take Section Quiz 19–3 from *Section Quizzes and Chapter Tests.*

Close

Evaluating Ask students to evaluate what restrictions, if any, they think the government should place on the Internet. **OL**

Taxing E-Commerce

Internet growth has led to the growth of e-commerce, or the sale of goods and services online. Along with this growth, questions have arisen about taxation of this new form of commerce. Because state sales tax laws are so cumbersome, the Supreme Court has blocked attempts by state governments to require online retailers to collect sales taxes. State governments claim that since e-commerce sales are projected to exceed $140 billion by the mid-2000s, they will lose billions of dollars if they cannot impose these taxes. A group of states supports a plan to use the same tax rate for all e-commerce sales, but online retailers, technology companies, and Congress have remained resistant to any such plan.

SECTION 3 Review

Section 3 Review

Vocabulary

1. **Explain** the significance of: partisan, electronic mailing list, action alert, electronic petition.

Main Ideas

2. **Identifying** What is the significance of the E-Government Act?

3. **Summarizing** Why has it been difficult for media companies to sue Internet file-swapping organizations?

Critical Thinking

4. **Differentiating** What are some benefits and weaknesses of electronic voting?

5. **Organizing** Use a table like the one below to analyze key features of the Internet.

Key Features	Benefits for Government
1.	
2.	
3.	

Writing About Government

6. **Expository Writing** Visit your local library and ask the librarians about their opinions on indecent Internet materials versus the right of free speech. Share the opinions you gather with your classmates.

CHAPTER 19: *Mass Media and the Internet* **549**

Answers

1. All definitions can be found in the section and the Glossary.
2. It established a federal office to help provide better online services to the public.
3. It is difficult because Internet activities and organizations are spread around the world, so it is often not clear which nation's laws should govern such activities.
4. Benefits include the ease and efficiency of electronic voting; weaknesses include the possibility of sabotage or vote stealing by hackers.

5. Widespread: government can provide services to nearly all Americans through the Internet; Interactive: makes it easy for people to tell their opinions to the government, and for the government to connect with people who need their services; Global scope: wide range of content for the government to draw from
6. Students should share their findings with the class.

CHAPTER
19 Assessment and Activities

ExamView®
Assessment Suite

This easy-to-use software includes extensive question banks and allows you to create fully customized tests that can be administered in print or online.

Reviewing Vocabulary

1. d
2. b
3. c
4. a

Reviewing Main Ideas

5. print and broadcast media
6. The president and Congress use television to share information with and present a certain image to their constituents. Television also helps set the public agenda by choosing which issues to cover and in how much detail.
7. First Amendment
8. The government classifies information as secret and limits press coverage of military actions.
9. The Internet makes it easier to gather information, to communicate with candidates, and to get involved in grassroots movements.
10. It has provided the public with more information. It helps like-minded people find each other and work toward a goal. It lets people contact their representatives more easily.
11. E-commerce taxation is difficult to resolve mainly because of the conflict between state governments —which support taxation as a source of revenue—and online retailers, technology companies, and Congress, which oppose taxes on e-commerce.

Reviewing Vocabulary

Choose the letter of the correct answer below to complete each sentence.

a. action alerts
b. fairness doctrine
c. prior restraint
d. news releases

1. Government officials prepare _____, ready-made stories for the press.
2. The _____ requires television and radio stations to present both sides of a controversial topic.
3. The First Amendment frees the U.S. print media from _____.
4. An interest group sends _____ that call on members to respond quickly to a political development.

Chapter Summary

Media and Government

★ President: Interacts with media through news releases and briefings, press conferences, background stories, leaks, and media events

★ Congress: Media coverage focuses on confirmation hearings, oversight activities, and the personal business of members

★ Court: Receives less media attention due to the remoteness of judges and the technical nature of their work

★ The Internet helps citizens gather information about political issues and government services and communicate with legislators and government leaders

Regulation of the Media

★ First Amendment protects freedom of the press
★ Federal Communications Commission (FCC) regulates media content and ownership
★ Telecommunications Act of 1996 updated regulations on cost, competition, and program content
★ Debates over regulation of Internet content and e-commerce taxation continue

Reviewing Main Ideas

Section 1 *(pages 527–534)*

5. **Identifying** What are the two traditional types of mass media?
6. **Analyzing** How has television's role in the political process developed?

Section 2 *(pages 536–541)*

7. **Stating** Which amendment protects the media?
8. **Describing** Which steps does the federal government take when attempting to control sensitive national security issues?

Section 3 *(pages 543–549)*

9. **Summarizing** How does the Internet assist citizen activists?

Critical Thinking

10. **Essential Question** How has the Internet opened up the political process to citizens? Explain.
11. **Speculating** Why is the issue of e-commerce taxation difficult to resolve?
12. **Demonstrating Reasoned Judgment** Should the media have been limited in its coverage of the 1991 Persian Gulf War? Explain.
13. **Synthesizing Information** Use a graphic organizer like the one below to list two or more arguments for and against this statement: "The media's greatest power is in the way they define reality for the American people." Then explain why you agree or disagree with the statement.

For	Against
1.	1.
2.	2.
Conclusion:	

Applying Technology Skills

14. **Using the Internet** Search the Internet to find Web sites that provide information about reactions to the Telecommunications Act of 1996. Find out which people or groups opposed the legislation, and identify the reasons for their opposition. Write a short report summarizing your findings.

---

12. Possible "yes" response: Because of the incidence of military personnel deaths from capture, "friendly fire," and the possibility of media personnel becoming POWs. Possible "no" response: It is within the rights of the media to take risks, barring breaches of national security, to cover the war independently.
13. For: Coverage largely determines which issues people think are important; the media influence people's attitudes and values. Against: People balance what they hear in the media with personal

observations; although the media may determine which issues are covered, they do not tell people what to think. Conclusion: Answers should reflect arguments made in the graphic organizer.

Applying Technology Skills

14. Students' reports should summarize what they found on the Web sites about opposition to the Telecommunications Act of 1996. Encourage students to share the addresses of the Web sites they found.

Government ONLINE Self-Check Quiz
Visit glencoe.com and enter *QuickPass*™ code USG9822c19.
Click on Self-Check Quizzes for additional test practice.

CHAPTER **Assessment and Activities**
19

Document-Based Questions

Analyzing Primary Sources

Read the excerpt below and answer the questions that follow.

Among the most famous campaign debates of the nineteenth century were the 1858 Abraham Lincoln–Stephen Douglas debates for one of Illinois' two seats in the U.S. Senate. Although he lost the election, the debates made Lincoln's a household name.

Douglas:

❝ Ladies and gentlemen: *I appear before you to-day for the purpose of discussing the leading political topics which now agitate the public mind. By an arrangement between Mr. Lincoln and myself, we are present here to-day for the purpose of having a joint discussion . . . in regard to the questions dividing us.* ❞

Lincoln:

❝ *MY FELLOW-CITIZENS: When a man hears himself somewhat misrepresented, it provokes him—at least, I find it so with myself; but when the misrepresentation becomes very gross and palpable, it is more apt to amuse him. [Laughter] The first thing I see fit to notice, is the fact that Judge Douglas alleges . . . that Judge Trumbull and myself made an arrangement in 1854 by which I was to have the place of Gen. Shields in the United States Senate, and Judge Trumbull was to have the place of Judge Douglas. Now all I have to say upon that subject is, that I think no man—not even Judge Douglas—can prove it, because it is not true. [Cheers.] I have no doubt he is 'conscientious' in saying it. [Laughter.]* ❞

15. How is the structure of these presidential debates different from those that take place on television today? Why do you think this structure has changed?

16. Based on the excerpt, how do you think the content of presidential debates has changed as a result of changes in the mass media?

Interpreting Political Cartoons

Analyze the cartoon and answer the questions that follow. Base your answers on the cartoon and your knowledge of Chapter 19.

17. During the 2008 presidential campaign, Senator Barack Obama said that it was to be expected that voters in small Midwestern towns had become bitter over the loss of jobs in their towns and, as a result, were against global trade or against immigration. Is the cartoon depicting voter sentiment in small Midwestern towns?

18. Does the cartoonist believe American voters are bitter, and is the bitterness justified?

19. How does this cartoon relate to the theory of agenda-setting discussed in this chapter? Do you think television stations today focus heavily on serious topics as the cartoonist suggests?

Participating IN GOVERNMENT

20. Interview local government officials and find out how and what type of media are involved in your local politics. Also find out how the media influence the public policy of the local government. Design a diagram to present your findings, and share it with your classmates.

CHAPTER 19: *Mass Media and the Internet* **551**

Government ONLINE

Have students use the *Chapter 19 Self-Check Quiz.* Visit glencoe.com and enter *QuickPass*™ code USG9085c19T to prepare for the Chapter Test.

Interpreting Political Cartoons

17. yes

18. The cartoonist appears to believe that American voters are bitter and that it is justified.

19. The media's role is to bring issues to the attention of the public and to shape the discussion between voters and government officials. The cartoon shows the news media bringing awareness to these issues. Students' answers will vary.

Participating IN GOVERNMENT

20. Students should interview local government officials to find out how media are involved in local politics and how the media influence public policy making at the local level. Students should illustrate their findings in a diagram.

Chapter Bonus Test Question

Ask: Which presidential election results were the first to be reported over the radio? *(the election of 1920 announcing Warren G. Harding's defeat of James M. Cox)*

Analyzing Primary Sources

15. Answers might include the fact that presidential debates today are less formal, without the statement-and-rebuttal structure. Rather, they are more in the form of question-and-answer sessions, with the mass media taking a more active part in these sessions. The structure has changed because the nature of media has changed. The debates in this excerpt could not have been televised, but instead would have been reported in newspapers.

16. Because news coverage is more immediate, debates can be shorter and the answers can take the form of "sound bites." But in the Lincoln-Douglas debates, the two candidates pointed out the flaws in each other's arguments, promoted their own party line, and made sure that the positive aspects of their candidacy were pointed out in detail, just as candidates do today.

Public Policies *and* Services

UNIT PACING CHART*		
Chapter 20	**Chapter 21**	**Chapter 22**
Day 1 Unit Opener Chapter Opener Section 1	Chapter Opener Section 1	Chapter Opener Section 1
Day 2 Section 2 Government Skills	Section 2	Section 2
Day 3 Section 3	Section 3 Supreme Court Cases to Debate	Section 3 Supreme Court Cases to Debate
Day 4 Supreme Court Cases to Debate	Section 4 Issues to Debate	Section 4 Issues to Debate
Day 5 Review Chapter Assessment	Review Chapter Assessment	Review Chapter Assessment

*Unit Pacing Chart based on year-long course; modify pacing by half for semester-long course

Teacher to Teacher

Rod Hanson

Redmond
School District
Redmond, OR

Balancing the Budget After students read Chapter 20 (Taxing and Spending), they will create a balanced budget. A current U.S. budget, put out by the Office of Management and Budget, can be downloaded from www.access.gpo.gov/ or found in the library. Have students take copies of the budget home and make the cuts in spending and/or the increases in revenue that are needed to balance the budget. Students must explain in writing the rationale for their proposed cuts and increases.

In class, organize students into groups of five. Each student will share his or her proposed budget and rationale with the group; then the groups must work together to create one overall balanced budget. Group votes must be unanimous to make a change in the budget. Requiring the votes to be unanimous helps students develop the art of political compromise.

After students have created a balanced budget, have them write a review of their group's budget process, addressing questions such as: What areas were the toughest to change? In what areas did the greatest controversy occur? How was compromise reached?

Author Note

Dear U.S. Government Teacher,

This unit examines the policies and services that the government maintains. But it begins at the beginning, that is, with how the revenues to pay for services are raised. Taxes are a subject of universal complaint, and perhaps that is appropriate since tax complaints set off the American Revolution.

Students may not be as interested in the topic of taxes as they will be in later life. Yet teachers can seize this opportunity to link tax issues to public policy and services. Without revenues, policies cannot be pursued or services provided. Even when revenues are more available, it is always necessary for government leaders to set policy priorities, and this is accomplished in a federal budget. The elements of the budget process are laid out in Section 2 of Chapter 20, while the important role of the Federal Reserve in regulating the flow of money is explained in the last section.

The policies and services that Americans often argue about are addressed in Chapter 21. The chapter opens with those policies that promote, protect, subsidize, or regulate business. After all, "The business of America is business," as President Calvin Coolidge famously said, and to a large extent that is still true.

In recent times, the government has taken a stronger role in consumer protection. Even more recently, with the threat of climate change, policies to preserve and protect the environment have become a higher priority. Since this is a topic many students are passionate about, it can serve as a model for teaching points on revenues versus services. The unit closes with the most basic government service of all—providing national security and implementing the foreign policies that support that goal.

Richard C. Remy, Ph.D.
Author

Focus

Making It Relevant

Preparing to Learn Ask students to skim through the unit, looking at visuals, captions and headings. Then have students write five facts they already know about the topics covered in the unit and five questions that they hope will be answered.

Unit Objectives

After studying this unit, students will be able to:

- **Describe** the federal government's methods of raising money and of budgeting and spending that money.

- **Discuss** social and domestic policy in such areas as business and labor, agriculture and the environment, health care and public assistance, and transportation.

- **Summarize** various aspects of foreign policy—goals, historical development, the roles of the executive and legislative branches, and tools.

Unit Overview

Unit 7 provides an overview of how public policies are formed and an overview of government services.

Chapter 20 describes how the federal government raises and spends money.

Chapter 21 provides an overview of social and domestic policy.

Chapter 22 provides an overview of foreign policy.

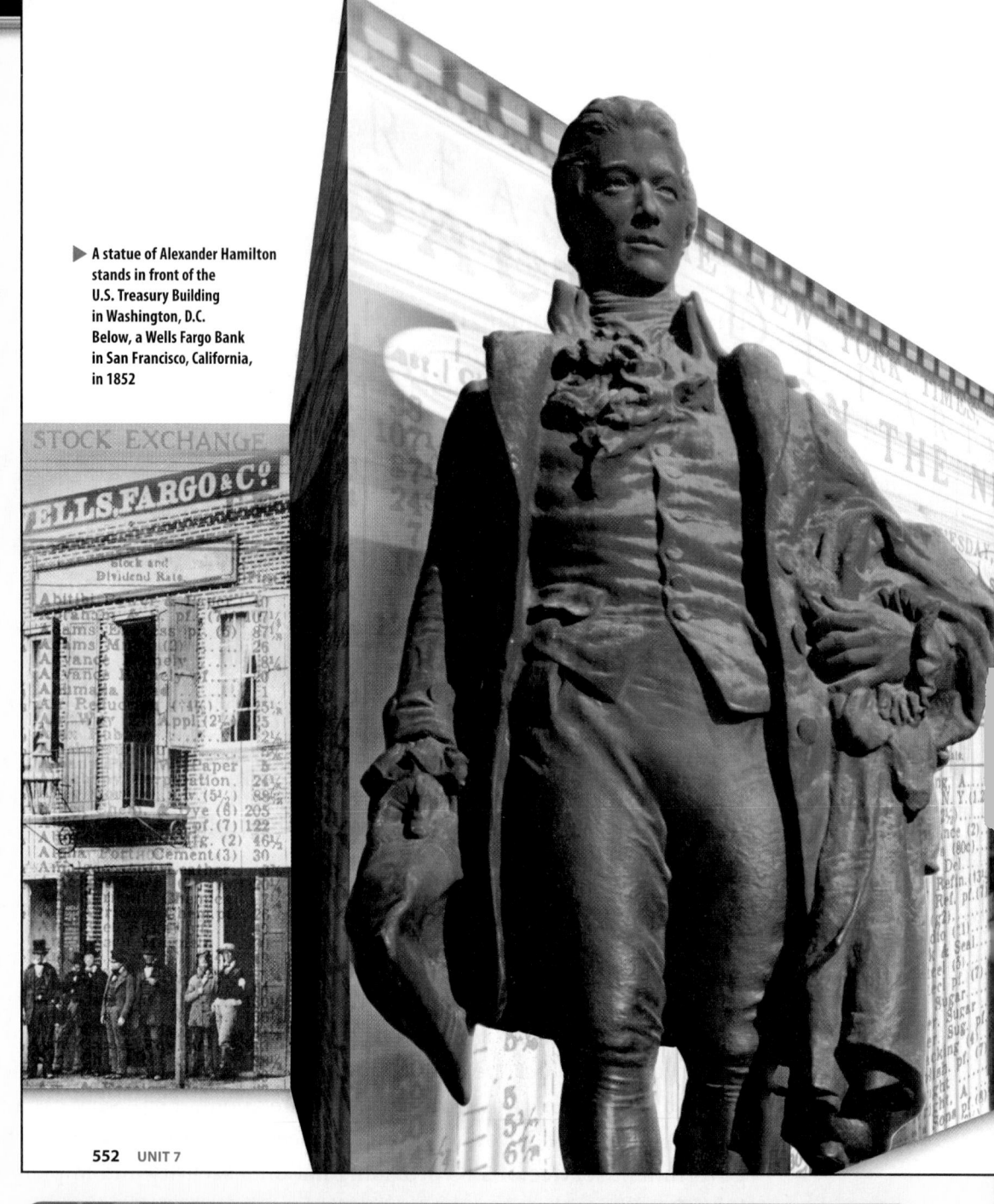

▶ A statue of Alexander Hamilton stands in front of the U.S. Treasury Building in Washington, D.C. Below, a Wells Fargo Bank in San Francisco, California, in 1852

552 UNIT 7

Activity: Launching the Unit

Reporting on the Arms Race During the Cold War, the Soviet Union and the United States engaged in an arms race that included not only bigger and more sophisticated weapons, but advances in aircraft and submarine technology. Have students read about other such results of the arms race and present their findings in an illustrated report. **OL**

UNIT 7

Public Policies *and* Services

Participating IN GOVERNMENT

BIG IDEA **Checks and Balances** The impact of the federal government can be balanced or checked by a citizen's access to Congress. As you read Chapters 20 and 21, list how specific federal policies affect you. At the end of the unit, write an essay on whether this impact is positive or negative on your economic welfare. If a policy negatively affects you, draft an e-mail message to your representatives.

▲ Soldiers carrying flags in an inaugural parade

553

Teach

S Skill Practice

Visual Literacy Have students examine the three images of the unit opener closely. **Ask:** Based on the style of dress, what time period does each image represent? How are these images related? *(Mid to late 1800s, early republic, and contemporary periods, respectively; students should suggest that all three images relate to public service of the government: a Wells Fargo bank suggests government regulation of currency and (today) of banking; Hamilton was the first Secretary of the Treasury and laid down the basics of its operation; soldiers represent the government's protection of national security.)*

Online Current Events Update
History happens every day. Visit Glencoe's Online Current Events Update at glencoe.com to find news reports, features, maps, graphs, and images about events that shape our lives. Students can connect those events to historical events in world and American history by exploring related events on an interactive time line—a time line that ends with today.

Graduation: Exit With Success

Teaching Tip Review with students the pros and cons of scanning and skimming and when each would be useful in studying this unit.

Extra Credit Project

Polling the Community Have students read newspapers and magazines for articles on topics related to taxing and spending, such as the IRS, the federal budget, the Federal Reserve, tax reform, or defense spending. Have them choose five articles and summarize the main points. Then ask students to choose one issue and write a position statement or a letter to the editor about the issue. **OL**

Key to Ability Levels

BL	Below level	AL	Above level
OL	On level	ELL	English Language Learners

Key to Teaching Resources

📁 Print Material 📀 CD-ROM or DVD 🖨 Transparency

Levels					Resources	Chapter Opener	Section 1	Section 2	Section 3	Chapter Assess
BL	OL	AL	ELL							
					FOCUS					
BL	OL	AL	ELL	🖨	Section Focus Transparencies		20-1	20-2	20-3	
					TEACH					
BL	OL		ELL	📁	Reading Essentials and Study Guide (and Answer Key)		p. 224	p. 227	p. 230	
BL	OL		ELL	📁	Guided Reading Activities		p. 71	p. 72	p. 73	
BL	OL		ELL	📁	Vocabulary Activities			p. 20		
BL	OL	AL	ELL	📁	Chapter Summaries				p. 58	
BL	OL			📁	American Biographies				p. 74	
BL	OL	AL	ELL	📁	Cooperative Learning Activities					
	OL	AL	ELL	📁	Government Simulations and Debate		p. 44			
BL	OL	AL	ELL	📁	Historical Documents and Speeches					
BL	OL	AL	ELL	📁	Interpreting Political Cartoons		p. 39			
BL	OL		ELL	📁	Skill Reinforcement Activities			p. 20		
BL	OL	AL	ELL	📁	Source Readings			p. 20		
BL	OL			📁	Supreme Court Case Studies					
BL	OL	AL	ELL	📁	Participating in Government Activities			p. 39		
BL	OL		ELL	📁	Spanish Declaration of Independence and U.S. Constitution	✓	✓	✓	✓	✓
BL	OL	AL	ELL	📁	NGS World Atlas, Spanish	✓	✓	✓	✓	✓
BL	OL	AL	ELL	🖨	Unit Overlay Transparencies, Strategies, and Activities	✓	✓	✓	✓	✓
BL	OL		ELL	🖨	Making It Relevant Transparencies	✓	✓	✓	✓	✓
BL	OL	AL	ELL	🖨	High School Writing Process Transparencies, Strategies, and Activities	✓	✓	✓	✓	✓
BL	OL	AL		🖨	American Art & Architecture Transparencies, Strategies, and Activities	✓	✓	✓	✓	✓

✓ Chapter- or unit-based activities applicable to all sections in this chapter

All-In-One Planner and Resource Center

- Interactive Lesson Planner
- Interactive Teacher Edition
- Fully editable blackline masters
- Chapter Spotlight Videos Launch

- Differentiated Lesson Plans
- Printable reports of daily assignments
- Standards tracking system

BL	OL	AL	ELL		Resources	Chapter Opener	Section 1	Section 2	Section 3	Chapter Assess
					TEACH (continued)					
BL	OL			◉	**American Music: Hits Through History**	✓	✓	✓	✓	✓
BL	OL		ELL	📁	**Reading Strategies for the Social Studies Classroom**	✓	✓	✓	✓	✓
			ELL	📁	**English Language Learner Handbook**	✓	✓	✓	✓	✓
BL	OL		ELL	📁	**Writer's Guidebook for Social Studies**	✓	✓	✓	✓	✓
BL	OL	AL	ELL	📁	**Living Constitution, SE**	✓	✓	✓	✓	✓
BL	OL	AL	ELL	📁	**Living Constitution, TAE**	✓	✓	✓	✓	✓
BL	OL			📁	**NGS World Atlas, English**	✓	✓	✓	✓	
BL	OL		ELL	📁	**The Constitution and You (poster set)**	✓	✓	✓	✓	✓
BL	OL	AL	ELL	📁	**Spanish Chapter Summaries**				p. 58	
BL	OL	AL	ELL	📁	**Spanish Vocabulary Activities**					
BL	OL		ELL	📁	**Spanish Reading Essentials and Study Guide (and Answer Key)**		p. 224	p. 227	p. 230	
BL	OL	AL	ELL	◉	**PresentationPlus! with MindJogger CheckPoint**	✓	✓	✓	✓	✓
					ASSESS					
BL	OL	AL	ELL	◉	*ExamView® Assessment Suite*		20-1	20-2	20-3	Ch. 20
BL	OL	AL	ELL	📁	**Authentic Assessment with Rubrics**		p. 27			p. 27
BL	OL	AL	ELL	📁	**Section Quizzes and Chapter Tests**		p. 245	p. 246	p. 247	pp. 249–256
BL	OL	AL	ELL	📁	**Spanish Section Quizzes and Tests**		p. 245	p. 246	p. 247	pp. 249–256
					CLOSE					
BL			ELL	📁	**Reteaching Activities**				p. 20	
BL	OL	AL	ELL	◉	**StudentWorks™ Plus with Audio Summaries**	✓	✓	✓	✓	✓
BL	OL		ELL	🖨	**Graphic Organizer Transparencies**		✓	✓	✓	
BL	OL		ELL	📁	**High School Government Reading and Study Skills Foldables®**		p. 63	p. 63	p. 63	

Teach With Technology

What is a Student Web Activity?

A Student Web Activity uses the Internet to enrich chapter content. It also helps students to enhance their online research skills.

How can a Student Web Activity help my students?

A Student Web Activity can teach students how to conduct research online and extends the content provided in the textbook. Features include:

- a research topic based on the chapter
- links to Web sites with more information on the topic
- short-answer questions to assess comprehension
- a form to e-mail answers to you or to themselves

Visit glencoe.com and enter a *QuickPass*™ code to go to a Student Web Activity.

TeacherWorks

Government ONLINE

Visit glencoe.com and enter *QuickPass*™ code USG9085c20T for Chapter 20 resources.

You can easily launch a wide range of digital products from your computer's desktop with the McGraw-Hill Social Studies widget.

	Student	Teacher	Parent
Media Library			
• Student Edition Section Audio	●		●
• Chapter Spotlight Videos	●	●	●
United States Government Online Learning Center (Web Site)			
• Chapter Overviews	●	●	●
• Multilingual Glossaries	●	●	●
• Study-to-Go	●	●	●
• Student Web Activities	●	●	●
• Self-Check Quizzes	●	●	●
• Online Student Edition	●	●	●
• Vocabulary eFlashcards	●	●	●
• Web Activity Lesson Plans		●	
• Vocabulary PuzzleMaker	●	●	●
• Landmark Supreme Court Cases	●	●	●
• Beyond the Textbook	●	●	●

READING SUPPORT FROM
JAMESTOWN EDUCATION

- **Timed Readings Plus in Social Studies** helps students increase their reading rate and fluency while maintaining comprehension. The 400-word passages are similar to those found on state and national assessments.

- **Reading in the Content Area: Social Studies** concentrates on six essential reading skills that help students better comprehend what they read. The book includes 75 high-interest nonfiction passages written at increasing levels of difficulty.

- **Reading Social Studies** includes strategic reading instruction and vocabulary support in Social Studies content for ELLs and native speakers of English.
www.jamestowneducation.com

Reading List Generator CD-ROM

GLENCOE BOOKLINK 3

Use this database to search more than 30,000 titles to create a customized reading list for your students.

- Reading lists can be organized by students' reading level, author, genre, theme, or area of interest.

- The database provides Degrees of Reading Power™ (DRP) and Lexile™ readability scores for all selections.

- A brief summary of each selection is included.

Economics Connection

Personal Finance Literacy

Understanding Nominal and Real Values

Remind students that inflation is a rise in the average price of goods and services, expressed as a percentage—or a decrease in the value of money. When inflation rises, government needs more revenue to provide the same programs. And the same goods and services cost consumers more. The rate of inflation varies from year to year and from one economy to another. In the United States and most industrialized nations, inflation in recent years has averaged about 2 to 5 percent per year.

When comparing costs in different years, it is important to remember that the current figure is the *nominal* cost. It does not take inflation into account. For example, if a city spends $10 million to repair highways this year and spent $8 million five years ago, it will not necessarily be repairing more miles of road. The same repairs may cost an extra $2 million because of inflation. For a true comparison, we must adjust for inflation to find the *real* cost.

Calculating real costs: The median family income in the United States in 2008 was about $62,000. In 2000 it was about $50,000. Were families better off financially in 2008? To find out, you have to know that inflation increased during that period by 25 percent. To calculate the real income difference, follow these steps:

1. First, find the nominal increase:

   $62,000 minus $50,000 = $12,000.

2. Find the percentage increase in nominal income by dividing the amount of increase by the original income. Then multiply by 100:

   $12,000 ÷ $62,000 = .24 × 100 = 24%

3. Determine the *real* percentage increase by subtracting the inflation percentage from the nominal percentage increase in income:

   24% minus 25% = −1%

As these calculations show, real incomes did not keep pace with inflation. In fact, families actually earned 1 percent less income in 2008 than in 2000.

Did You Know?

The most extreme modern example of inflation is Zimbabwe, with almost 15,000 percent in mid-2008. Historians blame the rise of the Nazis in 1930s Austria and Germany partly on the sudden poverty caused by extreme inflation.

Essential Question

Passing tax laws and monitoring how taxes are spent are functions that lie with Congress. Government expenditures, such as defense spending, have a huge effect on the economy by flowing tax revenues back into industries that receive government contracts. Federal grants to states for infrastructure and education are other ways that the government injects funds into the economy, providing services, research, and jobs in communities with fewer resources.

Chapter Spotlight Video

To generate student interest and provide a springboard for class discussion, access the Chapter 20 Video at glencoe.com or on the video DVD.

Dinah Zike's Foldables are three-dimensional, interactive graphic organizers that help students practice basic writing skills, review key vocabulary terms, and identify main ideas. Have students complete this chapter's Foldable activity or activities in *Dinah Zike's Reading and Study Skills Foldables* booklet. **OL**

Government ONLINE

Visit glencoe.com and enter *QuickPass*™ code USG9085c20T for Chapter 20 Resources including Chapter Overview, Student Web Activity, Self-Check Quiz, and other materials for students and teachers.

CHAPTER 20

Chapter Audio   Spotlight Video

Taxing and Spending

Essential Question

How does the government spend the taxes you pay, and how do government expenditures affect the economy?

Government ONLINE
Chapter Overview Visit glencoe.com and enter *QuickPass*™ code USG9822c20 for an overview, a quiz, and other chapter resources.

Engraving plate for a ten-dollar bill

554

Launching the Chapter

The Origin of Taxes The need for revenues, such as to raise and equip an army, lies behind a nation's imposition of taxes. The Civil War led to a tax on income, but this expired after the war. The Sixteenth Amendment to the Constitution, ratified in 1913, gave Congress the power to collect income taxes, in part because high tariffs and excise taxes had an unfair effect on poorer citizens. **Essential Question:** Could the federal government operate without the revenues of the income tax? Explain. *(Students should logically explain their answers.)* **OL**

Raising Money

Reader's Guide

Content Vocabulary
★ taxes *(p. 555)*
★ taxable income *(p. 555)*
★ dependent *(p. 556)*
★ withholding *(p. 556)*
★ securities *(p. 559)*
★ national debt *(p. 559)*

Academic Vocabulary
★ anticipate *(p. 556)*
★ estimate *(p. 556)*
★ impose *(p. 557)*

Reading Strategy
As you read, complete a graphic organizer similar to the one below to list the types of taxes the federal government uses for revenue.

Types of Taxes

Issues in the News

About 55 percent of Americans file their tax returns electronically, and the number is increasing. Most people file online because they think it is convenient, despite some concerns about Internet security. One polling firm reported that 50 percent of filers use a professional tax preparer, 25 percent use a software program, 15 percent still use pen and paper, and 8 percent rely on a friend or relative for help. Two-thirds of the people surveyed said that they expect to get a tax refund, and this is another reason to file online—it speeds up the turnaround time for receiving a refund. "We generally apply it [tax refund] to some kind of debt," said Sharon Caughron, a North Carolina schoolteacher.

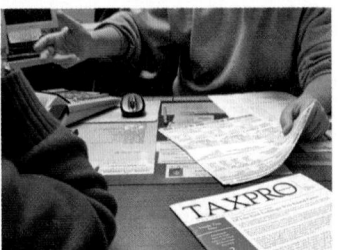

▲ E-filing has become an increasingly popular method of handling an unpopular activity.

Collecting taxes is one way the federal government affects the nation's economy. The government's budget is calculated in figures that are too large for most people to comprehend. In 2007 the federal government took in about $2.3 trillion in revenues—an average of nearly $8,024 for each person in the nation. Two major sources of this revenue are taxes and borrowing.

Taxes as a Source of Revenue

"In this world, nothing is certain but death and taxes," Benjamin Franklin once said. This quote sums up a universal feeling about taxes. **Taxes** are payments made by individuals and businesses to support government activities. The Constitution states the following:

❝ *The Congress shall have Power To lay and collect Taxes, Duties, Imposts and Excises, to pay the Debts and provide for the common Defence and general Welfare of the United States.* ❞
—Article I, Section 8

Individual Income Tax

The individual income tax is the federal government's biggest single source of revenue. About 45 cents of every dollar the government collects comes from this source. In a recent year, the individual income tax produced almost $1.16 trillion.

The federal income tax is levied on a person's **taxable income,** an individual's total income minus certain deductions and exemptions. People may elect to take deductions for contributions made to

---

Focus

Bellringer
Section Focus Transparencies 20-1

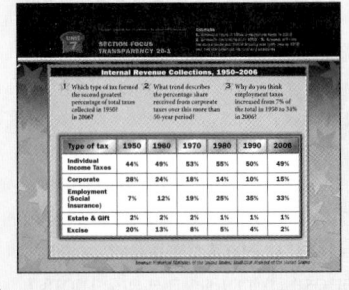

Reader's Guide

Answers to Graphic:
individual income tax, corporate income tax, social insurance taxes, excise taxes, customs duties, estate and gift taxes

Resource Manager

R Reading Strategies	**C** Critical Thinking	**D** Differentiated Instruction	**W** Writing Support	**S** Skill Practice
Additional Resources • Guid. Read. Act., p. 71 • Quizzes/Tests, p. 245	**Teacher Edition** • Identifying Alternatives, p. 556 • Making Inferences, p. 558 **Additional Resources** • Read. Essen., pp. 224–226	**Teacher Edition** • Interpersonal, p. 558 **Additional Resources** • Foldables, p. 63 • Gov. Sims. and Debates, pp. 44–49	**Additional Resources** • Authentic Assess., p. 27	**Teacher Edition** • Researching, p. 559 **Additional Resources** • Inter. Poli. Cartoons, pp. 39–40

Teach

C Critical Thinking

Identifying Alternatives
Remind students that the individual income tax is a progressive tax. Ask them if they favor or oppose the principle of a higher tax rate for people who make more money. Have students explain their opinions. *(Some students may say it is fairer to tax everyone at the same rate. Others may say that people with higher incomes can more easily afford a higher tax rate.)* Then ask students to develop an alternative way of taxing individual incomes. **OL**

Did You Know?

In the past few years the federal government's annual expenses have exceeded $1 trillion. If you were able to spend $1 million every day, you would need 2,740 years to spend $1 trillion.

Hands-On Chapter Project

Step 1

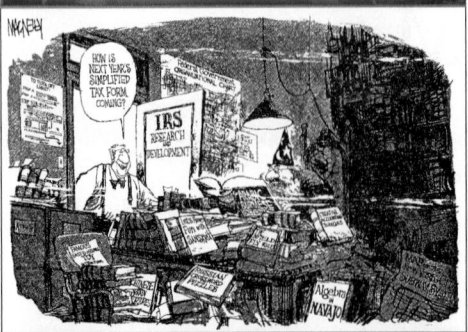

Taxes in America

Critical Thinking Reformers inside and outside government have often suggested ways to simplify the tax forms. *What is the cartoonist suggesting about the capacity of the IRS to revise tax forms in a way helpful to citizens?*

charity, for state and local income taxes, for home mortgage interest, and other expenses. Or, they may take a standard deduction that the government calculates. The government also allows personal exemptions that reduce the amount of taxable income, such as exemptions for the number of dependents. A **dependent** is someone who depends primarily on another person for basic items such as food, clothing, and shelter. Often dependents are children under the age of 18.

The income tax is a progressive tax based on a taxpayer's ability to pay. The higher a person's taxable income is, the higher his or her tax rate is. People with higher incomes can often take advantage of deductions that lower their taxes, but those with incomes above $250,000 pay about two-thirds of all taxes.

The deadline for filing income tax returns each year is April 15. Nearly everyone with taxable income in the preceding calendar year must file income tax returns by that date. During the year, employers withhold a certain amount of money from the workers' wages. This **withholding** pays the **anticipated** taxes ahead of the April 15 filing date. Self-employed people—including business owners, merchants, and professionals—who do not receive regular salaries are expected to file **estimates** of their income four times per year and make payments based on each estimate. In this way, these taxpayers avoid making one large payment for the

year on April 15, while the government receives a steady flow of income throughout the year.

The Internal Revenue Service (IRS), a bureau of the U.S. Treasury Department, collects taxes through regional centers that processed about 132 million individual income tax returns in 2006. IRS staff do a quick computer check on each return and audit, or check more closely, a small percentage of returns. Each year, the IRS investigates many suspected criminal violations of the tax laws.

Corporate Income Tax

Corporations also must pay income taxes. The federal government taxes all the earned income of a corporation beyond its expenses and deductions. In recent years, corporate income taxes have made up about 14 percent of federal revenues. Nonprofit organizations such as colleges, labor unions, and churches are exempt from this tax.

Social Insurance Taxes

The federal government collects huge sums of money each year to pay for Social Security, Medicare, and unemployment compensation programs. The taxes collected to pay for these major social programs are called social insurance taxes. Employees and employers share equally in paying the tax for Social Security and Medicare. Employers deduct it directly from each worker's paycheck, add an equal amount, and send the total to the federal government. The unemployment compensation program is a combined federal-state operation that is financed largely by a federal tax on business payrolls. All these social insurance taxes are often called payroll taxes.

Social insurance taxes are the fastest-growing source of federal income. In 1950 they amounted to $4 billion. In fiscal year 2004, these taxes brought in more than $700 billion. The second-largest source of federal tax income, social insurance taxes were expected to reach $950 billion by 2009.

Unlike other taxes, social insurance taxes do not go into the government's general fund. Instead, they go to Treasury Department special trust accounts. Congress then appropriates money from these accounts to pay benefits. These taxes are referred to as *regressive* because people with lower incomes pay a larger percentage of their income for these taxes than people with higher incomes.

Excise Taxes

Excise taxes are taxes on the manufacture, transportation, sale, or consumption of goods and the performance of services—gas and cigarette taxes are

Preparing a Nation's Budget

Step 1: Seeing the "Big Picture" Students will work in groups to form fictitious countries for which they will develop budgets. They may use the countries created in Chapter 1 or create new ones.

Directions Divide the class into several groups, representing these countries. Have students select a name for a fictitious country about the size of Sweden. Tell them they each have $100 billion in revenue to spend on all

government programs. In Step 1 they will create a poster showing the name and shape of their country, indicating its geographical features; natural resources; population distribution (urban, rural, or mixed); and, using icons to show major industries, its stage of development (developed or developing).

Putting It Together Ask each group to show the posters and acquaint the class with their country. **OL BL**

(Chapter Project continued in Section 2.)

excise taxes, for example. The Constitution permits levying excise taxes, and since 1789 Congress has placed excise taxes on many goods. Early targets included taxes on horse carriages, snuff (smokeless tobacco), and liquor. Today the government **imposes** excise taxes on gas, tobacco, and liquor, but also on airline tickets and highways. Sometimes excise taxes are called luxury taxes because they are levied on goods like exotic cars and boats. Excise taxes contribute about $65 billion per year to federal revenues. Highway and airport taxes bring in the most income.

Customs Duties

Taxes levied on imported goods are called customs duties, tariffs, or import duties. The federal government imposes them to raise revenue or to protect domestic business and agriculture from foreign competition. A high customs duty is called a protective tariff. Many business, labor, and farm groups support protective tariffs.

The Constitution gives Congress the authority to levy customs and to decide which imports will be taxed and at what rate. In turn, Congress has given the president authority to revise tariff rates through executive orders. In doing so, the president takes trade agreements with other nations into account.

After the income tax was passed in 1916, custom duties shrank as a source for federal revenues. In a recent period, they have produced about $26 billion, or 1 cent of every tax dollar collected.

Estate and Gift Taxes

An estate tax is on property and money left after someone has died. A gift tax is on money someone gives while they are living. First levied in 1916, the estate tax in 2007 and 2008 applied to estates worth more than $2 million. The goal of the gift tax is to prevent people from avoid paying the estate tax by giving money to family and friends before they die. (Different rules apply to money given to a spouse.)

Critics of the gift tax say it discourages savings and prevents families from passing on small businesses and farms to their heirs. Others argue that an estate tax can be structured only to apply to the super rich. In 2001, Congress repealed this tax gradually phasing it out over a number of years. But this provision has a "sunset" provision, in other words, it will expire in 2010 unless it is made permanent. Since Democrats are expected to dominate Congress, it is likely that the estate tax will be reinstated.

Taxes and the Economy

Governments at all levels can use taxes to influence the economy. Some tax laws aim to encourage an activity. Tax deductions for home mortgage interest, for example, encourage people to buy homes. That, in turn, helps the construction

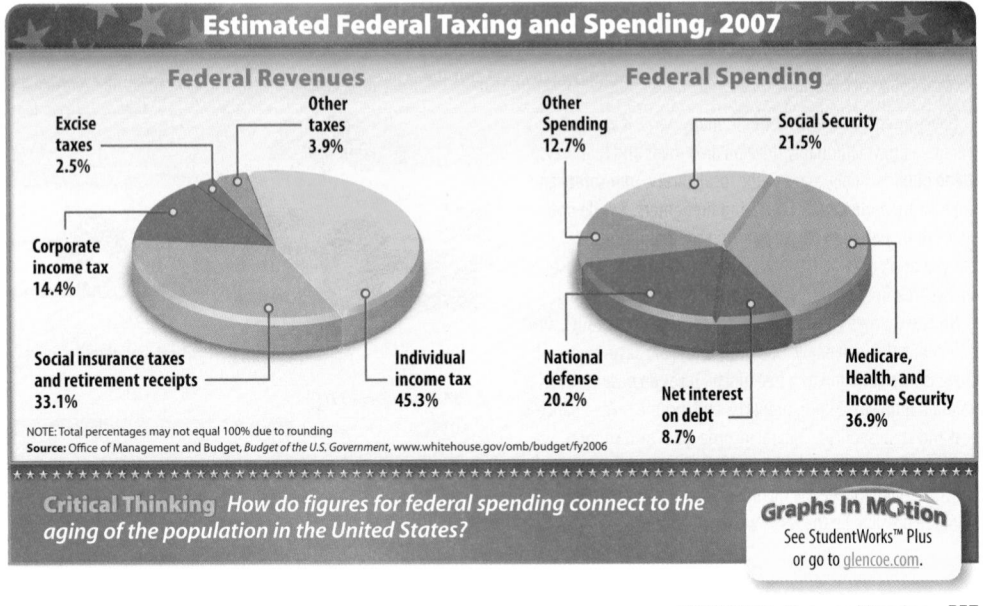

Estimated Federal Taxing and Spending, 2007

Federal Revenues
- Excise taxes 2.5%
- Other taxes 3.9%
- Corporate income tax 14.4%
- Social insurance taxes and retirement receipts 33.1%
- Individual income tax 45.3%

Federal Spending
- Other Spending 12.7%
- Social Security 21.5%
- National defense 20.2%
- Net interest on debt 8.7%
- Medicare, Health, and Income Security 36.9%

NOTE: Total percentages may not equal 100% due to rounding
Source: Office of Management and Budget, *Budget of the U.S. Government,* www.whitehouse.gov/omb/budget/fy2006

Critical Thinking *How do figures for federal spending connect to the aging of the population in the United States?*

Graphs In Motion
See StudentWorks™ Plus or go to glencoe.com.

CHAPTER 20: *Taxing and Spending* 557

Participating IN GOVERNMENT

Filling Out Tax Returns Obtain copies of income tax forms from the Internet, the local post office, or the library. Have students study and discuss them. Show students how to use the tax tables. Point out that tax rates increase with income levels. Note the kinds of deductions and exemptions that taxpayers may claim. Then provide students with the information they need to fill out a return for a hypothetical family. Have some students calculate the return using standard deductions and have others itemize deductions. Allow students to work in pairs if they like. **OL**

Critical Thinking

Answer: The cost of both the Social Security and Medicare programs tend to grow along with the number of senior citizens in the country.

Graph Skills Practice
What accounts for the largest percentage of federal spending? *(Medicare, Health, and Income Security, 36.9%)*

Differentiated Instruction

Activity: Multiple Learning Styles

Logical/Mathematical Have students create a bar graph showing the net amount received by the federal government from each of the various kinds of taxes discussed in the section. Assign different students several recent years so that they can compare one another's graphs to see what changes have occurred, if any, in each revenue source. Information for the graphs is available in *The World Almanac.* Tell students to look in the index for the subheading "Budget" under the main heading "United States." **OL**

C Critical Thinking

Making Inferences Many Americans feel that tax exemptions for certain people are unfair. One argument for exemptions is that some encourage activities that will benefit everyone in a society. **Ask:** Which entrepreneurs should receive a tax exemption—inventors of "green" technology or a creator of manufacturing jobs in the inner city? *(Answers will vary but students should consider the social benefits of both.)* **AL**

D Differentiated Instruction

Interpersonal Organize the class into three groups to find ways to reduce the federal deficit. Assign one group to raising taxes, another to reduce spending, and one group to brainstorm other ways of reducing the deficit. Then have representatives of each group present their ideas and work out a compromise solution. **OL**

Government *and* You

More About Government Benefits Taxes also support parks, monuments, school breakfast programs, disaster relief, and the space program.

Differentiated Instruction

industry and promotes stable communities. A tax exemption on oil exploration encourages people to invest their money in businesses that search for new energy sources. The government also can use taxes to discourage certain activities. Cigarettes are heavily taxed because smoking is dangerous to people's health.

Tax Exemptions

Tax exemptions are a privilege granted by government that legally frees certain types of property, sales, or income from taxpaying obligations. Most states, for example, exempt educational and religious groups from paying property taxes. Another type of exemption applies to the interest one might earn from investing in national, state, or local government bonds.

Tax exemptions function as a government subsidy to certain groups. Over the years, railroads, airlines, farmers, businesses, builders, defense contractors, the unemployed, the elderly, and veterans have received tax exemptions. In fact, the federal income tax is a complicated maze of exemptions. These so-called tax loopholes are usually discovered by attorneys and tax specialists who are hired for this purpose. Critics of the income tax system believe that such exemptions are unfair since only corporations or the wealthy can take

full advantage of them. Special-interest groups constantly lobby Congress to pass tax exemptions for them. Sometimes exemptions granted to one group negatively affect another group. Tax subsidies for the airline industry, for example, might adversely affect the railroad industry.

Tax Reforms

In 1985 President Reagan proposed tax changes to eliminate what he called a "source of confusion and resentment." The resulting Tax Reform Act of 1986 reduced tax deductions, tax credits, tax shelters, and the number of tax brackets or rates. In 2003 President George W. Bush signed the Job and Growth Act, which was intended to make the massive tax cuts of 2001 permanent. This reduced taxes for millions and increased the child tax credit from $600 to $1,000. In 2006 tax cuts were passed again, with most Democrats opposing the bill and most Republicans supporting it. These cuts were meant to stimulate spending and boost the economy but most of the provisions expire in 2009 so their future is uncertain.

Tax Credits

Today the federal government provides tax credits mostly to people with lower incomes. Tax credits allow taxpayers to reduce their income tax liability.

Government *and* You

Why We Pay Taxes

Government makes life better in many ways. If you are an average teen, you probably drive on area roads and highways, attend public schools, and use the local library. Your safety and property are protected by police and firefighters. You do not expect to be poisoned by the food you eat and the water that you drink or to be harmed by the products that you use. You live free from fear of foreign invasion or guerrilla attack.

No one charges you directly for these services, benefits, and protections that you enjoy. However, as the old saying goes, "there is no such thing as a free lunch." Taxes on gasoline maintain highways. Sales, property, and income taxes finance local and state services. Federal income taxes also support many programs and services. In fact, most government activities that enhance the quality of life in the United States are made possible by the taxes we pay.

▲ Taxes support critical ambulance services.

Participating IN GOVERNMENT ACTIVITY

Investigate Determine the role of government in providing and paying for some facility, program, or service that you enjoy in your community.

Interpreting Political Cartoons, p. 39

Taxing and Spending

Objective: Understand the relationship between employment and inflation.

Focus/Teach: Examine and discuss the cartoon with students.

Assess: Have students answer the "Analyzing the Cartoon" questions on page 40.

Close: Discuss with students the effect unemployment has on inflation.

Differentiated Instruction Strategies

BL Discuss why the "common person" in the cartoon keeps saying "That's great!"

AL Create a graph or chart showing the relationship between inflation and unemployment as a percentage.

ELL Discuss the meaning of the word *inflation* and how that meaning applies to the economy.

Tax Cut Debates

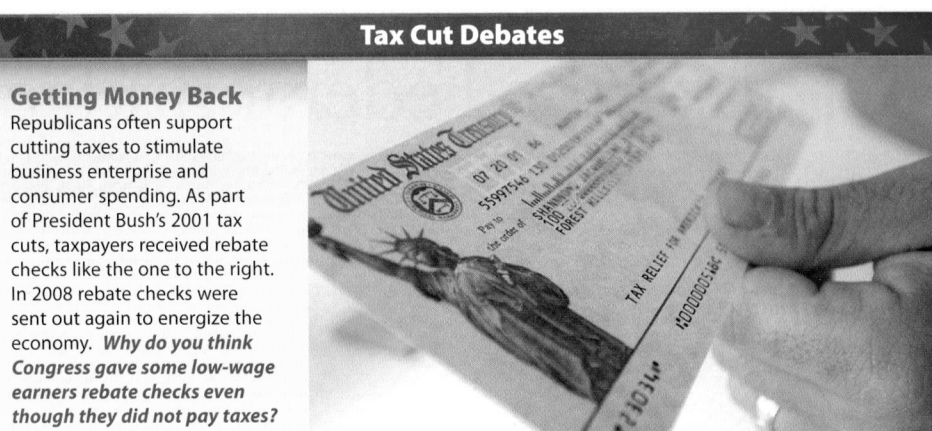

Getting Money Back
Republicans often support cutting taxes to stimulate business enterprise and consumer spending. As part of President Bush's 2001 tax cuts, taxpayers received rebate checks like the one to the right. In 2008 rebate checks were sent out again to energize the economy. *Why do you think Congress gave some low-wage earners rebate checks even though they did not pay taxes?*

Each dollar of tax credit offsets a dollar of tax liability. The earned-income credit enables many low-income families to receive refunds.

Workers who must pay for child care or claim dependents receive a tax credit for that expense. Certain elderly and retired people may be entitled to a tax credit, depending on the amount of their income.

Borrowing for Revenue

In addition to collecting taxes, the federal government borrows money. In 2007 the Bush administration estimated that borrowing was about $162 billion, with a projected $410 billion expected to be borrowed in 2008. The government borrows by selling federal **securities**—financial instruments that include bonds, notes, and treasury bills. Federal government securities are popular because they are among the safest securities in the world and because interest might not be taxable. The most popular bonds for small investors are savings bonds, which lend the government money and allow investors to earn interest on these bonds. The federal government pays a huge amount of interest.

When the government spends more than its income, it runs a deficit. Government borrowing to fund annual budget deficits over time creates the **national debt.** The size of the national debt affects the federal budget and the economy.

Caption Answer: Student answers will vary; some students may suggest that low-wage earners needed the rebate checks to help pay for necessities.

S Skill Practice

Researching Have students use a dictionary, the Internet, and library resources to research the definitions of *bonds, notes, treasury bills, deficit,* and *surplus.* When they are done, they should create a short glossary of these government revenue terms. **BL**

Assess

Assign the Section 1 Assessment as homework or as an in-class activity, or have students take Section Quiz 20-1 from *Section Quizzes and Chapter Tests.*

Close

Analyzing Have students list the three major sources of federal revenue. Then ask what they think the three most important sources *should* be, according to how each would affect the economy. **OL**

Section 1 Review

SECTION 1 Review

Vocabulary

1. **Explain** the significance of: taxes, taxable income, dependent, withholding, securities, national debt.

Main Ideas

2. **Explaining** What is the federal government's biggest single source of tax revenue?

3. **Describing** What are tax credits, and how do they affect taxpayers?

Critical Thinking

4. **Identifying Alternatives** Why does the government raise most of its revenues through taxing rather than borrowing?

5. **Organizing** Use a graphic organizer like the one below to show the steps in collecting federal income tax.

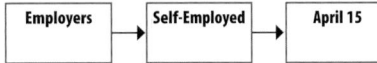

Employers	→	Self-Employed	→	April 15

Writing About Government

6. **Expository Writing** Obtain a paycheck stub—yours or a family member's. Note the categories and amounts of money that are deducted for city and state taxes, FICA, and Social Security. Create a graph that shows the percentage of the earned wages deducted in each category. Write a brief summary that explains the different taxes deducted from the check.

CHAPTER 20: *Taxing and Spending* **559**

Answers

1. All definitions can be found in the section and the Glossary.
2. individual income tax
3. Tax credits allow taxpayers to reduce their income tax liability. Each dollar of tax credit reduces taxes owed by a dollar.
4. Although taxes are unpopular, borrowing costs the government a huge amount of interest, adds to the national debt, and threatens the nation's economic security.
5. Employers withhold estimated taxed from workers' pay and send the money to the IRS;

self-employed people pay an estimated tax 4 times per year; by April 15 the following year, each taxpayer must file a return and send any amount still owed.
6. Tell students to complete this activity at home. (They should not bring the paycheck stub to school.) Remind students to drop the decimal point in expressing the amount in each category as a percentage. Students' summaries should explain the taxes deducted from the check.

Focus

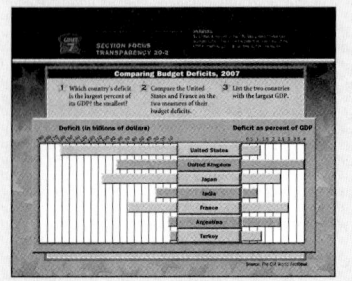
Reader's Guide

Answers to Graphic: Social Security, pensions for retired government employees, Medicare, Medicaid, and veterans' benefits

Preparing the Federal Budget

Reader's Guide

Content Vocabulary	Academic Vocabulary	Reading Strategy
★ fiscal year (p. 560)	★ confer (p. 560)	Create a graphic organizer similar to the one below to list entitlements provided by the government.
★ uncontrollables (p. 561)	★ preliminary (p. 561)	
★ entitlement (p. 561)	★ evaluate (p. 562)	
★ incrementalism (p. 564)		

Entitlements

Issues in the News

For two years running, Republican President George W. Bush wanted to trim or cut certain domestic programs from the annual budget. "I proposed a budget," Bush said, "that terminates or substantially reduces 151 wasteful or bloated programs. . . . And if Congress sends me [spending] bills that exceed the reasonable limits I have set, I will veto the bills." Many Democratic legislators were angry. Michigan's Democratic Senator Debbie Stabenow stated: "From cutting health care for the most vulnerable among us, to failing to make any real investments to support American manufacturing, this president's priorities are clear." As expected, congressional Democrats stated that they would oppose the president's budget plans.

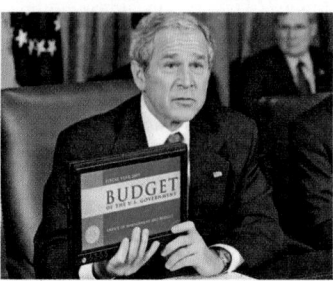

▲ President George W. Bush holding a tablet PC with the 2009 federal budget

Since its founding, the nation has always carefully accounted for its revenue and expenditures. Today, the federal budget is used to predict and control revenue and spending. The budget follows a **fiscal year**—the 12-month accounting period from October 1 to September 30 of the next year. The executive and legislative branches share in the responsibility of preparing the budget. Under the president's direction, the executive branch proposes a budget. Congress then uses this budget as a basis for preparing a tax and spending plan to submit to the president.

The President's Budget

The federal budget is not just numbers. The budget expresses important political choices by the president's administration. Each year's budget aims to promote the president's policies and priorities. In presenting the 2009 budget, White House staff highlighted such policy goals as combating terrorism, balancing the budget by 2012, and slowing the growth of entitlement spending.

The Budget and Accounting Act of 1921 makes the president responsible for directing the preparation of the budget and making key decisions about national budget priorities. The law requires the president to propose to Congress the budget for the entire federal government each fiscal year. This budget must be delivered within 15 days after Congress convenes each January.

The actual day-to-day preparation of the budget is the responsibility of the Office of Management and Budget (OMB). The OMB, along with the president's Council of Economic Advisers (CEA), **confers** with the president on a wide range of budgetary matters.

Resource Manager

Start of the Process

Budget making begins in early spring for the budget that will go into effect one year from the following October. Each federal agency draws up a list of its own spending plans and sends these requests to the OMB.

The director of the OMB takes the first set of figures to the president, along with OMB's analysis of the nation's economic situation. At this point, the president, assisted by the secretary of the treasury and the CEA, makes key decisions about the impact of the **preliminary** budget on the administration's general economic policy and goals. They discuss such questions as: Will the budget increase or reduce federal spending? Which federal programs will be cut back and which programs will be expanded? Will the federal government need to borrow more money? Should taxes be raised or lowered?

Agencies Review Their Budgets

The White House returns its decisions on the budget to the agencies and departments with guidelines to help them prepare their final budgets. The Department of Defense, for example, might be told to cut its budget by $5 billion, and the Transportation Department might be told it can increase its budget by $1 billion. Over the next few months, the executive departments and agencies work on detailed budget plans that fit the president's guidelines. During this time, OMB officials and agency heads negotiate cuts and additions to bring each agency's budget in line with the president's decisions.

Final Presidential Review

Sometime during the fall, the OMB submits a complete budget document to the president for final review and approval. Some last-minute juggling always takes place. Agency heads might make last-ditch efforts to convince the president to overrule an OMB decision and save a particular program. The president might order changes in parts of the budget in response to pressure from interest groups or political party members. Finally, the administration rushes the president's budget to the printer—often only days or perhaps hours before the January deadline. Then the president formally sends the budget to Congress along with an annual budget message. After receiving it, Congress takes the next steps in finalizing the federal budget.

Uncontrollables

Despite having a key role in the budget process, the president does not have complete freedom in making budgetary decisions. About 70 percent of the federal budget consists of what are called **uncontrollables.** Uncontrollables are expenditures required by law or resulting from previous budgetary commitments.

A major part of uncontrollable spending is the **entitlements.** Entitlements are benefits that Congress must by law provide to individuals. Entitlements include Social Security, pensions for retired government employees, Medicare, Medicaid, and veterans' benefits.

The other important uncontrollable item in the budget is the interest that must be paid on the national debt. As yearly budgets have forced the federal government to borrow more and more money, interest on the debt has grown. In fiscal year 2007, interest on the debt was equal to 8.7 percent of the total expenses for the federal government.

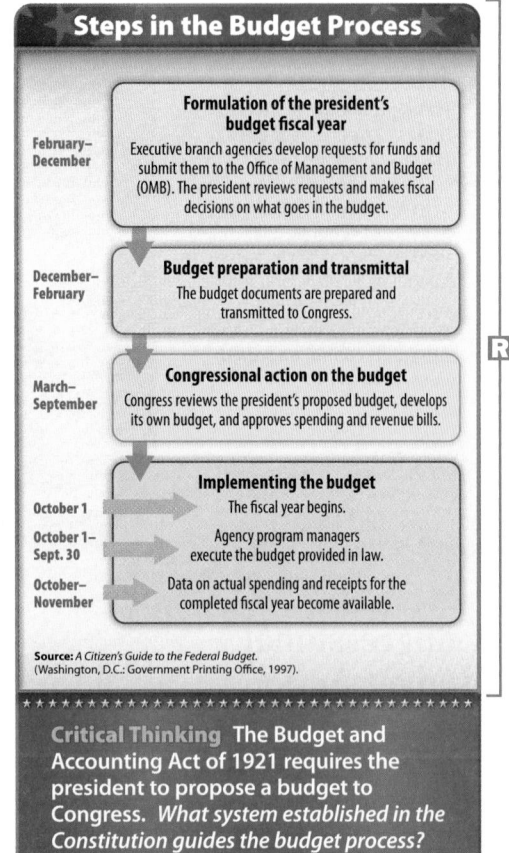

Steps in the Budget Process

February–December

Formulation of the president's budget fiscal year
Executive branch agencies develop requests for funds and submit them to the Office of Management and Budget (OMB). The president reviews requests and makes fiscal decisions on what goes in the budget.

December–February

Budget preparation and transmittal
The budget documents are prepared and transmitted to Congress.

March–September

Congressional action on the budget
Congress reviews the president's proposed budget, develops its own budget, and approves spending and revenue bills.

Implementing the budget
October 1 — The fiscal year begins.
October 1–Sept. 30 — Agency program managers execute the budget provided in law.
October–November — Data on actual spending and receipts for the completed fiscal year become available.

Source: *A Citizen's Guide to the Federal Budget.* (Washington, D.C.: Government Printing Office, 1997).

Critical Thinking The Budget and Accounting Act of 1921 requires the president to propose a budget to Congress. *What system established in the Constitution guides the budget process?*

Teach

R Reading Strategy

Reading Charts Students should carefully read the flowchart "Steps in the Budget Process," paying attention to the ways in which the budget involves both the executive and the legislative branches. **Ask:** How can students tell from the chart alone that the Office of Management and Budget is part of the executive branch? *(The OMB helps the president prepare the budget.)* How does the final step reflect the constitutional principle of checks and balances? *(When data on actual spending and receipts are published, Congress can monitor the performance of the executive branch.)* **OL**

Critical Thinking

Answer: checks and balances

Chart Skills Practice
When do agencies develop and submit requests for funds? *(February–December)*

Additional Support

Activity: Collaborative Learning

Making a Flowchart Organize the class into small groups and ask each group to devise an illustrated flowchart showing the steps in the budget-making process. Some students in each group may write the text of each component on the chart, others should design the layout of the chart, and others may illustrate, edit, and critique the chart. Post the charts on the bulletin board and have students compare them to one another for accuracy and clarity. **Ask:** Which ones are the most effective and clear? How could the others be improved? **OL**

S Skill Practice

Researching Have students research zero-based budgeting (ZBB) and explain how it differs from incrementalism. *(ZBB starts from a "zero base" and includes what is needed for the upcoming period, regardless of the previous budget. Incrementalism adds to or subtracts from the previous budget piece by piece.)* Have students list advantages and disadvantages of each system. Ask students to present arguments in favor of or opposing the use of each system with the federal budget. **Ask:** Which system of budgeting does the federal government use? *(There are aspects of both, but there is more incrementalism.)* **AL**

C Critical Thinking

Making Connections Ask: What is the check and balance for the Office of Management and Budget? *(The Congressional Budget Office)* **BL**

Hands-On Chapter Project

Step 2

Preparing a Nation's Budget

Step 2: Analyzing Needs Students will consider what factors determine the allocation of a country's resources.

Directions Before determining how their country should spend its money, students must identify its needs and problems. Have students consider demographics, such as income distribution; literacy, unemployment, and infant mortality rates; and major industries. Groups may want to look at the CIA's *World Factbook* for

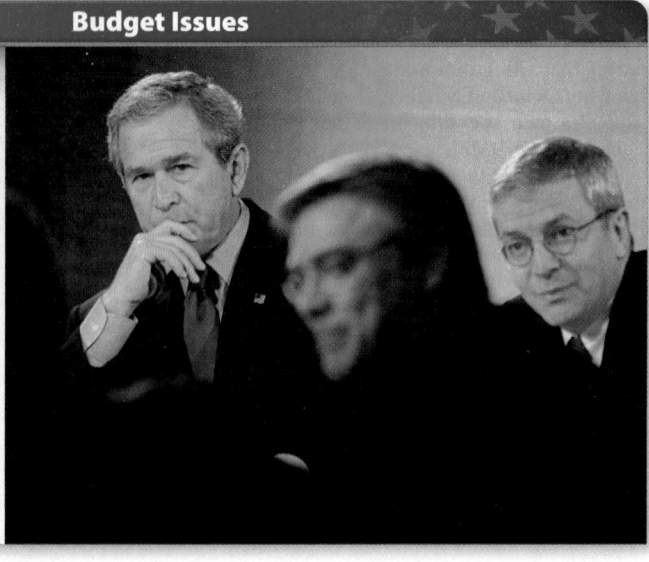

Discussing the Budget President George W. Bush (left) listens to a panelist at a White House conference on the economy. The costs of the war in Iraq and fighting terrorism, as well as economic challenges in the world market, intensified budget debates during the eight years of the Bush presidency. *Which domestic programs cannot be scaled back, even in wartime?*

Congressional Budget Action

Article I, Section 9, of the Constitution requires that Congress approve all federal spending. Thus, the president draws up budget proposals, but only Congress has the power to raise revenue and pass appropriations. No money may be spent and no taxes may be collected until Congress approves.

Congress can revise the president's budget proposals as it sees fit. Conflict between Congress and the president over the budget is inevitable. If the opposing party, not the president's party, controls either house of Congress, that house might criticize the president's budget.

Even if the president's party controls Congress, lawmakers may have different ideas than the president as to how money should be allocated. Key lawmakers and the president often must negotiate different parts of the budget. Compromises are usually necessary on both sides before a budget is passed.

Congressional Budget Act of 1974

For years, separate subcommittees of the Senate and House handled each agency's requested expenditures. This separation made it difficult for Congress to keep track of the total annual budget.

To remedy this situation, Congress passed the Congressional Budget Act in 1974. This law set up House and Senate Budget Committees and the Congressional Budget Office (CBO).

The CBO's job is to **evaluate** carefully the overall federal budget for Congress. The CBO has its own professional staff of experts. They report to Congress and act as a counterbalance to the OMB in the executive branch.

Gramm-Rudman-Hollings Act

By the mid-1980s, the size and growth of the national debt worried many economists. In 1985 Congress enacted the Balanced Budget and Emergency Deficit Control Act, known as the Gramm-Rudman-Hollings Act (GRH) after the senators who designed it. This law was intended to force the president and Congress to cooperate on programs that would reduce budget deficits.

GRH and later amendments required the OMB and CBO to issue a joint report each year estimating how much the proposed budget would exceed income and how much it should be cut to meet deficit-reduction targets. Yet the federal budget deficit continued to grow because the president and Congress could not agree on budgetary priorities and, therefore, on which programs could be cut or trimmed back. The failure to meet deficit-reduction targets prompted Congress to search for another remedy.

examples. Have groups list these major funding categories: Health; Education, Training, Employment, and Social Services; Social Security; Medicare; Income Security; Environment and Natural Resources; and Defense. Under each category, they will list the types of programs covered by that category. They will then highlight several programs that require extra funding and note why. For example, extra funding may be needed for "disease control" under the Health category due to a malaria epidemic affecting vast regions of the country. Or, a

population with a low literacy rate might require higher Education expenditures.

Putting It Together Ask the class to suggest the kinds of problems various countries around the world are currently experiencing that they think government should address. **OL AL**

(Chapter Project continued in Section 3.)

Budgetary Enforcement Act of 1990

When George H.W. Bush was in office, debates regarding what to do about the budget deficit continued. After lengthy negotiations, President George H.W. Bush and the Democratic Congress agreed on the Budgetary Enforcement Act (BEA). The BEA divided the budget into three areas: domestic policy, defense, and international affairs. It was decided that any spending that exceeded the budgeted limit in any area would come out of the next year's funding for that area.

A recession starting in 1990, however, temporarily derailed this deficit-cutting plan. When the economy improved beginning in 1993, partly as a result of the new Internet economy, tax receipts increased substantially. This made the job of reducing the deficit easier. Some members of Congress then called for a balanced budget. President Bill Clinton and other members of Congress, however, were satisfied that the annual deficits had been reduced from more than $300 billion to about $145 billion.

The booming economy of the Clinton administration created an impression that budget deficits were a thing of the past, but during the two terms of the George W. Bush administration,

deficits began to grow again. In 2007 the national debt was approximately $9 trillion. The debt represented about 64 percent of the nation's gross domestic product.

Steps in Congressional Budget Making

The budget-making process generally follows three steps:

- the House and Senate Budget Committees review;
- reconcile differences between the House and Senate versions of the budget bill;
- final budget aligns with the Budgetary Enforcement Act of 1990.

During the first step, House and Senate budget committees review the major features of the president's budget proposals. On April 15, these committees prepare a concurrent resolution. With the president's proposals as a starting point, this resolution identifies the total federal spending and tax plan for the coming fiscal year.

The next step, called reconciliation, occurs between April 15 and June 15. House and Senate committees reconcile, or fit, the spending and

We the People

Making a Difference

Taxes pay for many community services, but a private citizen can also step in to meet a need. Leonard Sanders, a retired mine worker in the tiny town of Elkville, Illinois, won the state lottery in 1995. Sanders had plenty of uses for the money. After dividing his winnings with his wife and children, however, he decided to direct some of his extra cash to improving his hometown. Sanders helped restore the 90-year-old church where his wife worshiped as a child. Then he bought and refurbished an empty grocery store to convert into a community center. He purchased two new pool tables, exercise equipment, furniture, and a television set for the center. Friends pitched in to build a small kitchen. The kitchen is stocked with free food and drinks that are paid for by a trust. Sanders set up the trust to fund the operation for future generations. The new community center provides a place for Elkville residents to gather for recreation and conversation. Sanders's additional plans for his town include a pavilion for the baseball park.

"Money will never change my attitude toward life," he said. "Elkville is really a nice place with a nice bunch of intelligent people. I've known most of them for 20 or 30 years, and we have always gotten along."

> "Money will never change my attitude toward life."
> —Leonard Sanders

Activity: Collaborative Learning

Drawing Conclusions Have students work individually or in groups to compose letters to the president of the United States regarding reducing the federal budget deficit. Students should address the problems associated with deficit spending and the impact it may have on their future and their families' future. Students may also pick a method of reducing federal budget deficits, such as raising taxes or cutting federal spending, and provide supporting reasons for one or both of these measures. Students should state their arguments and then use examples to support those arguments. **OL**

C Critical Thinking

Making Inferences Ask:
Why do you think a modern democracy tends to avoid radical proposals like the abolition of an agency? *(Modern nations include constituents of many backgrounds and outlooks; thus they favor moderate changes.)* **AL**

Assess

Assign the Section 2 Assessment as homework or as an in-class activity, or have students take Section Quiz 20-2 from *Section Quizzes and Chapter Tests.*

Close

Assessing Ask: What programs would you cut back or eliminate if you were trying to balance the budget? Who might oppose your proposed cuts? **OL**

Government ONLINE

Objectives and answers to the Student Web Activity can be found in the **Web Activity Lesson Plan** at glencoe.com. Enter *QuickPass*™ code USG9085c20T.

Section 2 Review

Taxing Problem Like any other citizen, U.S. presidents can choose to keep their tax records private. Still, since the early 1970s, most presidents have made at least part of their returns public. In 2007, for example, President and Mrs. George W. Bush reported a taxable income of $719,274; they paid $221,635 in federal taxes. Vice President Dick Cheney and wife Lynne had an even better year, with a taxable income of $2,528,068; they paid $602,651 in federal taxes.

taxing plans of the concurrent resolution with existing programs. Then the agreed-upon changes are put into a reconciliation bill that both the House and Senate must vote on and approve.

The House then passes an appropriations bill, officially setting aside money for expenditures approved during the reconciliation process. Congress is supposed to complete this bill by June 30, but the bill is often delayed.

Incremental Budget Making

Some analysts use the term *incrementalism* to explain how budgets tend to be made in American government. **Incrementalism** means that generally the total budget is changed only by an increment, or small amount. Based on the fact that historically budgets have increased incrementally, the best way to forecast what this year's budget will be is to assess last year's budget and add a little more.

Since incrementalism has been the usual practice, federal agencies assume they will get at least the same amount of money they received the previous year. Incrementalism also means that most budget debates focus on a proposed increment or reduction for an agency. For example, a battle over the FBI budget might be over whether its budget should increase by 2 or 5 percent from the previous year, not on whether the FBI should continue to exist.

Incrementalism means that most changes in our political system unfold gradually. This approach fits the need for predictability in bureaucratic operations and it helps administrators manage their agencies on a yearly basis.

Government ONLINE
Student Web Activity Visit glencoe.com and enter *QuickPass*™ code USG9822c20. Click on Student Web Activity and complete the activity about raising money.

SECTION 2 Review

Vocabulary

1. **Explain** the significance of: fiscal year, uncontrollables, entitlement, incrementalism.

Main Ideas

2. **Identifying** Which department is responsible for the day-to-day preparation of the federal budget?

3. **Describing** What did the Congressional Budget Act of 1974 establish?

Critical Thinking

4. **Expressing** Why does the federal government find it difficult to raise taxes or reduce spending to balance the budget?

5. **Organizing** Use a graphic organizer like the one below to show how the budget process is affected if Congress and the president are from different political parties.

Cause		Effect

Writing About Government

6. **Persuasive Writing** Imagine that you are part of a presidential committee that is set up to decide the spending priorities for next year's government budget. Your job is to list the four top areas that you think should have the greatest share of the budget. Prepare a supporting argument for the four areas you choose.

564 UNIT 7: *Public Policies and Services*

Answers

1. All definitions can be found in the section and the Glossary.
2. Office of Management and Budget (OMB)
3. It set up the House and Senate Budget Committees and the Congressional Budget Office (OMB) to streamline congressional review of the federal budget. The CBO (legislative branch) acts as a check on the OMB (executive branch).
4. Most people are opposed to increases in taxes, and the budget contains about 70 percent uncontrollables or entitlements, on which spending cannot be reduced.
5. Cause—president and Congress have different goals and priorities; Effect—budget is slowed due to the need for compromise
6. Allow students to present their arguments for the priorities they have listed.

Interpreting a Bar Graph

Bar graphs provide statistics in a visual format that makes it easy to understand how categories of information relate to each other. Some bar graphs are horizontal; others are vertical, depending on the type of information being shown and the purpose of the graph. Bar graphs have two axes that show the categories being compared. The *x*-axis is a horizontal list, and the *y*-axis is a vertical list of categories, such as time periods, quantities, percentages, items, programs, or events.

Why Learn This Skill?

Being able to interpret a bar graph is essential for understanding statistics about a wide range of subjects. Follow the steps on the left to interpret a bar graph:

1. Read the title, including dates and other qualifiers, to see what information the graph covers.

2. Read the column headings to see which categories are being presented.

3. Notice the source of the data. Ask yourself if the source is reliable.

4. State in sentences what trend or relationships the graph shows.

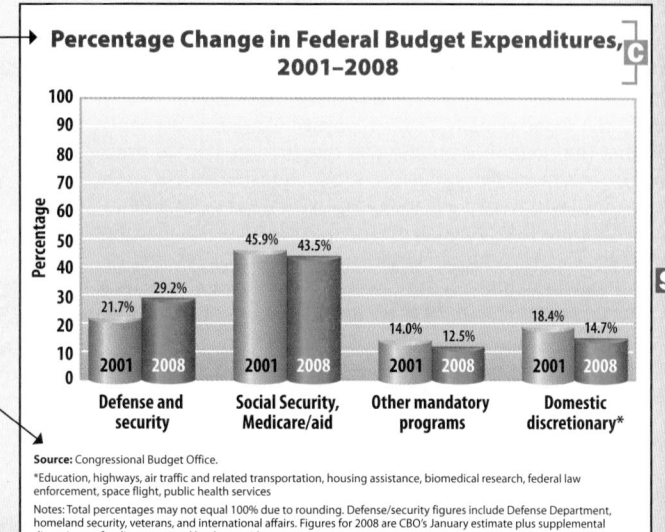

Percentage Change in Federal Budget Expenditures, 2001–2008

Source: Congressional Budget Office.

*Education, highways, air traffic and related transportation, housing assistance, biomedical research, federal law enforcement, space flight, public health services

Notes: Total percentages may not equal 100% due to rounding. Defense/security figures include Defense Department, homeland security, veterans, and international affairs. Figures for 2008 are CBO's January estimate plus supplemental discretionary funding requested by the president.

Practicing the Skill

Study the bar graph and answer the following questions.

1. What is the subject of the bar graph?

2. Which budget category increased from 2001 to 2008, and by what percentage?

3. Do you believe the figures in the chart are accurate? Why or why not?

4. Name some programs whose budgets were cut in 2008.

Applying the Skill

Ask 20 students which president (recent or historic) they most admire. Then create a bar graph showing the percentages for the top five presidents named and a bar labeled "Other."

Teach

S Skill Practice

Accessing Prior Knowledge
Have students brainstorm other types of graphs that they have used or seen. *(Examples can include line, circle or pie, scatter plot, and others.)* Have students try to present the same information from "Percentage Change in Federal Budget Expenditures, 2001–2008" in a different kind of graph. **Ask:** Is there another graph type that also works for presenting this information? Why or why not? *(The bar graph is probably the best option for this particular information because it allows for the comparison of two different dates for many different categories.)* **OL**

C Critical Thinking

Analyzing Information
Discuss with students the importance of properly labeling a bar (or any other kind of) graph. **Ask:** What if the numerical labels were left off one of the axes? *(There would be no reference point for magnitude.)* **OL**

Answers

Practicing the Skill

1. the percentage change in federal budget expenditures from 2001 to 2008

2. defense and security by 7.5%

3. Answers might vary, but students should note that the source, the Congressional Budget Office, is reliable.

4. Refer students to the footnote. Social Security, Medicare, education, highways, air traffic, housing assistance, biomedical research, federal law enforcement, space flight, and public health services.

Applying the Skill

Students should select an issue of concern, develop a nonbiased question to poll a selected sample, record the sample population's answers, and present the results of their poll in a chart, including their sample size and a brief summary.

Focus

Bellringer
**Section Focus Transparencies
20-3**

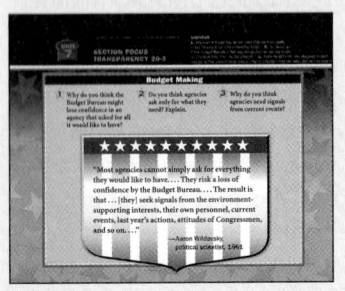

Reader's Guide

Answers to Graphic:

I. Where the Money Goes
   A. Direct Benefit Payments
   B. National Defense
   C. Discretionary Spending
II. Fiscal and Monetary Policy
   A. Fiscal Policy
   B. Monetary Policy

Resource Manager

Managing the Economy

Reader's Guide

Content Vocabulary
★ fiscal policy (p. 567)
★ monetary policy (p. 567)
★ gross domestic product (p. 568)
★ discount rate (p. 569)
★ reserve requirement (p. 569)
★ open-market operations (p. 570)

Academic Vocabulary
★ portion (p. 566)
★ objective (p. 567)
★ infrastructure (p. 567)

Reading Strategy
As you read, create a graphic organizer like the one to the right to help you take notes on managing the economy.

I. Where the Money Goes
   A. Direct Benefit Payments
   B.
   C.
II. Fiscal and Monetary Policy
   A.
   B.

Issues in the News

The main job for Ben Bernanke, chairman of the Federal Reserve since 2006, is to help manage the economy by regulating the money supply. In his report to Congress, Bernanke said that the sluggish economy was due in large part to problems in the mortgage industry. When housing values were increasing, loans were made too easily by banks and other financial institutions that hoped to make a quick buck. In 2008 reality has set in. Too many unsold homes were on the market, and too many people who took on risky loans were unable to make their mortgage payments. Bernanke promised that the Federal Reserve would "act in a timely manner as needed to support [economic] growth." In October 2008, the Federal Reserve cut interest rates yet again to combat the growing economic crisis.

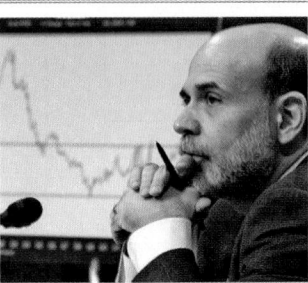

▲ Ben Bernanke, chairman of the Federal Reserve

Bernanke's promise to act is what the nation expects of the head of the Federal Reserve in troubled economic times. The Federal Reserve Board's decisions have a major impact on the economy. Other government officials also play a role in promoting a healthy economy.

Where the Money Goes

The federal government was spending about $4.6 billion per year when Franklin D. Roosevelt became president in 1933. Today, that amount would pay for less than one day of the federal government's expenditures. The government currently spends roughly $3 trillion per year, a figure that can be broken down into its four major components:

• direct benefit payments to individuals
• national defense
• discretionary spending
• interest on the national debt

Direct Benefit Payments

Spending for Social Security, health and welfare programs has become a big part of the federal budget. Almost half of every dollar goes for such items. In a recent budget, the federal government allocated about $960 billion for direct benefit payments of one kind or another. Uncontrollable expenditures are a large **portion** of this budget item. The biggest entitlement program is Social Security. In 2007 it accounted for about $586 billion.

R Reading Strategies	**C** Critical Thinking	**D** Differentiated Instruction	**W** Writing Support	**S** Skill Practice
Additional Resources • Guid. Read. Act., p. 73 • Quizzes/Tests, p. 247	**Teacher Edition** • Contrasting, p. 568 • Synthesizing, p. 569 **Additional Resources** • Read. Essen., pp. 230–232	**Additional Resources** • Foldables, p. 63 • Am. Biographies, p. 74	**Teacher Edition** • Personal Writing, p. 570 **Additional Resources** • Coop. Learning Act., pp. 13–14	**Additional Resources** • Reteaching Act., p. 20 • Ch. Summaries, pp. 58–60

National Defense

Spending for national defense was one of the biggest items in the budget beginning with World War II. When Ronald Reagan became president in 1981, he made increasing the Defense Department budget a major **objective** of his administration. He believed that the international climate at that time called for a raise in spending for military equipment and training.

When changes in the Soviet Union and Eastern Europe signaled an end to the Cold War, President George H.W. Bush announced adjustments in U.S. defense. He vowed to eliminate some nuclear weapons and to end the around-the-clock alert posture of strategic bombers, and he asked the Soviets to do the same. The Clinton administration reduced the share of the defense budget. In 2000 defense spending represented about 16.5 percent of total outlays, down from 22 percent in 1992.

By the 2000 election, many people believed that defense spending had been reduced too much. President George W. Bush fulfilled a campaign promise to increase spending for the military. In 2002 the defense budget increased by more than $11 billion to approximately 17.3 percent. The military response following the September 11, 2001, terrorist attacks demanded even more increases. By 2007, the defense budget had increased by about $100 billion from 2004 levels and was 20.5 percent of the budget.

Discretionary Spending

The federal government spends a sizable portion of tax revenues on the environment, transportation, criminal justice, and other areas. Much of this discretionary spending is in the form of grants to states and localities. State and local governments use federal grants for road repair, public housing, police training, school lunch programs, flood insurance, and so on.

States and communities have come to rely on this intergovernmental revenue for an increasing share of their total revenue. Between 1980 and 1989, however, federal grants to state and local governments declined. More recent federal budgets have increased federal aid to states while shifting federal grants away from **infrastructure** investments and toward public-welfare programs.

Fiscal and Monetary Policy

Beginning with the Great Depression of the 1930s, the federal government has played an increasing role in managing the nation's economy.

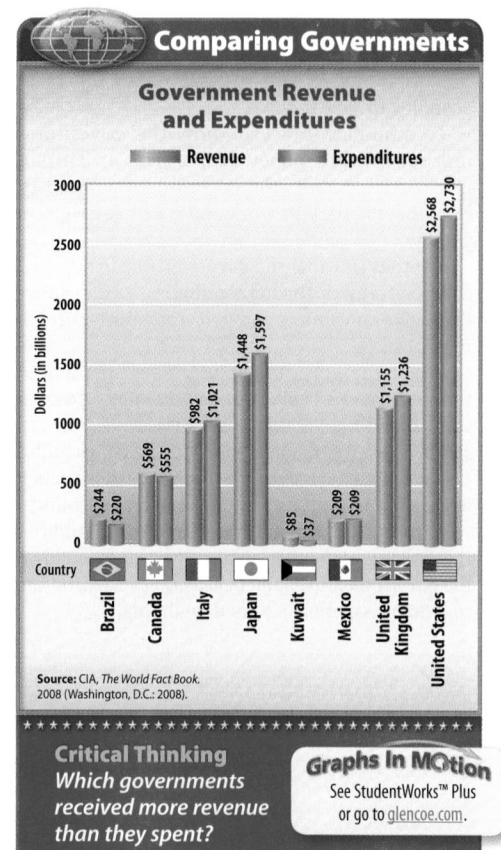

Comparing Governments

Government Revenue and Expenditures

Revenue ■ Expenditures ■

Dollars (in billions)

Country	Revenue	Expenditures
Brazil	$244	$220
Canada	$569	$555
Italy	$982	$1,021
Japan	$1,448	$1,597
Kuwait	$85	$37
Mexico	$209	$209
United Kingdom	$1,155	$1,236
United States	$2,568	$2,730

Source: CIA, *The World Fact Book.* 2008 (Washington, D.C.: 2008).

Critical Thinking
Which governments received more revenue than they spent?

Graphs In Motion
See StudentWorks™ Plus or go to glencoe.com.

Arguments continue over how large a part the government should play. Debates can be frequent because in the modified free-enterprise system control over the economy is divided between government and the private sector. Yet most Americans expect the federal government to play a significant role in moderating the economy's ups and downs and in promoting economic growth.

The government can influence the economy in two main ways: fiscal policy and monetary policy. **Fiscal policy** involves using government spending and taxation to influence the economy. **Monetary policy** involves controlling the supply of money and credit to influence the economy. This control is exercised through the Federal Reserve System.

Fiscal Policy

The federal budget is a major tool of fiscal policy because it shapes how much money the government will spend and how much it will collect through

CHAPTER 20: *Taxing and Spending* **567**

Teach

Comparing Governments

Answer: Brazil, Canada, Kuwait

Research Activity: Have students use an atlas to find each country shown on the graph. Then have them label them on an outline map. Ask students to select one of the countries, research how that country's government collects revenue, then present their findings to the class. **BL**

Should Government Intervene? Since the 1930s, the U.S. government has taken an increasing role in the nation's economy. *How large* a role should the government play in the economy? In this modified free-enterprise system, control of the economy is divided between the government and the private sector. Have students debate the following: Does fiscal or monetary policy conflict with the principles of free enterprise? What circumstances justify government intervention in the economy? **OL**

Additional Support

Activity: Cooperative Learning

Making a Bulletin Board Organize the class into small groups to create a bulletin board showing how federal grant money is used in your city or state. One group should be responsible for interviewing local government officials and another for calling the appropriate state government officials. Others may find information via the Internet. Some students in each group should be responsible for creating visuals (including graphs and maps) and for writing the captions that go with the visuals. **OL**

C Critical Thinking

Contrasting What is the difference between monetary policy and fiscal policy? **Ask:** How is monetary policy different from fiscal policy? *(Fiscal policy involves how the government spends and collects money. Monetary policy involves money supply and the cost of borrowing.)* **OL**

POLITICAL PROFILES **Ben Bernanke** (1953–) Ben Bernanke was appointed chair of the Federal Reserve by George W. Bush in 2006 to succeed Alan Greenspan. Whereas Greenspan never hesitated to weigh in on political issues, Bernanke has been generally more hesitant to do so. When faced with questions about fiscal policy, he insists that these issues should be left to politicians.

Critical Thinking

Answer: increased government spending and/or reduced taxes

Table Skills Practice
What is the percentage increase in public debt from 1990 to 2000? *(75.5%)* From 1990 to 2008? *(297.5%)* **AL**

Hands-On Chapter Project

Step 3

---

taxes and borrowing. The president and Congress can use the budget to pump money into the economy to stimulate it or to take money out of the economy to slow it down.

To stimulate the economy, the government may spend more money than it takes in. Through increased spending, the government aims to put more people back to work and increase economic activity.

Another way that the government can stimulate the economy is through reducing taxes. Lower taxes give consumers and investors more purchasing power.

When the government increases spending or reduces taxes, it is likely to run a deficit because it must spend money that it does not have. Since the 1930s, the United States has had deficit, or unbalanced, federal budgets. One reason for these deficits is that for many years these unbalanced budgets were thought to benefit the economy. In addition, this policy was popular politically because it allowed the government to spend heavily on social programs that many Americans were demanding.

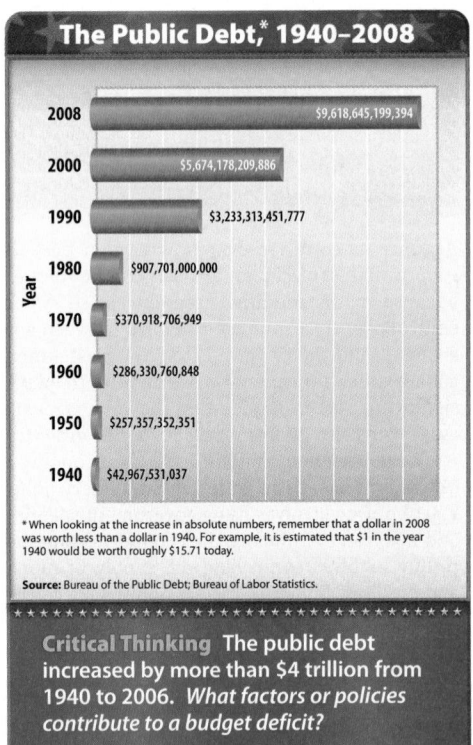

The Public Debt,* 1940–2008

Year	
2008	$9,618,645,199,394
2000	$5,674,178,209,886
1990	$3,233,313,451,777
1980	$907,701,000,000
1970	$370,918,706,949
1960	$286,330,760,848
1950	$257,357,352,351
1940	$42,967,531,037

* When looking at the increase in absolute numbers, remember that a dollar in 2008 was worth less than a dollar in 1940. For example, it is estimated that $1 in the year 1940 would be worth roughly $15.71 today.

Source: Bureau of the Public Debt; Bureau of Labor Statistics.

Critical Thinking The public debt increased by more than $4 trillion from 1940 to 2006. *What factors or policies contribute to a budget deficit?*

This policy of deficit spending led to increasingly large budget deficits and a growing national debt. During the 1970s and early 1980s, economists began to worry about the effects this would have on the nation's future.

Demands for cutting the deficit and even balancing the budget grew. Many economists, however, argued that a balanced budget would mean the federal government could not use fiscal policy to shape the economy. Some said that the deficit as a percentage of the **gross domestic product (GDP)** was more important than the deficit alone. The GDP is the sum of all goods and services produced in the nation in a year. They pointed out that the deficit still represented only 5 to 6 percent of the GDP.

Other economists disagreed. They pointed to the rapid growth of the deficit and the overall amount of national debt. When Congress promised to balance the budget in 1981, the gross federal debt was $930 billion. In 2008 it reached $5,252 billion ($5.25 trillion). Interest payments on the debt nearly equaled half of that spent for defense.

Monetary Policy

The American economy is a money economy. Americans exchange goods and services through a vast system of money and credit. The Constitution gives the national government authority to "coin money [and] regulate the value thereof." Today, the federal government also tries to regulate the economy through its monetary policy.

Monetary policy involves controlling the supply of money and the cost of borrowing money, or credit, according to the needs of the economy. The government controls the money supply through the Federal Reserve System.

The Federal Reserve System

The Federal Reserve System, known as the Fed, is the central banking system of the United States. When people or corporations need money, they borrow from a bank. When banks need money, they borrow from the Fed. Thus, in reality, the Federal Reserve System is a banker's bank.

Organization of the Fed

The United States is divided into 12 Federal Reserve Districts. Each district has one main Federal Reserve Bank. In addition, most Federal Reserve Banks have branch banks within their districts.

Preparing a Nation's Budget

Step 3: Presenting a Budget Students will determine how their country's $100 billion will be spent.

Directions Groups will draw a circle graph showing what percentage of the budget will be allocated to each major category. They should use the problems and program emphases they identified in Step 2 to help them determine priorities.

Putting It Together Have one member of each group present the circle graph to the class and another member explain the rationale for their allocations. **OL**

Federal Reserve Districts

Maps In Motion See StudentWorks™ Plus or go to glencoe.com.

Federal Open Market Governors

Chairman

Board of Governors (7 members) — Federal Advisory Council

12 Federal Reserve Banks

Commercial Banks (Members and nonmembers)

The Non-Banking Public

8 Federal Reserve District
◎ Board of Governors of the Federal Reserve System
● Federal Reserve Bank Cities

Source: Board of Governors of the Federal Reserve System, *The Federal Reserve System: Purposes & Functions* (Washington, D.C., 1994).

Critical Thinking The United States is divided into 12 Federal Reserve Districts. Federal Reserve Districts are privately owned but publicly controlled. *What do low discount rates from the Federal Reserve encourage banks to do?*

About 7,200 of the approximately 13,600 banks in the United States are members of the Federal Reserve System. These include all the large banks in the country. These member banks control the largest share of total bank deposits in the United States.

Board of Governors

A seven-member Board of Governors in Washington, D.C., supervises the entire Federal Reserve System. The president selects these members whose appointments must be ratified, or approved, by the Senate. The president selects one of the board members to chair the Board of Governors for a four-year term.

Once appointed, board members and the chairman are independent of the president. Even Congress exercises little control or influence over the board, since the board does not depend on Congress for an annual appropriation for operating expenses. This allows the Board of Governors to make economic decisions independent of political pressure.

Making Monetary Policy

The Board of Governors has two major responsibilities in forming monetary policy. First, and most

important, it determines the general money and credit policies of the United States. Second, it supervises the operations of the Federal Reserve Banks in the 12 districts across the country.

The Fed uses four main tools to control the financial activities of the nation's banks and, through them, the nation's monetary policy. First, the Fed can raise or lower the **discount rate.** The discount rate is the rate the Fed charges member banks for loans. Low discount rates encourage banks to borrow money from the Fed to make loans to their customers. High discount rates mean banks will borrow less money from the Fed.

Second, the Fed can raise or lower the **reserve requirement** for member banks. Member banks must keep a certain percentage of their money in their vaults or on deposit with the Federal Reserve Banks as a reserve against their deposits. If the Fed raises the reserve requirement, banks must leave more money with the Fed. Thus, they have less money to lend. The Fed has been reluctant to use the reserve requirement as a policy tool because other monetary policy tools work better. However, the reserve requirement can be powerful should the Fed decide to use it.

Critical Thinking

Answer: borrow money from the Fed to make loans to their customers

Map Skills Practice
What part of the country has the highest concentration of Federal Reserve Banks? *(The East Coast)* Why is this so? *(The higher population density creates more economic activity.)*

C Critical Thinking

Synthesizing Present the following economic problems. Ask how the Federal Reserve might react to each problem and why it would take that action.

1. prices rising rapidly *(raise reserve requirement/discount rate, sell securities—to cut money supply and inflation)*

2. unemployment rising *(lower reserve requirement/discount rate, buy securities—to increase money supply and borrowing for expansion and jobs)*

3. automobiles, houses, and other big-ticket items not selling well *(lower reserve requirement/discount rate—to reduce interest rates, encourage borrowing)* **AL**

Differentiated Instruction

Leveled Activities

ELL Source Readings, p. 20
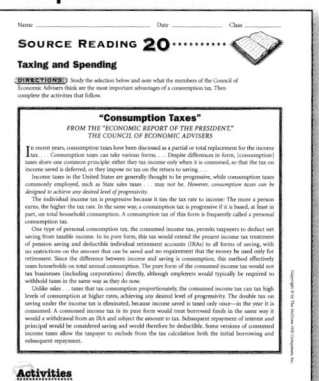

BL Cooperative Learning Activities, p. 13
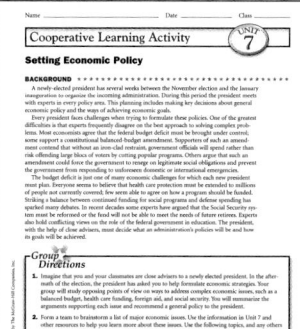

OL Participating in Government Activities, p. 39
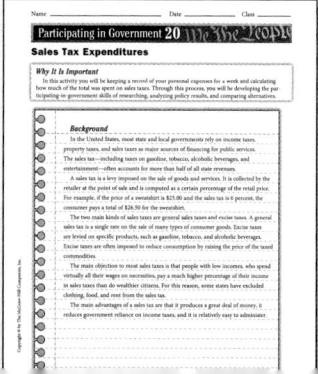

AL Historical Documents and Speeches, p. 20
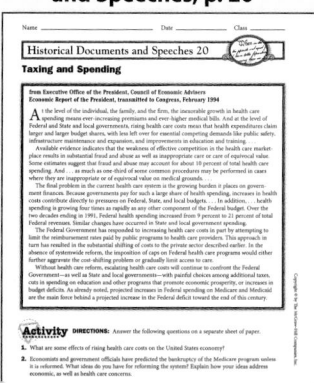

569

Section 3 Review

Teacher Sidebar

Caption Answer: The cartoon implies that Greenspan was so successful as chair of the Fed that his face replaced George Washington's on the one-dollar bill.

W Writing Support

Personal Writing Have students write a short essay in which they express an opinion on the following question: **Ask:** Do you think the Fed should be incorporated into one of the government branches to make it less independent? **AL**

Assess

Assign the Section 3 Assessment as homework or as an in-class activity, or have students take Section Quiz 20-3 from *Section Quizzes and Chapter Tests.*

Close

Evaluating The text states that recent federal grants to states have shifted from infrastructure projects toward public welfare programs. **Ask:** What is meant by infrastructure? **OL**

Chairs of the Fed

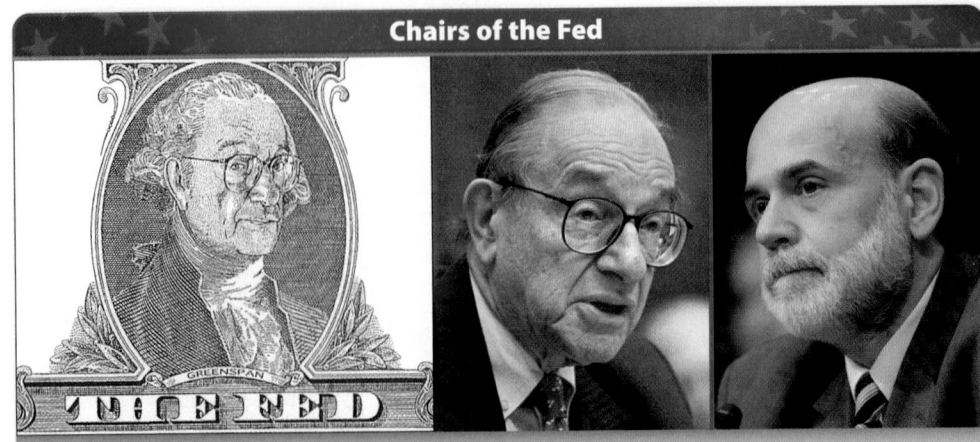

Passing the Baton Alan Greenspan (center above) had a record-long tenure as chairman of the Fed, from 1987 to 2006 when he was succeeded by Ben Bernanke, right. *Based upon the cartoon image at left, how would you judge the success of Greenspan's time at the Federal Reserve?*

Third, the Fed can put money into the economy by buying government bonds on the open market. These **open-market operations** stimulate and help expand the economy. Fourth, the Fed may also sell government securities. As investors spend their money on these securities, money is taken out of the economy, causing it to slow down.

Conflicting Policies

In recent years, the Fed has become an independent policy-making institution. While the president and Congress largely control taxing and spending, they have little control over the Fed. Thus, the Fed's policy might help or hinder the economic programs of the president and Congress. Sometimes when conflicting economic policies arise the president or Congress might complain that the Fed is interfering with their economic programs.

Because of conflicts like these, some people would like to limit the Fed's role and make it less independent. Others maintain that the nation needs an institution that is removed from political pressures to watch over monetary policy.

SECTION 3 Review

Vocabulary

1. **Explain** the significance of: fiscal policy, monetary policy, gross national product, discount rate, reserve requirement, open-market operations.

Main Ideas

2. **Analyzing** Why did the federal government adopt policies that created a huge debt?

3. **Explaining** How is the Federal Reserve District organized?

Critical Thinking

4. **Identifying Alternatives** What methods could the federal government use to stimulate the economy during a time when people were opposed to deficit spending?

5. **Organizing** Use a graphic organizer like the one below to compare recent federal grants with those in the 1980s.

Federal Grants	
1980s	Recently

Writing About Government

6. **Descriptive Writing** Research several back issues of *The Wall Street Journal* or selections from the *Readers' Guide to Periodical Literature* to analyze Federal Reserve Board decisions that affect the economy. Create a poster that displays headlines and captions that are suggestive of the Fed's actions.

Answers

1. All definitions can be found in the section and the Glossary.

2. For many years the government stimulated the economy by spending more money than it took in. The government cut taxes and spent heavily on social programs demanded by many Americans, causing a deficit.

3. The United States is divided into 12 Federal Reserve Districts; each district has one main Federal Reserve Bank. Most Federal Reserve Banks have branch banks.

4. The government could rely on monetary policy—controlling the supply of money and the cost of borrowing money by lowering the discount rate, lowering banks' reserve requirement, or expanding credit through open-market operations.

5. 1980s: Grants to local and state governments declined. Recently: Federal budgets increased federal aid to states; Federal grants shifted away from infrastructure investments and toward public-welfare programs

6. Students' posters should support their research and present how the Fed's actions affected the economy.

Is the Line-Item Veto Constitutional?

Clinton v. City of New York, 1998

*A*rticle I, Section 7, of the U.S. Constitution outlines how a bill becomes a law, grants the president a limited veto power, and explains how Congress can override a presidential veto. Should the president have the power to veto only parts of a bill rather than approving or rejecting the entire bill?

Facts of the Case

In 1992 Congressional Republicans announced a legislative agenda they called the "Contract With America." In it, they called for passage of a line-item veto that would allow the president to delete individual items from spending bills, without having to veto the entire bill. The goal was to reduce wasteful pork-barrel spending and tax breaks that benefit only a select few. The line-item veto was supported by President Bill Clinton and several previous presidents.

When President Clinton signed the line-item veto bill into law in 1996, he said that it would allow presidents to fight "special-interest boondoggles, tax loopholes, and pure pork." Opponents of the law, however, argued that it violated the separation of powers established in the Constitution and was, therefore, unconstitutional.

The law was challenged by several groups, including New York City, several health-care organizations, and Idaho potato growers. New York City sued because the president used the line-item veto to cancel a provision that gave tax breaks to hospitals caring for Medicaid recipients. In the case of the Snake River Potato Growers, the suit was brought because the president canceled a provision that would have deferred taxes for certain farmers' cooperatives.

The Constitutional Question

According to the Constitution, the president can veto bills passed by Congress. If he or she does, then Congress can decide to consider the president's objections and revise the bill, or it can vote on the original bill again. If two-thirds of the members of each house again vote for the original bill, it becomes law, overriding the president's veto.

Opponents believed that the line-item veto was unconstitutional because it effectively allowed the president to amend legislation passed by Congress. Supporters claimed that it provided the president with a degree of discretion in approving or rejecting bills passed by Congress, but that it did not violate the Constitution.

Debating the Issue

Questions to Consider

1. What was the purpose of the line-item veto?

2. Why did some members of Congress support it?

3. Why did some organizations argue that the line-item veto was unconstitutional?

You Be the Judge

When the line-item veto was enacted, the governors of many states had some form of a line-item veto. Should the president of the United States have this power? Why or why not?

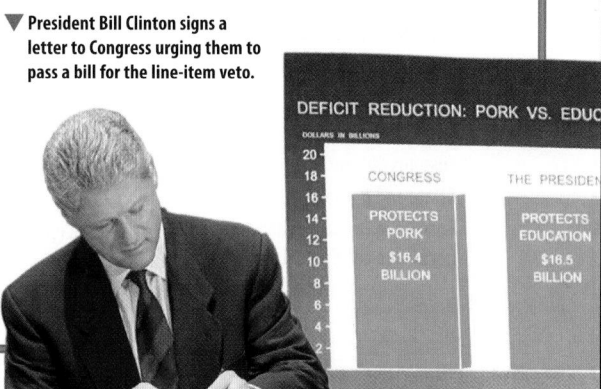

▼ President Bill Clinton signs a letter to Congress urging them to pass a bill for the line-item veto.

Class Debate

Organize students into three groups: one to represent members of Congress who support the line-item veto, another to represent members of Congress who are concerned that the line-item veto would give the president too much power, and the third group to serve as the jury and decide which point of view they find most persuasive.

The Court's Decision

In the case of *Clinton* v. *City of New York,* the Supreme Court ruled 6 to 3 that the president's use of the line-item veto to unilaterally amend or repeal parts of bills violated the Presentment Clause (Article I, Section 7, Clauses 2 and 3) of the Constitution. According to the Court, the Constitution allows the president only two choices: approve a bill by signing it or veto it and send it back to Congress. Justice John Paul Stevens, writing for the majority, declared: "If there is to be a new procedure in which the president will play a different role in determining the text of what may become a law, such change must come not by legislation but through the amendment procedures set forth in Article V of the Constitution."

Debating the Issue Answers

Questions to Consider

1. The purpose was to allow the president to reject certain parts of spending or revenue bills without having to veto the entire bill. This would allow the president to strike out provisions that were wasteful.

2. Supporters thought the executive branch needed the power in order to stop wasteful congresstional spending and reach a balanced budget.

3. They believed it violated the principle of separation of powers by taking lawmaking powers away from the legislative branch and giving them to the executive branch.

You Be the Judge

Answers will vary. In their responses, students should draw upon the relevant arguments presented in the feature.

CHAPTER
20 Assessment and Activities

ExamView®
Assessment Suite

This easy-to-use software includes extensive question banks and allows you to create fully customized tests that can be administered in print or online.

Reviewing Vocabulary

1. taxes
2. withholding
3. taxable income
4. fiscal year
5. uncontrollables
6. entitlements
7. national debt
8. GNP
9. fiscal policy
10. monetary policy

Reviewing Main Ideas

11. any three nonprofit organizations, such as churches, colleges, and labor unions
12. collect taxes, check tax returns, investigate suspected criminal tax law violations
13. The Office of Management and Budget (OMB)
14. road repair, public housing, police equipment and training, school lunches, flood insurance, mental health services, public welfare programs, and so on

Critical Thinking

15. uncontrollables, such as entitlements and interest on the national debt, disagreements between the president and Congress on budgetary priorities, recessions, and incrementalism and pressure from interest groups to maintain federal spending and programs

Reviewing Vocabulary

Insert the content vocabulary word(s) below into the following paragraph to describe how the federal government regulates the economy. Do not use a word more than once.

withholding	securities
national debt	taxes
taxable income	incrementalism
fiscal policy	GNP
monetary policy	fiscal year
entitlements	uncontrollables

The federal government collects more than $1 trillion in __(1)__ each year. Through __(2)__, wage earners pay taxes on their __(3)__ during the year. The government's __(4)__ begins on October 1. Because of __(5)__ such as __(6)__ in the budget, government spending often exceeds revenue, which enlarges the __(7)__. Some economists are not alarmed because deficits are only about 5 percent of the __(8)__. Others would like to see changes in __(9)__ to control spending or raise taxes. By its __(10)__, the Fed may stimulate economic growth to relieve some of these concerns.

Reviewing Main Ideas

Section 1 *(pages 555–559)*

11. **Identifying** Which three institutions are exempt from the federal income tax?

12. **Describing** What are three responsibilities of the Internal Revenue Service?

Section 2 *(pages 560–564)*

13. **Examining** Which executive agency is charged with preparing the federal budget?

Section 3 *(pages 566–570)*

14. **Stating** How do some state and local governments use intergovernmental revenues?

Critical Thinking

15. 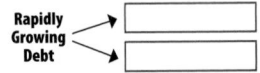 **Essential Question** Why has the United States been unable to balance the national budget most of the time beginning in the 1930s?

16. **Synthesizing** What kinds of banks are members of the Federal Reserve System?

17. **Making Generalizations** Why would business groups support protective tariffs?

18. **Analyzing** Why must the Federal Reserve operate free of pressure from the president or Congress?

19. **Organizing** Use a graphic organizer to show how the government might act if the debt is out of control.

```
Rapidly      →  [          ]
Growing
Debt         →  [          ]
```

Chapter Summary

Revenue
★ Individual income tax
★ Corporate income tax
★ Social insurance taxes
★ Excise taxes
★ Customs duties
★ Estate and gift taxes
★ Borrowing (by selling bonds, notes, and certificates)

Federal Budget
★ President directs budget preparation and sets budget priorities
★ Day-to-day budget preparation is carried out by the Office of Management and Budget (OMB) along with the Council of Economic Advisers (CEA)

Expenditures
★ Social Security
★ Social welfare programs
★ Health-care benefits
★ National defense
★ Discretionary spending (grants to state and local governments for road repair, public housing, police training, school lunch programs, etc.)

572 UNIT 7: *Public Policies and Services*

---

16. all of the largest U.S. banks
17. Protective tariffs help eliminate some foreign competition for domestic businesses.
18. so that it can make decisions based on sound monetary policy rather than political pressures
19. increase taxes, reduce spending

Government ONLINE Self-Check Quiz
Visit glencoe.com and enter QuickPass™ code USG9822c20.
Click on Self-Check Quizzes for additional test practice.

CHAPTER
20
Assessment
and Activities

Document-Based Questions

Analyzing Primary Sources

Read the excerpt below and answer the questions that follow.

One of the first major taxes the new constitutionally based government placed on the fledgling American republic was a 1794 tax on whiskey. Western farmers saw this tax as a direct attack on their business, and in Pennsylvania in particular, they revolted against this tax, often with arms. George Washington, the nation's first president, quelled the rebellion with troops. This excerpt is from Washington's proclamation about the Whiskey Rebellion.

❝ [C]ombinations to defeat the execution of the laws laying duties upon spirits distilled within the United States and upon stills have from the time of the commencement of those laws existed in some of the western parts of Pennsylvania. . . . the said combinations, proceeding in a manner subversive equally of the just authority of government and of the rights of individuals, have hitherto effected their dangerous and criminal purpose by the influence of certain irregular meetings whose proceedings have tended to encourage and uphold the spirit of opposition by misrepresentations of the laws calculated to render them odious . . . employing for these unwarrantable purposes the agency of armed [bandits] disguised in such manner as for the most part to escape discovery. ❞

20. What type of resistance did opponents of the whiskey tax employ to express their disapproval of the government's actions?

21. Why do you think taxes are not protested so violently today?

22. Washington's speech justified the government's forceful response to the Whiskey Rebellion. What words did he use that present a negative image of its leaders? How might the farmers have described their actions and purposes?

Interpreting Political Cartoons

Analyze the cartoon and answer the questions that follow. Base your answers on the cartoon and your knowledge of Chapter 20.

www.cartoonstock.com

23. What is the cartoonist saying about the Internal Revenue Service?

24. Do you think that the cartoonist's feelings are representative of the general feelings of taxpayers? Why might they feel that way?

Participating IN GOVERNMENT

25. Review the various kinds of taxes that are sources of revenue for local governments. Working in groups of three, complete the following tasks:

  1. Identify three needs that your community has.

  2. Estimate the amount of taxes that would need to be raised to meet these needs.

  3. Determine whether any current tax rate may be increased to meet one or more of these needs.

  4. Decide on any additional fair tax to raise money to benefit the needs that you have identified.

  5. Discuss whether people will be in favor of additional taxes to meet these needs. Summarize your findings in an informational brochure or flyer.

CHAPTER 20: *Taxing and Spending* **573**

Analyzing Primary Sources

20. Participants in the Whiskey Rebellion employed violent resistance, combining in groups to form what Washington called "banditti," or armed mobs, to fight against the tax. In Washington's opinion, they also misrepresented the tax's nature, stirring up public disapproval of the new law so that others might join their rebellion.

21. Students might answer that taxes are simply an accepted part of life today and that people recognize the need to have taxes to support government operations. Also, because there is now an income tax, which is paid by everyone in the nation, taxes might not seem as discriminatory as the tax on whiskey.

22. Washington used terms such as *subversive, just authority, dangerous and criminal, irregular, misrepresentations, armed banditti,* and so on. The farmers might have said that the tax on whiskey was unjust and discriminatory, that the new national government was becoming

---

Government ONLINE

Have students use the **Chapter 20 Self-Check Quiz.** Visit glencoe.com and enter QuickPass™ code USG9085c20T to prepare for the Chapter Test.

too powerful and destroying their independence, or that their rebellion was the only possible way to fight this injustice.

Interpreting Political Cartoons

23. The cartoonist is saying that it is difficult to navigate the IRS—that it is like a maze.

24. Possible Answer: Yes, most Americans dislike paying taxes and believe that the tax laws are unnecessarily complicated and difficult to understand.

Participating IN GOVERNMENT

25. You might compile class lists of the community's needs and the kinds of taxes students proposed.

Chapter Bonus Test Question

Ask: One nontax source of revenue for the federal government is seigniorage (seignorage). What is that? *(profit on the minting of coins)*

573

Planning Guide

Key to Ability Levels
BL Below level   **AL** Above level
OL On level   **ELL** English Language Learners

Key to Teaching Resources
📁 Print Material   📠 Transparency
💿 CD-ROM or DVD

Levels					Resources	Chapter Opener	Section 1	Section 2	Section 3	Section 4	Chapter Assess
BL	OL	AL	ELL								
					FOCUS						
BL	OL	AL	ELL	📠	Section Focus Transparencies		21-1	21-2	21-3	21-4	
					TEACH						
BL	OL		ELL	📁	Reading Essentials and Study Guide (and Answer Key)		p. 233	p. 238	p. 241	p. 245	
BL	OL		ELL	📁	Guided Reading Activities		p. 74	p. 75	p. 76	p. 77	
BL	OL		ELL	📁	Vocabulary Activities		p. 21				
BL	OL	AL	ELL	📁	Chapter Summaries					p. 61	
BL	OL			📁	American Biographies						
BL	OL	AL	ELL	📁	Cooperative Learning Activities					p. 13	
	OL	AL	ELL	📁	Government Simulations and Debate			p. 50			
BL	OL	AL	ELL	📁	Historical Documents and Speeches			p. 21			
BL	OL	AL	ELL	📁	Interpreting Political Cartoons			p. 41			
BL	OL		ELL	📁	Skill Reinforcement Activities						
BL	OL	AL	ELL	📁	Source Readings		p. 21			p. 21	
BL	OL			📁	Supreme Court Case Studies						
BL	OL	AL	ELL	📁	Participating in Government Activities				p. 41		
BL	OL		ELL	📁	Spanish Declaration of Independence and U.S. Constitution	✓	✓	✓	✓	✓	✓
BL	OL	AL	ELL	📁	NGS World Atlas, Spanish	✓	✓	✓	✓	✓	✓
BL	OL	AL	ELL	📠	Unit Overlay Transparencies, Strategies, and Activities	✓	✓	✓	✓	✓	✓
BL	OL		ELL	📠	Making It Relevant Transparencies	✓	✓	✓	✓	✓	✓
BL	OL	AL	ELL	📠	High School Writing Process Transparencies, Strategies, and Activities	✓	✓	✓	✓	✓	✓
BL	OL	AL		📠	American Art & Architecture Transparencies, Strategies, and Activities	✓	✓	✓	✓	✓	✓

✓ Chapter- or unit-based activities applicable to all sections in this chapter

All-In-One Planner and Resource Center

- Interactive Lesson Planner
- Interactive Teacher Edition
- Fully editable blackline masters
- Chapter Spotlight Videos Launch

- Differentiated Lesson Plans
- Printable reports of daily assignments
- Standards tracking system

Levels					Resources	Chapter Opener	Section 1	Section 2	Section 3	Section 4	Chapter Assess
BL	OL	AL	ELL								
					TEACH (continued)						
BL	OL			💿	**American Music: Hits Through History**	✓	✓	✓	✓	✓	✓
BL	OL		ELL	📁	**Reading Strategies for the Social Studies Classroom**	✓	✓	✓	✓	✓	✓
			ELL	📁	**English Language Learner Handbook**	✓	✓	✓	✓	✓	✓
BL	OL		ELL	📁	**Writer's Guidebook for Social Studies**	✓	✓	✓	✓	✓	✓
BL	OL	AL	ELL	📁	**Living Constitution, SE**	✓	✓	✓	✓	✓	✓
BL	OL	AL	ELL	📁	**Living Constitution, TAE**	✓	✓	✓	✓	✓	✓
BL	OL			📁	**NGS World Atlas, English**	✓	✓	✓	✓	✓	✓
BL	OL		ELL	📁	**The Constitution and You (poster set)**	✓	✓	✓	✓	✓	✓
BL	OL	AL	ELL	📁	**Spanish Chapter Summaries**					p. 61	
BL	OL	AL	ELL	📁	**Spanish Vocabulary Activities**		p. 21				
BL	OL		ELL	📁	**Spanish Reading Essentials and Study Guide (and Answer Key)**		p. 233	p. 238	p. 241	p. 245	
BL	OL	AL	ELL	💿	**PresentationPlus! with MindJogger CheckPoint**	✓	✓	✓	✓	✓	✓
					ASSESS						
BL	OL	AL	ELL	💿	*ExamView® Assessment Suite*		21-1	21-2	21-3	21-4	Ch. 21
BL	OL	AL	ELL	📁	**Authentic Assessment with Rubrics**		p. 28				p. 28
BL	OL	AL	ELL	📁	**Section Quizzes and Chapter Tests**		p. 257	p. 258	p. 259	p. 260	pp. 261–268
BL	OL	AL	ELL	📁	**Spanish Section Quizzes and Tests**		p. 257	p. 258	p. 259	p. 260	pp. 261–268
					CLOSE						
BL			ELL	📁	**Reteaching Activities**					p. 21	p. 21
BL	OL	AL	ELL	💿	**StudentWorks™ Plus with Audio Summaries**	✓	✓	✓	✓	✓	✓
BL	OL		ELL	🖨	**Graphic Organizer Transparencies**		✓	✓	✓	✓	
BL	OL		ELL	📁	**High School Government Reading and Study Skills Foldables®**		p. 64	p. 64	p. 64	p. 64	

Teach With Technology

What is Study-to-Go?
Study-to-Go provides portable textbook-based content direct from the Glencoe Web site to your students whenever and wherever they want!

How can Study-to-Go help my students?
Study-to-Go content can be downloaded to a personal digital assistant (PDA) or a cell phone. Students can download Study Sets that include:

- Self Quiz—a series of multiple-choice quizzes that provides instant answer feedback
- Key Terms—definitions for textbook vocabulary
- Flashcards—an assessment tool to help students study textbook key terms

Visit glencoe.com and enter a *QuickPass*™ code to go to Study-to-Go.

Government ONLINE
Visit glencoe.com and enter *QuickPass*™ code USG9085c21T for Chapter 21 resources.

You can easily launch a wide range of digital products from your computer's desktop with the McGraw-Hill Social Studies widget.

TeacherWorks

	Student	Teacher	Parent
Media Library			
• Student Edition Section Audio	●		●
• Chapter Spotlight Videos	●	●	●
***United States Government* Online Learning Center (Web Site)**			
• Chapter Overviews	●	●	●
• Multilingual Glossaries	●	●	●
• Study-to-Go	●	●	●
• Student Web Activities	●	●	●
• Self-Check Quizzes	●	●	●
• Online Student Edition	●	●	●
• Vocabulary eFlashcards	●	●	●
• Web Activity Lesson Plans		●	
• Vocabulary PuzzleMaker	●	●	●
• Landmark Supreme Court Cases	●	●	●
• Beyond the Textbook	●	●	●

READING SUPPORT FROM JAMESTOWN EDUCATION

- **Timed Readings Plus in Social Studies** helps students increase their reading rate and fluency while maintaining comprehension. The 400-word passages are similar to those found on state and national assessments.

- **Reading in the Content Area: Social Studies** concentrates on six essential reading skills that help students better comprehend what they read. The book includes 75 high-interest nonfiction passages written at increasing levels of difficulty.

- **Reading Social Studies** includes strategic reading instruction and vocabulary support in Social Studies content for ELLs and native speakers of English. www.jamestowneducation.com

Reading List Generator CD-ROM — GLENCOE BOOKLINK 3

Use this database to search more than 30,000 titles to create a customized reading list for your students.

- Reading lists can be organized by students' reading level, author, genre, theme, or area of interest.

- The database provides Degrees of Reading Power™ (DRP) and Lexile™ readability scores for all selections.

- A brief summary of each selection is included.

Leveled reading suggestions for this chapter:

- *Able To Work,* by Emily Mitchell
- *The Challenge of Clean Air,* by Martin J. Gutnik
- *Who Should Still Be on Welfare?,* by Adam Cohen

Review suggested books before assigning them.

Economics Connection

Personal Finance Literacy

Understanding Interest Rates

Explain to students: When you deposit money in a savings account, the bank *pays* you interest for the use of your money. Interest is expressed as a percentage of the principal that the money earns in one year—the annual percentage rate (APR). If you deposit $10,000 in an account that pays 5 percent APR, at the end of the year you will have $10,500.

When you borrow money, the lender *charges* you interest at a certain rate, which changes from lender to lender and from time to time. Since you have to pay the item's price plus interest, items you buy on credit cost more than if you paid cash.

The rate paid by banks and charged by lenders is affected by the federal funds rate set by the Federal Reserve Board. The federal funds rate is the rate banks charge each other for overnight loans. Some lenders charge—and pay—the same rate as the federal funds rate. Recently, some banks have begun charging borrowers more than the federal funds rate because of the number of mortgage loan defaults that occurred during the housing slump. The Fed raises or lowers the federal funds rate from time to time to control inflation or stimulate the economy.

These are some of the financial vehicles that pay or charge interest:

Savings Vehicles	Investment Instruments
Savings account	Stocks
Money market deposit account	Bonds
Certificates of deposit (CD)	Stock mutual funds
U.S. savings bonds	Bond mutual funds
Some checking accounts	U.S. Treasury notes

Types of Credit

Revolving: You continue to purchase items up to a specified limit and pay at least a minimum amount each month. Examples: Credit cards, store charge cards

Installment: The credit is for a specific item; you pay a specified amount each month, plus interest. Examples: Auto loans, mortgages

Did You Know?

If there are unauthorized charges on your credit card, you owe a maximum of $50 each. If charges appear after you report your card missing, you are not liable.

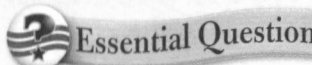

🔊 Chapter Audio   📹 Spotlight Video

CHAPTER 21

Essential Question

Political values and debate influence social and domestic policies that affect the welfare of all Americans. Whether it is through building highways, funding home loans, or providing health insurance, government policies shape your life.

Chapter Spotlight Video

To generate student interest and provide a springboard for class discussion, access the Chapter 21 Video at glencoe.com or on the video DVD.

FOLDABLES
Study Organizer

Dinah Zike's Foldables are three-dimensional, interactive graphic organizers that help students practice basic writing skills, review key vocabulary terms, and identify main ideas. Have students complete this chapter's Foldable activity or activities in *Dinah Zike's Reading and Study Skills Foldables* booklet. **OL**

Government ONLINE

Visit glencoe.com and enter *QuickPass*™ code USG9085c21T for Chapter 21 Resources including Chapter Overview, Student Web Activity, Self-Check Quiz, and other materials for students and teachers.

Social *and* Domestic Policy

Essential Question

How does politics affect social and domestic policies, and how do those policies affect your economic choices, your education, and even the air you breathe?

Government ONLINE
Chapter Overview Visit glencoe.com and enter *QuickPass*™ code USG9822c21 for an overview, a quiz, and other chapter resources.

► A cloverleaf interchange in Lexington, Massachusetts

574

Launching the Chapter

The Progressive Era The New Deal expanded the role of the federal government to an unprecedented extent. The movement toward greater government involvement in the economy and increased responsibility for the public welfare, however, dates to a generation earlier. During the Progressive Era of the late nineteenth and early twentieth centuries, the federal government began to regulate big business, enacted consumer protection laws, and established the first labor laws. **Essential Question:** How do you know that the food you eat and the medicine you take are safe? *(They are regulated, inspected, and tested by federal agencies such as the FDA and the USDA.)* **OL**

Business and Labor Policy

Reader's Guide

Content Vocabulary
* mixed economy (p. 575)
* laissez-faire (p. 577)
* trust (p. 578)
* monopoly (p. 578)
* interlocking directorate (p. 578)
* oligopoly (p. 579)
* securities (p. 581)
* collective bargaining (p. 581)
* injunction (p. 582)

Academic Vocabulary
* trend (p. 578)
* clarify (p. 578)
* investor (p. 581)

Reading Strategy
Create a time line to take notes about when the government started regulating business.

1879   1887 1890   1914

Issues in the News

Recently, the Federal Trade Commission (FTC) reported that identity theft affected 8.3 million Americans—about 3.7 percent of the adult population. The FTC points out that half of those victims discover the theft when they check their accounts, while another 26 percent are alerted by companies with which they do business. Experts predict that criminals will continue to use new technologies to commit identity theft. One new practice seems to invite identity theft: file sharing to download music, movies, and games. "We're concerned that consumers may accidentally share folders that contain private documents that they don't intend to share," said Mary Engel of the FTC. Engel urges people to use software protection as a precaution.

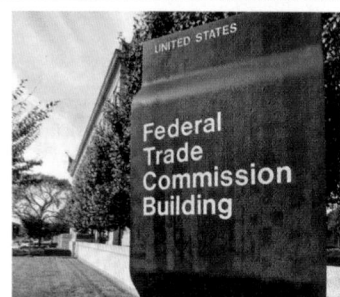

▲ The FTC headquarters

The Federal Trade Commission is just one of many government agencies that regulate the American economy. Although free enterprise is the foundation of the American economic system, ours is really a **mixed economy.** A mixed economy is one in which the government both supports and regulates private enterprise.

Promoting and Protecting Business

Regulating business is a relatively recent function of the federal government, but the promoting and protecting of business has been a major activity of United States government since George Washington was president. Washington's secretary of the treasury, Alexander Hamilton, claimed that emerging American manufacturers needed protection from foreign competition. He first proposed a protective tariff in 1791, but Congress shelved the request. After the War of 1812, British goods flooded American markets, threatening newly created industries. A member of Parliament in 1816 explained Britain's advantage:

> ❝ [I]t was well worth while to incur a loss upon the first exportation, in order, by the glut, to stifle, in the cradle, those rising manufactures in the United States, which the war has forced into existence, contrary to the natural course of things. ❞
>
> —Henry Brougham, Esq., 1816

The United States responded to this threat by imposing higher tariffs.

Bellringer
Section Focus Transparencies 21-1

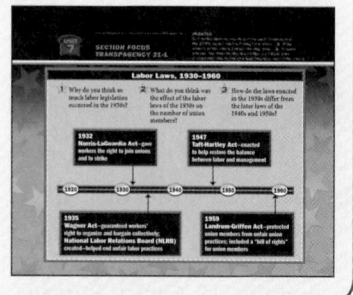

Reader's Guide

Answers to Graphic:
1879: Standard Oil Trust
1887: Interstate Commerce Act
1890: Sherman Antitrust Act
1914: Clayton Antitrust Act

Resource Manager

R Reading Strategies	**C** Critical Thinking	**D** Differentiated Instruction	**W** Writing Support	**S** Skill Practice
Teacher Edition • Identifying, pp. 577, 583 • Inferring, p. 581 **Additional Resources** • Guid. Read. Act., p. 74 • Quizzes/Tests, p. 257	**Teacher Edition** • Drawing Conclusions, p. 576 • Comparing and Contrasting, p. 578 • Predicting Consequences, p. 579 **Additional Resources** • Read. Essen., pp. 233–237	**Teacher Edition** • Visual/Spatial, p. 580 **Additional Resources** • Foldables, p. 64 • Source Readings, p. 21	**Teacher Edition** • Persuasive Writing, p. 582 **Additional Resources** • Authentic Assess., p. 28	**Teacher Edition** • Visual Literacy, p. 582 **Additional Resources** • Vocab. Act., p. 21

Teach

Caption Answer: Labor unions believe that NAFTA has led to a loss of jobs and lower wages in the United States.

C Critical Thinking

Drawing Conclusions Why is it valid to say that the U.S. census represents a subsidy to businesses? Students might want to visit the U.S. Census Bureau Web site in order to draw their conclusions. **Ask:** What is market research, and how would the census help in this endeavor? *(Students should be able to see the connection between businesses' need for information about their market niche or potential consumers and the detailed census information that is available online.)* **OL**

Additional Support

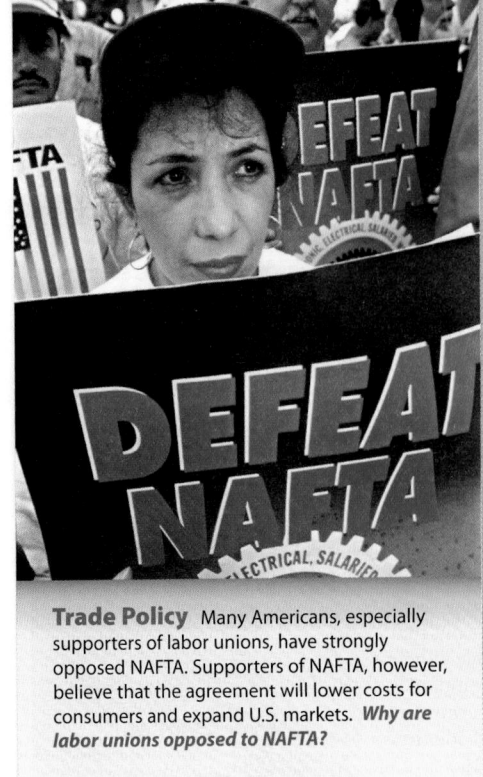

Trade Policy Many Americans, especially supporters of labor unions, have strongly opposed NAFTA. Supporters of NAFTA, however, believe that the agreement will lower costs for consumers and expand U.S. markets. *Why are labor unions opposed to NAFTA?*

Free Trade

The United States plays a leading role in promoting free trade around the world. In recent years, the federal government has emphasized lower tariffs and promoted free trade for many items. The North American Free Trade Agreement (NAFTA), signed by Canada, Mexico, and the United States in 1993, was designed to gradually eliminate trade restrictions among the trading partners beginning in 1994.

Consumers benefit from the lower cost of many imported goods. Although current tariff rates are at an all-time low, tariffs are still used to protect American industries from foreign competition. The government also restricts some products through quotas, or limits on the number that may be imported.

Types of Federal Subsidies

Today the federal government provides at least four types of subsidies, or forms of aid to business. One is tax incentives that allow businesses to deduct certain expenses from their annual tax returns. A second is government loans, or credit subsidies, that provide funds for businesses at low interest rates. A third type of subsidy is free services, such as weather

information, census reports, and other information that is valuable to businesses across the nation. Finally, the government provides direct cash payments to businesses whose products or services are considered vital to the general public. Businesses in the field of transportation often receive this type of subsidy.

Commerce Department Aid to Business

A separate department of the executive branch, the Department of Commerce, was formed in 1903 for the sole purpose of promoting business interests. Congress mandated that the department "foster, promote, and develop the foreign and domestic commerce of the United States."

The main functions of the Commerce Department are to provide information services, financial assistance, and research and development services. Several agencies within the Commerce Department supply businesses with valuable information and subsidies, particularly the Bureau of the Census, which provides important economic data to businesses.

Help for Small Businesses

Competition is important to the free-enterprise system, so the federal government tries to help small businesses. An important independent executive agency outside the Commerce Department that aids businesses is the Small Business Administration (SBA). In addition to offering credit subsidies, the SBA gives free advice and information to small business firms.

Regional offices of the SBA offer government-sponsored classes on sound management practices for owners of small businesses. Businesses also may seek advice from the SBA on how to overcome their problems. In addition, the SBA conducts programs to help women and minorities in business.

Regulating Business

People who are concerned about too much government regulation in the United States usually agree with the following sentiments expressed by President Ronald Reagan:

66 *We get onto dangerous ground when we allow government to decide what is good for us.* 99

—Ronald Reagan

★ Activity: Collaborative Learning ★

Role Playing Organize the class into groups of four, and assign each foursome an interest group mentioned in this section. Explain that each group is to publicize its assigned interest group. Allow groups to research their interest group to analyze its mission, goals, and main concern. Then have group members plan a publicity strategy. Students should choose from the following publicity tasks: write a letter to a government official to promote awareness, create a flyer to publicize their concerns to the community, design a bumper sticker to raise community awareness, or give a one-minute speech to the class on the major issues of the interest group. Allow each group time to present its publicity campaign to the class. **OL**

Consumer advocate Ralph Nader expressed the opposite point of view—that regulatory agencies are needed to protect the public interest. In Nader's opinion:

> 66 . . . it is important to look at regulation issues in terms of the human needs of society. . . . [W]e should ask ourselves what human purpose regulation fulfills, whether it is just or unjust, whether it is adequate or inadequate. . . . 99
>
> —Ralph Nader

Whether people agree with Reagan or Nader often depends on how regulation hurts or benefits them. Either way, federal regulation of economic activity springs from a constitutional provision.

Constitutional Basis of Regulation

The Constitution grants Congress the power to "lay and collect taxes" for the general welfare and to "regulate commerce . . . among the several states." Most regulatory laws enacted in the twentieth century are based upon these two powers.

The commerce clause in Article I, Section 8,[1] is the main basis for government regulation of the economy. ⌨ The Founders designed it to allow federal control of interstate commerce, eliminating a major weakness of the Articles of Confederation. Over the years, the Supreme Court has broadened the interpretation of interstate commerce to include a wide variety of economic activities. Citing the commerce clause, Congress has passed laws to regulate many economic activities. Besides restricting certain activities, regulation also prohibits, promotes, protects, and sets standards for many aspects of interstate commerce.

Demand for Reform

Until the late 1800s, the federal government for the most part took a hands-off, or **laissez-faire,** approach to the economy. The states passed the few regulations that limited business activities. Businesses were generally small, and locally owned, and they primarily served local markets.

📖 See the following footnoted materials in the **Reference Handbook:**
1. The Constitution, pages R42–R67.

Making a Difference

Since 2005, Janet Murguia has served as the first female president of La Raza, the largest national advocacy group for Latinos. (In Spanish, La Raza conveys the meaning of "our people" or "our community.") In the 1960s, La Raza, like other civil rights groups, often confronted government leaders to demand equal rights. Today, Murguia uses a more cooperative strategy. In her new job, she has devoted her efforts to improving relations with the White House when it serves the purposes of La Raza and especially to focusing programs on the needs of Latino women.

Murguia grew up in a small house in Kansas City, Kansas, where the children slept five to a room and lunched on bologna and powdered milk. Her parents did not go to high school, but they cut corners so their children could go to college. (Six of her siblings have law degrees, as does Murguia.)

Murguia got her feet wet in politics by working for a Kansas congressperson. She was asked to work in the legislative affairs office during the Clinton administration in the mid-1990s. "I'll never forget taking my parents into the Oval Office . . . My dad, standing up so straight and proud, stuck his hand out to meet President Clinton and said, 'Thank you for giving my daughter this opportunity.'" Clinton answered with: "I hired Janet, . . . but you're the ones who got her here."

Murguia says "I know the power of the American Dream, and I want to be able to give that to others."

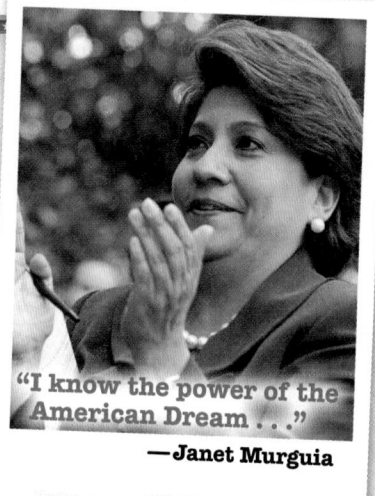

"I know the power of the American Dream . . ."
—Janet Murguia

R Reading Strategy

Identifying The term laissez-faire literally means "allow to do" in French and reflects the beliefs of Enlightenment thinkers who believed that free trade was the way to greater prosperity. **Ask:** Why did the development of big corporations inspire the government to pass laws to protect consumers? (Big corporations might monopolize resources and sales; after destroying competition, they would be able to raise prices.) **OL**

Making a Difference

Janet Murguia La Raza was founded in 1968, but it drew less attention than the NAACP. One writer has said that "the invisibility" of Latinos (or Mexican Americans to be more precise) was due to their being geographically concentrated in a few parts of the country. Latinos also lacked their own institutions or outside funding. La Raza was formed to fill the gaps.

Activity After doing online research, students can create a time line that compares the development of the NAACP and La Raza.

Differentiated Instruction

Activity: Multiple Learning Styles

Visual/Spatial Have students think about the impact on consumers if the Food and Drug Administration, the Federal Trade Commission, and the Consumer Product Safety Commission did not exist. Then have students choose one product or industry and draw a political cartoon reflecting its business practices or products if no regulatory body were in place. Use the cartoons for a bulletin board display. Some students might want to add to the display by finding and photocopying historical cartoons from the days before consumer protection laws were enacted. **OL**

People of the Same Trade Read aloud the following statement by economist Adam Smith in the 1700s: "People of the same trade seldom meet together, even for merriment or diversion, but the conversation ends in a conspiracy against the public or in some contrivance to raise prices." **Ask:** Does this assertion seem true or false? Have students debate their opinions.

C Critical Thinking

Comparing and Contrasting The Clayton Antitrust Act was passed to clarify the Sherman Antitrust Act. Have students compare the wording of each act. **Ask:** Why might the wording of the Clayton Act be more effective? *(Students may say that the Clayton Act is less sweeping and more specific. For example, it prohibits charging high prices in "certain areas," whereas the Sherman Act prohibits "every contract, combinations in the form of trust, or otherwise, or conspiracy, in restraint of trade," and so on.)* **OL**

Additional Support

By the late 1800s, the American economy had changed. Huge corporations dominated American industry. Rapid industrialization was accompanied by many abuses. Business combinations consolidated control of several industries in the hands of a few giant corporations that squeezed smaller companies out of business. Americans questioned the fairness of a system that allowed railroads to charge higher rates for farmers than for manufacturers. Because of these abuses, Americans began to demand government regulation of business.

Congress responded by passing the Interstate Commerce Act in 1887. This act established the first federal regulatory agency, the Interstate Commerce Commission (ICC), and placed certain limits on the freight rates that railroad companies charged. Congress later passed two measures to control corporations that threatened to destroy competition.

Sherman and Clayton Antitrust Acts

In the late 1800s, the trust became a popular form of business consolidation. In a **trust,** several corporations combined their stock and allowed a board of trustees to run the corporations as one giant enterprise. The trustees could set production quotas, fix prices, and control the market, thereby creating a monopoly. A **monopoly** is a single producer that controls so much of a product, service, or industry that little or no competition exists.

Monopoly Money The most high-profile antitrust case in recent years was against Microsoft. The federal government accused Bill Gates's computer-software company of unfair competition: forcing buyers of Microsoft's Windows operating system to use its packaged Web browser rather than competitors' browsers. A U.S. district judge declared Microsoft a monopoly, ordered a breakup of the company, and imposed penalties and restrictions. An appeals court overturned the breakup order but retained the rest of the previous rulings. Still, most experts believe Microsoft came out the winner.

The Standard Oil Trust, organized by John D. Rockefeller, was an example of such a trust. In 1879 it controlled the production and sale of 90 percent of the oil refined in the United States. The Standard Oil Trust consisted of several oil companies whose stock was held by a single board of trustees. Rockefeller was the chief stockholder and trustee. At the time, monopolistic trusts like Rockefeller's dominated many industries.

Congress's first attempt to halt monopolies came in 1890 with the passage of the Sherman Antitrust Act. The first two sections of the act stated the following:

> 66 *Every contract, combination in the form of trust or otherwise, or conspiracy, in restraint of trade or commerce among the several States, or with foreign nations, is hereby declared illegal.*
> *Every person who shall monopolize, or attempt to monopolize, or combine or conspire with any other person or persons to monopolize any part of the trade or commerce among the several States . . . shall be guilty of a felony.* 99
> —Sherman Antitrust Act, 1890

Today, violating the second section of the Sherman Antitrust Act is a felony.

The language of the Sherman Antitrust Act did not specify what was meant by restraint of trade. Thus, the act proved difficult to enforce, but it was successfully enforced in one notable case. In 1906 the federal government charged the Standard Oil Company with violating the first two sections of the act. Convicted, the company ultimately appealed to the Supreme Court, which upheld the conviction and ordered the company to be split into a number of smaller companies. For the first time in the nation's history, the government declared a major trust illegal.

Despite the conviction, the **trend** toward larger and larger business combinations continued. Then in 1914 Congress passed the Clayton Antitrust Act to **clarify** the Sherman Act. The Clayton Act prohibited charging high prices in an area where little competition existed, while at the same time charging lower prices in an area with strong competition. The act also said businesses could not buy stock in other corporations in order to reduce competition. Finally, the act addressed the control of companies by outlawing **interlocking directorates**—a circumstance in which the same people served on the boards of directors of competing companies.

Activity: Collaborative Learning

Identifying Central Issues Review with students the ways the federal government protects consumers' rights. Then have them form groups of two or three and answer the following questions:

- Are sufficient government regulations in place to protect consumers?
- Should more consumer protection regulations be enacted?

- Do too many such regulations exist already?

Ask students to cite examples that support their opinions. *(Answers should include considerations about product safety, labeling issues, and advertising; effect on competition and prices; and so on.)* **OL**

Enforcing the Antitrust Laws

In the same year that Congress passed the Clayton Act, it established the Federal Trade Commission (FTC), an independent regulatory agency, to prevent unfair trading practices. The commission may define unfair competitive practices, issue orders to halt these practices, examine corporate purchases of stock, and investigate trade practices. Since its creation, the FTC's duties have expanded. Today the FTC has many responsibilities in addition to enforcing antitrust laws. These include enforcing laws that prohibit false advertising and requiring truthful labels on textiles and furs. The FTC also regulates the packaging and labeling of certain consumer goods, requires full disclosure of the lending practices of finance companies and retailers who use installment plans, and checks consumer credit agencies.

Despite additional antitrust legislation passed since the Clayton Act, a few large corporations dominate several industries. Today, instead of trusts and monopolies, economic power belongs to oligopolies. An **oligopoly** exists when a few firms dominate a particular industry. By the 1990s, about 50 multibillion-dollar companies controlled approximately one-third of the manufacturing capacity in the United States.

Enforcing the country's antitrust laws is the responsibility of the Antitrust Division of the Department of Justice. Working with the Federal Trade Commission, this division has the legal authority to bring suit against suspected violators of antitrust laws. As a matter of practice, however, relatively few cases are brought against companies and those that are often are settled out of court.

Consumer Protection

Besides antitrust laws, Congress has passed other regulatory laws to protect consumers and ensure fair product standards. Congress also has established independent regulatory agencies that protect consumers or regulate certain economic activities. These regulatory agencies are independent in the sense that they are largely beyond the control of the executive branch.

To maintain this independence, Congress decided that each agency would have from 5 to 11 members, each appointed by the president and confirmed by the Senate. Normally the term of each of the commissioners is long enough to prevent a president from appointing enough new members to control the agency. The president may remove a member only for certain reasons specified by Congress.

The types of independent regulatory agencies vary widely. The Consumer Product Safety Commission, established in 1972, is just one of many. **C**

Consumer Protection Laws

Before 1900, many corporations were not overly concerned about whether their products were healthful or safe. Some truly deplorable practices were common in the food-processing and drug

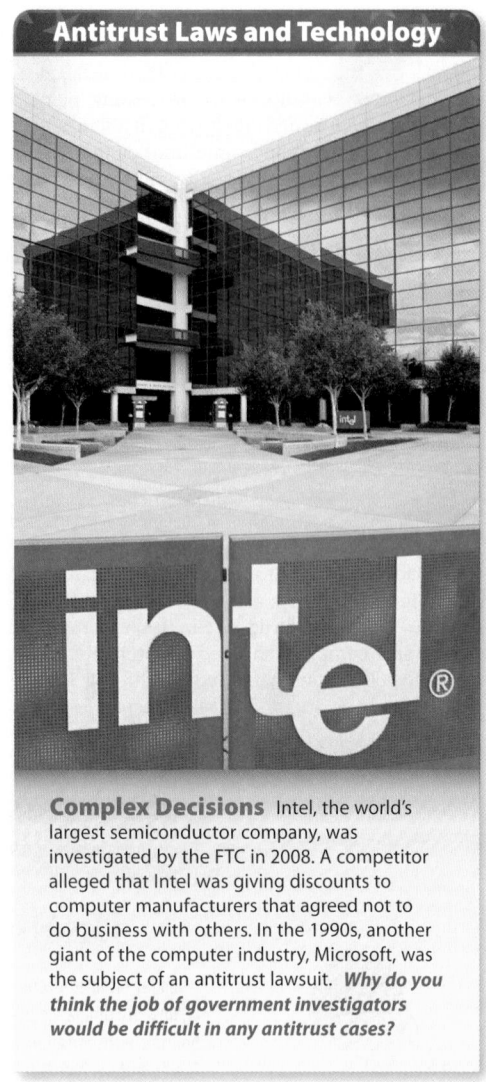

Antitrust Laws and Technology

Complex Decisions Intel, the world's largest semiconductor company, was investigated by the FTC in 2008. A competitor alleged that Intel was giving discounts to computer manufacturers that agreed not to do business with others. In the 1990s, another giant of the computer industry, Microsoft, was the subject of an antitrust lawsuit. *Why do you think the job of government investigators would be difficult in any antitrust cases?*

Linking ★ Past & Present

Meat Inspection In the late 1800s, many people called the impure meat they ate "embalmed beef." In 1906 the government required the inspection of meat in interstate commerce. Later, poultry inspection was mandated. Recent moves to increase the inspection of seafood show that government involvement in this area continues to expand.

Caption Answer: Corporations typically have greater financial resources with which to hire multiple lawyers and fight a prolonged legal battle.

C Critical Thinking

Predicting Consequences The heads of independent regulatory commissions are appointed by the president. Some of these appointees have experience working in the industry they are regulating. **Ask:** What effect might experience in a given field have on someone who is regulating that field? *(It might bias him or her in favor of that industry because he or she understands the problems and challenges.)* **AL**

Additional Support

Health Because of Food and Drug Administration regulations, Americans can almost always be assured that the medicines they take are safe if taken correctly. Some critics claim that FDA rules are too stringent, however, and that lives could be saved if new drugs were allowed on the market sooner. Have students find out about the testing that is required before new drugs are approved and about the controversy over the stringent regulations. Then have students write position statements on the issue. **Ask:** Which side do you support? If you believe that the time period should be shortened, would you drop certain tests? If not, how would you change the procedures? **OL**

More About the Americans with Disabilities Act The ADA defines *disability* as "a physical or mental impairment that substantially limits one or more of the major life activities of . . . [an] individual, a record of such impairment, or being regarded as having such an impairment." Among the conditions covered by the act are orthopedic, visual, speech, and hearing impairments; infection with the HIV virus; muscular dystrophy, diabetes, and learning disabilities.

D **Differentiated Instruction**

Visual/Spatial Have students peruse a national magazine with a target audience of teens or those younger than 30. **Ask:** Do any of the advertisements seem false or misleading? Would they be subject to FTC regulation? *(Students should point out specific ads and explain why they could be considered false or misleading.)* **OL**

Additional Support

industries. Some companies mislabeled foods and sold foods that were contaminated by additives. Other foods such as meat were tainted because of the unsanitary conditions in processing plants. Consumers were duped into buying medicines that were often worthless and sometimes dangerous.

Shortly after the turn of the century, Upton Sinclair described in his book *The Jungle* the conditions in a meatpacking house. He wrote:

> ❝ There would be meat stored in great piles in rooms; and the water from leaky roofs would drip over it, and thousands of rats would race about on it. . . . These rats were nuisances, and the packers would put poisoned bread out for them; they would die, and then rats, bread, and meat would go into the hoppers together. ❞
> —Upton Sinclair, 1906

In addition to Sinclair's stinging condemnation, magazine articles about similar conditions aroused public indignation. As a result, Congress passed the Pure Food and Drug Act in 1906 to make it illegal for a company engaged in interstate commerce to sell contaminated, unhealthful or falsely labeled foods or drugs. The Meat Inspection Act, also passed in 1906, provided for federal inspection of all meatpacking companies that sold meats across state lines.

The Food and Drug Administration (FDA) is responsible for protecting the public from poorly processed and improperly labeled foods and drugs. Scientists at FDA laboratories inspect and test prepared food, cosmetics, drugs, and thousands of other products every year. Agents from the FDA inspect factories, food-processing plants, and drug laboratories. They also check labels for accuracy. If a product fails to meet FDA standards, the FDA may force it off the market.

Protection Against False Advertising

The Federal Trade Commission (FTC) protects consumers from misleading and fraudulent advertising. The FTC has the power to review the advertising claims made about all products sold for interstate commerce. It may determine whether an **D** advertisement for a product is false or unfair. If it is, the FTC can order a company to change the ad to comply with FTC standards. As a result of one FTC ruling, cigarette manufacturers must place a health warning on cigarette packages. According to another FTC regulation, all manufacturers must clearly list the contents of packaged products on the label.

Disability and the Workplace

Today disabled people have recourse against discrimination in education, housing, transportation, and employment. The Americans With Disabilities Act (ADA) says that remedies under the Civil Rights Act of 1964 apply to ADA employment cases. The ADA bans inquiries about disabilities for job applicants. Also, employees are required to be provided with "reasonable accommodations" that are necessary to assist them in doing their jobs. The act also forbids employers to pay workers with disabilities less than nondisabled persons who do the same work, and it forbids discrimination in promotions.

◀ **Technology has helped many disabled people.**

Participating IN GOVERNMENT ACTIVITY

Make a List What would be considered "reasonable accommodations" for a person in a wheelchair working in a tall office building?

580

Extending the Content

Unions The strongest unions in the United States today have between 20 and 40 percent of the workers in a particular industry in their membership. The most powerful unions include Teamsters, automobile workers, steelworkers, machinists, electrical workers, and retail clerks. Generally, the weakest unions have been those in the service industries, especially those historically made up of minority groups and women, who are employed as domestic workers, farm laborers, and clerks. However, almost all unions have lost power due to increased global competition. Businesses now have the option to move to areas here or abroad that provide cheaper, nonunion labor. Discuss with students the pros and cons of labor unions from the perspective of workers and businesses.

Consumers and Product Safety

Books and articles about how consumers are cheated and deceived have always been popular. The book that really propelled consumer activism was Ralph Nader's *Unsafe at Any Speed,* published in 1965. Nader accused auto manufacturers of caring more about style than safety and neglecting to design cars to withstand crashes. Nader became a leader in the consumer movement.

As a result of this movement, Congress created the Consumer Product Safety Commission (CPSC) in 1972. It was set up to protect consumers from "unreasonable risk of injury from hazardous products." The CPSC establishes safety standards for a wide range of products, and when products fail to meet the standards, the CPSC can order it off the market. In a global economy, the CPSC faces new challenges to screen products from abroad that do not meet American safety standards. In 2008 toys from China were a special concern because they contained lead-based paint.

Regulating the Sale of Stocks

The Securities and Exchange Commission (SEC) has regulated the trading of **securities,** or stocks and bonds, since its creation during the Great Depression. Today the SEC regulates the nation's securities issued by public utility companies and requires all corporations that issue public stock to file regular reports on their assets, profits, sales, and other financial data. These reports must be made available to **investors** so they can judge the true value of a company's stock offerings.

Corporate accounting scandals became big news in 2001 when the Enron Corporation declared bankruptcy. This was, at the time, the largest single bankruptcy in American history. Employees lost their jobs, and millions of dollars in stock investment disappeared.

When Enron and several other corporations were investigated, it was revealed that fraudulent accounting was used to inflate stock value to hide the firms' weaknesses and to create the appearance of corporate success. The failure of the Securities and Exchange Commission to identify this problem led to the passage of the Sarbanes-Oxley Act of 2002. The act required chief executive officers and chief financial officers of publicly traded companies to personally sign SEC reports and pay penalties if improper accounting is later discovered.

Government and Labor

As large-scale businesses multiplied in the late 1800s, the relationship between employer and employee became strained. Corporations and businesses with national operations were more impersonal, and cooperation between business and labor deteriorated. Federal laws were created to regulate the relationship between employers and employees.

Protecting Unions and Workers

The first nationwide union was organized in the 1850s. Resisted by employers and with no support from government, early unions failed to survive for very long. The first successful national labor organization, the American Federation of Labor, was founded in the 1880s.

Workers organized unions and elected leaders to represent them in negotiations with employers for labor contracts that specified wages, hours, and working conditions. The practice of negotiating labor contracts is known as **collective bargaining.**

Employers generally refused to negotiate with unions. As a result, unions often resorted to strikes to obtain concessions. Between 1881 and 1905, American unions called about 37,000 strikes.

For many years, the government favored business over labor unions. Federal troops and state militia broke up some strikes. The courts even used the Sherman Antitrust Act, originally intended to regulate business, to prohibit union activities that restrained trade.

In the early 1900s, the government's attitude toward labor began to change. The Clayton Antitrust Act, passed in 1914, included a provision that labor unions were not to be treated as "conspiracies in restraint of trade." Before the 1930s, employers were often successful in challenging laws that regulated wages and working conditions. In 1937, however, the Supreme Court heard an appeal of a case in which a state had written a minimum wage law to protect women and children.

West Coast Hotel v. Parrish

Elsie Parrish, a hotel employee, brought suit to recover the difference between the wages paid to her and the state's minimum wage. The hotel owner claimed that the law deprived the employer of freedom of contract. The Court, however, upheld the minimum wage set by the Industrial Welfare Committee of the state of Washington:

POLITICAL PROFILES — **Frances Perkins** (1882–1965) became the first female cabinet member when President Franklin Roosevelt appointed her secretary of labor in 1933. Trade unionists vehemently opposed the appointment of a woman and made their opinions clear in a meeting with the president, but Roosevelt stood firm. According to a story at the time, he told his wife Eleanor (a firm supporter of women's rights) that he did not mind the controversy because, he quipped, "I'd rather have trouble with them for an hour than trouble with you for the rest of my life."

R Reading Strategy

Inferring The text notes that there were 37,000-plus strikes between 1881 and 1905. This was also the era of heavy immigration from Eastern Europe, Italy, and Russia. **Ask:** What kinds of connections might exist between a high number of strikes and cheap labor due to large-scale immigration of unskilled workers? *(Students might say that employers had no obligation to meet workers' demands for better wages and conditions, and workers responded by striking.)* **AL**

Additional Support

Extending the Content

The History of Organized Labor The American Federation of Labor (AFL) was a federation of craft unions in which all members belonged to the same skilled occupation. The Congress of Industrial Organizations (CIO) was a group of industrial unions to which all workers in a single industry belonged, regardless of the job they performed. In 1955 the two organizations merged, forming the AFL-CIO, thereby increasing the strength of organized labor. **Ask:** Is it more effective to have one large union as opposed to two separate, possibly competing ones? *(Students might mention greater negotiating power or less competition between unions.)*

S Skill Practice

Visual Literacy Have students examine the photograph of the picketers. **Ask:** Why do you think their signs and shirts all say "Unite Here"? Whom do they want to unite? *(Answers will vary. Students might suggest that the picketers want to unite with management in doing away with the "unfair labor practices" that can be seen on the signs.)* **AL**

W Writing Support

Persuasive Writing Have students write a short essay in which they reinforce Chief Justice Hughes's statement about the effects of the exploitation of workers on society and on the workers. **AL**

Hands-On Chapter Project

Step 1

Conducting Mini-Debates

Step 1: Researching the Issues
Student pairs will research issues addressed by domestic federal programs and conduct brief, one-on-one "mini-debates." Remind students that virtually every government program has supporters and critics. In these debates, each student will have three minutes to present one side of the issue.

Directions In Step 1, ask students to choose an issue from the chapter or one related to it and conduct research. Possible

---

Labor Force and Union Membership

Union Membership

Source: U.S. Bureau of the Census, Bureau of Labor Statistics, 2008.

Critical Thinking Hotel workers in Los Angeles organize a strike against their employer. *What can you infer about the strength of labor unions from this graph?*

---

66 *The exploitation of a class of workers who are in an unequal position with respect to bargaining power, and are thus relatively defenceless against the denial of a living wage, is not only detrimental to their health and wellbeing, but casts a direct burden for their support upon the community. . . . The community may direct its lawmaking power to correct the abuse.* 99

—Chief Justice Charles Evans Hughes, 1937

Today, federal laws set minimum wages and maximum working hours and prohibit child labor. In addition, the Department of Labor, established in 1913, helps people find jobs, trains workers for new jobs, collects data, and offers unemployment insurance.

Labor Laws of the 1930s

The greatest gains of organized labor occurred in the 1930s during the Great Depression when labor laws that seemed revolutionary at the time were enacted. Passed as part of President Franklin D. Roosevelt's New Deal, they are often called "labor's bill of rights." They guaranteed

labor's right to bargain collectively and to strike, and they generally strengthened labor unions.

In 1932 Congress passed the Norris-La Guardia Act, which gave workers the right to join unions and to strike. It outlawed yellow-dog contracts, which forced workers to sign contracts agreeing not to join a union. The act also restricted the use of federal court injunctions against labor unions. **Injunctions**—court orders to prevent an action from taking place—were often issued to force striking unions back to work.

In 1935 Congress passed the Wagner Act, guaranteeing the right of all workers to organize and bargain collectively. To achieve this goal, the law prohibited employers from engaging in certain unfair labor practices. Employers could not refuse to bargain collectively with recognized unions, they could not interfere in union organization, and they could not discharge or otherwise punish a worker for union activism.

To enforce these prohibitions, the Wagner Act created the National Labor Relations Board (NLRB). The board had power to supervise elections to determine which union a group of workers wanted to represent it. The NLRB could also hear labor's complaints and issue "cease and desist" orders to end unfair labor practices.

582 UNIT 7: *Public Policies and Services*

---

issues might be NAFTA, subsidies for airlines, 1930s labor laws, the 1989 savings and loan bailout, the Microsoft court case, price supports for farmers, the Works Progress Administration, protection of air and water quality, food stamps, Social Security, and so on. Pairs will take opposing sides of the issue they select. As they do their research, they will take notes to prepare debates that include: a) a concise resolution statement indicating the issue and their position on it; b) a brief history of the issue; c) a description of the

groups affected; and d) the rationale for their position.

Putting It Together Have students make posters for their debates that include a resolution statement and one or two photos relating to the issue. Discuss any problems they are having in conducting their research. **OL**

(Chapter Project continued in Section 2.)

Under the Wagner Act, unions gained tremendously in membership and strength.

Regulating Unions

Once the Wagner Act was passed, business leaders began protesting that unions were becoming too powerful. Critics of the act said that it favored the workers, that many workers were being forced to join unions, and that employers were being prevented from hiring nonunion employees. To avoid strikes, employers had to agree to establish a closed shop. In a closed shop, only members of a union can be hired.

Responding to these criticisms, Congress passed the Taft-Hartley Act in 1947, the government's first attempt to regulate certain practices of large unions. Its stated purpose was to restore the balance between labor and management. The act required unions to give 60 days' notice before calling a strike. This "cooling-off period" was intended to provide additional time for labor and management to settle their differences. The act also restored the limited use of injunctions. In strikes that endanger the nation, the president can obtain an injunction to stop the strike for 80 days. Under the Taft-Hartley Act, employers can sue unions for damages inflicted during a strike.

While the act prohibited the closed shop, it permitted the union shop. In a union shop, workers are required to join a union soon after they have been hired (but not before). Union shops can be formed if a majority of workers vote for them. They cannot be formed, however, in any state that has passed a right-to-work law. Right-to-work laws are state labor laws that prohibit both closed shops and union shops. They provide that all workplaces be open shops where workers may freely decide whether or not to join a union.

Protecting Union Members

At some periods in our history, a few labor unions were corrupt. In 1957, for example, a Senate investigating committee found that some leaders of the Teamsters union misused or stole union funds. These union officials were accused of associating with gangsters and racketeers and of using bribery, threats, and violence against their opponents.

These scandals led to passage of the Landrum-Griffin Act of 1959. It made it a federal crime to misuse union funds and also protected union members from being intimidated by union officials. It also helped eliminate fraud in union elections. The act included a bill of rights for union members. This guaranteed the right of members to nominate and vote by secret ballot in union elections, to participate and speak freely at union meetings, to sue their union for unfair practices, and to examine union records and finances.

SECTION 1 Review

Vocabulary

1. **Explain** the significance of: mixed economy, laissez-faire, trust, monopoly, interlocking directorate, oligopoly, securities, collective bargaining, injunction.

Main Ideas

2. **Identifying** Why was the Sherman Antitrust Act difficult to enforce?

3. **Examining** What are the government's main goals regarding competition and consumers?

Critical Thinking

4. **Identifying Central Issues** What general problems do the Federal Trade Commission, the Securities and Exchange Commission, and the Consumer Product Safety Commission address?

5. **Organizing** Use a graphic organizer like the one below to identify three laws passed by Congress that resulted in the growth of labor unions.

	Growth of Labor Unions

Writing About Government

6. **Persuasive Writing** Interstate commerce depends on an adequate system of highways funded by the federal government. Find out about the highway construction plans in your area. Create a bulletin board display with a map of the planned construction. Include a one-page written proposal that explains how the highway will improve or hinder the local economy. Include pertinent details and important financial information.

R **Reading Strategy**

Identifying Ask: What was the broad purpose of the Taft-Hartley Act? *(to restore the balance of power between labor and management)* **BL**

Assess

Assign the Section 1 Assessment as homework or as an in-class activity, or have students take Section Quiz 21-1 from *Section Quizzes and Chapter Tests*.

Close

Evaluating Ask: Why are groups such as the FDA, the FTC, and the CPSC called "watchdog agencies"? *(They "watch" businesses to ensure that federal rules and regulations are followed.)* **OL**

Section 1 Review

Answers

1. All definitions can be found in the section and the Glossary.
2. The act did not specify exactly what *restraint of trade* meant.
3. to maintain a competitive business environment and protect consumers' interests
4. protecting the public from deceit or physical harm, and ensuring fair product standards
5. Clayton Antitrust Act; Norris-LaGuardia Act; Wagner Act
6. Students may find the information they need to complete the display by checking local newspapers and by contacting local and state transportation departments.

Focus

Agriculture and Environment

Reader's Guide

Content Vocabulary

★ price supports (p. 586)
★ acreage allotment (p. 586)
★ marketing quotas (p. 586)

Academic Vocabulary

★ output (p. 584)
★ restore (p. 586)
★ environmental (p. 586)

Reading Strategy

As you read, create a graphic organizer that shows the three major ways the Department of Agriculture helps farmers.

Farmers

Issues in the News

As the cost of gas and energy rose in 2007 and 2008, food became more expensive. By mid-2008, according to the U.S. Department of Agriculture (USDA), food prices increased 3 to 4 percent as suppliers passed on the higher costs of fuel to consumers. The problem was made worse by the fact that many corn farmers decided to sell their corn to producers of ethanol, an alternative fuel, instead of selling it as food. Said Steve Gill, a USDA official: "Prices being where they're at, the food aid dollar is not buying as many products." To help the poor, the USDA decided to put more of its surplus wheat on the market to support food banks, school lunches, and meals for the elderly. The USDA also kept an eye on world shortages and famines. It has about 34 million bushels of wheat on hand for food-aid donations abroad.

▲ Wheat stockpile

The federal government has always encouraged American agriculture. In 1790 about 95 percent of Americans lived in rural areas, and most people were farmers. Farming remained the major occupation until early in the twentieth century. Today, however, the United States is an urban nation with more than 75 percent of the people living in towns and cities and only two percent working in agriculture.

From 1935 to the present, the number of farms in the United States has declined from 6.8 million to about 2 million because small family farms are disappearing. The average farm today is just under 500 acres, more than twice as large as the average farm 30 years ago. Large corporate farms are making agriculture big business. While the total number of farms has decreased, farm **output** per work hour has increased almost every year. In 1900 one farmer could feed about 7 people. Now the average farmer can feed approximately 80 people.

Farmers and Government

Despite being an urban nation, the federal government continues to support American agriculture because farming is vital to the nation.

Early Agricultural Legislation

In 1862 Congress passed three acts that were important to farmers. One law created the Department of Agriculture. Its original purpose was to show farmers how to improve and modernize their agricultural methods. The second law, the Morrill Act, aided northern states by granting them millions of acres in federal land to set up state-operated colleges of agriculture. The third law, the Homestead Act, gave land to those who were willing to farm it.

Farm Problems

In the 1920s, the nation's farms faced serious problems. A historian's view creates a bleak picture: **S**

66 *The golden era for farmers ended abruptly in 1920–21, when . . . Federal Reserve Board policies and lessening European demand for American agricultural produce inaugurated a decade-long agricultural depression. Signs of distress quickly became apparent. . . . Between 1920 and 1921 cotton prices fell from a dollar a pound to twenty cents a pound. . . . Many wheat farmers could not sell their produce even at the cost of production.* 99

—David Joseph Goldberg

As farm prices continued to decline, thousands of farmers lost their land. During the first years of the Great Depression, conditions became worse. Then in the 1930s, huge dust storms swept across the Great Plains, blowing away much of the region's soil. One account in the *Saturday Evening Post* described the scene in South Dakota: **D**

66 *When the wind died and the sun shone forth again, it was a different world. There were no fields, only sand drifting into mounds. . . . In the farmyard, fences, machinery, and trees were gone, buried. The roofs of sheds stuck out through drifts deeper than a man is tall.* 99

—R.D. Lusk, November 1933

Responding to this crisis, President Roosevelt's New Deal programs set out to raise the price of farm products by limiting the production of certain crops that were in oversupply. Under the Agricultural Adjustment Act (AAA), the government paid farmers for *not* producing their usual amount of corn, wheat, hogs, and other commodities. It also provided loans to help farmers keep their land. Although the Supreme Court declared the AAA unconstitutional in 1936, Congress quickly passed a similar act that overcame the Court's objections.

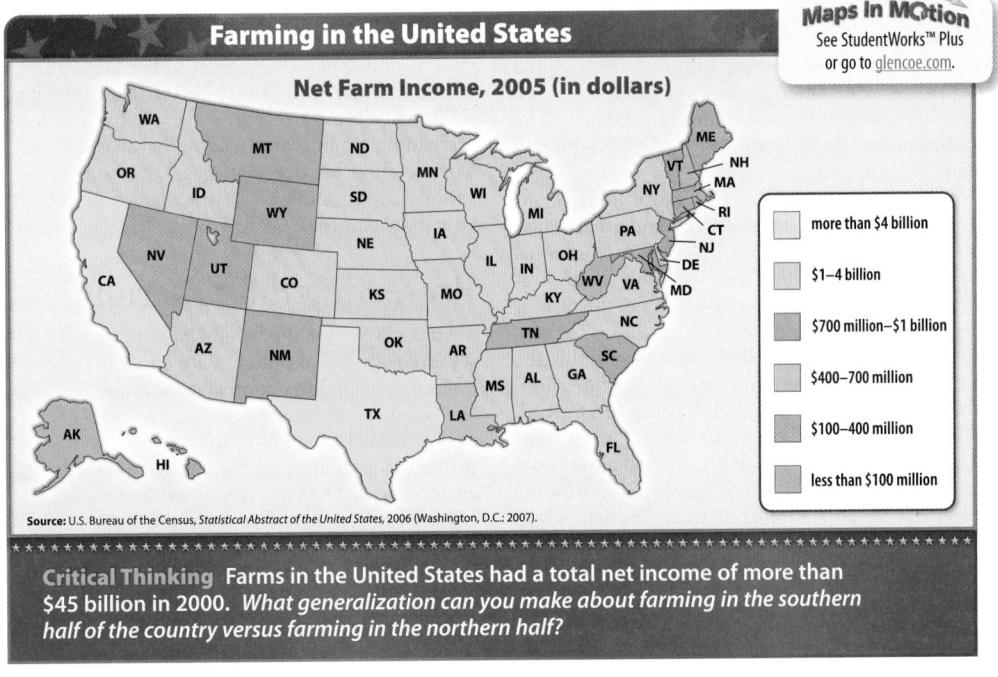

Farming in the United States

Maps in MOtion
See StudentWorks™ Plus or go to glencoe.com.

Net Farm Income, 2005 (in dollars)

- more than $4 billion
- $1–4 billion
- $700 million–$1 billion
- $400–700 million
- $100–400 million
- less than $100 million

Source: U.S. Bureau of the Census, *Statistical Abstract of the United States,* 2006 (Washington, D.C.: 2007).

Critical Thinking Farms in the United States had a total net income of more than $45 billion in 2000. *What generalization can you make about farming in the southern half of the country versus farming in the northern half?*

Teach

D Differentiated Instruction

Visual/Spatial Organize the class into small groups, and have each group choose one or two of the many agencies that make up the Department of Agriculture. Group members should do research on the activities and services of their agencies and design a visual to contribute to a bulletin-board display on the Department of Agriculture. Visuals should include labels and captions as appropriate. **OL**

S Skill Practice

Making a Time Line Work with students to make a time line of federal legislation enacted to support farmers. **BL**

Critical Thinking

Answer: Farming is more profitable in the southern half of the country. In 2005 the net farm income was greater in the southern half of the United States.

Differentiated Instruction

★ Activity: Multiple Learning Styles ★

Intrapersonal Have students investigate the Dust Bowl days of the 1930s through literature, videos, nonfiction, or the Internet. Possible sources include John Steinbeck's *The Grapes of Wrath;* Jerry Stanley's *Children of the Dust Bowl: The True Story of the School at Weedpatch Camp;* Michael L. Cooper's *Dust to Eat: Drought and Depression in the 1930s;* and PBS's *American Experience: Surviving the Dust Bowl.* Then have each student, in the role of a teenager of the time, write diary or journal entries describing the conditions, their effect on his or her family, and a personal reaction to the situation. **BL**

C **Critical Thinking**

Identifying Trends Have students use the U.S. *Statistical Abstract* to research changes in the number of farms in their state over the past two decades. Tell them to choose a table, a graph, or a summary paragraph to present their findings. **OL**

CURRICULUM CONNECTION

Literature In his novel *The Grapes of Wrath,* John Steinbeck chronicles the experiences of a farm family forced to leave Oklahoma as a result of the terrible dust storms that swept the Great Plains in the 1930s.

Did You Know?

During 2007 and 2008, the U.S. Forest Service, an agency of the Department of Agriculture, faced unprecedented challenges fighting large-scale fires. The cost of fighting these fires was very high. Students can get a sense of the cost of natural disaster relief at the U.S. Forest Service's Web site.

Differentiated Instruction

Source Readings, p. 21

Aid for Farmers Today

The Department of Agriculture provides many services to farmers. The chief functions are to help farmers market their produce, stabilize farm prices, conserve land, and promote research in agricultural science.

The Department of Agriculture also has helped develop rural areas. Rural Electrification Administration loans brought electricity and telephone service to many rural areas. The Farmers Home Administration was established to provide loans for farmers to buy land, livestock, seeds, equipment, and fertilizer; to build homes; to dig wells; and to obtain disaster relief.

Marketing Services

Several agencies of the Department of Agriculture are concerned with helping farmers find buyers for their crops. The Agricultural Marketing Service advises farmers on the demand for crops, current prices, and transportation methods. It also performs market research to help farmers know when and where to sell their products. The Foreign Agricultural Service promotes the sale of American farm goods in foreign markets.

Programs for Stabilizing Prices

The federal government has tried several methods for preventing farm prices from falling below a certain level. The current approach involves the coordination of three programs—price supports, acreage allotments, and marketing quotas. The Commodity Credit Corporation (CCC) administers these programs.

Under the program of **price supports,** Congress establishes a support price for a particular crop. The CCC then lends the farmer money equal to the support price for the crop. If the actual market price falls below the support price, the farmer repays the loan with the crop.

The Commodity Credit Corporation holds the surplus crops in government storage facilities until the market price goes up and the crop can be sold. It also uses surplus crops in welfare programs, for school lunches, and for famine relief overseas. Even so, from time to time, huge surpluses of some products have accumulated when market prices stayed at a low level.

To avoid large surpluses every year, the government has adopted the idea of acreage restriction, or acreage allotment. In this program, officials in the Department of Agriculture estimate the probable

demand for a crop in world and national markets. Then they estimate the number of acres that will produce that amount. Based on these estimates, the government assigns farmers **acreage allotments** and pays support prices for only the crops grown on the assigned number of acres.

When a crop has been overproduced and large surpluses threaten to lower prices, the government turns to **marketing quotas,** or marketing limits. Aided by Department of Agriculture officials, farmers set marketing quotas among themselves and agree to market only an assigned portion of their overproduced crop.

Not all observers agree with the government practices of having price supports and farm subsidies. In the early 1990s, critics said that the Department of Agriculture was overgrown and that its overlapping agencies were not efficient. In 1994 Congress responded to Agriculture secretary Mike Espy's proposal to reorganize the department. The resulting reorganization created the Farm Service Agency, which consolidated conservation programs and reduced the department's budget. The same legislation that created the Farm Service Agency also made participation in a federal crop insurance program mandatory for farmers who took part in federal price supports.

Promoting Conservation

C Conserving the nation's land and forests is a vital responsibility of agencies in the Department of Agriculture. The Forest Service has **restored** millions of acres of forests used for outdoor recreation, timber, and wildlife habitat. The Soil Conservation Service manages 3,000 soil conservation districts and works with farmers to manage conservation problems.

Protecting the Environment

For many years, the federal government did not set **environmental** policy. State and local governments developed few controls over air, water, land, and other natural resources.

Beginning in the 1950s, the federal government reacted to public concern over the deteriorating environment. The federal government passed legislation to clean up the air and water. In 1970 Congress issued a series of sweeping environmental laws. The Environmental Protection Agency (EPA) was created and charged with enforcing a host of regulations. Most of the regulations mandated changes in business and operations to comply with

Sustainable Development ★★★

Objective: Inform students about the dangers of environmental deterioration.

Focus/Teach: Students should complete the research activities.

Assess: Students should make a conclusion about sustainable development based on their research.

Close: Hold a class discussion to assess the need for sustainable development.

Differentiated Instruction Strategies

BL Have students determine, as a class, how much water they use on a daily basis. Brainstorm how to decrease that amount.

AL Have interested students discuss what would happen if the fresh water supply ran out.

ELL Discuss the differences between freshwater and salt water.

the law, but Congress provided no federal funds to states, localities, and businesses to pay for the improvements.

Air Pollution Policies

Congress first expressed concern about air pollution as early as 1955 when it passed the Air Pollution Act. This act, however, was limited to promoting research on air quality and to providing technical assistance to states and communities.

In the 1960s, Congress passed stronger laws requiring states to set clean air standards and to prepare plans for their enforcement. The 1970 Clean Air Amendments established the Environmental Protection Agency (1970), giving the federal government power to enforce air-quality standards.

The 1990 Clear Air Act mandated reductions in emissions. As a result, air quality in the United States improved between 1990 and 1999. Smog, sulfur dioxide, and carbon monoxide concentrations declined. In 1992 the Kyoto Protocol was presented at an international conference to set global greenhouse emissions standards. The United States signed the protocol, but Presidents Bill Clinton and George W. Bush never submitted it to the Senate for ratification. President Clinton disliked the fact that developing countries were exempt from some provisions, and President Bush favored voluntary actions by business to control gases.

During his eight years in office, President Bush argued that the government had no authority to regulate greenhouse gases because they are not specifically mentioned in the Clean Air Act. A Supreme Court decision in 2007 challenged this interpretation by the Bush administration. The Court said that the EPA has clear jurisdiction over "any air pollutant" that might be expected to endanger the public health.

Water Pollution Policies

The Water Pollution Control Act of 1948 first provided for federal technical assistance to the states, but, as with the early pollution laws, the act was weak. Congress then passed stronger measures. The Water Quality Improvement Act of 1970

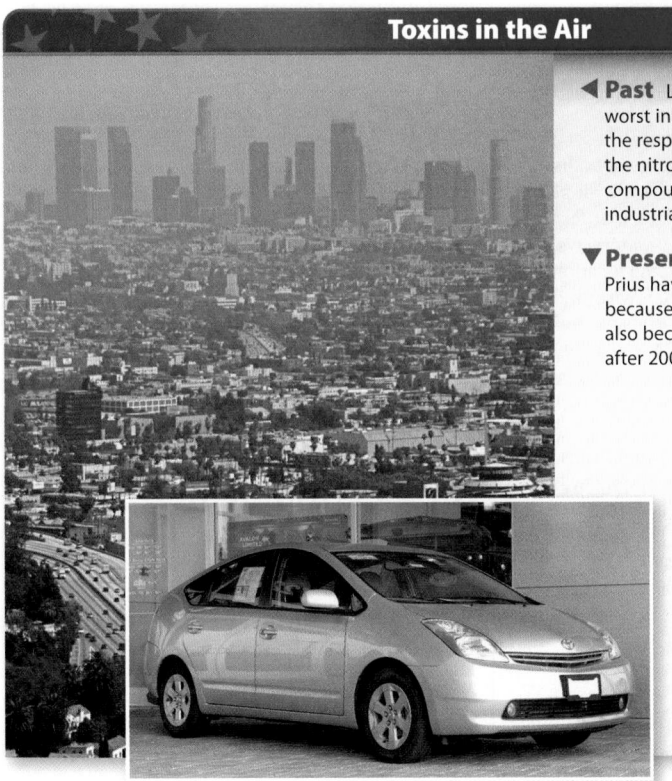

Toxins in the Air

◀ **Past** Los Angeles smog is among the worst in the nation. Smog, which irritates the respiratory system, is created when the nitrogen oxides and volatile organic compounds released from cars and industrial plants mix in the sunlight.

▼ **Present** Hybrid cars like this Toyota Prius have become popular not only because of environmental concerns, but also because the cost of fuel rose steeply after 2005.

Is Technology the Answer?

The automobile is the nation's chief source of air pollution. *Do you think more laws should be enacted to encourage Americans to use public transportation, or should the government promote new technology, such as hybrid and electric automobiles?*

CHAPTER 21: *Social and Domestic Policy* **587**

Participating IN GOVERNMENT

Improving Your School's Environment Have students identify a problem or an issue in the school's neighborhood. *(traffic problems, inadequate lighting, graffiti, or crime, for example)* Then have students formulate a plan for improvement. **Ask:** Do neighbors or nearby businesses need to be involved? The police? Community leaders? Are funds needed? Would a car wash or a bake sale provide enough funds to get started? If possible, have students carry out their plan. **BL**

S Skill Practice

Researching Industries are allowed a certain level of polluting emissions. If one industry does not use all of its allowance, it may sell its credits to another industry. Have students find out about this practice of "cap-and-trade" and explain why they agree or disagree with it. If they disagree, how would they change the law? **OL**

Caption Answer: Answers will vary. Students should defend their answers.

Hands-On Chapter Project

Step 2

Conducting Mini-Debates

Step 2: Organizing Notes Students will organize the notes they took in Step 1 by creating web diagrams.

Directions Have students make web diagrams, using the position statement as the main circle.

Putting It Together Ask students to compare diagrams and refine them for later use in their debates. **OL**

(Chapter Project continued in Section 3.)

W Writing Support

R Reading Strategy

Additional Support

The Human Footprint

Impact of Hurricane Katrina As these two images show, satellite imagery is able to monitor changes in surface water on land. The one on the left was taken of New Orleans in April 2004. The one on the right was taken in August 2005 after Hurricane Katrina had struck. *How do you think such photos affect the public debate on the environment?*

prohibited the discharge of harmful amounts of oil and other dangerous materials into navigable waters. The law concerned such pollution sources as ships, onshore refineries, and offshore oil-drilling platforms. It also controlled pesticide drainage into the Great Lakes.

The Water Pollution Control Act of 1972 set a goal of completely eliminating the discharge of pollutants into American waterways. Under the act, all polluters, whether they were cities, industries, or farmers, needed a permit to dump waste into waterways. The EPA was required to monitor dumping locations for compliance. Many lawsuits resulted. Environmentalists sued because they thought the EPA was too permissive. Industries sued the EPA because they thought the agency's standards were unreasonable.

In the decades since the act's passage, the law has been changed and amended so it remains effective. In 1981 treatment-plant capabilities were improved. In 1987 a new funding system was put in place to make it easier for states to comply with the act's standards. Separate laws have also impacted the government's efforts to ensure pollution-free water. For example, in 1990 an agreement between the United States and Canada ensured better water quality in the Great Lakes.

Unfunded Mandates

The EPA issued hundreds of regulations to implement environmental laws. As costs grew each year,

state and local leaders began to complain about these unfunded mandates—programs ordered but not paid for by federal legislation. The local share of environmental costs escalated from 76 percent of $35 billion in 1981 to a projected 82 percent of nearly $48 billion in 2000. Steven Walker, air-quality chief in Albuquerque, New Mexico, said, "It seems like every November from now to [forever] there's some deadline we have to meet."

Pressured by state and local governments and by businesses, Congress reviewed unfunded mandates in 1996. New laws restricted the ability of the federal government to impose additional requirements on governments without providing funds to pay for them. The problem has not been solved, however, since existing mandates remain in place.

Energy and the Environment

In the 1950s, most Americans were not familiar with terms like *energy crisis, environmental pollution,* or *ecology*. But a groundbreaking book *The Silent Spring* by Rachel Carson, published in 1962, alerted the public to the dangers of the pesticide DDT. Awareness about the declining quality of the environment, combined with concerns about energy costs in the 1970s, inspired the government to put environmental issues higher on its policy agenda.

Activity: Interdisciplinary Connection

In the early history of the continent, Native Americans and European settlers who came later found abundant natural resources—unending forests, clear lakes and rivers, and rich deposits of metals. As the nation grew, Americans developed increasingly sophisticated technologies to industrialize the economy. They gave little thought to the possibility that these resources might be depleted or that the careless exploitation of resources could seriously affect the environment.

By the early 1960s, however, the costs became obvious. Many rivers and lakes were dirty. Smog engulfed major cities, oil spills polluted the beaches, and the heavy use of pesticides endangered wildlife.

In the winter of 1973–1974, Americans found themselves in an energy crisis. Arab countries cut off shipments of oil because the United States supported Israel during an Arab-Israeli war. Industries that were dependent on oil laid off workers. Many gas stations closed, and long lines formed at the ones that were open. States lowered speed limits, and people set thermostats lower to save energy.

As the government fashioned a new energy policy in the mid-1970s to meet future energy crises, people began to recognize the costs of a cleaner environment, and conflicts among interest groups with different goals ensued. Americans discovered that preserving clean air might require them to drive cars with pollution-control devices that made the cars more costly to buy and operate. Oil companies wanted to drill for more offshore oil, while environmentalists believed that such drilling posed too great of a risk to the marine environment.

In 1991 the head of the Department of Energy said that the goals of a national energy strategy were to "reduce U.S. vulnerability to future disruptions in oil markets, improve the environment, and increase economic efficiency." These goals have proved hard to reach because there is disagreement over how to find a balance among them.

Competing interest groups often lobby to shape energy policy. This is illustrated by the debate over drilling in the Arctic National Wildlife Refuge, an oil-rich area that is home to some 40 species of mammals and about 180 species of birds, including the snow goose and peregrine falcon.

The usual policy fights between environmentalists and business groups have intensified recently for several reasons. First, there is a fear that terrorists or unfriendly governments might restrict access to Middle Eastern oil. Second, many people now worry that Americans' high consumption of oil contributes to global warming. They argue that finding new energy sources will protect the environment, while business activists argue that making the nation less dependent on foreign oil is the most important goal.

Government ONLINE

Student Web Activity Visit glencoe.com and enter **QuickPass**™ code USG9822c21. Click on Student Web Activity and complete the activity about agriculture and the environment.

SECTION 2 Review

Vocabulary

1. Explain the significance of: price supports, acreage allotment, marketing quotas.

Main Ideas

2. Identifying What are the main functions of the Department of Agriculture and the Environmental Protection Agency?

3. Describing How does the federal government attempt to stabilize farm prices?

Critical Thinking

4. Predicting Consequences Analyze the economic and environmental effects of recent air and water pollution legislation.

5. Comparing Use a graphic organizer like the one below to compare clean air legislation of the 1950s, 1960s, and 1990s.

1950s	1960s	1990s

Writing About Government

6. Expository Writing Choose a conservation project that you can do in your community. You might adopt a park, a pond, or a roadside to clean up and to keep attractive. Share your ideas with the class in the form of a proposal presentation.

Assess

Assign the Section 2 Assessment as homework or as an in-class activity, or have students take Section Quiz 21-2 from *Section Quizzes and Chapter Tests.*

Close

Analyzing Ask: Is a certain amount of risk or damage to the environment the price the nation has to pay to have jobs, profits, and a strong economy? *(Student answers will vary. Students may suggest that people's livelihoods are more important than protecting the environment at all costs. Other students may suggest that a strong economy doesn't need to damage the environment.)* **OL**

Government ONLINE

Objectives and answers to the Student Web Activity can be found in the *Web Activity Lesson Plan* at glencoe.com. Enter **QuickPass**™ code USG9085c21T.

Section 2 Review

Answers

1. All definitions can be found in the section and the Glossary.
2. Department of Agriculture: to help farmers market their produce, to stabilize farm prices, to conserve land, and to promote agricultural research
   Environmental Protection Agency: to enforce environmental regulations
3. with price supports, acreage allotments, and marketing quotas
4. It will provide cleaner air and water, but additional taxation might be required.

5. 1950s: Laws promoted research on air quality and provided technical assistance to states and communities.
   1960s: Laws required states to set clean-air standards and to prepare enforcement plans.
   1990s: Laws required reductions in automobile emissions and industrial toxic emissions.
6. Have students vote on which project they would like to pursue.

Focus

Bellringer
Section Focus Transparencies 21-3

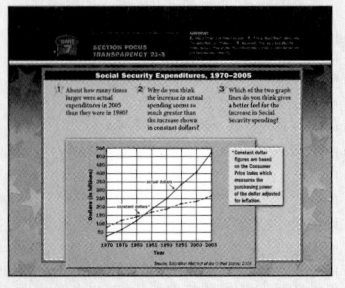

Reader's Guide

Answers to Graphic:

Medicare: medical assistance for senior citizens

Medicaid: medical assistance for low-income persons

Defense Department: medical care for military personnel and their families

Veterans Affairs: operates medical and dental care for veterans

HHS Department: programs to promote health

CDC: works to control the spread of infectious diseases

FDA: tests samples of food and drugs for safety

Resource Manager

Health and Public Assistance

Reader's Guide

Content Vocabulary	Academic Vocabulary	Reading Strategy
★ social insurance (p. 590) ★ public assistance (p. 590) ★ unemployment insurance (p. 591)	★ component (p. 591) ★ supplement (p. 592) ★ controversial (p. 593)	Create a graphic organizer similar to the one below to list and describe the programs the government uses to protect public health.

Government Program/Agency	Description

Issues in the News

Cloning is the process of creating genetic copies of animals with good characteristics in order to produce higher-quality foods. After several years of study and heated debate, the Food and Drug Administration (FDA) has declared that meat and milk from most cloned livestock is as safe as other food. The FDA announcement did not end the controversy as consumer anxiety drove several food companies to say they would not sell milk or meat from cloned animals. Meanwhile, some in Congress pushed for a law to label all food from cloned animals. Maryland Senator Barbara Mikulski, who sponsored the bill, said, "Just because something was created in a lab, doesn't mean we should have to eat it."

▲ Cloned calves born in Hokkaido, Japan

As this debate shows, the federal government has a major role in guaranteeing the safety of the food supply. It also makes sure that there is sufficient food in the market. This was not always the case. Well into the 1900s, most people were self-reliant when it came to finding food. When people were in need, they depended on their church or a few private charities.

The Depression's Impact

The Great Depression changed everything. After the stock market crash of 1929, the American economy continued to slump badly month after month for the next several years. During the worst period, unemployment increased from about 3 percent of the nation's workforce in 1929 to almost 25 percent in 1933. The song *Brother, Can You Spare a Dime?* expressed the mood of the early 1930s. Almost overnight, unemployment, hunger, and poverty became massive national problems. During this crisis, the federal government initiated two types of programs: **social insurance** and **public assistance**.

New Deal Programs

As the Depression deepened, private charities and local and state governments could not cope with the problems of the poor. To ease the nation's

R Reading Strategies	**C** Critical Thinking	**D** Differentiated Instruction	**W** Writing Support	**S** Skill Practice
Teacher Edition • Identifying Differences, p. 592 **Additional Resources** • Guid. Read. Act., p. 76 • Quizzes/Tests, p. 259	**Teacher Edition** • Drawing Conclusions, p. 593 **Additional Resources** • Read. Essen., pp. 241–243	**Teacher Edition** • English Learners, p. 592 • Logical/Mathematical, p. 595 **Additional Resources** • Foldables, p. 64	**Teacher Edition** • Narrative Writing, p. 591 **Additional Resources** • Part. in Gov. Act., pp. 41–42	**Teacher Edition** • Analyzing Research, p. 594 **Additional Resources** • Skill Reinforce. Act., p. 21

suffering, President Franklin D. Roosevelt proposed and Congress passed the Social Security Act in 1935. This act was the first of many government-supported social insurance, public assistance, and health-care programs. The government envisioned these programs as long-term ways to provide some economic security for all citizens.

Today the United States has two kinds of social programs. Social insurance programs are designed to help elderly, ill, and unemployed citizens. Public assistance programs distribute public money to poor people. The government uses general tax revenues to pay for these programs. Unlike social insurance, public assistance does not require recipients to contribute to the cost of the programs.

Social Insurance Programs

The Social Security Act and its later amendments created a social insurance system with three main **components.** The first component is Social Security, or Old Age, Survivors, and Disability Insurance (OASDI). The second component is a health-insurance program called Medicare, and the third is **unemployment insurance.**

The Social Security Administration, an independent executive agency, administers OASDI from its huge headquarters in Baltimore and from 1,300 local offices around the country. The Centers for Medicare and Medicaid Services, an agency within the Department of Health and Human Services, manages the Medicare program. The Department of Labor oversees the federal-state employment insurance program.

Social Security

More than 90 percent of American workers participate in the Social Security system. Employers and employees contribute to the system equally, but self-employed persons pay both portions of their Social Security tax. Retirees, disabled persons, and Medicare recipients are eligible for benefits. Survivors are spouses and children of deceased people who are covered by Social Security.

Changing the System

In the past several decades, the Social Security system has periodically been in crisis. The basic problem is that the number of workers who are retiring is putting a strain on the capacity of the system to pay out benefits. In 1981 the Social Security system faced a severe cash shortage as outgoing payments rose faster than incoming payroll taxes. Congress responded in 1983 with a law that gradually raised

Comparing Governments

Social Spending*

Country	Old age, invalidity, and death	Sickness and maternity	Work injury	Unemployment	Family allowances	Percent of total government spending
Australia	★	★	★	★	★	35.5
Colombia	★	★	★	★	★	12.1
Israel	★	★	★	★	★	28.0
Mexico	★	★	★	★	★	20.1
Thailand	★	★	★	★	★	6.0
United Kingdom	★	★	★	★	★	36.5
United States	★	★	★	★	★	28.3
Zimbabwe	★		★			18.2*

*For all countries, the data is for 2002 or 2003, with the exception of Zimbabwe, which is for 1997.
Source: Encyclopaedia Britannica, *2006 Book of the Year* (Chicago: Encyclopaedia Britannica, 2006).

Critical Thinking The majority of governments around the world provide some kind of social benefits for their citizens. *What is the relationship between social spending and a country's wealth?*

Charts In Motion
See StudentWorks™ Plus or go to glencoe.com.

Teach

W Writing Support

Narrative Writing Have students write a narrative piece about a futuristic, dystopian U.S. society in which funding for all social insurance and public assistance programs has run out, and these programs have collapsed. Encourage students to creatively compose a story while at the same time realistically discussing the societal problems that would result. **AL**

Comparing Governments

Answer: Though it is not necessarily evident in the chart, countries with higher levels of social spending are often relatively wealthy.

Research Activity Have students compare poverty levels in the countries that have unemployment insurance with poverty levels in countries that do not have unemployment insurance. **Ask:** Is there a correlation? *(Students might find a direct connection between lack of unemployment insurance and poverty.)* **OL**

Additional Support

Activity: Collaborative Learning

Explaining New Deal Laws Shortly after his first inauguration, in March 1933, President Franklin D. Roosevelt called Congress into a special session that lasted 100 days. During the so-called Hundred Days, Roosevelt sent 15 major bills to Congress. All were voted into law. Over the next few years other New Deal laws were enacted. Some of the programs that resulted from those laws still exist in some form; others lasted only a short time. Organize the class into small groups, each of which is to research one or two of the programs. Have the groups analyze the legacies of the New Deal. **OL**

Linking ★ Past & Present

Spending for Social Programs Since the end of World War II, the United States has greatly increased its funding for social insurance and public assistance. In 1950, for instance, the federal government spent $2.1 billion on social insurance. About 40 years later, the amount was nearly $400 billion. Public aid expenditures went from $1.1 billion to $80 billion during the same period.

D Differentiated Instruction

English Learners Have students read the conflicting views of Peter Peterson and Henry Aaron. **Ask:** Which economist is optimistic? Which one is pessimistic? *(Aaron is optimistic; Peterson is pessimistic.)* **ELL**

R Reading Strategy

Identifying Differences **Ask:** What is the difference between public assistance programs and social insurance programs? *(One large difference is that, although they are both federally funded, public assistance programs are run by state and local agencies.)* **OL**

Hands-On Chapter Project

Step 3

---

the retirement age to 67 by the year 2027. It required Social Security benefits of higher-income retirees to be subject to the federal income tax. To save additional money, the 1983 law also slowed the scheduling of the normal cost-of-living increases that the Social Security system pays to retirees.

Despite these changes, the dangers of cash shortages have continued to worry policymakers and the public. In the 2000 presidential campaign, the question of how to fix Social Security was prominent. Republican candidate George W. Bush proposed allowing people to invest a portion of their Social Security payroll taxes in stocks and bonds. Democratic candidate Al Gore said that the current level of benefits should be guaranteed by **supplementing** Social Security taxes with money from the general income tax. Any major changes in the system will require congressional action. Peter G. Peterson, who served on a bipartisan commission on entitlements, said:

> 66 The costs of Social Security and Medicare alone are projected to rise to between 35 and 55 percent of taxable payroll by 2040. . . . Balancing the budget by 2002 is a low-impact warm-up exercise compared with the grueling iron-man challenge that lies ahead when 76 million boomers retire. 99
> —Peter G. Peterson

D Henry J. Aaron, an economist at the Brookings Institution, has a different view of things:

> 66 Social Security does have a projected deficit over 75 years, but it can be easily managed. . . . Modest benefit reductions and small tax increases imposed gradually can bring revenues and expenditures into balance. The main factor driving up the combined cost of Medicare and Social Security is . . . growth in per capita medical costs. 99
> —Henry J. Aaron

Medicare

In 1965 Congress added Medicare to the social insurance system. The basic Medicare plan pays a major share of the total hospital bills for more than 30 million senior citizens.

A second portion of the Medicare program is voluntary. For those who choose to pay an extra amount, Medicare also helps pay doctors' bills and the costs of X-rays, surgical dressings, and so on. Nearly all the people covered by the basic plan are enrolled in the voluntary portion of the Medicare plan as well.

Unemployment Insurance

The 1935 Social Security Act also set up unemployment insurance programs for people who are out of work. Under these programs, federal and state governments cooperate to provide the needed help.

Workers in every state are eligible to receive unemployment payments if their employers dismiss them from their jobs. To fund the program, employers pay a tax to the federal government. Then, when workers are involuntarily laid off, they may apply for weekly benefits from a state, not a federal, employment office.

Public Assistance Programs

R Federal government public assistance programs began during the Depression. Although the federal government provides most of the money for these programs from general tax revenues, state and local welfare agencies actually run the programs. The major public assistance programs are Supplemental Security Income, food stamps, Medicaid, and the Job Opportunities and Basic Skills program (JOBS). A program called Aid to Families with Dependent Children ended in 1996 with the passage of a major welfare-reform bill.

Supplemental Security Income (SSI)

Set up by Congress in 1974, Supplemental Security Income, or SSI, brought all state programs for low-income persons who are elderly, blind, or disabled under federal control. Under the original Social Security Act, the states administered these programs, and benefits and procedures varied greatly from state to state. SSI sought to simplify these programs and streamline the administration of benefits.

The Social Security Administration runs the program. The federal government makes a monthly payment to anyone who is 65 or older, who is blind or disabled, or who has little or no regular income.

Food Stamps

President Kennedy started the food stamp program by executive order in 1961. Congress created a food stamp system by law in 1964. The purpose of the food stamp program was to increase the food-buying power of low-income families and to help dispose of America's surplus agricultural production. When the program started, about 367,000 people received food stamps. In 2008 almost 28 million Americans received food stamps at a cost to the government of approximately $34 billion.

Conducting Mini-Debates

Step 3: Presenting Debates Half of the pairs will present their mini-debates to the class. Debates should continue to be one-on-one format, but classmates may be allowed to choose a side to help support or defend. Allow time after each side of the debate for a limited number of comments or reinforcements from the supporters.

Directions Call on pairs to present their debates. Instruct the remaining students in class to choose a side to support.

Discussing Presentations Ask the class to discuss whether any of the debates changed their minds about an issue and, if so, how. **OL**

(Chapter Project continued in Section 4.)

Children's Health

The Cost of Care Through a federal program called the Children's Health Insurance Program (CHIP), individual states and the federal government provide health insurance coverage to many low-income children. These two Texas parents participated in a news conference celebrating changes in the program that helped insure their children. *Why has health insurance been a controversial issue in the United States?*

Caption Answer: It is costly, and there are numerous private insurance companies as well as public ones; any reform to increase coverage for so many people is complex.

C Critical Thinking

Drawing Conclusions It has been more than a decade since the 1996 welfare reform law was enacted. Have students think of some ways that they could try to measure its effects. Pose the following questions to get them started:

- Are fewer people receiving public assistance?
- Are fewer families living at the poverty level?
- Has unemployment dropped?

Have students find the statistics to answer these questions. As a class, discuss the results of their research. **OL**

Medicaid

Congress established the Medicaid program in 1965 as part of the Social Security system. Medicaid is designed to help pay hospital, doctor, and other medical bills for persons with low incomes. General federal, state, and local taxes fund this program that aids more than 35 million people at a cost of more than $150 billion each year.

Some observers have noted that both Medicaid and Medicare contribute to rising hospital and medical costs. The government pays the medical bills, so the patients, doctors, and hospitals have no incentive under this program to keep costs down. (Incentives for cost control are generally weak in the health-care sector, too, because supply and demand factors do not function in the same way as they do with other consumer choices.)

Family Assistance

During the Depression, the government designed a program to help families when the main wage earner died, was disabled, or left the family. A family with dependent children was eligible for assistance under the Aid to Families With Dependent Children program (AFDC) when the family's income fell below a level set by individual states. The AFDC program lasted until 1996 when it was replaced by Temporary Assistance for Needy Families (TANF).

In the early years of AFDC, about 75 percent of the aid went to the children of fathers who died or were disabled, but by the 1990s, more than 80 percent of the aid went to children whose fathers deserted their families or who never married the mothers of the children. Further, the 1994 Census Bureau showed that, despite AFDC aid, more than 21 percent of the nation's children under the age of 18 were living in poverty.

This situation roused criticism of the AFDC program. Some critics claimed that it created an incentive to have children outside marriage since they would then receive welfare payments. Others said the program might be encouraging men to leave their families to receive aid. For years, the program remained **controversial.**

The Need for Reform

Few people denied that society had a responsibility to help care for its disadvantaged, sick, and disabled. At the same time, many were unhappy with the public-assistance system. After more than 30 years of increasing program costs, the level of poverty remained high. In 2002 more than 34 million people, or 12.1 percent of Americans, were living in poverty.

Much of the public frustration over the welfare system stemmed from reports of welfare fraud and the cycle of dependence that developed among many welfare recipients. Many single parents on welfare had few strong incentives to work. Minimum-wage jobs provided less income than the welfare system, and working often meant paying additional day-care expenses.

CHAPTER 21: *Social and Domestic Policy* **593**

Differentiated Instruction

Leveled Activities

ELL Interpreting Political Cartoons, p. 41

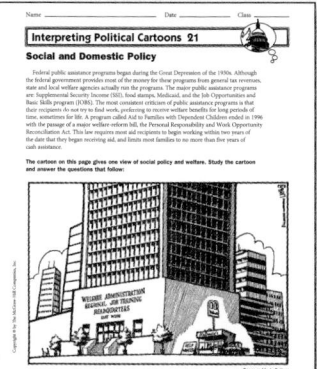

BL Guided Reading Activities, p. 76

OL Skill Reinforcement Activities, p. 21

AL Authentic Assessment with Rubrics, p. 28

S Skill Practice

Analyzing Research Point out to students that Article I, Section 8, of the U.S. Constitution gives Congress the power to grant patents. For more than 200 years, the policies of the Patent and Trademark Office have protected entrepreneurship leading to scientific discoveries. In recent years, perhaps the most dramatic discoveries that the patent process has promoted have come in the pharmaceutical industry. Drug companies know that a patent protects their discoveries, so they are encouraged to develop new drugs. The possibility of large profits motivates companies to develop medicines that benefit all Americans. Have students work in small groups to analyze how patents have fostered entrepreneurship and discoveries in other areas, such as agriculture, computers, chemicals, and biotechnology. Have students present their findings to the class. **OL**

Additional Support

Changes in Administrative Agencies
President Bill Clinton signed a welfare reform bill in 1996 that has commonly been called "workfare." Under the law, welfare benefits are paid only if a person fulfills certain requirements like working a certain number of hours per week, or job training. Clinton said the bill's goal was to create a path out of poverty. *What role did states play in the new workfare system?*

Congress first responded to calls for welfare reform in the Family Support Act of 1988. It required states to implement welfare-to-work programs by 1990 that would have the goal of moving people off the welfare rolls. The federal government promised to pay a share of education and job-training costs. This legislation provided child care and health benefits for one year to those people who took jobs and got off the welfare rolls.

Sweeping Changes in Welfare

In the 1992 election campaign, President Clinton vowed to "end welfare as we know it." In the 1994 elections, Republicans proposed broad welfare changes in their Contract With America. Although the president and Congress supported reform, it took two years to enact compromise legislation. After vetoing two previous Republican-sponsored bills and despite objections by liberals in his own party, the president signed a major welfare overhaul. On July 31, 1996, he announced:

> 66 *Today we have an historic opportunity to make welfare what it was meant to be: a second chance, not a way of life. . . . I believe we have a duty to seize the opportunity it gives us to end welfare as we know it.* 99
> —President Bill Clinton

The bill ended Aid to Families With Dependent Children (AFDC), a cash welfare program, and replaced it with the Temporary Assistance for Needy Families (TANF) program. TANF provides lump-sum payments to the states and gives states wide authority to design and operate their own welfare programs.

The bill, however, placed several restrictions on the states' use of federal welfare funding. The program established work requirements for welfare recipients and set a time limit for how long a family could remain eligible for assistance. The bill cut back on the food stamp program and limited the amount of food stamps available for people without children. The federal government agreed to provide $14 billion over the following six years for child care to families on welfare. TANF's goal was to make this aid a temporary solution until permanent work and self-sufficiency were reestablished.

Promoting Public Health

In 1792 Secretary of the Treasury Alexander Hamilton urged Congress to provide hospital care for sick and disabled sailors. Congress responded by establishing the United States Public Health Service. Today the government is deeply involved S in promoting public health.

Health Programs

Today the largest percentage of federal government spending on health goes for the Medicare and Medicaid programs. In addition to these, however, the government operates several programs designed to promote and protect public health.

★ ★ ★ Activity: Interdisciplinary Connection ★ ★ ★

Popular Culture During the 1930s radio became much more pervasive in American culture. President Franklin D. Roosevelt used the medium to broadcast his "fireside chats"— pep talks to reassure the public during the Depression. Many other radio programs were escapist—lighthearted romance, comedy, or action-packed adventure. Have students check the local library for archives of such shows— the comedies of Burns and Allen or of Jack Benny, or *Dick Tracy, Superman,* or *The Lone Ranger.* Play one or two of the recordings, and discuss why the genre would be popular during hard times. **OL**

The Department of Defense, for example, provides hospital and other medical care for active and retired American military personnel and their families. In addition, the Department of Veterans Affairs (VA) operates medical, dental, and hospital care programs for veterans.

The Public Health Service, part of the Department of Health and Human Services, promotes citizen's health by supporting research and health programs. Federal agencies, such as the Centers for Disease Control (CDC), focus on controlling the spread of infectious diseases like AIDS, flu, and tuberculosis. In a 2001 domestic terrorism event, the CDC helped detect and contain the spread of anthrax, a dangerous bacteria that was sent by mail, killing five Americans. (In 2008 the FBI finally tracked down the perpetrator of the anthrax scare, an Army scientist who worked at a federal biodefense laboratory.) The anthrax scare led to the creation of the Office of Public Health Preparedness to coordinate national responses to health emergencies.

Food and Drug Protection

The Food and Drug Administration (FDA) tests samples of food and drug products. The agency has the power to ban or withdraw from distribution drugs that it finds unsafe or ineffective. As a result, the FDA often finds itself involved in controversy. Some doctors, for example, claim that FDA policies are so restrictive that they make it difficult for Americans to receive the benefits of new drugs. Sometimes people who are suffering from a particular disease will travel outside the United States to obtain drugs that are permitted in other countries.

On the other hand, some consumer groups believe the FDA is not tough enough in banning drugs and food additives that might be harmful. The FDA has a difficult job because it must protect the public from dangerous substances while not denying people the drugs they need.

Stem Cell Research

The federal government funds some scientific research, and public policy can encourage research in one field compared to another. An example of this occurred in 2001 when President Bush established a policy for funding controversial research with embryonic stem cells. The researchers wanted federal funds to study stem cells from human embryos that were left over from couples seeking in-vitro fertilization. Some ethicists, however, said that out of respect for human life, embryonic stem cells should not be used in this way. For them, destroying a frozen embryo to obtain its stem cells was the moral equivalent of killing a person for research.

President Bush decided to compromise. He announced that federal funds could be used for embryonic stem cell research only if the researcher used already-existing lines of stem cells. Federal funds could not be used if a new embryo had to be destroyed to create the stem cells. Bush also announced increased funding for research using other types of stem cells that did not come from embryos. The policy thus limited research in one area and caused research to expand in a different area.

SECTION 3 Review

Vocabulary

1. **Explain** the significance of: social insurance, public assistance, unemployment insurance.

Main Ideas

2. **Contrasting** What is the primary difference between Medicare and Medicaid?

3. **Describing** How did welfare reform in 1996 affect Aid to Families With Dependent Children (AFDC)?

Critical Thinking

4. **Predicting Consequences** Research the ethical arguments over stem cell research. Analyze the information and predict the consequences of using or not using stem cells in research.

5. **Organizing** Use a graphic organizer like the one below to show who is eligible for Social Security benefits and Supplemental Security Income.

Social Security	Supplemental Security

Writing About Government

6. **Expository Writing** Interview three elderly persons who have used Medicare. Ask the following: How does the Medicare system benefit you? What problems have you had with the system? What improvements could be made to Medicare? Compare your answers with your classmates.

D ## Differentiated Instruction

Logical/Mathematical
Advances in medicine and health care in the United States have resulted in lower infant mortality rates, lower birthrates, and lower death rates. Have students find statistics to make line graphs showing the decline in one of those rates from 1900 to the present. Display the graphs on the bulletin board. **BL**

Assess

Assign the Section 3 Assessment as homework or as an in-class activity, or have students take Section Quiz 21-3 from *Section Quizzes and Chapter Tests.*

Close

Analyzing Ask: Why do people sometimes say that welfare is a trap that ensnares generations of a family? *(There are few strong incentives to find work, and minimum wage jobs provided less income than welfare, further reducing work incentives.)* **OL**

Section 3 Review

Answers

1. All definitions can be found in the section and the Glossary.
2. Medicare pays a major share of hospital bills for senior citizens and in some instances doctors' bills and other medical care expenses. Medicaid pays hospital bills, doctor bills, and other medical bills for persons with low incomes.
3. It replaced it with lump-sum payments to states. States were given authority to design and operate their own welfare programs.
4. Because a human embryo must be destroyed in order to use it for stem cell research, many people believe embryonic stem cell research is unethical. Stem cells can be used to treat a wide variety of cancers and conditions. Students should decide whether the potential ethical dilemma is worth the potential reward.
5. Social Security: retirees, survivors, disabled persons, Medicare recipients; Supplemental Security: anyone 65 or older, blind or disabled, anyone with little or no regular income
6. Make class time available for comparisons.

Can Congress Pressure the States to Raise Their Drinking Age?

South Dakota v. Dole, 1987

Class Debate

Organize the class into three groups: one to represent South Dakota, one for Secretary of Transportation Elizabeth Dole, and a third group to act as the Supreme Court justices. Allow class time to develop arguments; then have each side present its case. After the "justices" reach a decision, have them read it aloud. Also have the dissenting opinions, if any, read aloud.

The Court's Decision

To South Dakota, the Twenty-first Amendment constituted an "independent constitutional bar." The Court's decision hinged on its interpretation of an "independent constitutional bar" to congressional spending power. In earlier decisions, the Court had established the principle that an "independent constitutional bar" meant Congress could not use its spending power to force states to engage in activities that would be unconstitutional. The Court voted 7 to 2 that Congress had not violated the Constitution by requiring the states to adopt a minimum drinking age to receive federal highway funds. The Court said that restrictions on grants must meet four conditions: (a) the spending must be for the general welfare; (b) the restrictions must be unambiguous; (c) the grants must be related to "the federal interest in particular national projects or programs"; and, (d) the restrictions must not violate "other constitutional provisions . . . [that] provide an independent bar" to those restrictions. The Court concluded that if South Dakota did accept the condition set by Congress "and raise its drinking age to 21, the State's action in so doing would not violate the constitutional rights of anyone."

Drinking and driving is a serious national problem. Congress tried to deal with this problem when it required states to raise their legal drinking age to 21.

Facts of the Case

In the mid-1980s, Congress concluded that the nation's highways were not safe because states had different standards for a minimum drinking age. This lack of uniformity gave young people an incentive to drive to states where the drinking age was lower, and thus increased the number of alcohol-related accidents. In 1984 Congress passed a law directing the secretary of transportation to withhold 5 percent of federal highway funds from states that did not adopt 21 years old as the minimum drinking age. South Dakota, a state that permitted 19-year-olds to purchase alcohol, challenged the law as unconstitutional.

The Constitutional Question

Article I, Section 8, of the Constitution gives Congress the authority to "lay and collect Taxes, Duties, and Excises to pay the Debts and provide for the common Defence and general Welfare of the United States." In carrying out this spending power, the Supreme Court ruled in a 1936 case, *United States* v. *Butler,* that Congress could attach conditions to the receipt of federal funds.

While recognizing the right of Congress to set some conditions for federal funding, South Dakota argued that the Twenty-first Amendment barred Congress from requiring states to raise the drinking age. The amendment, South Dakota said, "grants the states virtually complete control over whether to permit importation or sale of liquor and how to structure the liquor distribution system."

The state also argued that setting a minimum drinking age was clearly within the "core powers" reserved to the states under the amendment.

Secretary of Transportation Elizabeth Dole conceded that the amendment gave the states authority to impose limits on the sale of alcohol. She argued, however, that it did not give states the power to allow sales that Congress wanted to stop in order to promote the important national goal of highway safety.

Debating the Issue

Questions to Consider

1. Did the congressional requirement to raise the drinking age contribute to a national goal?
2. Would South Dakota violate anyone's constitutional rights by making the drinking age 21 in order to get the federal funds?

You Be the Judge

In your analysis, was the Twenty-first Amendment an "independent constitutional bar" that prevented Congress from putting the condition of a minimum drinking age on federal highway funds? Explain your answer.

▶ **Former Secretary of Transportation Elizabeth Dole**

Debating the Issue Answers

Questions to Consider

1. yes, the goal of reducing accidents on the nation's highways
2. No, the Constitution does not set a drinking age.

You Be the Judge

yes, because the amendment gives states control over liquor laws; no, because the amendment does not deal with age limits

Education, Housing, and Transportation

Reader's Guide

Content Vocabulary
★ urban renewal (p. 600)
★ public housing (p. 600)
★ mass transit (p. 602)

Academic Vocabulary
★ undertake (p. 598)
★ decline (p. 600)
★ subsequent (p. 602)

Reading Strategy
As you read, create a table similar to the one below to list the different federal programs that promote education, housing, and transportation.

Education	Housing	Transportation

Issues in the News

In 2008 Secretary of Education Margaret Spellings announced $38 million in grants for 20 states to improve their schools. The goal is to make sure that students can read and do math at their proper grade level by 2014. Spellings, the first mother of school-aged children to serve as education secretary, helped draft the 2001 No Child Left Behind Act (NCLB). In making the grants, Spellings stated that NCLB "shines a spotlight on schools and holds them accountable for results." The new grants, she said, aim to support whatever steps low-performing schools are taking to improve "so that our nation's students can succeed in the classroom and beyond."

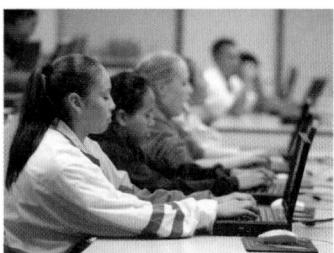

▲ Students using computers at a school on the Spokane Indian Reservation

In recent years, the federal government has been more active in trying to improve the performance of American students. Historically, however, public education has been an arena that the Constitution reserved for state authority. In turn, states for many years have deferred the main responsibility for education to local governments. In 1795 Connecticut created the first school fund with money from the sale of public lands. The first modern public school system was set up as early as 1816 in Indiana.

Public Education Programs

Today public education in the United States is a huge enterprise. In most states, elementary and high school education remains a local responsibility under state guidelines. The basic administrative unit for public schools is the local school district.

Federal Aid to Education

While public education remains under local control, the federal government plays an ever-increasing role, providing aid to local schools in several forms. In a recent year, the federal government contributed more than $1.6 billion in direct aid to local public schools and billions more in funds that are distributed through the states. The federal government provides even more support for higher education—about $17.6 billion to institutions of higher learning in a recent year.

Focus

Bellringer
Section Focus Transparencies 21-4

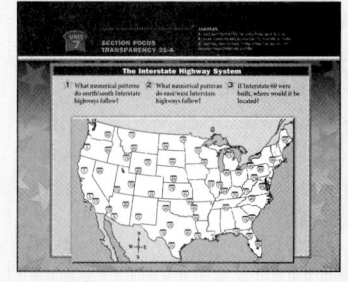

Reader's Guide

Answers to Graphic:
Education: Smith-Hughes Act of 1917, Elementary and Secondary Education Act, Morrill Act, Choice Program, Goals 2000, No Child Left Behind Act

Housing: Housing Act of 1949, Housing and Community Development Act of 1974

Transportation: Federal Road Aid Act of 1916, Federal Aid Highway Act of 1956, TEA-21

Resource Manager

R Reading Strategies	**C** Critical Thinking	**D** Differentiated Instruction	**W** Writing Support	**S** Skill Practice
Teacher Edition • Inferring, p. 600 • Activating Prior Knowledge, p. 601 **Additional Resources** • Guid. Read. Act., p. 67 • Quizzes/Tests, pp. 260–268 • Reteaching Act., p. 21	**Teacher Edition** • Making Generalizations, p. 598 • Identifying Alternatives, p. 600 **Additional Resources** • Read. Essen., pp. 245–246	**Teacher Edition** • Interpersonal, p. 601 **Additional Resources** • Foldables, p. 64 • Source Readings, p. 21	**Teacher Edition** • Personal Writing, p. 599 **Additional Resources** • Coop. Learning Act., pp. 13–14	**Teacher Edition** • Researching, p. 602 **Additional Resources** • Ch. Summaries, pp. 61–63

Teach

C Critical Thinking

Making Generalizations Ask students how an uneducated public can weaken a democracy. **Ask:** What can government do to ensure an educated citizenry? Should government deny uneducated people the right to vote? *(An uneducated public might not have the skills or knowledge to uphold the ideals of democracy. The government can create programs that reward quality education, give money to schools for good performance, and so on.)* **OL**

Caption Answer: Students, wanting to do well in these kinds of competitions, will be motivated to learn as much as possible about the subject matter. Also, by participating in a hands-on setting, they will gain valuable experience.

Additional Support

Aid to Public Schools

Congress began to provide aid for specific educational activities in the schools with the Smith-Hughes Act of 1917. This act set up matching grants to the states for teaching courses in agriculture and home economics. Since then, Congress has passed several laws directed toward other aspects of elementary and secondary education.

During the mid-1960s, President Lyndon B. Johnson made improved education in the United States a major goal of his Great Society program. In 1965, during the height of public support for Johnson's ideas, Congress passed the first general aid-to-education law—the Elementary and Secondary Education Act. This act, and later amendments, provided federal aid to most school districts.

Aid to Higher Education

Until 1862 higher education in the United States was a private **undertaking.** In that year, higher education received a major boost when Congress passed the Morrill Act. The act granted the states more than 13 million acres (about 32 million hectares) of public land for the endowment of colleges to teach agriculture and the mechanical arts. States established 69 of these so-called land-grant colleges under the Morrill Act and a second similar law.

In recent years, Congress has provided a number of specific programs to aid higher education. The best-known programs are several G.I. bills of rights that gave veterans of World War II, the Korean War, and the Vietnam War grants for college. The Office of Postsecondary Education also has many programs to provide financial assistance to students.

Education Issues

The policy of providing federal aid to public schools and colleges is controversial. Opponents say that education should be a state and local concern and worry that federal aid leads to federal control of what is taught and how it is taught. The president of a major university said: "Federal spending power is used indirectly to control colleges in ways the government could not use directly."

One event that propelled a greater federal interest in education occurred in 1983 when the National Commission on Excellence in Education (appointed by President Ronald Reagan) issued a report on American education. The report noted that on a series of tests, American students ranked below European and Asian students. In the face of this evidence, the commission called for reforms. The movement that resulted from the report did not reverse the trends. In the early 1990s, Barbara Lerner

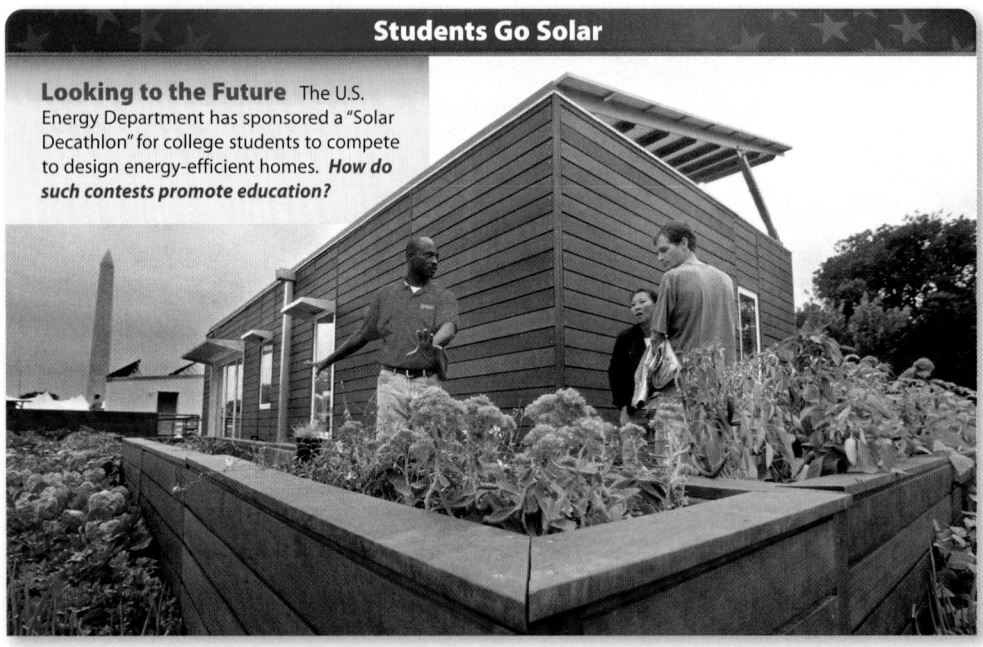

Students Go Solar

Looking to the Future The U.S. Energy Department has sponsored a "Solar Decathlon" for college students to compete to design energy-efficient homes. *How do such contests promote education?*

Activity: Collaborative Learning

Creating an Overhead Transparency
Organize the class into groups of three, called Home Teams. Assign each Home Team member the number 1, 2, or 3. Have all the same-numbered students from the Home Teams form an Expert Team. Assign each of the three Expert Teams one of the three main topics in the section—education, housing, or transportation. Have the Expert Teams create a teaching tool (chart, outline, concept web, or poster) that pertains to their topic. Then have the experts return to their Home Teams to share their teaching tools. **OL**

noted where students stood compared to foreign students at a comparable grade level:

> 66 *Data from good domestic tests . . . show that in an absolute sense we did not really get worse in the 1980s as we had done in the 1960s and 70s, but neither did we get much better. For the most part we stood still. . . . Our foreign competitors, however, did not stand still; they surged ahead. . . .* 99
>
> —Barbara Lerner, 1991

In 1991 President George H.W. Bush unveiled the Choice Program. This program allows students to attend any school, even private and parochial schools, at the state's expense. It also provided $30 billion to states to help them design Choice Programs and $200 million to enable disadvantaged children to participate in them. In 1994 Congress passed the Goals 2000: Educate America Act. The government set eight goals, including one to improve graduation rates. These reflected President Clinton's preference to develop public schools by setting benchmarks for performance.

In the 2000 election, President George W. Bush had a strong focus on education reform in his campaign. His administration created the No Child Left Behind (NCLB) legislation, which passed in 2002. Its goal was to close the "achievement gap" between white and minority students, as well as between the rich and poor. NCLB rewarded schools whose students showed improved test scores and punished schools whose students continued to fail. NCLB provided federal grants to states, but only if a state demonstrated steady improvement as measured by state-created educational standards.

Toward the end of the Bush administration, the future of NCLB was uncertain. Many educational experts criticized the bill. Some said that it relied too heavily on learning by repetition and teaching only to take a test, while critics cautioned that NCLB was setting expectations too high for inner-city schools. It was difficult to find hard evidence for the program's success, and many predicted that the next president would change the NCLB approach.

Housing and Urban Programs

Adequate housing is a basic requirement for the welfare of any society. The federal government has developed several programs to ensure that all citizens are able to afford decent housing.

Housing Policy

The government first became involved in housing policy during the Great Depression. Millions of Americans lost their homes or farms because they could not meet their mortgage payments. The government responded with a series of federally funded loan and housing support programs. After World War II, Congress passed the Housing Act of 1949. In this law, Congress declared its goal to provide "a decent home and a suitable living environment for every American family." **W**

Promoting Home Buying

The federal government has developed several programs to promote building and purchasing houses. The best-known program is the Federal Housing Administration (FHA). The FHA, a part of the Department of Housing and Urban Development (HUD), guarantees banks and other private lenders against losses on loans they make to those who want to build or buy homes. By acting as an insurer for these mortgages, the FHA has allowed many low- and middle-income families who might not have qualified for private loans to purchase their own homes. HUD also offers rent assistance to low-income families.

In addition, the federal government also sponsors two corporations, the Federal National Mortgage Association, nicknamed Fannie Mae, and the Federal Home Mortgage Corporation, nicknamed Freddie Mac. Fannie Mae was originally a government agency created in 1938 by the Roosevelt administration. Its purpose was to buy mortgages from banks and thereby free up bank money to go to other lenders. This enabled banks to reduce interest rates and make home loans to people who had lower incomes and were more of a credit risk. By 1968, Fannie Mae grew and began to cost the government so much money that President Johnson decided to make Fannie Mae into a government-sponsored enterprise. He also decided to create Freddie Mac so that Fannie Mae did not become a monopoly.

Fannie Mae and Freddie Mac are privately owned companies, but they are protected by the federal government. They are exempt from state and local income taxes and are regulated by HUD. In 2008 HUD had a standing line of credit with the federal government that allowed the agency to borrow up to $2.25 billion as needed for its operations. Both companies raise most of their funds

ISSUES to Debate

Federal Versus Local Funding of Education Have students find out more about the controversy over federal versus state or local funding of public education. Students may interview parents, teachers, administrators, and school board members and then hold a panel discussion to present students' views. **Ask:** Should one level of government fund public education, or should it be a combined effort? What advantages and disadvantages does each level have over the others? *(Answers will vary. Students should list the advantages and disadvantages of local, state, or federal funding of public education.)* **OL**

W Writing Support

Personal Writing Have students respond to the excerpt from the Housing Act of 1949. **Ask:** How much progress do you think has been made in 60 years? *(Students may note that the government has yet to find an effective housing policy, or may point out that local officials were given more control giving housing policy greater flexibility.)* **OL**

Differentiated Instruction

★ ★ Activity: Multiple Learning Styles ★ ★

Interpersonal Have students choose a project that they think will benefit the community—designing a new route for mass transit, building a minipark, or installing public computers with Internet access, for example.

Have them plan a campaign to convince community leaders of the need for their project. Ask volunteers to present their campaign speeches to the class. **OL**

Caption Answer: by rebuilding or repairing buildings and using them for low-income housing instead of for commercial needs or expensive living spaces

C Critical Thinking

Identifying Alternatives
Have students suppose that a new president proposes to respond to the need to cut federal spending by combining the Department of Transportation and the Department of Housing and Urban Development, and cutting back on the programs each administers. Have students propose which programs should be kept and which should be dropped and provide a rationale for their proposals. **AL**

R Reading Strategy

Inferring Ask: Why do you think public housing projects have the tendency to turn into "high-rise slums and centers for crime"? *(Students might mention that since the tenants are paying very little to live there, they might not treat the property with much respect.)* **OL**

Hands-On Chapter Project

Step 4

Rebuilding Cities In Houston, Texas, public housing stands in the shadow of the city. *How can urban renewal help lower-income families?*

from foreign governments, pension funds, and mutual funds that are willing to loan money to them at low interest rates because the two companies are backed by the federal government. This, in turn, allows them to give low-interest mortgages to low-income people.

In 2008 the sub-prime crisis in the financial industry created a crisis at Fannie Mae and Freddie Mac, which held hundreds of billions of dollars in mortgage loans that were unlikely to be paid back. To prevent the two companies from collapsing, the federal government took temporary control of them in late 2008. The companies received $200 billion in aid and were placed under the oversight of the Federal Housing Finance Agency.

Urban Renewal

To assist in the rebuilding of **declining** central cities, the federal government also supports **urban renewal** programs. Cities can apply for federal aid to clear and rebuild deteriorating areas. Most renewal projects begin by removing run-down properties. Private developers then buy the land at a reduced price and rebuild according to plans approved by the city and HUD. As part of urban renewal, federal mortgage insurance is available to the private developers.

600 UNIT 7: *Public Policies and Services*

The goal of urban renewal policies has been to restore slum areas and make cities more attractive places in which to live. Critics charge, however, that urban renewal neglects to rebuild an area to accommodate the housing needs of lower-income people. Instead, they say, urban renewal focuses new development on more affluent housing and commercial development. In turn, this forces the poor to move elsewhere, assuming they can find affordable housing nearby. As one advocate for the poor has said: "We're already living nowhere, and now they're going to move us out of that." Other critics say that urban renewal destroys older ethnic neighborhoods and uproots local businesses.

Urban renewal supporters see the issue differently. They say that the policy has been useful because it encourages local governments and private investors to work together to save crumbling inner cities. They also argue that a later federal initiative, the Housing and Community Development Act of 1974, focused on actually serving the needs of the disadvantaged when it redevelops inner cities.

Public Housing Programs

Since 1937 and especially after the 1949 Housing Act, the federal government has given aid to local governments to construct and operate **public housing** for low-income families. To implement the program, a city first sets up a "public housing authority" to which the federal government can make low-interest loans that may cover up to 90 percent of the housing construction costs. The government also grants subsidies to these agencies to allow them to operate by charging very low rents. Income from the rents is used to repay the federal loan. About 4 million Americans live in public housing.

Over the years, public housing projects have faced serious problems and opposition from many groups. Local authorities have mismanaged some public housing projects. Many such projects have turned into high-rise slums and centers for crime. The situation grew so grave that by 1973, President Nixon halted federal aid for public housing projects.

The government has yet to find a truly effective public housing policy. In 1976 Congress resumed federal aid for public housing projects on a limited scale. At the same time, HUD has experimented with rent subsidies as one alternative to public housing. Under this plan, lower-income families pay a percentage of the rent—normally 30 percent—for private housing, and the government pays the rest of the rent directly to the landlord.

Conducting Mini-Debates

Step 4: Presenting Debates Students who did not present their mini-debates in Step 3 will do so in Step 4.

Directions Have students present their debates to the class.

Analyzing Presentations Ask the class to vote on superlatives for the following three debate categories:

1. Which debate was the most thought-provoking?
2. Which debate had the cleanest, most professional presentation?
3. Which debate most changed their minds about the issue in question? **OL**

In the 1990s, Democrats and Republicans cooperated to improve the nation's housing policy. In 1994 state and local officials were given more control over housing decisions. In 1998 Congress agreed on more reforms that were intended to lessen the gap between the numbers of whites and minorities who own homes. HUD aims to place more than 5 million more minorities in homes by 2010.

Transportation Programs

In 1632 Virginia's legislature proclaimed: "Highways shall be laid out in such convenient places . . . as the parishioners of every parish shall agree." Governments at all levels in the United States have been concerned about improving transportation ever since.

The national government's first direct entry into the field of transportation began in 1811 with construction of the National Road that ultimately ran from Maryland to Illinois. The federal government continued to contribute, usually through some form of subsidy, to the building of channels, locks, dams, canals, ports, highways, railroads, and airports.

In 1966 Congress created the Department of Transportation (DOT) to coordinate national transportation policies and programs. This department brought together more than 30 agencies that dealt individually with transportation policies. These agencies were scattered throughout the government. Today the DOT operates through seven major agencies that reflect the various forms of transportation.

Other Agencies

Numerous agencies within the Department of Transportation provide important services. The Federal Aviation Administration works to ensure safety in aviation. It licenses pilots and enforces safety rules for air traffic. The Federal Highway Administration (FHWA) oversees the vast network of federal roads. The Federal Railroad Administration promotes and regulates the nation's railroad transportation. The National Highway Traffic Safety Administration is responsible for enforcing laws to protect drivers and promote highway safety.

Building and Maintaining Highways

The Federal Road Aid Act of 1916 set the pattern for the development of federal highway programs. Under this law, the federal government provided yearly grants for road building to the

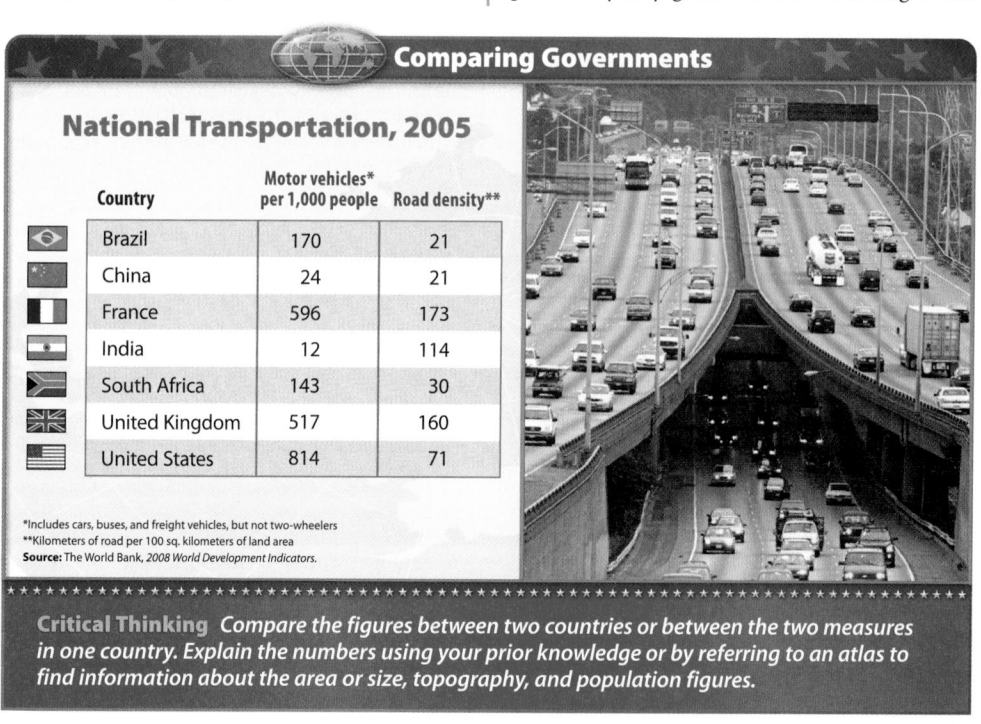

Comparing Governments

National Transportation, 2005

Country	Motor vehicles* per 1,000 people	Road density**
Brazil	170	21
China	24	21
France	596	173
India	12	114
South Africa	143	30
United Kingdom	517	160
United States	814	71

*Includes cars, buses, and freight vehicles, but not two-wheelers
**Kilometers of road per 100 sq. kilometers of land area
Source: The World Bank, *2008 World Development Indicators*.

Critical Thinking *Compare the figures between two countries or between the two measures in one country. Explain the numbers using your prior knowledge or by referring to an atlas to find information about the area or size, topography, and population figures.*

CHAPTER 21: *Social and Domestic Policy* **601**

CHAPTER 21, SECTION 4

R Reading Strategy

Activating Prior Knowledge
Discuss aviation safety. **Ask:** What federal agency assists the FAA with air travel safety? *(the Department of Homeland Security)* **OL**

D Differentiated Instruction

Interpersonal Have students interview neighbors to get a sense of their feelings toward surrounding roads and highways. **Ask:** Do people think that the highways and roads are "laid out in such convenient places," or are they dissatisfied? *(Answers will vary. If students find that people are unhappy with local roads, they should be able to explain why.)* **OL**

Comparing Governments

Critical Thinking

Answer: Students might note the density of India's population but that it has many roads that were probably developed during colonial times by the British, or they might refer to the fact that China has large areas in the interior or the west that are sparsely populated.

Additional Support

Activity: Interdisciplinary Activity

Architecture Modern city planners think the layout of neighborhoods and the type of architecture in them have a great deal to do with how livable the neighborhoods are. Planners tend to prefer low-rise dwellings of more human proportions over the high-rise apartment buildings and housing projects that are common in many cities. They advocate street plans that discourage vehicular traffic and encourage walking. Have students explore these ideas and suggest areas in their communities that would benefit by adopting such plans. **OL**

S Skill Practice

Researching Encourage students to conduct research on magnetic levitation (MAGLEV) technology. **Ask:** What are the advantages and disadvantages of incorporating MAGLEV into public transportation? How widespread is MAGLEV currently? *(Students' answers should reflect the results of their research.)* **OL**

Assess

Assign the Section 4 Assessment as homework or as an in-class activity, or have students take Section Quiz 21-4 from *Section Quizzes and Chapter Tests.*

Close

Making Generalizations Ask: Does every American have the right to adequate education, housing, and health care? Is federal involvement necessary to guarantee those rights? *(Students should pick a side and defend their answers.)* **OL**

Section 4 Review

---

states and required each state to match this aid on a dollar-for-dollar basis. These grants-in-aid, administered by the FHWA, form the basis of today's federal highway programs.

Under the Federal Aid Highway Act of 1956 and **subsequent** amendments, states receive billions of dollars every year to build and improve the Interstate Highway System that crisscrosses the nation. This system, begun in 1956, consists of more than 45,000 miles of 4- to 8-lane superhighways connecting nearly all of the nation's major cities. Federal funds cover 90 percent of the cost of the Interstate Highway System. The money for federal highway grants comes from the Highway Trust Fund. This fund is a special account that receives federal excise taxes on gasoline, tires, truck parts, and related items.

While the federal government provides the financial aid, the states do the work of constructing and improving the interstate highways. When the work has been completed, the interstate roads belong to the state or local governments, which have the responsibility of maintaining them.

Today the Federal Highway Administration oversees federal highways and their funding. The FHWA also applies federal safety standards to trucks and buses and does planning and research on highway construction and maintenance. The FHWA's main job, however, is to administer the massive federal-aid highway program that supports the construction and upkeep of about 25 percent of the nation's roads.

Since 1995, the Federal Highway Administration has succeeded in completing the 161,000 miles of highway in the National Highway System and has moved on to other transportation needs, including maintaining roads and bridges and reducing traffic fatalities and congestion.

Mass Transit

The streets and highways of large and small cities are clogged daily with automobile traffic. Could the urban transportation problem be solved with better **mass-transit** systems such as subways, commuter railroads, and bus lines? When properly operated, mass transit can transport more people than individual automobiles and help reduce congestion and air pollution. Beginning in the 1960s, the Urban Mass Transit Administration administered federal grant programs aimed at improving transit systems in urban areas. The federal government continues to help cities cope with the growing need for better mass-transit systems. The government also helps fund improvements in present transportation systems.

Efforts are underway to upgrade existing bus service, promote car and van pooling, and think of ways to make use of existing rail systems in and around cities. The Transportation Equity Act for the 21st Century (TEA-21), enacted in 1998, authorized $41 billion over six years to improve the national transit system. The funds included money to develop high-speed rail in some areas of the nation and to research magnetic levitation (MAGLEV) trains. In 2005 legislation was passed to reauthorize such funding for the five-year period between 2005 and 2009.

SECTION 4 Review

Vocabulary

1. **Explain** the significance of: urban renewal, public housing, mass transit.

Main Ideas

2. **Describing** What are three programs the government initiated to aid education in the 1990s?

3. **Explaining** What was the role of the FHA in helping individual families afford housing?

Critical Thinking

4. **Making Inferences** Why do governments at all levels spend so much money to support education?

5. **Contrasting** Use a graphic organizer like the one below to contrast the Democratic and Republican views on housing policy.

Democrats	Republicans

Writing About Government

6. **Expository Writing** The federal government has developed several programs to ensure adequate housing for the people living in the United States. Research programs that are established in your community that build or remodel homes for low-income families. Find out how the programs operate and who administers them. Write a summary of your findings.

Answers

1. All definitions can be found in the section and the Glossary.
2. Choice Program: students could choose any school; Goals 2000: adopted eight goals; charter schools: to raise performance standards
3. The FHA guarantees banks and other private lenders against losses on loans they make to people who want to build or buy homes. In so doing, the FHA has enabled many low- and middle-income families to get mortgages.
4. An educated public is a means to ensure democratic government; educated people usually earn better incomes and thus contribute more to the economy and pay more taxes.
5. Democrats: wanted the government to provide more low-income housing; Republicans: wanted to get the government out of the housing business
6. Students' summaries should include information about the groups that are responsible for the programs, where the funds come from, tax benefits, and so on.

Should the United States Regulate CO₂ Emissions?

As concern grew in the early 2000s that carbon dioxide (CO_2) emissions were contributing to global warming, a debate began as to whether the government should regulate the amount of CO_2 produced and, if so, how best to do it. One popular idea was cap-and-trade—a plan to put a cap on the overall amount of CO_2 allowed while permitting companies with low emissions to sell their CO_2 quota to companies with high emissions.

YES | **John McCain, U.S. Senator**

66 *Yet for all the good work of entrepreneurs and inventors in finding cleaner and better technologies, the fundamental incentives of the market are still on the side of carbon-based energy. . . . As a program under the Clean Air Act, the cap-and-trade system achieved enormous success in ridding the air of acid rain. And the same approach . . . can have an equally dramatic and permanent effect on carbon emissions. Instantly, automakers, coal companies, power plants, and every other enterprise in America would have an incentive to reduce carbon emissions, because when they go under those limits they can sell the balance of permitted emissions for cash. As never before, the market would reward any person or company that seeks to invent, improve, or acquire alternatives to carbon-based energy.* 99

—from *The New York Times*, May 12, 2008

NO | **Bjorn Lomborg, Professor of Economics**

66 *Politicians favor the cap-and-trade system because it is an indirect tax that disguises the true costs of reducing carbon emissions. . . . This message was recently backed up by the findings of the Copenhagen Consensus project, which gathered eight of the world's top economists—including five Nobel laureates. . . . The panel concluded that the least effective use of resources in slowing global warming would come from simply cutting carbon dioxide emissions. . . . [and] noted that spending $800 billion over 100 years solely on mitigating emissions would reduce inevitable temperature increases by just 0.4 degrees Fahrenheit. . . . [A] better response than cutting emissions would be to dramatically increase research and development on low-carbon energy—such as solar panels and second-generation biofuels.* 99

—from the *Washington Post*, June 26, 2008

Debating the Issue

1. **Analyzing** Why does John McCain think cap-and-trade is a good idea?

2. **Explaining** What is Lomborg's opinion about regulating CO_2?

3. **Deciding** Which argument is more effective in your opinion? Explain your reasoning.

▶ **CO₂ emissions from a coal power plant**

CHAPTER 21: *Social and Domestic Policy* **603**

Debating the Issue Answers

1. McCain thinks cap-and-trade will create incentives for businesses to cut emissions on their own and invent alternative technologies.

2. Lomborg does not think regulating CO_2 will make any difference for the environment and the money would be better used to research new technology.

3. Students should support their opinions with references to the quotes and with logical arguments.

Teach

Setting Up the Debate

Making Connections Have students research and compile a list of ways that individuals can reduce or offset their carbon footprint. *(turn off electronics when not in use, use energy-saving lightbulbs, turn down the furnace and water heater by one or two degrees, and so on)* **Ask:** Can any of these options carry over to businesses so that government regulation can be avoided? *(Answers will vary, but students might point out that most if not all of these techniques could carry over to businesses in some way.)* **OL**

Evaluating Have students research the arguments for and against regulation of carbon emissions. Students should give specific arguments to support both points of view. **OL**

Concluding the Debate

Discuss these questions with students:

- Have students brainstorm the pros and cons of the cap-and-trade system. Might the cap-and-trade system be vulnerable to corruption, or is it foolproof? Are there any ways that it can be tweaked?

- Which is a better option for the United States and the rest of the world: reducing emissions on a long-term basis or spending money on the research and development of low-carbon energy?

ExamView® Assessment Suite

This easy-to-use software includes extensive question banks and allows you to create fully customized tests that can be administered in print or online.

Reviewing Vocabulary

1. j
2. h
3. d
4. g
5. f
6. b
7. c
8. a
9. e
10. i

Reviewing Main Ideas

11. Large corporations abused workers, squeezed smaller companies out of business, fixed prices, and created monopolies.

12. price supports, acreage allotments, marketing quotas

13. The act was the first social insurance program to come out of the Depression. It was designed as a long-term solution to the problem of providing economic security for American citizens.

14. The federal government provides direct aid to local public schools and additional funds to be distributed through the states. The government also provides support for higher education.

Reviewing Vocabulary

Choose the letter of the correct content vocabulary word(s) below to complete the sentence.

a. mixed economy
b. public assistance
c. social insurance
d. laissez-faire
e. urban renewal
f. marketing quota
g. securities
h. oligopoly
i. mass transit
j. acreage allotment

1. The government tries the ___ method to avoid storing overproduced grain.
2. A small number of powerful companies controlling a market is called a(n) ___.
3. A hands-off government approach to the economy is called ___.
4. Stocks and bonds are forms of ___.
5. A(n) ___ is an agreement among farmers to sell only a portion of an overproduced crop.

Chapter Summary

Select Social and Domestic Policy Initiatives

- 1890 ★ Sherman Antitrust Act
- 1906 ★ Food and Drug Act
- 1914 ★ Clayton Antitrust Act; Federal Trade Commission created
- 1934 ★ Securities and Exchange Commission created
- 1935 ★ National Labor Relations Board; Social Security Act
- 1947 ★ Taft-Hartley Act
- 1965 ★ Medicare and Medicaid created
- 1970 ★ Environmental Protection Agency established
- 1972 ★ Consumer Product Safety Commission created; Water Pollution Control Act
- 1996 ★ Aid to Families With Dependent Children replaced by Temporary Assistance to Needy Families

(Timeline: 1850, 1900, 1950, 2000)

---

6. A federal program of ___ provides a certain minimum standard of living to those who do not earn enough income.
7. Federal ___ programs are designed to provide insurance for the elderly, sick, and unemployed.
8. A(n) ___ is one in which the government both supports and regulates private enterprise.
9. The federal government supports ___ in cities to help replace old buildings.
10. Cities build ___ systems to provide a substitute for automobiles.

Reviewing Main Ideas

Section 1 *(pages 575–583)*

11. **Describing** Explain the business environment that led to the Sherman and Clayton Antitrust Acts.

Section 2 *(pages 584–589)*

12. **Explaining** Which three programs does the federal government use to prevent low farm prices?

Section 3 *(pages 590–595)*

13. **Summarizing** Why did the government enact the Social Security Act of 1935?

Section 4 *(pages 597–602)*

14. **Discussing** How is the federal government involved in education?

Critical Thinking

15. 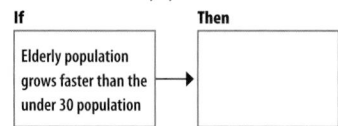 **Essential Question** Which clause of the U.S. Constitution underlies federal regulation of the economy? How do these regulations affect citizens?

16. **Identifying Central Issues** Which debates have made it hard to craft a national energy policy?

17. **Predicting** Use a graphic organizer like the one below to show how an increase in the elderly population would affect the Social Security system.

If	Then
Elderly population grows faster than the under 30 population →	

Critical Thinking

15. The Constitution grants Congress the power to "lay and collect taxes" for the general welfare and to "regulate commerce . . . among the several states." The commerce clause in Article I, Section 8, provides the constitutional basis for government regulation of the economy. Citizens must pay taxes and obey the laws concerning interstate commerce.

16. conflicts between saving the environment and saving jobs and money; conflicts among interest groups

17. Then: The reserve funds will be depleted by paying more benefits out of less income.

Government ONLINE Self-Check Quiz
Visit glencoe.com and enter QuickPass™ code USG9822c21.
Click on Self-Check Quizzes for additional test practice.

CHAPTER 21 Assessment and Activities
★★★★★★★★★★★★★★★★★★★★★★★★★★★

Document-Based Questions

Analyzing Primary Sources

Read the excerpt below and answer the questions that follow.

Ralph Nader, a political activist and recent candidate for the presidency, advocates protecting consumers from big business excesses. In this letter to the editor, Nader calls for greater government controls of big business.

> 66 *The relentless expansion of corporate control over our political economy has proven nearly immune to daily reporting by the mainstream media. Corporate crime, fraud and abuse have become like the weather; everyone is talking about the storm but no one seems able to do anything about it. This is largely because expected accountability mechanisms . . . are inert or complicit. . . .*
>
> *In 1938, in the midst of the Great Depression, Congress created the Temporary National Economic Committee to hold hearings around the country, recommend ways to deal with the concentration of economic power and promote a more just economy. World War II stopped this corporate reform momentum. We should not have to wait for a further deterioration from today's gross inequalities of wealth and income to launch a similar commission on the rampant corporatization of our country. At stake is whether civic values of our democratic society will prevail over invasive commercial values.* 99

18. What type of business practices is Nader criticizing?

19. What, in his opinion, is big business harming the most?

20. What further type of check on big business does Nader want?

21. Identify the words that Nader uses in this excerpt that reflect his negative characterization of big corporations.

Interpreting Political Cartoons

Analyze the cartoon and answer the questions that follow. Base your answers on the cartoon and your knowledge of Chapter 21.

22. How does the cartoonist present the difficulties of Social Security reform?

23. How does the cartoonist portray baby boomers?

24. According to the cartoon, who will financially support retired baby boomers?

25. In the cartoonist's view, how likely is it that Social Security reform will be accomplished?

Participating IN GOVERNMENT

26. Research how your local government protects consumers' rights. Find out which legislation protects consumers and how consumer complaints are handled. Also, find out which private community organizations work to protect consumers' rights. Prepare an oral report to share with the class.

CHAPTER 21: *Social and Domestic Policy* **605**

Security reform. (As baby boomers retire, a large segment of the population will not be working and contributing to Social Security, thereby depleting its funds.)

23. As large and bloated; baby boomers represent a large segment of the American population.

24. the U.S. government

25. Not likely—it is portrayed as a steep mountain to climb.

Participating IN GOVERNMENT

26. The content of students' reports depends on the legislation and organizations in the local community.

Chapter Bonus Test Question

Ask: What is OSHA? What does it do? *(The Occupational Safety and Health Administration, an agency of the Department of Labor, enforces federal laws concerning health and safety in the workplace.)*

Analyzing Primary Sources

18. Nader criticizes the idea that businesses are not accountable to checks from outside accounting firms and that state and regulatory agencies do not have enough power to make businesses follow the law.

19. He believes that big business is harming the democratic ideals of society and that democracy cannot flourish in a nation that does not hold businesses accountable.

20. Nader would like the reinstatement of the Temporary National Economic Committee to "promote a more just economy" with hearings on economic fairness.

21. relentless, inert, complicit, deterioration, gross, rampant, invasive

Interpreting Political Cartoons

22. The cartoonist presents Social Security reform as an uphill battle. The government is attempting to push the large (number of) baby boomers up the hill of Social

Key to Ability Levels

BL	Below level	**AL**	Above level
OL	On level	**ELL**	English Language Learners

Key to Teaching Resources

🗀 Print Material   🖳 Transparency
💿 CD-ROM or DVD

Levels					Resources	Chapter Opener	Section 1	Section 2	Section 3	Section 4	Chapter Assess
BL	OL	AL	ELL								
					FOCUS						
BL	OL	AL	ELL	🖳	**Section Focus Transparencies**		22-1	22-2	22-3	22-4	
					TEACH						
BL	OL		ELL	🗀	**Reading Essentials and Study Guide (and Answer Key)**		p. 247	p. 250	p. 254	p. 257	
BL	OL		ELL	🗀	**Guided Reading Activities**		p. 78	p. 79	p. 80	p. 81	
BL	OL		ELL	🗀	**Vocabulary Activities**		p. 22				
BL	OL	AL	ELL	🗀	**Chapter Summaries**					p. 64	
BL	OL			🗀	**American Biographies**						
BL	OL	AL	ELL	🗀	**Cooperative Learning Activities**					p. 15	
	OL	AL	ELL	🗀	**Government Simulations and Debate**						
BL	OL	AL	ELL	🗀	**Historical Documents and Speeches**			p. 22			
BL	OL	AL	ELL	🗀	**Interpreting Political Cartoons**			p. 43			
BL	OL		ELL	🗀	**Skill Reinforcement Activities**				p. 22		
BL	OL	AL	ELL	🗀	**Source Readings**		p. 22				
BL	OL			🗀	**Supreme Court Case Studies**						
BL	OL	AL	ELL	🗀	**Participating in Government Activities**			p. 43			
BL	OL		ELL	🗀	**Spanish Declaration of Independence and U.S. Constitution**	✓	✓	✓	✓	✓	✓
BL	OL	AL	ELL	🗀	**NGS World Atlas, Spanish**	✓	✓	✓	✓	✓	✓
BL	OL	AL	ELL	🖳	**Unit Overlay Transparencies, Strategies, and Activities**	✓	✓	✓	✓	✓	✓
BL	OL		ELL	🖳	**Making It Relevant Transparencies**	✓	✓	✓	✓	✓	✓
BL	OL	AL	ELL	🖳	**High School Writing Process Transparencies, Strategies, and Activities**	✓	✓	✓	✓	✓	✓
BL	OL	AL		🖳	**American Art & Architecture Transparencies, Strategies, and Activities**	✓	✓	✓	✓	✓	✓

✓ Chapter- or unit-based activities applicable to all sections in this chapter

TeacherWorks Plus™
All-In-One Planner and Resource Center

- Interactive Lesson Planner
- Interactive Teacher Edition
- Fully editable blackline masters
- Chapter Spotlight Videos Launch

- Differentiated Lesson Plans
- Printable reports of daily assignments
- Standards tracking system

Levels					Resources	Chapter Opener	Section 1	Section 2	Section 3	Section 4	Chapter Assess
BL	OL	AL	ELL								
TEACH *(continued)*											
BL	OL			💿	**American Music: Hits Through History**	✓	✓	✓	✓	✓	✓
BL	OL		ELL	📁	**Reading Strategies for the Social Studies Classroom**	✓	✓	✓	✓	✓	✓
			ELL	📁	**English Language Learner Handbook**	✓	✓	✓	✓	✓	✓
BL	OL		ELL	📁	**Writer's Guidebook for Social Studies**	✓	✓	✓	✓	✓	✓
BL	OL	AL	ELL	📁	**Living Constitution, SE**	✓	✓	✓	✓	✓	✓
BL	OL	AL	ELL	📁	**Living Constitution, TAE**	✓	✓	✓	✓	✓	✓
BL	OL			📁	**NGS World Atlas, English**	✓	✓	✓	✓	✓	✓
BL	OL		ELL	📁	**The Constitution and You (poster set)**	✓	✓	✓	✓	✓	✓
BL	OL	AL	ELL	📁	**Spanish Chapter Summaries**					p. 64	
BL	OL	AL	ELL	📁	**Spanish Vocabulary Activities**						
BL	OL		ELL	📁	**Spanish Reading Essentials and Study Guide (and Answer Key)**		p. 247	p. 250	p. 254	p. 257	
BL	OL	AL	ELL	💿	**PresentationPlus! with MindJogger CheckPoint**	✓	✓	✓	✓	✓	✓
ASSESS											
BL	OL	AL	ELL	💿	*ExamView® Assessment Suite*		22-1	22-2	22-3	22-4	Ch. 22
BL	OL	AL	ELL	📁	**Authentic Assessment with Rubrics**		p. 29				p. 29
BL	OL	AL	ELL	📁	**Section Quizzes and Chapter Tests**		p. 269	p. 270	p. 271	p. 272	pp. 273–280
BL	OL	AL	ELL	📁	**Spanish Section Quizzes and Tests**		p. 269	p. 270	p. 271	p. 272	pp. 273–280
CLOSE											
BL			ELL	📁	**Reteaching Activities**					p. 21	p. 21
BL	OL	AL	ELL	💿	**StudentWorks™ Plus with Audio Summaries**	✓	✓	✓	✓	✓	✓
BL	OL		ELL	🖐	**Graphic Organizer Transparencies**		✓	✓	✓	✓	
BL	OL		ELL	📁	**High School Government Reading and Study Skills Foldables®**		p. 65	p. 65	p. 65	p. 65	

Teach With Technology

What is a widget?

The McGraw-Hill Social Studies widget is a program for any computer with Internet access that acts as a one-stop launching pad for both software- and online-based programs.

How can the widget help my students and me?

The widget is a convenient way for you and your students to access McGraw-Hill's technology tools, both software-based and online. Some of the features of the widget include:

- customizable links to frequently used Glencoe Web pages
- recognition of, and compatibility with, Glencoe DVD and CD-ROM programs
- QuickPass™ entry for fast access to chapter content and activities

Visit glencoe.com to download the free student and teacher versions of the McGraw-Hill Social Studies widget.

Government ONLINE
Visit glencoe.com and enter *QuickPass*™ code USG9085c22T for Chapter 22 resources.

You can easily launch a wide range of digital products from your computer's desktop with the McGraw-Hill Social Studies widget.

	Student	Teacher	Parent
Media Library			
• Student Edition Section Audio	●		●
• Chapter Spotlight Videos	●	●	●
***United States Government* Online Learning Center (Web Site)**			
• Chapter Overviews	●	●	●
• Multilingual Glossaries	●	●	●
• Study-to-Go	●	●	●
• Student Web Activities	●	●	●
• Self-Check Quizzes	●	●	●
• Online Student Edition	●	●	●
• Vocabulary eFlashcards	●	●	●
• Web Activity Lesson Plans		●	
• Vocabulary PuzzleMaker	●	●	●
• Landmark Supreme Court Cases	●	●	●
• Beyond the Textbook	●	●	●

READING SUPPORT FROM JAMESTOWN EDUCATION

- **Timed Readings Plus in Social Studies** helps students increase their reading rate and fluency while maintaining comprehension. The 400-word passages are similar to those found on state and national assessments.

- **Reading in the Content Area: Social Studies** concentrates on six essential reading skills that help students better comprehend what they read. The book includes 75 high-interest nonfiction passages written at increasing levels of difficulty.

- **Reading Social Studies** includes strategic reading instruction and vocabulary support in Social Studies content for ELLs and native speakers of English. www.jamestowneducation.com

---

Reading List Generator CD-ROM

GLENCOE BOOKLINK 3

Use this database to search more than 30,000 titles to create a customized reading list for your students.

- Reading lists can be organized by students' reading level, author, genre, theme, or area of interest.

- The database provides Degrees of Reading Power™ (DRP) and Lexile™ readability scores for all selections.

- A brief summary of each selection is included.

Economics Connection

Personal Finance Literacy

The Secret of Compound Interest

Tell students that there are two types of interest: simple and compound. *Simple interest* is not added to the principal. If you deposit $10,000 in an account with 5 percent simple interest, at the end of the year you'll have $10,500:

$$.05 \times 10,000 = \$500 \text{ interest.}$$

Compound interest is interest that is periodically added to the principal so that the entire amount earns, or yields, more interest—the *annual percentage yield* (APY). The $9.5 trillion of national debt the federal government had incurred by mid-2008 for defense and other programs included compound interest that lenders charge.

Compound interest is a concept that can make *you* rich. In simplest terms, if you save a little for a long time, you end up with a lot. Interest may be compounded semi-annually, quarterly, or more often. The more frequent the compounding, the faster money grows.

Suppose your $10,000 deposit earns 5 percent interest *compounded twice a year*. In six months, your money will have earned half the annual interest:

$$\$10,000 \times 5\% \div 2 \text{ (½ year)} = \$250.$$

The bank adds that interest to your deposit, so the $250 interest also earns interest for the next half year: $250 × 5% ÷ 2 = $6.25. At year-end you have $10,506.25 instead of $10,500. The APY is 5.06 percent. The extra $6.25 does not seem like a lot but, thanks to compound interest, small amounts make a big difference over time!

Did You Know?

Albert Einstein is said to have called compound interest "the most powerful force in the universe." His Rule of 72 can be used to determine how long it will take for your money to double: Divide 72 by the underlined interest rate. For simplicity's sake, suppose you got 7.2 percent interest. Here's how your money would grow:

Age	Value of Account
25	$10,000
35	$20,000
45	$40,000
55	$80,000
65	$160,000

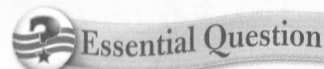

🔊 Chapter Audio   📺 Spotlight Video

Foreign Policy and Defense

Essential Question

Governments interact with other nations through trade, foreign aid, treaties, sanctions, and through military actions. Trade policies and sanctions affect the price of goods and affect workers. Military actions and foreign aid must be paid for through taxes.

Chapter Spotlight Video

To generate student interest and provide a springboard for class discussion, access the Chapter 22 Video at glencoe.com or on the video DVD.

Dinah Zike's Foldables are three-dimensional, interactive graphic organizers that help students practice basic writing skills, review key vocabulary terms, and identify main ideas. Have students complete this chapter's Foldable activity or activities in *Dinah Zike's Reading and Study Skills Foldables* booklet. **OL**

Visit glencoe.com and enter *QuickPass*™ code USG9085c22T for Chapter 22 Resources including Chapter Overview, Student Web Activity, Self-Check Quiz, and other materials for students and teachers.

Essential Question

How do governments interact with other nations? How do the choices made by these nations affect their citizens?

Government ONLINE

Chapter Overview Visit glencoe.com and enter *QuickPass*™ code USG9822c22 for an overview, a quiz, and other chapter resources.

◀ **A soldier who belongs to the Guards of Honor at the Tomb of the Unknowns at Arlington National Cemetery**

606

Launching the Chapter

Investigating the Hostage Crisis In 1979 a group of young extremists invaded the U.S. embassy in Tehran, Iran, took more than 60 American hostages, and held them for more than a year. Have students investigate this event and the diplomatic negotiations to free the hostages. **Essential Question:** What did the U.S. government do to free the American hostages? What might have been some repercussions for U.S. and Iranian citizens?

(After failed negotiations and an aborted rescue mission, the United States and Iran signed the Algiers Accords. Students might suggest that U.S. citizens could have considered the Algiers Accords to be negotiation with terrorists, and that most Iranian citizens did not want to be associated with people who used forceful takeovers and hostage situations to make political statements.) **OL**

Development of Foreign Policy

Focus

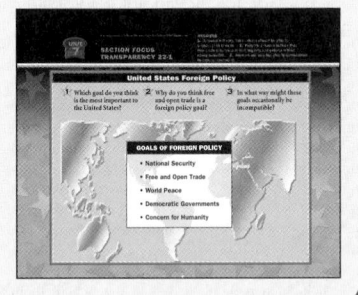
Reader's Guide

Content Vocabulary
★ foreign policy (p. 607)
★ national security (p. 607)
★ isolationism (p. 608)
★ internationalism (p. 608)
★ containment (p. 610)

Academic Vocabulary
★ fundamental (p. 607)
★ maintain (p. 608)
★ intervene (p. 611)

Reading Strategy
Create a time line similar to the one below to trace the transition of U.S. foreign policy from isolationism to internationalism.

1789   1823   1898   1914   1941

Issues in the News

In 2008 U.S. Deputy Secretary of State John Negroponte urged China to support a U.S. proposal at the United Nations for sanctions on Iran. China, which has close business ties to Iran, argued that negotiations were a better way to deal with the problem. In the face of Chinese resistance to the U.S. position, State Department spokesperson Sean McCormack stated the United States would not give up: "The whole strategy here is to use various kinds of diplomatic pressure at a gradually increasing rate to try to get a different set of decisions out of the Iranian leadership."

▲ Iranian President Mahmoud Ahmadinejad, at left, meets with Chinese President Hu Jintao in Shanghai.

China, with one-fifth of the world's population and its growing economy, is one of the major players on the international scene. As a result, U.S. government officials give special attention to China as they make and carry out U.S. foreign policy. Today, the United States confronts a global environment that is rapidly changing and marked by new challenges, such as increased economic competition and the spread of terrorism.

Goals of Foreign Policy

Foreign policy consists of the strategies and goals that guide a nation's relations with other countries and groups in the world. The specific strategies that make up U.S. foreign policy from year to year and even decade to decade change in response to changes in the international environment. However, the long-term goals of that policy remain constant, reflecting both the nation's ideals and its self-interest.

National Security

The principal goal of American foreign policy is to preserve the security of the United States. **National security** means protection of a nation's borders and territories against invasion or control by foreign powers. This goal is **fundamental** because no nation can achieve other aims such as improving its educational system or providing better health care if it is under attack.

Teach

R Reading Strategy

Analyzing Information Write the five main foreign policy goals on the board (national security, free and open trade, world peace, democratic governments, and concern for humanity). Ask volunteers to describe each goal and provide examples. **BL**

C Critical Thinking

Drawing Conclusions Ask: Do you think it is possible today for a world power such as the United States to maintain or return to a foreign policy of isolationism? *(Students might suggest that with today's globally interconnected societies, it would be difficult for the United States to return to a policy of isolationism.)* **OL**

Caption Answer: U.S. foreign policy, especially trade policy, can help or harm other nations' economies, which can affect the popularity of their leaders.

Hands-On Chapter Project

Step 1

Free and Open Trade

In today's global economy, national security means more than military defense. A nation's vital economic interests must also be protected. Thus, **maintaining** trade with other nations and preserving access to necessary natural resources have also been basic goals of U.S. foreign policy. Trade is an absolute necessity for the United States. Highly productive American factories and farms need foreign markets in which to sell their goods. The country also is in need of a number of natural resources, including oil. Generally, the United States supports trade that is free from both export and import restrictions.

World Peace

American leaders work for peace because they believe it helps the nation avoid outside conflicts and aids national security. The United States tries to help other nations settle disputes and has also supplied economic aid to at-risk countries, in part to prevent uprisings and revolutions. The United States helped organize the United Nations after World War II to promote world peace.

Democratic Governments

Throughout its history, the United States has been an example of democracy. In addition, the United States aids democratic nations and helps others create democratic political systems. With U.S. assistance, many formerly Communist nations in Europe began to form democratic political systems in the 1990s.

Concern for Humanity

The United States has often demonstrated its concern for others. Victims of natural disasters or starvation have looked to the United States for help, and the United States has often responded by providing food, medical supplies, and technical assistance for humanitarian reasons. At the same time, this aid serves the strategic interests of the United States by maintaining political stability in the world.

Development of U.S. Foreign Policy

Until the late 1800s, U.S. foreign policy was based on **isolationism**—avoiding involvement in world affairs. During the twentieth century, the nation shifted toward **internationalism.** Internationalists believed that involvement in world affairs was necessary for national security. A look at the history of U.S. foreign policy since 1789 shows how these different approaches developed.

Isolationism

When George Washington became president in 1789, the United States was a small nation, deeply in debt and struggling to build a new government. For this reason, U.S. leaders believed that the United States should not get involved in the politics and wars of Europe. Before leaving office, President Washington urged Americans to follow a path of isolationism.

Protesting American Beef

South Korean Discontent South Korea, a strong U.S. ally, was the scene of a fierce protest against trade policies with the United States. Thousands of South Koreans protested for days because their government resumed imports of American beef after a five-year ban. (In 2003 there was a case of mad cow disease.) The protests signaled general dissatisfaction with the government. *How can U.S. foreign policies affect the popularity of other nations' leaders?*

Analyzing Issues

Step 1: Researching the Issues

Divide the class into several groups and assign to each group a different area of the world (Africa south of the Sahara, Southwest Asia, East Asia, Europe, and so on).

Directions Ask groups to search the Internet, the library, and newspapers for information about U.S. foreign policy in their assigned area of the world.

Putting It Together Have students collect in a notebook the information they found and create a time line showing important dates and events relating to U.S. foreign policy in their area. Discuss any problems students are having in conducting their research. **OL**

(Chapter Project continued in Section 2.)

Humanitarian Assistance

Graphs In Motion
See StudentWorks™ Plus
or go to glencoe.com.

Disaster Relief by Region, 2007

Global
$88.9 million

The African
Nation of Sudan
$164.5 million

Africa except
for Sudan
$120.3 million

Asia
$28.5 million

EMCA (9 countries in
Europe, the Middle
East, and Central Asia)
$64 million

LAC (Latin America
and Caribbean)
$12.5 million

Disaster Assistance by Type, 2007

Agriculture and
Food Security 13%

Water, Sanitation
and Hygiene 17%

Humanitarian
Coordination and
Information
Management 6%

Nutrition 4%

Protection
5%

Health 14%

Other 16%

Shelter & Relief
Supplies 3%

Economy and Market
Systems 6%

Logistics and Relief
Supplies 16%

Source: The Office of U.S. Foreign Disaster Assistance (OFDA), USAID.

Critical Thinking The U.S. government supplies millions of dollars in aid for emergencies around the world. This aid reflects the American impulse to help others, but it is also a means of promoting foreign policy goals. *What percent of world aid went to the African continent in 2007? Why does so much aid go there? What are the three largest types of aid?*

ISSUES to Debate

Foreign Policy and Economics Have students research to find historical or current examples to argue the proposition that the most important factor in determining foreign policy is the nation's economy. **AL**

CURRICULUM CONNECTION

Law No world government exists to *enforce* international law, yet a body of laws is generally recognized and enforced through intervention by a neutral state, sanctions by the United Nations, the force of world opinion, or military force. International law was established in part at the Congress of Vienna (1815), the Geneva Convention (1864), and the Hague Conferences (1899, 1907).

The United States as a World Power

In the early nineteenth century, U.S. leaders continued to adhere to isolationism. In 1823 President James Monroe announced his Monroe Doctrine. It warned European powers that they should not attempt to extend their power or influence to the Americas.

This outlook changed in the 1890s as the United States became an industrial power and needed world markets for its products as well as sources for raw materials. Many leaders believed that the United States needed to play an active role in the world and even to expand and acquire a colonial empire.

In 1898 the United States fought the Spanish-American War, in part to free Cuba from Spanish rule. As a result, the United States acquired the Philippine Islands, Guam, and Puerto Rico. Hawaii was annexed in 1898 and Samoa in 1900. Although isolationist sentiments survived, the United States was now a major power in the Caribbean as well as in the Pacific region and East Asia.

Two World Wars

When World War I began in Europe in 1914, isolationist sentiment in the United States was still strong. After Germany sank neutral ships—includ-ing U.S. ships—President Woodrow Wilson asked Congress to declare war against Germany in 1917. American troops went overseas to fight in a European war for the first time.

Disillusioned by the terrible cost of war, Americans returned to isolationism. During the 1920s and 1930s, however, ruthless dictators came to power—Mussolini in Italy, Hitler in Germany, and military leaders in Japan. By the 1930s, these nations were using military force to invade other nations.

When World War II began in 1939, the United States officially remained neutral. The Japanese attack on Pearl Harbor in 1941, however, drew the United States into the war. Since World War II, U.S. foreign policy has been based on internationalism.

The Cold War

The United States emerged from World War II as the leader of the free nations of the world. The United States's new role soon brought it into conflict with the Soviet Union, which also emerged from the war as a world power. American government leaders viewed the power and ambitions of the Soviet Union as a threat to national security. Between 1945 and 1949, the Soviet Union imposed

CHAPTER 22: *Foreign Policy and Defense* **609**

Differentiated Instruction

Activity: Multiple Learning Styles

Verbal/Linguistic Have students use library resources or the Internet to find a recent speech by the president or secretary of state concerning foreign policy. Have them locate statements in the speech illustrating the five goals of foreign policy described in the student textbook. Ask students to write a brief essay explaining how the statements relate to foreign policy goals. Encourage students to include their own opinions about the main points of the speech, giving reasons to support their conclusions. **OL**

Did You Know?

Cold War The term *Cold War* was first used in a talk by journalist Herbert Bayard Swope in 1945 and then in a speech he wrote for Bernard Baruch in 1946. Thinking it was too strong a term, Baruch dropped it from that speech, only later saying, "Let us not be deceived—today we are in the midst of a cold war." The term was popularized by columnist Walter Lippmann.

We the People

Making a Difference

Douglas Engelbart finally received a financial reward for his work in 1997, when he was given the $500,000 Lemelson-MIT Prize for American inventors. Engelbart has received 20 patents for inventions that paved the way for e-mail, windows programs, and a research network for the U.S. government that was the predecessor of the Internet.

Activity: Have students brainstorm ideas for improvements in computers, TVs, refrigerators, cars, or other devices.

Differentiated Instruction

Interpreting Political Cartoons, p. 43

---

a communist system of government on the nations of Eastern Europe. Former British Prime Minister Winston Churchill warned that the Soviets would eventually look beyond Eastern Europe and try to spread communism to other parts of the world. Meanwhile, in 1949 Chinese Communists seized control of China. These events convinced U.S. leaders that they must halt Communist aggression.

As the rivalry between the United States and the Soviet Union intensified, it became clear that a "cold war" had begun. The Cold War was a war of words and ideologies with only a limited amount of military conflict.

Containment

To deal with communism, the United States introduced a new policy that had been proposed by George F. Kennan, an American diplomat and expert on the Soviet Union. The policy came to be called **containment.** Kennan argued that the United States did not have to go to war to defeat communism. Instead, all the United States had to do was to keep communism contained—prevent it from spreading—and eventually the Soviet Union would collapse from its own internal problems.

One approach to containment was to give aid to nations that appeared to be in danger of communist revolution or that had been threatened by communist countries. This policy became known as the Truman Doctrine because President Harry S. Truman first announced the policy in a speech in 1947:

> 66 *I believe that it must be the policy of the United States to support free peoples who are resisting attempted subjugation by armed minorities or by outside pressures. . . . I believe that our help should be primarily through economic and financial aid which is essential to economic stability and orderly political processes.* 99
>
> —Harry S. Truman, 1947

Three months later Congress passed the Marshall Plan, which provided badly needed economic aid for war-torn Europe. Within four years, the United States gave nations of Western Europe more than $13 billion.

Cold War tensions and fears also led to an arms race. At the end of World War II, the United States

We the People

★ Making a Difference ★

As technology develops, the world becomes a smaller place and U.S. foreign policy needs to be shaped accordingly. Some of the credit for expanding technology around the world belongs to Douglas Engelbart. In 1963 he invented what he called an "X-Y Position Indicator for a Display System"—in common language, the computer "mouse." "No one remembers who first called it that," Engelbart says, "but we all agreed that it looked like a mouse." He never received a profit from the invention of the mouse, which is essential for surfing the Web, but Engelbart chose research over wealth. "I made a conscious decision at age 25 that money would be secondary." (His employer, Stanford Research Institute, reaped the financial rewards.)

Since the invention of the mouse, Engelbart has enjoyed other victories. In 1989 he overcame lymphoma and retired to start his own think tank. With his daughter Christina, he formed the Bootstrap Institute, which operates out of an office donated by Logitech, the company that manufactures the mouse. Now in his 80s, Engelbart lectures on the benefits of yet another invention—his five-button, one-handed keyboard.

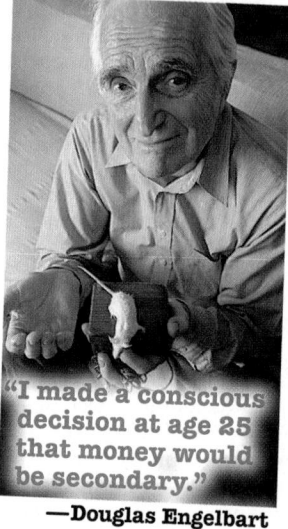

"I made a conscious decision at age 25 that money would be secondary."
—Douglas Engelbart

Interpreting Political Cartoons

Objective: To gain perspective on U.S. foreign policy toward China.

Focus/Teach: Ask students to identify the symbolism used in the cartoon.

Assess: Have students answer the questions on page 44 and then suggest other ways the cartoonist could have conveyed the same message.

Close: Discuss whether this cartoon exemplifies U.S. foreign policy.

Differentiated Instruction Strategies

BL Ask students why the United States helped protect Taiwan.

AL Discuss why China's foreign policy might threaten the interests of the United States.

ELL Discuss the concept of "scare tactics" with students. How do they compare to "bluffs"?

was the world's only nuclear power. However, by the late 1950s, the Soviet Union had developed nuclear weapons and large rockets that could reach the United States. To prevent nuclear war, the United States adopted a policy of deterrence. If any nation used nuclear weapons against the United States, the United States promised it would retaliate with nuclear weapons. The threat deterred nuclear war, but it meant that both sides began building a large stockpile of nuclear weapons.

The Korean and Vietnam Wars

The Cold War policy of containment drew the United States into two wars. In the Korean War, the United States aided pro-U.S. South Korea when that country was invaded by Communist North Korea. President Truman saw the invasion of South Korea as expansionism by the Soviet Union and sent U.S. troops to Korea under UN sponsorship.

In the Vietnam War, the United States committed troops for many years to fight on the side of the South Vietnamese government against Communist North Vietnam. Many U.S. policy makers and Presidents Lyndon Johnson and Richard Nixon said that U.S. involvement in the conflict was justified by the need to contain Communist expansion.

End of the Cold War

By the late 1980s, decades of competition with the United States had taken a toll, and in 1989 the Soviet Union began to collapse. Also that year, the Berlin Wall dividing Communist East Germany from democratic West Germany was torn down by demonstrators. A year later, the two Germanys **R** were reunited. Soon thereafter, the Eastern European countries of Poland, Czechoslovakia, Hungary, Romania, and Bulgaria overthrew their Communist governments. Then in 1991 the Soviet Union collapsed. It split into Russia and 14 other nations. The Cold War was over.

The Post–Cold War Era

The end of the Cold War changed global politics. Instead of a bipolar system in which the Soviet bloc of nations competed against the United States and its allies, a new multipolar system emerged with several major powers, including the United States, the European Union, China, India, Japan, and Russia competing with one another.

Under the leadership of Presidents George H.W. Bush and Bill Clinton, the United States shifted from the Cold War policy of containment to a policy of maintaining peace, building democracy, and promoting global trade. Important goals included maintaining stability in the Middle East, where much of the world's oil supplies are located, and helping Eastern Europe make the transition to democracy.

The Persian Gulf War

In August 1990, just as the Cold War was coming to an end, the dictator of Iraq, Saddam Hussein, decided to invade the tiny nation of Kuwait to gain control of its oil supplies. President George H.W. Bush quickly assembled a coalition of 34 nations, including Britain, France, and several Arab states, and won approval from the UN Security Council for action against Iraq. In early 1991, coalition troops, led by a massive American force, expelled Iraqi forces from Kuwait. A cease-fire was declared after Iraq agreed to allow UN weapons inspectors into Iraq to prevent Iraq from developing weapons of mass destruction.

During the 1990s, Saddam Hussein kept tensions high by failing to cooperate with the UN-mandated inspections. The UN maintained economic sanctions on Iraq, and in 1998 President Bill Clinton launched missile attacks against Iraqi installations related to the production of chemical, biological, and nuclear weapons. Despite the attacks, many believed Iraq was still secretly developing weapons of mass destruction.

Other Interventions

The Middle East was not the only region where the United States **intervened** to maintain order. In 1989 President Bush sent troops into Panama to topple Panama's dictator and help the Panamanians hold free elections. In 1992 U.S. troops joined a multinational UN force in Somalia to protect relief organizations operating during a civil war. In 1994 President Clinton sent U.S. troops to preserve order and restore democracy in Haiti after the elected president was toppled by Haiti's military.

Stabilizing the Balkans

In 1991 the collapse of communism in Yugoslavia led to a bloody ethnic and religious conflict in the former Yugoslav republic of Bosnia. Croats, Serbs, and Bosnian Muslims fought for control of parts of the country. Backed by the republic of Serbia, the Serbs living in Bosnia carried out a policy of ethnic cleansing, moving and sometimes killing non-Serbs to take control of the areas the Serbs wanted.

CHAPTER 22: *Foreign Policy and Defense* **611**

CHAPTER 22, SECTION 1

R Reading Strategy

Making Connections Have students check newspapers, newsmagazines, and online sources for articles about the former Soviet Union. Then have them reread the section "End of the Cold War" and discuss present relations among the countries that made up the U.S.S.R. **Ask:** Do the countries cooperate? Have their standards of living changed? Are they better off as independent countries? *(Answers will vary depending on the countries that students research.)* **AL**

Participating IN GOVERNMENT

Hosting a Foreign Exchange Student Have students investigate the available exchange programs and discuss them with their families. Perhaps some families might consider participating, or students could interview a foreign exchange host family in the community about their experiences. Other students might want to become exchange students. Discuss students' findings and opinions about foreign exchange programs as a class. **OL**

Additional Support

★ ★ ★ Activity: Interdisciplinary Connection ★ ★ ★

History Have students make a list of questions to ask friends and relatives who were adults or teenagers during the Vietnam War. For example: Did they support the war at the time? Why or why not? Have their views changed since then? How? Did they believe there were alternatives to sending U.S. combat troops to Vietnam? Do they think the war achieved any worthwhile purpose? If so, what was it? After students have conducted their surveys, tally the results on the board, and discuss the topic with the class. **BL**

S Skill Practice

Map Skills Ask: What country borders both Afghanistan and Iraq? *(Iran)* Have students research the state of current relations between the United States and Iran. **Ask:** How are these relations affected by Iran's border countries? *(U.S. relations with Iraq and Afghanistan might cause the United States to mistrust Iran, while simultaneously desiring their alliance, if only for geographic and strategic reasons.)* **BL** **AL**

W Writing Support

Expository Writing Have students write a short paper explaining how George W. Bush's "war on terror" compares to the idea of a "war on communism" in the 20th century. Suggest that students support their opinions with quotations from news sources and the Internet. **AL**

Additional Support

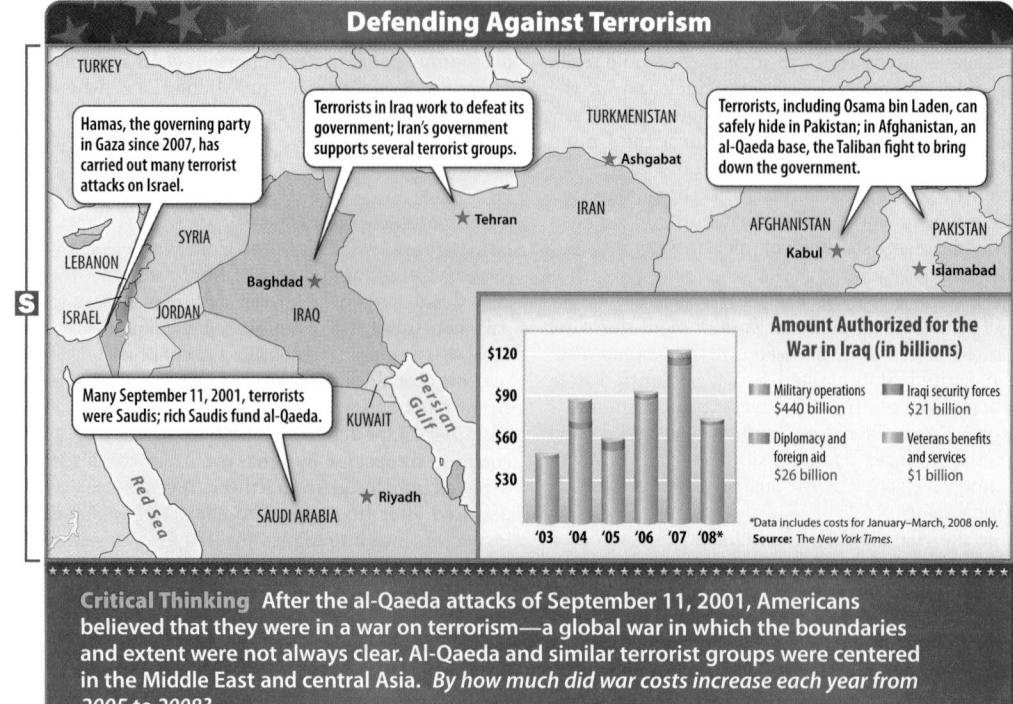

Defending Against Terrorism

TURKEY

Hamas, the governing party in Gaza since 2007, has carried out many terrorist attacks on Israel.

Terrorists in Iraq work to defeat its government; Iran's government supports several terrorist groups.

TURKMENISTAN

★ Ashgabat

Terrorists, including Osama bin Laden, can safely hide in Pakistan; in Afghanistan, an al-Qaeda base, the Taliban fight to bring down the government.

IRAN

★ Tehran

SYRIA

LEBANON

Baghdad ★

ISRAEL   JORDAN   IRAQ

AFGHANISTAN   PAKISTAN

Kabul ★

★ Islamabad

Many September 11, 2001, terrorists were Saudis; rich Saudis fund al-Qaeda.

KUWAIT

Persian Gulf

Red Sea

SAUDI ARABIA

★ Riyadh

Amount Authorized for the War in Iraq (in billions)

$120	
$90	
$60	
$30	

'03 '04 '05 '06 '07 '08*

Military operations $440 billion

Iraqi security forces $21 billion

Diplomacy and foreign aid $26 billion

Veterans benefits and services $1 billion

*Data includes costs for January–March, 2008 only.
Source: The *New York Times*.

Critical Thinking After the al-Qaeda attacks of September 11, 2001, Americans believed that they were in a war on terrorism—a global war in which the boundaries and extent were not always clear. Al-Qaeda and similar terrorist groups were centered in the Middle East and central Asia. *By how much did war costs increase each year from 2005 to 2008?*

To stop the fighting, NATO forces, led by the United States, attacked Serbia in 1995 to force the Serbs to negotiate. The Clinton administration then held peace talks in Dayton, Ohio. The Dayton Accords ended the war, and some 60,000 NATO troops headed into Bosnia to enforce the plan.

Three years later, war erupted in the Serbian province of Kosovo. Kosovo had two ethnic groups—Serbs and Muslim Albanians. The Albanians wanted Kosovo to be independent, and they formed a guerrilla army to fight the Serbs. In 1999, as the fighting escalated, NATO began bombing Serbia. In response, Serbia removed its troops from Kosovo. A NATO peacekeeping force was dispatched. In 2008 Kosovo formally declared its independence.

America's post–Cold War foreign policy agenda shifted abruptly on September 11, 2001, when terrorists hijacked commercial jetliners and crashed them into the World Trade Center and the Pentagon, resulting in the loss of nearly 3,000 lives. The FBI and intelligence sources traced the attack to al-Qaeda, a global network of Islamic terrorists. Al-Qaeda originated in Saudi Arabia, but trained many of its terrorists in Afghanistan. It works to maintain ties with other Islamic terrorist groups like Hamas, terrorists who fight to destroy the state of Israel.

The War in Afghanistan

In response to the attacks, President George W. Bush announced that the United States would pursue a global war on terror. He said it would target al-Qaeda, but would not end "until every terrorist group of global reach has been found, stopped and defeated." On October 7, 2001, the United States and its allies attacked Afghanistan. The Taliban, the militant Islamic government of Afghanistan, had refused to surrender al-Qaeda leaders there. In a few months, Taliban leaders were driven from power and retreated to the south. The United States helped the Afghani people elect a new government, but Taliban guerrillas continued to fight. Eight years after toppling the Taliban, the United States and its allies continued to fight the Taliban in Afghanistan and across the border in Pakistan.

Extending the Content

The Toll of the Vietnam War The loss of life and suffering were staggering. Between 1965 and 1975, an estimated 2 million Vietnamese civilians died. Vietnam lay in ruins, with whole villages completely destroyed. More than 58,000 Americans died, and about 300,000 suffered wounds resulting in permanent disabilities. Rather than receiving heroes' welcomes, returning U.S. veterans were ignored or even scorned by a public that had become increasingly critical of the war.

The Strategy of Preemption

Following the attacks of 9/11, the United States became concerned that terrorists might obtain weapons of mass destruction from rogue nations. During the Cold War, the American policy of deterrence reduced the likelihood that another nation might attack the United States with weapons of mass destruction. The rise of terrorist groups created a new problem. If a nation secretly gave such weapons to terrorists who used them on the United States, the American military might not know who to attack in response.

To counter this threat, the Bush administration adopted a strategy of preemption. Instead of waiting for an attack, the United States would strike first to prevent nations that support terrorism from developing weapons of mass destruction. Supporters argued that deterrence would no longer work in a world of suicide bombers and outlaw nations. Critics argued that preemption ignored international law and might lead to a series of wars, especially if other nations adopted the same policy.

The War in Iraq

Among the nations that sponsored terrorism and were suspected of developing weapons of mass destruction, President Bush believed that Iraq was the greatest threat. Iraq defied the UN and expelled its weapons inspectors. The president believed that overthrowing Iraq's dictator and helping Iraqis build a democratic nation would prevent Iraq from developing weapons of mass destruction, help stabilize the Middle East, and

reduce terrorism. With the help of Great Britain and several other nations, the United States invaded Iraq in March 2003. The coalition forces quickly defeated the Iraqi army and removed Saddam Hussein from power.

The quick victory did not end the fighting. Insurgents, or rebels, launched a guerrilla war against U.S. troops and the new Iraqi police forces. Some insurgents supported Saddam Hussein. Others were affiliated with al-Qaeda and wanted to establish a religious state. Still others belonged to militias organized by Iraq's different tribal groups. One strong divide among Iraqis was between the Shia and Sunni Muslims. Most Iraqis are Shias, but under Saddam Hussein, the minority Sunnis had ruled. In 2006 a civil war erupted between Shia and Sunni groups, causing even more casualties.

From 2003 to 2008, U.S. troops fought the insurgents. Billions of dollars in aid were spent to rebuild Iraq's infrastructure and economy. Iraqis voted for a new constitution and held their first free multiparty elections in 50 years. But the fighting continued. By 2007, more than 3,000 American soldiers had been killed, and a majority of Americans no longer supported the war. Congress, now controlled by the Democrats, tried to force the president to withdraw the troops, but President Bush decided on a new strategy involving a surge of additional troops to Iraq. By mid-2008, violence in Iraq had dropped and Iraqi Sunni and Shia groups seemed to be working together. Whether the situation would remain stable remained unclear.

SECTION 1 Review

Vocabulary

1. Explain the significance of: foreign policy, national security, isolationism, internationalism, containment.

Main Ideas

2. Describing What are the basic goals of U.S. foreign policy?

3. Explaining How did the United States carry out its policy of containment?

Critical Thinking

4. Drawing Conclusions Do you believe the United States could follow a policy of isolationism at this time? Support your answer.

5. Organizing Use a graphic organizer like the one below to show two foreign policy issues that are part of the nation's new global agenda.

Writing About Government

6. Persuasive Writing In recent years, the development of an interdependent global economy has led to an ongoing debate about the degree to which free trade helps or hurts the United States. Write a newspaper editorial about this topic illustrating either the benefits of free trade or the potential problems that may result from global interdependence.

C Critical Thinking

Comparing and Contrasting

Ask: What similarities and differences do you see in the policy of containment that followed WWII and the strategy of preemption that followed the terrorist attacks of September 11, 2001? *(Containment was more widely supported when employed in Korea than in Vietnam; the Persian Gulf War had more support than the later invasion of Iraq; both policies led to long wars that eroded the standing of the U.S. president. Encourage students to take notes during the discussion in the form of a simple chart. They may conclude that the two policies are similar.)* **OL AL**

Assess

Assign the Section 1 Assessment as homework or as an in-class activity, or have students take Section Quiz 22-1 from *Section Quizzes and Chapter Tests.*

Close

Evaluating Ask students to rank the objectives of U.S. foreign policy in order of importance. Discuss students' choices as a class. **OL**

Section 1 Review

Answers

1. All definitions can be found in the section and the Glossary.
2. national security, free and open trade, world peace, democratic governments, humanitarian concerns
3. The United States provided economic and military aid to nations threatened by communism, and sent combat troops to fight in Korea and Vietnam.
4. Answers should show an understanding of the global interdependence in today's world and of

the abundance of long-range weapons that make isolationism nearly impossible.
5. finding ways to open world markets to U.S. exports, dealing with the increased threat of terrorism
6. Students' editorial positions will vary and should be supported by facts organized in a reasonable argument.

Focus

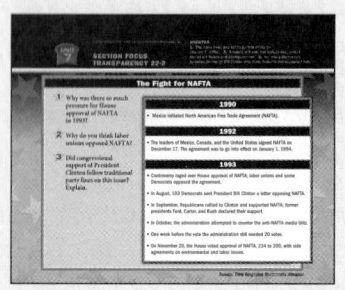
Reader's Guide

Answers to Graphic:

power to declare war

power to appropriate money

power to ratify treaties (Senate)

power to confirm appointments
of diplomats (Senate)

Resource Manager

Shared Foreign Policy Powers

Reader's Guide

Content Vocabulary	Academic Vocabulary	Reading Strategy
★ ambassador *(p. 615)* ★ treaty *(p. 615)* ★ executive agreement *(p. 619)* ★ bipartisan *(p. 620)*	★ regime *(p. 615)* ★ military *(p. 615)* ★ consult *(p. 616)*	As you read, create a graphic organizer like the one at the right to list the ways Congress can influence foreign policy.

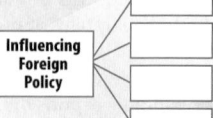

Influencing Foreign Policy

Issues in the News

As the Taliban continued its war to regain power in Afghanistan in 2008, the Bush administration tried to get reluctant European allies to send more troops to the war-torn country. U.S. officials believed that an increase in troops was needed to deal with the Taliban's ongoing attacks against Afghanistan's fledgling democratic government. During an unannounced visit to the Afghan capital of Kabul, U.S. Secretary of State Condoleezza Rice stressed progress in the country since the fall of the Taliban government in 2001. However, she also warned that Afghanistan faced "determined enemies" who would not be easy to defeat. Rice urged European leaders to convince their people that sending troops to Afghanistan was an important priority. She stated that "[P]opulations have to understand that this is not just a peacekeeping fight."

▲ Condoleezza Rice, U.S. Secretary of State, with Afghan president, Hamid Karzai

Condoleezza Rice is the first African American woman to serve as U.S. Secretary of State. A member of the president's cabinet, the U.S. Secretary of State helps the president formulate and execute the country's foreign policy. He or she often appears before Congress to explain or justify the actions of the administration on foreign policy issues. The Framers of the Constitution attempted to divide the responsibility for foreign affairs between the president and Congress. They did not, however, clearly outline the boundaries of power of each branch. As a result, on many occasions the president and Congress have vied for power.

Over the years, events have enabled the president to assume more responsibility in foreign policy. Today, according to one political scientist, "Any discussion of the making of United States foreign policy must begin with the president. He is the ultimate decider."

Presidential Powers and Responsibilities

The president derives power to formulate foreign policy from two sources. First, the Constitution

---

R Reading Strategies	**C** Critical Thinking	**D** Differentiated Instruction	**W** Writing Support	**S** Skill Practice
Teacher Edition • Accessing Prior Knowledge, p. 615 • Using Context Clues, p. 618 **Additional Resources** • Guid. Read. Act., p. 79 • Quizzes/Tests, p. 270	**Teacher Edition** • Making Inferences, pp. 615, 619 • Identifying Alternatives, p. 616 • Drawing Conclusions, p. 617 **Additional Resources** • Read. Essen., pp. 250–253	**Teacher Edition** • English Learners, p. 618 **Additional Resources** • Foldables, p. 65 • Hist. Docs. and Speeches, p. 22	**Additional Resources** • Part. in Gov. Act., pp. 43–44	**Teacher Edition** • Visual Literacy, p. 617 **Additional Resources** • Inter. Poli. Cartoons, pp. 43–44

lists certain presidential powers related to foreign policy. Second, the president functions as an important world leader.

The president's ability to commit U.S. troops abroad was well illustrated in the fall of 1994. When a military **regime** in Haiti continued to persecute supporters of a democratically elected leader, President Bill Clinton informed the American people that the United States would "lead a multinational force to carry out the will of the United Nations" to restore a legitimate government. Clinton's speech illustrates the president's foreign policy authority.

Commander in Chief

The Constitution grants the president the power to be the commander in chief of the nation's **military** forces. As such, the president may send troops, ships, and planes or even use nuclear weapons anywhere in the world, without congressional approval. For example, in 1991 President George H.W. Bush sent military forces to Saudi Arabia soon after Iraq invaded Kuwait.

Head of State

In addition to giving powers as commander in chief, Article II, Section 2,[1] grants the president certain diplomatic powers. 📖 The president appoints **ambassadors,** the government officials who represent the nation. The president also receives ambassadors from foreign governments. By receiving an ambassador or other diplomat from a country, the president formally recognizes that government. Conversely, by refusing to do so, the president can withhold diplomatic recognition of a government. Formal recognition is vital because it qualifies a foreign government for economic and other forms of aid. Article II, Section 2, also empowers the president to make treaties. A **treaty** is a formal agreement between the governments of two or more nations.

As head of state, the president plays an important part in controlling foreign policy. He or she represents the nation and stands as a symbol to the world for its policies. In an international crisis, Americans look to their president for leadership.

📖 *See the following footnoted materials in the **Reference Handbook**:*
1. *The Constitution, pages R42–R67.*

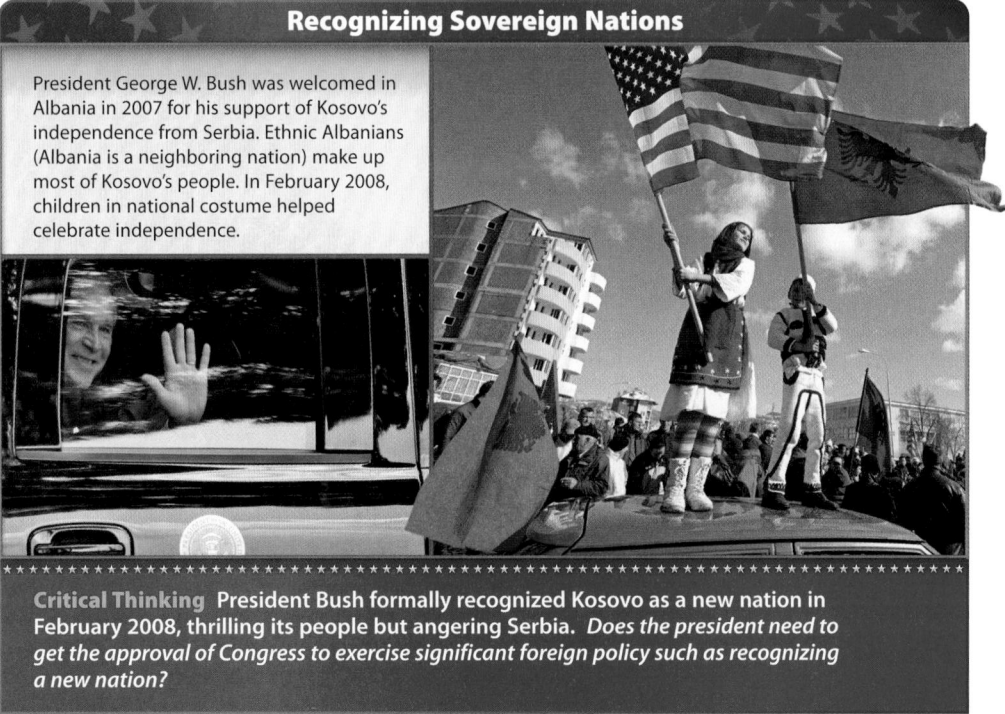

Recognizing Sovereign Nations

President George W. Bush was welcomed in Albania in 2007 for his support of Kosovo's independence from Serbia. Ethnic Albanians (Albania is a neighboring nation) make up most of Kosovo's people. In February 2008, children in national costume helped celebrate independence.

Critical Thinking President Bush formally recognized Kosovo as a new nation in February 2008, thrilling its people but angering Serbia. *Does the president need to get the approval of Congress to exercise significant foreign policy such as recognizing a new nation?*

CHAPTER 22: *Foreign Policy and Defense* **615**

C Critical Thinking

C Critical Thinking

Identifying Alternatives Have students look into the kinds of people who have been appointed to ambassadorships. Ask the following questions:

- What is their political background?

- Do they have business experience or knowledge of international law?

- Have they had previous diplomatic experience?

- Have they studied the culture and customs of the nation to which they are assigned?

Have students compare the qualifications for an ambassador with those of other appointed officials. **OL**

CURRICULUM CONNECTION

History Passed in 1944, the GI Bill, or the Servicemen's Readjustment Act, paid for veterans to attend college and provided guaranteed loans to buy or build a home.

Differentiated Instruction

Foreign Policy Advisers

The president has the final responsibility for establishing foreign policy. Before making foreign policy decisions, however, presidents usually **consult** advisers. Generally, chief executives rely upon the information and advice of the cabinet members, the White House staff, and officials in specialized agencies dealing with foreign policy. At times, presidents also go outside the government and seek advice from private individuals who have specialized knowledge in foreign affairs.

The Secretaries of State and Defense

C In their specialized fields, all cabinet members bring international problems to the president's attention and recommend how to deal with them. For two cabinet departments, however—the Department of State and the Department of Defense—foreign affairs are a full-time concern.

The secretary of state supervises all the diplomatic activities of the U.S. government. In the past, most presidents have relied heavily on their secretaries of state. In the early years of the Republic, four secretaries of state—Thomas Jefferson, James Madison, James Monroe, and John Quincy Adams—went on to become president.

Normally, the secretary of state carries on diplomacy at the highest level. The secretary frequently travels to foreign capitals for important negotiations with heads of state and represents the United States at major international conferences.

The secretary of defense supervises the government's military activities. He or she also informs and advises the president on the nation's military forces, weapons, and bases.

The National Security Advisor

The national security advisor—who is also the director of the National Security Council (NSC)—plays a major role in foreign affairs. President George W. Bush chose political scientist Dr. Condoleezza Rice for this office. She previously worked within the NSC between 1989 and 1991 and was the first woman to be chosen as national security advisor.

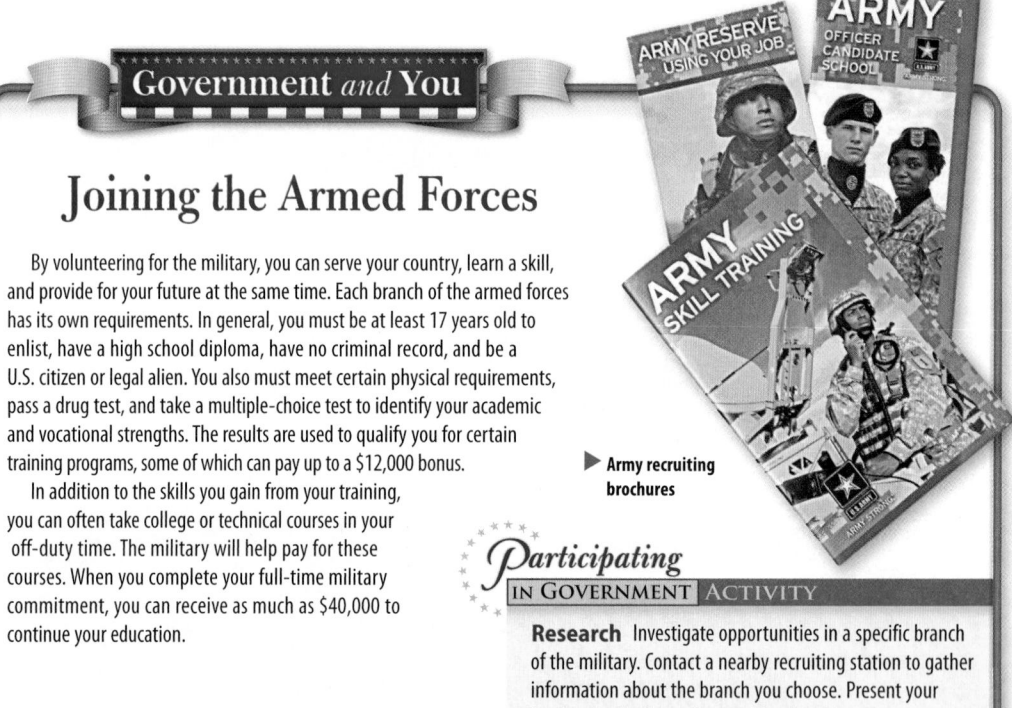

Government *and* You

Joining the Armed Forces

By volunteering for the military, you can serve your country, learn a skill, and provide for your future at the same time. Each branch of the armed forces has its own requirements. In general, you must be at least 17 years old to enlist, have a high school diploma, have no criminal record, and be a U.S. citizen or legal alien. You also must meet certain physical requirements, pass a drug test, and take a multiple-choice test to identify your academic and vocational strengths. The results are used to qualify you for certain training programs, some of which can pay up to a $12,000 bonus.

In addition to the skills you gain from your training, you can often take college or technical courses in your off-duty time. The military will help pay for these courses. When you complete your full-time military commitment, you can receive as much as $40,000 to continue your education.

▶ **Army recruiting brochures**

Participating IN GOVERNMENT ACTIVITY

Research Investigate opportunities in a specific branch of the military. Contact a nearby recruiting station to gather information about the branch you choose. Present your findings in the form of a recruiting brochure.

Activity: Multiple Learning Styles

Visual/Spatial Although Congress has not declared war since 1941, the United States has been involved in several conflicts—the Korean War, Vietnam War, and Persian Gulf War, for example. Students can better understand these conflicts by viewing one of the following documentaries: *Behind the Flag* considers the causes, the consequences, and the alternatives to the Gulf War (The Video Project, 1991); *Korea: The Forgotten War* is an in-depth documentary with archival combat footage (Fox Hills Videos, 1987); *Vietnam: After the Fire* is an award-winning two-part documentary on the conflict in Southeast Asia (The Cinema Guild, 1988); *Baghdad Day* presents an account of the war in Iraq from the perspective of an embedded American journalist and an Iraqi taxi driver (The History Channel, 2007). **BL**

A Senate Role in Foreign Policy

Spotlight on the Executive The president takes the lead in shaping foreign policy, but congressional committees ask executive branch officials to answer their questions. **S** Here Senators Joseph Biden and Barbara Boxer confer over statements of Secretary of State Condoleezza Rice to the Senate Foreign Relations committee. *How might this committee's work influence public opinion?*

Caption Answer: By raising questions and issuing reports, congressional committees can turn public attention to certain foreign policy problems.

S Skill Practice

Visual Literacy Senators Joseph Biden and Barbara Boxer are shown conferring during questioning of the secretary of state by the Foreign Relations Committee. **Ask:** What does the "body language" of Biden and Boxer suggest about the Senate's role? *(That as part of the system of checks and balances, the Senate monitors the actions of the executive branch. Committee members speak privately, then ask questions. In short, they are independent, not deferential.)* **AL**

C Critical Thinking

Drawing Conclusions Presidents have relied on a range of officials and friends for foreign policy advice. **Ask:** What does this tell you about the arena of foreign policy? *(Students might respond that expertise on foreign policy can come from a wide variety of sources.)* **AL**

The Central Intelligence Agency

To make foreign policy decisions, the president and the president's advisers need timely information about the activities of other nations along with data on non-state terrorist groups like al-Qaeda. The Central Intelligence Agency (CIA) was created in 1947 to gather and coordinate intelligence data for the president from across the world.

Today the CIA is only one of 15 intelligence agencies in the federal government. The largest, the National Security Agency (NSA), is responsible for code-breaking and electronic spying. The Pentagon has the Defense Intelligence Agency. The State, Energy, Treasury and Homeland Security Departments also have their own intelligence groups. Taken together, all of these agencies are known as the "intelligence community." More than 100,000 people work in these various intelligence agencies.

Each of these groups was created to collect information for a specific client, such as the president or the secretary of state. As a result, these agencies rarely share information with one another and often act like competitors, at times even hoarding vital information. The commission investigating the September 11, 2001, terrorist attacks reported that this lack of cooperation clearly affected the government's ability to prevent the attacks. In 2004 Congress tried putting one person in charge by creating the cabinet-level position of the Director of National Intelligence.

Making Foreign Policy

The government employs hundreds of foreign policy experts whom the president may consult before making a decision. In some cases, family members and trusted political friends have more influence on a president than the secretary of state. A mild-mannered Texan named Colonel Edward House was President Woodrow Wilson's most trusted adviser, especially during World War I, even though he held no cabinet post. **C**

In recent years, however, each president has taken a different approach to foreign policy. President Dwight D. Eisenhower relied heavily on Secretary of State John Foster Dulles for foreign policy advice. President John F. Kennedy, on the other hand, put together a team of foreign affairs experts who worked together in the basement of the White House. A group of advisers who lunched with the president in the White House every Tuesday often influenced President Lyndon B. Johnson's decisions on the Vietnam War. Included in these Tuesday cabinet luncheons were the director of the CIA and the White House press secretary. In contrast, the opinions of National Security Advisor Henry Kissinger were major influences on President Richard Nixon.

Finally, however, it is the president who determines the policies that are followed. As President Ronald Reagan wrote, only the president can "respond quickly in a crisis or formulate a coherent and consistent policy in any region of the world."

Powers of Congress

Although the president directs U.S. foreign policy, Congress plays an important role. The basis for this role lies in the Constitution. The Constitution gives Congress significant foreign policy powers,

---

Hands-On Chapter Project

Step 2

Analyzing Issues

Step 2: Identifying Connections Students will continue researching the areas of the world they were assigned.

Directions Ask groups to continue their research by identifying economic connections the United States has to their areas. Students should gather information about trade, foreign aid, the presence of multinational corporations in the area, local resources used by those corporations, and other relevant data. Their research should also include a "snapshot" synopsis of the area, including major industries and resources, economic and political conditions, standard of living, life expectancy, literacy and infant mortality rates, and so on.

Putting It Together Ask each group to draw a web diagram summarizing U.S. economic connections to their area. **OL**

(Chapter Project continued in Section 3.)

D Differentiated Instruction

English Learners Americans are often criticized for their ignorance of physical geography. To make sure that students know how to locate the places they are reading about, have them identify the countries discussed in the section (Panama, Colombia, Haiti, Israel, Britain, Mexico, Spain, Germany, Japan, Italy, Vietnam, Iraq, Kuwait, Somalia) on outline maps of the world. **ELL** **BL**

R Reading Strategy

Using Context Clues In the quote, Senator Jacob Javits argues that Congress should sometimes withhold its "unquestioning support of the presidency." **Ask:** What phrase does Javits used to point out potential dangers in the president's wartime powers? *("the fate of the nation in his hands" and "the awesome nature of the power over war")* **OL**

Differentiated Instruction

Risking American Lives

Presidential Actions

The United States sent food to war-torn Somalia. Although it was a humanitarian effort, the U.S.–led UN mission suffered casualties. President Clinton faced pressure to recall the troops, but he refused, believing that Somali lives and American credibility were at stake. *Do you think presidents should be able to ignore pressure from Congress in order to keep U.S. troops in foreign countries?*

including the power to declare war and appropriate money. The Senate must ratify treaties and confirm diplomatic appointments.

Power to Declare War

The Constitution balances the president's powers as commander in chief by granting Congress the power to declare war. Although the president may send troops anywhere in the world, only Congress may declare war. Despite this power, Congress has exercised its power to declare war only five times in our nation's history. It declared war in 1812 against Britain; in 1846 against Mexico; in 1898 against Spain; in 1917 against Germany; and in 1941 against Japan, Germany, and Italy. In these five cases, the United States was officially at war with a foreign government. In each instance, the president asked Congress for a declaration of war. Then, in accordance with the Constitution, both houses of Congress adopted the war resolution by a majority vote.

In other instances, instead of requesting a formal declaration of war, presidents have asked Congress to pass a joint resolution concerning the use of American troops. In 1964, for example, President Lyndon B. Johnson asked Congress for authority to use troops in Vietnam. In response to an alleged North Vietnamese attack on U.S. ships that occurred in the Gulf of Tonkin off Vietnam's coast, Congress

passed the Gulf of Tonkin Resolution.[1] The resolution authorized the president "to take all necessary measures to repel any armed attack against the forces of the United States."

Dismayed by the results of the Gulf of Tonkin Resolution, Congress tried to check the president's power to send troops into combat by passing the War Powers Act in 1973. The act declared that the president could not send troops into combat for more than 60 days without the consent of Congress. Seventeen years later, after the 1990 Iraqi invasion of Kuwait, some members of Congress questioned President George H.W. Bush's commitment of troops in the Middle East. The War Powers Act was not invoked, however. Instead, Congress authorized the use of force against Iraq. With this congressional approval, President Bush authorized Operation Desert Storm, which easily defeated the Iraqi forces.

Former Senator Jacob Javits explained the dilemma facing members of Congress who support the War Powers Act in this way:

66 *The reluctance to challenge the president is founded in an awareness that he holds, in large degree, the fate of the nation in his hands. We all wish to assist and sustain the presidency. But I have come to the conclusion that the awesome nature of the power over war in our time should require us to withhold, in relevant cases, that unquestioning support of the presidency.* 99
—Jacob Javits, 1985

See the following footnoted materials in the **Reference Handbook:**
1. *Gulf of Tonkin Resolution,* page R94.

Leveled Activities

Power to Appropriate Money

By far the greatest source of congressional power in foreign policy derives from the control that Congress has over government spending. Only Congress can appropriate the funds to equip American armed forces and to build new weapons. Congress must authorize funds for defense and foreign aid each year. If Congress disapproves of a president's action, such as committing troops to a particular war, it can refuse to provide the funds to maintain the force.

In a similar fashion, Congress may refuse to provide funds for aid to other nations. Congress also may decide not only the sum to be granted, but also the conditions that a foreign country must meet to be eligible for aid.

Power in Treaty Making

The Constitution also gives the Senate the power of advice and consent on all treaties. The president may make treaties with foreign governments, but a two-thirds vote of the Senate must ratify them.

The Senate's power in treaty making is real, however. The Senate has voted down or refused to consider more than 130 treaties since 1789. In 1978 President Jimmy Carter faced strong opposition from Senate conservatives regarding his proposed Panama Canal treaties. After much debate, the Senate eventually ratified both treaties.

Increasingly, presidents have turned to another tool for making binding commitments with foreign governments. **Executive agreements** are pacts between the president and the head of a foreign government that have the legal status of treaties but do not require Senate approval. Today, executive agreements make up more than 90 percent of all U.S. international agreements.

Most Favored Nation

Presidents have relied on executive agreements to enhance their foreign policy powers, and Congress has rarely objected. In fact, Congress authorized that all trade agreements be handled as executive agreements, requiring only a simple majority vote of both houses. Under U.S. law, the president may grant most-favored-nation (MFN) status to trading partners. Such agreements reduce tariff rates on all exports from that nation to the United States. By a two-thirds majority vote, Congress may overturn the president's decision to grant MFN status. In 1997, for example, the House voted to kill a bill that would have ended renewal of MFN status for China. In 2000 China was granted permanent MFN status.

A Historical Double Take

A Change of Policy President Jimmy Carter won Senate ratification of the Panama Canal treaties, which transferred control of the canal from the United States to Panama by the end of the century. Many Americans were outraged at the Panama "giveaway." *What do you think motivated the United States to make such a treaty and why would presidents prefer to use executive agreements?*

Power to Confirm Appointments

The Senate also must confirm presidential appointments to diplomatic posts. This power was intended to allow the Senate to screen applicants for foreign policy positions and thus help determine foreign policy. Usually the Senate is willing to accept the president's appointments to diplomatic posts.

The President Versus Congress

Congress has the power to block some of a president's foreign policies and even initiate policies of its own. Usually Congress lets the president set a direction in foreign policy. On most issues, Congress passes the foreign policy bills and treaties that the president and his advisers propose.

CHAPTER 22: *Foreign Policy and Defense* **619**

C Critical Thinking

Making Inferences Ask: Why might Congress's refusal to approve funds for certain foreign policies affect its own approval rating? *(If Congress denies a request for funding for weapons or troops, for example, its members may be seen as unpatriotic or unsupportive.)* **AL**

Caption Answer: The Panama Canal "giveaway" might have been a relatively easy way to maintain friendly relations with Panama. Executive agreements do not require Senate approval.

Did You Know?

Many scholars say that the Jay Treaty of 1794 represents the first time that the United States granted another country "most favored nation" status. The country in question was Great Britain, which received special trading status with the United States in return for settling some outstanding issues left over from the Revolutionary War.

Additional Support

Extending the Content

The National Security Council The NSC serves as an advisory board on matters of defense, foreign policy, and intelligence. It advises the president on security and supervises the Central Intelligence Agency. In 1986 the NSC was criticized for exceeding its role as an advisory board when it was revealed that NSC staff members sanctioned secret arms sales to Iran and used the proceeds to support the contras in Nicaragua. As a result of this criticism, President Ronald Reagan added a legal adviser to the NSC staff in 1987.

W **Writing Support**

Persuasive Writing Have students write a short story about an effective Vietnam War protest or series of protests. Students may choose to write from the perspective of the protesters, antiwar organizers, the president (Johnson or Nixon), a cabinet member, or another adviser. **Ask:** Why did the protest influence the president enough to consider a change of strategy or policy in Vietnam? **OL**

Assess

Assign the Section 2 Assessment as homework or as an in-class activity, or have students take Section Quiz 22-2 from *Section Quizzes and Chapter Tests.*

Close

Analyzing Ask: What might be the results if U.S. voters had to approve a declaration of war? **OL**

Section 2 Review

Especially in times of war and crisis, the president's foreign policies have enjoyed **bipartisan,** or two-party, support. This was true during World War II and the early Cold War. During the Vietnam War, however, Congress and the public became deeply divided about the war. Since then, Congress has often divided on foreign policy issues. There was substantial disagreement, for example on Ronald Reagan's policies toward the Soviet Union and toward George W. Bush's policies in Iraq.

Presidential Advantages

The president has advantages over Congress in conducting foreign policy. One is the president's position as the leader of the nation. Only the president—or a chosen spokesperson such as the secretary of state—can speak for the nation when dealing with other governments. It is the president to whom Americans look for leadership in foreign affairs.

A second advantage is that the president controls those agencies, such as the Department of State and the National Security Council, that help formulate and carry out foreign policy on a day-to-day basis. Consequently, the president has greater access to vital secret information about foreign affairs. Such information often is not readily available to members of Congress.

A third advantage is that the president is able to take quick decisive action. Today it is often necessary to respond to events rapidly, and at times extreme secrecy is essential. The House and Senate must discuss, vote, and take into consideration the opinions of many members. Congress simply cannot act as quickly as the president or maintain secrecy with so many people involved.

Finally, by using executive agreements, the president can bypass the Senate when making agreements with other nations. As a result of these advantages, the president's power over foreign policy matters has increased steadily.

The Role of Public Opinion

Although the president and Congress have the major responsibility for making foreign policy, their decisions are often influenced by the opinions of the American people. Public opinion, for example, directly influenced the Vietnam War. Mass protests and demonstrations in the 1960s and the early 1970s had a direct impact on foreign policy. Early on, most Americans supported the fighting in Vietnam. But as the number of Americans who were wounded and killed grew and media coverage heightened public awareness of the situation, public opinion slowly turned against the war. The growing discontent contributed heavily to President Lyndon B. Johnson's decision not to seek reelection in 1968 and later influenced President Richard Nixon's decision to pull troops out of Vietnam.

Besides public opinion, pressure from interest groups can also affect foreign policy. The votes of Congress on foreign policy questions are subject to the influence of organized interest groups. These groups, whose concerns range from trade to human rights issues, can have a substantial impact on legislation that affects their areas of interest.

SECTION 2 Review

Vocabulary

1. **Explain** the significance of: ambassador, treaty, executive agreement, bipartisan.

Main Ideas

2. **Identifying** Which cabinet members generally work most closely with the president on foreign policy?

3. **Explaining** What are the foreign policy powers of Congress?

Critical Thinking

4. **Forming an Opinion** Do you think the president has too much power in making foreign policy? Explain your answer.

5. **Organizing** Use a Venn diagram like the one below to compare executive agreements and treaties.

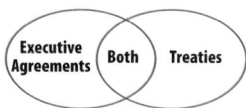

Writing About Government

6. **Descriptive Writing** Use library resources to find specific examples of how public opinion changed U.S. policy in Vietnam in the 1960s and 1970s. Prepare a one- to two-page report that illustrates the public's reaction to the war and the government's responses. You can include photos, captions, and headlines in your report.

Answers

1. All definitions can be found in the section and the Glossary.
2. the secretaries of state and defense
3. power to declare war, to appropriate money, to ratify treaties, to confirm diplomatic appointments
4. Some students may believe that certain situations need immediate action that Congress cannot provide; other students may believe that the longer time required by Congress to deliberate would help avoid rash or hasty actions.
5. executive agreements—do not require Senate approval; treaties—require Senate approval; both—the president uses them to execute foreign policy
6. Reports should reflect an understanding of events and adequate research of the topic.

State and Defense Departments

Reader's Guide

Content Vocabulary
★ embassy *(p. 623)*
★ consulate *(p. 623)*
★ consul *(p. 623)*
★ passport *(p. 623)*
★ visa *(p. 623)*
★ conscription *(p. 625)*

Academic Vocabulary
★ security *(p. 621)*
★ resolve *(p. 623)*
★ considerable *(p. 624)*

Reading Strategy
Use an outline similar to the one at the right to help you take notes about the State and Defense Departments.

State and Defense Departments
I. The Department of State
   A.
   B.
II. The Department of Defense
   A.
   B.

Issues in the News

The U.S. Embassy in Nairobi, Kenya, announced in 2008 that it was barring 10 prominent Kenyan politicians and businesspeople from traveling to the United States. U.S. diplomatic officials did not reveal the identity of the people affected, but all are believed to have been behind the ethnic violence that has engulfed Kenya following a disputed election. Following the announcement of the December 2007 election results, 10,000 people had been killed, and 350,000 others had been displaced from their homes. U.S. Ambassador to Kenya Michael Ranneberger confirmed the ban, stating that the United States "decided to apply . . . travel restrictions on individuals who we believe participated in the instigation of violence, violation of human rights, and breaking of democratic principles."

▲ Kenyans react to the period of intense violence in early 2008.

As the situation in Kenya illustrates, U.S. ambassadors and diplomats monitor and often respond to abuses against human rights around the world. It is their duty to put into practice the policies of the executive and the legislative branch, the two branches of government that establish the nation's foreign policy.

In the executive branch, two departments are mainly responsible for foreign policy. The Department of State, one of the smallest cabinet-level departments, carries out foreign policy. The Department of Defense, the largest of all of the executive departments, is responsible for guarding the national **security** of the United States.

The Department of State

Created by Congress in 1789, the Department of State was the first executive department. Originally known as the Department of Foreign Affairs, it was soon renamed the Department of State. The secretary of state, the head of this department, is generally considered the most important cabinet member, ranking just below the president and vice president. The State Department advises the president and formulates and carries out policy. Officially, its "primary objective in the conduct of foreign relations is to promote the long-range security and well-being of the United States." The Department

Focus

Bellringer
Section Focus Transparencies 22-3

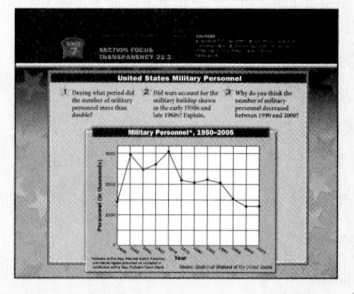

Reader's Guide

Answers to Graphic:
A. The Department of State
   1. informs president about international issues
   2. maintains diplomatic relations with foreign governments
   3. negotiates treaties
   4. protects U.S. business interests and travelers abroad
B. The Department of Defense
   1. supervises U.S. armed forces
   2. assists president in duties as commander in chief

Resource Manager

R Reading Strategies	C Critical Thinking	D Differentiated Instruction	W Writing Support	S Skill Practice
Teacher Edition	**Teacher Edition**	**Additional Resources**	**Teacher Edition**	**Teacher Edition**
• Comparing and Contrasting, p. 622	• Contrasting, p. 623 • Distinguishing Fact from Opinion, p. 624	• Foldables, p. 65	• Personal Writing, p. 625	• Visual Literacy, p. 622
Additional Resources	**Additional Resources**			**Additional Resources**
• Guid. Read. Act., p. 80 • Quizzes/Tests, p. 271	• Read. Essen., pp. 254–256			• Skill Reinforce. Act., p. 22

Teach

R Reading Strategy

Comparing and Contrasting
Have students compare and contrast the roles of the Departments of State and Defense in foreign policy. *(State: suggests, formulates, and carries out foreign policy; Defense: protects national security and carries out military aspects of foreign policy)* **BL**

S Skill Practice

Visual Literacy Have students examine the embassy buildings. **Ask:** What does the architecture tell you about the importance of embassies? *(Students might respond that the traditional, formal look commands respect.)* **OL**

Critical Thinking

Answer: Answers may vary but should indicate that embassies are the nerve centers of the countries they represent on foreign soil. They are the diplomatic and communications link to the home country. Either incoming or outgoing statements or actions made at embassies have a profound effect.

Additional Support

of State carries out four other important functions: (1) to keep the president informed about international issues, (2) to maintain diplomatic relations with foreign governments, (3) to negotiate treaties with foreign governments, and (4) to protect the interests of Americans who are traveling or conducting business abroad.

Organizational Structure

Six assistant secretaries direct the six geographic bureaus of the State Department. These bureaus are the Bureaus of African Affairs, European and Eurasian Affairs, East Asian and Pacific Affairs, Western Hemisphere Affairs, Near Eastern Affairs, and South and Central Asian Affairs. Other bureaus analyze information about specific foreign policy topics. One such bureau deals with educational and cultural affairs, another with political and military problems, and another with intelligence and research. The work of the State Department, therefore, is organized by topics and regions.

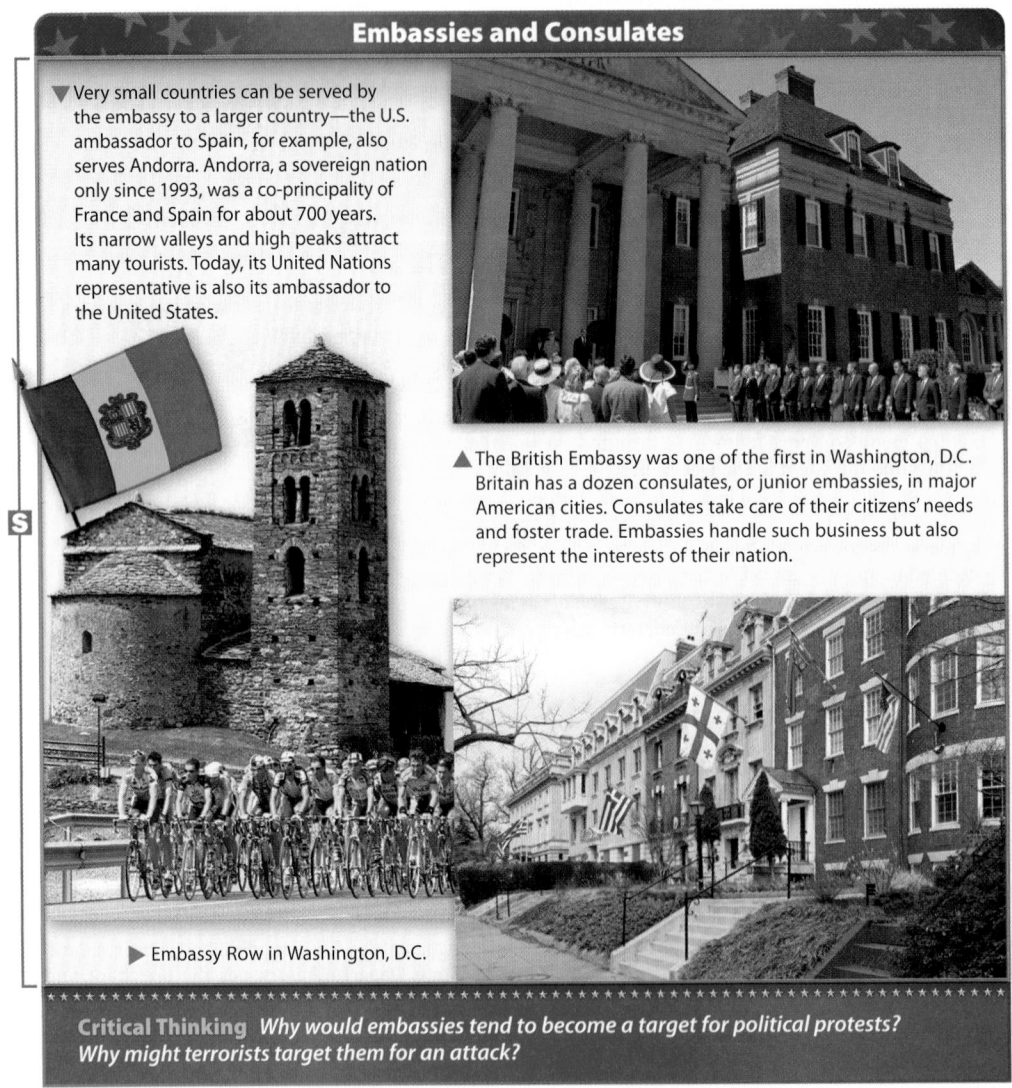

Embassies and Consulates

Very small countries can be served by the embassy to a larger country—the U.S. ambassador to Spain, for example, also serves Andorra. Andorra, a sovereign nation only since 1993, was a co-principality of France and Spain for about 700 years. Its narrow valleys and high peaks attract many tourists. Today, its United Nations representative is also its ambassador to the United States.

▲ The British Embassy was one of the first in Washington, D.C. Britain has a dozen consulates, or junior embassies, in major American cities. Consulates take care of their citizens' needs and foster trade. Embassies handle such business but also represent the interests of their nation.

▶ Embassy Row in Washington, D.C.

Critical Thinking *Why would embassies tend to become a target for political protests? Why might terrorists target them for an attack?*

Activity: Collaborative Learning

Making a Teaching Tool Organize the class into small groups and assign each one an agency or bureau of the Department of Defense or the Department of State. Have students use library resources or the Internet to find information on their assigned agency. (Internet addresses for the Departments of State and Defense may be found in the *World Almanac.)* After students have gathered information, have them choose a method of presenting it to the rest of the class—posters, videos, booklets, overhead transparencies, and so on. Students should divide the various tasks (researching, illustrating, using the Internet, writing, compiling, presenting) among group members. **OL**

The Foreign Service

More than half of the employees of the State Department serve in other countries. The officials who are assigned to serve abroad in foreign countries belong to the foreign service.

College graduates who seek a career in the Foreign Service must pass an extremely demanding civil service exam. Successful applicants then receive training in special schools. Foreign Service Officers (FSOs) usually spend several years abroad in a diplomatic post. Then they may be recalled to Washington, D.C., to participate in foreign policy discussions at the State Department.

For many FSOs, an overseas assignment is valued, but for others it may be a life of hardship. As one observer of the State Department noted:

❝ *Working at State demands far more than the usual 40-hour week. . . . Officers stationed overseas are almost never off duty. Not only may they be called on at any hour of the day or night, they also represent the government in every aspect of their lives and personal encounters. Even socializing is work. Attending parties, seemingly an attractive way of making a living, pales after weeks of mandatory and boring appearances following an intensive workday.* ❞

—Barry Rubin, 1985

In their service abroad, Foreign Service Officers are normally assigned either to an American embassy or to an American consulate.

Embassies

The United States maintains embassies in the capital cities of foreign countries—such as Tokyo, Japan; Paris, France; and Nairobi, Kenya. An **embassy** includes the official residence and offices of the ambassador and his or her staff. The primary function of an embassy is to make diplomatic communication between governments easier. Currently, the State Department directs the work of more than 200 American embassies and consulates.

Embassy officials keep the State Department informed about the politics and foreign policies of the host government. They also keep the host government informed about American policies.

An ambassador heads each American embassy. Most ambassadors today come from the ranks of the foreign service as experienced and highly qualified professional diplomats. Some ambassadors, however, may be political appointees, selected for reasons other than their diplomatic knowledge or experience. In every case, however, an ambassador is appointed by the president and must be confirmed by the Senate.

Each embassy includes specialists who deal with political and military matters, trade, travel, and currency. The specialists help **resolve** disputes that arise between the host country and the United States. Most disputes are minor enough to be settled by the embassy staff. In the case of major disagreements, governments may break off diplomatic relations by closing their embassies. Such action represents the strongest sign of displeasure that one government can show toward another.

Consulates

The United States also maintains offices known as consulates in major cities of foreign nations. **Consulates** are not normally involved in diplomatic negotiations with foreign governments. They function primarily to promote American business interests in foreign countries and to serve and safeguard American travelers in the countries where consulates are located.

Heading each consulate is a Foreign Service Officer called a **consul.** In the course of a routine day, the consul and staff handle individual problems and inquiries about such matters as shipping schedules, business opportunities, and travel needs.

Passports and Visas

For Americans who are traveling abroad, the State Department issues a document called a **passport.** The traveler whose photograph and signature appear on the passport is entitled to certain privileges and protection established by an international treaty. With a passport, an American citizen can expect to be granted entry into many countries.

In some cases, however, to be granted the right to enter another country, it is necessary to obtain another document called a visa. A **visa** is a special document issued by the government of the country that a person would like to enter. If a citizen of Kenya wants to visit the United States, for example, he or she must apply for a visa at an American embassy or consulate in one of the major cities in Kenya.

American immigration laws require nearly all foreign visitors to obtain visas prior to entering the United States. The countries of Western Europe, however, do not require American travelers to carry visas, only passports.

POLITICAL PROFILES

Madeleine Albright
(1937–) The first female secretary of state, Albright was appointed by President Bill Clinton in 1997. She was born in Czechoslovakia and emigrated to the United States with her family in 1949 to escape the Communist regime. She was exposed to many different cultures as a child because her father was in the Czechoslovakian diplomatic service. Albright has a B.A. in political science from Wellesley College, an M.A. in public law and government, and a doctorate from Columbia University. She was unanimously confirmed by the Senate in 1993 as ambassador to the United Nations. Described by one writer as an intellectual with a heart, she is known for her toughness and her no-nonsense approach to her duties.

C Critical Thinking

Contrasting Ask: How is an embassy different from a consulate? *(embassies: make communication between governments easier; consulates: promote U.S. business interests and safeguard Americans abroad)* **BL**

Differentiated Instruction

★ ★ ★ Activity: Multiple Learning Styles ★ ★ ★

Intrapersonal Have students investigate the Peace Corps to find the answers to the following questions:

• When was it founded?
• What is its purpose?
• What effect has it had on U.S. foreign relations?
• What are the requirements for volunteers?
• What training do volunteers receive?

Students also may read accounts of individual Peace Corps volunteers' experiences. Then have students choose a country in which they might like to work as a Peace Corps volunteer. Have students write essays explaining the reasons for their choices and the things they would do as a Peace Corps volunteer in that country. **OL**

★★★★★★★★★★★★★★★★★★★★★★★★★★
Critical Thinking

Answer: Spending increased most in operations and maintenance. An increase in technology and weapons research, increasingly expensive global wars, and expanding global involvement of U.S. military forces have all contributed to the growth of military spending.

C Critical Thinking

Distinguishing Fact from Opinion Women were not allowed to enter military schools such as West Point until the 1970s, and only recently have they been allowed to fly combat aircraft and to serve aboard warships. Women are still restricted from ground combat duty and have never been eligible for the draft. Ask volunteers why they would support or oppose including women in a military draft. Ask the class to identify facts and opinions in their explanations. **Ask:** Why do you think women currently are not eligible for conscription? Are there any civil rights issues at stake? *(Answers will vary, but students should point out that the Civil Rights Act of 1964 prohibited discrimination based on gender.)* **AL**

Hands-On Chapter Project

Step 3

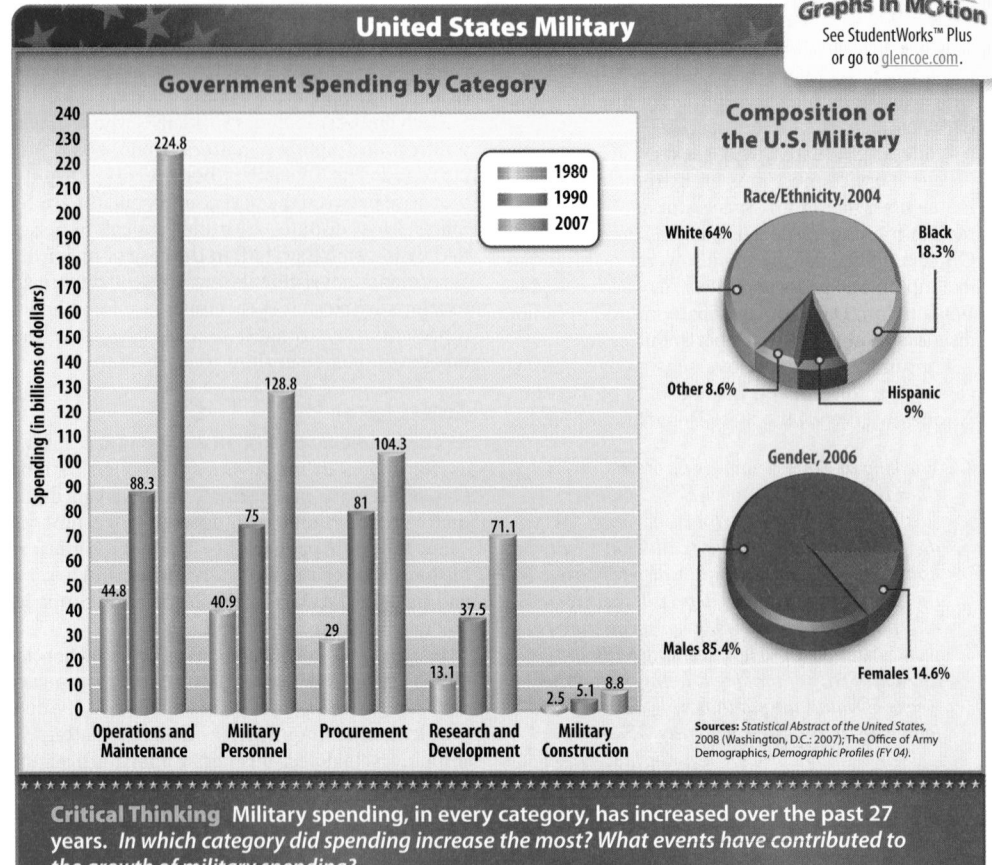

United States Military

Graphs In MOtion
See StudentWorks™ Plus or go to glencoe.com.

Government Spending by Category

Spending (in billions of dollars)

Legend: 1980, 1990, 2007

Operations and Maintenance: 44.8, 88.3, 224.8
Military Personnel: 40.9, 75, 128.8
Procurement: 29, 81, 104.3
Research and Development: 13.1, 37.5, 71.1
Military Construction: 2.5, 5.1, 8.8

Composition of the U.S. Military

Race/Ethnicity, 2004
White 64%
Black 18.3%
Other 8.6%
Hispanic 9%

Gender, 2006
Males 85.4%
Females 14.6%

Sources: Statistical Abstract of the United States, 2008 (Washington, D.C.: 2007); The Office of Army Demographics, Demographic Profiles (FY 04).

Critical Thinking Military spending, in every category, has increased over the past 27 years. *In which category did spending increase the most? What events have contributed to the growth of military spending?*

The Department of Defense

To protect national security, the Department of Defense supervises the armed forces of the United States and makes sure these forces are strong enough to defend American interests. The Department of Defense assists the president in carrying out the duties of commander in chief.

Establishing the Department of Defense

Before 1947, the Departments of War and the Navy were responsible for the nation's defense. The country's experiences in coordinating military forces in World War II, however, prompted a military reorganization. The result was the National Security Establishment, which two years later became the Department of Defense. From the out-

set, the secretary of defense was a member of the president's cabinet.

Civilian Control of the Military

The Founders wanted to ensure that the military would always be subordinate to the civilian leaders of the government. As a result, the ultimate authority for commanding the armed forces rests with the civilian commander in chief, the president of the United States.

Congress also exercises **considerable** authority over military matters. Because of its constitutional power over appropriations, Congress determines how much money the Department of Defense will spend each year.

Congress also has the power to determine how each branch of the armed forces will be organized and governed. In order to maintain civilian control

624 UNIT 7: *Public Policies and Services*

Analyzing Issues

Step 3: Preparing Presentations Groups will compile the information they have researched and prepare class presentations.

Directions Ask groups to divide tasks among themselves and prepare presentations that 1) summarize economic and political conditions in the area, 2) analyze U.S. foreign policy,

and 3) explain how economic connections and other factors affect U.S. foreign policy.

Visualizing Issues Groups will prepare visual aids to accompany their analyses. Discuss any problems they may be having in preparing the presentations. **OL**

(Chapter Project continued in Section 4.)

of the military, the top leaders of the Department of Defense all are required to be civilians.

Size of the Department of Defense

With more than 700,000 civilian employees and more than 1 million military personnel on active duty, the Department of Defense is the largest executive department. It is headquartered in the Pentagon in Arlington, Virginia, near Washington, D.C.

Army, Navy, and Air Force

Among the major divisions within the Department of Defense are the Departments of the Army, the Navy, and the Air Force. A civilian secretary heads each branch. The United States Marine Corps, under the jurisdiction of the Navy, maintains separate leadership, identity, and traditions.

The Joint Chiefs of Staff

The president, the National Security Council, and the secretary of defense rely on the Joint Chiefs of Staff (JCS) for military advice. This group is made up of the top-ranking officers of the armed forces. Included are the Chief of Staff of the Army, Chief of Staff of the Air Force, and the Chief of Naval Operations. The Commandant of the Marine Corps also attends meetings of the Joint Chiefs of Staff. The fifth and sixth members are the Chairperson and Vice Chairperson of the Joint Chiefs of Staff. The Chairperson is appointed for a two-year term by the president.

A Volunteer Military

The United States has used two methods of staffing its armed forces—by **conscription,** or compulsory military service, and by using volunteers. Conscription was first used during the Civil War and was implemented during World War I and World War II.

By executive order, President Richard Nixon **W** suspended conscription, or the draft, in 1973. Since then, membership in the military has been voluntary. Nixon's order, however, did not repeal the law that created the Selective Service System that administered the draft. For that reason, males between the ages of 18 and 25 could be required to serve if conscription is reinstated.

Military Registration

Since 1980, all young men who have passed their eighteenth birthdays are required to register their names and addresses with local draft boards. Though women are not eligible to be drafted, they may volunteer to serve in any branch of the armed services. All military services are now committed to the goal of increasing the number of female recruits.

> **Government ONLINE**
> **Student Web Activity** Visit glencoe.com and enter **QuickPass**™ code USG9822c22. Click on Student Web Activity and complete the activity about the State and Defense Departments.

W **Writing Support**

Personal Writing Have students write a short story in which the draft is reinstated. **Ask:** Are you drafted or is anyone you know drafted? How does the draftee react? Why has the government reinstated the draft? **OL**

Assess

Assign the Section 3 Assessment as homework or as an in-class activity, or have students take Section Quiz 22-3 from *Section Quizzes and Chapter Tests.*

Close

Accessing Prior Knowledge Have students think of countries in which the military is not controlled by civilians. **Ask:** What problems have resulted? **OL**

> **Government ONLINE**
> Objectives and answers to the Student Web Activity can be found in the **Web Activity Lesson Plan** at glencoe.com. Enter **QuickPass**™ code USG9085c22T.

SECTION 3 Review

Vocabulary

1. **Explain** the significance of: embassy, consulate, consul, passport, visa, conscription.

Main Ideas

2. **Describing** List the powers of Congress in military matters.
3. **Examining** How did the Founders ensure civilian control of the military?
4. **Identifying** Who are the members of the Joint Chiefs of Staff?

Critical Thinking

5. **Evaluating** Do you think a volunteer armed forces will perform better or worse than one of draftees?

6. **Organizing** Use a graphic organizer like the one below to show the organizational structure of the State Department.

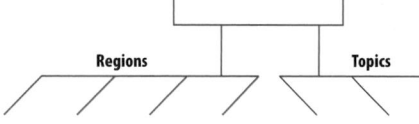

Writing About Government

7. **Persuasive Writing** What foreign policy goals do you think the State Department should carry out today? Review the major foreign policy goals of the United States outlined in Section 1. Choose the two goals that you think are most important today. Write and present a two-minute speech outlining why you think these goals are the most important.

CHAPTER 22: *Foreign Policy and Defense* **625**

Section 3 Review

★ Answers ★

1. All definitions can be found in the section and the Glossary.
2. Congress controls military spending and how the military will be organized and governed.
3. The Founders made the president the civilian commander in chief of the armed forces.
4. Chief of Staff of the Army, Chief of Staff of the Air Force, Chief of Naval Operations, the Commandant of the Marine Corps, and the Chairman and Vice Chairman of the Joint Chiefs, who are appointed by the president to a two-year term

5. Answers will vary, but may include the view that some volunteers may join for other than patriotic reasons.
6. Secretary of State: regions—African, European/Canadian, East Asian/Pacific, Inter-American, Near East/South Asian; topics—intelligence and research, political and military, education and culture
7. Students' speeches should logically outline why they believe the goals they have chosen are most important.

Class Debate

Organize students into three groups: the Bush administration, the attorneys representing Salim Hamdan, and the jury that will decide which point of view they find most persuasive.

The Court's Decision

On June 29, 2006, in a 5-to-3 decision, the U.S. Supreme Court ruled that the administration did not have the authority to establish military commissions without congressional authorization; that the military commission failed to meet the standards required by the Uniform Code of Military Justice; that preventing a detainee (and his counsel) from learning of the evidence of the crime for which he is on trial was unlawful.

The Court also ruled that the Geneva Conventions *do* apply to detainees at Guantanamo Bay. The military commission established by the administration was in violation of the Geneva Conventions, which require trials to take place before a "regularly constituted court." The commission, according to the Court, did not meet the standards of trial protections required by international law.

Do Enemy Combatants Have Rights?

Hamdan v. *Rumsfeld*, 2006

Do the federal courts have the authority to hear petitions filed by terrorist suspects detained at Guantanamo Bay? Is the military commission system set up by the Bush administration to try detainees legal? Are the Geneva Conventions enforceable in federal courts?

Facts of the Case

Salim Ahmed Hamdan, once the driver for al-Qaeda founder Osama bin Laden, was captured and turned over to the U.S. military during the 2001 invasion of Afghanistan. In 2002 he was sent to the U.S. military base at Guantanamo Bay, Cuba. Hamdan, a Yemeni citizen, was later charged with conspiracy "to commit . . . offenses triable by military commission."

Hamdan filed a writ of habeas corpus, challenging the legality of his imprisonment. Before his petition was ruled on, a military tribunal declared him an enemy combatant. Later, the district court ruled that before a military commission could try him, he must be given a hearing to determine if he was a prisoner of war as defined by the international Geneva Conventions. When the Circuit Court of Appeals reversed the decision, the U.S. Supreme Court agreed to hear the case.

The Constitutional Question

Hamdan argued that the military commission did not have the authority to try him. He challenged the legality of the military commission system established by the Bush administration on three grounds. First, its procedures did not follow the Uniform Code of Military Justice (UCMJ). Second, conspiracy was not a war crime and could not be considered one unless Congress passed a law to designate it as such. Third, the commission system violated Hamdan's right to a trial by a regularly constituted tribunal under the Geneva Conventions since the commission system could prevent a defendant from learning about the evidence against him or could exclude it from the actual trial.

The Bush administration rejected Hamdan's claims. It argued that the military commissions were legal and that they had implicitly been authorized by the 2001 Authorization for Use of Military Force Act. The administration further argued that the president had the authority to declare conspiracy a war crime and did not need explicit congressional approval to do so. As for the Geneva Conventions, the government maintained that these conventions could not be enforced through the federal courts.

Debating the Issue

Questions to Consider

1. Should enemy combatants have the right to petition in the federal courts?
2. Should a civilian court have the authority to rule on the legality of a military court proceeding?

You Be the Judge

Should enemy combatants have rights? Should they have access to the U.S. justice system? What limits, if any, should there be on the president's power in the war on terrorism?

▼ Lt. Commander Charles Swift, right, and Heal Katyal, were the lawyers for Salim Ahmed Hamdan.

Debating the Issue Answers

Questions to Consider

1. Yes: federal courts have safeguards to protect the innocent. No: federal courts lack the proper safeguards to deal with enemy combatants, and soldiers cannot collect evidence on the battleground.
2. Yes: civilian courts protect the rights of the accused and provide recourse through an appeals process.

No: military courts are set up to keep classified information secret and deal with the realities of battlefield captures, neither of which are covered in civilian courts.

You Be the Judge

Yes: combatants have rights given to them through signed treaties.

The U.S. justice system is the best place to assert those rights. No: Enemy combatants have no rights because they are not U.S. citizens and have fought against the United States. They should not gain access to the U.S. justice system. Students' answers will vary on limits to the presidential powers, but they should defend their answers.

Foreign Policy In Action

Reader's Guide

Content Vocabulary
- ★ mutual defense alliance *(p. 627)*
- ★ regional security pact *(p. 627)*
- ★ multilateral treaty *(p. 629)*
- ★ bilateral treaty *(p. 629)*
- ★ collective security *(p. 629)*
- ★ sanction *(p. 630)*

Academic Vocabulary
- ★ minimize *(p. 627)*
- ★ framework *(p. 628)*
- ★ nuclear *(p. 629)*

Reading Strategy
Use a graphic organizer like the one below to list the foreign policies the government uses to ensure the nation's security.

National Security

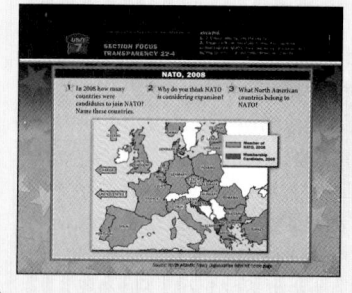

Issues in the News

Throughout 2008, President George W. Bush tried to get Congress to ratify a free-trade agreement with South Korea. "Free trade means good-paying jobs for Americans, and so Congress needs to pass [it and other trade agreements], for the sake of economic vitality," said Bush, but he also acknowledged that it would be an uphill struggle. Signed in June 2007 by the United States and South Korea, the trade deal faced stiff opposition in both countries. In the United States, congressional Democrats and organized labor refused to back the agreement because South Korea maintained restrictions on many U.S. beef imports. In 2003 South Korea banned U.S. beef imports because of concerns about mad cow disease in American beef products. The ban was partially lifted three years later, but continuing safety concerns among the South Koreans has kept South Korea's government from lifting all their restrictions on U.S. beef.

▲ President George W. Bush with South Korean President Lee Myung-bak near Camp David

Reader's Guide

Answers to Graphic:
- Alliances and pacts
- Foreign aid programs
- Economic sanctions
- Military action

In recent years, many nations have relaxed their international trade restrictions, but differences often develop between and within countries about which products to include—or not to include—in any agreement. In trade as well as other issues, the desire to preserve national security and economic well-being often can lead to disagreements and even conflicts among nations. To **minimize** the danger to national security, the United States tries to settle such conflicts peacefully and to negotiate agreements with foreign governments. The tools that are available include alliances, programs of foreign aid, economic sanctions, and, in extreme circumstances, military action.

Alliances and Pacts

Throughout history, when nations felt a common threat to their security, they came together to negotiate **mutual defense alliances.** Nations that became allies under such alliances usually agreed to support one another in case of an attack. The United States has signed mutual defense treaties with nations in three regions. Through such alliances, the United States has committed itself to defending Western Europe; the North Atlantic, Central and South America; and the island nations of the South Pacific. The treaties that protect these areas are referred to as **regional security pacts.**

CHAPTER 22: *Foreign Policy and Defense* **627**

R Reading Strategies	**C** Critical Thinking	**D** Differentiated Instruction	**W** Writing Support	**S** Skill Practice
Additional Resources • Guid. Read. Act., p. 81 • Quizzes/Tests, pp. 272–280	**Teacher Edition** • Analyzing Primary Sources, p. 629 **Additional Resources** • Read. Essen., pp. 257–259	**Teacher Edition** • Visual/Spatial, p. 629 **Additional Resources** • Foldables, p. 65	**Teacher Edition** • Narrative Writing, p. 630 **Additional Resources** • Coop. Learning Act., pp. 15–16	**Teacher Edition** • Map Skills, p. 628 **Additional Resources** • Ch. Summaries, pp. 64–66

Teach

S Skill Practice

Map Skills Call on volunteers to find on a world map the areas of the world involved in NATO. For fun or for extra credit, see if students can point out all 26 NATO members. *(Belgium, Bulgaria, Canada, the Czech Republic, Denmark, Estonia, France, Germany, Greece, Hungary, Iceland, Italy, Latvia, Lithuania, Luxembourg, the Netherlands, Norway, Poland, Portugal, Romania, Slovakia, Slovenia, Spain, Turkey, the United Kingdom, and the United States)* **OL**

Did You Know?

Iceland, the only member of NATO that does not have its own standing army, joined on the condition that membership in NATO did not mean it would be expected to establish one. The other members consented to these terms in part because of Iceland's strategic position on the Atlantic Ocean. Conversely, the United States, France, and the United Kingdom are the only three NATO members that have nuclear weapons.

Additional Support

TIME For the Record

Difficult Diplomacy A president's career often hinges on how he deals with international incidents. Just ask Jimmy Carter. In 1979 anti-American students in Iran held 52 members of the U.S. embassy hostage in Tehran. President Carter tried unsuccessfully to get the Americans released by using economic pressure, diplomacy, and finally military force. The frustrating situation angered Americans and is widely believed to have contributed to Carter's loss to Ronald Reagan in the 1980 election. After promising to release Iranian assets, Reagan got the hostages—who had spent 444 days in captivity—released, thus boosting his popularity.

The North Atlantic Treaty Organization

In 1945 the United States and leaders of the war-torn nations in Western Europe agreed to protect each other from domination by the Soviet Union. The mutual defense treaty that was the basis for the North Atlantic Treaty Organization (NATO) stated: "The parties agree that an armed attack against one or more of them in Europe or North America shall be considered an attack against them all."

During the Cold War, NATO countered the military might of the Soviet Union by stationing troops from the United States, West Germany, Great Britain, and other NATO nations on military bases across Western Europe under a single NATO commander. By providing this **framework** of military security, NATO gave the nations of Western Europe time to establish solid democratic governments and strong, free market economies. While primarily a military alliance, NATO also served as a useful place for American and European policymakers to meet regularly and discuss mutual problems.

The end of the Cold War also meant the end of NATO's original purpose, but it was not the end of NATO. Since the major military threat to its members ended in the early 1990s, the alliance has been redefining itself in two ways.

First, NATO has expanded its mission to include crisis intervention and peacekeeping in other areas of the world. When war broke out in Bosnia in 1995, NATO intervened with air strikes that brought an end to the fighting. Then, in 1999 NATO used a massive bombing campaign followed by the insertion of NATO peacekeeping troops to halt Serbian aggression in the province of Kosovo. Another crisis intervention occurred in 2001 when NATO troops moved into Macedonia to stop the fighting between the country's ethnic Macedonian majority and an ethnic Albanian minority. After the September 2001 terrorist attacks on the United States, NATO countries pledged military and other kinds of assistance in the war on terrorism.

Second, NATO has expanded its membership. In 1999 three former Warsaw Pact nations—Poland, Hungary, and the Czech Republic—were invited to join. Russia was made a NATO partner in 2002. While not the same as membership, partnership allows Russia to take an active role in alliance discussions. Seven other former Communist countries—Bulgaria, Estonia, Latvia, Lithuania, Romania, Slovakia, and Slovenia—entered the alliance in 2004. This growth in membership means that the global responsibilities of the United States have increased. Expansion also means that the United States could become involved in more peacekeeping missions such as those in Bosnia, Kosovo, and Macedonia. President George W. Bush has supported expansion of NATO membership. "All of Europe's new democracies," he stated, "should have the same chance for security and freedom and the same chance to join the institutions of Europe."

At the same time, many European leaders have observed that the United States is less interested in NATO now than it was during the Cold War. They note that the United States is becoming more concerned with threats to its national security that arise outside of Europe. Further, they note that in recent years, the United States has spent more than twice as much on national defense than all of the other NATO members combined. As a result, many European leaders believe that the United States is less concerned with cooperating with its allies and more willing to act on its own when it deals with global threats to American security.

Activity: Cooperative Learning Activity

Presenting Current Foreign Policy
Organize the class into seven groups and assign each group one of the following areas: Nigeria, China, Japan, Western Europe, Eastern Europe, Latin America, or the Middle East. Have each group present a report on current U.S. policy toward its assigned area. Have each student from each group take on a specific task such as obtaining resources, researching, writing, or presenting. Have a spokesperson for each group present a five-minute report and then open the topic for class discussion. **OL**

Latin America and the Pacific

In 1947 the United States and its Latin American neighbors signed the Rio Pact. Among its provisions is this statement:

> *An armed attack by any State against an American State shall be considered as an attack against all the American States, and, consequently, each one of the . . . Contracting Parties undertakes to assist in meeting the attack.*
>
> —Rio Pact, 1947

Since 1947 most Latin American nations and the United States have participated in the Rio Pact. Cuba withdrew from the pact in 1960 after the Cuban Revolution. In 1948 the United States signed a related treaty, establishing the Organization of American States (OAS). Unlike the Rio Pact, the OAS is primarily concerned with promoting economic development.

The United States also has a regional security pact with Australia and New Zealand. The ANZUS Pact, signed in 1951, obliged Australia, New Zealand, and the United States to come to one another's aid in case of attack. In 1984 New Zealand adopted a policy that excluded **nuclear** weapons and nuclear-powered ships from the nation's ports and waters. In response, the United States announced in 1986 that it would no longer guarantee New Zealand's security under the ANZUS treaty.

Bilateral Treaties of Alliance

NATO, the Rio Pact, OAS, and ANZUS are all examples of **multilateral treaties.** Multilateral treaties are international agreements signed by several nations. The United States has also signed bilateral treaties of alliance. A **bilateral treaty** is an agreement that involves only two nations.

One bilateral treaty, signed in 1951, makes the United States an ally of Japan. A similar treaty, also signed in 1951, pledges the United States to the defense of the Philippines. A third bilateral treaty, signed in 1953, makes the United States an ally of South Korea.

The United States has alliances with almost 50 nations. These nations can count on the military support of the United States in case of an attack. The goal of these treaties is to provide **collective security** for the United States and its allies. Collective security is a system by which member nations agree to take joint action against a nation that attacks any one of them.

U.S. Foreign Aid

Principal Recipients by Region, 2005

Other Unspecified 21.0%
Africa South of the Sahara 13.2%
Asia 6.8%
Middle East, North Africa, and Central Asia 44.9%
Western Europe 0.3%
Eastern Europe 3.2%
Russia 4.5%
Latin America 6.2%

Source: *Statistical Abstract of the United States,* 2008 (Washington, D.C.: 2007).

Critical Thinking The United States spent over $31 billion in foreign aid in the 2005 fiscal year. *Which regions receive the most aid from the United States? Why do you think this is so?*

Foreign Aid Programs

Military alliances are one benefit the United States can offer friendly nations. It can also offer military support for the purchase of American armaments. Economic aid is another benefit that American leaders can offer. Since the end of World War II, this aid has had two purposes: To establish friendly relations with other nations and to help them emerge as eventual economic partners.

Many developing nations have problems satisfying even the minimum needs of their people for food, housing, and education. They urgently need loans and technical assistance. Since 1946, the United States has provided more than $300 billion in economic aid worldwide and about $160 billion in military aid. Today the Agency for International Development (AID), an agency of the State Department, administers economic aid. AID has considerable independence and dispenses loans and technical assistance to countries throughout the world with very little direction from the U.S. secretary of state.

Critical Thinking

Answer: The Middle East, North Africa, and Central Asia receive the most aid. Many countries in these areas are impoverished and have few natural resources.

C Critical Thinking

Analyzing Primary Sources
Have students reread the excerpt from the Rio Pact. **Ask:** How does this excerpt show the influence of NATO? *(NATO stated: "The parties agree that an armed attack against one or more of them in Europe or North America shall be considered an attack against them all.")* **BL**

D Differentiated Instruction

Visual/Spatial The UN was at first severely limited by Cold War rivalries. Some people hope it will be better able to fulfill its mission in the post–Cold War world. Have students create charts showing the organization of the UN's main organs and agencies. To go with their charts, students should write a brief paragraph explaining the work of each major organ and agency. Allow students to work in pairs or small groups. **BL**

Hands-On Chapter Project

Step 4

Analyzing Issues

Step 4: Presenting Issues Groups will make presentations to the class.

Directions Have each group give its presentation. Some group members should present the visuals while others present their analyses.

Analyzing Presentations Have the class ask questions of each group. Then vote on which presentation was most effective and ask students to explain why. **OL**

Caption Answer: No, although Congress *does* have to approve funds to conduct military operations, which is why "the power of the purse" belongs to the legislative branch.

W Writing Support

Narrative Writing Ask students to write a short narrative from the point of view of a citizen of a country on which harsh economic sanctions have been imposed. **Ask:** Why are economic sanctions an effective tool in foreign policy? **OL**

Assess

Assign the Section 4 Assessment as homework or as an in-class activity, or have students take Section Quiz 22-4 from *Section Quizzes and Chapter Tests.*

Close

Analyzing Primary Sources It has been said that nations fall "from within," not "from without." **Ask:** To which tool of foreign policy does that statement relate? *(economic aid)* **OL**

Section 4 Review

War and Foreign Policy The war in Iraq began as a mission to remove its leader from power because he was alleged to have weapons of mass destruction. Here two American soldiers are seen leaving a Bradley Fighting Vehicle as they prepare to search a factory in Baghdad. *When the United States goes to war, does Congress have to pass a formal declaration of war?*

Economic Sanctions

Alliances and economic benefits are two methods of influencing other nations. The withdrawal or denial of benefits is a third diplomatic strategy. American policymakers sometimes use it to show that they oppose another nation's policies.

One way of withdrawing benefits is by applying sanctions. **Sanctions** are measures such as withholding loans, arms, or economic aid to force a foreign government to cease certain activities. During this century, the United States has employed sanctions more than 75 times. Sanctions were directed against Iraq beginning in 1990, but most were lifted in 2003 following the war between Iraq and U.S.–led coalition forces.

The United States may also restrict trade with another nation as an economic sanction. In the 1980s, President Reagan banned the use of American technology in building a natural gas pipeline in the Soviet Union. He did this to protest the Soviet Union's suppression of a Polish trade union.

The Use of Military Force

Using military force, or threatening to use force, has always been an important tool of foreign policy. Some argue that using force represents a complete breakdown of diplomacy. Others counter that using force, including covert operations, can be an effective way to avoid larger wars, ward off an impending attack, or protect human rights in other countries from brutal dictators.

The Constitution divides the war power between the president and Congress. Nevertheless, in the last 50 years presidents have sent U.S. troops into battle on numerous occasions without asking Congress for a formal declaration of war. In the Korean War, the Vietnam War, and other conflicts in recent decades such as the war in Iraq, the president has instead asked Congress to authorize funds for military action.

★ SECTION 4 Review ★

Vocabulary

1. **Explain** the significance of: mutual defense alliance, regional security pact, multilateral treaty, bilateral treaty, collective security, sanction.

Main Ideas

2. **Identifying** List two mutual defense alliances, besides NATO, in which the United States is a partner.

3. **Analyzing** Why is NATO so important to the United States?

Critical Thinking

4. **Making Inferences** Why would the stipulation of "an attack against one shall be considered as an attack against all" create a sense of security?

5. **Organizing** Use a graphic organizer like the one below to show the types and purposes of foreign aid programs.

Types of Aid	Purposes

Writing About Government

6. **Expository Writing** Research the requirements needed to be Peace Corps volunteers and the kinds of work they perform. Write a summary that you will use to present your findings to the class.

630 UNIT 7: *Public Policies and Services*

Answers

1. All definitions can be found in the section and the Glossary.
2. Any two of the following: OAS, Rio Pact, ANZUS Pact
3. NATO guarantees the security of Western Europe and other nations that support U.S. economic and political interests.
4. Nations know they will not have to fight alone. Opposing nations may not want to risk a full-scale war with many nations.
5. military alliances—give military support so countries do not have to fight alone; economic aid—establishes positive relations with nations and helps them emerge as eventual economic partners
6. After volunteers have made their presentations, discuss the value of the Peace Corps in maintaining good relations with other nations.

Should the Draft Be Reintroduced?

The United States ended the military draft in 1973. Since then, the military has relied on an all-volunteer force. The quality and performance of the all-volunteer force have been widely praised. In the early twenty-first century, however, extended military commitments in Afghanistan, Iraq, and elsewhere began to stretch the military rather thin. This led some to call for the reintroduction of the draft.

YES

Reintroduction of the draft would be good for the military and the nation in general. Service to one's country is a duty of citizenship. The need to reintroduce the draft has become urgent as the military faces a potential crisis in troop strength. Troop levels are already strained, and the armed forces may not have enough troops to accomplish future missions as they arise. Military personnel have already been shifted to Iraq from other overseas posts, leaving strategic locations (including the Korean peninsula) vulnerable.

Furthermore, the reliance on an all-volunteer force has meant that military service has fallen disproportionately on the sons and daughters of America's poor. Attracted by the economic and educational opportunities the military offers, African Americans in particular take on a disproportionate share of the risks of protecting the nation. A draft would ensure that the responsibility for national defense is shouldered by all economic segments of American society.

NO

A draft is fundamentally undemocratic and a violation of this nation's principles. Drafting people into the armed services is effectively forcing them into involuntary servitude. It is morally wrong to take away people's personal freedom and put their lives at risk. By relying on a volunteer force, the military has attracted recruits who are committed to serving their country. As the surge in enlistments after the attacks of September 11, 2001, demonstrates, the military has little trouble attracting recruits when Americans are united behind a cause. Reinstating the draft and forcing people into military service would allow the government to pursue unpopular or unnecessary wars. If too few Americans are willing to enlist to fight in a war, then the nation needs to reconsider its overseas commitments.

The all-volunteer force has been hugely successful. The military has attracted a force that, on average, is better educated than their peers. Why undermine its effectiveness by forcing unwilling individuals to serve?

Debating the Issue

1. **Identifying** What arguments are made in favor of bringing back the draft?

2. **Explaining** Why do some people believe that maintaining an all-volunteer force is preferable to reinstituting the draft?

3. **Evaluating** With which point of view do you tend to agree? Explain your reasoning.

▶ Marine recruits at boot camp

Debating the Issue Answers

1. The United States needs more troops to sufficiently cover all of the world's strategic locations; a draft would help evenly distribute the burden of national defense among all economic echelons.

2. Volunteers are not only committed to serving their country, but are also a good indicator of the appropriateness of overseas commitments.

3. Students should support their opinions with references to the quotes, evidence from individual research, and logical arguments.

Teach

Setting Up the Debate

Researching Have students research the global locations in which U.S. troops are currently committed. Have them find out how many troops are stationed in each place. **Ask:** Why are troops stationed at these locations? *(Answers might include conflicts with the United States or its allies, peacekeeping missions, and so on.)* Do enough troops appear to be available for these missions? Is it possible that too many are committed? **OL**

Evaluating Have students research the arguments for and against reintroduction of the draft. Students should give specific arguments to support both points of view. **OL**

Concluding the Debate

Discuss these questions with students:

- Imagine a hypothetical situation in which the draft is reinstituted and you are drafted for an unpopular war. Would you go to war, or would you resist the draft as some did in the Vietnam era?

- Consider Israel, a country in which the majority of citizens (men and women) are drafted upon turning age 18. Despite a relatively small population, Israel maintains one of the strongest, most advanced military forces in the world. Do you think this is due in part to the draft?

ExamView® Assessment Suite

This easy-to-use software includes extensive question banks and allows you to create fully customized tests that can be administered in print or online.

Reviewing Vocabulary

1. e
2. c
3. d
4. f
5. b
6. a

Reviewing Main Ideas

7. Since World War II, United States foreign policy has been based on active participation in world affairs and resistance to communism. Beginning in the 1970s, the United States and communist nations followed a policy of détente. After the Cold War, the United States adjusted its foreign policy to meet the world's changed political environment.

8. White House staff, National Security Council, CIA, private individuals with specialized knowledge

9. It is divided into geographic and topical bureaus. It implements foreign policy, conducts foreign relations, handles diplomatic missions, manages the foreign service, and oversees embassies and consulates.

10. Governments influence other nations by their trade policies, foreign aid, treaties, sanctions, and through military actions.

Reviewing Vocabulary

Choose the letter of the correct content vocabulary word(s) below to complete the sentences.

- **a.** executive agreement
- **b.** internationalism
- **c.** sanction
- **d.** consulate
- **e.** isolationism
- **f.** multilateral treaty

1. In the 1800s, the United States avoided involvement in world affairs, a policy known as ____.
2. Imposing an economic ____ on another nation restricts trade with that nation.
3. Located in foreign cities, a(n) ____ promotes American business interests and safeguards American travelers.
4. An international agreement signed by a group of several nations is called a(n) ____.
5. The United States now follows a policy of ____ regarding world affairs.
6. A pact between the president and a foreign government head, called a(n) ____, does not require Senate approval.

Reviewing Main Ideas

Section 1 (pages 607–613)

7. **Examining** What have been the major characteristics of U.S. foreign policy since 1945?

Section 2 (pages 614–620)

8. **Identifying** Who, in addition to the cabinet, advises the president on foreign policy?

Section 3 (pages 621–625)

9. **Discussing** Describe the structure and function of the Department of State.

Section 4 (pages 627–630)

10. **Summarizing** How can the United States influence the policies of other nations?

Critical Thinking

11. 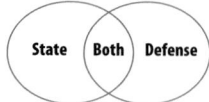 **Essential Question** Why do nations form bilateral and multilateral treaties?

12. **Synthesizing** Use a Venn diagram to show the overlapping roles of these departments.

State | Both | Defense

13. **Formulating** Many American presidents have achieved more success in foreign policy than in domestic policy. Explain why this might be so.

Chapter Summary

Foreign Policy Trends
- ★ **Isolationism**—The United States avoided foreign involvement until the late 1800s.
- ★ **Internationalism**—The United States expanded involvement after 1919 as it became a world power.
- ★ **Interdependence**—More emphasis since the end of the Cold War on cooperation to address global issues

Foreign Policy Powers
- ★ **President**—head of state and commander in chief
- ★ **Congress**—declares war, appropriates funds, ratifies treaties, confirms diplomatic appointments

Tools of Foreign Policy
- ★ Alliances and pacts
- ★ Foreign aid programs
- ★ Economic sanctions
- ★ Use or threat of military force

State and Defense Departments
- ★ **Department of State** advises president, conducts diplomacy, protects Americans abroad
- ★ **Department of Defense** supervises the armed forces and military missions under the president

Critical Thinking

11. Both provide collective security for nations that become allies.

12. State—makes foreign policy; Defense—provides military strength; Both—military strength helps make foreign policy effective

13. Answers will vary but may indicate that presidents have more freedom of action in foreign policy and are not as closely checked by Congress.

Government ONLINE Self-Check Quiz
Visit glencoe.com and enter *QuickPass*™ code USG9822c22.
Click on Self-Check Quizzes for additional test practice.

CHAPTER
22
Assessment
and Activities

Document-Based Questions

Analyzing Primary Sources

Read the excerpt below and answer the questions that follow.

George Kennan was an American diplomat in the Soviet Union in the 1940s and 1950s. The following excerpt details Kennan's vision of containment, the policy that was adopted by the United States during the Cold War.

66 *In these circumstances it is clear that the main element of any United States policy toward the Soviet Union must be that of a long-term, patient but firm and vigilant containment of Russian expansive tendencies. It is important to note, however, that such a policy has nothing to do with outward histrionics: with threats or blustering or superfluous gestures of outward 'toughness.' . . . [I]t is a sine qua non of successful dealing with Russia that the foreign government in question should remain at all times cool and collected and that its demands on Russian policy should be put forward in such a manner as to leave the way open for a compliance not too detrimental to Russian prestige.* 99

14. How does Kennan recommend that the United States deal with the Soviet Union's expansionist tendencies?

15. Do you think that this type of foreign policy practice is relevant today or similar to any ideas promoted by the U.S. government in its war on terror?

Applying Technology Skills

16. Using the Internet Go to the U.S. Department of State Web site and click on their Issues link. Choose a topic that interests you, or choose a particular country to read about or one of the "Popular Topics" listed, such as counterterrorism or women's issues. Take notes on what you read and then write a brief summary of what you have learned. Conclude your report by posing a question that you feel needs to be answered to clarify your understanding of the issue or country.

Interpreting Political Cartoons

Analyze the cartoon and answer the questions that follow. Base your answers on the cartoon and your knowledge of Chapter 22.

Daryl Cagle/Cagle Cartoons

17. How can you tell who the figure in the cartoon is and what is his apparent occupation?

18. By the symbolic image that cartoonist Daryl Cagle has chosen, what attitude is he displaying toward his subject?

19. What is the cartoonist saying about the role of the United States in the world?

Participating IN GOVERNMENT

20. Providing foreign aid is a way for the United States to maintain good relationships with other nations. Find out how you can contribute to an international relief effort. Outline the results of your research.

CHAPTER 22: *Foreign Policy and Defense* **633**

Interpreting Political Cartoons

17. The figure is President George W. Bush dressed as a juggling clown.

18. Students may say that by showing the president as a clown, Cagle is displaying a negative, irreverent attitude.

19. The United States has to juggle many tough, often baffling foreign policy issues.

Participating IN GOVERNMENT

20. Students may collect used textbooks for schools in developing nations, make personal care kits containing items such as soap and toothpaste, or raise money to donate to a world hunger fund. Note that the International Red Cross and church groups in the community may have suggestions for ways students can help.

Chapter Bonus Test Question

Ask: Which nation, though still a member of OAS, has been banned from all OAS activities since 1962? *(Cuba)*

Analyzing Primary Sources

14. Kennan recommends that U.S. foreign policy contain Soviet expansion around the world with a foreign policy that is firm but cool and straightforward. He also advises the United States to be sensitive to and careful not to harm Soviet prestige around the world, but he makes no direct military defense recommendations because those would be the responsibility of Congress and the president.

15. Answers may vary, but students should recognize that U.S. foreign policy shifted from containment to building democracy and promoting trade, then to preemption, or striking first to prevent terrorism.

Applying Technology Skills

16. Students' summaries should show an understanding of the chosen topic. Help students find a way to answer their question.

State *and* Local Government

UNIT PACING CHART*		
	Chapter 23	**Chapter 24**
Day 1	Unit Opener Chapter Opener Section 1	Chapter Opener Section 1
Day 2	Section 2	Section 2
Day 3	Section 3 Supreme Court Cases to Debate	Supreme Court Cases to Debate
Day 4	Section 4 Issues to Debate	Section 3 Issues to Debate
Day 5	Review Chapter Assessment	Review Chapter Assessment

*Unit Pacing Chart based on year-long course; modify pacing by half for semester-long course

 Teacher to Teacher

Al Fitzpatrick

Lincoln County School District Newport, OR

Issues of State and Local Governments
Students will arrange and conduct panel discussions about state and local issues. First, have students use media sources to prepare a list of current state and local issues, such as the following:

- Should drunk drivers who kill serve mandatory jail sentences?
- Should the state's bottle bill be expanded to require deposits on all bottled drinks?

Have pairs of students pick an issue. For each topic, provide the pair with a list of possible guest speakers (with phone numbers) in your area. Have each pair contact the speaker and explain the panel's topic and goals, invite him or her to speak to the class, and agree upon a date and time. (If the speaker is unavailable, encourage students to ask the person to suggest another speaker.)

Once speakers have accepted, each pair of students should prepare a list of questions and send it to their speaker. The day before each panel discussion, students should confirm the time and place with the speaker. Students should greet the speakers at the office, introduce them to the class, and conduct the panel discussion.

Author Note

Dear U.S. Government Teacher,

In teaching this unit, you might begin by asking students how well they feel they know their governor or mayor compared to the president. Students will probably have a much clearer idea of what the president stands for than they do of the governor. Is this because the media focus almost exclusively on the president and Congress in our great national pastime of politics? Or could it be that state and local leaders deal with more mundane issues—not war and peace, but local utilities or a 1 percent increase in the property tax?

When students become home owners and parents, they will recognize that local and state policies affect them directly. In any case, over their lifetime, students' civic duties will begin and end with the government closest to them. That is why this overview of the structure and responsibilities of state and local government is so important.

As you begin the unit, it might be useful to do a quick review with students on the definition of *federalism* (page 65) and the expanded discussion of that critical topic (Chapter 4, Sections 3 and 4) in order to gain perspective on the relationships between national, state, and local governments.

During the Reagan era, the attempt was made to de-emphasize the powers of the central government, and state governments were supposed to exercise more authority. Today the ideology of federalism has weakened, perhaps due to the threat of terrorism, perhaps due to budget stresses at every level. At the same time, state and local officials are initiating many policies to face economic and environmental challenges. Governors and mayors search overseas for investments and markets. Local activists pressure their community leaders to find innovative ways to be more efficient and thus protect the environment. The federalist tradition so central to the American republic continues.

Richard C. Remy

Richard C. Remy, Ph.D.
Author

Focus

Making It Relevant

Making Comparisons Write this list of federal officials on the board: president, vice president, attorney general, secretary of the treasury, Congress, House of Representatives, Senate, and Supreme Court. Briefly review the responsibilities of each. Then discuss how these responsibilities are carried out on the state and local levels, and by whom.

Unit Objectives

After studying this unit, students will be able to:

• **Discuss** the foundation, organization, and functions of state governments.

• **Summarize** the history, structure, and responsibilities of local governments.

Unit Overview

Unit 8 describes how state and local governments are organized as well as their powers and responsibilities.

Chapter 23 describes how state governments are organized and their powers and responsibilities.

Chapter 24 describes how local governments are organized and their powers and responsibilities.

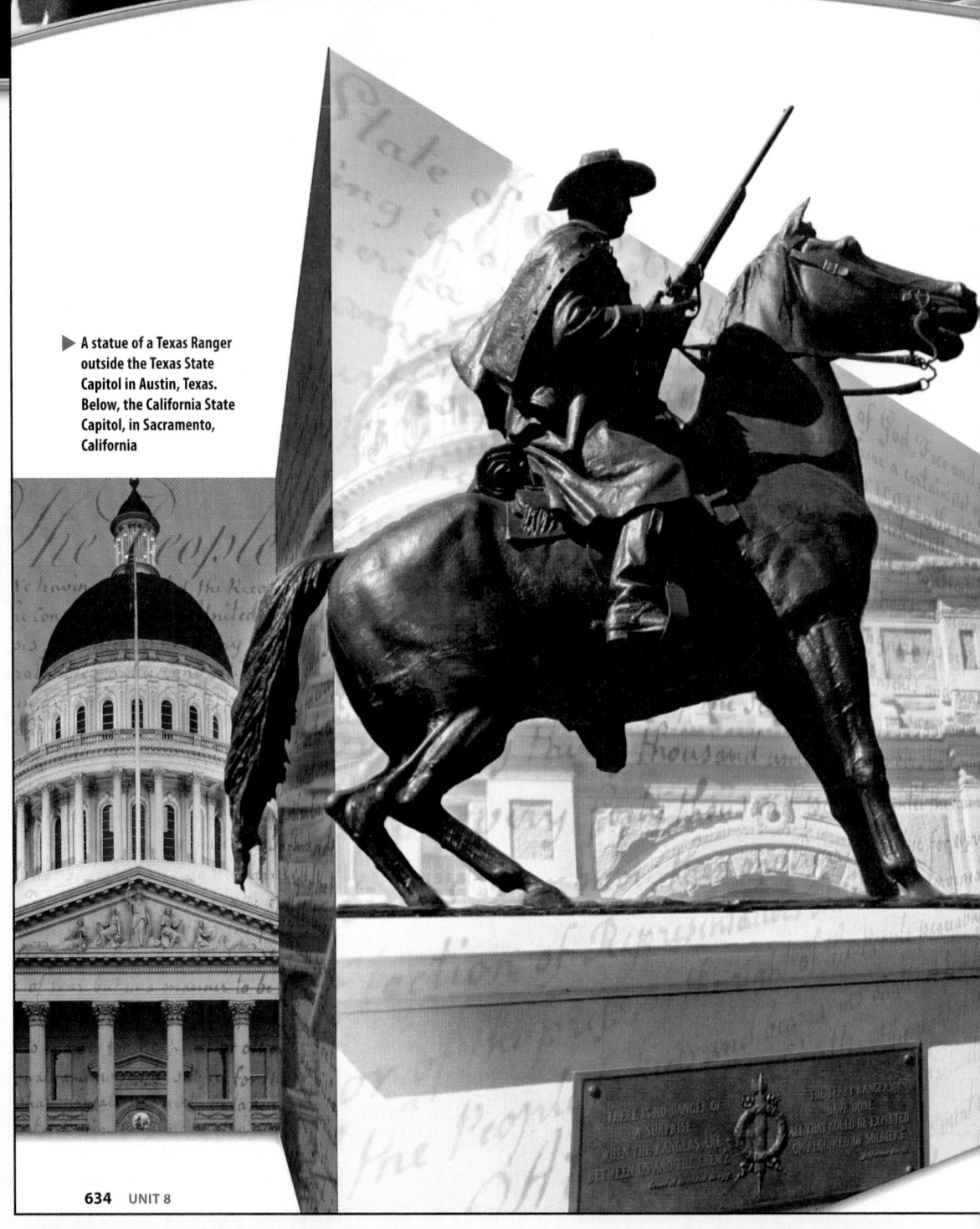

▶ A statue of a Texas Ranger outside the Texas State Capitol in Austin, Texas. Below, the California State Capitol, in Sacramento, California

634 UNIT 8

Activity: Launching the Unit

Researching Government Have students write a report that analyzes some aspect of their state or local government. Topics might include recent amendments to the state constitution, the governor's use of the line-item veto, relations between the mayor and the city council, and party politics in state or local government. Suggest that students illustrate their reports with quotations from leading state or local politicians and, where appropriate, charts, graphs, and diagrams. Select several students to present their reports to the class. **OL**

State *and* Local Government

Participating IN GOVERNMENT

BIG IDEA **Cultural Pluralism** The best way to appreciate how state officials and legislators consider the viewpoints of many groups is to visit the state capitol, a state agency, or court in your community. Make arrangements by calling ahead. Prepare questions in advance that ask your interviewee how he or she keeps in contact with all parts of your community. (You might ask them to give you an example of their agenda for an average week.)

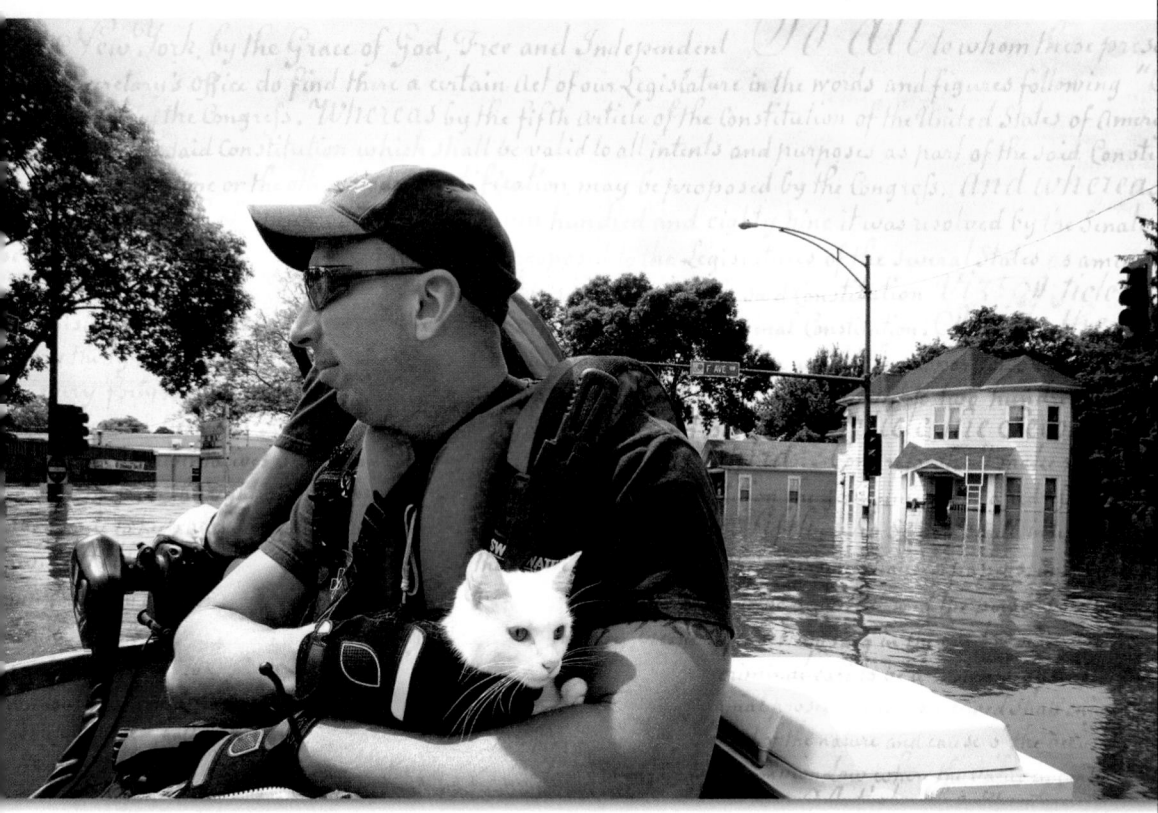

▲ A Cedar Rapids, Iowa, firefighter helping to evacuate victims of floodwaters.

635

Teach

S Skill Practice

Visual Literacy Students should examine the image about the flood evacuation on page 635. **Ask:** Why do you think the photographer chose this shot when he or she was sent to cover the Mississippi River flooding disaster? *(Students might comment that the angle of the photo is low so one can see how high and threatening the floodwaters are; also that the firefighters chose to save a helpless kitten in addition to its owner. This scene would rouse sympathy.)*

Online Current Events Update

History happens every day. Visit Glencoe's Online Current Events Update at <u>glencoe.com</u> to find news reports, features, maps, graphs, and images about events that shape our lives. Students can connect those events to historical events in world and American history by exploring related events on an interactive time line—a time line that ends with today.

Graduation: Exit With Success

Teaching Tip Assist students doing online research in selecting only reputable sources. For example, Web sites ending in *.gov, .org,* or *.edu* are generally trustworthy. Encourage students to look for historical museum sites and presidential libraries as they do their research for this chapter.

Extra Credit Project

Visualizing State and Local Governments
Supplement students' exploration of the unit by having them prepare posters that serve one or more of the following purposes:
- analyze the state or local government structure or a state or local government service
- campaign for a candidate for a state or local government office or for a state or local issue on the ballot

- encourage students to participate in their state or local government in various ways.

Encourage students to use a wide variety of media (for example, paint, photography, computer-generated artwork) to illustrate their topics. Display finished posters around the classroom as an aid to this chapter, or arrange for a "gallery walk" that groups posters by topic and allows student artists to explain their work. **OL**

Levels					Resources	Chapter Opener	Section 1	Section 2	Section 3	Section 4	Chapter Assess
BL	OL	AL	ELL		**FOCUS**						
BL	OL	AL	ELL	📠	**Section Focus Transparencies**		23-1	23-2	23-3	23-4	
					TEACH						
BL	OL		ELL	📁	**Reading Essentials and Study Guide (and Answer Key)**		p. 260	p. 263	p. 267	p. 271	
BL	OL		ELL	📁	**Guided Reading Activities**		p. 82	p. 83	p. 84	p. 85	
BL	OL		ELL	📁	**Vocabulary Activities**		p. 23				
BL	OL	AL	ELL	📁	**Chapter Summaries**					p. 67	
BL	OL			📁	**American Biographies**						
BL	OL	AL	ELL	📁	**Cooperative Learning Activities**						
	OL	AL	ELL	📁	**Government Simulations and Debate**				p. 50		
BL	OL	AL	ELL	📁	**Historical Documents and Speeches**			p. 23			
BL	OL	AL	ELL	📁	**Interpreting Political Cartoons**			p. 45			
BL	OL		ELL	📁	**Skill Reinforcement Activities**				p. 23		
BL	OL	AL	ELL	📁	**Source Readings**		p. 23				
BL	OL			📁	**Supreme Court Case Studies**						
BL	OL	AL	ELL	📁	**Participating in Government Activities**			p. 45			
BL	OL		ELL	📁	**Spanish Declaration of Independence and U.S. Constitution**	✓	✓	✓	✓	✓	✓
BL	OL	AL	ELL	📁	**NGS World Atlas, Spanish**	✓	✓	✓	✓	✓	✓
BL	OL	AL	ELL	📠	**Unit Overlay Transparencies, Strategies, and Activities**	✓	✓	✓	✓	✓	✓
BL	OL		ELL	📠	**Making It Relevant Transparencies**	✓	✓	✓	✓	✓	✓
BL	OL	AL	ELL	📠	**High School Writing Process Transparencies, Strategies, and Activities**	✓	✓	✓	✓	✓	✓
BL	OL	AL		📠	**American Art & Architecture Transparencies, Strategies, and Activities**	✓	✓	✓	✓	✓	✓

✓ Chapter- or unit-based activities applicable to all sections in this chapter

TeacherWorks™ Plus
All-In-One Planner and Resource Center

- Interactive Lesson Planner
- Interactive Teacher Edition
- Fully editable blackline masters
- Chapter Spotlight Videos Launch
- Differentiated Lesson Plans
- Printable reports of daily assignments
- Standards tracking system

Levels BL	OL	AL	ELL		Resources	Chapter Opener	Section 1	Section 2	Section 3	Section 4	Chapter Assess
					TEACH (continued)						
BL	OL			●	American Music: Hits Through History	✓	✓	✓	✓	✓	✓
BL	OL		ELL	📁	Reading Strategies for the Social Studies Classroom	✓	✓	✓	✓	✓	✓
			ELL	📁	English Language Learner Handbook	✓	✓	✓	✓	✓	✓
BL	OL		ELL	📁	Writer's Guidebook for Social Studies	✓	✓	✓	✓	✓	✓
BL	OL	AL	ELL	📁	Living Constitution, SE	✓	✓	✓	✓	✓	✓
BL	OL	AL	ELL	📁	Living Constitution, TAE	✓	✓	✓	✓	✓	✓
BL	OL			📁	NGS World Atlas, English	✓	✓	✓	✓	✓	✓
BL	OL		ELL	📁	The Constitution and You (poster set)	✓	✓	✓	✓	✓	✓
BL	OL	AL	ELL	📁	Spanish Chapter Summaries					p. 67	
BL	OL	AL	ELL	📁	Spanish Vocabulary Activities		p. 23				
BL	OL		ELL	📁	Spanish Reading Essentials and Study Guide (and Answer Key)		p. 260	p. 263	p. 267	p. 271	
BL	OL	AL	ELL	●	PresentationPlus! with MindJogger CheckPoint	✓	✓	✓	✓	✓	✓
					ASSESS						
BL	OL	AL	ELL	●	*ExamView® Assessment Suite*		23-1	23-2	23-3	23-4	Ch. 23
BL	OL	AL	ELL	📁	Authentic Assessment with Rubrics		p. 30				p. 30
BL	OL	AL	ELL	📁	Section Quizzes and Chapter Tests		p. 283	p. 284	p. 285	p. 286	pp. 287–294
BL	OL	AL	ELL	📁	Spanish Section Quizzes and Tests		p. 283	p. 284	p. 285	p. 286	pp. 287–294
					CLOSE						
BL			ELL	📁	Reteaching Activities					p. 23	p. 23
BL	OL	AL	ELL	●	StudentWorks™ Plus with Audio Summaries	✓	✓	✓	✓	✓	✓
BL	OL		ELL	🖨	Graphic Organizer Transparencies		✓	✓	✓	✓	
BL	OL		ELL	📁	High School Government Reading and Study Skills Foldables®		p. 66	p. 66	p. 66	p. 66	

Teach With Technology

What are Reproducible Lesson Plans?
Reproducible Lesson Plans (RLPs) are detailed lesson plans that teachers may use to prepare their lessons throughout the year.

How can RLPs help me teach?
RLPs are organized by chapter and also by section, suggesting where the wide variety of technology and ancillary products can be used within the book. RLPs are organized two ways:

- Teaching activities and ancillaries are presented using the FOCUS, TEACH, ASSESS, CLOSE organization of the Teacher Wraparound Edition.
- Teaching activities and ancillaries are also grouped by skill level, which helps you identify the activities that are appropriate for the students in your classroom.

RLPs are available on TeacherWorks™ Plus.

Government ONLINE
Visit glencoe.com and enter *QuickPass*™ code USG9085c23T for Chapter 23 resources.

You can easily launch a wide range of digital products from your computer's desktop with the McGraw-Hill Social Studies widget.

	Student	Teacher	Parent
Media Library			
• Student Edition Section Audio	●		●
• Chapter Spotlight Videos	●	●	●
***United States Government* Online Learning Center (Web Site)**			
• Chapter Overviews	●	●	●
• Multilingual Glossaries	●	●	●
• Study-to-Go	●	●	●
• Student Web Activities	●	●	●
• Self-Check Quizzes	●	●	●
• Online Student Edition	●	●	●
• Vocabulary eFlashcards	●	●	●
• Web Activity Lesson Plans		●	
• Vocabulary PuzzleMaker	●	●	●
• Landmark Supreme Court Cases	●	●	●
• Beyond the Textbook	●	●	●

READING SUPPORT FROM
JAMESTOWN EDUCATION

- **Timed Readings Plus in Social Studies** helps students increase their reading rate and fluency while maintaining comprehension. The 400-word passages are similar to those found on state and national assessments.

- **Reading in the Content Area: Social Studies** concentrates on six essential reading skills that help students better comprehend what they read. The book includes 75 high-interest nonfiction passages written at increasing levels of difficulty.

- **Reading Social Studies** includes strategic reading instruction and vocabulary support in Social Studies content for ELLs and native speakers of English.
www.jamestowneducation.com

Reading List Generator CD-ROM
GLENCOE BOOKLINK 3

Use this database to search more than 30,000 titles to create a customized reading list for your students.

- Reading lists can be organized by students' reading level, author, genre, theme, or area of interest.

- The database provides Degrees of Reading Power™ (DRP) and Lexile™ readability scores for all selections.

- A brief summary of each selection is included.

Economics Connection

Personal Finance Literacy

Cash or Credit?
Tell students that there are times when buying on credit may make financial sense, such as:

- When you need to buy something expensive before you have the money to pay for it, such as a car or college

- To establish a credit history, which is important to do as early as possible

- When you buy something over the Internet

- When you want a record of your purchase

- When you want to consolidate your bills into one payment

- When you don't want to carry cash with you

- When you want the legal protection of being able to return an item or reject something you did not order

Credit cards: Many people get into financial trouble because they think of credit cards as cash. When the monthly statement arrives, they pay only the minimum payment required—not the full balance. So their debt continues to grow. Here are the pitfalls of overusing credit cards:

- Higher cost of items (interest and finance charges are added to the original cost)

- Leads to impulse buying of unneeded items
- Can plunge a person into deep debt if the balance is not paid off every month
- Late payments damage credit ratings
- Prevents saving and investing

Calculating the True Cost
Suppose you see a jacket you want on sale for $200. You have a credit card that charges an 18 percent annual percentage rate (APR). What should you do? First, ask yourself: Do I really need the jacket? Do I need it now or could I wait until I can pay cash? If you buy the jacket now and take two years to pay off the balance (the total amount you owe), you'll pay $236 for the jacket ($200 + 18% = $236), plus tax.

Did You Know?

According to the Federal Reserve, one-fourth of American households do not have credit cards. Of those who do, 42 percent pay off the balances every month. The median balance for households with credit card debt was $2,200 in 2004, the latest data available, and 8.3 percent of card-holders owed $9,000 or more.

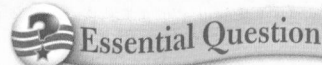

CHAPTER 23

🔊 Chapter Audio　　📺 Spotlight Video

State Governments

Essential Question

Like the federal government, every state has a constitution and three branches of government: an executive branch headed by a governor, a legislative branch (most state legislatures are bicameral), and a judicial branch capped by a supreme court. Key functions of state governments that directly affect citizens are regulating business, operating the criminal justice system, and financing and administering a state's educational system.

Chapter Spotlight Video

To generate student interest and provide a springboard for class discussion, access the Chapter 23 Video at glencoe.com or on the video DVD.

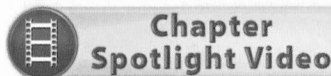

Dinah Zike's Foldables are three-dimensional, interactive graphic organizers that help students practice basic writing skills, review key vocabulary terms, and identify main ideas. Have students complete this chapter's Foldable activity or activities in *Dinah Zike's Reading and Study Skills Foldables* booklet. **OL**

▲ The Iowa State Capitol with its distinctive dome gilded in gold leaf

Essential Question

How is your state government structured, and why does it have more direct influence over citizens' lives than any other government unit?

Government ONLINE
Chapter Overview Visit glencoe.com and enter *QuickPass*™ code USG9822c23 for an overview, a quiz, and other chapter resources.

Government ONLINE
Visit glencoe.com and enter *QuickPass*™ code USG9085c23T for Chapter 23 Resources including Chapter Overview, Student Web Activity, Self-Check Quiz, and other materials for students and teachers.

Launching the Chapter

From Territory to State Many states began as territories. They were organized in order to govern land that was newly acquired by the United States, mostly in the 1800s. In 1959 two territories, Hawaii and Alaska, became states. The five remaining territories are American Samoa, Guam, Northern Mariana Islands, U.S. Virgin Islands, and Puerto Rico. Overall, 31 territories have applied for and won statehood. Organized territories have been in existence since 1789. The first was the Northwest Territory, from which Ohio, Indiana, Illinois, Michigan, and Wisconsin were carved. The process for granting statehood used for the Northwest Territory set the precedent by which the nation expanded west by adding new states. **Essential Question:** How might the structure of your state's government be different now than when it was first founded? *(Answers will vary for different states.)* **OL**

State Constitutions

Reader's Guide

Content Vocabulary
* ★ initiative (p. 639)
* ★ constitutional convention (p. 639)
* ★ constitutional commission (p. 640)

Academic Vocabulary
* ★ utility (p. 638)
* ★ aspect (p. 638)
* ★ revision (p. 640)

Reading Strategy
As you read, create a table similar to the one below to list the similarities and differences between the U.S. Constitution and state constitutions.

United States Constitution	Both	State Constitutions

Focus

Reader's Guide

Answers to Graphic:
U.S. Constitution: amendment process requires approval from each state, supreme above state constitutions, shorter than state constitutions;
Both: create structure of government, uphold separation of powers, contain bills of rights, can be amended;
State Constitutions: define power of local governments, regulate ways to raise and spend money, establish independent agencies

Issues in the News

For years, some groups in Alabama have tried to revise the state's 1901 constitution because they say it limits local government authority over land and tax policy. This limit, they claim, holds back economic growth. Opponents said that the limit is a healthy check on local government power. In 2008 the reformers again introduced a bill to give voters the chance to call for a convention to overhaul the constitution. "I guess we're eternal optimists," said Lenora Pate, a chairperson for the Alabama Citizens for Constitutional Reform. An opposing group, the Alabama Farmers' Federation, said that a convention was unnecessary and that article-by-article revision should be enough. "You already have representatives elected by the people, elected by a popular vote who can do that," said federation spokesperson Jeff Helms.

▲ Members of the Alabama House of Representatives in session

As Alabamans have learned, changing a state constitution is not an easy process. In North America, constitutional government began with colonial charters, long before there was a U.S. Constitution. When the colonies declared their independence in 1776, some states kept their colonial charters as their constitution. Other states drew up new constitutions. Since 1776, the 50 states have had a total of 146 constitutions. Only 20 states have kept their original documents, and all states have added many amendments.

Why Constitutions Matter

State constitutions are important for several reasons. First, state constitutions create the structure of state government. Like the federal Constitution, every state constitution provides for separation of powers among three branches of government—legislative, executive, and judicial. State constitutions outline the organization of each branch, the powers and terms of various offices, and the method of election for state officials.

Second, state constitutions establish the different types of local government, such as counties, townships, municipalities, special districts, parishes, and boroughs. State constitutions usually define the powers and duties as well as the organization of these different forms of local governments.

Third, state constitutions regulate the ways state and local governments can raise and spend money. In many states, for example, the state constitution

Resource Manager

R Reading Strategies	C Critical Thinking	D Differentiated Instruction	W Writing Support	S Skill Practice
Teacher Edition • Outlining, p. 638 **Additional Resources** • Guid. Read. Act., p. 82 • Quizzes/Tests, p. 283	**Additional Resources** • Read. Essen., pp. 260–262	**Teacher Edition** • Interpersonal, p. 639 **Additional Resources** • Foldables, p. 66 • Source Readings, p. 23	**Additional Resources** • Authentic Assess., p. 30	**Additional Resources** • Vocab. Act., p. 23

Teach

R Reading Strategy

Outlining Write *state constitutions* on the board, circle it, and draw four lines radiating from the circle. As students identify the four purposes of state constitutions, write each response along one of the lines. Ask students for an example of each purpose. **BL**

Linking ☆ Past & Present

Understanding State Principles In *Democracy in America,* French writer Alexis de Tocqueville (1805–1859) noted: "The great political principles which now rule American society were born and grew up in the state. . . . So one must understand the state to gain the key to the rest." Invite students to respond to this view.

Hands-On Chapter Project

Step 1

Governmental Transitions

State Constitutions
Citizens celebrated the inauguration of each new government as colonies adopted state constitutions. John L. Krimmel captures the excitement of a new state government on Election Day in Philadelphia in 1815. *Do you think every state needs a separate constitution? Why or why not?*

limits the taxing power of local governments. The state constitution usually specifies the kinds of taxes that state and local governments can impose. It may also specify how certain revenues must be used. In some states, for example, the constitution requires that money taken in through a state lottery must be earmarked for education.

Finally, state constitutions establish independent state agencies, boards, and commissions that have power in areas that affect citizens' lives directly. These include, for example, public **utility** commissions that regulate gas and electric rates, and state boards of education that help administer public schools throughout the state.

As the basic law of the state, the state constitution is supreme above all other laws made within the state. At the same time, the state constitution cannot contain provisions that clash with the U.S. Constitution.

Characteristics of Constitutions

R State constitutions show wide variations. Still, many of them share some basic characteristics that can be described.

Bill of Rights

Besides a provision for separation of powers among the three branches of state government, all state constitutions contain a bill of rights. This section includes all or most of the protections of the Bill of Rights in the Constitution of the United States. Many state constitutions contain additional protections not found in the U.S. Constitution. Examples of these protections are the workers' right to join unions, a ban on discrimination based on gender or race, and certain protections for the physically challenged.

Length

Originally, state constitutions were about the same length as the U.S. Constitution. Over the years, additions to state constitutions in many states have resulted in very long documents. While the U.S. Constitution is about 7,000 words long, the average state constitution today has more than 30,000 words. Very long constitutions are found in such states as Texas, with 80,000 words, and Alabama, with about 220,000 words, which is equal to about 250 pages of a textbook.

Detail

Long state constitutions are filled with details, often covering many varied and unusual **aspects** of life in a state. Such constitutions might include any of the following: a special tax to help veterans of the Civil War, a requirement that public schools teach agricultural subjects, fixed salaries for certain state and local officials, or a declaration of state holidays.

Drafting a Bill

Step 1: Finding the Issues Students will work in groups to write a bill to be introduced in a session of a mock state legislature.

Directions Ask students to locate a copy of your state's current budget to see what types of programs your state government supports. They also will check newspapers and other sources to get an idea of issues that are currently being considered, such as education spending or crime prevention.

Deciding As a class, brainstorm issues that students think need to be addressed in your state and vote on the one they would like to tackle. In Step 2, they will research a bill that addresses one aspect of the issue they select. **OL**

(Chapter Project continued in Section 2.)

Critics of state constitutions claim that such detailed, specific provisions are not needed in a constitution, but rather should be handled in state laws. Chief Justice John Marshall once wrote that a constitution "requires only that its great outlines should be marked, its important objects designated."

A major reason for lengthy and detailed state constitutions involves politics. State constitutions are sometimes very detailed because certain groups and individuals have lobbied hard for a provision. Including such provisions in the state constitution protects against their being changed by a simple vote of the legislature.

Amendments and Changes

Changing a constitution is sometimes necessary simply because societies change over time. Some states have amended their constitutions to give governors more power, for example, because it is felt that modern societies require a stronger executive than older societies did. Other amendments are made to allow for a very specific policy. Where this rule of thumb has been used, state constitutions tend to have an enormous number of amendments. These usually only add to the length and detail of the constitution. As of 2004, for example, Alabama has 742 amendments.

Proposing Amendments

The amendment process has two steps: proposal and ratification. Constitutions of the 50 states provide four different methods of proposing amendments. These include methods by state legislatures, by popular initiative, by a constitutional commission, or by a constitutional convention.

In every state, the state legislature has the power to propose an amendment to the state constitution. This method is the most commonly used. The actual practice of proposing a legislative amendment varies somewhat from state to state. In 17 states, a majority vote of the members of each house of the legislature must propose an amendment to the state constitution. In 18 states, a two-thirds vote of all members of each house is required. In 9 states, a three-fifths majority vote of the legislature is required. Finally, a few states require the legislature to vote for an amendment in two different sessions before the proposal is official.

Eighteen states also allow the people to propose constitutional amendments by popular initiative. An **initiative** is a method by which citizens propose an amendment or a law. The initiative process begins when an individual or a group writes a proposed amendment. People who are in favor of the amendment then circulate it as part of a petition to obtain the signatures of a required number of eligible voters. The number of signatures required varies from state to state. Constitutional initiatives account for only about 5 percent of the proposed amendments to state constitutions.

The third method of proposing amendments to a state constitution is by convening a state constitutional convention. A **constitutional convention** is a gathering of citizens who are usually elected by popular vote and who meet to consider changing or replacing a constitution.

D

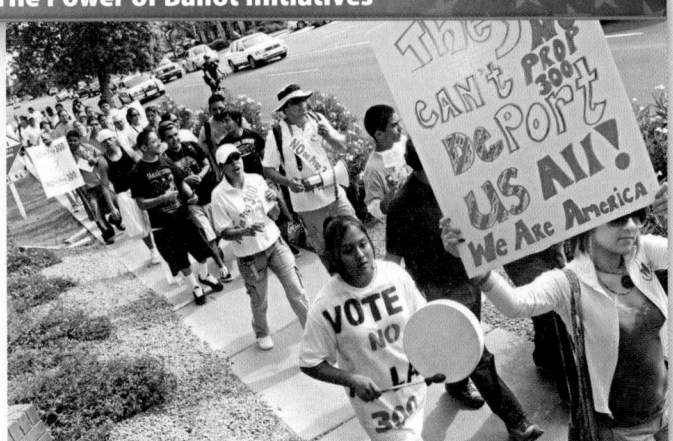

The Power of Ballot Initiatives

Proposition 300
In Arizona, Proposition 300 was put on the ballot in 2006 to discourage illegal immigration. After voters passed it, college students who could not prove they were legal residents could not get state financial assistance or qualify for in-state tuition. *Children who are born to illegal immigrants are U.S. citizens, but why might proving state residency be a problem?*

D Differentiated Instruction

Interpersonal Organize students into five or six groups to formulate a proposed amendment to their state constitution. Provide copies of amendments that already have been made to the state constitution as models. Have each group focus on a different area of concern, such as taxes, the structure of government, the power of business, the state's workforce, the environment, education, and so on. Within each group, have students choose a leader and agree on the division of the work into various research, writing, and editing tasks. A group spokesperson should report to the class on the final version of the amendment and the reasons behind it. Encourage students to ask questions after each presentation. Conclude the activity by holding a class vote on ratification of each proposal. **OL**

Caption Answer: Students should make a decision based on which is more important: college tuition assistance for all in need or discouraging illegal immigration.

Differentiated Instruction

Activity: Multiple Learning Styles

Interpersonal Have students survey classmates and neighbors, asking these two questions:
- What do you see as your most important right as a citizen of this state?
- What do you consider to be the most important responsibility that the state government has toward you?

Have students tabulate their responses. Then ask students to examine their state constitution to see which citizen rights and government responsibilities are addressed and what the specific constitutional provisions are in each case. **OL**

Assess

Assign the Section 1 Assessment as homework or as an in-class activity, or have students take Section Quiz 23-1 from *Section Quizzes and Chapter Tests*.

Close

Analyzing Ask students whether it should be easier or harder to amend state constitutions. Have them give reasons for their opinions. **OL**

Section 1 Review

Finally, many states have used a fourth method, the constitutional commission, to propose constitutional amendments. A **constitutional commission** is a group of experts who are appointed to study the state constitution and recommend changes. Eight states established constitutional commissions in the 1980s, but few of their recommendations resulted in amendments. Kentucky's commission recommended 77 changes in 1987. Only one was referred to the voters by 1988.

Methods of Ratification

All states except Delaware require ratification of amendments by popular vote. The kind of majority necessary to approve an amendment varies. Forty-four states require a simple majority of those who vote on the proposed amendment. Three other states require a majority of all voters who cast ballots in the election.

When the voters rather than the legislature vote on an issue, it is called a referendum. Some states allow voters to hold referendums on issues other than constitutional amendments. The practice is far more common at the county and local level than at the state level.

Criticism and Reform

Over the years, people have criticized state constitutions for being too long, too complicated, and too full of needless detail. What are the procedures by which new state constitutions could be enacted?

Constitutional Convention

In order to replace existing state constitutions, most states require a constitutional convention. In a few states, a special commission may also draft a new constitution that must be reviewed by the state legislature, followed by ratification by the people.

In every state, the process of calling a constitutional convention begins when the state legislature proposes a convention to the voters. If the people agree, the state holds an election to choose delegates. After they convene, the delegates may write a new constitution or suggest amendments in the existing document. The voters then must ratify the changes or the new constitution.

Although 14 states require that a popular vote be held periodically on the question of calling a convention, the voters in recent years have opposed the idea. Only five were held in the 1980s.

Although many state residents periodically call for reform, most states have kept their existing constitutions. Thirty-three states have constitutions that are more than 100 years old. Many, including Massachusetts (1780), Wisconsin (1848), and Oregon (1857), still have their original constitutions.

Judicial Interpretation

In the 1980s, the number of amendments and **revisions** to state constitutions declined. More state judges, however, began to interpret state constitutions independently of the U.S. Constitution. As it has for the U.S. Constitution, judicial review has become an important means of changing state constitutions.

SECTION 1 Review

Vocabulary

1. **Explain** the significance of: initiative, constitutional convention, constitutional commission.

Main Ideas

2. **Analyzing** In what ways are most state constitutions alike?

3. **Explaining** Why are state constitutions amended more frequently than the federal Constitution?

Critical Thinking

4. **Identifying Central Issues** Why do you think so many amendments to state constitutions have been adopted?

5. **Identifying** Use a graphic organizer like the one below to identify the purposes served by state constitutions.

Writing About Government

6. **Persuasive Writing** Many state constitutions contain historic provisions that are no longer applicable, such as a tax to help veterans of the Civil War. Identify provisions in the constitution of your state that appear to be outdated. Do you think states should take the time to eliminate these provisions? Write a one-page summary that explains your position.

Answers

1. All definitions can be found in the section and the Glossary.
2. They separate power into three branches, have a bill of rights, and include much specific detail.
3. Because state constitutions are more detailed and deal with more immediate and specific concerns, they go out of date more quickly, requiring further amendments. They are also easier to amend than the U.S. Constitution.
4. Students might suggest that people may fear major changes that would come with a new constitution; thus, they prefer to revise the old one.
5. create structure of state government, establish types of local government, regulate how state and local governments spend money, establish state bureaucracy
6. Examples of outdated provisions will vary. Students should support their opinions.

The Three Branches

Reader's Guide

Content Vocabulary
* bicameral (p. 641)
* lieutenant governor (p. 642)
* plurality (p. 643)
* item veto (p. 645)
* civil case (p. 646)
* criminal case (p. 646)

Academic Vocabulary
* area (p. 642)
* requirement (p. 642)
* obtain (p. 643)

Reading Strategy
As you read, use a graphic organizer like the one below to take notes about the different officials in the three branches of state government.

Executive	Legislative	Judicial

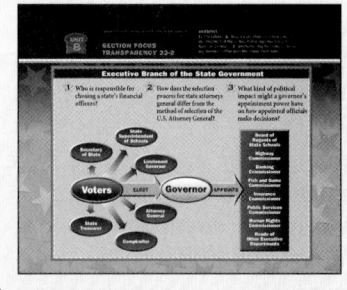
Issues in the News

The New Mexico legislature passed a spending bill to fund specific projects, some favored by legislators and others by the governor. The bill allocates about $14 million for various projects, many in legislators' home districts—local festivals and museums, police salaries, and sports programs. Another $7 million went to the governor's favorite projects, including one that provides breakfast for elementary students. Governor Bill Richardson, however, has threatened to veto the measure. His spokesperson said that the bill is "packed with unnecessary budget pork." Given his executive authority, Richardson could sign or veto the entire bill, or use his line-item veto to reject individual lines in the bill's budget.

▲ Governor Bill Richardson of New Mexico at a signing ceremony with a Native American resident.

The conflict between New Mexico Governor Bill Richardson and the state legislature is one played out in many American states—the chances for conflict can be greater when a governor and the legislature's majority are from different parties. To pass any laws, however, demands cooperation. Like the federal government, state government is divided into three separate branches: the legislature, the executive, and the judiciary.

The Legislative Branch

The state legislature passes laws that deal with a variety of matters, including health, crime, labor, education, and transportation. The state legislature has the power to tax and the power to spend and borrow money. Finally, the state legislature acts as a check on the power of the governor and the bureaucracy.

State legislatures are known by various names. In 19 states, the state legislature is called the general assembly. In New Hampshire and Massachusetts, the legislature is known as the general court. In North Dakota and Oregon, it is called the legislative assembly.

Almost every state has a **bicameral** state legislature—one with two houses, like the U.S. Congress. The upper house is always called the senate, and the lower house is usually called the house of representatives, but some states refer to it as the general assembly, the legislative assembly, or the general court. Nebraska has the only unicameral, or one-chambered, state legislature in the country.

Resource Manager

R Reading Strategies	**C** Critical Thinking	**D** Differentiated Instruction	**W** Writing Support	**S** Skill Practice
Teacher Edition • Outlining, p. 646 **Additional Resources** • Guid. Read. Act., p. 83 • Quizzes/Tests, p. 284	**Teacher Edition** • Making Comparisons, p. 644 • Determining Cause and Effect, p. 647 **Additional Resources** • Read. Essen., pp. 263–266	**Teacher Edition** • Interpersonal, p. 642 **Additional Resources** • Foldables, p. 66 • Hist. Docs. and Speeches, p. 23	**Teacher Edition** • Narrative Writing, p. 646 **Additional Resources** • Part. in Gov. Act., pp. 45–46	**Teacher Edition** • Researching, p. 643 **Additional Resources** • Inter. Poli. Cartoons, pp. 45–46

Teach

D Differentiated Instruction

Interpersonal To extend coverage of the committee system in state legislatures, organize the class into groups of three or four students each. Assign each group the task of investigating one of the committees in the state legislature. Encourage students to select areas of concern that are important to them personally or to their community. Have a student from each group focus on one specific task, such as researching, contacting state legislators, report writing, or presenting. Have a spokesperson for each group present a five-minute report on the committee. After each group's presentation, allow time for class discussion. **OL**

Government ONLINE

Objectives and answers to the Student Web Activity can be found in the **Web Activity Lesson Plan** at glencoe.com. Enter **QuickPass**™ code USG9085c23T.

Differentiated Instruction

The Road to the Legislature

Members of the state legislature are elected from legislative districts of relatively equal population. Until 1964, state voting was usually based on geographic **areas** rather than population, and most state constitutions used the county as the basic voting district for the upper house. When population growth occurred, it was, of course, not uniform by counties. As a result, striking differences arose in county representation. A county with 1,500 people and a county with 800,000 people were both entitled to one senator.

In 1964 the Supreme Court ruled that voting districts for both houses of state legislatures had to be based on roughly equal populations. Chief Justice Earl Warren stated the Court's position in the case of *Reynolds* v. *Sims*[1] (1964): "Legislators are elected by voters, not farms or cities or economic interests." In most states, voting districts were redrawn to comply with the Court's "one person, one vote" ruling. While cities gained from voting districts based on equal population, the suburbs gained many seats in the legislatures of states like Illinois, New York, and New Jersey.

Qualifications and Term of Office

The legal qualifications for state legislators are defined in a state's constitution. In most states, a person has to be a resident of the district that he or she wants to represent. To serve as a senator, a person usually must be at least 25 years old and a resident of the state for some specified time. To serve in the lower house, a person usually must be at least 21 years old and meet residency **requirements.**

Legal qualifications aside, the office of state legislator seems to attract certain kinds of professional people. Many state legislators are lawyers. A sizable number of state legislators also come from professions that state laws directly affect, such as real estate and insurance. Unlike members of the U.S. Congress, most state legislators work only part time at their office and are not well paid. (In eight states, legislators are paid only when the legislature is in session.) State senators often serve

Government ONLINE

Student Web Activity Visit glencoe.com and enter **QuickPass**™ code USG9822c23. Click on Student Web Activity and complete the activity about state constitutions.

---

four-year terms, and members of the lower house usually serve for two years. In Alabama, Maryland, Louisiana, and Mississippi, members of the senate and the lower house serve for four years.

Legislative Sessions

In the past, a typical state legislature met for one or perhaps two months of the year. Some state legislatures met as infrequently as every other year. To handle a growing workload, the length and frequency of legislative sessions has increased. In more than three-fourths of the states, the legislature now holds annual sessions. Only seven states have legislatures that still meet every other year.

Organization of Legislatures

Most state legislatures are organized like the U.S. Congress. The size and population of a state does not determine the size of its legislature as one might expect—California has 80 members in its lower house, whereas New Hampshire has 400. On average, lower houses have about 100 members, and state senates average about 40 members.

In the lower house, the presiding officer is called the speaker of the house—a position similar to that of the speaker in the House of Representatives. The majority party in the lower house usually chooses the speaker. The speaker has the power to appoint the chairpersons as well as all other members of house committees.

In 26 states, the presiding officer of the upper house is the **lieutenant governor.** He or she serves very much like the vice president of the United States, who presides over the U.S. Senate. In states without a lieutenant governor, senators usually elect their presiding officer.

Since state legislatures usually consider more than 1,000 bills each session, committees conduct much of the work.

The Course of Legislation

As in the U.S. Congress, a member of the state legislature introduces each bill. Unlike the Congress, however, the source for most bills is either the state's executive branch (the governor or state and local government agencies); or a wide range of private groups. The private groups that sponsor bills often are interest groups—an association of medical doctors, a labor union, or even a voluntary group of bird-watchers. These groups submit

See the following footnoted materials in the **Reference Handbook:**
1. *Reynolds* v. *Sims* case summary, page R33.

Federal Mandate versus States' Rights?

Government Simulations and Debates, p. 50

Objective: To learn about both sides of unfunded mandates issues.

Focus/Teach: Have students complete the steps and answer the questions in the activity.

Assess: Choose or have students vote on winners of the debate.

Close: Discuss the strengths and weaknesses of unfunded mandates.

Differentiated Instruction Strategies

BL Why do unfunded federal mandates potentially violate states' rights?

AL Have students create a compromise between unfunded mandates and fully funded federal mandates.

ELL Discuss synonyms for the words *mandate* and *unfunded*.

draft bills for the legislation that they want enacted into law. The same groups often come forward later to give expert testimony on their bill to committees.

A bill can be introduced in either house. The presiding officer sends the bill to the committee that specializes in the bill's subject matter. The committee discusses the bill and may hold public hearings. It may rewrite the bill or modify it and then sends it back to the full house with a recommendation to be passed or not passed. If one house passes a bill, it must go through a similar process in the other. Sometimes the second house changes a bill. In this case, a conference committee of both houses can meet to draft an acceptable version of the bill. Both houses then vote on this version. If it is passed, it goes to the governor for signature or veto. Of bills that are introduced, less than one-quarter become law.

The Executive Branch

Every state has an executive branch headed by a governor. In a sense, this office was created to be weak. Because of their bad experience with British colonial governors, states limited the powers of their governors. This practice continued through the nation's history, as most state constitutions severely restricted the governor's powers. Until 1965 most governors had short terms of office, a one-term limit on their service, and weak executive powers. Like the office of president, the office of governor has generally become more powerful in recent years. Because of the great differences in the area and population of states, one finds a vast difference among the states in the power and influence of the executive office.

Becoming a Governor

State constitutions spell out the few legal or formal qualifications for becoming governor. In most states, a governor must be at least 30 years old, an American citizen, and a state resident for 5 or more years. Citizenship and residency requirements differ widely.

In addition to these legal qualifications, however, a person must usually have certain political credentials. Most governors have served in state and local government before running for governor. Many have also served as lieutenant governor or as the state attorney general. Roughly half the governors recently elected were lawyers who had a law practice in their state.

State Budget Woes

Balancing State Needs and Resources State budgets affect residents in very direct ways; when their needs are not met, it is the executive branch that is usually singled out first for criticism. *What does the cartoonist imply about how states address urban problems?*

Election

In most states, the process of electing a governor has two basic steps. First, an individual must gain the nomination of a major political party, usually by winning a party primary. Only three states—Connecticut, Utah, and Virginia—still use the older convention method to nominate candidates for governor. Second, after he or she is chosen, the nominee runs in the general election.

In most states the candidate who wins a plurality vote is elected governor. A **plurality** is the largest number of votes in an election. (If three candidates ran for office and one had 35 percent of the vote, one had 45 percent, and one had 20 percent, the candidate with 45 percent would have a plurality.)

In five states, however, a majority (more than 50 percent) is needed to be elected. In Arizona, Georgia, and Louisiana, if no one receives a majority, a runoff election is held between the two candidates who receive the most votes in the general election. In Mississippi, the lower house of the state legislature chooses the governor if no candidate **obtains** a majority in the general election. In Vermont, the house and senate choose.

Caption Answer: Aid to cities has a difficult, or even impossible, job of surviving the state budget process.

ISSUES to Debate

Conflict of Interest Have students consider the ethical issues involved in having bills proposed by legislators who are also full-time professionals in areas such as insurance or real estate. Discuss some conflicts of interest that might develop. Then have students informally debate methods of preventing corruption in lawmaking based on this situation. **OL**

S Skill Practice

Researching Have students research celebrity governors and congresspersons in the United States. **Ask:** Why do you think these people chose to run for office? Did any of them have prior political or legal experience? Do you approve of celebrity politicians? **AL**

Differentiated Instruction

Auditory/Musical To reteach or extend section information, call on volunteers to assume the following roles: state legislator, governor, lieutenant governor, state attorney general, justice of the peace, state supreme court justice. After the volunteers form a panel, have each member do one or more of the following:

• give an oral summary of his or her responsibilities;

• take questions from the class about how the role varies from state to state;

• ask the class questions about the work of that official.

Some students are especially attuned to learning by listening, but encourage students to take notes during this activity to help them review the section later. **OL**

C **Critical Thinking**

Making Comparisons
Organize the class into two teams—one to represent the federal government and the other to represent your state government. Have a volunteer from one group make a statement, such as "The term limit for our chief executive is two." Then have a student from the other team respond to show either a similarity or a difference; for example, "There is no term limit for our chief executive." Have the teams alternate in presenting initial and responding statements. Statements should consider issues such as structure, qualifications, and procedures. Allow students from either group to challenge statements they believe to be in error. **OL**

Hands-On Chapter Project

Step 2

Replacing an Ousted Governor
California's Governor Arnold Schwarzenegger came to office after the sitting governor, Gray Davis, was recalled by voters. *What might be the advantages and disadvantages of using the recall method to remove a state official?*

Term of Office

Most governors serve four-year terms. In two states, Vermont and New Hampshire, the term of office is only two years. Many states also limit the number of terms a governor may serve in office. Twenty-seven states have a two-term limit.

Another factor that can influence the governor's term of office is recall, the process of voting to remove state officials from office. In 18 states, voters can **C** exercise recall at the polls. In 2003 Californian voters voted to recall their governor, Gray Davis. In the recall election, more than 100 people submitted the required fee of $3,500 to be on the ballot, but only a few were serious candidates. The winner was the actor and former bodybuilder Arnold Schwarzenegger, a Republican who attracted a range of voters. Schwarzenegger has been successful in addressing some of California's budget problems that were the source of dissatifaction with Gray Davis.

The Roles of the Governor

The governor's activities range from proposing and signing legislation to visiting foreign countries. The executive branch of state government carries out the laws that the state legislature passes. The governor's responsibilities may include budgeting, appointing officials, planning for economic growth, and coordinating the work of executive departments. The amount of control that a governor has over the executive branch varies widely from state to state.

People look to their state's governor for leadership. Therefore, the governor is expected to play an important legislative role. Theodore Roosevelt, who served as governor of New York State, said, "More than half of my work as governor was in the direction of getting needed and important legislation."

Governors are usually looked upon as the leaders of the party in their states. The governor attends political-party dinners, speaks at party functions, and might campaign for party candidates in local elections. In addition, governors participate in events such as the Democratic or Republican Governors' Conference.

Governors often try to obtain grants from the national government for their state's schools, highways, and urban areas. They also represent their states when they seek cooperation from other states in such areas as transportation and pollution control. More recently, governors have begun representing their states internationally. For example, they have tried to encourage foreign businesses to locate in their states and have sought foreign markets for products their states produce.

Managing the Executive Branch

The governor's executive powers include two basic components: the power to carry out the law and the power to supervise the executive branch of state government.

The constitutions of many states created a divided executive branch, making many executive officials politically and legally independent of each other. In more than half the states, for example, the people elect the governor, the lieutenant governor, the attorney general, and the secretary of state. In addition, they often serve for different terms of office and have specific and separate responsibilities that the state constitution defines.

As a result, officials from different political parties who have different ideas and conflicting political ambitions may head executive offices. Cooperation is often difficult, leaving the governor with limited control over the executive branch. Some states, such as Tennessee and New Jersey, give the governor considerable control over the executive branch. The constitutions of these states have created an executive branch with only one elected official or only a few such officials.

In all but eight states, the governor has full responsibility for preparing the state budget. After it is prepared, this budget is submitted to the state legislature for approval. The power to make up the budget allows a governor to push certain programs and policies.

All governors can exercise military powers through their role as commander in chief of the

Drafting a Bill

Step 2: Making Key Decisions Students will choose and research one aspect of the issue they selected in Step 1.

Directions As a class, discuss the components of the issue the class chose in Step 1. For example, if they chose education spending, have them list the programs the state currently funds. Then have them suggest areas they think need more funding or ideas for new programs. Divide the class into the House and the Senate. Then form one or two "committees" in each branch of the legislature, and ask each committee to select a program for which they want to draft legislation.

Researching Formats Have students use library sources or the Internet to locate examples of bills. **OL**

(Chapter Project continued in Section 3.)

state National Guard. The National Guard can be used in a national emergency, such as a war, if the president calls it into action. Normally, however, the National Guard serves as a state militia under the governor's control. State constitutions allow the governor to use the National Guard to maintain law and order during state emergencies.

Executive Reform

Since 1965, more than half the states have reformed their constitutions to give the governor more power. Methods of doing this include lengthening the governor's term of office, requiring the lieutenant governor to run on a joint ticket with the governor, and giving the governor more power to make appointments to departments and agencies.

Legislative Powers

Like the nation's president, a governor has legislative power without being part of the legislative branch. A governor can propose legislation to the state legislature, send messages to the state legislature or present new programs as part of the state budget. In addition, a governor can arouse public opinion to support these legislative proposals.

Today all governors have a veto power over legislation the state legislature passes. In 1996 North Carolina became the last state to grant this power to its governor. In most states, the governor has an **item veto,** the power to turn down one section or item without vetoing a bill completely. The use of the item veto has led to a controversy. Two Wisconsin legislators sued their governor over his veto of individual sentences, words, parts of words, single letters, and other minor details in a legislative bill. A federal appeals court sided with the governor. A state legislature can override a governor's veto under certain conditions. Usually a two-thirds vote of all the legislators in each house is required to override a governor's veto.

A third legislative power of the governor is the ability to call a special session of the legislature. Legislatures meet at regularly scheduled times, but the governor can call a special session to deal with legislation that he or she believes is vital to the state.

Judicial Powers

A governor normally has some limited powers over the state court system and the administration of justice. Governors appoint almost one-fourth of all state judges throughout the country. In addition, a governor might have one or more of the following powers over people who are convicted of crimes:

TIME For the Record

Two's a Crowd Most states make life a little simpler for their voters by holding the gubernatorial election in a different year from the presidential election. Currently, only 13 states elect governors and presidents in the same year.

the right to grant pardons, shorten sentences, waive fines, and release prisoners on parole.

Other Executive Officers

In all but four states—Maine, New Hampshire, New Jersey, and Tennessee—other elected officials are part of the executive branch. Less visible than the governor, these executives often hold important positions.

Forty-four states have a lieutenant governor, a position similar to that of the vice president of the United States. The lieutenant governor becomes governor when the office is vacated. The lieutenant governor also usually presides over the state senate.

In all but eight states, the people elect the attorney general, who is the top legal officer in state government. (In those eight states, the governor usually appoints the attorney general.) The attorney general supervises the legal activities of all state agencies, gives legal advice to the governor, and acts as a lawyer for the state in cases in which it is involved. Probably the most significant power of the attorney general is the power to issue opinions, or written interpretations of the state constitution or laws. These opinions carry legal authority unless a court overturns them.

At the federal level, the secretary of state deals with foreign relations. In state government, the position of secretary of state is very much what its name describes—the chief secretary or clerk of state government. The secretary of state is in charge of all state records and official state documents, including all the official acts of the governor and the legislature.

CHAPTER 23: *State Governments* **645**

POLITICAL PROFILES Minority Governors

The first female governor was Nellie Tayloe Ross of Wyoming, elected in 1924 to fill her deceased husband's unexpired term. The first woman to hold a state governorship without being preceded by her husband was Ella Grasso, who served as governor of Connecticut from 1975 to 1980. Virginia's Douglas Wilder, elected in 1989, was the nation's first African American elected governor.

Did You Know?

A governor's record can help a presidential candidate, but it also can be a hindrance. In 1976, Georgia governor Jimmy Carter used his state's economic growth to win the presidency. In 1988, Massachusetts governor Michael Dukakis lost the election after being blamed for the state's high taxes and environmental problems.

Additional Support

Activity: Interdisciplinary Connection

Literature The memoirs of governors can be fascinating reading. Invite students to read and present a report on one, commenting specifically upon insights they have gained into the nature of a governor's job. Some examples to offer include: *The Life and Times of Henry Bellmon* (Oklahoma) by Henry Bellmon and Pat Bellmon, Tulsa: Council Oak Books, 1992; *Diaries of Mario M. Cuomo: The Campaign for Governor* (New York) by Mario Cuomo, New York: Random House, 1984; *Living a Political Life* (Vermont) by Madeleine Kunin, New York: Knopf, 1994; *Straight from the Heart: My Life in Politics and Other Places* (Texas) by Ann Richards and Peter Knobler, New York: Simon and Schuster, 1989. **AL**

Charts in MOtion
See StudentWorks™ Plus
or go to glencoe.com.

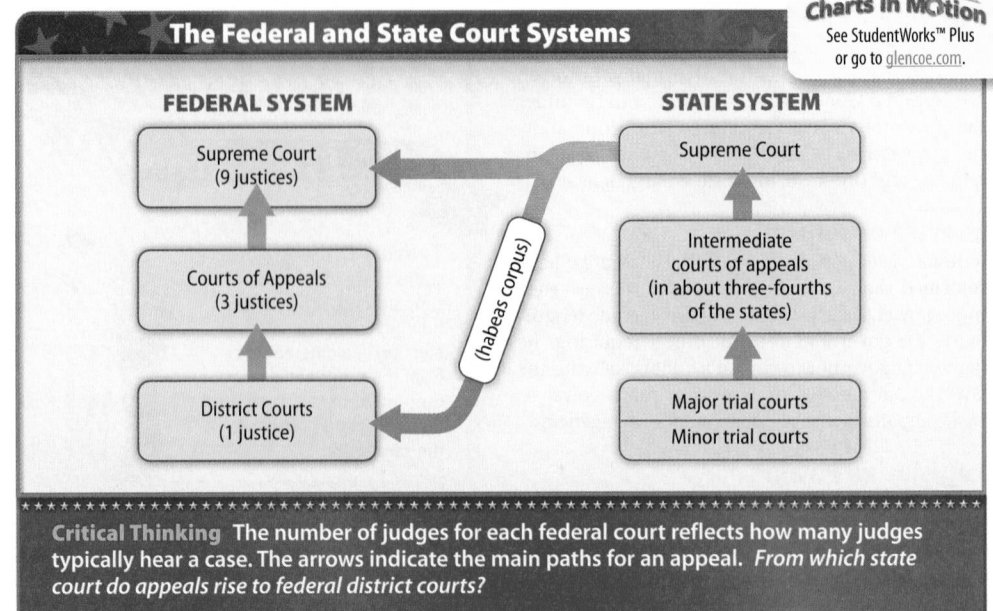

The Federal and State Court Systems

FEDERAL SYSTEM

Supreme Court
(9 justices)

Courts of Appeals
(3 justices)

District Courts
(1 justice)

(habeas corpus)

STATE SYSTEM

Supreme Court

Intermediate
courts of appeals
(in about three-fourths
of the states)

Major trial courts

Minor trial courts

Critical Thinking The number of judges for each federal court reflects how many judges typically hear a case. The arrows indicate the main paths for an appeal. *From which state court do appeals rise to federal district courts?*

W Writing Support

Narrative Writing Have students write a short narrative story about a civil or a criminal case that is tried in a state court. **OL**

Participating IN GOVERNMENT

Court Observers Explain that for the sake of judicial discipline, several states have volunteer court observers report on various aspects of daily courtroom activity. Encourage students to find out how a citizen can become a court observer. **OL**

R Reading Strategy

Outlining Ask: Have students create an outline of state courts' structure, with the alternate names for each court in parentheses. *(Answers will vary.)* **BL**

Additional Support

The state treasurer manages the money that a state government collects and pays out. He or she pays the bills of state government and often serves as the state tax collector. In most states, the state treasurer also has the power to invest state funds.

Many other executive officers work in state governments. Some of the more important offices commonly found in states are the state comptroller or auditor, the superintendent of public instruction, and the insurance commissioner.

The Judicial Branch

Vital to the operation of state governments, the judiciary interprets and applies state laws. In doing this, state courts help resolve conflicts such as business disagreements and grievances that citizens might have against each other. State courts also punish crimes that violate state laws.

The Importance of State Courts

State courts interpret and apply state and local laws. State courts decide most cases of murder, assault, and reckless driving, which are usually violations of state laws. State courts also decide cases that involve local laws, like littering or illegal parking. All local courts are part of a state court system. The local municipal court in which a person challenges a traffic ticket is also part of a state court system.

Two types of disputes can be heard in state courts: **civil cases,** which involve a dispute between two or more private individuals or organizations, and **criminal cases** in which the state brings charges against someone for violating the law. The state is always the prosecutor in criminal cases, but it is not usually involved in civil cases.

State Court Systems

State court systems vary in their structure. They also vary in the names the states give the courts. In general, state court systems include three types of courts: minor courts, general trial courts, and appeals courts.

In small towns and rural areas, the best-known minor court is often the justice court, which is presided over by a justice of the peace. Some common functions for justices of the peace are:

- performing marriages,
- handling minor civil and criminal cases, and
- legalizing documents.

In many cities, police courts, municipal courts, or magistrate courts handle minor legal matters like petty crimes and property disputes. (These courts are also referred to as minor courts of limited jurisdiction, local trial courts, or inferior trial courts.)

States include a range of minor courts. Small claims courts hear civil arguments that involve

Extending the Content

"States" Across the Border Canada is made up of 10 provinces and 3 territories. The central government in Ottawa represents all Canadians, but each province has its own government, which functions somewhat like a state government in the United States. Like states, for example, provinces are responsible for such matters as education and administration of justice. Each province has an elected unicameral legislature. Unlike states, however, each province has a lieutenant governor who is appointed by the governor general (who is appointed by the monarch—currently Elizabeth II—on the advice of the Canadian prime minister). The head of government in each of the provinces is a premier. The premier leads the majority party in the provincial legislature.

small amounts of money. Juvenile courts hear cases involving people under the age of 18. Domestic relations courts handle family disputes. Traffic courts hear cases dealing with traffic and parking violations. Probate courts handle cases involving the inheritance of property.

General trial courts are known by different names in different states: county courts, circuit courts, courts of common pleas, superior courts, and district courts. Such courts stand above minor courts and can hear any type of case, civil or criminal. Serious crimes such as murder, arson, and robbery are heard in these general trial courts.

Appeals courts review cases that a lower court has already decided. The highest state court is usually called the supreme court. The supreme court is the state court of final appeal. In Maryland and New York, this court is called the court of appeals. The state's supreme court performs another significant function: It interprets the state's constitution and laws. Three-fourths of the states have additional appeals courts, called intermediate appellate courts. These courts were created to relieve the state supreme court of the large number of cases that were being appealed.

Selecting State Court Judges

State judges are selected in four different ways: popular election, election by the legislature, gubernatorial appointment; or, the Missouri Plan method, which combines popular election and gubernatorial appointment. Popular election is the most common method.

People disagree over the various methods for selecting judges. Those who favor popular election believe that if government is "of the people, by the people, and for the people," then the people must be able to choose their judges directly in an election. Others say that having a popular election to choose judges will make them too worried about pleasing voters when they make rulings or that few voters know enough to choose a judge at the ballot box.

Removal of Judges

A judge must demonstrate a minimum level of competence, skill, and knowledge. The judge often makes the final ruling in a case and has the last word about very critical decisions in people's lives. If judges are so important, it should be possible to evaluate their performance and remove those who are unqualified. How is this done?

One method of removing judges is through impeachment. Impeachment is a procedure through which charges are brought against a judge or any public official accused of misconduct. Impeachment of judges, however, has proved to be inefficient and time-consuming.

In recent years most states have created disciplinary boards or commissions to investigate complaints about judges. These judicial conduct organizations are usually made up of both lawyers and nonlawyers. If a disciplinary board finds that a judge has acted improperly or unethically, it makes a recommendation to the state's supreme court. The court then may suspend or remove the judge.

C **Critical Thinking**

Determining Cause and Effect The text discusses two methods for removing judges. **Ask:** What was the reason many states decided to create disciplinary boards to review judicial conduct? *(States needed a way to remove poorly performing judges that was more efficient than the impeachment process.)* **BL**

Assess

Assign the Section 2 Assessment as homework or as an in-class activity, or have students take Section Quiz 23-2 from *Section Quizzes and Chapter Tests*.

Close

Analyzing Discuss how and why the power of various state government leaders and institutions has changed over time. **Ask:** What attitudes have allowed for these kinds of changes? *(Students might suggest that an increasing desire for states' and individuals' rights has forced state-based institutions to evolve.)* **OL**

SECTION 2 Review

Vocabulary

1. **Explain** the significance of: bicameral, lieutenant governor, plurality, item veto, civil case, criminal case.

Main Ideas

2. **Identifying** Why was *Reynolds* v. *Sims* significant for state legislatures?

3. **Describing** Why do some people question the wisdom of electing state court judges?

Critical Thinking

4. **Making Comparisons** How is the path a bill takes to become a law similar in a state legislature and in Congress?

5. **Organizing** Use a graphic organizer like the one below to show how the roles of president and governor differ in at least two ways.

President	Governor

Writing About Government

6. **Expository Writing** Look through local newspapers to find articles about the governor of your state. For each article, write a description of the role or roles the governor is filling in the newspaper article. Create a bulletin-board display called "The Role of the Governor" that includes a copy of each article and your description of the governor's role.

CHAPTER 23: *State Governments* **647**

Section 2 Review

Answers

1. All definitions can be found in the section and the Glossary.
2. It forced both houses of state legislatures to be proportionally representative.
3. They question whether people are informed enough to elect judges, and they fear political influences upon judges who are elected.
4. The bill is introduced by legislators, sent to a committee, reported back to the house, passed by both houses, and signed by the chief executive. A conference committee may resolve differences, and the legislature may pass a bill over an executive veto by a two-thirds majority vote in both houses.
5. Answers might include: president—makes foreign policy, does not have line-item veto; governor—does not make foreign policy, has line-item veto
6. Discuss how the articles on the bulletin board reflect the various roles of the governor.

Focus

Bellringer

Section Focus Transparencies 23-3

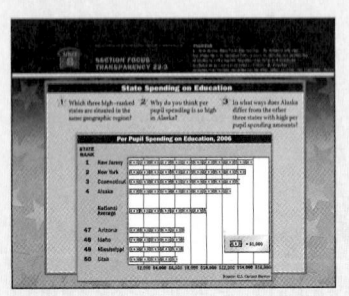

Reader's Guide

Answers to Graphic:

protecting consumers
protecting workers
promoting economic development
protecting the environment
regulating the criminal justice system
regulating education, health, and welfare

Resource Manager

State Government Policy

Reader's Guide

Content Vocabulary
- ★ corporate charter (p. 648)
- ★ public utility (p. 649)
- ★ workers' compensation (p. 649)
- ★ unemployment compensation (p. 649)
- ★ mandatory sentencing (p. 651)
- ★ victim compensation (p. 651)
- ★ extradition (p. 651)
- ★ parole (p. 652)
- ★ shock probation (p. 652)
- ★ shock incarceration (p. 652)
- ★ house arrest (p. 652)

Academic Vocabulary
- ★ restrict (p. 648)
- ★ prohibit (p. 649)
- ★ finance (p. 650)

Reading Strategy
Use a graphic organizer like the one below to list the areas that state governments regulate and protect.

Issues in the News

Criticism about the mistreatment of animals in pet stores has grown in recent years. In response, California increased regulation of pet stores within its borders. In late 2007, Governor Arnold Schwarzenegger signed into law the Pet Store Animal Care Act. Pet store owners were required to seek veterinary care for sick or injured animals and were given specific guidelines to follow when putting animals to sleep. Many Californians, however, believe the law does not go far enough. The director of the West Coast Region of the Humane Society of the United States stated that "[M]any people don't know what their rights are and what they're supposed to receive from the pet store."

▲ Citizens often turn to a state legislature if they are angry about an issue, such as mistreatment of animals.

A law to protect animals is only one of many examples of a subject on which a state can enact legislation. In most states, the major areas of legislative activity are business regulation, controlling and regulating natural resources, protecting individual rights, and implementing health, education, and public welfare programs.

State Business Regulation

In the United States, every business corporation must have a charter issued by a state government. A **corporate charter** is a document that grants certain rights, powers, and privileges to a corporation. A charter is important because it gives a corporation legal status. Before 1860, state charters greatly restricted the power of corporations. By the 1890s, however, courts and legislatures—influenced by business interests and believing that giant corporations were indispensable to the economy—relaxed such controls. States that continued to restrict corporations found their major businesses leaving for states with less regulation.

Types of Regulation

In response to citizen groups in the early 1900s, the government began to regulate corporations. Public pressure was successful at both the federal and state levels. States began regulating the interest rates that banks could charge, helped set insurance companies' rates, administered exams for doctors and other professionals to obtain licenses, and generally protected consumer interests.

R Reading Strategies	**C** Critical Thinking	**D** Differentiated Instruction	**W** Writing Support	**S** Skill Practice
Teacher Edition • Organizing, p. 649 • Identifying, p. 650 **Additional Resources** • Guid. Read. Act., p. 84 • Quizzes/Tests, p. 285	**Teacher Edition** • Recognizing Bias, p. 651 **Additional Resources** • Read. Essen., pp. 267–270	**Teacher Edition** • Interpersonal, p. 649 **Additional Resources** • Foldables, p. 66	**Teacher Edition** • Expository Writing, p. 654	**Additional Resources** • Skill Reinforce. Act., p. 23

Regulatory legislation affected many kinds of corporations, but laws regulating banks, insurance companies, and public utilities were especially rigorous. A **public utility** is an organization, either privately or publicly owned, that supplies such necessities as electricity, gas, telephone service, or transportation service. In the United States, most public utilities companies are owned by private stockholders. States can give public utility companies the right to supply service in the state or in a part of the state. In return for granting a company the right to provide a service, the state assumes the right to regulate the company. Beginning in the 1980s, many states worked to reduce their regulation in order to encourage competition, but since the early 2000s, there has been less enthusiasm for deregulation.

Protecting Consumers

Since the early 1900s, states have acted to protect consumers from unfair and deceptive trade practices such as false advertising. Almost all states have laws regulating landlord-tenant relations. Most states also regulate health-care industries. State governments have enacted legislation dealing with consumer sales and service—everything from regulating interest charges on credit cards to setting procedures for estimating the cost of automobile repairs. Most states also try to protect consumers in a number of housing-related areas, such as home-repair costs and home mortgages. In addition, several states require consumer education in the schools.

Protecting Workers

Nearly all states have laws that regulate the safety and sanitary conditions of factories. Federal child-labor rules limit the number of hours that 14- and 15-year-olds can work, and the rules place other restrictions on work for those under age 18. In addition to the federal rules, many states regulate the hours that 16- and 17-year-olds can work. Most states require minors to have work permits.

States also provide **workers' compensation**—payments to people who are unable to work as a result of job-related injury or ill health. Workers who lose their jobs may receive **unemployment compensation** under programs that are set up and regulated by their states.

Workers in all states have the right to join unions, but some states protect workers from being forced to join. More than one-third of the states have passed laws (often called right-to-work laws) that **prohibit** union shops. A union shop is an agreement between a union and an employer that all workers must join a union, usually within 30 days of being hired.

D Differentiated Instruction

Interpersonal Invite people from any of the following career fields to come to class and answer students' questions about the role that state regulations play in their jobs: banking, public utilities, pharmacy, law enforcement, or nursing. **BL**

Government *and* You

More About Licenses The origin of the word *license* provides an easy-to-remember definition. *License* comes from the Latin *lic*, "to be permitted," and a license grants authority to do something that otherwise would not be permitted.

R Reading Strategy

Organizing Government has passed consumer protection laws in some areas more than others. List major areas in which state governments have regulated on behalf of consumers. *(false advertising, rental practices, health care, credit card interest, home mortgages)* **BL**

Additional Support

Activity: Collaborative Learning

Preparing a Multimedia Presentation

Organize the class into groups, assigning each group one of the areas of state responsibility discussed in this section. Have each group give a multimedia presentation about its topic that (1) explains why states need to have authority in that area and (2) gives examples of how their state exercises its authority in that area. After initial planning, group members should assign the tasks—researching historical background and current issues, preparing artwork or slides, supervising computer activity, directing interviews or other video segments, writing, and presenting. Be available to offer advice, but allow students to work on their own as much as possible. Arrange to have students give their finished presentations for other classes, at a teachers' meeting, or at a parent-teacher activity. **OL**

We the People

Making a Difference

Elizabeth Wright Ingraham

In 1995 the American Institute of Architects (AIA) honored Elizabeth Wright Ingraham with a fellowship for her "significant contributions to the aesthetic, scientific, and practical efficiency of the profession; to the standards of architectural education, training, and practice; . . . [and] to the advancement of the living standards of people through their improved environment and to society through significant public service."

Activity: Ask: If you held a position of influence in this state, how might you use your "pull" to improve some aspect of life in the state?

R Reading Strategy

Identifying Trends in state action on the environment are traced broadly in the narrative.

Ask: What are some key actions states take to control pollution? *(They pass laws to control air pollution, require environmental impact statements, require businesses to get costly permits if they pollute, and regulate waste disposal.)* **OL**

Differentiated Instruction

We the People

Making a Difference

"I have met some really exciting young people at Taliesin."

—**Elizabeth Wright Ingraham**

Elizabeth Wright Ingraham, the granddaughter of famed architect Frank Lloyd Wright, became the first female architect licensed in Illinois in the 1950s. Although it was difficult to move out of the shadow of her grandfather, she has left an impressive legacy of her own. She's had her own firm since 1970, and has been at the forefront of trends in her profession for the last half century.

Not surprisingly, Wright Ingraham is deeply interested in architecture education. Her grandfather's career was energized by training aspiring young architects at his school, Taliesin West, in Arizona. (The first campus was in Spring Green, Wisconsin.) Wright Ingraham emphasizes that Taliesin cannot ride on past glories and that its future will lie with a new generation. "I have met some really exciting young people at Taliesin," she said.

One of her core ideas is that all things are interconnected. She has built more than 130 structures employing an economy of resources. Her Vista Grande Community Church was the first building in the nation to use the Thermo-Mass System—insulation contained within the structural concrete. Her long-held beliefs fit very well with today's emphasis on saving resources and preserving the environment.

Business Development

State governments are active in trying to attract new business and industry. Governors often travel in this country or abroad to bring businesses to their states, using television ads, billboards, brochures, and newspaper ads to promote travel or business opportunities.

Beginning in the 1930s, state governments sold bonds to promote economic development. The states used the income from bond sales to help **finance** industries that relocated or expanded in their borders. States were able to pay off the bonds in a specified time with the the the tax revenues from the new industries. Today states often give an incentive such as a tax credit, which reduces taxes, in return for a company's creation of new jobs or new business investment.

States and the Environment

In recent years, the quality of the physical environment has become a major concern of the public and state governments. Scientists have warned that air and water pollution can endanger public health in numerous ways.

Pollution Control

Before 1964, only nine states enacted regulations to control air pollution. In the 1960s, however, the federal government began passing pollution curbing laws. These laws set up federal standards for air and water quality and also provided federal money.

Today state governments are very concerned about pollution. Most states now require environmental impact statements for major governmental or private projects, describing how the project is likely to affect the environment. Many states require industries to secure permits if their wastes pollute the air or water. Often such permits are so costly that the industry finds it cheaper to install antipollution devices. Most have developed waste-management systems. Most regulate the disposal of radioactive wastes.

Climate Change

A critical issue facing the states today is climate change, sometimes called global warming. Climate change refers to the gradual warming of the Earth resulting from the release of greenhouse gases like carbon dioxide from the burning of fossil fuels into

---

Activity: Multiple Learning Styles

Visual/Spatial To help students better comprehend the range of interests that state governments oversee, bring in pictures of the following:

- banking: money, banks, ATM
- public utilities: gas meter reader, workers on telephone wires
- business development: construction work, young people on the job

- environmental concerns: people enjoying parks, native plants, and animals
- consumer concerns: people shopping, advertisements
- law enforcement: speed-limit sign, state police, courtroom scene

You might want to have students assist you with collecting the pictures. Call on volunteers to choose a picture and explain how state government has a role in what is depicted. **ELL** the atmosphere. Some people are skeptical that human activity plays a major role in climate change. Yet, in 2007 the Intergovernmental Panel on Climate Change (IPCC), a group of 600 scientists from 40 countries, reported that there was "unequivocal" evidence that the world was warming as a result of pollution from human-made heat trapping gases.

The federal government has been slow to respond to this problem. As a result, state governments have been acting on their own. More than half of the states have been moving aggressively to limit the pollution linked to global warming. In 2008 the counsel for the North Carolina General Assembly said: "There's a growing sense (global warming) is real and we've got to face up to it."

In 2008 six Midwestern states agreed to cut emissions of greenhouse gases within their borders up to 80 percent by 2050. Two similar coalitions involving 17 states in the Northeast and West set similar goals. These states are implementing a cap and trade system that allows companies that reduce their emissions below target levels to sell remaining credits to those that do not or cannot.

Some governors have also been pressing for tougher pollution standards. In 2007 California Governor Arnold Schwarzenegger promoted California's Global Warming Solutions Act. This law requires a 25 percent cut in the state's greenhouse gas emissions by the year 2020 and an 80 percent cut by 2050. Charlie Crist, Florida's governor, signed an executive order in 2008 setting a target of lowering emissions to 1990 levels by 2025. At the same time, Virginia Governor Tim Kaine released an energy plan that requires cutting greenhouse gases to 2000 levels by 2025.

State actions got a boost in 2007 from the Supreme Court's decision in *Massachusetts v. Environmental Protection Agency* (EPA). The Court ruled that the EPA has the authority to regulate carbon dioxide and other greenhouse gases emitted from new cars and trucks. The states had been calling for the EPA to act, but the agency claimed it lacked the authority to do so. The Court said: "the harms associated with climate change are serious and well recognized."

Conservation

The care and protection of natural resources, including the land, lakes, rivers, and forests; oil, natural gas, and other energy sources; and wildlife is called conservation. In recent years, state governments have increased their efforts to conserve these resources.

A number of states have laws that allow the state government to plan and regulate land use. Through a land-use law, for example, a state government can preserve certain land from industrial development and set aside other land for parks. Hawaii was the first state to enact a land-use law. Wyoming, Idaho, and Florida soon followed.

Other states have taken action to protect land and water resources. Oregon, for example, has taken steps to protect 500 miles of rivers and ban billboards and disposable bottles. Nearly half of the states have passed laws to control strip-mining, a form of mining that removes the topsoil.

Protecting Life and Property

For the most part, protecting life and property is the responsibility of state and local governments. They account for more than 90 percent of all employees in the criminal justice system. Laws dealing with most common crimes come from the state. The federal government has only limited jurisdiction over most crimes. Local governments usually do not make criminal laws, but they enforce state laws that protect life and property.

State Criminal Laws

Laws prohibiting such crimes as murder, rape, assault, burglary, and the sale and use of dangerous drugs are all part of the state criminal code. Local governments can only enact laws dealing with crime that their state governments allow them to pass.

The federal system allows for great variety in the ways that states deal with crime, permitting them to experiment with new programs. Each state sets its own system of punishment. Several states have introduced mandatory sentencing for drug-related crimes. **Mandatory sentencing** is a system of fixed, required terms of imprisonment for certain types of crimes. In most other states, a judge has greater flexibility in imposing sentences on drug offenders. To take another example, about four out of five states have passed **victim compensation** laws, whereby state government provides financial aid to victims of certain crimes.

Problems of Decentralized Justice

Because criminal justice is usually a state responsibility the justice system has often been described as decentralized, or fragmented. Generally, however, decentralization was regarded as an advantage. Different crime rates, along with different living conditions, may call for criminal laws that are specifically geared to a particular state.

Decentralized justice creates some problems, however. For example, **extradition** is a legal

Did You Know?

The word *environment* is used so often that its meaning can be lost. Literally, your environment is the conditions surrounding you. Discuss the connotation that one is "fenced in" by a physical environment—and the fact that pollution of the environment poses a danger that cannot easily be escaped.

C Critical Thinking

Recognizing Bias Have students look in local newspapers or magazines for editorials or letters that address law enforcement, education, public health, or welfare. Analyze examples by asking questions such as:

- What is the problem?
- Whom does the author blame?
- How does the author describe political views?
- What key words emerge?
- Do "loaded words" suggest attitudes that the author does not state outright?
- How does the author feel about minorities? How can you tell? **AL**

Hands-On Chapter Project

Step 3

Drafting a Bill

Step 3: Complete the Bill Student committees will write their bills.

Directions Ask each committee to divide the work among its members, do research, and write a bill addressing the program they selected in Step 2. They can use the examples of bills they researched in Step 2 to help them determine formatting and content, but remind students that their bills should use clear language the class can understand. Each committee member should make enough copies of his or her contribution for every committee member.

Putting It Together Have the committees meet to assemble their bills and agree on any changes or improvements they want to make. Each committee should select one person who will introduce the bill to the legislature in Step 4. **OL AL**

(Chapter Project continued in Section 4.)

CURRICULUM CONNECTION

Economics In many states, when people are convicted of certain crimes, they forfeit any property, such as cash, cars, boats, planes, and even houses, linked with the crime. Funds raised from such seizures often finance law enforcement activities.

Critical Thinking

Answer: State spending on criminal justice rose consistently until 2001, when it leveled off. The slowdown in prison population growth between 2002 and 2005 correlates with the slowdown in state spending.

Did You Know?

Extradition comes from a Latin term meaning "the act of handing over." The same Latin term, *traditio,* is the basis for the words *traitor* and *treason.*

GO TO To enrich the study of chapter content, remind students that footnoted materials appear in the *Reference Handbook.*

Additional Support

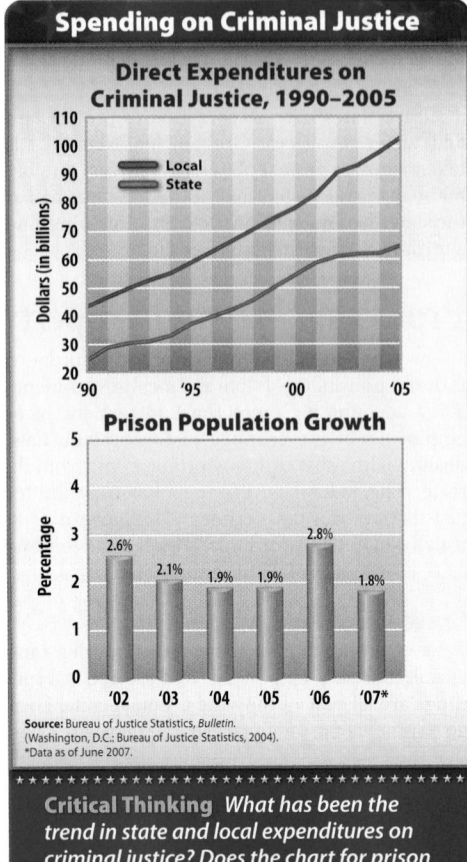

Spending on Criminal Justice

Direct Expenditures on Criminal Justice, 1990–2005

Dollars (in billions) — Local, State

Prison Population Growth

Percentage: '02 2.6%, '03 2.1%, '04 1.9%, '05 1.9%, '06 2.8%, '07* 1.8%

Source: Bureau of Justice Statistics, *Bulletin.* (Washington, D.C.: Bureau of Justice Statistics, 2004). *Data as of June 2007.

Critical Thinking *What has been the trend in state and local expenditures on criminal justice? Does the chart for prison population reflect these changes? Explain.*

procedure by which a person who is accused of a crime and has fled to another state is, on demand, returned to the state where the crime took place. While Article IV[1] of the U.S. Constitution specifically requires extradition, sometimes governors are reluctant to extradite people. 📖

State Police Forces

How long have states had established police forces? The well-known Texas Rangers were formed in 1835 as a border patrol. The first actual state police force, however, was the Pennsylvania State Constabulary, organized in 1905. As the automobile became more widely used, many states turned to mobile police forces. State police are normally limited in their functions. Most are basically highway patrol units. The state police have investigative

powers in many states, but they possess broad police responsibilities in only a few states.

Criminal Corrections

State courts handle the great majority of all criminal cases in the United States. State prisons, county and municipal jails, and other houses of detention throughout a state make up a state's correction system. In some recent years, state spending for corrections has grown faster than for education, public welfare, hospitals, or highways.

Judges, aware of the strains on the system, often choose probation as a sentence. Today more than 2 million people are on probation. Hundreds of thousands are on parole. **Parole** means that a prisoner serves the rest of the sentence in the community under the supervision of a parole officer. Because of probation and parole, three out of every four offenders who might otherwise be in prison are in the community.

Sentencing Options

Many states are giving judges more sentencing options, such as shock probation, shock incarceration, intensive supervision probation or parole, and house arrest. Several states introduced **shock probation** in the 1960s. It was designed to show young offenders how terrible prison life could be through a brief prison incarceration followed by supervised release. **Shock incarceration,** a relatively new program, involves shorter sentences in a highly structured environment where offenders participate in work, community service, education, and counseling.

Intensive supervision probation, or parole, keeps high-risk offenders in the community, but under close supervision. The offender might wear an electronic device that signals his or her location.

A related alternative sentence is **house arrest,** which requires an offender to stay at home except for certain functions the court permits. Several states are using this approach to incarceration.

Education, Health, and Welfare

Health, education, and welfare programs combined make up the largest part of state spending. In a recent year, for example, more than 60 percent

📖 *See the following footnoted materials in the **Reference Handbook:*** **1.** *The Constitution,* pages R42–R67.

Activity: Interdisciplinary Connection

The Environment What is being done in your state to reconcile economic growth with environmental protection? Have students work with partners or in small groups on any of the following investigative activities and then report their findings to the class:

• Research some of the early environmental legislation your state enacted as the federal government relinquished some of its regulatory control in the 1980s.

• Ask the state environmental protection office for information on preparing an environmental impact statement for a new project.

• Contact a national conservation organization and ask for information about topics that the organization believes are of concern in your state. **OL** of all state expenditures were in these three areas. Education accounted for the largest share; welfare was the next largest.

In education, local governments traditionally controlled and financed public schools. In 1900, for example, state governments contributed only 17 percent of public education costs to public schools; today they contribute about 45 percent. Yet there are vast differences among states in the percentages they contribute for public school funding. In Hawaii, the state contributes about 90 percent of public school funds. In New Hampshire, Oregon, and South Dakota, local funds make up the biggest share of school funding, with the state contributing less than 30 percent.

States also differ in per-pupil spending. Many factors affect this figure: the cost of living, the quality of facilities, busing costs, and property tax rates. In some states, differences between rich and poor school districts are so great that state courts have struck down their funding systems as unconstitutional. Yet the amount a state spends does not always lead to better student performance. Some states that spend less money have students who perform well on standardized tests.

State governments establish local school districts and give them the power to administer the schools, but the state regulates the taxes that school districts can levy or the amount of money they can borrow. States also establish many of the policies that school districts must follow. For example, nearly half of the states require a minimum competency test for graduation.

Other typical roles for the state in education include setting the number of days schools must stay open, the number of years a student must attend school, the types of courses that will be offered, the number and type of courses required for graduation, the minimum salaries of teachers, and general teacher qualifications. Some state governments also establish detailed course content, approve textbooks, and create statewide examinations.

In the area of health, the state's police power allows it to license doctors and dentists, regulate the sale of drugs, and require vaccines for schoolchildren. State governments provide a wide range of health services, and they support hospitals, mental health clinics, and institutions for the disabled.

State health agencies serve five broad areas: personal health, health resources, environmental health, laboratories, and aid to local health departments. State health agencies provide care for mothers and their newborn children, treatment of

Funding Issue In *DeRolph* v. *State of Ohio*—named after student Nathan DeRolph (above)—critics argued that relying heavily on the property tax for school funding leads to very unequal schools. *Why would using mostly property taxes for funding schools have this result?*

contagious diseases and chronic illnesses, mental health care, public dental clinics, and immunization against communicable and other diseases.

State governments are also involved in many activities related to the environmental health of its citizens. For example, states monitor air and water quality and manage the disposal of hazardous wastes.

State agencies provide laboratory services to local health departments that cannot afford separate facilities. State governments often pay the bill for public health services that local authorities deliver and administer.

A third major component in state budgets is public welfare, or human services. These terms refer to government efforts to maintain basic health and living conditions for people who cannot afford them. At every level of government, public welfare programs have grown in the last century. In 1900 welfare functions were few, and they were provided by local governments or private charities. By 1934, during the Great Depression, more than half the states had public-welfare programs. In the early 2000s, all three levels of government were spending

CHAPTER 23: *State Governments* **653**

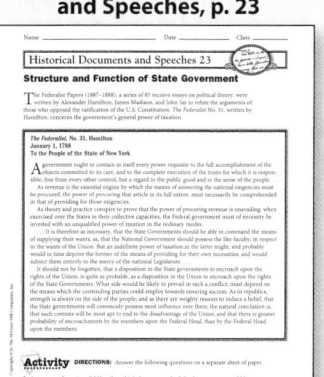

W Writing Support

Expository Writing Divide the class into four groups, and assign each group one of the TANF goals. Have each group write a plan that addresses their assigned goal. Remind students that the emphasis is on short-term assistance. **Ask:** Is it possible to help everybody who needs it? *(Students will probably agree that it is nearly impossible to help everyone in need.)* **AL**

Assess

Assign the Section 3 Assessment as homework or as an in-class activity, or have students take Section Quiz 23-3 from *Section Quizzes and Chapter Tests.*

Close

Predicting Ask: Which area of state government policy most affects your life right now? Do you think your answer will be different 10 years from now? Have students draw upon details from the section to support their responses. **OL**

Section 3 Review

---

billions of dollars on welfare programs from food stamps to cash payments.

Under the Social Security Act of 1935, the federal government created three areas of public assistance to provide financial help to state governments. These were Aid to Families With Dependent Children (AFDC), Aid to the Blind, and Old Age Assistance. Congress added Aid to the Permanently and Totally Disabled in 1950.

In the decades after 1950, these programs—especially AFDC—were criticized on the grounds that they reduced the incentive to work. Critics also said that AFDC contributed to the breakup of families since single mothers received payments, while families with employable fathers often did not.

In 1996 the AFDC system was ended. The new law replaced AFDC with Temporary Assistance for Needy Families (TANF). TANF provided federal payments or "block grants" to states to help needy families, but the emphasis was on short-term assistance. States were able to shape their TANF programs as long as they targeted four goals:

- to support needy families so their children can be cared for at home,
- to help parents in need by training them for jobs and successful parenting,
- to reduce the incidence of out-of-wedlock pregnancy,
- to support two-parent families overall.

Medicaid, a program that provides medical and health services to low-income people, is a program that is jointly funded by the state and federal governments. The federal government establishes guidelines for Medicaid, but each state can work within these guidelines to shape the program to fit its needs. Groups that receive Medicaid services include low-income elderly people, low-income families, and the visually and physically impaired.

Medicaid has become a major issue in recent years because many states have had a budget crisis. This is due to the fact that Medicaid is the second largest expenditure most states make—it accounts for roughly 20 percent of many state budgets. Looked at from the federal perspective, states contribute about 45 percent of the total cost of Medicaid.

State Welfare Programs

Most states have programs for needy people who do not fall into any of the federally mandated categories. Such programs are referred to as general assistance programs. States administer and finance them with some support from local governments. Their benefits vary from state to state. Heavily urbanized states such as New York, California, Michigan, and Massachusetts tend to have more generous programs. Since the early 1930s, state governments have spent more on general assistance programs in line with increases in public health, education, welfare, and environmental spending.

SECTION 3 Review

Vocabulary

1. **Explain** the significance of: corporate charter, public utility, workers' compensation, unemployment compensation, mandatory sentencing, victim compensation, extradition, parole, shock probation, shock incarceration, house arrest.

Main Ideas

2. **Identifying** What are some differences in how states control and fund public schools?

3. **Explaining** Why is a decentralized system of justice an advantage in the United States?

Critical Thinking

4. **Identifying Central Issues** What factors must a state legislature weigh when considering taxing or regulating large corporations?

5. **Organizing** Use the chart below to show the four major policy areas in which state governments enact legislation and an example of each.

Policy Area	Example

Writing About Government

6. **Persuasive Writing** States have distinctive policies in important policy areas such as education, the environment, housing, and welfare. Visit your state governor's Web site to learn about policies in one of these areas. Write a news article, including a chart or another graphic that lists serious problems in one of these areas, the governor's policies on the problems, and suggested solutions that you think should be considered.

Answers

1. All definitions can be found in the section and the Glossary.
2. Local governments tend to control and finance public schools. However, the percentage of states that fund education has increased since the early 1900s. States vary on the level of funding because of the cost of living, the quality of facilities, busing costs, property tax rates, and other circumstances.
3. Different crime rates and living conditions call for criminal laws that are specifically designed for each state.

4. States must consider the effect of taxation and regulation upon business and the possibility that the state might not be attractive to business if business taxes are too high or if business regulation is too severe.
5. business regulation—utilities, consumer protection; environment—clean air and water; crime—police and corrections; health, education, and welfare—school funding, TANF
6. Students' lists of problems and governor's policies should be legitimate, and their suggested solutions should be viable.

Do the Mentally Disabled Who Are Committed Against Their Will Retain Constitutional Rights?

O'Connor v. *Donaldson*, 1975

What guidelines does the state have to follow when mentally disabled people are deprived of their freedom without their consent? The Court referred to this case as raising "a single, relatively simple, but nonetheless important question concerning every man's constitutional right to liberty."

Facts of the Case

In 1957, during a visit to his father in Florida, Kenneth Donaldson began to talk of seeing things. His father then had his 43-year-old son committed to a Florida hospital for the mentally disabled after a sanity hearing before a county judge. Using provisions of a state statute, the judge ruled that Donaldson should be confined for care and treatment. Donaldson, who did not have a lawyer, spent the next 15 years in the understaffed hospital. Much of his time was spent in a large room with patients who had been convicted of crimes.

Donaldson often asked to be released, saying that he was not mentally disabled, was harmless, and that the hospital was not treating him for an illness. Hospital superintendent Dr. J.B. O'Connor refused, claiming that Donaldson could not adjust to normal life. After O'Connor retired, Donaldson achieved release, in part with the support of the hospital's staff. He then sued the state. The case ultimately made its way to the Supreme Court.

The Constitutional Issue

The Court considered a number of issues. The first concerned the rights of mentally disabled people who do no harm to others or to themselves. Can they be confined indefinitely, and does treatment have to be provided to justify such confinement? A second issue was whether state officials who are acting under a state law can be sued for violating the rights of the mentally disabled.

Debating the Issue

1. Did Donaldson have the right to claim damages from state officials if they were acting under existing state law?

2. To rule on O'Connor's suit, was it necessary to determine whether people have a right to treatment when they are committed against their will?

You Be the Judge

In your opinion, did the state of Florida violate the rights of Kenneth Donaldson? If the hospital actively treated Donaldson for a diagnosed mental disability, would his confinement have been justified?

▶ The cover of Kenneth Donaldson's memoir

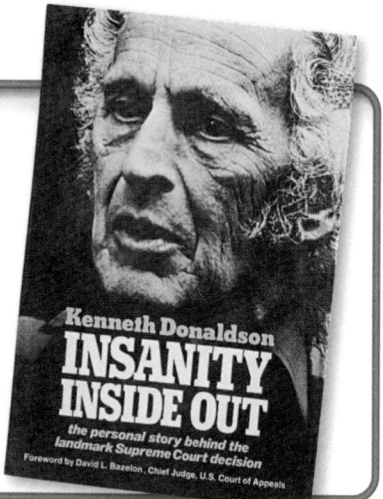

Kenneth Donaldson
INSANITY INSIDE OUT
the personal story behind the landmark Supreme Court decision
Foreword by David L. Bazelon, Chief Judge, U.S. Court of Appeals

---

Class Debate

Organize the class into three groups: one each to represent Kenneth Donaldson and Dr. J.B. O'Connor and one to act as the Supreme Court. Allow class time to develop arguments; have each side present its case; then have the "justices" read their decision and any dissenting opinions aloud.

The Court's Decision

The Supreme Court unanimously held that the state cannot forcibly confine non-dangerous individuals against their will if they are capable of surviving on their own or with the help of friends and family. Justice Stewart stated, "A finding of 'mental illness' alone cannot justify a State's locking a person up against his will and keeping him indefinitely in simple custodial confinement. Assuming that that term can be given a reasonably precise content and that the 'mentally ill' can be identified with reasonable accuracy, there is still no constitutional basis for confining such persons involuntarily if they are dangerous to no one and can live safely in freedom." The Court chose not to decide whether or not treatment had to be provided to dangerously mentally disabled patients.

Debating the Issue Answers

Questions to Consider

1. Yes: They knowingly violated his rights by following state law. No: Officials reasonably believed they were following the law and should not be held liable.

2. Yes: This was an important component in the case, showing that Donaldson was not dangerously mentally disabled. No: The Court does not need to reach a conclusion on this issue to determine whether Donaldson's rights were violated.

You Be the Judge

Students should state whether or not they believe Kenneth Donaldson's rights were violated and whether or not the confinement would be justified with treatment. Students should defend their answers.

Focus

Bellringer
Section Focus Transparencies
23-4

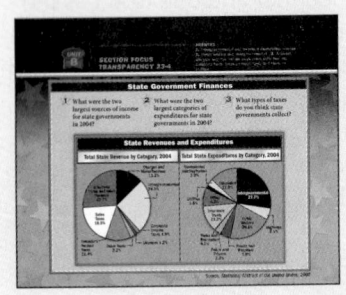

Reader's Guide

Answers to Graphic:

Sources of Revenue:
- Taxes: sales, income, and licensing fees
- Borrowing
- Lotteries
- Intergovernmental Revenue

Resource Manager

Financing State Government

Reader's Guide

Content Vocabulary
- ★ excise tax *(p. 657)*
- ★ regressive tax *(p. 657)*
- ★ progressive tax *(p. 657)*
- ★ proportional tax *(p. 657)*
- ★ intergovernmental revenue *(p. 657)*
- ★ block grant *(p. 658)*

Academic Vocabulary
- ★ export *(p. 656)*
- ★ income *p. 656*
- ★ registration *(p. 657)*

Reading Strategy
Use a graphic organizer similar to the one below to list the ways that states collect revenue.

Sources of Revenue

Issues in the News

Like many states, Georgia suffered revenue shortfalls as the nation faced an economic slowdown in early 2008. The state gets most of its money from two sources—income taxes and sales tax. In January 2008, Georgia's income tax collections dropped 7.7 percent from the year before, and sales tax revenues were off by 1.8 percent. The Georgia legislature, however, went ahead with plans to pass a bigger midyear budget. A spokesperson for Governor Sonny Perdue remained optimistic: "I don't think this is the time to panic. I think we've done a good job of conservative budgeting and spending. We've got a stable rainy day fund to help us through this if we have any trouble making our numbers."

▲ The state flag of Georgia

Taxes are an important source of revenue for most states, not just Georgia. State taxes raise nearly half of the general revenue of state governments. There are three other categories of revenue for states: federal funds of various types, revenues from state lotteries, and borrowed money.

Tax Revenue

Individual state constitutions limit state taxing powers. The federal Constitution also limits a state's taxing powers in three ways:

- A state cannot tax goods or products that move in or out of the state or the country. These imports and **exports** make up interstate and foreign commerce that only Congress can tax or regulate.
- A state cannot tax federal property.

- A state cannot use its taxing power to deprive people of "equal protection of the law," nor can it use its taxing power to deprive people of life, liberty, or property without "due process of the law."

State constitutions can also prevent states from taxing property used for educational, charitable, or religious purposes. Some state constitutions prohibit or limit certain taxes such as the sales tax and the **income** tax. In other states, voters have approved amendments limiting property taxes.

The Sales Tax

State governments began using the sales tax during the Great Depression in the 1930s. Today almost all states have a sales tax, which accounts for about half their tax revenue. Sales taxes are of two types: the general sales tax and the selective sales tax.

R Reading Strategies	**C** Critical Thinking	**D** Differentiated Instruction	**W** Writing Support	**S** Skill Practice
Teacher Edition • Outlining, p. 657 **Additional Resources** • Guid. Read. Act., p. 85 • Quizzes/Tests, pp. 286–294	**Teacher Edition** • Analyzing Information, p. 658 **Additional Resources** • Read. Essen., pp. 271–273	**Teacher Edition** • Visual/Spatial, p. 657 **Additional Resources** • Foldables, p. 66	**Additional Resources** • Gov. Sims. and Debates, p. 50	**Additional Resources** • Ch. Summaries, pp. 67–69 • Reteaching Act., p. 23

The general sales tax is imposed on items such as cars, clothing, household products, and other types of merchandise. In some states, food and drugs are not subject to this tax.

The selective sales tax is imposed on a narrower range of items, such as gasoline, liquor, or cigarettes. A selective sales tax is also called an **excise tax.**

People have strongly criticized the sales tax as a **regressive tax.** A regressive tax is a tax in which the percentage of income that is taxed drops as incomes rise. Because everyone buys necessary items such as clothing, the sales tax represents a higher percentage of the poorer person's income.

The State Income Tax

Today most states have individual income taxes and corporate income taxes. Despite much opposition, the state income tax now accounts for more than 30 percent of all state tax revenues, compared to 10 percent in 1956. The state imposes the income tax on the earnings of individuals and corporations.

When this tax rises as a person's income rises, it is called a **progressive tax.** Some states assess income taxes at the same rate for every wage earner. For example, each person's income might be taxed 10 percent. This type of tax is called a **proportional tax.**

Other Taxes

States have the ability to raise revenue from several other kinds of taxes. Many of these are imposed in the form of licensing fees. States require fees to be paid for many licenses. For example, in order to practice as a doctor, Realtor, or lawyer, a person must be licensed by the state, a process that often entails passing an exam and paying a fee. States also require licenses for hunting and fishing within their borders, as well as for bus lines, amusement parks, and other businesses. By far, the most tax revenue from licenses comes from driver's licenses and motor vehicle **registration.**

States impose severance taxes on the removal of natural resources such as oil, gas, coal, uranium, and fish from land or water. Severance taxes are good sources of revenue in oil- and gas-producing states, such as Oklahoma and Texas. For Kentucky, a severance tax on coal brings in significant revenues.

State governments are using the Internet to help collect delinquent taxes. More than 18 states have Web sites that post the names of people and businesses that have not paid their taxes. This "Internet shaming" has been very effective. In one year Georgia collected more then $19 million in back taxes.

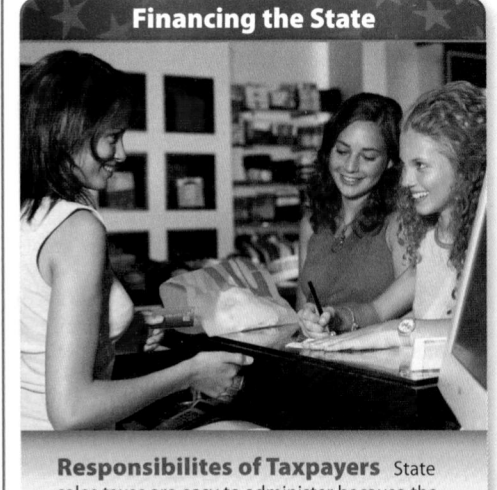

Financing the State

Responsibilites of Taxpayers State sales taxes are easy to administer because the person who sells the item, like the employee at this store, collects the tax. *Why is the sales tax a regressive tax?*

R Other Sources of Revenue

As noted above, taxes pay only a part of state government expenses. To pay for the rest of their expenses, states borrow money, hold a state lottery, and receive monies from the federal government.

Borrowing

States usually borrow money to pay for large, long-term expenditures such as highway construction or other building projects. State governments borrow by selling bonds. A bond is a contractual promise on the part of the borrower to repay a certain sum plus interest by a specified date. In most states, voters must be asked to approve new bond issues. **D**

Lotteries

Nearly three-fourths of the states run public lotteries to raise revenue. In the 1980s, lotteries became the fastest-growing source of state revenues. The states spend about half the lottery income on prizes and 6 percent on administering the lottery.

Intergovernmental Revenue

The federal government, with its vast revenue and taxing power, provides about 20 percent of all state revenues. **Intergovernmental revenue,** or

Teach

Caption Answer: because it represents a larger portion of a poorer person's income

R Reading Strategy

Outlining Have students construct charts that identify, with examples, the various kinds of taxes collected by states. Students can use the charts for section review. **BL**

D Differentiated Instruction

Visual/Spatial Have small groups of students choose one source of state revenue and create a flowchart that illustrates how the revenue is collected and used. (Groups might need to do additional research to find the details they need to prepare accurate flowcharts.) Some students can work on layout; some students can focus on research; some students can write the copy, and others can do the final drawing and lettering. Invite group representatives to explain the finished flowcharts to the class. **BL**

Hands-On Chapter Project

Step 4

Drafting a Bill

Step 4: Introducing the Bill Committees will introduce their bills.

Directions Appoint a Speaker of the House to open a session of the legislature and to call on speakers (using titles such as "Representative Smith" or "Senator Johnson"). Also appoint a

senate majority leader to conduct the votes. Each committee will present its bill, allowing the class to ask questions or contribute opinions for or against the bill.

Putting It Together Have the legislature vote on the bills. Discuss which parts of the process were the most difficult. **OL**

C Critical Thinking

Analyzing Information Have students reread the section about federal mandates. **Ask:** How did the UMRA relieve some state budgetary pressure? *(The UMRA required the issuers of federal mandates to outline the direct costs to the state or local government and to conduct cost-benefit analyses of private business mandates costing more than $100 million.)* **OL**

Assess

Assign the Section 4 Assessment as homework or as an in-class activity, or have students take Section Quiz 23-4 from *Section Quizzes and Chapter Tests.*

Close

Explaining Have students individually write definitions of each of the Key Terms in their own words. Then have students discuss and compare their definitions and decide on the best ones. **OL**

Section 4 Review

---

revenue distributed by one level of government to another, can come in the form of a federal grant. These grants, also called grants-in-aid, are monies given to the states for specific purposes.

By stipulating how federal money is supposed to be used, these grants influence the states in a number of ways. First, grants supply funds for programs that states might not otherwise decide to support. Grants also promote programs and goals that reflect national goals. Finally, because grants come with certain guidelines and requirements, they often set minimum standards for a service in the states. For example, the federal government provides grants to make sure that all states provide a minimum public welfare program.

Under categorical-formula grants, federal funds go to all the states on the basis of a formula. **C** Different amounts go to different states, often depending on the state's wealth. These grants usually require states to provide matching funds. Under project grants, state or local agencies or individuals may apply for funds for a variety of specific purposes: to fight crime, to improve a city's subway system, or to control air and water pollution, among other things.

State governments usually prefer block grants over categorical grants as a form of federal aid. A **block grant** is a large grant of money to a state or local government to be used for a general purpose, such as public health or crime control. Block grants have fewer guidelines, and state officials have considerably more choice over how the money will be spent.

Federal Mandates

In the 1980s and 1990s, the federal government's share of state and local government revenue declined, but federal regulatory mandates increased. A mandate is a formal order given by a higher authority, in this case by the federal government. Between 1980 and 1990, the federal government increased the number of mandated programs for which state and local governments had to raise their own revenue. State and local officials complained about the rising cost of federal mandates in areas such as health and the environment. Some people believed that the federal government had intruded on areas of state sovereignty.

In 1995 Congress passed the Unfunded Mandate Reform Act (UMRA) to address the unfunded requirements imposed by federal agencies. The law required congressional committees that approved a bill containing a federal mandate to describe its direct cost to the state, local, or tribal governments, or private companies. The committee was also required to estimate the mandate's total cost to the Congressional Budget Office (CBO). For private business mandates costing more than $100 million yearly, federal agencies must conduct cost-benefit analyses of new regulations. A 2003 study on state budget problems showed that the UMRA reduced state budgetary pressure. According to a CBO report, only 10 laws have been passed since 1996 that contain intergovernmental mandates that exceed the UMRA threshold ($50 million in 1996 dollars; adjusted annually for inflation, $68 million in 2008).

SECTION 4 Review

Vocabulary

1. **Explain** the significance of: excise tax, regressive tax, progressive tax, proportional tax, intergovernmental revenue, block grant.

Main Ideas

2. **Describing** What is a categorical-formula grant?

3. **Identifying** List the two main categories of state tax revenue.

Critical Thinking

4. **Understanding Cause and Effect** How does Congress influence state policies through its distribution of federal grants?

5. **Organizing** Use a graphic organizer like the one below to show why state officials prefer block grants as a form of federal aid.

Cause		Effect
	→	State officials have more control over funds

Writing About Government

6. **Expository Writing** Contact your state offices or use library reference materials to find out the major areas of your state's spending and the major sources of your state's revenue. Summarize your information in a multimedia presentation; you might want to include graphics like a circle graph to display relevant data.

Answers

1. All definitions can be found in the section and the Glossary.
2. Federal funds go to all the states on the basis of a formula that often depends on the state's wealth.
3. sales tax and income tax
4. by stipulating programs and goals that the federal government believes are necessary and by setting certain minimum standards in the states
5. cause: funds come with fewer guidelines
6. Have students show their presentations. Discuss with students the major sources of the state's revenue and the major areas of the state's spending.

Should State and Local Judges Be Appointed?

In some states, judges are appointed by the governor, the state legislature, or a governmental agency. In most states, however, judges are elected, either in partisan or nonpartisan elections. (A partisan election is one in which a candidate's political party is identified on the ballot.) Over the decades, critics have asked whether electing judges is the best way to get an independent and well-qualified judiciary.

YES

Appointment is a better system because most voters do not know enough about judicial candidates to make a reasonable choice. For ethical reasons, judicial candidates have to campaign without saying too much. The American Bar Association recommends that they be careful not to take any public position that might prevent them from being objective in a court case. In nonpartisan elections, voters do not even have a party ballot to go by. Proof that voters are uninformed can be seen in under-voting in judicial races—even when voters go to the polls, they often decide to withhold their vote in judicial races. The popular will would still be honored if judges were appointed by the legislature. After all, legislators themselves are elected by the people.

NO

States should continue to have their judges elected by popular vote. Our government is based on the principle of "the consent of the governed." Elected judges are more likely than appointed judges to make decisions that are in line with popular desires and interests. There is another very good reason for having voters elect judges—it is a much better guarantee of an independent judiciary. The American government system establishes three separate branches in order to preserve liberty: Each branch acts as a check and balance on the other. If, however, the state legislature appointed most judges, they would be too tempted to favor the dominant political party. Thus, it is popular election that ensures a government "of the people, by the people, and for the people."

Debating the Issue

1. **Analyzing** How does the No argument adapt the federal principle of "separation of powers" to support its position?

2. **Explaining** Why does the American Bar Association tell judicial candidates to be careful about how much they tell voters?

3. **Evaluating** Which opinion do you tend to agree with? Explain your reasoning.

▶ Was being photographed at the Cleveland Browns Stadium a way for Judge Dick Ambrose to connect to Cleveland voters?

Teach

Setting Up the Debate

Researching Remind students that U.S. Supreme Court justices are appointed, not elected. **Ask:** Is it appropriate that Supreme Court justices are appointed and most state and local judges are elected? *(Students might mention that the need for judges to be unaffected by partisan politics in court necessitates appointment as opposed to election.)* **OL**

Evaluating Have students research the arguments for and against appointment of state and local judges. Students should give specific arguments to support both points of view. **OL**

Concluding the Debate

Discuss these questions with students:

- Should the party affiliation of a state or a local judge be an important factor in his or her election campaign? Should it be a factor after he or she is elected? Why or why not?

- Are there any ways that state laws could be modified so that if judges were appointed instead of elected, there would be checks and balances on each appointment?

Debating the Issue Answers

1. It argues that if the state legislature (the legislative branch) were responsible for appointing judges (the judicial branch), it would wield too much power.

2. If a judge were too closely aligned either with or against a political figure or a public issue, it would be difficult for him or her to be unbiased in court.

3. Students should support their opinions with references to the quotes or with individual research and logical arguments.

CHAPTER 23 Assessment and Activities

Reviewing Vocabulary

Define each of the following content vocabulary words.

1. public utility
2. mandate
3. criminal case
4. initiative
5. civil case
6. item veto
7. regressive tax
8. intergovernmental revenue
9. bicameral
10. workers' compensation

Reviewing Main Ideas

Section 1 *(pages 637–640)*

11. **Analyzing** What is the method most states use to ratify an amendment to a state constitution?

12. **Classifying** In the federal system, how is sovereign power divided among state and federal laws and constitutions?

Section 2 *(pages 641–647)*

13. **Stating** What are the political qualifications that a person must meet to become governor?

14. **Identifying** What are four methods that states use to appoint state judges?

Section 3 *(pages 648–654)*

15. **Explaining** How do states regulate public utilities?

Section 4 *(pages 656–658)*

16. **Describing** In what three ways do federal grants influence the states?

Critical Thinking

17. 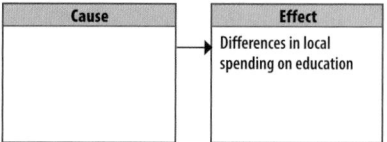 **Essential Question** How do state constitutions compare to the U.S. Constitution?

18. **Specifying** What legislative policymaking role is a governor expected to fill?

19. **Understanding Cause and Effect** Use a graphic organizer like the one below to show why spending for education differs among local districts.

Cause		Effect
	→	Differences in local spending on education

Chapter Summary

State Constitutions
★ Lay out the structure of state government
★ Establish different types of local government
★ Regulate how state and local governments can raise and spend money
★ Establish independent state agencies, boards, and commissions

State Government Policy
★ Regulate business—Protect consumers and workers, promote business and industry
★ Protect the environment—Pollution control, conservation of resources
★ Protect life and property—Set and enforce criminal laws, create police forces
★ Provide for education, health, and welfare

Branches of State Government
★ Legislative—All states except Nebraska have a bicameral legislature
★ Executive—Every state is headed by a governor, though the power and influence of the governor differs from state to state
★ Judicial—Interprets and applies state and local laws; state court systems vary

Financing State Government
★ Taxes—Sales tax, state income tax, severance tax, state property tax, inheritance tax
★ Borrowing—Selling bonds
★ Lotteries
★ Intergovernmental Revenue—Categorical grants and block grants from the federal government

Reviewing Vocabulary

1. an organization that supplies a necessity such as electricity
2. a formal order given by a higher authority
3. one in which the state brings charges against a citizen for violating the law
4. a method by which citizens propose a constitutional amendment or a law
5. a noncriminal lawsuit, usually between two private individuals or organizations
6. the power to turn down a particular item in a bill without vetoing the entire bill
7. tax in which people with lower incomes pay a larger portion of their income
8. revenue distributed by one level of government to another
9. two-house legislative body
10. payments received by people who are unable to work as a result of job-related injury or ill health

Reviewing Main Ideas

11. popular vote
12. State laws must be consistent with the state constitution, just as federal laws must agree with the U.S. Constitution. A state constitution or state law cannot contain provisions that clash with the U.S. Constitution.
13. A candidate should have experience in state government and knowledge of law.
14. popular election, election by state legislatures, appointment by the governor, and the Missouri Plan
15. States regulate the rates that utility companies may charge customers in return for granting the company the right to supply service in the state.
16. Federal grants fund programs that states otherwise cannot afford, advance goals the federal government believes are necessary, and set certain minimum standards in the states.

Critical Thinking

17. Most state constitutions are longer and much more detailed than the U.S. Constitution.
18. A governor is supposed to propose and sign legislation and to identify state needs.
19. Cause: Each local district has a different tax base that determines its ability to support education.

Government ONLINE Self-Check Quiz
Visit glencoe.com and enter QuickPass™ code USG9822c23.
Click on Self-Check Quizzes for additional test practice.

CHAPTER
23
Assessment
and Activities

Document-Based Questions

Analyzing Primary Sources

Read the excerpt below and answer the questions that follow.

Texas is the only state to have existed as a separate nation before being granted statehood. Adopted in 1876, this was the sixth constitution of the state of Texas since it declared its independence from Mexico in 1836, and it still forms the basis of the modern Texas state constitution.

66 **Article 1—BILL OF RIGHTS**
That the general, great, and essential principles of liberty and free government may be recognized and established, we declare:

Section 1—FREEDOM AND SOVEREIGNTY OF STATE
Texas is a free and independent State, subject only to the Constitution of the United States, and the maintenance of our free institutions and the perpetuity of the Union depend upon the preservation of the right of local self-government, unimpaired to all the States.

Section 2—INHERENT POLITICAL POWER; REPUBLICAN FORM OF GOVERNMENT
All political power is inherent in the people, and all free governments are founded on their authority, and instituted for their benefit. The faith of the people of Texas stands pledged to the preservation of a republican form of government, and, subject to this limitation only, they have at all times the inalienable right to alter, reform or abolish their government in such manner as they may think expedient. **99**

20. Why do you think it is important to have a state constitution and separate state governments?

21. Why do you think it was important to specify that the state government would be a republican form of government?

Interpreting Political Cartoons

Analyze the cartoon and answer the questions that follow. Base your answers on the cartoon and your knowledge of Chapter 23.

"The state decided to leave per pupil spending up to the individual."

22. What is the subject of this cartoon?

23. What dilemma faces the students in the cartoon?

24. Since most public schools rely on property taxes to operate, what is the cartoonist saying about that system?

Participating IN GOVERNMENT

25. The area in which state government makes decisions that might affect you most is education. As a person who is directly affected by the educational system, you are likely to have suggestions for improving it. As a class, brainstorm ideas for improving education in your state. Conduct research or a survey to gather more information. Organize your research into a coherent plan and draft a letter to your state representative suggesting a bill that addresses your concerns.

Government ONLINE

Have students use the ***Chapter 23 Self-Check Quiz.*** Visit glencoe.com and enter ***QuickPass***™ code USG9085c23T to prepare for the Chapter Test.

Interpreting Political Cartoons

22. state funding of education and schools

23. To participate in class, each student must pay the meter at his or her desk.

24. Property taxes are inadequate to support education as measured by "per pupil spending," so the cartoon depicts an absurd alternative.

Participating IN GOVERNMENT

25. Call on volunteers to present their letters to the class. Hold a class discussion to evaluate the suggestions. Students should share any responses they receive with the class.

Chapter Bonus Test Question

Ask: Why do state governments hold the right to issue occupational and professional licenses? *(Licenses are a form of consumer protection, helping to ensure that people working in various professions have the appropriate qualifications for doing so.)*

Analyzing Primary Sources

20. Answers may include that although the state is subject to the U.S. Constitution, local self-government is also a right. A state constitution can help protect the rights of local governments, but it can also help prevent other smaller governments from being established in certain regions. Additionally, state governments know local issues better than the federal government and can better and more efficiently manage those issues.

21. This amendment to the Texas State Bill of Rights would prohibit the state from establishing a government that might provide fewer freedoms than specified in the constitution, and it makes it clear that the government should not markedly differ from that established by the federal government. Students might suggest that this amendment prevents the state government from forming something like a totalitarian government, for instance.

Key to Ability Levels	
BL Below level	**AL** Above level
OL On level	**ELL** English Language Learners

Key to Teaching Resources	
📁 Print Material	🖇 Transparency
💿 CD-ROM or DVD	

Levels					Resources	Chapter Opener	Section 1	Section 2	Section 3	Chapter Assess
BL	OL	AL	ELL							
FOCUS										
BL	OL	AL	ELL	🖇	Section Focus Transparencies		24-1	24-2	24-3	
TEACH										
BL	OL		ELL	📁	Reading Essentials and Study Guide (and Answer Key)		p. 274	p. 277	p. 281	
BL	OL		ELL	📁	Guided Reading Activities		p. 86	p. 87	p. 88	
BL	OL		ELL	📁	Vocabulary Activities		p. 24			
BL	OL	AL	ELL	📁	Chapter Summaries				p. 70	
BL	OL			📁	American Biographies					
BL	OL	AL	ELL	📁	Cooperative Learning Activities				p. 15	
	OL	AL	ELL	📁	Government Simulations and Debate				p. 52	
BL	OL	AL	ELL	📁	Historical Documents and Speeches			p. 24		
BL	OL	AL	ELL	📁	Interpreting Political Cartoons			p. 47		
BL	OL		ELL	📁	Skill Reinforcement Activities				p. 24	
BL	OL	AL	ELL	📁	Source Readings		p. 24			
BL	OL			📁	Supreme Court Case Studies					
BL	OL	AL	ELL	📁	Participating in Government Activities			p. 47		
BL	OL		ELL	📁	Spanish Declaration of Independence and U.S. Constitution	✓	✓	✓	✓	✓
BL	OL	AL	ELL	📁	NGS World Atlas, Spanish	✓	✓	✓	✓	✓
BL	OL	AL	ELL	🖇	Unit Overlay Transparencies, Strategies, and Activities	✓	✓	✓	✓	✓
BL	OL		ELL	🖇	Making It Relevant Transparencies	✓	✓	✓	✓	✓
BL	OL	AL	ELL	🖇	High School Writing Process Transparencies, Strategies, and Activities	✓	✓	✓	✓	✓
BL	OL	AL		🖇	American Art & Architecture Transparencies, Strategies, and Activities	✓	✓	✓	✓	✓

✓ Chapter- or unit-based activities applicable to all sections in this chapter

CHAPTER 24

All-In-One Planner and Resource Center

- Interactive Lesson Planner
- Interactive Teacher Edition
- Fully editable blackline masters
- Chapter Spotlight Videos Launch
- Differentiated Lesson Plans
- Printable reports of daily assignments
- Standards tracking system

Levels BL	OL	AL	ELL		Resources	Chapter Opener	Section 1	Section 2	Section 3	Chapter Assess
					TEACH (continued)					
BL	OL			💿	American Music: Hits Through History	✓	✓	✓	✓	✓
BL	OL		ELL	📁	Reading Strategies for the Social Studies Classroom	✓	✓	✓	✓	✓
			ELL	📁	English Language Learner Handbook	✓	✓	✓	✓	✓
BL	OL		ELL	📁	Writer's Guidebook for Social Studies	✓	✓	✓	✓	✓
BL	OL	AL	ELL	📁	Living Constitution, SE	✓	✓	✓	✓	✓
BL	OL	AL	ELL	📁	Living Constitution, TAE	✓	✓	✓	✓	✓
BL	OL			📁	NGS World Atlas, English	✓	✓	✓	✓	✓
BL	OL		ELL	📁	The Constitution and You (poster set)	✓	✓	✓	✓	✓
BL	OL	AL	ELL	📁	Spanish Chapter Summaries				p. 70	
BL	OL	AL	ELL	📁	Spanish Vocabulary Activities		p. 24			
BL	OL		ELL	📁	Spanish Reading Essentials and Study Guide (and Answer Key)		p. 274	p. 277	p. 281	
BL	OL	AL	ELL	💿	PresentationPlus! with MindJogger CheckPoint	✓	✓	✓	✓	✓
					ASSESS					
BL	OL	AL	ELL	💿	*ExamView® Assessment Suite*		24-1	24-2	24-3	Ch. 24
BL	OL	AL	ELL	📁	Authentic Assessment with Rubrics		p. 31			p. 31
BL	OL	AL	ELL	📁	Section Quizzes and Chapter Tests		p. 295	p. 296	p. 297	pp. 299–306
BL	OL	AL	ELL	📁	Spanish Section Quizzes and Tests		p. 295	p. 296	p. 297	pp. 299–306
					CLOSE					
BL			ELL	📁	Reteaching Activities				p. 24	p. 24
BL	OL	AL	ELL	💿	StudentWorks™ Plus with Audio Summaries	✓	✓	✓	✓	✓
BL	OL		ELL	🖨	Graphic Organizer Transparencies		✓	✓	✓	
BL	OL		ELL	📁	High School Government Reading and Study Skills Foldables®		p. 67	p. 67	p. 67	

Teach With Technology

What is the Lesson Planner?

The TeacherWorks™ Plus Lesson Planner is a practical tool for creating and organizing daily lesson plans using an interactive calendar.

How can the Lesson Planner help me?

The Lesson Planner makes it easy to see, at a glance, the resources you have chosen to use for each class on any given day. Using a simple drag-and-drop format, you can generate lesson plans using any number of ancillary titles included in the TeacherWorks™ Plus software, as well as Internet links, documents, files, and programs of your choosing. Once a lesson plan is created, the Lesson Planner serves as a launching point for these resources.

The Lesson Planner is a feature of TeacherWorks™ Plus.

Government ONLINE

Visit glencoe.com and enter *QuickPass*™ code USG9085c24T for Chapter 24 resources.

You can easily launch a wide range of digital products from your computer's desktop with the McGraw-Hill Social Studies widget.

	Student	Teacher	Parent
Media Library			
• Student Edition Section Audio	●		●
• Chapter Spotlight Videos	●	●	●
***United States Government* Online Learning Center (Web Site)**			
• Chapter Overviews	●	●	●
• Multilingual Glossaries	●	●	●
• Study-to-Go	●	●	●
• Student Web Activities	●	●	●
• Self-Check Quizzes	●	●	●
• Online Student Edition	●	●	●
• Vocabulary eFlashcards	●	●	●
• Web Activity Lesson Plans		●	
• Vocabulary PuzzleMaker	●	●	●
• Landmark Supreme Court Cases	●	●	●
• Beyond the Textbook	●	●	●

READING SUPPORT FROM
JAMESTOWN EDUCATION

- **Timed Readings Plus in Social Studies** helps students increase their reading rate and fluency while maintaining comprehension. The 400-word passages are similar to those found on state and national assessments.

- **Reading in the Content Area: Social Studies** concentrates on six essential reading skills that help students better comprehend what they read. The book includes 75 high-interest nonfiction passages written at increasing levels of difficulty.

- **Reading Social Studies** includes strategic reading instruction and vocabulary support in Social Studies content for ELLs and native speakers of English. www.jamestowneducation.com

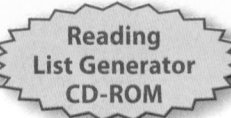

Reading List Generator CD-ROM

GLENCOE BOOKLINK 3

Use this database to search more than 30,000 titles to create a customized reading list for your students.

- Reading lists can be organized by students' reading level, author, genre, theme, or area of interest.

- The database provides Degrees of Reading Power™ (DRP) and Lexile™ readability scores for all selections.

- A brief summary of each selection is included.

Leveled reading suggestions for this chapter:

- *The Brawl Over Sprawl,* by Richard Lacayo

- *Man-Made America: Chaos or Control?,* by Christopher Tunnard and Boris Pushkarev

Review suggested books before assigning them.

Economics Connection

Personal Finance Literacy

Using Credit Wisely

Ask students: Are you creditworthy? Tell them that, before they can borrow money, lenders will want to know whether they are likely to be paid back. To determine this, lenders check a person's credit score. A credit score is a number from 300 to 900 that follows you throughout your life. It is determined by the history of all of your financial transactions. Whenever you borrow money, pay a bill, open or close an account, or carry a credit balance, your credit score is affected.

A credit score is kept by three private credit agencies. In 2007 the median score was 723; above 720 is usually considered good credit; below 600 is considered poor. Your credit score determines whether lenders allow you to borrow money and what interest rate you pay. Employers, too, check credit before hiring, and car rental agencies and landlords check credit before renting. It's important to establish credit as early as possible, since 15 percent of a credit score is determined by how long the credit has been established. Although you have to be at least 18 to have a credit card of your own, you can begin establishing credit sooner:

- Ask a parent to cosign for a low-limit card or a store card. Pay the balance off each month on time and, when you're 18, you can have the cosigner's name taken off and the limit increased.

- Have your parents put your name on the phone or utility bills and pay promptly.

- Open a checking and/or savings account.

How Do You Score?

Paying on time raises your credit score; paying late lowers it. Here's how:

Did You Know?

You should check your credit history for errors by requesting a report (one per year is free) from each credit agency.

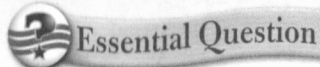

Essential Question

Local governments provide citizens with basic services such as education, fire and police protection, water, and sewage and sanitation. Local governments face challenges with urban decline, urban growth, funding services, and housing shortages.

Chapter Spotlight Video

To generate student interest and provide a springboard for class discussion, access the Chapter 24 Video at glencoe.com or on the video DVD.

FOLDABLES
Study Organizer

Dinah Zike's Foldables are three-dimensional, interactive graphic organizers that help students practice basic writing skills, review key vocabulary terms, and identify main ideas. Have students complete this chapter's Foldable activity or activities in *Dinah Zike's Reading and Study Skills Foldables* booklet. **OL**

Government ONLINE

Visit glencoe.com and enter *QuickPass*™ code USG9085c24T for Chapter 24 Resources including Chapter Overview, Student Web Activity, Self-Check Quiz, and other materials for students and teachers.

CHAPTER **24**

◀) **Chapter Audio**   📄 **Spotlight Video**

Local Governments

Austin City Hall in Austin, Texas

Essential Question

What are the main functions of local governments, and what are their greatest challenges today?

Government ONLINE
Chapter Overview Visit glencoe.com and enter *QuickPass*™ code USG9822c24 for an overview, a quiz, and other chapter resources.

662

Launching the Chapter

Limits on Local Governments It was an 1868 court case that definitively established that municipalities—cities, towns, counties, villages, and townships—are totally subordinate to the state. The theory of state preeminence has been called "Dillon's Rule," a term used in the 1868 case in which it was said: "Municipal corporations owe their origin to, and derive their powers and rights wholly from, the legislature. It breathes into them the breath of life, without which they cannot exist. As it creates, so may it destroy. If it may destroy, it may abridge and control." There is an opposing theory, but the Supreme Court has accepted the Dillon Rule in questions relating to the scope of municipal power. **Essential Question:** How does the Dillon Rule apply to local government functions? *(It states that a local government does not have the ultimate authority in any area.)* **OL**

Structure of Local Government

Focus

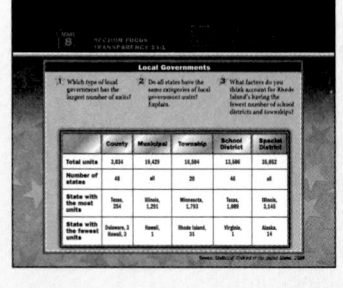
Reader's Guide

Content Vocabulary
* county (p. 664)
* county board (p. 664)
* township (p. 664)
* municipality (p. 665)
* special district (p. 665)
* incorporation (p. 666)
* referendum (p. 666)

Academic Vocabulary
* display (p. 664)
* administrator (p. 665)
* feature (p. 668)

Reading Strategy
Use a chart similar to the one below to list the roles of officials in the council-manager form of government.

Voters elect → [ ] → hires → [ ]

elects → [ ] appoints → [ ]

Reader's Guide

Answers to Graphic:
Voters elect→council
Council elects→mayor
Council hires→manager
Manager appoints→municipal workers

People in the News

New York City Mayor Michael R. Bloomberg received a leadership award from the U.S. Conference of Mayors. Bloomberg's peers recognized him for his leadership in helping New York City rise from the ashes of the 9/11 terrorist attacks. In accepting the award, Bloomberg emphasized that the nation's mayors are on the front lines of the American economy. Bloomberg, who led his own global media and financial data firm to success, has used his administrative skills to reduce crime, raise standards in the schools, and improve the environment. Political analysts have wondered if the popular and wealthy Bloomberg eventually will want to run for the New York governorship or perhaps for president of the United States.

▲ Michael Bloomberg campaigning for mayor of New York City in 2001

New mayors, such as Michael Bloomberg, can claim a national reputation. Most mayors, however, are known to only the residents of their own cities. In the United States, approximately 86,000 units of local government serve American residents.

Created by the State

Although the United States has a strong tradition of local self-government, local governments have no legal independence. Established by the state, they are entirely dependent on the state governments under which they exist. The state can assume control over them or even abolish them. A state government might, for example, assume control over a local school district that is in financial trouble. State constitutions usually set forth the powers and duties of local governments. They also might describe the form of government a locality can adopt based on its size and population or regulate the kinds of taxes a locality can levy.

Types of Local Government

The United States has four basic types of local government: the county, the township, the municipality, and the special district. It is important to

Resource Manager

R Reading Strategies	**C** Critical Thinking	**D** Differentiated Instruction	**W** Writing Support	**S** Skill Practice
Additional Resources • Guid. Read. Act., p. 86 • Quizzes/Tests, p. 295	**Teacher Edition** • Applying Information, p. 664 **Additional Resources** • Read. Essen., pp. 274–276	**Teacher Edition** • Interpersonal, p. 668 **Additional Resources** • Foldables, p. 67 • Source Readings, p. 24	**Additional Resources** • Authentic Assess., p. 31	**Teacher Edition** • Researching, p. 667 **Additional Resources** • Vocab. Act., p. 24

Teach

C Critical Thinking

Applying Information

Brainstorm with students a list of current topics in the news. Call on volunteers to identify any topics that involve local government or that they think will have an impact on local government. You might want to list students' responses and review the list again at the end of the section, having students refine their earlier comments. **BL**

CURRICULUM CONNECTION

Technology In most cases, town meetings are not televised; if they are, the broadcast is carried on a local cable channel. Politicians who are in the national spotlight, however—leading members of Congress, for instance, or presidential candidates—have learned that appearing at a town meeting will draw national media coverage and can boost their public image.

Additional Support

---

understand that these four types of local government are not found in every state and that they vary from state to state.

The County

The **county** is normally the largest territorial and political subdivision of a state. The county form of government is found in every state except Connecticut and Rhode Island. In Louisiana, counties are called parishes, and in Alaska they are called boroughs.

Counties of the United States **display** tremendous variety. The number of counties within a state varies from state to state, and counties differ in size and population. County governments also vary considerably in power and influence. In rural areas and in the South, early settlements were spread out over large areas, with few towns and villages. One town in each county became the seat of county government.

On the other hand, county government has never been very important in New England. In this region, people settled in towns, and each township, rather than the county, became the significant unit of local government.

Recently in some metropolitan areas, county governments have grown in importance as they assume some of the functions that municipalities once handled. For example, the government of Dade County, Florida, now administers transportation, the water supply, and other services for the Miami area. In many other places, county governments have declined in importance but continue to exist in spite of attempts to change or even abolish them.

Structure of County Governments

States provide county governments with a variety of organizational structures. A **county board** has the authority to govern most counties. The name of this board varies from state to state. It may be called the county board of supervisors, the board of county commissioners, or the board of freeholders. Board members are almost always popularly elected officials. State law strictly limits the legislative powers of county boards. For the most part, county boards decide on the county budget, taxes, and zoning codes.

In many counties, the county board has both executive and legislative powers. Board members often divide executive power, with each member being responsible for a different county department. In many counties, the county board shares executive power with other officials who are usually elected.

These officials may include the county sheriff, attorney, clerk, coroner, recorder of deeds, treasurer, auditor, assessor, surveyor, and superintendent of schools. County governments supervise elections, issue certain licenses, keep records of vital statistics, and provide many services, including hospitals, sports facilities, and public welfare programs.

The Township

Townships exist as units of local government in 20 states—mostly in New England and in the Midwest. In the 1600s, the early settlers in New England established the first townships in America. In New England, township is another name for town, a fairly small community with a population that usually numbers fewer than 5,000.

In many states, counties are subdivided into townships. The size and jurisdiction of townships vary greatly from one state to another. In New Jersey, the township covers a large area that may include several municipalities.

The services of township governments vary from state to state, too. In Nebraska and Missouri, the primary function of township government is road building and maintenance; in Pennsylvania, townships provide many government services, including police and fire protection.

In many rural areas, townships have lost population and power in the last few decades. For example, many townships in Kansas have lost power to county governments. In some other areas of the Midwest, such as Indiana, control over education has passed from the township to either the county or the local school district.

In some urban areas, however, township government has taken on increased importance. In areas with rapid metropolitan growth, townships have assumed some functions of city government, such as providing water, sewage disposal, and police protection. Urban townships in states such as Michigan and New Jersey also have become increasingly important.

The New England Town

Thomas Jefferson once described politics in the typical New England town as "the perfect exercise of self-government." With the strong community spirit fostered by their founders, these towns became models of citizen participation in local government.

The town meeting was the centerpiece of town government in New England. In the past, town meetings were open to all voters, and citizens

---

Activity: Collaborative Learning

Researching Local History How was the structure of government in your community established? How did it develop? Have students work in small groups to find out. Divide the coverage either chronologically or topically (perhaps following the flow of topics in the text) among the groups. Groups can choose their own leaders and presenters and then can divide the other tasks—for example, researching facts, researching historic

photographs and maps, interviewing local historians, outlining, writing, and editing—according to group members' strengths. Encourage students to include information about how the local government conforms to or varies from the information in their text. Devote one or more class periods to groups' presentations. Consider having students present the material in a community forum. **OL** participated in lawmaking, decided on taxes, and approved money for public projects they believed were needed. They elected selectmen, the town officials, who were responsible for administering the government between town meetings. As New England towns grew, this town meeting form of direct democracy became impractical. In a few very small towns, the town meeting is still used, but in larger towns and cities, voters elect representatives to attend the town meetings. Some towns have also hired town managers to perform duties that are similar to those of county **administrators.**

The Municipality

A **municipality** is an urban unit of government—a town, borough, city, or urban district that has legal rights granted by the state through its charter. The first charters were much like charters for private corporations, except that towns and cities were much more narrowly controlled. Each municipality had a charter until state legislatures began to pass general laws after 1850. These early charters and statutes contained powers that today seem outdated. For example, Ohio gave its cities the power to regulate the transportation of gunpowder; to prevent the excessive riding of horses; to provide for measuring hay, wood, coal, or other articles for sale; and to suppress riots, gambling, bowling, and billiards.

By the twentieth century, most states divided municipalities into classes, depending on their population. This way, the states could provide each class with a more standard type of charter.

The Special District

The **special district** is a unit of local government that deals with a specific function, such as education, the water supply, or transportation. Special districts are the most common type of local government, and they deal with a wide variety of special services. The local school district is the most common example of a special district.

Tribal Government

Some states have a separate level of government that serves the Native American population. The state of New Mexico established the Indian Affairs Department in 1953 to serve as a liaison between the tribal governments and the state government.

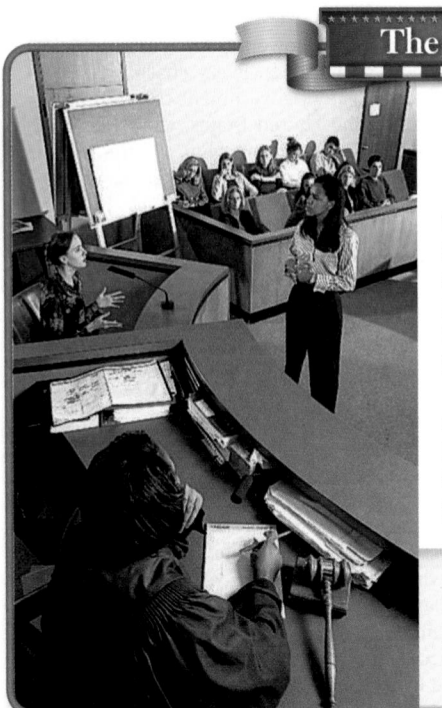

The Law *and* You

Teen Courts

Authorities have long sought ways to reduce teen crime. One approach that many communities have adopted is to establish teen courts. In teen courts, teenagers serve as jurors, defense attorneys, and prosecutors. The courts hear the cases of teens who have committed a minor, first-time offense. These offenders get a chance to avoid the record that would result from a juvenile court proceeding. They also learn a valuable lesson in how the law works.

Teen courts got their start in Texas in the 1970s and have since spread to more than 30 states. They often are supported by funds from school districts and traditional courts or by civic groups that hope to reach young offenders before they become hardened criminals. Statistics show that teen crime is generally reduced in communities where such programs exist.

Exploring the Law Activity

Research Call or write to municipal governments in your area to find out whether they have teen courts and how they work.

◀ **Teens conduct a trial.**

CHAPTER 24: *Local Governments* **665**

CURRICULUM CONNECTION

Economics Incorporation is usually associated more with business than with government. A business that incorporates is recognized as a "person" under the law, and it allows many individuals to invest their finances at relatively little risk. Interested students might enjoy comparing economic incorporation to government incorporation and sharing their insights.

The Law *and* You

More About Teen Courts In most cases, offenders cannot appear before a teen court unless they have admitted their guilt. In some teen court programs, teenagers serve not only as attorneys and jurors but as bailiffs, clerks of the court, and presiding judges. Opponents of the program suggest that teenagers do not have the maturity to render legal decisions, pointing to cases in which judges have had to step in and change an overly severe ruling from a teen court.

Differentiated Instruction

★ ★ ★ Activity: Multiple Learning Styles ★ ★ ★

Verbal/Linguistic Have students work individually or collaboratively to locate some of the documents that outline the structure of the community's form of government. Ask students to read the documents carefully and then answer the following questions:

• Think about the way in which these documents have been written. How easy is it to find the information you need?

• Are the details spelled out clearly, or are legal jargon and complex structure used? Why do you think such language and style choices were made?

Have students choose a passage from one of the documents and explain why they think it is worded effectively or how they would reword it to make it more effective. **AL**

POLITICAL PROFILES **Mayoral Reform** In the late nineteenth and early twentieth centuries, a trend toward reform in local government was echoed in the Midwest by the reforms instituted by several mayors of the time. In Detroit, Mayor Hazen Pingree established new schools, parks, and work programs. In Toledo, Ohio, Mayor Samuel "Golden Rule" Jones set up municipal ownership of public utilities and tackled police corruption. And in Cleveland, Mayor Tom Johnson reformed city services so much that Cleveland became known as the best-governed city in the United States.

Hands-On Chapter Project

Step 1

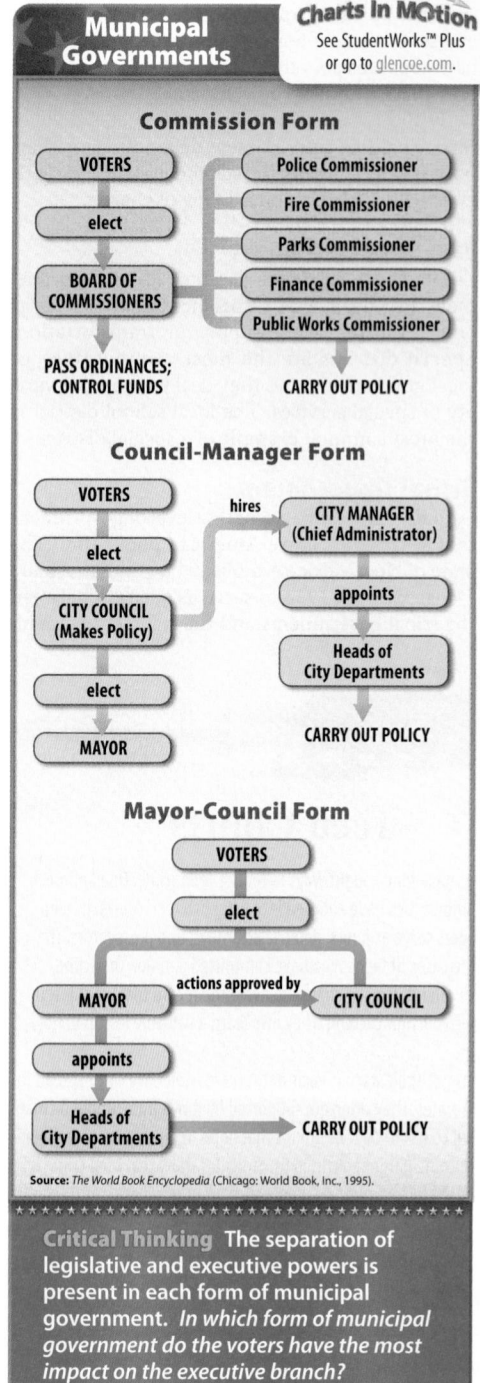

Municipal Governments

Charts In MOtion See StudentWorks™ Plus or go to glencoe.com.

Commission Form

VOTERS — elect — BOARD OF COMMISSIONERS

Police Commissioner
Fire Commissioner
Parks Commissioner
Finance Commissioner
Public Works Commissioner

PASS ORDINANCES; CONTROL FUNDS

CARRY OUT POLICY

Council-Manager Form

VOTERS — elect — CITY COUNCIL (Makes Policy) — elect — MAYOR

hires — CITY MANAGER (Chief Administrator) — appoints — Heads of City Departments — CARRY OUT POLICY

Mayor-Council Form

VOTERS — elect

MAYOR — actions approved by — CITY COUNCIL

MAYOR — appoints — Heads of City Departments — CARRY OUT POLICY

Source: *The World Book Encyclopedia* (Chicago: World Book, Inc., 1995).

Critical Thinking The separation of legislative and executive powers is present in each form of municipal government. *In which form of municipal government do the voters have the most impact on the executive branch?*

In New Mexico, for example, the Pueblo Native American culture is divided into 22 governing units operating on New Mexico's 19 pueblo land formations. Each tribal office has a governor and a lieutenant governor.

Forms of Municipal Government

A municipal government can be formed when a group of people asks the state legislature to permit its community to set up, or incorporate, legally. In this **incorporation** process, a community must usually meet certain requirements. These vary from state to state, but they typically include having a minimum population and a petition for incorporation signed by a certain number of residents. At times a **referendum,** or special election, may be held to determine whether residents want incorporation.

After a community is incorporated, the state issues it a charter granting legal status and allowing the community to have a separate government. The municipality now has the right to enter into contracts, to sue and be sued in court, and to purchase, own, and sell property. The state legislature can change the powers granted to a municipal government at any time. Every charter also provides for the type of government the community will have. In the United States, the three basic forms of municipal government are the mayor-council form, the commission form, and the council-manager form.

The Mayor-Council Form

The oldest and most widely used form of municipal government is the mayor-council form. Until the 1900s, it was used in most American cities, regardless of size. Today about half the cities in the United States use it, and it is preferred by the largest cities.

The mayor-council form follows the traditional concept of separation of powers. Executive power belongs to an elected mayor, and legislative power belongs to an elected council. A majority of cities have unicameral, or one-house, councils.

Most city councils have fewer than 10 members, who usually serve four-year terms, although some larger cities exceed that number—Chicago, for example, has a 50-member council, the largest in the nation. In most cities, council members are elected from the city at large, but individual wards or districts sometimes elect members, too.

Mock Council Meeting

Step 1: Organizing City Government
Using the form of city government of their city or town (or the nearest one), students will act as mayor, council president, department heads, legislative aids, or members of a research team.

Directions Tell students that later in the project, they will conduct a meeting of the city council or commission, playing the roles of various city government officials. In Step 1,

they will select a research team to find out how their city's government is organized. This team will draw a diagram indicating the organization and each department's responsibilities.

Presenting Have students who prepared the diagram present it to the class. Then assign other students to play the roles of department heads or legislative aides (members of a team that prepares briefings for the department heads). **OL AL**

(Chapter Project continued in Section 2.)

Two main types of mayor-council government exist, depending upon the power given to the mayor. These two types are the strong-mayor system and the weak-mayor system. In the strong-mayor system, the municipal charter grants the mayor strong executive powers. A strong mayor usually has the power to veto measures that the city council passes, and many of his or her actions might not require council approval. The mayor can appoint and fire department heads and high-ranking members of the municipal bureaucracy. In addition, a strong mayor can prepare the municipal budget, subject to council approval, and propose legislation to the city council. The mayor usually serves a four-year term. The strong-mayor system is most often found in large cities.

Many small cities, especially in New England, use the weak-mayor system of municipal government. In this form, the mayor has only limited powers. The mayor has little control over the budget or the hiring and firing of municipal personnel. The city council makes most policy decisions, and the mayor's veto power is limited. The mayor usually serves only a two-year term. In some small municipalities, the office of the mayor is only a part-time position.

The success of the mayor-council form of government depends to a large extent on the individual who serves as mayor. In the strong-mayor system, a politically skillful mayor can provide effective leadership. Under the weak-mayor plan, because official responsibility is in many hands, success depends upon the cooperation of the mayor and the council.

The Commission Form

The commission form of government combines executive and legislative powers in an elected commission. This commission is usually made up of five to seven members.

Each commissioner heads a specific department and performs all the executive duties related to that department. The most common departments are police, fire, public works, finance, and parks. The commissioners also meet as a legislative body to pass laws and make policy decisions. One of the commissioners usually has the title of mayor. The mayor has no substantial additional powers, however. Usually he or she merely carries out ceremonial functions like greeting important visitors to the city or officiating at the dedication or opening of hospitals and other public institutions.

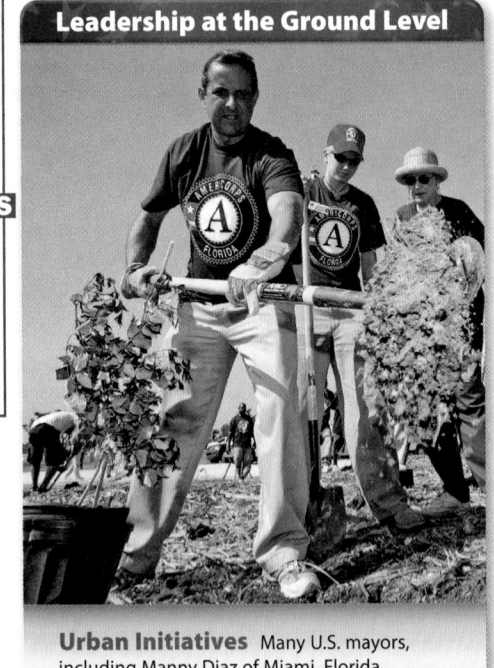

Leadership at the Ground Level

Urban Initiatives Many U.S. mayors, including Manny Diaz of Miami, Florida, actively promote "green" projects to revitalize their cities. *Why might the idea that pollution is bad for a child's asthma motivate city residents to respond more than a global issue?*

The commission form of municipal government developed in 1900 after a devastating tidal wave struck Galveston, Texas. As the citizens of Galveston tried to rebuild their city, they found that their mayor-council government was unable to handle the many urgent problems stemming from the disaster. As a result, the Texas state legislature decided to permit Galveston to elect five leading citizens to oversee the city's reconstruction. The commission form proved so successful in Galveston that other municipalities adopted the commission form in their communities. By 1920, more than 500 cities had this form of government.

Despite its early success, only a few American cities use the commission form today because over the years it was found to have some serious defects. First, in the absence of a powerful leader, the commission form can lead to a lack of cooperation and planning in government. This form of government has no strong executive to persuade or force the

S Skill Practice

Researching Have students research and write a report about Tammany Hall, the corrupt political machine headed by William M. "Boss" Tweed. Ask them to answer these questions in their analyses and share their findings and conclusions, perhaps in a panel-discussion format:

- What made it possible for someone like Tweed to gain, and keep, power?

- As a political "boss," how did Tweed take advantage of voters? How did he and the "Tweed Ring" benefit from their positions?

- Why would his administration be considered abusive by today's standards?

- How was the Tweed machine brought down at last? **OL**

Critical Thinking

Answer: City residents are more likely to take action on an issue that "hits home" than on an issue that does not.

Additional Support

Activity: Interdisciplinary Connection

Geography Bring to class a state map that shows counties. Have students characterize the state according to the number, size, and shape of counties. Discuss with students the possible reasons for differences in county characteristics. (*Answers include landforms, population densities, and state or international boundaries.*) Then have students identify county seats. **Ask:** Do these cities or towns tend to have the highest populations in their counties? What might be the reasons for this? (*Students may note that these cities or towns were established early or that they grew because of their role as government centers.*) **ELL**

D Differentiated Instruction

Interpersonal Find two adults in your community who follow local politics. Prepare three or more questions to learn about the form of government in your community. **Ask:** How satisfied are people in your community with their form of government? Why? *(Answers will vary, but students should make some attempt to inquire about the reasons for satisfaction or dissatisfaction in their interviews.)* **AL**

Assess

Assign the Section 1 Assessment as homework or as an in-class activity, or have students take Section Quiz 24-1 from *Section Quizzes and Chapter Tests.*

Close

Identifying Have students cite examples from the text to support this statement: **Units of local government have changed to meet the needs of communities.** *(Answers may include increased or decreased powers of some county governments and townships and the establishment of the commission form of government.)* **OL**

Section 1 Review

Conventional Wisdom Baltimore hosted the first national presidential convention, held by the Anti-Mason party, in 1831. In 1832, it also held the first conventions of the Democratic Party (known as Republican Delegates from Several States) and the National Republicans. The all-time top convention city, however, is Chicago. Since 1860 it has hosted 25 national conventions.

commissioners to act as an effective group. When commissioners disagree, it can be very difficult to make decisions or establish policies. Second, when commissioners agree, it might be only to support each others' budget requests. As a result, the municipal budget is sometimes far more generous than it should be.

The Council-Manager Form

Under a council-manager form of government, legislative and executive powers are separated. The council of between five and nine members acts as a legislative body and makes policy for the

municipality. A manager carries out the council's policies and serves as chief administrator. First used in 1912, the council-manager form is now one of the most common in the United States. More than 40 percent of cities, mostly in the West and the South, use this form.

The office of city manager is the key **feature** of the council-manager plan. Appointed by the council, the city manager is the chief executive. He or she appoints and fires municipal workers, prepares the budget, and runs the day-to-day affairs of the city. The city manager also might make policy recommendations to the council. Most city managers are professionals who are trained in public administration. They must answer to the council and are subject to dismissal by the council.

The council-manager form usually includes a mayor with limited powers. In most cases, the mayor is a council member whom the council elects for a two-year term.

Many political experts believe the council-manager form brings better management and business procedures to the government. Executive and legislative powers are clearly separated, and it is easy for the voters to assign praise or blame for what the government has done.

D Some critics point out disadvantages associated with council-manager government: Citizens do not elect the city manager, who might not be a city resident. In addition, this form of government might not provide the political leadership that is necessary in large cities with a diverse population.

SECTION 1 Review

Vocabulary
1. **Explain** the significance of: county, county board, township, municipality, special district, incorporation, referendum.

Main Ideas
2. **Identifying** Why and how have New England town meetings been replaced?
3. **Describing** How have the power and influence of county governments varied in the U.S. by geography or region?
4. **Comparing** What are the methods of selection for heads of departments in the three forms of city government?

Critical Thinking
5. **Drawing Conclusions** Why do many large cities prefer the council-manager form of municipal government?

6. **Organizing** Use a graphic organizer like the one below to compare the separation of powers in the mayor-council form of municipal government to that of the federal government.

Municipal	Federal

Writing About Government
7. **Expository Writing** The four basic types of local government that exist in the United States are the county, the township, the municipality, and the special district. Choose one type of local government that exists where you live. Create a diagram that shows how it is organized. Then write a one-page summary that identifies the officials who make up the government and their functions.

Answers

1. All definitions can be found in the section and the Glossary.
2. As towns grew and became more complex, direct democracy became impractical. Towns began to elect representatives to attend the town meetings.
3. In rural areas and the South where settlements were spread out, county governments were more powerful. In New England, towns and townships are the significant units. In some places, county governments have taken on metropolitan responsibilities, but in others they have been reduced to unimportance.
4. Mayor appoints heads in mayor-council form. City manager appoints heads in council-manager form, and elected commissioners are heads in the commission form.
5. Political experts believe it leads to better management and responsible government because executive and legislative powers are clearly separated, making it easy for voters to assign praise or blame.
6. Municipal: mayor has executive powers, council has legislative powers; Federal: president has executive powers, Congress has legislative powers.
7. Students' diagrams should clearly illustrate the organization of the chosen local government.

Serving Localities

Reader's Guide

Content Vocabulary
- ★ zoning (p. 669)
- ★ mass transit (p. 670)
- ★ metropolitan area (p. 671)
- ★ suburbs (p. 671)
- ★ real property (p. 674)
- ★ personal property (p. 674)
- ★ assessment (p. 674)
- ★ market value (p. 674)

Academic Vocabulary
- ★ disposal (p. 670)
- ★ maintenance (p. 671)
- ★ fee (p. 675)

Reading Strategy
As you read, create an outline similar to the one to the right to help you take notes on local governments.

Serving Localities
I. Local Government Services
   A. Education
   B.
   C.
II. Metropolitan Communities

Economics in the News

Unable to meet rising expenses, Mayor David Cohen is asking home owners in Newton, Massachusetts, for help. Cohen wants to raise property tax rates to fill the budget gap so two schools can be built or renovated. His request must now be approved by the Board of Aldermen before it goes to the voters. "It will have a big impact on a lot of people," said Alderman Susan Albright. "I'm not real confident it will be successful because we are looking at tough financial times." School officials emphasize that without this money, nearly 100 teachers and staff could lose their jobs, class sizes would grow, and programs would be reduced.

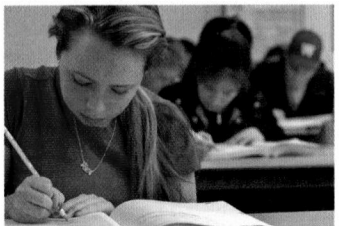
▲ A student in a Newton, Massachusetts, school

Supporting schools is just one of the many services of local government. Today most of these services are provided by taxes levied on everyone, rather than by fees paid by individuals.

Local Government Services

Local governments provide many critical services—education, fire and police protection, water service, sewage and sanitation services, trash collection, libraries, and recreation facilities.

Education

Providing education is one of the most important functions of government. In many states, a large share of local tax revenues fund public schools. Some states pay a large percentage of these costs, but local school districts generally provide most of the money and make the key decisions on public school policy. Local funding and local control of schools go hand in hand. However, local funding also contributes to inequality of education across the many districts of a state. Wealthier districts can provide much better educational opportunities. As a result, some states and state courts have begun to address this issue, raising questions about the way education is financed.

Zoning

Local governments use **zoning** to regulate the way land and buildings are used, thus shaping how a community develops. Zoning boards can regulate growth, preserve neighborhoods, and prevent the decline of land values. They can rule that certain districts (zones) be used only for homes, businesses, and parks.

Focus

Bellringer
Section Focus Transparencies 24-2

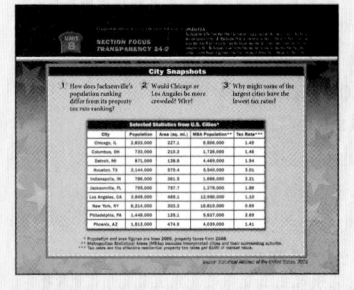

Reader's Guide

Answers to Graphic:
I. Local Government Services
   A. Education
   B. Zoning
   C. Police and Fire Protection
   D. Water Supply
   E. Sewage and Sanitation
   F. Transportation
   G. Social Services
   H. Recreation and Cultural Activities
II. Metropolitan Communities
   A. Cities
   B. Towns
   C. Suburbs

Resource Manager

R Reading Strategies	**C** Critical Thinking	**D** Differentiated Instruction	**W** Writing Support	**S** Skill Practice
Teacher Edition • Identifying, p. 675 **Additional Resources** • Guid. Read. Act., p. 87 • Quizzes/Tests, p. 296	**Teacher Edition** • Making Connections, p. 670 • Evaluating Alternatives, p. 673 **Additional Resources** • Read. Essen., pp. 277–280	**Teacher Edition** • Interpersonal, p. 671 **Additional Resources** • Foldables, p. 67 • Hist. Docs. and Speeches, p. 24	**Teacher Edition** • Expository Writing, p. 672 **Additional Resources** • Part. in Gov. Act., pp. 47–48	**Teacher Edition** • Researching, p. 670 **Additional Resources** • Inter. Poli. Cartoons, pp. 47–48

Teach

S Skill Practice

Researching Environmental concerns have prompted concerns about the availability of landfills. Have students research the specific issues that have concerned some communities. **Ask:** What regions of the country have the greatest issue with availability of landfills? Why do you think so? *(older urban areas because they have been densely populated for a long time)* **OL**

C Critical Thinking

Making Connections Ask each student to fold a sheet of paper in half lengthwise and on one side list activities in a typical school day. On the other side, have them link each activity to social services. (For example, the water used to brush teeth might come from public utilities.) As volunteers share their lists, use their responses to illustrate the types of local government. (For example, students probably came to school by traveling on city, township, and county roads.) **OL**

Additional Support

The concept of zoning has been criticized by some who claim that zoning is an excessive use of government power because it limits how people can use their property. Some criticize zoning laws that make it difficult for certain people, often minorities or families with children, to move into particular neighborhoods. Critics call this restrictive zoning. Advocates of zoning claim that without zoning, a community might develop in ways that would lower property values and make it an unpleasant place to live.

Police and Fire Protection

Police and fire services are expensive and make up a large part of the local budget. Police protection, for example, is the second-largest expense of many American cities, after public utilities.

Fire protection is a local function that varies with the size of the community. In small towns, volunteers usually staff the fire department. In large cities, professional, full-time fire departments provide the necessary protection. Professional fire departments also serve some small towns that have many factories and businesses.

Water Supply

Local governments make the vital decisions regarding water service. In smaller communities, they may contract with privately owned companies to supply water. The threat of water pollution and water shortages has prompted some local governments to create special water district arrangements. In case of a water shortage, such districts or local governments may attempt to limit the amount of water that is consumed.

Sewage and Sanitation

Local government is responsible for sewage **disposal.** Untreated sewage, if it is allowed to return to the natural water supply, can endanger life and property. Many local governments maintain sewage-treatment plants to deal with this problem.

Sewage and sanitation disposal are very expensive local services. For cities with populations of fewer than 50,000, sewage and sanitation, when combined, comprise the second-highest local governmental expenditure after police and fire protection. These costs have forced some smaller communities to contract with private companies to provide their sewage and sanitation services.

Because of environmental concerns, landfills are no longer the simple solution to sanitation that they once were. Some local governments use garbage-processing plants to dispose of the community's solid wastes.

Sewage and sanitation issues also often require that officials make difficult political decisions. For example, where should sewage-treatment plants be located? Although such plants are necessary, people often oppose having them near their homes. Another difficult decision involves how to pay for these services. While people want a clean and healthy community, they often object to paying taxes to improve sewage and sanitation services.

Transportation

As more people choose to live in suburban areas but continue to work in cities, transportation becomes a concern of city government. In addition, shopping centers often are located beyond walking distance from people's homes. To get to work and to shops, millions of Americans rely on either the automobile or **mass transit** facilities such as subways, trains, and buses.

Local governments spend millions of dollars each year to maintain more than 3 million miles of streets. In recent years, local governments have tried to encourage people to use mass transit rather than their own automobiles for three important reasons. First, mass transit is usually more efficient than the automobile. A high-speed rail system, for example, can transport about twice as many people each hour as a modern expressway. Second, mass transit causes less pollution than automobiles. Third, mass transit uses less energy per person than automobiles. However, many people prefer the independence of driving their own vehicles.

Social Services

Many local governments offer important services to citizens who cannot afford them. Normally, local governments provide services to people who have special needs that result from unemployment, low income, ill health, or permanent disabilities.

One type of social service provides aid to people who are temporarily unemployed. This aid consists of cash payments and help with finding new jobs. A second program is hospital care for people who need medical attention and cannot afford it. The third program is direct assistance to needy people in the form of cash payments. This type of social service is often referred to as public welfare.

Activity: Collaborative Learning

Conducting an In-Depth Study Organize students into groups, and have each group select a special district in their state for an in-depth study. Within each group, students can assume the roles of researchers, interviewer, writers, and editors. Researchers can use newspaper, Internet, and public library sources to identify the purpose of the district, how it is financed, how its officials are chosen, and how citizens can oversee its work and influence its decisions. The interviewer's job is to contact an official of the special district to find out how closely the researchers' findings match the actual work of the district. Writers and editors are responsible for creating a written report analyzing the group members' information. You might want to set aside time for group representatives to present the reports orally. **OL**

Local governments, especially cities, have a huge fiscal responsibility for social services. Paying for them is one of the biggest single expenditures for many large cities in the United States today. Although the federal and state governments pay part of the cost, the share that local governments pay toward these programs continues to rise.

Recreation and Cultural Activities

As the amount of Americans' leisure time increases, local governments have responded with recreational and cultural programs. Some local communities offer swimming, dancing, and arts and crafts programs. In addition, many localities provide baseball, football, and other sports programs. The **maintenance** of parks, zoos, and museums is also a function of local government. Many cities and counties have helped build stadiums, arenas, and convention centers that are used for sports and entertainment.

Metropolitan Communities

Cities, towns, and villages are metropolitan communities. These urban communities differ in size, ranging from a few thousand to millions of people.

The Census Bureau classifies any community with 2,500 people or more as an urban community. Whether an urban community is called a city, town, township, or village depends on local preference or sometimes on state charter classifications. The Office of Management and Budget has classified large urban areas as Metropolitan Statistical Areas. A **metropolitan area** or metropolis is a large city and its surrounding **suburbs.** This area also might include small towns that are located beyond the suburbs.

Cities

Cities are typically made up of commercial areas, industrial areas, and residential areas. States charter cities as municipal corporations.

Most major cities in the United States became urban centers during the 1800s when the country was being industrialized. Cities attracted African Americans, Americans from rural areas, and immigrants who sought jobs and better living conditions. After World War I, many more African American families migrated to large cities throughout the country in search of better opportunities. Since 1945 and the end of World War II, newcomers from Puerto Rico, Mexico, Cuba, and

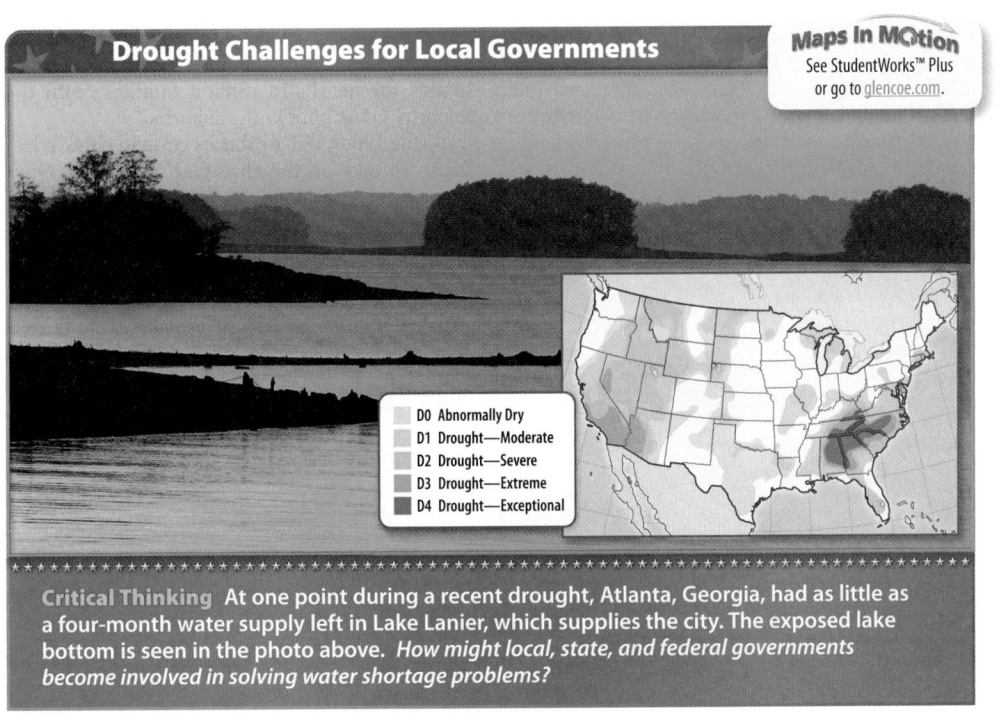

Drought Challenges for Local Governments

Maps In Motion
See StudentWorks™ Plus or go to glencoe.com.

D0 Abnormally Dry
D1 Drought—Moderate
D2 Drought—Severe
D3 Drought—Extreme
D4 Drought—Exceptional

Critical Thinking At one point during a recent drought, Atlanta, Georgia, had as little as a four-month water supply left in Lake Lanier, which supplies the city. The exposed lake bottom is seen in the photo above. *How might local, state, and federal governments become involved in solving water shortage problems?*

D Differentiated Instruction

Interpersonal A local government's services help establish a community's cultural distinctiveness. Have students work individually or collaboratively to prepare a presentation in which they try to define their town or community's cultural identity or distinctiveness. Questions such as the following may help them gather information: What reputation do the schools in your area have for academics, athletics, and so on? How might an environmentalist describe your community? What kinds of arts festivals, concerts, and the like are popular? What touring artists visit your community? How well maintained is the older "historic" part of your community? **OL**

Critical Thinking

Answer: Answers will vary, but students might mention that local, state, and federal governments can try to limit water consumption.

Differentiated Instruction

Activity: Multiple Learning Styles

Kinesthetic Local governments provide a wide variety of services that affect life on a daily basis. Ask students to collect and display items that represent these services (for example, a textbook for public education, a toy fire truck for fire protection, a toy bus for mass transit, a wastepaper basket for sanitation, want ads for unemployment services, and so

on). Call on volunteers to pick up various items from the display, identify the service that the item suggests, and explain the following:

• How do local governments attempt to finance and administer the service?
• What challenges do they face as they attempt to do so? **BL**

Participating
IN GOVERNMENT

Voters and School Policy
Have students prepare graphs, based on data from the local board of elections, showing the percentage of eligible voters taking part in school board elections over the past 10 years. Follow up by having students propose methods of increasing voter interest in school board elections. **AL**

Caption Answer: As gas prices rise, commuting to work from suburbs to cities will become increasingly expensive. People might consider moving closer to work. Cities also often have public transportation, which cannot be found in most suburbs.

W Writing Support

Expository Writing Have students write a paragraph explaining what the following prediction means to them and whether or not they agree with it: As transportation becomes more expensive, it will be necessary to build cities "up" rather than "out." **OL**

Hands-On Chapter Project

Step 2

---

other Spanish-speaking regions, as well as immigrants from many Asian nations, have contributed to rapid urban growth.

Beginning in the 1970s, cities in the South and West became the leaders in urban growth. Census statistics revealed a shift in urban population away from the Northeast and Midwest to cities in the region known as the Sunbelt. New industries attracted people to Sunbelt cities such as Jacksonville, Florida; Houston, Texas; and San Diego, California.

Meanwhile, older parts of the country were losing population. The 10 largest cities in the Northeast and Midwest—many of them in the so-called rust belt where the steel industry was dominant—all suffered a loss of population in the 1970s. In these cities, job opportunities and financial resources dried up. Detroit's population was 1.67 million in the 1960 census; by 2000 it was less than 1 million. Chicago lost 7.4 percent of its population in the 1980s. While the population of some Northeastern and Midwestern cities stabilized in the 2000s, 5 of the 10 largest cities were major Sunbelt cities that experienced tremendous growth.

Towns

In early U.S. history, most Americans lived in small towns and villages. After the 1860s, large cities grew faster than towns and villages. Between 1970 and 1990, as cities faced problems, several factors made rural areas and small towns attractive to Americans once again. Many towns and villages experienced growth, but the fastest-expanding areas were the suburbs.

Suburbs

After 2000, the Census Bureau classified 280 areas of the United States as metropolitan areas. The largest was New York City; the smallest was Enid, Oklahoma. These areas are made up of one or more central cities plus the adjacent, densely settled territory—the suburbs. Today more Americans live in suburbs than in cities or rural areas. A suburb may be called a village, a town, or a city, and it usually has a separate form of government.

Many people began to move to the suburbs after World War II. Between 1950 and 1990, many middle-class families bought homes in new residential suburbs. By 1970, an important population shift occurred—most people who previously lived in urban areas now resided in the suburbs. Even in the South, cities lost population to suburban areas. Atlanta, Georgia, experienced a 20.7 percent decline, while the population of the surrounding metropolitan area increased 173.1 percent.

The first rapid suburban growth took place close to the edge of cities in the 1950s and 1960s. Federal money for highways and home loans induced families to move to the suburbs, as the federal Urban Renewal Program demolished hundreds of thousands of low- and middle-income urban housing units in the cities. Federal Housing Administration and Veterans Administration programs subsidized homes for nearly 14 million families, with the majority being built in the suburbs.

By the 1980s, older suburbs close to cities' edges began to take on the character of the city. Once again people moved, this time to an outer suburban

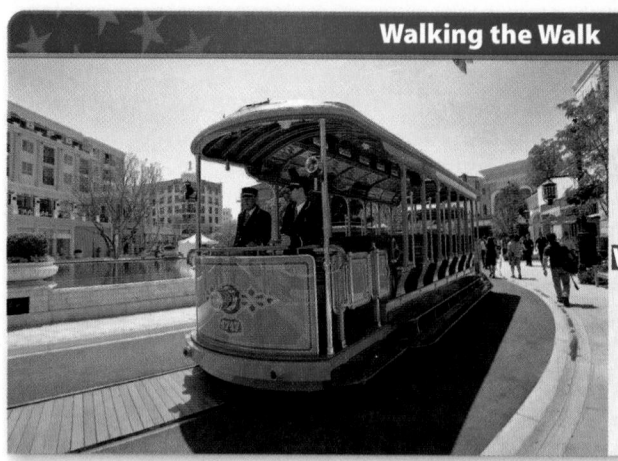

Walking the Walk

City Living For the last several decades, but more notably in recent years, city planners have taken steps to make cities more inviting for living and shopping. The goal is to make urban areas more "walkable," that is, less dependent on cars. Typical strategies to reach that goal include building bike paths and pedestrian overpasses above highways and limiting traffic in shopping areas. *How might rising gas prices affect attitudes about living in a city or a suburb? Why?*

Mock Council Meeting

Step 2: Preparing Presentations The legislative aides will prepare their briefings.

Directions Ask the legislative aides to decide on one issue related to the responsibilities listed by the research team. The aides will prepare a briefing for each department head to present at a council/commission meeting as a request for legislation or funding. Tell them that the issues will be put to a vote during the meeting, which will be held in Step 3. The aides will provide each department head with an opening statement (stating what he or she would like the commission to approve), the reason for the request, and at least two facts supporting the need for the request. One example might be a police commissioner who wants the city council to make it illegal for unspayed and unneutered cats to roam freely.

Reporting Have the legislative aides give an oral report telling the class which issues they will be recommending to the department heads. **OL AL**

(Chapter Project continued in Section 3.)

ring. These new suburban communities, 15 to 50 miles from the city center, attracted middle-class workers and professional people.

The growth of suburbia signaled political change. In an article titled "The Empowering of the Suburbs," Rob Gurwitt predicted:

> ❝ *Politics in the outer reaches of suburbia—the land of mega-malls and endless commuting—will soon attract the attention of a lot of people who never really had to think about it before. . . . In several legislatures, the suburbs as a whole will become the new heavyweights, outnumbering the urban or rural delegations that once held unquestioned sovereignty.* ❞
>
> —Rob Gurwitt, February 1991

Special Districts

Local governments face such problems as providing a safe water supply and an adequate transportation system. From time to time, local governments establish special districts that are better able to respond to specific problems than other units of local government.

The second reason for special districts derives from the financial limitations states impose on other units of local government. Most state governments limit the taxing and borrowing powers of local municipal governments. Some states also have laws that limit how much these local governments may spend. Creating a new special district that is not subject to such limitations becomes a practical solution for local leaders whose budgets are strained to meet local needs. Most special districts make their own policies, levy taxes, and borrow money.

The water commission and the port authority are two common types of special districts in the United States. The local school district is another such special unit. Other special districts are responsible for the administration of airports, sewage disposal, and roads. As the most common unit of local government, the special district is found in every state. Counting school districts, more than 47,000 special districts exist, comprising more than half of all the local governmental units in the country.

The School District

The school district is usually governed by an elected local body, the school board. The school board is responsible for setting school policies, hiring a superintendent of schools, and overseeing the day-to-day workings of schools. The board also makes up the school budget, decides on new school programs and facilities, and often has the final decision about hiring teachers and supervisory staff. In some places, the school board also decides on the amount of school taxes to levy.

Citizens often have strong feelings about how their schools should be run. In many communities, however, less than one-third of the eligible voters vote in school board elections. Turnout is usually higher when citizens vote on issues dealing with money, such as school bond referendums and school tax levies.

Regional Arrangements

In the 1990s, local governments began joining together to develop creative approaches to regional issues. Cooperative efforts addressed everything from waste management to law enforcement.

One example of this kind of regional approach occurred in Alabama, where five rural counties formed a waste management authority. Officials realized that they would have more bargaining power with the company that operated the landfills they used if they joined together.

Often city police departments and county sheriffs' offices join together to share crime laboratories, maintain joint records, operate joint radio bands, and share the cost of training personnel. Fire departments also have made agreements that require the closest fire station to answer the first alarm, ignoring political boundaries. Perhaps the most risky regional arrangement is Portland, Oregon's Metropolitan Service District (Metro). As the nation's only regional authority with multiple responsibilities run by elected officials, Metro covers three counties. Its main task is controlling growth under Oregon's land-use laws. Metro also does all the transportation and water-quality planning for the area, runs the zoo, manages the convention center and coliseum, and deals with solid waste disposal and recycling.

Financing Local Government

Local governments are the governments that are charged with providing costly services such as mass transit, airports, parks, water, sewage treatment,

C **Critical Thinking**

Evaluating Alternatives
Call on volunteers to list the advantages of special districts. *(Special districts can respond to specific problems; they can handle problems that cut across large areas; they can levy taxes and borrow money.)* Then have other volunteers list the disadvantages. *(Special districts are a source of fragmentation of local government; they reduce understanding of and citizen participation in local government.)* For each disadvantage, have students suggest and discuss ways to overcome it. **Ask:** What problems might stand in the way of creating regional governing bodies in our state, and how might those problems be resolved? **OL**

Did You Know?

Board might seem like an unusual term to describe a group of people (as in a school board), but it reflects an archaic meaning of *board* as a synonym for *table*. Councils or groups of magistrates once sat (and often sit today) at a table, or board, as they held their meetings.

Differentiated Instruction

Leveled Activities

ELL Historical Documents and Speeches, p. 24

BL Guided Reading Activities, p. 87

OL Interpreting Political Cartoons, p. 47

AL Authentic Assessment with Rubrics, p. 31

673

Linking ☆ Past & Present

Trash Talk In the late 1800s and early 1900s, residents of New York City dumped food, toilet waste, and coal or wood ash into sidewalk gutters. Trash was towed out to sea on barges and shoveled into the ocean to wash ashore on New Jersey beaches. Today most people take garbage collection for granted. For local officials, however, this service continues to pose a serious problem. "Everyone wants you to pick up their garbage," said one official, "but no one wants you to put it down." He might have added, ". . . especially in their backyard."

Critical Thinking

Answer: Local governments are mostly responsible for funding schools. The state makes payments to local governments and is also the pass-through for federal funds and grants that filter down to local governments.

Graph Skills Practices

Which two categories best reflect the critical importance of local government services? *(Police and Fire and Health and Hospitals)* **OL**

Additional Support

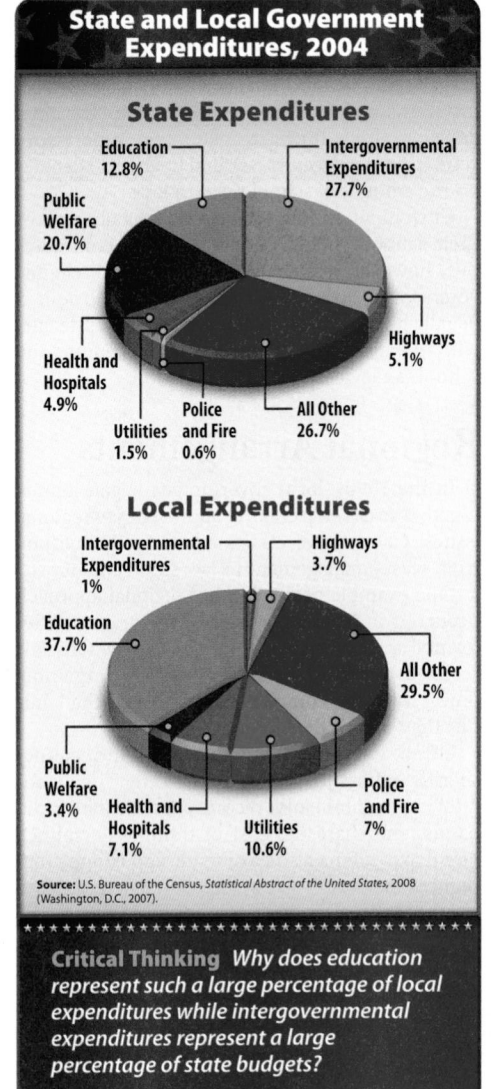

State and Local Government Expenditures, 2004

State Expenditures

- Education 12.8%
- Intergovernmental Expenditures 27.7%
- Public Welfare 20.7%
- Highways 5.1%
- Health and Hospitals 4.9%
- Utilities 1.5%
- Police and Fire 0.6%
- All Other 26.7%

Local Expenditures

- Intergovernmental Expenditures 1%
- Highways 3.7%
- Education 37.7%
- All Other 29.5%
- Public Welfare 3.4%
- Health and Hospitals 7.1%
- Utilities 10.6%
- Police and Fire 7%

Source: U.S. Bureau of the Census, *Statistical Abstract of the United States*, 2008 (Washington, D.C., 2007).

Critical Thinking Why does education represent such a large percentage of local expenditures while intergovernmental expenditures represent a large percentage of state budgets?

education, welfare, and correctional facilities. The costs for these services are enormous, and taxes provide the revenues necessary to supply these services.

The Property Tax

One of the oldest taxes—property taxes—once provided revenue for all levels of government. Today property taxes are the most important source of revenue for local governments, accounting for more than two-thirds of all their tax revenues.

Property taxes are collected on **real property** and **personal property.** Real property includes land and buildings. Personal property consists of such things as stocks and bonds, jewelry, furniture, automobiles, and works of art. Most local governments tax only real property. If personal property is taxed at all, the rate is usually very low.

How do local governments determine what the property tax rate will be? The process of calculating the value of the property is called **assessment.** It begins when the tax assessor appraises the **market value** of the homes and other real property in the community. The market value of a house or a factory is the amount of money the owner could expect to receive if the property were sold.

Most local governments do not tax property on its market value but on its assessed value, which is usually only a percentage of its market value. For example, a house that has an appraised value of $120,000 may have an assessed value of 30 percent of that figure, or $36,000.

Public opinion surveys indicate that most Americans view the property tax as unfair. A major complaint against the property tax is that it is regressive; it places a heavier burden on people with lower incomes than on those with higher incomes. The property tax also weighs heavily on retired home owners with fixed incomes who cannot afford constantly rising taxes.

The second criticism of the property tax is that it is often very difficult to determine property values on a fair and equal basis. Standards may vary with each tax assessor. Tax assessors are elected officials who are often underpaid and inadequately trained.

A third criticism is that reliance on the property tax results in unequal public services. A wealthy community with a large tax base can afford better public services than a less wealthy community with a small tax base. Based on this criticism, some state supreme courts have ruled against using the property tax to pay for local schools. They have held that using property taxes to support schools is a violation of the Fourteenth Amendment's guarantee of equal protection of the law.

Finally, property used for educational, religious, or charitable purposes and government property are exempt from the property tax. Some communities also give tax exemptions to new businesses and industries to encourage them to relocate there. As a result, the nonexempt property owners must bear a heavier share of the tax burden.

674 UNIT 8: *State and Local Government*

Extending the Content

A Taxing Problem Before it can establish a property tax rate, the local legislative body must determine how much money is needed from the property tax to pay for government services. For example, suppose that a city council decided that it needed to collect $800,000 from the property tax in a community whose total assessed property value was $40,000,000. The city would compute the tax rate by dividing the desired tax revenue—$800,000—by the total assessed value—$40,000,000—arriving at a tax rate of 2 percent. Each home owner then would receive a tax bill that was the product of the tax rate multiplied by the assessed value of his or her property; for example, the owner of a house assessed at $36,000 would have a tax bill of $720 ($36,000 × 0.02 = $720).

Other Local Revenue Sources

Local governments must have other revenue sources to meet their needs. They find these other revenue sources by imposing local income taxes, sales taxes, and fines and **fees,** as well as from operating government-owned businesses.

The local income tax is a tax on personal income. If the state and the local community each have an income tax, the taxpayer pays three income taxes: federal, state, and local. The sales tax is a tax on most items sold in stores; many states allow their local governments to use this tax. In some places, it is a selective sales tax—one that is applied to only a few items.

Fines paid for traffic, sanitary, and other violations as well as fees for special services provide some of the income for local governments. Special assessments are fees that property owners must pay for services that benefit them, for example, an assessment to a home owner when the city improves the sidewalk in front of the owner's home. Some cities also earn revenue through housing projects, markets, and parking garages.

States permit local governments to borrow money in the form of bonds—certificates that promise to repay the borrowed money with interest by a certain date. Some investors consider local government bonds to be good investments because their earned interest is not subject to federal income taxes. Municipal bonds raise money for large, expensive projects such as building a sports stadium, school buildings, or government office buildings.

Intergovernmental Revenue

In addition to local sources of revenue, most local governments receive economic aid from state and federal governments. This aid often comes in the form of grants.

When local governments carry out state laws or provide state programs, such as constructing highways or matching welfare payments, they receive state aid. State governments also grant funds to localities for specific functions that they perform, such as providing recreation and education services. Today, states are providing more than one-third of the general revenue of local governments. Most state aid comes in the form of categorical-formula grants—support for specific programs. Categorical-formula grants include grants designated for schools, highways, public welfare, and health and hospitals.

Federal financial aid comes to cities in two forms: categorical grants and block grants. Usually Congress includes guidelines for how categorical grants should be spent, for example, to help pay for a new highway or police training programs or to aid in sewage control. Local officials tend to prefer block grants, or unrestricted aid to cities for community development or social services.

Government ONLINE
Student Web Activity Visit glencoe.com and enter **QuickPass™** code USG9822c24. Click on Student Web Activity and complete the activity about serving localities.

CHAPTER 24, SECTION 2

R Reading Strategy

Identifying Ask: Other than property taxes, how do local governments raise money? *(Local income taxes, fines, assessments, parking garages, municipal bonds, and so on.)* **BL**

Assess

Assign the Section 2 Assessment as homework or as an in-class activity, or have students take Section Quiz 24-2 from *Section Quizzes and Chapter Tests.*

Close

Analyzing Have students explain and defend this statement: The economic decisions that governments make are more complicated than those the average citizen makes. **Ask:** What might be a local government leader's toughest economic decision? **OL**

Government ONLINE
Objectives and answers to the Student Web Activity can be found in the **Web Activity Lesson Plan** at glencoe.com. Enter **QuickPass™** code USG9085c24T.

Section 2 Review

SECTION 2 Review

Vocabulary

1. Explain the significance of: zoning, mass transit, metropolitan area, suburbs, real property, personal property, assessment, market value.

Main Ideas

2. Describing What are three goals of zoning?

3. Examining Why is the property tax considered by some people to be an unfair tax?

4. Identifying What is a Metropolitan Statistical Area?

Critical Thinking

5. Analyzing Why do local governments, with state and federal assistance, provide social services to residents?

6. Comparing Use a graphic organizer like the one below to compare the advantages of using mass transit or personal automobiles.

Advantages	
Mass Transit	Personal Auto

Writing About Government

7. Persuasive Writing Obtain a copy of your local government's most recent budget. Write an article identifying the services that account for most of the budget. Also, identify the main sources of your local government's revenue. Include your suggestions for change, either in spending priorities or in sources of revenue.

Answers

1. All definitions can be found in the section and the Glossary.
2. Students should discuss planning for regulated growth, preserving the character of neighborhoods, and preventing the decline of land values.
3. It is regressive and results in unequal public services. In addition, determining property values on a fair and equal basis is difficult. Property that some institutions own is exempt from property tax, so nonexempt property owners pay a larger share of the tax burden.
4. a large, urban area
5. People without jobs, without proper health care, or without money for food, clothing, or shelter need assistance.
6. Mass transit: more efficient, less polluting, uses less energy; Personal auto: independence, convenience
7. Articles should accurately and concisely discuss the local government's budget.

Class Debate

Organize the class into three groups: one to represent the home owners, one to represent the city of New London, and a third to act as the Supreme Court justices. Allow class time to develop arguments; then have each side present its case. After the "justices" reach a decision, have them read it aloud. Also have the dissenting opinions, if any, read aloud.

The Court's Decision

The Supreme Court, in a 5-to-4 decision, ruled that the city could use eminent domain to encourage commercial development. Justice Stevens, writing for the majority, stated that the "court long ago rejected any literal requirement that condemned property be put into use for the general public." The majority relied on the precedent set forth in *Berman* in reaching their decision. Sandra Day O'Connor, writing for the minority, wrote that the majority's decision removed "any distinction between private and public use of property—and thereby effectively delete[s] the words 'for public use' from the Takings Clause of the Fifth Amendment."

Should the Power of Eminent Domain Be Limited?

Kelo v. City of New London, 2005

The Fifth Amendment states that governments cannot take private property "for public use without just compensation." What constitutes public use? To what extent does the Constitution limit how broadly governments can define public use?

Facts of the Case

After years of economic decline in New London, Connecticut, the city moved ahead with a plan to build a conference center, a waterfront hotel, office space, and residential properties. In 2000 the city council agreed to allow the New London Development Corporation to acquire the property that it needed through eminent domain. Some home owners on the proposed site challenged the city's authority and refused to sell their homes. The city then began legal proceedings to condemn their homes so the properties could be taken. The home owners argued that these actions violated the public use restriction in the Fifth Amendment. The property owners argued taking private property to sell to private developers was not public use.

The Constitutional Question

Eminent domain is the right of government to take private property—usually land—for public use. This power is limited by the Fifth Amendment and by state constitutions; when the government takes private property for public use, it must pay a fair price to the owner.

Traditionally, governments used eminent domain to take private property only when it was used by the general public. Using land for a highway, a dam, or a park were common examples of public use. Governments also used eminent domain to improve areas that had deteriorated. More recently, governments have confiscated property that had not deteriorated to further economic development. To help decide *Kelo v. City of New London*, the Court looked at a 1954 decision, *Berman v. Parker*. In the earlier case, the Court ruled that the term *public use* does not mean that the property had to be used physically by the public. In *Berman*, the Court chose a broader definition of public use to include "public interest" or "public welfare."

Debating the Issue

Questions to Consider

1. Why did the city government want the property?
2. What does "public use" mean?
3. What national impact might the *New London* decision have?

You Be the Judge

Many cities face this issue when public projects are considered. What is the possible impact if the Court decides in favor of the city? In favor of the property owners? What limits, if any, should the Fifth Amendment place on a government's use of eminent domain?

▶ **Susette Kelo stands outside her former home with new owner Avner Gregory.**

Debating the Issue Answers

Questions to Consider

1. to build a conference center, a hotel, office space, and residential properties
2. Students may state that public use means that the space has to be used physically by the public, or they might choose to define it more broadly as the court did in *Berman*.
3. The *New London* decision might encourage more towns to use eminent domain for commercial interests, or it might cause a public backlash, leading states to increase protection of private property rights.

You Be the Judge

If the Court decides in favor of the city, the home owners will be forced to sell, and the city can build its commercial park. If the home owners win, the city will have to redesign its commercial park or increase the amount it is willing to spend to convince the home owners to move. Students' answers may vary on what limits the Fifth Amendment should place on the use of eminent domain. They should defend their answers.

Challenges of Urban Growth

Reader's Guide

Content Vocabulary
★ urban renewal *(p. 678)*
★ infrastructure *(p. 680)*
★ revitalization *(p. 681)*
★ gentrification *(p. 681)*
★ metropolitan government *(p. 682)*

Academic Vocabulary
★ inadequate *(p. 678)*
★ subsidize *(p. 678)*
★ displacement *(p. 681)*

Reading Strategy
As you read, use a graphic organizer similar to the one below to list the possible factors that contribute to social problems in urban areas.

Social Problems

Focus

Bellringer
Section Focus Transparencies 24-3

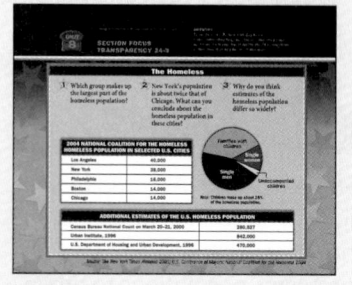

Reader's Guide

Answers to Graphic:
- Homelessness
- Drug Abuse
- Poverty
- Crime

Issues in the News

Richardson, a small inner-ring city near Dallas, Texas, was almost a boomtown from the 1950s to the 1980s. By 1990, growth had slowed and the city was losing its luster as urban blight affected some neighborhoods. City leaders worried about Richardson becoming less desirable than newer towns in outlying areas. Today, they are taking steps to ignite growth by enforcing building codes, providing tax breaks for businesses that make improvements, and supporting new stores and homes. One developer points out Richardson's continuing advantages—easy access to downtown Dallas, quality homes, and good jobs. "I want it to be reintroduced to people," he said. "Richardson is on the cusp of a renaissance."

▲ New condo construction has threatened older suburban towns such as Richardson.

Concentrating many people in a limited space creates problems. Today many urban areas in the United States confront a variety of problems—a lack of affordable housing and mass transportation systems, pollution, unemployment, and crime. Although these problems are most acute in big cities, they affect surrounding small towns and suburbs such as Richardson, Texas.

Population and Housing

Recall the kinds of population shifts that have taken place in recent years. Cities in the Northeast and Midwest have lost population while those in the South and West have grown rapidly. The population of small towns and rural areas has increased, and many people have moved from cities to nearby suburban areas. A number of cities have begun to attract older citizens to downtown living. The rising cost of gas has also alerted many people to the problems of living in suburbs that are distant from one's job or the central city. Yet it is unlikely that the American preference for suburban living will radically change anytime soon.

What challenges have these changing growth patterns presented for towns and cities? Studying the changes in housing offers a key to understanding many urban problems.

Managing Decline

As the population in an area increases, available land becomes more scarce and, hence, more costly. Local governments often have to decide whether available land should be used for new housing, industry, stores, or office buildings.

Resource Manager

R Reading Strategies	**C** Critical Thinking	**D** Differentiated Instruction	**W** Writing Support	**S** Skill Practice
Teacher Edition • Predicting, p. 682 **Additional Resources** • Guid. Read. Act., p. 88 • Quizzes/Tests, pp. 297–306 • Ch. Summaries, pp. 70–72	**Teacher Edition** • Predicting Consequences, p. 680 **Additional Resources** • Read. Essen., pp. 281–283 • Reteaching Act., p. 24	**Teacher Edition** • Naturalist, p. 681 **Additional Resources** • Foldables, p. 67 • Coop. Learning Act., pp. 15–16	**Teacher Edition** • Expository Writing, p. 679 **Additional Resources** • Gov. Sims. and Debates, pp. 52–56	**Teacher Edition** • Researching, p. 678 **Additional Resources** • Skill Reinforce. Act., p. 24

Teach

S Skill Practice

Researching Ask students to look for and share newspaper headlines that relate to urban problems or solutions to urban problems. (Alternatively, have students *suggest* newspaper headlines that they would consider typical of urban problems.) Discuss students' choices. **BL**

Linking ☆ Past & Present

Washington on Cities In 1791 George Washington wrote the following to the Marquis de Lafayette: "The tumultuous populace of large cities are ever to be dreaded. Their indiscriminate violence prostrates for the time all public authority, and its consequences are sometimes extensive and terrible."

Additional Support

Refurbishing Communities

Local Issues Through this redevelopment project in Englewood, New Jersey, local officials hope to transform older housing units into more functional and affordable housing. *Which local issue do you think is the most urgent in your community?*

Municipal governments attempt to manage land use to provide an environment for orderly growth. What action should be taken when an area begins to deteriorate?

In the 1950s, some inner cities showed signs of decline. People who could afford new housing left the inner cities and moved to the suburbs; poorer people remained. Jobs became scarce as industries moved to attractive suburban areas or to new locations in the South and West. Inner-city housing deteriorated, and slums multiplied. Residents endured **inadequate** heating, leaky pipes, poor sanitary conditions, and rising crime rates.

Urban Renewal

Aware of the growing inner-city problems, mayors of large cities appealed to the federal government for help. As a solution, the federal government offered an **urban renewal** program. Spending hundreds of millions of federal dollars

for new construction in the 1950s and 1960s, cities attempted to address their housing problems. Generally the approach was to tear down existing housing and build giant apartment complexes. Cities uprooted millions of people in an effort to renew disadvantaged areas. The original urban renewal program in the United States often forced residents out of their neighborhoods and replaced older buildings with new luxury apartment houses that the original residents could not afford.

A second factor in uprooting older neighborhoods was the construction of the Interstate Highway system. In many cases, freeways cut through inner-city neighborhoods, destroying housing and cutting links to other communities.

Since the 1990s, urban renewal has focused more on rebuilding existing neighborhoods. Involving residents and community groups has also become a much higher priority. Yet after years of federal spending, the results are not encouraging. It is still difficult to entice new employers and entrepreneurs to older parts of the city. When dilapidated structures are cleared, the result is sometimes just a vacant lot. In terms of inner-city housing, although urban renewal increased the amount of low-income and **subsidized** housing, it discouraged private investment. In the end, the lower overall supply resulted in higher average costs for rentals.

Housing Discrimination

Many Americans have been discriminated against when they try to rent or purchase a home. For years, smaller communities and suburban areas excluded African Americans and other groups, such as single mothers or gay couples.

At times, suburbs adopted policies that excluded the poor and the elderly. Some apartment owners flatly refused to rent to people with children. A 1981 study in Los Angeles found that owners excluded families with children from 71 percent of the apartments surveyed.

The courts have consistently ruled that discrimination in housing is illegal. Congress took action on this problem in 1968 when it passed the Open Housing Act, which barred discrimination in the sale and rental of housing. The problem persists, however, because housing discrimination can be difficult to prove, and the government has not always enforced the law effectively.

Coping With Housing Shortages

Many major cities, including Atlanta and Philadelphia, responded to the housing shortage

Activity: Collaborative Learning

Considering Problems and Solutions Organize the class into groups, and ask each group to select a leader. Assign each group an urban problem discussed in this section, or have them choose from a master list. Have the group as a whole agree upon a statement of the problem, identifying the issue. Next, provide time for all group members to do some preliminary research and create a list of possible solutions to the problem, sharing their lists with the group. Then the group leader can assign each group member one of the solutions for further study. After researching proposed solutions, each person can then summarize strengths and weaknesses of his or her solution. The group as a whole can choose the most promising solutions and present them to the class. **OL**

by renovating older housing. Home renovation projects include rewiring electricity, installing new plumbing, and rebuilding floors. In cities such as Baltimore and Des Moines, Iowa, funds from the city government along with federal, state, and private funds made some highly successful renovation programs possible.

The federal government also provided low-interest loans to local housing authorities. The loans were used to help build housing for low-income residents. Local housing authorities received federal aid to maintain rents at affordable levels.

Social Problems

Large cities face serious social problems. The concentration of poverty, homelessness, crime, and drug and alcohol abuse is easily identified in large cities. For those left in the inner city, life could easily develop into a cycle of related problems—dead-end jobs, or no job opportunities, poor housing, inferior schools, and inadequate transportation. The local and national media often report on these problems, raising the national awareness of their seriousness. City governments, however, must be more than aware of these social conditions. They must try to alleviate them.

Homelessness

Housing shortages are only one side of the housing problem in major cities. The other side is the human issue—homelessness. Hundreds of thousands of people spend their nights in shelters or on the streets. Unemployment and the housing shortage contribute to this problem. In addition, two-thirds of the homeless have a serious personal problem that contributes to their plight—alcoholism, drug addiction, or a criminal record. About one-third are mentally ill. The average homeless adult has been out of work for four years. Housing alone will not solve this problem. Rehabilitation programs are needed to address the personal problems that cause people to become homeless.

Private and religious charitable organizations contribute the most to relieving homelessness. In a recent year, the federal government provided about the same amount of assistance for the nation as New York City spent for its homeless people.

Drug Abuse

Closely associated with homelessness in many cities is drug abuse and addiction. Crack, a stronger form of cocaine, became the curse of the cities in the 1980s. Street gangs built a network for selling the drug in most of the nation's cities before the federal Drug Enforcement Administration realized the extent of the problem.

Inner-city teenagers, unable to find low-skill jobs, rationalized selling crack as a gateway to prosperity. Many worked long, hard hours in the drug trade with hopes of escaping the poverty cycle. The rewards, however, did not match the danger. Many crack dealers earned no more than what equates to minimum wage, and the earnings were often consumed by drug use.

The national media focused on drugs as a major problem in the United States. Some called it a $25 billion drain on the national wealth and implicated drugs in the renewed rising crime rates in the cities.

In November 1988, Congress responded to President Reagan's request for new antidrug legislation. A new law created the office of federal drug czar and increased spending for drug treatment and law enforcement. By 1991, the Justice Department's budget reached $10 billion, much of it targeted for fighting drug trafficking. Some evidence indicated that federal intervention was having an effect. A survey released in January 1990 reported a decline in the number of high school seniors who said they had tried illegal drugs. Use of crack showed the sharpest decline—a 50 percent drop from the 1985 figure.

The problem of drug abuse resurfaced in the media just a few years later. Teenage use of marijuana doubled between 1993 and 1996. While the number of hard-core drug users remained steady at about 3 million, the addicts were using an increasing amount of drugs. President Bill Clinton responded to the news by appointing Barry R. McCaffrey, a retired army general, as head of the Office of National Drug Control Policy.

A federal survey released in August 2000 showed that teenage drug use had declined; a 2006 survey confirmed that overall trend. Many teenagers, however, continued to use alcohol and marijuana, and the use of methamphetamine was beginning to become a serious concern.

Meeting Future Challenges

In the years ahead, municipal governments will face problems that demand imagination, citizen involvement, leadership—and, in most cases, large amounts of money. Municipalities continue to depend on help from state and federal governments. The level of aid might not satisfy big cities,

POLITICAL PROFILES

Clara Hale (1905–1992) In New York City's Harlem, Clara Hale was ready to retire from years of caring for foster children—and then a drug addict with a baby came to her door, sent by Hale's daughter Lorraine. Thus, in 1969 Hale began Hale House, a nonprofit children's center supported entirely by private donations. In 1985 President Ronald Reagan praised the work that "Mother" Hale and her daughter (who now directs Hale House) were doing to meet urban challenges. Today, Hale House specializes in caring for drug-addicted and HIV-positive babies.

W Writing Support

Expository Writing The National Coalition for the Homeless (NCH) is a prominent organization that works to solve this problem. Find their Web site online and review it. Have students write a brief summary of NCH explaining its origins, its current focus, and any other pertinent information they want to include. **OL**

Hands-On Chapter Project

Step 3

Mock Council Meeting

Step 3: Conducting a Meeting
Department heads will present requests and put them to a vote.

Directions Appoint a mayor or a council president to conduct the meeting. Have department heads present their requests, starting with their opening statements, based on the legislative aides' briefings.

Putting It Together Have the class vote on each issue. After voting is complete, discuss with class members why they voted the way they did. **OL**

C Critical Thinking

Predicting Consequences
Organize students in small groups to create a "best case" and a "worst case" scenario for life in American big cities in the year 2025. Encourage realistic predictions, based upon the information in this section and additional research and analysis that students might want to do. A "best case" scenario might, for example, include successful revitalization programs. A "worst case" scenario might describe the impact on city life of intensifying social and economic problems. Have students explain what factors today are responsible for the consequences in their predictions. **OL**

Making a Difference

Gillian Kilberg has continued to show that she is there for Grandma Rita's Children, enlisting volunteers to chaperone trips for children to various sites in the Washington, D.C., area.

Activity Ask students to imagine what they would do to help other people if they received an inheritance. Have them compile a master list of charitable works. **OL**

Differentiated Instruction

Participating in Government Activities, p. 47

680

---

however. Large cities usually have higher rates of poverty, crime, and unemployment than smaller localities. In 1979, for example, about one-third of all people living below the federally defined level of poverty resided in large cities.

Infrastructure

One essential duty for city leaders is maintaining **infrastructure.** The term *infrastructure* refers to the roads, bridges, and water and sewer systems that allow a city to function. In America's older cities, the infrastructure has been showing severe signs of wear for decades. In 1960 all levels of government together spent about $11 billion for airports, highways, railroads, and transit. By the 1990s, government spending for these forms of transportation surpassed $100 billion per year.

Cities face mounting costs for cleanup of polluted water, sewer-system replacement, and waste-treatment plants. Infrastructure costs are so enormous that local governments cannot do the job alone. State and federal aid is available for road building, water and sewage systems, bridge construction, and many other public works. Recent events suggest that problems with the nation's infrastructure will require a federal fix. First, in 2005 the American Society of Civil Engineers reported that it would take well in excess of a trillion dollars to restore the nation's bridges, roads, transit systems, and water and sewage plants. Then public attention was drawn to the issue of levees when Hurricane Katrina struck the Gulf Coast in 2005, and when severe storms flooded many towns along the Mississippi River in 2007 and 2008. Yet another 2007 catastrophe that highlighted infrastructure problems was the collapse of a bridge during rush hour traffic in Minneapolis.

In the view of New York City Mayor Michael Bloomberg, "the federal government is not investing enough in our infrastructure, and when it does, it's not investing wisely." The president of the U.S. Conference of Mayors, Manny Diaz, echoed this idea: "Plain and simple, Washington has abandoned us."

Mass Transit

Maintaining a sound transportation network is a serious challenge for local governments. Chronic

Making a Difference

What would you do if you inherited $20,000? Seventeen-year-old Gillian Kilberg decided to start a summer camp to help underprivileged children. Kilberg, from McLean, Virginia, received an inheritance when her grandmother died. "I wanted to do something with the money so people would remember my grandmother," she said.

Kilberg's plan was to create a "special trips" camp for children ages 5 to 12. The camp would give children from the Washington, D.C., area an opportunity to visit places that they could probably never afford to visit on their own. Although $20,000 seemed like a large sum of money, Kilberg soon realized she had to raise more. She worked with a local sheriff to create her program, and sent letters to friends and relatives explaining her project. "We ended up raising about $30,000, which was amazing," she said.

In 1996 Kilberg's summer camp, which she called Grandma Rita's Children, sent 47 children on 15 different day trips to places like the National Air and Space Museum and to a Baltimore Orioles baseball game. They went backstage at a Motown concert and paid a visit to Supreme Court Justice Clarence Thomas.

Five years later, the camp is thriving. Kilberg has continued to raise money, totaling $160,000 in 2001, and extended the camp age limit to 13. Camp graduates can also train to become camp counselors. At the end of summer 2001, Kilberg used any extra monies to create a college scholarship fund for former campers.

"We ended up raising about $30,000, which was amazing."
—**Gillian Kilberg**

680 **UNIT 8:** *State and Local Government*

Local Zoning

Objective: To understand the importance and scope of zoning laws.

Focus/Teach: Have students read the background information.

Assess: Complete the Questions to Consider and Activity.

Close: Have students speculate about the problems that might develop if there were no zoning laws.

Differentiated Instruction Strategies

BL Ask a city council member how zoning laws are created.

AL Have students evaluate local zoning laws and propose ways to improve or to simplify them.

ELL Discuss synonyms and different uses for the word *zone*.

traffic jams and air pollution have resulted from the millions of Americans who use their automobiles to commute to work. As noted earlier in this chapter, an alternative to automobile use in urban areas is mass transit—buses, subways, and rail lines. Mass transit moves large numbers of people, produces less pollution by consuming less fuel than automobiles, and uses less energy. Despite all the advantages of mass transit, however, most Americans prefer to drive to work in their automobiles. So far, higher gas prices have made only a modest impact on this cultural preference.

Many local leaders believe that more people would use mass-transit facilities if they were cleaner, faster, and more efficient. Elaborate mass-transit systems have been built in Washington, D.C., Atlanta, and in the San Francisco–Oakland area. San Francisco's Bay Area Rapid Transit system (BART) cost twice its original estimate to build. High costs discourage planners in other cities from taking on such projects.

The Need for Economic Development

Cities have tried various solutions to address their financial problems—state and federal aid, loans, budget cuts, and laying off city workers. Many cities, especially those that have lost businesses during the past 30 years, have also tried to stimulate economic development.

How can municipal governments stimulate such development? One approach is **revitalization.** Revitalization means that local governments make large investments in new facilities to promote growth. In recent years, a number of major cities have attempted to revitalize their downtowns. Baltimore built a $170 million office and residential complex. Detroit invested more than $200 million in a regional shopping mall and two giant office buildings. Funds usually come from local government and private investors. State and federal aid also might be available.

The second major approach to economic development is to create certain tax incentives for industries that relocate to a community. Tax incentives can take several forms. Especially in suburban areas, governments try to attract new businesses by offering lower property tax rates. Some states, such as Connecticut and Indiana, target their tax reductions for businesses that relocate to areas of high unemployment. Similarly, the federal government offers tax reductions, or credits, to businesses that move into areas of poverty and unemployment.

★ Light-Rail in Las Vegas ★

Light-Rail Light-rail—rail travel that handles fewer passengers and goes slower than trains or subways—is promoted as a way to revitalize cities and cut down on auto emissions. The Las Vegas monorail (above) moves tourists and residents between several hotels. *Why might cities be reluctant to invest in a monorail system?*

D Gentrification

One of the most debated issues of the revitalization movement concerns **gentrification.** Also called **displacement,** gentrification occurs when people with higher incomes move into and renovate an older neighborhood, changing the area's essential character. Beginning in the 1980s, some middle-income suburbanites and recent immigrants moved into the cities—often into areas where they could restore old houses and other buildings and take advantage of the lower housing costs while enjoying the benefits of city life. These areas often drew entrepreneurs who established upscale restaurants and small boutiques.

The positive side of gentrification is that it restores vitality to the city by reclaiming

Caption Answer: Startup costs would be extremely high, especially in well-established cities; the public might have doubts about its reliability.

D Differentiated Instruction

Naturalist Caring for the environment—and balancing that care with social and economic needs—is one of the many challenges that city governments face today. Have students research either their community or an urban area with which they are familiar. **Ask:** What does this area consider to be its greatest environmental strengths and greatest environmental challenges? How environmentally aware has this area's government been in the past, and what plans does it have for caring for the environment in the future? *(Encourage students to discuss the ways in which they can protect or improve the environment.)* **OL**

Additional Support

★ Activity: Interdisciplinary Connection ★

Photojournalism Photography can help raise public awareness about urban challenges and possible solutions. Have students choose one of these two activities and share the results with the class.

- Study the work of Jacob Riis, an urban reformer. Explain how he encouraged social reform in American cities through photographs and text in *How the Other Half Lives* (1890) and related books.

- Choose an urban problem today and document it with a series of photographs. (You may take them yourself or locate them in publications.) Organize your photographic essay around a theme or a motto—a memorable statement that encourages viewers to participate in a solution instead of merely observing the problem. **OL**

R Reading Strategy

Predicting Ask: What might be the national effect of energy conservation efforts at the mayoral level? *(a "bottom-up" effect; influential to legislators and other members of the federal government)* **AL**

Gentrification

Invite students to stage an informal debate about the gentrification of a hypothetical neighborhood. Encourage students to supplement the discussion in the text with additional research. **OL**

Assess

Assign the Section 3 Assessment as homework or as an in-class activity, or have students take Section Quiz 24-3 from *Section Quizzes and Chapter Tests.*

Close

Analyzing Have students draw upon details from the section as they discuss the following statement: The way we treat our cities tells us a great deal about our values and about our society as a whole. **OL**

Section 3 Review

---

deteriorating property and bringing new business to decayed areas. It also has a negative effect. By improving property values, housing prices inflate and taxes increase. Property taxes become too high for poorer residents who live in these neighborhoods. Some cities have defused this issue by passing legislation that reduces or prevents displacement. For example, Savannah, Georgia, preserved much of its social diversity by providing its limited-income residents with help in restoring their properties.

Energy Conservation

With huge concentrations of people, large cities across the nation could be drastically affected by air pollution and climate change. At the same time, cities have the opportunity to make significant contributions to solving these problems. Mayors are playing an important role in finding ways for city governments to cut their power use and to encourage citizens and businesses to do the same.

In 2005 Seattle Mayor Greg Nickels drafted a document called the U.S. Mayors Climate Protection Agreement. The agreement called for American cities to aim to cut greenhouse gas emissions by 2012 to 7 percent below the levels in 1990. Originally, the agreement was signed by eight mayors. By 2007, more than 435 mayors representing cities across the country had signed it and were implementing a wide variety of projects.

Arlington, Texas, mayor Robert Cluck has led his city to convert stoplights from incandescent bulbs to LEDs (light-emitting diodes). While LEDs are more expensive, they use 80 percent less energy than standard lights and last much longer. San Francisco officials are using recycled fat, oil and grease from restaurants to make biodiesel fuel for the city's garbage trucks. Boston has several programs under way to encourage the use of hybrid taxis. Such efforts are more than symbolic. Mayor Nickels notes that cities participating in the climate protection agreement represent 61 million people.

Metropolitan Government

One way to address urban problems is by reorganizing small areas into a **metropolitan government** that serves a larger region. Most problems do not affect just one local community. Instead, they are problems that affect an entire region. Air pollution, for example, is created in a city, but it quickly spreads to nearby suburbs and rural towns. Because a metropolitan area is interdependent, those who favor metropolitan government believe that one government for an entire metropolitan area would be better equipped to handle regional problems.

Many people believe that a metropolitan government would reduce waste and duplication of services. For example, one metropolitan sewage-treatment plant might serve many communities. Others point out that many people reside in the suburbs because the school systems and roads are better and crime is lower. They argue that creating metropolitan governments would simply bring urban problems to the suburbs.

SECTION 3 Review

Vocabulary

1. **Explain** the significance of: urban renewal, infrastructure, revitalization, gentrification, metropolitan government.

Main Ideas

2. **Summarizing** What are the positive and negative outcomes of gentrification?

3. **Describing** How would a metropolitan government address urban problems?

Critical Thinking

4. **Predicting Consequences** Analyze additional problems that cities will face if governments are unable to fund the replacement of urban infrastructures.

5. **Organizing** Use a graphic organizer like the one below to compare challenges that municipal governments faced in the 1950s to those they face today.

1950s	Today

Writing About Government

6. **Persuasive Writing** Mayors of large cities need strong arguments to get federal funding to address their problems. What could a mayor say to the president and Congress to support the city's cause? Research the types of projects that would benefit your community. Write a proposal explaining the need for federal money for a project in your community.

Answers

1. All definitions can be found in the section and the Glossary.
2. Positive: It restores vitality to the city by reclaiming deteriorating property and bringing new business to decayed areas. Negative: It accelerates property sales, inflating property values and increasing taxes; property becomes too expensive for poorer residents to remain in these neighborhoods.
3. A metropolitan government would reduce government waste and duplication of services; it also might provide services such as water, sewage disposal, and sanitation.
4. more traffic congestion; problems with services such as water, sewage disposal, and sanitation
5. 1950s: job losses, deteriorating housing, poor sanitary conditions, rising crime rates; Today: repairing infrastructure, maintaining and developing mass transit, providing for economic development, dealing with issues resulting from gentrification
6. Proposals will vary. Make sure that students have used facts to support their requests.

Should Cities Adopt Mass Transit as a Top Priority?

In 1991 Congress passed the Intermodal Surface Transportation Efficiency Act (ISTEA). The law's goal was to balance the need for transportation and clean air by promoting alternative forms of transportation. Pollution has declined in some cities, but these gains have come more from new emissions technology and vehicles and not from the fact that more people are using mass transit. Traffic congestion has worsened, and oil resources are diminishing. In the twenty-first century, should cities invest major resources in mass-transit systems?

NO

ISTEA gave states the ability to use highway funds for alternative transportation, but federal lawmakers cannot change the basic culture of Americans. The United States remains a car-dominated country. This point is clear from the fact that states spent almost the entire $23.9 billion for the ISTEA program for roads. Because of heavy spending from ISTEA funds and other sources, road conditions have steadily improved. The trucking industry, which moves a significant amount of the nation's commerce, relies on these roads. It is, therefore, essential to the economy to keep highways and bridges in good condition. Furthermore, the start-up resources necessary to build subways, railroads, and light-rail are massive. Diverting needed highway funds to mass transit when it is not clear that people will change their lifestyles is unwise.

YES

Now more than ever, American cities need to invest in alternative transportation systems. We have waited far too long to begin the transition to cleaner, more efficient, and less oil-depleting forms of transportation. We cannot continue to deny the problems of global warming and reliance on foreign energy. The transition will not be easy but we can begin by channeling transportation funds to any number of projects: elevated walkways, special lanes on freeways for High-Occupancy Vehicles, improvements in existing railroad lines, and light rail. Funds might also be used to give residents incentives to use mass transit. In the long run, these investments will pay off.

Debating the Issue

1. **Describing** How does each argument address the issue of whether Americans will use alternative transportation?

2. **Analyzing** Do the two arguments use the same time frame for their assumptions about transportation use?

3. **Evaluating** With which opinion do you tend to agree? Why?

▶ **Commuters using mass transit**

Debating the Issue Answers

1. The No argument asserts that without knowing for sure that people will embrace a new mass-transit system, it is a bad idea to commit to it; the Yes argument claims that the American people might need to be eased into the new system with incentives and so on.

2. No. The No argument implies a short-term focus, while the Yes argument is concerned with long-term results.

3. Students should support their opinion with references to the quotes or individual research and logical arguments.

Teach

Setting Up the Debate

Applying Research Have students research the mass-transit systems in two major U.S. or world cities. The first system should be a successful example. The second should be one that has failed miserably. **Ask:** Why did one succeed and the other fail? Is there a major difference between the two projects in the amount of time and money invested in them? Was either of the systems retrofitted to an already bustling city? Did each city effectively market the new mass-transit system to its citizens? (*Answers will vary, but students should start to understand the factors that make a successful mass-transit system.*) **OL**

Evaluating Have students research the arguments for and against the prioritization of mass transit. Students should give specific arguments to support both points of view. **OL**

Concluding the Debate

Discuss these questions with students:

- What are some ways to market a mass-transit system? Are there ways to convince the general commuting public that mass transit is a better alternative to cars? *Should they be convinced?*

- If a mass-transit system became available in your area (if there is not one already), would you use it even if it was a little less convenient than driving?

CHAPTER 24

Assessment and Activities

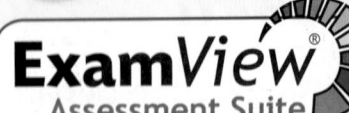

ExamView®
Assessment Suite

This easy-to-use software includes extensive question banks and allows you to create fully customized tests that can be administered in print or online.

Reviewing Vocabulary

1. infrastructure
2. market value
3. revitalization
4. county
5. zoning
6. real property
7. metropolitan government
8. municipality
9. special district
10. gentrification

Reviewing Main Ideas

11. mayor-council, commission, council-manager
12. public education
13. Cities and suburbs in the South and West grew rapidly, cities in the Northeast and Midwest lost population, the population of small towns and rural areas increased, and people moved from inner cities to suburbs.

Critical Thinking

14. The state creates the municipality by granting it a charter to govern.
15. Local Charter: provides structure and rules for local government.
State Constitution: provides structure and rules for state government.
Both: established by state officials.

Reviewing Vocabulary

From the list below, write the content vocabulary word(s) that best completes each sentence.

county
municipality
special district
zoning
market value

real property
infrastructure
revitalization
gentrification
metropolitan government

1. Basic facilities such as streets, water lines, and public buildings make up what is known as the ____ of a city.
2. The government does not tax property on the ____, which is the amount of money the owner may expect to receive if the property is sold.
3. To promote economic growth, local governments have tried ____ through large investments in new facilities.
4. In the South and in rural areas, ____ government is important.
5. Local governments might use ____ to control growth.
6. Local governments rely on ____ taxes as a main source of revenue.
7. Some people believe that the best way to address urban problems is reorganization using ____ that serves a large region.
8. Originally, a charter for a(n) ____ was much like one that states granted to corporations.
9. A public school district is a(n) ____ established by local government.
10. Sometimes called *displacement*, ____ has often changed the character of an urban area.

Reviewing Main Ideas

Section 1 *(pages 663–668)*

11. **Specifying** What are the three main forms of municipal government?

Section 2 *(pages 669–675)*

12. **Identifying** What is the single largest public service provided by local tax revenues?

Section 3 *(pages 677–682)*

13. **Describing** What are four kinds of population shifts in metropolitan areas since 1950?

Critical Thinking

14. **Essential Question** What is the relationship between a state and a municipality within that state?
15. **Making Comparisons** Use a Venn diagram to compare a local government's charter to a state constitution.

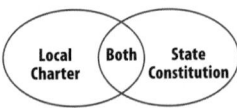

Local Charter — Both — State Constitution

Chapter Summary

Local Government

Structure and Finances	Services	Challenges
★ Created by and dependent on state government ★ Types—county, township, municipality, special district ★ Revenue—property, local income, and sales taxes, fines and fees, bonds, state and federal grants	★ Education ★ Zoning ★ Police and fire protection ★ Water, sewage and sanitation ★ Transportation ★ Social services ★ Recreation and cultural activities	★ Housing shortages, housing discrimination ★ Homelessness, drug abuse, poverty, crime, unemployment ★ Repairing and maintaining infrastructure ★ Stimulating development

Government ONLINE Self-Check Quiz
Visit glencoe.com and enter *QuickPass*™ code USG9822c24.
Click on Self-Check Quizzes for additional test practice.

Document-Based Questions

Analyzing Primary Sources

Read the excerpt below and answer the questions that follow.

In 1908, Staunton, Virginia, became the first city in the United States to adopt the council-manager form of local government. Below is an excerpt from the City of Staunton's Comprehensive Plan, which is updated every five years.

66 *Many factors must be taken into consideration when formulating a guide for the future development of a community. These factors help to determine the optimum pattern of development by balancing pursuit of residential, commercial, and employment opportunities with preservation of the natural environment, history, and character of the community.*

Over the years, an overriding concern voiced by many citizens at the public planning area meetings has been a desire to protect the 'quality of life'. . . . from providing more business opportunities downtown and constructing recreational facilities to protecting the scenic beauty and historic character . . .

Therefore, the Committee maintained the following guidelines as they conducted the update process for the Comprehensive Plan:

- *a desire to conserve and/or protect the City's natural resources, historic character, and scenic qualities;*

- *a desire to strengthen and broaden the City's economic base;*

- *a desire to insure adequate services and facilities . . . and*

- *a desire to encourage appropriate development and/or redevelopment of properties.* 99

16. How does this city plan resemble a business plan? What types of goals does this city have for its future?

17. Do you think that a council-manager form of government is the best way to achieve a city or a region's governmental goals? Explain.

Interpreting Political Cartoons

Analyze the cartoon and answer the questions that follow. Base your answers on the cartoon and your knowledge of Chapter 24.

SIGNE
PHILADELPHIA DAILY NEWS
Philadelphia
USA

18. Whom do the two figures represent?

19. What statement is the cartoonist making about the state of cities?

20. According to the cartoonist, what can the government do to help cities?

Participating IN GOVERNMENT

21. Attend a county, township, village, or special district meeting. Take notes on what you hear at the meeting and report to the class what happened.
Answer the following questions:
- Did the meeting follow an agenda?
- Were all members present at the meeting?
- How many local citizens attended the meeting?
- Were citizens allowed to speak on the issues?
- Did citizens' speeches affect the voting outcome?
- Was political partisanship evident? Explain.

Government ONLINE

Have students use the **Chapter 24 Self-Check Quiz.** Visit glencoe.com and enter *QuickPass*™ code USG9085c24T to prepare for the Chapter Test.

Interpreting Political Cartoons

18. Uncle Sam (the federal government) and U.S. cities

19. Cities are experiencing difficulties because of a lack of funding and unfunded mandates handed down from the federal government; cities are disabled and need federal attention.

20. The government can send more funds to cities and take a bigger role in solving urban problems.

Participating IN GOVERNMENT

21. Call on volunteers to share their reports. Interested students might write to local officials to present their views or suggestions about items discussed in the meeting.

Chapter Bonus Test Question

Ask: By population, what are the five largest cities in the United States? (*According to the 1990 and 2000 censuses, they are, in decreasing order: New York City, Los Angeles, Chicago, Houston, and Philadelphia.*)

Analyzing Primary Sources

16. Students might answer that this resembles a business plan in that it lays out a specific set of goals, like promoting the economy while protecting the environment, in a series of steps that should be achieved within a set period of time. It also focuses on developing the city rather than the actual governing of the city.

17. Students might say that a council-manager form of government is an efficient and businesslike way to manage a specific city or region, and there is a clear separation of powers as well as a chain of responsibility in this type of government. Its disadvantages include the fact that council members are not elected and are not always required to reside in the place they are governing. There is no clear leader in this form of government, which can make it difficult to set a defined path for a city or a region.

Political *and* Economic Systems

UNIT PACING CHART*		
	Chapter 25	**Chapter 26**
Day 1	Unit Opener Chapter Opener Section 1	Chapter Opener Section 1
Day 2	Supreme Court Cases to Debate Section 2	Section 2 Issues to Debate
Day 3	Section 3	Section 3
Day 4	Section 4 Government Skills	Section 4 Supreme Court Cases to Debate
Day 5	Review Chapter Assessment	Review Chapter Assessment

*Unit Pacing Chart based on year-long course; modify pacing by half for semester-long course

 Teacher *to* Teacher

Nicholas Petula

Scranton
School District
Scranton, PA

Global Economics Help students understand world economic interdependence by having them examine familiar products to identify imports. Organize the class into groups of three to five students, and have each group compile a list of imported items and their countries of origin. Have students check the labels on their clothing and list the countries of origin on the board. Then have them identify other imports by examining foods, electronics, automobiles, clothing, and other manufactured products at home or at drugstores, clothing stores, bookstores, or a shopping mall.

Discuss the variety of places from which imported products come and add them to the previous day's list. Then have students brainstorm a list of items, such as movies and CDs, that are exported from the United States. Create a list of major importers for U.S. products. Have each group pick an importer or exporter from the lists to research. The groups should present their findings to the class, identifying products that are traded with the United States and noting whether the United States has a trade surplus or a trade deficit with that country.

Author Note

Dear U.S. Government Teacher,

As you teach this final unit, students will cast their eyes abroad to survey other political and economic systems. It might be argued that there is no better way for students to understand U.S. traditions than to see them in context, and only an exposure to other political and economic systems will do that.

It hardly needs to be said that students in the twenty-first century learn more about and hear more about other nations than their parents or grandparents did. The Internet and the globalization of commerce have broadened their worldview. Yet much of this information and exposure is random and fractured. That is all the more reason for a U.S. Government teacher to provide the basic understanding of parliamentary and authoritarian government, of developing nations and the European Union, and of the transformations of Russia, China, and South Asia.

There are two other perspectives students will be able to take away from this unit. One is the coverage of international terrorism in Chapter 25. Students may hear many references to the topic in the news, but they need a cogent explanation of its origins and structure to comprehend the often sensationalized news reports. The other, quite different perspective will come from students' understanding of NGOs and IGOs (nongovernmental and intergovernmental organizations) increasing the role they play in world affairs. For many students, the idealism and vision of many NGOs will be appealing, and some students may even be drawn into public service—or at least responsible citizenship—by learning about global politics.

Richard C. Remy, Ph.D.
Author

Focus

Making It Relevant

Categorizing Politics and Economics Ask students to clip 10 articles about international events from the newspaper. Have them paste the articles on a sheet of paper. Then have them identify the following about each article: the countries involved, the type of political and economic systems, the political issues, and the economic issues. After students have marked up their articles, discuss the difficulties in separating political issues from economic issues.

Unit Objectives

After studying this unit, students will be able to:

- **Discuss** the characteristics of different types of political systems.

- **Evaluate** the relationship between economic decision making and political freedom.

- **Compare** capitalism, socialism, and communism.

Unit Overview

Unit 9 describes the different kinds of political systems around the world and explains the development of economic systems.

Chapter 25 describes various political systems and explains some global issues.

Chapter 26 describes how various economic systems developed as well as issues facing the global economy.

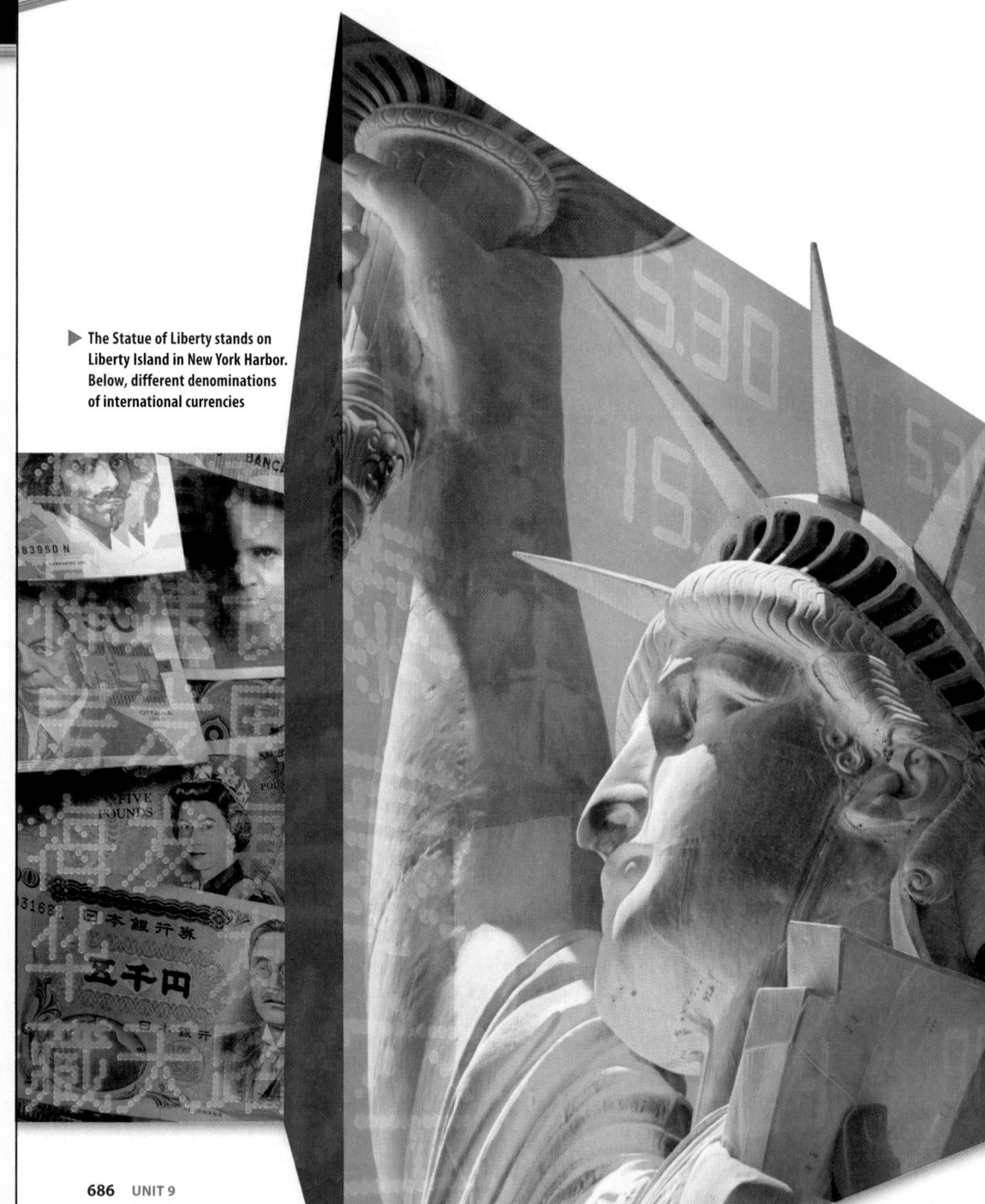

▶ The Statue of Liberty stands on Liberty Island in New York Harbor. Below, different denominations of international currencies

686 UNIT 9

Activity: Launching the Unit

Understanding Dictatorships Have interested students read a book about a dictator such as Benito Mussolini, Adolf Hitler, or Fidel Castro. Ask students to read with the purpose of trying to understand what type of personality fits the dictator role. Encourage students to consider whether a dictator could ever assume, or even wrest, power in the United States, and if so, under what conditions it could happen. Students should summarize their findings in a brief report. **OL**

UNIT 9

Political *and* Economic Systems

Participating IN GOVERNMENT

BIG IDEA **Global Perspectives** One of the most interesting ways to learn about political systems in other countries is to talk directly with a person from another country. Investigate your community to find out whether there is a foreign exchange student, visiting businessperson, or recent immigrant from another country. With the teacher's permission, invite that person to class to share information about his or her country.

▲ Beijing National Stadium, constructed in less than five years, is the largest steel structure in the world.

687

INTRODUCING UNIT 9

Teach

S **Skill Practice**

Visual Literacy Have students examine the photo of the Beijing National Stadium, nicknamed the Bird's Nest, and designed by a team of Swiss architects for the 2008 Summer Olympics. **Ask:** How might the stadium's design reflect internationalism or globalism? *(Students might suggest that the steel beams that are interconnected in one solid structure represent globalism.)*

Online Current Events Update

History happens every day. Visit Glencoe's Online Current Events Update at glencoe.com to find news reports, features, maps, graphs, and images about events that shape our lives. Students can connect those events to historical events in world and American history by exploring related events on an interactive time line—a time line that ends with today.

Graduation: Exit With Success

Teaching Tip One strategy that helps students who are having difficulty understanding information is to have them use graphic organizers, such as flowcharts, to understand the sequence of events in the text.

Extra Credit Project

Examining Trade Agreements Have students work in pairs to study the advantages and disadvantages of an American free trade agreement like NAFTA, CAFTA, or the Colombia Free Trade Agreement. Students should find sources that support trade agreements and sources that oppose them.

When students have compiled their sources, they should use a computer presentation program to prepare presentations on the trade agreements. After students present, engage the class in a problem-solving activity to address the concerns they raised. **AL**

Key to Ability Levels

BL Below level	**AL** Above level
OL On level	**ELL** English Language Learners

Key to Teaching Resources

Print Material   Transparency
CD-ROM or DVD

Levels					Resources	Chapter Opener	Section 1	Section 2	Section 3	Section 4	Chapter Assess
BL	OL	AL	ELL								
FOCUS											
BL	OL	AL	ELL	📽	Section Focus Transparencies		25-1	25-2	25-3	25-4	
TEACH											
BL	OL		ELL	📁	Reading Essentials and Study Guide (and Answer Key)		p. 284	p. 288	p. 291	p. 294	
BL	OL		ELL	📁	Guided Reading Activities		p. 89	p. 90	p. 91	p. 92	
BL	OL		ELL	📁	Vocabulary Activities		p. 24				
BL	OL	AL	ELL	📁	Chapter Summaries					p. 73	
BL	OL			📁	American Biographies						
BL	OL	AL	ELL	📁	Cooperative Learning Activities						
	OL	AL	ELL	📁	Government Simulations and Debate					p. 52	
BL	OL	AL	ELL	📁	Historical Documents and Speeches			p. 25			
BL	OL	AL	ELL	📁	Interpreting Political Cartoons			p. 49			
BL	OL		ELL	📁	Skill Reinforcement Activities				p. 25		
BL	OL	AL	ELL	📁	Source Readings						
BL	OL			📁	Supreme Court Case Studies						
BL	OL	AL	ELL	📁	Participating in Government Activities			p. 49			
BL	OL		ELL	📁	Spanish Declaration of Independence and U.S. Constitution	✓	✓	✓	✓	✓	✓
BL	OL	AL	ELL	📁	NGS World Atlas, Spanish	✓	✓	✓	✓	✓	✓
BL	OL	AL	ELL	📽	Unit Overlay Transparencies, Strategies, and Activities	✓	✓	✓	✓	✓	✓
BL	OL		ELL	📽	Making It Relevant Transparencies	✓	✓	✓	✓	✓	✓
BL	OL	AL	ELL	📽	High School Writing Process Transparencies, Strategies, and Activities	✓	✓	✓	✓	✓	✓
BL	OL	AL		📽	American Art & Architecture Transparencies, Strategies, and Activities	✓	✓	✓	✓	✓	✓

✓ Chapter- or unit-based activities applicable to all sections in this chapter

All-In-One Planner and Resource Center

- Interactive Lesson Planner
- Interactive Teacher Edition
- Fully editable blackline masters
- Chapter Spotlight Videos Launch

- Differentiated Lesson Plans
- Printable reports of daily assignments
- Standards tracking system

Levels					Resources	Chapter Opener	Section 1	Section 2	Section 3	Section 4	Chapter Assess
BL	OL	AL	ELL								
					TEACH *(continued)*						
BL	OL			💿	**American Music: Hits Through History**	✓	✓	✓	✓	✓	✓
BL	OL		ELL	📁	**Reading Strategies for the Social Studies Classroom**	✓	✓	✓	✓	✓	✓
			ELL	📁	**English Language Learner Handbook**	✓	✓	✓	✓	✓	✓
BL	OL		ELL	📁	**Writer's Guidebook for Social Studies**	✓	✓	✓	✓	✓	✓
BL	OL	AL	ELL	📁	**Living Constitution, SE**	✓	✓	✓	✓	✓	✓
BL	OL	AL	ELL	📁	**Living Constitution, TAE**	✓	✓	✓	✓	✓	✓
BL	OL			📁	**NGS World Atlas, English**	✓	✓	✓	✓	✓	✓
BL	OL		ELL	📁	**The Constitution and You (poster set)**	✓	✓	✓	✓	✓	✓
BL	OL	AL	ELL	📁	**Spanish Chapter Summaries**				p. 73		
BL	OL	AL	ELL	📁	**Spanish Vocabulary Activities**		p. 24				
BL	OL		ELL	📁	**Spanish Reading Essentials and Study Guide (and Answer Key)**		p. 284	p. 288	p. 291	p. 294	
BL	OL	AL	ELL	💿	**PresentationPlus! with MindJogger CheckPoint**	✓	✓	✓	✓	✓	✓
					ASSESS						
BL	OL	AL	ELL	💿	***ExamView® Assessment Suite***		25-1	25-2	25-3	25-4	Ch. 25
BL	OL	AL	ELL	📁	**Authentic Assessment with Rubrics**		p. 32				p. 32
BL	OL	AL	ELL	📁	**Section Quizzes and Chapter Tests**		p. 309	p. 310	p. 311	p. 312	pp. 313–320
BL	OL	AL	ELL	📁	**Spanish Section Quizzes and Tests**		p. 309	p. 310	p. 311	p. 312	pp. 313–320
					CLOSE						
BL			ELL	📁	**Reteaching Activities**					p. 23	p. 23
BL	OL	AL	ELL	💿	**StudentWorks™ Plus with Audio Summaries**	✓	✓	✓	✓	✓	✓
BL	OL		ELL	🖨	**Graphic Organizer Transparencies**		✓	✓	✓	✓	
BL	OL		ELL	📁	**High School Government Reading and Study Skills Foldables®**		p. 68	p. 68	p. 68	p. 68	

Combined Vocabulary Products

Teach With Technology

What Glencoe technology products improve students' vocabulary?

Vocabulary eFlashcards, ePuzzles and Games, and **Vocabulary PuzzleMaker** all build students' vocabulary and help students understand key words and concepts from the textbook.

How can these products help my students?

Vocabulary eFlashcards help students review and test their recall of content vocabulary, academic vocabulary, and people, places, and events for each chapter.
ePuzzles and Games are an entertaining way for students to study the key facts, concepts, and vocabulary introduced in each chapter. The **Vocabulary PuzzleMaker** lets you quickly create word searches, crosswords, and jumbles that students can use to practice vocabulary from each chapter.

For **Vocabulary eFlashcards** and **ePuzzles and Games,** visit glencoe.com and enter a student *QuickPass*™ code to go directly to student resources for the chapter. For **Vocabulary PuzzleMaker,** enter a teacher code to go to teacher resources.

Government ONLINE

Visit glencoe.com and enter *QuickPass*™ code USG9085c25T for Chapter 25 resources.

You can easily launch a wide range of digital products from your computer's desktop with the McGraw-Hill Social Studies widget.

	Student	Teacher	Parent
Media Library			
• Student Edition Section Audio	●		●
• Chapter Spotlight Videos	●	●	●
United States Government Online Learning Center (Web Site)			
• Chapter Overviews	●	●	●
• Multilingual Glossaries	●	●	●
• Study-to-Go	●	●	●
• Student Web Activities	●	●	●
• Self-Check Quizzes	●	●	●
• Online Student Edition	●	●	●
• Vocabulary eFlashcards	●	●	●
• Web Activity Lesson Plans		●	
• Vocabulary PuzzleMaker	●	●	●
• Landmark Supreme Court Cases	●	●	●
• Beyond the Textbook	●	●	●

- **Timed Readings Plus in Social Studies** helps students increase their reading rate and fluency while maintaining comprehension. The 400-word passages are similar to those found on state and national assessments.

- **Reading in the Content Area: Social Studies** concentrates on six essential reading skills that help students better comprehend what they read. The book includes 75 high-interest nonfiction passages written at increasing levels of difficulty.

- **Reading Social Studies** includes strategic reading instruction and vocabulary support in Social Studies content for ELLs and native speakers of English.
  www.jamestowneducation.com

Reading List Generator CD-ROM

GLENCOE BOOKLINK 3

Use this database to search more than 30,000 titles to create a customized reading list for your students.

- Reading lists can be organized by students' reading level, author, genre, theme, or area of interest.
- The database provides Degrees of Reading Power™ (DRP) and Lexile™ readability scores for all selections.
- A brief summary of each selection is included.

Leveled reading suggestions for this chapter:

- *Our Veils, Ourselves,* by Scott Macleod
- *The Haunted Land: Facing Europe's Ghosts After Communism,* by Tina Rosenberg
- *The Story of the United Nations,* by Katharine Savage

Review suggested books before assigning them.

Economics Connection

Personal Finance Literacy

Insurance Matters

Explain to students that you pay an insurance company monthly or quarterly premiums. If something bad happens, such as a traffic accident, insurance helps you stay afloat financially. If nothing bad happens, the company keeps the money.

The most common types of insurance are auto and health. People also buy many other types of insurance, including home-owner, flood, pet, and rental. Life insurance provides financial support to loved ones when a person dies. Disability insurance partially replaces income if a person is injured and cannot work.

Legal requirements: Most states require drivers to carry proof of basic liability insurance to cover property damage and injuries to others. Some also require personal injury coverage for the driver.

Auto insurance is important for teenage drivers. These drivers are involved in four times as many accidents as other age groups. Auto insurance helps pay the costs of injuries, car and property damage, and lawsuits.

A document detailing what your insurance covers is a policy. Most require a deductible, an amount you pay before insurance kicks in.

Major Types of Auto Insurance
Collision: Damage to driver's car
Comprehensive: Damage to driver's car not caused by an accident (theft, natural disasters)
Liability: Bodily injury and property damage to others, plus legal costs
Medical: Medical expenses for everyone involved
Personal injury: Medical expenses for driver
Uninsured motorist: Car damage in an accident caused by a driver with no liability insurance
Underinsured motorist: Car damage in an accident caused by an underinsured driver

Did You Know?

In the 1940s, movie studio 20th Century Fox insured the legs of World War II pinup Betty Grable; Irish dancer Michael Flatley insured his legs for $47 million in the 1990s. Rocker Bruce Springsteen insured his voice for $6 million.

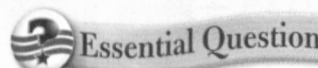

Essential Question

Governments around the world vary greatly, ranging from parliamentary and presidential democracies to authoritarian dictatorships. All governments face challenges with their economies, terrorism, nuclear proliferation, human rights, and the environment.

Chapter Spotlight Video

To generate student interest and provide a springboard for class discussion, access the Chapter 25 Video at glencoe.com or on the video DVD.

FOLDABLES **Dinah Zike's**
Study Organizer **Foldables** are
three-dimensional, interactive graphic organizers that help students practice basic writing skills, review key vocabulary terms, and identify main ideas. Have students complete this chapter's Foldable activity or activities in *Dinah Zike's Reading and Study Skills Foldables* booklet. **OL**

Government ONLINE

Visit glencoe.com and enter **QuickPass**™ code USG9085c25T for Chapter 25 Resources including Chapter Overview, Student Web Activity, Self-Check Quiz, and other materials for students and teachers.

CHAPTER 25

🔊 Chapter Audio   🎬 Spotlight Video

Political Systems *in* Today's World

▶ The people of Bhutan, a nation that shifted from monarchy to democracy in 2008, line up to vote.

Essential Question

How do governments vary around the world, and what collective challenges do they face in today's interdependent world?

Government ONLINE

Chapter Overview Visit glencoe.com and enter *QuickPass*™ code USG9822c25 for an overview, a quiz, and other chapter resources.

688

Launching the Chapter

Tracing the Development of Governments Have students choose a foreign country to research. Students should look for significant historical events that influenced the country's government and important or influential periods in the country's history. Have students try to place their chosen country's governmental structure into one of the following categories: long-standing democracy, emerging democracy, or authoritarian government. **Essential Question:** How does this country's government differ from that of the United States? How is it similar? *(Answers will vary greatly, but students should point out similarities and differences between their country of choice and the United States.)* **OL**

Democratic Governments

Reader's Guide

Content Vocabulary
★ consolidated democracy *(p. 689)*
★ parliamentary government *(p. 689)*
★ presidential government *(p. 691)*
★ apartheid *(p. 693)*
★ sanction *(p. 693)*

Academic Vocabulary
★ transition *(p. 689)*
★ widespread *(p. 689)*
★ ministry *(p. 691)*

Reading Strategy
Create a flowchart to list the process by which officials in a parliamentary government are chosen.

Voters → ☐ → ☐

People in the News

Possibly the world's last absolute monarchy, the mountain kingdom of Bhutan in the Himalayas, has at last embraced democracy. In 2005 King Jigme Singye Wangchuck announced that general elections would be held in 2008 to introduce a democratic constitution and that he would step down in favor of his son, the crown prince. One scholar commented that the move to constitutional monarchy was made because the king: "[T]hought that the way to safeguard Bhutan's sovereignty . . . is to give the people of Bhutan a say in the governance of this little country." The country is Buddhist and the king is devoted to a peaceful and harmonious transition. The nation's UN ambassador quotes the king as declaring that "'Gross national happiness is more important than gross national product.'"

▲ The king of Bhutan, Jigme Singye Wangchuck on a visit to India

There are more than 190 countries in the world. The history, culture, economics, natural resources, and geography of each country shape its government and politics. As a result, governments throughout the world vary greatly—no two are the same. We can, however, identify three basic types of government: long-standing democracies, nations that are in **transition** to democracy, and authoritarian governments.

The first democratic ideas originated in ancient Greece and Rome. The principles of representative government developed slowly over many centuries in Europe. English colonists eventually brought these principles to the Americas. Today, political scientists call countries like the United States with well-established democratic governments **consolidated democracies.** Such nations have fair elections, competing political parties, a constitutional government that guarantees individual rights, an independent judiciary, and some form of a market economy.

Parliamentary Systems

Democratic governments can take several forms. One of the most **widespread** is **parliamentary government.** In this form, executive and legislative functions both reside in the elected assembly, or parliament. Often the parliament selects the leaders of the executive branch of government, also known as the cabinet. Great Britain and Japan are consolidated democracies with a parliamentary form of government.

British Parliament

In Great Britain, the national legislature, called Parliament, holds almost all the governmental

Focus

Bellringer
Section Focus Transparencies 25-1

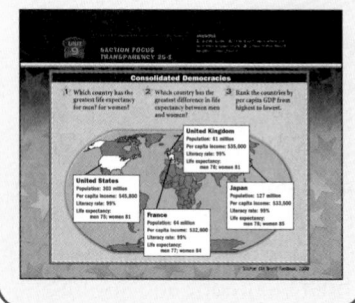

Reader's Guide

Answers to Graphic: Voters; Legislature; Chief Executive

Resource Manager

R Reading Strategies	C Critical Thinking	D Differentiated Instruction	W Writing Support	S Skill Practice
Teacher Edition • Comparing and Contrasting, p. 690 • Inferring, p. 692	**Teacher Edition** • Contrasting, p. 693 • Making Inferences, p. 694	**Teacher Edition** • Visual/Spatial, p. 691 • Auditory/Musical, p. 693	**Teacher Edition** • Expository Writing, p. 690	**Teacher Edition** • Using Geography Skills, p. 692
Additional Resources • Guid. Read. Act., p. 89 • Quizzes/Tests, p. 309	**Additional Resources** • Read. Essen., pp. 284–287	**Additional Resources** • Foldables, p. 68	**Additional Resources** • Authentic Assess., p. 32	**Additional Resources** • Vocab. Act., p. 24

Teach

W Writing Support

Expository Writing Ask students to select and research one member of the British House of Lords. Students will write a one-page report that includes a brief biography and any information available about the person's political actions or ideas. **Ask:** Despite the differences between the British Parliament and the U.S. Congress, are the ideals of the members that much different? *(Students will probably find that parliamentary ideals and congressional ideals are similar.)* **AL**

R Reading Strategy

Comparing and Contrasting Ask students to create a two-column table listing similarities and differences between the British Parliament and the Japanese Diet. **OL**

Additional Support

The Power of Parliament

The Government in Parliament In a parliamentary system like Great Britain's, the government depends on the legislature and regularly reports to it. Here, then Chancellor of the Exchequer Gordon Brown delivered his budget report to the House of Commons. Today, Brown is the prime minister, having replaced Tony Blair, seen at right. *How is the prime minister chosen in a parliamentary system?*

authority. Parliament is a bicameral, or two-house, legislature, consisting of the House of Commons and the House of Lords. Both have a role in enacting legislation, but the House of Commons has much greater power than the second chamber, the House of Lords.

The House of Commons is the British legislative body of elected representatives. The people elect members of the House of Commons, known as Members of Parliament (MPs), who then serve for five-year terms. Their terms may be shorter if Parliament is dissolved for new elections before the end of the five-year period.

The House of Commons determines Great Britain's legislative and financial policies. While any MP may introduce legislation, most bills are introduced by the majority party. Members debate bills on the floor of the Commons and then send them to one of eight standing committees to work out the final details. Committees must send their final bill back to the House of Commons, and a majority vote is then needed for passage.

In modern times, the House of Lords has had limited power. Since 1910, the House of Lords has been unable to initiate a bill or vote a bill down, but it can delay passage of a bill by voting against it. For centuries, only the first sons of "peers of the realm"— hereditary nobles—sat in the House of Lords. Until recently, it included about 1,200 members.

In 1999 a reform law allowed 92 hereditary nobles to remain in the Lords on a temporary basis, but the other 540 members were to become life peers. Life peers are people that the state appoints to the Lords because of their outstanding service or achievement. The reform process is continuing and it is expected that eventually all members of the House of Lords will be popularly elected.

The Prime Minister

Great Britain has no separation of powers between the executive and legislative branches of government. The leader of the majority party in the House of Commons becomes the prime minister and chooses other ministers to head executive departments and serve as cabinet members. Most ministers are members of the majority party in the House of Commons.

A prime minister who loses the support of his or her party resigns from office. The party then chooses another prime minister. If the majority party loses a vote on an important issue, it is said to have "lost the confidence of the House" and must resign. Parliament is dissolved, and new general elections are held to determine the party that will control the House of Commons.

Japanese Diet

Japan has a parliament of two houses, called the National Diet. The upper house is the House of Councillors, and the lower house is the House of Representatives. The Japanese constitution states that the National Diet shall be the "sole lawmaking organ of the state." In addition, the Diet has authority over the nation's fiscal policies. The House of

Activity: Collaborative Learning

Creating a Collage Organize the class into groups of three to create three-part collages that depict the governments of the countries mentioned in this section. Allow group members to choose Great Britain, Japan, or France to illustrate on their section of the collage. Encourage students to include tables, charts, graphs, pictures, sketches, and captions. **BL**

Councillors has only limited power to delay legislation. The House of Representatives has members who are chosen from election districts. Each district, with a single exception, elects three to five representatives. Each member of the lower house is elected for four years.

The House of Representatives elects the prime minister and has the power to vote "no confidence" in the prime minister or chief executive and the cabinet, just as in Great Britain. When considering legislation, the House of Representatives may override a negative vote in the House of Councillors by a two-thirds majority.

Members of the House of Councillors are chosen for six-year terms that cannot be dissolved with a no-confidence vote. As with the upper houses of other governments, the House of Councillors provides a calmer, more detached form of deliberation than the House of Representatives. In this way, it helps moderate any hasty actions that might be taken by the lower house.

Committees carry on much of the work of both houses of the Diet. Cabinet ministers often testify before committees, where they face penetrating questions from members of the opposition party. Committee proceedings tend to be very lively, and they are often televised.

When voting on legislation, members of the majority party are expected to vote with the government. If they do not agree with the legislation, they abstain. The opposing parties are rarely strong enough to do more than delay legislation, and most legislation is passed.

Function of the Cabinet

In parliamentary government, members of the cabinet preside over departments, or **ministries.** These may include justice, foreign affairs, finance, education, health and welfare, agriculture, and labor. Japan's system also includes other cabinet members known as ministers of state. They include the deputy prime minister and heads of various agencies, such as the Economic Planning Agency and the Science and Technology Agency.

Dissolving the Government

In Great Britain and other parliamentary systems, the prime minister and the cabinet together are referred to as the *government,* a word equivalent to the American use of the word *administration.* The government is responsible to the elected representatives. If the government should lose a vote on an important issue, it must resign.

The legislature is then dissolved, and new general elections are held.

Sometimes the government dissolves Parliament even while it still has a majority in the House of Commons. This dissolution may happen if a government senses that public support for it is so strong that it will elect more members of its party than it currently has. Then, at the prime minister's request, Parliament is dissolved and a general election is held to select members of the Commons.

Presidential Government

Another way to organize a democracy is by **presidential government.** In a presidential system of government, the president is chosen by the people to head the executive branch, which is distinct from the legislature. The United States has this type of government because its Constitution establishes a separate executive branch to carry out the laws of the nation. Only a small number of nations have a presidential government similar to that of the United States.

Many other nations have different types of presidential government. Sometimes these are referred to as semi-presidential systems. Such governments have a president as well as a prime minister (sometimes called a premier). The president has executive authority that is independent of the legislature, but the prime minister is the leader of the executive.

The power exercised by the president and the prime minister can vary. In France, the president is unusually powerful. It was the 1958 constitution that transformed the office of president into the most powerful office in the government. The president serves a seven-year term and is the only member of government who is elected directly by voters of the nation at large. As such, the president can claim to speak for the nation.

Similar to chief executives in other democracies, the French president is responsible for negotiating treaties, appointing high officials, and acting as chair of the high councils of the military.

Government ONLINE
Student Web Activity Visit glencoe.com and enter *QuickPass*™ code USG9822c25. Click on Student Web Activity and complete the activity about consolidated democracies.

CHAPTER 25: Political Systems in Today's World **691**

Did You Know?

The Chartists were a British reform group who proposed political changes in the early 1800s. They demanded voting rights for all adult men, a secret ballot, and salaries for representatives so that the middle and lower classes could serve. Parliament rejected their petitions, and the Chartist movement faded by the 1840s.

D Differentiated Instruction

Visual/Spatial Have students research the leader of a foreign country and create flyers that include a photo, the person's name, the name of the country, the date power was assumed, a short biography, and the person's political views. **BL**

Government ONLINE

Objectives and answers to the Student Web Activity can be found in the *Web Activity Lesson Plan* at glencoe.com. Enter *QuickPass*™ code USG9085c25T.

Differentiated Instruction

Activity: Multiple Learning Styles

Verbal/Linguistic Review with students the Preamble of the United States Constitution and the quote from the Japanese Constitution on page 690. Then have students assume the task of writing a preamble for the government of a newly formed democratic nation. Remind them that a preamble is an introduction to a constitution or statute that states its reasons and purposes. Call on volunteers to read their preambles to the class. **BL**

R Reading Strategy

Inferring Charles de Gaulle, a former French president, made the following statement during a speech in 1952: "The French will only be united under the threat of danger. Nobody can simply bring together a country that has 265 kinds of cheese." **Ask:** What do you think de Gaulle meant by the statement? **OL**

S Skill Practice

Using Geography Skills
Divide the class into three groups, and ask each group to research one type of democratic government: presidential, parliamentary, or democratic socialist. Each group will locate and photocopy a map of at least two countries having the type of government assigned to their group and color it with a distinctive color. Below the map they will list the population, literacy rate, and per capita income. Refer students to the CIA's *World Factbook* online for information. Display the maps in the classroom. **BL**

Critical Thinking

Answer: presidential government

Hands-On Chapter Project

Step 1

In addition, the French president has two special powers: the right to appeal directly to the people in a referendum, and the right to exercise dictatorial powers in a national emergency. In 1962 Charles de Gaulle ordered a referendum to approve a constitutional amendment providing for the direct election of the president, rather than by an electoral college. Voters approved the referendum with a 62 percent majority.

The president maintains contact with the legislative branch through a premier, whom the president appoints. (*Premier*, the French word for "first," is the French equivalent of a prime minister.) The premier, in turn, names the ministers who form the cabinet. Together they conduct the day-to-day government affairs. In theory, the premier and the cabinet are responsible to the National Assembly, or the lower house of the parliament; thus, if the cabinet loses legislative support, it must resign and the president appoints a new premier. In practice, however, the premier and the cabinet answer to the president. In regular meetings with the premier and the cabinet, the president makes sure that they continue to support the president's program.

Under the constitution, the president also has the authority to dissolve the National Assembly and call for new elections. This power may be used if the president loses the support of a majority of the Assembly. With this power, even the threat of dissolving the Assembly may be enough to force the deputies to accept the president's leadership.

Emerging Democracies

The spread of democracy around the world has increased in recent decades. Since the collapse of communism, a process that began in 1989, many of the countries of eastern Europe have been working to establish democratic governments. A number of countries in Latin America, Asia, and Africa have also been moving toward democracy. Poland, South Africa, and Mexico illustrate the types of challenges that confront nations that are trying to transition to democratic government.

Constitutional Government in Poland

In 1989 the people of Poland, East Germany, Czechoslovakia, Hungary, Romania, and Bulgaria threw out the Communist governments that were imposed on them at the end of World War II. Poland led the way in these revolutions when a

Charts In Motion
See StudentWorks™ Plus or go to glencoe.com.

Comparing Governments

Presidential versus Parliamentary Governments

Presidential: United States, Brazil, Argentina, Kenya

Presidential → Legislature → Senate and Congress → Judiciary → Chief Executive → Voters

Parliamentary: United Kingdom, Japan, Canada, India

Parliamentary → Legislature → Judiciary (Usually chosen by cabinet. In U.K. House of Lords provides highest appeals court) → Chief Executive (Chosen by legislature and holds office at their consent) → Voters

Critical Thinking Many of the parliamentary systems around the world derive their structure from the United Kingdom, the first parliamentary government. *In which form of government is the chief executive elected by the people?*

Museum Exhibit

Step 1: Researching Issues Student groups will research issues facing the world and prepare a museum exhibit explaining the issues and offering solutions.

Directions Tell students that some issues in the world can only be solved globally because they affect every country. Later in this project, they will create a museum exhibit that explains and suggests solutions to one of the world's

major issues: international terrorism, the threat posed by nuclear weapons, human rights, and protecting the environment. Divide the class into four groups and assign one of these issues to each group. Have students begin researching their issue.

Discussing Ask what problems students are having in doing their research. **OL**

(Chapter Project continued in Section 2.)

trade union called Solidarity emerged from an underground resistance movement. Solidarity swept the first democratic elections since World War II. It was supported by Pope John Paul II in its fight against Poland's Communist government. The pope, a native of Poland, quietly used his influence to strengthen Solidarity's opposition efforts. In 1990 Lech Walesa, the leader of Solidarity, became the first freely elected president of Poland. He won nearly 74 percent of the vote, and Solidarity won nearly all of the seats that were up for election in the parliament.

The collapse of communism did not ensure the development of democracy. Reformers who took office in Poland in the early 1990s faced two major challenges. First, they needed a written constitution that would place clear limits on governmental power. Second, they needed to strengthen local governments. Reformers believed that effective local governments would give citizens a chance to get directly involved in issues that immediately concerned them, such as education and transportation.

In 1992 President Walesa signed the "Little Constitution," which was intended to be a temporary measure until a new constitution could be developed. It took several more years of bitter debates to create a new constitution. New political parties, including some made up of former Communist officials, struggled to gain political advantage. Finally, on April 2, 1997, the National Assembly adopted the new Constitution of the Republic of Poland, and the voters approved it in May.

Chapter VII of the 1997 Polish constitution addressed the need to strengthen local governments. The constitution states:

66 *Local government shall perform public tasks not reserved by the Constitution or statutes to the organs of other public authorities. . . . [L]ocal government shall possess legal personality. . . . [L]ocal government shall be protected by the courts.* 99

This clause means that local governments became constitutionally responsible for such matters as education, municipal housing, waste collection, and firefighting.

Despite Poland's progress toward political democracy, the nation remains in a precarious position. A weakened economy in 2001 forced Solidarity members in the Polish Parliament to cut spending to reduce the government budget deficits. Voters responded to this action by voting Solidarity members out of Parliament. This shift in Poland's politics benefited many formerly Communist political supporters. Their political party, the Democratic Left Alliance (SLD), now holds a majority of the seats in the lower house of Poland's Parliament. Despite this, Poland joined the European Union in 2004.

Civil Rights in South Africa

Starting in 1948, South Africa followed a policy of **apartheid,** or strict segregation of the races enforced by the government. The South African populations of black South Africans, whites, coloreds (people of mixed European and African descent), and Asians were strictly segregated. Black Africans suffered the worst under this legalized segregation. Apartheid laws defined whom black Africans could marry and where they could travel, eat, and go to school. Black Africans could not vote or own property, and they could be jailed indefinitely without cause.

In response, black nationalist groups such as the African National Congress (ANC) pressed for reforms, but the government repeatedly crushed the resistance. By the 1960s, ANC leader Nelson Mandela formed a military operation. In 1962 South African officials charged Mandela with treason and jailed him for life. From his prison cell, Mandela became a world-famous symbol for freedom in South Africa. In the 1980s, the United States and the European Economic Community ordered economic **sanctions,** or the imposition of restrictions and the withholding of aid, against the South African government. This economic pressure helped bring a gradual end to apartheid. In 1990 President Frederik W. de Klerk released Mandela from prison. During the next few years, the South African government repealed the remaining apartheid laws.

In April 1994, South Africa held its first non-racial national election. Nineteen parties offered candidates for the National Assembly. The election went smoothly, and foreign observers declared that it was free and fair. The African National Congress won about 63 percent of the vote along with 252 of the 400 seats in the National Assembly, which then chose Nelson Mandela as president without opposition.

The ANC fostered national unity by allowing the Zulu Inkatha Party and the Afrikaner Nationalist Party to hold some cabinet positions. Since 1994, however, the ANC has dominated the government.

POLITICAL PROFILES **Lech Walesa** (1943–), the leader of Poland's Solidarity movement, was jailed in 1981 for his trade union activities. He was released in 1982 when all trade unions were dissolved. In 1983 Walesa won the Nobel Peace Prize for effectively preventing violence while trying to gain workers' rights.

C Critical Thinking

Contrasting Ask students to create graphic organizers showing the differences between the paths taken toward democracy in South Africa and Poland. OL

D **Differentiated Instruction**

Auditory/Musical Organize the class into small groups to write a song about South Africa. Have groups use a familiar tune as the melody for their song. Then have them write lyrics that might describe the sentiments of the South African people as the first free elections were held in 1994. Encourage students to include in the lyrics the names of significant people who helped make free elections possible. Call on volunteers to sing their song for the class. AL

Differentiated Instruction

Participating in Government Activities

Participating in Government Activities, p. 49

Objective: To figure out what *democracy* means to people.

Focus/Teach: First, have students reread Chapter 18, Section 4 (Measuring Public Opinion). Then ask them to read the Background and discuss the Questions to Consider.

Assess: Have students complete the Activity and discuss their results.

Close: Complete and discuss the Follow-up activity.

Differentiated Instruction Strategies

BL Have higher-level students help lower-level students write questions.

AL Have students figure out and evaluate the mean, median, mode, and standard deviation for their closed questions responses.

ELL Discuss some essentials of clearly worded questions.

693

C Critical Thinking

Making Inferences Refer students to the CIA's *World Factbook* online to research the economy of Mexico. **Ask:** Which data categories might indicate a need for reform in Mexico? *(Answers might include GDP versus national debt; percentage of population with access to potable water, electricity, or medical care; and so on.)* **Ask:** Despite having a governmental structure very similar to that of the United States, are there any major demographic or economic differences evident in the information presented about Mexico? **OL AL**

Assess

Assign the Section 1 Assessment as homework or as an in-class activity, or have students take Section Quiz 25-1 from *Section Quizzes and Chapter Tests.*

Close

Identifying Ask students to choose which country mentioned in this section they would want to live in if they could not live in the United States. Discuss the reasons for students' decisions. **OL**

Section 1 Review

Removing the legal structure of apartheid was an essential first step toward democracy in South Africa. Major challenges for the future include building a democratic civic culture, ensuring equal civil rights throughout society, and raising the standard of living for disadvantaged South Africans while maintaining economic growth.

Political Parties in Mexico

In 1917 Mexico adopted a constitution that divided the national government into three branches: executive, legislative, and judicial. The president heads the executive branch and is directly elected for one six-year term. The president exercises strong governmental control and is the dominant figure in politics.

The 1917 constitution also provided for a variety of individual, social, and economic rights. One political scientist described the 1917 constitution as the "most advanced labor code in the world at its time." However, the president's power and the control of the government by one political party, the Institutional Revolutionary Party (PRI), for more than 60 years has led political observers to describe the Mexican government as more authoritarian than democratic.

For decades, massive organizational resources, political patronage, and the support of the major media served to keep the PRI in power. In some cases, the PRI was accused of manipulating elec-

tions. In 1994, however, PRI candidate Ernesto Zedillo Ponce de León won the presidency and introduced nationwide electoral reforms that did much to end the PRI's long tradition of ballot box fraud. These reforms helped set the stage for other parties to compete fairly in Mexico's political process.

In July 2000, Mexico took a major step toward becoming a multiparty democracy when Vicente Fox, the candidate of the National Action Party, or PAN, defeated the PRI and became president. Although PAN was dominant, it did not have an outright majority and had to form coalitions to pass legislation. Fox brought significant economic progress, but many Mexicans were poor, and free trade and immigration policies were controversial. Class divisions between those who have prospered from global trade and the many who have not came to the surface in the July 2006 election for a new president. Conservative candidate Felipe Calderon of the PAN Party won a very narrow victory.

Since taking office Calderon has moved forcefully to reduce violence caused by drug traffickers along the U.S. border. He has also pledged to reform Mexico's tax system and to streamline the courts. Observers note that Calderon has shown a talent for negotiating with Congress. His biggest challenge will be to continue the economic progress begun under President Vicente Fox.

SECTION 1 Review

Vocabulary

1. **Explain** the significance of: consolidated democracies, parliamentary government, presidential government, apartheid, sanctions.

Main Ideas

2. **Identifying** What are the House of Commons, House of Lords, National Diet, and Solidarity?

3. **Examining** What happens when the majority party in Britain loses a vote in Parliament?

4. **Describing** Why is most of the legislation introduced in the Japanese National Diet ultimately passed?

Critical Thinking

5. **Understanding Cause and Effect** Which recent events in Mexico have contributed to making the country more democratic?

6. **Organizing** Use a graphic organizer like the one below to compare the most powerful parts of the British and French governments.

British	French

Writing About Government

7. **Persuasive Writing** Choose a country with a parliamentary system of government. Then draw a diagram comparing the organization of the U.S. government with the parliamentary system of government you have chosen. Write a brief assessment of which government you think is more effective in meeting people's needs.

Answers

1. All definitions can be found in the section and the Glossary.
2. House of Commons: elected lower house of the United Kingdom parliament; hereditary and appointed House of Lords: upper house of the United Kingdom parliament; National Diet: parliament of Japan; Solidarity: Polish trade union that was elected in 1990 in Poland's first democratic elections since World War II
3. It must resign. Parliament is then dissolved, and new general elections are held.

4. because the majority party members either approve the legislation or abstain, and the opposition party members are usually not strong enough to stop legislation
5. In 1994 PRI president Ernesto Zedillo Ponce de León introduced electoral reforms, and after Vicente Fox became president in 2000, he instituted more democratic policies.
6. British—Parliament serves the legislative and executive functions of government; French—the president appoints the premier, negotiates treaties, may appeal to the people

through referendum and dictatorial powers, may dissolve the National Assembly
7. Students' diagrams should compare the U.S. government with a parliamentary government.

If a Citizen Votes in a Foreign Election, Can Congress Revoke His or Her Citizenship?

Afroyim v. Rusk, 1967

Chief Justice Earl Warren once explained: "Citizenship is man's basic right for it is nothing less than the right to have rights." Can Congress take away the citizenship of an American who violates a law? Afroyim v. Rusk *dealt with this issue.*

Background of the Case

Beys Afroyim from Poland became a naturalized American citizen in 1926. In 1950 Afroyim went to Israel, and while there he voted in an election for the Israeli Parliament. In 1960 Afroyim wanted to renew his U.S. passport, but the U.S. State Department refused to grant him a new passport. The State Department informed Afroyim that under the terms of the Nationality Act of 1940, he had lost his American citizenship. The law stated that U.S. citizens shall lose their citizenship if they vote in a political election in a foreign state. Afroyim sued the U.S. Secretary of State Dean Rusk, and lost in both a federal district court and in an appeals court.

The Constitutional Issue

Afroyim's case raised the question of whether the Nationality Act's penalty for voting in foreign elections, thereby creating the loss of citizenship, was constitutional. The Court stated: "The fundamental issue before this Court . . . is whether Congress can . . . enact a law stripping an American of his citizenship which he has never voluntarily renounced or given up." Afroyim argued that neither the Fourteenth Amendment nor any other provision of the Constitution expressly grants Congress the power to take away a person's citizenship after it has been acquired. Thus, the only way he could lose his citizenship was to give it up voluntarily.

In 1958, in *Perez v. Brownell*, the Supreme Court upheld the Nationality Act, ruling that Congress could revoke citizenship because it had implied power to regulate foreign affairs. Further, Justice Felix Frankfurter rejected the argument that the Fourteenth Amendment denied Congress the power to revoke citizenship. Afroyim urged the Court to overturn its earlier decision and rule in his favor.

Class Debate

Organize the class into three groups: one to represent Beys Afroyim, one for Dean Rusk, and a third group to act as the Supreme Court justices. Allow class time to develop arguments; then have each side present its case. After the "justices" reach a decision, have them read it aloud. Also have the dissenting opinions, if any, read aloud.

The Court's Decision

The Court voted 5 to 4 that Congress did not have the power to revoke citizenship for voting in a foreign election. Thus, the Court overruled its decision in the case of *Perez v. Brownell* and accepted Beys Afroyim's argument that he could lose his citizenship only by voluntarily giving it up. As for the Fourteenth Amendment, the Court stated that in the citizenship clause, "There is no indication in these words of a fleeting citizenship, good at the moment it is acquired but subject to destruction by the government at any time."

Debating the Issue

Questions to Consider

1. What might be the consequences of allowing the government to determine if a person can keep his or her citizenship?

2. Could voting in a foreign election be considered the same as voluntarily giving up one's citizenship?

You Be the Judge

The Court had to determine whether to overrule the *Perez* decision. The choice depended on its interpretation of the so-called citizenship clause of the Fourteenth Amendment, which states: "All persons born or naturalized in the United States . . . are citizens of the United States. . . ." Does that imply that citizenship can be temporary? Or does the amendment mean that citizenship is permanent until a person voluntarily gives it up? State your opinion.

▲ Voting in Israel

Debating the Issue Answers

Questions to Consider

1. Answers will vary but may point out that in a worst-case scenario, the government could strip all citizens of their citizenship and become a dictatorship.

2. Students should state "yes" or "no." Possible "yes": voting implies citizenship and wherever someone votes should determine where he or she is a citizen; Possible "no": a person can choose to vote anywhere but that does not mean he or she is relinquishing citizenship or declaring it.

You Be the Judge

Students should decide whether they think citizenship is temporary or permanent, and whether it is voluntary, and explain their choices.

Focus

Authoritarian Governments

Bellringer

Section Focus Transparencies
25-2

Reader's Guide

Answers to Graphic:

1945: civil war breaks out between Chinese Nationalists and Communists

1949: Communists take over Nationalist areas of China

1959: Fidel Castro leads revolt against Batista

1961: anti-Castro exiles invade Cuba at the Bay of Pigs

1976: Mao Zedong dies

1989: Tiananmen Square massacre

Resource Manager

Reader's Guide

Content Vocabulary	Academic Vocabulary	Reading Strategy
★ Muslim (p. 699) ★ mullah (p. 700) ★ shah (p. 701)	★ civil (p. 696) ★ sustain (p. 698) ★ transform (p. 701)	Create a time line similar to the one below to list the important events in the history of Communist China and Cuba.

```
         1949      1961
    |-----|----|----|----|----|
  1945      1959        1976   1989
```

Issues in the News

As Raúl Castro began his tenure as president of Cuba in 2008, Cubans and Americans were excited. Raúl, the younger brother of Fidel Castro, is seen as less charismatic and more practical than Fidel, the dedicated Communist who has led Cuba ever since the 1959 revolution. One of Raúl's first moves was to decree that ordinary Cubans could have cell phones. "We have waited too long for this," said one housewife. Is the liberalization a sign of continuing reform? Many say "no." They point to the fact that Raúl just wants to make life more pleasant, not to restructure the communist system. "Suddenly, there will be a lot more people talking on the phone," said one retiree. "But not much else will change."

▲ Fidel Castro, left, then president of Cuba, and his brother Raúl in 2004. Raúl was elected president in 2008.

While the number of democratic nations around the world is increasing, many authoritarian governments still exist. Governments such as those in the People's Republic of China, Cuba, North Korea, Saudi Arabia, and Iran present a stark contrast to democracies.

The People's Republic of China

Modern China is a study in contrasts. A recent U.S. State Department report on human rights said that China was an authoritarian state in which citizens lack most **civil** rights and in which the government commits numerous abuses on human rights. At the same time, China's Communist Party government has pursued economic reforms that are reducing the government's tight grip on the people.

Political History

China was ruled by emperors until the late 1800s. In 1911 the last emperor was overthrown in an uprising. A year later, China became a republic, but rival factions divided the nation until 1929. The Nationalist Party, under the leadership of Chiang Kai-shek, defeated the Communists. The Nationalists, who tended to represent the urban middle class, controlled the urban areas. The Communists, who appealed to the peasants, resisted the Nationalist leadership and campaigned for a socialist revolution. When Japan invaded China in the 1930s, the Nationalists and Communists temporarily set aside their differences to

R Reading Strategies	**C** Critical Thinking	**D** Differentiated Instruction	**W** Writing Support	**S** Skill Practice
Teacher Edition • Explaining, p. 697 **Additional Resources** • Guid. Read. Act., p. 90 • Quizzes/Tests, p. 310	**Teacher Edition** • Making Inferences, p. 699 **Additional Resources** • Read. Essen., pp. 288–290	**Teacher Edition** • Visual/Spatial, p. 699 **Additional Resources** • Foldables, p. 68 • Hist. Docs. and Speeches, p. 25	**Teacher Edition** • Narrative Writing, p. 697 • Expository Writing, p. 700 **Additional Resources** • Part. in Gov. Act., pp. 49–50	**Teacher Edition** • Researching, p. 698 • Creating a Time Line, p. 701 **Additional Resources** • Inter. Poli. Cartoons, pp. 49–50

Protests for Tibet

Challenges to China's Human Rights Record

China has dominated neighboring Tibet since 1951 and Tibetans have often tried to resist China's rule. In 2008 China suppressed yet another Tibetan protest. During the Beijing Olympics in 2008, demonstrators in New York City's Grand Central Terminal criticized China's policies in Tibet. *Does China's strong economic position affect U.S. foreign policy toward China's human rights practices?*

resist the invaders. In 1945 when the Japanese were finally defeated at the end of World War II, a civil war broke out between the Nationalists and Communists over who would control the nation.

In 1949 the Communists, led by Mao Zedong, took control of the Nationalists areas of China—the Nationalists fled to the offshore island of Taiwan. (The Taiwanese maintained that they were the legitimate government of all of China until the early 1990s. The issue of when and if Taiwan and China will be unified has not been resolved.)

Mao then led China from 1949 until his death in 1976. He set up a totalitarian government under the Chinese Communist Party (CCP). China became a socialist state with government control of all major industries. The government also took control of agriculture, forcing peasants to work on collective farms that were run by the government.

Communist Party Government

Today China has two parallel systems of government. There is a ceremonial national government, which includes a legislature, a cabinet, and a president and vice president, but the government is **R** controlled by the CCP. The CCP's top governing body is the National Party Congress. It has about 3,000 party members from different provinces, but it meets for only about two weeks each year—

basically it is a "rubber stamp" for the policies of CCP leaders. Thus, the general secretary of the CCP is the nation's leader.

National policy is made by the party's Political Bureau—the Politburo. The Politburo has about 20 party leaders, and its standing committee is made up of the top 7 leaders. This small, elite group makes the key political, economic, and military decisions for China's 1.3 billion people.

Civil Liberties

Authoritarian governments tolerate little criticism or open disagreement of their policies. In China, a dramatic example of this intolerance occurred in 1989 when Chinese military forces **W** massacred hundreds of unarmed, pro-democracy students who were demonstrating in Beijing's Tiananmen Square. The government continues today to suppress criticism and oppress minorities.

Party leaders are especially suspicious of the growth of popular organizations. For example, the government has ruthlessly suppressed the Falun Gong, a spiritual movement that combines physical exercise with Buddhism and Taoism. It has cracked down on journalists and dissidents who are critical of the government. While citizens enjoy greater economic freedom and a measure of capitalism, freedom of expression remains limited.

CHAPTER 25: *Political Systems in Today's World* **697**

Activity: Collaborative Learning

Creating an Illustrated Time Line

Organize the class into groups of four to create illustrated time lines of the political development of a country mentioned in this section. Have each group decide which country to research, and how they want to illustrate the main events that led to the present system of government. Then have members choose from the following tasks: draw the time line, illustrate the events, write captions for the events, or write a brief summary of the present system of government including the names of its leader(s). Display completed time lines in the classroom. **OL**

Participating
IN GOVERNMENT

Persuasive Writing Have students review current newspapers and magazines to locate articles on U.S. relations with China, Cuba, North Korea, Iran, or Saudi Arabia. Then ask students to write editorials supporting or opposing the stance of the United States on the issue covered in their selected articles. Have students read their editorials to the class and/or send them to the local newspaper.

S Skill Practice

Researching Have students research the background of the Korean War and the events leading up to U.S. involvement. Then have them write a summary of what the North Korean government was like during the conflict, and compare and contrast the government then to Kim Jong Il's government in North Korea today. **AL**

Hands-On Chapter Project
Step 2

Authoritarian governments are committed to controlling ideas and information; thus, China has developed the world's most extensive system of Internet censorship. By using filtering technology, the government regularly denies local users access to many political and religious Web sites. The government allows Internet use for certain business, cultural, and educational purposes that it believes will make the nation economically competitive.

Relations With the United States

The United States ended official diplomatic relations with China in 1949 when the Communists gained control of the mainland. At the same time, the U.S. government maintained contact with the Nationalist government in Taiwan. China's foreign policy, however, began changing in 1960. A growing rift between China and the Soviet Union caused China's leaders to view the U.S.S.R. as the principal threat to its national security. China subsequently grew more willing to cooperate with the United States.

Meanwhile President Nixon was attempting to ease Cold War tensions with the Soviet Union and with China. In 1972 Nixon became the first U.S. president to visit China. During this meeting, both nations agreed to begin efforts to improve their diplomatic relationship. After several years of slow progress, in 1979 the United States recognized the Communist government in Beijing as the legitimate government of China. Tensions remain, however. While China seeks access to American technology and investments, the United States wants China to end its human rights abuses and to act as a stabilizing force in Asia.

Economic relations with China have changed dramatically over the years. By focusing on high-technology exports, China's exports grew to almost $1 trillion in 2007. The United States and China remain at odds about the status of Taiwan, and poverty and unemployment are continuing problems in rural China.

Communism in Cuba

In 1959 Fidel Castro led Cubans in a revolt that ousted dictator Fulgencio Batista. Under Castro, Cuba became a Communist dictatorship that was largely **sustained** by the Soviet Union. Castro maintained strict control over the Cuban people.

Tensions between Cuba and the United States boiled over in two crises. In 1961 anti-Castro exiles, trained by the United States, invaded Cuba

at the Bay of Pigs. The failed invasion embarrassed the United States. One year later, the United States discovered that Soviet missiles were being installed in Cuba. Tense negotiations with the Soviet Union brought the crisis to an end, but U.S.–Cuban relations were severely strained after this event that brought the world to the brink of nuclear war.

Economic Crisis

The end of the Cold War in the early 1990s left Cuba isolated. The loss of Soviet aid, combined with low prices for sugar exports, caused a deep economic crisis. The continuing American trade embargo against Cuba, which was in place since 1961, intensified the situation. The United States hoped the embargo would spur Fidel Castro into moving toward a more democratic system in exchange for better political and economic relations with the United States. So far, these efforts have failed to move the Cuban government toward instituting democratic reforms.

Cuba's Future

In 2008, Fidel Castro, in failing health, formally resigned as president and as commander of the military. The resignation produced little change, however, since Castro's brother, Raúl, along with communist officials loyal to the regime, had been running the country since 2006. Observers predict that Cuba will remain "a one-party communist state where political dissent is not tolerated and citizens' rights and the economy are tightly controlled."

North Korea

After World War II, the Korean peninsula was divided into North and South Korea. With U.S. aid, South Korea became a democracy with a strong, free market economy. North Korea became a Communist nation supported by the Soviet Union until its collapse. North Korea was led by dictator Kim Il Sung. Since 1994, Kim's son, Kim Jong Il, has ruled the country with an iron fist.

Cult of Personality

Today, North Korea's totalitarian government centers on unquestioning loyalty to Kim Jong Il. Kim's government controls all aspects of people's lives. This includes where people live and travel, what jobs they can have, and what schools their children will attend. North Koreans are almost totally cut off from outside sources of information.

698 UNIT 9: *Political and Economic Systems*

Museum Exhibit

Step 2: Taking Notes Students will continue research for their exhibits by taking notes as they read the section.

Directions As students read the section, have them note how the countries discussed may contribute to global issues or participate in the solutions.

Analyzing Issues Have the class discuss the notes they took in the section as they pertain to the global issues they will present later in the exhibits. **OL**

(Chapter Project continued in Section 3.)

Cult of Personality

A Totalitarian System
This North Korean poster depicts former leader Kim Il Sung, left, with son Kim Jong Il, the current North Korean leader, at an agricultural community outside the capital city of Pyongyang. North Korea experienced a famine in the 1990s and has faced major food shortages since. *What message is the poster conveying about the country's food supply?*

D Differentiated Instruction

Visual/Spatial Look at the North Korean poster, and note the style and the mood it conveys; then see if you can find a magazine ad that seems to convey a similar or the opposite message. **Ask:** How would you compare the messages intended by the poster and the ad you chose? What lies behind the differences? **OL**

C Critical Thinking

Making Inferences In North Korea hunger is widespread, but the military budget is large. **Ask:** What possible messages would North Korean propaganda send to citizens about the priority given to military spending? *(that food shortages are deemphasized; that the enemies of North Korea make military expenditures necessary; that some citizens must sacrifice so that the nation as a whole can be strong in the future)* **AL**

Propaganda glorifies Kim as the "Great Leader" who protects them against foreigners and will someday lead them to great prosperity.

A totalitarian regime like North Korea can cause great suffering. It is estimated that about 70 percent of the nation's children are malnourished. In the last decade, more than 2 million North Koreans starved to death because the economy could not produce enough food. Meanwhile much of the nation's money was spent on military weapons and on luxury items for Kim.

Tension With the United States

The first concern of totalitarian leaders is their own survival in power. Although North Korea's economy is weak, its military is strong. In the early 1990s, the country began to develop chemical, biological, and nuclear weapons. Few experts believe Kim would use such weapons directly against the United States, but Kim could sell the weapons to terrorists. Also, the existence of such weapons might lead other non-nuclear nations in the region to develop nuclear weapons. As a result, the United States has sought to limit North Korea's development of nuclear weapons.

Islamic Governments

Islam is a religion that was spread by Muhammad, who lived from A.D. 570 to A.D. 632. Muhammad claimed that he received the teachings of God (Allah) in a vision. These teachings were written in the Quran. A **Muslim,** or follower of Islam, is "one who submits" to Allah and the instructions of the Quran. For many Muslims, Islam is not only a religion, it is also an identity and a political loyalty that transcends all others.

Today, more than 1 billion Muslims are spread across the globe. Muslims form a majority in the Arab countries of the Middle East. However, only one in four Muslims is an Arab. Muslims also make up the majority of the population in some non-Arab countries including Iran, Pakistan, Turkey, and Indonesia. In a number of other countries, Muslims hold considerable political influence.

Religion and Government

In modern times, Islamic countries view the relationship between religion and the state differently than do most Western democracies. Since the beginning of Islam, many teachers of the Islamic faith have believed that political rulers should use Islamic tenets in shaping governmental authority. As a noted scholar of Islam, Bernard Lewis explains, "In the universal Islamic polity as conceived by Muslims, there is . . . only God, who is the sole sovereign and the sole source of law." Islamic leaders believe there is no need for a separation between religion and the state because Allah is inherent in politics. The Quran provides the guidance needed on issues such as what the duties of citizens and rulers are, what rights citizens have, what makes a government legitimate, and how the government should exercise power.

Since the American and French Revolutions, some Western nations have drawn a line of separation between religion and the authority of the state. The U.S. Constitution, for example, clearly states that "Congress shall make no law respecting an establishment of religion." Not all

CHAPTER 25: *Political Systems in Today's World* **699**

Differentiated Instruction

Activity: Multiple Learning Styles

Intrapersonal Ask students to choose one of the countries mentioned in this section about which to write a first-person narrative. Students should assume the role of a citizen of that country. Have them describe in their narratives what it feels like to live in that country, what their daily lives are like, what they dream about doing, how they feel toward the government and its leaders, and so on. You might want to have students do a dramatic reading of their narratives for the class. **OL**

We the People

Making a Difference

Mark, Dennis, and David Richard

Each year tens of thousands of wheelchairs are discarded in the United States. U.S. liability laws and insurance company rules prohibit the use of secondhand wheelchairs. However, other countries, especially developing ones, do not have these restrictions and are in dire need of wheelchairs. The mission of Wheels for Humanity is to "help the disadvantaged disabled around the world to re-enter their societies through the gift of a wheelchair."

Activity Organize the class into small groups to develop a nonprofit organization. Challenge group members to use Wheels for Humanity as an example and to think of an unfulfilled social need that their nonprofit can fill. Have each group create a name for their nonprofit and write a mission statement. **AL**

W Writing Support

Expository Writing Have students research the term *shari'ah*. Then have them write a one-paragraph explanation of the term's significance. **OL**

Additional Support

We the People

Making a Difference

In 1988 Mark Richard saw a disabled woman crawling along a roadside in Guatemala. He made up his mind to bring the woman a wheelchair. When he returned to the United States, Richard contacted the local chapter of the Spinal Cord Injury Association. Together they delivered 20 wheelchairs to Guatemala. Richard repeated the trip twice a year after that, distributing 2,000 wheelchairs. His older brother Dennis helped until he died in 1994. In July 1995, David Richard, another brother, began collecting wheelchairs throughout southern California. He created a nonprofit organization called Wheels for Humanity. In a California warehouse, volunteers restore battered wheelchairs to be distributed to disabled children in Vietnam, Guatemala, Bosnia, Costa Rica, Nicaragua, and other countries. In just 18 months, the Richards improved 987 lives with the gift of a wheelchair. "Once you put your hand on a used wheelchair, you're hooked," David Richard says.

The work of Wheels for Humanity continues. Various sources estimate that more than 21 million people worldwide are in need of wheelchairs.

> "Once you put your hand on a used wheelchair, you're hooked."
>
> —David Richard

Western nations follow this principle. The Church of England, also known as the Anglican Church, is the official church of Great Britain. The Evangelical Lutheran Church is the state church of Norway. Some democratic countries have political parties with religious identities, such as Germany's Christian Democratic Union. Although Western democracies may have official religions, they also protect free exercise of religion for those who do not belong to the established church.

Even when religion plays a role in Western democracies, that role is mostly symbolic. For example, many U.S. coins are imprinted with the phrase "In God We Trust." But religion is generally not the basis of authority in democracies, nor is it central to their political programs.

Views of Islam Today

Early in its history, Islam divided into two groups, Sunni Muslims and Shiite Muslims. Sunnis believe that the first four caliphs, or successors of the prophet Muhammad, were the rightful leaders of Islam. Shiites believe that only the heirs of the fourth caliph, Ali, are legitimate successors of Muhammad.

Today differences also exist in the political outlook of Muslims around the world. Some Muslims are moderates who believe that religious doctrine and secular, or civil, law can coexist. These Muslims are willing to work within a pluralistic society.

They might call for practical compromises between government and their religious beliefs, ultimately deferring to government authority on some key issues, such as declaring war. Moderate Muslims in the Middle East and Central and South Asia want to have friendly relations with Western nations. Some want democratic institutions and the benefits of capitalism in their own countries.

Muslim militants or radicals take a very different view. They believe that Islamic countries should base their legal systems strictly on the *shari'ah*, or law of the Quran, rather than on any Western legal principles. The goal of this group is that Muslims across the world will unite in one spiritual, cultural, and political community. Their commitment to this goal is often shown by the desire to preserve or bring back cultural traditions such as requiring women to cover their faces in public and banning modern movies and music. Although all Muslims have respect for specially trained Islamic religious leaders called **mullahs,** Islamic militants believe that Muslims should adhere to their rulings without question in every sphere of life. Finally, some militant Muslims say that it is the obligation of every Muslim to rebel against any society or ruler who does not follow Islamic principles.

For these militant or radical Muslims, Western culture and society represent a threat to their

---

Activity: Interdisciplinary Connection

Political Science Have students interview a person who has traveled to a foreign country. Ask students to include in the interview questions about the similarities and differences between that country's laws and political system and those of the United States. Then ask how the differences and similarities affected the interviewee as he or she traveled in that country. Call on volunteers to share the results of the interview with the class. **OL**

definition of Islamic culture. For this reason, they encourage negative attitudes toward Western democracies, especially the United States. Their main goal is to drive out moderate Islamic governments that have adopted foreign customs from power. In 1991, for example, fundamentalists murdered the moderate Egyptian President Anwar el-Sadat in a failed attempt to take over the government.

Revolution in Iran

To date, Iran provides the most successful example of a radical Islamic government. This government is the result of the revolution of 1979.

In the 1960s and 1970s, Iran began building a capitalistic economy based on oil revenues. The Iranian **shah,** or king, Mohammad Reza Pahlavi, led this effort, strengthening economic and cultural ties to the West. Religious leaders opposed these changes, but the shah's secret police were able to suppress them for many years. They began rallying around Ayatollah Ruhollah Khomeini, a religious and political leader who was living in exile. In 1979 his supporters forced the shah to flee to the United States. Khomeini then returned to Iran and formed an Islamic republic, a regime in which religious leaders had veto power over secular leaders.

The new Iranian government demanded that the shah be returned to Iran for trial, but the U.S. government refused. Anti-American sentiment increased and in late 1979, American diplomats in Iran were taken hostage. They were held for more than a year before their release. The 2000 elections gave some hope that Iran might begin to follow a more liberal path, but conservative forces have checked the reformists. President Mahmoud Ahmadinejad, an ultra-conservative who was elected in 2005, has aggressively promoted the nation's nuclear power program despite United Nations opposition. He has also supported Hezbollah, the Shiite group in Lebanon that is dedicated to eliminating the state of Israel.

Saudi Arabia

The struggle between militant Islam and the modern world has caused tension in Saudi Arabia, a country that has provided oil and important military bases to the United States. The Al Saud family established the country in 1932 and have ruled as absolute monarchs ever since. The government is based on a fundamentalist interpretation of Islam with no separation of religion and the state. Next to the royal family, the most powerful political force in the country has always been the mullahs, who impose traditional Islamic social and political ideas through government-sponsored organizations like the Committee for the Propagation of Virtue and the Prevention of Vice.

The discovery of oil in the 1950s **transformed** Saudi Arabia from an isolated desert nation to a wealthy urban one with thousands of foreign workers and a large middle class. Many Saudis began to demand an elected government. The royal family responded by modernizing the culture and government, but it also worked to placate conservative Muslim radicals. In fact, some American critics claim that one way they have done so is to funnel money to Islamic radicals.

CHAPTER 25, SECTION 2

S Skill Practice

Creating a Time Line Students should create a time line depicting Iran's revolution, including brief notes for each event listed. Students should add additional and/or more precise dates for recent years by drawing on Internet information or other outside research. **Ask:** What year did the Ayatollah Khomeini die? *(1989)* **BL**

Assess

Assign the Section 2 Assessment as homework or as an in-class activity, or have students take Section Quiz 25-2 from *Section Quizzes and Chapter Tests.*

Close

Analyzing Help students analyze the uneasy relationship between the United States and Islamic Middle Eastern countries. **OL**

Section 2 Review

SECTION 2 Review

Vocabulary

1. **Explain** the significance of: Muslim, mullah, shah.

Main Ideas

2. **Describing** What events in 1979 returned Iran to Muslim control?

3. **Explaining** How is China not a democratic nation? How does the government suppress criticism and disagreement?

4. **Examining** Why has Cuba been in a deep economic crisis since the early 1990s?

Critical Thinking

5. **Analyzing** How does the North Korean government promote its state leader to the people?

6. **Categorizing** Use a graphic organizer like the one below to profile each of the countries covered in this section, and indicate whether the country is moving toward or away from democracy.

Authoritarian States		
Country	Controlled by	+/− Democracy

Writing About Government

7. **Descriptive Writing** Choose a country discussed in this section and research recent political developments there. Imagine that you are traveling to the country. Write a letter to a friend describing the country, its government, and the extent to which the government affects people's lives.

Answers

1. All definitions can be found in the section and the Glossary.
2. Fundamentalist Islamists rallied around Ayatollah Khomeini and forced the shah of Iran to flee the country; they then set up a new government based on Islamic principles.
3. The Chinese Communist Party controls the government through the Politburo. The government censors information and uses force to silence dissent.
4. The collapse of the USSR left Cuba without a source for foreign aid, combined with low prices for sugar exports. The U.S. embargo helped intensify the situation.
5. North Korea's government promotes Kim Jong Il as the "Great Leader" and demands unquestioning loyalty to him from the people.
6. Students should list each country and leader discussed in the section, but their opinions may vary as to whether the countries are moving toward or away from democracy. Students should support their answers with evidence from the text.
7. Students' letters will vary but should include details from the text about their chosen countries.

Focus

Bellringer
Section Focus Transparencies 25-3

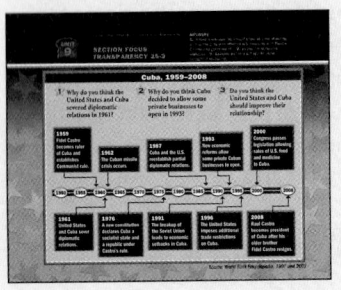

Reader's Guide

Answers to Graphic:
Council of the European Union, European Parliament, European Court of Justice, European Commission

Resource Manager

International Organizations

Reader's Guide

Content Vocabulary	Academic Vocabulary	Reading Strategy
★ nongovernmental organization (p. 702) ★ intergovernmental organization (p. 702) ★ supranational organization (p. 704)	★ scope (p. 702) ★ aid (p. 704) ★ unify (p. 705)	As you read, use a graphic organizer like the one below to list the various aspects of the government of the European Union.

```
          European Union
            Government
     ┌──────┬──────┬──────┐
   [   ] [   ] [   ] [   ]
```

Issues in the News

For many people around the globe, the image of the International Committee of the Red Cross and other relief agencies is a positive one. These are the good guys—the organizations whose dedicated staff help people who are starving and homeless after a disaster. Yet in May 2008, the military government of Myanmar (Burma) objected to the help of international relief agencies. The United Nations reported that aid sent to the victims of a cyclone was seized by the military government. In some cases, food and supplies were accepted, but workers were restricted. "There are problems to get the aid inside, and there are problems to get the aid out to the delta area," Denmark's Red Cross director said. "We are simply lacking transportation . . . This is really a nightmare to make this operation run."

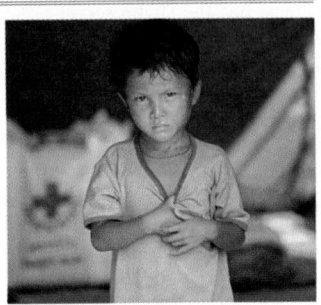

▲ This boy was displaced by the cyclone in Myanmar.

Nations such as the United States, Japan, and Saudi Arabia remain strong forces that are able to shape today's world. However, international organizations also play a key role in world politics. Two types of such organizations exist. **Nongovernmental organizations** (NGOs) are made up of individuals and groups outside the **scope** of government. The International Committee of the Red Cross is an example of an NGO. One of its major jobs is to monitor the treatment of prisoners during war. NGOs are funded largely by donations from private individuals and charitable foundations.

The second and most well-known type of international organization is one comprised of members of national governments. This type is called an **intergovernmental organization** (IGO). The United Nations (UN) is the most significant example of an IGO with a global membership and mission. The European Union (EU) is another example of an intergovernmental organization. IGOs are created through agreements, usually treaties, negotiated by the member states. The powers of an IGO are established and limited by its members.

The United Nations

In 1945 the United States and other nations established the United Nations to provide a forum to allow nations to settle their disputes peacefully. The Charter of the UN identifies the organization's three major goals. One is to preserve world peace and security. The second is to encourage nations

---

R Reading Strategies	C Critical Thinking	D Differentiated Instruction	W Writing Support	S Skill Practice
Teacher Edition • Inferring, p. 703 **Additional Resources** • Guid. Read. Act., p. 91 • Quizzes/Tests, p. 311	**Teacher Edition** • Distinguishing Fact from Opinion, p. 705 • Making Inferences, p. 706 **Additional Resources** • Read. Essen., pp. 291–293	**Teacher Edition** • Interpersonal, p. 703 • Visual/Spatial, p. 704 **Additional Resources** • Foldables, p. 68	**Teacher Edition** • Expository Writing, p. 704 **Additional Resources** • Gov. Sims. and Debates, pp. 52–56	**Additional Resources** • Skill Reinforce. Act., p. 25

Charts In MOtion
See StudentWorks™ Plus
or go to glencoe.com.

Organization of the United Nations

Selected Committees and Agencies of the UN

Military Staff Committee
Standing Committees
Peacekeeping Forces

SECURITY COUNCIL

TRUSTEESHIP COUNCIL

GENERAL ASSEMBLY

ECONOMIC AND SOCIAL COUNCIL

INTERNATIONAL COURT OF JUSTICE

SECRETARIAT

- United Nations Educational, Scientific, and Cultural Organization (UNESCO)
- World Health Organization (WHO)
- World Bank
- International Monetary Fund (IMF)

- United Nations Children's Fund (UNICEF)
- World Food Programme (WFP)
- United Nations Development Fund for Women (UNIFEM)
- United Nations Fund for Population Activities (UNFPA)
- United Nations Relief and Works Agency for Palestine Refugees in the Near East (UNRWA)

More than 8,900 people from 170 countries constitute the Secretariat staff, which is responsible for the day-to-day functions of the United Nations.

Source: www.UN.org

Critical Thinking The United Nations charter calls for the arrangement of the UN into six principal units, each with a specific set of responsibilities. *How might this type of council structure help the UN achieve its goals of preserving world peace?*

to deal fairly with one another. The third is to help nations cooperate in trying to solve their social and economic problems. United Nations membership is open to all "peace-loving states." Today, UN membership includes 192 nations from around the world.

Structure of the UN

The main headquarters of the UN is located in New York City. The UN is divided into a variety of units that help fulfill the organization's goals. The General Assembly is at the heart of the UN. It discusses, debates, and recommends solutions for major international problems presented to the United Nations. The Assembly also controls the UN budget by determining the members' yearly contributions and by setting expenditures for the many UN agencies. Each member nation has only one vote but may send a delegation of five representatives to the General Assembly.

The Security Council is a kind of executive board for the General Assembly. It has 15 members. The permanent members of the Security

Council are the United States, Russia, the People's Republic of China, France, and Great Britain. The General Assembly elects the other 10 members for two-year terms.

The Security Council has the authority to make peacekeeping decisions for the United Nations. The Council may call for breaking off relations with a nation, ending trade with a nation, or using military force. Because of its rules of procedure, however, the Security Council often has difficulty making such decisions. According to the UN Charter, in order to follow any course of action, 9 of the Council's 15 members must vote in favor of it. Furthermore, these 9 members must include all 5 permanent members. Thus, if a permanent member vetoes a measure, the Security Council is unable to act.

The Secretariat conducts the UN's day-to-day business with a staff of about 9,000 people who work under the direction of the secretary general. The secretary general is appointed by the General Assembly to a five-year term of office, with a two-term limit. This official is responsible for

CHAPTER 25: *Political Systems in Today's World* **703**

Teach

★★★★★★★★★★★★★★★★★★★★★★★★★★★
Critical Thinking

Answer: Each division of the UN is able to monitor world activities within the scope of its responsibilities, leading to efficiency.

D Differentiated Instruction

Interpersonal Organize the class into five groups, representing the five permanent members of the Security Council. Have the groups come up with proposals to deal with a worldwide security issue. You might want to give groups some time to research their country's opinions on the issue. Then see if all five groups can agree on a proposal. **AL**

R Reading Strategy

Inferring Ask: Why might the permanent members of the Security Council find it hard to agree on issues of peace and security? *(Answers will vary but should include that the foreign policy goals and international commitments of these countries are often varied.)* **OL**

Additional Support

Activity: Collaborative Learning

Creating a Board Game Organize the class into groups of five. Tell groups that their task is to create a game that tests their knowledge of the structure, purposes, and types of activities of the United Nations (UN). You might need to allow group members time to research more information about the UN. Once groups have

decided on the type of game they will create, have them write the directions for the game. Then group members should choose from the following tasks: create a game board, design playing pieces, or develop playing cards. Have groups exchange games to play and critique. **OL**

CURRICULUM CONNECTION

Economics For more than 50 consecutive years, the United States has been the largest contributor to the UN, both monetarily and in terms of supplying peacekeeping troops. The United States pays 25 percent of the UN's budget.

D Differentiated Instruction

Visual/Spatial Have students create a poster or a comic book that illustrates the work of the UN Economic and Social Council, the General Assembly, or the World Court. **AL**

W Writing Support

Expository Writing Direct students to research and write a report on one of the areas in which the United Nations works: peacekeeping, providing disaster aid, fighting disease, protecting the environment, or helping refugees. **OL**

Additional Support

carrying out the instructions of the Security Council and can be an important figure in world politics, especially when the UN is involved in controversial peacekeeping decisions.

The International Court of Justice, also called the World Court, is the judicial branch of the UN. Member nations may voluntarily submit disputes over international law to this court for settlement. The General Assembly and the Security Council select the 15 judges that sit on the International Court of Justice. The Court holds its sessions in The Hague, the Netherlands.

Finally, the Economic and Social Council (ECOSOC) is responsible for helping the UN promote social and economic progress around the world. It is concerned with such issues as improving education, health, and human rights. The Council has a membership of 54 countries elected by the General Assembly, with one-third of them being replaced by new members every three years.

Specialized Agencies

The United Nations also has units that carry out many of the organization's humanitarian activities under the supervision of the Economic and Social Council. These specialized agencies include the World Health Organization (WHO), the United Nations Children's Fund (UNICEF), the World Bank, and the International Monetary Fund (IMF).

Peacekeeping Activities

In addition to promoting alternatives to armed conflict, the UN has a limited ability to use military force for peacekeeping. The UN acts as a peacekeeper when its member states have approved a mission, volunteered troops, and agreed to pay for the mission. The UN has conducted 56 peacekeeping operations since 1948, but the majority of those operations were conducted after the end of the Cold War in the early 1990s. As of August 2008, the UN had 21 peacekeeping forces of different sizes at locations in Africa, Asia, Europe, and the Middle East. These forces totaled more than 88,576 troops and police drawn from 119 countries including the United States, Great Britain, France, China, Russia, Ireland, Canada, and several Scandinavian countries.

UN peacekeeping often involves inserting an international force of troops between combatants as a way to calm an explosive situation or to monitor a negotiated cease-fire. Sometimes lightly armed peacekeeping forces will undertake other missions, such as overseeing elections or providing humanitarian **aid** to help starving people in a war-torn country. More than 2,200 UN peacekeepers have been killed in such operations.

Although Americans tend not to think of it in such terms, the Persian Gulf War in 1990 was a UN peacekeeping operation. When Iraq invaded neighboring Kuwait in 1990 and then headed toward Saudi Arabia, the Saudis asked the United States for protection. The UN Security Council voted to condemn Iraq and authorized the United States to lead a coalition of seven nations to repel the invaders. The coalition forces quickly defeated Iraq. The UN then ordered Iraq to destroy its weapons of mass destruction and sent inspectors to Iraq to look for such weapons.

The European Union

Intergovernmental organizations, including the United Nations, traditionally have had little independent authority to make policies that would be binding on sovereign nations. Thus, IGOs do not act independently of the nations that make up their membership. Instead, nearly all IGOs are devices used by member states to promote their own diplomatic objectives or to accomplish nonpolitical tasks. Such IGOs include the International Civil Aviation Organization, which regulates civil aviation, and the International Criminal Police Organization (Interpol), which tracks down international criminals.

The European Union is a regional IGO that has evolved further than any other toward becoming a **supranational organization,** or an organization whose authority overrides or supercedes the sovereignty of its individual members. The EU was created in 1957 when six Western European nations saw an advantage in cooperating with each other politically and economically.

With the addition of Bulgaria and Romania in January 2007, the EU had a total of 27 members. Three other nations—Croatia, Macedonia, and Turkey—have applied for membership in the EU. According to one scholar, "The European Union is one of the great political and economic success stories of the twentieth century." Others worry that the EU is becoming a huge, stifling bureaucracy. In this chapter, we will look at the EU's political structure. In the next chapter, we will consider its economic endeavors.

Extending the Content

The European Union and the Euro
The euro became the official currency of most of the countries of the European Union on January 1, 2002. Its proponents believed that having a single currency would strengthen the EU's role in international forums and organizations such as the International Monetary Fund, the World Bank, and the Organization for Economic Cooperation and Development.

They also believed that the euro would make it easier for tourists to travel across Europe, because they would not have to exchange money in each new country in which they traveled. Not all EU countries embraced the euro, however. Today the member countries of Denmark, Sweden, and the United Kingdom still retain their own official currencies.

Integrating Europe

European Union Members		
Austria	Germany*	Netherlands*
Belgium*	Greece	Poland
Bulgaria	Hungary	Portugal
Cyprus	Ireland	Romania
Czech Republic	Italy*	Slovakia
Denmark	Latvia	Slovenia
Estonia	Lithuania	Spain
Finland	Luxembourg*	Sweden
France*	Malta	United Kingdom
Candidates for Membership		
Croatia	Former Yugoslav Republic of Macedonia	Turkey

*Original member when founded as the European Economic Community/Common Market in 1957.

Critical Thinking The Oresund Bridge links Sweden and Denmark by highway. When it opened in 2000, spokespeople for the European Union emphasized that travel times between the two countries would be reduced. *Why would this contribute to economic integration?*

Political Development

Since its founding, the EU has developed into a quasi-government with the authority to make and enforce some decisions that apply to all of its members even though they remain sovereign nations. In other words, these nations yield some of their sovereignty to the EU. How did the EU develop into a continent-wide political institution with a powerful economy that compares to that of the United States?

The original motivation for European integration was economic. In 1957 France, West Germany, Italy, Belgium, the Netherlands, and Luxembourg agreed to move toward a common trading market called the European Economic Community (EEC). In 1967 the EEC merged with two other organizations to become the European Community (EC). The goal of the EC was to remove all economic restrictions, permitting workers, capital, goods, and services to move freely throughout the member nations. By the late 1980s, the admission of Britain, Ireland, Denmark, Greece, Portugal, and Spain increased the EC's population to 370 million. In 1993 the EC was renamed the European Union; it became the world's largest **unified** market. Two years later, Austria, Finland, and Sweden joined to bring the total EU membership to 15 nations.

When Eastern European nations began to break free of Communist governments in the 1990s, their new leaders recognized the value of belonging to a unified European market. Almost immediately they began negotiating to join the organization in order to integrate their own emerging free market economies with those of Western Europe.

As more countries joined the European Union, pressure increased on the member states to implement greater political integration. Economic integration is less effective alone than it is when combined with political cooperation. A key step toward such integration was the 1993 Maastricht Treaty. Through this treaty, the member nations began to yield power to the European Union. This allowed the EU to start acting more as a political unit that is able to enforce common rules, not only for trade but also for crime fighting, immigration, citizenship, and other common concerns. This treaty also called for the eventual creation of a common foreign and defense policy. Two additional treaties since 1993 have further strengthened political integration by giving the EU government more authority.

European Union Government

The EU government is complex because of its need to combine many cultures, languages, and political traditions into a structure that is acceptable to all members. The Council of the European Union decides the key directions for EU policy. The Council is a gathering of foreign ministers or state

Critical Thinking

Answer: It is now quicker and easier for goods and people to travel between the two countries.

Chart Skills Practice How many countries are members of the European Union? How many European Union members were originally members of the European Economic Community? *(27; 6)* **OL**

C Critical Thinking

Distinguishing Fact from Opinion Have students scan this section or use outside research to find information about the European Union. Then have them write on a sheet of paper, in no particular order, five factual statements and five opinion statements describing the EU. Have students exchange papers with a partner to identify each statement as fact or opinion. Have the writer of the statements check the paper for correct answers and discuss any disagreement in answers. **OL**

Hands-On Chapter Project

Step 3

Museum Exhibit

Step 3: Organizing Information

Groups will compile the information they gathered in Steps 1 and 2.

Directions As students read the section, have them research the United Nations's Web site to see what is being done about the issue their group has been assigned. Have groups begin preparing their exhibits, which may include collages, objects with labels, audio recordings, or other elements they consider useful.

The exhibits should explain the issue and how it affects people in different parts of the world, include images and statistics, and offer specific solutions. In preparing the solutions section, they might want to use ideas they will formulate in the Collaborative Learning Activity in Section 4. Groups should determine which members will locate photos and objects, provide statistics, write captions and summaries of solutions, arrange the exhibit, and explain it to the class.

Putting It Together Have the groups prepare their exhibits. **OL**

(Chapter Project continued in Section 4.)

C Critical Thinking

Making Inferences Ask: From what you have read about the structure and the powers of the European Union, why do you think voters in France and the Netherlands rejected the proposed constitution? *(Students may suggest that they feared the EU had become too powerful and might overturn laws or exemptions that they hold dear.)* BL

Assess

Assign the Section 3 Assessment as homework or as an in-class activity, or have students take Section Quiz 25-3 from *Section Quizzes and Chapter Tests.*

Close

Analyzing Help students analyze the political and economic impact of international organizations on the global community. OL

Section 3 Review

Foreign Soil The United Nations sits on 18 acres of land in New York City. Donated by John D. Rockefeller, Jr., the land is not part of the United States. The UN is international territory and belongs to all members of the organization. The UN has its own security and firefighting forces and issues its own postage stamps. Mail a card from the UN, and you can say you sent a foreign letter!

secretaries chosen by each member nation. This group meets twice per year to discuss and vote on major issues. The larger EU countries have more votes on certain matters than smaller countries.

The European Parliament (EP) is the legislative branch of the EU, with 732 members divided among countries on the basis of population. Germany, the most populous country, has 99 seats; Malta, the smallest member, has 5 seats. EP members are elected to five-year terms by the voters in their own countries. The EP works alongside the Council to form the annual budget for the European Union and to supervise the operations of smaller EU institutions.

The European Court of Justice is the EU's highest judicial body and has one judge per member. The court hears many types of cases, often using EU treaties as a guide for its decisions. The court can declare laws of member nations invalid if they conflict with EU treaties. For example, the Court held that Great Britain had to eliminate certain tax exemptions that it had granted British citizens.

The European Commission does much of the EU's daily work. It drafts proposals for new laws, presents them to the European Parliament and the Council, and sees that decisions are implemented. The Commission was originally comprised of 20 individuals from member countries (2 from the larger countries and 1 per smaller country). Once the EU expanded in 2004, this number changed to 1 representative per nation, with the total never to exceed 27 commission members. If the number of member states exceeds 27, a rotation schedule will be established. The commissioners serve five-year terms. One commissioner is selected by the Council to be president of the Commission. The president directs the EU bureaucracy and oversees its annual budget of more than $86 billion.

C EU expansion led its leaders to draft a constitution in 2004 to codify various EU treaties and to more clearly define EU powers and member rights. When the ratification process went forward, however, voters in France and the Netherlands rejected the treaty. The "no" vote may have reflected a feeling that European integration had gone too far, or it might reflect opposition to specific EU policies and leadership.

SECTION 3 Review

Vocabulary

1. **Explain** the significance of: nongovernmental organizations, intergovernmental organizations, supranational organizations.

Main Ideas

2. **Listing** What are some incidences when the UN has acted as a peacekeeper in a nonmilitary setting?

3. **Describing** How has European Union expansion affected the European Commission?

Critical Thinking

4. **Analyzing** Should the five permanent members of the UN Security Council be able to override any UN decision? Why or why not?

5. **Summarizing** Use a graphic organizer like the one below to summarize the two international organizations described in this section.

Organization	Membership	Goals

Writing About Government

6. **Expository Writing** Identify and find out about the duties, responsibilities, and programs of the specialized agencies of the United Nations. Write a one- to two-page report that illustrates the work of these agencies. Share completed reports with the class.

Answers

1. All definitions can be found in the section and the Glossary.
2. Examples may include overseeing elections or providing humanitarian aid.
3. It has changed the makeup of the European Commission as far as how many members represent each participating nation.
4. Students' responses will vary but should be supported by evidence from the text.

5. UN—191 member nations; wants to preserve world peace, encourage nations to act fairly, and help nations cooperate in solving problems
   EU—27 member nations; formed to allow European nations to band together to cooperate politically and economically
6. Students' reports should accurately reflect the work of the UN agencies.

Global Issues

Reader's Guide

Content Vocabulary
- ★ terrorism *(p. 707)*
- ★ state-sponsored terrorism *(p. 708)*
- ★ nuclear proliferation *(p. 709)*
- ★ human rights *(p. 710)*

Academic Vocabulary
- ★ prime *(p. 707)*
- ★ monitor *(p. 709)*
- ★ comprehensive *(p. 710)*

Reading Strategy
Use a graphic organizer like the one below to list the promises made by major nuclear powers when they signed the nuclear Non-Proliferation Treaty.

> Non-Proliferation Treaty ▷

Issues in the News

The war on terrorism, an international effort led by the United States, began in Afghanistan where al-Qaeda forces have been training. The United States and its allies have joined in the fight to defeat the Taliban, the Islamic guerrillas who are trying to bring down Afghanistan's democratically elected government. Great Britain has been a staunch American ally. British Prime Minister Gordon Brown visited Afghanistan recently to show his commitment to the cause. "We are utterly resolute in our determination to support this new democracy in Afghanistan. We will not relax from our efforts . . . because we understand that . . . what happens in Afghanistan affects the rest of the world."

▲ British Royal Marines parade through a town in England to celebrate their return from Afghanistan.

In today's interdependent world, citizens, national leaders, and international organizations must increasingly adopt a global outlook. More and more, it is understood that many problems that affect significant numbers of people cannot be solved by a single nation. Cooperative action will be required to solve a variety of global issues including the defeat of terrorism, limiting the spread of nuclear weapons, and protecting the environment.

As the world becomes more interconnected, even the most powerful nations, including the United States, cannot escape the impact of global issues. As one leading American political scientist explains: "U.S. security and economic interests are inevitably tied to what happens in the rest of the world. Whether we like it or not."

Global issues pose a challenge to a nation's sovereignty, its ability to rule its own borders without interference from other nations. Responding effectively to global issues, however, sometimes means accepting the decisions or rules of an international body such as the United Nations or the World Trade Organization, even when those decisions or rules differ from those of an individual country.

Some global problems are so large in scope that a group of nations must work together to solve them. When this is the case, individual nations must give up some measure of national authority. For example, to combat worldwide pollution, nations might agree to participate in a treaty that limits a nation's economic choices. In other words, solving global issues might require international cooperation. A **prime** example came after the 2001 terrorist attacks when President George W. Bush met with nearly 80 foreign leaders to ask for their cooperation in fighting **terrorism.**

Focus

Bellringer
Section Focus Transparencies 25-4

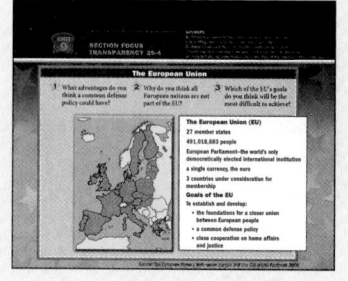

Reader's Guide

Answers to Graphic: not to provide nuclear weapons technology to other nations, to ensure the safe use of nuclear power, to encourage the general disarmament and destruction of existing nuclear weapons

Resource Manager

R Reading Strategies	**C** Critical Thinking	**D** Differentiated Instruction	**W** Writing Support	**S** Skill Practice
Teacher Edition • Identifying, p. 709 • Inferring, p. 712 **Additional Resources** • Guid. Read. Act., p. 92 • Quizzes/Tests, pp. 312–320	**Teacher Edition** • Making Inferences, p. 709 • Making Connections, p. 710 **Additional Resources** • Read. Essen., pp. 294–296	**Teacher Edition** • Visual/Spatial, p. 708 • Verbal/Linguistic, p. 710 **Additional Resources** • Foldables, p. 68	**Teacher Edition** • Persuasive Writing, p. 709	**Teacher Edition** • Conducting Internet Research, p. 708 • Researching, p. 711 **Additional Resources** • Ch. Summaries, pp. 73–75

Teach

★ Critical Thinking ★

Answer: Terrorist attacks are meant to cause fear in ordinary citizens and to get the government to change its policies to be more favorable to the terrorist group. Terrorists have achieved their goal of spreading fear, but U.S. policy has not changed in their favor.

D Differentiated Instruction

Visual/Spatial Have students create an illustrated time line depicting the events of one of the terrorist attacks in this section. **ELL**

S Skill Practice

Conducting Internet Research State-sponsored terrorism has been found in Libya, Syria, Iraq, and Iran. Conduct research at reliable sites, such as a U.S. State Department or academic site, on the terrorism linked to one of these countries. **Ask:** What is the alleged goal of the state-sponsored terrorism for the country you researched? **OL**

Hands-On Chapter Project

Step 4

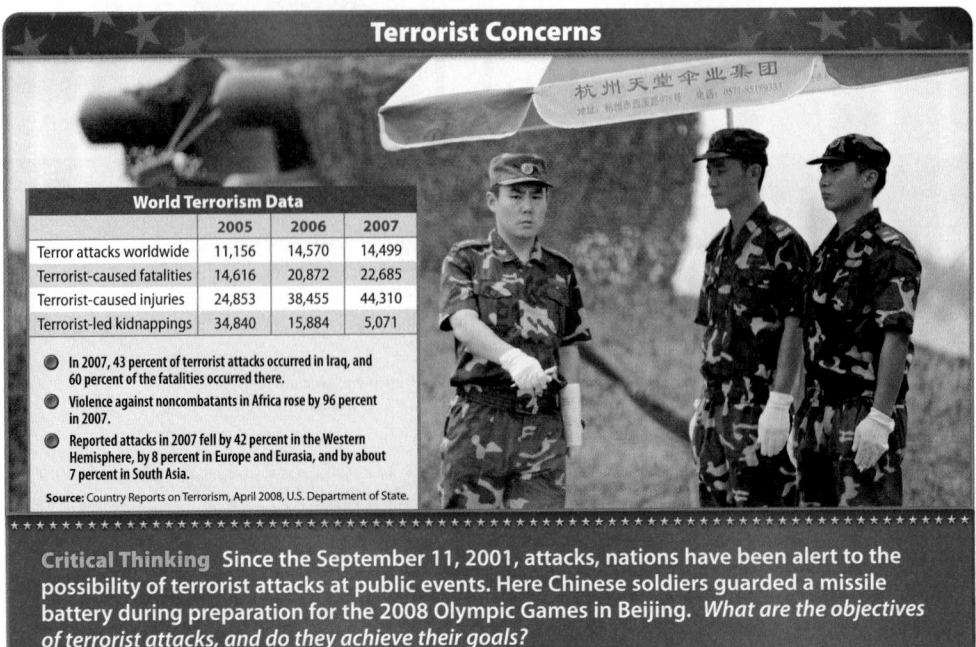

Terrorist Concerns

World Terrorism Data	2005	2006	2007
Terror attacks worldwide	11,156	14,570	14,499
Terrorist-caused fatalities	14,616	20,872	22,685
Terrorist-caused injuries	24,853	38,455	44,310
Terrorist-led kidnappings	34,840	15,884	5,071

● In 2007, 43 percent of terrorist attacks occurred in Iraq, and 60 percent of the fatalities occurred there.

● Violence against noncombatants in Africa rose by 96 percent in 2007.

● Reported attacks in 2007 fell by 42 percent in the Western Hemisphere, by 8 percent in Europe and Eurasia, and by about 7 percent in South Asia.

Source: Country Reports on Terrorism, April 2008, U.S. Department of State.

Critical Thinking Since the September 11, 2001, attacks, nations have been alert to the possibility of terrorist attacks at public events. Here Chinese soldiers guarded a missile battery during preparation for the 2008 Olympic Games in Beijing. *What are the objectives of terrorist attacks, and do they achieve their goals?*

International Terrorism

The U.S. State Department reports that in recent years, more than 300 attacks of terrorism have occurred per year across all regions of the world. Terrorism is the use of violence by nongovernmental groups against civilians to achieve a political goal.

International terrorism has become one of the greatest dangers of the new global era. This truth became very clear to Americans on September 11, 2001. On that day, terrorists launched their most devastating attack ever on the United States, hijacking commercial airliners and crashing them into the World Trade Center towers in New York City and the Pentagon in Washington, D.C. Another plane intended for a similar attack crashed in Pennsylvania.

Since World War II, most terrorist attacks on Americans have been carried out by Middle Eastern groups. One reason for such attacks stems from the history of American investment in the oil industry. Such investment enriched the ruling families of some Middle Eastern kingdoms but left most of the people poor. Some of these people became angry at the United States for supporting the wealthy ruling families. American support of Israel also angered many in the Middle East.

The global importance of the oil industry also increased cultural exchanges between Middle Eastern countries and the West. Many Muslim fundamentalists resented this contact, fearing that it weakened traditional Islamic values and beliefs. New movements arose that called for a strict interpretation of the Quran—the holy book of Islam—and a return to traditional Islamic religious laws. Eventually, some of the more militant fundamentalists began using terrorism to achieve their goals.

In the 1970s, several Middle Eastern nations realized that they could fight the United States by providing terrorist groups with money, weapons, and training. When a government secretly supports terrorism, this is called **state-sponsored terrorism.** The governments of Libya, Syria, Iraq, and Iran have sponsored terrorism.

A New Terrorist Threat

In 1979 the Soviet Union invaded Afghanistan. In response, a number of Muslims from the Middle East went to Afghanistan to join the fight against the Soviets. One of them was a 22-year-old Muslim named Osama bin Laden. Bin Laden came from one of Saudi Arabia's wealthiest families. He used his wealth to support the Afghan resistance.

Museum Exhibit

Step 4: Displaying Information Groups will finish and display their exhibits.

Directions Have groups explain their exhibits to the class. Encourage the class to ask difficult, critical thinking questions.

Discussing Presentations Have the class discuss which exhibit was most effective and why. **OL**

In 1988 he founded a group called al-Qaeda, or "the Base." Al-Qaeda recruited Muslims and channeled money and arms to the Afghan resistance. Bin Laden's experience in Afghanistan convinced him that superpowers could be beaten. He also believed that Western ideas had contaminated Islam. He was outraged when Saudi Arabia allowed American troops on Saudi soil after Iraq invaded Kuwait in 1990.

Operating first from Sudan and later Afghanistan—then under the control of the Taliban—bin Laden dedicated himself and al-Qaeda to driving Westerners, especially Americans, out of the Middle East. In 1998 he called on Muslims to kill Americans. Soon afterward, truck bombs exploded at the American embassies in Kenya and Tanzania.

In 1999 members of al-Qaeda were arrested while trying to smuggle explosives into the United States to bomb Seattle, Washington. Then, in October 2000, al-Qaeda terrorists crashed a boat loaded with explosives into the USS *Cole*, an American warship docked in Yemen. Finally in 2001 came the devastating attacks on New York City and Washington, D.C. The United States responded by going to war.

War on Terrorism

Experts on Islam point out that Islamic terrorists misrepresent the teachings of the Quran and that many of their statements contradict core Islamic principles. According to Bernard Lewis, an internationally recognized authority on Islam: "The callous destruction of thousands in the World Trade Center . . . has no justification in Islamic doctrine or law and no precedent in Islamic history." When the United States began bombing targets in Afghanistan in October 2001, President George W. Bush emphasized that he ordered the military to attack al-Qaeda's camps and the Taliban's military forces, and he reiterated that Islam and the Afghan people were not the enemy.

President Bush also vowed that although the war on terrorism began by targeting al-Qaeda, it would not end "until every terrorist group of global reach has been found, stopped, and defeated." In order for terrorism to be defeated on a global scale, many nations will have to work together toward that common goal.

Nuclear Weapons Threat

Another problem that the world faces is **nuclear proliferation**, or the spread of nuclear weapons.

Five nations—the United States, Russia, Great Britain, France, and China—have had nuclear weapons for many years. Israel, South Africa, Argentina, and Taiwan also are believed to possess nuclear weapons. More recently, India and Pakistan have acquired the capability to produce nuclear weapons.

The United States, in cooperation with many other developed nations, has taken several steps to limit the spread of nuclear weapons. In late 1956, a joint agreement of 81 nations created the International Atomic Energy Agency (IAEA). This organization oversees the safe operation of nuclear power plants and limits the export of plutonium processing technologies needed to build nuclear weapons.

In 1968 the major nuclear powers created the nuclear Non-Proliferation Treaty (NPT), in which they promised not to provide nuclear weapons technology to other nations. They also vowed to ensure the safe use of nuclear power and to encourage general disarmament and destruction of existing nuclear weapons. Since the NPT's creation, more than 180 parties have joined this treaty. On occasion the United Nations also has imposed sanctions on nations seeking to build nuclear weapons.

A new challenge to limiting the spread of nuclear weapons has arisen, making these international agreements more difficult to enforce. Scientists have revealed that it is possible to build small nuclear weapons using readily available, low-enriched uranium or spent nuclear fuel, the waste left over by reactors that are used to generate electric power. Previously it was thought that only plutonium or highly enriched uranium could be used. As a result, the treaties and **monitoring** programs that have been put into place so far have focused only on those two substances. The fact that these cheaper, more readily obtainable substances can be used to make weapons of mass destruction means that a wider range of nations might have access to the materials needed to build nuclear weapons. This means that the chance of terrorists obtaining weapons of mass destruction has increased.

North Korea signed the nuclear Non-Proliferation Treaty in 1985 as a non-nuclear weapons state. In 1992 both North and South Korea agreed to sign a Denuclearization Statement, which stated that neither country was allowed to test, manufacture, produce, receive, possess, store, deploy, or use nuclear weapons. It also forbade the possession of nuclear reprocessing and uranium

C Critical Thinking

Making Inferences **Ask:** Why might a scholar like Bernard Lewis be motivated to make this kind of statement about Islam? *(He wanted to explain to Americans who are unfamiliar with Islam that violence is not a part of that religion; thus, Lewis was encouraging tolerance for Muslims who are not terrorists.)* **OL**

W Writing Support

Persuasive Writing Research the background, mission, and activities of the IAEA at its Web site. Have students write a letter to the editor of a national newspaper urging financial support for the IAEA. **ELL**

R Reading Strategy

Identifying Nuclear weapons are spreading around the globe, despite the efforts to limit proliferation. **Ask:** Based on the text, what is the most important issue to solve if nuclear weapons are to be limited? *(The challenge is to figure out how to prevent proliferation, when small nuclear weapons can easily built by many nations—even without plutonium or highly enriched uranium.)* **BL**

Additional Support

Activity: Collaborative Learning

Resolving Disputes Have small groups of students consider possible approaches to resolving one of the global concerns mentioned in this section. After students list their ideas, have them discuss and develop a proposed solution. Then have them prepare a letter to the United Nations explaining the issue and the group's proposed solution. **OL**

C Critical Thinking

Making Connections The Universal Declaration of Human Rights is a document that bears some similarity to the Bill of Rights in the U.S. Constitution, but it includes many other and more specific rights. **Ask:** What rights are listed that tell you that the document dates from the late 1940s and not from the 1700s? *(Answers may vary, but a student might refer to its reference to trade unions or to "equal pay for equal work." In the 1700s, social egalitarianism was not well developed.)* **OL**

D Differentiated Instruction

Verbal/Linguistic The positive rights mentioned in the Universal Declaration of Human Rights have developed since the declaration was first drafted. Have students develop a speech that explains why the government needs to intervene—based on the human rights doctrine—in the economy to provide for its citizens. *(Students might point out that human rights such as the right to equal pay for equal work and the right to a decent standard of living might require some government intervention.)* **AL**

Differentiated Instruction

---

enrichment facilities. Also, plans were discussed for nuclear weapons inspections in both countries. After these promising beginnings, however, North Korea showed little progress in following up on these agreements with South Korea or the international community.

The United States tried a new round of negotiations with North Korea in 1993 and 1994. North Korea agreed to freeze use of its existing nuclear facilities and to allow international monitoring. In 2002, however, the United States discovered that North Korea was restarting some of its nuclear facilities. The North Korean government claims that these facilities are being used for power generation and not to manufacture nuclear weapons. The United States disputes this claim and is keeping a close watch on developments in North Korea.

The United States is also concerned about Iran, which appears to be in the very late stages of developing the capacity to manufacture nuclear weapons. Because North Korea and Iran were accused of sponsoring terrorism, the United States and international organizations are worried that nuclear weapons produced in these countries could be sold to international terrorist groups.

Continued efforts by the international community to tighten safeguards against the spread of nuclear weapons will be costly. The United States has won agreement from Britain, Canada, France, Germany, Italy, Japan, and Russia combined to match a U.S. pledge to spend $10 billion over the next 10 years on nonproliferation efforts.

Human Rights

Protecting **human rights** has become a major concern for the international community. Several important treaties on human rights have been signed by a majority of the world's nations, and various international courts have tried military and political leaders for human rights violations. Such international efforts to safeguard human rights have the potential to limit or interfere with the sovereignty of individual nations.

Universal Declaration of Human Rights

Human rights are the basic freedoms and rights that all people, regardless of age, gender, nationality, or ethnicity, should enjoy. In 1948 the United Nations adopted the Universal Declaration of Human Rights, which set forth in 30 articles a

comprehensive statement of "inalienable rights of all members of the human family."

The Declaration's early articles laid out a list of political and civil rights that all human beings should have. Many of these rights are the same as those found in the U.S. Constitution. Several other rights are also listed, including the freedom of movement, the right to seek asylum, the right to marry, and the right to own property. These articles list things a government should not do to limit people's freedoms.

The Declaration's later articles spell out economic, social, and cultural rights relating to a person's quality of life. These include the right to work, to receive equal pay for equal work, to form trade unions, to enjoy rest and leisure, to have a standard of living sufficient for health and well-being, and to receive an education. These so-called "positive rights" list things governments should provide for people.

Protecting Human Rights

The international community has developed numerous institutions and procedures for safeguarding human rights. The UN Commission on Human Rights monitors and reports on human rights violations. In addition, the UN Security Council has established several international criminal tribunals. These are temporary courts that are convened under UN authority to prosecute violators of international human rights laws. One such tribunal, created in 1993, has tried Yugoslavian leaders, including the former president of the country, for atrocities committed in the Balkans during the breakup of Yugoslavia. The United States is the largest financial contributor to this tribunal.

The European Union (EU) has also made a statement about the importance of protecting human rights. EU members stand behind the European Convention of Human Rights, which was signed in 1950 and remains a binding agreement on all current and future member states of the European Union. This treaty sets forth a long list of civil liberties that apply to all EU countries. The European Court of Human Rights has the power to enforce the Convention and rule on charges of abuses.

In 2002 a permanent International Criminal Court (ICC) was established as a result of the efforts of the UN and a group of nearly 50 countries led by Canada and Germany. The ICC has strong powers to investigate and prosecute those accused of major human rights violations and war

---

Activity: Multiple Learning Styles

Kinesthetic Organize the class into small groups to create museum exhibits that illustrate important political developments in any of the countries mentioned in this chapter. Suggest to group members that they divide their exhibits into three sections: an important person, a major event, an influential idea. Then have group members brainstorm items to include in each section of the exhibit and how they will display these items. Have groups display their finished exhibits for the class. **AL**

crimes. The United States participated in the treaty negotiations that created the ICC, but along with China, Russia, and several other nations has refused to sign the treaty.

The U.S. position against the ICC has drawn sharp criticism from many European governments. American critics of the ICC respond that as a superpower, the United States is frequently involved in controversial military actions across the globe. These critics claim that under the new ICC rules, American military troops as well as U.S. leaders could become targets of frivolous complaints of war crimes by enemies of the United States.

Protecting the Environment

Because the environment is a basic part of our daily lives, it is easy to take the air, water, and land upon which all life depends for granted. Yet the political issues and technical questions resulting from exploding population growth, increasing consumption of natural resources, and the growing discharge of pollution into the environment raise many difficult global issues. Policymakers and

scientists recognize that dealing effectively with such issues requires transnational programs that depend upon international cooperation.

The United States occupies a unique place in international debates and negotiations regarding the environment. As one group of scholars explains: "The United States is at the same time one of our world's leading promoters of environmental concerns and because of our size and extensive industrial wealth one of its major polluters."

Sustainable Development

The core dilemma for policymakers that cuts across specific environmental issues for air and water pollution is how to attain sustainable development; that is, how can the nations of the world, especially the less-developed nations, continue to develop their economies while protecting the environment and preserving the natural resources that are necessary for an industrial economy?

The choice between economic development and protecting the environment is different for already developed nations and poor developing nations. Only a minority of the world's population live in wealthy nations like the United States, Germany, and Japan. Before most people even

---

Government and You

Your Rights Overseas

If you visit another country, be aware that its laws may be very different from ours. Things that are no problem at home can cause you trouble overseas. For example, attempting to use a credit card that has exceeded its limit can get you arrested in some countries. Photographing police, military installations and personnel, and other subjects may also result in your detention.

If arrested, you have the right under international law to contact the U.S. consulate. Consular officials cannot get you out of jail, but they can recommend attorneys and will try to see that you are treated humanely. Most countries do not permit bail, so you might have to spend months in solitary confinement awaiting trial.

Remember that when you leave the United States, although you are a U.S. citizen, the Bill of Rights stays behind. The best way to protect your freedom overseas is to learn about a country's laws and customs before you visit.

▶ American students in France

Participating
IN GOVERNMENT ACTIVITY

Be Informed Visit the State Department's Web site on the Internet for advice about a country you want to visit.

S **Skill Practice**

Researching Ask students to research major environmental legislation that has been proposed or enacted in their state. Have them discuss why the legislation's proponents believed it was necessary, and also have them outline any objections to the legislation that might have come up from industry or other interests. Finally, have students draft a short essay discussing how best to balance the need to protect the environment with other interests that may be affected by environmental legislation. **AL**

Government and You

More About Preparing for Travel Overseas The State Department issues Consular Information Sheets about every country. They include information on the location of the U.S. embassy or consulate, passport and visa requirements, health conditions, and crime and security information. These sheets generally do not include advice; they present factual information so a traveler can make decisions concerning travel to a particular country.

Differentiated Instruction

Leveled Activities

ELL **Vocabulary Activities, p. 25**

BL **Guided Reading Activities, p. 92**

OL **Interpreting Political Cartoons, p. 49**

AL **Authentic Assessment with Rubrics, p. 32**

711

ExamView® Assessment Suite

This easy-to-use software includes extensive question banks and allows you to create fully customized tests that can be administered in print or online.

Reviewing Vocabulary

1. supranational organization
2. shah
3. terrorism
4. mullahs
5. consolidated democracy
6. state-sponsored terrorism
7. parliamentary government

Reviewing Main Ideas

8. Parliament; the national legislature
9. The National Party Congress has no real power, but instead serves as a rubber stamp for the Chinese Communist Party leaders' policies.
10. preserve world peace and security, encourage nations to be just in their actions toward one another, help nations cooperate in trying to solve their problems
11. Policymakers want nations of the world, especially less-developed nations, to continue to grow economically while protecting the environment and not exhausting the natural resources that fuel industrial growth.

Critical Thinking

12. The CCP determines governmental policies and ensures that the government carries out the party's policies and decisions. Most key officials are party members.

Reviewing Vocabulary

Insert the correct content vocabulary word(s) from the following list into the sentences below.

mullahs	consolidated democracy
shah	state-sponsored terrorism
terrorism	supranational organization
parliamentary government	

1. The European Union has evolved from a regional body into a(n) ____.
2. In the late 1970s, Muslims in Iran revolted against the ____, or king.
3. The use of violence by nongovernmental groups against civilians to achieve a political goal is known as ____.
4. Specially trained Islamic religious teachers called ____ interpret Islamic teaching.
5. A well-established government with fair elections, competing political parties, and some form of market economy is known as a(n) ____.
6. Terrorism that is secretly supported by a government is known as ____.
7. In a(n) ____, both the executive and the legislative functions are found in the elected assembly.

Reviewing Main Ideas

Section 1 *(pages 689–694)*

8. **Identifying** Who holds almost all governmental authority in Great Britain?

Section 2 *(pages 696–701)*

9. **Describing** What is the real role of China's National Party Congress?

Section 3 *(pages 702–706)*

10. **Identifying** What are the three major goals of the UN?

Section 4 *(pages 707–712)*

11. **Summarizing** What do policymakers hope to achieve with sustainable development?

Critical Thinking

12. **Essential Question** How does the role of the Communist Party show its importance in China's government?

13. **Organizing** Use a graphic organizer to identify the challenges that Poland faced after the overthrow of their Communist leaders.

Challenges Faced

Chapter Summary

Democratic Governments
★ These governments have free elections, competing parties, individual rights, and a market economy.
★ The elected body has both executive and legislative duties in **parliamentary governments;** these duties reside in separate branches in **presidential governments.**

Authoritarian Governments
★ In such governments, citizens have few civil rights and government criticism is restricted.
★ Examples include the **People's Republic of China,** the Communist government of **Cuba,** and the nonsecular Islamic government of **Iran.**

International Organizations
★ The **United Nations** seeks to preserve peace and encourages global cooperation to solve world problems.
★ The **European Union** promotes political and economic cooperation among members.

Global Issues
★ These issues include **terrorism, nuclear proliferation, human rights** and **environmental protection.**

13. create a written constitution that supports democratic values, decentralize power by creating local governments, strengthen the economy

Government ONLINE Self-Check Quiz
Visit glencoe.com and enter QuickPass™ code USG9822c25.
Click on Self-Check Quizzes for additional test practice.

CHAPTER 25 Assessment and Activities

Document-Based Questions

Analyzing Primary Sources

Read the excerpt below and answer the questions that follow.

The United Nations was formed in June 1945 at the end of World War II in an effort to provide a world forum for solving international political problems. The following excerpt is from the preamble to the United Nations Charter, signed on June 26, 1945, in San Francisco.

❝ *WE THE PEOPLES OF THE UNITED NATIONS DETERMINED*

- *to save succeeding generations from the scourge of war . . .*
- *to reaffirm faith in fundamental human rights, . . . in the equal rights of men and women and of nations large and small . . .*
- *to establish conditions under which justice . . . from treaties and other sources of international law can be maintained . . .*
- *to promote social progress and better standards of life in larger freedom . . .*
- *to practice tolerance and live together in peace . . .*
- *to unite our strength to maintain international peace and security . . .*
- *to ensure . . . that armed force shall not be used, save in the common interest, and*
- *to [promote] the economic and social advancement of all peoples*

HAVE RESOLVED TO COMBINE OUR EFFORTS TO ACCOMPLISH THESE AIMS ❞

14. What are some of the specific goals of the UN? How are these similar to and different from U.S. goals for national security?

15. What are the benefits of having such a worldwide cooperative organization? What are the drawbacks?

Interpreting Political Cartoons

Analyze the cartoon and answer the questions that follow. Base your answers on the cartoon and your knowledge of Chapter 25.

HENG
LIANHE ZAOBAO
Singapore
SINGAPORE

16. How are the United Nations and the various countries portrayed in this cartoon?

17. According to the cartoonist, does the UN seem equipped to handle the world's crises effectively? Explain your answer.

Participating IN GOVERNMENT

18. Take a poll of five or more adults in your community. Find out their opinion about the work of the United Nations. Ask them if they approve or disapprove of U.S. involvement in the UN. With one or two of the respondents, explore their ideas about the UN in greater depth through open-ended questions. For example, you might ask them: about the source of their information on the UN; when they first formulated their opinion on the UN; if they remember a particular activity or position of the UN that influenced their opinion.

CHAPTER 25: *Political Systems in Today's World* **715**

Interpreting Political Cartoons

16. The UN is portrayed as a nanny, attempting to clean and soothe various crying or troubled infants simultaneously; most countries are portrayed as helpless, crying infants that demand immediate attention. Somalia is crying for food, while Iraq is attempting to hamper the efforts in the UN.

17. Students might note that the UN seems stressed and unable to control the troubled infants. The cartoonist might be implying that the UN is not equipped to deal effectively with crises.

Participating IN GOVERNMENT

18. Students should poll adults about their opinions of the United Nations and whether they think the United States should be involved in it.

Chapter Bonus Test Question

Ask: How many countries were members of the United Nations when the charter went into effect on October 24, 1945? *(51)*

Analyzing Primary Sources

14. The UN wants, among other things, to promote peace, economic stability and cooperation, and human rights. All of these are similar goals in U.S. national security ideology. The United States seeks to advance these goals through the promotion of stable democratic republics around the world, whereas the UN would rather promote stability through economic cooperation.

15. The benefits include the idea that forming coalitions to promote peace ensures that it is not necessary to gather favorable international opinion when fighting aggression in the world. Additionally, it can be easier to gather larger fighting forces when working through a world organization. The drawbacks are that a worldwide organization like the UN often moves slowly, and not all members will always be satisfied with its goals or the manner in which they are achieved.

Planning Guide

Levels					Resources	Chapter Opener	Section 1	Section 2	Section 3	Section 4	Chapter Assess
BL	OL	AL	ELL								
					FOCUS						
BL	OL	AL	ELL	📽	**Section Focus Transparencies**		26-1	26-2	26-3	26-4	
					TEACH						
BL	OL		ELL	📁	**Reading Essentials and Study Guide (and Answer Key)**		p. 297	p. 300	p. 303	p. 306	
BL	OL		ELL	📁	**Guided Reading Activities**		p. 93	p. 94	p. 95	p. 96	
BL	OL		ELL	📁	**Vocabulary Activities**		p. 26				
BL	OL	AL	ELL	📁	**Chapter Summaries**					p. 76	
BL	OL			📁	**American Biographies**						
BL	OL	AL	ELL	📁	**Cooperative Learning Activities**						
	OL	AL	ELL	📁	**Government Simulations and Debate**				p. 57		
BL	OL	AL	ELL	📁	**Historical Documents and Speeches**			p. 26			
BL	OL	AL	ELL	📁	**Interpreting Political Cartoons**			p. 51			
BL	OL		ELL	📁	**Skill Reinforcement Activities**				p. 26		
BL	OL	AL	ELL	📁	**Source Readings**		p. 26				
BL	OL			📁	**Supreme Court Case Studies**						
BL	OL	AL	ELL	📁	**Participating in Government Activities**			p. 51			
BL	OL		ELL	📁	**Spanish Declaration of Independence and U.S. Constitution**	✓	✓	✓	✓	✓	✓
BL	OL	AL	ELL	📁	**NGS World Atlas, Spanish**	✓	✓	✓	✓	✓	✓
BL	OL	AL	ELL	📽	**Unit Overlay Transparencies, Strategies, and Activities**	✓	✓	✓	✓	✓	✓
BL	OL		ELL	📽	**Making It Relevant Transparencies**	✓	✓	✓	✓	✓	✓
BL	OL	AL	ELL	📽	**High School Writing Process Transparencies, Strategies, and Activities**	✓	✓	✓	✓	✓	✓
BL	OL	AL		📽	**American Art & Architecture Transparencies, Strategies, and Activities**	✓	✓	✓	✓	✓	✓

✓ Chapter- or unit-based activities applicable to all sections in this chapter

All-In-One Planner and Resource Center

- Interactive Lesson Planner
- Interactive Teacher Edition
- Fully editable blackline masters
- Chapter Spotlight Videos Launch

- Differentiated Lesson Plans
- Printable reports of daily assignments
- Standards tracking system

Levels					Resources	Chapter Opener	Section 1	Section 2	Section 3	Section 4	Chapter Assess
BL	OL	AL	ELL								
					TEACH (continued)						
BL	OL			💿	**American Music: Hits Through History**	✓	✓	✓	✓	✓	✓
BL	OL		ELL	📁	**Reading Strategies for the Social Studies Classroom**	✓	✓	✓	✓	✓	✓
			ELL	📁	**English Language Learner Handbook**	✓	✓	✓	✓	✓	✓
BL	OL		ELL	📁	**Writer's Guidebook for Social Studies**	✓	✓	✓	✓	✓	✓
BL	OL	AL	ELL	📁	**Living Constitution, SE**	✓	✓	✓	✓	✓	✓
BL	OL	AL	ELL	📁	**Living Constitution, TAE**	✓	✓	✓	✓	✓	✓
BL	OL			📁	**NGS World Atlas, English**	✓	✓	✓	✓	✓	✓
BL	OL		ELL	📁	**The Constitution and You (poster set)**	✓	✓	✓	✓	✓	✓
BL	OL	AL	ELL	📁	**Spanish Chapter Summaries**					p. 76	
BL	OL	AL	ELL	📁	**Spanish Vocabulary Activities**		p. 26				
BL	OL		ELL	📁	**Spanish Reading Essentials and Study Guide (and Answer Key)**		p. 297	p. 300	p. 303	p. 306	
BL	OL	AL	ELL	💿	**PresentationPlus! with MindJogger CheckPoint**	✓	✓	✓	✓	✓	✓
					ASSESS						
BL	OL	AL	ELL	💿	***ExamView® Assessment Suite***		26-1	26-2	26-3	26-4	Ch. 26
BL	OL	AL	ELL	📁	**Authentic Assessment with Rubrics**		p. 33				p. 33
BL	OL	AL	ELL	📁	**Section Quizzes and Chapter Tests**		p. 321	p. 322	p. 323	p. 324	pp. 325–332
BL	OL	AL	ELL	📁	**Spanish Section Quizzes and Tests**		p. 321	p. 322	p. 323	p. 324	pp. 325–332
					CLOSE						
BL			ELL	📁	**Reteaching Activities**					p. 26	p. 26
BL	OL	AL	ELL	💿	**StudentWorks™ Plus with Audio Summaries**	✓	✓	✓	✓	✓	✓
BL	OL		ELL	🖨	**Graphic Organizer Transparencies**		✓	✓	✓	✓	
BL	OL		ELL	📁	**High School Government Reading and Study Skills Foldables®**		p. 69	p. 69	p. 69	p. 69	

Teach With Technology

What is the Media Library?

The Media Library is an all-in-one online resource center that provides students with access to digital media associated with the textbook.

How can the Media Library help my students?

The Media Library contains Section Audio and Chapter Spotlight Videos. Section Audio can help struggling readers and English Language Learners better comprehend the textbook. Chapter Spotlight Videos engage visual learners and generate student interest. Students can download audio to their digital media player or listen from their computer screen.

Visit glencoe.com and enter a student *QuickPass*™ code to go to the Media Library.

Government ONLINE

Visit glencoe.com and enter *QuickPass*™ code USG9085c26T for Chapter 26 resources.

You can easily launch a wide range of digital products from your computer's desktop with the McGraw-Hill Social Studies widget.

	Student	Teacher	Parent
Media Library			
• Student Edition Section Audio	●		●
• Chapter Spotlight Videos	●	●	●
***United States Government* Online Learning Center (Web Site)**			
• Chapter Overviews	●	●	●
• Multilingual Glossaries	●	●	●
• Study-to-Go	●	●	●
• Student Web Activities	●	●	●
• Self-Check Quizzes	●	●	●
• Online Student Edition	●	●	●
• Vocabulary eFlashcards	●	●	●
• Web Activity Lesson Plans		●	
• Vocabulary PuzzleMaker	●	●	●
• Landmark Supreme Court Cases	●	●	●
• Beyond the Textbook	●	●	●

- **Timed Readings Plus in Social Studies** helps students increase their reading rate and fluency while maintaining comprehension. The 400-word passages are similar to those found on state and national assessments.

- **Reading in the Content Area: Social Studies** concentrates on six essential reading skills that help students better comprehend what they read. The book includes 75 high-interest nonfiction passages written at increasing levels of difficulty.

- **Reading Social Studies** includes strategic reading instruction and vocabulary support in Social Studies content for ELLs and native speakers of English.
www.jamestowneducation.com

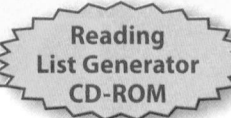

Reading List Generator CD-ROM

GLENCOE BOOKLINK 3

Use this database to search more than 30,000 titles to create a customized reading list for your students.

- Reading lists can be organized by students' reading level, author, genre, theme, or area of interest.
- The database provides Degrees of Reading Power™ (DRP) and Lexile™ readability scores for all selections.
- A brief summary of each selection is included.

Leveled reading suggestions for this chapter:
- *The Battle in Seattle,* by Margot Hornblower
- *Future Sources of Energy,* by Mark Lambert
- *A Wider Net,* by Jennifer Schenker

Review suggested books before assigning them.

Economics Connection

Personal Finance Literacy

Buying a Car
Explain to students that buying a car can be a challenging experience. Planning and research can help them get a good deal. Here are some tips for first-time buyers:

- **Making a choice:** Check the Internet or consumer publications for comparisons of various models' safety records, performance (fuel efficiency and environmental impact), and repair costs and frequency.

- **Financing:** Dealers make most of their profit on loans—not car sales. Research loans at banks and other financial institutions before discussing financing with dealers. If you apply for credit at more than one place, do it within 14 days to avoid damaging your credit rating.

- **New cars:** They're exciting and offer warranties, but depreciate in value the minute you drive them off the lot. Before making a deal, find the *factory invoice* price on the Internet. Ignore the higher "sticker" price on the window. Offer 3 to 5 percent over the factory invoice price. Get written bids from five dealers and use them as leverage to negotiate a good deal.

- **Used cars:** They're cheaper and some offer limited warranties. If you're buying from a dealer, ask for reference names and phone numbers of previous customers. Check the dealer's reputation with them and/or the Better Business Bureau. Whether buying from dealers, individuals, or over the Internet, drive the car, noticing how it handles and listening for any odd noises. Check the title to see if it was "salvaged" (declared a total loss by an insurer). Have a mechanic you trust or the American Automobile Association (AAA) test the car. Use the vehicle identification number (VIN) on the dash to check the car's history at the CARFAX Web site (www.carfax.com), and ask to see receipts for recent repairs.

Ask: What two considerations are most important when choosing a car to buy? Answers will vary.

Did You Know?
The average cost of driving a new sedan in the United States was $7,854 in 2006. Fuel and other costs have increased substantially since then. Sport utility vehicles and other cars with low miles cost considerably more.

Essential Question

As those nations industrialize and become wealthier, their demand for goods increases, opening new markets for trade. Manufacturers in the U.S. might be unable to compete with the low prices offered by competitors in those newly industrialized nations, causing some to go out of business or to press for trade barriers to protect their markets.

Chapter Spotlight Video

To generate student interest and provide a springboard for class discussion, access the Chapter 26 Video at glencoe.com or on the video DVD.

FOLDABLES
Study Organizer

Dinah Zike's Foldables are three-dimensional, interactive graphic organizers that help students practice basic writing skills, review key vocabulary terms, and identify main ideas. Have students complete this chapter's Foldable activity or activities in *Dinah Zike's Reading and Study Skills Foldables* booklet. **OL**

Government ONLINE

Visit glencoe.com and enter **QuickPass** code USG9085c26T for Chapter 26 Resources including Chapter Overview, Student Web Activity, Self-Check Quiz, and other materials for students and teachers.

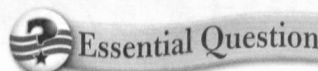

CHAPTER 26

Chapter Audio   Spotlight Video

Development *of* Economic Systems

Essential Question

How can changes in the economic power of a nation like China or India affect global trade and global politics?

Government ONLINE
Chapter Overview Visit glencoe.com and enter **QuickPass** code USG9822c26 for an overview, a quiz, and other chapter resources.

Stock market quotes on display on a Tokyo, Japan, street

716

Launching the Chapter

A Time Capsule Have each student create a time capsule that will tell future generations about economic issues at the beginning of the twenty-first century. Suggest that students search for photographs or other illustrations; published materials such as books, pamphlets, or slogans; original written or drawn materials such as a glossary of economic terms, a case study of a developing country, or a chart of the characteristics of major economic systems; or artifacts that illustrate some economic concept (such as free enterprise) or issue (such as free trade zones). **Essential Question:** How can American culture and economic ideals affect the behavior of other global superpowers? *(Answers will vary but might suggest that many global superpowers are at least partially dependent on the United States as a consumer of their goods and services.)* **OL**

Capitalist and Mixed Systems

Reader's Guide

Content Vocabulary
★ scarcity *(p. 717)*
★ traditional economy *(p. 717)*
★ command economy *(p. 717)*
★ market economy *(p. 718)*
★ factors of production *(p. 718)*
★ entrepreneur *(p. 718)*
★ monopoly *(p. 720)*
★ profit *(p. 720)*
★ mixed economy *(p. 721)*

Academic Vocabulary
★ resource *(p. 717)*
★ convert *(p. 718)*
★ domestic *(p. 721)*

Reading Strategy
Use an outline to take notes on economic systems.

Capitalist and Mixed Systems
I. Factors of Production
   A. Forms of Economic Organization
   B. Characteristics of Capitalism
II. Forms of Economic Organization

Issues in the News

Middle-class millionaire? That's the intriguing title of a 2008 book by Russ Prince and Lewis Schiff. The pair came up with the concept when they tried to identify the influence of the wealthy on the spending habits of ordinary Americans. What they found was that the very wealthy—people with more than $10 million—don't influence average consumers. For one thing, they don't mix much with those of lower socioeconomic classes. Also, ordinary Americans don't *talk* about what they buy. The middle-class millionaire—someone who makes between $1 and $10 million—is a very different type. (Roughly 8.4 million Americans fit this category.) Millionaires love to talk about what they buy. They operate with a belief that "most problems can be solved with a mix of creative thinking, the right people and an open wallet."

▲ The owners of this vessel could be middle-class millionaires.

American millionaires are a dramatic symbol of the opportunities that a capitalistic system can offer. Opportunity is a notable characteristic of capitalism, but like other economic systems, capitalism represents a method of making economic choices when **resources** are limited. Economic systems around the world are a response to the basic challenge of **scarcity.**

Scarcity is a condition that exists because society does not have all the resources to produce all the goods and services that everyone wants. Economic systems are an attempt to answer these questions: What should be produced? How should it be produced? For whom?

Economic systems can be classified into three major types—traditional, market, and command. In a **traditional economy,** habit and custom dictate the rules for all economic activity, determining what, how, and for whom goods and services are produced. A **command economy** has a central

Focus

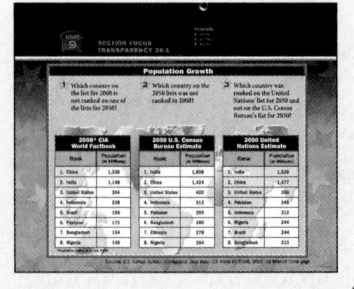
Reader's Guide

Answers to Graphic: Students' outlines may vary but should reflect the structure and content of the section.

Resource Manager

R Reading Strategies	**C** Critical Thinking	**D** Differentiated Instruction	**W** Writing Support	**S** Skill Practice
Teacher Edition • Activating Prior Knowledge, p. 721	**Teacher Edition** • Making Comparisons, p. 720	**Additional Resources** • Foldables, p. 69 • Source Readings, p. 26	**Teacher Edition** • Expository Writing, p. 718	**Teacher Edition** • Visual Literacy, p. 718 • Organizing, p. 719
Additional Resources • Guid. Read. Act., p. 93 • Quizzes/Tests, p. 321	**Additional Resources** • Read. Essen., pp. 297–299		**Additional Resources** • Authentic Assess., p. 33	**Additional Resources** • Vocab. Act., p. 26

Teach

Caption Answer: How economically powerful they are; student opinions may vary, but most students will likely suggest that the cartoon simply and clearly shows that theory.

S Skill Practice

Visual Literacy Organize the class into groups, and ask each group to design a cartoon that expresses an idea like Robert Mankoff's or an idea relating to factors of production. Groups can decide which members will be responsible for the concept, drawing, and captioning. **AL**

W Writing Support

Expository Writing Ask students to select one factor of production and one nation to research. Each student will write a one-page report that states who controls that factor in the selected country and explains a related issue. Someone might choose land use in Argentina, for example, and explain the environmental impact of the cattle industry. **OL AL**

Additional Support

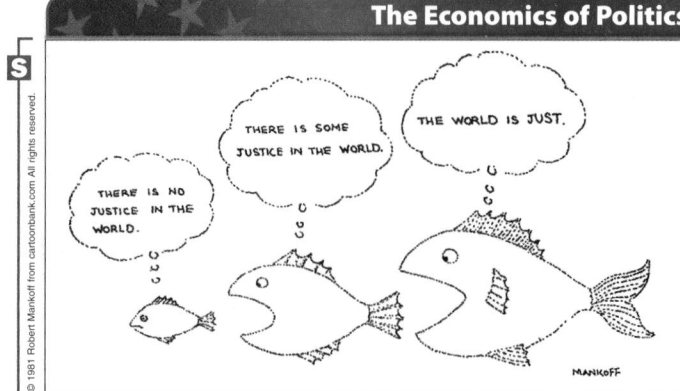

The Economics of Politics

Views of Economic Systems Robert Manikoff's cartoon presents an idea about why different people hold different opinions about economic systems. *What is Manikoff's theory about what determines a person's opinion? Is the cartoon clear and efficient in conveying the theory?*

authority—usually the government—that makes most of these economic decisions. State planning commissions or other agencies determine the needs of the people and direct resources to meet those needs. A **market economy** allows buyers and sellers acting in their individual interests to determine what, how, and for whom goods and services are produced. In a market economy, each individual's decisions are seen as acting like a vote. Consumers "vote" for a product when they purchase it, thus helping producers determine what to produce. Producers determine the best method for producing goods and providing services.

Factors of Production

The resources of an economic system are called **factors of production**—economies must have them in order to produce goods and services. The factors are usually identified by four categories:

- land
- capital
- labor
- entrepreneurs

Land includes all natural resources like water, air, and minerals such as copper. Capital is the means of production—factories, heavy machinery or tools—used to produce other products. The furnaces in a steel mill that **convert** iron ore to steel are capital. Labor is human resources: Factory workers, farmers, doctors, plumbers, teachers, and everyone else who is employed represent labor. The fourth factor of production are **entrepreneurs**—the risk-takers who organize and direct the other factors of production to produce goods and services to make a profit.

Forms of Economic Organization

Three major forms of economic organization—communism, socialism, and capitalism—represent the range of economic systems that determine how the factors of production are allocated. Communism is a command system in which the central government directs all major economic decisions. Socialism is a partial command system in which the government influences economic decisions. Under capitalism, consumers and private owners make the economic decisions in free markets.

People have strong opinions about the strengths and weaknesses of the three principal economic systems. For example, in a standard textbook, the authors of *Comparative Economic Systems* said:

> 66 *[Capitalism's] emphasis on the rights and freedoms of individuals . . . to pursue their individual goals seems to accord with our basic values and philosophic predilections [preferences]. It appears to many of us to be the form of economic organization that is most fundamentally consistent with the preservation of democratic political institutions.* 99
>
> —William Loucks and William Whitney

Although people often refer to the economies of different nations as being either capitalist, communist, or socialist, most countries in the world have a mixed economic system, meaning it has elements of more than one system. Furthermore, at any given time, a nation may be moving in the direction of a command economy or a market economy.

Activity: Collaborative Learning

Depicting Economic Roles Organize students into three groups and assign one of the following economic roles to each group: (1) government; (2) consumers; or (3) business. Explain that the task of each group is to produce some form of illustration—a billboard design, for example—that depicts their assigned role as it relates to the U.S. automobile industry. Have each group select a coordinator and brainstorm for five minutes to come up with an illustration idea. Then have group members share the tasks involved in producing the illustration; some might make preliminary designs, for example, others might write captions and explanatory materials, others might draw the illustration, and still others might provide finishing touches such as shading or color. Display the finished illustrations on the bulletin board. **OL**

Characteristics of Capitalism

The United States and a number of other industrialized nations have an economic system that is described as capitalism. In a capitalist system, the economy is based on private ownership of the factors of production and on individual economic freedom. A capitalist economic system is often called a free enterprise system.

In the free enterprise system, people who own the means of production are called capitalists. The owner of a small corner grocery store, the person who owns a few shares of stock in a huge corporation, industrialists who own large factories or coal mines, and those who own financial institutions are all capitalists.

Most capitalist economies today have five main characteristics. These include private ownership, individual initiative, competition, freedom of choice, and profit or loss.

Private Ownership

Capitalist economies depend on the right of private ownership of property and control of economic resources. Government provides some public services such as road building, water and sewers, parks, and libraries. In addition, the government may own land, as in the case of national parks.

Capitalism also emphasizes respect for personal property—personal property is property that is not used in producing goods and services. The Fifth Amendment of the Constitution embodies this value of the American system. It states that the government shall not deprive people of their property "without due process of law; nor shall private property be taken for public use, without just compensation." The right to inherit property is another aspect of private ownership under capitalism. In a pure capitalist system, no limit would be placed on this right, but inheritance taxes limit it in the United States. **S**

Individual Initiative

Under capitalism, the law does not prevent anyone from trying to be an entrepreneur. Each year, thousands of Americans go into business for themselves. In 2006, for example, Americans started more than 650,000 new businesses. Many start-ups were in fast-growing fields such as microcomputers, bioengineering, energy, and electronic communications.

Competition

Another essential aspect of capitalism is competition. Competition exists when a number of sellers sell a product or service and when no one seller exercises control over the market price.

Economic Terms	COMMAND ECONOMIES		MARKET ECONOMY
Related Political System	Communism	Socialism	Capitalism
Ownership of Resources	The government owns and operates all productive resources.	Government owns key industries like public utilities and steel; other resources are privately owned.	Productive resources are privately owned and operated.
Allocation of Resources	Centralized government plans for all resources.	Centralized government plans only key industries.	Resources are allocated by the market: The lure of profits attracts capital investment.
Role of Government	Government makes all major economic decisions.	Government directs its plans for key industries.	Government promotes competition and provides public goods where the market fails to do so.

Economic Systems in Theory

Critical Thinking The table shows economic systems in theory. In practice, no pure command or pure market economies exist. *Explain why both communism and socialism are considered command economies.*

Charts In MOtion
See StudentWorks™ Plus
or go to glencoe.com.

CURRICULUM CONNECTION

Economics Even under capitalism, private property rights are regulated in the public interest. In the United States, for example, taxes, zoning restrictions, health and building codes, and environmental regulations limit the uses of private property. Furthermore, federal laws prohibit using private property to make certain products, such as illegal drugs or alcohol.

S Skill Practice

Organizing Have students create a table with four columns labeled: *No Government Control, Regulation, Control, Potential Impact.* Ask students to list products and services, such as food, entertainment, schools, transportation, prescription drugs, and banking in one of the first three columns. Then have the class discuss what the impact of each item's placement would be. **OL** **AL**

Critical Thinking

Answer: The government has a role in the ownership and allocation of resources.

Differentiated Instruction

Activity: Multiple Learning Styles

Naturalist Remind students that land, as a factor of production, takes in far more natural resources than just the soil itself. Have students who are interested in natural science or environmental issues do research, individually or collaboratively, into the natural resources of their community, state, region, or another part of the world that interests them.

Invite students to use the information from their research to prepare a map or other visual and share their findings with the class. As they do so, encourage them to suggest how various natural resources such as water, minerals, vegetation, or wildlife might influence the economic system of the area in which they are found. **BL**

We the People
Making a Difference

Food From the 'Hood In its first four years, Food From the 'Hood put some $42,000—half of the net profits from the sale of its creamy Italian dressing—into scholarships. Food From the 'Hood received the 1996 Small Business Entrepreneurs Award, given by *Black Enterprise* magazine, in recognition of the students' achievement.

Activity Have students discuss how to set up a business in their community to help college-bound students.

C Critical Thinking

Making Comparisons Write the headings *Capitalism* and *the U.S. Economy* on the board. Ask students to list characteristics of each, them compare the "model" capitalist economy that they have developed with facts about the actual U.S. economy. **Ask:**

- How does the U.S. economy fit the capitalist model?

- What aspects of the U.S. economic system are not capitalistic? **OL**

Hands-On Chapter Project
Step 1

We the People
Making a Difference

When biology students at Crenshaw High School planted a small garden next to their football field, they had no idea that they were also planting the seeds for a successful business. The first year's harvest of herbs and vegetables was sold at local farmers' markets, generating $600 for college scholarships.

After the first year, students at the Los Angeles high school decided to create their own business. They called it Food From the 'Hood. Using herbs and produce from their garden, they concocted their own all-natural salad dressing called Straight Out 'the Garden. The dressing is now found on the shelves of more than 2,000 natural-food stores. In the words of their teacher, Tammy Bird, "Food From the 'Hood has helped these students apply what they are learning in the classroom."

The company is run just like any other successful company. Students must apply for the jobs through a rigorous process. Applicants have to write essays and participate in an internship program.

After 25 percent of the produce is donated each year to the homeless, profits are reinvested in the business or to establish scholarships. The company has earned an achievement award from *Newsweek* magazine, and has been visited by such well-known dignitaries as Great Britain's Prince Charles.

"Food From the 'Hood has helped these students apply what they are learning in the classroom."

—**Tammy Bird**

For example, competition exists when a city has a large number of gas stations that compete with one another. The gas station that offers the best combination of price, quality, and service is likely to get the largest share of the business.

A **monopoly** is the opposite of competition. A monopoly exists when an industry includes only one seller, resulting in no competition at all. Oligopoly, a situation in which only a few large firms compete in an industry, is more common. Businesses in such an industry often compete fiercely with each other, but there are also times when they might be tempted to limit competition by dividing the market or agreeing to raise prices. To ensure competition in free enterprise economies, governments pass laws against monopolies that try to control their markets.

Freedom of Choice

Buyers, sellers, and workers all have freedom of choice in a capitalist system. Consumers can buy the products they can afford from whatever companies they choose. At the same time, businesses are free to provide whatever legal goods and services they think people want. Workers can decide where they will work and what position they will hold.

When new jobs open up at better pay, workers can move to another job.

Profit or Loss

The capitalist system is based on the profit motive. **Profit** is the difference between the amount of money that is used to operate a business and the amount of money the business takes in. Profits are the fuel that keeps a free enterprise economy running.

Profits are part of the reward to the entrepreneur for assuming the risk. They also pay for future expansion and provide for unexpected events. Business owners use some profits for their own income. In addition, they might reinvest some of these profits in their business or in some other company.

In a capitalist economy, the risk of loss accompanies the potential for profits. Entrepreneurs must be willing to take chances and risk losses to be successful in a capitalist system.

Changes in Capitalism

The economic system of the United States is based on capitalism, yet it includes significant elements of a command economy. Especially since the 1930s, the federal government has played an important role in

---

Drawing a Special-Purpose Map

Step 1: Researching a Country Students will select a developing country to research in preparation for drawing a large special-purpose map that illustrates that country's current development. They may work alone or in pairs or groups.

Directions Have students select a developing country that interests them. They will use library resources and the Internet to learn about that country's current economic,

political, and social structure. The CIA *World Factbook* and the United Nations's Web site might be useful. For comparison, ask one student to select the United States or another developed country. Tell students they will be drawing and annotating a poster-sized map of the country.

Identifying Ask students to discuss what they have learned about the economic systems of the countries they chose. **OL**

(Chapter Project continued in Section 2.)

the economy. It protects the consumer, it regulates manufacturers and businesses of all kinds, and it is sometimes a direct producer of goods and services.

Regulation and Social Policies

For its first 100 years, the U.S. government role in the economy was limited, but in the late 1800s monopolies grew and workers endured long hours and low wages. The public demanded reform and some laws were passed to promote competition and protect workers. It was during the Great Depression, however, that federal policy truly shifted. The government was now seen as being responsible for insuring economic stability and citizen welfare. Since the 1930s, many laws have been passed to improve housing, health, and education. Given this larger economic role, the American economy today is described as a **mixed economy,** or modified capitalism.

In 2008 another financial crisis led to dramatic government intervention in the economy. The crisis began in the home mortgage industry. (Many believed that government deregulation allowed financial institutions to take on too many risky loans.) Investors lost trillions, stocks plunged, and many home owners could not pay their mortgages. Congress passed a law to provided $700 billion in "bailout" funds to buy up bad loans. The Federal Reserve and Treasury Department also bought out the ailing insurance company AIG (American International Group), the world's largest insurance company, to prevent damage to countless other investors and institutions. Days later, in early October, the government went even further.

It demanded that major banks accept $250 billion from the government and then make credit available. (This essentially gave the government shares in the banks.) The treasury secretary said these unusual actions were necessary to get banks lending money again and to restore the nation's economic health.

Capitalism Around the World

In Japan, the government works closely with business to limit foreign competition in the **domestic** market. The government spends relatively little on welfare, and taxes are low. Singapore and South Korea are other capitalist nations in Asia that have made remarkable progress in the last 20 years. In Singapore, the government has a close relationship with private business, which allows the government to target resources to certain industries.

Western European economies are generally more controlled and regulated than the American economy. Yet many of them have increased their commitment to free markets in recent years. In eastern European countries, many industries have been privatized in the years since the fall of the Soviet Union.

The 2008 financial crisis showed how connected world economies have become when turmoil in the American system quickly spread. Governments in Europe took steps to rescue their banks that had mortgage-backed securities from American banks. Stock markets in Indonesia, Russia, and Europe also plunged. The crisis led to an international effort to avoid a global recession by coordinating policy among a group of 20 nations.

SECTION 1 Review

Vocabulary

1. **Explain** the significance of: scarcity, traditional economy, command economy, market economy, factors of production, entrepreneur, monopoly, profit, mixed economy.

Main Ideas

2. **Identifying** What three forms of economic organization have emerged in the world?

3. **Explaining** How has the U.S. government played a growing role in the nation's economy since the late 1800s?

Critical Thinking

4. **Making Inferences** How does the free market system promote freedom of choice for consumers in the United States?

5. **Organizing** Use a graphic organizer like the one below to identify five characteristics of capitalist economies.

Writing About Government

6. **Expository Writing** Advocates of a planned economy and those who support a free market economy often debate whether democratic freedoms such as freedom of speech can exist in a nation without economic freedom. Write an essay explaining the connection between economic freedom and political freedom and then give your answer to this question.

CHAPTER 26: *Development of Economic Systems* **721**

R Reading Strategy

Activating Prior Knowledge Have students discuss and list on the board the ways in which a failure of banks and/or the lack of affordable credit might affect their lives and the U.S. economy. Encourage students to cite historical or current events that might help prove their points. **AL**

Assess

Assign the Section 1 Assessment as homework or as an in-class activity, or have students take Section Quiz 26-1 from *Section Quizzes and Chapter Tests.*

Close

Analyzing Lead a class discussion analyzing the economic significance to the United States of countries such as Singapore, Taiwan, and South Korea. **OL**

Section 1 Review

Answers

1. All definitions can be found in the section and the Glossary.
2. communism, socialism, and capitalism
3. It has taken responsibility for the well-being of individuals and for the financial condition of the nation. It has assumed increasing responsibility for social policies.
4. Consumers are free to choose which products they buy. Consumers may choose from a variety of sellers and products.

5. private ownership, individual initiative, competition, freedom of choice, profit and loss
6. Students' essays should show clear relationships between economic freedom and various civil liberties. You might have volunteers share their views in a panel discussion format or use the essays as the springboard for a class debate between regulatory economists and free market economists.

Focus

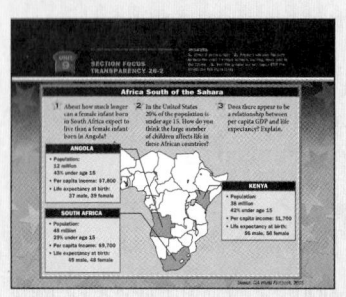
Reader's Guide

Answers to Graphic:

Investors fear their investment will be nationalized so they do not invest capital.

Large-scale planning has failed to meet the needs of consumers.

Western governments exert pressure to develop free markets.

Resource Manager

Emerging Economies

Reader's Guide

Content Vocabulary
★ developing nations *(p. 722)*
★ newly developed nations *(p. 722)*
★ welfare state *(p. 724)*
★ nationalization *(p. 724)*

Academic Vocabulary
★ redistribution *(p. 724)*
★ reliance *(p. 725)*
★ accumulate *(p. 725)*

Reading Strategy
As you read, create a graphic organizer similar to the one below to list the practical problems associated with socialism.

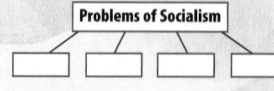

Problems of Socialism

Issues in the News

The education of girls remains a critical need in India. Despite dramatic economic progress, a substantial percentage of girls there cannot read and do not go to school. According to a United Nations report, in the poorest areas, girls are about 40 percent less likely to get a primary education. Government efforts to improve this figure have been disappointing. Many Indian families do not encourage a daughter's education because they think any economic benefits will only go to the family she marries into. Young student Geetha, for example, was pulled out of school at the age of nine to take care of the family's goats and to do housework. When a teacher tried to get her to return to the classroom, her father was unmoved. "This is the way it has always been, and it will not change."

▲ Many girls in rural India do not expect to get even a primary education.

By the late twentieth century, many developing countries faced common problems, but they used their resources in different ways. Turkey, for example, increased its defense spending even though the country only allotted $90 per student for education. This figure was far below the level in developed countries such as Greece ($240 per student) and Germany ($817 per student).

Developing and Newly Developed Nations

To understand the global economy, it is good to know the terms that are used to describe the economic level of nations. **Developing nations** are nations with little or no industry. The majority of

these countries are, of course, agricultural. A few of these developing nations, like Saudi Arabia and Kuwait, are rich because they possess a natural resource, such as oil. Many developing nations are former colonies of Western European nations and gained independence only after World War II. Developing nations contain much of the world's population.

Newly developed nations, on the other hand, are nations that have had significant or rapid industrial growth in recent decades. These countries can be found in several regions: Eastern Europe, the Middle East, Asia, and South America. They are playing a very influential role in shaping the world economy. Whether they can continue to expand their economies will depend on how they handle a number of economic issues.

R Reading Strategies	**C** Critical Thinking	**D** Differentiated Instruction	**W** Writing Support	**S** Skill Practice
Teacher Edition • Identifying, p. 726 **Additional Resources** • Guid. Read. Act., p. 94 • Quizzes/Tests, p. 322	**Teacher Edition** • Determining Cause and Effect, p. 725 **Additional Resources** • Read. Essen., pp. 300–302	**Teacher Edition** • Interpersonal, p. 723 **Additional Resources** • Foldables, p. 69 • Hist. Docs. and Speeches, p. 26	**Additional Resources** • Part. in Gov. Act., pp. 51–52	**Teacher Edition** • Researching, p. 723 **Additional Resources** • Inter. Poli. Cartoons, pp. 51–52

Comparing Governments

World Urbanization

- 51%
- 5%
- 14%
- 30%

Legend:
- ■ Rural areas
- □ Urban, under 1 million
- ■ Urban, 1–10 million
- ■ Urban, 10 million +

Development: Select Countries

COUNTRY	Percent Urban	GDP Per Capita*	Adult Literacy**
Bangladesh	26%	$1,300	43.1%
Bulgaria	70%	$11,300	98.2%
Chile	88%	$13,900	95.7%
Ethiopia	16%	$800	57.9%
Ghana	49%	$1,400	80%
Honduras	47%	$4,100	88.7%
Malaysia	68%	$13,300	88.7%
Turkey	68%	$12,900	87.4%
UNITED STATES	81%	$45,800	99%

*U.S. Dollars; **Population15 years and older

Source: CIA , *The World Fact Book*, 2008; for urbanization, United Nations, *World Population Prospects*, 2007.

Critical Thinking Based on the chart above, is it possible to say whether education or urbanization leads to a higher GDP per capita?

The Economic Choices

Some developing and newly developed nations have chosen to rely on free markets, trade, and contacts with the West to develop their economies. Their economic systems lean toward capitalism. The free market determines what goods and services are produced and at what prices. They are open to investment from capitalist countries.

Other developing and newly developed nations have chosen socialism as a model for their economies. What is socialism, and why did it develop? As was discussed in Chapter 1, under socialism, the government owns the basic means of production, determines the use of resources, distributes the products and wages, and provides for the welfare of the people.

The ideas for a socialist economy first developed in Europe after the Industrial Revolution. Social reformers witnessed the incredible wealth of goods that the new factories could produce. They reasoned that now it would be possible for all members of society to have enough to eat and to live comfortably. The basic motivation of socialists is to share wealth more equally in a society. For a socialist, this goal seems more important than maximizing the possibility of economic wealth for a few or preserving free markets.

Like socialism, communism is a command economy, meaning that the government has the power to command or direct the economy. Under communism, the government owns *all* factors of production and takes a much more direct role in deciding what, how, and for whom to produce. This is very different from many socialist economies where the command system is used to control only *parts* of their economy. For example, some socialist countries might operate important industries like mining and transportation but not industries that produce food and clothing. By contrast, communist systems usually draw up a detailed plan for production. A five-year plan would tell factory heads in every part of the country precisely how many units to manufacture and where these goods would be delivered.

Another important difference distinguishes the "command" democratic socialist economies and "command" communist economies. Under the first

CHAPTER 26: *Development of Economic Systems* **723**

Teach

Critical Thinking

Answer: The more urban and literate a society, the higher GDP tends to be.

S Skill Practice

Researching Have students look for economic news about countries in the chart, naming one economic problem that each country currently is facing and what solution the country is attempting. **OL**

D Differentiated Instruction

Interpersonal Organize the class into four groups—two to describe the advantages of socialism and two to describe the disadvantages. Some group members can do research, others can prepare key statements, and others can speak for the group. Urge students to support their views with facts. After each group has presented its work to the class, conduct a discussion to summarize students' major points. **OL**

Differentiated Instruction

Leveled Activities

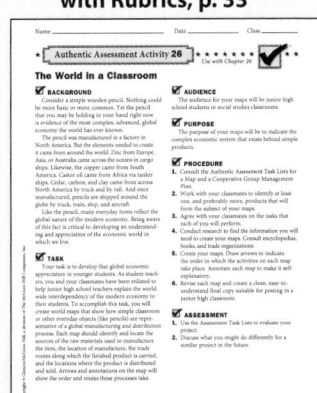

723

Linking ★ Past & Present

Collective Ownership The idea of collective ownership of property goes back at least to the ancient Greeks. Modern socialist theory—and the term *socialism*—was first advanced by French philosophers, notably the Comte de Saint-Simon, in the early 1800s. Robert Owen, Pierre-Joseph Proudhon, Giuseppe Garibaldi, John Stuart Mill, Auguste Comte, and Karl Marx were influenced by Saint-Simon's writings.

Did You Know?

Changes in Eastern Europe and the collapse of the Soviet Union have tainted the words *socialist* and *communist*. Some political parties have changed their names to Social Democrats or Democratic Left, for example, to avoid the negative connotations.

Caption Answer: Soy products are popular in Asian countries that have become more integrated into the global marketplace. The growth of vegetarianism has also helped make soybeans more profitable.

Differentiated Instruction

type, voters can replace the government leaders who are in command of the economy. In a Communist country, such as the former Soviet Union or Cuba, however, only one party exists, and the people have no control over the economic decisions.

Since socialists believe that wealth should be distributed as equally as possible, their policies are directed at making essential goods and basic social services available more or less equally to all.

Modern socialist governments also provide a wide array of so-called "cradle-to-grave" benefits for their citizens. In Western Europe, these kinds of government benefits developed in the first half of the twentieth century. Usually these benefits include free hospital, medical, and dental care; tuition-free education through college; generous retirement benefits; and low-rent public housing. Other government-provided services can include maternity allowances, free treatment for alcohol and drug abuse, and generous unemployment payments. Critics of socialism often use the term **welfare state** to describe this range of benefits and claim that it weakens people's work ethic. A welfare state, they say, discourages people from working to produce goods and services and makes citizens overly dependent on government. Socialists answer that every person should be able to receive such basic necessities as food, shelter, clothing, and medical care.

Cradle-to-grave services do not come free. Socialist governments require citizens to pay very high taxes to pay for social services. Businesses in socialist economies are also heavily taxed.

Searching for Economic Answers

Many developing and newly developed nations have adopted socialist economic policies, believing that this is the route to economic progress. Their policies aim to raise the standard of living of the large masses of people, most of whom are poor and uneducated. To date, however, these policies have not solved the problem of poverty.

Socialist governments in these countries often use centralized planning, or government control of the economy, to an even greater extent than developed socialist nations do. They believe that only centralized planning can achieve rapid industrial growth. In many of these nations, authoritarian governments take over economic planning. Many of these governments focus on welfare and education programs for the poor.

These socialist governments often turn to nationalization of existing industries, **redistribution** of land or establishment of agricultural communes, and a welfare system.

Socialist governments often take control of industry—usually selecting the country's most important industries—through a process called **nationalization.** When nationalization occurs in democratic countries, the government pays private owners of the businesses that it takes over. In less democratic countries, socialist governments have taken over private property with little or no compensation to the owners.

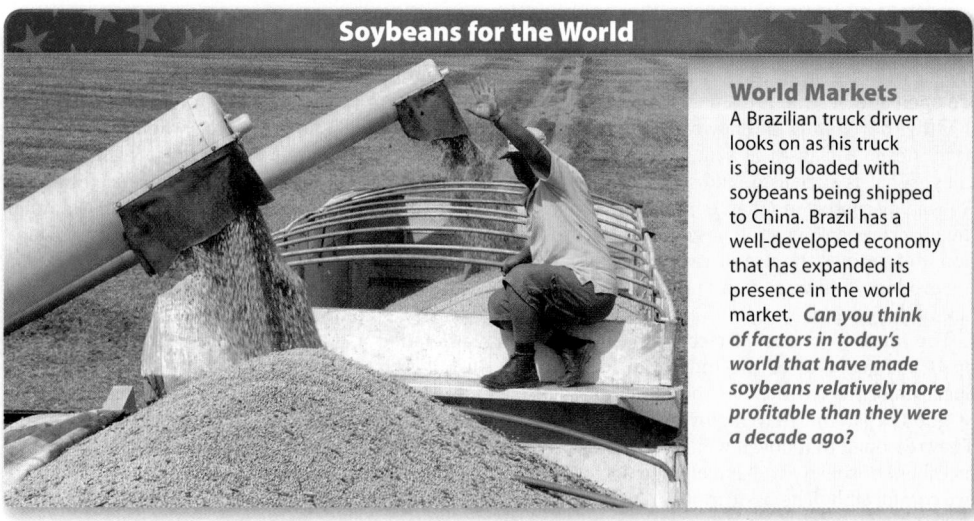

Soybeans for the World

World Markets
A Brazilian truck driver looks on as his truck is being loaded with soybeans being shipped to China. Brazil has a well-developed economy that has expanded its presence in the world market. *Can you think of factors in today's world that have made soybeans relatively more profitable than they were a decade ago?*

Activity: Multiple Learning Styles

Interpersonal People desiring economic well-being for their developing nations usually have had to argue for a change in the status quo. Have students experience the "persuasive spirit" by imagining themselves as one of the following: a socialist responding to a critic who claims that "cradle-to-grave" benefits weaken the national character; a Chilean government worker trying to persuade an industrialist not to reinvest funds in other countries; or an African leader explaining how his or her country can adopt socialism without giving up its own economic traditions.

Ask students to speak or write what they think the person would say. Interested students might enjoy turning this activity into a skit for classroom performance. **OL**

Nationalization in Latin America

Many developing nations have had foreign-owned industries because of their colonial history, or their **reliance** on foreign investment. This is especially true in Latin America. Nationalization of these industries by the government has been both an economic policy as well as a gesture of anticolonialism. In addition to foreign ownership of business, many developing countries have been ruled by wealthy elites. In these states, the poverty of masses of people could ignite revolution and civil war at almost any time.

The nation of Chile reflects the difficulties of a developing nation as it attempts to build a socialist democracy. In 1970 Chileans elected Salvador Allende as president. Allende, a Marxist socialist, took quick steps to nationalize businesses, including American copper mining companies. Wealthy Chileans, frightened by Allende's ties to Castro's Cuba and the government's efforts to nationalize industries, withdrew their money from Chile and invested it in other countries. As a result, the Chilean economy spiraled downward. In 1973 Chilean military leaders working with the CIA led a coup against Allende.

After Allende was found dead, a new government, led by General Augusto Pinochet, took over. Pinochet dissolved the congress, canceled civil liberties, and issued a new constitution. He also encouraged foreign investment. Inflation fell, consumer goods became available again, and the economy prospered. Mounting popular pressure against Pinochet, however, forced him to hold elections in 1988. The new leaders since then have increased government spending on education, health, and housing. Chile's economy has improved, and the nation is interested in joining the North American Free Trade Agreement.

Economic Development in Africa

After gaining their independence, many African nations tried to develop economies that were based on one cash crop or one resource for trade. Promoting the export of cash crops and raw materials while trying to industrialize did not produce sufficient capital. Seeking more funds for development, African nations then borrowed from foreign governments and banks. Some governments in Africa followed a capitalist model and developed close ties to the West. Others organized socialist economies.

Beginning in the 1970s, droughts, growing populations, lack of capital, and falling world prices for their exports weakened most African economies. African nations south of the Sahara relied heavily on foreign help, **accumulating** $130 billion worth of debt by the 1980s. Rising interest rates and economic stagnation compounded the region's debt, which reached $227 billion in 1996.

The World Bank identification of 33 African countries as Heavily Indebted Poor Countries (HIPC) provides them with some aid, but it is not enough. In 1996 nations south of the Sahara were

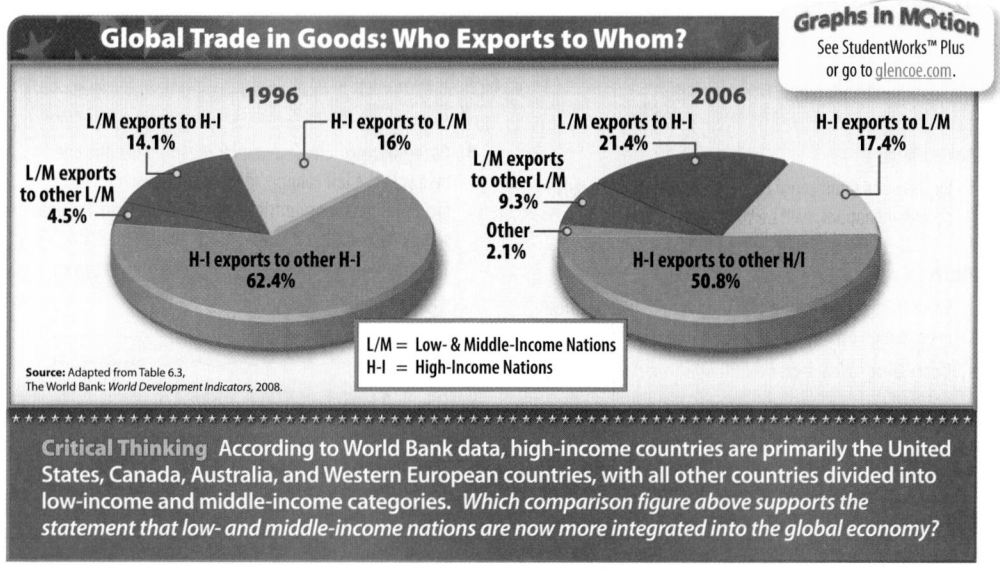

Global Trade in Goods: Who Exports to Whom?

Graphs In Motion See StudentWorks™ Plus or go to glencoe.com.

1996

L/M exports to H-I 14.1%

H-I exports to L/M 16%

L/M exports to other L/M 4.5%

H-I exports to other H-I 62.4%

2006

L/M exports to H-I 21.4%

H-I exports to L/M 17.4%

L/M exports to other L/M 9.3%

Other 2.1%

H-I exports to other H/I 50.8%

L/M = Low- & Middle-Income Nations
H-I = High-Income Nations

Source: Adapted from Table 6.3, The World Bank: *World Development Indicators*, 2008.

Critical Thinking According to World Bank data, high-income countries are primarily the United States, Canada, Australia, and Western European countries, with all other countries divided into low-income and middle-income categories. *Which comparison figure above supports the statement that low- and middle-income nations are now more integrated into the global economy?*

C Critical Thinking

Determining Cause and Effect As Section 2 indicates, it is common for an emerging nation's initial economic policies to do more harm than good, and ultimately those policies are reformed. Have pairs or small groups of students select one nation whose case is described in this section. For each case, have students create a flowchart or other kind of diagram that states the nation's initial economic policies, the needs or decisions that established those policies, the economic results, and the reforms produced by those results. Encourage comparisons between the finished diagrams, asking students to consider why some policies fail and others succeed. Also work with them to make generalizations about the economic policies that seem to work best for emerging nations. **ELL**

Critical Thinking

Answer: Low- and middle-income nations' exports to high-income nations have risen as a percentage of all other exports since 1996.

Hands-On Chapter Project

Step 2

Drawing a Special-Purpose Map

Step 2: Organizing Information Students will organize the information they researched in Step 1.

Directions Distribute poster paper, and have students draw their maps. On the map, students will indicate the following information: country name, major population centers, capital city, geographical features, natural resources, major industries. To indicate resources and industries, have students create or copy symbols. Adjacent to the map they will note: population, type of economy, type of government, literacy rate, unemployment rate, life expectancy, per capita GDP, number of phones per 100,000 people (to get this statistic, they will need to divide the population by 100,000; then, using the CIA's *World Factbook,* they will divide that number by the sum of the numbers of cell phones and phone lines).

Comparing Economies Explain that per capita GDP is a way to measure the wealth of a country. GDP, or Gross Domestic Product, is the value of all goods and services a country produces. Per capita GDP is that amount divided by the population. Have groups compare their country's per capita GDP with that of the other groups. **OL**

(Chapter Project continued in Section 3.)

Section 2 Review

Caption Answer: Students' answers will vary. Students might suggest attempting to impose embargoes on Russian goods or other ways to harm Russian investments.

R Reading Strategy

Identifying Ask: Why do emerging socialist economies often have difficulty raising capital? *(Foreign investors worry that they will not see any returns on their investments.)* **BL**

Assess

Assign the Section 2 Assessment as homework or as an in-class activity, or have students take Section Quiz 26-2 from *Section Quizzes and Chapter Tests.*

Close

Analyzing Have students identify what they believe is the greatest strength and the greatest weakness of capitalism and of socialism. **OL**

Section 2 Review

Russia's Ace in the Hole Gas and oil reserves in Russia have enhanced that nation's international power. In the photo, the first pipes for the gas pipeline between Germany and Russia are being transported in northern Germany. *Given Russia's resources, how will Germany or other Western nations address concerns about human rights in Russia?*

paying $1.30 toward debt for every $1.00 received in aid. A movement to cancel Africa's staggering debt has gained momentum around the world. Supporters argue that most African nations' current debt is so large that they will continue to pay more toward debt service than for health care and development unless their debt is canceled. Opponents argue that unless these nations end corruption, debt cancellation will only continue the cycle.

Socialism's Practical Problems

Socialist ideology is losing ground in the developing world because several practical problems have caused socialism to fail to live up to its promises. First, a primary need for developing economies is capital investments. The quickest route to capital is through foreign investors. Yet banks and private investors have been cautious when investing in developing nations. A major concern is whether the emerging economy will honor its obligations. Free market economies without a threat of nationalization of businesses attract capital. Emerging socialist economies may have trouble attracting the same capital.

Second, the failure of large-scale state planning to meet the needs of the consumers in Eastern European nations raises concern about socialism's ability to do so in other regions. Developing nations have large populations with basic consumer needs. Failure to meet these needs would risk revolt.

Finally, Western governments, particularly the United States, have exercised influence and pressure in favor of a combination of free markets and democracy in developing nations.

The interdependence of nations and a global communications network have made it very difficult for other nations to resist the West's economic leadership. Meanwhile, governments in industrialized nations have been willing to accept some government planning.

SECTION 2 Review

Vocabulary

1. **Explain** the significance of: developing nations, newly developed nations, welfare state, nationalization.

Main Ideas

2. **Examining** Why have many Latin American industries been foreign owned?

3. **Describing** What factor contributes to socialism in Africa?

4. **Identifying** What is centralized planning?

Critical Thinking

5. **Making Comparisons** Analyze the economic choices that developing and newly developed nations must make in an increasingly interdependent global economy.

6. **Categorizing** Create a graphic organizer like the one below. In the left column, identify the economic issues facing developing countries. In the right column, list policies some have adopted to promote economic progress.

Developing Nations	
Issues	Policies

Writing About Government

7. **Comparative Government** Review the characteristics of economies under socialist governments and under Communist governments. Create an organizational chart that illustrates decision making under each of these types of government. Write a summary for each type of government.

Answers

1. All definitions can be found in the section and the Glossary.
2. because of their colonial history or their reliance upon foreign investment
3. Some African leaders adopted socialism because they viewed Western capitalism as another form of colonialism.
4. government control of key segments of the economy
5. Developing nations may seek to industrialize as rapidly as possible, whereas newly developed nations may seek to sustain their rate of growth and influence the world economy.
6. Answers might include: Issues—foreign ownership of industry, how to achieve rapid industrial growth, development of cash crops for export; Policies—nationalization of industry, centralized planning, agricultural communes, acceptance of foreign aid and loans.
7. Call on volunteers to explain their charts to the class.

Should the United States Spend More on Foreign Aid?

Foreign aid represents a small percentage of the federal budget, yet many Americans think the money that goes to other counties is wasted. One of the most successful pleas for foreign aid came at the end of World War II from Secretary of State George C. Marshall. Marshall said that the devastated nations of Europe might fall to communism or fascism unless Americans helped them rebuild. In recent decades, similar arguments have been made for supporting economic development in poor African and Asian countries.

YES George W. Bush, President of the United States

Primary Source

❝ We are also sending a broader message about America's purpose in the world. In this new century, there is a great divide between those who place no value on human life, and rejoice in the suffering of others, and those who believe that every life has matchless value. . . .

The contrast is vivid—and the position of America is clear. . . . We believe in the timeless truth: To whom much is given, much is required. We also know that nations with free, healthy, prosperous people will be sources of stability, not breeding grounds for extremists and hate and terror. By making the world more hopeful, we make the world more peaceful—and by helping others, the American people must understand we help ourselves. ❞

—from a speech to the National Geographic Society, December 2006

NO William Easterly, Professor of Economics

Primary Source

❝ The governments of the poor countries, through which the aid is directed, often have little incentive to raise the productive potential of the poor, especially when doing so might engender political activism that threatens the current political elite. The [American] aid agencies themselves in this difficult environment do not have much incentive to achieve results, since the results are mostly unobservable. One can hardly monitor growth itself for a given country for a given year, since growth in any given year or even over a few years reflects too many other factors besides aid. ❞

—from "Can Foreign Aid Buy Growth?" *Journal of Economic Perspectives,* Summer 2003

Debating the Issue

1. **Identifying** How does President Bush connect foreign aid to the campaign against terrorism?

2. **Explaining** What is the main argument Easterly makes against giving aid to poor countries under the current system?

3. **Deciding** Which opinion do you agree with? Explain your reasoning.

▶ **American soldier distributing food aid**

727

Debating the Issue Answers

1. Helping other nations become prosperous and free makes them less likely to be breeding grounds for terrorism.

2. The aid is often wasted and fails to achieve any measurable results.

3. Students should support their opinion with references to the quotes or individual research and logical arguments.

Teach

Setting Up the Debate

Applying Research Have students research U.S. foreign aid sent to two different countries. The first should be an example of where foreign aid appeared to be successful. The second should be where foreign aid appeared to have no effect or made things worse. **Ask:** Why did one succeed and the other fail? Is there a major difference between the two projects in the amount of time and money spent? What efforts were made to make sure the aid made it to the right place? Was the aid distributed by the country's government, or did the aid bypass the government? *(Answers will vary, but students should show an understanding of the factors that make foreign aid successful.)*

Evaluating Have students research the arguments for and against the United States spending more on foreign aid. Students should give specific arguments to support both points of view.

Concluding the Debate

Discuss these questions with students:

- What standards should be set when determining the needs of foreign nations?

- If foreign aid is not effective, what other options does the U.S. have to help support economic development in poorer countries?

727

Focus

Bellringer

Section Focus Transparencies 26-3

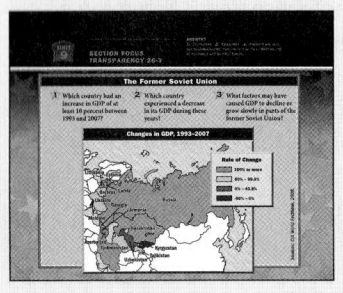

Reader's Guide

Answers to Graphic:

- resistance to reform by former Communists
- lack of commitment to democracy by citizens

Resource Manager

Major Economies in Transition

Reader's Guide

Content Vocabulary	Academic Vocabulary	Reading Strategy
★ state farm *(p. 729)* ★ collective farm *(p. 729)*	★ incentive *(p. 729)* ★ unparallel *(p. 730)* ★ investment *(p. 731)*	Create a graphic organizer similar to the one below to identify obstacles that slowed democratization in Russia.

Issues in the News

The new president of Russia, Dmitriy Medvedev, is a businessperson, and this might explain why he was chosen for the post by former president and current prime minister Vladimir Putin. The Russian economy boomed in an era of increasing oil prices, but it will take skilled management to sustain its economic gains. Russia's oil resources have seen a flood of foreign investment—more than any other major economy in the world. Its hold over the natural gas industry in Europe gave Putin confidence. In the words of one European leader: "Russia is getting stronger; we are getting weaker." Many economists predict that the boom conditions are nearly over and that unresolved social and political problems will cut into the nation's prosperity.

▲ **Russian President Dmitriy Medvedev, left, with Vladimir Putin, the former president and current prime minister**

Many nations today are transitioning from a command economy to a market economy. The two most significant nations in this group are Russia and China. Together they seem to be altering the shape of the global economy.

Transforming the Russian Economy

The Soviet Union collapsed in 1991 because its Communist leaders could not keep the economy going. Since then Russian leaders have been attempting to build a free enterprise system that can compete effectively in the global economy.

Collapse of Soviet Communism

Beginning in 1917, the Soviet Union built the world's leading communist economic system. Although Soviet leaders called their system a socialist economy, the Soviet system differed from that of democratic socialist countries. In the Soviet Union, the Communist Party closely controlled the government and made almost all the economic decisions. With few exceptions, enterprises were state owned and state operated. The government also controlled labor unions, wages, and prices.

R Reading Strategies	**C** Critical Thinking	**D** Differentiated Instruction	**W** Writing Support	**S** Skill Practice
Teacher Edition • Skimming, p. 729 **Additional Resources** • Guid. Read. Act., p. 95 • Quizzes/Tests, p. 323	**Teacher Edition** • Drawing Conclusions, p. 731 **Additional Resources** • Read. Essen., pp. 303–305	**Teacher Edition** • Logical/Mathematical, p. 730 **Additional Resources** • Foldables, p. 69	**Additional Resources** • Gov. Sims. and Debates, pp. 57–63	**Additional Resources** • Skill Reinforce. Act., p. 26

Under this system, the government controlled about 98 percent of all farmland. About two-thirds consisted of state farms. **State farms** are run like factories where farmworkers are paid wages. The remaining one-third of the farmland were collective farms. On a **collective farm,** the government owns the land but rents it to families. Farmworkers had little **incentive** to work hard, and inefficiency was widespread.

The huge, oppressive state bureaucracy that managed every detail of production bred economic stagnation. When the last Communist leader, Mikhail Gorbachev, came to power in 1985, he tried to reform the economy, while keeping an authoritarian government. The economy continued to decline, however. In 1991 amidst anti-government demonstrations, Gorbachev resigned as Communist Party leader. Several Soviet republics seized the opportunity to declare their independence, effectively ending the Soviet Union.

Incomplete Reforms

Since the collapse of communism, Russia has tried to move toward capitalism and democracy. Its leaders have broken up the huge, state-owned industries, created a stock market, and initiated other reforms, but progress has been slow. In many ways, the country is being run as it was under communism and by some of the same people. For example, the Russian president who was elected in 2000, Vladimir Putin, is a former officer of the KGB, or Soviet secret police. Putin believed that the cure for Russia's economic ills was strengthening of the state.

During Putin's administration, democratization slowed. The government shut down the only major independent television station and international observers asked whether parliamentary elections were truly free and democratic. In 2003 the Organization for Security and Cooperation in Europe noted that the Russian media gave more favorable coverage to the pro-state United Russia Party (Putin's party). That party went on to win more than 37 percent of the vote, and thus to control 37 percent of the seats in the Duma, or Russian parliament. (This number is about twice as large as the party held in the previous period.) The same flaws were noted in the 2007 elections: Many parties took part, but only Putin's United Russia Party received extensive media coverage.

Obstacles to Change

Several factors explain the slow pace of change in Russia. One has been resistance to reform by a group of former Communist bureaucrats. As the Soviet Union collapsed, these officials used inside knowledge to buy state properties—such as newspapers, banks, and oil and gas companies—at bargain rates. As a result, they became very wealthy and now control many of Russia's resources. Through bribes, mutual favors, and other strategies, they have found ways to slow reform to protect their newly acquired wealth and power.

In addition, many Russians do not have a deep understanding of democracy. Throughout their history, Russians have generally experienced order that was imposed from above. Public opinion polls have shown that the vast majority of Russians—79 percent in one poll—express regret for the breakup

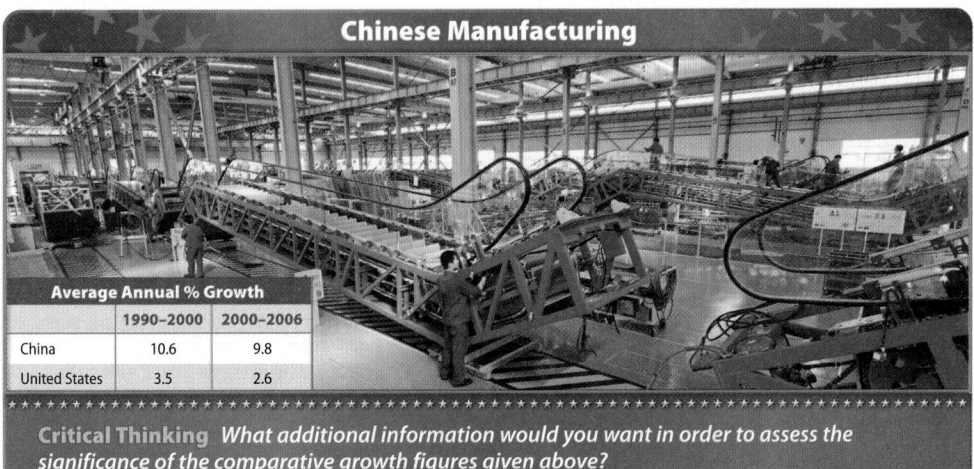

Chinese Manufacturing

Average Annual % Growth		
	1990–2000	2000–2006
China	10.6	9.8
United States	3.5	2.6

Critical Thinking *What additional information would you want in order to assess the significance of the comparative growth figures given above?*

Teach

R Reading Strategy

Skimming Write the following statement on the board: *Economic problems plagued the Soviet Union and continue to concern Russians today.* Have students work together to locate evidence that supports this opinion. **OL**

Participating IN GOVERNMENT

Consumer Advocacy Explain that the quality of goods produced in the United States is closely monitored by several organizations. Have students find out how the quality of one product they use frequently has been assessed. **AL**

Critical Thinking

Answer: Possible answers include population, GDP, or per capita GDP.

Additional Support

Activity: Collaborative Learning

Preparing a News Report Have students imagine themselves as journalists covering the collapse of the Soviet Union for an expanded television news program. Students should produce and present a segment of the show. Coverage could include the following: a retrospective on the history and recent problems of the Soviet Union; profiles of Mikhail Gorbachev and Boris Yeltsin; interviews with Soviet citizens; a panel discussion among diplomats, economists, and other experts; and a commentary about what the future might hold for the Soviet Union. **OL**

729

Conflict of Interest Have students consider the Soviet economy. **Ask:** What economic decisions might have kept the Soviet Union from political collapse? **OL**

D Differentiated Instruction

Logical/Mathematical Have students discuss these questions about China's transition away from a command economy:

- What difficulties might one experience going from a command to a socialist or capitalist economic system?

- How does rapid population growth affect a nation's economic system? **OL**

Government *and* You

More About Intercultural Exchange Programs Interested students can learn about the Council on International Educational Exchange at www.ciee.org or by writing to its headquarters at 205 East 42nd Street, New York, NY 10017.

Hands-On Chapter Project

Step 3

of the Soviet Union and respect for Vladimir Lenin, the leader of the Bolshevik Revolution that established Soviet communism. In the words of one Russian Parliament member: "The totalitarian mind-set is still an organic part of public consciousness."

The Russian experience suggests that a close relationship exists among capitalism, democracy, and the rule of law. In the words of leading economist Milton Friedman: "Economic freedom is an essential requisite for political freedom." Friedman pointed out that most politically free societies have a free market economy.

Changing the Chinese Economy

After World War II, the Chinese Communist government followed the Soviet model and created a planned economy. Over time, however, China found itself unable to compete economically with the market-based economies of its neighbors such as Taiwan, South Korea, Japan, Hong Kong, and Singapore.

In the late 1970s, China's Communist leaders began dismantling the centrally controlled economy and encouraging private enterprise. In recent years, the Chinese economy has grown between 5 and 8 percent per year. According to Nicholas Lardy of the Brookings Institute: "The pace of China's industrial development and trade expansion is **unparalleled** in modern economic history."

China's rapid development can be explained by several factors. First, its population of 1.3 billion provides a large labor pool. Companies all over the world have factories in China because the average factory wage is about 40 cents per hour. For example, 80 percent of shoes sold in the United States are made in China. Second, China's government promotes manufacturing by giving foreign companies tax breaks and cheap land. The government has also spent billions on highways, ports, and fiber-optic communications to assist manufacturers. The Pearl River Delta area of China, for example, has been turned into huge manufacturing zones. One of these zones alone has 22,000 factories with more than 4 million workers.

Economic, Not Political, Change

The Chinese government is attempting to move from a command to a market economy while maintaining the political control of the Communist Party.

Government *and* You

Hosting a Foreign Exchange Student

Does your school participate in a student exchange program? Has your family or anyone you know ever hosted a high school student from another country?

Families who support or participate in intercultural exchange programs believe that the experience promotes understanding and respect among the world's people. Hosting an exchange student provides your family with a chance to learn firsthand about another country, its government, and its culture. It also allows you to share your way of life with the visiting student.

Intercultural programs vary; families may host a student for a summer, a semester, or a year. Visiting students generally are members of the junior or

▶ Christina and Howard Pillot with son Carl and foreign student Charttraharn Chareonwong

senior class in high school. Some communities, however, participate in exchange programs for college students, teachers, or elementary school students. Host families may have members who are the same age as the visiting student. Families with young children, couples with no children, and single people also can host exchange students.

Organizations that sponsor exchange programs provide orientation meetings and staff to help make the experience valuable for everyone.

Participating IN GOVERNMENT ACTIVITY

Conduct an Interview Ask a foreign exchange student about his or her experiences in the United States and in their home country. Also discuss differences in forms of government that the students have experienced.

730

Drawing a Special-Purpose Map

Step 3: Creating a Chart Students will compare the statistics of their assigned country to those of the United States, Great Britain, or another highly developed nation.

Directions Have groups create a table or a graph that illustrates the huge disparity in economic statistics. Groups will present this visual aid with their maps.

Analyzing Information Have students discuss how their lifestyles would be different if one or more of their map-country's statistics suddenly became the statistics of the United States. For example, how would things change if tomorrow the United States had as many homes with Internet connections as Côte D'Ivoire or Nepal? **OL**

China's former president, Jiang Zemin, recently said: "Should China apply the parliamentary democracy of the Western world . . . the result will be great chaos."

Experts disagree about whether the current political system can keep up with the social changes that have resulted from China's economic boom. Its middle class has already grown substantially. In the old days, this group would have been punished as a counterrevolutionary threat, but in 2000, the Communist Party's general secretary stunned everyone by officially inviting members of the new middle class to join the party.

One danger to the Communist Party is that the growing middle class will want to have more say in how China is governed. Experts note that for the moment, there appears to be an unspoken deal. As long as the party can keep the economy booming, then the Communists can keep tight control over politics. If economic prosperity begins to falter, however, the party's authority might weaken.

Another danger is that China will remain a poor country. Two-thirds of Chinese still must live on less than $1 per day, and more than 26 million workers have lost jobs as old state-owned industries have closed down. Unemployed workers and farmers who were displaced by new technology are pouring into the cities. This is creating a new class of urban poor that is angry with the government. Finally, government corruption has become a bigger problem than ever. Without real political reform, Communist Party officials are able to reap the benefits of economic gains. For instance, officials might buy natural resources at fixed government prices and then sell them at a huge profit on the private market. They also might close a state factory, fire the workers without pay, and then sell the assets. Anyone who objects could be arrested.

Impact on the United States

Economic changes in China are having a huge effect on Americans. Trade with China is opening markets for American goods and new bases for American companies to expand. Along with Japan, the United States has been one of the largest investors in China's economy in recent years. China's growth is creating new sources of income for American lawyers, shippers, truckers, and many others. At the same time, many American manufacturers in areas such as textiles, furniture, and electronics have gone out of business or moved abroad because they cannot compete with the low labor costs of the Chinese.

Finally, some experts worry that an economically strong China might become a dangerous political and military rival if the United States does not maintain favorable relations with the Chinese government. China's attraction as a lucrative area of economic **investment** and the U.S. goal to promote democratic political practices to a repressive government creates tension between the United States and China. Other political observers argue that the economic development of China will create new opportunities for American business and could encourage the Chinese government to extend greater rights to its people.

CHAPTER 26, SECTION 3

C Critical Thinking

Drawing Conclusions Ask: Overall, do you think the growth of China's economy is good or bad for workers in the United States? (*Good: creates new sources of income for many U.S. workers; Bad: Low Chinese labor costs put U.S. manufacturers at a competitive disadvantage.*) **OL**

Assess

Assign the Section 3 Assessment as homework or as an in-class activity, or have students take Section Quiz 26-3 from *Section Quizzes and Chapter Tests.*

Close

Analyzing Considering the economic collapse of the Soviet Union and recent changes in China, have students discuss the meaning of the following statement by Peruvian novelist Mario Vargas Llosa: "You cannot be a modern man and a Marxist." **OL**

SECTION 3 Review

Vocabulary

1. Explain the significance of: state farm, collective farm.

Main Ideas

2. Describing What events in 1991 led to the collapse of the Soviet Union?

3. Identifying What was the main source of agricultural problems in the Soviet Union?

Critical Thinking

4. Examining Does the growing Chinese middle class threaten the current Chinese government?

5. Analyzing What policies in Russia suggest that democracy there remains limited?

6. Listing Use a graphic organizer like the one here to identify four reasons for China's rapid economic growth.

China's Growing Economy

Writing About Government

7. Expository Writing Before the 1980s, the Soviet economy was controlled by a central planning body of the Communist Party. Conduct research online or at your local library to find a political cartoon about how the Soviet economy worked. Write a paragraph explaining the cartoon, and present both to your classmates.

Section 3 Review

Answers

1. All definitions can be found in the section and the Glossary.
2. Six years of reform did not cure persistent problems in the Soviet economy. Citizens revolted and several Soviet republics declared their independence.
3. government mismanagement of production
4. Students may suggest that as the middle class grows, its members will want more say in how China is governed.
5. The government has shut down independent media outlets, and independent observers questioned whether the election was free and fair.
6. large labor pool, low production costs, tax breaks and cheap land given to foreign companies, billions spent by Chinese government on highways, ports, and communications
7. Students' paragraphs should clearly explain what the cartoon is showing.

Focus

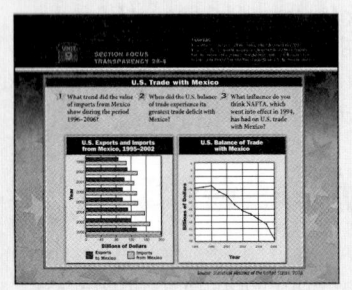
Reader's Guide

Answers to Graphic:

Tariffs

Quotas

Nontariff barriers (NTBs)

Embargoes

Resource Manager

The Global Economy

Reader's Guide

Content Vocabulary
* comparative advantage *(p. 732)*
* tariff *(p. 733)*
* quota *(p. 733)*
* trading bloc *(p. 734)*

Academic Vocabulary
* instance *(p. 733)*
* regional *(p. 734)*
* ideology *(p. 736)*

Reading Strategy
As you read, create a graphic organizer similar to the one below to list the ways in which governments may restrict international trade.

```
                      [        ]
                         ↑
[        ] ← Methods Used to → [        ]
              Restrict Trade
                         ↓
                      [        ]
```

Economics in the News

In the last decade, Wal-Mart® has gone global in a big way, opening stores in India, Brazil, European nations, China, and South Korea. Some of these ventures have failed. In 2006 Wal-Mart pulled out of South Korea because it did not localize its operations. It focused on clothing and electronics, the items Westerners prefer, instead of the food and beverages that South Korean housewives wanted. Probably the hardest cultural lesson Wal-Mart learned came in Germany where the company lost hundreds of millions of dollars because the chain did not adjust to the local culture. "We literally bought the two chains [there] and said, 'Hey, we are in Germany, isn't this great?'" Today, Wal-Mart tries to integrate into a country's culture. It has even been willing to sacrifice the Wal-Mart name if that's what it takes.

▲ A Wal-Mart in Hangzhou represents the company's effort to take advantage of the huge market in China.

In today's interdependent world, many forms of international economic activity take place. Participants in the global economy range from individuals who may invest directly in foreign companies or real estate to giant multinational corporations that employ tens of millions of workers. Global economic activities include investments, banking and financial services, and currency exchange. The major activity in the global economy is trade among nations.

International Trade

Since the end of World War II, the United States has been a dominant player in international trade. Congress and the president are constantly under pressure to manage trade policy in ways that will promote the American economy.

Purpose of Trade

Nations engage in international trade for several reasons. One is to obtain goods and services that they cannot produce themselves. For example, the United States buys, or imports, industrial diamonds from other countries because we do not have deposits of such minerals. The United States sells, or exports, computers and complex weapons like jet fighters to countries that do not have the technology to make their own.

Another reason nations trade is **comparative advantage.** This economic principle says that each country should produce those goods it can make more efficiently and purchase those that other nations produce more efficiently. When nations specialize in goods they can produce most efficiently, total world production is greater. This

---

R Reading Strategies	**C** Critical Thinking	**D** Differentiated Instruction	**W** Writing Support	**S** Skill Practice
Teacher Edition • Accessing Prior Knowledge, p. 733 • Identifying, p. 736 **Additional Resources** • Guid. Read. Act., p. 96 • Quizzes/Tests, pp. 324–332	**Teacher Edition** • Drawing Conclusions, p. 734 **Additional Resources** • Read. Essen., pp. 306–309	**Teacher Edition** • Visual/Spatial, p. 735 **Additional Resources** • Foldables, p. 69 • Reteaching Act., p. 26	**Teacher Edition** • Narrative Writing, p. 735	**Teacher Edition** • Researching, p. 733 **Additional Resources** • Ch. Summaries, pp. 76–78

Comparing Governments

Charts In Motion
See StudentWorks™ Plus
or go to glencoe.com.

Trade in the Global Economy

| Country | Largest Trade Partners, 2006 | | Value of Imports (billions of U.S. dollars) | Value of Exports (billions of U.S. dollars) |
	Imports	Exports		
United States	China, Canada, Mexico	Canada, Mexico, China	$1,965	$1,149
Japan	China, United States, Saudi Arabia	China, United States, South Korea	$572.4	$676.9
South Korea	China, Japan, United States	China, United States, Japan	$356.8	$371.5
China	Japan, South Korea, Taiwan	United States, Hong Kong, Japan	$901.3	$1,217
Russia	Germany, China, Italy	Germany, Netherlands, Turkey	$260.4	$365
Brazil	United States, China, Argentina	United States, China, Argentina	$120.6	$160.6
Jamaica	United States, Trinidad and Tobago, Venezuela	United States, Canada, United Kingdom	$5.784	$2.331
Cote d'Ivoire	Nigeria, France, China	Germany, Nigeria, Netherlands	$6.137	$18.5

Source: CIA Factbook, 2007.

Critical Thinking The global economy has expanded in recent decades. *What generalizations can you make from the list of main trading partners of the countries shown here?*

---

means that the total cost of all products is less, and therefore, the average cost of any product is less, which benefits all consumers.

Finally, nations trade to create jobs. For **instance,** the global market for automobiles is much larger than the market in the United States alone. More jobs will exist for American autoworkers if American automakers can sell their products abroad.

Barriers to International Trade

Unrestricted international trade promotes efficient production. At the same time, it can threaten domestic industries and the jobs of workers in those industries. As a result, policymakers in every nation are often under pressure to limit or control international trade. National governments use several methods to restrict international trade.

One trade barrier is **tariffs,** or taxes placed on imports to increase their price in the domestic market. The United States recently threatened to impose stiff tariffs on some Chinese goods if China did not end the illegal copying and distribution of U.S. intellectual property such as music and video compact discs by Chinese bootleggers.

Another barrier is **quotas.** These are limits on the quantities of a foreign product that can be imported. The United States placed quotas on the importation of Japanese cars in the 1970s in an effort to protect the jobs of American autoworkers. The United States also has import quotas on such products as peanuts, dairy products, sugar, and textiles.

Countries also can use nontariff barriers (NTBs) to limit or control unwanted imports. These are very strict health, safety, or other regulations that must be met before a foreign product can be offered for sale in a country. The Japanese, for example, have protected their automakers by requiring higher fuel efficiency standards and exhaust emission regulations on imported cars. This makes it harder to sell American cars there, although this is beginning to change as American manufacturers adapt to the need for fuel-efficient vehicles.

Finally, countries may use embargoes to totally bar trade with a specific country. An embargo is a complete prohibition of trade by law, and the use of one is considered an extreme measure.

CHAPTER 26: *Development of Economic Systems* **733**

Teach

Answer: Trading partners tend to include leading industrialized countries and regional neighbors; the United States and China are among the largest partners for these countries.

Research Activity
Have students focus upon the effects of international trade in their lives. Ask them to find out the origin of items they use daily (for example, athletic shoes made in South Korea or electrical appliances from Japan). **OL**

R Reading Strategy

Accessing Prior Knowledge
Ask: What is the name for someone who intentionally (and illegally) bypasses tariffs? *(a smuggler)* **OL**

S Skill Practice

Researching Have students research recent nontariff barriers used to protect U.S. consumers from health or safety violations.
Ask: Did the trade barrier damage U.S. foreign relations with this country? **AL**

Additional Support

Activity: Collaborative Learning

Reviewing Key Concepts Organize students into four groups, assigning each group one of the following topics: international trade agreements; economies in Asia; the role of developing nations in the world economy and the economic obstacles those nations face; or the role of multinational corporations. Each member of the group should become an "expert" on the group's topic. Students should summarize the text's discussion of the topic (background information and specific examples) and should exchange and answer questions within the group. Then form new groups, making sure that at least one representative from each "topic" group is in each new group, and have the "experts" teach their topics to fellow group members. **OL**

ISSUES to Debate

NAFTA Representative Maxine Waters of California asserted that "for every industry that goes [to Mexico] and opens a plant, there's a loss of jobs in our community." John Robinson of the National Minority Business Council countered that free trade would create more jobs in the minority community. Have students research and debate these positions. **AL**

C Critical Thinking

Drawing Conclusions The World Trade Organization has established "legal ground rules for international commerce."

Ask: Why do you think the WTO exists? Is it necessary? *(Students might point out that global trade can involve complex negotiations, and the WTO is needed as a mediator.)* **ELL**

Government ONLINE

Objectives and answers to the Student Web Activity can be found in the *Web Activity Lesson Plan* at glencoe.com. Enter *QuickPass*™ code USG9085c26T.

Hands-On Chapter Project

Step 4

Embargoes are often employed for political rather than economic reasons.

Besides these barriers, countries sometimes engage in unfair trade practices. The most common is dumping, or the practice of selling products in another country below their manufacturing cost or below their domestic cost in order to drive other producers out of a market. After the competition is gone, the price of the goods that are being dumped is then raised.

Financing Trade

Economists and policymakers look at a nation's balance of trade—also called the balance of payments—as an important measure of a nation's overall performance in the global economy. The balance of trade is the difference between the value of a country's imports and its exports. Thus, it is a measure of the entire flow of money in and out of a country. A nation has a trade deficit when the value of the products it imports exceeds the value of the products it exports. A nation has a trade surplus when the value of its exports is greater than the value of its imports.

Trade Agreements

High tariffs and trade wars between nations contributed to the Great Depression of the 1930s and to World War II. Since the end of World War II, the major nations have created a number of organizations and agreements aimed at limiting unfair trade practices. These agreements have created **trading blocs,** or groups of nations that trade with each other without barriers such as tariffs.

GATT and WTO

In 1947, 90 countries subscribed to a treaty, the General Agreement on Tariffs and Trade (GATT), in an effort to reduce trade barriers. Under this agreement and a revised series of trade regulations that were negotiated between 1986 and 1994, member nations meet in trade "rounds" to reduce or remove trade barriers, such as tariffs. In 1994 GATT was replaced by a regulatory body known as the World Trade Organization (WTO) to enforce the provisions of the treaty.

More than 100 nations signed the GATT between 1947 and 1994. Today 149 nations are members of the WTO, which is becoming an important player in the global economic community. The organization has its headquarters in Geneva, Switzerland, with a staff of more than 500 to oversee the various

trade agreements signed by its member countries. The WTO calls these agreements "the legal ground rules for international commerce."

The WTO hears complaints from member countries and has the authority to assess penalties against nations that violate the terms of the GATT treaty. Since the WTO's creation, the United States has brought many complaints against other nations and has also had to answer hundreds of complaints from other countries on trade issues.

Tariffs, import quotas, and subsidies for agriculture are a major issue in the WTO. A group of developing nations says that the United States and Europe are hurting the economies of developing nations by subsidizing their own farmers, thus making it impossible for farmers in poorer countries to compete.

The European Union

The EU has become the world's most important **regional** economic group. Twenty-five European nations currently make up the EU. Four additional countries—Bulgaria, Croatia, Romania, and Turkey—have applied for membership and will probably join the EU over the next few years. The gross national product (GNP) of the EU is almost as large as that of the United States. The EU imports and exports almost the same value of goods and services each year as the United States.

The European Union has been the means for the various countries of Europe to achieve full economic integration. No trade barriers exist among the EU nations. Goods, services, and workers can move freely among member countries. The EU achieved monetary integration in January 2002, when the euro became the official currency of most of the EU nations. The euro replaced many of the national currencies of Europe, including the German mark, the French franc, and the Italian lira.

North American Free Trade Agreement

The nations of North America constitute another large trading bloc. In December 1992, the United

---

Government ONLINE
Student Web Activity Visit glencoe.com and enter *QuickPass*™ code USG9822c26. Click on Student Web Activity and complete the activity about the development of economic systems.

Drawing a Special-Purpose Map

Step 4: Presenting Information

Visually Students will present their maps to the class and analyze the differences between developed and developing economies.

Directions Display the maps in the classroom. Have volunteers present a synopsis of the information their maps contain.

Analyzing Information Ask: What do these maps show that helps you understand how economic issues affect the lives of people in developing countries? **OL**

Trade-Offs in Trade?

A Continuing Debate When the United States considers trading with another country, the issue of human rights in that nation is considered. Some political leaders believe that trade benefits should be restricted if human rights are not respected. Others think that having strong economic ties eventually will influence a nation in the direction of democracy. *What does the cartoonist imply about how American businesses view this debate?*

"My government is very concerned about your government's torture and maiming of potential consumers."

States, Canada, and Mexico concluded negotiations for the North American Free Trade Agreement (NAFTA). This agreement eventually will remove all trade barriers among the three countries. Further, it ends restrictions on foreign investments among the NAFTA countries and gives shipping companies nearly free access across borders. The agreement established a standing commission with representatives from the member nations to resolve any trade disputes that may arise.

NAFTA created a large regional economic unit with more than 400 million people and a combined gross national product in 2002 of more than $12 trillion. Since the start of NAFTA, trade among the United States, Canada, and Mexico has expanded rapidly. At the same time, NAFTA has been controversial in all three countries. In Canada and Mexico, many people are worried about being overwhelmed by American culture and currency. In the United States, opponents of NAFTA fear that American workers will lose jobs as businesses move from the United States to Mexico to take advantage of lower labor costs and less strict environmental and workers' rights laws. Supporters of NAFTA have argued that the agreement provides an increase in lower-cost goods for Americans to buy and thereby decreases their cost of living. They also note that many Americans can take advantage of a growing Mexican market for goods and services.

Trade Alternatives for the United States

As global interdependence has increased, foreign trade has become ever more important to the American economy. Since World War II, the United States has generally wanted increased trade and fewer trade barriers. Yet lower trade barriers do not always benefit everyone. Sometimes workers in a particular industry may be hurt economically by the freer flow of trade. As a result, disagreements arise sometimes regarding the best approach to trade policy. The four major approaches include free trade, fair trade, managed trade, and protectionism.

Free Trade

A pure free-trade policy would mean businesses in different nations could buy and sell goods with no tariffs or other limitations of any kind. In theory, free trade would allow the principle of comparative advantage to work without interference. This would mean that all trading nations gain as each uses its scarce resources to produce those things, whether color televisions or bananas, that they produce more efficiently than other countries. The United States has never followed a pure free-trade policy because the government is always under pressure to protect domestic workers and industries from foreign competition.

Fair Trade

The United States has often advocated fair trade. This is trade that is regulated by international agreements that outlaw unfair business practices or limit tariffs. American participation in GATT, the WTO, and NAFTA are examples of the United States following a fair-trade policy. The key goal of a fair-trade policy is to create an orderly world market that does not give an unfair advantage to countries that are willing to use unfair business practices such as dumping.

CHAPTER 26: *Development of Economic Systems* **735**

W Writing Support

Narrative Writing Students will choose to write one of two short stories: (1) a personal account of a small business owner in the U.S. reflecting on the effect of NAFTA, or (2) a narrative from the point of view of the mayor of a large Mexican city, reflecting on the cultural changes occurring due to NAFTA. Encourage students to empathize with the protagonists of their stories. **AL**

D Differentiated Instruction

Visual/Spatial Point out that economists have suggested that three major trading blocs are developing—the European Union, the Pacific Rim, and the Western Hemisphere. After students mark on outline maps the boundaries of these three blocs, discuss which of the blocs they think other nations might join, and why. **BL**

Differentiated Instruction

Participating in Govern- ment Activities, p. 51

Participating in Government Activities

Objective: To gain a broad understanding of local importing and exporting.

Focus/Teach: Have students read the Background and discuss the questions to consider.

Assess: Have students complete the activity and discuss their results.

Close: Complete and discuss the follow-up activity.

Differentiated Instruction Strategies

BL Does your state or local area have any comparative advantages?

AL Discuss the concept of comparative advantage and its influence on trade.

ELL Discuss the etymology of the words *imports* and *exports*, and make a list of words with similar origins.

R Reading Strategy

Identifying Ask: What are some arguments posed by advocates of protectionism? *(Foreign investors and companies could gain too much influence in the U.S. economy; U.S. governing power would be lessened by conforming to international trade rules.)* What might be some arguments made by opponents of protectionism? *(Protectionism will interfere with the natural economic cycles of supply and demand or lull American businesses into a false sense of security, which could lead to greater problems in the future.)* OL AL

Assess

Assign the Section 4 Assessment as homework or as an in-class activity, or have students take Section Quiz 26-4 from *Section Quizzes and Chapter Tests.*

Close

Speculating Have students draw upon details from this section as they analyze the following question: How would life in the United States be affected if all international trade were suspended? OL

Section 4 Review

Advocates of fair trade claim that open exchange will promote prosperity by making available the largest number of markets for American goods. In their view, this eventually has the effect of creating new jobs for American workers. These advocates also argue that foreign competition is good for the overall health of the American economy. Competition spurs American manufacturers to modernize their production techniques to stay competitive. In the process, American consumers are offered better products at lower costs.

Finally, a few people on this side of the debate also argue that more open trade policies ultimately have a beneficial effect on international relations: By promoting economic interdependence, they say, it reduces the chances of military conflict or all-out war.

Managed Trade

Another approach to trade policy is managed trade. Here, the government intervenes in a trade arrangement to achieve a specific result. For example, in recent decades Japan has often used nontariff barriers such as very strict health, safety, and other regulations to limit or prevent American imports. As a result, the United States has had huge trade deficits with Japan. In order to reduce those deficits, the U.S. government negotiated trade agreements with Japan that required the Japanese government to allow American businesses to have a larger share of the Japanese market for certain products, such as auto parts.

Protectionism

A fourth trade policy is protectionism, the policy of using trade barriers to protect domestic industries from foreign competition and to prevent free trade. Former U.S. trade representative and secretary of commerce Mickey Kantor said the government's goal should be "to nurture American workers and industry. . . . not to adhere to some strict [free trade] **ideology.**" Some protectionists worry that foreign investors and companies will gain undue influence in the American economy if measures are not taken to prevent their entrance. Protectionists also argue that participation in international trade agreements is eroding American sovereignty by requiring the United States to accept rules that are made by organizations like the WTO.

Some advocates of managed trade and protectionism see international trade as a powerful foreign policy tool that should be used to promote American interests. The U.S. embargo on most trade with and travel to Cuba, in place since 1961, is an example of using trade to punish a hostile communist regime.

The globalization of the economy has brought many benefits to the American consumer, including new and more varied products and lower prices for goods. Yet globalization has also brought its share of challenges. The American worker must now compete with a much wider labor pool for some jobs, and economic and political decisions are now far more complicated for the federal policymakers and the U.S. Congress.

SECTION 4 Review

Vocabulary

1. **Explain** the significance of: comparative advantage, tariff, quota, trading bloc.

Main Ideas

2. **Describing** What is the purpose of the General Agreement on Tariffs and Trade (GATT) and the World Trade Organization (WTO)?

3. **Examining** Why do nations trade with one another?

Critical Thinking

4. **Drawing Conclusions** Which type of trade policy do you believe is the most appropriate for the United States to follow? Why?

5. **Organizing** Using a graphic organizer like the one below, identify factors that affect the stability of the global economy.

Writing About Government

6. **Descriptive Writing** Trade is becoming more international, and countries are linking their economic fortunes with trade agreements. However, barriers to international trade exist. Review these barriers and prepare a plan for helping nations overcome these barriers, and build their international trade opportunities.

Answers

1. All definitions can be found in the section and the Glossary.
2. GATT and the WTO exist to reduce trade barriers and keep international trade fair and regulated.
3. to benefit from comparative advantages
4. Answers will vary, but students should support their decisions with reasons based on facts.

5. Answers might include: Free Trade—quotas, tariffs, trading blocs; Economic Development—investment capital, stable markets, economic freedom, lack of national unity, military rule of government, rapid population growth.
6. Encourage students to share their plans.

Can the President Require a State to Comply With an International Court Ruling?

Medellín v. *Texas*, 2008

The president represents the nation when he or she signs international treaties. What happens, however, when presidential power, international law, and state judicial authority collide?

Facts of the Case

In 1993 Jose Medellín, a Mexican citizen, raped and murdered two girls in Houston, Texas. He was convicted and sentenced to death. Medellín appealed on the grounds that he was not informed that he had the right under an international treaty to receive assistance from the Mexican consulate. The international treaty was the Vienna Convention on Consular Relations, which the United States ratified in 1969.

While Medellín's appeal was pending, Mexico sued the United States in the World Court on behalf of Medellín and other Mexican citizens because they were not being informed of this right to assistance. The World Court agreed with Mexico and ordered Texas to review Medellín's case. Before Medellín's appeal reached the Supreme Court, President George W. Bush issued a memorandum that instructed Texas to reconsider Medellín's case.

The Texas courts refused to change their procedures for review, as requested by the president.

The Constitutional Question

In the case, the Supreme Court considered two issues. First, does the president of the United States have the constitutional authority to order states to comply with a judgment rendered by the World Court? A second issue concerned the authority of the states. Does the U.S. Constitution require state courts to follow the provisions of an international treaty ratified by the president and the Senate? Medellín's lawyer argued that if Texas did not do so, it would place the United States in breach of its international law obligation and it would frustrate the president's judgment about how to best serve the nation's foreign policy interests. On the other hand, the solicitor for the state of Texas said that it was unprecedented for the president to direct orders to state courts and state judges. If the federal government wanted to enforce a provision of an international body like the World Court, it would have to get the U.S. Congress to pass a law to that effect.

Debating the Issue

Questions to Consider

1. Was President Bush's memorandum to Texas equivalent to a directly enforceable federal law?

2. Can the president's power to ensure that treaties are enforced take precedence over the procedures of state courts?

You Be the Judge

Is the president's foreign policymaking power weakened if state courts can ignore treaties?

▶ **The World Court located at the International Court of Justice in The Hague**

Class Debate

Organize the class into three groups: one group to represent José Medellín, one group to represent the state of Texas, and a third group to act as the Supreme Court. Allow class time to develop arguments; then have each side present its case. After the "Court" reaches a decision, have them read it aloud. Also have the dissenting opinions, if any, read aloud.

The Court's Decision

The Court voted 6 to 3 that the president did not have the constitutional authority to order states to comply with a World Court judgment. Chief Justice Roberts wrote for the majority that "while a treaty may constitute an international commitment, it is not binding domestic law unless Congress has enacted statutes implementing it or the treaty itself conveys an intention that it be 'self-executing' and is ratified on that basis." Justice Breyer, writing for the minority, held that based on the history of other treaties, the Vienna Convention should be considered self-executing.

Debating the Issue Answers

Questions to Consider

1. Answers will vary but may note that although the president can make executive orders interpreting the law, only Congress has the power to pass laws.

2. Students should state "yes" or "no." Possible "yes" answer: The president has the power to enforce treaties in the states, because otherwise we would fail to meet international obligations. Possible "no" answer: the U.S. is a federal system, and the president has no power to interfere in decisions made in state courts.

You Be the Judge

Students should decide whether they think the president's foreign policy-making power is weakened if state courts can ignore treaties and explain their choices.

Reviewing Vocabulary

1. command economy
2. market economy
3. developing nations
4. newly developed nations
5. quotas
6. trading bloc

Reviewing Main Ideas

7. land, labor, capital, and entrepreneurs
8. Eastern Europe, the Middle East, Asia, and South America
9. Trade with China is opening new markets for U.S.-made products; U.S. investment in China is increasing; changes provide new sources of income for some American workers and professionals; some U.S. industries are harmed because they cannot compete with low Chinese labor costs; China's future relationship with the United States is uncertain.
10. When colonial rulers left, fears and hatreds based on ethnic, regional, religious, racial, and language ties surfaced.

Critical Thinking

11. Answers will vary but may include that by opening up their borders to trade, those countries can provide markets for U.S. products, but their increasing production also provides competition for U.S. manufacturing.

738

Reviewing Vocabulary

Match the following content vocabulary words with each of the descriptions given below.

newly developed nations   trading bloc
command economy   market economy
developing nations   quotas

1. an economy in which the government makes most of the economic decisions
2. an economy in which consumers make most of the economic decisions
3. nations with little or no industry
4. nations that have recently had significant or rapid industrial growth
5. limits on the quantities of a product that can be imported
6. a group of nations that trade without economic barriers

Reviewing Main Ideas

Section 1 *(pages 717–721)*

7. **Identifying** What are the four factors of production?

Section 2 *(pages 722–726)*

8. **Locating** Where are most newly developed nations located?

Section 3 *(pages 728–731)*

9. **Describing** How has China's growing economy impacted the United States?

Section 4 *(pages 732–736)*

10. **Synthesizing** What are the causes of a lack of national unity in some developing nations?

Critical Thinking

11. **Essential Question** How do the changes in economic policy in China or India affect the United States?

12. **Making Comparisons** Use a graphic organizer to compare land ownership in two economic systems.

Capitalist System	Planned Economy

Chapter Summary

Capitalist and Mixed Economies
★ Three major types of economic systems are traditional, market, and command.
★ Capitalist economies have private ownership, individual initiative, competition, freedom of choice.
★ Mixed economies blend capitalism with some government regulation.

Major Economic Transitions
★ Since 1991, Russia has been working toward capitalism and democracy, but change has been slow.
★ China's Communist government is trying to develop a market economy but at the same time maintain an authoritarian political system.

Emerging Economies
★ Some developing and newly developed nations rely on free markets, trade, and investment.
★ Others have chosen a socialist system, but socialism is losing popularity.

Global Economy
★ The main approaches to trade policy include free trade, fair trade, managed trade, and protectionism.
★ Trade barriers include tariffs, embargoes and unfair trade practices.
★ The World Trade Organization (WTO), European Union (EU), and North American Free Trade Agreement (NAFTA) encourage free trade.

12. Capitalist System—land is privately owned with some government ownership to provide public services; Planned Economy—all land is either owned by the government or privately owned under government regulation

Government ONLINE **Self-Check Quiz**
Visit glencoe.com and enter *QuickPass*™ code USG9822c26.
Click on Self-Check Quizzes for additional test practice.

CHAPTER **26** **Assessment and Activities**

Document-Based Questions

Analyzing Primary Sources

Read the excerpt below and answer the questions that follow.

Communist theory, which arose in Europe in the late 1800s, advocated the abolition of private property and government ownership of major industries. Read the excerpt below from Karl Marx and Frederick Engels's 1848 *Communist Manifesto.*

66 *Nevertheless, in most advanced countries, the following will be pretty generally applicable.*

1. *Abolition of property in land and application of all rents of land to public purposes.*

2. *A heavy progressive or graduated income tax. . . .*

5. *Centralization of credit in the banks of the state, by means of a national bank with State capital and an exclusive monopoly.*

6. *Centralization of the means of communication and transport in the hands of the State.*

7. *Extension of factories and instruments of production owned by the State; the bringing into cultivation of waste-lands, and the improvement of the soil generally in accordance with a common plan.*

8. *Equal obligation of all to work.* 99

13. What type of economy does communism advocate?

14. What elements of this type of economy do you think the U.S. capitalist economy has adopted, if any?

Applying Technology Skills

Evaluating Visit the Web site www.tradeagreements.gov and read about the latest global trade agreements between the United States and other nations. Prepare a one-page report that lists the pros and cons of at least three trade agreements. Include evidence to support your list.

Interpreting Political Cartoons

Analyze the cartoon and answer the questions that follow. Base your answers on the cartoon and your knowledge of Chapter 26.

"You drive a Japanese car, drink French wine, eat Chinese food, own an American computer, buy Canadian lumber and vacation in Mexico. How can you be AGAINST free trade?!"

15. Would an American trade union worker identify with the two men in trench coats who are having this exchange?

16. In the caption, one man supposes that the other is against free trade. Given that fact, what is the likely occupation or profession of the anti-free trader?

17. When you examine the list of products and services mentioned by the speaker, what additional common product can be added?

Participating IN GOVERNMENT

18. Nations of the world are increasingly interdependent. Find out what opportunities your community offers for individual involvement in world issues. For example, are there any organizations or programs that work to end world hunger? Find out how you might contribute to such efforts.

Government ONLINE

Have students use the **Chapter 26 Self-Check Quiz.** Visit glencoe.com and enter *QuickPass*™ code USG9085c26T to prepare for the Chapter Test.

Participating IN GOVERNMENT

18. Students might enjoy posting their findings on a bulletin board for class review. Call on volunteers to explain how they located the information and to comment upon the opportunities for involvement. Interested students might consider undertaking a project discovered through this activity's research.

Chapter Bonus Test Question

Ask: What is the formal name of the World Bank, and under whose authority does it operate? *(A United Nations agency, it is known formally as the International Bank for Reconstruction and Development.)*

Analyzing Primary Sources

13. Communist countries adopt a command economy, where the government owns the means of production, communication, and transportation.

14. The U.S. economy includes some regulation of businesses, a progressive income tax, and public lands for public use.

Interpreting Political Cartoons

15. No, because all they see is the products made available to consumers, without considering the effects on labor, the environment, or health and safety.

16. He could be a manufacturer who has to compete with cheaper foreign goods.

17. clothing, toys, and appliances

Reference
Handbook

Contents

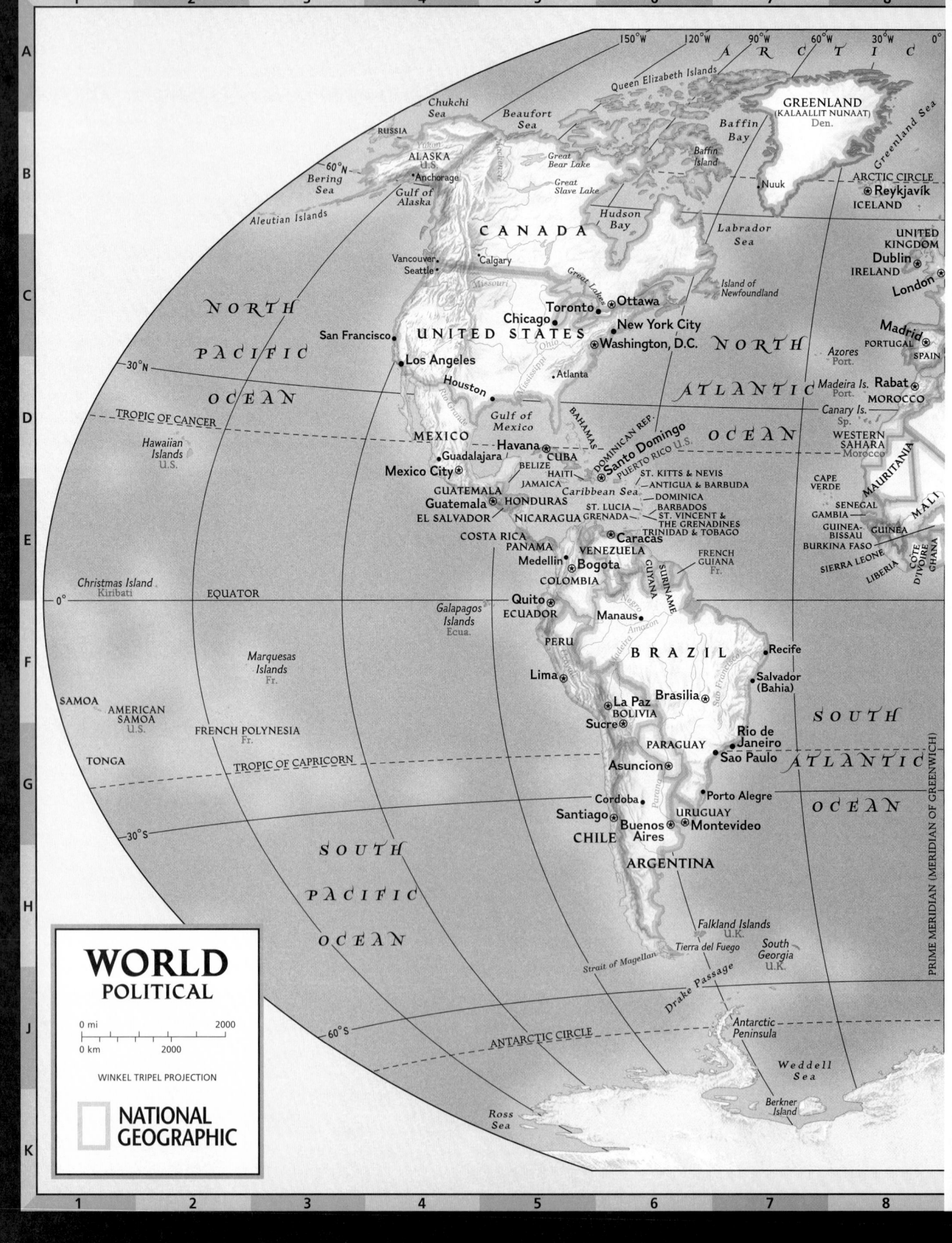

WORLD
POLITICAL

0 mi — 2000
0 km — 2000

WINKEL TRIPEL PROJECTION

NATIONAL
GEOGRAPHIC

The Atlantic, Indian, and Pacific Oceans merge around Antarctica. Some define this as an ocean, calling it the Antarctic Ocean, Austral Ocean, or Southern Ocean. While most accept four oceans (including the Arctic Ocean), there is little international agreement on the name and extent of a fifth ocean.

The People's Republic of China claims Taiwan as its 23rd province.

ABBREVIATIONS

AUST.	AUSTRIA
B.&H.	BOSNIA & HERZEGOVINA
BELG.	BELGIUM
CROAT.	CROATIA
CZECH REP.	CZECH REPUBLIC
DEM. REP. OF THE CONGO	DEMOCRATIC REPUBLIC OF THE CONGO
EQ. GUINEA	EQUATORIAL GUINEA
EST.	ESTONIA
HUNG.	HUNGARY
KOS.	KOSOVO
LITH.	LITHUANIA
MACED.	MACEDONIA
MOLD.	MOLDOVA
NETH.	NETHERLANDS
SERB.	SERBIA
MONT.	MONTENEGRO
SLOV.	SLOVENIA
SWITZ.	SWITZERLAND
U.A.E.	UNITED ARAB EMIRATES

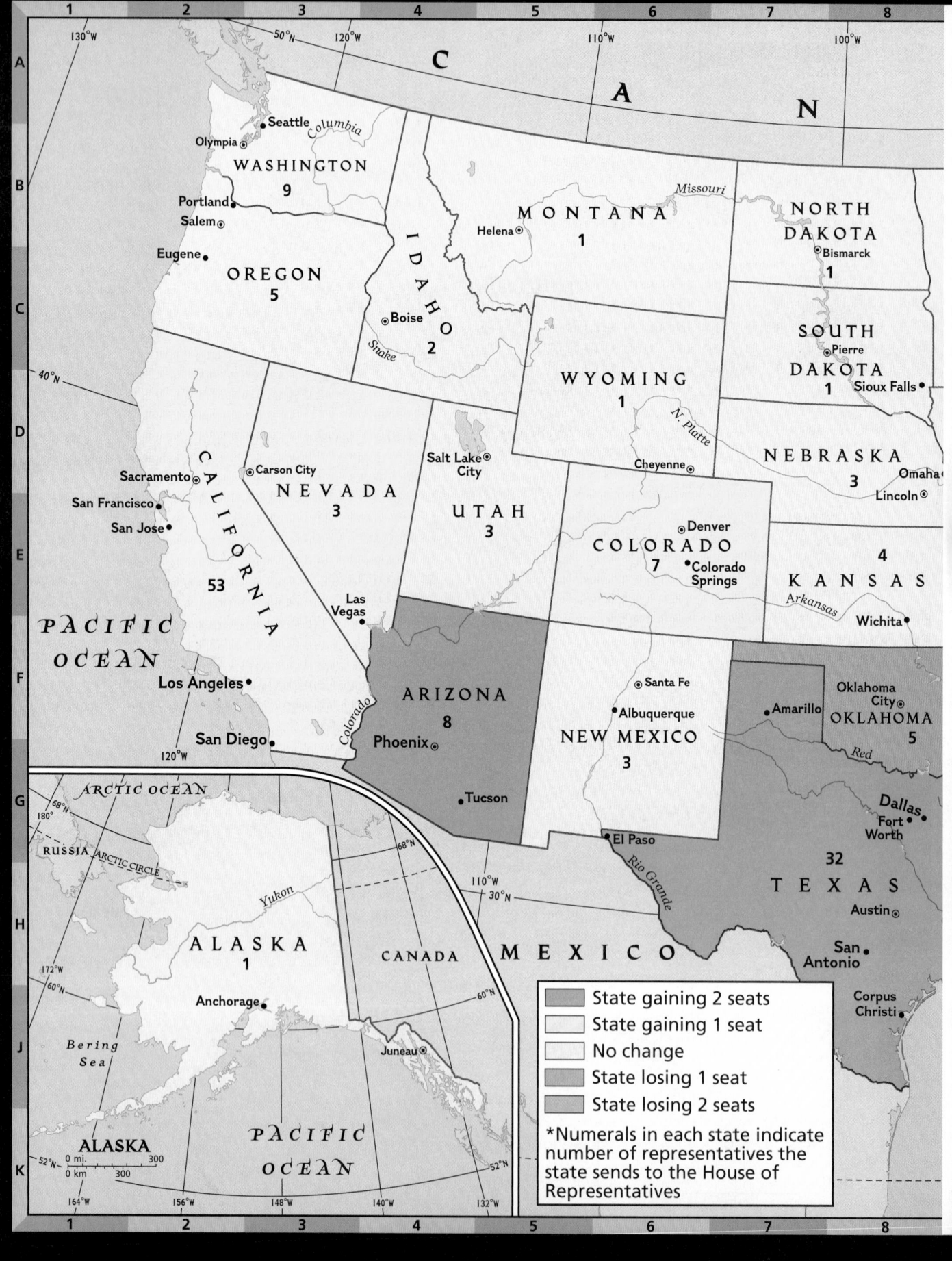

State gaining 2 seats
State gaining 1 seat
No change
State losing 1 seat
State losing 2 seats

*Numerals in each state indicate number of representatives the state sends to the House of Representatives

UNITED STATES

2000 CONGRESSIONAL REAPPORTIONMENT

0 mi. 300

0 km 300

ALBERS CONIC EQUAL-AREA PROJECTION

NATIONAL GEOGRAPHIC

PRINCIPAL HAWAIIAN ISLANDS

0 mi. 100

0 km 100

Presents of the United States

In this resource you will find portraits of the individuals who served as presidents of the United States, along with their occupations, political party affiliations, and other interesting facts.

**The Republican Party during this period developed into today's Democratic Party. Today's Republican Party originated in 1854.

1 George Washington

Presidential term: 1789–1797
Lived: 1732–1799
Born in: Virginia
Elected from: Virginia
Occupations: Soldier, Planter
Party: None
Vice President: John Adams

2 John Adams

Presidential term: 1797–1801
Lived: 1735–1826
Born in: Massachusetts
Elected from: Massachusetts
Occupations: Teacher, Lawyer
Party: Federalist
Vice President: Thomas Jefferson

3 Thomas Jefferson

Presidential term: 1801–1809
Lived: 1743–1826
Born in: Virginia
Elected from: Virginia
Occupations: Planter, Lawyer
Party: Republican**
Vice Presidents: Aaron Burr, George Clinton

4 James Madison

Presidential term: 1809–1817
Lived: 1751–1836
Born in: Virginia
Elected from: Virginia
Occupation: Planter
Party: Republican**
Vice Presidents: George Clinton, Elbridge Gerry

5 James Monroe

Presidential term: 1817–1825
Lived: 1758–1831
Born in: Virginia
Elected from: Virginia
Occupation: Lawyer
Party: Republican**
Vice President: Daniel D. Tompkins

6 John Quincy Adams

Presidential term: 1825–1829
Lived: 1767–1848
Born in: Massachusetts
Elected from: Massachusetts
Occupation: Lawyer
Party: Republican**
Vice President: John C. Calhoun

7 Andrew Jackson

Presidential term: 1829–1837
Lived: 1767–1845
Born in: South Carolina
Elected from Tennessee
Occupations: Lawyer, Soldier
Party: Democratic
Vice Presidents: John C. Calhoun, Martin Van Buren

8 Martin Van Buren

Presidential term: 1837–1841
Lived: 1782–1862
Born in: New York
Elected from: New York
Occupation: Lawyer
Party: Democratic
Vice President: Richard M. Johnson

9 William H. Harrison

Presidential term: 1841
Lived: 1773–1841
Born in: Virginia
Elected from: Ohio
Occupations: Soldier,
 Planter
Party: Whig
Vice President: John Tyler

10 John Tyler

Presidential term: 1841–1845
Lived: 1790–1862
Born in: Virginia
Elected as V.P. from: Virginia,
 Succeeded Harrison
Occupation: Lawyer
Party: Whig
Vice President: None

11 James K. Polk

Presidential term: 1845–1849
Lived: 1795–1849
Born in: North Carolina
Elected from: Tennessee
Occupation: Lawyer
Party: Democratic
Vice President: George M.
 Dallas

12 Zachary Taylor

Presidential term: 1849–1850
Lived: 1784–1850
Born in: Virginia
Elected from: Louisiana
Occupation: Soldier
Party: Whig
Vice President: Millard
 Fillmore

13 Millard Fillmore

Presidential term: 1850–1853
Lived: 1800–1874
Born in: New York
Elected as V.P. from: New York,
 Succeeded Taylor
Occupation: Lawyer
Party: Whig
Vice President: None

14 Franklin Pierce

Presidential term: 1853–1857
Lived: 1804–1869
Born in: New Hampshire
Elected from: New Hampshire
Occupation: Lawyer
Party: Democratic
Vice President: William R. King

15 James Buchanan

Presidential term: 1857–1861
Lived: 1791–1868
Born in: Pennsylvania
Elected from: Pennsylvania
Occupation: Lawyer
Party: Democratic
Vice President: John C.
 Breckinridge

16 Abraham Lincoln

Presidential term: 1861–1865
Lived: 1809–1865
Born in: Kentucky
Elected from: Illinois
Occupation: Lawyer
Party: Republican
Vice Presidents: Hannibal
 Hamlin, Andrew Johnson

17 Andrew Johnson

Presidential term: 1865–1869
Lived: 1808–1875
Born in: North Carolina
Elected as V.P. from: Tennessee,
 Succeeded Lincoln
Occupation: Tailor
Party: Democratic; National Unionist
Vice President: None

Presidents of the United States

18 Ulysses S. Grant

Presidential term: 1869–1877
Lived: 1822–1885
Born in: Ohio
Elected from: Illinois
Occupations: Farmer, Soldier
Party: Republican
Vice Presidents: Schuyler Colfax, Henry Wilson

19 Rutherford B. Hayes

Presidential term: 1877–1881
Lived: 1822–1893
Born in: Ohio
Elected from: Ohio
Occupation: Lawyer
Party: Republican
Vice President: William A. Wheeler

20 James A. Garfield

Presidential term: 1881
Lived: 1831–1881
Born in: Ohio
Elected from: Ohio
Occupations: Laborer, Professor
Party: Republican
Vice President: Chester A. Arthur

21 Chester A. Arthur

Presidential term: 1881–1885
Lived: 1830–1886
Born in: Vermont
Elected as V.P. from: New York, Succeeded Garfield
Occupations: Teacher, Lawyer
Party: Republican
Vice President: None

22 Grover Cleveland

Presidential term: 1885–1889
Lived: 1837–1908
Born in: New Jersey
Elected from: New York
Occupation: Lawyer
Party: Democratic
Vice President: Thomas A. Hendricks

23 Benjamin Harrison

Presidential term: 1889–1893
Lived: 1833–1901
Born in: Ohio
Elected from: Indiana
Occupation: Lawyer
Party: Republican
Vice President: Levi P. Morton

24 Grover Cleveland

Presidential term: 1893–1897
Lived: 1837–1908
Born in: New Jersey
Elected from: New York
Occupation: Lawyer
Party: Democratic
Vice President: Adlai E. Stevenson

25 William McKinley

Presidential term: 1897–1901
Lived: 1843–1901
Born in: Ohio
Elected from: Ohio
Occupations: Teacher, Lawyer
Party: Republican
Vice Presidents: Garret Hobart, Theodore Roosevelt

26 Theodore Roosevelt

Presidential term: 1901–1909
Lived: 1858–1919
Born in: New York
Elected as V.P. from: New York, Succeeded McKinley
Occupations: Historian, Rancher
Party: Republican
Vice President: Charles W. Fairbanks

27 William H. Taft

Presidential term: 1909–1913
Lived: 1857–1930
Born in: Ohio
Elected from: Ohio
Occupation: Lawyer
Party: Republican
Vice President: James S. Sherman

28 Woodrow Wilson

Presidential term: 1913–1921
Lived: 1856–1924
Born in: Virginia
Elected from: New Jersey
Occupation: College Professor
Party: Democratic
Vice President: Thomas R. Marshall

29 Warren G. Harding

Presidential term: 1921–1923
Lived: 1865–1923
Born in: Ohio
Elected from: Ohio
Occupations: Newspaper Editor, Publisher
Party: Republican
Vice President: Calvin Coolidge

30 Calvin Coolidge

Presidential term: 1923–1929
Lived: 1872–1933
Born in: Vermont
Elected as V.P. from: Massachusetts, Succeeded Harding
Occupation: Lawyer
Party: Republican
Vice President: Charles G. Dawes

31 Herbert C. Hoover

Presidential term: 1929–1933
Lived: 1874–1964
Born in: Iowa
Elected from: California
Occupation: Engineer
Party: Republican
Vice President: Charles Curtis

32 Franklin D. Roosevelt

Presidential term: 1933–1945
Lived: 1882–1945
Born in: New York
Elected from: New York
Occupation: Lawyer
Party: Democratic
Vice Presidents: John N. Garner, Henry A. Wallace, Harry S. Truman

33 Harry S. Truman

Presidential term: 1945–1953
Lived: 1884–1972
Born in: Missouri
Elected as V.P. from: Missouri, Succeeded Roosevelt
Occupations: Clerk, Farmer
Party: Democratic
Vice President: Alben W. Barkley

34 Dwight D. Eisenhower

Presidential term: 1953–1961
Lived: 1890–1969
Born in: Texas
Elected from: New York
Occupation: Soldier
Party: Republican
Vice President: Richard M. Nixon

35 John F. Kennedy

Presidential term: 1961–1963
Lived: 1917–1963
Born in: Massachusetts
Elected from: Massachusetts
Occupations: Author, Reporter
Party: Democratic
Vice President: Lyndon B. Johnson

Presidents of the United States

36 Lyndon B. Johnson

Presidential term: 1963–1969
Lived: 1908–1973
Born in: Texas
Elected as V.P. from: Texas, Succeeded Kennedy
Occupation: Teacher
Party: Democratic
Vice President: Hubert H. Humphrey

37 Richard M. Nixon

Presidential term: 1969–1974
Lived: 1913–1994
Born in: California
Elected from: New York
Occupation: Lawyer
Party: Republican
Vice Presidents: Spiro T. Agnew, Gerald R. Ford

38 Gerald R. Ford

Presidential term: 1974–1977
Lived: 1913–2006
Born in: Nebraska
Appointed as V.P. upon Agnew's resignation; succeeded Nixon
Occupation: Lawyer
Party: Republican
Vice President: Nelson A. Rockefeller

39 James E. Carter, Jr.

Presidential term: 1977–1981
Lived: 1924–
Born in: Georgia
Elected from: Georgia
Occupations: Business, Farmer
Party: Democratic
Vice President: Walter F. Mondale

40 Ronald W. Reagan

Presidential term: 1981–1989
Lived: 1911–2004
Born in: Illinois
Elected from: California
Occupations: Actor, Lecturer
Party: Republican
Vice President: George H.W. Bush

41 George H.W. Bush

Presidential term: 1989–1993
Lived: 1924–
Born in: Massachusetts
Elected from: Texas
Occupation: Business
Party: Republican
Vice President: J. Danforth Quayle

42 William J. Clinton

Presidential term: 1993–2001
Lived: 1946–
Born in: Arkansas
Elected from: Arkansas
Occupation: Lawyer
Party: Democratic
Vice President: Albert Gore, Jr.

43 George W. Bush

Presidential term: 2001–2009
Lived: 1946–
Born in: Connecticut
Elected from: Texas
Occupation: Business
Party: Republican
Vice President: Richard B. Cheney

44 Barack Obama

Presidential term: 2009–
Lived: 1961–
Born in: Hawaii
Elected from: Illinois
Occupation: Lawyer
Party: Democratic
Vice President: Joseph R. Biden, Jr.

Leaders of Government

Chief Justices of the United States

Name and Years of Service	State From Which Appointed	President by Whom Appointed
John Jay (1789–1795)	NY	Washington
John Rutledge (1795)*	SC	Washington
Oliver Ellsworth (1796–1800)	CT	Washington
John Marshall (1801–1835)	VA	John Adams
Roger B. Taney (1836–1864)	MD	Jackson
Salmon P. Chase (1864–1873)	OH	Lincoln
Morrison R. Waite (1874–1888)	OH	Grant
Melville W. Fuller (1888–1910)	IL	Cleveland
Edward D. White (1910–1921)	LA	Taft
William Howard Taft (1921–1930)	CT	Harding
Charles Evans Hughes (1930–1941)	NY	Hoover
Harlan F. Stone (1941–1946)	NY	F.D.Roosevelt
Fred M. Vinson (1946–1953)	KY	Truman
Earl Warren (1953–1969)	CA	Eisenhower
Warren E. Burger (1969–1986)	D.C.	Nixon
William H. Rehnquist (1986–2005)	AZ	Reagan
John C. Roberts, Jr. (2005–)	D.C.	Bush

* Rutledge was appointed Chief Justice on July 1, 1795, while Congress was not in session. He presided over the August 1795 term of the Supreme Court, but the Senate rejected his appointment on December 15, 1795.

Senate Majority Leaders

Congress	Years	Leader
62nd	1911–13	Shelby M. Cullom, R–IL
63rd–64th	1913–17	John W. Kern, D–IN
65th	1917–19	Thomas S. Martin, D–VA
66th–67th	1919–24	Henry Cabot Lodge, R–MA
68th–70th	1924–29	Charles Curtis, R–KS
71st–72nd	1929–33	James E. Watson, R–IN
73rd–75th	1933–37	Joseph T. Robinson, D–AR
75th–79th	1937–47	Alben W. Barkley, D–KY
80th	1947–49	Wallace H. White, Jr., R–ME
81st	1949–51	Scott W. Lucas, D–IL
82nd	1951–53	Ernest W. McFarland, D–AZ
83rd	1953–55	Robert A. Taft, R–OH
		William F. Knowland, R–CA
84th–86th	1955–61	Lyndon B. Johnson, D–TX
87th–94th	1961–77	Mike Mansfield, D–MT
95th–96th	1977–81	Robert C. Byrd, D–WV
97th–98th	1981–85	Howard H. Baker, Jr., R–TN
99th	1985–87	Robert Dole, R–KS
100th	1987–89	Robert C. Byrd, D–WV
101st–103rd	1989–95	George J. Mitchell, D–ME
104th	1995–96	Robert Dole, R–KS
104th–107th	1996–01	Trent Lott, R–MS
107th	2001–03	Tom Daschle, D–SD
108th–109th	2003–07	William H. Frist, R–TN
110th–111th	2007–	Harry Reid, D–NV

Speakers of the House of Representatives

Congress	Years	Speaker	Congress	Years	Speaker
1st	1789–91	Frederick A.C. Muhlenberg, F–PA	41st–43rd	1869–75	James G. Blaine, R–ME
2nd	1791–93	Jonathan Trumbull, F–CT	44th	1875–76	Michael C. Kerr, D–IN
3rd	1793–95	Frederick A.C. Muhlenberg, F–PA	44th–46th	1876–81	Samuel J. Randall, D–PA
4th–5th	1795–99	Jonathan Dayton, F–NJ	47th	1881–83	Joseph Warren Keifer, R–OH
6th	1799–1801	Theodore Sedgwick, F–MA	48th–50th	1883–89	John G. Carlisle, D–KY
7th–9th	1801–07	Nathaniel Macon, D–NC	51st	1889–91	Thomas Brackett Reed, R–ME
10th–11th	1807–11	Joseph B. Varnum, D–MA	52nd–53rd	1891–95	Charles F. Crisp, D–GA
12th–13th	1811–14	Henry Clay, R–KY	54th–55th	1895–99	Thomas Brackett Reed, R–ME
13th	1814–15	Langdon Cheves, D–SC	56th–57th	1899–1903	David B. Henderson, R–IA
14th–16th	1815–20	Henry Clay, R–KY	58th–61st	1903–11	Joseph G. Cannon, R–IL
16th	1820–21	John W. Taylor, D–NY	62nd–65th	1911–19	James B. Clark, D–MO
17th	1821–23	Philip P. Barbour, D–VA	66th–68th	1919–25	Frederick H. Gillet, R–MA
18th	1823–25	Henry Clay, R–KY	69th–71st	1925–31	Nicholas Longworth, R–OH
19th	1825–27	John W. Taylor, D–NY	72nd	1931–33	John Nance Garner, D–TX
20th–23rd	1827–34	Andrew Stevenson, D–VA	73rd	1933–34	Henry T. Rainey, D–IL*
23rd	1834–35	John Bell, W–TN	74th	1935–36	Joseph W. Byrns, D–TN
24th–25th	1835–39	James K. Polk, D–TN	74th–76th	1936–40	William B. Bankhead, D–AL
26th	1839–41	Robert M.T. Hunter, D–VA	76th–79th	1940–47	Sam Rayburn, D–TX
27th	1841–43	John White, W–KY	80th	1947–49	Joseph W. Martin, Jr., R–MA
28th	1843–45	John W. Jones, D–VA	81st–82nd	1949–53	Sam Rayburn, D–TX
29th	1845–47	John W. Davis, D–IN	83rd	1953–55	Joseph W. Martin, Jr., R–MA
30th	1847–49	Robert C. Winthrop, W–MA	84th–87th	1955–61	Sam Rayburn, D–TX
31st	1849–51	Howell Cobb, D–GA	87th–91st	1962–71	John W. McCormack, D–MA
32nd–33rd	1851–55	Linn Boyd, D–KY	92nd–94th	1971–77	Carl B. Albert, D–OK
34th	1855–57	Nathaniel P. Banks, R–MA	95th–99th	1977–87	Thomas P. O'Neill, Jr., D–MA
35th	1857–59	James L. Orr, D–SC	100th–101st	1987–89	Jim C. Wright Jr., D–TX**
36th	1859–61	William Pennington, R–NJ	101st–103rd	1989–95	Thomas S. Foley, D–WA
37th	1861–63	Galusha A. Grow, R–PA	104th–105th	1995–99	Newt Gingrich, R–GA
38th–40th	1863–68	Schuyler Colfax, R–IN	106th–109th	1999–07	J. Dennis Hastert, R–IL
40th	1868–69	Theodore M. Pomeroy, R–NY	110th–111th	2007–	Nancy Pelosi, D–CA

Party abbreviations: (D) Democrat, (F) Federalist, (R) Republican, (W) Whig

Teach

Introduction

The following Skills Handbook offers students the opportunities to practice a number of important critical thinking skills. By completing these lessons, students will benefit in several ways. First, being equipped with these skills makes students' reading more meaningful because it allows them to more fully understand the content. Second, students are getting practice in skills that they will need to do well on standardized tests.

You can use these lessons at any point in the course and in whatever order seems best to you. You can also use them as review for students who seem to need extra practice with particular skills.

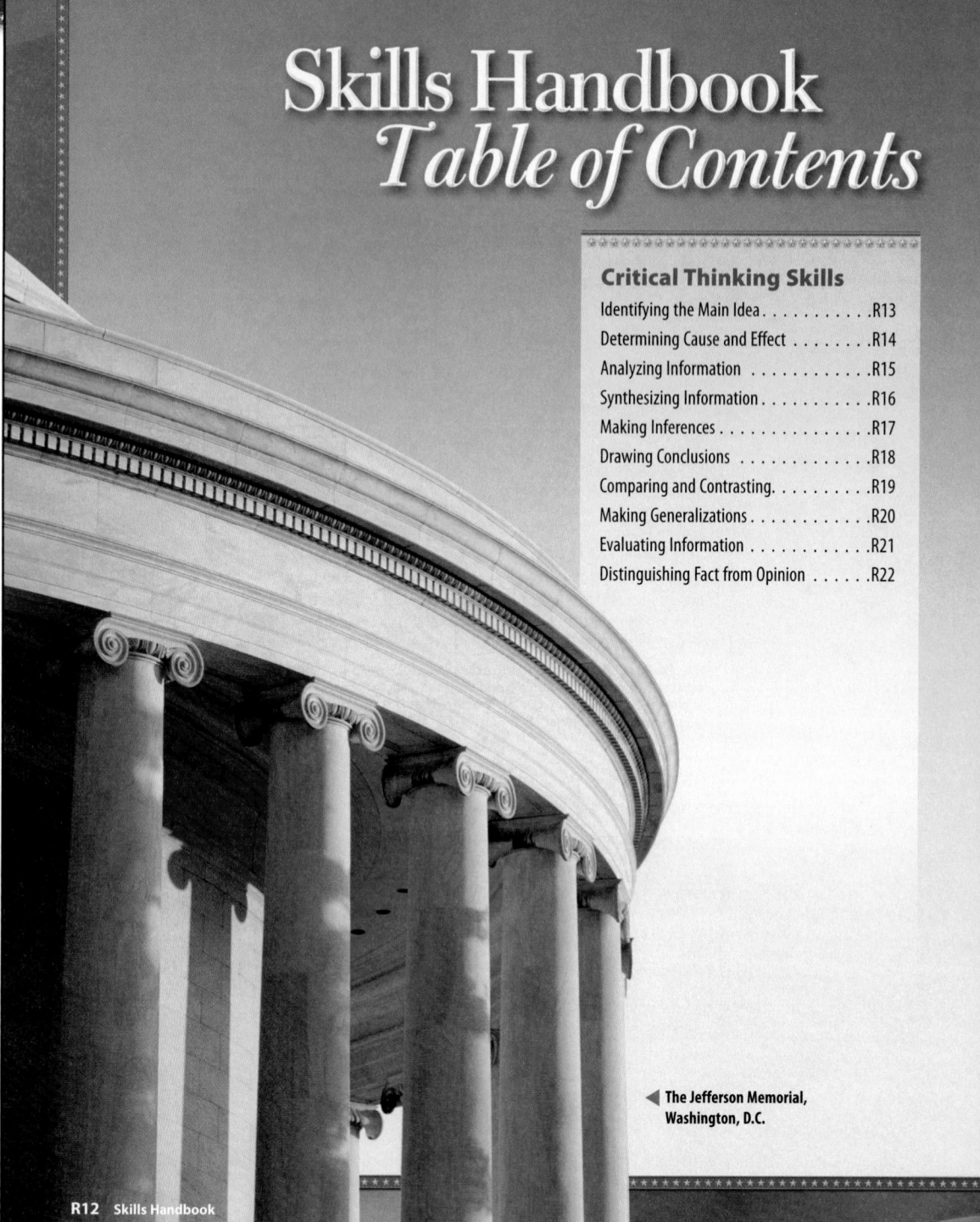

Skills Handbook
Table of Contents

Critical Thinking Skills

◀ The Jefferson Memorial, Washington, D.C.

Identifying the Main Idea

Why Learn This Skill?

Finding the main idea will help you see the "big picture." Organizing the information in front of you will help you determine the most important concepts.

Learning the Skill

When you read the excerpt below, follow the numbered steps to learn how to identify the main idea.

1. Skim the material to identify its general subject. Look at headings or recurring words to help you.

2. Determine the source and time frame for the passage.

66 *The basis of a democratic state is liberty; which, according to the common opinion of men, can only be enjoyed in such a state:—this they affirm to be the great end of every democracy. One principle of liberty is for all to rule and be ruled in turn . . . whence it follows that the majority must be supreme, and that whatever the majority approve must be the end and the just. Every citizen, it is said, must have equality, and therefore in a democracy the poor have more power than the rich, because there are more of them.* 99

—Aristotle, *Politics, 350 B.C.*

3. Notice any details that support a larger idea or issue.

4. Identify the central issue. Ask: Which sentence or phrase comes closest to capturing the main idea?

As you read, ask yourself what the author's goal was in writing the passage.

Practicing the Skill

1. Where did this passage appear?
2. What is the main topic or subject of the passage?
3. What details support the main idea?
4. Which part of the selection conveys the main idea best?

Applying the Skill

Bring to class an article about American government from the Internet or a passage from a library book on the subject. Identify the main idea and explain how you know that.

Teach

S Skill Practice

Analyzing Information Tell students that being able to identify the main idea is a key reading skill whether they are reading fact or fiction. Have students think about a fictional story they have read recently or about a movie they have seen. Students should tell their classmates the title of the book or movie and briefly explain its main idea. **Ask:** Was the main idea presented at the beginning of the story, or did it only become apparent at the story's end? **OL**

Practicing the Skill: Answers

1. The passage is from Aristotle's *Politics,* written in 350 B.C., and therefore dates from the classical period of ancient Greece; students might know that Greece had the first democracy and that Aristotle was an important Greek philosopher of politics. They can thus infer that such an excerpt is a classic statement on democracy.

2. democracy, a democratic state
3. Sentence beginning with "One principle of liberty . . ." is the beginning of Aristotle's detailed exploration of what *democracy* really means.
4. ". . . when it follows that the majority must be supreme, and that whatever the majority approve must be the end and the just." Aristotle is musing upon why the liberty of a democracy has the

consequence of majority rule and why it follows that people without great wealth will have relatively more power.

Teach

C Critical Thinking

Determining Cause and Effect The statement in item 3 under "Learning the Skill" says that "an effect can become the cause of yet another effect." This produces a cause-and-effect chain. Have students think about such chains and then come up with one that might occur in American political life or government. For example, an environmental or social problem might lead to a candidate's campaign message and election to office, the formation of a new policy, and additional budget outlays to solve the problem. Students should describe their cause-and-effect chains in as much detail as possible. They could also create a flowchart to illustrate the various causes and effects in their research problem. **AL**

Determining Cause and Effect

Why Learn This Skill?

Determining cause and effect involves considering how or why an event occurred. A cause is the action or situation that leads to an event. An effect is the result or consequence of an action or a situation.

Learning the Skill

To identify cause-and-effect relationships, follow these steps:

1. Identify two or more events or developments.

4. Look for logical connections between events or developments as in: "She overslept so she missed her bus."

Over the decades, government agencies have tended to multiply. Today a significant feature of all government levels is that there are a large number of agencies to administer programs and provide services. . . . Administrative law spells out their authority and procedures. During the 1930s, when the nation suffered the Great Depression, many new federal agencies were created in an effort to provide American citizens with basic security and health and unemployment insurance. Since then, administrative agencies have made a significant portion of our laws.

2. Decide whether one of the two events or developments caused the other. To help you do so, look for "clue words" like *because, led to, brought about, so that, since,* and *as a result.*

3. Identify the outcome or outcomes of an event. Remember that some effects have more than one cause and some causes lead to more than one effect. Also an effect can become the cause of yet another effect.

Practicing the Skill

Categorize the items below as *cause, effect, both,* or *neither.*

1. Over the decades, government agencies have tended to multiply.

2. During the 1930s, when the nation suffered the Great Depression, many new federal agencies were created in an effort to provide American citizens with basic security and health and unemployment insurance.

3. Today a significant feature of all government levels is that there are a large number of agencies to administer programs and provide services.

Applying the Skill

In a newspaper, read an article describing a current event. Determine at least one cause and one effect of that event and complete a flowchart like the one below.

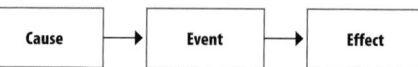

Practicing the Skill: Answers

1. neither
2. Both: The agencies' creation led to the provision of basic social services.
3. neither

Analyzing Information

Why Learn This Skill?

The ability to analyze information is important in deciding what you think about a subject. For example, you need to weigh the benefits of social services versus the benefits of small government to decide where you stand on the issue of Social Security.

Learning the Skill

To analyze information, use the following steps:

The great debate over ratification quickly divided the people in the states. . . . One group, known as the Federalists, favored the Constitution and was led by many of the Founders. . . . The other group, called the Anti-Federalists, opposed the new Constitution. . . .

The Anti-Federalists' strongest argument, however, was that the Constitution lacked a Bill of Rights. . . . Anti-Federalists warned that without a Bill of Rights, a strong national government might take away the human rights won in the Revolution.

The Federalists, on the other hand, argued that without a strong national government, anarchy or political disorder would triumph. . . . They also claimed that a Bill of Rights was not needed since eight states already had such bills in their state constitutions.

1. Identify the topic being discussed.

2. Examine how the information is organized. What are the main points?

3. Summarize the information in your own words, and then make a statement of your own based on your understanding of the passage.

Practicing the Skill

After reading the excerpt, answer the following questions:

1. What topic is being discussed?

2. What are the writer's main points?

3. Based on how the excerpt is developing and on what you already know, predict how the author will conclude the discussion of this topic.

Applying the Skill

Select an issue that is in the news, such as oil prices or climate change. Read an article or watch a news segment on the issue. Then analyze the information and make a brief statement of your own about the topic. Explain your thinking.

Teach

S Skill Practice

Analyzing Information Tell students that the Learning the Skill section talks about political issues. Have them work in groups to get additional information on the ideas and outlook of the Anti-Federalists and the Federalists. Students should be sure to indicate the sources they use for their research. When students have completed their research, they should summarize it for their classmates. It might be useful to display a map of the United States so it is clear where the Anti-Federalists and the Federalists were concentrated. **OL**

W Writing Support

Persuasive Writing Have students write a one-page persuasive argument for or against a particular response to a current political issue in the news. **OL**

Practicing the Skill: Answers

1. debate over ratification

2. that the debate turned on Anti-Federalists' insistence on protecting basic rights versus the Federalists' feeling that this was unnecessary and that national unity was most important

3. Students know that the Bill of Rights is part of the Constitution, so they can conclude that the discussion will close with a statement that it was added to placate the Anti-Federalists.

Teach

S Skill Practice

Synthesizing Information Tell students to research the issues surrounding the European Union's Parliament, to apply the critical thinking skill of synthesizing information, and to report on their conclusions. **Ask:** What are your sources? What did your sources add to your understanding of the European Union? Based on your synthesis, what are your conclusions? *(Answers will vary.)* **OL**

W Writing Support

Narrative Writing Have students write a one-page essay on the origins of the European Union based on online research. Tell them to be sure to reread their narrative when they are finished to see if it reads easily. **OL**

Synthesizing Information

Why Learn This Skill?

Synthesizing information involves combining information from two or more sources. Each source may shed new light on other information.

Learning the Skill

Follow these steps to learn how to synthesize information. Then answer the questions that follow.

Source A

. . . The main job of [the European] Parliament is to pass European laws. It shares this responsibility with the Council of the European Union, and the proposals for new laws come from the European Commission. . . . Members of the European Parliament (MEPs) do not sit in national blocks, but in seven Europe-wide political groups. The largest of these are the centre-right European People's Party (Christian Democrats), followed by the Socialists, the Liberals and the Greens. Between them, MEPs represent all views on European integration, from the strongly pro-federalist to the openly Eurosceptic.

—European Union online

> **1.** Analyze each source separately to understand its meaning.

Source B

What the constitution says:

The Union is said to be subsidiary to member states and can act only in those areas where "the objectives of the intended action cannot be sufficiently achieved by the member states but can rather . . . be better achieved at Union level." The principle is established that the Union derives its powers from the member states.

What it means:

The idea is to stop the Union from encroaching on the rights of member states other than in areas where the members have given them away. Critics say that the EU can act in so many areas that this clause does not mean much but supporters say it will act as a brake and is an important constitutional principle.

—BBCNews online

> **2.** Find relationships between the information in the sources.

> **3.** Identify points or topics that the two sources have in common. Ask: Do they agree, disagree, or supplement one another?

Practicing the Skill

1. What is the main subject of each passage?
2. What does Source A say about the subject?
3. What information does Source B add?
4. Summarize what you have learned from both sources.

Applying the Skill

Find two sources on a topic dealing with the climate change. What are the main ideas in each? How does each add to your understanding of the topic?

Practicing the Skill: Answers

1. Source A describes the EU Parliament; Source B tells what the EU constitution says about its powers and authority.
2. The EU Parliament represents all people who live in EU countries and passes laws for everyone; members are not grouped in national blocs, but in political groups, much like a national legislature.
3. It focuses on the language in the constitution regarding when the EU has the power to act—only in areas individual countries cannot affect—and that ultimately the EU must represent all the citizens of member countries.
4. Neither source makes it clear in what areas the EU Parliament will be able to pass laws, so that issue is open to interpretation. Sources suggest that it will be difficult for it to act in controversial areas.

Making Inferences

Why Learn This Skill?

To infer means "to evaluate information and arrive at a conclusion." When you make inferences, you "read between the lines," or use clues to figure out something that is not stated directly in the text.

Learning the Skill

Follow these steps to make inferences:

Because the suffrage is not a question of right or of justice, but of policy and expediency. . . .

. . . Because it means simply doubling the vote, and especially the undesirable and corrupt vote of our large cities.

. . . Because the great advance of women in the last century—moral, intellectual and economic—has been made without the vote; which goes to prove that it is not needed for their further advancement along the same lines.

. . . Because our present duties fill up the whole measure of our time and ability, and are such as none but us can perform. Our appreciation of their importance requires us to protest against all efforts to infringe upon our rights by imposing upon us those obligations which cannot be performed . . . without the sacrifice of the highest interests of our families and our society.

—from Northern California Association
Opposed to Woman Suffrage, 1912

1. Read carefully for statements of fact or opinion and list them.

2. Summarize the information.

3. Consider what you already know about the topic.

4. Use your knowledge and insight to develop logical conclusions.

Practicing the Skill

Read the statement above and answer the following questions.

1. What points do the authors make?

2. Which points does your experience contradict?

3. What inferences might you draw about the women who wrote the document?

Applying the Skill

Read an editorial printed in today's newspaper. What can you infer about the importance of the topic being addressed? Can you tell how the writer feels about the topic? Explain your answer.

Teach

S Skill Practice

Applying Bring a copy of the front page of a daily newspaper to class. Put it up on the board, and have students study it from their seats. Most students will not be able to read more than the headlines of the paper. Have them write a page of inferences they make based on what they can see. After they have had a chance to do this, have them share their inferences with the class. **Ask:** What does this exercise tell you about inferences? *(It tells you that what a person infers depends on prior knowledge and the facts at hand.)* OL

Practicing the Skill: Answers

1. Students would list the following statements of fact or opinion: Suffrage is not a right; women's suffrage would just double the vote and perhaps double the negative aspects of the vote; women have advanced without suffrage; women are too busy to vote without sacrificing their families.

2. Many students will understand that voting is a right and that an expanded franchise is associated with progress. They also will realize that wives and mothers can find the time to vote without harming their families.

3. that they were conservative, did not want suffrage, and saw it as placing an unnecessary additional duty on women

R17

Teach

D₁ Differentiated Instruction

Interpersonal Tell students that people often draw conclusions from facts they observe in everyday life. **Ask:** Consider these three facts: You hear the squealing of tires, then you hear a loud crash, and finally, you hear sirens. What is the conclusion you draw? *(that there was a car crash and possibly that someone was injured)* **OL**

D₂ Differentiated Instruction

Logical/Mathematical Ask students to research a measurable trend in the United States. Then have them explain the topic in terms of numbers and percentages. **Ask:** How can numbers support the conclusion?

Drawing Conclusions

Why Learn This Skill?

A conclusion is a logical understanding that you reach based on details or facts that you read or hear. When you draw conclusions, you use stated information to formulate ideas that are unstated.

Learning the Skill

Follow these steps to draw conclusions:

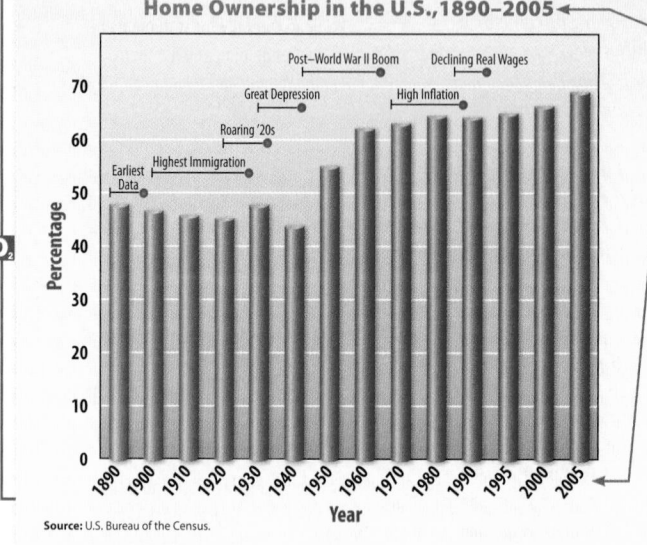

Home Ownership in the U.S., 1890–2005

Source: U.S. Bureau of the Census.

1. Read the text and labels carefully, looking for facts and ideas.

2. Summarize the information. List trends or important facts.

3. Apply related information that you already have.

4. Use your knowledge and insight to develop some logical conclusions.

Practicing the Skill

The bar graph above shows the percentage of Americans who owned their own homes during various time periods. Study the graph and answer the following questions:

1. When was the home-ownership rate the lowest? Why do you think this was so?

2. During which 20-year period did home-ownership rates increase the most? Why do you think this happened?

3. What conclusions can you draw about trends in home ownership?

Applying the Skill

Read one of the We the People profiles in this book. Using the information in the profile, what conclusions can you draw about the life of the person who is described?

Practicing the Skill: Answers

1. 1940; few people owned homes during this era of the Great Depression.

2. Home ownership increased the most between 1940 and 1950 as Americans moved out of the Depression and into an age of prosperity in the postwar boom.

3. Home ownership increases in times of prosperity.

Comparing and Contrasting

Why Learn This Skill?

When you make comparisons, you determine similarities among ideas, objects, or events. When you contrast, you are noting differences between ideas, objects, or events. Comparing and contrasting are important skills because they help you clarify your thinking on a topic or subject.

Learning the Skill

Follow these steps to draw conclusions. Then answer the questions below.

1. Select the items to compare or contrast.

2. To compare, determine a common area or areas in which comparisons can be drawn. (Typically in a table, similar elements will appear side-by-side.)

3. To contrast, look for differences that set the items apart from one another.

TYPES of LAW	
Civil Law	**Criminal Law**
Civil cases, or lawsuits, concern disputes among two or more people or between individuals and the government.	A crime breaks a criminal law and causes injury or harm to people or to society in general.
The person who brings charges in a lawsuit (called the complaint) is called the plaintiff.	In criminal cases, it is the government that charges a person with a crime.
The plaintiff seeks damages, an award of money, from the defendant.	The government, or state, seeks justice by winning a conviction in a trial and sentencing to prison or probation.

Practicing the Skill

1. How are civil and criminal law similar, if they are?

2. How do civil and criminal law differ?

Applying the Skill

Survey 10 of your classmates about an issue in the news and summarize their responses in a short document. Finally, compare and contrast their opinions in a paragraph, or if you prefer, a table.

Teach

S Skill Practice

Analyzing After students have read the lesson and practiced the skill, have them study the table on the page about civil and criminal law. Working with partners, have them compare and contrast the information on the two types of law. **BL**

Practicing the Skill: Answers

1. In both types of law, charges are brought before a court of law; in both, there is also the possibility of a punishment of some kind.

2. Criminal law concerns acts that society defines in the law as unjust and against the interests of an entire society; civil law concerns a narrower dispute, often between two individuals. Punishment in the case of criminal law can be prison time, whereas a payment of money is frequently the punishment in a civil trial.

Teach

C Critical Thinking

Making Generalizations Have students research print or online sources to find out more about the pre-Revolutionary era in American history. Then have them write three paragraphs that make generalizations about the pros and cons in the debate among American colonists over whether to rebel against the British Empire. **OL**

Making Generalizations

Why Learn This Skill?

Generalizations are judgments that are usually true based on the facts at hand. If you say, "We have a great soccer team," you are making a generalization. If you also say that your team is undefeated, you are providing evidence to support your generalization.

Learning the Skill

Follow these steps to learn how to make a valid generalization. Then answer the questions below.

1. Identify the subject matter.

2. Collect factual information and examples that are relevant to the subject.

The reins of government have been so long slackened that I fear the people will not quietly submit to those restraints which are necessary for the peace and security of the community. If we separate from Britain, what code of laws will be established? How shall we be governed so as to retain our liberties? Can any government be free which is administered by general stated laws? Who shall frame these laws? Who will give them force and energy? It is true your resolutions, as a body, have hitherto had the force of laws; but will they continue to have?

—Letter of Abigail Adams to John Adams, 1775

3. Identify similarities among these facts.

4. Use these similarities to form some general ideas about the subject.

Practicing the Skill

1. Based on the letter, what generalization is Abigail Adams making about the possibility of separating from Britain?

2. What evidence supports your generalization?

Applying the Skill

Read three editorials in a newspaper and make a generalization about each.

Practicing the Skill: Answers

1. that it will present a number of new challenges in governance
2. Adams says that if the colonies separate from Great Britain, there will be difficulties in finding a new code of laws, in making sure we "retain our liberties" under new laws, and in deciding who will "frame these laws" and who will enforce them.

Evaluating Information

Why Learn This Skill?

We live in an information age. Because the amount of information that is available can be overwhelming, it is sometimes difficult to tell which information is accurate and useful. To do this, you have to evaluate what you read and hear. **C**

Learning the Skill

To figure out how reliable information is, ask yourself the following questions as you read:

> *The single biggest factor in the inflation rate last year was from one cause: the skyrocketing prices of OPEC oil. We must take whatever actions are necessary to reduce our dependence on foreign oil—and at the same time reduce inflation.*
>
> —former president Jimmy Carter, January 23, 1980

> *Oil prices are so high, becuz big oil companys are tryng to goug us. Greedy oil executives, are driven up prices to get richer.*
>
> —on an individual's Internet "blog"

> *It's certainly clear that high oil prices aren't dulling demand for energy products. According to the Energy Dept.'s Energy Information Administration (EIA), U.S. demand for gasoline in June was 9.5 million barrels per day, a record.*
>
> —BusinessWeek, July 7, 2006

1. Is the author or speaker identified? Is he or she an authority on the subject?

2. Is there bias? Does the source unfairly present just one point of view, ignoring any arguments against it?

3. Is it well written and well edited? Writing filled with errors in spelling, grammar, and punctuation is likely to be careless in other ways, too.

4. Is the information printed in a credible, reliable publication? Also notice whether the information is up-to-date.

5. Is the information backed up by facts and other sources? Does it seem to be accurate?

Practicing the Skill

After reading the statements above, rank them in order of most reliable to least reliable. Explain why you ranked them as you did.

Applying the Skill

Find an advertisement that contains text and bring it to class. In a brief oral presentation, tell the class whether the information in the advertisement is reliable or unreliable, and why.

Teach

C Critical Thinking

Evaluating a Web Site This skill is increasingly valuable in the computer age. Point out to students that virtually anyone can create a Web page. So-called hosting sites allow people to post Web pages at no charge. This leads to a situation where a search for President Jimmy Carter will yield not only a site on his administration by noted historians, but also a site showcasing a homework assignment by someone in a class taught by someone named Carter. Ask students to search online for a topic or a person related to American government. Have them print its home page and explain why they think it is or is not authoritative. **OL**

Practicing the Skill: Answers

Students' rankings will vary. They should be ready to give an explanation for their rankings.

Teach

D Differentiated Instruction

Interpersonal Tell students that debates are forums in which facts and opinions are shaped into organized arguments for or against a specific question. Have students work in two groups to gather facts and form opinions about an issue at your school or from your community. Schedule a debate between the two sides. **AL**

R Reading Strategy

Activating Prior Knowledge Have students review the various critical thinking skills they have encountered to determine which skills rely more on facts and which rely more on opinions. **Ask:**

Which skills use facts to form an opinion? *(drawing conclusions, making generalizations, predicting, making inferences)* **AL**

Critical Thinking Skills

Distinguishing Fact from Opinion

Why Learn This Skill?

To make reasonable judgments about what others say or write, it is important to distinguish facts from opinions. Facts can be proved by evidence such as records, documents, or historical sources. Opinions are based on people's differing values and beliefs.

Learning the Skill

To learn how to separate facts from opinions, follow these steps:

1. Identify the facts. Ask: Which statements can be proved? Where would I find information to verify this statement? If the information is a statistic, it might sound impressive, but you won't know if it's accurate unless you check the source.

2. Identify opinions by looking for statements of feelings or beliefs. Opinions sometimes contain words like *should, would, could, best, greatest, all, every,* or *always.*

66 *In speaking of the consequences of a precipitate withdrawal [from Vietnam], I mentioned that our allies would lose confidence in America. Far more dangerous, we would lose confidence in ourselves. . . .*

In San Francisco a few weeks ago, I saw demonstrators carrying signs reading: "Lose in Vietnam, bring the boys home."

Well, one of the strengths of our free society is that any American has a right to reach that conclusion and to advocate that point of view. But as President of the United States, I would be untrue to my oath of office if I allowed the policy of this Nation to be dictated by the minority who hold that point of view and who try to impose it on the Nation by mounting demonstrations in the street. . . . If a vocal minority, however fervent its cause, prevails over reason and the will of the majority, this Nation has no future as a free society. 99

—Richard M. Nixon speech, November 3, 1969

Practicing the Skill

The excerpt above is from a televised speech given by President Richard M. Nixon in 1969, when a Gallup poll showed that 58 percent of Americans believed the Vietnam War was a mistake. Reread the excerpt and answer the questions that follow.

1. Which statements in the passage are factual?

2. Which statements are opinions? Explain.

3. What was the speaker's purpose?

Applying the Skill

Watch a television interview. Then list three facts and three opinions that you hear.

Practicing the Skill: Answers

1. The factual statements include:
   - Demonstrators were carrying signs in San Francisco.
   - Americans have the right to advocate their point of view.

2. The opinions include:
   - Our allies would lose confidence in America.
   - We would lose confidence in ourselves.
   - He would be untrue to his oath of office.
   - If a vocal minority prevails, this nation would not be a free society.

3. Nixon is defending his decision to not withdraw troops from Vietnam.

Supreme Court Case Summaries

The following case summaries explain the significance of important Supreme Court cases mentioned in the text narrative.

Abington School District v. *Schempp* and *Murray* v. *Curlett* (**1963**) struck down a Pennsylvania statute requiring public schools in the state to begin each school day with Bible readings and recitation of the Lord's Prayer. The Supreme Court ruled that the business of government is not to craft and mandate religious exercises. It held that the establishment clause leaves religious beliefs and practices to each individual's choice and commands that government not intrude into this decision-making process.

Adarand Constructors, Inc. v. *Peña* (**1995**) announced a major shift in the way the Court viewed federal affirmative action programs. Before this case, courts did not give the same level of scrutiny to federal programs as was given to state and local programs. After this case, all government affirmative action programs must be justified by a compelling interest.

Adderly v. *Florida* (**1966**) again applied the time-place-and-manner rationale. The Court held that demonstrators could be barred from public grounds near a jail. In so holding, the Court also pointed out that these grounds were not ordinarily open to the public.

Allegheny County v. *ACLU* (**1989**) held that a crèche (a Nativity scene) by a banner reading "Glory to God in the Highest" and centrally displayed in a city/county building violated the establishment clause because it endorsed a particular religious viewpoint.

Arizona v. *Fulminante* (**1991**) held that a confession given by one prison inmate, Oreste Fulminante, to another inmate, Anthony Sarivola, in exchange for Sarivola's promise of protection, was involuntary and could not be used as evidence at Fulminante's trial.

Arkansas v. *Sanders* (**1979**) held that a warrant was required to search luggage taken from a lawfully stopped automobile. The Supreme Court explained that a law enforcement emergency was necessary to dispense with the Fourth Amendment's warrant requirement. Because the search was unlawful, the evidence seized was inadmissible under the exclusionary rule (see *Mapp* v. *Ohio* discussed below).

Atwater v. *City of Lago Vista* (**2001**) held that the Fourth Amendment does not protect individuals from warrantless arrests for minor offenses. A Texas woman was arrested and jailed for violating the state's seat belt law, entailing a $50 fine. The Supreme Court recognized the arresting officer's lack of judgment but ruled that the arrest was not extraordinary or unusually harmful, adding that the problem of warrantless arrests for minor violations was best addressed by legislation.

Baker v. *Carr* (**1962**) established that federal courts can hear suits seeking to force a state to redraw electoral districts. In this case, the plaintiffs wanted the population of each district to be roughly equal to the population in all other districts. They claimed that where district populations differ, such an imbalance denied them equal protection of the laws. Before this case, it was thought that federal courts had no authority under the Constitution to decide issues of malapportionment.

Barron v. *Baltimore* (**1833**) held that the Fifth Amendment's provision that the government must pay if it takes private property did not apply to state governments. At the time, the decision supported the view that the Bill of Rights applied only to the federal government. However, the Supreme Court established that most of the rights contained in the Bill of Rights apply to all levels of government—states, counties, cities, towns, and agencies such as local school boards. This case has been effectively overruled by cases that apply Fourteenth Amendment protections to the Bill of Rights.

Bethel School District v. *Fraser* (**1986**) retreated from the expansive view of the First Amendment rights of public school students found in *Tinker* v. *Des Moines School District* (see below). Here the Supreme Court held that a public high school student did not have a First Amendment right to give a sexually suggestive speech at a school-sponsored assembly, and upheld the three-day suspension of the student who made the speech. In deciding the case, the Court made it clear that students have only a limited right of free speech. According to the Court, a school does not have to tolerate student speech that is inconsistent with its educational mission, even if the same speech would be protected elsewhere.

Betts v. *Brady* **(1942)** refused to extend the holding of *Powell* v. *Alabama* (see below) to noncapital, i.e., non-death penalty, cases. In this case, the Supreme Court held that poor defendants in noncapital cases are not entitled to an attorney at government expense.

Bigelow v. *Virginia* **(1975)** established for the first time that commercial speech—speech that proposes a commercial or business transaction—is protected by the First Amendment. The Court held that the Virginia courts had erred because "pure speech" rather than conduct was involved in the advertising.

Board of Education v. *Allen* **(1968)** upheld a state program that lent state-approved, secular textbooks to religious schools against an establishment clause (U.S. Const. Amend. I, cl. 1) challenge. The Supreme Court reasoned that the law had a valid secular purpose—teaching the state's secular curriculum—and that the primary effect of the program neither advanced nor inhibited religion.

Boumediene v. *Bush* **(2008)** addressed the rights of foreigners detained as terrorist suspects at Guantanamo Bay military base. The Court ruled that such suspects have the same habeas corpus rights under the Constitution as citizens; that is, they have the right to challenge their detention in American courts. Specifically, the Court ruled that operation of the military tribunals set up by the 2006 Military Commissions Act does not suspend their habeus corpus rights.

Brandenburg v. *Ohio* **(1969)** overruled *Whitney* v. *California* (see below). In this case, the Supreme Court held that laws that punish people for advocating social change through violence violate the First Amendment. The Court explained that advocacy of an idea, even an idea of violence, is protected by the First Amendment. What is not protected is inciting people to engage in immediate lawless conduct. The Court then reversed the conviction of a member of the Ku Klux Klan for holding a rally and making strong derogatory statements against African Americans and Jews.

Branzburg v. *Hayes* **(1972)** established that the press may be required to give information in its possession to law enforcement authorities. In this case the Supreme Court upheld findings of contempt against three journalists who refused to testify before grand juries investigating criminal activity. The Court recognized that an effective press must be able to keep the identity of news sources confidential but concluded that news-source confidentiality must yield to the needs of law enforcement.

Braswell v. *United States* **(1988)** held that the Fifth Amendment's protection against self-incrimination does not extend to an individual who is compelled by court order to surrender a corporation's records. First, the Supreme Court explained that the self-incrimination protection belongs only to an individual. Because a corporation is not an individual, it does not qualify for the protection. Second, the Court pointed out that the self-incrimination protection applies only to testimony, not to books and records.

Brown v. *Board of Education* **(1954)** overruled *Plessy* v. *Ferguson* (1896) (see below) and abandoned the "separate but equal" doctrine in the context of public schools. In deciding this case, the Supreme Court rejected the idea that truly equivalent but separate schools for African American and white students would be constitutional. The Court then held that racial segregation in public schools violates the equal protection clause because it is inherently unequal. In practical terms, the Court's holding in this case has been extended beyond public education to virtually all public accommodations and activities.

Buckley v. *Valeo* **(1976)** clarified the bearing that campaign finance laws had on the First Amendment's protection of free speech and association. In 1975 Congress attempted to eliminate sources of political campaign corruption with a law regulating and limiting campaign funds. The Court ruled that limiting the dollar amount contributed by individuals was allowable because the Court said it strengthened the "integrity of our system of representative democracy." The Court decided that other restrictions, such as limiting the total amount of money spent on a campaign, were not enough of a threat to government interests to justify limiting free speech.

Burstyn v. *Wilson* **(1952)** extended the protection of the First Amendment to motion pictures, overruling a 1915 case that held that motion pictures were unprotected. The Supreme Court went on to hold that a state may not ban a film on the ground that it is "sacrilegious," i.e., that it treats one, some, or all religions "with contempt, mockery, scorn and ridicule."

Bush v. *Gore* **(2000)** found that a manual recount of disputed presidential ballots in Florida lacked a uniform standard of judging a voter's intent, thus violating the equal protection clause of the Constitution. The court also ruled that there was not enough time to conduct a new manual recount that would pass constitutional standards. The case arose when Republican candidate George W. Bush asked the Court to stop a hand recount. This decision ensured that Bush would receive Florida's electoral votes and win the election.

Bush v. *Palm Beach Canvassing Board* (**2000**) was the first time the Supreme Court agreed to hear a case involving a presidential election. The Court reviewed a decision by the Florida Supreme Court to extend the deadline for recounting votes and returned the case to the Florida court for a better explanation of its reasoning.

California v. *Acevedo* (**1991**) held that the Fourth Amendment's prohibition of unreasonable searches and seizures does not require a warrant to search inside an automobile as long as police have probable cause to believe that the object to be searched contains contraband.

California v. *Greenwood* (**1988**) held that the Fourth Amendment's protection against unreasonable searches and seizures does not extend to the search of a person's garbage after that garbage has been placed outside of the home for trash collection. The Supreme Court explained that an individual does not have a reasonable expectation of privacy for trash that has been placed on public streets for disposal.

Chaplinsky v. *New Hampshire* (**1942**) announced the "fighting words" doctrine. The defendant, a Jehovah's Witness, was convicted under a state law making it a crime to address any person in public in an offensive manner; the offensive manner in this case was using profanity and name-calling in describing the town marshal. In upholding the conviction, the Supreme Court explained that the free speech clause does not protect fighting words—words that have a direct tendency to provoke the person to whom the words are addressed.

Chisholm v. *Georgia* (**1793**) stripped the immunity of the states to lawsuits in federal court. The Supreme Court held that a citizen of one state could sue another state in federal court without that state consenting to the suit. The Court's decision created a furor and led to the adoption of the Eleventh Amendment, which protected states from federal court suits by citizens of other states. In 1890 in *Hans* v. *Louisiana,* the Court extended this immunity; unless a state agreed, it could not be sued in federal court by its own citizens.

City of Boerne, Texas v. *Flores* (**1997**) struck down the Religious Freedom Restoration Act as an unconstitutional attempt by Congress to expand the Court's reading of the free exercise clause (U.S. Const., Amend. I, cl. 1). The Court then held that Congress could not pass legislation that would allow individuals and groups to disobey neutral laws of general application just because the laws might have the indirect effect of making religious practices more difficult.

Clinton v. *City of New York* (**1998**) consolidated two challenges to line-item vetoes President Bill Clinton issued in 1997. The Court ruled 6 to 3 in favor of New York City hospitals and Idaho's Snake River Potato Growers, who challenged separate vetoes. Justice John Stevens said Congress could not endow the president with power to alter laws without amending the Constitution.

Committee for Public Education v. *Regan* (**1980**) held that the establishment clause (U.S. Const., Amend. I, cl. 1) is not violated by a program that reimburses religious schools for routine record-keeping and testing services performed by the schools but required by state law.

Cox v. *Louisiana* (**1965**) upheld the constitutionality of a statute that prohibited parades near a courthouse. Acknowledging that the First Amendment generally protects marching or picketing, the Supreme Court explained that the special nature of courthouses—specifically, their central role in the administration of justice—justified the statute. The underlying principle justifying the statute is that while government may not be able to prohibit certain speech or speechlike conduct, it can control its time, place, and manner.

Cox v. *New Hampshire* (**1941**) upheld the convictions of 68 Jehovah's Witnesses for marching on a public sidewalk without a permit. The Court stressed that the defendants were not being punished for distributing religious leaflets or inviting passersby to a meeting of the religious group. The Court explained that local government officials have the authority to establish time, place, and manner restrictions on the use of public property for expressive purposes and that requiring a permit is a reasonable way for local officials to ensure that marching is not disruptive.

Dartmouth College v. *Woodward* (**1819**) held that the state of New Hampshire acted unconstitutionally when it attempted to transfer control of Dartmouth College from the trustees, the governing body of the college, to the state. When the college was created by a charter in 1769, the trustees were given all rights necessary to run the college. The charter, explained the Supreme Court, was a contract protected by the impairments of contracts clause (U.S. Const., Art. I, sec. 10, par. 1) from state interference. The Court then held that the trustees' contractual rights were violated when the state removed the trustees and replaced them with the governor and his appointees.

Debs v. United States (**1919**) followed the decision in *Schenck* v. *United States* (see below). The Supreme Court upheld labor leader Eugene V. Debs's convictions for violating the Federal Espionage Act and obstructing the draft. The basis of the convictions was a speech opposing war in general and World War I in particular. The Court held that Debs's speech was not protected by the free speech clause because it posed a clear and present danger to the nation's war effort.

DeJonge v. Oregon (**1937**) reinforced earlier Supreme Court holdings that the First Amendment's protection of peaceable assembly and association must be honored by the states. In this case, Dirk DeJonge, a member of the Communist Party, was convicted and sentenced to a seven-year prison term for speaking at a public meeting of the party. In reversing the conviction, the Court held that merely speaking at a meeting of the Communist Party was protected by the First Amendment.

Dennis v. United States (**1951**) upheld convictions of several Communist Party members for advocating the violent overthrow of the U.S. government in violation of the federal Smith Act. The Supreme Court applied the clear-and-present-danger test announced in the *Schenck* decision (see below) and once again rejected the claim that the free speech clause protects antigovernment speech and publications.

Dickerson v. United States (**2000**) overruled a federal law which stated that the admissibility of statements into evidence depended only on whether they were made voluntarily. In so doing, the Court upheld the standard set by the *Miranda* decision—statements were admissible only if the suspect had received Miranda warnings before being interrogated.

District of Columbia v. Heller (**2008**) held that a 1975 law banning handguns for most Washington, D.C., residents was unconstitutional. It was the first time that the Court ruled a law unconstitutional because it violated the Second Amendment. The Court said that the Second Amendment right to bear arms applies to individuals, not just to state militias. The Court said that, while the right to bear arms is not unlimited, the District law tried to ban an entire class of firearms that Americans often choose for the lawful purpose of self-defense.

Dred Scott v. Sandford (**1857**) was decided before the Fourteenth Amendment was added to the Constitution. (The Fourteenth Amendment provides that anyone who is born or naturalized in the United States is a citizen of the nation and of his or her state of residence.) In this case, the Supreme Court held that an enslaved person was property, not a citizen, and thus had no rights under the Constitution. The Court's decision was met with outrage in the North and was a prime factor precipitating the Civil War.

Edwards v. Aguillard (**1987**) struck down a Louisiana statute requiring public schools to teach creation science if they taught evolution. The Supreme Court explained that the effect of the statute was a clear violation of the establishment clause (U.S. Const., Amend. I, cl. 1), which is to keep government out of religion and religion out of government.

Engel v. Vitale (**1962**) held that the establishment clause (U.S. Const., Amend. I, cl. 1) was violated by a public school district's practice of starting each school day with a prayer that began: "Almighty God, we acknowledge our dependence upon Thee." The Supreme Court explained that under the establishment clause, religion is a personal matter to be guided by individual choice. In short, the Court concluded that the establishment clause was intended to keep government out of religion, thus making it unacceptable for government to compose prayers for anyone to recite.

Epperson v. Arkansas (**1968**) held that the state's anti-evolution law violated the establishment clause (U.S. Const., Amend I, cl. 1) because its sole purpose was to remove from the state's public school curriculum a scientific theory found objectionable by fundamentalist Christians. The Supreme Court explained that the law amounts to a clear violation of the establishment clause, which requires that government be neutral with respect to all religious views and practices.

Escobedo v. Illinois (**1964**) was the forerunner of *Miranda* v. *Arizona* (see below). In this case, the Supreme Court reversed the murder conviction of Danny Escobedo, who gave damaging statements to police during questioning. Throughout the questioning, Escobedo repeatedly but unsuccessfully asked to see his attorney. In holding that Escobedo's Sixth Amendment right to counsel had been violated, the Court explained that an attorney could have assisted Escobedo in invoking his Fifth Amendment privilege against self-incrimination. In other words, an attorney could have told Escobedo when to keep quiet.

Everson v. Board of Education (**1947**) concluded that a New Jersey township had not violated the establishment clause when it reimbursed parents for the cost of sending their children to school on public transportation. The reimbursement was made to all parents even if their children attended religious schools. The Supreme Court explained that the practice served the public purpose of getting children to school safely; was neutrally administered, neither favoring nor disfavoring anyone on the basis of their religious views; and was not intended to advance religion.

Ex parte Endo (**1944**) arose out of the detainment of Japanese Americans living on the West Coast during World War II when Japan was an enemy of the United States. The case began when a citizen of Japanese descent, whose loyalty to the United States was never in doubt, asked to be released from a relocation camp. In this case, the Supreme Court held that the federal government has no constitutional basis to detain a loyal citizen.

Ex parte Milligan (**1866**) established the primacy of the judicial branch in the absence of a bona fide national emergency. The case concerned the military trial of Lambdin Milligan, who was accused by the Army of conspiring to liberate Confederate prisoners from Union prisons during the Civil War. The Supreme Court held that the Constitution prohibits the federal government from trying a civilian in a military court as long as civilian courts are open and available.

Feiner v. New York (**1951**) upheld the disorderly conduct conviction of Irving Feiner. Feiner was arrested as he was giving a speech on a street corner in a predominantly African American section of the city. Among other things, Feiner suggested that if African Americans do not have equal rights, they should rise up in arms and fight for their rights. The Supreme Court said that the First Amendment protected free speech but not the right to use speech to incite a riot.

Fletcher v. Peck (**1810**) established the principle that a state could not interfere with or impair the value of lawful contract rights. In this case, the Georgia legislature enacted legislation that deprived a purchaser of land of the property. The Supreme Court held that the legislative action violated the impairment of contract clause (U.S. Const., Art. I, sec. 10, par. 1) and declared the Georgia statute null and void.

Florida v. J.L. (**2000**) established that an anonymous tip that a person is carrying a gun fails to justify a stop and frisk of the person by a police officer. Under the Fourth Amendment, such a search is unconstitutional.

Frisby v. Schultz (**1988**) upheld a picketing ordinance that prohibited protesters, such as antiabortion protesters, from picketing the house of a physician who performed abortions. However, the ordinance did not prohibit picketing in the general area of the physician's house. The Supreme Court explained that the ordinance was designed to preserve the privacy individuals expect at home. In addition, the ordinance was content-neutral and did not apply more broadly than necessary to protect residential privacy.

Furman v. Georgia (**1972**) invalidated imposition of the death penalty under state laws then in place. The Supreme Court explained that existing death penalty statutes did not give juries enough guidance in deciding whether or not to impose the death penalty; the result was that the death penalty in many cases was imposed arbitrarily, i.e., without a reasonable basis in the facts and circumstances of the offender or the crime.

Gannett Company, Inc. v. DePasquale (**1979**) established that neither the press nor the public have a First Amendment right to attend pretrial proceedings, such as a motion to suppress, or keep out, evidence in a criminal case.

Gibbons v. Ogden (**1824**) made it clear that the authority of Congress to regulate interstate commerce (U.S. Const., Art. I, sec. 8, cl. 3) includes the authority to regulate intrastate commercial activity that bears on, or relates to, interstate commerce. Before this decision, it was thought that the Constitution would permit a state to close its borders to interstate commercial activity—which, in effect, would stop such activity in its tracks. This case says that only Congress can regulate commercial activity that has both intrastate and interstate dimensions.

Gideon v. Wainwright (**1963**) overruled *Betts v. Brady* (see above) and held for the first time that poor defendants in criminal cases have the right to a state-paid attorney under the Sixth Amendment. This rule has been refined to apply when the defendant, if convicted, can be sentenced to more than six months in jail.

Gitlow v. New York (**1925**) upheld a conviction for publishing articles that advocated the violent overthrow of democratic governments, in general, and the U.S. government, in particular. In upholding the defendant's conviction under New York's so-called criminal anarchy law, the Court again rejected a free-speech defense while recognizing that the right of free speech is fundamental and that a state legislature is entitled to take steps to prevent public disorder.

Gratz v. *Bollinger* **(2003)** ruled that the use of racial preferences in the undergraduate admissions policy at the University of Michigan violated the Equal Protection Clause of the Fourteenth Amendment and Title VI of the 1964 Civil Rights Act. (Compare this with the *Grutter* v. *Bollinger* ruling discussed below.)

Grayned v. *City of Rockford* **(1972)** upheld the convictions of several hundred demonstrators charged with violating a city ordinance that prohibited demonstrations on or near schools while classes were being held. Once again the Court applied the time-place-and-manner doctrine (see *Cox* v. *Louisiana*). The First Amendment permits persons to demonstrate, but the government can regulate when, where, and how demonstrations are held.

Gregg v. *Georgia* **(1976)** specifically held that the death penalty is not necessarily unconstitutional. The Supreme Court went on to uphold the Georgia death penalty statute, explaining that the law provided sufficient safeguards to ensure that the penalty was imposed only as a rational response to the facts of the crime and the circumstances of the offender.

Grutter v. *Bollinger* **(2003)** upheld the University of Michigan Law School's use of racial preferences in its admissions policy. The Court ruled that the procedure's narrow focus did not violate the Equal Protection Clause of the Fourteenth Amendment.

Hamdan v. *Rumsfeld* **(2006)** ruled that the executive branch did not have the authority to set up special military commissions to try terrorist suspects without the authorization of Congress. As a result, Congress passed the Military Commissions Act, which provided for special military tribunals to try these suspects. The law, however, stated that noncitizens would not have the right to file writs of habeas corpus. (See *Boumediene* v. *Bush* for the Court's later ruling on that provision.)

Hazelwood School District v. *Kuhlmeier* **(1988)** held that public school officials are in control of the editorial content of a student newspaper published as part of the school's journalism curriculum. Students' First Amendment rights do not include deciding what will and will not be published in a student newspaper that is tied to the school's curriculum.

Heart of Atlanta Motel, Inc. v. *United States* **(1964)** upheld the Civil Rights Act of 1964, which prohibits racial discrimination by those who provide goods, services, and facilities to the public. The Georgia motel in the case drew its business from other states but refused to rent rooms to African Americans. The Supreme Court explained that Congress had the authority to ban such discrimination under both the equal protection clause (U.S. Const., Amend. XIV, sec. 1) and the commerce clause (U.S. Const., Art. I, sec. 8, cl. 3).

Hudson v. *United States* **(1997)** held 5 to 4 that the federal criminal charges in cases of regulatory wrongdoing could follow civil fines, if the fines were not punitive. The Supreme Court had ruled in *United States* v. *Halper* (see below) that civil and criminal penalties could not be imposed for the same act. The Court said Halper supported too broad a reading of the double jeopardy clause.

Hughes v. *Superior Court* **(1950)** upheld the contempt convictions of several individuals for picketing a grocery store in violation of a court order prohibiting the picketing. The picketers wanted the store to hire African Americans in proportion to the percentage of the store's African American customers. While recognizing that labor picketing is protected by the free speech clause, the Supreme Court explained that it does not enjoy the same protection as pure speech. The Court then held that the free speech clause does not bar a state from prohibiting labor picketing aimed at forcing an employer to adopt a hiring quota.

Hustler Magazine v. *Falwell* **(1988)** held that public officials or public figures subject to parody by the press cannot recover damages (i.e., money) for the emotional distress caused by the parody unless they can prove that the parody was false or was published in reckless disregard of the truth or falsity of its content.

Hutchinson v. *Proxmire* **(1979)** articulated the limits of the speech and debate clause (U.S. Const., Art. I, sec. 6), which provides that members of Congress cannot be held criminally or civilly liable for statements made in either house. In this case, however, the Supreme Court held that the clause did not protect Wisconsin Senator William Proxmire from being sued for libel. In a press release, at a news conference, and on television news programs, Proxmire claimed that federal funds were wasted in paying for a study of aggressive behavior in animals. Had the senator limited his remarks to a speech on the Senate floor, the speech and debate clause would have protected him from the libel suit; he lost the protection of the clause by making his remarks outside of Congress.

INS v. *Chadha* **(1983)** held that legislative action by Congress must comply with the Constitution. In this case, the Supreme Court concluded that the Constitution did not permit one house, acting unilaterally, to override the decision of the attorney general allowing an alien, Chadha, to remain in the United States. The Court said that the attorney general's decision could be set aside only by legislation passed by both houses and signed into law by the president, or passed a second time by a two-thirds vote of both houses in the event of a presidential veto.

International Brotherhood of Teamsters, Local 695 v. *Vogt* (**1957**) upheld a state court order prohibiting labor picketing aimed at nonunion employees and seeking to encourage them to join the picketers' union. The Supreme Court explained that a state cannot prohibit any and all labor picketing. (See *Thornhill* v. *Alabama* discussed below.) But, said the Court, a state can prohibit labor picketing in order to preserve the right of each nonunion employee to decide for himself or herself whether to join a union.

Jacobson v. *Massachusetts* (**1905**) upheld a state law requiring smallpox vaccinations against an individual's claim that submitting to a vaccination would violate his religious beliefs. The law was another example of a neutral law of general application intended to prevent the spread of a communicable disease that could kill. (See *Reynolds* v. *United States* discussed below.) The Supreme Court explained that the state's health and welfare interest took precedence over the individual's free exercise rights.

Jaffee v. *Redmond* (**1996**) held for the first time that federal rules of evidence recognize a psychotherapist-patient privilege, which protects confidential communications in that context from compelled disclosure at a criminal trial or in a civil trial. The Supreme Court, however, cautioned that the privilege is not absolute and might be required to yield if, for example, a therapist's disclosure is required to avert serious harm to the patient or another.

Johnson v. *Transportation Agency, Santa Clara County, California* (**1987**) held that Title VII of the Civil Rights Act of 1964 allows an employer to take gender into account in awarding promotions. The Supreme Court explained that this type of affirmative action is permissible as long as the employer is using the action to remedy the effects of past discrimination against women.

Katz v. *United States* (**1967**) overruled *Olmstead* v. *United States* (see below). In this case, the Supreme Court announced that the Fourth Amendment's protection against unreasonable searches and seizures applies to people, not places. In particular, the Court held that the

▲ **Supreme Court gavel**

Fourth Amendment applies to telephone wiretaps, and this means, as a general rule, that police must have a court order to place a wiretap.

Kiryas Joel Village School District v. *Grumet* (**1994**) struck down as a violation of the establishment clause (U.S. Const., Amend. I, cl. 1) a New York statute creating a public school district limited to a single Jewish village and controlled entirely by the leaders of an ultra-Orthodox Jewish sect. The Supreme Court explained that the statute gave the secular authority to educate to a specific religion. Also, because no other religious group had ever received such treatment, the Court said that the establishment clause was violated because the state had singled out the sect for favorable treatment.

Korematsu v. *United States* (**1944**) upheld the federal government's authority to exclude Japanese Americans, many of whom were citizens, from designated military areas that included almost the entire West Coast. The government defended the so-called exclusion orders as a necessary response to Japan's attack on Pearl Harbor, which widened World War II from a war against Germany to one against Japan as well. However, in upholding the exclusion orders, the Supreme Court established that courts will subject government actions that discriminate on the basis of race to the most exacting scrutiny, often referred to as strict scrutiny.

Lau v. *Nichols* (**1974**) held that the Civil Rights Act of 1964 was violated when San Francisco's public school district refused to instruct children of Chinese ancestry in English. The Supreme Court explained that the Chinese students in the case were not receiving the same education as non-Chinese students as required by the Civil Rights Act, which the school district had agreed to abide by in exchange for receiving federal funds.

Lee v. *Weisman* (**1992**) held that having clergy offer prayers as part of an official public school graduation ceremony is forbidden by the establishment clause of the First Amendment.

Lemon v. *Kurtzman* (**1971**) established a three-part test for determining if a particular government action violates the establishment clause (U.S. Const., Amend. I, cl. 1). First, the test asks if the government action has a primary *purpose* of advancing religion; second, if the action has a primary *effect* of advancing religion; and third, if the action risks entangling government in religious affairs or vice versa. The establishment clause is violated if the action fails any one of these tests.

Levitt v. *Committee for Public Education* (**1973**) struck down a New York law under which the state would reimburse religious schools for drafting, grading, and reporting the results of student achievement tests. Because teachers in religious schools prepared the tests, the tests could be used to advance the religious views of the school, a result prohibited by the establishment clause (U.S. Const., Amend. I, cl. 1).

Lloyd Corp. v. *Tanner* (**1972**) upheld a shopping center's refusal to allow anti–Vietnam War protesters to distribute flyers on its property. It is elemental that the First Amendment protects only against government action, not private action. The Court concluded that the First Amendment did not apply.

Lynch v. *Donnelly* (**1984**) held that a city-owned crèche (a Nativity scene) included in a Christmas display that also included reindeer, a Santa Claus, and a Christmas tree did not endorse a particular religious viewpoint and thus did not violate the establishment clause (U.S. Const., Amend. I, cl. 1). In the Supreme Court's view, the display was a secular holiday display.

Mapp v. *Ohio* (**1961**) extended the exclusionary rule announced in *Weeks* v. *United States* (see below) to state and local law-enforcement officers. After this case, evidence seized in violation of the Fourth Amendment could not be used by the prosecution as evidence of a defendant's guilt in any court—federal, state, or local.

Marbury v. *Madison* (**1803**) established one of the most significant principles of American constitutional law. In this case, the Supreme Court held that it is the Court itself that has the final say on what the Constitution means. It is also the Supreme Court that has the final say in whether or not an act of government—legislative or executive at the federal, state, or local level—violates the Constitution.

Marsh v. *Chambers* (**1983**) held that the establishment clause (U.S. Const., Amend. I, cl. 1) was not violated by the practice of the Nebraska legislature to begin its sessions with a prayer. The Supreme Court first noted that the practice had a long history in America, observing

that the first Congresses had chaplains. The Court also explained that such a practice when directed to adults is not likely to be perceived as advancing a particular religion or religion in general.

McCollum v. *Board of Education* (**1948**) held that the establishment clause was violated by a public school district's practice of allowing privately paid teachers to hold weekly religion classes in public schools. The Supreme Court explained that the practice used public funds to disseminate religious doctrine, a result flatly at odds with the purpose of the establishment clause.

McCulloch v. *Maryland* (**1819**) established the foundation for the expansive authority of Congress. The Supreme Court held that the necessary and proper clause (U.S. Const., Art. I, sec. 8, cl. 18) allows Congress to do more than the Constitution expressly authorizes it to do. This case says that Congress can enact nearly any law that will help achieve any of the ends set forth in Article I, Section 8. For example, Congress has the express authority to regulate interstate commerce; the necessary and proper clause permits Congress to do so in ways not specified in the Constitution.

Miller v. *California* (**1973**) established the test for determining if a book, movie, television program, etc., is obscene and thus unprotected by the First Amendment. A work is obscene if: 1) the average person would find that the work taken as a whole appeals to prurient interests; 2) the work defines or depicts sexual conduct in a "patently offensive way" as determined by state law; and 3) the work taken as a whole "lacks serious literary, artistic, political, or scientific value."

Minersville School District v. *Gobitis* (**1940**) held that a state could require public school students to salute the American flag. The Supreme Court explained that a general law (the flag-salute law in this case), not intended to restrict or promote religious views, must be obeyed. This decision did not last long; it was overruled three years later by *West Virginia State Board of Education* v. *Barnette,* discussed below.

Miranda v. *Arizona* (**1966**) held that a person in police custody cannot be questioned unless told that: 1) he or she has the right to remain silent, 2) he or she has the right to an attorney (at government expense if the person is unable to pay), and 3) that anything the person says after acknowledging that he or she understands these rights can be used as evidence of guilt at trial. These advisements constitute the well-known *Miranda* warnings and operate to ensure that a person in custody will not unknowingly give up the Fifth Amendment's protection against self-incrimination.

Mitchell v. *Helms* (**2000**) holds that Chapter 2 of the Education Consolidation and Improvement Act of 1981 does not violate the establishment clause of the First Amendment when it provides funds for religiously affiliated schools. The act distributes money to buy equipment and materials for public and private schools.

Mueller v. *Allen* (**1983**) upheld a Minnesota law that allowed parents of private school students, whether in sectarian or nonsectarian schools, to deduct educational expenses in computing their state income tax. The Supreme Court explained that the benefit flowed to parents and students and only indirectly, if at all, to religious schools. In addition, the benefit was neutral because it did not depend on the type of private school a student attended. The Court applied the three-prong Lemon test (see *Lemon* v. *Kurtzman* above) and concluded that the deduction had a neutral purpose, did not involve government in religious affairs, and, as noted, was neutral and so did not have the effect of advancing religion.

Munn v. *Illinois* (**1876**) held that the commerce clause (U.S. Const., Art. I, sec. 8, cl. 3) was not violated by an Illinois law that fixed the maximum prices grain elevators could charge farmers for the short-term storage of grain before it was shipped to processors. The Supreme Court explained that the operation of grain elevators was primarily an intrastate commercial enterprise. In addition, the Court noted that Congress had not acted with respect to interstate commerce in grain and so the Illinois law could not be said to interfere with Congress's authority to regulate interstate commerce.

Near v. *Minnesota* (**1931**) established the prior restraint doctrine. The doctrine protects the press (broadly defined to include newspapers, television and radio, filmmakers and distributors, etc.) from government attempts to block publication. Except in extraordinary circumstances, the press must be allowed to publish. If what is published turns out to be unprotected by the First Amendment, the government can take appropriate action.

Nebraska Press Association v. *Stuart* (**1976**) struck down a judge's order that the press covering a mass murder case could not report any facts that strongly implicated the defendant. The Supreme Court held that the press cannot be prohibited from reporting what transpires in a courtroom and that, in this case, there were no facts suggesting that press coverage would infringe upon the defendant's Sixth Amendment right to a fair trial.

New Jersey v. *T.L.O.* (**1985**) held that public school officials can search a student's property, such as a purse, for evidence of wrongdoing (i.e., violating the school's no-smoking policy) without having probable cause to believe that the student did anything wrong. It is enough, said the Supreme Court, if school officials have reason to believe that the student violated a rule and that the search will confirm or dispel that suspicion. The Court agreed, however, that the Fourth Amendment protects public school students from unreasonable searches and seizures but not to the degree that adults are protected.

New York Times Co. v. *Sullivan* (**1964**) extended the protections afforded to the press by the free press clause (U.S. Const., Amend. I). In this case, the Supreme Court held that a public official or public figure suing a publisher for libel (i.e., defamation) must prove that the publisher published a story that he or she knew was false or published the story in reckless disregard of its truth or falsity, which means that the publisher did not take professionally adequate steps to determine the story's truth or falsity.

New York Times Co. v. *United States (The Pentagon Papers Case)* (**1971**) reaffirmed the prior restraint doctrine established in *Near* v. *Minnesota* (see above). In this case, the Supreme Court refused to halt publication of the Pentagon Papers, which gave a detailed critical account of the United States's involvement in the Vietnam War. There was, however, considerable disagreement on the Court with four dissenting justices voting to halt publication temporarily to allow the president to show that the documents jeopardized the war effort.

Nix v. *Williams* (**1984**) announced the "inevitable-discovery rule," another example of a situation in which evidence that is otherwise inadmissible becomes admissible. Here the defendant told police where to find the body of a murder victim. The police, however, obtained this information by talking to the defendant without his attorney being present, in violation of the defendant's Sixth Amendment right to counsel. The Supreme Court excused the violation and allowed the information to be used as evidence of the defendant's guilt because the police inevitably would have discovered the body by other lawful means.

Olmstead v. *United States* (**1928**) held that the Fourth Amendment's prohibition against unreasonable searches and seizures applied only to searches and seizures of tangible property. The Court held that the protection did not apply to telephone calls placed from public telephones, which could be intercepted by police and used as evidence. This case was overruled some 40 years later by *Katz* v. *United States* (see above).

Oregon v. *Elstad* (**1985**) held that a defendant's voluntary but incriminating statement given before being told of his *Miranda* rights does not taint, ruin, or make inadmissible his later confession given after receiving his *Miranda* rights. (The first statement was never used against the defendant.)

Oregon v. *Smith* (**1990**), officially known as *Employment Division, Department of Human Services of Oregon* v. *Smith,* held that a state may deny unemployment benefits to a person who was fired for the religious use of an illegal drug called peyote. The Court followed the reasoning of an 1879 case, *Reynolds* v. *United States* (see below), that a person's free exercise rights are not violated by a neutral law of general application even though the law may penalize a person in the practice of his or her religion.

Parents Involved in Community Schools v. *Seattle School District No. 1, et al* (**2007**) held that public schools could not assign students purely for the purpose of achieving racial integration. In the Court's 5 to 4 ruling, the majority opinion argued that any school assignment plan that used race as a factor had to be very narrowly tailored and that factors besides race are involved in achieving a diverse student body.

Payton v. *New York* (**1980**) invalidated a New York statute authorizing police to make warrantless entries into homes to make routine, nonemergency felony arrests. The Court held that the Fourth Amendment requires a warrant for such routine arrests and that any evidence seized during the arrest and any statements made by the person arrested could not be used as evidence of guilt at any later criminal trial.

PGA Tour, Inc. v. *Martin* (**2001**) extended protection of the Americans With Disabilities Act of 1990 to professional golf tournaments. The PGA argued that allowing Casey Martin, a professional golfer with Klippel-Trenaunay-Weber Syndrome, the use of a golf cart would fundamentally alter the nature of the competition. However, the Supreme Court affirmed a Court of Appeals judgment that the ADA covered participation in professional competition and that Martin's use of a golf cart granted him equal access without changing the nature of the competition.

Pierce v. *Society of Sisters* (**1925**) held that parents have a right under the due process clause of the Fourteenth Amendment to send their children to religious schools as long as the schools meet the secular educational requirements established by state law. The Court also made it clear that although parents have the right to use religious schools, the Constitution forbids states from segregating public school students on the basis of religious affiliation.

Plessy v. *Ferguson* (**1896**) upheld the "separate but equal" doctrine used by Southern states to perpetuate segregation after the Civil War officially ended it. At issue was a Louisiana law requiring passenger trains to have "equal but separate accommodations for the white and colored races." The Court held that the Fourteenth Amendment's equal protection clause required only equal public facilities for the two races, not equal access to the same facilities. This case was overruled by *Brown* v. *Board of Education* (1954) (see above).

Police Department of Chicago v. *Mosley* (**1972**) struck down a Chicago ordinance that allowed peaceful labor demonstrations at or near public schools while classes were in session but prohibited all other demonstrations. The Court held that the ordinance was a content-based restriction; it allowed labor demonstrations but not Mosley's single-person demonstration in which he carried a sign alleging racial discrimination at a particular school. Content-based restrictions, the Court explained, almost always violate the First Amendment, but time-place-and-manner restrictions generally are accepted as placing reasonable limits on otherwise protected conduct.

Powell v. *Alabama* (**1932**) established that the due process clause of the Fourteenth Amendment guarantees the defendant in any death penalty case the right to an attorney. Accordingly, states are required to provide an attorney to poor defendants who face the death penalty if convicted.

Red Lion Broadcasting Co. v. *FCC* (**1969**) is one of a number of Supreme Court cases that make it clear that First Amendment rights of broadcasts are not as broad as the rights of the print media. In this case, the Court upheld two FCC regulations requiring broadcasters to give free reply-time to 1) persons criticized in political editorials and 2) persons who are attacked by others as the latter express their views on a controversial subject.

Reed v. *Reed* (**1971**) was the first Supreme Court case to hold that discrimination on the basis of sex violates the equal protection clause (U.S. Const., Amend. XIV, sec. 1). At issue in the case was a state law that preferred males to females as the administrators of estates, even though both might be equally qualified to serve as administrators. The Court held that such a mandatory preference serves no purpose but to discriminate—a basic violation of the equal protection clause.

Regents of the University of California v. Bakke (**1978**) was the first Supreme Court decision to suggest that an affirmative action program could be justified on the basis of diversity. The Supreme Court explained that racial quotas were not permissible under the equal protection clause (U.S. Const., Amend. XIV, sec. 1), but that the diversity rationale was a legitimate interest that would allow a state medical school to consider an applicant's race in evaluating his or her application for admission. (Several more recent Supreme Court cases suggest that the diversity rationale is no longer enough to defend an affirmative action program.)

Reno v. American Civil Liberties Union (**1997**) tested the Communications Decency Act that made it a crime to distribute "indecent" material over computer online networks. The Court said that protecting children from pornography did not supersede the right to freedom of expression, adding that the act was unenforceable with the current technology.

Reno v. Condon (**2000**) upheld The Driver's Privacy Protection Act of 1994. The law restricts the ability of a state to disclose a driver's personal information without the driver's consent. According to the Court, the law does not violate states' rights guaranteed in the Tenth Amendment or the Eleventh Amendment provision that suits against a state be tried in a state court.

Reynolds v. Sims (**1964**) extended the one-person, one-vote doctrine announced in *Wesberry* v. *Sanders* (see below) to state legislative elections. The Court held that the inequality of representation in the Alabama legislature violated the equal protection clause of the Fourteenth Amendment.

Reynolds v. United States (**1879**) was the first major Supreme Court case to consider the impact of neutral laws of general application on religious practices. (A neutral law of general application is one that is intended to protect the public health and safety and applies to everyone regardless of religious belief or affiliation. Such a law is not intended to affect adversely any religious belief or practice but may have indirect adverse effects.) The case presented a free exercise challenge by a Mormon to a federal law making it unlawful to practice polygamy (marriage in which a person has more than one spouse). The Mormon religion permitted a male to have more than one wife. The Court upheld the statute, saying that Congress did not have the authority to legislate with respect to religious beliefs but did have the authority to legislate with respect to actions that subvert good order.

Rhodes v. Chapman (**1981**) held that the Eighth Amendment's prohibition against cruel and unusual punishment is not violated when prison authorities house two inmates in a cell built for only one inmate.

Richmond Newspapers, Inc. v. Virginia (**1980**) established that both the public and the press have a First Amendment right to attend trials. The Supreme Court observed that the importance of a trial is the fundamental fact that the defendant's guilt or innocence is being determined and then explained that the fairness of the guilt/innocence determination is dependent, in part, on the openness of the proceeding.

Richmond v. J.A. Croson Co. (**1989**) held that state and local governments must have a compelling interest, i.e., an exceedingly important interest, in order to implement affirmative action programs. One such interest is remedying discrimination against racial minorities. However, the Supreme Court struck down a Richmond, Virginia, program that gave at least 30 percent of the city's construction contracts to minority-owned businesses. The Court said that there was no proof of racial discrimination, so nothing would be remedied by the program.

Roe v. Wade (**1973**) held that females have a constitutional right under various provisions of the Constitution—most notably, the due process clause (Amend. XIV, sec. 1)—to decide whether to terminate a pregnancy. The Supreme Court's decision in this case was the most significant in a long line of decisions over a period of 50 years that recognized a constitutional right of privacy, even though the word privacy is not found in the Constitution.

Santa Fe School District v. Doe (**2000**) ruled that the Santa Fe School District violated the establishment clause of the First Amendment when it allowed a student council member to deliver a prayer over the intercom before varsity football games.

Santobello v. New York (**1971**) put the Supreme Court's stamp of approval on plea bargaining. The Supreme Court explained that plea bargaining is an essential component in the administration of justice. The Court's decision established that a prosecutor must live up to the terms of a plea agreement, although the Court also made it clear that a defendant does not have an absolute right to have the trial judge accept a guilty plea or a plea agreement.

Schechter Poultry Corporation v. United States (**1935**) overturned the conviction of the employers, who were charged with violating wage and hour limitations of a law adopted under the authority of the National Industrial Recovery Act. The Court held that because the defendants did not sell poultry in interstate commerce, they were not subject to federal regulations on wages and hours.

Schenck v. Pro-Choice Network of Western New York (**1997**) upheld parts of an injunction aimed at antiabortion protesters and regulating the manner in which they could conduct their protests. The Supreme Court upheld the creation of a fixed 15-foot buffer zone separating protesters from clinic patrons and employees; the Court also upheld a cease-and-desist order under which a protester must move away from any person who indicates that he or she does not want to hear the protester's message. But the Court struck down the "floating buffer zone" that had allowed protesters who maintained a 15-foot distance to move along with patrons and employees.

Schenck v. United States (**1919**) upheld convictions under the Federal Espionage Act. The defendants were charged with distributing leaflets aimed at inciting draft resistance during World War I; their defense was that their antidraft speech was protected by the free speech clause (U.S. Const., Amend. I, cl. 2).

The Supreme Court explained that whether or not speech is protected depends on the context in which it occurs. Here, said the Court, the context was the nation's war effort. Because the defendants' antidraft rhetoric created a "clear and present danger" to the success of the war effort, it was not protected speech.

Sheppard v. Maxwell (**1966**) made it clear that a criminal defendant's Sixth Amendment right to a fair trial can justify restrictions on the press's First Amendment rights. The Supreme Court, however, was careful to explain that any restrictions on the press must be no broader than necessary to ensure that the defendant is tried in court and not in the press.

The Slaughterhouse Cases (**1873**) upheld Louisiana laws regulating the butcher trade. This decision was rendered shortly after the Civil War. It narrowly interpreted the privileges and immunities clause, as well as the due process and equal protection clauses. At the time, the Court saw these provisions as securing the rights of newly freed enslaved persons, not protecting the ordinary contract rights of businesspeople.

Texas v. Johnson (**1989**) held that burning an American flag is expressive conduct protected by the First Amendment. Expressive conduct, the Supreme Court explained, is conduct that is intended by the actor to convey a message, and the message that the actor intends to convey is one that observers likely would understand. The Court applied the O'Brien test (see *United States v. O'Brien*) under which the government can punish a person for conduct that might have an expressive component as long as the punishment advances an important government interest that is unrelated to the content of speech. The Court then reversed the conviction of Gregory Johnson for desecrating a venerated object—burning an American flag at the 1984 Republican National Convention to protest the policies of the Reagan administration. The Court explained that Johnson was convicted solely because of the content of his speech.

Thornhill v. Alabama (**1940**) reversed the conviction of the president of a local union for violating an Alabama statute that prohibited only labor picketing. Byron Thornhill was peaceably picketing his employer during an authorized strike when he was arrested and charged. In reaching its decision, the Supreme Court expressly held that the free speech clause protects speech about the facts and circumstances of a labor dispute.

Tinker v. Des Moines School District (**1969**) extended First Amendment protection to public school students in the now-famous statement that "it can hardly be argued that either students or teachers shed their constitutional rights of freedom of speech or expression at the schoolhouse gate." The Supreme Court then held that a public school could not suspend students who wore black armbands to school to symbolize their opposition to the Vietnam War. In so holding, the Court likened the students' conduct to pure speech and decided it on that basis.

Train v. City of New York (**1975**) held that if Congress directs the executive branch to spend funds that Congress has appropriated, the executive branch must do so. In this case, Congress, over a presidential veto, appropriated federal funds for state and local sewer projects. The president directed the head of the Environmental Protection Agency to distribute only some of the appropriated funds. The Supreme Court held that the president must comply with Congress's spending directives.

Turner Broadcasting System, Inc. v. *FCC* (**1997**) upheld the must-carry provisions of the Cable Television Consumer Protection and Competition Act against a challenge by cable television operators that the provisions violated their free speech rights. The must-carry provisions require a cable operator with 12 or more channels to set aside one-third of its capacity for use by broadcast television stations, such as CBS, at no cost. The provisions did not violate the First Amendment because they served several important government interests and did not restrict any more speech than necessary to achieve those interests.

United States v. *E.C. Knight Co.* (**1895**) gave a very narrow reading to the term *commerce* in deciding if a manufacturing monopoly violated the Sherman Antitrust Act. (Congress used its authority to regulate interstate commerce—U.S. Const., Art. I, sec. 8, cl. 3—to enact the Antitrust Act.) The Supreme Court held that commerce meant only the dollars and cents marketing of goods, not the production of goods that ultimately would be marketed. Note, however, that the Court's decision has been eroded over the years and is no longer valid.

United States v. *Eichman* (**1990**) struck down the Federal Flag Protection Act because it punishes the content of expressive speech. The Court concluded: "The Government may not prohibit the expression of an idea simply because society finds the idea itself offensive or disagreeable."

United States v. *Halper* (**1989**) held that the double jeopardy clause (U.S. Const., Amend. V, cl. 2), which prohibits multiple punishments for the same offense, can be violated by imposing a criminal and a civil penalty on an individual for the same conduct. In this case, the conduct was submitting false bills to the federal government. First the defendant received a criminal sanction (imprisonment) after a criminal trial; that penalty was followed by a civil sanction (a large fine) after a civil trial. The Court explained that the fine ($130,000) was punishment under the double jeopardy clause because it was grossly disproportionate to the total amount of the false bills ($585).

United States v. *Leon* (**1984**) created the good-faith exception to the exclusionary rule. In this case, a magistrate issued an arrest warrant that appeared to be valid but was later determined to be deficient because the facts on which it was based did not amount to probable cause.

However, officers served the warrant and, in the process, uncovered evidence used at Leon's trial. The Supreme Court explained that neither the officers nor the criminal justice system should be penalized for the magistrate's mistake. The good-faith exception transforms evidence otherwise inadmissible under the Fourth Amendment into admissible evidence.

United States v. *Nixon* (**1974**) made it clear that the president is not above the law. In the early 1970s, President Richard Nixon was named as an unindicted coconspirator in the criminal investigation that arose in the aftermath of a break-in at the offices of the Democratic Party in Washington, D.C. A federal judge ordered President Nixon to turn over tapes of conversations he had with his advisers. Nixon resisted the order, claiming that the conversations were entitled to absolute confidentiality by Article II of the Constitution. The Supreme Court disagreed and held that only those presidential conversations and communications that relate to performing the duties of the office of president are confidential and protected from a judicial order of disclosure.

United States v. *O'Brien* (**1968**) upheld the conviction of David Paul O'Brien for burning his draft card to dramatize his opposition to the Vietnam War, in violation of a regulation requiring a draft registrant to keep his card in his possession at all times. The Court held that symbolic speech was not a defense to a draft-card burning charge because the regulation: 1) served a valid government interest unrelated to the suppression of speech; 2) was narrowly drawn to serve the identified government interest; and 3) left open alternative channels of sending the same message.

United States v. *Playboy* (**2000**) struck down Section 505 of the Telecommunications Act of 1996 because it violated the First Amendment. The act required cable television operators to fully block channels devoted to sexually oriented programs or limit their transmission to hours when children are unlikely to be viewing television. The Court claimed that the way the law addressed the problem was too restrictive.

Vernonia School District 47J v. *Acton* (**1995**) held that the Fourth Amendment's prohibition of unreasonable searches and seizures was not violated by a public school district's policy of conducting random, suspicionless drug tests of all students participating in interscholastic athletics. The Supreme Court explained that the district's interest in combating drug use outweighed the students' privacy interests.

***Washington v. Davis* (1976)** held that the equal protection clause (U.S. Const., Amend. XIV, sec. 1) is not violated by government actions that have a disproportionate negative impact on members of a particular race or ethnic group. At issue in the case was a test given to police applicants on which white applicants scored higher than African American applicants. The Supreme Court explained that the equal protection clause is violated only by actions taken for the purpose of discriminating against individuals on the basis of race, ethnicity, or other improper factors.

***Watkins v. United States* (1957)** limited the authority of congressional committees to hold witnesses in contempt for refusing to answer questions. The Supreme Court explained that a witness can be required to answer questions posed by a committee of Congress, but only if the questions are relevant to the committee's purpose. The Court also held that a witness before a congressional committee can invoke the Fifth Amendment's privilege against self-incrimination.

***Weeks v. United States* (1914)** created the exclusionary rule as the remedy for an unconstitutional search or seizure (U.S. Const., Amend. IV). Under the exclusionary rule, evidence seized as a result of an unconstitutional search or seizure cannot be used as evidence of guilt at a later criminal trial. The Supreme Court applied the rule only against federal officers because, at that time, the Bill of Rights was thought to apply only to the federal government.

***Wesberry v. Sanders* (1964)** established the one-person, one-vote doctrine in elections for the U.S. House of Representatives. The doctrine ensures that the vote of each voter has the same weight as the vote of every other voter. This decision means that the voting population of each congressional district within a state must be as nearly equal as possible.

***West Coast Hotel Co. v. Parrish* (1937)** upheld a Washington state statute that authorized a state commission to fix the minimum wages of women and minors. The statute was challenged as a violation of the right to contract. The Supreme Court explained that the right to contract, like most of the rights protected by the due process clause (U.S. Const., Amend. XIV, sec. 1), is not absolute. The Court held that the right to contract was outweighed by the state's interest in protecting the health, safety, and security of vulnerable workers.

***West Virginia State Board of Education v. Barnette* (1943)** made it clear that the free exercise clause (U.S. Const., Amend. I)

forbids the government from requiring a person to swear to a belief. The Supreme Court struck down a state law requiring public school students to salute the American flag and recite the Pledge of Allegiance. Parents and students of the Jehovah's Witness faith claimed that the law violated their free exercise rights because their religion prohibits them from pledging allegiance to anything other than God. The Court agreed and held that the state had no interest compelling enough to justify the law.

***Westside Community Schools v. Mergens* (1990)** upheld the Federal Equal Access Act, which provides that public schools that open their facilities to noncurricular student groups must make their facilities equally available to student religious groups.

***Whitney v. California* (1927)** upheld the California Criminal Syndicalism Act against a claim that the statute violated First Amendment rights of speech and association. The statute made it a crime for anyone to become a member of any group known to espouse political change, particularly change that would affect the distribution of wealth in the country.

***Whren v. United States* (1996)** held that the Fourth Amendment's prohibition against unreasonable searches and seizures was not violated when police stopped an automobile for minor traffic violations and discovered illegal drugs in the process. In deciding this case, the Supreme Court rejected the defendant's claim that the real reason the police stopped the vehicle was to search for drugs and that the traffic violations were a pretext. The traffic violations provided probable cause for the stop and that, said the Court, is all the Fourth Amendment requires.

***Wisconsin v. Mitchell* (1993)** upheld a Wisconsin statute that increased the penalty imposed for certain crimes if the victim was selected on the basis of race. Here the victim of a severe beating was picked because he was African American. The Supreme Court explained that the enhanced penalty did not punish speech; Mitchell remained free to think or say what he pleased on matters of race. The Court also explained that penalties are enhanced in a variety of circumstances, such as when a murder victim is a police officer or under or over a certain age, and that the First Amendment is not violated when a murder sentence is enhanced from life imprisonment to death because race was a factor in the killing of the victim.

***Wisconsin v. Yoder* (1972)** ruled that Wisconsin's compulsory education laws must yield to the concerns of

Amish parents that sending their children to public school after the eighth grade exposed the children to influences that undermined their religious faith and religious practices.

Wolman v. *Walter* (**1977**) held that the establishment clause (U.S. Const., Amend. I, cl. 1) was not violated by an Ohio law that provided textbooks, testing services, and diagnostic and therapeutic services at state expense to all children, including children attending religious schools. The Supreme Court explained that a general program undertaken to ensure the health and welfare of all children was not unconstitutional simply because the program might provide an indirect benefit to religious schools. However, the Court struck down a provision that reimbursed religious schools for the cost of field trips, because the religious schools determined the purpose and destination of the trips and thus could select such trips based on the support they would lend to the schools' religious precepts.

Woodson v. *North Carolina* (**1976**) held that a state may not make the death penalty mandatory upon conviction for a particular offense. The Supreme Court explained that the death penalty is a particularized punishment; it can be imposed only after a jury (or a judge, in some instances) looks at the offender as an individual and at the facts of the crime and at the offender's character and life history.

Yates v. *United States* (**1957**) reversed the Smith Act convictions of five Communist Party officials. In reaching its decision, the Supreme Court distinguished between teaching and advocating an idea—the violent overthrow of the U.S. government—and teaching and advocating various concrete violent acts intended to overthrow the government. Speech advocating a violent idea is protected by the free speech clause, while speech advocating violent action is not.

Youngstown Sheet & Tube Co. v. *Sawyer (the Steel Seizure Case)* (**1952**) arose when a nationwide strike of steelworkers threatened to shut down the industry at the height of the Korean War. (Steel production was essential to the war effort.) To avert the strike, President Harry S. Truman ordered the secretary of commerce to take over the steel mills and keep them running. The Supreme Court held that the president must relinquish control of the mills because he had exceeded his constitutional authority. The Court specifically held that the president's authority as commander in chief did not justify his action. The Court explained that only Congress could "nationalize" an industry; if Congress did so, the president, who is constitutionally required to execute the law, would be authorized to seize and operate the mills.

Zemel v. *Rusk* (**1965**) placed a national-security limitation on a citizen's right to travel abroad. In this case, a citizen tried to get a visa to travel to Cuba, a Communist country with very tense relations with the United States in the early to mid-1960s. The State Department denied the visa request, and the Supreme Court affirmed, citing the "weightiest considerations of national security" as illustrated by the Cuban missile crisis of 1962 that had the United States on the brink of war with the Soviet Union.

Zorach v. *Clauson* (**1952**) upheld a New York City program that allowed students to be released early from school to attend religious classes in church buildings, not in public schools as in *McCollum* v. *Board of Education* (see above). The Supreme Court explained that all costs of the program were borne by the participating religions and that no public money, no public facility, and no public employee had any involvement with the program.

◄ **Scales of Justice**

Declaration of Independence

JULY 4, 1776

▲ Liberty Bell

DELEGATES AT THE SECOND CONTINENTAL CONGRESS faced an enormous task. The war against Great Britain had begun, but to many colonists the purpose for fighting was unclear. As sentiment increased for a complete break with Britain, Congress decided to act. A committee was appointed to prepare a document that declared the thirteen colonies free and independent from Britain. More important, the committee needed to explain why separation was the only fitting solution to long-standing disputes with Parliament and the British Crown. Thomas Jefferson was assigned to write a working draft of this document, which was then revised. It was officially adopted on July 4, 1776. More than any other action of Congress, the Declaration of Independence served to make the American colonists one people.

▲ *The Second Continental Congress* by Edward Savage

In Congress, July 4, 1776. The unanimous
Declaration of the thirteen united States of America,

Preamble

When in the Course of human events, it becomes necessary for one people to dissolve the political bands which have connected them with another, and to assume among the powers of the earth, the separate and equal station to which the Laws of Nature and of Nature's God entitle them, a decent respect to the opinions of mankind requires that they should declare the causes which impel them to the separation.—

Declaration of Natural Rights

We hold these truths to be self-evident, that all men are created equal, that they are endowed by their Creator with certain unalienable Rights, that among these are Life, Liberty, and the pursuit of Happiness.—

That to secure these rights, Governments are instituted among Men, deriving their just powers from the consent of the governed,—

That whenever any Form of Government becomes destructive of these ends, it is the Right of the People to alter or to abolish it, and to institute new Government, laying its foundation on such principles and organizing its powers in such form, as to them shall seem most likely to effect their Safety and Happiness. Prudence, indeed, will dictate that Governments long established should not be changed for light and transient causes; and accordingly all experience hath shewn, that mankind are more disposed to suffer, while evils are sufferable, than to right themselves by abolishing the forms to which they are accustomed. But when a long train of abuses and usurpations, pursuing invariably the same Object evinces a design to reduce them under absolute Despotism, it is their right, it is their duty, to throw off such Government, and to provide new Guards for their future security.—

List of Grievances

Such has been the patient sufferance of these Colonies; and such is now the necessity which constrains them to alter their former Systems of Government. The history of the present King of Great Britain is a history of repeated injuries and usurpations, all having in direct object the establishment of an absolute Tyranny over these States. To prove this, let Facts be submitted to a candid world.—

He has refused his Assent to Laws, the most wholesome and necessary for the public good.—

He has forbidden his Governors to pass Laws of immediate and pressing importance, unless suspended in their operation till his Assent should be obtained; and when so suspended, he has utterly neglected to attend to them.—

He has refused to pass other Laws for the accommodation of large districts of people, unless those people would relinquish the right of Representation in the Legislature, a right inestimable to them and formidable to tyrants only.—

He has called together legislative bodies at places unusual, uncomfortable, and distant from the depository of their public Records, for the sole purpose of fatiguing them into compliance with his measures.—

The printed text of the document shows the spelling and punctuation of the parchment original. To aid in comprehension, selected words and their definitions appear in the side margin, along with other explanatory notes.

impel *force*

endowed *provided*

People create governments to ensure that their natural rights are protected.

If a government does not serve its purpose, the people have a right to abolish it. Then the people have the right and duty to create a new government that will safeguard their security.

Despotism *unlimited power*

usurpations *unjust uses of power*

Each paragraph lists alleged injustices of George III.

relinquish *give up*
inestimable *priceless*

Annihilation *destruction*

convulsions *violent disturbances*

Naturalization of Foreigners *process by which foreign-born persons become citizens*

tenure *term*

Refers to the British troops sent to the colonies after the French and Indian War.

Refers to the 1766 Declaratory Act.

quartering *lodging*

Refers to the 1774 Quebec Act.

render *make*

abdicated *given up*

perfidy *violation of trust*

He has dissolved Representative Houses repeatedly, for opposing with manly firmness his invasions on the rights of the people.—

He has refused for a long time, after such dissolutions, to cause others to be elected; whereby the Legislative powers, incapable of Annihilation, have returned to the People at large for their exercise; the State remaining in the meantime exposed to all the dangers of invasion from without, and convulsions within.—

He has endeavoured to prevent the population of these States; for that purpose obstructing the Laws for Naturalization of Foreigners; refusing to pass others to encourage their migrations hither, and raising the conditions of new Appropriations of Lands.—

He has obstructed the Administration of Justice, by refusing his Assent to Laws for establishing Judiciary powers.—

He has made Judges dependent on his Will alone, for the tenure of their offices, and the amount and payment of their salaries.—

He has erected a multitude of New Offices, and sent hither swarms of Officers to harass our people, and eat out their substance.—

He has kept among us, in times of peace, Standing Armies without the Consent of our legislatures.—

He has affected to render the Military independent of and superior to the Civil power.—

He has combined with others to subject us to a jurisdiction foreign to our constitution, and unacknowledged by our laws; giving his Assent to their Acts of pretended Legislation:—

For quartering large bodies of troops among us:—

For protecting them, by a mock Trial, from punishment for any Murders which they should commit on the Inhabitants of these States:—

For cutting off our Trade with all parts of the world:—

For imposing Taxes on us without our Consent:—

For depriving us in many cases, of the benefits of Trial by Jury:—

For transporting us beyond Seas to be tried for pretended offences:—

For abolishing the free System of English Laws in a neighbouring Province, establishing therein an Arbitrary government, and enlarging its Boundaries so as to render it at once an example and fit instrument for introducing the same absolute rule into these Colonies:—

For taking away our Charters, abolishing our most valuable Laws, and altering fundamentally the Forms of our Governments:—

For suspending our own Legislatures, and declaring themselves invested with power to legislate for us in all cases whatsoever.—

He has abdicated Government here, by declaring us out of his Protection and waging War against us.—

He has plundered our seas, ravaged our Coasts, burnt our towns, and destroyed the Lives of our people.—

He is at this time transporting large Armies of foreign Mercenaries to compleat the works of death, desolation and tyranny, already begun with circumstances of Cruelty & perfidy scarcely paralleled in the most barbarous ages, and totally unworthy the Head of a civilized nation.—

He has constrained our fellow Citizens taken Captive on the high Seas to bear Arms against their Country, to become the executioners of their friends and Brethren, or to fall themselves by their Hands.—

He has excited domestic insurrections amongst us, and has endeavoured to bring on the inhabitants of our frontiers, the merciless Indian Savages, whose known rule of warfare, is an undistinguished destruction of all ages, sexes and conditions.

In every stage of these Oppressions We have Petitioned for Redress in the most humble terms: Our repeated Petitions have been answered only by repeated injury. A Prince, whose character is thus marked by every act which may define a Tyrant, is unfit to be the ruler of a free people.

Nor have We been wanting in attentions to our British brethren. We have warned them from time to time of attempts by their legislature to extend an unwarrantable jurisdiction over us. We have reminded them of the circumstances of our emigration and settlement here. We have appealed to their native justice and magnanimity, and we have conjured them by the ties of our common kindred to disavow these usurpations, which would inevitably interrupt our connections and correspondence. They too have been deaf to the voice of justice and of consanguinity. We must, therefore, acquiesce in the necessity, which denounces our Separation, and hold them, as we hold the rest of mankind, Enemies in War, in Peace Friends.—

Resolution of Independence by the United States

We, therefore, the Representatives of the united States of America, in General Congress, Assembled, appealing to the Supreme Judge of the world for the rectitude of our intentions, do, in the Name, and by Authority of the good People of these Colonies, solemnly publish and declare, That these United Colonies are, and of Right ought to be Free and Independent States; that they are Absolved from all Allegiance to the British Crown, and that all political connection between them and the State of Great Britain, is and ought to be totally dissolved; and that as Free and Independent States, they have full Power to levy War, conclude Peace, contract Alliances, establish Commerce, and to do all other Acts and Things which Independent States may of right do.—

And for the support of this Declaration, with a firm reliance on the protection of divine Providence, we mutually pledge to each other our Lives, our Fortunes and our sacred Honour.

---

insurrections *rebellions*

Petitioned for Redress *asked formally for a correction of wrongs*

unwarrantable jurisdiction *unjustified authority*

consanguinity *originating from the same ancestor*

rectitude *rightness*

The signers, as representatives of the American people, declared the colonies independent from Great Britain. Most members signed the document on August 2, 1776.

John Hancock
  President from
  Massachusetts

Georgia
Button Gwinnett
Lyman Hall
George Walton

North Carolina
William Hooper
Joseph Hewes
John Penn

South Carolina
Edward Rutledge
Thomas Heyward, Jr.
Thomas Lynch, Jr.
Arthur Middleton

Maryland
Samuel Chase
William Paca
Thomas Stone
Charles Carroll
of Carrollton

Virginia
George Wythe
Richard Henry Lee
Thomas Jefferson
Benjamin Harrison
Thomas Nelson Jr.
Francis Lightfoot Lee
Carter Braxton

Pennsylvania
Robert Morris
Benjamin Rush
Benjamin Franklin
John Morton
George Clymer
James Smith
George Taylor
James Wilson
George Ross

Delaware
Caesar Rodney
George Read
Thomas McKean

New York
William Floyd
Philip Livingston
Francis Lewis
Lewis Morris

New Jersey
Richard Stockton
John Witherspoon
Francis Hopkinson
John Hart
Abraham Clark

New Hampshire
Josiah Bartlett
William Whipple
Matthew Thornton

Massachusetts
Samuel Adams
John Adams
Robert Treat Paine
Elbridge Gerry

Rhode Island
Stephen Hopkins
William Ellery

Connecticut
Samuel Huntington
William Williams
Oliver Wolcott
Roger Sherman

Constitution of the United States

The Constitution of the United States is truly a remarkable document. It was one of the first written constitutions in modern history. The Framers wanted to devise a plan for a strong central government that would unify the country, as well as preserve the ideals of the Declaration of Independence. The document they wrote created a representative legislature, the office of president, a system of courts, and a process for adding amendments. For more than 200 years, the flexibility and strength of the Constitution have guided the nation's political leaders. The document has become a symbol of pride and a force for national unity.

The entire text of the Constitution and its amendments follows. For easier study, those passages that have been set aside or changed by the adoption of amendments are printed in blue. Also included are explanatory notes that will help clarify the meaning of each article and section.

The Capitol, Washington, D.C.

Preamble

We the People of the United States, in Order to form a more perfect Union, establish Justice, insure domestic Tranquility, provide for the common defence, promote the general Welfare, and secure the Blessings of Liberty to ourselves and our Posterity, do ordain and establish this Constitution for the United States of America.

Article I

Section 1

All legislative Powers herein granted shall be vested in a Congress of the United States, which shall consist of a Senate and House of Representatives.

Section 2

1. The House of Representatives shall be composed of Members chosen every second Year by the People of the several States, and the Electors in each State shall have the Qualifications requisite for Electors of the most numerous Branch of the State Legislature.

2. No person shall be a Representative who shall not have attained to the Age of twenty five Years, and been seven Years a Citizen of the United States, and who shall not, when elected, be an Inhabitant of that State in which he shall be chosen.

3. Representatives and direct Taxes shall be apportioned among the several States which may be included within this Union, according to their respective Numbers, which shall be determined by adding to the whole Number of free Persons, including those bound to Service for a Term of Years, and excluding Indians not taxed, three fifths of all other Persons. The actual Enumeration shall be made within three Years after the first Meeting of the Congress of the United States, and within every subsequent Term of ten Years, in such Manner as they shall by Law direct. The Number of Representatives shall not exceed one for every thirty Thousand, but each State shall have at Least one Representative; and until such enumeration shall be made, the State of New Hampshire shall be entitled to chuse three; Massachusetts eight, Rhode-Island and Providence Plantations one, Connecticut five,

The Preamble introduces the Constitution and sets forth the general purposes for which the government was established. The Preamble also declares that the power of the government comes from the people.

The printed text of the document shows the spelling and punctuation of the parchment original.

Article I. The Legislative Branch

Section 1. Congress

The power to make laws is given to a Congress made up of two chambers to represent different interests: the Senate to represent the states; the House to be more responsive to the people's will.

Section 2. House of Representatives

1. **Election and Term of Office** "Electors" means voters. Every two years the voters choose new Congress members to serve in the House of Representatives. The Constitution states that each state may specify who can vote. But the Fifteenth, Nineteenth, Twenty-fourth, and Twenty-sixth Amendments have established guidelines that all states must follow regarding the right to vote.

2. **Qualifications** Representatives must be 25 years old, citizens of the United States for 7 years, and residents of the state they represent.

3. **Division of Representatives Among the States** The number of representatives from each state is based on the size of the state's population. Each state is divided into congressional districts, with each district required to be equal in population. Each state is entitled to at least one representative. The number of representatives in the House was set at 435 in 1929. Since then, there has been a reapportionment of seats based on population shifts rather than on addition of seats.

   Only three-fifths of a state's slave population was to be counted in determining the number of representatives elected by the state. Native Americans were not counted at all.

The "enumeration" referred to is the census, the population count taken every 10 years since 1790.

4. **Vacancies** Vacancies in the House are filled through special elections called by the state's governor.

5. **Officers** The Speaker is the leader of the majority party in the House and is responsible for choosing the heads of various House committees. "Impeachment" means indictment, or bringing charges against an official.

Section 3. The Senate

1. **Number of Members, Terms of Office, and Voting Procedure** Originally, senators were chosen by the state legislators of their own states. The Seventeenth Amendment changed this, so that senators are now elected directly by the people. There are 100 senators, 2 from each state.

2. **Staggered Elections; Vacancies** One-third of the Senate is elected every two years. The terms of the first Senate's membership was staggered: one group served two years, one four, and one six. All senators now serve a six-year term.
   The Seventeenth Amendment changed the method of filling vacancies in the Senate.

3. **Qualifications** Qualifications for the Senate are more restrictive than those for the House. Senators must be at least 30 years old, residents of the states they represent, and citizens of the United States for at least nine years. The Framers of the Constitution made the Senate a more elite body to further check the powers of the House of Representatives.

4. **President of the Senate** The vice president's only duty listed in the Constitution is to preside over the Senate. The only real power the vice president has is to cast the deciding vote when there is a tie. However, modern presidents have given their vice presidents new responsibilities.

5. **Other Officers** The Senate selects its other officers, including a presiding officer (president pro tempore), who serves when the vice president is absent or has become president of the United States.

New York six, New Jersey four, Pennsylvania eight, Delaware one, Maryland six, Virginia ten, North Carolina five, South Carolina five, and Georgia three.

4. When vacancies happen in the Representation from any State, the Executive Authority thereof shall issue Writs of Election to fill such Vacancies.

5. The House of Representatives shall chuse their Speaker and other Officers; and shall have the sole Power of Impeachment.

Section 3

1. The Senate of the United States shall be composed of two Senators from each State, chosen by the Legislature thereof, for six Years; and each Senator shall have one Vote.

2. Immediately after they shall be assembled in Consequence of the first Election, they shall be divided as equally as may be into three Classes. The Seats of the Senators of the first Class shall be vacated at the Expiration of the second Year, of the second Class at the Expiration of the fourth Year, and of the third Class at the Expiration of the sixth Year, so that one third may be chosen every second Year; and if Vacancies happen by Resignation, or otherwise, during the Recess of the Legislature of any State, the Executive thereof may make temporary Appointments until the next Meeting of the Legislature, which shall then fill such Vacancies.

3. No Person shall be a Senator who shall not have attained to the Age of thirty Years, and been nine Years a Citizen of the United States, and who shall not, when elected, be an Inhabitant of that State for which he shall be chosen.

4. The Vice President of the United States shall be President of the Senate, but shall have no Vote, unless they be equally divided.

5. The Senate shall chuse their other Officers, and also a President pro tempore, in the Absence of the Vice President, or when he shall exercise the Office of the President of the United States.

6. The Senate shall have the sole Power to try all Impeachments. When sitting for that Purpose, they shall be on Oath or Affirmation. When the President of the United States is tried, the Chief Justice shall preside: And no Person shall be convicted without the Concurrence of two thirds of the Members present.

7. Judgment in Cases of Impeachment shall not extend further than to removal from Office, and disqualification to hold and enjoy any Office of honor, Trust or Profit under the United States: but the Party convicted shall nevertheless be liable and subject to Indictment, Trial, Judgment and Punishment, according to Law.

Section 4

1. The Times, Places and Manner of holding Elections for Senators and Representatives, shall be prescribed in each State by the Legislature thereof; but the Congress may at any time by Law make or alter such Regulations, except as to the Places of chusing Senators.

2. The Congress shall assemble at least once in every Year, and such Meeting shall be on the first Monday in December, unless they shall by Law appoint a different Day.

Section 5

1. Each House shall be the Judge of the Elections, Returns and Qualifications of its own Members, and a Majority of each shall constitute a Quorum to do Business; but a smaller Number may adjourn from day to day, and may be authorized to compel the Attendance of absent Members, in such Manner, and under such Penalties as each House may provide.

2. Each House may determine the Rules of its Proceedings, punish its Members for disorderly Behaviour, and, with the Concurrence of two thirds, expel a Member.

6. **Trial of Impeachments** When trying a case of impeachment brought by the House, the Senate convenes as a court. The chief justice of the United States acts as the presiding judge, and the Senate acts as the jury. A two-thirds vote of the members present is necessary to convict officials under impeachment charges.

7. **Penalty for Conviction** If the Senate convicts an official, it may only remove the official from office and prevent that person from holding another federal position. However, the convicted official may still be tried for the same offense in a regular court of law.

Section 4. Elections and Meetings

1. **Holding Elections** In 1842 Congress required members of the House to be elected from districts in states having more than one representative rather than at large. In 1845 it set the first Tuesday after the first Monday in November as the day for selecting presidential electors.

2. **Meetings** The Twentieth Amendment, ratified in 1933, has changed the date of the opening of the regular session of Congress to January 3.

Section 5. Organization and Rules of Procedure

1. **Organization** Until 1969, Congress acted as the sole judge of qualifications of its own members. In that year, the Supreme Court ruled that Congress could not legally exclude victorious candidates who met all the requirements listed in Article I, Section 2.

   A "quorum" is the minimum number of members that must be present for the House or Senate to conduct sessions. For a regular House session, a quorum consists of the majority of the House, or 218 of the 435 members.

2. **Rules** Each house sets its own rules, can punish its members for disorderly behavior, and can expel a member by a two-thirds vote.

3. **Journals** In addition to the journals, a complete official record of everything said on the floor, as well as the roll call votes on all bills or issues, is available in the *Congressional Record,* published daily by the Government Printing Office.

4. **Adjournment** Neither house may adjourn for more than three days or move to another location without the approval of the other house.

Section 6. Privileges and Restrictions

1. **Pay and Privileges** To strengthen the federal government, the Founders set congressional salaries to be paid by the United States Treasury rather than by members' respective states. Originally, members were paid $6 per day. Salaries for senators and representatives were $169,300 beginning in 2008.

   The "immunity" privilege means members cannot be sued or prosecuted for anything they say in Congress. They cannot be arrested while Congress is in session, except for treason, major crimes, or breaking the peace.

2. **Restrictions** "Emoluments" means salaries. The purpose of this clause is to prevent members of Congress from passing laws that would benefit them personally. It also prevents the president from promising them jobs in other branches of the federal government.

Section 7. Passing Laws

1. **Revenue Bills** "Revenue" is income raised by the government. The chief source of government revenue is taxes. All tax laws must originate in the House of Representatives. This ensures that the branch of Congress that is elected by the people every two years has the major role in determining taxes. This clause does not prevent the Senate from amending tax bills.

2. **How Bills Become Laws** A bill can become a law only by passing both houses of Congress and by being signed by the president. If the president disapproves, or vetoes, the bill, it is returned to the house where it originated, along with a written statement of the president's objections.

3. Each House shall keep a Journal of its Proceedings, and from time to time publish the same, excepting such Parts as may in their Judgment require Secrecy; and the Yeas and Nays of the Members of either House on any question shall, at the Desire of one fifth of those Present, be entered on the Journal.

4. Neither House, during the Session of Congress, shall, without the Consent of the other, adjourn for more than three days, nor to any other Place than that in which the two Houses shall be sitting.

Section 6

1. The Senators and Representatives shall receive a Compensation for their Services, to be ascertained by Law, and paid out of the Treasury of the United States. They shall in all Cases, except Treason, Felony and Breach of the Peace, be privileged from Arrest during their Attendance at the Session of their respective Houses, and in going to and returning from the same; and for any Speech or Debate in either House, they shall not be questioned in any other Place.

2. No Senator or Representative shall, during the Time for which he was elected, be appointed to any civil Office under the Authority of the United States, which shall have been created, or the Emoluments whereof shall have been encreased during such time; and no Person holding any Office under the United States, shall be a Member of either House during his Continuance in Office.

Section 7

1. All Bills for raising Revenue shall originate in the House of Representatives; but the Senate may propose or concur with Amendments as on other Bills.

2. Every Bill which shall have passed the House of Representatives and the Senate, shall, before it become a Law, be presented to the President of the United States; If he approve he shall sign it, but if not he shall return it, with his Objections to that House in which it shall have originated, who shall enter the Objections at large on their Journal, and proceed to reconsider it. If after such Reconsideration two thirds of that House

shall agree to pass the Bill, it shall be sent, together with the Objections, to the other House, by which it shall likewise be reconsidered, and if approved by two thirds of that House, it shall become a Law. But in all such Cases the Votes of both Houses shall be determined by yeas and Nays, and the Names of the Persons voting for and against the Bill shall be entered on the Journal of each House respectively. If any Bill shall not be returned by the President within ten Days (Sundays excepted) after it shall have been presented to him, the Same shall be a Law, in like Manner as if he had signed it, unless the Congress by their Adjournment prevent its Return, in which Case it shall not be a Law.

3. Every Order, Resolution, or Vote to which the Concurrence of the Senate and House of Representatives may be necessary (except on a question of Adjournment) shall be presented to the President of the United States; and before the Same shall take Effect, shall be approved by him, or being disapproved by him, shall be repassed by two thirds of the Senate and House of Representatives, according to the Rules and Limitations prescribed in the Case of a Bill.

Section 8

1. The Congress shall have the Power To lay and collect Taxes, Duties, Imposts and Excises, to pay the Debts and provide for the common Defence and general Welfare of the United States; but all Duties, Imposts and Excises shall be uniform throughout the United States;

2. To borrow Money on the credit of the United States;

3. To regulate Commerce with foreign Nations, and among the several States, and with the Indian Tribes;

4. To establish an uniform Rule of Naturalization, and uniform Laws on the subject of Bankruptcies throughout the United States;

5. To coin Money, regulate the Value thereof, and of foreign Coin, and fix the Standard of Weights and Measures;

6. To provide for the Punishment of counterfeiting the Securities and current Coin of the United States;

If two-thirds of each house approves the bill after the president has vetoed it, it becomes law. In voting to override a president's veto, the votes of all members of Congress must be recorded in the journals or official records. If the president does not sign or veto a bill within 10 days (excluding Sundays), it becomes law. However, if Congress has adjourned during this 10-day period, the bill does not become law. This is known as a "pocket veto."

3. **Presidential Approval or Veto** The Framers included this paragraph to prevent Congress from passing joint resolutions instead of bills to avoid the possibility of a presidential veto. A bill is a draft of a proposed law, whereas a resolution is the legislature's formal expression of opinion or intent on a matter.

Section 8. Powers Granted to Congress

1. **Revenue** This clause gives Congress the power to raise and spend revenue. Taxes must be levied at the same rate throughout the nation.

2. **Borrowing** The federal government borrows money by issuing bonds.

3. **Commerce** The exact meaning of "commerce" has caused controversy. The trend to expand its meaning and, consequently, the extent of Congress's powers have been reversed to some extent since 1995.

4. **Naturalization and Bankruptcy** "Naturalization" refers to the procedure by which a citizen of a foreign nation becomes a citizen of the United States.

5. **Currency** Control over money is an exclusive federal power; the states are forbidden to issue currency.

6. **Counterfeiting** "Counterfeiting" means illegally imitating or forging.

7. **Post Office** In 1970 the United States Postal Service replaced the Post Office Department.

8. **Copyrights and Patents** Under this provision, Congress has passed copyright and patent laws.

9. **Courts** This provision allows Congress to establish a federal court system.

10. **Piracy** Congress has the power to protect American ships on the high seas.

11. **Declare War** While the Constitution gives Congress the right to declare war, the United States has sent troops into combat without a congressional declaration.

12. **Army** This provision reveals the Framers' fears of a standing army.

13. **Navy** This clause allows Congress to establish a navy.

14. **Rules for Armed Forces** Congress may pass regulations that deal with military discipline.

15. **Militia** The "militia" is now called the National Guard. It is organized by the states.

16. **National Guard** Even though the National Guard is organized by the states, Congress has the authority to pass rules for governing its behavior.

17. **Nation's Capital** This clause grants Congress the right to make laws for Washington, D.C.

18. **Elastic Clause** This is the so-called "elastic clause" of the Constitution and one of its most important provisions. The "necessary and proper" laws must be related to one of the 17 enumerated powers.

---

7. To establish Post Offices and post Roads;

8. To promote the Progress of Science and useful Arts, by securing for limited Times to Authors and Inventors the exclusive Right to their respective Writings and Discoveries;

9. To constitute Tribunals inferior to the supreme Court;

10. To define and punish Piracies and Felonies committed on the high Seas, and Offences against the Law of Nations;

11. To declare War, grant Letters of Marque and Reprisal, and make Rules concerning Captures on Land and Water;

12. To raise and support Armies, but no Appropriation of Money to that Use shall be for a longer Term than two Years;

13. To provide and maintain a Navy;

14. To make Rules for the Government and Regulation of the land and naval Forces;

15. To provide for calling forth the Militia to execute the Laws of the Union, suppress Insurrections and repel Invasions;

16. To provide for organizing, arming, and disciplining, the Militia, and for governing such Part of them as may be employed in the Service of the United States, reserving to the States respectively, the Appointment of the Officers, and the Authority of training the Militia according to the discipline prescribed by Congress;

17. To exercise exclusive Legislation in all Cases whatsoever, over such District (not exceeding ten Miles square) as may, by Cession of particular States, and the Acceptance of Congress, become the Seat of Government of the United States, and to exercise like Authority over all Places purchased by the Consent of the Legislature of the State in which the Same shall be, for the Erection of Forts, Magazines, Arsenals, dock-Yards, and other needful Buildings;—And

18. To make all Laws which shall be necessary and proper for carrying into Execution the foregoing Powers, and all other Powers vested by this Constitution in the Government of the United States, or in any Department or Officer thereof.

Section 9

1. The Migration or Importation of such Persons as any of the States now existing shall think proper to admit, shall not be prohibited by the Congress prior to the Year one thousand eight hundred and eight, but a Tax or duty may be imposed on such Importation, not exceeding ten dollars for each Person.

2. The Privilege of the Writ of Habeas Corpus shall not be suspended, unless when in Cases of Rebellion or Invasion the public Safety may require it.

3. No Bill of Attainder or ex post facto Law shall be passed.

4. No Capitation, or other direct, Tax shall be laid, unless in Proportion to the Census or Enumeration herein before directed to be taken.

5. No Tax or Duty shall be laid on Articles exported from any State.

6. No Preference shall be given by any Regulation of Commerce or Revenue to the Ports of one State over those of another: nor shall Vessels bound to, or from, one State, be obliged to enter, clear, or pay Duties in another.

7. No Money shall be drawn from the Treasury, but in Consequence of Appropriations made by Law; and a regular Statement and Account of the Receipts and Expenditures of all public Money shall be published from time to time.

8. No Title of Nobility shall be granted by the United States: And no Person holding any Office of Profit or Trust under them, shall, without the Consent of the Congress, accept of any present, Emolument, Office, or Title, of any kind whatever, from any King, Prince, or foreign State.

Section 10

1. No State shall enter into any Treaty, Alliance, or Confederation; grant Letters of Marque and Reprisal; coin Money; emit Bills of Credit; make any Thing but gold and silver Coin a Tender in Payment of Debts; pass any Bill of Attainder, ex post facto Law, or Law impairing the Obligation of Contracts, or grant any Title of Nobility.

Section 9. Powers Denied to the Federal Government

1. **Slave Trade** This paragraph contains the compromise the Framers reached regarding regulation of the slave trade in exchange for Congress's exclusive control over interstate commerce.

2. **Habeas Corpus** *Habeas corpus* is a Latin term meaning "you may have the body." A writ of habeas corpus issued by a judge requires a government official to bring a prisoner to court and show cause for holding the prisoner. The writ may be suspended only during wartime.

3. **Bills of Attainder** A "bill of attainder" is a bill that punishes a person without a jury trial. An "ex post facto" law is one that makes an act a crime after the act has been committed.

4. **Direct Taxes** The Sixteenth Amendment allowed Congress to pass an income tax.

5. **Tax on Exports** Congress may not tax goods that move from one state to another.

6. **Uniformity of Treatment** This prohibition prevents Congress from favoring one state or region over another in the regulation of trade.

7. **Appropriation Law** This clause protects against the misuse of funds. All of the president's expenditures must be made with the permission of Congress.

8. **Titles of Nobility** This clause prevents the development of a nobility in the United States.

Section 10. Powers Denied to the States

1. **Limitations on Power** The states are prohibited from conducting foreign affairs, carrying on a war, or controlling interstate and foreign commerce. States are also not allowed to pass laws that the federal government is prohibited from passing, such as enacting ex post facto laws or bills of attainder. These restrictions on the states were designed, in part, to prevent an overlapping in functions and authority with the federal government that could create conflict and chaos.

Constitution of the United States

2. **Export and Import Taxes** This clause prevents states from levying duties on exports and imports. If states were permitted to tax imports and exports, they could use their taxing power in a way that weakens or destroys Congress's power to control interstate and foreign commerce.

3. **Duties, Armed Forces, War** This clause prohibits states from maintaining an army or navy and from going to war, except in cases where a state is directly attacked. It also forbids states from collecting fees from foreign vessels or from making treaties with other nations. All of these powers are reserved for the federal government.

Article II. The Executive Branch

Section 1. President and Vice President

1. **Term of Office** The president is given power to enforce the laws passed by Congress. Both the president and the vice president serve four-year terms. The Twenty-second Amendment limits the number of terms the president may serve to two.

2. **Election** The Philadelphia Convention had trouble deciding how the president was to be chosen. The system finally agreed upon was indirect election by "electors" chosen for that purpose. The president and vice president are not directly elected. Instead, the president and vice president are elected by presidential electors from each state who form the electoral college. Each state has a number of presidential electors equal to the total number of its senators and representatives. State legislatures determine how the electors are chosen. Originally, the state legislatures chose the electors, but today they are nominated by political parties and elected by the voters. No senator, representative, or any other federal officeholder can serve as an elector.

3. **Former Method of Election** This clause describes the original method of electing the president and vice president. According to this method, each elector voted for two

2. No State shall, without the Consent of the Congress, lay any Imposts or Duties on Imports or Exports, except what may be absolutely necessary for executing it's inspection Laws: and the net Produce of all Duties and Imposts, laid by any State on Imports and Exports, shall be for the Use of the Treasury of the United States; and all such Laws shall be subject to the Revision and Controul of the Congress.

3. No State shall, without the Consent of Congress, lay any Duty of Tonnage, keep Troops, or Ships of War in time of Peace, enter into any Agreement or Compact with another State, or with a foreign Power, or engage in War, unless actually invaded, or in such imminent Danger as will not admit of delay.

Article II

Section 1

1. The executive Power shall be vested in a President of the United States of America. He shall hold his Office during the Term of four Years, and, together with the Vice President, chosen for the same Term, be elected, as follows

2. Each State shall appoint, in such Manner as the Legislature thereof may direct, a Number of Electors, equal to the whole Number of Senators and Representatives to which the State may be entitled in the Congress: but no Senator or Representative, or Person holding an Office of Trust or Profit under the United States, shall be appointed an Elector.

3. The Electors shall meet in their respective States, and vote by Ballot for two Persons, of whom one at least shall not be an Inhabitant of the same State with themselves. And they shall make a List of all the Persons voted for, and of the Number of Votes for each; which List they shall sign and certify, and transmit sealed to the Seat of the Government of the United States, directed to the President of the Senate. The President of the Senate shall, in the Presence of the Senate and House of Representatives, open all the Certificates, and the Votes shall then be counted. The Person having the greatest Number of Votes shall be the President, if such Number be a Majority

of the whole Number of Electors appointed; and if there be more than one who have such Majority, and have an equal Number of Votes, then the House of Representatives shall immediately chuse by Ballot one of them for President; and if no person have a Majority, then from the five highest on the List the said House shall in like Manner chuse the President. But in chusing the President, the Votes shall be taken by States, the Representation from each State having one Vote; A quorum for this Purpose shall consist of a Member or Members from two thirds of the States, and a Majority of all the States shall be necessary to a Choice. In every Case, after the Choice of the President, the Person having the greatest Number of Votes of the Electors shall be the Vice President. But if there should remain two or more who have equal Votes, the Senate shall chuse from them by Ballot the Vice President.

4. The Congress may determine the Time of chusing the Electors, and the Day on which they shall give their Votes; which Day shall be the same throughout the United States.

5. No Person except a natural born Citizen, or a Citizen of the United States, at the time of the Adoption of this Constitution, shall be eligible to the Office of President; neither shall any Person be eligible to that Office who shall not have attained to the Age of thirty five Years, and been fourteen Years a Resident within the United States.

6. In Case of the Removal of the President from Office, or of his Death, Resignation, or Inability to discharge the Powers and Duties of the said Office, the Same shall devolve on the Vice President, and the Congress may by Law provide for the Case of Removal, Death, Resignation or Inability, both of the President and Vice President, declaring what Officer shall then act as President, and such Officer shall act accordingly, until the Disability be removed, or a President shall be elected.

7. The President shall, at stated Times, receive for his Services, a Compensation, which shall neither be encreased nor diminished during the Period for which he shall have been elected, and he shall not receive within that Period any other Emolument from the United States, or any of them.

candidates. The candidate with the most votes (as long as it was a majority) became president. The candidate with the second-highest number of votes became vice president. In the election of 1800, the two top candidates received the same number of votes, making it necessary for the House of Representatives to decide the election. To prevent such a situation from recurring, the Twelfth Amendment was added in 1804.

4. **Date of Elections** Congress selects the date when the presidential electors are chosen and when they vote for president and vice president. All electors must vote on the same day. The first Tuesday after the first Monday in November has been set as the date for presidential elections. Electors cast their votes on the Monday after the second Wednesday in December.

5. **Qualifications** The president must be a citizen of the United States by birth, at least 35 years old, and a resident of the United States for 14 years. See the Twenty-second Amendment.

6. **Vacancies** If the president dies, resigns, is removed from office by impeachment, or is unable to carry out the duties of the office, the vice president becomes president. (Amendment 25 deals with presidential disability.) If both the president and vice president are unable to serve, Congress has the power to declare by law who acts as president. Congress set the line of succession in the Presidential Succession Act of 1947.

7. **Salary** Originally, the president's salary was $25,000 per year. The president's current salary of $400,000 plus a $50,000 taxable expense account per year was enacted in 1999. The president also receives numerous fringe benefits including a $100,000 nontaxable allowance for travel and entertainment, and living accommodations in two residences—the White House and Camp David. However, the president cannot receive any other income from the United States government or state governments while in office.

8. **Oath of Office** The oath of office is generally administered by the chief justice, but can be administered by any official authorized to administer oaths. All presidents-elect except Washington have been sworn into office by the chief justice. Only Vice Presidents John Tyler, Calvin Coolidge, and Lyndon Johnson in succeeding to the office have been sworn in by someone else.

Section 2. Powers of the President

1. **Military, Cabinet, Pardons** Mention of "the principal officer in each of the executive departments" is the only suggestion of the president's cabinet to be found in the Constitution. The cabinet is a purely advisory body, and its power depends on the president. Each cabinet member is appointed by the president and must be confirmed by the Senate. This clause also makes the president, a civilian, the head of the armed services. This established the principle of civilian control of the military.

2. **Treaties and Appointments** The president is the chief architect of American foreign policy. He or she is responsible for the conduct of foreign relations, or dealings with other countries. All treaties, however, require approval of two-thirds of the senators present. Most federal positions today are filled under the rules and regulations of the civil service system. Most presidential appointees serve at the pleasure of the president. Removal of an official by the president is not subject to congressional approval. But the power can be restricted by conditions set in creating the office.

3. **Vacancies in Offices** The president can temporarily appoint officials to fill vacancies when the Senate is not in session.

Section 3. Duties of the President

Under this provision, the president delivers annual State of the Union messages. On occasion, presidents have called Congress into special session to consider particular problems.

The president's duty to receive foreign diplomats also includes the power to ask a foreign country to withdraw its diplomatic officials from this country. This is called "breaking diplomatic relations" and often carries with it the implied threat of more drastic action, even war. The

8. Before he enter on the Execution of his Office, he shall take the following Oath or Affirmation:—"I do solemnly swear (or affirm) that I will faithfully execute the Office of President of the United States, and will to the best of my Ability, preserve, protect and defend the Constitution of the United States."

Section 2

1. The President shall be Commander in Chief of the Army and Navy of the United States, and of the Militia of the several States, when called into the actual Service of the United States; he may require the Opinion, in writing, of the principal Officer in each of the executive Departments, upon any Subject relating to the Duties of their respective Offices, and he shall have Power to grant Reprieves and Pardons for Offences against the United States, except in Cases of Impeachment.

2. He shall have Power, by and with the Advice and Consent of the Senate, to make Treaties, provided two thirds of the Senators present concur; and he shall nominate, and by and with the Advice and Consent of the Senate, shall appoint Ambassadors, other public Ministers and Consuls, Judges of the supreme Court, and all other Officers of the United States, whose Appointments are not herein otherwise provided for, and which shall be established by Law: but the Congress may by Law vest the Appointment of such inferior Officers, as they think proper, in the President alone, in the Courts of Law, or in the Heads of Departments.

3. The President shall have Power to fill up all Vacancies that may happen during the Recess of the Senate, by granting Commissions which shall expire at the End of their next Session.

Section 3

He shall from time to time give to the Congress Information of the State of the Union, and recommend to their Consideration such Measures as he shall judge necessary and expedient; he may, on extraordinary Occasions, convene both Houses, or either of them, and in Case of Disagreement between them, with Respect to the Time of Adjournment, he may adjourn them to such Time as he shall think proper; he shall receive

Ambassadors and other public Ministers; he shall take Care that the Laws be faithfully executed, and shall Commission all the Officers of the United States.

Section 4

The President, Vice President and all civil Officers of the United States, shall be removed from Office on Impeachment for, and Conviction of, Treason, Bribery, or other high Crimes and Misdemeanors.

Article III

Section 1

The judicial Power of the United States, shall be vested in one supreme Court, and in such inferior Courts as the Congress may from time to time ordain and establish. The Judges, both of the supreme and inferior Courts, shall hold their Offices during good Behaviour, and shall, at stated Times, receive for their Services, a Compensation, which shall not be diminished during their Continuance in Office.

Section 2

1. The judicial Power shall extend to all Cases, in Law and Equity, arising under this Constitution, the Laws of the United States, and Treaties made, or which shall be made, under their Authority; to all Cases affecting Ambassadors, other public Ministers and Consuls; to all Cases of admiralty and maritime Jurisdiction; to Controversies to which the United States shall be a Party; to Controversies between two or more States; between a State and Citizens of another State; between Citizens of different States, between Citizens of the same State claiming Lands under Grants of different States, and between a State, or the Citizens thereof, and foreign States, Citizens or Subjects.

2. In all Cases affecting Ambassadors, other public Ministers and Consuls, and those in which a State shall be Party, the supreme Court shall have original Jurisdiction. In all the other Cases before mentioned, the supreme Court shall have appellate Jurisdiction, both as to Law and Fact, with such Exceptions, and under such Regulations as the Congress shall make.

president likewise has the power of deciding whether or not to recognize foreign governments.

Section 4. Impeachment

This section states the reasons for which the president and vice president may be impeached and removed from office. (See annotations of Article I, Section 3, Clauses 6 and 7.)

Article III. The Judicial Branch

Section 1. Federal Courts

The term *judicial* refers to courts. The Constitution set up only the Supreme Court but provided for the establishment of other federal courts. Presently nine justices serve on the Supreme Court. Congress has created a system of federal district courts and courts of appeals, which review certain district court cases. Judges of these courts serve during "good behavior," which means that they usually serve for life or until they choose to retire.

Section 2. Jurisdiction

1. **General Jurisdiction** Use of the words *in law* and *equity* reflects the fact that American courts took over two kinds of traditional law from Great Britain. The basic law was the "common law," which was based on more than five centuries of judicial decisions. "Equity" was a special branch of British law that was developed to handle cases where common law did not apply.

   Federal courts deal mostly with "statute law," or laws passed by Congress, treaties, and cases involving the Constitution itself. "Admiralty and maritime jurisdiction" covers all sorts of cases involving ships and shipping on the high seas and on rivers, canals, and lakes.

2. **The Supreme Court** When a court has "original jurisdiction" over certain kinds of cases, it means that the court has the authority to be the first court to hear a case. A court with "appellate jurisdiction" hears cases that have been appealed from lower courts. Most Supreme Court cases are heard on appeal from lower courts.

3. **Jury Trials** Except in cases of impeachment, anyone accused of a crime has the right to a trial by jury. The trial must be held in the state where the crime was committed. Jury trial guarantees were strengthened in the Sixth, Seventh, Eighth, and Ninth Amendments.

Section 3. Treason

1. **Definition** Knowing that the charge of treason often had been used by monarchs to get rid of people who opposed them, the Framers of the Constitution defined treason carefully, requiring that at least two witnesses to the same treasonable act testify in court.

2. **Punishment** Congress is given the power to determine the punishment for treason. The children of a person convicted of treason may not be punished, nor may the convicted person's property be taken away from the children. Convictions for treason have been relatively rare in the nation's history.

Article IV. Relations Among the States

Section 1. Official Acts

This provision ensures that each state recognizes the laws, court decisions, and records of all other states. For example, a marriage license or corporation charter issued by one state must be accepted in other states.

Section 2. Mutual Duties of States

1. **Privileges** The "privileges and immunities," or rights of citizens, guarantee each state's citizens equal treatment in all states.

2. **Extradition** "Extradition" means that a person convicted of a crime or a person accused of a crime must be returned to the state where the crime was committed. Thus, a person cannot flee to another state hoping to escape the law.

3. **Fugitive-Slave Clause** Formerly this clause meant that enslaved people could not become free persons by escaping to free states.

3. The Trial of all Crimes, except in Cases of Impeachment, shall be by Jury; and such Trial shall be held in the State where the said Crimes shall have been committed; but when not committed within any State, the Trial shall be at such Place or Places as the Congress may by Law have directed.

Section 3

1. Treason against the United States, shall consist only in levying War against them, or in adhering to their Enemies, giving them Aid and Comfort. No Person shall be convicted of Treason unless on the Testimony of two Witnesses to the same overt Act, or on Confession in open Court.

2. The Congress shall have Power to declare the Punishment of Treason, but no Attainder of Treason shall work Corruption of Blood, or Forfeiture except during the Life of the Person attainted.

Article IV

Section 1

Full Faith and Credit shall be given in each State to the public Acts, Records, and judicial Proceedings of every other State. And the Congress may by general Laws prescribe the Manner in which such Acts, Records and Proceedings shall be proved, and the Effect thereof.

Section 2

1. The Citizens of each State shall be entitled to all Privileges and Immunities of Citizens in the several States.

2. A Person charged in any State with Treason, Felony, or other Crime, who shall flee from Justice, and be found in another State, shall on Demand of the executive Authority of the State from which he fled, be delivered up, to be removed to the State having Jurisdiction of the Crime.

3. No Person held to Service of Labour in one State, under the Laws thereof, escaping into another, shall, in Consequence of any Law or Regulation therein, be discharged from such Service or Labour, but shall be delivered up on Claim of the Party to whom such Service or Labour may be due.

Section 3

1. New States may be admitted by the Congress into this Union; but no new State shall be formed or erected within the Jurisdiction of any other State; nor any State be formed by the Junction of two or more States, or Parts of States, without the Consent of the Legislatures of the States concerned as well as of the Congress.

2. The Congress shall have Power to dispose of and make all needful Rules and Regulations respecting the Territory or other Property belonging to the United States; and nothing in this Constitution shall be so construed as to Prejudice any Claims of the United States, or of any particular State.

Section 4

The United States shall guarantee to every State in this Union a Republican Form of Government, and shall protect each of them against Invasion; and on Application of the Legislature, or of the Executive (when the Legislature cannot be convened) against domestic Violence.

Article V

The Congress, whenever two thirds of both Houses shall deem it necessary, shall propose Amendments to this Constitution, or, on the Application of the Legislatures of two thirds of the several States, shall call a Convention for proposing Amendments, which, in either Case, shall be valid to all Intents and Purposes, as Part of this Constitution, when ratified by the Legislatures of three fourths of the several States, or by Conventions in three fourths thereof, as the one or the other Mode of Ratification may be proposed by the Congress; Provided that no Amendment which may be made prior to the Year One thousand eight hundred and eight shall in any Manner affect the first and fourth Clauses in the Ninth Section of the first Article; and that no State, without its Consent, shall be deprived of its equal Suffrage in the Senate.

Article VI

1. All Debts contracted and Engagements entered into, before the Adoption of this Constitution, shall be as valid against the United States under this Constitution, as under the Confederation.

Section 3. New States and Territories

1. **New States** Congress has the power to admit new states. It also determines the basic guidelines for applying for statehood. One state, Maine, was created within the original boundaries of another state (Massachusetts) with the consent of Congress and the state.

2. **Territories** Congress has power over federal land. But neither in this clause nor anywhere else in the Constitution is the federal government explicitly empowered to acquire new territory.

Section 4. Federal Protection for States

This section allows the federal government to send troops into a state to guarantee law and order. The president may send in troops even without the consent of the state government involved.

Article V. The Amending Process

There are now 27 amendments to the Constitution. The Framers of the Constitution deliberately made it difficult to amend the Constitution. Two methods of proposing and ratifying amendments are provided for. A two-thirds majority is needed in Congress to propose an amendment, and at least three-fourths of the states (38 states) must accept the amendment before it can become law. No amendment has yet been proposed by a national convention called by the states, though in the 1980s a convention to propose an amendment requiring a balanced budget was approved by 32 states.

Article VI. National Supremacy

1. **Public Debts and Treaties** This section promised that all debts the colonies had incurred during the Revolution and under the Articles of Confederation would be honored by the new United States government.

2. **The Supreme Law** The "supremacy clause" recognized the Constitution and federal laws as supreme when in conflict with those of the states. It was largely based on this clause that Chief Justice John Marshall wrote his historic decision in *McCulloch* v. *Maryland.* The Fourteenth Amendment reinforced the supremacy of federal law over state laws.

3. **Oaths of Office** This clause also declares that no religious test shall be required as a qualification for holding public office.

Article VII. Ratification of the Constitution

Unlike the Articles of Confederation, which required approval of all thirteen states for adoption, the Constitution required approval of only nine of thirteen states. Thirty-nine of the 55 delegates at the Constitutional Convention signed the Constitution. The Constitution went into effect in June 1788.

2. This Constitution, and the Laws of the United States which shall be made in Pursuance thereof; and all Treaties made, or which shall be made, under the Authority of the United States, shall be the supreme Law of the Land; and the Judges in every State shall be bound thereby, any Thing in the Constitution or Laws of any State to the Contrary notwithstanding.

3. The Senators and Representatives before mentioned, and the Members of the several State Legislatures, and all executive and judicial Officers, both of the United States and of the several States, shall be bound by Oath or Affirmation, to support this Constitution; but no religious Test shall ever be required as a Qualification to any Office or public Trust under the United States.

Article VII

The Ratification of the Conventions of nine States, shall be sufficient for the Establishment of this Constitution between the States so ratifying the Same.

Done in Convention by the Unanimous Consent of the States present the Seventeenth Day of September in the Year of our Lord one thousand seven hundred and Eighty seven and of the Independence of the United States of America the Twelfth. In witness whereof We have hereunto subscribed our Names,

Signers

George Washington, **President and Deputy from Virginia**

New Hampshire
John Langdon
Nicholas Gilman

Massachusetts
Nathaniel Gorham
Rufus King

Connecticut
William Samuel Johnson
Roger Sherman

New York
Alexander Hamilton

New Jersey
William Livingston
David Brearley
William Paterson
Jonathan Dayton

Pennsylvania
Benjamin Franklin
Thomas Mifflin
Robert Morris
George Clymer
Thomas FitzSimons
Jared Ingersoll
James Wilson
Gouverneur Morris

Delaware
George Read
Gunning Bedford, Jr.
John Dickinson
Richard Bassett
Jacob Broom

Maryland
James McHenry
Daniel of St. Thomas Jenifer
Daniel Carroll

Virginia
John Blair
James Madison, Jr.

North Carolina
William Blount
Richard Dobbs Spaight
Hugh Williamson

South Carolina
John Rutledge
Charles Cotesworth Pinckney
Charles Pinckney
Pierce Butler

Georgia
William Few
Abraham Baldwin

Attest:
William Jackson,
Secretary

Amendment I

Congress shall make no law respecting an establishment of religion, or prohibiting the free exercise thereof; or abridging the freedom of speech, or of the press; or the right of the people peaceably to assemble, and to petition the Government for a redress of grievances.

Amendment II

A well regulated Militia, being necessary to the security of a free State, the right of the people to keep and bear Arms, shall not be infringed.

Amendment III

No Soldier shall, in time of peace be quartered in any house, without the consent of the Owner, nor in time of war, but in a manner to be prescribed by law.

Amendment IV

The right of the people to be secure in their persons, houses, papers, and effects, against unreasonable searches and seizures, shall not be violated, and no Warrants shall issue, but upon probable cause, supported by Oath or affirmation, and particularly describing the place to be searched, and the persons or things to be seized.

Amendment V

No person shall be held to answer for a capital, or otherwise infamous crime, unless on a presentment or indictment of a Grand Jury, except in cases arising in the land or naval forces, or in the Militia, when in actual service in time of War or public danger; nor shall any person be subject for the same offence to be twice put in jeopardy of life or limb; nor shall be compelled in any criminal case to be a witness against himself, nor be deprived of life, liberty, or property, without due process of law; nor shall private property be taken for public use without just compensation.

Amendment 1.
Freedom of Religion, Speech, Press, and Assembly (1791)

The First Amendment protects the civil liberties of individuals in the United States.

Amendment 2.
Bearing Arms (1791)

This amendment is often debated. For many years, some scholars argued it protected only the right of the states to have militias, not an individual's right to own a weapon. In 2008 the Court supported an individual's right to own a weapon by striking down a District of Columbia's ban on handguns, but it said this right was not unlimited.

Amendment 3.
Quartering Troops (1791)

This amendment is based on the principle that people have a right to privacy in their own homes. It also reflects the colonists' grievances against the British for quartering (housing) troops in private homes.

Amendment 4.
Searches and Seizures (1791)

Like the Third Amendment, the Fourth Amendment reflects the colonists' desire to protect their privacy. Britain had used writs of assistance (general search warrants) to seek out smuggled goods. Americans wanted to make sure that such searches and seizures would be conducted only when a judge believed that there was "reasonable cause" to conduct them. The Supreme Court has ruled that evidence seized illegally without a search warrant can not be used in court.

Amendment 5.
Rights of Accused Persons (1791)

It is the function of a grand jury to bring a "presentment" or "indictment," which means to formally charge a person with committing a crime, if enough evidence is found to bring the accused person to trial. A person may not be tried more than once for the same crime (double jeopardy). Members of the armed services are subject to military law. They may be tried in a court martial. In times of war or a natural disaster, civilians can also be put under martial law. The Fifth Amendment also guarantees that accused persons may refuse to answer questions on the ground that the answers might tend to incriminate them.

Amendment 6.
Right to Speedy, Fair Trial (1791)

The requirement of a "speedy" trial ensures that an accused person will not be held in jail for a lengthy period as a means of punishing the accused without a trial. A "fair" trial means that the trial must be open to the public and that a jury must hear witnesses and evidence on both sides before deciding the guilt or innocence of a person charged with a crime. This amendment also provides that legal counsel must be provided to a defendant. In 1963 the Supreme Court ruled in *Gideon* v. *Wainwright* that if a defendant charged with a felony cannot afford to hire a lawyer, the government must provide one.

Amendment 7.
Civil Suits (1791)

"Common law" means the law established by previous court decisions. In civil cases where one person sues another for more than $20, a jury trial is provided for. But customarily, federal courts do not hear civil cases unless they involve a good deal more money.

Amendment 8.
Bail and Punishment (1791)

"Bail" is money that an accused person provides to the court as a guarantee that he or she will be present for a trial. This amendment ensures that neither bail nor punishment for a crime shall be unreasonably severe.

Amendment 9.
Powers Reserved to the People (1791)

This amendment provides that the people's rights are not limited to those mentioned in the Constitution.

Amendment 10.
Powers Reserved to the States (1791)

This amendment protects the states and the people from an all-powerful federal government. It provides that the states or the people retain all powers except those denied them or those specifically granted to the federal government. This "reserved powers" provision is a check on

Amendment VI

In all criminal prosecutions, the accused shall enjoy the right to a speedy and public trial, by an impartial jury of the State and district wherein the crime shall have been committed, which district shall have been previously ascertained by law, and to be informed of the nature and cause of the accusation; to be confronted with the witnesses against him; to have compulsory process for obtaining Witnesses in his favor, and to have the assistance of counsel for his defence.

Amendment VII

In Suits at common law, where the value in controversy shall exceed twenty dollars, the right of trial by jury shall be preserved, and no fact tried by a jury, shall be otherwise reexamined in any Court of the United States, than according to the rules of common law.

Amendment VIII

Excessive bail shall not be required, nor excessive fines imposed, nor cruel and unusual punishments inflicted.

Amendment IX

The enumeration in the Constitution, of certain rights, shall not be construed to deny or disparage others retained by the people.

Amendment X

The powers not delegated to the United States by the Constitution, nor prohibited by it to the States, are reserved to the States respectively, or to the people.

Amendment XI

The Judicial power of the United States shall not be construed to extend to any suit in law or equity, commenced or prosecuted against one of the United States by Citizens of another State, or by Citizens or Subjects of any Foreign State.

Amendment XII

The electors shall meet in their respective states and vote by ballot for President and Vice-President, one of whom, at least, shall not be an inhabitant of the same state with themselves; they shall name in their ballots the person voted for as President, and in distinct ballots the person voted for as Vice-President, and they shall make distinct lists of all persons voted for as President, and of all persons voted for as Vice-President, and of the number of votes for each, which lists they shall sign and certify, and transmit sealed to the seat of the government of the United States, directed to the President of the Senate;—The President of the Senate shall, in the presence of the Senate and House of Representatives, open all the certificates and the votes shall then be counted;—The person having the greatest number of votes for President, shall be the President, if such number be a majority of the whole number of Electors appointed; and if no person have such majority, then from the persons having the highest numbers not exceeding three on the list of those voted for as President, the House of Representatives shall choose immediately, by ballot, the President. But in choosing the President, the votes shall be taken by states, the representation from each state having one vote; a quorum for this purpose shall consist of a member or members from two-thirds of the states, and a majority of all the states shall be necessary to a choice. And if the House of Representatives shall not choose a President whenever the right of choice shall devolve upon them, before the fourth day of March next following, then the Vice-President shall act as President, as in the case of the death or other constitutional disability of the President. The person having the greatest number of votes as Vice-President, shall be the Vice-President, if such number be a majority of the whole number of Electors appointed, and if no person have a majority, then from the two highest numbers on the list, the Senate shall choose the Vice-President; a quorum for the purpose shall consist of two-thirds of the whole number of Senators, and a majority of the whole number shall be necessary to a choice. But no person constitutionally ineligible to the office of President shall be eligible to that of Vice-President of the United States.

Amendment XIII

Section 1

Neither slavery nor involuntary servitude, except as a punishment for crime whereof the party shall have been duly convicted, shall exist within the United States, or any place subject to their jurisdiction.

the "necessary and proper" power of the federal government provided in the "elastic clause" in Article I, Section 8, Clause 18.

Amendment 11.
Suits Against States (1795)

This amendment provides that a lawsuit brought by a citizen of the United States or a foreign nation against a state must be tried in a state court, not in a federal court. This amendment was passed after the Supreme Court ruled that a federal court could try a lawsuit brought by citizens of South Carolina against a citizen of Georgia. This case, *Chisholm v. Georgia,* decided in 1793, was protested by many Americans, who insisted that states would lose authority if they could be sued in federal courts.

Amendment 12.
Election of President and Vice President (1804)

This amendment changes the procedure for electing the president and vice president as outlined in Article II, Section 1, Clause 3.

To prevent the recurrence of the election of 1800 whereby a candidate running for vice president (Aaron Burr) could tie a candidate running for president (Thomas Jefferson) and thus force the election into the House of Representatives, the Twelfth Amendment specifies that the electors are to cast separate ballots for each office. The votes for each office are counted and listed separately. The results are signed, sealed, and sent to the president of the Senate. At a joint session of Congress, the votes are counted. The candidate who receives the most votes, providing it is a majority, is elected president. Other changes include: (1) a reduction from the five to three candidates receiving the most votes among whom the House is to choose if no candidate receives a majority of the electoral votes, and (2) provision for the Senate to choose the vice president from the two highest candidates if neither has received a majority of the electoral votes.

The Twelfth Amendment places one restriction on electors. It prohibits electors from voting for two candidates (president and vice president) from their home state.

Amendment 13.
Abolition of Slavery (1865)

This amendment was the final act in ending slavery in the United States. It also prohibits the binding of a person to perform a personal service due to debt. In addition to imprisonment for crime, the Supreme Court has held that the draft is not a violation of the amendment.

This amendment is the first adopted to be divided into sections. It is also the first to contain specifically a provision granting Congress power to enforce it by appropriate legislation.

Amendment 14.
Rights of Citizens (1868)

The clauses of this amendment were intended (1) to penalize Southern states that refused to grant all citizens the vote, (2) to keep former Confederate leaders from serving in government, (3) to forbid payment of the Confederacy's debt by the federal government, and (4) to ensure payment of the war debts owed the federal government.

Section 1. Citizenship Defined By granting citizenship to all persons born in the United States, this amendment granted citizenship to former slaves. The amendment also guaranteed "due process of law." By the 1950s, Supreme Court rulings used the due process clause to protect civil liberties. The last part of Section 1 establishes the doctrine that all citizens are entitled to equal protection of the laws. In 1954 the Supreme Court ruled, in *Brown* v. *Board of Education of Topeka,* that segregation in public schools was unconstitutional because it denied equal protection.

Section 2. Representation in Congress This section reduced the number of members a state had in the House of Representatives if it denied its citizens the right to vote. This section was not implemented, however. Later civil rights laws and the Twenty-fourth Amendment guaranteed the vote to African Americans.

Section 3. Penalty for Engaging in Insurrection The leaders of the Confederacy were barred from state or federal offices unless Congress agreed to revoke this ban. By the end of Reconstruction, all but a few Confederate leaders were allowed to return to public life.

Section 2

Congress shall have power to enforce this article by appropriate legislation.

Amendment XIV

Section 1

All persons born or naturalized in the United States, and subject to the jurisdiction thereof, are citizens of the United States and of the State wherein they reside. No State shall make or enforce any law which shall abridge the privileges or immunities of citizens of the United States; nor shall any State deprive any person of life, liberty, or property, without due process of law; nor deny to any person within its jurisdiction the equal protection of the laws.

Section 2

Representatives shall be apportioned among the several States according to their respective numbers, counting the whole number of persons in each State, excluding Indians not taxed. But when the right to vote at any election for the choice of electors for President and Vice President of the United States, Representatives in Congress, the Executive and Judicial officers of a State, or the members of the Legislature thereof, is denied to any of the male inhabitants of such State, being twenty-one years of age, and citizens of the United States, or in any way abridged, except for participation in rebellion, or other crime, the basis of representation therein shall be reduced in the proportion which the number of such male citizens shall bear to the whole number of male citizens twenty-one years of age in such State.

Section 3

No person shall be a Senator or Representative in Congress, or elector of President and Vice President, or hold any office, civil or military, under the United States, or under any State, who, having previously taken an oath, as a member of Congress, or as an officer of the United States, or as a member of any State legislature, or as an executive or judicial officer of any State, to support the Constitution of the United States, shall have engaged in insurrection or rebellion against the same, or given aid or comfort to the enemies thereof. But Congress may by a vote of two-thirds of each House, remove such disability.

Section 4

The validity of the public debt of the United States, authorized by law, including debts incurred for payment of pensions and bounties for service in suppressing insurrection or rebellion, shall not be questioned. But neither the United States nor any State shall assume or pay any debt or obligation incurred in aid of insurrection or rebellion against the United States, or any claim for the loss or emancipation of any slave; but all such debts, obligations and claims shall be held illegal and void.

Section 5

The Congress shall have power to enforce, by appropriate legislation, the provisions of this article.

Amendment XV

Section 1

The right of citizens of the United States to vote shall not be denied or abridged by the United States or by any State on account of race, color, or previous condition of servitude.

Section 2

The Congress shall have power to enforce this article by appropriate legislation.

Amendment XVI

The Congress shall have power to lay and collect taxes on incomes, from whatever source derived, without apportionment among the several States and without regard to any census or enumeration.

Amendment XVII

Section 1

The Senate of the United States shall be composed of two Senators from each State, elected by the people thereof, for six years; and each Senator shall have one vote. The electors in each State shall have the qualifications requisite for electors of the most numerous branch of the State legislatures.

Section 4. Public Debt The public debt incurred by the federal government during the Civil War was valid and could not be questioned by the South. However, the debts of the Confederacy were declared to be illegal. In addition, former slaveholders could not collect compensation for the loss of their slaves.

Section 5. Enforcement Congress was empowered to pass civil rights bills to guarantee the provisions of the amendment.

Amendment 15.
The Right to Vote (1870)

Section 1. Suffrage for All Citizens The Fifteenth Amendment replaced Section 2 of the Fourteenth Amendment in guaranteeing all citizens the right to vote; that is, the right to vote was not to be left to the states. Despite this prohibition, African Americans as well as other groups, including Hispanics and Asians, were often denied the right to vote by such means as poll taxes, literacy tests, and white primaries.

Section 2. Enforcement Congress was given the power to enforce this amendment. During the 1950s and 1960s, it passed successively stronger laws to end racial discrimination in voting rights.

Amendment 16.
Income Tax (1913)

The origins of this amendment went back to 1895, when the Supreme Court declared a federal income tax unconstitutional. To overcome this Supreme Court decision, this amendment authorized an income tax that was levied on a direct basis.

Amendment 17.
Direct Election of Senators (1913)

Section 1. Method of Election The right to elect senators was given directly to the people of each state. It replaced Article I, Section 3, Clause 1, which empowered state legislatures to elect senators. This amendment was designed not only to make the choice of senators more democratic but also to cut down on corruption and to improve state government.

Section 2. Vacancies A state must order an election to fill a Senate vacancy. A state may empower its governor to appoint a person to fill a Senate seat if a vacancy occurs until an election can be held.

Section 3. Time in Effect This amendment was not to affect any Senate election or temporary appointment until it was in effect.

Amendment 18.
Prohibition of Alcoholic Beverages (1919)

This amendment prohibited the production, sale, or transportation of alcoholic beverages in the United States. This amendment was later repealed by the Twenty-first Amendment.

Amendment 19.
Woman Suffrage (1920)

This amendment, extending the vote to all qualified women in federal and state elections, was a landmark victory for the woman suffrage movement, which had worked to achieve this goal for many years. The women's movement had earlier gained full voting rights for women in four Western states in the late nineteenth century.

Section 2

When vacancies happen in the representation of any State in the Senate, the executive authority of such State shall issue writs of election to fill such vacancies: Provided, That the legislature of any State may empower the executive thereof to make temporary appointments until the people fill the vacancies by election as the legislature may direct.

Section 3

This amendment shall not be so construed as to affect the election or term of any Senator chosen before it becomes valid as part of the Constitution.

Amendment XVIII

Section 1

After one year from ratification of this article, the manufacture, sale, or transportation of intoxicating liquors within, the importation thereof into, or the exportation thereof from the United States and all territory subject to the jurisdiction thereof for beverage purposes is hereby prohibited.

Section 2

The Congress and the several States shall have concurrent power to enforce this article by appropriate legislation.

Section 3

This article shall be inoperative unless it shall have been ratified as an amendment to the Constitution by the legislatures of the several States, as provided in the Constitution, within seven years from the date of the submission hereof to the States by the Congress.

Amendment XIX

Section 1

The right of citizens of the United States to vote shall not be denied or abridged by the United States or by any State on account of sex.

Section 2

Congress shall have power by appropriate legislation to enforce the provisions of this article.

Amendment XX

Section 1

The terms of the President and Vice President shall end at noon on the 20th day of January, and the terms of the Senators and Representatives at noon on the 3d day of January, of the years in which such terms would have ended if this article had not been ratified; and the terms of their successors shall then begin.

Section 2

The Congress shall assemble at least once in every year, and such meeting shall begin at noon on the 3d day of January, unless they shall by law appoint a different day.

Section 3

If, at the time fixed for the beginning of the term of the President, the President elect shall have died, the Vice President elect shall become President. If a President shall not have been chosen before the time fixed for the beginning of his term, or if the President elect shall have failed to qualify, then the Vice President elect shall act as President until a President shall have qualified; and the Congress may by law provide for the case wherein neither a President elect nor a Vice President elect shall have qualified, declaring who shall then act as President, or the manner in which one who is to act shall be selected, and such person shall act accordingly until a President or Vice President shall have qualified.

Section 4

The Congress may by law provide for the case of the death of any of the persons from whom the House of Representatives may choose a President whenever the right of choice shall have devolved upon them, and for the case of the death of any of the persons from whom the Senate may choose a Vice President whenever the right of choice shall have devolved upon them.

Section 5

Sections 1 and 2 shall take effect on the 15th day of October following the ratification of this article.

Section 6

This article shall be inoperative unless it shall have been ratified as an amendment to the Constitution by the legislatures of three-fourths of

Amendment 20.
"Lame-Duck" Amendment (1933)

Section 1. New Dates of Terms This amendment had two major purposes: (1) to shorten the time between the president's and vice president's election and inauguration, and (2) to end "lame-duck" sessions of Congress.

When the Constitution first went into effect, transportation and communication were slow and uncertain. It often took many months after the election in November for the president and vice president to travel to Washington, D.C., and prepare for their inauguration on March 4. This amendment ended this long wait for a new administration by fixing January 20 as Inauguration Day.

Section 2. Meeting Time of Congress "Lame-duck" sessions occurred every two years, after the November congressional election. That is, the Congress that held its session in December of an election year was not the newly elected Congress but the old Congress that had been elected two years earlier. This Congress continued to serve for several more months, usually until March of the next year. Often many of its members had failed to be reelected and were called "lame-ducks." The Twentieth Amendment abolished this lame-duck session, and provided that the new Congress hold its first session soon after the November election, on January 3.

Section 3. Succession of President and Vice President This amendment provides that if the president-elect dies before taking office, the vice president-elect becomes president. In the cases described, Congress will decide on a temporary president.

Section 4. Filling Presidential Vacancy If a presidential candidate dies while an election is being decided in the House, Congress may pass legislation to deal with the situation. Congress has similar power if this occurs when the Senate is deciding a vice-presidential election.

Section 5. Beginning the New Dates Sections 1 and 2 affected the Congress elected in 1934 and President Roosevelt, elected in 1936.

Section 6. Time Limit on Ratification The period for ratification by the states was limited to seven years.

Amendment 21.
Repeal of Prohibition Amendment (1933)

This amendment nullified the Eighteenth Amendment. It is the only amendment ever passed to overturn an earlier amendment. It remained unlawful to transport alcoholic beverages into states that forbade their use. It is the only amendment ratified by special state conventions instead of state legislatures.

▶ **Presidential campaign button**

Amendment 22.
Limit on Presidential Terms (1951)

This amendment wrote into the Constitution a custom started by Washington, Jefferson, and Madison, whereby presidents limited themselves to two terms in office. Although both Ulysses S. Grant and Theodore Roosevelt sought third terms, the two-term precedent was not broken until Franklin D. Roosevelt was elected to a third term in 1940 and then a fourth term in 1944. The passage of the Twenty-second Amendment ensures that no president is to be considered indispensable. It also provides that anyone who succeeds to the presidency and serves for more than two years of the term may not be elected more than one more time.

the several States within seven years from the date of its submission.

Amendment XXI

Section 1

The eighteenth article of amendment to the Constitution of the United States is hereby repealed.

Section 2

The transportation or importation into any State, Territory, or possession of the United States for delivery or use therein of intoxicating liquors, in violation of the laws thereof, is hereby prohibited.

Section 3

This article shall be inoperative unless it shall have been ratified as an amendment to the Constitution by conventions in the several States, as provided in the Constitution, within seven years from the date of the submission hereof to the States by the Congress.

Amendment XXII

Section 1

No person shall be elected to the office of the President more than twice, and no person who had held the office of President, or acted as President, for more than two years of a term to which some other person was elected President shall be elected to the office of the President more than once. But this Article shall not apply to any person holding the office of President when this Article was proposed by the Congress, and shall not prevent any person who may be holding the office of President, or acting as President, during the term within which this Article becomes operative from holding the office of President or acting as President during the remainder of such term.

Section 2

This article shall be inoperative unless it shall have been ratified as an amendment to the Constitution by the legislatures of three-fourths of the several States within seven years from the date of its submission to the States by the Congress.

Amendment XXIII

Section 1

The District constituting the seat of Government of the United States shall appoint in such manner as the Congress may direct:

A number of electors of President and Vice President equal to the whole number of Senators and Representatives in Congress to which the District would be entitled if it were a State, but in no event more than the least populous State; they shall be in addition to those appointed by the States, but they shall be considered, for the purposes of the election of President and Vice President, to be electors appointed by a State; and they shall meet in the District and perform such duties as provided by the twelfth article of amendment.

Section 2

The Congress shall have power to enforce this article by appropriate legislation.

Amendment XXIV

Section 1

The right of citizens of the United States to vote in any primary or other election for President or Vice President, for electors for President or Vice President, or for Senator or Representative in Congress, shall not be denied or abridged by the United States or any State by reason of failure to pay any poll tax or other tax.

Section 2

The Congress shall have power to enforce this article by appropriate legislation.

Amendment XXV

Section 1

In case of the removal of the President from office or his death or resignation, the Vice President shall become President.

Amendment 23.
Presidential Electors for the District of Columbia (1961)

This amendment granted people living in the District of Columbia the right to vote in presidential elections. The District casts three electoral votes. The people of Washington, D.C., still are without representation in Congress.

Amendment 24.
Abolition of the Poll Tax (1964)

A "poll tax" was a fee that persons were required to pay in order to vote in a number of Southern states. This amendment ended poll taxes as a requirement to vote in any presidential or congressional election. In 1966 the Supreme Court voided poll taxes in state elections as well.

Amendment 25.
Presidential Disability and Succession (1967)

Section 1. Replacing the President The vice president becomes president if the president dies, resigns, or is removed from office.

Section 2. Replacing the Vice President The president is to appoint a new vice president in case of a vacancy in that office, with the approval of the Congress.

The Twenty-fifth Amendment is unusually precise and explicit because it was intended to solve a serious constitutional problem. Sixteen times in American history, before passage of this amendment, the office of vice president was vacant, but fortunately in none of these cases did the president die or resign.

This amendment was used in 1973, when Vice President Spiro Agnew resigned from office after being charged with accepting bribes. President Richard Nixon then appointed Gerald R. Ford as vice president in accordance with the provisions of the Twenty-fifth Amendment. A year later, President Nixon resigned during the Watergate scandal, and Ford became president. President Ford then had to fill the vice presidency, which he had left vacant upon assuming the presidency. He named Nelson A. Rockefeller as vice president. Thus, both the presidency and vice presidency were held by men who had not been elected to their offices.

Section 3. Replacing the President With Consent If the president informs Congress, in writing, that he or she cannot carry out the duties of the office of president, the vice president becomes acting president.

Section 4. Replacing the President Without Consent If the president is unable to carry out the duties of the office but is unable or unwilling to so notify Congress, the cabinet and the vice president are to inform Congress of this fact. The vice president then becomes acting president. The procedure by which the president may regain the office if he or she recovers is also spelled out in this amendment.

Section 2

Whenever there is a vacancy in the office of the Vice President, the President shall nominate a Vice President who shall take the office upon confirmation by a majority vote of both Houses of Congress.

Section 3

Whenever the President transmits to the President pro tempore of the Senate and the Speaker of the House of Representatives his written declaration that he is unable to discharge the powers and duties of his office, and until he transmits to them a written declaration to the contrary, such powers and duties shall be discharged by the Vice President as Acting President.

Section 4

Whenever the Vice President and a majority of either the principal officers of the executive departments or of such other body as Congress may by law provide, transmit to the President pro tempore of the Senate and the Speaker of the House of Representatives their written declaration that the President is unable to discharge the powers and duties of his office, the Vice President shall immediately assume the power and duties of the office of Acting President.

Thereafter, when the President transmits to the President pro tempore of the Senate and the Speaker of the House of Representatives his written declaration that no inability exists, he shall resume the powers and duties of his office unless the Vice President and a majority of either the principal officers of the executive department or of such other body as Congress may by law provide, transmit within four days to the President pro tempore of the Senate and the Speaker of the House of Representatives their written declaration that the President is unable to discharge the powers and duties of his office. Thereupon Congress shall decide the issue, assembling within forty-eight hours for that purpose if not in session. If the Congress, within twenty-one days after receipt of the latter written declaration, or, if Congress is not in session, within twenty-one days after Congress is required to assemble, determines by two-thirds vote of both Houses that the President is unable to discharge the powers and duties of his office, the Vice President shall continue to discharge the same as Acting President; otherwise, the President shall resume the power and duties of his office.

Amendment XXVI

Section 1

The right of citizens of the United States, who are eighteen years of age or older, to vote shall not be denied or abridged by the United States or by any State on account of age.

Section 2

The Congress shall have power to enforce this article by appropriate legislation.

Amendment XXVII

No law, varying the compensation for the services of Senators and Representatives, shall take effect, until an election of representatives shall have intervened.

Amendment 26.
Eighteen-Year-Old Vote (1971)

This amendment made 18-year-olds eligible to vote in all federal, state, and local elections. Until then, the minimum age had been 21 in most states.

Amendment 27.
Restraint on Congressional Salaries (1992)

Any increase in the salaries of members of Congress will take effect in the subsequent session of Congress.

▲ Joint session of Congress

Historical Documents

Contents

The Code of Hammurabi

Hammurabi, a Mesopotamian ruler, developed his code of laws around 1700 B.C. This development of written law was a major advance toward justice and order.

Anu and Bel called by name me, Hammurabi, the exalted prince, who feared God, to bring about the rule of righteousness in the land, to destroy the wicked and the evil-doers; so that the strong should not harm the weak; so that I should . . . further the well-being of mankind. . . .

2. If any one bring an accusation against a man, and the accused go to the river and leap into the river, if he sink in the river his accuser shall take possession of his house. But if the river prove that the accused is not guilty, and he escape unhurt, then he who had brought the accusation shall be put to death, while he who leaped into the river shall take possession of the house that had belonged to his accuser. . . .

8. If any one steal cattle or sheep, or an ass, or a pig or a goat, if it belong to a god or to the court, the thief shall pay thirtyfold therefor; if they belonged to a freed man of the king he shall pay tenfold; if the thief has nothing with which to pay he shall be put to death. . . .

21. If any one break a hole into a house (break in to steal), he shall be put to death before that hole and be buried.

22. If any one is committing a robbery and is caught, then he shall be put to death.

23. If the robber is not caught, then shall he who was robbed claim under oath the amount of his loss; then shall the community, and . . . on whose ground and territory and in whose domain it was compensate him for the goods stolen. . . .

53. If any one be too lazy to keep his dam in proper condition, and does not so keep it; if then the dam break and all the fields be flooded, then shall he in whose dam the break occurred be sold for money, and the money shall replace the corn which he has caused to be ruined. . . .

(continued)

117. If any one fail to meet a claim for debt, and sell himself, his wife, his son, and daughter for money or give them away to forced labor: they shall work for three years in the house of the man who bought them, or the proprietor, and in the fourth year they shall be set free. . . .

136. If any one leave his house, run away, and then his wife go to another house, if then he return, and wishes to take his wife back: because he fled from his home and ran away, the wife of this runaway shall not return to her husband. . . .

▲ **Ruins of ancient Babylon**

142. If a woman quarrel with her husband . . . the reasons for her prejudice must be presented. If she is guiltless, and there is no fault on her part, but he leaves and neglects her, then no guilt attaches to this woman, she shall take her dowry and go back to her father's house.

143. If she is not innocent, but leaves her husband. . . this woman shall be cast into the water. . . .

195. If a son strike his father, his hands shall be hewn off.

196. If a man put out the eye of another man, his eye shall be put out.

197. If he break another man's bone, his bone shall be broken. . . .

199. If he put out the eye of a man's slave, or break the bone of a man's slave, he shall pay one-half of its value.

200. If a man knock out the teeth of his equal, his teeth shall be knocked out. . . .

202. If any one strike the body of a man higher in rank than he, he shall receive sixty blows with an ox-whip in public. . . .

215. If a physician make a large incision with an operating knife and cure it, or if he open a tumor (over an eye) with an operating knife, and saves the eye, he shall receive ten shekels in money. . . .

218. If a physician make a large incision with the operating knife, and kill him, or open a tumor with the operating knife, and cut out the eye, his hands shall be cut off. . . .

229. If a builder build a house for some one, and does not construct it properly, and the house which he built fall in and kill its owner, then that builder shall be put to death. . . .

Laws of justice which Hammurabi, the wise king, established. A righteous law, and pious statute did he teach the land. Hammurabi, the protecting king am I. . . . The king who ruleth among the kings of the cities am I. My words are well considered; there is no wisdom like unto mine. By the command of Shamash, the great judge of heaven and earth, let righteousness go forth in the land. . . .

The Magna Carta

The Magna Carta, signed by King John in 1215, marked a decisive step forward in the development of constitutional government in England. Later it served as a model for colonists who carried its guarantees of legal and political rights to America.

John, by the grace of God, king of England, lord of Ireland, duke of Normandy and Aquitaine, and count of Anjou: to the archbishops, bishops, abbots, earls, barons, justiciaries, foresters, sheriffs, reeves, ministers, and all bailiffs and others his faithful subjects, greeting. . . .

1. We have, in the first place, granted to God, and by this our present charter confirmed for us and our heirs forever that the English church shall be free. . . .

9. Neither we nor our bailiffs shall seize any land or rent for any debt so long as the debtor's chattels are sufficient to discharge the same. . . .

12. No scutage [tax] or aid [subsidy] shall be imposed in our kingdom unless by the common counsel thereof . . . .

14. For obtaining the common counsel of the kingdom concerning the assessment of aids . . . or of scutage, we will cause to be summoned, severally by our letters, the archbishops, bishops, abbots, earls, and great barons; we will also cause to be summoned generally, by our sheriffs and bailiffs, all those who hold lands directly of us, to meet on a fixed day . . . and at a fixed place. . . .

20. A free man shall be amerced [punished] for a small fault only according to the measure thereof, and for a great crime according to its magnitude. . . . None of these amercements shall be imposed except by the oath of honest men of the neighborhood.

21. Earls and barons shall be amerced only by their peers, and only in proportion to the measure of the offense. . . .

38. In the future no bailiff shall upon his own unsupported accusation put any man to trial without producing credible witnesses to the truth of the accusation.

39. No free man shall be taken, imprisoned, disseised [seized], outlawed, banished, or in any way destroyed, nor will we proceed against or prosecute him, except by the lawful judgment of his peers and by the law of the land.

40. To no one will we sell, to none will we deny or delay, right or justice. . . .

42. In the future it shall be lawful . . . for anyone to leave and return to our kingdom safely and securely by land and water, saving his fealty to us. Excepted are those who have been imprisoned or outlawed according to the law of the land. . . .

61. Whereas we, for the honor of God and the amendment of our realm, and in order the better to allay the discord arisen between us and our barons, have granted all these things aforesaid. . . .

63. Wherefore we will, and firmly charge . . . that all men in our kingdom shall have and hold all the aforesaid liberties, rights, and concessions . . . fully, and wholly to them and their heirs. . . in all things and places forever . . . . It is moreover sworn, as well on our part as on the part of the barons, that all these matters aforesaid will be kept in good faith and without deceit. Witness the abovenamed and many others. Given by our hand in the meadow which is called Runnymede. . . .

The English Bill of Rights

▲ **Seal of William and Mary**

In 1689 William of Orange and his wife, Mary, became joint rulers of England after accepting what became known as the Bill of Rights. This document assured the people of certain basic civil rights.

An act declaring the rights and liberties of the subject and settling the succession of the crown. Whereas the lords spiritual and temporal and commons assembled at Westminster lawfully fully and freely representing all the estates of the people of this realm did upon the thirteenth day of February in the year of our Lord one thousand six hundred eight-eight [-nine] present unto their majesties . . . William and Mary prince and princess of Orange . . . a certain declaration in writing made by the said lords and commons in the words following viz

Whereas the late king James the second by the assistance of divers evil counsellors judges and ministers employed by him did endeavor to subvert and extirpate the protestant religion and the laws and liberties of this kingdom.

By assuming and exercising a power of dispensing with and suspending of laws and the execution of laws without consent of parliament. . . .

By levyng money for and to the use of the crown by pretence of prerogative for other time and in other manner than the same was granted by parliament.

By raising and keeping a standing army within this kingdom in time of peace without consent of parliament and quartering soldiers contrary to law. . . .

By violating the freedom of election of members to serve in parliament. . . .

And excessive bail hath been required of persons committed in criminal cases to elude the benefit of the laws made for the liberty of the subjects.

And excessive fines have been imposed.

And illegal and cruel punishments inflicted. . . .

And thereupon the said lords spiritual and temporal and commons . . . do . . . declare

That the pretended power of suspending of laws or the execution of laws by regal authority without consent of parliament is illegal. . . .

That levying money for or to the use of the crown . . . without grant of parliament for longer time or in other manner than the same is or shall be granted is illegal.

That it is the right of the subjects to petition the king and all commitments and prosecutions for such petitioning are illegal.

That the raising or keeping a standing army within the kingdom in time of peace unless it be with consent of parliament is against law. . . .

That election of members of parliament ought to be free. . . .

That excessive bail ought not to be required nor excessive fines imposed nor cruel and unusual punishments inflicted. . . .

The said lords . . . do resolve that William and Mary prince and princess of Orange be and be declared king and queen of England France and Ireland. . . .

The Mayflower Compact

On November 21, 1620, 41 men aboard the Mayflower *drafted this agreement. The Mayflower Compact was the first plan of self-government ever put in force in the English colonies. The original compact has been lost. Mourt's Relation (1622) is the earliest source of the text reprinted here.*

This day, before we came to harbor, observing some not well affected to unity and concord, but gave some appearance of faction, it was thought good there should be an association and agreement that we should combine together in one body, and to submit to such government and governors as we should by common consent agree to make and choose, and set our hands to this that follows word for word.

In the name of God, Amen. We whose names are underwritten, the loyal subjects of our dread sovereign lord, King James, by the grace of God, of Great Britain, France, and Ireland, King, Defender of the Faith, etc.

Having undertaken for the glory of God, and advancement of the Christian faith and honor of our king and country, a voyage to plant the first colony in the northern parts of Virginia, do by these present, solemnly and mutually, in the presence of God and one of another, covenant and combine ourselves together into a civil body politic, for our better ordering and preservation and furtherance of the ends aforesaid; and by virtue hereof to enact, constitute, and frame such just and equal laws, ordinances, acts, constitutions, offices from time to time as shall be thought most meet and convenient for the general good of the colony; unto which we promise all due submission and obedience. In witness whereof we have hereunder subscribed our names, Cape Cod, 11th of November, in the year of the reign of our sovereign lord, King James, of England, France, and Ireland 18, and of Scotland 54. Anno Domini 1620.

▲ *Signing of the Compact on the* Mayflower *by Edward Percy Moran, c. 1900*

Fundamental Orders of Connecticut

In January 1639, settlers in Connecticut, led by Thomas Hooker, drew up the Fundamental Orders of Connecticut—America's first written constitution. It is essentially a compact among the settlers and a body of laws.

Forasmuch as it has pleased the Almighty God by the wise disposition of His Divine Providence so to order and dispose of things that we, the inhabitants and residents of Windsor, Hartford, and Wethersfield are now cohabiting and dwelling in and upon the river of Conectecotte and the lands thereunto adjoining; and well knowing where a people are gathered together the Word of God requires that, to maintain the peace and union of such a people, there should be an orderly and decent government established according to God, . . . do therefore associate and conjoin ourselves to be as one public state or commonwealth. . . . As also in our civil affairs to be guided and governed according to such laws, rules, orders, and decrees as shall be made, ordered, and decreed, as follows:

1. It is ordered . . . that there shall be yearly two general assemblies or courts; . . . The first shall be called the Court of Election, wherein shall be yearly chosen . . . so many magistrates and other public officers as shall be found requisite. Whereof one to be chosen governor . . . and no other magistrate to be chosen for more than one year; provided aways there be six chosen besides the governor . . . by all that are admitted freemen and have taken the oath of fidelity, and do cohabit within this jurisdiction. . . .

4. It is ordered . . . that no person be chosen governor above once in two years, and that the governor be always a member of some approved congregation, and formerly of the magistracy within this jurisdiction; and all the magistrates freemen of this Commonwealth. . . .

5. It is ordered . . . that to the aforesaid Court of Election the several towns shall send their deputies. . . . Also, the other General Court . . . shall be for making of laws, and any other public occasion which concerns the good of the Commonwealth. . . .

7. It is ordered . . . that . . . the constable or constables of each town shall forthwith give notice distinctly to the inhabitants of the same . . . that . . . they meet and assemble themselves together to elect and choose certain deputies to be at the General Court then following to [manage] the affairs of the Commonwealth; which said deputies shall be chosen by all that are admitted inhabitants in the several towns and have taken the oath of fidelity. . . .

10. It is ordered . . . that every General Court . . . shall consist of the governor, or someone chosen to moderate the Court, and four other magistrates, at least, with the major part of the deputies of the several towns legally chosen. . . . In which said General Courts shall consist the supreme power of the Commonwealth, and they only shall have power to make laws or repeal them, to grant levies, to admit of freemen, dispose of lands undisposed of to several towns or person, and also shall have power to call either Court or magistrate or any other person whatsoever into question for any misdemeanor. . . .

In which Court, the governor or moderator shall have power to order the Court to give liberty of speech, . . . to put all things to vote, and, in case the vote be equal, to have the casting voice. . . .

Two Treatises of Government

John Locke's Two Treatises of Government *was published in 1690. The "Second Treatise of Government" states his belief that government is based on an agreement between the people and ruler.*

Of the State of Nature.

To understand Political Power right, and to derive it from its Original, we must consider what State all Men are naturally in, and that is, a State of perfect Freedom to order their Actions, and dispose of their Possessions, and Persons as they think fit, within the bounds of the Law of Nature, without asking leave, or depending upon the Will of any other Man.

A State also of Equality, wherein all the Power and Jurisdiction is reciprocal, no one having more than another. . . .

▲ John Locke

Of the Beginning of Political Societies.

Men being, as has been said, by Nature, all free, equal and independent, no one can be put out of this Estate, and subjected to the Political Power of another, without his own Consent. The only way whereby any one divests himself of his Natural Liberty, and puts on the bonds of Civil Society is by agreeing with other Men to joyn and unite into a Community, for their comfortable, safe, and peaceable living one amongst another, in a secure Enjoyment of their properties, and a greater Security against any that are not of it. This any number of Men may do, because it injures not the Freedom of the rest; they are left as they were in the Liberty of the State of Nature. . . .

For when any number of Men have, by the consent of every individual, made a Community, they have thereby made that Community one Body, with a Power to Act as one Body, which is only by the will and determination of the majority. . . .

Whosoever therefore out of a state of Nature unite into a Community, must be understood to give up all the power, necessary to the ends for which they unite into Society, to the majority of the Community. . . .

Of the Dissolution of Government.

. . . Governments are dissolved from within . . . when the Legislative is altered. . . . First, that when such a single Person or Prince sets up his own Arbitrary Will in place of the Laws, which are the Will of the Society, declared by the Legislative, then the Legislative is changed. . . . Secondly, when the Prince hinders the legislative from . . . acting freely, pursuant to those ends, for which it was Constituted, the Legislative is altered. . . . Thirdly, When by the Arbitrary Power of the Prince, the Electors, or ways of Election are altered, without the Consent, and contrary to the common Interest of the People, there also the Legislative is altered. . . .

In these and the like Cases, when the Government is dissolved, the People are at liberty to provide for themselves, by erecting a new Legislative, differing from the other, by the change of Persons, or Form, or both as they shall find it most for their safety and good. For the Society can never, by the fault of another, lose the Native and Original Right it has to preserve itself. . . .

The Wealth of Nations

Adam Smith, a Scottish economist and philosopher, published An Inquiry into the Nature and Causes of the Wealth of Nations *in 1776. The book offered a detailed description of life and trade in English society. It also scientifically described the basic principles of economics for the first time.*

But it is only for the sake of profit that any man employs a capital in the support of industry; and he will always, therefore, endeavour to employ it in the support of that industry of which the produce is likely to be of the greatest value, or to exchange for the greatest quantity either of money or of other goods. . . .

As every individual, therefore, endeavours as much as he can both to employ his capital in the support of domestic industry, and so to direct that industry that its produce may be of the greatest value; every individual necessarily labours to render the annual revenue of the society as great as he can. He generally, indeed, neither intends to promote the public interest, nor knows how much he is promoting it. . . . By pursuing his own interest he frequently promotes that of the society more effectually than when he really intends to promote it. . . .

What is the species of domestic industry which his capital can employ, and of which the produce is likely to be of the greatest value, every individual, it is evident, can, in his local situation, judge much better than any statesman or lawgiver can do for him. . . .

To give the monopoly of the home-market to the produce of domestic industry, in any particular art or manufacture, is in some measure to direct private people in what manner they ought to employ their capitals, and must, in almost all cases, be either a useless or a hurtful regulation. If the produce of domestic can be brought there as cheap as that of foreign industry, the regulation is evidently useless. If it cannot, it must generally be hurtful. It is the maxim of every prudent master of a family, never to attempt to make at home what it will cost him more to make than to buy. The taylor does not attempt to make his own shoes, but buys them of the shoemaker. The shoemaker does not attempt to make his own clothes, but employs a taylor. The farmer attempts to make neither the one nor the other, but employs those different artificers. All of them find it in their interest to employ their whole industry in a way in which they have some advantage over their neighbours, and to purchase with a part of its produce . . . whatever else they have occasion for.

What is prudence in the conduct of every private family, can scarcely be folly in that of a great kingdom. If a foreign country can supply us with a commodity cheaper than we ourselves can make it, better buy it of them with some part of the produce of our own industry, employed in a way in which we have some advantage. . . . It is certainly not employed to the greatest advantage, when it is thus directed towards an object which it can buy cheaper than it can make.

▲ Adam Smith

Articles of Confederation

In 1776, Richard Henry Lee moved that Congress appoint a committee to draw up articles of confederation among the states. One member of each state was selected. The committee of state delegates revised and adopted John Dickinson's plan of union in 1781.

Articles of Confederation and Perpetual Union Between the States of New Hampshire, Massachusetts Bay, Rhode Island and Providence Plantations, Connecticut, New York, New Jersey, Pennsylvania, Delaware, Maryland, Virginia, North Carolina, South Carolina, and Georgia.

▲ **The Articles of Confederation**

Article I. The style of this confederacy shall be "The United States of America."

Article II. Each state retains its sovereignty, freedom, and independence, and every power, jurisdiction, and right which is not by this confederation expressly delegated to the United States in Congress assembled.

Article III. The said states hereby severally enter into a firm league of friendship with each other, for their common defense, the security of their liberties, and their mutual and general welfare, binding themselves to assist each other against all force offered to, or attacks made upon them, or any of them, on account of religion, sovereignty, trade, or any other pretense whatever.

Article IV. The better to secure and perpetuate mutual friendship and intercourse among the people of the different states in this union, the free inhabitants of each of these states, paupers, vagabonds, and fugitives from justice excepted, shall be entitled to all privileges and immunities of free citizens in the several states; and the people of each state shall have free ingress and regress to and from any other state and shall enjoy therein all the privileges of trade and commerce, subject to the same duties, impositions, and restrictions as the inhabitants thereof respectively, provided that such restrictions shall not extend so far as to prevent the removal of property imported into any state, to any other state of which the owner is an inhabitant; provided also that no imposition, duties, or restriction shall be laid by any state on the property of the United States, or either of them.

If any person guilty of or charged with treason, felony, or other high misdemeanor in any state shall flee from justice, and be found in any of the United States, he shall, upon demand of the governor or executive power of the state from which he fled, be delivered up and removed to the state having jurisdiction of his offense.

Full faith and credit shall be given in each of these states to the records, acts, and judicial proceedings of the courts and magistrates of every other state.

Article V. For the more convenient management of the general interests of the United States, delegates shall be annually appointed in such manner as the legislature of each state shall direct, to meet in Congress on the first Monday in November, in every year, with a power reserved to each state to recall its delegates, or any of them, at any time within the year and to send others in their stead for the remainder of the year.

No state shall be represented in Congress by less than two nor by more than seven members; and no person shall be capable of being a delegate for more than three years in any term of six years; nor shall any person, being a delegate, be capable of holding any office under the United States for which he, or another for his benefit, receives any salary, fees, or emolument of any kind.

Each state shall maintain its own delegates in a meeting of the states and while they act as members of the Committee of the States.

In determining questions in the United States in Congress assembled, each state shall have one vote.

Freedom of speech and debate in Congress shall not be impeached or questioned in any court or place out of Congress, and the members of Congress shall be protected in their persons from arrests and imprisonments during the time of their going to and from, and attendance on, Congress, except for treason, felony, or breach of the peace.

Article VI. No state, without the consent of the United States in Congress assembled, shall send any embassy to, or receive any embassy from, or enter into any conference, agreement, alliance, or treaty with any king, prince, or state; nor shall any person holding any office of profit or trust under the United States, or any of them, accept of any present, emolument, office, or title of any kind whatever from any king, prince, or foreign state; nor shall the United States in Congress assembled, or any of them, grant any title of nobility.

No two or more states shall enter into any treaty, confederation, or alliance whatever between them without the consent of the United States in Congress assembled, specifying accurately the purposes for which the same is to be entered into and how long it shall continue.

No state shall lay any imposts or duties which may interfere with any stipulations in treaties entered into by the United States in Congress assembled with any king, prince, or state, in pursuance of any treaties already proposed by Congress, to the courts of France and Spain.

No vessels of war shall be kept up in time of peace by any state except such number only as shall be deemed necessary by the United States in Congress assembled for the defense of such state or its trade; nor shall any body of forces be kept up by any state in time of peace except such number only as in the judgment of the United States in Congress assembled shall be deemed requisite to garrison the forts necessary for the defense of such state; but every state shall always keep up a well-regulated and disciplined militia, sufficiently armed and accoutered, and shall provide and constantly have ready for use, in public stores, a due number of field pieces and tents and a proper quantity of arms, ammunition, and camp equipage.

No state shall engage in any war without the consent of the United States in Congress assembled unless such state be actually invaded by enemies, or shall have received certain advice of a resolution being formed by some nation of Indians to invade such state, and the danger is so imminent as not to admit of a delay till the United States in Congress assembled

Articles of Confederation

can be consulted; nor shall any state grant commissions to any ships or vessels of war, nor letters of marque or reprisal, except it be after a declaration of war by the United States in Congress assembled, and then only against the kingdom or state and the subjects thereof against which war has been so declared and under such regulations as shall be established by the United States in Congress assembled, unless such state be infested by pirates, in which case vessels of war may be fitted out for that occasion and kept so long as the danger shall continue or until the United States in Congress assembled shall determine otherwise.

Article VII. When land forces are raised by any state for the common defense, all officers of or under the rank of colonel shall be appointed by the legislature of each state respectively, by whom such forces shall be raised, or in such manner as such state shall direct, and all vacancies shall be filled up by the state which first made the appointment.

Article VIII. All charges of war and all other expenses that shall be incurred for the common defense or general welfare, and allowed by the United States in Congress assembled, shall be defrayed out of a common treasury, which shall be supplied by the several states in proportion to the value of all land within each state, granted to or surveyed for any person, as such land the buildings and improvements thereon shall be estimated according to such mode as the United States in Congress assembled shall from time to time direct and appoint. The taxes for paying that proportion shall be laid and levied by the authority and direction of the legislatures of the several states within the time agreed upon by the United States in Congress assembled.

Article IX. The United States in Congress assembled shall have the sole and exclusive right and power of determining on peace and war, except in the cases mentioned in the sixth article—of sending and receiving ambassadors—entering into treaties and alliances, provided that no treaty of commerce shall be made whereby the legislative power of the respective states shall be restrained from imposing such imposts and duties on foreigners as their own people are subjected to or from prohibiting the exportation or importation of any species of goods or commodities whatsoever—of establishing rules for deciding in all cases what captures on land or water shall be legal, and in what manner prizes taken by land or naval forces in the service of the United States shall be divided or appropriated—of granting letters of marque and reprisal in times of peace—appointing courts for the trial of piracies and felonies committed on the high seas and establishing courts for receiving and determining finally appeals in all cases of captures, provided that no member of Congress shall be appointed a judge in any of the said courts.

The United States in Congress assembled shall also be the last resort on appeal in all disputes and difference now subsisting or that hereafter may arise between two or more states concerning boundary, jurisdiction, or any other cause whatever. . . . Provided, also, that no state shall be deprived of territory for the benefit of the United States.

All controversies concerning the private right of soil claimed under different grants of two or more states, whose jurisdictions as they may respect such lands, and the states which passed such grants are adjusted, the said grants or either of them being at the same time claimed to have originated antecedent to such settlement of jurisdiction shall, on the petition of either party to the Congress of the United States, be finally determined as near as may be in the same manner as is before prescribed for deciding disputes respecting territorial jurisdiction between different states.

The United States in Congress assembled shall also have the sole and exclusive right and power of regulating the alloy and value of coin struck by their own authority or by that of the respective states—fixing the standard of weights and measures throughout the United States—regulating the trade and managing all affairs with the Indians not members of any of the states, provided that the legislative right of any state within its own limits be not infringed or violated—establishing or regulating post offices from one state to another, throughout all the United States, and exacting such postage on the papers passing through the same as may be requisite to defray the expenses of the said office—appointing all officers of the land forces in the service of the United States excepting regimental officers—appointing all the officers of the naval forces, and commissioning all officers whatever in the service of the United States—making rules for the government and regulation of the said land and naval forces, and directing their operations.

The United States in Congress assembled shall have authority to appoint a committee, to sit in the recess of Congress, to be denominated "A Committee of the States," and to consist of one delegate from each state; and to appoint such other committees and civil officers as may be necessary for managing the general affairs of the United States under their direction—to appoint one of their number to preside, provided that no person be allowed to serve in the office of President more than one year in any term of three years; to ascertain the necessary sums of money to be raised for the service of the United States, and to appropriate and apply the same for defraying the public expenses—to borrow money or emit bills on the credit of the United States, transmitting every half-year to the respective states an account of the sums of money so borrowed or emitted—to build and equip a navy—to agree upon the number of land forces, and to make requisitions from each state for its quota, in proportion to the number of white inhabitants in such state, which requisition shall be binding. . . .

Thereupon the legislature of each state shall appoint the regimental officers, raise the men and clothe, arm, and equip them in a soldier-like manner, at the expense of the United States; and the officers and men so clothed, armed, and equipped shall march to the place appointed and within the time agreed on by the United States in Congress assembled. . . .

The United States in Congress assembled shall never engage in a war, nor grant letters of marque and reprisal in time of peace, nor enter into any treaties or alliances, nor coin money, nor regulate the value thereof, nor ascertain the sums and expenses necessary for the defense and welfare of the United States, or any of them, nor emit bills, nor borrow money on the credit of the United States, nor appropriate money, nor agree upon the number of vessels of war to be built or purchased or the number of land or sea forces to be raised, nor appoint a commander in chief of the Army or Navy, unless nine states assent to the same; nor shall a question on any other point, except for adjourning from day to day, be determined unless by the votes of a majority of the United States in Congress assembled. . . .

Article XI. Canada acceding to this Confederation, and joining in the measures of the United States, shall be admitted into and entitled to all the advantages of this union; but no other colony shall be admitted into the same unless such admission be agreed to by nine states.

Article XII. All bills of credit emitted, moneys borrowed, and debts contracted by or under the authority of Congress, before the assembling of the United States, in pursuance of the present Confederation, shall be deemed and considered as a charge against the United States, for payment and satisfaction whereof the said United States and the public faith are hereby solemnly pledged.

The Federalist, No. 10

James Madison wrote several articles supporting ratification of the Constitution for a New York newspaper. In the excerpt below, Madison argues for the idea of a federal republic.

▲ **James Madison**

Among the numerous advantages promised by a well-constructed Union, none deserves to be more accurately developed than its tendency to break and control the violence of faction. The friend of popular governments never finds himself so much alarmed for their character and fate as when he contemplates their propensity to this dangerous vice. . . . The instability, injustice, and confusion introduced into the public councils have, in truth, been the mortal diseases under which popular governments have everywhere perished. . . . It will be found, indeed, on a candid review of our situation, that some of the distresses under which we labor have been erroneously charged on the operation of our governments; but it will be found, at the same time, that other causes will not alone account for many of our heaviest misfortunes; and, particularly, for that prevailing and increasing distrust of public engagements and alarm for private rights which are echoed from one end of the continent to the other. These must be chiefly, if not wholly, effects of the unsteadiness and injustice with which a factious spirit has tainted our public administration.

By a faction I understand a number of citizens, whether amounting to a majority or minority of the whole, who are united and actuated by some common impulse of passion, or of interest, adverse to the rights of other citizens, or to the permanent and aggregate interests of the community.

There are two methods of curing the mischiefs of faction: the one, by removing its causes; the other, by controlling its effects.

There are again two methods of removing the causes of faction: the one, by destroying the liberty which is essential to its existence; the other, by giving to every citizen the same opinions, the same passions, and the same interests.

It could never be more truly said than of the first remedy that it was worse than the disease. Liberty is to faction what air is to fire, an aliment without which it instantly expires. But it could not be a less folly to abolish liberty, which is essential to political life, because it nourishes faction than it would be to wish the annihilation of air, which is essential to animal life, because it imparts to fire its destructive agency.

The second expedient is as impracticable as the first would be unwise. As long as the reason of man continues fallible, and he is at liberty to exercise it, different opinions will be formed. . . .

The latent causes of faction are thus sown in the nature of man; and we see them everywhere brought into different degrees of activity, according to the different circumstances of civil society. A zeal for different opinions concerning religion, concerning government, and many other points . . . ; an attachment to different leaders ambitiously contending for pre-eminence and power . . . have, in turn, divided mankind into parties, inflamed them with mutual animosity, and rendered them much more disposed to vex and oppress each other than to cooperate for their common good. . . . But the most common and durable source of factions has been the verious and unequal distribution of property. Those who hold and those who are without property have ever formed distinct interests in society. Those who are creditors, and those who are debtors, fall under a like discrimination. A landed interest, a manufacturing interest, a mercantile interest, a moneyed interest, with many lesser interests, grow up of necessity in civilized nations, and divide them into different classes, actuated by different sentiments and views. The regulation of these various and interfering interests forms the principal task of modern legislation and involves the spirit of party and faction in the necessary and ordinary operations of government. . . .

[Y]et what are many of the most important acts of legislation but so many judicial determinations, not indeed concerning the rights of single persons, but concerning the rights of large bodies of citizens? And what are the different classes of legislators but advocates and parties to the causes which they determine? . . .

It is in vain to say that enlightened statesmen will be able to adjust these clashing interests and render them all subservient to the public good. Enlightened statesmen will not always be at the helm. Nor, in many cases, can such an adjustment be made at all without taking into view indirect and remote considerations, which will rarely prevail over the immediate interest which one party may find in disregarding the rights of another or the good of the whole.

The inference to which we are brought is that the causes of faction cannot be removed and that relief is only to be sought in the means of controlling its effects.

If a faction consists of less than a majority, relief is supplied by the republican principle, which enables the majority to defeat its sinister views by regular vote. It may clog the administration, it may convulse the society; but it will be unable to execute and mask its violence under the forms of the Constitution. When a majority is included in a faction, the form of popular government, on the other hand, enables it to sacrifice to its ruling passion or interest both the public good and the rights of other citizens. To secure the public good and private rights against the danger of such a faction, and at the same time to preserve the spirit and the form of popular government, is then the great object to which our inquiries are directed. . . .

By what means is this object attainable? Evidently by one of two only. Either the existence of the same passion or interest in a majority at the same time must be prevented, or the majority, having such coexistent passion or interest, must be rendered, by their number and local situation, unable to concert and carry into effect schemes of oppression. If the impulse and the opportunity be suffered to coincide, we well know that neither moral nor religious motives can be relied on as an adequate control. They are not found to be such on the injustice and violence of individuals, and lose their efficacy in proportion to the number combined together. . . .

From this view of the subject it may be concluded that a pure democracy, by which I mean a society consisting of a small number of citizens, who assemble and administer the government in person, can admit of no cure for the mischiefs of faction. A common passion or interest will, in almost every case, be felt by a majority of the whole; a communication and concert results from the form of government itself; and there is nothing to check the inducements to sacrifice the weaker party or an obnoxious individual. Hence it is that such democracies have ever been spectacles of turbulence and contention; have ever been found incompatible with personal security or the rights of property; and have in general been as short in their lives as they have been violent in their deaths. . . .

A republic, by which I mean a government in which the scheme of representation takes place, opens a different prospect and promises the cure for which we are seeking. Let us examine the points in which it varies from pure democracy, and we shall comprehend both the nature of the cure and the efficacy which it must derive from the Union.

The two great points of difference between a democracy and a republic are: first, the delegation of the government, in the latter, to a small number of citizens elected by the rest; secondly, the greater number of citizens and greater sphere of country over which the latter may be extended.

The effect of the first difference is, on the one hand, to refine and enlarge the public views by passing them through the medium of a chosen body of citizens, whose wisdom may best discern the true interest of their country and whose patriotism and love of justice will be least likely to sacrifice it to temporary or partial considerations. Under such a regulation it may well happen that the public voice, pronounced by the representatives of the people, will be more consonant to the public good than if pronounced by the people themselves. . . . On the other hand, the effect may be inverted. Men of factious tempers, of local prejudices, or of sinister designs, may, by intrigue, by corruption, or by other means, first obtain the suffrages, and then betray the interests of the people. The question resulting is, whether small or extensive republics are most favorable to the election of proper guardians of the public weal; and it is clearly decided in favor of the latter by two obvious considerations.

In the first place it is to be remarked that however small the republic may be the representatives must be raised to a certain number in order to guard against the cabals of a few; and that however large it may be they must be limited to a certain number in order to guard against the confusion of a multitude. Hence, the number of representatives in the two cases not being in proportion to that of the constituents, and being proportionally greatest in the small republic, it follows that if the proportion of fit characters be not less in the large than in the small republic, the former will present a greater option, and consequently a greater probability of a fit choice.

In the next place, as each representative will be chosen by a greater number of citizens in the large than in the small republic, it will be more difficult for unworthy candidates to practise with success the vicious arts by which elections are too often carried; and the suffrages of the people being more free, will be more likely to center on men who possess the most attractive merit and the most diffusive and established characters.

It must be confessed that in this, as in most other cases, there is a mean, on both sides of which inconveniencies will be found to lie. By enlarging too much the number of electors, you render the representative too little acquainted with all their local circumstances and lesser interests; as by reducing it too much, you render him unduly attached to these, and too little fit to comprehend and pursue great and national objects. The federal Constitution forms a happy combination in this respect; the great and aggregate interests being referred to the national, the local and particular to the State legislatures. . . .

In the extent and proper structure of the Union, therefore, we behold a republican remedy for the diseases most incident to republican government. And according to the degree of pleasure and pride we feel in being republicans ought to be our zeal in cherishing the spirit and supporting the character of federalists.

The Federalist, No. 51

▲ Eagle and crossed flags

To what expedient, then, shall we finally resort, for maintaining in practice the necessary partition of power among the several departments as laid down in the Constitution? . . .

In order to lay a due foundation for that separate and distinct exercise of the different powers of government, which to a certain extent is admitted on all hands to be essential to the preservation of liberty, it is evident that each department should have a will of its own; and consequently should be so constituted that the members of each should have as little agency as possible in the appointment of the members of the others. Were this principle rigorously adhered to, it would require that all the appointments for the supreme executive, legislative, and judiciary magistracies should be drawn from the same fountain of authority, the people. . . .

It is equally evident that the members of each department should be as little dependent as possible on those of the others for the emoluments [finances] annexed to their offices. Were the executive magistrate, or the judges, not independent of the legislature in this particular, their independence in every other would be merely nominal.

But the great security against a gradual concentration of the several powers in the same department consists in giving to those who administer each department the necessary constitutional means and personal motives to resist encroachments of the others. . . . Ambition must be made to counteract ambition. The interest of the man must be connected with the constitutional rights of the place. It may be a reflection on human nature that such devices should be necessary to control the abuses of government. But what is government itself but the greatest of all reflections on human nature? If men were angels, no government would be necessary. If angels were to govern men, neither external nor internal controls on government would be necessary. In framing a government which is to be administered by men over men, the great difficulty lies in this: you must first enable the government to control the governed; and in the next place oblige it to control itself. A dependence on the people is, no doubt, the primary control on the government; but experience has taught mankind the necessity of auxiliary precautions. . . .

But it is not possible to give to each department an equal power of self-defense. In republican government, the legislative authority necessarily predominates. The remedy for this inconveniency is to divide the legislature into different branches; and to render them, by different modes of election and different principles of action, as little connected with each other as the nature of their common functions and their common dependence on the society will admit. It may even be necessary to guard against dangerous encroachments by still further precautions. As the weight of the legislative authority requires that it should be thus divided, the weakness of the executive may require, on the other hand, that it should be fortified. An absolute negative [veto] on the legislature appears, at first view, to be the natural defense with which the executive magistrate should be armed. But perhaps it would be neither altogether safe nor alone sufficient. On ordinary occasions it might not be exerted with the requisite firmness, and on extraordinary occasions it might be perfidiously abused.

The Federalist, No. 51 *(continued)*

May not this defect of an absolute negative be supplied by some qualified connection between this weaker department and the weaker branch of the stronger department, by which the latter may be led to support the constitutional rights of the former, without being too much detached from the rights of its own department? . . .

There are, moreover, two considerations particularly applicable to the federal system of America, which place that system in a very interesting point of view.

First. In a single republic, all the power surrendered by the people is submitted to the administration of a single government; and the usurpations are guarded against by a division of the government into distinct and separate departments. In the compound republic of America, the power surrendered by the people is first divided between two distinct governments, and then the portion allotted to each subdivided among distinct and separate departments. Hence a double security arises to the rights of the people. The different governments will control each other, at the same time that each will be controlled by itself.

Second. It is of great importance in a republic not only to guard the society against the oppression of its rulers, but to guard one part of the society against the injustice of the other part. Different interests necessarily exist in different classes of citizens. If a majority be united by a common interest, the rights of the minority will be insecure. There are but two methods of providing against this evil: the one by creating a will in the community independent of the majority—that is, of the society itself; the other, by comprehending in the society so many separate descriptions of citizens as will render an unjust combination of a majority of the whole very improbable, if not impracticable. The first method prevails in all governments possessing an hereditary or self-appointed authority. This, at best, is but a precarious security; because a power independent of the society may as well espouse the unjust views of the major as the rightful interests of the minor party, and may possibly be turned against both parties. The second method will be exemplified in the federal republic of the United States. Whilst all authority in it will be derived from and dependent on the society, the society itself will be broken into so many parts, interests and classes of citizens, that the rights of individuals, or of the minority, will be in little danger from interested combinations of the majority. In a free government the security for civil rights must be the same as that for religious rights. It consists in the one case in the multiplicity of interests, and in the other in the multiplicity of sects. The degree of security in both cases will depend on the number of interests and sects; and this may be presumed to depend on the extent of country and number of people comprehended under the same government. This view of the subject must particularly recommend a proper federal system to all the sincere and considerate friends of republican government, since it shows that in exact proportion as the territory of the Union may be formed into more circumscribed Confederacies, or States, oppressive combinations of a majority will be facilitated; the best security, under the republican forms, for the rights of every class of citizen, will be diminished; and consequently the stability and independence of some member of the government, the only other security, must be proportionally increased. Justice is the end of government. It is the end of civil society. It ever has been and ever will be pursued until it be obtained, or until liberty be lost in the pursuit. . . .

The Federalist, No. 59

The natural order of the subject leads us to consider . . . that provision of the Constitution which authorizes the national legislature to regulate, in the last resort, the election of its own members. . . . Its propriety rests upon the evidence of this plain proposition, that every government ought to contain in itself the means of its own preservation. . . . Nothing can be more evident, than that an exclusive power of regulating elections for the national government, in the hands of the state legislatures, would leave the existence of the union entirely at their mercy. . . .

It is certainly true that the state legislatures, by forbearing the appointment of senators, may destroy the national government. But it will not follow that, because they have a power to do this in one instance, they ought to have it in every other. . . . [I]t is an evil; but it is an evil which could not have been avoided without excluding the states . . . from a place in the organization of the national government.

The Federalist, No. 78

Under the name of "Publius," Alexander Hamilton wrote many of the Federalist Papers. Here he argues that an independent judiciary is critical to liberty. Two things are necessary to guarantee an independent judiciary, he said: judges must be able to hold office for as long as they show good behavior, and the judiciary must be independent of other branches of government. It is no accident that two of his footnotes cite the French philosopher baron de Montesquieu, the first thinker to theorize on the importance of separate branches of government.

According to the plan of the convention, all judges who may be appointed by the United States are to hold their offices DURING GOOD BEHAVIOR; which is conformable to the most approved of the State constitutions and among the rest, to that of this State. . . . The standard of good behavior for the continuance in office of the judicial magistracy, is certainly one of the most valuable of the modern improvements in the practice of government. In a monarchy it is an excellent barrier to the despotism of the prince; in a republic it is a no less excellent barrier to the encroachments and oppressions of the representative body. And it is the best expedient which can be devised in any government, to secure a steady, upright, and impartial administration of the laws.

Whoever attentively considers the different departments of power must perceive, that, in a government in which they are separated from each other, the judiciary, from the nature of its functions, will always be the least dangerous to the political rights of the Constitution; because it will be least in a capacity to annoy or injure them. The Executive not only dispenses the honors, but holds the sword of the community. The legislature not only commands the purse, but prescribes the rules by which the duties and rights of every citizen are to be regulated. The judiciary, on the contrary, has no influence over either the sword or the purse; no direction either of the strength or of the wealth of the society; and can take no active resolution whatever. It may truly be said to have neither FORCE nor WILL, but merely judgment; and must ultimately depend upon the aid of the executive arm even for the efficacy of its judgments.

The Federalist, No. 78   (continued)

This simple view of the matter suggests several important consequences. It proves incontestably, that the judiciary is beyond comparison the weakest of the three departments of power;[1] that it can never attack with success either of the other two; and that all possible care is requisite to enable it to defend itself against their attacks. It equally proves, that though individual oppression may now and then proceed from the courts of justice, the general liberty of the people can never be endangered from that quarter; . . . . For I agree, that "there is no liberty, if the power of judging be not separated from the legislative and executive powers."[2] And it proves, in the last place, that as liberty can have nothing to fear from the judiciary alone, but would have every thing to fear from its union with either of the other departments.

Some perplexity respecting the rights of the courts to pronounce legislative acts void, because contrary to the Constitution, has arisen from an imagination that the doctrine would imply a superiority of the judiciary to the legislative power. It is urged that the authority which can declare the acts of another void, must necessarily be superior to the one whose acts may be declared void. As this doctrine is of great importance in all the American constitutions, a brief discussion of the ground on which it rests cannot be unacceptable.

If it be said that the legislative body are themselves the constitutional judges of their own powers, and that the construction they put upon them is conclusive upon the other departments, it may be answered, that this cannot be the natural presumption, where it is not to be collected from any particular provisions in the Constitution. It is not otherwise to be supposed, that the Constitution could intend to enable the representatives of the people to substitute their WILL to that of their constituents. It is far more rational to suppose, that the courts were designed to be an intermediate body between the people and the legislature, in order, among other things, to keep the latter within the limits assigned to their authority. The interpretation of the laws is the proper and peculiar province of the courts. A constitution is, in fact, and must be regarded by the judges, as a fundamental law. It therefore belongs to them to ascertain its meaning, as well as the meaning of any particular act proceeding from the legislative body. If there should happen to be an irreconcilable variance between the two, that which has the superior obligation and validity ought, of course, to be preferred; or, in other words, the Constitution ought to be preferred to the statute, the intention of the people to the intention of their agents.

Nor does this conclusion by any means suppose a superiority of the judicial to the legislative power. It only supposes that the power of the people is superior to both; and that where the will of the legislature, declared in its statutes, stands in opposition to that of the people, declared in the Constitution, the judges ought to be governed by the latter rather than the former. They ought to regulate their decisions by the fundamental laws, rather than by those which are not fundamental.

If, then, the courts of justice are to be considered as the bulwarks of a limited Constitution against legislative encroachments, this consideration will afford a strong argument for the permanent tenure of judicial offices, since nothing will contribute so much as this to that independent spirit in the judges which must be essential to the faithful performance of so arduous a duty.

1 The celebrated Montesquieu, speaking of them, says: "Of the three powers above mentioned, the judiciary is next to nothing."
   "Spirit of Laws," vol. i., page 186.
2 Idem, page 181.

(continued)   *The Federalist, No. 78*

This independence of the judges is equally requisite to guard the Constitution and the rights of individuals from the effects of those ill humors, which the arts of designing men, or the influence of particular conjunctures, sometimes disseminate among the people themselves, and which, though they speedily give place to better information, and more deliberate reflection, have a tendency, in the meantime, to occasion dangerous innovations in the government, and serious oppressions of the minor party in the community. Though I trust the friends of the proposed Constitution will never concur with its enemies,[3] in questioning that fundamental principle of republican government, which admits the right of the people to alter or abolish the established Constitution, whenever they find it inconsistent with their happiness, yet it is not to be inferred from this principle, that the representatives of the people, whenever a momentary inclination happens to lay hold of a majority of their constituents, incompatible with the provisions in the existing Constitution, would, on that account, be justifiable in a violation of those provisions; . . . . Until the people have, by some solemn and authoritative act, annulled or changed the established form, it is binding upon themselves collectively, as well as individually; and no presumption, or even knowledge, of their sentiments, can warrant their representatives in a departure from it, prior to such an act. But it is easy to see, that it would require an uncommon portion of fortitude in the judges to do their duty as faithful guardians of the Constitution, where legislative invasions of it had been instigated by the major voice of the community.

PUBLIUS

▲ Statue of Alexander Hamilton

3 Vide "Protest of the Minority of the Convention of Pennsylvania," Martin's Speech, etc.

Seneca Falls Declaration

One of the first documents to express the desire for equal rights for women is the Declaration of Sentiments and Resolution, issued in 1848 at the Seneca Falls Convention.

We hold these truths to be self-evident: that all men and women are created equal; that they are endowed by their Creator with certain inalienable rights; that among these are life, liberty, and the pursuit of happiness; that to secure these rights governments are instituted, deriving their just powers from the consent of the governed.

▲ Elizabeth Cady Stanton

Whenever any form of government becomes destructive of these ends, it is the right of those who suffer from it to refuse allegiance to it, and to insist upon the institution of a new government, laying its foundation on such principles, and organizing its powers in such form, as to them shall seem most likely to effect their safety and happiness. . . .

The history of mankind is a history of repeated injuries and usurpations on the part of man toward woman, having in direct object the establishment of an absolute tyranny over her.

Now, in view of this entire disfranchisement . . . we insist that they have immediate admission to all the rights and privileges which belong to them as citizens of the United States. . . .

Fourth of July Address

As the city's most distinguished resident, Frederick Douglass was requested to address the citizens of Rochester on the Fourth of July celebration in 1852. The speech he delivered, under the title "What to the Slave is the Fourth of July?," is excerpted below.

▲ **Frederick Douglass**

Fellow Citizens: Pardon me, and allow me to ask, why am I called upon to speak here today? What have I or those I represent to do with your national independence? Are the great principles of political freedom and of natural justice, embodied in that Declaration of Independence, extended to us? And am I, therefore, called upon to bring our humble offering to the national altar, and to confess the benefits, and express devout gratitude for the blessings resulting from your independence to us? . . .

I say it with a sad sense of disparity between us. I am not included within the pale of this glorious anniversary! Your high independence only reveals the immeasurable distance between us. The blessings in which you this day rejoice are not enjoyed in common. The rich inheritance of justice, liberty, prosperity, and independence bequeathed by your fathers is shared by you, not by me. . . . This Fourth of July is yours, not mine. You may rejoice, I must mourn. . . .

I do not hesitate to declare, with all my soul, that the character and conduct of this nation never looked blacker to me than on this Fourth of July. Whether we turn to the declarations of the past, or to the professions of the present, the conduct of the nation seems equally hideous and revolting. America is false to the past, false to the present, and solemnly binds herself to be false to the future. . . . I will, in the name of humanity, which is outraged, in the name of liberty, which is fettered, in the name of the Constitution and the Bible, which are disregarded and trampled upon, dare to call in question and to denounce, with all the emphasis I can command, everything that serves to perpetuate slavery—the great sin and shame of America! "I will not equivocate; I will not excuse"; I will use the severest language I can command, and yet not one word shall escape me that any man, whose judgment is not blinded by prejudice, or who is not at heart a slave-holder, shall not confess to be right and just. . . .

Would you have me argue that man is entitled to liberty? That he is the rightful owner of his own body? You have already declared it. Must I argue the wrongfulness of slavery? . . . There is not a man beneath the canopy of heaven who does not know that slavery is wrong for him.

What! Am I to argue that it is wrong to make men brutes, to rob them of their liberty, to work them without wages, to keep them ignorant of their relations to their fellow men, to beat them with sticks, to flay their flesh with the lash, to load their limbs with irons, to hunt them with dogs, to sell them at auction, to sunder their families, to knock out their teeth, to burn their flesh, to starve them into obedience and submission to their masters? . . . The feeling of the nation must be quickened; the conscience of the nation must be roused; the propriety of the nation must be startled; the hypocrisy of the nation must be exposed; and its crimes against God and man must be denounced. . . .

The Emancipation Proclamation

On January 1, 1863, President Abraham Lincoln issued the Emancipation Proclamation, which freed all slaves in states under Confederate control. The Proclamation was a significant step toward the Thirteenth Amendment (1865) that ended slavery in the United States.

▲ **Abraham Lincoln**

Whereas, on the 22nd day of September, in the year of our Lord 1862, a proclamation was issued by the President of the United States, containing, among other things, the following, to wit:

That on the 1st day of January, in the year of our Lord 1863, all persons held as slaves within any state or designated part of a state, the people whereof shall then be in rebellion against the United States, shall be then, thenceforward, and forever free; and the executive government of the United States, including the military and naval authority thereof, will recognize and maintain the freedom of such persons and will do no act or acts to repress such persons, or any of them, in any efforts they may make for their actual freedom.

That the executive will, on the first day of January aforesaid, by proclamation, designate the states and parts of states, if any, in which the people thereof, respectively, shall then be in rebellion against the United States; and the fact that any state or the people thereof shall on that day be in good faith represented in the Congress of the United States by members chosen thereto at elections wherein a majority of the qualified voters of such states shall have participated shall, in the absence of strong countervailing testimony, be deemed conclusive evidence that such state and the people thereof are not then in rebellion against the United States.

Now, therefore, I, Abraham Lincoln, President of the United States, by virtue of the power in me vested as commander in chief of the Army and Navy of the United States, in time of actual armed rebellion against the authority and government of the United States, and as a fit and necessary war measure for suppressing said rebellion, do, on this 1st day of January, in the year of our Lord 1863, and in accordance with my purpose so to do, publicly proclaimed for the full period of 100 days from the day first above mentioned, order and designate as the states and parts of states wherein the people thereof, respectively, are this day in rebellion against the United States. . . .

And, by virtue of the power and for the purpose aforesaid, I do order and declare that all persons held as slaves within said designated states and parts of states are, and henceforward shall be, free; and that the executive government of the United States, including the military and naval authorities thereof, will recognize and maintain the freedom of said persons. . .

And upon this act, sincerely believed to be an act of justice, warranted by the Constitution upon military necessity, I invoke the considerate judgment of mankind and the gracious favor of Almighty God.

The Fourteen Points

▲ Leaders (left to right) David Lloyd George of Great Britain, Vittorio Orlando of Italy, Georges Clemenceau of France, and Woodrow Wilson of the United States

On January 8, 1918, President Woodrow Wilson went before Congress to offer a statement of aims called the Fourteen Points.

We entered this war because violations of right had occurred. . . . What we demand in this war, therefore, is . . . that the world be made fit and safe to live in. . . . The only possible programme, as we see it, is this:

I. Open covenants of peace, openly arrived at, after which there shall be no private international understandings of any kind but diplomacy shall proceed always frankly and in the public view.

II. Absolute freedom of navigation upon the seas, outside territorial waters, alike in peace and in war. . . .

III. The removal, so far as possible, of all economic barriers and the establishment of an equality of trade conditions among all the nations. . . .

IV. Adequate guarantees given and taken that national armaments will be reduced to the lowest point consistent with domestic safety.

V. A free, open-minded, and absolutely impartial adjustment of all colonial claims, based upon a strict observance of the principle that in determining all such questions of sovereignty the interests of the populations concerned must have equal weight with the equitable claims of the government whose title is to be determined.

VI. The evacuation of all Russian territory and . . . opportunity for the independent determination of her own political development and national policy. . . .

VII. Belgium . . . must be evacuated and restored. . . .

VIII. All French territory should be freed and the invaded portions restored, and the wrong done to France by Prussia in 1871 in the matter of Alsace-Lorraine should be righted. . . .

IX. A readjustment of the frontiers of Italy should be effected along clearly recognizable lines of nationality.

X. The peoples of Austria-Hungary . . . should be accorded the freest opportunity of autonomous development.

XI. Rumania, Serbia, and Montenegro should be evacuated; occupied territories restored . . . the relations of the several Balkan states to one another determined by friendly counsel along historically established lines of allegiance and nationality. . . .

XII. The Turkish portions of the present Ottoman Empire should be assured a secure sovereignty. . . .

XIII. An independent Polish state should be erected which should include the territories inhabited by indisputably Polish populations. . . .

XIV. A general association of nations must be formed under specific covenants for the purpose of affording mutual guarantees of political independence and territorial integrity. . . .

The Four Freedoms

President Franklin D. Roosevelt delivered this address on January 6, 1941, in his annual message to Congress. Roosevelt called for a world founded on "four essential human freedoms": freedom of speech and expression, freedom of worship, freedom from want, and freedom from fear.

Just as our national policy in internal affairs has been based upon a decent respect for the rights and dignity of all our fellowmen within our gates, so our national policy in foreign affairs has been based on a decent respect for the rights and dignity of all nations, large and small. And the justice of morality must and will win in the end.

Our national policy is this:

First, by an impressive expression of the public will and without regard to partisanship, we are committed to all-inclusive national defense.

Second, by an impressive expression of the public will and without regard to partisanship, we are committed to full support of all those resolute peoples, everywhere, who are resisting aggression and are thereby keeping war away from our Hemisphere. . . .

▲ Roosevelt (left) and British Prime Minister Winston Churchill

Third . . . we are committed to the proposition that principles of morality and considerations for our own security will never permit us to acquiesce in a peace dictated by aggressors. . . .

Let us say to the democracies, "We Americans are vitally concerned in your defense of freedom. We are putting forth our energies, our resources, and our organizing powers to give you the strength to regain and maintain a free world. We shall send you, in ever increasing numbers, ships, planes, tanks, guns. This is our purpose and our pledge."

In fulfillment of this purpose we will not be intimidated by the threats of dictators that they will regard as a breach of international law and as an act of war our aid to the democracies which dare to resist their aggression. . . .

In the future days, which we seek to make secure, we look forward to a world founded upon four essential human freedoms.

The first is freedom of speech and expression everywhere in the world.

The second is freedom of every person to worship God in his own way everywhere in the world.

The third is freedom from want, which, translated into world terms, means economic understandings which will secure to every nation a healthy peacetime life for its inhabitants everywhere in the world.

The fourth is freedom from fear—which, translated into world terms, means a worldwide reduction of armaments to such a point and in such a thorough fashion that no nation will be in a position to commit an act of physical aggression against any neighbor—anywhere in the world. . . .

Charter of the United Nations

The United Nations Charter was signed on June 26, 1945. It formally established the United Nations, a new international peace organization to succeed the League of Nations. The following excerpt contains Article I of the charter.

▲ **United Nations flag**

We the peoples of the United Nations determined

to save succeeding generations from the scourge of war, which twice in our lifetime has brought untold sorrow to mankind, and

to reaffirm faith in fundamental human rights, in the dignity and worth of the human person, in the equal rights of men and women and of nations large and small, and

to establish conditions under which justice and respect for the obligations arising from treaties and other sources of international law can be maintained, and

to promote social progress and better standards of life in larger freedom,

And for these ends

to practise tolerance and live together in peace with one another as good neighbours, and

to unite our strength to maintain international peace and security, and

to ensure, by the acceptance of principles and the institution of methods, that armed force shall not be used, save in the common interest, and

to employ international machinery for the promotion of the economic and social advancement of all peoples,

Have resolved to combine our efforts to accomplish these aims.

Accordingly, our respective Governments, through representatives assembled in the city of San Francisco, who have exhibited their full powers found to be in good and due form, have agreed to the present Charter of the United Nations and do hereby establish an international organization to be known as the United Nations. . . .

Article 1. The Purposes of the United Nations are:

1. To maintain international peace and security, and to that end: to take effective collective measures for the prevention and removal of threats to the peace, and for the suppression of acts of aggression or other breaches of the peace, and to bring about by peaceful means and in conformity with the principles of justice and international law, adjustment or settlement of international disputes or situations which might lead to a breach of the peace;

2. To develop friendly relations among nations based on respect for the principle of equal rights and self-determination of peoples, and to take other appropriate measures to strengthen universal peace;

3. To achieve international co-operation in solving international problems of an economic, social, cultural, or humanitarian character, and in promoting and encouraging respect for human rights and for fundamental freedoms for all without distinction as to race, sex, language, or religion; and

4. To be a centre for harmonizing the accusations of nations in the attainment of these common ends.

"I Have a Dream"

On August 28, 1963, while Congress debated wide-ranging civil rights legislation, Martin Luther King, Jr., led more than 200,000 people in a march on Washington, D.C. On the steps of the Lincoln Memorial, he gave a stirring speech in which he eloquently spoke of his dreams for African Americans and for the United States.

Five score years ago, a great American, in whose symbolic shadow we stand, signed the Emancipation Proclamation. This momentous decree came as a great beacon light of hope to millions of Negro slaves who had been seared in the flames of withering injustice. It came as a joyous daybreak to end the long night of captivity.

But one hundred years later, we must face the tragic fact that the Negro is still not free. One hundred years later, the life of the Negro is still sadly crippled by the manacles of segregation and the chains of discrimination. . . .

There are those who are asking the devotees of civil rights, "When will you be satisfied?"

We can never be satisfied as long as the Negro is the victim of the unspeakable horrors of police brutality.

We can never be satisfied as long as our bodies, heavy with the fatigue of travel, cannot gain lodging in the motels of the highways and the hotels of the cities.

We cannot be satisfied as long as the Negro's basic mobility is from a smaller ghetto to a larger one.

We can never be satisfied as long as a Negro in Mississippi cannot vote and a Negro in New York believes he has nothing for which to vote.

No, no, we are not satisfied, and we will not be satisfied until justice rolls down like waters and righteousness like a mighty stream. . . .

I say to you today, my friends, that in spite of the difficulties and frustrations of the moment I still have a dream. It is a dream deeply rooted in the American dream.

I have a dream that one day this nation will rise up and live out the true meaning of its creed: "We hold these truths to be self-evident; that all men are created equal."

I have a dream that one day on the red hills of Georgia the sons of former slaves and the sons of former slaveowners will be able to sit down together at the table of brotherhood.

I have a dream that one day even the state of Mississippi, a desert state sweltering with the heat of injustice and oppression, will be transformed into an oasis of freedom and justice.

I have a dream that my four little children will one day live in a nation where they will not be judged by the color of their skin but by the content of their character. . . .

When we let freedom ring, when we let it ring from every village and every hamlet, from every state and every city, we will be able to speed up that day when all of God's children, black men and white men, Jews and Gentiles, Protestants and Catholics, will be able to join hands and sing in the words of the old Negro spiritual, "Free at last! Free at last! Thank God Almighty, we are free at last!"

▶ **Martin Luther King, Jr.**

Gulf of Tonkin Resolution

The Gulf of Tonkin Resolution was a joint resolution passed overwhelmingly by Congress on August 7, 1964. It became the basis for President Johnson's escalation of the war in Southeast Asia. A 1968 U.S. Senate investigation questioned the alleged Gulf of Tonkin attacks, and the resolution was repealed in May 1970.

PUBLIC LAW 88—408; 78 STAT. 384
[H.J. Res 1145]
JOINT RESOLUTION

To promote the maintenance of international peace and security in southeast Asia.

Whereas naval units of the Communist regime in [North] Vietnam, in violation of the principles of the Charter of the United Nations and of international law, have deliberately and repeatedly attacked United States naval vessels lawfully present in international waters, and have thereby created a serious threat to international peace; and

Whereas these attacks are part of a deliberate and systematic campaign of aggression that the Communist regime in North Vietnam has been waging against its neighbors and the nations joined with them in the collective defense of their freedom; and

Whereas the United States is assisting the peoples of southeast Asia to protect their freedom and has no territorial, military or political ambitions in that area, but desires only that these peoples should be left in peace to work out their own destinies in their own way: Now, therefore, be it

Resolved by the Senate and House of Representatives of the United States of America in Congress assembled,

That the Congress approves and supports the determination of the President, as Commander in Chief, to take all necessary measures to repel any armed attack against the forces of the United States and to prevent further aggression.

Sec. 2. The United States regards as vital to its national interest and to world peace the maintenance of international peace and security in southeast Asia. . . . The United States is, therefore, prepared, as the President determines, to take all necessary steps, including the use of armed force, to assist any member or protocol state of the Southeast Asia Collective Defense Treaty requesting assistance in defense of its freedom.

Sec. 3. This resolution shall expire when the President shall determine that the peace and security of the area is reasonably assured by international conditions created by action of the United Nations or otherwise, except that it may be terminated earlier by concurrent resolution of the Congress.

Approved August 10, 1964.

▲ **The Vietnam Memorial**

George W. Bush's Address to Congress, September 20, 2001

▲ President George W. Bush

On September 11, 2001, terrorists destroyed the World Trade Center in New York City and damaged the Pentagon. President Bush responded in a message to Congress on September 20.

. . . Tonight we are a country awakened to danger and called to defend freedom. Our grief has turned to anger, and anger to resolution. Whether we bring our enemies to justice, or bring justice to our enemies, justice will be done.

. . . On September 11th, enemies of freedom committed an act of war against our country. Americans have known wars—but for the past 136 years, they have been wars on foreign soil, except for one Sunday in 1941. Americans have known the casualties of war—but not at the center of a great city on a peaceful morning. Americans have known surprise attacks—but never before on thousands of civilians. All of this was brought upon us in a single day—and night fell on a different world, a world where freedom itself is under attack.

. . . Americans are asking: Who attacked our country? The evidence we have gathered all points to a collection of loosely affiliated terrorist organizations known as al Qaeda. They are the same murderers indicted for bombing American embassies in Tanzania and Kenya, and responsible for bombing the USS *Cole.*

. . . This group and its leader—a person named Osama bin Laden—are linked to many other organizations in different countries.

. . . Americans are asking, why do they hate us? They hate what we see right here in this chamber—democratically elected government. . . . They hate our freedoms—our freedom of religion, our freedom of speech, our freedom to vote and assemble and disagree with each other.

. . . We are not deceived by their pretenses to piety. We have seen their kind before. They are the heirs of all the murderous ideologies of the 20th century. By sacrificing human life to serve their radical visions—by abandoning every value except the will to power—they follow the path of Nazism, and totalitarianism. And they will follow that path all the way to where it ends: in history's unmarked grave of discarded lies.

. . . We will direct every resource at our command—every means of diplomacy, every tool of intelligence, every instrument of law enforcement, every financial influence and every necessary weapon of war—to the disruption and to the defeat of the global terror network.

. . . Every nation, in every region, now has a decision to make. Either you are with us, or you are with the terrorists.

. . . This is not, however, just America's fight. And what is at stake is not just America's freedom. This is the world's fight. This is civilization's fight.

. . . We are in a fight for our principles, and our first responsibility is to live by them. No one should be singled out for unfair treatment or unkind words because of their ethnic background or religious faith.

. . . Great harm has been done to us. We have suffered great loss. And in our grief and anger we have found our mission and our moment. Freedom and fear are at war. The advance of human freedom—the great achievement of our time, and the great hope of every time—now depends on us. Our nation—this generation—will lift a dark threat of violence from our people and our future.

. . . I will not forget this wound to our country or those who inflicted it. I will not yield; I will not rest; I will not relent in waging this struggle for freedom and security for the American people.

United States Data Bank

Contents

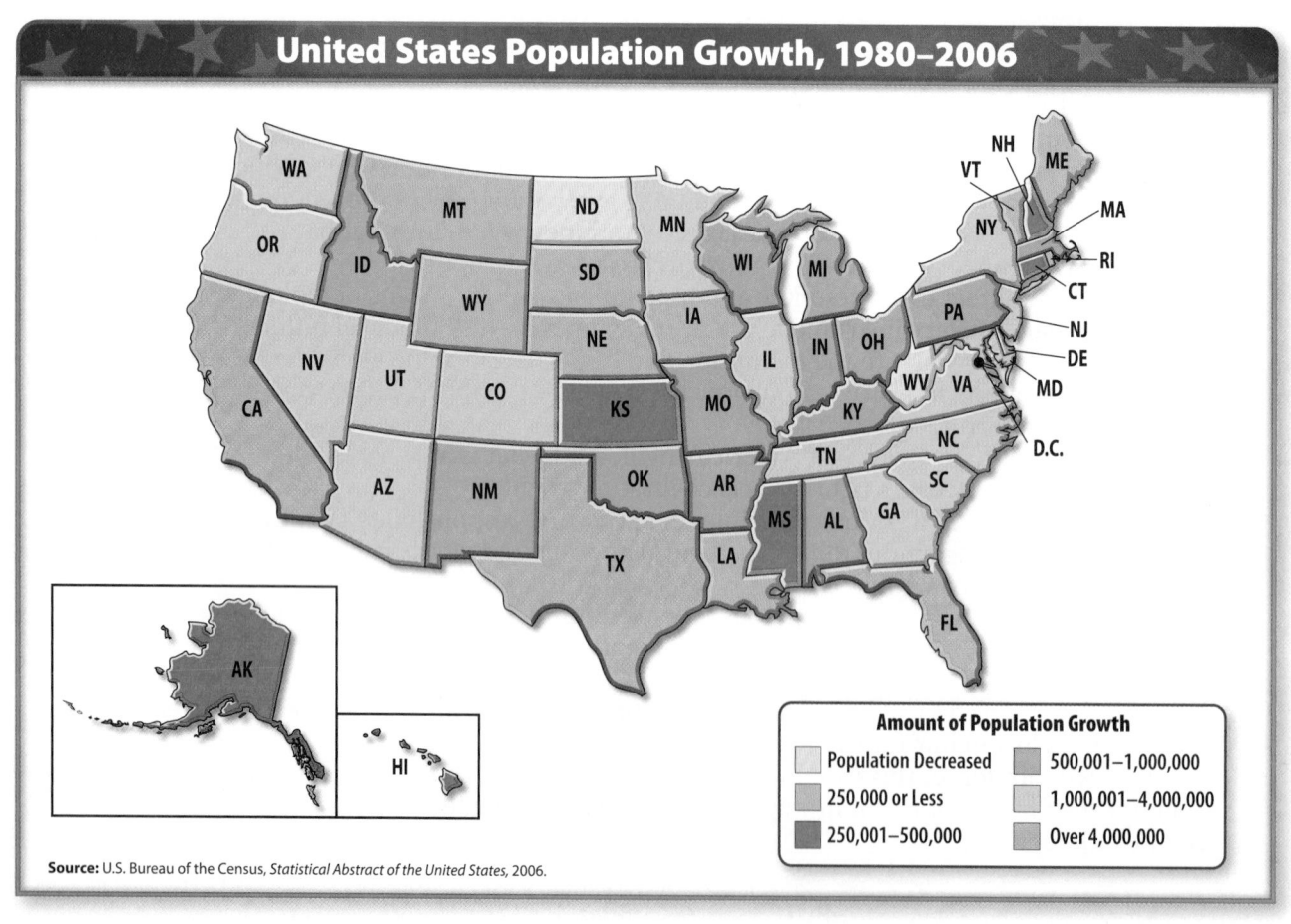

United States Population Growth, 1980–2006

Amount of Population Growth

- Population Decreased
- 250,000 or Less
- 250,001–500,000
- 500,001–1,000,000
- 1,000,001–4,000,000
- Over 4,000,000

Source: U.S. Bureau of the Census, *Statistical Abstract of the United States,* 2006.

Crime and the Justice System

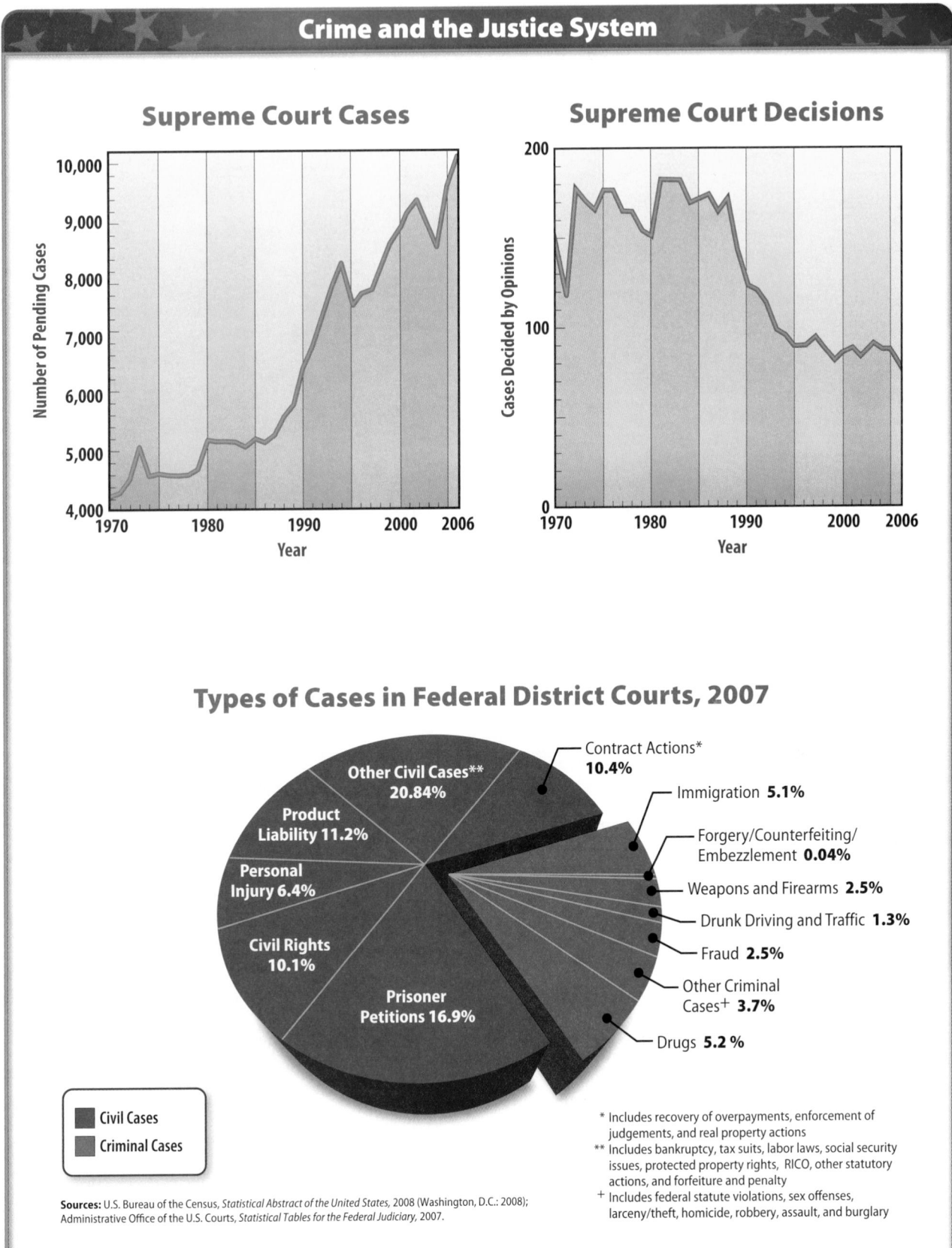

Supreme Court Cases

Number of Pending Cases vs. Year

Supreme Court Decisions

Cases Decided by Opinions vs. Year

Types of Cases in Federal District Courts, 2007

Other Civil Cases** 20.84%

Product Liability 11.2%

Personal Injury 6.4%

Civil Rights 10.1%

Prisoner Petitions 16.9%

Contract Actions* 10.4%

Immigration 5.1%

Forgery/Counterfeiting/ Embezzlement 0.04%

Weapons and Firearms 2.5%

Drunk Driving and Traffic 1.3%

Fraud 2.5%

Other Criminal Cases+ 3.7%

Drugs 5.2 %

Civil Cases

Criminal Cases

* Includes recovery of overpayments, enforcement of judgements, and real property actions
** Includes bankruptcy, tax suits, labor laws, social security issues, protected property rights, RICO, other statutory actions, and forfeiture and penalty
+ Includes federal statute violations, sex offenses, larceny/theft, homicide, robbery, assault, and burglary

Sources: U.S. Bureau of the Census, *Statistical Abstract of the United States,* 2008 (Washington, D.C.: 2008); Administrative Office of the U.S. Courts, *Statistical Tables for the Federal Judiciary,* 2007.

Bills Introduced, Passed, and Enacted by Congress, 1967–2008

CONGRESS (Years)	BILLS INTRODUCED*		BILLS PASSED*		BILLS ENACTED
	House	Senate	House	Senate	
90th (1967–68)	24,227	4,906	1,659	1,731	1,002
91st (1969–70)	23,575	5,466	1,712	1,676	941
92nd (1971–72)	20,458	4,896	1,469	1,371	768
93rd (1973–74)	21,095	5,127	1,524	1,564	774
94th (1975–76)	19,371	4,913	1,624	1,552	729
95th (1977–78)	17,800	4,513	1,615	1,596	803
96th (1979–80)	10,400	4,194	1,478	1,482	736
97th (1981–82)	9,175	3,172	1,058	1,209	528
98th (1983–84)	8,104	4,097	1,348	1,322	677
99th (1985–86)	7,522	4,080	1,368	1,330	690
100th (1987–88)	7,269	4,013	1,502	1,430	758
101st (1989–90)	7,611	4,184	1,370	1,321	666
102nd (1991–92)	7,771	4,245	1,338	1,277	609
103rd (1993–94)	6,647	3,177	1,126	938	473
104th (1995–96)	5,329	2,661	1,012	822	337
105th (1997–98)	5,982	3,161	1,186	891	404
106th (1999–2000)	6,942	3,898	1,534	1,245	604
107th (2001–2002)	7,029	3,762	1,215	953	383
108th (2003–2004)	6,953	3,716	1,424	1,259	504
109th (2005–2006)	8,152	4,920	1,457	1,260	483
110th (2007–2008)	9,341	4,531	1,621	889	436

Source: thomas.loc.gov
*Includes House and Senate resolutions, joint resolutions, and concurrent resolutions.

Federal Revenue and Expenditures, 2007

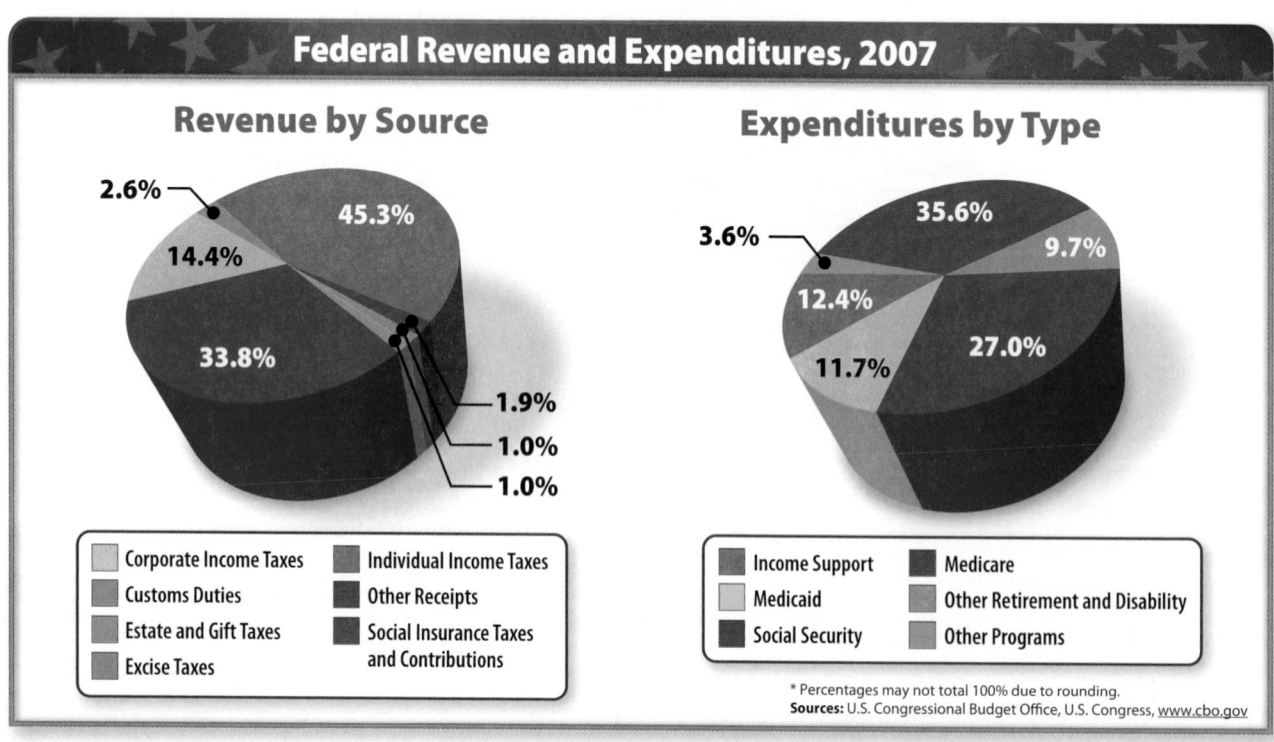

Revenue by Source

- 2.6%
- 14.4%
- 45.3%
- 33.8%
- 1.9%
- 1.0%
- 1.0%

Legend:
- Corporate Income Taxes
- Individual Income Taxes
- Customs Duties
- Other Receipts
- Estate and Gift Taxes
- Social Insurance Taxes and Contributions
- Excise Taxes

Expenditures by Type

- 3.6%
- 35.6%
- 9.7%
- 12.4%
- 11.7%
- 27.0%

Legend:
- Income Support
- Medicare
- Medicaid
- Other Retirement and Disability
- Social Security
- Other Programs

* Percentages may not total 100% due to rounding.
Sources: U.S. Congressional Budget Office, U.S. Congress, www.cbo.gov

Federal Government Revenues and Expenditures, 1965–2005

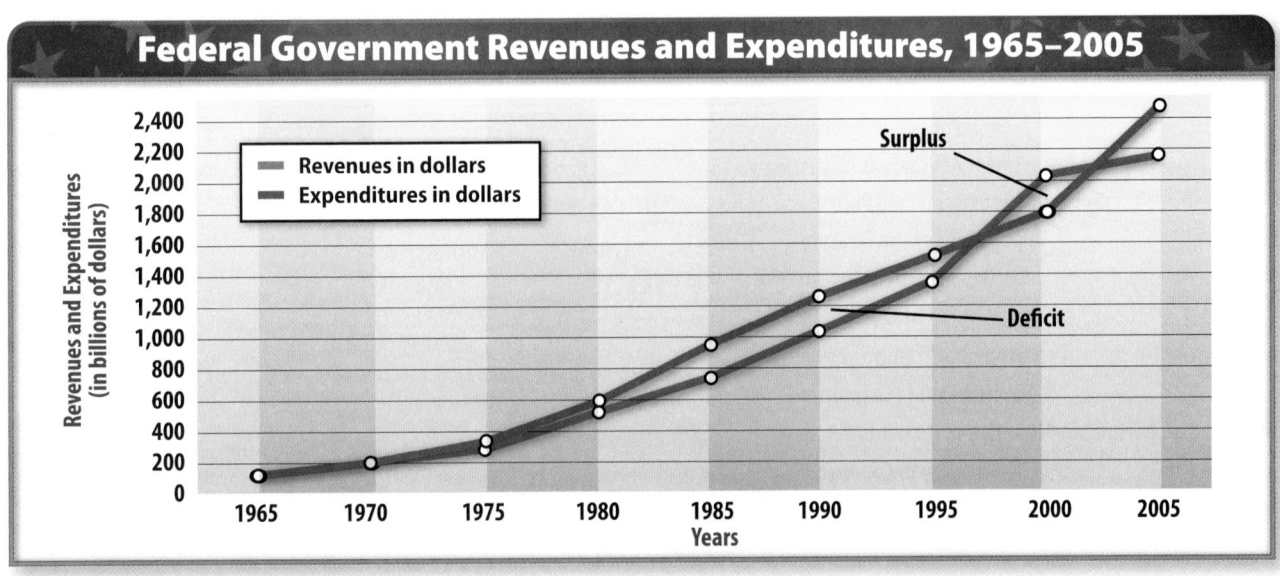

Gross Federal Debt, 1965–2005

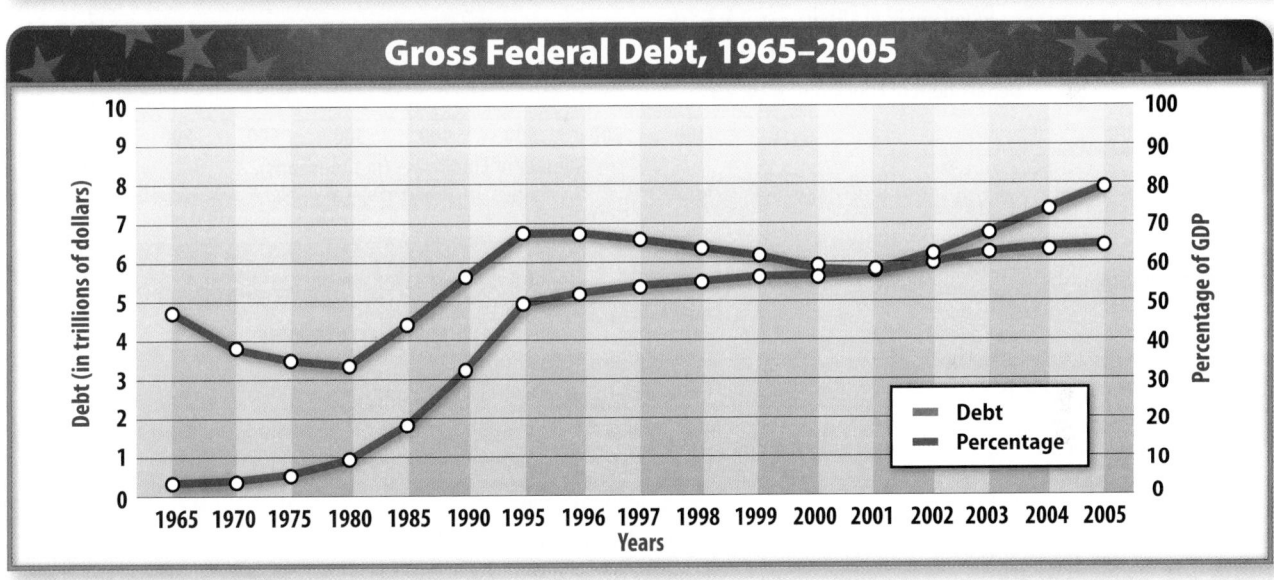

National Debt per Capita, 1960–2006*

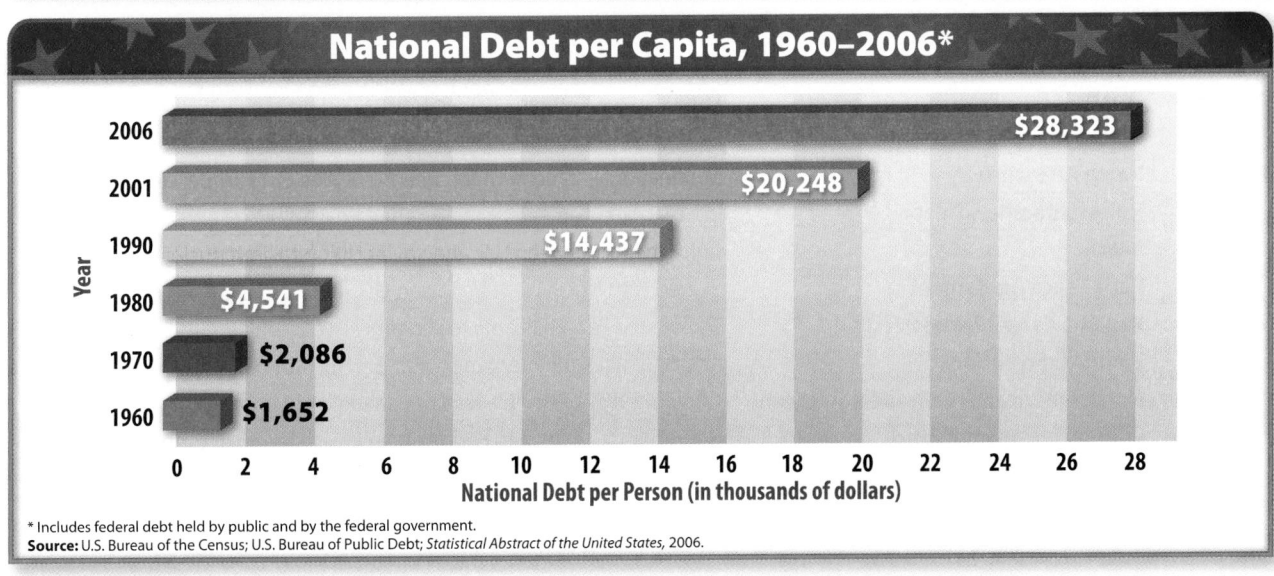

* Includes federal debt held by public and by the federal government.
Source: U.S. Bureau of the Census; U.S. Bureau of Public Debt; *Statistical Abstract of the United States,* 2006.

Executive Department Civilian Employees*

Department	Number of Employees
Department of Defense	676,452
Department of Veterans Affairs	236,938
Department of Homeland Security	151,771
Department of the Treasury	112,000
Department of Justice	106,159
Department of Agriculture	101,887
Department of Transportation	53,573
Department of the Interior	71,593
Department of Health and Human Services	60,756
Department of Commerce	40,335
Department of State	33,968
Department of Labor	15,434
Department of Energy	14,838
Department of Housing and Urban Development	9,814
Department of Education	4,257

Number of Employees (in thousands)

* as of September 2006
Source: U.S. Bureau of the Census, *Statistical Abstract of the United States*, 2008 (Washington, D.C.: 2008).

Major United States Treaties

Year	Treaty	Major Provisions
1783	Treaty of Paris	Great Britain recognized U.S. independence
1795	Pinckney's Treaty	Spain granted U.S. navigation rights on Mississippi River
1803	Louisiana Purchase	U.S. gained Louisiana Territory from France
1818	Convention of 1818	Set border with Canada west from Great Lakes as the 49th parallel
1819	Adams-Onís Treaty	Spain ceded Florida; U.S. border set with Spanish territory in West
1846	Oregon Treaty	Signed with Great Britain to settle claims to Oregon Country
1848	Treaty of Guadalupe Hidalgo	Ended Mexican War; U.S. gained Southwest and California
1867	Alaska Purchase	U.S. gained Alaska from Russia
1898	Treaty of Paris	Ended Spanish-American War; U.S. gained Puerto Rico and Philippines
1903	Hay-Buneau-Varilla Treaty	Signed with Panama to give U.S. right to build Panama Canal
1949	North Atlantic Treaty	Multinational agreement for defense of Western Europe; created NATO
1968	Nonproliferation Treaty	International agreement to prevent spread of nuclear weapons
1972	SALT I	Agreements between U.S. and Soviet Union to limit nuclear weapons
1973	Paris Peace Agreement	Signed with North Vietnam to end U.S. involvement in Vietnam War
1977	Panama Canal Treaties	Transferred Panama Canal to Panama effective in 1999
1985	Vienna Convention	International agreement to protect Earth's ozone layer
1993	North American Free Trade Agreement	Established duty-free trade with Canada and Mexico
1996	Counterterrorism Accord	Israel and U.S. agreed to cooperate in investigation of terrorist acts
1997	Mutual Recognition Agreement	Reduced trade barriers between the U.S. and European Community

Sources: U.S. State Department, *Treaties in Force; Findling, Dictionary of American Diplomatic History,* 2nd ed. (New York: Greenwood Press, 1989).

State Facts

State*	Year Admitted	Population 2006	Land Area (sq. miles)	Capital	Largest City	House Rep. 2000**
1. Delaware	1787	853,000	1,955	Dover	Wilmington	1
2. Pennsylvania	1787	12,441,000	44,820	Harrisburg	Philadelphia	19
3. New Jersey	1787	8,725,000	7,419	Trenton	Newark	13
4. Georgia	1788	9,364,000	57,919	Atlanta	Atlanta	13
5. Connecticut	1788	3,505,000	4,845	Hartford	Bridgeport	5
6. Massachusetts	1788	6,437,000	7,838	Boston	Boston	10
7. Maryland	1788	5,616,000	9,775	Annapolis	Baltimore	8
8. South Carolina	1788	4,321,000	30,111	Columbia	Columbia	6
9. New Hampshire	1788	1,315,000	8,969	Concord	Manchester	2
10. Virginia	1788	7,643,000	39,598	Richmond	Virginia Beach	11
11. New York	1788	19,306,000	47,224	Albany	New York City	29
12. North Carolina	1789	8,857,000	48,718	Raleigh	Charlotte	13
13. Rhode Island	1790	1,068,000	1,045	Providence	Providence	2
14. Vermont	1791	624,000	9,249	Montpelier	Burlington	1
15. Kentucky	1792	4,206,000	39,732	Frankfort	Louisville	6
16. Tennessee	1796	6,039,000	41,220	Nashville	Memphis	9
17. Ohio	1803	11,478,000	40,953	Columbus	Columbus	18
18. Louisiana	1812	4,288,000	43,566	Baton Rouge	Baton Rouge	7
19. Indiana	1816	6,314,000	35,870	Indianapolis	Indianapolis	9
20. Mississippi	1817	2,911,000	46,914	Jackson	Jackson	4
21. Illinois	1818	12,832,000	55,593	Springfield	Chicago	19
22. Alabama	1819	4,599,000	50,750	Montgomery	Birmingham	7
23. Maine	1820	1,322,000	30,865	Augusta	Portland	2
24. Missouri	1821	5,843,000	68,898	Jefferson City	Kansas City	9
25. Arkansas	1836	2,811,000	52,075	Little Rock	Little Rock	4
26. Michigan	1837	10,096,000	56,809	Lansing	Detroit	15
27. Florida	1845	18,090,000	53,997	Tallahassee	Jacksonville	25
28. Texas	1845	23,508,000	261,914	Austin	Houston	32
29. Iowa	1846	2,982,000	55,875	Des Moines	Des Moines	5
30. Wisconsin	1848	5,557,000	54,314	Madison	Milwaukee	8
31. California	1850	36,458,000	155,973	Sacramento	Los Angeles	53
32. Minnesota	1858	5,167,000	79,617	St. Paul	Minneapolis	8
33. Oregon	1859	3,701,000	96,003	Salem	Portland	5
34. Kansas	1861	2,764,000	81,823	Topeka	Wichita	4
35. West Virginia	1863	1,818,000	24,087	Charleston	Charleston	3
36. Nevada	1864	2,496,000	109,806	Carson City	Las Vegas	3
37. Nebraska	1867	1,768,000	76,878	Lincoln	Omaha	3
38. Colorado	1876	4,753,000	103,730	Denver	Denver	7
39. North Dakota	1889	636,000	68,994	Bismarck	Fargo	1
40. South Dakota	1889	782,000	75,898	Pierre	Sioux Falls	1
41. Montana	1889	945,000	145,556	Helena	Billings	1
42. Washington	1889	6,396,000	66,582	Olympia	Seattle	9
43. Idaho	1890	1,466,000	82,751	Boise	Boise	2
44. Wyoming	1890	515,000	97,105	Cheyenne	Cheyenne	1
45. Utah	1896	2,550,000	82,168	Salt Lake City	Salt Lake City	3
46. Oklahoma	1907	3,579,000	68,679	Oklahoma City	Oklahoma City	5
47. New Mexico	1912	1,955,000	121,365	Sante Fe	Albuquerque	3
48. Arizona	1912	6,166,000	113,642	Phoenix	Phoenix	8
49. Alaska	1959	670,000	570,374	Juneau	Anchorage	1
50. Hawaii	1959	1,285,000	6,423	Honolulu	Honolulu	2
District of Columbia	—	582,000	61	—	—	—
Puerto Rico	—	3,928,000	3,425	San Juan	San Juan	—
United States***	—	303,331,000	3,539,703	Washington, D.C.	New York City	—

* Numbers denote the order in which states were admitted   ** Number of members in U.S. House of Representatives based on the 2000 U.S. Census   *** Including Puerto Rico
Source: The *World Almanac and Book of Facts,* 2008.

State Revenues and Expenditures, 2004

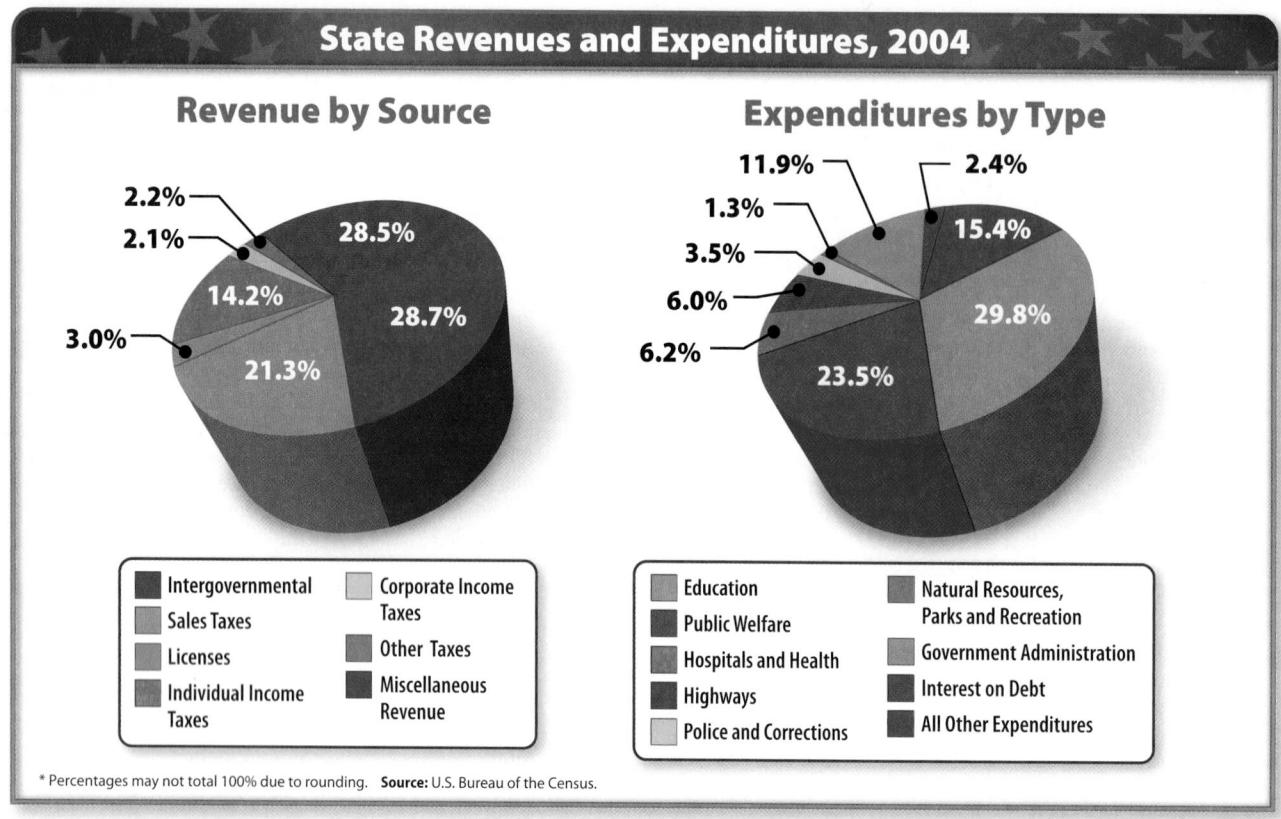

Revenue by Source

- 2.2%
- 2.1%
- 28.5%
- 14.2%
- 28.7%
- 3.0%
- 21.3%

Legend:
- Intergovernmental
- Sales Taxes
- Licenses
- Individual Income Taxes
- Corporate Income Taxes
- Other Taxes
- Miscellaneous Revenue

Expenditures by Type

- 11.9%
- 2.4%
- 1.3%
- 15.4%
- 3.5%
- 6.0%
- 29.8%
- 6.2%
- 23.5%

Legend:
- Education
- Public Welfare
- Hospitals and Health
- Highways
- Police and Corrections
- Natural Resources, Parks and Recreation
- Government Administration
- Interest on Debt
- All Other Expenditures

* Percentages may not total 100% due to rounding. **Source:** U.S. Bureau of the Census.

State Expenditures for Public Education, 2002

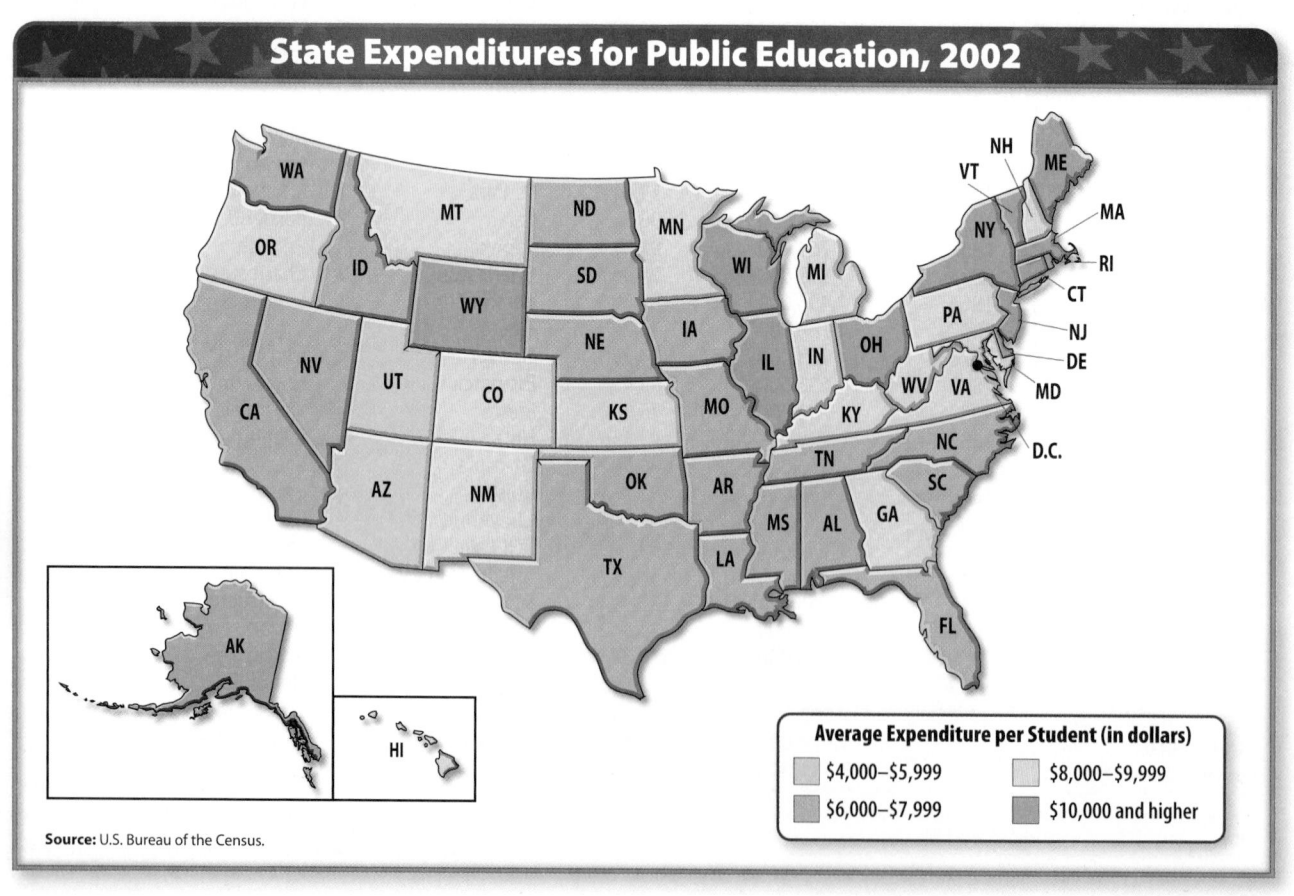

Average Expenditure per Student (in dollars)
- $4,000–$5,999
- $6,000–$7,999
- $8,000–$9,999
- $10,000 and higher

Source: U.S. Bureau of the Census.

Size of State Legislatures

State	House Members	Senate Members
Alabama	105	35
Alaska	40	20
Arizona	60	30
Arkansas	100	35
California	80	40
Colorado	65	35
Connecticut	151	36
Delaware	41	21
Florida	120	40
Georgia	180	56
Hawaii	51	25
Idaho	70	35
Illinois	118	59
Indiana	100	50
Iowa	100	50
Kansas	125	40
Kentucky	100	38
Louisiana	105	39
Maine	151	35
Maryland	141	47
Massachusetts	160	40
Michigan	110	38
Minnesota	134	67
Mississippi	122	52
Missouri	163	34
Montana	100	50
Nebraska	N/A	49
Nevada	42	21
New Hampshire	400	24
New Jersey	80	40
New Mexico	70	42
New York	150	62
North Carolina	120	50
North Dakota	94	47
Ohio	99	33
Oklahoma	101	48
Oregon	60	30
Pennsylvania	203	50
Rhode Island	75	38
South Carolina	124	46
South Dakota	70	35
Tennessee	99	33
Texas	150	31
Utah	75	29
Vermont	150	30
Virginia	100	40
Washington	98	49
West Virginia	100	34
Wisconsin	99	33
Wyoming	60	30

Source: *The World Almanac and Book of Facts*, 2007.

State Legislators' Compensation

State	Salary	Expense allowance during session
Alabama	$10/day*	$2,280/month
Alaska	$24,012	$163–218/day
Arizona	$24,000	$35–60/day
Arkansas	$14,765	$130/day
California	$113,098	$162/day
Colorado	$30,000	$45–99/day
Connecticut	$28,000	$0
Delaware	$42,000	$0
Florida	$30,996	$126/day
Georgia	$17,342	$173/day
Hawaii	$35,900	$10–120/day
Idaho	$16,116	$49–122/day
Illinois	$57,619	$125/day
Indiana	$11,600	$137/day
Iowa	$25,000	$88–118/day
Kansas	$84.80/day*	$99/day
Kentucky	$180.54/day*	$108.90/day
Louisiana	$16,800	$138/day
Maine	$12,713	$70/day
Maryland	$43,500	$157/day
Massachusetts	$58,237.15	$10–100/day
Michigan	$79,650	$12,000/year
Minnesota	$31,140.90	$77–96/day
Mississippi	$10,000	$91/day
Missouri	$31,351	$79.20/day
Montana	$82.67/day+	$98.75/day
Nebraska	$12,000	$39–99/day
Nevada	$137.90/day*	federal rate
New Hampshire	$200	$0
New Jersey	$49,000	$0
New Mexico	$0	$142/day
New York	$79,500	varies
North Carolina	$13,951	$104/day
North Dakota	$125/day*	up to $900/month
Ohio	$58,933.56	$0
Oklahoma	$38,400	$122/day
Oregon	$18,408	$99/day
Pennsylvania	$73,613	$129/day
Rhode Island	$13,089.44	$0
South Carolina	$10,400	$119/day
South Dakota	$6,000	$110/day
Tennessee	$18,123	$153/day
Texas	$7,200	$139/day
Utah	$130/day*	$144/day
Vermont	$600.78/week+	$51–139/day
Virginia	$18,000	$135–140/day
Washington	$36,311	$90/day
West Virginia	$15,000	$115/day
Wisconsin	$47,413	$88/day
Wyoming	$150/day+	$85/day

* calendar day
+ legislative day
Source: National Conference of State Legislatures, www.ncsl.org, 2007.

abridge to limit (p. 363)

absentee ballot one that allows a person to vote without going to the polls on Election Day (p. 491)

*abstract dealing with a subject in its theoretical aspects; not concrete (p. 513)

*access to get at (p. 519)

*accessible easy to contact (p. 234)

*accompany to go along with (p. 332)

*accumulate to gather or pile up, esp. little by little (p. 725)

*acknowledge to admit to be true (p. 361)

acreage allotment the program under which the government pays support prices for farmers' crops grown on an assigned number of acres (p. 586)

action alert a message from an interest group to its members, calling upon them to respond immediately by telephone, fax, or e-mail to a specific lawmaker, group of lawmakers, or other official (p. 546)

*adapt to make suitable for a new or different situation (p. 76)

administrative assistant member of a lawmaker's personal staff who runs the lawmaker's office, supervises the schedule, and gives advice (p. 148)

administrative law law that spells out the authority, procedures, rules, and regulations to be followed by government agencies (p. 417)

*administrator one who performs executive duties or manages (p. 665)

adversary system a judicial system in which opposing lawyers present their strongest cases (p. 419)

advisory opinion a ruling on a law or action that has not been challenged (p. 339)

*advocate a supporter (p. 54)

*affect to influence (pp. 6, 101, 515)

affidavit a statement that is written and sworn to in the presence of an authorized person, such as a notary public (p. 426)

affirmative action government policies that award jobs, government contracts, promotions, admission to schools, and other benefits to minorities and women in order to make up for past discriminations (p. 404)

*aid help (p. 704)

alien a person who lives in a country where he or she is not a citizen (p. 391)

*allocate to assign a portion of something (p. 109)

*alternative a different choice (p. 224)

ambassador an official of the government who represents the nation in diplomatic matters (p. 615)

*amend to change, alter (p. 14)

privar limitar (pág. 363)

papeleta ausente permite a una persona votar sin ir a la urna electoral en el día de elección (pág. 491)

*abstracto trata del sujeto en sus aspectos teóricos; no concreto (pág. 513)

*acceso llegar a algo (pág. 519)

*accesible fácil de contactar (pág. 234)

*acompañar ir junto con algo/alguien (pág. 332)

*acumular juntar o apilar, especialmente, poco a poco (pág. 725)

*aceptar admitir que es cierto (pág. 361)

asignación de acres programa bajo el cual el gobierno paga precios de apoyo para las cosechas de los agricultores cultivadas en un número de acres asignado (pág. 586)

alerta para entrar en acción mensaje de un grupo de interés a sus miembros pidiéndoles que respondan inmediatamente por teléfono, fax o correo electrónico a un dirigente político específico, grupo de congresales u otros funcionarios públicos (pág. 546)

*adaptar adecuar para una situación nueva o diferente (pág. 76)

auxiliar administrativo miembro del personal propio de un legislador que dirige la oficina del legislador, supervisa el calendario, y da asesoramiento (pág. 148)

ley administrativa ley que estipula la autoridad, procedimientos, y reglas para ser seguidos por agencias gubernamentales (pág. 417)

*administrador aquel que lleva a cabo deberes ejecutivos o que administra (pág. 665)

sistema adversario sistema judicial en el cual los abogados opositores presentan sus casos más sólidos (pág. 419)

opinión asesorada decisión sobre una ley o acción que no ha sido desafiada (pág. 339)

*defensor partidario (pág. 54)

*afectar influenciar (págs. 6, 101, 515)

affidávit una declaración que es escrita y jurada ante una persona autorizada, tal como un notario público (pág. 426)

acción afirmativa política de gobierno que les asigna trabajos, contratos gubernamentales, promociones, admisiones a escuelas, y otros beneficios a minorías y mujeres con el fin de enmendar discriminaciones pasadas (pág. 404)

*ayuda asistencia (pág. 704)

extranjero persona que vive en un país donde no es ciudadano (pág. 391)

*adjudicar asignar una porción de algo (pág. 109)

*alternativa una opción diferente (pág. 224)

embajador oficial del gobierno que representa la nación en asuntos diplomáticos (pág. 615)

*enmendar cambiar, alterar (pág. 14)

amendment a change to the Constitution (pp. 65, 102)

amicus curiae (uh•mee•kuhs KYUR•ee•eye) Latin for "friend of the court"; a written brief from an individual or group claiming to have information useful to a court's consideration of a case (p. 333)

amnesty a group pardon to individuals for an offense against the government (pp. 254, 390)

*analyst one who studies the parts and nature of something (p. 115)

anarchy political disorder (p. 57)

*annual yearly (p. 247)

answer a formal response by a defendant to the charges in a complaint (p. 425)

*anticipate to give advance thought or treatment to; to foresee or deal with in advance (p. 556)

apartheid strict segregation of the races (p. 693)

appellate jurisdiction authority held by a court to hear a case that is appealed from lower court (p. 307)

appropriation approval of government spending (p. 191)

appropriations bill a proposed law to authorize spending money (p. 160)

*arbitrary seemingly random or by chance rather than by reason (p. 407)

*area part of a place (p. 642)

arrest warrant an order signed by a judge naming the individual to be arrested for a specific crime (pp. 86, 430)

article one of seven main divisions of the body of the Constitution (p. 64)

*aspect a certain view; an element of (p. 638)

*assembly a gathering (p. 20)

assessment the complicated process involved in calculating the value of property to be taxed (p. 674)

*assign to appoint to a duty (p. 203)

*assist to help or aid (p. 213)

*assistant a helper (p. 138)

at-large as a whole; for example, statewide (p. 127)

*authority the right to command or lead (pp. 19, 96)

authorization bill a bill that sets up a federal program and specifies how much money may be appropriated for the program (p. 191)

autocracy a system of government in which the power to rule is in the hands of a single individual (p. 19)

*automatic happening by itself, without intervention or special process (p. 393)

*available present or ready for use, accessible, obtainable (p. 133)

*aware knowing (p. 195)

enmienda cambio en la Constitución (págs. 65, 102)

amicus curiae término latino que significa "amigo de la corte"; un informe escrito por un individuo o un grupo afirmando tener información útil para la consideración de la corte de un caso (pág. 333)

amnistía indulto a un grupo de individuos por una ofensa en contra del gobierno (págs. 254, 390)

*analista alguien que estudia las partes y la naturaleza de algo (pág. 115)

anarquía desorden político (pág. 57)

*anual cada año (pág. 247)

respuesta contestación formal por un acusado a los cargos en una demanda (pág. 425)

*anticipar pensar o tratar de antemano, prever o tratar con antelación (pág. 556)

apartheid segregación estricta de las razas (pág. 693)

jurisdicción de apelación autoridad que tiene por una corte para oír un caso que es apelado de una corte menor (pág. 307)

asignación de fondos aprobación de gastos gubernamentales (pág. 191)

proyecto de ley de asignación de fondos ley propuesta para autorizar el gasto de dinero (pág. 160)

*arbitrario aparentemente al azar o por casualidad, en vez de usar la razón (pág. 407)

*área parte de un lugar (pág. 642)

orden de detención orden firmada por un juez nombrando al individuo a ser arrestado por un crimen determinado (págs. 86, 430)

artículo una de las siete divisiones principales de la Constitución (pág. 64)

*aspecto una visión determinada, un elemento de algo (pág. 638)

*asamblea reunión (pág. 20)

tasación proceso complicado de calcular el valor de propiedad para el impuesto (pág. 674)

*asignar designar un deber (pág. 203)

*asistir ayudar o auxiliar (pág. 213)

*asistente ayudante (pág. 138)

en general como un todo; por ejemplo, por todo el estado (pág. 127)

*autoridad derecho a comandar o dirigir (págs. 19, 96)

proyecto de ley presupuestaria proyecto de ley que establece un programa federal y especifica cuánto dinero le puede ser asignado (pág. 191)

autocracia sistema de gobierno en el cual el poder para dirigir está en manos de un solo individuo (pág. 19)

*automático que ocurre por sí mismo, sin intervención o un proceso especial (pág. 393)

*disponible presente o listo para usar, accesible, obtenible (pág. 133)

*consciente que sabe (pág. 195)

B

balanced budget plan requiring that what the government spends will not exceed its income (p. 77)

*beneficiary an individual who benefits from something (p. 488)

*benefit something that adds to well-being, an aid (p. 15)

biased sample in polling, a group that does not accurately represent the larger population (p. 520)

bicameral relative to a two-house legislative body (p. 641)

bicameral legislature a two-chamber legislature (p. 123)

bilateral treaty agreement between two nations (p. 629)

bill a proposed law (p. 135)

bipartisan consisting of members of both major political parties (p. 620)

bloc coalition that promotes a common interest (p. 344)

block grant a grant of money to a state or local government for a general purpose (p. 658)

*bond a government security (p. 160)

boss a powerful party leader (p. 465)

bourgeoisie capitalists who own the means of production (p. 29)

brief a written statement setting forth the legal arguments, relevant facts, and precedents supporting one side of a case (p. 333)

bureaucracy government administrators (p. 115)

bureaucrat one who works for a department or agency of the federal government; a civil servant (p. 275)

presupuesto balanceado plan financiero requiriendo que lo que el gobierno federal gasta no excederá su ingreso (pág. 77)

*beneficiario individuo que se beneficia de algo (pág. 488)

*beneficio algo que aporta al bienestar, una ayuda (pág. 15)

muestra sesgada en votación, un grupo que no representa exactamente la mayor población (pág. 520)

bicameral legislatura de dos cámaras (pág. 641)

legislatura bicameral legislatura de dos cámaras (pág. 123)

tratado bilateral acuerdo firmado por dos naciones (pág. 629)

proyecto de ley ley propuesta (pág. 135)

bipartidario que consta de miembros de los dos partidos políticos más grandes (pág. 620)

bloque coalición unida para promocionar un interés común (pág. 344)

otorgación general gran donación de dinero a un gobierno estatal o local para un propósito general (pág. 658)

*bono valores del gobierno (pág. 160)

jefe poderoso líder de partido (pág. 465)

burguesía capitalistas que poseen los medios de producción (pág. 29)

informe declaración escrita exponiendo los argumentos legales, hechos relevantes, y precedentes apoyando un lado de un caso (pág. 333)

burocracia administradores gubernamentales (pág. 115)

burócrata aquél que trabaja para un departamento o agencia del gobierno federal—servidor civil (pág. 275)

C

cabinet secretaries of the executive departments, the vice president, and other top officials that help the president make decisions and policy (p. 228)

calendar a schedule that lists the order in which bills will be considered in Congress (p. 136)

campaign manager the person responsible for the overall strategy and planning of a campaign (p. 476)

canvass the vote count by the official body that tabulates election returns and certifies the winner (p. 487)

canvassing board the official body that counts votes and certifies the winner (p. 490)

*capacity the power to produce or provide (p. 28)

capitalism an economic system providing free choice and individual incentive for workers, investors, consumers, and business enterprises (p. 27)

gabinete secretarios de los departamentos ejecutivos, el vicepresidente, y otros altos funcionarios que ayudan al presidente a tomar decisiones y hacer políticas (pág. 228)

calendario horario que enumera el orden en el cual los proyectos de ley serán considerados en el Congreso (pág. 136)

director de campaña persona responsable de la estrategia global y la planeación de una campaña (pág. 476)

escrutinio el conteo de votos hecho por el cuerpo oficial que tabula las devoluciones electorales y certifica al ganador (pág. 487)

consejo de escrutinio cuerpo oficial que cuenta los votos y certifica al ganador (pág. 490)

*capacidad poder para producir o proveer (pág. 28)

capitalismo un sistema económico que proporciona la libertad de acción y el incentivo individual para trabajadores, inversionistas, consumidores y empresas de negocios (pág. 27) casework the work a lawmaker does to help constituents with problems (p. 200)

caseworker a member of a lawmaker's personal staff who handles requests for help from constituents (p. 148)

*category a classification (p. 366)

caucus a private meeting of party leaders to choose candidates for office (pp. 134, 464)

cede to yield (p. 50)

censure a vote of formal disapproval of a member's actions (p. 128)

census a population count (p. 124)

central clearance Office of Management and Budget's review of all legislative proposals that executive agencies prepare (p. 236)

*challenge to formally question the legality of (p. 188)

checks and balances the system where each branch of government exercises some control over the others (p. 66)

*circumstance an accessory fact or detail; state of affairs (p. 422)

*citation an official summons to appear, as before a court (p. 430)

*civil relating to citizens, and to the state and its citizenry (p. 696)

civil case one usually involving a dispute between two or more private individuals or organizations (p. 646)

civil law one relating to disputes among two or more individuals or between individuals and the government (pp. 103, 422)

civil rights movement the efforts to end segregation (p. 401)

civil service system practice of government employment based on competitive examinations and merit (p. 286)

*clarify to free of confusion, make understandable (p. 578)

client group individuals and groups who work with a government agency and are most affected by its decisions (p. 295)

closed primary an election in which only members of a political party can vote (p. 465)

closed rule rule that forbids members of Congress to offer amendments to a bill from the floor (p. 190)

cloture a procedure that allows each senator to speak only 1 hour on a bill under debate (p. 140)

cluster sample a polling method that groups people by geographical divisions (p. 521)

coalition government one formed by several parties who combine forces to obtain a majority (p. 454)

*code a collection of laws (p. 415)

trabajo particular trabajo que un legislador hace para ayudar a los constituyentes con sus problemas (pág. 200)

asistente social miembro del equipo de trabajo de un legislador que se encarga de las peticiones de ayuda de los constituyentes (pág. 148)

*categoría clasificación (pág. 366)

junta electoral reunión privada de dirigentes del partido para escoger candidatos al gobierno (págs. 134, 464)

ceder renunciar (pág. 50)

censura voto de desaprobación formal de las acciones de un miembro (pág. 128)

censo conteo de población (pág. 124)

despacho central revisión por la Oficina de Dirección y Presupuesto de todas las propuestas legislativas que las agencias ejecutivas preparan (pág. 236)

*disputar cuestionar formalmente la legalidad de algo (pág. 188)

control y balances sistema en que cada rama del gobierno ejercita algún control sobre los otros (pág. 66)

*circunstancia hecho accesorio o detalle; situación actual (pág. 422)

*emplazamiento una citación oficial para comparecer ante un tribunal (pág. 430)

*civil relacionado a los ciudadanos, estado y ciudadanía (pág. 696)

caso civil caso generalmente tiene que ver con una disputa entre dos o más individuos privados u organizaciones (pág. 646)

ley civil relacionada a disputas entre dos o más individuos o entre individuos y el gobierno (págs. 103, 422)

movimiento de derechos civiles esfuerzos para acabar con la segregación (pág. 401)

sistema de servicio civil práctica de empleo gubernamental basada en exámenes competitivos y mérito (pág. 286)

*clarificar sin confusiones, hacer comprensible (pág. 578)

grupo de clientes individuos y grupos que trabajan con una agencia gubernamental y que son los más afectados por sus decisiones (pág. 295)

elección preliminar cerrada una elección en que sólo los miembros de un partido político pueden votar (pág. 465)

norma cerrada regla que prohíbe a miembros del Congreso ofrecer enmiendas a un proyecto de ley haciendo uso de la palabra (pág. 190)

clausura procedimiento que permite a cada senador hablar sólo una hora sobre un proyecto de ley bajo debate (pág. 140)

muestra regional método de votación que agrupa a personas por división geográfica (pág. 521)

gobierno de coalición formado por varios partidos que unen fuerzas para obtener una mayoría (pág. 454)

*código conjunto de leyes (pág. 415)

collective bargaining–conference committee

collective bargaining the practice of negotiating labor contracts (p. 581)

collective farm farm in which the land is owned by the government but rented to a family (p. 729)

collective naturalization a process by which a group of people become American citizens through an act of Congress (p. 395)

collective security a system by which the participating nations agree to take joint action against a nation that attacks any one of them (p. 629)

command economy an economic system in which the government controls the factors of production (pp. 30, 717)

*commentator one who reports and discusses news on radio or television (p. 530)

committee staff the people who work for House and Senate committees (p. 147)

*commodity an economic good, such as an agricultural product (p. 505)

common law law made by judges in the process of resolving individual cases (p. 418)

*communicate to convey information about; to make known (p. 515)

communism an economic system in which the central government directs all major economic decisions (pp. 29, 718)

*community people with common interests living in a particular area (p. 113)

comparative advantage economic principle that each country should produce those goods it can make more efficiently and trade for other goods (p. 732)

compensation salary (p. 214)

complaint a legal document filed with the court that has jurisdiction over the problem (p. 425)

*complex involved, not simple (p. 146)

*component a part (p. 591)

*comprehensive including much; covering completely (p. 710)

*compromise to come to agreement by mutual concession (p. 462)

*concept idea (p. 68)

*conclude to determine or make up one's mind (p. 238)

concurrent jurisdiction authority shared by both federal and state courts (p. 306)

concurrent powers powers that both the national government and the states have (p. 97)

*conduct to manage, direct (p. 79)

confederacy a loose union of independent states (p. 13)

*confer to compare views, consult (p. 560)

conference committee a temporary joint committee set up when the House and the Senate have passed different versions of the same bill (p. 144)

negociación colectiva práctica de negociar contratos laborales (pág. 581)

granja colectiva ejido en el cual la tierra es propiedad del gobierno pero arrendada a una familia (pág. 729)

naturalización colectiva proceso por el cual los miembros de un grupo llegan a ser ciudadanos americanos por medio de un acto del Congreso (pág. 395)

seguridad colectiva un sistema en el cual las naciones participantes acuerdan tomar acción unida en contra de una nación que ataque a cualquiera de ellas (pág. 629)

economía de mando un sistema económico en el cual el gobierno controla los elementos de producción (págs. 30, 717)

*comentarista alguien que informa y discute las noticias en radio o televisión (pág. 530)

personal del comité personas que trabajan para los comités de la Cámara y el Senado (pág. 147)

*mercancía bienes económicos, tales como un producto agrícola (pág. 505)

ley común ley hecha por jueces en el proceso de resolver casos individuales (pág. 418)

*comunicar transmitir información de algo; dar a conocer algo (pág. 515)

comunismo sistema económico en el cual el gobierno central dirige todas las importantes decisiones económicas (págs. 29, 718)

*comunidad personas con intereses en común que viven en un área en particular (pág. 113)

ventaja comparativa principio económico en el cual cada país debe hacer aquellos productos que puede elaborar eficientemente e intercambiar por otros productos (pág. 732)

compensación salario (pág. 214)

queja documento legal presentado en la corte que tiene jurisdicción sobre el problema (pág. 425)

*complejo complicado; que no es simple (pág. 146)

*componente una parte (pág. 591)

*comprensivo que incluye mucho; que cubre completamente (pág. 710)

*compromiso llegar a un acuerdo por concesión mutua (pág. 462)

*concepto idea (pág. 68)

*concluir determinar o decidirse (pág. 238)

jurisdicción conjunta autoridad compartida por las cortes federales y estatales (pág. 306)

poderes comunes poderes tanto del gobierno nacional como de los gobiernos estatales (pág. 97)

*conducir manejar, dirigir (pág. 79)

confederación unión suelta de estados independientes (pág. 13)

*conferir comparar puntos de vista, consultar (pág. 560)

comité de conferencia comité común temporal creado cuando la Cámara y el Senado han aprobado diferentes versiones del mismo proyecto de ley (pág. 144) *confirm to make sure of (p. 487)

conscription compulsory military service; also called a draft (p. 625)

consensus an agreement about basic beliefs (p. 6)

*consequence something produced by a cause or action (p. 191)

*considerable of substantial size or importance (p. 624)

consolidated democracy a nation that has democratic elections, political parties, constitutional government, an independent judiciary, and usually a market economy (p. 689)

constituent a person whom a member of Congress has been elected to represent (p. 133)

*constitute to make up, form, compose (p. 137)

*constitution a plan that provides the rules for government (pp. 13, 47)

constitutional commission a group of experts appointed to study a state constitution and recommend changes (p. 640)

constitutional convention a gathering of citizens elected to consider changing or replacing a constitution (p. 639)

constitutional government a government in which a constitution has authority to place clearly recognized limits on the powers of those who govern (p. 13)

constitutional law law that involves the interpretation and application of the U.S. Constitution and state constitutions (pp. 14, 416)

consul a government official who heads a consulate in a foreign nation (p. 623)

consulate office that promotes American business and safeguards its travelers in a foreign country (p. 623)

*consult to ask for advice (p. 616)

*consumer a buyer and user (p. 27)

containment the policy designed to keep the Soviet Union from expanding its power (p. 610)

contempt willful obstruction of justice (p. 168)

*contract a set of voluntary promises, enforceable by the law, between two or more parties (pp. 37, 422)

*contradict to assert the contrary of, to imply the opposite of (p. 417)

*contrast the difference between things that are of similar natures (p. 72)

*contribute to give or supply in company with others (p. 196)

*controversial debatable; arousing differences of opinion (p. 593)

*convention a meeting (p. 77)

*confirmar demostrar o verificar (pág. 487)

conscripción servicio military obligatorio, tambien llamada la quinta (pág. 625)

consenso acuerdo sobre creencias básicas (pág. 6)

*consecuencia algo que se produce por una causa o acción (pág. 191)

*considerable que tiene un tamaño o importancia sustancial (pág. 624)

democracia consolidada nación que tiene elecciones democráticas, partidos políticos, gobierno constitucional, judicatura independiente, y generalmente una economía de mercados (pág. 689)

constituyente persona a la cual un miembro del Congreso ha elegido para representar (pág. 133)

*constituir inventar, formar, componer (pág. 137)

constitución plan que provee las normas para el gobierno (págs. 13, 47)

comisión constitucional grupo de expertos designados para estudiar la constitución de un estado y recomendar cambios (pág. 640)

convención constitucional junta de ciudadanos electos para considerar el cambio o reemplazo de una constitución (pág. 639)

gobierno constitucional gobierno en el cual una constitución tiene la autoridad de establecer límites claramente reconocidos en los poderes de aquellos que gobiernan (pág. 13)

ley constitucional ley que involucra la interpretación y la aplicación de la Constitución de EE.UU. y constituciones estatales (págs. 14, 416)

cónsul funcionario gubernamental que encabeza un consulado en una nación extranjera (pág. 623)

consulado oficina que promueve los intereses comerciales americanos en un país extranjero y guarda a los viajeros de su nación en ese país (pág. 623)

*consultar pedir consejos (pág. 616)

*consumidor comprador y usuario (pág. 27)

contención política diseñada para prohibir que la Unión Soviética expandiera sus poderes (pág. 610)

rebeldía obstrucción voluntaria de la justicia (pág. 168)

*contrato conjunto de promesas voluntarias, que se pueden hacer cumplir a fuerza de ley, entre dos o más partidos (págs. 37, 422)

*contradecir afirmar lo contrario de algo, insinuar lo opuesto de algo (pág. 417)

*contraste diferencia entre las cosas que tienen una naturaleza similar (pág. 72)

*contribuir dar o suplir en compañía de otros (pág. 196)

*controversial debatible; suscitar las diferencias de opinión (pág. 593)

*convención reunión (pág. 77)

*convert to alter the nature or properties of, especially in manufacturing; to change from one form or function to another (p. 718)

*convince to make someone believe something (p. 106)

*cooperate to act together for mutual benefit (p. 458)

*coordinate to arrange and organize (p. 149)

*core the basic, essential part; the essential meaning (p. 392)

corporate charter a document that gives a corporation legal status (p. 648)

counsel an attorney (p. 439)

county the largest political subdivision of a state (p. 664)

county board the governing body of most counties (p. 664)

covert secret (p. 266)

criminal case one in which the state brings charges against a citizen for violating the law (p. 646)

criminal justice system system of state and federal courts, police, and prisons that enforces criminal law (p. 429)

criminal law one that defines crimes and provides for their punishment (p. 429)

cross-pressured voter one who is caught between conflicting elements in his or her own life (p. 493)

*convertir alterar la naturaleza o las propiedades de algo, especialmente en la manufactura; cambiar de una forma o función hacia otra (pág. 718)

*convencer hacer que alguien crea en algo (pág. 106)

*cooperar actuar juntos para el beneficio mutuo (pág. 458)

*coordinar arreglar y organizar (pág. 149)

*núcleo parte básica, esencial; significado esencial (pág. 392)

estatuto de corporación documento que da el estatus legal a una sociedad anónima (pág. 648)

asesor jurídico abogado (pág. 439)

condado la mayor subdivisión territorial y política de un estado (pág. 664)

consejo del condado organismo de gobierno de la mayoría de los condados (pág. 664)

cubierto secreto (pág. 266)

caso criminal uno en el cual el estado lleva cargos contra un ciudadano por violar la ley (pág. 646)

sistema de justicia criminal sistema de cortes estatales y federales, policías y prisiones que hacen cumplir la ley criminal (pág. 429)

ley criminal aquella que define crímenes y provee para su castigo (pág. 429)

votante bajo presión aquel que se encuentra atrapado entre elementos conflictivos en su propia vida (pág. 493)

D

*data facts, information (p. 277)

*decline to become less, change to poorer condition (p. 600)

de facto existing "in fact" rather than legally (p. 266)

defamatory speech false speech that damages a person's good name, character, or reputation (p. 369)

defendant the person against whom a civil or criminal suit is brought in court (p. 424)

delegated powers powers the Constitution grants or delegates to the national government (p. 95)

democracy government in which the people rule (p. 20)

*demonstration a public display of feelings about a cause or person (p. 85)

denaturalization the loss of citizenship through fraud or deception during the naturalization process (p. 395)

*deny to refuse to grant (p. 357)

dependent one who relies primarily on another person for basic needs (p. 556)

deregulate to reduce regulations (p. 281)

*derive to come from; are given by (p. 306)

*design a pattern (p. 253)

*datos hechos, información (pág. 277)

*declinar hacerse menos, cambiar a una condición más pobre (pág. 600)

de facto existiendo de hecho en vez de legalmente (pág. 266)

expresión difamatoria discurso falso que deteriora el buen nombre, carácter o reputación de una persona (pág. 369)

acusado persona contra la cual una demanda civil o criminal es traída (pág. 424)

poderes delegados poderes que la Constitución otorga o delega al gobierno nacional (pág. 95)

democracia gobierno en el cual la gente manda (pág. 20)

*demostración muestra pública de los sentimientos relacionados a una causa o persona (pág. 85)

desnaturalización pérdida de la ciudadanía por causa de fraude o decepción durante el proceso de naturalización (pág. 395)

*denegar rehusarse a conceder (pág. 357)

dependiente aquel que depende principalmente de otra persona para la necesidades básicas (pág. 556)

desregular reducir los reglamentos (pág. 281)

*derivar venir de; estar dado (pág. 306)

*diseñar patrón (pág. 253)

developing nation a nation that is only beginning to develop industrially (pp. 16, 722)

*device a piece of equipment or a mechanism designed to serve a special purpose or perform a special function (p. 483)

*devote to commit to an activity (p. 139)

*diminish to lessen the impact or reduce (p. 484)

direct primary an election in which party members select people to run in the general election (p. 465)

discount rate the interest rate the Federal Reserve System charges member banks for loans (p. 569)

discovery process in which both sides prepare for a trial by gathering evidence to support their case (p. 425)

discrimination unfair treatment of individuals based solely on their race, gender, ethnic group, age, physical disability, or religion (p. 399)

*displacement substitution of one thing or group for another (p. 681)

*display to put or spread before the view, to make evident (p. 664)

*disposal the act of getting rid of (p. 670)

dissenting opinion the opinion expressed by a minority of justices in a Supreme Court case (p. 335)

*distribute to give out or disburse to clients, customers, or members of a group (p. 476)

*diverse different, unlike (p. 405)

*domestic of, relating to, or originating within a country, esp. one's own country (p. 721)

*dominant being in a state or position of command or control over all others (p. 481)

double jeopardy retrial of a person who was acquitted in a previous trial for the same crime (p. 441)

*draft rough copy of a written piece (p. 46)

*dramatically excitingly, strikingly (p. 42)

due process principle in the Fifth Amendment stating that the government must follow proper constitutional procedures in trials and in other actions it takes against individuals (pp. 86, 419)

due process clause Fourteenth Amendment clause stating that no state may deprive a person of life, liberty, or property without due process of law (p. 309)

*dynamic forceful, energetic (p. 67)

país en desarrollo nación apenas comenzando a desarrollarse industrialmente (págs. 16, 722)

*aparato mecanismo diseñado para un propósito específico o para llevar a cabo una función especial (pág. 483)

*dedicar comprometerse con una actividad (pág. 139)

*disminuir mermar el impacto o reducir (p. 484)

elección preliminar directa elección en la cual miembros del partido seleccionan a personas para postularse en la elección general (pág. 465)

tipo de descuento tasa de interés que el Sistema de Reserva Federal les cobra a los bancos que son miembros por préstamos (pág. 569)

descubrisemiento proceso cuando ambos lados preparan para un juicio reuniendo evidencia para apoyar su caso (pág. 425)

discriminación tratamiento injusto de individuos basado sólo en su raza, género, grupo étnico, edad, incapacidad física o religión (pág. 399)

*desplazamiento sustituir una cosa o grupo por otro (pág. 681)

*mostrar poner o propagar a la vista, hacer evidente (pág. 664)

*disponer deshacerse de algo (pág. 670)

opinión disidente opinión expresada por una minoría de jueces en un caso de la Corte (pág. 335)

*distribuir dividir o repartir un grupo (pág. 476)

*diverso diferente, distinto (pág. 405)

*doméstico de o relacionado a, o que se origina dentro de un país, especialmente en el país propio (pág. 721)

*dominante estar en un estado o posición de mando o control sobre todos los demás (pág. 481)

doble riesgo nuevo juicio de una persona que fue absuelto en un juicio previo por el mismo crimen (pág. 441)

*borrador escrito provisional (pág. 46)

*dramáticamente apasionadamente, notablemente (pág. 42)

debido proceso un principio en la Quinta Enmienda que establece que el gobierno debe seguir los procedimientos constitucionales propios en juicios y en otras acciones que toma en contra de individuos (págs. 86, 419)

cláusula de proceso legal correspondiente cláusula en la Decimocuarta Enmienda que establece que ningún estado puede privar a una persona de vida, libertad o propiedad sin el proceso legal correspondiente (pág. 309)

*fuerte enérgico (pág. 67)

economics the study of human efforts to satisfy seemingly unlimited wants through the use of limited resources (p. 26)

economía estudio de los esfuerzos humanos para satisfacer los deseos aparentemente ilimitados por el uso de recursos limitados (pág. 26)

elastic clause clause in Article I, Section 8, of the Constitution that gives Congress the right to make all laws "necessary and proper" to carry out the powers expressed in the other clauses of Article I (pp. 69, 96)

elector member of a party chosen in each state to formally elect the president and vice president (p. 220)

electoral vote the official vote for president and vice president by electors in each state (p. 220)

electronic mailing list an automated e-mail notification that provides subscribers with current information on a topic (p. 545)

electronic petition a message that asks the recipient to "sign" his or her name electronically to a request that will be sent to an official (p. 546)

*eliminate to remove from further competition by defeating (p. 468)

embargo an agreement prohibiting trade (p. 44)

embassy an ambassador's official residence and offices in a foreign country (pp. 276, 623)

eminent domain the power of the government to take private property for public use (p. 86)

*emphasize to stress, give importance to (p. 308)

enabling act the first step in the state admission procedure, which enables the people of a territory to prepare a constitution (p. 99)

enemy alien a citizen of a nation with which the United States is at war (p. 391)

*enforce to carry out effectively (p. 245)

*ensure to make sure; to guarantee (p. 377)

entitlement a required government expenditure that continues from one year to the next (pp. 192, 561)

entrepreneur a person who takes a risk to produce goods and services in search of profit (p. 718)

enumerated powers the expressed powers of Congress that are itemized and numbered 1–18 in Article I, Section 8, of the Constitution (p. 69)

*environmental having to do with air, water, land, and other natural resources (p. 586)

*equip to furnish for action, prepare (p. 504)

equity a system of rules by which disputes are resolved on the grounds of fairness (p. 418)

*establish to set up (p. 36)

establishment clause the First Amendment guarantee that "Congress shall make no law respecting an establishment of religion" (p. 358)

*estimate an approximate calculation (p. 556)

*ethics set of moral principles; system of moral values (p. 167)

cláusula elástica cláusula en el Artículo I, Sección 8 de la Constitución que otorga al Congreso el derecho de hacer todas las leyes "necesarias y propias" para llevar a cabo los poderes expresados en las otras cláusulas del Artículo I (págs. 69, 96)

elector miembro de un partido político escogido en cada estado para elegir formalmente al presidente y vicepresidente (pág. 220)

voto electoral voto oficial para presidente y vicepresidente por los electores en cada estado (pág. 220)

lista de correo electrónico notificación automática por correo electrónico que provee a los suscriptores información al día acerca de un tema (pág. 545)

petición electrónica mensaje en que se le pide a quien lo recibe que "firme" su nombre electrónicamente en una petición que se le enviará a un funcionario público (pág. 546)

*eliminar descartar de una futura competencia por medio de la derrota (pág. 468)

embargo acuerdo que prohibe el comercio (pág. 44)

embajada residencia y oficinas oficiales de un embajador en un país extranjero (págs. 276, 623)

dominio eminente poder del gobierno de tomar propiedades privadas para el uso público (pág. 86)

*enfatizar recalcar, dar importancia a algo (pág. 308)

acto capacitador primer paso en el procedimiento de admisión de un estado el cual permite a la gente de un territorio preparar una constitución (pág. 99)

enemigo extranjero ciudadano de una nación contra la cual Estados Unidos está en guerra (pág. 391)

*imponer llevar a cabo efectivamente (pág. 245)

*asegurar afirmar; garantizar (pág. 377)

derecho obligatorio gasto gubernamental requerido que continúa de un año al otro (págs. 192, 561)

empresario persona que se arriesga a producir bienes y servicios en busca de ganancias (pág. 718)

poderes enumerados poderes expresados del Congreso que son especificados y numerados de 1 al 18 en el Artículo I, Sección 8 de la Constitución (pág. 69)

*ambiental relacionado al aire, agua, tierra y otros recursos naturales (pág. 586)

*equipar proporcionar para la acción, preparar (pág. 504)

equidad sistema de normas por el cual las disputas son resueltas basado en lo que es justo (pág. 418)

*establecer fundar (pág. 36)

cláusula de establecimiento garantía de la Primera Enmienda que el Congreso "no hará ninguna ley respecto al establecimiento de religión" (pág. 358)

*estimar cálculo estimado (pág. 556)

*ética conjunto de principios morales; sistema de valores morales (pág. 167) *evaluate to determine the significance or worth of through careful study (p. 562)

*evidence an outward sign; something that furnishes proof (p. 436)

excise tax tax on the manufacture, transportation, sale, or consumption of certain items such as gasoline, liquor, or cigarettes (p. 657)

*exclusion keeping out (p. 373)

exclusionary rule a law stating that illegally obtained evidence cannot be used in a federal court (p. 437)

executive agreement an agreement made between the president and a head of state (pp. 80, 257, 619)

executive order a rule issued by the president that has the force of law (p. 253)

executive privilege the right of the president and other high-ranking executive officers to refuse to testify before Congress or a court (p. 266)

expatriation giving up one's citizenship by leaving to live in a foreign country (p. 395)

*expert an individual who has mastered a particular subject or skill (p. 147)

*explicit fully expressed without vagueness; leaving no question as to meaning or intent (p. 423)

*export something that is sold and sent to another country as part of international trade (p. 656)

*expose to make known, bring to light, disclose the faults of (p. 529)

expressed contract a contract in which the terms are specifically stated, usually in writing (p. 422)

expressed powers powers directly stated in the Constitution (pp. 69, 95, 157)

extradite to return a criminal or fugitive who flees across state lines back to the original state (p. 103)

extradition the legal procedure through which a person accused of a crime who has fled to another state is returned to the state where the crime took place (p. 651)

extralegal not sanctioned by law (p. 57)

*evaluar determinar el significado o valor de algo a través de un estudio cuidadoso (pág. 562)

*evidencia signo externo; algo que sirve como prueba (pág. 436)

impuesto indirecto impuesto en la manufactura, transportación, venta o consumo de ciertos artículos tales como gasolina, licor o cigarrillos (pág. 657)

*excluir dejar fuera (pág. 373)

norma de exclusión ley que establece que cualquier evidencia obtenida ilegalmente no puede ser usada en una corte federal (pág. 437)

acuerdo ejecutivo acuerdo hecho entre el presidente y un jefe de estado (págs. 80, 257, 619)

orden ejecutiva norma emitida por el presidente que tiene fuerza de ley (pág. 253)

privilegio ejecutivo derecho del presidente y otros altos funcionarios a rehusarse testificar ante el Congreso o una corte (pág. 266)

expatriación renunciar a la ciudadanía al irse a vivir en un país extranjero (pág. 395)

*experto individuo que ha dominado un tema o destreza particular (pág. 147)

*explícito sin vaguedad; expresado en su totalidad, sin dejar cuestionamientos sobre el significado o la intención (pág. 423)

*exportar algo que se vende y se envía a otro país como parte del comercio internacional (pág. 656)

*exponer dar a conocer, sacar a la luz, revelar las faltas de algo/alguien (pág. 529)

contrato expresado contrato en el cual los términos son específicamente establecidos, generalmente por escrito (pág. 422)

poderes expresados poderes establecidos directamente en la Constitución (págs. 69, 95, 157)

extraditar traer de vuelta a su estado de origen a un criminal o fugitivo que cruza los límites estatales al huir (pág. 103)

extradición proceso legal a través del cual una persona acusada de un crimen que ha huido a otro estado es regresado al estado que no está donde el crimen tuvo lugar (pág. 651)

extralegal no permitido por ley (pág. 57)

*facility something built or established to serve a particular purpose (p. 192)

*factor part of a product or concept (p. 514)

factors of production resources that an economy needs to produce goods and services (p. 718)

fairness doctrine rule requiring broadcasters to provide opportunities for the expression of opposing views on issues of public importance (p. 538)

*feature a prominent part or characteristic (p. 668)

*instalaciones algo que se construye o se establece para servir un propósito particular (pág. 192)

*factor parte de un producto o concepto (pág. 514)

elementos de producción recursos que una economía necesita para producir bienes y servicios (pág. 718)

doctrina justa norma que requiere que los medios de difusión proporcionen oportunidades para la expresión de ideas opuestas en temas de importancia pública (pág. 538)

*rasgo parte o característica prominente (pág. 668)

federal bureaucracy departments and agencies of the federal government—mostly the executive branch (p. 72)

federalism a system in which power is divided between the national and state governments (p. 65)

federal system a government that divides the powers of government between the national government and state or provincial governments (p. 13)

*fee a cost for service (p. 675)

felony a major crime (p. 430)

*file to register as a candidate; to place among official records as prescribed by law (p. 465)

filibuster a method of defeating a bill in the Senate by stalling the legislative process and preventing a vote (p. 139)

*finance to provide necessary funds for (p. 650)

fiscal policy a government's use of spending and taxation to influence the economy (p. 567)

fiscal year a 12-month accounting period (p. 560)

foreign policy the strategies and goals that guide a nation's relations with other countries (p. 607)

*format general plan of organization, arrangement, or choice of material (p. 540)

*formula a set method for doing or calculating something (p. 389)

*formulate to put into a systematized statement or expression (p. 123)

forum medium for discussion (p. 249)

*foundation basis (p. 343)

*framework basic structure (p. 628)

free enterprise the opportunity to control one's own economic decisions (p. 24)

free exercise clause the First Amendment guarantee that prohibits government from unduly interfering with the free exercise of religion (p. 358)

free market economic system in which buyers and sellers make free choices in the marketplace (p. 27)

front-runner the early leader in an election (p. 531)

*function to serve, to operate (p. 344)

*fund financial capital (p. 216)

*fundamental basic (p. 607)

fundamental right a basic right of the American system or one that is indispensable in a just system (p. 399)

burocracia federal departamentos del gobierno federal, en su mayoría de la rama ejecutiva (pág. 72)

federalismo sistema en el cual el poder es dividido entre los gobiernos nacionales y estatales (pág. 65)

sistema federal gobierno que divide los poderes del gobierno entre el gobierno nacional y los gobiernos de los estados o provincias (pág. 13)

*honorario costo por servicio (pág. 675)

crimen delito grave (pág. 430)

*presentar registrarse como candidato; colocar entre registros oficiales como prescribe la ley (pág. 465)

obstruccionismo método de derrotar un proyecto de ley en el senado al demorar el proceso legislativo y evitar un voto (pág. 139)

*financiar proveer los fondos necesarios (pág. 650)

política fiscal uso por parte del gobierno de gastos e impuestos para influenciar la economía (pág. 567)

año fiscal período de contabilidad de 12 meses (pág. 560)

política exterior estrategias y metas que guían las relaciones de una nación con otros países (pág. 607)

*formato plan general de organización, arreglo o selección de material (pág. 540)

*fórmula método establecido para hacer o calcular algo (pág. 389)

*formular poner en un hecho o expresión sistematizada (pág. 123)

foro medio para discusión (pág. 249)

*fundamento base (pág. 343)

*armazón estructura básica (pág. 628)

empresa libre oportunidad de controlar sus propias decisiones económicas (pág. 24)

cláusula de libre ejercicio garantía en la Primera Enmienda que prohibe al gobierno interferir sin causa con el libre ejercicio de la religión (pág. 358)

mercado libre sistema económico en el cual los compradores y los vendedores hacen decisiones libres en el mercado (pág. 27)

candidato favorito líder a principios de una elección (pág. 531)

*función servir, operar (pág. 344)

*fondo capital financiero (pág. 216)

*fundamental básico (pág. 607)

derecho fundamental derecho básico del sistema estadounidense o uno que es indispensable en un sistema justo (pág. 399)

gag order an order by a judge barring the press from publishing certain types of information about a pending court case (p. 373)

orden de supresión orden de un juez que prohibe a la prensa publicar ciertos tipos de información sobre un caso judicial pendiente (pág. 373) *gender an individual's sex, male or female (p. 228)

*generate to produce; to be the cause of (p. 262)

gentrification the phenomenon of new people moving into a neighborhood, forcing out those who live there, and changing the area's essential character (p. 681)

gerrymander to draw a district's boundaries to gain an advantage in elections (p. 126)

*global worldwide (p. 544)

*goal aim, purpose (p. 14)

government the institution through which the state maintains social order, provides public services, and enforces binding decisions on citizens (p. 8)

government corporation a business that the federal government runs (p. 279)

grandfather clause an exemption in a law for a certain group based on previous conditions (p. 483)

grand jury group that hears charges against a suspect and decides whether there is sufficient evidence to bring the person to trial (pp. 312, 431)

gross domestic product (GDP) the sum of all goods and services produced in a nation in a year (p. 568)

*guarantee to assure fulfillment of a condition; to promise (p. 355)

*guideline an indication or outline of policy or conduct (p. 292)

*sexo género, masculino o femenino, de un individuo (pág. 228)

*generar producir, ser la causa de algo (pág. 262)

gentificación fenómeno de nueva gente mudándose a un vecindario, echando afuera aquellos que viven ahí, y cambiando el carácter esencial del área (pág. 681)

gerrymander trazar los límites de un distrito para ganar ventaja en las elecciones (pág. 126)

*global mundial (pág. 544)

*meta objetivo, propósito (pág. 14)

gobierno institución por medio de la cual el estado mantiene el orden social, proporciona servicios públicos, e impone decisiones obligatorias para los ciudadanos (pág. 8)

corporación gubernamental empresa dirigida por el gobierno federal (pág. 279)

cláusula abuelo exención en una ley para un cierto grupo basada en condiciones previas (pág. 483)

gran jurado grupo que escucha cargos en contra de una persona sospechosa y decide si hay suficiente evidencia para someter la persona a juicio (págs. 312, 431)

producto nacional bruto total de bienes y servicios producidos en una nación en un año (pág. 568)

*garantizar asegurar el cumplimiento de una condición; prometer (pág. 355)

*pauta indicación o bosquejo de una política o conducta (pág. 292)

H

hearing a session at which a committee listens to testimony from people interested in the bill (p. 184)

heckler's veto public veto of free speech and assembly rights of unpopular groups by claiming demonstrations will result in violence (p. 379)

house arrest a sentence that requires an offender to stay at home except for certain functions the court permits (p. 652)

human rights fundamental freedoms (pp. 355, 710)

hung jury a jury that is unable to reach a decision (p. 434)

audiencia sesión en la cual un comité escucha el testimonio de gente interesada en el proyecto de ley (pág. 184)

heckler's veto veto público de la libre expresión y derechos de asamblea de grupos impopulares al declarar que las demostraciones resultarán en violencia (pág. 379)

arresto domiciliario sentencia que requiere a un ofensor quedarse en casa a excepción de ciertas funciones que la corte permite (pág. 652)

derechos humanos libertades fundamentales (págs. 355, 710)

jurado indeciso jurado que no puede tomar una una decisión (pág. 434)

I

*ideology a set of basic beliefs about life, culture, government, and society (pp. 454, 736)

*ignore to pay no attention to (p. 285)

*illegal against the law (p. 399)

image mental picture (p. 476)

ideología conjunto de creencias básicas sobre la vida, cultura, gobierno y sociedad (págs. 454, 736)

*ignorar no prestar atención (pág. 285)

*ilegal en contra de la ley (pág. 399)

imagen representación mental (pág. 476)

immunity–inherent powers

immunity freedom from prosecution for witnesses whose testimony ties them to illegal acts (p. 169)

*impact a significant or major effect (p. 399)

impeach to accuse a public official of misconduct in office (p. 79)

impeachment a formal accusation of misconduct in office against a public official (p. 164)

*implement to put into effect (p. 291)

implied contract a contract in which the terms are not expressly stated but can be inferred from the actions of the people involved and the circumstances (p. 422)

implied powers powers the government requires to carry out its expressed constitutional powers (pp. 96, 157)

*impose to establish or apply by authority (p. 557)

impound to refuse to spend (p. 337)

impoundment the president's refusal to spend money Congress has voted to fund a program (pp. 175, 253)

*inadequate insufficient (p. 678)

*incentive something that has a tendency to incite to determination or action; motive (p. 729)

*income money taken in by an individual or a corporation (p. 656)

income tax the tax levied on individual and corporate earnings (p. 108)

*incorporation the process by which a municipal government can be formed when a group of people asks the state legislature to legally set up a government in their community (pp. 357, 666)

*incorporation doctrine a process that extended the protections of the Bill of Rights against the actions of state and local governments (p. 84)

incrementalism the term used to explain that the total budget changes little from year to year (p. 564)

incumbent elected official who is already in office (p. 129)

independent a voter who does not support any particular party (p. 459)

*indication something that points out, as a sign or symbol (p. 520)

indictment a formal charge by a grand jury (pp. 313, 431)

industrialized nation a nation with large industries and advanced technology that provides a more comfortable way of life than developing nations (p. 16)

information a sworn statement by the prosecution that there is sufficient evidence for a trial (p. 432)

*infrastructure the basic facilities of a city, such as paved streets and sidewalks, water pipes, sewers, bridges, and public buildings (pp. 567, 680)

*inherently of the essential character of something (p. 347)

inherent powers powers the national government may exercise simply because it is a government (p. 96)

inmunidad libertad de enjuiciamiento de los testigos, cuyo testimonio los vincula a actos ilegales (pág. 169)

*impacto efecto significativo o notable (pág. 399)

acusar acusar a un funcionario público de mala conducta en su cargo (pág. 79)

acusación acusación formal por mala conducta en un cargo en contra de un oficial público (pág. 164)

*implementar entrar en vigor (pág. 291)

contrato implícito contrato en el cual los términos no son expresamente citados pero pueden ser deducidos de las acciones de la gente involucrada y las circunstancias (pág. 422)

poderes implícitos poderes que el gobierno requiere para llevar a cabo los poderes constitucionales expresados (págs. 96, 157)

*imponer establecer o aplicar por autoridad (pág. 557)

confiscar rehusar a gastar (pág. 337)

confiscamiento negativa del presidente de gastar el dinero que el Congreso ha votado para financiar un programa (págs. 175, 253)

*inadecuado insuficiente (pág. 678)

*incentivo algo que tiene una tendencia a incitar hacia la determinación o acción; motivo (pág. 729)

*ingresos dinero ganado por un individuo o una corporación (pág. 656)

impuesto a los ingresos impuesto recaudado en ganancias individuales y corporativas (pág. 108)

*incorporación proceso por el cual un gobierno municipal puede ser formado cuando un grupo de personas solicita a la asamblea legislativa estatal que establezca legalmente un gobierno en su comunidad (págs. 357, 666)

*doctrina de incorporación proceso que extiende la protección de la Declaración de Derechos en contra de las acciones de gobiernos estatales y locales (pág. 84)

incrementalismo término usado para explicar que el presupuesto total cambia poco de un año al otro (pág. 564)

titular funcionario gubernamental que ya ocupa e cargo (pág. 129)

independiente votante que no apoya a un partido político en particular (pág. 459)

*indicación algo que señala, como un símbolo o signo (pág. 520)

acusación acusación formal por un gran jurado (págs. 313, 431)

nación industrializada nación con grandes industrias y tecnología avanzada que proporciona una forma de vida más cómoda que la de las naciones en desarrollo (pág. 16)

información declaración jurada por la fiscalía que afirma que hay suficiente evidencia para un juicio (pág. 432)

infraestructura instalaciones básicas de una ciudad, tales como calles y aceras pavimentadas, tubería de agua, puentes, y edificios públicos (págs. 567, 680)

*inherente carácter esencial de algo (pág. 347)

poderes inherentes poderes que el gobierno nacional puede ejercitar simplemente porque es un gobierno (pág. 96) *initial the first (p. 335)

*initiate to begin (p. 157)

*initiative a method by which citizens propose a constitutional amendment or a law (pp. 73, 639)

injunction an order that will stop a particular action or enforce a rule or regulation (pp. 297, 424, 582)

*innovative tending to introduce newness (p. 280)

*inspect to look at closely (p. 259)

*instance example, illustration (p. 733)

*institution establishment, practice, or social organization (p. 21)

*integrate to open to all races (p. 405)

*intense existing in an extreme degree (p. 475)

*interact to act upon one another (p. 103)

*interactive relating to a two-way electronic communication system (p. 184)

interest group a group of people with common goals who organize to influence government (p. 503)

intergovernmental organization (IGO) an international organization composed of members of national governments (p. 702)

intergovernmental revenue revenue distributed by one level of government to another (p. 657)

interlocking directorate the same people serving on the boards of directors of competing companies (p. 578)

internationalism involvement in world affairs (p. 608)

*interpretation explanation (p. 338)

interstate commerce trade among the states (pp. 55, 161)

interstate compact a written agreement between two or more states (p. 105)

*intervene to come between (p. 611)

*investigation a systematic examination of related facts (p. 143)

*investment outlay of money for income or profit, capital outlay (p. 731)

*investor one who commits money in order to make a financial return (p. 581)

*invoke to appeal to or cite as authority (p. 415)

*involve to engage as a participant (p. 200)

iron triangle a relationship formed among government agencies, congressional committees, and client groups who work together (p. 297)

isolationism the avoidance of involvement in world affairs (p. 608)

*issue topic for consideration (p. 141)

*item veto the power to turn down a particular item in a bill without vetoing the entire bill (p. 645)

*inicial primero (pág. 335)

*iniciar empezar (pág. 157)

*iniciativa método por el cual los ciudadanos proponen una enmienda constitucional o una ley (págs. 73, 639)

mandato judicial orden que detendrá una acción en particular o hará cumplir una norma o reglamentación (págs. 297, 424, 582)

*innovador con tendencia a introducir la novedad (pág. 280)

*inspeccionar mirar de cerca (pág. 259)

*instancia ejemplo, ilustración (pág. 733)

*institución establecimiento, práctica u organización social (pág. 21)

*integrar abrirse a todas las razas (pág. 405)

*intenso que existe a un grado extremo (pág. 475)

*interactuar actuar uno con otro (pág. 103)

*interactivo relacionado a un sistema de comunicación electrónico de dos vías (pág. 184)

grupo de intereses grupo de personas con objetivos comunes que se organizan para influenciar al gobierno (pág. 503)

organización intergubernamental organización internacional compuesta por miembros de gobiernos nacionales (pág. 702)

ingresos intergubernamentales ingresos distribuidos de un nivel de gobierno a otro (pág. 657)

dirección entrelazada misma gente sirviendo en juntas directivas de compañías competidoras (pág. 578)

internacionalismo involucramiento en asuntos mundiales (pág. 608)

*interpretación explicación (pág. 338)

comercio interestatal intercambio entre los estados (págs. 55, 161)

pacto interestatal acuerdo escrito entre dos o más estados (pág. 105)

*intervenir interponerse (pág. 611)

*investigación examen sistemático de hechos relacionados (pág. 143)

*inversión desembolso de dinero para ingresos o ganancias, gastos de capital (pág. 731)

*inversionista alguien que compromete dinero con el propósito de tener un retorno financiero (pág. 581)

*invocar apelar o citar como autoridad (pág. 415)

*involucrar convertirse en un participante (pág. 200)

triángulo de hierro relación formada entre agencias gubernamentales, comités congresistas, y grupos de clientes que trabajan juntos (pág. 297)

aislacionismo evasión del involucramiento en asuntos mundiales (pág. 608)

*asunto tema para ser considerado (pág. 141)

veto de artículo poder de rechazar un artículo particular en un proyecto de ley sin vetar el proyecto entero (pág. 645)

Jim Crow laws laws requiring racial segregation in such places as schools, buses, and hotels (p. 400)

joint committee a committee of the House and the Senate that usually acts as a study group and reports its findings back to the House and the Senate (p. 143)

*journal a personal record of experiences, ideas, and reflections (p. 547)

judicial activism the philosophy that the Supreme Court should play an active role in shaping national policies by addressing social and political issues (p. 80)

judicial circuit a region containing a United States appellate court (p. 313)

judicial restraint the philosophy that the Supreme Court should avoid taking the initiative on social and political questions (p. 80)

judicial review the power of the Supreme Court to declare laws and actions of local, state, or national governments unconstitutional (pp. 66, 336)

jurisdiction the authority of a court to rule on certain cases (p. 64)

jury a group of citizens who hear evidence during a trial and give a verdict (p. 433)

jus sanguinis (YOOS SAHN•gwuh•nuhs) Latin phrase meaning "law of blood"; the principle that grants citizenship on the basis of the citizenship of one's parents (p. 394)

jus soli (YOOS SOH•lee) Latin phrase meaning "law of the soil"; the principle that grants citizenship to nearly all people born in a country (p. 393)

*justify to show to be right or reasonable (p. 363)

ley Jim Crow ley que requiere la segregación racial en lugares tales como escuelas, autobuses, y hoteles (pág. 400)

comité conjunto comité de la Cámara y el Senado que generalmente actúa como grupo de estudio y reporta sus descubrimientos de regreso a la Cámara y el Senado (pág. 143)

*diario registro personal de experiencias, ideas y reflexiones (pág. 547)

activismo judicial filosofía que la Suprema Corte debe tomar un papel activo en darle forma a políticas nacionales que traten cuestiones sociales y políticas (pág. 80)

circuito judicial región que contiene una corte de apelación de Estados Unidos (pág. 313)

represión judicial filosofía que la Suprema Corte debe evitar tomar la iniciativa en cuestiones sociales y políticas (pág. 80)

revisión judicial poder de la Suprema Corte de declarar leyes y acciones del gobierno local, estatal y nacional inconstitucionales (págs. 66, 336)

jurisdicción autoridad de una corte para dictaminar en ciertos casos (pág. 64)

jurado grupo de ciudadanos que escuchan evidencias durante un juicio y dan el veredicto (pág. 433)

jus sanguinis frase latina que quiere decir "ley de sangre"; principio que otorga ciudadanía en base de la ciudadanía de los padres (pág. 394)

jus soli frase latina que quiere decir "ley de la tierra"; principio que otorga ciudadanía a casi toda persona nacida en un país (pág. 393)

*justificar mostrar que está correcto o que es razonable (pág. 363)

*labor an economic group composed of those who do manual labor or who work for wages (p. 181)

laissez-faire the philosophy that government should keep its hands off the economy (pp. 27, 577)

lame duck an outgoing official serving out the remainder of a term, after retiring or being defeated for reelection (p. 90)

law set of rules and standards by which a society governs itself (p. 415)

leak the release of secret information by anonymous government officials to the media (pp. 230, 529)

legislative assistant a member of a lawmaker's personal staff who makes certain that the lawmaker is well informed about proposed legislation (p. 148)

*mano de obra grupo económico compuesto por aquellos que llevan acabo labores manuales o que trabajan por un salario (pág. 181)

laissez-faire filosofía que el gobierno debe mantener sus manos fuera de la economía (págs. 27, 577)

lame duck funcionario saliente sirviendo el resto de un período después de su retiro o derrota en reelecciones (pág. 90)

ley conjunto de normas y estándares por los cuales una sociedad se gobierna a sí misma (pág. 415)

divulgación anuncio de información secreta por funcionarios gubernamentales anónimos a los medios de comunicación (págs. 230, 529)

asistente legislativo miembro del equipo de trabajo de un legislador que se asegura que el legislador esté bien informado de legislación propuesta (pág. 148)

legislative veto the provisions Congress wrote into some laws that allowed it to review and cancel actions of executive agencies (p. 170)

*legislature governing body that creates laws (p. 49)

*levy to impose a tax (p. 49)

liaison officer a cabinet department employee who helps promote good relations with Congress (p. 296)

libel false written or published statements intended to damage a person's reputation (pp. 369, 537)

*license a permit issued by an official agency (p. 103)

lieutenant governor the presiding officer of the upper house in some state legislatures (p. 642)

limited government a system in which the power of the government is limited, not absolute (p. 36)

*link a connection (p. 532)

litigant a person engaged in a lawsuit (p. 307)

lobbying direct contact made by lobbyists to persuade government officials to support the policies their interest group favors (pp. 198, 508)

lobbyist interest group representative (pp. 198, 508)

*location a place (p. 87)

logrolling an agreement by two or more lawmakers to support each other's bills (p. 202)

veto legislativo provisiones que el Congreso escribió dentro de algunas leyes que le permitieron revisar y cancelar acciones de las agencias ejecutivas (pág. 170)

*legislatura organismo de gobierno que crea las leyes (pág. 49)

*recaudar colectar un impuesto (pág. 49)

oficial de enlace empleado de un departamento de gabinete que ayuda a promover las buenas relaciones con el Congreso (pág. 296)

difamación declaración falsa escrita o publicada con intención de dañar la reputación de una persona (págs. 369, 537)

*licencia permiso emitido por una agencia (pág. 103)

vicegobernador oficial que preside en la cámara alta en algunas legislaturas estatales (pág. 642)

gobierno limitado sistema de gobierno en el cual el poder del gobierno es limitado, no absoluto (pág. 36)

*enlace conexión (pág. 532)

litigante persona comprometida en una demanda (pág. 307)

cabildeo contacto directo hecho por un cabildero con el fin de persuadir a los funcionarios gubernamentales para apoyar la política que su grupo de interés favorece (págs. 198, 508)

cabildero representante de un grupo de interés (págs. 198, 508)

*lugar sitio (pág. 87)

convenio de ayuda mutua un acuerdo entre dos o más legisladores para apoyarse el uno al otro en sus proyectos de ley (pág. 202)

*maintain to keep the same (p. 608)

*maintenance the upkeep of property or equipment (p. 671)

*major prominent or significant in size, amount, or degree (p. 158)

*majority greater number (p. 221)

majority leader the Speaker's top assistant whose job is to help plan the majority party's legislative program and to steer important bills through the House (p. 134)

majority opinion a Supreme Court decision expressing the views of the majority of justices (p. 335)

mandate a formal order given by a higher authority (p. 248)

mandatory sentencing a system of fixed, required terms of imprisonment for certain types of crimes (p. 651)

*margin the limit or bare minimum (p. 222)

market economy an economic system that allows buyers and sellers acting in their individual interests to control the factors of production (p. 718)

*mantener conservar igual (pág. 608)

*mantenimiento cuidado de propiedad o equipos (pág. 671)

*mayor prominente o importante en tamaño, cantidad, o grado (pág. 158)

*mayoría mayor número (pág. 221)

líder mayoritario asistente máximo del presidente de la Cámara, cuyo trabajo es ayudar a planear el programa legislativo del partido mayoritario y dirigir importantes proyectos de ley a través de la Cámara (pág. 134)

opinión mayoritaria decisión de la Corte Suprema expresando la perspectiva de la mayoría de los jueces (pág. 335)

mandato orden formal dada por una autoridad superior (pág. 248)

sentencia mandataria sistema de términos de encarcelamiento fijos y requeridos por ciertos tipos de crímenes (pág. 651)

*margen límite o lo mínimo (pág. 222)

economía mercadera sistema económico que permite a compradores y vendedores actuar en sus propios intereses para controlar los elementos de producción (pág. 718)

marketing quota–municipality

marketing quota a limit set among farmers to market only an assigned portion of an overproduced crop (p. 586)

market value the amount of money an owner may expect to receive if property is sold (p. 674)

mass media means of communication, such as television, newspapers, movies, books, and the Internet, that influence large audiences (pp. 515, 527)

mass transit systems such as buses and subways that are used to transport large numbers of people (pp. 602, 670)

*media source of information including television, print, and the Internet (p. 230)

media event a visually interesting event designed to reinforce a politician's position on some issue (p. 529)

mediation a process in which each side is given the opportunity to explain its side of dispute and must listen to the other side (p. 425)

*medium system of communication, such as newspaper or radio (p. 249)

*method a procedure or process for accomplishing something (p. 429)

metropolitan area a large city and its surrounding suburbs (p. 671)

metropolitan government a type of government that serves several different communities in the same region (p. 682)

*military referring to armed forces (p. 615)

*minimize to make less important (p. 627)

*ministry a government department (p. 691)

misdemeanor a minor crime that is usually punished by a fine or a jail sentence of less than one year (p. 430)

mixed economy a system in which the government regulates private enterprise (pp. 575, 721)

*modification minor change (p. 54)

monarchy autocracy in which a king, queen, or emperor exercises supreme powers of government (p. 19)

monetary policy a government's control of the supply of money and credit to influence the economy (p. 567)

*monitor to watch, keep track of, oversee (p. 709)

monopoly a business that controls so much of an industry that little or no competition exists (pp. 578, 720)

mortgage a loan taken out to pay for a house (p. 423)

*motivate provide a reason for (p. 399)

mullah a specially trained Islamic religious leader (p. 700)

multilateral treaty international agreement signed by several nations (p. 629)

municipality an urban unit of government chartered by a state (p. 665)

cupo mercader límite establecido entre agricultores para vender sólo una porción asignada de una cosecha sobreproducida (pág. 586)

valor de mercado cantidad de dinero que un propietario espera recibir si su propiedad es vendida (pág. 674)

medios informativos medios de comunicación, tales como televisión, periódicos, películas, libros, e Internet, que influencian a grandes audiencias (págs. 515, 527)

tránsito público sistemas tales como el metro, que son usados para transportar a grandes números de personas (págs. 602, 670)

*medios de comunicación fuente de información que incluye la televisión, impresos e Internet (pág. 230)

evento para los medios informativos evento de interés visual diseñado para reforzar la posición de un político en algún tema (pág. 529)

mediación proceso en el cual cada partido tiene la oportunidad de explicar su lado de la disputa y debe escuchar al otro lado (pág. 425)

*medio sistema de comunicación, tales como los periódicos o emisoras de radio (pág. 249)

*método procedimiento o proceso para lograr algo (pág. 429)

área metropolitana ciudad grande y sus suburbios alrededores (pág. 671)

gobierno metropolitano tipo de gobierno que sirve a varias comunidades en la misma región (pág. 682)

*militar que se refiere a las fuerzas armadas (pág. 615)

*minimizar hacer menos importante (pág. 627)

*ministerio departamento del gobierno (pág. 691)

delito menor crimen menor que normalmente es castigado con una multa o sentencia de cárcel por menos de un año (pág. 430)

economía mixta sistema en el cual el gobierno regula empresas privadas (págs. 575, 721)

*modificación cambio menor (pág. 54)

monarquía autocracia en la cual un rey, reina, o emperador, ejercita los poderes supremos del gobierno (pág. 19)

política monetaria control del gobierno del abastecimiento de dinero y crédito para influenciar la economía (pág. 567)

*observar mirar, hacer un seguimiento, supervisar (pág. 709)

monopolio negocio que controla tanto una industria que existe poco o nada de competencia (págs. 578, 720)

hipoteca préstamo solicitado para pagar una casa (pág. 423)

*motivar proveer una razón para algo (pág. 399)

mullah líder religioso islámico con entrenamiento especializado (pág. 700)

tratado multilateral acuerdo internacional firmado por varias naciones (pág. 629)

municipalidad unidad urbana de gobierno establecida por un estado (pág. 665)

Muslim a follower of the religion of Islam (p. 699)

mutual defense alliance an agreement between nations to support each other in case of an attack (p. 627)

musulmán adepto a la religión islámica (pág. 699)

alianza de defensa mutua acuerdo entre naciones para apoyarse la una a la otra en caso de ataque (pág. 627)

nation group of people united by bonds of race, language, custom, tradition, and, sometimes, religion (p. 6)

national budget the yearly financial plan for the federal government (p. 175)

national committee representatives from the 50 state party organizations who run a political party (p. 460)

national convention a gathering of local and state party members chosen to nominate presidential and vice-presidential candidates (p. 460)

national debt the total amount of money the government owes at any given time (p. 559)

nationalist position a position that favors national action in dealing with problems (p. 107)

nationalization the process by which a government takes control of industry (p. 724)

national security protection of a nation's borders and territories against invasion or control by foreign powers (p. 607)

National Security Advisor director of the National Security Council staff (p. 236)

nation-state a country in which the territory of both the nation and the state coincide (p. 6)

naturalization the legal process by which a person is granted citizenship (p. 392)

necessary and proper clause Article I, Section 8, of the Constitution, which gives Congress the power to make all laws that are necessary and proper for carrying out its duties (p. 157)

***network** an interconnected or interrelated chain, group, or system (p. 312)

***neutral** not favoring either side in a quarrel, contest, or war (p. 287)

newly developed nation a nation that has had significant or rapid industrial growth in recent years (p. 722)

news briefing a meeting during which a government official makes an announcement or explains a policy, decision, or action (p. 528)

news release a ready-made story that government officials prepare for members of the press (p. 528)

nominating convention an official public meeting of a party to choose candidates for office (p. 464)

nongovernmental organization (NGO) an international organization composed of individuals and groups outside the scope of government (p. 702)

nación grupo de personas unidas por lazos de raza, lenguaje, costumbre, tradición y a veces religión (pág. 6)

presupuesto nacional plan financiero anual para el gobierno federal (pág. 175)

comité nacional representantes de las 50 organizaciones estatales dirigen un partido político (pág. 460)

convención nacional reunión de miembros locales y estatales de un partido escogidos para nominar a los candidatos para presidente y vicepresidente (pág. 460)

deuda nacional total de dinero que el gobierno debe en cualquier momento (pág. 559)

posición nacionalista posición que favorece la acción nacional en tratar problemas (pág. 107)

nacionalización proceso por el cual el gobierno toma control de la industria (pág. 724)

seguridad nacional protección de las fronteras y territorios de una nación en contra del control o invasión de poderes extranjeros (pág. 607)

consejero de seguridad nacional director del personal del Consejo de Seguridad Nacional (pág. 236)

estado nación país en el cual el territorio de ambos la nación y el estado coinciden (pág. 6)

naturalización proceso legal por el cual se le otorga a una persona la ciudadanía (pág. 392)

cláusula de necesario y propio Artículo I, Sección 8 de la Constitución, la cual le da al Congreso el poder de aprobar todas las leyes que sean necesarias y propias para hacer cumplir sus deberes (pág. 157)

***red** cadena, grupo o sistema interconectado o interrelacionado (pág. 312)

***neutral** que no favorece ningún lado en una discusión, contienda o guerra (pág. 287)

nación nuevamente desarrollada nación que ha tenido rápido crecimiento industrial en años recientes (pág. 722)

sesión noticiera junta durante la cual un funcionario gubernamental anuncia o explica una política, decisión o acción (pág. 528)

comunicado de prensa historia preparada que los funcionarios gubernamentales escriben para los miembros de la prensa (pág. 528)

convención de nominación junta oficial pública de un partido para escoger candidatos para un cargo (pág. 464)

organización no gubernamental organización internacional compuesta por individuos y grupos fuera del ámbito del gobierno (pág. 702)

nonresident alien a person from a foreign country who expects to stay in the United States for a short, specified period of time (p. 391)

*nuclear atomic (p. 629)

nuclear proliferation the spread of nuclear weapons (p. 709)

extranjero no residente persona de un país extranjero que espera quedarse en Estados Unidos por un período corto y específico (pág. 391)

*nuclear atómico (pág. 629)

proliferación nuclear expansión de armas nucleares (pág. 709)

*objective something toward which effort is directed; end, goal (p. 567)

*objectivity ability to deal with facts or situations as they exist without distortion of personal feelings or prejudices (p. 322)

*obtain to get (p. 643)

*obvious easily discovered, seen, or understood (p. 433)

*occupation having control or possession of a location (p. 492)

*occur to happen (p. 124)

office-group ballot one that lists the candidates together by the office for which they are running (p. 488)

oligarchy a system of government in which a small group holds power (p. 20)

oligopoly situation in which only a few firms dominate a particular industry (p. 579)

open-market operations the means the Federal Reserve System uses to affect the economy by buying or selling government securities on the open market (p. 570)

open primary an election in which all voters may participate (p. 465)

opinion a written explanation of a Supreme Court decision; also, in some states, a written interpretation of a state constitution or state laws by the state's attorney general (p. 322)

ordinance a law (pp. 50, 417)

original jurisdiction the authority of a trial court to be first to hear a case (p. 307)

*outcome result, consequence (p. 372)

*output amount produced (p. 584)

*overlap to extend over or past; to have something in common (p. 306)

*objetivo algo a lo que se dirigen los esfuerzos; fin, meta (pág. 567)

*objetividad capacidad para lidiar con los hechos o situaciones tal y como existen, sin ser distorsionados por las emociones personales o prejuicios (pág. 322)

*obtener adquirir (pág. 643)

*obvio que se descubre con facilidad, visto o entendido (pág. 433)

*ocupación profesión o carrera (pág. 492)

*ocurrir acontecer (pág. 124)

papeleta de grupo por cargo aquella que enumera los candidatos juntos por el cargo al cual se están postulando (pág. 488)

oligarquía sistema de gobierno en el cual un pequeño grupo mantiene el poder (pág. 20)

oligopolio situación en la cual sólo unas cuantas empresas dominan una industria particular (pág. 579)

operaciones de mercado abierto lo medios que el Sistema de Reserva Federal usa para afectar la economía comprando o vendiendo bonos del gobierno u otras seguridades en el mercado abierto (pág. 570)

elección primaria abierta elección en la cual todos los votantes pueden participar (pág. 465)

opinión explicación escrita de una decisión de la Suprema Corte; también, en algunos estados, una interpretación escrita de la constitución estatal o leyes estatales por el fiscal del estado (pág. 322)

ordenanza ley (págs. 50, 417)

jurisdicción original autoridad de un tribunal para ser el primero en escuchar un caso (pág. 307)

*resultado efecto, consecuencia (pág. 372)

*rendimiento cantidad producida (pág. 584)

*traslapar extenderse más allá o pasarse, tener algo en común (pág. 306)

*panel group of persons selected for some service (p. 313)

*parallel similar, analogous, having corresponding positions (p. 135)

pardon a release from legal punishment (p. 254)

*panel grupo de personas seleccionadas para un servicio (pág. 313)

*paralelo similar, análogo, que tiene posiciones que corresponden (pág. 135)

indulto liberación de castigo legal (pág. 254)

parliamentary government form of government in which executive and legislative functions both reside in an elected assembly, or parliament (p. 689)

parochial school a school operated by a church or religious group (p. 359)

parole means by which a prisoner is allowed to serve the rest of a sentence in the community under the supervision of a parole officer (p. 652)

partisan adhering to or supporting a particular party, faction, cause, or person (p. 544)

party-column ballot one that lists each party's candidates in a column under the party's name (p. 489)

passport a document that shows citizenship and entitles a traveler to certain protections established by international treaty (p. 623)

patronage the practice of granting favors to reward party loyalty (pp. 256, 462)

peer group an individual's close friends, religious group, clubs, or work groups (p. 515)

*perceive the capacity, degree, and accuracy of one's consciousness, awareness, or comprehension (p. 495)

*percent one unit of 100 (p. 284)

per curiam opinion (puhr KYUR•ee•ahm) a brief, unsigned statement of a Supreme Court decision (p. 333)

*period a portion of time (p. 174)

*periodic occurring at intervals (p. 331)

perjury lying under oath (p. 168)

personal property movable belongings such as clothes and jewelry, as well as intangible items such as stocks, bonds, copyrights, and patents (pp. 423, 674)

personal staff the people who work directly for individual senators and representatives (p. 147)

petition an appeal (p. 77)

petit jury a trial jury, usually consisting of 6 or 12 people, that weighs the evidence presented at a trial and renders a verdict (p. 313)

petty offense a minor crime, usually punished by a ticket rather than being arrested (p. 430)

*phase a distinguishable part in a cycle; an aspect or part (p. 422)

*philosopher one who engages in the pursuit of wisdom (p. 5)

picket to patrol an establishment to convince workers and the public not to enter it (p. 378)

plaintiff person who brings charges in court (p. 424)

plank a section of a political party platform (p. 469)

platform a statement of a political party's principles, beliefs, and positions on vital issues (p. 469)

gobierno parlamentario tipo de gobierno en el cual las funciones ejecutiva y legislativa residen en la asamblea electa, o parlamento (pág. 689)

escuela parroquiana escuela operada por una iglesia o grupo religioso (pág. 359)

libertad condicional forma por la cual se le permite a un prisionero servir el resto de una sentencia en la comunidad bajo la supervisión de un oficial (pág. 652)

prosélito que se adhiere o apoya un partido, facción, causa o persona en particular (pág. 544)

balota de la columna del partido aquella que enumera a cada candidato de partido en una columna bajo el nombre del partido (pág. 489)

pasaporte documento que muestra la ciudadanía y el derecho de un viajero a cierta protección establecida por tratado internacional (pág. 623)

patrocinio práctica de otorgar favores para recompensar la lealtad al partido (págs. 256, 462)

grupo paritario amigos cercanos, grupo religioso, clubes, o grupos de trabajo de un individuo (pág. 515)

*percepción capacidad, grado y precisión del conocimiento, conciencia o comprensión de una (pág. 495)

*porcentaje unidad de 100 (pág. 284)

opinión per curiam breve declaración no firmada de una decisión de la Suprema Corte (pág. 333)

*período porción del tiempo (pág. 174)

*periódico que ocurre en intervalos (pág. 331)

perjurio mentir bajo juramento (pág. 168)

propiedad personal pertenencias movibles tales como ropa y joyas, así como artículos intangibles tales como acciones, bonos, derechos de autor, y patentes (págs. 423, 674)

personal propio personas que trabajan directamente para senadores y representantes individuales (pág. 147)

petición solicitud (pág. 77)

jurado pequeño jurado generalmente de 6 o 12 personas, que considera la evidencia presentada en un juicio y rinde un veredicto (pág. 313)

ofensa menor crimen menor, generalmente castigado con una multa en vez de arresto (pág. 430)

*fase parte que se distingue en un ciclo; aspecto o parte (pág. 422)

*filósofo alguien que se dedica a la búsqueda de la sabiduría (pág. 5)

hacer piquete patrullar un establecimiento para convencer a trabajadores y al público de no entrar (pág. 378)

demandante persona que presenta cargos en una corte (pág. 424)

puntal un sección individual de la plataforma partidiaria de un partido polítco (pág. 469)

plataforma declaración de los principios, creencias, y posiciones en asuntos vitales de un partido político (pág. 469)

plea bargaining–president pro tempore

plea bargaining the process in which a defendant pleads guilty to a lesser crime than the one with which the defendant was originally charged (p. 432)

plurality the largest number of votes in an election (pp. 465, 643)

pocket veto when a president kills a bill passed during the last 10 days Congress is in session by simply refusing to act on it (p. 187)

*policy a plan that includes general goals and procedures (p. 336)

political action committee (PAC) an organization formed to collect money and provide financial support for political candidates (p. 478)

political culture a set of shared values and beliefs about a nation and its government (p. 516)

political party a group of individuals with broad common interests who organize to nominate candidates for office, win elections, conduct government, and determine public policy (pp. 23, 453)

politics the effort to control or influence the conduct and policies of government (p. 14)

polling place the location in a precinct where people vote (p. 488)

poll tax money paid in order to vote (pp. 90, 483)

popular sovereignty rule by the people (p. 65)

pork-barrel legislation laws passed by Congress that appropriate money for local federal projects (p. 202)

*portion an often limited part of a whole (p. 566)

*potential possible (p. 377)

preamble a statement in a constitution that sets forth the goals and purposes of government (p. 14)

*precedent a model on which to base later decisions or actions (pp. 50, 338, 364, 426)

precinct a voting district (pp. 459, 488)

precinct captain a volunteer who organizes party workers to distribute information about the party and its candidates and to get the voters to the polls (p. 459)

*precise exact (p. 436)

*predict to tell in advance of an event (p. 493)

*preemption the federal government's ability to take over a state government function (p. 109)

*preliminary coming before something else (p. 561)

presidential government a form of democratic government in which a president heads the executive branch (p. 691)

presidential succession the order in which officials fill the office of president in case of a vacancy (p. 217)

president pro tempore the Senate member, elected by the Senate, who stands in as president of the Senate in the absence of the vice president (p. 139)

negociación de alegato proceso en el cual el acusado se declara culpable a un crimen menor a la acusación original (pág. 432)

pluralidad mayor cantidad de votos en una elección (págs. 465, 643)

veto indirecto cuando un presidente se deshace de un proyecto de ley aprobado durante los últimos 10 días que el Congreso está en session, simplemente negándose a cumplirlo (pág. 187)

*política plan que incluye objetivos generales y procedimientos (pág. 336)

comité de acción política organización formada para recolectar dinero y proporcionar ayuda financiera a candidatos políticos (pág. 478)

cultura política conjunto de valores y creencias compartidos sobre una nación y su gobierno (pág. 516)

partido político grupo de individuos con intereses comunes que se organizan para nominar candidatos para un cargo, ganar elecciones, conducir el gobierno, y determinar la política pública (págs. 23, 453)

política esfuerzo para controlar o influenciar la conducta y política del gobierno (pág. 14)

lugar de votación área en un recinto donde la gente vota (pág. 488)

impuesto al voto dinero pagado para votar (págs. 90, 483)

soberanía popular gobernado por la gente (pág. 65)

legislación de favoritismo político leyes aprobadas por el Congreso que asignan dinero para proyectos federales locales (pág. 202)

*porción parte limitada de un todo (pág. 566)

*potencial posible (pág. 377)

preámbulo declaración en una constitución que estipula los objetivos y propósitos del gobierno (pág. 14)

precedente modelo en el cual basar decisiones o acciones posteriores (págs. 50, 338, 364, 426)

recinto distrito electoral (págs. 459, 488)

capitán de recinto voluntario que organiza los trabajadores del partido para distribuir información acerca del partido y sus candidatos y para urgir a los votantes a las urnas (pág. 459)

*preciso exacto (pág. 436)

*predecir decir antes de un evento o adivinar (pág. 493)

*derecho de prioridad capacidad del gobierno federal de asumir una función del gobierno estatal (pág. 109)

*preliminar que viene antes de algo más (pág. 561)

gobierno presidencial forma de gobierno democrático en la cual el presidente encabeza la rama ejecutiva (pág. 691)

sucesión presidencial orden en el cual funcionarios ocupan el cargo del presidente en caso de vacante (pág. 217)

presidente pro tempore miembro del Senado, electo por el Senado, que actúa como presidente del Senado en la ausencia del vicepresidente (pág. 139)

press secretary one of the president's top assistants who is in charge of media relations (p. 239)

secretario de prensa uno de los asistentes máximos del presidente que se encarga de las relaciones con los medios de comunicación (pág. 239)

*presume to expect or assume (p. 369)

*presumir esperar o asumir (pág. 369)

presumed innocence the presumption that a person is innocent until proven guilty (p. 420)

inocencia presunta presunción de la inocencia de una persona hasta que se compruebe lo contrario (pág. 420)

price supports the program under which Congress buys farmers' crops if the market price falls below the support price (p. 586)

apoyo de precios programa bajo el cual el Congreso compra la cosecha a los agricultores si el precio del mercado cae por debajo del precio de apoyo (pág. 586)

*prime foremost, significant (p. 707)

*principal más importante, significativo (pág. 707)

*principle an underlying doctrine or assumption (p. 63)

*principio doctrina o presunción subyacente (pág. 63)

prior restraint government censorship of information before it is published or broadcast (pp. 85, 371, 537)

restricción anterior censura de información por el gobierno antes de ser publicada o emitida (págs. 85, 371, 537)

private bill a bill dealing with individual people or places (p. 181)

proyecto de ley privado proyecto de ley que trata de personas o lugares individuales (pág. 181)

probable cause a reasonable basis to believe a person or premises is linked to a crime (p. 86)

causa probable base razonable para creer que una persona o un lugar está ligado a un crimen (pág. 86)

procedural due process principle that prohibits arbitrary enforcement of the law, and also provides safeguards to ensure that constitutional and statutory rights are protected by law enforcement (p. 419)

proceso de procedimiento correspondiente principio que prohibe la aplicación arbitraria de la ley, y también provee resguardos para asegurar que los derechos constitucionales y legales estén protegidos por la policía (pág. 419)

*procedure a way of doing (p. 64)

*procedimiento forma de hacer algo (pág. 64)

*process a continuing action or series of actions; a way of doing (p. 392)

*proceso acción o serie de acciones continuas; forma de hacer algo (pág. 392)

*professional an individual with intense preparation and knowledge in a specific field of work (p. 235)

*profesional individuo con preparación y conocimiento intensos en un área de trabajo específico (pág. 235)

profit the difference between the amount of money used to operate a business and the amount of money the business takes in (p. 720)

ganancia diferencia entre la cantidad de dinero usado para operar un negocio y la cantidad de dinero que el negocio recibe (pág. 720)

progressive tax tax based on a taxpayer's ability to pay (p. 657)

impuesto progresivo impuesto basado en la habilidad del contribuyente para pagar (pág. 657)

*prohibit to forbid (p. 649)

*prohibir vedar (pág. 649)

proletariat workers who produce the goods (p. 29)

proletariado trabajadores que producen los bienes (pág. 29)

propaganda the use of ideas, information, or rumors to influence opinion (p. 495)

propaganda uso de ideas, información o rumores para influenciar la opinión (pág. 495)

proportional representation a system in which several officials are elected to represent the same area in proportion to the votes each party's candidate receives (p. 457)

representación proporcional sistema en el cual varios oficiales son electos para representar la misma área en proporción a los votos que cada candidato de partido recibe (pág. 457)

proportional tax tax that is assessed at the same rate for everyone (p. 657)

impuesto proporcional impuesto fijado a la misma tasa para todos (pág. 657)

public assistance government programs that distribute money to poor people (p. 590)

asistencia pública programas gubernamentales que distribuyen dinero a los pobres (pág. 590)

public bill a bill dealing with general matters and applying to the entire nation (p. 182)

proyecto de ley público proyecto de ley relacionado con asuntos generales y que aplican a toda la nación (pág. 182)

public housing government-subsidized housing for low-income families (p. 600)

vivienda pública alojamiento subsidiado por el gobierno para familias de bajos ingresos (pág. 600)

public-interest group a group that seeks policy goals that it believes will benefit the nation (p. 506)

grupo de interés público grupo que busca realizar metas políticas que cree que beneficiarán a la nación (pág. 506)

public opinion the ideas and attitudes a significant number of Americans hold about issues (p. 514)

opinión pública ideas y actitudes que un número significativo de americanos tiene a cerca de temas (pág. 514)

public utility–regulation

public utility an organization that supplies such necessities as electricity, gas, or telephone service (p. 649)

empresa de servicio público organización que administra necesidades tales como electricidad, gas, o servicio telefónico (pág. 649)

*publish to print (p. 58)

*publicar imprimir (pág. 58)

pure speech the verbal expression of thought and opinion before an audience that has chosen to listen (p. 366)

expresión pura expresión verbal de pensamiento y opinión ante una audiencia que ha escogido escuchar (pág. 366)

*pursue to employ measures to obtain or accomplish (p. 357)

*perseguir emplear medidas para obtener o lograr algo (pág. 357)

quorum the minimum number of members who must be present to permit a legislative body to take official action (p. 137)

quórum número mínimo de miembros que deben estar presente para permitir a un grupo legislativo tomar acción oficial (pág. 137)

quota a limit on the quantity of a product that may be imported (p. 733)

cuota limitación de la cantidad de un producto que puede ser importado (pág. 733)

random sampling a polling technique in which everyone in the "universe" has an equal chance of being selected (p. 521)

muestreo al azar técnica de votación en la cual cada uno en el universo tiene una oportunidad equitativa de ser escogido (pág. 521)

*range the extent of options (p. 454)

*alcance magnitud de las opciones (pág. 454)

ratify to approve (pp. 48, 76)

ratificar aprobar (págs. 48, 76)

real property land and whatever is attached to or growing on it (pp. 423, 674)

propiedad real tierra y lo que esté unido o creciendo en ella (págs. 423, 674)

reapportionment the process of reassigning representation based on population, after every census (p. 124)

nueva distribución proceso de reasignar representación basada en la población, después de cada censo (pág. 124)

*recover to bring back to normal (p. 218)

*recuperar traer de vuelta a la normalidad (pág. 218)

*redistribution spreading to other areas; reallocation (p. 724)

*redistribución que se propaga a otras zonas; reasignación (pág. 724)

redistrict to set up new district lines after reapportionment is complete (p. 125)

delimitar nuevos distritos establecer nuevas líneas de distrito después de concluida la reasignación (pág. 125)

referendum a special election (p. 666)

referéndum elección especial (pág. 666)

refugee a person fleeing a country to escape persecution or danger (p. 391)

refugiado persona huyendo de un país para escapar del peligro y la persecución (pág. 391)

*regime system of rule (p. 615)

*régimen sistema de gobierno (pág. 615)

*regional having to do with a geographic area (p. 734)

*regional relacionado a una zona geográfica (pág. 734)

regional security pact a mutual defense treaty among nations of a region (p. 627)

pacto de seguridad regional tratado de defensa mutua entre las naciones de una región (pág. 627)

*register make a record of (p. 277); to enroll one's name with the appropriate local government in order to participate in elections (p. 487)

*registrar hacer un registro de algo (pág. 277); inscribirse enlistar su nombre con el gobierno local apropiado con el fin de participar en las elecciones (pág. 487)

*registration signing up (p. 657)

*inscripción registrarse (pág. 657)

regressive tax tax whereby people with lower incomes pay a larger portion of their income (p. 657)

impuesto regresivo impuesto por el cual personas de bajos recursos pagan una mayor porción de sus ingresos (pág. 657)

*regulation rule or procedure that has the force of law (p. 28)

*regulación norma o procedimiento que tiene fuerza de ley (pág. 28) *relevant significant (p. 230)

*reliance dependence (p. 725)

*reluctant hesitant, unwilling, disinclined (p. 439)

representative government a system of government in which people elect delegates to make laws and conduct government (p. 37)

representative sample a small group of people, typical of the universe, that a pollster questions (p. 520)

reprieve the postponement of legal punishment (p. 254)

republic a government in which voters hold sovereign power; elected representatives, responsible to the people, exercise that power (p. 20)

*require to call for, need (p. 367)

*requirement something that is necessary (p. 642)

reserved powers powers that belong strictly to the states (p. 96)

reserve requirement the percentage of money member banks must keep in Federal Reserve Banks as a reserve against their deposits (p. 569)

*residency determined as where one lives and is legally eligible to vote (p. 104)

resident alien a person from a foreign nation who has established permanent residence in the United States (p. 391)

*resolve to deal with, clear up, settle (p. 623)

*resource a source of supply or support, available means (p. 717)

*restore to return to original condition, rebuild (p. 586)

*restrict to limit (p. 648)

*retain to keep in one's pay or service (p. 508)

revenue the money a government collects from taxes or other sources (pp. 43, 189)

revenue bill a law proposed to raise money (p. 158)

*reverse to overturn, as an earlier decision (p. 89)

*revise to correct or improve (p. 173)

*revision change, especially to a document (p. 640)

revitalization investments in new facilities in an effort to promote economic growth (p. 681)

*revolution a fundamental change in political organization, esp. by overthrow of a government (p. 453)

*revolutionary causing sudden and dramatic change (p. 38)

rider a provision included in a bill on a subject other than the one covered in the bill (p. 183)

riding the circuit traveling to hold court in a justice's assigned region of the country (p. 320)

*role the part played by someone or something (p. 112)

*relevante significativo (pág. 230)

*dependencia necesidad (pág. 725)

*reacio que vacila, poco dispuesto, renuente (pág. 439)

gobierno representativo sistema de gobierno en el cual la gente elige delegados para hacer leyes y dirigir el gobierno (pág. 37)

muestra representativa pequeño grupo de gente, típica del universo, al que un encuestador cuestiona (pág. 520)

indulto postergación de un castigo legal (pág. 254)

república gobierno en el cual los votantes mantienen el poder soberano; los representantes electos, responsables a la gente, ejercitan ese poder (pág. 20)

*requerir avisar, necesitar (pág. 367)

*requisito algo que es necesario (pág. 642)

poderes reservados poderes que pertenecen estrictamente a los estados (pág. 96)

requerimiento de reserva porcentaje de dinero que los bancos miembros deben guardar en Bancos de Reserva Federal como una reserva contra sus depósitos (pág. 569)

*residencia determinada en relación a donde vive alguien y donde es legalmente apto para votar (pág. 104)

extranjero residente persona de una nación extranjera que ha establecido residencia permanente en Estados Unidos (pág. 391)

*resolver lidiar con algo, aclarar, solucionar (pág. 623)

*recurso fuente de suministros o apoyo, medios disponibles (pág. 717)

*restablecer regresar a la condición original, reconstruir (pág. 586)

*restringir limitar (pág. 648)

*retener quedarse con algo como forma de pago o servicio (pág. 508)

ingresos dinero que un gobierno cobra de impuestos u otras fuentes (págs. 43, 189)

proyecto de ley de ingresos ley propuesta para juntar dinero (pág. 158)

*invalidar anular una decisión previa (pág. 89)

*revisar corregir o mejorar (pág. 173)

*revisión cambio, especialmente en un documento (pág. 640)

revitalización inversiones en nuevas instalaciones en el esfuerzo de promover el crecimiento económico (pág. 681)

*revolución cambio fundamental en una organización política, especialmente al derrocar un gobierno (pág. 453)

*revolucionario que causa un cambio repentino y dramático (pág. 38)

cláusula añadida provisión incluida en un proyecto de ley sobre un tema diferente al abarcado en el proyecto (pág. 183)

recorriendo el circuito viajes para presidir un tribunal en la región del país asignada a un juez (pág. 320)

*rol papel desempeñado por algo o alguien (pág. 112)

runoff primary a second primary election between the two candidates who received the most votes in the first primary (p. 465)

elección de desempate segunda elección entre los dos candidatos que recibieron la mayor cantidad de votos en la primera elección (pág. 465)

sampling error a measurement of how much the sample results may differ from the sample universe (p. 521)

error de muestreo medida de cuánto los resultados de la muestra pueden diferenciarse del universo de la muestra (pág. 521)

sanction a measure, such as withholding economic aid, intended to influence a foreign government's activities (pp. 630, 693)

sanción medida tal como embargar la asistencia económica para influenciar las actividades de un gobierno extranjero (págs. 630, 693)

scarcity a condition that exists because society does not have all the resources to produce all the goods and services that everyone wants (p. 717)

escasez condición que existe porque la sociedad no tiene todos los recursos para producir todos los bienes y servicios que todos quieren (pág. 717)

*schedule to appoint or designate for a specific time (p. 167)

*programar fijar o asignar para un momento específico (pág. 167)

*scheme a plan of action, esp. a crafty or secret one (p. 168)

*esquema plan de acción, especialmente si es uno elaborado o secreto (pág. 168)

*scope range or extent (p. 702)

*alcance rango o grado (pág. 702)

search warrant an order signed by a judge describing a specific place to be searched for specific items (p. 86)

orden de cateo orden firmada por un juez describiendo un lugar específico para buscar artículos específicos (pág. 86)

secular nonreligious (p. 360)

profano no religioso (pág. 360)

securities financial instruments, including bonds, notes, and certificates, that are sold as a means of borrowing money with a promise to repay the buyer with interest after a specific time period (pp. 559, 581)

seguridades instrumentos financieros, incluyendo bonos, notas, y certificados, que son vendidos como medios de pedir dinero prestado con la promesa de volver a pagarlo al comprador con intereses después de un período específico (págs. 559, 581)

*security safety (p. 621)

*seguridad seguro (pág. 621)

security classification system the provision that information on government activities related to national security and foreign policy may be kept secret (p. 408)

sistema de clasificación de seguridad provisión que establece que la información sobre las actividades gubernamentales relacionadas a la seguridad nacional y la política exterior pueden mantenerse en secreto (pág. 408)

seditious speech speech urging resistance to lawful authority or advocating the overthrow of the government (p. 368)

expresión sediciosa discurso urgiendo resistencia a las autoridades legales o el derrocamiento del gobierno (pág. 368)

select committee a temporary committee formed to study one specific issue and report its findings to the Senate or the House (p. 143)

comité selecto comité temporal formado para estudiar un tema específico y reportar sus descubrimientos al Senado o a la Cámara (pág. 143)

self-incrimination testifying against oneself (p. 440)

autoincriminación atestiguar en contra de sí mismo (pág. 440)

senatorial courtesy a system in which the president submits the name of a candidate for judicial appointment to the senators from the candidate's home state before formally submitting it for full Senate approval (p. 317)

cortesía senatorial sistema en el cual el presidente somete el nombre de un candidato para una asignación judicial a los senadores del estado del candidato antes de someterlo formalmente para la aprobación de todo el Senado (pág. 317)

seniority system a system that gives the member of the majority party with the longest uninterrupted service on a particular committee the leadership of that committee (p. 145)

sistema de antigüedad sistema que da el liderazgo de un comité al miembro del partido mayoritario con el servicio ininterrumpido más largo en ese comité (pág. 145)

sentence the punishment to be imposed on an offender after a guilty verdict (p. 434)

sentencia castigo a ser impuesto a un acusado después de un veredicto de culpable (pág. 434)

separate but equal doctrine a policy that held that if facilities for different races were equal, they could be separate (p. 400)

doctrina de separación pero equitativa política que mantuvo que si las instalaciones para las diferentes razas fueran iguales podrían ser separadas (pág. 400)

separation of powers the division of power among the legislative, executive, and judicial branches of government (pp. 40, 66)

sequester to keep isolated (p. 373)

session a period of time during which a legislature meets to conduct business (p. 123)

shah a king (p. 701)

shield law a law that gives reporters some means of protection against being forced to disclose confidential information or sources in state courts (pp. 374, 537)

*shift a change of position (p. 389)

shock incarceration a prison program involving shorter sentences in a highly structured environment where offenders participate in work, community service, education, and counseling (p. 652)

shock probation program designed to show young offenders how terrible prison life is, by means of brief incarceration followed by supervised release (p. 652)

*significant important, meaningful (p. 358)

simple resolution a statement adopted to cover matters affecting only one house of Congress (p. 182)

single-member district electoral district in which only one candidate is elected to each office (p. 457)

*site location (p. 544)

slander false speech intended to damage a person's reputation (p. 369)

social contract theory that by contract, people surrender to the state the power needed to maintain order and the state, in turn, agrees to protect its citizens (p. 8)

social insurance government programs designed to help elderly, ill, and unemployed citizens (p. 590)

socialism an economic system in which the government owns the basic means of production, distributes the products and wages, and provides social services such as health care and welfare (p. 28)

soft money money raised by a political party for general purposes, not designated for a candidate (p. 479)

*source origin, point of procurement; one who supplies information (pp. 203, 537)

sovereignty the supreme and absolute authority within territorial boundaries (p. 6)

special district a unit of local government that deals with a specific function, such as education, water supply, or transportation (p. 665)

*specific distinct or particular characteristics (p. 138)

splinter party a political party that splits away from a major party because of some disagreement (p. 455)

spoils system the practice of victorious politicians rewarding their followers with government jobs (p. 285)

separación de poderes división de poder entre las ramas del gobierno legislativo, ejecutivo, y judicial (págs. 40, 66)

secuestrar mantener aislado (pág. 373)

sesión período durante el cual una legislatura se reúne para hacer negocios (pág. 123)

shah rey (pág. 701)

ley protectora ley que da a los reporteros alguna forma de protección en contra de ser forzados a revelar información o fuentes de información confidenciales en cortes estatales (págs. 374, 537)

*cambiar dejar una posición por otra (pág. 389)

encarcelamiento a choque programa de encarcelamiento que involucra sentencias más cortas en un ambiente altamente estructurado donde los acusados participan en trabajos, servicio a la comunidad, educación, y asesoramiento (pág. 652)

libertad condicional a choque programa diseñado para mostrar a los delincuentes juveniles lo terrible de la vida en la prisión por medio de un breve encarcelamiento seguido de libertad supervisada (pág. 652)

*significativo importante, valioso (pág. 358)

resolución simple informe adoptado para cubrir asuntos que afectan solamente una cámara del Congreso (pág. 182)

distrito de un solo miembro distrito electoral en el cual sólo un candidato es electo para cada cargo (pág. 457)

*sitio lugar (pág. 544)

calumnia expresión falsa con la intención de dañar la reputación de una persona (pág. 369)

contrato social teoría que, por contrato, la gente entrega al estado el poder necesario para mantener el orden y el estado, a cambio, acuerda proteger a sus ciudadanos (pág. 8)

seguro social programas gubernamentales diseñados para ayudar a los ciudadanos ancianos, enfermos, y desempleados (pág. 590)

socialismo sistema económico en el cual el gobierno es dueño de los elementos básicos de producción, distribuye los productos y salarios, y proporciona servicios sociales tales como cuidado de salud y asistencia social (pág. 28)

dinero no asignado dinero recaudado por un partido político para propósitos generales que no es asignado a un candidato (pág. 479)

*fuente origen, punto de obtención; alguien que provee información (págs. 203, 537)

soberanía lautoridad absoluta y suprema dentro de los límites territoriales (pág. 6)

distrito especial unidad de gobierno local que realiza una función específica tal como educación, abastecimiento de agua, o transportación (pág. 665)

*específico características distintivas o particulares (pág. 138)

partido disidente partido político que se separa de uno de los grandes partidos a causa de algún desacuerdo (pág. 455)

sistema del botín práctica de políticos victoriosos que compensan a sus seguidores con puestos gubernamentales (pág. 285)

spot advertising the brief, frequent, positive descriptions of a candidate or a candidate's major themes broadcast on television or radio (p. 531)

*stability remaining steady (p. 462)

standing committee a permanent committee in Congress that oversees bills that deal with certain kinds of issues (p. 142)

stare decisis (stehr•ee dih•SY•suhs) a Latin term meaning "let the decision stand"; the principle that once the Court rules on a case, its decision serves as a precedent on which to base other decisions (p. 338)

state a political community that occupies a definite territory and has an organized government with the power to make and enforce laws without approval from any higher authority (p. 5)

state central committee committee usually composed largely of representatives from the party's county organizations (p. 460)

state farm farm owned by the government and run like a factory, with farmworkers being paid wages (p. 729)

state-sponsored terrorism terrorism that is secretly supported by a government (p. 708)

states' rights position a position that favors state and local action in dealing with problems (p. 107)

statute a law written by a legislative branch (p. 417)

statutory law a law that is written down so that everyone might know and understand it (p. 417)

straight party ticket one in which a voter has selected candidates of his or her party only (p. 493)

*strategy a plan or method for achieving a goal (p. 476)

subcommittee a group within a standing committee that specializes in a subcategory of its standing committee's responsibility (p. 142)

*submit to present or propose for consideration (p. 256)

*subordinate of less importance (p. 107)

subpoena a legal order that a person appear or produce requested documents (p. 168)

*subsequent following, coming after (p. 602)

*subsidize to assist in payment with public money (p. 678)

substantive due process certain rights of individuals in the application of laws, some that are specified in the Constitution (like free speech) and some that are not specified (like the right of privacy in making personal decisions) (p. 419)

suburb a densely settled territory adjacent to a central city (p. 671)

*sufficient enough; satisfactory in amount (p. 313)

suffrage the right to vote (p. 482)

summons an official notice of a lawsuit that includes the date, time, and place of the initial court appearance (p. 425)

espacio publicitario descripciones breves, frecuentes, y positivas de un candidato o de sus importantes temas transmitidos por televisión o radio (pág. 531)

*estabilidad que se mantiene constante (pág. 462)

comité permanente comité permanente en el Congreso que supervisa los proyectos de ley que tratan de cierta clase de temas (pág. 142)

stare decisis término latino que significa "que permanezca la decisión"; el principio que dice que una vez que la Corte dictamina en un caso, su decisión sirve como precedente en el cual basar otras decisiones (pág. 338)

estado comunidad política que ocupa un territorio definido y tiene un gobierno organizado con el poder de hacer leyes y hacerlas cumplir sin la aprobación de cualquier autoridad superior (pág. 5)

comité central estatal comité generalmente compuesto en gran parte de representantes de organizaciones del partido de los condados (pág. 460)

granja estatal granja propiedad del gobierno, administrada como una fábrica con granjeros asalariados (pág. 729)

terrorismo apoyado por un gobierno apoyo secreto del terrorismo por parte de un gobierno (pág. 708)

posición de derechos estatales posición que favorece acción estatal y local al tratar problemas (pág. 107)

estatuto ley escrita por una rama legislativa (pág. 417)

ley estatutaria ley escrita de una manera que todo el mundo pueda conocer y entenderla (pág. 417)

papeleta partidaria aquella en que el votante selecciona a candidatos de su partido solamente (pág. 493)

*estrategia plan o método para lograr una meta (pág. 476)

subcomité grupo dentro de un comité permanente que se especializa en una subcategoría de la responsabilidad del comité permanente (pág. 142)

*presentar ofrecer o proponer para ser considerado (pág. 256)

*subordinado de menos importancia (pág. 107)

citación orden legal para que una persona comparezca o produzca documentos requeridos (pág. 168)

*subsiguiente que sigue, que viene después (pág. 602)

*subsidiar ayudar en el pago con dinero público (pág. 678)

proceso substantivo correspondiente ciertos derechos de individuos en la aplicación de leyes, algunos de los que son especificados en la Constitución (como la libre expresión) y otros que no son especificados, (como el derecho de privacidad al tomar decisiones personales) (pág. 419)

suburbio territorio muy poblado adjunto con una ciudad central (pág. 671)

*suficiente bastante, cantidad satisfactoria (pág. 313)

sufragio derecho al voto (pág. 482)

citación judicial notificación oficial de una demanda que incluye la fecha, tiempo, y lugar de la aparición inicial en la corte (pág. 425) sunset law a law that requires periodic checks of laws or of government agencies to see if they are still needed (p. 112)

sunshine law a law prohibiting public officials from holding meetings not open to the public (p. 113)

*supplement to add to (p. 592)

supranational organization an organization whose authority overrides the sovereignty of its individual members (p. 704)

supremacy clause statement in Article VI of the Constitution establishing that the Constitution, laws passed by Congress, and treaties of the United States "shall be the supreme Law of the Land" (pp. 65, 97)

*survey a poll; a collection of data (p. 261)

*survivor one who remains alive (p. 379)

suspect classification classification made on the basis of race or national origin that is subject to strict judicial scrutiny (p. 399)

*suspension a temporary removal or withholding (p. 337)

*sustain to support, keep up (p. 698)

swing vote the deciding vote (p. 344)

*symbol something that stands for something else (p. 387)

symbolic speech the use of actions and symbols, in addition to or instead of words, to express opinions (p. 366)

ley de puesta del sol ley que requiere inspecciones periódicas de leyes o de agencias gubernamentales para ver si todavía son necesarias (pág. 112)

ley del sol ley que prohibe a funcionarios públicos tener reuniones no abiertas al público (pág. 113)

*complementar añadir a algo (pág. 592)

organización supranacional organización cuya autoridad anula la soberanía de sus miembros individuales (pág. 704)

cláusula de supremacía declaración en el Artículo VI de la Constitución estableciendo que la Constitución, las leyes aprobadas por el Congreso, y los tratados de Estados Unidos "serán la Ley suprema de la Tierra" (págs. 65, 97)

*encuesta sondeo; colección de datos (pág. 261)

*sobreviviente alguien que sigue vivo (pág. 379)

clasificación de sospecho clasificación hecha en la base de raza u origen nacional que es sujeto al severo escrutinio judicial (pág. 399)

*suspensión remoción o retención temporaria (pág. 337)

*sustentar apoyar, mantener (pág. 698)

voto ganador voto decisivo (pág. 344)

*símbolo algo que representa otra cosa (pág. 387)

expresión simbólica uso de acciones y símbolos, junto con o en lugar de palabras, para expresar opiniones (pág. 366)

*target an object of criticism (p. 507)

tariff a tax placed on imports to increase their price in the domestic market (p. 733)

tax the money that people and businesses pay to support the activities of the government (pp. 189, 555)

taxable income the total income of an individual minus certain deductions and personal exemptions (p. 555)

*technical highly detailed (p. 292)

*technique method of accomplishing desired aim (p. 508)

*temporary lasting a short amount of time (p. 143)

*tension strain or conflict (p. 261)

terrorism the use of violence by nongovernmental groups against civilians to achieve a political goal (p. 707)

theocracy a government dominated by religion (p. 454)

*theory speculation based on study (p. 8)

*thereby by that means, in that way (p. 453)

third party any political party other than one of the two major parties (p. 455)

ticket a party's candidates for president and vice president (p. 466)

ticket-splitting voting for candidates from different parties for different offices (p. 488)

*blanco objeto de la crítica (pág. 507)

tarifa impuesto sobre importaciones para aumentar su precio en el mercado doméstico (pág. 733)

impuesto dinero que la gente y los negocios pagan para apoyar las actividades del gobierno (págs. 189, 555)

ingresos imponibles total de ingresos de un individuo menos ciertas deducciones y exenciones personales (pág. 555)

*técnico muy detallado (pág. 292)

*técnica método para lograr el objetivo deseado (pág. 508)

*temporario que dura muy poco tiempo (pág. 143)

*tensión presión o conflicto (pág. 261)

terrorismo uso de violencia por parte de grupos no gubernamentales contra los ciudadanos con el propósito de alcanzar una meta política (pág. 707)

teocracia gobierno dominado por la religión (pág. 454)

*teoría especulación basada en un estudio (pág. 8)

*así de tal modo, de esa manera (pág. 453)

tercer partido cualquier partido político además de los dos partidos mayores (pág. 455)

candidatura candidatos para presidente y vicepresidente de un partido (pág. 466)

papeleta no partidaria votar por candidatos de diferentes partidos para cargos diferentes (pág. 488)

tort a wrongful act, other than breach of contract, for which an injured party has the right to sue (p. 423)

agravio acto injusto, aparte del incumplimiento de contrato, por el cual el partido ofendido tiene derecho de demandar (pág. 423)

township a unit of local government found in some states, usually a subdivision of a county (p. 664)

municipio unidad de gobierno local encontrada en algunos estados, generalmente una subdivisión de un condado (pág. 664)

*trace to discover by going backward over the evidence (p. 126)

*localizar descubrir revisando de nuevo la evidencia (pág. 126)

trading bloc a group of nations that trade without barriers such as tariffs (p. 734)

bloque comerciante grupo de naciones que comercian sin barreras tales como tarifas (pág. 734)

*traditional time-honored or established (p. 491)

*tradicional que honra el tiempo o que está establecido (pág. 491)

traditional economy economic system in which customs dictate the rules for economic activity (p. 717)

economía tradicional sistema económico en el cual el hábito y la costumbre dictan las normas para toda actividad económica (pág. 717)

*transform to change completely or radically (p. 701)

*transformar cambiar por completo o radicalmente (pág. 701)

*transition change (p. 689)

*transición cambio (pág. 689)

*transmission broadcasting, as by television or radio (p. 374)

*emisión transmitir por radio o televisión (pág. 374)

*transportation public conveyance of passengers or goods (p. 174)

*transportación transporte público de pasajeros o mercancía (pág. 174)

treaty a formal agreement between the governments of two or more countries (pp. 79, 257, 615)

tratado acuerdo formal entre los gobiernos de dos o más países (págs. 79, 257, 615)

*trend a prevailing tendency (p. 578)

*tendencia una inclinación predominante (pág. 578)

trust a form of business consolidation in which several corporations combine their stock and allow a board of trustees to operate as a giant enterprise (p. 578)

fundación forma de consolidación de negocios en la cual varias sociedades anónimas unen sus acciones y permiten que una mesa directiva las dirija como una sola empresa gigante (pág. 578)

U

*unaffected not influenced or changed (p. 197)

*inalterado que no ha sido influenciado o cambiado (pág. 197)

*unconstitutional not consistent with a nation's constitution; against highest law (p. 321)

*inconstitucional que no es consistente con la constitución de un país; en contra de las leyes supremas (pág. 321)

uncontrollable government expenditure required by law or resulting from previous budgetary commitments (p. 561)

incontrolable gasto gubernamental requerido por ley o como resultado de previos compromisos presupuestarios (pág. 561)

undocumented alien one who entered the country illegally, or one whose permit for residency has expired (p. 391)

extranjero indocumentado alguien que entró ilegalmente al país, o uno cuyo permiso de residencia ha expirado (pág. 391)

*undertake to agree to do or attempt (p. 598)

*emprender llegar a un acuerdo para hacer o intentar (pág. 598)

unemployment compensation payments by a state to workers who lose their jobs (p. 649)

compensación de desempleo pagos por parte de un estado a los trabajadores que pierden su trabajo (pág. 649)

unemployment insurance programs in which the federal and state governments cooperate to provide help for people who are out of work (p. 591)

seguro de desempleo programas en los cuales el gobierno federal y estatal cooperan para proporcionar ayuda a personas que no tienen empleo (pág. 591)

unfunded mandates programs ordered but not paid for by federal legislation (p. 588)

mandatos sin fondos programas requeridos pero sin pagar por la legislación federal (pág. 588)

unicameral a single-chamber legislature (p. 48)

unicameral legislatura de una cámara (pág. 48)

*unify to form into one (p. 705)

*unificar formarse en uno (pág. 705)

unitary system a government that gives all key powers to the national or central government (p. 12)

sistema unitario gobierno que da todos los poderes claves al gobierno nacional o central (pág. 12)

universe in polling, the group of people who are to be studied (p. 520)

universo en votación, el grupo de gente que será estudiada (pág. 520)

*unparalleled having no equal or match; unique in kind or quality (p. 730)

*incomparable que no tiene igual o par; único en calidad o en su clase (pág. 730)

urban renewal programs under which cities apply for federal aid to clear slum areas and rebuild (pp. 600, 678)

*utility a service such as gas, water, etc. (p. 638)

renovación urbana programas bajo los cuales las ciudades pueden solicitar asistencia federal para limpiar áreas deterioradas y reconstruirlas (págs. 600, 678)

*servicios esenciales públicos servicios tales como gas, agua, etc. (pág. 638)

*variation difference, change (p. 521)

*vary to differ (p. 464)

verdict decision (p. 433)

veto rejection of a bill (pp. 66, 187)

*via by way of (p. 539)

victim compensation a program in many states whereby the state government provides financial aid to victims of certain crimes (p. 651)

*violate to disregard, disrespect (p. 321)

visa a special document, required by certain countries, issued by the government of the country that a person wishes to enter (p. 623)

voir dire a preliminary examination to determine the competency of a witness or juror (p. 420)

*variación diferencia, cambio (pág. 521)

*variar cambiar (pág. 464)

veredicto decisión (pág. 433)

veto rechazo de un proyecto de ley (págs. 66, 187)

*vía por medio de (pág. 539)

compensación de víctima programa en varios estados a través del cual el gobierno proporciona ayuda financiera a las víctimas de ciertos crímenes (pág. 651)

*violar hacer caso omiso, falta de respeto (pág. 321)

visa documento especial, requerido por ciertos países, emitido por el gobierno del país al que la persona desea entrar (pág. 623)

voir dire preliminar para determinar la capacidad de un testigo o jurado (pág. 420)

ward a large district comprising several adjoining precincts (p. 459)

welfare state a nation that has an economic system, such as socialism, that provides many welfare programs (p. 724)

whip an assistant to the party floor leader in the legislature (p. 135)

*widespread covering many areas (p. 689)

withholding the money an employer holds back from workers' wages as payment of anticipated income tax (p. 556)

workers' compensation payments by a state to people who are unable to work as a result of job-related injury or ill health (p. 649)

writ of certiorari (suhr•shee•uh•RAR•ee) an order from the Supreme Court to a lower court to send up the records on a case for review (p. 332)

distrito gran distrito que consta de varios recintos adjuntos (pág. 459)

estado benefactor nación que tiene un sistema económico, tal como el socialismo, que proporciona varios programas de bienestar social (pág. 724)

caudillo de partido asistente al jefe de partido en la legislatura (pág. 135)

*extenso que cubre muchas áreas (pág. 689)

impuesto retenido dinero que un empleador retiene del salario de los trabajadores para pagar los impuestos anticipados (pág. 556)

compensación del trabajador pagos por parte del estado que reciben las personas imposibilitadas para trabajar como resultado de una herida o mala salud relacionada con el trabajo (pág. 649)

orden de certiorari orden de la Suprema Corte a una corte menor para mandar los registros de un caso para su revisión (pág. 332)

zoning the means a local government uses to regulate the way land and buildings may be used in order to shape community development (p. 669)

restricciones de edificación medios que un gobierno local utiliza para regular la manera en que la tierra y los edificios pueden ser utilizados para dar forma al desarrollo de una comunidad (pág. 669)

Index